Spartanburg County South Carolina Deed Abstracts

Books A-T

-1785-1827-

(Volume #1)

Compiled by:
Albert Bruce Pruitt

Book Publishers

Southern Historical Press, Inc.
Greenville, South Carolina

Please direct all correspondence and book orders to:
www.southernhistoricalpress.com
or
SOUTHERN HISTORICAL PRESS, Inc.
1071 Park West Blvd.
Greenville, SC 29611

Southernhistoricalpress@gmail.com

ISBN #978-0-89308553-7
Printed in the United Sattes of America

FOREWORD

This book began as a much smaller project to provide material for an article for The Carolina Herald (by the South Carolina Genealogical Society). However, it has grown to its present size--abstracts of Spartanburg County/District deeds in Books A through T. This amounts to 7917 pages from deed books. This number of pages doesn't include places where page numbers were duplicated or page numbers were omitted. In the latter case, it never appeared that a page had been torn from the book causing loss of information; someone had just skipped a number or two in the page numbering process. Abstracts from Books A and B were published in The Carolina Herald. Abstracts for most of Book C have also been published (by Mrs. Hazel A MacIvor) in the Carolina Genealogist (beginning in the Spring 1970 issue).

When this work was begun, there appeared to be no standard method of stating an abstract. The method here has been adopted from several places. The primary purpose of the abstract is to give all pertinent information in an abbreviated (understandable) form. The form used in this book is outlined below:
(1) the page numbers indicate the page on which the deed begins and the page on which the next deed begins, i.e. p. 4-5 means the deed begins on p. 4 and the next deed begins on p. 5;
(2) locations such as "(Union Dist)" after the date indicate the deed was written in another county. Similarily "(Union Dist)" in the witness oath or the dower renunciation indicate they were made outside Spartanburg Dist;
(3) the first date indicated is the date of the transaction, i.e. Dec. 5, 1812 indicates the property was sold on Dec. 5, 1812;
(4) the grantor's name and place of residence is indicated next, i.e. Samuel Bobo (Spartanburgh) indicates Samuel Bobo was the grantor and he was living in Spartanburgh Dist/Co at the time of the transaction; I have chosen to present the places of residence in the following manner: (a) Spartanburgh is used for Spartanburgh Co or Dist, (b) Spartanburgh, SC is used for the town (similarily for other towns--Columbia, SC indicates the town), (c) for other counties or districts in South Carolina, only the name of the district or county is given--Laurens Dist--and the "SC" is omitted, (d) for districts, counties, or cities outside South Carolina, the name of the county or city is followed by the state--Rutherford Co, NC;
(5) following the grantor and the word "to" is the grantee's name and place of residence; "(same)" indicates grantor and grantee were from the same county;
(6) the body of the abstract follows beginning with the amount paid and the number of acres (if given); semicolons have been used to separate phrases or parts of the description of the land; there has been no effort to use complete sentences in the description; this was done primarily to conserve space; the order in which I have tried to present the description is: (a) the amount paid (dollars or pounds), (b) the number of acres sold, (c) the creek or branch or river on which the land was located, (d) the bounding property owners, (e) the title chain beginning with the original grant (if given), (f) any additional information. "(ac omitted)" or "(money omitted)" imply the number of acres or amount of money were not indicated. Unfortunately, sometimes very little beside the purchase price and number of acres was given in the deed;
(7) the names of witnesses are given next; I didn't try to indicate which witness signed his name and which witness signed with "his mark"; there appeared to be very little variation in the "marks" from one person to the next--most were very similar to an "X".
(8) the name of the grantor is given next as he signed it--his signed name or name followed by "his mark"; occasionally a wife will make her mark even though she is mentioned nowhere in the body of the deed (and may not have given a dower renunciation); in these cases, "Elizabeth's mark" was typed since her last name was the same as her husband's.

(9) the witness oath is given next--place (if different from Spartanburgh), witness' name, name of the judge who listened and signed, and the date; most of the time this was one of the witnesses in (6) above; witness oaths are not given for every deed because they were not regularily recorded until about Book B p. 281; occasionally a judge would "certify" he had witnessed the transaction in which case only the judge's name and the date are given;
(10) the date recorded in the deed book is given next; these dates start regularily about Book B p. 430;
(11) dower renunciation is given next--name of wife (or mother), name of judge, and the date; dower rights were the wife's rights to the property by state law and do not always indicate she originally owned the property; there should have been a dower to renounce every time a man with a wife (or perhaps mother) sold property; the dowers are not recorded in anywhere near that frequency (unless a large percentage of babies were born in Spartanburg County without female help); this lack of information is unfortunate;
(12) the titles JP (justice of the peace) and JQ (justice of Quarterly Sessions Court) have been omitted; it should be understood that the person listening to the witness oath or dower oath was (or should have been) a JP or JQ. Abbreviations which are used include--SSD, sheriff of Spartanburg Dist, SM, Spartanburg Magistrate, and SAD, sheriff of Abbeville Dist.

The deeds in this book were recorded in books from about 1785 to 1827. The money changed hands from 1752 to 1827. Only a few transactions between 1752 and about 1774 are recorded. During this period, the state line was indeterminate. So some transactions may have been recorded in North Carolina (Mecklinburg Co, Tryon Co, etc) even though the land was later judged to be in Spartanburg Co. Some transactions may also have been properly recorded in Charleston, SC. Because of the uncertainty of which state may have claimed the land when it was granted, the governor's name is followed by the state if the governor was from outside South Carolina.

As would be expected, most of the land described is in present day Spartanburg and Cherokee Counties which comprised the old Spartanburg County. Some land is in Union Co. which was, for a time, part of Spartanburgh Dist. Also there is land on the boundary between Spartanburg and Union or Greenville Counties. However, for some reason, there are also a few deeds for land in Pendleton Dist, Edgefield Dist, and various other districts in South Carolina, land in North Carolina (primarily Rutherford Co), Tennessee, and Georgia. The transactions are not restricted to selling land. There are sales of Negro slaves, household articles (when the whole house and contents are sold), a few apprenticeships (Book B p. 404), bonds given for the first set of judges and sheriffs of the county, the sale of a cotton mill (or manufacturing company) (Book T p. 282), and even a few stills (for liquid corn). There are various ways in which land was sold--the usual exchange of money, a deed of gift, a mortgage, or a sheriff's same (Common Pleas Court cases) or Equity Court sales.

The information given in these abstracts is as complete a distillation from the original "legalese" as was possible in the time allotted. Please refer to North Carolina Research Appendix A (by H. F. M. Leary and M. R. Stirewalt) for definitions of legal terms. The reader may wish to consult the microfilm (available at the Greenville County Library, South Carolina Archives in Columbia, and other places) or the original books which are still at the Spartanburg County Court House, Spartanburg, SC. A closer, slower reading of a deed may reveal misinterpretated handwriting or other things of interest to the reader. In some cases, however, there is just a lack of detail in the description of the parcels of land.

INDEX

The following is a brief description of the indexing methods used in this book. As appears to be the custom, the index is of every name appearing in the text with the slaves separated because they are only referred to by one name. The names of the major rivers--Broad, North, South, and Middle Tyger, Enoree, Saluda, and North and South Pacolet--have been omitted because at least one seems to appear on every page of the book. All the creeks and branches have been indexed. Spartanburg Dist or County and the town Spartanburg have not been indexed. Each name appears in the index in its most complete form, i.e. Fortunatus H Legg is listed in the index even though the text may mention him as F. H. Legg or Fortunatus H Legg. The various spellings of creeks and counties have been grouped, as nearly as possible, under the more modern spelling, i.e. Jimmy's or James' Cr instead of Jiemmies, Jimmies, etc, and Laurens Co instead of Lawrence, Laurence, etc

ACKNOWLEDGEMENTS

The author wished to thank the staff of the Gerrnville County Library and especially the librarian and staff of its South Carolina Room for the use of one microfilm reader and replacement of burned out bulbs and the use of their microfilm copy of the Spartanburg Deed Books A through T. He also wishes to thank the staff of the Spartanburg County Registrar of Means Conveyance office for their tolerance of an occasional visitor who needed to look at the original deed books when the microfilm was faded or hard to understand. Also thanks to Debbie Salyor for preparing the map which accompanys this book and to the publisher for having the index typed. It is also necessary to thank The Carolina Herald (and its editors Mrs. Beverly Shuler and Dr. Eugene C Sneary) for publishing my first efforts and various members of the South Carolina Genealogical Society for their encouraging words during the hours of abstracting. Most important, this book would have never reached its present form without the advice, prodding and encouragement of Mrs. A. O. Hendrix. Thanks Jo, I think.

NORTH CAROLINA
MIDDLE TYGER RIVER
NORTH FORK SALUDA RIVER
MUSH CR.
S. TYGER RIVER
CLEAR CR.
PARIS MOUNTAIN
MIDDLE FORK
S. FORK TYGER RIVER
BRUSHY CR.
ROCK CR.
REEDY RIVER
GREENVILLE
BRUSH CR.
LAUREL CR.
HORSEPEN CR.
GREENVILLE COUNTY
REEDY FORK
GOLDEN GROVE CR.
REEDY RIVER
SALUDA RIVER
MOUNTAIN CR.

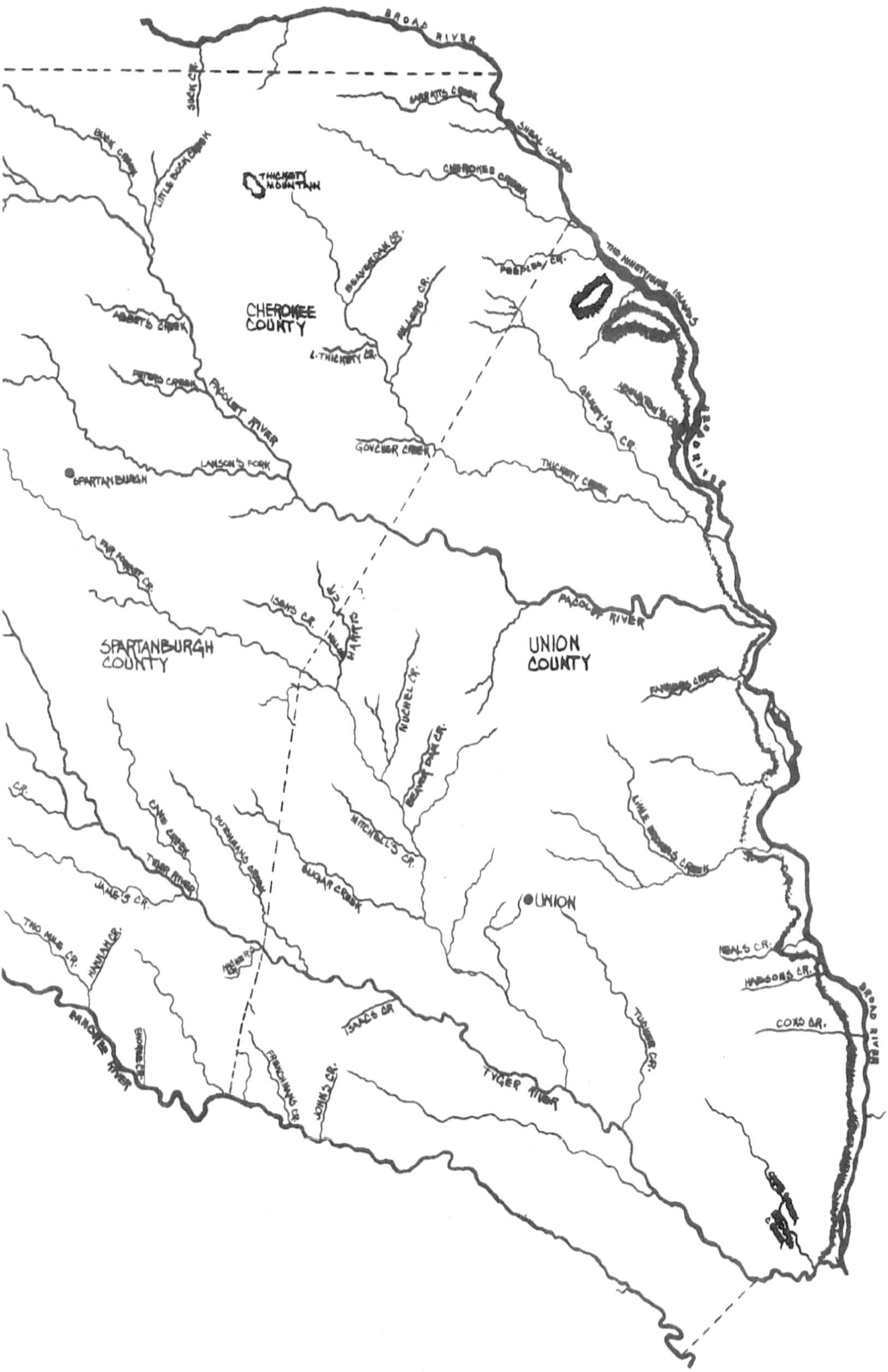

BROAD RIVER
SUCK CR.
BUCK CREEK
LITTLE BUCK CREEK
THICKETY MOUNTAIN
CHEROKEE CREEK
BEAVERDAM CR.
PEOPLES CR.
THE NINETY-NINE ISLANDS
CHEROKEE COUNTY
L. THICKETY CR.
PETERS CREEK
PACOLET RIVER
GILKEY'S CR.
GONCHER CREEK
THICKETY CREEK
LAWSON'S FORK
SPARTANBURGH
FAIR FOREST CR.
ISBENS CR.
PACOLET RIVER
UNION COUNTY
SPARTANBURGH COUNTY
NUCHEL CR.
BEAVER DAM CR.
MITCHELL'S CR.
CANE CREEK
SUGAR CREEK
TYGER RIVER
JANE'S CR.
UNION
TWO MILE CR.
HANNAH CR.
NEALS CR.
HADSONS CR.
COXS CR.
ISAACS CR.
JOHNS CR.
FRENCHMANS CR.
TYGER RIVER
TUCKER CR.
BROAD RIVER

Book A 1785-1787

p. 1-3 Nov. 8, 1785 Charles Moore (Spartanburgh) yoeman to Thomas Moore, son of Charles (same) yoeman; for 1£ 5s sterling sold (1) 150 ac grant Aug. 11, 1784 by the King to Charles Moore; border: W-North fork Tyger R; and (2) 300 ac; part of two grants--(a) May 13, 1763 to Charles Moore and (b) Aug. 11, 1774 to Charles Moore; border: S-Richard Barry, W-vacant, N-Andrew Barry and land sold to Thomas Bullion, and E-N fork Tyger R. Witness by Thomas Moon, Wm Ford and Richard Barry. Signed Cha Moore

p. 3-6 Feb. 10, 1785 William Wood (96 Dist) to Thomas Williamson (96 Dist); for 75£ Virginia money and 10s SC money sold 440 ac below the Fair Forest line; border: S-William Wood, and other sides vacant; where William Wood now lives; grant Jan. 28, 1785 Gov. Benjamin Guarrard to William Wood. Witness by William Williamson, Rebekah Wood, and Moses Wood. Signed William Wood's mark.

p. 6-10 Oct. 14, 1785 John Patton (Camden Dist, York Co) to Zadok Ford (Spartanburgh); for 388£ 17s 9p 3f SC money sold 600 ac on S side Broad R and both sides of Kings R; grant Jun. 29, 1753 Gov. Matthew Rowan (NC) to Samuel Gulkey in Anson Co, NC and recorded in SC Book L #11, p 92 and sold Jan. 9, 1755 to John Dickinson who sold to John Patton. Witness Duncan McCrowen (?), Thomas Brandon, and Christopher Brandon. Signed John Patton

p. 10-11 Jan. 20, 1784 Thomas Farrow (96 Dist) to Samuel and William Farrows (96 Dist); for "good causes and valuable considerations" sold 300 ac on Cedar Shoal Cr branch on N side Enoree R; grant to Henry Hamilton who sold to John Farrow, desc, and to Thomas Farrow, John's son, by heirship; buyers "not to molest my mother Rosanna Farrow while she lives on the land". Witness Mary Waters and Thomas W. Waters. Signed Thomas Farrow

p. 11-14 Jan. 7, 1785 David Cook (96 Dist) to Michael Sprinkle (96 Dist); for 50£ sterling sold 136 ac on Fairforrest and Buffalloe lick Crs; border: W-a corner John Gibbs sold to Peter Elder; grant "by a North Right reference to King's Records in that State" to Giles Tittet who evidently sold to John Gibbs, sr, desc, who sold to David Cook. Witness John Smith, Robin Head, and Ephriam Elder. Signed David Cook

p. 14-17 Jun. 22, 1784 John Elder, planter (settlement of Tyger R, 96 Dist) to Samuel Farrow, gentn (settlement of Enoree, 96 Dist); for 200£ sterling sold 450 ac; border: NW, NE, and S-Daniel Huger, and S-William Williamson; grant Aug. 14, 1775 Gov. William Campbel to John Elder in Craven Co on Brown's Cr of Broad R. Witness Andrew Thomson and Phillemon Waters, sr. Signed John Elder and wife Mary's mark

p. 17-21 Oct. 29, 1776 Henry Hamilton and wife Agness (settlement of Enoree R) to John Farrow (same); for 350£ 5s SC money sold 300 ac in Barkley Co on Cedar Shoals Cr of Enoree R; border: SE-John Stone and vacant, N and other sides-vacant; grant Jul. 21, 1770 Gov. Chas G. Montague to Henry Hamilton. Witness Thomas Farrow, Joshua Collins, and James Head. Signed Henry Hamilton and Agness' mark

p. 21-23 The following transaction is marked out; the information is from the lease since the release was never recorded: Mar. 5, 1779 Matthew Tate, eldest son and heir of Joseph Tate (late of Lancaster Co, Penn.) to James Lusk (Thickety Cr); for 5s SC money leased 432 ac on Fairforrest Cr; border: N-Shands Goteghtly, E-Moses Foster and John Thomas, S-Henry White, and

W-Handcock Smith and Peter Smith. Witness James McCleveane, John Thompson, and Andrew Thompson. Signed Matt Tate

p. 23-27 Nov. 29, 1785 Samuel Porter (Spartanburgh) to Uriah Conner (same); for 100 guineas sold 313 ac on N side Saluda R on Golden Grove Cr; border: W-Capt. William Wood, E-Maj. Bowie, and NE and NW-vacant; grant Jan. 21, 1785 Gov. Benjamin Guarrard to Samuel Porter. Witness Maximillian Conner and John Conner. Signed Samuel Porter and Anne Porter

p. 27-29 Mar. 20, 1786 Joseph Wofford (Spartanburgh) to William Linch; for 100£ SC money sold 100 ac on Patterson's Br on N fork Saluda R; border: SE-Robert Henderson and others vacant; grant Jan. 28, 1785 Gov. Benjamin Guerard to JW. Witness George Roebuck and James Wofford. Signed Joseph Wofford

p. 29-31 Dec. 29, 1784 John Walker (Camden Dist) to Jesse Connell (96 Dist); for 80£ 10s sterling sold 175 ac that is ½ of land on Fairforest called McClure's tract; border: Robert Walker who sold to David Golightly; grant by NC Right (see King's Records of NC) to Arthur McClure. Witness John Smith, Robert Walker, and Frances Connell. Signed John Walker

p. 31-35 Jan. 31, 1785 Austin Clayton and wife Katherine (96 Dist) to George Newman (same); for 50£ 2s sterling sold 200 ac; border: E-Tygar R, SE-George Newman and vacant, W-Benjamin Wofford, SW-a branch; part of 300 ac grant Oct. 15, 1784 to Austin Clayton. Witness Thomas Tod and Jonathan Lenard. Signed Austin and Katherine Clayton's marks

p. 35-39 Oct. 4, 1785 William Dickson (Duptin Co, NC) to Thomas Farrar (Spartanburgh); for 60£ NC money sold 300 ac on head branch of Fairforest Cr middle grounds of Tygar R and Pacolate R; border--John Prince; grant Oct. 26, 1767 George III via Gov. Wm Tryon (NC) to William Dickson; recorded first in Mecklinburg Co, NC and on Apr. 28, 1773 in SC. Witness Mary Slavaul (?), James Poole, and Curtis Turry. Signed William Dickson

p. 39-42 Nov. 10, 1785 Daniel Symms (Spartanburgh, 96 Dist) to Thomas Wadsworth and William Turpin (Charleston Co), merchants; for 100£ 5s sterling and SC money sold 640 ac East of ancient boundary on Green's Cr branch of Lawson's Fork waters of Pacolet R; border: S-William Brandon, E-Mr. Wilcock and Mr. Nevil, and others vacant; grant May 2, 1785 Gov. William Moultrie to Daniel Symms. Witness John Thomas, jr and Patrick McDowall. Signed Daniel Symmes

p. 42-44 Mar. 24, 1785 Gov. William Moultrie appoints the following Justices of the Peace for Spartanburgh Co: Bayles Earle, John Thomas, jr, Henry White, John Ford, James Jordan, William Wood and Henry Machan Wood. Refer to legislative act of Mar. 24, 1785

p. 44-45 Sept. 19, 1785 a bond of 1000£ SC money for John Young to be clerk of court. Bond secured by John Thomas, jr, Richard Harrison, William Prince, and William Smith.

p. 45 Sept. 19, 1785 a bond of 1500£ sterling (to be paid in gold or silver specie at the rate of 4s 8p per dollar or 1£ 1s 9p per guinea) for William Young to be sherriff of Spartanburgh Co. Bond secured by William Young, John Young, sr, and William Wood.

p. 45-46 Sept. 20, 1785 William Neel (Spartanburgh) to Daniel Jackson (Union CO); for 200£ sterling sold three Negroes: woman Lue, girl Riner, and boy Limas; also the following: a feather bed and furniture, a wagon and gear, a white horse (branded). Witness John Motlow and Wm Prince. Signed Wm Neal

p. 46-50 May 20, 1779 Nathaniel Miller (formerly 96 Dist) to John Miller (late of Cumberland Co, Pa and now of 96 Dist); for 1550£ SC money sold 116 ac on N side of N fork Tygar R on Lawson's Cr; border: E-John Miller (desc), S-the River, W-Samuel Neely, and N-vacant; grant May 30, 1763 Gov. Thomas Boone to Robert Miller and given to Robert's son Nathaniel Miller (see will of Robert). Witness Thomas Bullin, Thomas Moore, and Andrew Thomson. Signed Nathaniel Miller

p. 50-53 Mar. 18, 1786 Jesse Connell (Spartanburgh) to George Connell (same); for 100£ 10s sold 250 ac that is half of 500 ac where Jesse Connell and George Connell now live on E side of Fairforrest Cr; grant Dec. 24, 1770 Gov. Wm Tryon (NC) to Jesse Connell (500 ac). Witness Henry Wells, David Golightly, and William Fort. Signed Jesse Connell and his wife Anne

p. 53-55 Oct. 19, 1785 Benjamin Wofford and wife Mary and Burwell Thomson and wife Ann (Spartanburgh) to Henry Meridith (same); for 300£ sterling sold 500 ac a part of 600 ac on both sides of Enoree R and W of 100 ac sold on N side of Enoree R to Matthew Couch; land on N side of River in Spartanburgh Co and land on S side of River in Laurens Co; border: Matthew Couch and Fort Shoal; grant Mar. 26, 1755 Gov. Arthur Dobbs (NC) to Thomas Irwin who sold on May 11, 1755 to Bartlett Brown. Witness James Allison and John Couch. Signed Benjamin and Mary Wofford and Burwell and Ann Thomson

p. 55-58 Mar. 8, 1785 Austin Clayton and wife Katherine (96 Dist) to Stephen Wilson, farmer (96 Dist); for 100£ 1s sterling sold 100 ac on S side Tryon R; border: NW-Benjamin Wofford, SW-Richard Young, SE-George Newman, and NE-a branch; part of 300 ac grant Oct. 15, 1784 to Austin Clayton. Witness William Harris and Rubin Newman. Signed Austin and Katherine Clayton's marks

p. 58-61 Feb. 14, 1786 Thomas Tod and wife Ann (Spartanburgh) to Tilman Bobo (same); for 50£ 1s sterling sold 500 ac on Cedar Shoals Cr-Enoree R; border: NE-Christopher Casey and James McDowall, NW-vacant, SE-Nathaniel Kellan (Kellon) and vacant; grant Jun. 15, 1775 Lt. Gov. Wm Bull to Thomas Tod. Witness Wm Clayton and Edward Hooker. Signed Thomas and Ann Todd

p. 61-63 Mar. 17, 1786 James Fanning and wife Elizabeth (Thickety Cr, Spartanburgh) to William Lipscomb (same); for 50£ SC money sold 27¼ ac on Thickety Cr; grant Mar. 8, 1763 Gov. Bull to James Fanning. Witness Wm Thomson, Phil Martin, Isham Lafote, Daniel Joslen, and Jeremiah Thomson. Signed James and Elizabeth Fanning

p. 63-66 Mar. 28, 1786 court is held at plantation of John Woods; present are John Ford, James Jordan, and Henry M Wood. The following transaction was proved: Dec. 23, 1785 Samuel Bell (Spartanburgh) to Sampson Bobo (same); for 500£ 10s SC money sold 200 ac on Cedar Shoals Cr-Enoree R; border: vacant and NE-unknown; grant Sept. 25, 1763 Gov. Charles Granville Montague to Samuel Cannon (land in Craven Co) and sold by Samuel Cannon and wife Lide to Samuel Bell on Aug. 15 & 17, 1776 for 500£ SC money. Witness Burwell Bobo, Thos Tod, and Joseph Howell. Signed Samuel Bell

p. 66-69 May 23, 1786 court is held at plantation of John Wood; present are Bayles Earle, James Jordan, and Henry M. Wood. The following transaction is proved: Sept. 5, 1782 Nathaniel Miller (Craven Co) to Robert Miller (same); for 100 guineas SC money sold 160 ac on Middle and N fork Tyger R; grant May 30, 1763 by the King to Robert Miller and to Nathaniel Miller by the will of Robert Miller, his father. Witness John Nicoll, John Berry, and Andrew Thomson. Signed Nathaniel Miller

p. 69-71 Dec. 30, 1785 Thomas Tod and wife Ann (Spartanburgh) to Edward Musgrove (Laurens Co); for 32£ 2s SC money sold 100 ac on Enoree R; former owner Wm Cox, desc, sold land to John Briggs, desc, and Thomas Tod bought land from Thos Briggs, heir of John Briggs. Witness George Roebuck and John Roebuck. Signed Thomas Tod and Anne Tod

p. 71-73 Jul. 14, 1785 John Timmons (Spartanburgh) to Abner Timmons, son of John (same); for love and affection sold 150 ac on N side Brown's Br; part of 1000 ac where John Timmons now lives and in possession of Abner Timmons. Witness David Goodlett, William Goodlett, and Frances Howel. Signed John Timmons

p. 73-76 Jan. 11, 1786 Samuel Langston (state of Ga) and wife Sarah, John Stanford and wife Rachal, heirs of Reuben Young (late of Tygar R, 96 Dist) to Thomas Tod (96 Dist); for 50£ sterling and 2s Ga money sold 200 ac on S side Tygar R; border: N-Tygar R, E-James Spears, S-estate of Edward Arnett, W-Thomas Tod; grant to Phillip Mulkie and sold to Reuben Young. Witness Wm Clayton, Edward Hooker, and Hezekiah Bussey. Signed Samuel Langston, Sarah's mark, John Stanford, and Rachal's mark

p. 76-79 Oct. 2, 1782 Nathaniel Miller (96 Dist) to Robert Miller (same); for 50£ and 50 guineas sold 80 ac between Middle and North fork Tygar R; part of 100 ac grant Dec. 22, 1768 Gov. William Tryon (NC) to Nathaniel Miller; border: E-Nathaniel Miller. Witness John Nicoll, John Barry, Andrew Thomson. Signed Nathaniel Miller

p. 79-82 Mar. 20, 1785 Thomas Tod and wife Ann to John Thomas, sr, esq (all of Spartanburgh), commissioner for locations on N side Saluda R; for 146£ 2s sterling sold 440 ac on S fork Tygar R; most of 640 ac grant Jan. 21, 1785 to Maj. Parsons; border: E-John Thomas, sr, S-S fork Tygar R; the river divides it from the other 200 ac including land where Maj. Parsons now lives. Witness Samuel Porter and George Roebuck. Signed Thomas and Ann Tod

p. 82-85 Jan. 17, 1785 Martin Armstrong (96 Dist) to Richard Harrison (same); for 100£ sterling and 10s SC money sold 200 ac on both sides of Fairforrest Cr; border: Robert Dugan; grant Oct. 26, (?) Gov. William Tryon (NC) to Thomas Case who sold to Martin Armstrong. Witness Wm Wood,JP. Signed Martin Armstrong

p. 85-89 Apr. 21, 1785 William Benson (Spartanburgh) to Richard Harrison (same); for 50£ 10s SC money sold 200 ac on both sides of Fairforrest Cr; border: E-land disputed between Thomas Dugan and John Golightly, S-John Golightly, W-Richard Harrison; grant Gov. Charles Montague to Archd. Robinson and by renewal of grant (?) to William Benson. Witness John Holcom and Thomas Wingo. Signed Wm Benson

p. 89-93 Jan. 5, 1785 James Bruton (96 Dist) to Thomas Williamson (same); for 60£ sterling and 10s SC money sold 132 ac on Ferguson's Cr waters of Tygar R; border: N-David Bruton, S-by "north land", and others vacant; contains place where James Bruton now lives; E part of 200 ac grant (in Craven Co) Feb. 12, 1776 Gov. Charles Granville Montague to James Bruton. Witness John Ford,

William Ford, and William Williamson. Signed James Bruton

p. 93-98 Jun. 5, 1785 James Bruton (96 Dist) to Thomas Williamson (same); for 65£ sterling and 10s SC money sold 300 ac on S side Tygar R and N fork Furgeson's Cr; border: James Bussel; grant Mar. 13, 1756 Gov. Athur Dobbs (NC) to Alexander Foguson (Ferguson) in Anson Co (now SC) on S side Little R and N fork of Antigouorum (?) Cr now called Tygar R and Ferguson's Cr; sold to James Bruton Jun. 12, 1784. Witness John Ford, William Ford, and William Williamson. Signed James Bruton

p. 98-101 Jun. 1, 1786 James Jordan (Spartanburgh) to George Debors (same); for 40£ sterling sold 150 ac on N side Lawson's fork waters of Pacolate R; border: Jonathan Newman; grant for 300 ac on both sides Lawson's Fork on May 4, 1769 Gov. Wm Tryon (NC) to Robert Henderson who sold on Dec. 23, 1773 to James Jordan; release shows James Jordan sold to heirs of Robert Bishop, desc, with George Debours' name marked out. Witness none. Signed James Jordan

p. 101-104 Aug. 1, 1783 William Wofford (NC) to Willis Griffith (96 Dist); for 100£ 5s sterling sold 200 ac on both sides Lawson's Fork "including a mill seat deemed to be in Tryon Co, NC"; grant Nov. 25, 1771 (?) Gov. Josiah Martin (NC) to James Hammett. Witness Jas Ainworth, Arthur Crocker, Ginnouisun (?) Pyend, and Amos Space. Signed William Wofford

p. 104-109 Nov. 14, 1785 Thomas Briggs (son of John Briggs, late of Enoree, 96 Dist, desc) (Edgecomb Co, NC) and wife Katherine to Thomas Tod (Spartanburgh); for 80£ 4s sterling sold 200 ac and grist mill; property of John Briggs, miller of Enoree; one tract--100 ac N side Enoree R sold by Wm Cox, desc, to John Briggs and where John lived and Thomas Briggs lives; second tract--100 ac in Union Co on N side Enoree R opposide land surveyed for Wm Briggs and granted to John Briggs. Witness Edward Musgrove, Thomas Layton, and Westwood Waters. Signed Thomas and Katherine Briggs' marks

p. 109-110 Jul. 28, 1786 Edward Dickson (Duplin Co, NC) to Bagel Lee (Spartanburgh); for 50£ NC money sold 100 ac on S side Lawson's Fork of Pacolate R; border: S-formerly owned by Alexander Dickson. Witness Dirkerd Grand, Alexr. Dickson, and Joseph Dickson. Signed Edward Dickson

p. 110-113 __?__ 1786 James McDowall and wife Mary (Laurens Co) to Richard Fryar (Spartanburgh); for 57£ 12s 10p SC money sold 150 ac on Cedar Shoals Cr waters of Enoree R; grant May 20, 1768 Gov. Ch. Granville Monte (SC) to James McDowall; border vacant at time of grant. Witness Thomas Gorman and John Couch. Signed James and Mary McDowall's marks

p. 113-117 Jul. 8, 1786 William McKowan (Union Co) to William Tate, sr (Spartanburgh); for 150£ 10s sterling sold 250 ac on Cherokee Cr and S side of main Broad R; border: SE-Alexr Martin, esq, NE-John Fendrin, and others vacant; grant Apr. 21, 1775 Gov. William Bull to William McKowan; release mentions William's wife Martha. Witness Michael Hogan, Reubin Blanton, and Wm Tate, jr. Signed William McKowan and Martha's mark

p. 117-120 Nov. 8, 1785 Joseph Morris, farmer (SC) to William Morris, sr; for __?__ £ sterling and 10s SC money sold 60 ac on both sides Buck Cr of Pacolate R; grant May 22, 1772 Gov. Josiah Martin (NC) to John Kircinnell 200 ac in Tryon Co (now Spartanburgh Co) and bordering: S-Robert Nilson and others vacant; later sold by John Kircinnell to Joseph Morris. Witness Necodimus

Thomson, John Morris, and William Morriss, jr. Signed Joseph and Jemima Morris' marks

p. 120-122 Jan. 23, 1782 Jesse Tate (96 Dist) to John Arnold (96 Dist); for 200£ SC money sold 300 ac on Big and Little Cherokee Cr; where John Arnold now lives; part of 800 ac grant to Wm Downs who sold in 1775 to George Blanton who sold to Jesse Tate; land sold is W part of grant. Witness Charles Hester and Henry Robinson. Signed John Arnold's mark

p. 122-125 Jun. 13, 1786 Thomas Garvin (96 Dist) to Thomas Wadsworth and William Turpin, merchants (Charleston, SC); for 50£ 10s sterling SC money sold 195 ac on both sides Camp Br of Lawson's Fork; border: N-Edmond Bishop, SE-Robert McMurdy, and others vacant; grant Jan. 21, 1785 Gov. Benjamin Guerrard to Thomas Garvin. Witness Daniel Symmes and Thomas Farrar. Signed Thomas and Jane Garvin's marks

p. 125-128 Jun. 1, 1786 Peggy Lewis (Spartanburgh) to Thomas Wadsworth and William Turpin, merchants (Charleston, SC); for 100£ 5s SC money sold 400 ac on Enoree R; border: N-Moore, W-Smith, and others vacant; grant Nov. 7, 1785 from Gov. William Moultrie to Peggy Lewis. Witness Thomas Farrar and Isaiah Lewis. Signed Peggy Lewis

p. 128-131 Jun. 2, 1786 John Clemons (96 Dist) to Thomas Wadsworth and William Turpin, merchants (Charleston, SC); for 100£ (?)s sterling SC money sold 344 ac on Peters Cr of Cherokee Cr of Pacolate R; border: vacant; grant Jul. 4, 1785 Gov. William Moultrie to John Clemons. Witness Danl Symmes and Thomas Benson. Signed John and Mary Clemons' marks

p. 131-134 Jun. 1, 1785 Polly Lewis (Spartanburgh) to Daniel Symmes (same); for 300£ 5s sterling SC money sold 640 ac in two tracts both on N side of Saluda R and S fork of Brushy Cr of Reedy R; (a) 320 ac border vacant and granted Nov. 7, 1785 Gov. William Moultrie to Polly Lewis; (b) 320 ac border: S-Chandler and others vacant; granted Nov. 7, 1785 Gov. William Moultrie to Polly Lewis. Witness Thomas Farrar and Isaiah Lewis. Signed Polly Lewis

P. 134-137 Nov. 15, 1783 William Nevel (Green R, NC) to Christaphor Long (Lawson's Fork of Pacolate R); for 20£ SC money sold 150 ac on N side of Lawson's Fork; part of 300 ac where William Nevel lives; grant May 15, 1772 Gov. Josiah Martin (NC) to William Nevel in Tryon Co. Witness Henry Hays, George Devors, and Gabriel Moffatt. Signed William Nevil. Witness oath Aug. 27, 1785 George Devors to William Wood, JP

p. 137-138 Sept. 19, 1786 Israel Morris (Spartanburgh) to James Jordan; for 80£ sterling sold a Negro man Peter of Cromateo (?) Nation 19 years old 5' 8". Witness none. Signed Israel Morris

p. 138-141 Apr. 25, 1786 John McCullock (Charleston, SC) to Spencer Bobo (Spartanburgh); for 100£ 15s sterling sold 150 ac between Enoree and Tygar R; border: NE-Sampson Bobo, S-Moses Casey and William Whitaker; part of 1000 ac grant to James Sample and sold to John McCullock. Witness Sampson Bobo, Jas Casey, and Burrell Bobo. Signed John McCullock

p. 141-142 Oct. 27, 1784 James Holland (NC) to Thomas Davis (96 Dist); for _?_ sold a Negro woman Dinah. Witness Henry Moffatt and Sarah Bird. Signed James Holland

p. 142-145 Dec. 8, 1786 Edmund Bishop (Spartanburgh) to William Bishop (same); for 100£ 5s sterling SC money sold 250 ac on Lawson's Fork of Pacolate R; border: NE-Robert McMurdy, E-vacant and Moultrie, W-vacant and Wm Dickson; grant Jan. 21, 1785 Gov. Benjamin Guerrard to Edmund Bishop. Witness Stephen Miller, William Messkelly, and John Bishop. Signed Edmund and Ama Bishop

p. 145-147 Nov. 5, 1785 John Kirkonnell (NC) to Joseph Morris (SC); for 55£ 10s NC money sold 200 ac on both sides Buck Cr of Pacolate R; grant May 22, 1770 Gov. Josiah Martin (NC) to John Kirkonnell then bordering N-Robert Nelson and vacant. Witness Daniel Gilbert and John Morris. Signed John Kirkonnell

p. 147-150 Sept. 6, 1785 John Mapp (96 Dist) to John Atkison (96 Dist); for 50£ 7s 3p sterling SC money sold 247 ac on both sides Gooher Cr; border: NW-David Allen, SE-late John Anderson, desc, and others not known. Witness Lewis Tanner and Jonathan Gilkey. Signed John Mapp

p. 150-153 May 9, 1786 Joseph Wofford (96 Dist) to Thomas Brown (96 Dist); for 80£ 10s sterling sold 175 ac on S side Pacolate R including the mouth of Rich Land Cr; grant Apr. 2, 1768 Gov. William Tryon (NC) to Joseph Wofford; release mentions "Capt" Joseph Wofford and wife Martha. Witness John Brown and James Wofford. Signed Joseph Wofford and Martha's mark

p. 153-156 Sept. 17, 1786 Nicholas Jasper (Union Co, 96 Dist) to Peter Howard (Spartanburgh); for 40£ 10s sold 200 ac on both sides Tygar R; border: N-Thomas Davis; grant Jan. 21, 1785 Gov. Benjamin Guerrard to Nicholas Jasper. Witness Nevil Wayland and John Thomas. Signed Nicholas Jasper

p. 156-159 Dec. 15, 1786 William Sterling and wife Jannet (Spartanburgh) to Thomas Cearey; for 20£ 10s SC money sold 150 ac; border: Alexander Elder, Samuel Morrow, and John Elder; part of 350 ac grant Apr. 3, 1786 Gov. William Moultrie to William Sterling. Witness John Elder and Andrew Thomson. Signed William Sterling and Jannet's mark

p. 159-161 Oct. 14, 1785 Benjamin Brown, heir of Bartlett Brown, desc, of Burk Co, Ga, to Henry Hammilton (96 Dist); for 30£ sterling sold 200 ac on N side Enoree R; part of two tracts: (a) 600 ac and (b) 400 ac bordering Jacob Pennington and granted May 11, 1753 Gov. Matthew Rowen (NC) to Bartlett Brown. Witness Andrew Cunningham, John Lindsey, and Abraham Gray. Signed Benjamin Brown

p. 161-164 Oct. 25, 1783 James Jordan (96 Dist) to Thomas Davis (same); for 210£ SC money sold 200 ac on both sides of Tyger R; border: Jonathan Newman; grant Oct. 28, 1767 Gov. William Tryon (NC) to David Davis and wife Eloner who sold Jan. 4, 1772 to Henry Hurtle who sold Feb. 17, 1775 to James Jordan. Witness Bayles Earle and Nevil Wayland. Signed Thomas Jordan

p. 164-167 May 24, 1786 John Pedan (Fairfield Co) to John Tippins (96 Dist); for 30£ 10s SC money sold 150 ac on branch of Furguson's Cr; border: NE and SW-Thomas Pendan and vacant; grant Mar. 17, 1775 Lt. Gov. Wm Bull to John Pendan. Witness Samuel Pendan and David Pendan. Signed John Pendan's mark

p. 167-169 May 10, 1785 John Elder (96 Dist) to Alexander Elder (same); for 110 guineas sold "all horses, cows, beds, pots, pewter, and household goods" that John Elder now possesses. Witness Robert Elder and Thomas Clary. Signed John Elder

p. 169-172 Oct. 24, 1785 Uriah Conner (Spartanburgh) to Jeremiah Dutton (same); for 200£ sterling sold 300 ac on both sides Tygar R; land is known "by the name Kings improvement"; border: S-Robert Nelson; where Solomon King now lives; grant Jan. 21, 1785 Gov. Benjamin (Guerrard?) to Uriah Conner. Witness John Conner and Maximilliam Conner. Signed Uriah and Margret Conner

p. 172-174 Oct. 18, 1785 Benjamin Brown (Burk Co, Ga), heir of Bartlett Brown, desc, to Mary Hannah, widow of Robert Hannah, desc; for 50£ sterling sold 200 ac; part of 600 ac on N side of Enoree R formerly Kings R; grant May 11, 1753 Gov. Matthew Rowan (NC) to Bartlet Brown, sr; border: Mary Hannah, NE-Jacob Pennington. Witness John Lindsey, Henry Hammitton, and Peter Hammitton. Signed Benjamin Brown

p. 174-177 Dec. 30, 1784 Richard Chesney (96 Dist) to Paul Castleberry (96 Dist); for 50£ Va money 10s SC money sold 150 ac on Jemison's Cr of Tygar R between Broad and Saluda R forks; border John Highlers and vacant; grant Nov. 20, 1772 Gov. Chas Granville Montague to (not given). Witness Richd. Chesney, jr, and Wm Earnest. Signed Richard Chesney's mark and Jane's mark

p. 177-181 Feb. 25, 1786 John Hightown, minister, and wife Christiana (Spartanburgh) to Thomas Jourdan (same); for 16£ 10s sterling sold 75 ac on N side of Buck Cr; grant Jan. 21 (or 25), 1785 Gov. Benjamin Guerrard to John Hightown 150 ac near John Hightown's mill; border John Hightown. Witness Wm Morris and Abraham Cantral. Signed John and Christiana Hightown

p. 181-182 Mar. 15, 1787 Thomas Tod (Tygar R, Spartanburgh) to William Swanson (Blackwater R, Franklin Co, Va), blacksmith; power of attorney to get a Negro woman Nan (Thomas Tod's property) purchased from Hampton Lillybridge and ran away in Mar. 1778; Nan to be returned (plus cost) from Christopher Harwood (King and Queen Co, Va) who has Nan and holds her for ransom, for prison charges, as Jaillor of King and Queen Co. Signed Thos Tod. Witness oath Mar. 20, 1787 before James Jordan, Richard Harrison, and Obediah Tremier, justices

p. 182-185 Mar. 17, 1787 Joshua Smith and Elizabeth Osheal, his wife (Spartanburgh) to William Swanson (Blackwater R, Franklin Co, Va), blacksmith; power of attorney to obtain from Mr. Jones a tract of land on Shokoe Cr, NC; former owner Danl Osheal who sold by gift to Elizabeth Osheal, daughter of Sarah Walker and now wife of Joshua Smith, by deed recorded in Granville Co, NC; William Swanson also empowered to sell land; Sarah Osheal signs statement that she is mother of Elizabeth Osheal Smith and Joshua Smith is Elizabeth's only husband. Witness Sarah Osheal, Joseph Wofford, and Thos Tod. Signed Joshua and Elizabeth Smith's marks. Witness oath before James Jordan, Richard Harrison, and Obediah Trimier, justices

p. 185-188 Mar. 18, 1787 John Golightly (Spartanburgh) to Shands Golightly (same); for 30£ 5s sold 100 ac on both sides of Fairforrest Cr; border: S-James Lusk, W-Peter Smith, N-Shands Golightly, and E-Moses Foster(?). Witness none. Signed John Golightly

p. 188-189 Mar. 10, 1787 Article of agreement between Robert Evens (Rutherford Co, NC), Vardry McBee and William Young (Spartanburgh), and Tabez Evens (Rutherford Co, NC); on Jun. 13, 1786, a survey was made of 402 ac on Shoals Cr of N Pacolet R "supposed to be a copper mine"; all the above to be joint partners and Robert Evens to make good title to land; there is a bond of 10,000 pounds sterling to aid Robert Evens and land can only be sold by mutual agreement. Witness George Henning, Rhoda McBee, and Matthias McBee. Signed Robert Evens, Vardry McBee, William Young, and Tabez Evens

p. 189-190 May 10, 1785 Francis Ballinger (96 Dist) to Leonard Adcock (same); for 100£ Va money "of SC" sold 200 ac on N side Pacolet R; border: Leonard Adcock and John Larkey. Witness Wm Wood, Margret Wood, and John Ballinger. Signed Francis Ballinger's mark

p. 190-194 Jan. 18, 1787 Stephen Vaughan (Rutherford Co, NC) to Alexander Walker (Spartanburgh); for 90£ 10s SC money sold 361 ac on Fairforrest Cr near its head; border: E-David Goodlett and Isham Foster, S-Thos Wyatt, W-Thomas Farrar, and N-William Foster; grant Mar. 6, 1766 Gov. William Moultrie to Stephen Vaughan. Witness Isham Foster, William Foster, and John Walker. Signed Stephen Vaughan

p. 194-197 Dec. 23, 1786 John Ford, esq (Spartanburgh) to James White (same); for 20s SC money sold 2/3 of 400 ac on Tates Br; the 2/3 is on SW side of the 400 ac; grant Apr. 27, 1767 NC governor to James Tillett (?) and regranted Sept. 1774 by Gov. William Bull. Witness Charles Bruce, Samuel Porter, Henry White, and Jesse Connell. Signed John Ford and Ann's mark

p. 197-199 Jul. 5, 1786 Robert Evens (Rutherford Co, NC) to Bayles Earle (Spartanburgh); for 100£ sterling sold 400 ac on both sides of Brutess Cr, a branch of N Pacolet R. Witness Felix Walker and Samuel Earle. Signed Robert Evens

p. 199-201 Jun. 18, 1787 Mary Wood, widow of James Wood, esq, desc. (Spartanburgh) to William Poole (same), iron master; for 500£ 5s sterling sold 400 ac on both sides Lawson's Cr of Pacolate R. Witness Henry White and William Young. Signed Mary Wood

p. 201-203 Sept. 12, 1779 John Earle (NC) to Richard Raburn (SC); for 1000£ SC money sold 200 ac on both sides Lawson's Ford; grant Aug. 31, 1774 Lt. Gov. William Bull to (not given) in Craven Co; border: NW-John Earle, SE-William Nevil, and SE-John Earle. Withess John Anthony and Thomas Rodin. Signed John Earle

p. 203-204 Sept. 12, 1799 John Raburn (SC) to Henry Hays (SC); for 1000£ SC money sold 200 ac on both sides Lawson's Cr; grant Aug. 31, 1774 Lt. Gov. William Bull to John Earle, land then in Craven Co; border: NW-John Earle, SE-William Nevil, and SE-John Earle. Witness Moses Wood and Thomas Hays. Signed John Raburn

p. 204-205 Edward Dickson (Duplin Co, NC) to Zachariah Robison (Spartanburgh); for 75£ NC money sold 200 ac on both sides of Lawson's Fork of Pacolate R "including small improvement above James Alexander's land"; grant Apr. 25, 1767 to Alexander Dickson. Witness Derkin Grant, Joseph Dickson, and Alexr Dickson. Signed Edwd Dickson

p. 205-206 Aug. 19, 1786 Vardry McBee (Thickety Cr, Spartanburgh) to William Rickman (same); for 20£ SC money sold 392 ac on Poplar Cr of Broad R; see survey Feb. 6, 1784 by Thomas Warren. Witness Phillemon Martin, Robert Harper, and Joseph Tanner. Signed Vardry McBee

p. 206-209 Jul. 26, 1785 James Bright and wife Sarah (Spartanburgh) to James Nesbit (same); for 80£ 20s sterling sold 200 ac on S side of Tygar R about 3 mi from Joseph Jones on

Middle Fork Tygar R; ½ of 400 ac grant on both sides of S Fork Tygar R; grant (Mecklinburgh Co, NC) Oct. 26, 1767 Gov. William Tryon (NC) to William Sharp who sold Jan. 18, 1771 to James Bright. Witness Robert Nesbit and Geo. Thomson. Signed James Bright and Sarah's mark

p. 209-212 Dec. 23, 1786 George Connell and wife Frances (Spartanburgh) to John Ford, esq (Saluda R, Spartanburgh); for 10s sterling and 10s SC money sold 153 1/3 ac on Tates Br; joins Tates line and is on SW corner of a 400 ac grant; grant Apr. 27, 1767 by "a NC governor" to James Tillett. Witness Chas. Bruce, Samuel Porter, Henry White, and Jesse Connell. Signed George and Frances Connell

p. 212-214 Jun. 20, 1786 Israel Morris (96 Dist) to Thomas Wadsworth and William Turpin (Charleston, SC); for 100£ 5s sterling sold 200 ac on Buck Br of Fairforrest Cr; border: vacant; grant Jun. 5, 1786 Gov. William Moultrie to Israel Morris. Witness Daniel Symmes and Edmund Walker Clement. Signed Israel Morris and Latta's mark

p. 214-216 Jun. 15, 1786 William Venable (96 Dist) to Daniel Symmes (Spartanburgh); for 100£ 5s sterling SC money sold 457 ac on both sides of Peters Cr of Lawson's Fork of Pacolate R; border: vacant; grant Nov. 20, 1785 Gov. William Moultrie to William Venable. Witness Thos. Farrar and George Petters. Signed William Venable

p. 216-217 Oct. 4, 1786 George Blanton (Rutherford Co, NC) to James Powell (York Co, SC); for 20£ sterling sold 300 ac on W side of Cherokee Dr of Broad R; part of 800 ac grant Jan. 6, 1775 by "SC governor" to William Downs; sold by Downs to George Blanton on Jan. 10, 1775. Witness John Cooper and Nathl Robison. Signed George Blanton

p. 217-220 Sept. 20, 1786 Phillip Gibbs (Wilks Co, Ga) to Henry Ayres (Spartanburgh); for 100£ 10s sterling and SC money sold 200 ac on Fairforrest Cr where Henry Ayres now lives; border: E-Wm Prince, S-Peter Elder, W-Rowland Cornelius, and N-vacant; except for ½ of land where Susannah Gibbs, mother of Phillip Gibbs, now lives and ½ of the orchard to be Susannah's as long as she pleases or lives; John Gibbs, desc, gave his place to his son Phillip Gibbs by a will. Witness Robin Head, Ephraim Elder, and Peter Elder. Signed Phillip and Phebe Gibbs

p. 220 Dec. 5, 1786 Laurens Reddy (96 Dist) to William Poole (same); for 25£ sterling sold 150 ac on N side of Pacolate R "including Troft Shoals and portions of an old Mill Seat"; border: Trembling Shoals Br; grant Nov. 2, 1784. Witness Adam Potter, Laurence Esterwood, and Joseph Gibson. Signed Laurence Reddy's mark

p. 220-223 Dec. 21, 1786 James Jones and wife Elizabeth (Spartanburgh) to Burwell Bobo (same); for 20£ 10s sterling sold 25 ac on Cedar Shoal of Enoree R; border: N-Moses Casey, W-William McDowell, S-Sampson Bobo; grant Nov. 24, 1767 Gov. Charles Granville Montague to James Bright (150 ac) and sold Dec. 26, 1788 for 200£ SC money by James Bright to Thomas Jones and after Jones' death to his son James Jones. Witness Christopher Casey, Joseph Howell, and Sampson Bobo. Signed James Jones and Elizabeth's mark

p. 223-226 Dec. 21, 1786 James Jones and wife Elizabeth (Spartanburgh) to Burwell Bobo (same); for 57£ SC money and 10s sterling sold 100 ac on Cedar Shoal of Enoree R; border: NW-James

Bright, NE-Moses Casey, SW-Samuel Cannon; grant May 13, 1768 Gov. Charles Montague to William McDowell then bordering S-Samuel Cannon, SE-William Whitaker, N-Moses Casey and W-James Bright; sold in 1776 William McDowell to Thomas Jones, desc and by lineal descent to James Jones, son of Thomas. Witness Christopher Casey, Joseph Howell, and Sampson Bobo. Signed James Jones and Elizabeth's mark

p. 226-229 Jan. 14, 1786 Thomas Davis (Spartanburgh) to Matthias Sulcer (same); for 110£ sterling sold 440 ac on both sides of S Tygar R including mouth of Wildcat Cr; border: vacant; grant Oct. 15, 1784 Gov. Benjamin Guarrard to Thomas Davis. Witness James Jordan, Nevil Wayland, and Alexander Ray. Signed Thomas Davis

p. 229-230 Jan. 25, 1787 George Turner (SC) to William Wilkins (Spartanburgh); for 100£ SC money sold 100 ac on both sides of Thickety Cr; border: Gabriay Brown's corner, Thomas Hathaway, and Robert Moore; grant NC governor to Thomas Nickols who sold to George Turner. Witness John Keadon, Saml Turner, and Amolera Austell. Signed George Turner

p. 230-232 May 7, 1785 Alexander Alexander and Ann McCorry, his wife (Craven Co, 96 Dist) to John Nicoll (same); for 4£ 10s sterling sold 100 ac on N side of Middle Fork of Tygar R; border: John Nicoll, Nathaniel Miller, and John Barry; grant Oct. 15, 1784 Gov. Benjamin Guarrard to Ann McCoory. Witness Richard Nally and Andrew Thomson. Signed Alexander Alexander and Ann's mark

p. 232-235 Mar. 19, 1787 Thomas Hightower (Spartanburgh) to Joel Traylor (same); for 25£ 10s sterling sold 100 ac on N Fork of Tygar R; border: Jno Timmons; part of 150 ac grant Oct. 26, 1767 Gov. William Tryon (NC) to Wm McMahan who sold to David Calhoun who sold to Thomas Hightower. Witness William Benson and Thos Wyatt. Signed Thomas Hightower

p. 235-237 Mar. 11, 1787 James Foster (Spartanburgh) to John Foster; for 40£ 10s SC money sold 195 ac on S side Fairforrest Cr; border: NE-Richd Price and others vacant; grant in 1785 Gov. William Moultrie to James Foster. Witness Isham Foster and Thomas Wyatt. Signed James Foster

p. 237-240 May 23, 1786 James Bruton and wife Mary (Spartanburgh) to Thomas Williamson (same); for 95£ sterling and 10s SC money sold 200 ac on Ferguson's Cr of Tygar R; border: N-David Bruton and other vacant; grant Feb. 12, 1770 Gov. Charles G. Montague to James Bruton; sale is exclusive of 20 ac on E side of 200 ac included in a tract formerly granted by NC governor to Alexr Ferguson. Witness George Bruton and Enoch Bruton. Signed James Bruton

p. 240-243 Sept. 7, 1781 James Hardin (Thickity Cr, 96 Dist) to Vardry McBee, esq (same); for 10£ SC money [note: James Hardin acknowledges receipt of 250£] sold 150 ac on Thickity Cr; 100 ac is part of grant to Thomas Nickolls who sold to George Turner who sold to James Hardin; 50 ac is part of 400 ac grant Apr. 21, 1767 "also" from Gov. William Tryon (NC) to William Marchbanks and William Symes who sold to Robert Moore who sold to James Hardin; border: Gabrial Brown, Thos Hattaway, Robert Moore, and Thos Nickols. Witness Wm Wier, Rhoda McBee and Josiah Tarner. Signed Jas Hardin and Jean Hardin

p. 243-245 Jun. 7, 1787 Jacob Earnest and wife Nancey (Jimmy's Cr) to Thomas Dorg; for 25£ 5s sold 160 ac on S side of Tygar R; border: S-James Crow, N-Thomas White, S-Robert Rogers, NNE-John Crow, and E-James Stone; grant Nov. 6, 1786 Gov. William Moultrie to Jacob Earnest and surveyed (?) Mar. 11, 1786. Witness Alexr. Alexr. and David McCarley. Signed Jacob and N Earnest

p. 245-246 Jun. 21, 1785 Last will and testament of Moses McCarley (96 Dist) now 77 years old: (1) to son David McCarley, 100 ac where Moses now lives; David is to pay 500£ Va money to Moses' son Abram McCarley and pay grandson Thomas McCarley (son of Abram) 10£ Va money when Thomas comes of age; (2) to daughter Elizabeth Cavin, a feather bed and furniture "where I and my wife now lies" and pewter Moses possesses after the death of Moses' wife; (3) to daughter Jean Heddleston, 3£ Va money; (4) to son James McCarley, 3£ Va money; (5) residue to wife Ruth McCarley. Witness John Ford, Samuel Ford, and Spencer Ford. Signed Moses McCarley

p. 246-250 Mar. 17, 1787 William Smith (Wiley's Fork, Spartanburgh) to Abram Moore (same); for 50£ 5s sterling sold 47 ac on Wiley's Fork of Dutchman's Cr; border: James Ham; part of 250 ac grant Apr. 3, 1786 Gov. William Moultrie to William Smith then bordering Abraham Moor, William Elder, Thornton, and Isaac Patan. Witness James McLean, James Ham, and John Moore. Signed William Smith

p. 250-253 Jul. 25, 1787 Joshua Smith and wife Elizabeth OSheal to Owen Forrester; for 200£ sterling sold 100 ac on S side of Tygar R; border: NW-Richard Young, SE-Benjamin Wofford and Tygar R; grant Mar. 6, 1787 to Joshua Smith. Witness James Hewet and Thos Tod. Signed Joshua and Elizabeth Smith's marks

p. 253-254 Sept. 14, 1787 Owen Forrester and wife Eleaner to Joshua Smith; for 100£ sterling sold 103 ac on N side of Tyger R; border: NW-David Grimmes, SE-Samuel Cathcart, E-Joel Hembree, and NW-Spring Br where Owen Forrester "now takes his water"; grant of 174 ac Feb. 5, 1787 Gov. William Moultrie to Owen Forrester. Witness Joseph Wofford and Thos Tod. Signed Owen and Eleaner Forrester's marks

p. 254-256 Apr. 4, 1787 William Clayton and wife Elizabeth to Joseph Wofford; for 100£ sterling sold 497 ac on a branch of Two Mile Cr of Enoree R; border: E-William Crow, W-William Miles; grant Jan. 1, 1787 Gov. William Moultrie to William Clayton. Witness Joshua Smith and Thomas Tod. Signed William and E Clayton

p. 256-260 Sept. 21, 1787 Charles Bruce, carpenter (Spartanburgh) to James Lusk (same); for 100£ 5s sterling sold 80 ac on Fairforrest Cr where Charles Bruce lives; border: John Smith, Peter Smith, Henry White, and James Lusk; grant Aug. 1, 1785 Gov. William Moultrie to Charles Bruce; Thomas Young is "given freedom of the land". Witness Chas Moore, Wm Poole, and Josiah Culbertson. Signed Charles Bruce

p. 260-261 Agreement Sept. 20, 1787 William Thomason, poor boy and son of John Thomason, desc,(Spartanburgh) and William Poole (same), bloomer and blacksmith; Thomason to be apprentice to Poole until Thomason is 21; judges signing: Bayles Earle, James Jordan, and Obadieh Trimmier. Witness W. Shaw and Thomas Farrar. Signed William Thomason's mark and Wm Poole

p. 261-264 Feb. 20, 1787 Jacob Demard (Washington Co, Ga) to Swann Thomson (Spartanburgh); for 200£ 5s SC money sold 100 ac on Gocher's Cr of Thickity Cr; border: N-Wm More, E-David Allen, and S-vacant. Witness Theophilus Thompson, Isham

Thompson, and James Thurston. Signed Jacob Demard's mark

p. 264-265 Apr. 11, 1787 Betty Thompson (Thickety, Spartanburgh) to Wm Poole (same); Betty owes William 8£ 15s 10½p sterling and interest from Oct. 10, 1786; now to secure this loan plus 5s, Betty sells a red cow and calf, a brinded(?) cow, and 2 feather beds for 1000 years to William. Witness Edward Balinger and Jeremiah Walker. Signed Betty Thompson's mark

p. 265-268 Jun. 27, 1787 James Head (Spartanburgh), yoeman to David Vinson (Richmond Co, Ga); for 60£ sterling sold 150 ac on Fules(?) Br of Cedar Shoals Cr; grant Aug. 14, 1772 Gov. Charles Montague to Eleazer Benton for 300 ac; Eleazer sold for 50£ on Jul. 30, 1773 to Nathaniel Hillin; Nathaniel, desc, by his heirs and executors, Mary Hillin and John Hillin, sold for 40£ on Jan. 15, 1787 to James Head. Witness Ralph Jackson, Lucrisa Head, and Charity Smith. Signed James Head and Ann's mark. Witness oath Sept. 11, 1797 Ralph Jackson to George Bruton

p. 268-271 Jul. 3, 1787 John McCullock (Charleston, SC) to James Casey (Spartanburgh); for 100£ 10s sterling sold 107 ac; border: Richard Fryar; grant of 1000 ac Jul. 21, 1785 Gov. William Cambell to James Semple between Enoree and Tygar R; sold by Rattery Semple, heir of James Semple, to John McCullock on Dec. 5 & 6, 1785. Witness Sarah Brooks, Peter Brooks, and Spencer Bobo. Signed Jno McCulloch

p. 271-272 Jun. 13, 1787 Vardery McBee (Thickety Cr, Spartanburgh) to William Wier (same); for 10s sterling sold 100 ac on both sides of Thickety Cr; border: J. Wade and Jno Watson. Witness John Gasser. Signed Vardery McBee

Book B 1787-1792

p. 1-3 Mar. 1, 1786 David McRee (Mecklinburgh Co, NC) to John Smith (Burk Co, NC); for 65£ sterling sold 200 ac on both sides of Middle Fork of Tygar R; border: John McRee. Witness Ja Robertson, Wm Young, George Peters, and Wm Wells. Signed Dd. McRee

p. 3 Jul. 5, 1787 John McCullock to Robert Kilpatrick; a mortgage for 5£ SC money on 1000 ac; condition of mortgage is that John McCullock repay in 6 months a Negro 16 yrs old whom John has borrowed (Negro not named). Witness Joseap Elliott and Hugh Baid. Signed Jno McCullock

p. 3-7 Dec. 4, 1785 Thomas Bonner (Spartanburgh) to Vardrey McBee (same); power of attorney to convey 2 tracts of land to William Tate esq in fee simple; first tract 150 ac and second tract 144 ac; land is on Cherokee Cr and S side of Broad R; both were granted to Thomas Bonner. Witness Wm Tate sr, Thomas Camp, and William Tate. Signed Thomas Bonner

Jun. 16, 1787 Thomas Bonner (formerly SC now Ga) to William Tate, sr, esq (Spartanburgh); for 100£ sterling sold 150 ac on both sides of Cherokee Cr waters of Broad R; grant May 1, 1786. Witness Ola(?) Trimmer and J(?) Thomson. Signed Thomas Bonner by atty Vardry McBee

Jun. 16, 1787 Thomas Bonner (formerly SC now Ga) to William Tate, sr, esq (Spartanburgh); for 60£ sterling sold 143 ac on both sides of Cherokee Cr waters of Broad R; granted May 1, 1786. Witness Ola(?) Trimmer and J(?) Thomson. Signed Thomas Bonner by atty Vardry McBee

p. 7-8 Mar. 4, 1787 Samuel Knox and wife Mary (Mecklinburgh Co, NC) to Henry Wells (Spartanburgh); for 30£ sterling sold 200 ac on N Fork Tygar R; border: John Miller and David Knox.

Witness George Petters and Wm Wells. Signed Samuel Knox and Mary's mark

p. 8-9 Jan. 20, 1787 John McRee (Mecklinburgh Co, NC) to James Jordan, esq (Spartanburgh); for 40£ "proclamation money" of NC sold 400 ac on Middle Fork Tyger R; on lower end of 540 ac grant Sept. 7, 1766 Gov. William Tryon (NC) to John McRee. Witness Ruth McRee and Nevel Wayland. Signed John McCree

p. 9-12 Sept. 18, 1787 Nathaniel Miller to Zachariah Walker; for 55£ sterling sold 300 ac; grant Nov. 7, 1785 Gov. William Moultrie to Nathaniel Miller. Witness Nevel Wayland and James Jordan. Signed Nathaniel Miller

p. 12-13 Aug. 7, 1787 John McCulloch to Edward Hooker; for 40£ sterling sold 250 ac; part of 1000 ac grant to James Semple, jr; "on ridge between Tyger and Enoree Rivers above the road from Blackstock Ford on Tyger to Musgrove Ford on Enoree". Witness Absalom Bobo and Thos Tod. Signed Jno McCullock

p. 13-14 Sept. 4, 1787 Joseph Powers and wife Rachel to Edward Smith; for 20£ sterling sold 80 ac on N side Tyger R about 3 mi above Blackstock's Ford; part of 250 ac grant Jan. 21, 1785 Gov. Ben Guerrard to Joseph Powers; border: S-rest of grant, E-estate of Col. Benjamin Roebuck, N-Thomas Prewit, and W-Timothy Tonie. Witness John Roebuck and Thos Tod. Signed Joseph Power and Rachel's mark

p. 14-15 Sept. 5, 1787 Joseph Powers and wife Rachel to James Crowther; for 20£ sterling sold 80 ac on N side Tyger R about 3 mi above Blackstock's Ford; part of 250 ac grant Jan. 21, 1785 Gov. Benjamin Guerrard to Joseph Powers; border: W-Timothy Tonie, E-estate of Benjamin Roebuck, S-Joseph Power, and N-Edward Smith. Witness John Roebuck and Thos Tod. Signed Joseph Powers and Rachel's mark

p. 15-16 Sept. 20, 1787 Peter Smith (Spartanburgh) and wife Agnes to William Smith (same); for 50£ sold (ac not given); west of boundary run by Col. Philemon Waters for Peter Smith; Peter and William Smith were both granted some or all this land by mistake; border: William Smith, Hancock Smith, Flemming Smith. Witness Jas Lusk, Flemming Smith, and Josiah Culbertson. Signed Peter Smith and Agnes' mark

p. 16-18 Sept. 20, 1787 William Smith and wife Catherine (Spartanburgh) to James Smith (same); for 20£ sterling sold 350 ac "taken up by William and James"; part of 640 ac grant Jan. 21, 1785 to William Smith; in two parts (1) 200 ac border: George Skove(?), Connel, William Smith, Peter Smith, Flemming Smith, Kelsoe's Cr, Dod, and Story; (2) 150 ac border: Story. Witness Felmming Smith and Josiah(?) Culbertson. Signed William Smith and Catherine's mark

p. 18-20 Jul. 30, 1787 Elisha Ford and wife Sarah (Newberry Co) to John Posey (Spartanburgh); for 50£ sterling sold 250 ac; border: W-waggon road; E part of 400 ac grant May 2, 1785 Gov. William Moultrie to Elisha Ford. Witness Charles Moore, Robert Goodgeon, and Wm Ford. Signed Elisha and Sarah Ford

p. 20-22 Mar. 17, 1788 William McDowall (Spartanburgh) makes oath that he was at plantation, called Mount Pleasant, of Adam Crane Jones, esq (Abaville Co) with Adam Crane Jones, Richard Hodges, jr (late of Va) and others; Richard Hodges, jr acted as attorney for Richard Hodges, the elder (Va), father of Richard Hodges, jr; Adam Crane Jones paid a debt to Richard

Hodges, the elder, and Richard Hodges, jr gave a receipt on Aug. 13, 1774 for 2500£ as a "security to Long, Brown, Lawden, Baley, and others"; Adam Crane Jones signed a bond Aug. 29, 1774 for 700£ SC money to Richard Hodges, jr for Adam to deed 150 ac on Mulbery Cr, Abaville Co, to Richard Hodges, jr whenever Richard gives Adam complete release from the debt for which Richard, sr is the Securitor. Signed J Thomas, jr and Wm McDowell

p. 22-24 Jul. 30 1787 Elisha Ford (Newberry Co) to Robert Goodgeon (Spartanburgh); for 40£ 10s current money sold 187 ac where Robert Goodgeon lives; part of 400 ac grant May 2, 1785 Gov. William Moultrie to Elisha Ford; border: E-waggon road. Witness Charles Moore, John Posey, and Wm Ford. Signed Elisha and Sarah Ford

p. 24-25 Aug. 30, 1774 exhibit No. 1 of Adam Crane Jones' debt to Richard Hodges, jr; payment of 2500£

p. 25 Aug. 29, 1774 exhibit No. 2 of Adam Crane Jones' debt to Richard Hodges, jr; 150 ac of land border: William Hallum; Adam bought land from Richard Andrews Rapley, esq

p. 25-27 Sept. 1, 1787 James Miller (Spartanburgh) to Robert and William Miller (same), his sons; for 50£ sterling sold 200 ac on both sides S fork Tyger R; land N of river goes to Robert, and land S of river goes to William; border: wagon road from Robert Miller's to Charleston; grant Oct. 24, 1767 Gov. William Tryon (NC) to James Miller; then in Meclenburgh Co, NC and now Spartanburgh Co. Witness Robert Miller, Samuel Miller, and James Jordan. Signed James Miller

p. 27-28 Apr. 7, 1787 Joseph Burchfield (96 Dist) to James Tanner (Spartanburgh); for 50£ sterling sold 100 ac on N fork Thickety Cr; border: James Tanner, Mapp, Miller (now Wm ?); S end of 250 ac grant Nov. 25, 1771 Gov. Josiah Martin (NC) to Joseph Burchfield. Witness Vardry McBee and Isham Saffold. Signed Joseph Burchfield

p. 28-30 Apr. 19, 1784 William Lewis (Burke Co, NC) to John Young, sr (96 Dist); for 200£ 10s NC money sold 200 ac on both sides of Brutes Cr of N Pacolett R; grant May 15, 1772 Gov. Josiah Martin (NC) to Thomas McKnight, then bordering: Obed Roberts and in Tryon Co; Thomas McKnight sold land to William Lewis. Witness Wm Wood, jr and Saml Porter. Signed William Lewis

p. 30-31 Jun. 9, 1787 William Wier (Spartanburgh) to Silas McBee; power of attorney for good causes to recover 6000£ Va money from John Wilson and Peter Perkins, esqrs and recover debts from Dugold McKichan (Burke Co, NC) due to estate of Thomas Wier, desc and from others who have debts with estate of Thomas Wier, desc. Witness Obadiah Trimmer. Signed William Wier

p. 31-32 Sept. 18, 1787 Thomas Brown, sr (Spartanburgh) to Thomas Brown, jr and Jno Brown (same), his sons; give "all goods, chattels, and household stuff" he owns. Witness Hugh Price and Reuben Lawson. Signed Thomas Brown's mark

p. 32-33 Sept. 10, 1786 James Ross (96 Dist) to John Tolison, sr (same); for 50£ sterling sold 200 ac on S side of Packolate R "including improvements where Jno Pigs formerly lived". Witness Adam Potter, Zachariah Bullock, Thomas Draper, and Anthony Crocker. Signed James and Ellis Ross' marks

p. 33-35 Jan. 22, 1787 Seth Lewis (late of Spartanburgh), carpenter to John Gossett (late of Va); for 100£ 10s sterling sold

405 ac on Harress Cr waters of Fairforrest Cr; where Seth Lewis lived and where John Gossett lives; grant Apr. 3, 1786 Gov. William Moultrie to Seth Lewis. Witness John Lemaster, James Lusk, and J. Thomas, jr. Signed Seth Lewis

p. 35-38 Jul. 2, 1787 John McCullock (Charleston, SC) to Spensor Bobo, jr (Spartanburgh); for 100£ sterling 10s SC money sold 100 ac; part of 1000 ac grant Jul. 21, 1775 Gov. William Campbell to James Sample, desc, between Enoree and Tyger R, and sold by Rattery Semple, adm. of James Sample's estate, to John McCullock on Dec. 5 & 6, 1785. Witness Sarah Brookes and Peter Brookes. Signed Jno McCullock

p. 38-40 Mar. 29, 1787 William Hendrix, heir of late James Hendrix (96 Dist) and Frankey Hendrix, wife of James, to Ebenezer Morse, blacksmith (same); for 210£ sterling sold 150 ac on Two Mile Cr of Enoree R; border: vacant; W half of 250 ac grant Nov. 27, 1770 Lt. Gov. William Bull to James Hendrix, sr. Witness Abraham Gray, Travis Morse, and John Erven. Signed William Hendrix and Frankey's mark

p. 40-42 Aug. 18, 1787 David Goodlet, joiner (Spartanburgh) to John Foster (Amelia Co, Va); for 150£ sterling and 10s SC money sold 250 ac on N side of N fork Tyger R and both sides of Hannon's Br; grant Nov. 25, 1771 Gov. Josiah Martin (NC) to William Hannons in Tryon Co and bordering Francis Wilson and Francis Prince; William Hannons sold to Isaac Penning who sold to David Goodlet. Witness Isham Foster and John Foster. Signed David Goodlet

p. 42-45 Dec. 24, 1784 James Jones and wife Elizabeth (Enoree, 96 Dist) to Jesse Casey (same); for 100£ sterling and 10s SC money sold 50 ac on Cedar Shoals Cr of Enoree R; border: N-Christopher Casey, sr, E-Moses Casey, and remainder of tract; part of 150 ac grant Nov. 24, 1757 Gov. Charles Montague to James Bright with border then vacant. Witness Sarah Brookes and Peter Brookes. Signed James and Elizabeth Jones' marks

p. 45-47 Mar. 18, 1788 Samuel Farrow, esq, high sherriff (Spartanburgh) to James Jordan, esq (same); for 20£ 10s sold 300 ac on Rock Br of S fork of N fork Tyger R; land sold Oct. 23, 1787 due to writ from county court (held at farm of Thomas Williamson) with Bayles Earle presiding on 3rd Monday in Sept. last and returnable to court 3rd Monday in Dec. 1788; John Thomson is assessed 19£ 17s 9p sterling plus 2£ 5s 1p court cost in argument with James Jordan; so John Thomson's land is sold; plat attached shows land border: N-Joseph Thomson, E-Morgan and Jones, S-Daniel Monroe and Wm Ford, and W-land disputed between Neisbitt and Ford. Witness J. Thomas, jr and W. Shaw. Signed Saml Farrow

p. 47-50 Christopher Casear and wife Susanah (Enoree, 96 Dist) to Moses Casey (same); for 100£ sterling and 10s SC money sold 100 ac on Cedar Shoals Cr waters of Enoree R; border: NW-James McDowell, S-James Bright, and others vacant; part of 250 ac grant Jun. 23, 1774 Lt. Gov. William Bull to Christopher Casear. Witness Peter Brookes, Aaron Casey, and Moses Croffer. Signed Christopher Casear's mark (Susanah doesn't sign)

p. 50-52 Oct. 11, 1787 Jesse Casey and wife Mary (Spartanburgh) to Moses Casey (same); for 100£ 10s sterling sold 50 ac on Cedar Shoals Cr of Enoree R; border: N-Christopher Casey, sr, E-Moses Casey, and remainder of tract; part of 150 ac grant to James Bright of which 50 ac sold Dec. 23 & 24, 1784 James Jones to Jesse Casey. Witness Peter Brookes and Sarah Brookes. Signed Jesse Casey and Mary's mark

p. 52-53 Jun. 18, 1787 Josiah Tanner and wife Martha (Union Co, 96 Dist) to Jonathan Harris (Spartanburgh); for 100£ SC money sold 34 ac on both sides McBee's Cr; it is called Tanner's place and is where Jonathan Harris lives; grant Feb. 6, 1786 Gov. William Moultrie to Josiah Tanner. Witness Michael Hogan, Wm Thomson, and Vardry McBee. Signed Josiah and Martha Tanner

p. 53-54 Dec. 17, 1787 Thomas Doeg and wife Agnes (Spartanburgh) to James Crow (same); for 20£ sterling sold 160 ac on S side Tyger R; border: N-James Crow, S-Robert Rodgers, E-James Sloane and Thomas White, and NE-Tyger R; grant Nov. 6, 1786 Gov. William Moultrie to Jacob Earnest; sold Jun. 8, 1787 Jacob Earnest and wife Nancy to Thomas Doeg and recorded Sept. 10, 1787 in Spartanburgh Co by Samuel Porter for John Thomas, clerk; Witness John Chesney and Andrew Thomson. Signed Thomas Doeg and Agnes' mark

p. 54-57 Dec. 14, 1787 Richard Chesney (Spartanburgh) to James Chesney (same); for 44£ 10s sold 100 ac on Jamyes Cr of Tyger R between Broad and Saluda Rivers; border: vacant; grant Dec. 24, 1772 Gov. Charles G. Montague to Richard Chesney. Witness Richard Chesney and Jonathan Floyd. Signed Richard Chesney's mark

p. 57 Sept. 17, 1787 Jeremiah Lucus (Spartanburgh) to John Lucus (same); for 28£ 16s 8p sterling sold 50 ac on N fork Tyger R; border: John Timmons. Witness John Osling. Signed Jeremiah and Sarah Lucus

p. 57-58 Dec. 17, 1787 John Snoddy (Spartanburgh) to John Lucus (same); for 38£ 17s 9p sterling sold 100 ac on N fork Tyger R; border: John Timmons. Witness Jeremiah Lucus and John Osling. Signed John and Jean Snoddy

p. 58-60 Jan. 14, 1785 Mary Hellin and son John Hellin (Spartan- to James Head (same); for 42£ 27s 2p sterling sold 300 ac on Fulse's Br of Cedar Shoals Cr of Enoree R; border: vacant; grant to Eleazer Benton in Berkeley Co between Broad and Saluda Rivers and sold Jul. 30, 1773 to Nathaniel Hillin. Witness Moses Casey, Abigail Casey, and William Head. Signed Mary and John Hillin

p. 60-61 Jun. 11, 1787 Daniel Kelley and wife Sarah (Greenville Co) to John Childs (Spartanburgh); for a Spanish milled dollar sold 225 ac on Lawson's Fork of Pacolate R; border: S-William Moultrie, W-Peter Lewis, N-vacant, and E-rest of tract but sold by Daniel Kelley to John Childs' father; part of grant Jan. 21, 1785 Gov. Benjamin Guerard to John Bennet. Witness H. M. Woods, John Kelley, Henry Turner. Signed Daniel Kelley and Sarah's mark

p. 61-64 Jun. 11, 1787 Daniel Kelley (Greenville Co) to Hezekiah Childs (Spartanburgh); for 50£ 19s sterling sold 225 ac on both sides Lawson's Fork; border: SE-Mary Woods, W-Moultrie, E-William Woods, and N-John Childs; grant of 450 ac Gov. Benjamin Guerard to John Bennett. Witness H. Mechan Woods, John Kelley, and Henry Turner. Signed Daniel Kelley

p. 64-65 Apr. 8, 1786 Jesse Casey (Enoree, Spartanburgh) to Joseph Couch (same); for 22£ 10s sterling sold 100 ac on Two Mile Cr of Enoree R; border: William Crow and vacant; grant in 1785 Gov. William Moultrie to Jesse Casey. Witness John Watson and Benjamin Couch. Signed Jesse Casey and Mary's mark

p. 65-66 Nov. 19, 1787 Richard Prince and wife Edeth (Union Co) to William Wood (Spartanburgh); for a Spanish milled dollar sold 32 ac on Fairforrest Cr of Tyger R; border: William Wood and Richard Harrison, esq; part of grant Mar. 6, 1786 Gov. William Moultrie to Richard Prince; rest of grant sold by Richard Prince to John White and Thomas Maize. Witness Alexr Walker and Henry Walden. Signed Richard and Edeth Prince's marks

p. 66 Oct. 17, 1787 John Steen (Union Co) to James Lusk (Spartanburgh); for 16£ 8s sterling sold 8 year old horse with blaze in face called Holland branded "I" on left buttock and a rifle; condition of sale is that John Steen pays John Thomas, jr 8£ 4s 3p sterling on 3rd Monday of Dec. 1787 and take a note of John Steen to John Thomas, jr for 8£ 4s 3p sterling. Witness J Thomas, jr. Signed John Steen

p. 66-67 Jun. 18, 1787 Desken Grant (Spartanburgh) to Littleton Bagwell (same); for 30£ sold 100 ac on branch of Lawson's Fork of Pacolate R; border: Dixon; part of 284 ac grant Mar. 6, 1786 to John Holcomb; plat shows border: S-Grant, W-Dixon, N-Dixon, N-Littleton Bagwell, and E-White. Witness Jas Smith, Basel Lee, and John Robeson. Signed Desken Grant

p. 67-68 Nov. 20, 1786 Henry Hays (96 Dist) to John Caldhous (same); for 300£ SC money sold 300 ac on Mill Cr of Tyger R; grant Jun. 4, 1772 to John Snoddy who sold to Henry Hays; border: vacant. Witness Nathaniel Hakes(?), Samuel Miller, and James Jordan. Signed Henry Hayes

p. 68-69 Dec. 19, 1787 Samuel Farrow, sherrif, (Spartanburgh) to Ebezener Moses (same); for 14£ sterling sold (ac not given) on Two Mile Cr of Enoree R; border: Isaac Hendrix, George Lawder, and William Cleaton; Ebezener Moses was attorney for Isaac Hendileks in a case against John Cooper; settlement of case was that John Cooper's land was sold. Witness Thos P. Carnes and Daniel Brown. Signed Saml Farrow

p. 69-72 Jun. 14, 1787 Michael Sprinkle (Spartanburgh) to William Prince (same); for 50£ 5s SC money sold 136 ac on Fairforrest and Bufflow Creeks; "former owner John Gibbs, sr, desc"; grant by "a North right" to Giles Tillet; border: land sold by John Gibbs to Peter Elder and by land of McClure. Witness Peter Elder, Broadrick Mason, and Thomas Rees. Signed Michael Sprinkle and Patty's mark

p. 72-73 Nov. 2, 1785 Jeremiah Neasbett (SC) to Henry Morgan (Spartanburgh); for 125£ SC money sold 100 ac on a branch of S fork of N fork of Tyger R; border: W-Joseph James, John Nichols, and vacant; grant Sept. 12, 1768 Lt. Gov. William Bull to Jeremiah Neasbett. Witness Samuel Miller and Christopher Taylor. Signed Jeremiah Nesbitt

p. 73-76 Aug. 23, 1787 Mason Cox Smithson (Greenville Co) to Joel Traylor (Spartanburgh); for 50£ 10s sterling sold 237 ac on N fork Tyger R above mouth of Cub Br; border: W-Thomas Hightower and others unknown; grant Mar. 6, 1786 Gov. William Moultrie to Mason Cox Smithson. Witness David Goodlett and Isham Foster. Signed Marion Cox Smithson

p. 76-78 Oct. 20, 1786 Jesse Connell and wife Ann (Spartanburgh) to Giles Smith (same); for 20£ 5s SC money sold 100 ac on branch of Fairforrest Cr where Jesse Connell lives; border: brother, George Connell;part of 500 ac grant Dec. 24, 1770 from King's Land Office (NC) to Jesse Connell. Witness John Smith, Flemming Smith, and Patty Sprinkles. Signed Jesse Connell

p. 78-79 Apr. 25, 1786 John McCullock (Charleston, SC) to Samson Bobo (Spartanburgh); for love and affection sold 130 ac; border: SE-Samson Bobo, NE-Ezekiah Backler, NW-Thos Miles, and SW-John McCulloch; grant to James Sample and sold by an heir to John McCullock. Witness James Casey, Spencer Bobo, and Burrell Bobo. Signed John McCullock

p. 79-80 Oct. 4, 1787 John Young (York Co, Campden Dist) to Robert Foster (Spartanburgh); for 120£ sold 350 ac on S side of Pacolate R; part of 800 ac grant Nov. 18, 1752 to Robert Miller; sold Apr. 20, 1769 by John Miller and William Nealy, executors of Robert Miller's will, to John Young. Witness John Hammett, Samuel Miller, James Jordan. Signed John Young

p. 80 Feb. 7, 1788 Arthur Crocker (96 Dist) to William Crocker (same); for 25£ sterling sold 250 ac on branch of Richland Cr; grant Feb. 6, 1786 Gov. William Moultrie to (not given). Witness Stovaiel Poole and William Poole. Signed Arthur Crocker's mark

p. 80-83 Jun. 18, 1787 John McCarter, heir of Alexander McCarter, desc to James Amos; for 28£ 6s 8p sterling sold 150 ac on both sides S fork of N fork of Tyger R; above John Sharps; grant Apr. 29, 1768 Gov. William Tryon (NC) to Alexander McCarter in Meclenburgh Co, NC. Witness Nevil Wayland and John Leech. Signed John McCarter

p. 83-85 Feb. 21, 1787 David Prewet (Spartanburgh) to William Brown (same); for 200£ sterling sold 150 ac on Forgerson's Cr of Tyger R; N part of 300 ac grant May 2, 1770 Gov. William Bull to D. Pruitt in Craven Co; border: NW-James Wofford, W-Isaac Crow, S-Enoch Floyd, and others vacant; rent in lease to be paid to David Bruton. Witness Aaron Floyd, Ben Rhodes, and James Wofford. Signed David Prewett

p. 85-88 Feb. 21, 1787 David Pruett (or Bultt) (Dutchman's Cr) to Benjamin Rhodes (or Roads) (Forgurson's Cr); for 200£ sterling sold 150 ac on Fougerson's Cr of Tyger R; part of 300 ac grant May 2, 1770 Lt. Gov. Wm Bull to D Pruett in Craven Co; border: NW-James Wofford, W-Isaac Crow, S-Enoch Floyd, and others vacant. Witness Aron Floyd, William Brown, James Wofford, and Enoch Floyd, sr. Signed David Pruett

p. 88-89 Jan. 10, 1787 John Crow (Brown's settlement of Broadmouth of Saluda R) to Isaac Crow (Spartanburgh); for 60£ 10s sterling sold 125 ac on Tewes Fork of Two Mile Cr of Enoree R; lower part of 250 ac grant May 25, 1779 Lt. Gov. William Bull to John Crow with border vacant. Witness Joseph Marler, John Grizel, Richard Rodgers, Nicholas White, Benjamin Beison, and Benjamin Carley. Signed John and Charity Crow's marks

p. 89-92 Jan. 12, 1788 William Bradshaw (or Bracher) and wife Sarah (Spartanburgh) to Nathaniel Wooten (same); for 30£ 10s SC money sold 100 ac on both sides Duchman's Cr; part of 270 ac grant to William Bratcher then bordering: NE-David Prewitt, N-vacant, W-Samuel Lancaster, and S-Ralph Smith; now border: Ralph Smith's old line and William Clayton. Witness Ja Smith, Samuel Ward, and James Ward. Signed William Bracher and Sarah's mark

p. 92 May 21, 1786 William McDowell and wife Mary (SC) to David Lewis (same); for 80£ sterling sold 250 ac on Willcock's Cr of Lawson's Fork; border: NE-John Rotten and NW-John Earle. Witness Robert McDowell, David Lewis, jr, and David McDowell. Signed William and Mary McDowell

p. 92-94 Aug. 20, 1785 George Alexander (Mecklenburgh Co, NC) to William McMillin (96 Dist); for 100£ North currency sold 300 ac on both sides of N fork Packolate R including mouth of Mill Cr; grant Sept. 25, 1766 to George Alexander. Witness Wm Johnston, jr and James Brown. Signed Geo Alexander. Witness oath Apr. 2(?), 1787 (Mecklenburgh Co, NC) William Johnston to James Martin Clark

p. 94-96 Jan. 5, 1786 Charles Hunt (Enoree) to John Couch (same); for 3£ 10s sterling sold 50 ac on a branch of Enoree R; grant Dec. 5, 1785 Gov. William Moultrie to Charles Hunt for 176 ac bordering Mary Couch Spring; now border: Charles Hunt, John Couch, John Bevit, Thomas Couch, desc. Witness Henry Merideth, George Hunt, and Jesse Couch. Signed Charles and Millie Hunt

p. 96-99 Feb. 28, 1788 John Livingston and wife Isabel (Newberry Co) to Richard Chesney (James Cr, Spartanburgh); for 100£ 10s sterling sold 150 ac on Tommey's Cr of Tyger R; grant Jun. 7, 1768 Lt. Gov. William Bull to Martin Lewis; border: W-Jacob Earnest and others vacant. Witness Robert Rutherford, John Chesney, and Andrew Brown. Signed John and Isabel Livingston

p. 99-100 Mar. 5, 1788 Cable Stone and wife Easter (Spartanburgh) to Mark Powell (same); for 100£ sterling sold 50 ac; grant Jan. 21, 1785 Gov. Benjamin Guerard to Cable Stone on Cedar Shoals Cr of Enoree R below Indian Boundary; border: SE and SW-John Stone and others vacant. Witness Moses Casey and James Casey. Signed Cable and Easter Stone's marks

p. 100-101 Dec. 11, 1787 John Blailock (96 Dist) to William Thomson (same); for 75£ SC money sold 200 ac on Thickety Cr. Witness Joseph Buffington, Richard Thomson, and Mourning Mitchell. Signed John Blailock's mark

p. 101-106 Oct. 2, 1787 Robert Prince (Greenville Co) to Wade Hampton, esq (Congaree's); for 200£ 5s sterling sold 350 ac on Willson's Mill Cr of N fork of Tyger R; part of 640 ac grant Apr. 29, 1768 Gov. William Tryon (NC) to John Prince and bordering Francis Wilford, John Neisbett, and William Dickson; John Prince, late of Spartanburgh, (late Mecklenburgh Co, NC) desc gave 350 ac (where John lived) to his son Robert by last will and testament Feb. 7, 1782. Witness Bayles Earle, Thomas Benson, and Wm Benson. Signed Robert and Jane Prince. Dower oath Oct. 3, 1787 Mary Prince, widow of John, to Bayles Earle and Thos Benson

p. 106-107 Mar. 6, 1788 William Himmeluright (Philadelphia, Pa) to James Fannen (Spartanburgh); for 10£ sterling SC money sold 23 ac on N side Blue Br of Thickety Cr; part of 400 ac grant May 14, 1774 Gov. Montague to Daniel Berkmeyor; border: old path to Adam Thomson's, William Himmeluright, and James Fannen. Witness Littleton Mapp, jr, Anne Mapp, and Sarah Fannen. Signed William Himmeluright

p. 107-109 Jun. 24, 1774 Charles Moore (96 Dist) to Thomas Bullion (same); for 225£ currency sold 200 ac on both sides Tyger Cr formerly Lawson's Cr; border Andrew Barry; where Thomas Bullion lives; part of 550 ac grant May 30, 1763 to Charles Moore. Witness John Coulhoun, Moses Mendry(?), and Alexander Henderson. Signed Chas Moore

p. 109-111 Mar. 18, 1788 William Ford (Spartanburgh) to Daniel Monroe (same); for 20£ 10s sterling sold 183 ac; N half of 366 ac grant May 7, 1787 Gov. Thomas Pinckney to William Ford on N fork of N fork of Tyger R; border: Thomas Brooks, Thomas Davis, Daniel Monroe, Jeremiah Nesbit, Moses Thomson, and on N side of branch where Elias Johnston lives. Witness none. Signed William Ford

p. 111-114 Mar. 17, 1788 Daniel Monroe (Spartanburgh) to James Abonatha (Newberry Co); for 75£ sterling sold 270 ac on branch of N fork of Tyger R; grant Oct. 3, 1785 Gov. William Moultrie to Daniel Monroe. Witness Elias Johnston, Nevil Wayland, and Henry Morgan, sr. Signed Daniel Monroe

p. 114-116 Mar. 17, 1788 Vardry McBee (Spartanburgh) to David Allen; for 40£ SC money sold 250 ac on both sides of Goacher Cr of Thickety Cr. Witness Joseph Morriss and Jordan Gibson. Signed Vardry and Hannah McBee

p. 116 Jan. 31, 1788 Ann White, administrix for estate of Henry White, esq, desc (Spartanburgh) to Maj. James Lusk and Capt. James Smith (same); power of attorney to administer the estate. Witness Peter Smith and Spencer Smith. Signed Ann White

p. 116-117 Mar. 10, 1788 William and Hancock Smith (Spartanburgh) to William Sutherd (same); for 5£ to H Smith and 20£ to W Smith sold 63 ac on Fairforrest Cr; border: ford on Fairforrest Cr between W Smith and William Suthard. Witness Ja Smith, William Smith, and Jane Smith. Signed Hancock and William Smith

p. 117-118 Nov. 19, 1787 Richard Prince and wife Edith (Union Co) to Ann White, Alexander Walker, and Richard Harrison, execs. of estate of John White, desc (Spartanburgh); for 70£ sold 300 ac on Fairforrest Cr of Tyger R; part of 440 ac grant Mar. 6, 1786 to Richard Prince; border: S-John Foster and Obadiah Wingo, E-Richard Harrison and William Wood, N-William Wood and Thomas Hayes, sr, and W-Thomas Hayes, sr. Witness William Wood and Henry Walden. Signed Richard and Edith Prince's marks

p. 118-120 Mar. 19, 1788 Thomas Hayze (on waters of Beaverdam Cr of Fairforrest Cr, Spartanburgh) to John Foster (same); for 30£ 10s sterling sold 160 ac on Beaver dam Cr of Fairforrest Cr; grant Sept. 4, 1786 Gov. William Moultrie to Thomas Hayze. Witness none. Signed Thomas Hayze

p. 120-121 Feb. 20, 1788 Timothy Toney to Daniel Grant; for 100£ sterling sold 414 (sic) ac on N side Tyger R in two parts: (1) 240 ac border: S-Tyger R, W-Joel Hembrie, N-James Hembrie, and E-by tract (2); grant Jul. 3, 1772 Gov. Chas G. Montague to Timothy Toney; and (2) 165 ac border: S-Tyger R, W-tract (1), N-vacant, and E-Joseph Power; grant Nov. 17, 1785 Gov. Chas G. Montague to Timothy Toney. Witness Joel Hembrie, James Crowder, Beckner Smith, and Thos Tod. Signed Timothy Toney

p. 121-122 Jun. 16, 1788 Josiah Tanner (Union Co) to William Thompson (Spartanburgh); for 100£ sterling sold 300 ac on Beaverdam Cr of Thickety Cr; grant Mar. 6, 1786 Gov. William Moultrie to Josiah Tanner. Witness Turner Thomason. Signed Josiah Tanner

p. 122-125 Jun. 15, 1787 Reuben Lawson (Spartanburgh) to Joseph Mitchell (same); for 20£ sterling sold 100 ac; part of 400 ac grant Feb. 5, 1787 Gov. William Moultrie to Reuben Lawson on Herrican Cr of Pacolet R and border vacant. Witness Zachariah S. Sparks and Wm Poole. Signed Reuben Lawson's mark

p. 125-127 Jun. 15, 1787 Reubin Lawson (Spartanburgh) to Zachariah Sparks (same); for 20£ sterling sold 100 ac; part of 400 ac grant Feb. 1, 1786 (sic) Gov. William Moultrie to Reubin Lawson on Herrican Cr of Packolate R. Witness Joseph Mitchell and Wm Poole. Signed Reubin Lawson's mark

p. 127 Apr. 23, 1788 George Storey makes oath that a Black Gum tree about 2 chains on S side of Fairforrest Cr was marked as a corner for tract of 432 ac surveyed by Frances McElerayn in 1752 for John Wilson. Sworn before Samuel Lancaster

p. 127-128 Jun. 16, 1788 Zachariah Bullock (Union Co) to Josiah Tanner (Spartanburgh); for 150£ sterling sold 270 ac on both sides of Thickety Cr known as Bullock's Mills; border: John Johnston. Witness none. Signed Zachariah Bullock

p. 128-131 Jun. 16, 1788 John Roson (Spartanburgh) to William Poole (same); for 15£ 10s sold 100 ac on S side of S fork of Tyger R; grant Jun. 5, 1786 Gov. William Moultire to John Roson. Witness James Jordan and Nevil Wayland. Signed John Roson

p. 131-132 Nov. 17, 1787 Richard Sanders (Spartanburgh) to Luke Browning (same); for 30£ sterling sold 150 ac on Buck Cr of Packolet R; grant Jan. 1, 1787 from the State to Richard Sanders. Witness John Nelson, John Henderson, and Joice Sanders. Signed Richard and Ann Sanders

p. 132-133 Apr. 25, 1788 William Williamson (Spartanburgh) to John Alexander (Greenville Co); power of attorney to sell lnad on Saluda R in Abbeville Co. Witness Lunsford Beuford and Philemon Beuford. Signed Wm Williamson

p. 133 Oct. 26, 1787 John Tippen (Spartanburgh) to Thomas Williamson; for 10£ an agreement to sell 76 ac; John has only a conveyance from George Bruton and heirs to whom land was granted; both parties agree that sale is legal unless it appears on an older survey whereupon Thomas gets his money back; John is to have 6 months to return money with interest. Witness Wm Williamson and George Bruton. Signed Thomas Williamson and John Tippen

p. 133-135 Feb. 6, 1787 Ambrose Barnett and wife Sarah (Spartanburgh) to Abram Nalley (same); for 20£ 10s sterling sold 135 ac on S side of Cain Cr of Tyger R; grant Nov. 6, 1786 Gov. William Moultrie to Ambrose Barnett. Witness Richard Nalley, David Grimes, and John Butter. Signed Ambrose and Sarah Barnett's marks

p. 135-138 Jul. 30, 1786 James McCarley (Laurens Co) to John Bragg (Spartanburgh); for 100£ 10s sterling sold 50 ac on Jemmy's Cr of Tyger R; part of 150 ac grant to William Hendrix (memorial auditor's book G-7 p. 395) who sold to Moses McCarley on Jan. 13, 1772; Moses then sold to James McCarley Oct. 18, 1783; the 50 ac is on W end of the 150 ac grant. Witness Peter Bragg, Moses Cavin, and Thomas Doig. Signed James McCarley

p. 138-141 Jul. 30, 1786 James McCarley (Laurens Co) to John Bragg (Spartanburgh); for 100£ 10s sterling sold 50 ac on Hendrix Br of Jemmy's Cr; border: SE-John Lindsey and others vacant; part of 150 ac grant to William Hendrix (auditor's book H-8 p. 277); Moses McCarley sold land to James McCarley Oct. 18, 1783. Witness Peter Bragg, Moses Cavin, and Thomas Doig. Signed James McCarley and Jean's mark

p. 141-144 Dec. 7, 1786 Robert Sims (Enoree R, Spartanburgh) to Jeremiah Moore (same); for 10£ 5s sterling sold 100 ac on N side of Deldine's Br on N side of Enoree R; part of 200 ac grant Jul. 10, 1769 Gov. Charles G. Montague to William Sims and bordering: SW-Enoree R and other sides vacant; sold Mar. 21, 1778 William Sims to Robert Sims for 50£ currency. Witness Thomas Moore, Thomas Gunter, and Joseph Lyon. Signed Robert Sims

p. 144-147 Feb. 6, 1787 Ambrose Barnett and wife Sarah (Spartanburgh) to Nathaniel Davis (same); for 20£ 10s sterling sold 125 ac on N side Cain Cr of Tyger R; grant Nov. 6, 1786 Gov. William Moultrie to Ambrose Barnett. Witness Richard Nelley, David Grims, and John Butter. Signed Ambrose and Sarah Barnett's marks

p. 147-149 Dec. 26, 1786 Thomas Brooks and wife Elizabeth (Spartanburgh) to Robert Kimbell; for 50£ 15s sterling sold 67 ac on Fairforrest Cr; grant Apr. 3, 1786 Gov. William Moultrie to Thomas Brooks. Witness Nevil Wayland and Wm Fields. Signed Thomas and Elizabeth Brooks' marks

p. 149-152 May 5, 1779 Nathaniel Miller (96 Dist) to Samuel Neely (Campden Dist); for 1550£ SC money sold 160 ac on N side of Tyger R or Lawson's Cr including mouth of Mill Cr; part of grant May 30 (or 3), 1763 Gov. Thomas Boone to Robert Miller and to Nathaniel by will of Robert Miller; border: S-Tyger R or Lawson's Cr, E-John Miller. Witness Thomas Bullion, Thomas Moore, and Andrew Thomson. Signed Nathaniel Miller

p. 152-156 Jun. 3, 1786 Westwood Waters and wife Abby (Enoree, Spartanburgh) to Elizabeth Waters (same); for 40 guineas 31s 9p SC money sold 100 ac in fork between Broad and Saluda Rivers on Cedar Shoal Cr of Enoree R; grant Apr. 17, 1764 Gov. Thomas Boone to Westwood Waters; border: NW-Rosanna Farrows and S-Thomas Scurrie (or Scurry); heirs of Elizabeth listed as Landon, Rosanna, Boardwine, and Thomas Waters. Witness Thomas Gormon, Mary Gormon, and Rachel Fryer. Signed Westwood Waters and Abby's mark. On Jun. 3, 1786 Elizabeth Waters received full consideration of title bond from Westwood Waters; bond was dated May 20, 1786 and the penalty was 500£ sterling.

p. 156-159 Mar. 20, 1787 William Smith (Wyley's Fork, Spartanburgh) to James Ham (Spartanburgh); for 20£ 5s sterling sold 116 ac N of Wyley's Fork of Duchman's Cr of Tyger R; grant Apr. 3, 1786 Gov. William Moultrie to William Smith for 250 ac bordering Abraham Moore, William Elder Thornton, and William Smith. Witness Dudley Sneedy, Thos Russell, and Jas McElwean. Signed William Smith

p. 159-161 Jan. 18, 1787 William Alldridge (Spartanburgh) to Matthew McBee (same); for 50£ 1s sterling sold 200 ac on S side of Packolate R; border: SW-Benjn Mehaney, NW-vacant, NE-McBee; grant Jan. 21, 1785 Gov. Benjamin Guerard to William Aldridge. Witness Jas Wofford and Jas Lusk. Signed William Alldridge and Hannah's mark

p. 161-162 Mar. 17, 1787 Vardry McBee (Spartanburgh) to William Wilkins (same); for 10£ sterling sold 400 ac on both sides Gotes Cr of Thickety Cr; grant Apr. 26, 1767 Gov. William Tryon (NC) to William Sims and William Marchbanks. Witness Wm Thomson, Rhoda McBee and Joshua Preslidge. Signed Vardry and Hannah McBee

p. 162-163 Dec. 25, 1786 George Turner and wife Nancy (Spartanburgh) to Milly Austill (same); for 5£ sterling sold 200 ac; part of 400 ac grant to Thomas Nichols on Thickety Cr; border: N-John Steen and Anderson and remainder of grant; where Milly Austill lives. Witness John Headen, William Wilkins, and

Samuel Turner. Signed George Turner

p. 163-165 Mar. 13, 1787 Daniel Walker (96 Dist) to Elisha Smith (same); for 40£ sold 100 ac on S side of Packolate R; grant Aug. 31, 1784 to Daniel Walker. Witness Ellis Cannon and Mason Cannon. Signed Daniel Walker

p. 165 Nov. 14, 1786 Susannah Hollaway and George Turner (Spartanburgh) to John Haden (same); for 5£ sold 100 ac on Gotes Cr of Thickety Cr; border: Robert Moor, Melea Auston, and Charles McDade. Witness Henry Turner, Phil Martin, William Headen and William Wilkins. Signed Susannah's mark, George Turner, and Ann Turner's mark

p. 165-166 Feb. 26, 1786 Samuel Sarratt (96 Dist) to John Byars (same); for 100£ sterling sold 200 ac on W side of "Main" Broad R; half of grant Nov. 14, 1771 Gov. Josiah Martin (NC) to Samuel Sarratt. Witness James Byars, Thomas Wilson, and John Humphrey. Signed Samuel Sarratt

p. 166-167 Jun. 1, 1787 John Kelley (Spartanburgh) to John Turner (same); for good causes sold a bed and a white cow. Witness Samuel Porter and Wm Young. Signed John Kelley

p. 167-168 Mar. 5, 1787 John Atkinson (Spartanburgh) to Henry Turner (same); for 5£ sold 247 ac on Gocher Cr of Thickety Cr; border: David Allen, John Headen, and Robert Wilkens. Witness John Headen, William Headen, and David Jones. Signed John Atkinson and Rebekah's mark

p. 168-169 Apr. 21, 1787 Leonard Adcock (Spartanburgh) to Jonathan Low (same); for 5£ SC money sold 100 ac on N side of Packolate R; this is upper end of 300 ac grant to Frances Ballenger. Witness Aaron Templeton. Signed Leonard Adcock

p. 169 Aug. 25, 1788 John Mapp (SC) to William Thomson (Spartanburgh); for 120£ sterling sold Negro named Doll, Negro girl Dinah, sorrel horse branded with "8" on shoulder and buttock, 2 cows and calves, and a feather bed and furniture. Witness Jerem. Thomson and Richd. Thomson. Signed John Mapp

p. 169-170 Oct. 27, 1788 Obadiah Trimmier (Spartanburgh) to Elizabeth Trimmier (same); for 5£ sold a Negro girl. Witness John Trimmier and Henry Wells. Signed Obadiah Trimmier

p. 170-171 Aug. 24, 1788 John Cambell (Spartanburgh) to John Forester (same); for 50£ sterling sold 100 ac on N side Tyger R; border: S-Tyger R, W-John Cambell, and by Samuel Kithcart. Witness Brittain Willeford, Thomas Forester, and Moses Clayton. Signed John Cambell

p. 171 Mar. 1, 1788 John Campbell and wife Sarah (Spartanburgh) to John Walker (same); for 120£ sterling sold 2 tracts totaling 200 ac on N side Tyger R; 100 ac grant (blank) 20, 1772 to Daniel Bush and 100 ac grant Feb. 2, 1773 to John Gowen. Witness John Forrester, James Hewat, and John Hembree. Signed John Campbell and Sarah's mark

p. 171-173 Jan. 23, 1787 Richard Hampton (Spartanburgh) to Peter Elder (same); for 100£ sterling sold 150 ac; part of 296 ac grant Jul. 4, 1785 Gov. William Moultrie to Richard Hampton on Reedy Br of Fairforrest Cr; border: W-Richard Hampton, S-vacant and Richard Hampton, NE-John Gibbs, N-Rowland Cornelius and James Keen. Witness John Watson and George Connell. Signed Richard Hampton

p. 173-174 Apr. 30, 1788 James Smith (Spartanburgh) to Nathaniel Wooton (same); for 30£ sterling sold 100 ac on N side of Cane Cr of Tyger R; part of 200 ac grant to James Hembrie; border: Timothy Toney. Witness Leonard Smith and William Evett. Signed James Smith

p. 174-176 Aug. 20, 1788 Henry Meredith and wife Milley and Thomas Meredith (Spartanburgh) to Landon Farrow (same); for 150£ sold 333 ac on N bank of Enoree R; border: Matthew Couch and Bebty Coxen; part of 600 ac grant Mar. 26, 1755 Gov. Arthur Dobbs (NC) to Thomas Erwine in Anson Co on both sides of Enoree R about 4½ miles below Bartlett Brown; 333 ac was sold by Thomas Erwine to Bartlett Brown, sr, desc, May 7, 1755 who sold to Benjamin Wofford and Burrell Thomson who then sold to Henry Meredith. Witness Thomas Farrow and John Farrow. Signed Henry Meredith, Milley's mark, and Thomas Meredith

p. 176-177 Mar. 29, 1788 Vardry McBee (Spartanburgh) to Joseph Morris (same); power of attorney to collect debts owed Vardry McBee. Witness John Lefever, Silas McBee, and Peter Edwards. Signed Vardry McBee

p. 177 Jan. 24, 1788 John Fincher (Union Co) to John Pace (Spartanburgh); for 50£ sterling sold 100 ac on N fork of Tyger R; where John Fincher lives; part of grant Oct. 24, 1767 to Francis Dod who sold to John Fincher. Witness Jeremiah Lucus, John Often, and John Fowler. Signed John Fincher's mark

p. 177-178 Sept. 16, 1788 Spence Ford (Spartanburgh) to William Prince (same); for 100£ sold 310 ac on a branch of Fairforrest Cr "below the line"; grant Jan. 21, 1785 Gov. Benjamin Guerard to Spence Ford. Witness George Salmon and Samuel Ford. Signed Spence Ford

p. 178-179 Sept. 16, 1788 William Ford (Spartanburgh) to William Prince (same); for 100£ SC money sold 247 ac on a branch of N Tyger R; grant May 1, 1786 Gov. Thomas Pinckney to William Ford. Witness Charles Bruce and Frederick Eisen. Signed William Ford

p. 179-180 Sept. 16, 1788 John Gibbs (Spartanburgh) to William Prince (same); for 50£ sold 40 ac; part of 640 ac grant to John Gibbs, sr, desc; the 40 ac was bequeath to John Gibbs by John Gibbs, sr's will; border: Sprinkle. Witness Charles Bruce and Wm Ford. Signed John Gibbs

p. 180-181 Aug. 8, 1788 John Holcomb and wife Keziah (Spartanburgh) to Dickin Grant (same); for 6£ sterling sold 284 ac on Lawson's fork of Packolate R; border: Dixon; grant Mar. 6, 1786 with plat drawn by George Salmon. Witness Ja Smith, Jas Lusk, and William Thomas. Signed John Holcomb and Keziah's mark

p. 181-183 Sept. 16, 1788 William Prince and Henry Wells (Spartanburgh) to John Hammett (same); for 40£ SC money sold 107 ac; part of 247 ac grant May 1, 1786 Gov. Thomas Pinckney to William Ford on branches of N Tyger R; also sold Thomas Salmon 100 ac from the same tract with a division by line from Lawson's corner to a stake on Parker's line. Witness Wm Ford and Jno Brown. Signed Wm Prince and Henry Wells

p. 183-185 Sept. 16, 1788 William Allen (Spartanburgh) to Daniel Allen (same); for 100£ sterling sold 320 ac; East half of grant Dec. 3, 1787 Gov. Thomas Pinckney to William Allen on branches of Forgerson's Cr of Tyger R; border: S-an old line, E-Henry Middleton, and others vacant. Witness Thomas Grant, William

Duncan, and John Duncan. Signed William Allen's mark

p. 185-188 Sept. 15, 1788 Israel and John Morriss (Spartanburgh) to Daniel White (same); for 100£ 5s sold 267 ac on both sides of Thickety Cr of Packolate R; border: John Johnson; grant Jun. 5, 1786 Gov. William Moultrie to John Morriss. Witness George Salmon, David Lewis, and Joseph Venable. Signed John Morriss and Israel Morriss

p. 188-191 Sept. 8, 1788 Mary Hannah (Spartanburgh) to John Owens (Va); for 100£ sterling sold 160 ac on N side of King's R (now Enoree R); border: Robert Hanna; part of 600 ac grant May 4, 1753 Gov. Matthew Rowan (NC) to Bartlett Brown and "by a lawful right made to Mary Hannah by Benjamin Brown, right heir of Bartlett Brown." Witness Jas Wofford, Jno Brockman, and Peter Hamilton. Signed Mary Hannah's mark

p. 191-193 May 31, 1788 Francis Bremar, esq (Charleston, SC) and David Hopkins, esq (Chester Co) to James Fannen (Spartanburgh); for 10£ sterling sold 38 ac on Thickety Cr; part of grant Mar. 6, 1786 Gov. Moultrie to Francis Bremar and David Hopkins; border: Hamelright (formerly granted to Daniel Burkmire), Fannen, and Burchfield. Witness Abner Coleman, Christy Fraser, and Moses Lewis. Signed F. Bremar and Dd Hopkins

p. 193-194 Sept. 18, 1788 Robert Kimbel and wife Frances (Spartanburgh) to Samuel Ward (same); for 40£ sold 67 ac on Fairforrest Cr; grant Apr. 3, 1786 to Thomas Brooks. Witness James Laxson, James Ward, and John Hayes. Signed Robert Kimbel and Frances Kimbel

p. 194-197 Sept. 17, 1788 William Prince (Spartanburgh) to David Golightly (same); for 101£ sterling sold 384 ac in two tracts on S side of Fairforrest Cr and both sides of Buflow Lick Cr; one tract granted from North Carolina to Giles Tillet; second tract granted Jan. 21, 1785 Gov. Benjamin Guerard to Spencer Ford who sold to William Prince; border: SW-Henry Acres and Ephraim Elder, SE-Michael Sprinkle, NE & NW-David Cook, David Golightly and Maryan Otes; plat also shows border: S-Hancock Smith and vacant land. Witness Larkin Lancaster and Tosher Smith. Signed William Prince and Elizabeth Prince

p. 197-199 Nov. 24, 1788 Thomas White and wife Sarah (Spartanburgh) to Isham Chote (or Choat) (same); for 50£ SC money sold 98 ac on a branch of Tyger R; part of 300 ac grant Apr. 3, 1786 Gov. William Moultrie to Thomas White on S side of Tyger R; border: E-John White and by rest of grant. Witness John Whitten, Charles Whitten, and Luke Thornton. Signed Thomas White and Sarah White. Witness oath Luke Thornton and John Whitten to Saml Lancaster Dec. 15, 1788

p. 199-200 Nov. 24, 1788 Thomas White and wife Sarah (Spartanburgh) to Luke Thornton (same); for 50£ sterling sold 140 ac on S side of Tyger R; part of grant Apr. 3, 1786 Gov. William Moultrie to Thomas White. Witness John Whitten, Isham Choat, and Charles Whitten. Signed Thomas White and Sarah White. Witness oath Isham Choat and John Whitten to Saml Lancaster Dec. 15, 1788

p. 200-203 Dec. 5, 1788 Benjamin Rhodes to Obadiah Gravet; for 112£ sterling sold 150 ac on Ferguson's Cr of Tyger R; sold Feb. 21, 1787 David Pruett to Benjamin Rhodes and recorded in Spartanburgh Court March 1788; border: N-James Wofford, W-Isaac Crow, S-Enoch Floyd, and others vacant. Witness John Bragg, John Whitten, and John Even. Signed Benjamin Rhodes. Witness oath Dec. 15, 1789 John Bragg and John Whitten to Saml Lancaster

p. 203-204 Dec. 6, 1788 Vardry McBee, surveyor (Thickety Cr) to William McDowell esq (same); for 40£ sterling sold 144 ac on both sides of N Packolate R below mouth of Roberts Cr; grant Sept. 18, 1785 to Vardry McBee. Witness T Thomas, jr, David McDowell, and James Wofford. Signed Vardry McBee. Certified Dec. 17, 1788 by Saml Lancaster

p. 204-205 Sept. 8, 1788 Robert White and wife Isbel (Spartanburgh) to Robert Starling (same); for 40£ sterling sold 100 ac on branch of Kelsoe's Cr of Fairforrest; plat shows border: White, Foster, Golightly, and vacant. Witness Samuel Morrow, William Stevenson, and A Lancaster. Signed Robert White, jr and Isabell White. Witness oath Dec. 16, 1788 Samuel Morrow, William Stevenson, and Absalom Lancaster to Saml Lancaster

p. 205-206 Dec. 13, 1788 William Austen (Greenville Co) to Thomas Collins (Spartanburgh); for love and affection sell "all goods, chattels, leases, debts, lands, etc and other substances" as follows: 183 ac, 196 ac, a stud colt, 2 bay geldings, 2 cows and yearlings, 25 hogs, 40 barrels of corn, a note from William Richards for 1000 wt of tobacco, a Book of Acrompts (?), a note Richard Jones, a note Asey Estes, a note Richard Scruggs, all household furniture, and a hogshead of rum. Witness James Taylor White and John Collins. Signed Wm Austin. Witness oath Dec. 16, 1788 James Taylor White and John Collins to Wm Smith

p. 206-207 Dec. 15, 1788 Rowland Cornelius (Spartanburgh) to his son Rowland Cornelius, jr (same); for love and affection sold 300 ac at Reedy Br; part of grant to Giles Connell and part of grant to Rowland Cornelius, sr. Witness Nimrod Underwood and Thomas Underwood. Signed Rowland Cornelius. Witness oath Dec. 15, 1788 Thomas Underwood to David Goodlett

p. 207-211 May 1, 1788 William Weakfield, sr and wife (not named) (Spartanburgh) to William Weakfield, jr (same); for 40£ 10s sterling sold 75 ac on Panther's Cr of Enoree R; about 3 miles below the Indian line and 2½ miles above mouth of Panther's Cr; half of 150 ac grant Dec. 22, 1768 Gov. William Tryon (NC) to Charles Moore on N side Panthers Cr in Tryon Co, NC; sold Apr. 7, 1784 by Charles Moore to William Weakfield; release refers to buyer as John Wakefield. Witness John Nisbett and Jonathan Nisbitt. Signed William Weakfield

p. 211-216 May 3, 1775 Samuel Spencer esq (Anson Co, NC) to Alexander Kilpatrick (96 Dist); for 80£ Proclamation money and 5s Great Britian money sold 300 ac on a branch of S fork of Pacolate R; grant Apr. 27, 1767 King George III (NC seal) to Samuel Spencer then in Mecklenburgh Co, NC now in 96 Dist, SC. Witness John Clark, Peter Watkins, David Miller, Wm Nevill, and James Hooper. Signed Saml Spencer. Witness oath Wm Nevill, David Miller, and James Hooper to Bayles Earle Jun. 25, 1788 and John Clark to John Tagert May 5, 1775

p. 216-217 Dec. 15, 1788 John Pack, heir of Samuel Pack, desc, and mother Jean (Spartanburgh) to Thomas Davis (same); for 100£ sold 200 ac on N branch of N fork of Tyger R; grant Apr. 29, 1766 Gov. William Tryon (NC) to Elisha Thomson then in Craven Co, SC and now in Spartanburgh; sold by Elisha Thomson and wife Rachel to Samuel Pack and wife Jean. Witness Nevil Wayland, Rowland Burks, and William Barton. Signed John Pack and Jean Pack

p. 217-221 Mar. 29, 1788 John McElheny and wife Anne Armstrong (Spartanburgh) to John and William Armstrong (same); for 5s SC money sold 500 ac on N side of Saluda R in Greenville Co; grant May 2, 1785 Gov. William Moultrie to Ann Armstrong.

Witness MRtin Armstrong, Wm Stiggs, and James Jordan. Signed John and Anne McElheny

p. 221-222 Dec. 15, 1788 James Fannen (Spartanburgh) to Littleton Mapp, jr (same); for 5£ sterling sold 100 ac between Thickety and Goties Cr; grant Nov. 1, 1787 Gov. Thomas Pinckney to James Fannen; border: E-Alotel (?), S-old fort land, W-Anderson, and N-Thonson and Lipscomb. Witness Joseph Venible, William Headen, and Abner Coleman. Signed James Fannen. Witness oath Dec. 16, 1788 Joseph Venible to Obadiah Trimmier

p. 222 Nov. 11, 1788 William Prince (Spartanburgh) and Henry Wells to Thomas Selmon (same); for 30£ sold 100 ac on a branch of N Tyger R; grant May 1, 1786 to William Ford (according to note at bottom of transaction). Witness Nimrod Underwood and Enoch Jones Underwood. Signed Wm Prince and Henry Wells. Witness oath Mar. 16, 1789 Nimrod Underwood to Thomas Farrow

p. 222-225 Dec. (blank), 1788 Greenham Crowder (Spartanburgh) to John Johnson; for 85£ sold 150 ac on branches of Thomson's Cr; border: Kimball; plat made Jun. 4, 1787 for Greenham Crowder. Witness James Smith, Robert Kimbell, and Thomas Crowther (or Crowder). Signed Greenham Crowder. Wit. oath Dec. 14, 1789 Thomas Crowther to D. Goodlett

p. 225-226 Mar. 9, 1788 David Henry (96 Dist) to Elizabeth Graham (same); for 20£ sterling sold 50 ac on N (or S) of Packolate R including improvements where Samuel Feljor (or Feyas) lived; part of 200 ac grant Nov. 14, 1771 Gov. Josiah Martin (NC) to James Alley on both sides of Pacolate R then in Tryon Co, NC. Witness Hugh Pierce and Nathaniel Hammett. Signed David Henry. Wit. oath Feb. 24, 1789 Hugh Pierce to Obadiah Trimmier

p. 226-228 May 16, 1780 John Wood (96 Dist) to William Benson (same); for 7,000£ SC money sold 200 ac on both sides of Fairforrest Cr; grant May 15, 1772 Gov. Josiah Martin (NC) to Benjamin Thomson then in Tryon Co, NC and sold to Lambath Lain who sold to John Wood. Witness George Selmon, Ephraim Rees, and Isham Foster. Signed John Wood. Wit. oath Mar. 4, 1789 Isham Foster to D. Goodlett

p. 228-230 Feb. 11, 1788 Robert Crowder (Lawrence Co) to Thomas Kimbol (Spartanburgh); for 20£ 10s sterling sold 200 ac on both sides of Thomson's Cr of Pacolate R "below the forks"; grant Jun. 4, 1788 (sic) Gov. Thomas Pinckney to Robert Crowder; border: W-Thomas Bennet and others vacant. Witness John Johnson, Joseph Venible, and William Vinable. Signed Robert Crowder. Wit. oath Mar. 16, 1789 Joseph Venible to D. Goodlett

p. 230-232 Feb. 11, 1789 William Wier (Thickety Cr, Spartanburgh) to William Bostick (York Co); for 50£ sterling sold two tracts: (a) 100 ac on both sides Thickety Cr bordering John Watson and Wade; and (b) 50 ac on S side of Thickety Cr joining (a) and bordering Wade and Matthew Guttery. Witness Obadiah Trimmier and Matthew Guttery. Signed William and Judith Wier. Wit. oath Feb. 12, 1789 Matthew Guttery to Obadiah Guttery

p. 232-233 Mar. 3, 1789 Reubin Matthis and wife Judith (Spartanburgh) to Joseph Lively (same); for 50£ sterling sold 100 ac on Lindsey's Cr of Packolate R; grant Feb. 5, 1787 to Reubin Matthis (or Matthews); plat attached shows border: vacant. Witness Robert Obarr, Joseph Barnett, and Elisha McAbee. Signed Reubin and Judah Matthis. Wit. oath Mar. 16, 1789 Joseph Barnett and Elisha McAbee to Saml Lancaster

p. 233-234 Jan. 27, 1789 John Langston and wife Elizabeth (Greenville Co) to James Beard (Spartanburgh); for 110£ sterling sold 150 ac on S side of Tyger R where John Langston use to live; border: NE-Tyger R, SE-Delany Carroll, and others vacant; grant May 13, 1768 Gov. Charles G. Montague to David Dunaman. Witness John Beard and Fanny McElroy. Signed John and Elizabeth Langston. Wit. oath Mar. 12, 1789 John Beard to Saml Lancaster

p. 234-238 Mar. 16, 1788 William Ford (Spartanburgh) to Thomas Brooks, sr (same); for 20£ sold 183 ac on S side of small branch of N fork of Tyger R where Elias Johnston now lives; border: Thomas Brooks, Nevil Wayland, John Leech, Joseph Jones, Henry Morgan, and Monroe;half of 366 ac grant May 7, 1787 Gov. Thomas Pinckney to William Ford. Witness G. Salmon and Ellis Johnson. Signed Wm Ford

p. 238-239 Oct. 19, 1784 Charles Waters, constable (Enoree, SC) to William Hinton (Tyger R); bond for 500£ sterling; Charles is to make a title for 225 ac on N side of Enoree R; border: James Benton, Charles Waters, "the Irish line", and land laid out for James Couch; part of 450 ac surveyed by Charles Waters. Witness Edwd Musgrove. Signed Charles Waters. Wit. oath Apr. 16, 1789 Edwd Musgrove to Saml Lancaster

p. 239-240 Sept. 5, 1788 William Clayton and wife Elizabeth (Spartanburgh) to James Clayton (same); for 50£ sterling sold 150 ac on S side Tyger R;part of 200 ac grant Sept. 16, 1774 Lt. Gov. William Bull to William Clayton; border: N-James Sample and remainder of grant. Witness Francis Clayton and Moses Clayton. Signed William and Bettey Clayton. Wit. oath Mar. 5, 1789 Francis Clayton to Thomas Farrow

p. 240-241 Apr. 13, 1786 Joseph Buffington (Spartanburgh) to Caroline Matilda Buffington (same); for 20£ sterling sold a Negro girl named Rose about 9 mo. old. Witness H. White. Signed Joseph Buffington

p. 241-242 Feb. 5, 1789 James Spears and wife Mary (Charleston, SC) to James Gibbs (Union Co); for 70£ sterling sold 250 ac on S side of Tyger R; part of 350 ac grant Aug. 11, 1774 Lt. Gov. William Bull to Demund Beardan; border: E-Thomas Tod, S-remainder of grant, and W-James Semple and Philip Mulkie. Witness Thos. Brandan and James Jordan. Signed Jas and Mary Spears

p. 242-243 Dec. 21, 1773 John Ford (96 Dist) to his son-in-law, Philip Ford (same); for love and affection sold 300 ac on Fairforrest Cr; where John Ford use to live; grant Jun. 1, 1767 Gov. Charles G. Montague to John Ford. Witness William Akridge, Thomas Laxon, and John Caan. Signed John Ford. Wit. oath Sept. 4, 1783 Thomas Laxon to J. Thomas, jr

p. 243-246 Feb. 16, 1789 Robert Goodgion (Greenville Co) to Isham Foster (Spartanburgh); for 47£ 10s sterling sold 180 ac on S side of Ridge Rd between Tyger R and Fairforrest Cr; part of 400 ac grant May 2, 1785 Gov. William Moultrie to Elisha Ford who sold part on S side of Ridge Rd to Robert Goodgion. Witness David Goodlett, William Goodgion, and Robert Goodgion. Signed Robert Goodgion. Certified Mar. 17, 1787 D. Goodlett

p. 246-248 Feb. 1, 1787 Ann Holloway (Spartanburgh) to William Tinsley (same); for 100£ 10s sterling sold 550 ac on Ford's Br of Fairforrest Cr; border: NE and SW-Ford and others vacant; grant May 5, 1773 Lt. Gov. William Bull to John Parker who sold to Joseph Kirkland who sold to Ann Holloway. Witness

Isham Foster, Thomas Cimbell, and Thomas Crowder. Signed Ann Holloway. Wit. oath Mar. 18, 1789 Isham Foster to D. Goodlett

p. 248-249 Mar. 16, 1789 Giles Smith and wife Mary (Spartanburgh) and Absalom Lancaster (same);for 50£ sold 100 ac on branch of Fairforrest Cr of Tyger R; border: Joseph Buffington, Jesse Connell, and George Connell; part of grant Dec. 24, 1770 Gov. William Tryon (NC) to Jesse Connell. Witness Jesse Connell, George Connell, and Frances Connell. Signed Giles and Mary Smith. Wit. oath Mar. 16, 1789 Jesse Connell to Saml Lancaster

p. 249-251 Mar. 12, 1789 Landon Farrow and wife Rachel (Spartanburgh) to John Farrow (same); for 100£ sterling sold 167 ac on N side of Enoree R; part of tract sold by William Brown to Benjamin Wofford who sold to Henry Meredith who sold to Landon Farrow; border: Matthew Couch. Witness Peter Brocks and Thomas Farrow. Signed Landon and Rachel Farrow. Wit. oath Mar. 12, 1789 Thomas Farrow to Wm Smith

p. 251-252 Oct. 12, 1788 Francis Balenger (Spartanburgh) to John Lackey (same); for 4£ 5s sterling sold 100 ac on N side of Pacolate R; lower part of 300 ac; border: John Lackey and Leonard Adcock. Witness none. Signed Francis Balenger

p. 252-253 Jan. 24, 1789 Samuel Jackson, sr (Spartanburgh) to Samuel Jackson, jr (N fork of Packilate R); for 50£ sterling sold 100 ac on S side of N fork of Packolate R; border: Nathaniel Henderson; part of 250 ac sold in 1773 by Jabez Evans to Samuel Jackson, sr. Witness Moses Foster and Saml Culbertson. Signed Saml Jackson. Wit. oath Mar. 17, 1789 Moses Foster to D. Goodlett

p. 253-254 Nov. 10, 1788 William Prince and wife Elizabeth (Spartanburgh) to Michael Sprinkle (same); for 50£ sold 112 ac on Fairforrest Cr near Buflow Cr; part of 310 ac grant Jan. 21, 1785 to Spence Ford. Witness Jesse Connell and Salley Connell. Signed Wm and Elizabeth Prince. Wit. oath Mar. 16, 1789 Salley Connell to Wm Smith

p. 254-256 Mar. 3, 1789 John Gibbs and wife Ann (Spartanburgh) to Michael Sprinkle; for 10£ SC money sold 16 ac on Fairforrest Cr and Buflow lick Cr; part of 640 ac grant North Carolina to Giles Trillett. Witness John Smith, Robert Roberts, and Thomas Roberts. Signed John and Anne Gibbs. Wit. oath Mar. 16, 1789 Robert Roberts to Wm Smith

p. 256-257 Aug. 1, 1788 Peter Johnson, executor of John Curconel's estate, (Rutherford Co, NC) to James Brown (SC); for 40£ sold 200 ac on both sides of Grias Cr of Packolate R; border: Jacoles Gribn (?); survey on Mar. 23, 1772; grant May 23, 1772 to John Corconel. Witness John McKinney and William McKinney. Signed Peter Johnson. Wit. oath Apr. 10, 1789 John McKinney to Obadiah Trimmier

p. 257-259 Jan. 13, 1789 John Thomas, jr (Greenville Co) to Josiah Culbertson (Spartanburgh); for 100£ sterling sold two tracts: (a) 50 ac on S side of Fairforrest Cr and on Dugars Br; grant Jun. 5, 1786 Gov. William Moultrie to John Thomas, jr; includes adjoining saw mill, pond and mill room; and (b) 960 ac on Fairforrest and Storey's Creeks; grant Feb. 5, 1787 Gov. William Moultrie to John Thomas, jr. Witness Keziah Holcomb, Daniel McMillan, and Celia Culbertson. Signed J. Thomas, Jr. Wit. oath May 29, 1789 Keziah Holcomb to Wm Smith

p. 259 Oct. 11, 1782 Nancy Dandy, widow of Charles Dandy, desc,

(96 Dist) to John Barry; sold a bay mare "pretty much in the English blood about 8 years old" natural trotter, blaze face, and two or three white feet for which she received "payment and satisfaction". Witness Thos. Moore and Chas Moore. Signed Nancy Dandy. Wit. oath Oct. 11, 1782 Thos Moore to James Jordan

p. 259-260 Jun. 8, 1789 Francis Amos, sr (late of Va now of Spartanburgh) to his son, James Amos; give a brown horse called Waldon, a feather bed and furniture, 3 pewter casons, a pewter dish, 6 pewter plates and a pot. Witness William Brooks and Archer Brooks. Signed Francis Amos. Wit. oath Jun. 15, 1789 William Brooks to David Goodlett

p. 260 May 15, 1789 Joshua Hawkins (Spartanburgh) to Rowland Johnson (same); for 20£ sold a black cow with white streak along her back and young calf and all household furniture and other property. Witness John Walker and Polley Ford. Signed Joshua Hawkins

p. 260-261 Jan. 29, 1787 John Sanders (Louisa Co) to Jordan Gibson (same); for 10£ 7s Va money sold a waggon and harness for four horses. Witness John Brown, John Boswell, and Henry Gibson. Signed John Sanders

p. 261-262 Nov. 3, 1785 Jeremiah Dotton and wife Sarah (96 Dist) to John Cannon (same); for 100£ sterling sold 200 ac on Peter's Cr of Packolate R; grant May 27, 1762 Gov. Josiah Martin (NC) to John Rock (?) Connell who sold Jul. 9, 1773 to Jeremiah Dotton. Witness Samuel Nesbitt, Henry Prince, and James Jordan. Signed Jeremiah and Sarah Dotton. Wit. oath Jun. 15, 1789 Henry Prince to James Jordan

p. 262-265 Mar. 14, 1787 Nathaniel Davis and wife Piety (Spartanburgh) to Samuel Cathcart (same); for 300£ 10s SC money sold 150 ac on Cane Cr of Broad R; grant Aug. 2, 1768 Lt. Gov. William Bull to Nathaniel Davis, heir to assigns of Richard Harris (grantee); border: SE-Timothy Toney and John Campbell, and others vacant. Witness Richard Nelley, John Butter, and David Grimes. Signed Nathaniel and Piety Davis. Wit. oath May 31, 1789 John Butter to Wm Smith

p. 265-266 Dec. 9, 1788 David Grimes and wife Agnes to Samuel Hindman; for 30£ sterling sold 100 ac on N side of Tyger R; border: Joseph Wofford and Joshua Smith. Witness John Walker and Joshua Smith. Signed David and Agnes Grimes. Wit. oath May 14, 1789 John Walker to Wm Smith

p. 266-267 Dec. 9, 1788 Joshua Smith and wife Elizabeth to Samuel Hindman; for 80£ sold 130 ac on N side of Tyger R; part of 170 ac grant Feb. 5, 1787 Gov. William Moultrie to Owen Forest "a party to these presents"; border: NW-David Grimes, and by Joshua Smith and his improvements, Samuel Cathcart, John Beard, and John Walker. Witness John Walker and David Grimes. Signed John and Elizabeth Smith. Wit. oath May 14, 1789 John Walker to Wm Smith

p. 267-268 Apr. 6, 1789 William Crocker (Spartanburgh) to John Lukeroy (same); for 20£ sold 100 ac on Richland Cr of Packolate R; border: Minehole Spring Branch; grant Oct. 6, 1788 Gov. Thomas Pinckney to William Crocker. Witness Michael McGunghy and George Basitt. Signed William Crocker

p. 268-269 Dec. 20, 1788 Adam Potter (Union Co) to Jesse Austin (Spartanburgh); for 31£ sterling sold 100 ac on N side of Packolate R; including improvements where Jacob Green formerly lived; border: David Smith; half of 200 ac grant to James Green on both sides of Green's Cr. Witness David Smith and Zachariah Bullock. Signed Adam Potter. Wit. oath Jun. 15, 1789 David Smith to John Lancaster

p. 269-271 Feb. 24, 1789 John Brawley, shoemaker, eldest son of William Brawley and heir-at-law to Ann Brownlee, alias Brawley, desc (Rowan Co, NC) to James McGowen (same); for 20£ NC money sold 100 ac on Wards Cr of N fork of Tyger R; border: SW-James McGowen; grant Aug. 12, 1768 to Anne Brownlee (alias Brawley) on bounty. Witness Robert Rogers, John Hudgens, and Wm Smith. Signed John Braley. Wit. oath Jan. 26, 1789 Robert Rogers to Wm Smith

p. 271-272 Jun. 26, 1789 Jun. 26, 1789 James McGowan (Rowan Co, NC) to William Adams (Spartanburgh); for 50£ sterling sold two tracts of 100 ac each (adjoining each other) on Wards Br of N fork of Tyger R; border: James McGowan; one lot granted to Anne Brownlee; second lot granted Aug. 12, 1768 to James McGowan on bounty. Witness Robert Rogers, John Hudgens, and Wm Smith. Signed James McGowen. Wit. oath Jan. 26, 1789 Robert Rogers to Wm Smith

p. 272-273 Aug. 7, 1789 Ephraim Rees (Spartanburgh), captain, to Samuel Jackson, jr (same); for 70£ sterling sold 150 ac on branch on S side of N fork of Packolate R; border: James Howard and Kilpatrick. Witness John Spence and Wm D. Thomas. Signed Ephraim Rees. Wit. oath (Greenville Co) Aug. 17, 1789 Wm D. Thomas to Robert Nilson

p. 273-275 Oct. 28, 1788 John McCullock (Charleston, SC), merchant, to Austin Clayton (Spartanburgh); for 20£ sterling sold 200 ac on S side of Tyger R about 2 miles above Blackstock's ford; border: John Gibbs, Thomas Miles, and Samuel Bobo; part of 1,000 ac grant Jul. 21, 1785 Gov. William Campbell to James Sample, jr and sold by Ratery Sample to John McCullock on Dec. 6, 1785. Witness Samson Bobo and Tilman Bobo. Signed Jno McCullock. Wit. oath Sept. 23, 1789 Samson Bobo to Wm Smith

p. 275 Sept. 9, 1789 Will of Henry Hargrove: first debts to be paid; second to wife, Martha Hargrove, during her widowhood remainder of estate and "at the end of her widowhood to sale and to descend to children". Executors Joseph Barnett, a friend, and son Thomas. Witness William Hammett and William Thomson. Signed Henry Hargrove

p. 275-277 Mar. 16, 1789 Elias Legate (Spartanburgh) to John Cobb (same); for 42£ sold 200 ac on Buch Cr; grant May 1, 1786 State Office to Elias Legate, blacksmith; part of land was surveyed for Montague and another part by John Turner for Robert Nelson; border: "John line", "Hightower line", Thomas Warren, and Elijah Green; Elias Legate has questions about the validity of "said Nelson's survey". Witness Ralph Cobb and Elijah Green. Signed Elias Legate and Sarah Legate's mark

p. 277-278 Jan. 20, 1789 Thomas Jordan (Spartanburgh) to Elias Legate (same); for 3£ 10s sold 200 ac on Buck Cr of Packolate R; border: John Hightower, Thomas Warren, Isaac Young, John Cantrel, and Grasy fork; grant Dec. 3, 1787 States Office to Thomas Jordan. Witness Ralph Cobb and John Cantrell. Signed Thomas and Mary Jordan's marks

p. 278-280 Sept. 21, 1789 Thomas Farrar, sherriff, (96 Dist) to Thomas Farrar; for 20£ sterling sold 243 ac on Brown's Br of Lawson's fork; this sale due to case in Charleston Common

Pleas Court Nov. term 1784 with James Brown and Jesse Brown; judgement was for 60£ 19s 10p sterling on Dec. 3, 1787 signed Jul. 1, 1788 by John Fawherard Grimbie, assoc. judge; sale was held Aug. 13, 1788; survey attached Mar. 13, 1789 by James Smith shows border: Wofford's Iron Works, Reubin Matthews, McGray, and Sasafras Swamp; land called Cainbrake tract on Lawson's Fork. Witness James Smith and Ann Williamson. Signed Thomas Farrar

p. 280-281 Jan. 19, 1788 Noel Johnson (Spartanburgh) to John Nelson (same); for 10s sterling sold 150 ac on W side of Buch Cr; grant Jan. 1, 1787 States Office to Noel Johnson. Witness Luke Browning, William Jordan, and Jesse Shoemaker. Signed Nowel and Agness Johnson

p. 281 Sept. 23, 1789 Sarah Boyd, administrix for John Boid, desc, to Benjamin Wofford; power of attorney to help administer estate of her late husband. Witness Chas Goodwin. Signed Sarah Boyd

p. 281-283 Mar. 14, 1789 Joseph Buffington (Spartanburgh) to Ninian Barret (same); for 37£ 6s 8p sterling sold a Negro fellow, Will; 21£ of sum is borrowed; if 21£ is paid by May 1, 1790 in money or a way judged equitable by Capt. Charles James or James Smith or an agreed third party, then this sale is null and void; if not, then Ninian Barret pays the remaining 16£ 6s 8p; Ninian Barret is to hire Will to Joseph Buffington until May for one barrel of (page torn). Witness Jas Smith and Charles James. Signed Joseph Buffington. Wit. oath Sept. 22, 1789 Jas Smith and Charles James to John Lancaster

p. 283 Dec. 16, 1788 Ann White, widow and administrix of Henry White, esq (Spartanburgh) to Ann White, Daniel White, Reuben White, Frances White, and Henry White; give her dower right to land warrant between Ann White and James White, late of Spartanburgh, desc; land is on Tyger R. Witness Joseph Buffington, William Clayton, and James Smith. Signed Ann White. Wit. oath Sept. 22, 1789 James Smith to Samuel Lancaster

p. 283-285 Aug. 24, 1789 Robert W. Night (or Knight) (York, SC) to Benjamin Bonner (same); for 25£ sterling sold 300 ac on S side of Broad R and both sides of Surratt's Cr; border: John Givan and Mathew Gutrey; grant Jun. 15, (blank) from SC to John W. Knigh, desc, and now sold by John's oldest son Robert. Witness David Wiley, Jas Pirketon, and James Herbeson. Signed Robt W. Night. Wit. oath Sept. 16, 1789 David Wiley to Obadiah Tremier

p. 285-287 Sept. 7, 1789 Matthew Guttry (Spartanburgh) to Benjamin Bonner (York Co); for 20£ sterling sold 122 ac on S side of Broad R and on Surratt's Cr; border: N & E-Harkley, S-W. Knight, and W-vacant; grant Oct. 6, 1788 SC Office to Matthew Guttry. Witness Obadiah Trimmier and Frederick Guttey. Signed Mathew Guttry and Elizabeth Guttry's mark. Wit. oath Sept. 6, 1789 Frederick Guttey to Obadiah Trimmier

p. 287-288 Dec. 25, 1788 Patrick Moore (Union Co) to Philimon Martin (Spartanburgh); for 50£ sterling sold 246 ac on Goties Cr; part of 400 ac grant Apr. 25, 1767 Gov. William Tryon (NC) to William Sims and William Marchbanks and sold to Patrick Moore; border: William Williams, who owns the remainder of the 400 ac. Witness John Headen, William Wilkins, and William Hargrove. Signed Patrick Moore. Wit. oath Jun. 25, 1789 William Wilkins to Obadiah Trimmier

p. 288-289 Sept. 21, 1789 Abraham Byce (Spartanburgh) to Jane Byce (same); for 10£ SC money sold 196 ac on Dam Cr of Thickety Cr; where Jane Byce now lives; grant May 1, 1786 Gov. William Moultrie to Abraham Byce. Witness Isham Safold, Elizabeth Prestage, and Josiah Edwards. Signed Abraham Byce's mark

p. 289 (blank), 1789 Joel Blackwell (96 Dist) to Patrick Sanders (Rutherford Co, NC); for 35£ Va money sold 154 ac; border: Gutry and William Morris. Witness Matthew Gutry and William Hirn. Signed Joel Blackwell. Wit. oath Aug. 15, 1789 Matthew Gutry and William Hirn to Obadiah Trimmier

p. 289-291 Aug. 26, 1789 Samuel Miller, son and heir of John Miller, desc, (Spartanburgh) to James Jordan (same); for 100£ sterling sold 400 ac on S side of Broad R and N fork of N fork of Little R (now Tyger R) above Patrick Campbel's survey; grant Sept. 3, 1753 Gov. Matthew Rowan (NC) to John Miller then in Anson Co, NC. Witness John Tinny, Lod Tulin, and Nevil Wayland. Signed Samuel Miller

p. 291 Sept. 20, 1789 Abraham Nally and wife Crissy (Spartanburgh) to Thomas Rogers (same); for 20£ sterling sold 135 ac on S side of Cane Cr of Tyger R; grant Nov. 6, 1786 Gov. William Moultrie to Ambrose Barnet. Witness David Grimes, Abraham Williams, and Benjamin Spencer. Signed Abraham and Crissy Nally's marks. Wit. oath Sept. 21, 1789 Benjamin Spencer to Sam Lancaster

p. 291-294 Mar. 12, 1789 Thomas Davis (Spartanburgh) to William Fields (same); for 100£ 10s sold 200 ac on main N fork of N fork of Tyger R; border: David Davis; grant Apr. 29, 1768 Gov. William Tryon (NC) to Elisha Thompson and wife Rachel, who sold to Samuel Pack and wife Jean and sold by their heir John Pack to Thomas Davis. Witness Elis Gohntor, Mary Broks, and Thomas Brooks. Signed Thos Davis. Wit. oath Aug. 29, 1789 Thomas Brooks to James Jordan

p. 294-296 Mar. 4, 1789 John Conner (Ga) to Moses Timmons (Spartanburgh); for 100£ 10s sterling sold 350 ac on Fann Br of Lawson Fork of Pacolet R; part of 400 ac grant May 23, 1772 Gov. Josiah Martin (NC) to Thomas Hatherway who sold for 60£ sterling to John Conner; the other 50 ac on NW corner was sold to Uriah Conner. Witness Martin Armstrong, Saml Porter, and William Wood. Signed John Conner. Wit. oath Aug. 3, 1789 Martin Armstrong to David Goodlet

p. 296-297 Apr. 10, 1789 Hopkins Bright (Spartanburgh) to Charles Burton (same); for 200£ SC money sold 283 ac on N side of Saluda R and on Ward's Cr of Tyger R; grant Nov. 4, 1786 Gov. William Moultrie to Hopkins Bright. Witness William Burton, Nath Burton, and Aaron Pinson. Signed Hopkins Bright. Wit. oath Jun. 9, 1789 Nath Burton to Wm Smith

p. 297-298 Apr. 10, 1789 Allbartus Bright (Spartanburgh) to Charles Burton (same); for 300£ SC money sold 400 ac on S side of Tyger R; grant Dec. 5, 1785 Gov. William Moultrie to Allbartus Bright. Witness William Burton, Nath Burton, and Aaron Pinson. Signed Allbartus Bright. Wit. oath Jun. 9, 1789 Nath Burton to Wm Smith

p. 298-299 Jun. 3, 1789 Daniel Grant and wife Catherine (Spartanburgh) to James Crowder (same); for 10£ sterling sold 76 ac on N side of Tyger R; part of grant Nov. 7, 1785 to Timothy Toney; border: S & W-Daniel Grant, N-vacant, and E-Joseph Powers. Witness Joseph Power and Buckner Smith. Signed Daniel and Catherine Grant's marks. Wit. oath Sept. 19, 1789 Buckner Smith to Wm Smith

p. 299-300 Jun. 5, 1789 John McCullock (SC), trader, to George Divine (Spartanburgh); for 10£ sterling sold 100 ac on S side of Tyger R; part of 1,000 ac grant to James Sample, jr; border: N-William Clayton, and the rest of the grant; below Merchants Field. Witness William Clayton and Francis Clayton. Signed Jno McCullock. Wit. oath Aug. 6, 1789 William Clayton to Saml Lancaster

p. 300-302 Oct. 20 (or 24), 1788 John McCullock to Sampson Bobo (Spartanburgh); for 200£ 10s sterling sold 350 ac between Tyger and Enoree Rivers; border: Sampson Bobo; part of 1,000 ac grant Apr. 14, 1775 Lt. Gov. William Bull to J. Sample then bordering: James Whitaker, Ezekiel Backler, Philip Waters, Edmd Bearden, Samuel Lankston, Vardry McBee (?), Moses Casey, and Sampson Bobo; sold Dec. 6, 1788 (or 85 or 86) for 600£ sterling to John McCullock. Witness Burwell Bobo, George Robuck, and Tilmon Bobo. Signed Jno. McCullock. Wit. oath Jun. 23, 1789 Burwell Bobo to Thomas Farron

p. 302-303 Dec. 27, 1787 Richard Die (96 Dist) to Joel Blackwell (Spartanburgh); for 35£ Va money sold 154 ac; border: Gentry and William Morris. Witness Joseph Price and Fredrick Gutry. Signed Richard Die's mark. Wit. oath Aug. 15, 1789 Fredrick Gutry to Obadiah Trimmier

p. 303-305 Sept. 21, 1789 Thomas Thornton and wife Martha (Spartanburgh) to John Smith (same); for 60£ sold 150 ac on E branch of Wiley's fork of Dutchman's Cr of Tyger R; grant Apr. 2, 1773; plat attached shows border: W-Moore. Witness John Shands, Larkin Lancaster, and Thomas Williams. Signed Thomas and Martha Thornton's marks. Wit. oath Sept. 21, 1789 John Shands and Larkin Lancaster to Saml Lancaster

p. 305-307 Mar. 7, 1789 William McDowel and wife Sarah (Spartanburgh) to William Poole, ironmaker; for 100£ sterling sold 700 ac in two tracts on Lawson's fork of Packolet R; (1) 500 ac grant Jun. 4, 1787; border: John Conner, William Poole, and Steadman; plat attached shows border: Waddleton; and (2) 200 ac granted May 1, 1787; border: John Conner and Turner Thomason. Witness William Poole, PS, Jas Smith and William Marchbanks. Signed William McDowel and Sarah's mark. Certified Sept. 23, 1789 by Sam Lancaster. Dower renounced by Sarah McDowel to Bayles Earle, esq

p. 307-308 Oct. 31, 1789 Richard Speake (Newberry Co) to Abraham Andrews (Spartanburgh); for 40£ SC money sold 200 ac on S Pacolet R and on Richland Cr; border: William Links; grant Gov. William Moultrie to Richard Speake. Witness John Mason, John Lindsey, and James Lindsey. Signed Richard Speake. Wit. oath Dec. 22, 1789 John Mason to D. Goodlett

p. 308-309 Mar. 15, 1789 Greenham Crowder (Spartanburgh) to John Mason (same); for 30 (?) £ sterling sold 280 ac on Thomson's Cr of Pacolet R; border: NW-George Bonnet, SW-Speaks, and others vacant; grant Jun. 4, 1787 to Greenham Crowder. Witness David Goodlett, James Johnson, and John Butler. Signed Greenham Crowder's mark. Certified Sept. 5, 1789 by D. Goodlett

p. 309-310 Dec. 25, 1788 Patrick Moore (Union Co) to William Wilkins (Spartanburgh); for 20£ sterling sold 103 ac; part of 400 ac grant Apr. 25, 1767 Gov. William Tryon (NC) to William Simms and William Marchbanks who sold to Robert Moore and to Patrick Moore by heirship; part of tract is now possessed by Philemon Martin and noted by a line drawn between Wilkins and Martin. Witness John Headen, Philemon Martin, and William

Hargrove. Signed Patrick Moore. Wit. oath Jun. 25, 1789 Philemon Martin to Obadiah Trimmier

p. 310-311 Dec. 21, 1789 John Kimbol (Spartanburgh) to John Johnson (same); for 40£ sterling sold 100 ac on Thompson Cr of S Pacolet R; below Indian line; grant in 1786 Gov. William Moultrie to John Kimbol (see Book 4H p. 265). Witness D. Goodlett, Thos Crowder, and Stephen Miller. Signed John and Sarah Kimbol's marks. Wit. oath Dec. 21, 1789 by D. Goodlett

p. 311-312 Aug. 17, 1789 Abraham Nally and wife Crisey (Spartanburgh) to Nathaniel Burton; for 100£ sterling sold 189 ac on N side of Tyger R; part of 423 ac grant Nov. 6, 1786 Gov. William Moultrie to Abraham Nally. Witness Charles Burton, Richd Nalley, and Thom. Butler. Signed Abraham anc Crisey Nally's marks. Wit. oath Aug. 22, 1789 Thom Butler to Wm Smith

p. 312-313 Mar. 20, 1789 John Hightower, minister, (Spartanburgh) to John Cantrell (same); for 80£ sterling sold 75 ac on Buck Cr; grant Jan. 21, 1785 States Office to John Hightower; border: Thomas Warren and Thomas Jordan. Witness Sampson Bethel, Elijah Green, and Isaac Young. Signed John Hightower and Christen's mark. Wit. oath Dec. 22, 1789 Isaac Young to R. Harrison

p. 313 Feb. 5, 1789 William Wofford (Spartanburgh) to James Wyatt, jr; for 60£ SC money sold 360 ac on Peter's Cr of Pacolet R; grant Jun. 5, 1786 Gov. William Moultrie to William Wofford. Witness James Wofford, Benjamin Wofford, and William Dailey. Signed W Wofford. Wit. oath Dec. 22, 1789 William Wofford to Saml Lancaster

p. 313-314 Dec. 11, 1789 John Woodward (Fairfield Co) to Isaac Young (Spartanburgh); for 60£ sold 400 ac on Buck Cr and N side of Pacolet R; grant Dec. 16, 1769 to Daniel McDaniel. Witness John Cantrell, Samson Bethel, and Mary Bethel. Signed Jno Woodward. Wit. oath Dec. 22, 1789 John Cantrell to Rich. Harrison

p. 314-315 Feb. 26, 1789 Joseph Pack (or Park) (Camden Dist) to Jacob Casey (Spartanburgh); for 100£ sold 100 ac on Cedar Shole Cr of Enoree R; grant Jul. 13, 1777 Lt. Gov. William Bull to Joseph Pack. Witness Aaron Casey to Moses Casey. Signed Joseph Pack. Wit. oath Dec. 22, 1789 Aaron Casey to D Goodlett

p. 315-316 Aug. 6, 1789 Philip Martin (Spartanburgh) to William Wilkins, Erin Davis, Charles Littlejohn, and John Headen; for 1s SC money sold 1 ac on S side of Gosher Cr where old meeting house stood and where new one is to stand. Witness Charles Littlejohn, John Humphrey, and Edmund Ellis. Signed Philemon Martin. Wit. oath Aug. 7, 1789 Charles Littlejohn to Obadiah Trimmier

p. 316-317 Jul. 24, 1789 Reuben Dickson (Spartanburgh) to John Hightower (same); for 137£ sterling sold 426 ac on both sides of Pacolet R; grant Jan. 21, 1785 State Office to Reuben Dickson; border: Thomas Warren and Edward Stubblefield. Witness Sampson Sether, John Cantrell, and Mathew Bailey. Signed Reuben and Anna Dickson's marks. Wit. oath Dec. 21, 1789 John Cantrell to Rich. Harrison

p. 317-318 Aug. 17, 1789 William Bostick (York Co) to James Wood (Spartanburgh); for 8,000 weight of tobacco sold 100 ac on both sides of Thickety Cr and sold 50 ac adjoining on S side of Thickety Cr; border: Wade and Mathew Guttray. Witness Wm Lipscomb, George Hening, and Richd Thomson. Signed William Bostick. Wit. oath Dec. 23, 1789 Wm Lipscomb to Saml Lancaster

p. 318-322 May 20, 1788 Daniel Bourdeaux (SC), merchant, to Pierce Butler, esq; Pierce Butler bound to Herculas Daniel Bize and others as security for Daniel Bourdeaux for 15,371£ 4s 10p; to secure Pierce Butler, Daniel Bourdeaux mortgages to Pierce the following property: (1) for 5£ sells a fourth of 5,000 ac on Thickety Cr of Broad R bought from Vardry McBee; (2) a third of 14,582 ac on Thickety Cr of Broad R surveyed in two parts for Daniel Bourdeaux, Col. David Hopkins, and Francis Bremar and bordering: Malachy Jones, Matthew Giothigly, Vardry McBee, Thomas Gordan, and unknown; (3) "individual moiety" of 16,569 ac at lower three runs of Savannah R where saw mills are erected being part of land originally property of Andrew Irwin and sold by Commissioners of Forfieted Estates and other part was land surveyed for Daniel Bourdeaux and for Daniel Bourdeaux and Robert McHenrath and for Pierce King, Jonathan Turner, and William Green; (4) two tracts of 500 ac each on Turkey Cr of Broad R surveyed for Daniel Bourdeaux and borders partly land surveyed for John Banfield; (5) tract in St. Thomas' Parish of 287 ac bordering: Thomas Kanvon, Nathl. Lavinsan, and William Wells; (6) a fourth of 10,000 ac in York Co, Camden Dist with William Hill, and Joseph Atkison on which is a furnace known as Aera Furnace and Forge with four fires, a lot of steel works, and various other improvements for manufacture of iron and steel; (7) 100 ac on Savannah R and Tybee Cr opposite Island Cockspur in Ga; all above done to insure Daniel Bourdeaux pays the debt. Witness John Payne and William Payne. Signed Daniel Bourdeaux. Wit. oath (in Charleston) Feb. 19, 1790 John Payne to L Drayton

p. 322-323 Jun. 3, 1789 Daniel Grant and wife Catherine (Spartanburgh) to Buckner Smith (same); for 10£ sterling sold 127 ac on Cane Cr of Tyger R; border: N and W-Joel Hembree, E and N-James Crowder, and S-Daniel Grant. Witness Joseph Power and James Crowder. Signed Daniel and Catherine Grant's marks. Wit. oath Sept. 19, 1789 James Crowder to Wm Smith

p. 323-324 Jul. 30, 1789 Daniel Grant and wife Catherine (Spartanburgh) to Thomas Beddington (same); for 20£ sterling sold 101 ac on N side of Tyger R and N of Cane Cr; part of 249 ac grant Jul. 3, 1772 to Timothy Toney; border: S-Tyger R, W-Joel Hembree, N-Samuel Cathcart, and E-Daniel Grant. Witness Thomas James and James Crowder. Signed Daniel and Catherine Grant's marks. Wit. oath Sept. 19, 1789 James Crowder to Wm Smith

p. 324 Oct. 26, 1789 in Iredell Co, NC Hugh Terrence (Iredell Co, NC), heir of Adam Terrence, desc, to William Banister, jr, heir of William Banister, desc; Hugh Terrence says Adam Terrence sold William Banister some land on S Pacolet R known as Maden Meadows; refer to records dated Dec. 12, 1786 and recorded Jun. 19, 1786 (sic); original grant has been burned; now Hugh Terrence assigns his rights to the land to William Banister, jr. Witness James McKnight and Benjn Irgram. Signed Hugh Terrence. Wit. oath Oct. 30, 1789 Benjn Irgram to Baylis Earle

p. 324-325 Mar. 6, 1790 Rebecca Berry (Spartanburgh) to Andrew Berry (same); for 44£ 6s 4p sterling sold 4 horses branded "ƗB", 15 cows marked with smooth cross on left ear and a nich and on right ear a steupel fork, 8 sheep, 13 hogs marked same as cows and their increase, 3 beds with furniture, weavers loom with tackle and other appurtenances, and all household furniture, woman's saddle and bridle and her wearing apperel, and plantation tools: plows, hoes, axes, and mallocks. Witness John Barry and

Thos Moore. Signed Rebekah Barry. Wit. oath Mar. 8, 1790 Thos Moore to James Jordan

p. 325-326 Dec. 2, 1789 Nathan Gibson (Spartanburgh) to Henry Gibson (same); for 40£ sold following: a large bay horse 7 years old, 2 feather beds and furniture, 3 cows and calves, 2 heffers, 3 young stears, 17 hogs, a large iron pot, a dutch oven, 6 pewter pleats, 2 "diches" for basons, and a crib of corn. Witness John Sanders, George Gibson, Masten Sanders, and Lewis Sanders. Signed Nathan Gibson's mark. Wit. oath Dec. 21, 1789 Lewis Sanders to Wm Smith

p. 326 Dec. 23, 1789 Ann White to James Lusk and James Smith; revokes power of attorney first given Jan. 31, 1789 to settle Henry White's estate. Witness none. Signed Ann White

p. 326-328 Mar. 18, 1790 William Moore (Spartanburgh) to Reuben Hatten (same); sold 180 ac on ____no (faded) Cr and goods and chattels and household furniture, 25 mares and 11 cattle marked (faded) and two slits in each ear; this done to secure payment by Nov. 3, 1790 of 20£ sterling William Moore owes Reuben Hatten (see note of Dec. 24, 1789) because of a horse Reuben sold William. Witness Thomas Hadden and James Hadden. Signed William Moore. Wit. oath Mar. 19, 1790 James Hadden to Andrew Barry

p. 328-329 Mar. 15, 1790 Benjamin Piper (Spartanburgh) to John Hammett Faugerson (Forqiere Co, Va); power of attorney to collect debts in Virginia. Witness Peter Carnes and W Lancaster. Signed B Piper

p. 329 Feb. 9, 1790 John Holcomb (Spartanburgh) to Charles Bruce (same); power of attorney to receive a conveyance of title to tract of land from Richard Harrison, esq that was sold to John Holcomb. Witness John Golightly and John White. Signed John Holcomb. Wit. oath Mar. 17, 1790 John Golightly to Wm Smith

p. 329 (second)-330 Apr. 29, 1789 Tobias Bright and wife Jane (Spartanburgh) to William Meadows; for 142£ 10s SC money sold 250 ac on small branches of Cane Cr of Tyger R; grant Nov. 7, 1785 Gov. William Moultrie to Tobias Bright. Witness Gideon Harelson, Thomas Meadows, and Aaron Pinson. Signed Tobias and Jane Bright. Wit. oath Jan. 30, 1790 Thomas Meadows to Wm Smith

p. 330-333 Jun. 29, 1789 Hugh Quinn (96 Dist) to Daniel McClaren (same); for 800£ SC money sold 200 ac on W side of Broad R; border: John Dill, now owned by John Ross, gentl; grant Aug. 31, 1774 Gov. William Bull to Daniel McClaren (sic). Witness Jesse Tate, Mary Tate, and James Collins. Signed Hugh Quinn's mark. Wit. oath Jan. 30, 1779 James Collins to William Tate

p. 333-334 Nov. 10, 1789 Daniel Monroe (Spartanburgh) to William Ford (same); for 42£ 14s sterling sold a bay horse which Daniel Monroe bought from John Tap (or Tass) and saddle and bridle, 5 head of cattle (all Daniel owns), 2 beds and furniture, 2 pots and oven, 3 pewter plates, 1 pewter bason and all implements of husbandry and trade, 3 staks of forrage, a table, a chest and loom, a flax wheel, 2 mares in the hands of his brother Nat, a roan and a sorrel; above sale void if Daniel pays William 42£ 14s by Mar. 5, 1790. Witness Nevil Wayland. Signed Daniel Monroe. Wit. oath Nov. 24, 1789 Nevil Wayland to James Jordan

p. 334-335 Mar. 7, 1778 James Collins, schoolmaster, to Daniel McClary; for 300£ SC money sold 60 ac which is an island in the Broad R and part of tract granted to James Collins on E side of Broad R. Witness Newberry Stockton and John Stockton. Signed James Collins. Wit. oath Mar. 7, 1778 John Stockton to John Tagert

p. 335 Nov. 22, 1788 James Philips (Rutherford Co, NC) to James Saunders (Spartanburgh); for 87£ 10s sterling sold 264 ac on both sides of Packolate R; grant Nov. 25, 1771 North Carolina to (not given); border: Isaac Young. Witness Thos Warren, William Sheid, and Isaac Young. Signed James and Jean Philips. Wit. oath Dec. 18, 1789 Thos Warren to William McDowell

p. 335 (second)-337 Jan. 22, 1790 Tilley Merrick (Pendleton Co) to John Golightly (Spartanburgh); for 5£ 5s sterling sold 264 ac on branches of Ford's Cr of Fairforrest Cr; grant Feb. 5, 1787 to Augustus Merrick; E of ancient boundary. Witness Thomas Farrar and W Cunnington. Signed Tilley Merrick

p. 337-338 Dec. 3, 1789 John Whittemore (Spartanburgh) to Samuel Neasbitt (same); for 27£ 5s sold 200 ac on S fork Tyger R; border: N-Tyger R, NW-Frances Powers and "an old line", SW-John Neasbitt and David Anderson. Witness Mary Vernon, Alexr Red, and James Jordan. Signed John Whittemore

p. 338-339 Mar. 11, 1790 William Wofford (Turkey Cove, Burk Co, NC) to Josiah Thornton (Spartanburgh); for 335£ SC money sold 300 ac on both sides of Dugan's Br of Fairforrest Cr; grant Dec. 23, 1768 Gov. William Tryon (NC) to John Gibbs then in Tryon Co, NC. Witness Samuel Gray, Thomas Thornton, and James Bernard. Signed W Wofford. Wit. oath Mar. 16, 1790 James Bernard to Samuel Lancaster

p. 339-340 Mar. 8, 1790 Wills Griffith (Spartanburgh) to George McDowell (same); for 40£ SC money sold 200 ac on both sides of Lawson's fork of Packolate R; border: Bishop and others vacant; grant Jan. 25, 1785 Gov. Benjamin Guerard to Willis Griffith. Witness Eli Griffith and Wm Rotten. Signed Wills and Elizabeth Griffith. Wit. oath Mar. 16, 1790 Eli Griffith to David Goodlett

p. 340-342 Dec. 2, 1779 Abraham Clemons (Broad River, Rutherford Co, NC) to Thomas Jackson (Pacolate River, 96 Dist); for 1,000£ 10s SC money sold 150 ac on both sides of N fork of Pacolate R; where Thomas Jackson now lives; grant Apr. 25, 1767 Gov. William Tryon (NC) to Samuel Young who sold to Bayles Earle, esq. Witness Samuel Jackson, jr and Saml Jackson. Signed Abraham Clements. Wit. oath Mar. 9, 1790 Samuel Jackson, jr to James Jordan

p. 342-343 Jan. 1 (or 12), 1790 Cranshaw Camp (Rutherford Co, NC) to John Turner (Spartanburgh), blacksmith; for 20£ sterling sold 100 ac on branch of Ashworth Cr; part of grant Oct. 6, 1788 to Cranshaw Camp; conditional boundary for tract is at head of Serratt's Cr at upper corner of Margret Green's improvement. Witness Matthis Turner and John Turner. Signed Cranshaw Camp. Wit. oath Mar. 3, 1790 Matthis Turner to Obadiah Trimmier

p. 343-344 Jan. 30, 1790 Jonathan Dildine, heir of Hermon Dildine, desc, (Spartanburgh) to John Cross (same); for 30£ sterling sold 100 ac on branch of Enoree R; grant Jun. 3, 1773 Lt. Gov. William Bull to Hermon Dildine; border: SW-William Sloutanburgh, N-Samuel Baden, and others vacant. Witness Joshua Lindsey, James Wofford, and John Hamley. Signed Jonathan Dildine. Wit. oath Mar. 16, 1790 James Wofford to Zadock Ford

p. 344-345 Jan. 19, 1790 Richard Hampton (Lexington Co) to Stephen Cantrell (Spartanburgh); for 50£ sterling sold 500 ac on N side of Enoree R; grant Oct. 5 & 6, 1785 from Commission of Confiscated Estates to William Staotlowe (or Vaottowe) who sold to Richard Hampton. Witness James Harrison and John Bowers. Signed Richard Hampton. Wit. oath (Greenville Co) Feb. 14, 1790 James Harrison to L. T. Alston

p. 345-348 Oct. 3, 1789 James Rainey (SC) to Ebenezer Morse; for 30£ sterling sold 140 ac on branch of Enoree R; border: N-Ebenezer Morse, E-James Hendrix (or Hendricks), S-Thomas Farrows; grant Jan. 21, 1785 to John Farrow and sold at public sale by Commission of Treasury to James Rainey. Witness Henry Wells and James Garner. Signed James Rainey. Wit. oath Mar. 16, 1790 Henry Wells to David Goodlett

p. 348-349 (not given), 1790 James Jordan (Spartanburgh) to William Hendrix (same); for 100£ sterling sold 300 ac on branches of Enoree R and Fougerson's Cr of Tyger R; grant Aug. 1, 1785 Gov. William Moultrie to James Jordan. Witness none. Signed James Jordan

p. 349-350 Jan. 2, 1790 Josiah Tanner (Spartanburgh) to William Wilkins (same); for 2,000£ sterling sold the following: 2 Negroes: Will about 40 years old and Peter about 19 years old; a large bay mare 10 or 12 years old branded "To", a sorrel horse 12 or 13 years old brand unknown, 4 cattle, 6 hogs marked with shallow fork in right ear and nick in each side of left ear, 3 geather beds with furniture, 3 pewter dishes and 11 plates, 2 basons, a tin pan, a pot and hooks, a set of mill irons, 2 pole axes, 3 billing (?) hoes and other plantation tools; above sold to William Wilkins for 10 years so Josiah Tanner can keep William free of trouble during time William is security for Josiah in Josiah's administration of estate of Mark Skelton in which Josiah has an interest. Witness John Thompson, Philemon Martin, and James Robinson. Signed Josiah Tanner. Wit. oath Jan 4, 1790 Philemon Martin to Obadiah Trimmier

p. 350-352 Jan. 1, 1790 Josiah Tanner (Spartanburgh) to William Wilkins (same); for 2,000£ sterling sold 1,000 ac on both sides of Thickety Cr where Josiah now lives; border: E-John Thompson, N-vacant, W-Brown, and S-Shippy; sold (or leased) for 10 years (rent of 1 pepper corn due Jan. 1 of each year); sale void if Josiah gives orphans of Mark Skelton, desc, their due from his estate and if Josiah keeps William clear of bond that William is security for Josiah as administrator of estate. Witness John Thompson, Philemon Martin, and James Robinson. Signed Josiah Tanner. Wit. oath Jan. 5, 1790 Philemon Martin to Obadiah Trimmier

p. 352-353 Feb. 4, 1789 John Swann (Campden Dist) to Joseph Boren (96 Dist); for 100£ SC money sold 100 ac on Serratt's Cr; border: Thomas Harrison; one third of grant Aug. 19, 1774 Lt. Gov. William Bull to James Gilchesta who sold to Robert Swann who sold to John Swann. Witness Alexander Elliot, Reubin Brock, Thomas Harrison, and Wm Johnson. Signed John Swann. Wit. oath Jan. 11, 1790 Thomas Harris (sic) to Obadiah Trimmier

p. 353 Mar. 14, 1790 Henry Hayes to James Jordan; power of attorney to recover a Negro from James Wood; Henry has a note of hand from James Wood selling the Negro to Henry. Witness John Hayes, Nath. Stokes, and Thomas Jackson. Signed Henry Hayes

p. 353-354 Jan. 4, 1789 John Swann (Campden Dist) to Thomas Harris (96 Dist); for 200£ SC money sold 200 ac on Serratt's Cr; two-thirds of grant Aug. 19, 1774 Lt. Gov. William Bull to

James Gilchista who sold to Robert Swann who sold to John Swann. Witness William Johnson, Joseph Boring, and Charles Boring. Signed John Swann. Wit. oath Jan. 11, 1790 Joseph Boring to Obadiah Trimmier

p. 354 Mar. 17, 1790 Ann White, widow of Henry White, desc, to William Shaw (Edgefield Co), attorney; for 50£ sterling sold a Negro Isaac. Witness Peter Carns. Signed Ann White

p. 354-355 Mar. 16, 1790 Thomas Williamson (Spartanburgh) to John Thomas, clerk of Spartanburgh Co, (same); an agreement: Thomas leases to John a ¼ ac lot where John's office is now; lot to be used as clerk's office while John is clerk; Thomas reserves use of shed adjoining SE side of office; Thomas will pay John for the house and lot (exclusive of shed) when John ceases to be clerk; Thomas and John to pick two judicious men to set the price to be paid if they can't agree on a price. Witness Obadiah Trimmier and W Lancaster. Signed Thomas Williamson and J Thomas, jr. Wit. oath Mar. 18, 1790 W Lancaster to Saml Lancaster

p. 355-356 Mar. 4, 1790 Arnis Brown (Spartanburgh) to Reubin Hatten (same); for 80£ sterling sold 100 ac on N side of Middle fork of Tyger R; border: Floyd. Witness Richard Lewis, Fields Lewis, and Beverly Lewis. Signed Aries Brown. Wit. oath Mar. 24, 1790 Beverly Lewis to David Goodlett

p. 356-357 Jan. 16, 1790 William White (Greenville Co) to William Traylor (Spartanburgh); for 20£ sold 315 ac on a branch of Tyger R; grant "see Book 4E". Witness Joel Trayton, Richard Trayton, and William Moore. Signed William White. Wit. oath May 28, 1790 Joel Trayton to David Goodlett

p. 357-358 Jan. 25, 1790 Ann White (Spartanburgh) to Brittian Willeford (same); for 20£ sterling sold the following: a black horse, a sorrel horse, a sorrel mare and colt, 3 cattle, 2 feather beds, all her household furniture and the "thirds" of land; sale is void if Ann pays Brittian 70£ principle and the interest from Mar. 15, 1790. Witness Wm Alldridge, Larkin Davis, Josiah Culbertson, and Daniel White. Signed Ann White. Wit. oath Jun. 21, 1790 Josiah Culbertson to Saml Lancaster

p. 358-360 Dec. 25, 1789 Jacob Earnest, sr and wife Agness (Abaville Co) to Robert Hammon (Spartanburgh); for 50£ sterling sold 100 ac on a branch of Jamey's Cr of Tyger R; border: S-Jacob Earnest and others vacant; surveyed Apr. 4, 1769 (in Barcley Co) for William Hendricks and grant Dec. 23, 1771 Gov. Charles G. Montague to William Hendricks. Witness John Collyer, William Hogges, and William Earnest. Signed Jacob and Agnes Earnest. Wit. oath Jun. 1, 1790 John Collyer and William Earnest to Thomas Farrow

p. 360-361 Dec. 25, 1789 Jacob Earnest, sr and wife Agnes (Abaville Co) to Robert Hammon (Spartanburgh); for 200£ sterling sold 150 ac on Jamey's Cr of Tyger R; border: W-John Lindsey, and others vacant; grant Mar. 22, 1769 Gov. Charles G. Montague to Jacob Earnest. Witness John Collyer, William Haggers, and William Earnest. Signed Jacob and Agnes Earnest. Wit. oath Jun. 1, 1790 John Collyer and William Earnest to Thomas Farrow

p. 361-363 Sept. 26, 1789 Christopher Long (Pendleton Co) to George West (Spartanburgh); for 60£ sterling sold 150 ac on N side of Lawson's Fork where George West now lives; sold Nov. 22, 1783 by William Nevil (Rutherford Co, NC) to George West (sic) see Spartanburgh Co deed Book A p. 134. Witness John Young, jr, James Burnett, and Wm West. Signed Christopher Long. Wit. oath

Jun. 20, 1790 James Burnett to Wm McDowell

p. 363 Jun. 1, 1790 William Brown (Winton Co) to Catherine Grace (Spartanburgh); for 50£ sterling sold 150 ac on both sides of Faugerson's Cr of Tyger R; W part of grant May 2, 1770 Lt. Gov. William Bull to David Prewit; border: NW-James Wofford, W-Isaac Crows, S-Enoch Floyd, and others vacant. Witness Zachariah Grace and Peter Bragg. Signed Wm Brown. Wit. oath Jun. 21, 1790 Peter Bragg to Thomas Farrow

p. 363-365 Sept. 5, 1769 William Nelly (Tryon Co, NC) to John Ward (Craven Co); for 6£ 5s NC money sold 200 ac on N fork of Tyger R; border: Charles Moore; grant Oct. 24, 1767 Gov. William Tryon (NC) to William Neely. Witness Thomas Collins and John Miller. Signed William Neely. Wit. oath Mar. 28, 1788 Thomas Collins to James Jordan

p. 365-366 May 20, 1790 (Rutherford Co, NC) George Walker to Mary Walker (SC); for 140£ sterling sold 3 Negroes: Fann (female) and her children, James about 10 years old and Mary about 2 years old. Witness Edw Scarbrough and Reubin Brock. Signed George Walker. Wit. oath Jun. 20, 1790 Edw Scarbrough to William McDowell

p. 366 May 25, 1790 George Walker to Mary Walker (Spartanburgh); for 100£ sold the following: 4 horses, a Negro Jack about 60 years old, a bright bay about 14 hands 1 in, 6 years old with a white star on forehead and branded "b", a bright bay with a large ball face glase eyes 5 years old 14 hands and branded "S" on near shoulder, a roan horse 15 years old 15 hands and branded "D" on near shoulder, and a large brown bay horse 12 years old about 14½ hands branded "D" on shoulder. Witness Edw Scarbrough and Reubin Brock. Signed George Walker. Wit. oath Jun. 20, 1790 Edw Scarbrough to William McDowell

p. 366-368 Sept. 17, 1789 Christopher Long (Pendleton Co) to George West (Spartanburgh); for 60£ sterling sold 150 ac on N side of Lawson's Fork where George now lives; tract was sold Nov. 15, 1783 by William Nevil (Rutherford Co, NC) to Christopher Long see Spartanburgh Co deed Book A p. 134. Witness John Young, jr, James Burnett, and Wm West. Signed Christopher Long. Wit. oath Jun. 20, 1790 James Burnett to William McDowell

p. 368-369 Mar. 9, 1790 William Rush (Montgomery Co, NC) to Philemon Martin (SC); power of attorney to recover debts from people living in South Carolina and to sell all his lands in SC. Witness James Garner and Mark Davis. Signed Wm Rush. Wit. oath Jun. 22, 1790 James Garner to Obadiah Trimmier

p. 369-370 Jan. 22, 1790 Martin Armstrong and wife Mary (Spartanburgh) to Henry Wells (same); for 80£ sold 377 ac on branches of Tyger R below the old boundary line; border: Knox, Clerk(?), Moffett, and vacant; grant for 370 ac(sic) Nov. 7, 1785 Gov. William Moultrie to Martin Armstrong. Witness Henry Moffett, Margret Moffett, and Jno. C. Armstrong. Signed Martin and Mary Armstrong. Wit. oath Feb. 9, 1790 Henry Moffett to James Jordan

p. 370-373 Oct. 23, 1789 James Jones and wife Elizabeth (Abaville Co) to Spencer Bobo, jr (Spartanburgh); for 10s sold 75 ac on Cedar Shoals Cr of Enoree R and on Camp Br; part of 150 ac grant Nov. 24, 1768 Gov. Charles G. Montague to James Bright who sold on Dec. 26 & 27, 1768 to Thomas Jones and to James Jones by heirship. Witness John Newman and Moses Hayes. Signed James and Elizabeth Jones. Wit. oath Apr. 7, 1790 Moses Hayes to Saml Lancaster

p. 373-375 Apr. 1, 1789 John Huger, Thomas Jones, and John Postell, Commissioners of SC Loan Office authorized by General Assembly act passed Oct. 12, 1785, to William Drayton; for 77£ 5s sold 400 ac on Shoaly Cr of Lawson's fork of Packolate R; John Conner borrowed 66£ with the land as security (see Loan Office Book A p. 145) due to General Assembly's act "An Act to Establish a Medium of Circulation by way of Loan and to Secure its Credit and Utility"; John Conner failed to pay interest on loan due Mar. 4, 1789, so land was auctioned Apr. 1, 1789 and bought by William Drayton; date of original loan was May 6, 1786. Witness F. Bremar, esq and Peter Martin. Signed Jno Huger, Thos Jones, and Jno Postell. Wit. oath (Columbia, SC) May 17, 1790 F Bremar esq to Peter Freneau

p. 375-376 Jun. 25, 1790 John Ward (Spartanburgh) to Richard Barry (same); for 160£ sterling sold 200 ac on N fork of Tyger R; grant Oct. 24, 1767 to William Neely who sold to John Ward; border: Charles Moore. Witness James Scott, David Watson, and Thos Moore. Signed John Ward. "Wit. oath" Jun. 25, 1790 John Ward delivered deed to Andrew Barry

p. 376-378 Mar. 22, 1790 John D. Young (Spartanburgh) to Thomas Moore (same); for 50£ sold 200 ac; border: John Smith, Thomas Cook, and Daniel Barnett; and sold a white horse, a sorrel colt, 4 cows and calves marked with a cross and slit on right ear and cross and hole in left ear, a man's and woman's saddle, 2 beds and their furniture, and all household furniture. Witness Charles Moore and Patrick Rodgers. Signed John D. Young. Wit. oath Mar. 22, 1790 Charles Moore to Andrew Barry

p. 378-379 Dec. 28, 1789 Richard Harrison (Spartanburgh) to John Holcomb (same); for a pepper corn sold 93 ac on N side of Fairforrest Cr; border: Harrison and Wells; part of 200 ac grant in 1785 Gov. Montague to Richard Harrison. Witness Diskin Grant, James Harrison, and Elizabeth Harrison. Signed Richard Harrison. Wit. oath (Greenville Co) Jun. 12, 1790 James Harrison to R. Maxwell

p. 379 Jul. 29, 1782 Robert Walker, sr (Mecklinburgh Co, NC) to son Robert Walker (same); half of land in Craven Co, SC above John Wilson's entry on Big Cr of Little R of Broad R and on S side of Broad R; 175 ac. Witness Jno Walker, jr and Jno Walker, sr. Signed Robert Walker. Wit. oath Dec. 30, 1784 John Walker to John Thomas, jr

p. 379-382 Dec. 29, 1784 Robert Walker (96 Dist) to David Golightly (same); for 50£ 5s sterling sold 175 ac on both sides of Fairforrest Cr; lower half of 350 ac known as McClure's tract; plat attached. Witness Jas Smith, Jesse Connell, George Connell, Fairfax Handcock, and Giles Connell. Signed Robert Walker. Wit. oath Jul. 20, 1790 Jas Smith to Saml Lancaster

p. 382 Jul. 2, 1790 Elizabeth Stewart (96 Dist) to Owen Bowen (Spartanburgh); power of attorney to recover from William Headen (Spartanburgh) two colts (one 4 years old and the other 2 years old) and their increase if any; the colts are of a sorrel mare that William Headen "had of a certain Montgomery" which Elizabeth proved was hers two years ago this fall before Squire Harrison. Witness George Campbell. Signed Elizabeth Stewart. Wit. oath (Newberry Co) Jul. 2, 1790 George Campbell to Thos Waters

p. 382-383 Apr. 1, 1790 John Bullion (Spartanburgh), son of Thomas Bullion, desc, and his heir, to Thomas Shirley (same); for 20£ sterling sold 200 ac on both sides of Tyger R; border: W-

Andrew Thomson, S-Thomas Moor, E-Charles Moore, and N-John Parker; tract was sold Jun. 24, 1774 by Charles Moore to Thomas Bullion; Condition of sale: sale is void if John delivers to Thomas on Dec. 25, 1790 200 pounds of good merchantable tobacco; tobacco to be delivered in Charleston; after it is inspected, if tobacco doesn't bring 20£ sterling at market, then John pays the remainder in Indian corn delivered at Charleston at the customary price. Witness Charles Burton and Andrew Thomson. Signed John Bullion. Wit. oath Jun. 17, 1790 Andrew Thomson to Wm Smith

p. 383-386 Apr. 8, 1789 John Edwards and William Hort, esqs, Treasurers of SC, to John Gray (Spartanburgh); for 5£ sold 200 ac on Buffington's Br below ancient boundary; border: SE-Joseph Buffington; by several acts of General Assembly, the said Treasurers are empowered to sell lands of people who don't pay "purchase money" for grants in specified time; Phebe Buffington on Oct. 15, 1784 was granted above land and didn't comply with the act of the Assembly; the land was sold Apr. 7, 1790; surveyed for Phebe Jul. 6, 1784 and plat attached signed Apr. 18, 1789 by F Bremar, surv. gen. Witness Abm Alexander and Edward Edwards. Signed John Edwards and Wm Hort. Wit. oath (in SC) Jan. 5, 1789 (sic) Edward Edwards to Zachariah Bullock

p. 386-388 Feb. 18, 1790 William Rickman (Spartanburgh) to John Gray (same); for 12£ 12s 9p sold 392 ac on People's Cr of Broad R; grant Sept. 7, 1785 Gov. William Moultrie to Vardry McBee. Witness Vardry McBee and David Lipscomb. Signed William Rickman. Wit. oath Jun. 19, 1790 Vardry McBee to Obadiah Trimmier

p. 388-390 Mar. 9, 1790 William Rickman (Spartanburgh) to John Gray (same); for 47£ 7s sold following: 7 horses: a bay horse with bald face, paces and trots, branded on near jaw and shoulder "ƗO", 14 hands and 6 years old; a chunky black horse with star in forehead and branded on near shoulder "M" named Cubb Horse; a black mare about 15 years old branded on near shoulder "GR" natural pacer; a pacer, branded on neck "ƗT" and near buttock "EC"; a sorrel branded on near shoulder and buttock "W"; a bright bay filley 2 years old last August, branded on near shoulder and buttock "W"; a black filley one year old not branded; and 36 hogs, 12 sheep, 21 geese, cotton wheels, a flax wheel, a large oven and large pot, a quantity of flax (all that is on the plantation), a side saddle, a man's saddle, all pewter about the house, a loom and jars, two pair of cotton cards, a case of knives and forks, and a grindstone. Witness Vardry McBee and Elizabeth Scot. Signed William Rickman. Wit. oath Jun. 19, 1790 Vardry McBee to Obadiah Trimmier

p. 390-392 Dec. 20, 1779 Richard Henderson, esq (NC) to Robert Henderson (SC); for 305£ SC money sold 300 ac on both sides of Cub Cr of S fork of Packolate R. Witness George Salmon and William Wood, jr. Signed Richard Henderson. Note: Col. William Henderson as attorney signed for his brother Richard Henderson. Wit. oath Feb. 29, 1780 George Salmon to James Wood

p. 392-394 Mar. 17, 1790 William Dickson (Duplin Co, NC) to William Poole (healing springs, Packolate R, Spartanburgh); for 70£ NC money sold 300 ac on S side of Packolate R and both sides of Richland Cr; formerly in Mecklinburgh Co, NC; about a mile above where John Dennis formerly settled. Witness Benjamin Burnes, James Dickson, and James Poole. Signed Wm Dickson. Wit. oath Sept. 3, 1790 James Poole to Obadiah Trimmier

p. 394-396 Apr. 12, 1790 William Poole (Spartanburgh) to James Poole (same); for 50£ sterling sold 300 ac on S side of

Packolate R and both sides of Richland Cr; about a mile above where John Dennis formerly settled; formerly in Mecklinburgh Co, NC. Witness John Stovaul, Henry Pettit, and George Poole. Signed William Poole. Wit. oath Sept. 3, 1790 John Stovaul to Oba Trimmier

p. 396 Aug. 27, 1790 Seth Lewis and Elizabeth Lewis (Spartanburgh) to James Neasbitt (same); Agness Nesbitt, wife of James, is in bad health and Seth and Elizabeth Lewis agree to take "their" mother Agness and keep her as long as she lives and bury her decently; for their care and trouble and expense James Neasbitt agrees to give them a cow and calf valued at 3£ sterling; Seth and Elizabeth Lewis and Agness Nesbitt give James Neasbitt acquittance of all debts or dower claims. Witness Jonathan Nisbett. Signed Seth Lewis, Elizabeth Lewis, and Agness Nisbitt

p. 396-397 Dec. 22, 1773 Zachariah Gibbs and John Ward (96 Dist) to John Pinkstone (late of Va); a bond for 850£ SC money; bond void if Zachariah conveys 300 ac on Ready Br of Fair-forrest Cr where Zachariah lives; a "north patent land"; and Zachariah's wife (not named) is to relinquish her dower rights. Witness John Ford and William Ford. Signed Zachrs Gibbs and John Ward. Wit. oath Mar. 22, 1791 John Ford to Zadock Ford

p. 397-398 Jul. 22, 1790 Jesse Connell and wife Ann (Spartanburgh) to Vincent Wyatt (same); for 10£ sold 260 ac on May___(faint) Br of S side of Pet___(page torn) Cr; SW end of grant Dec. 3, 1787 Gov. Thomas Pinckney to Jesse Connell. Witness George Connell and James Wyatt. Signed Jesse Connell and Ann. Wit. oath Sept. 21, 1790 Jesse Connell to Richard Harrison

p. 398-400 Sept. 21, 1790 Jesse Connell and wife Ann (Spartanburgh) to Vincent Wyatt (same); for 10£ sold 220 ac on a ridge between Peter's Cr and Packolate R; part of a grant Gov. Thomas Pinckney to Jesse Connell. Witness Benj Wofford, Jno Hightower, and James Wyatt. Signed Jesse Connell and Ann. Wit. oath Sept. 21, 1790 Jesse Connell to Richard Harrison

p. 400-401 Jun. 26, 1790 James Wyatt and wife Molly (Spartanburgh) to Vincent Wyatt (same); for 60£ sold 360 ac on Peter's Cr of Packolate R; grant Jun. 5, 1786 Gov. William Moultrie to William Wofford who sold to James Wyatt. Witness Robert Armour, Mason Cannon, and James Wyatt. Signed James Wyatt and Molly's mark. Wit. oath Sept. 21, 1790 James Wyatt to Rich. Harrison

p. 401-402 Jun. 26, 1790 Lacy McAbee (Spartanburgh) to Vincent Wyatt (same); for 3£ sterling sold 25 ac on both sides of Peter's Cr of Packolate R; part of grant Jan. 5, 1789 Gov. Thomas Pinckney to Lacy McAbee. Witness Mason Cannon and James Wyatt. Signed Lacy McAbee's mark. Wit. oath Sept. 21, 1790 James Wyatt to Ric. Harrison

p. 402-403 Dec. 15, 1790 Thomas Barton (Greenville Co) to William Barton (Spartanburgh); for 30£ sterling sold 674 ac on both sides of Pacolate R; granted Oct. 1, 1787 State's Office to Thomas Barton. Witness Mason Bennet, William Bennett, and Elizabeth McDowell. Signed Thomas Barton's mark. Wit. oath Dec. 15, 1790 Mason Bennet, William Bennett, and Elizabeth McDowell to Wm McDowell

p. 403-404 Dec. 15, 1790 Thomas Barton (Greenville Co) to William Barton (Spartanburgh); for 40£ sterling sold 100 ac on both sides of Packolate R; grant Apr. 25, (year not given) N. Carolina to Thomas Williamson who sold to Thomas Barton on Aug. 29, 1769. Witness Mason Bennett, Wm Bennett, and

Elizabeth McDowell. Signed Thomas Barton's mark. Wit. oath Dec. 15, 1790 Mason Bennett, Wm Bennett, and Elizabeth McDowell to William McDowell

p. 404-405 Jan. 6(?), 1790 Richard Barry (Spartanburgh) to John Davison and "present" wife Margret (York Co); John with consent of his wife and her son Nathan Cooper binds Nathan as apprentice to Richard, sadler, until Nathan is 21; Nathan is now 15 years old since Aug. 5, 1789; Nathan can't play cards or dice or frequent taverns or the ale house or get married or practice fornication; Richard is to provide clothes, meat, drink, washing, and lodging with one year of schooling and, when the time expires, one suit. Witness D. Gordon, Thos Moore, and Robert Hanna. Signed Richard Barry, John Davison, Nathan Cooper's mark, and Margret Davison's mark. Wit. oath Sept. 21, 1790 Thos Moore to Andrew Barry

p. 405-406 Apr. 7, 1791 William Rush (NC) to John Gowen (Pinckney Dist); for 30£ sterling sold 200 ac on both sides of Mill Cr on N side of S Packolate R; including place where John McNeel formerly lived; grant Nov. 25, 1771 Gov. Josiah Martin (NC) to Timothy Terrell and to William Rush by heirship. Witness Wm Benson, Vinson Anderson, and W Lancaster. Signed Philemon Martin attorney for William Rush

p. 406-409 Feb. 8, 1790 Martin Armstrong and Henry Moffett (Spartanburgh) to Clayborn Johnson (same); for 70£ 5s sterling sold 200 ac on both sides of Lawson's fork of Packolate R above John Rotton's land; grant Apr. 12, 1768 Gov. William Tryon (NC) to John Alexander (Mecklinburgh Co, NC) who sold to Martin Armstrong and Henry Moffett. Witness Rowland Johnson, Henry Wells, and William Check. Signed Martin Armstrong and Henry Moffett. Wit. oath Oct. 11, 1791 Rowland Johnson to D. Goodlett

p. 409-410 Feb. 11, 1790 John Foster (Union Co) to Josiah Culbertson (Spartanburgh); for 50£ SC money sold 352 ac on Fairforrest Cr; grant Jan. 1, 1787 Gov. William Moultrie to Charles Kempton who sold to John Foster on Feb. 4, 1789; border: Henry Foster, Joseph Kelso, and Col. John Thomas. Witness Thomas Brandon, James Bell, and Zachariah Bell. Signed John Foster. Wit. oath Sept. 29, 1790 Thomas Brandon and James Bell to Thos. M. Junkin

p. 410-412 Jun. 18, 1790 Rowland Cornelius, jr and wife Phebe (Spartanburgh) to William Underwood (same); for 116£ 13s 4p sold 100 ac on W side of Ready Br of Fairforrest Cr; grant Dec. 5, 1785 Gov. William Moultrie to Rowland Cornelius, sr and to Rowland Cornelius, jr by deed of gift from his father Dec. 15, 1788; also sold 280 ac on W side of Ready Cr; all(sic) of 300 ac grant Dec. 23, 1768 NC Gov. to Giles Connell and regranted by SC Gov. Sept. 9, 1774; sold by Giles Connell to Rowland Cornelius, sr who sold to Rowland Cornelius, jr. Witness David Cook and John Underwood. Signed Roland and Phebe Cornelius. Wit. oath Oct. 11, 1790 David Cook to Wm Smith

p. 412-413 Apr. 27, 1782 Giles Connell (96 Dist) to John Golightly (same); for 200£ SC money sold 155 ac on both sides of Fairforrest Cr; plat attached shows 155 ac is part of 500 ac survey Jan. 16, 1775 by John Smith; Giles Connell retains 345 ac. Witness George Brooks and Amey Brooks. Signed Giles Connell. Wit. oath Sept. 21, 1790 Giles Connell to Zadock Ford

p. 413-414 Aug. 26, 1789 James Blackwood and wife Anna (Mecklinburgh Co, NC) to Roland Johnson (SC); for 60£ Va money sold (ac not given) on S side of Lawson's fork of Pacolet

R; border: John Rolons (or Rottons); except half of all gold and silver mines. Witness Eli McVay. Signed James and Anna Blackwood. Wit. oath Oct. 6, 1789 Eli McVey(sic) to David Goodlet

p. 414-415 Feb. 24, 1789 Charles Kempton (Charleston, SC) to John Foster (Union Co); for 10£ sold 352 ac on Fairforrest Cr; grant Jan. 1, 1787 Gov. William Moultrie to Charles Kempton; border: Henry Foster, Joseph Kelsoe, and Col. John Thomas. Witness Thomas Brandon and John Gray. Signed Charles Kempton. Wit. oath (Union Co) Sept. 29, 1790 Thomas Brandon to Joseph McJunkin

p. 415-416 Sept. 21, 1790 Major Passons to Thomas Tod; in Spartanburgh Court (Sept. 1790 term) Major Passons makes oath that Thomas Tod gave his bond to Major when Major sold Thomas the land where Col. John Thomas, sr now lives; the bond obliges Thomas to return the land to Major if Major repays debt to Thomas (date not given); the penality to Thomas for not returning land is 200£ sterling to be paid to Major; but Major never repaid his debt to Thomas, so the bond is void but has been lost or mislayed. Witness W Lancaster. Signed Major Passons

p. 416-417 May 11, 1790 Littleton Mapp, jr (Spartanburgh) to Joseph Austell (same); for 11£ sterling sold 100 ac between Thickety Cr and Gochen Cr; border: E-Austell, S-old fort land, W-Anderson, and N-Thompson; grant in 1787 Gov. Thomas Pinckney to James Fannen. Witness James Garner and Elizabeth Humphrey. Signed Littleton Mapp. Wit. oath Sept. 13, 1790 James Garner to Obadiah Trimmier

p. 417-418 Sept. 12, 1790 George Story (Spartanburgh) to John Story (same); for love and affection to his son gives 85 ac on both sides of Storey's Cr of Fairforrest Cr (see attached plat); border: W & S-Henry Story and others by George Story; part of 448 ac grant Nov. 18, 1752 Gov. Nathaniel Rice (NC) to George Story and in Auditor's book (SC?) Jun. 20, 1774 formerly in Anson Co, NC and now in Spartanburgh Co, SC on S side of Broad R and on Fairforrest Cr. Witness Henry Story, John White, and Jas Lusk. Signed George Story. Wit. oath Sept. 21, 1790 Jas Lusk to William Smith

p. 418-420 Sept. 15, 1789 Ephraim Lewis (Spartanburgh) to George Bishop, sr (same); for 60£ SC money sold 300 ac on branch of Lawson's fork of Packolet R. Witness George Bishop, jr, Wm Liles, and George Miller. Signed Ephraim Lewis. Wit. oath Sept. 21, 1790 Wm Liles to D Goodlett

p. 420-421 Jun. 5, 1790 Roland Johnson and wife Milley (Spartanburgh) to William Wood, sr (same); for 30£ Va money sold 125 ac; border: Rotton; exclusive of half of gold and silver mines; sold by James Blackwood and wife Anna to Roland Johnson Aug. 26, 1789. Witness John Young, jr and James Wood, jr. Signed Roland and Milley Johnson. Wit. oath Jul. 17, 1790 James Wood, jr to D Goodlett

p. 421 Oct. 26, 1789 Handcock Smith (Spartanburgh) to William Smith (same); for 70£ sterling to be paid on or before Dec. 25, 1790 sold 192 ac on both sides of Fairforrest Cr; border: Suddoth, Wm Smith, Peter Smith, John Smith, and others; grant Jan. 21, 1785 (by not given) to Handcock Smith. Witness Jas Smith, Jane Smith, and Ann Smith. Signed Handcock Smith. Wit. oath Sept. 22, 1790 Jane Smith to Saml Lancaster

p. 421-423 Apr. 20, 1790 John Beardan and wife Ann (Spartanburgh) to John Shands (same); for 75£ sterling(? page torn) sold 271 ac on branch of Tyger R and on N side of Tyger R; grant to John Beardan. Witness Zopher (or Tossher) Smith and Saml Smith. Signed John and Ann Beardan. Wit. oath Sept. 9, 1790 Zopher Smith and Saml Smith to Saml Lancaster

p. 423-424 May 20, 1789 John Evans, jr (Caroline Co, Va) to William Benson, esq (Spartanburgh); power of attorney to make deeds for two tracts of land sold by John Evans to Reubin Samuel (Caroline Co, Va) because John cannot travel to South Carolina; one tract is in Greenville Co and one tract is in Spartanburgh Co. Witness Robert Gilchrist, Edward Evans, and John Evans. Signed John Evans, jr. Wit. oath (Caroline Co, Va) Aug. 4, 1789 Robert Gilchrist and John Evans to Thomas Miller. Wit. oath Aug. 4, 1789 Edward Evans to Thomas Miller

p. 424-425 Sept. 21, 1790 Thomas Williamson (Spartanburgh) to Baylis Earle, James Jordan, William Smith, David Goodlett, Zadock Ford, William McDowell, Andrew Barry, James Farrow, Richard Harrison, Obadiah Trimmier, and Samuel Lancaster, esqs, Justices of Spartanburgh Co Court; for 5 s sold 2 ac part of land where Thomas Williamson lives and where county buildings have been erected; Thomas also gives people at the courthouse free use of nearby spring; this sale due to an act of General Assembly Mar. 12, 1785, "An Act for laying off the Several Counties Herein mentioned and to appoint Commissioners to erect public buildings"; the Justices of such Counties among other things are vested with full power to purchase or receive by annexation two ac of land whereon to erect the county buildings; by act of the Governor and Council (date not written in), the county buildings are to be erected on land owned by Thomas Williamson. Witness W. Shaw and Thos Moore. Signed Thomas Williamson

p. 425-426 May 11, 1790 Jesse Reams and wife Agness (Spartanburgh) to Robert Kimbell (same); for 50£ sold 200 ac on E side of Old Indian Line; grant Jan. 21, 1785 Gov. Benjamin Guerard to Jesse Reams and wife. Witness Thomas Brooks and Mary Brooks. Signed Jesse and Agness Reams. Wit. oath Sept. 20, 1790 Thomas and Mary Brooks to Saml Lancaster

p. 426-427 Jul. 9, 1790 James Rainey, surveyor (SC) to John Wilson (Spartanburgh); for 40£ sterling sold 640 ac on S side of Tyger R; grant to James Semple, sr; border: SE-James Smith, SW-Rustine Young, NW-Benjamin Wofford and Tyger R. Witness Martin Newman and Reubin Newman. Signed James Rainey. Wit. oath Dec. 31, 1790 Reubin Newman to Andrew Barry

p. 427-428 Aug. 10, 1789 Patrick March (Spartanburgh) to Francis Ward (same); for 50£ sterling sold 150 ac on N side of N fork of Tyger R; grant Jan. 21(?), 1785 Gov. Benjamin Guerard to Patrick March; surveyed Sept. 29, 1773; border: S-Tyger R, N-John Ward and John Ford. Witness John Ward and John Brown. Signed Patrick March's mark. Wit. oath Nov. 3, 1790 John Ward and John Brown to Andrew Barry

p. 428-430 Dec. 17, 1790 Rowland Cornelius and wife Mary (Spartanburgh) to David Cook (same); for 55£ SC money sold 120 ac on S side of Reedy Cr of Fairforrest Cr; on a line with 100 ac Rowland received (?by grant) Dec. 5, 1785; border: Tillet (including part of 640 ac granted Giles Tillet), below mouth of Cornelius Spring Br, and land sold by Roland Cornelius, jr to William Underwood; includes part of grants to Giles Tillet and Rowland Cornelius. Witness John Golightly, Peter Kimsey, and Mariam Oats. Signed Roland and Mary Cornelius' marks. Wit. oath Mar. 1, 1791 John Golightly to Isham Harrison

p. 430-431 Jan. 31, 1791 William Brandon (Spartanburgh) to John Ginnings (same); for 150£ sterling sold 300 ac on both sides of Lawson's Fork; part of 400 ac grant Jul. 4, 1785 Gov. William Moultrie to William Brandon. Witness James Perry and Jeremiah Garner. Signed William Brannon and Searbary Brannon's mark. Wit. oath Mar. 22, 1791 James Perry to D Goodlett. Rec. May 24, 1791.

p. 431 Jun. 12, 1777 Susannah Spencer (Anson Co, NC) to son Jesse Spencer (same); for love and affection give Jesse all her estate except 1/8 of land; Susannah is to give Jesse an inventory of the estate dated "evan date"; condition of this gift: that Jesse keep and rear her three youngest children as best he can. Witness Jno McInvaile and Griffen Hogan. Signed Susannah Spencer's mark. Rec. May 24, 1791

p. 431-432 Oct. 1, 1790 William Crocker (Spartanburgh) to Benjamin Howard (same); for 25£ SC money sold 100 ac; border: William Crocker and Arthur Crocker's old line. Witness Mich Megaughy and John Luckroy. Signed William Crocker. Wit. oath Apr. 11, 1791 William Crocker to Isham Harrison. Rec. May 25, 1791

p. 432-434 Mar. 28, 1790 Alexander Kilpatrick and wife Judith (Pendleton Co) to Benjamin Clock (Spartanburgh); for 150£ sterling sold 300 ac on a branch of S fork of Packolate R; grant Apr. 27, 1767 Gov. William Tryon (NC) to Samuel Spencer who sold to Alexander Kilpatrick, deed is in Spartanburgh Co. Clerk's Office. Witness John C. Kilpatrick and John Young, jr. Signed Alexander and Judith Kilpatrick. Rec. May 25, 1791

p. 434-435 Apr. 7, 1791 John Hammett (96 Dist) to William Hammett (same); for 10£ sterling sold 94 ac on Packolate R; border: John Harris; grant Nov. 10, 1786 Gov. William Moultrie to John Hammett. Witness Wm Underwood, Francis Mason, and Thos Posey. Signed John Hammett. Wit. oath Apr. 11, 1791 John Hammett to Isham Harrison. Rec. May 26, 1791

p. 435-436 Jan. 15, 1791 Minor Winn, esq (Fairfield Co) to John Ford, jr (Spartanburgh); for 50£ SC money sold 500 ac "at the line" on a branch of Tyger R; formerly Robert Wills' land and sold by Commissioners of Forfieted Estates to Minor Winn, esq Oct. 5 & 6, 1785; plat made by Malcolm Clark, dept. surv. Jul. 13, 1772; land originally in Craven Co. Witness Robert Rabb, Spence Ford, and Thomas Bell. Signed M Winn. Wit. oath May 26, 1791 Spence Ford to Thos Moore. Rec. May 26, 1791

p. 436-437 Nov. 9, 1790 John Beardan (Spartanburgh) to son-in-law William Smith, esq (same); for love and affection sells a Negro girl, Violet. Witness John Beardan and Moses Clayton. Signed John Beardan. Wit. oath Apr. 11, 1791 John Beardan to D Goodlett. Rec. May 26, 1791

p. 437-439 Nov. 16, 1790 William Calwell (Newberry Co) to Martha McCrory (Sparting Co); for 10£ 5s sold 100 ac on Jamey's Cr; grant Aug. 11, 1774 Lt. Gov. William Bull to John Dunkin (or Duncan) who sold to William Calwell Jan. 19 & 20, 1787; when granted border: W-Marting Livingstone, E-"an old survey", and others vacant. Witness Phebe French, John Rodgers, and Andrew Thomson. Signed William Caldwell. Rec. May 27, 1791

p. 439-440 Oct. 11, 1790 John Bagwell (Spartanburgh) to Littleton Bagwell and George Parkison (same); for 4£ 9s 7p sold 3 (?page torn) cows and calves, 3 heifers, 2 steers, a dark bay horse with bald face and all stock, 2 beds and furniture, 6 pewter plates and all household furniture, all corn and fodder and all tools. Witness Samuel Ward, sr and Giles Connell. Signed John Bagwell's mark. Wit. oath Apr. 11, 1791 Samuel Ward to Isham Harrison

p. 440-443 Jan. 6, 1791 John Bullion (Spartanburgh), heir and oldest son of Thomas Bullion, desc (same), to Andrew Thomson (same); for 126£ 6s 8p sterling sold 200 ac on both sides of Tyger Cr, formerly Lawson's Cr; border: Andrew Barry; part of 550 ac grant May 13, 1763 to Charles Moore who sold 200 ac to Thomas Bullion Jun. 24, 1774. Witness Charles Burton, Thomas Shurly, and John Ford. Signed John Bullion. Wit. oath Apr. 12, 1791 Charles Burton to Wm Smith

p. 443-444 Dec. 28, 1790 William Moore (Spartanburgh) to John Durham (same); for 50£ sterling sold 171 ac on Reedy fork of S Tyger R; border: John Nisbett and John Anderson; E part of 271 ac grant Mar. 6, 1786 to William Moore. Witness Philip Johnson, John Jeffers, and Thos Hadden. Signed William Moore. Rec. May 28, 1791

p. 444-446 (not given), 1790 Luke Thornton and wife Martha (Spartanburgh) to Nicholas Keating (Union Co); for 50£ sterling sold 140 ac on S side of Tyger R; part of grant Apr. 3, 1786 Gov. William Moultrie to Thomas White who sold to Luke Thornton in 1788. Witness Thomas Price, Joseph Venable, and Andrew Thomson. Signed Luke Thornton and Martha's mark. Rec. May 28, 1791

p. 446-447 Mar. 4, 1791 William Traylor (Spartanburgh) to Elizabeth Williams, jr (same); for 40£ sold 200 ac on N end of 315 ac grant Aug. 1, 1785 to William White who sold to William Traylor. Witness Isham Foster, Milley Traylor, and Elizabeth Williams, jr. Signed Wm Traylor. Wit. oath Apr. 12, 1791 Isham Foster to D Goodlett. Rec. Jun. 2, 1791

p. 447-449 Mar. 9, 1790 Samuel Farrow, high sheriff (Spartanburgh Co) to Thomas Tod (same); for 5£ sold 300 ac on N side of Enoree R; grant Oct. 2, 1786 Gov. William Moultrie to (not given) and recorded in Secretary's grant book 4-o p. 43; sale is due to a court case of Charles Waters vs. John Couch which was won by John Couch; writ from Spartanburgh Co Court, Baylis Earle presiding, on third Monday in Mar. 1789 to collect 6£ 10s 5p sterling from Charles Waters; sale of land was held Mar. 18, 1789. Witness W Lancaster and Brittain Willeford. Signed Saml Farrow. Wit. oath Mar. 9, 1790 W Lancaster to Obadiah Trimmier. Rec. Jun. 2, 1791. plat attached

p. 449-450 Mar. 15, 1790 Thomas Tod (Spartanburgh) to Samuel Farrow, high sheriff (same); for 5£ sold 300 ac on N side of Enoree R; border: S-Enoree R, E-James Benton, W-James Couch; part of 450 ac grant Oct. 2, 1786 Gov. William Moultrie to Charles Waters; 300 ac were seized and sold for a debt of Charles Waters and bought from Samuel Farrow by Thomas Tod. Witness Thomas Farrow and W Lancaster. Signed Thomas Tod. Rec. Jun. 10, 1791

p. 450-451 Feb. 24, 1789 Thomas Stribling and William Buckhannon (Union Co) to Samuel Farrow (Spartanburgh); a bond for 1,000£ sterling; "some time past" Samuel sold Thomas and William some land in Union Co on Brown's Cr in two parts: Thomas got 300 ac on Apr. 9, 1785 and William got 150 ac on Apr. 8, 1785; but Samuel's right to land proved deficient; but transactions are recorded and the whole matter is now "compremised and settled"; this bond is void if the transactions deemed null and void. Witness Wm Smith and Wm Farr. Signed Thos Stribling and Wm Buckhannon

p. 451-452 May 24, 1791 Joel Hembree and wife Hannah to Lee Clark; for 60£ sterling sold 230 ac on N side of Tyger R near Cane Cr. Witness John Hyndman (or Hindman) and John Walker. Signed Joel Hembree and Hannah's mark. Wit. oath May 28, 1791 John Hindman to Wm Smith. Rec. Aug. 23, 1791

p. 452-455 Dec. 10, 1774 John Kissler and wife Hanna to David Dunamore; for 500£ SC money sold 250 ac in Craven Co on Jamey's Cr of Tyger R; border: all vacant; grant May 2, 1770 Lt. Gov. William Bull to John Kissler. Witness James Wofford, Mary Crow, and James Driver. Signed John Kisseler and Hanna's mark. Rec. Aug. 23, 1791

p. 455-456 May 24, 1791 Samuel Hindman and wife Jean to John Hindman; for 30£ sterling sold 100 ac on N side of Tyger R; border: Joseph Wofford and Joshua Smith. Witness Joel Hembree and William Hyndman. Signed Samuel Hindman and Jean's mark. Wit. oath May 28, 1791 Joel Hembree to William Smith. Rec. Aug. 23, 1791

p. 456-457 Mar. 16, 1789 Obadiah Edwards (Union Co) to Aaron Pinson; for 40£ sterling sold 200 ac on N side of Tyger R; border: S-Tobias Bright and others vacant; grant Nov. 6, 1786 Gov. William Moultrie to Obadiah Edwards. Witness Tobias Bright, Rachel Bright, and James Bright. Signed Obadiah Edwards. Wit. oath Jun. 13,1791 Tobias Bright to David Goodlett. Rec. Aug. 25, 1791

p. 457-458 Mar. 19, 1791 Michael McGaughey (Spartanburgh) to Enos Land (same); for 15£ sterling sold 150 ac on Packolet R; border: Thomas Brown, Luckroy's Branch, and McGaugh. Witness Aaron Land and John Megaughy. Signed Michael Megaughh's mark. Wit. oath Jun. 13, 1791 Michael McGaughey to Isham Harrison. Rec. Aug. 25, 1791

p. 458-459 (not given), 1790 John Ward (Spartanburgh) to Daniel Barnett, blacksmith (same); for 20£ sold 100 ac on N side of N fork of Tyger R and on Ward's Br; border: all vacant; grant Aug. 21, 1776 Gov. Charles G. Montague to (not given). Witness John Ford and Thomas Hightower. Signed John Ward. Rec. Aug. 26, 1791

p. 459-460 Mar. 30, 1790 Stephen Miller (Spartanburgh) to George Bishop (same); for 15£ SC money sold 100 ac on N side of Lawson's Fork of Packolate R; grant Nov. 25, 1774 Lt. Gov. William Bull to Stephen Miller. Witness Hance Harper and Edward Bishop, jr. Signed Stephen Miller. Wit. oath Jun. 13, 1791 Hance Harper to David Goodlett. Rec. Sept. 1, 1791

p. 460-462 Apr. 11, 1791 Robert Patten (Burk Co, NC) to Jesse Spencer (Spartanburgh); for 20£ sterling sold 100 ac on Ward's Br of N fork of Tyger R; border: all vacant; grant Aug. 24, 1779 to Alexander Curry who sold to Robert Patten on Jan. 12, 1775. Witness Lawson Thomson and James Scott. Signed Robert Patten. Wit. oath Jun. 13, 1791 Lawson Thomson to Thos Moore. Rec. Sept. 1, 1791

p. 462-463 Jan. 14, 1791 Ellis Cannon (96 Dist) to Daniel Walker (same); for 20£ sterling sold 100 ac on Peter's Cr; grant Dec. 28, 1787 Gov. Thomas Pinckney to Ellis Cannon. Witness George Lamkin, sr, James Wyatt, and John Cannon. Signed Ellis Cannon. Wit. oath Jun. 13, 1791 Ellis Cannon to Samp Bethel. Rec. Sept. 6, 1791

p. 463-464 Mar. 5, 1790 John McCulloch to Edward Hooker; for 10£

sterling sold 300 ac which is all of the unsold land from a 1,000 ac grant to James Simple, jr between Tyger and Enoree Rivers. Witness Edmund Clayton and Thos Tod. Signed Jno McCullock. Wit. oath Sept. 2, 1791 Thos Tod to Wm Smith. Rec. Sept. 6, 1791

p. 464-465 Dec. 17, 1790 John Elder (Spartanburgh) to Robert Elder (same); for 100£ SC money sold 300 ac on Crowdan's Cr of Broad R; it is half of land John bought from Robert Cowden Jan. 16, 1765 and recorded in Mecklinburgh Co, NC Quarterly Sessions Court Jul. 4, 1789; grant Sept. 3, 175(? page torn) Gov. Matthew Rowan (NC) to (not given) and recorded in Charleston Surveyor Book 9 p. 520 on Sept. 12, 1786 and examined by Peter Bremar, surv. gen. Witness Alexander Elder and Thomas Carey. Signed John Elder. Wit. oath Dec. 20, 1790 Alexander Elder to D Goodlett. Rec. Sept. 7, 1791

p. 465-466 May 11, 1790 John Lindsey (Spartan Co) to John McMahan (same); for 30£ sold 100 ac on N side of Enoree R (formerly Kings R) where Mary Hanna now lives; border: "along a line of a minor date Pennington's land"; part of a "north survey" of 600 ac granted May 11, 1753 Gov. Matthew Rowan (NC) to Bartlett Brown. Witness John Ambler Johnson, Nathan Childs, and Carlton Lindsey. Signed John Lindsey. Wit. oath Mar. 1, 1791 John Ambler Johnson to Thomas Farrow. Rec. Sept. 7, 1791

p. 466-468 May 30, 1791 Randolph Johnson (Spartanburgh) to John Snoddy (same); (money not given) sold 148 ac on Jamey's Br; border: Sadler; part of grant to John Leech and sold to Randolph Johnson. Witness Samuel Miller, Samuel Snoddy, and Isaac Snoddy. Signed Randolph Johnson's mark. Wit. oath Jun. 14, 1791 Samuel Miller to D Goodlett. Rec. Sept. 7, 1791

p. 468-469 Feb. 21, 1791 Reubin Lawson (Spartanburgh) to Thomas Hughes (same); for 40£ SC money sold 100 ac on S side of Packolate R; border: Hurrican Br, Wild Cat Br, Mr Milhank's line, and Robinson. Witness Ellis Cannon, Jesse Cannon, and Mason Cannon. Signed Reubin Lawson's mark. Wit. oath Jun. 14, 1791 Ellis Cannon to Isham Harrison. Rec. Sept. 9, 1791

p. 469-470 Jan. 15, 1791 Nichodemus Thomson and wife Sarah (Spartanburgh) to James Wood (same); for 35£ SC money sold 200 ac on both sides of Big Br of Thickety Cr; border: N-Vardry McBee and others vacant; grant Jan. 1789 SC office to Nichodemus Thomson. Witness Obadiah Watson and Jno Trimmier. Signed Nichodemus Thomson and Sarah's mark. Wit. oath Jun. 15, 1791 Obadiah Watson to D Goodlett. Rec. Sept. 9, 1791

p. 470-472 Aug. 9, 1791 Augustin Clayton to Edward Hooker; for 10£ sterling sold 200 ac; part of 1,000 ac grant Jul. 21, 1775 Gov. William Campbell to James Simple, jr and sold Dec. 6, 1785 by Rattey Simple to John McCulloch who sold to Augustin Clayton; between Tyger and Enoree R about two miles above Blackstock's farm on Tyger R; border: John Gibbs, Thomas Milus, and Samson Bobo. Witness Absalom Bobo, William Simmons, and Thomas Tod. Signed Augustine Clayton. Wit. oath Sept. 2, 1791 Thomas Tod to Wm Smith. Rec. Sept. 9, 1791

p. 472 Apr. 11, 1791 William Lancaster, David Golightly, John Golightly, and James Terrill to Treasurers of State of SC; a bond for 1,000£ sterling; Condition: that William Lancaster perform duties of County Court Clerk to which he was elected. Witness none. Signed W Lancaster, David Golightly, John Golightly, and James Terrill

p. 472-473 Apr. 11, 1791 John Gowen, William Benson, and Andrew

Thomson to Commissioners of Treasury of SC; a bond of 1,500£; Condition: that John Gowen be a good sherriff, an office to which he has been appointed. Witness none. Signed Jno Gowan, Wm Benson, and Andrew Thomson

p. 473-476 Jan. 9, 1755 Samuel Gilkey to Adam Dickeson; for 30£ Va money sold (ac not given) in Anson Co, NC on S side of Broad R and both sides of Kings R; Samuel agrees to go 300 miles (if necessary) in the next 50 years at Adam's expense to prove this transaction; entered in SC Auditor's Book L #11 p. 92 on Nov. 7, 1771. Witness Alexander Lockhart and Wm Wilkinson. Signed Samuel Gilkey. Wit. oath Sept. 15, 1791 Alexander Lockhart to S Bethel. Rec. Nov. 11, 1791

p. 476-477 Aug. 13, 1790 William Dickson, captain (Spartanburgh) to John Kirklain (same); for 35£ sterling sold 100 ac on N side of Packolate R; border: Henry Turner; grant Nov. 7, 1785 SC office to William Dickson. Witness Samson Bethel and John Cantrill. Signed William Dickson. Wit. oath Jul. 20, 1791 John Cantrill to S Bethel. Rec. Nov. 22, 1791

p. 477-478 Mar. 18, 1791 Robert Hammon and wife Elizabeth (Spartanburgh) to Alexander Alexander (same); for 50£ sterling sold 100 ac on Jamie's Cr of Tyger R; border: S-Jacob Earnest and others vacant; survey for William Hendrix Apr. 4, 1769 in Barkley Co; grant (date not given) Gov. Charles G. Montague to (not given). Witness David McCarley, William Kesley, and Richard Chesney. Signed Robert Hammon and Elizabeth's mark. Wit. oath Sept. 10, 1791 David McCarley to Thomas Farrow

p. 478-479 Mar. 8, 1791 Robert Hammon and wife Elizabeth (Spartanburgh) to Alexander Alexander (same); for 100£ sterling sold 150 ac on Jamie's Cr of Tyger R in Berkly Co; border: W-John Lindsey and others vacant when granted by Gov. Charles G. Montague. Witness David McCarley, William Kesley, and Richard Chesney. Signed Robert Hamon and Elizabeth's mark. Wit. oath Sept. 10, 1791 David McCarley to Thomas Farrow. Rec. Nov. 25, 1791

p. 479-482 Dec. 25, 1786 Charles Waters and wife Mary (Spartanburgh) to Samuel Farrow (same); for 100£ 10s sterling sold 150 ac on Enoree R; part of 450 ac grant Oct. 2, 1786 Gov. William Moultrie to Charles Waters; border: James Couch, Edward Linch, Samuel Farrow, and Westwood Waters, and Thomas Scurry. Witness Mrs Betsy Ham, Mrs. Mary Blasingame, and Miss Polley Blasingame. Signed Charles Waters' mark and Mary Waters. Wit. oath (Greenville Co) Oct. 22, 1791 Polley Blasingame to Blasingame. Rec. Nov. 28, 1791

p. 482-483 Mar. 17, 1791 Henry Foster, sr (Lancaster Co) to John Foster and Henry Foster, jr (Spartanburgh); for 100£ sterling sold 170 ac in two parts: (1) 150 ac granted Aug. 25, 1769 Gov. William Bull to Henry Foster; and (2) 20 ac part of grant Nov. 18, 1752 Gov. Nathaniel Rice (NC) to James Mitchell on both sides of Fairforrest Cr; the total 170 ac includes a Great Shoal where Henry Foster, jr now lives. Witness Adam Potter, John White, and Hugh Means. Signed Henry Foster. Wit. oath (Union Co) Sept. 9, 1791 John White to H Means. Rec. Nov. 29, 1791

p. 483-485 Mar. 17, 1791 Henry Foster, sr (Lancaster Co) to John Foster (same); for 100£ sterling sold 180 ac on both sides of Fairforrest Cr; border: a line between John and Henry Foster, jr; part of 380 ac grant Nov. 18, 1752 Gov. Nathaniel Rice (NC) to James Mitchell who sold to Henry Foster, sr. Witness Adam Potter, John White and Henry Foster. Signed Henry Foster. Wit. oath (Union Co) Sept. 9, 1791 John White to H Means. Rec.

BOOK B

Nov. 29, 1791

p. 485-486 Mar. 17, 1791 Henry Foster, sr (Lancaster Co) to Henry Foster, jr (Spartanburgh); for 100£ sterling sold 180 ac on both sides of Fairforrest Cr just above mouth of Pounding (or Rounding) Mill Br; part of grant Nov. 18, 1752 Gov. Nathaniel Rice (NC) to James Mitchell who sold to Henry Foster, sr. Witness Adam Potter, John White, and John Foster. Signed Henry Foster. Wit. oath (Union Co) Sept. 9, 1791 John White to H Means. Rec. Nov. 29, 1791

p. 486-487 Nov. 21, 1789 Charles Carter (Spartanburgh) to Samuel Farrow, sheriff (same); a bond of 100£ sterling; Condition: bond void if Charles Carter makes deed for one-third of Thomas Scurry's (desc) land to Polley Scurry when Polley is of age; Thomas Scurry's will leaves land equally divided between his daughters: Liddy Carter, Katey Scurry, and Polley Scurry. Witness Peter Brooks and Landon Waters. Signed Charles Carter's mark. Wit. oath Aug. 21, 1791 Peter Brooks to Thomas Farrow. Rec. Dec. 3, 1791

p. 487-488 Apr. 26, 1790 James Lusk (Spartanburgh) to Josiah Culbertson (same); for 300£ sterling sold 430 ac on Fairforrest Cr and a Negro man Charles; sale is void if James Lusk pays Josiah Culbertson 300£ sterling principle and 21£ annual interest at the end of 5 years. Witness Robert Davison. Signed Jas Lusk. Rec. Dec. 3, 1791

p. 488 Apr. 26, 1790 James Lusk (Spartanburgh) to Robert Davison (same); for 45£ sterling sold 20 cattle, 3 horses, 20 hogs, and 15 sheep; sale is void if James pays Robert 45£ sterling principle and 3£ 3s annual interest in 5 years. Witness Samuel Clouney and Archibald Cloney. Signed Jas Lusk. Rec. Dec. 3, 1791

p. 488-489 Dec. 15, 1790 Ebenezer Morse (Spartanburgh) to Benjamine Busey (same); for 200£ sterling sold 100 ac on E side of Two Mile Cr of Enoree R; border: George Lawther, Isaac Hendrix, William Cleaton, and William Miles. Witness James Morse and James Wofford. Signed Ebezener Morse's mark. Rec. Dec. 12, 1791

p. 489-491 Dec. 18, 1789 William Hargrove (Spartanburgh) to John George Reiner (or Riner) (same); for 50£ SC money sold 100 ac on Green Cr of Packolate R; grant Oct. 6, 1788 Gov. Thomas Pinckney to William Hargrove. Witness John Headen and Ignatius Griffin. Signed William Hargrove's mark. Wit. oath Sept. 12, 1791 Ignatius Griffin to S Bethel. Rec. Dec. 12, 1791

p. 491 Oct. 15, 1789 John Evans, jr (Caroline Co, Va) to Reubin Samuel (same); for 100£ sterling sold 500 ac on Holeson's Br of Fairforrest Cr. Witness Thomas Farrar and Obadiah Wingo. Signed John Evans, jr and Wm Benson, by virtue of power of attorney. Wit. oath Sept. 12, 1791 Wm Benson, esq to D Goodlett. Rec. Dec. 13, 1791

p. 491-493 Apr. 8, 1790 Michael McGaughy (Spartanburgh) to Thomas Brown (same); for 30£ SC money sold 150 ac on branches of Packolet R; border: Solomon Crocker and McGaughy's Spring Br; part of grant Jun. 2, 1788 Gov. Thomas Pinckney to Michael McGaughy. Witness John Peterson and Jacob Wholmes. Signed Michael McGaughy. Wit. oath Sept. 12, 1791 Michael McGaughy to D Goodlett. Rec. Dec. 13, 1791

p. 493-494 Oct. 9, 1790 William Clayton and wife Elizabeth to William Parker (Spartanburgh); for 100£ sterling sold 100 ac on Prater's Cr of Tyger R; part of 200 ac grant Sept. 16,

1774 Gov. William Bull to William Clayton; border: N-James Simple, W-late survey for William Clayton, S-John Daniel Kern, E-remainder of grant. Witness Jonathan Linard and James Clayton. Signed William Clayton and Elizabeth's mark. Wit. oath Sept. 26, 1791 Jonathan Linard to Thomas Farrow. Rec. Dec. 13, 1791

p. 494-495 Jun. 5, 1790 James Gibbs and wife Anne (Union Co) to Peter Elder (Spartanburgh); for 70£ sold 200 ac on S side of Fairforrest Cr and both sides of Lick Br about a mile below Miller's Waggon Road; border: Giles Tillet. Witness Ephraim Elder and Thomas Paces. Signed James Gibbs and Anne's mark. Wit. oath Sept. 21, 1790 Ephraim Elder to Wm Smith. Rec. Dec. 14, 1791

p. 495-496 Mar. 22, 1791 Thomas Warren (Spartanburgh) to Isaac Young (same); for 70£ sterling sold 200 ac on N side of Packolate R; grant Aug. 23, 1774 State's office to Hugh Warren who sold to Thomas Warren on Feb. 16, 1787. Witness Samson Bethel, John Cantrell, and Richard Turner. Signed Thomas Warren. Wit. oath (not dated) Thomas Warren to Samp Bethel. Rec. Dec. 14, 1791

p. 496-498 Apr. 23, 1788 Israel Morris (Spartanburgh) to William Brannon (same); for 100£ 5s sterling sold 240 ac on both sides of Lawson's Fork of Packolate R; border: SW-David Lewis and NE-granted to Stephen Miller; grant Jun. 5, 1786 Gov. William Moultrie to Israel Morris. Witness Stephen Miller, Thomas Whitehead, and Edmund Bishop. Signed Israel Morriss and Lettice's mark. Wit. oath Sept. 12, 1791 Stephen Miller to D Goodlett. Rec. Dec. 14, 1791

p. 498 Sept. 6, 1791 Philemon Martin and wife Molley (Spartanburgh) to John Lipscomb (Union Co); for 100£ sterling sold 245 ac on Gotie's Cr where Philemon now lives; divided from remainder of grant by a line between John Lipscomb and William Wilkins, who own remainder of grant; part of 400 ac grant Apr. 25, 1767 Gov. William Tryon (NC) to William Sims and William Marchbanks who sold to Robert Moore. Witness John Shippy and Samuel Shippy. Signed Philemon Martin (Molley doesn't sign). Wit. oath Sept. 12, 1791 John Shippy to Isham Harrison. Rec. Dec. 14, 1791

p. 498-499 Sept. 7, 1791 Federick Eisen (Union Co), blacksmith to John D. Young (Spartanburgh); for 20£ sterling sold 238 ac on S side of Fairforrest Cr; border: N-Richard Hampton, NE-John Smith, and others vacant; grant in Secretary's book 4Z p. 40. Witness Jothn Bowen and John Haile. Signed Fredrick Eisen. Rec. Dec. 21, 1791

p. 499-500 Dec. 7, 1791 David Golightly (Spartanburgh) to William Lancaster (same); for 50£ sold a Negro girl named Sukey 16 years old. Witness Amey Golightly and James Golightly. Signed David Golightly. Wit. oath Sept. 3, 1792 Amey Golightly to Sam Lancaster. Rec. Sept. 8, 1792

p. 500-501 Dec. 22, 1790 Moses Ward (Spartanburgh) to William McDaniel (same); for 40£ sterling sold 200 ac between S and N forks of Tyger R and on small branch of S fork of Tyger R; grant May 1, 1786 Gov. William Moultrie to Moses Ward. Witness Drury McDaniel and James Cook. Signed Moses Ward. Wit. oath Jul. 25, 1791 James Cook to Thos Moore. Rec. Dec. 22, 1791

p. 501-502 Nov. 25, 1791 Mary & Margaret Smith, daughters of Edward Smith, (Edgefield Co) to Isham Bobbitt; power of attorney to recover from Mary Cornelius of Spartanburgh, executrix for Edward Smith, desc, 2£ each as their legacy from Edward Smith; Mary and Margaret are absent from Spartanburgh Co. Witness John Smith, Drucallen Bobbett, and John Vardit. Signed Mary and

Margaret Smith's marks. Wit. oath Dec. 10, 1791 John Smith to Saml Lancaster. Wit. oath (Edgefield Co) Jan. 21, 1792 John Vardit to John Thomas Fair Charles. Rec. Mar. 14, 1792

p. 502-503 (not given) 11, 1791 James Russel (Mecklinburgh Co, NC) to James Bruton (Spartanburgh); for 20£ NC money sold 310 ac on S side of Little R (now Tyger R) and on Anloquorum Cr (now Ferguson's Cr); grant Nov. 18, 1757 Gov. Arthur Dobbs (NC) to James Russell then in Anson Co, NC; border: Alexander Ferguson. Witness James Purvians, James Russell, and Jacob Bruton. Signed James Russell. Wit. oath Nov. 2, 1791 Jacob Bruton to Zadock Ford. Rec. Mar. 14, 1792

p. 503-505 Oct. 20, 1785 Benjamin Brown (Buck Cr, Ga), oldest son of Bartlett Brown, sr, desc, and his heir, to Benjamin Wofford (Spartanburgh); for 108£ sterling sold 600 ac on both sides of Enoree R (formerly King's R); grant May 11, 1753 Gov. Matthew Rowan (NC) to Bartlett Brown, sr; where Benjamin Wofford now lives. Witness John Lindsey, Abraham Gray, and Henry Hamilton. Signed Benjamin Brown. Wit. oath Feb. 19, 1782 John Lindsey to Dan Wright. Rec. Mar. 14, 1792

p. 505-506 Feb. 25, 1792 John Golightly (Spartanburgh) to Francis Mason (same); for 20£ SC money sold 100 ac on Fairforrest Cr; border: Widow Wilkins, Tinsley, Underwood, Ford, and Connell; grant Jun. 5, 1786 Gov. William Moultrie to John Golightly for 437 ac. Witness Isham Harrison. Signed John Golightly. Wit. oath Feb. 25, 1795 John Golightly to Isham Harrison. Rec. Mar. 19, 1792

p. 506-507 Feb. 25, 1792 John Golightly (Spartanburgh) to Broadrick Mason (same); for 25£ sterling sold 125 ac on Fairforrest Cr. Witness Frances Golightly and Joel Hurt. Signed John Golightly and Winnefred's mark. Wit. oath Feb. 25, 1792 Joel Hurt to Isham Harrison. Rec. Mar. 20, 1792

p. 507-508 Aug. 10, 1791 Michael McGaughy (Spartanburgh) to Richard Whittey (same); for 55£ sterling sold 308 ac; border: John Nailes, Thomas Brown, and Enos Land. Witness John Tollison, John Gosset, and John Lemaster. Signed Michael McGaughy and Susannah's mark. Wit. oath Jan. 14, 1792 John Lemaster to D Goodlett. Rec. Mar. 21, 1792

p. 508-509 Sept. 20, 1791 Frederick Eisen (SC) to David Stephens; for 40£ sterling sold 140 ac on branch of Ward's Cr of Tyger R; border: NW-David Stephens and others vacant; grant Oct. 1, 1787 Gov. Thomas Pinckney to Frederick Eisen. Witness Rowland Jennings and Jacob Ison. Signed Frederick Eisen. Wit. oath Jan. 13, 1792 Rowland Jennings to Thos Moore. Rec. Mar. 23, 1792

p. 509-510 Nov. 23, 1790 Abraham Nalley and wife Creasy (Spartanburgh) to John Barnett (same); for 130£ sterling sold 169½ ac which is remainder of 403 ac after Nathaniel Burton and Benjamin Spencer's lands were sold to them; grant Nov. 6, 1786 Gov. William Moultrie to Abraham Nalley for 403 ac on N side of Tyger R. Witness Nathl Burton, Richd Nalley, and David Grimes. Signed Abraham's mark and Creasy Nally. Wit. oath Jan. 12, 1792 Nathl Burton to Thomas Moore. Rec. Mar. 31, 1792

p. 510-512 Mar. 11, 1791 William Barton (Spartanburgh) to Dan Gilbert (same); for 35£ sterling sold 514 ac on S side of Packolate R; border: Barton's old corner; grant Oct. 1, 1787 State's office to Thomas Barton. Witness Joseph Morris, S Bethel, and George Gilbert. Signed William Barton. Wit. oath Jul. 30, 1791 Joseph Morris to W Smith. Rec. Mar. 31, 1792

p. 512-513 Mar. 8, 1791 William Barton (Spartanburgh) to Dan Gilbert (same); for 35£ sterling sold 100 ac on S side of Pacolate R; grant Apr. 25, 1767 State's Office to Thomas Williamson. Witness S Bethel, George Gilbert, and Joseph Morris. Signed William Barton. Wit. oath (not dated) Joseph Morris to S Bethel. Rec. Apr. 3, 1792

p. 513-514 Mar. 8, 1791 Isham Chote (or Clove) and wife Elizabeth (Spartanburgh) to James Crow (same); for 57£ sterling sold 98 ac on Tyger R; border: E-John White, N-Tygar R, and by remainder of grant; part of 300 ac grant Apr. 3, 1786 Gov. William Moultrie to Thomas White who sold to Isham Chote in 1788. Witness Nicholas Keating and Wm Crow. Signed Isham and Elizabeth Chote's marks. Wit. oath Jan. 12, 1792 Nicholas Keating to D Goodlett. Rec. Apr. 4, 1792

p. 514-515 Mar. 18, 1791 William Barton (Spartanburgh) to Joseph Morris (same); for 20£ sterling sold 200 ac on N side of Packolate R; border: Barton's old line; grant Oct. 1, 1787 State's Office to Thomas Barton. Witness S Bethel, Dan Gilbert, and George Gilbert. Signed William Gilbert. Wit. oath (not dated) Dan Gilbert to S Bethel. Rec. Apr. 4, 1792

p. 515-516 Mar. 18, 1791 William Barton (Spartanburgh) to Joseph Morris (same); for 20£ sterling sold 100 ac on N side of Packolate R; grant Apr. 25, 1767 State's Office to Thomas Williamson who sold Aug. 29, 1769 to Thomas Barton. Witness S Bethel, Dan Gilbert, and George Gilbert. Signed William Barton. Wit. oath (not dated) Dan Gilbert to S Bethel. Rec. Apr. 4, 1792

p. 516-518 Aug. 30, 1791 John Smith to John Grist; for 20£ sterling sold 80 ac on N side of Tyger R about 3 miles above Blackstock's Ford; border: S-remainder of grant, E-estate of Col. len(?) Robuck, N-Thomas Prewitt, W-Timothy Tony; part of 250 ac grant Jan. 21, 1785 Gov. Benjamin Guerard to Joseph Powers. Witness John Robuck and Ephraim Elder. Signed John Smith's mark. Wit. oath (not dated) Ephraim Elder to James Jordan. Rec. Apr. 5, 1792

p. 518-519 (not given), 1791 Joseph Morris (Spartanburgh) to John Morris (same); for 10£ sold 40 ac on Buck Cr; grant May 22, 1772 States Office to Cur D(?) Connal. Witness Samp Bethel, Thos Jordan, and James Jordan. Signed Joseph Morris' mark. Certify Sept. 12, 1791 by S Bethel. Rec. Apr. 5, 1792

p. 519 Feb. 18, 1791 Joseph Morris (Spartanburgh) to John Morris (same); for 20£ sold 53 ac on Buck Cr of Packolet R; grant Jan. 1, 1787 States Office to Joseph Morris. Witness Samp Bethel, Thomas Jordan, and James Morris. Signed Joseph Morris' mark. Certified Sept. 12, 1791 by S Bethel. Rec. Apr. 5, 1792

p. 519-521 Aug. 5, 1791 William Bratcher (Spartanburgh) to Joseph Reader (Union Co); for 9£ sterling sold 200 ac on both sides of Dutchman's Cr where William now lives; border: E-William Prewit, W-Nathaniel Wooten; Condition: deed void if William pays Joseph 9£ sterling by Nov. 15, 1791 with no interest. Witness Robt Donaldson and Mills Summer. Signed William Bratcher. Wit. oath (not dated) Mills Summer to Saml Lancaster. Rec. Apr. 6, 1792

p. 521 Sept. 8, 1791 William Morris, sr (Spartanburgh) to John Morris (same); for 20£ sterling sold 80 ac on Buck Cr of Packolate R and at mouth of Back Br; border: Joseph Morris; grant States Office to William Morris. Witness Sampson Bethel, Joseph Morris, and James Morris. Signed William Morris' mark. Certified Sept. 12, 1791 by S Bethel. Rec. Apr. 6, 1792

p. 521-523 Feb. 24, 1791 Nathan Smith (96 Dist) to Richard Beardon (Spartanburgh); for 60£ sold 200 ac on E side of Dutchman's Cr of Tygar R; border: Thos Thornton's old ford; grant Aug. 11, 1774 Gov. William Bull to Ralph Smith and left to Nathan Smith by his father's will. Witness Larkin Lancaster and Thos Blasingame. Signed Nathan Smith and Mary's mark. Wit. oath (not dated) Larkin Lancaster to Saml Lancaster

p. 523-524 May 1, 1789 William Morris, sr (Spartanburgh) to his son James Morris (same); for 10£ sterling sold 280 ac on Buck Cr; border: John Cantrel and Thos Warren; grant Oct. 6, 1788 States Office to William Morris, sr. Witness John Morris and John Hightower. Signed William Morris' mark. Certified Sept. 12, 1791 S Bethel. Rec. Apr. 7, 1792

p. 524-525 Dec. 27, 1790 William and Elizabeth Clayton to Jonathan Leonard; for 80£ sterling sold 140 ac on S side of Tyger R; part of 2 tracts: (a) 250 ac and (b) 200 ac granted to William Clayton; 140 ac borders: Edwd Arnett, Robt Irwin, E-E Arnett and part of (a), N-Robt Irwin, W-James Clayton and part of (a) and (b). Witness Edmond Clayton and Thos Tod. Signed William Clayton and Elizabeth's mark. Wit. oath (not dated) Edmond Clayton to Wm Smith. Rec. Apr. 7, 1792

p. 525-526 Aug. 20, 1791 John Gibbs and wife Anne (Spartanburgh) to Ephraim Elder (same); for 10£ SC money sold 20 ac on E side of Buffalo Lick Cr of Fairforrest Cr; border: Michael Sprinkle; part of 640 ac grant NC governor to Giles Tillit (date not given). Witness Peter Elder and Caty Smith. Signed John and Anne Gibbs. Wit. oath Jan. 13, 1792 Peter Elder to Thos Moore. Rec. Apr. 12, 1792

p. 526-528 Dec. 20, 1790 Thomas B. Wyatt (Spartanburgh) to William Benson (same); for 20£ sterling sold 89 ac on branch of Tyger R; border: Dixon, Francis Prince, William Hannon, Timmons, and John Prince. Witness Obadiah Wingo and William Lancaster. Signed Thomas B. Wyatt. Wit. oath Oct. 7, 1791 Obadiah Wingo to David Goodlett. Rec. Apr. 30, 1792

p. 528-529 Jul. 25, 1791 William Mackey (Pendleton Co) to Henry Young (Spartanburgh); for 5s sterling sold 100 ac on both sides of Meadows Cr of Packolate R; border: N & NW-William Gilbert and others vacant; grant May 6, 1786 to William Mackey. Witness Benjamin Ingram, William Banister, and John C Kilpatrick. Signed William Mackey's mark. Wit. oath (not dated) William Banister to Bayles Earle. Rec. May 5, 1792

p. 529-531 Nov. 22, 1791 William Shurley (Spartanburgh) to John Skiggs; for 50£ SC money sold 100 ac on E side of N fork of Tyger R; E part of 450 ac grant Apr. 17, 1788 Gov. Thomas Pinckney to William Shurley; border: Tobias Bright. Witness Tobias Bright, James Bright, and Thomas Shurley. Signed William Shurley. Wit. oath Apr. 10, 1792 Tobias Bright to Isham Harrison. Rec. May 8, 1792

p. 531-532 Dec. 31, 1791 Bayles Earle (Spartanburgh) to John Anderson (same); for 100£ sold (ac not given) on Obed's Cr of Packolate R. Witness John Moore and Bayles Earle, jr. Signed Bayles Earle. Wit. oath Jan. 26, 1792 Bayles Earle to David Goodlett. Rec. May 8, 1792

p. 532-533 Nov. 20, 1791 Thomas Wadsworth and William Turpin, merchants (SC) to Henry Turner (same); for 30£ sold 350 ac on both sides of Shoally Cr of Lawson's fork of Packolate R; border: Thomas Bennett on two sides; grant Feb. 5, 1787 to Thomas

Wadsworth and William Turpin and surveyed Oct. 22, 1784 by George Salmon for William Wood, son of Moses. Witness John Trotter and James Young. Signed Thos Wadsworth. Wit. oath Dec. 24, 1791 John Trotter to John Hunter. Rec. May 8, 1792

p. 533-536 May 12, 1791 John Rotton, sr and William Rotton, sr, brothers (SC) to Edward Ballanger (Spartanburgh); for 60£ 10s sterling sold 300 ac on both sides of Lawson's fork where Edward Ballanger lives; grant (date not given) Gov. William Tryon (NC) to John Rotton in Mechlinburgh Co, NC, who sold to William Rotton, sr but transaction was lost. Witness Wm Wood, David Lewis, John Young, jr, Henry Macher, and James Macher. Signed John and William Rotton's marks. Wit. oath Jun. 15, 1791 Henry Macher to David Goodlett. Rec. May 8, 1792

p. 536-538 Jan. 16, 1791 Irby Duberry and wife Molly (96 Dist) to William Thomson (same); for 250£ SC money sold (ac not given) in 2 tracts on both sides of Bullock's Cr of Thickety Cr; (a) 150 ac granted to James Bridges who sold to Irby Duberry and (b) (ac not given) granted in 1786 Gov. William Moultrie to Irby Duberry. Witness Richard Thomson, Wm Duberry, and Betty Duberry. Signed Irby Duberry and Molly's mark. Wit. oath Apr. 18, 1792 Richard Thomson to Isham Harrison. Rec. May 10, 1792

p. 538 Feb. 17, 1792 Henry OKean (Spartanburgh) to William Austin; for several debts William has discharged to Henry, sold one still with fixtures now on Jno McClrath(?)'s land on Tyger R. Witness John Muckelwrath and James Collins. Signed Henry OKean. Wit. oath Feb. 26, 1792 John Muckelwrath to James Jordan. Rec. May 24, 1792

p. 538-540 Aug. 13, 1791 Patrick Moore and wife Bettsy and mother Sarah (Union Co) to William Thomson (Spartanburgh); for 100£ SC money sold 300 ac in 2 tracts: (a) 200 ac granted Apr. 27, 1767 Gov. William Tryon (NC) to Hugh Moore on both sides of Bullock's Cr of Thickety Cr and (b) 100 ac grant Nov. 25, 1771 Gov. Martin (NC) to Hugh Moore. Witness Richd Thomson, David Brock, and Margaret Thomson. Signed Patrick Moore and Betsey and Sarah's marks. Wit. oath Apr. 18, 1792 Richd Thomson to Isham Harrison. Rec. May 29, 1792

p. 540-542 Dec. 24, 1791 Drury Prewit and wife Linna to Thomas Evatt; for 20£ sterling sold 100 ac on both sides of Dutchman's Cr and N side of Tyger R; border: E-Drury Prewit, and others vacant; grant Dec. 3, 1787 Gov. Thos Pinckney to Drury Prewit. Witness William Prewitt, Moses Prewitt, and David Prewitt. Signed Drury and Linna Prewit's marks. Wit. oath Feb. 9, 1792 William and Moses Prewitt to Saml Lancaster. Rec. May 30, 1792

p. 542-543 Mar. 12, 1792 Henry Turner, sr (SC) to Henry Turner, jr (same); for 24£ sold 70 ac on W side of Sholy Cr; border: W-John Boley, S-Henry Childs, E-Darby Turner, and NW-Henry Turner, sr; part of survey Oct. 22, 1784 by George Salmon for Wm Wood, son of Moses Wood. Witness Wills Griffith and Darby Turner. Signed Henry Turner, sr's mark. Wit. oath Apr. 30, 1792 Darby Turner to D Goodlett. Rec. Jun. 6, 1792

p. 543-544 Dec. 1, 1791 Swan Thomson (Ga) to Ezekiel Howard (Spartanburgh); for 200£ sterling sold 90 ac on head branches of Gotie's Cr. Witness Henry Pettet and Charles Barnett. Signed Swan Thomson. Wit. oath May 26, 1792 Henry Pettet to Isham Harrison. Rec. Jun. 6, 1792

p. 544-545 Dec. 1, 1791 Swan Thomson (Ga) to Ezekiel Howard (Spartanburgh); for 20£ sterling sold 200 ac at head branches of Gotie's and Green's Creeks. Witness Henry Pettet and Charles Barnett. Signed Swan Thomson. Wit. oath May 26, 1792 Henry Pettet to Isham Harrison. Rec. Jun. 8, 1792

p. 545 Jun. 12, 1792 Joseph Thompson (Spartanburgh), husband of Jane Dill, to John Sloan (same); power of attorney to sell a tract of land (ac not given) in York Co, Pa on branches of Yellow Breeches Cr of Susquehannah R; border: James Dill and Matthew Dill; was late property of John Dill, desc, father of James, the heir of the land. Witness James Jordan and Nevil Wailand. Signed Joseph Thompson

p. 545-547 May 13, 1799 James Hanna (Camden Dist) to William Floyd (96 Dist); for 1,500£ SC money sold 300 ac on S side of Broad R of Middle fork of Little R about 3 miles above Robert Miller; grant Feb. 3, 1754 to David Park. Witness John Gordon, Cathrin Gordon, and Elizabeth Lawson. Signed James Hanna. Wit. oath Sept. 13, 1779 John Gordon to David Gordon. Rec. Jul. 2, 1792

p. 547-549 May 13, 1779 James Hanna (Camden Dist) to William Floyd (96 Dist); for 100£ SC money sold (ac not given) on S side of Broad R of Middle fork of Little R about 3 miles above Robert Miller; grant May 4, 1769 to James Hanna. Witness John Gordon, Cathrin Gordon, and Elizabeth Lawson. Signed James Hanna. Wit. oath (Camden Dist) Sept. 13, 1779 John Gordon to David Gordon. Rec. Jul. 5, 1792

Book C 1792-1795 begun Jul. 7, 1792 by Wm Lancaster
p. 1-2 Jun. 13, 1792 William Floyd (Pendleton Co) to Berryman Shumate (Spartanburgh); for 150£ (sic) sterling sold 200 ac on S side of Broad R and Middle fork of Little R (known as Tygar R) about 3 miles above Robert Miller; border: second line of 300 ac tract sold by John Hanna (Camden Dist) to William Floyd; part of 300 ac grant Feb. 3, 1754 to David Park. Witness Nevil Wailand, Benjamin P. McMakin, and James Taylor White. Signed William Floyd. Wit. oath Jun. 13, 1792 James Taylor White to D Goodlett. Rec. Jul. 7, 1792

p. 2-6 Oct. 4, 1790 John Daniel Kearn, merchant, (96 Dist) to William Clayton (Spartanburgh); for 5s sterling sold 139 ac in 2 tracts: (a) 63 ac on Tygar R; border: NE-Edward Arnett, SE-James Cliphant, SE-Edward Bearden, and NW-McCullock and (b) 76 ac on branch of Tygar R; border: SW-John McCullock, NW-Edward Hooker, SW, E, and NE-William Clayton, and SW-Edward Arnett. Witness Robert Hanna, Absalom Bobo, James Clayton, and James McCarley. Signed John Daniel Kearn. Wit. oath Feb. 15, 1792 James Clayton to Thomas Farrow. Rec. Jul. 24 and 26, 1792

p. 6-8 Apr. 23, 1792 William Storke Jett, executor of Richard Bernard, desc, and a son and executor of William Bernard, sr, desc, and guardian of orphans of Richard Bernard, and William Bernard, the other surviving son of William Bernard, sr, to William Benson; power of attorney to recover slave John, property of William Bernard, sr,who escaped or has been stolen and to sell slave for 30£ Va money to Wm Benson, when slave is recovered. Witness Lan Berry and Matthew Tully. Signed Wm Storke Jett and Wm Bernard. Proved (Westmoreland Co, Va) Apr. 24, 1792 to Jas Bland. Rec. Jul. 26, 1792

p. 8-9 Apr. 16, 1792 Catherine Grace (Spartanburgh) to George Grace (same); for 40£ sterling sold 125 ac on Forgeson's Cr at mouth of Hooper's School House Br; SW part of grant May 2, 1770 Gov. William Bull to David Prewit. Witness John Ford, Richard Cox, and Catherine Bruton. Signed Catherine Grace's mark. Wit. oath Jun. 9, 1792 Richard Cox to Thos Moore. Rec. Jul. 26, 1792

p. 9-10 Dec. 22, 1790 Alexander Robison, sr (Fairfield Co) to James Sutherland (Spartanburgh); for 4 hogsheads of tobacco sold 200 ac in Craven Co on branches of Tyger R; border: E-Joseph Brown, W-Thomas Seston, N-Enoch Floyd, and others vacant; grant Aug. 19, 1774 to Benjamin Mahanah. Witness Burr Harrison, Zebulon Bragg, and Henry Moore. Signed Alexander Robison. Wit. oath Jul. 23, 1791 Zebulon Bragg to Saml Lancaster. Rec. Jul. 26, 1792

p. 10-11 Mar. 17, 1791 William Morris, sr (Edgefield Co) to Thomas Jordan (Spartanburgh); for 18£ sold 50 ac on Little Buck Cr on N side of Packolate R; border: Thomas Jordan; grant Jan. 1, 1787 State Office to William Morris. Witness S Bethel, George Gilbert, and Joseph Morris. Signed William Morris' mark. Certified Jan. 7, 1792 by (not signed). Rec. Jul. 27, 1792

p. 11-13 Apr. 13, 1792 Reuben Matthis and wife Judith (Spartanburgh) to Wills Griffith (same); for 60£ sterling sold 204 ac on Lawson's fork of Packolate R; grant Sept. 7, 1789 Gov. Charles Pinckney to Reuben Matthis; border: Lucy McAbee, Wofford and Co, land formerly James Brown, land formerly Samuel Ward, and William Pool. Witness Henry McCray and William Pool. Signed Reuben Matthis and Judith's mark. Wit. oath Jun. 13, 1792 William Pool to D Goodlett. Rec. Jul. 31, 1792

p. 13-14 Nov. 23, 1791 Austin Clayton and wife Catharine (Spartanburgh) to Jesse Spann; for 80£ sterling sold 200 ac on Cedar School Cr of Enoree R; grant Oct. 15, 1784 to Austin Clayton; border: all sides vacant. Witness John Layton and John Harris. Signed Austin Clayton and Catharine's mark. Wit. oath Mar. 30, 1792 John Layton to Thomas Farrow. Rec. Jul. 31, 1792

p. 14-15 Jan. 13, 1787 Robert Nelson, doctor, (Spartanburgh) to Joseph Morris (same); for 60£ SC money sold 200 ac on Buck Cr of Packolate R; grant May 15, 1772 State Office to Robert Nelson. Witness Thomas Jordan, Elias Legate, and Sampson Bethel. Signed Robert Nelson and Rebeckah's mark. Wit. oath Jun. 21, 1791 Sampson Bethel to Thomas Jordan. Rec. Jul. 31, 1792

p. 15-16 May 3, 1792 John Watson (Union Co) to Obadiah Trimmier (Spartanburgh); for 22£ 17s 4p sterling sold 174 ac on N fork Thickety Cr; part of 350 ac grant in Dec. 1774 Gov. William Bull to Vardry McBee. Witness John Trimmier, Obadiah Watson, and John Headon. Signed John Watson. Wit. oath May 3, 1792 John Headon to Edwd Goode. Rec. Aug. 1, 1792

p. 16-17 Dec. 27, 1791 Littleton Mapp and wife Mary (SC) to William Lipscomb; for 100£ sold 326 ac on both sides of Thickety Cr; border: William Lipscomb, Burchfield, and Thomson. Witness Vardry McBee and Wm Lipscomb, jr. Signed Littleton and Mary Mapp. Wit. oath Jun. 11, 1792 Vardry McBee to Edwd Goode. Rec. Aug. 1, 1792

p. 17-19 Dec. 23, 1791 James Fannin and wife Elizabeth (SC) to William Lipscomb (SC); for 180£ sold 161 ac on N side of Thickety Cr; border: William Lipscomb, Map, and a little blue branch. Witness John Headen and Smith Lipscomb. Signed James Fannin and Elizabeth's mark. Wit. oath (not dated) John Headen to Edwd Goode. Rec. Aug. 2, 1792

p. 19 Jun. 22, 1790 Thomas Jordan (Spartanburgh) to Elijah Green (same); for 20£ sterling sold 192 ac on Buck Cr; border: Cobb; grant Dec. 3, 1787 State Office to Thomas Jordan. Witness S Bethel and Thos Warren. Signed Thomas Jordan's mark. Certified Dec. 2, 1792 by S Bethel. Rec. Aug. 2, 1792

p. 19-20 Jan. 30, 1792 James Compton to John Wofford; mortgages the following to secure debt of 7£ 1s 9p James owes John: a mare and colt, 9 cattle, 2 beds and funrniture, 3 pewter dishes, 12 plates, 2 iron pots, a kittle, a frying pan, 6 knives and forks, and a chest; mortgage valid until James pays the debt. Witness William Smith and Mourning Smith. Signed James Compton's mark. Rec. Aug. 4, 1792

p. 20-21 Jan. 13, 1792 Elijah Green (Rutherford Co, NC) to Abraham Cantrell (Spartanburgh); for 40£ sold 192 ac on Buck Cr; border: Cobb; grant Dec. 3, 1787 State Office to Thomas Jordan. Witness S Bethel, Mary Bethel, and Larkin Bethel. Signed Elijah Green. Certified Feb. 3, 1792 by S Bethel. Rec. Aug. 4, 1792

p. 21-22 Feb. 10, 1792 John Cobb (Spartanburgh) to John Cantrell (same); for 28£ sold 200 ac on Buck Cr of Packolate R; border: Isaac Young, Thomas Jordan, Elias Legate's line, and Abraham Cantrell; grant May 1, 1786 State Office to Elias Legart. Witness Sampson Bethel, Solomon Abbett, and Hutchens Forrestor. Signed John Cobb's mark. Certified Feb. 14, 1792 by Samp Bethel. Rec. Aug. 4, 1792

p. 22-24 Nov. 10, 1791 Andrew Brown and wife Margery (Ga) to Richard Harris (Spartanburgh); for 10£ sterling sold 200 ac on branch of Fergerson's Cr of Tyger R; border: N-David Templeton and others vacant; plat Feb. 20, 1775 by James Wofford, dept. surveyor; grant to Andrew Brown (Secretary's grant book 3Y p. 447). Witness Joseph Morris, Thomas Harris, and John Hellion. Signed Andrew Brown and Margery's mark. Wit. oath May 5, 1792 Joseph Harris (sic) to Thomas Moore. Rec. Aug. 7, 1792

p. 24-25 Mar. 29, 1792 John D. Young (Spartan Co) to Daniel Finch (same); for 20£ sterling sold 230 ac on S side of Fairforrest Cr; border: N-Richard Hampton, NE-John Smith, and others vacant when surveyed; sold by Fredrick Eisen to John D Young; grant in Secretary's book 4Z p. 40. Witness Jesse Spencer and Roland Ginnins. Signed John D. Young. Wit. oath Jun. 12, 1792 Jesse Spencer to D Goodlett. Rec. Aug. 7, 1792

p. 25-27 Dec. 10, 1791 Absalom Bobo (Spartanburgh) to John Frederick Harmoning (Laurens Co); for 30£ sterling sold 250 ac on "draught" of Cedar Shoal Cr of Enoree R; border: NE-Sampson Bobo and vacant, SW-Joseph Kershaw and vacant, NW-John Robinson, and others vacant; grant Aug. 19, 1774 Gov. William Bull to Joseph Kershaw then in Berkly Co. Witness John Robinson, Geo Whitmire, and John Head. Signed Absalom Bobo. Wit. oath (Laurens Co) May 29, 1792 John Robinson to Rogers Brown. Rec. Aug. 13, 1792

p. 27-29 Dec. 10, 1791 William Castleburry and Wife Elizabeth (Spartanburgh) to Charles McCarter (same); for 30£ SC money sold 150 ac on White's Br of Fairforrest Cr; part of 460 ac grant Jan. 21, 1785 "State" to John Smith. Witness James Smith, Paul Castlebury, and Jerimah Smith. Signed William and Elizabeth Castlebury's marks. Wit. oath Jun. 12, 1792 Jerimah Smith to Isham Harrison. Rec. Aug. 15, 1792

p. 29-30 Jun. 8, 1792 Diskin Grant and wife Susannah (Spartanburgh) to Bazel Lee (same); for 50£ sterling sold 184 ac on Lawson's fork of Packolate R; part of grant Jul. 24, 1784 to John Holcom who sold to Diskin Grant; border: Dickson, Bull, and Littleton Bagwell. Witness Thomas Underwood and Jesse Cannon. Signed Diskin Grant and Susannah's mark. Wit. oath Jun. 13, 1792 Thomas Underwood to D Goodlett. Rec. Aug. 17, 1792

p. 30-31 Feb. 21, 1792 William Roberts and wife Martha (Spartanburgh) to David Golightly (same); for 15£ sold 150 ac on Fairforrest Cr; border: Peter Elder, William Wofford, Robert Head, and David Golightly; formerly land of Michael Sprinkle, desc, former husband of Martha Roberts, and since to his heirs; Condition: deed void if William pays David 30 barrels of corn or 5 good lively cows and calves on Dec. 25, 1792 for which William has received full value. Witness W Lancaster and A Lancaster. Signed Wm Roberts and Martha's mark. Rec. Aug. 17, 1792

p. 31-32 Mar. 12, 1792 Henry Turner, sr (SC) to Darby Turner (SC); for 24£ sold 100 ac on E and W of Sholy Cr; border: W-road from William McDowell's to Spartanburgh Court House, N-Henry Turner, sr; part of survey Oct. 22, 1784 by George Salmon for William Wood, son of Moses Wood. Witness Wills Griffith and Henry Turner (signature). Signed Henry Turner's mark. Wit. oath Apr. 30, 1792 Henry Turner, sr (signature) (sic) to D Goodlett. Rec. Aug. 21, 1792

p. 32-35 Dec. 8, 1787 Shadrach Nowland and wife Anna Stacy (96 Dist) to Edward Williams (same); for 50£ SC money sold 200 ac on Luck (or Suck) Br of Broad R; grant May 6, 1769 Gov. William Tryon (NC) to Daniel McDaniel then in Tryon Co, NC. Witness Stephen Nowland and Reubin Warren. Signed Shadrach and Anna S Nowland's marks. Certified Jul. 27, 1792 by S Bethel

p. 35-36May 6, 1792 Spencer Bobo, sr and wife Judah to their son Absalom Bobo; for 50£ sterling sold 220 ac between Tygar and Enoree R; border: Sampson Bobo, Jno Frederick Harmoning, Moses Casey, James Casey, and Absalom Bobo; part of 1,000 ac grant to James Semple, jr and sold by Rottry Simple, heir-at-law of James, to John McCullock who sold to Spencer Bobo, sr. Witness Edward Hooper and John Fryer. Signed Spencer Bobo and Judith's mark. Wit. oath Jul. 6, 1792 Edward Hooper to Wm Smith. Rec. Aug. 27, 1792

p. 36-38 Nov. 4, 1791 John Williams (Spartanburgh) to Samuel Cawley (same); for 40£ sterling sold 150 ac on branches of Tygar R; grant for 158 ac Feb. 5, 1787 Gov. William Moultrie to John Williams. Witness Michael Br Roberts, Drury McDaniel, and John Williams. Signed John and Hannah Williams. Wit. oath Aug. 4, 1792 Drury McDaniel to Thomas Moore. Rec. Aug. 30, 1792

p. 38-39 Nov. 22, 1790 John Brown (Spartanburgh) to David Pulliam (same); for 50£ sterling sold 310 ac; border: James Miller and English; W part of 606 ac grant Feb. 4, 1788 to John Brown on both sides of Tyger R and bordering NW-Adam Meek, SW and S-old line, and S-James Miller. Witness Isham Pulliam, Wm Ford, and Drury McDaniel. Signed John Brown. Wit. oath Apr. 1791 Isham Pulliam to Thos Moore. Rec. 30, 1792

p. 39-41 Aug. 1, 1792 David Pulliam (Spartanburgh) to William and Drury McDaniel (same); for 65£ sterling sold 310 ac; border: James Miller and Old English line; part of 606 ac grant Feb. 4, 1788 to John Brown on both sides of S fork of Tyger R and bordering NW-Adam Meek, SW and S-old line, and S-James Miller; sold Nov. 22, 1790 by John Brown to David Pulliam 310 ac. Witness James Crook, Michael Barrier, and Abraham Barrier. Signed David Pulliam's mark. Wit. oath Aug. 4, 1792 James Crook to Thos Moore. Rec. Aug. 31, 1792

p. 41-42 Jan. 26, 1792 Spencer Bobo, sr (Spartanburgh) to Aaron Casey (same); for 50£ sterling sold 507 ac known by name of Peace (or Rase) path survey; grant Oct. 1786 Gov. William Moultrie to (not given); border: former land of Nath Hillim, Thomas Couch, and John Burt. Witness Absalom Bobo and Levenston Bobo.

Signed Spencer Bobo. Wit. oath Jun. 25, 1792 Levenston Bobo to Saml Lancaster. Rec. Sept. 2, 1792

p. 42-43 Dec. 4, 1784 Philip Langfitt, sr (Fairfield Co, Va) to James Smith (SC); for 250£ Va money sold 6 Negroes: Nace, Rose, Lewes, Nathan, Flora, and Simon. Witness Yelverton Reardon, Francis Langfitt, and Mason Foley. Signed Philip Langfitt. Wit. oath Sept. 11, 1792 Yelverton Reardon to D Goodlett. Rec. Sept. 11, 1792

p. 43 Apr. 2, 1792 William Farrow, dept. sheriff (96 Dist) to Josiah Culbertson; for 20£ 5s sold "land" of Maj. Lusk on Fairforrest Cr at public sale (Apr. 2, 1792) due to levy Isakim Bulow vs Robt Lusk and James Lusk. Witness Saml Davidson, Signed William Farrow. Wit. oath Sept. 10, 1792 Saml Davidson to Saml Lancaster. Rec. Sept. 19, 1792

p. 43-44 Apr. 16, 1792 John Ford, sr and Catherine Grace, widow (Tyger R, Spartanburgh); a marriage contract: John gives Catherine all property she now has and John disclaims his rights he might have had by marriage; Catherine relinquishes dower rights to John's estate. Witness John Bruton, Catherine Bruton, Richard Cox, and George Grace. Signed John Ford and Catherine Grace's mark. Wit. oath Sept. 10, 1792 John Bruton to Thos Moore. Rec. Sept. 19, 1792

p. 44-48 Mar. 9, 1778 Jerimiah Fowler (96 Dist), laborer to Thomas Compton, shoemaker (same); for 100£ 10s SC money sold 200 ac on branch of Dutchman's Cr of Tyger R; border: N-Thomson, E-Abraham Moore, and others vacant; grant Aug. 11, 1774 Lt. Gov. William Bull to Jerimiah Fowler. Witness William Simpson, James White, and Mary McElevean. Signed Jerimiah Fowler's mark. Wit. oath Mar. 10, 1778 William Simpson to John Thomas, jr. Rec. Sept. 20, 1792

p. 48-52 Apr. 16, 1789 Robert Sterling and wife Sarah (Spartanburgh) to Bazel Trail (same); for 110£ sold 240 ac on Dutchman's Cr of Tyger R; part of 440 ac grant Mar. 6, 1786 Gov. William Moultrie to Sarah Elder now Sterling; border: N and E-William Smith and S-grant to Ralph Smith. Witness Wm Smith, Moses Purvines, and Elizabeth Purvines. Signed Robert and Sarah Sterling. Wit. oath Sept. 11, 1792 Wm Smith, esq to D Goodlett. Rec. Sept. 26, 1792

p. 52-53 Nov. 3, 1790 Moses Purvines and wife Elizabeth (Spartanburgh) to Ausburn West (same); for 70£ sold 140 ac on S side of Dutchman's Cr of Tyger R; border: William Elder's old line now William Smith's line and Butler; part of grant Mar. 6, 1786 to Moses Purvines. Witness Benjamin Peak, Samuel Morrow, Bazel Trail. Signed Moses Purvines and Elizabeth's mark. Wit. oath Dec. 28, 1790 Bazel Trail to Wm Smith. Rec. Sept. 28, 1792

p. 53-55 Oct. 22, 1790 Thomas Haney and wife Jane (Spartanburgh) to David Trail (same); for 100£ sold 300 ac on N side of Tyger R and both sides of Dutchman's Cr including a shoal; border: Andrew Simeson; grant Apr. 29, 1768 Gov. William Tryon (NC) to Robert Henderson. Witness Benjamin Peak, Bazel Trail, and Andrew Thomson. Signed Thomas Heany and Jean's mark. Wit. oath Dec. 28, 1790 Benjamin Peak to Wm Smith. Rec. Sept. 29, 1792

p. 55-58 Oct. 10, 1775 William Sergant and wife Susanna (96 Dist) to Edward Nash (Orange Co, NC); for 400£ 10s SC money sold 300 ac on Two Mile Cr of Enoree R; grant Jan. 20, 1773 Gov. Charles G. Montague to Daniel Mooring who sold to William Sergant on Jan. 20, 1773(sic). Witness Andrew Hendricks, Ebezener Morse, and Isaac Hendricks. Signed William Sergant and Susanna's mark.

Wit. oath Oct. 11, 1775 Andrew Hendricks to John Ford. Rec. Oct. 2, 1792

p. 58-61 Nov. 9, 1773 Daniel Moreing and wife Mary (96 Dist) to William Sergant, blacksmith (same); for 400£ 10s SC money sold 300 ac on Two Mile Br of Enoree R; grant Jan. 20, 1773 Gov. Charles G. Montague to Daniel Moreing. Witness Jos Barnett, Andrew Hendricks, and Tobias Hendricks. Signed Daniel and Mary Moreing's marks. Wit. oath Oct. 10, 1775 Andrew Hendricks to John Ford. Rec. Oct. 3, 1792

p. 61-63 Oct. 15, 1791 Roland Cornelius, sr and wife Mary (Spartanburgh) to David Cook (same); for 100£ sterling sold 218 ac on Reedy Br of Fairforrest Cr; border: Elder, Tillet, S corner of 129 ac grant Dec. 5, 1785 to Roland Cornelius, grant to Giles Connell, upper crossing of Reedy Br below mouth of Cornelius' Spring Br, and Cook; parts of "different tracts". Witness Samuel Casey, Henry Ayres, and Thomas Cook. Signed Roland and Mary Cornelius' marks. Wit. oath Feb. 18, 1792 Henry Ayres to Isham Harrison. Rec. Oct. 19, 1792

p. 63-65 Mar. 12, 1792 Nathaniel Wooten and wife Mary to Samuel Sharbut; for 30£ sterling sold 100 ac on N side of Cane Cr and N side of Tyger R; border: Timothy Tonie; part of 200 ac grant to James Hembree. Witness Benjamin Grist, John Chumble, and John Grist. Signed Nathaniel and Mary Wooten's marks. Wit. oath Mar. 19, 1792 Benjamin Grist to Wm Smith. Rec. Oct. 19, 1792

p. 65-66 Aug. 13, 1792 Benjamin Clerk and wife Rhoda to Mary Clerk; for 70£ sterling sold 132 ac where Mark lives; border: NE-unknown, NW-John Young, and S and SE-"part of same tract". Witness John Young, jr and John Clerk. Signed Benjamin and Rhoda Clerk. Wit. oath Sept. 10, 1792 John Clerk to D Goodlett. Rec. Oct. 19, 1792

p. 66-67 Aug. 7, 1792 Joseph Mitchell (Tyger R, Spartanburgh) to Nathan Ward (same); for 50£ sterling sold 100 ac on S side of Packolate R and N side of Lawson's fork; part of grant Gov. William Moultrie to Reubin Lawson (date not given); border: Old Iron Works Rd and land sold by John Gray and entered by James Lee. Witness Elisha McAbee, Zachariah Sparks, and Thomas Mitchell. Signed Joseph Mitchell's mark. Wit. oath Sept. 10, 1792 Elisha McAbee to D Goodlett. Rec. Oct. 20, 1792

p. 67-68 Dec. 24, 1790 William Barnett to mother Sarah Barnett; in return for a legacy Sarah gives William, William gives the right and title to 300 ac where his father lived before he died on N side of Two Mile R; land now belongs to Sarah. Witness Joseph Barnett, Moses Ward, and James Landford. Signed William Barnett. Rec. Oct. 22, 1792

p. 68-69 Apr. 16, 1792 Catherine Grace (Spartanburgh) to John Grace (same); for 10£ sterling sold 25 ac on Forgeson's Cr opposite mouth of Cooper's School House Br; border: Patton; NW part of grant May 2, 1770 Gov. William Bull to David Prewit. Witness George Bruton, Richard Cox, George Grace. Signed Catherine Grace's mark. Wit. oath Aug. 16, 1792 Richard Cox to Zadock Ford. Rec. Oct. 22, 1792

p. 69-70 Aug. 18, 1792 Daniel Gilbert (Spartanburgh) to Lucy Hearne (same); for 26£ sterling sold 120 ac on Thickety Cr of Broad R; border: N-Hopkins, W-"old land", S-Mense, E-vacant; grant Jan. 1, 1786 SC Office to Daniel Gilbert. Witness James Wood, Matthew Gullry, and Frederick Gullry. Signed Dan Gilbert. Wit. oath Aug. 24, 1792 Matthew Gullry to Edwd Goode. Rec. Oct. 23, 1792

p. 70-72 Aug. 8, 1792 George Poole (Spartanburgh) to Thomas Jones (same); for 60£ sterling sold 148 ac; 100 ac of which is SW end of land where Eli Lemaster lives on head waters of Goucher's Cr; 48 ac of which borders: Ezekiel Howard and David Allen. Witness Henry Jones, John Lemaster, and Griffin Carter. Signed George Poole and Elizabeth's mark. Wit. oath Oct. 5, 1792 Griffin Carter to Isham Harrison. Rec. 23, 1792

p. 72-73 Aug. 7, 1790 William Banister (Wilks Co, Ga) to Hugh Stevenson (Spartanburgh); for 25£ sterling sold 200 ac on both sides of S fork of Packolate R; half of 400 ac grant May 17, 1759 to Richard Lyons; border: William Dickson and James Gilmore. Witness John Young, jr, James Norris, and William Gilmore. Signed William Banister. Wit. oath Apr. 14, 1792 John Young, jr to James Jordan, jr. Rec. Oct. 24, 1792

p. 73-75 Mar. 18, 1789 Thomas Ceary and wife Mary (Spartanburgh) to James Lee (same); for 50£ SC money sold 137½ ac; border: Wm Sterling, James Lee, Samuel Morrow, and John Elder; part of 350 ac grant Apr. 3, 1786 Gov. William Moultrie to William Sterling who sold 150 ac to Thomas Ceary. Witness Wm Smith, John McPherson, and Abram Poole. Signed Thomas and Mary Ceary's marks. Wit. oath Apr. 7, 1789 John McPherson to Wm Smith. Rec. Oct. 24, 1792

p. 75-76 (not given), 1791 Francis Howell (Greenville Co) to John Timmons (Spartanburgh); for 100£ sold 160 ac on both sides of N fork of N Tyger R; border: Samuel Timmons; part of 1,000 ac tract where John Timmons lives; sold by John Timmons to Francis Howell. Witness Moses Timmons, John Morris, and Abner Timmons. Signed Francis Howel's mark. Wit. oath Sept. 10, 1792 Moses Timmons to D Goodlett. Rec. Oct. 31, 1792

p. 76-78 May 7, 1792 Thomas Farrow (Pendleton Co) to Wills Griffith (Spartanburgh); for 50£ sterling sold 365 ac on Lawson's fork; part of two tracts granted to James Brown. Witness Vincent Davis and Vincent Lewis. Signed Thomas Farrar. Wit. oath May 29, 1792 (Pendleton Co) Vincent Davis to Robert Anderson. Rec. Nov. 1, 1792

p. 78 Oct. 11, 1792 David Golightly (Spartanburgh) to William Lancaster (same); for 40£ sterling sold a Negro girl Doll. Witness A Lancaster, Christopher Golightly, and Wm F Golightly. Signed David Golightly. Wit. oath Oct. 12, 1792 Christopher Golightly. to Isham Harrison. Rec. Nov. 2, 1792

p. 78-79 Oct. 11, 1792 David Golightly (Spartanburgh) to Mary Golightly, minor and heir of William Golightly, desc; sold a Negro wench Rose and Negro girl child Dilce for consideration of ½ of Negro wench Tiller and ½ of her increase, a legacy left Mary by her father William Golightly, which was made use of by David, executor, to pay a debt due from William Golightly's estate to Nathan Barnett (Ga) "for purchase of above named Negroes"; Condition: sale void if Mary brings suit for Negro Tiller or her increase. Witness W Lancaster, A Lancaster, and Christopher Golightly. Signed David Golightly. Wit. oath Oct. 12, 1792 Christopher Golightly to Isham Harrison. Rec. Nov. 2, 1792

p. 79-81 Oct. 5, 1792 Jesse Reams (Spartanburgh) to George Anderson (same); for 50£ sterling sold 152 ac on both sides of McMillen's Br of N Packolate R; border: E-McMillin, N-James Millican, W-William McWilliams, SW and W-John Young, sr: survey for Jesse Reams Aug. 12, 1789. Witness Isham Harrison. Signed Jesse Reams' mark. Rec. Nov. 6, 1792

p. 81-82 May 19, 1792 Charles Moore (Spartanburgh) to son Andrew

Moore (same); for 100£ SC money sold 385 ac on E side of Tyger R; border: Andrew Thomson, an old line (owner unknown), and Andrew Moore; part of 3 grants SC governor to Charles Moore (dates not given). Witness Thomas Doing and Andrew Thomson. Signed Charles Moore. Wit. oath Oct. 5, 1792 Thomas Doing to Thos Moore. Rec. Nov. 6, 1792

p. 82-84 Aug. 17, 1792 Amelia Austill and Joseph Austill (Spartanburgh) to William Lipscomb (same); for 30£ sold 150 ac between Thickety Cr and Gocher's Cr; border: E-Austill, S-old Fork land, W-Anderson, N-Thomson and Lipscomb and Milley Austill and road in Haden's line. Witness John Lipscomb and Amos Austill. Signed Amelia and Joseph Austill. Wit. oath Oct. 8, 1792 John Lipscomb to Isham Harrison. Rec. Nov. 8, 1792

p. 84-85 May 23, 1792 Edward Hooker and wife Millie (Spartanburgh) to Thomas Tod (same); for 50£ sterling sold 150 ac between Tyger and Enoree R and on Publick Rd from Isaac Crow's to Sampson Bobo's old place; part of 1,000 ac grant to James Semple, jr and sold by Rottry Semple, heir-at-law of James, to John McCullock who sold to Edward Hooker; plat attached. Witness Henry Huff and Jesse Parker. Signed Edward Hooker and Millie's mark. Wit. oath Oct. 9, 1792 Jesse Parker to James Jordan. Rec. Nov. 10, 1792

p. 85-86 Nov. 2, 1790 Benjamin Clerk to Samuel Jamison; for 50£ sterling sold 370 ac on N fork of N fork of Tygar R; on W side of 578 ac grant Feb. 6, 1786 Gov. William Moultrie to Benjamin Clerk; remaining 200 ac (sic) of grant excepted from this sale. Witness Allen Wakefield, Alexander Roddy, and John Crawford. Signed Benjn Clerk. Wit. oath Oct. 23, 1792 Alexander Roddy to James Jordan. Rec. Nov. 15, 1792

p. 86-88 Mar. 12, 1792 Henry Turner, sr (SC) to Samuel Turner (SC) for 24£ sold 70 ac on E side of Sholy Cr; border: Henry Turner; part of survey Oct. 22, 1784 by George Salmon for William Wood, son of Moses Wood. Witness Wills Griffith and Darby Turner. Signed Henry Turner's mark. Wit. oath May 8, 1792 Darby Turner to D Goodlett. Rec. Nov. 15, 1792

p. 88-89 Oct. 17, 1791 Jeremiah Walker (Elbert Co, Ga) to friend Henry McCray (Spartanburgh); power of attorney to collect a note dated Feb. 19, 1790 for 3,000 pounds of tobacco due Jeremiah from Wilm Poole. Witness Littleton Bagwell. Signed Jeremiah Walker's mark. Wit. oath Dec. 12, 1792 Littleton Bagwell to Isham Harrison. Rec. Dec. 18, 1792

p. 89-90 Feb. 11, 1791 John Conner and wife Winefred (Franklin Co, Ga) to Benjamin Bratcher (Spartanburgh); for 50£ sterling sold 100 ac on E side of branch of Richland Cr; part of grant to Thomas Hatteway; border: conditional line with William Wood, "across the ridge to head of Fawn Br, Clemmons, and Jesse Remes. Witness Daniel Cornwell and Larkin (or Parkin) Venable. Signed John Conner and Winefred's mark. Wit. oath Feb. 5, 1793 Daniel Cornwell to Isham Harrison. Rec. Feb. 5, 1793

p. 90 Dec. 10, 1792 (Pasquotank Co, NC) Joseph Kinyon to William Lancaster; for 57£ 10s NC money sold a Negro boy Mustavo. Witness Samuel Welliforn and J Banks. Signed Joseph Kinyon. Wit. oath (Warren Co, NC) Dec. 18, 1792 Samuel Welliforn to Will Johnson. Rec. Feb. 15, 1793

p. 90-91 Sept. 25, 1787 Thomas Wadsworth and William Turpin to George Lewis; for 100£ sterling sold 150 ac on both sides of Beaverdam Cr of Tyger R; survey Jun. 21, 1784 for George Lewis; grant Feb. 5, 1787 to Augustus Merrick (see Public Register Book

Z p. 23-25) who sold to Thomas Wadsworth and William Turpin. Witness John Cuningham and John Young, jr. Signed Thomas Wadsworth and Wm Turpin. Wit. oath Jan. 14, 1793 John Young, jr to Thos Moore. Rec. Feb. 15, 1793

p. 91-92 Oct. 15, 1791 Edward Hooker to James McClure; for 50£ sterling sold 200 ac; part of 600 ac grant May 7, 1774 to John Brodie on itlex (or Alex) Cr of Packolate R and N of Packolate R; sold by John Brodie to David Baty who sold to Edward Hooker. Witness Thomas White, John McClure, and Richard Saunders. Signed Edward Hooker. Wit. oath Jan. 16, 1793 John McClure to James Hooper. Rec. Mar. 1, 1793

p. 92-93 Mar. 14, 1791 William Anderson, yoeman (Spartanburgh) to James Alexander, jr (same); for 100£ sterling sold 245 ac on Mollie's Cr of S fork of Packolate R; on upper part of a line through 491 ac marked by Jn Clayton; grant Jun. 6, 1785. Witness Robert Harper and James Alexander. Signed William Anderson. Wit. oath Jan. 14, 1793 Robert Harper and James Alexander to James Hooper. Rec. Mar. 1, 1793

p. 93-94 Oct. 6, 1791 Thomas Tod to Edward Hooker; for 50£ sterling sold 200 ac; part of 600 ac grant May 7, 1774 to John Bodie on Alex's Cr of S Packolate R and N of Packolate R; sold by John Bodie to David Baty who sold to Thomas Tod. Witness Stephen Layton, Thomas Wright, and John McClure. Signed Thos Tod. Wit. oath Jan. 15, 1793 John McClure to James Hooper. Rec. Mar. 2, 1793

p. 94-95 Dec. 24, 1791 Isaac Young (Spartanburgh) to John Bankson (same); for 110£ SC money sold 200 ac on N side of Packolate R; grant Aug. 23, 1774 State Office to Hugh Warren. Witness Larkin Bethel, Richard Cox, and John Mure. Signed Isaac Young's mark. Certified Dec. 24, 1791 by Sampson Bethel. Rec. Mar. 7, 1793

p. 95-98 Oct. 9, 1792 William Poole (Spartanburgh), iron monger and founder to William Shaw (Abbeville Co), attorney; for 200£ sterling sold 200 ac on branches of Fairforrest Cr near the Court House; border: 100 ac of William Shaw (formerly Jeremiah Walker's), Thomas Williamson, heirs of late Richard Harrison, esq, Bull, and Williford; Condition: William's wife (not named) must remounce her dower in 6 months. Witness Andw Torrance and Esther Torrance. Signed William Poole. Wit. oath Oct. 8, 1791 Andw Torrance to Thomas Blasingame. Rec. Mar. 7, 1793

p. 98-100 Jan. 10, 1792 William Shurley and wife Elizabeth (Spartanburgh) to Richard Cox (same); for 40£ sterling sold 150 ac where Richard lives on N side of Tygar R; border: James Scaggs, Tobias Bright, and Thomas Shurley; grant Apr. 7, 1780 Gov. Thomas Pinckney to William Shurley. Witness Thomas Shurley, James Skiggs, and Isaac Philpot. Signed William Shurley and Elizabeth's mark. Wit. oath Feb. 1, 1793 Thomas Shurley to Thos Moore. Rec. Mar. 12, 1793

p. 100-101 Oct. 9, 1792 David Benson (Spartanburgh) to James Mason (same); for 55£ sold 205 ac on Mollie's Cr of Packolate R; part of 255 ac grant Jun. 6, 1785 Gov. William Moultrie to John Clayton. Witness William Calwell and James Alexander. Signed David Benson's mark. Wit. oath Jan. 14, 1793 James Alexander to James Hooper. Rec. Mar. 13, 1793

p. 101-102 Jan. 27, 1791 Willis Whitaker (Kershaw Co) to Absalom Bobo (Spartanburgh); for 50£ sterling sold 250 ac on Cedar Shoals Cr of Enoree R; border: NE-Sampson Bobo and vacant, SW-Joseph Kershaw and vacant, NW-John Roberson, and others vacant; grant Aug. 19, 1774 Gov. William Bull to Joseph Kershaw who sold on

May 20, 1775 to James Whitaker and to Willis Whitaker by descent about Aug. 1, 1780. Witness John Rainwater, Benja Rainwater, and Burrell Bobo. Signed Willis Whitaker. Wit. oath Dec. 12, 1792 John Rainwater to Thomas Farrow. Rec. Mar. 15, 1793

p. 102-103 Jan. 15, 1793 Isham Foster (Spartan Co) to Thomas Foster (same); for 50£ sold 180 ac; part of 400 ac grant May 2, 1785 Gov. William Moultrie to Elisha Ford on both sides of Ridge Road between Tyger R and Fairforrest Cr; sold by Elisha Ford to Robert Goodgion who sold part on S side of road to Isham Foster. Witness Alexander Montgomery, William Ballow, and David Goodlett. Signed Isham Foster. Certified Jan. 14, 1793 by D Goodlett. Rec. Mar. 20, 1793

p. 103-104 Jul. 2, 1792 William Morris, sr (Spartanburgh) to James Morris (same); for 300£ SC money sold 50 ac on Buck Cr of Packolate R; border: James Morris and Joseph Morris; grant May 22, 1772 NC Office to John herconnel. Witness S Bethel, John Morris, and Noel Johnston. Signed William Morris' mark. Certified Jul. 6, 1792 by S Bethel. Rec. Mar. 21, 1793

p. 104-105 Jan. 9, 1793 Stephen Wilson and wife Mary (Spartanburgh) to George Newman (same); for 30£ sterling sold 100 ac; border: S Wilson and near "the" Meeting House; part of 640 ac grant to James Sample, sr and sold Jul. 9, 1790 by James Rainey to Stephen Wilson. Witness Reuben Newman and Martin Newman. Signed Stephen Wilson and Mary's mark. Wit. oath Jan. 12, 1793 Reuben Newman to D Goodlett. Rec. Mar. 21, 1793

p. 105-107 Jan. 14, 1793 James Gibbs and wife Anne (Union Co) to Ephraim Elder (Spartanburgh); for 150£ sterling sold 50 ac on W side of Buffalowlick Br of Fairforrest Cr; border: James Gibbs' clearing and David Cook's old line; part of grant to Gilles Tillet and willed to James Gibbs by his father, John Gibbs, sr. Witness Spencer Casey and Peter Elder. Signed James Gibbs and Anne's mark. Wit. oath Jan. 14, 1793 Spencer Casey to Isham Harrison. Rec. Mar. 21, 1793

p. 107-110 Jan. 12, 1793 John Burnett and wife Sary (or Sarah) (Spartanburgh) to Adam Kilby (late of NC); for 114£ 10s sterling sold 400 ac on both sides of Fawn Br of Lawson's fork of Packolate R; grant Jan. 1, 1787 Gov. William Moultrie to John Burnett; border: SW-Israel Morris and others vacant. Witness James Wood, Joseph Venable, and Stephen Miller. Signed John and Sally Burnett's marks. Wit. oath Jan. 14, 1793 Joseph Venable to D Goodlett. Rec. Mar. 21, 1793

p. 110-111 (not dated) Richard Harrison and Charles Bruce; each give up award made previously because it was conceived in error in accounts; controvercy was a suit Charles brought against Richard in Court of Common Pleas in 96 Dist for false and scandulous words said by Richard to damage Charles and a breach of covenant where Charles was bound to build the Court House; Richard acknowledges words "occasioned by" Charles swearing Richard "bargained to saw upon an average plank, scantling and featheridge" for house for Bazel Lee at the rate of 4s per hundred feet which Richard said was false; Charles didn't hear the bargin and pled justification; upon investigation Richard was shown to be right; therefore Richard should pay no part of a suit at Cambridge or pay Charles the horse adjudged in the former award; but Charles should pay Richard 13£ 14s Va money which is the balance due Richard; and Charles shouldn't pay rent for Richard since Charles did the equivalent amount of work on Richard's plantation and wintering of stock; Charles expected to have that given him since Charles undertook the work "on the goal" at 2/4 per day. Signed Bayles Earle and Wm Benson, arbitrars.

Rec. Mar. 27, 1793

p. 111-112 Nov. 9, 1792 John Foster, sr (Rutherford Co, NC) to Ezekiel Stanly (Green Co, Ga); for 100£ sterling sold 100 ac on both sides of Thickety Cr; grant Mar. 6, 1786 Gov. William Moultrie to John Foster. Witness John Foster and Philip Cox. Signed John Foster. Wit. oath Nov. 10, 1792 John Foster to James Hooper. Rec. Apr. 13, 1793

p. 112-113 Jan. 5, 1792 John Couch (Spartanburgh) to Joseph Couch (same); for 100£ sold 150 ac on Enoree R; half of 300 ac grant May 7, 1767 Gov. Charles G Montague to Thomas Couch, desc; <u>and</u> 50 ac on E side of Enoree R; grant to Charles Hunt and leased to John Couch. Witness Aaron Casey and Isaac Couch. Signed John Couch. Wit. oath Oct. 22, 1792 John Couch to Thomas Farrow. Rec. Apr. 15, 1793

p. 113-114 Nov. 23, 1792 William Marks (Southampton Co, Va) to William Lancaster (Spartanburgh); for 27£ 10s sold a Negro boy Shrewsberry 8 years old next Spring. Witness Brittain Williford, Joel Harris, and Juday Harris. Signed William Marks. Wit. oath Feb. 21, 1793 Brittain Williford to Saml Lancaster. Rec. Apr. 19, 1793

p. 114-115 Feb. 16, 1791 Tilman Bobo to William Waldrop; for 6£ sterling sold 60 ac; part of 250 ac grant Dec. 3, 1787 to Tilman Bobo on N side of Enoree R; border: S-Enoree R, W-Patrick Cunningham's grant, E-Mechael Waldrop, and N-remainder of grant. Witness Christopher Rhodes and Moses Casey. Signed Tilman Bobo. Wit. oath Jul. 26, 1791 Tilman Bobo to Thomas Farrow. Rec. Apr. 19, 1793

p. 115-116 Jul. 6, 1792 William Jamison (Washington Dist) to John Gowen (Pinckney Dist); for 30£ sterling sold 249 ac on both sides of N fork of Mill Cr of S fork Paccolate R; grant Apr. 5, 1792 Gov. Charles Pinckney to William Jamison. Witness James Jordan, Thomas Benson, and William Martin. Signed William Jamison. Rec. May 8, 1793

p. 116-117 Feb. 28, 1793 William Patton to Saml Archibald; for 20£ sterling sold 40 ac on McElevean's Cr; upper end of grant NC governor to James McElevean. Witness Hugh Donaldson, Robt Donaldson, and Alexander McCarter. Signed Wm Patton. Wit. oath Mar. 1, 1793 Hugh Donaldson to Wm Smith. Rec. May 13, 1793

p. 117-118 Apr. 8, 1793 Peter Smith and wife Agnes (Spartanburgh) to James Smith (same); for 13£ sterling sold 12 ac on SW side of Kilsoe's Cr; part of grant to Peter Smith (see Book 32 p. 255); border: James Smith; plat attached. Witness Daniel White, James Allen, and M Lovina Smith. Signed Peter Smith. Wit. oath Apr. 8, 1793 Daniel White to David Goodlett. Rec. May 14, 1793

p. 118-119 Oct. 9, 1790 William Dickson (Spartanburgh) to Soloman Abbitt (same); for 5£ SC money sold 125 ac on S side of Paccolate R; part of 534 ac "taken up" by William Dickson; border: a branch between Jeremiah Dickson and Elizabeth Dickson. Witness Samuel Turner, Richard Turner, and John Fowler. Signed William and Mary Dickson's marks. Wit. oath Oct. 11, 1790 Samuel Turner to Obadiah Trimmier. Rec. May 14, 1793

p. 119-121 Jan. 4, 1785 Adam Potter (96 Dist) to David Smith (same); for 20£ 1s sterling sold 100 ac on N side of Paccolate R; border: Jacob Green; lower or E end of 200 ac grant Nov. 25, 1777 Gov. Joseph Moultrie (NC) (sic) to Jacob Green who sold Oct. 20, 1782 to Adam Potter. Witness Stephen Potter, Robert Franks, and Angelica Mitchel. Signed Adam Potter. Rec. May 16, 1793

p. 121-122 Dec. 9, 1790 Zachariah Bullock (Union Co) to David Smith (Spartanburgh); for 10£ sterling sold 160 ac on N side of Paccolate R; part of a new survey granted to Zachariah Bullock; border: island above Easterwood fish trap, Matthew Sparks, and Jacob Green's old line. Witness Adam Potter, John Lipscomb, and Nehemiah Norton. Signed Zacha Bullock. Rec. May 17, 1793

p. 122-124 Jan. 8, 1791 David Smith (Spartanburgh) to Nehemiah Norton (Union Co); for 55£ sterling sold 170 ac on N side of Pacolate R where David Smith lives; part of old survey granted to Jacob Green and part of new survey granted to Zacharias Bullock joining each other; border: Matthew Sparks, Sparks' Spring Br, Thomas Norton, and Jesse Austin. Witness Adam Potter, Matthew Sparks, and John Sparks. Signed David Smith. Rec. May 17, 1793

p. 124-125 Sept. 3, 1792 John Case (Rutherford Co, NC) to James Turner (Spartanburgh); for 80£ SC money sold 200 ac on S side of Pacolate R; border: Case's Cr; grant May 12, 1772 NC governor to (not given). Witness William Tunnel, Drury Abbitt, and Jase Case, jr. Signed John Case's mark. Wit. oath Apr. 16, 1793 William Tunnel to S Bethel. Rec. May 20, 1793

p. 125-126 Nov. 20, 1792 Isham Safford (Washington Co, Ga) to William Murray (Spartanburgh); for 50£ sterling sold 196 ac on Island Cr; border: Leonard Adcock; part of 396 ac grant Jan. 2, 1792 Gov. Charles Pinckney to Isham Safford. Witness Leonard Adcock and Wm Walker. Signed Isham Safford. Wit. oath Apr. 5, 1793 Leonard Adcock to S Bethel. Rec. May 22, 1793

p. 126-127 Nov. 28, 1792 Isham Safford (Washington Co, Ga) to Leonard Adcock (Spartanburgh); for 50£ sterling sold 200 ac on Island Cr of Packolate R; border: Leonard Adcock and William Murrey; part of 396 ac grant in 1792 Gov. Charles Pinckney to Isham Safford. Witness William Walker and William Murray. Signed Isham Safford. Wit. oath Apr. 5, 1793 William Murray to S Bethel. Rec. May 22, 1793

p. 127-128 Feb. 26, 1793 Peter Elder and wife Elizabeth (Spartanburgh) to William Lancaster (same); for 30£ sterling sold 50 ac on S side of Fairforrest Cr and on Buffalo Lick Cr; border: SW-John Smith, SE-Wofford or the Mountain tract, NE and NW-Alexander Autry; including improvements where William Lancaster lives; part of grant State Office to Thomas Bullion who sold to Zach Gibbs who sold to James Gibbs who sold to Peter Elder. Witness Christopher Golightly, Levi Lancaster, and Henry Ayres. Signed Peter and Elizabeth Elder's marks. Wit. oath Apr. 8, 1793 Christopher Golightly to Isham Harrison. Rec. May 23, 1793

p. 128-131 Nov. 20, 1775 Henry Sunday (Craven Co) to Joseph Reice (same), clergyman; for 500£ 10s SC money sold 150 ac on branch of Lawson's fork; border: SW-Wm Moultrie, SE-Henry Prince, and others vacant; grant (date not given) Gov. William Bull to Henry Sunday. Witness Derrell Hart, Hargrove Arthur, and Nathan Center. Signed Henry Sunday's mark. Wit. oath (Orangeburgh Dist) Jan. 8, 1793 Hargrove Arthur to Alear Blair. Rec. May 24, 1793

p. 131-132 Jun. 14, 1793 John and Pressila Pepes to children Presscilla, Ruth, and Sarah Pipes, equally; give 11 cattle: 2 cows, 2 calves, 3 heifers, 2 bulls, and 2 yearlings; 3 horses, 7 sheep, a loom, 2 feather beds with furniture, "thereunto belonging pewter and all household furniture". Witness Thos Wmson and Wm Poole. Signed John Pepes and Pressilla's mark. Wit. oath Jun. 14, 1793 Wm Poole to D Goodlett. Rec. Jul. 16, 1793

p. 132-135 Jul. 14, 1790 Joseph Thompson (Spartanburgh) to Edward Stewart (same); for 50£ sold 200 ac on S fork of N fork of Tyger R and E of Indian boundary; survey Jul. 15, 1785 for Joseph Thompson "in the name John Davis" and afterwards released to Augustus Murdock. Witness Nevil Wayland, Allen Wakefield, and Henry Wayland. Signed Joseph Thompson. Wit. oath Jul. 17, 1793 Nevil Wayland to Isham Harrison. Rec. Jul. 17, 1793

p. 135-136 Feb. 1, 1793 Sampson Bobo and wife Sarah to Anthony Foster, sr; for 150£ sterling sold 400 ac on Cedar Shole Cr between Enoree and Tygar R; ½ ac reserved for a burying ground "in the old plantation for Bobo family"; plat attached shows border: Whitaker, Sampson Bobo, and Spencer Bobo. Witness Robert Hanna and Fielding Foster. Signed Sampson and Sarah Bobo's marks. Wit. oath Jul. 16, 1793 Fielding Foster to Thomas Farrow. Rec. Jul. 23, 1793

p. 136-137 Oct. 9, 1790 William Dickson (Spartanburgh) to Henry Turner (same); for 5£ sold 150 ac on N side of Pacolate R; part of 533 ac where William Dickson lives; border: Anthony Coulter, Elizabeth Dickson, and Soloman Abbitt. Witness Samuel Turner, Richard Turner, and John Fowler. Signed William and Mary Dickson's marks. Wit. oath Oct. 11, 1790 Samuel Turner to Obadiah Trimmier. Rec. Jul. 25, 1793

p. 137-139 Jun. 8, 1792 (Loundon Co, Va) Joseph Wildman states Benjamin McMikin, son of Alexander McMikin who married Mary Caru (or Carae or Carr) and moved to SC, at 14 years old was a drummer in Militia Company commanded by Alexander McMikin until he was old enough to be enrolled on the Muster List when he served in militia when called until discharged because of a "complaint of the leg which as well as I recollect in Apr. 1780" in militia company where Joseph was an Ensign. Signed Joseph Wildman. Certified by Gustavas Elgin (not dated), who served as a lieutenant in the militia company and lived 1½ miles from Benjamin McMikin. Certified by John Alexander on Jun. 8, 1792 who says the militia company belonged to the Third Battalion of Loundon Co, Va of which John Alexander was Lt. Colonel and battalion commander.
Apr. 1, 1780 a Court Martial of the Third Battalion of Landoun Co Militia held at Capt. Fergansis; present--William Brenaugh, esq (Col and Presd), Alexander McMakin, Jacob Reid, William Owsley, Simon Hancock, John Davis, and Daniel Fegans (all gentelmen and captains); Benjamin McMikin "labours" under infirmity in his leg and is ordered to be discharged from mustering during the continuance of the infirmity. Signed William Brenaugh
Jun. 8, 1792 This is to certify the above is true copy of records of the Court Martial, and that Benjamin McMikin was about 15 and until he moved his residence was about 2 miles from Benjamin McMikin, that Benjamin had a strong interest in the county and an aversion for Toryism and was honest. Signed Chas Binns, jr, late clerk of Loudn Militia
Jun. 8, 1792 (Loundoun Co, Va) Certify that Joseph Wildman, Gustavus Elgin, John Alexander, and Charles Binns, jr bore the respective offices mentioned and John Alexander was duly authorized to keep the peace in Loundoun Co. Signed Charles Binn
Apr. 17, 1783 Benjamin McMikin and wife Mary have unblemished character and "leave these parts" with reputation and are commended to any "crystian" Society where God cast their lot. Signed David Bard

p. 139-140 Jun. 11, 1793 Richard Harrison, desc, and Charles Bruce now settle accounts and disputes; Charles is to deliver to Isham Harrison, administrator for estate of Richard, two bonds: a letter from James Harrison and an award awarded him by the arbitrators Bayles Earle, esq and Capt. William Benson and John

Blasingame, esq; the two bonds are (a) a bond Richard gave John Holcom to make a title to land adjoining Richard's land and (b) arbitration bond James Harrison gave Charles and all other paper of their dispute; Isham Harrison will give Charles his arbitration bond that he gave James Harrison and all other papers and the last award to Richard by the arbitrators; all agree settlement shall stand for receipt from "beginning of the world to today"; all debts between Charles and Richard are to be recorded in Spartanburgh. Witness none. Signed Chas Bruce and Isham Harrison. Certified by Thomas Moore. Rec. Jul. 31, 1793

p. 140-141 Feb. 18, 1793 Thomas Davis (Wilkes Co, Ga) to John Davis (Spartanburgh); for 100£ sold 200 ac on N fork of Tygar R; grant Oct. 20, 1767 Gov. William Tryon (NC) to Davis Davis who sold to Henry Hartle who sold to James Jordan, esq who sold to Thomas Davis. Witness James Vernon, Samuel Jamison, and Samuel Miller. Signed Thomas Davis. Wit. oath May 15, 1793 Samuel Jamison to James Jordan. Rec. Aug. 1, 1793

p. 141-143 Mar. 9, 1793 John Nail and wife Nancy (Union Co) to Henry ONaill (same); for 100£ sterling sold 506 ac on S side of Pacolate R and on Trough Shoal Br of Pacolate R; including land where widow Collins formerly lived; grant Feb. 6, 1786 Gov. William Moultrie to John Nail. Witness Robert Donaldson, John McDowel, and Andrew Thomson. Signed John and Agnes Nail's marks. Rec. Aug. 1, 1793

p. 143-144 May 28, 1793 Samuel Jamison (Spartanburgh) to John Davis (same); for 50£ sold 378 ac on N fork of N Tygar R; part of 578 ac grant Feb. 6, 1786 Gov. William Moultrie to Benjamin Clark who sold 378 ac to Samuel Jamison; remaining 200 ac of grant (on W side) excepted. Witness Nevil Wayland, Samuel Miller, and Robert Jamison, jr. Signed Samuel Jamison. Wit. oath May 28, 1793 Samuel Miller to James Jordan. Rec. Aug. 5, 1793

p. 144-145 Feb. 25, 1793 Peter Elder (Spartanburgh) to Ephraim Elder (same); for 30£ SC money sold 48 ac on W side of Buffelow lick Cr; border: Tillet. Witness William Roberds and Thomas Underwood. Signed Peter Elder's mark. Wit. oath Mar. 7, 1793 Thomas Underwood to Isham Harrison. Rec. Aug. 6, 1793

p. 145-146 Apr. 18, 1793 Thomas Wright (Spartanburgh) to Andrew Barry (same); for 11£ 4s sterling sold a Negro girl Jude about 8 years old if Andrew pays the money by Dec. 25, 1794. Witness Richard Barry and Thomas Moore. Signed Thomas Wright. Rec. Aug. 6, 1793

p. 146-148 May 21, 1790 William Wofford (Broad R, Franklin Co, Ga) to Malachi Jones (Pacolate R, Spartanburgh); for 100£ sterling sold 200 ac on both sides of Pacolate R; including a large shoal, the mouth of Lindsay's Br, and Doctor's Bottom; grant from North Carolina to Isaac Lindsay then in Tryon Co, NC. Witness Benjamin Wofford and Owen Bowen. Signed William Wofford. Wit. oath Oct. 24, 1792 Benjamin Wofford to I Harrison. Rec. Aug. 9, 1793

p. 148-149 Apr. 8, 1793 Jesse Tate (Spartanburgh) to William Sanders (same); for 32£ 2s sterling sold 103 ac on Thickety Cr of Broad R; border: SE-Hopkins, N-William Morris, and SW-Dunaway; grant Oct. 6, 1788 Gov. Thomas Pinckney to Jesse Tate. Witness Samuel Clark and Patrick Sanders. Signed Jesse Tate's mark. Wit. oath Jun. 12, 1793 Samuel Clark to S Bethel. Rec. Aug. 9, 1793

p. 149-151 May 27, 1793 Josiah Tanner and wife Martha (Spartanburgh) to John Lipscomb (same); for 10£ sterling sold 85 ac on

Gocher's Cr; border: Obediah Olephout, Moore, and John Sheppey. Witness William Lipscomb. Signed Josiah and Martha Tanner. Wit. oath Jun. 10, 1793 William Lipscomb to Isham Harrison. Rec. Aug. 13, 1793

p. 151-152 Feb. 16, 1793 John Hightower (Spartanburgh) to Lawrence Bankson (same); for 100£ sterling sold 426 ac on both sides of Pacolate R; border: Edward Stubblefield; grant Jan. 21, 1785 State Office to Reuben Dickson who sold to John Hightower. Witness Sampson Bethel, John Cantrell, and James Turner. Signed John Hightower and Cristan's mark. Certified Feb. 16, 1793 by Sampson Bethel. Rec. Aug. 13, 1793

p. 152-154 Oct. 6, 1779 David McDowel and wife Elizabeth (Craven Co) to Benjamin Simmons (same); for 3,000£ SC money sold 200 ac on S side of S fork of Pacolate R; border: William Dickson; commonly called Maiden Meadows; part of 500 ac grant Dec. 23, 1768 North Carolina to John Pfifer on both sides of S fork Pacolate R and sold by John Pfifer to James Huggins Jun. 14, 1775 who sold on Nov. 30, 1778 to David and Elizabeth McDowel. Witness Thomas Roden and James Ken. Signed William and Elizabeth McDowel. Wit. oath Oct. 15, 1779 James Cain to James Wood. Rec. Aug. 15, 1793

p. 154-157 Dec. 24, 1790 Benjamin Simmon and wife Mary (Union Co) to Wm McWilliams (Spartanburgh); for 60£ SC money sold 200 ac; border: William Dickson; called Meaden Meadows; part of 500 ac grant Sept.(sic) 23, 1768 North Carolina to John Pfifer in Craven Co, SC on both sides of S fork Packolate R and sold by John Pfifer to James Huggans Jun. 14, 1776 who sold Nov. 30, 1778 to David and Elizabeth McDowel who sold 200 ac on S side of S fork Pacolate R to Benjamin Simmons. Witness Harrell Cain and William Kelly. Signed Benjamin and Mary Simmons' mark. Wit. oath (Union Co) Nov. 9, 1792 Harrell Cain to John Pearson. Rec. Aug. 16, 1793

p. 157-158 Jul. 22, 1789 John Butler and wife Mary (Spartanburgh) to John Beard (same); for 80£ sterling sold 200 ac on both sides Cane Cr of Tyger R; grant Dec. 5, 1785 Gov. William Moultrie to John Butler. Witness Richard Nalley, James Beard, and John Butler, jr. Signed John Butler and Mary's mark. Wit. oath Feb. 23, 1793 James Beard to Samuel Lancaster. Rec. Aug. 19, 1793

p. 158-159 Jan. 19, 1793 William Reid (Spartanburgh); a will: he gives his soul to God and body to the earth; and (1) all debts to be paid, (2) to wife, during her widowhood, all land where William lives on S side of Pacolate R and all stock and all household furniture, (3) when wife marrys or dies, land goes to son, John Reid, (4) to daughter, Sarah George, 5s sterling, (5) to son, William Reid, 5s sterling, (6) to son Thomas all land on N side of Pacolate R on provision Thomas builds his mother as good a house where she now lives as now is on land on N side of Pacolate R, (7) to son, Joseph Reid, 5s sterling, (8) to son, Isaac Reid, 5s sterling, (9) to daughter, Jane Reid, 5s sterling, (10) to daughter, Mary Reid, 5s sterling; William Poole, sr and son William Reid appointed executors. Witness John Stovaul and John Poole. Signed William Reid. Rec. Aug. 20, 1793

p. 159-160 Mar. 7, 1793 Daniel Stillwell (Spartanburgh) to Samuel Donnway (same); for 50£ SC money sold 100 ac on both sides of Island Cr of Pacolate R; grant Sept. 4, 1786. Witness Leonard Adcock and John Wootan. Signed Daniel Stillwell. Wit. oath May 4, 1793 Leonard Adcock to Sampson Bobo. Rec. Aug. 20, 1793

p. 160-161 Jan. 23, 1793 John Cobb (Spartanburgh) to William Garret (same); for 30£ sterling sold 182 ac on Buck Cr of Pacolate R; border: Abraham Cantrell and Thomas Warran; grant May

1, 1786 State Office to (not given). Witness Abraham Cantrell, Elijah Thompson, and John Pipers. Signed John Cobb's mark. Wit. oath Jun. 11, 1793 Abraham Cantrell to Sampson Bethel. Rec. Aug. 21, 1793

p. 161-162 Jan. 28, 1793 William Armstrong (Spartanburgh) to Alexander Keenum (same); for 30£ sterling sold 188 ac on both sides of Fawn Br of Lawson's fork of Pacolate R; grant Nov. 27, 1784 to William Armstrong. Witness Stephen Miller, William Brandon, and John Kennum. Signed William Armstrong. Wit. oath Mar. 30, 1793 Stephen Miller to D Goodlett. Rec. Aug. 22, 1793

p. 162-164 Dec. 31, 1792 Henry Pettit (Spartanburgh) to William Reid (same), schoolmaster; for 25£ sterling sold 200 ac on both sides Pacolate R below Healing Springs; border: conditional line with William Poole, sr; grant Sept. 16, 1784 Gov. William Moultrie to (not given). Witness William Poole, Jane Reid, and Thomas Reid. Signed Henry Pettit. Wit. oath Jun. 12, 1793 William Poole to Isham Harrison. Rec. Aug. 22, 1793

p. 164-165 Dec. 26, 1792 Richard Lewis (late of Spartanburgh but now of Ga) to James Vernon (Spartanburgh); for 50£ sterling sold 88 ac on Jimmy's Cr of N Tyger R; border: SE-Nesbitt, NE-Collins, NW & NE-Snoddy, NW-Lucan, SW & NW-Alex Vernon, and SW & SE-vacant; grant Jun. 4, 1787 Gov. Thomas Pickney to Richard Lewis. Witness Beverly Lewis, Fields Lewis, and Nevil Wayland. Signed Richard Lewis. Wit. oath Jun. 7, 1793 Beverly Lewis to James Jordan. Rec. Aug. 23, 1793

p. 165-167 Jun. 24, 1788 Andrew Thompson (Tyger R) to William Miller (same); for 5£ SC money sold 100 ac on S side of S fork of Tyger R; border: N-William Miller and S-unknown; grant Aug. 26, 1774 to Andrew Thompson. Witness Duncan McCreevan, John Nicoll, and Alexander Vernon. Signed Andrew Thompson. Wit. oath Jun. 29, 1778 Duncan McCreevan to James Wood. Rec. Aug. 24, 1793

p. 167-168 Jun. 11, 1793 David McCarley (Spartanburgh) and wife Ursilla to Alexander Alexander (same), merchant; for 120£ sterling sold 100 ac on both sides Jamie's Cr of Tyger R; border: Jacob Earnest, Henerey Cearley, and John Bragg; part of 150 ac grant Jun. 25, 1765 to William Hendricks who sold Jan. 13 & 14, 1772 to Moses McCarley who "sold" 100 ac to his son David McCarley in his will. Witness Nicholas Keating, Moses Cavin, and Francis Doig. Signed David and Ursilla McCarley's marks. Rec. Aug. 27, 1793

p. 168-170 Sept. 7, 1790 William Benson (Spartanburgh), sheriff, to William Shaw (Cambridge, Abbeville Co); for 10£ 6s sold 100 ac near the Court House; border: Thomas Williamson; sale due to writ from court held at Thomas Williamson's place Baylis Earle presiding on their Monday in Mar. 1790 and returnable the third Monday in June 1791; writ was to assess 2£ 13s 6p sterling from Jeremiah Walker and Reubin Mathews and 2£ 1s 6p to county treasurer for costs; land sold belonged to Jeremiah Walker. Witness William Poole and Christopher Golightly. Signed Wm Benson. Rec. Aug. 27, 1793

p. 170-173 Jul. 8, 1793 John Golightly and wife Winnefred (Spartanburgh) to Christopher Golightly, William Shands Golightly, and David Golightly, sons and heirs of William Golightly, desc (same); for 200£ sterling sold 1,500 ac on Kilsoe's and Dennis' Creeks; from three surveys: (1) 600 ac grant to James Hammett on "the Rich Hill", (2 & 3) grant to John Golightly and adjoining Rich Hill, (2) is 500 ac and (3) is 400 ac; border: SW-Amey Golightly, Robert Sterling, and Robert White, S-unknown, E-William Crocker, James Poole, and Joseph Barnett, and W-Richard Williss; plat attached divides land into 3 parts: 438 ac, 589 ac, and Christopher Golightly's 568 (or 508) ac. Witness Philip Hoofman, David Golightly, and William Lancaster. Signed John Golightly and Winnefred's mark. Wit. oath Jul. 16, 1793 William Lancaster to Isham Harrison. Rec. Aug. 29, 1793

p. 173-176 Feb. 26, 1793 Joshua English, jr, eldest son and heir of Thomas English, desc to John and Robert English, the other sons of Thomas English; for 15s sterling sold 300 ac (or 200 ac) on S fork of Tyger R; border: N-Isaac Ross and others vacant; grant May 13, 1763 Gov. Thomas Boone (SC) to Thomas English, desc; Thomas English had 200 ac when he died without a will and Joshua English now sells the land. Witness Saml Tomlinson and Thomas English. Signed Joshua English and Ann's mark. Wit. oath (Kershaw Co) Mar. 7, 1793 Saml Tomlinson to Francis Boykin. Rec. Aug. 29, 1793

p. 176-177 Jan. 20, 1792 Enos Land (Spartanburgh) to John Burk (same); for 30£ sterling sold 100 ac on Pacolate R; border: Nicholas Oldridge and Richardson Whitbey. Witness Richardson Whitbey, John Vandiver, and Isham Harrison. Signed Enos Land's mark. Rec. Aug. 30, 1793

p. 177-178 Sept. 10, 1793 Robert Foster (Spartanburgh) to George McDowell, jr, son of Wm McDowell, desc; for 50£ sold 202 ac on both sides of Lawson's fork; survey for Thomas Wood and grant Feb. 6, 1786 Gov. William Moultrie to Robert Prince who sold to Robert Foster. Witness Isham Foster, John Walker, and Jeremiah Selmon. Wit. oath Sept. 9, 1793 Isham Foster to D Goodlett. Rec. Sept. 18, 1793

p. 178-179 Jul. 19, 1793 Edward Stewart (Spartan Co) to Willey S Brown (same); for 100£ sterling sold 200 ac on S fork of N fork Tyger R; survey Jul. 15, 1785 for John Davis and granted Feb. 5, 1787 to Augustus Merrick who sold to Joseph Thompson who sold to Edward Stewart. Witness William Ford, Elizabeth Larrance, and James Larrance. Signed Edward Stewart. Wit. oath Sept. 9, 1792 William Ford to James Jordan. Rec. Sept. 19, 1793

p. 179-180 Feb. 25, 1793 Samuel Elder (Spartan Co) to James Hicky (same); for 20£ sterling sold 100 ac on Dutchman's Cr of Tyger R; border: Drewry Smith; part of 525 ac grant Apr. 3, 1786 Gov. William Moultrie to Drewry Smith. Witness William Roberts and Jacob Ison (or Json). Signed Samuel Elder's mark. Wit. oath Aug. 30, 1793 William Roberts to I Harrison. Rec. Sept. 19, 1793

p. 180-182 Mar. 25, 1793 James Cantrell (Spartanburgh) to Elijah Thompson (same); for 50£ SC money sold 200 ac on Meaden Br of Buck Cr of Pacolate R; border: Isaac Young, Thomas Jordan, Elias Legett. Witness S Bethel, Mary Bethel, and Larken Bethel. Signed James Cantrell. Certified Mar. 26, 1793 by S Bethel. Rec. Sept. 20, 1793

p. 182-184 May 4, 1790 William Banister and wife Elizabeth (Spartanburgh) to James Gilmore (same); for 70£ sterling sold 200 ac on both sides of S Pacolate R in Berkley Co; including the "first great bottoms called Meaden's Meadows"; lower half of grant May 17, 1759 to Richard Lyon and 200 ac sold by James Woods to Adam Terrance and to James Woods by power of attorney from Richard Lyon. Witness David McDowel, James McDowel, and Thomas McKnight. Signed William and Elizabeth Banister. Wit. oath Jul. 13, 1793 David McDowel to James Hooper. Rec. Sept. 30, 1793

p. 184-186 Jul. 25, 1793 John McCarter, heir of father Alexander McCarter, desc (Spartanburgh) to Alexander McCarter, jr, his brother; for 50£ sterling sold 300 ac on S side of N fork of

Tyger R and both sides of a branch; grant Apr. 26, 1768 Gov. William Tryon (NC) to Alexr McCarter, sr then in Meclenburgh Co, NC; 200 ac in center of tract surveyed for Jno Sharp and granted Oct. 20, 1767 Gov. William Tryon (NC) to (not given) who sold to Alexander McCarter, sr Dec. 1, 1769. Witness N Wayland, John Davis, and Robert McEntire. Signed John McCarter. Wit. oath Jul. 25, 1793 John McCarter to James Jordan. Rec. Oct. 4, 1793

p. 186-187 Oct. 8, 1793 Wells Griffith (Spartanburgh) to Jordan Holcome (Greenville Co); for 10£ sold 60 ac on N side Losson's Fork of Pacolate R; border: Jordan Holcome; grant Jan. 21, 1785 Gov. Benjamin Guerard to Wells Griffith; deed not warranted for any part of land in a grant before Jan. 21, 1785. Witness Bazel Lee, Israel Robertson, and James Holcome. Signed Wells Griffith. Wit. oath Oct. 8, 1793 James Holcome to I Harrison. Rec. Oct. 9, 1793

p. 187-188 Jan. 25, 1793 John McCarter, heir and son of Alexander McCarter, desc, to Esther McCarter; for 50£ sterling sold 160 ac on S branch of N fork of Tyger R; border: Alexander Vernon, John Miller, and James Miller; grant Oct. 6, 1767 Gov. William Tryon (NC) to John Orr in Mecklinburgh Co, NC, who sold to Alexander McCarter. Witness N Wayland, John Faris, and Robert McEntire. Signed John McCarter. Wit. oath Jul. 25, 1793 John McCarter to James Jordan. Rec. Oct. 15, 1793

p. 188-190 Mar. 2, 1793 Moses Timmons to William Wood, sr; for 100£ sterling sold 350 ac where William Wood lives on both sides Fawn Br of Lawson's fork of Pacolate R; part of 400 ac grant (date not given) Gov. Joseph Martin (NC) to Thos Hatherway who sold to John Conner who sold 350 ac to Moses Timmons; the remaining 50 ac of grant on E side sold to Uriah Conner. Witness Abner Howel and Wm Benson. Signed Moses Timmons. Wit. oath Sept. 9, 1793 Wm Benson to D Goodlett. Rec. Oct. 16, 1793

p. 190-191 Aug. 1, 1793 William Wood, sr to James Burnett; for 73£ sterling sold 150 ac where James Burnett lives on both sides Fawn Br of Lawson's fork of Pacolate R; border: "main road" and William Wood; part of 400 ac grant (date not given) Gov. Joseph Martin (NC) to Thos Hatherway who sold to John Conner who sold 350 ac to Moses Timmons who sold to William Wood. Witness Joseph Venible and Robert Kimble. Signed Wm Wood. Wit. oath Sept. 9, 1793 Joseph Venible to D Goodlett. Rec. Oct. 17, 1793

p. 191 Sept. 9, 1793 Samuel Morrow (Spartanburgh) to his Negro wench, Poll; gives her her freedon if she will "be her own woman". Witness Wm Smith, Jason Moore, and Brittain Willeford. Signed Samuel Morrow. Rec. Oct. 17, 1793

p. 191-193 Dec. 7, 1792 William Shurley and wife Elizabeth (Spartanburgh) to John Meadown (same); for 30£ sterling sold 100 ac near N fork Tyger R; border: N-Andrew Thomson, E-Tobias Bright and Robert Rogers and Thomas Shurley, and SW-Tyger R; part of 450 ac grant Apr. 7, 1788 Gov. Thomas Pinckney to William Shurley. Witness Joseph Meadows, Zephniah Pinson, and Jesse Meadows. Signed William Shurley. Wit. oath Aug. 1, 1793 Jesse Meadows to Wm Smith. Rec. Oct. 18, 1793

p. 193-194 Feb. 2, 1793 Peter Elder (Spartanburgh) to Robert Sprincle (same); for 6£ SC money sold 12 ac on Buffilow Lick Cr of Thickety Cr; part of land sold by Thomas Bullion to James Gibbs and part of land sold by James Gibbs to Peter Elder; border: land formerly owned by Michel Sprincle, desc and now Robert Sprincle's land. Witness Thos Underwood and Alexander Autry. Signed Peter Elder's mark. Wit. oath Sept. 6, 1793 Alexander Autry to I

Harrison. Rec. Oct. 22, 1793

p. 194-195 Sept. 2, 1793 James Brown (Spartanburgh) to Peter Peterson (same); for 40£ sold 100 ac on N side Pacolate R and both sides Green Cr of Pacolate R; lower part of 200 ac where James Brown lives; part of 200 ac grant May 23, 1792(sic) Gov. Josiah Martin (NC) to John Kirkconnel. Witness W Lancaster, A Lancaster, and D Goodlett. Signed James Brown's mark. Wit. oath Sept. 14(?), 1793 A Lancaster to I Harrison. Rec. Oct. 25, 1793

p. 195-196 Oct. 8, 1792 David Milhanks (Spartanburgh) to Deskin Grant (same); a bond for 60£; Condition: that David makes a title to Deskin for a tract that is part of land surveyed by Reubin Lawson and sold by Zachariah Sparks to David Milhanks. Witness Ellis Cannon and James Gibbs. Signed David Milhanks. Wit. oath Nov. 11, 1793 Ellis Cannon to I Harrison. Rec. Jan. 1, 1794

p. 196-197 Feb. 4, 1794 John Boley (Spartanburgh) to Blake Massingale (same); for 30£ sterling sold 100 ac on E side of Shoally Cr of Lawson's fork; part of 547 ac grant Oct. 3, 1785 Gov. William Moultrie to Boley Conner who sold to John Boley. Witness John Killey, Nathan Bishop, and Thomas Massingale. Signed John Boley. Wit. oath Feb. 15, 1794 Thomas Massingale to D Goodlett. Rec. Feb. 15, 1794

p. 197-198 Jan. 2, 1794 Thomas Massingale (Spartan Co) to his children James, Mary, Nancy, Sally, and Betsy, in equal parts; for love and affection give: 2 cows and heifers, a black mare, 2 sows and pigs marked with slit in left ear and staple fork in right ear. Witness John Boley, Henry Turner, and James Wyatt. Signed Thomas Massingale's mark. Wit. oath Jan. 25, 1794 James Wyatt to D Goodlett. Rec. Feb. 15, 1794

p. 198-199 Sept. 23, 1793 Moses McCartey (Spartanburgh) to Daniel Bragg (same); for 150£ sterling sold 200 ac on Forgeson's Cr; border: George Bruton and Little Forgeson's Cr; grant May 9, 1771 Gov. William Bull to John McCarley. Witness Zachariah Grace and Moore Bragg. Signed Moses McCarley. Wit. oath Feb. 28, 1794 Zachariah Grace to Thos Moore. Rec. Mar. 6, 1794

p. 199-201 Oct. 8, 1793 Jordan Holcome (Greenville Co) to Zachariah Robinson (Spartanburgh); for 10£ sold 60 ac on N side Lawson's fork of Pacolate R; grant Jan. 21, 1785 Gov. Benjamin Guerard to Wells Griffith; border: Wells Griffith, Jordan Holcome, and Wm Dickson. Witness Alley Robinson and Wm Robinson. Signed Jordan Holcome. Wit. oath Jan. 17, 1794 Wm Robinson to D Goodlett. Rec. Mar. 12, 1794

p. 201-202 Jan. (not given), 1794 Clayborn Johnson (Spartan Co) to William Johnston (same); for 30£ sterling sold 80 ac; part of 200 ac grant Apr. 28, 1768 Gov. William Tryon (NC) to John Alexander in Mecklenburgh Co, NC on both sides Lawson's fork of Pacolate R above John Roden's land; sold by John Alexander to Martin Armstrong and Henry Moffeit who sold to Clayborn Johnson. Witness Joshua Hawkins, Roland Johnson, and Roling Cook. Signed Claborne Johnson. Wit. oath Jan. 13, 1794 Roland Johnson to D Goodlett. Rec. Mar. 13, 1794

p. 202-203 Mar. 15, 1794 Ebezener Morse (Spartanburgh) to Obadiah Morse (same); for 100£ sterling sold 60 ac; border: Benjamin Beausey, Spencer Colbert, Wm Miles, Still House Br, and Two Mile Cr; grant in 1765 to John Hendrix. Witness Travis Morris and Worrington Spiller. Signed Ebezener Morse. Wit. oath Mar. 15, 1794 Ebezener Morse to I Harrison. Rec. Mar. 18, 1794

p. 203-206 Apr. 7, 1789 John Edwards and William Hort, treasurers of South Carolina, to James Rainey; for 1£ 8s 4p sold 140 ac on branches of Enoree R; land granted Jan. 21, 1785 to John Farrow but no purchase money was paid in the prescribed time so it is now sold. Witness Abraham Alexander and Edward Edwards. Signed John Edwards and Wm Hort. Wit. oath (Charleston Dist) Mar. 11, 1793 Abraham Alexander to Stephen Ravenel. Rec. Mar. 18, 1794

p. 206-209 May 15, 1793 John Elder (Spartanburgh) to Thomas Beardan (same); for 100£ SC money sold 200 ac on W side Crowder's Cr; border: Robert Elder, Ephraim Hill, and John Elder, jr; where Thomas Beardan lives; plat attached dated Jan. 1, 1793 by Andrew Thomson, D. S.; part of 600 ac grant Sept. 3, 1753 Gov. Matthew Rowan (NC) to Robert Crowden. Witness James Lee, Alexander Elder, Isaac Bearden, and Samuel Morrow. Signed John Elder. Wit. oath Jan. 10, 1793 Isaac Bearden to (not given). Rec. Mar. 20, 1794

p. 209-210 Dec. 11, 1792 Elizabeth Lewis (Spartanburgh) to Daniel Cornwell (same); for 60£ sterling sold 200 ac on N side Lawson's fork; part of two tracts granted Aug. 31, 1774 Gov. William Bull to John Earle; border: N-John West, S-Wm Brannan, and W-remainder of the two tracts. Witness John Bennett, Joel Lewis, David Lewis. Signed Elizabeth Lewis' mark. Wit. oath Feb. 4, 1793 John Bennett to Wm Smith. Rec. Mar. 26, 1794

p. 210-211 Aug. 8, 1793 William Crocker (Spartanburgh) to Luke Lekeroye (same); for 10£ sterling sold 75 ac; border: Thomas Crown, Anthony Crocker, and Poole; part of 415 ac grant Oct. 6, 1788 Gov. Thomas Pinckney to (not given). Witness Richisson Whitbey, John Lekeroy, and Seth Lewis. Signed William Crocker's mark. Wit. oath Jan. 14, 1794 John Lekeroy to I Harrison. Rec. Mar. 26, 1794

p. 211-212 Jun. 15, 1793 William Dalton (Rutherford Co, NC) to Presley Garrett (Spartan Co); for 20£ SC money sold 640 ac on Back Br of Buch Cr of Pacolate R; grant Oct. 6, 1788 States Office to William Dalton. Witness Wm Jordan and Elizabeth Dalton. Signed William Dalton. Wit. oath Jan. 14, 1794 Wm Jordan to S Bethel. Rec. Mar. 27, 1794

p. 212-213 Aug. 31, 1792 Cranshaw Camp (Rutherford Co, SC (sic)) to John Turner (Spartan Co); for 26£ sterling sold 100 ac on both sides Ashworth Cr; deed good as long as grant for 555 ac to Cranshaw Camp "holds"; grant Oct. 6, 1788; border: Cranshaw Camp, John Turner, Bradick's Br and path from John Turner's to Peter Watkins. Witness Mary Turner, John Turner, jr, and Samuel Turner. Signed Cranshaw Camp. Wit. oath Mar. 4, 1793 Samuel Turner to Edwd Goode. Rec. Mar. 27, 1794

p. 213-215 Nov. 28, 1793 David Pruitt and wife Anna to William Farmer; for 25£ sterling sold 50 ac on N side Tyger R and both sides Dutchman's Cr; part of 150 ac grant Apr. 27, 1767 Gov. William Tryon (NC) to Moses Wylie. Witness John Grist, Samuel Pruitt, and Jesse Chistain. Signed David Pruitt and Anna's mark. Wit. oath Dec. 28, 1793 John Grist to Saml Lancaster. Rec. Mar. 28, 1794

p. 215-216 Oct. 31, 1793 Josiah Culbertson (Spartanburgh) to Henry Neal (same); for 120£ sold 207 ac on Culbertson's Cr Dugan's Cr of Fairforrest Cr; part of 497 ac grant Feb. 23, 1754 Gov. Matthew Rowan (NC) to George Gillaspy and entered in South Carolina Feb. 27, 1775 and eventually sold to Samuel Culbertson, sr who sold on Aug. 24, 1773 to Josiah Culbertson; <u>and</u> 50 ac on Dugan's Br below the first tract and including a mill, pond, mill room, saw mill; grant Jun. 5, 1786 Gov. William Moultrie to John Thomas, jr who sold Jan. 8, 1789 to Josiah Culbertson. Witness Andrew Culbertson, Hugh Donaldson, and John McDowel. Signed Josiah and Martha Culbertson. Wit. oath Jan. 13, 1793 Josiah and Martha Culbertson to Wm Smith. Rec. Apr. 1, 1794

p. 216-217 Jan. 13, 1793 Randal Johnson (Spartanburgh) to Samuel Miller (same); for (money not given) sold 148 ac on both sides James Cr; half of land formerly owned by John Leech; see grant Dec. 11, 1770 for 240 ac (actual survey shows 296 ac) then in Tryon Co, NC. Witness Isaac Snoddy, John Snoddy, and Margot Snoddy. Signed Randal Johnson's mark. Wit. oath Jan. 14, 1794 Isaac Snoddy to Thomas Moore. Rec. Apr. 1, 1794

p. 217-221 Jan. 7, 1793 Elizabeth Woodard (Union Co), spinster, to John McElwrath (Spartanburgh); for 150£ sold 500 ac on Middle fork Tyger R; formerly in Craven Co; border: all vacant when granted; where John McElwrath lives; grant Dec. 24, 1772 Gov. Charles Montague to Edward Bleak and sold Mar. 2, 1774 to Thomas Woodward and by his will to Thomas Mary who sold Feb. 12, 1785 to Elizabeth Woodard. Witness John Ponny, Robert Gregrory, and Michael McElwrath. Signed Elizabeth Woodard's mark. Wit. oath Jan. 2, 1794 John Ponny to James Jordan. Rec. Apr. 2, 1794

p. 221-223 Sept. 7, 1793 William Davis Thomson, survivor of Candace Jones, jr, desc, James Clark and wife Mary, Elijah Stephens and wife Anna, heirs of Joseph Jones, sr, desc, to Michael Miller; for 75£ sterling sold 200 ac on branches of N fork Tygar R; grant (not dated) Gov. William Tryon to Samuel Neasbit who sold Jan. 21, 1793 to Joseph Jones and by his will dated Sept. 12, 1794 to his daughters: Candace, who married William D. Thomas, Mary, who married James Clarke, and Anna who married Elijah Stephens; border: Miller, David Davis, Joseph Jones, and Jean Knox. Witness N Wayland, James Reynolds, and J. L. McCulloch. Signed W. D. Thomas, James Clark, Mary Clark's mark, Elijah Stephens, and Anna Stephens' mark. Rec. Apr. 3, 1794

p. 223-225 Jan. 27, 1702 (sic 1792) Abraham Hembrey and wife Winey (Spartanburgh) to Thomas Meadows (same); for 20£ SC money sold 117 ac; border: Tobias Bright and Alleutus (or Albutus) Bright; part of 265 ac grant Jan. 7, 1788 Gov. Thomas Pinckney to Abraham Hembrey on branch of Dutchman's and Cane Creeks and N side Tygar R. Witness Gideon Hearleson, Jesse Meaders (or Meadows), and William Meadows. Signed Abraham Hembrey and Winey's mark. Wit. oath Jan. 10, 1793 Jesse Meaders to Wm Smith. Rec. Apr. 3, 1794

p. 225-226 Aug. 12, 1791 Abraham Nally (Spartanburgh) to Nathaniel Burton (same); for 20£ sterling sold 50 ac on N side Tygar R; border: Nathaniel Burton and John Vice; part of 424 ac grant Nov. 6, 1786 Gov. William Moultrie to Abraham Nally. Witness Matthew Mullineaux, James Smith, and Jonathan Moore. Signed AN. Wit. oath Jan. 11, 1794 Matthew Mullineaux to Thos Moore. Rec. Apr. 4, 1794

p. 226-227 Jan. 17, 1793 Charles Burton (Spartanburgh) to Cutbert Burton (same); for 300£ SC money sold 400 ac on N side Tygar R; grant Dec. 5, 1785 Gov. William Moultrie to Allburtus Bright. Witness John Cates, Andrew Thomson, and John Esterwood. Signed Charles Burton. Wit. oath Nov. 12, 1793 Andrew Thomson to Thos Moore. Rec. Apr. 4, 1794

p. 227-229 Oct. 9, 1793 John Williams (Spartanburgh) to Charles Burton; for 60£ SC money sold 300 ac on S fork Tyger R; border: SW-William Hendricks and others vacant; grant May 13, 1763 Gov. Thomas Boon to John Millhaen in Barkly Co. Witness Cutbert Burton, Charles Burton, and Andrew Thomson. Signed John Williams.

Wit. oath Nov. 12, 1793 Andrew Thomson to Thos Moore. Rec. Apr. 4, 1794

p. 229-230 Dec. 19, 1793 Richard Chesney, sr and wife Jane (Spartanburgh) to Richard Chesney, jr (same); for 62£ 10s sterling sold 100 ac on James' Cr; border: W-widow McCrary; grant Jul. 15, 1768 Gov. William Bull to Martin Livingston and sold to Richard Chesney, sr and recorded in Spartanburgh. Witness Richard Young and William Earnest. Signed Richard and Jane Chesney's marks. Wit. oath Jan. 12, 1794 William Earnest to D Goodlett. Rec. Apr. 4, 1794

p. 230-231 Dec. 21, 1790 in North Carolina Peter Bennett, attorney for Thomas Wheelright Pearson, to John Gowen (Spartanburgh); power of attorney to sell land in Spartanburgh Co of late Abner Nash, esq of Craven Co; the will of Abner Nash dated Nov. 22, 1786 appoints Jacob Blunt, sr, Alfred Moore, Thomas Pearson, and William Blunt as executors; Abner Nash died soon after date of his will. Witness William Eafley and Allen Gowen. Signed P Bennett. Rec. Apr. 4, 1794

p. 231-233 Oct. 1, 1785 William Lucas (Bladen Co, NC) to William Gee (Lunenburg Co, Va); for 55£ NE money sold 200 ac on S side Lawson's fork of Pacolate R and on head of Reedy Br above Jones' Waggon Road; border: Robert McMurdy; grant Oct. 26, 1767 Gov. William Tryon (NC) to William Lucas then in Meclenburgh Co, NC and now Burkley Co, SC; see also South Carolina memorial Apr. 24, 1773. Witness Geo Lucus, John Osling, and George Gee. Signed William Lucus. Wit. oath Apr. 4, 1794 John Osling to James Jordan. Rec. Apr. 5, 1794

p. 233 Jul. 26, 1793 Arthur Crocker, sr (Spartanburgh) to Arthur Crocker, jr (same); for 10£ sold a bay horse and saddle, 15 hogs, 2 feather beds and furniture, a Dutch oven, skillett, tea kettle, 2 cows and calves, and a two year old heifer. Witness James Paole and Anthony Crocker. Signed Arthur Crocker's mark. Wit. oath Apr. 24, 1794 James Paole to I Harrison. Rec. Apr. 24, 1794

p. 233-236 Jan. 21, 1778 Ebenezer Moss (96 Dist) to William Miles (same); for 25 (£ ?) 10s SC money sold 60 ac on N side Enoree R and on Two Mile Cr where William Miles lives; part of 400 ac grant Nov. 19, 1772 to John Hendrix. Witness Edwd Stone, jr, William Caughon, sr, and William Miles, sr. Signed Ebenezer Moss' mark. Wit. oath Mar. 18, 1794 William Miles, sr to Zadock Ford. Rec. Apr. 25, 1794

236-238 Feb. 25, 1793 Peter Elder and wife Elizabeth (Spartanburgh) to Alexander Autry (same); for 100£ sold 200 ac; part of two grants: (1) 296 ac grant Jul. 4, 1785 Gov. William Moultrie to Richard Hampton who sold part to Peter Elder on Reedy Br of Fairforrest Cr and (2) 200 ac grant Dec. 16, 1769 on Buffelow Br of Fairforrest Cr North Carolina governor to Thomas Bullion and regranted by South Carolina governor and sold by Thomas Bullion to Zacharias Gibbs who sold to James Gibbs who sold to Peter Elder and bordering: David Cook and Bullion. Witness Thos Underwood and Wm Roberds. Signed Peter and Elizabeth Elder's marks. Wit. oath Mar. 7, 1793 Thos Underwood to Isham Harrison. Rec. May 1, 1794

p. 238-240 Jan. 23, 1794 Alexander Autry and wife Martha (Spartanburgh) to William Lancaster (same); for 17£ 10s sterling sold 75 ac on S side Fairforrest Cr and E side Bufloelick Cr; border: SW-William Lancaster, SE-Sprinkle (old Bullion line), N-William Roberds, and W-Alexander Autry; also includes land on W side of Bufloelick Cr for William Lancaster to run a fencenear the creek from upper part of his field, which Alexander Autry sold him to the beginning for William's convenience; part of grant to Thomas Bullion who sold to Zachariah Gibbs who sold to James Gibbs who sold to Peter Elder who sold to Alexander Autry; plat attached shows William Lancaster ownes 50 ac adjoining. Witness David Golightly and James Moore. Signed Alexander and Martha Autry's marks. Wit. oath Jun. 13, 1794 James Moore to Baylis Earle. Rec. May 1, 1794

p. 240-241 Dec. 17, 1791 in Franklin Co, Ga John Conner (Franklin Co, Ga) to James Wyatt (Spartanburgh); for 16£ sterling sold 100 ac on Lawson's fork of Pacolate R; grant Mar. 6, 1786. Witness Maxn Conner, Charles Sullivant, and Boley Conner. Signed John Conner. Wit. oath Dec. 27, 1791 Boley Conner to D Goodlett. Rec. May 2, 1794

p. 241-244 Nov. 1, 1775 James Gibbs (96 Dist) to James Smith (same); for 200£ SC money and 5s sterling Great Britian money sold 200 ac on W side Fairforrest Cr; border: Zachariah Gibbs; part of 640 ac grant May 15, 1772 North Carolina governor to James Gibbs and regranted Sept. 9, 1774 by Lt. Gov. William Bull. Witness James Tillet, John Calahan, and James Lanman. Signed James Gibbs. Wit. oath Feb. 19, 1776 John Calahan to J Thomas, jr. Rec. May 2, 1794

p. 244-245 (not dated) William Hammet (Spartanburgh) to Messr. Alexander McBeth & Co; a bond dated Feb. 12, 1791 for 5£ 18s 6p sterling has been secured by the following: William sells 591 ac on Peter's Cr, grant is lodged with Alexander, and sells 70 ac on Lindsey's Cr adjoining Malachi Jones and sells a bay horse branded on off shoulder, buttock and highthers "2" and a saddle and bridle, a cow and calf and yearling, a feather bed and furniture, a sow, 5 shoats, and remainder of his estate; Condition: sale is void if William pays the bond with interest before Dec. 1, 1791. Witness Male Jones and Ben Haile. Signed Wm Hammett. Wit. oath May 5, 1794 Male Jones to I Harrison. Rec. May 7, 1794

p. 245-246 Aug. 4, 1792 Daniel Walker (96 Dist) to George Martain (same); for 40£ sterling sold 100 ac on Peter's Cr; grant Dec. 28, 1787 Gov. Thomas Pinckney to Ellis Cannon. Witness Ellis Cannon, George Lamkin, and Jesse Cannon. Signed Daniel and Mary Walker's marks. Wit. oath Apr. 14, 1794 Daniel Walker to I Harrison. Rec. May 8, 1794

p. 246-248 Mar. 2, 1793 Samuel Ross (Kershaw Co) to James Crook (Spartanburgh); for 50£ sterling sold 88 ac on S fork Tyger R; grant Nov. 24, 1762 Gov. William Bull to Samuel Ross then border was all vacant. Witness Nancy Crook, Joshua Crook, and Thos Neely. Signed Saml Ross. Rec. May. 9, 1794. Dower renounced Nancy Crook to Thos Moore Jan. 28, 1794

p. 248-250 Oct. 16, 1793 John Boyd (Fairfield Co) to Henry Jamison (Spartanburgh); for 50£ 5s sterling sold 100 ac on Nichols Br of Tyger R; grant Aug. 12, 1768 Gov. William Bull to Danl McCoy who sold Mar. 1, 1780 to John Boyd. Witness Charles Miller, Samuel Miller, and James Kennedy. Signed John Boyd. Wit. oath Mar. 7, 1794 Samuel Miller to James Jordan. Rec. May 10, 1794

p. 250-253 Aug. 13, 1775 John Hendrix (Tryon Co, NC) to William Miles (96 Dist); for 100£ 10s SC money sold 50 ac on E side of Two Mile Cr of Enoree R; part of 400 ac grant Dec. (or Nov.) 19, 1772 Gov. Charles G Montague to John Hendrix; where William Miles lives; border: Miles' Spring Br. Witness Andrew Hendrix, Andrew Banckson, and Isaac Hendrix. Signed John Hendrix's mark. Wit. oath Oct. 14, 1775 Isaac Hendrix to John Ford

p. 253-256 Mar. 20, 1775 Richard Nalley and wife Elizabeth (Jamemy's Cr, 96 Dist) to William Miles (Two Mile Cr, 96 Dist); for 500£ 10s SC money sold 150 ac on Two Mile Cr of Enoree R; border: W-John Hendricks, S-James Hendricks, E-John Crow; grant Jun. 19, 1772 Gov. Charles G Montague to Richard Nalley. Witness John Huse (or Hues) and Thomas Stuckey. Signed Richard Nally and Elizabeth's mark. Wit. oath Oct. 14, 1775 John Huse to John Ford. Rec. May 21, 1794

p. 256-257 Jan. 11, 1794 Benjamin Bonner (Spartanburgh) to son Demsey Bonner (same); for love and affection and $1 sell 100 ac where Demsey lives on N side of Benjamin's land. Witness Leonard D Shaw, Briant Bonner, and Obadiah Cook. Signed Benjamin Bonner's mark. Wit. oath Apr. 15, 1794 Briant Bonner to Wm Smith. Rec. May 23, 1794

p. 257-258 Jan. 11, 1794 Henry Prince (Greenville Co) to John Wood (Spartanburgh); for 105£ sterling sold 350 ac on Willson Mill Cr of N Tygar R; border: William Benson and Robert Hail, esq. Witness D Goodlett, William Foster, and William Foster of Fair-forrest. Signed Henry Prince. Wit. oath Jan. 11, 1794 William Foster (no distinction) to D Goodlett. Rec. May 28, 1794

p. 258-260 Sept. 18, 1793 James Amos to John Brooks; for 5£ sold 167 ac; part of 400 ac grant Dec. 5, 1791 Gov. Charles Pinckney to James Amos on S fork of N fork of Tygar R above John Sharp's line. Witness John Young, jr and William Brooks. Signed James Amos. Wit. oath Apr. 24(?), 1794 James Amos to I Harrison. Rec. May 29, 1794

p. 260-261 Jul. 10, 1792 George Martin (Spartanburgh) to Sarah and Elender Martin; sold all goods and chattels and house-hold "stuff" and 100 ac where Elender now lives and rest of land and stuff to Sarah Martin. Witness George Lamken, Mathew Gutry, and Daniel Walker. Signed George Martin's mark. Wit. oath Apr. 25, 1794 Daniel Walker to I Harrison. Rec. May 30, 1794

p. 261-262 Jun. 6, 1793 Henry Chiles (Spartanburgh) to John High-tower, minister (same); for 30£ SC money sold 80 ac on Lasson's fork of Pacolate R; border: Henry Chiles; grant Jan. 1, 1785 States Office to John Bennett. Witness S Bethel, Henry Turner, and Darby Turner. Signed Henry Chiles' mark. Certified Jun. 6, 1793 by S Bethel. Rec. May 30, 1794

p. 262-263 Nov. 15, 1791 Philip Wells (Laurens Co) to Edward Arnold, jr (Spartanburgh); for 75£ sterling sold 200 ac on N side Enoree R; border: William Lindsey and including a grice mill; where Edward now lives; grant Sept. 22, 1769. Witness Thomas Hamilton and Benjamin Arnold. Signed Philip Wells. Wit. oath (Greenville Co) Dec. 30, 1793 Benjamin Arnold to Joseph Dunklin. Rec. Jun. 2, 1794

p. 263-265 Jan. 3, 1794 Joel Hembree and wife Hannah (Spartanburgh) to Thomas Price (same), merchant; for 25£ sterling sold 165 ac on branch of Cane Cr; border; John Butter, William Rumply, and Lee Clark; part of 815 ac grant May 2, 1791 Gov. Charles Pinckney to Joel Hembree. Witness Henry Pettit and Andrew Thomson. Signed Joel Hembree and Hannah's mark. Wit. oath May 10, 1794 Andrew Thomson to Thomas Moore. Rec. May 3, 1794 (sic)

p. 265-266 Sept. 16, 1793 Abraham Barrier and wife Elizabeth (Spartanburgh) to Thomas Price (same), merchant; for 60£ sterling sold 140 ac between N and S forks Tygar R; border: Aaron Floyd and Richard Barrier; part of 200 ac grant May 1, 1786 Gov. William Moultrie to Francis Ward and sold Jul. 5, 1791 to Abraham

Barrier. Witness Andrew Thomson, Thomas Shurley, and Daniel Barnett. Signed Abraham Barrier and Elizabeth's mark. Wit. oath May 20, 1794 Andrew Thomson to Thos Moore. Rec. Jun. 4, 1794

p. 266-268 Apr. 5, 1794 Samuel Sherbert (Spartanburgh) to Thomas Price, merchant (same); for 50£ sterling sold 100 ac on N side Cain Cr and N side of Tyger R; border: Toney; part of 200 ac grant to James Hembree. Witness Lawson Thomson, Andrew Thomson, and Charles Burton. Signed Samuel Sherbett. Wit. oath May 10, 1794 Andrew Thomson to Thos Moore. Rec. Jun. 6, 1794

p. 268-289 Jul. 26, 1793 Abram Markley (Charles(ton?)) to William Poole (the Healing Springs, Spartanburgh); power of attorney to rent or lease Abram's land in Pinckney Dist and receive the rent. Witness John Stovaut, James Poole, and Anthony P(marked through). Signed Abrm Markley. Rec. Jun. 6, 1794

p. 269-270 Jan. 18, 1794 Anthony Pearson (Spartanburgh) to William Benson (same); for 70£ sterling sold 200 ac on Jamey's Cr of N Tygar R; border: Alexander Vernon and Leach. Witness N Wayland, Willey Brown, and Jonathan Nisbett. Signed Anthony and Mary Pearson's marks. Wit. oath Apr. 14, 1794 N Wayland to I Harrison. Rec. Jun. 7, 1794

p. 270-271 Feb. 4, 1794 William Wofford and wife Mary (Franklin Co, Ga) to Reuben Daniel (Spartanburgh); for 70£ sterling sold 300 ac on NW side of Poison Br and Big Br; part of 500 ac grant to William Wofford on Fairforrest Cr; two small parts excepted: (1) a corner of old survey called Dugan's land and (2) a small piece sold to George Parkison including George Parkison's improvements and a place called Hill's old field. Witness Benj. Wofford, James Wofford, and George Parkison. Signed W Wofford and Mary's mark. Wit. oath Feb. 8, 1794 George Parkison to I Harrison. Rec. Jun. 11, 1794

p. 271-272 Feb. 14, 1794 James Burnett (Spartanburgh) to George Rowland (same); for 73£ sterling sold 150 ac where "Burnett" now lives; part of 400 ac grant Gov. Joseph Martin (NC) to Thomas Hatherway on both sides Fawn Br of Lawson's fork of Pacolate R and on Rich Run; border: on N side of the "Main Road". Witness Benjamine Rowland, Robert Kimble, and John Johnston. Signed James and Elizabeth Burnett's marks. Wit. oath Apr. 14, 1794 Robert Kimble to Saml Lancaster. Rec. Jun. 11, 1794

p. 272-274 Jan. 10, 1794 Thomas McKnight (Spartanburgh) to Thomas Crumly (Newberry Co); for 75£ sterling sold 300 ac on both sides Brutter's Cr of N Pacolate R; grant May 15, 1772 Gov. Josia Martin (NC) to Thomas McKnight in Tryon Co, NC. Witness Nevil Wayland, John McCarrol, and Henry Morgan. Signed Thomas Mcknight. Wit. oath Feb. 8, 1794 Nevil Wayland to James Jordan. Rec. Jul. 1, 1794

p. 274-275 Oct. 21, 1793 Enoch Floyd (Spartanburgh) to Allen Gentry (same); for 30£ sterling sold 50 ac; part of grant to Enoch Floyd on both sides of Fergeson's Cr. Witness Nathaniel Floyd and Ester Hyndes. Signed Enoch Floyd. Wit. oath Dec. 14, 1793 Nathaniel Floyd to Thos Moore. Rec. Jul. 20, 1794

p. 275-276 Sept. 2, 1793 Alexander Martin, esq (Rockingham Co, NC) to Joseph Dill (Spartanburgh); for 200£ NE money sold 200 ac on both sides Cherokee Cr and W side of Broad R about 2 miles from the mouth of Cherokee Cr; grant Apr. 25, 1767 to Alexander Martin. Witness Jesse Tate and William McGown. Signed Alex Martin. Wit. oath Apr. 14, 1794 Jesse Tate to Saml Lancaster. Rec. Jul. 22, 1794

p. 276-278 Jan. 20, 1794 Alexander Autrey and wife Martha (Spartanburgh) to William Roberds (same); for 15£ SC money sold 25 ac on E side of Buffaloe Lick Cr of Fairforrest Cr; part of grant to Alexander Autrey. Witness W Lancaster and Jesse Connell. Signed Alexander and Martha Autrey's marks. Wit. oath Apr. 15, 1794 W Lancaster to I Harrison. Rec. Jul. 22, 1794

p. 278-279 Feb. 12, 1794 George Parkison (Spartanburgh) to Robert Belcher (same); for 25£ sterling sold 27 or 25 ac on Fairforrest Cr where Robert Belcher lives; border: Parkison, Duggan, and corner formerly Armstrong's. Witness James Saunders and William Bagwell. Signed George Parkison. Wit. oath Apr. 14, 1794 James Saunders to I Harrison. Rec. Jul. 23, 1794

p. 279 Aug. 22, 1794 James Gilmore, sr (Spartanburgh) to son William Gilmore (same); for love and affection sold all goods, chattels, and lands. Witness John Mason Price CDS, James Gilmore, jr, and Alexander Copeland. Signed James Gilmore's mark. Wit. oath Aug. 23, 1794 James Gilmore, jr to James Hooper. Rec. Aug. 25, 1794

p. 279-281 Jul. 5, 1794 Edward Hooker and wife Millay (Spartanburgh) to Thomas Tod (same); for 50£ sterling sold 100 ac; part of 1,000 ac grant to James Simple and sold by Rottry Simple, heir-at-law of James Simple, to John McCulloch who sold to Thomas McClurkin who sold to Edward Hooker; border: Spencer Bobo, Thomas Tod, on a ridge between Tygar and Enoree Rivers, and above a road from Isaac Crow to Anthony Foster. Witness Humphry Yarbrough and William Wilson. Signed Edward Hooker and Millay's mark. Wit. oath Jul. 10, 1794 Humphry Yarbrough to Wm Smith. Rec. Aug. 26, 1794

p. 281-282 Nov. 18, 1793 Thomas Jordan (Spartan Co, NC (sic)) to Susannah Ashley (same); for 10£ sterling sold 30 ac on Little Buck Cr; border: John Contrell, School House Spring Br, and Richard Morris; grant Jan. 1, 1787 State Office to William Morris. Witness S Bethel, William Morris, and Francis Jordan. Signed Thomas Jordan's mark. Certified (not dated) by S Bethel. Rec. Aug. 26, 1794

p. 282-284 Apr. 14, 1794 John Shands (Spartanburgh) to Thomas Williams (same); for 50£ sold 200 ac on Dutchman's Cr of Tygar R; grant Nov. 7, 1785 Gov. William Moultrie to John Shands. Witness John Smith, Thomas Spann, and Joseph Smith. Signed John Shands. Wit. oath Apr. 14, 1794 Joseph Smith to Wm Smith. Rec. Aug. 30, 1794

p. 284-285 Jan. 20, 1794 Zadock Ford, esq (Spartanburgh) to John Ford (Tyger R, same); for 20£ SC money sold the slaves: a Negro woman Bett and her female child Judy; Condition: sale void if Zadock pays John 20£ SC money before Dec. 25, 1794. Witness George Grace, Burges McFearson, and Wm Ford. Signed Zadock Ford. Wit. oath May 6, 1794 Wm Ford to Thos Moore. Rec. Jun. 15, 1794

p. 285-287 Aug. 5, 1794 Thomas Wright (Spartanburgh) to John Ford (same); for 140£ SC money sold a Negro woman Mary about 29 years old, black complexion, and her five children--a boy named Lewis, girls Bett, Rose, and Ester and a boy called Archer; Condition: sale void if Thomas Wright pays John 35£ SC money May 1, 1796, 35£ on May 1, 1797, and 35£ May 1, 1798 for a total of 140£. Witness Robert Belcher, Wm Ford, and John Wright. Signed Thomas Wright. Wit. oath Sept. 15, 1794 Wm Ford to Thos Moore. Rec. Sept. 16, 1794

p. 287-289 Sept. 6, 1794 John Ford (Spartanburgh) to George Bruton (same); power of attorney to receive payment of debt for Negroes from Thomas Wright and to execute a deed of mortgage if

Thomas Wright fails to pay the debt. Witness William McDaniel, James Southerland, and Wm Ford. Signed John Ford. Wit. oath Sept. 15, 1794 Wm Ford to Thos Moore. Rec. Sept. 16, 1794

p. 289-290 Sept. 15, 1794 William Rucher (Spartanburgh) to "heirs of the body" of daughter Sarah Wingo, desc; gives a Negro woman Milley and her "increase": Sam, Ben, Nan, Charles, Beck, Lewis, Reubin, Edy, and Moses; all now in possession of John Wingo, sr in Amelia Co, Va; William ment to dispose of slaves only to his daughter and her heirs; William also authorizes Sherwood Fowler to recover the slaves. Witness Elisha Rucher and William Wilson. Signed William Rucher. Wit. oath Sept. 16, 1794 Elisha Rucher to Isham Foster. Rec. Sept. 24, 1794

p. 290-294 Apr. 5, 1794 Edward Lacy, sheriff (Pinckney Dist) to John Golightly (same); for 57£ sterling sold 400 ac on both sides Lawson's fork of Pacolate R; border: W-Mary Wood and others vacant; grant Oct. 22, 1784 in grant book 4E p. 35 and sold by Mary Wood, desc, to William Poole, iron monger, on Jun. 18 & 19, 1787 (Spartanburgh Co Book A p. 199-201); includes an ironworks and mill known as Poole's iron works; William Poole had a debt to Henry Lancaster dated Jan. 1, 1790 for 132£ 15s 9p; Henry Lancaster sued in April term of Common Pleas Court and won 100£ sterling and court costs by judgment signed by John Rutledge, esq, Chief Justice, at Pinckneyville Nov. 1, 1793; sale of land held Mar. 3, 1794. Witness James Lusk and William Lancaster. Signed Edwd Lacy. Wit. oath Apr. 15, 1794 William Lancaster to Wm Smith. Rec. Oct. 5, 1794. Apr. 8, 1794 Edward Lacy sold 400 ac to John Golightly to settle a suit of Henry Lancaster vs. William Poole. Signed Wm Poole. Witness William Wells and John Lancaster. Wit. oath Apr. 15, 1794 William Wells to Wm Smith

p. 294-296 May 16, 1794 Randolf Laurens (Spartanburgh) to John Lefevour, jr (same); for 64£ SC money sold 196 ac on Beaverdam Cr of Thickety Cr; grant May 1, 1787 Gov. William Moultrie to Abraham Breis (or Briars). Witness Vardry McBee, Wm Tate, and Jno Wilkinson. Signed Randolf and Allis Laurens. Wit. oath Jun. 2, 1794 Jno Wilkinson to Edwd Goode. Rec. Oct. 10, 1794

p. 296-297 Apr. 29, 1794 Michael Brown Roberds (Spartanburgh) to Robert Roberds (same); for 46£ sterling sold a black horse branded on near shoulder (a backward S) trots and canters, some few saddle spots and about 8 years old; a black mare branded (same) with blaze in her face, some saddle spots and 3 white feet and a glass eye trots and canters about 6 years old; 6 cattle with separate marks, 10 hogs marked with a (blank) heal or Keal and slit in left ear, 2 feather beds and furniture, 8 pewter plates, 2 pewter dishes, 2 pewter basons, 12 spoons, a parcel of earthen ware, a spinning wheel, table, 6 chairs, wash tub, 2 water pales, 2 pigging, an iron pot, a flat iron, a case of knives and forks, 3 pair of cottor cards, a set of shoe tools, a man's saddle, 2 axes, 4 hoes, 2 powderine tubs, a hogshead, 150 wt of bacon, 20 barrels of corn, 20 bu of sheat, a parcel of fother, and all other real and personal articles to Michael B Roberds. Witness John Jefferies, Thomas Roberds, and Nancy Roberds. Signed Michael Bro Roberds. Wit. oath May 8, 1794 John Jefferies to Thos Moore. Rec. Oct. 14, 1794

p. 297-299 Nov. 4, 1794 Samuel Farrow (Spartanburgh) to Robert Goodloe Harper (Charleston, SC); for 700£ sterling sold (1) 298 ac on Forkshoal Cr of Enoree R and grant Dec. 4, 1786 Gov. William Moultrie to Samuel Farrow; and (2) 450 ac on N side Enoree R grant Gov. William Moultrie to Charles Waters who sold to Samuel Farrow; and (3) 430 ac on N side Enoree R where J Head now lives grant to Philemon Waters who sold to John Head who sold to Samuel

Farrow; see book C p. 391 for "relinquishing of this deed". Witness Obadiah Trimmier, John Lancaster, and Wm Thompson. Signed Saml Farrow. Wit. oath Nov. 4, 1794 Obadiah Trimmier to I Harrison. Rec. Nov. 8, 1794

p. 299-300 Feb. 3, 1794 William Wofford (Franklin Co, Ga) to Solomon Hayes (Spartanburgh); for 25£ sterling sold 150 ac on SE side of Poison Br; part of 540 ac on Fairforrest Cr and divided from the 540 ac by Poison Br; border: NW-Big Br and remainder of 540 ac. Witness George Parkison, James Wofford, Benja Wofford. Signed W Wofford. Wit. oath Feb. 8, 1794 George Parkison to I Harrison. Rec. Nov. 9, 1794

p. 300-302 Mar. 8, 1794 Jonathan Low (Spartanburgh) to Henry McCrary (same); for 50£ sterling sold 100 ac on N side of Pacolate R; upper end of 300 ac grant to Francis Ballinger. Witness Thomas Green, Leonard Adcock, and John Trimmier. Signed Jonathan Low. Wit. oath Jun. 14, 1794 Leonard Adcock to I Harrison. Rec. Nov. 10, 1794

p. 302-304 Aug. 20, 1793 Joseph Wofford and wife Martha to Spencer Calbert; for 60£ sold 200 ac on branch of Two Mile Cr of Enoree R; border: William Crow and William Miles; part of 497 ac grant Jan. 1, 1787 Gov. William Moultrie to William Clayton who sold to Joseph Wofford. Witness James Lanford, John Leatherwood, and Isaac Crow. Signed Jos Wofford and Martha's mark. Wit. oath Jun. 10, 1794 John Leatherwood to Thomas Farrow. Rec. Nov. 10, 1794

p. 304-305 Dec. 20, 1790 William Wofford (Franklin Co, Ga) to son Benjamin Wofford; for 50£ sterling sold 20 ac on N side Lawson's fork including dwelling and "chief"(?) of the orchard where William Wofford once lived near where the main road crosses Lawson's fork and the shoals; part of 350 ac grant on both sides Lawson's fork from North Carolina to James McElroy who sold 100 ac to William Wofford. Witness Thomas Baker, Charlotte Baker, and James Wofford. Signed W Wofford. Wit. oath Jan. 15, 1794 James Wofford to Edwd Goode. Rec. Nov. 11, 1794

p. 305-307 Sept. 19, 1793 John Burt (Laurens Co) to Drury Couch (Spartanburgh); for 200£ sterling sold 150 ac on Fort Shoals Br of Enoree R; grant Dec. 4, 1786 Gov. William Moultrie to John Burt. Witness Aaron Casey and Joseph Couch. Signed John Burt's mark. Wit. oath Oct. 4, 1793 Joseph Couch to Thomas Farrow. Rec. Nov. 11, 1794

p. 307-308 Apr. 2, 1794 Thomas McClerkin to Edward Hooker; for 20£ sterling sold 100 ac; part of 1,000 ac grant Jul. 21, 1775 Gov. William Bull to James Sample, jr and sold by Rotry Sample to John McCullock Dec. 6, 1785 who sold to Thomas McClerkin; grant between Tygar and Enoree R; border: Spencer Bobo, Tod (since sold to John Rainwater), John Stone, Whitiker, Kirne(?), and McCullock (leased to Edward Hooker). Witness Fielding Foster, Sarah Casey, and John Foster. Signed Thomas McClurkin. Wit. oath Jun. 9, 1794 Fielding Foster to Thomas Farrow. Rec. Nov. 11, 1794

p. 308-310 Apr. 13, 1789 Samuel Ford (Spartanburgh) to John Ford, sr (same); for 200£ SC money sold 332 ac between N and S forks of Tygar R; grant May 1, 1786 Gov. William Moultrie to Samuel Ford. Witness Wm Ford, Spencer Ford, and Casander Ford. Signed Samuel Ford. Wit. oath May 6, 1794 Wm Ford to Thos Moore. Rec. Nov. 12, 1794

p. 310-311 Mar. 26, 1794 Matthew Landry (Union Co) and James Crook (Spartanburgh) to David White (Spartanburgh); for 65£ sterling sold 100 ac on S side of S fork Tygar R; border: land formerly of Matthew Sanders and Drummond's Spring Br. Witness Wm Hightower, Samuel Colley, and Drury McDaniel. Signed James Crook and Matthew Landry's mark. Wit. oath Aug. 12, 1794 Drury McDaniel to Thos Moore. Rec. Nov. 12, 1794

p. 311-313 Mar. 17, 1794 Adam Meek (Mecklenburgh Co, NC) to James Crook (Spartanburgh); for 150£ sterling sold 400 ac on S fork of Little R. Witness Wm Hightower, James Pickens and James Crook, jr. Signed Adam Meek. Wit. oath Aug. 12, 1794 James Crook, jr to Thos Moore. Rec. Nov. 12, 1794

p. 313-314 Feb. 28, 1794 Adam Markly, merchant (Charlestown, SC) to Sampson Trammel (Spartanburgh); for 15£ SC money sold 310 ac; border: James Phillips, William Dickson, and Isaac Young; part of 1,000 ac grant State Office to Adam Markly on N side of Pacolate R. Witness Reubin Warren and John Kirkland. Signed William Poole, agent for Mr. Markley. Wit. oath May 18, 1794 Reubin Warren and John Kirkland to S Bethel. Rec. Nov. 13, 1794

p. 314-316 Jan. 6, 1794 John McNight (Spartanburgh) to John Millican (same); for 300£ NC money sold 336 ac on N fork Pacolet R where John Millican lives; grant by "North Patent" to Robert Tate and sold by his heir John Tate to John McNight Jan. 13, 1785. Witness Alexander Copeland, James Hooper, and Hugh McMillian. Signed John McNight. Wit. oath Jan. 13, 1794 James Hooper to Edwd Goode. Rec. Nov. 13, 1794

p. 316-320 Sept. 5, 1793 John Hunter, esq (Laurens Co) to Thomas Williamson (Greenville Co); for 25£ 10s sterling sold 200 ac on Fergeson's Cr of Tygar R; border at original survey: David Huger, James Bruton, James Wofford, and vacant; grant Jan. 5, 1773 to Pierce Butler who sold to Hurcules Daniel Baze (or Beze) Jul. 9, 1792 and now sold by John Hunter by virtue of power of attorney from H. Daniel Baze Jun. 1, 1793. Witness J. F. Wolff and Wm Dunlap. Signed John Hunter attorney for Hercules Baze. Wit. oath Sept. 5, 1793 Wm Dunlap to Jonthn Down (Laurens Co). Rec. Nov. 14, 1794

p. 320-321 Sept. 31, 1794 Daniel Joslin (Spartanburgh) to daughter Nancy Joslin (same); for 5s sterling give (or sell) grey mare branded on near shoulder "D", near buttock "N", and off shoulder "as"; a hunting saddle and bridle, 11 cattle: 4 cows, 4 yearlings, 3 heifers marked with cross and slit in right ear and "under heel (or underkul) in the left" ear, 50-60 hogs old and young marked as the cattle, 3 feather beds, with pots, ovens, and all household furniture. Witness Samuel Joslin and Curtis Gray. Signed Daniel Joslin. Wit. oath Dec. 17, 1794 Samuel Joslin to S Bethel. Rec. Jan. 15, 1795

p. 321-322 Jun. 4, 1787 William Morris (Spartanburgh) to Thomas Jordan (same); for 2£ 7s 4p sterling sold 100 ac on Little Buck Cr of Pacolate R; border: John Hightower, William Wamock, William Morris, and Jordan; grant Jan. 1, 1787 States Office to William Morris. Witness Sampson Bethel, John Hightower, and Elias Leggett. Signed William and Barbara Morris' marks. Certified (not dated) by S Bethel. Rec. Jan. 15, 1795

p. 322-323 Jan. 10, 1795 Samuel Culbertson (Spartanburgh) to Henry ONail; for 13£ 10s 2p sterling sold a bay mare about 7 years old, 2 coults about 1 year old, 5 cows and calves, and a still containing 40 gal. now in possession of Samuel Culbertson; Condition: sale void if Samuel pays Henry 13£ 10s 2p before Feb. 1, 1795 with interest. Witness Abm(?) Nott and Ben Haile. Signed Saml Culbertson. Rec. Mar. 7, 1795

p. 323-325 Dec. 10, 1789 Michah Maddox and wife Jane (Spartanburgh) to Nathan Veal (same); for 80£ sterling sold 146 2/3 ac on Fairforrest Cr where Michah Maddox lives; a third of grant Sept. 9, 1774 SC office to James Tillet, desc, father of Jane Maddox and given to Jane Maddox and her 2 sisters as co-heirs; border: James White, desc and Josiah Culbertson. Witness John Smith, William Aldridge, and Larkin David. Signed Michah and Jane Maddox's marks. Wit. oath Apr. 14, 1794 John Smith to I Harrison. Rec. Nov. 15, 1794

p. 325-327 Apr. 14, 1794 John Smith, blacksmith (Spartanburgh) to Thomas Williams (same); for 50£ sold 100 ac on N side Dutchman's Cr; border: Wm Smith, esq, and John Shands; part of 300 ac grant Apr. 3, 1786 Gov. William Moultrie to John Smith. Witness John Shands, Thomas Spann, and Joseph Smith. Signed John Smith. Wit. oath Apr. 14, 1794 John Shands to Wm Smith. Rec. Nov. 16, 1794

p. 327-328 Sept. 8, 1794 William T Thomason (Spartanburgh) to Blake Massingale (same); for a pepper corn sold 200 ac at head branches of Walker's Cr. Witness I Harrison. Signed William T Thomason's mark. Certified Sept. 9, 1794 by I Harrison. Rec. Nov. 16, 1794

p. 328-330 Apr. 30, 1794 David Goodlett (Greenville Co) to Isham Foster (Spartanburgh); for 55£ sterling sold 150 ac on Fairforrest Cr where Isham Foster lives; border: William Foster, Alexander Walker, and John Woods; grant to James McElwean. Witness Thomas Foster, William Foster, and James Foster. Signed D Goodlett. Wit. oath May 31, 1794 William Foster to I Harrison. Rec. Nov. 17, 1794

p. 330-331 Nov. 17, 1794 John Watson, sr (Union Co) to John Watson, jr (same); give 93½ ac on Thickety Cr; border: mouth of Price's Cr and Mulberry; part of 300 ac grant in Dec. 1774 Gov. William Bull to Vardry McBee; contains remainder of grant not sold to Obadiah Trimmier and Obadiah Watson. Witness Obadh Trimmier, Henry McCray, and Obadiah Watson. Signed John Watson. Wit. oath Jan. 21, 1795 Obadh Trimmier to Henry McCray. Rec. Mar. 27, 1795

p. 331-333 Nov. 17, 1794 John Watson, sr (Union Co) to Obadiah Watson (Spartanburgh); give 93½ ac on N fork of Thickety Cr; border: mouth of Price's Cr, Mulberry, and Trimmier; part of 350 (sic) ac grant in Dec. 1774 Gov. William Bull to Vardry McBee. Witness Obadiah Trimmier, Henry McCray, and John Watson, jr. Signed John Watson. Wit. oath Mar. 27, 1795 Obadiah Trimmier to Henry McCray. Rec. Mar. 27, 1795

p. 333-335 Feb. 8, 1794 Joseph Lively and wife Sarah (Spartanburgh) to William Hammett (same); for 40£ sold 70 ac on Lindsey's Cr of Pacolate R; border: Malica Jones; grant Feb. 5, 1787 to Reubin Matthews. Witness Charles Hammett, William Hammett. Signed Joseph Lively and Sarah's mark. Wit. oath Apr. 14, 1794 William Hammett to I Harrison. Rec. Nov. 17, 1794

p. 335-337 May 10, 1794 Abraham Markley (Charleston, SC) to Joseph Robertson (Spartanburgh); for 40£ sterling sold 273 ac on Chiquepin Br on S side of Lawson's fork; border: NE-Wells Griffith and Duskin Grant and SE-Thomas Williamson. Witness Isham Foster, Wells Griffith, and Bazel Lee. Signed Abram Markley. Wit. oath Dec. 13, 1794 Bazel Lee to Isham Harrison. Rec. Dec. 13, 1794

p. 337-338 Jul. 25, 1793 Matthew Landres (Union Co) to James Crook (Spartanburgh); for 40£ sterling sold 50 ac on S fork of Tygar R; border: Ross' old line, Drummen's Spring Br; grant Jan. 7, 1788 Gov. Thomas Pinckney to Matthew Landres. Witness Drury

McDaniel, Jesse Crook, and Nancy Crook. Signed Matthew Landres' mark. Wit. oath Mar. 4, 1794 Drury McDaniel to Thos Moore. Rec. Dec. 13, 1794

p. 338-340 Jun. 6, 1792 James Pool (Spartanburgh) to William Pool (same); for 50£ sterling sold 300 ac on S side Pacolate R and both sides of Richland Cr about a mile from where John Dennis formerly settled; formerly in Mecklinbergh Co, NC. Witness Henry Pettit, Elizabeth Pool, and Mary Pool. Signed James Pool

p. 340-342 Apr. 12, 1794 William Faris, Thomas Faris, and Agnes Faris (Spartanburgh and Chester Cos) to Thomas Hanna (same); for 100£ sold 200 ac on branch of Dutchman's Cr; border: W-vacant, N-Edward Lownd, E-vacant, S-John Elder; grant Jan. 1, 1785 South Carolina to James Faris. Witness Wm Lancaster and John Lancaster. Signed Wm Fearys, Thomas Fearis, and Agnes' mark. Wit. oath Apr. 14, 1794 Wm Lancaster to Saml Lancaster. Rec. Dec. 13, 1794

p. 342-343 Jan. 9, 1793 Benjamin Bradshaw and wife Hannah (Spartanburgh) to Simon Pack (same); for 70£ sterling sold 100 ac on E side of branch of Richland Cr; part of grant to Thomas Hatteway; agreeable to conditional line between John Conner and Wm Wood; border: Fawn Br, Clement, and Jesse Reames. Witness James Wood and Wm Kenum. Signed Benjamin and Hannah Bradshaw's marks. Wit. oath (not dated) Wm Kenum to S Bethel. Rec. Dec. 14, 1794

p. 343-344 Mar. 8, 1792 Samuel Farrow (Spartanburgh) to Burrel Bobo (same); for 10£ sterling sold 10 ac on the corner of 298 ac grant nearest to the Creek; grant Dec. 4, 1786 Gov. William Moultrie to Samuel Farrow between Enoree R and Cedar Shoal Cr and on Cedar Shoal Br; border: Sampson Bobo on all sides. Witness Sampson Bobo (his mark), Sampson Bobo (signature), and Barram Bobo. Signed Saml Farrow. Wit. oath Dec. 2, 1793 Sampson Bobo (signature) to Thomas Farrow. Rec. Dec. 14, 1794

p. 344-345 Mar. 17, 1794 George Parkison (Spartanburgh) to Bazel Lee (same); for 10£ sold 100 ac; border: a line between George Parkison and Randolph Brown. Witness I Harrison and Saml Ward, jr. Signed George Parkison. Certified Mar. 18, 1794 by I Harrison. Rec. Dec. 14, 1794

p. 345-346 Mar. 17, 1794 George Parkison (Spartanburgh) to Littleton Bagwell (same); for 10£ sold 186 ac. Witness I Harrison and Saml Ward, jr. Signed Geo Parkison. Certified Mar. 18, 1794 by I Harrison. Rec. Dec. 14, 1794

p. 346-347 Feb. 14, 1794 Alexander Autry (Spartanburgh) to Ephraim Elder (same); for 10£ SC money sold 5 ac on W side Buffaloe Lick Cr of Fairforrest Cr; border: Ephraim Elder's Spring; part of 200 ac grant North Carolina to Thomas Bullun (date not given). Witness John Autry and John Gritman. Signed Alexander Autry's mark. Wit. oath Jun. 13, 1794 John Gritman to S Bethel. Rec. Dec. 15, 1794

p. 347-349 Nov. 21, 1794 John Child (Elbert Co, Ga) to John Hightower (Spartanburgh); for a Spanish milled dollar sold 100 ac on S side Lawson's fork of Pacolate R; border: S-William Morttre and NW-Peter Lewis; half of grant Jan. 21, 1785 Gov. Benjamin Guerard to John Bennett. Witness Jeston Childs and Richard Childs. Signed John Child. Wit. oath Mar. 14, 1795 Richard Child to S Bethel. Rec. Apr. 4, 1795

p. 349-350 Jan. 6, 1795 Thomas Jordan (Spartanburgh) to John Martin (same); for 65£ sold 200 ac on little Buck Cr; grant Dec.

3, 1787 State Office to Thomas Jordan. Witness S Bethel, Richard Cantrell, and Francis Jordan. Signed Thomas Jordan's mark. Certified (not dated) by S Bethel. Rec. Apr. 15, 1795

p. 350-351 May 5, 1794 Stephen Cantrell (Pendleton Co) to John Jones (Spartanburgh); for 70£ sterling sold 100 ac on N side Enoree R; border: conditional line with Kevel; part of 500 ac grant to Thomas Scottow who sold to Richard Hampton who sold to Stephen Cantrell Feb. 27, 1775. Witness Curttes Moore and Levy Moore. Signed Stephen Cantrell. Wit. oath Jun. 12, 1794 Curttes Moore to Zadock Ford. Rec. Dec. 15, 1794

p. 351-352 Oct. 19, 1794 William and John Young, gentlemen, (Spartanburgh) to Gen. Richard Winn; power of attorney to sell ten 1,000 ac grants granted Oct. 6, 1794 by Gov. William Moultrie; land in Greenville Co, Washington Dist on N fork of Saluda R, Tygar R, Oilcamp Cr and branches thereof. Witness C Bradford and J. L. Bradford. Signed William and John Young. Wit. oath (Fairfield Co) Oct. 19, 1794 William and John Young to H Milling. Rec. May 18, 1795

p. 352-354 Oct. 4, 1794 William and John Young, gentlemen (Spartanburgh) to Gen. Richard Winn; power of attorney to sell (1) 11,200 ac tract in Washington Dist on both sides of Middle fork of Saluda R and border: SW-William and John Young and others vacant; and (2) 8,640 ac in Greenville Co, Washington Dist on Middle fork Saluda R and Oilcamp Cr and border: William and John Young and others vacant. Witness C. D. Bradford and J. L. Bradford. Signed Wm and John Young. Wit. oath (Fairfield Co) Oct. 4, 1794 William and John Young to Hugh Milling. Rec. May 18, 1795

p. 354-355 Aug. 22, 1794 William Patton to Robert Patton; for 20£ sterling sold 75 ac on a fork of McElwean's Cr; border: E-a prong of the creek and Samuel Archabald and by George Story; part of grant North Carolina to James McElwean who sold to William Patton. Witness Robert Donaldson, Alexander McCarter, and Samuel Archabald. Signed William Patton. Wit. oath Aug. 23, 1794 Samuel Archabald to Wm Smith. Rec. Sept. 29, 1794

p. 355 Jul. 9, 1795 Daniel Evins to I Harrison, JP; swears his brand is a cross in the left ear and a shallow fork in right ear. Signed Daniel Evins' mark.

p. 355-357 Apr. 8, 1795 Samuel Culbertson and wife Celia (Spartanburgh) to Henry ONeil (same); for $1 per ac sold 26.6 ac on Dogan (or Dougan) Br of Fairforrest Cr; border: Tittel's Br, Henry ONeil, and a line of Gillaspy's old survey; part of 497 ac grant Feb. 23, 1754 North Carolina to George Gillaspy who sold to Robert Dougan who sold to Samuel Culbertson who sold to Samuel Culbertson, jr; recorded in South Carolina Feb. 27, 1775; plat attached. Witness Andrew McBride, Jas Smith, and Jas Lusk. Signed Samuel Culbertson and Celia's mark left out. Wit. oath Apr. 14, 1795 Jas Smith to James Jordan. Rec. Apr. 16, 1795

p. 357-359 Apr. 26, 1794 Abram Markley, merchant (Charlestown, SC) to Reubin Warren (Spartanburgh); for 90£ SC money sold 1,000 ac; part of "sundry" thousand ac grant States Office to Abram Markley on N side Pacolate R; border: John Cobb and William Garret. Witness Samuel Turner, John Headen, and Abram Wyatt. Signed Abram Markley by William Pool, attorney for Abram. Wit. oath Jul. 10, 1795 Samuel Turner to James Turner. Rec. (not given) 15, 1795

p. 359-361 Feb. 6, 1792 John Gibbs, W Lancaster, Absalom Lancaster, and Jesse Connell (SC); agreement among them: John binds himself to make a deed to Jesse for all rights to land surveyed by warrant in John's name with border: W & SW-Jesse Spencer, and adjoining Stephens, McDol, Charles Moore, Porcher, and part joins Jesse Spencer on E and formerly surveyed for Richard Hampton; John promises to divide the money from the sale equally with Absalom and W Lancaster; Jesse is to survey the land; John Absalom and W are to bear all other expenses of getting the grant for the land; the land can be divided after the grant by mutual agreement. Witness Wilie Williford, Charles Trale, and D Golightly. Signed James Gibbs, W Lancaster, A Lancaster, and Jesse Connell. Wit. oath Apr. 14, 1795 D Golightly to I Harrison. Rec. Jul. 1795

p. 361-363 Sept. 13, 1794 Robert Waring (Columbia, Camden Dist) to Wade Hampton (Camden Dist); for 5s lease: (1) 600 ac surveyed Apr. 17, 1792 for Daniel McClaren; (2) 1,000 ac surveyed Apr. 17, 1792 for Daniel McClaren; (3) 883 ac surveyed May 16, 1792 for Daniel McClaren; (4) 930 ac surveyed Sept. 18, 1792 for John Bagnal; (5) 5,000 ac surveyed Jul. 23, 1792 for Benjamin Davis; (6) 6,000 ac surveyed Jun. 4, 1792 for Daniel Reels; (7) 3,200 ac surveyed Jul. 18, 1792 for Benjamin Davis; (8) 476 ac surveyed May 10, 1785 for Bibby Bush; (9) 1,000 ac surveyed May 17, 1792 for Daniel McClaren; and (10) 1,000 ac surveyed Jan. 4, 1792 for Cushman Edson; all granted Aug. 5, 1793 to Robert Waring and totaling 20,089 ac. Witness H Hampton and Jas White. Signed Robt. Waring. Rec. Aug. 15, 1795. release mentioned but not found.

p. 363-369 Nov. 14, 1794 Wade Hampton, esq (Camden Dist) to Robert Smock and Eden Shotwell, merchants (Philadelphia, Pa) and Abraham Morehouse, merchant (Alexandria, Va); for 10s Pennsylvania money sold (1) 600 ac surveyed for Daniel McClarin on W side Broad R and on Mike's Cr; border: S-Charles Hester, E-William Tate, John Ross, and Daniel McClarin's old line, N-Samuel, John, and Leonard Saratt; (9) 1,000 ac surveyed for Daniel McClaren on Cherokee and Saratt's Cr of Broad R; border: S & W-Hopkins Bremar and Co, N-Bonner, and E-McClain and Swan; (3) 883 ac surveyed for Daniel McClaren on Cherokee and Saratt's Cr of Broad R; border: N-Swan and Mrs. Walker, S-Martin, and E & W-McClain; (4) 930 ac surveyed for John Bagnal in Camden Dist at head of Broad Br of Black R; border: NW-Abner Bagnal, SE-Edward Lown; (5) 5,000 ac surveyed for Benjamin Davis in Camden Dist between Santee and Black R at a place called Junkyard Bay; border: SE & SE-Edward Lown and William Burnson, NW & SW-William McGonery, NE-James Davis and Plat, N & NE-William Crosserus, NW, NE & SE-Willis, N, NW & NE-James Davis, SW-John Bagnal, and N & E-Early; (6) 6,000 ac surveyed for Daniel Keels in Camden Dist at head of Pudding Swamp; border: NW & NE-Daniel Keels, SW-Story, SE-Welcher, and others vacant; (7) 3,200 ac surveyed for Benjamin Davis in Camden Dist on head branches of Wyleoo Cr of Santee R and head branches of Bear Cr of Black R; border: SW & NW-James Winn, Malcom Carr, and A Clemmons, SE & SW-William Clemmons, Joseph Kitton and West, NE & SE-Joseph Mechum (or Mitcham), NE-Davis, Frierson, and P Brooks; (8) 476 ac surveyed for Bibby Burt in Edgefield Co on branches of Edisto R; border: NE & NW-Edward Couch, Cobb, Clinton Squir, Bibby Bush, Fredrick Holm, and Widow Melton, NE-vacant; (2) 1,000 ac surveyed for Daniel McClaren on W side Broad R and both sides Saratt's Cr; border: E-McClaren, S-James Martin, N-James Bayas, and W-Joseph Champion, William Davison, and Reubin Blanton; (10) 1,000 ac surveyed for Cushman Edson on Sandy Run of Pacolate R; border: NE & SE-Daniel Huger, esq, SW-John Hail, esq, and NW-John Henderson, esq; tracts numbered according to listing in the immediately previous deed; granted Aug. 5, 1793 Gov. William Moultrie to Robert Waring who sold to Wade Hampton Sept. 13 and 15, 1794; Wade Hampton defends above tracts against prior granting or being too small for next 6 years. Witness Peter Lohra and Jacob Hoffman. Signed W Hampton. Wit. oath (Philadelphia, Pa) Nov. 27, 1794 Wade Hampton to Matthew Clarkson, mayor. Rec. Aug. 15, 1795

p. 369-377 Jan. 17, 1795 Robert Smock, merchant and Eden Shotwell, merchant and wife Mary Shotwell (all of Philadelphia, Pa) and Abraham Morehouse, merchant (Alexandria, Va) to John Nicholson, esq (Philadelphia, Pa); for 50s Pa money sold 20,089 ac (as described above); grants are in following books: tract 8 in book 5H p. 68, tract 9 book 5I p. 40, in book 5L: tract 1 on p. 88, tract 2 on p. 87, tract 3 p. 89, tract 4 p. 90, tract 5 p. 191, tract 6 p. 190, tract 7 p. 192, and tract 10 p. 38; all granted to Robert Waring and sold Sept. 13 & 15, 1794 to Wade Hampton who sold to Robert Smock, Eden Shotwell, and Abraham Morehouse Nov. 14, 1794; sellers warrant the grants for 6 years. Witness Daniel Jones and William Schenek. Signed Robert Smock, Eden and Mary Shotwell, and A Morhouse. Wit. oath (Philadelphia, Pa) Robert Smock, Eden and Mary Shotwell, and A Morhouse to Isaac Howell, judge of Common Pleas Jan. 21, 1795. Rec. Aug. 15, 1795. Jan. 23, 1795 Gov. Thomas Mufflin of Pa says Isaac Howell was and is a judge in said court signed by James Trimble, dept. sec.

p. 377-379 Jun. 23, 1794 John Clayton (Spartanburgh) to David McCarley; for 50£ sterling sold 150 ac in Greenville Co on both sides Fortenberry Beaverdam Cr; border: Alxander McDanold, Joseph Evans, and John Burk; part of grant State patent to Wm Swift. Witness Matthew Patton and John Clayton. Signed John Clayton and Hannah's mark. Wit. oath Nov. 14, 1795 Matthew Patton to George Brewton. Rec. Nov. 24, 1795

p. 379-382 Jan. 16, 1795 William Crocker (Spartanburgh) to John Gray (same); for 20£ sold 650 ac on Losson's fork of Fairforrest Cr; grant Sept. 29, 1772 Gov. Charles G. Montague to Arthur Crocker. Witness Ellis Cannon, John Cannon, and Joshua Wiatt. Signed William Crocker's mark. Wit. oath Nov. 28, 1795 Ellis Cannon to I Harrison. Rec. Dec. 1, 1795

p. 382-384 Jan. 3, 1794 David Floyd and wife Jean (Union Co) to Thomas Price, merchant (Spartanburgh); for 50 (£ ?) sterling sold 144 ac; border: Tygar R, John Patton, and Enoch Floyd; part of 257 ac grant Dec. 4, 1786 Gov. William Moultrie to David Floyd. Witness William Lamb, Jonathan Floyd, and Andrew Thomson. Signed David Floyd and Jean's mark. Wit. oath Sept. 3, 1795 Andrew Thomson to Thos Moore. Rec. Dec. 1, 1795

p. 384-385 Oct. 3, 1791 Philip Wells (Laurens Co) to Martha McCrorey; for 50£ sterling sold a Negro woman Dinah, born in this country, blind in left eye, and 26 years old. Witness William Earnest. Signed Philip Wells. Rec. Dec. 1, 1795. Jan. 16, 1794 Anthony Wilson assigns his interest in Dianah to William Earnest. Witness Thos Tod. Signed Anthony Wilson. Wit. oath Apr. 30, 1794 Anthony Wilson to Thomas Farrow

p. 385-388 Apr. 29, 1794 John Chesney to wife Sarah (Spartanburgh) to Alexander Alexander, merchant (same); for 30£ sterling sold 223 ac on both sides Jamie's Cr between Tygar and Enoree Rivers; border: N-Moses McCarley, E-Henry Kerley, and others vacant; survey Aug. 17, 1786 to John Chesney and granted by Gov. Thomas Pinckney. Witness Jeremiah Wofford, Luke Thornton, and Thomas Doig. Signed John Chesney and Sarah's mark. Wit. oath Jun. 14, 1794 Thomas Doig to Thos Moore. Rec. Dec. 11, 1795

p. 388-389 Nov. 13, 1793 Jane Buis (Spartanburgh) to Randolph Laurens (same); for 60£ Va money sold 196 ac on Beaverdam Cr of Thickety Cr; where Jane Buis lives; grant May 1, 1787 Gov. William Moultrie to Abraham Buis. Witness Vardry McBee, John Wilkinson, and Essex Capshaw. Signed Jane Buis' mark. Wit. oath Apr. 12, 1794 John Wilkinson to Edwd Goode. Rec. Dec. 11, 1795

p. 389-391 Nov. 22, 1793 Henry Wells and wife Catherine (Spartanburgh) to Joseph Hurt (same); for 50£ sterling sold 200 ac on N fork of Tygar R; border: John Miller and David Knox. Witness I Harrison. Signed Henry and Catherine Wells. Certified Nov. 22, 1793 by I Harrison. Rec. Dec. 12, 1795

p. 391 Dec. 20, 1794 Robt G. Harper to Saml Farrow; Robert acknowledges a deed was made to him for "a particular purpose" and that purpose is now served, so he cancels the deed and relinquishes it to Samuel; see deed in Book C p. 297. Witness Obadiah Trimmier. Signed Robt G Harper

Book D 1794-1797

p. 1-2 May 13, 1794 Jarvis Cornwell (Spartanburgh) to Baylis Earle (same); for 100£ sterling sold 458 ac on McBee's Cr of Pacolate R where Jarvis lives; border: Andrew Cally; survey by William Benson, dept. surv. and granted Feb. 13, 179(2? page torn) Gov. Charles Pinckney to Jarvis Cornwell. Witness Jno Lancaster, Allan McDougall, and Jno(?) Gowen. Signed Jarvis Cornwell's mark. Rec. Sept. 9, 1794

p. 2-5 Oct. 9, 1793 Alexander Ray (Spartanburgh) to Benjamin McMakin (same); for 5£ sold 250 ac on both sides Tyger R; border: NE-John K(page torn), Hugh Barnet, and Joseph Jones and SW-Hugh Barnet; grant May 5, 1773 Lt. Gov. William Bull to Alexander Ray. Witness Samuel Miller, Ann Brown, and Martha Miller. Signed Alexander Ray's mark. Wit. oath Sept. 22, 1794 Samuel Miller to James Jordan. Rec. Oct. 14, 1794

p. 5-6 Jan. 21, 1792 Drury Couch (Spartanburgh) to Benjamin Rhodes (same); for 40£ 10s sterling sold 150 ac on both sides Fort Shoals Cr; grant Gov. Charles G. Montague to Thomas Couch, desc, and by will to Drury Couch. Witness Christopher Rhodes and John Gorzvel. Signed Drury Couch's mark. Wit. oath Oct. 4, 1793 Drury Couch to (not given). Rec. Oct. 13, 1794

p. 6-9 Sept. 17, 1793 John Gray (Spartanburgh) to Henry Pettit (same); for 50£ sterling sold 300 ac on both sides of Graham's Br on N side Pacolate R; part of 620 ac grant May 2, 1791 Gov. Charles Pinckney to John Gray. Witness Ellis Cannon, G. Lamkin,jr, and William Pool. Signed John Gray. Rec. Sept. 9, 1794

p. 9-11 May 18, 1794 John Gowen (SC) to Bartholomew Grogin (SC); for 50£ sold 150 ac(?) on both sides Beaverdam Cr of S Pacolate R including land John bought from Isaac Spivey (see Court records at Cambridge); grant Nov. 25, 1771 Gov. Joseph Martin (NC) to Abigail Terrel. Witness Isaac Spivey and James Gowen. Signed Jon Gowen. Rec. Sept. 9, 1794

p. 11-13 Aug. 15, 1793 John Nicoll (Greenville Co) to James Vernon and Michael Miller (Spartanburgh); for 60£ sterling sold 300 ac on both sides Middle fork Tyger R; border: Thomas Penny's upper line; part of 400 ac grant Apr. 29, 1768 Gov. William Tryon (NC) to Elisha Thomson in Mechlinburgh Co, NC who sold to William Sharp who sold to Thomas Price who sold to John Nicoll; about 100 ac from grant excepted on upper of W side which is "laid off" to John Slone. Witness Adam Slone, Jone Bigwell, and Mary Vernon. Signed John Nichol. Wit. oath Sept. 8, 1794 Mary Vernon to James Jordan. Rec. Sept. 9, 1794

p. 13-15 Apr. 24, 1794 Enoch Floid (Spartanburgh) to Thomas Price, merchant (SC); for 75£ sterling sold two Negroes: Phillis about 47 years old and her son Harry 9 years old; Phillis is African and has her country marks; Harry is South Carolina born. Witness Wm Easley and Andrew Thomson. Signed Enoch Floid. Wit. oath Sept. 3, 1794 Andrew Thomson to Thos Moore. Rec. Sept. 8, 1794

p. 15-21 Jul. 15, 1773 Elizabeth Bailey (Craven Co) to Thomas Pendan (or Peden) (Barkley Co); for 50£ 10s SC money sold 100 ac on Forgisson's Cr of S fork of Tyger R; border: W-Edward Bayles and others vacant; grant Aug. 12, 1768 Lt. Gov. William Bull to Elizabeth Bailey. Witness William Peden and John Turner. Signed Elizabeth Bailey's mark. Wit. oath (Chester Co) Sept. 3, 1793 William Peden to John Bell. Rec. Nov. 18, 1794

p. 21-28 Jul. 15, 1773 Robert Bealey and Elizabeth Bealey (Craven Co) to Thomas Peden (Berkley Co); for 50£ 10s SC money sold 100 ac on Forgesson's Br of S fork of Tyger R; border: vacant; grant Aug. 12, 1773 Lt. Gov. William Bull to Edward Baley and to Robert and Elizabeth Bealey by heirship. Witness William Peden and John Turner. Signed Robert and Elizabeth Bealey's marks. Wit. oath Sept. 3, 1793 (Chester Co) William Peden to John Bell. Rec. Nov. 18, 1794

p. 28-30 Dec. 4, 1794 Spencer Bobo and wife Nancy (Spartanburgh) to Anthony Foster, sr (same); for 50£ sterling sold 100 ac where Spencer and Nancy Bobo live between Tyger and Enoree Rivers on a ridge about 3 miles above blackstock's ford on Tyger R; part of 1,000 ac grant to James Semple, jr and sold by Rutry Semple, heir-at-law to James Semple, jr, to John McCullock who sold to Spencer Bobo. Witness Anthony Foster, jr and Absalom Bobo. Signed Spencer Bobo and Nancy Berrey's (sic) mark. Wit. oath Apr. 18, 1795 Anthony Foster, jr to Saml Lancaster. Rec. Feb. 20, 1795

p. 30-31 Sept. 29, 1794 John Ford (Spartanburgh) to son William Ford; for love and affection gives 400 ac on E side Tyger R where William lives and 50 ac adjoining the 400 ac on W side; both granted to Robert Miller who sold to John Ford. Witness Thomas Grace, James Southerlin (or Southerland), and Daniel Bragg. Signed John Ford. Wit. oath Jan. 13, 1795 James Southerlin to Zadock Ford. Rec. Feb. 20, 1795

p. 31-33 Sept. 8, 1794 Willey J Brown (Spartanburgh) to Alexander Thomson (same); for 70£ sterling sold 200 ac on S fork of N Tyger R and E of Indian Boundary; surveyed Jul. 15, 1785 for John Davis and granted Feb. 15, 1787 to Augustus Merrick who sold to Joseph Thompson who sold to Edward Stewart who sold to Willey J Brown. Witness none. Signed Willey J Brown. Rec. Feb. 20, 1795

p. 33-35 Dec. 4, 1792 West Harris (Edgefield Co) to William Ussery (Spartanburgh); for 100£ sterling sold 200 ac on Buck Cr; grant Dec. 4, 1792 State Office to West Harris. Witness Philip Ussery, Saml Ussery, and James Morris. Signed West Harris. Certified Feb. 23, 1793 by S Bethel. Rec. Feb. 21, 1795

p. 35-37 Apr. 14, 1794 Samuel Brice (Spartanburgh) to Thomas Pedan; for 10£ due to Samuel sold 7 cattle marked with swallow fork in near ear and upper keel in right ear, 4 horses: a sorrel mare branded "S" on near shoulder, a bay horse branded "S" on near shoulder, and 2 young bay mare colts (sic) branded same, 6 sheep marked with shallow fork in near ear and upper keel in right ear, household furniture, and farming tools; Condition: above sale void if Samuel pays Thomas 10£ by Mar. 21, 1795. Witness John Barry. Signed Samuel Brice's mark. Wit. oath Jul. 13, 1794 John Barry to Thomas Moore. Rec. Feb. 21, 1795

p. 37-40 Jun. 6, 1792 Aaron Moore (Pendleton Co) to Phillip Johnson (Spartanburgh); for 100£ sterling sold 208 ac where Phillip lives on Ben's Cr of S Tygar R; border: John Neasbitt, James Jordan, John McDowell, William Moore, and remainder of grant; part of 290 ac grant Jul. 1, 1785 to Aaron Moore. Witness John Durham, Howell Johnson, and Mary Durham. Signed Aaron and Jean Moore. Wit. oath Oct. 10, 1792 Howell Johnson to D Goodlett. Rec. Feb. 22, 1795

p. 40-42 Jan. 15, 1795 James Bruton (Spartanburgh) to Thomas Williamson (same); for 85£ sterling sold 310 ac on Antiquorum Cr (now Fergison's Cr) on S side of Little R (now Tyger R); border: Alexander Fergison; grant Nov. 18, 1757 Gov. Arthur Dobbs (NC) to James Russell in Anson Co, NC. Witness Margeret Moore, Martha Moore, and Thos Moore JP. Signed James Burton. Rec. Feb. 22, 1795

p. 42-44 Sept. 29, 1794 Richard Cox, sr (Spartanburgh) and wife Hannah to Samuel Shurbut (or Sherbutt) (same); for 70£ sterling sold 150 ac on N side Tygar R; border: James Scagg, Tobias Bright, and Thomas Shurley; part of grant Apr. 7, 1778 Gov. Thomas Pinckney to Wm Shurley; "see p. 50 for rest of deed" (some of following signatures on p. 50). Witness Tobias Bright, Benj Shurbutt, and Arthur Faulkner. Signed Richard Cox and Hannah's mark. Wit. oath Jan. 9, 1795 Tobias Bright to Samuel Lancaster. Rec. Feb. 23, 1795

p. 44-46 Jan. 24, 1795 Alexander Autrey and wife Martha (Spartanburgh) to Jesse Connell (same); for 20£ sold 66 ac on W side of Bufelowlick Cr of Fairforest Cr; border: Ephraim Elder; grant to Richard Hampton who sold to Peter Elder who sold to Alexander Autrey. Witness John Autry and Francis Connell. Signed Alexander and Martha Autrey's marks. Wit. oath Apr. 13, 1796 Francis Connell to Wm Smith. Rec. Apr. 21, 1796

p. 46-48 Apr. 4, 1796 Zacheriah Gibbs (Union Co) to Jesse Connell (Spartanburgh); for 5s sold 150 ac; border: Jesse Spencer and Charles Moore; grant May 7, 1792 Gov. Charles Pinckney to James Gibbs. Witness George Connell and Francis Connell. Signed Zacheriah Gibbs. Certified Apr. 12, 1796 by Wm Smith. Rec. Apr. 21, 1796

p. 48-50 Feb. 4, 1795 Isham Bobbitt (Spartanburgh) to Jesse Connell (same); for 46£ 13s 4p sold a Negro boy James. Witness I Harrison JP. Signed Isham Bobbit. Certified Feb. 4, 1795 by I Harrison. Rec. Apr. 21, 1796

p. 50-52 Dec. 8, 1794 John Fincher (Union Co) to Nicholas Waters (same); for 50£ sold (ac not given) on N side of S fork Tygar R; border: Thomas Collins, John Leech, and John McElhany; grant May 4, 1769 to John McElhany. Witness Absalom Stokes, John Fapp, and Samuel Martindille. Signed John Fincher's mark. Wit. oath Jun. 6, 1795 Absalom Stokes to Ism Foster. Rec. Apr. 24, 1795

p. 52-54 May 26, 1795 William Goodwin (Greenville Co) to Nathaniel Walker (Spartan Co); for 35£ sterling sold 148 ac on S Tygar R; border: David McCoy and others vacant; grant Aug. 1, 1785 to William Goodwin. Witness Wm Silversides, Ann Watkins, and John Thomas, jr. Signed William Goodwin's mark. Wit. oath Sept. 10, 1795 John Thomas, jr to B. D. Shumate. Rec. Sept. 12, 1795

p. 54-56 Apr. 25, 1795 John Thomas, jr (Greenville Co) to Nathaniel Walker (Spartan Co); for 20£ sterling sold 60 ac on S and Middle Tygar Rivers; border: Nathaniel Walker, McCoy, Jos Edwards, and John Vaughn; part of 1,000 ac grant Jun. 2, 1788 to John Thomas, jr. Witness Charles Bruce, Jonathan Nisbett, and W. D. Thomas. Signed Jo Thomas, jr. Wit. oath Sept. 10, 1795 John Thomas jr to Berryman D Shumate. Rec. Sept. 12, 1795

p. 56-58 Jun. 9, 1794 William Ussery (Spartanburgh) to William Jordan (same); for 50£ sold 200 ac on Little Buck Cr; grant Dec. 4, 1792 State Office to (not given). Witness S Bethel, Joseph Morris, and Larkin Bethel. Signed William Ussery's mark. Certified Aug. 25, 1794 by S Bethel. Rec. Sept. 13, 1795

p. 58 Nov. 5, 1795 W Shaw to Wm Wells; there is a contract between

W Shaw and Wm Wells relating to a lot at Spartan Courthouse whereby W Shaw received an "obligation" to sell the lot; the contract or bargin is now voided. Witness I Harrison. Signed W Shaw. Rec. Sept. 13, 1795

p. 58-60 Jun. 25, 1794 Col Thomas Sabb (Matthews Parish, Orangeburgh Dist) to Robert Lee (Spartanburgh); for 20£ sterling sold 2,719 ac on Buck, Horse, and McKinney's Creeks of Pacolet and Broad R; border: E & SE-Richard Saunders, NW & NE-David Forrest, NE, SE & SW- Wm Dotton, NE & SE-James Forrest, E-Jas Stedman and Haney, W, NW & N-Andrew Ray, and W-NC state line; grant Jul. 5, 1778 Gov. Thomas Pinckney to Thomas Sabb. Witness Jothn Bowen, Arthur Crocker, and Richard Lee. Signed Thomas Sabb. Wit. oath Jan. 14, 1795 Richard Lee to Saml Lancaster. Rec. Sept. 13, 1795

p. 60-62 Jun. 25, 1794 Col. Thomas Sabb (Mathews Parish, Orangeburgh Dist) to Robert Lee (Spartanburgh); for 15£ sterling sold 1,870 ac on S side Pacolate R; border: Col. Winns, Edwd Stubblefield, Thomas Barton, and Kimbol; grant Jul. 7, 1788 Gov. Thomas Pinckney to Thomas Sabb. Witness Jothn Bowen, Arthur Crocker, and Richard Lee. Signed Thom Sabb. Wit. oath Jan. 14, 1795 Richard Lee to Saml Lancaster. Rec. Sept. 18, 1795

p. 62-64 May 16, 1795 Robert Lee (Spartanburgh) to Anne Lee (same); for 10£ sterling sold 300 ac on waters of Pacolet and Broad R; part of grant Jul. 5, 1788 to Thomas Sabb. Witness Matthew Mackbee, Arthur Crocker, and John Pearce. Signed Robt Lee. Wit. oath Jul. 23, 1795 John Pearce to I Harrison. Rec. Sept. 18, 1795

p. 64-66 May 16, 1795 Robert Lee (Spartanburgh) to John Pearce (same); for 10£ sterling sold 350 ac on waters of Pacolet and Broad R; part of grant Jul. 5, 1788 to Col. Thomas Sabb. Witness Matthew Mackbee, James Wofford, and Arthur Crocker. Signed Robt. Lee. Wit. oath Jul. 23, 1795 James Wofford to I Harrison. Rec. Sept. 18, 1795

p. 66-68 Mar. 8, 1795 Robert Lee (Spartanburgh) to Bazel Scott (same); for 10£ sterling sold 200 ac on W side of Little Cherokee Cr; part of 2,100 ac grant Apr. 2, 1787 to James Stedman on both sides Cherokee Cr. Witness John Wallace, Anne Lee, and Martha Reason. Signed Robt Lee. Wit. oath Nov. 9, 1795 Martha Reason to I Harrison. Rec. Nov. 20, 1795

p. 68-69 Mar. 23, 1791 Wm Wofford (Turkey Cove, Burk Co, NC) to John Harris (Spartanburgh); a bond of 100£ sterling; Condition: bond from William to John void if William makes deed to John for 200 ac on S side of Pacolet R where John lives; William to make deed for land when John pays him 45£. Witness Henry McCray and Arthur Crocker. Signed W Wofford. Wit. oath Jun. 16, 1795 Henry McCray to I Harrison. Rec. Nov. 20, 1795

p. 69-71 Mar. 20, 1795 Thomas Hightower (Spartanburgh) to Thomas Underwood; for 160£ SC money sold 640 ac where Thomas lives except 25 ac sold to Zachariah Grace in SW corner; grant Jan. 1, 1787 Gov. William Moultrie to Thomas Hightower. Witness Wm Ford, John Underwood, and James Ford. Signed Thomas Hightower's mark. Wit. oath Sept. 10, 1795 Wm Ford to W Lancaster. Rec. Nov. 20, 1795

p. 71-74 Apr. 21, 1795 Thomas Brown and wife Hannah (Spartanburgh) to John Lee (same); for 60£ sterling sold 87½ ac; N part of 175 ac grant Apr. 2, 1768 Gov. William Tryon (NC) to Joseph Wofford on S side Pacolate R including mouth of Richland Cr and sold by Joseph Wofford to Thomas Brown. Witness James Wofford, Anne Lee, and Martha Reason. Signed Thomas Brown. Wit. oath Jul. 23, 1795 James Wofford to Isham Harrison. Rec. Nov. 23, 1795

p. 74-75 Jan. 20, 1792 Wells Griffith (Spartanburgh) to Justice Reynolds (Stokes Co, NC); a bond of 800£ SC money; Condition: bond void if Wells makes deed to Justice for 200 ac "bearing date" Nov. 25, 1771 and a "parcel" on N side of Lawson's fork joining the 200 ac and continuing down the creek to first long Branch between the 200 ac and Zachariah Robertson; deed to be made after Justice pays 200£ to Wells. Witness Bazel Lee and William McDowell. Signed Wells Griffith. Wit. oath Sept. 14, 1795 Bazel Lee to I Harrison. Rec. Nov. 23, 1795

p. 75-77 Sept. 14, 1795 John Lefever, sr (Spartanburgh) to Sarah Wooton (same); for 50£ sterling sold a sorrel stud horse, 3 cows and calves, 2 grass heifers and a yearling, 10 year old hogs, 15 shoats, a grey mare, a sorrel mare and colt, a woman's saddle, and all household and kitchen furniture and plantation tools: a mattress and furniture, puter dish, a bason, 6 plates, a case of knives and forks, a large iron pot, a small oven, a small pot, an iron braid pan. 5 sheep, 2 axes, 2 hoes, a plow, and an iron wedge. Witness Thomas Cole and Gideon Gibson. Signed John Lefever. Wit. oath Sept. 15, 1795 Thomas Cole to I Harrison. Rec. Nov. 23, 1795

p. 77-79 Sept. 11, 1795 James Dillingham (Greenville Co) to David McDowell; for 20£ sterling sold 400 ac on branch of Lawson's fork near head of Fawn Br; border: Daniel White, McDowell, and Gowen; grant Nov. 26, 1790 Gov. William Moultrie to James Dillingham. Witness John Young, jr and James Young. Signed Jas Dillingham. Wit. oath Sept. 14, 1795 John Young, jr to I Harrison. Rec. Nov. 24, 1795

p. 79-82 Jan. 17, 1795 Arthur Simpson and wife Jane (Spartanburgh) to Arthur Simpson McCarter (same); for 5s sterling sold 181 ac; border: William Simpson; grant Apr. 3, 1786 Gov. William Moultrie to Arthur Simpson. Witness Samuel Clouney, Richard Cruse, and Robert Harris. Signed Arthur and Jane Simpson's marks. Wit. oath Mar. 5, 1795 Richard Cruse to Isham Foster. Rec. Nov. 24, 1795

p. 82-83 Jan. 17, 1795 Arthur Simpson (Spartanburgh) to grandson Arthur Simpson McCarter (same); for love and affection sold his black mare, 2 cows: Whiteface and Mulberry, a black stear, a brown "Ditto", 3 sheep, and all farming tools of which Arthur Simpson has presented an inventory. Witness Samuel Clauny and Robert Harris. Signed Arthur Simpson's mark. Wit. oath Mar. 5, 1795 Robert Harris to Isham Foster. Rec. Nov. 25, 1795

p. 83-87 Jan. 25, 1796 William Wells and wife Martha (Spartanburgh) to William Thompson (same); for 350£ sterling sold 355 ac on branch of Fairforrest and Lawson's fork Cr where Spartanburgh Court House now stands; part of two grants: (1) Jan. 21, 1785 to William Wood and (2) Jun. 4, 1787 to Thomas Williamson who sold to William Wells; E end of 440 ac grant Gov. William Guerard to William Wood who sold to Thomas Williamson who sold to William Wood; border: Old Trail. Witness Joshua Downs, Isabella Rodgers, and John Wood. Signed Wm Wells and Martha's mark. Wit. oath Apr. 13, 1796 Joshua Downs to I Harrison. Rec. Jul. 1, 1796. Dower renounced Martha Wells to Isham Harrison Jun. 11, 1800 recorded in Book G p. 2

p. 87-89 Feb. 19, 1795 Thomas Green (Spartanburgh) to Robert Dunnaway (same); for 30£ sterling sold 84½ ac on S side Thickety Cr; part of 400 ac grant to John Headen. Witness Richard Proctor, John Gibbs, and John Reece. Signed Thomas Green. Wit. oath Feb. 11, 1795 John Gibbs to H McCray. Rec. Nov. 25, 1795

p. 89-90 Feb. 2, 1790 James Brown (Charleston, SC)to Samuel Dunnaway (Spartanburgh); a bond for 220£ sterling; Condition: bond void if James makes a deed to Samuel for 1,000 ac at head branches Thickety Cr of Broad R called Thickety Meadows; Feb. 20, 1790 James

Brown receives 110£ from Samuel Dunnaway for the land. Witness Obadiah Trimmier. Signed James Brown. Wit. oath Mar. 26, 1795 Obadiah Trimmier. Rec. Nov. 25, 1795

p. 90-92 Jan. 10, 1795 James Jordan (Spartanburgh) to Philip Johnson, jr (same); for 50£ sterling sold 286 ac on Provoy's Cr of Tyger R; grant Apr. 21, 1785 Gov. William Moultrie to James Jordan. Witness (signed in open court). Signed James Jordan. Rec. Nov. 26, 1795

p. 92-94 Jul. 19, 1794 John Atkins (Laurens Co) to Thomas Posey (Spartanburgh); for 100£ SC money sold 300 ac on S fork Tygar R; border: NW-John Ford, W & S-James Miller, and E-Kirkland; grant Aug. 19, 1774 to Joseph Atkins in Craven Co and to John Atkins, heir-at-law of Joseph Atkins, desc. Witness Geo Anderson and John Ford. Signed John Adkins. Wit. oath Sept. 27, 1794 John Ford to Thos Moore. Rec. Nov. 26, 1795

p. 94-96 Jan. 13, 1793 Samuel Miller (Spartanburgh) to Randolph Johnson (same); for (money not mentioned) sold 200 ac on both sides Provise Cr except 40-50 ac "that was run away by an old right". Witness Isaac Snoddy, John Snoddy, and Marget Snoddy. Signed Samuel Miller. Wit. oath Jan. 14, 1794 Isaac Snoddy to Thos Moore. Rec. Nov. 27, 1795

p. 96-97 Feb. 16, 1789 John Leech (Spartanburgh) to Randolph Johnson (same); for (money not mentioned) sold 240 ac where Randolph lives on James Cr; border: Saddler; grant Dec. 11, 1770 to John Leech in Tryon Co, NC. Witness Isaac Snoddy, James Vernon, and John Reynolds (or Runnels). Signed John Leech. Wit. oath Jun. 10, 1791 Isaac Snoddy to D Goodlett. Rec. Nov. 27, 1795

p. 97-100 Mar. 18, 1795 Robert Lee (Spartanburgh) to Richard Lee (same); for 50£ sterling sold 712 ac; NE part of 2,100 ac grant Apr. 2, 1787 to James Stedman; border: where Main Rd fords Cherokee Cr. Witness John Wallace, Anne Lee, and Martha Reason. Signed Robt Lee. Wit. oath Apr. 14, 1795 John Wallace to Thomas Moore. Rec. Nov. 28, 1795

p. 100-101 Mar. 4, 1791 Thomas Collins (Spartanburgh) to William Traylor (same); for 60£ sold 143 ac; border: Randolph Johnson; part of 193 ac on branch of Middle fork Tyger R. Witness Isham Foster, David Leech, and Elizabeth Williams. Signed Thom Collins. Wit. oath Sept. 15, 1791 Isham Foster to D Goodlett. Rec. Nov. 28, 1795

p. 101-104 May 7, 1794 Ephraim Elder and wife Sally (Spartanburgh) to Mark Swadley (same); for 60£ SC money sold 100 ac on both sides Buffelow lick Cr of Fairforrest Cr; border: Mark Swadley's Spring, William Roberts, David Golightly, Henry Ayres, and Jesse Connell; part of grant on "day of 17" to Jailes (sic) Tillett who sold part to Richard Hampton who sold part to Thomas Bullan. Witness William Roberds and Charles ewil White. Signed Ephraim Elder and Sally's mark. Wit. oath Jan. 12, 1795 William Roberds to I Harrison. Rec. Nov. 28, 1795

p. 104-106 Jan. 10, 1795 Charles James and wife Mary (Spartanburgh) to Edward Barnett (SC); for 50£ sterling sold 100 ac on Lawson's fork of Pacolate R; border: William Wofford & Co, William Poole, land formerly Reubin Matthews, and Henderson & Co; grant Oct. 3, 1785 Gov. William Moultrie to Charles James. Witness Joroyal Barnett and Charles James, jr. Signed Charles James and Mary's mark. Wit. oath Jan. 12, 1795 Joroyal Barnett to I Harrison. Rec. Nov. 29, 1795

p. 106-108 Dec. 22, 1794 John Golightly (Spartanburgh) to Isham Harrison (same); for 20 guineas sold 35 ac on Fairforrest Cr; border: Richard Harrisons Deicast formerly called Druggan's and another Richard Harrisons Deicast formerly Benson's, and Benson. Witness Henry Wells, and W Wells. Signed John Golightly. Wit. oath Jan. (not given), 1795 Henry Wells to Baylis Earle. Rec. Nov. 29, 1795

p. 108-110 Jul. 4, 1793 Charles Hester (Spartanburgh) to Thomas Cole (same); for 70£ SC money sold (ac not given); on both sides Beaverdam fork of Thickety Cr; grant Gov. William Moultrie to Charles Hester. Witness Jesse Tate and Mary Tate. Signed Charles Hester. Wit. oath Jan. 2, 1794 Jesse Tate to Edwd Goode. Rec. Nov. 29, 1795

p. 110-112 Jul. 30, 1796 Morris Veal (Oglethrope Co, Ga) to James Smith (Spartanburgh); release and quit claim judgments or claims Morris has against James. Witness Natham Williford, W Wofford, and Sherewood Halcombe. Signed Morris Veal. Wit. oath (Franklin Co, Ga) Aug. 1, 1796 Natham Williford to James Ferrell, and (Spartanburgh) Aug. 4, 1796 Sherewood Halcombe to Isham Foster. Rec. Aug. 4, 1796

p. 112-116 Nov. 10, 1794 Thomas Cole (Spartanburgh) to Benjamin Arindle (same); for 50£ SC money sold 200 ac on Beaverdam Cr of Thickety Cr of Broad R. Witness Obadh Watson and John Trimmier. Signed Thomas Cole. Wit. oath Jan. 12, 1795 Obadh Watson to S Bethel. Rec. Nov. 29, 1795. Dower renounced Martha Cole to John Trimmier and Obadh Watson (witness) Nov. 10, 1794

p. 116-120 Sept. 25, 1784 Wm Embry (Camden Dist) to Jane Fowler (Fairforrest, 96 Dist); for 150£ "formerly currency" of SC sold 150 ac on Wilie's Br of Fairforrest Cr; grant May 17, 1774 Lt. Gov. William Bull to William Embry; "said William Hembree (sic)" sells the 150 ac. Witness James Ham, Abraham Moore, and Jonathan Moore. Signed W Embry. Wit. oath Dec. 18, 1784 James Ham to Jo Thomas, jr. Rec. Nov. 29, 1795

p. 120-123 Feb. 7, 1795 William Burton and wife Mary (Spartanburgh) to Henry Foster (same); for 50£ sterling sold 788 ac on both sides Henry Foster's Cr of Fairforrest; grant Feb. 4, 1788 Gov. Thomas Pinckney; border: E-Neasbitt and vacant, S-vacant and Henry Foster, and N-vacant. Witness Charles Burton, Lawson Thomson, and Aaron Froyd (or Floyd). Signed William and Mary Burton. Wit. oath Mar. 11, 1795 (Union Co) Lawson Thomson to Hugh Means. Rec. Nov. 29, 1795

p. 123-126 Jan. 2, 1794 Samuel Saxon (sheriff, 96 Dist) to Joachim (or Isachim) Bulow (Charleston, SC); for 186£ sterling sold 440 ac on Big Cr of Little R; sold by Mr. Tate to James Lusk; Joachim brought case against Robert and James Lusk in Cambridge Common Pleas Court (Union and Spartan Co) and was awarded 149£ 12s 6p by a writ from Court Jan. 3, 1792 signed by Hon. John Rutledge; as result of this case, above land sold on a Monday in Oct. 1792. Witness Joshua Downs and James Saxon. Signed S Saxon, sheriff. Wit. oath Oct. 1, 1796 Joshua Downs to I Harrison. Rec. Oct. 6, 1796

p. 126-128 Jul. 26, 1794 Charles Hunt (Pendleton Co) to Joseph Couch (Spartanburgh); for 10s SC money sold 126 ac on Enoree R; grant Dec. 5, 1785 to Charles Hunt and 50 ac of "same" grant Jan. 5, 1786 to John Couch; Charles warrants all the land except part held and claimed by Landon Farrow by a "north wright". Witness Henry Hardin and Mark Stroud. Signed Charles Hunt. Wit. oath Feb. 26, 1795 Henry Hardin to Thos Farrow. Rec. Oct. 6, 1796

p. 128-129 Apr. 9, 1795 Thomas Matthews (Spartanburgh) to Andrew Barry (same); a bond of 500£; Condition: Thomas to deed Andrew 640 ac; land is due Thomas by Georgia Assembly act at Augusta Dec. 24, 1789 "compensation to troops in service of state of Georgia" and due Thomas as appears in a certificate; land is to be laid out where Georgia Assembly directs. Witness Thos Moore. Signed Thomas Matthews. Rec. Nov. 29, 1795

p. 129-131 Jan. 24, 1795 Solomon Hays (Spartanburgh) to Reubin Daniel (same); for 30£ sold 150 ac on SC side Poison Br of Big Br; part of 540 ac on Fairforrest Cr granted to Wm Wofford; 150 ac is divided from 540 ac by Poison Br until it runs into Big Br. Witness I Harrison. Signed Solomon Hays's mark. Certified Apr. 13, 1795 by I Harrison. Rec. Nov. 29, 1795

p. 131-133 Mar. 25, 1795 Henry Foster (Spartanburgh) to Henry Amberson (same); for 20£ sterling sold 225 ac on E side Henry Foster's Cr of Fairforrest Cr; border: E-Joseph Nesbitt; part of grant Feb. 4, 1788 Gov. Thomas Pinckney to Wm Burton. Witness Matthew Patton, Samuel Kelso, and James Farris. Signed Henry Foster. Wit. oath Apr. 10, 1795 (Union Co) Matthew Patton to W Means. Rec. Nov. 29, 1795

p. 133-134 Apr. 13, 1795 John Hightower (Spartan Co) to George Lewis (same); for a Spanish milled dollar sold 112 ac on S side Lawson's fork of Pacolet R; border: S-William Moultrie, NW-Peter Lewis, and Standing Stone Br; part of grant Jan. 21, 1785 Gov. Benjamin Guerard to John Bennett. Witness S Bethel, Ephraim Lewis, and Christopher Golightly. Signed John Hightower. Certified Apr. 13, 1795 by S Bethel. Rec. Nov. 29, 1795

p. 134-135 Apr. 9, 1795 Bazel Scott (Spartanburgh) to his only child Mary Scott; for love and affection give 2 mares, 7 cattle, 15 hogs, 3 beds and furniture, a dish and 6 plates. Witness Richard Lee and Nancy Lee. Signed Bazel Scott's mark. Wit. oath Apr. 14, 1795 Richard Lee to Thos Moore. Rec. Nov. 29, 1795

p. 135-136 Feb. 5, 1795 Edward Hooker (Spartanburgh) to John Williams (same); for 50£ sterling sold 100 ac on Cedar Shoal Cr of Enoree R; border: John Stone; SW end of grant to James Sample. Witness Burrell Bobo and Richard Fryer. Signed Edward Hooker. Wit. oath Feb. 6, 1795 Burrell Bobo and Richard Fryer to Thomas Farrow. Rec. Nov. 29, 1795

p. 136-138 Mar. 24, 1794 Drury McDonald, "attorney for Gee" (Spartanburgh) to William Foster (same); for 50£ sterling sold 200 ac on Lawson's fork; border: William Foster and Robert McMurdy; grant to William Dickson. Witness Elisha Heddin, Samuel Hedden, and David Hedden. Signed Drury McDonald. Wit. oath Apr. 11, 1795 Elisha Hedden to Isham Foster. Rec. Nov. 29, 1795

p. 138-139 Feb. 27, 1795 Joseph Warren (Rutherford Co, NC) to Nathaniel Parris (Spartanburgh); for 75£ sterling sold 300 ac on both sides Horse Cr of Broad R; border: North Carolina state line; grant Jan. 1, 1787 States Office to Joseph Warren. Witness Drury Scruggs, Andrew Rea, and James Saunders. Signed Joseph Warren. Wit. oath Apr. 13, 1795 Andrew Rea to I Harrison. Rec. Nov. 29, 1795

p. 139-141 Feb. 12, 1794 Dennis Lindsay (Spartanburgh) to Richard Harris (same); a bond of 50£ sterling; Condition: bond void if Dennis deeds Richard before Aug. 10, 1794 124 ac; half of 248 ac grant to Dennis on branches of Jammy's Cr and Ferguson's Cr called Lockhart's land. Witness David Bruton and Ephraim Parmely. Signed Daniel Lindsey. Wit. oath Apr. 13, 1795 David Bruton to George Bruton. Rec. Nov. 29, 1795

p. 141-143 Feb. 11, 1795 John Brooks (Spartanburgh) to James Sutton (same); for 90£ sold 191 ac on S fork of N fork Tygar R; grant May 1, 1786 Gov. William Moultrie to John Brooks. Witness Hance Harper, jr, Eliz Oliver, and James Amos. Signed John and Liliam Brooks' marks. Wit. oath Apr. 22, 1795 Hance Harper, jr to James Jordan. Rec. Nov. 29, 1795

p. 143-145 Aug. 30, 1791 Jesse Tate (Spartanburgh) to Joseph Champion (same); for 100£ SC money sold 302 ac on S side Broad R and on Sarat's Cr; border: grant State Office to Thomas Wilson; granted in 1787 South Carolina office to Jesse Tate. Witness Charles Hester and Ezekiel Standly. Signed Jesse Tate's mark. Wit. oath Mar. 18, 1796 Charles Hester to H McCray. Rec. Apr. 25, 1796

p. 145-146 Feb. 13, 1796 Joseph Champion (Spartanburgh) to Jesse Davidson (same); for 5£ sterling sold 12 ac where Jesse lives and laid off conditionally. Witness John Turner to Sion Cooper. Signed Joseph Champion's mark. Wit. oath Mar. 18, 1796 John Turner to H McCray. Rec. Apr. 25, 1796

p. 146-150 Dec. 10, 1795 Robert Waring (Columbia, SC) to Jesse Davidson (Seratt Cr); for 14s 4p sterling sold 111 ac on Seratt's Cr; border: N-Joseph Champion; land is part of survey by Daniel McClarin and "relapsed" by Robert Waring. Witness John Turner and John Brown. Signed Robt H Waring. Wit. oath Mar. 18, 1796 John Turner to H McCray. Rec. Apr. 25, 1796

p. 150-151 Feb. 24, 1795 John Shands (Spartanburgh) to son Willis Shands (same); for love and affection give 118 ac on Tygar R where John lives; border: road from Grant's ford on Tyger R to Joel Smith's. Witness Augustine Bumpas, Joel Smith, and Bazzel Compton. Signed John Shands. Wit. oath Feb. 24, 1795 Joel Smith to Wm Smith. Rec. Apr. 26, 1795

p. 151-152 Aug. 13, 1794 William Garrett, sr (Spartanburgh) to Laurence Bankson (same); for 112£ SC money sold 150 ac on S side Pacolate R; border: Charleston old road; grant Aug. 20, 1784 State Office to William Garrett. Witness S Bethel, John Barkson, and John Mitchell. Signed William and Sarah Garrett's marks. Certified Sept. 23, 1794 by S Bethel. Rec. Apr. 26, 1796

p. 152-154 Feb. 9, 1795 Brittain Williford (Spartanburgh) to Samuel Lancaster (same); for 10£ sterling sold 162 ac in Union Co on Bogan's Br of Sugar Cr; border: Samuel Lancaster. Witness William Williford, Larkin Lancaster, and Levi Lancaster. Signed Brittain Williford. Wit. oath May 7, 1795 William Williford to Wm Smith. Rec. Apr. 26, 1796

p. 154-156 Feb. 9, 1795 Brittain Williford (Spartanburgh) to Samuel Lancaster (same); for 10£ sterling sold 142 ac on N side Dutchman's Cr of Tygar R; border: Thomas Spann and Samuel Lancaster. Witness Willis Williford, Larkin Lancaster, and Levi Lancaster. Signed Brittain Williford. Wit. oath May 7, 1795 William Williford to Wm Smith. Rec. Apr. 26, 1796

p. 156-158 Sept. 17, 1794 Mary Sadler (Pa) to Thomas Collins; for 45£ sterling sold 100 ac on N fork Tygar R; border: Samuel Nesbitt, Daniel Brice, and Alexr McCarter; granted from King George III. Witness Wm Austin and Agness Collins. Signed Mary Sadler's mark. Wit. oath Jan. 12, 1795 Wm Austin to Thomas Moore. Rec. Apr. 26, 1796

p. 158-159 Dec. 15, 1794 Henry Walker (Green Co, Ga) to William T Thomason (Spartanburgh); for 55£ sold 150 ac between Lawson's fork and Pacolate R; border: Thomas Wells. Witness Bazel

Lee and I Harrison JP. Signed Henry Walker. Certified Dec. 15, 1794 by I Harrison. Rec. Apr. 26, 1796

p. 159-161 Oct. 10, 1794 William Gee (Luenburgh Co, Va) to William Foster (Spartanburgh); for a "valuable consideration" sold 200 ac on Standing Springs Stone (sic) of Lawson's fork; border: McMurdy; grant to William Dickson; also Drury McDonald (Spartanburgh) given power of attorney to execute this deed. Witness Wm Benson and Richard Pace. Signed Wm Gee. Wit. oath (date not given) Richard Pace to Thos Moore. Rec. Apr. 26, 1796

p. 161-162 Sept. 8, 1796 John White, Reubin White, Francis White, Richard James, Thomas James, John Mapp, and Ann Cook, for her son Henry White (children and representatives of children of Henry White, esq, desc, late of Spartanburgh Co) to brother Daniel White; power of attorney to call Henry White's administrator to account for final settlement to Henry White's estate. Witness James Smith and M Lovina Smith. Signed Reubin and John White, Richard and Thomas James, Francis White, John Mapp, and Ann Cook. Wit. oath Nov. 21, 1796 James Smith to Isham Foster. Rec. Nov. 21, 1796

p. 162-165 Nov. 21, 1796 Daniel White (Spartanburgh) for John White, Reubin White, John Mapp, Richard James, Thomas James, and Francis White (by power of attorney of Sept. 8, 1796) to settle with Mrs. Ann Cook, administrix for Henry White, esq, desc and to finish administration of estate quit claims obligations including a bond given by Ann Cook (then Ann White), James Smith, James Lusk, John Mapp, and Wifford Junior for administration of said estate; Daniel White now takes the books of the estate after above quit claim. Witness James Smith, M Lovina Smith, and Letice Smith. Signed Daniel White, Reubin White, John White, Richard James, Thomas James, Frances White, and John Mapp. Wit. oath Nov. 21, 1796 James Smith to Isham Foster. Rec. Nov. 21, 1796

p. 165 Dec. 3, 1796 John D Young to Ism Foster JP; John says the following is his brand; a hold and cross in left ear and a cross and slit in right ear; horses branded "DY". Signed John D Young

p. 165-168 Jan. 15, 1793 Joel Hembree and wife Hannah (Spartanburgh) to William Rumpley (same); for 80£ SC money sold 104 ac on both sides Cane Cr; border: Joel Hembree, John Butter (or Butler), James Hewett, and Joshua Smith; part of 815 ac grant May 2, 1791 Gov. Charles Pinckney to Joel Hembree. Witness Walter Barrell and Andrew Thomson. Signed Joel Hembree and Hannah's mark. Wit. oath Jul. 20, 1793 Walter Barrel to Samuel Lancaster. Rec. Apr. 26, 1796

p. 168-169 Jan. 8, 1795 John Hightower (Spartanburgh) to William Cockrell (same); for 60£ SC money sold 80 ac on Lasson's fork of Pacolate R; border: Henry Childs; grant Jan. 1, 1785 State Office to John Burnett. Witness John Underwood, Aaron Youngblood, and Anderson Cockell. Signed John Hightower and Christian's mark. Certified Jan. 13, 1794 by S Bethel. Rec. Apr. 26, 1796

p. 169-171 Sept. 7, 1794 Jesse Laxon (Spartanburgh) to Ephraim Elder (same); for 20£ sterling sold 100 ac on S side Pacolate R; border: Jesse Turner and John Cobb. Witness William Shed and Elizabeth Shed. Signed Jesse Laxon. Wit. oath Sept. 17, 1794 William Shed to S Bethel. Rec. Apr. 26, 1796

p. 171-172 Jan. 12, 1795 Zachariah Robertson (or Robinson) (Spartanburgh) to Bazel Lee (same); for 50£ sold 100 ac on S side Lawson's fork. Witness I Harrison, Signed Zachariah Robertson's mark. Certified Jan. 12, 1795 by I Harrison. Rec. Apr. 26, 1796

p. 172-174 Nov. 19, 1794 Thomas Scurry (Edgefield Co) to William Farrow (Spartanburgh); for 100£ sterling sold 100 ac on Cedar Shoals Cr of Enoree R; border: N-Cedar Shoals Cr, W-Samuel Farrow, S-a waggon road to "heads" ford on Enoree R, and E-Isaac Linch (or Linak); part of 450 ac grant to Robert Howard and known as land where William Stewart lives. Witness Joseph Herndon and William Berry. Signed William Scurry. Wit. oath Jan. 15, 1795 Joseph Herndon to Thomas Farrow. Rec. Apr. 26, 1796

p. 174-181 Oct. 21, 1790 Francis Adams, esq (York Co) to William Bostick (same); for 300£ 10s SC money sold 600 ac on Cherokee Cr about 2 miles from Cherokee fork of Broad R; includes a shoal on lower end and the forks of the creek at the upper end and Joseph Clement's improvements about the middle of the place; grant Apr. 21, 1764 to Thomas Henry. Witness John McCaw, Floyd Bostick, and Wm McCaw. Signed Fras Adams. Wit. oath (York Co) John McCaw to Peter Quin

p. 181-183 Jan. 13, 1797 William Bostick (Spartanburgh) to Nathaniel Robertson (same); for $600 sold 600 ac on Cherokee Cr of Broad R including a shoal on lower end, William Bostick's improvements and where William lives; grant Apr. 21, 1764 to Thomas Henry who sold to Joseph Henry who sold to Francis Adams who sold to William Bostick; William excepts from warrant of this sale 40-50 ac that is part of older grant to Matthew Caldwell and Curtiss Caldwell. Witness John Arendel, Peter Quin, and Dennis Sullivan. Signed William Bostick and Ann's mark. Wit. oath Jan. 19, 1797 John Arendel to H McCray. Rec. Jan. 21, 1797

p. 183 Jan. 10, 1795 Priscilla Underwood (Spartanburgh) to son Willis Underwood; for love and affection give Negro girl Sarah, 2 cows, and a "mare colt"; note: Jan. 10, 1795 Thomas Underwood now has the 2 cows and "mare colt" valued at 6£ 6s which he is obliged to pay Willis when Willis becomes 21. Witness John Underwood and Enoch Jones Underwood. Signed Priscilla Underwood's mark. Wit. oath Jan. 13, 1795 John Underwood to I Harrison. Rec. Apr. 26, 1796

p. 183-184 Apr. 18, 1794 John Hunt and wife Martha (Greenville Co) to William Smith (Spartanburgh); for 100£ sterling sold 200 ac on S side Tyger R and on branch of Jamie's Cr; border: W-Jonathan Linard and others vacant; grant Oct. 2, 1786 Gov. William Moultrie to John Hunt. Witness Samuel Townsen and Jonathan Linard. Signed John and Martha Hunt. Wit. oath Jan. 3, 1795 Jonathan Linard to Thomas Farrow. Rec. Apr. 26, 1796

p. 184-185 Nov. 19, 1794 Thomas Scurry (Edgefield Co) to William Farrow (Spartanburgh); for 100£ sterling sold 100 ac on Cedar Shoal Cr of Enoree R; border: N-Cedar Shoal Cr, W-Samuel Farrow, S-a waggon road from Head's ford on Enoree R, and E-Isaac Linch; part of 450 ac grant to Robert Howard (or Haward); known "by the land" where William Stewart lives. Witness Joseph Herndon and William Berry. Signed Thomas Scurry. Wit. oath Jan. 5, 1795 Joseph Herndon to Thomas Farrow. Rec. Apr. 26, 1796

p. 185-187 Nov. 24, 1794 Alexander Keenum and wife Jenny (Spartanburgh) to John Nicholas Cruse (same); for 38£ sterling sold 53 ac on E side of branch of Richland Cr; part of grant to Thomas Hathoway. Witness Geo Rowland, Edmund Fowler, and Henry Woody. Signed Alexander Keenum and Jenny's mark. Wit. oath Jan. 13, 1794 John Woody (sic) to Ism Foster. Rec. Apr. 27, 1796

p. 187-188 Sept. 7, 1795 David Allen (Spartanburgh) to David Allen, jr (same); for 100£ sterling sold 300 ac on N side Goocher's Cr. Witness John Lipscomb and Englis King. Signed David Allen's mark. Wit. oath Sept. 14, 1795 Englis King to William Lancaster.

Rec. Apr. 27, 1796

p. 188-189 Oct. 20, 1793 Alexander Brown (Chester Co) to Jason Moore (Spartanburgh); for 12£ SC money sold 100 ac on small branch of Ward's Cr of Tyger R; border: W-Andrew Cowen and others vacant; grant Aug. 19, 1774 Lt. Gov. William Bull to (not given) in Craven Co. Witness James Paden and Samuel Brown. Signed Alexander Brown. Wit. oath Oct. 30, 1793 Samuel Brown to Thos Moore. Rec. Apr. 27, 1796

p. 189-191 Aug. 13, 1790 William Paden, yoeman, and wife Mary (Chester Co) to Jason Moore, yoeman (Spartanburgh); for 20£ SC money sold 100 ac on Ward's Br; border: all vacant; grant May 4, 1775 Lt. Gov. William Bull to (not given). Witness Robert Morrow, William Essler, and Thomas Essler. Signed William Paden and Mary's mark. Wit. oath (Union Co) Aug. 14, 1790 Robert Morrow to Thomas Brandon. Rec. Apr. 27, 1796

p. 191-192 Jul. 23, 1790 Alexander Paden and wife Rebekah (Greenville Co) to Jason Moore (Spartanburgh); for 30£ SC money sold 100 ac on Ward's Br of Tyger R; border: E-Currie and others vacant; grant Mar. 17, 1775 Lt. Gov. William Bull to (not given). Witness Robert Morrow, Samuel Brown, and James Morton (Jason Moore marked out). Signed Alexander Paden and Rebekah's mark. Wit. oath Aug. 5, 1790 Robert Morrow to Andrew Barry. Rec. Apr. 28, 1796

p. 192-194 Apr. 10, 1795 Elijah Kelly and wife Margaret (Spartanburgh) to Robert Beard (same); for 15£ sterling sold 50 ac; border: Benjamin Hooker and a waggon road; part of 250 ac grant Sept. 14, 1784 Gov. William Moultrie to Jonathan Linard on S side Tyger R. Witness Thomas Young and Jesse Spann. Signed Elijah Kelly and Margaret's mark. Wit. oath Apr. 13, 1795 Thomas Young to George Bruton. Rec. Apr. 28, 1796

p. 194-196 Apr. 4, 1795 William Young and wife Patience (Laurence Co) to Thomas Young (Spartanburgh); for 50£ sterling sold 100 ac on Jamie's Cr of Tyger R; border: E-Wm Young, sr, W-George Crawford, and others vacant; grant Feb. 17, 1767 to William Young. Witness Thomas Harris, Joseph Harris, and Robert Beard. Signed William and Patience Young's marks. Wit. oath Apr. 13, 1795 Robert Beard to George Bruton. Rec. Apr. 28, 1796

p. 196-197 Jan. 20, 1791 Zachariah Sparks (Spartanburgh) to David Millhanks (same); for 40£ SC money sold 100 ac on Harasan's Cr; border: a waggon road and Robertson. Witness Ellis Cannon and Reubin Lawson. Signed Zachariah Sparks' mark. Wit. oath Oct. 13, 1794 Ellis Cannon to S Bethel. Rec. Apr. 28, 1796

p. 197-198 Aug. 18, 1795 Richard Hampton (Edgefield Co) to Zacharias Gibbs (Spartanburgh); for 50£ sterling sold 400 ac on Ward's Cr of Tyger and waters of Fairforrest Cr; called Cool Springs tract; grant Gov. Josiah Martin (NC) to Richard Hampton; border: 500 ac sold by Richard to Edward Michison. Witness Jesse Connell, John Gibbs, and Francis Connell. Signed Richd Hampton. Wit. oath Apr. 12, 1796 Jesse Connell to I Harrison. Rec. Apr. 12, 1796

p. 198-200 Feb. 12, 1795 Jesse Christian and wife Rachel to Buckner Smith; for 50£ sterling sold 126 ac; border: William Farmer; part of 2 tracts (1) 150 ac grant Apr. 27, 1767 Gov. William Tryon (NC) to Moses Wylie and (s) 120 ac grant Mar. 6, 1786 Gov. William Moultrie to David Pruet; both on N side Tyger R and on Dutchman's Cr. Witness Robert Young, Thos Evatt, and Nancy Smith. Signed Jesse and Rachel Christian's marks. Wit. oath Apr.

11, 1795 Thos Evatt to Saml Lancaster. Rec. Apr. 29, 1796

p. 200-201 Feb. 7, 1795 Lucy Hearne (Spartanburgh) to Joseph Price (same); for 18£ sterling sold 120 ac on branch of Thickety Cr; border: Hopkins and vacant; grant in Jan. 1786 Gov. William Moultrie to Daniel Gilbert. Witness Matthew Gutery, Shadrach Gutery, and John Proctor. Signed Lucy Hearne's mark. Wit. oath Feb. 7, 1795 Matthew Gutery to H McCray. Rec. Apr. 29, 1796

p. 201-202 Jan. 20, 1795 Thomas Bennett to Ezekiel Young; for 5s sterling sold 43 ac on Richland Cr of S Pacolet R; border: Andrews, Daniel White, John Young, sr, and Benjamin Clerk; grant Oct. 3, 1791 Gov. Charles Pinckney to Thomas Bennett. Witness Dan Bennett and Wm Bennett. Signed Thomas Bennett. Wit. oath Apr. 14, 1795 Wm Bennett to W Lancaster. Rec. Apr. 30, 1796

p. 202-203 Nov. 5, 1793 Thomas Williamson and wife Anne (Spartanburgh) to William Wells (same); for 50£ sterling sold 107 ac; border: E-Poole, S-Harrison, W-William Wells, N-vacant. Witness Thomas McKnight, John Lancaster, Moses Shield, and Henry Wells. Signed Thomas and Anne Williamson. Wit. oath Apr. 14, 1795 John Lancaster and Henry Wells to I Harrison. Rec. Apr. 30, 1796

p. 203-204 Nov. 5, 1793 Thomas Williamson and wife Anne (Spartanburgh) to William Wells (same); for 240£ sold 440 ac on Fairforrest Cr where William Wells lives; border: S-William Woods and others vacant. Witness Thomas McKnight, John Lancaster, Moses White, and Henry Wells. Signed Thomas and Anne Williamson. Wit. oath Apr. 14, 1795 John Lancaster to Henry Wells to I Harrison. Rec. Apr. 30, 1796

p. 204-206 Jan. 5, 1789 Gov. Thomas Pinckney to Thomas Hayes; for 4£ 8p sterling to treasurer of SC granted 174 ac on branches of Peter's Cr of Pacolet R; border: N-James Stedman, and S & SE-William Poole and Wm Wofford; survey Oct. 21, 1788 for Thomas Hayes; plat attached certified by F (or P) Bremar, surv. Gen; on Jun. 12, 1789 Thomas Hayes assigned his rights to this grant to Robert Armour. Witness R Harrison and Diskin Grant. Signed Thos Pinckney. Wit. oath Jun. 13, 1794 Diskin Grant to I Harrison. Rec. Apr. 30, 1796

p. 206-207 Oct. 17, 1796 John Ford (Shelby Co, Ky) to son Jesse Ford (same); power of attorney to sell 150 ac on Tyger R; border: E-Tyger R, N-Richd Barry, S & SW-John Ford and John Posey; and sell 420 ac; border: E-Richd Barry, W-land granted to James Miller, and S-Jno Posey; both tracts granted to John Ford. Signed John Ford. Wit. oath (Shelby Co, Ky) Oct. 18, 1796 John Ford to William Butler and William Johnson. Certified Oct. 18, 1796 (Shelby Co, Ky) that William Butler and William Johnson are justices of peace for Shelby Co, Ky signed by James Craig. Certified Oct. 18, 1796 (Shelby Co, Ky) that James Craig is Clerk of Court signed by Abraham Owen, first Justice of Commission of Pease. Rec. Feb. 15, 1797

p. 207-208 Feb. 11, 1797 Wells Griffith and wife Elizabeth (Spartanburgh) to Justice Reynolds (same); for 200£ sterling sold 200 ac on both sides Lawson's fork of Pacolet R including a mill seat; grant North Carolina to James Hammett who sold to Wm Wofford who sold to Wells Griffith; and sold a second tract "quantity not assertained"; part of 187 ac grant to Wells Griffith on N side Lawson's fork. Witness Wm Foster, Wm Wells, and Zachariah Robinson. Signed Wells Griffith and Elizabeth. Wit. oath Feb. 14, 1797 Wm

Wells to I Harrison. Rec. Feb. 20, 1797. Dower renounced Elizabeth Griffith to I Harrison Feb. 16, 1797

p. 208-210 Feb. 22, 1797 Patrick Hinds to Joseph Woodruff (Spartanburgh); for 200£ sterling sold 600 ac on N side Enoree R; border: NE-John Woods, SW-Wm Sims, NW-"land claimed", and SE-Enoree R; grant Jul. 26, 1774 Lt. Gov. William Bull. Witness David Bruton and John Woodruff. Signed Pat Hinds. Wit. oath Mar. 4, 1797 David Bruton to George Brewton. Rec. Mar. 4, 1797

p. 210-211 Jul. 14, 1795 Robert Piper (Spartanburgh) to John Bolin (same); for 20£ sterling sold a gray mare and her increase, a white cow and calf and 3 yearlings and their increase, 3 sows and 11 shoats and their increase, 2 beds and furniture, a pot and oven and puter chest, table chairs, knives, forks, water vessels, a plow, how, ax, corn and meat and crop that is growing; Condition: sale void if Robert Piper pays John Bolin 40£ sterling by Dec. 25, 1797. Witness John Autry and Deskin Grant. Signed Robert Piper. Wit. oath Jul. 18, 1795 John Autry to I Harrison. Rec. Apr. 30, 1796

p. 211-214 Mar. 17, 1794 Owen Forester and wife Eleanor (Spartanburgh) to Samuel Hindman Taylor (same); for 30£ sterling sold 44 ac on N side Tyger R; part of 174 ac grant Feb. 5, 1778 Gov. William Moultrie to Owen Forester with survey signed by J Bremar; border: Samuel Cathcart, Joel Henbree, and David Grimes. Witness Charles Maybery and William Hindman. Signed Owen and Eleanor Foster's marks. Wit. oath Jul. 22, 1794 William Hindman to Samuel Lancaster. Rec. Apr. 30, 1796

p. 214-216 Sept. 23, 1795 James Wyatt (Spartanburgh) to Job Sosbree (same); for 100£ sold 200 ac on both sides Peter's Cr; border: all vacant; grant Aug. 13, 1784 Gov. Benjamin Guerard to James Wyatt. Witness Wells Griffith, William Bagwell, and Littleton Bagwell. Signed James Wyatt and Mary's mark. Wit. oath Feb. 13, 1796 Wells Griffith to Isham Foster. Rec. Apr. 30, 1796

p. 216-217 Mar. 7, 1795 Robert Lee (Spartanburgh) to Aaron Templeman (same); for 20£ sterling sold 306 ac; border: near where "main road" fords Cherokee Cr; E part of 2,100 ac grant Apr. 2, 1787 to James Stedman on both sides Cherokee Cr. Witness Richard Lee, Anne Lee, and Martha Reson. Signed Robert Lee. Wit. oath Jun. 1, 1795 Richard Lee to James Turner. Rec. Apr. 30, 1796

p. 217-219 Oct. 8, 1796 James Wofford (Spartanburgh) to David Moore (same); for 10£ sterling sold 200 ac on both sides Ferguson's Cr of Tyger R where Aaron Arnold formerly lived; border: Nimrod House, James Wofford, and John Paden. Witness William Rhodes and Christopher Rhodes. Signed James Wofford. Wit. oath Oct. 19, 1796 Christopher Rodes to Thomas Farrow. Rec. Mar. 11, 1797

p. 219-221 Dec. 29, 1794 James Amos (Spartanburgh) to Job Loftis (same); for 20£ sterling sold 94 ac on S fork of N fork Tyger R and East of ancient boundary; border: all vacant; grant May 7, 1787 Gov. Thomas Pinckney to James Amos. Witness James Powell and Charles Amos. Signed James Amos. Wit. oath Feb. 21, 1794 James Amos to Isham Foster. Rec. Apr. 30, 1796

p. 221-223 May 21, 1795 Daniel White (Spartanburgh) to John Nicholas Cruse (same); for 40£ sterling sold 137 ac on head branches of Rich Run of S Pacolate R; border: E-Robert Kimboll and Abraham Andrews, NW-Daniel White and Henry Wooddy, SW-Thomas Hatherway, and S-Leonard Carden; grant May 5, 1794 Gov. William Moultrie to Daniel White. Witness James White and Samuel Woody. Signed Daniel and Susannah White's marks. Wit. oath Aug. 18, 1795 Samuel Woody to

Ism Foster. Rec. May 1, 1796

p. 223-225 Mar. 1, 1795 Rev. Austin Clayton (Spartanburgh) to Thomas Price (same); for 20£ sterling sold 400 ac on Middle Tyger R; part of 872 ac grant Jul. 1, 1793 Gov. William Moultrie to Austin Clayton in Greenville Co and border: Forkenberry, Elisha Thomson, and Bever Davis; 400 ac borders: John Foster and Nicholas Jasper. Witness John Wright, Charles Burton, and Andrew Thomson. Signed Austin Clayton. Wit. oath Apr. 24, 1795 Andrew Tnomson to Thomas Moore. Rec. Mayl, 1796

p. 225-227 Feb. 23, 1795 Anthony Wilson and wife Jean (Spartanburgh) to Thomas Price (same); for 50£ sterling sold 100 ac on Jamie's Cr of Tygar R; grant Aug. 11, 1774 Gov. William Bull to Johnn Dunkins in Craven Co who sold Jan. 19 & 20, 1787 to William Caldwell who sold Nov. 16 & 17, 1790 to Marth McCrorey who bequeathed by will Oct. 2, 1793 to Anthony Wilson. Witness Nicholas Keating and Andrew Thomson. Signed Anthony Wilson and Jean's mark. Wit. oath Apr. 24, 1795 Andrew Thomson to Thos Moore. Rec. May 1, 1796

p. 227-229 Dec. 13, 1793 John Hewie (Iredale Co, NC) to George McWilliams; for 4£ 7s sold 150 ac on N Pacolet R; border: S-Joseph French, SE & E-Zacharias Bullock, and others vacant; grant Sept. 13, 1774 Lt. Gov. William Bull to John Hewie. Witness Wm McWilliams, John Huey, and Nancy Huey. Signed John Hewie. Wit. oath Jun. 14, 1795 Wm McWilliams to Isham Foster. Rec. May 1, 1796

p. 229-230 Jul. 12, 1793 John Forrister and wife Hannah (Spartanburgh) to Millenton Smith (same); for 30£ sterling sold 224 ac on Tygar R; border: John Walker, Samuel Cathcart, and Toney's line to Negro Branch; grant Feb. 5, 1787 to John Campbell. Witness James Hewet and Thos Crow. Signed John and Hannah Forrister's marks. Wit. oath Jun. 10, 1794 James Hewet to Wm Smith. Rec. May 1, 1796

p. 230-231 Mar. 5, 1796 William Sturges (Charleston, SC), attorney for Francis Lee (same), to Smith Lipscomb (Spartanburgh); for 50£ sold 400 ac on Blue Br of Thickety Cr; grant in May 1774 to Daniel Buckoneyer. Witness Gideon Gibson and Wm Gibson. Signed Wm Sturges, atty for Francis Lee. Wit. oath Jul. 18, 1796 Gideon Gibson to John Lipscomb. Rec. Aug. 12, 1796

p. 231-233 Feb. 14, 1795 Joseph Morris (Spartanburgh) to John Jordan (same); for 40£ sterling sold 100 ac on Buck Cr; grant (date not given) States Office to Robert Neilson. Witness S Bethel and Hezekiah Garrett. Signed Joseph Morris' mark. Certified Feb. 4, 1795 S Bethel. Rec. May 1, 1796

p. 233-234 Feb. 6, 1792 John Cannon and wife Rebekah (Spartanburgh) to Thomas Springfield (Laurens Co); for 100£ sterling sold 100 ac on N side Enoree R of Broad R; where John Cannon lives; part of grant to William Cox who sold 100 ac to John Brigs who sold to his brother Thomas Briggs who sold to Thomas Tod who sold to Edward Musgrove "a party to these 'resents" (sic). Witness Solomon Langston and Ephraim Christorfer. Signed John Cannon and Rebekah's mark. Wit. oath (Laurens Co) Dec. 24, 1793 Solomon Longston to Roger Brown. Rec. May 1, 1796

p. 234-236 Apr. 4, 1796 Jesse Connell (Spartanburgh) to Jesse Hammett (same); for 14£ sold 291 ac; border: Thomas Cook, Calvert, Daniel Finch, and near Thomas Vaugh's line; grant Jul. 1, 1793. Witness Wm Ford and A Lancaster. Signed Jesse Connell. Wit. oath Apr. 11, 1796 Wm Ford to I Harrison. Rec. May 1, 1796. Dower renounced Ann Connell to James Jordan Apr. 11, 1796

p. 236-238 May 8, 1794 Jesse Tate, jr (Spartanburgh) to Charles Hester (same); for 150£ SC money sold 250 ac on Cherokee Cr and on S side Broad R; includes a mill and improvements known as Wm Tate's mill and now in possession of Charles Hester; border: S-Alexander Martin, esq (where Joseph Dills now lives) and SE-John Fondred; grant Apr. 21, 1775 to William McKowen who sold to William Tate, desc and to his son Jesse Tate by a will. Witness Jas Laurence, George Taylor, and Joseph Dill. Signed Jesse Tate. Wit. oath Jun. 12, 1795 George Talyor to H McCray. Rec. May 1, 1796

p. 238-242 Jul. 8, 1789 Delany Carroll (SC) to Rezine Holland (96 Dist); for 100£ 50s SC money sold 181 ac on S side Tygar R; border: NE-Joseph Wofford, SW-John Langston, and others vacant; grant Feb. 5, 1788 South Carolina to Delany Carroll. Witness Joseph Wofford and Abraham Campbell. Signed Delany Carroll's mark. Wit. oath Jul. 13, 1789 Joseph Wofford to Saml Lancaster. Rec. May 2, 1796

p. 242-243 Feb. 7, 1794 James Martin, esq (York Co) to John Ross (Spartanburgh); for 10£ SC money sold 118 ac on a ridge between Cherokee and Saratt's Creeks on Gutry's waggon road. Witness Charles Hester and Newman Wilson. Signed James Martin. Wit. oath Jun. 12, 1795 Charles Hester to H McCray. Rec. May 2, 1796

p. 243-245 Nov. 13, 1794 Joel Hembree and wife Hannah (Spartan Co) to James Burns and Solomon Hill (same); for 30£ sold the Brigwood Iron Works and 60 ac on N side Tyger R including four small islands in the river; border: John Vise. Witness Stanly Fewell, James Hewett, and George Galbraith. Signed Joel Hembree and Hannah's marks. Wit. oath Jun. 15, 1795 James Hewett to B. D. Shumate. Rec. May 2, 1796

p. 245-246 Dec. 13, 1796 James Bitterton (Spartanburgh) to Mary Bryant and Sarah Bitterton (same); for 50£ sterling sold 150 ac in Greenville Co on branch of Guilder's Cr of Enoree R. Witness John Grist and Daniel Grant. Signed James Bitterton's mark. Wit. oath Apr. 20, 1797 Daniel Grant to Wm Smith. Rec. Apr. 24, 1797

p. 246-247 Dec. 13, 1796 James Bitterton (Spartanburgh) to Mary Bryant and Sarah Bitterton (same); for 50£ sterling sold 125 ac on Dutchamn's Cr; border: Joshua Bitterton, James Bitton, and Samuel Prewit; part of 350 ac grant to Thomas Bitterton, desc. Witness John Grist and Daniel Grant. Signed James Bitterton's mark. Wit. oath Apr. 20, 1797 Daniel Grant to Wm Smith. Rec. Apr. 24, 1797

p. 247-248 Union Court House Dec. 18, 1795 John Watson, jr to Alexander Macbeth and Co; John promises to pay 15£ 3s 6p sterling which is balance due on settlement of his account to date; to secure this debt, John bonds 93½ ac on Thickety Cr which John received from his father, John Watson, sr, Nov. 17, 1794 and recorded in Spartanburgh Mar. 25, 1795. Witness Ben Haile. Signed John Watson. Wit. oath (Union Co) Apr. 19, 1797 Ben Haile to Thomas Vance. Rec. Apr. 28, 1797

p. 248-251 Sept. 5, 1796 William Beatton, sheriff (Pinckney Dist) to William Lipscomb (Spartanburgh); for 55£ sold 300 ac; Vardry McBee (late of Spartanburgh) owned 300 ac on Thickety Cr including a limestone quarry and was in debt to estate of Moses Cherry, desc, and Samuel Talbert, Thos Weir, Elizabeth Weir, executors of Moses Cherry; case heard in Common Pleas Court April 1796 with judgment that Vardry McBee owes 88£ 2p 1 fathing sterling and court costs; due to writ from court, land sold Dec. 5, 1796 by sheriff. Witness Willis Williford and Alexr McKie. Signed W Bratton. Wit. oath Apr. 16, 1797 Alexr McKie to Ism Foster. Rec.

Apr. 28, 1797

p. 251-252 Mar. 3, 1797 Wilie Williford (Spartanburgh) to Samuel Williams (same); a bond for $2,000; Condition: bond void if Wilie lets Samuel and wife Selan(?) have property given by them to their daughter Betsy, wife of Wilie, by deed of gift in North Carolina; land to be returned for lifetime of Samuel and wife Selan. Witness John Lancaster and Saml Lancaster JP. Signed Wilie Williford. Rec. Mar. 5, 1797

p. 252-253 Feb. 15, 1795 Thomas Burges (Spartanburgh) to Alston Edney (Davidson Co, teretory S of Ohio R); power of attorney to get a title to 640 ac agreeable to a certificate now in "his" possession and make Thomas Huggings a title to 320 ac. Witness I Harrison JP. Signed Thos Burges. Rec. May 9, 1797

p. 253-254 Apr. 2, 1796 William Lancaster (Spartanburgh) to Jesse Connell (same); for 5s sold (1) 291 ac; border: Thomas Cook, Colbert, Daniel Finch, and near Thomas Vaughn; grant Jul. 1, 1793 Gov. William Moultrie to William Lancaster; and (2) 18 ac part of same grant; border: Elizabeth Autry and John Smith. Witness A Lancaster and John Gritman. Signed W Lancaster. Wit. oath (not dated) W Lancaster to I Harrison. Rec. May 3, 1796

p. 254-255 Oct. 16, 1795 Luke Browning (Spartanburgh) to Samuel Donaway, jr (same); for 50£ SC money sold 150 ac on Buck Cr of Pacolate R; grant Jan. 1, 1787 States Office to Richard Saunders. Witness S Bethel, Joseph Morris, and Elijah Thompson. Signed Luke Browning. Certified Oct. 17, 1795 S Bethel. Rec. May 3, 1796

p. 255-256 Dec. 9, 1794 William Wilkins (Spartanburgh) to Joseph Austill (same); for 5£ sterling sold 30 ac on both sides Thickety Cr; border: W-Joseph Austill, N-Lipscomb, and E-Wilkins; part of grant in 1792 Gov. Thomas Pinckney to William Wilkins. Witness D Goudelock, John Headen, and Larkin Bethell. Signed William Wilkins. Wit. oath Mar. 11, 1795 John Headen to H McCray. Rec. May 3, 1796

p. 256-257 Dec. 3, 1796 John Brown (Laurens Co) to Jenny and Nelley Poole, daughters of Abram and Nancy Poole, as a guardance (Spartanburgh); for love and affection give 2 feather beds and furniture, 6 pewter plates, a dish, a bason, 4 cups, a coffee can, a large wheel, a little wheel, a cotton gin, 4 knives and forks, 6 spoons, 2 pales, 2 locks, 2 pots, a dutch oven, a skillet, a wire sifter, a table, chest, churn, Indian basket, a pickleing tub, 2 club axes, a broad ax, 3 augers, 6 chissels, a drawing knife, 4 planes, a side saddle, a loom, harnish and 3 slays, 2 cows and a calf, 8 hogs, and all corn upon the premises and in the present dwelling house of Abram Poole known as Brigg's old place; note: John Brown conveys "only" his right and title to above articles. Witness Richard Fryar and John Farrow. Signed John Brown's mark. Wit. oath May 3, 1797 Richard Fryar to Moses Casey. Rec. May 23, 1797

p. 257-260 May 11, 1795 James Crow (Spartanburgh) to Samuel Crow (same); for 100£ sold 80 ac on branch of Two Mile Cr of Enoree R; SE part of 200 ac grant Sept. 5, 1780 Gov. William Moultrie to James Crow. Witness Aaron Casey, Jas Wofford, and Moses Casey. Signed James Crow. Wit. oath May 24, 1797 Aaron Casey to Moses Casey. Rec. May 27, 1797

p. 260-261 May 11, 1795 James Crow (Pinckney Dist) to Randolph Crow (same); for 5£ sterling sold 120 ac; part of 200 ac grant in 1785 to James Crow; border: John Casey. Witness Aaron

Casey, James Wofford, and Moses Casey. Signed James Crow. Wit. oath May 24, 1797 Aaron Casey to Moses Casey. Rec. May 27, 1797

p. 261-268 Jan. 22, 1787 Vardry McBee (Thickety Cr) to Francis Bremar, esq (Charleston, SC); a bond of 614£ sterling; Condition: Vardry to pay at different periods 307£ sterling and interest; to secure thid debt Vardry sells the following land for 5s SC money (1) 1,740 ac on Miller's fork on N side of Thickety Cr of Broad R; border: S & W-Mapp and Thompson, N & W-Tanner and Middleton, E-vacant; surveyed Dec. 20, 1774 for Vardry McBee; (2) 240 ac on both sides Goucher's Cr of Thickety Cr of Broad R and S of Saluda R (sic); survey for David Allen; (3) 114 ac on Pacolate R; border: vacant; (4) 140 ac on Thickety Cr of Broad R; border: W-John Hogan and others vacant; survey Feb. 8, 1774 for Robert Loony; (5) 240 ac (or 140 ac) in Camden Dist on Certains Cr and on W side Broad R; border: E-Wm Dawbins, S-John Wade, N-Wm Dawbins, and W-vacant; survey Jan. 10, 1785 for Vardry McBee; all land granted Sept. 18, 1785 Gov. William Moultrie to Vardry McBee; above bond void if Vardry pays the debt. Witness Alexander Petrie and Peter Bremar. Signed Vardry McBee. Wit. oath (Charleston Dist) Feb. 9, 1787 Peter Bremar to D Mazyck. Rec. Jun. 3, 1797

p. 268-271 May 2, 1795 Jason Moore (Spartanburgh) to son James Moore (same); for 25£ sterling sold 263 ac in two parts on Wards Cr of Tygar R; (1) 163 ac border: N-Thomas Moore, W-William Ford, S-Daniel Barnett, and E-Robert Morrow; grant Dec. 3, 1787 Gov. Thomas Pinckney to (not given); and (2) 100 ac on branch of Ward's Cr of Tygar R; border: W-Andrew Cowens and others vacant; grant Aug. 19, 1774 Lt. Gov. William Bull to (not given) and sold Oct. 25, 1793 by Alexr Brown to Jason Moore. Witness John Otts, William Otts, and Samuel Otts. Signed Jason Moore. Wit. oath May 7, 1795 John Otts to Thos Moore. Rec. May 3, 1796

p. 271-273 May 2, 1795 Jason Moore, sr (Spartanburgh) to son Jason Moore, jr (same); for 30£ sterling sold 200 ac in two parts; (1) (ac not given) on Ward's Br of Tygar R; border: E-Currey and others vacant; grant Mar. 17, 1775 Lt. Gov. William Bull to (not given) and sold Jul. 23, 1790 by Alexander Peden and wife Rebekah to Jason Moore, sr; and (2) 100 ac on Ward's Br; border: vacant; grant May 4, 1775 Lt. Gov. William Bull to (not given) and sold Aug. 13, 1790 by William Peden and wife Mary to Jason Moore, sr. Witness John Otts, Wm Otts, and Samuel Otts. Signed Jason Moore. Wit. oath May 7, 1795 John Otts to Thos Moore. Rec. May 3, 1796

p. 273-275 May 2, 1795 Jason Moore (Spartanburgh) to James Moore and Jason Moore, jr (same); for 40£ sell all goods: 5 horses: a gray, a bay horse, 2 bay mares, and a rone mare all branded "‡M", 29 cattle marked with cross in left ear and half cross in right ear, 20 hogs, 5 sheep, 11 goats all marked with cross in left ear and half cross in right ear, a still and all her vessels and implements, 2 weaver's looms with all their tackling and harness, a waggon with her geers and harness etc, 5 ploughs with their geers and tackling, axes, hoes, etc, and all plantation and mechanical tools, 6 beds with their stands and furniture, all tables chairs, dishes, ovens, pots, etc, and all other household stuff and furniture. Witness John Otts, William Otts, and Samuel Otts. Signed Jason Moore. Wit. oath May 7, 1795 John Otts to Thos Moore. Rec. May 4, 1796

p. 275-276 Jul. 26, 1794 John Davis (Spartanburgh) to Richard Cantrell (same); for 21£ SC money sold 200 ac on little Buck Cr of Pacolate R; border: Wade; grant Jun. 4, 1787 States Office to John Jones. Witness S Bethel, Moses Procter, and John Mason. Signed John Davis. Certified Jul. 26, 1794 by S Bethel.

Rec. May 4, 1796

p. 276-278 Jan. 14, 1793 Jan. 14, 1793 John McElhany (Spartanburgh) to Absalom Stokes (same); for 100£ sterling sold 200 ac on both sides Brown's Br of N fork Tyger R; border: John Prince; grant May 4, 1769 Gov. William Tryon (NC) to (not given). Witness John Vaughn, Thos Moore, and D Goodlett. Signed John McElhenny. Wit. oath Aug. 17, 1795 Thos Moore to I Harrison. Rec. May 5, 1796

p. 278-279 Aug. 17, 1795 Absalom Stokes (Spartanburgh) to John Chapman (same); for 100£ sterling sold 200 ac on Brown's Br of Timmon's Mill Cr of N Tygar R; border: Robert Goodlett, Knox, and John Prince; grant to John McElhenny who sold to Absalom Stokes. Witness James Jordan, Brittain Williford, and Thos Moore JP. Signed Absalom Stokes. Rec. May 16, 1796

p. 279-280 Aug. 17, 1795 John Wofford (Spartanburgh) to son William Wofford; for love and affection give 101 ac on Sugar Cr. Witness James Jordan JP and James Saunders. Signed John Wofford's mark.

p. 280-281 May 9, 1795 Samuel Elder (Spartanburgh) to James Moore (same); for 10£ SC money sold 50 ac; part of 150 ac on W side of a creek formerly called Ward's Cr; grant Aug. 11, 1774 to Thomas Moore who sold to Samuel Elder. Witness William Otts, Samuel Otts, and Samuel Elder, jr. Signed Samuel Elder's mark. Wit. oath May 26, 1795 Samuel Otts to Thos Moore. Rec. May 7, 1796

p. 281-283 May 14, 1795 David Anderson (Spartanburgh) to John Waldrop (same); for 50£ sterling sold 350 ac on Provis Cr of S Tyger R; where John Waldrop lives; grant May 17, 1787 to David Anderson. Witness John Durham and John Moore. Signed David Anderson. Wit. oath Aug. 18, 1795 David Anderson to Barryman D Shumate. Rec. May 7, 1796

p. 283-285 Apr. 28, 1795 Thomas Betterton and wife Palaiah (Spartanburgh) to James Betterton; for 50£ sterling sold 175 ac; border: S-Joshua Betterton; half of 350 ac grant Apr. 21, 1774 to Thomas Betterton, desc. Witness Thos Tod and James Crowder. Signed Thomas Betterton and Palaiah's mark. Wit. oath May 2, 1795 James Crowder to Wm Smith. Rec. May 7, 1796

p. 285-287 Jun. 9, 1795 James Betterton (Spartanburgh) to Daniel Palmore (or Polmer) (Union Co); for 51£ sterling sold 50 ac on Dutchman's Cr; border: "mouth of first branch above the mill" Witness Ransom King, Thomas Spann, and Buckner Smith. Signed James Betterton. Wit. oath Jun. 10, 1795 Ransom King to Saml Lancaster. Rec. May 8, 1796

p. 287-292 May 8, 1777 James Mayson, esq to James Dyson; for 500£ 10s SC money sold 400 ac in Craven Co on forks of Tyger R; border: N-a fork of Tyger R, Samuel Brize's bounty land and old lines and S-other fork of Tyger R and Randolph Casey; grant Jun. 23, 1774 Lt. Gov. William Bull to James Mayson. Witness John Coury Smith, John Ritchey, and Peter Hubbard. Signed Jas and Henrietta Mayson. Wit. oath (Laurens Co) Mar. 26, 1796 John Ritchey to Zach Bailey. Rec. Feb. 7, 1797

p. 292-293 (not given), 1795 Nathaniel Parris (Spartanburgh) to John Southerlin (same); for 30£ sterling sold 100 ac; part of 300 ac on both sides Horse Cr of Broad R grant Jan. 1, 1787 States Office to Joseph Warren who sold to Nathaniel Parris. Witness James Black and Varison Brammel. Signed Nathaniel Parris' mark. Certified Sept. 17, 1795 S Bethel. Rec. May 8, 1796

p. 293-295 Feb. 10, 1795 Daniel Obar (SC) to William Childress (Spartanburgh); for 20£ sterling sold 200 ac; border: N-Paden and James Wofford; part of 640 ac on branches of Fergerson's Cr of Tyger R granted Nov. 6, 1796 to Daniel Obar. Witness Jeremiah Snow, Mary Bradberry, and Thomas Childress. Signed Daniel Obar. Wit. oath Jun. 5, 1795 Jeremiah Snow to Zadock Ford. Rec. May 8, 1796

p. 295-297 Oct. 14, 1785 Benjamin Brown, heir of Bartlet Brown, desc (Burke Co, Ga) to John Lindsey (Laurens Co); for 30£ sterling sold 100 ac where Mary Hanna resides on N side of Enoree R formerly King's R; border: Pennington; part of 600 ac grant May 11, 1753 Gov. William Rowan (NC) to Bartlett Brown. Witness Andw Cunningham, Abraham Gray, and Henry Hamilton. Signed Benjamin Brown. Wit. oath Jul. 31, 1789 Henry Hamilton to Thomas Farrow. Rec. May 8, 1796

p. 297-298 Aug. 19, 1786 William Rickman (Spartanburgh) to Capt. Vardry McBee; William given limestone and wood to be burned on 392 ac which Vardry sold to William except for the limestone and wood; 100£ sterling penality if agreement is broken. Witness Thomas Cole and John Martin. Signed William Rickman. Wit. oath Apr. 20, 1796 Thomas Cole to H McCray. Rec. May 8, 1796

p. 298-299 Sept. 26, 1793 John Hunter, esq (Laurens Co) to Peneywell Wood (Spartanburgh); a bond of 400£ sterling: Condition: bond void if John gives Peneywell title "to an estate of inheritance" of 1,340 ac on Rockey field Cr of Enoree R; border: old Indian boundary line; N half of 2,600 ac (sic) grant to William (blank) who sold to John Rutledge, jr, Frederick Cloerhs(?), and William Rutledge and divided by John Brockman, Henry Wood, William Willson, John Redman, and Henry Brockman; titles to be made when the first instalment or part if paid and "then in complyance with this condition the above obilgation is to be void". Witness Henry Wood and William Willson. Signed John Hunter, attorney for John Rutledge, jr. Wit. oath Apr. 10, 1797 Henry Wood to W Lancaster. Rec. Apr. 15, 1797

p. 299-300 May 7, 1796 Richard Lee (Spartanburgh) to Nathan Waldin (same); for 20£ sterling sold 160 ac on Pacolate R; border: Robert Armour. Witness Aaron Timpleman and Nancy Lee. Signed Richard Lee. Wit. oath Jul. 19, 1796 Richard Lee to I Harrison. Rec. May 9, 1796

p. 300-301 May 17, 1795 Robert Lee (Spartanburgh) to George Poole (same); for 10£ sterling sold 300 ac; part of grant Jul. 5, 1788 to Thomas Sabb (or Labb) on Pacolate R and Broad R who sold to Robert Lee. Witness William Bagwell, James Wofford, and John Lee. Signed Robt Lee. Wit. oath Jan. 13, 1796 William Bagwell to I Harrison. Rec. May 9, 1796

p. 301-303 Jul. 13, 1795 William Wood (Greenville Co) to Amos Spese (Lincoln Co, NC); for 5s sterling sold 430 ac on both sides Cherokee Cr of Broad R; grant Sept. 4, 1786 to William Wood. Witness George Salmon and Wm Young. Signed Wm Wood. Wit. oath Jul. 23, 1796 George Salmon to Robert Cooke. Rec. Sept. 12, 1796

p. 303-305 Dec. 22, 1794 Edward Williams (Spartanburgh) to son George Williams; for love and affection give 784 ac where Edward lives and 24 cattle and all increase thereof, 12 sheep and increase, all stock of hogs and increase, all beds and furniture and household furniture, ploughs, hows, axes and all kind of work tools, firearms etc, and a sorrel horse "now present" 4' 11" high 7 years old branded on the near shoulder and jaw with "W", and other horses and increase. Memorandom Dec. 22, 1794 Sorrell horse described above delivered to George Williams with witnesses as follows. Witness Edward Curry and Robert Cook. Signed Edward Williams. Wit. oath Nov. 13, 1795 Edward Curry and Robert Cook to H McCray. Rec. May 9, 1796

p. 305-307 Dec. 17, 1790 William Dickson (Spartanburgh) to Daniel Joslin (same); for 5£ SC money sold 125 ac; part of 534 ac grant to William Dickson on S side Pacolet R; lower border: Solomon Abbett. Witness Solomon Abbett and Wm Abbett. Signed William Dickson's mark. Wit. oath Jan. 13, 1796 Solomon Abbett to H McCray. May 9, 1796

p. 307-308 Aug. 1, 1795 Leonard Adcock (Spartanburgh) to William Adcock (same); for 100£ Va money sold 100 ac on N side Pacolate R; border: John Lackey; where "said" Adcock lives; middle part of 300 ac grant to Francis Ballinger. Witness Henry Adcock, Jonathan Low, and John Low. Signed Leonard Adcock. Wit. oath Oct. 17, 1795 Jonathan Low to H McCray. Rec. May 9, 1796

p. 308-309 Jan. 29, 1795 Holloway Power (Laurens Co) to John Wells (Spartanburgh); for 20£ sold a third of a saw mill now in partnership between Holloway and John and six "rood" square of Holloway's land on S side Enoree R. Witness Joseph Woodruff. Signed Holloway Power. Wit. oath Jan. 13, 1796 Joseph Woodruff to Thos Moore. Rec. May 10, 1796

p. 309-310 May 27, 1795 Robert Lee (Spartanburgh) to Robert Armour (same); for 70£ sterling sold 730 ac; part of grant Apr. 2, 1787 to James Stedman, on both sides Cherokee Cr of Pacolate R, who sold to Robert Lee. Witness George Poole, Arthur Crocker, and Richard Lee. Signed Robert Lee. Wit. oath Jan. 13, 1796 George Poole to I Harrison. Rec. May 9, 1796

p. 310-313 Apr. 9, 1795 James Huggins (Spartanburgh) to Leffert French (same); for 45£ sold 75 ac on NE side of N Pacolet R; part of grant Oct. 13, 1765 to Ebenezer Alexander who sold May 19, 1774 to Thomas Harris and sold Oct. 13, 1783 by Thomas Harris' executor to Hugh Lewis who sold Apr. 1, 1784 to John McClure. Witness Hugh McMillin, David Leech, and Andrew McMillan. Signed James Huggins. Wit. oath Aug. 10, 1795 Hugh McMillin to James Hooper. Rec. May 9, 1796

p. 313-315 Jan. 13, 1796 John Timmons and wife Elizabeth (Spartanburgh) to Moses Timmons (same); for 100£ sterling sold 330 ac on Timmon's Mill Cr of N Tyger R; border: Abner Timmons, Samuel Timmons, Robert Connor, Francis Dodd, and Robert Jamison; part of 1,000 ac grant May 16, 1754 to Francis Wilson who sold to John Timmons. Witness Wm Benson, John Walker, and Absalom Stokes. Signed John and Elizabeth Timmons' marks. Wit. oath Jan. 12, 1796 Absalom Stokes to Isham Foster. Rec. May 10, 1796

p. 315-316 Jan. 10, 1792 Philimon Waters, sr to John Tackett (Spartanburgh); for "good causes and a valuable consideration" sold 100 ac on N side Enoree R; grant Jan. 6, 1786 (see Book 4G p. 422). Witness Charles Waters and John Summers. Signed P Waters. Wit. oath Jan. 29, 1792 Charles Waters to Thomas Farrow. Rec. May 10, 1796

p. 316-318 Dec. 31, 1788 Hugh McWilliams and wife Jane (Laurens Co) to John Tackett (Spartanburgh); for 30£ sterling sold 100 ac; border: Waters and Enoree R; S part of 377 ac grant Jan. 1, 1787 to Hugh McWilliams. Witness Henry Hamilton, William Tacket, and John Lindsey. Signed Hugh and Jane McWilliams' marks. Wit. oath Mar. 21, 1789 Henry Hamilton and William Tacket to Thomas Farrow. Rec. May 10, 1796

p. 318-320 Nov. (not given), 1792 Henry McWood (Greenville Co) to Daniel Hackney (same); for 100£ sterling sold 200 ac on Lawson's fork of Pacolate R below Jones' Wagon Road; grant Sept. 25, 1766 Gov. William Tryon (NC) to (not given). Witness John Morris, Absalom Stokes, and Moses Timmons. Signed H McWood. Wit. oath Jan. 12, 1796 Moses Timmons to Isham Foster. Rec. May 10, 1796

p. 320-322 Jan. 4, 1796 James Martin, esq to Micajah Cooper (Spartanburgh); for 10£ 18s 8p sterling sold 150 ac on both sides Beaverdam Cr; border: William Cooper and Lipscomb; part of a "large" grant to James Martin, esq. Witness George Taylor and Moses Guyton. Signed James Martin. Wit. oath Mar. 28, 1796 George Taylor to H McCray

p. 322-323 Jul. 22, 1795 John Timmons (Spartanburgh) to Richard Fraylor (same); for 80£ SC money sold 160 ac on both sides N fork Tygar R; border: Samuel Timmons; part of 1,000 ac where John Timmons lives. Witness Jas T White, Danl Carmichael, and Absalom Stokes. Signed John Timmons' mark. Wit. oath Jan. 12, 1796 Danl Carmichael to Isham Foster. Rec. May 10, 1797 (sic)

p. 323-324 Nov. 20, 1790 Richard Harrison to Samuel Ward; for 60£ sold 130 ac; border: John James; where Charles Bruce formerly lived. Witness John James. Signed Richard Harrison. Wit. oath Dec. 5, 1795 John James to I Harrison. Rec. May 10, 1797

p. 324-326 Aug. 7, 1795 Elisha Garland (Pendleton Co) to Daniel Rogers (Spartanburgh); for 30£ sterling sold 230 ac; border: James Paden; S part of 640 ac on N fork Forgeson's Cr of Tyger R grant Dec. 3, 1787 to Elisha Garland. Witness James Wofford, Samuel Jones, Moses Fowler. Signed Elisha Garland's mark. Wit. oath Aug. 10, 1795 Moses Fowler to Thos Moore. Rec. May 10, 1796

p. 326-329 Feb. 10, 1795 Daniel Obar (SC) to Jeremiah Snow (Spartanburgh); for 10£ sterling sold 88 ac; part of 640 ac grant Nov. 6, 1786 to Daniel Obar on branches of Furgeson's Cr on Tyger R. Witness William Childress, Mary Bradberry, and Thomas Childress. Signed Daniel Obar. Wit. oath Jun. 5, 1795 William Childress to Zadock Ford. Rec. May 10, 1796

p. 329-330 Dec. 17, 1789 David Neal (or Neell) (Spartanburgh) to Ancil Doller (same); for 17£ sterling sold 50 ac; border: Benjamin Rhodes and William Waldrop; part of 557 ac on N side of Enoree R and on Danceing Br granted Mar. 3, 1788 Gov. Thomas Pinckney to David Neal. Witness John Grizrel and Reubin Doller. Signed David Neal's mark. Wit. oath Aug. 13, 1791 Reubin Doller and John Grizrel to Thomas Farrow. Rec. May 10, 1796

p. 330-332 May 4, 1795 John Elder (Spartanburgh) to Samuel Morrow, jr (same); for 100£ sterling sold 125 3/4 ac on W side Dutchman's Cr; border: Alexander Elder, Samuel Morrow, and Thomas Beardan; part of 600 ac grant Sept. 3, 1753 Gov. Matthew Rowan (NC) to Robert Cowden who sold Jan. 16, 1765 to John Elder. Witness Saml Lancaster, Augustine Bumpass, and Archebel McCrury. Signed John Elder. Certified (not dated) by Wm Smith. Rec. May 11, 1796

p. 332-334 Dec. 3, 1793 Alexander Keenum (Spartanburgh) to John Keenum (same); for 50£ sterling sold 188 ac on both sides Fawn Br of Lawson's fork of Pacolet R; grant Nov. 27, 1784 to Alexander Keenum. Witness Leonard Burnett, John Johnson, and Luke Bennett. Signed Alexander Keenum. Wit. oath Jun. 16, 1795 Leonard Burnett to Isham Foster. Rec. May 11, 1796

p. 334-336 Jul. 8, 1795 Robert Armour (Spartanburgh) to Richard Lee (same); for 30£ sterling sold 360 ac; part of grant on both sides Cherokee Cr of Pacolate R Apr. 2, 1787 to James Stedman who sold to Richard Lee who sold to Robert Armour. Witness James Wofford, Blackburn Quinn, and Elizabeth Armour. Signed Robert Armour. Wit. oath Oct. 31, 1795 Blackburn Quinn to I Harrison. Rec. May 11, 1796

p. 336-338 Jan. 26, 1794 Drury Couch (Spartanburgh) to Thomas Stroud (same); for 50£ sold 50 ac W of Hunt's Path including upper ford of Fort Shoal Cr; part of 150 ac on Fort Shoal Cr of Enoree R granted in 1786 Gov. William Moultrie to John Burt who sold Sept. 19, 1793 to Drury Couch (see Book C p. 305). Witness Mark Stroud and Aaron Casey. Signed Drury Couch's mark. Wit. oath Jan. 11, 1796 Mark Stroud to Thomas Farrow. Rec. May 11, 1796

p. 338-339 Aug. 18, 1795 Austin Clayton (Spartanburgh) to John Foster (same); for 25£ sterling sold 200 ac in Greenville Co, Pinckney Dist (sic), on Falkenbury's Beverdam Cr of Middle Tyger R; border: Price and Varnon; part of 873 ac grant Jul. 1, 1793 to Austin Clayton. Witness William Foster, Nathan Walden, and Ism Foster. Signed Austin Clayton. Wit. oath Aug. 18, 1795 Austin Clayton to Ism Foster. Rec. May 11, 1796

p. 339-340 Jun. 23, 1795 James Pack (Spartan Co) to Thomas Massingale (same); for 2£ 10s SC money sold 15 ac. Witness John Boley and James Massingale. Signed James Pack. Wit. oath Aug. 14, 1795 James Massingale to Ism Foster. Rec. May 11, 1796

p. 340-341 Jun. 4, 1795 John Pipes (Spartan Co) to Thomas Massingale (same); for a Spanish mill Dollar sold 2 ac on Sholly Cr. Witness Levi Burchum and Jeremiah Massingale. Signed John Pipes. Wit. oath Aug. 14, 1795 Levi Burchum to Ism Foster. Rec. May 11, 1796

p. 341-344 Aug. 6, 1784 William Whitaker, gentleman, and wife Mary (Camden Dist) to Sampson Bobo (96 Dist); for 10s SC money sold 100 ac on Cedar Shoal Cr of Enoree R in Craven Co; border: Samuel Cannon. Witness Thomas Whitaker and John Williams. Signed Wm Whitaker and Mary's mark. Wit. oath (Kershaw Co) Feb. 10, 1796 Thomas Whitaker to A. B. Ross. Rec. May 12, 1796

p. 344-346 Aug. 5, 1784 William Whitaker and wife Mary (Camden Dist) to Sampson Bobo (96 Dist); for 100£ sterling sold 100 ac; border: Cannon; part of 500 ac on Cedar Shoal Cr of Enoree R granted Sept. 25, 1773 Gov. Charles Montieggre (sic) to John Cashaw then bordering: SW-Cannon, N, NW, & SW-Thomas Jones, and SE & NE-vacant; and sold by John Cashaw Aug. 12, 1778 to William Whitaker. Witness Thomas Whitaker and John Williams. Signed William Whitaker and Mary's mark. Rec. May 12, 1796

p. 346-351 Dec. 19, 1782 Isaac Hendrix and wife Nancy (96 Dist) to Col Benjamin Roebuck, esq (same); for 200£ 10s SC money sold 100 ac on Two Mile Cr of Enoree R; border: vacant; grant Dec. 23, 1771 Gov. Charles G Montague to Isaac Hendrix. Witness Peter Brookes and Hugh Smith. Signed Isaac and Nancy Hendrix's marks. Wit. oath (Union Co) Jul. 8, 1796 Peter Brookes to Thos Blassingame. Rec. Apr. 11, 1797

p. 351-356 Dec. 19, 1782 Isaac Hendrix and wife Nancy (96 Dist) to Col Benjamin Roebuck, esq (same); for 500£ 10s SC money sold 250 ac on Two Mile Cr of Enoree R; border: NW-George Lowther, S-Daniel Morning and John Hendrix, N-Isaac Hendrix, and E-vacant; grant (not given) 19, 1774 Lt. Gov. William Bull to Isaac Hendrix. Witness Peter Brookes and Hugh Smith. Signed Isaac Hendrix. Wit. oath (Union Co) Jul. 8, 1796 Peter Brookes to Thomas Blassingame. Rec. Apr. 11, 1797

p. 356-357 Apr. 8, 1790 George Roebuck and wife Lovina, heirs-at-law to estate of brother Col Benjamin Roebuck, desc (Spartanburgh) to Sampson Bobo; for 100£ sold 350 ac on Two Mile Cr of Enoree R of Broad R in two tracts both sold by Isaac Hendrix to Benjamin Roebuck; (1) 100 ac grant Dec. 23, 1771 Gov. Charles G. Montague to Isaac Hendrix with border vacant; and (2) 250 ac grant Aug. 19, 1774 Lt. Gov. William Bull to Isaac Hendrix with border: NW-George Lowther, S-Daniel Morning and John Hendrix, N-Isaac Hendrix, and E-vacant. Witness Spencer Bobo, jr and William Wilder. Signed George Robuck and Lovina's mark. Wit. oath in 1797 William Wilder to Moses Casey. Rec. Jul. 10, 1797

p. 357-359 Dec. 21, 1795 Jonathan Harris (Spartanburgh) to Henry Cocks (or Cox) and William Neal (Ga); for 20£ SC money sold 200 ac on Bullock's fork of Thickety Cr; part of 380 ac grant Apr. 16, 1785 Gov. William Moultrie to Jonathan Harris. Witness Vardry McBee, Joseph Harris (or Morris), and Vardry McBee, jr. Signed Jonathan Harris' mark. Wit. oath Apr. 12, 1796 Vardry McBee to H McCray. Rec. May 12, 1796

p. 359-361 Nov. 7, 1795 Reuben Samuel (Caroline Co, Va) to Nathan Walden (Spartanburgh); for 55£ sterling sold 500 ac on Holston Br of Fairforrest Cr. Witness I Harrison JP. Signed for Reubin Samuel by Nicholas Samuel by power of attorney. Wit. oath Nov. 7, 1795 Nicholas Samuel to I Harrison. Rec. May 14, 1796

p. 361-362 Oct. 23, 1795 Malichi Jones (Spartanburgh) to Ignatious Griffin (same); for 30£ sterling sold 140 ac on both sides Gocher's Cr. Witness John H Jones and John Humphrey. Signed Malichi Jones. Wit. oath Apr. 11, 1796 John H Jones to John Lipscomb. Rec. Apr. 12, 1796

p. 362-365 Mar. 24, 1795 Josiah Tanner (or Fanner) (Spartanburgh) to William Lipscomb (same); for 60£ sold (1) 1,000 ac where Josiah lives on N side of Thickety Cr; grant in 1787 to Josiah Tanner; and (2) 452 ac on Goucher's Cr; border: John Shippis; grant Jul. 2, 1792 to Josiah Tanner. Witness Abraham Lamaster and Nathan Lipscomb. Signed Josiah and Martha Tanner. Wit. oath Mar. 30, 1796 Abraham Lamaster and Nathan Lipscomb to H McCray. Rec. May 14, 1796

p. 365-367 Jul. 13, 1795 Samuel Culbertson and wife Silah (Spartanburgh) to Henry O'Nail (same); for 5£ 19s sterling sold 25½ ac on Culbertson's Still House Br of Fairforrest Cr; part of land where Samuel lives; border: Henry O'Nail. Witness Samuel Lancaster, Wm Smith, and Brittain Williford. Signed Saml Culbertson. Certified Jul. 30, 1795 by Wm Smith. Rec. May 14, 1796. Dower renounced Silah Culbertson to Wm Smith Mar. 22, 1796

p. 367-369 Oct. 30, 1795 William Wilder (Spartanburgh) to John Frederick Harmoning and Co (same); a bond: for 15£ 17s 7p SC money sold a roun horse named Paddy, a black cow unmarked, 2 red and white cows, a red cow and calf, 3 yearlings two of which are heifers and one a stear, a red heifer with calf, a black heifer yearling, 2 man's saddles, and 25 hogs--nine cattle and the hogs marked with a swallow in each ear; Condition: bond void if William pays John 15£ 17s 7p SC money with interest by Nov. 8, 1795. Witness Jesse Chamblan and Liviston Bobo. Signed William Wilden. Wit. oath Feb. 22, 1796 Jesse Chamblan to Moses Casey. Rec. May 15, 1796

p. 369-371 Dec. 20, 1795 David Humphrey and wife Jane (Spartanburgh) to Henry Gibson (same); for 60£ sterling sold 185 ac on both sides Gocher's Cr; part of 200 ac grant Dec. 6, 1771 North Carolina to Hugh Moore who sold to Charles Ray who sold to William

Thompson and sold by his son Sevan Thompson to David Humphrey; 15 ac from grant excluded from this sale on N side of Goucher's Cr and on E corner of grant. Witness George Gibson, Young Allen, and William Wilkins. Signed David Humphrey and Jane's mark. Wit. oath Apr. 12, 1796 Young Allen to John Lipscomb. Rec. May 15, 1796

p. 371-373 Feb. 20, 1796 James Simmons and wife Elizabeth (Spartanburgh) to Terrell Wilkins (same); for 50£ sterling sold 127 ac on both sides Goaches Cr; part of 247 ac. Witness Thomas Gillenwaters and Wm Wilkins. Signed James Simmons and Elizabeth's mark. Wit. oath Apr. 11, 1796 Thomas Gillenwaters to John Lipscomb. Rec. May 16, 1796. Dower renounced Elizabeth Simmons to James Jordan Apr. 11, 1796

p. 373-376 Oct. 14, 1793 John West, sr and wife Mary (Spartanburgh) to Robert McDowell; for 100£ sterling sold 150 ac on N side Lawson's fork; where John and Mary live; grant to Francis Ross and sold Feb. 23 & 24, 1792 by George West to John West, sr. Witness John Bennett, Daniel Cornwell, and George Bennett. Signed John and Mary West's marks. Wit. oath Apr. 10, 1795 John West to Isham Foster. Rec. May 16, 1796

p. 376-378 Apr. 21, 1794 John Headen (Spartanburgh) to Thomas Green (same); for 80£ sterling sold 400 ac on both sides Thickety Cr; border: E-Malichi Jones and others vacant; grant Apr. 3, 1785 Gov. William Moultrie to John Headen. Witness Obadh Trimmier, John Trimmier, and Leonard Adcock. Signed John Headen. Wit. oath Apr. 21, 1794 John Trimmier to Edwd Goode. Rec. May 16, 1796

p. 378-380 Feb. 12, 1795 James Huggins (Spartan Co) to Hugh McMillian (same); for 40£ "paid down" sold 75 ac on SW side of N Pacolate R; border: Thomas McKnight; grant Oct. 13, 1765 to Ebezener Alexander who sold May 19, 1774 to Thomas Hiris and sold Oct. 13, 1783 by Thomas Hiris' executors to Hugh Lewis who sold Apr. 1, 1784 to John McClure. Witness Andrew McMillian and William McKnight. Signed James Higgins. Wit. oath Aug. 10, 1795 William McKnight to James Hooper. Rec. May 17, 1796

p. 380-382 Oct. 7, 1795 Daniel Barnett (Spartanburgh) to Francis Mayson (same); for 20£ sold 100 ac on Ward's Br on N side of N fork of Tygar R; grant Aug. 21, 1776 Gov. Charles G Montague to John Ward. Witness Michael Barnett, John James, and Wm Ford. Signed Daniel Barnett. Wit. oath Apr. 11, 1796 John James to I Harrison. Rec. May 17, 1796

p. 382-384 Nov. 14, 1795 Randolph Laurence (SC) to Mary Harris (SC); for 30£ SC money sold 146 ac at head branches of Miller's Br of Beaverdam Cr; grant Mar. 22, 1792 Gov. Charles Pinckney to Randolph Laurence. Witness Vardry McBee and Betsy McBee. Signed Randolph and Allis Laurence. Wit. oath Apr. 12, 1796 Vardry McBee to H McCray. Rec. May 17, 1796

p. 384-386 Aug. 28, 1793 Stephen Miller and wife Mary (Spartanburgh) to Robert McDowell (same); for 100£ sterling sold 150 ac on a fork of Lawson's fork; border: George Bishop; half of grant Nov. 25, 1774 to Stephen Miller. Witness George Bishop, jr, Wm Saunders, and Wm West. Signed Stephen Miller and Mary's mark. Wit. oath Apr. 10, 1795 Wm West to Isham Foster. Rec. May 18, 1796

p. 386-387 Aug. 10, 1795 David Humphrey (Spartanburgh) to Ignatious Griffin (same); for 5£ sterling sold 50 ac; border: Malichi Jones. Witness John Lipscomb and Thomas Gore. Signed David Humphrey. Wit. oath Apr. 11, 1796 John Lipscomb to George Lamkin. Rec. May 18, 1796

p. 387-388 Feb. 26, 1796 Catey Johnson (Spartanburgh) to Betsy Dunkin and Polly Dunkin (same); for $25 sold 3 cattle: a black cow, a two year old hiefer, moild and pyded(?), and a yearling heifer pyded, a bed and furniture, a pot, a dutch oven and a skillet, a pewter bason, 9 plates, 6 earthen plates, a set of knives and forks, 4 chairs, and all goods and household stuff. Witness William Duncan, Ruth Duncan, and Drury McDaniel. Signed Catey Johnson's mark. Wit. oath Apr. 9, 1796 Drury McDaniel to Thos Moore. Rec. May 18, 1796

p. 388-389 Dec. 17, 1795 Baylis Earle to Richard Barry; for $60 sold a Negro girl 14 years old called Nutty; note: said girl free of any disorders and impediments as far as Baylis knows except loss of sight in one eye. Witness Alexr Alexander. Signed Baylis Earle. Wit. oath Apr. 11, 1796 Alexr Alexander to Thos Moore. Rec. May 18, 1796

p. 389-392 Jul. 14, 1796 James Crow, sr and wife Elizabeth (Spartanburgh) to Asahel Beeson (same); for 30£ SC money sold 80 ac on S side Tygar R; part of 300 ac grant Apr. 3, 1788 Gov. William Moultrie to Thomas White "a party to these presents" (sic) who sold in 1788 to Isham Chote who sold in 1791 to James Crow, sr. Witness Nicholas Keating, Thomas Chumley, and Alexr Alexander. Signed James Crow and Elizabeth's mark. Wit. oath Sept. 10, 1796 Thomas Chumley to George Bruton. Rec. Sept. 20, 1796

p. 392-393 Oct. 21, 1795 Presley Garrett (Spartanburgh) to William Haney (same); for 18£ SC money sold 640 ac on Buck Br of Buck Br of Pacolate R; grant Oct. 6, 1788 States Office to William Daulton. Witness S Bethel and Joseph Morris. Signed Presley Garrett's mark. Certified Oct. 21, 1795 by S Bethel. Rec. Sept. 20, 1796

p. 393-395 Sept. 5, 1796 Abraham Andrews and wife Nancy (Spartanburgh) to Daniel White (same); for 26£ sold 100 ac on Richland Cr and E of Indian Boundary; grant Oct. 2, 1786 Gov. William Moultrie to Richard Speakes; where John Andrews lives and W of "main" creek. Witness Robert Kimble, James White, and Martha Andrews. Signed Abraham and Nancy Andrews' marks. Wit. oath Sept. 9, 1796 James White to Ism Foster. Rec. Sept. 21, 1796

p. 395-396 Apr. 13, 1796 Thomas Wright (Spartanburgh) to Thomas Price (same); for 140£ sterling sold a Negro woman Mary 30 years old and her three children: Rose 6 years old, Easther 4 years old, and Arch about 2 years old "all country born". Witness John Wright and Andrew Thomson. Signed Thomas Wright. Rec. Sept. 21, 1796

p. 396-397 Sept. 12, 1796 Bazel Lee (Spartanburgh) to William Robertson (same); for $100 sold 100 ac on Lawson's fork; border: Zacheriah Robertson, Bull, and Wells Griffith. Witness I Harrison JP. Signed Bazel Lee. Rec. Sept. 22, 1796

p. 397-398 Aug. 22, 1796 John Timmons (Spartanburgh) to grandson James Lamiel Timmons (same); for love and affection give a Negro boy named Ben, son of Cate. Witness John Bowen and John Tap. Signed John Timmons' mark. Wit. oath Sept. 12, 1796 John Tap to Ism Foster. Rec. Sept. 22, 1796

p. 398-399 Aug. 13, 1796 Zadock Baker Thackston (Prince Edward Co, Va) to Thomas Davidson (Spartanburgh); for $50 sold 100 ac; border: E-George McCarter, W-John Foster, NW-David Brown's new survey, and S-Arthur Simpson. Witness William Simpson and George McCarter. Signed Z. B. Thackston. Wit. oath Sept. 12, 1796 William Simpson to Thos Moore. Rec. Sept. 23, 1796

p. 399-400 Apr. 16, 1796 James Brown (Spartanburgh) to Evan Davis (same); for 5s sold 423 ac; part of 990 ac grant Jan. 6, 1794 Gov. William Moultrie to James Brown. Witness Jesse Connell, Jonathan Davis, and John Asd Gore. Signed James Brown's mark. Wit. oath Sept. 10, 1796 Jonathan Davis to John Lipscomb. Rec. Sept. 24, 1796

p. 400-401 Feb. 12, 1796 Thomas Wmson (Spartanburgh) to Henry O'Nail; for 60£ sold a Negro girl Sall age 17. Witness William Patton. Signed Thos Wmson. Rec. Sept. 24, 1796

p. 401-405 Sept. 2, 1785 William Young (Union Co) to William Simpson (Spartanburgh), guardian of person and estate of Agness Bird; for 30£ 5s sterling sold 200 ac on Foster's or Hanes' Mill Cr on N side Fairforrest Cr;for Agness Bird's use where Samuel Bird, desc lives; border: land belonging to the State by an old survey; grant May 5, 1769 Gov. William Tryon (NC) to John Foster and sold Mar. 29, 1770 by John Foster and wife Ann to William Young. Witness Turner Rountree, Christopher Brandon, and Frederick Layne. Signed William Young. Wit. oath (Union Co) Sept. 3, 1796 Christopher Brandon to Thos Brandon. Rec. Sept. 25, 1796

p. 405-407 Aug. 15, 1796 Daniel Rogers (Spartanburgh) to George Rogers, William Rogers, Darling Rogers, James Rogers, and Leweresey(?) Rogers (same); for love and affection give all goods, chattels, and household stuff and "all my other substance"; no list. Witness David Moor, John Adams, and James Wofford. Signed Daniel Rogers' mark. Wit. oath Aug. 15, 1796 John Adams to Thos Moore. Rec. Sept. 25, 1796

p. 407-408 Nov. 5, 1793 James Martin, esq (York Co) to James Ballenger (Spartanburgh); for 50£ SC money sold 300 ac on both sides Cherokee Cr. Witness Thomas Cook and George Walker. Signed James Martin. Wit. oath Oct. 30, 1794 George Walker to Edwd Goode. Rec. Sept. 26, 1796

p. 408-410 Jan. 10, 1795 Joseph Wofford and wife Martha (Spartanburgh) to William Pugh (same); for 100£ sterling sold 100 ac on S side Tyger R; border: James' Cr, Thomas Young, and William Young; part of 300 ac grant Aug. 11, 1774 Lt. Gov. William Bull to Luke Luckory (or Suckory). Witness Jno Grist, Wm Britain, and Benjm Grist. Signed Jos Wofford and Martha's mark. Wit. oath Feb. 29, 1796 Wm Britain to Moses Casey. Rec. Sept. 27, 1796

p. 410-411 Mar. 3, 1795 Joseph Wofford (Spartanburgh) to William Crow (same); for 60£ sterling sold 270 ac; border: N & E-Isaac Crow, W-Spencer Culbert, and S-William Crow. Witness James Lanford (or Sanford), James Higgins, and Isaac Crow. Signed Joseph Wofford and Martha's mark. Wit. oath Jul. 19, 1796 Isaac Crow to Saml Lancaster. Rec. Sept. 27, 1796

p. 411-412 Dec. 10, 1795 James Johnson (Union Co) to Nathan Walden (Spartanburgh); for 50£ sold 162 ac on Holston Br of Fairforrest Cr. Witness Richd Barry. Signed James Johnson. Wit. oath Apr. 11, 1796 Richd Barry to I Harrison. Rec. Sept. 28, 1796

p. 412-413 Mar. 1, 1796 Edward Herring (Spartanburgh) to George Thomason (same); for 50£ SC money sold 178 ac on Lawson's fork; border: James Steadman. Witness I Harrison JP. Signed Edward Herring. Wit. oath Jul. 14, 1796 Edward Herring to I Harrison. Rec. Sept. 28, 1796

p. 413-415 Mar. 1, 1796 William T Thomason (Spartanburgh) to Edward Herring (same); for 25£ SC money sold 50 ac; part of grant Jan. 21, 1785 Gov. Benjamin Guerard to William T

Thomason. Witness I Harrison JP. Signed William T Thomason's mark. Wit. oath Jul. 18, 1796 William T Thomason to I Harrison. Rec. Sept. 28, 1796

p. 415-416 Apr. 9, 1796 William Lancaster and wife Clarimont (Spartanburgh) to Thomas Vaughn (same); for 25£ sterling sold 174 ac on Wilies' fork of Dutchman's Cr; border: N-Daniel Finch, John Smith and the Mountain tract, E-James Hickey, S-Lowden(?), and W-Thomas Cook; includes improvements where Thomas Vaughn lives. Witness David Golightly and Alexander Autry. Signed W and Clary Lancaster. Wit. oath Apr. 12, 1796 David Golightly to I Harrison. Rec. Sept. 28, 1796

p. 416-418 Oct. 21, 1795 Ephraim Rees and James Clark (Spartanburgh) to Job Loftis (same); for 15£ SC money sold 100 ac; border: McElhenny, Ladson, and James Powell; part of 270 ac on Middle fork Tyger R granted Sept. 2, 1793 Gov. William Moultrie to Ephraim Rees and James Clark. Witness James Powell and Benjamin Jones. Signed Ephraim Rees and James Clark. Wit. oath (Greenville Co) Jan. 9, 1796 James Powell to J Thomas, jr. Rec. Sept. 29, 1796

p. 418-420 Oct. 19, 1795 Ephraim Reese and James Clark (Spartanburgh) to James Powell (same); for 10£ sold 70 ac; border: NE & SE-Benjamin Perine McMakin, W & N-Hugh Barnett, NW-Ladson, SW-James Powell and Ephraim Reese, SE-unknown, and NE, SE & SW-Jno McElhaney; part of 270 ac on both sides Middle fork Tyger R granted Sept. 2, 1793 Gov. William Moultrie to Ephraim Reese and James Clark; survey Jul. 16, 1793. Witness Job Loftis and Edwd Mitchenson. Signed Ephraim Reese and James Clark. Wit. oath (Greenville Co) Jan. 9, 1796 Job Loftis to J Thomas, jr. Rec. Sept. 28, 1796

p. 420-422 Oct. 11, 1793 James Cantrell (Pendleton Co) to Thomas Kevil (Laurens Co); for 20£ sterling sold 400 ac on Little Rockey Cr of Enoree R; grant Feb. 6, 1786 Gov. William Moultrie to James Cantrell. Witness Joab League, Benjamin Kevil, and Edward Dial. Signed James Cantrell. Wit. oath Jul. 16, 1796 Edward Dial to Zadock Ford. Rec. Sept. 29, 1796

p. 422-424 Oct. 1, 1790 Stephen Cantrell (Pendleton Co) to Thomas Kevil (Laurens Co); for 20£ sterling sold 350 ac on Enoree R; border: Thomas Kevil; part of 500 ac grant to Thomas Skolton who sold to Richard Hampton who sold Feb. 27, 1795 to Stephen Cantrell. Witness Henry Brockman, Joel Deen, and John Deen. Signed Stephen Cantrell. Wit. oath Oct. 1, 1792 John Deen to Zadock Ford. Rec. Sept. 29, 1796

p. 424-426 Feb. 29, 1796 William Peugh (Spartanburgh) to Isaac Crow; for 100£ sterling sold 100 ac on S side Tyger R; border: James' Cr, Thomas Young, and Wm Young; part of 300 ac grant Aug. 11, 1774 Lt. Gov. William Bull to Luke Vicary(?). Witness John Hudgens, Wm Britain, and John Saxton. Signed William Peugh. Wit. oath Feb. 29, 1796 Wm Britain to Moses Casey. Rec. Sept. 30, 1796

p. 426-428 Jan. 22, 1796 Zadock Ford (Spartanburgh) to America Fowler (same); for 20£ sterling sold 100 ac; border: Thomas Harves and a waggon road; SE part of 548 ac on branches of Enoree R granted Jul. 16, 1784 to Zadock Ford. Witness Nicholas Garrol, Aaron Fowler, and Zadock Ford. Signed Zadock Ford. Wit. oath Apr. 23, 1796 Aaron Fowler to George Brewton. Rec. Sept. 30, 1796

p. 428-429 Dec. 22, 1794 Alexander Keenum (Spartanburgh) to Matthew Harper (same); for 25£ sterling sold 100 ac on E side of branch of Richland Cr agreeable with a conditional line between John Conner and William Wood; border: Fawn Br, Clement, Jones, and Jesse Rease; grant to Thomas Hollaway. Witness Ephraim Lewis, John Sanders, and John Crease. Signed Alexander Keenum. Wit. oath Jul. 10, 1796 John Sanders to Ism Foster. Rec. Sept. 30, 1796

p. 429-431 Oct. 15, 1795 Philip Johnston (Spartanburgh) to Cary Traylor; for 25£ sterling sold 50 ac on Ben's Cr; border: William Gray, Moses Wakefield, and Henry Crow. Witness Joseph Fowler and Curtis Gray. Signed Philip Johnston's mark. Wit. oath Jul. 18, 1796 Philip Johnston to Thomas Moore. Rec. Sept. 30, 1796

p. 431 Dec. 30, 1797 John Sloan to Adam Sloan; for $250 sold a Negro Isaac. Witness Richard Barry. Signed John Sloan. Wit. oath Jan. 3, 1798 Richard Barry to Thomas Moore

p. 431-433 Jan. 4, 1796 James Robertson (Spartanburgh) to Theophilus Hews; a bond of 80£; Condition: bond void if James deeds (ac not given) on Harican Cr to (not given); where James lives; border: Thomas Hews. Witness Ellis Cannon and Nathan Ward. Signed James Robertson's mark. Wit. oath Jan. 14, 1797 Ellis Cannon to H McCray. Feb. 23, 1796 Theophelus Hewes assigns above to Zachariah Sparks. Witness Thos Hews

p. 433-434 Jul. 18, 1796 Joseph Wofford (Spartanburgh) to James Barnett (same); for 60£ sterling sold 250 ac on both sides Fairforrest Cr; including land where John Thomas, jr formerly lived; border: John Thomas sr, Josiah Culbertson, and James Tillett; "a few" ac excepted that were previously sold to Josiah Culbertson; grant in 1771 Gov. William Tryon (NC) to John Thomas, jr. Witness David Wells, John Wofford, and John Hammett. Signed Joseph Wofford. Wit. oath Jul. 18, 1796 John Hammett to H McCray. Rec. Sept. 30, 1796

p. 433-435 Jul. 14, 1796 Edward Hooker and wife Milley to John David Neleuhe (same); for 22£ sterling sold 100 ac; border: Sampson Bobo sr's South corner, Thomas Miles, Jonathan Pennell, and George Divine; part of 1,000 ac between Tyger and Enoree R granted to James Sample, jr and sold by Rathry Sample, heir-at-law of James Sample jr, to John McCullock who sold to Edward Hooker. Witness Livinston Bobo. Signed Edward Hooker and Milley's mark. Rec. Oct. 1, 1796

435-438 Nov. 28, 1795 John Thomas jr (Greenville Co) to Joseph Wofford (Spartanburgh); for 60£ sterling sold 250 ac on both sides Fairforrest Cr; where John Thomas jr formerly lived; "a few" ac excepted that were sold to Josiah Culbertson; grant in 1771 Gov. William Tryon (NC) to John Thomas jr. Witness George Roebuck and Andrew Thompson. Signed J Thomas jr. Wit. oath Jul. 18, 1796 George Roebuck to Ism Foster. Rec. Oct. 1, 1796

p. 438-440 Jan. 11, 1796 Thomas Terry (Greenville Co) to Aaron Fowler (Spartanburgh); for 30£ sterling sold 200 ac on both sides Fergerson's Cr; grant in 1785 Gov. William Moultrie to James Blenefield. Witness Moses Fowler, Johon Baker, and John Adair. Signed Thomas Terry. Wit. oath Mar. 5, 1796 Moses Fowler to Zadock Ford. Rec. Oct. 1, 1796

p. 440-441 Dec. 22, 1794 Alexander Keenum (Spartanburgh) to Matthew Harper (same); for 25£ sterling sold 70 ac on E side of a branch of Richland Cr; agreeable with conditional line between John Conner and William Wood; border: Fawn Br, Clemont, and Jesse Reaves; part of 100 ac grant to Thomas Hatteway. Witness Ephraim Lewis, John Sanders, and John N Crease. Signed Alexander Keenum. Wit. oath Jul. 18, 1796 John Sanders to Ism Foster. Rec. Oct. 2,

1796

p. 441-445 Jan. 6, 1794 Gov. William Moultrie to Col Thomas Brandon, esq; a grant for 793 ac on both sides Storey Cr of Fairforrest Cr and both sides Wilie's fork of Dutchman's Cr; border: S-Thomas Compton and Jacob Fowler, W-Charles Smith and vacant, N-an old line, and E-Thomas Brandon; survey Mar. 7, 1793 with plat attached signed by Peter Bremar and witnessed by Andw Thomson, dept surv; this grant due to act passed Feb. 19, 1791 by the Legislature--"to grant lands now vacant and to allow commutation to be received for some lands that have been granted". Signed Wm Moultrie. Rec. Oct. 3, 1796. Dec. 25, 1795 (Union Co) Thomas Brandon (Union Co) assigns to Andrew Mayo (same) title and rights to above grant. Witness John Huckaby and Oliver Hart. Signed Thomas Brandon. Wit. oath (Union Co) Dec. 25, 1795 John Huckaby to Thos Brandon

p. 445-446 Jul. 31, 1794 Tilman Bobo (Union Co) to Richard Fryer; for 20£ sterling sold (ac not given) on branches of Enoree R; border: Fars, David Neel, Christopher Rhodes, Spencer Bobo, Thomas Tod, and Whittaker; plat attached shows also bordering John David; except all white pine trees, if any, and except a tenth of gold and silver mined. Witness John Fryer and James Casey. Signed Tilman Bobo. Wit. oath Dec. 29, 1796 James Casey to Moses Casey. Rec. Jul. 15, 1797

p. 446-448 Dec. 1, 1795 Edward Hooker and wife Millie (Spartanburgh) to Richard Fryer; for 30£ sold 100 ac on Enoree R and on the ridge on W of a road from Tyger R to Enoree R; border: Spencer Bobo, Thomas McCurken, Thomas Tod, Whittaker, John Williams, Richard Fryer, and James Casey; part of grant to James Simple jr and sold by Rattry Simple to John McCulloch who sold to Thomas McCurken who sold to Edward Hooker. Witness Moses Casey and Absalom Bobo. Signed Edward Hooker and Millie's mark. Wit. oath Mar. 28, 1797 Absalom Bobo to Moses Casey. Rec. Jul. 15, 1797

p. 448-450 Oct. 28, 1793 Thomas Childress (Spartan Co) to Thomas House (same); for 100£ sterling sold 270 ac on N side Enoree R; border: S-Enoree R, E-John Hemby, W-land surveyed for William Lindsey now Spurgen's land, and John Hemby's Spring Br, David Childress, and Thomas House; NW part of 350 ac grant Aug. 23, 1774 to Thomas Childress. Witness Thomas Holden and John Heaton. Signed Thomas and Unydice Childress' marks. Wit. oath Mar. 10, 1794 Thomas Holden to Zadock Ford. Rec. Oct. 4, 1796

p. 450-453 Jul. 15, 1796 Robert Connell and wife Ruth (Spartanburgh) to Samuel Stewart (same); for 90£ sterling sold 200 ac on S fork Tyger R; border: below Frances Powers. Witness Robert Jamison jr and Richard Pace. Signed Robert Connell's mark. Wit. oath Jul. 16, 1796 Robert Connell to James Jordan. Rec. Oct. 4, 1796

p. 453-454 Jul. 30, 1795 James Reaves (Spartanburgh) to Samuel Jamison (same); for 50£ sterling sold 237 ac on both sides Beaverdam Cr of S Pacolate R; grant Aug. 4, 1794 Gov. William Moultrie to James Reaves. Witness Michael Miller, Jno Gowen, and Wm Reaves. Signed James Reaves' mark. Wit. oath Jul. 19, 1796 Jno Gowen to Ism Foster. Rec. Oct. 5, 1796

p. 454-456 Jan. 4, 1796 Reubin Warren (Spartanburgh) to William Morrow (same); for "half the expenses of saving 655 ac" sold 328 ac on ridge between Horse and Buck Cr including some branches of each; border: Drury Scruggs; part of 655 ac grant Dec. 2, 1793 States Office to Reubin Warren. Witness Henry Turner, Richard Proctor, and Joseph Turner. Signed Reuben Warren. Wit. oath Jan. 5, 1796 Henry Turner to James Turner. Rec. Oct. 6, 1796

p. 456-458 Nov. 13, 1795 Nicholas Waters (Union Co) to Richard Pace (Spartanburgh); for 50£ sterling sold 100 ac on S side of N fork of Tyger R; border: Thomas Collins, John Leech, and John McElhany; grant May 4, 1769 to John McElhoony. Witness Joshua Downs, John Pace, and William Kelley. Signed Nicholas Waters. Wit. oath Jul. 17, 1795 Joshua Downs to Isham Foster. Rec. Oct. 6, 1796

p. 458-462 May 24, 1790 John Whittemore and wife Rachel (Spartanburgh) to Robert Connell (same); for 60£ 10s sterling sold 200 ac on S fork of Tyger R where John Whittemore lives; border: on S side and below Francis Powers; grant (date not given) Gov. William Moultrie to John Whittemore. Witness David Goodlett, Howell Johnson, and Randolph Johnson. Signed John Whittemore. Certified Oct. 28, 1790 by D Goodlett. Rec. Oct. 6, 1796

p. 462-464 Jul. 18, 1796 John Jackson, Thomas Jackson, Robert White, Samuel Kelso, and William and Isanna Kelso, heirs of Samuel Jackson sr, desc (Spartanburgh) to John Jackson (same); for 250£ sold 100 ac on N side of N fork Pacolate R; border: Nathaniel Henderson; part of 250 ac tract sold in 1773 by Jabez Evans to Saml Jackson sr. Witness John McGough, Thomas Stephenson, jr and James Anderson. Signed James Jackson, Thomas Jackson, Robert White, Saml Kelso, William Kelso, and Isanna Kelso. Wit. oath Aug. 16, 1796 Thomas Stephenson jr to James Jordan. Rec. Oct. 6, 1796

p. 464-465 Oct. 1, 1795 James Wyatt jr (Spartanburgh) to Samuel Hays (same); for 20£ sold 100 ac on Lawson's fork of Pacolate R; grant Mar. 6, 1786 to John Conner. Witness Edward Prince, Henry Wyatt, and Anne Wyatt. Signed James Wyatt, jr. Wit. oath Oct. 1, 1795 James Wyatt to Ism Foster. Rec. Oct. 7, 1796

p. 465-467 Mar. 7, 1795 William Bratcher (Greenville Co) to Moses Pruett (Spartanburgh); for 10£ sterling sold 60 ac on Dutchman's Cr of Tyger R; border: N-Nathanl Wooten, W-Joel (or Joseph) Smith, S & E-Dutchman's Cr and John Grist, and N-Wooten's Spring Branch; grant Dec. 4, 1786 to William Bratcher. Witness John Grist, Moses Lewis, and Elizabeth Harrison. Signed William Bratcher. Wit. oath Oct. 30, 1795 John Grist to Saml Lancaster. Rec. Oct. 7, 1796

Book E 1796-1798

p. 1-3 Oct. 22, 1792 David Morton, heir of John Morton, desc (Greenville Co) to Francis Fowler (Spartanburgh); for 75£ sterling sold 300 ac on Forgeson's Cr of Tygar R; border: E-Thomas Paden and others vacant; grant Sept. 1, 1768 Lt. Gov. William Bull to John Morton, desc. Witness Moses Fowler, Thomas House, and Aris Fowler. Signed David Morton. Wit. oath Jan. 8, 1796 Moses Fowler to Zadock Ford. Rec. Oct. 15, 1796

p. 3-4 Jul. 29, 1795 Matthew Harper (Spartanburgh) to James Boyd (same); for 30£ sold 70 ac on E side of branch of Richland Cr; border: head spring of branch of Fawn Br, Clemmons, and conditional line between John Conner and William Wood; part of 100 ac grant to Thomas Hatteway. Witness Ephraim Lewis, Hance Harper jr, and Nancy Harper. Signed Matthew Harper. Wit. oath Jul. 18, 1796 Hance Harper jr to Ism Foster. Rec. Oct. 15, 1796

p. 4-5 Feb. 1795 Hance Harper sr (Spartanburgh) to Hance Harper jr (same); for a Spanish milled dollar sold 100 ac on Lawson's fork of Pacolate R; part of 200 ac tract sold by John Kerconnel to Hance Harper sr. Witness Ephraim Lewis, Isaiah Lewis, and Peter Lewis. Signed Hance Harper sr. Wit. oath Jul. 19, 1795 Peter Lewis to Ism Foster. Rec. Oct. 16, 1796

p. 5-7 Oct. 27, 1795 William Jordan (Spartanburgh) to Leonard Adcock (same); for 80£ sold 200 ac on Little Buck Cr; grant Dec. 4, 1792 States Office to West Harris. Witness Berry Young, Elijah Thompson, and William Garrett. Signed William Jordan. Wit. oath (not dated) William Garrett to George Lampkin. Rec. Oct. 16, 1796

p. 7-8 Feb. 16, 1796 Absalom Bobo and wife Ann to father Spencer Bobo; for 20£ sterling sold (ac not given) "all" of Absalom's land where Spencer Bobo lives between Tygar and Enoree R; border: W-"a branch", N-remainder of Absalom's land (sic), E-Sampson Bobo, Wm Whitaker, and Moses Casey; part of 150 ac sold Apr. 5, 1786 by John McCullock to Spencer Bobo. Witness Aaron Casey and Leviston Bobo. Signed Absalom Bobo and Ann's mark. Wit. oath Jul. 11, 1796 Leviston Bobo to M Casey. Rec. Oct. 16, 1796

p. 8-10 Jul. 21, 1795 John Earle (Greenville Co) to Thomas Jackson (Spartanburgh); for 10£ 10s sterling sold 35 ac on S side of N Pacolate R where Thomas Jackson lives; part of 68 ac grant Oct. 25, 1784 Gov. William Moultrie to John Earle. Witness Alexander Stevenson, Thomas Prince Earle, Samuel Earle, and Hugh Stevenson, jr. Signed John and Nancy H. Earle. Wit. oath Dec. 28, 1795 Hugh Stevenson to James Hooper. Rec. Oct. 16, 1796

p. 10-12 Apr. 8, 1796 in Meclinburgh Co, NC Samuel Watson and Jean McDowel, executors of estate of John McDowell, desc, to James Powel (Spartanburgh); for 88£ sterling sold 400 ac on Middle fork of Tygar R below David McKee; grant Gov. William Tryon (NC) to Hugh Park in Rowan Co, NC and regranted Mar. 1775 Gov. William Bull to Hugh Parks (sic) and bequeathed to John McDowell by Hugh Park's will. Witness Hugh Parks, Ephraim Reese, and John McDowel. Signed Samuel Watson and Jean McDowel's mark. Wit. oath (Greenville Co) May 2, 1796 Ephraim Reese to J Thomas jr. Rec. Oct. 17, 1796

p. 12-14 Feb. 16, 1795 Ephraim Reese (Greenville Co) to James Powel (Spartanburgh); for 20£ sterling sold 167 ac on Middle fork Tygar R; border: John Smith; part of 267 ac grant Gov. William Moultrie to Ephraim Reese (date not given). Witness Jno Loftis and Elijah Oliver. Signed Ephraim Reese. Wit. oath Feb. 21, 1794 Jno Loftis to Ism Foster. Rec. Oct. 17, 1796

p. 14-15 Oct. 24, 1795 Elias Jordan (Spartan Co) to Isaac Young (same); for 80£ SC money sold 350 ac on Buck Cr of Pacolate R; grant Oct. 6, 1788 States Office to (not given). Witness S Bethel, Reubin Warren, and Elijah Thompson. Signed Elias Jordan's mark. Certified Oct. 24, 1795 by S Bethel. Rec. Oct. 17, 1796

p. 15-17 Sept. 16, 1796 Malichi Monk (Union Co) to Micajah Barnett (Spartanburgh); for 20£ sterling sold 200 ac on S side Pacolate R; where Jacob Holmes formerly lived; about 30 ac excepted on upper end previously sold to Thomas Hunter; border: Thomas Brown, John Tolleson, and Stone; grant to Jacob Holmes (date not given). Witness Thomas Brown and James Poole. Signed Malichi Monk's mark. Wit. oath Oct. 10, 1796 Thomas Brown to H McCray. Rec. Oct. 18, 1796

p. 17-19 Mar. 21, 1795 John Lemaster (Spartanburgh) to John Ashford Gore (same); for 25£ sterling sold 200 ac on N side Pacolate R and on Dennan Cr; part of tract surveyed by Jesse Connel for John Lemaster. Witness Thomas Jones, Griffin Carter, and Joseph Lively. Signed John Lemaster's mark. Wit. oath Dec. 15, 1796 Thomas Jones to John Lipscomb. Rec. Oct. 18, 1796

p. 19-20 May 17, 1790 Henry Turner (Spartanburgh) to James Simmons (same); for 50£ sold 127 ac; border: David Allin, David Jones, Philip Martin, and John Headen; part of 247 ac on a branch of Goucher's Cr of Thickety Cr. Witness John Headen and John George

Reiner. Signed Henry Turner. Wit. oath May 21, 1790 John Headen to Obadiah Trimmier. Rec. Oct. 19, 1796

p. 20-21 Nov. 21, 1796 Ann Cook (Edgefield Co), administrator of Henry White's (Spartanburgh) estate, to friend Daniel White; power of attorney to administer and settle Henry White's estate. Witness Jas Smith, M Lovina Smith, and Wm R Smith. Signed Ann Cook. Wit. oath Nov. 21, 1796 Jas Smith to Ism Foster. Rec. Nov. 29, 1796

p. 21-22 Nov. 21, 1796 Ann Cook (Edgefield Co), sold surviving administrator of estate of Randolph Mitchel (Laurens Co), desc, and son Samuel Mitchell and James Hardy, surviving husband of daughter Patty Mitchel, desc, (all other Mitchel children being desc), Daniel White and his brothers and sisters: John White, Reubin White, Richard James, Thomas James, John Mapp, and Francis White ("in consideration of release and discharge from administration of estate of Henry White, esq, Spartanburgh, desc" received from Daniel White and his brothers and sisters) to John White; release and quit claim of John White's security for administration of estate of Randolph Mitchel. Witness Jas Smith, M Lovina Smith, and Lettice Smith. Signed Ann Cook. Wit. oath Nov. 21, 1796 Jas Smith to Ism Foster. Rec. Nov. 29, 1796

p. 22-24 Jan. 10, 1797 John Gowen (Spartanburgh) to Abner Hona (same); for 50£ sold 100 ac on both sides S fork of Mill Cr; border: Ridge between N and S forks of Mill Cr and includes McNeal's old place. Witness Jo Easley and John Robuck. Signed Jon Gowen. Rec. Nov. 29, 1797

p. 24-27 Feb. 16, 1795 William Hasel Gibbs, esq, master of Equity Court (Charleston, SC) to John McDowell (same); for 70£ sold 700 ac on Maple Swamp Cr of Tryer R; border: N-old Indian line, E-Heyward, and others vacant; grant to Thomas Farr; Ralph Izard, the younger, and Joshua Ward two of the qualified executors of will of Thomas Farr (St. Andrews Parish), esq, desc, on Mar. 13, 1793 filed a complaint in Equity Court against William Bradford Farr, son and qualified executor of Thomas Farr and on behalf of the other children; Court is asked to sell Thomas Farr's estate to settle the debts--refer to "bill of record" in clerk's office; decision in Mar. term 1793; land sold on Feb. 16, 1795. Witness Oliver Cromwell and Cs Stewart. Signed W Hasel Gibbs. Wit. oath Mar. 18, 1797 Oliver Cromwell to John Johnson. Rec. Mar. 31, 1798

p. 27-29 Jun. 1, 1797 Vardry McBee (Spartanburgh) to James Ross, jr (York Co); for 300£ sold 1,740 ac on Miller's fork of Thickety Cr; grant Sept. 18, 1785 to Vardry McBee; includes "several ancient surveys allowed to Vardry McBee by Counsel of State of SC". Witness John Bailey, Moses Carroll, and Humphrey Baker. Signed Vardry McBee. Wit. oath Jun. 1, 1797 Moses Carroll to Jos Kerr. Rec. Nov. 29, 1797

p. 29-30 Dec. 28, 1796 John Robuck and wife Sarah (Spartanburgh) to Joseph Powers (same); for 30£ sterling sold 47 ac on both sides Motley's Cr and N side Tyger R; border: Benja Grist and John Chumley. Witness Jon Gowen and John Chumley. Signed John Robuck and Sarah's mark. Wit. oath Jan. 18, 1797 Jon Gowen to H McCray. Rec. Feb. 6, 1797

p. 30-31 Oct. 1, 1795 Richard Cantrell (Spartanburgh) to Charles Cantrell (same); for 20£ SC money sold 200 ac on Little Buck Cr; grant Jan. 12, 1789 States Office to John Jones. Witness S Bethel, Cantrell Bethell, and John Cantrell, sr. Signed Richard Cantrell. Certified Oct. 31, 1795 by S Bethel. Rec. Feb. 6, 1797

p. 31-32 Jan. 1, 1798 Maxamillian Conner to Isaac Bishop; for 70 (or 75) £ sold 140 ac where Seth Lewis lives six miles from Spartan Co Court, a black horse 4' 10" high, a saddle, 2 feather beds and furniture, 2 pots, an oven, 2 dishes and 6 plates, a set of knives and forks, a plough and set of harnes, an ax, 2 spinning wheels, a large framed table, 6 chairs, 9 hogs marked with cross and split in each ear, and a cow and calf. Signed Maxn Conner. Certified Feb. 6, 1798 James Jordan. Rec. Apr. 30, 1798

p. 32-34 Nov. 4, 1794 Edward Lacy, esq, sheriff (Pinckney Dist) to Samuel Lancaster, esq (Spartanburgh); for 30£ 3s 2p sold 266 ac SW part of grant in 1774 to James Tillett; John Ford, esq, obtained judgment in Nov. term of court in 1793 against Brittain Williford and John Shands, executors of James White, desc for 47£ 7s 5p sterling Judge John Rutledge, presiding; above 266 ac of James White sold Jul. 7, 1794. Witness Obadiah Trimmier, John Gowen, and James A Whyte. Signed Edwd Lacey. Wit. oath Nov. 4, 1794 John Gowen to I Harrison. Rec. Feb. 7, 1797

p. 34-36 Sept. 2, 1797 Thomas Smith (Spartanburgh) to Thomas Cook (same); for 50£ SC money sold 147 ac on Dutchman's Cr where Thomas Smith lives; on NW side of Edward Rollin's land; grant May 7, 1787 Gov. Thomas Pinckney to Thomas Smith. Witness Augustine Bumpass and John Smith. Signed Thomas Smith. Certified Sept. 2, 1797 by Wm Smith. Rec. Feb. 7, 1797

p. 36-37 Sept. 20, 1796 John Cooper (Spartanburgh) to William Cooper (same); for 40£ sold 100 ac on Beverdam Cr of Thickety Cr; border: William Cooper, Tanner, Cowpen's Road; part of 600 ac grant Jan. 1, 1787 to John Cooper. Witness Matthew Cooper and Micajah Cooper. Signed John Cooper. Wit. oath Nov. 30, 1796 Macajah Cooper to Henry McCray. Rec. Sept. 17, 1797

p. 37-39 Aug. 26, 1796 Abraham Andrews (Spartanburgh) to James Boyd (same); for 50£ SC money sold 100 ac on Richland Cr; part of 200 ac grant Oct. 2, 1786 States Office to Richard Speaks. Witness Dan Bennett, John Hasty, and Mary White. Signed Abraham Andrews' mark. Wit. oath Sept. 7, 1796 Dan Bennett to William McDowell. Rec. Sept. 17, 1797

p. 39-40 Aug. 22, 1796 Obadiah Oliphant (Spartanburgh) to Isaac Chapman (Union Co); for 90£ sterling sold 200 ac on Goucher's Cr; border: Wm Wilkins; where Obadiah Oliphant lives. Witness Richard Simmonds and James Harrison. Signed Obadiah Oliphant. Wit. oath Aug. 22, 1796 Richard Simmonds to John Lipscomb. Rec. Sept. 18, 1797

p. 40-42 Feb. 6, 1795 Charles Benson (Greenville Co) to William Benson (Spartanburgh); for 10£ sterling sold 118 ac on Fairforrest Cr of Tygar R; border: Benjamin Thompson and others unknown; grant Feb. 6, 1786 Gov. William Moultrie to (not given). Witness Wm Gowen, Michael Miller, and Joseph Benson. Signed Charles Benson. Wit. oath Jan. 13, 1797 Michael Miller to Isham Foster. Rec. Sept. 18, 1797

p. 42-43 Jun. (not given), 1796 Capt. James Martin (Lincoln Co, NC) to Alexander Cooper; for 30£ SC money sold 200 ac on branches of Beverdam Cr of Thickety Cr and on Cherokee Cr and on both sides of Cowpens Road. Witness Saley Taylor and George Taylor. Signed James Martin. Wit. oath (not dated) George Taylor to H McCray. Rec. Sept. 18, 1797

p. 43-45 Sept. 8, 1796 Wells Griffith (Spartanburgh) to Bazel Lee (same); for 50£ sterling sold 100 ac on S side Lawson's fork of Pacolet R; border: Wm Dickson's old line; grant Jan. 21,

1785 Gov. Benjamin Guerard to Wells Griffith. Witness Joseph Robertson and Richd Cruce. Signed Wells Griffith. Wit. oath Dec. 8, 1796 Joseph Robertson to I Harrison. Rec. Sept. 18, 1797

p. 45-46 Jan. 26, 1796 Ignatious Griffin and wife Mavel (Spartanburgh) to George Gibson (same); for 30£ sterling sold 140 ac on both sides Goucher's Cr. Witness Young Allen and Sarah Croyley. Signed Ignatious and Mavel Griffin's marks. Wit. oath Young Allen to John Lipscomb. Rec. Sept. 19, 1797

p. 46-48 Apr. 12, 1796 Simon Park (Spartan Co) to Adam Johnson (same); for 15£ sold 50 ac on Barton's Br and Shoaly Cr. Witness John Pipes, Priscilla Pipes, and Levi Burchum. Signed Simon Park's mark. Wit. oath Apr. 13, 1796 John Pipes to William McDowell. Rec. Sept. 19, 1797

p. 48-50 May 23, 1795 Alexander Elder and wife Mary (Spartanburgh) to Zopher Smith (same); for 100£ sold 151 ac on Dutchman's Cr and on N side Tyger R; border: Samuel Morrow; part of 468 ac grant Mar. 5, 1787 Gov. Thomas Pinckney to Alexander Elder. Witness Jonathan Smith, Robert Elder, and John Elder. Signed Alexander Elder and Mary's mark. Wit. oath Jan. 13, 1796 Jonathan Smith to I Harrison. Rec. Sept. 19, 1797

p. 50-51 Jan. 6, 1791 Leonard Sparks (Spartanburgh) to Samuel Wilkins (same); for 40£ sold 75 ac on N side Pacolate R and above the mouth of Tumbling Shoal Br. Witness I Harrison. Signed Leonard Sparks. Rec. Sept. 19, 1797

p. 51-52 Jan. 7, 1797 Josiah Culbertson (Greenville Co) to Samuel Culbertson (Spartanburgh); for 20£ sold 179 ac on a branch of Fairforrest Cr; border: NE & NW-Samuel Culbertson, SE & SW-old lines, and W-vacant; grant Jan. 21, 1785 Gov. Benjamin Guerard to Josiah Culbertson. Witness Elin Smith, Andrew Culbertson, and Wm Davis Thomas. Signed Josiah Culbertson. Wit. oath (Greenville Co) Jan. 13, 1797 Wm Davis Thomas to J Thomas jr. Rec. Sept. 20, 1797

p. 52-54 Nov. 28, 1795 John George Reiner (Franklin Co, Ga) to Peter Peterson (Spartanburgh); for (page torn) £ sold 100 ac on Green's Cr of Pacolet R; grant to William Hargrove. Witness John Headen (? page torn) and Walker Walker. Signed John George Reiner. Wit. oath Jan. 13, 1797 John Headen to Ism Foster. Rec. Sept. 20, 1797

p. 54-56 Nov. 3, 1796 John McDowell (Union Co), heir to estate of Benjamin McDowell (96 Dist), desc to Andrew Thomson (Spartanburgh); for 75£ sterling sold 200 ac on both sides Ward's Cr; border: Charles Moore and Martin Otts; grant NC governor to Joseph Alexander, minister, (then in Tryon, NC) who sold to Benjamin McDowell, desc. Witness William Burton, David Tanner, and George Isom. Signed John McDowell. Wit. oath Nov. 24, 1796 George Isom to Thos Moore. Rec. Sept. 20, 1797

p. 56-58 Jan. 14, 1794 Thomas Hunter (Spartanburgh) to Richeson Whitley (same); for 20£ sterling sold 75 ac; border: Thomas Brown, Richeson Whitley's Spring Br, John Lukeroy's Br, and John Burke; part of 608 ac grant Jun. 2, 1788 Gov. Thomas Pickney to Michael Megaughy who sold to "Thomas Brown, Enos Land and Richeson Whitley". Witness William Crocker, Anthony Crocker, and Richard Lee. Signed Thomas Hunter. Wit. oath Apr. 23, 1796 William Crocker to William Simpson. Rec. Sept. 20, 1797

p. 58-60 Jan 26, 1796 Ignatious Griffin (Spartanburgh) to George Gibson (same); for 5£ sterling sold 15 ac; border: Malichi Jones. Witness Young Allen and Sarah Croyley. Signed Ignatious

Griffin's mark. Wit. oath Jan. 12, 1797 Young Allen to John Lipscomb. Rec. Sept. 20, 1797

p. 60-61 Aug. 4, 1796 Gideon Heraldson and wife Elizabeth (Spartanburgh) to John Hendman jr (same); for 50£ sterling sold 50 ac on branches of Dutchman's Cr and N side of Tyger R; border: Samuel Morrow, Zopher Smith, Fuller, John Hendman, Abraham Hembree, and George Sloan; part of 200 ac where Gideon Heraldson lives granted in 1786 Gov. William Moultrie to William Weir. Witness Jesse Meaders, Thomas Meaders, and Joseph Meaders. Signed Gideon and Elizabeth Heraldson. Wit. oath Jan. 11, 1797 Jesse Meaders to Wm Smith. Rec. Sept. 21, 1797

p. 61-64 Apr. 17, 1795 Thomas Jordan (Spartanburgh) to John Cantrell (same); for 150£ SC money sold 186 ac on Big and Little Buck Cr; border: School House Br; granted "three times" on Dec. 3, 1787 States Office to Thomas Jordan, on Jan. 21, 1785 to John Hightower, and on Jan. 1, 1787 to William Morris. Witness S Bethel, Larkin Bethel, and Cantrell Bethel. Signed Thomas Jordan's mark. Certified Apr. 17, 1795 by S Bethel. Rec. Sept. 21, 1797

p. 64-65 Jan. 5, 1797 Richard Chesney (Spartanburgh) to Richard Chesney jr (same); for 25 (? £) sold 50 ac on James' Cr; border: W-Jacob Earnest, N-William Earnest, and E-Richard Chesney jr; part of 150 ac grant to Martin Leviston and sold by John Leviston, an heir, to Richard Chesney. Witness John Chesney, Thomas Richards, and Paul Castleberry. Signed Richard Chesney's mark. Wit. oath Jan. 12, 1797 John Chesney to George Bruton. Rec. Sept. 21, 1797

p. 65-66 Dec. 26, 1796 Solomon Hays (Union Co) to Edward Herring (Spartanburgh); for 20£ sold 100 ac on Lawson's fork of Pacolet R; grant Mar. 6, 1796 to John Conner. Witness I Harrison. Signed Solomon Hays' mark. Rec. Sept. 21, 1797

p. 66-67 Jan. 4, 1796 James Martin (York Co) to Moses Guyton (Union Co); for 200£ sold 500 ac on Beverdam Cr of Thickety Cr including improvements where George Taylor lives; in two grants: (1) for 300 ac on John Hogan and (2) for 250 ac to Vardry McBee. Witness George Taylor and Isham Fannin. Signed James Martin. Wit. oath (Union Co) Apr. 2, 1796 George Taylor to Nicholas Corry. Rec. Sept. 22, 1797

p. 67-70 Nov. 10, 1795 Reubin Bryant (Spartanburgh) to Peter Peterson; for 30£ sterling sold 640 ac on N side Pacolet R; border: E-Jesse Catin, Peter Peterson, George Reiner, and James Brown, N-Jones and Howard, W-John Stovaul, SW-Arthus Debardelaban and John Peterson. Witness Joshua Elliot, Daniel Lenalen, and William Pool. Signed Reubin Bryant's mark. Wit. oath Jan. 10, 1797 Joshua Elliot to John Lipscomb. Rec. Sept. 22, 1797

p. 70-72 Mar. 7, 1795 William Bratcher (Greenville Co) to John Grist (Spartanburgh); for 60£ sterling sold 120 ac on Dutchman's Cr of Tyger R; border: S-Carns, E-William Farmer, N-Samuel Lancaster, and W-Dutchman's Cr; Nathan Wooton and Moses Pruett's lands are a mioty of the same tract; part of 270 ac grant Dec. 4, 1786 Gov. William Moultrie to (not given). Witness Moses Pruett, Moses Lewis, and Elizabeth Harrison. Signed William Bratcher. Wit. oath Oct. 30, 1795 Moses Pruett to Saml Lancaster. Rec. Sept. 22, 1797

p. 72-73 Jan. 13, 1797 Edward Barnett (Spartanburgh) to William Bagwell (same); for 30£ sold 100 ac on Lawson's fork; grant to Charles James. Witness I Harrison. Signed Edward Barnett. Rec. Sept. 22, 1797

p. 73-74 Jul. 14, 1796 John Kirkland (Spartanburgh) to Ephraim Elder (same); for 65£ sterling sold 100 ac on N side Pacolate R; border: Henry Turner; grant Nov. 7, 1785 States Office to William Dickson. Witness James Turner, William Saunders, and James Saunders. Signed John Kirkland's mark. Wit. oath Oct. 11, 1796 William Saunders to I Harrison. Rec. Sept. 22, 1797

p. 74-75 Dec. 22, 1796 Daniel Bragg (Spartanburgh) to Alexander Autry (same); for 20£ sterling sold 73 ac except 3/4 ac on SW corner; on S side of S fork Tyger R; plat attached shows border: Thomas Hightower, George Bruton, and Tyger R; grant Gov. William Moultrie to Daniel Bragg. Witness Paul Castlebury and Catherine Brewton. Signed Daniel Bragg. Wit. oath Dec. 22, 1796 Paul Castlebury to George Brewton. Rec. Sept. 23, 1797

p. 75-77 Oct. 20, 1796 Allen Gowen (Davison Co, Tenn) to Burrell Bobo (Spartanburgh); for 150£ sterling sold 300 ac on N side Tyger R; border: NE-Thomas Fletcher and others vacant; grant Dec. 23, 1771 Gov. Charles G Montague to Joseph Gowen and to Allen Gowen by descent. Witness Martin Newman, Charity Newman, and Simpson Newman. Signed Allen Gowen. Wit. oath Oct. 22, 1796 Martin Newman to Moses Casey. Rec. Sept. 23, 1797

p. 77-78 Aug. 3, 1794 Reubin Blanton (Rutherford Co, NC) to Thomas Clary; for 50£ sold 292 ac on Sarratt's Cr of Broad R; border: N-North Carolina line, S-William Davidson, and E & W-vacant; grant Oct. 6, 1788 Gov. Thomas Pinckney to Reubin Blanton. Witness James Laurence and David Tate. Signed Richard Blanton. Wit. oath Apr. 27, 1797 David Tate to H McCray. Rec. Sept. 23, 1797

p. 78-80 Mar. 28, 1796 James T White (Spartanburgh) to John James (Pinckney Dist, same); for 23£ sterling sold 143 ac where James T White lives; border: John Timmons, Jeremiah Lucas, and John Lucas; part of grant to Thomas Collins. Witness Wm Foster and John Walker. Signed James T White. Wit. oath May 9, 1797 John Walker to Thos Moore. Rec. Sept. 24, 1797

p. 80-81 Sept. 10, 1796 John James (Spartanburgh) to John D Young (same); for $173 sold 143 ac on W side of N fork Tyger R; border: John Timmons, Jeremiah Lucus, and John Lucus; part of grant to Thomas Collins; sold by James T White to John James. Witness Lowrie McDaniel and Thos Moore JP. Signed John James. Wit. oath Apr. 15, 1797 Lowrie McDaniel to Thos Moore. Rec. Sept. 24, 1797

p. 81-82 Sept. 12, 1796 Jason Moore, sr (Spartanburgh) to James Moore (same); for $40 sold 72 ac on both sides Ward's Cr of Tyger R; border: NW-Thomas Moore, W-Charles Moore, S-William Ford, and "others" including Jason Moore. Witness John Otts, Samuel Otts, and William Otts. Signed Jason Moore. Wit. oath Oct. 8, 1796 William Otts to Thos Moore. Rec. Sept. 24, 1797

p. 82-83 Dec. 20, 1796 Laurence Bankson (Spartanburgh) to Isaac Cantrell sr (same); for 70£ sterling sold 426 ac on both sides Pacolate R; border: John Bankson and Edward Stubblefield; grant Jan. 21, 1785 States Office to Reubin Dickson who sold to John Hightower who sold to Laurence Bankson. Witness Joseph Turner, John Bankson, and Mary Burgess. Signed Laurence Bankson's mark. Wit. oath Jan. 13, 1797 Laurence Bankson to George Lamkin. Rec. Sept. 24, 1797

p. 83-85 Jan. 22, 1796 William Simpson (Spartanburgh) to Aaron Lan (same); for 15£ sterling sold 300 ac on Fairforrest Cr; border: William Golightly, Noblet, McCord, and Thomas; part of 365 ac grant Jan. 6, 1794 to William Simpson. Witness William Crocker, John Lukeroy, and Richeson Whittery. Signed William Simson. Wit. oath Apr. 23, 1796 William Simson esq to I Harrison. Rec. Sept. 24,

1797

p. 85-87 Jul. 30, 1796 John Bolen sr (Spartanburgh) to John Giding (Spartanburgh); for 10£ sterling sold 40 ac on both sides of Old Iron Rd and on Ford's Cr; border: land Henry Wells sold to Travice Reece, John Bolin, Thomas Reece, and Bolin's Spring Br. Witness Francis Mason and John Mason. Signed John Bolen's mark. Wit. oath Oct. 10, 1796 Francis Mason to I Harrison. Rec. Sept. 24, 1797

p. 87-88 Jun. 24, 1797 James Ward and wife Susannah (Spartanburgh) to Solomon Ward; for a Spanish milled dollar sold 72 ac on both sides Fairforrest Cr of Tyger R; border: Wells, Tan trough Br, John White, and Nathan Ward. Witness Wm Foster and Nathan Ward. Signed James and Susannah Ward's marks. Wit. oath Jul. 1, 1797 Wm Foster to I Harrison. Rec. Sept. 24, 1797

p. 88-90 Jul. 11, 1796 Henry Wells (Spartanburgh) to John Giding (same); for 20£ sterling sold 70 ac on Ford's Cr; border: John Bolin, Josiah Hatchel, William Tindsley, and land Robert Piper sold to Thomas Reese; "part of it" Henry Wells sold to Travice Reece and part "takeing of" William Tindsley's land. Witness John Mason and Jesse Wells. Signed Henry Wells. Wit. oath Oct. 10, 1796 John Mason to I Harrison. Rec. Sept. 24, 1797

p. 90-92 Dec. 31, 1796 Wells Griffith and wife Elizabeth (Spartanburgh) to Richard James (same); for 100£ SC money sold (1) 204 ac on Lawson's fork of Pacolate R where Wells Griffith lives; border: Lacey McAbee, Wofford and Co, land formerly James Brown's, land formerly Samuel Wards', and land formerly William Pool's; grant Sept. 7, 1789 Gov. Charles Pinckney to Reubin Matthews; and (2) 365 ac on Lawson's fork of Tyger R (sic) in two tracts granted to James Brown and sold May 27, 1792 by Thomas Farrow to Wells Griffith. Witness Joroyal Barnett and Jesse Matthews. Signed Wells Griffith and Elizabeth's mark. Wit. oath Apr. 10, 1797 Jesse Matthews to I Harrison. Rec. Sept. 25, 1797. Dower renounced Elizabeth Griffith to I Harrison Apr. 20, 1797

p. 92-94 Mar. 10, 1797 Alexander McMekin (Loudoun Co, Va) to son Benjamine Perrine McMekin; for love and affection and 5s sterling sold a Negro woman Linn and her child Jack. Witness Gust Eggin, Thos Janney, Jno Mathias. Signed A McMakin. Wit. oath (Loudoun Co, Va) Mar. 11, 1797 Thos Janney and Jno Mathias to Joseph Smith. Mar. 11, 1797 Certified that Joseph Smith is a justice of peace by Chas Binns, clerk Loudoun Co, Va.

p. 94-96 Oct. 9, 1795 Edward Stubblefield (Spartanburgh) to Thomas Burgess, minister (same); for 25£ SC money sold 114 ac on Pacolet R; grant Jan. 21, 1785 States Office to Reubin Dickson. Witness S Bethel, Reubin Warren, and Elijah Thompson. Signed Edward Stubblefield's mark. Certified Oct. 10, 1795 by S Bethel. Rec. Sept. 25, 1797

p. 96-97 Jan. 23, 1797 Hansel Dollar (Spartanburgh) to William Waldrope (same); for 50£ sold 50 ac on W side Danceing Br; border: David Neel and William Waldrope. Witness Aaron Casey and Benjamin Rhodes. Signed Hansel Dollar. Wit. oath Mar. 29, 1797 Aaron Casey to Moses Casey. Rec. Sept. 25, 1797

p. 97-98 Nov. 22, 1794 John Leech (Spartanburgh) to William Benson (same); for 40£ sterling sold 167 ac on branches of N fork Tyger R; border: Alexander Vernon; grant May 4, 1769 Gov. William Tryon (NC) to John Leech. Witness John Vaughan, Michael Waldan, and Daniel Evans. Signed John Leech. Wit. oath May 9, 1797 John Vaughan to H McCray. Rec. Sept. 25, 1797

p. 98-100 Nov. 29, 1791 William Tate, sr (Spartan Co) to Andrew Hopkins; for 60£ sterling sold 143 ac on both sides of "main" Cherokee Cr of Broad R; grant May 1, 1786. Witness Joseph Dill and James Clarke. Signed William Tate. Wit. oath Mar. 11, 1797 Joseph Dill to Henry McCray. Rec. Sept. 25, 1797

p. 100-102 Jan. 4, 1797 Isaac Tindsley (Spartan Co) to Francis Mason (same); for 40£ SC money sold 211 ac on both sides Ford's Cr after 39 ac taken off lower line to run parallel with upper line; part of grant Gov. William Bull to John Parker who sold to Joseph Kirkland who sold to Ann Holloway who sold to William Tindsley who sold to Isaac Tindsley. Witness Wm Foster and John Mason. Signed Isaac Tindsley. Wit. oath Mar. 11, 1797 Wm Foster to I Harrison. Rec. Sept. 26, 1797

p. 102-103 Oct. 31, 1796 George Taylor (Spartan Co) to Dennis Sullivan (same); power of attorney to collect from Alexander McBeth (Union Co) the balance of three notes given after satisfying an account due from George Taylor to Alexander McBee. Witness Wm Thomson and John Watson jr. Signed George Taylor's mark. Wit. oath Jan. 16, 1797 John Watson to Henry McCray. Rec. Sept. 26, 1797

p. 103-105 Mar. 22, 1797 Joseph Morris (Edgefield Co) to William Morris (Spartanburgh); for 20£ sterling sold 200 ac on N side Pacolate R; grant Oct. 1, 1787 States Office to Thomas Barton. Witness William Burckhalter, Jeremiah Burckhalter, and Abraham Burckhalter. Signed Joseph Morris' mark. Wit. oath (Abbeville Co) Mar. 25, 1797 Joseph Morris to Jno Trotter. Rec. Sept. 26, 1797

p. 105-106 Mar. 22, 1797 Joseph Morris (Edgefield Co) to William Morris (Spartanburgh: for 20£ sterling sold 100 ac on N side Pacolet R; grant Apr. 25, 1767 States Office (NC) to Thomas Williamson who sold Aug. 29, 1769 to Thomas Barton. Witness William Burckhalter, Jeremiah Buckhalter, and Abraham Buckhalter. Signed Joseph Morris' mark. Wit. oath (Abbeville Co) Mar. 25, 1797 Joseph Morris to Jno Trotter. Rec. Sept. 26, 1797

p. 106-108 Nov. 4, 1791 Jesse Connell and wife Ann (Spartanburgh) to Ransom Tinsly (same); for 41£ 15s sold 83½ ac on NE side Fairforrest Cr; part of 175 ac sold by John Walker to Jesse Connell. Witness William Foster and Thomas Tinsly. Signed Jesse Connell and Ann's mark. Wit. oath Mar. 2, 1792 William Foster to D Goodlett. Rec. Sept. 26, 1796

p. 108-110 Feb. 6, 1797 John Ford (Shelby Co, Ky) to Henry Cannon (Spartanburgh); for $170 sold two tracts: (1) 150 ac border: E-Tyger R, N-Richard Barry, S & SW-John Ford and John Poesey; and (2) 420 ac border: E-Richard Barry, W-James Mivoron(?), and S-John Poesey; both granted to John Ford: (1) in May 1774 and (2) Jun. 2, 1794; plat attached shows additional border: (1): vacant and tract (2); and (2): James Miller, Charles Moore, Alexander, and Jos Akins. Witness Clary Lancaster and William Lancaster. Signed Jesse Ford, attorney for John Ford. Wit. oath Apr. 10, 1797 William Lancaster to Isham Foster. Rec. Sept. 26, 1797

p. 110-111 May 18, 1798 John Ross (Spartanburgh) to James Tate (same); for 50£ sterling sold (1) 46 ac and (2) 200 ac in two tracts on W side Broad R below Tate's Ferry and bordering Tate's old line; (1) part of 200 ac grant Dec. 23, 1768 Gov. William Tryon (NC) to John Tygert; (2) is half of grant Apr. 2, 1792 Gov. Charles Pinckney to John Ross and bordering Tate's old line, Gowen, and Tate's Mill tract. Witness Jas Smith and William Gibson. Signed John Ross. Wit. oath May 18, 1798 Jas Smith to

BOOK E

H McCray

p. 111-113 May 17, 1798 James Tate (Spartanburgh) to John Ross (same); for 10£ sold 23 ac on W side Broad R including Tate's Ferry; part of grant Oct. 26, 1767 NC governor to Frances Batey and eventually sold to William Tate (late of Spartanburgh) and by his will to his son James Tate. Witness Jas Smith and William Gibson. Signed James Tate. Wit. oath May 18, 1798 Jas Smith to H McCray

p. 113-114 Sept. 10, 1796 David Jones (Spartanburgh) to John Robertson (same); for 26£ sterling sold 175 ac; NW half of 350 ac grant to David Jones. Witness David Jones, jr and William Morris. Signed David Jones. Wit. oath Sept. 10, 1796 David Jones, jr to John Lipscomb. Rec. Sept. 27, 1797

p. 114-116 Mar. 12, 1797 Joel Hembree and wife Hannah (Spartanburgh) to Thomas Betterton (same); for 60£ sterling sold 78 ac on N side Tyger R; border: John Campbell and Timothy Toney. Witness Levi Lancaster and Samuel Wilson. Signed Joel Hembree and Hannah's mark. Wit. oath Mar. 25, 1797 Samuel Wilson to Wm Smith. Rec. Sept. 27, 1797

p. 116-118 Mar. 28, 1797 William Moore (Spartanburgh) to William Earnest (same); for 55£ sterling sold 100 ac exclusive of a small piece taken by Brown's line; border: S-Enoree R, SE-Benjn Wofford, and NW-Joseph Wofford; grant Jul. 4, 1769 Gov. Chas G. Montague to Zachariah Gibbs. Witness Holloway Power and Joseph Woodruff. Signed William Moore. Certified Mar. 28, 1797 by Wm Smith. Rec. Sept. 27, 1797. Dower renounced Betty Moore to Wm Smith Mar. 28, 1797

p. 118-119 Dec. 20, 1793 John Hamby (Spartanburgh) to William Moore (same); for 110£ sterling sold 100 ac exclusive of a small piece taken by Brown's line; border: S-Enoree R and others vacant; grant in 1769 Gov. Charles G Montague to Zachariah Gibbs. Witness Holloway Powers, James Higgins, and Simon Gentry. Signed John Hamby's mark. Wit. oath Mar. 28, 1797 Holloway Powers to Wm Smith. Rec. Sept. 27, 1797

p. 119-120 Oct. 26, 1796 John Gray (Spartanburgh) to Nathan Ward (same); for a Spanish milled dollar sold 240 ac on branches of Lawson's fork; border: Reubin Lauson. Witness Curtis Gray, Casandra Gray, and Ann Mathis. Signed John Gray. Wit. oath Apr. 10, 1797 Curtis Gray to I Harrison. Rec. Sept. 28, 1797

p. 120-122 Aug. 18, 1796 Reubin Warren (Spartanburgh) to Thomas Wyatt (same); for 5£ sterling sold 100 ac on Pacolet R; part of 1,000 ac grant to Abram Markley who sold to Reubin Warren. Witness Samuel Turner, Henry Adcock, and William Adcock. Signed Reubin Warren. Wit. oath Aug. 24, 1796 Samuel Turner to George Lamkin. Rec. Sept. 28, 1797

p. 122-124 Mar. 3, 1795 William Hamby (Pendleton, SC) to Joseph Woodruff (Spartanburgh); for 40£ sterling sold 180 ac on Enoree R; border: William Moore, Lick Cr, John Hamby, Isaac Hamby, and Henry Cole; part of grant Aug. 17, 1774 Gov. William Bull to William Hamby. Witness James Lindsey, John Allen, and William Allen. Signed William Hamby's mark. Wit. oath Apr. 8, 1797 James Lindsey to Zadock Ford. Rec. Sept. 28, 1797. Dower renounced (Greenville Co) Cealia Hamby, wife of William Hamby, to Robert Maxwell May 14, 1796. Dower renounced Anne Hamby, widow of "within named" William Hamby, sr, desc, to William Smith Aug. 15, 1797

p. 124-127 Nov. 30, 1789 William Hamby (Spartanburgh) to Joseph Woodruff (same); for 55£ sterling sold 200 ac on Jamey's

Cr; W part of grant Aug. 19, 1774 Gov. Bull to Thomas Laxton. Witness William Moore, Moses Moore, and Thomas House. Signed William Hamby's mark. Wit. oath Mar. 28, 1797 William Moore to Wm Smith. Rec. Sept. 28, 1797. Dower renounced (Greenville Co) Cealia Hamby, wife of William Hamby, to Robert Maxwell May 14, 1796. Dower renounced Ann Hamby, wife of "within named" William Hamby, sr to Wm Smith. Aug. 15, 1796

p. 127-128 Dec. 14, 1792 John Gibbs and wife Ann to John Hacker; for 30£ sterling sold 100 ac; part of 350 ac on Rocky Cr and S side of Tyger R grant Aug. 11, 1774 to Edmond Bearden; border: N-Peter Pennell, E-Thomas Tod, S-Thomas Miles, and W-James Simples; plat attached. Witness Peter Pennell and James Anderson. Signed James Gibbs and Ann's mark. Wit. oath Jul. 19, 1793 Peter Pennell and James Anderson to Saml Lancaster

p. 128-133 Nov. 8, 1788 William Hamby (96 Dist) to John Hamby (same); for 20£ sterling sold 100 ac on N side Enoree R; border: all vacant; if there is an earlier claim to the land, John looses the land; grant Jul. 4, 1769 Gov. Charles G. Montague to Zachariah Gibbs who sold to William Hamby, desc and to William Hamby by heirship. Witness Jonathan Dildine, John Cross, James Wofford. Signed William and Sealey Hamby's marks. Wit. oath Mar. 28, 1797 John Cross to Wm Smith. Rec. Sept. 30, 1797

p. 133-134 Jul. 31, 1796 Feneter Wilkins (Spartanburgh) to William Vincent (same); for 45£ sold 104 ac on Beverdam Cr. Witness I Harrison. Signed Feneter Wilkins' mark. Wit. oath Jul. 31, 1796 Feneter Wilkins to I Harrison. Rec. Sept. 30, 1797

p. 134-135 Apr. 20, 1797 William Vincent (Spartanburgh) to John Cantwell (same); for 30£ sold 104 ac on Beverdam Cr of Fairforrest Cr. Witness I Harrison. Signed William Vincent. Rec. Oct. 1, 1797

p. 135-136 Mar. 29, 1797 Abraham Moore (Spartanburgh) to James Moore (same); for 20£ sold 50 ac on Dutchman's Cr; border: Thomas Compton; part of 150 ac grant Jun. 20, 1770 to Abraham Moore. Witness James Ham and John Shands. Signed Abraham Moore's mark. Certified Mar. 30, 1797 by Wm Smith. Rec. Oct. 1, 1797. Dower renounced Mary Moore to Wm Smith Mar. 30, 1797

p. 136-138 Mar. 29, 1797 Thomas Thornton (Spartanburgh) to James Moore (same); for 10£ sold 37 ac on Dutchman's Cr; border: Thomas Compton and Samuel Morrow; part of 236 ac grant Jun. 5, 1786 to Thomas Compton. Witness Saml Morrow and Willis Williford. Signed Thomas Thornton's mark. Certified Mar. 29, 1797 by Wm Smith. Rec. Oct. 1, 1797. Dower renounced Martha Thornton to Wm Smith Apr. 10, 1797

p. 138-140 Dec. 21, 1791 Ezekiel Howard and wife Mary (Spartanburgh) to Griffin Carter (same); for 15£ sterling sold 90 ac on head branches of Goties Cr. Witness James Simmons and Thomas Jones. Signed Ezekiel Howard's mark and Mary Ann Howard. Wit. oath Jun. 16, 1792 Thomas Jones to Isham Harrison. Rec. Oct. 1, 1797

p. 140-142 Aug. 7, 1793 Jesse Barker (Laurens Co) to James Wofford (Spartanburgh); for 10s sterling sold 820 ac on Maple Swamp Cr and Rockfield Cr of Tygar and Enoree R; border: E-Williamson and others vacant or old lines; grant Mar. 4, 1793 to Jesse Barker. Witness Nathaniel Wofford, John Barker, and Mary Barker. Signed Jesse Barker's mark. Wit. oath Nov. 5, 1796 Nathaniel Wofford to Zadock Ford. Rec. Oct. 1, 1797

p. 142-143 Jun. 27, 1796 John Morgan, heir of John Morgan, desc, and wife Sarah (Spartanburgh) to James Wofford (same); for 60£ sterling sold 450 ac on Forgeson's Cr of Tyger R; border: James Wofford, James Bruton, and Henry Earnest; grant in 1773 to John Morgan, desc in Craven Co. Witness John Hambey, jr, John Hambey, and Aaron Baulcomb. Signed John Morgan and Sarah's mark. Wit. oath Nov. 5, 1796 John Hambey jr to Zadock Ford. Rec. Oct. 2, 1797

p. 143-145 Dec. 5, 1796 Joseph Morris (Edgefield Co) to John Morris (Spartanburgh); for 25£ sterling sold 100 ac on Buck Cr of Pacolet R; border: formerly Robert Nelson's land and William Morris, sr; part of grant May 22, 1772 North Carolina to John Kirkconell who sold to Joseph Morris. Witness John Bankson, Isaac Young, and Abraham Cantrell. Signed Joseph Morris' mark. Wit. oath May 17, 1797 John Bankson to William McDowell. Rec. Oct. 2, 1797

p. 145-146 Nov. 11, 1796 Aaron Floyd (Spartanburgh) to George Isom (same); for 60£ sterling sold 195 ac between N and S forks of Tyger R; border: W-Samuel Floyd, E-Francis Ward, S-S fork Tyger R, and N-N fork Tyger R; survey Dec. 17, 1792 for Aaron Floyd. Witness Matthew Patton and John Patton. Signed Aaron Floyd. Wit. oath Apr. 10, 1797 Matthew Patton to Thos Moore. Rec. Oct. 2, 1797

p. 146-147 Jun. 23, 1797 Phillip Johnson (Spartanburgh) to Cary Traylor (same); for 18£ sterling sold 50 ac on Brushey fork where Phillip Johnson lives; border: William Geary and Alexander Wakefield. Witness William Gray, Curtis Gray, and Reubin Traylor. Signed Phillip and Jamina Johnson's marks. Wit. oath Jul. 18, 1797 Reubin Traylor to George Brewton. Rec. Oct. 2, 1797

p. 147-149 Jul. 30, 1797 George Divine and wife Mary (Spartanburgh) to Stephen Layton (same); for 10£ sterling sold 100 ac on Prather's Cr where James Sinard (or Sirard) lives; border: Stephen Layton; grant to James Sample jr. Witness John Layton and James Vessell. Signed George Divine and Mary's mark. Wit. oath Jul. 13, 1797 James Vessell to Moses Casey. Rec. Oct. 2, 1797

p. 149-150 May 21, 1797 Burgess West (Union Co) to Alexander Elder (Spartanburgh); for 75£ sterling sold a Negro woman Dinah about 20 years old born in Maryland. Witness Osborn West and Andrew Thomson. Signed Burgess West's mark. Wit. oath May 30, 1797 Osborn West to Thos Moore. Rec. Oct. 3, 1797

p. 150-151 Feb. 14, 1797 Joseph Kelso, sr (Spartanburgh) to Samuel Kelso (same); for 30£ sterling sold (ac not given); part of grant on both sides Fairforrest Cr Nov. 18, 1752 to George Storey who sold to Joseph Kelso sr. Witness James Story, John Story, and William Watson. Signed Joseph Kelso's mark. Wit. oath Jul. 18, 1797 William Watson to William Simpson. Rec. Oct. 3, 1797

p. 151-153 May 12, 1797 John Wofford, sr (Spartanburgh) to William Wofford (same); for 10£ sterling sold 150 ac; border: William Thomson, John Smith, and Benja West; part of 300 ac grant Jul. 8, 1774 to Jeremiah Barnet who sold to Jo Wofford sr; grant on Muckelwain's Cr of Fairforrest Cr and border: N-William Thomson, SE-Wm Browley, and others vacant. Witness James Wofford, John Wofford (a different mark), and Isaac Wofford. Signed John Wofford's mark. Wit. oath Jul. 16, 1798 Isaac Wofford to George Lamkin. Rec. Oct. 3, 1797

p. 153-154 Mar. 3, 1797 Samuel Dunaway sr (Spartanburgh) to Reubin Warren (same); for 10£ SC money sold 40 ac on W side Island Cr; part of 100 ac grant Sept. 4, 1786 States Office to Daniel Stilwell. Witness Robert Dunaway, William Anders, and Robert Proctor. Signed Samuel Dunaway. Wit. oath Mar. 4, 1797 Robert Proctor to Geor Lamkin. Rec. Oct. 3, 1797

p. 154-155 May 8, 1797 Peter Peterson (Spartanburgh) to George Connel (same); for $59 sold 170 ac on N side Pacolet R about a mile from Gollison's Shoals or "perhaps something more" on Green's Cr; border: Thomas Jones, David Jones, James Brown, George Ryner, and E side of a line now surveyed for Bryant and George Connell. Witnes Jas Smith, Jas Barnett, and James Kickey. Signed Peter Peterson. Wit. oath Jul. 18, 1797 Jas Smith to Ism Foster. Rec. Oct. 4, 1797

p. 155-157 Apr. 5, 1796 Jesse Connell (Spartanburgh) to John Ligon (same); for 5s sold 150 ac; border: Jesse Spencer, Daniel Stevens, McDole, and Charles Moore; part of grant May 7, 1792 Gov. Charles Pinckney to James Gibbs. Witness Francis Connell and George Connell. Signed Jesse Connell. Certified Apr. 12, 1796 by Wm Smith. Rec. Oct. 4, 1797. Dower renounced Ann Connell to Wm Smith Apr. 13, 1796

p. 157-158 Jun. 6, 1797 Robert Miller (Spartanburgh) to Samuel Miller (same); for 63£ sterling sold 63 ac on S side of Middle fork Tyger R; part of 160 ac grant to Robert Miller, sr and sold by Nathaniel Miller to Robert Miller. Witness Nathaniel Miller, James Otts, and Samuel Neely. Signed Robert Miller. Rec. Oct. 4, 1797

p. 158-161 Mar. 28, 1796 Samuel Miller, sheriff (Spartanburgh) to William Wells (same); for 6£ sterling sold 540 ac on Chinquapin Cr; plat attached shows border: James Stedman, Diskin Grant, W Williamson, and unknown and vacant; survey by Jesse Connell; land sold due to writ from Spartan County Court held Jul. 27, 1795 at Wells Griffith's place and returnable to the court Jan. 12, 1795 (sic); judges: Baylis Earle, James Jordan, and William Smith; suit by William Pool against Jeremiah Walker due to promise Jeremiah Walker made but didn't "perform"; so Jeremiah Walker is assessed 25£ 6s and 2£ 3s 9p for William Pool's cost; land sold Nov. 7, 1795. Witness Joshua Downs and James Carmichael. Signed Samuel Miller. Wit. oath Nov. 23, 1796 Joshua Downs to Isham Harrison. Rec. Oct. 5, 1797

p. 161-163 Dec. 3, 1795 John Muckelwrath (Spartanburgh) to John Perry (same); for 60£ sterling sold 150 ac on S side of S fork Tyger R; border: Samuel Nesbitt, William Reaves, and Nathaniel Muckelwrath; part of grant to Frances Dodds who sold to Henry Leach who sold to John Muckelwrath. Witness Benjamin D. Shumate JP, Robert Canuth (or Carruth) and John Collins. Signed John Muckelworth. Rec. Oct. 5, 1797

p. 163-165 Feb. 5, 1796 William Ford (Spartanburgh) to Robert Ligon (late of Amelia Co, Va); for $500 sold (a) 400 ac on E side Tyger R; where William Ford lives; grant Sept. 3, 1753 to Robert Miller; and (b) 50 ac adjoining W side of (a); grant May 15, 1771 to Robert Miller. Witness William Lancaster, Robert Foster, and John Golightly. Signed Wm Ford. Wit. oath Apr. 11, 1796 William Lancaster to Zadock Ford. Rec. Oct. 7, 1797. Dower renounced Cassandar Ford to James Jordan

p. 165-168 Mar. 31, 1796 Jesse Connell (Spartanburgh) to Robert Ligon (late of Amelia Co, Va); for $635 sold 575 ac where Jesse Connell lives; border: Tinsley, David Golightly, William Smith, and the Meeting House tract surveyed for Giles Connell; part of 3 grants: (1) for 401 ac Feb. 6, 1786 Gov. William Moultrie to Jesse Connell, (2) Dec. 24, 1770 Gov. William Tryon (NC) to (not given), and (3) Sept. 4, 1753 Gov. Matthew Rowan (NC) to Arthur McClower. Witness Wm Smith and A Lancaster. Signed Jesse Connell. Certified Apr. 13, 1796 by Wm Smith. Rec. Oct. 7, 1797. Dower renounced Ann Connell to Wm Smith Apr. 13, 1796

p. 168-170 May 2, 1797 William Turpin, merchant (SC) to Thomas Wadsworth; for "land of equal value" sold William's rights to the following land which goes to Thomas due to division of land held previously jointly by William and Thomas; (1) 195 ac bought from Thomas Gravin on Lawson's fork; surveyed Oct. 7, 1784 by George Salmon and granted "by" (sic) Benjamin Garrett Jan. 21, 1785 and sold by Benjamin Garrett (sic) to William and Thomas; (2) 302 ac on Nesbit's Br of Tyger R survey Mar. 10, 1787 by Andrew Thomson for Elkanah Hutchison and granted Feb. 5, 1787 Gov. William Moultrie to Augustus Merrick; (3) 300 ac on Fairforrest Cr survey Nov. 20, 1784 by James Seaborn and granted Feb. 5, 1787 Gov. William Moultrie to Thomas Wadsworth; (4) 184 ac on N side Enoree R survey Dec. 19, 1784 by Robert Hannah for Samuel Thomson and granted Feb. 5, 1787 to Thomas Wadsworth; (5) 640 ac on Green's Cr of Lawson's fork granted May 2, 1785 Gov. William Moultrie to Daniel Symmes who sold to William Turpin and Thomas Wadsworth; (6) 200 ac on Tuckey Cr of Lawson's fork survey Jul. 11, 1785 for Peggy Lewis and granted Aug. 7, 1786 to William Turpin and Thomas Wadsworth; (7) 200 ac on Buch Br of Fairforrest Cr grant Jun. 5, 1786 Gov. Moultrie to Israel Morris who sold on Jul. 20, (1786?) to William Turpin and Thomas Wadsworth. Witness James Boyce and William Turpin sr. Signed Willm Turpin. Wit. oath (Laurens Co) Aug. 21, 1797 James Boyce to William Neil. Dower renounced Mary Turpin to Peter Bounetheaw May 8, 1797

p. 170-172 May 13, 1797 George Robuck and wife Lavina (Spartanburgh) to Jacob Ortner (same); for 50£ sterling sold 100 ac; border: Burrell Bobo, Charles Hotts (or Hold), Robert Wallas, and Daniel Langston. Witness Daniel Langston and William Evatt. Signed George Robuck. Wit. oath May 31, 1797 Daniel Langston and William Evatt to Saml Lancaster. Rec. Oct. 10, 1797

p. 172-173 Apr. 17, 1797 Dower renounced Mary Allen (late Mary Lindsey), wife of Dennis Lindsey, desc to William Smith; deed Dennis Lindsey to Richard Harris on Feb. 12, 1794 for 124 ac; part of 248 ac on Forgeson's and James Cr. Rec. Oct. 10, 1797

p. 173-175 Sept. 12, 1797 John Foster (Spartanburgh) to William Wingo (same); for 40£ sterling sold 330 ac on Beaverdam Cr. Witness Jacob Utley, Ism Foster, and Robert Belcher. Signed Josh Foster's mark. Rec. Oct. 10, 1797

p. 175-176 Oct. 27, 1796 Samuel Ward and wife Susana (Spartanburgh) to Jacob Utley (same); for a Spanish milled dollar sold 100 ac on N side Fairforrest Cr; border: William Wells and William Thompson. Witness John Kelley and James Ward. Signed Samuel Ward and Susana's mark. Wit. oath Mar. 4, 1797 James Ward to I Harrison. Rec. Oct. 10, 1797

p. 176-177 Nov. 28, 1796 Andrew McRee and Robert Barnett, executors of estate of John McRee, desc (Mecklinburgh Co, NC) to Joseph and Alexander Thompson, heirs of Elisha Thompson, desc (Spartanburgh); "by virtue of a contract between John McRee and Elisha Thompson" convey 200 ac on Beverdam Cr and on S side of the Indian Path; grant to John McRee. Witness Benjamin Prince McMakin and John McClure. Signed Andrew McRee and Robert Barnett, executors. Wit. oath Feb. 1, 1797(? page torn) Benjn Prince McMakin to James Jordan. Rec. Oct. 10, 1797

Book F 1797-1800

p. 1-2 Mar. 3, 1797 Samuel Dunaway, sr and Reubin Warren (both Spartanburgh) to Hiram Proctor (same); for 25£ SC money sold 100 ac in two parts: (1) 60 ac on E side Island Cr; part of 100 ac grant States Office to Daniel Stilwell who sold to Samuel Dunaway; and (s) 40 ac adjoining (1) and part of 1,000 ac grant States Office to Abraham Markley who sold to Reubin Warren. Witness Robert Dunaway and William Sanders. Signed Samuel Dunaway and Reubin Warren. Wit. oath Mar. 4, 1797 Robert Dunaway to Geor Lampkin. Rec. Oct. 10, 1797

p. 2-3 Jun. 14, 1797 James Ward and wife Susannah (Spartanburgh) to Nathan Ward (same); for a Spanish milled dollar sold 50 ac on S side Fairforrest Cr; border: Harrison and White. Witness William Foster and Solomon Ward. Signed James and Susannah Ward's marks. Wit. oath Jul. 1, 1797 William Foster to I Harrison. Rec. Oct. 10, 1797

p. 3-4 Apr. 12, 1796 Zacharias Gibbs (Union Co), son and executor of James Gibbs, desc to John Finch (Spartanburgh); for 50£ sterling paid to James Gibbs during his lifetime sold 200 ac on Fairforrest Cr of Tyger R; border: Hampton; part of 400 ac grant Gov. Josiah Martin (NC) to Richard Hampton who sold to James Gibbs, desc. Witness Shads Golightly, James Keen, and John Golightly. Signed Zacharias Gibbs. Wit. oath Apr. 12, 1796 Zacharias Gibbs to I Harrison. Rec. Oct. 10, 1797

p. 4-5 Apr. 25, 1797 Robert Elder (Spartanburgh) to James Crowder (same); for 30£ sterling sold 157 ac on both sides Dutchman's Cr; grant 150 ac (sic) Sept. 3, 1753 to (not given). Witness John Grist and Daniel Pruett. Signed Robert Elder and Sarah's mark. Rec. Oct. 10, 1797. Dower renounced Sarah Elder to Isham Harrison Jul. 17, 1797

p. 5-6 Feb. 24, 1797 (Pendleton Co) David Pruett (Pendleton Co) to Daniel Pruett (Spartanburgh); for 50£ sold 125 ac; part of 2 tracts: (1) 150 ac grant Apr. 27, 1767 to Moses Wiley who sold to Abraham Balow (or Balue) who sold Mar. 13, 1792 to David Pruett; and (2) grant Gov. William Moultrie to David Pruett see Book 4H p. 268. Witness Snoden Pruett, Jesse Burrell, and Robert Caldwell. Signed David Pruett and Amey's mark. Wit. oath Jun. 17, 1797 Snoden Pruett to Saml Lancaster. Rec. Oct. 10, 1797

p. 6-7 Nov. 9, 1795 Edward Curry (SC) to Jacob Davis (Spartanburgh); for "a likely Negro woman" sold (ac not given) on both sides Suck Cr; all of grant Oct. 26, 1767 to William Shark then in Mecklinburgh Co, NE on W side of Broad R and sold Mar. 28, 1769 to (not given). Witness Evan Watkins, William Watkins, and David Blackwell. Signed Edward Curry. Wit. oath Feb. 25, 1796 Evan Watkins to Isham Foster. Rec. Oct. 11, 1797

p. 7-8 Jan. 25, 1797 Dan Gilbert (Spartanburgh) to son Samuel Gilbert (same); for 15£ sterling sold 188 ac on S side Pacolate R; border: Barton's old line and Thomson's Cr; part of 2 grants: (1) Apr. 25, 1767 States Office to Thomas Williamson and (2) Oct. 1, 1787 States Office to Tho Barton. Witness Dan Gilbert, jr, Jarvis (or Garvis) Gilbert, and John Gilbert. Signed Dan Gilbert. Wit. oath Mar. 8, 1797 Garvis Gilbert to William McDowell. Rec. Oct. 11, 1797

p. 8-9 Apr. 17, 1797 Isaac Lansdale (Camden Dist) to Jonas Bayles (SC); for 50£ sterling sold 273 ac on S side Pacolet R; border: NW-Solomon Abbett, SW-vacant, SE-Cherokee Cr and James Stedman, NE, SE & S-James Stedman, and NE & SE-Turner and "others" (including Pacolet R); survey Jul. 29, 1795 for Richard Lee and granted Oct. 3, 1796 Gov. Arnoldus VanderHorst to Isaac Lansdale. Witness Theodore Stark and Richd H Homan. Signed Isaac Lansdale. Wit. oath (Richland Co) Apr. 20, 1797 Richd H Homan to Marty Atkins. Rec. Oct. 11, 1797

p. 9-10 Jul. 28, 1797 Jonas Bayles (York Co) to Bazel Lee (Spartanburgh); for 25£ sterling sold 273 on S side Pacolet R;

border: NW-Solomon Abbett, SW-vacant, SE-Cherokee Cr and James Stedman, NE, SE & S-James Stedman, and NE & SE-Turner and "others" (including Pacolet R); survey Jul. 29, 1795 for Richard Lee and granted Oct. 3, 1796 Gov. Arnoldus VanderHorst to Isaac Lansdale who sold Apr. 17, 1797 to Jonas Bayles. Witness Joshua Downs and Joseph Robinson. Signed Jonas Bayles. Wit. oath Jul. 29, 1797 Joshua Downs to Geor Lamkin. Rec. Oct. 12, 1797

p. 10-11 Nov. 6, 1796 Samuel Sexton (or Lexton) (Spartanburgh), heir by will to Thomas Sexton, desc, to James Taylor (same); for 20£ sterling sold 77 ac on Forgeson's Cr of Tyger R; grant Jun. 5, 1786; border: Enoch Floyd, Charles Whitten, and James Wofford. Witness William Rhodes and James Wofford. Signed Samuel Sexton. Wit. oath Aug. 14, 1797 William Rhodes to Thos Moore. Rec. Oct. 12, 1797

p. 11-13 May 20, 1797 Francis Bremar (Charleston, SC) to David Cooper, desc (Thickety); for 10s and "consideration of David assisting in finding and searching for the best beds of ore on the survey made on Thickety Cr for Daniel Bourdeaux, David Hopkins, John Vanderhorst, and Francis Bremar as by an agreement given David by Francis" sell to Elizabeth Cooper, widow of David, 365 ac; border: NE & NW-Obadiah Trimmier, NE-Mackley and other sides by survey for Daniel Bourdeaux, David Hopkins, John Vanderhorst, and Francis Bremar; Daniel Bourdeaux, David Hopkins, John Vanderhorst, and Francis Bremar reserve all iron ore, wood, or water for carrying on an Iron works for themselves; plat attached shows two adjoining tracts of 217 ac and 148 ac. Witness VardryMcBee and Wm Henderson. Signed F Bremar (at Pacolate). Wit. oath Aug. 30, 1797 Vardry McBee to H McCray. Rec. Oct. 13, 1797

p. 13-14 Sept. 13, 1797 James Stedman (Charleston, SC), house carpenter, to Thomas Tod (Tyger R); power of attorney to take possession of (1) 2,482 ac at head branches Island Cr of Broad R and on Buck Cr; border: West Harris and "Doctor"; grant Apr. 2, 1787 to James Stedman; (2) 767 ac on both sides Chenquepin Cr and other branches of Lawson's fork; grant May 7, 1787 to James Stedman; and (3) 426 ac on Pacolet R; border: George Turner, Solomon Abbot, Edmund Bellenger, and James Stedman; grant Oct. 7, 1793 to James Stedman; and all other land of James Stedman in Pinckney Dist. Witness John Kelsey and Thomas Steedman. Signed James Steedman (at Charleston). Wit. oath (Charleston, SC) Sept. 30, 1797 John Kelsey to John Johnson. Rec. Oct. 15, 1797

p. 14-15 Nov. 26, 1796 Robert Barnett, heir and executor of Hugh Barnett, desc, and David Freeman, executor of Hugh Barnett (Mecklinburgh Co, NC) to Benjamin Perine McMakin (Spartan Co); for 500£ sterling sold 150 ac on N side Middle fork Tyger R and "on a branch at upper end of Jones' line". Witness John Hayes, William Allison, and Joseph Thompson. Signed Robert Barnett and David Freeman's mark. Wit. oath Feb. 1, 1797 Joseph Thompson to James Jordan. Rec. Oct. 15, 1797

p. 15-16 Jan. 16, 1797 Henry Turner (Spartanburgh) to Lewis Cockrell (same); for 50£ sold 100 ac on N side Lawson's fork of Pacolet R; border: Peter Lewis; grant Jan. 21, 1785 States Office to John Bennett. Witness I Harrison JP. Signed Henry Turner. Rec. Oct. 15, 1797

p. 16-17 Nov. 26, 1796 Robert Barnett, heir and executor of Hugh Barnett, desc, and David Freeman, executor of Hugh Barnett (Mecklinburgh Co, NC) to Benjamin Perin McMakin (Spartan Co); for 500£ sterling sold 200 ac on Middle fork of Tyger R; where Benjamin lives; border: Joseph Jones and Alexander McCarter. Witness John Hayes, William Allison, and Joseph Thomson. Signed Robert

Barnett and David Freeman's mark. Wit. oath Feb. 1, 1797 Joseph Thomson to James Jordan. Rec. Oct. 16, 1797

p. 17-19 Oct. 15, 1795 Thomas Green (Spartanburgh) to James Dewberry (same); for 40£ sterling sold 165½ ac; border: Haden and Dunaway; part of 400 ac grant to John Haden. Witness William Dewberry, Rolley Horton, and John Low. Signed Thos. Green. Wit. oath Jul. 2, 1796 Rolley Horton and William Dewberry to George Lamkin. Rec. Oct. 16, 1796

p. 19-20 Sept. 25, 1795 Thomas Green (Spartanburgh) to John Low (same); for 30£ sterling sold 150 ac on Thickety Cr; border: J Headen and Malichi Jones; grant Apr. 3, 1786 Gov. William Moultrie to John Headen. Witness Frederick Gutry, Joseph Price, and Wm Thomson. Signed Thos Green. Wit. oath Jul. 2, 1796 Frederick Gutry to John Lipscomb. Rec. Oct. 16, 1797

p. 20-22 Mar. 11, 1797 Thomas Hays and wife Sarah (Spartanburgh) to John Underwood (same); for 50£ sterling sold 250 ac on S side Fairforrest Cr; border: Wm Benson, Widow White and James Ward. Witness John Lancaster, Joshua Downs, and Wm Wells. Signed Thomas and Sarah Hays' marks. Wit. oath Mar. 18, 1797 Joshua Downs to I Harrison. Rec. Oct. 16, 1797. Dower renounced Sarah Hays to I Harrison Mar. 18, 1797

p. 22-23 Jan. 19, 1797 John Wood (Spartan Co) to Moses Timmons (same); for 100£ sterling sold 230 ac on both sides Fairforrest Cr where Moses Timmons lives; border: Isham Foster and Thomas Burton; survey for John Wood. Witness Isham Foster and Jon Gowen. Signed John Wood. Wit. oath Jan. 19, 1797 John Wood to Ism Foster. Rec. Oct. 17, 1797

p. 23-24 Jan. 10, 1792 Dennis Lindsey (Spartanburgh) to George Bruton (same); a bond of 50£ sterling; Condition: bond void if Dennis deeds George half of 248 ac survey by Andrew Thomson for Dennis; on branches of Forgeson's and James Cr of Tyger R formerly called Lackhart's land; deed to be made after Dennis obtains grant from Lindsey. Signed Dennis Lindsey. Wit. oath Apr. 25, 1796 William Pearson to Zadock Ford. Rec. Oct. 17, 1797. Dower renounced Mary Allen (late Mary Lindsey), widow of Dennis, to William Smith. Apr. 17, 1797. Dower renounced Mary Allen to George Bruton Oct. 17, 1797

p. 24-25 Oct. 6, 1797 David White (Spartanburgh) to James White (same); for 100£ sold 117 ac where James lives and is lower part of tract of land where David lives. Witness Robert Kinble, John Hasty, and Abraham Andrews. Signed David White's mark. Wit. oath (not given) 10, 1797 John Hasty to Ism Foster. Rec. Oct. 17, 1797

p. 25-26 Aug. 29, 1796 Thomas Jones and wife Hester (Spartanburgh) to Thomas Gillenwaters (same); for 12£ sterling sold 148 ac in two tracts: (1) 100 ac (that is SW end of the 148 ac) on Gocher's Cr and (2) 48 ac border: Ezekiel Howard and David Allen. Witness Richard Simmonds and James Harrison. Signed Thomas Jones. Wit. oath Aug. 29, 1796 Richard Simmonds to John Lipscomb. Rec. Nov. 30, 1797

p. 26-27 May 13, 1797 George Robuck and wife Levina (Spartanburgh) to David Langston (same); for 25£ sterling sold 100 ac; border: Burrell Bobo, Nathan Langston, Robt Wallas, and Blackstock Rd. Witness William Evatt and Jacob Ortner. Signed George Robuck. Wit. oath May 31, 1797 William Evatt and Jacob Ortner to Saml Lancaster. Rec. Nov. 30, 1797

p. 27-28 Aug. 13, 1795 Daniel Barnet and wife Sarah (Spartanburgh) to Rolley Calvert (same); for 60£ SC money sold 435 ac on both sides Dutchman's Cr and N side Tyger R; grant Dec. 4, 1786 Gov. William Moultrie to Daniel Barnet. Witness David Golightly and Reubin White. Signed Daniel Barnett and Sarah's mark. Wit. oath Oct. 21, 1797 David Golightly and Reubin White to W Lancaster. Rec. Nov. 30, 1797

p. 28-29 Oct. 7, 1796 Thomas Gillenwaters and wife Molley (Spartanburgh) to William Cantrell (same); for 35£ sterling sold 148 ac in two parts: (1) 100 ac (that is SW end of the 148 ac) on Gocher's Cr and (2) 48 ac border: Ezekiel Howard and David Allen. Witness David Goudelock and Nathan Gibson. Signed Thomas Gillenwaters and Molley's mark. Wit. oath Nov. 18, 1797 Nathan Gibson to John Lipscomb. Rec. Nov. 30, 1797

p. 29-30 Apr. 27, 1792 Edward Mitcheson (Laurence Co) to John Wood (same); for 25£ sterling sold 53 ac on N side Enoree R; border: Edward Arnold; "assigned" Jul. 2, 1787 Gov. Thomas Pinckney to Edward Mitcheson. Witness Thos Holden and Margaret Holden. Signed Edward Mitcheson. Wit. oath Feb. 28, 1797 Thos Holden to Zadock Ford. Rec. Nov. 30, 1797

p. 30-31 Nov. 23, 1784 James Keen (SC) to Rowland Jennings; for 50£ sterling sold 100 ac on branch of Dutchman's Cr of Tyger R; border: all vacant; grant Jan. 1, 1792 Gov. William Moultrie to James Keen. Witness Jesse Spencer and William Jennings. Signed James Keen. Wit. oath Jul. 1, 1797 Jesse Spencer to Thos Moore. Rec. Jan. 1, 1798

p. 31-32 Oct. 19, 1796 John Low (Spartanburgh) to son Jonathan Low and to two youngest daughters Hannah and Dice Low; for "good cause" give all household furniture. Witness Adam Thompson, Rolley Horton, and George Horton. Signed John Low. Wit. oath Oct. 19, 1796 Rolley Horton to Geor Lamkin. Rec. Jan. 6, 1798

p. 32-33 May 11, 1795 Thomas Kivil (Spartanburgh) to Reubin Gunn (same); for 42£ 10s sterling sold 180 ac on Enoree R including mouth of Abner's Cr; border: Stephel (sic) Cantrel; part of 500 ac survey Feb. 27, 1775 by James Wofford and granted to Thomas Sitton, esq who sold to Col. Richard Hampton who sold to Stephen Cantrell who sold 350 ac to Thomas Kivil. Witness John Kitcheb, Elizabeth Jackson, and Edward Dial. Signed Thomas Kivil. Wit. oath Jun. 27, 1795 Edward Dial to Zadock Ford. Rec. Jan. 16, 1798

p. 33-34 Jan. 12, 1798 Henry Wells (Spartanburgh) to John Foster (same); for 40£ sterling sold 200 ac near David Wells; border: a 1,000 ac tract and Beaverdam Cr. Witness Wm Foster and Wm Foster "FF". Signed Henry Wells. Certified Jan. 13, 1798 by Ism Foster. Rec. Jan. 17, 1798

p. 34-35 Oct. 10, 1797 John Lefever (Spartanburgh) to Sarah Wooten; for 72£ 16s sold a dark chesnut stud horse with star and stripe 10 years old and a sorrel stud colt with small star in forehead 16 mo old. Witness Rice Ross, Gideon Gibson, and Jordan Gibson. Signed John Lefever. Wit. oath Oct. 24, 1797 Gideon Gibson to Henry McCray. Rec. Jan. 17, 1798

p. 35 Jan. 13, 1798 Moses Timmons (Spartanburgh) to John Crawford (same); for $400 sold a Negro man Wil. Witness B. D. Shumate JP. Signed Moses Timmons. Rec. Jan. 17, 1798

p. 35-36 Aug. 14, 1797 William Wofford (Franklin Co, Ga) to David Qualls (Spartanburgh); for 80£ sterling sold 200 ac on S side Pacolate R; border: all vacant; survey Sept. 10, 1785. Witness

John Storn and John Harris. Signed William Wofford. Wit. oath Jan. 11, 1798 John Harris to James Jordan. Rec. Jan. 17, 1798

p. 36-38 Dec. 14, 1797 John Meadows and wife Elizabeth (Spartanburgh) to Aaron Pinson (same); for 50 Spanish milled dollars sold 50 ac near N side Tygar R; border: Aaron Pinson, Andrew Thompson, William Meadows, and Joel Hambree; part of 240 ac grant Jan. 6, 1794 Gov. William Moultrie to John Meadows. Witness Andrew Thomson, Thomas Shurley, and Zephaniah Pinson. Signed John Meaders and Elizabeth's mark. Wit. oath Jan. 2, 1798 Thomas Shurley to Thomas Moore. Rec. Jan. 18, 1798

p. 38-39 Jan. 6, 1798 Elisha Smith (Spartanburgh) to Abraham Wyatt (same); for 5£ sold 100 ac on S side Pacolet R; formerly belonged to Daniel Walker. Witness Richard Turner and Mason Cannon. Signed Elisha and Elizabeth Smith's marks. Wit. oath Jan. 13, 1798 Richard Turner to Geor Lamkin. Rec. Jan. 18, 1798

p. 39-40 Feb. 8, 1792 Buckner Smith and wife Dina to Benjamin Grist; for 40£ sterling sold 127 ac on Cain Cr of Tyger R; border: N & W-Joel Hembree, E & N-James Crowder, S-Daniel Grant, and by a mill dam; part of two tracts granted Jul. 3, 1772 and Nov. 7, 1785 to Timothy Toney. Witness John Robuck, Samuel Sherbertt (or Shubutt), and James Evatt. Signed Buckner and Dina Smith's marks. Wit. oath Mar. 19, 1792 Samuel Sherbertt to Wm Smith. Rec. Jan. 19, 1798

p. 40-41 Nov. 17, 1795 Jacob Pennington (Spartanburgh) to Samuel Burns (same); for 60£ sterling sold 100 ac on both sides Maple Swamp Cr of Tyger R; grant Nov. 6, 1786 Gov. William Moultrie to Jacob Pennington. Witness William Boctor and Robert Neisbitt. Signed Jacob Pennington. Wit. oath Dec. 26, 1797 William Boctor to B. D. Shumate. Rec. Jan. 19, 1798

p. 41-42 Nov. 17, 1795 Jacob Pennington (Spartanburgh) to Samuel Burns (same); for 60£ sterling sold 100 ac on branch of S Tyger R; border: vacant; grant in Aug. 1774 Lt Gov. William Bull to William Earnest. Witness Robert Nisbit and William Boctor. Signed Jacob Pennington. Wit. oath Dec. 26, 1797 William Bull to B. D. Shumate. Rec. Jan. 19, 1798

p. 42-44 Feb. 13, 1788 Tilmon Bobo (Spartanburgh) to John Rainwater (same); for 100£ sterling sold 500 ac on Cedar Shoal Cr of Enoree R; grant Jun. 15, 1775 Lt. Gov. William Bull to Thomas Tod and sold Feb. 15, 1775 to Tilmon Bobo; border: NE-Christopher Case and James McDowell, NW-"land laid out" and vacant, and SE-Nathaniel Hilliam and vacant. Witness Joseph Wofford and Moses Casey. Signed Tilmon Bobo. Wit. oath Dec. 22, 1797 Joseph Wofford to Moses Casey. Rec. Jan. 20, 1797

p. 44-45 Jul. 1, 1789 Spencer Bobo and wife Judath (Spartanburgh) to John Rainwater (same); for 50£ sold 50 ac; border: Hillin and Tod; part of 446 ac grant Oct. 2, 1786 Gov. William Moultrie to Spencer Bobo; grant on Cedar Shoal Cr and N side Enoree R. Witness Peter Brooks and Solomon Rainwater. Signed Spencer and Judath Bobo's marks. Wit. oath Dec. 14, 1797 Spencer Bobo to Moses Casey. Rec. Jan. 20, 1798

p. 45-46 Jan. 28, 1791 Willis Whitaker (Kershaw Co) to John Rainwater (Spartanburgh); for 75£ sterling sold 300 ac on a branch of Cedar Shoal Cr of Enoree R; border: E-Edward Stone and Thomas Stone, S-Robert Skelton, W-John Ford, and others vacant; grant Aug. 31, 1774 Gov. William Bull to James Whitaker, desc and to his son Willis Whitaker by descent about Aug. 1, 1780. Witness Burrell Bobo and Benjamin Rainwater. Signed Willis Whitaker. Wit.

oath Dec. 13, 1797 Burrell Bobo to Moses Casey. Rec. Jan. 20, 1798

p. 46-47 Dec. 23, 1797 Thomas Clark (Newberry Co) to William Ford (Spartanburgh); for $270 sold 270 ac on branch of N Tyger R; border: James Newman, Thomas Davis, and vacant and unknown. Witness James Jordan and Thomas Dois. Signed Thomas Clark. Certified (not dated) by Jas Jordan. Rec. Jan. 22, 1798

p. 47-48 Nov. 21, 1797 Nathaniel Robertson (Spartanburgh) to Charles Morgin (same); for 50£ SC money sold 196 ac on Beverdam Cr of Thickety Cr. Witness John Arendell, John Cooper, and Vardry McBee. Signed Nathaniel Robertson. Wit. oath Jan. 12, 1798 John Cooper to Geor Lamkin. Rec. Jan. 22, 1798

p. 48-49 Dec. 30, 1797 William Garrot (Spartanburgh) to John Martin (same); for 75£ SC money sold 75 ac on both sides Case's Cr and S side Pacolet R including a Griss Mill; grant Aug. 20, 1784 States Office to William Garrot. Witness Isaac Cantrell and Nimrod Cantrell. Signed William Garrot. Wit. oath Jan. 13, 1798 Isaac Cantrell to George Brewton. Rec. Jan. 23, 1798

p. 49-51 Dec. 30, 1797 Isaac Young (Spartanburgh) to Isaac Cantrell, jr (same); for 70£ SC money sold 410 ac; grant Oct. 6, 1788 States Office to William Jordan on Buck Cr; border: Jordan and Walles; and a "compliment" grant Mar. 17, 1771 States Office to (not given); border: William Jordan and Buck Cr. Witness Berry Young, James Cantrell, and John Young. Signed Isaac Young's mark. Wit. oath Jan. 15, 1798 Berry Young to George (blank) JP. Rec. Jan. 23, 1798

p. 51-52 Jan. 12, 1798 Broadrick Mason (Spartanburgh) to William Baver (same); for 35£ sterling sold 125 ac on Fairforrest Cr; border: Tinsley. Witness Roaland Johnson and John Williams. Signed Broadrick Mason. Wit. oath Jan. 12, 1798 Francis Mason (sic) to Ism Foster. Rec. Jan. 23, 1798

p. 52-53 Oct. 1, 1795 Isaac Hamby (Spartanburgh) to Elijah Hendrix (same); for 75£ sterling sold 150 ac on Lick Cr; border: John Hambey and William Moore; grant Aug. 19, 1774 Lt. Gov. William Bull to Isaac Hamby. Witness Isaac Hamby (signature), William Hendrix, and Aaron Bakron. Signed Isaac Hamby's mark. Wit. oath Aug. 15, 1796 Aaron Bakron to I Harrison. Rec. Jan. 23, 1798

p. 53-54 Dec. 21, 1797 Malachi Jones (Spartanburgh) to John Low (same); for 75£ sterling sold 200 ac on Thickety Cr; grant by Gov. (blank) to (not given). Witness Patrick Tylor and John H. Jones. Signed Malachi Jones. Wit. oath Jan. 12, 1798 John H Jones to Geor Lamkin. Rec. Jan. 23, 1798

p. 54-55 Sept. 22, 1797 John Low (Spartanburgh) to James Dewberry (same); for 100£ sterling sold 100 ac; grant Apr. 3, 1786 to John Hadin. Witness none. Signed John Low. Witness Jan. 12, 1798 John Low to Goer Lamkin. Rec. Jan. 23, 1798

p. 55-56 Jan. 13, 1798 William Cantrell (Union Co) to Henry Gibson (Spartanburgh); for 40£ sterling sold 148 ac in two parts: (1) 100 ac on Goucher's Cr and SW side of 148 ac; and (2) 48 ac border: Ezekiel Howard and David Allen. Witness Griffin Carter and Nathan Gibson. Signed William Cantrell. Wit. oath Jan. 13, 1798 Griffin Carter to John Lipscomb. Rec. Jan. 23, 1798

p. 56-57 Jan. 28, 1796 John Cobb (Spartanburgh) to John Murry (same) for 5£ SC money sold 125 ac on S side Pacolate R; border: Solomon Abbit; part of 534 ac grant to Wm Dickson. Witness William Murry, Drury Abbitt, and Henry Turner. Signed John Cobb's mark.

Wit. oath Jan. 16, 1798 William Murry to Geor Lamkin. Rec. Jan. 23, 1798

p. 57-65 Jul. 6, 1792 Pierce Butler, esq (SC) to Harceles Daniel Bize, esq; for (money left blank) "in settlement of accounts today" and 5s sold the following 23 pieces of land: (1) 500 ac in Craven Co on Beaverdam Br of Ready R; border: S & SW-Elias Brock and James Pen, N-Jonathan Downs and others vacant; (2) 500 ac between Broad and Saluda R; border: NE-Pierce Butler, SW & SE-Richard Winn, NW-Benjamin Williams, NE & NW-Benjamin Elliot and Samuel Elliot, NW-Kit Shoat(?); (3) 500 ac between Broad and Saluda R; border: NW-Benjamin Elliot and Samuel Elliot, SW & NW-Paddy Cunningham, S-granted land, E, S & W-James Lindsey, and SE-Peirce Butler; (4) 500 ac between Broad and Saluda R; border: NE & NW-Pierce Butler, W-James Lindsey and granted land, SE & S-surveyed land; (5) 500 ac on branch of Brown's Cr; border: SW & S-Daniel Hugir, N & E-Philip Watters, N-William Grant, NW-William Palmor, and others vacant; (6) 300 ac on Dutchman's Cr of Tygar R; border: SE-Isaac Peters; (7) 300 ac on Forgerson's Cr of Tyger R; border: SW-David Brewton; (8) 500 ac on branches of Little R of Saluda R; border: NE-Thomas Woodward, NW-John Rogers and vacant, SE-Robert Tweedy; (9) 500 ac on branch of Buffion Cr; border: SE & SW-Jonathan Parker, W-Killey Gee, and others vacant; (10) 500 ac on Dry Branch of Enoree R; border: N & W-Alexander Fraser, W-Robert Goodwin, and others vacant; (11) 200 ac on branch of Elisha Cr; border: NW, SW, SE & NE-William Dodd and NE-Whitaker; (12) 200 ac on branch of Fergerson's Cr; border: SE-Daniel Hugin, SW-Jones Brewton, NW & SW-James Wofford; (13) 500 ac in fork of Broad and Saluda R; border: SW-Benjamin Elliot and Pierce Butler, NW & NE-John Holmes and Roger Brown, and NW-Benjamin Williamson; (14) 500 ac on S side Reedy R; border: NE & NW-Hugh Beard, NE-John Read, SE & NE-Richard Pen, SW & SE-Elias Brooks, and NW-Paddy Cunningham; (15) 200 ac on branches of Fairforrest Cr; border: all vacant; (16) 500 ac on Buffelow Cr of Camping Cr of Saluda R; border: N-Michael Wryat and others vacant; (17) 500 ac in fork of Broad and Saluda R; border: NE & NW-Paddy Cunningham, S & W-James Lindsey, and S-Gant; (18) 500 ac on branch of Little R; border: SE-John Caldwell, SW-unknown, W & S-John Hunter, NW-Deek Neely, NW-Lowry, NE & NW-Williamson, NE-George Ankin, and others vacant; (19) 200 ac on Widow Stewart Br of Broad and Saluda R; to be surveyed Jul. 6, 1785 but previously surveyed in 1775; (20) 200 ac on Beaverdam Cr on NE side of Wateree R; survey Jun. 27, 1775 for Pierce Butler; (21) a town lot in Charleston; border: W-most of a line next to a lot previously sold to William Miller, and by Perapet line, John Edwards, esq, desc, John Morris, and Josiah Smith; all on high ground; (22) a low water lot except about 60 feet left for Parepet or a street; border: Ashley R; (23) 1,167 ac in St. Andrew Parish; border: NW-William Wood and Maj. Fuller, desc, NW-Benjamin Fuller, esq, Isaac Debosta, and Ashley R, SW & SE-Edmond Petree (now belonging to Christopher Williman). Witness Thomas Marshal and Edward Rutledge. Signed Pierce Butler. Wit. oath (Charleston, SC) Mar. 21, 1793 Edward Rutledge, attorney of Charleston, to D Mazyck. Rec. Jan. 24, 1798. Jul. 7, 1792 Harceles Daniel Bize releases Maj. Butler from "covenant" respecting previous 23 pieces of land except those of Aray Viles(?) and the lot in Charleston. Witness Ed Rutledge. Signed Hercules Danl Bizel, in Charleston. Wit. oath Mar. 21, 1793 Edward Rutledge to D Mazyck

p. 65-66 Jan. 15, 1798 William Thompson (Spartanburgh) to Edward Smith (same); for 100£ sterling sold two tracts on both sides Bullock's Cr of Thickety Cr and on Rocky fork: (1) 150 ac grant to James Bridges who sold to Irby Denberry who sold to William Thompson; and (2) (ac not given) adjoining a grant in 1786 Gov. William Moultrie to Irby Denberry. Witness William Anderson and Joroyal Barnett. Signed Wm Thomson. Wit. oath Jan. 17, 1798 Joroyal Barnett to Geor Lamkin. Rec. Jan. 26, 1798

p. 66-67 Dec. 23, 1797 Malachi Jones (Spartanburgh) to John Low (same); for 31£ sold 88 ac on Thickety Cr. Witness John H Jones and Patrick Tylor. Signed Malachi Jones. Wit. oath Jan. 12, 1798 John H Jones to Geor Lamkin. Rec. Jan. 26, 1798

p. 67-68 Jul. 19, 1798 Robert Black to Sheriff of Newcastle Co, Delaware; Robert requests Sheriff to stop judgment and execution obtained by Robert in Newcastle Co and proceed no further until Dec. 25, 1798 or afterwards or until Robert gives orders. Witness Waddy Thomson, esq. Signed Robert Black. Wit. oath Jul. 20, 1798 Waddy Thomson, esq to William Lancaster. Rec. Jul. 25, 1798

p. 68-70 Apr. 2, 1798 John Watson, jr (Spartanburgh) to James Woods (same); for 55£ sterling sold 93 ac on Thickety Cr; border: south of Price's Cr; includes all of the grant not sold by John Watson jr to Obadiah Trimmier and Obadiah Watson; part of 350 ac grant Gov. Bull to Vardry McBee. Witness Obadh Trimmier, James Dunaway, and Catherine Dunaway. Signed John Watson jr. Wit. oath Jul. 16, 1798 Obadh Trimmier to Henry McCray. Rec. Aug. 14, 1798

p. 70-71 Sept. 22, 1797 James Dewberry (Spartanburgh) to Rolley Horton (same); for 35£ sterling sold 130 ac; border: Dunaway; part of grant Apr. 3, 1786 to John Haden. Witness John Low and Rosannah Low. Signed James Dewbery. Wit. oath Sept. 22, 1797 John Low to Geor Lamkin. Rec. Jan. 27, 1798

p. 71-72 Aug. 29, 1797 Mary Bryant and Sarah Betterton (Spartanburgh) to James Betterton (same); for 60£ sterling sold 150 ac in Greenville Co on branch of Guilder's Cr of Enoree R; border: James Puk. Witness John Grist, Ezekiah Burrell, and Rebekah Burrell. Signed Mary Bryant's and Sarah Betterton's marks. Wit. oath Sept. 6, 1797 Ezekiah Burrell to Wm Smith. Rec. Jan. 27, 1798

p. 72-74 Jan. 13, 1798 Alexander Thomson (Spartan Co) to James Ballinger (same); for 100£ sterling sold 200 ac on N fork of Tyger and E of Indian boundary line; border: Alexander Ray; survey Jul. 15, 1785 for John Davis and grant to Augustus Merrick. Witness Lewis Cockrill, Edward Ballinger, and Daniel Bragg. Signed Alex Thompson. Certified Jan. 13, 1798 by Ism Foster. Rec. Jan. 27, 1798

p. 74-75 Feb. 9, 1797 John Robertson (or Robinson) (Spartanburgh) to Grove Cole (same); for 30£ sterling sold 175 ac; NW half of 350 ac grant to David Jones. Witness Hugh Moore and John Laurence. Signed John Robinson. Wit. oath Jan. 15, 1798 John Laurence to John Lipscomb. Rec. Jan. 28, 1798

p. 75-76 Aug. 29, 1797 Mary Bryant to Sarah Betterton (Spartanburgh) to James Betterton (same); for 60£ sterling sold 125 ac on N side Tyger R and on Dutchman's Cr; border: Joshua Betterton, James Betterton, Betterton's Spring Br, and Samuel Pruett; part of 350 ac grant to Thomas Betterton, desc. Witness John Grist, Ezekiah Burrell, and Rebeckah Burrell. Signed Mary Bryant's and Sarah Betterton's marks. Wit. oath Sept. 6, 1797 Ezekiah Burrell to Wm Smith. Rec. Jan. 29, 1798

p. 76-77 Jun. 13, 1797 Evan Davis (Spartanburgh) to Jonathan Davis (same); for 5£ sold 100 ac where Jonathan Davis lives; border: David Jones, Howell, and Connell; part of grant from the State to James Brown. Witness Grove Cole, Evan Davis jr, and William Poole. Signed Evan Davis sr. Wit. oath Jan. 3, 1798 Grove Cole to John Lipscomb. Rec. Jan. 29, 1798

p. 77-78 Oct. 3, 1797 Rebeckah Arindell (Spartanburgh) to son Redick Arindell (same); for love and affection give a Negro boy

Bartley about 11 years old. Witness John Turner and William Morgan. Signed Rebeckah Arindell's mark. Wit. oath Jan. 13, 1798 John Turner to H McCray. Rec. Jan. 29, 1798

p. 78-79 Jan. 9, 1797 Jonathan Pinnell and wife Jamima (Spartanburgh) to Humphry Yarbrugh (same); for 40£ sterling sold 150 ac on S of Tyger R where Jonathan Pinnell lives; border: S-land granted to Joseph Peek (or Peck), E-grant to Edmond Bearden, and by remainder of 1,000 ac grant; part of 1,000 ac grant to James Simple jr and sold by Rottny Simple, heir to James Simple jr, to John McCullock who sold to Edward Hooker who sold to Jonathan Pinnell. Witness Jno Bryant and Thos Tod. Signed Jonathan Pinnell and Jamima's mark. Wit. oath Jan. 25, 1797 Jno Bryant to Moses Casey. Rec. Jan. 29, 1798

p. 79-81 May 26, 1797 Alexander Elder (Spartanburgh) to Burgess West (Union Co); for 150£ sterling sold 325 ac on both sides Dutchman's Cr where Alexander Elder lives; border: N-survey for James Faris, W-"by L, division line of land sold to Zopher Smith", S-Capt. Samuel Morrow, and by grant to William Sterling; part of 460 ac grant Mar. 5, 1787 Gov. Charles Pinckney to Alexander Elder; 150 ac of grant sold to Zopher Smith. Witness Osborn West and Andrew Thomson. Signed Alexander Elder. Wit. oath May 30, 1797 Osborn West to Thos Moore. Rec. Jan. 30, 1798. Dower renounced Mary Elder to I Harrison Oct. 7, 1797

p. 81-83 Sept. 28, 1789 Vardry McBee (Thickety, Spartanburgh) to William Wofford (Turky Cove, Burk Co, NC); for 100£ sterling sold 1,224 ac in three tracts: (1) 579 ac on both sides N Pacolate R including part of Walnut Mt; survey May 26, 1787 for Robert Evans; (2) 205 ac on N fork of Trall Cr of N fork Saluda R; survey May 28, 1787 for Robert Evans; and (3) 440 ac on Trall Cr of N Pacolate R including part of Walnut Mt; survey May 26, (year not given); all were replated and returned to the SC Office of Granting Lands in Vardry McBee's name and it is expected that all have been granted to Vardry McBee. Witness Lacyannie McBee and Elizabeth McBee. Signed Vardry McBee. Rec. Jan. 30, 1798

p. 83-84 Sept. 26, 1789 Vardry McBee to William Wofford; William is security for a "suit of debt" for Vardry and, by a "misconduct" judgment Col Odlina(?) Osborn vs William Wofford, William has to pay 400£ SC money; Vardry can't pay William a like sum, so Vardry mortgages the following land to William: (1) 300 ac on branch of Thickety Cr; including place called Sline (sic) Kilns and where "subscriber" now lives; (2) 400 ac on Fall Cr of Pacolate R in Greenville Co called copper mines; (3) 300 ac in Camden Dist on branch of Buffeloe Cr near mouth of it; border: Peper Quin and John Bridges; (4) three other grants for 2,900 ac on both sides Doolittle's Cr on E side of Broad R; including three places of iron ore and some slime (sic) stone; and (5) 1,120 ac in three tracts at head of Pacolate R in Greenville Co; bought to Vardry McBee from Jabez Evans and Robert Evans. Witness Z Taliferro and Henry McCray. Signed Vardry McBee. Rec. Jan. 30, 1798. Jan. 5, 1794 William Wofford assigns rights to above mortgage to James Wofford for 100£ sterling. Witness Thos Baker. Signed W Wofford

p. 84-85 Jan. 15, 1798 David Quarles (Spartanburgh) to John Harris (Greenville Co); for 60£ sterling sold 100 ac on N side Enoree R; border: Abner's Cr and Scott. Witness James Jordan and William McAbee. Signed David Quarles. Rec. Jan. 30, 1798

p. 85-86 Jan. 27, 1798 William Smith (Jackson Co, Ga) to James Smith (Spartanburgh); for 25£ sold 150 ac on Fairforrest Cr; border: William Smith, Peter Smith, Handcock Smith, Meeting house tract, and Golightly; part of 640 ac grant Jan. 21, 1785 Gov.

Benjamin Guerard to William Smith and part of Handcock Smith's 220 ac tract on Fairforrest Cr. Witness William R Smith, M Lovina Smith, and Lettice Smith. Signed William Smith. Wit. oath Feb. 3, 1798 M Lovina Smith to I Harrison. Rec. Feb. 30 (sic), 1798

p. 86-88 Feb. 20, 1797 Thomas Price (Spartanburgh), merchant, to Thomas Wright (same); for 60£ sterling sold (ac not given, maybe 140 ac) between N and S forks Tyger R; border: Aaron Floyd and N fork Tyger R; part of 200 ac grant May 1, 1786 Gov. William Moultrie to Francis Ward who sold to Abraham Barryer on Jul. 1, 1791 who sold 140 ac to Thomas Price. Witness Matthew Patton and John Wright. Signed Thomas Price. Wit. oath Aug. 5, 1797 John Wright to Thos Moore. Rec. Feb. 30, (sic), 1798

p. 88-89 Jul. 15, 1797 James Crook (Spartanburgh) to Drury McDaniel (same); for 100£ sterling sold 160 ac on N side of S fork Tyger R. Witness Joseph Massey, John Ward, and Thos Moore. Signed James Crook. Rec. Mar. 10, 1798. Dower renounced by Mary Crook (not dated)

p. 89-90 Oct. 17, 1791 John McCoole (Chester Co) to John Vandever (Spartanburgh); for 17£ sterling sold 135 ac on both sides Story's Mill Cr; border: Lemaster; part of 500 ac grant May 4, 1789 Gov. Charles Pinckney to John McCoole. Witness John Gossel, William Burton, and Thomas Wells. Signed Jno McCoole. Wit. oath Jan. 13, 1798 John Lamaster (sic) to William Simpson. Rec. Mar. 11, 1798

p. 90-92 Jul. 15, 1797 James Crook (Spartanburgh) to William McDaniel (same); for 100£ sterling sold 171 ac on N side of S fork Tyger R. Witness Drury McDaniel, John Ward, and Thomas Moore. Signed James Crook. Rec. Mar. 11, 1798. Dower renounced by Mary Crook to (not given and not dated)

p. 92-93 Feb. 7, 1797 John Head to Samuel Farrow (Spartanburgh); for 400£ sterling sold 1,075 ac in three tracts: (1) 375 ac on N side of Enoree R granted Aug. 4, 1770 Lt. Gov. William Bull to Robert Howard; border: John Billops, Isaac Lynck, and land formerly of James Benton now held by James Adair; (2) 60 ac adjoining (1) on Enoree R; grant to John Head; border: John Billops, William Stone, and including "a little mount"; and (3) 640 ac on both sides Lyahias Cr of Enoree R; border: John Head on two sides; grant Jul. 26, 1784 Gov. William Moultrie to John Head. Witness Stephan Heard, Wm Easley, and Josiah N Kennedy. Signed John Head. Wit. oath Feb. 7, 1798 Wm Easley to Reuben Barrett. Rec. Apr. 3, 1798. Dower renounced (Greenville Co) Sarah Head to John Thomas, jr Feb. 7, 1797

p. 93-95 Jan. 13, 1798 John Leonard Anderson and wife Keziah (Union Co) to Jacob Peeler (York Co); for $13 sold 200 ac on Shelton's Cr of Miller's fork of Thickety Cr of Broad R; border: SW-Obrian Smith and others vacant. Witness Stephen Chaffin, Wm Parker, and Thomas Quarles. Signed John Leonard and Keziah Anderson's marks. Wit. oath Feb. 20, 1798 Wm Parker to William McDowel. Rec. Apr. 8, 1798

p. 95-97 Feb. 10, 1797 Joseph Robertson and wife Drucilla (Spartanburgh) to Absalom Lancaster (same); for 100£ sterling sold 273 ac on Chinquepin Br on S side of Lawson's fork; border: NE-Wells Griffith and Duskin Grant and SE-Thomas Williamson. Witness Joshua Downs and Isham Foster. Signed Joseph Roberson and Drucilla's mark. Wit. oath Sept. 12, 1797 Joshua Downs to Ism Foster. Rec. Apr. 8, 1798

p. 97-98 Dec. 1, 1797 Henry ONail (Spartanburgh) to John Stone (same); for 50£ sold 560 ac on S side Pacolett R and on

Trough Shoal Br; border: Toleson and Homes; grant Feb. 6, 1788 Gov. William Moultrie to John Nail; Note: Henry Onail pays John Stone "2 and 2p" per ac for any land lost due to dispute. Witness John McDowell, William Stone, and Stephen Cruise. Signed Henry ONail. Wit. oath Apr. 9, 1798 William Stone to William Simpson. Rec. Apr. 12, 1798

p. 98-99 Oct. 17, 1791 John McCoole (Chester Co) to John Lamaster (Spartanburgh); for 34£ sterling sold 291 ac on both sides Stry's Mill Cr and both sides of a road from Spartanburgh to Union Court House; border: Lemaster's field, Bird, Vandever, Whitley (or Whittey), Nail, and Gosset; part of 500 ac grant May 4, 1789 Gov. Charles Pinckney to John McCoole. Witness John Gosset, William Burton, and John Vandever. Signed John McCoole. Wit. oath Mar. 10, 1798 John Vandever to William Simpson. Rec. Apr. 13, 1798

p. 99-101 Jan. 20, 1798 John Ford, heir to estate of Philip Ford, desc (Montgomery Co, Tenn) to James Ford jr (same); for 100£ sterling sold 300 ac on Fairforrest Cr; border: Giles Connell; grant Jun. 7, 1767 Gov. Charles G Montague to John Ford. Witness Edwd Lacy, Richd Miles, and James Ford. Signed John Ford. Wit. oath Jul. 23, 1798 Edwd Lacy to James Hooper. Rec. Sept. 24, 1798

p. 101-103 Mar. 21, 1798 John Thomas (Spartanburgh) to Moses Foster (same); for $200 sold 400 ac on N side Fairforrest Cr and on Rich Hill; border: Long Branch, Henry's Br, and Robert White; grant Dec. 11, 1770 Gov. William Tryon (NC) to Peter Johnston and signed by Wm Palmer, dept. surv; in NC auditor's book Jan. 3, 1771 signed John Frohock(?), aud; and memorial in SC auditor's book Oct. 12, 1773 signed R Lambton, d. aud. Witness Jas Smith, John Foster, and M Lovina Smith. Signed John Thomas, Shands Golightly and Martha Golightly (as relinquishment of dower). Wit. oath Mar. 21, 1798 John Foster to I Harrison. Rec. Apr. 14, 1798. Dower renounced Martha Golightly, mother of John Thomas, to I Harrison Apr. 9, 1798

p. 103-104 Apr. 10, 1798 Vincent Wyatt and wife Elizabeth (Spartanburgh) to Zachariah Wyatt (same); for 10£ sold 200 ac on Mayer's Br and S side of Peter's Cr; grant Dec. 3, 1787 States Office to Jesse Connell who sold to Vincent Wyatt (see Book B, p. 397-398). Witness Reubin Warren and George Thomason. Signed Vincent Wyatt and Elizabeth's mark. Wit. oath Apr. 10, 1798 Reubin Warren to Geor Lamkin. Rec. Apr. 14, 1798

p. 104-106 Jan. 12, 1796 Charles Wood (Spartanburgh) to John Lemaster (same); for 30£ sterling sold 100 ac on waters of Pacolate R; border: John Lukeroy's Spring Br, Michael McGaughy's grant on Jun. 2, 1788, Mine Spring Br, Seth Lewis, Lewis' Spring Br, and Richeson Whitley. Witness Mathias Bates, John Gossett, and Richeson Whitley. Signed Charles Wood. Wit. oath Mar. 10, 1798 Mathias Bates to William Simpson. Rec. Apr. 15, 1798

p. 106-107 Aug. 1, 1798 Thomas Carver (Spartanburgh) to Joseph Carver jr (same); for 50£ sterling sold "his whole estate" except the land: a bay horse, a young black mare, a sorrell colt, 2 cows and calves, and all household furniture--beds and furniture, tables, pewter, earthenware, potts, ovens, chairs, and all farming utensils--mattocks, axes, ploughs, hoes, etc. Witness Mitley Carver and Richard Carver. Signed Thomas Carver. Wit. oath Oct. 17, 1798 Thomas Carver and Ism Foster. Rec. Oct. 20, 1798

p. 107-111 Jun. 15, 1788 in Newberry Co William Johnston (Newberry Co) to James Smith (same); for 100£ 10s SC money sold 500 ac on Middle Tygar R; border: NW & SW-Elias Vanderhorst, N-Capt. Blake, and others vacant; grant Dec. 24, 1772 in Craven Co Gov. Charles G Montague to Elias Foysin who sold Nov. 1 & 2, 1789 to

William Johnston. Witness Thomas Johnston and David Johnston. Signed William Johnston. Wit. oath (Newberry Co) Sept. 19, 1794 David Johnston to Charles Griffin

p. 111-113 Jun. 29, 1797 Justice Reynolds and wife Mary (Spartanburgh) to Alexander Alexander (same); for 100£ sterling sold (1) 200 ac on both sides Lawson's fork of Pacolate R; including Saw and Grist Mills; grant North Carolina to James Hammett who sold to William Wofford who sold to Wells Griffith who sold to Justice Reynolds; and (2) (unknown) ac part of 187 ac on N side Lawson's fork; grant to Wells Griffith. Witness I Harrison and Geor Lamkin. Signed Justus Reynolds. Rec. Oct. 10, 1798. Dower renounced Mary Reynolds to Isham Harrison Jul. 20, 1797

p. 113-115 Jan. 25, 1798 Alexander Alexander (Spartanburgh) to Isham Harrison (same); for 200£ sold (1) 200 ac on both sides Lawson's fork of Pacolate R including Mill Seat; grant North Carolina to James Hammett who sold to William Wofford who sold to Wells Griffith; and (2) (unknown) ac part of 187 ac on N side Lawson's fork; grant to Wells Griffith. Witness Moses Timmons, Osburn West, and Turner Thomason. Signed Alexr Alexander. Wit. oath Jan. 3, 1799 William T Thomason to James Jordan. Rec. Jan. 5, 1799

p. 115-117 Jan. 5, 1799 Samuel Miller, sheriff (Spartanburgh) to Alexander McKie (same); for 41£ 10s sold 200 ac; Justice Reynolds had the land on both sides of Lawson's fork including Saw and Grist Mills; grant North Carolina to James Hammett who sold to Wm Wofford who sold to Wells Griffith who sold to Justice Reynolds; Hampton and Matthews obtained a judgment against Justice Reynolds in Spartanburgh Co Court Jul. term 1798 for 78£ 7s 11p sterling; dept. sheriff Britain Williford seized the land and sold it Dec. 1, 1798. Witness Wm Wells, Bazel Lee, and Wm T Thomason. Signed Samuel Miller. "acknowledged in open court" Jan. term 1799. Rec. Jan. 12, 1799

p. 117-119 Dec. 15, 1798 Isham Harrison (Spartanburgh) to Alexander McKie (same); for $183.25 sold (1) 200 ac on both sides Lawons's fork of Pacolate R including Saw and Grist Mills; grant North Carolina to James Hammett who sold to William Wofford who sold to Wells Griffith who sold to Justice Reynolds who sold to Alexander Alexander who sold to Isham Harrison; and (2) (unknown) ac part of 187 ac on N side of Lawson's fork;grant to Wells Griffith and "sold as previous tract". Witness John Lancaster and Wm T Thomason. Signed I Harrison. Wit. oath Jan. 3, 1799 Wm T Thomason to James Jordan. Rec. Jan. 3, 1799

p. 119-121 Apr. 2, 1787 (Charleston, SC) Gov. Thomas Pinckney to James Steadman; a grant; for 49£ sterling granted 2,100 ac on both sides Cherokee Cr and other branches of Pacolate R; border: Wadsworth and vacant or unknown; plat on Oct. 10, 1786 shows land on both sides Green River Rd signed Jesse Connell, DS and F Bremar, Surv. Gen. Signed Thomas Pinckney. Rec. Jan. 12, 1799. Feb. 20, 1795 James Steadman assigns rights to above grant to Robert Lee for 5s sterling. Witness Thomas Steadman and Richard Lee. Signed James Steadman. Wit. oath Mar. 10, 1795 Richard Lee to S Bethel

p. 121-122 Nov. 3, 1797 John Peterson (Pendleton Co) to James Wilkins (Spartanburgh); for 30£ sold 75 ac on Pacolate R; border: grant May 1, 1786 Gov. William Moultrie to Laurence Reddy. Witness Joshua Eliott, John Brown sr, and John Brown jr. Signed John Peterson. Wit. oath Apr. 14, 1798 Joshua Eliott to I Harrison. Rec. Oct. 20, 1798

p. 122-123 Sept. 14, 1798 Justus Reynolds (Spartanburgh) to Gideon

Reynolds; for 30£ sterling sold all horses, cattle, hogs, sheep, waggon and giers, all beds and furniture, all pots, ovens, pewter, all knives, forks and all "Delfware". Witness Benjamin Church and Jean Church. Signed Justus Reynolds. Wit. oath Mar. 14, 1799 Benjamin Church to A Lancaster. Rec. Mar. 14, 1799

p. 123-124 Feb. 15, 1799 Samuel Lancaster (Spartanburgh) to William Lancaster (same); for 105£ sold 266 2/3 ac on both sides Tates Br and S side of Fairforrest Cr; border: N-Nathan Veal, S-Charles Smith, E-Henry Nail, W-Gibbs or Smith; part of grant to James Tillet and "transfered" to James White who sold to Samuel Lancaster. Witness Britton Williford esq and Thomas Sarrart. Signed Saml Lancaster. Wit. oath Mar. 2, 1799 Britton Williford to I Harrison. Rec. Mar. 30, 1799. Dower renounced Agnes Lancaster to Wm Smith Mar. 25, 1799

p. 124-126 May 22, 1798 Moses Guyton (Union Co) to William Bostick (Spartanburgh); for 141£ sterling sold 375 ac on Beverdam Cr of Thickety Cr; border: Hogan and Hagan; of which 179½ ac is on S side of Creek and granted May 15, 1772 Gov. John Martin (NC) to John Hogans and eventually sold to Moses Guyton; remainder of 375 ac is on N side of Creek and part of the same grant and part of a grant Sept. 18, 1785 Gov. William Moultrie to Vardry McBee and eventually sold to Moses Guyton. Witness Richard Thomson, James Fowler, and Jas Smith. Signed Moses Guyton. Wit. oath Jul. 17, 1798 Jas Smith to Ism Foster Rec. Oct. 20, 1798

p. 126-127 Mar. 7, 1786 James Martin (Lincoln Co, NC) to William Bostick (Spartanburgh); for $400 sold (ac not given) on branch of Thickety Cr; border: grant to John Hogan, W & N-Thomas Cole, Higgins, and "may lie" between McBee and Cole; includes a corner of grant to Vardry McBee; grant Mar. 6, 1786 South Carolina to Robert Montgomery who sold Mar. 28, 1786 to James Martin. Witness Jas Smith and Archd Patterson. Signed James Martin. Wit. oath Jul. 17, 1798 Jas Smith to Ism Foster.

p. 127-128 Apr. 29, 1797 David Allen (Spartanburgh) to Young Allen (same); for 50£ sterling sold 150 ac; border: Gocher's Cr, George Gibson, David Allen's Spring Br, and Jones; part of 543 ac grant Oct. 6, 1788 Gov. Thomas Pinckney to David Allen. Witness David Jones and Willis Allen. Signed David Allen's mark. Wit. oath Jul. 15, 1797 David Allen to John Lipscomb. Rec. Oct. 20, 1798

p. 128-129 Dec. 15, 1795 John Cavin (Spartanburgh) to Joseph Cavin (same); for 50£ sterling sold 200 ac; grant Mar. 15, 1787 State Patent to John Cavin. Witness Zachariah Grace and Peter Bragg. Signed John Cavin. Wit. oath Jul. 30, 1796 Zachariah Grace to George Breuton. Rec. Oct. 21, 1798

p. 129-130 Nov. 8, 1797 Henry Kerley (Burke Co, NC) to Moses Cavin (Spartanburgh); for 40£ sold 150 ac on S fork Jimmey's Cr; border: N-William Hendrick, W-Alexander Alexander, S-Isaac Crow, and E-Henry Kerley. Witness James Kerley, Joseph Cavin, and Jno White. Signed Henry and Sarah Kerley's marks. Wit. oath Jan. 26, 1798 Joseph Cavin and George Breuton. Rec. Oct. 21, 1798

p. 130-132 Nov. 4, 1794 Edward Lacy esq, sheriff (Pinckney Dist) to William Wells (Spartanburgh); for 12£ 2s 8p sold 200 ac; James White had 240 ac on branches of Fairforrest Cr; granted in 1787 to Henry White; in Pinckney Dist Court Nov. term 1793, John Ford esq got a judgment against Briton Williford and John Shands, executors for James White desc, for 47£ 7s 5p sterling; writ signed by Chief Justice John Rutledge;sale Jul. 7, 1794. Witness Obediah Trimmier, Jno Gowen, and Jno Lancaster. Signed Edwd Lacy. Wit. oath Apr. 26, 1799 Jno Lancaster to A Lancaster. Rec. Apr. 26, 1799

p. 132-134 Mar. 28, 1797 Benjamin Wofford (Spartanburgh) to William Earnest (same); for 50£ sterling sold 170 ac on N side Enoree R; border: mouth of Lick Cr. Witness James Wofford and Benjamin Wofford jr. Signed Benja Wofford. Rec. Oct. 22, 1798. Dower renounced Mary Wofford to Wm Smith Aug. 14, 1797

p. 134 Mar. 2, 1798 Reubin Lawson to I Harrison; Reubin says he was present when land was surveyed for William Wofford with a warrant in name of Arther Crocker; the line left out John Gray's Spring "about 40 steps as they came on Westerwardly and cornered on the side of a hill on the other side"; Reubin says the stake he stuck in the side of the hill was corner of the tract. Signed Reubin Lawson's mark. Certified Mar. 2, 1798 by I Harrison

p. 134-135 Nov. 25, 1797 Henry Wyatt (Tencey) to John Pitman (Spartanburgh); for 25£ sterling sold 240 ac on E side of Pacolate R and head of Doctor's Branches; border: John Landford Dart; part of 267 ac grant Nov. 19, 1795 to Henry Wyatt. Witness William Murry and Abraham Wyatt. Signed Henry Wyatt's mark. Wit. oath Apr. 9, 1798 Abraham Wyatt to Geor Lamkin. Rec. Oct. 22, 1798

p. 135-137 Apr. 4, 1795 James Martin (Pinckney Dist) to George Walker (same); for 50£ sterling sold 51½ ac on N side Cherokee Cr; grant Apr. (not given), 1786 to James Martin. Witness Cushman R Edson and James Fanning. Signed James Martin. Wit. oath Jul. 1, 1795 James Fanning to H McCray. Rec. Oct. 22, 1798

p. 137-138 Dec. 27, 1796 Rezin Holland and wife Mary (Spartanburgh) to Richard Young (same); for 50£ sterling sold 181 ac on S side Tyger R; grant Feb. 5, 1787 Gov. William Moultrie to Delany Carrell who sold to Rezin Holland as recorded in Spartanburgh Co deeds. Witness Joseph Wofford and Owen Forester. Signed Rezin Holland and Mary's mark. Certified Dec. 27, 1796 by Wm Smith. Rec. Oct. 23, 1798. Dower renounced Mary Holland to Wm Smith Dec. 27, 1796

p. 138-140 Dec. 27, 1796 Owen Forrester and wife Eleoner (Spartanburgh) to Richard Young (same); for 5£ sold 10 ac; border: Millinton Smith; part of 100 ac on S side Tyger R grant Mar. 6, 1780 Gov. William Moultrie to Joshua Smith who sold to Owen Forrester; border: Benjamin Wofford and land grant to Wm Young. Witness Joseph Wofford and Rezin Holland. Signed Owen and Eleoner Forrester's marks. Certified Dec. 27, 1796 by Wm Smith. Rec. Oct. 23, 1798. Dower renounced Dleonor Forrester to Wm Smith Dec. 27, 1796

p. 140-141 Jan. 29, 1798 William Smith (Jackson Co, Ga) to Spencer Smith (Spartanburgh); for 75£ sold 191 ac on Fairforrest Cr; border: Hancock's Br; grant to Hancock Smith. Witness Jas Smith, Peter Smith, and William R Smith. Signed William Smith. Wit. oath May 11, 1798 Jas Smith to I Harrison. Rec. Oct. 23, 1798

p. 141-143 Dec. 23, 1796 Joseph Wofford and wife Martha (Spartanburgh) to Richard Young (same); for 25£ sterling sold 45 ac on S side Tyger R; border: Wofford's field and grant to Delany Currol; on S side of 300 ac grant Aug. 11, 1774 Lt. Gov. William Bull to Luke Vickry who sold Aug. 7, 1777 to Joseph Wofford. Witness Owen Forrester, Rezin Holland, and Richard Holland. Signed Joseph Wofford. Certified Dec. 27, 1796 Wm Smith. Rec. Oct. 24, 1798. Dower renounced Martha Wofford to Wm Smith Dec. 27, 1796

p. 143-144 Nov. 3, 1791 Hugh Pierce (Spartanburgh) to William Poole (same); for 60£ sterling sold 312 ac on N side of Pacolate R about a mile above the Healing Springs; border: E-David Henry, W-Hammet's old line, and others vacant. Witness William Poole jr, Blackburn Guin, and John Stovaul. Signed Hugh Pierce. Wit. oath

Apr. 9, 1798 John Stovaul to I Harrison. Rec. Oct. 24, 1798

p. 144-146 Aug. 12, 1789 Philemon Waters (Newbery Co) to Thomas Niles (Spartanburgh); for 200£ sterling sold 350 ac on Rocky Br of Tyger R and on S side Tyger R; border: all vacant; grant Mar. 22, 1769 Gov. Charles G Montague to Joseph Pack. Witness Saml Farrow and James Rainwater. Signed Philn Waters. Wit. oath Jan. 29, 1791 James Rainwater to Thomas Farrow. Rec. Oct. 24, 1798

p. 146-147 Feb. 20, 1798 William Dottan (Spartanburgh) to William Kelso (same); for $88 sold (ac not given) on N Pacolate R; border: Hugh Moris' old field, Mells Welch, and Any Hooper's Cr; part of grant in 1777 to Alexander Kilpatrick. Witness Thos Jackson, Enoch Hooper, and John Dottan. Signed Wm Dottan. Wit. oath Apr. 14, 1798 Thos Jackson to James Hooper. Rec. Oct. 24, 1798

p. 147-148 Oct. 26, 1795 George Story sr (Spartanburgh) to George Story jr, son of Anthony Story, desc (same); for 35£ sterling sold 200 ac; grant Dec. 23, 1771 SC governor to George Story sr and part of grant Nov. 18, 1752 NC governor to George Story sr. Witness R Donaldson, Saml Kelso, James Story. Signed George Story's mark. Wit. oath Apr. 29, 1798 James Story to William Simpson. Rec. Oct. 24, 1798

p. 148-149 Mar. 31, 1798 George Story sr (Spartanburgh) to James Story (same); for 30£ sterling sold 76 ac on branch of Fairforrest Cr; part of two grants Nov. 10, 1752 and Dec. 16, 1769 both to George Story sr; see survey to Andrew Thomson and plat made from it. Witness John Story, George Story jr, and William Patton. Signed George Story's mark. Wit. oath Apr. 9, 1798 John Story to William Simpson. Rec. Oct. 25, 1798

p. 149-150 Mar. 8, 1798 William Wells (Spartanburgh) to George Campbell (same); for 5£ sold 100 ac on branches of Chinquemin Cr of Lawson's fork of Pacolate R; border: Reynolds, Lancaster, and Thompson. Witness Absolom Lancaster and John Lancaster. Signed William Wells. Wit. oath Apr. 9, 1798 Absolom Lancaster to George Lamkin. Rec. Oct. 24, 1798

p. 150-152 Jun. 10, 1791 William Garret (Wilks Co, Ga) to John Sloan (Spartanburgh), ironmaster; for 50£ SC money sold 146 ac on Middle fork of Tyger R known as Long Br; grant (date left blank) to William Garret. Witness Samuel Niesbett, Peter Tramel, and Nansey Gentry. Signed William Garret. Wit. oath Feb. 5, 1799 Samuel Niesbett to B. D. Shumate. Rec. Jun. 8, 1799

p. 152-153 Mar. 31, 1796 Robert Neisbet (Spartanburgh) to John Sloan (same); for 70£ sterling sold 200 ac; grant Apr. 3, 1786 to Robert Neisbet. Witness John Nisbett and James Bright. Signed Robert Neisbett. Wit. oath Feb. 2, 1799 John Nisbett to B. D. Shumate. Rec. Jun. 8, 1799

p. 153-154 Dec. 10, 1796 Richard Lee to Blackbourn Guim; for 25£ sold 360 ac on waters of Cherokee Cr. Witness Jon Low and Bazzel Scott. Signed Richard Lee. Wit. oath Jan. 28, 1797 Bazzel Scott to George Lamkin. Rec. Oct. 25, 1798

p. 154-155 Oct. 31, 1793(or 8) John Martin esq (York Co) to Lewis Standley (Spartanburgh); for 50£ SC money sold 250 ac on both sides Cherokee Cr; part of grant of "large tract" to John Martin esq. Witness Gideon Brown and James Ballinger. Signed James Martin. Wit. oath May 6, 1794 James Ballinger to Edward Goode. Rec. Oct. 25, 1798

p. 155-157 Mar. 5, 1798 Francis Clark (Spartanburgh) to William

Bonner (Lincoln Co, NC); for $400 sold 600 ac in two tracts on waters of Sarralle's Cr of Broad R: (1) 180 ac; border: S-Francis Clark, E-Guinn, W-Markley, N-vacant; grant Oct. 6, 1788 Gov. Thomas Pinckney to Francis Clark; and (2) 420 ac; border: Gibbs, Clark, and others vacant; grant Jan. 5, 1795 Gov. Arnoldus Vanderhorst to Francis Clark. Witness Obadiah Trimmier, Samuel McCraw, and David Tate. Signed Francis Clark's mark. Wit. oath Mar. 24, 1798 Obadiah Trimmier to H McCray. Rec. Oct. 26, 1798

p. 157-158 Oct. 21, 1793 Allen Sarratt (Rutherford Co, NC) to Raydeck Arndell (Spartanburgh); for 9£ 11s sterling sold 150 ac on Mike's Cr on W side Broad R; border: Buflow Ridge Path, Raydeck Arndell, and Samuel Sarratt; part of 450 ac "laid out" to Allen Sarratt. Witness Samuel Sarratt and William Sarratt. Signed Allen Sarratt. Wit. oath Jan. 11, 1798 William Sarratt to H McCray. Rec. Oct. 26, 1798

p. 158-160 Mar. 9, 1795 Allen Sarratt (Spartanburgh) to Raydeck Ardell (same); for 15£ 11s sterling sold 148 ac on W side Broad R; border: N-John Sarratt, Raydeck Ardell, and Buflow Path; where "he" now lives; grant to Allen Sarratt. Witness William Sarratt and Samuel Sarratt. Signed Allen Sarratt. Wit. oath Jan. 11, 1798 William Sarratt to H McCray. Rec. Oct. 26, 1798

p. 160-161 Feb. 1, 1793 Nathaniel Robertson and James Byars (Pinckney Dist) to Raydeck Arnald (Spartanburgh); for 10£ sterling sold 143½ ac on Mike's Cr; border: William Tate, William Byars, Vardry McBee's line between William Byars and Raydeck Arnald, and includes improvements where Henry Robertson sr and Raydeck Arnald lived at the same time; half of grant Jan. 1, 1787 to Henry Robertson sr, desc and James Byars. Witness Obadiah Trimmier, Jos Jno Martin, and Peter Quinn. Signed Nathaniel Robertson and James Byars. Wit. oath Jan. 8, 1798 Obadiah Trimmier to H McCray. Rec. Oct. 26, 1798

p. 161-163 Oct. 25, 1798 Zacharias Gibbs (Union Co) to John Otts (Spartanburgh); for 30£ 6s 8p sterling sold 200 ac; part of 500 ac grant to Richard Hampton on branch of Ward's Cr of Fairforrest Cr of N Tygar R. Witness William Otts, Thomas Cook, and Jesse Spencer. Signed Zacharias Gibbs. Wit. oath Apr. 9, 1798 Jesse Spencer to B. D. Shumate. Rec. Oct. 26, 1798

p. 163-164 Sept. 23, 1797 William Turner (Spartanburgh) to James Philips (Rutherford Co, NC); for 25£ SC money sold 340 ac on Ashworth's Cr; border: Camp and Evan Wadkins. Witness Patrick Sullivan and John Turner. Signed William Turner's mark. Wit. oath Mar. 8, 1798 Patrick Sullivan to H McCray. Rec. Oct. 27, 1798

p. 164-165 Aug. 16, 1796 Thomas Thompson (Spartanburgh) to William Turner (same); for 17£ sterling sold 340 ac on both sides Ashworth's Cr; border Camp and Evan Wadkins. Witness John Turner, William Morrow, and Samuel Turner. Signed Thomas Thompson. Wit. oath Mar. 8, 1798 John Turner to H McCray. Rec. Oct. 27, 1798

p. 165-166 Mar. 6, 1798 Thomas Cook (Spartanburgh) to Christopher Orenduff (same); for $100 sold 147 ac on waters of Dutchman's Cr; border: Edward Rollins; grant to Thomas Soreth (or Sorett). Witness George Head, Clary Lancaster, and William Lancaster. Signed Thomas Cook. Wit. oath Mar. 13, 1799 William Lancaster to Samuel Lancaster. Rec. Mar. 15, 1799

p. 166-167 Feb. 19, 1797 Zacharias Gibbs (Union Co) to William Calvert (Spartanburgh); for 15£ sold 134 ac; plat attached shows border: Daniel Stephens, Jesse Spencer, Richd Hampton, Roland Jinnings, and Constable; grant May 17, 1792 Gov. Charles Pinckney to James Gibbs, Zacharias Gibbs' father. Witness William Burton,

Alexander Elder, Rolley Calvert, and Nelley Calvert. Signed Zacharias Gibbs. Wit. oath Feb. 24, 1798 Rolley Calvert to W Lancaster. Rec. Oct. 27, 1798

p. 167-168 Feb. 12, 1799 Thomas Penny (Spartanburgh) to James Vernon (same); for $43 sold (ac not given) on both sides Middle fork Tygar R; border: Elisha Thompson's grant; part of 400 ac grant Aug. 19, 1774 to Robert Nisbet who sold Jul. 28, 1793 to Thomas Penny. Witness James Templeton, Gab Benson, and Jesse Cooper. Signed Thomas Penny's mark. Wit. oath Apr. 8, 1799 Gab Benson to W Lancaster. Rec. Oct. 27, 1798

p. 168-169 Mar. 25, 1799 William Dalton (Spartanburgh) to William and Foster Jackson, sons of Samuel Jackson jr, desc (Same); for 8£ 15s sterling sold 8 3/4 ac on S side of N fork Pacolet R; border: E side of William Kelsoe's Cr; part of grant to Alexander Kilpatrick who sold to Joseph Moore. Witness Thos Jackson, John Dalton, and William Kelsoe. Signed William Dalton. Wit. oath (not dated) Thos Jackson to John Anderson. Rec. Apr. 15, 1799

p. 169-170 Mar. 1, 1796 Augustine Clayton (Sparting Co) to Elisha Hedden (same); for 200£ sterling sold 248 ac on waters of Tyger R; border: John Barry; "low end" of 500 ac grant to James Alexander. Witness William Harris, Charles Hide, and David Drummon. Signed Augustine Clayton. Wit. oath Mar. 27, 1799 William Harris to Drury McDaniel. Rec. Apr. 15, 1799

p. 170-171 Oct. 20, 1798 Stephen Wilson and wife Mary (Pinckney Dist) to son Reubin Wilson; for 10£ sold 100 ac on S side Tyger R; border: N of Methodist Meeting House, W-Austin Clayton, S-Wm Lindsey, N-Tyger R, and S & E-Stephen Wilson. Witness Reubin Newman, William Qualls, and William Smith. Signed Stephen Wilson and Mary's mark. Wit. oath Mar. 20, 1799 Reubin Newman to H McCray. Rec. Apr. 16, 1799

p. 171-172 Jan. 4, 1799 John Pitman (Spartanburgh) to Jesse Vincent (same); for $100 sold 240 ac on E side Pacolet R; border: Dart; grant Mar. 17, 1796 to Henry Wyatt. Witness Briton George and Susanna Lamkin. Signed John Pitman's mark. Wit. oath Feb. 22, 1799 Briton George to George Lamkin. Rec. Jun. 1, 1799

p. 172-173 Nov. 27, 1798 Benjamin Jones (SC) to Michael Miller (Spartanburgh); for 200£ sold 300 ac on both sides N fork Tyger R; part of 350 ac grant to Samuel Nisbett who sold to Joseph Jones and by his will to Benjamin Jones. Witness Thomas Brevard, James Jordan, and James Vernon. Signed Benjamin Jones. Rec. Jun. 1, 1799

p. 173-174 Nov. 17, 1795 Isham Matthews and wife Drusilla (Spartanburgh) to Danid Golightly (same); for 45£ sterling sold 100 ac on Fairforrest Cr; border: SE-Hancock Smith, SW-David Golightly, N & NW-William Mitchel, NE-William Smith, and at the mouth of a hollow near ford on the Creek between Isham Matthews and William Smith. Witness William Lancaster and Absalom Lancaster. Signed Isham Matthews and Drusilla's mark. Wit. oath Feb. 13, 1799 William Lancaster to I Harrison. Rec. Jun. 1, 1799

p. 174-175 (not given), 1793 Ephraim Elder (Spartanburgh) to Henry Ayres (same); a bond of 50£ sterling; Condition: Ephraim deeds Henry 7 ac on NW corner of Ephraim's land; border: David Golightly and Henry Ayres. Witness William Roberds and Mark Swadley. Signed Ephraim Elder. Wit. oath Feb. 13, 1799 William Roberds to W Lancaster. Rec. Jun. 1, 1799

p. 175-177 Jul. 26, 1798 Henry Ayres (Spartanburgh) to David Golightly (same); for $200 sold 211 ac on S side Fairforrest Cr; border: N-heirs of William Wheeler, desc, S-George Connell, E-David Golightly, W-David Cook, and Tillet's old line. Witness Ephraim Elder and William Lancaster. Signed Henry Ayres. Wit. oath Feb. 13, 1799 William Lancaster to I Harrison. Rec. Jun. 1, 1799. Dower renounced Susannah Ayres to I Harrison Sept. 19, 1798

p. 177-178 Jul. 1, 1795 William Bird (Spartanburgh) to Thomas Brandon (Union Co); for 30£ SC money sold 145 ac on both sides S Pacolet R; border: NE-Young; grant Oct. 3, 1785 Gov. William Moultrie to William Bird. Witness James Bird, William Bird, jr, and James M Price. Signed William Bird. Wit. oath (Union Co) Jul. 9, 1795 James M Price to Andrew Tarrance. Rec. Oct. 27, 1798

p. 178-180 Jul. 19, 1797 Jno Gowen, late sheriff (Spartanburgh) to William Dalton (same); for 86£ 5(s?) 3p sterling sold 200 ac on both sides of N Pacolet R; formerly owned by John Moore; judgment was obtained by Winthrop Todd and Winthrop & Co in Spartanburgh Co Court Jan. term 1792 for 86£ 19s sterling; writ was issued in 1792; and sale was June. 13, 1792 to William Dalton. Witness Samuel Farrow esq and Jas Lancaster. Signed Jno Gowen. Wit. oath Jul. 19, 1798 Samuel Farrow to William Lancaster. Rec. Oct. 28, 1798

p. 180-181 May 26, 1798 John Johnston (Spartanburgh) to John Morris (same); for 10£ sold 215 ac on Thompson's Cr of Pacolet R; border: N-Thomas Bennett, W-vacant, S-Joseph Vennable, and E-vacant. Witness William Bennett and Vinct Bennett. Signed John Johnston. Wit. oath Jul. 16, 1798 John Johnston and wife Salley to Ism Foster. Rec. Oct. 28, 1798. Dower renounced Salley Johnston to William and Vinct Bennett May 26, 1798

p. 181-183 Dec. (not given), 1797 Robert White (Spartanburgh) to James Riely (same); for 10£ sterling sold 50 ac on Kelsoe's Br of Kelsoe's Cr of Fairforrest Cr of Tyger R; border: still house and dam, White, and Rich Hill Br; plat attached shows border: Robert White, Moses Foster, and Jno Thomas or vacant and includes Jas Riely's house; part of grant NC governor to Jno Gibbs and eventually sold to Robert White. Witness Robert Sterling, Wm S Golightly, and Jno Foster. Signed Robert White. Wit. oath Dec. 30, 1797 Wm S Golightly to I Harrison. Rec. Oct. 28, 1798. Dower renounced Ezebell White to I Harrison Jun. 16, 1798

p. 183-184 Mar. 20, 1798 David Allen and wife Martha (Spartanburgh) to Drury Allen (same); for 30£ sterling sold 130 ac; border: Allen's Spring Br and Jones; part of grant Oct. 6, 1788 Gov. Thomas Pinckney to David Allen. Witness Abigail Allen and Reynold Allen. Signed David Allen's mark (Martha doesn't sign). Wit. oath Mar. 20, 1798 Reynold Allen to John Lipscomb. Rec. Oct. 28, 1798

p. 184-185 Mar. 2, 1795 Reubin Warren (Spartanburgh) to Drury Scruggs (same); for "a third of expenses of saving 655 ac" sold 177 ac a part of said 655 ac on both sides Horse Cr of Broad R; border: conditional line between Reubin Warren and Drury Scruggs, and by Richard Haney; grant Dec. 2, 1793 States Office to Reubin Warren. Witness John Cobbs and Samuel Teal. Signed Reubin Warren. Wit. oath Apr. 6, 1795 Samuel Teal to S Bethel. Rec. Oct. 28, 1798

p. 185-187 Aug. 25, 1796 George Story sr (Spartanburgh) to Henry Story (same); for 10£ sterling sold 73 ac on branch on Fairforrest Cr; survey by Andrew Thompson; part of two grants Nov. 20, 1752 and Dec. 16, 1769 both to George Story sr. Witness Robert Donaldson, Saml Kelso, and James Muckleware jr. Signed George Story's mark. Wit. oath Jul. 17, 1798 Saml Kelso to William Simpson.

Rec. Oct. 28, 1798

p. 187-188 Sept. 17, 1794 William Clayton (SC) to James Linard (Spartanburgh); for 10£ sold 76 ac on S side Tyger R; border: John McCullocks, Edward Hooker, William Clayton, and Edward Arnett; grant to J(?) Daniel Kern (or Rem) who sold to William Clayton. Witness George Divine and Robert Harrison. Signed William Clayton. Wit. oath Jul. 17, 1798 George Divine to H McCray. Rec. Oct. 28, 1798. Feb. 27, 1798 James Linard and wife Margaret assign rights to above land to Stephen Clayton. Witness George Divine and Solomon Pennel. Signed James Linard and Margaret's marks

p. 188-189 Mar. 2, 1795 Reubin Warren (Spartanburgh) to Drury Scruggs (same); for 23£ 9s SC money sold 150 ac on both sides Horse Cr of Broad R; border: conditional line between Reubin Warren and Drury Scruggs; part of 655 ac grant Dec. 2, 1793 States Office to Reubin Warren. Witness John Cobbs and Samuel Teal. Signed Reubin Warren. Wit. oath Apr. 6, 1795 Samuel Teal to S Bethell. Rec. Oct. 29, 1798

p. 189-191 Sept. 23, 1796 Joseph Couch (Spartanburgh) to John Petty Poole (Union Co); for 100 (£ ?) sold 200 ac on Enoree R and part of two tracts: (1) 150 ac is part of 300 ac grant May 7, 1767 Gov. Charles G Montague to Thos Couch desc; and (2) 50 ac is part of grant to Charles Hunt; one ac excepted where Joseph Couch's father is buried and one of "his" children. Witness Spencer Brown, Seth Petty Pool, and Jesse Petty Pool. Signed Joseph Couch's mark. Wit. oath May 15, 1798 Spencer Brown to Thos Farrow. Rec. Oct. 29, 1798

p. 191-192 Dec. 10, 1797 Nancy Ward (Spartanburgh) to John Ward (same); for 15£ sterling sold 50 ac on N side Tyger R; border: N-John Ward and W-Ward's Cr; survey Sept. 29, 1783 (or 1773) and grant Gov. Benjamin Guerard to Patrick March who sold to Nancy Ward. Witness Aaron Pinson and Thomas Shearley. Signed Nancy Ward's mark. Wit. oath Jan. 2, 1798 Aaron Pinson to Thos Moore. Rec. Oct. 30, 1798

p. 192-194 Jul. 14, 1798 James Sanders (Spartanburgh) to Lawrence Bankson (same); for 10£ sterling sold 13 ac on S side Pacolet R; border: Lawrence Bankson; part of grant Nov. 25, 1771 NC States Office to James Philips. Witness James Turner, William Abbett jr, and Isaac Young. Signed James Sanders' mark. Wit. oath Jul. 17, 1798 Isaac Young to Wm McDowell. Rec. Oct. 30, 1798

p. 194 Jun. 13, 1788 Henry Turner (Spartanburgh) to Thos Gillenwaters (Union Co); for 5£ sold 120 ac on Gocher's Cr of Thickety Cr; upper end of 247 ac. Witness William Wright and James Simmons. Signed Henry Turner. Wit. oath Aug. 2, 1796 James Simmons to John Lipscomb. Rec. Nov. 1, 1798

p. 194-196 Jan. 28, 1793 Nathaniel Henderson (York Co) to James and Daniel Henderson; for 20£ SC money sold 400 ac on N fork Pacolet R; border: Robert Tate; grant Sept. 26, 1766 to Belvey Clark. Witness Jas Alexander and Joshua C Alexander. Signed Nathl Henderson. Wit. oath Feb. 27, 1798 Joshua C Alexander to James Hooper. Rec. Nov. 1, 1798

p. 196-197 Jan. 28, 1793 Nathl Henderson (York Co) to Saml and Robert Henderson (same); for 20£ sterling sold 400 ac on N of Pacolet R below Beaverdam Br; including "rich land bottom"; grant Sept. 26, 1766 to Jno Clark. Witness James Alexander and Joshua C Alexander. Signed Nathl Henderson. Wit. oath Feb. 27, 1798 Joshua C Alexander to James Hooper. Rec. Nov. 1, 1798

p. 197-198 Aug. 20, 1797 George Ewing's will (Spartanburgh): (1) all just debts and funeral charges to be paid; (2) wife Catherine--a sorrel horse and all other stock of cattle, furniture and otherwise and houses and improvements and farming tools and she can dispose of it at her death, but if she marrys, she gets a third of a dividend of the personal property; (3) to son Hugh--$10; (4) to daughter Mary--$10; (5) to daughter Catherine--a young horse called Bob not cut; (6) to two daughters, Ann and Margret--all land where George Ewing lives 240 ac; (7) to Ann--a mare called Sal with a bed and furniture; (8) to Margaret--young horse called Herculus with a bed and furniture; Note: wife Catherine and son Hugh are appointed executors. Witness David Alexander, Mary Logan, and Jas Logan. Signed George Ewing. Wit. oath Jun. 16, 1798 David Alexander to James Hooper. Rec. Nov. 1, 1798

p. 198-199 Jul. 2, 1798 John Golightly (Spartanburgh), iron monger to John Williams (same); for "one Eagle" sold 70 ac near Beaverdam Cr on S side Fairforrest Cr; border: Williams, Tinsley, and taking (or assertaining) 12 ac from corner of Tinsley's survey; including Foster's Spring. Witness none. Signed John Golightly. Wit. oath Jul. 14, 1798 John Golightly to Ism Foster. Rec. Nov. 1, 1798

p. 199-200 Jul. 12, 1798 Thomas Brandon (Union Co) to Thomas Jackson (Spartanburgh); for $80 sold 145 ac on S Pacolate R; border: NE-Young. Witness James White, D. M. Duff, and James Davis. Signed Thomas Brandon. Wit. oath (Union Co) Jul. 12, 1798 James White to Thos Brandon. Rec. Nov. 1, 1798

p. 200-202 Apr. 18, 1798 Richard Barry (Spartanburgh) to Adam Sloan (same); for 100£ sold 185 ac on W side of N fork Tyger R; border: Cannon; includes Adam Sloan's house where he lives; part of two tracts: (1) E end is part of grant Oct. 24, 1767 to William Nealy who sold to John Ward who sold to Richard Barry; and (2) W end is part of grant May 15, 1772 to Charles Moore who sold to Richard Barry. Witness Charles Moore and Thos Moore JP. Signed Richard Barry. Certified Apr. 18, 1798 Thos Moore. Rec. Nov. 2, 1798

p. 202-203 Aug. 14, 1797 James Taylor (Spartanburgh) to James Southerlin (same); for $77 sold 77 ac on Floyd's Cr; border: Enoch Floyd, Charles Whitton, and James Wofford; grant Jun. 5, 1786 Gov. William Moultrie to Thomas Sexton and by his will to Samuel Sexton who sold to James Taylor. Witness William Rhodes, Thos Westmorland, and Thos Moore JP. Signed James Taylor. Certified Aug. 14, 1797 by Thos Moore. Rec. Nov. 2, 1798. Dower renounced Rebekah Taylor to Wm Smith Oct. 11, 1797

p. 203-205 Feb. 18, 1793 Adam Potter (Union Co) to William Reed (Spartanburgh); for 27£ sterling sold 100 ac on Clark's Mill Cr; border: Norton. Witness John Lyle and Angelica Mitchell. Signed Adam Potter. Wit. oath Jul. 16, 1798 John Lyle to William Simpson. Rec. Nov. 3, 1798

p. 205-206 Mar. 2, 1798 David Allen (Spartanburgh) to Reynolds Allen (same); for 50£ sterling sold 159½ ac; half (sic) of 390 ac grant Oct. 6, 1788 Gov. Thomas Pinckney to David Allen sr; border: Gibson. Witness Young Allen and George Gibson. Signed David Allen's mark. Wit. oath Mar. 16, 1798 Young Allen to John Lipscomb. Rec. Nov. 3, 1798

p. 206-207 Jul. 14, 1798 James Sanders (Spartanburgh) to Lawrence Bankson (same); for 10£ sterling sold 13 ac on S side Pacolate R; border: Lawrence Bankson; part of grant Nov. 25, 1771 States Office to James Phillips then in North Carolina; "by mistake deed recorded on p. 192 and 193". Witness James Turner, William

Abbit jr, and Isaac Young. Signed James Sanders' mark. Wit. oath Jul. 17, 1798 Isaac Young to Wm McDowell

p. 207-209 May 6, 1794 Nehemiah Norton (Union Co) to William Reed (Spartanburgh); for 10£ sterling sold 110 ac on Mill Cr in Union and Spartanburgh Counties; border: James Gosset; grant to Adam Potter and sold to Nehemiah Norton. Witness John Hodge and George Kenit. Signed Nehemiah Norton. Wit. oath Jul. 14, 1798 George Kenit to William Simpson. Rec. Nov. 2, 1798

p. 209-210 May 8, 1798 John Meckelwrath (Spartanburgh) to Alexander Evins (same); for $260 sold 100 ac on N side of S fork Tyger R; grant "oct etc" Gov. William Tryon (NC) to Francis Dodds who sold in 1770 to Henry Leech who sold Nov. 25, 1773 to John Meckelwrath. Witness Samuel Neisbett, John Wilson, Thomas McKelwrath. Signed John Meckelwrath. Wit. oath Jul. 18, 1798 John Wilson to B. D. Shumate. Rec. Nov. 2, 1798

p. 210-211 Jul. 14, 1798 John Wright (Spartanburgh) to Henry Onail; for $240 sold a Negro girl Comfort about 9 years old. Witness Thos Moore JP and John Oniell. Signed John Wright. Rec. Nov. 2, 1798

p. 211-212 Apr. 13, 1796 Henry Chiles (Spartan Co) to William Cockrill (same); for a Spanish dollar sold 40 ac on S side Lawson's fork; border: Moultrie; part of 450 ac grant in 1785 Gov. Benjamin Guerard to John Bennett. Witness Henry Turner, Anderson Cockrill, and Darby Turner. Signed Henry Chiles' mark. Wit. oath May 29, 1796 Anderson Cockrill to Ism Foster. Rec. Nov. 2, 1798

p. 212-213 Feb. 17, 1798 Henry Pettit (Spartanburgh) to Christopher Scaggs (same); for 24£ sterling sold 150 ac; border: Graham's Br, Joshua Pettit, and Joshua Pettit's Spring Br; grant May 2, 1791 Gov. Charles Pinckney to John Gray. Witness Thomas Robison and William Morris. Signed Henry Pettit. Wit. oath Jul. 4, 1798 William Morris to John Lipscomb. Rec. Nov. 3, 1798

p. 213-214 Mar. 29, 1797 William Kelso and wife Joanah (Spartanburgh) to Thomas Jackson (same); for 50£ sterling sold 125 ac on small branch of Cuttabah R in Lancaster Co; part of grant Oct. 7, 1767 to Joseph Kelso sr and wife Joanah; survey by John Gaston. Witness James Hooper, Wm Dalton, and James Anderson. Signed William and Joanah Kelso. Wit. oath Dec. 25, 1797 Wm Dalton to James Hooper. Rec. Nov. 3, 1798

p. 214-217 Dec. 18, 1790 James Abernathy (Newberry Co) to John and Thomas Clark, both sons of Thomas Clark sr; for 80£ sterling sold 270 ac on branches of N fork of Tyger R; grant Oct. 3, 1785 Gov. William Moultrie to Daniel Monro who sold Mar. 16 & 17, 1788 for 70£ sterling to James Abernathy; land to be equally divided between John and Thomas Clark. Witness James Lindsey, George Abernathy, and Abraham Long. Signed James Abernathy and Jane's mark. Wit. oath Apr. 11, 1798 James Lindsey to James Jordan. Rec. Nov. 3, 1798

p. 217-219 Oct. 1, 1794 Benjamin Wofford (Spartanburgh) to William Wofford; for 150£ sterling sold 500 ac on both sides Enoree R in Spartanburgh and Laurens Counties; border: land where Benjamin Wofford lives; part of grant May 11, 1753 Gov. Matthew Rowan (NC) to Bartlett Brown sr, desc. Witness Thomas Wallace and Pattsy Wofford. Signed Benja Wofford. Wit. oath Oct. 31, 1795 Thomas Wallace to George Bruton

p. 219 Feb. 10, 1798 Robert Henry Waring (Columbia, SC) to Daniel

McClaren (Spartanburgh); for (money not given) sold 200 ac; border: S & E-where Daniel McClaren lives, and by "a large survey elapsed to me" surveyed originally by Daniel McClaren. Witness Martyn Allren(?) CRC and R. H. Homan. Signed R. H. Warren. Rec. Nov. 2, 1798

p. 219-221 Nov. 27, 1798 Zachariah Robinson (Spartanburgh) to John Rainwater (same); for $250 sold 200 ac on Lawson's fork Cr; border: Wells Griffith, Jordan Holcomb, Wofford, and John Gray. Witness I Harrison JP. Signed Zachariah Robinson. Certified Nov. 27, 1798 by I Harrison. Rec. Jan. 20, 1799. Dower renounced Elizabeth Robinson to Isham Harrison Dec. 14, 1798

p. 221-222 Sept. 3, 1798 James Wofford and wife Catherine (Spartanburgh) to Thomas Price (same); for 20£ sterling sold 100 ac on S side Tyger R. Witness Samuel Jones and David McCarly. Signed James and Catherine Wofford. Wit. oath Sept. 3, 1798 David McCarly to George Brewton. Rec. Oct. 30, 1798

p. 222-223 Mar. 14, 1796 David Jones, jr (Spartanburgh) to Thomas Gillinwaters (same); for 41£ sterling sold 225 ac on Gum Root Br of Gocher's Cr. Witness Terrell Wilkins and William Wright. Signed David Jones jr. Wit. oath Aug. 2, 1796 Terrell Wilkins to John Lipscomb. Rec. Oct. 30, 1796

p. 223-224 Mar. 23, 1794 Thomas Wadsworth esq (Lawrence Co) to John Wingo (Spartanburgh); for 50£ sold 445 ac, except about 20 ac claimed by Rowland Johnston, on waters of Tyger R; border: S-Henry Prince's old line, N-Rowland Johnston; grant to Mary Turpin and sold to Thomas Wadsworth and William Turpin. Witness D Goodlett, James Boyce, and James Young. Signed Thos Wadsworth for Wadsworth and Turpin. Wit. oath Apr. 2, 1794 D Goodlett to I Harrison. Wit. oath for editorial additions to deed Jan. 15, 1798 D Goodlett to Ism Foster. Rec. Oct. 30, 1798

p. 224-229 Jun. 14, 1787 Drew Smith (Ga) to Arthur Hutchins (Spartanburgh); for 50£ 5s sterling sold 275 ac on branch of Dutchman's Cr of Tyger R; part of 525 ac grant Apr. 3, 1786 Gov. William Moultrie to Drew Smith; border: all vacant. Witness John Richardson, John Camperson, and Thomas Bond. Signed Drew Smith. Wit. oath Feb. 17, 1790 John Camperson to Wm Smith. Rec. Oct. 30, 1798

p. 229-231 Aug. 14, 1787 Drew Smith (Ga) to Samuel Elder (Spartanburgh); for 50£ sterling sold 250 ac on branch of Dutchman's Cr of Tyger R; border: Arthur Hutchins; part of 525 ac grant Apr. 3, 1786 Gov. William Moultrie to Drew Smith and then having vacant border. Witness James Robinson, Elisha Smith, and William Jackson. Signed Drew Smith and Jane's mark. Wit. oath Aug. 28, 1790 James Robinson to Richd Harrison. Rec. Oct. 30, 1798

p. 231-233 Jun. 22, 1798 David Allen (Spartanburgh) to William Rickman (same); for 50£ sterling sold 159½ ac; W half of 319 ac grant Oct. 6, 1788 Gov. Thomas Pinckney to David Allen. Witness Vardry McBee and Abigail Allen. Signed David Allen's mark. Wit. oath Jun. 22, 1798 Vardry McBee to H McCray. Rec. Oct. 30, 1798

p. 233-234 Jan. 25, 1798 Alexander Evins jr (Spartanburgh) to Broadrick Mason (same); for 60£ sterling sold 150 ac on S side of S fork Tyger R; part of 300 ac grant Jan. 21, 1785 Gov. Benjamin Guerard to John Patton who sold to Alexr Evins, sr who sold to his son Alexr Evins jr. Witness David Bruton and Zephaniah Posey. Signed Alexr Evins. Wit. oath Jan. 21, 1798 Zephaniah Posey to George Bruton. Rec. Oct. 30, 1798

p. 234-236 Mar. 23, 1791 Alexander Evins sr (Spartanburgh) to Alexander Evins jr (same); for 50£ sterling sold 150 ac on S side of S fork of Tyger R; border: John Patton; part of 300 ac grant Jan. 21, 1785 Gov. Benjamin Guerard to John Patton who sold 150 ac to Alexander Evins sr. Witness Matthew Patton, John Callaham, and Andrew Thomson. Signed Alexr Evins. Wit. oath Aug. 18, 1798 Geor Brewton. Rec. Nov. 1, 1798

p. 236-237 Feb. 19, 1787 John Patton to Alexander Evins sr; for 30£ sold 150 ac on both sides of Forgeson's Cr of Tyger R of Santee R; border: N-John Patton, W-George Brewton, and E-David Pruett. Witness Alexr Evins, John Evins, and William Lamb. Signed John Patton. Wit. oath none. Rec. Nov. 1, 1798

p. 237-240 Feb. 19, 1787 John Patton (Tyger R, SC) to Alexander Evins sr (Forgason's Cr); for 30£ Va money sold 150 ac on S side of S fork Tygar R of Santee R; part of 300 ac grant Jan. 21, 1785 Gov. Benjamin Guerard to John Patton. Witness Alexr Evins, John Evins, and William Lamb. Signed John Patton. Wit. oath Apr. 5, 1798 Alexr Evins to George Brewton. Rec. Nov. 1, 1798

p. 240-242 Mar. 17, 1798 Andrew Millican (Elbert Co, Ga) to William Millican (Spartanburgh); for $214 sold 114 ac on S side of N fork Pacolate R; part of land where Andrew Millican lived; border: conditional line between Robert and William Millican; grant Apr. 3, 1786 Gov. William Moultrie to Andrew Millican. Witness Thomas Crumly, Robt Millican, and Jesse Dougles. Signed A Millican. Wit. oath Jul. 28, 1798 Thomas Crumly to James Hooper. Rec. Nov. 1, 1798

p. 242-243 (not given), 1797 Elizabeth Williams (Spartanburgh) to William Moore (same); for 30£ sold 150 ac; part of 315 ac grant Aug. 1, 1785 to William White. Witness Austan Clayton, Nancy Clayton, and Drury McDaniel. Signed Elizabeth Williams' mark. Wit. oath Sept. 10, 1798 Drury McDaniel to Ism Foster. Rec. Jan. 20, 1799

p. 243-244 Jul. 17, 1798 William Moore (Spartanburgh) to Barnett W Sweeney (same); for $300 sold 150 ac; border: Elizabeth Williams; part of 315 ac grant Aug. 1, 1785 to William White. Witness none. Signed William Moore's mark. Wit. oath Jul. 16, 1798 William Moore to Isham Foster. Rec. Jan. 20, 1798

p. 244-245 Dec. 27, 1797 John Jones (Greenville Co) to Reubin Gunn (Spartanburgh); for 64£ in trade sold 100 ac on Enoree R including land where Curtis Moore now lives; border: conditional corner between Thomas Keville and Stephen Cantrell and Little Rocky Cr; part of 500 ac grant to Thomas Scotts esq and sold by Richard Hampton to Stephen Cantrell who sold to John Jones; plat attached dated Feb. 27, 1775. Witness Curtis Moore, William Jones, and Saml Jones. Signed John Jones. Wit. oath Jun. 2, 1798 William Jones to Zadock Ford. Rec. Jan. 20, 1799

p. 245-247 Mar. 17, 1798 Andrew Millican (Elbert Co, Ga) to Robert Millican (Spartanburgh); for $214 sold 60 ac on S side of N fork Pacolate R; part of land where Andrew Millican use to live; border: conditional corner between Robert and William Millican; grant Apr. 3, 1786 Gov. William Moultrie to Andrew Millican. Witness Thomas Crumly, Wm Millican, and Jesse Douglas. Signed A Millican. Wit. oath Jul. 28, 1798 Thomas Crumly to James Hooper. Rec. Nov. 3, 1798

p. 247-248 Mar. 15, 1799 William Lancaster (Spartanburgh) to David Golightly (same); for 50£ sold 125 ac on E bank of Buffelow Cr where William Lancaster lives; border: S-John Smith,

N-William Roberts, E-old Mountain tract survey, and W-Autry. Witness Robert Wilson, and Mary Shands. Signed W Lancaster. Wit. oath Mar. 15, 1799 Mary Shands to W Lancaster. Rec. Apr. 15, 1799. Dower renounced Claremont Lancaster to I Harrison May 20, 1799

p. 248-250 Apr. 8, 1795 William Thomson (Spartanburgh) to John Cannon (same); for 10£ sterling sold 38 ac on waters of Pacolate R; border: Nathaniel Hammitt, Cannon, and Quarles; grant Nov. 10, 1786 Gov. William Moultrie to John Hammitt. Witness Wm Hammett, Ellis Cannon, and David Quarles. Signed William Thomson. Wit. oath Apr. 8, 1799 David Quarles to H McCray. Rec. Apr. 15, 1799

p. 250-251 Mar. 31, 1798 John Billups and wife Chloe (Spartanburgh) to John Fredrick Harmening (same); for 100£ sterling sold 100 ac on Enoree R and Cedar Shoal Cr; border: Whitaker and William Stone. Witness John Rainwater and David Jones. Signed John Billups and Chloe's mark. Wit. oath Apr. 6, 1799 John Rainwater to A Casey. Rec. Apr. 15, 1799

p. 251-252 Jul. 31, 1798 Drury Scruggs (Spartanburgh) to James Black (same); for 11£ 11s sterling sold 85 ac on fork of Horse Cr; border: conditional line between Drury Scruggs to Richard Haney; part of 655 ac grant Dec. 2, 1793 State's Office to Reubin Warren. Witness William Morrow and Nathan Byars. Signed Drury Scruggs. Wit. oath Aug. 18, 1798 William Morrow to Wm McDowell. Rec. Apr. 15, 1799

p. 252-253 Nov. 12, 1794 Robert Lee (Spartanburgh) to John Ashford Gore (same); for 50£ sterling sold 650 ac on S side of Pacolate R; border: Thomas Barton and Edward Stubblefield; part (sic) of 650 ac grant Jul. 7, 1788 Gov. Thomas Pinckney to Thomas Sabb. Witness John Lee, John Brown, and John Pearce. Signed Robert Lee. Wit. oath Jan. 15, 1799 John Lee to John Lipscomb. Rec. Apr. 15, 1799

p. 253-254 Jun. 13, 1798 Thomas Underwood and "legitimate" wife Elizabeth (Spartanburgh) to David McCarley (same); for $80 sold 100 ac; border: Zachariah McDaniel; NW part of grant Jan. 1, 1787 to Thomas Hightower. Witness Zachariah Grace and Peter Bragg. Signed Thos Underwood and Elizabeth's mark. Wit. oath Jun. 28, 1798 Zachariah Grace to Geor Brewton. Rec. Apr. 15, 1799

p. 254-255 Jun. 9, 1798 Francis Mason (Spartanburgh) to John Williams (same); for $100(?) sold 100 ac on waters of Fairforrest Cr; border: Widow Wilkins, Tinsley, Underwood, Ford, and Connel; where John Williams lives; part of grant to John Golightly. Witness I Harrison JP. Signed Francis Mason. Certified Jun. 9, 1798 by I Harrison. Rec. Apr. 15, 1798

p. 255-256 May 31, 1798 Hugh Donaldson (Union Co) to Samuel Archabald (Spartanburgh); for 5£ sterling sold 170 ac on SW side Lick Br of McElwain's Cr; part of grant to Hugh Donaldson. Witness R Donaldson, Mack Harris, and James Donaldson. Signed Henry Donaldson. Wit. oath Jan. 15, 1799 R Donaldson to Thos Moore. Rec. Apr. 15, 1799

p. 256-258 Jul. 7, 1791 Richard Sanders (Spartanburgh) to Thomas Goor (same); for 200£ sterling sold 690 ac on Buck Cr of Pacolate R; border: Luke Browning; part of two grants States Office to Richard Sanders: (1) 400 ac survey by James Seaborn(?) on Oct. 8, 1784 and (2) 440 ac survey May 22, 1788 by Vardry McBee; Richard Sanders sold 150 ac of above grants to Luke Browning. Witness John Gowen and Marah Sanders. Signed Richard Sanders' mark and Ann Sanders. Wit. oath Jan. 15, 1799 John Gowen to John Anderson. Rec.

Apr. 20, 1799

p. 258-260 Feb. 3, 1779 William Safford sr (Thickety, SC) to William Buis (same); for 1,000£ SC money sold 200 ac on both forks of Bullock's Cr of Thickety Cr; grant Apr. 27, 1767 Gov. William Tryon (NC) to William Twitty, then in Mecklinburgh Co, who sold to William Safford. Witness Robert Lee and John Busk. Signed Wm Safford. Wit. oath Feb. 3, 1779 Robert Lee to William Wofford. Rec. Apr. 20, 1799

p. 260-261 Nov. 13, 1798 William Baghton (Spartanburgh) to William Duncan (same); for love and affection give (until Dec. s5, 1799) all his Negroes: Rachal, Isham, Ned, Harrey, Lewis, and Isham (sic); whereever they may be found. Witness Thornton McDaniel, Drury McDaniel, and John Cooper. Signed William Baghton's mark. Wit. oath Nov. 23, 1798 Drury McDaniel to Thos Moore. Rec. Apr. 20, 1799

p. 261-262 Jan. 12, 1799 (Georgia) Matilda Buffington (Warren Co, Ga) to Joseph Hays (SC); for $100 sold (ac not given) on Foster's Cr; remainder of grant Oct. 15, 1784 to Matilda Buffington. Witness Thos Friend and Samuel Flowrney. Signed Matilda Buffington. Wit. oath Jan. 19, 1799 Thos Friend to W Lancaster. Rec. Apr. 20, 1799

p. 262-264 Oct. 9, 1798 John Earle jr (Greenville Co) to Hugh Henderson (Lawrence Co); for $400 sold 200 ac on Henry Wolf Cr; border: North Carolina line; grant Gov. William Moultrie to John Earle jr. Witness Thos Edwards and George Williams. Signed John Earle. Wit. oath Mar. 30, 1799 George Williams to James Hooper. Rec. Apr. 20, 1799

p. 264-265 Oct. 27, 1798 John Shands (Spartanburgh) to John Hewitt (same); for 70£ sterling sold 153 ac N of Tygar R; border: Joel Smith and Grant's Road; part of grant to John Bearden. Witness John Osheals, James Hewet, and Anthony Shands. Signed John Shands. Wit. oath Oct. 29, 1798 John Osheals to Wm Smith. Rec. Apr. 20, 1799. Dower renounced Margaret Shands to Wm Smith Oct. 29, 1798

p. 265-266 Oct. 5, 1798 Thomas Gillinwaters (Hawkins Co, Tencey) to James Harrison (Spartanburgh); for $60 sold 112½ ac; border: William Morris; part of 225 ac survey in 1784 for James Thomson. Witness Terrell Wilkins and William Morris. Signed Thomas Gillinwater and Molley's mark. Wit. oath Jan. 14, 1799 Terrell Wilkins to John Lipscomb. Rec. Apr. 20, 1799

p. 266-267 Aug. 1, 1798 Jonathan Gibbs (Pendleton Co) to William Bonner; for 10£ sold 137 ac on Surrat's Cr of Broad R; border: N-state line, S-survey for Markley, E-Clark, and W-Borings; grant Oct. 6, 1788 Gov. Thomas Pinckney to (not given). Witness Benjamin Clark and Thos P Earle. Signed Jonathan Gibbs. Wit. oath Oct. 20, 1798 Benjamin Clark to Geor Lamkin. Rec. Apr. 21, 1799

p. 267-269 Jul. 8, 1794 Samuel Elder and wife Patience (Spartanburgh) to Thomas Moore (same); for 12£ SC money sold 35 or 40 ac on "other" side of Vice's Spring Br and on branch of Ward's Cr of Tyger R; border: SE-Jason Moore, E-Thomas Moore, NE-Thomas Moore, and NE-Samuel Elder; grant Aug. 17, 1774 Lt. Gov. Bull to (not given). Witness Jason Moore, James Moore, and Hammonds Elder. Signed Samuel and Patience Elder's marks. Wit. oath Oct. 14, 1794 Hammonds Elder to Thomas Moore. Rec. Apr. 21, 1799

p. 269-270 Nov. 20, 1797 Elijah Brice (Spartanburgh) to Ephraim Jackson (same); for 20£ SC money sold 100 ac on S fork Thickety Cr at mouth of Rocky fork; border: E & W-William Brice,

W-Irby Dubury, E & N-David Hopkins, and vacant; half of 200 ac grant May 24, 1788 Gov. Thomas Pinckney to Elijah Brice. Witness Ezekiel Silleven and John Loving. Signed Elijah Brice. Wit. oath Oct. 8, 1798 Ezekiel Silleven to H McCray. Rec. Apr. 21, 1799

p. 270-271 Nov. 27, 1797 George McCarter, James McElwain, jr, and Jean Simpson (Pinckney Dist) to William Simpson (same); for a Spanish milled dollar sold (1) 200 ac grant Mar. 4, 1768 Gov. William Tryon (NC) to Arthur Simpson; and (2) 150 ac grant May 5(?), 1788 Gov. Thomas Pinckney to Arthur Simpson. Witness Matthew Patten and James Jordan. Signed Jean Simpson's mark, James McElwain and George McCarter. Certified Nov. 27, 1797 by H Means. Rec. Apr. 21, 1799

p. 271-272 Jan. 3, 1799 John McMordie (Franklin Co, Pa) to James Templeton and Samuel Miller (Spartanburgh); for $600 sold 300 ac on S side Lawson's fork of Pacolate R and both sides Reedy Br and both sides of Jones' Waggon Road; border: a "Spring at a Gladson" John Mallar's corner; grant in Dec. 1768 North Carolina to Robert McMordie, in Lincoln Co, NC, and sold May 11, 1797 by heirs of Robert McMordie to John McMordie. Witness James Jordan and David Jordan. Signed John McMordie. Certified Jan. 14, 1799 by James Jordan. Rec. Apr. 21, 1799

p. 272-273 Nov. 14, 1797 John W Wood (Greenville Co) to Reuben Lissenber; for 100£ sold 300 ac on both sides Lawson's fork including mouth of Shoal Cr; grant May 22, 1772 Gov. Josiah Martin (NC) to John Wood who sold to Wm Wood who sold to Mary Wood. Witness Wm Pearson and Betsy Camp. Signed John W Wood. Rec. Apr. 21, 1799

p. 273-274 Aug. 24, 1798 Matthias Turner (Spartanburgh) to John Sutherland (or Southerland) (same); for 50£ sterling sold 100 ac on Surratt's Cr; border: Thomas Harris. Witness Nathan Byars and Zachariah Blackwell. Signed Matthias Turner's mark. Wit. oath Jan. 10, 1799 Nathan Byars to Geor Lamkin. Rec. Apr. 21, 1799

p. 274-275 Jan. 4(?), 1799 David Henry and wife Hannah (Spartanburgh) to "son" Benjamin Hammett; power of attorney to recover all debts and legacies coming to them by heirship and to sell "the" land if he wants to. Witness Elijah Hammett, Elisha Lindsey, and Ann Henry. Signed David Henry's mark and Hanah Henry. Wit. oath Jan. 4, 1799 Elijah Hammett to I Harrison. Rec. Apr. 21, 1799

p. 275-276 Jan. 15, 1799 James Barnett and wife Sarah (Spartanburgh) to Richard Barnett (same); for 30£ sold (ac not given) on S side Fairforrest Cr; part of tract formerly belonging to John Thomas. Witness H McCray and Micajah Barnett. Signed Jas Barnett. Certified Jan. 15, 1799 by H McCray. Rec. Apr. 21, 1799

p. 276-278 Oct. 1, 1798 Jas Boyd (Spartanburgh) to Jesse Adams, sr (Wilks Co, NC); for 50£ sold 100 ac; border: Richland Cr; part of 200 ac grant Oct. 2, 1786 States Office to Richard Speeks(?). Witness Robert Kimble and Benjamin Bradshaw. Signed Jas Boyd's mark. Wit. oath Nov. 22, 1798 Benjamin Bradshaw to Wm McDowell. Rec. Apr. 22, 1799

p. 278-279 Dec. 13(?), 1797 James Martin (Lincoln Co, NC) to Nicholas Merryman (Montgomery Co, NC); for 40£ sterling sold 216 ac on Cherokee Cr; border: Col Isaac Mott. Witness Polley Alexander and Abednego Merryman. Signed James Martin. Wit. oath Nov. 22, 1798 Abednego Merryman to H McCray. Rec. Apr. 22, 1799

p. 279-280 Feb. 14, 1797 Maryan Crocker (Spartanburgh) to Solomon

Crocker (same); for 10£ sterling sold 60 ac on waters of Lawson's fork; border: John Bagwell, Tackwell, Arthur Crocker, and "her" third of grant to Arthur Crocker, desc. Witness Richesson Whitley and Sarah Whitley. Signed Maryan Crocker's mark. Certified Nov. 17, 1797 William Simpson. Rec. Apr. 22, 1799

p. 280-281 Nov. 20, 1798 Jesse Adams sr (Spartanburgh) to James Burnett (same); for 55£ sterling sold 100 ac; border: Richland Cr of Pacolate R; part of 200 ac grant to Richard Speeks; "grant" Oct. 2, 1786 to Jesse Adams sr. Witness Edmond Clement and Edward Clement. Signed Jesse Adams. Wit. oath Nov. 22, 1798 Edward Clement to Wm McDowell. Rec. Apr. 22, 1799

p. 281-282 Jul. 13, 1796 Samuel Swann (Rutherford Co, NC) to Joseph Borin (Spartanburgh); for 50£ NC money sold 200 ac on Sarratt's Cr; "called the Buck Ponds"; border: all vacant; grant Sept. 9, 1774 Gov. William Bull to (not given). Witness G Wm Winey (or Htiney), Wm Millican, and William Camp. Signed Saml Swann. Wit. oath Feb. 16, 1799 William Camp to H McCray. Rec. Apr. 21, 1799

p. 282-283 Jun. 6, 1798 Edward Herring (Spartanburgh) to Isham Bobbitt (same); for 20£ sold 100 ac on Lawson's fork Cr of Pacolate R; grant Mar. 6, 1786 to John Cannon. Witness Allin Bobbitt and William Jean Bobbitt. Signed Edward Herring. Wit. oath Sept. 29, 1798 William Jean Bobbitt to Geor Lamkin. Rec. Apr. 23, 1799

p. 283-284 Sept. 13, 1796 Samuel Ward and wife Susannah (Spartanburgh) to John Kelley (same); for 40£ sold 120 ac on N side of Fairforrest Cr; border: John James. Witness James Saunders, James Ward, Jacob Utley, and Wm Wells. Signed Samuel Ward and Susannah's mark. Wit. oath Mar. 4, 1797 Jacob Utley to I Harrison. Rec. Apr. 23, 1799

p. 284 Mar. 15, 1798 David Wells (Spartanburgh) to Henry Wells (same); for "(blank) hundred sixty" dollars sold a gray horse, a black horse, and a Negro man named Jack. Witness Wm Wells. Signed David Wells. Certified Dec. 1, 1798 by I Harrison. Rec. Dec. 28, 1798

p. 284-285 Sept. 25, 1797 David Wells (Spartanburgh) to Henry Wells (same); for $400 sold a bay stud horse, 10 cattle and all "Books of Acts", 3 feather beds and furniture, and 4 sheep. Witness I Harrison. Signed David Wells. Rec. Dec. 1, 1799 (sic)

p. 285 Oct. 26, 1796 William Wood (Lawrence Co) to Henry Walden (Spartanburgh); for $100 sold 150 ac; part of grant to Richard Harrison and William Wood. Witness James Ward and John Kelley. Signed William Wood's mark. Wit. oath Mar. 11, 1797 James Ward to I Harrison. Rec. Apr. 23, 1799

p. 285-287 Oct. 10, 1798 Duskin Grant (Spartanburgh) to Bazel Lee (same); for $15 sold 60 ac; border: Harrison; grant Aug. 4, 1794 to Duskin Grant. Witness I Harrison. Signed Diskin Grant. Certified Oct. 10, 1798 by I Harrison. Rec. Apr. 23, 1799

p. 287-288 Aug. 26, 1798 Nathl Stokes (Greenville Co) to Isham Foster (same); for 100£ sterling sold 289 ac on Hanson's Br of Tyger R; where Gideon Seay (or Leay) lived; except one ac where Meeting House stands; border: John Foster, William Benson desc, William Foster, Alexander Walker, and Robert Wood; of which 200 ac was surveyed Nov. 25, 1771 for Francis Prince and 89 ac was half of 178 ac grant to Thomas Wyatt who sold half to William Benson and the other half to Nathl Stokes. Witness Gabl Bumpass, Jesse Traylor, and Dabney Brooks. Signed Nathl Stokes. Wit. oath Oct.

9, 1798 Gabl Bumpass to Wm Smith. Rec. Apr. 23, 1799

p. 288-289 May 2, 1798 Joseph Fowler (Spartanburgh) to John Johnson (same); for 110£ sold 253 ac on Reedy fork Cr of S Tyger R; border: John Durham; includes "all but 2 (?) ac toward land where Joseph Fowler now lives". Witness Wm Gray, Randolph Johnson, and Newbell Johnson. Signed Joseph Fowler. Wit. oath Jun. 9, 1798 Randolph Johnson to Thos Moore. Rec. Jan. 20, 1799

p. 289-290 Mar. 5, 1798 James Hickey (Spartanburgh) to Thos Vaughan (same); for 25£ sold 100 ac on waters of Dutchman's Cr where James Hickey lives; border: Drewry Smith, N & W-Thos Vaughan, S & E-Lowns and Elijah Smith. Witness Judah Head, Christopher Orenduff (or Brenduff), and W Lancaster. Signed James Hickey. Certified Jul. 12, 1798 by I Harrison. Rec. Jan. 21, 1799. Dower renounced Elizabeth Hickey to I Harrison Jul. 12, 1798

p. 290-291 May 10, 1798 John McElrath (Spartanburgh) to Alexander Evins (same); for $400 sold 400 ac on N side of S fork Tyger R; border: Samuel Nesbett to McElrath; grant Mar. 6, 1786 Gov. William Moultrie to John McElrath. Witness Samuel Neisbett, Michaiel McElrath, and Thos McElrath. Signed John McElrath. Wit. oath Oct. 8, 1798 Samuel Neisbett to I Harrison. Rec. Jan. 21, 1799

p. 291-292 Jul. 20, 1798 John Wright (Spartanburgh) to Charles Moore jr (same); for $350 sold a Negro man named Cesar under 20 years old. Witness Richard Barry and Thomas Wright. Signed John Wright. Wit. oath Aug. 25, 1798 Richard Barry to Thos Moore. Rec. Jan. 21, 1799

p. 292-293 Dec. 29, 1797 William Moore (Spartanburgh) to James Hadden (same); for 30£ sterling sold 100 ac; where James Hadden lives; border: John McDole and John Durham. Witness David White and Thos Hadden. Signed William Moore. Wit. oath Oct. 9, 1798 David White to Thos Moore. Rec. Jan. 22, 1799

p. 293-294 Jan. 16, 1798 Samuel Hampton (Stokes Co, NC) to William Bostick (Spartan Co); power of attorney to get from Justice Reynolds (Spartan Co) the amount of a judgment due Samuel Hampton and James Matthews, for whom Samuel Hampton is attorney; William Bostick can appoint another attorney to help him. Witnes Dennis Sullivan and Richard Thomson. Signed Samuel Hampton. Wit. oath Jan. 17, 1798 Dennis Sullivan to I Harrison. Rec. Jan. 22, 1799

p. 294-295 Oct. 17, 1797 Micajah Cooper to Margaret Cooper (Spartanburgh) to William Cooper (same); for 25£ sterling sold 150 ac on both sides Beaverdam Cr; border: William Cooper and Lipscomb; part of grant to James Martin who sold to Micajah Cooper. Witness Dennis Sullivan and Benjamin Arindale. Signed Micajah and Margaret Cooper's marks. Wit. oath Nov. 28, 1797 Dennis Sullivan to H McCray. Rec. Jan. 22, 1799

p. 295 Nov. 18, 1798 William Parker to Geor Brewton JP (Spartanburgh); William Denys he gave a report that James Southerlin was "conserned" with James Southerlin's Negro woman (not named) in a carnal way, and William never saw James Southerlin in such an act or had grounds to think James Southerlin guilty. Witness Geor Brewton. Signed William Parker

p. 295-296 Jul. 28, 1798 John Woldrop (Spartanburgh) to John Durham (same); for 50£ sterling sold 183 ac on both sides Provis Cr of S Tyger R; border: Anderson, James Woldrop, Benjamin Woldrop, Still House Br, and Phillip Johnson; where John and Ezekel Woldrop live. Witness Randolph Johnson, Phillip Johnson, and George Durham. Signed John Woldrop's mark. Wit. oath Feb. 28, 1799 Randolph Johnson to Isham Foster. Rec. Apr. 22, 1799

p. 296-297 Jan. 25, 1798 George Pettis (York Co) to Thomas Wells (Spartanburgh); for 75£ sold 200 ac on branch of Lawson's fork of N side Pacolate R; about two miles above "the old Ironworks"; grant Dec. 16, 1769 North Carolina to (not given). Witness Jas Smith and Wm Wells. Signed George Pettis. Wit. oath Jul. 17, 1798 Jas Smith to Geor Lamkin. Rec. Apr. 23, 1799

p. 297-299 Apr. 8, 1795 William Hammett sr and wife Rosannah (Spartanburgh) to David Quarles (same); for 38£ 17s 9p sold 94 ac on Pacolate R; border: John Harris; grant Nov. 10, 1786 Gov. William Moultrie to William Hammett sr. Witness Ellis Cannon, John Cannon, and William Thomson. Signed William Hammett. Wit. oath Feb. 14, 1798 Ellis Cannon to George Lamkin

p. 299-300 Oct. 9, 1797 Nathaniel Hammett (Spartanburgh) to Moses Quarles (same); for 25£ sold 65 ac on waters of Pacolet R; border: John Harris and John (no last name); part of survey for John Hammett sr (Spartanburgh). Witness Dishen Grant, David Quarles, and Susannah Grant. Signed Nathaniel Hammett. Wit. oath Nov. 28, 1797 David Quarles to George Lamkin. Rec. Apr. 23, 1799

p. 300-301 Sept. 12, 1798 Joseph Champain (Spartanburgh) to William Hollaway (Person Co, NC); for 100£ SC money sold 290 ac on S side of main Broad R on Serat's Cr; border: grant South Carolina to Thomas Wilson; grant in 1787 South Carolina to Jesse Tate who sold to Joseph Champain. Witness David Tate and Chesley Bostick. Signed Joseph Champain's mark. Wit. oath Feb. 16, 1799 David Tate to H McCray. Rec. Apr. 24, 1799

p. 301-302 Feb. 9, 1799 Thomas Wood (Greenville Co) to Hugh Meanes; for $150 sold 350 ac on both sides Lawson's fork. Witness James Gage, Alexander McNaughton, and James McClure. Signed Thomas Woods. Wit. oath Feb. 9, 1799 James Gage to John Alexander. Rec. Apr. 24, 1799

p. 302-303 Nov. 6, 1793 David Millhanks (NC) to David Quarles (Spartan Co); for 30£ sold 100 ac on Pacolet R; border: Thomas Hughes, Pettrie's Cr, James Robinson, near "the three Springs", and Losson; part of survey for Reubin Lasson. Witness Dishen Grant, George Lamkin, and John Robinson. Signed David Millhanks. Wit. oath Nov. 20, 1797 Dishen Grant to George Lamkin. Rec. Apr. 24, 1799

p. 303-304 Feb. 2, 1799 Joseph Borin (Logan Co, Ky) to William Hollaway (Spartanburgh); for $100 sold 200 ac on Sarratt's Cr; called the buck pond; border: all vacant; grant Sept. 9, 1773(?) Gov. William Bull to (not given). Witness Joseph Camp, Bishai Camp, Benjamin Bonner, and H McCray. Signed Joseph Borin. Wit. oath Feb. 16, 1799 William Camp, on behalf of power of attorney from Joseph Borin, to H McCray. Rec. Apr. 24, 1799

p. 304-305 Apr. 8, 1795 William Thomson (Spartanburgh) to David Quarles (same); for 20£ sterling sold 50 ac on Pacolet R; grant Nov. 10, 1786 Gov. William Moultrie to John Hammett sr; border: Nathl Hammett and Wofford. Witness Ellis Cannon, Henry Cannon, and Elizabeth Cannon. Signed William Thomson. Wit. oath Feb. 14, 1798 Ellis Cannon to Geor Lamkin. Rec. Apr. 25, 1799

p. 305-306 Oct. 25, 1797 John Cannon (Spartanburgh) to David Quarles (same); for 5£ sterling sold 38 ac on waters of Pacolet R; border: Nathl Hammett; grant Nov. 10, 1786 Gov. William Moultrie to John Hammett sr. Witness Ellis Cannon, Elizabeth Cannon, and Disken Grant. Signed John Cannon. Witness oath Feb. 14, 1796 Disken Grant to George Lamkin. Rec. Apr. 25, 1799

p. 306-307 Mar. 15, 1798 Ignatious Griffin and wife Mavel (Spartanburgh) to Thomas Reid (same); for 30£ sterling sold 90 ac on head branches of Gocher's Cr. Witness George Gibson and Young Allen. Signed Ignatious and Mavel Griffin's marks. Wit. oath Mar. 16, 1798 Young Allen to John Lipscomb. Rec. Apr. 25, 1799

p. 307-308 Jan. 24, 1799 Charles Steedman and David Haig, executors of will of James Steedman desc, to Richard Lee; for a horse valued at 21£ sterling that Richard Lee paid James Steedman during his lifetime sold 150 ac on Pacolet R; plat attached shows border: Solomon Abbett, Pacolet R, heirs of James Steedman, Cherokee Cr, Charleston Road, and Edmund Bellinger; part of 426 ac grant Sept. 16, 1793 to James Steedman. Witness Thomas Tod and Peter Fisher. Signed Charles Steedman and David Haig. Wit. oath Apr. 8, 1799 Thomas Tod to John Lipscomb. Rec. Apr. 25, 1799

p. 308-309 Jan. 24, 1799 Charles Steedman and David Haig, executors of will of James Steedman desc, to John Lee, executor of will of Robert Lee desc; for surveying Robert Lee did for James Stedman sold 573 ac; plat attached shows border: waters of Island Cr, heirs of James Steedman, and branch of Suck Cr; part of 2,482 ac grant Oct. 12, 1786 to James Steedman. Witness Thomas Todd and Peter Fisher. Signed Charles Steedman and David Haig. Wit. oath Apr. 8, 1799 Thomas Todd to John Lipscomb. Rec. Apr. 25, 1799

p. 309-311 Feb. 9, 1790 William Duncan, heir of William Duncan desc (Spartanburgh) to Moses Boiter (same); for 100£ sterling sold 100 ac on N side Tyger R; border: William Hendrix; part of 300 ac grant May 7, 1763 to John Milhoun (or Millhouse) who sold to William Duncan desc. Witness John Duncan, James Wofford, and William Boiter. Signed William Duncan's mark. Wit. oath Mar. 25, 1799 John Duncan to Drury McDaniel. Rec. Apr. 25, 1799

p. 311 Nov. 11, 1797 John Timmons (Spartanburgh) to nephew, Levi Timmons, son of Catherine, and now living with John Timmons; for love and affection give 2 cows named Brindy and Whiteface; to Delilah Timmons, daughter of Moses, John gives his young gray horse. Witness Daniel Timmons, Eliza Stokes, and Peter Gray. Signed John Timmons' mark. Wit. oath Apr. 8, 1799 Peter Gray to W Lancaster. Rec. Apr. 25, 1799

p. 311-313 Aug. 4, 1788 Spencer Bobo sr and wife Judah (Spartanburgh) to Christopher Rhodes sr (same); for 10£ sterling sold 146 ac; border: Thomas Todd, John Hillin, John Couch, Christopher Rhodes sr, Tilmon Bobo, and John Rainwater; part of 446 ac grant in 1786 Gov. William Moultrie to Spencer Bobo sr on Seedarshoal Cr of Enoree R. Witness Spencer Bobo (signed) and Benjamin Hooker. Signed Spencer and Judah Bobo's marks. Wit. oath Apr. 10, 1790 Spencer Bobo (signed) to Thomas Farrow. Rec. Apr. 26, 1799

p. 313-315 Dec. 26, 1799 Margaret Underwood, widow of Thomas Underwood desc, Henry Cannon, William Underwood, Thomas Wells, Thomas Underwood, Prescilla Underwood, Enoch Jones Underwood, John Underwood, and William Robinson (all of Spartanburgh), legates of Thomas Underwood's estate, to Solomon Rainwater (same); bond of 100£; Condition: bond void if Solomon Rainwater gets title to 100 ac on S side Fairforrest Cr where Widow Underwood now lives; title to be made when youngest legate is of age. Witness John Williams and Frederick Williams. Signed Margaret Underwood's mark, Wm Underwood, and John Underwood. Mar. 14, 1799 Solomon Rainwater assigns his rights to Benjamin Rainwater "for value received". Witness John Williams and I Harrison. Signed Solomon Rainwater. Wit. oath (to both transactions) Mar. 14, 1799 John Williams to I Harrison. Rec. Apr. 26, 1799

p. 315-316 Dec. 14, 1798 James Anderson (Chester Co) to James Fanning

(Spartanburgh); power of attorney to sell 300 ac granted May 25, 1774 Gov. William Bull to William Anderson. Witness Dennis Sullivan and Thomas Brown. Signed James Anderson. Wit. oath (Union Co) Dec. 15, 1798 Dennis Sullivan to Wm McCullock. Rec. Apr. 26, 1799

p. 316 Nov. 23, 1792 Nathaniel Gentry (Spartanburgh) to Zabulon Bragg (same); bond of 200£ sterling; Condition: bond void if Nathaniel deeds Zabulon 100 ac on S fork Tyger R; border: a pine tree Nathaniel sawed in presence of Allen Gentry and David McCarley and by Miry Br; deed to be made in the next fifteen years. Witness Zachariah Grace and David McCarley. Signed Nathaniel Gentry's mark. Wit. oath (omitted) 20, 1799 Zachariah Grace to George Brewton. Rec. Apr. 26, 1799

p. 316-318 Oct. 24, 1796 Austin Clayton (Spartanburgh) to Joseph Pinson (same); for 40£ sterling sold 200 ac; border: E-David Drummon, W-Hugee, and by Elisha Hadden; where Joseph Pinson lives; part of grant Feb. 6, 1773 Gov. Charles G Montague to James Alexander who sold Dec. 17, 1795 to Austin Clayton. Witness William Harris, Elisha Hedden, and David Drummon. Signed--not signed. Wit. oath Feb. 9, 1799 Elisha Hedden to Drury McDaniel. Rec. Apr. 26, 1799

p. 318-320 Apr. 8, 1799 Michael Miller (Spartanburgh) to James Vernon (same); for $7 sold all moiety share of 400 ac sold Aug. 15, 1793 by John Nicholl to Michael Miller and James Vernon jointly; on both sides Middle fork Tygar R; except about 100 ac sold from W side to John Sloan; that leaves 300 ac bordering: S-Thomas Penney and including a shoals on the river where there is now a Grist Mill and Saw Mill; 400 ac was granted Apr. 29, 1768 to Elisha Thompson, in Mecklinburgh Co, NC, who sold to William Sharp who sold to Thomas Price who sold to John Nicholl. Witness Peter Gray and Alexr McCarter. Signed Michael Miller. Rec. Apr. 26, 1799

p. 320-322 Dec. 21, 1798 James Fannen (Spartanburgh) to William Brock (Union Co); for 30£ sold 300 ac on both sides Gochers Cr; border: Robert Wilkins; surveyed Jan. 3, 1773 and grant Mar. 11, 1773 Gov. William Bull to "William Anderson, James Anderson heir-at-law, James Fannen" impowered Dec. 14, 1798 by John Anderson. Witness H McCray, Elizabeth McCray, and Ann Trimmier. Signed James Fannin. Certified Dec. 25, 1798 by H McCray. Rec. Jun. 12, 1799

p. 322-323 Oct. 10, 1798 Diskin Grant (Spartanburgh) to William Robinson (same); for $30 sold 185 ac; border: Harrison; part of grant Aug. 4, 1794. Witness I Harrison. Signed Diskin Grant. Certified Oct. 10, 1798 by I Harrison. Rec. Jun. 12, 1799. Dower renounced Susannah Grant to I Harrison Oct. 18, 1798

p. 323-326 Aug. 25, 1798 Benjamin Wofford sr (Spartanburgh) and Daniel McKie (Newberry Co); an agreement: Benjamin Wofford is to deed Daniel McKie 700 ac on Enoree R; if resurvey shows more that 875 ac, then Daniel pays Benjamin "523£ 6 & 8p dollars at 4 & 8p" with $100 to be paid in a horse, half the balance paid in cash by Nov. 1, and balance by Apr. 1; titles to land to be made on first payment; if less than 700 ac, then Benjamin to make up the balance; Benjamin gives up a small survey of 17 ac (title warranted only from Benjamin) and all profits accruing from 17 ac to remain with Benjamin until dispute with John Brockman is settled; plat attached shows 823 ac; Apr. 29, 1799 Benjamin Wofford sr rented the land of Daniel McKie, where Benjamin Wofford lives, and promises to give Daniel McKie half of corn and fodder raised on the Bottom field adjoining John Wright's land; the field to be well tended. Witness Pillmon B Waters and Fanny Wofford. Signed Benj Wofford and Daniel McKie. Wit. oath (Newberry Co) Jun. 3, 1799 Pillmon B Waters to Fred Nance. Witness, to Apr. 29, 1799 part, James Simms and Robert Sims and Signed Benja Wofford. Wit. oath Jul. 10, 1799 Robert Sims to George

Brewton. Benjamin Wofford receives $1,100 from Daniel McKie for 799 ac (sic) as resurvey shows

p. 326-328 Apr. 16, 1796 Giles Connell sr (Spartanburgh) to Absalom Lancaster (same); for 5s sold 198 ac; border: Giles Connell, George Connell, Draton, and Absalom Lancaster; grant Jan. 6, 1794 Gov. William Moultrie to Giles Connell. Witness William Underwood and Wm T. Golightly. Signed Giles Connell. Wit. oath Jul. 17, 1799 Wm T Golightly to William Lancaster. Rec. Aug. 8, 1799

p. 328 Sept. 8, 1798 John Sloan (Spartanburgh) to Adam Sloan (same); for $200 sold a Negro girl Sarah about 10 years old. Witness Thos Moore JP. Signed John Sloan. Rec. Aug. 8, 1799

p. 328-330 Sept. 10, 1798 Samuel Elder (Spartanburgh) to Elijah Smith (same); for 50£ sterling sold 137 ac on waters of Dutchman's Cr of Tyger R; border: N-the mountain tract, E-Arthur Hutchins, S-Edward Lowndes, and W-Thomas Vaughan; plat attached; grant Apr. 3, 1786 Gov. William Moultrie to Drew Smith. Witness William Smith and Landford (or Sandford) Smith. Signed Samuel Elder. Wit. oath Feb. 18, 1799 William Smith to William Lancaster. Rec. Aug. 8, 1799

p. 330-331 May 23, 1799 Abraham Motte (Charleston, SC) to William Camp; for $500 sold 1,000 ac; plat attached shows border: Ashworth Cr, Cherokee Cr of Broad R, and Cherokee Meadows, and vacant land when granted; survey Jun. 12, 1772 certified by John Bremar, dept. surv. gen. and signed by Jas Cook, d. surv; warrant dated Mar. 15, 1772 and grant Oct. 20, 1772 Gov. Charles G Montague to Isaac Motte, esq in Craven Co. Witness Andw Boddan, S (or L) Quince, and Jacob Drayton. Signed Abraham and Mary S. W. Motte. Wit. oath Jun. 11, 1799 Andw Boddan to H McCray. Rec. Aug. 8, 1799. Dower renounced (Charleston, SC) Mary Sarah Washington Motte to Jacob Drayton May 23, 1799

p. 331-333 Oct. 19, 1798 William Stubs and wife Jeane (Spartanburgh) to Levy Penneton (same); for $190 sold 100 ac on both sides People's Cr; part of grant to William Taylor who sold to "said" John Stubs. Witness William Thompson, John Stubs, and Nichlas Stubs. Signed William Stubs' mark and Jean Stubs. Wit. oath Apr. 18, 1799 William Thompson to H McCray. Rec. Aug. 8, 1799

p. 333-334 Dec. 13, 1792 James Spears and wife Mary (Charleston, SC) to Thomas Miles (Spartanburgh); for 20£ sterling sold 100 ac on Rocky Cr and S side Tygar R; border: S-Thomas Miles, W-James Samples, N-John Hacker, and E-Thomas Tod; part of 350 ac grant Aug. 11, 1774 to Edmond Beardan; blank space in book for plat which was left out. Witness Joseph Gist, Alexander Gordan, and Saml Farrow. Signed James and Mary Spears. Rec. Aug. 8, 1799

p. 334-335 Apr. 7, 1798 John Stubs and wife Mary (Spartanburgh) to William Stubs (same); for 40£ SC money sold (ac not given) on both sides People's Cr; part of grant to William Taylor who sold to John Stubs. Witness Vardry McBee and Dennes Stubs. Signed John Stubs and Mary's mark. Wit. oath Apr. 12, 1798 Vardry Mc Bee to H McCray. Rec. Aug. 8, 1799

p. 335-336 Aug. 6, 1798 William Bratton, sheriff (Pinckney Dist) to Elizabeth Weir (Chester Co); for $25 sold 1,000 ac on Thickety Cr; where Vardry McBee use to live; border: William Lipscomb; land was sold due to Common Pleas Court cast Apr. term 1796 to collect debt Vardry McBee owes estate of Moses Chery, desc; suit by Samuel Talbert, Thomas Weir, and Elizabeth Weir, executors of estate; executors are awarded 88£ 2p 1 fathing sterling; sale of land was on Aug. 6, 1798; Vardry McBee listed as "late" of Spartanburgh. Witness John Lancaster and William Wells. Signed William Bratton. Wit. oath Apr. 26, 1799 John Lancaster to Absalom Lancaster. Rec. Aug. 8, 1799

p. 336 Jun. 17, 1799 Burgess West to Isham Harrison; Burgess West says his brand on cattle, hogs, and sheep is a smooth cross in each ear. Witness Isham Harrison. Signed Burgess West's mark. Rec. Aug. 8, 1799

p. 336-337 Nov. 7, 1787 William Taylor and wife Ann (Spartanburgh) to John Stubs (same); for 75£ SC money sold (ac not given) on both sides of People's Cr. Witness Vardry McBee, Micajah Taylor, and John Taylor. Signed William and Ann Taylor's marks. Wit. oath Apr. 12, 1798 Vardry McBee to H McCray. Rec. Aug. 8, 1799

p. 337-338 Nov. 12, 1798 John Lewis (Christian Co, Ky) to William Embry (Rutherford Co, NC); for $150 sold 200 ac on N Pacolet R; grant Jan. 1, 1785 Gov. Benjamin Guerard to (not given), Witness John McGough and Wm Bruce. Signed John Lewis. Wit. oath May 7, 1799 Wm Bruce to James Hooper. Rec. Aug. 8, 1799

p. 338-339 Dec. 16, 1798 William Tinsley (Clark Co, Ky) to George Roaland (Spartanburgh); for $155 sold 250 ac on waters of Pacolet R; except unknown amount taken by Jesse Remes from SE part of tract; border: Jesse Rhemy and Samuel Porter; grant Mar. 8, 1786 Gov. William Moultrie to Lewis Turner. Witness Robert Foster, William Foster, and Jno Morton. Signed William Tinsley. Wit. oath Jan. 7, 1799 William Foster to Isham Foster. Rec. Aug. 8, 1799

p. 339-340 Feb. 13, 1799 David Lewis (Spartanburgh) to Adam Kelby (same); for 120 (? £ or $) sold 400 ac; border: W-John West and Elizabeth Lewis, S & SE-James Barnett, and E-Smith. Witness Maxn Conner. Signed David Lewis. Wit. oath Jul. 17, 1799 David Lewis to Isham Foster. Rec. Aug. 8, 1799

p. 340-341 Jul. 17, 1799 John Rainwater (Spartanburgh) to William Casey (same); for 100£ sold (ac not given); border: Jno Stone; part of grant Aug. 31, 1774 to James Whittaker and sold Jan. 28, 1791 by heir-at-law, Willis Whittaker, to John Rainwater. Witness Randolph Casey and Wm Rainwater. Signed John Rainwater. Wit. oath Jul. 17, 1799 Randolph Casey to A Casey. Rec. Aug. 8, 1799

p. 341-342 Mar. 5, 1799 Jonathan Harris (Spartanburgh) to William Darwin (Union Co); for 27£ 3s SC money sold 340 ac on both sides of McBee's Cr; known as Tanner's place; 69 ac excluded for Horts and McBee's old survey; grant (date not given) Gov. William Moultrie to Josiah Tanner. Witness Joseph Adams and James Ballenger. Signed Jonathan Harris' mark. Wit. oath Jul. 15, 1799 Joseph Adams to H McCray. Rec. Aug. 8, 1799

p. 342-343 Jul. 2, 1799 William Gaston (Greenville Co) to James Cowen (Spartanburgh); for 100£ sold 100 ac; border: N-N fork Tyger R, S-John Calwell "granted to" Elizabeth Peden; grant May 4, 1775 to William Gaston. Witness James Alexander and Nathaniel Miller. Signed William Gaston. Wit. oath Jul. 16, 1799 Nathaniel Miller to George Brewton. Rec. Aug. 8, 1799

p. 343-344 Mar. 18, 1799 George McDowell (Spartanburgh) to William Ford (same); for $50 sold (ac not given) at head of Holly Spring Br where William Ford lives; border: John Beard, Richard Carver, Sarah McDowell, Isaac Bishop, and George Deavours. Witness Armstead Shumate, Edward Stewart, and Culvin Ford. Signed George McDowell's mark and Mary McDowell.Wit. oath Mar. 29, 1799 Armstead

Shumate to James Jordan. Rec. Aug. 8, 1799

p. 344-345 Mar. 8, 1796 John Williams (Spartanburgh) to William Parker (same); for 50£ SC money sold 100 ac on Cedar Shoal Cr of Enoree R; border: John Stone; SW part of grant to James Sample. Witness I Harrison. Signed John Williams. Certified Mar. 8, 1799 by I Harrison. Rec. Aug. 8, 1799. Dower renounced Nancy Williams to I Harrison Mar. 25, 1799

p. 345-346 Jan. 18, 1799 Samuel Elder (Spartanburgh) to Samuel Otts (same); for 20£ sold 70 ac on E side of Ward's Cr; part of 150 ac grant Aug. 11, 1774 to Thomas Moore who sold to Samuel Elder. Witness William Acree and William Otts. Signed Samuel Elder. Wit. oath May 1, 1799 William Acree to Thos Moore. Rec. Aug. 8, 1799

p. 346-347 Apr. 20, 1799 Thomas Wright (Spartanburgh) to Andrew Thomson (same); for 800 Spanish milled dollars sold two Negroes: a man Moses about 17 years old and another named Billey not described; both born in Va. Witness Thos Wright and Michael Barnett. Signed Thomas Wright. Wit. oath May 21, 1799 Michael Barnett to Drury McDaniel. Rec. Aug. 8, 1799

p. 347 Jan. 9, 1799 Margret McCarter (Spartanburgh) to Alexander McCarter; for 30£ SC money sold two Negro boys George and Willis, but Margret reserves right to use Negroes during her lifetime. Witness James Jordan. Signed Margret McCarter's mark. Rec. Aug. 8, 1799

p. 347-348 Jan. 9, 1799 Margret McCarter (Spartanburgh) to Mary McCarter and her daughter Mateldy, in joint contract; for 5£ sold a Negro girl Dollie to be Mary's during her lifetime and Mateldy's when Mary dies. Witness James Jordan. Signed Margret McCarter's mark. Rec. Aug. 8, 1799

p. 348-349 Apr. 27, 1799 Thomas Wright (Spartanburgh) to Michael Barnett (same); for 300 Spanish milled dollars sold a Negro girl Levinah about 13 years old born in Virginia. Witness Andrew Thomson and Absalom Blundell. Signed Thomas Wright. Wit. oath May 21, 1799 Andrew Thomson to Drury McDaniel. Rec. Aug. 8, 1799

p. 349-350 Mar. 25, 1799 Thomas Wright (Spartanburgh) to Thomas Wright jr; for 800 Spanish milled dollars sold two Negroes: George 21 years old and a woman Judith 14 years old both born in Virginia. Witness Andrew Thomson and Michael Barnett. Signed Thomas Wright. Wit. oath May 21, 1799 Andrew Thomson to Drury McDaniel. Rec. Aug. 8, 1799

p. 350 Mar. 20, 1799 Richard Lee (Spartanburgh) to James James Scott; for $50 sold 105 ac on Cherokee Cr; part of grant to James Stedman. Witness Isham Foster. Signed Richard Lee. Certified Mar. 20, 1799 by Isham Foster. Rec. Aug. 9, 1799

p. 350-351 Mar. 20, 1799 Aaron Templeman (Spartanburgh) to James James Scott; for $10 sold 20 ac on Cherokee Cr; part of grant to James Stedman. Witness none. Signed Aaron Templeman's mark. Certified Mar. 20, 1799 by Isham Foster. Rec. Aug. 9, 1799

p. 351-352 Jan. 18, 1792 Bayles Earle esq (Spartanburgh) to Andrew Colley (same); for 12£ sterling sold 45 ac where Bayles Earle lives; border: Maple Swamp; part of 400 ac grant on N fork Pacolet R. Witness Wm Benson and James Rogers. Signed Bayles Earle. Acknowledged in open court Jul. term 1799. Rec. Aug. 9, 1799

p. 352-353 Oct. 22, 1798 Stephen Wilson and wife Mary to William Wilson; for 10£ sterling sold 100 ac on S of Tyger R;

plat attached shows on Horshoe Br; grant Oct. 15, 1784 to Austin Clayton. Witness James Smith, Catrondy Wilson, and Lucy Potter Wilson. Signed Stephen Wilson and Mary's mark. Wit. oath Oct. 22, 1798 James Smith to Moses Casey. Rec. Aug. 9, 1799

p. 353-354 Oct. 20, 1798 Edward Rutledge (Charleston, SC) to Pennywell Wood (Spartanburgh); for 200£ sterling sold 1,340 ac on Rocky field Cr of Enoree R; border: Old Indian Line; half of 2,600 ac (sic) grant divided by writ of Petition between heirs of John Ruledge and heirs of Thos Woodward; half is near Tygar R and other half (N part) is the part now sold. Witness Jno Hunter. Signed Edward Rutledge. Wit. oath Apr. 2, 1799 Jno Hunter to Isham Foster. Rec. Aug. 15, 1799

p. 354 Jun. 29, 1799 Zachariah McDaniel, heir of William Golightly (Spartanburgh) to estate of William Golightly desc (same); for 75£ sold a Negro girl Rose. Witness Martha McDougal. Signed Z McDaniel. Wit. oath Jun. 29, 1799 Martha McDougal to William Lancaster. Rec. Aug. 15, 1799

p. 354-356 Jul. 11, 1786 Benjamin Wofford (Spartanburgh) to Christopher Rodes (same); for 50£ sterling sold 200 ac on Two Mile Cr of Enoree R; border: S-William Hendrix, N-Samuel Corkin and James Hendrix, and others vacant; grant Dec. 24, 1772 Gov. Charles G Montague to Joshua Morgan; "refer to p. 362 for lease" (sic p. 361 for lease for half a year). Witness Burwell Thompson, William Wofford, and James Wade. Signed Benjamin and Merry (or Meny) Wofford. Wit. oath Jan. 28, 1789 Benjamin Wofford to Thomas Farrow. Rec. Aug. 15, 1799

p. 356-357 Aug. 22, 1796 Thomas Collins renounces for "good consideration" claim to land where William Auston lives and other "things" William Auston gave Thomas Collins by deed of gift "evidenced" by John Collins and Thos T White and recorded in Spartanburgh Co Court. Witness John Collins. Signed Thos Collins and James Jordan JJC "certify the above". Rec. Aug. 15, 1799

p. 357 Aug. 23, 1799 Thomas Davidson (Spartanburgh) to Matthew Bates (or Betes) (same); for $123 sold 100 ac; border: E-George McCarten, W-John Foster, NW-David Brown's new survey, and S-Arthur Simpson. Witness George McCarter. Signed Thos Davidson. Certified Apr. 23, 1799 by William Simpson. Rec. Aug. 15, 1799

p. 357-359 Feb. 14, 1774 James Martin and wife Hannah (Fargason Cr, SC) to James Wofford (same); for 400£ SC money sold 200 ac; grant Dec. 23, 1771 Gov. Charles G Montague to James Marin (sic) on Forgason's Cr of Tygar R and then bordering vacant land. Witness William Sierria Norris, James Martin jr, and Edward Sparks. Signed James Martin and Hannah's mark. Wit. oath Feb. 11, 1775 Edward Sparks to William Wofford. Rec. Aug. 15, 1799

p. 359-361 Nov. 10, 1794 Frederick Ison (Union Co) to John Sloan jr (Spartanburgh); for 40£ sterling sold 200 ac on S side of N fork Tyger R and on Jammies Cr; grant May 5, 1769 to Daniel Brice (or Bruce) and sold by Thomas Davis to Frederick Ison. Witness Berryman Shumate and Jacob Eisen. Signed Frederick Eisen. Wit. oath Jun. 27, 1799 Benjamin D. Shumate (sic) to Thos Moore. Rec. Aug. 17, 1799

p. 361-362 Jul. 11, 1786 Benjamin Wofford to Christopher Rodes; for 50£ sterling leased for one year 200 ac on Two Mile Cr of Enoree R; border: S-William Hendrix, N-Samuel Corkin and James Hendrix, and others vacant; release for this deed on p. 354. Witness Burwell Thompson, William Wofford, and Jas Wade. Signed Benjamin and Mary Wofford

p. 362-363 Sept. 29, 1798 Josiah Culbertson and wife Martha (Greenville Co) to Daniel White (Spartanburgh); for $300 sold 80 ac on Fairforrest Cr; border: John Smith, James Lusk, Handcock Smith; grant Aug. 1, 1784. Witness Jno White and Jas Lusk. Signed Josiah Culbertson (Martha doesn't sign). Wit. oath Jul. 17, 1799 Jno White to William Simpson. Rec. Aug. 19, 1799

p. 363-364 Oct. 27, 1798 Leonard Adcock (Spartanburgh) to Cornelius Rogers (Lincoln Co, NC); for $130 sold 200 ac on Gland Cr of Pacolet R; border: William Murry; part of grant in 1792 States Office to Isham Saffald. Witness William Adcock and Jeremiah Wyatt. Signed Leonard Adcock. Wit. oath May 18, 1799 Jeremiah Wyatt to Geo Lamkin. Rec. Aug. 20, 1799

p. 364-365 Mar. 28, 1793 Philip Johnson (or Johnston) (Spartanburgh) to William Gray (same); for 80£ sterling sold 108 ac where William Gray lives; border: John Nesbit, James Jordan, Brushy fork Cr, Ben's Cr, John McDowel, and John Durham. Witness John Durham and John Whittemore. Signed Philip Johnson's mark. Wit. oath May 29, 1797 John Durham to Thos Moore. Rec. Aug. 20, 1799

p. 365-367 May 17, 1787 John Stone and wife Sarah (Spartanburgh) to William Casey (same); for 100£ 10s sterling sold 100 ac on branch of Cedar Shoal Cr of Enoree R; border: James Whitaker and Thomas Todd; part of 250 ac grant Oct. 20, 1772 Gov. Charles G Montague to John Stone then bordering vacant land. Witness George Grizsel and Peter Brooks. Signed John Stone and Sarah's mark. Wit. oath Jul. 15, 1799 George Grizsel to A Casey. Rec. Aug. 20, 1799

p. 367-368 Apr. 13, 1799 Elijah Hammet and William Hammet to William Smith; for $110 sold 100 ac on both sides Thomson's Br of Kelsoe's Cr of Fairforrest Cr; border: N-Micajah Barnett, S-James Smith, W-Charles James, E-Fleming Smith. Witness Joroyal Barnett and Elijah Barnett. Signed Elijah and Wm Hammett. Wit. oath Jul. 17, 1799 Elijah Barnett to H McCray. Rec. Aug. 26, 1799

p. 368-369 Feb. 28, 1799 Sampson Trammell (Spartanburgh) to Ephraim Elder (same); for 5£ sold 60 ac; border: Ephraim Elder, Henry Turner, and Markley. Witness James Sanders and William Sanders. Signed Sampson Trammell's mark. Wit. oath Jul. 17, 1799 James Sanders to Isham Foster. Rec. Aug. 26, 1799

p. 369-370 Apr. 14, 1796 James Reynolds (Spartanburgh) to Joshua Edwards (same); for 10£ SC money sold 40 ac on S side of Thompson's Beaverdam Cr; part of 340 ac on both sides Middle fork Tyger R grant Aug. 6, 1787 Gov. Thomas Pinckney to James Reynolds. Witness Nathaniel Walker, Daniel Evan, and John Vaughan. Signed James Reynolds. Wit. oath Jul. 17, 1799 John Vaughan to B. D. Shumate. Rec. Aug. 26, 1799

p. 370-371 Jul. 15, 1799 William Thomson (Union Co) to John Tollison (Spartanburgh); for $130 sold 100 ac on waters of Mills Cr of Fairforrest Cr; border: John Foster. Witness Andrew Thompson and Matthias Beates. Signed William Thomson and Agnes' mark. Wit. oath Jul. 17, 1799 Matthias Beates to William Simpson. Rec. Aug. 27, 1799

p. 371 Mar. 6, 1799 George Newman (Spartanburgh) to Martin Newman; for 40£ sold a Negro winch Jude about 22 years old; sale to occur when George and his wife die. Witness William Wilson and Stephen Wilson. Signed George Newman's mark. Wit. oath Mar. 6, 1799 William Wilson to Aaron Casey. Rec. Aug. 27, 1799

p. 371-372 Mar. 20, 1799 John McDowell (Charleston, SC) to Thomas Hadden (Spartanburgh); for 60£ sterling sold 331 ac on

Ben's Cr; where Thomas Hadden lives. Witness James Hadden and Jesse Page. Signed John McDowell. Wit. oath Jul. 29, 1799 James Hadden to Drury McDaniel. Rec. Aug. 28, 1799

p. 372-373 Jul. 15, 1799 William Thompson (Union Co) to Matthias Bates (Spartanburgh); for $100 sold 100 ac on waters of Mill Cr of Fairforrest Cr; part of grant to John Foster. Witness Andrew Thomson and John Tollison. Signed William Thomson and Agnes' mark. Wit. oath Jul. 17, 1799 John Tollison to William Simpson. Rec. Aug. 30, 1799

p. 373-374 Apr. 8, 1799 William Smith Melson (Spartanburgh) to Jesse Traylor; for $112 sold a brown bay mare--branded on right buttock "BB", sorrel horse--about 13½ hands tall, a bald face, and four white feet, 4 cows and calves, 2 feather beds and furniture, 6 sheep--5 ewes and a ram. Witness Gabriel Benson. Signed William Smith Melson's mark. Wit. oath Aug. 14, 1799 Gabriel Benson to Isham Foster. Rec. Aug. 30, 1799

p. 374-375 Dec. 4, 1798 Obadiah Trimmier (Spartanburgh) to Joseph Champain (same); for $650 sold 174 ac on N fork of Thickety Cr; part of 350 ac grant in Dec. 1774 Gov. William Bull to Vardry McBee. Witness John Trimmier, William Hollowdy, and John Champain sr. Signed Obadiah Trimmier. Wit. oath Jul. 16, 1799 John Trimmier to H McCray. Rec. Aug. 30, 1799

p. 375-376 Apr. 13, 1799 Elijah Hammett and William Hammett (Spartanburgh) to Micajah Barnett (same); for $110 sold 130 ac on both sides Thomson's Br of Kelsoe's Cr of Fairforrest Cr; border: N-Micajah Barnett, W-Charles Jame, and S-William Smith. Witness Elijah Barnett and Joroyal Barnett. Signed Elijah and William Hammett. Wit. oath Jul. 17, 1799 Elijah Barnett to H McCray. Rec. Aug. 30, 1799

p. 376-377 Dec. 23, 1794 Nathaniel Davis (Spartanburgh) to Thomas Sarratt (same); for 50£ sterling sold 100 ac on Cain Cr of Tyger R; border: N & E-Abraham Williams, N & W-Amanuel Mullinax, and other sides by remainder of grant; part of 260 ac grant Nov. 6, 1786 Gov. William Moultrie to Ambrose Barnett. Witness John Grist, Jesse Christain, and William Wilson. Signed Nathaniel Davis' mark. Wit. oath Apr. 28, 1798 John Grist to Saml Lancaster. Rec. Aug. 30, 1799

p. 377-378 Sept. 7, 1798 Eren Lands (or Haron Land) (SC) to Richard Cruse (Spartanburgh); for 50£ sterling sold (ac not given) on both sides Henry Br of Fairforrest Cr; border: William Golightly; land was sold by William Simpson to Eren Lands; 60 ac on upper corner excepted that was laid off for his brother Johep Lands. Witness Matthias Bates and Isaac Cruce. Signed Eren Lands' mark. Certified (not dated) by William Simpson. Rec. Sept. 2, 1799

p. 378-379 Mar. 16, 1799 Abraham Markley (Charleston, SC), merchant to Ephraim Elder (Spartanburgh); for 7£ SC money sold 65 ac; border: Ephraim Elder, Sampson Trammell, and James Sanders formerly Philips; part of 1,000 ac grant on N side of Pacolet R States Office to Abraham Markley. Witness John Brokshire and Benjamin Poole. Signed Abraham Markley by William Pool as lawful (atty?). Wit. oath Mar. 20, 1799 John Brokshire to Isham Foster. Rec. Sept. 2, 1799

p. 379 Apr. 12, 1799 James McCluer (Spartanburgh) to John Clerke (same); for 100£ sold 104 ac on waters of Alien Cr. Witness Abraham Andes. Signed James McCluer. Wit. oath Apr. 12, 1799 James McCluer to John Anderson. Rec. Sept. 2, 1799

p. 379-380 Jul. 11, 1798 Carie Traylor (Spartanburgh) to Thomas Moore (same); for $50 sold 176 ac on branches of Provey's Cr of Tyger R; border: SW & SE-Jas Jordan, NW-old line, NE & NW-Aaron Moore, and vacant; grant to Carrie Traylor (date not given). Witness John Ramsey and John Pace. Signed Carie Traylor's mark. Wit. oath Aug. 14, 1799 John Pace to Drury McDaniel. Rec. Sept. 2, 1799

p. 380-382 Feb. 28, 1788 John Hendrix (96 Dist) to Samuel Woodruff (same); for 70£ 10s sterling sold 180 ac on N side Enoree R and on waters of Two Mile Cr; border: James Megoun and others vacant. Witness Burrell Pace and William Bramlet. Signed John Hendrix's mark. Wit. oath Aug. 12, 1799 Burrell Pace to William Lancaster. Rec. Sept. 2, 1799

p. 382-384 Mar. 9, 1795 Matthew Guttry (Spartanburgh) to Frederick Guttry (same); for 5£ sterling sold 100 ac; upper part of 200 ac on both sides Thickety Cr grant in Apr. 1786 Gov. William Moultrie to Matthew Guttry. Witness John Trimmier, Betsy McCray, and Ann Trimmier. Signed Matthew Guttry. Wit. oath Mar. 9, 1795 John Trimmier to H McCray. Rec. Sept. 13, 1799

p. 384-385 Jun. 13, 1799 Peter Gray (Spartanburgh) to Gabriel Benson (same); for 5£ sold 7½ ac; border: Gabriel Benson and estate of William Benson desc. Witness John Walker and Eaton Walker. Signed Peter Gray. Wit. oath Sept. 9, 1799 Eaton Walker to Isham Foster. Rec. Sept. 13, 1799

p. 385-386 May 31, 1799 Isham Bobbett and wife Betty (Spartanburgh) to Charles Kimbol; for $160 sold 100 ac on both sides Lawson's fork below Golightly's Ironworks. Witness Geo Bishop and William Turner Thomason. Signed Isham Bobbett and Betty's mark. Wit. oath Nov. 2, 1799 William Turner Thomason to A Lancaster. Rec. Nov. 2, 1799

p. 386 Oct. 5, 1799 James Crook (Spartanburgh) to Daniel Allen (same); for 100£ sterling sold 130 ac on S side Tyger R and mouth of Mile Br; border: Meeks and (David?) Rogers. Witness John Durham, Elijah Tompson, and Drury McDaniel JP. Signed James Crook. Rec. Dec. 2, 1799

p. 386-387 Oct. 5, 1799 William Duncan (Spartanburgh) to Daniel Allen (same); for 100£ sterling sold 88 ac on S side Tyger R; border: James Crook, John Massey, and Daniel Allen. Witness John Durham, Elijah Thompson, and Drury McDaniel JP. Signed William Duncan's mark. Rec. Dec. 2, 1799

p. 387-389 Oct. 1, 1799 William Wells and wife Martha (Spartanburgh) to Richard Thompson (same); for $1,200 sold 270 ac on both sides Fairforrest Cr and branches thereof; where William Wells lives; W end of 440 ac grant Jan. 21, 1785 to William Wood. Witness Jas Smith, John Toney, and Nancy Arnet. Signed William Wells and Martha's mark. Wit. oath Oct. 9, 1799 John Toney to A Lancaster. Rec. Dec. 2, 1799. Dower renounced Martha Wells to Thos Moore Oct. 1, 1799

p. 389-390 May 18, 1798 Robin Head (Spartanburgh) to George Connell (same); for $100 sold 90 ac on Buffaloe Lick Cr on S side Fairforrest Cr; border: S-Elizabeth Autry and William Roberds, N-David Golightly, Henry Ayres, and David Cook, and by Head's Spring Br and Ephraim Elder; where Robin Head lives; sold by Mary Swadley to Robin Head. Witness Jacob Autry and W Lancaster. Signed Robin Head. Wit. oath Nov. 2, 1799 Jacob Autry to William Lancaster. Rec. Dec. 3, 1799. Dower renounced Patty Head to I Harrison Oct. 15, 1798

p. 390-392 Jun. 27, 1798 William Dickson (Duplin Co, NC) to son James Dickson (same); for love and affection and for James Dickson's promotion and advancement in life give 1,100 ac in three tracts: (1) 600 ac on S fork Pacolet R including Hutchens' cabin; grant Dec. 23, 1768 Gov. William Tryon (NC) to William Dickson; (2) 300 ac on both sides Pacolet R "about" Hutchens' Cabin and including the pretty meadow and on Meadow Br; grant Dec. 23, 1768 Gov. William Tryon (NC) to William Dickson; and (3) 200 ac on both sides S fork Pacolet R; joining (1) and (2); grant May 4, 1769 Gov. William Tryon to William Dickson. Witness Lewis Dickson, David Hooks, Joseph Dickson, and James Barfield. Signed Wm Dickson. Wit. oath Oct. 15, 1799 Joseph Dickson to Isham Foster. Rec. Dec. 3, 1799

p. 392-393 Oct. 4, 1799 James Crook (Spartanburgh) to Ephraim Drummon (same); for 100£ sterling sold 100 ac on S side Tyger R; border: Addams Meeks' old tract, Landres, Landres' Spring Br, Long Br, Ephraim Drummon, and Daniel Alling(?). Witness James Crook jr, Joseph Crook, and Drury McDaniel JP. Signed James Crook. Rec. Dec. 4, 1799

p. 393-394 Oct. 14, 1793 Robert McDowell and wife Mary (Spartanburgh) to John West (same); for 100£ sterling sold 150 ac on forks of Lawson's fork; border: George Bishop; half of grant Nov. 25, 1774 to Stephen Miller. Witness John Bennett, Daniel Cornwel, and George Bennett. Signed Robert McDowell and Mary's mark. Wit. oath Apr. 10, 1795 Robert McDowell to Isham Foster. Rec. Dec. 4, 1799

p. 394-395 Feb. 1, 1798 Joseph Hale Ramsey and William Clarkson, executors of will of Aaron Loocock esq desc (Charleston, SC) to John McClure; for (money not given) sold (ac not given) on branch of Roberts Cr of N Pacolet R; border: N-W Roberts, NW-Thomas Shirly, and others vacant; grant Sept. 26, 1772 to Thomas Shirley. Witness Thomas Cook, Saml McClure, and William McWilliams. Signed Will Clarkson and Jos H Ramsey. Wit. oath Dec. 7, 1799 Saml McClure to John Anderson. Rec. Dec. 16, 1799

p. 395-396 Nov. 26, 1799 John Roebuck and wife Sarah (Greenville Co) to Drury Parkham (Union Co); for $350 sold 179 ac on N side of Tyger R. Witness Benjamin Grist, William Evatt, and Joseph Cavin. Signed John Roebuck and Sarah's mark. Wit. oath Nov. 28, 1799 Benjamin Grist to Saml Lancaster. Rec. Dec. 27, 1799

p. 396-398 Feb. 15, 1788 James Henderson (Spartanburgh) to William Alexander (same); for 27£ sterling sold 120 ac on both sides Bridge Br of S Pacolet R; grant Nov. 6, 1786 to James Henderson. Witness Mathew Alexander and David Alexander. Signed James Henderson. Wit. oath Sept. 23, 1795 David Alexander to James Hooper. Rec. Dec. 27, 1799

p. 398-400 Mar. 30, 1793 Mathew Harper (Spartanburgh) to William Reeves sr (same); for 150£ sterling sold 200 ac on both sides S fork Pacolet R; where William Reeves lives; border: NW & SE-remainder of grant, SW-Samuel Fowler, and NE-William McClure; part of grant to Joseph White then in North Carolina and granted again Feb. 3, 1775 Gov. William Bull to Mathew Harper sr. Witness John Reeves and Jacob Fleming. Signed Mathew Harper. Wit. oath Sept. 22, 1795 John Reeves to James Hooper. Rec. Dec. 30, 1799

p. 400-401 Jul. 20, 1792 William Alexander (Spartanburgh) to James Smith (same); for 30£ sold 120 ac on both sides Bridge Br; grant to James Henderson. Witness Robert McDowell, Hugh Stevenson sr, and Alexander Stevenson. Signed James Alexander for William Alexander by virtue of power of attorney. Wit. oath Nov. 30, 1795

Robert McDowell to James Hooper. Rec. Dec. 30, 1799

p. 401-402 Aug. 19, 1795 William Reeves (Spartanburgh) to James Smith (same); for 100£ sterling sold 200 ac on both sides of S fork Pacolet R; border: NW & SE-remainder of grant, SW-Samuel Fowler, and NE-William McClure; where William Reeves lives; part of grant to Joseph White then in North Carolina and granted "again" Feb. 3, 1775 Gov. William Bull to Mathew Harper sr. Witness John McGuyne, Thomas Alexander, and James Reeves. Signed William Reeves' mark. Wit. oath Nov. 30, 1795 John McGuyne to James Hooper. Rec. Dec. 30, 1799

p. 402-403 Jun. 4, 1787 Gov. Thomas Pinckney to Granger Camp; a grant for 10£ 3s sterling paid to Treasury of South Carolina granted 435 ac on waters of Horse Cr of Broad R; border: N-North Carolina line, S-unknown, and others vacant; plat attached shows land on Camp fork of Horse Cr May 18, 1786 signed Vardry McBee, dept. surv. and F Bremar Surg. Gen. Witness none. Signed none. Rec. Dec. 30, 1799

p. 403-405 Oct. 6, 1788 Gov. Thomas Pinckney (Charleston, SC) to Cranshaw Camp; a grant for 19 (? £) sterling paid to Treasury of South Carolina granted 555 ac; border: S-David Hopkins, and others vacant; plat attached shows land on Camp fork of Suck Cr and on Ashworth Cr May 22, 1788 signed Vardry Mc Bee, dept. surv. and F Bremar, surv. gen. Witness none. Signed none. Rec. Dec. 30, 1799

p. 405-406 Jan. 18, 1800 James Jordan (Spartanburgh) to Job Hanson (Greenville Co); for 10£ sterling sold 35 ac on Middle fork of Tyger R below Indian boundary; border: John Smith; part of grant to John McRee who sold to James Jordan. Witness William Hanson and Edward Smith. Signed James Jordan. Wit. oath Jan. 18, 1800 William Hanson to Ism Foster. Rec. Mar. 11, 1800

p. 406-407 Aug. 17, 1799 Richard Lee (Spartanburgh) to John Brookshire; for 30£ SC money sold 200 ac; border: shoal on Cherokee Cr, Bazel Scot, and Little Cherokee Cr; part of grant to James Steadman. Witness Ephraim Elder and Henry Turner. Signed Richard Lee. Wit. oath Jan. 12, 1800 Henry Turner to Ism Foster. Rec. Mar. 11, 1800

p. 407-408 Jun. 25, 1799 Rolley Horton (Spartanburgh) to James Dewberry (same); for 35£ sterling sold 130 ac; border: Dunaway; part of grant Apr. 3, 1786 to John Hadin. Witness John Low and Jean Low. Signed Rolley Horton's mark. Wit. oath Jan. 9, 1800 John Low to Geor Lamkins. Rec. Mar. 12, 1800

p. 408-409 Sept. 10, 1799 Cornelius Rogers (Spartanburgh) to John Low (same); for $130 sold 200 ac on Island Cr of Pacolet R; border: William Morrow and Leonard Adcock; part of grant in 1792 to Isam Safford. Witness Jonathan Low and Leonard Low. Signed Cornelius Rogers' mark. Wit. oath Oct. 29, 1799 Leonard Low to Geor Lamkins. Rec. Mar. 12, 1799

p. 409-410 Nov. 26, 1799 William Camp (York Co) to Abishai Camp (same); for $500 sold 1,000 ac on Cherokee Cr; known as Cherokee Meadows; grant Oct. 20, 1772 Gov. Charles G Montague to Isaac Motte. Witness Joseph Camp and Vardry Camp. Signed William Camp. Wit. oath Jan. 4, 1800 Joseph Camp to H McCray. Rec. Mar. 12, 1800

p. 410-411 Nov. 25, 1789 Robert Cooper (Lawrence Co) to Henry Cole (Spartanburgh); for 30£ sterling sold 330 ac on N side Enoree R below Indian Boundary; border: Thomas Childres; grant Dec.

5, 1785 Gov. William Moultrie to Robert Cooper. Witness James Childres, Peter Childres, and William Taylor. Signed Robert and An Cooper. Wit. oath May 10, 1794 Peter Childres to Thomas Farrow. Rec. Mar. 13, 1800

p. 411-412 Sept. 21, 1795 John Neel (Union Co) to Andrew Hermon (same); for 30£ sterling sold 332 ac on Mary's Mill Cr of Fairforrest Cr of Tyger R; border: NW-Ash, NE-Burch and Crocker, S & SE-Deyoung, SW-Bird, NW, SW & SE-Brown. Witness John McDowel. Signed John Neel's mark. Wit. oath (not dated) John McDowel to William Simpson. Rec. Mar. 14, 1800

p. 412-413 Dec. 17, 1772 a plat for a grant; precept date: Dec. 1, 1772 John Bremar, dept. Surv. Gen. to James Wofford, dept. surv.; 350 ac on Dutchman's Cr of Tyger R in Craven Co granted to Thomas Betterton; border: all vacant; recorded in Surv. Gen. office (Columbia, SC) Sept. 27, 1794. Signed James Wofford and Peter Bremar, Surv. Gen.
Nov. 7, 1799 William Betterton, heir of Thos Betterton desc, assigns his rights to above land to Thomas Betterton. Witness Surrat Wilson and Thos Tod. Signed William Betterton. Wit. oath Dec. 14, 1799 Surrat Wilson to Wm Smith. Rec. Mar. 14, 1800

p. 413-414 Aug. 10, 1799 Richard Bullock, heir of Leonard Hendley Bullock desc (Greenville Co, NC) to Richard Willis (Spartanburgh); for $320 sold 400 ac on both sides S fork Tygar R; border: N-George Floyd and Jeremiah Gentry, S-James Crow and Robert Rogers, E-Jonathan Crow and Nicholas Gentry, and W-James Southerland. Witness Richard Barnet, Adam Chisholm and Thomas Littlejohn. Signed Richard Bullock by Adam Potter, attorney for Richard Bullock. Wit. oath Jan. 14, 1800 Richard Barnett to A Lancaster. Rec. Mar. 17, 1800

p. 414-415 Oct. 3, 1797 William Penington Spurgin and wife Margaret (Laurence Co) to Thomas Holden (same); for 110£ sterling sold 300 ac on N side Enoree R; border: vacant; surveyed "to" Robert Bailey and now in Thomas Holden's possession (sic); grant to William Lindsey who sold to Jacob Pennington who sold to John Spurgin and by right of heirship to his son William P Spurgin, John Spurgin died intestate. Witness Jno Penington, John Holden, and Jno Power. Signed Wm Penington Spurgin and Margaret's mark. Wit. oath Apr. 27, 1798 John Holden to Zadock Ford. Rec. Mar. 17, 1800

p. 415-416 Aug. 24, 1794 Thomas Holden (Laurence Co) to Isaac Hamby sr (same); for 200£ SC money sold 300 ac on N side of Enoree R; border: vacant; grant to Wm Lindsey who sold to Jacob Penington who sold to John Spurgin, who died intestate, and by heirship to his son William Spurgin who sold to Thomas Holden. Witness John Holden and Aaron Baughcom. Signed Thomas Holden. Wit. oath Sept. 20, 1799 John Holden to Thos Moore. Rec. Mar. 18, 1800. Dower renounced Margaret Holden to Thos Moore Sept. 20, 1799

p. 416-417 Nov. 23, 1799 John Kelley (Spartanburgh) to James Lecay (or Leeay) (same); for $300 sold 120 ac on N side Fairforrest Cr. Witness I Harrison JP and Thomas Tinsley. Signed John Kelley. Wit. oath (not dated) John Kelley to I Harrison. Rec. Mar. 18, 1800. Dower renounced Leah Kelley to I Harrison Dec. 13, 1799

p. 417-418 Nov. 1, 1799 John Cantwell (Spartanburgh) to James Bagwell (same); for $214 sold 104 ac on both sides of Beaverdam Cr of Fairforrest Cr; grant to Phannatta Wilkins. Witness I Harrison JP. Signed John Cantwell. Certified Nov. 1, 1799 by I Harrison. Rec. Mar. 19, 1800. Dower renounced Jane Cantwell to I Harrison Nov. 25, 1799

p. 418-419 Oct. 12, 1795 James Wyatt jr (Spartanburgh) to George Lamkin (same); for 6£ sold 60 ac; border: Dort; part of 304 ac on S side of Pacolet R grant Feb. 5, 1787 to James Wyatt. Witness Vincent Wyatt and Wm McAbee. Signed James Wyatt. Wit. oath Jan. 13, 1800 Wm McAbee to A Lancaster. Rec. Mar. 19, 1800

p. 419-420 Oct. 31, 1793 James Martin esq (York Co) to Gideon Brown (Spartanburgh); for 30£ SC money sold 162 ac on both sides Little Cherokee Cr. Witness Lewis Standley and James Balenger. Signed James Martin. Wit. oath May 6, 1794 Lewis Standley to Edwd Goode. Rec. Mar. 21, 1800

p. 420-421 Feb. 6, 1794 Gideon Brown (Spartanburgh) to Jesse Temples (same); for 80£ SC money sold 162 ac on both sides Little Cherokee Cr; part of survey by James Martin for Charles Miles. Witness Lewis Standley, James Balinger, and Dennis Bonner. Signed Gideon Brown's mark. Wit. oath May 6, 1794 Lewis Standley to Edwd Goode. Rec. Mar. 22, 1800

p. 421-422 Jan. 16, 1800 James Jordan esq (Spartanburgh) to Edward Balinger; for $50 sold 50 ac on N fork of Tyger R; border: SW-William Fields' old tract and Thomas Brooks; survey Nov. 21, 1785 for Wm Ford and grant May 17, 1787 Gov. Thomas Pinckney to Wm Ford. Witness James Balinger and David Jordan. Signed James Jordan. Wit. oath Mar. 26, 1800 James Balinger to Thomas Moore. Rec. Apr. 1, 1800

p. 422-423 Nov. 27, 1784 Thomas Miles and wife Sarah (Tyger R, 96 Dist) to Thomas Farrow (Enoree R, 96 Dist); for 100£ sterling sold 150 ac on N side Enoree R; border: W-Robert Hannah, E-Michael Waldrop, and vacant; grant Dec. 4, 1771 Gov. Charles G Montague to Philemon Waters; previously surveyed for Francis Hastting. Witness William Wood and John Beardin. Signed Thomas and Sarah Miles. Wit. oath (Laurence Co) Aug. 13, 1799 Thomas Miles to Starling Tucker. Rec. Apr. 1, 1800

p. 423-425 Sept. 5, 1796 William Bratton, sheriff (Pinckney Dist) to Thomas Farrow (Spartanburgh); for 10£ sold 250 ac on waters of Enoree R; George Souther desc (late of Spartanburgh) owned the land and was indebted to Ebenezer Moss; Pinckney Dist Common Pleas Court Apr. term 1796 awarded Ebenezer Moss 44£ 5s 5p sterling; sale Sept. 5, 1796 subject to mortgages and incumberances. Witness S Farrow and Thomas Wells. Signed W Bratton. Wit. oath Oct. 28, 1799 S Farrow to A Casey. Rec. Apr. 2, 1800

p. 425-426 Sept. 5, 1796 William Bratton, sheriff (Pinckney Dist) to Thomas Farrow (Spartanburgh); for 10£ sold 100 ac on Enoree R; George Souther desc (late of Spartanburgh) owned the land and was indebted to Ebenezer Moss; Pinckney Dist Common Pleas Court Apr. term 1796 awarded Ebenezer Moss 44£ 5s 5p sterling; sale Sept. 5, 1796 subject to mortgages and incumberances. Witness S Farrow and Thomas Wells. Signed W Bratton. Wit. oath Oct. 28, 1799 S Farrow to A Casey. Rec. Apr. 3, 1800

p. 426-427 Feb. 27, 1800 Charles Morgan (Spartanburgh) to James Hunter (same); for $200 sold 196 ac on both sides of branch of Beaverdam Cr of Thickety Cr; grant to Abram Bays. Witness Wm Thomson, Wm Bostick, and Wm Weber. Signed Charles Morgan's mark. Wit. oath Mar. 21, 1800 Wm Thomson to H McCray. Rec. Apr. 3, 1800

p. 427 May 13, 1790 George Grace (Greenville Co) to John Hammon (Spartanburgh); for $300 sold 150 ac on both sides Forgeson's Cr of Tyger R; border: N-Thomas Prince and Matthew Patton, W-Broadrick Mason and George Bruton, E-Milley Gravia (?), and S-unknown; part of grant May 2, 1770 States Office to David Prewett. Witness

David Bruton and John Bruton. Signed George Grace. Wit. oath Mar. 22, 1800 John Bruton to George Brewton. Rec. Apr. 3, 1800

p. 427-429 Jan. 14, 1800 James Dewberry (Spartanburgh) to Thomas Betterton (same); for $300 sold 265 ac; border: Dunaway; part of grant Apr. 3, 1786 to John Headin. Witness Tho Moore and Martha Moore. Signed James Dewberry and Mary's mark. Wit. oath Jan. 14, 1800 Martha Moore to Tho Moore. Rec. Apr. 4, 1800. Dower renounced Mary Dewberry to Thomas Moore Jan. 21, 1800

p. 429 Feb. 10, 1800 Joseph Austell (Union Co) to Wm Austell (Spartanburgh); for $30 sold 30 ac; border: W-Milley Austell, N-Wm Lipscomb, E-Wm Wilkins; grant in 1792 to Wm Wilkins. Witness Amos Austell and Robert Stacey. Signed Joseph Austell. Wit. oath Mar. 21, 1800 Amos Austell to John Lipscomb. Rec. Apr. 4, 1800

p. 429-430 Jan. 1, 1800 Drury McDaniel (SC) to Luke Thornton (SC); for $160 sold 100 ac on waters of Furgeson's Cr; border: Thomas Williamson, Griffey, David McKurly, and Measerline. Witness Zachariah McDaniel and Thornton McDaniel. Signed Drury McDaniel. Wit. oath Jan. 13, 1800 Zachariah McDaniel to Drury McDaniel. Rec. Apr. 7, 1800

p. 430-432 Jul. 13, 1798 John Hamby (Spartanburgh) to Joseph Woodruff (same); for 47£ sterling sold 82 ac in two tracts: (1) 20 ac on Lick Cr;part of grant Aug. 19, 1774 Lt. Gov. William Bull to William Hamby; and (2) 62 ac; border: Amos Pilgrim and Kirge's old line; part of grant Mar. 4, 1793 Gov. William Moultrie to Jno Hamby. Witness Amos Pilgrim and Thomas Woodruff. Signed John Hamby's mark. Wit. oath Sept. 14, 1798 Amos Pilgrim to Wm Smith. Rec. Apr. 7, 1800. Dower renounced Braddy (or Bradbrock) Hamby to Wm Smith Sept. 13, 1798

p. 432 Feb. 22, 1800 William Moore and wife Elizabeth (Spartanburgh) to William Hendrix (same); for $50 sold 100 ac on branch of Lick Cr of Enoree R; W half of 200 ac grant to William Moore. Witness Peter Bragg, Henry Cannon, and Jason Moore. Signed William Moore and Betty's mark. Wit. oath Mar. 22, 1800 Peter Bragg to G Brewton. Rec. Apr. 7, 1800

p. 432-433 Mar. 4, 1798 John Couch (Greenville Co) to Drewry Couch (same); for 50£ sold 108 ac on N side Enoree R. Witness Aaron Casey and Moses Couch. Signed John Couch and Ann's mark. Wit. oath Dec. 26, 1799 Moses Couch to A Casey. Rec. Apr. 8, 1800

p. 433-434 Jan. 6, 1797 Landon Farrow (Spartanburgh) to John Couch (Greenville Co); for 10£ sold (ac not given) on Old Fied Br; "all of land NW of conditional line between Landon Farrow and John Couch"; border: Brown. Witness John Farrow and Aaron Casey. Signed Landon Farrow. Wit. oath Mar. 22, 1800 Aaron Casey to G Brewton. Rec. Apr. 8, 1800

p. 434-435 Jan. 10, 1800 John Robuck and wife Sarah (Greenville Co) to Daniel Sims (Spartanburgh); for 23£ 6s 8p sterling sold 70 ac on N side Tyger R; border: William Evatt, Richard Blackstock, Richard Bearden, and Drury Pariam; part of grant to Thos Fletcher. Witness Lewis Evatt and Willie Brown. Signed John Robuck and Sarah's mark. Wit. oath (omitted) 21, 1800 Lewis Evatt to A Casey. Rec. Apr. 8, 1800

p. 435 Mar. 8, 1800 Young Allen (Spartanburgh) to William Allen (same); for 100£ sterling sold 300 ac on N side of Goacher Cr; William is son of David Allen jr. Witness Willis Allen and Drury Allen. Signed Young Allen and Elizabeth's mark. Wit. oath Mar. 17, 1800 Willis Allen to John Lipscomb. Rec. Apr. 9, 1800

p. 435-436 Jul. 14, 1797 Baylis Earle (Spartanburgh) to John Otts (Greenville Co); for 50£ sold 245 ac on both sides Colley's Cr of N Pacolet R; lower end of 458 ac grant Mar. 5, 1792 to Jervis Cornwell who sold to Baylis Earle. Witness Lewis Spencer, Robt Goodgion, and Mirram Gowen. Signed Baylis Earle. Wit. oath Feb. 20, 1800 Robt Goodgion to James Jordan. Rec. Apr. 9, 1800

p. 436-437 Aug. 22, 1799 Hance Harper (Spartanburgh) to George Hughey (Union Co); for $25 sold (1) 100 ac on Lawson's fork; border: Hance Harper jr, son of Hance Harper; sold by John Kerconnel to Hance Harper sr; and (2) 108 ac E of Lawson's fork; grant Mar. 3, 1794 Gov. William Moultrie to Hance Harper sr. Witness Ephraim Lewis, John Reenum, and James Johnson. Signed Hance Harper. Wit. oath Mar. 26, 1800 Ephraim Lewis to Geor Lamkin. Rec. Apr. 9, 1800

p. 437-438 Nov. 8, 179(2 or 8) John Cannon and wife Rebecahah (Spartanburgh) to Benjamin Couch (same); for 20£ sold 50 ac on N side Enoree R; border: Edward Lyaeh's Spring Br; part of 300 ac grant in 1773 Gov. William Bull to John Couch who sold to Addam Garman who sold to John Cannon. Witness Henry Merideth and Addam Garmon. Signed John Cannon and Rebecahah's mark. Wit. oath Jul. 27, 1799 Henry Merideth to A Casey. Rec. Apr. 10, 1800

p. 438-439 Jan. 21, 1800 William Wells (Spartanburgh) to Gannaway Johnson (same); for $86 sold 128 ac; where Gannaway Johnson lives; border: N-David Golightly, S-the mountain lands, E-part of same grant, and N-John Smith; part of grant to Col Henry White desc and by heirship to son James White and at the instance of Maj John Ford's execution sold by Edward Lacy, sheriff of Pinckney Dist. Witness William Roberds and Curtis Gray. Signed Wm Wells. Wit. oath Mar. 24, 1800 William Roberds to I Harrison. Rec. Apr. 11, 1800. Dower renounced Martha Wells to I Harrison Mar. 24, 1800

p. 439-441 Jan. 20, (not given) William Wells (Spartanburgh) to Rhodham Daffem (same); for 10£ sold 112 ac on waters of Fairforrest Cr; border: land sold by William Wells to Gannaway Johnson; part of grant to Col Henry White desc and due to suit of John Ford esq, desc, vs. executors of James White, son of Henry White, sold Jul. 17, 1794 by Edward Lacy, sheriff of Pinckney Dist, to William Wells. Witness William Roberds and Curtis Gray. Signed Wm Wells. Wit. oath Mar. 24, 1800 William Roberds to I Harrison. Rec. Apr. 12, 1800. Dower renounced Martha Wells to I Harrison Mar. 24, 1800

p. 441 Sept. 28, 1799 William Fields (Spartanburgh) to Edward Ballenger (same); for $400 sold 200 ac on N Tyger R; border: John David and William Ford. Witness John James and Atd Shumate. Signed William Fields' mark. Certified Sept. 28, 1799 by Ism Foster. Rec. Apr. 14, 1800. Dower renounced Any Fields to James Jordan Dec. 26, 1799

p. 441-442 Sept. 13, 1799 James McBee (Franklin Co, Ga) to Andrew Colley (Spartanburgh); for $300 sold 400 ac on McBee's Cr (formerly Plumtree Br) on N Pacolate R and "on S side of S Pacolate R"; border: Saml Young; grant May 24, 1770 Gov. William Tryon (NC) to James McBee. Witness William Cawley and Isham McBee. Signed James McBee. Wit. oath Sept. 30, 1799 William Cawley to John Anderson. Rec. Apr. 14, 1800

p. 442-443 Sept. 2, 1799 Warrington Spiller and Travis Morss (Laurence Co) to Sampson Bobo jr (Spartanburgh); a bond of $500; Condition: Warrington and Travis to deed 86 ac granted Jun. 5, 1786 to Warrington Spiller desc and left to his children; deed to be made in the next 7 years. Witness James Morss and Nathaniel Hamby. Signed Worington Spillor and Travis Morss. Wit. oath Oct.

27, 1799 James Morss to A Casey. Rec. Apr. 15, 1800

p. 443-444 Sept. 4, 1799 Benjamin Wofford to Daniel McKee; for $943 "last payment in full" sold 800 ac on Enoree R; where Daniel McKee lives; except a small part of N side belonging to an "old" grant to Joseph Woodruff; see sale Apr. 25, 1798; Note--the above receipt of $943 not against "book account" Daniel McKee has against Benjamin Wofford but to be "accounted for" by Benjamin Wofford. Witness John Spirgin and Wm Glen. Signed Benj Wofford. Wit. oath Mar. 3, 1800 John Spirgin to G Brewton. Rec. Apr. 16, 1800

p. 444 (not dated) William Wofford (Spartanburgh) relinquishes rights to land his father Benjamin Wofford sold Daniel McKee agreeable to title Aug. 25, 1798; where Daniel McKee lives; and William Wofford rents the land where William Wofford lives to Daniel McKee for three months for a pepper corn paid by Daniel McKee "today" as long as Daniel McKee doesn't injure William Wofford's crop; Daniel McKee can seed the land; Note--William Wofford certifies he will sign "article" at any time called. Witness John Spurgin and Wm Glenn. Signed William Wofford. Wit. oath Mar. 3, 1800 John Spurgin to G Brewton. Rec. Apr. 16, 1800

p. 444-445 Oct. 14, 1799 Hance Harper jr (Spartanburgh) to Jesse Hammett (same); for $200 sold 100 ac on Lawson's fork of Pacolate R; part of 200 ac sold by John Kerconel to Hance Harper sr who sold to Hance Harper jr. Witness William Cockrill jr, Anderson Cockrell, and William Cockrell. Signed Hance Harper jr. Wit. oath Mar. 25, 1800 William Cockrell to John Anderson. Rec. Apr. 16, 1800

p. 445-446 Aug. 8, 1798 a letter from Thomas Wadsworth to Capt. Daniel McClary; Thomas Wadsworth says he had titles to land he sold to Thomas Wilson "wrote here and took to Charleston" for William Turpin to sign; Thomas also signed the titles; William Turpin, late partner of Thomas, was to return same to Spartanburgh Co clerk and Thomas doesn't know why he didn't. Signed Thomas Wadsworth.Dec. 10, 1799 (Charleston, SC) Books of Wadsworth and Turpin show 200 ac on both sides Sarat's Cr of Broad R was sold and Thomas received full payment on Sept. 26, 1789; border: all vacant; grant Feb. 5, 1787 Gov. William Moultrie to Augustus Mirrick who sold to Wadsworth and Turpin, see Charleston deeds; survey Nov. 24, 1784 by George Salmon for Thos Wilson. Witness Claton Smith and James Boyle. Signed Wm Turpin, surviving partner of Wadsworth and Turpin. Wit. oath Mar. 24, 1800 Claton Smith to I Harrison. Rec. Apr. 18, 1800

p. 446-448 Mar. 4, 1799 Capt. Robert White (Spartanburgh) to John Foster (same); for $150 sold 100 ac on Kelso's Cr; border: Sterling and Ryly;part of 250 ac grant Dec. 23, 1768 Gov. William Tryon (NC) to John Gibbs who sold Dec. 16, 1776(or 8) to Moses White and at Moses White's death to son Robert White; border: Moses Foster; South Carolina Memorial Feb. 12, 1774; 100 ac of grant was sold to Robert Sterling and 50 ac more was sold to John Riley. Witness Jas Smith, Moses Foster, and Wm P Smith. Signed Robert White. Certified Mar. 12, 1799 by I Harrison. Rec. Apr. 18, 1800. Dower renounced Isable White to I Harrison Mar. 12, 1799

p. 448-449 Feb. 21, 1796 Mark Swadley and wife Elizabeth (Spartanburgh) to William Roberds (same); for 3£ sterling sold 10 ac on Buffalo Lick Cr on S side of Fairforrest Cr; plat attached shows border: Roberds and Sprinkle; part of land sold by Ephraim Elder to Mark Swadley. Witness D Golightly and Alexander Autry. Signed Mark Swadley and Elizabeth's mark. Wit. oath Oct. 10, 1796 D Golightly to I Harrison. Rec. Apr. 19, 1800

p. 449-450 Nov. 2, 1799 John Peden (Greenville Co) to Alexander Sweeney (Spartanburgh); for $500 sold 100 ac on Mill Cr of Tyger R; where Alexander Sweeney lives; grant in 1775 Gov. Bull to John Peden. Witness John W Wood and Eaton Walker. Signed John Peden. Wit. oath Nov. 8, 1799 Eaton Walker to Ism Foster. Rec. Apr. 21, 1800

p. 450 Aug. 17, 1799 Andrew Hopkins (Spartanburgh) to Ezekial Stanley (Pendleton Co); for $320 sold 143 ac on "main" Cherokee Cr of Broad R. Witness George Walker and Richard Robertson. Signed Andrew Hopkins. Wit. oath Nov. 28, 1799 Richard Robertson to H McCray. Rec. Apr. 23, 1800

p. 450-451 Mar. 27, 1800 John Utley (Spartanburgh) to John Robnett (same); for $300 sold 160 ac on waters of Pacolet R. Witness Ism Foster. Signed John Utley. Wit. oath Mar. 27, 1800 John Utley to Ism Foster. Rec. Apr. 24, 1800

p. 451-452 Sept. 8, 1794 Benjamin Wofford and wife Mary (Spartanburgh) to Joseph Wofford (same); for 100£ sterling sold 200 ac on S side Tyger R at mouth of Jamey's Cr; border: N-Tyger R, NW-William Young; survey Jun. 7, 1768 when it bordered vacant land. Witness William Wofford and Jeremiah Wofford. Signed Benj Wofford and Mary Wofford. Wit. oath Jan. 15, 1795 Jeremiah Wofford to William Lancaster. Rec. Apr. 25, 1800

p. 452-453 Oct. 19, 1799 John Gossett (Spartanburgh) to John Tollison (same); for $260 sold 255 ac on waters of Pacolet R and Fairforrest Cr; border: Bird, road to Grondal Shoal, Thomas Minry, John Stone, George Kinnett, and George McCarter; part of grant to Seth Luis. Witness George McCarter and Nicholas Murry (or Murray). Signed John Gossett and Emna's mark. Wit. oath Oct. 19, 1799 Nicholas Murry to William Simpson. Rec. Apr. 25, 1800

p. 453-454 Oct. 19, 1799 John Lemaster (Spartanburgh) to John Tollison (same); for $30 sold 5 ac on waters of Mill Cr of Fairforrest Cr; border: Pickney Road at John Tollison's house, Pattle or Peittle, and Inglishmaor's line; part of grant to John Meuete who sold to John Lemaster. Witness Thomas Deon (or Deen) and George McCarter. Signed John Lemaster. Wit. oath Oct. 19, 1799 Thomas Deon to William Simpson. Rec. Apr. 26, 1800

p. 454-455 Dec. 21, 1799 Young Griffin (Greenville Co) to James Loftis (Spartanburgh); for $150 sold 286 ac. Witness John Loftis and James Powell. Signed Young Griffin. Wit. oath (Greenville Co) Dec. 26, 1799 John Loftis to Reuben Barrett. Rec. Apr. 26, 1800

p. 455-456 Nov. 20, 1799 James Powel (Spartanburgh) to John Loftis (same); for $300 sold 200 ac on Middle fork Tyger R; plat attached shows border: Tyger R, John Smith, Landson, and Powell; part of two grants: (1) to Ephraim Rease, and (2) to Hugh Parks and eventually sold to James Powel. Witness Lambert Loftis, James Loftis, and William Atkins. Signed James Powel. Wit. oath (Greenville Co) Dec. 26, 1799 James Loftis to Reubin Barrett. Rec. Apr. 26, 1800

p. 456-457 Mar. 14, 1775 John Young (Craven Co) to James Peden (SC); for 35£ SC money sold 100 ac on S side of N fork Tyger R; border: Charles Moore; includes "his" improvements where "he" lives; grant May 4, 1769 Gov. William Tryon (NC) to John Young. Witness Alex Brown, Alex Peden, and Thos Dula. Signed John Young. Wit. oath (Greenville Co) Mar. 22(?), 1800 Alex Peden to John Alexander. Rec. Apr. 28, 1800

p. 457-458 Jul. 15, 1799 John Reese (Spartanburgh) to John Tollison (same); for $60 sold 100 ac on Big Br of Island Cr of Pacolet R; border: Markley's old line and Murray; Condition: deed void if John Reese pays John Tollison $60 in three years. Witness Muse Tollison, Thomas Dean, and Richeson Whitbey. Signed John Reese's mark. Wit. oaths Apr. 23, 1800 Muse Tollison and Thomas Dean to William Simpson and Apr. 23, 1800 Richeson Whitbey to William Simpson Apr. 23, 1800 William Poole (the Healing Springs) gave oath that in Mar. 1799 John Reese bought 100 ac from William Poole on N side of Pacolet R and N side of Island Cr and on Big Br; border: William Slunow, Markley's old corner, and Murrow (sic); part of 886 ac belonging to Abram Markley, merchant (Charleston); Abram Markley has empowered William Poole to sell 100 ac of the 886 ac; John Reese told William Poole the deed wasn't good and John Reese had James Smith, surveyor, to write another deed in "his" son's Hubburd's name; William Poole asked if John Reese had mortgaged land to Capt John Tollison before William Poole assigned him the deed in his son's name; John Reese said he hadn't nor did he intend to; William Poole then assigns the second deed in Mar. 1800. Witness William Simpson JP. Signed William Poole

p. 458-459 Oct. 11, 1799 John West (Spartanburgh) to Cyrus Leay (or Leecy) (same); for $416.64 sold 150 ac on Lawson's fork of Pacolate R; border: David Hicks, John West, and William Brannan. Witness Gabriel Benson, John Wingo, and Zachariah Wingo. Signed John West's mark. Wit. oath Apr. 25, 1800 Gabriel Benson to Isham Foster. Rec. May 6, 1800

p. 459-460 Apr. 30, 1796 Henry Coon (Spartanburgh) to John Durham (same); for 60£ sterling sold 200 ac on two forks of Ben's Cr, one called Brushey fork; border: James Jordan, Aaron Moor, William Moor, and David Anderson; where Henry Coon lives. Witness William Gray, George Durham, and Curtis Gray. Signed Henry Coon. Wit. oath Jul. 27, 1797 William Gray to Thos Moore. Rec. May 7, 1800

p. 460-461 Jan. 16, 1800 Robert Watkins (Union Co) to John and Margarett Hendricks, administrators of Wm Hendricks, desc (Spanish Province of E Florday); for $100 sold 100 ac on Two Mile Cr of Enoree R; land for legates of Wm Hendricks; border: E-Wm Hendricks and Benj Wofford, W-Michael Waldrip and vacant, S-Edward Musgrove, and N-vacant. Witness Peter Philips, Thomas Davis, and John Coldwell. Signed Robert Watkins. Wit. oath (Union Co) Jan. 16, 1800 Peter Philips to Josiah Darby. Rec. May 9, 1800

p. 461-462 Oct. 8, 1799 Thomas Sarratt (Spartanburgh) to Gideon Reynolds (same); for 50£ sterlins sold 100 ac on Coin Cr of Tyger R; part of 250 ac grant Nov. 6, 1786 Gov. William Moultrie to Ambrose Barrett. Witness John Grist and Thomas Powers. Signed Thomas Sarratt's mark. Wit. oath Oct. 8, 1799 John Grist to Saml Lancaster. Rec. May 26, 1800. Dower renounced Sarah Sarratt to Thomas Moore Jan. 7, 1800

Book G 1800-1801

p. 1-2 Dec. 20, 1799 John Peice and Richard Peice (Spartanburgh) to John D Young (same); for $239.44 sold 100 ac on S side Tygar R; border: Sheilds Booker, John D Young, estate of Wm Benson, desc, and Richard Peice; half of two tracts granted to John McElhany and Francis Dodds. Witness Gab Benson and John Jamison. Signed John and Richard Peice. Wit. oath May 22, 1800 John Jamison to James Jordan. Rec. Jun. 23, 1800

p. 2-3 Jun. 11, 1800 dower renounced Martha Wells to Isham Harrison for deed from Wm Well and wife Martha to Wm Thompson; deed recorded in Book D p. 83. Rec. Jun. 23, 1800

p. 3 Apr. 16, 1800 Armstead Shumate (Spartanburgh) to B. D. Shumate (same); for $430 sold a Negro James about 20 years old. Witness William Hopkins and Townley Redfearn. Signed Atd Shumate. Wit. oath May 7, 1800 Townley Redfearn to Thos Moore. Rec. Jun. 24, 1800

p. 3-5 Jan. 27, 1800 John McCluen (or McCluer), sr (Greenville Co) to Henry Young (Spartanburgh); for 200£ sold 200 ac on both sides S Pacolate R; grant Jun. 5, 1786 Gov. William Moultrie to John McCluen. Witness Walter McChesney, Edw Jemmes, and William McCluer. Signed John McCluen's mark. Wit. oath Jan. 28, 1800 William McCluer to John Anderson. Rec. Jun. 24, 1800

p. 5-7 Jan. 18, 1800 Thomas Farrow (Spartanburgh) to Isham Harrison (same); for $250 sold 83 ac on Fairforrest Cr; called Dugan's land; border: Isham Harrison, Rubin Daniel, and "line dividing Widow's distribution from that of the children". Witness Reuben Daniel, Sophia Daniel, and Priscilla Harrison. Signed Thos Farrow. Wit. oath May 24, 1800 Reuben Daniel to A Lancaster. Rec. Jun. 25, 1800

p. 7-8 Jan. 18, 1800 Thomas Farrow (Spartanburgh) to Reuben Daniel (same); for $350 sold 254 ac on both sides Fairforrest Cr; called Duggan's land; border: Duggan, Belsher, James, and "widow's distribution"; part of a lot drawn for Emily Harrison. Witness Isham Harrison, Sophia Daniel, and Pricilla Harrison. Signed Thos Farrow. Wit. oath May 24, 1800 Isham Harrison to A Lancaster. Rec. Jun. 25, 1800. Dower renounced (recorded in Book G p. 64) Ann Farrow to James Kilgore Aug. 11, 1800 and Rec. Sept. 4, 1800

p. 8-9 Mar. 7, 1800 William Hunger Torrans (Charleston, SC) to William Turner (same); for $500 sold 500 ac "old measure" on waters of Pacolet R and Lawson's fork; border: W-William Moultrie, and others vacant; grant May 4, 1773 to Robert Smith; sale due to power of attorney to William Hunter Torrans from Hugh Clark, son and heir of Malcom Clark (late of Orangeburgh), dept. surveyor. Witness Edward Wells, Isaac Jeurdon, and M J Moon. Signed Wm H Torrans, atty for Hugh Clark. Wit. oath (Charleston Dist) Mar. 7, 1800 Isaac Jeurdon to Benj Boyd. Rec. Jun. 26, 1800

p. 9-10 Mar. 12, 1800 William Wofford (Franklin Co, Ga) to Benjamin Wofford (Spartanburgh); for $300 sold 400 ac on Fairforrest Cr; grant to Zachariah Giles and sold to William Wofford. Witness Garmett Smethers and Benjn Wofford (of Ga). Signed W Woford. Wit. oath Mar. 22, 1800 Benjn Wofford (of Ga) to G Brewton. Rec. Jun. 27, 1800

p. 10-11 Apr. 4, 1800 Benjamin Wofford (Spartanburgh) to George Connell (same); for $300 sold 400 ac on Fairforrest Cr; border: Duggan. Witness I Harrison, James Bagwell, Anney Harrison. Signed Benj Wofford. Certified Apr. 4, 1800 by I Harrison. Rec. Jun. 27, 1800. Dower renounced Apr. 11, 1800 Mary Wofford to I Harrison

p. 11-13 Sept. 12, 1798 Samuel Culbertson sr (Washington Co, Tenn) to Samuel Culbertson jr (Spartanburgh); for 20£ sold 290 ac where Samuel Culbertson jr lives on Culbertson's Br of Fairforrest Cr; part of 297 ac grant Gov. Matthew Rowan (NC) to George Gillaspie Feb. 23, 1754 and South Carolina Memorial in book M13 p. 158 on Feb. 27, 1775; eventually sold to Samuel Clubertson sr; border: Josiah Culbertson and Henry ONeil. Witness Wm Pickens, Josiah Culbertson, and John Swingle. Signed Samuel Culbertson. Wit. oath May 26, 1800 Josiah Culbertson to Wm McDowell. Rec. Jun. 27, 1800. Dower renounced (Washington Co, Tenn) Jane Culbertson to James Stewart Sept. 18, 1798

p. 13-14 May 25, 1798 Obadiah Watson (Spartanburgh) to Thomas Moore, merchant (Rutherford Co, NC); for $1278 worth of goods sold to Obadiah by Thomas mortgage 250 ac where Obadiah lives, 150 ac adjoining bought from Obadiah Trimmier, 3 Negroes: boy Arch, boy Billey, and girl Hester; Condition: mortgage void if Obadiah pays Thomas $1278 by Nov. 15, 1799; security: land and Negroes are Obadiah's. Witness David Watson and John Amos. Signed Obadiah Watson. Wit. oath Jun. 27, 1800 John Amos to H McCray. Rec. Jun. 30, 1800

p. 14-18 Apr. 2, 1800 Daniel Bordeaux (Barnwell Dist) esq to Thomas Fitzsimmons (Philadelphia, Pa) esq; for $2,000 sold 1/3 of (a) 7,582 ac on Main Thickety Cr and both sides Bullocks Fork of Thickety Cr; border: Irby Dewberry,William Bice, unknown, Isom Saffold, Vardry McBee, Thomas Gardau (or Gordau), William Weir, Matthew Guthrey, William Haven, Malachi Jones; surrounding 200 ac grant to Nichodemus Thompson; original survey for Daniel Bordeaux, David Hopkins, and Francis Bremar by Zachariah Bullock, dept. surv. Nov. 3, 1785; 1/3 of (b) 7,000 ac on both sides Jarret's and Cherokee Creeks of Thickety Cr; border: NW & N-Mary Horton and unknown, E-Col Hopkins & Co and Vardry McBee, S-Col Hopkins & Co, Mary Horton, and unknown, SE-Mathew Guthrey; surrounding 200 ac grant to Price and two tracts of 640 ac each grant to Col Hopkins & Co; original survey Oct. 27, 1785 for Daniel Bordeaux, David Hopkins, and Francis Bremar by Zachariah Bullock, dept. surv; both a and b granted to Daniel Bordeaux, David Hopkins, and Francis Bremar. Witness Alexander Juhan and Isaac Bordeaux. Signed Daniel Bordeaux. Wit. oath Apr. 2, 1800 (Barnwell Dist) Isaac Bordeaux to Chas Goodwin. Rec. Jul. 1, 1800. Dower renounced (Barnwell Dist) Martha Bordeaux to Chas Goodwin Apr. 2, 1800

p. 18-19 Mar. 10, 1799 Christopher Orrenduff (Spartanburgh) to James Hickey (same); for $100 sold 147 ac on waters of Dutchman's Cr; border: Edward Rollins; grant to Thomas Smith and sold to Thomas Cook who sold to Christopher Orrenduff. Wit. oath William Lancaster and Absolum Lancaster. Signed Christopher Orrenduff's mark. Wit. oath Mar. 13, 1799 Absolum Lancaster to Saml Lancaster. Rec. Jul. 2, 1800. Dower renounced Elizabeth Orrunduff to I Harrison Sept. 10, 1799

p. 19-21 Jan. 13, 1799 William Moore (Spartanburgh) to Leonard Burnett (same); for 40£ sterling sold 148 ac on Barton's Br and Connor's Br of Sholey Cr of Lawson's fork of Pacolet R; part of grant Aug. 1, 1785 to Bolly Connor. Witness I Harrison and Elisha Hedden. Signed William Moore. Wit. oath Mar. 31, 1800 I Harrison to John Anderson. Rec. Jul. 2, 1800

p. 21-22 Mar. 13, 1800 Dudley Wooton and wife Tubitha (Spartanburgh) to William Prewett sr (same); for 10£ sterling sold 50 ac in Union Co; border: Wotton's Spring Br and Charles Hotts; part of 158 ac grant Nov. 7, 1796 Gov. Arnoldus Vanderhorst to Dudley Wotton. Witness Samuel Pruett and John Grist. Signed Dudley and Tubitha Wotton's marks. Wit. oath Mar. 15, 1800 John Grist to Ism Foster. Rec. Jul. 2, 1800

p. 22-23 Apr. 17, 1800 Benjamin Wofford (Spartanburgh) to Thomas Foster sr (same); for $100 sold 240 ac on S Branch of Fairforrest Cr; known as Gibbs' Mountain; part of grant to Zachariah Gibbs. Witness I Harrison and George Connell. Signed Benj Wofford. Certified Apr. 17, 1800 by I Harrison. Rec. Jul. 3, 1800

p. 23-24 Sept. 9, 1797 Ransom Tinsley and wife Sarah (Spartanburgh) to John Barnett, son of Joseph (same); for 41£ 15s sterling sold 83½ ac on NE side Fairforrest Cr; part of 175 ac that John Walker sold to Jesse Connell. Witness George Connell and Frances Connell. Signed Ransom Tinsley and Sarah's mark. Wit. oath Oct.

2, 1797 Ransom Tinsley to I Harrison. Rec. Jul. 4, 1800. Dower renounced Sarah Tinsley to I Harrison Oct. 2, 1797

p. 24-27 Nov. 11, 1799 Michael Brown Roberds (Spartanburgh) to Charles Waddle Hide (same); for 30 silver dollars sold 50 ac on Branch of Tyger R; border: John Jeffres and David Anderson. Witness Jesse Page, John Shadduck, and Gannaway Johnson. Signed Michael Bro Roberds. Wit. oath May 1, 1800 Jesse Page to Drury McDaniel. Rec. Jul. 5, 1800

p. 27-28 Nov. 12, 1799 Michael Brown Roberds (Spartanburgh) to Charles Waddle Hide (same); for 30 silver dollars sold 160 ac on branch of Tygar R; border: William Allen, Jesse Payge's Spring Br, Benjamin Waldrop, Ceeps Miller, and Randolph Johnson. Witness Jessee Page and Caty Page. Signed Michael Bro Roberds. Wit. oath May 16, 1800 Jessee Page to Drury McDaniel. Rec. Jul. 5, 1800

p. 28-30 Apr. 4, 1792 Henry Turner (Spartanburgh) to Samuel McClure (same); for 50£ sold 100 ac; part of 183 ac grant Jun. 5, 1786 Gov. William Moultrie to George Thomson on both sides of Pacolet R; border: NE- Edward Haeuton and others vacant. Witness William Metcalf and David Benson. Signed Henry Turner's mark. Wit. oath (Greenville Co) Jun. 24, 1800 William Metcalf to Robert Cooke. Rec. Jul. 7, 1800

p. 30-31 Dec. 23, 1799 William Morris (Spartanburgh) to Gibson Oliver (same); for 56£ 10s sterling sold 100 ac; part of two tracts: (1) granted Apr. 25, 1767 North Carolina to Thomas Williamson who sold Aug. 29, 1769 to Thomas Barton; and (2) granted Oct. 1, 1787 South Carolina to Thomas Barton; on N side of N Pacolet R; border: Barton's Cr. Witness William McDowel, John Nolen, and Kendal Savage. Signed William Morris. Certified Dec. 23, 1799 by William McDowel. Rec. Jul. 8, 1800

p. 31-33 Mar. 7, 1794 Matthew Harper (Spartanburgh) to James Fowler (same); for 15£ 10s sterling sold 90 ac; part of 200 ac grant Jun. 5, 1786 Gov. William Moultrie to Thomas Morah on Holston's Cr of Pacolet R; border: all vacant. Witness William Jameson, John McClroy, and John Harper. Signed Matthew Harper. Wit. oath Aug. 22, 1799 John Harper to John Anderson. Rec. Jul. 11, 1800

p. 33-35 Jun. 11, 1800 Britain Williford, sheriff (Spartanburgh) to Alexander McKee and Gabriel Benson (same); for 4£ sterling sold 815 ac; Joel Hembrie had 815 ac on both sides Cain Cr near the N side of Tygar R; border: NW-old lines, owner unknown, NE-Sarah Elder and Ralph Smith esq, S-Joel Henbrie, SW-Owing Forrister, David Grimes, and John Butler; grant May 2, 1791 Gov. Charles Pinckney to Joel Hembrie; Gabriel, administrator for William Benson desc had a judgment agaînes Joel Hembrie in court Jul. 1799 for $32.45; sale of land on Dec. 7, 1799. Witness I Harrison JP, W Lancaster, and Ab Benson. Signed Britn Williford, sheriff. Rec. Jul. 14, 1800

p. 35-36 Oct. 6, 1798 Joseph Davis (Green Co, Tenn) to friend Vinson Wyatt (Spartanburgh); power of attorney to sell or rent 200 ac on S side Pacolate R; part of survey for Jesse Connell; border: Aaron Templeman and sold to Joseph Davis. Witness Ellis Cannon, Lewis Cannon, and William Cannon. Signed Joseph Davis' mark. Wit. oath Nov. 3, 1798 Lewis Cannon to Geor Lamkins. Rec. Jul. 14, 1800

p. 36-37 Mar. 21, 1789 Jesse Connell (Spartanburgh) to Joseph Davis (same); for 30£ SC money sold 200 ac on Pacolet R. Witness Ellis Cannon and Daniel Walker. Signed Jesse Connell. Wit. oath Jul. 29, (not given) Ellis Cannon and Daniel Walker to Richd Harrison. Rec. Jul. 15, 1800

p. 37-39 Mar. 24, 1800 Peter Gray (Spartanburgh) to Gabriel Benson (same); for $102.50 sold 22 ac on N side Willson's Mill Cr of N Tygar R; border: William Foster's M (sic) Spring Br, Peter Gray, Gabriel Benson, and Estate of William Benson desc. Witness Robert Miller and John Jordan. Signed Peter Gray. Wit. oath Jul. 12, 1800 John Jordan to Ism Foster. Rec. Jul. 18, 1800. Dower renounced Hannah Gray to James Jordan May 24, 1800

p. 39-40 Jan. 28, 1800 Obadiah Watson (Spartanburgh) to John Champion (same); for $350 sold 100 ac on N fork Thickety Cr; border: mouth of Prices Cr and John Champion. Witness John Cooper and William Byors. Signed Obadh Watson. Wit. oath Jul. 16, 1800 John Cooper to H McCray. Rec. Jul. 23, 1800

p. 40-42 Aug. 8, 1795 James Bruton (Spartanburgh) to Nathaniel Woodruff (same); for 20£ sterling sold 100 ac; grant Oct. 3, 1785 Gov. William Moultrie to James Bruton; border: E-where Nathaniel Woodruff lives, W-Susannah Hambey, S-Burrell Pace, and N-John Woodruff. Witness Burrel Pace, John Woodruff, and Samuel Woodruff. Signed James Bruton. Wit. oath Jul. 15, 1800 Burrel Pace to George Bruton. Rec. Jul. 24, 1800

p. 42-44 Jul. 10, 1792 James Woodruff (Spartanburgh) to Nathaniel Woodruff (same); for 30£ sterling sold 200 ac; W part of 400 ac grant Apr. 2, 1773 to Joseph Brown on Jeamey's Cr of Tygar R; border: E-John Keighler and others vacant; sold by William Brown, heir of Joseph Brown desc, to James Woodruff. Witness Charles Whitten, David Bruton, Samuel Woodruff, Burrel Pace, and Paul Casle Bury. Signed James Wodruff. Wit. oath Jul. 15, 1800 Samuel Woodruff to George Bruton. Rec. Jul. 24, 1800

p. 44-45 Jun. 21, 1799 Giles Connell (Spartanburgh) to Anthony Foster jr (same); for $300 sold 400 ac; part of two tracts granted to Giles Connell; border: Lancaster; includes cross road about 3 miles below Court House. Witness I Harrison JP. Signed Giles Connell. Wit. oath Jun. 21, 1799 Giles Connell to I Harrison. Rec. Jul. 25, 1800. Dower renounced Elizabeth Connell to I Harrison Apr. 5, 1800

p. 45-46 Oct. 15, 1798 Richard Traylor (Spartanburgh) to Edward Boman (same); for 50£ sold 160 ac on waters of N Tygar R; border: Samuel Timmons. Witness none. Signed Richard Traylor and Elizabeth's mark. Wit. oath Oct. 15, 1798 Richard Traylor to Ism Foster. Rec. Jul. 25, 1800

p. 46-47 Mar. (blank), 1800 John Turner (Spartanburgh) to William Hollaway (same); for $125 SC money sold 100 ac on branch of Ashworth Cr; part of Cranshua Camp's tract granted Oct. 6, 1788; border: Sarrat's Cr and Margaret Green's improvements. Witness Gashim Lee and Matthias Turner. Signed John Turner. Wit. oath Jul. 18, 1800 Gashim Lee to Geor Lamkin. Rec. Jul. 25, 1800

p. 47-48 Jan. 6, 1800 Elizabeth Cooper (Spartanburgh) to John Ardnold jr (same); for $150 sold 148 ac on waters of Thickety Cr; part of tract sold by Francis Bremar to Elizabeth Cooper; border: Obadiah Trimmier. Witness John Arendell sr and John Amos. Signed Elizabeth Cooper's mark. Wit. oath Jan. 6, 1800 John Arendell sr to H McCray. Rec. Jul. 26, 1800

p. 48-50 Mar. 29, 1800 David White (Spartanburgh) to James Crook jr (same); for $350 sold 100 ac on S side of S fork Tygar R; border: Drummond's Spring Br. Witness Robt McCord, Jesse Crook, and James Crook. Signed David White. Wit. oath Apr. 4, 1800 James Crook to Drury McDaniel. Rec. Jul. 28, 1800

p. 50-51 Aug. 22, 1799 Samuel Casey to Thomas Todd; for $300 sold 125 ac and crops thereon and all hogs; between Enoree and Tygar R; border: E-Henry Williamson, N-Thomas Todd, W-James Hill and Robert Wilson, and S-Stephen Layton. Witness Edmo (or Edward) Williams and Peter Pennell. Signed Samuel Casey's mark. Wit. oath Apr. 19, 1800 Peter Pennell to John Martindale. Rec. Aug. 18, 1800

p. 51 Jul. 16, 1799 John Wright (Spartanburgh) to John Barnett (same); for $275 sold a Negro girl Jene about 14 years old. Witness Elijah Barnett. Signed John Wright. Wit. oath Aug. 14, 1800 Elijah Barnett to I Harrison. Rec. Aug. 18, 1800

p. 51-53 Jul. 19, 1800 Bernard Wm Sweeney, taylor (Spartanburgh) to Edward Bomar (same); for $100 sold 150 ac part of 315 ac grant Aug. 1, 1785 to William White; border: Elizabeth Williams and William Moore. Witness Samuel Caldwell and John Jordan. Signed Bernard W Sweeney. Wit. oath Jul. 19, 1800 Samuel Caldwell to Drury McDaniel. Rec. Aug. 19, 1800

p. 53-54 Jul. 8, 1797 Jeremiah Salmon (Spartanburgh) to Re . Auston Claton and members of Baptist Church (same); for 5s sold 1 ac on waters of N fork Tygar R; border: N-unknown and other sides by Jeremiah Salmon; "house of religious worship" to be built there by subscriptions of Baptist members and other denominations; house to be free and open to the members and open for Gospel Ministers of every denomination for preaching and land to be free burying ground to all religious "societies" that may chose (sic) to bury there with preference to members of the Baptist Chruch. Witness Robert Foster and Jeremiah Salmon. Signed Jeremiah Salmon. Wit. oath Jul. 19, 1800 Jeremiah Salmon to Drury McDaniel. Rec. Aug. 19, 1800

p. 54-55 Apr. 28, 1800 John McDowell (Charleston, SC) to Thomas Terry (Greenville Co); for 5£ sold 140 ac on Ferguson's Cr of Tygar R; original "older" survey for 200 ac reduced to 140 ac and granted Jul. 14, 1785. Witness Willim Turpin and Hewlet Sullivant. Signed John McDowell. Wit. oath (Greenville Dist) May 23, 1800 Hewlet Sullivant to Hudson Berry. Rec. Aug. 20, 1800. Dower renounced Barbara McDowell to Willm Turpin Apr. 28, 1800

p. 55-56 Feb. 27, 1800 Aaron Smith (Spartanburgh) to Buckner Smith (same); for 6£ 2s 3p sold 2 cows and yearlings: a red and white cow and a "dark" both branded under bit and hole in right ear and under sloap(?) in the left, yearlings marked with swallow fork in left ear and hole in right; and a black sow with "a list" and 6 pigs, 9 geese, sow marked with cross and hold in each ear. Witness William Farmer and Moses Lancaster. Signed Aaron Smith's mark. Wit. oath Feb. 27, 1800 William Farmer to Saml Lancaster. Rec. Aug. 23, 1800

p. 56-58 Jan. 15, 1797 Robert Foster (Spartanburgh) to Rev "learned and pious" Austin Clayton, minister (same); for 75£ SC money sold 100 ac on S side of N fork Tyger R; border: Andrew Thomson and Samuel Miller esq; part of 800 ac grant North Carolina governor to Robert Miller and due to Robert Miller's will sold to John Young who sold to Robert Foster. Witness Thomas Foster and Robert Foster jr. Signed Robert Foster's mark. Wit. oath Jul. 19, 1800 Thomas Foster to Drury McDaniel. Rec. Aug. 23, 1800

p. 58-59 Jul. 14, 1800 Joseph Wofford (Spartanburgh) to Reuben Newman (same); for $100 sold 100 ac on N side Tygar R; border: Horseshoe Br, George Newman, and part of grant to Benjamin Wofford. Witness Anthony Shands and William Willson. Signed Joseph Wofford. Wit. oath Jul. 30, 1800 Anthony Shands to A Casey. Rec.

Aug. 25, 1800

p. 59-60 May 6, 1800 Reuben Wilson to Reuben Newman; for $120 sold 100 ac on S side Tyger R; border: near the meeting house, Wilson's meeting house Spring Br, Reuben Newman, and George Newman; part of grant in 1774 to James Simple. Witness Anthony Shands and William Willson. Signed Reubin Willson and Elizabeth's mark. Wit. oath Jul. 30, 1800 Anthony Shands to A Casey. Rec. Aug. 25, 1800

p. 60 Jun. 27, 1798 George Newman (Spartanburgh) to Reuben Newman (same); for 10£ sterling sold 100 ac part of 300 ac on S side Tyger R granted Oct. 15, 1784 to Austin Clayton; plat attached shows border: George Newman, Horseshoe Br, and Ben Wofford. Witness Martin Newman and Randal Casey. Signed George Newman's mark. Wit. oath Jul. 7, 1798 Randal Casey to Moses Casey. Rec. Aug. 25, 1800

p. 60-61 Jun. 28, 1798 George Newman (Spartanburgh) to Reuben Newman (same); for 10£ sterling sold 100 ac on S side of Tygar R; plat attached shows border: Tygar R and Ben Wofford; part of 300 ac grant Oct. 15, 1784 Gov. Benjamin Guerard to Austin Clayton. Witness Martin Newman and Randal Casey. Signed George Newman's mark. Wit. oath Jul. 7, 1798 Randal Casey to Moses Casey. Rec. Aug. 25, 1800

p. 61-63 Mar. 20, 1800 Penwell Wood sr (Spartanburgh) to Henry Wood (same); for $275 sold 439 ac W of Rockfield Cr; part of grant Gov. Rutledge to Penwell Wood sr. Witness Benjamin Wood and Barnett Wood. Signed Penewell Wood. Wit. oath Jun. 7, 1800 Benjamin Wood to Zadock Ford. Rec. Aug. 30, 1800

p. 63-64 Mar. 7, 1800 William Pool (Spartanburgh), attorney for Adam Markley, merchant (Charleston, SC) to Hubard Reese (Spartanburgh); for $43 paid by father John Reese sold 100 ac on Big Br of Island Cr of Pacolet R; border: Markley. Witness William Willis, James Smith, Samuel Dunaway. Signed William Pool, attorney for sd Markley. Wit. oath Mar. 24, 1800 James Smith to Geor Lamkin. Rec. Sept. 1, 1800

p. 64-65 Two dower renouncements Anne Farrow to James Kilgore Aug. 11, 1800; deeds recorded in Book G p. 5-7 and 7-8. Rec. Sept. 4, 1800

p. 65-66 Mar. 7, 1800 Giles Connell sr (Spartanburgh) to daughter Susannah Yews; give 200 ac; border: mouth of Mother's Spring Br, George Connell, Lancaster, and Wildcat (or Weldeat) Br. Witness I Harrison JQ, John Connell, and John Young. Signed Giles Connell. Wit. oath Aug. 21, 1800 Giles Connell to I Harrison. Rec. Sept. 6, 1800

p. 66-67 Mar. 4, 1800 Giles Connell sr (Spartanburgh) to daughter Lettice Yews; give 200 ac; border: mouth of Alder Br, road from Anthoney Foster's to Giles Connell's, Reuben Daniel, and Anthoney Foster. Witness I Harrison JQ, Nathan Yaes, and John Connell. Signed Giles Connell. Wit. oath Aug. 21, 1800 Giles Connell sr to I Harrison. Rec. Sept. 6, 1800

p. 67 Mar. 12, 1800 William Wofford (Franklin Co, Ga) to Benjamin Wofford (Spartanburgh); for $200 sold 200 ac on South Br of Fairforrest Cr; known as Gibbs mount; part of grant to Zachariah Gibbs. Witness Garnett Smethers and Benjn Wofford. Signed W Wofford. Wit. oath Mar. 22, 1800 Benjn Wofford (of Ga) to G Brewton. Rec. Sept. 9, 1800

p. 67-69 Sept. 19, 1798 Daniel Hammett (Spartanburgh) to Elizabeth Quarles (same); for 48£ sold 47 ac on Pacolet R; part of

50 ac tract with 3 ac excepted for Mary Drummon anywhere she pleases "outside the enclosed" (boundary?); border: Haraiam Shoal, Dart, Charles Hammett, and John Pitman. Witness James Lee and Nancy Quarles. Signed Daniel Hammett's mark. Wit. oath Sept. 15, 1800 Nancy Quarles to A Lancaster. Rec. Sept. 16, 1800

p. 69-70 Mar. 9, 1793 James William Lindsey (Rutherford Co, NC) to James Lindsey (Spartanburgh); for 10£ sterling sold 75 ac on Lick Cr of Enoree R; grant Mar. 5, 1792 Gov. Charles Pinckney to James William Lindsey; border: SW & SE-William Rives and John Hamley, S-Thomas Childers, E-Isaac Hamley, and NW-William More. Witness Burrel Pace, Joshua Lindsey, and Samuel Woodruff. Signed James Wm Lindsey. Wit. oath Sept. 19, 1800 Burrel Pace to G Brewton. Rec. Sept. 22, 1800

p. 70-71 Aug. 7, 1797 James Lindsey (Spartanburgh) to Micajah Lindsey (same); for 10£ sterling sold 175 ac on branches of Lick Cr of Enoree R; where James Lindsey lives; border: N-Hambey and Reeves, E-Joseph Woodruff, S-Amos Pilgrim and Alijah Hendrix, and W-William Moore; 100 ac is half of 200 ac grant Jun. 5, 1786 Gov. William Moultrie to William Moore jr; 75 ac joins W part of 100 ac and was granted Mar. 1, 1792 Gov. Charles Pinckney to James William Lindsey. Witness Isaac Brewton and Philip Bruton. Signed James Lindsey. Wit. oath Sept. 18, 1800 Isaac Brewton to G Bruton. Rec. Sept. 22, 1800

p. 71-72 Oct. 25, 1799 Micajah Lindsey (Spartanburgh) to William Hendrix (same); a bond of 70£ sterling; Condition: bond void if Micajah makes good deed for 70 ac granted to James Lindsey, 50 ac where Micajah Lindsey lives, and 30 ac; total of 150 ac except what John Lindsey owns on S side of Meeting House Br where James Lindsey sr lives. Witness David Moor and Thomas Woodruff III. Signed Micajah Lindsey. Wit. oath Sept. 19, 1800 Thomas Woodruff III to G Brewton. Rec. Sept. 22, 1800

p. 72-74 Jan. 25, 1798 (Camden Dist) Henry Rives (Richland Co) to William Hendrix (Spartanburgh); for 70£ sold 500 ac; grant to William Rives; on waters of Tyger R. Witness Isaac Tucker, Aaron Bochium, and Michael French. Signed Henry Rives. Dower renounced (Richland Cr) Jenny Rives to Isaac Tucker JRC Feb. 7, 1798. Rec. Sept. 26, 1800

p. 74-76 Feb. 21, 1787 William Brown, heir of Joseph Brown desc (Spartanburgh) to James Wofford (same); for 200£ sterling sold 200 ac; border: E-John Keighler, S-Richard Chesney, and others vacant; W part of 400 ac grant Apr. 2, 1773 Lt. Gov. William Bull to Joseph Brown in Craven Co on Jeamey's Cr. Witness Aron Floyd, Ben Rhodes, and David Pruett. Signed William Brown. Wit. oath Sept. 24, 1800 Aron Floyd to G Brewton. Rec. Sept. 27, 1800

p. 76-77 May 17, 1795 Robert Lee (Spartanburgh) to James Wofford (same); for 10£ sterling sold 245 ac; border: Ray and Haney; part of grant Jul. 5, 1788 to Thomas Sabb on waters of Pacolet and Broad R and sold to Robert Lee. Witness William Bagwell, George Poole, and John Lee. Signed Robt Lee. Wit. oath May 8, 1797 William Bagwell to I Harrison. Rec. Sept. 29, 1800

p. 77-78 Aug. 20, 1800 Thomas Wright (Spartanburgh) to Thomas Wright jr (same); for $300 sold 200 ac; border: W-Aaron Floyd, S-an old line, E-Andrew Thomson, N-N fork Tygar R; grant South Carolina governor to Francis Ward who sold to Abraham Barrier who sold to Thomas Price who sold to Thomas Wright. Witness John Thomas, Joel Marchbanks, Andrew Thomson. Signed Thomas Wright. Wit. oath Sept. 27, 1800 Andrew Thomson to G Brewton. Rec. Sept. 29, 1800

p. 78-80 Sept. 20, 1800 William McDaniel (Spartanburgh) to daughter

Betsey McDaniel (same); for love and affection give a Negro Ambus. Witness Joseph Barnett and John Ward. Signed Wm McDaniel. Wit. oath Oct. 3, 1800 Joseph Barnett to Drury McDaniel. Rec. Oct. 7, 1800

p. 80-81 Mar. 11, 1800 Nathaniel Power (Laurens Co) to Sampson Bobo (Spartanburgh); for $250 sold 160 ac on Two Mile Cr of Enoree R; part of two tracts granted to Richard Neeley and John Hendrix; Richard Neeley sold 150 ac to William Miles and it went at his death to daughter Uncey now married to Nathaniel Power of which 50 ac at upper end is now sold; 50 ac was sold to W Miles and eventually got to Nathaniel Power; 60 ac was sold to Ebenezer Morse who sold to William Miles and eventually got to Nathaniel Power; three tracts border: Joseph Casey, Crow, Colbert, and Jesse Brown. Witness Burrell Bobo and Burrell Wiledn. Signed Nathl and Unicey Power. Wit. oath Oct. 14, 1800 Burrell Bobo to I Harrison. Rec. Oct. 17, 1800. Dower renounced Unicy Power to Daniel Wright Sept. 27, 1800

p. 81-82 Jan. 10, 1799 Thomas Tod to John Layton; for 5£ sterling sold 100 ac; plat attached shows border: Thomas Tod, John Spear, and Tygar R. Witness John Yarbrough and Robt Anderson. Signed Thos Tod. Wit. oath Jul. 27, 1799 Robt Anderson to A Casey. Rec. Oct. 17, 1800

p. 82-84 Jun. 2, 1797 James Wofford (Spartanburgh) to William Rhodes (same); for 10£ sterling sold 180 ac; border: David More, James Wofford, and Richard James; grant of 266 ac to James Wofford on Forgeson's Cr of Tygar R bordering James Wofford, Charles James, and Richard James. Witness Martin Cole, Nathaniel Wofford, and Catherine Wofford. Signed James Wofford. Wit. oath Jun. 2, 1798 Martin Cole to Zadack Ford. Rec. Oct. 27, 1800

p. 84-85 Sept. 20, 1800 William McDaniel (Spartanburgh) to daughter Nancey Barnett (same); for love and affection give Negro Jeney. Witness John Ward and Polly Ward. Signed Wm McDaniel. Wit. oath Sept. 22, 1800 John Ward to Drury McDaniel. Rec. Oct. 18, 1800

p. 85-87 Apr. 24, 1797 Sarah Barnett (Hancock Co, Ga) to Joseph Barnett (Spartanburgh); for 70£ sterling sold 200 ac; border: Shillus(?) and John Leathewood; part of grant Nov. 5, 1771 to Joseph Barnett desc on branch of Two Mile Cr of Enoree R. Witness John Brown and Benjamin Barnett. Signed Sarah Barnett's mark. Wit. oath Jul. 1, 1799 Benjamin Barnett to George Brewton. Rec. Oct. 18, 1800

p. 87-88 Sept. 17, 1800 William McDaniel and Drury McDaniel (Spartanburgh) to Zachariah McDaniel (same); for 50£ sold 150 ac on S side of Tyger R; border: Inglish. Witness John Ward, James McDaniel, and Polley McDaniel. Signed Wm and Drury McDaniel. Wit. oath Sept. 17, 1800 John Ward to Drury McDaniel. Rec. Oct. 18, 1800

p. 88-89 Jan. 10, 1800 John Roebuck and wife Sary (Greenville Co) to Wilie Cook (Spartanburgh); for $200 sold 100 ac on N side Tygar R; border: Burrell Bobo, Richard Bearden, a ridge path, and Drury Parram; part of grant to Thos Fletcher. Witness Lewis Evatt and Willey Brown. Signed Jno Roebuck and Sary's mark. Wit. oath Jan. 21, 1800 Lewis Evatt to A Casey. Rec. Oct. 18, 1800

p. 89-90 Sept. 20, 1800 William McDaniel (Spartanburgh) to daughter Polley Ward (same); for love and affection give Negro Aney. Witness Joseph Barnett and Nancey Barnett. Signed Wm McDaniel. Wit. oath Sept. 22, 1800 Joseph Barnett to Drury McDaniel. Rec. Oct. 20, 1800

p. 90-91 Sept. 17, 1800 William and Drury McDaniel (Spartanburgh) to John Ward (same); for 50£ sold 160 ac on S side Tygar

R; border: Inglish, Mill Shoal, and Miller; part of grant Feb. 4, 1788 to John Brown. Witness Zachariah McDaniel, James McDaniel, and Polly McDaniel. Signed Wm and Drury McDaniel. Wit. oath Sept. 17, 1800 Zachariah McDaniel to Drury McDaniel. Rec. Oct. 20, 1800

p. 91-92 Sept. 3, 1800 Moses Guyton (Union Co) to Joseph Adams (Spartanburgh); for 50£ sold 144 ac on N side Beaverdam Cr of Thickety Cr. Witness Jas Smith and William Bostick. Signed Moses Guyton. Wit. oath Oct. 4, 1800 William Bostick to I Harrison. Rec. Oct. 20, 1800

p. 92-93 Mar. 18, 1800 William Hammett (Spartanburgh) to Richardson Vincent (same); for $100 sold 106 ac on Pacolet R; border: Elizabeth Quarles and Charles Hammett; part of grant to John Hammett. Witness Sabirey Hammett and John Hammett. Signed William Hammett. Wit. oath Oct. 13, 1800 William Hammett to I Harrison. Rec. Oct. 20, 1800

p. 93-94 Oct. 25, 1800 Rachel Snow to grandson Baley Adams and granddaughter Mary Adams; for love and affection give to Baley a bay horse about 14 hands high 5 years old and a gray mare about 13 hands high 14 years old; and give to Mary a red cow with white face and a calf and a feather bed and furniture. Witness Thomas Alexander and Polley Jones. Signed Rachel Snow. Wit. oath Oct. 25, 1800 Thomas Alexander to Thos Moore. Rec. Nov. 4, 1800

p. 94-96 Oct. 20, 1791 Nicholas Holley (Spartanburgh) to George Robuck (same); for 200£ sterling SC money sold 200 ac; border: SE-William Hendrix and others vacant; surveyed Nov. 24, 1767 for David Hambey in Craven Co on Jamey's Cr of Tygar R; grant Nov. 24, 1767 Gov. Charles G Montague to David Hambey. Witness Alexr Alexander, John Thornton, and William Earnest. Signed Nicles Holley. Wit. oath Oct. 23, 1800 Alexr Alexander to G Brewton. "came to hand" Oct. 25, 1800. Rec. Nov. 4, 1800

p. 96-98 Nov. 17, 1791 George Robuck (Spartanburgh) to Sampson Bobo (same); for 200£ sterling sold 200 ac; border: SE-William Hendrix and others vacant; survey Nov. 24, 1767 for David Hambey in Craven Co on Jamey's Cr of Tyger R; grant Nov. 21 (sic), 1767 Gov. Charles G Montague to David Hambey. Witness Jesse Casey, William Wileder, and Burrell Bobo. Signed George Robuck. Wit. oath Feb. 6, 1792 William Wileder to Thomas Farrow. "came to hand" Oct. 25, 1800. Rec. Nov. 4, 1800

p. 98-99 Jun. 26, 1800 William Brannan (Spartanburgh) to Jesse Davis (same); for $60 sold 121 ac on waters of Lawson's fork; border: Frances Balenger and Edward Balenger; part of grant May 17, 1799 Gov. Edward Rutledge to Samuel Fley. Witness Joshua Hawkins and Lewis Brown. Signed William Brannan. Certified Jun. 26, 1800 by Ism Foster. Rec. Nov. 4, 1800

p. 99-100 Nov. 26, 1784 Thomas Miles (Tyger R, 96 Dist) to Thomas Farrow (Enoree, 96 Dist); for 10s SC money sold 150 ac on N side Enoree R; border: W-Robert Hannah, E-Michael Waldrup and vacant, S-Enoree R; grant to Philemon Waters and survey by Frances Hostting. Witness William Wood and John Beardin. Signed Thomas Miles. Rec. Nov. 5, 1800

p. 100-101 Sept. 20, 1800 Abram Markley, merchant (Charleston, SC) to William Adcock (Spartanburgh); for 10£ sterling sold 100 ac on N side Pacolet R; border: Samuel Turner and Reuben Warren. Witness Reuben Warren, Bazel Scott, and Thos Wyatt. Signed Abram Markley. Wit. oath Oct. 25, 1800 Thos Wyatt to Geo Lamkin. Rec. Nov. 5, 1800

p. 101-102 Aug. 4, 1800 John Lee (Spartanburgh) to George Poole; for 10£ sterling sold 620 ac on branches of Pacolate R; border: Barton and Kimble. Witness James Wofford, Richard Lee, and Matthew McAbee. Signed John Lee. Wit. oath Oct. 31, 1800 Richard Lee to A Lancaster. Rec. Nov. 4, 1800

p. 102-104 Dec. 17, 1798 Jonathan Lenard and wife Ann to Henry Huff; for 80£ sterling sold 140 ac on Prather's Cr of Tygar R and on S side Tygar R; part of two tracts (1) 250 ac and (2) 200 ac; grant to William Clayton who sold to Jonathan Lenard; border: Edwd Arnett, Robert Irwin, E-heirs of Edwd Arnett and part of 250 ac, N-Robert Irwin, W-James Clayton, S-part of (1) and (2). Witness Christopher Stone and James Leonard. Signed Jonathan Lenard and Ann's mark. Wit. oath Dec. 6, 1798 James Leonard to Moses Casey. Rec. Nov. 5, 1800

p. 104-106 Dec. 5, 1798 Edmund Clayton and wife Heneritta to Henry Williamson; for 50£ sterling sold 50 ac on Prather's Cr of Tygar R on S side Tygar R; part of 250 ac grant to William Clayton who sold to Edmund Clayton; border: Robert Irwin, Philip Mulkie, John Spears, Henry Huff, E-part of 250 ac grant, S-Prather's Cr, N-Irwin and Todd, and W-Henry Huff. Witness Stephen Williamson and James Pelphrey. Signed Edmund Clayton and Heneritta's marks. Wit. oath Dec. 24, 1799 James Pelphrey to A Casey. Rec. Nov. 6, 1800

p. 106-107 Dec. 28, 1790 William Clayton and wife Elizabeth to Edmund Clayton; for 50£ sterling sold 100 ac in two tracts of 50 ac each: (1) on Prather's Cr of Tyger R and on S side Tyger R; part of 250 ac grant to William Clayton; border: Robt Irwin, Philip Mulkie, Nathl Henderson, John Linord, W-Jonathan Leonard, N-Robert Irwin and T Tod, E-part of 250 ac grant, and S-Prather's Cr; and (2) part of two tracts (a) 250 ac and (b) 200 ac on Prather's Cr granted to William Clayton; border: Jonathan Lenard, Wm Parker, James Clayton, E-heirs of Edwd Arnett, S-John Daniel, W-Wm Parker, N-James Clayton and Jonathan Lenord. Witness Jonathan Lenard and Thos Tod. Signed William Clayton. Wit. oath Dec. 31, 1790 Jonathan Lenard to Wm Smith. Rec. Nov. 7, 1800

p. 107-109 Dec. 6, (not given) Henry Huff to Henry Williamson; for 80£ sold 140 ac on Prather's Cr of S side Tyger R part of two tracts (1) 250 ac and (2) 200 ac grant to William Clayton who sold to Jonathan Linard who sold to Henry Huff; border: E-Edward Arnett and part of 250 ac, N-Robert Irwin, W-James Clayton, and S-part of (1) and (2). Witness Aaron Casey and Jas Lenard. Signed Henry Huff. Wit. oath Dec. 6, 1798 Aaron Casey to Moses Casey. Rec. Nov. 10, 1800

p. 109-110 Oct. 3, 1797 Rebecah Arendell (Spartanburgh) to son Richard Arendell (Rutherford Co, NC) and Bridges Arendell (Spartanburgh); for love and affection give all her Negroes: a woman Doll about 36 years old, boy Morris about 11 years old, boy George 5 years old, boy Luke 5 years old, and all goods and chattles in dwelling house of Rebecah Arendell; Condition: Oct. 3, 1797 Rebecah has above Negroes and goods for her lifetime and afterwards to be equally divided between Richard and Bridges Arendell (signed Richard and Bridges Arendell). Witness Saml Sarratt and William Morgan. Signed Rebecah Arendell. Wit. oath Oct. 12, 1797 William Morgan to H McCray. Rec. Nov. 10, 1800

p. 110-112 Apr. 15, 1799 Thomas Foster (Spartanburgh) to Mark Swadly (same); for 200£ sold 180 ac on S side of Road; part of grant to Elisha Ford then bordering all vacant land on both sides Ridge Road between Tygar R and Fairforrest Cr; where Mark Swadly lives. Witness David Cook and William Cook. Signed Thomas Foster's mark. Wit. oath Aug. 3, 1799 William Cook to I Harrison. Rec.

Nov. 10, 1800

p. 112-114 Jul. 23, 1795 Charles Hide (Spartanburgh) to Daniel David (same); for 25£ sterling sold 50 ac; S part of 158 ac grant Feb. 5, 1787 to John Williams on branch of Tygar R. Witness James Waldrop, John Ward, and Jesse Crook. Signed Charles Hide's mark. Wit. oath Feb. 29, 1796 James Waldrop to Ism Foster. Rec. Nov. 11, 1800

p. 114-115 Dec. 12, 1793 Samuel Colley (Spartanburgh) to Thomas Stone (same); for 40£ sterling sold 108 ac; border: Seiward (or Seeward) and Duncan; N part of 158 ac grant Feb. 5, 1787 to John Williams on branch of Tyger R. Witness James Crook, Charles Hide, and John McCord. Signed Samuel Colley's mark. Wit. oath Jan. 29, 1793 Charles Hide to Zadock Ford. Rec. Nov. 12, 1800

p. 115-116 Mar. 21, 1800 William Traylor (Spartanburgh) to Isaac Snoddy (same); for $250 sold 143 ac; part of 193 ac on E branch of Middle Tygar R sold by Thomas Collins to William Traylor; border: Randolph Johnson and Bough. Witness John Traylor and Jesse Cooper. Signed William Traylor and Mary's mark. Wit. oath Mar. 24, 1800 Jesse Cooper to Drury McDaniel. Rec. Nov. 12, 1800

p. 116-117 Mar. 1, 1800 John Sutherlin (Spartanburgh) to William Morrow (same); for 30£ sterling sold 100 ac; on both sides of Horse Cr of Broad R; part of 300 ac grant Jan. 1, 1787 States Office to Joseph Warren and sold by Nathaniel Pacace (or Perrace) to John Sutherlin. Witness Nathan Byars, Jno Bonner, and David Paris. Signed John Sutherlin. Wit. oath May 10, 1800 David Paris to Geo Lamkin. Rec. Nov. 13, 1800

p. 117-118 Jan. 31, 1800 John White (Spartanburgh) to Moses Foster (same); for $45 sold 37 ac and 144 ac on waters Henry's Br of Kelsy's Cr on Rich Hill; border of 37 ac: Golightly, Simpson, and Thomas; border of 144 ac: Tilly Buffington, Simpson, and Thomas; part of 347 ac grant Sept. 3, 1798 but an "old survey" takes 166 ac away from middle and leaves 37 ac on waters of Henry's Br and Kelsy's Cr near the narrow passage and 144 ac on Henry's Br and waters of Fairforrest Cr on E side of Rich Hill. Witness Jas Smith and John Foster. Signed John White. Wit. oath Feb. 5, 1800 John Foster to I Harrison. Rec. Nov. 13, 1800. Dower renounced Agnes White to I Harrison Apr. 5, 1800

p. 118-119 Mar. 7, 1797 John Waldrop (Spartanburgh) to Rachel Dickson (same); for 20£ sterling sold 120 ac; N part of a "tract"; border: Daniel Rogers' land that is also part of same "tract"; where John Waldrop lives. Witness Thomas Stone, Daniel Rogers, and John Anderson Everton. Signed John Waldrop's mark. Wit. oath Oct. 25, 1800 Daniel Rogers to Tho Moore. Rec. Nov. 13, 1800

p. 119-120 Oct. 29, 1800 Solomon Crocker (Spartanburgh) to Thomas Wells (same); for $150 sold 100 ac on Lawson's fork of Pacolet R; border: Pool's old IronWorks, Robertson, Tackwell, Thompson, and Thomas Wells. Witness Jas Smith and Francis Mason. Signed Solomon Crocker's mark. Wit. oath Oct. 29, 1800 Jas Smith to James Jordan. Rec. Nov. 14, 1800

p. 120-121 Apr. 22, 1797 David McDowell (Spartanburgh) to James McDowel (same); for 20£ sterling sold 200 ac on branches of S Pacolate R; grant "state" to David McDowell; David "reserves" a moiety of the 200 ac above N side of Rockey Br. Witness Capt William Anderson and John Clark. Signed David McDowell. Wit. oath Oct. 28, 1800 William Anderson to Ism Foster. Rec. Nov. 15, 1800

p. 121-122 Feb. 1, 1800 Ezechial Howard (Union Co) to Thomas Reed

(Spartanburgh); for $65 sold 200 ac on head branches of Gocher's Cr and Green's Cr. Witness Jonathan Davis and Ann Briant. Signed Ezekiel Howard's mark. Wit. oath Apr. 5, 1800 Jonathan Davis to John Lipscomb. Rec. Nov. 17, 1800

p. 122-123 Oct. 28, 1800 Robert Dunaway (Spartanburgh) to Edward Smith (same); for $80 sold 84½ ac; part of 400 ac grant to John Headon on both sides Thickety Cr "near head of same tract"; Witness David Jones and William Austell. Signed Robert Dunnaway. Wit. oath Oct. 28, 1800 David Jones to H McCray. Rec. Nov. 17, 1800

p. 123-124 Aug. 18, 1794 John Sarratt (Spartanburgh) to John Byras (or Byros) (same); for 30£ sterling sold 100 ac on W side Broad R; lower half of grant Nov. 14, 1771 Gov. Josiah Martin (NC) to Samuel Sarratt; an acre reserved for "the grave". Witness James Byros, John Bryas, and John Grist. Signed John Sarratt. Wit. oath Apr. 23, 1796 John Byras to H McCray. Rec. Nov. 18, 1800

p. 124-125 Aug. 8, 1800 Thomas Pruett (Spartanburgh) to William Pruett (same); for 20£ sterling sold 50 ac on Molley's Cr of Tygar R; half of 100 ac grant Mar. 5, 1787 Gov. Thomas Pinckney to Thomas Pruett. Witness Samuel Pruett and John Grist. Signed Thomas Pruett's mark. Wit. oath (Union Co) Oct. 8, 1800 Samuel Pruett to John Martindale. Rec. Nov. 18, 1800. Dower renounced (Union Co) Sarah Pruett to John Martindale Oct. 8, 1800

p. 125-126 May 15, 1800 Jacob Ortner (Union Co) to Burrell Bobo (Spartan Co); for $200 sold 100 ac; border: Burrell Bobo, Charles Holt, Robert Wallace desc, and Daniel Langston. Witness Daniel Palmer, Benj Grist, and Richard Palmer. Signed Jacob Ortner's mark. Wit. oath Oct. 24, 1800 (Union Co) Richard Palmer to John Martindale. Rec. Nov. 18, 1800. Dower renounced (Union Co) Phebe Ortner to John Martindale Oct. 24, 1800

p. 126-127 Aug. 7, 1800 Joshua Betterton (Spartanburgh) to Samuel Pruett (same); for 20£ sterling sold 70 ac on Dutchman's Cr of Tygar R; border: S-Joseph Butterton and William Grant, E-Mills Sumner and Dudley Wooten, W-Dutchman's Cr; part of 350 ac grant Apr. 21, 1774 to Thomas Butterton desc. Witness William Pruett and Daniel Palmer. Signed Joshua Betterton's mark. Wit. oath (Union Co) Oct. 8, 1800 William Pruett to John Martindale. Rec. Nov. 19, 1800. Dower renounced (Union Co) Cassa Butterton to John Martindale Oct. 8, 1800

p. 127-129 Aug. 7, 1800 Daniel Palmer (Union Co) to Samuel Pruett (Spartanburgh); for 60£ sterling sold 50 ac on Dutchman's Cr of Tygar R; part of 350 ac grant Apr. 21, 1774 to Thomas Betterton desc; border: line between James and Joshua Betterton made by Samuel Lancaster esq and James Betterton's Spring Br. Witness William Pruett and Joshuaway Betterton. Signed Daniel Palmer. Wit. oath (Union Co) Oct. 8, 1800 William Pruett to John Martindale. Rec. Nov. 19, 1800. Dower renounced (Union Co) Elizabeth Palmer to John Martindale Oct. 8, 1800

p. 129-130 Nov. 13, 1790 Jesse Temple (Carren (sic) Co, Ky) to Charles Morgan (Spartanburgh); for $666 2/3 SC money sold 420 ac on both sides Little Cherokee Cr; border: Bonner; grant 1784 to Jesse Temple and survey by George Salmon. Witness John Arendell and John Cooper. Signed Jesse Temple. Wit. oath Aug. 19, 1800 John Arendell to H McCray. Rec. Nov. 21, 1800

p. 130-131 Sept. 8, 1796 Thomas Gillenwaters (Spartanburgh) to William Morris (same); for 85£ sterling sold 232½ ac on S side Goochies Cr; part (sic) of 200 ac survey 1769 for John Dennard. Witness James Simmons and Griffen Carter. Signed Thomas Gillenwaters and Molley's mark. Wit. oath Sept. 15, 1796 James Simmons to John Lipscomb. Rec. Nov. 21, 1800

p. 131-132 Jun. 3, 1800 Joseph Barnett and wife Lucy (Spartanburgh) to Anthony Bates (same); for $95 sold 100 ac on waters of Richland Cr of Pacolate R; part of a survey for David Lewis; border: the Ironworks and Golightly, Pinckney Rd, and near "place known by the Indian Graves"; where Anthony Bates lives. Witness Joroyal Barnett and Joseph Barnett jr. Signed Joseph Barnett and Lucy's mark. Wit. oath Oct. 13, 1800 Joroyal Barnett to I Harrison. Rec. Nov. 21, 1800

p. 132-133 Jul. 14, 1800 James Morris (Edgefield Co) to John Morris (Spartanburgh); for $100 sold 70 ac of which 50 ac was granted May 22, 1772 States Office to John Kirconnell on Buck Cr of Pacolate R; border: James Morris and John Morris; and 20 ac of which was part of grant Oct. 6, 1788 States Office to William Morris sr; border: James Morris. Witness William Connelley, George Gilbert, and John Bankson. Signed James Morris' mark. Wit. oath Oct. 27, 1800 William Connelley to Wm McDowell. Rec. Nov. 22, 1800

p. 133-134 Oct. 17, 1800 William Rich (Spartanburgh) to Vincent Wyatt (same); for $24 sold 40 ac on S side Pacolet R; part of grant Dec. 3, 1787 States Office to Jesse Connell. Witness Reuben Warren and Zachariah Wyatt. Signed William Rich's mark. Wit. oath Oct. 29, 1800 William Rich to I Harrison. Rec. Nov. 22, 1800

p. 134-135 Oct. 28, 1800 John Gowen (Spartanburgh) to James McDowell (same); for 50£ sterling sold 250 ac on branches of S Pacolate R and Lawson's fork; grant States Office to James Rutherford and sold Jan. 19, 1793 to Maj John Gowen. Witness William Anderson CDS and Robert McDowell. Signed Jno Gowen. Wit. oath Oct. 28, 1800 Maj John Gowen to Ism Foster. Rec. Nov. 24, 1800

p. 135-136 Oct. 5, 1797 John Jackson (Knox Co, Tenn) to Zacheriah Leathewood (Spartanburgh); for $450 sold 200 ac on James' Cr of Tygar R; part of 400 ac grant Apr. 2, 1773 to Joseph Brown and sold by heir-at-law William Brown to John Jackson; other part of grant now owned by Nathaniel Woodruff; border: S-Richd Chesney, E-John Kighler, N-Susanna Taylor, and W-Nathl Woodruff. Witness Thos Tod and Isaac Crow. Signed John Jackson. Wit. oath Jan. 22, 1799 Isaac Crow to Aaron Casey. Rec. Nov. 24, 1800

p. 136-137 Sept. 19, 1797 William Brown (Winton Co) to John Jackson (Knox Co, Tenn); for 5£ sold all rights to 200 ac tract on Jamey's Cr of Tygar R; half of 400 ac grant to William Brown's father and sold to Joseph Erwin who sold to James Erwin who sold to John Jackson "but Lecri (or Lere) never proved to each other"; William Brown now assigns his rights to land. Witness Daniel McMurphy and Thomas Proctor. Signed William Brown. Wit. oath Sept. 19, 1797 (Orangeburgh Dist) Daniel McMurphy to W Bunbar. Rec. Nov. 25, 1800

p. 137-138 Mar. 20, 1800 Richard Pace (Spartanburgh) to William Traylor (Spartanburgh); for $250 sold 60 ac; part of grant to John McElhonny on S side of N fork Tyger R; border: Leech, John D Young, and McElhenny. Witness Isaac Snoddy, John Pace, and John Traylor. Signed Richard Pace. Wit. oath Apr. 26, 1800 Isaac Snoddy to Ism Foster. Rec. Nov. 25, 1800

p. 138-139 Mar. 20, 1800 John Pace (Spartanburgh) to William Traylor (same); for $250 sold 40 ac; part of grant to Frances Dodds on S side of N fork Tygar R; border: McElhenny. Witness Isaac Snoddy, John Traylor, and Richard Pace. Signed John Pace. Wit.

oath Apr. 26, 1800 Isaac Snoddy to Ism Foster. Rec. Nov. 25, 1800

p. 139-140 Jan. 1, 1800 James McDowell to William Lewis (Spartanburgh); for 50£ sold 200 ac on both sides Lawson's fork of Pacolet R near the head including Redman's improvements; border: all vacant; surveyed in 1784. Witness Wm Anderson CDS and John Clark. Signed James McDowell. Wit. oath Aug. 11, 1800 Wm Anderson to William McDowell. Rec. Nov. 26, 1800

p. 140-141 Aug. 7, 1800 Robert McDowell (Spartanburgh) to William Lewis (same); for 80£ sterling sold 200 ac; on N side of 500 ac grant to Francis Ross on waters of Lawson's fork of Pacolet R; border: John Lackey and William Foster. Witness John Anderson esq, James Galt, and William Kelso. Signed Robert McDowell. Wit. oath Aug. 11, 1800 John Anderson to Wm McDowell. Rec. Nov. 26, 1800

p. 141-143 Dec. 2, 1800 Jesse Page (Spartanburgh) to children Neetty, William, Nancy, Michael, Jesse jr, and Betsey Page; for love and affection give all his goods and chattels in "my present" dwelling house, goods which he has given children before signing this, and 20 hogs, 5 cattle, 2 horses kind creatures and all corn and fodder and tobacco and all property. Witness Michael B Roberds, Daniel Rogers, and William Cox. Signed Jesse Page's mark. Wit. oath Dec. 4, 1800 Michael B Roberds to Drury McDaniel. Rec. Dec. 23, 1800

p. 143-144 Dec. 20, 1797 James Robinson jr (Lancaster Co) to James Robinson sr (same); for 50£ SC money sold 100 ac on waters of Pacolet R; sold Mar. 15, 1788 by Reubin Lawson to James Robinson. Witness Wm Robinson, John Hammett, and Marget Robinson. Signed James Robinson. Wit. oath Jan. 10, 1798 Wm Robinson to I Harrison. Rec. Feb. 6, 1801

p. 144-146 Jan. 9, 1801 Benjamin Clark (Spartanburgh) to Mary Davis (same); for 10£ sterling sold 300 ac on both sides N fork Tygar R; above Joseph Jones' land. Witness Joshua Hunt, John Davis jr and Isham Burks. Signed Benjm Clark. Wit. oath Jan. 10, 1801 Isham Burks to James Jordan. Rec. Jan. 12, 1801

p. 146-147 Jan. 17, 1799 (Union Co) John Fincher (Union Co) to Samson Bobo; for (money not mentioned) sold 200 ac on Lyhas Cr of Enoree R; grant to Jesse Dodd who sold Nov. 15, 1791 to John Fincher. Witness Burrell Bobo, Fredrick Jackson, and Sollomon Bobo. Signed John Fincher's mark. Wit. oath Jan. 6, 1801 Burrell Bobo to I Harrison. Rec. Jan. 13, 1801

p. 147-148 May 27, 1797 Charles Whitten sr (Spartanburgh) to James Southerland (same); for 125£ sterling sold 300 ac--200 ac for value received and 100 ac as a gift; on branch of Furgeson Cr; border: N-vacant, E-Enoch Floyd sr, S-vacant, and W-vacant; 300 ac grant Dec. 4, 1770 to Thomas Sexton who sold Jul. 17, 1784 to Charles Whitten sr, Witness John Duncan, William Parker, and Janney Parker. Signed Charles Whitten sr. Wit. oath May 13, 1798 John Duncan to George Bruton. Rec. Jan. 17, 1801

p. 148-149 Feb. 13, 1799 Samuel Busey (Spartanburgh) to Jonas Lenard (same); for 10 silver dollars sold 140 ac; part of 414 ac grant to Samuel Busey on branches of Ben's Cr of Tygar R. Witness Townley Redfern, James Wofford, and Stephen Raines. Signed Samuel Busey's mark. Wit. oath Dec. 16, 1800 Stephen Raines to Drury McDaniel. Rec. Jan. 17, 1801

p. 149-151 Feb. 13, 1799 Samuel Busey (Spartanburgh) to William Beacham (same); for 10 silver dollars sold 100 ac; part of 414 ac grant to Samuel Busey on branches of Ben's Cr of Tygar R.

Witness Jonas Lenard, James Wofford, and Stephen Rains. Signed Samuel Busey's mark. Wit. oath Dec. 16, 1800 Jonas Lenard to Drury McDaniel. Rec. Jan. 20, 1801

p. 151-152 Feb. 13, 1799 Samuel Busey (Spartanburgh) to Stephen Raines (same); for 100 silver dollars sold 174 ac; part of 414 ac grant to Samuel Busey on branches of Ben's Cr of Tygar R. Witness James Wofford, Townley Redfern, and Jonas Lenard. Signed Samuel Busey's mark. Wit. oath Dec. 16, 1800 Jonas Lenard to Drury McDaniel. Rec. Jan. 20, 1801

p. 152-153 Dec. 27, 1800 William Duncan (Spartanburgh) to John Massey (same); for $340 sold 60 ac on S side of S Tygar R; border: Thomas Stone. Witness David Anderson, James Duncan, and Rosannah Brodway. Signed William and Ruth Duncan's marks. Wit. oath Dec. 29, 1800 David Anderson to Drury McDaniel. Rec. Jan. 20, 1801

p. 153-155 Oct. 18, 1800 John Durham (Spartanburgh) to Jonas Lenard (same); for 35£ sterling sold 40 ac on waters of Ben's Cr of Tygar R; part of grant to Henry Coon; border: John Durham, Brushy Fork, Aron(?) Moore, and Anderson. Witness William Beacham and Drury Reins. Signed John Durham. Wit. oath Dec. 16, 1800 William Beacham to Drury McDaniel. Rec. Jan. 20, 1801

p. 155-157 Dec. 10, 1798 Alexander Evins and wife Elizabeth, William McElrath and wife Mary, and Mary Patton (all Spartanburgh) to William Beacham (same); for $300 sold 300 ac on both sides Ben's Cr of Tygar R; below old Indian Boundary; grant Jan. 21, 1785 Gov. Benjamin Guerard to John Patton. Witness Jonas Lenard, John McCord, and John Patton. Signed Alexr Evins, Elizabeth's mark, William McElrath, Mary's mark, and Mary Patton's mark. Wit. oath Dec. 16, 1800 Jonas Lenard to Drury McDaniel. Rec. Jan. 21, 1801

p. 157-159 Aug. 7, 1797 John Durham (Spartanburgh) to Jonas Lenard (same); for 35£ sterling sold 150 ac on fork of Ben's Cr of Tygar R; border: David Anderson. Witness William Beacham, Elijah Johnson, and George Durham. Signed John Durham. Wit. oath Dec. 16, 1800 William Beacham to Drury McDaniel. Rec. Jan. 21, 1801

p. 159 Jan. 17, 1801 Mary Hutchins received from Elisha Smith "full satisfaction" concerning the maintainance of her child for which Mary Hutchins had "proceeded against Elisha Smith. Witness William Smith. Signed Mary Hutchins' mark. Wit. oath Jan. 18, 1801 William Smith to I Harrison. Rec. Jan. 21, 1801

p. 159-161 Nov. 19, 1799 Jane McClurkin (Spartanburgh) to Paul Castelberry (same); for $200 sold 100 ac on Jamey Cr; border: N-John King, E-Margaret Dunmore (or Dinsmore), S-Teseor (or Tesior) Kirk, W-Charles Bragg; grant May 2, 1785 Gov. William Moultrie to Jane McClurkin. Witness James Allen and Samuel Woodruff. Signed Jane McClurkin's mark. Wit. oath Jan. 15, 1801 Samuel Woodruff to George Bruton. Rec. Jan. 22, 1801

p. 161-162 Feb. 23, 1799 Shadrah Waldrop sr (Spartanburgh) to sons Shadrah, Ely, and Ira Waldrop; for good causes give all his land where he lives except about 30 ac that Col Waters laid out for Thomas Farrow at upper end of tract; border: Thomas Farrow; and give a piece of land bought from Thomas Farrow on lower side of first tract suppose to be 31 ac; border: Thomas Farrow. Witness Thomas Farrow, Emily Harrison, and Mary Harrison. Signed Shadrah Waldrop sr's mark. Wit. oath (Laurens Dist) Dec. 8, 1800 Emily Harrison to Starling Tucker. Rec. Jan. 22, 1801

p. 162-164 Mar. 21, 1799 William Moore and wife Elizabeth (Spartanburgh) to George Isham (same); for 250 Spanish milled dollars sold 104 ac on S side of N fork Tygar R; border: Michael Barrett; part of 332 ac grant May 1, 1796 South Carolina governor to Samuel Ford who sold to John Ford who sold Mar. 15, 1799 to William Moore. Witness Absolom Blundett and Thos Moore JQ. Signed William Moore and Elizabeth's mark. Rec. Jan. 26, 1801

p. 164-165 Apr. 23, 1773 Thomas McCroy (Spartanburgh) to Alexander Alexander (same); for 10£ sterling sold 65 ac on small branch of Two Mile Cr of Enoree R; border: Joseph Barrett and Pamely; N part of 640 ac grant Jun. 5, 1786 to William Barrett. Witness Aaron Casey and John Anderson. Signed Thomas McCrory. Wit. oath Mar. (sic) 24, 1801 Aaron Casey and John Anderson to Absolom Lancaster. Rec. Jan. 17, 1801

p. 165-166 Jan. 28, 1801 William Smith (Charleston Dist) to Joshua Smith (Franklin Co, NC); for $1,500 sold 1,000 ac on Beaverdam Cr of Fairforrest Cr and waters of Mill Cr of Tygar R; grant Jul. 8, 1774 to Samuel Granville. Witness Jas Smith and John Cantwell. Signed W Smith. Wit. oath Jan. 28, 1801 Jas Smith to A Lancaster. Rec. Jan. 28, 1801

p. 166-167 Sept. 30, 1800 Henry Wells (Spartanburgh) to John Cantwell (same); for $300 sold 160 ac on branches of Fords Cr of Beaverdam Cr of Fairforrest Cr. Witness Jas Smith and Wm Smith. Signed Henry Wells. Wit. oath Oct. 12, 1800 Jas Smith to Geor Lamkin. Rec. Jan. 29, 1801

p. 167-168 Oct. 23, 1799 Joseph Davice (Green Co, Tenn) to William Rich (Spartanburgh); for $130 sold 200 ac on S side Pacolet R; part of grant to Jesse Comrell (or Connell or Comsell) who sold to Joseph Davice; border: Aaron Templeman. Witness Robert Armour and Zacheriah Wyatt. Signed Joseph Davice's mark. Wit. oath Oct. 29, 1800 Vincent Wyatt (sic) to I Harrison. Rec. Feb. 3, 1801

p. 168-169 Oct. 16, 1799 Lafonte to Charles Berry (Spartanburgh); for $500 sold Negro boy Peter age 16 years old and girl 16 years old (not named); Witness John Barry. Signed Lafonte. Wit. oath Jan. 2, 1801 John Barry to Thos Moore. Rec. Feb. 4, 1801

p. 169-170 Feb. 8, 1800 Charles Barry to Isaac Snoddy; for $350 sold a Negro boy Peter. Witness Andrew Barry and Andrew Coan. Signed Charles Barry. Wit. oath Jan. 2, 1801 Andrew Barry to Thos Moore. Rec. Feb. 4, 1801

p. 170-171 Oct. 18, 1799 John Tolleson (Spartanburgh) to Thomas Deen (same); for 50£ sterling sold 230 ac on S side Pacolet R; border: Jacob Hombres, Ross, John Stone, and Shole Br; part of two tracts. Witness John Poole and George McCarter. Signed John Tolleson. Wit. oath Oct. 19, 1799 John Poole to William Simpson. Rec. Feb. 12, 1801

p. 171-172 Oct. 19, 1799 John Lemaster (Spartanburgh) to Thomas Deen (same); for $200 sold 150 ac on waters of Pacolet R; border: Whitter and Crocker; part of three tracts granted to "departed persons". Witness John Tolleson and George McCarter. Signed John Lemaster. Wit. oath Oct. 19, 1799 John Tolleson to William Simpson. Rec. Feb. 13, 1801

p. 172-174 Nov. 6, 1800 Thomas Bearden (Spartanburgh) to Benjamin Nichols (same); for $141 sold 70½ ac on S side Dutchman's Cr; border: S & W-Samuel Morrow and Ephrain Mills (or Hills) and Thomas Bearden, S-Thomas Bearden, and N-Benjamin Peaks; plat attached. Witness Wilie Williford and Levi Lancaster. Signed Thos Bordun. Wit. oath Nov. 6, 1800 Wilie Williford and Levi Lancaster to Saml Lancaster. Rec. Feb. 14, 1801. Dower renounced Abigal (or Abesila)

Bearden to Wm Smith Nov. 10, 1800

p. 174-175 Feb. 3, 1801 Aaron Land (Spartanburgh) to Anthoney Bates (same); for $40 sold 60 ac on Henry's Br of Fairforrest Cr; border: W-Golightly, N-Samuel McCleth, E-Joseph Ash, and SE-Richard Cruse. Witness Muse Tollison and Christopher Golightly. Signed Aaron Land's mark. Wit. oath Feb. 6, 1801 Christopher Golightly to William Simpson. Rec. Feb. 16, 1801

p. 175-176 May 15, 1800 Richard Lee (Spartanburgh) to John Lee (same); for $400 sold 100 ac on Cherokee Cr; border: land formerly Richard Lee's; part of 2,100 ac grant Apr. 2, 1787 to James Stedman who sold to Richard Lee; border: John Bruckshuer, Bazel Scot, Aaron Templeman, and James Scoot. Witness James Lee and Elizah Mackbee. Signed Richard Lee. Wit. oath Jan. 18, 1801 Elijah Mackbee to William Simpson. Rec. Feb. 25, 1800

p. 176-177 May 15, 1800 Richard Lee(Spartanburgh) to John Lee (same); for $400 sold 100 ac on S side Pacolet R and both sides Cherokee Cr and both sides of Waggon Rd from Cotten Ford on Pacolet R to old Iron works on Lawson's fork; border: Sollomon Abbet, Edward Ballenger, and James Stedman. Witness James Lee and Elijah Macbee. Signed Richard Lee. Wit. oath Jan. 18, 1801 Elijah Mackbee to William Simpson. Rec. Feb. 25, 1801

p. 177-179 Sept. 25, 1800 Richard Barnett (Spartanburgh) to William Lancaster (same); for 75£ sold 167 ac on S side Fairforrest Cr and both sides Tates Br; where Richard Barnett lives; border: Veal and Henry ONaol. Witness Elizabeth Shends and Nathan Veal. Signed Richd Barnett. Wit. oath Feb. 12, 1801 Nathan Veal to I Harrison. Rec. Mar. 18, 1801. Dower renounced Susannah Barnett to I Harrison Jun. (sic) 24, 1800

p. 179-180 Jun. 10, 1800 John Hill (Spartanburgh) to Daniel McKee; for $100 sold a bay "guilden"; horse was left with Samuel Bellenslee on Holeson R 7 miles above Long Islands to be fattened for $9; same horse John Sims "made a race on" last fall at Mr Joseph in Spartanburgh Co; Samuel Bellenslee or whoever has the horse is requested to give it to Daniel McKee when "he" is paid $9. Witness Britn Williford. Signed John Hill's mark. Wit. oath Mar. 24, 1801 Britn Williford to Thomas Moore. Rec. Mar. 25, 1801

p. 180-181 Dec. 15, 1800 Samuel Nesbet and wife Nancy (Spartanburgh) to Hosea Camp (same); for money not mentioned sold 200 ac; sale "according to contract made with James Jordan esq"; grant "No. grant" to Samuel Nesbet on waters of N fork Tyger R. Witness John Robnett, Thomas Penny, and James Clowney. Signed Samuel and Nancy Neisbett. Wit. oath Feb. 20, 1801 Thomas Penny to James Jordan. Rec. Mar. 31, 1801

p. 181-182 Mar. 14, 1801 John Gray (Spartanburgh) to John Fredric Harmening (same); for $200 bond sold Negro woman Sarah about 35 years old; bond void if John pays John F Harmening $200 by Mar. 14, 1803. Witness Wm Steward and Wm Ranwater. Signed John Gray. Wit. oath Mar. 20, 1801 Wm Stewart to Aaron Casey. Rec. Mar. 31, 1801

p. 182-184 Sept. 13, 1800 Abram Markley, merchant (Charleston, SC) to William Wood (Rutherford Co, NC); for $360 sold 360 ac on waters of Thickety Cr and Broad R; border: SE-John Wade. Witness Richard Thomson and Obadh Watson. Signed William Poole agent for Abram Markley. Wit. oath Mar. 16, 1801 Obadh Watson to George Lamkin. Rec. Mar. 31, 1801

p. 184-185 Nov. 29, 1799 Jesse Spann (Union Co) to Thomas B Hunt (same); for $300 sold 200 ac on Cedar Shoal Cr; known as Banyan's old place on head branch of Jemmey's Cr. Witness Solomon Spann and Absalom Bobo. Signed Jesse Spann. Wit. oath Feb. 19, 1800 Solomon Spann to John Martindale. Rec. Apr. 1, 1801

p. 185-186 Oct. 8, 1800 Benjamin Jones (Leviston (sic) Co, KY) to Michael Miller (same); for $80 sold 228 ac on branch of S fork of N fork Tygar R; grant Oct. 3, 1785 Gov. William Moultrie to (not given). Witness John Montgomery, James Renolds, and James Edington. Signed Benjamin Jones. Wit. oath Mar. 24, 1801 John Montgomery to Drury McDaniel. Rec. Apr. 1, 1801

p. 186-189 Oct. 18, 1800 William West and wife Susanah (Spartanburgh) to Zacheriah Wingo (same); for $80 SC money sold 50 ac; border: a line formerly between Thomas Hays and son William Hays, Fairforrest Cr, and Benson. Witness Isham Foster, Joshua Hawkins, and William Lewis. Signed William West's mark. Certified Oct. 18, 1800 by Isham Foster. Rec. Apr. 2, 1801

p. 189-190 Apr. 14, 1800 Isham Foster (Spartanburgh) to John Wingo (same); for $100 sold 240 ac on waters Lawson's fork of Pacolet R; grant Gov. Benjamin Guerard to Isham Foster; except part taken by old survey sold to Rowland Johnson (quantity unknown). Witness Wm Foster and John James. Signed Ism Foster. Wit. oath Oct. 29, (not given) John James to James Jordan. Rec. Apr. 2, 1801

p. 190 Jul. 17, 1800 Dan Gilbert sr and wife Molley (Spartanburgh) to John Gilbert (same); for 20£ sterling sold 70 ac; border: N & W-Dan Gilbert and S-Sam Gilbert; part of 514 ac grant to Thos Barton and sold to Wm Barton and sold to Dan Gilbert; on S side Pacolet R below the fork. Witness Daniel Bennett, George Horton, and Mary Gilbert. Signed Dan Gilbert sr and Molley's mark. Wit. oath Aug. 5, 1800 Daniel Bennett to Wm McDowell. Rec. Apr. 2, 1801

p. 190-191 Nov. 6, 1799 John Morrow (Spartanburgh) to John Cantrell (same); for 20£ SC money sold 125 ac; border: Sollomon Abbett; part of 534 ac grant to Wm Dickson on S side Pacolet R. Witness John E Morrow, Mary Morrow, and Elizabeth Morrow. Signed John Morrow. Wit. oath Apr. 11, 1800 John E Morrow to Geor Lamkin. Rec. Apr. 2, 1801

p. 191-192 Dec. 6, 1800 John Dill (Spartanburgh) to Richard Robertson; for $200 sold 200 ac on waters of Cherokee Cr; border: Gibson, Wm Reckman, Beuton, and Bostick. Witness Danl McCray and Jesse Fondrin. Signed John Dill's mark. Wit. oath Dec. 22, 1800 Danl McCray to H McCray. Rec. Apr. 3, 1801

p. 192-193 Oct. 3, 1797 Rebekah Arendell (Spartanburgh) to Richard Arendell (Rutherford Co, NC); for 22£ 16s 1p sold a Negro boy Jacob 16 years old. Witness Readick Arendell and Saml Sarratt. Signed Rebekah Arendell's mark. Wit. oath Jan. 11, 1798 Readick Arendell to H McCray. Rec. Apr. 3, 1801

p. 193-195 Jan. 16, 1801 James Vernon (Spartanburgh) to Thomas McKnight (same); for $50 sold 62 ac on waters of N Pacolet R; border: George Allexander and Hugh McMillin; grant Jan. 1, 1787 to William Frence. Witness James Templeton and Hugh McMillin. Signed James Vernon. Wit. oath Jan. 16, 1801 Hugh McMillin to James Jordan. Rec. Apr. 3, 1801

p. 195-196 Feb. 19, 1801 Nathaniel Wofford (Spartanburgh) to Micajah Purvis (same); for $35 sold 40 ac on branch of Dildines Cr of Enoree R; border: Samuel Woodruff, Page, Wm Stoutten, and Hagus; grant Jun. 4, 1798 to Nathaniel Wofford. Witness Joseph Woodruff and Nat Woodruff. Signed Nathaniel Wofford. Wit. oath Mar. 24,

1801 Joseph Woodruff to John Anderson. Rec. Apr. 3, 1801

p. 196-197 Mar. 8, 1800 John Cross (Spartanburgh) to Jos Woodruff (same); for $200 sold 100 ac on branch of Enoree R; border: SW-William Stonttanburgh, N-Samuel Pedan, and others vacant; grant Jun. 3, 1773 Lt Gov William Bull to Normon Dildine. Witness William Earnest, James Allen, and Thomas Woodruff III. Signed John Cross' mark. Wit. oath Mar. 3, 1801 Thomas Woodruff III to Ism Foster. Rec. Apr. 6, 1801

p. 197-199 Nov. 17, 1800 John Dickson jr (NC) to William Easley (SC); for $1,500 sold 600 ac on S fork Pacolet R; includes Hukkin's cabin; grant Dec. 23, 1768 Gov. William Tryon to William Dickson. Witness John Gowen esq, Robert McDowell, and William Sanders. Signed James Dickson jr. Wit. oath Mar. 23, 1801 John Gowen esq to Samuel Lancaster. Rec. Apr. 7, 1801

p. 199-200 Aug. 4, 1800 John Lee (Spartanburgh) to Matthew Mackbee (same); for 10£ sterling sold 275 ac on branches of Pacolet R. Witness James Wofford, Ann Lee, and Richard Lee. Signed John Lee's mark. Wit. oath Mar. 23, 1801 James Wofford to Drury McDaniel. Rec. Apr. 7, 1801

p. 200-201 May 16, 1795 Robert Lee (Spartanburgh) to Mathew McAbee (same); for 10£ sterling sold 350 ac on waters of Pacolet R; grant Jul. 5, 1788 to Thomas Sabb who sold to Robert Lee. Witness James Wofford, Arthor Crocker, and John Pearce. Signed Rbt Lee. Wit. oath Mar. 23, 1801 James Wofford to Drury McDaniel. Rec. Apr. 7, 1801

p. 201-202 Jun. 6, 1799 James Wofford (Spartanburgh) to William Borough; for 5£ sterling sold 100 ac on S side Fergeson's Cr of Tygar R and on Tate's Br; deed void if William Borough sells land within 10 years. Witness Nathaniel Wofford, Sary Albrighty, and Jacob Albrighty. Signed James Wofford. Wit. oath Mar. 6, 1800 Sary Albrighty or Sary Westmoreland (sic) to Zadock Ford. Rec. Apr. 8, 1801

p. 202-203 Apr. 11, 1799 John Lipscomb (Spartanburgh) to Robert Stacey (same); for $13 sold 13 ac. Witness David Lipscomb and Griffen Carter. Signed John Lipscomb. Wit. oath Aug. 1, 1799 David Lipscomb to H McCray. Rec. Apr. 8, 1801

p. 203-204 Dec. 30, 1800 (Union Dist) Isaac Hawkins (Union Dist) to John Thornton (Spartanburgh); for 25£ sterling sold 100 ac on S side Tygar R; grant Aug. 2, 1768 Gov. William Bull to Ralph Humphreys who sold to Isaac Hawkins. Witness John Hawkins, Benjamin Hawkins, and James Crow. Signed Isaac Hawkins. Wit. oath Jan. 22, 1801 James Crow to George Brewton. Rec. Apr. 8, 1801

p. 204-206 Jul. 20, 1800 Grove Cole (Spartanburgh) to Griffen Carter (same); for $150 sold 175 ac; NW half of 350 ac grant to David Jones. Witness David Jones and Jonathan Davis. Signed Grove Cole and Elizabeth's mark. Wit. oath Aug. 2, 1800 David Jones to John Lipscomb. Rec. Apr. 9, 1801. Dower renounced Elizabeth Cole to I Harrison Mar. 2, 1801

p. 206-207 Jan. 30, 1801 John Yews (Spartanburgh) to John Simons (same); for $200 sold 200 ac on waters Fairforrest Cr; border: road from Anthoney Foster's to Giles Connell's, Reuben Daniel, and Wild Cat Br. Witness I Harrison JQ. Signed John Yews' mark. Certified Jan. 30, 1801 by I Harrison. Rec. Apr. 9, 1801. Dower renounced Lettice Yews to I Harrison Feb. 9, 1801

p. 207-209 Jan. 2, 1801 Abel Lewis (Rutherford Co, NC), schoolmaster,

Isaiah Lewis (Greenville Co), Ephraim Lewis, Peggy Lewis, Polley Boley, widow (Spartan Dist) to George Lewis (Spartan Dist); for a Spanish milled dollar sold 50 ac; includes Shoals and Grist Mill except a rood square which includes graves of "our" father and mother on S side of "the Hill"; E half of 100 ac grant Oct. 6, 1767 Gov. William Tryon (NC) to Peter Lewis. Witness Abel A Lewis, Peter Lewis, and Polley Beaver. Signed Ab Lewis, Isaiah Lewis, Ephriam Lewis, Peggy Lewis, and Polly Boly. Wit. oath Jan. 24, 1801 "Peggy" (sic) to Ism Foster. Rec. Apr. 9, 1801

p. 209-210 Mar. 5, 1800 John Cook and David Cook (Spartanburgh) to Joseph Barnett (same); for $500 sold 450 ac on E side Fairforrest Cr and on Kelsoe's Cr; called meeting house tract; survey for Giles Connell; land warranted against all except James Smith and a corner (not exceeding 10 to 12 ac) taken by Charles James. Witness Joroyal Barnett and Elijah Barnett. Signed John and David Cook. Wit. oath Oct. 13, 1800 Joroyal Barnett to I Harrison. Rec. Apr. 13, 1801. Dower renounced Sarah Cook, wife of John, to I Harrison Feb. 28, 1801

p. 210-211 Nov. 27, 1800 Matthew Guttry (Spartanburgh) to Joseph Price (same); for 100£ sold 100 ac; lower part of 200 ac on both sides Thickety Cr granted Apr. (not given), 1786 Gov. William Moultrie to Matthew Guttry. Witness Frederick Guttey, Shadreck Gutry, and William Hearn (or Heam). Signed Matthew Gutry and Elizabeth's mark. Wit. oath Feb. 7, 1801 Frederick Guttey to John Lipscomb. Rec. Apr. 14, 1801

p. 211-213 Nov. 4, 1798 John and William Braly (Rowan Co, NC) to James Wofford (Spartanburgh); for 125£ sterling sold 300 ac on waters of McElevain's Cr and Sugar Cr of Fairforrest Cr; border: all vacant; left to John and William Braly by will of their father William Braly desc who had obtained bounty patent for the land. Witness Mordicai Fowler, Thos Williams, and James Ham. Signed John and William Braly. Wit. oath Nov. 4, 1800 Mordicai Fowler to Wm Smith. Rec. Apr. 14, 1801

p. 213-214 Sept. 11, 1800 Rhoda Daffein (Spartanburgh) to John Wilson (same); for $60 sold 58 ac; border: "road near Herrican" on W end of William Lancaster's land, Nathan Veal, Col Thomas Taylor, Charles McCarter, and Thomas Smith; where John Wilson lives. Witness William Lancaster and Thomas Smith. Signed Rhoda Daffein's mark. Wit. oath Sept. 11, 1800 William Lancaster to Saml Lancaster. Rec. Apr. 15, 1801

p. 214-215 Sept. 11, 1800 William Bostick (Spartanburgh) to William Weber (same); for $333 sold 195½ ac on N side Beaverdam Cr of Thickety Cr; border: Hogan; part of two tracts: (1) grant May 15, 1772 North Carolina to John Hogin and (2) grant Sept. 18, 1785 South Carolina to Vardry McBee. Witness Joseph Adams and Thomas Philips. Signed William Bostick. Wit. oath Dec. 26, 1800 Joseph Adams to H McCray. Rec. Apr. 15, 1801

p. 215-216 Mar. 24, 1800 Thomas Hadden (Spartanburgh) to David White (same); for 24£ sterling sold 50 ac on Ben's Cr; border: Moor, John Darham, and Deny (or Deuy) Anderson; where Cary Traylor lives. Witness Curtes Gray and Cary Traylor. Signed Thomas Hadden. Wit. oath Mar. 2, 1801 Cary Traylor to Drury McDaniel. Rec. Apr. 15, 1801

p. 216-217 Nov. 7, 1800 Barnett Dempsey and wife Winiferd (Spartanburgh) to William Dempsey (same); for $150 sold 150 ac; border: Lockart and Flanagin; N part of 392 ac grant Dec. 1, 1795 to Barnett Dempsey on branch of Abner's Cr of Enoree R. Witness Absalom Blundell, William Tippins, and David Childress. Signed

Barnett and Winiferd Dempsey's marks. Wit. oath Mar. 2, 1801 Absalom Blundell to Drury McDaniel. Rec. Apr. 15, 1801

p. 217-219 Nov. 8, 1800 William Demsey and wife Betsey (Spartanburgh) to Henry House (same); for $150 sold 150 ac; border: Lockard and Flanagin; N part of 392 ac grant Dec. 1, 1795 to Barnett Demsey on branch of Abner's Cr of Enoree R. Witness Absalom Blundell, David Childress, and William Tippins. Signed William Demsey's mark and Elizabeth Demsey. Wit. oath Mar. 2, 1801 Absalom Blundell to Drury McDaniel. Rec. Apr. 17, 1801

p. 219-220 Oct. 6, 1800 Charles Morgan (Spartanburgh) to John Sarratt sr (same); for $120 sold 424 ac on W side Broad R; border: "old Rights land", Harris, Sarratt; grant Mar. 5, 1798 Gov. Charles Pinckney to Charles Morgan. Witness John Phillips, Anthony Sarratt, and Wm Carter. Signed Charles Morgan's mark. Wit. oath Oct. 16, 1800 John Phillips to H McCray. Rec. Apr. 17, 1801

p. 220-221 Nov. 10, 1800 Charles Morgan (Spartanburgh) to John Arendell jr (same); for $250 sold 100 ac on Cherokee Cr. Witness John Arendell and Benet Arendell. Signed Charles Morgan's mark. Wit. oath Nov. 29, 1800 John Arendell to H McCray. Rec. Apr. 20, 1801

p. 221-223 Dec. 5, 1789 David Neell (Spartanburgh) to Benjamin Rhodes (same); for 3£ sterling sold 200 ac; border: Danung Br, Christopher Rodes, and John Couch; part of 557 ac grant Mar. 3, 1788 Gov. Charles Pickney to David Neel on N side Enoree R. Witness John Grezsel and Christopher Rodes sr. Signed David Neell's mark. Wit. oath Fev. 15, 1794 Christopher Rodes sr to Thomas Farrow. Rec. Apr. 20, 1801

p. 223-224 Mar. 23, 1801 Edward Smith sr (Spartanburgh) to Edward Smith jr (same); for $100 sold 370 ac; border: Rock House on Bullock's fork of Thickety Cr; part of grant to Irbey Dewbery and all of grant to Edward Smith sr. Witness Reubin Smith and Holmon Smith. Signed Edwd Smith sr. Wit. oath Mar. 18, 1801 Holmon Smith to John Lipscomb. Rec. Apr. 20, 1801

p. 224-225 Oct. 4, 1799 Samuel Farrow (Spartanburgh) to William Farrow (same); for 200£ sterling sold (1) 300 ac on Tulkses Br of Enoree R; grant in 178(blank) to Samuel Farrow; where William Farrow lives; (2) 100 ac where William Farrow lives; part of 300 ac grant to Henry Hamble on N side of Cedar Shoal Cr of Enoree R; and (3) 40 ac on Cedar Shoal Cr and both sides Tulkse's Br (or Fulkse's); grant to Landon Farrow who sold to Samuel Farrow. Witness Aaron Casey and Reuben Doller. Signed S Farrow. Wit. oath Mar. 23, 1801 Aaron Casey to George Brewton. Rec. Apr. 20, 1801

p. 225-226 Mar. 13, 1801 Thomas Foster (Spartanburgh) to Joel Hurt (same); for $300 sold 100 ac on waters Fairforrest Cr; border: Ford's Cr; grant to John Ford. Witness Isham Foster, William Foster, and John Williams. Signed Thomas Foster's mark. Certified Mar. 13, 1801 by Isham Foster. Rec. Apr. 21, 1801

p. 226-228 Mar. 13, 1801 Thomas Foster (Spartanburgh) to William Foster (same); for $500 sold 253 ac on waters Fairforrest Cr; border: Thomas Foster's Spring, Underwood, Ford, Gibs' old line, Barnett, mouth of Beaverdam Cr, and Fords upper Cr; grant to John Ford. Witness Ism Foster, Joel Hurt, and John Williams. Signed Thomas Foster's mark. Certified (Mar?) 13, 1801 by Ism Foster. Rec. Apr. 21, 1801

p. 228-229 Mar. 12, 1799 (Union Co) William Haney (Union Co) to Jonathan Cud (same); for $140 sold 640 ac on Back Br of

Buck Cr of Pacolet R; grant Oct. 6, 1788 States Office to William Dotton. Witness James Foster, John Bailey, and Aberam Haney. Signed William Haney's mark. Wit. oath (Union Co) Apr. 9, 1799 James Foster to Wm McCulloch. Rec. Apr. 21, 1801

p. 229-230 Mar. 13, 1801 John Williams (Spartanburgh) to Thomas Foster (same); for $150 sold 100 ac on waters Fairforrest Cr; border: John Bagwell, Connell, Beaverdam Cr, and Ford's old line; part of 430 ac grant Gov. William Moultrie to John Golightly; where John Williams formerly lived. Witness Ism Foster, Joel Hurt, and William Foster. Signed J Williams. Certified Mar. 13, 1801 Ism Foster. Rec. Apr. 22, 1801

p. 230-231 Mar. 28, 1795 Robert Harper (Spartanburgh) to James Fowler (same); for 20£ sterling sold 100 ac on S side S Pacolet R and on Holston's Cr of S Pacolet R; border: Matthew Harper and Horn. Witness Andrew Bouland, Mary Harper, and Phebe Harper. Signed Robt Harper. Wit. oath Mar. 24, 1801 Phebe Harper to John Anderson. Rec. Apr. 22, 1801

p. 231-232 Jan. 13, 1800 Thomas Selman (or Salmon) (Elbert Co, Ga) to David Burton (Spartanburgh); for 30£ sold 100 ac on branches of N Tygar R. Witness James Selman and Jeremiah Selman jr. Signed Thos Selman. Wit. oath Mar. 24, 1801 Jeremiah Selman jr to G Brewton. Rec. Apr. 22, 1801

p. 232-234 May 12, 1797 John Wofford sr (Spartanburgh) to John Wofford jr (same); for 10£ sterling sold 50 ac; border: Benjn West and Browley; part of 300 ac grant Jul. 8, 1794 Jeremiah Barnut on Muckewain's Cr of Fairforrest Cr and bordering: NW-Wm Thomson, E-Wm Browley, and others vacant. Witness James Wofford, Isaac Wofford, and Wm Wofford. Signed John Wofford's mark. Wit. oath Mar. 19, 1801 Wm Wofford to Saml Lancaster. Rec. Apr. 22, 1801

p. 234-235 Oct. 20, 1800 Charles Morgan (Spartanburgh) to William Morgan; for $215 sold 98 ac on waters Cherokee Cr of Broad R; border: John Arrendale. Witness Danl McCray and John Arendell. Signed Charles Morgan's mark. Wit. oath Nov. 29, 1800 John Arendell to H McCray. Rec. Apr. 25, 1801

p. 235-236 Mar. 7, 1801 Thomas Williams (Spartanburgh) to daughter Elizabeth Williams, "alias" Meadows; for love and affection give a Negro girl about 2 years old Massey, for Elizabeth's lifetime and then Negro goes back to "the family" unless Elizabeth has heirs in which case Negro goes to Elizabeth's heirs. Witness Joseph Smith and Lettice Smith. Signed Thos Williams. Wit. oath Mar. 7, 1801 Joseph Smith to Wm Smith. Rec. Apr. 25, 1801

p. 236-237 Mar. 20, 1801 Thomas Williams (Spartanburgh) to daughter Fanny Williams; for love and affection give a Negro girl Nancy about 4 years old; Negro goes to Fanny's heirs if Fanny had heirs otherwise Negro goes to Fanny for her lifetime and then goes back to "the family". Witness Joseph Smith and Lettice Smith. Signed Thos Williams. Wit. oath Mar. 7, 1801 (sic) Joseph Smith to Wm Smith. Rec. Apr. 27, 1801

p. 237-238 Apr. 7, 1798 William Brown (Laurens Co) Michael Wood (Spartanburgh); for $75 sold 57 ac; border: Abner's Cr and John Redman; part of 500 ac on branch of Enoree R; survey Jan. 6, 1775 "on warrant granted" Dec. 8, 1774; grant Oct. 15, 1784 to Daniel Huger esq and sold by Arnold Vanderhorst and Thomas Waring sr, executors of will of John Vanderhorst desc (late of Charleston, SC), to William Brown. Witness Gabriel Jones and Joseph Lyon. Signed William Brown. Wit. oath Apr. 11, 1798 Gabriel Jones to Zadock Ford. Rec. Apr. 27, 1801

p. 238-239 Mar. 4, 1801 Amey Golightly (Spartanburgh) to Robert Sterling (same); for $24 sold 24 ac on branch of Kelsoe's Cr of Fairforrest Cr; border: N-Amey Golightly, SE-Robert Sterling, and others vacant. Witness Christi Golightly and David Golightly. Signed Amey Golightly. Wit. oath Mar. 25, 1801 Christi Golightly to Wm Smith. Rec. Apr. 27, 1801

p. 239-241 Feb. 13, 1798 Arnoldus Vanderhorst and Thomas Waring sr, executors of will of John Vanderhorst esq desc (late of Charleston, SC), to Andrew Boddan and Robert Lethgow (Camden Dist); for 226£ 13s 4p sterling sold 640 ac on N side of Middle Fork Tygar R; border: SW-John Nichols, W-William Garrard and an old line, N-Alexander Vernon, E-Thomas Penny; grant Aug. 1, 1785 to Robert Torrance; see power of attorney in John Vanderhorst's will in Charleston Ordinary's Office. Witness John Frances Chion and Oliver Cromell for Arnoldus Vanderhorst , George Mathews and Daniel Smith esq for Thomas Waring sr. Signed A Vanderhorst esq and Thos Waring sr esq. Wit. oath Jun. 11, 1798 Oliver Cromell to Stephen Ravenel and Daniel Smith to Stephen Ravenel. Rec. Apr. 28, 1801

p. 241-242 Jan. 3, 1798 David Quarles (Spartanburgh) to Michael Wood (same); for $105 sold 130 ac on S side Abner's Cr where James Johnson lives; border: Vanderhorst "above" and Thos Scottow "below"; part of grant Feb. 3, 1791 Gov. Charles Pinckney to David Quarles. Witness Reuben Gunn, James Johnson, and Charles Gunn. Signed David Quarles. Wit. oath May 11, 1799 Charles Gunn to Zadock Ford. Rec. Apr. 28, 1801

p. 242-244 Mar. 2, 1801 David Anderson (Spartanburgh) to Samuel Jamison (same); for 20£ sterling sold 116 ac on S side S fork Tygar R; border: Wm Hendricks and Prowey's Cr. Witness John Crawford, John Durham, and William Anderson. Signed David Anderson. Wit. oath Mar. 2, 1801 John Crawford to Drury McDaniel. Rec. Apr. 28, 1801

p. 244-245 Jan. 16, 1801 Andrew Thomson DM (Spartanburgh) to George Thomas Sloan (same); for 20£ sterling sold 140 ac on waters Dutchman's Cr and on main road to Blackstock ford on Tygar R; border: Ephraim Hill, Gidion Haroldson, and Samuel Morrow; grant Aug. 4, 1794 Gov. William Moultrie to Andrew Thomson. Witness Ignatious Turley and Jesse Meaders. Signed Andrew Thomson. Wit. oath Jan. 31, 1801 Jesse Meaders to Wm Smith. Rec. Apr. 30, 1801

p. 245-246 Jan. 12, 1801 Thomas Davidson (Spartanburgh) to George Vandiver (same); for $75 sold 50 ac on both sides Prielepere Br of Storie's Mill Cr; border: Ash and John King; part of 266 ac grant Mar. 5, 1798 Gov. Charles Pinckney to Thomas Davidson. Witness Simpson McCarter and Richeson Whitbey. Signed Thos Davison. Wit. oath Jan. 12, 1801 Richeson Whitbey to William Simpson. Rec. Apr. 30, 1801

p. 246-248 Apr. 2, 1796 Pearceful Nicholls (Richland Cr) to Jacob Smith (same); for $106 sold 212 ac on N side Saluda and N side Dutchman's Cr of Tygar R; border: E & N-James Burnet, N & W-Samuel Lancaster, W & E-Thos Evatt, W & S-Wm Bracher, and others vacant; survey Jul. 13, 1793 for Larkin Lancaster and granted Mar. 7, 1796 Gov. Arnoldus Vanderhorst to Pearceful Nicholls. Witness Jno Halliday and James Sanders Guignard. Signed Pearsefull Nicholls. Wit. oath (Camden Dist) Apr. 18, 1796 James Sanders Guignard to Martyn Alken. Rec. May 1, 1801

p. 248-249 Jan. 1, 1800 Jacob Smith (Columbia, SC) to James Sanders Guignard (Columbia, SC); for $212 sold 212 ac on N side Dutchman's Cr; border: E & NE-James Bennett, N & W-Samuel Lancaster, S-Thomas Evatt, W-William Bracher, and others vacant; survey Jul. 13,

1793 for Larkin Lancaster and granted Mar. 7, 1796 Gov. Arnoldus Vanderhorst to Pearceful Nicholls and sold Apr. 2, 1796 to Jacob Smith. Witness John Hampton and Jacob J Faust. Signed Jacob Smith. Wit. oath (Richland Co) Feb. 13, 1801 Jacob J Faust to R Witherspoon. Rec. May 1, 1801

p. 249-251 Jul. 14, 1800 Jacob Smith (Charleston, SC) to James Sanders Guignard (Columbia, SC); for 175£ sterling sold (1) 112 ac on Dutchman's Cr; border: NW-Thomas Cook and Wm Lancaster esqs, E-Lowndes, SE-John Robinson; survey Nov. 26, 1798 for Christopher Ornduff and granted Jul. 7, 1800 Lt. Gov. John Drayton to Jacob Smith; (2) 300 ac on branches of Middle Tygar R; border: W-the ancient boundary line, Robb, and Watson, E-John McElhaney and survey for Reese and Clark, NE-Dabney Brooks, and others unknown; survey Dec. 24, 1793 for Dabney Brookes and granted Oct. 7, 1799 Gov. Edward Rutledge to Jacob Smith; and (3) 409 ac on waters of Thickety Cr; border: NE-Wm Heston, E-Joseph Dill, SE-Limekiln, SW-Harres, W-Thomas Cole; survey Jan. 16, 1797 for Sarah Wooten and granted Oct. 7, 1799 Gov. Edward Rutledge to Jacob Smith. Witness John Hampton and Jacob J Faust. Signed Jacob Smith. Wit. oath (Richland Co) Feb. 13, 1801 Jacob J Faust to R Witherspoon. Rec. May 1, 1801

p. 251-253 Mar. 13, 1801 Charles Williamson (Columbia, SC) to James Sanders Guignard (same); for $396 sold (1) 166 ac on Lawson's fork of Pacolet R; border: NE-Stephens Miller, NW-Francis Bellinger, SW-William Wood, and others unknown; survey Apr. 8, 1785 for William Hogan and granted Jun. 3, 1799 Gov. Edward Rutledge to Charles Williamson; (2) 178 ac on fork of Raybenn's Cr; border: NE-Samuel Peeden, E-David Peeden and McClintock, S-Andrew McKnight, NW-John Peeden, John Morton, and James Nesbit; survey Nov. 8, 1797 for John Peeden and granted Oct. 7, 1799 Gov. Edward Rutledge to Charles Williamson; and (3) 52 ac on Pacolet R; border: E-James Phillips, S-Pacolet R and William Garrot, N-vacant, and W-Reubin Dixon; survey Mar. 25, 1786 for Amos Speice and granted Feb. 1, 1796 Gov. Arnoldus Vanderhorst to Charles Williamson. Witness Peter Bremar and Samuel Green. Signed Chas Williamson. Wit. oath (Richland Co) Apr. 8, 1801 Peter Bremar to Sicu(?) Taylor. Rec. May 1, 1801

p. 253-254 Mar. 14, 1801 John Gray (Spartanburgh) to Minar Winn (same); for $375 sold a Negro man Stephen about 23 years old; Negro is redeemable until Mar. 14, 1803 if John pays Minar $375 by then. Witness John Fredk Harmining and James Whutley. Signed John Gray. Wit. oath Apr. 10, 1801 John Fredk Harmining to Aaron Casey. Rec. May 6, 1801

p. 254-255 Feb. 21, 1801 Robert Armour (Spartanburgh) to John Tolleson (same); for $50 sold 174 ac on Peter's Cr and waters of Pacolet R; border: NE-James Stedman, S & SE-Wm Poole and Wofford; where Robert Armour lives; grant Jan. 5, 1789 to Thomas Hays who sold to Robert Armour; sold for 10 months; Condition: deed void in 10 months if Robert pays John $50. Witness Muse Tolleson, William Gossett jr, and Thomas Lemaster. Signed Robert Armour. Wit. oath May 11, 1801 Muse Tolleson to I Harrison. Rec. May 12, 1801

p. 255-256 Feb. 15, 1801 Isaac Tinsley (Spartanburgh) to Gabriel Bumpass; for $100 sold a Negro boy Jack; sale conditioned for due and faithful discharge of bond from Isaac Tinsley to Gabriel Bumpass and tested by John James Feb. 18, 1801 for $100; Condition: if bond paid then this sale is void. Witness Ism Foster. Signed Isaac Tinsley. Certified May 20, 1801 by Ism Foster. Rec. May 28, 1801

p. 256-259 Feb. 28, 1801 Moses Timmons to Gabriel Bumpass; a bond for $10,000; Condition: bond void if Moses Timmons pays all debts due by copartnership of Timmons and Bumpass and "keep from all harm" Gabriel Bumpass due to copartnership. Witness none.

Signed Moses Timmons. Rec. May 28, 1801. Feb. 28, 1801 Moses Timmons (Spartanburgh) to Gabriel Bumpass (same); for $5 sell a cupboard and furniture, 4 feather beds and furniture and beadsteads, 5 trunks, 2 fine tables, 2 spinning wheels, 10 charis, a looking glass, 5 tongues and shovels and 5 dogs, a chest, 2 flat irons, 3 iron pots, 3 dutch ovens, a skillet, a tea kittle, a waggon and 3 pair of grars complete, a yoke of oxen, 10 head of cattle, 20 hogs, 3 horses, 7 Negroes: Pompey, Leah, Peter, Harey, Jean, Jude, Peter (little), and a boy Ben, and "my part" in company with my two daughters; all above sold to futher secure Gabriel Bumpass from debt--see bond of $10,000 Moses Timmons to Gabriel Bumpass; debts from copartnership of Timmons and Bumpass of which Gabriel has given his share to Moses; this sale void if Moses fulfills conditions of bond to Gabriel. Signed Moses Timmons. Wit. oath May. 15, 1801 Moses Timmons to Drury McDaniel. Rec. May 28, 1801

p. 259-261 Apr. 30, 1801 James Barnett (Spartanburgh) to William Lancaster (same); for 5£ sold 3 ac includes part of the shoal on Fairforrest Cr where wagon road crosses and rights to cut timber on remainder of James Barnett's land to build a mill on Fairforrest Cr and shoal; except for "Rail and Board Timber"; plat attached shows border: Buffington's old tract, Barnett, and Thomas. Witness James Riely and John White. Signed Jas Barnett. Wit. oath Apr. 30, 1801 John White to William Simpson. Rec. Jun. 23, 1801. Dower renounced Sara Barnett to Wm Smith May 22, 1801

p. 261-262 Jan. 25, 1797 Henry Wells (Spartan Co) to William Pollard (same); for 40£ sterling sold 150 ac on branch of Lawson's fork border: SW-William Moutrie (sic), SE-Henry Prince, and others vacant; grant Sept. 9, 1774 to Henry Sunday. Witness David Wells, Obadiah Wingo, and James Foster. Signed Henry Wells. Wit. oath May 17, 1797 James Foster to Ism Foster. Rec. Jun. 29, 1801

p. 262-264 Oct. 17, 1796 James Seay (Amelia Co, Va) to William Pollard (Spartanburgh); for 60£ Va money sold 200 ac on waters of Tygar R; border: John Wood; grant (no date given) to James Seay. Witness Waller Ford, Moses Pollard, Thos Burton, and Curus Seay. Signed James Seay. Wit. oath Nov. 7, 1796 Thos Burton to Isham Foster. Rec. Jun. 29, 1801

p. 264-265 May 13, 1801 John Stone (Spartling (sic) Dist) to William Stone (same); for $100 sold 100 ac on waters of Pacolet R; border: Tolleson, Stone Spring Br, Murray's Spring Br, Murray, and Gosset. Witness William Reid and John Gosset. Signed John Stone. Wit. oath May 13, 1801 William Reid to William Simpson. Rec. Jun. 29, 1801

p. 265-268 Jul. 3, 1801 Samuel Miller, sheriff (Spartanburgh) to Burrell Bobo (same); for $47 sold 95 ac; William Farrow "shewed me" 95 ac on waters Enoree R near Cedar Shoal Cr; border: N-part of same tract, E-Widow Warters, S-Mathias Couch, and W-James Clayton; execution levied obtained by George Robuck vs William Farrow in Spartanburgh Co Court for $125.85; sale Sept. 1, 1798 for $47. Witness Drury McDaniel, Anthony Foster, and John Anderson. Signed Saml Miller. Wit. oath Jul. 3, 1801 Anthony Foster to Drury McDaniel. Rec. Jul. 4, 1801

p. 268-269 Sept. 25, 1800 Nathan Veal (Spartanburgh) to Thomas Davison (same); for 100£ sold 147 ac where Nathan Veal lives; border: William Lancaster, Culbertson, Henry O'Nail, and Col White or Taylor. Witness Henry O'Neill and William Lancaster. Signed Nathan Veal. Wit. oath Jul. 3, 1801 William Lancaster to Drury McDaniel. Rec. Jul. 4, 1801

p. 269-271 Jan. 22, 1799 William Pinson (Spartanburgh) to Hugh Moore (same); for $165 sold 262 ac on Bullock's fork of Thickety Cr; border: N & E-Ann Moor, S & E-John Wooten. Witness James Poole, Elijah Bruice, and Joshua Pettett. Signed William Penn's mark. Wit. oath Jul. 18, 1799 Elijah Bruice to Geor Lamkin. Rec. Jul. 17, 1801

p. 271-272 Feb. 28, 1801 Rebecah Arundell to John Arundell sr; give all her dower rights for consideration of free use of the part of land where Rebecah lives and land goes to John when Rebecah dies. Witness John Cooper and Richard Arendell. Signed Rebecah Arundell's mark. Wit. oath Apr. 18, 1801 John Cooper to Geor Lamkin. Rec. Jul. 17, 1801

p. 272-274 Jun. 3, 1801 Henry Young (Spartan Dist) to Baylis Earle (same); for $240 sold 242 ac in Pendleton Dist on 23 mile Cr; border: NW-William Mackie and other sides by old survey and vacant land; grant Feb. 7, 1791 Gov. Charles Pinckney to Henry Young. Witness John Hooper, Hugh Ewing, and Abraham Baker. Signed Henry Young. Wit. oath Jun. 4, 1801 Hugh Ewing to John Anderson. Rec. Jul. 22, 1801

p. 274-276 (not dated--see below) John Anderson to Baylis Earle; John assigns a grant from himself to Baylis; grant for 294 ac; plat attached shows border: on Evans Cr of Pacolet R, SE & SW-Robert Evans, and others vacant. Rec. Jul. 23, 1801
Survey Jan. 19, 1792 by Wm Benson dept surv for John Anderson; signed Feb. 13, 1792 by Peter Bremar pro. Serv. Gen.
Mar. 5, 1792 Gov. Charles Pinckney to John Anderson; a grant--see Legislature act of Feb. 19, 1791 for granting vacant land; 294 ac surveyed Jan. 19, 1792 on Evan's Cr of N Pacolet R; border: SW-Robert Evans and others vacant. Signed Charles Pinckney
Dec. 10, 1800 John Anderson assigns grant to Baylis Earle jr. Witness Wm Gilmore and Benjamin Anderson. Signed John Anderson

p. 276-279 Sept. 18, 1800 Andrew Colley (Spartan Dist) to Baylis Earle (same); for $600 sold 445 ac on McBee's Cr of N Pacolet R; of which 400 ac was granted May 24, 1770 Gov. William Tryon (NC) to James McBee bordering: formerly Sam Young and now Baylis Earle; and other 45 ac formerly Baylis Earle's and sold to Andrew Colley. Witness William Anderson, John Jackson, and Andrew Hopkins. Signed Andrew Colley. Wit. oath Jun. 5, 1801 William Anderson to John Anderson. Rec. Jul. 25, 1801

p. 279-280 Feb. 24, 1801 Robert Carter (Greenville Dist) to Baylis Earle (Spartan Dist); for $100 sold 286 ac on waters of N Pacolet R and branch of Obed's Cr; border: John Anderson esq; grant Jan. 7, 1799 Gov. Edward Rutledge to Robert Carter. Witness John Anderson and Charles Bruce. Signed Rot Carter. Wit. oath Jan. 7, 1801 Robert Carter to John Anderson. Rec. Jul. 28, 1801

p. 280-282 Nov. 7, 1799 Thomas Betterton to Joshua Betterton; for 50£ sterling sold 175 ac on Dutchman's Cr and N side Tygar R; half of 350 ac grant to father Thomas Betterton except for 1 ac where father and mother are buried which remains of Thomas Betterton's land. Witness Surratt Wilson and Thos Tod. Signed Thomas Betterton. Wit. oath Dec. 14, 1799 Surratt Wilson to Wm Smith. Rec. Jul. 28, 1801. Dower renounced Palateah Betterton to Wm Smith Dec. 14, 1799

p. 282-284 Jun. 3, 1801 John Cantrell (Spartanburgh) to Henry Wells (same); for $209 sold 160 ac on branches of Ford's Cr of Beaverdam Cr of Fairforrest Cr. Witness Isaac Tinsley and Jeremiah Selman. Signed John Cantwell. Wit. oath Jun. 13, 1801 Jeremiah Selman to I Harrison. Rec. Jul. 31, 1801

p. 284-286 Feb. 7, 1801 John Golightly (Spartanburgh) to William Lancaster (same); for $10 sold 2½ ac including shoal on Fairforrest Cr near where waggon road crosses; border: James Barnett, Moses Foster, and Tate. Witness Nancy Williams and Susannah Williams. Signed John Golightly. Wit. oath Jul. 30, 1801 Nancy Williams to I Harrison. Rec. Aug. 5, 1801

p. 286-288 Jun. 12, 1801 Thomas Foster (Spartanburgh) to William Roberds (same); for $50 sold 30½ ac; border: mountain tract, N-Sprinkle, S & E-lies (sic) Brown, W-David Golightly. Witness Joel Hurt and John Foster. Signed Thomas Foster's mark. Wit. oath Jul. 20, 1801 Thomas Foster to I Harrison. Rec. Aug. 7, 1801. Dower renounced Sary Foster to I Harrison Jul. 20, 1801

p. 288-289 Mar. 17, 1801 Sampson Bethell ("state" of Cumberland (sic)) to Larrance Bankston (Spartan Co); for 5£ sterling sold 270 ac on waters of Buck Cr and Island Cr; grant Sept. 3, 1794 States Office to Sampson Bethell. Witness Leonard Adcock, Jeremiah Nichols, and William Adcock. Signed Sampson Bethell. Wit. oath Apr. 17, 1801 Leonard Adcock to Geor Lamkin. Rec. Aug. 13, 1801

p. 289-291 Sept. 15, 1800 Henry Morgan (Spartanburgh) to son William Morgan (same); for $100 sold 100 ac on branch on N side of N fork Tygar R; border: W-Joseph Jones and others vacant; grant Sept. 20, 1768 Gov. William Bull to Jeremiah Nesbett who sold Nov. 2, 1785 to Henry Morgan; where Henry Morgan lives. Witness Michael Miller, John Montgomery, and Alexander Thompson. Signed Henry Morgan's mark. Wit. oath Feb. 4, 1801 Alexander Thompson to James Jordan. Rec. Aug. 14, 1801

p. 291-293 Jan. 26, 1801 John Morris (Spartanburgh) to David Lewis (same); for $268.21 sold 200 ac on waters Lawson's fork of Pacolet R; where John Morris lives; formerly John Bennett's land being part of land David Lewis sold to John Bennett; deed void if John Morris pays David Lewis $268.21 by Oct. 1, 1802. Witness Peter Hawkins. Signed John Morris. Certified Jul. 31, 1801 by Ism Foster. Rec. Aug. 15, 1801

p. 293-294 Mar. 8, 1800 Peter Peterson (Spartanburgh) to Henry Pettet (same); for 12£ sold 12 ac; part of 640 ac grant State to Reuben Brion (no date given) on N side Pacolet R; border: Henry Pettet and below "the mill". Witness Reuben Richards and Thos Robinson. Signed Peter Peterson. Wit. oath Jul. 30, 1801 Thos Robinson to John Lipscomb. Rec. Aug. 15, 1800

p. 294-295 Mar. 4, 1801 Abram Markley (Charleston, SC), merchant to Henry Pettet (Spartanburgh); for 50£ sterling sold 200 ac on N side Pacolet R above mouth of Tumbling Shoals Br; border: Polston; includes mill and improvements where Henry Pettet lives. Witness Thomas Robison, Leuresey Wilkins, and Henry Pettet. Signed William Poole. Wit. oath Jul. 30, 1801 Thomas Robison to John Lipscomb. Rec. Aug. 17, 1801

p. 295-297 Jun. 21, 1799 John Williams (Spartanburgh) to Giles Connell (same); for $8 sold 10 ac on E side Beaverdam Cr; border: Giles Connell and John Ford; part of grant to John Golightly who sold to Francis Mason who sold to John Williams. Witness I Harrison JQ. Signed John Williams. Certified Jun. 21, 1799 by I Harrison. Rec. Aug. 18, 1799. Dower renounced Nancy Williams to I Harrison Aug. 14, 1801

p. 297-298 Feb. 9, 1801 Morgan Darnell to Mrs. Maryan Cole, widow; for $20 sold a dark brended cow and calf marked with cross and under tut in both ears, a brown cow with white spot in forehead, and calf marked with half cross in right ear, 12 hogs marked with cross and slit and under tut in each ear. Witness Ebel Darnel and Henry Cole. Signed Morgan Darnell's mark. Wit. oath May 25, 1801 Henry Cole to G Brewton. Rec. Aug. 19, 1801

p. 298-299 Sept. 1, 1801 Jane Goore, wife of Thos Goor, (Spartanburgh) and Mary Goore, daughter of Thos Goore, to Thomas Moore; "deliver" a black mare about 9 years old about 14 hands high branded "O" on left shoulder and on left thigh and on right shoulder--horse is security for "book account" of 16£ 16s 10½p; and a bull now among cattle and at residence of Mr McWilliams about 5 years old not branded; and another bull among cattle of Thomas Goore and present before us about 4 years old--color white except head, neck, and legs which are black; Thomas Moore can "sell at public sale or make them his property" for satisfaction of the debt. Witness John Harrison and Thos McCarrell. Signed Jane Goore's mark and Mary Goore. Wit. oath Sept. 4, 1801 John Harrison to A Lancaster. Rec. Sept. 7, 1801

p. 299-301 May 11, 1801 letter from Daniel Doyley (office of State Treasury, Charleston)--refer to "act to raise supplies and make appropriations for 1800"--due to said act, described land will be put up for public sale by sheriff first Monday and Tuesday of Sept. 1801 (if land is in another county, then paper work is to be sent to sheriff of the other county); ¼ of purchase price must be paid in cash, remaining 3/4 paid in one and two years with land as security for bond (approved by Benjamin D Shumate, Isham Harrison, and James Jordan esqs, Commissioners for "your" district); copy of paper work after sale to be sent to Daniel Doyley; bearer of this letter to be given receipt for letter and paperwork; adressed to William Wells esq, sheriff (Spartanburgh) and signed Daniel Doyley, State Treasurer at Charleston. P. S. if any land is "redeemed according to law" Daniel Doyley will notify "you". List of enclosed: Plat #221 Joseph Buffinton, four advertisements, and 4 extracts of the law. Rec. Sept. 9, 1801

p. 301-302 Apr. 14, 1801 Josiah Culbertson (Greenville Co) to Jesse Rakestraw; quit claim to 80 ac Josiah Culbertson formerly claimed granted to Charles Bruce; Jesse Rakestraw brought counter claim that land was sold to him by Thomas Young and his heirs; if Jesse Rakestraw's claim proves out, then Josiah Culbertson agrees to leave land by Jan. 1, 1802. Witness Saml Culbertson and Jas Smith. Signed Josiah Culbertson. Wit. oath Sept. 8, 1801 Jas Smith to A Lancaster. Rec. Sept. 24, 1801

p. 302-303 Mar. 2, 1801 Thomas Reece (Spartanburgh) to David Golightly (same); for $75 sold 127 ac where Thomas Reece lives on waters of Dutchman's Cr; border: Thomas Cook, James Hickey, and Calvert. Witness James Reese and William Lancaster. Signed Thomas Rees. Wit. oath Sept. 7, 1801 William Lancaster to A Lancaster. Rec. Sept. 24, 1801

p. 303-305 Sept. 14, 1801 Charles Morgan (Spartanburgh) to son Anthony Morgan; for love and affection give "all goods and chattles" now in his possession and delivered the ones on a list Charles Morgan made; inventory: Negro fellow Jacob, a horse sadle and bridle, mamed sorrel, a sorrel mare, a black horse, 8 head of horned cattle, 22 hogs great and small, my whold crop as it stands, 4 feather beds and furniture, all household furniture, the wearing apparrell excepted, all plantation and carpenter tools, and a rifle gun (list signed Sept. 14, 1801 by Charles Morgan's mark). Witness John Arendell, Richard Arendell, and Jesse Temple. Signed Charles Morgan's mark. Wit. oath Sept. 23, 1801 Richard Arendell to John Lipscomb. Rec. Sept. 24, 1801

p. 305-306 Oct. 17, 1800 William Hendrix (Spartanburgh) to John Lindsey (same); for $300 sold (195 ac?) on waters of Lick

Cr of Enoree R; 25 ac is part of grant to William Reaves; 70 ac was granted to John W Lindsey on Lick Cr; border: Aron Bawkums, James Allen, and Elijah Hendrix; and 100 ac is on W side of 200 ac grant to William Moore; border: Reaves. Witness William S Allen, Matthew Sparks, and Elijah Hendrix. Signed William Hendrix. Wit. oath Sept. 24, 1801 William S Allen to George Brewton. Rec. Sept. 25, 1801

p. 306-307 Aug. 31, 1801 William Shands Golightly (Spartanburgh) to David Golightly jr (same); for 100£ sold 675 ac where David Golightly lives; border: N-Christopher Golightly, S-Widow Golightly, E-Anthony Bates, and W-William S Golightly; on waters of Fairforrest Cr. Witness Clary Lancaster and William Lancaster. Signed W. S. Golightly. Wit. oath Sept. 7, 1801 William Lancaster to Absalom Lancaster. Rec. Sept. 25, 1801

p. 307-309 Aug. 31, 1801 David Golightly jr (Spartanburgh) to William Shands Golightly (same); for 100£ sold 591 ac on waters of Fairforrest Cr; part of where William S Golightly lives; border: E-Christopher Golightly, N-James Poole, W-William S Golightly, and W-Joroyal Barnett. Witness Clary Lancaster and William Lancaster. Signed David Golightly. Wit. oath Sept. 7, 1801 William Lancaster to Absalom Lancaster. Rec. Sept. 26, 1801

p. 309-311 Jul. 1, 1801 Absalom Lancaster (Spartanburgh) to William Burton (same); for $214 sold (1) 100 ac on branches of Fairforrest Cr; border: George Connel; and (2) 103 ac on waters of Fairforrest Cr; border: Giles and George Connell. Witness Joseph Barnett, George Connell, and Robert Ligon. Signed A Lancaster. Wit. oath Aug. 7, 1801 George Connell to I Harrison. Rec. Sept. 26, 1801. Dower renounced Sally Lancaster to I Harrison Sept. 7, 1801

p. 311-313 Sept. 28, 1801 John DeYoung (Spartanburgh) to daughters Mary Anne DeYoung, Jenny DeYoung, Sary DeYoung, and Elizabeth DeYoung; for love and affection give 300 ac where John DeYoung lives on N fork of Tygar R; border: Joseph Collins, Moses Timmons, Babley Lewis; grant to Lucas who sold to Taylor White who sold to John Walker who sold to John James who sold to John DeYoung; and give all plantation tools and utensels and all goods and chattles, horses, cattle, and whatever kind of stock and household furniture within South Carolina. Witness Joseph Collins, John Bettes, and James Jordan JQ. Signed John D Young. Rec. Sept. 30, 1801

p. 313-315 Aug. 29, 1801 John Willson (Spartanburgh) to Charles Rogers (same); for $60 sold 58 ac where John Willson lives; border: road near Hurrican Cr, Wm Lancaster, Nathan Veal, Col Thomas Taylor, Charles McCarter, and Thomas Smith. Wit. oath Daniel White and John White. Signed John Willson's mark. Wit. oath Sept. 7, 1801 John White to William Simpson. Rec. Oct. 1, 1801

p. 315-316 Aug. 6, 1798 Robert Smyth (Abbeville, SC) to Thomas Davison (Spartanburgh); for 20£ sterling sold 200 ac; survey Jul. 20, 1785 for Wm Simpson on Foster's Mill Cr of Fairforrest Cr; grant Gov. Wm Moultrie to (not given). Witness James Mordock and James Walker. Signed Robert Smyth and Jean's mark. Wit. oath (Edgefield Co) Oct. 8, 1798 James Walker to Wm Robinson. Rec. Oct. 1, 1801

p. 316-318 Aug. 12, 1797 Jesse Hammett (Spartanburgh) to Thomas Reece (same); for 15£ sold 130 ac; W part of grant Jul. 1, 1793 Gov. William Moultrie to Wm Lancidor; border: Thomas Cook, Thomas Reece, Calvert, Daniel Finch, and Thomas Vaughn. Witness Daniel Finch and William Hammett. Signed Jess Hammett. Wit. oath Aug. 11, 1800 Daniel Finch to George Brewton. Rec. Oct. 2, 1801

p. 318-321 Sept. 14, 1801 Charles Morgan (Spartanburgh) to Richard

Arendell (same); for 500 Spanish milled dollars sold 220 ac on both sides Cherokee Cr; border: John Arendell jr, Bonnus, John Arendell, William Morgan (who has 100 ac out of original tract); grant in 1784 to Jesse Temple and survey by George Salmon. Witness Danl McCay and William Morgan. Signed Charles Morgan's mark. Wit. oath Sept. 15, 1801 William Morgan to John Lipscomb. Rec. Oct. 2, 1801

p. 321-322 Oct. 12, 1800 John Eaves Murray (Spartanburgh) to William Murray (same); for $150 sold 190 ac on Big Br of Island Cr of Pacolate R; where John E Murray lives; border: Hubard Reece, John Reece, and "others". Witness James Smith and Osborn Reece. Signed John E Morrow (sic). Wit. oath Oct. 12, 1800 James Smith to Geor Lamkin. Rec. Oct. 2, 1801

p. 322-325 Sept. 14, 1801 William Wells, sheriff (Spartanburgh) to Alexander McKee (same); for $150 sold 250 ac; Joseph Buffington mortgaged to South Carolina for "valuable consideration" 250 ac on Fairforrest Cr of Broad R survey by David Hopkins and granted Sept. 9, 1774 to Zacheriah Bullock who sold Oct. 16, 1776 to John Thomas who sold Feb. 29, 1780; mortgage was forfieted; see act to make appropiations for 1800 and decree from Daniel Doyle, state Treasurer at Charleston; sale on Sept. 8, 1801; plat attached shows border: vacant, vacant (now Foster), vacant (now Joseph Wade), Jno Gibbs, Jno Thomas; plat signed J Thomas Jr. Witness I Harrison JQ and James Jordan. Signed Wm Wells SSD. Rec. Oct. 3, 1801

p. 325-327 Sept. 14, 1801 William Wells, sheriff (Spartanburgh) to Alexander McKee (or Mackee) (same); for $212 sold 300 ac; Joseph Buffington mortgaged to South Carolina 300 ac for "a valuable consideration" on Fairforrest Cr of Broad R; survey by Daniel Thomas and granted Oct. 12, 1770 to Giles Tillet who sold Jul. 5, 1771 to John Thomas who sold Feb. 29, 1780 to Joseph Buffington; mortgage was forfieted; see act to make appropiations for 1800 and decree from Daniel Doyley, state Treasurer at Charleston; Sale Sept. 8, 1801; plat attached shows border: Barnett (granted to Thomas), Foster, Kelsoe's Cr, Bullock, Fairforrest Cr, Duggan's Br; plat signed by J Thomas jr and certified May 23, 1801 by Daniel Doyley. Witness I Harrison JQ and James Jordan. Signed Wm Wells SSD. Rec. Oct. 3, 1801

p. 327-329 Sept. 22, 1801 Thomas Lancaster, son of Absolom Lancaster esq, to William Boman, bricklayer (Rutherford Co, NC); a bond to be taught a trade of brick laying; Thomas of his own free will gives bond with advice of his father for 3 years; Thomas can't embezzel or waste William, can't consent at cards, dice, or other unlawful games, can't play taverns, can't frequent matumony, can't contract without William's consent, and can't leave; William is to teach Thomas and give Thomas meat, drink, washing, lodging, and apparel (linen and woolen), and other necessities. Witness W Lancaster and I Harrison JQ. Signed Thos Lancaster, A Lancaster, and Wm Bowman. Rec. Oct. 8, 1801

p. 329-331 Sept. 14, 1801 William Wells, sheriff (Spartanburgh) to James Smith (same); for $150 sold 640 ac; Joseph Buffington mortgaged to South Carolina 640 ac on Kelsoe's Cr of Broad R; survey by Philemon Waters and granted Oct. 15, 1784 Gov. Benjamin Guerard to Joseph Buffington; mortgage forfieted; see act to raise appropiations in 1800 and decree from Daniel Doyley, state Treasurer at Charleston; sale Sept. 8, 1801; plat attached shows border: David Mott, Connell, vacant, both sides Buffington's Br, Hammell's Br of Kelsoe's Cr; plat certified by J Thomas jr (not dated). Witness I Harrison JQ and James Jordan. Signed Wm Wells SSD. Rec. Oct. 9, 1801

p. 331-332 Nov. 6, 1799 Thomas Penny sr (Spartanburgh) to John McElrath (same); for $400 sold 200 ac on S side of Middle Fork Tygar R; border: James Vernon and Samuel Nesbett; of which 50 ac is part of old survey where Thomas Perry sr lives and 150 ac was granted Fev. 24, 1773 to Robert Nesbett. Witness B. D. Shumate JP. Signed Thomas Penny's mark. Rec. Oct. 13, 1801

p. 332-334 Nov. 6, 1799 Thomas Penny jr (Spartanburgh) to John Mackelrath (same); for 100£ sterling sold 192 ac on N side of Middle Fork Tygar R; border: Penny, Norman, and Benson; of which 50 ac is part of grant Feb. 17, 1785 to Thomas Penny sr and 150 ac was part of a new survey. Witness B. D. Shumate JP. Signed Thomas Penney. Rec. Oct. 13, 1801

p. 334-335 Mar. 7, 1797 John Waldrop (Spartanburgh) to Rachel Dickson (or Dixson) (same); for 10£ sold 50 ac part of Daniel Rogers' tract. Witness Thomas Stone and Daniel Rogers. Signed John Waldrop's mark. Wit. oath Oct. 25, 1800 Daniel Rogers to Thos Moore. Rec. Oct. 13, 1801

p. 335-336 Jul. 21, 1801 James Leech (Levingston Co, Ky) to friend David Leech (same); power of attorney to receive money owed him in South Carolina and to sell his land in South Carolina. Acknowledged to Wm Prince JQC and William Dobbins JQC. Certified Jul. 22, 1801 by Enoch Prince, clerk in Levingston Co, Ky that Wm Prince and Wm Dobbins are judges. Signed James Leech. Rec. Oct. 22, 1801

p. 336-338 Jul. 7, 1801 William Leech (Levingston Co, Ky) to friend David Leech (same); power of attorney to receive money owed him in South Carolina and sell his land in South Carolina. Acknowledged to Wm Dobbins JQC and Wm Miles JQC. Certified Jul. 7, 1801 by Enoch Prince, CLC in Levingston Co, Ky that Wm Prince and Wm Dobbins are judges. Signed Wm Leech. Rec. Oct. 22, 1801

p. 338-339 Aug. 25, 1801 John Leech (Barren Co, Ky) to David Leech (Levigston Co, Ky); power of attorney to receive money owed to him in South Carolina and sell his land in South Carolina. Acknowledged to John Buford and William Richardson. Certified Aug. 22, 1801 by W Logan in Barren Co, Ky that John Buford and William Richardson are judges. Signed John Leech. Rec. Oct. 22, 1801

p. 339-340 Aug. 23, 1801 Rachel Dickson (or Dixon) (Spartanburgh) to Reuben Traylor (same); for 15£ sterling sold 50 ac on branch of Provey's Cr; includes N part of Rachel Dickson's land. Witness Curtis Gray, John Patten, and William Gray. Signed Rachel Dickson's mark. Wit. oath Oct. 19, 1801 William Gray to Drury McDaniel. Rec. Oct. 24, 1801

p. 340-342 Apr. 13, 1801 Anthony Shands, Elizabeth Shands, Rebekah Shands, and Mary Shands (Spartanburgh) to Edward Smith (same); for $155 sold 142 ac on branches of Dutchman's Cr and Tyger R; border: Moses Pruitt, Caron, and Mottow. Witness Solomon Spann and William Wilson. Signed Anthony Shands, Elizabeth Shands, and Rebekah and Mary Shands' marks. Wit. oath Oct. 25, 1801 William Wilson to Wm Smith. Rec. Nov. 7, 1801. Dower renounced Catherine Shands, wife of Anthony, to William Wilson Apr. 22, 1801

p. 342-344 Oct. 17, 1801 (NC) John Campbell and wife Sary (Iredell Co, NC) to Owen Forrester (Spartanburgh); for 15£ sterling sold 40 ac on Tygar R; border: William Marten, Negro Br, Millington Smith; part of grant Feb. 5, 1787 to John Campbell. Witness John Campbell jr, John Wasson, and John Hewatt. Signed John Campbell and Sary's mark. Wit. oath Oct. 24, 1801 John Hewatt to Wm Smith. Certified (Iredell Co, NC) by Archd Sloan JP. Rec. Nov. 7, 1801 p.344-346 Mar. 25, 1801 Justice Reynolds and wife Mary (Spartanburgh) to James English (Lincoln Co, NC); for $1,000 sold (1) 200 ac on both sides Lawson's fork of Pacolet R; including Grist and Saw Mills; grant North Carolina to James Hammett who sold to Wm Wofford who sold to Wells Griffeth who sold to Justice Reynolds; and (2) 187 ac on N side Lawson's fork; grant to Wells Griffeth. Witness John Gray, Gideon Reynolds, and Thos Brock. Signed Justice Reynolds and Mary's mark. Wit. oath Sept. 29, 1801 Thos Brock to I Harrison. Rec. Nov. 9, 1801

p. 346-348 Feb. 4, 1793 Nathaniel Robertson and James Byras (Pinckney Dist) to William Byras (Spartanburgh); for 23£ sterling sold 143½ ac; half of grant Jan. 1, 1787 to Henry Robertson sr desc and James Byras; where James Byras lived and where William Byras lives; border: Daniel McClaren, Samuel Scurall, Arendell, and line between Raydeck Arendell and James Byras made by Vardry McBee. Witness Obadh Trimmier, Jos Jno Martin, and Peter Quin esq. Signed James Byras and Nathaniel Robertson. Wit. oath Dec. 23, 1800 Peter Quin to H McCray. Rec. Nov. 9, 1801

p. 348-349 Feb. 26, 1796 Readick Arendell (Spartanburgh) to William Byras (or Byers) (same); for 40£ Va money sold 140 ac on Meeks Cr of Broad R; grant Jan. 1, 1787 to James Byars and Henry Robertson; border: N-Danl McClarin and William Byras. Witness Dennis Sullivan and Wm Hester. Signed Readick Arendell. Wit. oath Dec. 23, 1800 Wm Hester to H McCray. Rec. Nov. 9, 1801

p. 349-351 Oct. 10, 1799 Samuel Farrow (Spartanburgh) to James Clayton (same); for 25£ sterling sold 150 ac on Fort Shoal Cr of Enoree R; part of 298 ac grant Dec. 4, 1786; that part of grant on S side of Charleston Rd; where James Clayton lives. Witness Isaac Mills and Rosannah Farrow. Signed S Farrow. Wit. oath Dec. 24, 1799 Isaac Mills to A Casey. Rec. Nov. 9, 1801

p. 351-352 Feb. 24, 1801 James Kilgore (Greenville Dist) to Newman Wilson (Spartanburgh); for $21 sold 242 ac; where Newman Wilson lives; part of 392 ac grant Dec. 1, 1800 to James Kilgore on both sides Vines Fork of Abner's Cr of Enoree R. Witness Daniel Branson and Robert Greer. Signed James Kilgore. Wit. oath (Greenville Dist) Mar. 17, 1801 Robert Greer to Jo Thomas jr. Rec. Nov. 10, 1801

p. 352-354 Feb. 7, 1794 James Martin esq (York Co) to Charles Hester (Spartanburgh); for 30£ SC money sold 100 ac on both sides Cherokee Cr; border: John Arendell and Charles Hester. Witness Newman Wilson and Robt Murphey. Signed James Martain. Wit. oath Oct. 26, 1801 Newman Wilson to Thos Moore. Rec. Nov. 10, 1801

p. 354-355 Sept. 12, 1801 Henry Jamison (Spartanburgh) to John Patton (same); for $200 sold 100 ac on Ready fork (called Nicholas Cr in Plat) of Tygar R; border: Samuel Stewart and Moses Wakefield; grant to Daniel McCoy who sold to John Boyd who sold to Henry Jamison. Witness Thomas Hadden, William McElrath, and Nathaniel McElrath. Signed Henry Jamison. Wit. oath Oct. 26, 1801 Nathaniel McElrath to Drury McDaniel. Rec. Nov. 10, 1801

p. 355-356 Dec. 30, 1797 Howard Bailey (Spartanburgh) to Robert Goodgion (Greenville Co); for $375 sold Negro boy Catto about 17 years old and healthy. Witness Capt William Anderson and William Rollins. Signed Howard Bailey. Rec. Nov. 10, 1801

p. 356-357 Jan. 15, 1801 Leonard Adcock (Spartanburgh) to Jonathan Low (same); for 30£ sold 100 ac on N side Pacolet R; part of grant Mar. 16, 1787 States Office to Francis Ballinger; border: Wm Adcock and Jonathan Low. Witness Henrey Adcock and Thos Wyatt.

Signed Leod Adcock. Wit. oath Oct. 24, 1801 Thos Wyatt to Geor Lamkin. Rec. Nov. 11, 1801

p. 357-359 Aug. 15, 1799 Matthew Harper (Sumner Co, Tenn) to Alexander Anderson (Greenville Co); for 40£ 13s 4p sold 200 ac on both sides S Pacolet R; upper end of 640 ac grant Feb. 3, 1775 Lt. Gov. William Bull to Matthew Harper sr who sold 200 ac on Feb. 20, 1776 to Matthew Harper. Witness David McCollure and Samuel McClure. Signed Matthew Harper. Wit. oath Aug. 24, 1801 Samuel McClure. Rec. Nov. 16, 1801

p. 359-360 Mar. 7, 1801 Moses Timmons and wife Hannah to Abner Wingo; for $50 sold 200 ac on Holson's Br of Fairforrest Cr; part of grant to D Goodlett bordering Roberson and Wm Moore; grant sold by "said Moore" (sic) to Hill. Witness Gabl Bumpass and Aniel Allin. Signed Moses Timmons and Hannah's mark. Wit. oath Aug. 15, 1801 Gabl Bumpass to John Collins. Rec. Nov. 23, 1801

p. 360-361 Apr. 26, 1796 Zacheriah Robinson (Spartanburgh) to John Gray (same); for 5£ sold 5 ac on N side Lawson's fork; border: Gray; part of land where Zacheriah Robinson lives; part of North Carolina grant survey by Dixon and part of South Carolina grant to Wells Griffeth. Witness Casandra Gray, Elizabeth Robinson, and Curtis Gray. Signed Zacriah Robinson. Wit. oath Apr. 28, 1796 Casandra Gray to Geor Lamkin. Rec. Nov. 27, 1801

p. 361-363 Jan. 26, 1795 James Henry and wife Anne (Spartanburgh) to John Gray; for 30£ sold 50 ac on S side Pacolet R; including a small improvement; part of 200 ac grant Nov. 14, 1771 Gov. Josiah Martin (NC) to James Alley. Witness John Henry, Elizabeth Henry, and Curtis Gray. Signed James and Anne Henry's marks. Wit. oath Apr. 23, 1796 Curtis Gray to Geor Lamkin. Rec. Nov. 27, 1801

p. 363-365 Aug. 7, 1801 George Connell (Spartanburgh) to Thomas Foster (same); for $400 sold 372 ac on Fairforrest Cr; border: Ligon, Barnett, Foster,Giles Connell. Witness William Burton, John Connell, and Wm Foster. Signed George Connell. Wit. oath Aug. 7, 1801 William Burton to I Harrison. Rec. Nov. 28, 1801. Dower renounced Frances Connell to I Harrison Sept. 8, 1801

p. 365-367 Sept. 1, 1801 George Connell (Spartanburgh) to Obadiah Wingo (same); for $400 sold 400 ac on Fairforrest Cr; border: Duggan. Witness I Harrison JQ and A Foster. Signed George Connell. Wit. oath (not dated) George Connell to I Harrison. Rec. Nov. 30, 1801. Dower renounced Sept. 8, 1801 Fracis Connell to I Harrison Sept. 8, 1801

p. 367-368 Feb. 14, 1799 Peter Gray (Spartan Co) to John Wood sr (same); for $500 sold 500 ac; border: Henry Prince, Knox, and others vacant. Witness Gab Benson and James Boyd. Signed Peter Gray. Wit. oath May 25, 1799 Peter Gray to I Harrison. Rec. Dec. 1, 1801

p. 368-369 Feb. 24, 1801 Austin Clayton (Spartanburgh) to John Collins (same); for $50 sold about 40 ac; part of 244 ac grant in 1798 to Auston Clayton on N side of S fork Tygar R; border: Collins. Witness Martha Miller and Samuel Miller. Signed Auston Clayton. Wit. oath Oct. 27, 1801 Samuel Miller to Drury McDaniel. Rec. Dec. 1, 1801

p. 369-370 Oct. 29, 1800 Richard Lee (Spartanburgh) to Jesse Hester (same); a bond of 40£ sterling; Condition: bond void if Richard Lee deeds Jesse Hester 200 ac on branches of Cherokee Cr; border: Clayburn Holt, James Skots, and Bazel Skots. Witness Thomas Betterton and James Ray. Signed Richard Lee. Wit. oath Oct.

27, 1801 Thomas Betterton to A Lancaster. Rec. Dec. 1, 1801

p. 370-372 Oct. 13, 1801 George Newman and wife Francis (Spartanburgh) to Martin Newman (same); for 30£ sterling sold 100 ac; border: Wilson on 3 sides; part of 640 ac grant to James Samples and sold by James Rainey to "said Wilson" Jul. 9, 1790. Witness Moses Casey and Simson Newman. Signed George Newman's mark. Wit. oath Oct. 23, 1801 Moses Casey to A Casey. Rec. Dec. 2, 1801

p. 372 Jan. 29, 1805 "Probate of R Goodgion Bill of Sale Recorded" Wit. oath William Rollins to Ism Foster for sale by Howard Bailey to Robert Goodgion

Book H 1801-1803

p. 1 (not dated) Sampson Bethel to John Bankston (Spartan Co); power of attorney to assign grant for land (270 ac on Maple Swamp) to Laurance Bankston. Witness Abraham Cantrell. Signed S Bethel. Wit. oath Apr. 19, 1801 Abraham Cantrell to George Lamkin. Rec. Dec. 1, 1801

p. 1-3 Mar. 18, 1801 William Hammett (Spartanburgh) to John Duncan (same); for $100 sold 100 ac except 5 ac reserved for Mary McBee where she lives; part of 440 ac grant States Office to William Hammett; on Peter's Cr of Pacolet R. Witness William Rich and Rachel McAbee. Signed William Hammett. Wit. oath Oct. 27, 1801 William Rich to Wm Smith. Rec. Dec. 3, 1801

p. 3-5 Nov. 10, 1801 William Hurt (Spartanburgh) to Gabriel Bumpass (same); for $90 sold a black horse, 2 cows and calves, 2 beds, bedstead and furniture, a chest, a Flax wheel, a count reel, a pot, an oven; Condition: to secure debt owed to Gabriel Bumpass by William Hurt (same date) for $90 payable in 3 months. Witness Edward Cornwel. Signed William Hurt's mark. Nov. 10, 1801 William Hurt agrees to pay Gabriel Bumpass $90 in 3 months. Witness Edward Cornwil. Signed William Hurt's mark. Wit. oath Nov. 30, 1801 Edward Cornwil to Drury McDaniel. Rec. Dec. 4, 1801

p. 5-6 May 14, 1801 Capt John James and wife Nancy to Gabriel Bumpass; for 10£ sold about 50 ac in fork between N and Middle Tygar R; part of 2 tracts: (1) 100 ac grant to Ann McCrory in grant book 4A p. 223; border: W-Middle Tyger R, S-John Barry, N-Thomas Doig; and (2) grant (joining (1) on NW) to John Nichols; border: James McMahan and branch near Capt James' house. Witness William Calwall and John Hugues. Signed John James and Nancy's mark. Wit. oath Nov. 30, 1801 William Calwall to Drury McDaniel. Rec. Dec. 4, 1801

p. 6-7 Jul. 22, 1801 Thomas Posey (Spartanburgh) to William Posey (same); for $200 SC money sold 100 ac on S fork Tygar R; E part of grant Aug. 19, 1774 States Office to Joseph Alkins. Witness Zephaniah Posey and Richard Posey. Signed Thos Posey. Wit. oath Oct. 27, 1801 Zephaniah Posey to John Collins. Rec. Dec. 5, 1801

p. 7-9 Jul. 22, 1801 Thomas Posey (Spartanburgh) to Richard Posey (same); for $300 sold 100 ac on S fork of Tygar R at Thomas Posey's Spring Br; part of grant Aug. 19, 1774 to Joseph Alkin. Witness William Posey and Zephaniah Posey. Signed Thos Posey. Wit. oath Oct. 27, 1801 Zephaniah Posey to Drury McDaniel. Rec. Dec. 5, 1801

p. 9-11 Nov. 1, 1800 Richard Lee (Spartanburgh) to Richard Cantrell (same); for $30 sold 100 ac on N side Cherokee Cr; border: John Bookshare and Blackburn Quin; part of grant States Office to James Steadman. Witness James Poole and Abraham Cantrell. Signed Richard Lee. Wit. oath Apr. 17, 1801 Abraham Cantrell to Geor Lamkin. Rec. Dec. 5, 1801

p. 11-12 Sept. 29, 1801 Jordan Gibson (Logan Co, Ky) to Robert Stacey (Spartanburgh); for 47£ sold 200 ac on waters Cherokee Cr of Broad R. Witness Amos Austell and Samuel Austell. Signed Jordan Gibson's mark. Wit. oath Oct. 26, 1801 Amos Austell to John Lipscomb. Rec. Dec. 5, 1801

p. 12-13 Aug. 29, 1801 James Brown to Peter Peterson; for $100 sold 250 ac on waters of Pacolet R; part of grant to James Brown. Witness I Harrison JQ, Thomas Vaughn, and Josiah Sparks. Signed James Brown's mark. Wit. oath Aug. 29, 1801 James Brown to I Harrison. Dec. 8, 1801

p. 13-14 Mar. 26, 1801 James Martin (Lincoln Co, NC) to Matthew Cooper (Spartanburgh); for $100 sold 150 ac; border: William Cooper and Cyon Cooper. Witness William Bostick, John Philips, and Zachariah Cooper. Signed James Martin. Wit. oath Apr. 18, 1801 Zachariah Cooper to John Lipscomb. Rec. Dec. 8, 1801

p. 14-15 Apr. 18, 1801 Isaac Tinsley (Spartanburgh) to Josiah Hatchet (same); for $200 sold 100 ac on Ford's Cr; border: W-Francis Mason, N-James Seay and James Hunt, E-Benjamin Rainwater, and SE-Underwood. Witness John Cantwell and Jess Wells. Signed Isaac Tinsley. Wit. oath Oct. 29, 1801 Isaac Tinsley to I Harrison. Rec. Dec. 8, 1801

p. 15-17 (Pendleton Dist) Dec. 19, 1800 James Jett (Pendleton Dist) to John Cantwell sr (Spartanburgh); for $12 sold 490 ac on Island Cr of Pacolet R; grant Apr. 1, 1799 Gov. Edward Rutledge to (not given). Witness Abraham Cantrell, Richard Harris, and Reuben Cantrell. Signed James Jett. Wit. oath Apr. 17, 1801 Abraham Cantrell to Geor Lamkin. Rec. Dec. 8, 1801

p. 17-18 Feb. 28, 1801 Peter Peterson (Spartanburgh) to James Wilkins (same); for $20 sold 80 ac. Witness John Sarratt and Jesse Fondren. Signed Peter Peterson. Wit. oath Feb. 28, 1801 John Sarratt to John Lipscomb. Rec. Dec. 9, 1801

p. 18-20 Jan. 9, 1801 George Vandiver (Spartanburgh) to Demps Bonner (same); for $100 sold 100 ac; part of 500 ac grant Feb. 28, 1794 to Thomas Harris on N fork Sarratt's Cr of Broad R. Witness John Turner and Matthew Turner. Signed George Vandiver's mark. Wit. oath Apr. 18, 1801 John Turner to Geor Lamkin. Rec. Dec. 9, 1801

p. 20-21 Mar. 27, 1801 Benjamin Hammett (Spartanburgh) and brother Elijah Hammett, attorneys for Nathaniel Dodd (Fauquire Co, Va) to Micajah Barnett (Spartanburgh); for $100 sold 130 ac on Thomson's Br of Kelsey's Cr of Fairforrest Cr; border: Dodd. Witness James Harrison and William Hammet. Signed Benjamin Hammett. Wit. oath Oct. 30, 1801 James Harrison to A Lancaster. Rec. Dec. 10, 1801

p. 21-23 Oct. 12, 1801 Fleming Smith (Spartanburgh) to Henry Brown (same); for $300 sold 199 ac on waters of Kelsey's Cr; where Fleming Smith lives; border: Peter Smith, Shands Golightly, James Smith, Dodd, and Moses Foster. Witness Wm Lancaster and Lewis Brown. Signed Fleming Smith. Wit. oath Oct. 30, 1801 Wm Lancaster to Jno Anderson. Rec. Dec. 10, 1801

p. 23-24 Mar. 25, 1801 James Martin (Lincoln Co, NC) to Ezekiel Standley (Spartanburgh); for $50 sold 139 ac on Cherokee Cr; border: Ezekiel Standley, Lewis Stanley, and Richard Arnold. Witness Lewis Stanley and Rhoda Stanley. Signed James Martin. Wit. oath May 16, 1801 Lewis Stanley to Geor Lamkin. Rec. Dec. 10, 1801

p. 24-25 Nov. 14, 1800 Mark Swadley (Spartanburgh) to William Hammett (same); for $200 sold 100 ac between Tygar R and Fairforrest Cr and on S side of Ridge Road; where William Hammett lives; part of grant to Elizha Ford on both sides Ridge Rd. Witness James Hammett, Robert Foster, and Thomas Foster. Signed Mark Swadley. Wit. oath Oct. 27, 1801 James Hammett to A Lancaster. Rec. Dec. 10, 1801

p. 25-30 Mar. 31, 1788 James Hall and wife Mary (Spartanburgh) to Joshua Edwards and wife Fanny (Fairfield Co); for 150£ sterling sold 96 ac on branches of Elisha Thomson's Beaverdam Cr of Middle fork Tygar R; grant Dec. 5, 1785 Gov. William Moultrie to James Hall. Witness Samuel Miller and James Jordan JP. Signed James and Mary Hall's marks. Rec. Dec. 11, 1801

p. 30-31 Apr. 10, 1801 George Williams (Spartanburgh) to Matthew Abbett (same); for $200 sold 350 ac on Island Cr; lower end of 500 ac grant Aug. 12, 1796 to George Williams. Witness Reuben Warren and William Adcock. Signed George Williams. Wit. oath Apr. 17, 1801 Reuben Warren to Geo Lamkin. Rec. Dec. 17, 1801

p. 31-32 Oct. 1, 1801 Ephraim Elder and Thomas Reece (Spartanburgh), heir of John Smith desc (late of Spartanburgh), to Mary Smith, wife of John Smith; since Mary has given up her dower rights to John Smith's land, Ephraim and Thomas give Mary the part of John's personal estate assigned her by David Golightly, William Lancaster, and William Roberds, executors of John's estate; and Mary gets part of land given her by same executors about 170 ac. Witness Jas Smith and D Golightly. Signed Ephraim Elder and Thomas Reece. Wit. oath Oct. 27, 1801 Jas Smith to William Simpson. Rec. Dec. 19, 1801

p. 32-34 Oct. 28, 1800 Richard Lee (Spartanburgh) to William Holt (same); for 20£ sold 200 ac on waters Cherokee Cr; part of 2,100 ac grant to James Steadman; border: Daniel Walden, Richard Lee, and Job Lozbee. Witness Robert Armour and John Martin. Signed Richard Lee. Wit. oath Oct. 27, 1801 Robert Armour to A Lancaster. Rec. Dec. 19, 1801. Dower renounced Nancy Lee to I Harrison Oct. 26, 1801

p. 34-35 Apr. 17, 1801 Reuben Warren (Spartanburgh) to William Garrott (same); for 5£ sold 100 ac on N side of Pacolate R. Witness Samuel Turner, Ephraim Potter, and Henry Turner. Signed Reuben Warren. Wit. oath Apr. 17, 1801 Reuben Warren to Ism Foster. Rec. Dec. 19, 1801

p. 35-37 Mar. 12, 1801 Alexander Autry (Spartanburgh) to Thomas Finch (same); for $80 sold 80 ac on waters of S Tygar R; part of grant Jan. 1, 1787 to Thomas Hightower. Witness Thos Underwood and John Smith. Signed Alexander Autry's mark. Wit. oath Aug. 8, 1801 Thos Underwood to George Brewton. Rec. Dec. 21, 1801

p. 37-38 Jun. 10, 1800 John Hammonds and wife Milley (Spartanburgh) to Thomas Price (same); for $150 sold 48 ac on N side of Fairforrest Cr; border: NW & N-John Patten and W-Thomas Price; part of 300 ac grant to Daniel Prewtt who sold to (not given). Witness Andrew Thomson and William Hammonds. Signed John and Milley Hammonds' marks. Wit. oath Dec. 12, 1801 William Hammonds to George Brewton. Rec. Dec. 21, 1801

p. 38-40 Feb. 20, 1801 Alexander Autry (Spartanburgh) to Thomas Price (same); for 20£ sold 73 ac on S side of S Tygar R; 3/4 ac on SW corner excepted; grant Gov. William Moultrie to Daniel Bragg; border: S-George Bruton, N-Thomas Hightower, and S (sic)-South Tygar R. Witness William Hammons and Margrat Floyd. Signed Alexander Autry's mark. Wit. oath Dec. 12, 1801 William Hammons to George Burton. Rec. Dec. 21, 1801

p. 40-42 Jun. 10, 1799 George Floyd and wife Esther (Spartanburgh) to Thomas Price (same); for 50 Spanish milled dollars sold 18 ac on S side of S Fork of Tyger R; border: Thomas Price, Allen Gentry, branch of Fergeson's Cr; part of two tracts given to George Floyd by will of his father Enoch Floyd desc. Witness James Southerlin, Nathaniel Floyd, and Samuel Floyd. Signed George Floyd and Heaster Floyd's marks. Wit. oath Sept. 13, 1799 James Southerlin to George Brewton. Rec. Dec. 21, 1800

p. 42-43 Aug. 26, 1801 George Gilbert (Spartan Dist) to Gassham Lee (same); for $142 sold 200 ac on waters Buck Cr; where George Gilbert lives; border: ridge path from Thomas Henderson's to Gilmore's old place. Witness Dan Gilbert jr. Signed George Gilbert and Jervis Gilbert. Wit. oath Oct. 2, 1801 Dan Gilbert to Wm McDonald. Rec. Dec. 21, 1801

p. 43-45 Nov. 9, 1801 Thomas Williams (Spartanburgh) to Wilie Willeford (same); for $60 sold 75 ac on Dry fork Br of Dutchman's Cr; part of grant Nov. 7, 1785 to John Shands who sold to Thomas Williams; border: Esquire Smith and Brittain Willeford. Witness Willis Williford, Aaron Smith, and Langster (or Langston) Williams. Signed Thos Williams. Wit. oath Nov. 9, 1801 Willis Williford to Wm Smith. Rec. Dec. 22, 1801. Dower renounced Jane Williams to Wm Smith Nov. 27, 1801

p. 45-47 Oct. 27, 1801 Jonathan Low, John Low sr, and John Low jr to Thomas Betterton (Spartanburgh); for $200 sold 100 ac on both sides of branch of Thickety Cr; border: SE-John Haden and remainder of grant; part of grant in 17(blank) to John Haden. Witness John Alexander, Rolly H Horton, and Gideon Reynolds. Signed Jonathan Low, John Low sr, and John Low jr's mark. Wit. oath Oct. 27, 1801 Rolly H Horton to A Lancaster. Rec. Dec. 22, 1801

p. 47-49 May 26, 1801 Joseph Cavin (Spartanburgh) to George Irwin Beard (same); for $160 sold 100 ac; border: W & E-remainder of grant, S-George Robuck, N-James Southerland, and Peter Bragg; part of 525 ac grant to Joseph Cavin on S side Tygar R and on branches of Fergeson's and James' Creeks. Witness Wm Easley and Jon Gowen. Signed Joseph Cavin. Wit. oath none. Rec. Dec. 22, 1801. Dower renounced Elizabeth Caven to Reuben Barrett May 26, 1801

p. 49-50 Nov. 10, 1799 John Eades Morrow (Spartanburgh) to Jesse Morrow (Rutherford Co, NC); for 50£ sold 141 ac on E side Island Cr. Witness Wm Little, Isaac Morrow, James Morrow, and Orsborn (or Ausborn) Reese. Signed J.E. Morrow. Wit. oath Oct. 26, 1801 Orsborn Reese to A Lancaster. Rec. Dec. 23, 1801

p. 50-52 Jan. 26, 1801 John Eades Morrow (Pinckney Dist) to Philip Jean sr (same); for 10£ sterling sold 100 ac on branch of Island Cr of Pacolet R; border: Abram Markley; part of 431 ac grant States Office to John Eades Morrow. Witness Reuben Warran and William Morrow. Signed John E Morrow. Wit. oath Mar. 3, 1801 William Morrow to Geor Lamkin. Rec. Dec. 23, 1801

p. 52-53 Apr. 6, 1795 John Boley (Spartan Co) to John Pipes (same); for one Spanish milled dollar sold 200 ac on W side Sholey Cr. Witness Levi Burcham and Parsiller Pipes. Signed John Boley. Wit. oath Apr. 25, 1795 Levi Burcham to Ism Foster. Rec. Dec. 23, 1801

p. 53-56 Oct. 23, 1789 Thomas Farrar (Spartanburgh) to William Foster Amelia Co, Va); for 117£ sterling sold 300 ac on both sides Fairforrest Cr; border: W-William Benson and by John Prince; grant Oct. 26, 1767 to William Dikson in Mecklenburgh Co, NC and recorded in South Carolina Apr. 24, 1773; sold by William Dickson to Thomas Farrar. Witness Isham Foster, William Foster, and David Goodlett.

Signed Thomas and Peggy Farrier. Wit. oath Nov. 10, 1790 Thomas Farrier to D Goodlett. Rec. Dec. 23, 1801

p. 56-58 Nov. 29, 1800 William Hammett sr (Spartanburgh) to David Milhanks (same); for 3£ sold 80 ac on waters of Pacolet R and on Turkey pen Br; border: Jones. Witness Ellis Cannon, Benjamin Hammett, John Milhanks. Signed Wm Hammett. Wit. oath Nov. 25, 1801 John Milhanks to A Lancaster. Rec. Dec. 24, 1801

p. 58-60 Jan. 9, 1799 William Earnest and wife Rachel (Spartanburgh) to Thompson Chumley (same); for 55£ sold 150 ac; border: Alexander Alexander and Richard Stone; and sold "piece of land" William Earnest bought from Richard Chesney sr; otherwise William "forfiets" 55£ to Thompson Chumley. Witness Jacob Earnest and Isaac Crow. Signed William Earnest and Rachel's mark. Wit. oath Mar. 23, 1802 (sic) Isaac Crow to John Dean. Rec. Dec. 24, 1801

p. 60-62 Apr. 15, 1801 Robert English (Sumter Dist) to Samuel Tomlinson (Roan Co, NC); for $100 sold (ac not given); half of land on S fork of Tygar R granted May 13, 1763 Gov. Thomas Boon to Thomas English. Witness G Cooper, Gates Harris, and John Perry esq. Signed Robert English. Wit. oath (Sumter Co) Apr. 15, 1801 John Perry to G Cooper. Rec. Jan. 8, 1802. Dower renounced (Sumter Co) Elizabeth English to G Cooper Apr. 15, 1801

p. 62-63 Oct. 12, 1801 Henry Brown (Spartanburgh) to Fleming Smith (same); for $300 sold 199 ac which Henry Brown "lately" bought from Fleming Smith; border: Peter Smith, Shands Golightly, James Smith, Dodd, and Moses Foster; on waters of Kelsoe's Cr. Witness William Lancaster and Lewis Brown. Signed Henry Brown's mark. Wit. oath Jan. 4, 1802 William Lancaster to I Harrison. Rec. Jan. 12, 1802

p. 63-65 Aug. 24, 1801 Capt John James (Spartanburgh) to Robert Foster (same); for $500 sold 2 horses, 4 feather beds and furniture, a set of blacksmith tools, 6 cattle, 25 hogs, 3 pots, 2 dutch ovens, 2 walnut tables, a chest, 6 water vessells, 10 chairs, 4 casks, 10 still vessells, a woman's saddle, a man's saddle, a cupboard, 2 dishes, 10 plates, 5 basons, a turene(?), a set of tea ware, coffee pot, sooking glass, a cotton machine, 4 axes, a mattock, 2 shovel plows, a spaid, 2 spinning wheels, 2 pair of drawing gear, and a hogshead of tobacco. Witness I Harrison JQ. Signed John James. Certified Aug. 24, 1801 by I Harrison. Rec. Jan. 12, 1801

p. 65 Jan. 16, 1802 Job Sosbee to I Harrison; Job says his ear marks on cattle, hogs, and sheep is slit and under tut or keel in right ear and smooth cross in left ear. Rec. Jan. 18, 1802. Signed Job Sosbee's mark

p. 65-66 Dec. (blank), 1800 Moses Timmons (Spartanburgh) to John Hill (same); for $30 sold 150 ac on Cub Br and on waggon road from Spartanburgh to Greenville Court House; known as Agg Traylor's old place. Witness Thomas James and John James. Signed Moses Timmons. Wit. oath Jan. 15, 1802 John James to Ism Foster. Rec. Jan. 18, 1802

p. 66-68 Jul. 29, 1801 John Hill (Spartanburgh) to Richard Traylor (same); for $30 sold 150 ac on Cub Br and waggon road from Spartanburgh to Greenville Court House; known as Agg Traylor's old place. Witness John Underwood, Henry Walden, and John James. Signed John Hill's mark. Wit. oath Jan. 15, 1802 John James to Ism Foster. Rec. Jan. 18, 1802

p. 68-69 Aug. 26, 1801 Christopher Golightly (Spartanburgh) to Richard Daniel (same); for $200 sold 93 ac on Fairforrest Cr. Witness I Harrison JQ and Reuben Daniel. Signed Christi Golightly. Rec. Jan. 18, 1802. Dower renounce Jane Golightly to I Harrison Jan. 11,1802

p. 69-70 Jan. 9, 1802 Jesse Vincent (Spartanburgh) to Richardson Vincent (same); for $100 sold 200 ac on E side Pacolet R; border: Dart; grant Mar. 17, 1796 to Henry Wyatt. Witness I Harrison JQ and Reuben Daniel. Signed Jesse Vincent. Rec. Jan. 19, 1802

p. 70-71 Jan. 16, 1802 Benjamin Hammett (Spartanburgh) to William Smith (same); for $110 sold 100 ac on both sides Thomson's Br of Kelsoe's Cr of Fairforrest Cr; border: N-Micajah Barnett, S-James Smith, W-Charles James, and E-Fleming Smith. Witness Wm Hammett and I Harrison JQ. Signed Benjamin Hammett. Rec. Jan. 19, 1802

p. 71-73 Oct. 5, 1801 Terrell Wilkins (Spartanburgh) to Robert Wilkins (same); for 60£ sterling SC money sold 127 ac on both sides Gocher's Cr; part of 247 ac. Witness William Wilkins and Jane Wilkins. Signed Terrell Wilkins. Wit. oath Nov. 26, 1801 Jane Wilkins to Jno Lipscomb. Rec. Jan. 19, 1802

p. 73-74 Jan. 25, 1802 Jacob Earnhart (Spartanburgh) to John Wright (Laurens Dist); for $3,000 sold 14 Negroes: Hager, Sinder, Cole, Charlote, Rosetter (children of Hager), Alisey and her child, Sophe, Philis and her child Hannah, Sary, Fanny, Matt, Merinah, and Charles. Witness John Hembrick and Sarratt Wilson. Signed Jacob Earnhart. Wit. oath Jan. 26, 1802 John Hembrick to A Lancaster. Rec. Jan. 26, 1802

p. 74-75 Jan. 21, 1802 John Whittemore (Spartanburgh) to Thomas Price (same); for 65 Spanish milled dollars sold (ac not given) on S side Fergeson's Cr; border: Allen Gentry, Obadiah Gravel, James Southland, and Samuel Floyd. Witness Ignatius Twiley, and Thomas Shirley. Signed John Whittemore. Wit. oath Jan. 26, 1802 Thomas Shirley to Geor Lamkin. Rec. Jan. 27, 1802

p. 75-76 Jan. 4, 1802 William Taff (Spartanburgh) to son John Taff; for love and affection give all goods and chattles in William Taff's dwelling house known as McMahan's place on Tygar R and all stock and corn. Witness Samuel Snoddy and James McMahan. Signed William Taff. Wit. oath Jan. 27, 1802 James McMahan to A Lancaster. Rec. Jan. 27, 1802

p. 76-78 Jan. 15, 1802 David Allen jr (Spartanburgh) to Willis Allen (same); for $33 sold "part of tract of 30 ac" on N side Gocher's Cr; border: Willis Allen and William Brock. Witness Charles Evans and Charlott Evans. Signed David Allen. Wit. oath Jan. 15, 1802 Charles Evans to John Lipscomb. Rec. Jan. 27, 1802

p. 78 Feb. 1, 1802 Thomas Betterton to Geor Lamkin; Thomas says his ear brand on cattle, hogs, and sheep is half cross in each ear out of back part of ear. Signed Thomas Betterton. Rec. Feb. 4, 1802

p. 78-80 Dec. 13, 1800 George Floyd (Spartanburgh) to Thomas Shurley (same); for $500 sold 171 ac where Thomas Shurley lives; border: mouth of Forgeson's Cr on S side Tygar R, mouth of Floyd's Cr, Samuel Floyd, and Richard Willis. Witness John Ward and Andrew Thomson. Signed George Floyd's mark. Wit. oath Jan. 27, 1802 John Ward to George Bruton. Rec. Feb. 5, 1802

p. 80-82 Feb. 3, 1801 Gannaway Johnson (Spartanburgh) to Lewis Brown (same); for $100 sold 128 ac where Gannaway Johnson lives; border: N-David Golightly, S-Lewis Brown, and E-rest of grant; grant to Col Henry White who sold to Gannaway Johnson; on waters of Fair-forrest Cr. Witness William Lancaster and Clary Lancaster. Signed Gannaway Johnson's mark. Rec. Feb. 5, 1802. Dower renounced Nancy Johnson to Isham Harrison Feb. 22, 1802

p. 82-84 Oct. 3, 1801 William Adcock (Spartanburgh) to Henry Adcock (same); for $100 sold 100 ac on N side Pacolet R; part of 300 ac "run" by Frances Ballenger; border: Leonard Adcock and John Larkey. Witness Leo Adcock and Henry Adcock. Signed William Adcock's mark. Wit. oath Dec. 5, 1801 Leo Adcock to Geor Lamkin. Rec. Feb. 12, 1802

p. 84-85 Nov. 1, 1801 Bridges Arendell (Spartan Co) to mother Rebecca Arendell; for love and good will give all Negroes and other property she gave him in deed Oct. 3, 1797; he has given her an inventory of property. Witness Daniel McCay and William Morgan. Signed Bridges Arendell. Wit. oath Feb. 19, 1802 William Morgan to John Lipscomb. Rec. Feb. 20, 1802

p. 85-86 Nov. 30, 1801 Robert Ligon sr (Spartanburgh) to son Robert Ligon jr (same); for love and affection give 225 ac; all of upper half of tract Robert sr bought from William Ford including improvements made by William Ford; on E side of Tygar R; border: his sons John Ligon and Robert Ligon jr; Robert sr bought 450 ac from William Ford. Witness Elijah Barnett and Giles Connell. Signed Robert Ligon. Wit. oath Feb. 8, 1802 Giles Connell to I Harrison. Rec. Feb. 22, 1802

p. 86-87 Oct. 16, 1801 William Dodds, executor of Francis Dodds desc (late of SC) to Shields Booker; for $600 sold 300 ac; border: Robert Jamison, Collins, Traylor, and Tanner. Witness Ism Foster JP, John Collins, and Alexr McCarter. Signed William Dodds executor. Rec. Feb. 24, 1802

p. 87-89 Jun. 10, 1799 Samuel Fley (Spartanburgh) to John Mullinex (same); for $110 sold 220 ac on N side Tygar R and branches of Cain Cr; border: E & N-an old survey, NW-Ephraim Hill and Alexander McBeth, and SW-Benjamin Spence and an old line; survey Jul. 31, 1786 for Abraham Williams and granted Jun. 3, 1799 Gov. Edward Rutledge to Samuel Fley. Witness Wm Murrell and Christian C Thode. Signed Saml Fley. Wit. oath (Claremont Co, SC) Christian C Thode to John Horan. Rec. Feb. 26, 1802

p. 89-90 Feb. 20, 1802 Jesse Traylor (Spartanburgh) to Mason Shumate (same); for 10£ sold 2 ac on S side of N fork Tygar R. Witness Ism Foster and James Foster. Signed Jesse Traylor. Wit. oath Feb. 21, 1802 James Foster to Ism Foster. Rec. Feb. 27, 1802

p. 90-91 Feb. 13, 1802 Joel Traylor (Spartanburgh) to Mason Shumate (same); for 50£ sold 137 ac on N side of N fork Tygar R; part of grant Mar. 6, 1786 to Mason Coxsmithson who sold to Joel Traylor. Witness Isham Foster and James Foster. Signed Joel Traylor's mark. Wit. oath Feb. 27, 1802 James Foster to Ism Foster. Rec. Feb. 27, 1802

p. 91-92 (not given) 19, 1802 George Roebuck (Spartanburgh) to Burrell Bobo (same); for $200 sold 100 ac on Enoree R; border: NW-Burrell Bobo and river "nearly all around". Witness Absalom Bobo and Nathaniel Burton. Signed George Roebuck. Wit. oath Feb. 19, 1802 Nathaniel Burton to John Dean. Rec. Mar. 4, 1802

p. 92-93 Jan. 11, 1802 George Eslinger (Spartanburgh) to Thomas Moore (same); mortgage for 27£ 16s 3p for 230 ac where George Eslinger lives on Morgan's Br; border: Anderson, McClure, and Morgan; Condition: deed void if George pays Thomas 27£ 16s 3p in 12 months; Thomas takes $20 in cash and remainder to be paid in grain or horse flesh. Witness Nathaniel McCarrol and John Belford. Signed George Eslinger. Wit. oath Feb. 25, 1802 Nathaniel McCarrol to John Anderson. Rec. Mar. 4, 1802

p. 93-94 Dec. 26, 1800 John Lindsey (Spartanburgh) to Elijah Hendrix (same); for $100 sold 30 ac; grant to James Lindsey; on fork of Lick Cr; border: John Hambey. Witness Wm Hendrix and Nancy Hendrix. Signed John Lindsey. Wit. oath Feb. 24, 1802 Wm Hendrix to Ism Foster. Rec. Mar. 4, 1802

p. 94-96 Sept. 24, 1801 John Lindsey (Spartanburgh) to Amos Pilgrim (same); for $300 sold 170 ac on both sides Lick Cr of Enoree R; part of two grants (1) to William Moore and (2) James William Lindsey; border: W-Aaron Bawkins and Elijah Hendrix, S-Elijah Hendrix and Amos Pilgrim, E-Josey Woodruff, and N-Wm Hendrix. Witness Amos Pilgrim and Philip Pilgrim. Signed John Lindsey. Wit. oath Sept. 25, 1801 Philip Pilgrim to G Brewton. Rec. Mar. 5, 1802

p. 96-97 Jan. 15, 1802 John Ervin (Spartanburgh) to Isaac Crow; bond for $75 with security: 2 cows and calves, a hiefer, 2 yearlings, 2 beds and furniture, 2 bedsteads, a chest, a table, all his pewter and crockeryware, a lomb, an oven, 2 pots, a flax wheel, and a cotton wheel. Witness Nancy Erven and James Sills. Signed John Ervin. Wit. oath Feb. 24, 1802 James Sills to Ism Foster. Rec. Mar. 5, 1802

p. 97-99 May 18, 1801 Anthony Bates (Spartanburgh) to William Golightly (same); for $80 sold 100 ac on Richland Cr of Pacolet R; border: S-William Golightly, W & NW-Richard and Joroyal Barnett, E-by Iron Works land and borders road from Spartan Court House to Pinckneyville. Witness James Smith and Joroyal Barnett. Signed Anthony Bates' mark. Wit. oath Mar. 1, 1802 James Smith to A Lancaster. Rec. Mar. 5, 1802

p. 99-100 Oct. 19, 1797 Richard Willis and wife Drusilla (Spartanburgh) to William Shands Golightly (same); for 50£ sterling sold 164 ac on Thomson's Br of Kelsoe's Cr of Fairforrest Cr; border: N-William S Golightly, S-unknown, E-widow Golightly, and W-Michajah and Joroyal Barnett. Witness Joroyal Barnett and William Lancaster. Signed Richard and Drusilla Willis. Wit. oath Mar. 1, 1802 William Lancaster to A Lancaster. Rec. Mar. 5, 1802

p. 100-101 Jul. 25, 1801 Joseph Thomson (Ky and late of SC) to Alexander Thompson (Spartanburgh); for $1,000 sold (1) 200 ac on S fork of N fork Tygar R; grant to David Davis who sold to Nathaniel Miller who sold to Joseph Thomson; and (2) 307 ac adjoining granted Jun. 22, 1785 to Joseph Thomson. Witness John Hurt, Joseph Thompson, and James Jordan. Signed Joseph Thomson's mark. Rec. Mar. 8, 1802

p. 101-103 Nov. 4, 1801 David Leech and for John, William, and James Leech as "by power" Sarah and Joseph Leech, John Vaughan, Samuel Underwood, and Lamuel Loftis (all Spartanburgh except John, William, and James Leech) to Alexander Thompson (same); for $150 sold 200 ac on Middle fork Tygar R; border: David Evans (part of same tract); grant to John Leech sr desc. Witness Alexr Jordan, James Sornon, and certified by John Collins JP. Signed David and Joseph Leech, Sarah's mark, John Vaughan, Samuel Underwood and Lemuel Loftis. Rec. Mar. 9, 1802

p. 103-104 Dec. 13, 1801 James Millican (Spartanburgh) to William Millican (same); for $500 sold 220 ac on S side of N fork Pacolet R; including where James and William Millican live; border: Tate; grant "North" patent to Robert Tate and sold Jan. 13, 1785 by his heir John Tate to John McKnight who sold Jan. 6, 1794 to James Millican. Witness Thomas Chumly, Jesse Duglas, and Robt Millican. Signed James Millican's mark. Wit. oath Mar. 13, 1802 Jesse Duglas to John Anderson. Rec. Apr. 17, 1802

p. 104-106 Feb. 24, 1801 Hugh Means (Spartanburgh) to Anderson Cockrill (same); for $50 sold 60 ac on S side Lawson's fork of Pacolet R; part of grant Aug. 7, 1786 Gov. William Moultrie to Thomas Wood. Witness William Cockrill jr and Joshua McPharson. Signed Hugh Means. Wit. oath Mar. 23, 1802 William Cockrill to John Anderson. Rec. Apr. 20, 1802

p. 106-107 Dec. 28, 1801 James Crow (Spartanburgh) to Nicholas Jentice; for $140 sold 52½ ac on S side Tygar R; border: Bullox. Witness Jeremiah Gentry, John Crow, and John Thornton. Signed James Crow. Wit. oath Feb. 23, 1802 John Thornton to Saml Lancaster. Rec. Apr. 20, 1802

p. 107-108 Feb. 3, 1802 Basil Trail (Spartanburgh) to Joseph Lannam (same); for $240 sold 240 ac on both sides Dutchman's Cr; Basil bought land from Robert Sterling and wife Sary; part of 440 ac South Carolina governor to Sary Elder. Witness Aaron Smith and Lettice Smith. Signed Basil Trail. Wit. oath Mar. 22, 1802 Aaron Smith to Wm Smith. Rec. Apr. 20, 1802. Dower renounced Elizabeth Trail to Wm Smith Feb. 10, 1802

p. 108-110 Feb. 5, 1801 James Jordan (Spartanburgh) to Roubin Boman (same); for 65£ SC money sold (1) 167 ac on N fork Tygar R; border: John Snody and "others"; of which 50 ac is part of grant in 1767 Gov. William Tryon (NC) to Wm McMarkan on S side of N fork Tygar R; and (b) 117 ac adjoining granted in 1786 Gov. William Moultrie to Thomas Hightower. Witness John Pace and Wm Moore. Signed John Jordan. Wit. oath Mar. 13, 1802 Wm Moore to John Collins. Rec. Apr. 21, 1802

p. 110-112 Jan. 26, 1802 Benjamin Buey and wife Lucy (Spartanburgh) to Augustine Bumpass (same); for $164 sold 74 ac on S side of Two Mile Cr; border: W-Ebn Moses, S-William Hendrix, E-Christopher Rhodes, and land originally granted to James Hendrix and by James Casey. Witness John Moses and Ebenezer Moses. Signed Benjamin and Lucy Buey's marks. Wit. oath Jan. 27, 1802 John Moses to Chas Allen. Rec. Apr. 22, 1802. Dower renounced Lucy Buey to Charles Allen Jan. 27, 1802

p. 112-113 Aug. 29, 1798 James Blackwell (Spartanburgh) to Edward Wyatt (NC); for 30£ SC money sold 150 ac on Suck Cr near Null Shoal; border: John Dulback and Wdward Wyatt. Witness Leonard Adcock and Drury Scruggs. Signed James Blackwell. Wit. oath Jun. 1, 1799 Leonard Adcock to Geor Lamkin. Rec. Apr. 22, 1802

p. 113-114 Mar. 13, 1802 Rebecah Arendell (Spartan Co) to Bridges Arendell; for 16s 1p Va money sold a Negro girl named Mill about 14 years old who has been in possession of Bridges Arnedell "upwards" of 4 years. Witness Daniel McCay and Charles Hester. Signed Rebecah Arendell's mark. Wit. oath Mar. 22, 1802 Charles Hester to John Lipscomb. Rec. Apr. 23, 1802

p. 114-115 (not given), 1801 Charles Holt (Spartanburgh) to John Storye (or Stony) (same); for $200 sold 180 ac; grant Jul. 1, 1793 Gov. William Moultrie to (not given); border: James Betterton and David Prewet. Witness Absalom Bobo and James Winter. Signed Charles Holt's mark. Wit. oath Dec. 23, 1801 Absalom Bobo to Wm Smith. Rec. Apr. 23, 1802. Dower renounced Martha Holt to Wm Smith Dec. 23, 1801

p. 115-116 Mar. 17, 1802 David Allen jr (Spartanburgh) to Young Allen (same); for $30 sold 30 ac at fork of Gocher's Cr. Witness Drury Allen and Jesse Griffin. Signed David Allen. Wit. oath Mar. 13, 1802 Jesse Griffin to John Lipscomb. Rec. Apr. 23, 1802

p. 116-117 Oct. 29, 1801 Josiah Hatchet (Spartanburgh) to James Mayson (same); for $200 sold 100 ac on Ford's Cr; border: W-Francis Mayson, N-James Seay and James Hurt, E-Benjamin Rainwater, and SE-Mrs. Underwood. Witness John Ligon, Elizabeth Mason, and Francis Mason. Signed Josiah Hatchett. Wit. oath Mar: 22, 1802 Francis Mason to John Lipscomb. Rec. Apr. 23, 1802

p. 117-119 Oct. 7, 1800 David Wardlaw, sheriff (Abbeville Dist) to John Sims, by his agent John Brunnum (same); for $30 sold 300 ac on waters Enoree R; border: NE-Philmon Waters and Cox, NW-John Ford, and SW-"land laid out"; grant Feb. 3, 1775 to Paul Sehatatter; see writ from Charleston Common Pleas Court Wm Clarkson, surviving executor of Aaron Looebek desc, against Jas Hall Ramsey, administrator of Solurll Beaufort desc; sale Oct. 7, 1800. Witness Orange David and Frederick Burtz. Signed Dd Wardlaw sheriff AD. Wit. oath Mar. 15, 1802 (Laurens Dist) Frederick Burtz to Starling Tucker. Rec. Apr. 24, 1802

p. 119-120 Sept. 19, 1801 Daniel White (Spartanburgh) to Reuben Richards (same); for $70 sold 170 ac on waters of Green's Cr and on N side Pacolate R; border: Thomas Jones, David Jones, James Brown's land surveyed for George Ryner, Bryant, and Connell. Witness James Bryant and James Moore. Signed Daniel White. Wit. oath Mar. 19, 1802 James Bryant to John Lipscomb. Rec. Apr. 24, 1802

p. 120-121 Apr. 24, 1802 Absalom Lancaster, Samuel Lancaster, Brittain Willeford, Mary Haselwood, Aaron Lancaster, and Samuel Williams (all Spartanburgh) to Thomas C Williams esq (Montgomery Co, NC); power of attorney to obtain from estate of Lawrence Lancaster (Warren and Franklin Co, NC) their equal parts of Lawrence Lancaster's estate and to sign all necessary papers. Witness John Golightly and Willis Williford. Signed A Lancaster, Samuel Lancaster, Brittain Williford, Mary Haselwood's mark, and Saml Williams (Aaron Lancaster doesn't sign). Wit. oath Apr. 24, 1802 Willis Williford to I Harrison. Rec. Apr. 24, 1802

p. 121-122 Jul. 13, 1799 James Blackwell (Rutherford Co, NC) to Peter Gosnell (Lincoln Co, NC); for $80 sold 150 ac on Suck Cr near Mill Shoal; border: Peter Gosnell and Edward Wyatt. Witness Leonard Adcock and John Debback. Signed James Blackwell's mark. Wit. oath Mar. 4, 1802 Leonard Adcock to (not signed). Rec. Apr. 26, 1802

p. 122-124 Feb. 21, 1800 Thomas Betterton (Spartanburgh) to William Martindale (Union Co); for $500 sold (1) 78 ac on N side Tygar R; border: John Campbell and Timothy Toney; (2) 101 ac on N side Tygar R; part of 249 ac grant Jul. 3, 1772 to Timothy Toney; border: S-Tygar R, W-Joel Hembree, N-Samuel Cathcart, E-Daniel Grant, and at mouth of Cach Cr. Witness John Blasingame, Henry Birdson, and Kindred Bobo. Signed Thomas Betterton. Wit. oath Feb. 22, 1800 John Blasingame to John Martindale. Rec. Apr. 26, 1802. Dower renounced Patitiah Betterton to John Martindale Feb. 22, 1800

p. 124 Mar. 4, 1802 Ephraim Elder (Spartanburgh) to Wm Garrott (same); for 5£ sold 349 ac; border: Col Winn. Witness Ism Foster and John Cantrell. Signed Ephraim Elder. Wit. oath Mar. 4, 1802 Ephraim Elder to Ism Foster. Rec. Apr. 26, 1802

p. 124-125 Apr. 24, 1802 Thomas McKnight (Spartanburgh) to son Wm McKnight; for 80£ sold "all personal property": a roand horse, a black mare, 8 cows 6 years old, a calf (cattle marked with swallow fork in right ear and cross in left), 20 hogs (of the above mark), household furniture, 3 feather beds, and their furniture. Witness Hugh McMillin and Mary McDowell. Signed Thomas McKnight. Wit. oath Apr. 24, 1802 Hugh McMillin to Wm McDowell. Rec. Apr. 27,

1802

p. 125-126 Apr. 24, 1802 Thomas McKnight (Spartanburgh) to son Wm McKnight; for 100£ sterling SC money sold 322 ac on both sides N Pacolate R; grant to George Alexander "including his own improvements"; "including" 61 ac on S side N Pacolate R sold by James Varner to Thomas McKnight. Witness Hugh McMillin, Mary McDowell, and Margret Forbus. Signed Thomas McKnight. Wit. oath Apr. 24, 1802 Hugh McMillin to Wm McDowell. Rec. Apr. 27, 1802

p. 126-127 Feb. 21, 1801 James Smith (Spartanburgh) to William Ross Smith (same); for $500 sold 1,000 ac on branches of Island Cr of Pacolet R and waters of Thickety Cr; brant Apr. 26, 1801 Gov. John Drayton to James Smith; border: Markley and Dunnaway. Witness William Shands Golightly, John Smith, and Hancock Smith. Signed Jas Smith. Wit. oath Apr. 24, 1802 John Smith to A Lancaster. Rec. Apr. 27, 1802. Dower renounced Jane Smith to Isham Harrison Mar. 23, 1802

p. 127-129 Jul. 31, 1801 Penywell Wood (Spartanburgh) to Ism Hendrix (same); for $362.50 sold 200 ac on N side Rockfield Cr of Enoree R; including where Elishua Rucker lives; border: James Wheelor. Witness Henry Wood and Benjamin Wood. Signed Penuwell Wood. Wit. oath Feb. 22, 1802 Henry Wood to Denney Anderson. Rec. Apr. 28, 1802

p. 129-130 Jul. 31, 1801 Penuwell Wood (Spartanburgh) to Benjamin Wood (same); for 40£ sold 100 ac on N branch Rockeyfield Cr of Enoree R; border: Isham Hendrix; where Benjamin Wood lives; part of 1,340 ac sold by Edward Rutledge to Penuwell Wood. Witness Henry Wood and Isham Hendrix. Signed Penuwell Wood. Wit. oath Feb. 22, 1802 Henry Wood to Ism Foster. Rec. Apr. 28, 1802

p. 130-131 Nov. 18, 1801 James Burns and Solomon Hill (Spartanburgh) to Thomas Moore (same); for $300 sold 330 ac on small branches of Dutchman's Cr and Ward's Cr of Tygar R and both sides waggon road from Blackstock's ford on Tygar R to Charleston; border: W-Thomas Moore, N-Daniel Barnett, E-James Facres and Thomas Robinson, and S-"old line owner unknown"; grant Jan. 4, 1796 Gov. Arnoldus Vanderhorst to James Burns, Solomon Hill, and George Gilbreath and survey "for them" Dec. 18, 1794. Witness George Normon, Jason Moore, and James Robosin. Signed James Burnes and Solomon Hill. Wit. oath Mar. 23, 1802 Jason Moore to Drury McDaniel.

p. 131-133 Feb. 10, 1802 Joseph Lannam, carpenter (SC) to Bazzil Trail; for 500 Spanish milled dollars sold 240 ac on both sides Dutchman's Cr; part of 440 ac grant (date not given) South Carolina governor to Sarah Elder and sold 240 ac to Bassil Trail (sic); Condition: deed void if Joseph (sic) pays Bazzil $40 by Dec. 25, 1802 and $46 by Sept. 1, 1803. Witness Aaron Smith and Lettice Smith. Signed Joseph Lannam's mark. Wit. oath Mar. 16, 1802 Aaron Smith to Wm Smith. Rec. Apr. 28, 1802

p. 133-136 Jul. 17, 1798 Samuel Farrow, sheriff (Spartanburgh) to William Ford (same); for 71£ 10s sold 200 ac on Tygar R; writ from Spartanburgh Co Court (by Baylis Earle, esq) Dec. 23, 1789 and returnable to Court third Monday in Jun. 1790; from estate of Joseph Jones desc assess 42£ 13s 11p sterling; this due to John McEllehanye's debt vs Thomas and Candice Jones, administrators for Joseph Jones. Witness Joseph C Gist and Shepard Mize. Signed S Farrow, "late" sheriff Spartanburgh Co. Wit. oath Mar. 22, 1802 Joseph C Gist to John Anderson. Rec. Apr. 30, 1802

p. 136-137 Aug. 25, 1801 Shadrach Waldrop and Rachel Waldrop (Spartan Dist) to Obadiah Moss (same); for 125 silver dollars sold 50 ac; agreeable with plat "down" by Jas Wofford; on Enoree R. Witness

Jarrot Moss, Augustin Bumpass, and John Folley Moss. Signed Shadrach and Rachel Waldrop's marks. Wit. oath Jan. 27, 1802 Jarrot Moss to Chas Allen. Rec. May 1, 1802

p. 137-139 Dec. 1, 1801 John Gray (Spartanburgh) to William Patterson (same); for $220 sold (ac not given); remainder of 620 ac sold to Henry Pettet by John Gray and now owned by Joshua Pettet and Christopher Shags; see line drawn in deed from Gray to Pettet; 620 ac was surveyed for Joshua Pettet and John Hembree Nov. 15, 1788 on N side Pacolate R opposite the Healing Springs and bordering: SW, SE & NE-vacant. Witness Thomas Gore, Joshua Pettet, and William Saggs. Signed John Gray. Wit. oath Mar. 23, 1802 Thomas Gore to John Lipscomb. Rec. May 5, 1802

p. 139-140 Nov. 15, 1800 George Poole and wife Elizabeth (Spartan Dist) to Mark Gilbert (same); for $70 sold 100 ac "of Woodland land"; part of tract where George Poole lives; border: Joseph Venable and Joseph Bennet. Witness Dan Bennett, Samuel Gilbert, and Thomas Kimbel. Signed George Poole and Elizabeth's mark. Wit. oath Nov. 18, 1800 Dan Bennett to Wm McDowell. Rec. May 10, 1802

p. 140-142 Nov. 4, 1800 William Pruett and wife Mary (Spartanburgh) to Jeduthun Woodson (same); for $100 sold 50 ac on Motley's Cr of Tygar R; border: Thomas Pruett and Jeduthun Woodson; half of grant Mar. 5, 1787 Gov. Thomas Pinckney to Thomas Pruett. Witness John Grist, Samuel Pruett, and Alexander Pruett. Signed William and Mary Pruett's marks. Wit. oath Mar. 21, 1801 John Grist to Wm Smith. Rec. May 12, 1802

p. 142-143 Jan. 1, 1(omitted)02 John Morris (Spartanburgh) to David Lewis (same); for $268 sold 200 ac on waters Lawson's fork and on N side of Twilly's Br; where John Morris lives; formerly owned by John Bennett; part of tract bought from John Bennett. Witness Peter Hawkins and James Lewis. Signed John Morris. Wit. oath Mar. 6, 1802 Peter Hawkins and James Lewis to Ism Foster. Rec. May 13, 1802

p. 143-144 Sept. 19, 1801 James Saunders (Spartanburgh) to Lawrence Bankston (same); for $133 sold 50 ac on N side Pacolet R; border: Isaac Young and Buck Cr; part of grant Nov. 25, 1771 States Office to James Philips who sold to James Saunders. Witness Abraham Cantrell, John Brokshire, and William Sheed. Signed James Saunders' mark. Wit. oath (not given) 4, 1802 John Brokshire to Ism Foster. Rec. May 14, 1802

p. 144-145 Feb. 24, 1802 Hosea Camp (Spartanburgh) to Thomas Booker (same); for 150£ sold 300 ac on waters N fork Tygar R; border: Joseph Alexander and McCarter; grant Oct. 26, 1767 to John Knox now wife (sic) of George Pettis. Witness David Jordan, William Jordan, and James Jordan JQ. Signed Hosea Camp. Rec. May 15, 1802

p. 145-146 Aug. 20, 1801 George Petters (York Dist) to Hosea Camp (Spartanburgh); for 150£ sold 300 ac on waters N fork Tygar R; border: Joseph Alexander and McCarter; grant Oct. 26, 1767 to Jane Knox now wife of George Pettus. Witness James Jordan JQ, Alexr Candish, and Wm Kerr. Signed George Petters. Dower renounced (York Dist) Jane (or Jenny) Petters to James Jordan Aug. 21, 1801. Rec. Mar. 17, 1802

p. 146-148 Nov. 7, 1800 Elizabeth Weir (Chester Dist), widow,to Francis Bremar (Charleston Dist); for 30£ sold (1) 150 ac on waters Thickety Cr adjoining "the limestone land"; and (2) 1,740 ac on Miller's fork on N side Thickety Cr of Broad R; border: S & W-Mapp and Thompson, N & W-Tanner and Steddleton, E-vacant; survey Dec. 20, 1774 for Vardry McBee; both (1) and (2) sold by William Bratton esq late sheriff Pinckney Dist to Elizabeth Weir. Witness Thomas Beuford, Thomas Cherry, and Daniel Huger. Signed Elizabeth Weir's mark. Wit. oath Mar. 30, 1802 Daniel Huger to Stephen Ravenel. Rec. May 18, 1802

p. 148-149 Apr. 29, 1793 Thomas Philips and wife Mary (Spartanburgh) to William Gibson (same); for 15£ SC money sold 142 ac on branches of Cherokee Cr and S side Broad R; border: NW-Powel, S-Taylor, and E-vacant; grant Oct. 6, 1788. Witness Joseph John Martin, Nathaniel Robertson, and Thomas Robertson. Signed Thomas and Mary Philips' marks. Wit. oath Jan. 23, 1796 Nathaniel Robertson to H McCray. Rec. May 19, 1802

p. 149-150 Oct. 12, 1801 William Gibson (Spartanburgh) to Smith Lipscomb (same); for $30 sold 142 ac on branches of Cherokee Cr and S side Broad R; border: N-Powel and S-Taylor; grant Oct. 6, 1788 to Matthew Jones. Witness William Lipscomb and Elizabeth Lipscomb. Signed William Gibson's mark. Wit. oath Apr. 3, 1802 William Lipscomb to John Lipscomb. Rec. May 20, 1802

p. 150-151 Jul. 24, 1801 William Dodds (Levinston Co, Ky), a single man, to James McMacken and James Jordan for James Jordan McMacken (Spartanburgh); for $100 sold (ac not given) on both sides N fork Tygar R including place called the narrow passage; border: Middle fork Tygar R; grant Oct. 26, 1767 to William McMaken who sold to William Dodds. Witness Mordaccai Clark, John Jordan, and James Jordan JQ. Signed William Dodds. Rec. May 20, 1802

p. 151-152 Mar. 16, 1802 Thomas Foster (Spartanburgh) to John Barnett (same); for $80 sold 40 ac on N side of Fairforrest Cr; border: John Barnett and Ford's old line. Witness Capt. James Smith and William Foster. Signed Thomas Foster's mark. Wit. oath Mar. 19, 1802 James Smith to I Harrison. Rec. May 25, 1802

p. 152-154 Dec. 6, 1801 John Young sr and Ezekiel Young (both Spartanburgh) to Jonathan Wall (same); for $500 sold 250 ac on Jacob's Br of S fork Pacolet R; border: Danl White, Bennett, Andrew, E and W branch of Richland Cr, Benjamin Clark, and Bodley's Br; part of two grants to William Young and Thomas Bennett who sold to John Young and Ezekiel Young. Witness Sarh Young, Daniel White, and James White. Signed John Young's mark and Ezekel Young. Wit. oath Apr. 5, 1802 Daniel White to John Anderson. Rec. May 25, 1802

p. 154-155 Sept. 19, 1801 James Brown (Spartanburgh) to Reuben Richards (same); for $100 sold 100 ac on N side Pacolate R and on waters of Green's Cr; border: Jesse Connell. Witness James Moore and James Bryant. Signed James Brown's mark. Wit. oath Mar. 19, 1802 James Bryant to John Lipscomb. Rec. May 28, 1802

p. 155-156 Jul. 23, 1800 John Reid (Union Dist) to William Willis (Spartanburgh); for $60 sold 40 ac on S side Pacolate R below Pacolet Springs; border: Henry Pettet and William Poole sr; includes cleared land on River that William Reid sr bought from Henry Pettet. Witness George Hatfield, William Poole, and Phillipp Zeller (or Zoller). Signed John Reid's mark. Wit. oath Feb. 19, 1801 George Hatfield to John Lipscomb. Rec. Jun. 1, 1802

p. 156-158 Jan. 2, 1801 Willis Whitaker (Kershaw Dist) to John Dean (Spartan Dist); for $214.30 sold 250 ac on branch of Two Mile Cr of Enoree R; border: Andrew Hendrix and Daniel Morine; survey by James Wofford for James Whitaker and granted in 1774 Gov. Bull to James Whitaker. Witness Isaac Arthur Brown Ross and Hannah Ross. Signed Willis Whitaker. Wit. oath (Kershaw Dist) Jan. 2, 1801 Isaac A Brown Ross to A. B. Ross. Rec. Jun. 3, 1802. Dower renounced (Kershaw Dist) Sarah Whitaker to A. B. Ross Jan. 2, 1801

p. 158-160 Nov. 27, 1801 Brittain Williford (Spartanburgh) to Thomas Williams (same); for $100 sold 89 ac on waters of Dutchman's Cr; part of 456 ac grant Nov. 6, 1786 to Brittain Williford. Witness Wilie Williford, Gideon Reynolds, and Lettice Smith. Signed Britain Williford. Wit. oath Nov. 27, 1801 Wilie Williford to Wm Smith. Rec. Jun. 4, 1802. Dower renounced Ludy Williford to Wm Smith Nov. 27, 1801

p. 160-161 Aug. 19, 1799 Isaac Hendrix (Spartanburgh) to John Dean (same); for $150 sold 100 ac on S side Two Mile Cr; half of survey by E Pearson for Andrew Hendrix and granted in 1773 Gov. Bull to Andrew Hendrix. Witness Thomas Clarke, Nicholas Smith, and Thomas Farrow. Signed Isaac Hendrix's mark. Wit. oath Mar. 23, 1800 Thomas Farrow to A Lancaster. Rec. Jun. 5, 1802. Dower renounced Fallaby (or Falleby) Hendrix to Thomas Moore Apr. 29, 1800

p. 161-162 Dec. 19, 1801 James Tracy (Spartanburgh) to John Tolleson (same); for $60 sold two oxen both 3 years old next Spring: one is red with white face and other is red with "white pided one"; 2 heifers 2 years old both red pided, 3 stears 2 years old: one black and one white pided; a brown cow and young calf: cow is red and has white face and was bought from Edward Auason; a cow and yearling: cow is black and red and was bought from Wm Lipscomb; a small bundle cow bought from John Auston; no condition on sale. Witness John Gossett and Major Gossett. Signed James Tracy's mark. Wit. oath Mar. 29, 1802 John Gossett and Major Gossett to William Simpson. Rec. Jun. 9, 1802

p. 162-163 (blank), 1801 Joseph Barnett (Spartanburgh) to John Leatherwood (same); for $18 sold 12 ac on branches of Enoree R; part of grant to Joseph Barnett desc. Witness B. W. Waters and William Landford. Signed Joseph Barnett. Wit. oath Mar. 20, 1802 Joseph Barnett to John Dean. Rec. Jun. 11, 1802

p. 163-165 Nov. 14, 1801 George Newman (Spartanburgh) to John Smith (same); for 20£ sterling sold 100 ac on N side Tygar R and on branches of Coin's Cr; border: Joel Smith, John OSheal(?), and Jno Hewett; grant Mar. 2, 1789 to George Newman. Witness Drury Smith and John Red. Signed George Newman's mark. Wit. oath Feb. 26, 1802 John Red to Saml Lancaster. Rec. Jun. 11, 1802

p. 165-166 Mar. 9, 1801 William and Solomon Hill (Spartanburgh) to Henry Gray (same); for 60£ sterling sold 200 ac on Middle fork Tygar R; grant Apr. 3, 1786 to Robert Nisbitt jr who sold to John Sloan who sold to William and Solomon Hill. Witness Aries Brown and Charles Moore. Signed Wm Hill jr, Solomon Hill, and Nancy Hill. Wit. oath Mar. 20, 1802 Aries Brown to John Collins. Rec. Jun. 11, 1802

p. 166-168 Nov. 24, 1795 Sarah Barnett (Hancock Co, Ga) to John Leatherwood (Spartanburgh); for 40£ sterling sold 100 ac on branch of Two Mile Cr of Enoree R; border: Thomas McCroy and Henry Corley; part of grant May 15, 1772. Witness Joseph Barnett, Miles Nash, and Benjamin Barnett. Signed Sarah Barnett's mark. Wit. oath Mar. 20, 1802 Joseph Barnett to John Dean. Rec. Jun. 14, 1802

p. 168-169 Oct. 1, 1790 Matthew Jones (Lincoln Co, NC) to Thomas Philips (Spartanburgh); for 15£ SC money sold 142 ac on branches of Cherokee Cr and S side Broad R; border: NW-Powel, S-Jarfer (sic), E-vacant, and Taylor. Witness Vardry McBee, Nathaniel Robertson, and Stephen Rainey. Signed Matthew Jones. Wit. oath Oct. 2, 1790 Vardry McBee to Obadiah Trimmier. Rec. Jun. 14, 1802

p. 169-171 Oct. 25, 1800 Charles Kimble and wife Sukkey (Spartanburgh) to William Poole (same); for $500 sold 100 ac on both sides Lawson's Fork. Witness A Lancaster JP and Jeremiah Garner. Signed Charles Kimberl and Sukkey's mark. Certified Apr. 21, 1802 by A Lancaster. Rec. Jun. 17, 1802

p. 171-172 Oct. 31, 1801 Sarah Leach, David Leach, powers of attorney for John and William Leach, and James Leach, Joseph Leach, John Vaughn, Samuel Underwood, and Lemuel Loftis (for ourselves) (Spartanburgh) to Thomas Booker; for $800 sold (1) 150 ac; grant Oct. 1, 1767 Gov. William Tryon (NC) to Alexander McCarter who sold to John Leach; and (2) 219 ac grant Jan. 19, 1790 Gov. Charles Pinckney to John Leach. Witness Michael Miller, Mary Jones, and Rebekah Culbertson. Signed Sarah Leach's mark, David Leach, John Leach, William Leach, James Leach, John Vaughn, Saml Underwood, Joseph Leach, and Lemuel Loftis' mark. Wit. oath Jun. 8, 1802 Michael Miller to Ism Foster. Rec. Jun. 18, 1802

p. 172-173 Feb. 27, 1802 Peter Peterson (Spartanburgh) to John Tollison (same); for 100£ sold 2(page torn)8 ac on N side Pacolate R; border: N-George Runer and Jas Brown, W-Jonas and Howard, S-Robert Thompson and Henry Pettet, and E-James Wilkins. Witness Muse Tollison and John Gossett. Signed Peter Peterson. Wit. oath Mar. 1, 1802 John Gossett to William Simpson. Rec. Jun. 18, 1802

p. 173-174 Nov. 25, 1801 David Golightly (Spartanburgh) to Elijah Barnett (same); for $200 sold 77 ac on S dide Fairforrest Cr; border: E-David Golightly, W & N-Robert Ligon, and S-Oruendough; where David Golightly formerly lived; upper end of tract sold by Robert Walker to David Golightly known as McCloore's land. Witness Capt. James Smith and Joseph Barnett. Signed D Golightly. Wit. oath May 15, 1802 James Smith to I Harrison. Rec. Jun. 19, 1802

p. 174-176 May 4, 1799 Benjamin Busey (Spartanburgh) to Benjamin Wofford (same); for 5£ SC money sold 600 ac on N side Enoree R; part of which is included in Wm Hambey's grant with title not warranted. Witness Wm Wofford, Mason Morse, John Pennington, and Panaman Tate. Signed Benjamin Busey's mark. Wit. oath Apr. 27, 1802 Panaman Tate to John Dean. Rec. Jun. 21, 1802. Dower renounced Lucy Busey to Thomas Moore May 24, 1799

p. 176-178 Jun. 1, 1799 Benjamin Wofford sr (Spartanburgh) to Daniel McKie (same); for 500£ sold 790 ac; plat attached shows border: on N of Enoree R, Wm Earnest, William Hambey, Joseph Wofford, "old line owney unknown", Wm Stratonburg, vacant, and Patrick Hynds; part of two grants on both sides Enoree R to Bartlett Brown sr (1) May 11, 1753 and sold to Benjamin Wofford sr by Benjamin Brown on Oct. 12, 1785 (see Book B p. 503, 504, and 505 rec. Mar. 5, 1792) and (2) Oct. 3, 1785 and sold to Benjamin Wofford sr by "said" Busey May. 4, 1799. Witness Laban P Poole and Paraman Tate. Signed Benj Wofford. Wit. oath Apr. 29, 1802 Paraman Tate to John Dean. Rec. Jun. 22, 1802

p. 178-180 Feb. 18, 1801 Joseph Woodruff (Spartanburgh) to Daniel McKie (same); for $50 sold 100 ac on Dildine's Cr of Enoree R; border: SW-William Stauttenburgh, N-Samuel Padan and others vacant; grant Jun. 3, 1773 to Norman Dildine; where John Cross formerly lives and now Morgan Darnall lives; sold Mar. 8, 1800 by John Cross to Joseph Woodruff. Witness Henry Jones and Paraman Tate. Signed Joseph Woodruff's mark. Wit. oath Apr. 29, 1802 Paraman Tate to John Dean. Rec. Jun. 23, 1802. Dower renounced Anne Woodruff to Daniel Wright Apr. 6, 1802

p. 180-181 Jan. 1, 1802 Joseph Dill (Spartanburgh) to Thomas Philips sr; a bond of $400; condition: bond void if Joseph makes deed to Thomas for tract on People's Cr; see plat now in Joseph's possession; title to be made on Jan. 2, 1802 and Thomas pays $134 2/3. Witness Daniel McCay and William Tate. Signed Joseph Dill. Wit. oath (Union Co) William Tate to John Jefferies. Rec. Jun. 28, 1802

p. 181-182 Dec. 13, 1801 Hosea Camp (Spartanburgh) to Joseph Scales (Rockingham Co, NC); for $1,100 sold 296 ac on N fork Tygar R; in two tracts: (1) grant to Samuel Nesbett and (2) grant to Hoseah Camp. Witness John Dodd, John Jamison, James Scales, and James Ballinger. Signed Hosea Camp. Wit. oath Jun. 26, 1802 John Dodd to James Jordan. Rec. Jun. 28, 1802

p. 182-183 Nov. 13, 1799 Jesse Temple (Carron Co, Ky) to William Hester (Spartanburgh); for 80£ SC money sold 162 ac on both sides Little Cherokee Cr; part of survey by James Martin for Charles Miles. Witness John Arendell sr and John Cooper. Signed Jesse Temple. Wit. oath Jun. 25, 1802 John Arendell to John Kukman. Rec. Jun. 28, 1802

p. 183-185 Jan. 15, 1800 William Hester (Spartanburgh) to John Hester (same); for 80£ SC money sold 162 ac on both sides Little Cherokee Cr; part of survey by James Martan (sic) for Charles Miles. Witness Thomas Phillips and John Ruckman. Signed Wm Hester. Wit. oath Jun. 24, 1802 Thomas Phillips to John Kukman. Rec. Jun. 29, 1802

p. 185-186 Feb. 1, 1802 Jonathan Davis (Spartanburgh) to David Jones (same); for 20£ sold 100 ac; where "he" now lives; border: David Jones, Howel, and Connell; grant "state" to James Brown. Witness Judith Davis and Sary Davis. Signed Jonathan Davis. Wit. oath Feb. 10, 1802 Judith Davis to John Lipscomb. Rec. Jul. 19, 1802

p. 186-188 Sept. 10, 1796 David Jones (Spartanburgh) to William Brock (same); a bond of 120£ sterling; Condition: bond void if David Jones makes title to William Brock for two tracts--(1) 421 ac and (2) 175 ac part of 350 ac "the said William Brock has paid of (sic) the 3-20£ notes" then David Jones to make titles. Witness John Lipscomb and David Jones. Signed "name cut out of original". Rec. Jul. 20, 1802. Wit. oath Feb. 2, 1802 John Brock to John Lipscomb--John Brock says he bonds to titles for land that David Jones desc gave William Brock and met "the old gentleman with his son David Jones" on the road, and the old man said if David Jones, his son, would give the 10£ horse he should have the land as his property. Wit. oath Apr. 3, 1801 William Brock to John Lipscomb--William says David Jones desc and his son David Jones came and asked him if William would let him have the land back; William said they could have it if David Jones would give William 10£; David said he couldn't and William said he couldn't take less; son, David Jones, said he would give 10£ and William said he could have land; "old man" siad "David the land is yourn" and David Jones jr sent William the 10£ horse by John Brock.

p. 188-189 (not given), 1801 David Leech for self and for John Leech for William Leech and James Leech "(as by Power)", Joseph Leech, John Vaughan, and Lamuel Loftis (all Spartanburgh except John, William, and James Leech whose residence is in power of attorney to David Leech) to Samuel Underwood (same); for $250 sold 117 ac on S fork of N fork Tygar R; grant to John Leech and then bordering vacant land. Witness Richard Willing and John Collins JP. Signed David Leech, by Power-John Leech, Wm Leech, James Leech, Joseph Leech, John Vaughan, Lamuel Loftis' mark, and Sarah Leech's mark. Rec. Jul. 20, 1802

p. 189-190 Feb. 13, 1802 John Mottey (Greenville Dist) to Lemuel Loftis (Spartanburgh); for $200 sold 200 ac where Lemuel

Loftis lives. Witness B. P. McMakin and Howard Bailey. Signed John Mottey. Wit. oath Apr. 19, 1802 B. P. McMakin to Ism Foster. Rec. Jul. 20, 1802

p. 190-191 Jun. 15, 1801 Joseph Collins (Spartanburgh) to Aries Brown (same); for $50 sold 16 ac; border: James Nesbett's Spring Br and Aries Brown. Witness Gabriel Benson and John Collins. Signed Joseph Collins. Wit. oath (not dated) John Collins to James Jordan. Rec. Jul. 22, 1802

p. 191-193 Apr. 13, 1802 Minor Winn (Winnsborough, SC) to William Wells esq (Spartanburgh); for $800 sold 1,000 ac on branches of Tygar R; border: NE & SE-John Ford, NW-Porcher and Lawson; includes crossroads where Georgia and Blackstock roads pass eachother; grant to John Parker and sold Nov. 3 & 4, 1773 to Joseph Kirkland and sold Feb. 12 & 13, 1789 to Minor Winn. Witness Abner Benson, Noah Wells, and Lewis Cockrell. Signed M Winn. Wit. oath Aug. 2, 1802 Abner Benson to A Lancaster. Rec. Aug. 11, 1802

p. 193-195 Apr. 5, 1802 William Thompson (Spartanburgh) to William Wells (same); for $130 sold half an ac on W side of the Court House; border: S-"public land", E-Public street, N-Thomson (lot #2), and W-lot #3 on plat of Spartanburgh, SC; plat attached shows border: "Main Cross Street"; Thomson's lot #3 border: lot 2, Public land, lot 4 (2/3 ac sold to William Wells by another deed) and Thomson; lot 4 border: lot 3, Public land, McKie's land, and Thomson; lots 2, 3, and 4 in a row side by side. Witness Abner Benson, A Lancaster JP, and Richard Thomson. Signed Wm Thomson. Rec. Aug. 11, 1802

p. 195-196 Apr. 5, 1802 William Thomson (Spartanburgh) to William Wells (same); for $170 sold 2/3 ac; lot 4 in Spartanburgh, SC; border: near old Jail and Public ground. Witness Abner Benson, A Lancaster JP, and Richard Thomson. Signed Wm Thomson. Rec. Aug. 12, 1802

p. 196-198 Mar. 16, 1802 Joseph Wade (Spartanburgh) to grandson William Thomas, minor son of Richard Thomas (same); for love and affection give 125 ac; includes "small" improvements made by Richard Thomas; border: N-Henry Foster and Joseph Hayes, E & S-Henry Foster, W-Joseph Wade; on N side Fairforrest Cr. Witness Joseph Hayes and Jas Barnett. Signed Joseph Wade. Wit. oath Aug. 10, 1802 Joseph Hayes to I Harrison. Rec. Aug. 13, 1802

p. 198-199 Jun. 8, 1799 Zacheriah Robinson (Mongumery Co, Tenn) to John Robinson (Spartanburgh); "for value received this date" sold Negro man named Aaron. Witness Diskin Grant and John Hammett. Signed Zacheriah Robinson. Wit. oath Aug. 18, 1802 John Hammett to A Lancaster. Rec. Aug. 19, 1802

p. 199-201 Jul. (blank), 1801 Jeremiah Stokes (Greenville Dist) to Samuel Hunt (Spartanburgh); for $100 sold 50 ac on N side of S fork Pacolate R; part of grant Sept. 25, 1766 to John Crawford and sold to Joab Mitchell and sold to Robert Wilkins, and sold to George Blanton, and sold to James McElory and sold to Edward Hampton whose daughter (not named) Jeremiah Stokes married. Witness Baylis Earle and Edward H Earle. Signed Jeremiah Stokes. Wit. oath Jun. 5, 1802 Baylis Earle sr to John Anderson. Rec. Aug. 19, 1802

p. 201-202 May 31, 1802 Edmond Bishop (Spartanburgh) to George Lewis (same); for $60 sold 50 ac; W half of 100 ac grant to Peter Lewis; border: George Lewis III; includes "upper" improvements. Witness Lewis Cockrell and Ephraim Lewis. Signed Edmund Bishop. Wit. oath Aug. 25, 1802 Ephraim Lewis to Ism Foster. Rec. Sept. 2, 1802

p. 202-203 Oct. 26, 1801 William Poole (Spartanburgh), iron master, to Stephen Pace (same); for $100 sold 100 ac on S side of S fork Tygar R; grant Jun. 5, 1786 to John Rosin who sold to William Poole. Witness John Wood and Aries Brown. Signed William Poole. Wit. oath Aug. 24, 1802 John Wood to Isham Foster. Rec. Sept. 3, 1802

p. 203-204 Feb. 5, 1802 William Dunkin (Spartanburgh) to John Jordan (same); (money not mentioned) sold a white horse known as Bull, a colt named Whisler, all his cows and yearlings with their calves, a quantity of corn, all "goods" household stuff, implements and furniture therein, 5 hogs in the pen at the "above" property; delivered in presence of David Jordan and Henry Gray. Witness David Jordan and Henry Gray. Signed William Dunkin. Wit. oath Aug. 22, (not given) David Jordan to James Jordan. Rec. Sept. 14, 1802

p. 204-205 Jan. 22, 1802 Obadiah Watson (Spartanburgh) to Joshua Richards (same); for $50 sold 51 ac; part of 393 ac grant Nov. 28, 1798 to Obadiah Watson. Witness Jacob Crocker and George Walker. Signed Obadh Watson. Wit. oath May 15, 1802 Jacob Crocker to John Lipscomb. Rec. Sept. 14, 1802

p. 205-206 (not given), 1801 James McElwean (Union Dist) to daughter Agnes Storey; for love and affection give a Negro boy named Abram which James McElwean delivered to Agnes Storey. Witness Thomas Compton, Moses White, and James Storey. Signed James McElwean's mark. Wit. oath May 15, 1802 James Storey to Wm Smith. Rec. Sept. 14, 1802

p. 206-207 Dec. 19, 1801 Reuben Newman (Spartanburgh) to Thomas Gn Potter (or Pottor); for one Eagle (or $10) sold 100 ac on S side Tyger R; border: below Grant's ford, Mary Wilson, and "the" meeting house. Witness Reuben Wilson and Anthony Shands. Signed Reuben Newman. Wit. oath Dec. 24, 1801 Anthony Shands to Wm Smith. Rec. Sept. 15, 1802

p. 207-209 Oct. 20, 1801 Charles Rodgers (Spartanburgh) to James Finch (same); for $100 sold 58 ac on waters of Fairforrest Cr and on N side of "old" road; border: William Lancaster, Thomas Davidson, Col. Thomas Taylors, Charles McCarter, and Thomas Smith. Witness Daniel White and James Gourley. Signed Charles Rodgers' mark. Wit. oath Apr. 13, 1802 Daniel White to Saml Lancaster. Rec. Sept. 17, 1802

p. 209-210 Mar. 7, 1800 James Wofford (Spartanburgh) to Benjamin Griffith (Greenville Co); for 80£ sterling sold 300 ac on N fork Furgeson's Cr of Tygar R; border: Henry Middleton on two sides and Francis Fowler on other side. Witness Benjamin Griffith jr and Catey Wofford. Signed James Wofford. Wit. oath Mary 27, 1802 (Greenville Dist) Benjamin Griffith jr to Kilgore. Rec. Sept. 17, 1802

p. 210-212 Mar. 20(?), 1802 Moses Timmons (Spartanburgh) to Robert Foster (same); for $1,000 sold 330 ac on waters of Tygar R; border: Abner Timmons, Samuel Timmons, Shields Booker, Bob Jamison, Brown's Cr, and including Mill Shoal. Witness James Reece, Henry Wells, and David Tanner. Signed Moses Timmons. Wit. oath Sept. 11, 1802 Henry Wells to T Harrison. Rec. Sept. 18, 1802. Dower renounced Hannah Timmons to I Harrison Nov. 17, 1802

p. 212-213 Dec. 24, 1798 John Luckeroy (96 Dist) to William Gossett sr (same); for 40(£ ?) sold 135 ac on waters of Storey's Mill Cr; border: John King and Widow Lemaster. Witness John Gossett, John Gossett (sic), and William Gossett jr. Signed John Luckeroy's mark. Wit. oath Feb. 27, 1802 William Gossett jr to William Simpson. Rec. Sept. 20, 1802

p. 213-215 Aug. 18, 1802 Lucy Barnett, Joroyal Barnett, Micajah Barnett, Richard Willis, Nathaniel Burton, John Barnett, James Barnett, and Elijah Barnett (all Spartanburgh) to Richard Barnett (same); for $400 sold 369 ac; remainder of the meeting house tract on waters of Kelsoe's Cr of Fairforrest Cr; border: Legan, James, Meeting House Br, Smith, Elijah Barnett. Witness Jas Smith and William Lancaster. Signed Lucy Barnett's mark, Joroyal Barnett, Michael Barnett, John Barnett, James Barnett, and Elijah Barnett, Nathl Burton, and Richard Willis. Wit. oath Sept. 14, 1802 William Lancaster to A Lancaster. Rec. Sept. 20, 1802

p. 215-216 Sept. 7, 1802 Christopher Orenduff (Spartanburgh) to Robert Legan (or Ligan) (same); for $50 sold 10 ac on N side Fairforrest Cr; border: Robert Legan and Barnett. Witness Richard Barnett and William Lancaster. Signed Christopher Orenduff's mark. Wit. oath Sept. 14, 1802 William Lancaster to Absalom Lancaster. Rec. Sept. 21, 1802

p. 216-217 Dec. 24, 1793 Tilman Bobo (Spartanburgh) to Ebenezer Moss (or Morse) (same); a bond of 100£ sterling sell all right and claim to "tract" on N side Enoree R joining Mountain Shoal. Witness none. Signed Tilman Bobo. Dec. 24, 1793 if Ebenezer Moss looses land, then he can't recover anything from Tilman Bobo. Witness Edward Arnold and Edward Hooper. Signed Ebenezer Moss' mark. Wit. oath Mar. 23, 1802 Edward Arnold to John Dean. Rec. Sept. 27, 1802

p. 217-218 Jan. 3, 1800 Johnston Smith (Jackson Co, Ga) to Samuel Nesbett (Spartanburgh); for $342 sold 192 ac on both sides S Tygar R; grant Jan. 21, 1785 to Rodger Smith; Johnston Smith is heir-at-law of Rodger Smith desc; part included in 400 ac grant to James Mayson excepted from this sale. Witness Samuel F Thomson, Joseph Culbertson, and William D Thomas. Signed Johnston Smith. Wit. oath Sept. 24, 1802 William D Thomas to James Jordan. Rec. Oct. 4, 1802

p. 218-220 Oct. 8, 1801 Richard Cruce (Spartanburgh) to Anthony Bates (same); for $60 sold 60 ac on Henry's Br of Fairforrest Cr; border: W-Moses Foster and John White, N-Anthony Bates, S & SE-Charles Rodgers. Witness Charles Rogers and Matthias Bates. Signed Richard Cruce. Wit. oath Oct. 21, 1801 Charles Rogers to William Simpson. Rec. Oct. 4, 1802

p. 220-221 Mar. 17, 1801 Laurence Banckston (Spartanburgh) to Jeremiah Nickles (same); for 80£ sold 100 ac on branch of Little Buck Cr; border: Abraham Cantrell and Leonard Adcock; grant Sept. 3, 1794 States Office to Sampson Bethel. Witness Leonard Adcock and Andrew Rea. Signed Laurence Banckston. Wit. oath Apr. 17, 1801 Leonard Adcock to George Lamkin. Rec. Oct. 15, 1802

p. 221-225 Nov. 8, 1788 Vardry McBee (Thickety, SC) to Francis Bremar, surveyor General of SC; a bond of 510£; Condition: Vardry is to pay 255£ with interest at different periods; to secure that payment and for 5s Vardry sells 300 ac on Miller's fork of Thickety Cr including Hannah's Cowpens and lime quary; bought from Col. Adley Osburn (NC); where Vardry McBee lives; Condition: if Vardry pays 255£ with interest, then sale is void. Witness Archd McLaughton and Peter Bremar. Signed Vardry McBee. Wit. oath Nov. 10, 1788 (Charleston Dist) Peter Bremar to Peter Treneau (or Preneau?). Rec. Oct. 22, 1802

p. 225-227 Feb. 23, 1789 William Crocker and wife Ann (Spartanburgh) to William Poole ("of the iron works", same); for 20£ sold 53 ac on dividing ridge between waters of Pacolate R and Fairforrest Cr; including "oarbanks"; part of two tracts: (1) grant Feb.

6, 1786 to Arthur Crocker and (2) grant Oct. 6, 1788 to William Crocker. Witness Thomas Gordon and Lacy McAbee. Signed William and Ann Crocker's marks. Wit. oath Oct. 26, 1802 Lacy McAbee to Geo Lamkin. Rec. Jan. 5, 1803

p. 227 Jul. 29, 1802 Thomas Goore (SC) to Gaasham (or Gursham) Lee (Spartanburgh); for $70 sold 100 ac on both sides of road to Mill's Gap; border: road to William McDowell's; upper part of tract where Gaasham Lee lives. Witness Moses Henderson and Salley Henderson. Signed Thos Gore. Wit. oath Oct. 20, 1802 Moses Henderson to William McDowell. Rec. Jan. 5, 1803

p. 227-228 Oct. 19, 1802 Blake Massingale (Spartanburgh) to William T Thomason (same); for $150 sold 200 ac on head branches of Walker's Cr; border: William T Thomason. Witness I Harrison JQ. Signed Blake Masingale. Rec. Jan. 5, 1803

p. 228-229 Jan. 24, 1801 John Chesney (Spartanburgh) to Robert Beard (same); a mortgage of 25£ sterling for 100 ac on James' Cr; grant to Richard Chesney sr; sold until John Chesney pays 25£ with interest from today (Jan. 24, 1801) until Dec. 25, 1801. Witness Capt. Richard Young and Isabel Young. Signed John Chesney. Wit. oath Dec. 16, 1802 Richard Young to A Casey. Rec. Jan. 6, 1803

p. 229-230 Nov. 13, 1801 William Brannan and John Wood; William and John agree to build a mill on William's land on Lawson's fork Cr and share expenses and profits equally; John is to do the woodwork; William is to find workmen while building; copartnership is to continue while mill lasts except by sale from each other; Note: each one is to have privilege of mill seat during "pleasure". Witness Isham Foster JP. Signed William Brannan and John Wood's mark. Rec. Jan. 25, 1802

p. 230-231 (not given), 1802 William Ford (Spartanburgh) to John Ballenger (same); for $300 sold 200 ac on both sides N fork of N fork Tygar R; grant to Joseph Jones sr and by will to Joseph Jones jr who sold to Samuel Farrow esq (late sheriff Spartanburgh) and sold "by his office" to William Ford. Witness Jno Jamison, Henry Jamison, and James Jordan JQ. Signed Wm Ford. Dower renounced Peggy Ford to James Jordan (not given), 1802. Rec. Jan. 25, 1803

p. 231-233 (not given), 1802 George Washington Brown (Union Dist) to William Lipscomb (Spartanburgh); for 20£ sterling sold 200 ac on both sides Thickety Cr of Broad R; grant Oct. 28, 1765 to Gabriel Brown jr, son of John Brown. Witness Rice Mills and James Ballenger. Signed G. W. Brown. Wit. oath Aug. 27, 1802 James Ballenger to John Lipscomb. Rec. Jan. 25, 1803

p. 233-235 Oct. 6, 1802 David Jones (Spartanburgh) to John Tollison (same); for $100 sold 100 ac at head of Green's Cr of Pacolate R; border: Howell and Connel; part of grant by "state" to James Brown who sold to Evan Davis who sold to Jonathan Davis who sold to David Jones. Witness Muse Tolleson, James Wilkins, and William Hill. Signed David Jones. Wit. oath Oct. 12, 1802 Muse Tolleson to I Harrison. Rec. Jan. 25, 1803

p. 235-236 Jan. 21, 1802 Obadiah Watson (Spartanburgh) to Jacob Crocker (same); for $100 sold 101 ac; part of 393 ac grant Nov. 28, 1798 to Obadiah Watson. Witness Joshua Richards and George Walker. Signed Obadiah Watson. Wit. oath May 15, 1802 Joshua Richards to John Lipscomb. Rec. Jan. 25, 1803

p. 236-237 Aug. 1, 1801 (NC) John Nicoll (or Nicholl) (Buncomb Co, NC) to John Sloan (Greenville Dist); for $100 sold 100 ac on N side Middle Tygar R; below and joining lands where Hill's

Iron Works are erected; upper end of grant Apr. 29, 1768 to Elisha Thomson. Witness Willey S Brown and Polly Nicoll. Signed John Nicoll. Wit. oath Nov. 19, 1802 Willey S Brown to James Jordan. Rec. Jan. 25, 1803

p. 237-238 Oct. 12, 1802 Mathias Rush (Spartanburgh), planter or taylor, to James Wood (same); for $40 sold 20 ac; part of grant to Robert Goodlett jr who sold to James Lawrence who sold to Joseph Lawrence who sold to Mathias Rush; border: John Prince's old line and Knox. Witness James Jordan JQ. Signed Mathias Rush. Rec. Jan. 26, 1803

p. 238-240 Oct. 25, 1802 William Hester (Spartanburgh) to Charles Hester (same); for $900 sold 5,429 ac on Cherokee Cr and Mike's Cr of Broad R; border: W-Vardry McBee, N-granted land, E-McClaren, S-Cooper and Tanner, and SE-Tate, Temple, and Arnold; grant to Charles Miles. Witness Smith Lipscomb and William Lipscomb. Signed William Hester. Wit. oath Oct. 26, 1802 William Lipscomb to John Lipscomb. Rec. Jan. 26, 1803

p. 240-241 Sept. 6, 1802 William Wells, sheriff (Spartanburgh) to William Hester (same); for $900 sold 5,429 ac on Cherokee and Mike's Cr of Broad R; border: W-Vardry McBee, N-granted land, E-McClaren, S-Cooper and Tanner, and SE-Tate, Temple, and Arnold; see writ from Pinckney Dist Common Pleas Court William Milligan, executor of William Lindsey desc, vs Maj. Charles Miles desc. Witness W Smith and Abner Benson. Signed Wm Wells SSD. Wit. oath Oct. 26, 1802 Abner Benson to John Lipscomb. Rec. Jan. 26, 1803

p. 241-243 Jul. 12, 1802 James Crow (Spartanburgh) to Nathaniel Burton (same); for $1,100 sold 440 ac on N & S forks of Tygar R; border: Thornton, Rogers, and Jonathan Crow. Witness Zephaniah Pinson, John Thornton, and William Willis. Signed James Crow. Wit. oath John Thornton to Wm Smith. Rec. Jan. 26, 1803. Dower renounced Elizabeth Crow to Wm Smith Oct. 18, 1802

p. 243-245 Jun. 1, 1802 William Parker and wife Elizabeth (Spartanburgh) to John F Harmening (same); for $250 sold 100 ac on SW side of grant to James Sample; on Cedar Shoal Cr of Enoree R; border: John Stone. Witness John Brooks and William Rainwaters. Signed William Parker and Elizabeth's mark. Wit. oath Jul. 17, 1802 John Brooks to A Casey. Rec. Jan. 27, 1803

p. 245-246 Sept. 2, 1802 Alexander Alexander (Spartanburgh) to John Lindsey (same); for $150 sold 65 ac on branch of Two Mile Cr of Enoree R; border: Joseph Barnet; N part of 648 ac grant Jun. 5, 1786 to William Barnett. Witness Josiah Woodruff, Thomas Woodruff, and Robert Alexander. Signed Alexander Alexander. Wit. oath Oct. 22, 1802 Thomas Woodruff to George Brewton. Rec. Jan. 27, 1803

p. 246-248 Mar. 20, 1802 Joseph Wade (Spartanburgh) to Richard Willis (same); for $850 sold 425 ac on both sides Fairforrest Cr; border: N-Joseph Hayes. Witness Ignatius Turley and Thomas Shurley. Signed Joseph Wade. Wit. oath Dec. 14, 1802 Ignatius Turley to G Brewton. Rec. Jan. 27, 1803

p. 248-249 Jan. 17, 1801 George Williams (Spartanburgh) to John Paris (same); for $50 sold 100 ac on both sides Long Br of Island Cr. Witness William Hall and John Williams. Signed George Williams. Wit. oath Oct. 22, 1802 John Williams to George Lamkin. Rec. Jan. 27, 1803

p. 249-250 Jul. 22, 1802 David Allen (Spartanburgh) to George Gibson (same); for 20 (£ or $?) sold 10 ac; border: on N side Goches Cr; part of grant to David Allen sr. Witness Michael Gafney and William Wilkins. Signed David Allen. Wit. oath Nov. 15, 1802 Michael Gafney to George Lamkin. Rec. Jan. 27, 1803

p. 250-251 Sept. 21, 1801 Alexander Anderson (Spartanburgh) to John Ridings (Rutherford Co, NC); for 60£ sterling sold 200 ac on both sides S Pacolate R; upper end of 240 ac grant Feb. 3, 1775 Lt. Gov. William Bull to Mathew Harper sr who sold 200 ac to Mathew Harper jr Feb. 20, 1776. Witness Robert Harper, James Blackwell, and Joseph Veneble. Signed Alexander Anderson. Wit. oath May 13, 1802 Robert Harper to Isham Foster. Rec. Jan. 28, 1803

p. 251-253 Mar. 27, 1802 Henry Storey (Spartanburgh) to Henry Cunningham (same); for $100 sold 139 ac on S side Storey's Cr; part of grant to Henry Storey. Witness Thomas Patton and James Storey. Signed Henry Storey. Wit. oath Mar. 27, 1802 (Union Dist) James Storey to H Means. Rec. Jan. 28, 1803

p. 253-254 Feb. 17, 1802 Vincent Wyatt sr and wife Elizabeth (Spartanburgh) to Vincent Wyatt jr (same); for $1 sold (1) 220 ac on ridge between Peter's Cr and Pacolate R; and (2) 40 ac adjoining upper end of (1) and sold by William Rich sr to Vincent Wyatt sr; (1) and (2) are part of grant Dec. 3, 1787 State Office to Jesse Connell. Witness Robert Armour and Elizabeth Armour. Signed Vincent Wyatt and Elizabeth's mark. Wit. oath Oct. 26, 1802 Robert Armour to George Lamkin. Rec. Feb. 1, 1803

p. 254-255 Oct. 22, 1802 Charles Cantrell (Spartanburgh) to John Purkle (same); for $40 SC money sold 50 ac of wooded land; on branch of Little Buck Cr; part of grant Jan. 20, 1789 State Office to John Jons. Witness Moses Cantrell and Isham Bobbitt. Signed Charles Cantrell. Wit. oath Oct. 26, 1802 Moses Cantrell to George Lamkin. Rec. Feb. 1, 1803

p. 255-257 Sept. 5, 1800 Solomon Forester (Spartanburgh) to Daniel Cantrell (same); for $150 sold 100 ac on branch of Little Buck Cr; border: Hutchens and Mark Forester; part of grant in 1787 States Office to James Forester. Witness James Turner, Laure Bankson, and John Bankson. Signed Solomon Forester's mark. Wit. oath Apr. 17, 1801 James Turner to George Lamkin. Rec. Feb. 1, 1803

p. 257-258 Feb. 2, 1802 Thomas Evett and wife Mellender to Daniel Sims; for 50£ sterling sold 100 ac on N side Tygar R and both sides branch of Dutchman's Cr; grant Dec. 3, 1787 Gov. Thomas Pinckney to Drury Prewitt then bordering: vacant land and joining "the four squares". Witness Hundley Evett and Lewis Evett. Signed Thomas and Mellender Evett's marks. Wit. oath Feb. 8, 1802 Hundley Evett to Samuel Lancaster. Rec. Feb. 1, 1803

p. 258-260 Jul. 21, 1802 Thomas Underwood (Spartanburgh) to Zachariah Grace (same); for $50 sold 39 ac between Tygar R and Forgerson's Cr; border: John Means and Thomas Finch; on S side of and part of grant Jan. 1, 1787 to Thomas Hightower. Witness Peter Bragg and David McCarely. Signed Thos Underwood. Wit. oath Dec. 15, 1802 Peter Bragg to George Brewton. Rec. Feb. 2, 1802

p. 260 Oct. 10, 1802 James Landford jr to sister Mary Leathewood; for love and affection give 94 ac; border: Thomas Farrow and Sampson Bobo. Witness Paul Castleberry and Nathaniel Woodruff. Signed James Landford. Wit. oath Oct. 20, 1802 Paul Castleberry to John Dean. Rec. Feb. 2, 1802

p. 260-262 Apr. 9, 1802 James Vessals (Spartanburgh) to Willis Williford (same); for $131 sold 50 ac on S side Tygar R; border: Benjamin Hooker and waggon road; part of land originally belonging to Jonathan Linard. Witness Wilie Williford and Edward

Hooker. Signed James Vessals' mark. Wit. oath Jun. 19, 1802 Wilie Williford to Wm Smith. Rec. Feb. 2, 1803. Dower renounced Ellender Vessals to William Smith May 4, 1802

p. 262-263 Feb. 18, 1802 David Vinson (Richmond Co, Ga) to James King (Spartanburgh); for $200 sold 150 ac on Fulee's Br of Cedar Shoal Cr; part of 300 ac grant to Eleazor Benton who sold to Nathaniel Hillon and sold by Nathaniel Hillon's heirs to James Head who sold to David Vinson. Witness Fredk Jackson and William Berry. Signed David Vinson and Hanna's mark. Wit. oath Apr. 8, 1802 William Berry to A Casey. Rec. Feb. 2, 1803

p. 263-264 Oct. 1, 1802 William Smith (Spartanburgh) to Willis Williford (same); for $10 sold 100 ac on N side Tygar R and branches of Cain Cr; part of grant Jan. 7, 1793 to William Smith. Witness Aaron Smith and Isaac Smith. Signed Wm Smith. Wit. oath Oct. 12, 1802 Aaron Smith to I Harrison. Rec. Feb. 3, 1803

p. 264-266 Mar. 9, 1801 William and Solomon Hill (Spartanburgh) to Charles Moore (same); for 50£ sold 200 ac on S side of N fork Tygar R and on Jamies Cr; including "his" improvements; grant May 5, 1769 to Daniel Brice who sold to Thomas Davis who sold to Fredrick Isham who sold to John Sloan who sold to William and Solomon Hill. Witness Aries Brown and Henry Gray. Signed Wm Hill, Solomon Hill, and Nancy Hill. Wit. oath Oct. 12, 1802 Aries Brown to John Collins.

p. 266-267 Dec. 4, 1801 Daniel Cantrell (Spartanburgh) to John Pirkle (same); for $100 SC money sold 100 ac on Little Buck Cr; grant Jan. 21, 1798 States Office to George Pirkle. Witness Charles Cantrell and Nathaniel Pirkle. Signed Daniel Cantrell. Wit. oath Oct. 16, 1802 Charles Cantrell to A Lancaster. Rec. Feb. 3, 1803

p. 267-268 Jan. 24, 1801 Peggy Lewis (Spartanburgh) to Edmund Bishop (same); for $60 sold 50 ac; border: George Lewis III; W half of 100 ac grant to Peter Lewis. Witness Allen Bishop. Signed Peggy Lewis. Certified Jan. 24, 1801 by Isham Foster. Rec. Feb. 4, 1803

p. 268-269 Dec. 27, 1801 Obadiah Watson and John Champion (Spartan Dist) to Joshua Richards (same); for $500 sold 300 ac on waters of Thickety Cr; border: Joseph Champion and Marley; part of tract Obadiah Watson bought from Wm Pool and John Arnold. Witness Joseph Champion and Benjamin Champion. Signed Obadiah Watson and John Champion. Wit. oath May 15, 1802 Joseph Champion to John Lipscomb. Rec. Feb. 4, 1803

p. 269-270 Mar. 8, 1802 James King (Spartanburgh) to Spencer Bobo (same); for $200 sold 150 ac on Fullee's Br of Cedar Shoal Cr; part of 300 ac grant to Eleazor Benton who sold to Nathaniel Hillon and from his heirs sold to James Head who sold to David Vinson who sold to James King. Witness John Brooks and Nancy Bobo. Signed James and Rachel King's marks. Wit. oath Apr. 8, 1802 John Brooks to A Casey. Rec. Feb. 4, 1803

p. 270-272 Jan. 7 (or 8), 1801 John Hammett (Spartanburgh) to William Haskins; for $40 sold 47 ac on Lick Cr; part of 247 ac grant on branches of N Tygar R Gov. Thomas Pinckney to William Ford. Witness Jesse Hammett to James Hammett. Signed John Hammett. Wit. oath Oct. 11, 1802 James Hammett to Drury McDaniel. Rec. Feb. 4, 1803

p. 272-273 Apr. 5, 1802 William Bartan (sic) (Spartanburgh) to Abraham Nelson (same); for 50£ sold 150 ac on W side Buck Cr; grant Oct. 6, 1788 South Carolina to William Jordan. Witness John

Cantrell and Sarah Bartan. Signed William Barton. Wit. oath May 20, 1802 John Cantrell to William McDowell. Rec. May 9, 1803

p. 273-275 Aug. 7, 1001 (sic) Thomas Gore (Spartanburgh) to John Nelson (same); for 40£ SC money sold 100 ac on W side Buck Cr; border: Apple orchard; grant Jan. 1, 1787 States Office to Richar Sanders. Witness Henry McKinney and Nowel (or Noel) Johnson. Signed Thos Gore. Wit. oath Sept. 3, 1801 Nowel Johnson to William McDowell. Rec. Mar. 9, 1803

p. 275-276 Dec. 20, 1802 David Fleming (Richland Dist) to Edward Smith (Greenville Dist); for $100 sold 100 ac on both sides Thompson's Beaverdam Cr of Middle Tygar R; border: James Reynalds and Dunlap; S end of grant Jan. 6, 1794 to David Fleming. Witness William Anderson and John Center. Signed Dd Fleming. Wit. oath (Greenville Dist) Feb. 3, 1803 William Anderson to Reuben Barrett. Rec. Mar. 14, 1803

p. 276-277 Jan. 22, 1802 Lewis Brown and wife Patsey (Spartanburgh) to Samuel Gideons (same); for $128 sold 128 ac on waters of Fairforrest Cr; border: N-David Golightly, S-David Golightly, E-rest of grant; part of grant to Henry White desc who sold to Johnson who sold to Lewis Brown. Witness Isham Foster JP and William Traylor. Signed Lewis Brown and Patsey Brown. Rec. May 14, 1803

p. 277-279 Jul. (not given), 1796 James Ballenger and wife Elizabeth (Spartan Co) to William Fondren (same); for 70£ Va money sold 300 ac on both sides Cherokee Cr of Broad R. Witness Dens Sullivan and Mathew Fondren. Signed James and Elizabeth Ballenger's marks. Wit. oath Sept. 9, 1796 Mathew Fondren to Henry McCray. Rec. Mar. 14, 1803

p. 279-280 Feb. 22, 1802 Christopher Stone (Spartanburgh) to Anthony Foster (same); for $125 sold 50 ac on branch of Jamie's Cr; border: NE-Calley, Hunt, and Kern; part of 250 ac grant Apr. 3, 1780 to Jonathan Linard. Witness John Brooks and John Fedk Harmony. Signed Christopher Stone and Martheu's mark. Wit. oath Jul. 17, 1802 John Brooks to A Casey. Rec. Mar. 14, 1803

p. 280-282 Mar. 7, 1801 Ebenezer Moss (Spartanburgh) to Benjamin Busy (same); for 330 silver dollars sold 150 ac on Two Mile Cr; border: N-Ebenezer Moss, E-Christopher Rhodes, and S-Wm Hendrix. Witness Obadiah Moss and Levi Crow. Signed Ebenezer Moss' mark. Wit. oath Jan. 27, 1802 Obadiah Moss to Chas Allen. Rec. Mar. 16, 1803. Dower renounced Agness Moss to Charles Allen Jan. 27, 1802

p. 282-283 Sept. 7, 1802 John Low (Spartanburgh) to James Lard (same); for $150 sold 200 ac on Island Cr of Pacolate R; border: William Morrow and Leonard Adcock; part of grant in 1792 to Isham Saffolo (or Saffold). Witness Wm McKenney and William Morrow. Signed John Low. Wit. oath Nov. 19, 1802 William Morrow to George Lamkin. Rec. Mar. 16, 1803

p. 283-284 Oct. 3, 1801 Jonathan Smith (Ky) to Isaac Wofford (Spartanburgh); for $300 sold 150 ac on branches of McElwain's Cr of Fairforrest Cr; half of 300 ac grant Apr. 28, (1767?) Gov. William Tryon (NC) to William Thomson who sold to Ralph Smith esq and 150 ac was left to Jonathan Smith by will of Ralph Smith esq. Witness Aaron Smith, Jesse Meadows, and Thos Williams. Signed Jonathan Smith. Wit. oath Oct. 3, 1801 Jesse Meadows to Wm Smith. Rec. Mar. 16, 1803

p. 284-285 Feb. 17, 1801 James Sanders (Spartanburgh) to James Turner (same); for 5£ sold 13 ac on S side Pacolate R near the old ford; border: James Turner and Lawrance Bankston. Witness Reubin

Cantrell and William Sanders. Signed James and Mary Sanders' marks. Wit. oath Apr. 17, 1801 James Sanders to Isham Foster. Rec. Mar. 16, 1803

p. 285-286 Feb. 17, 1801 Ephraim Elder (Spartanburgh) to James Turner (same); for 20£ sold 100 ac; border: James Turner and John Cantrell. Witness Henry Turner and Mathew Abbott. Signed Ephraim Elder and Sarah's mark. Wit. oath Apr. 17, 1801 Henry Turner to Isham Foster. Rec. Mar. 17, 1803

p. 286-288 Apr. 26, 1779 William Coapland (Camden Dist) to William Walker (same); for 4,000£ (sic) SC money sold 100 ac; includes forks of Sarrat's Cr on S side Broad R; grant May 4, 1775 to William Coapland. Witness John Fondren, Joseph Collins, and Hugh Quin sr (or Quenns). Signed William Capland. Wit. oath (York Dist) Mar. 29, 1802 Joseph Collins to Peter Quin. Rec. Mar. 17, 1803

p. 288-289 Mar. 23, 1801 Ebenezer Moss (Spartan Dist) to Benjamin Busey (same); for $50 sold 25 ac on branch of Two Mile Cr; border: James Hendrix. Witness Obadiah Moss and Levi Crow. Signed Ebenezer Moss' mark. Wit. oath Jan. 27, 1802 Obadiah Moss to Chas Allen. Rec. Mar. 17, 1803

p. 289-291 Apr. 22, 1800 Jonathan Crow (Spartanburgh) to James Crow (same); for $50 sold 30 ac; border: N-N fork Tygar R, S-S fork Tygar R, E-James Crow, and W-division line at the narrow passage between the two rivers; part of 166 ac grant Mar. 3, 1788 Gov. Thomas Pinckney to Jonathan Crow. Witness Elizabeth Span, Elizabeth Crow, and Andrew Thomson. Signed Jonathan Crow. Wit. oath Jan. 5, 1802 Elizabeth Crow to John Dean. Rec. Mar. 17, 1803

p. 291-292 Mar. 20, 1799 William Moore and wife Elizabeth (Spartanburgh) to Michael Barnett (same); for 220 Spanish milled dollars sold 91 ac on N side of S fork Tygar R; border: George Isham, William Moore, and vacant; part of 332 ac grant May 1, 1796 South Carolina governor to Samuel Ford who sold to John Ford who sold Mar. 15, 1799 to William Moore. Witness Absolom Blundett and Thomas Moore JQ. Signed William Moore and Elizabeth's mark. Wit. oath Oct. 12, 1802 Thomas Moore to A Lancaster. Rec. Mar. 18, 1803

p. 292-294 Jan. 7, 1800 Joseph Wofford and wife Martha (Spartanburgh) to Thomas Leatherwood; for $64 sold 150 ac on branch of Two Mile Cr of Enoree R; border: Morning; part of 470 ac grant Apr. 20, 1795 Gov. Arnoldus Vanderhorst to Joseph Wofford; title of land not warranted against older rights. Witness Spencer Calvert, Lewis Landford, and James Landford. Signed Jos and Martha Wofford. Wit. oath Oct. 26, 1801 Spencer Calvert to Drury McDaniel. Rec. Mar. 18, 1803

p. 294-295 Sept. 23, 1802 William Lancaster (Spartanburgh) to Zachariah McDaniel (same); for 75£ sold 167 ac on both sides Tate's Br and S side Fairforrest Cr; where Zachariah McDaniel lives; border: Davison and Henry ONeil. Witness Christi Golightly and William S Golightly. Signed W Lancaster. Wit. oath Oct. 11, 1802 William S Golightly to Drury McDaniel. Rec. Mar. 19, 1803

p. 295-297 Sept. 23, 1802 William Lancaster (Spartanburgh) and Zachariah McDaniel (same); an agreement: William sells half of mill and mill seat which parties have and intend to build agreeable with deed from James Barnett to William Lancaster; profits and expenses and loss share equal between partners for grist mill already built and in future mills; mill seat bought from James Barnett. Witness Christi Golightly and William S Golightly. Signed W Lancaster and Z McDaniel. Wit. oath Oct. 11, 1802 William S Golightly to Drury McDaniel. Rec. Mar. 19, 1803

p. 297-298 Jan. 2, 1801 Abel Lewis (Rutherford Co, NC), Isaiah Lewis (Greenville Dist), George Lewis (Spartan Dist), and Ephraim Lewis and Polly Boley (Spartan Dist) to Peggy Lewis (Spartan Dist); for one Spanish milled dollar sold 50 ac; border: George Lewis III; W half of 100 ac grant to Peter Lewis. Witness Peter Lewis, Mary Lewis, Polly Beaver. Signed A Lewis, George Lewis, Isaiah Lewis, Ephraim Lewis, and Polly Boley. Wit. oath Jan. 24, 1801 George Lewis to Ism Foster. Rec. Mar. 19, 1803

p. 298-301 Jan. 5, 1801 William Wells, sheriff (Spartanburgh) to Elias Earle (Greenville Dist); for $200 sold 1,000 ac on Pacolate R including place called Hammett's bottom; border: W-Pacolate R, S & E-James Hammett, and N-vacant; John Sandford Dart desc, Isaac Molle Dart administrator, late of Charleston,SC owned the land and owed John Juger, executor of Jacob Motte desc,and John Huger sued in Common Pleas Court of Charleston; writ is for 4,076£ 10s 2p sterling and cost; sale of land on Oct. 7, 1800 at Spartanburgh between 11 AM and 5 PM; price of sale was $200 and mortgages and incumberances. Witness Bazel Lee and John Lancaster. Signed Wm Wells SSD. Wit. oath Oct. 30, 1802 John Lancaster to A Lancaster. Rec. Mar. 19, 1803

p. 301-304 Dec. 13, 1794 William Adams (Combahee, Charleston Dist) to William Rogers (Tygar R, Spartanburgh Co); for "good-will" and 20£ sterling sell two adjoining tracts on Wards Cr and N side Tyger R; each has 100 ac survey Jul. 7, 1768 and granted Aug. 12, 1768: (1) to James McGown and (2) to Ann Brownlee. Witness Thomas Patterson and Ashford Ginkins. Signed William Adams. Wit. oath (Beaufort Dist) Jan. 3, 1795 Ashford Ginkins to John Lightwood. Rec. Mar. 21, 1803. Dower renounced (Colleton Dist) Sarah Adams to John Smyly Dec. 21, 1802

p. 304-306 May 19, 1802 William Wells, sheriff (Spartanburgh) to Elizabeth Legee (SC) by Abner Benson, her agent; for $257 sold 4,000 ac on waters of Pacolate R and Broad R; border: Benjamin Huger esq, Roberts, and vacant; writ from Charleston Common Pleas Court Elizabeth Legee vs William Skirving, executor to John Ward desc; sale first Monday in May 1802 at Spartanburgh. Witness Elizabeth Love Hutcheson and Gabriel Benson. Signed Wm Wells SSD. Wit. oath Mar. 30, 1803 Gabriel Benson to A Benson. Rec. Mar. 30, 1803

p. 306-308 Jan. 13, 1801 David Alexander (Spartanburgh) to James Galt (same); for $190 sold 150 ac on lower side of line through said tract on Mottley's Cr to Easley Cr; border: Jno Clayton; lower part of grant Jun. 6, 1785 Robert Gogiant. Witness Hugh Ewing, James Fowler, and William Alexander. Signed David Alexander. Wit. oath Jan. 31, 1801 William Alexander to William McDowell. Rec. Mar. 29, 1803

p. 308-311 Jun. 3, 1793 John Lewis (Spartanburgh) to Drury Hutcherson (same); for 80£ sterling sold 140 ac where Drury Hutcherson lives on S side Twilley's Br and S side Lawson's fork; part of 300 ac grant to William Nevel who sold to David Lewis sr and part of Henry Hayes tract sold to David Lewis sr and David Lewis sr "gave" it to John Lewis; border: Thomas Wadsworth. Witness Joshua Hawkins, John Jennings, John Bennett. Signed John Lewis. Wit. oath Feb. 27, 1804 Joshua Hawkins to Wm McDowell. Rec. Mar. 29, 1803

p. 311-313 Dec. 6, 1802 Drury Hutcherson (SC) to Joel Lewis (SC); for $167 sold 100 ac; bought from John Lewis except 20 ac that Joel Lewis bought from Drury Hutcherson "some time ago". Witness John Harris, James Lewis, David Lewis. Signed Drury Hutcherson's mark. Wit. oath Mar. 31, 1803 James Lewis to William Simpson. Rec. Apr. 20, 1803

p. 313-314 Jun. 20, 1802 Drury Hutcherson (SC) to Joel Lewis (SC); for $61 sold 20 ac on S side Meadow Cr; border: David Lewis; leaving out "therewit ground that's not tendable". Witness William Harris, James Lewis, and David Lewis. Signed Drury Hutcherson's mark. Wit. oath Mar. 31, 1803 James Lewis to William Simpson. Rec. Apr. 20, 1803

p. 314-317 Jul. 5, 1802 William Washington (Larance Dist), attorney for Burdue, Sherlot, and Burdue, merchants (London) to James Crow (Sparlingburgh Dist); for $150 sold 150 ac on SW side of Tygar R; border: NE-Tyger R, SE-Tobias Bright, and others vacant. Witness Isaac Crow, Elizabeth Thornton, and John Thornton. Signed William Washington, attorney for Burdue, Sherlot, and Burdue of London. Wit. oath Mar. 28, 1803 Isaac Crow to John Dean. Rec. Apr. 20, 1803

p. 317-319 Dec. 8, 1802 William Wood (Spartanburgh) to William Lipscomb (same); for $600 sold 360 ac where William Wood lives on Thickety Cr; border: SE-John Wade. Witness Smith Lipscomb and Jesse Fondren. Signed William Wood. Wit. oath Apr. 2, 1803 Smith Lipscomb to John Lipscomb. Rec. Apr. 21, 1803. Dower renounced Elizabeth Wood to John Simpson Apr. 2, 1803

p. 319-321 Mar. 3, 1798 John Hammett (Spartanburgh) to Jeremiah Salmon (same); bond of 100£ sterling; Condition: bond void if Jeremiah Salmon obtains John Hammett's 921 ac grant now at Surveyor General's office and Jeremiah pays all fees and John to give deed to Jeremiah for land. Witness John Williams and Malachi Eskrige. Signed John Hammett. Wit. oath Mar. 28, 1803 John Williams and Malachi Eskrige to John Collins. Rec. Apr. 21, 1803

p. 321-323 Mar. 1, 1803 Thomas Penney (Spartanburgh) to Joseph McMillin (same); for one guinea sold 125 ac on Middle Tyger R; where Thomas Penney lives; part of 300 ac grant to Thomas Penney; Thomas Penney and wife get to remain there for their lifetimes. Witness Samuel Brice and Thomas Brice. Signed Thomas and Sarah Penney's marks. Wit. oath Mar. 29, 1803 Thomas Brice to John Anderson. Rec. Apr. 21, 1803

p. 323-325 May 16, 1797 Nathaniel and Nancy Power (Lawrence Co) to Joseph Casey (Spartanburgh); for 30£ sterling sold 100 ac on N side of T Mile Cr of Enoree R; part of 150 ac grant to Richard Nalleey. Witness Christopher Rodes and Elisha Attaway. Signed Nathl Power and Nancy's mark. Wit. oath Feb. 28, 1801 Christopher Rodes to A Casey. Rec. Apr. 25, 1803

p. 325-327 Mar. 2, 1803 Robert Kimble and wife Frances (Spartanburgh) to James Boyd (same); for $300 sold 200 ac E of old Indian boundary on head branches of Richland Cr; grant to "said" Reams; Note: land to be Robert's until January "eight hundred and four" as his own. Witness Edmond Clement and John Clement. Signed Robert Kimble and Frances' mark. Wit. oath Mar. 31, 1803 Edmond Clement to John Lipscomb. Rec. Apr. 26, 1803

p. 327-328 Mar. 22, 1803 Isaac Creece and wife Jane (Greenville Dist) to Stephen Creece (Spartanburgh); for $100 sold 350 ac on NE side of Fairforrest Cr; between Robert Anderson on SE and George McCarter on N and Nesbet on W; grant in 1774 Lt. Gov. Thomas Winsday (NC?) to Robert Creece and memorial in Auditor General's Book 13M p. 433 Apr. 4, 1775 and Sec. Book 3T p. 109. Witness Hugh Means and Wm Thomson. Signed Isaac Creece and Jean's (sic) mark. Wit. oath Mar. 29, 1803 Wm Thomson to William Simpson. Rec. Apr. 26, 1803

p. 328-330 May 12, 1802 Mathew Macbee (Spartanburgh) to John Pearce (same); for (not given) sold 185 ac on S side of Pacolate

R; border: John Lee; part of 200 ac grant Jan. 21, 1785 to William Oldrige. Witness John Lee and Richeson Whitbey. Signed Mathew Macbee. Wit. oath Mar. 29, 1803 Richeson Whitbey to John Lipscomb. Rec. Apr. 21, 1803

p. 330-332 Jan. 23, 1801 David Forrester (SC) to Acheles (or Achulles) Durham (Spartanburgh); for $100 sold 100 ac on both sides branch of Little Buck Cr. Witness Beryman Hicks and Charles Cantrell. Signed David Forrester. Wit. oath Mar. 4, 1802 Beryman Hicks to Georg Lampkin. Rec. Apr. 27, 1803

p. 332-334 Nov. 12, 1802 David Allen jr (Spartanburgh) to William Lipscomb (same); for $200 sold 300 ac; where David Allen jr lives; border: Pol's Spring Br, Brock, and Willis Allen; deeded by David Allen sr to son David; on Gocher's Cr; except a small part at lower end sold to Willis Allen. Witness Smith Lipscomb and Ignatios Griffin. Signed David Allen. Wit. oath Apr. 15, 1803 Smith Lipscomb. Rec. Apr. 27, 1803

p. 334-336 Apr. 9, 1803 Zachariah Robinson (Spartanburgh) to son William Roberson (same); for love and affection give a Negro woman Kezza and her young child Fetney. Witness Absalom Lancaster and John Lancaster. Signed Zachariah Roberson. Wit. oath Apr. 9, 1803 John Lancaster to A Lancaster. Rec. Apr. 28, 1803

p. 336-338 Apr. 17, 1802 Armsterd Shewmate and wife Betsy (Spartanburgh) to James Jordan (same); for $200 sold 71 ac on both sides N branch of N fork Tygar R; border: Millar (or Miller); part of grant to Alexander Rea and to his wife by will, and wife married Armsterd Shewmate. Witness James Bright and John Jordan sr. Signed Armsterd Shewmate and Betsey's mark. Wit. oath Mar. 29, 1803 John Jordan sr to John Collins. Rec. Apr. 28, 1803

p. 338-339 Jul. 20, 1801 Spencer Bobo sr (Spartanburgh) to Leveston Bobo (same); for 50£ sold 75 ac; border: Absalom Bobo, Moses Casey, John F Harmony, and Anthony Foster; part of grant to James Sample. Witness Edward Hooker and Aaron Casey. Signed Spencer Bobo. Wit. oath Mar. 29, 1803 Aaron Casey to Wm Smith. Rec. Apr. 28, 1803

p. 339-342 Nov. 15, 1802 Thomas Moore (Spartanburgh) to Joseph Rogers (same); for $162 sold 130 ac on N side Tyger R and N side Ward's Cr; border: Vicker's Spring Br. Witness Samuel Elder and Samuel Oats. Signed Thomas Moore and Edy's mark. Wit. oath Nov. 15, 1802 Samuel Elder to Tho Moore. Rec. Apr. 29, 1803. Dower renounced Edy Moore to William Lancaster Mar. 30, 1803

p. 342-344 Mar. 7, 1802 Thomas Miles and wife Sarah (Spartanburgh) to James Rainwaters (same); for $100 SC money sold 100 ac on Rocky Cr on S side Tyger R; border: S-Thomas Miles, W-James Sample, N-John Hacker, E-Thos Tod; near where James Rainwaters lives; part of 350 ac grant Aug. 11, 1774 to Edmond Beardan. Witness Benjamin Hooker and Moses Casey jr. Signed Thomas Miles. Wit. oath Dec. 11, 1802 Moses Casey to A Casey. Rec. Apr. 29, 1803

p. 344-345 Aug. 26, 1797 Thomas Brandon (Union Co) attorney for William Hendricks (east. (sic) florady) to Christopher Rods (Spartanburgh); for $100 sold 100 ac; sold by James Hendricks to William Hendricks Feb. 25, 1773 see Charleston Book 5X p. 55 & 57. Witness John Casey and Isaac Edwards. Signed Thomas Brandon attorney. Wit. oath Oct. 31, 1800 John Casey to A Casey. Rec. Apr. 29, 1803

p. 345-348 Apr. 2, 1803 Ignatious Griffin (Spartanburgh) to William Lipscomb (same); for 50£ sold 121 ac on waters of Buises fork Thickety Cr; grant Mar. 2, 1801 to Ignatious Griffin. Witness

William Bostick and William Wilkins. Signed Ignatious Griffin's mark. Wit. oath Apr. 2, 1803 William Bostick to John Lipscomb. Rec. Apr. 30, 1803. Dower renounced Mavel Griffin to John Lipscomb Apr. 4, 1803

p. 348-350 Mar. 29, 1803 Peter Smith (Spartanburgh) to Henry Smith (same); for $50 sold 50 ac on Kelsoe's Cr of Fairforrest Cr; where Henry Smith lives; part of grant Oct. 15, 1785 by "state" to Peter Smith. Witness James Smith jr. Signed Peter Smith. Certified Mar. 29, 1803 by William Simpson. Rec. Apr. 30, 1803

p. 350-352 Nov. 15, 1802 Jason Moore (Spartanburgh) to Joseph Rogers (same); for $52 sold 35 ac on N side Ward's Cr of Tygar R; border: Thomas Moor and Jason Moore. Witness Samuel Elder and Samuel Oats. Signed Jason Moore. Wit. oath Nov. 15, 1802 Samuel Elder to Thomas Moore. Rec. May 2, 1803. Dower renounced Edy Moore, wife of Thomas Moore (sic), to W Lancaster Mar. 30, 1803

p. 352-353 Feb. 22, 1803 William Hammett and wife Rosomon (Spartanburgh) to Caleb Jones (same); for $70 sold 80 ac on S side Pacolate R and both sides Lindsay's Cr. Witness John Hunter Jones, John Millhanks, and Malt Jones. Signed William Hammett and Rosomon's mark. Wit. oath Mar. 29, 1803 John Hunter Jones to Georg Lampkins. Rec. May 2, 1803

p. 353-356 Feb. 26, 1800 William Hammett (Spartanburgh) to Caleb Jones (same); for $70 sold 20 ac on waters Lindsay's Cr of Pacolate R; border: David Millhanks on line granted to Reuben Mathus. Witness John Hunter Jones, John Millhanks, and Malt Jones. Signed William Hammett. Wit. oath Mar. 29, 1803 John Hunter Jones to Georg Lamkins. Rec. May 2, 1803

p. 356-358 Aug. 9, 1800 John Lee and wife Elizabeth (Spartanburgh) to William Willis (same); for $200 sold 200 ac on S side Pacolate R and on Cherokee Cr; border: Bazzel Lee, Solomon Abbet, and Richard Turner; where Richard Lee formerly lives. Witness William Pool, William Crocker, and Georg Hatfield. Signed John and Elizabeth Lee's marks. Wit. oath Feb. 19, 1801 Georg Hatfield to John Lipscomb. Rec. May 3, 1803

p. 358-360 Nov. 4, 1801 Benjamin Busy and wife Lucy (Spartanburgh) to Christopher Rods (same); for $168 sold 75 ac; border: Christopher Rods; E part of grant to James Hendricks on Two Mile Cr of Enoree R. Witness Joseph Casey, John Guzsef, and James Werford. Signed Benjamin and Lucy Busy's marks. Wit. oath (blank). Rec. May 3, 1803

p. 360-362 Nov. 8, 1802 Washington Spiller, James Sims, John Spiller, and William Spiller (all Spartanburgh) to Sampson Bobo (same); for $120 sold 86 ac on both sides Two Mile Cr of Enoree R; grant Jun. 5, 1786 to William Spiller desc. Witness John Dean and David Sims. Signed Washington Spiller, John Spiller, and William Spiller, and James Sims. Wit. oath Nov. 8, 1802 David Sims to John Dean. Rec. May 3, 1803

p. 362-364 Sept. 8, 1802 Zachariah Leatherwood (Spartanburgh) to James Leatherwood (same); for $10 sold 50 ac on N side Jammy (or Jommy) Cr of Tyger R; if James sells land, Zachariah or "his" brother Georg is to have chance to buy it back for same or larger price. Witness John Edwards and James Wofford. Signed Zachariah Leatherwood's mark. Wit. oath Mar. 28, 1803 James Wofford to John Dean. Rec. May 4, 1803

p. 364-367 Oct. (not given), 1802 James Blackwood (Spartanburgh) to to Alexander Copeland; for $30 SC money sold 30 ac on waters of Gelmore's Cr and N side of N Pacolate R; border: John Woods; part of grant Feb. 8, 1796 to James Blackwood. Witness James Copeland and Charles Copeland. Signed James Blackwood. Wit. oath blank. Rec. May 4, 1803

p. 367-368 Oct. 22, 1802 John Pearce (Spartanburgh) to Mathew Macbee; for 10£ sterling sold 275 ac on waters of Pacolate R; border: George Pool. Witness Elijah Mcbee and Jacob Land. Signed John Pearce's mark. Wit. oath Mar. 29, 1803 Elijah Mcbee to John Lipscomb. Rec. May 5, 1803

p. 368-370 Oct. 22, 1802 John Pearce (Spartanburgh) to Mathew Mcbee (same); for 15£ sold 350 ac on waters Pacolate R and Broad R; part of grant Jul. 5, 1788 to Col. Thomas Sable (or Sabb). Witness Elijah Mcbee and Jacob Land. Signed John Pearce's mark. Wit. oath Mar. 29, 1803 Elijah Mcbee to John Lipscomb. Rec. May 5, 1803

p. 370-374 Mar. 26, 1803 Edward Hooker and wife Amelia (Spartanburgh) to Golden Tinsley; for $500 sold 200 ac on Publick Road from Isaac Crow's to Anthony Foster's; between Tyger and Enoree Rivers; part of 1,000 ac grant to James Sample jr and sold by Rottry Sample (heir-at-law of James Sample) to John McCulloch and sold to Edward Hooker. Witness Aaron Smith, Samuel Smith, and Benjamin Hooker. Signed Edward Hooker. Wit. oath Apr. 23, 1803 Aaron Smith to Wm Smith. Rec. May 5, 1803. Dower renounced Amelia Hooker to William Smith Apr. 23, 1803

p. 374-376 Feb. 6, 1802 Philip Jean sr (Spartanburgh) to Samuel Loveless (same); for $30 sold 100 ac on branch of Island Cr of Pacolate R; border: J. E. Morrow, Abraham Markley, and remainder of grant; part of 431 ac granted States Office to John Eades Morrow who sold to Philip Jean sr. Witness William Garrett, Elijah Thompson, and John Bankson. Signed Philip Jean's mark. Wit. oath Nov. 1, 1802 Elijah Thompson to Wm McDowell. Rec. May 6, 1803

p. 376-378 Feb. 24, 1803 Anderson Cockrill (Spartanburgh) to Hugh Means (same); for $50 sold 60 ac on S side of Lawson's fork of Pacolet R; part of grant Aug. 7, 1786 to Thomas Wood and sold by Hugh Means to Anderson Cockrill and now sold by Anderson Cockrill to Hugh Means. Witness William Turner and John Speers. Signed Anderson Cockrill. Wit. oath Mar. 30, 1803 John Speers to William Simpson. Rec. May 9, 1803

p. 378-381 Nov. 22, 1802 William Brock (Spartanburgh) to William Lipscomb (same); for $300 sold 300 ac on both sides Goucher's Cr of Thickety Cr; border: Robert Wilkins; survey Jan. 3, 1773 certified Mar. 11, 1773 and granted in 1774 Gov. William Bull to "Wm Anderson James Anderson heir-at-law James Fannin power of attorney" dated Dec. 14, 1798. Witness William Thompson, William Wilkins, and William Bostick. Signed William Brock's mark. Wit. oath Nov. 22, 1802 William Bostick to John Lipscomb. Rec. May 9, 1803. Dower renounced Patsy Brock to John Lipscomb Apr. 4, 1803

p. 381-383 Mar. 28, 1802 James Boyd (Spartanburgh) to Joseph Veneble jr (same); for 30£ sterling sold 75 ac or 70 ac on E side of branch of Richland Cr; border: John Connen, Wm Wood, Fawn Br, and Edmd Clement; grant to Thos Hatteway. Witness Edmond Clement and Robert Kemble. Signed James Boyd's mark. Wit. oath May 9, 1803 Edmond Clement to A Lancaster. Rec. May 11, 1803

p. 383-384 Dec. 9, 1802 Nancy Simpson to son Samuel Piercy Simpson; for love and affection give a Negro child Lucinda about 8 months old and $100 with interest now in hands of her brother Burrel Bobo; if Samuel dies before he is 21 or before marrying, then Negro goes to Nancy; if Nancy dies, then Negro goes to "my daughter and sister of him my said son Sarah Holland"; interest to $100 to be applied to schooling of Samuel. Witness Aaron Casey and John Luke. Signed Nancy Simpson's mark. Wit. oath May 3, 1803 John Luke to Wm Smith. Rec. May 13, 1803

p. 384-385 Mar. 11, 1803 Isham Harrison and James Smith, arbitrators chosen by John Golightly and William Pool to determine damages William has sustained by John by cutting timber and "colewood" on William's land; a decision of $15 due to William Pool. Signed I Harrison and Jas Smith; Mar. 11, 1803 William Pool receives $15 from John Golightly. Signed Wm Pool. Witness Jas Smith and Jno Golightly jr. Wit. oath Mar. 11, 1803 Jas Smith to A Benson. Rec. May 13, 1803

p. 385-386 Apr. 9, 1802 Thomas Tod to Martin Newman; Thomas indemnifys Martin (to secure against loss or damage) for sale of slave; Martin sold Negro boy Jame to Thomas "from" expiration of Widowhood or natural life of Mrs. Mary Wilson; Negro was taken by virtue of execution obtained by Dr. Andrew Thomson against estate of Stephen Wilson desc and "shewed" by Reuben Wilson, executor of Stephen Wilson's estate, to belong to estate; Negro was advertised and sold agreeable to law and Thomas binds self and heirs to indemnify Martin against all persons. Witness Anthony Shands. Signed Thos Tod. Wit. oath Apr. 9, 1802 Anthony Shands to Aaron Casey. Rec. May 13, 1803

Book I 1803-1805

p. 1-3 Dec. 13, 1792 James Spears and wife Mary (Charleston, SC) to Thomas Miles (Spartanburgh); for 20£ sterling sold 100 ac on Rocky Cr on S side Tygar R; border: S-Thomas Miles, W-James Sample, N-John Hacker, and E-Thomas Tod; plat attached; part of 350 ac grant Aug. 11, 1774 to Edmund Beardan. Witness Joseph Gist, Alexander Gordon, and Samuel Farrow. Signed Jas and Mary Spears. Wit. oath Oct. 28, 1799 Samuel Farrow to A Casey. Rec. May 19, 1803

p. 3-5 Mar. 6, 1800 Spencer Smith (Spartanburgh) to James Smith (same); for $93 sold 93 ac on Fairforrest Cr; grant to Hancock Smith. Witness John Smith, William Smith, and Henry Smith. Signed Spencer Smith. Wit. oath Oct. 26, 1802 Henry Smith to Ism Foster. Rec. May 19, 1803. Dower renounced Mary Smith to Ism Foster Oct. 26, 1802

p. 5-6 Apr. 24, 1802 Thomas Burgess (Spartanburgh) to John Morris (same); for $12 sold 24 ac on waters of Pacolate R; border: Joseph Morris and John Morris. Witness Georg Gilbert, John Carter, and John Bankson. Signed Thomas Burgess. Wit. oath Aug. 28, 1802 Georg Gilbert to Wm McDowell. Rec. May 19, 1802

p. 6-9 Sept. 7, 1801 William Wells, sheriff (Spartanburgh) to John Murrell (Union Dist); for $44 sold 337 ac on waters Tyger R; grant to Elisha Hadden who sold to William Hill; writ from Spartanburgh Common Pleas Court suit of Thomas McMakin and "others" orders sale first Monday in Sept. 1802. Witness Noah Wells and Abner Benson. Signed Wm Wells. Wit. oath May 20, 1803 Abner Benson to A Lancaster. Rec. May 20, 1803

p. 9-10 Mar. 1, 1803 John Murrell (Union Dist) to Henry O'Neill (Spartanburgh); for $170.75 sold 337 ac on waters of Tyger R and Mill Cr; grant in 1794 to Elijah Hadden who sold to William Hill and taken by "execution" by William Wells, sheriff (Spartanburgh) and sold to John Murrell. Witness Ann A Murrell, David Murrell, and Robert Love. Signed John Murrell. Wit. oath Apr. 6, 1803 Robert Love to A Benson. Rec. May 20, 1803

p. 10-12 Mar. 15, 1803 Henry O'Neill (Spartanburgh) to bodily heirs of Agness Love; for $180 sold 337 ac; grant Elijah Hadden and sold to William Hill and sold by William Wells, sheriff, to John Morrel (Union Dist) who sold to Henry O'Neill. Witness Hanah O'Neill, John McDowel, and Robert Love. Signed Henry O'Neill. Wit. oath Apr. 6, 1803 Hanah O'Neill to Abner Benson. Rec. May 23, 1803

p. 12-13 Mar. 4, 1803 James Rodgers (Spartanburgh) to Robert Love; for $50 sold a feather bed, the "wright 30 (pounds?) of feathers" and furniture belonging to bed now, chaff bed and furniture, a table, a big wheel and a pair of cards, a pot, a fish pan with 20 (pounds?) of pewter consisting of plates, dished, and basons. Witness Henry O'Neill. Signed James Rodgers' mark. Wit. oath Apr. 6, 1803 Henry O'Neill to A Benson. Rec. May 23, 1803

p. 13-15 Jan. 12, 1803 Reuben Richards (Spartanburgh) to Thomas Hill (same); for $125 sold 100 ac on waters of Green's Cr on N side Pacolate R; border: Jesse Connell and James Brown. Witness Abner Benson and John Cantwell. Signed Reuben Richards. Wit. oath May 23, 1803 Abner Benson to A Lancaster. Rec. May 23, 1803

p. 15 Nov. 20, 1802 Drury McDaniel to Tho Moore; Drury says his brand for stock is a swlow fork in right ear and slit in left ear. Signed Drury McDaniel. Rec. May 27, 1803

p. 15-17 (not dated) Isham Harrison to James Seay; for $16 sold 75 ac on E side of branch of Richland Cr; border: John Conner, William Wood, Fon Br, Edmond Clement; writ from Spartanburgh Common Pleas Court suit of Joseph Venable jr orders sale first Monday in Apr. 1803; grant to Thomas Hatteway. Witness Obadiah Watson and Alexr McKee. Signed I Harrison. Wit. oath May 30, 1803 Obadiah Watson to A Lancaster. Rec. Jun. 3, 1803

p. 17-19 Jul. 9, 1802 Allen Gentry (Spartanburgh) to Thomas Price (same); for $150 SC money sold 50 ac on both sides Forgeson's Cr; part of grant to Enoch Floyd. Witness John Freeman and James Isham. Signed Allen Gentry's mark. Wit. oath Jun. 4, 1803 John Freeman to Drury McDaniel. Rec. Jun. 7, 1803

p. 19-21 Mar. 23, 1801 Simpson Newman (Spartanburgh) to Thomas Price; for 20£ sold 150 ac; border: Hog back Mountains, Jonathan Floyd, Thomas Masifield, Thomas White, and James Jonston; grant to William Clayton (Greenville Co). Witness Samuel Crow, James Askew, and Isaac Crow sr. Signed Simpson Newman's mark. Wit. oath Nov. 20, 1802 James Askew to G Brewton. Rec. Jun. 7, 1803

p. 21-23 Jun. 9, 1803 Jesse Traylor (Spartanburgh) to Isaac Snoddy (same); for $250 sold 153 ac; border: John Timmons, Jeremiah Lucas, and John Lucas, and Timmons; part of grant to Thomas Collins. Witness Moses Timmons, Samuel Miller, and Thomas Doig. Signed Traylor. Wit. oath Jun. 24, 1803 Moses Timmons to A Lancaster. Rec. Jun. 27, 1803

p. 23-25 Apr. 17, 1802 James Harrison and wife Rhoda (Spartanburgh) to Joroyall Barnett; for $200 sold 206 ac on "dividing waters between" Lawson's fork and Fairris Cr; border: Joroyall Barnett, Richard Barnett, old Iron Works, Wm Bagwell, Wm Pool, and Charlses and Jameses old path; part of survey for Wm Pool; land warranted except for claims from Joseph Buffenston's old Iron Works (a small quantity). Witness Micajah Barnett and Joseph Barnett. Signed James Harrison and Rhoda's mark. Wit. oath May 5, 1803 Micajah Barnett to William Lancaster. Rec. Jul. 2, 1803. Dower renounced May 5, 1803 Rhoda Harrison to William Lancaster

p. 25-31 Mar. 18, 1803 John Martain (Union Dist) to John and Charles Bulow, merchants (Charleston, SC); a bond of $2,240; Condition:

deed void if John pays $1,220 to be paid at different periods; to secure payment and for 5s sell 440 ac on Big Cr of Little R; sold "from" one tract to James Lusk and sold Jan. 2, 1794 as James Lusk's land by sheriff of 96 Dist to Joachim Bulow. Witness William Farnandes and James Farnandes. Signed John Martin. Wit. oath May 31, 1803 William Farnandes to John Lipscomb. Rec. Jul. 13, 1803

p. 31-32 Jul. 15, 1803 Robert Love (Spartanburgh) to Henry O'Neil (same); for $700 sold all books and account books, 72 notes of different amounts and on different people. Witness John McDowel. Signed Robert Love. Rec. Jul. 14, 1803.
Jul. 13, 1803 Robert Love (Spartanburgh), merchant, to Henry O'Neil (same); for $500 sold a Negro "Nench" Peg about 13 years old, a mare and colt, 2 beds and furniture formerly Henry O'Neil's, a bay horse about 5 years old, 4 cows, 3 calves, and a silver watch. Witness John McDowel. Signed Robert Love. Wit. oath Jul. 14, 1803 John McDowel to Abner Benson

p. 32-35 Feb. 5, 1801 John Gore (Spartanburgh) to James Carter (same); for $60 sold 100 ac on S side Pacolate R; border: Stubblefield Cr and Mathew Morkaboy; part of grant States Office to Robert Lee who sold to John Gore. Witness William Garret and John Bankson. Signed John Gore's mark. Wit. oath Oct. 25, 1802 John Bankson to Ism Foster. Rec. Jul. 15, 1803

p. 35-37 Sept. 28, 1802 Baylis Earle (Spartanburgh) to Andrew Hopkins (same); for $260 sold 300 ac (or 200 ac) on McBris Cr of N Pacolate R including mouth of the creek; border: E-Thos Jackson, N & W-Baylis Earle sr, S-Baylis Earle; and 300 ac (or 200 ac) part of 400 ac formerly Andrew Calley's land who sold to Jane (or Jame) Hopkins who sold to Baylis Earle; North of where Molly Hooper lives; some of the land was divided by Baylis Earle and Andrew Calley by agreement so each had 42 or 45 ac. Witness Thos Jackson and Hugh Henderson. Signed Baylis Earle. Wit. oath May 6, 1803 Hugh Henderson to John Anderson. Rec. Jul. 19, 1803

p. 37-38 Nov. 13, 1798 (Chestain (sic) Co, SC) John Lewis (Chestain Co) to Baylis Earle (Spartanburgh); (money omitted) sold 100 ac on S fork of Woolf's Cr; border: William Emry and land formerly of William Bird. Witness Hugh McMullin and William Bruce. Signed John Lewis. Wit. oath (Pendleton Dist) Jun. 4, 1803 William Bruce to Colin Campbell. Rec. Jul. 19, 1803

p. 38-40 Jul. 28, 1801 Elizabeth Autry (Spartanburgh) to Jacob Autry (same); for $103 sold 83 ac; border: Jacob Autry and Robert Hedd; part of two adjoining tracts: (1) grant to Richard Hampton and (2) grant to William Lancaster. Witness Thomas Underwood and William Wheel. Signed Elizabeth Autry's mark. Wit. oath Oct. 11, 1802 Thomas Underwood to I Harrison. Rec. Jul. 20, 1803

p. 40-42 Jul. 28, 1801 Alexander Autry (Spartanburgh) to Jacob Autry (same); for $103 sold 60 ac on Buffalow Br of Fairforrest Cr; where Jacob Autry lives; part of grant Dec. 16, 1769 to Thomas Bullem. Witness Thomas Underwood and William Wheely. Signed Alexander Autry's mark. Wit. oath Oct. 11, 1802 Thomas Underwood to I Harrison. Rec. Jul. 20, 1803

p. 42-44 (date omitted) William Wells, sheriff (Spartanburgh) to John Murrell; for (money omitted) sold 280 ac on branch of Mill Cr of Tyger R; border: SW, SE, N, & W-Elisha Hadden, SW-Thomas Clayton, NE-Sallard(?) White, and vacant land; grant Dec. 1, 1794 to Samuel Hedden and sold to Wm Hill; writ from Spartanburgh Common Pleas Court with Wm Hill defendant orders sale first Monday in Sept. 1801. Witness Abner Benson and Noah Wells. Signed Wm Wells SSD. Wit. oath Jul. 21, 1803 Abner Benson to John Lipscomb. Rec. Jul.

21, 1803

p. 44-47 (not dated) William Wells, sheriff (Spartanburgh) to Henry O'Neill; for $30 (sic) sold 146 ac on waters of Tyger R and E of ancient boundary; grant Apr. 3, 1786 to William Garrett who sold to John Sloan; writ from Spartanburgh Common Pleas Court on suit of Thomas McMackin and "others" ordered sale first Monday in Sept. 1801; sale price $80. Witness Abner Benson and Noah Wells. Signed Wm Wells. Wit. oath May 20, 1803 Abner Benson to John Lipscomb. Rec. Jul. 22, 1803

p. 47-49 (not dated) William Wells to Henry O'Neill; for $100 sold 300 ac on Mill Cr of Tyger R; border: all vacant land; known as Nell's Furnace; writ from Spartanburgh Common Pleas Court on suit with William Hill defendant ordered sale first Monday in (not given) 1802; granted Jun. 4, 1772 to John Snoddy. Witness Noah Wells and Abner Benson. Signed Wm Wells SSD. Wit. oath May 20, 1803 Abner Benson to John Lipscomb. Rec. Jul. 22, 1803

p. 49-51 Apr. 22, 1803 Robert Legon (or Ligon) (Spartanburgh) to Walter (or Waller) West; for 100 Spanish milled dollars sold 56 ac; border: John Barnett, Fairforrest Cr, and Robert Legan. Witness Thomas Tinsley and Andrew Thomson. Signed Robert Ligon. Wit. oath Jul. 26, 1803 Thomas Tinsley to A Lancaster. Rec. Jul. 27, 1803

p. 51-54 Apr. 22, 1803 Robert Ligon (Spartanburgh) to Thomas Tinsley, administrator of estate of Thomas Foster desc; for 70 Spanish milled dollars sold 35 ac; border: Thomas Foster and William Barton. Witness Walter West and Andrew Thomson. Signed Robert Legan. Wit. oath Jul. 26, 1803 Walter West to Absalom Lancaster. Rec. Jul. 27, 1803. Dower renounced Edith Legan to William Lancaster Jul. 23, 1803

p. 54-56 Feb. 12, 1803 John Sarratt (Spartanburgh) to John McKee (York Dist); for $250 sold 805 ac in two tracts: (1) 424 ac where John Lefever formerly lived and granted Mar. 5, 1798 to Charles Morgan who sold Oct. 16, 1800 to John Sarratt; and (2) 381 ac granted Feb. 4, 1799 to John Sarratt; includes improvements where John Lefever now lives. Witness Thomas Kitchen and Richard Quin. Signed John Sarratt. Wit. oath Jun. 27, 1803 Thomas Kitchen to John Richman. Rec. Jul. 28, 1803

p. 56-59 Feb. 12, 1803 John Sarratt (Spartanburgh) and John McKee (York Dist); an agreement: John Sarratt sold John McKee two tracts where John Lefever formerly lives and Richard Fondren now lives and tract where John Lefever now lives at crossroads called Little Meadows--805 ac in all; John McKee paid John Sarratt $250 for land and Sarratt returns money if older claim is found in seven years; if older claim arises, McKee sues at his own cost or refers judgment to three honest men chosen by Sarratt and McKee; if in either case McKee loses, then Sarratt returns money; if McKee wins, Sarratt keeps money. Witness Thomas Kitchen and Richard Quin. Signed John Sarratt and John McKee. Wit. oath Jun. 27, 1803 Thomas Kitchen to John Richman. Rec. Jul. 28, 1803

p. 59-60 Oct. 28, 1800 William Ford (Spartanburgh) to George McDowell (same); for $50 sold 100 ac on Lawson's fork; border: Isaac Bishop and John Beard;part of 200 ac grant to George McDowell. Witness Isham Foster JP. Signed Wm Land (sic). Rec. Aug. 3, 1803

p. 60-62 Feb. 2, 1803 George Vandever sr (Spartanburgh) to John Tolleson (same); for $100 sold 50 ac on waters of Story's Mill Cr and both sides Pruelepare(?) Br; border: John King and Ash; part of 266 ac grant Gov. Charles Pinckeny to Thomas Davison who sold Jan. 13, 1801 to George Vandever. Witness Muse Tolleson and Edward (or Edmon) Chapman. Signed George Vandever's mark. Wit. oath Jul. 30, 1803 Muse Tolleson to William Simpson. Rec. Aug. 3, 1803

p. 62-64 Mar. 28, 1803 James Lackee (or Lackey) (Spartanburgh) to John Tolleson (same); for $200 sold 100 ac on N side Pacolate R; where James Lackee lives; border: Leonard Adcock. Witness Muse Tolleson and James Moore. Signed James Lackee's mark. Wit. oath Jul. 3, 1803 Muse Tolleson to William Simpson. Rec. Aug. 3, 1803

p. 64-66 Feb. 1, 1802 Austin Clayton (Spartanburgh) to Thomas Price (same); for $17 sold 100 ac on Middle fork Tyger R in Greenville Dist; border: W-Bass's Br, N-Chail Clayton, E-John Foster and Thomas Price, and S-Alexander Jordan; part of 872 ac grant Feb. 19, 1791. Witness John Brewton and Mathew Patton. Signed Austin Clayton. Wit. oath Jun. 14, 1803 Mathew Patton to Drury McDaniel. Rec. Aug. 3, 1802

p. 66-68 Mar. 8, 1803 Mathias Bates (Spartanburgh) to John Tolleson (same); for $455 sold 200 ac in two adjoining tracts on waters of Fairforrest Cr and Storey's Mill Cr: (1) 100 ac part of grant to John Foster; and (2) 100 ac border: E-George McCarter, NW & W-John Foster, NW-David Brown, and S-Arthur Simpson. Witness Henry Foster and M Tolleson. Signed Mathias Bates and Chanle's mark. Certified Mar. 9, 1803 by William Simpson. Rec. Aug. 4, 1803

p. 68-71 Jan. 26, 1802 William McDaniel (Spartanburgh) to Enoch Underwood (same); for $570 sold 300 ac on E side of S fork of Tyger R; border: James Miller, Sterling Staforn, William Allen, Thornton McDaniel, Drury McDaniel, Moses Wood's old line, and Meek's old line; part of grant to "William McDaniel, Moses Ward, Adam Meek, and James Crook". Witness John Underwood, Thornton McDaniel, and William McDaniel. Signed William McDaniel. Wit. oath Jan. 26, 1802 John Underwood to Drury McDaniel. Rec. Aug. 8, 1803. Dower renounced Judah McDaniel to William Lancaster Jul. 16, 1803

p. 71-72 Oct. 1, 1798 dower renounced Lely Martin (Lincoln Co, NC) to John McClenleham, judge (York Co); for two tracts sold to Maj Moses Guiton (York Co): (1) 300 ac on Beaverdam Cr of Thickety Cr including George Taylor's old improvements;grant to (a) John Hogan and (b) to Capt. James Martin; and (2) 250 ac adjoining (1) on N side of grant to Vardry McBee who sold to Lely Martin. Signed Lely Martin. (no witness or recording date)

p. 72-73 Nov. 29, 1800 William Hort (SC) to Moses Guyton; for $700 sold 1,250 ac on head branches Beaverdam Cr of Thickety Cr of Broad R in Craven Co; border: E-William Hort, N & W-vacant, and S-unknown; survey for William Hort Sept. 13, 1772 and granted Feb. 17, 1773. Witness James Goodman and John Guyton. Signed Wm Hort. Wit. oath Feb. 5, 1803 James Guyton to John Richman. Rec. Aug. 13, 1803

p. 73-75 Aug. 12, 1803 Capt. John Murrell (Union Dist) to Henry O'Neill (Spartanburgh); for $100 sold 280 ac on branch of Mill Cr of Tyger R; border: SW, SE, N & W-Elisha Hadden, SW-Thomas Clayton, NE-Latice Miles (or Neles) and vacant; grant Dec. 1, 1794 to Samuel Hedden who sold to William Hill. Witness none. Signed John Murrell and Ann Murrell. Wit. oath (Union Dist) Aug. 12, 1803 John Murrell to Thomas B Hunt. Rec. Aug. 19, 1803

p. 75-76 Nov. 15, 1802 John Low (Spartanburgh) to William Rook (same); for $50 sold 88 ac on waters of Thickety Cr; grant Gov. William Moultrie to (not given). Witness Henry Adcock and Leonard Low. Signed John Low. Wit. oath Jan. 12, 1803 Henry Adcock to Geor Lamkin. Rec. Aug. 25, 1803

p. 76-78 Aug. 23, 1803 Jonathan Low (Spartanburgh), schoolmaster, to Thomas Wyatt (same); for $43 sold 100 ac on Long Br of Island Cr of Pacolate R; border: Rueben Warren; part of grant States Office to Jonathan Low. Witness Reuben Warren and James Lard. Signed Jonathan Low. Wit. oath Aug. 24, 1803 Reuben Warren to Geor Lamkens. Rec. Aug. 25, 1803

p. 78-80 Aug. 23, 1803 Jonathan Low, schoolmaster (Spartanburgh) to Reuben Warren (same); for $28 sold 134 ac on branches of Island Cr of Pacolate R; border: Thos Wyatt and Reuben Warran; part of grant States Office to Jonathan Low. Witness Thomas Wyatt and James Lard. Signed Jonathan Low. Wit. oath Aug. 24, 1803 Thomas Wyatt to Geor Lamkens. Rec. Aug. 26, 1803

p. 80-82 Jun. 8, 1803 Thomas Goore (Spartanburgh) to Philip Johnson (Rutherford Co, NC); for $300 sold 240 ac on both sides N Pacolate R and at fork of Pacolate R; border: Barton's Spring Br and S Pacolate R. Witness Robert Davis, John Pullam, and William Vaughn. Signed Thomas Goor. Wit. oath Jul. 28, 1803 John Pullam to William McDowell. Rec. Aug. 29, 1803

p. 82-83 Aug. 15, 1803 John Gray (Spartanburgh) to William Rickman (same); for 12£ 12s 9p sold 392 ac on Peoples Cr of Broad R; grant Sept. 17, 1785 Gov. William Moultrie to Cardry (sic) McBee. Witness Curtis G Gray, Casandra Gray, and Mary Lovell. Signed John Gray. Wit. oath Aug. 29, 1803 Curtis G Gray to A Lancaster. Rec. Aug. 29, 1803

p. 83-85 Mar. 20, 1803 Moses Guyton (Spartanburgh) to John Dill (same); for $500 sold 295 ac on Thickety Cr of Broad R; border: Bostick and mouth of Beaverdam Cr; part of grant in 1773 to William Hort. Witness Thomas Collins and Jesse Fondren. Signed Moses Guyton. Wit. oath Apr. 18, 1803 Thomas Collins to John Lipscomb. Rec. Aug. 31, 1803

p. 85-87Apr. 5, 1803 Moses Guyton (Spartanburgh) to Thomas Collins (same); for $559 sold 392 ac on Thickety Cr; part of grant in 1773 to William Hort. Witness John Greyton and John Dill. Signed Moses Guyton. Wit. oath Apr. 18, 1803 John Dill to John Lipscomb. Rec. Aug. 31, 1803. Dower renounced Tabetha Guyton to John Lipscomb Apr. 18, 1803

p. 87-91 Mar. 15, 1803 John Joachim Bulow and Charles William Bulow, executors of will of Joachim Bulow desc (all merchants of Charleston, SC) to John Martin (Union Dist); for $1,320 sold 440 ac on Big Cr of Little R; see will of Joachim Bulow Jun. 9, 1795 for naming of executors; land sold by M Tate to James Lusk and sold as James Lusk's property Jan. 2, 1795 by Samuel Saxon, sheriff (Union Dist) to Joachim Bulow. Witness Henry Farnandes and Robert Hemming. Signed John J Bulow and Charles Wm Bulow. Wit. oath Aug. 26, 1803 Henry Farnandes to William Simpson. Rec. Aug. 31, 1803

p. 91-93 Jul. 22, 1793 Stephen Miller (Spartanburgh) to David Hix (same); for 40£ SC money sold 50 ac on both sides Lawson's fork of Pacolate R; grant Nov. 25, 1774 Gov. William Bull to Stephen Miller. Witness Ephraim Lewis, Georg Bishop, and Mary Lewis. Signed Stephen Miller. Wit. oath Nov. 10, 1797 Ephraim Lewis to Ism Foster. Rec. Sept. 1, 1803

p. 93-95 Nov. 13, 1797 David Hix (Spartanburgh) to William Brannon (same); for $60 sold 50 ac on both sides Lawson's fork of Pacolate R; part of grant Nov. 25, 1774 Gov. William Bull to Stephen Miller who sold to David Hix. Witness John Sanders, Nancy Harper, and Hance Harper jr. Signed David Hix's mark. Wit. oath Feb. 8, 1803 Hance Harper jr to A Lancaster. Rec. Sept. 1, 1803

p. 95-96 Apr. 8, 1800 George Deavers (Spartanburgh) to William Brannon (same); for $90 sold 500 ac on little Sholy Cr of Pacolate R; border: John Kelley, William Venable, and Ballenger; survey Feb. 15, 1797 for Maxn Conner and granted Feb. 15, 1797 Gov. Edward Rutledge to George Deavers. Witness John Bobbett. Signed Georg Deavers. Wit. oath Dec. 1, 1802 John Bobbett to A Lancaster. Rec. Sept. 2, 1803

p. 96-98 Mar. 13, 1799 Henry Machen (Gruolle (or Greenville) Co) to William Brannon (Spartanburgh); for $200 sold 467 ac on Sholy Cr of Lawson's fork; grant Apr. 3, 1797 Gov. Charles Pinckney to Henry Machen. Wit. oath Adam Kelly, John Keenum, and Dudly Brannon. Signed Henry Machen. Wit. oath Aug. 24, 1803 John Keenum to James Jordan. Rec. Sept. 2, 1803

p. 98-100 Jun. 19, 1799 Samuel Fley (Spartanburgh) to William Brannon (same); for $100 sold 106 ac on Lawson's fork of Pacolate R; border: S-Stephen Miller, SE-Edmund Bishop and Hance Harper, W-Stephen Miller, and others vacant; survey for Georg West Jul. 22, 1786 and granted Jun. 3, 1799 Gov. Edward Rutledge to Samuel Fley. Witness William Murrell and Christian Cornelius Thode. Signed Samuel Fley. Wit. oath (Claremont Co, Camden Dist) Christian C Thode to John Horan. Rec. Sept. 3, 1803

p. 100-101 Jun. 19, 1799 Samuel Fley (Spartanburgh, SC) to William Brannon (Spartanburgh); for $121 sold 242 ac on Lawson's fork of Pacolate R; border: N-Stephen Miller, NE-Edmond Bishop, NW-Frances Balenger, and others vacant; survey Jul. 22, 1786 for Stephen Miller and granted Jun. 3, 1799 Gov. Edward Rutledge to Stephen Fley. Witness William Murrell and Christian Cornelious Thode. Signed Samuel Fley. Wit. oath (Claremont Co, Camden Dist) Christian C Thode to John Horan. Rec. Sept. 3, 1803

p. 101-102 Sept. 4, 1803 John Roberson to William Roberson; for $500 sold a Negro man Aron. Witness John Lancaster and Curtis G Gray. Signed John Roberson. Wit. oath Sept. 4, 1803 John Lancaster to A Lancaster. Rec. Sept. 7, 1803

p. 102-103 Sept. 4, 1803 William Roberson to John Roberson; for $500 sold a Negro woman Kiz and her child Fetney. Witness John Lancaster and Curtis G Gray. Signed William Roberson. Wit. oath Sept. 4, 1803 John Lancaster to A Lancaster. Rec. Sept. 7, 1803

p. 103-104 Nov. 9, 1802 Roaland Johnson and wife Milly (Spartanburgh) to John Dodd (same); for $1,000 sold 200 ac on waters of Lawson's fork. Witness John Chapman, John Wingo, and James Foster. Signed Roaland Johnson. Wit. oath Nov. 9, 1802 John Chapman to Ism Foster. Rec. Sept. 7, 1803

p. 104-106 Aug. 17, 1803 Reynold Allen (Spartanburgh) to John Henry (same); for $200 sold 159 ac; border: Gibson; grant Oct. 6, 1788 Gov. Thomas Pinckney to David Allen sr. Witness John H Gray and Curtis G Gray. Signed Reynold Allen. Wit. oath Sept. 5, 1803 John H Gray to Geor Lamkins. Rec. Sept. 8, 1803

p. 106-108 May 24, 1803 William Ford (Spartanburgh) to John Dodd (same); for $180 sold 109 ac on both sides N fork Tyger R; border: SW & NE-Samuel Nesbett and Moses Thompson, SE & NE-Daniel Monroe and Benjamin Clark, SW-"old North survey" for Joseph James Dust. Witness James Young, John Wood, and John Harkens. Signed William Ford. Wit. oath Aug. 19, 1803 John Harkens to James Jordan. Rec. Sept. 8, 1803

p. 108-109 Aug. 20, 1803 John Kelly (Spartanburgh) to Elizabeth

Whitby (same); for love and affection give 2 cows now in John Kelly's possession: (a) red and (b) red and white; cows to be delivered to Elizabeth before singing. Witness John Dunlap and Elizabeth Dunlap. Signed John Kelly's mark. Wit. oath Aug. 30, 1803 John Kelly to Geor Lamkin. Rec. Sept. 9, 1803

p. 190-110 Jan. 19, 1803 Ignatious Griffin (Spartanburgh) to Daniel Forwellen (same); for $30 sold 30 ac. Witness George Gibson and Hubbard Qualls. Signed Ignatious Griffin's mark. Wit. oath Sept. 6, 1803 George Gibson to Geor Lamkins. Rec. Sept. 13, 1803

p. 110-113 Mar. 10, 1802 William Wells to Gabriel Benson, agent for Gabriel Bumpass; for $109 sold 190 ac in two tracts: (a) 100 ac grant to Michael Miller and (2) 90 ac part granted to John Nichols and part granted to James Nicols; border: (1) mouth of Conwell's Spring Br near Mill Shoal, Thomas Foster, and James Nicols; (2) William McMahan's old corner; see writ from Spartanburgh Common Pleas Court Moses Timmons defendant; sale first Monday in Mar. 1802; Isham Harrison's name replaced by William Wells' name before deed is executed. Witness John Lancaster and Noah Wells. Signed William Wells. Wit. oath Sept. 22, 1803 John Lancaster to A Lancaster. Rec. Sept. 23, 1803

p. 113-114 Dec. 6, 1802 Robert McDowell (Spartanburgh) to William Foster (same); for 250£ sterling sold 461 ac on waters Lawson's fork; border: John Lackey, William Lewis, John Bennett; part of three tracts: (1) large grant to Francis Boys and (2) and (3) "State" to David Lewis and Daniel White. Witness William Lewis and John Lackey. Signed Robert McDowell. Wit. oath Aug. 26, 1803 John Lackey to John Anderson. Rec. Oct. 4, 1803

p. 114-116 Aug. 2, 1803 John Arendell jr (Spartan Dist) to John Arendell sr; for $415 sold (ac not given) on waters Cherokee Cr of Broad R; border: John Arendell sr, Martin, and Walker. Witness Daniel McCay and Lot(?) Arendale. Signed John Arendal. Wit. oath Oct. 21, 1813 (sic) Daniel McCay to John Richman. Rec. Oct. 29, 1803

p. 116-117 May 14, 1803 James Betterton (Spartanburgh) to Daniel Prewett (same); for $200 sold 125 ac on N side Tyger R; border: Joshua Betterton, Betterton Spring Br, and Saml Pruitt; part of 350 ac grant to Thomas Betterton desc. Witness John Gust, Samuel Pruitt, and Alexander Pruitt. Signed James Betterton's mark. Wit. oath May 31, 1803 Samuel Pruitt to Wm Smith. Rec. Oct. 29, 1803

p. 117-119 Feb. 7, 1803 Thomas Gore (Spartanburgh) to Zachariah Green Cud (sic) (same); for 60£ sterling sold 150 ac on Buck Cr of Pacolate R; border: Zachariah Green and Sanders; part of two grants Jan. (not given), 1787 to Richard Sanders. Witness John Nelson and Andrew McMillen. Signed Thomas Gore. Wit. oath Oct. 18, 1803 John Nelson to Wm McDowell. Rec. Oct. 29, 1803

p. 119-121 Sept. 10, 1803 James Moore (Spartanburgh) to William Acue (or Acree) (same); for $90 sold 80 ac on NE side of Tyger R and N side Ward's Cr of Tyger R; border: N-Martin Oats, W-Charles Moore, S-William Ford, SE-Casons Moor, and E-Thomas Moore; part of two tracts: (1) granted Aug. 11, 1774 Gov. William Bull to Thomas Moore and (2) granted Jul. 6, 1795 Gov. Arnoldus Vanderhorst to Casons Moore. Witness Samuel Oats and Samuel Elder. Signed James Moore. Wit. oath Sept. 24, 1803 Samuel Oats to Drury McDaniel. Rec. Oct. 31, 1803

p. 121-122 Sept. 21, 1803 Lacy McAbee (Spartanburgh) to Charles McAbee (same); for 25£ sold 60 ac on N side Lawson's fork; survey Jun. 2, 1772 and W end of grant to Lacy McAbee; border: Cole Water Br and Thomson. Witness William McAbee jr, Blackburn Quinn, and Michael Obare. Signed Lacy McAbee's mark. Wit. oath Oct. 31, 1803 Michael Obare to A Lancaster. Rec. Oct. 31, 1803

p. 122-123 Dec. 19, 1799 Ezekiel Wyatt (Spartanburgh) to Ephram Potter (same); for 4(?) £ SC money sold 147 ac on N side Pacolate R. Witness Henry Turner and Richard Turner. Signed Ezekiel Wyatt's mark. Wit. oath Mar. 4, 1802 Richard Turner to Ism Foster. Rec. Oct. 31, 1803

p. 123-125 Oct. 31, 1803 Charles McAbee and wife Cela (Spartanburgh) to Richard Thomson (same); for $100 sold 60 ac on N side Lawson's fork; W end of 450 ac grant Jun. 2, 1772 to Lacy McAbee on Colewater Br. Witness Michael Obare and Susanna Hopson. Signed Charles McAbee and Cela's mark. Wit. oath Oct. 31, 1803 Michael Obare to A Lancaster. Rec. Nov. 1, 1803

p. 125-127 Dec. 7, 1797 James and Nancy Casey (Spartanburgh) to Abner Casey (same); for 170£ sterling sold 107 ac; border: Richard Fryar; part of 1,000 ac grant Jul. 21, 1775 to James Sample and sold by Rattary Sample, heir-at-law,to John McCullock Dec. 5 & 6, 1786 who sold to James Casey Jul. 4, 1787. Witness Aron Casey and John Casey. Signed James Casey and Nancy's mark. Wit. oath Oct. 24, 1803 Aron Casey to John Lipscomb. Rec. Nov. 2, 1803

p. 127-128 Jan. 11, 1802 Joseph Morris (Edgefield Dist) to John Jordan (Spartanburgh); for $100 sold 200 ac on S side Buck Cr; border: John Morris. Witness William Morris, John Morris, and George Gilbert. Signed Joseph Morris' mark. Wit. oath Aug. 28, 1802 John Morris to William McDowell. Rec. Nov. 3, 1803

p. 128-130 Oct. 3, 1803 Nicholas Keating (Spartanburgh) to John Thornton (same); for $220 sold 140 ac; part of grant to Thomas White who sold to Luke Thornton who sold to Nicholas Keating. Witness James Sells, Isaac Crow jr, and Levi Lamb. Signed Nichoals Keating. Wit. oath Oct. 7, 1803 James Sells to A Casey. Rec. Nov. 3, 1803

p. 130-131 Oct. 25, 1803 John Rickman (Spartanburgh) to Daniel McClaren (same); for $2,000 sold 2485 ac on waters of Cherokee and Sarratt's Creeks of Broad R; in three surveys Jan. 18, 1803 for John Rickman. Witness John McHenry and Joseph Clark. Signed John Rickman. Wit. oath Oct. 25, 1803 John McHenry to John Lipscomb. Rec. Nov. 3, 1803

p. 131-133 Oct. 20, 1803 Thomas Williams (Spartanburgh) to Elisworth Moore (same); for $100 sold 114 ac on waters Dutchman's Cr; part of two tracts: (1) 456 ac grant to Brittin Williford Nov. 6, 1786 and (2) 200 ac grant Nov. 7, 1785 to John Shands. Witness John Vise and Aron Smith. Signed Thomas Williams. Wit. oath Oct. 20, 1803 John Vise to Wm Smith. Rec. Nov. 4, 1803. Dower renounced Jane Williams to William Smith Oct. 20, 1803

p. 133-135 Feb. 22, 1803 Isaac Young and Abraham Cantrell (Spartanburgh) to Moses Cantrell (same); for $208 sold 250 ac on waters of Island Cr of Pacolate R. Witness Leonard Adcock and Benny Young. Signed Abraham Cantrell and Isaac Young's mark. Wit. oath Oct. 25, 1803 Leonard Adcock to Geor Lamkins. Rec. Nov. 4, 1803

p. 135-136 Oct. 17, 1803 Benjamin Brown (Spartanburgh) to Bryant Bonner (same); for $200 sold 200 ac on Sarratt's Cr of Broad R. Witness John Rickman and Sina (or Lina) Williams. Signed none. Wit. oath Oct. 17, 1803 Sina Williams to John Rickman (or

Rukman). Rec. Nov. 4, 1803

p. 136-138 Aug. 15, 1803 John Robnet (Spartanburgh) to James Wilson (same); for ($?)450 sold 299 ac on both sides Middle fork Tyger R; grant to Joseph Nisbet desc and part of 299 ac is "held by a new warrant". Witness James Gilleland, Jeremiah Nisbet, and Andrew Nesbit. Signed John and Margert Bell Robert. Wit. oath Oct. 20, 1803 Andrew Nesbit to James Jordan. Rec. Nov. 4, 1803. Dower renounced Margret Bell Robert to James Jordan Oct. 20, 1803

p. 138-140 Oct. 17, 1802 Dudley Walton (Spartanburgh) to Jesse Story (same); for $110 sold 108 ac; burder: John Story; part of 158 ac grant Nov. 7, 1796 Gov. Androus Vanderhorst to Dudley Walton; "reserving" about 50 ac for William Pruett. Witness John Grist and James K Benson. Signed Dudley Walton's mark. Wit. oath Oct. 20, 1803 John Grist to Wm Smith. Rec. Nov. 5, 1803. Dower renounced Tabitha Wilton to Wm Smith Oct. 19, 1802

p. 140-142 Oct. 24, 1803 William Duncan (Spartanburgh) to John Duncan (same); for $300 sold 80 ac on S side Tygar R; border: John Massey, Thomas Stone, and Hendrake. Witness James Duncan, Daniel Daviar (or David), and David Fowler. Signed William and Ruth Duncan's marks. Wit. oath Oct. 24, 1803 James Duncan to Drury McDaniel. Rec. Nov. 7, 1803

p. 142-144 Nov. 13, 1802 James Wofford (Spartanburgh) to John Wofford (same); for $200 sold 50 ac on waters of McClevean's Cr and Sugar Cr of Fairforrest Cr; part of 300 ac grant to William Brownlee who sold to James Wofford; border: John Wofford. Witness William Wofford and Benjamin Bearden. Signed James Wofford's mark. Wit. oath Oct. 21, 1803 William Wofford to Wm Smith. Rec. Nov. 7, 1803. Dower renounced Mary Wofford to Wm Smith Dec. 7, 1802

p. 144-145 May 2, 1803 Bayles Earle (Spartanburgh) to Thomas Jackson (same); for $30 sold 3 ac in a bend of N Pacolet R and on S side of N Pacolet R and on N side of river; border: a canal cut through a small neck and separated by canal from Gilbert Bowman; whole 3 ac is an island. Witness Theron Earle and John Hopkins. Signed Bayles Earle. Wit. oath Oct. 22, 1803 John Hopkins to John Anderson. Rec. Nov. 7, 1803

p. 145-147 Jan. 19, 1803 John Odle and wife Rebekar (Spartanburgh) to John Duncan (same); for $50 sold 25 ac on S side Tygar R. Witness Georg Massy, Wm Massey, and James Wofford. Signed John Odle's mark. Wit. oath Oct. 21, 1803 James Wofford to Drury McDaniel. Rec. Nov. 7, 1803

p. 147-149 Sept. 27, 1803 Thomas Brooks (Spartanburgh) to son Moses Brooks (same); for $50 sold 213 ac on N fork of N fork Tyger R; border: Jesse Reames, Miller (or Milles), and Ballenger; grant in 1786 Gov. William Moultrie to Thomas Brooks. Witness John Davis (Scll or Sck?), Ellis Johnson, and Polly Brooks. Signed Thomas Brooks' mark. Wit. oath (not dated) John Davis to Jas L Burd. Rec. Nov. 8, 1803

p. 149-150 Jan. 6, 1802 John Meadows (Spartanburgh) to William Meadows (same); for 200 Spanish milled dollars sold 45 ac; border: Tobias Bright, Charles Burton, Andrew Thomson, Aaron Pinson, and William Meadows; part of 240 ac grant Jan. 6, 1794 Gov. William Moultrie to John Meadows. Witness Joseph Smith and James Wofford. Signed John Meadows. Wit. oath Jan. 25, 1802 Joseph Smith to Wm Smith. Rec. Nov. 8, 1803

p. 150-152 Apr. 2, 1803 Aaron Lancaster (Spartanburgh) to Lamuel Lancaster (same); for $180 sold 112 ac on both sides Sugar

Cr of Fairforrest Cr; border: SW-Samuel Lancaster, NW-John Varnan, E-John Wofford, and others vacant. Witness John Tolleson and Muse Tolleson. Signed Aaron Lancaster's mark. Wit. oath Apr. 2, 1803 John Tolleson to Saml Lancaster. Rec. Nov. 8, 1803. Dower renounced Elizabeth Lancaster to William Lancaster Oct. 26, 1803

p. 152-154 Jun. 5, 1802 John Ridings (Rutherford Co, NC) to John Burn (Spartanburgh); for $250 sold 200 ac on both sides S Pacolate R; upper end of 640 ac grant Feb. 3, 1775 Lt. Gov. William Bull to Matthew Harper sr who sold 200 ac to Matthew Harper jr Feb. 20, 1776. Witness Samuel Hunt and Theron Earle. Signed John Ridings. Wit. oath Aug. 5, 1803 Samuel Hunt to James L Burd. Rec. Nov. 8, 1803

p. 154-155 May 26, 1803 Malachi Eskridge (Spartanburgh) to Drury McDaniel (same); for $30 sold 6 cattle, 25 hogs of different marks "tho my mark" is a cross and slit in right ear and swallow in left ear, 2 beds and furniture, and all household furniture. Witness John Hughes and William McDaniel. Signed Malachi Eskridge. Wit. oath Oct. 25, 1803 William McDaniel to William Simpson. Rec. Nov. 8, 1803

p. 155-157 Oct. 9, 1800 Thomas Burgess (Spartanburgh) to Edward Stublefield (same); for $80 sold 50 ac on S side Pacolate R; border: Edward Stublefield; part of grant Sept. 2, 1799 States Office to Thomas Burgess. Witness William Morris, John Morris, and West Harris. Signed Thomas Burgess. Wit. oath Oct. 25, 1803 West Harris to Ab Benson. Rec. Nov. 9, 1803

p. 157-159 Aug. 10, 1803 Vincent Wyatt and wife Elizabeth (Spartanburgh) to Zachariah Wyatt (same); for 16£ sold 60 ac on Mayes Br on S side Peter Cr; border: Mill dam, Mare Br; part of SW end of grant Dec. 3, 1787 Gov. Thomas Pinckney to Jesse Connel. Witness Robert Armour and Vincent Wyatt jr. Signed Vincent Wyatt and Elizabeth's mark. Wit. oath Oct. 21, 1803 Vincent Wyatt jr to Geor Lamkins. Rec. Nov. 9, 1803

p. 159-178 missing when microfilmed Jul. 15, 1791 "book skips from p. 158 to 179" written in book.

p. 179-181 Mar. 31, 1803 John Odel (Spartanburgh) to James Vernon (same); for $1,000 sold 275 ac on both sides S fork Tygar R; part of 300 ac grant to John Duncan and sold by Robert Starkes, sheriff (6 Dist, to Wm Hendricks and then to daughter Rebecah Hendricks wife of John Odell. Witness Thomas Hendricks and John Jordan. Signed John Odell's mark. "acknowledged before James Jordan" (not dated). Rec. Nov. 9, 1803. Dower renounced (Newberry Co) Rebeca Odell to Levi Casey Apr. 22, 1803

p. 181 Feb. 23, 1803 Alexander Macbeth to William Hammett; a receipt in full satisfaction "for the account of the within mortgage". Witness John H Jones and Caleb Jones. Signed Alex Macbeth. Wit. oath Oct. 24, 1803 John H Jones to Wm Lancaster. Rec. Nov. 9, 1803

p. 181-182 Oct. 24, 1803 Caleb Jones to Geor Lamkins: Caleb says his brand on ear of cattle, hogs, and sheep is two smooth crosses and a slit in left ear. Signed Caleb Jones. Rec. Nov. 9, 1803

p. 182 Oct. 24, 1803 John Hunter Jones to Geor Lamkins; John says his brand on cattle, sheep, and hogs is two smooth crosses and two slits in left ear. Signed John H Jones. Rec. Nov. 9, 1803

p. 182-184 Apr. 7, 1803 John Cook (Spartanburgh) to Isaac Toomer (same); for $100 sold 70 ac on Caen Cr of Tygar R; border:

Timothy Toney's old line, Samuel Shearbutt, James Hembree, and Belews Beaner (or Bianu); grant Nov. 20, 1772 Gov. "G Montagu" to James Hembree. Witness Willis Willeford, John Grist, and W. S. Willeford. Signed John Clark's mark. Witness Willis Willeford to Wm Smith. Rec. Nov. 9, 1803. Dower renounced Deborah Cook to Wm Smith Apr. 7, 1803

p. 184-185 May 28, 1803 Malachi and Elizabeth Eskridge (Spartanburgh) to Wm Allen (same); for $400 sold a Negro woman Sall. Witness Enoch Underwood and Michael Barnett. Signed Malachi Eskridge and Elizabeth's mark. Wit. oath Oct. 24, 1803 Enoch Underwood to A Lancaster. Rec. Nov. 17, 1803

p. 185-187 Oct. 20, 1800 Solomon Hill (Spartanburgh) to Michael McElrath (same); for 50£ sterling sold 186 ac on Middle and S forks of Tygar R; border: Jno Vanderhos,through which lands runs the road from Mountains to Charleston, unknown, Blakes, and James Bright; grant Jan. 5, 1795 to John Thomas. Witness Henry Gray and James McElrath. Signed Solomon Hill. Wit. oath Nov. 14, 1803 James McElrath to John Collins. Rec. Nov. 26 or 25, 1803

p. 187-189 Nov. 20 (or 10), 1803 Philip Evins (Greenville Dist) to John Anderson (Spartanburgh); for 100£ sold 640 ac on both sides Obed's Cr of Pacolate R and E of old Indian boundary; border: all vacant and "marked lines and corner trees being a mile square (sic) each way"; survey Oct. 4, 1784 by George Sammon and granted to Thomas Evans. Witness Benjamin C Anderson, William Anderson, and Isaac Anderson. Signed Philip Evins. Wit. oath Nov. 25, 1805 Benjamin C Anderson to Ism Foster. Rec. Nov. 25, 1803

p. 189-190 Jun. 21, 1803 Zachariah McDaniel and William Lancaster (Spartanburgh) to Daniel White (same); for $370 sold 3 ac including part of a shoal on Fairforrest Cr where "the" wagon road crosses; border: Alexander McKee; plat attached shows border: Barrett, Thomas' old corner, and Buffington's old tract now McKee's. Witness Thomas Davison and James Finch. Signed Z McDaniel and Wm Lancaster. Wit. oath Nov. 28, 1803 Thomas Davison to A Lancaster. Rec. Nov. 28, 1803

p. 190-191 Apr. 19, 1803 Thomas Gore (Spartanburgh) to Thomas Henderson (same); for 10£ sold 100 ac on both sides Buck Cr. Witness John Henderson and Maly Henderson. Signed Thomas Gore. Wit. oath Jul. 27, 1803 John Henderson to Wm McDowell. Rec. Nov. 29, 1803

p. 191-192 Mar. 8, 1796 James Dukes (Richland Co), tanner, to William McWilliams (Spartanburgh); for 20s sold 124 ac on Suck Cr of Broad R; border: W-NC line, E-Alexander, and others vacant; survey Jun. 3, 1785 for John Blackwell and granted Mar. 7, 1796 Gov. Arnoldus Vanderhorst to James Dukes. Witness Andrew Boddan and John Holliday. Signed James Duke. Wit. oath Dec. 1, 1801 Andrew Boddan to Isaac Motte Dach(?). Rec. Nov. 29, 1803

p. 192-194 Nov. 3, 1803 John Paul Thomson (Orangeburgh Dist) to William McWilliams (Spartanburgh); for $6 sold 18 ac; border: W-John Jackson, N-NC line, E-James Henderson, and S-N Pacolate R; part of 500 ac grant Jul. 8, 1774 to Col. William Thomason between NC line and N Pacolate R then bordering: N-NC line, S-N Pacolate R, W-Col. W Thomson, and E-Hon. Thomas Knox Gordon; balance of grant "taken away by older grants" now property of John Jackson and Jas Henderson. Witness James Jordan esq and Andrew Boddan. Signed J. P. Thomson. Wit. oath Nov. 4, 1803 Andrew Boddan to Wm McDowell. Rec. Nov. 29, 1803

p. 194-195 May 18, 1803 Ephram Elder (Spartanburgh) to Laurence Bankston (same); for 7£ SC money sold 100 ac on S side

Pacolate R and on Cherokee Cr; part of 449 ac grant States Office to Ephram Elder. Witness James Turner and Jehu Wells. Signed Ephram Elder. Wit. oath Dec. 16, 1803 Jehu Wells to Abner Benson. Rec. Dec. 16, 1803

p. 195-197 Mar. 12, 1803 Thomas Gore (Spartanburgh) to West Harris (same); for $500 sold 590 ac on Buck Cr of Pacolate R; border: Lukes Browning and John Nelson; part of two tracts granted States Office to Richard Sanders: (1) survey Oct. 8, 1784 by James Seaborn and (2) 440 ac survey May 22, 1788 by Vardry McAgby (sic); both grants sold to Thomas Gore. Witness William Bridges and Richard Morris. Signed Thos Gore. Wit. oath Dec. 7, 1803 William Bridges to Wm McDowell. Rec. Dec. 16, 1803

p. 197-199 Dec. 24, 1803 Thomas Williams (Spartanburgh) to Wilie Willeford (same); for $450 sold 250 ac on waters of Dutchman' Cr; where Thomas Williams lives; part of two tracts: (1) 300 ac grant to Thomas Thornton bordering Moore and (2) 330 ac grant to John Smith bordering John Shands. Witness Joseph Smith, Aaron Smith, and Wm T. Hewett. Signed Thomas Williams. Wit. oath Dec. 25, 1803 Joseph Smith to Wm Smith. Rec. Dec. 27, 1803. Wit. oath Jane Williams to Wm Smith Dec. 26, 1803

p. 199-200 Jun. 15, 1803 John Williams (Spartanburgh) to John Keenum (same); John Williams is bound to John Keenum by "several" notes for $60; to secure those notes John Williams sells a still capacity of 60 gal and sale is void if John Williams pays off notes. Witness Thomas Beannon. Signed John Williams. Wit. oath Aug. 24, 1803 Thomas Beannon to James Jordan. Rec. Jan. 2, 1804

p. 200-202 Sept. 14, 1801 James Smith (Spartanburgh) to Henry Young (same); for $30 sold 30 ac on N side S Pacolate R; border: Alexander, NE-Henry Young, and on three sides by remainder of grant; part of grant North Carolina to Joseph White and "again" granted Feb. 3, 1775 Lt. Gov. William Bull to Matthew Harper sr; where Henry Young lives. Witness James Redens, Elisha Cornwell, and John Huth. Signed James Smith. Wit. oath May. 13, 1802 James Redens to Ism Foster. Rec. Jan. 2, 1804

p. 202-203 Apr. 26, 1803 Robert McDowell (Spartanburgh) to James McDowell (same); for $115 sold 46 ac on S side of S Pacolate R; border: Dickson; grant to William Dickson. Witness William Lewis, David Alexander, and David McDowell. Signed Robert McDowell. Wit. oath Dec. 17, 1803 David McDowell to Wm McDowell. Rec. Jan. 4, 1804

p. 203-205 Dec. 1, 1803 Benjamin Grist (Spartanburgh) to Mills Sumner (Union Co); for $250 sold 126 ac on N side Tygar R and on Dutchman's Cr; border: William Farmer; part of two tracts (1) 150 ac grant Apr. 27, 1767 Gov. William Tryon (NC) to Moses Miller and (2) 120 ac grant Mar. 6, 1786 Gov. William Moultrie to David Pruitt. Witness John Grist, Aaron Smith, and Isaac Smith. Signed Benjamin Grist's mark. Wit. oath Dec. 1, 1803 John Grist to Wm Smith. Rec. Jan. 23, 1804. Dower renounced Fanny Grist to Wm Smith Dec. 19, 1803

p. 205-206 Feb. 13, 1801 Buckner Smith (Spartanburgh) to Benjamin Grist (same); for $200 sold 126 ac on N side Tygar R and on Dutchman's Cr; border: William Farmer; part of two tracts (1) 150 ac grant Apr. 27, 1767 Gov. William Tryon (NC) to Moses Williu (sic) and (2) 120 ac grant Mar. 6, 1786 Gov. William Moultrie to David Pruitt. Witness John Grist and Osburn West. Signed Buckner Smith's mark. Wit. oath Feb. 13, 1801 John Grist to Wm Smith. Rec. Jan. 23, 1804. Dower renounced Dinah Smith to Wm Smith Feb. 13, 1801

p. 206-208 Jan. 12, 1804 Samuel Hunt (Spartanburgh) to James Sanderl

Guignard (Columbia, SC); for $5 sold 421 ac on S Pacolate R; border: N-Magby's Cr, E-Gilbert, Roddy and Hunt, S-S Pacolate R, SW-Stokes, W-Grogan, and NW-Goodair; half of 892 ac (50 ac "expected" being an old survey and bought by Samuel Hunt from Jeremiah Stokes) survey Apr. 13, 1803 for Samuel Hunt and granted Jun "seath", 1803 Gov. James B Richardson to Samuel Hunt. Witness Lucy Hunt and Gabriel Benson. Signed Samuel Hunt. Wit. oath Jan. 17, 1804 Gabriel Benson to Wm McDowell. Rec. Jan. 24, 1804

p. 208-210 Jan. 7, 1803 Thomas Posey (Spartanburgh) to Burguk McPherson (same); for $200 sold 217 ac on branches of Fairforrest Cr; grant May 11, 1787 to Thomas Posey; border: N-Henry Wells, NW-John Posey, and SW & SE-unknown. Witness William Posey and John Cantwell. Signed Thomas Posey. Wit. oath Nov. 1, 1803 John Cantwell to William Lancaster. Rec. Jan. 27, 1804. Dower renounced Polly Posey to William Lancaster Nov. 1, 1803

p. 210-211 Jan. 26, 1804 Henry Monro (Spartanburgh) to William Fields (same); for 25£ sold 50 ac on N fork Tygar R; border: Elisha Thompson, David Davis, Jonathan Newman, Wm Fields, and Danial Monroe; part of 366 ac grant Nov. 21, 1785 Gov. Thomas Pinckney to William Ford. Witness Mary McDowell and Fedrick Andrews. Signed Henry Monro. Wit. oath Jan. 30, 1804 Mary McDowell to Wm McDowell. Rec. Jan. 30, 1804

p. 211-213 Jan. 13, 1804 Henry Young sr (Spartanburgh) to Gabriel Benson (same); for $100 sold 100 ac on S Pacolate R; border: Robert Young, Robert Henderson, James Smith, and Gabriel Benson. Witness William Lewis and William Bennett. Signed Henry Young. Wit. oath Jan. 17, 1804 William Bennett to Wm McDowell. Rec. Jan. 30, 1804

p. 213-215 Mar. 10, 1803 Isham Harrison, sheriff (Spartanburgh) to James Galt; for $81 sold 150 ac; border: near a coal kiln, Twitty's Br and Meadow Cr; writ from Spartanburgh Common Pleas Court William Turpin, survivor of Thomas Wadsworth, and during Thomas' lifetime called Wadsworth and Turpin, merchants, vs Drury Hutchison; judgment was for 80£ 6p sterling; land sold first Monday in Mar. 1803. Witness D. J. Puckett, Henry Wells, and Thomas McElhiney. Signed I Harrison. Wit. oath Feb. 2, 1804 Henry Wells to George Lamkins. Rec. Feb. 2, 1804

p. 215-216 Feb. 2, 1804 Henry Gray (Spartanburgh) to David Jordan (same); for $261.74 sold 132 ac on S side Middle Tygar R; border: Vanderhorst; plat attached shows border: Vanderhorst or Hill; grant to Robert Newbell jr. Witness I Harrison, Obediah Watson, and Solomon Hill. Signed Henry Gray. Wit. oath Feb. 2, 1804 I Harrison to Geor Lamkins. Rec. Feb. 2, 1804

p. 216-218 Feb. 4, 1804 James Dickson (Craven Co, NC) to Gabriel Benson (Spartanburgh); for $600 sold 300 ac on both sides S Pacolate R; plat attached signed by Gabl Benson DS shows includes Clear and Meadow Creeks of S Pacolate R; part of two tracts granted to William Dickson bordering William Easley, Young, McDowell, and Gabriel Benson. Witness William Bennett and James Young. Signed James Dickson. Wit. oath Feb. 4, 1804 James Young to Wm McDowell. Rec. Feb. 6, 1804

p. 218-221 Oct. 17, 1803 Benjamin Clark (Spartanburgh) to John Clark (same); for $300 sold 168 ac on branch of S fork Pacolate R; grant Apr. 27, 1767 Gov. William Tryon (NC) to Samuel Spencer who sold to Alexander Kilpatrick who sold to Benjamin Clark. Witness William Anderson, Luke Burnett, and John Lewis. Signed Benjamin Clark. Wit. oath Feb. 13, 1804 Luke Burnett to Wm McDowell. Rec. Feb. 13, 1804

p. 221-222 Apr. 7, 1803 John Fleming (Spartan Dist) to Jesse Wells; for $200 sold a sorrel horse about 14 hands 1" high with blaze in her face and white foot, e feather beds and furniture, "sundrys of delshware", a desk, an oven, a skillet, a teakettle, a set of saddle tools, and 2 pots. Witness Wesley Arry Smith and Wm West. Signed John Fleming. Wit. oath Feb. 12, 1804 Wm West to Jacob Utley. Rec. Feb. 14, 1804

p. 222-224 Jul. 19, 1803 Thomas Davison (Spartanburgh) to William Lancaster (same); for $400 sold 147 ac where Thomas Davison lives; border: William Lancaster, Culbertson, Henry ONeill, and Col. Taylor; part of 400 ac grant Sept. 9, 1774 to James Tillet and to heirs of James Tillet or (sic) Michael Maddock who sold to Nathan Veal who sold to Thomas Davison. Witness James Riely and Zacheriah McDaniel. Signed Thomas Davison. Wit. oath Sept. 9, 1803 Zacheriah McDaniel to William Simpson. Rec. Feb. 18, 1804. Dower renounced (see Book K p. 140) Mary Davison to Absolom Lancaster Aug. 15, 1805 (Rec. Aug. 17, 1805)

p. 224-225 Feb. 21, 1804 Robert Swann (Laurens Co) to Daniel McClaren (Spartanburgh); for $150 sold 500 ac on Sarratt's Cr; border: NW-Hugh Quin and others vacant. Witness Benjamin Bonner and Susana Hamrick. Signed Robert Swann. Wit. oath Feb. 21, 1804 Benjamin Bonner to Jno Rukman. Rec. Feb. 27, 1804

p. 225-227 Feb. 17, 1804 William Robertson (Spartanburgh) to Alexander McKee, carpenter (same); for $47 sold 47 ac on branch of Lawson's fork of Pacolate R; border: Alexander McKee, Isham Harrison, and Widow Lee; part of 350 ac grant Aug. 4, 1794 South Carolina Office to Diskin Grant who sold to William Robertson; plat attached shows border: Wells; resurvey Feb. 15, 1804 by Richd Thomson DS. Witness Noah Wells and Abner Benson. Signed William Robinson. Wit. oath Feb. 18, 1804 Noah Wells to Jacob Utley. Rec. Mar. 1, 1804

p. 227-229 Mar. 11, 1803 George Campbell (Spartanburgh) to William Wells (same); for $100 sold 100 ac on branch of Chinqupin Cr of Lawson's fork of Pacolate R; border: Lancaster and Thompson. Witness Duglas Josiah Puckett and Stephen Thomason. Signed George Campbell's mark. Wit. oath Feb. 18, 1804 Duglas J Puckett to Jacob Utley. Rec. Mar. 1, 1804

p. 229-230 Jul. 26, 1803 William Morrow (Spartanburgh) to Richard Haney sr; for $200 sold 328 ac between Hors and Buck Cr; border: Reuben Warren and Drury Scruggs; part of 655 ac grant Dec. 2, 1793 States Office to Reubun Warren. Witness Mathew Abbett, Richard Haney, and John Haney. Signed William Morrow and Ruth's mark. Wit. oath Feb. 4, 1804 Richard Haney to Wm McDowell. Rec. Mar. 9, 1804

p. 230-232 Jun. 1, 1789 Arther Crocker (Pacolate R, Spartanburgh) to Vardry McBee; for 45£ sterling sold (ac not given) on N side Pacolate R; Arther to defend title to land for next twenty years. Witness Jesse Rakestraw, William Patterson, and Micajah Barnett. Signed Arther Crocker's mark. Wit. oath Aug. 1, 1789 Jesse Rakestraw to Richard Harrison. Rec. Mar. 13, 1804

p. 232-235 Jul. 1, 1789 Vardry McBee (near Thickety Cr, Spartanburgh) to Abram Markley (Charleston, SC) and Arthur deBardeleben (Amelia Township (SC?)); for 45£ sterling sold 200 ac on N side Pacolate R; border (when surveyed): N & W-Maths McMacklie, E-Polslon, and N-vacant; Vardry defends title to land for next twenty years. Witness William Askew and Gobloa (or Gelson) Goodman. Signed Vardry McBee. Wit. oath Aug. 4, 1789 William Askew to Obediah Trimmier. Rec. Mar. 13, 1804

p. 235-236 Nov. 26, 1803 William Anderson (Spartanburgh) to James

Galt (same); for $500 sold 316 ac. Witness James Sharp and Gaberal Benson. Signed William Anderson. Wit. oath Nov. 26, 1803 Gaberal Benson to John Anderson. Rec. Mar. 14, 1804

p. 236-238 Nov. 1, 1801 Bayles Earle (Spartanburgh) to Gilbert Bowman (Burk Co, NC); for $400 sold 150 ac on N side of N Pacolate R near an old bridge; border: land where Bayles Earle lives and bought by Bayles from Samuel Young, Thomas Jackson, and a large canal. Witness Henry Gray, James Hooper, and Henry B Baker. Signed Bayles Earle. Wit. oath Dec. 4, 1801 Henry B Baker to John Anderson. Rec. Mar. 16, 1804

p. 238-240 Sept. 23, 1803 John Jackson (Spartanburgh) to Peter Free (NC); for $1,000 sold (1) 250 (or 202) ac on N side of N fork Pacolate R; part of land sold by Jobes Evans to Samuel Jackson sr in 1773 and by James Jackson, Thomas Jackson, Robot White, Samuel Kelso, and William and Janna Kelso, heirs of Samuel Jackson desc, sold to John Jackson in 1790; border: Nathaniel Henderson; and (2) 98 ac grant Apr. 7, 1800 Gov. John Drayton to John Jackson. Witness Hugh Ewing, James Beaay (sic), and Drewrey Bowman. Signed John Jackson. Wit. oath Feb. 10, 1804 Drewrey Bowman to John Anderson. Rec. Mar. 16, 1804

p. 240-242 Jul. 17, 1803 William Morgan (Spartanburgh) to John Arendell jr; for $215 sold 98 ac on waters of Cherokee Cr of Broad R; border: John Arendell. Witness Daniel McCay and Lot Arendell. Signed William and Elizabeth Morgan's marks. Wit. oath Jul. 18, 1803 Daniel McCay to John Rickman. Rec. Mar. 20, 1804

p. 242-244 Apr. 15, 1774 Alexander McCarter and wife Margret and son John McCarter (Craven Co, SC) to grandson Alexander Keller (SC); for love and affection give 300 ac on S side of N fork Tygar R; grant Apr. 29, 1768 Gov. William Tryon (NC) to John McCarter in Mecklinburgh Co, NC now in Craven Co, SC; border: Mr Alexander's upper line. Witness Elisha Thompson, Alexander Vernon, and James Jordan. Signed Alexander, Margret, and John McCarter. Certified Oct. 29, 1803 by James Jordan. Rec. Mar. 20, 1804

p. 244-246 Feb. 4, 1804 James Hunter (Spartanburgh) to Frances Littlejohn (same); for $300 sold 196 ac on both sides branch of Beaverdam Cr of Thickety Cr; grant to Abraham Buys. Witness William Bostick and Joseph Austell. Signed James Hunter. Wit. oath Feb. 4, 1804 William Bostick to John Lipscomb. Rec. Mar. 23, 1804. Dower renounced Rachel Hunter to John Lipscomb Mar. 10 or 20, 1804

p. 246-248 Jan. 7, 1804 Patterson Thompson (Spartanburgh) to Leonard Sparks (Union Dist); for $80 sold 100 ac; part of 326 ac grant Jan. 17, 1801 Gov. John Drayton to Patterson Thompson. Witness Henry Littlejohn and Henry Littlejohn jr. Signed Patterson Thompson. Wit. oath Jan. 7, 1804 Henry Littlejohn to John Lipscomb. Rec. Mar. 23, 1804

p. 248-250 Oct. 19, 1797 John Lefever jr (Handcock Co, Ga) to Nathaniel Robertson (Spartanburgh); for 30£ SC money sold 196 ac on both sides Beaverdam Cr; grant May 1, 1786 Gov. William Moultrie to Abram Bris. Witness Solomon Mangum, James Lamar, and Charles Morgan. Signed John and Lucy Lefer's marks. Wit. oath Nov. 8, 1797 Charles Morgan to H McCray. Rec. Mar. 23, 1804

p. 250-251 Dec. 10, 1800 George Bishop (Spartanburgh) to Ephram Lewis; for $50 sold 50 ac; part of 74 ac grant Dec. 7, 1795 to Edmond Bishop who sold to George Bishop. Witness George Hughey and Meleson Bishop (female). Signed George Bishop. Wit. oath Apr. 20, 1801 George Hughey to Isham Foster. Rec. Mar. 24, 1804

p. 251-253 Feb. 25, 1795 John Keenum (Spartanburgh) to Ephram Lewis (same); for 20£ sterling sold 60 ac on both sides Fawn Br of Lawson's fork; border: Bever Pon Br; part of grant to William Armstrong who sold to Alexander Keenum who sold to John Keenum. Witness David Hix, Hance Harper, and Elizabeth Hix. Signed John Keenum's mark. Wit. oath Nov. 10, 1797 David Hix to Isham Foster. Rec. Mar. 24, 1804

p. 253-254 Jan. 14, 1804 Frances Fowler (Sparklingburgh) to son Moses Fowler (same); for love and affection give all her legacy from estate of Ares(?) Fowler desc; Frances has given an inventory (not included) of legacy. Witness John House, Nathaniel Jacobs, and William House. Signed Frances Fowler's mark. Wit. oath Jan. 21, 1804 John House to Denny Anderson. Rec. Mar. 26, 1804

p. 254-256 Jan. 5, 1804 Frances Fowler (Spartanburgh) to Moses Fowler (same); for $150 sold 150 ac on Forgeson's Cr of Tygar R; border: E-Thomas Padens and on N side Forgeson's Cr; part of 300 ac grant Sept. 1, 1768 to John Martain. Witness David Moore and Samuel Jones. Signed Frances Fowler's mark. Wit. oath Jan. 21, 1804 David Moore to Denny Anderson. Rec. Mar. 26, 1804

p. 256-258 Jan. 1, 1804 Jacob Smith (Columbia, SC) to Thomas Gilbert (SC); for $90 sold 228 ac on Barton's Cr of Pacolate R; border: NE-John Mason, E-Thomas Barton, S-Lewis Bamett, and others vacant; survey Mar. 8, 1798 for Thomas Gilbert and granted Oct. 7, 1799 Gov. Edward Rutledge to Jacob Smith. Witness Samuel Green and Peter Bremar. Signed Jacob Smith. Wit. oath Mar. 10, 1800 Samuel Green to R Witherspoon. Rec. Mar. 26, 1804

p. 258-260 Oct. 21, 1803 William Dalton (Spartanburgh) to Robert Davis (Rutherford Co, NC); for $600 sold 140 ac; border: Howard; part of grant to Alexander Kilpatrick. Witness Jesse Dalton and John Ridings. Signed William Dalton. Wit. oath Feb. 10, 1804 Jesse Dalton to John Anderson. Rec. Mar. 26, 1804

p. 260-261 Aug. 25, 1803 Robert Legon (Spartanburgh) to son John W Legan (same); for love and affection give 225 ac; border: Wm Moore; half of land on E side of Tygar R which Robert bought from William Ford "including lower end". Witness George Lamkins JP. Signed Robert Legon. Certified Aug. 25, 1803 by George Lamkins. Rec. Mar. 26, 1804

p. 261-263 Nov. 13, 1795 James Clark (Spartanburgh) to Michael Miller (same); for 20£ sterling sold 75 ac on branches of N fork Tygar R; border: Miller, Jones, Luch, A Jordan, and Wadsworth; grant to James Clark by (left blank). Witness Nevel Wayland, Benjamin Jones, and William Fields. Signed James Clark. Wit. oath Feb. 2, 1804 William Fields to John Collins. Rec. Mar. 26, 1804

p. 263-265 Nov. 19, 1795 Abraham Emery and wife Winnefred (Spartanburgh) to Thomas Price (same); for 50£ sterling sold 200 ac on Brown's Br of Keowee R of Savannah R in Pendleton Co; Border: vacant; grant May 7, 1792 Gov. Charles Pinckney to Abraham Emery. Witness Ephraim Jackson and Andrew Thomson. Signed Abraham and Winnefred Emery's marks. Wit. oath Mar. 26, 1804 Andrew Thomson to Drury McDaniel. Rec. Mar. 26, 1804

p. 265-267 Mar. 6, 1797 Henry Wayland (late of Spartanburgh) to Benjamin Jones (Spartanburgh); for 30£ sold 228 ac on branch of S fork of N fork Tygar R; grant Oct. 3, 1786(or 6) by Gov. William Moultrie. Witness Alexander Jordan, James Clark, and Moses Brooks. Signed Henry Wayland. Wit. oath Apr. 19, 1802 Moses Brooks to Ism Foster. Rec. Mar. 26, 1804

p. 267-268 Mar. 18, 1799 Peter Peterson (or Paterson) (Spartanburgh) to James Brown (Spartanburgh); for $30 sold 100 ac on Green's Cr of Pacolate R; grant to William Hartgrove who sold to John George Riner who sold to Peter Peterson. Signed Paterson Thomson and John Woods. Signed Peter Peterson. Wit. oath (not given) 23, 1799 Paterson Thomson to John Lipscomb. Signed Mar. 26, 1804

p. 268-270 Jan. 20, 1803 Matthew Abbett (Spartanburgh) to William Dobbins (same); for $200 sold 290 ac on both sides Island Cr of Pacolate R; border: Pool and Lee; including an old house with a small improvement; part of 500 ac grant Jan. 2, 1797 to George Williams. Witness Wm Abbett jr and Richard Scrugs. Signed Matthew Abbett. Wit. oath Aug. 6, 1803 Richard Scrugs to Geor Lamkins. Rec. Mar. 26, 1804

p. 270-271 Dec. 27, 1799 Milley Gravet, widow of Obediah Gravet desc, and her sons William Gravet and Randolph Gravet (all Spartanburgh) to Thomas Price (same); a bond of 500 Spanish milled dollars; Condition: bond void if Milley, William, and Randolph Gravet deliver in 6 months to Thomas a deed for 80 ac; border: S-Forgeson's Cr, W-John Hammend, and N & E-Thomas Price. Witness Andrew Thomson and Stephen Hyde. Signed Milley, William, and Randolph Gravet's marks. Wit. oath Mar. 26, 1804 Andrew Thomson to Drury McDaniel. Rec. Mar. 26, 1804

p. 271-273 Dec. 24, 1798 Benjamin Busey (Spartanburgh) to Jesse Brown (same); for $500 sold 100 ac on E side of Two Mile Cr of Enoree R; border: George Lowther, Isaac Hendrix, William Clayton, and William Miller. Witness Sterling and James Attaway. Signed Benjamin Busey's mark. Wit. oath Oct. 19, 1799 James Attaway to A Casey. Rec. Mar. 27, 1804

p. 273-275 Feb. 25, 1804 James Wofford (Spartanburgh) to Manley Ford (same); for $250 sold 350 ac on branches of Rockeyfield and Maple Swamp Creeks of Enoree and Tygar Rivers. Witness Isham Hendrick and Jacob Perington. Signed James Wofford. Wit. oath Mar. 12, 1804 Isham Hendrick to Denny Anderson. Rec. Mar. 27. 1804

p. 275-276 Nov. 20, 1801 James Young (Spartanburgh) to Gabriel Benson (same); for $100 sold 300 ac on branches of S Pacolate R; border: road from McWilliams Bridge to Spartanburgh Court House, John Young White, Walls Woody, and McDowell; grant to James Dillingham. Witness Eaton Walker and Wm Foster. Signed James Young. Wit. oath Mar. 27, 1804 Eaton Walker to James Jordan. Rec. Mar. 27, 1804

p. 276-278 Oct. 20, 1803 William Dalton (Spartanburgh) to John Ridings (same); for $329.25 and 7p SC money sold 77½ ac; border: Milse and Kelso; part of grant to Alexander Killpatrick. Witness Robert Davis, Wm Kelso, and Jesse Dalton. Signed Wm Dalton. Wit. oath Robert Davis (signed by Wm Davis, sic) to James L Burd. Rec. Mar. 27, 1804

p. 278-279 Nov. 9, 1802 Thomas Brooks (Spartanburgh) to Michael Miller (same); for $200 sold 180 ac on branches of N Tygar R; border: near Brooks Br, Brooks, and Morgan; part of grant Nov. 21, 1785 to William Ford. Witness Gabriel Benson and Moses Brooks. Signed Thomas Brooks' mark. Wit. oath Mar. 26, 1804 Gabriel Benson to John Collins. Rec. Mar. 27, 1804

p. 279-281 Apr. 2, 1803 Mathias Rush (Spartanburgh) to Michael Miller (same); for $125 sold 241 ac on branches of Middle and N Tygar R; border: Miller, Neisbett, and Thompson; part of 500 ac grant to Richd Robert Smith. Witness Gabriel Benson, Joseph Collins, and Wm R Smith. Signed Mathias Rush. Wit. oath Mar. 26, 1804 Gabriel Benson to John Collins. Rec. Mar. 27, 1804

p. 281-283 Feb. 4, 1804 William Fields (Oglethorpe Co, Ga) to Jesse Reams (Spartanburgh); for $50 sold 260 ac on N fork of N fork Tygar R; border: Thomas Brooks, Nevel Wayland, Thomas Davis, and vacant; grant in 1792 Gov. Charles Pinckney to William Fields. Witness Ellis Johnson, Moses Brooks, and Mary Brooks. Signed William Fields' mark. Wit. oath Mar. 27, 1804 Moses Brooks to Ism Foster. Rec. Mar. 27, 1804

p. 283-285 Aug. 2, 1794 George Bishop (Spartanburgh) to David Hix (same); for 40£ SC money sold 100 ac on N side Lawson's fork; where George Bishop lives; part of grant Nov. 25, 1774 Gov. William Bull to Stephen Miller who sold to George Bishop. Witness Alexander Keenum, John Keenum, and Stephen Miller. Signed Georg Bishop. Wit. oath Aug. 30, 1799 John Keenum to Wm McDowell. Rec. Mar. 28, 1804

p. 285-286 Jul. 10, 1796 William Fields (Spartanburgh) to Jesse Reams (same); for 50£ sold 174 ac on N fork Tygar R; grant Jan. 21, 1785 Gov. Benjamin Guerard to William Fields. Witness Robert Kimble and William Brooks. Signed William Fields' mark. Wit. oath Jul. 18, 1797 Robert Kimble to Isham Foster. Rec. Mar. 28, 1804

p. 286-288 (Edgefield Co, SC) Jan. 20, 1789 John Huse sr to John Casey sr; a bond of 100£ sterling; Condition: bond void if John Huse sr deeds John Casey sr 150 ac on Twome Cr; grant in 1772 to Samuel Oorkings; John Casey to live on land and build house and clear land for tobacco and can't waste land; deed to be made by Dec. 25, 1791. Witness Jacob Smith, Kelley Salle, and Rebecah Hogans. Signed John Huse sr. Wit. oath (Edgefield Co) Feb. 23, 1795 Jacob Smith to Russel Wilson. Rec. Mar. 28, 1804

p. 288-289 Feb. 5, 1804 William Fields (Ogelthorpe Co, Ga) to Edward Ballenger (Spartanburgh); for 25£ sold 50 ac on N fork of Tygar R; border: Jonathan Newman, David Davis, Elijah Thompson, and Tanul (or Sanul) Monroo; part of 266 ac grant Nov. 21, 1785 Gov. Thomas Pinckney to William Ford. Witness Isaac Bishop, James Ballenger, and James Vernon. Signed William Fields' mark. Wit. oath Apr. 2, 1804 James Vernon to James Jordan. Rec. Apr. 2, 1804

p. 289-290 Sept. 24, 1803 John Reese (Spartanburgh) to John Tolleson (same); for $175 sold 100 ac on Big Br of Island Cr; border: Markley's old line, Smith, Murry. Witness David Brook, John Gossett, and Jas Smith. Signed John and Maryann Reese's marks. Wit. oath Sept. 24, 1803 John Gossett to William Simpson. Rec. Apr. 2, 1804

p. 290-292 Dec. 6, 1803 Thomas Wyatt (Spartanburgh) to John Tolleson (same); for $62.50 sold 100 ac on branch of Pacolate R; border: Reuben Warren. Witness Muse Tolleson and Thomas Chapman. Signed Thomas Wyatt. Wit. oath Feb. 11, 1804 Muse Tolleson to John Lipscomb. Rec. Apr. 2, 1804

p. 292-293 Oct. 30, 1803 William Gossett sr (Spartanburgh) to John Tolleson (same); for $300 sold (1) 135 ac on waters of Storey's Mill Cr; border: Widow Lemaster; where William Gossett sr lives; and (2) 8 cattle of different sizes, 16 hogs, a bed and furniture, 2 walnut tables, 6 pewter plates, 2 pewter basons and all William Gossett sr's estate; all sold for 9 months; Condition: sale void if William Gossett pays John Tolleson $300 in 9 months.

Witness Muse Tolleson and John Kirbey jr. Signed William Gossett's mark. Wit. oath Feb. 11, 1804 Muse Tolleson to John Lipscomb. Rec. Apr. 2, 1804

p. 293-295 Aug. 20, 1803 James Harrison (Spartanburgh) to Austin Wright (or Right) (same); for $72 sold 112 ac; border: William Morris; part of 200 ac survey in 1784 for Adam Thomson. Witness James Campbell and Joroyal Barnett. Signed James Harrison. Wit. oath Aug. 20, 1803 Joroyal Barnett to John Lipscomb. Rec. Apr. 2, 1804

p. 295-297 Apr. 21, 1802 James Hooper (Spartanburgh) to Hugh Ewing (same); for $1,000 sold (1) 250 ac on both sides N Pacolate R; border: W-Thomas Jackson; grant Apr. 27, 1767 Gov. William Tryon (NC) to Samuel Young and regranted May 4, 1775 Gov. William Bull to Samuel Young who sold Dec. 9, 1777 to James Hooper; and (2) 104 ac granted Jul. 6, 1801 Gov. John Drayton to James Hooper and William Davis. Witness Isaac Disheroon, William Hooper and Baylis Earle. Signed James Hooper. Wit. oath Feb. 20, 1804 Baylis Earle to John Anderson. Rec. Apr. 2, 1804

p. 297-299 Feb. 16, 1802 Richard James (Spartanburgh) to James Campbell (same); for $300 sold 204 ac on waters of Brown's Br of Lawson's fork of Pacolate R; grant Sept. 7, 1789 to Reuben Matthews. Witness Joroyal Barnett and James Harrison. Signed Richard James. Wit. oath May 5, 1803 Joroyal Barnett to William Lancaster. Rec. Apr. 9, 1804. Dower renounced Elizabeth James to William Lancaster May 5, 1803

p. 299-300 Apr. 5, 1804 Patterson Thomson (Spartanburgh) to James Ballenger (same); for $100 sold 196 ac; border: Sparks, Sheppey, and Evin Davis; part of grant Feb. 2, 1801 Gov. John Drayton to Patterson Thomson. Witness Joseph Camp and William Lipscomb. Signed Patterson Thomson. Wit. oath Apr. 5, 1804 Joseph Camp to John Lipscomb. Rec. Apr. 13, 1804

p. 300-302 (not given), 1804 Mathias Rush (Charleston, SC), taylor, to John Chapman (Spartanburgh); for $56 sold 27 ac on branch of N Tygar R; border: John Chapman, Gray, Wood, and Knox; grant to Robert Goodlett sr. Witness Peter Gray and Hannah Gray. Signed Mathias Rush. Wit. oath Apr. 28, 1804 Peter Gray to Ism Foster. Rec. Apr. 28, 1804

p. 302-303 Apr. 2, 1804 Betsey Brown receives $30 from Joseph Austell in full payment for dower rights to 200 ac on both sides Thickety Cr and below mouth of Blue Br; sold by son George Warronton Brown to William Lipscomb. Witness Philip Colman and William Austell. Signed Betsey Brown. Wit. oath Apr. 7, 1804 Philip Colman and William Austell to John Lipscomb. Rec. May 3, 1804. (not dated) Joseph Austell signs over his right to land to William Lipscomb. Witness John Lipscomb JQ. Signed Joseph Austell. Rec. May 3, 1804

p. 303-304 Dec. 7, 1803 Nathaniel Yoes (or Yews) (Robertson Co, Tenn) to John Connell (Spartanburgh); for $150 sold 200 ac; border: George Connell, Lancaster, and Wild Cat fork Br; part of grant Jan. 6, 1794 to Giles Connell and part "given" to Nathaniel Yoes. Witness William Burton, Richard James, and Giles Connell. Signed Nathan Yoes. Wit. oath Feb. 17, 1804 Giles Connell to William Lancaster. Rec. May 5, 1804

p. 304-306 Jan. 24, 1797 Daniel Hackney (Spartanburgh) to William Turner (same); for 100£ SC money sold 200 ac on both sides Lawson's fork of Pacolate R; grant Sept. 25, 1766 Gov. William Tryon (NC) to Thomas Williamson. Witness William Cockrell, Anderson

Cockrell, and Henry Turner. Signed Daniel Hackney's mark. Wit. oath Dec. 23, 1799 Anderson Cockrell to Ism Foster. Rec. May 5, 1804

p. 306-307 Nov. 24, 1802 Jeremiah Nichols (Rockinham Co, NC) to William Adcock (Spartanburgh); for $42.50 sold 100 ac on branch of Little Buck Cr; border: Leonard Adcock, Abraham Cantrel, Stedman, and a road; part of grant Sept. 3, 1794 States Office to Sampson Bethel. Witness Leonard Adcock and David Adcock. Signed Jeremiah Nichols. Wit. oath Apr. 6, 1804 Leonard Adcock to Geor Lamkins. Rec. May 7, 1804

p. 307-309 Apr. 7, 1804 William Wells, tavern keeper, (Spartanburgh) to James Ward sr (same); for $40 sold 40 ac on branches of Fairforrest Cr about a mile from Spartanburgh Court House; border: Richard Thomson, road to Greenville Court House, James Ward, James Benson, and Hays; part of 457 ac grant in 1799 to William Wells. Witness Jacob Utley and Noah Wells. Signed Wm Wells. Wit. oath Apr. 21, 1804 Noah Wells to Jacob Utley. Rec. May 7, 1804

p. 309-310 Nov. 16, 1803 West Harris (Spartanburgh) to Leonard Adcock (same); for $100 sold 200 ac on middle fork of Little Buck Cr; part of grant Oct. 6, 1788 to West Harris. Witness John Harris and William Adcock. Signed West Harris. Wit. oath Apr. 6, 1804 John Harris to Geor Lamkin. Rec. May 7, 1804

p. 310-312 Dec. 16, 1803 William Murry (Spartanburgh) to John Tolleson sr (same); for $200 sold 190 ac on Big Br of Island Cr of Pacolate R; border: John Tolleson; part of grant to John E Morrow who sold to William Murry; sold for 9 months; Condition: deed void if William pays John $200 in 9 months. Witness Muse Tolleson and Jonathan Low jr. Signed William Murry's mark. Wit. oath May 4, 1804 Muse Tolleson to H Means. Rec. May 7, 1804

p. 312-313 May 3, 1804 James Enoch (Spartanburgh) to John Tolleson sr (same); for $300 sold a roan horse about 13½ halds high, 3 years old, a natural trotter, which James bought from John Tolleson, 2 cows and calves marked with a swallow fork in right ear and hatchet in left ear, 13 hogs marked same, 3 feather beds and furniture, 2 pots, a dutch oven, a weaving loom, 6 puter plates, 3 puter basons, 2 puter dishes, 2 large cotton wheels, 2 small flax wheels, and all household furniture; sold for 2 months; Condition: sale void if James pays John $300 in 2 months. Witness Muse Tolleson and Robert Donaldson. Signed James Enoch's mark. Wit. oath Mar. 4, 1804 Muse Tolleson to H Means. Rec. May 7, 1804

p. 313-314 Aug. 18, 1802 James Smith (Spartanburgh) to Richard Barnett (same); for $400 sold 419 ac on waters of Fairforrest Cr and Kealsy's Cr; called meeting house tract; where Mrs. Lucy (or Lury) Barnett lives; border: James and William Smith, James, and Leagain's path; remainder of 462 ac after 43 ac taken out. Witness Richard Wells and John Barnett. Signed Jas Smith. Wit. oath Oct. 9, 1802 John Barnett to I Harrison. Rec. May 7, 1804

p. 314-316 Jun. 11, 1802 Reuben Lessenbee (Spartanburgh) to William Turner (same); for $200 sold 300 ac on both sides Lawson's fork including mouth of Sholey Cr; grant May 22, 1772 Gov. Josiah Martin (NC) to James Wood. Witness Gabriel Benson and Samuel Turner. Signed Reuben Lessenbee's mark. Wit. oath May 7, 1804 Samuel Turner to Ism Foster. Rec. May 7, 1804

p. 316-317 Feb. 10, 1804 Henry Turner (Spartanburgh) to Samuel Turner; for $45 sold 30 ac on N side of Lawson's fork; border: E-Hugh Means, N-Darby Turner, W-Henry Childs, and S-Lawson's fork; grant Gov. William Moultrie to Henry Turner. Witness William

Turner, John Spears, and James Turner. Signed Henry Turner and Henry Childs' mark (sic). Wit. oath May 7, 1804 William Turner to Ism Foster. Rec. May 7, 1804

p. 317-319 Feb. 17, 1804 William Wells (Spartanburgh) to Alexander McKie (same); for $145 sold 100 ac on branches Chinquepin Cr of Lawson's fork of Pacolate R; border: Alexander McKie, Absalom Lancaster, William Thomson, road from Spartanburgh Court House to Bridges's (or Budgers) ferry on Broad R; part of 350 ac grant Aug. 4, 1794 South Carolina to Diskin Grant who sold 100 ac to William Wells Nov. 15, 1797 who sold Mar. 8, 1798 to George Campbell who sold Mar. 11,1803 to William Wells. Witness Noah Wells and Abner Benson. Signed Wm Wells. Wit. oath Feb. 18, 1804 Noah Wells to Jacob Utley. Rec. May 16, 1804

p. 319-321 Oct. 20, 1796 Thomas McKnight (Pinckney Dist) to John McKnight (same); for 150£ SC money sold 200 ac on N side of N fork of N Pacolate R; part of two grants in 1765 to George Alexander who sold Mar. 11, 1773 to Hugh McKnight who sold Mar. 21, 1778 to Thomas McKnight. Witness Georg Kesee, William McKnight, and Charles McKnight. Signed Thomas McKnight. Wit. oath Mar. 23, 1798 William McKnight to Geor Lamkins. Rec. May 23, 1804

p. 321-323 Apr. 2, 1803 Mathias Rush (Spartanburgh) to Alexander Thompson (same); for $125 sold 241 ac on branches of N and Middle Tygar R; border: Alexander Thompson, Miller, and McElrath; half of 500 ac (sic) grant to Rev. Robert Smith. Witness Wm Smith, John Jones, and Gideon Tilman. Signed Mathias Rush. Wit. oath (not dated) John Jones to John Collins. Rec. May 30, 1804. Dower renounced Ann Rush to Samuel House Mar. 24, 1804

p. 323-324 Oct. 5, 1803 Willis Benson (Greenville Dist) to Robert Sloan (Spartanburgh); for $30 sold 265 ac on Holeson's Cr of S Pacolate R. Witness Gabriel Benson and Eaton Walker. Signed Willis Benson. Wit. oath Jun. 4, 1804 Eaton Walker to Ism Foster. Rec. Jun. 4, 1804

p. 324-325 May 11, 1804 Adam Sloan (Greenville Dist) to Esther Sloan (same or Spartanburgh); for $300 sold a Negro girl Sarah born and raised under his father John Sloan's direction; about 15 years old. Witness Alexr Roddy and Willey S Brown. Signed Adam Sloan. Wit. oath May 12, 1804 Willey S Brown to James Burd. Rec. Jun. 4, 1804

p. 325 Aug. 24, 1803 Robert Legon (Spartanburgh) to William Burton (same); for $112 sold 119 ac; border: Ceader Spring. Witness Elijah Barnett and Walter West. Signed Robert Legon. Wit. oath Oct. 25, 1803 Elijah Barnett to William Lancaster. Rec. Jun. 4, 1804

p. 325-328 Mar. 19, 1803 Robert McDowell (Spartanburgh) to John Sloan jr (same); for $150 sold 276 ac on Burd's Cr of S Pacolate R; border: NE-James Alexander; grant Mar. 3, 1794 to Robert McDowell. Witness William Stevenson and John Sloan sr. Signed Robert McDowell. Wit. oath Jun. 4, 1804 John Sloan to Ism Foster. Rec. Jun. 4, 1804

p. 328-331 Dec. 22, 1803 James Tate and wife Sally and mother Elizabeth (York Dist) to Thomas Dear (Spartanburgh); for $3,000 sold (1) 318 ac where William Tate lived and died on W side of Broad R; at upper end of small part excepted; willed to James Tate and his mother Elizabeth; (2) two tracts (a) 46 ac sold by John Ross desc to James Tate on W side Broad R; part of 200 ac grant Dec. 23, 1768 Gov. William Tryon (NC) to John Tygret and part of grant Apr. 2, 1792 South Carolina governor to John Ross; and (b) 200 ac; border: Tate's Mill tract and John Ross. Witness Peter Quin, John Trimmier,

Abraham Green, and James Wight. Signed James Tate, and Sally and Elizabeth's marks. Wit. oath May 19, 1804 Abraham Green to John Rickman. Rec. Jun. 4, 1804

p. 331-333 Jan. 20, 1804 John McKie (Spartanburgh) to Michael Gaffney (York Dist); for $600 sold (1) 381 ac on Peoples Cr of Broad R; known as little meadows; including fork of Cherokee ford and Tate's ferry road; grant Feb. 4, 1799 Gov. Edward Rutledge to John Sarratt; and (2) 424 ac; border: John Sarrat and Harris; grant Mar. 5, 1798 Gov. Charles Pinckney to Charles Morgan who sold to John Sarrat who sold Feb. 12, 1803 to John McKie. Witness Abraham Green and Abner McAfee. Signed John McKee. Wit. oath May 19, 1804 Abraham Green to John Rickman. Rec. Jun. 4, 1804

p. 333-334 Jan. 14, 1804 Frances Bremar (Charleston, SC) to Thomas McCartan (Thickety); for $200 sold 1,740 ac on Miller's fork of Thickety Cr of Broad R; border: SW-Masass (or Mapp) and Thomson, NW-Turner and Middleton, and E-vacant; survey Dec. 20, 1774 to Vardry McBee and mortgaged by Vardry McBee to Frances Bremar Jan. 23, 1787 and sold by Mrs. Elizabeth Ware to Frances Bremar who bought tract at sheriff William Bratton's sale. Witness Artemas B Darby and James Crawford. Signed F Bremar. Wit. oath Jan. 17, 1804 Artemas B Darby to Daniel Hager. Rec. Jun. 7, 1804

p. 334-336 Jan. 7, 1804 Jesse Hammett (Spartanburgh) to Joroyal Barnett; for $200 sold 100 ac on Lawson's fork of Pacolate R; border: N-Brannon and Bobett, E & S-George Hughey, and W-Edward Bishop. Witness Micajah Barnett and George Hughey. Signed Jesse Hammett. Wit. oath Mar. 27, 1804 Micajah Barnett to William Lancaster. Rec. Jun. 8, 1804. Dower renounced Danna Hammett to William Lancaster Mar. 27, 1804

p. 336-338 Nov. 30, 1803 James Harrison and wife Rhoda (Spartanburgh) Joroyal Barnett (same); for $200 sold 176 ac on "dividing waters" of Fairforrest Cr and Lawson's fork; border: Joroyal Barnett, Richard James, James Campbell, and Locock. Witness Reuben Harrison and Thomas Barnett. Signed James Harrison and Rhoda's mark. Wit. oath Feb. 7, 1804 Thomas Barnett to William Lancaster. Rec. Jun. 8, 1804. Dower renounced Rhoda Harrison to William Lancaster Feb. 7, 1804

p. 338-339 May 10, 1801 George Graham and Jane Graham (Greenville Co) to Alexander Thompson (Spartanburgh); for 400 Spanish milled dollars sold a Negro woman named Cloath about 23 years old. Witness Henry Prince and William Prince. Signed George and Janney Graham. Wit. oath Jun. 9, 1804 Henry Prince to John Collins. Rec. Jun. 13, 1804

p. 339-341 Apr. 28, 1804 Alexander McKie (Spartanburgh) to three daughters Salley, Narcissa, and Nancy McKie; for good-will and affection give a Negro woman Winney, Negro girl Rhody, Negro girl Eady, Negro girl Mary, Negro boy Henry, children of Winney, another small girl Harriot, three feather beds and furniture; property remains undivided until Salley, oldest daughter, is 18 years old or until she marrys; each then gets 1/3; should Salley die, property goes to Narcissa and Nancy, and when Narcissa is 18 or marrys before that she gets 1/3 of original property or ½ of what's left after Salley gets her part; if Narcissa dies, property goes to Salley and Nancy; Nancy gets 1/3 at age 18 or when she marrys. Witness Robert Benson and Richard Thomson. Signed Alexr McKie. Wit. oath Jun. 23, 1804 Robert Benson to Jacob Utley. Rec. Jun. 23, 1804

p. 341-343 Mar. 26, 1804 William Thomson (Spartanburgh) to Abner Benson (same); for $31 sold ½ac on S side Spartanburgh

Court House; border: S-Thomson, W-William Smith, E-Alexander McKie, and N-Publick Street; lot number 13. Witness Richard Thomson, Robert Benson, and William Ross Smith. Signed Wm Thomson. Wit. oath Jun. 23, 1804 William R Smith to Jacob Utley. Rec. Jun. 23, 1804

p. 343-345 (date omitted) William Thomson (Spartanburgh) to Duglass Josephas Puckett (same); for $48.50 sold two lots (number 8 and 9) of ½ ac each in Spartanburgh; border: E-Noah Wells, W-William Thomson, N-William Thomson, and S-Main St; plat attached shows border: lot 10 and 7. Witness W. R. Smith and Robert Benson. Signed Wm Thomson. Wit. oath Jun. 23, 1804 Robert Benson to Jacob Utley. Rec. Jun. 25, 1804

p. 345-346 Dec. 31, 1803 William Thomson (Spartanburgh) to Sally McKie, daughter of Alexander McKie (same); for $100 sold lot 19 that is ½ ac in Spartanburgh including house next to Spartanburgh Court House. Witness Richard Thomson and Alexander McKie. Signed Wm Thomson. Wit. oath Jun. 23, 1804 Alexander McKie to Jacob Utley. Rec. Jun. 26, 1804

p. 346-348 Dec. 31, 1803 William Thomson (Spartanburgh) to Narcissa McKie, daughter of Alexander McKie (same); for $100 sold ½ ac on S side Spartanburgh Court House. Witness Richard Thomson and Alexander McKie. Signed Wm Thomson. Wit. oath Jun. 23, 1804 Alexander McKie to Jacob Utley. Rec. Jun. 26, 1804

p. 348-349 Dec. 31, 1803 William Thomson (Spartanburgh) to Nancy McKie, daughter of Alexander McKie (same); for $90 sold ½ ac on S side Spartanburgh Court House. Witness Richard Thomson and Alexander McKie. Signed Wm Thomson. Wit. oath Jun. 23, 1804 Alexander McKie to Jacob Utley. Rec. Jun. 26, 1804

p. 349-352 Feb. 6, 1804 Isham Harrison, sheriff (Spartanburgh) to Alexander McKie and Abner Benson (same); for $115 sold 100 ac on both sides Thomson's Br of Kelsoe's Cr of Fairforrest Cr of Tygar R; border: N-Stories' old line and Micajah Barnett, S-James Smith, W-Charles James, E-Fleming Smith; William Smith owned the land but due to Spartanburgh Common Pleas Court case William Hammett vs Wm Smith on fourth Monday in Oct. 1803 a writ of $129.19 and 7 mills was entered in sheriff's office Jan. 5, 1804; sale by Dept. William Wells on first Monday Feb. 6, 1804. Witness Obadiah Watson and Richard Thomson. Signed I Harrison SSD. Wit. oath Jun. 23, 1804 Obadiah Watson to Jacob Utley. Rec. Jun. 26, 1804

p. 352-354 Dec. 21, 1803 Robert Boyce (Newberry Dist) to John Crawford (Spartanburgh); for $200 sold 100 ac on Middle Tygar R; border: John Crawford, "Esquire" Collins, Isaac Snoddy; grant in 1772 to Alexander Boyce. Witness John McMorries, Edward Phillips, and William Wilson. Signed Robert Boyce. Wit. oath Feb. 4, 1804 William Wilson to John Collins. Rec. Jul. 2, 1804

p. 354-355 Aug. 10, 1803 Isham Harrison, sheriff (Spartanburgh) to Henry Wells, agent for Thomas McCartan; for $11 sold 400 ac on head branch Thickety Cr and Clark's fork; where James Clark formerly lives; sale due to writ from Spartanburgh Common Pleas Court McCartan and Gafney vs James Clark and John Clark. Witness William Wells and George T Sloan. Signed I Harrison SSD. Wit. oath Jul. 2, 1804 William Wells to Jacob Utley. Rec. Jul. 2, 1804

p. 355-356 Jun. 26, 1798 Jonathan Nesbett (Spartanburgh) and Elizabeth McRarry (same); an agreement: when Jonathan dies, Elizabeth is to have all his property--a Negro wench Tan, Negro boy Jack, and all Jonathan's land and stock; Elizabeth agrees to marry Jonathan. Witness B. D. Shumate JP. Signed Jonathan Nesbett and Elizabeth McRarry. Wit. oath Jul. 9, 1804 John Collins recognizes B. D.

Shumate's signature to Geor Lamkins. Rec. Jul. 9, 1804

p. 356-358 Mar. 24, 1804 John Brown jr (Chester Dist) to Hugh Calwall (Spartanburgh); for $150 sold 350 ac on N side of N fork Tygar R; border: S-N Tygar R, N-Samuel Snody, and others vacant; grant Aug. 19, 1774 Gov. William Bull to John Brown sr and then to heir John Brown jr. Witness Samuel Calwall and Gabriel Bumpass. Signed John Brown. Wit. oath Apr. 20, 1804 Samuel Calwall to John Collins. Rec. Jul. 16, 1804

p. 358-360 Jul. 4, 1804 Joseph Collins (Spartanburgh) to James Vernon (same); for $237 sold 130 ac on branches of N Tygar R; part of grant to Alexander Collins. Witness Ism Foster and John Jordan. Signed Joseph Collins. Wit. oath Jul. 4, 1804 Joseph Collins to Ism Foster. Rec. Jul. 18, 1804. Dower renounced Jul. 4, 1804 Elizabeth B Collins to Ism Foster

p. 360-361 Feb. 10, 1804 John Anderson (Spartanburgh) to William Dalton (same); for $400 sold (ac not given) on waters of Obed's Cr of Pacolate R. Witness Peter Fry, John Dalton, and Drury Bowman. Signed John Anderson. Wit. oath Mar. 3, 1804 Peter Fry to James R Burd. Rec. Jul. 20, 1804

p. 361-364 Jun. 9, 1792 William McMillin and wife Elizabeth (Spartanburgh) to George Keese (same); for 150£ sterling sold 300 ac on both sides N fork Pacolate R including mouth of Mill Cr; grant Sept. 25, 1766 to George Alexander who sold Aug. 28, 1785 to William McMillin. Witness Thomas McKnight, Charles Smith, and Levice Smith. Signed William and Elizabeth McMillin's marks. Wit. oath Sept. 15, 1798 Thomas McKnight to William McDowell. Rec. Jul. 21, 1804

p. 364-367 Aug. 31, 1799 George Keesee and wife Agnes (Spartanburgh) to Thomas Keesee (same); for $700 sold 390 ac (sic) on both sides N fork of Pacolate R including mouth of Mill Cr; grant Setp. 25, 1766 to George Alexander who sold Aug. 28, 1785 to William McMillin who sold Jun. 9, 1792 to George Keesee. Witness Thomas McKnight and James Smith. Signed George Keesee and Agnes' mark. Wit. oath Aug. 2, 1803 Thomas McKnight to Wm McDowell. Rec. Jul. 21, 1804

p. 367-369 Sept. 5, 1803 Thomas Keesee and wife Mary (Spartanburgh) to James Camp (Rutherford Co, NC); for $580 sold 298 ac (by "late" survey) on S side of N Pacolate R; border: Thomas McKnight, Wm McKnight, and McWilliams; sold Aug. 20, 1785 George Alexander to William McMillin who sold Jun. 9, 1792 to George Keesee who sold Aug. 31, 1799 to Thomas Keesee. Witness George McWilliams and Margret McWillians. Signed Thomas and Mary Keesee. Wit. oath Jul. 18, 1804 George McWilliams to Wm Kelso. Rec. Jul. 21, 1804

p. 369-370 Apr. 4, 1803 John McKinney and Daniel Madden (Rutherford Co, NC) to James Camp (same); for $400 sold 400 ac in Rutherford Co, NC on both sides Buck Cr of Pacolate R; joining "south state line"; survey Sept. 27, 1774 by John Kerconell and granted Mar. 2, 1775 to John McKinney. Witness John Hopson and Christy Money (or Christopher Mooney). Signed John McKinney and Daniel Madden. Wit. oath (Rutherford Co, NC) Apr. 1803 Christy Money in open court. Rec. Jul. 21, 1804

p. 370-372 Apr. 15, 1803 Richard Bearden (Spartanburgh) to John Blasingame (Union Dist); for $150 sold 142 ac on branches of Dutchman's Cr and Tygar R; border: Grant's Rd, Moses Prewitt, Cron, Mollow's Br. Witness Philip Blasingame and Benjamin Woten. Signed Richard Bearden. Wit. oath (Union Dist) Nov. 17, 1803 Philip Blasingame to Thos B Hunt. Rec. Jul. 27, 1804

p. 372-374 Nov. 9, 1801 Edward Smith (Spartanburgh) to Richard Beardan (same); for $200 sold 142 ac on branches of Dutchman's Cr and Tygar R; border: Grant's Rd, Moses Prewitt, Caron, and Mollow's Br. Witness Willis Williford and John Hewett. Signed Edward Smith. Wit. oath Nov. 10, 1801 John Hewett to Wm Smith. Rec. Jul. 27, 1804. Dower renounced Mary Smith to Wm Smith Nov. 9, 1801

p. 374-375 Jul. 25, 1804 Gallent Easters (Spartanburgh) to William Nelson (same); for $112 sold a bay horse, one year old colt, 3 cows and calves, 2 yearlings, 2 beds and furniture, a pot, and an oven. Witness John Brown and John Collins. Signed Gallent Easters' mark. Wit. oath Jul. 25, 1804 John Brown to John Collins. Rec. Jul. 27, 1804

p. 375-376 Jan. 13, 1802 Thomas Foster (Spartanburgh) to William Foster (same); for $300 sold 100 ac on Ford's Cr of Fairforrest Cr. Witness I Harrison JQ. Signed Thomas Foster's mark. Wit. oath Aug. 6, 1804 I Harrison to Georg Lamkin. Rec. Aug. 6, 1804

p. 376-377 Feb. 6, 1790 Henry Moffett to Alexander Roddy; for 100£ sterling sold 320 ac on both sides Moffett's Br of Tyger R; grant Jul. 13, 1784 Gov. William Moultrie to Henry Moffett. Witness Henry Wells and Martin Armstrong. Signed Henry Moffett. Wit. oath Feb. 6, 1790 Martin Armstrong to James Jordan. Rec. Aug. 6, 1804

p. 377-379 Aug. 27, 1803 West Harris (Spartanburgh) to Daniel Harris (same); for $225 sold 295 ac on Buck Cr of Pacolate R; part of grant States Office to Richard Sanders who sold to Thomas Gore who sold to West Harris; border: Thomas Gore and John Nelson. Witness William Bridges and John Harris. Signed West Harris. Wit. oath Dec. 7, 1803 William Bridges to William McDowell. Rec. Aug. 6, 1804

p. 379-380 Jul. 31, 1804 Henry Hutcheson (Spartanburgh) to Turner Hutcheson (same); for $60 sold "household furniture": a woman's saddle, a man's saddle, 2 pots, an oven, a skillet, a tea kettle, 6 pewter plates, 2 basons, a dish, 2 bed steds, 5 counter pins, 5 bed covers, a chest, 2 sets of cups and saucers, 11 earthen plates, a sugar canister, a coffee pot, a tea pot, 6 chairs, a cotton wheel, a stear, 6 hogs, and 3 earthen bowls. Witness William Foster sr and William Bennett jr. Signed Henry Hutcheson. Wit. oath Aug. 6, 1804 William Bennett jr to Ism Foster. Rec. Aug. 6, 1804

p. 380-381 Apr. 20, 1804 John Calwell and wife Mary (Spartanburgh) to William Calwell; for 10£ sold 98 ac on S side Middle Tygar R; grant to John Calwell (see grant Book 4-O p. 415). Witness Samuel Calwell, Hugh Calwell, and John Collins JP. Signed John Calwall and Mary's mark. Wit. oath Apr. 20, 1804 Samuel Calwell to John Collins. Rec. Aug. 6, 1804

p. 381-383 Jul. 2, 1804 Ezekiel Sulivan (Spartanburgh) to John Tolleson (same); for $80 sold 71 ac on waters of Bullock's fork of Thickety Cr; where Ezekiel Sulivan lives; sold for 3 months; Condition: sale void if Ezekiel pays John $80 in 3 months. Witness Muse Tolleson and Abraham Brus. Signed Ezekiel Sulivan. Wit. oath Jul. 3, 1804 Muse Tolleson to John Lipscomb. Rec. Aug. 6, 1804

p. 383-384 Jul. 2, 1804 Ruben Mathis (Spartanburgh) to John Tolleson (same); for $250 sold a sorrel horse about 12 or 13 years old and saddle, a cow and 3 yearlings marked with cross and slit in each ear, a red cow with a large bell marks unknown, 2 sows with cross and slit in each ear, a sow marks unknown with a black lest(?)

around her, 7 small hogs marked with two smooth crosses in each ear, 3 small hogs marks unknown, 2 beds and furniture, a weaving loom, 2 pots, a dutch oven, a large spinning wheel, a small lening wheel, and all household furniture, all his crop of wheat, rye, oats, and corn; sold for 2 months; Condition: sale void if Ruben pays John $250 in 2 months; (within goods delivered to Muse Tolleson for John Tolleson Jul. 14, 1804; witness Jesse Rakestraw). Witness Muse Tolleson and Beverly Bagwell. Signed Ruben Mathias' mark. Wit. oath Jul. 3, 1804 Muse Tolleson to John Lipscomb. Rec. Aug. 6, 1804

p. 384-386 Mar. 26, 1804 Henry ONeill (Spartanburgh) to Solomon Hill (same); for $125 sold 146 ac on waters of Tygar R and E of ancient boundary; grant Apr. 3, 1786 to William Garrett and sold to John Sloan. Witness D. J. Puckett and John ONeile. Signed Henry O'Neill. Wit. oath Aug. 6, 1804 D. J. Puckett to Ism Foster. Rec. Aug. 6, 1804

p. 386-387 Mar. 20, 1804 Edward Penman and Alexander McDowell (Charleston, SC) to Thomas Payden (Spartanburgh); for 100£ sold 100 ac on branch Forgason's Cr of Tygar R; border: E-James Payden and S-Thomas Payden. Witness John Dunlap and Wm Dunlap. Signed Edward Penman and Alexr McDowell by their attorney J McCrackan. Wit. oath Mar. 20, 1804 (Laurens Dist) Wm Dunlap to W Burnside. Rec. Aug. 6, 1804

p. 387-389 Aug. 5, 1803 Henry Cannon (Spartanburgh) to Richard Barry (same); for $101 sold 101 ac on Forks of Tygar R; border N & E-grant to Charles Moore and W-James Miller; part of grant Jun. 2, 1794 to John Ford. Witness Theopheles Cannon and Thos Moore. Signed Henry Cannon. Wit. oath Jul. 2, 1804 Thos Moore to Drury McDaniel. Rec. Aug. 10, 1804

p. 389-391 Apr. 26, 1804 William Williamson,preacher (Spartanburgh, but residing in Union Dist) to Abner Benson (Spartanburgh); for $62.50 sold 62½ ac on waters of N side Forrest Cr of Tygar R; near Spartanburgh Court House; survey by Richard Harrison, Dept. Surv. for William Williamson Oct. 27, 1785 and granted Mar. 6, 1786 Gov. William Moultrie to William Williamson then bordering vacant land. Witness Thos Moore and Thomas Williamson. Signed Wm Williamson. Wit. oath Aug. 6, 1804 Thos Moore to John Collins. Rec. Aug. 14, 1804

p. 391-393 Aug. 18, 1804 John Sloan sr and wife Mary (Spartanburgh) to Willey S Brown (Greenville Dist); for $1,000 sold 300 ac on both sides N fork of N fork Tygar R; above Joseph Jones' survey; grant Sept. 6, 1766 Gov. William Tryon (NC) to Jonathan Newman who sold to John Clark, son of Benjamin Clark, Nov. 2, 1779 and sold by Benjamin Clark to Mary Sloan Jan. 9, 1801; including land rented to "Melson" where he lives. Witness John Sloan jr (or Slone) and James L Burd. Signed John and Mary Slone. Wit. oath Aug. 18, 1804 John Sloan jr to James L Burd. Rec. Aug. 21, 1804

p. 393-402 Jul. 7, 1803 William Miller (Columbia, SC) to Lewis Ogrier (Foster?) (Charleston, SC); for $1,750 sold (1) 1,000 ac Reedy fork of William's Cr in Craven Co; border: SW, S & SE-unknown and N-Joshua Edwards and Jordan Esq.; and (2) 400 ac between S and Middle fork Tygar R; border: NE-McBright, SW-Saml and Jonathan Nesbett, and N-Michael and John McElrath. Witness Thos Broughton and William Wilson. Signed William Miller. Wit. oath (Charleston Dist) Jul. 9, 1803 Thos Broughton to Chars Glover. Rec. Aug. 25, 1804 Release: Jul. 7, 1803 William Miller to Lewis Ogier Foster; William is bound to Lewis for $2,400; Condition: William must pay $1,750; to secure debt and for 5s sells 1,400 ac above; two plats attached: (1) 1,000 ac granted Apr. 2, 1773 to Daniel Haywood and resurveyed Apr. 9, 1802 for Lewis Saxon, attorney for Capt. Lewis Ogier; and

(2) 400 ac survey Mar. 15, 1773 for James Mayson and resurvey Apr. 10, 1802 for Lewis Saxon, attorney for Capt. Lewis Ogier.

p. 402-403 Oct. 13, 1798 Henry McGowen (Columbia, SC) to William Wells esq (Spartanburgh); for 20s sold 300 ac on branch of Pacolate R; border: SE, NE & SW-William Wofford and Lheere and NW-vacant; survey Mar. 12, 1796 for George Lamkins and granted Jan. 19, 1798 Gov. Charles Pinckney to Henry McGowen. Witness Robert Weston and Andrew Heatly. Signed H McGowen. Wit. oath (Richland Co) Nov. 30, 1798 Robt Weston to J Hoodwyl(?). Rec. Aug. 27, 1804

p. 403-405 Feb. 10, 1804 William Wells (Spartanburgh) to George Lamkin (same); for $100 sold (ac not given) on branch of Pacolate R; border: Wofford and Lheree. Witness Isham Harrison and T(?) W. Winne (?). Signed Wm Wells. Wit. oath Aug. 6, 1804 I Harrison to John Utley. Rec. Aug. 27, 1804

p. 405-406 Sept. 2, 1801 Ann McElhaney, administor for John McElhaney (Spartanburgh) to John Leech (York Co); power of attorney to recover from Samuel Farrow, esq, attorney (Spartan Dist) 42£ 13s 11p sterling which is due John McElhaney from administration of Joseph Jones (see Spartanburgh Court) and Samuel Farrow collected the money from William Ford (Spartanburgh). Witness John Armstrong. Signed Ann McElhaney administor for John McElhaney. Wit. oath (Hancock Co, Ga) Sept. 2, 1801 John Armstrong to Zephaniah Harvey. Rec. Sept. 13, 1804

p. 406-408 Feb. 21, 1804 Peter Smith (Spartanburgh) to James Harrison (same); for $290 sold 130 ac on Fairforrest and Kelsey's Creeks; border: Capt. James Smith, Hancock Smith, Bels or Belos, and Shands Golightly; part of 270 ac grant Oct. 15, 1784 Gov. Benjamin Guerard to Peter Smith. Witness James Smith and Elijah Barnett. Signed Peter Smith. Wit. oath Mar. 27, 1804 Elijah Barnett to John Lipscomb. Rec. Sept. 14, 1804. Dower renounced Agatha Smith to William Lancaster Mar. 15, 1804

p. 408-409 Dec. 9, 1803 James Sanders Guignard (Columbia, SC) to Gabriel Benson (Spartanburgh); for $5 sold (1) 1,000 ac on Peters Cr of Pacolate R; survey Apr. 28, 1801 for James S Guignard; border: E-Simms, W-Scott, and others unknown; grant Sept. 7, 1801 Gov. John Drayton to James S Guignard; and (2) 313 ac on Clear Cr; border: N-Wm Gilbert, E-Henry Morgan, SE-Hugh Stephenson, S-Dickson, and W-Henry Young; resurvey Sept. 1, 1801 for Abner Benson and granted Jan. 3, 1803 James S Guignard to Gabriel Benson (sic). Witness William Taylor jr and William Lancaster. Signed James S Guignard. Wit. oath Sept. 15, 1804 William Lancaster to Jacob Utley. Rec. Sept. 17 or 14, 1804

p. 409-411 (not given), 1804 Andrew McMullen (Abington Dist (sic), Va) and Hugh McMullen (Spartanburgh) to Alexander Cunningham (Spartanburgh); for $100 sold 69 ac; border: William Renfrow and Coningham. Witness Wm McDowell and Mary McDowell. Signed Andrew and Hugh McMullen. Certified Jan. 9, 1804 by Wm McDowell. Rec. Sept. 15, 1804

p. 411-412 (omitted), 1801 David Leech for self and John Leech, William Leech, and James Leech, by power, Joseph Leech, John Vaughn, Samuel Underwood, and Lemeul Loftis (all Spartanburgh except John, William and James Leech) to Alexander Cunningham (same); for $400 sold 340 ac on both sides Obed's Cr; grant to John Leech; border: W-W McMillin, SE-John Young, NE-John Daniels. Witness Wm Anderson and Isereat (or Isairail) Easterwood. Signed David Leech, power for John, William and James Leech, Joseph Leech, John Vaughn, Saml Underwood, Lamuel Loftis, and Sarah Leech's mark. Wit. oath Jul. 23, 1803 Wm Anderson to Wm McDowell. Rec. Sept. 15, 1803

p. 412-414 Jan. 24, 1804 Burrel Pace (Spartanburgh) to John Shands (same); for $150 sold 100 ac; border: W & S-old survey, E-vacant, and N-Burrel Pace; part of grant Jan. 1, 1787 Gov. William Moultrie to Burrel Pace. Witness William Lindsey Allen and Thomas Woodruff III. Signed Burrel Pace. Wit. oath Aug. 13, 1804 William L Allen to W Lancaster. Rec. Sept. 15, 1804

p. 414-417 Mar. 21, 1778 Hugh McKnight and wife Margret (Rowan Co, NC) to Thomas McKnight (Rowan Co, NC); for 291£ "America" money sold 312 ac in Berkley Co on both sides N Pacolate R; grant Oct. 13, 1765 to George Alexander who sold Mar. 11, 1773 to Hugh McKnight. Witness James Aston and Stephen Cowen. Signed Hugh and Margret McKnight. Wit. oath Mar. 17, 1780 James Aston to James Wood. Rec. Sept. 15, 1804

p. 417-419 Sept. 20, 1804 John Wood (Spartanburgh) to Gabriel Benson (same); for $50 sold (1) 80 ac on branch of N Tygar R; and (2) 10½ ac; both granted to John Prince; (2) border: near Wilson's Mill Cr, Peter Gray, and Gabriel Benson. Witness John Wood jr and John Bankston. Signed John Wood's mark. Wit. oath Sept. 20, 1804 John Wood to Wm McDowell. Rec. Sept. 21, 1804

p. 419-420 Sept. 20, 1804 Gabriel Benson (Spartanburgh) to John Wood, carpenter (same); for $50 sold 29 ac on branch of N Tygar R; border: road to Prince's old road; part of grant to Gabriel Benson. Witness John Wood sr and John Bankston. Signed Gab Benson. Wit. oath Sept. 20, 1804 John Wood to Wm McDowell. Rec. Sept. 21, 1804

p. 420-422 Jul. 18, 1804 Absolem Hestey and John Hestey to Hugh McMillen and Alexander Cunningham; for $36.25 sold a "serten lies" of land with crop as it stands for 4 years; land was leased from Alexander Cuningham; and sold all household and "perashable" property from Dec. 25, 1804; Condition: sale void if Absolem and John Hestey pay $32.25 before Dec. 25, 1804. Witness David Logan Cunningham and Jean (or Jane) Cunningham. Signed Absolem and John Hestey's marks. Wit. oath Sept. (omitted), 1804 David L. Cunningham to Wm McDowell. Rec. Sept. 21, 1804

p. 422-423 Aug. 9, 1804 Daniel McClaren (Spartanburgh) to Benjamin Bonner (same); for $400 sold 150 ac on waters of Sarratt's Cr of Broad R; border: Turner and Long Br. Witness Wm Walker and John McClaren. Signed Daniel McClaren. Wit. oath Aug. 10, 1804 John McClaren to John Rickman. Rec. Oct. 8, 1804

p. 423-424 May 29, 1804 James Phillips (Rutherford Co, NC) to Reuben Phillips (Spartanburgh); for $50 sold 170 ac on both sides Ashworth Cr; border: N-North Carolina line, S-Camp; on lower end of 300 ac grant to Thomas Thomson; survey Sept. 23, 1794 for Thomas Thomson. Witness Jacob Phillips and Nathan Byars. Signed James Phillips' mark. Wit. oath Jul. 21, 1804 Jacob Phillips to Jno Rickman. Rec. Oct. 8, 1804

p. 424-426 May 26, 1804 Hugh Calwall to Samuel Snoddy; for $45 sold 51 ac on N side of N fork Tygar R; part of grant to John Brown who sold to Hugh Calwall. Witness Gabriel Bumpass and Nancy Buchanan. Signed Hugh Calwall. Wit. oath Aug. 18, 1804 Gabriel Bumpass to John Collins. Rec. Oct. 8, 1804

p. 426-427 Mar. 20, 1804 William Rook (Spartanburgh) to Thomas Sterling (same); for 50£ sold 98 ac on waters of Thickety Cr; grant in 1784 Gov. William Moultrie to (not given). Witness John Low and Rolly Horton. Signed William Rook's mark. Wit. oath Oct. 8, 1804 Rolly Horton to John Lipscomb. Rec. Oct. 8, 1804

p. 427-429 Aug. 9, 1804 Daniel McClaren (Spartanburgh) to Bryant

Bonner (same); for $100 sold 50 ac on waters of Sarratt's Cr of Broad R; border: Benjamin Bonner. Witness William Walker and John McClaren. Signed Daniel McCaren. Wit. oath Aug. 10, 1804 John McClaren to John Rickman. Rec. Oct. 8, 1804

p. 429-431 Sept. 27, 1804 Henry Smith (Spartanburgh) to Henry Brown (same); for $125 sold 50 ac on waters Fairforrest Cr and Kelsoe's Cr; part of grant Oct. 15, 1785 "state" to Peter Smith. Witness John Smith and Thomas Smith. Signed Henry Smith. Wit. oath Oct. 5, 1804 John Smith to W Lancaster. Rec. Oct. 8, 1804. Dower renounced Lydia Smith to William Lancaster Oct. 5, 1804

p. 431-433 Aug. 3, 1804 Robert Sterling (Spartanburgh) to James Bennet (same); for $200 sold 200 ac on both sides Dutchman's Cr; part of 440 ac grant to Sarah Elder now Robert Sterling's wife. Witness Clary Lancaster and William Lancaster. Signed Robert Sterling. Wit. oath Oct. 8, 1804 William Lancaster to John Collins. Rec. Oct. 8, 1804. Dower renounced Sarah Sterling to William Lancaster Sept. 17, 1804

p. 433-434 Sept. 8, 1804 John Smith (Spartanburgh) to Thomas Smith (same); for $60 sold 60 ac on waters of Fairforrest Cr; border: Henry Smith; part of grant in Jan. 1785 "state" to John Smith. Witness John Connell, William Rakestraw, and Henry Smith. Signed John Smith. Wit. oath Oct. 5, 1804 Henry Smith to W Lancaster. Rec. Oct. 8, 1804

p. 434-435 Mar. 8, 1804 Samuel Sarratt (Spartanburgh) to Readick Arendell (same); for $200 sold 83½ ac; border: William Sarratt. Witness Joseph Camp and John Saratt. Signed Saml Surratt and Elizabeth's mark. Wit. oath May 19, 1804 Joseph Camp to John Rickman. Rec. Oct. 8, 1804

p. 435-436 Jan. 10, 1804 Fleming Smith receives payment of $160 Oct. 12, 1801 from Henry Brown; Fleming is one of parties to "annexed" deed as grantee (deed not annexed). Witness Richard Brown and Anthony Foster. Signed Fleming Smith. Wit. oath Oct. 8, 1804 Richard Brown to William Lancaster. Rec. Oct. 8, 1804

p. 436-437 Apr. 15, 1804 Hightower Dotson (Spartanburgh) to friend Samuel Collet; for love and affection and other good causes give a mare called Cate, a bed, a cow, and calf. Witness Daniel Bragg and William Otts. Signed Hightower Dotson. Wit. oath Oct. 9, 1804 Daniel Bragg to A Casey. Rec. Oct. 9, 1804

p. 437-438 Sept. 8, 1804 James Rnox (Wilks Co, Ga) to John Chapman (Spartanburgh); for $400 sold 300 ac on waters of N fork Tygar R; border: David Rnox, John Brown, and John McThennes (or Hennes); grant Apr. 28, 1768 Gov. William Tryon (NC) to James Rnox in Mecklinburgh Co, NC. Witness Isham Foster, William Traylor, and Robert Foster. Signed James Rnox. Certified (not dated) by Ism Foster. Rec. Oct. 9, 1804

p. 438-439 Sept. 11, 1804 George Story (Spartanburgh) to son James Story and daughter Hannah Story; for love and affection give to Hannah a Negro girl Bett which George delivered to her. Witness Samuel Archibald, Samuel Kelso, and William Cunningham. Signed George Story's mark. Wit. oath Sept. 11, 1804 William Cunningham to William Simpson. Rec. Oct. 9, 1804

p. 439-441 Jun. 2, 1804 Edward Smith (Spartanburgh) to William Smith (same); for $80 sold 84½ ac; part of 400 ac grant on both sides Thickety Cr to John Headon. Witness Sally Lipscomb and Holmon Smith. Signed Edward Smith. Wit. oath Jun. 2, 1804 Holmon Smith to John Lipscomb. Rec. Oct. 9, 1804

p. 441-442 Oct. 4, 1799 Jason Moore (Spartanburgh) to William Moore (same); for $110 SC money sold 90 ac on W side Ward's Cr; border: William Ford; includes 1 ac on E side of creek joining the shoal; part of 163 ac grant Dec. 3, 1787 to Jason Moore. Witness William Otts and Thomas Cook. Signed Jason Moore. Wit. oath Oct. 9, 1804 Thomas Cook to W Lancaster. Rec. Oct. 9, 1804

p. 442-444 Nov. 25, 1794 James Amos (Spartanburgh) to Patrick Hogan (same); for 100£ sterling sold 383 ac in two tracts on each side of N fork Tygar R: (1) 150 ac where James Amos lives; grant Apr. 9, 1768 Gov. William Tryon (NC) to Alexander McCarter and sold by John McCarter to James Amos; and (2) 233 ac; part of 400 ac grant Dec. 1, 1791 Gov. Charles Pinckney to James Amos; excludes 167 ac "grant" by James Amos to John Brooks: border: Young Griffeth, Ams Br, Broadtree Br, Meeting house path. Witness Nevil Wayland, Benjamin Shumate, and Jonathan Nesbett. Signed James Amos. Wit. oath Oct. 9, 1804 Jonathan Nesbett to W Lancaster. Rec. Oct. 9, 1804

p. 444-446 Jan. 6, 1804 Mathew Waldrop (Spartanburgh) to John Owens (same); for $150 sold 100 ac on branch of Buffelow Cr and branch of Two Mile Cr of Enoree R; border: Whittaker, James Landford, and Thomas Clerk. Witness Thomas Farrow, Jordan Massay, and Rebekah Farrow. Signed Mathew Waldrop's mark. Wit. oath Aug. 23, 1804 Thomas Farrow to John Dean. Rec. Oct. 9, 1804. Dower renounced Elizabeth Waldrop to Daniel Wright Sept. 15, 1804

p. 446-449 Mar. 30, 1804 James Askew (Spartanburgh) to John Thomas (same); for 60 Spanish milled dollars sold 35 ac between N and S fork Tygar R; border: Andrew Thomson and Andrew Broughtor; part of 100 ac grant "state" to Abuatus Bright who sold to Samuel Gentry. Witness Thomas Wright, Lawson Thomson, and Andrew Thomson. Signed James Askew. Wit. oath Sept. 28, 1804 Thomas Wright to Drury McDaniel. Rec. Oct. 9, 1804. Dower renounced Mary Askew to William Lancaster Apr. 13, 1804

p. 449-450 Aug. 25, 1799 Peter Gray (Spartan Co) to John Chapman (same); for 8¼ guineas sold 8¼ ac; border: Prince's old line. Witness Henry Gray and Mathias Rush. Signed Peter Gray. Wit. oath Oct. 9, 1804 Mathias Rush to William Lancaster. Rec. Oct. 9, 1804

p. 450-452 May 8, 1804 Thomas Gore (Spartanburgh) to Thomas Pope (same); for $277.25 sold 371 ac on both sides Buck Cr of Pacolate R; border: Henderson, Arrow Wood, and a waggon road; part of 692 ac grant to "said Gore McWilliams". Witness Charles Crocker and John Henderson. Signed Thos Gore. Wit. oath May 24, 1804 Charles Crocker to Wm McDowell. Rec. Oct. 9, 1804

p. 452-454 Sept. 24, 1804 John Legon (Spartanburgh) to Thomas Cook (same); for $570 sold 100 ac on N Tygar R; border: W-Joseph Hatchet and S, E & N-Robert Legon jr; part of tract sold by William Ford to Robert Legon sr who sold to John Legon. Witness Samuel Moore, Jason Moore jr, and Phillips Otts. Signed John W Legon. Wit. oath Oct. 9, 1804 Jason Moore jr to William Lancaster. Rec. Oct. 9, 1804. Dower renounced Mary Legon to William Lancaster Oct. 9, 1804

p. 454-456 Sept. 2, 1801 Thomas Wilson (Rutherford Co, NC) to John Murrell (Union Dist); for $100 sold 30 ac on Cain Cr of Tygar R; border: Belwo's Br and James Hembree; part of grant to James Hembree; Elizabeth Grist has 1/3 of land until her death. Witness Charles Wilkins JP and John Grist. Signed Thomas Wilson's mark. Wit. oath (Union Dist) Sept. 24, 1803 John Grist to Thos B Hunt. Rec. Oct. 10, 1804. Dower renounced (Rutherford Co, NC) Jemime Wilson to Charles Wilkins JP Sept. 2, 1801

p. 456-458 Jul. 20, 1802 Thomas Gore (SC) to William Crocker (Spartanburgh); for 200 ($?) sold 100 ac on both sides of two small branches of Buck Cr of Pacolate R and Buck Cr; border: all vacant land; grant Oct. 7, 1793 to Thomas Gore. Witness John Gore, John Gore (sic), and Motley Gore. Signed Thomas Gore. "Acknowledged" Feb. 12, 1803 by Thomas Gore to Wm McDowell. Rec. Oct. 20, 1804

p. 458-459 May 4, 1803 Charles Moore (Spartanburgh) to grandson Charles Hamilton Moore (same); for love and affection and "good causes" gave a Negro boy Prince about 5 years old, son of Phillip. Witness Andrew B Moore and Charles Moore jr. Signed Charles Moore. Wit. oath Mar. 20, 1803 Andrew B Moore to Drury McDaniel. Rec. Oct. 22, 1804

p. 459-second p. 458 May 14, 1803 John Parris (Spartanburgh) to Richard Scruggs (same); for $80 sold 100 ac on both sides Long Br of Island Cr. Witness Mathew Abbett and William Dobbins. Signed John Parris. Wit. oath Aug. 6, 1803 Mathew Abbett to Geor Lamkin. Rec. Oct. 22, 1804

second p. 458-p. 460 Aug. 6, 1803 William Dobbins (Spartanburgh) to Richard Scruggs (same); for $80 sold 127 ac; border: Richard Scruggs; part of land where William Dobbins lives. Witness Mathias Abbett and Susanna Lamkin. Signed William Dobbins. Wit. oath Aug. 6, 1803 Mathias Abbet to Geor Lamkin. Rec. Oct. 22, 1804

p. 460-461 Apr. 12, 1801 Thomas Moore (Spartanburgh) to Carie Traylor (man) (same); for $176 sold 176 ac on branches of Provey's Cr of Tygar R; border: SW & SE-James Jordan, NW-an old line, NE & NW-Aaron Moore, and E-vacant; grant Mar. 6, 1797 Gov. Charles Pinckney to Carie Traylor (sic) who sold to Thomas Moore. Witness Berryman D Shumate and James Acre. Signed Thos Moore. Wit. oath Apr. 12, 1801 Berryman D. Shumate to Drury McDaniel. Rec. Oct. 22, 1804

p. 461-463 Oct. 13, 1804 Thomas Compton (Spartanburgh) to James Moore (same); for $225 sold 100 ac on waters of Dutchman's Cr; part of grant Aug. 11, 1774 to Jeremiah Fowler. Witness John Bearden and Aaron Moore. Signed Thomas Compton. Wit. oath Oct. 13, 1804 John Bearden to Wm Smith. Rec. Oct. 22, 1804. Dower renounced Rachel Compton to Wm Smith Oct. 20, 1804

p. 463-465 Feb. 13, 1804 John Low to Henry Adcock sr; for $50 sold 50 ac on N side Pacolate R; border: Henry Adcock; part of grant in 1803 States office to John Low. Witness John Dunlap, Tohos Wyatt and John Low jr. Signed John Low. Wit. oath Mar. 20, 1804 John Dunlap to Geor Lamkin. Rec. Oct. 22, 1804

p. 465-466 Jan. 9, 1804 John Wells (Spartanburgh) to Richard Shackelford (same); for $350 sold 100 ac on N side Enoree R and at mouth of Wells' Spring Br; part of grant to William Hamby. Witness Thomas Woodruff III to Caleb Woodruff. Signed Jno Wells. Wit. oath Jan. 9, 1804 Thomas Woodruff III to Dan Wright. Rec. Oct. 22, 1804. Dower renounced Sarah Wells to Daniel Wright Jan. 9, 1804

p. 466-468 May 4, 1803 John McDowell (Charleston, SC), merchant to John Hobby (Spartanburgh); for $333 sold 333 ac on Two Mile Cr of Enoree R; border: Fooler and Croas; part of 500 ac grant in 1774 to Thomas Farr jr esq. Witness William Shackelford and Joseph Woodruff. Signed John McDowell. Wit. oath Jun. 11, 1803 Joseph Woodruff to John Dean. Rec. Oct. 22, 1804. Dower renounced Barbara McDowell to James Jordan May 5, 1803

p. 468-470 Aug. 4, 1800 John Lee (Spartanburgh) to James Wofford (same); for $10 sold 55 ac on waters of Pacolate R; border: James Stedman, James Wofford, Forrester, and Sabb; part of grant Jul. 5, 1788 to Thomas Sabb. Witness Richard Lee, Ann Lee, and William Brown. Signed John Lee's mark. Wit. oath Oct. 22, 1804 Ann Lee to Drury McDaniel. Rec. Oct. 22, 1804

p. 470-471 Aug. 4, 1800 John Lee (Spartanburgh) to James Wofford; for $20 sold 300 ac on waters of Pacolate R and Broad R; border: John Arrowood, North Carolina state line, Robert Lee, Thomas Sabb, Arthur Crocker, and Cad; part of grant to Thomas Sabb. Witness Richard Lee, Ann Lee, and William Brown. Signed John Lee's mark. Wit. oath Oct. 22, 1804 Ann Lee to Drury McDaniel. Rec. Oct. 22, 1804

p. 471-473 Mar. 24, 1803 Abraham Nelson (Spartanburgh) to John Jordan (same); for $10 sold 20 ac on S side Buck Cr; border: "the big Sarry line" and John Jordan. Witness William Morris and Sally Morris. Signed Abraham Nelson. Wit. oath Dec. 30, 1803 William Morris to Wm McDowell. Rec. Oct. 23, 1804

p. 473-475 Apr. 3, 1804 Frances Fowler (Spartanburgh) to Lucy Fowler (same); for $10 sold 65 ac on branches Forgeson's Cr of Tygar R. Witness America Fowler, Thomas Childress, Moses W Peden. Signed Frances Fowler's mark and Moses Fowler. Wit. oath Jun. 19, 1804 America Fowler to Denny Anderson. Rec. Oct. 23, 1804

p. 475-476 Nov. 2, 1803 Zachariah Arrowood (SC) to Joseph Woods (Spartanburgh); for $100 sold 100 ac on S side Buck Cr of Pacolate R; grant Mar. 10, 183 (sic) to Zachariah Arrowood. Witness Charles Crocker and William Crocker. Signed Zachariah Arrowood. Wit. oath May 24, 1804 William Crocker to Wm McDowell. Rec. Oct. 23, 1804

p. 476-478 Oct. 13, 1804 Thomas Compton (Spartanburgh) to Basel Compton (same); for $200 sold 100 ac on waters of Dutchman's Cr; border: James Moore; part of grant Aug. 11, 1774 to Jeremiah Fowler. Witness Aaron Moore and John Bearden. Signed Thomas Compton. Wit. oath Oct. 13, 1804 Aaron Moore to Wm Smith. Rec. Oct. 23, 1804. Dower renounced Rachel Compton to Wm Smith Oct. 20, 1804

p. 478-479 Apr. 10, 1804 John Low sr (Spartanburgh) to James Lackey (same); for 10s sold 100 ac on N side Pacolate R; border: J. L. Adcock, John Lackey, and Buk's Br; grant to John Low. Witness Jonathan Low jr and Clabourn Holl. Signed John Low. Wit. oath Oct. 23, 1804 Clabourn Holl to John Lipscomb. Rec. Oct. 23, 1804

p. 479-481 Feb. 24, 1801 Elijah Bruce (Spartanburgh) to Ezekeal Sillivan (same); for $74 sold 100 ac; border: Ephraim Jackson and Edwd Smith; part of 200 ac grant Oct. 6, 1788 to Elijah Bruce. Witness Joseph Austell and Patterson Thomson. Signed Elijah Brue (sic). Wit. oath Feb. 24, 1801 Patterson Thomson to John Lipscomb. Rec. Oct. 23, 1804

p. 481-483 Mar. (not given), 1804 Barnet Demsey (Spartanburgh) to William Wilson (same); for 10£ sterling sold 106 ac on branch of Abnor's Cr of Enoree R; part of grant to Charles Wakefield. Witness William Medford and Newman Wilson. Signed Barnet Demsey's mark. Wit. oath Jun. 19, 1804 Newman Wilson to Denny Anderson. Rec. Oct. 23, 1804

p. 483-484 Feb. 2, 1804 William Morris (Spartanburgh) to John Jordan (same); for $6.75 sold 150 ac on waters of Buck Cr of Pacolate R; border: John Jordan. Witness John Morris, Richard Morris, and Elizabeth Morris. Signed William Morris. Wit. oath Feb. 4, 1804 John Morris to Wm McDowell. Rec. Oct. 23, 1804

p. 484 Jun. 8 1804 John Sloan received $475 from Michael Miller for a Negro man Frank. Witness William Traylor and Carm Barry. Signed John Sloan. Wit. oath Oct. 23, 1804 Cham Barry to Wm Kelso. Rec. Oct. 23, 1804

p. 484-486 Oct. 24, 1804 George Lamkin (Spartanburgh) to Thomas Deer (same); for $200 sold 300 ac on branch of Pacolate R; border: Wofford and Leheree. Witness Richard Turner and David Quals. Signed Geor Lamkin. Wit. oath Oct. 24, 1804 David Quals to J Utley. Rec. Oct. 24, 1804

p. 486-488 Aug. 28, 1804 Joshua Prout (Anson Co, NC) to Isaac Young (Spartanburgh); for $150 sold 200 ac on both sides Island Cr of Pacolate R; grant to Peter Howard and eventually sold to Thomas Wades and to Joshua Prout, heir of Thomas Wade. Witness William Abbett jr, Berry Young, and Mathew Abbett. Signed Joshua Prout. Wit. oath Oct. 23, 1804 William Abbett jr to John Lipscomb. Rec. Oct. 24, 1804
land surveyed by William Abbot "included in my patent" and he relinquishes his claim to land. Signed William Abbot's mark. Witness Berry Young. Wit. oath (not given) 23, 1804 Berry Young to John Lipscomb

p. 488-490 Jul. 12, 1803 Thomas McCartan (Thickety, Spartanburgh) to Frances Bremar; a bond of $3,200 consideration to pay $1,600 in two installments: (1) Dec. 1, 1803 of $1,000 and (2) Dec. 1, 1804 of $600; to secure that payment and for 5s sold 1,740 ac on Millers Fork on N side Thickety Cr of Broad R; border: SW-Mapp and Thomson, N & W-Tanner and Middleton, and E-vacant; survey Dec. 20, 1774 by Vardry McBee and mortgaged by Vardry McBee to Frances Bremar Jan. 23, 1787 and since sold to Frances Bremar by Mrs. Weare who bought land from William Bratton esq, sheriff (Pinckney Dist); "words £780 erased". Witness William Beard and Jales Neely. Signed Thos McCarten. Wit. oath (?Charleston Dist)Oct. 2, 1804 William Beard to Danl Jas Ravenel. Rec. Nov. 10, 1804

p. 490-492 Jan. 12, 1795 John Hammett (96 Dist) to William Thomson (same); for 10£ sterling sold 208 ac on waters of Pacolate R; border: William Hammett, Wofford; grant Nov. 10, 1786 Gov. William Moultrie to John Hammett. Witness I Harrison JP. Signed John Hammett. Certified Jan. 12, 1795 by I Harrison. Rec. Nov. 28, 1804

p. 492-493 May 24, 1804 Reuben Richards (Spartanburgh) to Thomas Hill (same); for $70 sold 170 ac on N side Pacolate R and waters of Green's Cr; border: Thomas Jones, David James, James Brown's land, survey for George Ryner, Bryant, and Conner. Witness James Hudson and Wilia Walker. Signed Reuben Richards. Wit. oath Nov. 21, 1804 Wilia Walker to John Lipscomb. Rec. Nov. 28, 1804

p. 493-495 Aug. 28, 1804 David Quarles and wife Ann (Spartanburgh) to Isaac Hill (same); for $300 sold 250 ac on waters of Pacolate R; grant to John Hammett sr. Witness Thomas Hill and James Brown. Signed David Quarles. Wit. oath Nov. 21, 1804 Thomas Hill and James Brown to John Lipscomb. Rec. Nov. 28, 1804

p. 495-497 Jan. 11, 1796 William Thomson (Spartanburgh) to Nathaniel Hammett; for 80£ sterling sold 100 ac on S side Pacolate R; border: branch of Peter's Cr and "the Great Survey"; grant Nov. 10, 1786 Gov. William Moultrie to John Hammett sr. Witness Elias Cannon, John Low, and Henry Cannon. Signed William Thomson. Wit. oath Jan. 1, 1803 Elias Cannon to Geor Lamkin. Rec. Dec. 3, 1804

p. 497 Nov. 7, 1804 Dower renounced Mary Sloan to Isham Foster for deed John Sloan to Willey S Brown. Rec. Dec. 11, 1804

p. 497-501 Jun. 30, 1804 James Smith (Spartanburgh) to David Lynch (same); for $150 sold (1) 64½ ac on both sides Kelsey's Cr; and (2) 70 ac part of Cedar Spring tract; both border: James, Buffington, and Bennet; total 134 ac; plat for both attached shows border: Bardon; grant Dec. 7, 1795 to Jas Smith. Witness James Harrison and Cynthia Smith. Signed Jas Smith. Wit. oath Dec. 26, 1804 James Harrison to William Lancaster. Rec. Dec. 27, 1804. Dower renounced Jane Smith to William Lancaster Dec. 26, 1804

p. 501-521 Oct. 23, 1779 William Wofford, the elder, and wife Mary (Lawson's fork) to Simon Berwick, John Berwick, and Charles Elliot esqs (Charleston, SC); for 70,000£ SC money sold (1) 3/4 (undivided) of 300 ac; where Iron Works are erected; part of 350 ac grant Dec. 22, 1768 Gov. William Tryon (NC) to James Mackelroy then in Tryon Co, NC; 300 ac is on both sides Lawson's fork of Pacolate R including a large shoal and mill seat; (2) 3/4 of 450 ac on Lawson's fork of Pacolate R; grant Sept. 26, 1772 Gov. Charles G Montague to Lacy McAbee; border: E-James Mackelroy and others vacant; (3) 3/4 of 650 ac on Fairforrest Cr; border: N-unknown, S-Lewis Tackwell, and E-"surveyed for North Carolina owner unknown", and others vacant; grant Apr. 2, 1773 Lt. Gov. William Bull to Arthur Crocker; (4) 3/4 of 200 ac on both sides Pacolate R in Tryon Co, NC including a large shoal and place called Doctors Bottom; border: Lindsey's Br; grant Nov. 14, 1771 Gov. Josiah Martin to Isaa Lindsey; (5) 3/4 of 300 ac on Duggon's Br of Fairforrest Cr in Tryon Co, NC; border: Duggon (or Duggin); grant Dec. 23, 1768 Gov. William Tryon (NC) to John Gibbes; (6) 3/4 of 400 ac on both sides Fairforrest Cr in Tryon Co, NC; border: Duggin; grant Dec. 23, 1768 Gov. William Tryon (NC) to Zachariah Gibbes; (7) 3/4 of 300 ac in Tryon Co, NC; part of 640 ac grant May 15, 1772 Gov. William Tryon (NC) to James Gibbes and by order of Councel of State regranted Sept. 9, 1774 to James Gibbes by Lt. Gov. William Bull; 300 ac includes a mountain near Miller's road now called "Mount Zion" and borders: S-land sond to Henry White, W-land sold to John Smith by James Gibbes; (8) 3/4 of 150 ac on Sugar Cr in Craven Co between Broad and Saluda R; grant Aug. 3, 1765 Lt. Gov. William Bull to William Wofford; border: vacant on three sides and other by "northsurvey" John Lattas' (or Lattis') land; (9) 3/4 of 211 ac on S fork Pacolate R; grant Lt. Gov. William Bull to John Nickols then bordering: W-John Lyon, S-David McDowell, E-John Feser (or Fefor), and others vacant; and (10) 3/4 of all buildings; William and Mary Wofford reserve 20 ac part of tract (1) for their lifetimes including house where they live; if anyone of parties desires to sell his share, then others have first refusal at buying. Witness James Ladson esq and Alexander Walker. Signed William Wofford. Wit. oath (Charleston Dist) Sept. 26, 1804 James Ladson esq to Chs Glover. Rec. Jan. 1, 1805

p. 521-523 Sept. 8, 1804 Spencer Smith (Spartanburgh) to Henry Smith (same); for $120 sold 96 ac on waters of Fairforrest Cr; land formerly belonged to Henry Smith; border: John Smith, Handcock's Br, and James Smith; grant in Sec. Book 4A (or 4H) p. 360. Witness John Connell, William Rakestraw, and Robert Rakestraw. Signed Spencer Smith. Wit. oath Jan. 3, 1805 Robert Rakestraw to William Lancaster. Rec. Jan. 3, 1804

p. 523-525 Sept. 8, 1804 John Smith (Spartanburgh) to Henry Smith (same); for $70 sold 50 ac on waters Fairforrest Cr; grant to John Smith. Witness John Connell, William Rakestraw, and Robert Rakestraw. Signed John Smith. Wit. oath Jan. 3, 1805 Robert Rakestraw to William Lancaster. Rec. Jan. 3, 1805

p. 525-527 Dec. 17, 1804 Abner Benson and Alexander McKie (Spartanburgh) to Micajah Barnett (same); for $150 sold 100 ac on both sides Thompson's Br of Kelsoe's Cr of Fairforrest Cr; border: N-Micajah Barnett, S-James Smith, W-Charles James, and E-Fleming Smith; deed warranted against all except claim that Micajah Barnett has from Elijah Benjamin and William Hammett. Witness Gabriel Bumpass and Robert Benson. Signed Alexr McKie and Abner Benson. Wit. oath Jan. 5, 1805 Robert Benson to Jacob Utley. Rec. Jan. 5, 1805

p. 527-529 Nov. 2, 1804 Nathan Ward and Suseanner Ward (Spartanburgh) to James Trail; for a Spanish milled dollar sold 62½ ac on S side Cherokee Cr; border: a road near ford of creek; part of tract bought from James Scott. Witness Jery McMellon and John Brooksheer. Signed Nathan Ward and Suseanner's mark. Wit. oath Jan. 7, 1805 John Brooksheer to Jacob Utley. Rec. Jan. 7, 1805

p. 529-530 Sept. 10, 1804 William Beter (Spartanburgh) to granddaughter Betsey Mathers, wife of Daniel Mathias (same); for love and affection give a Negro boy Harry about 12 years old. Witness John Cooper, James McDaniell and Susanna McDaniell. Signed William Beter's mark. Wit. oath Jan. 8, 1805 Susanna McDaniell to Drury McDaniell. Rec. Jan. 8, 1805

p. 530-532 Oct. 6, 1804 Thomas McCarryl (or McCarrel) (Spartanburgh) to Nathaniel McCarryl; for $150 sold 100 ac on N side Obed's Cr of N Pacolate R; survey Mar. 5, 1768 for Obediah Roberts who sold to John McCarrel sr and bequeathed to Thomas McCarrel. Witness James Young, John Holdiebey (or Holdiabey), and James McKnight. Signed Thos McCarryl. Wit. oath Dec. 20, 1804 James Young to Wm McDowell. Rec. Jan. 10, 1805

p. 532-534 Nov. 26, 1803 James Scott and wife Rebecah (Spartanburgh) to Nathan Ward; for $50 sold 150 ac on Cherokee Cr; border: "the main road"; part of grant to James Stedman. Witness George Thomason and John Dunlap. Signed James Scott's mark. Wit. oath Jan. 18, 1805 John Dunlap to Geor Lamkin. Rec. Jan. 19, 1805

p. 534-535 Nov. 20, 1803 James Scott and wife Rebecah (Spartanburgh) to Nathan Ward; for a Spanish milled dollar sold 20 ac on S side Cherokee Cr; border: "the main road"; part of grant to James Stedman. Witness George Thomason and John Dunlap. Signed James Scott's mark. Wit. oath Jan. 18, 1805 John Dunlap to Geor Lamkin. Rec. Jan. 19, 1805

p. 535-537 Mar. 9, 1804 (or Feb. 17, 1804) Thomas Penny sr (Spartanburgh) to Michael Maclerath (same); for $80 sold 150 ac on N side of Middle fork Tygar R; border: N & W-James Vernon, S & E-John Maclerath and Gabriel Benson. Witness Abner Wingo, Joseph McMullen, and William McElrath. Signed Thomas and Sarah Penny's marks. Wit. oath Mar. 15, 1804 William McElrath to James Kilgore. Rec. Jan. 21, 1805

p. 537-539 Jan. 9, 1805 Edward Herren (or Hering) (Spartanburgh) to Alexander McKie, shopkeeper (same); for $102 sold 153 ac on waters of Lawson's fork; border: Crocker and Alexander McKie; part of two tracts: (1) grant in 1785 to William Turner Thomason who sold to Edward Herren and (2) grant in 1804 to Edward Herren. Witness George Thomason, Robert Benson, and William West jr. Signed Edward Hering and Maryan's mark. Wit. oath Feb. 5, 1805 Robert Benson to Jacob Utley. Rec. Feb. 5, 1805

p. 539-541 Feb. 5, 1805 Dudley Brannan, heir of William Brannan desc (Davison Co, Tenn) to Cyrus Seay, carpenter (Spartanburgh); for $70 sold 40 ac on Lawson's fork; border: Edward Bollinger, Cyrus Seay, and Thomas Brannan; part of grant to Samuel Fleay (or Tleay) and admeasured number 4 by Isham Foster(?), William Foster, Rowland Johnson, Gabriel Benson, and Peter Gray, commissioners appointed by Spartanburgh Common Pleas Court to divide estate of William Brannan desc. Witness Abner Benson, Jacob Utley, and Robert Benson. Signed Dudley Brannan. Wit. oath Feb. 5, 1805 Abner Benson to Jacob Utley. Rec. Feb. 5, 1805

p. 541-543 Jul. 10, 1804 William Connell and Giles Connel for selves and by power of attorney from Milley Connell, Alus Adhens, Susanna Connel, Alus Yews, Lettice Connell, Alus Yews (sic), Elisa Connell, John Connell, and Elisabeth Connell, mother of above children and widow of late Giles Connel desc to Elijah Barnett (Spartanburgh); for $500 sold 200 ac on both sides Fairforrest Cr; border: Beaverdam Cr, Foster's old line, and Ford. Witness John Barnett and Richard Barnett. Signed Wm Connell, Giles Connell, Wm Alkins, Nathan Yoes, John Yoes, John Connell, Elizabeth Connell's mark, and Elizabeth Connell (sic), William Connell and Giles Connell for Milly Allkins, Sarah Yoes, and Lettice Yoes. Wit. oath Jan. 19, 1805 John Barnett to Geor Lamkin. Rec. Feb. 5, 1805

p. 543-545 Feb. 23, 1804 Jonathan Cud (Rutherford Co, NC) to Moses Proctor (Spartanburgh); for $400 sold 540 ac on both branches of Buck Cr of Pacolate R; grant Oct. 6, 1788 States Office to William Dotton. Witness Besy Hicks and Jane Henderson. Signed Jonathan Cud's mark. Wit. oath Feb. 1, 1805 Besy Hicks to Wm McDowell. Rec. Feb. 11, 1805

p. 545-551 Dec. 4, 1787 George Storey sr and wife Hannah (Spartanburgh) to Charles James (same); for 100£ SC money sold 200 ac on Kelsoe's Cr on N side Fairforrest Cr; grant Apr. 25, 1767 Gov. William Tryon (NC) to George Storey and regranted Mar. 1, 1775 Lt. Gov. William Bull to George Storey. Witness Wm Lancaster, Hugh Means, and David Golightly. Signed George and Hannah Storey's marks. Wit. oath Nov. 7, 1804 David Golightly to William Lancaster. Rec. Feb. 11, 1805

p. 551-553 Mar. 15, 1804 Joel Smith, son and one of legates of Ralph Smith esq desc, (Spartanburgh) to William Palmore (same); for $370 sold 183 except 20 feet square containing some graves that reamins Joel Smith's land; on waters of Dutchman's and Cain Creeks of Tygar R; grant to Ralph Smith and by his will to Joel Smith; 183 ac in 150 ac and part of another tract of Ralph Smith's land. Witness John Hewett, James Bearden, and William Hewett. Signed Joel Smith. Wit. oath Aug. 1, 1804 John Hewett to Wm Smith. Rec. Feb. 19, 1805. Dower renounded Mary Smith to William Smith. Mar. 24, 1804

p. 553-554 Mar. 21, 1804 John Arrendel sr (Spartan Dist) to John Arrendel jr; for $415 sold (ac not given) on waters of Cherokee Cr of Broad R; border: Marlen and Walker. Witness Daniel McCay and Lot Arrendell. Signed John Arrendell. Wit. oath Apr. 28, 1804 Daniel McCay to John Lipscomb. Rec. Feb. 28, 1805

No Book J
Book K 1805-1807
p. 1-2 Feb. 4, 1805 Eaton Walker (SC) to Thomas Burton; for $100 sold 118 ac on Fairforrest Cr of Tyger R; grant Feb. 6, 1795 to Charles Benson who sold to William Benson and "drawn" by Eaton Walker, heir of Wm Benson desc, "as a distributive part of original tract". Witness Abner Benson and Robert Benson. Signed Eaton Walker. Wit. oath Mar. 1, 1805 Robert Benson to Jacob Utley. Rec. Mar. 1, 1805

p. 2-3 Jan. 11, 1805 Nathan Ward (Spartanburgh) to Solomon Ward; for $50 sold 62½ ac on S side Cherokee Cr. Witness John

Utley and Samuel Ward. Signed Nathan Ward. Wit. oath Mar. 7, 1805 Samuel Ward to Jacob Utley. Rec. Mar. 7, 1805

p. 3-4 Feb. 19, 1805 Nathan Ward (Spartanburgh) to Solomon Ward; for (money not mentioned) sold "a black horse saddle and bridle", a red cow and red yearling, 2 pots, an oven, a Spider, a pewter dish, 3 pewter basons, 3 pewter plates, 6 "delph" plates, a set of tea ware, 4 pit chers, 2 boles, a chest, a flat iron, a case of knives and forks, 3 beds and furniture. Witness James Trail and Samuel Ward. Signed Nathan Ward. Wit. oath Mar. 7, 1805 Samuel Ward to Jacob Utley. Rec. Mar. 7, 1805

p. 4 Jan. 17, 1804 Thomas Bennett (Spartanburgh) to son Vincent Bennett (same); for love and affection give a Negro man Richard about 23 years old now in Thomas' possession. Witness Andw B Moore. Signed Thomas Bennett. Wit. oath Mar. 4, 1805 Andw B Moore to Jacob Utley. Rec. Mar. 8, 1805

p. 4-6 Feb. 18, 1805 Joseph Fleming (Spartan Dist) to Joseph Collins; Joseph Fleming is bound to Joseph Collins for $1,000 and to secure the bond (for payment of $500) Joseph Fleming sells Joseph Collins 58 ac; Condition sale void if Joseph Fleming pays $500 with interest. Witness Peter Gray, James Thomson, and John Fleming. Signed Jos Fleming. Wit. oath Mar. 11, 1805 Peter Gray to Ism Foster. Rec. Mar. 12, 1805

p. 6-7 Mar. 15, 1804 West Harris (Spartanburgh) to William Bridges (same); for $100 sold 25 ac on Little Buck Cr; border: Charles Cantrell. Witness Leonard Adcock and John Harris. Signed West Harris. Wit. oath Apr. 5, 1804 John Harris to Wm McDowell. Rec. Mar. 23, 1805

p. 7-8 Sept. 15, 1804 Austin Clayton (Spartanburgh) to James Moss (same); for $600 sold 100 ac on N fork Tyger R; border: William Clayton's fence and Samuel Miller's Spring Br. Witness Richard Daniel and William Moss. Signed Austin Clayton. Wit. oath Mar. 20, 1805 Richard Daniel to Jacob Utley. Rec. Mar. 25, 1805. Dower renounced Caty Clayton to William Lancaster Feb. 10, 1805

p. 8-9 Apr. 2, 1800 James McElwean (SC) to James Mayes (Spartanburgh); for $300 sold 200 ac on McElwean Cr of Fairforrest Cr; grant Sept. 9, 1774 to (not given). Witness Henry Storey and Moses White. Signed James McElwean's mark. Wit. oath Aug. 14, 1804 Henry Storey to William Simpson. Rec. Mar. 25, 1805

p. 9-11 Dec. 4, 1804 James Millican (Spartanburgh) to Thomas Millican (Rutherford Co, NC); for $500 sold 100 ac on N side of N fork Pacolate R; part in Spartanburgh Dist and part in North Carolina; including improvements where Thomas Millican lives near Millican's ford; part of grant Jan. 13, 1785 North Carolina governor to Robert Tate "to John McKnight" and sold Jan. 6, 1794 by John McNight to James Millican. Witness Wm Millican, Alexander Copeland, and Robert Millican. Signed James Millican's mark. Wit. oath Mar. 20, 1805 Robert Millican to Wm Kelso. Rec. Mar. 25, 1805

p. 11-12 Nov. 3, 1804 Joshua Gordan (Rutherford Co, NC) to Samuel Adams (Spartanburgh); for 20£ sold 50 ac on Beaverdam Cr of Thickety Cr; part of two tracts: (1) grant in North Carolina to John Hogan and (2) "in" South Carolina to Vardry McBee; border: Hogan and Joseph Adams. Witness Moses Guyton and John Guyton. Signed Joshua Gordan's mark. Wit. oath Mar. 25, 1805 Moses Guyton to John Lipscomb. Rec. Mar. 25, 1805

p. 12-13 Mar. 29, 1803 Nathaniel Miller (Spartanburgh) to Joshua

Edwards (same); for $200 sold 250 ac; remainder of 300 ac that lost 50 ac due to claim of "an old survey"; grant Nov. 7, 1785 to Nathaniel Miller; on Reedy fork of Tyger R. Witness John Collins JP and James Jordan JQ. Signed Nathaniel Miller. Wit. oath Sept. 13, 1804 John Collins to Drury McDaniel. Rec. Mar. 25, 1805

p. 13 May 19, 1804 Amous Speace (Spartanburgh) to William Shedd (or Shead) (same); for $30 sold 60 ac on both sides Casus Cr. Witness Edmond Cooley and Henry Turner. Signed Amous Speace's mark. Wit. oath Mar. 16, 1805 Henry Turner to Ism Foster. Rec. Mar. 25, 1805

p. 13-15 Jan. 16, 1805 Thomas Paden (Spartanburgh) to David Morton (same); for $214 sold 500 ac on branch of Forgeson's Cr of Tygar R; E part of 1,000 ac. Witness John Morton and James Morton. Signed Thomas Paden. Wit. oath Jan. 18, 1805 James Morton to John Collins. Rec. Mar. 25, 1805

p. 15-16 Jan. 23, 1805 Simpson McCarter (Spartanburgh) to George McCarter (same); for $250 sold 181 ac on Mile Cr; border: William Simpson. Witness David Chapman and Isaac Chapman. Signed Simpson McCarter. Wit. oath Jan. 23, 1805 David Chapman to John Lipscomb. Rec. Mar. 25, 1805. Dower renounced Polley McCarter to John Lipscomb Jan. 30, 1805

p. 16-17 Feb. 29, 1804 Benjamin Bonner Simons and Anthony Simons (Charleston, SC) to John Gowen (Spartanburgh); for $500 sold 1,450 ac in two tracts in Craven Co granted (date omitted) to Henry Bonneau and Peter Cedean; (1) 1,000 ac; border: NW-Lord Charles G Montague, W-Cherokee land, S-S Pacolate R, SE-Anthony Simons, and SE-vacant; (2) 450 ac; border: NW & SW-Henry Bonneau, NE-vacant, and S-S Pacolate R; both tracts sold by Henry Bonneau and Peter Cedean to Anthony Simons Oct. 10, 1774 and Apr. 2 & 3, 1788. Witness Jeremiah Brown and William Gowen. Signed Benj B Simons and A Simons. Wit. oath (Charleston, SC) Feb. 29, 1804 Jeremiah Brown to Isaac Motte (or Molle) Duel(?) JQ. Rec. Mar. 25, 1805

p. 17-19 Jan. 24, 1800 Zadock Ford (Spartanburgh) to John Cantrell (same); for $128 sold 100 ac on N side Enoree R; border: Snortrer Cr. Witness James Chambler, Zadock Ford jr, and Mary Ford. Signed Zadock Ford. Wit. oath Jun. 18, 1802 Zadock Ford jr to Kilgore. Rec. Mar. 25, 1805. Dower renounced Casander Ford to James Kilgore Jan. 24, 1802

p. 19-20 Feb. 9, 1801 James McDowell (Spartan Dist) to William Renfro (same); for $260 sold 75 ac on N fork Pacolate R; half of grant Oct. 13, 1765 by Henry Lewis (sic) to Robert McMillian and sold by James McDowell to William Renfro May 19, 1774 "by James McDowell, executor of will of Robert McMillian desc, to William Renfro Oct. 13, 1783"(sic). Witness John Vaughn, Thomas Cruly (or Crumley), and John McClure. Signed James McDowell. Wit. oath Jul. 4, 1801 John McClure to Wm McDowell. Rec. Mar. 25, 1805

p. 20-21 Nov. 10, 1803 Samuel Archebald (Spartanburgh) to James Mayes sr (same); for 10£ sterling sold 47 ac; border: James Mayes and George Storey; part of grant to Hugh Donaldson (date omitted). Witness Henry Storey, George Storey, and James McElwean. Signed Samuel Archebald. Wit. oath Aug. 14, 1804 Henry Storey to William Simpson. Rec. Mar. 25, 1805

p. 21-23 Dec. 18, 1804 James Crowder (Spartanburgh) to Alexander Pruwett (same); for 60£ sterling sold 156 ac on N side Tygar R; border: Daniel Grant; part of two tracts: (1) granted Jan. 21, 1785 to Joseph Powers and (2) grant Nov. 7, 1785 to Timothy Toney. Witness Isaac Bearden and John Grist. Signed James Crowder. Wit.

oath Dec. 18, 1804 John Grist to Wm Smith. Rec. Mar. 25, 1805. Dower renounced Ama (or Lorhamah) Crowder to Wm Smith Mar. 22, 1805

p. 23-24 Dec. 1, 1804 Gideon Reynolds (Spartanburgh) to Zacheriah Moore (same); for $150 sold 100 ac on Cain Cr of Tygar R; part of grant Nov. 6, 1786 Gov. William Moultrie to Ambrose Barnett. Witness Nathaniel Burton, Andrew Culbertson, and Aaron Smith. Signed Gideon Reynolds. Wit. oath Jan. 5, 1805 Andrew Culbertson to Wm Smith. Rec. Mar. 25, 1805. Dower renounced Mary Reynolds to Wm Smith Dec. 1, 1804

p. 24-25 (not given), 1804 Alexander Cunningham (Spartanburgh) to William Renfro (same); for $50 sold 34½ ac; border: William Renfro. Witness Thomas Gore and Isaac Cantrell. Signed Alexr Cunningham. Wit. oath Dec. 27, 1804 Thomas Gore to Wm McDowell. Rec. Mar. 25, 1805

p. 25-26 Dec. 22, 1800 Thomas Keesee (Spartanburgh) to Lefford French (same); for $100 sold 70 ac on N side of N Pacolate R; part of grant Sept. 24, 1766 to George Alexander. Witness Thomas McKnight and Margret McKnight. Signed Thomas Keesee. Wit. oath Jun. 12, 1801 Thomas McKnight to Wm McDowell. Rec. Mar. 25, 1805

p. 26-28 Feb. 13, 1804 Mellington Smith and wife Sarah (Spartanburgh) to Voletine Smith (same); for 18£ sterling sold 53 ac on N side Tygar R; border: Edward Hooker, Samuel Cathcart, Mellington Smith, and Jeremiah Wofford; part of 284 ac grant Feb. 5, 1788 (or 1787) to John Campbell who sold Jul. 12, 1793 to Mellington Smith. Witness Jeremiah Wofford and Drury Smith. Signed Mellington Smith's mark and Sarah Smith. Wit. oath Apr. 3, 1804 Jeremiah Wofford to Wm Smith. Rec. Mar. 25, 1805. Dower renounced Sarah Smith to Wm Smith Apr. 3, 1804

p. 28-29 Feb. 13, 1804 Jeremiah Wofford and wife Elizabeth to Voluntine Smith; for $50 sold 40 ac on N side Tygar R and on Negro Br; border: Voluntine Smith, Mellington Smith, Forrester's ford on Tygar R, E-Edward Hooker, S-Tygar R, other sides by remainder of grant; part of 284 ac grant Feb. 5, 1787 to John Campbell. Witness Drury Smith and Solomon Smith. Signed Jeremiah Wofford. Wit. oath Sept. 8, 1804 Drury Smith to Wm Smith. Rec. Mar. 25, 1805. Dower renounced Elizabeth Wofford to Wm Smith Apr. 3, 1804

p. 29-30 Jan. 9, 1805 Francis Robertson (Charleston, SC) to William Humphreys jr and Alexander Davidson (Spartanburgh); for $600 sold 400 ac; border: W-Thimothy Philips, "now to" Francis Robertson, N-North Carolina border, E-George Walker, and S-Robert Swan; bought by Francis Robertson from William Bonner Mar. 12, 1803; only 300 ac is warranted and "as much more as conveyed" to Francis Robertson. Witness William Walker and John Rukman. Signed Francis Robertson. Wit. oath Jan. 9, 1805 William Walker to John Rukman. Rec. Mar. 25, 1805

p. 30-31 Mar. 20, 1805 John Low and son Jonathan Low (Spartanburgh) to Rolley H Horton (same); for $100 sold 100 ac on E side Pacolate R; grant Jun. 5, 1786 to Michael Jones. Witness Samuel Sherbert and Thomas Betterton. Signed John and Jonathan Low. Wit. oath Mar. 22, 1805 Thomas Betterton to Geor Lamkin. Rec. Mar. 25, 1805

p. 31-32 Oct. 23, 1804 Jonathan Low, schoolmaster (Spartanburgh) to William Johnson (same); for $60 sold 100 ac on waters of and S side of Lawson's fork of Pacolate R; grant to James Young; border: Clabourn Johnson, Turpin, John Wood, William Johnson, and Thomas Wadsworth. Witness Ephraim Lewis and Robert Foster. Signed Jonathan Low. Wit. oath Jan. 20, 1805 Robert Foster to Isham Foster.

Rec. Mar. 25, 1805

p. 32-33 Jan. 16, 1800 James Vernon (Spartanburgh) to Hugh McMillin (same); for $50 sold 61 ac on waters of N Pacolate R; border: John Howey and George Alexander; part of grant Jan. 1, 1787 to William French. Witness James Templeton and Thomas McKnight. Signed James Vernon. Wit. oath Jan. 16, 1801 Thomas McKnight to James Jordan. Rec. Mar. 25, 1805

p. 33-34 Feb. 17, 1801 Nathaniel Dodd (Faquere Co, Va) to nephews Elijah Hammett and Benjamin Hamet (Spartanburgh); give power of attorney to sell 200 ac on Thompson's Br of Kellsoy's Cr; border: George Storey; "taken up" by Nathaniel Dodd and surveyed by Zacheriah Bullock. Witness Jas Lewis attorney at law, George Kemper jr, and Thomas Fisher. Signed Nathaniel Dodd. Wit. oath (Fouquere Co, Va) Feb. 17, 1801 Nathaniel Dodd to W Edmonds. Rec. Mar. 25, 1805. Feb. 17, 1801 Francis Booker, clerk Foquier Co, Va, certifies William Edmonds is acting magistrate. Feb. 17, 1801 William Edmonds, presiding justice Fouquier Co, Va, certifies Francis Booker is clerk.

p. 34-36 Feb. 20, 1805 James Smith (Newberry Co) to John McElrath (Spartanburgh); for $650 sold 500 ac on Middle fork Tygar R; border: S-Elias Vandehorst, W-Capt. Blake, and N & E-vacant when surveyed; grant Dec. 24, 1772 Gov. Charles Montague to Elias Foesen (?); plat attached. Witness Charles Friffen, John Sells jr, and William McElrath. Signed James Smith's mark. Wit. oath Mar. 2, 1805 William McElrath to Michael Miller. Rec. Mar. 25, 1805. Dower renounced (Newberry Dist) Elizabeth Smith to Jacob R Brown Feb. 21, 1805

p. 36-37 Feb. 28, 1805 Abisha Camp (Spartanburgh) to William Camp (York Dist); for $500 sold 1,000 ac on Cherokee Cr of Broad R. Witness Joseph Camp and Vardry Camp. Signed Abisha Camp. Wit. oath Mar. 16, 1805 Joseph Camp to John Rukman. Rec. Mar. 25, 1805

p. 37-38 Sept. 5, 1803 John Cooper (Spartanburgh) to John Champion, Wm Hester, Nathan Byars, and Vardry Camp, deacons of Church of Providence; for $5 sold 4 ac; plat attached. Witness Abisha Camp and Joseph Camp. Signed John Copper. Wit. oath Mar. 25, 1805 Abisha Camp to William Lancaster. Rec. Mar. 25, 1803

p. 38-39 Mar. 17, 1804 Richard Thomas and Robert Rakestraw (Spartanburgh) to Arthur Hutchesens (same); for $150 sold 125 ac on N side Fairforrest Cr with improvements made by Richard Thomas; border: S, E & N- Henry Foster, N-Joseph Hays, and W-Joseph Wade. Witness Christopher Johnson and James D Johnson. Signed Richard Thomas' mark and Robert Rakestraw. Wit. oath Mar. 25, 1805 Christopher Johnson to William Simpson. Rec. Mar. 25, 1805

p. 39-40 Oct. 14, 1804 Thomas Goodune (or Goodure) (Spartanburgh) to Bartley Grogan (same); for $100 or value thereof sold 216 ac on branch of Mubery Cr of N Pacolate R. Witness John Byen, John Ridings, and Samuel Hunt. Signed Thomas Goodune's mark. Wit. oath Mar. 22, 1805 Samuel Hunt to Jas L Burd. Rec. Mar. 26, 1805

p. 40-41 Sept. 19, 1804 Joseph Pinson (Pendleton Dist) to Gowen Harris (Spartanburgh); for $252 sold 200 ac; border: Elisha Headdy; W end of tract on Middle Tygar R and on Bridge Cr; survey for James Alexander. Witness David Drummon and William Harris jr. Signed Josep Penson. Wit. oath Feb. 23, 1805 William Harris jr to Drury McDaniel. Rec. Mar. 26, 1805

p. 41-42 Apr. 10, 1800 Samuel Harmon (Spartanburgh) to Isaac Brown (same); for $80 sold 10 ac; border: WSW-Thompson's old line and David Brown; if some of land is taken away by old survey, Isaac Brown won't charge Samuel Hermon more per acre than is now given. Witness Samuel Brown and George McCarter. Signed Samuel Hermon. Wit. oath Mar. 26, 1805 George McCarter to William Simpson. Rec. Mar. 26, 1805

p. 42-43 Dec. 10, 1804 Samuel Sarratt (Spartanburgh) to John Sarratt; for $10 sold 7 ac "covered with water" on main Broad R; border: John Sarratt. Witness Nancy Sarratt and Joseph Camp. Signed Samuel Sarratt. Wit. oath Mar. 16, 1805 Joseph Camp to Jno Rukman. Rec. Mar. 26, 1805

p. 43-44 Mar. 9, 1805 Benjamin Bonner (Spartanburgh) to Thomas Cook (Montgomery Co, NC); for $150 sold 100 ac on waters of Sarratt's Cr; border: Bryant Bonner and Canebrake. Witness William Walker and Briant Bonner. Signed Benjamin Bonner's mark. Wit. oath Mar. 11, 1805 Briant Bonner to Jno Rukman. Rec. Mar. 26, 1805

p. 44-45 Nov. 5, 1790 William Wakefield jr and John Wakefield (Spartanburgh) to William Tippin (same); for 110£ sterling sold 150 ac on Peter's Cr now called Abner's Cr; part of grant Dec. 22, 1768 Gov. William Tryon (NC) to Charles Moore who sold Apr. 17, 1784 to William Wakefield sr who sold May 1, 1788 to William Wakefield jr and John Wakefield. Witness William Wakefield sr, David Bruton, and Joseph Hughs. Signed William Wakefield's mark and John Wakefield. Wit. oath Dec. 18, 1790 Joseph Hughs to Zadock Ford. Rec. Mar. 26, 1805

p. 45-47 Mar. 23, 1804 Aaron Pinson (Spartanburgh) to John Meadows (same); for $150 sold 150 ac on N side Tygar R; border: NE & S-Tobias Bright, SE-a division of Zepaniah Pinson's land, E-grant to Joel Hembree, N-John Meadows, NW-Andrew Thomson, and SW-John Meadows; part of two grants: (1) Nov. 6, 1786 Gov. William Moultrie to Obediah Edwards and (2) "other" part about 50 ac granted Jan. 6, 1794 Gov. William Moultrie to John Meadows. Witness Aaron Smith and Isaac Smith. Signed Aaron Pinson. Wit. oath Mar. 24, 1804 Aaron Smith to Wm Smith. Rec. Mar. 26, 1805. Dower renounced Elizabeth Pinson to Wm Smith Mar. 24, 1804

p. 47 (Union Dist) Feb. 1, 1804 Hugh Donaldson sr (Union Dist) to Robert Donaldson (same); for 5s sold 138 ac on Harris Cr of Fairforrest Cr; border: McCartan, Gossett, and Stephen Cruie. Witness Margaret Donaldson and Jane Donaldson. Signed Hu Donaldson. Wit. oath Jan. 15, 1805 Margaret Donaldson to William Simpson. Rec. Mar. 26, 1805

p. 47-48 Aug. 25, 1803 Samuel McClue (Greenville Dist) to John Kirkland (Spartanburgh); for $300 sold 94 ac on S fork Pacolate R; where John Kirkland lives; S part of 183 ac grant Jun. 5, 1786 to George Thompson. Witness Daniel Kirkland, John Brook, and Winn B Gowen. Signed Samuel McClue's mark. Wit. oath Mar. 3, 1805 Daniel Kirkland to James L Burd. Rec. Mar. 26, 1805

p. 48-49 Oct. 20, 1803 Daniel Comwell and wife Polley (Spartanburgh) to James White (same); for $100 sold 200 ac where Daniel Comwell lives on N side Lawson's fork; part of two grants to John Earle; border: N-John West and S-Wm Brannon. Witness David Lewis, William Kelbey, and Salia Kelbey. Signed Daniel and Polley Comwell's marks. Wit. oath Feb. 25, 1804 David Lewis to Jas L Burd. Rec. Mar. 26, 1805

p. 49-50 Nov. 25, 1801 Daniel White (Spartanburgh) to Rowland Jennings (same); for $100 sold 110 ac on waters of Fairforrest Cr; border: Wm Castleberry, Col. White's Br, and John Smith; sold Oct. 22, 1801 by Thomas Smith to Daniel White; part of 460 ac grant Feb. 21, 1785 Gov. Thomas Pinckney to John Smith. Witness Daniel Smith and James Gourley. Signed Daniel White. Wit. oath May 17, 1803 Daniel Smith to Samuel Lancaster. Rec. Mar. 26, 1806

p. 50-51 Jul. 9, 1804 Joseph Woodruff (Spartanburgh) to Baptist Bethel Church; for $10 sold 12½ ac on branch of Enoree R; including old former Bethel Meeting House; border on all sides: Joseph Woodruff; sold to Baptist Bethel Church and Successors as long as said Church shall continue the worship of God; plat attached. Witness David Moore, James Wofford, Nathaniel Wofford, and Jonathan Moore. Signed Joseph Woodruff's mark. Wit. oath Jul. 9, 1804 Jonathan Moore to John Dean. Rec. Mar. 26, 1805

p. 51-52 Apr. 3, 1804 Frances Fowler and Lucy Fowler (Spartanburgh) to Moses Fowler (same); for $10 sold 65 ac on branches of Forgeson's Cr of Tygar R. Witness America Fowler, Thomas Childrews, and Moses W Paden. Signed Frances and Lucy Fowler's marks. Wit. oath Jun. 19, 1804 America Fowler to Denny Anderson. Rec. Mar. 26, 1805

p. 52-53 Dec. 31, 1804 Frances Fowler (Spartanburgh) to Moses Fowler (same); for $150 sold 150 ac on S of Forgeson's Cr; border: Thomas Peden; part of 300 ac grant Sept. 1, 1768 to John Martin on Forgeson's Cr. Witness George Thornton, John Reeves, and Joseph Thornton. Signed Frances Fowler's mark. Wit. oath Feb. 16, 1805 John Reeves to Denny Anderson. Rec. Mar. 26, (omitted)

p. 53-54 Feb. 16, 1804 Rowland Ginnings (or Jennings) (Spartanburgh) to Hugh White (same); for $21 sold 21 ac on waters of Fairforrest Cr; border: William Lancaster and a waggon road. Witness Christopher Johnson and Charles Smith. Signed Rowland Ginnings' mark. Wit. oath Mar. 5, 1804 Christopher Johnson to William Lancaster. Rec. Mar. 26, 1805

p. 54-55 Feb. 18, 1805 William French (Spartanburgh) to Hugh White (same); for $50 sold 58 ac on waters of Fairforrest Cr; where Hugh White lives; border: Charles Smith and William Lancaster. Witness John Smith and James Kean. Signed William French's mark. Wit. oath Feb. 27, 1805 John Smith to William Lancaster. Rec. Mar. 26, 1805

p. 55-57 Mar. 11, 1805 Daniel Bragg (Spartanburgh) to Elias Corder; for $100 sold 50 ac on waters Forgeson's Cr; border: where Elias Corder lives, Georgia Road, and Floyd's Br. Witness William Otts and Samuel Brewton. Signed Dan Bragg. Wit. oath (not dated) William Otts to George Grace. Rec. Mar. 26, 1805. Dower renounced Elisabeth Bragg to George Grace Mar. 11, 1805

p. 57-58 Sept. 19, 1804 William Gray (Spartanburgh) to Carie Traylor (same); for $200 sold 108 ac on Ben's Cr of Tygar R; where William Gray lives; border: Jno Neisbett, James Jordan, Brushy Fork Cr, Penman, and John Durham. Witness James Hadden and Curtes Gray. Signed William Gray. Wit. oath Oct. 4, 1804 James Hadden to Denny Anderson. Rec. Mar. 26, 1805

p. 58-59 Sept. 19, 1805 James Hadden (Spartanburgh) to Carie Traylor (same); for $100 sold 30 ac on S side Poin's Cr; border: Penman, William Gray, John Durham, and Aaron Moore. Witness Curtes Gray and Joshua Johnson. Signed James Hadden. Wit. oath Oct. 4, 1804 Curtes Gray to Denny Anderson. Rec. Mar. 26, 1805

p. 59 Aug. 17, 1804 John Bazwell (Spartanburgh) to Carie Traylor (same); for $10 sold 5 ac on branch of Ben's Cr; border: John McDowell, Aaron Moore, and Carie Traylor; includes half of water of Spring. Witness Curtes Gray and James Anderson. Signed John

Bazwell. Wit. oath Oct. 4, 1804 Curtes Gray to Denny Anderson. Rec. Mar. 26, 1804

p. 59-60 Nov. 17, 1804 Reuben Traylor (Spartanburgh) to John Johnson (same); for $120 sold 143 ac on branch of Provey's Cr of Tygar R. Witness John Johnson and Salley Johnson. Signed Reuben and Susanna Traylor's marks. Wit. oath Mar. 26, 1805 John Johnson to Drury McDaniel. Rec. Mar. 26, 1805

p. 60-61 Jan. 11, 1803 Carie Traylor (Spartanburgh) to William Brice (same); for $18 sold 12 ac on Camp Br of Ben's Cr of S Tygar R; border: David Morton. Witness James Hadden and David White. Signed Carie Traylor's mark. Wit. oath Mar. 26, 1805 James Hadden to Drury McDaniel. Rec. Mar. 26, 1805

p. 61-62 Apr. 18, 1802 William Moore (SC) to Thomas Cook (Spartanburgh); for $110 sold 90 ac on W side Ward's Cr; border: Benett and a Shoal; part of 260 ac grant Dec. 3, 1787 to Jason Moore; and sold ½ ac on W side of Shoal. Witness William Cook and Simmon Yewel. Signed William Moore. Wit. oath Mar. 26, 1805 William Cook to Wm Hendrix. Rec. Mar. 26, 1805

p. 62-63 May 3, 1804 Brittin Williford (Spartanburgh) to Elsworth Moore (same); for $50 sold 40 ac on Dry Fork Br of Dutchman's Cr; border: Esquire Smith, "above" Williford's field, and Elsworth Moore; part of grant Sept. 20, 1784 to Brittin Williford. Witness William Patton, Hardy Williford, and Wm L Williford. Signed Brittin Williford. Wit. oath Dec. 22, 1804 William Patton to Wm Smith. Rec. Mar. 26, 1805. Dower renounced Elizabeth Williford to Wm Smith Dec. 29, 1804

p. 63-65 Aug. 21, 1804 James Campbell (Spartanburgh) to Richard James (same); for $52.50 sold 21 ac on waters Lawson's fork of Pacolate R; border: N & W-Richard James, E-James Campbell, and formerly Brown's Pond. Witness Joroyal Barnett and Bartho Conus Stovall. Signed James Campbell. Wit. oath Sept. 17, 1804 Joroyal Barnett to William Lancaster. Rec. Mar. 26, 1805. Dower renounced Molley Campbell to William Lancaster Sept. 17, 1804

p. 65-66 Mar. 4, 1805 John Hammett (Spartanburgh) to Jeremiah Selman (same); for 100£ sterling sold 921 ac on Lick Cr of N Tygar R; border: Prince, Pos, and Selman. Witness Christopher Johnson, Sandford Smith, and Frances Mason. Signed John Hammett. Wit. oath Mar. 26, 1805 Frances Mason to Absalom Lancaster. Rec. Mar. 26, 1805

p. 66-67 Feb. 15, 1804 Wilie Williford (Spartanburgh) to Elsworth Moore (same); for $75 sold 75 ac on Dry fork Br of Dutchman's Cr; border: Esquire Smith and Britain Williford; part of grant Nov. 7, 1785 to John Shands who sold to Thomas Williams who sold to Wilie Williford. Witness William Patton, Absalom Langston, and Margret Patton. Signed Wilie Williford. Wit. oath Dec. 22, 1804 William Patton to Wm Smith. Rec. Mar. 26, 1805

p. 67-68 Dec. 13, 1804 George Anderson (Spartanburgh) to Robert Wall (same); for $150 sold 152 ac on Mellekin's Br of N Pacolate R; border: E-McMillin, N-James Mellekin, W-Wm McWilliams, and SW & S-John Young sr. Witness Jonathan Wall and John Crawford. Signed George Anderson. Wit. oath Mar. 20, 1805 Jonathan Wall to Wm McDowell. Rec. Mar. 26, 1805

p. 68-69 Jan. 17, 1805 Zachariah Grace (Spartanburgh) to Peter Bragg (same); for $400 sold 160 ac on branches of Forgeson's Cr; border: John Means, Thomas Underwood, and George Brewton. Witness Matthew Patton and John Bragg. Signed Zachariah Grace and Ruth's mark. Wit. oath Mar. 4, 1805 Matthew Patton to A Casey. Rec. Mar. 26, 1805. Dower renounced Ruth Grace to George Grace Mar. 11, 1805

p. 69-70 Mar. 9, 1802 David Brown (Spartanburgh) to Isaac Brown (same); for $200 sold (1) 150 ac on both sides Moses Cr of Fairforrest Cr; surveyed in 1788 by William Wofford for David Brown and granted by Gov. Charles Montague (date not given); border: SE-Mayus (or May) and others vacant; and (2) 100 ac surveyed in 1787 by Zachariah Bullock and granted Gov. Thomas Pinckney to David Brown; on Mayus Br of Fairforrest Cr; border: NW-Col. Thompson, N-unknown, SE-McNuse, SW-David Brown, and NW-Brown. Witness Samuel Hays and Henry Emerson. Signed David Brown. Wit. oath Mar. 26, 1805 Henry Emerson to William Simpson. Rec. Mar. 26, 1805

p. 70-71 Feb. 15, 1805 John Foster for self and for Stephen Foster, Thomas Tinsley for self and heirs of Polley Pollard desc, and William Foster, all legatees of Thomas Foster desc (Spartanburgh) to Joel Hurt (same); for $150 sold 100 ac on waters of Fairforrest Cr; border: Spring branch where "said" Williams formerly lived, James Bagwell, Connell, Beaverdam Cr, and Ford's old line; part of 430 ac grant Gov. William Moulley (sic) to John Golightly. Witness Ism Foster and Reuben Daniel. Signed John Foster, Thomas Tinsley, and William Foster's marks. Wit. oath Mar. 26, 1805 Ism Foster to Jacob Utley. Rec. Mar. 27, 1805

p. 71-73 Feb. 25, 1792 John Golightly (Spartanburgh) to Joel Hurt (same); for 40£ SC money sold 200 ac on branches of Ford's Cr; part of grant Gov. William Moultrie to John Golightly. Witness Broadrick Mason and Frances Golightly. Signed John Golightly and Winefred's mark. Wit. oath Feb. 25, 1792 Broadrick Mason to Isham Harrison. Rec. Mar. 27, 1805

p. 73-74 Jan. 10, 1805 Matthew Lyle and wife Janet (Kershaw Dist) to John Crawford (Spartanburgh); for 5s sold 400 ac "devolved" to Matthew Lyle by father-in-law John Robertson; in Barkley Co (now Spartanburgh); on Cub Br of Tyger R; then bordering vacant land; now border: Daniel Timmons, Joel Traylor, Samuel Timmons, and vacant. Witness William Crawford and Ann Hory (or Hoy). Signed Matthew Lyle and Janet's mark. Wit. oath Mar. 28, 1805 William Crawford to Michl Miller. Rec. Mar. 28, 1805. Wit. oath (Kershaw Dist) for Janet's signature Mar. 18, 1805 Richard Drakeford

p. 74-75 Mar. 12, 1803 William Bonner (Spartanburgh) to Frances Robinson (Charleston, SC), factor; for $500 sold 500 ac; border: W-Timothy Phillips' grant Dec. 9, 1774 now Frances Robinson's land, N-North Carolina border, E-George Walker, and S-Robert Swan. Witness Samuel Chapman and E Pain. Signed W Bonner. Wit. oath Mar. 30, 1805 William Walker (sic) to John Rukman. Rec. Apr. 1, 1805

p. 75-76 Mar. 21, 1803 John Pipes (Spartanburgh) to Sarah Pipes (same); for $200 sold 200 ac on W side Sholey Cr. Witness Leonard Burnett and Addman Johnson. Signed John Pipes' mark. Wit. oath Oct. 24, 1803 Leonard Burnett to John Anderson. Rec. Apr. 1, 1805

p. 76-77 Apr. 5, 1803 Michael Barnett (Spartanburgh) to Matthew Patton (same); for $300 sold 91 ac on S fork Tygar R; border: James Isom, William Moore, and vacant; part of grant May 1, 1796 to Samuel Ford. Witness Zachariah Grace and Ruth Grace. Signed Michael Barnett. Wit. oath Mar. 11, 1805 Zachariah Grace to George Grace. Rec. Apr. 1, 1805. Dower renounced Jenny Barnett to George Grace Mar. 11, 1805

p. 77-78 Mar. 11, 1805 George Brewton (Spartanburgh) to Matthew

Patton (same); for $100 sold 40 ac on S fork Tygar R; border: Matthew Patton, Broadrick Mason, and Peter Bragg. Witness Zachariah Grace and John Brewton. Signed George Brewton. Wit. oath Mar. 11, 1805 John Brewton to George Grace. Rec. Apr. 1, 1805

p. 78-79 Nov. 6, 1804 Samuel Woodruff and wife Nancy (Spartanburgh) to John Smith (same); for $102 sold 18 ac on S side Two Mile Cr of Enoree R; border: James Whittuar and Ford; part of grant Oct. 6, 1786 Gov. William Moultrie to John Hendrix. Witness John Dean and John Lindsey. Signed Samuel Woodruff and Nancy's mark. Wit. oath Mar. 15, 1805 John Lindsey to Wm Hendrix. Rec. Apr. 1, 1805

p. 79-80 Oct. 18, 1803 John Smith (Spartanburgh) to William Patton (same); for $100 sold 120 ac on waters of Dutchman's Cr; border: Thomas Williams and Wm Wofford; part of 330 ac grant to John Smith. Witness John Vise and Aaron Smith. Signed John Smith. Wit. oath Jan. 7, 1805 John Vise to Wm Smith. Rec. Apr. 1, 1805. Dower renounced Mary Smith to Wm Smith Oct. 18, 1803

p. 80-81 Oct. 20, 1803 Thomas Williams (Spartanburgh) to William Patton (same); for $100 sold 100 ac on waters of Dutchman's Cr; border: William Smith;part of grant Nov. 7, 1785 to John Shands. Witness John Vise and Aaron Smith. Signed Thomas Williams. Wit. oath Jan. 7, 1805 John Vise to Wm Smith. Rec. Apr. 1, 1805

p. 81-82 Aug. 20, 1804 James Wofford (Spartanburgh) to William Patton (same); for $60 sold 57 ac on branch of Dutchman's Cr; part of grant Feb. 3, 1800 to James Wofford. Witness Levi Lancaster, Benjamin Bearden, and John Wofford. Signed James Wofford's mark. Wit. oath Jan. 7, 1805 Benjamin Bearden to Wm Smith. Rec. Apr. 1, 1805

p. 82-83 Oct. 17, 1804 Moses Proctor (Spartanburgh) to Arthur Crocker (same); for $100 sold 540 ac on Back Br of Buck Cr of Pacolate R; grant Oct. 6, 1788 States Office to William Dalton. Witness Charles Crocker and Sarah Crocker. Signed Moses Proctor's mark. Wit. oath Apr. 13, 1805 Charles Crocker to William Lancaster. Rec. Apr. 13, 1805

p. 83-84 Feb. 5, 1805 Stephen Thomason (Spartanburgh) to Alexander McKie (same); for $199 sold 165 ac on waters of Lawson's fork; border: Salley Thomason, Nathan Ward, Delelia Thomason, John Thomason; part of 1,000 ac grant May 7, 1887 (sic) to William Turner Thomason and allotted and numbered "7" to Stephen Thomason as William T Thomason's estate by Isham Harrison, William Smith, Aaron Foster, Reuben Daniel, and William esqs (sic) Commissioners of Spartanburgh Common Pleas Court to divide William T Thomason's estate to his heirs. Witness Abner Benson, Robert Benson, and Cyrus Seay. Signed Stephen Thomason. Wit. oath Apr. 24, 1805 Robert Benson to Abner Benson. Rec. Apr. 24, 1805

p. 84-85 Apr. 14, 1803 James Barnett (Spartanburgh) to Alexander McKie (same); for $390 sold 147 ac on Dougan's Br of Fairforrest Cr below shoal on Fairforrest Cr; border: waggon road, Thomas, "leaving a timber yard to the old saw mill seat", Christopher Buffington's old corner; plat attached shows border: McDowell's Mill on Fairforrest Cr, old mill pond, Neel, and saw mill. Witness Anthony Foster and Richard Barnett. Signed James Barnett. Wit. oath Feb. 18, 1804 Anthony Foster to Jacob Utley. Rec. Apr. 24, 1805

p. 85 Apr. 16, 1805 Arnold Thomason, son and heir of William Turner Thomason desc (Spartanburgh) to Alexander McKie (same); for $204 sold 204 ac on waters of Lawson's fork of Pacolate R; border:

William Thomason and Polley Thomason; part of 1,000 ac grant May 7, 1787 to William T Thomason and allotted to Arnold Thomason as his share of William T Thomason's estate by Isham Harrison, William Smith, Reuben Daniel, Anthony Foster, and William Wells esqs, Commissioners of Spartanburgh Court to divide William T Thomason's estate to his heirs. Witness Robert Benson and Abner Benson. Signed Arnold Thomason. Wit. oath Apr. 24, 1805 Robert Benson to Abner Benson. Rec. Apr. 24, 1805

p. 85-86 Dec. 25, 1804 Richard Thomason (Spartanburgh) to Alexander McKie and Obadiah Watson (same); for $55 sold 1 ac on a branch of Fairforrest Cr near Spartanburgh Court House; includes Tan yard on S side of branch that was formerly William Wells'. Witness Abner Benson and William Robertson. Signed Richard Thomson. Wit. oath Apr. 24, 1805 William Robertson to Abner Benson. Rec. Apr. 24, 1805

p. 86-87 Apr. 22, 1802 David Culberson (Spartanburgh) to John McElrath (same); for $40 sold 93 ac on both sides Piggeon Rust Cr of S fork Tygar R; grant Dec. 22, 1800. Witness James Kilgore and John Pearson. Signed Dd Culberson. Wit. oath Apr. 12, 1805 James Kilgore to Michl Miller. Rec. May 1, 1805

p. 87-88 Feb. 2, 1805 Armstead Shumate (Spartanburgh) to John McElrath (same); for (money not mentioned) sold a bay mare and colt, 3 feather beds and furniture, 2 cows and a heiffer, 18 pewter plates, 3 dishes, a bason, 3 earthen pans, 2 dishes, 2 tin pans, 2 sets otu(?) ware, a trunk, 4 pots, an oven, a spider, a stone jugg, a pair of drawing chains, a looking glass, 102 choping axes, 2 iron wedges, and other utensils belonging to Armstead Shumate. Witness Hugh Beley. Signed Armstead Shumate. Wit. oath Apr. 29, 1805 Hugh Beley to Michl Miller. Rec. May 1, 1805

p. 88-89 May 26, 1804 William Thomson (Spartanburgh) to William Ross Smith (same); for $20 sold ½ ac lot number 12 in Spartanburgh , SC; border: Main St. Witness Richard Thomson, Robert Benson, and Duglas J Puckett. Signed Wm Thomson. Wit. oath May 6, 1806 Richard Thomson to Abner Benson. Rec. May 6, 1805

p. 89-90 Dec. 3, 1804 John Eddington (Spartanburgh) to William Ross Smith (same); for $30 sold 2 feather beds, a "Straw under bed", a Cattarl under bed", 2 white sheats, 3 checked sheats, 2 dutch blankets, 2 handmade blankets, an oven and lid, a pot and "Koocks", a skillet, 3 pewter basons, 6 pewter plates, a dish, 10 pewter spoons, 8 dish pans, 16 cups, a sugar canister, 2 quart bottles, a big wheel, a pair of cotton cards, a bread tray, a water pail, a "Piggin", 2 plows, 2 "swingtestaus", 2 clevises, an open "wring", an ax, a hand saw, a "post add", a draw knife and shoe tools, a curey comb, 2 men's saddles, 2 bridles, 3 bells and collars, 2 meal bags, a "sack" bag, a trunk, men's and women's wearing appareal, 2 weeding hoes, traces, collars, harnes, etc. Witness Robert Benson. Signed John Eddington. Wit. oath May 6, 1805 Robert Benson to Abner Benson. Rec. May 6, 1805

p. 90-91 May 20, 1804 William Thomson (Spartanburgh) to Noah Wells (same); for $60 sold (ac not given); lot 7 in Spartanburgh, SC; border: Main St. Witness Richard Thomson, Robert Benson, and William Ross Smith. Signed Wm Thomson. Wit. oath May 6, 1805 William R Smith to Abner Benson. Rec. May 6, 1805

p. 91-92 Nov. 15, 1804 Samuel White (Spartanburgh) to Abner Benson (same); for $68.82 sold 4 cows and 3 calves marked with smooth cross in right ear and two slits in left ear, a heifer unmarked, 4 two year old stears with "same" mark, 2 one year old stears with "same" mark, 3 feather beds anf furniture and bed steads, 6 hogs with "same" mark as cattle, all pewter and dishware, and all household furniture. Witness Robert Benson. Signed Samuel White's mark. Wit. oath May 6, 1805 Robert Benson to Abner Benson. Rec. May 6, 1805

p. 92 Feb. 20, 1804 Moses Timmons (Spartanburgh) to Eaton Walker; for $330 sold a Negro wench Jane. Witness John Walker. Signed Moses Timmons. Wit. oath May 6, 1804 John Walker. Rec. May 6, 1805

p. 92-93 Mar. 27, 1805 Elias Earle (Greenville Dist) to James Campbell (Spartanburgh); for $500 sold 1,000 ac on N side of Pacolate R; border: SE or W-Pacolate R including Hammett's "botton", S & E-James Hammett, and N-vacant. Witness Anthony Foster and Henry Wells. Signed Elias Earle. Wit. oath May 6, 1805 Anthony Foster to to Isham Foster. Rec. May 6, 1805

p. 93-94 Jul. 8, 1803 Drury Allen (Spartanburgh) to William Paterson (same); for $188 sold 94 ac; part of two tracts: (1) grant to John Elliot and (2) grant to David Allen who sold to Drury Allen. Witness Wm Smith to Austin Wright. Signed Drury Allen. Wit. oath Jul. 18, 1803 Austin Wright to John Lipscom. Rec. May 6, 1805

p. 94-95 Oct. 3, 1804 Henry Brown (Spartanburgh) to Reuben Harrison (same); for $200 sold (1) 48 ac where Morduca Brown lives and (2) 40 ac where Henry Brown lives; on E side of Kelsoe's Cr; border: W-Smith and Harrison, SE-Golightly, and NE-Henry Brown. Witness Hancock Smith and James Smith jr. Signed Henry Brown. Wit. oath Mar. 21, 1805 Hancock Smith to William Lancaster. Rec. May 6, 1805. Dower renounced Susannah Brown to William Lancaster Apr. 27, 1805

p. 95-96 Feb. 19, 1805 Thomas McKnight and William McKnight (Spartanburgh) to William McKnight sr (same); for $530 sold 112 ac on N side of N Pacolate R; border: Lefferton French, John McKnight's land, and land sold by Thomas McKnight to John McKnight; part of grant to George Alexander. Witness Gabriel Benson to James Camp. Signed Thomas and William McKnight. Wit. oath Apr. 20, 1805 Gabriel Benson to Wm McDowell. Rec. May 6, 1805

p. 96-97 Feb. 22, 1805 Mark Swadley (Spartanburgh) to Moses Tapp; for $500 sold 75 ac on S side of Georgia Rd. Witness Robert Miller and Nathaniel Miller. Signed Mark Swadley and Elizabeth's mark. Wit. oath Mar. 20, 1805 Nathaniel Miller to Jacob Utley. Rec. May 6, 1805

p. 97-98 (not given), 1804 John Connell (Spartanburgh) to Lewis Huskey (same); for $200 sold 236 ac. Witness William Burton, George Thomason, and Allen Bobbett. Signed John Connèll and Francis' mark. Wit. oath Mar. 20, 1805 William Burton to Jacob Utley. Rec. May 6, 1805

p. 98-99 Apr. 2, 1804 John Walker (Spartanburgh) to Thomas Burton (same); John is to deliver to Thomas a Negro boy Phil on Dec. 25, 1804 for Thomas to sell for $100 "lent" money to John in case John doesn't pay $100 by then; Note: "balance" of sale money is to be delivered by John Walker. Witness Isham Foster. Signed John Walker. Wit. oath May 6, 1805 Isham Foster to Abner Benson. Rec. May 8, 1805

p. 99-100 May 9, 1805 William Willis (Spartanburgh) to son Thomas Willis; gives a note from John Pool for $100 with interest, and two notes on George Hatfield (1) for $25 and (2) for $10, and note on John Lee for 2£ 16s 4p, and note on Bartholamew Stovall for $11, and two notes on James Pool (1) for $12.50 and (2) for $2.75, and give 2 horses: a sorrel horse and bay colt, 25 hogs, a work oxen, a cow and heifer, and all plantation tools, and "wearking" gear and a saddle, an iron pot, 40 ac where William Willis lives, and another note on Thomas Gore for 10 barrels of corn, and a shotgun. Witness John Brock and Salley Lipscomb. Signed William Willis. Wit. oath May 9, 1805 John Brock to John Lipscomb. Rec. May 10, 1805

p. 100 May 9, 1805 William Willis (Spartanburgh) to Mourning Shores; gives a loom, a feather bed, a small iron pot, a cow and yearling; to Betsey Shores gives a Dutch oven, a cow and yearling and a feather bed; to Nancy Shores give a cow and yearling, 4 basons and 6 pewter plates, a saddle, and "flesh fork", 3 chairs, 3 "piggins", and rest of household furniture; above property to remain with son Thomas Willis until each of three girls becomes of age or marries and then it goes to the girls. Witness John Brock and Salley Lipscomb. Signed William Willis. Wit. oath May 9, 1805 John Brock to John Lipscomb. Rec. May 10, 1805

p. 100-102 Feb. 19, 1805 James Seay (Spartanburgh) to John Nicholas Cruce (same); for $60 sold 75 ac on E side of branch of Richland Cr; agreeable to conditional line between John Conner and William Wood; border: branch of Fawn Br and Edmond Clemont; land was sold by Spartanburgh sheriff to James Seay due to an "execution" as property of Joseph Venable at instance of James Boyd. Witness William Wyatt, Abner Benson, and Robert Benson. Signed James Seay. Wit. oath May 11, 1805 Abner Benson to Jacob Utley. Rec. May 15, 1805

p. 102-103 Oct. 16, 1804 Henry Brown (Spartanburgh) to Shands Golightly (same); for $159 sold 159 ac on waters of Kelsoe's Cr on N side Fairforrest Cr; border: NW-Dodd, SE-Moses Foster, S-Shands Golightly, and SW-Harrison and Smith. Witness David Golightly and John Thomas "the". Signed Henry Brown. Wit. oath Apr. 26, 1805 John Thomas "the" to Dal White. Rec. May 23, 1805

p. 103-104 Feb. 14, 1803 Robert Jamison (Spartanburgh) to John James (same); for $850 sold 230 ac on waters of N fork Tygar R; border: Timmons, road from Prince's old place to Timmons, and John James. Witness Isham Foster, William Foster, and Eaton Walker. Signed Robert Jamison. Wit. oath Apr. 5, 1804 Isham Foster and William Foster to John Collins. Rec. May 24, 1805

p. 104-105 Jan. 20, 1805 Thomas Timmons (Greenville Dist) to Jesse Traylor (Spartanburgh); for $310 sold 150 ac on N fork Tygar R; where Jesse Traylor lives; left by deed to "my father" Thomas Timmons by his father John Timmons. Witness Isham Foster and Mason Shumate. Signed Thomas Timmons' mark. Wit. oath May 24, 1805 Isham Foster to Abner Benson. Rec. May 24, 1805

p. 105-106 Dec. 13, 1804 James Ward (Spartanburgh) to Duglass Josephus Puckett (same); for $40 sold 40 ac on branches of Fairforrest Cr about a mile from Spartanburgh Court House; border: Richard Thomson, near a road to Greenville Court House, "said" Wells, James Benson, and Hays; part of 447 ac grant in 1799 to William Wells. Witness Jacob Utley, Solomon Ward, and William Smith. Signed James Ward's mark. Wit. oath May 25, 1805 Jacob Utley to Abner Benson. Rec. May 27, 1805

p. 106-107 Jan. 5, 1805 James Moss (Spartanburgh) to Richard Daniel (same); for $67.30 sold 37 ac on waters of Fairforrest Cr; part of lot "laid off" for Emily Harrison. Witness Isham Harrison and Reuben Daniel. Signed Jas Moss. Wit. oath May 31, 1805 Reuben Daniel to A Lancaster. Rec. Jun. 1, 1805. Dower renounced Emily Moss to Absalom Lancaster May 31, 1805

p. 107-108 Jan. 5, 1805 James Moss (Spartanburgh) to Reuben Daniel (same); for $132 sold 73 ac on waters of Fairforrest Cr; part of lot "laid off" for Emily Harrison. Witness Isham Harrison and Richard Daniel. Signed Jas Moss. Wit. oath Mar. 20, 1805 Richard Daniel to Jacob Utley. Rec. Jun. 1, 1805. Dower renounced Emily Moss to Absalom Lancaster May 31, 1805

p. 108-109 Dec. 26, 1801 William Crocker (Spartanburgh) to Anthony Bates (same); for $20 sold 30 ac on Richland Cr of Pacolate R; border: Arthur Crocker. Witness Benjamin Howard and Samuel Noblet. Signed William Crocker's mark. Wit. oath Dec. 27, 1802 Benjaman Howard to William Simpson. Rec. Jun. 3, 1805

p. 109-110 Jan. 28, 1805 Thomas Wells (Spartanburgh) to John Cantwell (same); for $200 sold 75 ac on waters of Fairforrest Cr; border: Bull (or Ball), Parkinson, Doggan, and Armsrong; where Robert Betteher formerly lived. Witness William Wells and Noah Wells. Signed Thomas Wells. Wit. oath Jan. 28, 1805 Noah Wells to Abner Benson. Rec. Jun. 3, 1805

p. 110-111 Mar. 17, 1802 Samuel Giddens (Spartanburgh) to William Roberds (same); for $60 sold 40 ac; border: near the Ridge path, S & N-David Golightly, E-rest of grant; part of grant to Henry White desc who sold to Wm Wells who sold to Johnson who sold to Brown who sold to Samuel Giddens. Witness William Sprinkle and Ameyden Sprinkle. Signed Samuel Giddens' mark. Wit. oath Jun. 1, 1805 William Sprinkle to Daniel White. Rec. Jun. 3, 1805

p. 111-112 Dec. 20, 1801 William Crocker (Spartanburgh) to Anthony Bates (same); for $150 sold 150 ac on Richland Cr of Pacolate R; border: Howard, ironwork, W-John Burk and Arthur Crocker, William Crocker's Spring Br, Maypole corner between William and Arthur Crocker, and William Poole's Hammerman. Witness Benjamin Howard and Samuel Nobelt. Signed William Crocker's mark. Wit. oath Dec. 27, 1802 Benjamin Howard to William Simpson. Rec. Jun. 3, 1805

p. 112-113 Feb. 9, 1804 William Crocker (Spartanburgh) to Anthony Bates (same); for $20 sold 40 ac on branch of Richland Cr of Pacolate R; border: Iron work and Big Br. Witness Charles Corcker and Benjamin Howard. Signed William Crocker's mark. Wit. oath Mar. 27, 1804 Benjamin Howard to William Simpson. Rec. Jun. 3, 1805

p. 113-114 Oct. 24, 1796 Augustin Clayton (Spartanburgh) to David Drummon (same); for 50£ sterling sold (ac not given) on branch of Middle Tygar R; border: SE-Elisha Hadden and SW-Jas Pinson; part of survey for James Alexander. Witness William Harris, Elisha Hadden, and Austin Grisham. Signed Agustin Clayton. Wit. oath Feb. 9, 1799 Elisha Hadden to Drury McDaniel. Rec. Jun. 3, 1805

p. 114-115 Apr. 21, 1804 John Sloan sr (Spartanburgh) to James Burns (same); for $200 sodl 150 ac on N side of Middle Tygar R; border: Hill's Ironworks and Elish Thompson; upper end of grant Apr. 29, 1786 to Elisha Thompson. Witness Willey S Brown and James Blassingame. Signed John Sloan. Wit. oath Apr. 21, 1804 Willey S Brown to Jas Burd. Rec. Jun. 10, 1805

p. 115-116 Dec. 18, 1804 Anthony Foster to William Blackstock; agree to dividing line of land; border: Miles, tree marked ‡WHY, and Barkler; NW of line is Anthony Foster's land and SE of line is William Blackstock's land. Witness James Wofford and Humphey Yarborough. Signed Anthony Foster's mark and Wm Blackstock.

Wit. oath Jun. 11, 1805 Humphey Yarborough to A Casey. Rec. Jun. 15, 1805

p. 116-117 Jun. 1, 1805 Thomas McCarten (Spartanburgh) to Benjamin King (same); for $300 sold 400 ac on N fork Thickety Cr of Broad R; grant in 1787 to James Clark. Witness Edward Smith and Samuel Dunaway. Signed Thomas McCartan. Wit. oath Jun. 1, 1805 Samuel Dunaway to John Lipscomb. Rec. Jun. 17, 1805

p. 117 Nov. 20, 1796 Ann Cook to Daniel White; for Daniel White's clearing and exonerating Ann Cook of any claim against her due to settlement of Henry White desc's estate, Ann Cook sells Daniel White her dower right to Henry White's estate. Witness Lettice Smith. Signed Ann Cook. Wit. oath Jun. 26, 1805 Lettice Lynch (sic) to Jacob Utley. Rec. Jun. 22, 1805

p. 117-118 Oct. (omitted), 1804 George Eslinger (Spartanburgh) to Thomas Moore (same); for $120 sold 230 ac on Morgan's Br of S Pacolate R and on N side of S Pacolate R; border: NE-Anderson, SE-McClure, S-Anderson, N-Morgan, and NW-Gilbert; grant Nov. 2, 1801 Gov. John Drayton to George Eslinger. Witness Nathaniel McCarrel, Henry Eslinger, and John Bas. Signed George Eslinger. Wit. oath Dec. 8, 1804 Nathaniel McCarrel to Wm McDowell. Rec. Jun. 25, 1805

p. 118-119 Jun. 6, 1805 John Sloan and "Rhoda John Sloan" (or Johnson); give a Negro Rachel; John Sloan got Negro by marriage contract; Rachel to remain property of John Sloan's wife during her lifetime, then Negro goes to Rhoda Sloan at death of Mrs John Sloan; Rhoda pays "one of her value and her increase" if any to Betsy Davis 1/3 to Salley Davis in 12 months "after division of their mother". Witness Samuel Evans. Signed John Sloan. Wit. oath Jun. 15, 1805 Samuel Evans to James L Burd. Rec. Jun. 28, 1805

p. 119-121 Jan. 9, 1805 William Humphrys jr and Alexander Davison (both of Spartanburgh) to Frances Robertson (Charleston, SC); a bond of $800; Condition: $400 to be paid--$200 by Jan. 9, 1806 and $200 Jan. 9, 1805; to secure payment they sell 300 ac on Sarratt's Cr; border: W-Frances Robertson, N-"the" boundary line, E-George Walker, and S-Robertson; deed void if debt paid. Witness John Rukman and Wm Walker. Signed William Humphrys' and Alexander Davison's marks. Wit. oath Jan. 9, 1805 Wm Walker to John Rukman. Rec. Jul. 5, 1805

p. 121-122 Nov. 13, 1801 James Fowler (Spartanburgh) to Samuel Fowler "elorn" (same); for $175 sold 190 ac on branch of Holslen's Cr on S side of S Pacolate R; part of two tracts (1) 100 ac sold by Robert Harper to James Fowler and (2) 90 ac bought from Matthew Harper. Witness Andrew Fergeson and Mark Fowler. Signed James Fowler. Wit. oath Jul. 4, 1805 Andrew Fergeson to James L Burd. Rec. Jul. 13, 1805

p. 122-123 Aug. 26, 1803 Hugh Means "futter" (Spartanburgh) to John Spears (same); for $190 sold 100 ac on Lawson's fork; border: William Turner. Witness Frund Spears and Lewis Turner. Signed Hugh Means. Wit. oath Jul. 13, 1805 Lewis Turner to Abner Benson. Rec. Jul. 15, 1805

p. 123-124 Apr. 5, 1805 John Spears (Spartanburgh) to James Barrett (same); for $120 sold 100 ac; border: William Turner; in possession and occupied by Henry Means; plat attached shows border Court House road. Witness Abner Benson and Thomas Tinsley. Signed John Spears. Wit. oath May 25, 1805 Abner Benson to Jacob Utley. Rec. Jul. 15, 1805

p. 124-125 Mar. 14, 1805 Thomas Bearden (Spartanburgh) to Benjamin

Nicholls (same); for $210 sold 100 ac on S side Dutchman's Cr; border: Robert Elder, Ephram Hill, and Benjamin Nicholls. Witness Benjamin Peak and James Lee. Signed Thomas Barden (sic). Wit. oath Jul. 15, 1805 Benjamin Beak (sic) to William Lancaster. Rec. Jul. 15, 1805

p. 125-126 Dec. 16, 1804 William Turner (Spartanburgh) to Lewis Turner (same); for $350 sold 392 ac; border: SE-Thomas Woods and unknown, NE & NW-John Golightly, and SW-William Turner. Witness Henry Turner and James Barrett. Signed William Turner. Wit. oath Mar. 27, 1805 Henry Turner to Ism Foster. Rec. Jul. 19, 1805

p. 126-128 Nov. 8, 1788 William Hamby, heir of William Hamby desc (Spartanburgh) to John Wells (same); for 20£ sterling sold 100 ac on N side Enoree R; border: Wells Spring Br; W part of 300 ac grant Aug. 19, 1774 Gov. William Bull to William Hamby desc then bordering S-Enoree R, N-Isaac Hamby, S-Wm Hamby, and others vacant. Witness James Wofford, Jonathan Dildin, and John Hamby. Signed William and Salley Hamby's marks. Wit. oath Mar. 3, 1801 James Wofford to Ism Foster. Rec. Jul. 22, 1805

p. 128-129 Jan. 30, 1801 William Childress and wife Tabitha (Spartanburgh) to John Wells (same); for $350 sold 250 ac on branches Forgeson's Cr of Tygar R; border: James Wofford; part of grant to Daniel Obare (or Obone). Witness James Wofford and Martin Cole. Signed William Childress and Tabitha's mark. Wit. oath Mar. 3, 1801 James Wofford to Ism Foster. Rec. Jul. 22, 1805

p. 129-130 Jul. 25, 1805 George Lamkin (Spartanburgh) to Isham Harrison (same); for $500 sold a Negro man Jess about 29 years old. Witness Anthony Foster and William Ross Smith. Signed Geo Lamkin. Wit. oath Jul. 26, 1805 William R Smith to Abner Benson. Rec. Jul. 26, 1805

p. 130-131 (not given), 1804 David Quals (Spartanburgh) to Moses Quals, son of Thomas Quals desc; for $100 sold 75 ac; border: John Edenton, Hankin Cr, Brock, and Pacolate R. Witness Abram Brock, John Quals, and Frances Brock. Signed David Quals. Wit. oath Mar. 18, 1805 Frances Brock to Geor Lamkin. Rec. Jul. 27, 1805

p. 131-133 Jan. 30, 1805 William Vincent (Spartanburgh) to Moses Vincent; for 20£ sold 180 ac in two adjoining tracts: (1) 100 ac on branch of Lawson's fork and (2) 80 ac bordering Daniel Walling; part of grant to Joseph Carver by Gov. William Moultrie and part of grant to John Kerkennel. Witness John Davis SM, William Davis, and Polly Davis. Signed William Vincent. Wit. oath Jul. 27, 1805 John Davis SM to Michael Miller. Rec. Jul. 29, 1805

p. 133-135 Apr. 29, 1805 William Thomson (Spartanburgh) to Richard Thomson (same); for $5,000 sold 355 ac on branches of Fairforrest Cr and Lawson's fork; where Spartanburgh Court House stands; part of two grants: (1) E end of 440 ac grant Jan. 21, 1785 to William Wood who sold to Thomas Williamson who sold to William Wells who sold to William Thomson and (2) part of grant Jan. 4, 1787 to Thomas Williamson who sold to William Wells; (1) and (2) adjoin; 7 ac excepted: 2 ac given to publick where Court House and Joal stand and about ten ½ ac lots sold by William Thomson to the following: two (2 and 4) to Wm Wells, #7 to Noah Wells, #8 & 9 to Duglass Puckett, #12 to William Smith, #13 to Abner Benson, #17 to Nancy McKie, #18 to Narcissa McKie, and #19 to Sally McKie; 7 ac is near center of 355 ac. Witness Leonard Adcock and Nancy Nickolls. Signed Wm Thomson. Wit. oath Aug. 5, 1805 Leonard Adcock to Abner Benson. Rec. Aug. 5, 1805

p. 135-136 Aug. 3, 1805 William Burton (Spartanburgh) to John Connell (same); for $25 sold 63.8 ac on waters of Kelsy Cr. Witness Wm Robinson. Signed William Burton. Wit. oath Aug. 3, 1805 Wm Robinson to Daniel White. Rec. Aug. 5, 1805

p. 136-137 Aug. 6, 1806 James Burns and Solomon Hill (Spartanburgh) to Samuel Shurbett (or Shurbutt) (same); for 40£ sterling sold 171 ac; border: Gideon Reynolds, Gideon Hanall, Thomas Price, and Mullinet; part of grant Dec. 19, 1795 South Carolina governor to (not given) on both sides Cain Cr of Tygar R. Witness William Rogers, Thomas Betterton, and D Puckett. Signed James Burnes and Solomon Hill. Wit. oath Aug. 5, 1805 Thomas Betterton to Geor Lamkin. Rec. Aug. 5, 1805

p. 137-138 Apr. 3, 1805 Thomas Brice (Spartanburgh) to Samuel Brice (same); for $50 sold 100 ac on waters of Tygar R; on NE side of 200 ac grant Apr. 6, 1767 to Thomas Penny who sold to Daniel Brice Apr. 29, 1771 and to Thomas Brice by inheritance from his father Daniel Brice; Thomas Brice lives on SE side of same tract; division line is agreed upon by Thomas and Samuel Brice. Witness James Templeton and Peggy Vernon. Signed Thomas Brice and Mary's mark. Wit. oath Aug. 12, 1805 James Templeton to Ism Foster. Rec. Aug. 12, 1805

p. 138-139 Dec. 1, 1801 John Brown (Spartanburgh) to Isaac Sinclair (same); for $150 sold 300 ac on N side Pacolate R; border: Joshua Pettet (100 ac), William Lands, James Poole, and John Gray. Witness William Poole and Beoen(?) Patterson. Signed John Brown. Wit. oath Jun. 19, 1802 William Poole to John Lipscomb. Rec. Aug. 14, 1805

p. 139-140 Aug. 15, 1805 Dower renounced Clarey Lancaster to Absalom Lancaster for deed William Lancaster to Zachariah McDaniel. Rec. Aug. 17, 1805

p. 140 Aug. 15, 1805 Dower renounced Mary Davison to Absalom Lancaster for deed Thomas Davison to William Lancaster. Rec. Aug. 17, 1805

p. 140-141 (May? ?), 1800 Robert Hail (Orangeburgh Dist) to Mathias Rush (Spartanburgh); for $257.12 sold 50 ac on branch of N Tygar R; border: Peter Gray, John Chapman, Robert Goodlett, and Robert Jamison. Witness John Rush and Jane Gibson. Signed Robert Hail. Wit. oath (Orangeburgh Dist) Dec. 31, 1800 John Rush to Wm Heally. Rec. Aug. 19, 1805

p. 141-143 Sept. 21, 1803 Mathias Rush (Spartanburgh) to Joseph Fleming (Richland Dist); for $200 sold (1) 50 ac sold Dec. 30, 1800 (sic) by Robert Hail to Mathias Rush; border: Peter Gray, John Chapman, Robert Goodlett, and Robert Jamison; and (2) 9 adjoining ac sold Aug. 26, 1799 John Chapman to Mathias Rush. Witness James S Guignard and Thomas Gardner. Signed Mathias Rush. Wit. oath (Richland Dist) May 16, 1803 James S Guignard to Claiborn Clifton. Rec. Aug. 19, 1805. Dower renounced Dec. 15, 1803 Ann Rush to William Lancaster

p. 143-144 Jul. 11, 1805 Joseph Fleming (Spartan Dist) to William Wells (same); for $500 sold (1) 50 Ac sold Dec. 30, 1800 (sic) by Robert Hail to Mathias Rush; border: Peter Gray, John Chapman, and Robert Goodlett, and Robert Jamison; and (2) 9 adjoining ac sold Aug. 26, 1799 John Chapman to Mathias Rush. Witness Andrew B Moore and Noah Wells. Signed Joseph Fleming. Wit. oath Aug. 19, 1805 Noah Wells to Abner Benson. Rec. Aug. 19, 1805

p. 144-145 Aug. 19, 1805 William Wells (Spartanburgh) to John Jones (same); for $400 sold (1) 50 ac border: Peter Gray, John Chapman, Robert Goodlett, Robert Jamison; sold Dec. 30, 1800 (sic) by Robert Hail to Mathias Rush who sold to Joseph Fleming who sold to William Wells; and (2) 9 ac adjoining (1) and sold Aug. 20, 1799 by John Chapman to Mathias Rush. Witness Noah Wells and Gideon Reynolds. Signed Wm Wells. Wit. oath Aug. 19, 1805 Noah Wells to Abner Benson. Rec. Aug. 19, 1805

p. 145-147 Feb. 23, 1805 Thomas Phillips (Spartanburgh) to Joseph Dill, John Dill, and Richard Robertson (same); for $324.66 sold 200 ac where Thomas Phillips lives on E of Indian boundary and both sides of Peoples Cr; grant Sept. 5, 1791 to James Martin; border: NW-William Rickman; Condition: deed void if Thomas pays Joseph, John, and Richard $162.66 in one year. Witness William Bostick, Abisha Camp, and John Phillips. Signed Thomas Phillips' mark. Wit. oath Aug. 20, 1805 John Phillips to A Camp. Rec. Aug. 21, 1805

p. 147-148 Feb. 23, 1805 Joseph Dill, John Dill, and Robert Robertson (Spartanburgh) to Thomas Phillips sr (same); for $134.66 sold 200 ac on E of Indian boundary and both sides of People's Cr; includes where Thomas Phillips lives; border: NW-Wm Rukman; grant Sept. 5, 1791 to James Martin. Witness William Bostick, Abisha Camp, and John Phillips. Signed Joseph Dill, John Dill's mark, and Richard Robertson. Wit. oath Aug. 17, 1805 John Phillips to John Lipscomb. Rec. Aug. 21, 1805

p. 148-149 Oct. 22, 1804 James Wofford (Spartanburgh) to Austin Clayton (same); for 100£ sterling sold 382 ac on Mill Cr of N Tygar R. Witness Thomas Tinsley and Thomas Foster. Signed James Wofford's mark. Wit. oath Mar. 26, 1805 Thomas Foster to Drury McDaniel. Rec. Aug. (blank), 1805

p. 149-150 Sept. 4, 1805 James Lee and wife Ellenoer Lee and Jane West (Spartanburgh) to Solomon West (same); power of attorney to get their share of estate of father James Trail desc from administrator James Trail (late of Maryland and now of Ky). Witness Aaron Smith and Mark Thornton. Signed James Lee, Ellenoer's mark, and Jane West's mark. Wit. oath Sept. 4, 1805 Mark Thornton to Wm Smith. Rec. Sept. 7, 1805

p. 150-151 Dec. 3, 1804 Isham Harrison, sheriff (Spartanburgh) to Elijah Barnett (same); for $35 sold 116 ac on branches of Ward's Cr and Dutchman's Cr of Tygar R; border: SW-Barnett, N & W-Stephens, SE-Thomas Moore, NE-James Hakey, and NW-unknown; grant Aug. 17, 1797 to Thomas Moore; sale due to writ from Spartanburgh Common Pleas Court Hill and Burns vs Thomas Moore. Witness Anthony Foster, William R Smith, and William Wells. Signed I Harrison SSD. Wit. oath May 18, 1805 William Wells to D White. Rec. Sept. 7, 1805

p. 151-152 Jan. 28, 1805 Edward Barnett (Spartanburgh) to William Wells (same); for $250 sold 100 ac on both sides Ford's Cr; border: John Pouy, John Bowling, Thomas Reid, William Tinsley, Brodrick Mayson, Henry Wells, and Benjamin Pipor; part of tract sold by Henry Wells to Travice Reece. Witness Noah Wells and John Cantrell. Signed Edward Barnett. Wit. oath Sept. 21, 1805 John Cantrell to Abner Benson. Rec. Sept. 21, 1805

p. 152-153 Feb. 15, 1805 Andrew Crawford (Chester Dist) to Thomas Cole (Spartanburgh); for $120 sold 193 ac on Beaverdam Cr of Thickety Cr; border: E-"Doctor old rights", N-William Dooper and William Thomson, and S-Thomas Coole; grant Jan. 1, 1798 to Samuel Armstrong who sold Dec. 4, 1804 to Andrew Crawford. Witness John Brown and Thomas Cole jr. Signed Andw Crawford. Wit. oath Sept. 20, 1805 Thomas Cole to A Camp. Rec. Sept. 23, 1805

p. 153-154 Sept. 23, 1801 Jonathan Cudd (Spartanburgh) to James Cudd (same); for $50 sold 100 ac on branch of Buck Cr; part of 650 ac grant Oct. 6, 1788 to William Dalton and eventually sold to Jonathan Cudd. Witness Zacheriah Arrowood and James Smith. Signed Jonathan Cudd's mark. Wit. oath Sept. 5, 1805 Zacheriah Arrowood to Jno Rukman. Rec. Sept. 30, 1805

p. 154-156 Oct. 2, 1805 Mellington Smith and wife Sarah (Spartanburgh) to Volentine Smith (same); for $300 sold 194 ac on Tyger R; border: John Walker, John Campbell, Samuel Cathcart, and Volentine Smith; part of grant Feb. 5, 1787 to John Campbell. Witness Reuben Wilson and Solomon Smith. Signed Mellington Smith's mark. Wit. oath Oct. 3, 1805 Solomon Smith to Wm Smith. Rec. Oct. 4, 1805

p. 156-157 Mar. 26, 1805 Henry Cannon, William Underwood, Thomas Wells, Enoch Jones Underwood, William Robinson, Abner Underwood, William McDaniel, and Polly Underwood, legates of Thomas Underwood desc to John Underwood; for $500 sold 292 ac in two tracts: (1) 92 ac granted Gov. William Moultrie to Thomas Underwood and (2) 200 ac part of tract sold by John Ford to Thomas Underwood; border: Benjamin Rainwater. Witness Benjamin Rainwater and Jacob Utley. Signed Henry Cannon, William Underwood, Thos Wells, Enoch S Underwood, Abner Underwood, William McDaniel, William Robinson, Thos Underwood, and Polly Underwood. Wit. oath Oct. 7, 1805 Jacob Utley to George Lamkin. Rec. Oct. 7, 1805

p. 157-158 Sept. 17, 1805 James Sharpe (Rutherford Co, NC) to Gowen Harris (Spartanburgh); for $50 sold a Negro woman Jenny. Witness William Harris jr and William Harris sr. Signed James Sharp. Wit. oath Oct. 2, 1805 William Harris jr to Drury McDaniel. Rec. Oct. 7, 1805

p. 158-159 Sept. 9, 1804 Samson Trammel (Spartan Dist) to James Gum (same); for $10 sold 100 ac on N side Pacolate R; border: Isaac Young and Sanders. Witness Richard Turner and John Brookshure. Signed Samson Trimmel. Wit. oath Mar. 28, 1805 John Brookshure to Ism Foster. Rec. Oct. 7, 1805

p. 159-161 Aug. 23, 1803 Robert Leggon (Spartan Dist) to Elijah Barnett (same); for $100 sold 70 ac on branch of Fairforrest Cr; border: David Golightly formerly called McClure's old line, Golightly, Smith and Connell, old Meeting House tract, Elijah Barnett, Spring formerly called School House Spring. Witness Christopher Golightly and Richard Willis. Signed Robert Legon. Wit. oath Jun. 7, 1804 Christopher Golightly to William Lancaster. Rec. Oct. 7, 1805

p. 161-162 Oct. 11, 1802 Henry Gibson (Spartanburgh) to Jarrett Patterson (same); for $300 sold (148 ac?); SW end of tract (100 ac?); border : corner marked ID and C; on Gocher's Cr and 48 ac bordering Ezekiel Howard and David Allen. Witness George Gibson and Ezekiel Swillivan. Signed Henry Gibson's mark. Wit. oath Oct. 11, 1803 George Gibson to John Lipscomb. Rec. Oct. 16, 1805. Dower renounced Nancy Gibson to John Lipscomb Nov. 2, 1804

p. 162-163 Oct. 3, 1803 Ephram Hill (Lexington Co, Ky) to Robin Rogers (Spartanburgh); power of attorney to sell two tracts: (1) 257 ac and (2) 319 ac. Witness Wm Prince, Enoch Prince, and Anthony Mayes. Signed Ephram Hill. Wit. oath Dec. 7, 1803 Anthony Mayes to Wm Smith. Rec. Oct. 10, 1805

p. 163-164 Apr. 16, 1805 Andrew McMullin (Taswell Co, Va) to Hugh McMullin (Spartanburgh); for $300 sold 394 ac on both sides of N Pacolate R; border: Renfrow, Foster, Cunningham, and

John McMullin; grant Oct. 31, 1793 to Andrew McMullin. Witness Jonathan Wall and Mary McDowell. Signed Andrew McMillin. Wit. oath Apr. 17, 1805 Mary McDowell to Wm McDowell. Rec. Oct. 12, 1805

p. 164-166 Sept. 7, 1805 Thomas McKnight and William McKnight jr (Spartanburgh) to William Wilkins (same); for $1,000 sold total of 300 ac: (1) 53 ac granted Dec. 13, 1784 Gov. William Moultrie to Thomas McKnight, (2) 15 ac granted Oct. 13, 1765 Gov. William Tryon (NC) to George Alexander including William McKnight jr's Spring, (3) 62 ac part of grant Jan. 1, 1787 Gov. William Moultrie to William French, (4) 170 ac part of two tracts granted Oct. 13, 1765 Gov. William Tryon (NC) to George Alexander; 300 ac borders: Camp, McWilliams, McMillin, and N Pacolate R. Witness James Camp and William Cantrell. Signed Thomas and William McKnight. Wit. oath Sept. 7, 1805 William Cantrell to Gab Benson. Rec. Oct. 12, 1805. Dower renounced Abigal McKnight, wife of Thomas, and Rhoda McKnight, wife of William, to Gabriel Benson Sept. 28, 1805

p. 166-167 May 4, 1803 Thomas Gore (Spartanburgh) to Isaac Wood (same); for $80 sold 100 ac on both sides Cartor's Cr; upper end of tract surveyed for James (blank) and cleared out for Thomas Gore; containing David Johnson's land; border: McDowell's Path. Witness William Barton and Zachariah Cudd. Signed Thos Gore. Wit. oath Oct. 1, 1805 William Barton to Gab Benson. Rec. Oct. 14, 1805

p. 167-169 Oct. 17, 1800 David Wardlaw, sheriff (Abbeville Dist) to Daniel Garvin (same), merchant; for $73 sold 650 ac on Island Cr of Pacolate R of Broad R in Craven Co, SC Mark's Parish, when surveyed; border: N-Thomas Loughton Smith esq, S-Roger P. H. Hatley esq, W-Capt Miller, and others vacant; sale due to writ from Charleston Common Pleas Court William Clarkson, surviving executor of Aaron Loocock desc, vs Joseph Hale Ramsey, administrator of Solur de Beaufort desc; sale in Abbeville, SC. Witness Frances Ross, Gilbert Smith, and William Little. Signed Dd Wardlaw Shff AD. Wit. oath (Abbeville Dist) Aug. 17, 1801 Frances Ross to Andrew Hamilton. Rec. Oct. 17, 1805

p. 169-171 May 3, 1805 John and Thomas Smith (Spartanburgh) to William Rakestraw (same); for $180 sold 150 ac where John and Thomas Smith live; on waters of Fairforrest Cr; border: James Fleming, Henry Smith, Col. Thomas Taylor; "note: original of this" bears date Jun. 21, 1785 recorded in Secretary's Grant book 4Z p. 1. Witness Robert Rakestraw and Henry Smith and Giles Smith. Signed John Smith and Thomas Smith's mark. Wit. oath Oct. 4, 1805 Henry Smith to D White. Rec. Oct. 18, 1805

p. 171 Aug. 19, 1805 Thomas Paden (Spartanburgh) to Samuel Brice (late of same); quit claim to (ac not given) on both sides of N fork Tygar R; grant to Samuel Brice; border: S-William McMahan and W-John Calwell. Witness William Brice and Andrew Paden. Signed Thomas Paden. Wit. oath Aug. 27, 1805 William Brice to Daniel McDaniel. Rec. Oct. 22, 1805

p. 171-173 Jul. 29, 1805 Samuel and Jennet Brice (Spartanburgh) to Andrew Cowen (same); for $150 sold 80 ac on both sides N fork of Tygar R; border: Middle Tyger R; half of tract left by will of Samuel Brice to his son Samuel Brice; grant Dec. 4, 1786 Gov. William Moultrie to Samuel Brice desc. Witness William Brice and Thomas Moore. Signed Samuel Brice and Jennet's mark. Wit. oath Aug. 27, 1805 William Brice to Drury McDaniel. Rec. Oct. 22, 1805

p. 173-175 Jul. 10, 1805 Ann Stewart and Margaret Stewart (Charleston, SC), spinsters, to William Smith ("St. George Parish Bacon bridge"); for $100 sold 1,000 ac on Beaverdam Cr of Fairforrest

Cr and waters of Hill Cr of Tyger R; grant Jul. 8, 1774 to Samuel Gravell and survey in 1774 (sic) by James Wood dept surv.; plat attached shows border: all vacant (survey Mar. 1773 by James Wood DS); copy of survey from Surveyor Gen. office (Columbia) Jan. 6, 1798 by F Bremar, Surv. Gen. Witness Robert McNeele and M McDonald. Signed Ann and M Stewart. Wit. oath (SC) Jul. 17, 1805 Robert McNeele to J Bentham. Rec. Oct. 23, 1805

p. 175-177 Dec. 12, 1804 James Henderson (Rutherford Co, NC) to Daniel Henderson (Pendleton Co); for $400 sold 200 ac on N fork Pacolate R; border: Robert Cates; part of grant in 1766 to Betsey Clark; now in possession of James Henderson. Witness Robert Henderson and Abigail Henderson. Signed James Henderson. Wit. oath Jul. 2, 1805 Robert Henderson to James L Burd. Rec. Nov. 5, 1805

p. 177-178 Mar. 29, 1805 Obadiah Watson (Spartanburgh) to Col. Elias Alexander and Stephen Camp (Rutherford Co, NC); for $700 sold two Negro men: Owens about 25 years old and Uoy(?) about 21 years old; Condition: Elias Alexander and Stephen Camp are security for Obediah Watson to William Casius, sheriff (Rutherford Co, NC) for $700 and if Obadiah pays debt with interest and cost, sale is void. Witness Abner Benson. Signed Obadiah Watson. Wit. oath Nov. 12, 1805 Abner Benson to Gab Benson. Rec. Nov. 12, 1805

p. 178-180 Mar. 23, 1805 Joel Hembree (Spartanburgh) to Drury Parham (same); for $280 sold 280 ac on N side Tygar R and on Cane Cr; part of 480 ac grant Oct. 3, 1785 Gov. William Moultrie to Joel Hembree. Witness James Bennett and John Hewett. Signed Joel Hembree. Wit. oath Mar. 22, 1805 James Bennett to Wm Smith. Rec. Nov. 11, 1805. Dower renounced Hannah Hembree to William Smith Nov. 2, 1805

p. 180-181 Jan. 12, 1805 Vincent Bennett (Spartanburgh) to Marke Gilbert (same); for 10£ sold 100 ac on Thompson's Cr of Pacolate R; border: S & N-vacant, W-Thomas Bennett, and E-Joseph Venable. Witness William Carter and Samuel Gilbert. Signed Vinct Bennett. Wit. oath Jan. 19, 1805 William Carter to Wm McDowell. Rec. Nov. 11, 1805

p. 181-182 (not given), 1805 Elizabeth Cooper, widow of David Cooper desc, to Daniel Amos (Spartanburgh); for $300 sold 217 ac on "main" Thickety Cr of Broad R; border: NE & NW-Champion, NE-Abm Markley, and others by survey for Daniel Burdeaux and Co; where Elizabeth Cooper lives. Witness William Amos and Sarah Amos. Signed Elizabeth Cooper's mark. Wit. oath Jul. 6, 1805 William Amos to A Camp. Rec. Nov. 11, 1805

p. 182-183 Jun. 6, 1805 Jesse Duglas (Rutherford Co, NC) to Thomas Crumley (Spartanburgh); for $200 sold 183 ac on branch of Obed's Cr of Pacolate R; border: McClure, Galt, Young, and McCarroll; grant to Isaac Anderson. Witness Gabriel Benson and Henry Morgan. Signed Jesse Duglas. Wit. oath Jun. 13, 1805 Henry Môrgan to Wm Kelso. Rec. Nov. 11, 1805

p. 183-185 Dec. 5, 1801 Isaac Anderson (Spartanburgh) to Jesse Duglas (same); for $163 sold 183 ac on branch of Obed's Cr of Pacolate R; border: N-John McCarroll, NE-John Young sr, S-William Anderson, and W-Locock; grant Jan. 2, 1797 Gov. Charles Pinckney to Isaac Anderson. Witness Thomas Crumley, William Bennett, and Henry Easlinger. Signed Isaac Anderson's mark. Wit. oath Jun. 13, 1805 Thomas Crumley to Wm Kelso. Rec. Nov. 11, 1805

p. 185-186 Mar. 21, 1805 Joshua Betterton (Spartanburgh) to Joseph Betterton (same); for $300 sold 200 ac on both sides of

Dutchman's Cr; border: N-"hill" Summers, W-Samuel Pruit, and E & S-Thomas Sarratt; part of grant to Thos Betterton sr. Witness Reuben S Sanders and Thomas V Nance. Signed Joshua Betterton's mark. Wit. oath Nov. 10, 1805 Reuben S Sanders to Gab Benson. Rec. Nov. 11, 1805

p. 186-187 Nov. 11, 1805 Edward Smith (Spartanburgh) to Wolman Smith (same); for $190 sold (ac not given); where Edward Smith lives in fork of Bullock's and Rock Fork Creeks. Witness Charles Smith and Collins Smith. Edward Smith. Wit. oath Nov. 11, 1805 Charles Smith to John Lipscomb. Rec. Nov. 11, 1805

p. 187-188 Sept. 14, 1805 John Cantrell (Spartanburgh) to James Turner (same); for $235 sold 125 ac on S side Pacolate R; border: on upper side of Solomon Abbett; part of 534 ac grant to William Dickson. Witness Henry Turner and Edward Turner. Signed John Cantrell. Wit. oath Nov. 12, 1805 (sic) Henry Turner to Gab Benson. Rec. Nov. 11, 1805. Dower renounced Sarah Cantrell to Gabriel Benson Nov. 12, 1805

p. 188-189 Nov. 6, 1805 Frances Robertson (Kershaw Dist) to John Wilson (Spartanburgh); for $300 sold 150 ac; border: E-William Humphreys and Alexander Davidson, S-Maj. McClarin, and W & S-Frances Robertson; SE corner of "large tract" granted Dec. 9, 1774 to Timothy Philips. Witness John Sarratt and Samuel Sarratt. Signed Frances Robertson. Wit. oath Nov. 11, 1805 John Sarratt to Jno Rukman. Rec. Nov. 11, 1805

p. 189-191 Nov. 8, 1805 Moses Foster (Spartanburgh) to John Kelso (same); for $45 sold 181 ac in two tracts on Henrus Br of Kelso's Cr of Fairforrest Cr "on or about the rich hill"; border: Golightly, Simpson, Thomas Tilley Buffington, Ash, Simpson, Thomas, and Wade; two tracts are (1) 37 ac and (2) 144 ac; grant Sept. 3, 1798 for 347 ac but older grant through middle removed 166 ac and leaves 37 ac on Henrus Br near narrow passage and 144 ac on Henrus Br and waters of Fairforrest Cr and on E side of rich hill. Witness Thomas Lancaster and Clary Lancaster. Signed Moses Foster. Wit. oath Nov. 8, 1805 Thomas Lancaster to William Lancaster. Rec. Nov. 12, 1805

p. 191-192 Feb. 8, 1805 Jeremiah Wofford (Spartanburgh) to Jacob Davis (same); for $65 sold 80 ac on waters of Suck Cr; border: James Shoeman, Moultrie's old line, and Zacheriah Blackwell. Witness Peter Gausnell and Joel Blackwell. Signed Jeremiah Wofford. Wit. oath Aug. 26, 1805 Peter Gausnell to A Camp. Rec. Nov. 12, 1805

p. 192-193 Jan. 19, 1804 Agnes Storey, widow of John Storey desc, (Spartanburgh) to Henry Storey; for $10 sold 6¼ ac; where Henry Storey's house stands; see plat by Richard Thomson. Witness Hugh Means and Henry Cunningham. Signed Agnes Storey. Wit. oath Nov. 12, 1805. Rec. Nov. 12, 1805

p. 193-194 Sept. 17, 1805 Isaac Wood (Spartanburgh) to Thomas Gilbert (same); for $90 sold 100 ac on both sides Cartain's Cr; border: McDowell's path; upper end of survey for James Huggains and cleared out for Thomas Gore; containing David Johnson's land. Witness Philip Johnson and William Gilbert. Signed Isaac Wood. Wit. oath Nov. 12, 1805 Philip Johnson to Wm Hendrix. Rec. Nov. 12, 1805

p. 194-195 Mar. 26, 1804 Gabriel Benson (Spartanburgh) to Daniel White (same); for $55 sold 90 ac E of conditional line made by Gabriel Benson and Daniel White; border: S-Henry Woody, N-Jonathan Watt, E-Daniel White; part of grant to James Dillingham who sold to James Young who sold to Gabriel Benson. Witness Frederick

Andrews, Edward Clemont,and Robert Kimble. Signed Gab Benson. Wit. oath Nov. 12, 1805 Edward Clemont and Robert Kimble to Jacob Utley. Rec. Nov. 12, 1805

p. 195-196 Mar. 10, 1803 Zachariah McDaniel (Spartanburgh) to William Lancaster (same); for $148 sold 74 ac; border: Davidson, Henry O'Neil, and Henry White desc. Witness William Fince and Daniel White. Signed Z McDaniel. Wit. oath Nov. 12, 1805 Daniel White to William Hendrix. Rec. Nov. 12, 1805. Dower renounced Mary McDaniel to Absalom Lancaster Aug. 13, 1805

p. 196-197 Oct. 8, 1805 John Arrendell (Spartanburgh) to William Williams (same); for $400 sold 200 ac; border: John Arrendell sr, Martain, and Walker's line now called Hester's line. Witness Daniel McCay and Lewis Stanley jr. Signed John Arrendell and Elizabeth's mark (who "firmly agrees" to deed Nov. 4, 1805). Wit. oath Nov. 8, 1805 Daniel McCay to A Camp. Rec. Nov. 12, 1805

p. 197-198 Feb. 14, 1805 Thomas Gore (Spartanburgh) to John Mathias (same); for $150 sold 212 ac on both sides Cartain's Cr; border: old road from Gore's old mill to Esq. McDowell and Isaac Wood. Witness Isaac Wood and John Mason. Signed Rhos Gore. Wit. oath Aug. 3, 1805 Isaac Wood to Wm McDowell. Rec. Nov. 12, 1805

p. 198-200 Aug. 1, 1805 Samuel Woodruff to William Shackelford (Spartanburgh); for $345 sold 50 ac; border: Enoree R, Joseph Woodruff, and James Allen; part of grant Aug. 19, 1774 Gov. William Bull to William Hambey. Witness James Allen and Joseph Woodruff. Signed Samuel Woodruff "th 3". Wit. oath Nov. 11, 1805 Joseph Woodruff to Wm Hendrix. Rec. Nov. 12, 1805. Dower renounced Polley Woodruff to Daniel Wright Oct. 12, 1805

p. 200-201 Oct. 7, 1805 Jarrett Patterson (Spartanburgh) to Willis Allen (same); for $300 sold (ac not given, maybe 149 ac) on waters of Goucher's Cr; SW side of 149 ac (sic) and corner marked "ƗD"; and 48 ac border: Ezekiel Howard and David Allen. Witness William Morris and Caty Lipscomb. Signed Jarrett Patterson. Wit. oath Oct. 7, 1805 William Morris to John Lipscomb. Rec. Nov. 12, 1805. Dower renounced Jean (or Jenney) Patterson to John Lipscomb Nov. 2, 1805

p. 201-202 Feb. 9, 1805 Dan Gilbert sr (Spartanburgh) to Samuel Gilbert (same); for 5£ sold 50 ac on Pacolet R; border: NE & W-Pacolet R, S-John Gilbert, agreeable with line run by John Gilbert and Mark Gilbert to divide John Gilbert's land. Witness Thomas Kimbol and Isaiah Gilbert. Signed Dan Gilbert. Wit. oath Feb. 16, 1805 Thomas Kimbol to Wm McDowell. Rec. Nov. 12, 1805

p. 202-204 Dec. 4, 1804 Samuel Omelvemey (Chester Dist) to Andrew Crawford (same); for $120 sold 193 ac on waters Beverdam Br of Thickety Cr; border: E-"Doctor old Rights", N-William Cooper and William Thomson, and S-Thomas Cole; survey Apr. 20, 1793 for Thomas Cole and granted Jan. 1, 1798 Gov. Charles Pickney to Samuel and William Omelvemey. Witness Robert Gibson and Samuel Gibson. Signed Samuel Omelvenney and William Omelvenney. Wit. oath (Chester Dist) Jan. 23, 1805 Robert Gibson to James Strong. Rec. Nov. 12, 1805.

p. 204-205 Jan. (blank), 1805 Elijah Barnett (Spartanburgh) to John Cantrell (same); for $50 sold 116 ac on waters Wards Cr of Dutchman's Cr; border: SW-Barnett, N & W-Stephens, SE-Thomas Moore, NE-James Hukey, and NW-unknown. Witness Wm Wells and John Connell. Signed Elijah Barnett. Wit. oath (blank space). Rec. Nov. 12, 1805

p. 205-206 Nov. 6, 1805 John Rukman (Spartanburgh) to Luck Lefever (same); for $187 sold 187 ac on waters Sarratt's Cr of Broad R. Witness William Cox and Robert McClaren. Signed John Rukman. Wit. oath Nov. 6, 1805 William Cox to John Rukman. Rec. Nov. 13, 1805

p. 206-207 Aug. 8, 1803 Elizabeth Tate (Spartanburgh) to son-in-law Abner McAfee (Lincoln Co, NC); for love and affection give "all goods and chattles": Hugh, Eudy, Bet, Willis, and their increase. Witness Arthur Graham "Jucatsonz", William Martan, and William Collins. Signed Elizabeth Tate's mark. Wit. oath Aug. 20, 1805 Elizabeth Tate to John Rukman. Rec. Nov. 13, 1805

p. 207-208 Oct. 19, 1800 James Carson (NC) to John Spence (Greenville Co); for $130 sold 250 ac on Middle fork Tygar R; border: SW-James Pearson and others vacant; grant Sept. 30, 1774 to Andrew Carson. Witness Henry Gray, Ann Gray, and Thomas Spence. Signed James Carson. Wit. oath Nov. 14, 1805 Thomas Spence to John Lipscomb. Rec. Nov. 13, 1805

p. 208-209 Nov. 1, 1800 John Blasingame (Union Dist) to Joseph Betterton (same); for 40£ sterling sold 200 ac on both sides Dutchman's Cr; border: Thomas Fletcher and Gowen; part of 451 ac grant Aug. 17, 1786 Gov. William Moultrie to Absalom Lancaster. Witness John Lancaster, Richd Bearden, and Joseph Venable. Signed Jno Blasingame. Wit. oath Apr. 15, 1805 Richd Bearden to Wm Smith. Rec. Nov. 13, 1805

p. 209-210 Jun. 22, 1805 Thomas Hadden (Spartanburgh) to James Hadden; for 20£ SC money sold 100 ac; border: Aaron Moore. Witness David Morton and David White. Signed Thomas Hadden. Wit. oath Nov. 13, 1805 David Morton to Drury McDaniel. Rec. Nov. 13, 1805

p. 210-212 Oct. 6, 1802 George Pool (Rutherford Co, NC) to Samuel Gilbert (Spartanburgh); for $25 sold 100 ac; border: Samuel Gilbert, Thomas Kimble, Lee's old line, Gore, and Macaboy; part of grant to Robert Lee. Witness Thomas Kimble, Dann Gilbert, and John Gilbert. Signed George Pool. Wit. oath Feb. 16, 1805 Thomas Kimble to Wm McDowell. Rec. Nov. 13, 1805

p. 212-213 Mar. 30, 1805 George Lamkin (Spartanburgh) to Joseph Wade (same); for $75 sold 60 ac on E side Pacolate R; border: Dart; part of 304 ac grant Feb. 5, 1787 to James Wyatt. Witness John Dunlap and Susannah Lamkey(?). Signed George Lamkin. Wit. oath Mar. 30, 1805 John Dunlap to Geor Lamkin. Rec. Nov. 13, 1805

p. 213-214 Sept. 8, 1801 James Smith (Spartanburgh) to Ralph Danger (or Danggar) (same); for 50£ sterling sold 479 ac on both sides Bridge Br of S Pacolate R; where James Smith lives; "run in two surveys T Henderson" 120 ac and 359 ac "run by" James Smith partly around Henderson's survey--refer to "Smith grant". Witness Wm Bishop, Joseph Carver, and Charles Smith. Signed James Smith. Wit. oath Jun. 24, 1805 Wm Bishop to James L Burd. Rec. Nov. 26, 1805

p. 214-215 Jun. 7, 1803 William Willis (Spartanburgh) to John Pool (same); for $200 sold 200 ac on Cherokee Cr on S side Pacolate R; where John Pool lives; border: James Scott, Bazel Lee, Solomon Abbett, and Richard Turner. Witness John Matthis, Thomas Gore, and William Pool. Signed William Wells. Wit. oath Dec. 2, 1805 William Pool to John Lipscomb. Rec. Dec. 2, 1805

p. 215-217 Nov. 15, 1805 Volentine Allen to William Austin; Volentine is bound to William for $400 for payment of $200; to secure payment, Volentine sold William: a gray mare and colt, 3 cows and calves, and all his other "movable" property with future issue and increase thereof; Condition: sale void if Volentine pays debt. Witness Peter Gray and Joseph Collins. Signed Volentine Allen. Wit. oath Dec. 2, 1805 Joseph Collins to Ism Foster. Rec. Dec. 2, 1805

p. 217-218 Nov. 15, 1805 Volentine Allen (Spartan Dist) to William Allen; bond of $200 "at rate of" 4s 8p per dollar; Condition: if Volentine pays $100 Sept. 1, 1806 and $100 Jan. 1, 1807, then bond is void. Witness Peter Gray and Joseph Collins. Signed Volentin Allen. Wit. oath Dec. 2, 1805 Joseph Collins to Ism Foster. Rec. Dec. 2, 1805

p. 218-219 Sept. 20, 1805 Amos Speace (Spartanburgh) to Leonard Cardan (same); for $500 sold 630 ac on both sides Pacolate R; border: Thomas Bennett, Wm Halley, Phillip Johnson, Luke Burnett, and Larken Carden. Witness Jordan Carden and Hetty (or Milley) Carden. Signed Amos Speace. Wit. oath Nov. 22, 1805 Jordan Carden to A Lancaster. Rec. Dec. 3, 1805

p. 219-220 Apr. 13, 1805 Elijah Barnett (Spartanburgh) to Joel Hurt (same); for $94.50 sold 3¼ (or 3/4) ac on Fairforrest and Beverdam Creeks; border: Joel Hurt. Witness Isham Harrison and Wm Robinson. Signed Elijah Barnett. Wit. oath Apr. 13, 1805 Isham Harrison to Geor Lamkin. Rec. Dec. 9, 1805

p. 220-221 Nov. 3, 1805 Frances Robertson (Kershaw Dist) to Cabred McCraw (Spartanburgh); for ($?) 300 sold 150 ac; border: North Carolina line and Alexander Davidson; NE corner of grant Dec. 9, 1774 to Timothy Phillips. Witness Daniel McClaren and James Owens. Signed Frances Robertson. Wit. oath Nov. 21, 1805 Daniel McClaren to John Rukman. Rec. Dec. 9, 1805

p. 221-222 Dec. 16, 1805 John Gowen (Spartanburgh) to daughter Elizabeth Woodson, wife of Obediah Woodson esq (Greenville Dist); for love and affection give two Negroes: Fany about 22 years old and Mary about 15 years old. Witness Isham Harrison and Obadh Watson. Signed Jon Gowen. Wit. oath Dec. 16, 1805 Isham Harrison to A Lancaster. Rec. Dec. 16, 1805

p. 222-223 Nov. 11, 1805 John Williams (Spartanburgh) to Sarah Rainwater, Susanna William, Rhode William, Silas Williams, Elizabeth Williams, John Wyatt, William Eleat, and William Tate "tho Cumewilliams" (same); for $150 sold a mare, 3 cattle, 31 hogs, a crib of corn, a fother stack, 2 feather beds anf furniture, a chest and trunk, and all household furniture and the "catchin" furniture. Witness John Golightly sr and John Duncan. Signed John William (sic). Wit. oath Dec. 20, 1805 John Duncan to Jacob Utley. Rec. Dec. 21, 1805

p. 223-224 Nov. 26, 1805 Ralph Danger (Spartanburgh) to his children: Nancy, Salley, Henry, and Nathaniel; for "good causes and valuable considerations" give all his estate real and personal "goods and chattles, household stuff and other of my substance". Witness Abner Benson and Robert Benson. Signed Ralph Danger's mark. Wit. oath Dec. 27, 1805 Robert Benson. Rec. Dec. 27, 1805

p. 224 Feb. 19, 1805 Thomas Brannon (Spartanburgh) to Reuben Seay; for $76 sold 72 ac on S side Lawson's fork; border: Reuben Seay, Edmond Bishop, Rolley Fauset, and Cyrus Seay; land was "a part" Thomas Brannon obtained as a legasee. Witness John Keenum, Edmond Bishop, and Thomas Burnett. Signed Thomas Brannon. Wit. oath Dec. 30, 1805 John Keenum to Jacob Utley. Rec. Dec. 30, 1805

p. 224-225 Jan. 8, 1802 Cyrus Seay (Spartanburgh) to Reuben Seay (same); for $209 sold 106 ac on Lawson's fork of Pacolate R; border: Cyrus Seay, Dudley Brannon, and David Hix; granted to Stephen Miller. Witness Gabriel Benson and Winkfield Bagwell. Signed Cyrus Seay. Wit. oath Feb. 16, 1802 Winkfield Bagwell to Ism Foster. Rec. Dec. 30, 1805

p. 225-226 Oct. 24, 1804 John Bobbett (Christian Co, Ky) to Reuben Seay; for $11 sold 10 ac; border: Thomas Brannon and Reuben Seay. Witness William Rollins and Thompson Fosett (or Fausett). Signed John Bobbett and Esther's mark. Wit. oath Dec. 30, 1805 William Rollins to Jacob Utley. Rec. Dec. 30, 1805

p. 226 Aug. 26, 1805 Amos Spuce (Spartanburgh) to Edmond Cooley (same); for $600 sold 500 ac on both sides of S and N Pacolate R; border: Johnson, William Barton, Luke Burnett, Leonard Cardin's fish trap, Thomas Burnett (or Bennett), Thomas Kimble, John Gilbert, and William Holley. Witness Jarvis (or Garvis) Gilbert and Sarah Gilbert. Signed Amos Spruce. Wit. oath Jan. 1, 1806 Jarvis Gilbert to James L Burd. Rec. Jan. 2, 1806

p. 226-229 Aug. 11, 1801 Matthew Patton (Union Dist) to Samuel Archibald (Spartanburgh); for 65£ sterling sold 130 ac on S fork McElevean's Cr; border: N-formerly Wm Patton sr's land and others vacant; granted to Matthew Patton. Witness Robert Donaldson, Robert Sterling, and James Riely (or Redly). Signed Matthew Patton. Wit. oath Oct. 12, 1802 Robert Sterling to William Simpson. Rec. Jan. 6, 1806

p. 229-230 Aug. 3, 1805 William Wells (Spartanburgh) to Dr Samuel Todd ("village of Laurence Dist"); for $130 sold ½ ac that is lot 2 in Spartanburgh, SC; border: Main St, S-Publick land, E-Publick St, N-William Thomson, and W-lot 3 belonging to Wm Thomson. Witness Abner Benson, Robert Belcher, and Noah Wells. Signed Wm Wells. Wit. oath Jan. 7, 1806 Robert Belcher to Abner Benson. Rec. Jan. 7, 1806. Dower renounced Martha Wells to Gabriel Benson Jan. 6, 1806

p. 230-231 Aug. 14, 1805 Duglas J Puckett (Spartan Dist) to Josiah Edenton; for love and affection give a white and red cow which Duglas delivered (hereby) to Josiah. Witness Robert Todd. Signed D. J. Puckett. Wit. oath Jan. 6, 1806 Robert Todd to A Lancaster. Rec. Jan. 6, 1806

p. 231-232 Jan. 3, 1806 Thomas Hill (Spartanburgh) to Henry Littlejohn (same); for $250 sold 75 ac on N side Pacolate R; border: Samuel Wilkins; E side of grant to Laurence Ready. Witness Peter Peterson and James Mitchell. Signed Thomas Hill's mark. Wit. oath Jan. 6, 1806 Peter Peterson to John Lipscomb. Rec. Jan. 8, 1806

p. 232-233 Oct. 5, 1797 John White (Spartanburgh) to Henry Walden (same); for 50£ sold 290 ac on branches of Fairforrest Cr of Tygar R; border: S-John Foster and Obediah Wingo, E-Richard Harrison and William Wood, N-William Wood and Thomas Hays sr, and W-Thomas Hays sr; grant Mar. 6, 1786 to Richard Prince. Witness John Foster and Samuel Ward jr. Signed John White. Wit. oath Jun. 16, 1798 Samuel Ward jr to I Harrison. Rec. Jan. 9, 1806

p. 233-235 Mar. 12, 1805 (North Carolina) William Tomlinson, John Ruddock, and Joshua Tomlinson, esecutors of estate of Samuel Tomlinson desc, and John English (Rowan Co, NC) to Jesse Crook (Spartanburgh); for 500£ NC money sold 300 ac on S fork Tygar R; granted to Thomas English; border: NW-Isaac Ross and vacant and others vacant. Witness James Crook jr, William Boornhamer, and

Matthew Burn. Signed Wm Tomlinson, Josiah Tomlinson, Jno Ruddack, and John English. Wit. oath Dec. 27, 1805 James Crook to Drury McDaniel. Rec. Jan. 11, 1806

p. 235-236 Oct. 1, 1805 John Brown (Spartanburgh) to William Willis (same); for $212 sold 148 ac on S side Pacolate R and on Lawson's fork; border: William Pool. Witness Solomon Garritson and Ezekiel Sellivan (or Swellivan). Signed John Brown's mark. Wit. oath Oct. 1, 1805 Solomon Garritson to John Lipscomb. Rec. Jan. 14, 1806

p. 236-238 Dec. 12, 1805 William Roberts (Spartanburgh) to David Golightly (same); for $150 sold 65½ ac in three tracts: (1) 25 ac on Bufflow Lick Cr; sold by Alexander Autry and Marthy Autry to William Roberts; (2) 10 ac sold by Mark Swadley and Elizabeth Swadley to William Roberts; adjoins (1) on Buffloe Lick Cr; and (3) 30½ ac; sold by Thomas Foster to William Roberts; border: mountain tract, S-Sprinkle, S & E-Lewis Brown, and S-David Golightly. Witness Christopher Johnson, John White, and Rolly Calvert. Signed Wm Roberds. Wit. oath Jan. 11, 1806 Christopher Johnson to William Lancaster. Rec. Jan. 18, 1806. Dower renounced Martha Roberds to William Lancaster Jan. 11, 1806

p. 238-240 Dec. 12, 1805 William Roberds (Spartanburgh) to David Golightly (same); for $37 sold (ac not given) in "several tracts"; two tracts were "lesst" by Michael Sprinkle desc and one was sold by William and Elexr Prince to Michael Sprinkle (122 ac); another was sold by John and Ann Gibbs to Michael Sprinkle (16 ac); and another was sold by Peter Elder to Robert Sprinkle (12 ac). Witness Christopher Johnson, John White, and Rolly Calvert. Signed William Roberds. Wit. oath Jan. 11, 1806 Christopher Johnson to William Lancaster. Rec. Jan. 18, 1806. Dower renounced Martha Roberds to William Lancaster Jan. 11, 1806

p. 240-241 Jan. 18, 1806 William Willis (Spartanburgh) to son Thomas Willis (same); for love and affection give 148 ac where John Brown lives on S side Pacolate R; border: Lawson's fork and William Pool. Witness Robert Benson and Duglas J Puckett. Signed William Willis. Wit. oath Jan. 23, 1806 Robert Benson to Abner Benson. Rec. Jan. 23, 1806

p. 241-243 Jul. 14, 1799 John Copeland, Maryann Trimbel, William Copeland, Elizabeth Copeland, and Charles Gilmore (all York Co) to John McKee (same); for $170 sold 350 ac on People's Cr; grant Dec. 8, 1774 Gov. William Bull to William Copeland sr. Witness John McFarlen and Abisha Camp. Signed Maryann Trembel, John Copeland, William Copeland. Wit. oath Jan. 20, 1806 John McFarlen to Jno Rukman. Rec. Jan. 23, 1806

p. 243-244 Dec. 1, 1803 James Nichols (Lancaster Dist) to Thomas Gaston (same), waggon maker; for $400 sold 250 ac on Nichols Cr of Tygar R; border: all vacant; grant Jan. 12, 1768 to James Nichols. Witness Richard Ussery and John Keziah. Signed James and Elizabeth Nichols' marks. Wit. oath (Lancaster Dist) Jan. 7, 1804 Richard Ussery to William Ward. Rec. Jan. 27, 1806

p. 244-246 Jan. 27, 1806 John Carr (or Kerr) (York Dist) to Lemuel Loftis (Spartanburgh); for $50 sold 200 ac on Middle fork Tygar R; "nearly joining above (sic) Jones land"; grant Oct. 26, 1767 Gov. William Tryon to John Kerr. Witness John Vaughn and Roger Berry. Signed John Carr. Wit. oath Jan. 27, 1806 John Vaughn to Abner Benson. Rec. Jan. 27, 1806. Dower renounced (York Dist) Jan. 27, 1806 Ruth Kerr to Robert McCaw.

p. 246-247 Nov. 15, 1804 (Greenville Dist) Adam Sloan (Greenville

Dist) to John Gowen (same); for $212.70 sold a Negro man man Isaac; Condition: sale void if Adam pays $212.70 with interest by Apr. 1, 1805. Witness Jos Blassingame, James Gowen, and John Sloan jr. Signed Adm Sloan. Wit. oath (Greenville Dist) Jan. 20, 1806 John Sloan jr to Reuben Barrett. Rec. Feb. 1, 1806. Mar. 26, 1805 John Gowen assigns above mortgage to Andrew B Moore. Witness Richard Berry. Signed Jon Gowen

p. 247-248 Nov. 9, 1805 William Wells (Spartanburgh) to Henry Wells (same); for $1,000 sold 1,000 ac on branch of Tygar R; border: NE & SE-John Ford and NW-Porcher and Lawson; includes cross-roads where Georgia and Blackstock's Roads pass each other; grant to John Parker who sold Nov. 3 & 4, 1773 to Joseph Kirkland who sold Feb. 12 & 13, 1789 to Minor Winn who sold Apr. 30, 1802 to William Wells. Witness Andrew B Moore, Noah Wells, and Henry Wells jr. Signed Wm Wells. Wit. oath Feb. 1, 1806 Noah Wells to Abner Benson. Rec. Feb. 1, 1806

p. 248-250 Oct. 1, 1805 Richard Willis (Spartanburgh) to Joseph Wade (same); for $200 sold 400 ac on Fairforrest Cr; border: Joseph Meas (or heas), Henry Foster, and Arthur Hutchings; formerly belonged to Joseph Wade. Witness John Willis and Cary Whitlock. Signed Richard Willis. Wit. oath Jan. 25, 1806 John Willis to John Brewton. Rec. Feb. 3, 1806. Dower renounced Drusilla Willis to William Smith Feb. 1, 1806

p. 250-251 Jan. 15, 1806 Joseph Wade (Spartanburgh) to Obediah Wingo (same); for $190 sold 190 ac on both sides Fairforrest Cr; border: Henry Foster, Gibbs' old corner, and Wade's old field. Witness James Smith and John White. Signed Joseph Wade. Wit. oath Feb. 3, 1806 John Wade to Ism Foster. Rec. Feb. 3, 1806. Dower renounced Mary Wade to Isham Foster Feb. 3, 1806

p. 251-252 Nov. 9, 1805 William Wells (Spartanburgh) to Jesse Wells (same); for $50 sold 50 ac on Fairforrest Cr; border: James Ward (where Nathan Ward formerly lived). Witness John Otts and Jehu Wells. Signed Wm Wells. Wit. oath Feb. 3, 1806 Jehu Wells to Abner Benson. Rec. Feb. 3, 1806

p. 252-253 Nov. 9, 1805 William Wells (Spartanburgh) to Jesse Wells (same); for $155 sold 100 ac on both sides Ford's Cr; border: John Posey, John Bouling, Thomas Price, William Tinsley, Brodrick Mayson, Henry Wells, and Benjamin Peper; part of tract sold by Henry Wells to Travis Reese. Witness Andrew B Moore, John Otts, and Jehu Wells. Signed Wm Wells. Wit. oath Feb. 3, 1806 Jehu Wells to Abner Benson. Rec. Feb. 3, 1806

p. 253-255 Feb. 20, 1802 William Wells, sheriff (Spartanburgh) to Jesse Wells; for $34 sold 100 ac on Lawson's fork of Pacolate R; border: Peter Lewis; part of grant to John Bennett; sale due to writ from Spartanburgh Common Pleas Court suit of Jesse Wells "indorsee" of William Wells; sale first Monday in Dec. 1801. Witness Jehu Wells and Noah Wells. Signed Wm Wells SSD. Wit. oath Feb. 3, 1806 Jehu Wells to Abner Benson. Rec. Feb. 3, 1806

p. 255-256 Nov. 11, 1805 William Wells (Spartanburgh) to Thomas Wells (same); for $400 sold 895 ac on Chinquepin Cr; border: NE-Golightly, NW-unknown, SW-William Wells, and SE-Lancaster. Witness Noah Wells, Jehu Wells, and Henry Wells. Signed Wm Wells. Wit. oath Feb. 3, 1806 Jehu Wells to A Lancaster. Rec. Feb. 3, 1806

p. 256-257 Dec. 10, 1805 John Gray (Spartanburgh) to William Burton (same); for $400 sold 500 ac on both sides Cain Cr of Tygar R; grant Jan. 5, 1789 to John Gray. Witness Richard Thomson and John Robinson. Signed John Gray. Wit. oath Feb. 3, 1806

Richard Thomson to Ism Foster. Rec. Feb. 3, 1806

p. 257-259 Mar. 27, 1805 James Smith (Spartanburgh) to James Fleming (same); for $140 sold 93 ac on Fairforrest Cr; grant to Hencock Smith (see Sec. book 4A p. 306). Witness John Smith and James Harrison. Signed James Smith. Wit. oath Feb. 3, 1806 John Smith to William Lancaster. Rec. Feb. 3, 1806. Dower renounced Jemimah Smith to William Lancaster Feb. 1, 1806

p. 259-260 Dec. 30, 1805 Reuben Harrison (Spartanburgh) to Henry Smith (same); for $200 sold 90 ac on Kelso's Cr. Witness Thomas James and Hancock Smith. Signed Reuben Harrison. Wit. oath Feb. 3, 1806 Hancock Smith to William Lancaster. Rec. Feb. 3, 1806

p. 260-261 Feb. 3, 1806 William and Elizabeth Biter (or Beter) (Spartanburgh) to Moses Biter (or Beter); for love and affection give "all our Negroes": Rachel, Ned, Lewis, Tim or Aleck, Gob, and John. Witness Ephram Moore, Rosamon Hammett, and Kesiah Biter. Signed William and Elizabeth Biter's marks. Wit. oath Feb. 3, 1806 Ephram Moore to Drury McDaniel. Rec. Feb. 4, 1806

p. 261-262 May 10, 1802 John McElrath (Spartanburgh) to Jacob Bridges (same); for $825 sold 250 ac on S side Middle fork Tygar R; part of 500 ac grant to Edward Blake and sold by Elizabeth Woodard to John McElrath. Witness James Gilleland, Charles Moore, and John Wm Keepers. Signed John McElrath. Wit. oath Jan. 27, 1806 James Gilleland to Michl Miller. Rec. Feb. 4, 1806

p. 262-263 Sept. 7, 1805 John Keenum (Spartan Dist) to Jeremiah Burnett (same); for $110 sold 267 ac on Little Shoaly Cr of Lawson's fork; part of grant "in the year 97" to Henry Mitchen and part of legacy obtained at death of William Brannon; border: Edmond Bishop. Witness Thomas Burnett, John Burnett sr, and John Burnett jr. Signed John Keenum and Mary Keenum. Wit. oath Feb. 5, 1806 John Burnett sr and John Burnett jr to Abner Benson. Rec. Feb. 5, 1806

p. 263-264 Sept. 9, 1805 James Martin (Lincoln Co, NC) to William Rukman (Spartanburgh); for 60£ sterling sold 640 ac on People's Cr; granted to George Taylor. Witness Michael Gaffney and Robert Love. Signed James Martin. Wit. oath Dec. 2, 1805 Michael Gaffney to Jno Rukman. Rec. Feb. 12, 1806

p. 264-265 Jan. 1, 1806 Isaac Tinsley (Clerk Co, Ky) to James Mason (Spartanburgh); for $300 sold 100 ac where James Mason lives; border: E-John Gidson, N & S-William Wells, and W-Buyick McPhearson. Witness Thomas Tinsley, Moses Foster, and Stephen Foster. Signed Isaac Tinsley. Wit. oath Jan. 1, 1806 Thomas Tinsley, Moses Foster, and Stephen Foster to Ism Foster. Rec. Feb. 12, 1806

p. 265-267 Feb. 6, 1806 Tobias Bright (Spartanburgh) to Benjamin Nichols; for $660 sold 250 ac on N side Tygar R and W of Thompson's Br; where Tobias Bright lives; border: James Bright and Arthur Former; sold in 1773 by Michael Prewett to Tobias Bright and granted May 5, 1772 to Michael Prewett then bordering: all vacant land and now bordering: Middleton Shurbet, John Meadows, Mr Hudgins, Arthur Forkner, Nathaniel Vice, Robert Rodgers, and James Bright. Witness Thomas Johnson, Saml Morrow, and Elisha West. Signed Tobias Bright. Wit. oath Feb. 6, 1806 Saml Morrow to Wm Smith. Feb. 12, 1806. Dower renounced Rachel Bright to William Smith Feb. 6, 1806

p. 267-268 Feb. 6, 1806 Benjamin Nichols (Spartanburgh) to Samuel Morrow (same); for $200 sold 70½ ac on S side Dutchman's Cr; border: W-Samuel Morrow, Ephram Hill, and Thomas Bearden, S-

Thomas Bearden, and N-Benjamin Peek (or Pick). Witness Thomas Johnson, Elisha West, and Tobias Bright. Signed Benjamin Nicholls. Wit. oath Feb. 6, 1806 Elisha West to Wm Smith. Rec. Feb. 12, 1806. Dower renounced Anna Nicholls to William Smith Feb. 6, 1806

p. 268-270 Aug. 23, 1805 Littleton Bagwell (Spartanburgh) to Richard Thomson (same); for $600 sold total of 436 ac: (1) 150 ac on both sides branch of Lawson's fork of Pacolate R; where Littleton Bagwell lives; except a small corner that runs into Dixon's old grant; (2) 100 ac joining (1); border: Dixon's old corner; part of 284 ac grant Mar. 6, 1786 to John Holcom; (3) 186 ac joining (1) and (2); grant Jan. 7, 1793 to George Parkison. Witness Abner Benson, William Robinson, and Robert Benson. Signed Littleton Bagwell's mark. Wit. oath Feb. 24, 1806 Robert Benson to Abner Benson. Rec. Feb. 25, 1806. Dower renounced Nelly Bagwell to John Lipscomb Nov. 12, 1805

p. 270-272 Aug. 23, 1805 Richard Thomson (Spartanburgh) to Littleton Bagwell (same); for $400 sold 254 ac on branches of Lawson's fork of Pacolate R; where Reuben Matthis lives; border: James Wofford, a waggon road to Hammet's ford on Pacolate R, road to Wyatt's mill; grant Jun. 4, 1804 to William H Thomson; if Littleton looses land to older grant, Richard pays him $400. Witness Abner Benson, Robert Benson, and William Robinson. Signed Richard Thomson. Wit. oath Feb. 24, 1806 Robert Benson to Abner Benson. Rec. Feb. 25, 1805

p. 272-273 Feb. 17, 1806 William Boiter to son Moses Boiter; for love and affection give all household and kitchen furniture, all beds, chests, tables, chairs, pots, and everything thereunto belonging, all horse, cattle, sheep, hogs, corn, fodder, plantation tools, and all other substance (movable). Witness Martha McDaniel, Polley McDaniel, and Susanna McDaniel. Signed William Boiter's mark. Wit. oath Feb. 20, 1806 Susanna McDaniel to Drury McDaniel. Rec. Feb. 26, 1806

p. 273-274 Oct. (blank), 1803 Isaac Tinsley (Spartanburgh) to Benjamin Rainwaters (same); for $30 sold 30 ac on S side Fairforrest Cr; border: Ford's Cr, Ford's old line, and John Williams' Spring Br. Witness John Barnett and Richard Daniel. Signed Isaac Tinsley. Wit. oath Oct. 24, 1803 John Barnett to A Casey. Rec. Mar. 3, 1806

p. 274-276 Mar. 26, 1805 Margaret Underwood, widow of Thomas Underwood desc, Henry Cannon, William Underwood, Thomas Wells, Thomas Underwood, William Whealer, Enoch Jones Underwood, John Underwood, William Robinson, William McDaniel, Abner Underwood, and Mary Underwood (all Spartanburgh) to Benjamin Rainwater (same); for $200 sold 100 ac on S side Fairforrest Cr; part of tract where "the" widow lives. Witness Jacob Utley and William Burton. Signed Abner Underwood, John Underwood, Wm Underwood, Enoch J Underwood, Thos Underwood, Mary Underwood, William Robinson, Thos Wells, Margaret Underwood's mark, Wm McDaniel, and Henry Cannon. Wit. oath Mar. 3, 1806 Jacob Utley to John Lipscomb. Rec. Mar. 3, 1806

p. 276-277 Jan. 30, 1805 Isaac Chapman (Spartanburgh) to William Lipscomb (same); for $400 sold 200 ac on Gocher's Cr; where Isaac Chapman lives; border: Brown and William Wilkins; "escepting the land W Lipscomb's line runs unto the land". Witness Solomon Garretson and Henry Littlejohn jr. Signed Isaac Chapman. Wit. oath Jan. 30, 1805 Solomon Garretson to John Lipscomb. Rec. Mar. 8, 1806. Dower renounced Nancy Chapman to John Lipscomb Feb. 8, 1805

p. 277-278 Nov. 10, 1804 James Martin (Lincoln Co, NC) to William

Lipscomb (Spartanburgh); for $200 sold 115 ac on McBee's Cr of Thickety Cr; grant Jul. 4, 1785 Gov. William Moultrie to Wm Cotter who sold Dec. 3, 1786 to James Martin. Witness Smith Lipscomb and Jesse Fondren. Signed James Martin. Wit. oath Apr. 30, 1805 Smith Lipscomb to John Lipscomb. Rec. Mar. 8, 1806

p. 278-279 Feb. 16, 1804 Charles Smith (Spartanburgh) to Hugh White (same); for $50 sold 45 ac on waters of Fairforrest Cr; border: William Lancaster. Witness Christopher Johnson and Aaron Smith. Signed Charles Smith. Wit. oath May 5, 1804 Christopher Johnson to William Lancaster. Rec. Mar. 16, 1806

p. 279-280 Oct. 13, 1805 Hugh Thomson (Spartanburgh) to John Haems (Pendleton Dist); for $500 sold 150 ac on waters of Bea Cr of N Pacolate R of Broad R; border: Alexr Copeland, James Blackwood, and John Pullham. Witness John Crownover and Joseph Crownover. Signed Hugh Thomson's mark. Wit. oath Nov. 6, 1805 John Crownover to John Lipscomb. Rec. Mar. 24, 1806. Dower renounced Sarah Thomson to Ism Foster Mar. 3, 1806

p. 280-281 Mar. 19, 1806 Laurence Rambo (Granby Dist, SC) to Meriman Burns (Spartanburgh); power of attorney to secure a Negro; Laurence owns Negro Elick and hired him to George Culberson for a year which is over Apr. 2, 1806; Laurence thinks George Culberson sold Elick and "is carried towards the western country"; Meriman is to search for Elick and return him to Laurence. Witness Martha McDaniel, Polley McDaniel, and Susanna McDaniel. Signed Laurence Rambo's mark. Wit. oath Mar. 19, 1806 Susanna McDaniel to Drury McDaniel. Rec. Mar. 24, 1806

p. 281-283 Sept. 14, 1801 James Smith (Spartanburgh) to James Ridings (same); for $170 sold 170 ac on S side of S Pacolate R; border: NW & SE-remainder of grant and NE-Henry Young; including land where Elijah Cornwel lives; part of grant North Carolina to Joseph White and regranted Feb. 3, 1775 Gov. William Bull to Matthew Harper sr; border: Capt. Harper and SW-Samuel Fowler. Witness Henry Young, Elijah Cornwell, and John Huth. Signed James Smith. Wit. oath May 13, 1802 Henry Young to Ism Foster. Rec. Mar. 27, 1806

p. 283-284 Nov. 28, 1804 Henry Young (Spartanburgh) to Sterling Ingram (Greenville Dist); for $300 sold (1) 200 ac on Pacolate R; grant Sept. 23, 1784 to John McClure; (2) 118 ac on waters of Pacolate R; grant Dec. 1, 1806 to Henry Young; and (3) 30 ac; part of grant Feb. 3, 1775 North Carolina to Joseph White; border: Alexander. Witness William Easley, James Blasingame, and B. B. Byan. Signed Henry Young. Wit. oath (Greenville Dist) Mar. 26, 1806 James Blasingame to Reuben Barrett. Rec. Mar. 27, 1806

p. 284-285 Sept. 13, 1805 William Smith (Charleston Dist) to Joshua Smith (Franklin Co, NC); for $1,500 sold 1,000 ac on waters of Beverdam Cr of Fairforrest Cr and waters of Tygar R; grant Jul. 8, 1774 to Saml Gravell. Witness Reddick Rutland and Joseph Lawy. Signed William Smith. Wit. oath Mar. 26, 1806 Reddick Rutland to Abner Benson. Rec. Mar. 27, 1806

p. 285-286 Feb. 15, 1805 Charles Hester (Spartanburgh) to John Hester; for $200 sold 200 ac on both sides Little Cherokee Cr; border: Stanlee (or Stanler) and Arndel. Witness Benjamin Camp and Bridges Arendell. Signed Charles Hester. Wit. oath Feb. 27, 1806 Benjamin Camp to John Rukman. Rec. Apr. 7, 1806

p. 286-287 Feb. 15, 1806 William Burton (Spartanburgh) to Benjamin Pettet (same); for ($?) 100 sold 112½ ac grated Jan. 5, 1789 to John Gray and sold Dec. 5, 1805 to William Burton. Witness Malachi Eskridge and Lawson Thomson. Signed William Burton. Wit.

oath Mar. 1, 1806 Lawson Thomson to William Lancaster. Rec. Apr. 7, 1806

p. 287-289 Sept. 19, 1804 William Hester (Spartan Dist) to Jesse Fondren (same); for $200 sold 200 ac on waters of Cherokee Cr; border: Lewis Stanley; part of grant to Charles Miles. Witness Joseph Dill and John Hester. Signed William Hester. Wit. oath Feb. 19, 1806 John Hester to John Rukman. Rec. Apr. 7, 1806

p. 289-290 Nov. 21, 1805 Jesse Fondren (Spartan Dist) to John Hester (same); for $300 sold 200 ac on waters of Cherokee Cr; border: Lewis Stanley; part of grant to Charles Miles. Witness Daniel McCay and Robert McClaren. Signed Jesse Fondren and Sarah's mark. Wit. oath Mar. 3, 1806 Daniel McCay to John Rukman. Rec. Apr. 7, 1806

p. 290-291 Feb. 7, 1806 Thomas Kevil (Laurence Co) to Robert McFadden (Spartanburgh); for 30£ sterling sold 250 ac on waters of Little Rock Cr of Enoree R; border: Cantrell, John Kitchens, Wilson Bryand, and Robert McFadden; part of 500 ac grant to Thomas Scotton who sold to Richard Hampton who sold to Stephen Cantrell who sold to Thomas Kevil. Witness Pennewell Wood and Charles McCain. Signed Thomas Kevel and Agga's mark. Wit. oath Feb. 15, 1806 Pennewell Wood to James Kilgore. Rec. Apr. 7, 1806

p. 291-292 Oct. 15, 1805 Stephen Raens (Spartanburgh) to Jonas Leonard; for $135 sold 174 ac on branches of Ben's Cr of Tygar R; grant to Samuel Busey. Witness William Brice and Noah Sincler. Signed Stephen Raens's mark. Wit. oath Oct. 19, 1805 William Brice to Denny Anderson. Rec. Apr. 7, 1806

p. 292-294 Feb. 11, 1806 Lee Clark (Spartanburgh) to Osbern West (same); for $300 sold 213 ac on waters of Cain Cr. Witness Aaron Smith and Willis Williford. Signed Lee Clark's mark. Wit. oath Feb. 11, 1806 Willis Williford to Wm Smith. Rec. Apr. 7, 1806. Dower renounced Mary Clark to William Smith Feb. 11, 1806

p. 294-295 Nov. 9, 1785 Samuel Shurbut (or Sharbutt) (Spartanburgh) to John Williams (same); for $200 sold 171 ac; border: Gideon Reynolds, Gideon Harrall, Thomas Ross, and Mullinn; part of grant Dec. 19, 1795 to (not given); on both sides Cain Cr of Tygar R. Witness Aaron Moore and Rebecah Rogers. Signed Sam Sharbutt. Wit. oath Apr. 5, 1806 Aaron Moore to Wm Smith. Rec. Apr. 7, 1806

p. 295-296 Nov. 22, 1805 John Williams (Spartanburgh) to Zacheriah Moore (same); for $300 sold 2½ ac; border: John Williams, John Rogers, and Zacheriah Moore; part of 194 ac grant (date not given) Gov. Arnoldus Vanderhorst to James Byrns, Solomon Hill, and George Gabbrath. Witness John Rogers and Aaron Moore. Signed John Williams. Wit. oath Feb. 8, 1806 Aaron Moore to Wm Smith. Rec. Apr. 7, 1806

p. 296-297 Sept. 2, 1805 Richard Venable (Spartanburgh) to Andrew Furgeson (same); for $300 sold 100 ac on S side of S Pacolate R; border: Mollow's Cr, Robert Harper, John Mguise (or Mguese), and Robert Black; part of grant Jun. 6, 1800 to John Gowen; except enough rail timber to keep up a fence now built on S side of Pacolate R. Witness John Spencer and Thomas Venable. Signed Richard Venable. Wit. oath Sept. 3, 1805 John Spencer to James L Burd. Rec. Apr. 7, 1806

p. 297-298 Dec. 5, 1805 John Sutherland (Pendleton Dist) to Thomas Harris (Spartanburgh); for $100 sold (ac not given) on waters of Sarratt's Cr; border: W-Thomas Harris and E-Robertson. Witness James Ellis, James Sutherland, and George Trout. Signed

John Sutherland. Wit. oath Dec. 24, 1805 James Ellis to John Rukman. Rec. Apr. 8, 1806

p. 298-300 Jan. 21, 1806 James McClure (Spartanburgh) to Lewis Branham (same); for $700 sold 708 ac on S Pacolate R and both sides Ellick's Cr; border: Robert Henderson, William Bishop (called Gilbert's), Sterling Ingram, Robert Venable, James Alexander, and land sold to John Miller; all of John Brody's grant May 7, 1774 of 600 ac resurveyed as 708 ac by Gabriel Benson esq and sold by John Brody to David Baty who sold to Thomas Todd who sold Oct. 6, 1791 to Edward Hooker (or Hocker) who sold Oct. 15, 1791 to James McClure. Witness Thomas Venable, Andrew Venable, and Samuel Venable. Signed James McClure. Wit. oath Feb. 22, 1806 Thomas Venable to Gab Benson. Rec. Apr. 8, 1806. Dower renounced Jocuy McClure to Gabriel Benson Feb. 22, 1806

p. 300-301 Nov. 23, 1805 Basel Compton (Spartanburgh) to James Hamm (same); for $215 sold 100 ac on waters of Dutchman's Cr; where Basel Compton lives; part of grant Aug. 11, 1774 to Jeremiah Fowler; border: James Moore. Witness Aaron Smith to Benjamin Peak. Signed Basel Compton. Wit. oath Nov. 23, 1805 Benjamin Peak to Wm Smith. Rec. Apr. 8, 1806. Dower renounced Sally Compton to William Smith Nov. 23, 1805

p. 301-302 Jan. 15, 1806 William Farris (Fairfield Dist) and Thomas Farris (Chester Dist) to Thomas Meaden (Spartanburgh); for $132.50 sold 100 ac on waters of Dutchman's Cr; border: Abraham Hembrie; part of 200 ac grant to James Farris desc and then to William and Thomas Farris, his surviving heirs (half of grant to each). Witness Samuel Smith, Thomas Reid, and Thomas Farris McFadden. Signed Wm Farris and Thos Farris. Wit. oath Apr. 5, 1806 Samuel Smith to Wm Smith. Rec. Apr. 8, 1806

p. 302-304 Dec. 12, 1805 John Foster (Lancaster Dist) to Henry Foster (Spartanburgh); for $800 sold 265 ac on both sides Fairforrest Cr; in three parts: (1) 180 ac part of grant Nov. 18, 1752 Gov. Nathaniel Reece (NC) to James Mitchell who sold to Henry Foster sr who sold part of John Foster; (2) 75 ac John Foster's half of 150 ac grant Aug. 25, 1769 Gov. William Bull to Henry Foster sr; and (3) 10 ac John Foster's half of 20 ac including Great Shoal on Fairforrest Cr (see sale from Henry Foster to John Foster and Henry Foster jr. Witness John O'Niell, Hannah Means, and Thomas Patton. Signed John Foster. Wit. oath Apr. 8, 1806 Thomas Patton to Wm Kelso. Rec. Apr. 8, 1806

p. 304-305 Jul. 25, 1805 Gilbert Boman (Spartanburgh) to Samuel Smith (same); for $260 sold 70 ac on N side of N Pacolate R; border: James Barry and Baylis Earle. Witness Hugh Ewing, Emy (or Emny) Boman, and Nancy Boman. Signed Gilbert Boman's mark. Wit. oath Mar. 6, 1806 Hugh Ewing to Wm Kelso. Rec. Apr. 8, 1806

p. 305-306 Nov. 6, 1805 William McKnight and James McKnight (Spartanburgh) to William Cantrell (same); for $900 sold (total ac not given); where William Cantrell lives; part of three grants: (1) and (2) both 200 ac (ea ?) granted in 1765 to George Alexander; (2) borders Laffordton French and John McKnight; on N side Pacolet R; and (3) 160 ac border: (1) and (2); grant May 12, 1794 to John McKnight; on N side of N fork Pacolet R. Witness John McCarrel and Nathan McCarrel. Signed William McKnight and James McKnight. Wit. oath Apr. 8, 1806 John McCarrel to Wm Kelso. Rec. Apr. 8, 1806

p. 306-307 Feb. 15, 1806 William Burton (Spartanburgh) to Samuel Smith (same); for $250 sold 275 ac on both sides Cain Cr of Tygar R; part of grant Jan. 5, 1787 to John Gray who sold Dec. 10, 1805 to William Burton. Witness Lawson Thomson, George Isom, and Leonard George. Signed William Burton. Wit. oath Apr. 5, 1806 Lawson Thomson to Wm Smith. Rec. Apr. 8, 1806

p. 307-308 Feb. 26, 1805 Edward Hoocker (Spartanburgh) to Benjamin Hoocker (same); for 100£ sold (ac not given) on S side Tygar R; border: Golden Tinsley, Joel Foster, Simson Newman, Willis Willeford, J. D. Hem, William Morton, James Samples, and Robert Harmour. Witness William Morton and Jesse Lamb. Signed Edward Hoocker. Wit. oath Jan. 4, 1806 William Morton to A Casey. Rec. Apr. 8, 1806

p. 308-309 Jan. 7, 1805 Simson and Susanna Newman (Spartanburgh) to John McForson (same); for $250 sold 200 ac on S of Tygar R; border: Benjamin Hoocker, Willis Willeford, Thomas Todd, and Robert Criswell; part of tract sold by William Clayton to Simpson Newman and part of tract sold by Edmond Clayton to Simson Newman. Witness Richard Fryer and Benjamin Hoocker. Signed Simson and Susanna Newman's marks. Wit. oath Jan. 29, 1806 Richard Fryer to A Casey. Rec. Apr. 8, 1806

p. 309-311 Nov. 1, 1803 Joseph Lannum (Spartanburgh), waggonmaker, to John Wofford (same); for $100 sold 240 ac on both sides of Dutchman's Cr; part of 440 ac grant to Sarah Elder. Witness Joseph Smith and Aaron Smith. Signed Joseph Lannum's mark. Wit. oath Jan. 28, 1806 Aaron Smith to Wm Smith. Rec. Apr. 9, 1806. Dower renounced Sally Lannum to William Smith Nov. 23, 1803

p. 311-312 Jan. 21, 1800 William Duncan (Spartanburgh) to David Duncan (same); for $194 sold 50 ac on branch of S Tygar R; border: Moses Boiter, waggon road from William Duncan's to the stoney hill. Witness Joseph Massey and James McDaniel. Signed William Duncan's mark. Wit. oath Jan. 21, 1800 Joseph Massey to Drury McDaniel. Rec. Apr. 9, 1806

p. 312-313 May 25, 1805 Robert Legon sr (Spartanburgh) to Richard Barnett (same); for $10 sold (ac not given); including spring formerly called School House Spring; border: Richard Barnett. Witness Robert Legon jr and John Barnett. Signed Robert Legon. Wit. oath Jan. 25, 1806 John Barnett to William Lancaster. Rec. Apr. 9, 1806

p. 313-314 Dec. 6, 1805 William Land (Spartanburgh) to Ephram Jackson (same); for $120 sold 100 ac on N side Pacolate R; border: Joshua Pettet and a new waggon road; where William Land lives. Witness Ezekiel Swellivan and George Hatford (or Hatfield). Signed William Land's mark. Wit. oath Feb. 8, 1806 Ezekiel Swellivan to John Lipscomb. Rec. Apr. 9, 1806. Dower renounced Rachal Land to John Lipscomb Feb. 18, 1806

p. 314-315 Nov. 25, 1805 Shands Golightly (Spartanburgh) to Daniel White (same); for $200 sold 37 3/4 ac on Fairforrest Cr; plat attached shows border: Alexander Mackey, McDaniel, White, Young, Martin, Golightly, and Foster. Witness Hancock Smith and John French (or linch). Signed Shands Golightly. Wit. oath Apr. 8, 1806 Hancock Smith to Wm Hendrix. Rec. Apr. 9, 1806

p. 315-316 Jan. 2, 1806 Isaac Tinsley (Ky) to George Wright (Spartanburgh); for $200 sold 60 ac on waters of Fairforrest Cr; border: E-John Hurt, S-Frances Mason, N-John Golightly, and W-Wm Baber. Witness Isham Foster, James Seay, and Moses Foster. Signed Isaac Tinsley. Wit. oath Apr. 8, 1806 James Seay to Jacob Utley. Rec. Apr. 12, 1806

p. 316 Apr. 8, 1806 John Golightly (Spartanburgh) to George Wright; for $200 sold 100 ac on branch of Ford's Cr; border: Joel

Hurt, George Wright, a waggon road, and William Baber. Witness James Seay and Abner Wingo. Signed John Golightly. Wit. oath Apr. 8, 1806 James Seay to Jo Utley. Rec. Apr. 12, 1806

p. 316-317 Apr. 19, 1800 John Sloan and wife Mary (Spartanburgh) to Sarah Davis; for love and affection give a Negro girl Charlot with half of issue in our lifetimes to Sarah and half to Alexander Sloan; Condition: Charlot remains with John and Mary Sloan during their lifetimes and sale is void if Mary Sloan has issue. Witness Wm Dannelly and Anna Dannelly. Signed John Sloan and Mary Sloan. Wit. oath Apr. 19, 1800 Wm Dannelly to Jas L Burd. Rec. Apr. 21, 1806

p. 317-318 Oct. 26, 1804 James Sims (Spartanburgh) to William Stone (same); for $600 sold 300 ac on N side of Enoree R; border: E-William Sims, NW-Horman Dildine, SW-Daniel McKee, and S-Enoree R; grant to John Potter and sold Apr. 19, 1803 by William Rouse to James Sims. Witness James Arnold and Daniel McKee. Signed James Sims. Wit. oath Oct. 26, 1804 Daniel McKee to Danl Wright. Rec. Apr. 21, 1806. Dower renounced Dolley Sims to Daniel Wright Oct. 27, 1804

p. 318-320 Oct. 26, 1804 Robert Sims (Spartanburgh) to William Stone sr (same); for $200 sold 100 ac on N side of Enoree R; border: E-Daniel McKie, NW-John Potter, and S-Enoree R; grant Sept. 1772 to William Sims who sold Mar. 21, 1778 to Robert Sims. Witness James Arnold and Danl McKie. Signed Robert Sims. Wit. oath Oct. 25, 1804 Danl McKie to Danl Wright. Rec. Apr. 21, 1806. Dower renounced Gressey Sims to Daniel Wright Oct. 26, 1804

p. 320-321 Nov. 10, 1801 Jeremiah Moore (Spartan Dist) to William Stone (same); for 24£ sterling sold 100 ac on N side of Deldine's Br; part of grant Jul. 10, 1769 Gov. Charles Gevell to William Sims. Witness Daniel McKie and Anderson Page. Signed Jeremiah Moore's mark. Wit. oath Feb. 22, 1802 Anderson Page to George Brewton. Rec. Apr. 21, 1806

p. 321-322 Dec. 12, 1805 James Sprinkle, William Sprinkle, Amma Sprinkle, and Milley Sprinkle (Spartanburgh) to Rev. David Golightly (same); for $225 sold 150 ac in three parts on Buffelo lick Cr on S side Fairforrest Cr: (1) sold by William and Elear Prince to Michael Sprinkle 122 ac; (2) 16 ac adjoining (1) sold by John and Ann Gibbs to Michael Sprinkle; and (3) 12 ac bordering (1) and (2) sold by Peter Elder to Robert Sprinkle; border: Peter Elder, formerly Michael Sprinkle desc's land now Robert Sprinkle's land, and William Robinson. Witness Christopher Johnson, Zacheriah McDaniel, John White, and Rolley Calvert. Signed James, William, Amma, and Milley Sprinkle's marks. Wit. oath Mar. 29, 1806 John White to William Lancaster. Rec. May 6, 1806

p. 322-324 Mar. 22, 1806 James Harrison (Spartanburgh) to James Fleming (same); for $30 sold 10 ac on S side of Fairforrest Cr; part of grant to Peter Smith who sold to James Harrison. Witness William Rakestraw and Polly (or Potty) Fleming. Signed James Harrison. Wit. oath Mar. 31, 1806 William Rakestraw to William Lancaster. Rec. May 10, 1806. Dower renounced Rhodah Harrison to William Lancaster Apr. 23, 1806

p. 324-325 Jan. 11, 1806 James Hickey (Spartanburgh) to Thomas Vaughn (same); for $180 sold 140 ac; where James Hickey lives; border: formerly Edward Bolens' land; sold by Christopher Orenduff to James Hickey; grant to Thomas Smith. Witness Christopher Johnson and Thomas Johnson. Signed James Hickey. Wit. oath Apr. 8, 1806 Christopher Johnson to A Casey. Rec. May 10, 1806. Dower renounced Elizabeth Hickey to William Lancaster Jan. 30, 1806

p. 325-326 Nov. 8, 1805 William Wells (Spartanburgh) to Obediah Watson (same), tavernkeeper; for $600 sold 2/3 ac; lot number 4 in Spartanburgh, SC; border: old jail and publick ground; plat attached shows border: Thomson's land or lot and publick land. Witness Thomas Goode, Stephen Thomason, and William R Smith. Signed Wm Wells. Wit. oath Apr. 2, 1806 Thomas Goode to A Lancaster. Rec. May 10, 1806

p. 326-327 Nov. 11, 1805 William Wells (Spartanburgh) to Obediah Watson (same); for $400 sold 540 ac on waters of Chenquepin Cr; border: old Court House tract; see plat in deed from Samuel Miller to William Wells. Witness George Walker, Thomas Goode, and Joseph Watson. Signed Wm Wells. Wit. oath Apr. 2, 1806 Thomas Goode to A Lancaster. Rec. May 10, 1806

p. 327-328 Jan. 29, 1806 James Sutherland (Pendleton Dist) to John Skinner (Spartanburgh); for $300 sold 100 ac on S side of Floyd's Br; border: part of grant for "the mas Sexton" (or Sixteon) and "babts hunton Shope". Witness Matthew Patton and James Arnold. Signed James Sutherland. Wit. oath Mar. 29, 1806 Matthew Patton to John Brewton. Rec. May 17, 1806

p. 328-329 Jan. 29, 1806 James Sutherland (Pendleton Dist) to Elias Corder (Spartanburgh); for $600 sold 200 ac on Floyd's Br; border: Enoch Floyd. Witness James Arnold and Matthew Patton. Signed James Sutherland. Wit. oath Mar. 29, 1806 Matthew Patton to John Brewton. Rec. May 17, 1806

p. 329-330 Apr. 2, 1806 Elias Corder (Spartanburgh) to Young Scott (same); for $300 sold 100 ac on Floyd's Br; border: Corder Spring Br, Georgia Road, Gravell, and Samuel Floyd; part of tract sold by James Sutherland to Elias Corder. Witness James Yates and Vincent Tapp. Signed Elias Corder. Wit. oath Apr. 5, 1806 James Yates to John Brewton. Rec. May 17, 1806

p. 330-332 May 15, 1805 Alexander McDowell (or McDowall) (Charleston, SC), merchant, to James Hadden (Spartanburgh); for $60 sold 80 ac on Ben's Cr of Tygar R; plat attached shows border: Tho Hadine and John Drummon; part of 300 ac grant Jun. 23, 1774 to John Phillips. Witness Wm Dunlap and John Barells (or Bardle). Signed Alex McDowall. Wit. oath Apr. 15, 1805 Wm Dunlap to R Criswell. Rec. May 24, 1806

p. 332 Mar. 7, 1800 Thomas Hendrix (Warren Co, Ky) to Richard Collins (same); power of attorney ; Thomas Hendrix is heir-at-law of John Hendrix desc (late of Spartanburgh); Richard is to get land or settle claim to 400 ac in Spartanburgh Co. Witness Edward Bradshaw. Signed Thomas Hendrix. Wit. oath (Warren Co, Ky) Mar. 7, 1800 Thomas Hendrix to William Chaplin, clerk of County Court. Rec. Jun. 2, 1800

p. 332-second p. 322 Feb. 6, 1804 (Warren Co, Ky) Rachal Hendrix (Warren Co, Ky) to Hudspath (sic) and William Milton, JP (same); dower renounced for 400 ac in Spartanburgh on Two Mile Cr of Enoree R; renouncement to Thomas Hendrix (now in Warren Co, Ky). Witness none. Signed David Hudspath and Wm Milton. Rec. Jun. 2, 1806. Feb. 2, 1804 (Warren Co, Ky) William Chaplin, clerk of county, certifys David Hudspath and Wm Milton were justices when they signed

p. (2nd) 322-333 Feb. 13, 1806 John Quarles (Spartanburgh) to Samuel Ward; for love and affection give a black cow and black yearling and deliver them to Samuel Ward. Witness Jesse Mathis, Abraham Brock, and Nathan Ward. Signed John Quarles. Wit. oath Jun. 2, 1806 Nathan Ward to Abner Benson. Rec. Jun. 4, 1806

p. 333-334 Jan. 13, 1806 James Lackey (Spartanburgh) to James Campbell (same); for $60 sold 100 ac; border: John Low, Pacolate R, and Dart's old line. Witness Levi Rainwater and James Cannon. Signed James Lackey's mark. Wit. oath Feb. 7, 1806 Levi Rainwater to John Lipscomb. Rec. Jun. 5, 1806. Dower renounced Loranah Lackey to John Lipscomb Feb. 7, 1806

p. 334-335 Jul. 26, 1802 Austin Clayton (Spartanburgh) to Austin Grisham (same); for $150 sold 200 ac on N side of Tygar R; border: Mucklerath, Evans, Collins, and old survey. Witness Robert Foster and James Foster. Signed Austin Clayton. Wit. oath Jun. 10, 1806 Robert Foster. Rec. Jun. 10, 1806

p. 335-336 Mar. 21, 1776 (sic) Spencer Bobo (Spartanburgh) to Calton Greer (same); for $500 sold 300 ac on both sides Cedar Shoal Cr of Enoree R; border: Nathan Langston, Wilks B Waters, J. F. Harmoning, Musgrove's Road, S-Samuel Farrow, E-M Chanlers and J. F. Harmoning, N-Spencer Bobo, and W-N Langston. Witness Nathan Langston and Richard Harrison. Signed Spencer Bobo. Wit. oath (Union Dist) May 10, 1805 Richard Harrison to David Floyd. Rec. Jun. 14, 1806

p. 336-338 Jan. 19, 1802 Spencer Bobo (Spartanburgh) to Mordica Chandler (same); for $300 sold 84 ac on Cedar Shoal Cr; border: J. F. Harmoning and William Stone. Witness James Newman and William Stone. Signed S Bobo. Wit. oath (Union Dist) May 10, 1805 James Newman to David Floyd. Rec. Jun. 14, 1806. Dower renounced Jane Bobo to J. F. Grimke sr (not dated)

p. 338-339 Feb. 13, 1806 Samuel Smith (Spartanburgh) to William Parmer (same); for $80 sold 40.2 ac on waters of Dutchman's Cr; part of grant to Ralph Smith. Witness Aaron Smith and Joseph Smith. Signed Saml Smith. Wit. oath Feb. 13, 1806 Joseph Smith to Wm Smith. Rec. Jun. 20, 1806. Dower renounced Sarah Smith to William Smith Feb. 13, 1806

p. 339-340 Oct. 10, 1805 William Lewis (Spartanburgh) to James Lewis (same); for $200 sold 190 ac on Lawson's fork of Pacolate R; border: William Gilmore, William Foster, and Capt. McDowell. Witness James McDowell and William Gilmore. Signed William Lewis. Wit. oath Jun. 13, 1806 William Gilmore to Gab Benson. Rec. Jun. 30, 1806

p. 340-342 Oct. 10, 1805 Austin Clayton (Spartanburgh), minister, to Andrew Berry (same); for $200 sold 50 ac on S side of N fork Tygar R; where William Clayton lives; border: Andrew Thomson, Andrew Berry, Samuel Miller, James Moore; part of 800 ac grant North Carolina governor to Robert Miller. Witness Gowen Harris to John Brewton. Signed Austin Clayton. Wit. oath May 10, 1806 John Brewton to Drury McDaniel. Rec. Jul. 2, 1806

p. 342-343 Jan. 18, 1805 Austin Clayton (Spartanburgh) to Andrew Berry (same); for $160 sold 40 ac on W side of N fork Tygar R; includes Austin Clayton's improvements; sold by Andrew Thomson to Robert Foster who sold to Austin Clayton. Witness John Berry and Charles M Berry. Signed Robert Foster's mark (sic). Wit. oath May 10, 1806 Charles M Berry to Drury McDaniel. Rec. Jul. 2, 1806

p. 343-344 Dec. 24, 1805 Benjamin Nichols (Spartanburgh) to Thomas Bearden (same); for $210 sold 100 ac on S side Dutchman's Cr; border: Robert Elder and Ephram Hill. Witness Isaac Bearden and James Bearden. Signed Benj Nicholls. Wit. oath Apr. 15, 1806 Isaac Bearden to Wm Smith. Rec. Jul. 3, 1806

p. 344 Jun. 26, 1806 Margaret McCarter (Spartanburgh) to son-in-law John Hurt (same); for love and affection give a Negro girl Nutty (or Mutty). Witness Alexander McCarter, Mary McCarter, and James Vernon. Signed Margaret McCarter's mark. Wit. oath Jun. 27, 1806 James Vernon, Alexander McCarter and Mary McCarter to Ism Foster. Rec. Jul. 7, 1806

p. 344-346 May 15, 1804 Isaac Linch desc (late of Spartanburgh), by Aaron Casey esq (same), to Samuel Farrow (same); for $300 sold 100 ac on S side Cedar Shoal Cr of Enoree R; border: NE-Cedar Shoal Cr, E, S & SW-Samuel Farrow, and N-William Stewart; where Isaac Linch lived; part of 450 ac grant Aug. 24, 1770 Gov. William Bull to Robert Howard; Isaac Linch's sill signed Apr. 1804 appointed Aaron Casey esq executor and Aaron sold the land; Isaac Linch died May 1804. Witness Landon Waters and Nancy Herendon. Signed A Casey esq. Wit. oath Jan. 23, 1805 Landon Waters to J Puckett. Rec. Jul. 7, 1806

p. 346-347 Sept. 17, 1804 James Adear (late of Spartanburgh) to John Puckett esq (Laurens Dist); for $250 sold 165 ac on N side Enoree R; border: Samuel Farrow and William Stewart; grant 150 ac (sic) May 15, 1771 to James Burton. Witness William Craig and William Jones. Signed James Adear sr. Wit. oath (Laurens Co) Sept. 17, 1804 William Craig to J. A. Elmore. Rec. Jul. 7, 1806

p. 347-348 Oct. 4, 1804 John Puckett esq (Laurence Dist) to Samuel Farrow (Spartanburgh); for $250 sold 165 ac on N side Enoree R; border: Samuel Farrow and William Stewart; grant 150 ac (sic) Mar. 15, 1771 to James Burton and sold by James Adiar to John Puckett. Witness J. A. Elmore and Edmond Puckett. Signed John Puckett. Wit. oath May 11, 1805 Edmond Puckett to J. A. Elmore. Rec. Jul. 7, 1806. Dower renounced (Laurence Dist) May 11, 1805 Ana Puckett to J. A. Elmore

p. 348-349 Jan. 29, 1796 James Head (Pendleton Co) to Samuel Farrow (Spartanburgh); for 50£ sterling sold 574 ac on waters of Enoree R; border: Philemon Waters on two sides and John Head and Hendrix on other two sides; grant Aug. 7, 1786 Gov. William Moultrie to James Head. Witness John Head and Landon (or Leonard) Farrow. Signed James Head. Wit. oath Nov. 21, 1799 John Head to Adm Cr Jones. Rec. Jul. 7, 1806. Dower renounced Stacy Head to John Thomas jr Feb. 7, 1797

p. 349-352 Feb. 27, 1790 Lazaras Benton (96 Dist) to James Adair (same); for 30£ sold 150 ac on N side Enoree R; border: NW-James Bouch; grant Mar. 15, 1771 Lt. Gov. Bull to James Benton desc and Lazaras Benton is James' brother "next in birth" to James and the land is now his by heirship. Witness Joshua Hill, Jesse Benton, and Elizah Benton. Signed Lazaras and Faney Benton's marks. Wit. oath (Laurence Co) May 14, 1790 Elijah Benton to James Montgomery. Rec. Jul. 7, 1806

p. 352-353 Jan. 23, 1806 Moses Guyton (Spartanburgh) to Thomas Littlejohn (same); for $425 sold 324 ac on N side Thickety Cr; border: John Dills, Collins, Thomas Collins, and mouth of Beaverdam Cr; part of grant in 1773 to William Hert. Witness Smith Lipscomb and William Weber. Signed Moses Guyton. Wit. oath Jun. 7, 1806 William Weber to John Lipscomb. Rec. Jul. 17, 1806. Dower renounced Tabitha Guyton to John Lipscomb Jun. 21, 1806

p. 353-2nd 353 Jul. 11, 1806 John Murrell (Spartanburgh) to his two children John (Murrell?) and Elizabeth Dabney, who now lives with my father-in-law Christopher Johnson (same); for love and affection give: a Negro woman Sukey, a Negro girl Vine and all futher increase equally divided between them when they come of age or marry; if either dies before coming of age or marrying, that part is to be divided equally by his other three sons: David, William, and James; also he gives Elizabeth a Negro girl Amy, Suckey's child; all are given to father-in-law for support of John and Elizabeth and father-in-law is to rear the children at his discression (?discretion). Witness David Johnson and Justice Reynolds. Signed Jno Murrell. Wit. oath Jul. 11, 1806 David Johnson to Abner Benson. Rec. Jul. 20, 1806

p. 2nd 353-354 May 10, 1803 Arthur Hutchins (Spartanburgh) to Christopher Johnson (same); for $500 sold 200 ac where Arthur lives; border: Charles Smith, Lown, and mountain tract. Witness Thomas Hutchins and Elijah Smith. Signed Arthur Hutchins' mark. Wit. oath May 10, 1803 Elijah Smith to William Lancaster. Rec. Jul. 20, 1806. Dower renounced Jean Hutchins to William Lancaster Jul. 9, 1803

p. 354-356 Jan. 23, 1805 John Lee (Spartanburgh) to Aaron Templeman; for $200 sold 150 ac on both sides Thickety Cr of Broad R; border: Rolley Horton and Betterton. Witness Jonathan Low sr and Nancy Templeman. Signed John Low. Wit. oath Jan. 2, 1806 Nancy Templeman to Geor Lamkin. Rec. Jul. 21, 1806

p. 356-358 Feb. 8, 1806 Elizabeth Bounetheau, Gabriel Manegault Bounetheau and Edward Weyman Bounetheau (Charleston, SC) to Moses Guyton (Spartanburgh); for $400 sold 1,250 ac at head branches Thickety Cr of Broad R; border: N & E-vacant, S-unknown, and W-William Hort esq; survey Sept. 12, 1772 by James Cook; plat attached indicates granted "order of Council today" to William Hort dated Feb. 2, 1772 by John Bremar dept Surv. Gen. and signed C. G. Montague, governor. Witness John Smelly and Robert Larrey. Signed Elizabeth, G. M. & E. W. Bounetheau. Wit. oath (Union Dist) Jul. 19, 1806 John Smelly to Wm McCulloch. Rec. Jul. 30, 1806

p. 358-359 Feb. 17, 1806 Richard Arndell and wife Polley to John Arndell (all Spartan Dist); for $400 SC money sold 120 ac on S side Cherokee Cr; border: Elizabeth Stanley, John Arndell, and William Morgan. Witness Charles Hester and Daniel McCay. Signed Richard Arndell and Polley's mark. Wit. oath Feb. 19, 1806 Daniel McCay to John Rukman. Rec. Aug. 4, 1806

p. 359-360 Feb. 26, 1806 Thomas Phillips (Spartanburgh) to William Philips (same); for $155 sold 200 ac on both sides People's Cr and E of Indian Boundary; where Thomas Phillips lives; border: NW-William Rukman; grant Sept. 5, 1791 to James Martin; Condition: sale void if Thomas pays William $155.25 by Nov. 20, 1806 agreeable to two notes Thomas gives (1) Richard Arnold $155.25 and (2) James Lockhart $50. Witness John Leek, John Philips, and Samuel Vist. Signed Thomas Phillips' mark. Wit. oath Jul. 22, 1806 Samuel Vist to John Lipscomb. Rec. Aug. 4, 1806

p. 360-361 Jan. 1, 1806 John Hester and wife Salley (Spartanburgh) to John Vineset (same); for $100 sold 100 ac on W side of Cherokee Cr of Broad R; border: Standley and Arndell. Witness Benjamin Camp and Bridges Arendell. Signed John Hester and Salley's mark. Wit. oath Feb. 27, 1806 Benjamin Camp to John Rukman. Rec. Aug. 4, 1806

p. 361-362 Jan. 1, 1806 John Hester ane wife Salley (Spartanburgh) to Edmond Green (same); for $102 sold 102 ac on W side Cherokee Cr of Broad R; border: John Vineset. Witness Bridges Arndell and Benjamin Camp. Signed John Hester and Salley's mark. Wit. oath Feb. 27, 1806 Benjamin Camp to John Rukman. Rec. Aug. 4, 1806

p. 362-364 Jul. 21, 1806 James Crow (Buncom Co, NC) to son Levi Crow (Spartanburgh); for $150 sold 124 ac on Jemmey's Cr on S side Tygar R; border: Robert Rogers, NW-John Caven, S-Widow Alexander, and E- Longshuse(?) Lamb, or NW-Robert Rogers, S-John Caven, E-Widow Alexander, and Longshuse Lamb. Witness John Crow, Middleton Shurbutt, and John Thornton. Signed James Crow. Wit. oath Aug. 4, 1806 John Thornton to William Hendrix. Rec. Aug. 4, 1806

p. 364-365 Feb. 21, 1804 James Kennedy (Charleston, SC) to Hugh McMillen (Spartanburgh); for $200 sold 271 ac on both sides of N Pacolate R; border: Cunningham, Renfro, and John McWilliams; part of 280 ac sold by Commissioners of Forfieted Estates to James Kennedy resurvey shows 271 ac; sold as property of Lord Charles G Montague. Witness George Dener and William McKnight. Signed James Kennedy. Wit. oath Aug. 4, 1806 William McKnight to Ism Foster. Rec. Aug. 4, 1806

p. 365-366 Apr. 26, 1806 Thomas Peden (Spartanburgh) to Andrew Paden (same); for $200 sold 100 ac on Furgeson's Cr of S Tygar R; border: E-Edward Bealley and others vacant. Witness David Templeton and John Paden. Signed Thomas Paden. Wit. oath Aug. 4, 1806 David Templeton to David Morton. Rec. Aug. 4, 1804

p. 366-367 Nov. 3, 1803 James Crow (Spartanburgh) to John Thornton; for $20 sold 17 ac on S side Tygar R; part of 160 ac grant Nov. 6, 1786 to Jacob Earnest who sold to John Doig who sold to James Crow. Witness Moses White, Asahu Buson, and John White. Signed James Crow. Wit. oath Feb. 3, 1806 John White to John Brewton. Rec. Aug. 4, 1806

p. 367-369 Oct. 26, 1775 Elijah Thompson, Joseph Thompson, Joseph Keller, William Motley, and John McCarter (all 96 Dist) to Margaret McCarter, Sarah Alexander, Mary Alexander, Elizabeth Alexander, Rebecah Alexander, and Esther McCarter, widow and children to late Alexr McCarter desc; a ond of 1,000£ SC money each; Condition: Alex McCarter desc died "in a state" and before death gave Elisha Thompson, his stepson, Joseph Thompson, his son-in-law and sons-in-law: Joseph Keller and William Motley or their wives, daughters of Alexr McCarter (except stepson Elijah Thompson) their shares of Alexr McCarter's estate and Alexr gave John McCarter, his son, all his share of estate; so the men are to be satisfied with what they have received and they aren't to "molest" widow and younger children. Witness John Prince, Thos (or Charles) Moore, and Andrew Berry. Signed Elisha Thompson, Joseph Thompson, Joseph Keller, William Motlow (sic), and John McCarter. Witness Wit. oath Jun. 22, 1806 Andrew Berry to Drury McDaniel. Rec. Aug. 4, 1806

p. 369-370 Apr. 24,1806 John Low sr (Spartanburgh) to John Tolleson (same); for $200 sold 340 ac on waters of Pacolet R; border: Buk's Br, Henry Adcock, Bremar, Richard Thomas, and James Lackey; where John Low lives; part of 446 ac grant Sept. 14, 1803 Gov. John B Richardson to John Low. Witness Muse Tolleson and William Murrey. Signed John Low. Wit. oath Jul. 24, 1806 Muse Tolleson to John Lipscomb. Rec. Aug. 4, 1806

p. 370-371 Mar. 6, 1806 John Lackey (Spartanburgh) to John Tolleson (same); for $83.83 and 5 mills sold 100 ac on waters of and on N side of Pacolate R; border: Buk's Br and Leonard Adcock; lower end of 300 ac grant to Frances Ballinger who sold to John Lackey. Witness Muse Tolleson and Willis Dean. Signed John Lackey's mark. Wit. oath Jul. 24, 1806 Muse Tolleson to John Lipscomb. Rec. Aug. 4, 1806

p. 371-372 Jul. 5, 1806 Samuel Fowler (Spartanburgh) to John Sloan (same); for $250 sold total of 245 ac: (1) 185 ac on S side of Holeston's Cr of S Pacolet R; except part taken by an older grant; grant Mar. 3, 1794 to Robert Harper who sold to James Fowler who sold to Samuel Fowler; and (2) 60 ac on N side of (1) between (1) and Holeston's Cr; part of grant Jun. 5, 1786 to Thomas Murrow who sold to Matthew Harper who sold to James Fowler who sold to Samuel Fowler. Witness Wm Donnelly and Edward Fowler. Signed Samuel Fowler's mark. Wit. oath Jul. 10, 1806 Wm Donnelly to James L Burd. Rec. Aug. 9, 1806

p. 372-373 Mar. 21, 1806 John Sloan jr (Greenville Dist) to Robert Sloan (Spartanburgh); for $150 sold 276 ac on Bird's Cr of Pacolet R; border: NE-James Alexander; grant Mar. 3, 1794 to Robert McDowell who sold to John Sloan jr. Witness Jane Shumate and William Brown. Signed John Sloan jr. Wit. oath Jul. 28, 1806 Jane Shumate to John Collins. Rec. Aug. 9, 1806

p. 373-374 Dec. 26, 1805 Robert Love (Spartanburgh) to Henry ONeill (same); for $710.06 sell (at Publick Vandew) a Negro Winch about 16 or 17 years old, 2 bedsteads and furniture, a bay mare about 10 years old, a cupboard anf furniture, 2 cows and calves, 12 chairs, a desk, 2 tables, a knife box, and a tract of 280 ac. Witness John Foster. Signed Robt Love. Wit. oath Aug. 10, 1806 John Foster to Abner Benson. Rec. Aug. 11, 1806

p. 374-375 Feb. 22, 1806 Thomas Philips sr (Spartanburgh) to John Philips (same); for $162.66 sold 200 ac on both sides People's Cr and E of Indian boundary; where "said" Philips lives; border: NW-Wm Ruckman; grant Sept. 5, 1791 to James Martin. Witness Edward Evans and James Bullock. Signed Thomas Philips' mark. Wit. oath Aug. 19, 1806 Edward Evans to William Simhson (sic). Rec. Aug. 20, 1806

p. 375-377 Dec. 6, 1806 John Rainwaters (Spartanburgh) to John Frederick Harmoning (same); for $500 sold (1) 500 ac on Cedar Shoal Cr of Enoree R; grant to Thomas Tod and sold to Tilman Bobo who sold to John Rainwaters; (2) 50 ac on S of Chesnut Br; grant to Spencer Bobo; on N of (1); (3) 300 ac adjoining "former" on W; grant to James Whitaker and at his death to William Whitaker (by primogenitor) and sold to John Rainwaters; except 100 ac that John Rainwaters sold to William Casey. Witness Burrell Bobo and David Neel. Signed John Rainwaters. Wit. oath Dec. 23, 1805 Burrell Bobo to Samuel Lancaster. Rec. Aug. 22, 1806. Dower renounced Susannah Rainwaters to Abner Benson Aug. 22, 1806

p. 377-378 Nov. 13, 1805 Daniel White (Spartanburgh) to John Smith (same); for $150 sold 80 ac on waters of Fairforrest Cr; border: Hugh White, William Roberts, mountain tract, and a road; formerly "settled" by Rhoaham Daffim (or Daffun) except 2 ac of an old field claimed by Thomas Smith; border: John White; part of grant South Carolina to Col. Henry White desc. Witness Henry Smith and Lydia Smith. Signed Daniel White. Wit. oath Feb. 3, 1806 Henry Smith to William Lancaster. Rec. Aug. 27, 1806. Dower renounced Susanna White to William Lancaster Feb. 3, 1806

p. 378-381 Jul. 21, 1806 Edmond Bishop sr (Spartanburgh) to Abner and Robert Benson (same); for $1,000 sold (1) 200 ac on S side Lawson's fork of Pacolate R; border: McMurdy and John Miller; grant Apr. 25, 1765 Gov. William Tryon (NC) to John Miller; (2) 100 ac on Rady Br (now called Standing Stone Br) on S side Lawson's fork of Pacolate R; part of 200 ac grant in 1767 to John Miller; adjoins (1) on W of Standing Stone Br; (1) and (2) sold Feb. 1, 1772 by John Miller to Edmond Bishop sr; except 20 ft square in center for graveyard. Witness Robert A Todd, Alexander McKie, and Obadiah Watson. Signed Edmond Bishop's mark. Wit. oath Sept. 1, 1806 Alexander McKie to Jacob Utley. Rec. Sept. 1, 1806

p. 381-382 May 29, 1806 William Garrett (Spartanburgh) to Mary Cantrell (same); for $100 sold 78 ac on both sides Cases Cr of Pacolate R; border: John Martain, a road, Laurence Bankston, and James Turner; grant Jan. 21, 1785 States Office to William Garrett. Witness James Turner and Henry Turner. Signed William Garrett's mark. Wit. oath Jul. 30, 1806 James Turner to Henry Turner. Rec. Sept. 1, 1806

p. 382-383 Aug. 18, 1806 Mary Burton sr (Spartanburgh), widow, to daughter Mary Bright; for love and affection give a Negro girl Suck about 6 years old. Witness Arthur Faulkner and Drury Burton. Signed Mary Burton. Wit. oath Aug. 30, 1806 Arthur Falkner to Wm Smith. Rec. Sept. 6, 1806

p. 383-384 Aug. 18, 1806 Mary Burton sr (Spartanburgh), widow, to Nancy Burton; for love and affection give a Negro boy Dick about 8 years old. Witness Arthur Faulkner and Drury Burton. Signed Mary Burton. Wit. oath Aug. 30, 1806 Arthur Faulkner to Wm Smith. Rec. Sept. 6, 1806

p. 384-385 Aug. 18, 1806 Mary Burton sr (Spartanburgh), widow, to son Drury Burton; for love and affection give a Negro boy Phill about 10 years old. Witness Arthur Faulkner and Nancy Burton. Signed Mary Burton. Wit. oath Aug. 30, 1806 Arthur Faulkner to Wm Smith. Rec. Sept. 6, 1806

p. 385-386 Aug. 26, 1806 Frances Powers (Spartanburgh) to William McElrath (same); for $150 sold 120 ac; border: Nichols and Widow Powers; part of grant of 538 ac Mar. 6, 1786 South Carolina governor to Frances Powers. Witness Reuben Traylor and James Powers. Signed Frances Powers. Wit. oath Aug. 26, 1806 Reuben Traylor to David Morton. Rec. Sept. 20, 1806

p. 386-387 Aug. 3, 1805 William Lewis (Spartanburgh) to Samuel Knight (same); for $340 sold 170 ac on branches Lawson's fork of Pacolate R; border: "the great road", William Foster, unknown, and David McDowell. Witness Robert McDowell, James Lewis, and John Knight. Signed William Lewis. Wit. oath Jun. 14, 1806 James Lewis to Gal Benson. Rec. Sept. 13, 1806

p. 387-388 Jan. 8, 1806 Robert McDowell (Spartanburgh) to William Lewis (same); for $120 sold 200 ac on waters of Lawson's fork; border: S-500 ac grant, W-Woody, N-McDowell, and W-Lewis; grant to Daniel White who sold to Robert McDowell. Witness J Lewis and John Lackey. Signed Robert McDowell. Wit. oath Sept. 13, 1806 J Lewis to Jacob Utley. Rec. Sept. 13, 1806

p. 388-389 Jun. 28, 1806 Larkin Rylle to Joshua Ingram; for (money not mentioned) sold 232 ac. Witness James Smith and Ann Thomas. Signed Larkin Rylle and William D Thomas, his attorney. Wit. oath (Greenville Dist) Jul. 4, 1806 James Smith to Elisha Green. Rec. Oct. 6, 1806

p. 389-390 Dec. 24, 1804 Ephram Jackson and wife Rebecah (Spartanburgh) to Charles Smith (same); for $140 sold 100 ac on S fork Thickety Cr and at mouth of Rocky fork of Thickety Cr; border: E & W-William Byers, W-Irby Dewberry, N-David Hopkins and vacant; half of 200 ac grant May 24, 1788 Gov. Thomas Pinckney to "said" Elijah Byce. Witness Edward Smith and Isham Sethmon. Signed Ephram Jackson's mark and Rebecah Jackson. Wit. oath Nov. 11, 1805 Edward Smith to John Lipscomb. Rec. Oct. 13, 1806

p. 390-391 Sept. 7, 1805 Richardson Vincent (Spartanburgh) to Charles Smith (same); for $197 sold 200 ac on E side of Pacolate R; border: Dart; grant Mar. 17, 1796 to Henry Wyatt. Witness Edward

Smith and Holeman Smith. Signed Richardson Vincent and Jessee Vincent. Wit. oath Nov. 11, 1805 Edward Smith to John Lipscomb. Rec. Oct. 13, 1806

p. 391-392 Oct. 10, 1805 James Campbell (Spartanburgh) to Charles Smith (same); for $250 sold 500 ac on E side of Pacolate R; border: Big Canebrake Br, Big Spring Br, Dart, and Hurrican Shoal; part of Dart's survey. Witness Ellis Cannon and James Cannon. Signed James Campbell. Wit. oath Feb. 6, 1806 Ellis Cannon to John Lipscomb. Rec. Oct. 13, 1806

p. 392-393 May 13, 1805 Edward Smith (Spartanburgh) to Charles Smith (same); for $100 sold 50 ac on both sides Rocky fork near its mouth; border: Jackson; sold by Ezekeal Sullivan to Edward Smith. Witness Wm Smith and Holeman Smith. Signed Edward Smith. Wit. oath Nov. 11, 1805 Holeman Smith to John Lipscomb. Rec. Oct. 13, 1806

p. 393-394 Dec. 7, 1805 Basel Scott (Spartanburgh) to John Broockshier (same); for 10£ sold (ac not given) on waters of Cherokee Cr; grant to Jasstead(?) Manley. Witness Mannering Broockshier and William Scott. Signed Basel Scott's mark. Wit. oath Oct. 14, 1806 William Scott to Ism Foster. Rec. Oct. 14, 1806

p. 394-395 Aug. 22, 1805 Richard Cantrell (Spartanburgh) to John Broockshier (same); for 5£ sold 100 ac on N side of Cherokee Cr; border: John Broockshier, Blackburn Quinn, and a new road; part of grant to James Steadman. Witness Henry Turner and John Stone. Signed Richard Cantrell. Wit. oath Oct. 14, 1806 Henry Turner to Ism Foster. Rec. Oct. 14, 1806

p. 395-397 Sept. 2, 1789 Henry Hamilton (Spartanburgh) to Levi Casey (Newberry Co); a bond of 1,000£ sterling; Condition: bond void if Henry deeds Levi: (1) (ac not given) on N side of Enoree R; where Henry lives; grant "by North Right" to Bartlett Brown and "S side by William Cannon"; and (2) 100 ac adjoining N side of (1); grant to Isaac Gray and sold by Joseph Burton to Henry Hamilton; deed to be made when Levi delivers a Negro man "equal as good" on Oct. 28, 1789. Witness Abram Gray, John Hellion, and Moses Casey. Signed Henry Hamilton. Wit. oath Nov. 7, 1806 Moses Casey to A Casey. Rec. Nov. 10, 1806

p. 397-398 May 23, 1806 John Cooper (Spartanburgh) to Anthony Login (same); for $100 sold 105 ac on branch of Roberson's Cr; border: near the meeting House and Thomson. Witness Lewis Stanley and Joseph Camp. Signed John Cooper. Wit. oath Nov. 3, 1806 Lewis Stanley to John Lipscomb. Rec. Nov. 10, 1806

p. 398-399 (blank), 1806 Charles Hester (Spartanburgh) to Abraham Hester (same); for $300 sold 300 ac on Cherokee Cr; border: Wm Fondren. Witness John Arndell and William Fondren. Signed Charles Hester. Wit. oath Sept. 27, 1806 John Arndell to John Lipscomb. Rec. Nov. 10, 1806

p. 399-400 Aug. 20, 1806 Willis Allen (Spartanburgh) to Thomas Reid (same); for $300 sold 148 ac(?); border: tree marked ED & C; part of a tract (of 148 ac?). Witness Robert Thomson and Young Allen. Signed Willis Allen's mark. Wit. oath Aug. 20, 1806 Young Allen to John Lipscomb. Rec. Nov. 10, 1806. Dower renounced (not dated) Salley Allen to John Lipscomb

p. 400-402 Aug. 6, 1803 David Bruton (Spartanburgh) to Isaac Bruton (same); for $100 sold 98 ac on Forgason's Cr of Tygar R; border: Williamson, David Burton's Spring Br and George Bruton; of which 75 ac is part of grant Oct. 23, 1756 to Robert Russell and 23 ac was granted Dec. 3, 1792 to David Burton (sic). Witness John Means, Enoch Bruton, and Phillip Bruton. Signed David Bruton. Wit. oath Nov. 8, 1806 Phillip Bruton to John Bruton. Rec. Nov. 10, 1806

p. 402 Feb. 15, 1806 David and Susannah Bruton to Samuel Tater, son of James Tater (Spartanburgh); for love and good will give a "firy" year old horse about 13 hands high, kind of chesnut sorrell with a blase face, and no brand. Witness James Leatherwood. Signed David Bruton and Susannah's mark. Wit. oath Nov. 7, 1806 James Leatherwood to William Hendrix. Rec. Nov. 10, 1806

p. 402-404 Aug. 6, 1803 David Bruton (Spartanburgh) to Enoch Bruton (same); for $100 sold 77 ac on Forgeson's Cr of Tygar R; border: James Bruton, Thomas Woodruff's Spring Br and George Bruton; part of grant Oct. 23, 1756 to Robert Russell and recorded Dec. 23, 1774 and other part (27 ac) grant Dec. 3, 1792 to David Bruton. Witness John Means, Isaac Bruton, and Phillip Bruton. Signed David Bruton. Wit. oath Nov. 8, 1806 Phillip Bruton to John Bruton. Rec. Nov. 10, 1806

p. 404-405 Aug. 6, 1803 David Bruton (Spartanburgh) to Philip Bruton (same); for $100 sold 92 ac on Forgason's Cr of Tygar R; border: head of David Bruton's Spring Br, Isaac Bruton, and Williamson; part of grant Oct. 23, 1756 to Robert Russell and recorded Dec. 23, 1774. Witness John Means, Enoch Bruton, and Isaac Bruton. Signed David Bruton. Wit. oath Nov. 8, 1806 Enoch Bruton to John Bruton. Rec. Nov. 10, 1806

p. 405-406 Sept. 1, 1806 John and Abner Hendrix (Jackson Co, Ga), Elijah Hendrix, Larken Hendrix, and William Bramblet (Spartanburgh) to friend William Hendrix (Spartanburgh); power of attorney to recover from William Lee desc's (grandfather--NC) executors their part of estate. Witness Robert Miller and James Otts. Signed John and Abner Hendrix's marks, Larken Hendrix, and Wm Bramblet. Wit. oath Sept. 1, 1806 James Otts to Drury McDaniel. Rec. Nov. 10, 1806

p. 406-407 Nov. 6, 1806 Amely Austell (Spartanburgh) to Amos Austell (same); for $500 sold 200 ac on Thickety Cr; border: N-William Lipscomb and W-Robert Wilkins; where Amely Austell lives; part of 400 ac grant to Thomas Nichols. Witness Joseph Austell and William Austell. Signed Miley(sic) Austell. Wit. oath Nov. 9, 1806 Joseph Austell to John Lipscomb. Rec. Nov. 10, 1806

p. 407-408 May 8, 1806 Peter Frye (Spartanburgh) to Drury Boman (same); for $300 sold 80 ac on N side of N Pacolate R; border: W & N-Peter Frye; part of tract sold in 1773 by Jabis Evans to Samuel Jackson and sold by James Jackson, Thomas Jackson, Robert White, Samuel Kelso, William Kelso, and Joanna Kelso, heirs of Samuel Jackson desc, to John Jackson who sold to Peter Frye. Witness Hugh Ewing, George Alexander, and Gilbert Bowman. Signed Peter Frye's mark. Wit. oath May 8, 1806 Hugh Ewing to Wm Kelso. Rec. Nov. 10, 1806

p. 408-410 Nov. 6, 1804 Moses Guyton (Spartanburgh) to Joab Heslin (same); for $720 sold 336 ac on Thickety Cr; border: Collins; part of grant Feb. 17, 1773 to William Hort. Witness John Guyton and Jonathan Heslin. Signed (none). Wit. oath Jun. 1, 1805 John Guyton to John Lipscomb. Rec. Nov. 11, 1806. Dower renounced Tabitha Guyton to John Lipscomb Jun. 21, 1806

p. 410-411 Apr. 14, 1806 Robert Stacey (Spartanburgh) to William Brock (same); for $250 sold 187 ac border: John Lipscomb; part of a tract. Witness William Hudson and John Brock. Signed

Robert Stacey. Wit. oath Apr. 4, 1806 William Hudson to John Lipscomb. Rec. Nov. 11, 1806. Dower renounced Salley Stacey to John Lipscomb Jun. 21, 1806

p. 411-413 Apr. 14, 1806 Robert Stacey (Spartanburgh) to William Brock (same); for $13 sold 13 ac. Witness William Hudson and John Brock. Signed Robert Stacey. Wit. oath Apr. 14, 1806 William Hudson to John Lipscomb. Rec. Nov. 11, 1806. Dower renounced Salley Stacey to John Lipscomb Jun. 21, 1806

p. 413-414 (blank), 1893 John Storey (Spartanburgh) to John Huckeby (same); for $190 sold 180 ac; border: James Betterton and David Prewet; grant Jul. 1, 1793 by Wm Marshall esq to (not given). Witness Burrell Bobo, Alexander Prewett, and William Martin. Signed John Storey's mark. Wit. oath Dec. 19, 1803 Alexander Prewett to Wm Smith. Rec. Nov. 11, 1806. Dower renounced Elizabeth Storey to William Smith Mar. 20, 1804

p. 414-415 Mar. 7, 1806 William Shed (or Shead) (Spartanburgh) to Andrew Ray (same); for $50 sold 50 ac; part of grant Oct. 23, 1784 States Office to William Shed. Witness John Cantrell and William Garrott. Signed William Sheed. Wit. oath Nov. 11, 1806 William Garrott to Leonard Adcock. Rec. Nov. 11, 1806

p. 415-416 Feb. 7, 1806 William Shead (Spartanburgh) to Andrew Ray (same); for $325 sold 260 ac on Case's Cr of Pacolate R and "for complements" add a piece of land William Shead bought from Amos Speare; border: William Shead; on both sides Case's Cr. Witness James Turner and John Bankston. Signed William Shead. Wit. oath Nov. 11, 1806 James Turner to Leonard Adcock. Rec. Nov. 11, 1806

p. 416-417 Jan. 12, 1802 Blackburn Quin to John Stone; for $155 sold 360 ac on waters of Cherokee Cr. Witness William Stone and Leonard Murry. Signed Blackburn Quin. Wit. oath Oct. 13, 1802 William Stone to William Simpson. Rec. Nov. 11, 1806

p. 417-418 May 3, 1806 John Dobney (Spartanburgh) to Nancy Saunders (same); for $50 sold 100 ac on branch of Thickety Cr of Broad R; border: Samuel Dunnaway and Brown. Witness John Brock and Patrick Saunders. Signed John Dobey's mark. Wit. oath Aug. 2, 1806 Patrick Saunders to John Lipscomb. Rec. Nov. 11, 1806

p. 418-419 Nov. 8, 1805 David White (Spartanburgh) to John Andrews (same); for 26£ sold 100 ac E of old Indian Boundary on Richland Cr; grant Oct. 2, 1786 Gov. William Moultrie to Richard Sparks and sold by Abraham Andrews to David White; except part taken by David White's grant. Witness Robert Kimble and John Hasley. Signed David White's mark. Wit. oath Nov. 1, 1806 John Hasley to Ism Foster. Rec. Nov. 11, 1806

p. 419-421 May 10, 1806 William Millican (Spartanburgh) to James Berry (same); for $200 sold 100 ac on N side of N Pacolate R; where James Berry lives; border: Tate's old line, a ditch cut near the river, Robert Tate, Thomas Millican, and below ford between William Millican and Thomas Millican; part of grant to Robert Tate and sold by John Tate, his heir, to Robert Tate who sold to John McKnight Jan. 13, 1785 who sold to James Millican Jan. 6, 1794. Witness Thomas Millican, Jesse Deshawon, and Isaac Dishawon. Signed Wm Millican. Wit. oath Oct. 6, 1806 Jesse Deshawon to Wm Kelso. Rec. Nov. 11, 1806

p. 421-422 Sept. 13, 1805 William Morris sr (Spartanburgh) to John Doby (same); for $40 sold 100 ac on branch of Thickety Cr of Broad R; border: Samuel Dunnaway and Brown. Witness Richard Morris and John Morris. Signed William Morris' mark. Wit. oath

May 1, 1806 Richard Morris to Leonard Adcock. Rec. Nov. 11, 1806

p. 422-423 Mar. 21, 1801 John Hammon (Spartanburgh) to George Isom (same); for $150 sold 50 ac on Forgeson's Cr; border: Milley Gravet and George Bruton. Witness Zach Grace and Matthew Patton. Signed John Hammon's mark. Wit. oath Oct. 27, 1804 Matthew Patton to Drury McDaniel. Rec. Nov. 11, 1806

p. 423-424 Oct. 10, 1806 Josiah Thornton (Spartanburgh) to George West (same); for $100 sold 100 ac on ridge between waters of Fairforrest and Dutchman's Creeks; grant (not dated) South Carolina governor to Josiah Thornton. Witness Thomas Lancaster and James Vernon. Signed JT. Wit. oath Oct. 24, 1806 James Vernon to William Lancaster. Rec. Nov. 11, 1806. Dower renounced Salley Thornton to William Lancaster Oct. 24, 1806

p. 424-425 Nov. 10, 1806 James Wofford (Spartanburgh) to John Vernon (same); for $50 sold 50 ac on branch of Sugar Cr. Witness Willis Willeford and Aaron Smith. Signed James Wofford's mark. Wit. oath Nov. 10, 1806 Willis Willeford to Wm Smith. Rec. Nov. 11, 1806. Dower renounced Cecly Wofford (or Cecla) to Wm Smith Nov. 10, 1806

p. 425-426 Aug. 6, 1806 Adam Kelbey (Spartanburgh) to William Bishop (same); for $150 sold 200 ac on Lawson's fork; border: E-Adam Kelbey and W-John White. Witness James White and Nancy Kelbey. Signed Adam Kelbey's mark. Wit. oath Oct. 17, 1806 James White to Ism Foster. Rec. Nov. 11, 1806

p. 426-427 Nov. 19, 1805 James Byars (Spartanburgh) to William Ellis; for $40 sold 42 ac on W side of Broad R. Witness Thomas Byans and William Wilson. Signed James Byars. Wit. oath Mar. 1, 1806 William Wilson to Jno Rukman. Rec. Nov. 11, 1806

p. 427-428 Oct. 28, 1806 William Wheeler (Spartanburgh) to James Pike (same); for $80 sold 100 ac on E side of Rockfield Cr. Witness Joshua Benson, Manley Ford, and William McDade. Signed William Wheeler's mark. Wit. oath Nov. 10, 1806 William McDade to Michl Miller. Rec. Dec. 11, 1806 (sic)

p. 428-429 Oct. 25, 1806 James Rucker and William Wheeler (Spartanburgh) to Joshua Benson and Robert Redmon (Greenville Dist); for $300 sold 200 ac on S side of Rockyfield Cr. Witness Manly Ford, James Pike, and William McDeade. Signed James Rucker and William Wheeler's marks. Wit. oath Nov. 10, 1806 William McDeade to Michl Miller. Rec (omitted)

p. 429-431 Oct. 16, 1806 Josiah Thornton (Spartanburgh) to John Varner (same); for $100 sold 100 ac on head waters Sugar Cr of Fairforrest Cr; part of grant Feb. 5, 1787 to Josiah Thornton; border: Wofford; plat attached shows 178 ac bordering Elsworth Moore. Witness James Vernon and Thomas Lancaster. Signed Josiah Thornton's mark. Wit. oath Oct. 24, 1806 James Vernon to William Lancaster. Rec. Nov. 11, 1806. Dower renounced Salley Thornton to William Lancaster Oct. 24, 1806

p. 431-433 Nov. 27, 1802 William Bowen (Laurence Dist) to James Hornbuckle (Spartanburgh); for $124 sold 147 ac on branch of Enoree R; part of 500 ac survey Jan. 6, 1775 and warrant for grant dated Dec. 8, 1774 and granted Oct. 15, 1784 to Daniel Huger esq and sold by Arnold Vanderhorst and Thomas Waring sr, executors of will of John Vanderhorst (late of Charleston), to William Bowen. Witness Joseph Lyon and John Redman. Signed William Bowen. Wit. oath Dec. 24, 1803 John Redman to James Kilgore. Rec. Nov. 12, 1806. Dower renounced Mary Bowen to Danl Wright Dec. 22, 1802

p. 433-434 Oct. 29, 1801 John Redman (Spartanburgh) to James Hornbuckle (same); for 50£ sold 130 ac; where John Redman lives; border: Enoree R and Abner's Cr; part of 265 ac grant Apr. 2, 1792 to David Qualls. Witness William Hornbuckle and George Sondus (or Sonders). Signed John Redman and Nancy's mark. Wit. oath Feb. 28, 1803 William Hornbuckle to James Kilgore. Rec. Nov. 12, 1806

p. 434-435 Sept. 26, 1806 James Hornbuckle (Spartanburgh) to Tracy Glenn (Greenville Dist); for $600 sold 250 ac; where James Hornbuckle lives; border: S-Enoree R, E-Reuben Gun and Abner's Cr, N-John Redman, and W & NW-Robert Greer and John McCollester; sold Nov. 27, 1802 by William Bowens to James Hornbuckle and on Oct. 29, 1801 by John Redmon to James Hornbuckle. Witness John Redman and Henry Brockman. Signed James Hornbuckle. Wit. oath Sept. 26, 1806 John Redman to James Kilgore. Rec. Nov. 12, 1806. Dower renounced Frances Hornbuckle to James Kilgore (not dated)

p. 435-437 Oct. 15, 1798 John Harris (Spartanburgh) to John Redman (same); for 50£ sold 130 ac on N side Enoree R and on Abner's Cr; where Mr Russ lives; part of 265 ac grant Apr. 2, 1792 to David Qualls. Witness Pennel Wood and Traves Rees (or Reece). Signed John Harris' mark. Wit. oath Sept. 29, 1801 Traves Rees to John Collins. Rec. (omitted)

p. 437-438 Aug. 29, 1806 John Dill (Spartanburgh) to Abraham Green (SC); for $218 sold 111½ ac on S side Cherokee Cr; where John Dill formerly lived; border: E-Nathaniel Robertson, S-Gibson and land formerly belonging to Powell, and W & N-John Avndele and Joseph Dill; part of 400 ac grant to John Dill. Witness Peter Quin, Joseph Camp, Richard Quin. Signed John Dill's mark. Wit. oath Aug. 30, 1806 Joseph Camp to John Lipscomb. Rec. Nov. 12, 1806. Dower renounced Ellender Dill to John Lipscomb Aug. 20, 1806

p. 438-440 Mar. 9, 1805 Giden Gibson (Knox Co, Tenn) to Michael Gaffney (SC); for $200 sold 250 ac; border: Thomas Philips, Obigen Smith, and Dr Odwight; part of 500 ac grant Oct. 30, 1795 Gov. Arnoldus Vanderhorst to William Ruckman. Witness John Amos and William Darvin. Signed Gideon Gibson. Wit. oath Sept. 27, 1806 John Amos to John Lipscomb. Rec. Nov. 12, 1806

p. 440-441 May 8, 1798 William Ruckman (Spartanburgh) to Gideon Gibson; for 5£ SC money sold 250 ac; border: Thomas Philips, Obuant Smith, and Dr Oldwight; part of 500 ac grant Oct. 30, 1795 Gov. Arnoldus Vanderhorst to William Ruckman. Witness Vardry McBee and Elizabeth Ruckman. Signed William Ruckman. Wit. oath Jun. 1, 1798 Vardry McBee to Henry McCray. Rec. Nov. 12, 1806

p. 441-442 Oct. 19, 1805 Robert Rogers (Spartanburgh) to Herum Harrelson (same); for $117 sold 188 ac on waters of Dutchman's Cr of Tygar R; part of grant 319 ac Apr. 5, 1790 Gov. Charles Pinckney to Ephram Hill. Witness William Hase and Arthur Faukner. Signed Robert Rogers. Wit. oath Oct. 3, 1806 William Hase to Wm Smith. Rec. Nov. 12, 1806

p. 442-443 Jul. 25, 1805 Isaac Sinkler (Iredel Co, NC) to Beven Patterson (Spartanburgh); for $100 sold 175 ac on N side of Pacolate R; part of 300 ac sold by John Brown to Isaac Sinkler and Jarret Patterson gets 125 ac (remainder of 300 ac). Witness William Patterson jr and Duglas Sinkler. Signed Isaac Sinkler. Wit. oath Dec. 12, 1805 William Patterson to John Lipscomb. Rec. Nov. 12, 1806

p. 443-445 Oct. 19, 1805 Robert Rogers sr (Spartanburgh) to William Hase (same); for $242.50 sold (1) 257 ac on branch of

Dutchman's Cr of Tygar R; border: Samuel Morrow; grant Jan. 21, 1785 Gov. Benjamin Guerard to Ephram Hill; and (2) 131 ac adjoining (1); border: Herum Harrelson; part of grant Mar. 25, 1790 Gov. Charles Pinckney to Ephram Hill. Witness John Bright, Arthur Faulkner, and Herum Harrelson. Signed Robert Rogers. Wit. oath Oct. 3, 1806 Herum Harrelson to Wm Smith. Rec. Nov. 28, 1806

p. 445-446 Oct. 28, 1806 James Harrison (SC) to James Reyley (same); for $481 sold 204 ac on Fairforrest and Kelso Creeks; border: Golightly, Hancock Smith's old line, and James Smith. Witness James Smith and Hancock Smith. Signed James Harrison. Wit. oath Nov. 15, 1806 James Smith to William Lancaster. Rec. Jan. 1, 1806 (sic)

p. 446-448 Sept. 13, 1806 George Parkinson (Spartanburgh) to Henry Brown (same); for $333 sold 222 ac on waters of Fairforrest Cr; resurvey by Richard Thomson; where George Parkinson lives; part of 361 ac grant to Thomas Luhee (or Luhu) who sold to Abraham Markley who sold to Gabriel Benson who sold to Duglas Josephas Puckett who sold to George Parkinson. Witness D. J. Puckett, Beverly Lewis, and Obadiah Watson. Signed George Parkinson. Wit. oath Dec. 30, 1806 Obadiah Watson to Abraham Lancaster. Rec. Jan. 3, 1807. Dower renounced Frances Parkinson to Absalom Lancaster Dec. 30, 1806

p. 448-450 Jan. 17, 1794 William Pool (Spartanburgh) to Elisha Lindsey (same); for 15£ sterling sold 100 ac on N side Pacolate R; border: 2 ac of William Pool's; lower end of where George Pool lives. Witness John H. Jones, John Pool, and John Headen. Signed William Pool. Wit. oath Jan. 5, 1807 John H. Jones to Jacob Utley. Rec. Jan. 5, 1807

p. 450-451 Nov. 26, 1806 Jesse Hester (Spartanburgh) to John Broockshier (same); for $100 sold 200 ac on waters of Pacolate R; border: Bassel Scott. Witness Manniung Broockshier and Abraham Potter. Signed Jesse Hester's mark. Wit. oath Dec. 10, 1806 Abraham Potter to Henry Tuani (or Turner). Rec. Jan. 13, 1807

p. 451-452 Jul. 7, 1806 Isham Harrison, sheriff (Spartanburgh) to James Camp (same); for $108.50 sold 500 ac on both sides Big Buck Cr of Pacolate R; border: Luke Browning, Sander, Thomas Gore, and John Nelson; part of two tracts granted to Richard Saunders who sold to Thomas Gore who sold to West Harris; sale due to writ from Spartanburgh Common Pleas Court suit Noble Hamilton vs. West Harris; land known as Thomas Gore's old mill place; sale on Jul. 7, 1806. Witness Obadiah Watson, Henry Turner, and Joseph Watson. Signed I Harrison SSD. Wit. oath Jan. 19, 1807 Obadiah Watson to Abner Benson. Rec. Jan. 20, 1807

p. 452-453 Jan. 22, 1807 Dower renounced Martha Wells to Abner Benson; for deed William Wells to Obadiah Watson; 540 ac on waters of Chinquepin Cr; adjoining Court House tract; see plat in deed from Samuel Miller to William Wells. Rec. Jan. 22, 1807

p. 453-454 Jan. 22, 1807 Dower renounced Martha Wells to Abner Benson; for deed William Wells to Obadiah Watson; 2/3 ac lot #4 in Spartanburgh, SC; border: Old Jail and Publick land. Rec. Jan. 22, 1807

p. 454-455 Apr. 15, 1806 Lacy McAbee (Spartanburgh) to Vincent Wyatt sr (same); for $78 sold 55 ac; border: Vincent Wyatt and Connell. Witness John Quarles and Muse Tolleson. Signed Lacy McAbee's mark. Wit. oath Jan. 15, 1807 Muse Tolleson to Henry Turner. Rec. Jan. 26, 1807

p. 455-456 Mar. 1, 1806 Sterling Ingram (Spartanburgh) to Alfred

S. E. Slken (Greenville Dist); for $400 sold (1) 318 ac on both sides of S Pacolate R; grant Jun. 5, 1786 to John McClure; and (2) (ac not given); grant in 1800 Gov. John Drayton to Henry Young. Witness John B. E. Elken, John Vaughn, and Betsey Vaughn. Signed Sterling Ingram. Wit. oath Dec. 15, 1806 John B. E. Elken to John Collins. Rec. Jan. 26, 1807

p. 456-458 Nov. 5, 1806 Joseph Champeon (Spartanburgh) to William Lipscomb (same); for $1,200 sold 174 or 164 ac on N fork of Thickety Cr; part of 350 ac grant in Dec. 1774 Gov. William Bull to Vardry McBee who sold to Obadiah Trimmier who sold to Joseph Champeon. Witness Smith Lipscomb, Richard Thomson, and William Thomson. Signed Joseph Champeon's mark. Wit. oath Dec. 1, 1806 Smith Lipscomb to John Lipscomb. Rec. Feb. 2, 1807. Dower renounced Nancy Champeon to John Lipscomb Dec. 1, 1806

p. 458-459 Oct. 22, 1799 Richard Lee (Spartanburgh) to Richard Turner (same); for 5£ sterling sold 60 ac on S side of Pacolate R; border: Solomon Abbett, Cherokee Cr, and James Steadman. Witness Claborn Holt and Susanna Holt. Signed Richard and Nancy Lee. Wit. oath Feb. 9, 1807 Claborn Holt to Leonard Adcock. Rec. Feb. 2, 1806 (sic)

p. 459-460 Mar. 9, 1805 Thomas Woodruff (Spartanburgh) to Richard Daniel (same); for $230 sold 125 ac on Beverdam Cr of Fairforrest Cr. Witness Thomas Tinsley and James Wofford. Signed Thomas Woodruff. Wit. oath Feb. 2, 1807 Thomas Tinsley to Jacob Utley. Rec. Feb. 2, 1807. Dower renounced Mary Woodruff to William Lancaster Jan. 10, 1806

p. 460-461 Dec. 2, 1805 John Duncan (Spartanburgh) to Daniel Daved (same); for $8 sold 6 ac on branch of Tygar R. Witness Thomas Stone, James David, and James Wofford. Signed John Duncan. Wit. oath Feb. 24, 1806 Thomas Stone to Denny Anderson. Rec. Feb. 2, 1807

p. 461-463 Nov. 8, 1804 John Hamby (Spartanburgh) to John Johnson (same); for $200 sold 205 ac on branch of Luk (or Lick) Cr of Enoree Cr; part of 400 ac grant in 1773 to John Hamby. Witness Moore Bragg and James Wofford. Signed John Hamby's mark. Wit. oath Jan. 22, 1807 James Wofford to Wm Hendrix. Rec. Feb. 6, 1807

p. 463-464 Dec. 7, 1802 Jesse Smith (Richland Dist) to John H Harrison (Greenville Dist); for $155 sold 500 ac on Williams' Cr of Tygar R; border: David Culberson sr; survey for David Culberson and granted Jan. 5, 1801 Gov. John Drayton to Jesse Smith. Witness Moses Kelley, Samuel Douglas, and Elizabeth Smith. Signed Jesse Smith. Wit. oath (Greenville Dist) May 28, 1803 Moses Kelley to Hudson Berry. Rec. Feb. 9, 1807

p. 464-465 Oct. 1, 1805 John Keenum (Spartanburgh) to Hezekiah Seay (same); for $150 sold 200 ac on Faun Br of Lawson's fork; border: John Burnett, Ephram Lewes, Isarell Woods, bever pond, and Thomas Brannon. Witness Thomas Burnett and David Hicks. Signed John Keenum. Wit. oath Jan. 5, 1807 David Hicks to Jacob Utley. Rec. Feb. 12, 1807

p. 465-466 Jan. 18, 1806 Hugh Means (Spartanburgh) to Samuel Turner (same); for $30 sold 48½ ac; border: Samuel Turner and a waggon road; on N side Lawson's fork; part of grant to Thomas Wood. Witness John Spearse and Lewis Turner. Signed Hugh Means. Wit. oath Jan. 17, 1807 John Spearse to Jacob Utley. Rec. Feb. 12, 1807

p. 466-467 Dec. 29, 1806 Keah Seay (Spartanburgh) to Scarbary (or

Searbary) Brannon (same); for $45 sold 50 ac on both sides of Lawson's fork; part of survey for James Morris and granted Oct. 24, 1784 to Isarel Morris. Witness David Hicks and James Brannon. Signed Keah and Elizabeth Seay's marks. Wit. oath Jan. 5 (or 6), 1807 David Hicks to Jacob Utley. Rec. Feb. 12, 1807

p. 467-469 Mar. 3, 1806 Isham Harrison, sheriff (Spartanburgh) to Aaron Templeman (same); for $51 sold 300 ac on N side Pacolate R; plat attached; sale due to writ from Spartanburgh Common Pleas Court suit Abraham Nott vs Jonathan Low; sale Mar. 3, 1806. Witness Jacob Utley, Robert A Todd, and Thomas Lancaster. Signed I Harrison. Wit. oath Feb. 12, 1807 Robert A Todd to Abner Benson. Rec. Feb. 12, 1807

p. 469-471 Aug. 6, 1804 Moses Guyton (Spartanburgh) to Joshua Gordan (Rutherford Co, NC); for 20£ sold 50 ac on Beverdam Cr of Thickety Cr; part of two tracts: (1) grant in North Carolina to Samuel Hogan and (2) grant in South Carolina to Vardry McBee; border: Hogan and Joseph Addams. Witness Joseph Addams and John Guyton. Signed Moses Guyton. Wit. oath Nov. 6, 1806 Joseph Addams to John Lipscomb. Rec. Feb. 16, 1807. Dower renounced Tobetha Guyton to John Lipscomb Nov. 6, 1806

p. 471-473 Jan. 26, 1792 James Terrell and wife Frances (Spartanburgh) to John Lock (or Loek) (Union Dist); for 100£ sold 496 ac on S fork of Gilkee's Cr; grant (not dated) South Carolina governor to James Terrell. Witness Powers Lamken, Hezekiah Terrell, and John Border. Signed James Terrell and Frances' mark. Wit. oath Feb. 23, 1807 John Border to Henry Turner. Rec. Feb. 24, 1807

p. 473-475 Jan. 3, 1807 William Thomason (Spartanburgh) to Alexander McKie (same); for $100 sold 164 ac on ridge between Lawson's fork and Peter's Cr; border: land Alexander McKie bought from Arnold Thomason, Mary Thomason, Zachariah Wyatt, and William Poole; allotted to William Thomason as one of heirs of William Turner Thomason desc; see records of Spartanburgh Common Pleas Court. Witness Robert Alexr Tod, Abner Benson, and Robert Benson. Signed Wm Thomason. Wit. oath Feb. 21, 1807 Robert A Todd to A Benson. Rec. Feb. 25, 1807

p. 475-476 Sept. 30, 1806 Duglas J Puckett to George Parkinson (Spartan Dist); for $20 sold 222 ac on waters of Fairforrest Cr; where George Parkinson lives; survey by Richard Thomson; part of 361 ac grant to Thomas Luhu who sold to Absalom Markley who sold to Gabriel Benson who sold to Duglas J Puckett; "within a line of grant" to George Parkinson. Witness Bevel Lewis and Robert Benson. Signed D. J. Puckett. Wit. oath Feb. 26, 1807 Robert Benson to A Benson. Rec. Feb. 26, 1807

p. 476-478 Feb. 18, 1807 Zachariah Wyatt (Spartanburgh) to Alexander McKie (same); for $70 sold 165 ac on waters of Lawson's fork of Pacolate R; allotted to Zachariah Wyatt as heir of William Turner Thomason desc by Isham Harrison, William Smith, Reuben Daniel, Anthony Foster, and William Wells, commissioners appointed by Spartanburgh Court. Witness Robert Benson and Abner Benson. Signed Zacharc Wyatt. Wit. oath Feb. 28, 1807 Robert Benson to Abner Benson. Rec. Feb. 28, 1807

p. 478-479 Oct. 22, 1799 John Lancaster (Spartanburgh) to Lucy Lancaster (same); for $100 sold 286 ac on waters of Fairforrest Cr; border: Sells, Whilboey (or Whetboey), Murrey, Vandiver(?), Bird, Tollenson; part of grant to John Macoule (or Macoale) who sold to John Lancaster. Witness John Goftis (or Gossett) and John Vandiver. Signed John Lancaster. Wit. oath Feb. 8, 1806 John Goftis to William

Simpson. Rec. Mar. 2, 1807

p. 479-480 Sept. 23, 1791 William and Solomon Crocker (Spartanburgh) to Anthony Crocker (same); for 5£ SC money sold (1) 50 ac on S side Pacolate R; (William Crocker's land ?); part of 250 ac grant Jul. 10, 1789 Gov. William Moultrie to Arthur Crocker sr; border: John Burke's Spring Br, William Poole ironmaster, Arthur Crocker's old line, and Solomon Crocker; and for 5£ SC money sold 50 ac E of (1); border: John Burks' Spring Br and Solomon Crocker; part of grant Oct. 26, 1786 to Solomon Crocker. Witness John Crocker and James Ross. Signed William and Solomon Crocker's marks. Wit. oath Feb. 24, 1792 William and Solomon Crocker to Isham Harrison. Rec. Mar. 2, 1807

p. 480-482 Dec. 10, 1806 Elijah Barnett (Spartanburgh) to Samuel Barton (same); for $600 sold 200 ac on both sides of Fariforrest Cr and on Cold Springs Br. Witness William Burton and Leonard George. Signed Elijah Barnett. Wit. oath Feb. 17, 1807 William Burton to Danl White. Rec. Mar. 4, 1807

p. 482-483 Jan. 30, 1807 William Foster (Spartanburgh) to John Foster (same); for $250 sold 140 ac on Mile Cr of Tygar R. Witness William Wingo, William Foster, and John Foster. Signed William Foster. Wit. oath Jan. 30, 1807 William Foster(?) to Jacob Utley. Rec. Mar. 2, 1807

p. 483-484 Jan. 1, 1807 Lemuel Loftis (Spartanburgh) to Alexander McCarter jr, son of John McCarter (same); for $300 sold 200 ac on both sides Middle Tygar R; grant to John Keen (or Keer) who sold to Lemuel Loftis. Witness Daniel Welbanks, Joseph Brown, and Stephen Paece (or Pace). Signed Lemuel Loftis' mark. Wit. oath Jan. 10, 1807 Stephen Paece to John Collins. Rec. Mar. 6, 1807

p. 484 Feb. 24, 1807 Dower renounced Elizabeth Demsy to David Morton; for deed William Demsey to Henry House. Rec (omitted)

p. 484-486 Mar. 13, 1807 William Lewis (Spartanburgh) to James Boyd (same); for $300 sold 115 ac on both sides Lawson's fork; border: Cudd, Foster, and Knight; part of two surveys granted to Frances Ross and James McDowell. Witness Robert McDowell, Wm Gilmore, and James Lewis. Signed William Lewis and Sarah's mark. Wit. oath Mar. 14, 1807 James Lewis to Ab Benson. Rec. Mar. 14, 1807

p. 486-487 Mar. 5, 1806 Edmond Cooley (Spartanburgh) to Leonard Carden jr (same); for $10 gave quit claim to 500 ac on both sides Pacolate R; border: Philip Johnson, N Pacolate R, William Barton, Luke Burnett, Leonard Carden's fish trap, Thomas Barnett, Thomas Kimbal, John Gilbert, William Holley; and Edmond Cooley gives Leonard Carden jr title to land obtained from Amos Speace. Witness D. J. Puckett esq, David Johnson, and Lawson Thomson. Signed Edmond Cooley's mark. Wit. oath Mar. 20, 1807 D. J. Puckett to A Benson. Rec. Mar. 20, 1807

p. 487-488 Mar. 16, 1807 Barnard W Sweney (Spartanburgh) to Robert Miller and Laban P Pool (same); for $850 sold a bay stud horse named Cab (or Cub), a bay mare, 2 cows and calves, a cow, 4 sows and 12 pigs marked with an under "peal" (or seal" on right ear and oaveheal in left ear; 6 shotes marked same, 3 beds and furniture, all household furniture, 10 geese, 500 ac where Richard Roberts formerly lived called Green Pond; Condition: sale void if Barnard pays $850 in one year. Witness Harbert Hawkins and William Neely Miller. Signed B. W. Sweney. Wit. oath Mar. 16, 1807 William N Miller to Drury McDaniel. Rec. Mar. 21, 1807

p. 488-489 Mar. 20, 1807 John Young (Spartanburgh) to James Young (same); for $500 sold 200 ac on both sides Obed's Cr of N Pacolate R; grant Mar. 5, 1771 to Thomas McKnight. Witness Jonathan Wall and Robert Wall. Signed John Young's mark. Wit. oath Mar. 23, 1807 Jonathan Wall to Geo Salmon. Rec. Mar. 23, 1807

p. 489-490 Jul. 26, 1806 William Easley (Greenville Dist) to Reuben Bowman (Spartanburgh); for $600 sold 250 ac on both sides S Pacolate R; border: Shields Booker and Reuben Bowman's Spring Br; part of grant to William Dickson. Witness Baylis Earle and Pleasant Easley. Signed Wm Easley. Wit. oath Aug. 8, 1806 Baylis Earle to Gal Benson. Rec. Mar. 30, 1807

p. 490-491 Nov. 27, 1806 Isham Burks (Pendleton Dist) to Baylis Earle (Spartanburgh); for $200 sold 75 ac on N fork of Beverdam Cr of S Pacolate R; part of 100 ac grant Oct. 1, 1787 to William Bird. Witness Josiah Foster and Robert Lingleton Crews Foster. Signed Isham Burks. Wit. oath (Greenville Dist) Feb. 17, 1807 Robert L. C. Foster to John Goode. Rec. Mar. 30, 1807

p. 491-493 Jan. 11, 1806 William Calvaret (Spartanburgh) to Rowland Jennings (same); for $120 sold 134 ac; plat attached shows border: Rowland Jennings or Constable, Daniel Stephens, Jesse Spencer, and Richd Hampton; grant Gov. Charles Pinckney to James Gibbs and sold by Zacheriah Gibbs, son of James Gibbs, to William Calvaret. Witness Willis Bobo and Elisha Gennings (or Jennings). Signed William Calvaret. Wit. oath Jan. 15, 1806 Elisha Jennings to William Lancaster. Rec. Apr. 6, 1807

p. 493-494 Mar. 18, 1807 William Bridges (Spartanburgh) to William Gilbert (same); for $60 sold 25 ac on Meadow fork of Little Buck Cr; border: Charles Conlwell (or Cantwell); part of grant State office to West Harris who sold to William Bridges. Witness Mourning Gilbert and George Gilbert. Signed Wm Bridges. Wit. oath Apr. 6, 1807 George Gilbert to Leonard Adcock. Rec. Apr. 6, 1807

p. 494-495 Jan. 13, 1807 John Jordan (Spartanburgh) to William Morrow (same); for $210 sold 100 ac on Buck Cr; grant States office to Robert Nelson. Witness Abraham Nelson and John Cantrell. Signed John Jordan's mark. Wit. oath Apr. 4, 1807 John Cantrell to Leonard Adcock. Rec. Apr. 6, 1807

p. 495-496 Oct. 28, 1805 Aaron Pinson to Sterling Hudgeon; for (money not mentioned) sold 70 ac on "small" Tygar R; border: Zephaniah Pinson, son of Aaron Pinson; S end of 200 ac grant in 1786 to Obadiah Edwards. Witness John Ward and Thomas Shurley. Signed Aaron Pinson. Wit. oath Oct. 13, 1806 John Ward to Drury McDaniel. Rec. Apr. 6, 1807

p. 496-497 Mar. 14, 1807 William Meadows and wife Ann (Spartanburgh) to Joseph Meadows (same); for $140 sold 140 ac on branch Cane Cr of Tygar R; where Joseph Meadows lives; grant Nov. 7, 1785 Gov. William Moultrie to Tobias Bright. Witness Samuel Smith, James Meadows, and George T Sloan. Signed William and Ann Meadows' marks. Wit. oath Mar. 14, 1807 Samuel Smith to William Lancaster. Rec. Apr. 6, 1807

p. 497-499 Jan. 1, 1806 Zachariah Gibbs (Union Dist) to Rowland Ginnings (Spartanburgh); for $500 sold 398 ac on Ford's Cr of Fairforrest Cr and Ward's Cr of Tygar R; border: Jesse Spencer and both sides of "main" waggon road; agreeable with will of Zachariah Gibbs' father, James Gibbs. Witness Elisha Ginnings and Joseph White. Signed Zachariah Gibbs. Wit. oath Jan. 15, 1806 Elisha Ginnings to William Lancaster. Rec. Apr. 6, 1807

p. 499-500 Dec. 11, 1806 William Morris sr (Spartanburgh) to William Sanders (same); for $20 sold 40 ac at head of Thickety Cr; border: Samuel Dunaway sr; grant Jan. 1, 1787 States Office to William Morris. Witness John Morris, Richard Morris, and John Bankston. Signed William Morris' mark. Wit. oath Dec. 27, 1806 John Morris to Leonard Adcock. Rec. Apr. 6, 1807

p. 500-501 Mar. 9, 1807 Gideon Harreldson (or Harelson) (Spartanburgh) to Abraham Hembey (same); for $100 sold 50 ac on branch of Dutchman's Cr of Tygar R; part of 200 ac grant Jun. 5, 1786 to William Wier who sold Jan. 27, 1792 to Gideon Harreldson. Witness David Trail and Mark Bennett. Signed Gideon Harelson. Wit. oath Mar. 7, 1807 David Trail to William Lancaster. Rec. Apr. 6, 1807. Dower renounced Elizabeth Herelson to William Lancaster Mar. 7, 1807

p. 501-503 Sept. 8, 1806 Joseph Adams (Spartanburgh) to William Webber (same); for $400 sold 144 ac on N side Beverdam Cr of Thickety Cr; border: Bostick; part of two tracts: (1) grant May 15, 1772 North Carolina governor to John Hogan and (2) grant Sept. 7, 1785 to Vardry McBee. Witness Daniel Amos and Moses Guyton. Signed Joseph Adams. Wit. oath Oct. 4, 1806 Moses Guyton to John Lipscomb. Rec. Apr. 6, 1807. Dower renounced Jean Adams to John Lipscomb Oct. 11, 1806

p. 503-504 Jan. 13, 1807 John Jordan (Spartanburgh) to William Morrow (same); for $40 sold 20 ac on S side of Buck Cr; border: "the Big Survey" and Abraham Nelson. Witness Abraham Nelson and John Cantrell. Signed John Jordan's mark. Wit. oath Apr. 4, 1807 John Cantrell to Leonard Adcock. Rec. Apr. 6, 1807

p. 504-506 Sept. 6, 1805 Benjamin Busey (Spartanburgh) to James Stone; for $350 sold 160 ac on Two Mile Cr; border: Joseph Casey, Samuel Crow, Spence Calbert, Sampson Bobo, Joseph Brown; part of two tracts granted to John Hendrex and Richard Nelson. Witness Augusten Bumpass, Mary Owens, and John Dean. Signed Benjamin Busey's mark. Wit. oath (Laurence Dist) Mar. 7, 1806 Augusten Bumpass to Sterling Tucker. Rec. Apr. 6, 1807. Dower renounced Lucy Busey to Sterling Tucker Mar. 7, 1806 (Laurence Dist)

p. 506-507 Apr. 20, 1803 Edward Wyatt (Spartanburgh) to Peter Gosnell (same); for 30£ sold 140 ac on Suck Cr; border: includes Mile Shoal and Peter Gosnell. Witness Leonard Adcock and David Adcock. Signed Edward Wyatt's mark. Wit. oath Mar. 4, 1806 Leonard Adcock to Ism Foster. Rec. Apr. 6, 1807

p. 507-508 Feb. 11, 1807 Drury McDaniel (Spartanburgh) to Robert Miller Hughes and Ann Hughes (same); for $80 sold 80 ac on waters of Tygar R; border: James Miller, Andrew Cowen, vacant, Elisha Hadden, Samuel Miller, and Hughes. Witness John Hughs, Margaret Hughs, and Mary Hughs. Signed Drury McDaniel. Wit. oath Mar. 11, 1807 John Hughs to John Collins. Rec. Apr. 7, 1807

p. 508-509 Feb. 13, 1807 Solomon Crocker (Spartanburgh) to son-in-law William Gore (same); for love and affection give 111 ac on S side of Pacolate R; border: James Poole, Solomon Crocker, and Benjamin Pool. Witness Anthony Baites and Anthony Crocker. Signed Solomon Crocker's mark. Wit. oath Apr. 4, 1807 Anthony Bailes to William Simpson. Rec. Apr. 7, 1807

p. 509-510 (Laurence Dist) May 4, 1805 Nathan Bramlett (Laurence Dist) to John Robinson (same); for $85 sold 70 ac on Beverdam Cr of Enoree R in Laurence Dist; border: Cutchfield, William Brown, and Joseph Alleson; part of two grants: (1) to Ezekiel Griffith and (2) to Richard Fowler. Witness George Sims and Ephram Moore.

Signed Nathan Bramlett. Wit. oath (Laurence Dist) May 4, 1804 George Sims to Wm Rountree. Rec. Apr. 7, 1807

p. 510-511 Aug. 13, 1804 John Young, Joseph Young, and Thomas Young (Spartanburgh) to Daniel McKie (same); for $180 sold 200 ac on N side Enoree R; border: SE-William Stone and W-Robert Sims; grant Aug. 16, 1784 to William Young desc and "conveyed" by will Oct. 13, 1787. Witness Labouror P. Pool and Isaiah Hembree. Signed John Young, Joseph Young, and Thomas Young. Wit. oath Mar. 21, 1807 Labouror P Pool to John Dean. Rec. Apr. 7, 1807

p. 511-513 Feb. 24, 1804 William Earnest (Spartanburgh) to Daniel McKie (same); for $1,200 sold 270 ac; part of two grants: (1) 100 ac to Zachariah Gibbs Jul. 4, 1769 on N side Enoree R and sold to William Hamley and sold Nov. 8, 1788 to John Hamley (see Book E p. 130) and sold Dec. 20, 1793 to William Moore (see Book E p. 118) and sold Mar. 20, 1797 to William Earnest (Book E p. 116); and (2) 170 ac sold Mar. 28, 1797 by Benjamin Wofford sr to William Earnest (see Book F p. 132) on N side Enoree R and adjoining (1) and on Luk Cr; where William Earnest lives; plat attached. Witness Laborn P Pool and Joseph Rogers. Signed William Earnest's mark. Wit. oath Mar. 21, 1807 Laborn P Pool to John Dean. Rec. Apr. 7, 1807. Dower renounced Rachel Earnest to Daniel Wright Feb. 26, 1804

p. 513-515 Feb. 19, 1799 Robert Hembree sr (Spartanburgh) to James Bright jr (same); for 42£ sold 100 ac on E of Tygar R; below mouth of Thompson's Br; border: Tobias Bright; part of 450 ac grant Apr. 7, 1788 Gov. Thomas Pinckney to William Shurley. Witness Arthur Faulkner, Tobias Bright, and Sarah Hembree. Signed Robert Hembree's mark. Wit. oath Feb. 3, 1806 Tobias Bright to John Brewton. Rec. Apr. 7, 1807

p. 515-516 Feb. 1, 1806 Tobias Bright (Spartanburgh) to James Bright jr (same); for 30£ sold 50 ac; border: on W bank of Thompson's Br; part of 300 ac grant May 15, 1772 to Michael Prewett. Witness Benjamin Nichols and John Thornton. Signed Tobias Bright. Wit. oath Feb. 3, 1806 John Thornton to John Brewton. Rec. Apr. 7, 1807. Dower renounced Rachel Bright to William Smith Feb. 6, 1806

p. 516-517 Feb. 22, 1800 Samuel Young and James Young (Spartanburgh) to Daniel McKie; for $60 sold 2/7 of 200 ac due Samuel and James Young's father's will--William Young desc; border: E-Stone, W-Robert Simson, and S-Enoree R; where Widow Young lives. Witness James Smith and Labon P Pool. Signed Samuel and James Young's marks. Wit. oath Mar. 21, 1807 Labon P Pool to John Dean. Rec. Apr. 7, 1807

p. 517-518 Oct. 29, 1806 William McElrath (Spartanburgh) to Thomas Hadden (same); for $250 sold 120 ac on S fork Tygar R; border: Francis Powers, Nichols, Widow Powers; part of 538 ac grant Mar. 6, 1786 South Carolina governor to Francis Powers. Witness David White and Nathaniel McElrath. Signed William McElrath. Wit. oath Apr. 7, 1807 Nathaniel McElrath to David Morton. Rec. Apr. 7, 1807

p. 518-519 Mar. 30, 1807 James Laurence and William Tate (Union Dist), executors of will of William Tate desc (Spartanburgh), to George Walker (Spartanburgh); for $500 sold 150 ac on both sides Cherokee Cr of Broad R; grant May 1, 1786 to Thomas Bonner and sold by William Tate in his lifetime to George Walker--see a bond given by William Tate to George Walker, "assenee" to Jesse Tate desc. Witness Samuel Tate to Frances Laurence. Signed Jas Laurence and William Tate. Wit. oath Apr. 6, 1807 Samuel Tate to Danl Wilbanks. Rec. Apr. 7, 1807

p. 519-520 Jan. 11, 1806 Joel Blackwell (Spartanburgh) to Richard Scruggs (same); for $40 sold 100 ac if not taken by an older survey; on Island Cr of Pacolate R; border: E-Edward Williams and W-Matthew Abott and Robert Lee; part of 500 ac grant Feb. 19, 1796 to George Williams and 100 ac sold Dec. 24, 1801 to Joel Blackwell. Witness L Adcock and William Dobbins. Signed J Blackwell. Certified Apr. 1, 1807 by L Adcock. Rec. Apr. 7, 1807

p. 520-522 Apr. 8, 1807 (sic) John Sloan (Greenville Dist) to Alexander Roddy (Spartanburgh), trustee; for $1,000 "made use of Mary Sloan's private property and to hold it for Mary Sloan" (ac not given) on S side Cumberland R and near E fork of Yellow Cr; about 1¼ miles below Chickesaw Trace in Tenn; deed Jan. 4, 1792 by Gov. Alexander Martin; border: James Pickens; Alexander Roddy is trustee for support of John Sloan's wife Mary during her lifetime; Mary Sloan can sell or will the land or appoint another trustee to do the work. Witness John Davis SM and Rowland Johnson. Signed John Sloan and Alexr Roddy, a trustee. Wit. oath Feb. 8, 1807 John Davis SM to Henry Turner. Rec. Apr. 7, 1807 (sic)

p. 522-523 Dec. 5, 1806 Thomas Taylor (Columbia, SC) to Christopher Golightly (Spartanburgh); for $400 sold 200 ac (original survey calls for 240 ac); on S side Fairforrest Cr of Broad R; or 240 ac by resurvey; grant to James Tettle (or Tittle) and sold to Daniel Thomas and "to Henry White mortgaged to Commissioners of loan Office of South Carolina" and by William Hort, treasurer of South Carolina, agreeable to General Assembly act, sold to Thomas Taylor. Witness Andrew B Moore and Thomas Taylor jr. Signed Thomas Taylor. Wit. oath Apr. 6, 1807 Andrew B Moore to William Lancaster. Rec. Apr. 7, 1807. Dower renounced Ann Taylor to William Lancaster Dec. 13, 1806

p. 523-525 Jul. 31, 1805 William Stone (Spartanburgh) to Samuel Woodruff (same); for $230 sold 100 ac on N side of Dilden's Cr; part of grant Jul. 10, 1769 Gov. Charles Gravel (sic) to William Sims. Witness James Allen, Simon Stone, and William Shackelford. Signed William Stone's mark. Wit. oath Mar. 30, 1807 William Shackelford to Daniel Wright. Rec. Apr. 8, 1807. Dower renounced Salley Stone to Daniel Wright Mar. 30, 1807

p. 525-526 Jan. 24, 1803 John Davis (Spartanburgh) to Edward Ballenger (same); for $70 sold 87 ac on N side of Lawson's fork; includes mill seat; border: Edward Ballenger, Jesse Davis, Cyrus Seay, and Dudly Brannon. Witness David Lewis, John James, and James Ballenger. Signed John Davis' mark. Wit. oath Jan. 25, 1803 James Ballenger to Ism Foster. Rec. Apr. 8, 1807

p. 526-527 Dec. 2, 1806 Robert McFadden (Spartanburgh) to James Hammett (same); for $100 sold 100 ac on N of Enoree R; where Robert McFadden lives; border: Reuben Gunn, John Herren, Absalem Blundell, Richard Woods; part of two tracts of 500 ac granted to Thomas Scott esq who sold to Richard Hampton who sold to Sephen Cantrell who sold to Thomas Kivel who sold to Robert McFadden. Witness Frances Hamby and Jesse Demsey. Signed Robert McFadden. Wit. oath Jan. 3, 1807 Jesse Demsey to James Kilgore. Rec. Apr. 8, 1807. Dower renounced Mary McFadden to Daniel Wright Dec. 4, 1806

loose sheet in microfilm copy not in original book--sheed marked "S"--"Warrants and Recognizances not included by the Grand Jury"--nothing on page

p. 527-528 Oct. 13, 1806 Joshua Ingram (Greenville Dist) to Edward Ballenger (Spartanburgh); for $50 sold 232 ac on Camp Br of Lawson's fork of Pacolate R; border: S-William Wood, SE-Isham Foster, NE-unknown, NW & NE-Thomas Garvin, and NW- Edward Ballenger;

survey Jul. 22, 1797 for Edward Ballenger and granted Jan. 7, 1799 Gov. Edward Rutledge to Larkin Rylu and by assignment "on back of grant" to Joshua Ingram Jun. 28, 1806. Witness Bevely Daniel, Henry Muhen, and James Payn. Signed Joshua Ingram. Wit. oath (Greenville Dist) Oct. 16, 1806 Bevely Daniel to Willis Benson. Rec. Apr. 9, 1807

p. 528-529 Mar. 5, 1807 Edward Arnold jr (Spartanburgh) to Edward Arnold sr (same); for $2,000 sold 345 ac on N side Enoree R; includes a mill and land where Edward Arnold sr lives; border: John Westmoreland and a road. Witness William Massey, James Wofford, and William Arnold. Signed Edward Arnold jr's mark. Wit. oath Mar. 6, 1807 William Arnold to Wm Hendrix. Rec. Apr. 9, 1807

p. 529-530 Apr. 7, 1807 Edmond Clemont (Spartanburgh) to Ephram Lewis (same); for $120 sold 114 ac on N side Lawson's fork; border: Woolf Br, Meadow Br, Edmond Bishop, George Hughey, and Ephram Lewis; grant Sept. 20, 1784 by Gov. Benjamin Guerard; part of two tracts "including in one deed the second part" signed Nov. 6 (or 16), 1795 by Gov. Arnoldus Vanderhorst. Witness James L Burd and William Bishop. Signed Edmond Clemont. Wit. oath Apr. 7, 1807 James L Burd to David Morton. Rec. Apr. 9, 1807

p. 530-532 Aug. 2, 1806 William Quin (Spartanburgh) to Joseph Quin sr (same); for $150 sold a bay mare 3 years old last Spring branded "00" on near shoulder, natural pacer, 4' 8" or 9" high, a road colt 2 years old last Spring natural trotter brands unknown, 2 cows and calves one white all (or ace) on the head, the other red to the best of William Quin's knowledge "all to the Bolley", 14 hogs 2 beds and furniture, a walnut chest, a walnut table, a large wheel, 6 sitting chairs, and all Willian Quin's part of crop where he lives and all Willian Quin's other property; Condition: sale void if William Quin pays $150 in a month. Witness Muse Tollenson and John Quin. Signed William Quin. Wit. oath Nov. 11, 1806 Muse Tollenson to Daniel White. Rec. Apr. 9, 1807

p. 532-533 Nov. 14, 1805 William Camp (York Dist) to Zachariah Cooper (same); for $333.33 sold 166.6 ac on Cherokee Cr of Broad R; includes where Abisha Camp lives. Witness John Quin and Nathan Boulden. Signed William Camp. Wit. oath Mar. 31, 1806 Nathan Boulden to John Lipscomb. Rec. Apr. 10, 1807

p. 533-534 Oct. 6, 1806 Leonard Carden sr (Spartanburgh) to Vincent Bennett (same); for $200 sold 286 ac on S side Pacolate R; at mouth of Mulles Br and border: S-Thomas Bennett and Thomas Kimbel, E-John Gilbert, N-William Holley, and W-Leonard Carden; part of two tracts granted to Amos Speace. Witness William Bennett, John Woody, and Robert Standford. Signed Leonard Carden. Wit. oath Apr. 9, 1807 William Bennett to Ism Foster. Rec. Apr. 10, 1807

p. 534-536 Feb. 1, 1806 Moses Guyton (Spartanburgh) to William Bostick (same); a bond of $2,000; Condition: William to deliver at his house 2,000 lbs of clean cotton to Moses by Dec. 25, 1806; otherwise William gives up part of 1,250 ac granted in 1772 to William Hort, "part" amounts to 583 ac where William lives described in two "younger" grants to Robert Montgomery: 213 ac and to William Bostick 370 ac. Witness Joseph Peace and Samuel W Smith. Signed Moses Guyton. Wit. oath Mar. 2, 1807 (Charleston, SC) Joseph Peace to C(?) Reid. Rec. May 1, 1807

p. 536-538 Oct. 13, 1806 Ebezener Moss (Spartanburgh) to Caleb Woodruff (same); for $322 sold 116 ac on S side of Two Mile Cr; plat attached shows border: John Moss and Thos Farrow; money paid to Ebezener Moss' son William Moss; part of 400 ac grant to John Hendrix on both sides Two Mile Cr of Enoree R and sold to

Ebezener Moss. Witness Augusten Bumpass and Samuel Farrow. Signed Ebezener Moss' mark. Wit. oath Feb. 21, 1807 Augusten Bumpass to John Dean. Rec. May 1, 1807. Dower renounced Agness Moss to Drury McDaniel Oct. 13, 1806

p. 538 Nov. 1, 1806 Alexander Alexander (Davidson Co, Tenn) to William Alexander (Spartanburgh); power of attorney to collect debts due Alexander Alexander as heir of Alexander Alexander desc. Witness John Hall, D Anderson, and Jno Coffee. Signed Alexr Alexander. Wit. oath (Tenn) Nov. 1, 1806 Alexander Alexander to John Overton, Supreme Court judge. Rec. May 11, 1807

p. 538-540 Oct. 21, 1806 John Alexander (Green Co, Ohio) to William Alexander (Spartanburgh); power of attorney to collect his due from estate of Alexander Alexander desc. Witness Samuel (J or I?) Martin and Abraham Chuse jr. Signed John Alexander. Wit. oath (Green Co, Ohio) Oct. 21, 1806 John Alexander to Josiah Grover, Assoc justice of Common Pleas Court. Oct. 21, 1806 (Green Co, Ohio) John Paul, clerk of Common Pleas Court, certifies Josiah Grover is Assoc judge. Oct. 23, 1806 (Green Co, Ohio) James Barrett, senior Assoc judge of Common Pleas Court, certifies John Paul is clerk. Rec. May 11, 1807

p. 540-541 Jan. 13, 1807 John Low, sr (Spartanburgh) to James Campbell (same); for $50 sold 50 ac on NE side Pacolate R; border: Kelley, Dart, and James Lackey. Witness Charles Smith and Ellis Cannon. Signed John Low. Wit. oath Apr. 18, 1807 Charles Smith to William Lancaster. Rec. May 15, 1807

p. 541 Nov. 10, 1806 Richard Barnett (Spartanburgh) to James Campbell (same); for $60 sold 65 ac on E side Pacolate R; border: Dart; part of 300 ac grant to James Wyatt. Witness William Bagwell and Jesse Mathis. Signed Richard Barnett. Wit. oath Nov. 10, 1806 William Bagwell to William Lancaster. Rec. May 11, 1807 (sic May 15 scratched out)

BOOK L 1807-1809

p. 1-2 Jan. 17(?), 1807 Rowland (or Roland) Ginnings (Spartanburgh) to James Keen (same); for $100 sold 175 ac; border: Finch and James Keen. Witness Christopher Johnson and Thomas Thornton. Signed Rowland Ginning's mark. Wit. oath Christopher Johnson to William Lancaster May 9, 1807. Rec. May 11, 1807. Dower renounced Doanna Ginnings to William Lancaster May 9, 1807(? page torn)

p. 2-3 Apr. 20, 1807 Henry Adcock (Spartanburgh) to John Tollinson (same); for $356 sold 100 ac on waters of and N side of Pacolate R; border: Leonard Adcock and John Lackey; part of 300 ac "run by" Frances Ballinger; sold for 8 months; Condition: sale void if Henry pays John $146 in 8 months. Witness Muse Tollinson and Reuben Harrison. Signed Henry Adcock's mark. Wit. oath Apr. 28, 1807 Muse Tollinson to William Simpson. Rec. May 11, 1807

p. 3-4 Oct. 22, 1806 William Miller (Spartanburgh) to James Patterson (same); for $200 sold 75 ac on N side Enoree R; where James Patterson lives; part of 500 ac grant to Thomas Scott who sold to Richard Hampton who sold to Stephen Cantrell who sold to William Towns and by plat Feb. 27, 1775 to John McCormick "by deed Nov. 8, 1799 from John McCormick to William Miller by deed Apr. 15, 1801"; border: Gals and Kevel. Witness Barnett H Algood and Samuel Walker. Signed William Miller. Wit. oath Oct. 22, 1806 Barnett H Algood to James Kilgore. Rec. May 11, 1807

p. 4-5 Jun. 12, 1794 John Henry and wife Elizabeth (Spartanburgh) to James Henry (same); for 20£ sold 50 ac on S side Pacolate R; including "a small" improvement; part of 200 ac grant Nov. 14,

1791 Gov. Josiah Martin (NC) to James Allen. Witness William Hammett, John Pool, and James Simpson. Signed John Henry and Elizabeth's mark. Wit. oath May 15, 1807 William Hammett to John Walker. Rec. May 15, 1807

p. 5-6 Mar. 23, 1807 Moses Wood (Greenville Dist) to John Young sr (Spartanburgh); for $1.25 sold 220 ac on S side Lawson's fork of Pacolate R; border: Rowland Johnson and Isham Foster; grant Jan. 21, 1785 to Moses Wood. Witness John Wood and George Salmon. Signed Moses Wood. Wit. oath (Greenville Dist) Mar. 28, 1807 George Salmon to John Young. Rec. Jun. 1, 1807

p. 6-7 Mar. 28, 1807 John Young sr (Spartanburgh) to John Dodd (same); for $600 sold 220 ac on S side Lawson's fork of Pacolate; border: Edward Ballinger, Isham Foster, and Moses Wood; part of grant to James Blackwood and grant to Moses Wood; 10 ac is reserved for Edward Ballinger. Witness William Young and Sarah (or Salley) Young. Signed John Young's mark. Wit. oath Mar. 28, 1807 William Young to Geo Salmon. Rec. Jun. 1, 1807

p. 7 Feb. 23, 1807 William Stewart (Spartanburgh) to Richard Fryer (same); to secure Richard Fryer from loss due to note of $150 payable Jan. 2, 1806 with interest, William sold (ac not given) where William Stewart lives; grant to George Wright and Ebenezer Moss and sold by George Wright to Patrick Cunningham and sold to Thomas Morngieger and sold to Henry Harding and sold to William Stewart; border: as on original plat except on E-bordered by 30 ac of grant sold by Henry Harden to David Niel. Witness Burrell Bobo, Aaron Casey, and Chaney Bobo. Signed Wm Stewart. Wit. oath May 21, 1807 Aaron Casey to Burrell Bobo. Rec. Jun. 1, 1807

p. 7-9 Jul. 1, 1805 Isham Harrison, sheriff (Spartanburgh) to James Roley (same); for $30.25 sold 56 ac on branch of Fairforrest Cr of Tygar R; border: N-Huskey, S-John Foster another legate, E-William Burton, W-John Connell; plat attached from "return of commissioners nominated in the writ of partition" drawn by W. R. Smith DS; part of land formerly owned by Thomas Foster desc and to William Foster by writ of division of property from Spartanburgh Common Pleas Court; sale due to writ from Spartanburgh Common Pleas Court suit Richard Love indorsee vs William Foster; sale Jul. 1, 1805. Witness Thomas Lancaster, Hugh Means, William Robinson. Signed I Harrison SSD. Wit. oath Jun. 1, 1807 William Robinson to D. T. Puckett. Rec. Jun. 1, 1807

p. 9-10 May 20, 1807 John Low sr (Spartanburgh) to John Tollinson (same); for $51.86 sold 520 ac on branches of Dewberry's Mill Cr of Thickety Cr; border: N-"lines laid out", NE-Low and the Creek, SE-Dewberry, NW-Moore, and SW-vacant and Dewberry; survey Feb. 3, 1799 for John Low and granted Gov. Edward Rutledge to Samuel Fley. Witness Muse Tollinson and Joseph Gist. Signed John Low. Wit. oath May 20, 1807 Muse Tollinson to Jos Gist. Rec. Jun. 1, 1807

p. 10-11 May 19, 1807 William Garrett (Spartanburgh) to John Tolleson (same); for $23.62 sold 100 ac on N side Pacolate R; sale for 7 months; Condition: sale void if William Garrett pays John Tolleson $23.62 in 7 months. Witness Muse Tolleson and William Murry. Signed William Garrett's mark. Wit. oath Jun. 1, 1807 William Murry to Michl Miller. Rec. Jun. 1, 1807

p. 11-12 Nov. 1, 1806 Henry Wells (Spartanburgh) to Moses Tapp (same); for $360 sold 180 ac; border: John Hammett. Witness Jas Smith, Noah Wells, and Henry Wells jr. Signed Henry Wells. Wit. oath Jun. 1, 1807 Noah Wells to Danl White. Rec. Jun. 1, 1807. Dower renounced Catherine Wells to Isham Foster Feb. 20, 1807

p. 12-13 Feb. 10, 1807 Alesent Seay (Amelia Co, Va) to William Pollard (96 Dist); power of attorney to obtain part of father's estate in hands of Gideon Seay, administrator for John Seay desc. Witness Dabney Miller and John Jeter. Signed Alesent Seay's mark. Wit. oath (Amelia Co, Va) Feb. 10, 1807 Alesent Seay to Thos Ellmore. Rec. Jun. 1, 1807. Feb. 11, 1807 James Towns, clerk of Amelia Co, Va, certifys Thos Ellmore is Justice of Peace

p. 13 Aug. 4, 1800 John Lee (Spartanburgh) to Anne Lee (same); for 10£ sterling sold 286 ac on Slend or Thuck(?) Cr of Pacolate R and Broad R; border: Island Cr. Witness James Wofford, Matthew McBee, and Richard Lee. Signed John Lee's mark. Wit. oath May 30, 1807 James Wofford to William Hendrex. Rec. Jun. 1, 1807

p. 13-14 Nov. 3, 1806 William Thomson (Spartanburgh) to John Gray (same); for 40£ sterling sold 60 ac on Lawson's fork of Pacolate R; border: Richard Thomson and John Gray; part of 700 ac grant Nov. 18, 1752 to James Alexander. Witness William Lipscomb, Margaret McKie, and Nancy Nichols. Signed Williamson (sic). Wit. oath May 20, 1807 William Lipscomb to John Lipscomb. Rec. Jun. 2, 1807

p. 14-15 Mar. 21, 1807 William Young (Greenville Dist) to John Young sr (Spartanburgh); for $2 sold 1,130 ac on both sides of S Pacolate R; where John Young lives; grant Sept. 4, 1786 to William Young. Witness William McWilliams, William Foster, and John Young jr. Signed Wm Young. Wit. oath Mar. 21, 1807 William McWilliams to Geo Salmon. Rec. Jun. 6, 1807

p. 15-16 Mar. 21, 1807 George Salmon (Greenville Dist) to John Young (Spartanburgh); for $2 sold 500 ac on both sides Pacolate R; border: N & W-vacant, SE-unknown and formerly Alexander Kilpatrick, and SW-formerly Isarel Morris; sold Jul. 9 & 10, 1783 John Burwick, Thomas Warring, and John E. Colhoun, commissioners of forfieted estates, to George Salmon. Witness William McWilliams, William Foster, and John Young jr. Signed Geo Salmon. Wit. oath May 21, 1807 William McWilliams to Geo Salmon. Rec. Jun. 6, 1807

p. 16-18 Apr. 16, 1807 Daniel White (Spartanburgh) to John Martin (same); for $550 sold (1) 3 ac which was sold Jun. 21, 1803 by William Lancaster and Zachariah McDaniel to Daniel White; border: Alexander McKie; including Daniel White's grist mill and saw mill; and (2) 37 3/4 ac which was sold Nov. 25, 1805 by Shands Golightly to Daniel White; border: Alexander McKie, Fairforrest Cr near end of Mile Dam, Moses Foster, White or Young, and McDaniel. Witness Elisha James and Peter Smith. Signed Daniel White. Wit. oath Jun. 1, 1807 Elisha James to William Lancaster. Rec. Jun. 13, 1807. Dower renounced Susannah White to William Lancaster Jun. 5, 1807

p. 18-19 Mar. 1, 1807 Matthew Harper (Smith Co, Tenn) to Robert Harper (Spartanburgh); for $200 sold 240 ac on both sides of S Pacolate R. Witness John Hale, William B. Harper, and Calesy Harper. Signed Matthew Harper. Wit. oath Mar. 20, 1807 William B. Harper to James Ballow. Rec. Jun. 23, 1807

p. 19-20 Apr. 6, 1807 Edward Herring (or Herrin) and wife Mary (Spartanburgh) to John Gray (same); for a Spanish milled dollar sold 100 ac on branches of Lawson's fork and E of Ancient boundary; border: Arthur Crocker and Rainwater. Witness William Herring and E Herring (female). Signed Edward and Maryan Herring. Wit. oath Jun. 16, 1807 William Herring to John H Jones. Rec. Jun. 23, 1807

p. 20 Jun. 15, 1807 Dower renounced Polly Thomson to Abner Benson; for deed from Richard Thomson to Littleton Bagwell. Rec.

Jun. 24, 1807

p. 20-21 Oct. 19, 1805 Isham Harrison, sheriff (Spartanburgh) to Jesse Wells; for $45.50 sold (ac not given) in Spartanburgh, SC; border: Main Street; formerly Noah Wells' land; sale due to writ from Spartanburgh Common Pleas Court suit John Underwood vs Noah Wells; sale Oct. 7, 1805. Witness Richard Thomson and Robert Alexander Todd. Signed I Harrison SSD. Wit. oath Jun. 24, 1807 Robert A Todd to Abner Benson. Rec. Jun. 24, 1807

p. 21-22 Nov. 12, 1806 Richard Thomson (Spartanburgh) to Samuel Farrow (same); for $80 sold ½ ac; lot #14 on S side of Spartanburgh Court House; border: S-Thomson, W-Abner Benson, E-Thomson, and N-Publick St. Witness John Wood Farrow and Andrew Harrison. Signed Richard Thomson. Wit. oath Jun. 23, 1807 John W Farrow to A Benson. Rec. Jun. 24, 1807

p. 22-23 Mar. 20, 1802 Robert Hanna (Spartanburgh) to Thomas Farrow (same); for $219 sold 146 ac on N side Enoree R; border: NE-Thomas Clark, SE-Thomas Farrow, SW-Moss, and W-Robert Hanna; plat attached shows 146.34 ac; part of 300 ac grant Oct. 7, 1762 Gov. Thomas Boone to Jacob Pennington who sold to Robert Hanna. Witness Ebenezer Moss and John Wood Farrow. Signed Robert C Hanna. Wit. oath Jun. 24, 1807 John W Farrow to A Benson. Rec. Jun. 24, 1807

p. 23-24 Jan. 1, 1803 Robert H Waring (Columbia, SC) to Daniel McClaren esq (Spartanburgh); for $500 sterling sold (1) 1,000 ac; border: NE-Tate, NW-Champion, NE-Davidson, SE-Boyes, and SW & NW-McClaren and Martin; and (2) three other tracts totaling 2,403 ac; border: SW-Charles Hester and Joseph Dill, E-Daniel McClaren's old tract on the River, E-William Byers and Arnold, Byers, Joseph Byers, and John Byers, E-William Wilson, Sarratt, Benner, and unknown, and S-Francis Breman and Co and James Martin; on branch of Cherokee Cr. Witness Benjamin Harrison and Jonathan Harrison. Signed R. H. Waring. Wit. oath Jan. 3, 1803 Benjamin Harrison to John Taylor. Rec. Jul. 1, 1807

p. 24 Mar. 30, 1807 William Wilkins (Spartanburgh) to daughter Sarah Wilkins; give 80 ac including where William McKnight formerly lived on Pacolate R; part of land William Wilkins bought from William McKnight. Witness John Lipscomb, Smith Lipscomb, and Joshua Richards. Signed William Wilkins. Wit. oath Jul. 6, 1807 Smith Lipscomb to A Benson. Rec. Jul. 6, 1807

p. 24-25 Oct. 9, 1805 Thomas Gore (Spartanburgh) to Thomas Pope (same); for $50 sold 100 ac on Buck Cr; border: Thomas Henderson, George Gilbert, and William McWilliams. Witness Pater Harris, Mary Buck, and Charles Crocker. Signed Thos Gore. Wit. oath Aug. 23, 1807 Charles Crocker to William Lancaster. Rec. Jul. 6, 1807

p. 25-26 Dec. 16, 1805 William Roberds (Spartanburgh) to Jesse Rakestraw (same); for $50 sold 50 ac on S side of Fairforrest Cr; border: Samuel Geddins, John Smith, "mountain line" and ridge path. Witness Christopher Johnson and Hugh White. Signed William Roberds. Wit. oath Jul. 6, 1807 Christopher Johnson to D. T. Puckett. Rec. Jul. 6, 1807. Dower renounced Martha Roberds to William Lancaster Jan. 11, 1806

p. 26-27 Jan. 6, 1807 Henry Wells (Spartanburgh) to Elijah Barnett (same); for $250 sold 156 ac on waters of Fairforrest Cr. Witness Isham Harrison, William Wells, and Noah Wells. Signed Henry Wells. Wit. oath Apr. 7, 1807 Isham Harrison to Daniel White. Rec. Jul. 6, 1807. Dower renounced Catherine Wells to Isham Foster

Feb. 20, 1807

p. 27-28 Feb. 22, 1807 Henry Wells (Spartanburgh) to Elijah Barnett (same); for $100 sold 60 ac; border: a waggon road on Daniel Wells' south line of fork of peper's path. Witness William Wells, John Wells, and James Turner. Signed Henry Wells. Wit. oath Apr. 7, 1807 William Wells to Daniel White. Rec. Jul. 6, 1807

p. 28-29 Dec. 29, 1806 Henry Wells (Spartanburgh) to Elijah Barnett (same); for $800 sold 295 ac; border: Richard Thomson; part of grant to Henry Wells. Witness Isham Harrison, Wm Ross Smith, and A Foster. Signed Henry Wells. Wit. oath Apr. 7, 1807 Isham Harrison to Danl White. Rec. Jul. 6, 1807. Dower renounced Catherine Wells to Isham Foster Feb. 20, 1807

p. 29-30 Feb. 16, 1807 Thomas Bennett (Spartanburgh) to Jonathan Wall (same); for $100 sold 50 ac on E side Richland Cr of Pacolate R; border: S-James Burnett, W-Richland Cr, and N-Clark; part of 743 ac grant to Thomas Bennett. Witness Vincent Bennett and George Gilbert. Signed Thomas Bennett's mark. Wit. oath May 29, 1807 Vincent Bennett to Wm Kelso. Rec. Jul. 6, 1807

p. 30-31 Jan. 1, 1807 Gasham Lee (Spartanburgh) to James Camp (same); for $150 sold 200 ac on Buck Cr; border: old ridge path, Thomas Henderson, and Gilmore's old place. Witness George McWilliams and Margaret McWilliams. Signed Gasham Lee's mark. Wit. oath Jul. 7, 1807 George McWilliams to Wm Kelso. Rec. Jul. 9, 1807

p. 31-32 Sept. 30, 1804 Mary Walker (Rutherford Co, NC) to George Walker (Spartanburgh); for $3,000 sold following Negroes: winch Fann, four girls: Mary, Rachel, Sarah, and Casey, a boy Matthew, and a young child. Witness William Walker. Signed Mary Walker. Wit. oath Jul. 16, 1807 William Walker to Abner Benson. Rec. Jul. 16, 1807

p. 32-33 Jan. 12, 1807 Augustin Bumpass (Spartanburgh) to Robert Bumpass (same); for $200 sold 90 ac on S side of Two Mile Cr; border: Casey. Witness Philip Massey, James Leatherwood, and Obadiah Moss. Signed Augt Bumpass. Wit. oath (Laurens Dist) May 9, 1807 James Leatherwood to Sterling Tucker. Rec. Jul. 21, 1807

p. 33 a plat for 74 ac on "Creek"

p. 33-34 Jun. 13, 1806 Sampson Tramel (Spartanburgh) to Ephram Elder (same); for 25£ SC money sold 150 ac on N side Pacolate R; border: Ephram Elder, a waggon road, Thomas Reese, and James Saunders; part of 1,000 ac grant States Office to Abraham Markley. Witness Peter Elder and John Wyatt. Signed Sampson Tramel's mark. Wit. oath Jan. 7, 1807 John Wyatt to Henry Turner. Rec. Jul. 29, 1807

p. 34-35 Jan. 22, 1807 Thomas Underwood (Spartanburgh) to Thomas Williamson (same); for $300 sold 88 ac between Furgason's Cr and Tygar R; on SW side of ridge road; part of tract sold by Hightower (or Hidhtower) to Thomas Underwood. Witness Thornton McDaniel, Thomas Williamson jr, and John Means. Signed Thos Underwood. Wit. oath Apr. 16, 1807 Thornton McDaniel to Drury McDaniel. Rec. Aug. 3, 1807. Dower renounced Elizabeth Underwood to Drury McDaniel May 7, 1807

p. 35-36 Aug. 6, 1803 William McDaniel (Spartanburgh) to Malichi Eskridge; for $52 sold 140 ac; border: Malicha Eskridge, Enoch Underwood, Berry, and William McDaniel jr. Witness John Ward, Edward McDaniel, and Thornton McDaniel. Signed Wm McDaniel.

Wit. oath Mar. 9, 1807 John Ward to Drury McDaniel. Rec. Aug. 3, 1807

p. 36-37 Aug. 19, 1806 John Hester and wife Sally (Spartanburgh) to Thomas Crutchfield (same); for $75 sold 75 ac on both sides Little Cherokee R; border: Edward Green, George Walker, Richard Arnold, and Venetts (or Venutt); part of "big survey" belonging to Charles Hester. Witness John Venetts and Thomas Farmer. Signed John Hester and Sally's mark. Wit. oath Sept. 27, 1806 Thomas Farmer to John Lipscomb. Rec. Aug. 3, 1807

p. 37-38 Dec. 24, 1800 James Wofford (Spartanburgh) to Joseph Wofford (same); for $50 sold 112 ac; border: NE, NW & SE-Joseph Woodruff and SE & SW-Revers and Hughes; grant Mar. 4, 1793 Gov. William Moultrie to Joseph Woodruff. Witness Daniel Wright, William Rhodes, and Thomas Woodruff III. Signed James Wofford. Wit. oath Aug. 3, 1807 Thomas Woodruff III to Drury McDaniel. Rec. Aug. 3, 1807. Dower renounced Caty Wofford to Daniel Wright Jul. 16, 1807

p. 38-39 Feb. 28, 1807 Thomas Williamson (Spartanburgh) to John Means (same); for $300 sold 300 ac on N side of N fork Forgeson's Cr. Witness Thomas Williamson jr, John Warde, and Samuel Colley. Signed Thomas Williamson. Wit. oath Apr. 10, 1807 John Warde to Drury McDaniel. Rec. Aug. 3, 1807

p. 39-41 Feb. 28, 1807 Samuel Colly (Spartanburgh) to Thomas Williamson (same); for $150 sold 45 ac between Tygar R and Forgason's Cr; border: N-Daniel Bragg, NW-Hightowers, SW-Drury McDaniel, and SE-Thomas Williamson; survey Apr. 17, 1799. Witness John Ward, Thomas Williamson jr, and John Means. Signed Samuel Colly's mark. Wit. oath Apr. 10, 1807 John Ward to Drury McDaniel. Rec. Aug. 3, 1807. Dower renounced Obedience Colly to Drury McDaniel May 7, 1807

p. 41-42 Feb. 19, 1807 Henry Wells (Spartanburgh) to Thomas Wells (same); for $1,000 sold 1,000 ac except 180 ac sold by Henry Wells to Moses Tapp; on branch of Tygar R; border: NE & SE-John Ford, NE-Porcher and Lawson and includes crossroads where Georgia and Blackstock's Roads cross; grant to John Parker who sold Nov. 3 & 4, 1773 to Joseph Kirkland who sold Feb. 12 & 13, 1789 to Minor Winn who sold Apr. 13, 1802 to William Wells who sold Nov. 9, 1805 to Henry Wells. Witness Burger McFearson, Jehu Wells, and Henry Wells jr. Signed Henry Wells. Wit. oath Aug. 3, 1807 Jehu Wells to Danl White. Rec. Aug. 3, 1807

p. 42-43 Nov. 8, 1806 James Hadden (Spartanburgh) to William Bice (same); for $430 sold 236 ac on Camp Br of Ben's Cr of S Tygar R; border: Elijah Johnson, N & NW-John Bonwell, James Hadden, William Hoy, and Denny Anderson, and W-John Durham. Witness William Beacham and William Fusham. Signed James Hadden. Wit. oath Mar. 11, 1807 William Beacham to John Collins. Rec. Aug. 3, 1807

p. 43-44 Dec. 28, 1804 Thomas Finch (Spartanburgh) to William Cook (same); for $150 sold 80 ac on waters of S Tygar R; part of grant to Thomas Hightower. Witness Thomas Underwood and Zachariah Grace. Signed Thomas Finch's mark. Wit. oath Jun. 28, 1805 Thomas Underwood to Drury McDaniel. Rec. Aug. 3, 1807

p. 44-45 Dec. 10, 1803 Thomas Shurley (or Shurby) (Spartanburgh) to John Martin (Union Dist); for (money not mentioned) sold 100 ac where Ignatious Surly lives; border: Tygar R, Andrew Thomson, and E-John Meadows, Samuel Shurburt, and S-N fork Tygar r. Witness Ignatious Turley and Rachel Turley. Signed Thomas Shurbey. Wit. oath Feb. 4, 1805 Ignatious Turley to Wm Smith. Rec. Aug. 3, 1807. Dower renounced Milley Shurbey to Wm Smith

BOOK L

Oct. 13, 1804

p. 45-46 Nov. 16, 1799 Daniel Draper and wife Susanna and Marthy Philips Gibbs (Spartanburgh) to John Cook (same); for $300 sold 450 ac on Kelsoe's Cr; land comes to Daniel and Susanna Draper and Marthy P Gibbs by heirship; grant to Giles Connel and sold by "our" father Zachariah Gibbs and "bound for titles governing the bond falling to us". Witness Anthony Foster and George Connell. Signed Daniel Draper and Susanna and Marthy's marks. Wit. oath Aug. 3, 1807 Anthony Foster to Daniel White. Rec. Aug. 3, 1807

p. 46-47 Mar. 13, 1807 Elijah Barnett (Spartanburgh) to James Selmon (same); for $75 sold 60 ac; border: a waggon road, David Wells, and fork of Piper's path. Witness Frederick Williams, John Williams, and William Selman. Signed Elijah Barnett. Wit. oath Apr. 18, 1807 Frederick Williams to Danl White. Rec. Aug. 3, 1807

p. 47-48 Jan. 21, 1807 Mathew Lile and wife Jenett (Kershaw Dist) to Edmond Bomar; for $400 sold 400 ac on Cub Br of Tygar R; survey Jun. 9, 1772 by John Robertson and then bordering vacant land. Witness Ism Foster, John Crawford, and Mary Crawford. Signed Mathew Lile and Jenett's mark. Wit. oath Aug. 3, 1807 Ism Foster to J Walker. Rec. Aug. 3, 1807. Dower renounced Jenett Lile to Isham Foster Jan. 21, 1807

p. 48-49 Feb. 5, 1807 Stephen Foster (Spartanburgh) to Edith Legon; for $60 sold 27 ac; border: William Burton; includes improvements where Edith Berry lives; "originally belonging to" Jessy Connell who sold to Robert Legon who sold to Thomas Foster desc and is Stephen Foster's legacy; between dower of Stephen Foster's mother and dower of Edith Legon. Witness Robert Legon and Lewis Huskey. Signed Stephen Foster. Wit. oath Apr. 6, 1807 Robert Legon to Drury McDaniel. Rec. Aug. 3, 1807. Dower renounced Jane Foster to Ism Foster (not dated)

p. 49-50 Sept. 17, 1805 Henry Smith (Spartanburgh) to David Golightly sr (same); for $180 sold (1) 96 ac on waters of Fairforrest Cr; border: John Smith, Hancock's Br, James Smith, and Spencer Smith; grant to Hancock Smith; and (2) 50 ac adjoining (1) on waters of Fairforrest Cr; border: formerly Hancock Smith; grant to John Smith. Witness Christopher Johnson, Jame (or Saml) Williams, and Robin Head. Signed Henry Smith. Wit. oath Aug. 3, 1807 Christopher Johnson to Danl White. Rec. (not given). Dower renounced Lydia Smith to William Lancaster Aug. 3, 1807

p. 50-51 Aug. 17, 1807 Jacob Autry (Spartanburgh) to David Golightly (same); for $90 sold 61½ ac on Buffeloelick Cr on S side Fairforrest Cr; border: Buleon's old line and Hampton's old line; part of two tracts: (1) grant to Thomas Buleon and (2) grant to Jesse Connell. Witness Abner Underwood and William Crook. Signed Jacob Autry. Wit. oath Aug. 3, 1807 William Crook to Danl White. Rec. Aug. 3, 1807

p. 51-52 Mar. 23, 1802 William Wheeler (Spartanburgh) to John Cook (same); for $50 sold (ac not given) on both sides Fairforrest Cr; border: N-Robert Legon, S & SE-David Golightly, and W-Thomas Foster; land "fell by heirship" to James Zachious and Wm Wheeler and belonged to "our" father William Wheeler desc. Witness Jacob Autry and Solomon Autry. Signed William Wheeler. Wit. oath Aug. 3, 1807 Solomon Autry to D. J. Puckett. Rec. Aug. 3, 1807

p. 52-53 Mar. 18, 1807 David Golightly jr (Spartanburgh) to John Foster (same); for $80 sold 47 ac on branch of Fairforrest Cr of Tygar R; border: S-John Foster, W-Shands Golightly, and N & E-David Golightly; part of grant to William Wofford who sold to

Robert White who sold to Robert Sterling who sold to David Golightly. Witness Christopher Golightly and Joseph Kelso. Signed David Golightly. Wit. oath Mar. 18, 1807 Joseph Kelso to William Lancaster. Rec. Aug. 3, 1807

p. 53-54 Feb. 24, 1800 Giles Connell (Spartanburgh) to John Cook (same); for $300 sold 450 ac on E side Fairforrest Cr; called Meeting House tract; tract Giles Connell gave Zachariah Gibbs a bond to make a title. Witness Gabriel Benson and Henry Wells. Signed Giles Connell. Wit. oath Aug. 26, 1800 Henry Wells to I Harrison. Rec. Aug. 3, 1807

p. 54-55 Jan. 22, 1800 Ignatious Turley (Spartanburgh) to John Cook (same); for $200 sold 90 ac on Buffeloe lick Cr on S of Fairforrest Cr; border: S-Elizabeth Autry and William Roberds, N-David Golightly and David Cook, and Henry Ayres and Ephram Elder; sold by Robin Head to George Connell. Witness William Cook and David Cook. Signed Ignatious Turley's mark. Wit. oath May 23, 1801 David Cook to Wm Smith. Rec. Aug. 3, 1807

p. 55-56 Dec. 17, 1805 Jesse Morrow (Rutherford Co, NC) to Isaac Young (Spartanburgh); for $71.50 sold 141 ac on E side Island Cr; Jesse Morrow pays Isaac Young if older right takes some of the land. Witness William Young, John Young, and Isaac Young. Signed J Morrow. Wit. oath Jul. 18, 1807 William Young to Leonard Adcock. Rec. Aug. 3, 1807

p. 56-57 Aug. 3, 1807 Gabriel Benson, sheriff (Spartanburgh) to Samuel Morrow; for $41 sold 50 ac on W side Dutchman's Cr of Tygar R; part of grant to William Ware; sale due to writ from Spartanburgh Common Pleas Court suit Reuben S Saunders vs Hezekiah Burrell; sale Jul. 6, 1807. Witness Benjamin Peak and David Trail. Signed Gab Benson SSD. Wit. oath Aug. 3, 1807 Benjamin Peak to Danl White. Rec. Aug. 3, 1807

p. 57-58 Feb. 4, 1807 John Cantwell (Spartanburgh) to Edith Berry (same); for $150 sold 102 ac on E side Fairforrest Cr; border: E of Reubin Daniel, S of Henry Brown, N of Mrs. Lee. Witness Robert Legon and Henry Brown. Signed John Cantwell. Wit. oath Apr. 6, 1807 Robert Legon to William Simpson. Rec. Aug. 3, 1807. Dower renounced Jane Cantwell to Burrell Bobo Apr. 7, 1807

p. 58-59 Feb. 7, 1806 John Tolleson (Spartanburgh) to Reuben Bryant (same); for $100 sold 150 ac on S side Pacolate R; border: Richard Kirby (or Keeley), John Harvy, Richard Harvy, William Reed, John Easterwood, Reuben Bryant's Spring Br; grant to John Tolleson. Witness Muse Tolleson and Major Gossett. Signed John Tolleson. Wit. oath Feb. 8, 1806 Muse Tolleson to William Simpson. Rec. Aug. 3, 1807

p. 59-60 Jan. 16, 1806 John Easterwood (Spartanburgh) to Reuben Bryant (same); for $70 sold 50 ac on S side of Pacolate R; border: Reuben Bryant, Reuben Bryant's Spring Br, and Harvy; part of tract "leased" to John Easterwood. Witness William Chesney and John Cates. Signed John Easterwood's mark. Wit. oath Feb. 8, 1806 William Chesney to William Simpson. Rec. Aug. 3, 1807

p. 60-61 May 2, 1807 John Tolleson (Spartanburgh) to Major Gossett (same); for $100 sold 100 ac on waters of Fairforrest Cr; border: George Kennet, George McCarter, and Charleston Rd. Witness Muse Tolleson and John Chisholm. Signed John Tolleson. Wit. oath Aug. 1, 1807 Muse Tolleson to William Simpson. Rec. Aug. 3, 1807

p. 61-62 Aug. 3, 1807 John Tolleson (Spartanburgh) to Richard Kirby (or Kerby) (same); for $500 sold 350 ac on S side Pacolate

R; border: Mile Cr, Josiah Sparks' Spring Br, path to William Bryant, path to Richard Kirby, Roaring Springs, John Harvy's shoal, William Bryant, Troaght Shoals Br, Joseph Quin, and Ready Br; John Tolleson keeps half of "fishery"; part of two grants to John Tolleson. Witness Joshua Draper and Reubin Bryant. Signed John Tolleson. Wit. oath Aug. 3, 1807 Joshua Draper to John Lipscomb. Rec. Aug. 3, 1807

p. 62-63 Dec. 27, 1806 John Huckabee (Spartanburgh) to Jobe Sims (same); for $80 sold 80 ac; part of 180 ac grant Jun. 17, 1793 Gov. William Moultrie to Charles Holt. Witness James K Benson and John Grist. Signed John Huckabee's mark. Wit. oath Jun. 6, 1807 John Grist to Saml Lancaster. Rec. Aug. 21, 1807

p. 63-64 Feb. 19, 1807 John Tolleson (Spartanburgh) to Bennett Dafforn (same); for $125.20 sold 100 ac on N side of grant Dec. 4, 1786 to William Bratcher; border: "said" Wooten, John Grist, Wooten Spring, Dutchman Cr, and Moses Prewett. Witness Samuel Lancaster JP and John Gossett. Signed John Tolleson. Wit. oath Jul. 4, 1807 Samuel Lancaster to William Lancaster. Rec. Aug. 21, 1807

p. 64-65 Dec. 27, 1806 John Huckaby (Spartanburgh) to Daniel Sims (same); for $100 sold 100 ac; part of 180 ac grant Jun. 17, 1793 Gov. William Moultrie to Charles Holt. Witness James K Benson and John Grist. Signed John Huckaby's mark. Wit. oath Jun. 6, 1807 John Grist to Saml Lancaster. Rec. Aug. 24, 1807

p. 65-66 Mar. 7, 1807 Samuel Dunaway sr and Samuel Dunaway jr (Spartanburgh) to Nimrod Lunceford (same); for $200 sold 202 ac on branches of Thickety Cr; border: William Haden. Witness Lot Warren and Reuben Warren. Signed Samuel Dunnaway sr and Samuel Dunnaway jr. Wit. oath Mar. 7, 1807 Lot Warren to Henry Turner. Rec. Aug. 31, 1807

p. 66-67 May 14, 1805 J. W. Legon (Laurence Dist) to Josiah Hatchett (Spartanburgh); for $500 sold 139½ ac; border: ford in "the" river, William Moore, Thomas Cook, a waggon road, and Robert Legon. Witness Thomas Cook and Judah Hatchett. Signed J. W. Legon. Wit. oath Aug. 31, 1807 Thomas Cook to Jacob Utley. Rec. Sept. 1, 1807

p. 67-68 Dec. 22, 1804 John Knox (Spartanburgh) to William Abbett (same); for $100 sold 225 ac on Island Cr of Pacolate R; grant Mar. 1, 1802 States Office to John Knox. Witness William Young and Mathew Abbett. Signed James Knox. Wit. oath Aug. 25, 1807 William Young to Henry Turner. Rec. Sept. 7, 1807

p. 68-70 Jan. 27, 1807 John White (Spartanburgh) to Obadiah Wingo (same); for $18 sold 18 ac on Dugan's Br of Fairforrest Cr; border: SE-Henry Oniell and Obadiah Wingo and NW-Alexander McKie; grant Jan. 6, 1806 to John White. Witness William Lancaster and William Simpson. Signed John White. Wit. oath Sept. 7, 1807 William Simpson to D. J. Puckett. Rec. Sept. 7, 1807. Dower renounced Agatha White to William Lancaster Jun. 12, 1807

p. 70-71 Mar. 12, 1807 David Burton, Drury Burton, Nancy Burton, James Bright and wife Polley, Charles Burton, Samuel Burton, Culbert Burton, and Nathaniel Burton (all Spartan Dist) to William Burton; for $100 sold (1) all "our part" or 300 ac on both sides of N Tygar R; grant to John Meehouse who sold to John Williams who sold to Charles Burton; and (2) 116 ac "all our part" within bounds of (1); grant to John Williams who sold to Charles Burton. Witness Thomas Meadow and Sterling Hudgins. Signed David Burton, Drury Burton, Nancy Burton, Charles Burton, Samuel Burton, Colbert

Burton, and James Bright. Wit. oath Aug. 29, 1807 Thomas Meadow to John Burton. Rec. Sept. 10, 1807

p. 71-72 Jul. 15, 1807 Mark Thomason (Spartan Dist) to William West; for $65 sold 165 ac; lot #4 that Mark Thomason "drew" from his father's real estate. Witness D. J. Puckett and Thomas Bennett. Signed Mark Thomason's mark. Wit. oath Aug. 15, 1807 Thomas Bennett to D. J. Puckett. Rec. Sept. 11, 1807. Dower renounced Hannah Thomason to D. J. Puckett Sept. 11, 1807

p. 72-73 Apr. 26, 1807 Obadiah Wingo (Spartanburgh) to Willis Wingo (same); for $100 sold 100 ac on Paddy's Br of Fairforrest Cr; border: Culbertson's old line and Gibbs' old line; plat attached shows 102 ac. Witness Thomas Wingo and Hamilton Willis (or Wilson). Signed Obadiah Wingo. Wit. oath Sept. 16, 1807 (sic) Hamilton Wingo to William Lancaster. Rec. Sept. 15, 1807

p. 73-74 Apr. 26, 1807 Obadiah Wingo (Spartanburgh) to Willis Wingo (same); for $200 sold a Negro boy Enoch about 6 or 7 years old. Witness Hamilton Wilson and Thomas Wingo. Signed Obadiah Wingo. Wit. oath Sept. 16, 1807 Hamilton Wilson to William Lancaster. Rec. Sept. 15, 1807

p. 74-75 Oct. 28, 1803 Henery Jamison (Spartanburgh) to Reuben Traylor (same); for $100 sold 61 ac on Nichols Cr of S Tygar R; border: NW-Frances Powers, SE-James Nichols, and NE-John Patton. Witness James Ford and Nowbell Johnson. Signed Henery Jamison. Wit. oath Apr. 7, 1807 Nowbell Johnson to David Morton. Rec. Sept. 18, 1807

p. 75-76 Aug. 8, 1807 John Patton (Spartanburgh) to Reuben Traylor (same); for $200 sold 100 ac on Reedy fork; border: Frances Powers. Witness Austin Grisham and James Powers. Signed John Patton and Jeney Patton. Wit. oath Sept. 16, 1807 James Powers to David Morton. Rec. Sept. 18, 1807

p. 76 Jun. 10, 1803 Samuel Moore (Spartanburgh) to Hezekiah Burrell (same); a bond of 32£ 14s 6p; Condition: bond void if Samuel Moore deeds Hezekiah Burrell part of grant to William Ware on W side Dutchman's Cr "where said land is paid for". Witness Milley Burrel and Nancy Hembe (or Henbny). Signed Saml Moore. Wit. oath Aug. 12, 1807 Milley Burrel to Danl White. Rec. Sept. 18, 1807

p. 76-78 Mar. 13, 1805 William Clarkson (Charleston, SC) to James Smith (Spartanburgh); for $200 sold 900 ac on Kelsoe's Cr of Fairforrest Cr and Brown's Br of Lawson's fork of Pacolate R; border: NE-James Brown and others vacant; survey Nov. 23, 1773 by William Gist and granted Feb. 8, 1773 to "said" Locock and memorial in Auditor Gen Office Book M #12 p. 240 Jun. 9, 1773; plat attached with note--Brown tract takes about 10 ac, Cedar Spring tract takes about 30 ac "which were excepted by Mr Brannan because they were older than Locock's and agreed by me" signed James Smith. Witness Hancock Smith and Tucker Harris. Signed Will Clarkson. Wit. oath Sept. 19, 1807 Hancock Smith to Dan White. Rec. Sept. 19, 1807

p. 78-79 Mar. 8, 1806 William Burton (Spartanburgh) to James Smith (same); for $100 sold 110 ac on branch of Kelsoe's Cr of Fairforrest Cr; border: Old Cedar Spring tract, Court House Road near Cedar Spring Crossroads, Jesse Connell, Legon now Burton, and Smith; plat attached. Witness William Bagwell and David Linch (or Lynch). Signed William Burton. Wit. oath Sept. 19, 1807 David Linch to Danl White. Rec. Sept. 19, 1807

p. 79-80 Mar. 27, 1807 Michael French to John Dean (Spartanburgh); for $50 sold a bay mare called "Jin" branded "A"; and a sorrel colt two years old this Spring. Witness John W Farrow. Signed Michael French's mark. Wit. oath Sept. 25, 1807 John W Farrow to Abner Benson. Rec. Sept. 25, 1807

p. 80-81 Mar. 22, 1807 William Austell (Spartanburgh) to Amos Austell (same); for $30 sold 30 ac on both sides of Thickety Cr; grant "to Amos to William Wilkins 1792"; border: W-Milly Austell, N-William Lipscomb, and E-William Wilkins. Witness Joseph Austell and William Wilkins. Signed William Austell. Wit. oath Sept. 4, 1807 William Wilkins to John Lipscomb. Rec. Sept. 25, 1807

p. 81-82 Jan. 6, 1807 John Brannon (Spartanburgh) to James Brannon (same); for $75 sold 50 ac on Lawson's fork; grant Nov. 25, 1774 Gov. William Bull to Stephen Miller. Witness Thomas Brannan, Drury Hutcheson, and William Rollins. Signed John Brannon. Wit. oath Feb. 9, 1807 Thomas Brannan to Ism Foster. Rec. Oct. 1, 1807

p. 82-83 Oct. 5, 1807 Reuben Bomar to Benjamin High (Spartanburgh); for $400 sold 167 ac on N fork Tygar R; border: John Snoddy and others. Witness Thomas Bomar and Edward Bomar. Signed Reuben Bomar's mark. Wit. oath Oct. 5, 1807 Thomas Bomar to D. J. Puckett. Rec. Oct. 5, 1807

p. 83-84 Sept. 15, 1807 David Bruton (Spartanburgh) to Jean Thomson (same); for $369 sold 123 ac; border: N side of N Tygar R; part of grant Jan. 5, 1786 to Andrew Thomson. Witness Lewis Furguson and Lawson Thomson. Signed David Burton. Wit. oath Sept. 29, 1807 Lewis Furguson to Drury McDaniel. Rec. Oct. 5, 1807

p. 84-85 Oct. 2, 1807 John Simmons (Spartanburgh) to Frances Robertson (Kershaw Dist); by promissary note of same date payable Jan. 1, 1810 there is bond to pay $120 to Frances Robertson; to secure payment of that debt, John sells Frances 100 ac on Sarratt's Cr; border: N-North Carolina line, S-Frances Robertson, E-Calbert McGraw, and Thomas Harris; Condition sale void if John pays his debt. Witness Bryant Bonner and Batus (or Batees) Harris. Signed John Simmons. Wit. oath Oct. 4, 1807 Bryant Bonner to L Adcock. Rec. Oct. 5, 1807

p. 85-86 Apr. 25, 1807 Thomas Bennett (Spartanburgh) to Vincent Bennett (same); for $160 sold 643 ac on branches of Thomson's and Richland Creeks of Pacolate R; border: Jonathan Wall (Thomas Bennett sold some part of tract to Jonathan Wall) E-land sold by Thomas Bennett to William Bennett, S-Greenham Crowder and Abram Andrews, W & NW-Daniel White and John Young sr, and N-Alexr Kilpatrick and unknown. Witness William Bennett, Robert Stanford, and William Sentell. Signed Thomas Bennett's mark. Wit. oath Sept. 26, 1807 William Bennett to William Kelso. Rec. Oct. 5, 1807

p. 86-87 Apr. 10, 1807 Thomas Bennett (Spartanburgh) to William Bennett (same); for $200 sold 340 ac on both sides Thomson's Cr of Pacolate R; where Thomas Bennett lives; at time of grant bordered: NE-vacant, N-confiscated land, W-vacant, and SE-John Kimble. Witness Larkin Carden and Thomas Kimble. Signed Thomas Bennett. Wit. oath Jul. 25, 1807 Larken Carden to William Kelso. Rec. Oct. 5, 1807

p. 87-88 Feb. 13, 1799 John Barnet and wife Nancy (Spartanburgh) to Gideon Harrelson (same); for 33£ sterling sold 95 ac on N side Tygar R; border: Thos Rogers, John Vice, and Nathl Burton; part of 420 ac grant Nov. 6, 1786 Gov. William Moultrie to Abraham Notty (or Notly). Witness I Harrison. Signed John and Nancy Barnett. Wit. oath Feb. 13, 1799 John Barnett to I Harrison and Oct. 5, 1807 I Harrison to D. J. Puckett. Rec. Oct. 5, 1807.

p. 88-90 Feb. 6, 1802 Nathaniel Burton (Spartanburgh) to Gideon Harrelson (same); for 50£ 6s 8p sterling sold 125 ac; border: John Vince, Thomas Rogers, and Gideon Harrelson. Witness Arthur Faulkner, Tephance Pinson, and Tobias Bright. Signed Nathl Burton and Martha's mark. Wit. oath Oct. 3, 1807 Arthur Faulkner to William Lancaster. Rec. Oct. 5, 1807. Dower renounced Martha Burton to William Smith Oct. 2, 1802

p. 90-91 Jun. 3, 1807 Christopher Johnson (Spartanburgh) to Lawson Thomson (same); "by note of hand" a bond of $1,100; to secure the bond, Christopher sells a Negro man Bob, a Negro winch Doll, Negro girl Watsey, boy Will, and boy Obey; Condition: sale void if Christopher pays debt. Witness Lewis Shelton and Sarah Thomson. Signed Christopher Johnson. Wit. oath Aug. 31, 1807 Lewis Shelton to Drury McDaniel. Rec. Oct. 5, 1807

p. 91-93 Mar. 17, 1807 William Gibson (Spartanburgh) to Abraham Green (York Dist); for $200 sold 142 ac; border: NW-Powell and S-Taylor; grant Oct. 6, 1788 to Matthew Jones. Witness Michael Gaffney and Smith Lipscomb. Signed William Gibson's mark. Wit. oath Aug. 29, 1807 Smith Lipscomb to John Lipscomb. Rec. Oct. 5, 1807. Dower renounced Salley Gibson to John Lipscomb Sept. 22, 1807

p. 93-94 May 16, 1806 Smith Lipscomb (Spartanburgh) to William Gibson (same); for $10 sold 142 ac on branch of Cherokee Cr on S side Broad R; border: NW-Powell and S-Taylor; grant Oct. 6, 1788 to Matthew Jones. Witness William Lipscomb and Joseph Collins. Signed Smith Lipscomb. Wit. oath Sept. 1, 1807 William Lipscomb to John Lipscomb. Rec. Oct. 5, 1807. Dower renounced Agness Lipscomb to John Lipscomb Aug. 29, 1807

p. 94-95 (omitted), 1804 William Crocker (Spartanburgh) to Joseph Gibson Olliver (same); for $100 sold 100 ac on both sides of Branch of Buck Cr of Pacolate R and both sides of Ridge Road between Buck Cr and Pacolate R; where William Crocker lives; border: all vacant land when granted. Witness Thomas Gilbert, Mark Gilbert, and William Rollins. Signed William Crocker's mark. Wit. oath Oct. 17, 1804 Thomas Gilbert to Wm McDowell. Rec. Oct. 5, 1807

p. 95-96 Aug. 28, 1800 John and Margaret Densmore (Spartanburgh) to Nathaniel Woodruff (same); for $196 sold 82 ac on Jeamy's Cr of Tygar R; border: Leatherwood, Calesberry, and Myres Br; W part of 250 ac grant to John Kiehler. Witness David Brewton, John Woodruff, James Taylor. Signed John Densmore and Margaret's mark. Wit. oath Sept. 12, 1807 John Woodruff to John Brewton. Rec. Oct. 14, 1807

p. 96-97 Apr. 11, 1807 Jesse Spencer (Union Dist) to John Stephens (Spartanburgh); for $450 sold 100 ac; border: grant to John Gibbs and Model; grant in 1770 to Curuce(?) "a part of another grant to John Gibbs". Witness Robert Legon, Reuben Jentry, and Robert Hammett. Signed Jesse and Elizabeth Spencer. Wit. oath Aug. 31, 1807 Robert Legon to Daniel White. Rec. Oct. 24, 1807

p. 97-98 Apr. 11, 1807 John Stevens (Spartanburgh) to Daniel Stevens (same); for $225 sold (1) 50 ac and (2) "part of a half" of a 50 ac grant to James Gibbs ("half" is 25 ac) "which I also sell to my father". Witness Robert Legon, Reuben Jentry, and Robert Hammett. Signed John Stevens. Wit. oath Aug. 31, 1807 Robert Legon to Daniel White. Rec. Oct. 24, 1807

p. 98-99 Dec. 26, 1806 John Otts (Spartanburgh) to Daniel Stevens; for $200 sold 129 ac on waters of Ward's Cr; border: Philip Otts and John Fench; W end of tract John Otts bought from Zachariah Gibbs; part of grant to Richard Hampton. Witness Christopher Johnson and John Stevens. Signed John Otts. Wit. oath Aug. 31, 1807 John Stevens to Daniel White. Rec. Oct. 24, 1807

p. 99-100 Oct. 24, 1807 James Robertson (Spartanburgh) to William Morgan (same); for $107 sold 2 beds and furniture, 35 barrels of corn, 1,000 bundles of fodder shuks, 2 cows and calves, 4 pots and an oven, 500 wt. of cotton, and a hat; Condition: sale void if James pays William $107 by Dec. 25, 1807. Witness P. M. Tate, Andrew Calwall and Jacob Hedden. Signed James Robinson's mark. Wit. oath Oct. 24, 1807 P. M. Tate to Drury McDaniel. Rec. Oct. 26, 1807

p. 100-101 Oct. 14, 1807 Mason Shumate (Spartanburgh) to John Crawford (same); for $700 sold (1) 2 ac on S side of N fork Tygar R; and (2) 137 ac on N fork Tygar R. Witness Abner Benson and Robert Benson. Signed Mason Shumate. Wit. oath Oct. 26, 1807 Robert Benson to Abner Benson. Rec. Oct. 26, 1807

p. 101-102 Apr. 11, 1804 Alexander Alexander (Spartanburgh) to Gideon Reynolds (same); a bond of 600 Spanish milled dollars; Condition: bond void if Alexander deeds Gideon 68 ac on James Cr including a Grist Mill and water pond; border: John Cowen; deed to be made by Dec. 25, 1805. Witness Andrew Thomson. Signed Alexr Alexander. Wit. oath Nov. 9, 1807 Nathaniel Burton recognizes Andrew Thomson's and Alexander Alexander's handwriting to John Dean. Rec. Nov. 9, 1807

p. 102-103 Jun. 7, 1806 Daniel Grant (Spartanburgh) to Alexander Prewett (same); for $130 sold 60 ac on Cainy fork Cr; border: Edward Hoocker and Alexander Prewett's fence. Witness Drury Parham and William Grant. Signed Daniel Grant's mark. Wit. oath Jun. 28, 1806 Drury Parham to William Smith. Rec. (omitted). Dower renounced Catherine Grant to William Grant Sept. 16, 1806

p. 103-105 Sept. 13, 1806 Volentine Smith (Spartanburgh) to Asey Collecot (same); for $300 sold 194 ac; border: John Walker, Benjamin Grist, Samuel Cathcart, and John Red; part of 284 ac grant Feb. 5, 1787 to John Campbell. Witness Daniel Grant to Ralph Smith. Signed Volentine Smith. Wit. oath Sept. 16, 1806 Daniel Grant to Wm Smith. Rec. Nov. 9, 1807. Dower renounced Catherine Smith to William Smith Sept. 16, 1806

p. 105-106 Jul. 28, 1807 James Sanders (Spartanburgh) to Casper Webber (same); for $350 sold 264 ac on N side Pacolate R at mouth of Buck Cr; border: Isaac Young; grant(?) Nov. 25, 1771 then in North Carolina. Witness John Morrow and William Webber. Signed James Sanders' mark. Wit. oath Jul. 28, 1807 John Morrow to Henry Turner. Rec. Nov. 9, 1807

p, 106-107 Jan. 13, 1807 James Morris (Edgefield Dist) to Abraham Cantrell (Spartanburgh); for $127 sold 170 ac on S side Buck Cr of Pacolate R; border: School house Br, Bankston, and John Morris; grant May 10, 1788 States Office to William Morris sr who sold to James Morris. Witness James Bankston, John Morris, and John Bankston. Signed James Morris' mark. Wit. oath Nov. 5, 1807 John Morris to Leonard Adcock. Rec. Nov. 9, 1807

p. 107-108 Jun. 18, 1804 Henry Wood (Spartanburgh) to James Wheeler (same); for 10£ sold 194 ac on W side Rocky field Cr of Enoree R. Witness Manly Ford and John Jones. Signed Henry Wood. Wit. oath Sept. 10, 1804 John Jones to James Kilgore. Rec. Nov. 9, 1804

p. 108-109 Nov. 29, 1806 Sterling Hugins (Spartanburgh) to John Meaders (same); for $100 sold 70 ac on S Tyger R; border:

Aaron Pinson and "his" son Sepheniah; part of 200 ac grant in 1786 to Obadiah Edwards. Witness Daniel Hammett and Joseph Meaders. Signed Sterling Hugins' mark. Wit. oath Oct. 3, 1807 Joseph Meaders to William Lancaster. Rec. Nov. 9, 1807

p. 109-110 Oct. 29, 1806 John Cooper (Spartanburgh) to Isaac Gorden; for $400 sold 400 ac on Beverdam and Cherokee Creeks of Broad R; part of 600 ac grant in 1787 to John Cooper. Witness Jacob Crocker and Nathaniel Robertson. Signed John Cooper. Wit. oath Nov. 5, 1806 Jacob Crocker to John Lipscomb. Rec. Nov. 9, 1807. Dower renounced Nancy Cooper to John Lipscomb Nov. 5, 1806

p. 110 Oct. 29, 1806 John Cooper (Spartanburgh) to Isaac Gorden; "for value received" sold 100 ac; border: a road, Robertson, and Cooper's old line. Witness Jacob Crocker and Nathaniel Robertson. Signed John Cooper. Wit. oath Nov. 5, 1806 Jacob Cooper to John Lipscomb. Rec. Nov. 9, 1807

p. 110-111 Nov. (omitted), 1804 John Hampton (Orangeburgh Dist) to Lemuel Loftis (Spartanburgh); for 65£ sterling sold 175 ac. Witness James Kilgore and David McClanahan. Signed John Hampton. Wit. oath (Greenville Dist) Nov. 4, 1807 James Kilgore to Reuben Barrett. Rec. Nov. 9, 1807. Dower renounced Margaret Hampton to John Adam Turner Apr. 1, 1806

p. 111-113 Jul. 28, 1801 William Stubbs and wife Jean (Spartanburgh) to Joseph Dill (same); for $4 sold 200 ac in Spartanburgh and Union Dists and on both sides of road near Cherokee ford on Broad R "of" Cherokee Cr and People's Cr. Witness Richard Thomson and Nicholas Stubbs. Signed William Stubbs' mark and Jane Stubbs. Wit. oath Mar. 2, 1802 Richard Thomson to John Lipscomb. Rec. Nov. 10, 1807

p. 113 Jan. 13, 1807 John Chisholm (Jefferson Co, Tenn) to John Amos; for $160 sold 146 ac on waters of Beverdam Cr; grant Gov. Charles Pinckney to Randolph Laurence. Witness Michael Gaffney and Reuben Morgan. Signed John Chisholm. Wit. oath Jun. 8, 1807 Michael Gaffney to John Lipscomb. Rec. Nov. 10, 1807

p. 113-114 Jul. 27, 1805 James Gilmore (Spartanburgh) to James Gilmore jr (same); for $300 sold 100 ac on Bare Cr of Pacolate R; border: McKnight and Calfpen Br; part of grant Aug. 11, 1784 to James Gilmore. Witness Gabriel Benson to James Lewis. Signed James Gilmore's mark. Wit. oath Jul. 27, 1805 James Lewis to Wm McDowell. Rec. Nov. 10, 1807

p. 114-115 Sept. 15, 1806 Dower renounced Sarah Smith to William Smith; for deed Millington Smith to Volentine Smith. Rec. Nov. 10, 1807

p. 115-116 Sept. 26, 1807 John Tolleson (Spartanburgh) to John Low (same); for $50 sold 420 ac on branch of Durberry's Mile Cr of Thickety Cr; border: NE-Low and creek, SE-Dewberry, NE-Moore, and SW-vacant and Dewberry; survey Feb. 3, 1799 for John Tolleson and granted Gov. Edward Rutledge to Saml Fly. Witness John Gossett and Ely Tolleson. Signed John Tolleson. Wit. oath Nov. 9, 1807 John Gossett to Leonard Adcock. Rec. Nov. 10, 1807

p. 116-117 Aug. 11, 1807 William and John Philips (Spartanburgh) to John Old Hance (same); for $27.50 sold 30 ac E of Old Indian Boundary; border: on E side of People's Cr and E-William Rukman; part of grant Sept. 5, 1791 to James Martin. Witness William Rukman and John Daffron. Signed Jno Philips and William Philips' mark. Wit. oath Nov. 5, 1807 John Daffron to John Lipscomb. Rec. Nov. 10, 1807

p. 117-118 Jun. 20, 1807 James Galt (Spartanburgh) to George Alexander (same); for $150 sold 150 ac on both sides of Motley's Cr; on lower end of line from Motley's Cr to Esley Cr; lower part of grant Jun. 6, 1785 to Robert Goodjuant; except "the situation" of a machine now built on the land and enough land to support a dam and seat of the saw machine not to exceed 6 ac; the machine is James Galt's. Witness Hugh Ewing and Ibey Galt. Signed James Galt. Wit. oath Nov. 5, 1807 Hugh Ewing to Wm Kelso. Rec. Nov. 10, 1807

p. 118-119 Jun. 10, 1807 James Wofford (Spartanburgh) to John Wofford (same); for $200 sold 100 ac on head branches of Sugar Cr; border: Varnel. Witness John Wofford jr and Mary Wofford. Signed James Wofford's mark. Wit. oath Nov. 11, 1807 John Wofford jr to William Wofford. Rec. Nov. 10, 1807. Dower renounced Selah Wofford to William Lancaster Nov. 7, 1807

p. 119-120 Mar. 3, 1800 Thomas Hews (Spartanburgh) to John Quarles (same); for 50£ SC money sold 100 ac on S side Pacolate R; border: Hurican Cr, mouth of Wild Cat Br, Milhanks, and Robertson. Witness Ellis Cannon, David Quarles, and Mary Hughes. Signed Thomas Hews and Nancy's mark. Wit. oath Oct. 27, 1804 David Quarles to George Lamkin. Rec. Nov. 11, 1807

p. 120-121 Aug. 12, 1807 (Union Dist) Henry ONiell to Nancy ONeill; for $200 sold 122 ac on waters of Fairforrest Cr and branch of Harris Cr; border: Hugh Donaldson, Samuel Simpson, and vacant. Witness Thomas Sullivan and Richard Cruse. Signed Henry ONiell. Wit. oath Nov. 3, 1807 Thomas Sullivan to William Simpson. Rec. Nov. 11, 1807

p. 121-122 Feb. 17, 1807 Frances Robertson (Kershaw Dist) to Benjamin Bonner (Spartanburgh); for $200 sold 200 ac on waters of Sarratt's Cr; border: N-Thomas Harris, E-Frances Robertson, S-Benjamin and Dempsey Bonner, and W-William Holloway. Witness Thomas Harris and Charles Jones. Signed Frances Robertson. Wit. oath May 10, 1807 Charles Jones to L Adcock. Rec. Nov. 11, 1807

p. 122-124 Oct. 7, 1807 William Davidson (Spartanburgh) to Anthony Sarratt (Rutherford Co, NC); for $500 sold 120 ac on waters of Sarratt's Cr; grant to William Holoway who sold(?) Sept. 12, 1798 to William Davidson. Witness John Sarratt and Casper Webber. Signed William Davidson's mark. Wit. oath Nov. 10, 1807 John Sarratt to John Lipscomb. Rec. Nov. 12, 1807

p. 124-125 Oct. 7, 1807 Anthony Sarratt (Rutherford Co, NC) to Samuel Sarratt (Spartanburgh); for $200 sold 135 ac on W side Broad R; border: John Sarratt, Buffaloe path, and "said" Sarratt. Witness John Sarratt and John Sarratt jr. Signed Anthony Sarratt's mark. Wit. oath Nov. 10, 1807 John Sarratt to John Lipscomb. Rec. Nov. 12, 1807

p. 125-126 Aug. 12, 1801 Redick Arrendell (Spartanburgh) to Anthony Sarratt (same); for $102 sold 135 ac on W side of Broad R; border: John Sarratt, Buffaloe path, and Anthony Sarratt; grant Oct. 1, 1792 Gov. Charles Pinckney to Allen Sarratt who sold to Redick Arrendell. Witness John Sarratt and John Rukman. Signed Readick Arrendell. Wit. oath Feb. 13, 1802 John Sarratt to John Lipscomb. Rec. Nov. 12, 1807

p. 126-127 Oct. 7, 1807 William Davidson sr (Spartanburgh) to Anthony Sarratt (Rutherford Co, NC); for $500 sold 200 ac on wathers of Sarratt's Cr; grant Dec. 5, 1785 to William Davidson sr. Witness John Sarratt and Casper Webber. Signed William Davidson's mark. Wit. oath Nov. 10, 1807 John Sarratt to John Lipscomb. Rec.

Nov. 12, 1807

p. 127 Nov. 7, 1807 Burrell Bobo (Spartanburgh) to Miles Rainwaters (same); a bond of $1,000; Condition: bond void if Burrell "warrant and defends" 300 ac (sic) "leased" (sic) by William Stone to Miles Rainwaters; land near cleared part of 418 ac grant to William Stone. Witness Robert McCord and James Rainwaters. Signed Burrell Bobo. Wit. oath Nov. 13, 1807 James Rainwaters to Burrell Bobo. Rec. Nov. 16, 1807

p. 127-129 Nov. (omitted), 1807 William Stone (Spartanburgh) to Miles Rainwaters (same); for $400 sold 418 ac where William Stone lives; grant to William Stone. Witness Robert McCord, James Rainwaters, and Burrell Bobo. Signed William Stone. Certified (not dated) by Burrell Bobo. Wit. oath Nov. 16, 1807 James Rainwaters to Abner Benson. Rec. Nov. 16, 1807. Dower renounced Mary Stone to Burrell Bobo Nov. 7, 1807

p. 129-131 Feb. 12, 1788 George Thomson (Spartanburgh) to John Salley (same); for 32£ 10s sold 83 ac on Pacolate R; border: Edward Hampton; part of 183 ac grant Jun. 5, 1786 Gov. William Moultrie to George Thomson on both sides Pacolate R and bordering: NE-Edward Hampton and others vacant. Witness William Jamison, William Turner, and Luke Burnett. Signed George Thomson. Wit. oath (Pendleton Dist) Sept. 4, 1807 William Jamison to Wm Edmondson. Rec. Nov. 19, 1807.
Aug. 31, 1802 John Salley (Pendleton Dist) assigns rights to David Mosley "for value received from him". Witness John Gowen and John Gowen sr. Signed John Salley's mark. Wit. oath Nov. 18, 1807 John Gowen sr to A Benson.

p. 131 Jan. 6, 1807 Isham Harrison and Richard Daniel agree line between their lands on both sides Fairforrest Cr will be "main bed" of Fairforrest Cr; Isham's land is on W side of creek and Richard's land is on E side ofcreek. Witness William Underwood, John H Jones, and Gal Bumpass. Signed I Harrison and Richard Daniel. Wit. oath Jan. 5, 1807 (sic) John H Jones to Jacob Utley. Rec. Nov. 25, 1807

p. 131-133 Oct. 1, 1807 William McKnight (Spartanburgh) to William Chapmon (same); for $900 sold 330 ac on N side of N Pacolate R and Bare Cr. Witness John Chapmon and Moses Foster. Signed William McKnight. Wit. oath Nov. 18, 1807 Moses Foster to Ism Foster. Rec. Nov. 27, 1807

p. 133-134 Sept. 28, 1807 Moses Brooks (Spartanburgh) to John Ballenger (same); for $405 sold 213 ac on N fork of N fork Tygar R; border Jesse Reames, Wayland, Miller, and Edward Ballenger; grant in 1786 Gov. William Moultrie to Thomas Brooks. Witness John Davis SM, John Cargell, and Elizabeth Cargell. Signed Moses Brooks and Mary's mark. Wit. oath Dec. 11, 1807 John Davis to D. J. Puckett. Rec. Dec. 14, 1807. Dower renounced Elizabeth Brooks, wife of Thomas Brooks, and Mary Brooks, wife of Moses Brooks, to D. J. Puckett Dec. 11, 1807

p. 134-135 Aug. 22, 1807 Matthew Couch and wife Elizabeth (Spartanburgh) to James Clayton (same); for $200 sold 150 ac on N side Enoree R; where Matthew Couch lives; border: N-James Clayton, E-Solomon Smith, S-Benjamin Stone, and N(sic)-John Farrows; part of two grants to (1) William Cox and (2) Matthew Couch sr. Witness Henry Meredith and Fielding Clayton. Signed Matthew and Elizabeth Couch's marks. Wit. oath Sept. 16, 1807 Fielding Clayton to Burrell Bobo. Rec. (not given)

p. 135-136 Jan. 23, 1807 Carie Traylor (Spartanburgh) to William

Grisham (same); for $150 sold 60 ac on N side Ben's Cr of S Tygar R; where William Grisham lives; border: John Nisbett. Witness William Brice and Samuel Brice. Signed Carie Traylor's mark. Wit. oath Mar. 17, 1807 William Brice to David Morton. Rec. Dec. 7, 1807

p. 136-137 Sept. 1, 1807 Samuel Burton (Spartanburgh) to Daniel White (same); for $715 sold 200 ac on both sides of Fairforrest Cr; sold by Elijah Barnett to Samuel Burton; part of grant to Giles Connell. Witness Colbert Burton and Martha Burton. Signed Samuel Burton. Wit. oath Oct. 6, 1807 Colbert Burton to John Burton. Rec. Dec. 15, 1807

p. 137-138 Dec. 13, 1806 James and John Brannon (Spartanburgh) to Joroyal Barnett (same); for $75 sold 50 ac on E side of Fawn Br; border: J Barnett (bought from Jesse Hammett). Witness William Rollins and Thomas Barnett. Signed James Brannon and John Brannon. Wit. oath Nov. 10, 1807 Thomas Barnett to Burrell Bobo. Rec. Dec. 15, 1807. Dower renounced Sarah Brannon, wife of James, to Burrell Bobo Nov. 10, 1807

p. 138-140 Nov. 17, 1806 James Alexander sr (Spartanburgh) to Thomas Burton (same), bricklayer; for $700 sold 200 ac on waters of S Pacolate R; border: John Clark. Witness Robert Benson, Andw Furgason, and Jesse A Burton. Signed Jas Alexander. Wit. oath Dec. 15, 1807 Robert Benson to A Benson. Rec. Dec. 16, 1807

p. 140-141 Mar. 9, 1807 Adaman Johnson (Spartanburgh) to James Johnson (same); for $50 sold 50 ac; border: Barton's Br. Witness Ephram Lewis and Nathaniel Bishop. Signed Adaman Johnson. Wit. oath Jun. 1, 1807 Ephram Lewis to Danl White. Rec. Dec. 19, 1807

p. 141-142 Sept. 27, 1805 John Johnson (Spartanburgh) to William Hendrix (same); for $200 sold 205 ac on branch of Suk Cr of Enoree R; SW part of 400 ac grant in 1773 to John Hamby. Witness William Lindsey and Emley Hendrix. Signed John Johnson. Wit. oath Dec. 26, 1807 Unicy (sic) Hendrix to John Brewton. Rec. Dec. 27, 1807. Dower renounced Dicey Johnson to David Morton Jan. 22, 1807

p. 142-144 Dec. 19, 1807 Thomas Philips sr (Spartanburgh) and John and William Philips (Union Dist) to Samuel Old Hance (Union Dist); for $147 sold 180 ac on waters of People's Cr; border: William Ruckman and John Hance; grant Sept. 5, 1781 Gov. Charles Pinckney to James Martin and sold to Joseph Dill and sold to Thomas Philips and sold to son William Philips. Witness Smith Lipscomb and William Wood. Signed Thomas, John, and William Philips' marks. Wit. oath Dec. 19, 1807 Smith Lipscomb to John Lipscomb. Rec. Dec. 27, 1807

p. 144-145 Apr. 25, 1807 Samuel Lancaster (Spartanburgh) to William Palmer (same); for $250 sold 70 ac on S side Dutchman's Cr; part of grant to Samuel Lancaster. Witness John Grist and Thomas Prewett. Signed Saml Lancaster. Wit. oath Sept. 5, 1807 John Grist to William Lancaster. Rec. Dec. 31, 1807. Dower renounced Agness Lancaster to William Lancaster Sept. 5, 1807

p. 145-146 Jul. 25, 1805 Henry Wells (Spartanburgh) to John Wood (same); for $300 sold 377 ac on waters of Tygar R; grant Mar. 5, 1785 Gov. William Moultrie to Martin Armstrong. Witness Isham Foster and Nancy Foster. Signed Henry Wells. Wit. oath Nov. 7, 1807 Isham Foster to J Walker. Rec. Jan. 1, 1808

p. 146-148 Dec. 10, 1807 James Lee (Spartanburgh) to Samuel Morrow (same); for $20 paid by Nancy Pool, wife of Abraham Pool Samuel Morrow gets "interest" and Nancy Pool gets 92½ ac for "sole use and benefit" of Nancy Pool until her son John Pool is 21 years old; land on waters of Dutchman's Cr; part of 350 ac grant Apr. 3, 1786 to William Sterling; John Pool gets land when he is 21, but if he dies first, then Peggy and Cassey Pool, Scotes (or Scates?) of John Pool get the land; plat attached shows border: William Lewis, Thompson, James Lewis, and West. Witness Thomas Meaders (or Meadows), John Wofford, and William N Morrow. Signed James Lee. Wit. oath Dec. 26, 1807 Thomas Meaders to Saml Lancaster. Rec. Jan. 1, 1808

p. 148-149 Aug. 28, 1807 John H Arnold (Spartanburgh) to Stone and Herring (or Hearing); for $130 sold 135 ac on Suk (or Luk) Cr of Enoree R; border: Isaac Hembey; part of 400 ac grant to John Hambey. Witness John Crocker and William Hendrix. Signed John H Arndeld. Wit. oath Aug. 29, 1807 John Crocker to Denny Anderson. Rec. Jan. 1, 1808

p. 149-150 Dec. 31, 1802 John Hamby sr (Spartanburgh) to John Arnold jr; for $130 sold 135 ac on Luk Cr of Enoree R; border: Isaac Hamby; part of 400 ac grant to John Hamby. Witness James Wofford, John Crocker, and John Hamby. Signed John Hamby's mark. Wit. oath Aug. 29, 1807 John Crocker to Denny Anderson. Rec. Jan. 1, 1808

p. 150-152 Sept. 10, 1803 Thomas Moore (Spartanburgh) to James Moore (same); for $100 sold 100 ac on N side Tygar R and branch of Ward's Cr; border: NW-James McGowen, SE-Joseph Rogers, E-Robert Morrow, E-"an old line", and by Hammon Elder; part of 285 ac grant Dec. 3, 1787 Gov. Thomas Pinckney to Thomas Moore. Witness Samuel Otts and William Acree. Signed Thomas Moore. Wit. oath Sept. 24, 1803 William Acree to Drury McDaniel. Rec. Jan. 4, 1808. Dower renounced Edy Moore to William Lancaster Mar. 27, 1804

p. 152-153 Dec. 16, 1806 William Gilmore (Spartanburgh) to John Clark (same); for $400 sold 416 ac on both sides Lawson's fork and branches of Meadow Cr; border: N-McDowell, E-Cudd, S-Sackey (or Lackey), and W-Carr (or Carves); grant Nov. 20, 1801 to William Gilmore. Witness James Lewis and William Lewis. Signed William Gilmore. Wit. oath Jan. 2, 1808 James Lewis to William Kelso. Rec. Jan. 4, 1808

p. 153-154 Oct. 9, 1807 John Simmons (Spartanburgh) to Anthony Foster (same); for $250 sold 200 ac at mouth of Alder Br; border: road from Anthony Foster to Giles Connell and Reuben Daniel. Witness James Smith sr, James Smith jr, and John Lancaster. Signed John Simmons. Wit. oath Oct. 23, 1807 John Lancaster to D. J. Puckett. Rec. Jan. 15, 1808. Dower renounced Agness Simmons to D. J. Puckett Oct. 23, 1807

p. 154-156 Feb. (omitted), 1807 Lewis Husky (Spartanburgh) to Anthony Foster (same); for $200 sold 236 ac. Witness D. J. Puckett, Fielding Foster, and John Foster. Signed Lewis Hasky. Wit. oath Feb. 15, 1807 Fielding Foster to Isham Foster. Rec. Jan. 15, 1808

p. 156-157 Jan. 14, 1808 John Johnson (Spartanburgh) to James Medford (same); for $80 sold 40 ac; border: James Allon, Henry Cole, and Aaron Baughcom. Witness John Cantrell, William Massey, and Thomas House. Signed John Johnson. Wit. oath Jan. 19, 1808 William Massey to David Morton. Rec. Jan. 18, 1808

p. 157-158 Jan. 14, 1808 Henry Wells (Summer Co, Tenn) to Thomas Wells (Spartanburgh); for $80 sold 126 ac on road from Spartanburgh Court House to Anthony Foster's and about 2 miles from the Court House. Witness Abner Benson and Robert Benson. Signed Henry Wells. Wit. oath Jan. 22, 1808 Robert Benson to Abner Benson. Rec. Jan. 22, 1808

p. 158-159 Sept. 9, 1795 Benjamin Rowland (Spartanburgh) to George Rowland (same); for 50£ Va money sold a Negro man Lewis about 35 years old. Witness Robert Kimbol and Edward Clement. Signed Benjamin Rowland. Wit. oath Jan. 13, 1808 Robert Kimbol to Ism Foster. Rec. Jan. 25, 1808

p. 159-160 Jan. 23, 1808 John Andrews (Spartanburgh) to George Rowland (same); for $75 sold 100 ac E of old Indian Boundary and on Richland Cr of S Pacolate R; grant Oct. 2, 1786 Gov. William Moultrie to Richard Sparks and sold by Abraham Andrews to Daniel White; except part taken by Daniel White's old grant. Witness Alexander Austin and Elizabeth Rowland. Signed John Andrews. Wit. oath Jan. 25, 1808 Alexander Austin to James Young. Rec. Jan. 25, 1808

p. 160-162 Dec. 5, 1807 George Salmon (Greenville Dist), executor of will of William Wood jr desc, (late of Spartanburgh) to George Rowland (Spartanburgh); for $500 sold 245 ac on head branch of Fawn Br of Lawson's fork of Pacolate R; border: School House Spring Br; known as Boiling Green (or Grun); sale due to instructions in William Wood jr's will; notice of 21 days was given and land sold Mar. 7, 1795; land was sold for 37£ to George Salmon (sic) and on Dec. 9, 1806 "set over" by purchase to George Rowland. Witness Alexander Austin and Elizabeth Rowland. Signed Geo Salmon. Wit. oath Jan. 25, 1808 Alexander Austin to James Young. Rec. Jan. 25, 1808

p. 162-164 Jan. 6, 1806 Charles Hester (Spartanburgh) to William Champeon (York Dist); for $800 (or $8,000?) sold two adjoining tracts: (1) 250 ac on Cherokee Cr on S side Broad R; Tate's old mill tract; border: S-Alexander Martin esq that Joseph Dill lives on, SE-John Fondren, and includes the mill and all its benefits and meadow above the mill--formerly Tate's mill then Hester's; grant Apr. 21, 1775 to William McKowen who sold to William Tate desc and left by his will to son Jesse Tate who sold to Charles Hester; and (2) 222 ac adjoins (1) on SE; border: S-Nathaniel Robertson and Slaysy, E-William McCowen, and N-Thomas Dace (or Doies); grant Jun. 4, 1798 to Charles Hester. Witness John Trimmier and Peter Quin. Signed Charles Hester. Wit. oath Aug. 23, 1806 John Trimmier to John Lipscomb. Rec. Jan. 25, 1808

p. 164-165 Jan. 15, 1807 Arnold Thomason (Spartanburgh) to John Cantwell (same); for $350 sold 200 ac on S side Pacolate R; where Arnold Thomason lives; part of grant to Jesse Connell who sold to Joseph Davis and sold by Vincent Wyatt, attorney for Joseph Davis, to William Rich who sold to Arnold Thomason. Witness Richard Thomson, David Linch, and A Foster. Signed Arnold Thomason. Wit. oath Jan. 12, 1808 Richard Thomson to Jno H Jones. Rec. Jan. 12, 1808

p. 165-166 Dec. 5, 1808 (sic) John Cantrell (Spartanburgh) to Aaron Templemon (same); for $300 sold 200 ac on S side Pacolate R; part of grant to Jesse Connel who sold to Joseph Davis and sold by Vincent Wyatt, attorney for Joseph Davis, to William Rich who sold to Arnold Thomason who sold to John Cantrell. Witness Abner Benson and Jno H Jones. Signed John Cantrell. Wit. oath Jan. 12, 1808 Abner Benson to Jno H Jones. Rec. Jan. 12, 1808

p. 166-167 Dec. 1, 1807 Jonathan Low (Spartanburgh) to Aaron Templemon (same); for $50 sold 100 ac on N side Pacolate R; part of grant Mar. 16, 1787 States Office to Frances Ballenger;

border: William Adcock. Witness Thomas Wyatt and Hugh Moore. Signed Jonathan Low. Wit. oath Jan. 6, 1808 Thomas Wyatt to Henry Turner. Rec. Jan. 12, 1808

p. 167-168 Jan. 25, 1804 Samuel Dunnaway sr (Spartanburgh) to Samuel Dunnaway jr (same); for $200 sold 150 ac on branch of Thickety Cr; border: Robert Dunnaway and Morres; part of 1,000 ac grant States Office to Thomas English. Witness Robert Dunnaway and Reuben Warren. Signed Samuel Dunnaway. Wit. oath Jul. 24, 1804 Robert Dunnaway to Ger Lamkin. Rec. Jan. 30, 1808

p. 168-169 Nov. 21, 1801 John Turner (Spartanburgh) to William Turner (same); for 15£ sold 100 ac on both sides of "buck Suck Cr"; taken from lower end of John Turner's survey on Suck Cr. Witness Vardry Camp and Mathias Turner. Signed John Turner. Wit. oath Oct. 22, 1802 Mathias Turner to Geor Lamkin. Rec. Jan. 30, 1808

p. 169-171 Mar. 4, 1805 Isham Harrison, sheriff (Spartanburgh) to William Morris (same); for $81 sold 794 ac on head branch Suck Cr of Pacolate R; border: SW-Poole and Turner, SE & NE-Speares (or Speaces), NW-Camp, and others vacant; sale due to writ from Spartanburgh Common Pleas Court suit James Harrison vs John Bonner; sale Mar. 4, 1805. Witness John Semmons, James Camp, and Charles James. Rec. I Harrison SSD. Wit. oath Feb. 1, 1808 (sic) John Semmons to Abner Benson. Rec. Jan. 30, 1808

p. 171-172 Nov. 25, 1807 James Moore (Spartanburgh) to John Tolleson (same); for $260 sold 240 ac on waters of John Isom's (or Tims') Mill Cr; border: Stephen Cruse, Samuel Simon's old line, Robert Harris, Story, Nesbett, John Isham, John McDowell, McGray, and Robenett; "taken off 26 ac adjoining McDowell". Witness Muse Tolleson and John Gossett. Signed James Moore's mark. Wit. oath Dec. 3, 1807 John Gossett to H Means. Rec. Feb. 1, 1808. Dower renounced Nancy Moore to H Means Dec. 3, 1807

p. 172-174 James Crowder (Spartanburgh) to John Morrow (same); for $380 sold 157 ac on both sides Dutchman's Cr; grant Sept. 3, 1753. Witness James Hamm, Joseph Lanmum (or Lamnum), and William N Morrow. Signed James Crowder. Wit. oath Dec. 19, 1807 James Hamm to Samuel Morrow. Rec. Feb. 3, 1808. Dower renounced Lowhamah Crowder to William Lancaster Jan. 9, 1808

p. 174-175 Aug. 7, 1807 Andrew Berry (Spartanburgh) to Samuel Miller (same); $100 sold 65 ac on S side of N fork Tygar R; border: Andrew Berry. Witness Charles Moore, Charles M Berry, and Andrew Berry jr. Signed Andrew Berry. Wit. oath Aug. 17, 1807 Charles Moore to Michael Moore. Rec. Feb. 5, 1808

p. 175-176 Feb. 5, 1808 Jacob Bright (Spartanburgh) to Page Rork (Greenville Dist); for $100 sold "all my property": a sorrell mare 4 years old, 2 cows, 2 heffers, 2 sows and pigs and 2 other hogs, and all household furniture--2 beds and bed clothes, pots and ovens, and "even from a pin or upwards" belonging to the house, a set of blacksmith and gun smith tools; Condition: Page lets Jacob have use of above property until Jan. 1, 1809 and sale void if Jacob pays Page $100 or Page can keep what he can pay for. Witness Henry old Hance and Elizabeth Bright. Signed Jacob Bright. Wit. oath Feb. 8, 1808 Henry old Hance to A Benson. Rec. Feb. 8, 1808

p. 176-177 Jan. 14, 1808 John Martin (Spartanburgh) to Robert Martin (same); for $603.12 sold 179.1 ac on both sides Fair-forrest Cr; part of tract sold by Mr Tate to James Lusk. Witness D. J. Puckett and Vincent Bennett. Signed John Martin. Wit. oath

Jan. 19, 1808 Vincent Bennett to D. J. Puckett. Rec. Feb. 9, 1808. Dower renounced Peggy Martin to William Lancaster Feb. 3, 1808

p. 177-178 Jan. 15, 1808 Benjamin King (Spartanburgh) to Benjamin Champion (same); for $500 sold 400 ac on N fork Thickety Cr of Broad R; grant in 1787 to James Clark. Witness Moses Guyton and Thomas Collins. Signed Benjn King. Wit. oath Jan. 30, 1808 Thomas Collins to John Lipscomb. Rec. Feb. 9, 1808

p. 178-181 Apr. 3, 1793 William Hort, treasurer of South Carolina, (Charleston, SC) to Thomas Taylor (Columbia, Camden Dist); for 120£ sold (1) 200 ac below ancient boundary on Fairforrest Cr and (2) 500 ac on Middle fork Tygar R; border: Vernon (or Vunon), Sowen, and unknown; Henry White (Spartanburgh) on May 11, 1786 borrowed from John Huger, Thomas Jones, and John Postell, Commissioners of Loan Office, by virtue of Legislature act passed Oct. 12, 1785; loan was for 163£ sterling with interest; to repay the loan Henry White mortgaged to Commissioners his land and Henry failed to pay interest due Mar. 1, 1793; so land was sold Apr. 3 due to act of Legislature passed Feb. 19, 1791; loan was recorded in Book A p. 209 of Loan Office. Witness Wm Skrine and Absalem Alexander. Signed Wm Hort. Wit. oath (Charleston, SC) Aug. 18, 1807 Absalem Alexander to Tup (or Puss) Lee jr JP. Rec. Feb. 15, 1808.

p. 181-183 Aug. 5, 1806 Elizabeth Connell, John Rossan, and Sampson Connell (Spartanburgh) to Anthony Foster (same); for $1,000 sold 475 ac on Fairforrest Cr; border: Anthony Foster, Fairforrest Cr, and mouth of Alder Br; on Aug. 5, 1806 received $300 and a Negro boy "at $400". Witness James Smith, James Reeley, and James Smith jr. Signed Elizabeth Connell, John Rossan, and Simpson Connell. Wit. oath Feb. 13, 1808 James Smith jr to Danl White. Rec. Feb. 18, 1808. Dower renounced Nancy Rossan, wife of John, to Absalem Lancaster Aug. 28, 1806

p. 183-187 Feb. 12, 1789 Joseph Kirkland (Camden Dist) to Minor Winn esq (same); for 200£ 2s sterling sold (1) 1,000 ac in Craven Co on branch of Tygar R; border: NE & SE-John Ford and NW-Porcher and Lawson; grant to John Parker who sold Nov. 3 & 4, 1773 to Joseph Kirkland; (2) 1,300 ac; half of 2,600 ac in fork of Enoree and Tygar R; border: W-Indian land and S-"surveyed land" and others vacant; grant to Benjamin Williamson and sold Oct. 3 & 4, 1773 by William Williamson to Joseph Kirkland; and (3) 300 ac; grant to John Hope who sold to Joseph Kirkland. Witness John Means and Geo Brown. Signed Jo Kirkland. Wit. oath (Fairfield Dist) Dec. 11, 1807 John Means to Wiles Nooell (or Novell). Rec. Mar. 1, 1808

p. 187 Dec. 8, 1807 James and Joseph Black (Albermace Co, Va) to James Vernon (Spartanburgh); for $300 sold a Negro boy Ben. Witness Samuel Crowder. Signed James and Joseph Black. Wit. oath Mar. 7, 1808 Samuel Crowder to Ism Foster. Rec. Mar. 7, 1808

p. 187-2nd 188 (after 1st 189) Dec. 13, 1806 Joel Hembrie (Tenn) to John Browning (Spartanburgh); for $86 sold 122 ac on both sides Cain Cr on N side Tygar R; grant by Gov. William Moultrie; Joel deeded John this land but it was "mislaid or lost" and Joel gives this deed in lew of the first one. Witness John Thornton, Levi Crow, and Peter Hamilton. Signed Joel Hembrie. Wit. oath May 20, 1807 John Thornton to Saml Lancaster. Rec. Mar. 7, 1808

p. 2nd 188-189 Mar. 2, 1808 Samuel Noblet (Spartanburgh) to John Tolleson (same); for $78.12 sold 164 ac on waters of Fairforrest Cr; border: Simpson and Joseph Asken; Condition deed void if Samuel pays John $78.12 in 10 months. Witness Muse Tolleson and Philip Tackett. Signed Samuel Noblet. Wit. oath Mar. 4, 1808 Muse Tolleson to William Simpson. Rec. Mar. 7, 1808

p. 189-2nd 189 Mar. 3, 1808 David Brock (Spartanburgh) to John Tolleson (same); for $145.25 sold a waggon with horse tacklings and other "appertenences" belonging to it, a black mare about 8 years old a natural trotter, a "Dun" bay horse about 10 years old with a ball face, a bright bay horse about 7 years old, another bright bay horse about 10 years old all natural trotters, 4 feather beds, bedsted, and all their furniture; Condition: sale void if David pays John $145.25 in 9 months. Witness Muse Tolleson and James Harrison. Signed David Brock. Wit. oath Mar. 4, 1808 Muse Tolleson to William Simpson. Rec. Mar. 7, 1808

p. 2nd 189-193 Jul. 13, 1779 James Millican Barnard (96 Dist) to Benjamin West (same); for 100£ sold 100 ac on McElwain's Cr of Fairforrest Cr; border: NW-William Thomson, SE-William Brawley, and others vacant; N or lower end of 300 ac grant Aug. 11, 1774 Gov. William Bull to Jeremiah Barnard and descended to James M Barnard, eldest son of "James Barnard"; border: the other 200 ac sold to John Wofford. Witness Simon Sackett and Arthur Hutchens. Signed James Millican Barnard. Wit. oath Feb. 26, 1808 Arthur Hutchens to William Lancaster. Rec. Mar. 3, 1808

p. 193 Feb. 24, 1808 Dower renounced Jane Cantrell to A Benson; for deed John Cantrell to Aaron Templemon. Rec. Mar. 4, 1808

p. 193-195 Dec. 18, 1807 William Darvin (Spartanburgh) to Amos Austell (same); for $270 sold 340 ac with 69 ac excluded that is held by Horts and McBee old survey; on both sides McBee's Cr; known as Tanner's place; grant Gov. William Moultrie to Joshua Tanner. Witness Joseph Austell, William Bostick, and Thomas Harrison. Signed Wm Darvin. Wit. oath Mar. 2, 1808 Joseph Austell to John Lipscomb. Rec. Mar. 4, 1808. Dower renounced Gran Darvin to John Lipscomb Jan. 26, 1808

p. 195-196 Dec. 21, 1807 Richard Thomson (Spartanburgh) to Thomas Allison (Rutherford Co, NC), merchant; for $250 sold ½ ac at Spartanburgh Court House; on S side Main St; border: Publick land and McKie's lower lot. Witness Gabriel Benson and Abner Benson. Signed Richard Thomson. Wit. oath Mar. 4, 1808 Abner Benson to D. J. Puckett. Rec. Mar. 4, 1808

p. 196-197 Mar. 4, 1808 George Hewey (Spartanburgh) to Abner and Robert Benson (same); for $65 sold 23 ac on Lawson's fork; border: Abner Benson, Robert Benson, and Camp Br. Witness Robert A Todd, John G Bostick, and Thomas Poole. Signed George Hewey's mark. Wit. oath Mar. 4, 1808 John G Bostick to D. J. Puckett. Rec. Mar. 4, 1808

p. 197-198 Jan. 28, 1808 James Hays (Pendleton Dist) to Solomon Ward (Spartanburgh); for $50 sold (ac not given) on branch of Fairforrest Cr; border: Benson and James Ward; part of grant to William Wood. Witness Robert Benson, James Ward sr, and Abner Benson. Signed James Hays. Wit. oath Mar. 4, 1808 Robert Benson to A Benson. Rec. Mar. 4, 1808

p. 198-199 Oct. 22, 1807 Christopher Orrenduff (Spartanburgh) to Walter West (same); for $15 sold 7(?) ac on N side of Fairforrest Cr; border: Walter West; upper part of where Christopher Orrenduff lives and border: John Barnett. Witness Daniel White and James Smith jr. Signed Christopher Orrenduff's mark. Wit. oath Oct. 22, 1807 James Smith jr to Danl White. Rec. Mar. 7, 1808

p. 199-200 Dec. 24, 1806 John Trail (Spartanburgh) to David Trail, Sandford Smith, and Daniel Smith (same); for $30 sold a small bay mare about 3 years old, saddle, and bridle. Witness Moses Smith and John Stevens. Signed John Trail's mark. Wit. oath Mar. 7, 1808 Moses Smith to Samuel Morrow. Rec. Mar. 7, 1808

p. 200-201 Mar. 2, 1807 Joroyal Barnett (Spartanburgh) to Reuben Harrison (same); for $150 sold 107 ac except 4 ac taken by Locock's old survey near the highland pond. Witness James Barnett and Thomas James. Signed Joroyal Barnett. Wit. oath Mar. 7, 1808 Thomas James to Danl White. Rec. Mar. 7, 1808. Dower renounced Agness Barnett to William Lancaster Feb. 27, 1808

p. 201-202 Jan. 20, 1808 Jacob Land (Spartanburgh) to John Tolleson (same); for $27 sold a bay colt about one year old, a red sow and 9 shotes, a feather bed and furniture, a large grinestone, a corner cubbard and all its furniture, a pine table, a handsaw, a lennent (or Tannent) saw, a quantity of carpenter's tools such as jack planes, jointing plains, smoothing plains, drawing knives and augurs; Condition: sale void if Jacob pays John $27 "in time above mentioned". Witness Muse Tolleson, Abraham Lancaster, and Isham Briant. Signed Jacob Land. Wit. oath Jan. 21, 1808 Muse Tolleson to William Simpson. Rec. Mar. 7, 1808

p. 202-203 Feb. 6, 1808 Charles Gravett (Spartanburgh) to Thomas Price (same); for $250 sold 100 ac on S side Furgason's Cr; border: Salley Chesney. Witness William Otts, William Hammonds, and Ransel Gravett. Signed Charles Gravett's mark. Wit. oath Feb. 17, 1808 William Otts to John Brewton. Rec. Mar. 7, 1808

p. 203-204 Oct. 26, 1806 Robert Harper (Spartanburgh) to Jonathan Stokes (same); for $200 sold 100 ac on waters of S Pacolate R; border: S-Samuel Fowler, W-vacant, N-Hampton, and NE & E-Alston; grant Apr. 26, 1788 Gov. Charles Pinckney to Robert Harper. Witness Edward Fowler and John Spencer. Signed Robert Harper. Wit. oath Nov. 6, 1807 John Spencer to Wm Kelso. Rec. Mar. 7, 1808

p. 204-206 Jan. 27, 1808 James Hays (Pendleton Dist) to Abner Benson esq (Spartanburgh); for $10 sold 287 ac on branch of Fairforrest Cr; grant to John Hays and willed to James Hays. Witness John G Bostick, Robert Benson, and Solomon Ward. Signed James Hays. Wit. oath Mar. 5, 1808 John G Bostick to D. J. Puckett. Rec. Mar. 8, 1808

p. 206-207 Jan. 19, 1807 Samuel Smith (Spartanburgh) to James Sarratt (same); for $75 sold 70 ac on both sides of Ephram Wells Still House Br; part of grant Jan. 5, 1789 to John Gray who sold Dec. 10, 1805 to William Burton who sold Feb. 15, 1806 to Samuel Smith; border: Ephram Hill. Witness George T Sloan and Ezekiah Burrell. Signed Samuel Smith. Wit. oath Mar. 17, 1807 George T Sloan to Saml Lancaster. Rec. Mar. 12, 1808

p. 207-208 Oct. 21, 1805 Henry Morrow (Spartanburgh) to Alexander Evins (same); for $30 sold 168 ac on both sides N fork of Tygar R; border: N-Edward Ballenger, "nearly" W-Moses Brooks, NE-John Davis, "nearly" S-Michael Miller, SE-William Morgan, and E-John Jordan; grant to William Ford and sold to Daniel Morrow. Witness James McHughes, Samuel Pearson, and William Morgan. Signed Henry Morrow. Wit. oath Mar. 10, 1808 Samuel Pearson to John Collins. Rec. Mar. 14, 1808

p. 208-209 Oct. 14, 1805 Augustin Clayton (Spartanburgh) to Alexander Evins (same); for $50 sold 50 ac on both sides S fork of Tygar R; border: W-Alexander Evins, NW-James Gilleland, N-John

Collens, SE-Austin Grisham (or Gusham), and near waggon road; grant Gov. Edward Rutledge to Augustin Clayton. Witness Richard Foster and Gowen Clayton. Signed Austin Clayton. Wit. oath Apr. 6, 1807 Richard Foster to Drury McDaniel. Rec. Mar. 14, 1808

p. 209-210 Sept. 28, 1807 Levi Crow (SC) to John Sims (Spartanburgh); for $60 sold 50 ac; border: Grimes and William Rampley; part of 850 ac grant May 17, 1791 Gov. Charles Pinckney to Joel Hembrie. Witness John Red and Michael Sims. Signed Levi Crow. Wit. oath Feb. 12, 1808 John Red to Wilie Willeford. Rec. Mar. 14, 1808

p. 210-211 Aug. 13, 1805 James Alexander jr (Spartanburgh) to George Campbell (or Camell) (same); for $200 sold 200 ac on N side of Easley Cr; part of where James Alexander lives; border: survey by John Cleaton, James Alexander jr, and James Mason; part of grant Jun. 6, 1785 to Robert Goode. Witness Andrew Furgason and William Camel. Signed Jas Alexander. Wit. oath Feb. 7, 1808 Andrew Furgason to Jas L Burd. Rec. Mar. 21, 1808

p. 211-213 Sept. 22, 1807 William Crow jr (Spartanburgh) to William Posey (same); for $460 sold 150 ac on S fork of Jame's Cr; border: N-William Hendrix, W-Alexander Alexander, S-Isaac Crow, and E-"said" K Kearley; grant Oct. 30, 1767 Gov. L(sic) Montague to Charles Dunham who sold to Daniel Moring Aug. 16 & 17, 1771 who sold to Henry Keacley (or Kearley) Jun. 10, 1774 who sold Nov. 8, 1797 to Moses Caven who sold Mar. 9, 1807 to William Crow jr. Witness Zephaniah Posey and James Crow jr. Signed William Crow. Wit. oath Mar. 4, 1808 Zephaniah Posey to Drury McDaniel. Rec. Mar. 21, 1808. Dower renounced Mary Crow to Burrell Bobo Feb. 13, 1808

p. 213-214 Feb. 8, 1806 James Campbell (Spartanburgh) to Joseph Simmons (same); for $400 sold 200 ac on waters Brown's Cr of Lawson's fork of Pacolate R; border: "the" old ford and high-land pond. Witness Anthony Foster and John Simmons. Signed James Campbell. Wit. oath Apr. 8, 1806 John Simmons to Jacob Utley. Rec. Mar. 31, 1808

p. 214 Jan. 12, 1807 Thomas Jackson (Spartanburgh) to James Quin (same); for $145 sold 145 ac on S Pacolate R; border: Young. Witness William Foster and Samuel Turner. Signed Thos Jackson. Wit. oath Aug. 21, 1807 Samuel Turner to Henry Turner. Rec. Apr. 1, 1808

p. 214-215 Apr. 28, 1807 Amos Speace (Spartanburgh) to Daniel McClaren (same); for $125 sold 125 ac on Cherokee Cr of Broad R. Witness William Cox and James Goodall. Signed Amos Speace. Wit. oath Mar. 4, 1807 James Goodall to Henry Turner. Rec. Apr. 2, 1808

p. 215-216 Apr. 28, 1807 Amos Speace (Spartanburgh) to Daniel McClaren (same); for $430 sold 430 ac on both sides of Cherokee Cr; sold by William Wood to Amos Speace. Witness William Cox and James Goodall. Signed Amos Speace. Wit. oath Mar. 4, 1807 James Goodall to Henry Turner. Rec. Apr. 2, 1808

p. 216-218 Sept. 12, 1807 George Walker (SC) to son William Walker, a son of Clara Miraman (or Mireman) (sic); for love and affection give 150 ac on both sides Cherokee Cr of Broad R; grant May 1, 1786. Witness Clara Mireman and Daniel McClaren. Signed George Walker. Wit. oath Apr. 2, 1808 Daniel McClaren to A Benson. Rec. Apr. 2, 1808

p. 218-219 Dec. 19, 1807 Patrick Sanders jr and Abey David King

(Spartanburgh) to James Furgason (same); for $18 sold 104 ac on Thickety Cr of Broad R; border: Mathew Guttery. Witness Federick Guttery and Jonathan Guttery. Signed Patrick Sanders' mark and Aly d King. Wit. oath Apr. 2, 1808 Jonathan Guttery to John Lipscomb. Rec. Apr. 4, 1808

p. 219-220 May 6, 1801 Henry Pettet (Spartanburgh) to Joshua Petet (same); for 40£ sterling sold 150 ac on N side of Pacolate R at mouth of the big branch and a little below Pacolate Springs; border: Joshua Fektre. Witness John Pettet and James Hewet. Signed Henry Pettet. Wit. oath Apr. 24, 1802 John Pettet to John Lipscomb. Rec. Apr. 5, 1808

p. 220-221 Nov. 28, 1807 John Gray (Spartanburgh) to Richard Thomson (same); for $350 sold (1) 100 ac on both sides Lawson's fork; border: Richard Thomson and John Rainwater; where John Gray lives; part of two adjoining tracts: (a) grant Nov. 18, 1752 to James Alexander and sold by Wm Thomson to John Gray and (b) grant Jan. 6, 1794 to John Gray on N side of Lawson's fork; border: Tackcoll (or Taekcoll) and Crocker; and (2) 33 ac granted to John Gray; on S side Lawson's fork between Richard Thomson and Widow Lee; border: formerly Littelton Bagwell; and (3) 15 ac joining Tackwell. Witness Charles McAbee and Marshal Seay. Signed John Gray. Wit. oath Apr. 8, 1808 Charles McAbee to A Benson. Rec. Apr. 8, 1808

p. 221-222 Jan. 22, 1807 William Hendrix (Spartanburgh) to Henry Cole (same); for $60 sold 50 ac on branch of "lack" Cr of Enoree R; S part of 400 ac grant in 1773 to John Hamby. Witness Martin Cole and James Cole. Signed William Hendrix. Wit. oath Jan. 22, 1807 Martin Cole to David Morton. Rec. Apr. 11, 1808. Dower renounced Nancy Hendrix to David Morton Jan. 22, 1807

p. 222-223 Nov. 8, 1803 John Arrendell sr (Spartanburgh) to Isam Arrendell; for $480 sold 200 ac on waters of Little Cherokee Cr; border: Downs, Big Cr, and little Cr. Witness Danl McCay and James Byars. Signed John Arrendell and Grace's mark. Wit. oath Jan. 15, 1804 James Byars to Jno Rickman for sale John Arrendell sr to Bridges(sic) Arrendell. Rec. Apr. 11, 1808

p. 223-224 Sept. 22, 1807 Charles Hester (Spartanburgh) to Bridges Arendel (same); for $200 sold 200 ac; border: Gorden, John Arendell, and Stanley. Witness Thomas Farrow and Joseph Camp. Signed Chs Hester. Wit. oath Oct. 15, 1807 Thomas Farrow to John Lipscomb. Rec. Apr. 11, 1808

p. 224-226 Mar. 14, 1808 John P Poole (Spartanburgh) to John Stroud jr (same); for $300 sold 100 ac on N side of Enoree R; border: E-Drury Couch, W-land sold today to Benjamin Rhodes by John P Poole, and N-land sold by Drury Couch to Benjamin Rhodes; part of 300 ac grant to Thomas Couch and sold Sept. 23, 1796 by Joseph Couch to John P Poole. Witness Aaron Casey and William Higgins. Signed John P Poole. Wit. oath Mar. 10, 1808 Aaron Casey to Burrell Bobo. Rec. Apr. 11, 1808. Dower renounced Elender Poole to Burrell Bobo Mar. 14, 1808

p. 226-227 Jan. 29, 1807 James Wofford (Spartanburgh) to Littleton Bagwell (same); for $110.25 sold 231 ac on both sides of branch of Lawson's fork of Pacolate R and on N side Lawson's fork; border: recent survey by Richard Thomson; grant to James Wofford. Witness Clary Lancaster and William Lancaster. Signed James Wofford's mark. Wit. oath Mar. 14, 1808 William Lancaster to Danl White. Rec. Apr. 11, 1808

p. 227-228 Feb. 6, 1807 Frances Robertson (Kershaw Dist) to Thomas Harris (Spartanburgh); for $150 sold 150 ac on branch of

Sarratt's Cr; border: S-Frances Robertson and E & W-Thomas Harris; part of grant Dec. 9, 1774 to Thomas Philips. Witness Balus Harris and Joseph Johnston. Signed Frances Robertson. Wit. oath Jul. 12, 1807 Balus Harris to Leonard Adcock. Rec. Apr. 11, 1808

p. 228 Mar. 2, 1808 Joseph Austell (Spartanburgh) to Thomas Thompson (same); for 10£ sold 70 ac on Harris Cr of Thickety Cr; border: Thompson; part of grant to Joseph Austell. Witness Robert Storey, Moses Wilkins, and Jesse Fondren. Signed Joseph Austell. Wit. oath Mar. 2, 1808 Moses Wilkins to John Lipscomb. Rec. Apr. 11, 1808

p. 228-229 Sept. 26, 1807 Matthew Abbet (Spartanburgh) to William Daubbins (or Daubins) (same); for $3 sold 60 ac on both sides of Island Cr; border: William Daubbins. Witness Richard Scruggs and Isaac Williams. Signed Matthew Abbet. Wit. oath Oct. 10, 1807 Richard Scruggs to L Adcock. Rec. Apr. 11, 1808

p. 229-230 Jan. 5, 1808 James Reynolds (Spartanburgh) to John Reynolds (same); for $150 sold 145 ac on N side of Thompson's beverdam Cr; border: McMeckin (or McMukin), James Reynolds, and Edward Smith; plat attached. Witness William Thomas, John McMukin, and Edward Smith. Signed James Reynolds. Wit. oath Jan. 5, 1808 William Thomas to Danl Willbank. Rec. Apr. 11, 1808

p. 230-231 Sept. 8, 1805 Sampson Bobo (Spartanburgh) to Sarah Bobo (same), widow of Sampson Bobo desc, and her five present children; for love and affection give 150 ac; border: John Hendrix, Two Mile Cr, Joseph Barnett's Spring Br, and Calvert's improvement; given during Sarah's widowhood; then given to children and if they die before coming of age, then land reverts to Sampson Bobo. Witness William Steward and Chancy Bobo. Signed Sampson Bobo's mark. Wit. oath Mar. 5, 1808 Chancy Bobo to Burrell Bobo. Rec. Apr. 11, 1808

p. 231-232 Jan. 21, 1808 Jesse Fondren (Spartanburgh) to Allen Sarratt (same); for $100 sold 200 ac on branch of Quen's Cr of Thickety Cr; border: Crocker, Markley, Price, and Byers. Witness William Fondren and Ransom Frazier. Signed Jesse Fondren. Wit. oath Mar. 12, 1808 Ransom Frazier to John Lipscomb. Rec. Apr. 11, 1808

p. 232-233 Jan. 10, 1807 William Fondren (Spartanburgh) to Jesse Davidson (same); for $150 sold 300 ac on Cherokee Cr of Broad R. Witness Ransom Frazier and William Blanton. Signed William Fondren and Elizabeth's mark. Wit. oath Jan. 16, 1808 Ransom Frazier to John Lipscomb. Rec. Apr. 11, 1808

p. 233-234 Apr. 13, 1799 William Beshears (Spartanburgh) to John Wadkins; for 20£ sold 50 ac on N fork of Tygar R; border: Thomas Wadsworth, John Amos, and Wm Beshears jr. Witness Howard Bailey, John Loftis, and Job Loftis. Signed William Beshears's mark. Wit. oath Nov. 8, 1807 John Loftis to Danl Willbanks. Rec. Apr. 11, 1808

p. 234-235 Sept. 20, 1807 John McForson (or McPhearson) (Spartanburgh) to Benjamin Hoocker (same); for $300 sold 200 ac on S of Tyger R; where John McForson lives; border: Benjamin Hoocker, Thomas Todd, Robert Criswell (or Cuswell), and Willis Willeford; part of two tracts: (1) from William Clayton and (2) from Edmond Cleaton; both sold to Simson Newman and "wife" who sold to John McForson. Witness Stephen J Casey, Humphey Yarborough, and Burrell Bobo. Signed John McPheason. Wit. oath Apr. 11, 1808 Burrell Bobo to John Lipscomb. Certified (not dated) by Burrell Bobo. Rec. Apr. 11, 1808. Dower renounced Marjory McForson to Burrell Bobo Sept. 30, 1807

p. 235-236 Oct. 27, 1806 William Burton (Spartanburgh) to John Mullenax (same); for $180 sold 180 ac on waters of Cain Cr of Tygar R; part of grant Jan. 5, 1789 to John Gray who sold Dec. 15, 1805 to William Burton. Witness Thomas Meadows, Gideon Harrelson, and David Burton. Signed William Burton. Wit. oath Jul. 14, 1807 Thomas Meadows to William Lancaster. Rec. Apr. 12, 1808

p. 236-237 Apr. 4, 1808 Dower renounced Judeth Gray to Abner Benson; for deed John Gray to Richard Thomson for (1) 100 ac on N side Lawson's fork; where John Roberson formerly lived; border: Richard Thomson and John Rainwaters; part of two grants: (a) Nov. 18, 1752 to James Alexander and sold by William Thomson to John Gray and (b) Jan. 6, 1794 to John Gray adjoining (a); border: Tackwell and Crocker; (2) 133 ac on S side of Lawson's fork; border: Richard Thomson and Widow Lee; grant to John Gray; and (3) 15 ac on N side Lawson's fork; border: Tackwell. Rec. Apr. 12, 1808

p. 237-238 Feb. 28, 1805 George Brewton (Spartanburgh) to Broadrick Mason (same); for $100 sold 48 ac on Forgason's Cr; part of grant to George Brewton. Witness Peter Bragg and Samuel Brewton. Signed George Brewton. Wit. oath Aug. 5, 1807 Samuel Brewton and John Brewton. Rec. Apr. 12, 1808

p. 238-240 Sept. 22, 1775 (sic) William Sterling and wife Jane (Spartanburgh) to William Lewis (same); for 50£ sold 200 ac on Dutchman's Cr of Tygar R; border: Alexander Elder; part of grant Apr. 3, 1786 (sic) Gov. William Moultrie to William Sterling. Witness Saml Lancaster, William Patterson, and Augustin Bumpass. Signed Wm Sterling and Jane's mark. Wit. oath Sept. 22, 1795 Saml Lancaster to Wm Smith. Rec. Apr. 12, 1808

p. 240-241 Dec. 31, 1808 (sic) James Byars sr (Spartanburgh) to James Byars jr (same); for $300 sold 130 ac on Broad R. Witness William Wilson and William Byars. Signed James Byars. Wit. oath Jan. 16, 1808 William Wilson to John Lipscomb. Rec. Apr. 12, 1808

p. 241-242 Jan. 6, 1808 William Lewis (Spartanburgh) to Sandford Smith (same); for $160 sold 212½ ac on waters of Dutchman's Cr; border: Nancy Poole, Miss Poole, S-Poole and Lee, E-Smith (or Swith) Brooks, and W-West Hannah, and N-"oldroid". Witness Daniel Smith and Robert Page. Signed William Lewis' mark. Wit. oath Jan. 13, 1808 Daniel Smith to William Lancaster. Rec. Apr. 12, 1808. Dower renounced Drusillah Lewis to William Lancaster Jan. 13, 1808

p. 242-243 Feb. 1, 1808 Thomas Bearden (Spartanburgh) to Isaac Bearden (same); for $200 sold 100 ac on S side of Dutchman's Cr; border: E-John Marrow, S-Herum Harrelson, N-Samuel Marrow and Benjamin Peak. Witness John Morrow and William N Morrow. Signed Thos Bearden. Wit. oath Feb. 2, 1808 John Morrow to Saml Morrow. Rec. Apr. 12, 1808. Dower renounced Abigal Bearden to Saml Lancaster Apr. 2, 1808

p. 243-245 Mar. 5, 1808 Amos Speace (Spartanburgh), hammerman, to Daniel White (same); for $300 sold 300 ac on S side Pacolate R; border: ford at Wading Shoals, Thomas Bennett, Thomas Burnett, and Mullesses (or Mulresses) Br; part of two grants to Amos Speace. Witness Jonathan Wall, Daniel Gilbert, and William Bennett. Signed Amos Speace. Wit. oath Apr. 12, 1808 William Bennett to James Young. Rec. Apr. 12, 1808. Dower renounced Mary Speace to James Young Apr. 12, 1808

p. 245-246 Mar. 12, 1808 Amos Speace (Spartanburgh, hammerman, to

Jonathan Wall (same); for $100 sold 100 ac on W side of Pacolate R; border: Philip Johnson, "the burnt cabin", S Pacolate R, Jordan Carden, Daniel White, and Wading Shoal; part of grant to Amos Speace. Witness William Bennett, Thomas Bennett, and Edmond Cooley. Signed Amos Speace. Wit. oath Apr. 12, 1808 William Bennett to James Young. Rec. Apr. 12, 1808. Dower renounced Mary Speace to James Young Apr. 12, 1808

p. 246-247 Apr. 9, 1808 Jean Thomson, widow (Spartanburgh) to Lawson Thomson (same); for $500 sold 160 ac on N Tygar R; plat attached shows border: Busy (or Bury), L Thomson, Parker, and Hught (or Wright); part of two grants: (1) Feb. 23, 1754 to Hugh Lawson and (2) May 20, 1763 to Charles Moore. Witness Joseph Rodgers and George Floyd. Signed Jean Thomson. Wit. oath Apr. 12, 1808 Joseph Rodgers to Drury McDaniel. Rec. Apr. 12, 1808

p. 247-248 Mar. 13, 1806 Aaron Moore (Pendleton Dist) to James Hadden (same); for $174 sold 200 ac on branch of Ben's Cr of Tygar R; border: David Anderson and William Moore. Witness John Moore and Alexander Moore. Signed Aaron Moore. Wit. oath Apr. 5, 1806 John Moore to David Morton. Rec. Apr. 12, 1808

p. 248-249 Feb. 8, 1808 Henry ONiell to John Hindmon (Spartanburgh); for $100 sold 260 ac on N side Tygar R; border: John Beard, John Hindmon, and John Viece (or Vuce); part of grant Feb. 5, 1786 Gov. William Moultrie to David Grimes who sold to Gustavus Boswell who sold to Samuel Moore and attached by David Golightly against Samuel Moore and sold by Gabriel Benson, sheriff (Spartanburgh) to Henry ONiell. Witness Sterling Tucker and Joshua Doyal. Signed Henry ONiell. Wit. oath Jan. 8, 1808 Sterling Tucker to William Lancaster. Rec. Apr. 12, 1808

p. 249-250 Apr. 4, 1808 Henry Cole sr (Spartanburgh) to David Childress (same); for $44 sold 50 ac on N side of Enoree R; border: W-Thomas Childress, N-vacant, E-Henry Cole, and S-Enoree R; W part of 330 ac grant Dec. 5, 1785 Gov. William Moultrie to Robert Cooper. Witness Henry Cole jr and Jesse Childress. Signed Henry Cole sr. Wit. oath Apr. 12, 1808 Jesse Childress to Danl Willbanks. Rec. Apr. 12, 1808

p. 250-251 Nov. 20, 1807 Thomas Childress (Jackson Co, Ga) to David Childress (Spartanburgh); for $200 sold 80 ac on N side of Enoree R; border: John Hamby's Spring Br. Witness Martin Cole and Jesse Childress. Signed Thomas Childress' mark. Wit. oath Mar. 12, 1808 Martin Cole to John Brewton. Rec. Apr. 12, 1808

p. 251-252 Oct. 3, 1807 Ephram Storey (Spartanburgh) to John Hindmon (same); for $92 sold 92 ac on branch of Cain Cr of Tygar R; part of grant Feb. 5, 1787 to Owen Forrester. Witness William Hindmon and Lawson Thomson. Signed Ephram Storey's mark. Wit. oath Feb. 13, 1808 William Hindmon to William Hendrix. Rec. Apr. 12, 1808

p. 252 Mar. 5, 1807 Charles Hester (Spartanburgh) to Matthew Cooper (same); for "so much money as shall or hath been expended in the South Carolina Office for surveying the grant of 150 ac" paid to Charles Hester by Matthew Cooper, sold 150 ac; border: William Cooper and Scon Cooper. Witness Jacob Gordan and Joseph Camp. Signed Charles Hester. Wit. oath Mar. 12, 1808 Jacob Gordan to John Lipscomb. Rec. Apr. 12, 1808

p. 252-253 Mar. 4, 1808 Charles Hester (Spartanburgh) to James Cooper (same); for 10£ sold 150 ac on both sides Beaverdam Cr; border: William Cooper and Lipscomb. Witness William McGowen and Isaac Dill. Signed Charles Hester. Wit. oath Apr. 12, 1808

William McGowen to John Lipscomb. Rec. Apr. 12, 1808

p. 253-254 Oct. 28, 1805 John Nesbett (late of Spartanburgh and now of Dickson Co, Tenn) to Alexander Evins (Spartanburgh); for $300 sold 200 ac on S side of S fork Tygar R; half of 400 ac grant survey May 23, 1767 for William Sharp and granted to William Sharp. Witness James Gilleland, James Nesbett, and Robert Sloan. Signed John Nesbett. Wit. oath Apr. 12, 1808 James Nesbett to William Simpson. Rec. Apr. 12, 1808

p. 254-256 Jan. 30, 1806 James Sutherlin (Pendleton Dist) to John Arnold (Spartanburgh); for $1,050 sold 400 ac on branch of Tygar R; border: Enoch Floyd, Skinner, Elis Corder, and Young Scott. Witness William Shackelford, Barnett H Allgood, and Richard Harrison. Signed James Sutherlin. Wit. oath Apr. 9, 1808 William Shackelford to John Brewton. Rec. Apr. 12, 1808. Dower renounced Mary Sutherlan to John Cochran Apr. 7, 1807

p. 256 Apr. 12, 1808(?) Isaac Williams to John Williams; for $140 sold 139 ac on head branches of "Souh" Cr; border: Dilbeck; part of grant to Isaac Williams. Witness Joseph Camp and Zacheriah Blackwell. Signed Isaac Williams. Wit. oath Apr. 12, 1808 Zacheriah Blackwell to Leonard Adcock. Rec. Apr. 12, 1808

p. 256-258 Apr. 12, 1807 Isaac Williams to John Williams; for $165 sold (1) 100 ac on Island Cr of Pacolate R; and (2) 65 ac adjoining (1). Witness Joseph Camp and Zacheriah Blackwell. Signed Isaac Williams. Wit. oath Apr. 12, 1808 Zacheriah Blackwell to Leonard Adcock. Rec. Apr. 12, 1808

p. 258-259 Apr. (blank), 1808 John McKie to Joseph Camp; power of attorney to sell two tracts: (1) 350 ac granted to William Copeland sr and sold by William Copeland sr's legatees to John McKie; and (2) 500 ac granted to John McKie; both on Proctor's Cr. Witness William Fondren and Jesse Fondren. Signed John McKie. Wit. oath Apr. 13, 1808 William Fondren to John Lipscomb. Rec. Apr. 12, 1808

p. 259-260 Jan. 24, 1807 Benjamin Bonner (Spartanburgh) to Charles Cook; for $100 sold 100 ac on Long Br of Sarratt's Cr; border: Daniel McClaren. Witness Joseph Camp and Bryant Bonner. Signed Benjamin Bonner's mark. Wit. oath Apr. 13, 1808 Joseph Camp to John Lipscomb. Rec. Apr. 13, 1808

p. 260-261 Mar. 16, 1808 Reuben Warren (Spartanburgh) to Henry Turner (same); for $401 sold 401 ac on both sides of Island Cr. Witness David Adcock and Edward Turner. Signed Reuben Warren. Wit. oath Apr. 12, 1808 David Adcock to Leon Adcock. Rec. Apr. 13, 1808

p. 261-262 Jan. 3, 1807 Samuel Lancaster (Spartanburgh) to John Varnel (same); for $150 sold 112 ac on waters of Sugar Cr; grant Jan. 4, 1793 to Aaron Lancaster. Witness James Howell and Aaron Smith. Signed Samuel Lancaster. Wit. oath Apr. 2, 1808 James Howell to Samuel Lancaster. Rec. Apr. 13, 1808. Dower renounced Silah (or Lelah) Lancaster to Samuel Lancaster Apr. 9, 1808

p. 262-263 Jul. 3, 1807 John and James Barry (Warren Co, Ky) to Gen. Thomas Moore (Spartanburgh); for $800 sold adjoining tracts on Middle fork Tygar R: (1) 200 ac; border: Robert Miller and both sides Middle Tygar R; grant Oct. 24, 1767 to John Miller who sold to John Barry desc, father of John and James Barry, and left by will to John and James Barry; and (2) 100 ac on W bank of Middle Tygar R; grant Sept. 1, 1768 to James Gillespie who sold to

James McGowen who sold to John and James Barry. Witness Charles M Barry, Peggy Moore, and Polly Moore. Signed John Barry and James Barry. Wit. oath Charles M Barry to Drury McDaniel Feb. 18, 1808. Rec. Apr. 13, 1808

p. 263-264 Feb. 10, 1808 Samuel Kimmins (Spartanburgh) to William Carter (same); for $100 sold 115 ac on Thompson's Cr of Pacolate R; border: John Kimbol. Witness William Bennett, William R Watson, and Thomas Kimboll. Signed Samuel Kimmins' mark. Wit. oath Feb. 27, 1808 William Bennett to L Adcock. Rec. Apr. 13, 1808

p. 264-265 Apr. 17, 1807 Robert Harper, attorney for Samuel Wire, (Macklenburgh Co, Ky(sic)) to Owen Hembree (Spartanburgh); for $100 sold 96 ac; border: William M(or W) Hembrie, Thomas Moore, and Smith; on waters of Dutchman's Cr; grant to William Wire and "transfered" to Samuel Wire. Witness Clarey Lancaster to William W Hembree. Signed Robert Harper, attorney for Saml Wire. Wit. oath Apr. 17, 1807 William W Hembree to William Lancaster. Rec. Apr. 14, 1808

p. 265-266 Oct. 9, 1807 Owen Hembrie to Robert Page jr (Spartanburgh); for $200 sold 96 ac on waters of Dutchman's Cr; border: William W Hembree, Thomas Moore, and Smith; grant to William Wire and "transfered" to Samuel Wire. Witness Zacheriah McDaniel and William Lancaster. Signed Owen Hembrie. Wit. oath Mar. 2, 1808 Zacheriah McDaniel to William Lancaster. Rec. (omitted)

p. 266 Apr. 17, 1808 Lewis Turner (Spartanburgh) to James Kendricks (or Kindrix) (same); for $150 sold 150 ac on S side of Lawson's fork; part of grant May 3, 1799 Gov. Edward Rutledge to William Turner. Witness William Owens to Elisha Turner. Signed Lewis Turner's mark. Wit. oath Apr. 18, 1808 Elisha Turner to Hugh Means. Rec. Apr. 21, 1808

p. 266-267 Dec. 16, 1807 William West (Spartanburgh) to daughter Patsey May or Burkett, widow (same); for love and affection give "all my possessions" at "my present dwelling" known as McKie's Mill and a tract of 165 ac bought(?) from Marharh (or Mcrharh) Thomason; on Lawson's fork of Pacolate R. Witness William Rainwater and Betsy Wood. Signed William West. Wit. oath Apr. 25, 1808 Betsy Wood to A Benson. Rec. Apr. 25, 1808

p. 267-268 Jan. 10, 1807 Henry Wells (Spartanburgh) to Richard Daniel (same); for $450 sold 180 ac on Beverdam fork of Fairforrest Cr; border: head of a Mill Pond, old road, and a new road. Witness Thomas Tinsley and William Moss. Signed Henry Wells. Wit. oath Apr. 14, 1808 Thomas Tinsley to John Lipscomb. Rec. Apr. 26, 1808

p. 268-269 Oct. 31, 1807 Newsum Cooper (Spartanburgh) to Isaac Hamby (same); for $200 sold 163 ac on N side of Enoree R; border: Charles Pearson, Henry Tate, Thomas Westmoreland; part of grant to John Pruat. Witness John Crocker and Obed Whitamore. Signed Newsum Cooper. Wit. oath Feb. 22, 1808 John Crocker to Wm Hendrix. Rec. Apr. 30, 1808. Dower renounced Isabel Cooper to David Morton Nov. 18, 1807

p. 269-270 Oct. 23, 1806 Elijah Hendrix (Spartanburgh) to William Hendrix (same); for $400 sold 200 ac on both sides "Bek" (or leek) Cr; border: James Lindsey and John Hamby; grant to Isaac Hamby and part of grant to James Lindsey; leaves about 4 ac in corner to James Allen. Witness James Allen and Caleb Woodruff. Signed Elijah Hendrix's mark. Wit. oath Mar. 12, 1807 James Allen to David Morton. Rec. May 2, 1808. Dower renounced Ann Hendrix to David Morton Mar. 12, 1807

p. 270-271 Mar. 7, 1808 Thomas Murray (Union Dist) to Thomas Cook (same); for $100 sold 200 ac; border: all vacant when originally surveyed; grant to Edward Kelly desc and by heirship to Mary and Masten Kelley and "leased" to William Chesny who sold to Thomas Murray. Witness Davis Goudelock and Christopher Cook. Signed Thomas Murry. Wit. oath Mar. 17, 1808 Christopher Cook to Davis Goudelock. Rec. May 2, 1808

p. 271-272 Feb. 9, 1808 Richard Harrison (Spartanburgh) to Reuben Daniel (same); for $220 sold 165 ac on waters Beverdam Cr of Fairforrest Cr; border: Thomas Tinsley, Reuben Daniel, Laxton's Br, and near Court House Road. Witness Christopher Golightly and James Harrison. Signed Richard Harrison. Wit. oath Apr. 11, 1808 Christopher Golightly to William Lancaster. Rec. May 2, 1808

p. 272-273 Aug. 15, 1807 John Browning (Spartanburgh) to William Hase (same); for $50 sold 122 ac on both sides Cane Cr and N side Tygar R; border: Francis Bremar, William Meaows, and Aaron Pinson; grant Dec. 4, 1794 Gov. William Moultrie to Joel Hembrie. Witness Nathaniel Burton, John Thornton, and Samuel Busey. Signed John Browning's mark. Wit. oath Aug. 15, 1807 John Thornton to John Brewton. Rec. May 2, 1808

p. 273-274 Feb. 9, 1808 Henry Harrison (Spartanburgh) to Reuben Daniel (same); for $235 sold 168 ac on waters of Fairforrest Cr; border: Thomas Tinsley and Court House Rd. Witness Christopher Golightly and James Harrison. Signed Henry Harrison. Wit. oath Apr. 11, 1808 Christopher Golightly to William Lancaster. Rec. May 2, 1808

p. 274-276 May 2, 1808 Gabriel Benson (Spartanburgh) to Isham Foster (same); for $900 sold (1) 300 ac on Wilson's Mill Cr of N Tygar R and a branch of Fairforrest Cr; grant Jan. 18, 1785 to Gabriel Benson; (2) 29½ ac; refer to deeds given by Peter Gray to Gabriel Benson; 50 ac of which was "allotted" Gabriel Benson at division of lands of William Benson desc; (3) 10 ac sold by John Wood to Gabriel Benson; and (4) 8 ac sold by John Wood to Gabriel Benson; total of 398 ac (sic); border: Peter Gray, John Wood, John Wingo, William Foster, and estate of William Benson. Witness Josiah Watson and Andrew Harrison. Signed Gab Benson. Wit. oath May 2, 1808 Andrew Harrison to D. J. Puckett. Rec. May 2, 1808

p. 276-277 Feb. 2, 1798 William Ford (Spartanburgh) to Edward Stewart (same); for $260 "say £60.13.4" sold 270 ac; border: Benjamin Clark, James Laurence, John Davis, Hosea Camp, and David Monroe. Witness William Laurence, James Laurence, and Colvin (or Calvin) Ford. Signed William Ford. Wit. oath Feb. 23, 1799 James Laurence to B. D. Shumate. Rec. May 9, 1808

p. 277-278 Feb. 13, 1808 Vincent Simmons (Spartanburgh) to Reuben Daniel (same); for $215 sold 165 ac on branch of Beverdam Cr of Fairforrest Cr; border: Harrison and Holley Spring Br. Witness Daniel White and Isham Harrison. Signed Vinson Simmons. Wit. oath May 5, 1808 Isham Harrison to Danl White. Rec. May 13, 1808. Dower renounced Elizabeth Simmons to D. J. Puckett May 2, 1808

p. 278-279 Aug. 1, 1806 Willis Williford (Spartanburgh) to Moses Lancaster (same); for $90 sold 100 ac at head branches of Cane Cr on N side Tygar R; part of grant Jan. 7, 1793 to William Smith. Witness Brittin Williford and Hardy Williford. Signed Willis Williford. Wit. oath Nov. 15, 1808 Brittin Williford to Wm Smith. Rec. May 28, 1808. Dower renounced Polley Williford to Samuel Lancaster Feb. 27, 1808

p. 279-280 Aug. 1, 1806 Willis Williford (Spartanburgh) to Moses Lancaster (same); for $15 sold 61 ac on head branches of Cane Cr and on N side Tygar R; grant Feb. 7, 1805 to Willis Williford. Witness Britin Williford and Hardy Williford. Signed Willis Williford. Wit. oath Nov. 15, 1806 Brittin Williford to Wm Smith. Rec. May 28, 1808. Dower renounced Polley Williford to Samuel Lancaster Feb. 27, 1808

p. 280-281 Mar. 30, 1801 Samuel Turner (Spartanburgh) to Justin Childs; for $90 sold 80 ac on N side of Shoaly Cr; border: "my brother" Richard Childs, Darby Turner, and Thomas Wadsworth desc; survey Oct. 22, 1784 by George Salmon for Wm Wood, son of Moses Wood. Witness Anderson Cockrell and Jacob Sarten. Signed Samuel Turner's mark. Wit. oath Mar. 27, 1802 Anderson Cockrell to Ism Foster. Rec. Jun. 2, 1808

p. 281-282 Feb. 6, 1808 William Hase, blacksmith (Spartanburgh) to Hearon Meadows (same); for $100 sold 122 ac on both sides Cane Cr and on N side of Tygar R; grant Dec. 4, 1794 Gov. William Moultrie to Joel Hembrie; border: Frances Bremar, William Meadows, and Aaron Pinson. Witness George T Sloan and John Meadows. Signed William Hase. Wit. oath Feb. 13, 1808 John Meadows to Wilie Williford. Rec. Jun. 6, 1808

p. 282-283 Sept. 24, 1801 Nathaniel Walker (Greenville Dist) to Alexander Thompson (Spartanburgh); for $90 sold (1) 60 ac on waters of S and Middle Tygar R; border: Wm Atkins, McCay, Wm McClannahan, and Alexander Thompson; part of 1,000 ac grant to Jno Thomas sr who sold to Nathaniel Walker; "the same tract he once sold to Moses Moore"; and (2) 1 ac including Spring which Shadrack Farmer used when he lived on said tract. Witness Abraham Thomas, William McDade, and John Pennington. Signed Nathaniel Walker. Wit. oath May 28, 1808 John Pennington to (not given). Rec. Jun. 6, 1808

p. 283-284 Jan. 26, 1808 Charles James (Spartanburgh) to John Connell (same); for $300 sold 333 ac on branch of Kelso's Cr of Fairforrest Cr; "½ ac around the graves" excepted. Witness Charles James jr and James Smith jr. Signed Charles James. Wit. oath Jan. 26, 1808 James Smith jr to Danl White. Rec. Jun. 6, 1808

p. 284-285 Dec. 28, 1807 Thomas Price (Spartanburgh) to Seth Clark; for (money not mentioned) sold 165 ac on branch of Cane Cr; border: John Butler, William Rampley, and Lee Clark; part of 815 ac grant May 2, 1791 Gov. Charles Pinckney to Joel Hembree. Witness Osborn West and James Hendman. Signed Thomas Price. Wit. oath Feb. 4, 1808 James Hendman to Wilie Williford. Rec. Jun. 13, 1808

p. 285-286 Mar. 7, 1808 James Young (Spartanburgh) to James Galt (same); for $200 sold 140 ac on waters of Lawson's fork; border: N-William Foster, S-Twitty's branch, E-Midow Cr of Lawson's fork, and W-Joel Lewis; part of tract sold by Isham Harrison, sheriff (Spartanburgh), to James Young Jul. 7, 1806 to satisfy suit of James Galt vs John Morris. Witness John ONiell and Alexander McMillin. Signed James Young. Wit. oath (not dated) Alexander McMillin to James Young. Rec. Jun. 14, 1808

p. 286-287 Jan. 16, 1808 William Abbett (Spartanburgh) to Susanna Walker; for $200 sold 225 ac on Island Cr of Pacolate R; border: NE & NW-William Abbett, E & SE-Wade (Wad), and others vacant; part of grant to James Knox. Witness William Walker and George Brock. Signed William Abbett. Wit. oath Jan. 17, 1808 William Walker to L Adcock. Rec. Jun. 20, 1808

p. 287-288 Aug. 20, 1799 George Toor (Clermont Co, SC) to Thomas Betterton (Spartanburgh); for $1 sold 330 ac on Rece's fork of Thickety Cr; border: NE-Rook and vacant, NW-Low, SW-Hadden's old tract, and others vacant; survey Jan. 1, 1799 for Rolley Horton and granted Aug. 5, 1799 Gov. Edward Rutledge to George Toor. Witness Samuel Fley and Charles Richardson. Signed Geo Toor. Wit. oath (Clermount Co, Camden Dist) Aug. 29, 1799 Samuel Fley to John Haron. Rec. Jun. 20, 1808

p. 288-290 Dec. 24, 1807 Mary Taggart and Mary Haly (Charleston, SC), widow and only daughter respectively of Dr John Haly, to Nicholas Herbemont (Columbia, SC); for $1,000 sold five tracts: (1) 500 ac in Craven Co on Toms Cr of Congaree R; 7 miles from McCord's ford and border: SW-Nicholas McCartney and others vacant; (2) 500 ac in Craven Co on Tom's Cr about 10 miles from McCord's ferry; border: all vacant land; (3) 400 (ac?) in Craven Co on waters of Wateree Cr of Wateree R; border: SE-John Wigfall and SW-vacant; (4) 500 ac in Craven Co at head of Persemon Br; 1 mile from Lane's Mill and 13 miles from McCord's ford; border: all vacant land; and (5) 500 ac in Craven Co on Glard's Br of Tygar R; border: NE-Edward Savage esq and others vacant. Witness Eleanora Bredu and L. N. G. Danzlord. Signed Marry Taggart and Mary Haley. Wit. oath (Charleston Dist) Dec. 28, 1807 L N G Danzlord to Chas Glover. Rec. Jun. 25, 1808

p. 290-292 May 6, 1808 John Hurt (Spartanburgh) to James Vernon (same); for $100 sold 50 ac on N fork of branch of Tygar R; border: S-Alexander McCarter, E-James Vernon, and N-line mentioned below; part of 160 ac grant to John Orr but presently owned by John Hurt; except land between "head of a pond" and a line to N fork of Tygar R. Witness William Perrin, Andrew Vernon, and Moses Richardson. Signed John Hurt. Wit. oath May 7, 1808 William Perrin to Ism Foster. Rec. Jun. 24, 1808. Dower renounced Ester Hurt to Isham Foster May 7, 1808

p. 292-293 Mar. 16, 1808 Austen Wright (Spartanburgh) to John Tolleson (same); for $67.35 sold 112½ ac on waters of Gouchy Cr; border: Gumroat Br and William Morres; sale for 10 months; Condition: sale void if Austen pays John $67.35 in 10 months. Witness Muse Tolleson and Jacob Land. Signed Austen Wright. Wit. oath May 10, 1808 Muse Tolleson to William Simpson. Rec. Jul. 4, 1808

p. 293 Mar. 29, 1808 George Wright (Spartanburgh) to Nathan Wright (same); for $200 sold 100 ac on branches of Ford's Cr; border: Joel Hurt, John Golightly, waggon road, and William Beaver. Witness Elijah Barnett, Martin Hemperly, and Levi Wright. Signed George Wright's mark. Wit. oath Jun. 11, 1808 Elijah Barnett to Danl Wright. Rec. Jul. 4, 1808

p. 293-295 Sept. 15, 1807 Richard Thomson (Spartanburgh) to Robert A Todd (same); for $200 sold ½ ac; lot #3 at Spartanburgh Court House; border: Publick land, Samuel Todd, and Obadiah Watson. Witness Charles Edwards and Abner Benson. Signed Richard Thomson. Wit. oath Jul. 4, 1808 Abner Benson to Henry Turner. Rec. Jul. 4, 1808. Dower renounced Polly Thomson to William Lancaster May 16, 1808

p. 295-296 Jun. 10, 1808 Benjamin Wofford (Flint R, Tenn) to William Bagwell (Spartanburgh); for $200 sold 120 ac on Lawson's fork Cr; border: William Bagwell and Brown's Br; lower end of grant to James McCleroy. Witness Isham Harrison and Charles Mathis. Signed Benjamin Wofford. Wit. oath (omitted) 4, 1808 Charles Mathis to Henry Turner. Rec. Jul. 4, 1808

p. 296-297 Jun. 10, 1808 Benjamin Wofford (Flint R, Tenn) to Charles Mathias (Spartanburgh); for $200 sold 137½ ac on both sides of Lawson's fork Cr; border: William Bagwell; upper part of 350 ac grant to James McCleroy. Witness Isham Harrison and William Bagwell. Signed Benjn Wofford. Wit. oath Jul. 4, 1808 William Bagwell to Henry Turner. Rec. Jul. 4, 1808

p. 297-298 Mar. 3, 1806 Isham Harrison, sheriff (Spartanburgh) to William McWilliams (same); for $62 sold 338 ac on waters of Buck Cr and Barton's Br and other branches of Main Pacolate R; border: Thomas Goore, Wm Wells, and James Smith; half of grant to William Wells and James Smith; sale due to writ from Spartanburgh Common Pleas Court suit Felen Warley vs William Wells. Witness William Burto, J Crocker, and William Ross Smith. Signed I Harrison SSD. Wit. oath Jul. 4, 1808 William R Smith to A Benson. Rec. Jul. 4, 1808

p. 298-299 Jun. 20, 1808 Joseph Morris (Edgefield Dist) to Isarel Morris (Spartanburgh); for $200 sold 250 ac on Buck Cr of Pacolate R; border: William Jordan, John Morris, and grant to John Curonnel. Witness William Morris and John Turden. Signed Joseph Morris' mark. Wit. oath Jul. 29, 1808 William Morris to Abner Benson. Rec. Jul. 29, 1808

p. 299-2nd 299 Sept. 7, 1801 John Pennington (Spartanburgh) to Denny Anderson (same); for $20 sold 7 ac on Enoree R; part of 600 ac grant Jun. 29, 1752 to Samuel Gilkey. Witness William Massey and Thomas Kevil. Signed Jno Pennington. Wit. oath Oct. 12, 1807 William Massey to David Morton. Rec. Aug. 1, 1808

p. 2nd 299-300 Mar. 18, 1807 Gabriel Bumpass (Spartanburgh) to Thomas Doig (same); for $9 sold 20 ac; border: S-Middle fork Tygar R, E-David Tanner, and N-James McMucan. Witness Labon P Poole and Hugh Caldwell. Signed Gal Bumpass. Wit. oath Aug. 1, 1808 Labon P Poole to D McDaniel. Rec. Aug. 1, 1808

p. 300-302 Oct. 7, 1800 David Wardlow, sheriff (Abbeville Dist) to John Brannon, agent for James McWilliams (Spartanburgh); for $13 sold 500 ac on Robert's Cr of N Pacolate R; border: SE-Thomas Shurly and others vacant when granted Sept. 26, 1772 to Thomas Shurley; sale due to writ from Charleston Common Pleas Court suit executors of Aaron Locock desc vs administrator of Soleuel(?) (or Solem deBeauford) Buford desc; sale at Abbeville. Witness William McWilliams, John Sanders, and Hugh Morrah. Signed Dd Wardlow SAD. Wit. oath Nov. 26, 1807 William McWilliams to Wm Kelso. Rec. Aug. 1, 1808

p. 302-303 Jun. 3, 1808 Gabriel Benson, sheriff (Spartanburgh) to Capt. William Read; for $105.50 sold 170 ac where David Smith formerly lived on Pacolate R; border: Mathew Sparks; sale due to writ from Spartanburgh Common Pleas Court suit Reuben Richards vs Joseph Read. Witness Alexr R. Gray and Thomas Harrison. Signed Gal Benson SSD. Wit. oath Aug. 1, 1808 Alexr R Gray to Hugh Means. Rec. Aug. 1, 1808

p. 303-304 Sept. 15, 1807 Jean and Sarah Thompson (Spartanburgh) to David Burton (same); for $456 sold 152 ac on N side of N Tygar R; part of grant Jan. 7, 1799 to Andrew Thomson. Witness Lewis Furgason and Lawson Thompson. Signed Jean and Sarah Thomson. Wit. oath Sept. 26, 1807 Lewis Furgason to John Brewton. Rec. Aug. 1, 1808

p. 304-305 Feb. 8, 1808 James Ezell (Spartanburgh) to James Scott (same); for $100 sold 100 ac on N side of Pacolate R; border: John Bankston, Abraham Cantrell, and John Morris. Witness

John Bankston and Laurence Bankston. Signed James Ezell. Wit. oath Jul. 6, 1808 John Bankston to Leon Adcock. Rec. Aug. 1, 1808

p. 305-306 Apr. 1, 1807 Jonathan Cud sr (Spartanburgh) to Negro woman Abby (or Abby Cud); for "good causes and valuable considerations" give her her freedom and bequeath Abby 15 ac in Rutherford Co, NC including his dwelling house and other out houses and give Abby 5 cattle, a pewter dish, 3 plates, 3 basons, a walnut bedstead and furniture, an iron (blank), an oven, "all my corn and Meat now ready" and the rent of above land, a loom and tacklery, 5 chairs, a churn, 2 pails, a barrow, a sow and pigs, 9 pewter spoons, 2 punch boles, a mug, a black jack (or jark), a flat iron, all cotton, one bee gum, a basket etc; given during her lifetime. Witness William Lewis, James Boyd, and Nathaniel Lewis. Signed Jonathan Cud's mark. Wit. oath Jul. 4, 1808 James Boyd to Wm Kelso. Rec. Aug. 1, 1808

p. 306-307 Jul. 5, 1808 Obadiah Watson (Spartanburgh) to Maj John Tolleson (same); for $800 sold 2/3 ac; lot #4 in Spartanburgh, SC; border: Old Jail and Publick land. Witness Thomas Harrison, Duglas J Puckett, and William Ross Smith. Signed Obadh Watson. Wit. oath Jul. 5, 1808 Thomas Harrison to D. J. Puckett. Rec. Aug. 2, 1808. Dower renounced Sally Watson to Duglas J Puckett Aug. 2, 1808

p. 307-308 Feb. 3, 1808 John Finch (Spartanburgh) to son John Finch jr (same); for good will and affection give 200 ac; sold by James Gibbs desc to John Finch sr; border: N-James Kean, S-Philip Otts, E-James Cook, and W-Elisha Jennings; and give all (or 4) horses, 10 cattle, 10 hogs, 10 sheep, and all household furniture and working tools and all property of all kinds. Witness Hugh White, James Finch, and Josiah Thornton. Signed John Finch. Wit. oath Feb. 3, 1808 James Finch to William Lancaster. Rec. Aug. 3, 1808. Dower renounced Jany Finch to William Lancaster Aug. 2, 1808

p. 308-309 Jan. 12, 1807 James Morris (Edgefield Dist) to John Morris (Spartanburgh); for $30 sold 40 ac on S side Buck Cr of Pacolate R; grant May 10, 1788 State Office to William Morris sr who sold to James Morris. Witness Nimrod Cantrell and John Bankston. Signed James Morris' mark. Wit. oath Nov. 5, 1807 Nimrod Cantrell to Leonard Adcock. Rec. Aug. 4, 1808

p. 309 Jan. 12, 1808 Margaret McCarter (Spartanburgh) to Mary McCarter (Greenville Dist); for $1 sold a Negro girl Fanny. Witness William Perrin and John Hurt. Signed Margaret McCarter's mark. Wit. oath Jul. 4, 1808 John Hurt to Danl Willbanks. Rec. Aug. 8, 1808

p. 309-312 Jul. 7, 1806 Isham Harrison, sheriff (Spartanburgh) to James Young (same); for $57 sold 140 ac on waters of Lawson's fork; border: N-William Foster, S-Twitter's Br, E-Meadow Cr, and W-Joel Lewis; sale due to writ from Spartanburgh Common Pleas Court suit James Galt vs John Morris. Witness John Lancaster, Allen Lancaster, and William Ross Smith. Signed I Harrison SSD. Wit. oath Aug. 8, 1808 Allen Lancaster to D. J. Puckett. Rec. Aug. 9, 1808

p. 312-313 Oct. 12, 1807 George Bishop (Clay Co, Ky) to Jacob Chapmon (Spartanburgh); for $40 sold 160 ac on N side of Lawson's fork; border: Richard Childes; grant Jul. 18, 1805 Gov. Paul Hamilton (SC) to (not given). Witness John Moore, John West, and Wm Bishop. Signed George Bishop. Wit. oath Feb. 3, 1808 Wm Bishop to J. L. Burd. Rec. Aug. 15, 1808

p. 313-314 Feb. 22, 1808 Franklin Foster (Spartanburgh) to Anthony

Foster; for $683.84 and 2 mills penal sum of a bond for payment of $341.92 and 1 mill SC money and to secure the bond sold a bay horse about 5 years old, a brown bay mare about 14½ hands high about 11 years old, a cow and calf and yearling, 2 beds and furniture, all household furniture, all plantation utensils, a loom, all sadler's tools, all corn, meat, and fodder, and all cotton, a sow and 5 pigs; Condition: sale void if Franklin pays his debt. Witness John Lancaster and John Foster. Signed Franklin Foster. Wit. oath Oct. 22, 1808 John Lancaster to William Lancaster. Rec. Aug. 25, 1808

p. 314-315 Jun. 4, 1808 Samuel Sparks (Spartanburgh) to Thomas Hill (same); for $300 sold 417 ac on waters of Gilkie's and Shelton's Creeks of Thickety Cr; border: SE-Sparks and Lampkin, SW-Wright, and NE-vacant. Witness Isaac Hill and Liuat Sparks. Signed Samuel Sparks' mark. Wit. oath Aug. 20, 1808 Isaac Hill to Jno H Jones. Rec. Aug. 29, 1808

p. 315-316 Jun. 4, 1808 Samuel Sparks (Spartanburgh) to Isaac Hill (same); for $500 sold 600 ac at head of Scot's Cr of Broad R. Witness Thomas Hill and Lauah Sparks. Signed Samuel Sparks' mark. Wit. oath Aug. 20, 1808 Thomas Hill to John H Jones. Rec. Aug. 29, 1808

p. 316-317 Jun. 11, 1808 Isaac Hill and wife Betsy (Spartanburgh) to Samuel Sparks (same); for $300 sold 250 ac on waters of Pacolate R; grant to John Hammett sr. Witness Thomas Hill and Jno H Jones. Signed Isaac Hill. Wit. oath Aug. 20, 1808 Thomas Hill to Jno H Jones. Rec. Aug. 29, 1808

p. 317-318 (not dated) Lewis Brandon and wife Margaret (Spartanburgh) to Thomas Jackson (same); for $700 sold 780 ac on N side of Pacolate R and both sides of Elax Cr; "all the land within 600 ac" grant May 7, 1774 to John Brodey (and by resurvey of Gabriel Benson esq as 780 ac) who sold to Thomas Todd who sold Oct. 6, 1791 to Edward Hoocker who sold Oct. 15, 1791 to James McClure; border: Robert Henderson, William Bishop, "land called" Gilbord's, Sterling Ingram, Richard Vennable, James Alexander, and land sold to John Mimelton. Witness James Ridings, David Hall, and William Jackson. Signed Lewis Brandon and Margaret's mark. Wit. oath Aug. 27, 1808 William Jackson to Wm Kelso. Rec. Aug. 29, 1808

p. 318-320 Mar. 24, 1806 Thomas Murray (Spartanburgh) to William Stone (same); for $144 sold 100 ac; border: John Stone, Richardson Whitby, and "Great Road"; part of 500 ac grant to Seth Lewis and part of 500 ac grant to John McCoole. Witness Fielder Norton and John Stone. Signed Thomas Murray. Wit. oath Jul. 26, 1806 John Stone to Wm Simpson. Rec. Aug. 30, 1808

p. 320-321 Aug. 20, 1808 William Stone (Spartanburgh) to John Tolleson (same); for $125 sold 100 ac on waters of Pacolate R; border: "big road", John Tolleson, Aaron Stone, and Richard Whitby; lower part of grant to Seth Lewis who sold to John Gosset who sold to John Lemaster and upper part of grant to John McCoole who sold to Robert Lemaster who sold to John Lemaster who sold to John Murray who sold to Thomas Murray who sold to William Stone. Witness Muse Tolleson and Richard Kearby (or Kirby). Signed Wm Stone. Wit. oath Aug. 26, 1808 Muse Tolleson to William Simpson. Rec. Aug. 30, 1808

p. 321-322 Sept. 2, 1808 Gabriel Benson, sheriff (Spartanburgh) to William Walker Meremon; for $12,50 sold 150 ac on both sides Cherokee Cr of Broad R; grant May 1, 1786 to Thomas Bonner; sale due to writ from Spartanburgh Common Pleas Court suit Susanna Walker vs George Walker; sale Mar. 7, 1808; sold to Susanna Walker but she doesn't want "titles to be made to her only" so titles made to William W Meremon. Witness Vincent Bennett and George Walker. Signed Gab Benson. Wit. oath Sept. 2, 1808 George Walker to Abner Benson. Rec. Sept. 2, 1808

p. 322-324 Feb. 3, 1808 Thomas Wright (Spartanburgh) to Andrew B Moore; for $350 sold 134 ac on both sides of N fork Tygar R; border: Gen. T Moore and Andrew B Moore. Witness Vincent Tapp and Charles Moore. Signed Thomas Wright. Wit. oath Feb. 16, 1808 Charles Moore to Drury McDaniel. Rec. Sept. 5, 1808. Dower renounced Mary Wright to Drury McDaniel Aug. 20, 1808

p. 324-325 Feb. 23, 1808 (Greenville Dist) William McDowell (Greenville Dist) to Underwood and Green (same); for $200 sold 350 ac on both sides Green's Cr of Lawson's fork; border: Widow West; part of 500 ac grant Dec. 2, 1793 to William McDowell sr. Witness Daniel Walling and Polley Underwood. Signed William McDowell. Wit. oath (Greenville Dist) Sept. 1, 1808 Polley Underwood to George Green. Rec. Sept. 5, 1808

p. 325-326 Aug. 19, 1808 William Moore (Spartanburgh) to Thomas Wright (same); for $200 sold 100 ac in fork of Tygar Rivers. Witness Vincent Tapp and John Ward. Signed William Moore. Wit. oath Aug. 20, 1808 John Ward to Drury McDaniel. Rec. Sept. 5, 1808. Dower renounced Betsy Moore to Drury McDaniel Aug. 20, 1808

p. 326-328 Jan. 24, 1807 David Burton (Spartanburgh) to Thomas Wright; for $108 sold 36 ac on S side of N fork of Tygar R. Witness John Ward and Buyuk McFerson. Signed David Burton. Wit. oath Aug. 31, 1807 John Ward to Drury McDaniel. Rec. Sept. 5, 1808. Dower renounced Esther Burton to Drury McDaniel (not dated)

p. 328-329 Mar. 12, 1808 James Wofford (Spartanburgh) to John Wofford (same); for $377.75 "written obligation" from James Wofford to John Wofford payable Mar. 1, 1809 and to secure payment of obligation sold 100 ac where James Wofford lives; border: John Wofford; grant to William Braley of North Carolina; and sold a Negro woman Soock (or Sooch) about 26 years old. Witness William Lancaster esq and John Lancaster. Signed James Wofford's mark. Wit. oath Sept. 5, 1808 John Lancaster to Wilie Willeford. Rec. Sept. 5, 1808

p. 329-330 Apr. 23, 1808 Arthur Faulkner (Spartanburgh) to loving friend Benjamin Nichols (same); for love and affection give 110 ac on branch of Cain Cr of Tygar R; grant Feb. 2, 1795 Gov. Arnoldus Vanderhorst to Arthur Faulkner. Witness Lawson Thomson and John Meadows. Signed Arthr Faulkner. Wit. oath Jul. 29, 1808 John Meadows to Wilie Willeford. Rec. Sept. 5, 1808

p. 330-331 (omitted) 2, 1804 Ezekiel Swillivan (Spartanburgh) to Edward Smith (same); for $70 sold 50 ac; border: Edward Smith; part of 200 ac grant to Elijah Buice who sold to Edward Smith. Witness William Bostick and William W Hembrie. Signed Ezekiel Swillivan. Wit. oath Oct. 23, 1804 William Bostick to John Lipscomb. Rec. Sept. 12, 1808

p. 331-332 Apr. 26, 1806 Jonathan Harris (Rutherford Co, NC) to Edward Smith (Spartanburgh); for $200 sold 200 ac on waters of Bullock's fork of Thickety Cr; part of 385 ac grant to Jonathan Harris; border: Jonathan Byars. Witness Holeman Smith and Collens Smith. Signed Jonathan Harris' mark. Wit. oath Jul. 27, 1807 Holeman Smith to John Lipscomb. Rec. Sept. 12, 1808

p. 332-333 Apr. 4, 1806 Abraham Markley (Charleston, SC), merchant, to Gabriel Benson (Spartanburgh); for $100 sold 361 ac on waters of Fairforrest Cr; border: NW-Bazel Lee, NE & N-John Holcomb and William Wofford, SE-Richard Harrison, and SW-George Bull; grant to Thomas Luher. Witness Peter R Staunton and Samuel Earle. Signed Abm Markley. Wit. oath (Pendleton Dist) Aug. 5, 1808 Samuel Earle to Jno George. Rec. Sept. 20, 1808

p. 333-334 Jun. 7, 1806 Gabriel Benson (Spartanburgh) to Duglass J Puckett (same); for $100 sold 361 ac on waters of Fairforrest Cr; border: NW-Bazel Lee, NE & N-John Holcomb and William Wofford, SE-Richard Harrison, and SW-Govenor Bull; grant to Thomas Leher. Witness Abner Benson and Robert Benson. Signed Gab Benson. Wit. oath Sept. 20, 1808 Robert Benson to A Benson. Rec. Sept. 20, 1808

p. 334-335 Feb. 13, 1808 William Fowler (Spartanburgh) to James Compton (same); for $300 sold 70 ac; border: Thomas Thornton. Witness Ralph Compton and Thomas Compton. Signed William Fowler. Wit. oath Apr. 2, 1808 Ralph Compton to Danl Willbanks. Rec. Sept. 29, 1808

p. 335-336 Apr. 19, 1805 John Gowen sr (Spartanburgh) to Richard Vennable (same); for 100£ sold 582 ac on S Pacolate R; border: Robert Harper, John McGuire, Robert Black, and James McClure; part of grant Jun. 6, 1800 to John Gowen; except 250 ac only warranted from claims of John Gowen's heirs and himself. Witness Gabriel Benson and Jno Gowen jr. Signed Jno Gowen. Wit. oath Oct. 3, 1808 Gabriel Benson to W Lancaster. Rec. Oct. 3, 1808

p. 336-337 Jan. 12, 1807 Andrew Hopkins (Spartanburgh) to Joseph and Saul Camp (same); for $600 sold 200 ac on McRees Cr of N Pacolate R; border: E-Thomas Jackson and S, N & W-Baylis Earle; part of 400 ac. Witness Abisha Camp and John Hopkins. Signed Andrew Hopkins. Wit. oath Feb. 17, 1807 John Hopkins to Wm Kelso. Rec. Oct. 3, 1808

p. 337 Dec. 9, 1807 Jacob Crocker (Spartanburgh) to Joseph Byars (same); for $300 sold 286 ac; border: Camp, Cherokee Cr, Watson, Markley, and Green's Cr. Witness Nathan Byars and Thomas Byars. Signed Jacob Crocker. Wit. oath Aug. 27, 1808 Thomas Byars to John Lipscomb. Rec. Oct. 3, 1808

p. 337-339 Mar. 20, 1807 Richard Vennable (Spartanburgh) to Rice F Ross (Lincoln Co, NC); for $1,000 sold 582 ac on S Pacolate R; border: Robert Harper, John McGuire, Robert Black, and James McClure; part of grant Jun. 6, 1800 to John Gowen. Witness Andrew Furgason and John Boham. Signed Richard Vennable. Wit. oath Jun. 28, 1808 Andrew Furgason to Jas L Burd. Rec. Oct. 3, 1808

p. 339-340 Oct. 8, 1808 Thomas Farrow (Spartanburgh) to son John Wood Farrow (same); for love and affection give (1) 100 ac survey Jul. 20, 1788 for George Louther; on both sides of Two Mile Cr and on N side of Enoree R; border: N-Isaac Hendrex, E & SE-Ebenerzar Morss, and W-George Louther; and (2) 100 ac adjoining (1) on branch of Two Mile Cr of Enoree R; border: N-Isaac Hendrex, NW-Robert Pringle, S-a big branch and remainder of grant, and E-John Hendrix; plat attached; part of 250 ac grant to George Louther. Witness Caleb Woodruff and Jordan Monjoy. Signed Thos Farrow. Wit. oath Oct. 8, 1808 Jordan Monjoy to John Dean. Rec. Oct. 9, 1808

p. 340-342 Apr. 2, 1808 Ebsworth Moore (Spartanburgh) to Henry Golightly (same); for $63 sold 229 ac on waters of Dutchman's Cr; part of three tracts: (1) 200 ac grant Nov. 7, 1785 to John Shands, (2) 456 ac grant Nov. 6, 1786, and (3) 240 ac grant

Jan. 21, 1785; grants (2) and (3) to Brittain Williford; 229 ac borders: William Smith and Williford field. Witness William W Hembrie and Samuel Lancaster. Signed Ebsworth Moore. Wit. oath Apr. 2, 1808 William W Hembrie to Saml Lancaster. Rec. Oct. 10, 1808. Dower renounced Elizabeth Moore to Saml Lancaster Apr. 2, 1808

p. 342-343 May 29, 1807 Samuel Smith (Spartanburgh) to James Meaders (same); for $350 sold 120 ac on both sides Dutchman's Cr of Tygar R; part of grant Sept. 22, 1769 to Ralph Smith. Witness John Meaders, Hiram Harrelson, and John Rogers. Signed Saml Smith. Wit. oath Feb. 13, 1808 John Rogers to Saml Lancaster. Rec. Oct. 11, 1808. Dower renounced Sarah Smith to Samuel Lancaster Feb. 13, 1808

p. 343-345 Jul. 25, 1808 James Crow (Spartanburgh) to Asael Beason (same); for $95 sold 48 ac on S side Tygar R; part of grant to Thomas White. Witness James W Reynolds and John Thornton. Signed James Crow. Wit. oath Oct. 10, 1808 James W Reynolds to John Brewton. Rec. Oct. 11, 1808

p. 345-346 Jul. 18, 1808 John Shands (Spartanburgh) to Shands Golightly (same); for $150 sold 100 ac; border: W & S-an old survey, E-vacant, and N-Burrell Pace; part of grant Jan. 1, 1787 Gov. William Moultrie to Burrel Pace. Witness Henry Golightly and Abraham Shands. Signed John Shands. Wit. oath Aug. 1, 1808 Henry Golightly to Samuel Lancaster. Rec. Oct. 11, 1808. Dower renounced Margaret Shands to Burrell Bobo Sept. 11, 1808

p. 346-347 Feb. 4, 1808 John Budd (Charleston, SC), heir of William Mitchell desc (Charleston, SC) by marriage and by power of attorney from rest of heirs, to David Golightly (Spartanburgh); for $100 sold 133 ac near Fairforrest Cr and on Buflow Lick Cr; border: David Golightly on all sides; former owner was Wm Mitchell. Witness Robert Martin and Polly Golightly. Signed John Budd. Wit. oath Oct. 11, 1808 Robert Martin to Wilie Willeford. Rec. Oct. 11, 1808

p. 347-348 Sept. 25, 1807 David Hix (Spartanburgh) to Reuben Seay (same); for $150 sold 100 ac on N side of Lawson's fork; grant Nov. 25, 1774 Gov. William Bull to Steven Miller. Witness Ephram Lewis and John Bird. Signed David Hix's mark. Wit. oath Oct. 11, 1808 Ephram Lewis to Ism Foster. Rec. Oct. 11, 1808

p. 348-349 Feb. 3, 1808 John Budd (Charleston, SC), heir of William Mitchel desc (Charleston, SC) by marriage and by power of attorney from rest of heirs, to David Golightly (Spartanburgh); for $300 sold 200 ac on S side of Fairforrest Cr; border: Esquire Lancaster, N-David Golightly, E-Hugh Wright, S-Christopher Johnson, and W-Thomas Vaughan; part of 640 ac grant to James Gibbs who sold to William Mitchel. Witness Robert Martin and Polly Golightly. Signed John Budd. Wit. oath Oct. 11, 1808 Robert Martin to Wilie Williford. Rec. Oct. 11, 1808

p. 349-350 Jun. 14, 1804 James Bagwell and wife Rebeca (Spartanburgh) to Micajah Barnett (same); for $300 sold 129 ac on both sides Beverdam Cr. Witness Akellis Foster and John Connell. Signed James and Rebeca Bagwell's marks. Wit. oath Oct. 11, 1808 John Connell to Danl White. Rec. Oct. 11, 1808. Dower renounced Rebeca Bagwell to William Lancaster Sept. 24, 1808

p. 350-351 Feb. 17, 1804 John Chesney (Spartanburgh) to James Smith (same); for 50£ sold 100 ac on James Cr of Tygar R; border: vacant when granted to Richard Chesney who sold to son John Chesney. Witness James Sills and Isaac Crow jr. Signed John Chesney. Wit. oath Jan. 11, 1806 Isaac Crow jr to A Casey. Rec. Oct. 11, 1808

p. 351-352 Jan. 25, 1808 Isaac Shurley (Spartanburgh) to John Means (same); for $50 sold 50 ac; border: W-branch of Forguson's Cr, S-Thomas Williamson, E & NE-John Means, and N-David McClarley (or McCearley); part of grant to Drury McDaniel and sold Jan. 1, 1800 to Look Thornton (see Book F p. 429) who sold Aug. 22, 1807 to Isaac Shurley. Witness Joseph Johnston, Andrew Otts, and James Otts. Signed Isaac Shurley. Wit. oath May .7, 1808 James Otts to Drury McDaniel. Rec. Oct. 11, 1808

p. 352-354 Feb. 11, 1805 John W Legon (Spartanburgh) to Jesse Spencer (same); for $100 sold 150 ac; border: Jesse Spencer, Danis Stephens, McSiles (or Mr. Siles), and Charles Moore; part of grant May 7, 1792 Gov. Charles Pinckney to James Gibs. Witness Samuel Otts and Samuel Moore. Signed J. W. Legon. Wit. oath Sept. 17, 1808 Samuel Otts to William Lancaster. Rec. Oct. 13, 1808

p. 354-355 Jan. 24, 1806 Benjamin Waldrop (Spartanburgh) to Elijah Johnson (same); for $200 sold 134 ac on branch of Provis Cr of S Tygar R; border: Elijah Johnson, Morten, William Brice, and Aaron Moore's old line; where Benjamin Waldrop lives. Witness Philip Johnson and George Durham. Signed Benjamin Waldrop's mark. Wit. oath Apr. 17, 1806 Geroge Durham to Drury McDaniel. Rec. Oct. 14, 1808

p. 355-356 Oct. 19, 1804 Cary Traylor (Spartanburgh) to Benjamin Waldrop (same); for $200 sold 134 ac on branches of Provis Cr of Tygar R; border: Elijah Johnson, William Brice, and Aaron Moore's old line. Witness Reuben Traylor and James Hadden. Signed Cary Traylor's mark. Wit. oath Mar. 1, 1805 Cary Traylor to Ism Foster. Rec. Oct. 14, 1808

p. 356-357 Jun. 3, 1808 Henry ONeal (Spartanburgh) to grandson Henry ONeal Love (same); for love and affection give a Negro boy Jim about 18 years old. Witness A Benson, John ONiell, and John McDowell. Signed Henry ONeall. Wit. oath Oct. 17, 1808 John McDowell to A Benson. Rec. Oct. 17, (omitted)

p. 357-358 Jun. 3, 1808 Henry ONeal (Spartanburgh) to grandson John ONeal Love (same); for love and affection give a Negro boy Perry about 18 years old. Witness A Benson, John ONiell, and John McDowell. Signed Henry ONiell. Wit. oath Oct. 17, 1808 John McDowell to A Benson. Rec. Oct. 17, 1808

p. 358-359 Mar. (omitted), 1808 Moses Crow (Christian Co, Ky) to William Clark (Spartanburgh); for $150 sold 100 ac on branch of James Cr of Tygar R; border: Charles Denem and vacant; grant to Mary Dunlap who sold to Moses Crow. Witness Thomas Waters, Henry Martor (or Markor), and John Thornton. Signed Moses Crow's mark. Wit. oath Mar. 10, 1808 Thomas Waters to John Dean. Rec. Oct. 17, 1808

p. 359-360 Sept. 13, 1807 James Mason (Spartanburgh) to Nathaniel Simmons (same); for $300 sold 126 ac on branch of Fairforrest Cr; border: Buryuk McFerson, Posey, Richardson Vincent, John Gideon, and William Wells; where James Mason lives. Witness William Ross Smith, John Simmons, and Joseph Simmons. Signed James Mason. Wit. oath Jan. 1, 1808 John Simmons to D. J. Puckett. Rec. Oct. 20, 1808

p. 360-361 Dec. 28, 1805 "Cowford" Province of E. Florida Isaac Hendricks (Prov. of E. Fla) to brother Thomas Hendricks (SC); power of attorney " in relation a tract of land" (ac not given) on Two Mile Cr of Enoree R; now occupied by John Grissel and Ebenezer Moss and others; Thomas can rent or sell the land. Witness

Rebeca Odell and Abner Broadaway. Signed Isaac Hendrix. Wit. oath (Laurence Dist) Mar. 8, 1806 Rebeca Odell to Robert Long. Rec. Oct. 24, 1808

p. 361-362 Mar. 9, 1805 Nathaniel Guiton (Spartanburgh) to Robert Storey (same); for $250 sold 200 ac on W side of Cherokee Cr; border: Jesse Fondren; grant to Nathaniel Guiton. Witness Fendol Robertson and Jacob Guyton. Signed Nathaniel Guiton's mark. Wit. oath Oct. 10, 1805 Fendol Robertson to John Rukman. Rec. Oct. 29, 1808

p. 362-363 Aug. 14, 1807 James Kilgore (Greenville Dist) to William Nelson (Spartanburgh); for $312 sold 156 ac where William Nelson lives; on branch of Abnor's Cr; border: William Jones, Samuel Jones, William Mayfield, and James Kilgore; part of 500 ac grant Jun. 23, 1774 to Robert Philip. Witness Robert Mason and Felix Vaughan. Signed James Kilgore. Wit. oath Nov. 7, 1808 Robert Mason to Danl Willbanks. Rec. Nov. 7, 1808

p. 363-366 Apr. 3, 1793 Edward Lacy, sheriff (Pinckney Dist) to William Darby, merchant; for 40£ sterling sold 300 ac on S fork of Pacolate R; border: William Dixon, William Anderson, and Col. Thomas Brandon; Thomas Rawdon owned the land; Common Pleas Court at 96, SC Nov. term in 1784 with case John Stokes vs Hugh Fruman, administrator of Thomas Rawdon desc, for breach of contract between John Stokes and Thomas Rawdon (during his lifetime); judgment on Apr. 26, 1786 against Hugh Fruman of 40£ 9s sterling and costs and Hugh asked to show cause by Nov. 26, 1789 why John Stokes shouldn't get money; John Stokes gest judgment Apr. 8, 1792 to be paid by Hugh Fruman by writ signed by Chief Justice, John Rutledge and signed by clerk at Cambridge Apr. 18, 1792--67£ 10s 8p sterling; sale Aug. 6, 1792. Witness Allen De Graffenrudh and Andrew Tarrance. Signed Edwd Lacey. Wit. oath Jul. 18, 1803 Andrew Tarrance esq to H Means. Rec. Nov. 8, 1808.
Apr. 16, 1808 (Charleston Dist) Julus Petsch (or Petech) assigns his rights (to land) obtained by his wife Jane H Petich, formerly Jane H Darby; land assigned to James W Darby (Union Dist). Witness W Muir (or Miuer)

p. 366-367 Jun. 5, 1807 John Wright (Spartanburgh) to Vincent Tapp (same); for $400 sold 100 ac on N side of S fork of Tygar R; border: a road; in two tracts. Witness William Moore and Charles Moore. Rec. John Wright. Wit. oath Sept. 1, 1808 William Moore to Drury McDaniel. Rec. Nov. 8, 1808

p. 367-368 Apr. 31, 1807 Joseph Hall (Cumberland Co, Ky) to Daniel McKie (Spartanburgh); for $30 sold 50 ac; border: NE-Jean Berrey and S-Barkey Brown. Witness Robt Anderson and Lod Dulen. Signed Joseph Hall. Wit. oath (Laurence Dist) Apr. 14, 1807 Lod Dulen to Stephen Garrett. Rec. Nov. 12, 1808

p. 368-369 Jan. 16, 1800 Adam and William Young (Spartanburgh) to Daniel McKie; for $120 sold 2/7 of 200 ac; border: E-William Stone, W-Robert Sims, and S-Enoree R; where Widow Young now lives; land willed to Adam and William Young by their father William Young. Witness William McKie, Amos Cutchfield, and Stephen Herndon. Signed Adam Young and William Young's mark. Wit. oath Jun. 15, 1807 Stephen Herndon to John Dean. Rec. Nov. 12, 1808

p. 369-370 Feb. 18, 1806 Abraham Poole (Spartanburgh) to Matthew Couch (same); for $800 sold 133 ac on N side Enoree R; where Abraham Poole lives; including Grist Mill on River; part of two tracts: (1) grant to William Cox and (2) grant to Benjamin Stone; border: S-Enoree R, E-John Coush, N-Benjamin Couch, and W-Benjamin Stone. Witness Samuel Farrow. Signed Abram Poole. Wit. oath Nov.

(blank), 1808 Samuel Farrow to D. J. Puckett. Rec. Nov. 12, 1808. Dower renounced Nancy Poole to William Smith Aug. 23, 1806

p. 370-372 Mar. 5, 1808 Amos Speace (Spartanburgh), hammerman, to Dan Gilbert (same); for $200 sold 200 ac on S side of Pacolate R; border: John Gilbert, William Holley, Mullesoy's Br, Thomas Bennett, and Thomas Kimbol. Witness Wm Bennett, Jonathan Wall, and Danl White. Signed (a scrawl). Wit. oath Apr. 13, 1808 Wm Bennett to John Lipscomb. Rec. Nov. 12, 1808. Dower renounced Mary Speace to John Lipscomb Apr. 13, 1808

p. 372-374 Oct. 26, 1808 John Low sr (Spartanburgh) to George Curling (Charleston, SC);for $180 sold 230 ac on waters of Pacolate R; border: Buk's Br; plat attached shows border: Dry Br, vacant, and "Boundry" line and on both sides of "Court House" road. Witness Reuben Warren and Samuel Turner. Signed John Low. Wit. oath Oct. 26, 1808 Samuel Turner to Henry Turner. Rec. Nov. 12, 1808. Dower renounced Jane Low to Abner Benson Nov. 14, 1808

p. 374 Nov. 14, 1808 John Tolleson received "full of all demand" in mortgage against John Low; John Low mortgaged land; mortgage is at clerk's office. Witness John Gossett. Signed John Tolleson. Wit. oath Nov. 14, 1808 John Gossett to Hugh Means. Rec. Nov. 2, 1808

p. 374-375 Jul. 8, 1808 John Nolen (Spartanburgh) to John Carter (same); for $60 sold 32 ac on waters of Pacolate R; border: James Carter and Edward Stublefield. Witness John Bankston and James Carter. Signed John Nolen. Wit. oath Nov. 8, 1808 John Bankston to Leon Adcock. Rec. Nov. 12, 1808

p. 375-376 Sept. 8, 1808 Edward Stublefield (Spartanburgh) to John Carter (same); for ($?)35 sold 50 ac on waters of Pacolate R; border: Burgess and John A Gore; part of grant to Thomas Burgess sr who sold to Edward Stublefield. Witness George Gilbert, Dan Gilbert, and Samuel Gilbert. Signed Edward Stublefield's mark. Wit. oath Nov. 8, 1808 George Gilbert to Leon Adcock. Rec. Nov. 12, 1808

p. 376-377 Aug. 22, 1808 Thomas Cowden (Williamson Co, Tenn) to James Hammett (Spartanburgh); for $100 sold 129 ac on W side Rocky Cr of Enoree R; border: Thomas Kevil, Stephen Cantrel, and Curtis Moore; where Feten Vaughan lives. Witness Lyn Walker and Theophelus Cannon. Signed Thomas Cowden. Wit. oath (Greenville Dist) Aug. 22, 1808 Lyn Walker to James Kilgore. Rec. Nov. 12, 1808. Dower renounced (Greenville Dist) Cattern Cowden to J. P. Hudson Aug. 25, 1808

p. 377-379 Aug. 3, 1808 John H Akins, John Powel, William Darvin, John Leech, and Benjamin Rollins (York Dist) to Abraham Green (same); for $165 sold 127 ac on waters of Little Cherokee Cr; border: Downn; half or W end of Powel's tract that is part of 800 ac grant to William Downs. Witness John Smith and Henry Smith. Signed John H Akin, John Powel, William Darvin, and John Leech's and Benjamin Rollins' marks. Wit. oath Oct. 8, 1808 John Smith to Jno H Jones. Rec. Nov. 12, 1808

p. 379-380 Sept. 19, 1808 Jesse Fondren (Spartanburgh) to John Hester (same); for $250 sold (1) 191 ac on Cherokee Cr and (2) 7 ac "a small slip of land" border: Lewis Stanly and Wm Hester. Witness Michael Gaffney and Daniel Hogan. Signed Jesse Fondren. Wit. oath Nov. 8, 1808 Michael Gaffney to John Lipscomb. Rec. Nov. 12, 1808

p. 380-381 Nov. 7, 1808 David Trail (Spartanburgh) to John Trail (same); for $300 sold 150 ac on both sides Dutchman's Cr of Tygar R; part of 300 ac grant Apr. 29, 1768 to Robert Henderson. Witness Sandford Smith and Robert Page jr. Signed David Trail. Wit. oath Nov. 8, 1808 Sandford Smith to Saml Morrow. Rec. Nov. 12, 1808

p. 381-382 Jun. 10, 1801 Reuben Gunn (Spartanburgh) to Thomas Cowden (same); for 64£ sold 100 ac on N side Enoree R; border: Thomas Kevil, Stephen Cantrel, and Little Rock Cr; where Thomas Cowden lives; part of 500 ac grant Feb. 27, 1775 to Thomas Scott esq and sold by Richard Hampton to Stephen Cantrell who sold to John Jones who sold to Reuben Gunn. Witness Charles Gunn and William Miller. Signed Reuben Gunn. Wit. oath Jun. 10, 1801 William Miller to James Kilgore. Rec. (not given). Dower renounced Mary Gunn to James Kilgore Jun. 10, 1801

p. 382-383 Nov. 23, 1808 Joseph Camp to Feritee, Lenny, Tobitha, and Debither Meremon; grantees disclaim 140 ac on Cherokee Cr left them by Nicholas Meremon desc; grantor gives 207 ac on Cherokee Cr; border: Holloway and Tinner. Witness Briant Bonner and George Walker. Signed Joseph Camp. Wit. oath Nov. 28 1808 George Walker to A Benson. Rec. Nov. 28, 1808

p. 383-385 Sept. 29, 1808 Rice F Ross (Spartanburgh) to Andrew Furgason (same); for $200 sold 100 ac on S side of S Pacolate R; border: near Motley's Cr and Robert Black; part of grant Jun. 6, 1800 to John Gowen. Witness Edward Fowler and John Lucas. Signed Rice F Ross. Wit. oath Nov. 18, 1808 Edward Fowler to Jas L Burd. Rec. Dec. 5, 1808

p. 385-386 Apr. 28, 1807 Obadiah Watson (Spartanburgh), tavern keeper, to Alexander McKie (same); for $100 sold 1 ac; half of land on branch of Fairforrest Cr near Spartanburgh Court House; including Tan yard on S side of branch; sold by Richard Thomson to Obadiah Watson and Alexander McKie and now Obadiah sells Alexander his (Obadiah's) half. Witness Anthony Foster, John Green Bostick, and Richard Daniel. Signed Obad Watson. Wit. oath Apr. 28, 1807 Richard Daniel to Abner Benson. Rec. Dec. 5, 1808. Dower renounced Sarah Watson to Abner Benson May 8, 1807

p. 386-388 Nov. 19, 1808 Samuel Kelso (Spartanburgh) to Thomas Foster (same); for $105 sold 100 ac on waters of Fairforrest Cr; border: "District Road", James Hurt, Benjamin Rainwaters, Joel Hurt, Michael Burnett, John Golightly, and Ridge Road; where John Williams desc formerly lived; grant to John Golightly; "I say bargained and sold" to Nancy widow of John Williams during her lifetime or widowhood for her and family's support and then to Elizabeth Williams the "deformer" daughter of John Williams during her lifetime for her support by her legal guardian and then to be deposed by public sale by Commissioners of the Poor of Spartanburgh at 12 months credit. Witness Joel Hurt and Elijah Barnett. Signed Saml Kelso. Wit. oath Nov. 19, 1808 Elijah Barnett to Danl White. Rec. Dec. 5, 1808

p. 388-389 Oct. 4, 1808 Obadiah Watson (Spartanburgh) to John Tolleson sr (same); for $400 sold 540 ac on Chinquepin Cr joining the Old Court House tract; sold by Samuel Miller to William Wells and sold to Obadiah Watson; except about 50-60 ac claimed by Abner Benson and except John Moorehouse's claim during John Moorehouse's life or his stay on the land--see deed from Obadiah Watson to John Moorehouse. Witness D. J. Puckett and Muse Tolleson. Signed Obad Watson. Wit. oath Dec. 10, 1808 Muse Tolleson to D. Puckett. Rec. Dec. 11, 1808. Dower renounced Sarah Watson to D. J. Puckett Nov. 16, 1808

p. 389-391 Sept. 1, 1808 Henry Brown (Spartanburgh) to John Tolleson (same); for $450 sold 222 ac on waters of Fairforrest Cr; part of 361 ac grant to Thomas Lehee who sold to Abraham Markley who sold to Gabriel Benson who sold to Duglas Josephas Puckett who sold to George Parkeson who sold to Henry Brown. Witness Muse Tolleson and Anthony Foster. Signed Henry Brown. Wit. oath Sept. 10, 1808 Muse Tolleson to William Simpson. Rec. Dec. 11, 1808. Dower renounced Susanna Brown to D. J. Puckett Oct. 1, 1808

p. 391-393 Oct. 15, 1808 James Boyd (Spartanburgh) for love and affection and $5 to wife Elizabeth Boyd, James sells to William Dunlap in trust for support of Elizabeth during her lifetime: (1) 150 ac on both sides of Lawson's fork; border: Cud, Foster, and Knight; sold Mar. 13, 1807 by William and Sarah Lewis to James Boyd; (2) 3 horses: a bay mare 8 years old, a bay horse 5 years old, and a sorrel filly 2 years old, 4 cattle, 18 hogs, 2 beds and bedsteads and furniture, pewter and crockery ward, table, chairs, wheels, rials, pails, potts, ovens, and all other kitchen or household furniture. Witness John McCarroll, Paul Cox, and John McKnight. Signed James Boyd's mark. Wit. oath Dec. 7, 1808 John McCarroll to James Young. Rec. Dec. 14, 1808

p. 393-394 Dec. 19, 1808 Gabriel Gossett (Spartanburgh) to John Tolleson (same); Gabriel gave John three notes for $138 due "at this time" and to secure payment he sells John the following: 2 feather beds, 3 bedsteads and furniture, an iron bound trunk, a spinning wheel, 12 pewter plates, 4 pewter basons, 2 pewter dishes, a pine cubbard and all his furniture, 2 ovens, 2 pots, one froh pan (sic), 3 axes, a mattock, 2 plows, a "cottu" or cotter, a pair of chain traces, a lock chain, 2 bee gums, a sorrel mare, saddle and bridle, a small colt, 2 cows and calves, 2 heifers, 20 barrels of corn, 1,000 bundles of fodder, 15 hogs, a hand saw, a drawing knife, 3 screw augers, a pine table and 6 chairs; Condition: sale void if Gabriel pays John $138 with interest by Dec. 19, 1809. Witness Muse Tolleson and Isham Briant. Signed Gabriel Gossett's mark. Wit. oath Dec. 24, 1808 Muse Tolleson to William Simpson. Rec. Dec. 24, 1808

p. 394-395 Dec. 24, 1808 Joseph Quin sr (Spartanburgh) to John Tolleson (same); Joseph executed 3 notes for $263.44 and to secure payment of money Joseph sells John the following: a bay horse, 4 cattle, 15 hogs, 2 sheep, 30 barrels of corn, 1,500 bundles of fodder, 2 beds, bedsteads, anf furniture, 3 pots, an oven, a skillet, 8 pewter plates, 3 basons, 2 dishes, a trunk, a large spinning wheel, 5 chairs, 3 plows, 2 axes, 2 "grubbing" hoes, 2 augers, a drawing knife, 2 pair of chain traces, a side cubbard and all furniture, 1,000 weight of cotton and table; Condition: sale void if Joseph pays money and interest by Jun. 25, 1809. Witness Muse Tolleson and Isham Briant. Signed Joseph Quin. Wit. oath Dec. 24, 1808 Muse Tolleson to William Simpson. Rec. Dec. 24, 1808

p. 395-396 Nov. 10, 1807 Richardson Vincent (Spartanburgh) to Benjamin Hammett (same); for $100 sold 100 ac on N side of Pacolate R; border: Doctor Br and Elizabeth Quarles. Witness John H Jones and William Hammett. Signed Richardson Vincent. Wit. oath Oct. 10, 1808 William Hammett to Jno H Jones. Rec. Dec. 31, 1808

p. 396-399 Jun. 30, 1808 Henry ONiell (Spartanburgh) to Hamilton Wilson (same); for $300 sold (1) 50 ac; border: Alexander McKie, N-John G(?) Buffington, E-John Gibbs, S-Samuel Culbertson, and W-John Thomas jr; grant to John Thomas jr who sold to Josiah Culberson who sold to Henry Oniell; (2) 23.6 ac on E side of Dugan's Br; border: Samuel Culbertson, Henry ONiell, Gallaspie's old survey; part of grant Feb. 23, 1754 North Carolina governor to George

Gallespie who sold to Robert Dugan who sold to Samuel Culberson sr who sold to Samuel Culbertson jr who sold to Henry ONiell; (3) (unknown) ac under the high water mark of a mill pond built by John Thomas jr who sold to Josiah Culbertson who sold to Henry ONiell; and (4) (unknown) ac at fork of Dugan's and Tate's Branches; border: Zachariah McDaniel, Alexander McKie, and "high water mark of saw mill bottom land" or pond; part of where Henry ONiell lives; grant to George Gillespie; all land on Dugan's Br of Fairforrest Cr. Witness John McDowell, Mary McDowell, and Andrew Harrison. Signed Henry ONiell. Wit. oath Dec. 31, 1808 Andrew Harrison to A Benson. Rec. Dec. 31, 1808

p. 399 Jun. 10, 1808 Sterling Tucker to Benjamin Wofford; Sterling relinquishes his claim to land where he lives and promises to give Benjamin 25¢ rent for present year. Witness Isham Harrison. Signed Sterling Tucker's mark. Wit. oath Jan. 2, 1809 Isham Harrison to A Benson. Rec. Jan. 2, 1809

p. 399-400 Dec. 9, 1808 John Tolleson (Spartanburgh) to Richard Kirby (same); for $60 sold 100 ac on S side Pacolate R; border: Old Spring Br, School House Br, Richard Kirby, Roaring Springs, and a road from Meeting House to "the River"; part of grant to John Tolleson. Witness John Gossett and Stephen Tolleson. Signed John Tolleson. Wit. oath Dec. 9, 1808 John Gossett to William Simpson. Rec. Jan. 2, 1809

p. 400-401 Mar. 5, 1808 James Reely (Spartanburgh) to John Foster (same); for $75 sold 50 ac on waters Kelsoe's Cr of Fairforrest Cr; border: White. Witness William S Golightly to Joseph Kelso. Signed James Reely. Wit. oath Mar. 14, 1808 Joseph Kelso to William Lancaster. Rec. Jan. 11, 1809. Dower renounced Mary Reely to William Lancaster Mar. 14, 1808

p. 401-403 Mar. 23, 1798 Hugh Moore (Spartanburgh) to William McKnight (same); for 14£ sterling sold 100 ac on S side of N Pacolate R; border: Robert Tate; part of 400 ac grant Apr. 27, 1767 to Patrick Moore. Witness John McCarroll to John Dunlap. Signed Hugh Moore. Wit. oath Mar. 23, 1798 John McCarroll to Geor Lamkin. Rec. Jan. 14, 1809

p. 403-404 Nov. 5, 1808 James Smith (Spartanburgh) to Sandford Smith (same); for $400 sold 100 ac on both sides James Cr of Tygar R; grant to Richard Chesny who sold to his son John Chesney who sold to James Smith. Witness William Smith and Henry Smith. Signed James Smith. Wit. oath Dec. 13, 1808 Henry Smith to Saml Morrow. Rec. Jan. 14, 1809

p. 404-405 Apr. 9, 1808 Abraham Hester (Rutherford Co, NC) to William Lipscomb (same); for $300 sold 300 ac on both sides of Cherokee Cr; border: Charles Miles' old line and William Fondren. Witness Smith Lipscomb and Jesse Fondren. Signed Abraham Hester's mark. Wit. oath Oct. 13, 1808 Smith Lipscomb to (omitted). Rec. Jan. 21, 1809. Dower renounced Sarah Hester to John Lipscomb Oct. 13, 1808

p. 405-407 Jan. 14, 1809 Charles Mathews (or Mathis) (Spartanburgh) to William Ross Smith (same); for $150 sold (1) 50 ac on N side Lawson's fork of Pacolate R; border: McElray; and (2) 150 ac on N side Lawson's fork adjoining (1) on E side; border: Benjamin Wofford jr, Littleton Bagwell, and William R Smith. Witness Anthony Foster, Isham Harrison, and David Linch (or Lynch). Signed Charles Mathis. Wit. oath Jul. 3, 1815 (sic) David Lince to Thomas Poole. Rec. Jan. 26, 1809. Dower renounced Nancy Mathias to William Lancaster Jan. 23, 1809

p. 407-408 Mar. 3, 1808 Amos Speace (Spartanburgh) to Luke Burnett (same); for $500 sold 40 ac on N side fo S Pacolate R. Witness William Standford and William Littlefield. Signed Amos Speace. Wit. oath Jul. 4, 1808 William Standford to James Young. Rec. Feb. 2, 1809

p. 408-409 Feb. 3, 1809 Baxter Gilbert (Spartanburgh) to John Nobles (same); for love and affection give a horse, a cow and calf, a loom, a table, a trunk, 2 beds and furniture, a "stan of cartens", 2 wheels, a pair of cards, clothing of all kinds, 2 saddles, all his crockery ware, a pot, an ax, "shoomaking" tools, and 5 sides of tanned leather. Witness John Robnett and Charles P Noble. Signed Baxter Gilbert. Wit. oath Feb. 3, 1809 John Robnett to William Simpson. Rec. Feb. 4, 1808

p. 409-410 Oct. 20, 1808 Daniel McClaren (Spartanburgh) to Wilson Nesbett (same); for $730 sold (1) 730 ac on both sides of Cherokee Cr of Broad R; grant in 1786 to William Wood who sold to Amos Spearce who sold to Daniel McClaren; and (2) 300 ac on Island Cr and Suck Cr of Pacolate R; border: John Williams. Witness John Sarratt and James Swaney. Signed Daniel McClaren. Wit. oath Feb. 4, 1809 James Swaney to John Collins Feb. 4, 1809. Rec. Feb. 6, 1809. Dower renounced Mary McClaren to Leon Adcock Nov. 7, 1808

p. 410-411 Oct. 18, 1808 Daniel McClaren (Spartanburgh) to Wilson Nesbett (same); for $125 sold 125 ac on both sides Cherokee Cr of Broad R; grant Jun. 5, 1786 to Amos Speace who sold Oct. 18, 1806 to Daniel McClaren. Witness John Sarratt and James Swaney. Signed Daniel McClaren. Wit. oath Feb. 4, 1809 James Swaney to John Collins. Rec. Feb. 6, 1809. Dower renounced Mary McClaren to Leon Adcock Nov. 7, 1808

p. 411-413 Oct. 18, 1808 Daniel McClaren (Spartanburgh) to Wilson Nesbett (same); for $100 sold 2,000 ac on waters of Suck Cr, Camp Cr, Horse Cr, Island Cr, and Buck Cr of Broad R; includes part of Cowpens Battleground; border: NE & NW-Williams, NW-Moultrie and unknown, SW, W & N-vacant, S-Scruggs, SW-William Abbott, NW-Cantrell, and "other sides"-Mathew Abbott; in two 1,000 ac tracts in two grants Feb. 10, 1791 to Daniel McClaren; except 150 ac border: Cantrell and William Abbot; and another 150 ac border: the Battleground, Scruggs, Hainey, Earle, and Williams. Witness John Sarratt and James Swaney. Signed Daniel McClaren. Wit. oath Feb. 4, 1809 James Swaney to John Collins. Rec. Feb. 6, 1809. Dower renounced Mary McClaren to Leond Adcock Nov. 7, 1808

p. 413-414 Oct. 19, 1808 Daniel McClaren (Spartanburgh) to Wilson Nesbett (same); for $1,000 sold 343 ac on S side of Broad R; border: John Dill, John Tugart, Samuel Sarratt, and vacant when surveyed; and border: Ross; and sold (2) 60 ac an island on E side of Broad R; grant to James Collins who sold in 1778 to Daniel McClaren. Witness John Sarratt and James Swaney. Signed Daniel McClaren. Wit. oath Feb. 4, 1809 James Swaney to John Collins. Rec. Feb. 6, 1809. Dower renounced Mary McClaren to Leon Adcock Nov. 7, 1808

p. 414-416 Oct. 18, 1808 Daniel McClaren (Spartanburgh) to Wilson Nesbett (same); for $2,650 sold (1) 2,650 ac on S side of Sarratt's Cr; and (2) 453 ac border: Bonner; and (3) (ac not given) on both sides Sarratt's Cr; border: Walker; grant in 1804 to Daniel McClaren. Witness James Swaney and John Sarratt. Signed Daniel McClaren. Wit. oath Feb. 4, 1809 James Swaney to John Collins. Rec. Feb. 6, 1809. Dower renounced Mary McClaren to Leon Adcock Nov. 7, 1808

p. 416 Oct. 11, 1802 William Stubs (Spartanburgh) to John Hance (same); for $60 sold 276 ac on branch of Cherokee Cr and on S side of Broad R; border: William Wrukman (or Rukman). Witness Fendol Robertson and Nathaniel Robertson. Signed William Stubs' mark. Wit. oath Dec. 16, 1808 Fendol Robertson to John Lipscomb. Rec. Feb. 6, 1809

p. 416-417 Nov. 2, 1808 Jacob (or John) Oldhance (Spartanburgh) to Michael Gaffney; for $274 sold 274 ac on Pewter and People's Creeks on S side Broad R; grant Gov. Charles Pinckney to Jacob Oldhance; border: Gaffney. Witness George Walker and John Arendell. Signed Jacob Oldhance's mark. Wit. oath Dec. 16, 1808 George Walker to John Lipscomb. Rec. Feb. 6, 1809

p. 417-418 Dec. 24, 1800 John Cooper and wife Ann (Spartanburgh) to William Stubs (same); for $10 sold 276 ac on branch of Cherokee Cr on S side Broad R; border: Rukman. Witness John Phillips and Nicholas Stubs. Signed John Cooper. Wit. oath Dec. 29, 1800 Nicholas Stubs to H McCray. Rec. Feb. 6, 1809

p. 418-419 Sept. 2, 1808 John Oldhance (Spartanburgh) to Michael Gaffney (same); for $552 sold 276 ac on branch of Cherokee Cr on S side Broad R; border: William Rukman. Witness Joseph Daffron and James Byars. Signed John Oldhance's mark. Wit. oath Oct. 8, 1808 Joseph Daffron to John H Jones. Rec. Feb. 6, 1809

p. 419-420 Aug. 10, 1800 William Clark (Spartanburgh) to William Posey (same); for $170 sold 100 ac on branch of Jameys Cr of Tygar R; border: Charles Dinim and vacant; grant to Mary Dunlap who sold to Moses Crow who sold to William Clark. Witness Samuel Enocks (or Enox) and James Crow. Signed William Clerk. Wit. oath Jan. 31, 1809 Samuel Enocks to John Brewton. Rec. Feb. 6, 1809

p. 420-421 Dec. 7, 1805 Solomon Crocker (Spartanburgh) to James Poole (same); for $5 sold 244 ac on Lawson's fork of Pacolate R; border: NE-Solomon Crocker, SE-James Poole, W-William R Smith and James Barnett, and N-Lawson's fork; platt attached. Witness William Willis, William Crocker, and Elizabeth Poole. Signed Solomon Crocker's mark. Wit. oath Dec. 14, 1805 William Willis to John Lipscomb. Rec. Feb. 6, (omitted)

p. 421-422 Mar. 5, 1808 John Low (Spartanburgh) to Stephen White (same); for $100 sold 320 ac on waters of Thickety Cr; border: N-formerly owned by Lewis, NE-Lewis and Thickety Cr, SE-Duberry, NW-Templemon, and SW-vacant; part of tract John Low "took" and "relapsed" by Samuel Fley and sold by Samuel Fley to John Low; 100 ac of tract excluded from upper part of tract. Witness Thomas Betterton, Warren Shurbutt, and Towmans (or Townens) Horton. Signed John Low. Wit. oath Oct. 22, 1808 Warren Shurbutt to John Lipscomb. Rec. Feb. 6, 1809

p. 422-423 Feb. 11, 1805 Joseph Wofford (Spartanburgh) to Middleton Shurbutt (same); for $108 sold 61 ac on S side Tygar R; border: N-Solomon Littlefield and Isaac Crow, W-Joseph Wofford, and SE-Alexander Dunlap. Witness Joseph Wofford jr and John Tucker. Signed Joseph Wofford. Wit. oath Aug. 6, 1805 John Tucker to Wm Smith. Rec. Feb. 6, 1809

p. 423-424 Jan. 10, 1806 Middleton Shurbutt (Spartanburgh) to Samuel Jones (same); for $200 sold 61 ac on S side of Tygar R; border: N-Solomon Littlefield and Isaac Crow, W-Joseph Wofford, and SE-Alexander Dunlap. Witness John Wright and Thomas Wright. Signed Middleton Shurbutt. Wit. oath Aug. 31, 1807 Thomas Wright to Drury McDaniel. Rec. Feb. 6, 1809

p. 424 Oct. 2, 1808 Amos Speace (Spartanburgh) to stepdaughter Nancy Holder (same); for love and affection give: a feather bed and bedstead, 12 pewter plates, a pewter dish and bason, a tin pan and large trunk, a bedstead, 6 chairs, 2 pots, an oven, a skillet, 2 "piggins", a water pail, a table, 6 knives and forks, 5 pewter spoons, 2 hoes, a pair "stityards", a pair of fire tongs, a spinning wheel, a "falling" ax, a "dun" coulered cow with her yearling calf, a red cow and calf, and an iron potrack. Witness Archelans Fore and Rachal Fore. Signed Amos Speace. Wit. oath Feb. 3, 1809 Archelans Fore to Henry Turner. Rec. Feb. 6, 1809

p. 424-425 Dec. 14, 1807 Rolly H Horton (Spartanburgh) to Warren Shurbutt (same); for $120 sold 100 ac on E side Pacolate R; grant Jun. 5, 1786 to Malichi Jones. Witness John Low and James Lackey. Signed Rolly H Horton's mark. Wit. oath Oct. 22, 1808 John Low to John Lipscomb. Rec. Feb. 6, 1809

p. 425-427 Jan. 21, 1809 Samuel Colley (Spartanburgh) to John Means (same); for $200 sold (1) (ac not given) on S side of S fork Tygar R; part of grant Jan. 1, 1787 to Thomas Hightower; and (2) 165 ac adjoining (1) and on N side of S fork Tygar R; border: E-Peter Bragg and W-Samuel Colley; grant to Daniel Bragg. Witness Robert Scott, James Scott, and Usela (or Usley) Colley. Signed Samuel Colley's mark. Wit. oath Jan. 21, 1809 Robert Scott to Drury McDaniel. Rec. Feb. 6, 1809

p. 427-428 Dec. 13, 1802 William Poole (Spartanburgh) to James Poole (same); for $500 sold 300 ac on Richland Cr on S side Pacolate R; where James Poole lives. Witness Anthony Bates, Sterling Tucker, and Elijah Poole. Signed William Poole. Wit. oath Aug. 19, 1803 Anthony Bates to John Lipscomb. Rec. Feb. 6, 1807

p. 428-429 Jul. 4, 1808 Henry Turner (Spartanburgh) to Joroyal Burnett (same); for (money not mentioned) sold 73 ac on N side Lawson's Cr; border: E-Henry Turner and W-Noah Wells. Witness Thomas James and Caleb Jones. Signed Henry Turner. Wit. oath Nov. 8, 1808 Thomas James to Danl White. Rec. Feb. 6, 1809

p. 429-430 Mar. 29, 1807 Thomas Moore (Spartanburgh) to William Cantrell; for $100 sold 136 ac on Sefford's Cr of N Pacolate R; border: W-Sefford French, S-McMillen, and others vacant; survey Mar. 12, 1798 for John Hall and granted Dec. 2, 1799 Gov. Edward Rutledge to Elias Earle. Witness John Marten and Nathan Lovelass. Signed Thomas Moore. Wit. oath Feb. 3, 1808 John Marten to Leonard Adcock. Rec. Feb. 6, 1809

p. 430-431 Jan. 9, 1809 William Coan (Spartanburgh) to John Traylor; for $100 sold a bay horse, saddle and bridle, a sorrel mare and sucking colt, a "sawd" horn cow and calf, 4 hogs marked with swallow fork in left ear and half cross in right ear, all household and kitchen furniture, all plantation tools and gear, all saddler's tools, a watch, all corn, fodder, oats, and all goods whatsoever. Witness Robert Hughs and Samuel Crowder. Signed William Coan. Wit. oath Jan. 9, 1809 Samuel Crowder to Drury McDaniel. Rec. Feb. 6, 1809

p. 431-432 Oct. 5, 1808 Gowen Harris (Greenville Dist) to Samuel Crowder (Spartanburgh); for $270 sold 200 ac on Bridges Cr of Middle Tygar R; border: Elisha Hadden; W end of survey for James Alexander. Witness John Traylor and Howell Johnson. Signed Gowen Harris. Wit. oath Feb. 6, 1809 John Traylor to Drury McDaniel. Rec. Feb. 6, 1809

p. 432 Jan. 21, 1809 Samuel Colly (Spartanburgh) to Robert Miller; for $75 sold a sorrel horse about 5 feet high 7 years old a "staer" in his forehead, a cream colored mare 7 years old 15½ hands high branded on near shoulder "TB"; Condition: sale void if Samuel pays $75 in two years. Witness Labon P Poole and Joshua Brown. Signed Samuel Colly's mark. Wit. oath Jan. 21, 1809 Labon P Poole to Drury McDaniel. Rec. Feb. 6, 1809

p. 432-434 Aug. 1, 1808 John McElrath (Spartanburgh) to Abner Wingo (same); for $300 sold 192 ac on N side of Middle Tygar R; border: Penny, Vernon, and Benson; 50 ac of which is part of grant Feb. 17, 1785 to Thomas Penny and remainder is part of "a new survey". Witness William Perrin, John Smith, and Adam McElrath. Signed John McElrath. Wit. oath Jan. 25, 1809 Adam McElrath to Michl Miller. Rec. Feb. 7, 1809. Dower renounced Rachal McElrath to Isham Foster Aug. 11, 1808

p. 434-435 Dec. 15, 1808 Christopher Orrenduff (Spartanburgh) to David Golightly sr (same); for $150 sold 105 ac; border: Fairforrest Cr, David Golightly, and David Cook; plat attached. Witness Robert Martin and William Orrenduff. Signed Christopher Orrenduff's mark. Wit. oath Feb. 10, 1809 William Orrenduff to D. J. Puckett. Rec. Feb. 6, 1809. Dower renounced Elizabeth Orenduff to D. J. Puckett Feb. 10, 1809

p. 435-436 Feb. 13, 1809 Edith Berry (Spartanburgh) to John Tolleson (same); for $150 sold 102 ac on W side Fairforrest Cr; border: E-Reuben Daniel, S-Henry Brown, and N-Mrs. Lee; sold by Thomas Wells to John Cantrell who sold to Edith Berry. Witness Muse Tolleson and Robert Legon. Signed Edith Berry's mark. Wit. oath Feb. 13, 1809 Muse Tolleson to D. J. Puckett. Rec. Feb. 10, 1809

p. 436-437 Jan. 9, 1809 James McDaniel to Ralph Danger; for $395 sold (ac not given) on both sides Meadow Cr of S Pacolate R; border Marky and Robert Young. Witness William Durham and Sina Durham. Signed James McDaniel's mark and Sarah McDaniel. Wit. oath Jan. 31, 1809 William Durham to Andrew Fergerson. Rec. Feb. 10, 1809

p. 437-439 Apr. 13, 1803 Henry Young (Spartanburgh) to James McDaniel (same); for $300 sold 395 ac on both sides Meadow Cr of S Pacolate R; in two tracts; border: Markey and Robet Young; except what "lies in Henderson's and Gilbert's". Witness Walter McChesny Margaret McChesny, and Hugh Stevenson. Signed Henry Young. Wit. oath Sept. 27, 1803 Walter McChesny to James L Burd. Rec. Feb. 10, 1809

p. 439-440 Feb. 13, 1809 Ransom Golightly (Spartanburgh) to Peter Best (Union Dist); for $600 sold 1,000 ac on Lawson's fork of Pacolate R; border: a mill pond. Witness John Golightly and John Golightly jr. Signed Ransom Golightly. Wit. oath Feb. 13, 1809 John Golightly jr to A Benson. Rec. Feb. 13, 1809

p. 440 Feb. 13, 1809 Duglas J Puckett to Edith Berry; for $5 quit claim to part of "her tract" where Edith Berry lives. Witness Muse Tolleson and Robert Legon. Signed D. J. Puckett. Wit. oath Feb. 13, 1809 Muse Tolleson to J Walker. Rec. Feb. 13, (omitted)

p. 440-441 Feb. 13, 1809 Richard Thomson (Spartanburgh) to son Henry Hopson Thomson (same); for love and affection give ½ ac that is corner lot at Spartanburgh Court House on N side of Court House; border: Alexr Todd and "the cross street". Witness George Walker and Holmon Smith. Signed Richard Thomson. Wit. oath Feb. 13, 1809 Holmon Smith to A Benson. Rec. Feb. 13, 1809

p. 441-442 Feb. 13, 1809 Richard Thomson (Spartanburgh) to son

William Halten Thomson (same); for love and affection give ½ ac that is corner lot (#26) at Spartanburgh Court House on S side of Court House; border: Alexr McKie, publick ground, "cross street", and Bostick. Witness George Walker and Holmon Smith. Signed Richard Thomson. Wit. oath Feb. 13, 1809 Holmon Smith to A Benson. Rec. Feb. 13, 1809

p. 442-444 Feb. 14, 1809 Gabriel Benson, sheriff (Spartanburgh) to John Cook; for $560 sold 206 ac on Fairforrest Cr; 2/3 of estate of Robert Legon desc; sale due to writ from Spartanburgh Common Pleas Court Nov. term 1807 suit John Cook vs Edith Legon, administrix of Robert Legon desc; sale Mar. 7, 1808. Witness John G Bostick and Richard Barnett. Signed Gab Benson SSD. Wit. oath Feb. 14, 1809 John G Bostick to A Benson. Rec. Feb. 14, 1809

p. 444-445 Oct. 3, 1808 Daniel McClaren (Spartanburgh) to John Brown (same); for $862 sold 862 ac on both sides Sarratt's Cr of Broad R; grant to John Prukmon (or Rukmon) who sold to Daniel McClaren. Witness John Sarratt and James Swaney. Signed Daniel McClaren. Wit. oath Feb. 15, 1809 James Swaney to John Collins. Rec. Feb. 14, 1809. Dower renounced Mary McClaren to Leon Adcock Nov. 7, 1808

Book M 1809-1811
p. 1 Oct. 20, 1808 Daniel McClaren (Spartanburgh) to John McClaren (same); for $200 sold 200 ac on waters of Broad R; border: Daniel McClaren; grant Apr. 3, 1786 to Daniel McClaren and "sold to me" Oct. 20, 1808. Witness James Swaney and Wilson Nesbett. Signed Daniel McClaren. Wit. oath Feb. 17, 1809 James Swaney to John Collins. Rec. Mar. 2, 1809

p. 1-2 Mar. 27, 1807 Gabriel Benson (Spartanburgh) to Paul Cox (Lincoln Co, NC); for $900 sold 333 ac on S Pacolate R; grant to William Dixon who sold to James Dixon who sold to Gabriel Benson. Witness Wm Ramsey and Abraham Bannister. Signed Gal Benson. Wit. oath Sept. 26, 1807 Wm Ramsey to Wm Kelso. Rec. Mar. 6, 1809

p. 2-4 Oct. 11, 1803 Henry Gibson (Spartanburgh) to Jarret Patterson (same); for $250 sold 180 ac on both sides of Goocher's Cr; "there is a line made between Jarret Patterson and George Gibson"; part of 200 ac grant Dec. 6, 1771 North Carolina to Hugh Moore who sold to Charles Ray and sold to "William Thomson Swan Thomson's son her at" sold to David Humphreys who sold to Henry Gibson. Witness George Gibson to Ezekiel Swillivan. Signed Henry Gibson's mark. Wit. oath Oct. 11, 1803 George Gibson to John Lipscomb. Rec. Mar. 6, 1809

p. 4-5 Jul. 22, 1805 Isaac Sincler (or Cincler) (Iredel Co, NC) to Jarrett Patterson (Spartanburgh); for $50 sold 125 ac on N side of Pacolate R; border: Joshua Petet and John Gray. part of 300 ac. Witness Sally Lipscomb and Elizabeth Lipscomb. Signed Isaac Sincler. Wit. oath Jul. 22, 1805 Sally Lipscomb to John Lipscomb. Rec. Mar. 6, 1809

p. 5-6 Sept. 13, 1806 Jessey Tate sr (Spartanburgh) to Nathaniel Robertson (same) (or Reuben Morgan); for $250 sold 200 ac on waters of Cherokee Cr of Broad R; border: Little Cr, Little Cherokee Cr, Powell, and English; grant "from" George Blanton to Jessey Tate who sold to Nathaniel Robertson who sold to Reuben Morgan. Witness Fondel Robertson and Nathaniel Robertson. Signed Marry Tate's mark, Samuel Tate, John Hester, Cabrid McCran's mark, Fondel Tate's mark, Reuben Tate's mark, James Tate, and Kossia Tate's mark. Wit. oath Jan. 13, 1807 Nathaniel Robertson to John Lipscomb. Rec. Mar. 6, 1807

p. 6 Nov. 16, 1808 James Barnett (Spartanburgh) to Eli Tolleson (same); for $100 sold 170 ac; border: William Golightly, Solomon Crocker, Wm Bagwell, and Eli Tolleson. Witness Richard James and John Lancaster. Signed Jas Barnett. Wit. oath Mar. 6, 1809 Richard James to Danl White. Rec. Mar. 6, 1809

p. 6-7 May 5, 1808 John Connell (Spartanburgh) to Ely Tolleson (same); for $130 sold 50 ac on branch of Kelsoe's Cr of Fairforrest Cr. Witness Elizabeth James and Richard James. Signed John Connell. Wit. oath Mar. 6, 1809 Richard James to Danl White. Rec. Mar. 6, 1809

p. 7-9 Dec. 22, 1807 Elijah Barnett (Spartanburgh) to Eli Tolleson (same); for $220 sold 200 ac; border: branch of Richland Cr; where James Barnett lives. Witness Isham Harrison and Richard James. Signed Elijah Barnett. Wit. oath Mar. 6, 1809 Richard James to Danl White. Rec. Mar. 6, 1809. Dower renounced Polly Barnett to D. J. Puckett Aug. 31, 1808

p. 9-10 May 29, 1806 Cary Traylor (Spartanburgh) to James Hadden (SC); for $200 SC money sold 100 ac; border: Pinmon, Ben's Cr, John Durham, and William Gray. Witness Jonathan N Hadden and Reuben Traylor. Signed Cary Traylor's mark. Wit. oath Nov. 30, 1808 Jonathan N Hadden to David Morton. Rec. Mar. 6, 1809

p. 10 Mar. 6, 1809 Frances Mason (Spartanburgh) to Joseph Rodgers (same); for $300 sold 100 ac on Ward's Cr of Tygar R; now bordering: Jean Thomson, S-John Otts, N-Jason Moore, and W-Lewis Furgason. Witness Lawson Thomson and Lewis Furgason. Signed Frances Mason. Wit. oath Mar. 6, 1809 Lawson Thomson to William Lancaster. Rec. Mar. 6, 1809

p. 10-11 Mar. 4, 1809 Lewis Furgason (Spartanburgh) to Joseph Rodgers (same); for $80 sold 29 ac on branch of Ward's Cr of Tygar R; grant Mar. 28, 1804. Witness Lawson Thomson and John Ward. Signed Lewis Furguson. Wit. oath Mar. 6, 1809 Lawson Thomson to William Lancaster. Rec. Mar. 6, 1809

p. 11-13 Mar. 4, 1809 John Ward (Spartanburgh) to Joseph Rodgers (same); for $100 sold 36 ac on N fork Tygar R; part of 150 ac grant Nov. 10, 1784 to Patrick March. Witness Lewis Furguson and Lawson Thomson. Signed John Ward. Wit. oath Mar. 6, 1809 Lawson Thomson to William Lancaster. Rec. Mar. 6, 1809

p. 13-14 Feb. 25, 1809 Thomas Thornton (Spartanburgh) to Gideon Harrelson (same); for $39.72 and to secure payment thereof sell a mare bridle and saddle, a set of smith's tools, a belos, anvell, vise, hammer, tongs, and other articles of the set, a bed, bedstead, and furniture, a cow and yearling, a pot and oven, a dish and bason, 2 plates, a pair of "dressers" and table, a gun, a shot bag, a cotton wheel, a barrel, 4 chairs, 2 flat irons, 2 cotton cards, a bee gum, a plow and "clives", 2 weeding hoes; debt is $39.72 and 7% interest per year; Condition: sale void if debt is paid by Dec. 25, 1809. Witness Hiram Harrelson and John Meadows. Signed Thomas Thornton. Wit. oath Mar. 4, 1809 Hiram Harrelson to Saml Morrow. Rec. Mar. 6, 1809

p. 14-15 Apr. 4, 1808 Patrick Saunders jr (Spartanburgh) to Abby D King (same); for $110 sold 120 ac on Thickety Cr of Broad R; border: Guttery, Sanders, vacant, and William Hopkins; if there isn't 120 ac, then "we take" 30 ac from land given by Patrick Saunders sr to son Patrick with border: at mouth of Morris Spring Br, Patrick Saunders sr, and Sanders; "portion of land I, Mary King" give to daughter Abby D King with Mary King to live on land for her lifetime if she chooses. Witness Joseph Forgerson and James Forgerson. Signed Patrick Saunder's mark. Wit. oath Oct. 10, 1808 James Forgerson to Henry Turner. Rec. Mar. 17, 1809

p. 15-16 Feb. 17, 1809 Ralph Dangard (Spartanburgh) to Henry and Nathaniel Dangard (same); for $300 sold 395 ac; grant to Henry Young. Witness James Brannon and Alexander McKie. Signed Ralph Dangard's mark. Wit. oath Mar. 17, 1809 James Brannon to A Benson. Rec. Mar. 17, 1809

p. 16-17 Sept. 29, 1808 Pleasent Easley (Greenville Dist) to John Dodd (Spartanburgh); for $350 sold 100 ac on both sides of S Pacolate R; border: a waggon road; where John Henrey lives; part of 640 ac grant Feb. 3, 1775 to Matthew Harper sr. Witness John Gowen jr and John Henry. Signed Pleasent Easley. Wit. oath Oct. 28, 1808 John Henry to Jas L Burd. Rec. Feb. 15, 1809

p. 17-18 Feb. 21, 1807 Henry Wells (Spartanburgh) to John and Richard Foster (same); for $200 sold 100 ac on Beverdam Cr of Fairforrest Cr; border: Elijah Barnett, John Foster, and Richard Foster. Witness John Mason, Jesse Wells, and James Wofford. Signed Henry Wells. Wit. oath Mar. 24, 1809 Jesse Wells to D. J. Puckett. Rec. Mar. 24, 1809

p. 18-19 Mar. 18, 1809 Robert Kimble (Spartanburgh) to Shands Golightly (same); for $100 sold 250 ac at head of N Tygar R; border: where Dry Pond Path crosses Parson's Road. Witness James Hanna and William Hanna. Signed Robert Kimble. Wit. oath Mar. 29, 1809 William Hanna to Danl White. Rec. Mar. 28, 1809

p. 19-21 Apr. 29, 1801 William McDaniel (Spartanburgh) to Thornton McDaniel (same); for love and affection give 120 ac on E side of S Tygar R; border: Drury McDaniel, Ward, English, William Allen, and Thornton McDaniel; part of grant to Adam Meek. Witness Jesse Crook, James Crook jr, and Henry Cannon (or Cannors). Signed William McDaniel and Juday's mark. Wit. oath Apr. 29, 1801 Jesse Crook to Drury McDaniel. Rec. Apr. 3, 1809

p. 21-22 Mar. 10, 1809 Daniel White (Spartanburgh) to Samuel Burton (same); Daniel owes Samuel $400 until Feb. 1, 1810 so Daniel mortgages 200 ac where Daniel lives; on both sides of Fair-forrest Cr; sold by Samuel Burton to Daniel White; part of land formerly owned by Giles Connell desc. Witness Drury Burton. Signed Daniel White. Wit. oath Mar. 28, 1809 Drury Burton to John Brewton. Rec. Apr. 3, 1809

p. 22-24 Nov. 4, 1809 James Templeton (Spartanburgh) to Darney Bishop (same); for $150.50 sold 43 ac on Standing Stone Cr of Lawson's fork; border: William Bishop sr's Spring Br; part of grant in 1768 North Carolina to Robert McMurdy and sond by his heirs to son John McMurdy in 1797 who sold in 1799 to James Templeton and Samuel Miller and Samuel Miller sold his part to James Templeton in 1800. Witness James Barrett and Edmond Bishop. Signed Jas Templeton. Wit. oath Mar. 11, 1809 James Barrett to J Walker. Rec. Apr. 3, 1809

p. 24-25 Apr. 23, 1787 Reubin Dickson (Spartanburgh) to Edward Stubblefield (same); for 3£ sterling sold 214 ac on both sides Milse's Br of Pacolate R; grant Jan. 21, 1785 States Office to Reubin Dickson. Witness Sampson Bethel, Thos Warrin, and Hannah Warren. Signed Reubin Dickson's mark. Certified Mar. 4, 1794 by S Bethel. Rec. Apr. 3, 1809

p. 25-26 Feb. 20, 1809 Richard Gentry (Spartanburgh) to John Meaders (same); Richard owes John $60 with interest; Richard sells John 199 ac where Richard Gentry lives, 2 cows and calves, 2 feather beds and furniture, 14 barrels of corn, 2 stacks of "bleads" fodder, 2 stacks of oats, 300 weight of bacon, 2 pewter basons, 6 pewter plates, a dish, a chest, a box, a loom, 7 hogs, a pair of chair traces; debt is for $60 with "legal interest of 7 and 60% per year";

Condition of sale: sale void if Richard pays John $60 with interest by Feb. 20, 1800 (sic). Witness George T Sloan and James Meadors. Signed Richard Gentry's mark. Wit. oath Mar. 29, 1809 George T Sloan to Saml Morrow. Rec. Apr. 3, 1809

p. 26-28 Feb. 25, 1809 Thomas Woodruff III (SC) to Joseph Woodruff sr (Spartanburgh); a bond dated Feb. 1, 1809 for $3,000 to pay $1,500 with interest; to secure payment of bond Thomas sells to Joseph Negro slaves: woman Winny and "her furniture issue", her boy York, 4 sorrel horses, 11 cattle, 21 hogs, a cotton machine and cotton packing screw, 4 feather beds and furniture, 5 bedsteads, 12 chairs, a loom, 2 tables, a large wheel, a small flaxwheel, a clock reel(?), a man's and woman's saddle, 2 trunks, a small assortment of family books, 3 plows, 3 pair of iron gears, 2 axes, "the wood of waggon and Iron to put on her", some household and kitchen furniture; Condition: sale void if Thomas pays the debt. Witness Archibald McCravy and Thomas Farrow. Signed Thomas Woodruff III. Wit. oath Apr. 7, 1809 Archibald McCravy to John Brewton. Rec. Apr. 7, 1809

p. 28-29 Feb. 28, 1809 George Arnold (Spartanburgh) to Joseph Woodruff sr (same); for $88 sold two tracts on waters of Deldine's Cr: (1) 50 ac; border: N-Stoutingburgh, E-Samuel Woodruff, S-Anderson Page, and W-Morgan Darnet; and (2) 40 ac; border: Samuel Woodruff, Robert Page, Wm Stoutingburgh, and Huger. Witness John Crocker, John Wells, and William Hendrix. Signed George Arnold. Wit. oath Apr. 7, 1809 William Hendrix to John Brewton. Rec. Apr. 7, 1809

p. 29 Mar. 11, 1809 Sarah Foster (Spartanburgh) to Thomas Tinsley (same); for $500 sold a Negro woman Sarah and Negro boy Edom 3 years old, and Negro girl Jud 2 or 3 months old, both children of Sarah, and feather bed and furniture. Witness Richard Daniel and Thomas James. Signed Sarah Foster's mark. Wit. oath Apr. 8, 1809 Richard Daniel to Danl White. Rec. Apr. 7, 1809

p. 29-30 Feb. 23, 1809 James Miller (Spartanburgh) to Josiah Miller (same); for $96 sold (ac not given) on S side of Middle Tygar R; border: Buffalo Br, W-Josiah Miller and other sides-Samuel Miller. Witness Robert Miller, Samuel Neely, and Hugh Caldwell. Signed James Miller. Wit. oath Apr. 11, 1809 Samuel Neely to John Collins. Rec. Apr. 7, 1809

p. 30-32 Nov. 29, 1808 (Laurence Dist) Augustus F Durkie (Laurence Dist) to William Calvert (Spartanburgh); Augustus F and Nathaniel Durkie are bound to William Calvert for $1,800 to pay $300 Dec. 1, 1809, $500 Dec. 1, 1810, $500 Dec. 1, 1811 and $500 Dec. 1, 1812; to secure payment and for 5s Augustus mortgages 150 ac on Enoree R; formerly known as Moss's Mills; border: James Leatherwood, Shaderich Woodruff, Spencer Brown, Nathan Watson, John Gresel, Christophers Rhoas, William Hendricks, and Mr Waldrop; Condition: sale void if Augustus and Nathaniel Durkie pay debt. Witness Uriah Leatherwood and Thomas Porter. Signed Augs F Durkie. Wit. oath (not dated) Thomas Poole to James Young. Rec. Apr. 10, 1809

p. 32-33 May 20, 1808 (Rutherford Co, NC) Charles Wilkins (Rutherford Co, NC) to Anthony Sarratt (Spartanburgh); for $140 sold 80 ac on Sarratt's Cr of Broad R; border: William Davidson, William Holloway, and Wilson's old line; part of two grants (1) to Joseph Champeon and (2) to Robert Warren. Witness John Sarratt and Saul Camp. Signed Charles Wilkins. Wit. oath Apr. 10, 1809 John Sarratt to John Lipscomb. Rec. Apr. 10, 1809

p. 33-34 Aug. 8, 1808 Joseph Austell to Casper K Webber; for $196 sold 147 ac on waters of Thickety Cr; border: Amos. Witness Joseph Camp and Wm Weber. Signed Joseph Austell. Wit. oath Mar. 21, 1809 Wm Weber to John Lipscomb. Rec. Apr. 10, 1809

p. 34-35 Mar. 3, 1807 Thomas Underwood (Spartanburgh) to James Otts (same); for $575 sold 215 ac on S side of S fork Tygar R; part of grant Jan. 1, 1787 Gov. William Moultrie to Thomas Hightower. Witness Robert Miller, William Otts, and Samuel Cally. Signed Thomas Underwood. Wit. oath Mar. 7, 1808 Robert Miller to Drury McDaniel. Rec. Apr. 10, 1809

p. 35-36 Oct. 17, 1799 William Miller (Spartanburgh) to James Otts (same); for $550 sold (1) 50 ac on S side S Tygar R; part of grant Oct. 24, 1767 Gov. William Tryon (NC) to James Miller who sold to William Miller; (2) 100 ac; grant Aug. 26, 1774 Lt. Gov. William Bull to Andrew Thomson who sold to William Miller; and (3) 62 ac; grant Gov. William Moultire to William Miller. Witness Robert Miller and Thos Moore JQ. Signed William Miller. Wit. oath May 7, 1808 Robert Miller to Drury McDaniel. Rec. Apr. 10, 1809

p. 36-37 Apr. 15, 1808 Henry Cannon and wife Elizabeth (Spartanburgh) to Robert Miller (same); for $1,600 sold 469 ac on S side of N Tygar R; border: N-Richard Barry and Charles Barry, W-Robert Miller, S-Mrs. Posey, and E-William Moore (or Morris). Witness Jesse Cannon, Joseph Johnston, and James Otts. Signed Henry and Elizabeth Cannon. Wit. oath Aug. 20, 1808 James Otts to Drury McDaniel. Rec. Apr. 10, 1809

p. 37-39 Jun. 9, 1802 Spencer Bobo jr (Spartanburgh) to London Miles (same); for $500 sold 150 ac on Letches Cr of Enoree R; border: where Benson and Bobo line cross Reedy fork, James Chamblain, Groves Yarbor, Joseph Woolbanks; part of 640 ac to John Head; known as where James Chamblain lives. Witness Mordica Chandler and William Farrow. Signed S Bobo jr. Wit. oath (Union Dist) May 10, 1805 Mordica Chandler to David Floyd. Rec. Apr. 10, 1809. Dower renounced Jane Bobo to J. F. Gremke (not dated)

p. 39-40 Jan. 18, 1809 Malechi Eskrididge (Spartanburgh) to Daniel McKie; for $200 sold 140 ac; border: Enock Underwood, Berry, and William McDaniel jr. Witness Labon P Poole and William N Miller. Signed Malechi Eskridge. Wit. oath Jan. 19, 1809 Labon P Poole to Drury McDaniel. Rec. Apr. 10, 1809

p. 40 Jan. 25, 1809 William Webb to James Vernon; for $420 sold a Negro slave Sam about 23 years old. Witness John Wood. Signed William Webb. Wit. oath Apr. 11, 1809 John Wood to John Collins. Rec. Apr. 11, 1809

p. 40-41 Apr. (omitted), 1809 Lawson Thomson (Spartanburgh) to Dr. Andrew B Moore (same); for $200 sold 62 ac on branch on N side of N fork Tygar R;part of grant May 20, 1763 to Charles Moore. Witness Elijah Barnett and John Cook. Signed Lawson Thomson. Wit. oath Apr. 11, 1809 Elijah Barnett to W Lancaster. Rec. Apr. 11, 1809

p. 41-42 Nov. 19, 1808 Thomas Reid (Spartanburgh) to Willis Allen (same); for $300 sold 148 ac; border: oak marked "ID & C"; "part of a tract". Witness Frances Littlejohn and David Lipscomb. Signed Thomas Reid. Wit. oath Nov. 19, 1808 Frances Littlejohn to John Lipscomb. Rec. Apr. 11, 1809. Dower renounced Judith Reid to John Lipscomb Dec. 15, 1808

p. 42-44 Feb. 23, 1809 James Miller (Spartanburgh) to Samuel Miller; for $205 sold 110 ac on S side of Middle Tygar R and on Buffalo Br; border: W-Josiah Miller and other sides-Samuel Miller.

Witness Samuel Neely, Robert Miller, and Hugh Caldwell. Signed James Miller. Wit. oath Apr. 11, 1809 Samuel Neely to John Collins. Rec. Apr. 11, 1809

p. 44-45 Oct. 18, 1808 William Gossett (Spartanburgh) to Henry Farnandis (Union Dist); for $120 sold 135 ac on waters of Story's Mill Cr; where William Gossett lives; border: John King, a road, and Widow Lemaster. Witness William Kennedy and William Reid. Signed William Gossett's mark. Wit. oath Apr. 10, 1809 William Reid to John Lipscomb. Rec. Apr. 11, 1809

p. 45-46 Oct. 26, 1795 Elijah Stevens (Spartanburgh) to William Beshears (same); for 30£ sterling sold 300 ac; border: Fields, Wadsworth, and Amos; grant in 1791 to Elijah Stevens. Witness Nevel Wayland and Betsy Wayland. Signed Elijah Stevens. Wit. oath Oct. 10, 1808 Betsy Wayland to James L Burd. Rec. Apr. 11, 1809

p. 46-47 Mar. 7, 1809 Robert Davis (SC) to William Kelso (Spartanburgh); for $700 sold 150 ac; border: Howard; sold by William Dalton to Robert Davis. Witness John Ridings, Arthur F Jackson, and Joseph Kelso. Signed Robert Davis' mark. Wit. oath Apr. 11, 1809 Arthur F Jackson to James Young. Rec. Apr. 11, 1809

p. 47-48 May 27, 1808 (Laurence Dist) Samuel Chew (Laurence Dist) to James Cook (Spartanburgh); for $400 sold 468 ac on Ready Br of Buffalow lick Br of Fairforrest Cr; border: N-David Cook, W-John Finch, S-"a big survey, and E-David Golightly and Edward Barnet; grant to Richard Hampton who sold to Edward Mitchusson who sold to Samuel Chew. Witness William Shackelford, William Allen, and Thomas Woodruff III. Signed Saml Chew. Wit. oath Apr. 10, 1809 William Shackelford to Danl White. Rec. Apr. 11, 1809

p. 48-49 Jul. 14, 1807 Amos Speace (or Peice) (Spartanburgh) to Edmond Cooley (same); for $100 sold 100 ac on both sides Bartin's Cr; border: Wm Bartin, Philip Johnson, Thomas Gibbert, John Mathews, Wm McWilliams, and David Cunningham; lower end of survey for Amos Speace. Witness John Mathews and John Mason. Signed Amos Speace. Wit. oath Aug. 29, 1807 John Mason to Leonard Adcock. Rec. Apr. 11, 1809

p. 49-50 Nov. 12, 1808 Lewis Burnett (Spartanburgh) to Edmond Cooley (same); for $200 sold 150 ac on Pacolate R. Witness William R Watson, Samuel Centell (or Sattle), and Absolem Littlefield. Signed Lewis Burnett's mark. Wit. oath Nov. 26, 1808 William R Watson to James Young. Rec. Apr. 11, 1809

p. 50-51 Sept. 25, 1807 John Blasingame (Spartanburgh) to Jethro Osheal (same); for $200 sold 142 ac on branch of Dutchman's Cr; border: Grant's Road, Moses Prewitt, and Motlow's Br. Witness John Lancaster jr and John Rochell. Signed Jno Blassingame and Rachal's mark. Wit. oath Apr. 11, 1809 John Lancaster to W Lancaster. Rec. Apr. 11, 1809

p. 51-52 Oct. 29, 1807 Edward Arnold (Spartanburgh) to John Cantral (same); for $2,000 sold 500 ac on both sides of Enoree R; border: John Westmoreland, Henry Earnest, and William Childress; includes "the mill and houses" where Edward Arnold lives. Witness William Arnold, James Wofford, and Thomas Grant. Signed Edward Arnold. Wit. oath Oct. 29, 1807 William Arnold to David Morton. Rec. Apr. 11, 1809. Dower renounced Catren Arnold to David Morton Oct. 29, 1807

p. 52-53 Dec. 28, 1808 Jonathan Wall (Spartanburgh) to Zacheriah Wall (same); for $100 sold 50 ac on E side Richland Cr of

Pacolate R; border: S-James Barnett, W-Richland Cr, N-Clark, and Thomas Bennett; part of 743 ac grant to Thomas Bennett. Witness Henry White and Jesse Woody. Signed Jonathan Wall. Wit. oath Feb. 20, 1809 Henry White to James Young. Rec. Apr. 11, 1809

p. 53-54 Dec. 22, 1808 John Hames (Spartanburgh) to Edmond Chapmon and John Lucas (same); for $320 sold 150 ac; border: Alexander Copeland, James Blackwood, and John Pullins; original owner was Hugh Thompson. Witness Robert Millican and Robert McDowell. Signed John Hames' mark. Wit. oath (not dated) Robert McDowell to James Young. Rec. Apr. 11, 1809. Dower renounced Charity Hames to John Young Dec. 22, 1808

p. 54-55 Mar. 27, 1806 John Lindsey (Spartanburgh) to John Smith (same); for $130 sold 50 ac on waters of Two Mile Cr; border: Schoolhouse Br and Ford's old line; part of grant to John Ford jr on S side of Two Mile Cr. Witness William Shackelford, William L Allen, and Richard Shackelford jr. Signed John Lindsey. Wit. oath Mar. 12, 1807 William Shackelford to William Hendrix. Rec. Apr. 11, 1809. Dower renounced Jememah Lindsey to Burrell Bobo Sept. 20, 1808

p. 55-56 Jan. 16, 1809 James and Eleanor Littlefield to John Ward; for $55 sold 1/6th of 150 ac in a grant and 230 ac by resurvey on N side of N Tygar R; border: S-N Tygar R, E-Andrw Thomson, N-John Ward, and W-Wm Moore; 1/6th is "our" part or dowery of grant to Patrick March who sold to Frances Ward desc and to James and Eleanor Littlefield to heirship. Witness Thomas Wright and John Otts. Signed James and Eleanor Littlefield's marks. Wit. oath Apr. 12, 1809 Thomas Wright to Drury McDaniel. Rec. Apr. 11, 1809

p. 56-57 Jan. 23, 1809 Thomas Shurley (Spartanburgh) to three granddaughters Matildia Ward, Abigail Ward, and Cynthia Ward (same); for good cause give 2 cows and heifers: a large reddish bundle cow with star in her forehead, a small white spot on her shoulders and some white on her flanks and a pide (or side) cow red and white with a white face, the heifer "molley yellow" with some white. Witness Thomas Wright and Robert Shurley. Signed Thomas Shurley. Wit. oath Apr. 12, 1809 Thomas Wright to Drury McDaniel. Rec. Apr. 12, 1809

p. 57-58 Apr. 11, 1809 Samuel Floyd and Aaron Shurley to John Ward; for $100 sold (ac not given) on N side of N Tygar R; "our" part of grant Nov. 10, 1784 to Patrick March who sold to Frances Ward desc. Witness Thomas Wright and George Floyd. Signed Aaron Shurley and Samuel Floyd. Wit. oath Apr. 12, 1809 Thomas Wright to Drury McDaniel. Rec. Apr. 12, 1809

p. 58-59 Apr. 11, 1809 John Ward (Spartanburgh) to George Floyd (same); for $300 sold 102 ac on both sides Ward's Cr of Tygar R; part of 115 ac grant Nov. 10, 1784 to Patrick March. Witness Thomas Wright and Aaron Shurley. Signed John Ward. Wit. oath Apr. 12, 1809 Thomas Wright to Drury McDaniel. Rec. Apr. 12, 1809

p. 59-60 Jan. 12, 1809 Elijah McBee (Spartanburgh) to Mathew McBee (same); for $200 sold for two years 2 cows and calves, a heifer of different marks, a bay mare, a sorrel colt, 12 hogs, some yearlins, and some pigs; Condition: sale void if Elijah pays Mathew $200 in two years. Witness James Crocker and James Lands. Signed Elijah Machbee. Wit. oath Apr. 7, 1809 James Crocker to Jno H Jones. Rec. Apr. 12, 1809

p. 60-61 Mar. 25, 1809 John Duncan (Newberry Dist) to James Vernon (Spartanburgh); for $100 sold 79 ac on S fork of a branch

Tygar R; border: SW-Hughes, SE-William Hendricks, NE-William Duncan, NW-Thomas Doeg, and others vacant. Witness Isaac Crow and Saml Miller. Signed John Duncan's mark. Wit. oath Apr. 11, 1809 Saml Miller to John Collins. Rec. Apr. 12, 1809

p. 61-62 Dec. 9, 1795 Thomas Reid (Spartanburgh) to William Loan (same); for 12£ sterling sold 75 ac; border: Hacom's Br, ridge road, Jean Reid, William Loan, and Poole's Island; on N side of Pacolate R; part of grant Sept. 16, 1784 Gov. William Moultrie to (not given) and part of 200 ac sold by Henry Pettit to William Reid sr; leaves 50 ac on lower end to Jean Reid. Witness William Crocker, Arthur Crocker, and Richardson Whitbey. Signed Thomas Reid. Wit. oath Jan. 27, 1809 Richardson Whitbey to Jno H Jones. Rec. Apr. 12, 1809

p. 62-63 Mar. 1, 1806 Thomas Warren (Franklin Co, Ga) to John Bankston (Spartanburgh); for $21.50 sold 276 ac on branch of Pacolate R; grant Oct. 6, 1788 States Office to Thomas Warren. Witness James Bankston, Reuben Warren, and Lamuel Waters. Signed Thomas Warren. Wit. oath Mar. 20, 1809 James Bankston to Henry Turner. Rec. Apr. 20, 1809

p. 63-64 Dec. 12, 1804 Mary Buffington (Warren Co, Ga) to James Smith (Spartanburgh); for $100 relinquishes dower rights to 640 ac granted to Joseph Buffington on Kelsoe's Cr; border: Connel, "others", and known as Cedar Spring tract. Witness Thomas Frund and Samuel Buffington. Signed Mary Buffington. Wit. oath Dec. 17, 1804 Samuel Buffington to Wm Smith. Rec. Apr. 23, 1809

p. 64-65 Oct. 25, 1808 (Laurence Dist) Nathaniel Durkie (Laurence Dist) to Hugh Young (same); to secure notes of $500 mortgaged two tracts of 50 ac each on Enoree R in Spartanburgh Dist; sold today by James Leatherwood to Nathaniel Durkie; Condition: sale void if Nathaniel pays his debt. Witness Robert Hutcheson and Joseph Hall. Signed N Durkie. Wit. oath (Laurence Dist) Feb. 6, 1809 Robert Hutcheson to Sterling Tucker. Rec. Apr. 23, 1809

p. 65-66 Aug. 15, 1806 John Tolleson (Spartanburgh) to John King (same); for $76 sold 50 ac on waters of Story's Mill Cr and both sides of Purplepain Br; border: Asher and King; part of 266 ac grant Gov. Charles Pinckney to Thomas Davidson. Witness Muse Tolleson and Edmond Chapmon. Signed John Tolleson. Wit. oath Mar. 1, 1808 Edmond Chapmon to William Simpson. Rec. Apr. 27, 1809

p. 66 Jul. 31, 1799 Thomas Davison (or Davidson) (Spartanburgh) to John King (same); for $150 sold 200 ac; border: S-Christopher Golightly, SE-Samuel Noblet and Davison, and NW-Harmon. Witness James Gosset and James Moore. Signed Thomas Davison and Mary's mark. Wit. oath Dec. 16, 1807 James Gosset to William Simpson. Rec. Apr. 27, 1809

p. 66-68 Dec. 4, 1094(sic) Thomas Price (Spartanburgh), merchant to Andrew Hendricks (same); for 10£ sterling SC money sold 50 ac on Two Mile Cr; part of 350 ac grant Jan. 21, 1785 Gov. Benjamin Guerard to John Ford who sold 50 ac Sept. 29, 1794 to Thomas Price. Witness Isaac Hendricks, Aaron Casey, and Andrew Thomson. Signed Thomas Price. Wit. oath Apr. 27, 1809 Isaac Hendricks to John Dean. Rec. Apr. 28, 1809

p. 68-69 Apr. 27, 1809 Andrew Hendricks (Spartanburgh) to Micajah Allen (same); for $140 sold 50 ac; part of 350 ac grant Jan. 21, 1785 Gov. Benjamin Guerard to John Ford. Witness John Ervin, John Allen jr, and James Taylor. Signed Andrew Hendricks' mark. Wit. oath Apr. 27, 1809 John Allen jr to John Dean. Rec.

Apr. 28, 1809

p. 69 Nov. 12, 1804 George McDowell jr (Spartanburgh), son of William McDowell desc, to George McDowell sr (same); for 50£ sterling sold 200 ac on both sides of Lawson's fork; border: NW-Isaac Bishop, W-Daniel Warlling, N-William McDowell, and E-John Beard; land was "sold to" George McDowell jr. Witness William McDowell and Margaret Burd. Signed George McDowell. Wit. oath Nov. 12, 1804 William McDowell to Jas L Burd. Rec. May 1, 1809

p. 69-70 Aug. 27, 1808 John Moore (Spartanburgh) to George McDowell sr (same); for $40 sold 10 ac on N of George McDowell; border: Long Br of Lawson's fork; part of land sold by William Satefield to John Moore. Witness William Ford and Edmond Bishop. Signed John Moore. Wit. oath Jan. 21, 1809 Edmond Bishop to Ism Foster. Rec. May 1, 1809

p. 70-71 Dec. 3, 1808 David Tanner to Floyd Tanner; for $300 sold (ac not given); on Holeson Br of Fairforrest Cr; grant to John Evans. Witness William T Tanner, Lucy Tanner, and Betsy Tanner. Signed David Tanner. Wit. oath Dec. 17, 1808 William T Tanner to Drury McDaniel. Rec. May 2, 1809

p. 71-72 Mar. 25, 1807 Daniel McKie (Spartanburgh) to John Arnold sr (same); for $600 sold 200 ac on N side of Enoree R; where William Young desc lived; grant Aug. 16, 1784 to Wm Young desc and by his will Oct. 13, 1787 to his seven sons: Adam, Samuel, William, James, John, Joseph, and Thomas and sold to Daniel McKie Jan. 16, 1800 and Feb. 22, 1800 and Aug. 30, 1804. Witness Simon Stone, Zachariah Gray, and Thomas Stone. Signed Daniel McKie. Wit. oath Feb. 26, 1809 Thomas Stone to John Brewton. Rec. May 2, 1809. Dower renounced Francis McKie to Burrell Bobo Sept. 19, 1808

p. 72-73 Nov. 10, 1808 Daniel McClaren (formerly of Spartanburgh and now of state of Tenn) to Wilson Nesbett (Spartanburgh); power of attorney to collect debts and goods and effects due Daniel and sell his land. Witness James Gilleland, John Brown, and Samuel Nesbett. Signed Daniel McClaren. Wit. oath May 8, 1809 James Gilleland to John Collins. Rec. May 8, 1809

p. 73-74 Jan. 11, 1809 Jesse Spencer (Union Dist) to William Acre (Spartanburgh); for $100 sold 34 ac on W side of Ward's Cr of Tygar R; part of 684 ac grant May 7, 1792 to James Gibbs. Witness Burton Acre and Reuben Gentry. Signed Jesse Spencer and Elizabeth's mark. Wit. oath Jan. 13, 1809 Burton Acre to Saml Morrow. Rec. May 8, 1809

p. 74-75 Jan. 12, 1809 Charles Moore (Spartanburgh) to William Acre (same); for $65 sold 60 ac on W side Ward's Cr of Tygar R; border: McDowell; part of tract from C Moore sr desc by heirship to Charles Moore in May 1773. Witness Andrew B Moore and Burton Acre. Signed Chas Moore. Wit. oath Jan. 14, 1809 Burton Acre to Saml Morrow. Rec. May 8, 1809

p. 75-76 Nov. 1, 1808 Gideon Seay (Spartanburgh) to William Traylor (same); for $400 sold (1) 70 ac on S side of Fairforrest Cr adjoining the mill; and (2) the mill with 10 ac on both sides of creek; (border?) land sold by Gideon Seay to Marshal Seay. Witness Ism Foster, Robert Foster, Marshal Seay. Signed Gideon Seay's mark. Wit. oath May 10, 1809 Ism Foster to J Walker. Rec. May 25, 1809

p. 76-77 Dec. 29, 1808 Willis Willeford (Spartanburgh) to Moses Lancaster (same); for $130 sold 50 ac on S side Tygar R; part of grant to Jonathan Senard; border: Benjamin Hooker and waggon road. Witness Thomas Lancaster and William Lancaster. Signed Willis Willeford. Wit. oath Dec. 30, 1808 Thomas Lancaster to Saml Lancaster. Rec. May 25, 1809

p. 77-78 Nov. 29, 1808 John Giddings (Spartanburgh) to James Yates (same); for $200 sold 110 ac; border: Wells, Simmons, old Iron Road, Simmons' Spring Br, Richardson Vincent, and Frances Mason. Witness Joshua Tapp and Joel Yates. Signed John Giddings. Wit. oath May 13, 1809 Joshua Tapp to Drury McDaniel. Rec. May 27, 1809

p. 78-79 Nov. 28, 1808 Robert Redman (Spartanburgh) to Joshua Benson (Greenville Dist); for $150 sold 200 ac on S side Rocky Field Cr; sold by William Wheeler and James Bucken to Robert Redman and Joshua Benson and now Robert Redman is selling his share of the land. Witness Benjamin Benson to Barley Bruice. Signed Robert Redman's mark. Wit. oath Mar. 3, 1809 Benjamin Benson to Danl Wilbanks. Rec. May 30, 1809

p. 79-80 Jul. 31, 1799 Christopher Rhodes (Pinckneyville Dist) to Thomas Rhodes (SC); for 50£ sold (ac not given); border: Thomas Couch and a waggon road; sold Aug. 4, 1788 by Spencer Bobo sr to Christopher Rhodes. Witness Shadrack Waldrop and Judeth Rhodes. Signed Christopher Rhodes. Wit. oath Jul. 31, 1799 Shadrack Waldrop to A Casey. Rec. Jun. 3, 1809

p. 80-81 Dec. 14, 1808 Leonard Carden (Spartanburgh) to John Burnett (same); for $118 sold 100 ac; border: Cart road Br and Vennable's fork of crossroads. Witness James Burnett and John Carden. Signed Leonard Carden. Wit. oath Feb. 6, 1809 James Burnett to James Young. Rec. Jun. 5, 1809

p. 81-82 Mar. 18, 1809 Thomas Cave (Spartanburgh) to Thomas Redman (SC); for $100 sold 282 ac, a cow and yearling, 9 hogs, 2 feather beds and furniture, 10 pewter plates, 2 dishes, and 3 basons; Condition: sale void if Thomas pays $100 by Mar. 3, 1810. Witness John Ward, James Hendricks, and Dennis Tippens. Signed Thomas Cave. Wit. oath Mar. 18, 1809 John Ward to Tyru Glen. Rec. Jun. 5, 1809

p. 82-83 Feb. 7, 1809 Arthur Falkner (Spartanburgh) to Benjamin Nichols (same); for $182 sold 110 ac on branch of Cain Cr of Tygar R; grant Feb. 2, 1795 Gov. Arnoldus Vanderhorst to Arthur Faulkner. Witness Lawson Thomson and Elisha West. Signed Arthr Faulkner. Wit. oath Apr. 7, 1809 Elisha West to Saml Morrow. Rec. Jun. 5, 1809

p. 83-84 Dec. 26, 1808 John Champion (Spartanburgh) to Nancy Wood (same); for $400 sold 100 ac on N fork Thickety Cr at mouth of and on E side of Price's Cr; border: Mulberry, Quin's Cr, Joshua Richards, and William Lipscomb. Witness William Wood and Joshua Richards. Signed John Champion. Wit. oath Jan. 25, 1809 William Wood to John Lipscomb. Rec. Jun. 5, 1809. Dower renounced Keziah Champion to John Lipscomb Jan. 24, 1809

p. 84-85 Oct. 28, 1808 John Finch (Jackson Co, Ga) to Micajah Barnett (Spartanburgh); for $300 sold 200 ac on Ready and Ford's Creeks of Fairforrest Cr; border: N-James Keen (or Kun), E-Thompson's new survey, S-remainder of tract, W-"old survey", and Hampton. Witness Richard Barnett and William H Cook. Signed John Finch's mark. Wit. oath Jan. 25, 1809 William H Cook to Danl White. Rec. Jun. 6, 1809

p. 85-86 Jan. 15, 1807 James Paden (Spartanburgh) to Andrew Berry (same); for $200 sold 100 ac on S side of N Tyger R; border: Charles Moore and Mr. Berry. Witness John Peden, Thomas Peden, and

Thomas Marrow. Signed Jamed Paden. Wit. oath Jun. 16, 1807 Thomas Marrow to David Morton. Rec. Jun. 10, 1809

p. 86-87 Nov. 29, 1808 Robert Giddes (Charleston, SC) to William Roads and Thomas House (Spartanburgh); for $700 sold 1,000 ac on branches of Furgason's Cr of Tygar R; grant Jun. 9, 1775 to George Savage and then bordering: S-William Rivers and others vacant. Witness Frs Millegan and Isaac Underwood. Signed Robert Giddes. Wit. oath Dec. 16, 1808 (Charleston Dist) Isaac Underwood to Henry Gray. Rec. Jun. 13, 1809

p. 87-88 Dec. 22, 1808 Nathan Wright (Spartanburgh) to Silus Williams; for $150 sold 100 ac on branch of Ford's Cr; border: Joel Hurt, John Golightly, George Wright, waggon road, and William Beaver. Witness John Underwood and Benjamin Rainwaters. Signed Nathan Wright. Wit. oath May 24, 1809 Benjamin Rainwaters to Danl White. Rec. Jun. 22, 1809

p. 88-89 May 9, 1806 Daniel Henderson (Pendleton Dist) to William Wade (Spartanburgh); for $1,000 sold 400 ac on N side of Pacolate R; part in Spartanburgh Dist and part in Rutherford Co, NC; grant to Betsy Clarke; border: Thomas Millican, Frey, Widow Jackson, and N Pacolate R. Witness Thomas Henderson and John Cansler. Signed Danl Henderson. Wit. oath (Pendleton Dist) May 9, 1806 Thomas Henderson to Wm Edmondson. Rec. Jul. 3, 1809. Dower renounced (Pendleton Dist) Isabel Henderson to Wm Edmondson May 9, 1806

p. 89-90 Apr. 4, 1806 James Henderson (Spartanburgh) to William Wade (same); for $1,000 sold 400 ac on N side of N Pacolate R; border: Thomas Millican, Widow Jackson, and Peter Frey; grant to Betsy Clarke. Witness Gabriel Benson and Robert Henderson. Signed James Henderson. Wit. oath Jul. 3, 1809 Gabriel Benson to Hugh Means. Rec. Jul. 3, 1809. Dower renounced Frances Henderson to Gabriel Benson Apr. 4, 1806

p. 90-92 May 10, 1809 Zachariah McDaniel (Spartanburgh) to Robert Smith (same); for $300 sold 150 ac; border: English, John Ward, Jesse Crook, James Crook, Ephram Drummon, and Mrs Charles; on S side of Tygar R. Witness Elizabeth Mathus and William Lancaster. Signed Z McDaniel. Wit. oath May 17, 1809 Elizabeth Mathus to W Lancaster. Rec. Jul. 3, 1809. Dower renounced Mary McDaniel to William Lancaster May 18, 1809

p. 92-93 Mar. 18, 1809 Thomas Shurley (Spartanburgh) to Thomas Price (same); for $256 sold 171 ac on S side of S Tygar R; border: E-Richard Willis, S-Sam Floyd, W-Furgason Cr, and N-S Tygar R; Condition: deed void if Thomas pays $256 by Mar. 1, 1810. Witness John Ward and Robert Shurley. Signed Thomas Shurley. Wit. oath Jul. 1, 1809 John Ward to Drury McDaniel. Rec. Jul. 4, 1809

p. 93-94 Mar. (omitted), 1809 Vincent Tapp (Spartanburgh) to Thomas Price (same); for $212 sold (1) 100 ac on N side of S Tygar R; and (2) 57 ac joining (1) on S side. Witness William Moore and John Ward. Signed Vincent Tapp. Wit. oath Jul. 3, 1809 John Ward to Drury McDaniel. Rec. Jul. 4, 1809

p. 94-95 Jun. 6, 1809 Robert Elder (Spartanburgh) to Benjamin Peak (same); for 75£ sold 150 ac on waters of Dutchman's Cr; where Robert Elder formerly lived; border: John Morrow; grant in 1753 to Robert Cowden; Note: this is second deed from Robert Elder to Benjamin Peak for this land, first one was lost. Witness Joseph West and William N. Morrow. Signed Robert Elder's mark. Wit. oath Jun. 6, 1809 Joseph West to Saml Morrow. Rec. Jul. 4, 1809

p. 95-96 May 16, 1809 Jeane Jordan (Spartanburgh) to William Brown (same); for $400 sold 200 ac on N side of S Tygar R; border: Andrew F Nesbett and great road. Witness Wilson Nesbett, Samuel Nesbett, and Andrew F Nesbett. Signed Jeane Jordan's mark. Wit. oath Jul. 4, 1809 Wilson Nesbett to Michael Miller. Rec. Jul. 4, 1809

p. 96-97 Mar. 6, 1809 Samuel Hindman (Spartanburgh) to Thomas Pruitt (same); for $200 sold 100 ac on waters of Tygar R; border: Thomas Pruitt and James Hindman; part of 174 ac grant Feb. 5, 1787 Gov. William Moultrie to Owing Forester. Witness Wilson Nance and Jesse Palmer. Signed Samuel Hindman. Wit. oath May 5, 1809 Jesse Palmer to Saml Morrow. Rec. Jul. 13, 1809

p. 97 Dec. 12, 1808 Malachi Eskridge (Spartanburgh) to Thomas Eskridge (same); for $75 sold 2 cows and "earlings", 5 hogs, 2 beds and furniture, 2 bedsteads, "a parcel" of earthenware and glass, a saddle and bridle, an iron pot, an oven, some pewter and watter vessels, all his iron tools, a hogskin trunk and contents, and three chairs. Witness William Wood and Tolliver Scott. Signed Malachi Eskridge. Wit. oath Jan. 19, 1809 William Wood to John Brewton. Rec. Jul. 15, 1809

p. 97-98 Jan. 23, 1809 John Penington (Spartanburgh) to John Wood (same); to secure loan of $200 John Penington gives John Wood a Negro boy James about 9 years old until Dec. 25, 1810; Condition: sale void if Penington pays debt. Witness Benjamin Wood and William Wilson. Signed John Penington. Wit. oath Apr. 28, 1809 William Wilson to Tyru (or Tyrce) Glenn. Rec. Jul. 21, 1809

p. 98-99 Feb. 18, 1809 Isham Harrison (Spartanburgh) to Hayes Bagwell (same); for $450 sold 300 ac on Tygar R and on E side of McMican's big Branch; where Hayes Bagwell lives; formerly claimed by George Wright and William Hurt "under" sale of Gabriel Bumpass. Witness Elizabeth Harrison and Daniel White. Signed I Harrison. Wit. oath Jul. 29, 1809 Elizabeth Harrison to Danl White. Rec. Jul. 29, 1809

p. 99-100 Aug. 23, 1806 Thomas Wilson to John OShields; for $100 sold 150 ac on branch of Cain Cr; border: John Smith; part of 224 ac grant Mar. 2, 1789 Gov. Charles Pinckney to George Newman. Witness Valentine Smith and Aaron Smith. Signed Thomas Wilson. Wit. oath Aug. 23, 1806 Valentine Smith to William Smith. Rec. Aug. 5, 1809

p. 100-101 Dec. 11, 1799 Joel Hembrie (SC) to John Osheals (same); for 40£ sterling sold 100 ac on N side Cain Cr of Tygar R; border: Stephen Wilson, Mittington Smith, John Osheals, and James Smith; part of 165 ac grant Dec. 1, 1794 Gov. William Moultrie to (not given). Witness John Grist, John Red, and Reuben Willson. Signed Joel Hembree. Wit. oath Feb. 19, 1800 John Grist to John Martindale. Rec. Aug. 5, 1809. Dower renounced Hannah Hembree to William Smith Dec. 11, 1799

p. 101-102 Mar. 14, 1809 John Cargill (Spartanburgh) to William Tippins (same); for $40 sold 150 ac on waters of Abner's Cr of Enoree R; where John Cargill lives; and sold a sorrel mare, 2 sows and pigs, a cow and calf, all household furniture; Condition: sale void if John pays $40 by Dec. 25, 1810. Witness James Hammett and William Hughes. Signed John Cargill's mark. Wit. oath Jul. 11, 1809 James Hammett to Tyrce Glenn. Rec. Aug. 7, 1809

p. 102-103 Apr. 5, 1809 Andrew Bodden (Columbia, SC) to Michael Miller (Spartanburgh); for $713.75 sold 571 ac on N side of Middle Tygar R and branches thereof; when granted border was: William Garrard, John Nichols, Thomas Penny, and unknown; grant of

640 ac Aug. 1, 1785 to Robert Tarrance and resurvey in 1797 by Gabl Benson dept. surv. as 571 ac. Witness John Davis SM, Thomas Roddy, and Alexander Montgomery. Signed Andrew Bodden. Wit. oath Aug. 7, 1809 John Davis SM to Drury McDaniel. Rec. Aug. 7, 1809

p. 103-104 Mar. 18, 1809 John Easterwood to William Reid; to secure note of $16 (included and on same date), John "pledges" and makes chargable to William a chesnut sorrel mare 18 years old this Spring branded "ĪE" on left buttock and a sorrel horse 6 years old this Spring same brand. Witness John Cates and Woday Brock. Signed John Easterwood's mark. Wit. oath Aug. 5, 1809 Woday Brock to John Lipscomb. Rec. Aug. 7, 1809

p. 104-105 Apr. 6, 1809 Francis Hambey jr (Spartanburgh) to James Hammett and company (same); for $15 sold (1) 140 ac where Francis and Nathan Hambey jr's live on Rock Cr of Enoree R; and (2) 11 ac adjoining (1); Condition: deed void if Francis pays James $15 by Dec. 25, 1804. Witness Nathan Hambey sr and Theophelus Cannon. Signed Francis Hambey's mark. Wit. oath Jul. 20, 1809 Theophelus Cannon to Tyrce Gleen. Rec. Aug. 7, 1809

p. 105-106 Mar. 23, 1809 William Willson (Spartanburgh) to James Hammett (same); for $29.36 sold 106 ac where William Willson lives on Abner's Cr of Enoree R; Condition: sale void if William pays James $29.36 by Dec. 25, 1809. Witness Henry Brockman and Theophelus Cannon. Signed William Willson. Wit. oath Jul. 20, 1809 Theophelus Cannon to Tyrce Gleen. Rec. Aug. 7, 1809

p. 106-107 Mar. 24, 1809 William Morgan (Spartanburgh) to James Hammett (same); for $123 sold 200 ac where William Morgan lives; Condition: sale void if William pays James $123 with interest by Dec. 25, 1809. Witness John Brockman and Thomas Mehaffey. Signed William Morgan. Wit. oath Aug. 7, 1809 John Brockman to Tyre Gleen. Rec. Aug. 7, 1809

p. 107 May 2, 1809 John Golightly sr (Spartanburgh) to Elihu Golightly and Frances Golightly (same); for love and good will and $100 sold 430 ac on Beverdam Cr on W side of Fairforrest Cr; where John Golightly sr lives; border: an old road. Witness Ransom Golightly and John Golightly jr. Signed John Golightly. Wit. oath Jun. 13, 1809 Ransom Golightly to Daniel White. Rec. Aug. 7, 1809

p. 107-108 Jun. 9, 1809 John Simmons to Maj. John Tolleson; to secure bond of $65 sold a sorrel horse 5 years old about 13½ hands high, 2 featherbeds anf furniture, 3 bedsteads, and cords, a cubbard, Table furniture, 2 tables, a loom, a chest, 2 cows and calves; Condition: sale void if John Simmons pays John Tolleson $65 with interest by Sept. 1, 1809. Witness D. J. Puckett and Muse Tolleson. Signed John Simmons. Wit. oath Aug. 7, 1809 Muse Tolleson to D. J. Puckett. Rec. Aug. 7, 1809

p. 108-109 Mar. 20, 1809 Isaac Hamby (Spartanburgh) to Thomas Westmoreland sr (same); for $140 sold 163 ac on Enoree R; border: Thomas Westmoreland. Witness John Kemp and John Cantrell. Signed Isaac Hamby and Elender's mark. Wit. oath Mar. 29, 1809 John Kemp to John Ford. Rec. Aug. 28, 1809

p. 109-110 Sept. 2, 1809 Jeremiah Gregory (Union Dist) to Edward Clement (Spartanburgh); for $90 sold 44 ac on waters of Tygar R; formerly owned by William Benson and drawn by Therza Benson, legatee of William Benson. Witness Abner Benson and Robert Stanford. Signed Jeremiah Gregory's mark. Wit. oath Sept. 2, 1809 Robert Stanford to A Benson. Rec. Sept. 2, 1809

p. 110-111 Mar. 15, 1809 George McDowell sr (Spartanburgh) to John

Bankston (same); for $400 sold 240 ac of which 202 ac was grant Feb. 6, 1786 States Office to Robert Prince (survey for Thomas Wood) who sold to Robert Foster who sold to George McDowell jr, son and heir of William McDowell desc who sold to George McDowell sr; and other 40 ac(sic) grant State Office to Daniel Walling and William McDowell desc; land is on both sides Lawson's fork; border: Long Br, John Moore, James Walling, Elijah Bishop, Daniel Walding, and William Ford. Witness Edmd Bishop, William McDowell, and Laurence Bankston. Signed George McDowell's mark. Wit. oath Sept. 4, 1809 Laurence Bankston to Ism Foster. Rec. Sept. 4, 1809. Dower renounced Mary McDowell to Ism Foster Sept. 4, 1809

p. 111-112 Sept. 4, 1809 Jobe Sosebee (Spartanburgh) to Ransom Golightly (same); for $200 sold 200 ac on branch of Cherokee Cr; border: Ransom Golightly. Witness Robert Benson and Andrew Ray. Signed Jobe Sosebee's mark. Wit. oath Sept. 4, 1809 Andrew Ray to James Young. Rec. Sept. 4, 1809

p. 112-113 Oct. 26, 1808 John Poole (Spartanburgh) to Richard Turner; for $300 sold 182 ac on S side Pacolate R and on Cherokee Cr; border: Soloman Abbett, James Trail, and little Cherokee Br. Witness Jeremiah McMillin and Drury McMillin. Signed John Poole and Polley Poole. Wit. oath Oct. 29, 1808 Jeremiah McMillin to Henry Turner. Rec. Sept. 4, 1809

p. 113 May 16, 1809 Beverly Lewis and John Lucas (Spartanburgh) to Isaac Snoddy (same); for $500 sold 50 ac on N Tygar R; border: Jesse Traylor. Witness Mason Shumate and Nancy Lewis. Signed Beverly Lewis, Rachal Lewis, and John Lucas. Wit. oath May 19, 1809 Mason Shumate to Isham Foster. Rec. Sept. 4, 1809

p. 113-114 May 10, 1809 Beverly Lewis and John Lucas (Spartanburgh) to Isaac Snoddy (same); for $500 sold 100 ac on N Tygar R; border: Jesse Traylor. Witness Mason Shumate and Nancy Lewis. Signed Beverly Lewis, Rachel Lewis, and John Lucas. Wit. oath May 19, 1809 Mason Shumate to Ism Foster. Rec. Sept. 4, 1809

p. 114-115 May 9, 1809 Thomas Thornton, blacksmith (Spartanburgh) to Moses Fowler (same); to repay $42 with interest of 7% per year sold a saddle and bridle, a set of smith tools, a bellos, an anvil, vice, hammer, and tongs, other articles belonging to the set, a feather bed and bedstead and furniture, a cow and yearling, a pot, an oven, a dish, 9 plates, a pair of dressers and tables, a tin pan, a gun and shot bag, a cotton wheel, a barrel, 4 chairs, 2 flat irons, a "pair of cotten", a bee hive, a plow anc chains, and 2 weeding hoes; Condition: sale void if Thomas Thornton pays $42 with interest by Dec. 25, 1810. Witness James Childress (or Childrews) and America Fowler. Signed Thomas Thornton. Wit. oath Jul. 4, 1809 James Childress to James Ford. Rec. Sept. 4, 1809

p. 115-116 Aug. 3, 1803 John Mathies (or Mathus) and wife Susannah (Spartanburgh) to William Scraggs (same); for $20 sold 70 ac on N side Pacolate R; border: Gray, Kennedy, a road, William Land, and Joshua Pettet. Witness William Patterson and Benjamin Poole. Signed John Mathus. Wit. oath Aug. 20, 1803 Benjamin Poole to John Lipscomb. Rec. Sept. 4, 1809

p. 116 Jun. 23, 1809 Joseph Scales (Davidson Co, Tenn) to William Foster (Spartanburgh); for $861 sold 287 ac in two tracts (1) grant to Samuel Nesbett and (2) grant to Hosea Camp; on N Tygar R. Witness John Dodd and William Pollard. Signed Joseph Scales. Wit. oath Sept. 4, 1809 William Pollard to James Young. Rec. Sept. 4, 1809

p. 116-117 Jul. 17, 1809 Richard Kerby (Spartanburgh) to "brothers-in-law" Berdsong Tolleson and Joseph Berryman Tolleson, youngest sons of Maj John Tolleson; for love and affection give to Berdsong a Negro woman Alic and her child Gilberd and her future increase and to Joseph a Negro woman Rachal and her future increase; if Berdsong or Joseph die without heirs, slaves go to their two brothers living; James Tolleson and Berdsong or Joseph and otherwise slaves go to sole surviving brother; slaves bought in Virginia from Mr. Rodgers. Witness Muse Tolleson and D. J. Puckett. Signed Richard Kerby. Wit. oath Sept. 5, 1809 Muse Tolleson to D. J. Puckett. Rec. (not given)

p. 117-118 Jul. 17, 1809 John Tolleson, late merchant (Spartanburgh) to James Tolleson; for love and affection give a yeallow Negro winch Bet and her child Malinda and her future increase; if James dies without an heir, then slave goes to his brothers Birdsong and Joseph Tolleson (equally divided). Witness Muse Tolleson and D. J. Puckett. Signed John Tolleson. Wit. oath Jul. 17, 1809 Muse Tolleson to D. J. Puckett. Rec. Sept. 5, 1809

p. 118 Apr. 10, 1809 Joseph White (Spartanburgh) to James Keen (same); for $12.50 sold 25 ac. Witness Robert Legon and Solomon Austry. Signed Joseph White's mark. Wit. oath Apr. 10, 1809 Robert Legon to Danl White. Rec. Sept. 11, 1809

p. 118-119 Aug. 9, 1808 James Ridings (Spartanburgh) to John Dodd (same); for $30 sold 40 ac on S side of Pacolate R; border: John Dodd; part of grant Feb. 3, 1775 Lt. Gov. William Bull to Matthias Harper sr; an acre reserved to James Ridings around the Meeting House. Witness Andrew Furguson, John Hammitt, and James L Burd. Signed James Ridings' mark. Wit. oath Aug. 9, 1808 Andrew Furguson to James L Burd. Rec. Sept. 11, 1809

p. 119-120 Nov. 28, 1808 Richard Thomson (Spartanburgh) to William Bostick (same); for $18 sold 18 feet square in Spartanburgh, SC; border: the lot of McKie and cross street from Court House to James Seay's. Witness Vincent Bennett and John G Bostick. Signed Richd Thomson. Wit. oath Jul. 24, 1809 Vincent Bennett to A Benson. Rec. Sept. 11, 1809

p. 120-121 Mar. 11, 1809 Catherine Porters Sloan (Spartanburgh) to Charles Moore (same); for $55 sold 3 beds and their furniture, "my" riding saddle and a little wheel, reel, and "my" kitchen furniture. Witness Andrew B Moore and Charles M Berry. Signed Cathrine Porters Sloan. Wit. oath Sept. 15, 1809 Charles M Berry to Drury McDaniel. Rec. Sept. 15, 1809

p. 121-122 Jun. 9, 1809 John Simmons to James Seay; to secure a note of Feb. 21, 1807 to Jesse Wells for $30 and note was transferred to James Seay and a note to James Seay for $33.15 sold a small horse 4 years old about 14(?) hands high, 10 hogs marked with cross and stapple fork in each ear, a bed and furniture and bedstead, 6 chairs, an 8 gal. pot, a 3 gal. pot, a dutch oven, a 1 gal. pot, 2 fish pans, and a frying pan; Condition: sale void if John pays James $33.15 by Oct. 1, 1809. Witness Muse Tolleson and D. J. Puckett. Signed John Simmons. Wit. oath (not dated) Muse Tolleson to D. J. Puckett. Rec. Sept. 16, 1809

p. 122-123 Aug. 29, 1808 William West (Spartanburgh) to Lewis Brown (same); for $50 sold 150 ac on branch of Lawson's Cr; border: William Bishop, Bishop's Spring Br, and John Beard; grant Dec. 2, 1793 Gov. William Moultrie to William McDowell. Witness John Brown, Richard Brown, and Willis Burton. Signed William West's mark. Wit. oath Oct. 2, 1809 Richard Brown to Ism Foster. Rec. Oct. 2, 1809

p. 123 Sept. 26, 1809 Nathaniel Wright (Spartanburgh) to John Dunkin (same); for $50 sold 65 ac on waters of Fairrest Cr; border: E-James Hurt, S-Francis Mason, N-John Golightly, and W-William Baber (or Batier); grant to Isaac Tinsley who sold Jan. 2, 1806 to George Wright and sold as George Wright's property by suit of Eaton Walker by Vincent Bennett, sheriff (Spartanburgh)--land sold to Nathaniel Wright Sept. 9, 1809. Witness Henry Hurt and Elizabeth Hurt. Signed Nathaniel Wright's mark. Wit. oath Oct. 2, 1809 Elizabeth Hurt to Danl White. Rec. Oct. 2, 1809

p. 123-124 Aug. 29, 1808 John Dodd (Spartanburgh) to William Foster (same); for $190 sold 180 ac; border: Nesbitt, Clabourn Johnson, and Jones; part of two grants (1) Mar. 4, 1793 to William Ford and (2) Apr. 7, 1806 to John Dodd; land on N fork of N Tygar R. Witness John Davis SM and Gabriel Benson. Signed John Dodd. Wit. oath Sept. 18, 1809 John Davis SM to Michl Miller. Rec. Oct. 2, 1809

p. 124-125 Feb. 25, 1809 Alexander M Thompson and Joseph Thompson (Spartanburgh) to Lemuel Loftis (same); for $25 sold 12 ac on S side Beverdam Cr; border: Lemuel Loftis and Beverdam Swamp; part of grant "for" John McRie and conveyed by governor to Alexander and Joseph Thompson. Witness Alexr Robbs and William Robbs. Signed Alexr M Thompson and Joseph Thompson. Wit. oath Oct. 2, 1809 William Robbs to Michael Miller. Rec. Oct. 2, 1809

p. 125-126 Nov. 20, 1805 Hugh Gorley (Spartanburgh) to Joshua Thomas (Union Dist); for $300 sold 200 ac on both sides of Storey's Cr; border: S-Cunningham, W-Brandon, N-Hucheon, and E-Hucheon and Cuningham. Witness Aaron Smith and Benjamin Peak. Signed Hugh Gorley. Wit. oath Nov. 23, 1805 Benjamin Peak to Wm Smith. Rec. Oct. 2, 1809. Dower renounced Murphy Gorley to William Smith Nov. 23, 1805

p. 126-127 Apr. 5, 1809 William Ballinger (Spartanburgh) to Elizabeth Ballinger (same); for $5,000 bond to leave Elizabeth along and let her sell her property without molestation; this done as a material consent separation of marriage agreement. Witness John Jordan and Jeremiah Owen. Signed Wm Ballenger. Wit. oath Sept. 30, 1809 Jeremiah Owen to Michael Miller. Rec. Oct. 2, 1809

p. 127 Apr. 5, 1809 John Owen (Spartanburgh), for daughter Elizabeth Ballinger, to William Ballenger (same); for $5,000 bond to leave William alone and let him sell his property; this done as settlement of mutual consent separation of marriage agreement. Witness John Ballenger and Thomas Bomar. Signed John Owen's mark. Wit. oath Oct. 2, 1809 John Ballenger to James Young. Rec. Oct. 2, 1809

p. 127-128 Oct. 2, 1809 Alexander McKie (Spartanburgh) to Richard Thomson (same); for $80 sold one ac on branch of waters of Fairforrest Cr; near the Court House; includes a tanyard on S side of branch formerly owned by William Wells. Witness John Crafford and Jack Lumkin. Signed Alexr McKie. Wit. oath Oct. 2, 1809 John Crafford to A Benson. Rec. Oct. 2, 1809

p. 128-129 Jul. 12, 1809 Joseph Davis (Jackson Co, Ga) to Aaron Wilkins (Spartanburgh); for $160 sold 80 ac on Pacolet R; was the land William Wilkins desc (late of Spartanburgh) gave his daughter Sarah Wilkins (now Sarah Davis) Mar. 13, 1807 and recorded Jul. 6, 1807 in "registers office". Witness Joshua Draper and Stephen Tolleson. Signed Joseph Davis and Sarah's mark. Wit. oath Aug. 24, 1809 Stephen Tolleson to John Lipscomb. Rec. Oct. 7, 1809

p. 129-130 Feb. 21, 1805 William Allen (Spartanburgh) to John Duncan (same); for $120 sold 100 ac on Mile Br of Tygar R; border: N-John Duncan, E-Thomas Stone, S-"the big survey", and W-Samuel Jamison. Witness James Crook jr, Randolph Johnson, and Thomas Stone. Signed William Allen and Rachel's mark. Wit. oath Feb. 25, 1806 James Crook to Drury McDaniel. Rec. Oct. 26, 1809

p. 130-131 Oct. 24, 1809 Thomas Betterton (Spartanburgh) to Stephen White (same); for $150 sold 233 ac on waters of Thickety Cr. Witness William Dewberry and Warner Shearbutt. Signed Thomas Betterton. Wit. oath Oct. 24, 1809 William Dewberry to Henry Turner. Rec. Oct. 27, 1809

p. 131-132 Oct. 24, 1809 Thomas Betterton (Spartanburgh) to Stephen White (same); for $700 sold 265 ac on waters of Thickety Cr; border: Dunway. Witness William Dewbery and Rolley Horton. Signed Thomas Betterton. Wit. oath Oct. 24, 1809 William Dewbery to Henry Turner. Rec. Oct. 27, 1809

p. 132 Oct. 24, 1809 Thomas Betterton (Spartanburgh) to Warner Shurbutt (same); for $25 sold 25 ac on waters of Thickety Cr. Witness Stephen White and William Dewbery. Signed Thomas Betterton. Wit. oath Oct. 24, 1809 William Dewbery to Henry Turner. Rec. Oct. 27, 1809

p. 132-133 Oct. 28, 1809 John Thomason (Spartanburgh) to daughter Juliet (or Julia or Jabel) Thomason; for love and affection give 140 ac on Taylor's Cr; border: Thomas Wells, Solomon Crocker, Franklin Foster, Swaney McKie, and Dibly Thomason; where John Thomason lives; grant to Henry Walker and given by William Turner Thomason to son John Thomason; and give a brown bay mare, about 14 hands high and 2 years old, 2 cows and calves, 14 hogs, 2 feather beds and all household stuff and his "other" goods. Witness Samuel Turner, Thomas Holt, and William Garret. Signed John Thomason. Wit. oath Nov. 1, 1809 Thomas Holt to James Young. Rec. Nov. 1, 1809

p. 133-134 Sept. 10(?), 1805 Adam Sloan (Pendleton Dist) to Richard Berry (Spartanburgh) for $300 sold a Negro woman Amy about 24 years old. Witness Aaron Hill and William Castury. Signed Adam Sloan. Wit. oath Aaron Hill to John McMillan on Sept. 21, 1805 and to Drury McDaniel (not dated). Rec. Nov. 2, 1809

p. 134-135 Oct. 22, 1809 Clayborn Holt (Spartanburgh) to son William Holt; for love and affection give a gray horse about 14 hands high 5 years old branded "TT" on near shoulder, a bridle and saddle, a sorrel horse colt, 2 feather beds, and all his chattles. Witness Thomas Holt and George Tucker. Signed Clayborn Holt's mark. Wit. oath Oct. 27, 1809 Thomas Holt to Henry Turner. Rec. Nov. 3, 1809

p. 135-136 Nov. 6, 1809 William Kelso (Spartanburgh) to John McCarroll (same); for $50 sold 25 ac on Ann Hooper's Cr of Pacolate R; part of grant Dec. 4, 1797 Gov. Charles Pinckney to William Kelso. Witness Robert Millican, William Millican, and Henry Hutcheson. Signed Wm Kelso. Wit. oath Nov. 6, 1809 Robert Millican to James Young. Rec. Nov. 6, 1809

p. 136-137 Oct. 15, 1805 Joseph Woodruff (Spartanburgh) to Thomas Woodruff and William Shackelford; for $100 sold 16 3/4 ac on main road; border: Joseph Woodruff on all sides. Witness Jas Chumblain and Barnett H Allgood. Signed Joseph Woodruff's mark. Wit. oath none. Rec. omitted. Dower renounced Ann Woodruff to Daniel Wright Oct. 12, 1805

p. 137-138 Feb. 27, 1807 Thomas Woodruff (Spartanburgh) to William Shackelford (same); for $400 sold 14 3/4 ac on main road; border: Joseph Woodruff on all sides and Thomas Woodruff; NW part of 16 3/4 ac that Joseph Woodruff sold to Thomas Woodruff (sic). Witness Simon Lavender, James Harrison, and Richard Shackelford. Signed Thomas Woodruff. Wit. oath Apr. 10, 1809 James Harrison to Daniel White. Rec. Nov. 6, 1809. Dower renounced Mary (or Polly) Woodruff to Daniel White (not dated)
The following marked out: Vincent Bennett to Wm Kelso recorded Nov. 6, 1809

p. 138-139 Feb. 3, 1809 James Dunnaway (Spartanburgh) to Noble Hamilton (Rutherford Co, NC); for $33.81 sold 120 ac on waters of Thickety Cr; border: John Turner; part of 1,000 ac grant States Office to Thomas English. Witness Leonard Adcock and John Bess. Signed James Dunnaway. Wit. oath Oct. 5, 1809 Leonard Adcock to Henry Turner. Rec. Nov. 6, 1809

p. 139-140 Apr. 22, 1809 Michael McElrath (Spartanburgh) to James Vernon (same); for $10 sold 150 ac on N side of Middle Tygar R; border: W & N-James Vernon and S & E-John McElrath and Gabriel Benson. Witness William Moore, William Cornwell, and Alexr Jordan. Signed Michael McElrath. Wit. oath Nov. (omitted), 1809 William Moore to John Collins. Rec. Nov. 7, 1809

p. 140-141 Oct. (omitted), 1796 William Reeves (Spartanburgh) to William Morgan (same); for 100£ sterling sold 311 ac on Williams Cr of S Tygar R; where William Reeves lives. Witness Samuel Nesbett, John Collins, and James Vernon. Signed William Reeves and Margaret's mark. Wit. oath Nov. 7, 1809 John Collins to Daniel McKie. Rec. Nov. 8, 1809

p. 141-142 Dec. 16, 1808 Christopher Johnson (Spartanburgh) to present members of Philadelphia Baptist Church (same); for $10 sold 1 3/4 ac at fork of road from Christopher Johnson's to Maj. William Smith's and John Wofford's; plat attached shows triangular shaped land; border: Arthur Hutchins. Witness Elijah Smith and James D Johnson. Signed Christopher Johnson. Wit. oath Dec. 16, 1808 James D Johnson to Danl Wilbanks. Rec. Nov. 8, 1809

p. 142-143 Feb. 22, 1802 John Berry (Spartanburgh) to William Morgan (same); for $200 sold 75 ac on S side of S Tygar R; border: Sarah Patton, Samuel Nesbitt, Nathaniel McElrath; part of grant to Frances Dodd who sold to Henry Leech who sold to John McElrath who sold to John Berry. Witness G Culberson, Nathaniel McElrath, and Alexander Evins. Signed John and Elizabeth Berry. Wit. oath Nov. 7, 1809 Alexander Evins to Danl McKie. Rec. Nov. 8, 1809

p. 143-144 May 9, 1809 Bartholomew Stovall (Spartanburgh) to Samuel Kelso (same); for $90 sold 210 ac on N side Pacolate R of Broad R; border: NE-McBee, SW-Pacolate R, N & NW-Jane Reid, William Spencer, and Rachal Duncan, and on other sides--Robert Thomson and Holemes Br and branch that George Poole formerly settled; grant to Bartholomew Stovall and part of grant to William Poole who sold to George Poole who sold to John Brown who sold to Bartholomew Stovall. Witness Christopher Golightly and James Poole. Signed Bartholowmew Stovall. Wit. oath Oct. 25, 1809 Christopher Golightly to W Lancaster. Rec. Nov. 8, 1809. Dower renounced Keziah Stovall to W Lancaster Oct. 25, 1809

p. 144-145 Feb. 8, 1809 William Ellis (Spartanburgh) to Benjamin Ellis; for $170 sold 139 ac in two tracts on W side of Broad R--(1) 42 ac and (2) 97 ac; border: North Carolina line and Ellis. Witness William Camp jr. Signed William Ellis and Mary's mark. Wit. oath Jul. 29, 1809 William Camp jr to John Lipscomb. Rec. Nov. 8, 1809

p. 145-146 Oct. 16, 1809 John Duncan (Spartanburgh) to Samuel Snoddy (same); for $850 sold 370 ac on S side of S Tygar R; border: Vernon, Samuel Jamison, William Allen, Leary, Croock. Witness John Snoddy, James Woodruff, and John Woodruff. Signed John and Mary Duncan. Wit. oath Nov. 7, 1809 John Snoddy to Ism Foster. Rec. Nov. 8, 1809

p. 146-147 Jan. 18, 1787 John Williams and wife Hanna (Spartanburgh) to William Reevs (same); for 300£ sterling sold 311 ac on Williams Cr of Tygar R; border: N & S-"old lines" and E-John McElrath; grant Apr. 3, 1786 Gov. William Moultrie to John Williams. Witness Elisha Gorland and Jesse Gorland and James Woodruff. Signed John and Hanna Williams. Wit. oath Aug. 30, 1796 James Woodruff to Zadock Ford. Rec. Nov. 8, 1809

p. 147-148 Nov. 7, 1809 Isaac Brown (Culwell Co (sic), Tenn) to John Gossett (Spartanburgh); for $150 sold (1) 150 ac on both sides Mayses Cr of Fairforrest Cr; border: SE-Mays and other sides vacant; survey in 1768 by William Wofford for David Brown and granted "for the time then being" by Gov. Charles Montague; and (2) 33 ac bordering David Brown. Witness Eli Tolleson and Reubin Bryant. Signed Isaac Brown. Wit. oath Nov. 8, 1809 Eli Tolleson to Jno H Jones. Rec. Nov. 9, 1809

p. 148-149 Nov. 7, 1809 Isaac Brown (Culwell Co (sic), Tenn) to Gabriel Gossett (Spartanburgh); for $273 sold (1) 140 ac on branch of Fairforrest Cr; border: NW-Col Thompson, N-unknown, SE-Neacce, and NW-Brownd; grant in 1787 Gov. Thomas Pinckney to David Brown; and (2) 20 ac between Thompon and Brown. Witness Eli Tolleson and Reuben Briant. Signed Isaac Brown. Wit. oath Nov. 11, 1809 (sic) Eli Tolleson to John Gossett. Rec. Nov. 9, 1809

p. 149-151 Oct. 3, 1808 William Champeon and wife Francis (Spartanburgh) to Thomas Dare (same); for $800 sold 472 ac in two adjoining tracts: (1) 250 ac on Cherokee Cr on S side of Broad R; Tate's Old Mill tract; border: S-Alexander Morton esq where Joseph Dill lives and SE-John Fondren; includes a mill and its benefits and meadow above the mill formerly called Tate's Mill then Hester's Mill and then Champion's Mill; grant Apr. 21, 1775 to McKown who sold to William Tate desc and by his will to son Jesse Tate who sold to Charles Hester who sold to William Champeon; and (2) 222 ac adjoining (1) on SE; border: S-Nathaniel Robertson and Stacy, E-Wm McGown, and N-Dare; grant Jun. 4, 1798 to Charles Hester. Witness Jesse Tate and Nathaniel Robertson. Signed William Champeon. Wit. oath Nov. 7, 1809 Jesse Tate to Jno H Jones. Rec. Nov. 9, 1809. Dower renounced (Union Dist) Frances Champeon to John Jeffries Oct. 12, 1808

p. 151 Feb. 3, 1809 John Golightly (Spartanburgh) to son Ransom Golightly (same); for love and affection give (1) 1,400 ac on E side of Lawson's fork; border: where Ransom Golightly lived and originally granted to Mary Wood, Billy Grun (or Green), Pool, Connel, Golightly, and Peter's Cr; (2) (ac not given) half of grant to Job Sosbary and John Golightly on E side of Peter's Cr and on Cherokee Cr. Witness Elihu Golightly and John Golightly jr. Signed John Golightly. Wit. oath Jun. 13, 1809 Elihu Golightly to Danl White. Rec. Dec. 4, 1809

p. 151-152 Sept. 24, 1809 John Barnett (Spartanburgh) to Reubin Daniel (same); for $200 sold 200 ac; border: Obediah Wingo's Spring Br, John Foster, Richard Foster, Elijah Barnett, Richard Daniel. Witness Isham Harrison and Amey Harrison. Signed

John Barnett. Wit. oath Oct. 13, 1809 Isham Harrison to Danl White. Rec. Dec. 4, 1809

p. 152-153 Dec. 7, 1800 Solomon Crocker (Spartanburgh) to Benjamin Poole (same); for $5 sold 244 ac on Lawson's fork; border: NE-Benjamin Poole, SE-John Lee, SE & SW-Solomon Crocker, and NW-Lawson's fork; plat attached. Witness William Willis, James Poole, and William Crocker. Signed Solomon Crocker's mark. Wit. oath Dec. 14, 1805 William Willis to John Lipscomb. Rec. Dec. 4, 1809

p. 153-154 Jul. 26, 1808 Isaac Williams to James Wells; for $50 sold 80 ac on waters of Suck Cr. Witness John Williams and Joseph Camp. Signed Isaac Williams. Wit. oath Nov. 22, 1809 John Williams to Leonard Adcock. Rec. Dec. 7, 1809

p. 154-155 Jul. 11, 1809 Cassandra Gray (Spartanburgh) to John Hammet (same); for $65 sold 50 ac on S side Pacolate R; part of 200 ac grant to James Alley. Witness James Brannon and John Simmons. Signed Cassandra Gray. Wit. oath Sept. 23, 1809 James Brannon to A Benson. Rec. (not given)

p. 155 Dec. 13, 1809 James Kendrix (Spartanburgh) to Jacob Certin (same); for $40 sold 30 ac on Lawson's fork of Pacolate R. Witness John Sperner and Edmond Bishop. Signed James Kendrix's mark. Wit. oath Dec. 13, 1809 Edmond Bishop to Hugh Means. Rec. (not given)

p. 155-157 Aug. 14, 1809 Thomas Posey (Spartanburgh) to Richard Berry (same); for $350 sold 100 ac on fork of Tygar R; border: E-William Posey, N-John Ford, NW-Richard Basey (or Barry), and S-S Tygar R; part of grant Aug. 19, 1774 Gov. William Bull to Joseph Atkins and sold by John Atkins to Thomas Posey. Witness Thomas Moore, Charles M Barry, and A Sloan. Signed Thomas Posey. Wit. oath Dec. 11, 1809 Charles M Narry to Drury McDaniel. Rec. Dec. 16, 1809. Dower renounced Polly Posey to Drury McDaniel Dec. 11, 1809

p. 157-158 Feb. 22, 1806 William Lindsey jr and wife Rachal (Spartanburgh) to Nathaniel Woodruff (same); for $76 sold 38 ac on branch of Forgason's Cr of Tygar R; border: Samuel Woodruff. Witness John Crocker, Thomas Woodruff, and Joseph Woodruff. Signed William Lindsey's mark and Rachal Lindsey. Wit. oath Jan. 30, 1807 John Crocker to William Hendrix. Rec. Jan. 1, 1810

p. 158-159 Mar. 4, 1809 John Thomas (Spartanburgh) to Broughton Thomas (same); for $90 sold "all my property": 4 horses, 2 cows, 14 hogs, 5 beds and furniture, 4 bedsteads, chest, a pot, an oven, frying pay, "some" pewter and earthenware, 2 spinning wheels, 2 pair of cards, 5 chairs, 3 water vessels, 5 tubs, 3 axes, a pair of wedges, 2 guns, 7 geese, a cask, all corn fodder, all bacon, a bable, 2 saddles, 2 bedsteads, a loom and gear, all the wheat growing, all cotton, all tobacco, a plow and gear, a cow "tongace", and a cut real(?). Witness Malichi Eskridge and Thomas Eskridge. Signed John Thomas. Wit. oath Mar. 13, 1809 Thomas Eskridge to Drury McDaniel. Rec. Jan. 1, 1810

p. 159 Jul. 29, 1809 Daniel Timmons (Greenville Dist) to John Bomar (Spartanburgh); for $105 sold 100 ac on Cub Br; border: E-Edward Bomar and N-Joel Traylor. Witness Elisha Bomar and Edward Allen. Signed Daniel Timmons' mark. Wit. oath Dec. 27, 1809 Elisha Bomar to J Walker. Rec. Jan. 1, 1810

p. 159-160 Aug. 19, 1809 Elijah Barnett (Spartanburgh) to John Wofford (same); for $300 sold 326 ac on waters of Fairforrest Cr; border: Foster; part of two grants to Henry Wells.

Witness Daniel White JP and John Connel. Signed Elijah Barnett. Wit. oath Aug. 9, 1809 John Connel to Danl White. Rec. Jan. 1, 1810

p. 160-161 Jan. 10, 1808 Spencer Bobo (Spartanburgh) to Nathan Langston (same); for $850 sold 300 ac on Seader Shoal Cr of Enoree R. Witness Mordicai Chandler and William Langston. Signed Spencer Bobo. Wit. oath (Union Dist) May 10, 1808 Mordicai Chandler to David Floyd. Rec. Jan. 1, 1810. Dower renounced Jane Bobo to J. F. Grimke (not dated)

p. 161-162 Sept. 15, 1807 James McGowen (Roan Co, NC) to John Lindsey (Spartanburgh); for $370 sold 321 ac on both sides Two Mile Cr of Enoree R; border: S & W-Samuel Woodruff, N-Nathaniel Woodruff and Zachariah Leatherwood, and E-Paul Castleberry; grant Feb. 5, 1787 Gov. William Moultrie to James McGowen. Witness Thomas Woodruff III and Lewis Landford. Signed James McGowen. Wit. oath Nov. 27, 1809 Thomas Woodruff III to John Brewton. Rec. Jan. 1, 1810

p. 162-163 Apr. 25, 1808 Alexander McKie (Spartanburgh) to Zacheriah McDaniel (same); for $126 sold 42 ac on S side Fairforrest Cr and W side of waggon Road; border: McKie's field and road from Martin's Mill to Henry ONeill; the part of land sold by James Barmet to Alexander McKie; grant to John Thomas jr. Witness Richard Thomson and William Lancaster. Signed Alexr McKie. Wit. oath Apr. 25, 1809 Richard Thomson to William Lancaster. Rec. Jan. 1, 1810

p. 163-164 Nov. 6, 1809 Vincent Bennett, sheriff (Spartanburgh) to William Hirley (or Kirley); for $3 sold 130 ac on waters of Pacolet R; sold due to writ from Spartanburgh Common Pleas Court suit Thomas Dien vs administrator of John Hirley (or Kirley) desc; sale Oct. 2, 1809. Witness William Bennett and William Wood. Signed Vincent Bennett SSD. Wit. oath Jan. 6, 1810 William Bennett to Hugh Means. Rec. Jan. 6, 1810

p. 164-165 Jan. 8, 1810 Robert Benson (Spartanburgh) to Mason Shumate (same); for $800 sold a total of 403 ac (sic) on waters of Tygar R: (1) 200 ac; border: John Cooper, James Vernon, and John McElrath; (2) 160 ac on waters of Tyger R; and (3) 36 ac on waters of Tygar R; all allotted to Robert Benson as heir of William Benson desc; (1) was granted to Anthony Pearson (2) granted to John Leech, and (3) granted to William Benson; except about 3 ac that is Bevely Lewis' land; Robert Benson pays Mason Shumate if older claims take any more land. Witness Peter Gray, Nathaniel McElrath, and Thomas McCarley. Signed R Benson. Wit. oath Jan. 8, 1810 Thomas McCarley to A Benson. Rec. Jan. 8, 1810

p. 165-166 Nov. 6, 1809 Moses Foster (Spartanburgh) to son Andrew Foster (same); for love and affection give 200 ac on Long Branch on N side Fairforrest Cr; border: N-Moses Foster, S-John Foster and Moses Foster,E & W-John Kelso, and by Thomas; part of Rich Hill and part of grant Dec. 11, 1770 Gov. William Tryon (NC) to Peter Johnson who sold to Robert Thomas and by heirship to John Thomas who sold to Moses Foster. Witness Absolem Lancaster and Clarey Lancaster. Signed Moses Foster. Wit. oath Nov. 6, 1809 Absolem Lancaster to W Lancaster. Rec. Jan. 9, 1810

p. 166-167 Jun. 24, 1808 Abraham Nott (Columbia, SC) to Reuben Bomar (Spartanburgh); for $30 sold 21 ac near S Pacolate R; border: William Dickson and William Gilbert; sold by William Bratton, former sheriff (Pinckney Dist), as property of Hugh Stevenson as suit of William Dickson vs Hugh Stevenson, to Abraham Nott. Witness An B Moore and William Lipscomb. Signed Abm Nott. Wit. oath Jan. 9, 1810 William Lipscomb to Andrew Furgason. Rec. Jan.

9, 1810

p. 167-168 Apr. 5, 1809 Rice F Ross (Greenville Dist) to James Clark (Lincoln Co, NC); for $600 sold 320 ac on both sides of S Pacolate R; border: a lake, Dempsy Fowler, and Furgason; part of grant (150 ac (sic)) Jul. 7, 1800 to John Gowen; where Richard Vennable formerly lives. Witness John Lucas and Edmond Fowler. Signed Rice F Ross. Wit. oath Apr. 5, 1809 John Lucas to Andw Fugason. Rec. Jan. 9, 1810

p. 168-169 Sept. 5, 1808 Elias Vanderhorst (Bristol, England), by John Stanyarn Vanderhorst, his attorney, to David Dantzler (Orangeburgh Dist); for $944 sold 944 ac; border: NW-David Jordan, SW-Melwrath, and SE & NE-James Bright; grant Dec. 24, 1772 to Elias Vanderhorst. Witness John Collins and John Crawford. Signed Elias Vanderhorst by his attorney John S Vanderhorst. Wit. oath Sept. 5, 1808 (Charleston, SC) John Crawford to J(?) Reid. Rec. Jan. 9, 1810

p. 169-170 Dec. 17, 1809 John Smith (Spartanburgh), blacksmith, to Basel Compton (same); for $300 sold 150 ac on waters of Dutchman's Cr; part of 300 ac grant to Thomas Thornton. Witness William Wofford, Isaac Smith, and Ralph Smith. Signed John Smith. Wit. oath Jan. 9, 1810 William Wofford to W Lancaster. Rec. Jan. 7, 1810. Dower renounced Mercey Smith to William Lancaster Jan. 6, 1810

p. 170-171 Sept. 27, 1807 Alexander Sweaney (Spartanburgh) to John Foster (same); for $500 sold 100 ac on Mill Cr of Tygar R; where Alexander Sweaney lives; "grant" in 1799 by John Paden to Alexander Sweaney. Witness Labon P Poole, Herbertt Hawkins, and Samuel Neely. Signed Alexr Sweaney. Wit. oath Oct.3, 1807 Labon P Poole to John Collins. Rec. Jan. 11, 1810

p. 171-173 Oct. 12, 1808 Edward Hoocker (Spartanburgh) to Buckner Smith (same); for$50 sold (1) 78 ac on N side Tygar R; border: John Campbell and Timothy Toney; (2) 101 ac on N side Tygar R; border: S-Tygar R, W-Joel Hembree, N-Samuel Ketchcart, and E-Daniel Grantz; on Cain Cr; part of 249 ac grant Jul. 3, 1772 to Timothy Toney. Witness John Young and Samuel Farrow. Signed Edward Hoocker. Wit. oath Oct. 12, 1808 John Young to Burrell Bobo. Rec. Jan. 11, 1810. Dower renounced Milley Hoocker to Burrell Bobo Oct. 12, 1808

Oct. 12, 1808 Samuel Farrow to Edward Hoocker; Samuel bought land at sheriff's sale for Edward and Edward now repays Samuel; see case of Samuel Hindman vs Edward Hoocker; now Samuel gives up his claim to the land; where Edward Hoocker lives. Signed S Farrow. Rec. Jan. 11, 1810

p. 173-174 Dec. 23, 1808 John Young (Spartanburgh) to Archebald Smith (same); for $300 sold 66 ac; on NW corner of 200 ac grant to George Croford; border: James Cr. Witness John Holley and Buckner Smith. Signed John Young. Wit. oath Dec. 23, 1808 Buckner Smith to Burrell Bobo. Rec. Jan. 11, 1810. Dower renounced Nancy Young to Burrell Bobo Dec. 23, 1818 (sic)

p. 174 Jan. 27, 1809 John Arnold and wife Elizabeth (Spartanburgh) to Susanna Walker (same); for $525 sold 120 ac on S side of Cherokee Cr; border: Ezekiel Standley, John Arnold sr, and William Morgan. Witness Abner Benson and John G Bostick. Signed John Arnold. Wit. oath Jan. 11, 1810 Abner Benson to Drury McDaniel. Rec. Jan. 11, 1810

p. 174-175 Jul. 10, 1807 John Posey (Spartanburgh) to Daniel McCarley (same); for $330 sold 213 ac on Ford's Cr; border: a waggon road and remainder of grant; SE side of grant May 2, 1785 to Elisha Ford. Witness Zephaniah Posey and Matthew Patton. Signed John Posey's mark. Wit. oath Jan. 11, 1810 Matthew Patton to Drury McDaniel. Rec. Jan. 11, 1810

p. 175-177 Oct. 10, 1809 Nathaniel Walker (Greenville Dist) to John McMakin (same); for $304.50 sold 203 ac on N side of "the" river; border: Goodwin and Anderson; except one ac Nathaniel sold to Moses Moore; part of 140 ac grant Aug. 1, 1785 to William Goodwin and part of 500 ac grant Jan. 7, 1799 to Nathaniel Walker. Witness Shaderick Farmer and William T Walker. Signed Nathaniel Walker. Wit. oath Jan. 23, 1810 Shaderick Farmer to Michl Miller. Rec. Jan. 24, 1810. Dower renounced (Greenville Dist) Milley Walker to William T Walker Oct. 10, 1809

p. 177-178 Jan. 24, 1810 William Barton (Spartanburgh) to Hannah Barton (same); for $200 sold 200 ac on both sides of Pacolate R; grant Dec. 24, 1796 to Thomas Gore. Witness Milton Davis and Henry Davis. Signed William Barton. Wit. oath Jan. 25, 1810 Henry Davis to Andw Furgason. Rec. Jan. 28, 1810

p. 178-179 Jun. 14, 1809 Ransom Golightly (Spartanburgh) to Jobe Sosebee; for $200 sold 200 ac on Peter's Cr; border: Sosebee. Witness John Golightly jr and Elihu Golightly. Signed R Golightly. Wit. oath Sept. 4, 1809 John Golightly jr to Michl Miller. Rec. Jan. 28, 1810

p. 179-180 Jul. 26, 1809 Leonard and Jordan Carden (Spartanburgh) to Vincent Bennett (same); for $120 sold 360 ac on branch of Shoaley Cr; border: road from Spartanburgh Court House to Galt's old Store on S Pacolate R, Boiling Spring Br, Maverick, and Guelyard; part of grant Dec. 6, 1802 Gov. John Drayton to Leonard Carden sr and Jordan Carden. Witness John Watson and Frances Watson. Signed Leonard Carden and Jordan Carden. Wit. oath Jan. 28, 1810 John Watson to A Benson. Rec. Jan. 28, 1810

p. 180-181 Sept. 8, 1792 David Knox (Mecklenburgh Co, NC) to James McCall (York Co); for 20£ NC money sold 300 ac in Ireson Co (sic) on waters of N Tygar R; border: John Miller, John Brown, and Samuel Knox; grant Dec. 16, 1769 to David Knox. Witness Thomas Green esq, Robert Bigham, and Robt Jesm(?). Signed David Knox. Wit. oath (Mecklenburgh Co, NC) Sept. 8, 1809 Thomas Green to James Spratt. Rec. Jan. 29, 1810

p. 181-182 Jan. 27, 1810 Leonard Sparks sr (Spartanburgh) to John Tolleson (same); to secure a note of $80.40, Leonard sells John 196 ac; border: Shippy and Evan Davis; grant to Patterson Thomson; Condition: sale void if Leonard pays $80.40 with interest by Aug. 1, 1810. Witness Muse Tolleson and Keziah Tolleson. Signed Leonard Sparks' mark. Wit. oath Jan. 27, 1810 Muse Tolleson to D. J. Puckett. Rec. Jan. 27, 1810

p. 182 Mar. 14, 1808 Solomon Garrison (Spartanburgh) to Leonard Sparks (Union Dist); for $200 sold 196 ac; border: Shippy and Evan Davis; part of grant Feb. 2, 1080 (sic) Gov. John Drayton to Patterson Thomson. Witness Moses Stubs and Zarah Sparks. Signed Solomon Garrison. Wit. oath Mar. 18, 1809 Moses Stubs to John Lipscomb. Rec. Jan. 27, 1810

p. 182-184 Mar. 8, 1809 Pleasant Branham (Spartanburgh) to Robert Millican (same); to secure a note of $255.04, Pleasant sells Robert a Negro man Peter, a bay mare and colt, 2 cows and calves, all his wife's land from her desc husband (where Pleasant lives), and household furniture; Condition: sale void if Pleasant pays Robert the debt. Witness Arthur F Jackson and Joseph Kelso.

Signed Pleasant Banham's mark. Wit. oath Feb. 2, 1810 Joseph Kelso to Wm Kelso. Rec. Feb. 5, 1810

p. 184-185 Feb. 2, 1807 David Anderson (Spartanburgh) to John Durham (same); for 5£ sold 232 ac on waters of Ben's Cr of S Tygar R; border: David Anderson. Witness George Durham and William Hay. Signed David Anderson. Wit. oath Feb. 10, 1808 George Durham to Drury McDaniel. Rec. Feb. 5, 1810

p. 185-186 Feb. 16, 1809 William Pearson (Spartanburgh) to William Shackelford (same); for $800 sold 99 ac on James Cr of Tygar R; part of 250 ac formerly owned by David Densmore. Witness Jonathan Moore and Wm L Allen. Signed William Pearson's mark. Wit. oath Feb. 5, 1810 Wm L Allen to Burrell Bobo. Rec. Feb. 5, 1810

p. 186 Aug. 1, 1809 William Morgan and wife Nancy (Spartanburgh) to Daniel McKie (same); for $1,000 sold 400 ac on both sides Williams Cr of S Tygar R; where William and Nancy Morgan live; part (sic) of 311 ac grant Apr. 3, 1786 to John Williams and sold to William Reavs Jan. 18, 1787 who sold to William Morgan Oct. 1, 1796; and 75 ac part of grant to Frances Dodd who sold to Henry Leech who sold to John McElrath who sold to John Berry who sold to William Morgan, and 14 ac granted to William Morgan. Witness Andrew Harrison and John Rodgers. Signed William Morgan and Nancy's mark. Wit. oath Jan. 4, 1810 John Rodgers to Danl McKie. Rec. Feb. 5, 1810

p. 186-187 Aug. 22, 1809 Allen Bishop (Spartanburgh) to John Bird (same); for $60 sold 50 ac; border: Peter Lewis, Gov. Moultrie, Henry Bishop, and John Bird; half of 100 ac divided by joint purchase with Henry Bishop or agreed by Henry Bishop and John Bird. Witness James Barrett and John Bishop. Signed Allen Bishop. Wit. oath Jan. 9, 1810 John Bishop to Hugh Means. Rec. Feb. 10, 1810

p. 187-188 Dec. 1, 1809 James Clayton (Spartanburgh) to Fielding Clayton (same); for $500 sold 100 ac on Fort Shoal Cr of Enoree R; where Mathew Couch formerly lived; part of survey by his father Mathew Couch; border: John Farrow; grant Nov. 22, 1771 Gov. Charles G Montague to Mathew Couch. Witness John W Farrow and William Clayton. Signed John Clayton. Wit. oath Jan. 2, 1810 William Clayton to Burrell Bobo. Rec. Feb. 12, 1810

p. 188-190 Feb. 18, 1773 Mathew Couch and wife Fanny (Enoree, SC) to Beverly Cox (same); for 50£ SC money sold 50 ac on branch of Enoree R; NW part of 100 ac grant Jun. 16, 1700 (sic) Gov. Charles G Montague to Mathew Couch in Craven Co. Witness Peter Brooks, John Rainwaters, and Moses Casey. Signed Mathew and Fanny Couch's marks. Wit. oath none. Rec. Feb. 12, 1810

p. 190-191 Sept. 8, 1809 William Duncan (Spartanburgh) to Daniel McKie (same); for $600 sold 204 ac on N side of S Tygar R; where William Duncan jr lives; part of grant May 13, 1763 to John Millhouse who sold Nov. 3, 1777 to William Duncan and "to" William Duncan jr; plat attached shows border: Moses Barton, Cowen, and McDaniel; resurvey Aug. 16, 1809 by James Wofford. Witness Labon P Poole and James Duncan. Signed William Duncan's mark. Wit. oath Feb. 19, 1810 Labon P Poole to Drury McDaniel. Rec. Feb. 19, 1810. Dower renounced Ruth Duncan to Drury McDaniel Nov. 2, 1809

p. 191-193 Oct. (omitted), 1809 William Duncan jr (Spartanburgh) to Daniel McKie (same); for $158 sold 158 ac on branch of Tygar R; border: SW & NW-William Duncan, SE & NE-Alexander, SW-Cowen; grant Apr. 16, 1807 to William Duncan jr. Witness Labon P

Poole, Asa Mitchel, and Lowry McDaniel. Signed William Duncan's mark. Wit. oath Feb. 19, 1810 Labon P Poole to Drury McDaniel. Rec. Feb. 19, 1810. Dower renounced Ruth Duncan to Drury McDaniel Nov. 17, 1809

p. 193-194 Dec. 20, 1809 Ralph Danger, Henry Danger, and Gnat Danger (Spartanburgh) to James McDaniel (same); for $300 sold 390 ac on Meadow Cr of S Pacolate R; border: S-Henry Young and William Dixson, EW (sic), NE & NW-William Gilbert and William Marks, and SW-vacant; grant Sept. 10, 1793 to Henry Young. Witness Alexander McMillin and James Galt. Signed Ralph, Henry, and Gnat Danger's marks. Wit. oath Sept. 30, 1809 Alexander McMillin to James Young. Rec. Feb. 22, 1810.
Dec. 27, 1809 James McDaniel assigns the deed to John Dalton "for intent within mentioned". Witness Alexr McMillin and Wm Dalton. Signed James McDaniel's mark

p. 194-195 Dec. 17 (or 7), 1809 James McDaniel (Spartanburgh) to John Dalton (same); for $400 sold 390 ac on Meadow Cr of S Pacolate R; border: S-Henry Young and William Dixon, EW (sic), NE & NW-William Gilbert and William Marks, SW-vacant; grant Sept. 10, 1793 to Henry Young. Witness Alexander McMillin and William Dalton. Signed James and Sarah McDaniel's marks. Wit. oath Jan. 7, 1810 William Dalton to Wm Kelso. Rec. Feb. 22, 1810

p. 195-196 Jan. 4, 1809 Thomas Reece (Spartanburgh) to Thomas Vaughn (same); for $100 sold 124 ac on ridge between branches of Buffalow lick Cr of Fairforrest Cr and Dutchman's Cr. border: D Golightly, old mountain tract, SW & W-Thomas Vaughn, E-David Golightly, N & NW-E Barnett and Golightly; plat attached; part of the mountain tract. Witness Robert Martin esq and D Golightly. Signed Thomas Rees. Wit. oath Feb. 18, 1810 Robert Martin to W Lancaster. Rec. Mar. 2, 1810. Dower renounced Jan. 17, 1809 Mary Rees to William Lancaster

p. 196-197 Oct. 14, 1809 Pereman Tate (Spartanburgh) to Daniel McKie (same); for a $290 debt, Pereman sells Daniel the following: a dark bay horse 6 years old with large scar on his near side and back occasioned by a burn and lost his hear eye at same time, 2 cows--a brown or "Brendle" one and the other red, 6 hogs, 3 beds and furniture and all household and kitchen furniture--pots, wheels, pewter wheels, and all crop of corn, fodder, and cotton. Witness William Readen and Zacheriah Leatherwood. Signed P. W. Tate. Wit. oath Feb. 17, 1810 William Readen to Danl White. Rec. Mar. 4, 1810

p. 197-198 Feb. 27, 1810 Samuel Crowder (Spartanburgh) to Daniel McKie (same); for $500 sold 104 ac where Pearman W Tate lives; border: David Drummon, Hadden, the big survey, and an old road. Witness Thomas Tinsley and Henry Utley. Signed Saml Crowder. Wit. oath Feb. 27, 1810 Thomas Tinsley to Drury McDaniel. Rec. Mar. 4, 1810. Dower renounced Neomy Crowder to Drury McDaniel Feb. 27, 1810

p. 198-199 Apr. 15, 1809 Samuel Smith (Spartanburgh) to Money Southern (Rutherford Co, NC); for $300 sold 70 ac on N side of N Pacolate R; border: road from Gilbert Bomar's to James Berry's and by Baylis Earle. Witness Jo B Earle and William Prince. Signed Samuel Smith and Susa's mark. Wit. oath Feb. 1, 1810 William Prince to Wm Kelso. Rec. Mar. 5, 1810

p. 199 Jul. 8, 1809 Jane Smith (Spartanburgh) to James Fleming (same); for $30 sold dower rights to 31 ac; border: William Smith and Hancok Smith's tract; where James Fleming lives; part of 200 ac formerly property of Jane's husband Hancok Smith 93 ac of which was sold by James Smith to James Fleming. Witness Robert Rakestraw and John Smith. Signed Jane Smith's mark. Wit. oath Feb. 27, 1810 Robert Rakestraw to W Lancaster. Rec. Mar. 5, 1810

p. 199-200 Apr. 24, 1809 William Lewis (Spartanburgh) to James Gilmore (same); for $100 sold 100 ac; border: great survey near head of Lawson's fork, great road to Branning's Mill, David McDowell, and Knight. Witness William Gilmore and Elizabeth Gilmore. Signed William Gilmore. Wit. oath Mar. 2, 1810 William Gilmore to James Young. Rec. Mar. 5, 1810

p. 200-202 Jan. 18, 1809 Thomas Layton (Spartanburgh) to Robert Creswell (Laurens Dist); to secure bond of $207 dated "today" to pay $103.50 with interest from Dec. 28, 1807--a third on Jan. 1, 1810, a third Jan. 1, 1810 (sic), and a third Jan. 1, 1812, and for $1 Thomas Layton sells Robert Creswell 125 ac where Thomas lives; border: Stephen Wilson, Simpson Newman, and Casey; land sold Feb. 28, 1804 by Robert Creswell to James Sills and sold today by Robert Creswell, attorney for James Sils, to Thomas Layton; Condition: sale void (from Layton to Creswell) if Thomas pays the debt. Witness Aaron Casey and L. J. Casey. Signed Thomas Layton. Wit. oath Mar. 5, 1810 Aaron Casey to D. J. Puckett. Rec. Mar. 5, 1810

p. 202-203 Feb. 25, 1804 Robert Wilson (Spartanburgh) to James Sills (same); for $127 sold 125 ac on branch on S side of Tygar R; border: Stephen Wilson, Simpson Newman, and Casey; part of two tracts granted to William Grist. Witness John Tucker and John Grist. Signed Robert Wilson's mark. Wit. oath Feb. 4, 1809 John Grist to M Casey. Rec. Mar. 5, 1810. Dower renounced Anne Wilson to Wm Smith. Dec. 21, 1804

p. 203-204 Dec. 18, 1809 Richard Traylor (Spartanburgh) to Thomas Bomar (same); for $8 sold 150 ac on waters of Cub Br of Tygar R; border: road from Spartanburgh to Greenville Court House; known as Agg Traylor's old place. Witness Jesse Traylor and Robert Foster. Signed Richard Traylor's mark. Wit. oath Jan. 12, 1810 Jesse Traylor to J Walker. Rec. Mar. 5, 1810

p. 204-205 Sept. 12, 1809 William Monrow (Spartanburgh) to Nancy Monrow (same); for $65 sold 100 ac; border: a waggon road, Young, McWilliams, McDowell, and Benjon; part of grant to James Dillingham. Witness Peterson Borrum and Henry Monrow. Signed William Monrow. Wit. oath Feb. 24, 1810 Peterson Borrum to James Young. Rec. Mar. 5, 1810

p. 205 Feb. 28, 1810 John Scott (Spartanburgh) to daughter Sally Scott; for good causes give all my chattels and substance. Witness Samuel Turner and James Gunn. Signed John Scott's mark. Wit. oath Mar. 5, 1810 Samuel Turner to Jno H Jones. Rec. Mar. 5, 1810

p. 205-207 Nov. 25, 1809 Vincent Bennett, sheriff (Spartanburgh) to Daniel White esq; for $20 sold 130 ac on Mile Cr of N Tygar R; where Thomas Foster formerly lived; sale due to writ from Spartanburgh Common Pleas Court suit James Cooper vs Gabriel Bumpass; sale Sept. 4, 1809. Witness John Barnett and James Cooper. Signed Vincent Bennett SSD. Wit. oath Mar. 5, 1810 James Cooper to D. J. Puckett. Rec. Mar. 5, 1810

p. 207 Mar. 29, 1808 John Gowen (Spartanburgh) to James Sutherland (Pendleton Dist); for $300 sold 150 ac on both sides Mile Cr; border: Emey (or Emry); where Nelly White lives. Witness John Whitten and Willey S Brown. Signed Jno Gowen. Wit. oath Mar. 2, 1810 Willey S Brown to Andrew Furgason. Rec. Mar. 6, 1810

p. 207-209 Nov. 1, 1800 John Robuck (Greenville Dist) to James Sutherland (Spartanburgh); for $60 sold 20 ac on Mile Cr; border: John Gowen and "others" and John Woods; part of grant Nov. 25, 1771 Gov. Joshua Martin (NC) to Timothy Terrell and by heirship to William Rush who sold to John Gowen who sold to John Robuck. Witness John Whitten, Willey S Brown, and William Parks. Signed John Robuck. Wit. oath Mar. 2, 1810 Willey S Brown to Andrew Furgason. Rec. Mar. 6, 1810

p. 209 Sept. 15, 1808 Benjamin Champion (Spartanburgh) to Samuel Clark (same); for $70 sold 53 ac; border: mouth of Crockey Br of Thickety Cr. Witness Reuben Warren and William King. Signed Benjamin Champion's mark. Wit. oath Mar. 3, 1810 William King to Henry Turner. Rec. Mar. 6, 1810

p. 209-210 Sept. 26, 1809 James Cook (Spartanburgh) to Elizabeth Autery (same); for $80 sold 40 ac on branch of Fairforrest Cr; border: N-James Keen, W-Barnett, and S & E-Thomas Cook. Witness Joseph Thomas Cook and Jacob Autry. Signed James Cook. Wit. oath Oct. 20, 1809 Joseph T Cook to W Lancaster. Rec. Mar. 6, 1810

p. 210-212 Nov. 13, 1809 Vincent Bennett, sheriff (Spartanburgh) to Gen. Thomas Moore; for $4 sold 18 ac on both sides of Middle Tygar R; grant to Gabriel Bumpass; border: SW-Gen. Thomas Moore, N-David Tanner, E-Robert Miller and David Tanner; and sold 3 ac border: S & N-Gen. Thos Moore and W-Elisha Haddy; sale due to writ from Spartanburgh Common Pleas Court suit James Cooper vs Gabriel Bumpass; sale Nov. 6, 1809. Witness Abner Benson and William Bennett. Signed Vincent Bennett SSD. Wit. oath Apr. 2, 1810 Abner Benson to James Young. Rec. Apr. 2, 1810

p. 212-213 Sept. 3, 1808 Noah Wells (Spartanburgh) to Joroyal Barnett; for $100 sold 100 ac on Lawson's fork of Pacolate R; border: George Lewis, Edmond Clemment, Josiah Blackwell, and Joroyal Barnett. Witness James Blackwell and Joseph Barnett. Signed Noah Wells. Wit. oath Jan. 8, 1810 James Blackwell to Danl White. Rec. Apr. 2, 1810

p. 213-214 Dec. 1, 1809 John Broockshier (Burk Co, NC) to Solomon Abbott (Spartanburgh); for $300 sold 200 ac; border: the shoal on Cherokee Cr, a waggon road, Bazel Scott, and Little Cherokee Cr; part of grant to James Steedman. Witness James Trail and Ephraim Potter. Signed John Broocksher. Wit. oath Dec. 1, 1809 Ephraim Potter to Henry Turner. Rec. Apr. 2, 1810

p. 214 Jan. 23, 1810 Samuel Turner (Spartanburgh) to Demps Murry (same); for love and affection give all my goods and chattels--a bay mare and sorrel mare, 2 feather beds and furniture, a loom with all its utenseals for weaving, a pot and oven and skillet, 6 plates, a dish, and bason. Witness Ephraim Potter and Elizabeth Garrett. Signed Samuel Turner. Wit. oath Jan. 23, 1810 Ephraim Potter to Henry Turner. Rec. Apr. 2, 1810

p. 214-215 Nov. 10, 1809 Joshua Edwards (Spartanburgh) to John Jordan (same); for $50 sold 136 ac on branch on S side of Elisha Thompson's Beverdam Cr of Middle Tygar R; grant to James Hall and James Reynolds. Witness Wilson Nesbett, John Jordan, and John Collins. Signed Joshua and Kelurah Edwards' marks. Wit. oath Nov. 10, 1809 Wilson Nesbett to John Collins. Rec. Apr. 3, 1810

p. 215-216 Sept. 17, 1807 Nancy Nichols, Richard Thomson, and Charles Littlejohn, administrators of estate of John Nichols desc (Union Dist and Spartanburgh) to William McNite; agreeable with bond John Nichols gave William McNite Dec. 31, 1800 for $20 sold (ac not given) on S side of N Pacolate R; where Charles McNite lived in 1800; known as Nichols land. Witness John McCarrol and Thomas Belsher. Signed Nancy Nichols, Richard Thomson, and Charles Littlejohn. Wit. oath Mar. 9, 1810 John McCarrol to James Young. Rec. Apr. 3, 1810

p. 216 Nov. 17, 1808 William McKnight (Spartanburgh) to John McClure; for (a bond?) dated Nov. 17, 1808 for $20 sell 300 ac on S side of N Pacolate R; where Charles McKnight formerly lives. Witness Henry Monrow and Alexander Copeland. Signed William McKnight. Wit. oath Mar. 9, 1810 Henry Monrow to James Young. Rec. Apr. 3, 1810

p. 216-218 Dec. 2, 1799 William Bratton, the younger, sheriff (Pinckney Dist) to Abraham Nott esq (Union Dist); for 2£ sold 50 ac on waters of Pacolate R; where Hugh Stevenson lives; sale due to writ from Pinckney Common Pleas Court signed by John Martin, clerk on Nov. 1, 1797 assessing 300£ awarded to William Dickson and 11£ 17s 8p court cost; land belongs to Hugh Stevenson; sale Dec. 2, 1799. Witness D. R. Evans and John McCaw. Signed Wm Bratton SPD. Wit. oath Mar. 23, 1809 (Union Dist) D. R. Evans to R. S. Saunders. Rec. Apr. 6, 1810

p. 218-219 Mar. 31, 1810 Abraham Hembrie (Spartanburgh) to John Tolleson (same); to secure a bond of $111.19 sold (1) 159 ac on N side of Pacolate R; grant to David Allen; and (2) 159½ ac; border: Dickson; W half of 319 ac grant Oct. 6, 1788 to David Allen; Condition: sale void if Abraham pays bond by Oct. 1, 1810. Witness Muse Tolleson and William Reid. Signed Abraham Hembrie's mark. Wit. oath Apr. 7, 1810 Muse Tolleson to A Benson. Rec. Apr. 7, 1810

p. 219-220 Nov. 1, 1809 John Henry (Spartanburgh) to Abraham Hembrie (same); for $220 sold 159½ ac on N side of Pacolate R; border: Whitteton's Cr; part of grant Oct. 6, 1788 Gov. Thomas Pinckney to David Allen; "increasing" all the land where Abraham Hembrie lives on Goucher's Cr. Witness Leonard Low and William Lands. Signed Abraham Henry and John Henry. Wit. oath Nov. 3, 1809 William Lands to John Gossett. Rec. Apr. 7, 1810

p. 220-221 Apr. 8, 1809 William Rickmon to Abraham Hembrie; for $150 sold 159½ ac; border Dickson; W half of 319 ac grant Oct. 6, 1788 Gov. Thomas Pinckney to David Allen. Witness Ezekiel Swillivan to Joseph Camp. Signed William Rickmon. Wit. oath Jan. 27, 1810 Ezekiel Swillivan to John Lipscomb. Rec. Apr. 7, 1810

p. 221-222 Jan. 10, 1809 John Wilson (Spartanburgh) to Thomas Allison (Rutherford Co, NC); for $54.53½ sold a bay mare 4 years old, a sorrel mare 3 years old, a brown "mare colt" a year old, a "Maly Dun" cow, a red cow unmarked, a "speckled" cow and calf, a red heifer 2 years old, a "dum" heifer 2 years odl, a "Bundle" heifer a year old, 6 sheep--3 yeaues, 2 "Moathers" and a roan, a spotted sow and 5 pigs, a sandy sow and 6 pigs, 8 year old shoats of different colors, 3 feather beds and furniture, a 9 gallon pot, a middle sized oven, 10 pewter dishes, 12 pewter plates, 6 white plates, and 6 blue edged plates. Witness Richard Blanton and Sils Odam. Signed John Wilson's mark. Wit. oath Apr. 7, 1810 Richard Blanton to D. J. Puckett. Rec. Apr. 7, 1810

p. 222-223 Oct. 3, 1804 Samuel Sarratt, sr (Spartan Dist) to Rederick Arendell (same); for $10 sold (ac not given) a fishing place on big Broad R; border: Rederick Arendell, McClaren's Island, a little island, and John Sarratt. Witness William Sarratt and John Williams. Signed Samuel Sarratt. Wit. oath Apr. 16, 1810 William Sarratt to John Lipscomb. Rec. Apr. 7, 1810

p. 223-224 Sept. 18, 1809 James and Elizabeth Hewett (Spartanburgh) to Benjamin Rainwaters (same); for $50 sold 80 ac on Ford's Cr; border: Williams Spring Br and Mason. Witness Ransom Golightly and John Golightly jr. Signed James Hewett and Elizabeth's mark. Wit. oath Apr. 9, 1810 John Golightly jr to Burrell Bobo. Rec. Apr. 9, 1810

p. 224-225 Oct. 7, 1809 Thomas Young sr (Spartanburgh) to William Young (same); for $100 sold 25 ac on Jamey's Cr on S side of Tygar R; border: Thomas Young and Richard Young; W end of 150 ac grant Feb. 7, 1767 Gov. Montague to William Young sr, father of Thomas Young sr, and willed to Thomas Young sr. Witness Richard Young and Sarah Young. Signed Thos Young. Wit. oath Mar. 16, 1810 Richard Young to Burrell Bobo. Rec. Apr. 9, 1810. Dower renounced Mary Young to Burrell Bobo Mar. 16, 1810

p. 225-226 Jan. 14, 1803 William Waldrop (Spartanburgh) to Benjamin Rhodes (same); for $60 sold 50 ac on Enoree R; border: William Waldrop, Benjamin Rhodes, David Neil; formerly owned by Hansel Dollar; part of grant to David Neill. Witness Curtus Burton and Aaron Casey. Signed William Waldrop's mark. Wit. oath Mar. 14, 1808 Aaron Casey to Burrell Bobo. Rec. Apr. 9, 1810

p. 226-227 Mar. 4, 1808 John P Poole (Spartanburgh) to Benjamin Rhodes (same); for $100 sold 50 ac; border: John D Neil (now owned by Benjamin Rhodes); W of branch that runs through a grant May 7, 1767 to Thomas Couch who sold Sept. 23, 1796 to John P Poole. Witness Aaron Casey and William Higgins. Signed John P Poole. Wit. oath Mar. 14, 1808 Aaron Casey to Burrell Bobo. Rec. Apr. 9, 1810. Dower renounced Elender Poole to Burrell Bobo Mar. 14, 1808

p. 227-228 Oct. 28, 1808 Rowland Jennings (Spartanburgh) to John Stephens (same); for $125 sold 100 ac; border: John Otts; grant Gov. Charles Pinckney to James Gibbs and "to" his son Zachariah Gibbs who sold to Rowland Jennings. Witness Jesse Jennings and William Jennings. Signed Rowland Jennings' mark. Wit. oath Apr. 11, 1809 Jesse Jennings to John Brenton. Rec. Apr. 10, 1810

p. 228-229 Oct. 28, 1808 Rowland Jennings (Spartanburgh) to John Stephens (same); for $350 sold 134 ac; grant Gov. Charles Pinckney to James Gibbs desc and "to" his son Zachariah Gibbs who sold to William Calvert who sold to Rowland Jennings. Witness Jesse Jennings and William Jennings. Signed Rowland Jennings' mark. Wit. oath Apr. 11, 1809 Jesse Jennings to John Brenton. Rec. Apr. 10, 1810

p. 229-230 Mar. 10, 1802 John Brooks to Thoddus Owen; for 20£ sold 167 ac; part of 400 ac on S fork of N Tygar R "above" John Sharp's land; grant Dec. 5, 1791 Gov. Charles Pinckney to James Amos. Witness James L Burd, Matthew Burd, and Miles Brooks. Signed John Brooks sr's mark. Wit. oath Jun. 8, 1802 James L Burd to James Jordan. Rec. Apr. 10, 1810

p. 230-231 Mar. 20, 1810 Thomas Collens (Spartanburgh) to Samuel Adams; for $97 sold 97 ac on S side of Thickety Cr; border: Jacob Hofler (or Hoflin). Witness Joseph Collens and Hugh Moore. Signed Thomas Collens. Wit. oath Mar. 20, 1810 Hugh Moore to John Lipscomb. Rec. Apr. 10, 1810

p. 231-232 Jan. 13, 1810 Pencel Wood (Spartanburgh) to Benjamin Wood (same); for $22 sold 100 ac; border: E-land sold by John Wood to Benjamin Wood and NW-land sold by Pencel Wood to Benjamin Wood; part of where Pencel Wood lives and part of 1,340 ac grant Gov. Edward Rutledge to Pencel Wood. Witness John Wood sr and James Wood. Signed Pencel Wood sr's mark. Wit. oath Jan.

14, 1810 John Wood to Tyre Glen. Rec. Apr. 10, 1810

p. 232-233 Dec. 21, 1809 John Wood sr to Benjamin Wood; for $100 sold 100 ac; includes head of branch of Rocky field Cr of Enoree R and head branch of Abner's Cr; border: Pencel Wood, Benjamin Wood, John Jones, and Reuben Mayfield; N part of 200 ac sold by Pencel Wood sr to John Wood sr. Witness John Jones and Reuben Green. Signed John Wood. Wit. oath Jan. 5, 1810 Robert (sic) Green to Tyre Glenn. Rec. Apr. 10, 1810

p. 233-234 Jan. 1, 1810 Samuel Elder (Spartanburgh) to John Stevens (same); for $80 sold 40 ac on N side Wards Cr and N side of Tygar R; border: Paden and James McGowen. Witness Jesse Jennings and William Jennings. Signed Samuel Elder. Wit. oath Apr. 10, 1810 Jesse Jennings to Drury McDaniel. Rec. Apr. 10, 1810

p. 234-235 Apr. 10, 1810 John Wofford jr (Spartanburgh) to Thomas Posey (same); for $500 sold 200 ac in two tracts: (1) 100 ac on head branches of McElwayn's Cr and Sugar Cr of Fairforrest Cr; part of 300 ac grant Sept. 12, 1768 to William Brownlee--see mortgage of James Wofford to John Wofford jr; and (2) 100 ac; part of 222 ac grant Feb. 3, 1800 to James Wofford. Witness James Ham jr and Benjamin Peak. Signed John Wofford jr's mark. Wit. oath Apr. 10, 1810 James Ham jr to Danl White. Rec. Apr. 10, 1810

p. 235-236 Jan. 18, 1810 John Arnold (Spartanburgh) to William Arnold (same); for $345 sold 135 ac on waters of branch of Tygar R; part of 400 ac grant Jan. 30, 1806 to James Sutherland. Witness Richard Shackelford, Willis Arnold, and James Arnold jr. Signed John Arnold. Wit. oath Apr. 10, 1810 Richard Shackelford to Daniel McKie. Rec. Apr. 10, 1810

p. 236-237 Dec. 11, 1809 Moses Wilkins (Spartanburgh) to William and Aaron Wilkins (same); for $310 sold (ac not mentioned) on S side of N Pacolate R; willed by William Wilkins sr to William, Aaron, and Moses Wilkins; border: Camp, McWilliams, McMillin, and N Pacolate R. Witness David Lipscomb and Nilson Brock. Signed Moses Wilkins. Wit. oath Mar. 20, 1810 David Lipscomb to John Lipscomb. Rec. Apr. 10, 1810

p. 237-238 Apr. 5, 1810 Jane Thomson, David Burton, Thomas Wright, and Sarah Thomson (Spartanburgh) to Lawson Thomson (same); for $600 sold 200 ac on both sides Ward's Cr of Tygar R; border: William Rodgers, Martin Otts, and Charles Moore; grant North Carolina to Rev. Joseph Alexander and sold by Andrew Thomson desc and title bond given which is warranted by Jane Thomson, David Burton, Thomas Wright, and Sarah Thomson, heirs of Andrew Thomson. Witness Daniel Hammett and George Floyd. Signed Joan Thomson, Sarah Thomson, David Burton, and Thomas Wright. Wit. oath Apr. 10, 1810 Daniel Hammett to Hugh Means. Rec. Apr. 11, 1810

p. 238-239 Oct. 13, 1806 Henry Brockman and Isaac Crow, commissioners of Thomas Leatherwood (Spartanburgh) to John Leatherwood (same); for $200 sold 217 ac on S side of Two Mile Cr; border: N-James Langford, E-Thomas Farrow, S-John Terry and Robert Hanna, and W-David Owen; where Thomas Leatherwood lives. Witness Daniel McKie and Richard Shackelford. Signed Henry Brockman and Isaac Crow's mark. Wit. oath Apr. 3, 1810 Richard Shackelford to Danl McKie. Rec. Apr. 11, 1810

p. 239-240 Oct. 25, 1809 William Foster (Spartanburgh) to James Ballenger jr (same); for $309 sold 103 ac on N Tygar R; plat attached shows border: J Ballenger sr and Bankston; plat dated Oct. 25, 1809 and signed by Hubbard Hawkins; part of grant to Samuel Nesbett who sold to Hosea Camp who sold to Joseph Scales who sold to William Foster. Witness John Johnson, Lawrence Banckston, and Jeremiah Owen. Signed William Foster. Wit. oath Apr. 12, 1810 (sic) Jeremiah Owen to James Young. Rec. Apr. 11, 1810

p. 240-241 Dec. 30, 1809 John King (Spartanburgh) to James W Reynolds (SC); for $300 sold 90 ac; border: Elizabeth Cavens, Gideon Reynolds, Sampson Bobo desc, Mark Langston, and John Arnold; part of three tracts; where James W Reynolds. Witness Benjamin Robuck and John Henry. Signed John King's mark. Wit. oath Apr. 10, 1810 John Henry to Jno H Jones. Rec. Apr. 11, 1810

p. 241-242 Mar. 29, 1810 Nathaniel Woodruff sr (Spartanburgh) to William L Allen (same); power of attorney to collect debts owed him and sell all real and personal property. Witness William Shackelford and Jonathan Moore. Signed Nathaniel Woodruff sr. Wit. oath Mar. 29, 1810 William Shackelford to Danl McKie. Rec. Apr. 11, 1810

p. 242-243 Jul. 16, 1806 William Grant (Spartanburgh) to Thomas Sarratt (same); for $200 sold 200 ac on both sides Dutchman's Cr of Tygar R; border: John Ham, James Betterton's old line, Bery's old line, Drury Parham, heirs of Wilie Cook desc, and Blackstock's road. Witness John Grist (or Gust), Lewis Parham, and Elias Parham. Signed William Grant. Wit. oath Apr. 9, 1808 John Grist to Wilie Williford. Rec. Apr. 11, 1810. Dower renounced Mary Grant to Burrell Bobo Jan. 19, 1810

p. 243-245 Apr. 13, 1809 Gabriel Benson, sheriff (Spartanburgh) to David Johnson; for $150 sold 794 ac on branches of Storey's Cr of Fairforrest Cr; grant Jan. 6, 1794 Gov. William Moultrie to Thomas Brandon and then border: E-Hugh Gouchy (or Gousley), Robert Erwin, and old line, S-Thomas Compton, W-Thomas Brandon, and N-old line; land belonged to Gen. Thomas Brandon; land sold due to suit May 4, 1808 Union Dist Common Pleas Court by James McElroy (or Clay) vs Dr. James Davis and Maj. Thomas Young, administrators of estate of Gen. Thomas Brandon for $213.60; writ dated third Monday of Mar. 1808; sale Aug. 1, 1808. Witness John W Farrow esq and Thomas Porter. Signed Gab Benson SSD. Wit. oath Apr. 12, 1810 John W Farrow to John Taylor. Rec. Apr. 12, 1810

p. 245-246 Aug. 31, 1809 David Childres (Spartanburgh) to Thomas House (same); for $300 sold 130 ac on N side of Enoree R; border: John Hamby's Spring Br; part of two grants: (1) to Thomas Childres and (2) to Robert Cooper. Witness Thomas Thornton and William House. Signed David Childres. Wit. oath Oct. 21, 1809 William House to Drury McDaniel. Rec. Apr. 12, 1810. Dower renounced Aga Childres to Drury McDaniel Oct. 7, 1809

p. 246-247 Sept. 15, 1807 Robert Mason (Greenville Dist) to Richard Brown (Spartanburgh); for $100 sold 208 ac; border: Widow Storey, Nox, Rowland Johnson, and John Wood. Witness Col. Ism Foster and Eaton Walker. Signed Robert Mason. Wit. oath May 10, 1809 Ism Foster to J Walker. Rec. Apr. 13, 1810

p. 247-248 Mar. 25, 1810 Richard Robertson (Spartanburgh) to Robert Stacy (same); for 5£ sold 52 ac on waters of Cherokee Cr and Broad R; border: Stacy. Witness Anderson Boyd and Thomas Robertson. Signed Richard Robertson. Wit. oath Apr. 11, 1810 Anderson Boyd to Jno H Jones. Rec. Apr. 13, 1810

p. 248-249 Apr. 9, 1810 Nehemiah Norton (Spartanburgh) to John Tolleson; a bond of 5£ 5s 5p by note of Oct. 12, 1809; to secure the bond Nehemiah sold a sorrel horse, a gray mare, a cow and calf, 2 feather beds and furniture, 6 pewter plates, a pewter dish, 3 pewter basons, an oven, a skillet, and a spider; Condition:

sale void if Nehemiah pays debt by Nov. 1, 1810. Witness Muse Tolleson and Charles McAbee. Signed Nehemiah Norton. Wit. oath Apr. 14, 1810 Muse Tolleson to D. J. Puckett. Rec. Apr. 14, 1810

p. 249-250 Oct. 22, 1809 Isham Harrison (Spartanburgh) to Anthony Foster (same); for $1,700 sold 380 ac on Fairforrest Cr; border: Reuben Daniel and a beech tree marked "IH". Witness Richard Foster, John Rainwater, and Reuben Harrison. Signed I Harrison. Wit. oath Nov. 4, 1809 John Rainwater to D. J. Puckett. Rec. May 7, 1810. Dower renounced Amey Harrison to D. J. Puckett Nov. 4, 1809

p. 250-252 May 7, 1810 Vincent Bennett, late sheriff (Spartanburgh) to Labon P Poole; for $70 sold 300 ac on N Tygar R just above Tanner's Mill; sale due to writ from Spartanburgh Common Pleas Court suit David Crews vs Gabriel Bumpass; sale Sept. 4, 1810. Witness Wm R Smith and Alexr McCarter. Signed Vincent Bennett. Wit. oath May 7, 1810 Alexr McCarter to John Lipscomb. Rec. May 7, 1810

p. 252-253 Apr. 21, 1810 Michael McElrath (Spartanburgh) to John McElrath and Page Rork (or Rook) (same); for $150 sold a black horse, a bay horse, a sorrel colt, 6 cows and 6 calves 3 years old, a bason, a pewter dish, 2 sets of cups and sausers, 2 large "Delf" dishes, 11 gallon pot, 6 gallon pot, 2 ovens, a skillet, a spider, 9 sheep, all plantation utenseals, a flax wheel, a cotton wheel, and 3 pair of cotton cards. Witness Wm McElrath and Peggy Thompson. Signed Michl McElrath. Wit. oath May 5, 1810 Wm McElrath to John Collens. Rec. May 7, 1810

p. 253-254 Apr. 26, 1810 William Kelso (Spartanburgh) to Thomas Jackson (same); for $115 sold 92 ac; mill and mill race excepted. Witness Mary W Kelso, Jenny Kelso, and William Jackson. Signed William Kelso. Wit. oath (not dated) William Jackson to Wm Kelso. Rec. May 7, 1810

p. 254 Jan. 26, 1808 William Kelso (Spartanburgh) to Thomas and William Jackson (same); for $1 sold a "piece of land" on Ann Hooper's Cr; border: Mill house. Witness Thomas Divine and Jane Kelso. Signed Wm Kelso. Wit. oath May 5, 1810 Jane Kelso to Wm Kelso. Rec. May 7, 1810

p. 254-255 May 8, 1810 Samuel Clark (Spartanburgh) to John Tolleson (same); for $53 sold 53 ac at mouth of Lackey's Br of Thickety Cr. Witness Muse Tolleson and Wm R Smith. Signed Samuel Clark's mark. Wit. oath May 8, 1810 Muse Tolleson to D. J. Puckett. Rec. May 8, 1810

p. 255-256 Feb. 17, 1810 Laurence Krouse (Spartanburgh) to Hugh Means; a bond of $89.17 by two notes: (1) Dec. 10, 1808 and (2) Dec. 10, 1808; to secure the bond Laurence sold a white mare about 6 years old, 6 cattle 14 hogs marked with "under bet" in each ear, a number of carpenter's tools--jack, smoothing and jointing plains, chissels and 5 or 6 augers, 2 large hand saws, a tenant saw, a copper kettle, 2 pots, and 2 ovens; Condition: sale void if Laurence pays debt by Oct. 1, 1810. Witness William Turner and John Turner. Signed Laurence Krous. Wit. oath May 9, 1810 William Turner to J Walker. Rec. May 9, 1810

p. 256-257 Nov. 13, 1809 Robert Wood (Spartanburgh) to Thomas Bomar (same); for $25 sold 10 ac on Cub Br of Tygar R on S side of road from Spartanburgh Court House to Greenville; part of 387 ac grant Sept. 15, 1784 Gov. William Moultrie to Thomas Crowther. Witness William Bomar and John Burton. Signed Robert Wood. Wit. oath May 14, 1810 William Bomar to D. J. Puckett. Rec. May 15, 1810

p. 257-258 Mar. 8, 1809 Edward Bomar (Spartanburgh) to Thomas Bomar (same); for $100 sold 115 ac on waters of Cub Br of Tygar r; border: Robert Wood. Witness Thomas Wingo and William Bomar. Signed Edward Bomar. Wit. oath May 14, 1810 William Bomar to D. J. Puckett. Rec. May 15, 1810

p. 258-259 Nov. 25, 1809 Vincent Bennett, sheriff (Spartanburgh) to Daniel White esq; for $6.25 sold 50 ac on N Tygar R; border: above where Hays Bagwell lives; sale due to writ from Spartanburgh Common Pleas Court suit David Crews vs Gabriel Bumpass; sale Sept. 4, 1809. Witness James Cooper and John Barnett. Signed Vincent Bennett. Wit. oath May 7, 1810 James Cooper to James Young. Rec. May 7, 1810

p. 259-260 Nov. 25, 1809 Daniel White (Spartanburgh) to Stephen Foster (same); for $50 sold 50 ac on waters of Tygar R; border: where Hays Bagwell lives; sold by attachment of property of Gabriel Bumpass at suit of James Cooper by Vincent Bennett, sheriff (Spartanburgh). Witness John Foster and Richard Daniel. Signed Daniel White. Wit. oath May 7, 1810 John Foster to James Young. Rec. May 7, 1810

p. 260-261 Jan. 24, 1807 Armstead Shumate (Spartanburgh) to Samuel Burns (same); for $30 sold 86 ac on S side Tygar R; border: W-Samuel Burns, S-James Kilgore, and E-Armstead Shumate; grant May 17, 1803 to Armstead Shumate. Witness Michael McElrath and Nancy Ford. Signed Atd Shumate and Elizabeth's mark. Wit. oath Mar. 29, 1809 Michael McElrath to Michl Miller. Rec. May 28, 1810

p. 261-262 Feb. 17, 1808 John Durham (Spartanburgh) to William Frazure (or Frasure) (same); for $60 sold 125 ac on waters of Ben's Cr of S Tygar R; border: Leonard, Brushy Fork Cr, Frasure, William Anderson, and Alexander Wakefield. Witness John Durham and Philip Johnson. Signed John Durham. Wit. oath Nov. 12, 1808 Philip Johnson to Drury McDaniel. Rec. Jun. 4, 1810

p. 262 Dec. 25, 1809 Rachal Duncan (Spartanburgh) to son Jesse Duncan; for love and affection give a mare and colt, a cow and calf, 4 hogs, "what corn and fodder I have", a feather bed and furniture, a side saddle, a walnut table, 2 spinning wheels and plantation tools and "what pewter I have" and all household furniture. Witness William Gore and Rachal Gore. Signed Rachal Duncan's mark. Wit. oath Feb. 14, 1810 William Gore to John Lipscomb. Rec. (not given)

p. 262-263 Feb. 7, 1810 Thomas Shurly to Thomas Price (Spartanburgh); for $300 sold 171 ac at mouth of Furgason's Cr on S side of Tygar R; border: mouth of Floyd's Cr, Samuel Floyd, and Richard Miller. Witness John Ward, William Wood, and Robert Shurley. Signed Thomas Shurly. Wit. oath May 5, 1810 William Wood to Drury McDaniel. Rec. Jun. 4, 1810

p. 263-264 Sept. 16, 1809 James Quin (Spartanburgh) to Henry Turner (same); for $250 sold 140 ac on both sides of Pacolate R. Witness James Turner and Margaret Turner. Signed James Quin. Wit. oath Mar. 31, 1810 James Turner to James Young. Rec. Jun. 4, 1810

p. 264-265 Feb. 4, 1810 John Brice (Caldwell Co, Ky) to brother James Brice (same); power of attorney to sell land on N Tygar R; his part of inheritance by will of his father Samuel Brice. Witness none. Signed John Brice. Wit. oath (Caldwell Co, Ky) Feb. 4, 1810 John Brice to John H Philips. Rec. Jun. 4, 1810. May 4, 1810 (Caldwell Co, Ky) William Mitchusson JP in Caldwell certifys John H Philips is clerk of court

p. 265-266 Jan. 4, 1810 Joseph Rodgers (Spartanburgh) to Marshal Piper (same); for $480 sold 165 ac on both sides Ward's Cr; border: S-John Otts, S & E-George Floyd, and W & S-William Moore and N Tygar R. Witness William Hammett, Lawson Thomson, and Alexr McKie. Signed Joseph Rogers. Wit. oath Jun. 4, 1810 William Hammet to Durry (sic) McDaniel. Rec. Jun. 4, 1810

p. 266-267 Dec. 22, 1809 Baylis Earle (Spartanburgh) to Theron Earle (same); for $500 sold (1) 130 ac on both sides N Pacolate R; part of 400 ac grant to Samuel Young who sold to Baylis Earle; border: Vardry Camp, grant to Baylis Earle, Theron Earle, and Alpasia (or Asspasio) Earle; and (2) 45 ac Baylis Earle bought from Andrew Colley; and (3) 225 ac grant to Baylis Earle. Witness Gabriel Benson and E. W. McVay. Signed Baylis Earle. Wit. oath Jun. 4, 1810 Gabriel Benson to William Reid. Rec. Jun. 4, 1810

p. 267-268 Aug. 8, 1809 Josiah Culbertson (Greenville Dist) to Joseph Kelso (Spartanburgh); for $400 sold 800 ac on S side of Fairforrest Cr; border: Henry Foster, N-Obadiah Wingo and Samuel Culbertson, SW-Josiah Thomas, NW-Henry Cuningham and Nancy Story and James Storey and Thomas Kelso, and by Halley. Witness Christopher Golightly and Mark Crocker. Signed Josiah Culbertson. Wit. oath Mar. 5, 1810 Christopher Golightly to William Reid. Rec. Jun. 4, 1810. Dower renounced (Greenville Dist) Mathew Culbertson (wife) to Reuben Parrett Feb. 24, 1810

p. 268-269 Nov. 25, 1809 Daniel White (Spartanburgh) to John Foster (same); for $30 sold 130 ac on Tygar R; part of tract where John Foster lives; sold as Gabriel Bumpass' property by attachment in suit of James Cooper and sold by Vincent Bennett, sheriff (Spartanburgh) to Daniel White. Witness Thomas Tinsley and Richard Daniel. Signed Daniel White. Wit. oath Mar. 5, 1810 Richard Daniel to D. J. Puckett. Rec. Jun. 4, 1810

p. 269-270 Jan. 4, 1810 Leonard Carden (Spartanburgh) to William Sentell (same); for $300 sold 200 ac on waters of Shoaly and Thomson's Creeks; border: a waggon road, John Burnett, Hardy Flaker, Samuel Sentell, and survey for Joseph Vennable; part of 890 ac survey Jan. 21, 1793 for Leonard Carden and granted by Gov. William Moultrie to (not given). Witness Gideon Stevens and John Carden. Signed Leonard Carden. Wit. oath Jan. 28, 1810 Gideon Stephens to Hugh Means. Rec. Jun. 4, 1810

p. 270-271 May 28, 1810 James Brice (Caldwell Co, Ky), by power of attorney from John Brice, legate of Samuel Brice desc (Spartanburgh) to Andrew Coan (Spartanburgh); for $75 sold 80 ac on both sides N Tygar R; border: Middle Tygar R; half of tract left by will of Samuel Brice to son John Brice; grant Dec. 4, 1786 Gov. William Moultrie to Samuel Brice. Witness John Snoddy Coan and Wm McM. Brice. Signed James Brice's mark. Wit. oath Mar. 30, 1810 John S Coan to Drurry McDaniel. Rec. Jun. 4, 1810

p. 271-273 Feb. 21, 1809 ("Eastern Circuit", SC) William Hasell Gibbs, master of Equity Court for Eastern Circuit at Charleston, SC, to John Bulow and Charles Bulow (same); for (money omitted) sold (1) 2,482 ac at head branches of Island Cr, branches of Broad R, Buck Cr; border: SE & SW-West Harris and SE-Doctor; Elizabeth Steedman and other legates of James Steedman on Nov. 19, (year omitted) had complaint in Oct. term in Charleston Equity Court and said they were entitled to property of James Steedman's estate and asked court to partition land and partition couldn't be made advantageously and land was sold; sale Feb. 21, 1809; 523 ac "deducted" that was sold by executors of James Steedman to estate of Robert Lee; (2) "remainder" of 426 ac on Pacolate R; grant to James Steedman; border: NW-George Turner, SW-Solomon Abbett, and

SE & SW- Edmond Ballenger; 150 excepted that was sold by executors to Richard Lee; and (3) 767 ac on both sides of Chinquepin Cr; border: SW & NW-McDowell and Wadleton and NE-Dickins and Edward Herring; grant to James Steedman. Witness Horatea Griffen esq and J. H. Dendy. Signed Wm Hasell Gibbs, master in equity. Wit. oath Jun. 14, 1810 Horatea Griffen to D. J. Puckett. Rec. Jun. 15, 1810

p. 273-274 Mar. 16, 1805 Laurence Bankston (Spartanburgh) to Abraham Cantrell (same); for $28 sold 100 ac on waters of Little Buck Br; border: Bethell; grant Sept. 3, 1794 States Office to Sampson Bethell. Witness Reuben Warren and Isham Foster JQ. Signed Laurence Bankston's mark. Wit. oath Jul. 2, 1810 Isham Foster to James Young. Rec. Jul. 2, 1810

p. 274-275 Sept. 15, 1808 John Martin (Spartanburgh) to Abraham Cantrell (same); for $166 sold 200 ac on Little Burk Cr; border: Thomas Jordan and Richard Morris; grant Dec. 3, 1787 States Office to Thomas Jordan. Witness John Durham and John Cantrell. Signed John Martin. Wit. oath Nov. 15, 1808 John Durham to Leonard Adcock. Rec. Jul. 2, 1810

p. 275-276 Oct. 22, 1807 Samuel Hays (Spartanburgh) to Isaac Harris (same); for $200 sold 212 ac on waters of Fairforrest Cr; border: S-Joseph Hays, W-Moses Foster, N-Joseph Ash, and E-Henry Emerson. Witness James Robenett and Christopher Golightly. Signed Samuel Hays. Wit. oath Oct. 22, 1807 James Robenett to William Simpson. Rec. Jul. 2, 1810. Dower renounced Mary Hays to William Lancaster Jun. 12, 1810

p. 276-277 Oct. 11, 1809 Isaac Harris (Spartanburgh) to Mark Crocker (same); for $180 sold 212 ac in two adjoining grants to Samuel Hays who sold to Isaac Harris; on N side Fairforrest Cr and on Henry's Br; border: Sympson and Joseph Hays. Witness Christopher Golightly, Richard Daniel, and Thomas Merredi. Signed Isaac Harris. Wit. oath Jun. 9, 1810 Christopher Golightly to W Lancaster. Rec. Jul. 2, 1810. Dower renounced Nancy Harris to William Lancaster Jun. 9, 1810

p. 277-278 Feb. 15, 1810 Isaac Young sr (Spartanburgh) to Ephraim Potter (same); for $225 sold 200 ac on both sides of Island Cr just below William Abbott; includes where Wm Young lives; "part of littlefield over the creek" excluded. Witness Isaac Young, Moses Young, and James Young. Signed Isaac Young's mark. Wit. oath May 15, 1810 James Young to Henry Turner. Rec. Jul. 4, 1810

p. 278-279 May 30, 1810 William Morris (Spartanburgh) to James Harrison (same); for $50 sold 350 ac on head branches of Suck Cr of Broad R; border: Turner and Poole. Witness William Lipscomb and John Lipscomb. Signed William Morris. Wit. oath Jul. 2, 1810 William Lipscomb to John Lipscomb. Rec. Jul. 4, 1810

p. 279-280 Apr. 9, 1810 Mason Shumate (Spartanburgh) to Joseph Rodgers (same); for $300 sold 172 ac on both sides Jamey's Cr of N Tygar R; border: on N side "District Rd" and Snody; part of two grants: (1) May 4, 1769 North Patent to John Leech and (2) to Anthony Peason. Witness Peter Legon, David Burton, and Lawson Thomson. Signed Mason Shumate. Wit. oath Jun. 4, 1810 Lawson Thomson to Drury McDaniel. Rec. Jul. 7, 1810. Dower renounced Ann Shumate to Duglas Josephus Puckett Jul. 7, 1810

p. 280-281 Jul. 26, 1810 Jacob Sartin (Spartanburgh) to Elisha Turner (same); for $75 sold 30 ac on Lawson's fork. Witness Vincent Bennett and J. W. Farrow. Signed Jacob Sartin. Wit. oath Jul. 26, 1810 Vincent Bennett to A Benson. Rec. Jul.

26, 1810

p. 281-282 Apr. 13, 1810 Henry Emerson (Spartanburgh) to James Campbell (same); to secure a bond: notes of "12th day of this instant" for $375 to be paid annually with first payment Oct. 15, 1810 Henry sells a bay horse, a black mare, a waggon and all rigging belonging to it, 6 sheep, 13 hogs, 3 axes, 2 mattocks, 3 weading hoes, 2 augers, a wedge, a coatter, a shovel, plow, a cowtoring plow, 3 cows and yearlings, 2 big wheels, a little wheel, a loom, 4 feather beds and furniture, a chest, a cupboard, a table, 17 geese and all household and kitchen furniture; Condition: sale void if Henry pays debt by Oct. 15, 1813; property remains with Henry until Oct. 15, 1813. Witness Charles Smith. Signed Henry Emerson. Wit. oath Jul. 21, 1810 Chas Smith to W Lancaster. Rec. Jul. 28, 1810

p. 282-283 Jan. 20, 1810 Jonathan Nesbett (Spartanburgh) to James Nesbett, John Robenet, and their wives (same); for love and affection give 109 ac on N side of Middle Tygar R; grant to Jonathan Nesbett. Witness William Brown, John Robinson, and Edmond Staggs. Signed Jonathan Nesbett. Wit. oath Jul. 28, 1810 William Brown to Michl Miller. Rec. Jul. 29, 1810

p. 283-284 Mar. 16, 1810 Richard Roberts (Spartanburgh) to William Tippins (same); for $88 sold 210 ac on branch of Williams Cr of Tygar R; border: Langford and Edwards McKie; grant to "R Roberts"; Condition: sale void if Richard pays William or Dennis Tippins $44 by Dec. 25, 1810; note given by Richard Roberts to Dennis Tippins but now in possession of William Tippins. Witness James Kilgore and Tyrce Glenn. Signed Richard Roberts. Wit. oath Jul. 4, 1810 Tyrce Glenn to James Ford. Rec. Aug. 2, 1810

p. 284-285 Mar. 6, 1810 Joshua Thomas (Spartanburgh) to John Wright, tanner (same); for $250 sold 234 ac on both sides Story's Cr of Fairforrest Cr; border: E, N & W-Henry Cuningham and Joseph Kelso, SE & S-David Johnson; plat attached; part of 200 ac (sic) grant to Joshua Thomas and all of 200 ac grant to Hugh Gorely (or Gouly) who sold to Joshua Thomas. Witness Daniel Wilbanks, John Blasingame, and Isaac Bogan. Signed Joshua Thomas. Wit. oath Jul. 3, 1810 Isaac Bogan to W Lancaster. Rec. Aug. 6, 1810. Dower renounced Rebekah Thomas to William Lancaster Mar. 22, 1810

p. 285-286 Feb. 15, 1810 William Morgan (Spartanburgh) to John Jordan jr (same); for $70 sold (ac not given) on S fork of N Tygar R; grant to James Nesbett who sold to Henry Morgan who sold to William Morgan. Witness James Vernon and Jesse Cooper. Signed William Morgan. Wit. oath Aug. 6, 1810 James Vernon to John Collins. Rec. Aug. 6, 1810

p. 286-287 Nov. 24, 1809 William Hurt (Spartanburgh) to James Vernon (same); for $100 sold 150 ac on waters of Tygar R; on S side of "original tract" including mill seat; separated from remainder of grant by road from Spartanburgh to Greenville; part of where William Hurt lives. Witness William Perrin and Peggy Jordan. Signed William jurt (sic). Wit. oath Aug. 6, 1810 William Perrin to D. J. Puckett. Rec. Aug. 6, 1810. Dower renounced Jane Hurt to D. J. Puckett Aug. 6, 1810

p. 287-288 Mar. 6, 1810 Elizabeth Autery (Spartanburgh) to James Keen (same); for $40 sold 40 ac on branch of Fairforrest Cr; border: N-James Keen, W-Barnett, and S & E-Thomas Cook. Witness Robert Martin and Polly Martin. Signed Elizabeth Autery's mark. Wit. oath Apr. 10, 1810 Robert Martin to Danl White. Rec. Aug. 6, 1810

p. 288-289 Apr. 18, 1810 William Adcock (Spartanburgh) to Jeane Henderson (same); for $50 sold 100 ac on waters of Horse Cr of Broad R. Witness Noble Hamilton and Leonard Adcock. Signed William Adcock. Wit. oath Apr. 18, 1810 Noble Hamilton to Leonard Adcock. Rec. Aug. 6, 1810

p. 289-290 Feb. 16, 1810 Elisha Lindsey (Spartanburgh) to John Ward; for $50 sold 50 ac on S side Pacolate R; below mouth of Hurrekin Br; border: Patrick Tylor and Jones; grant to Henry McCray. Witness Jonathan Low sr and James Ward. Signed Elisha Lindsey. Wit. oath Feb. 16, 1810 James Ward to Jno H Jones. Rec. Aug. 6, 1810

p. 290-291 Jan. 20, 1808 Tilmon Bobo and wife Beulah to Humphry Yarborough; for $400 sold (ac not given) S of Tygar R; border: N-Thomas Todd and Widow Taylor, E-John Gurry, S-heirs of James Anderson and William Edwards, and by a pond, the Story Ridge, and Edmond Bearden; where Ephraim Smith lives. Witness Samuel Hurt and Thomas Smith. Signed Tilmon Bobo and Beulah's mark. Wit. oath Jan. 29, 1818 (sic) Samuel Hurt to Burrel Bobo. Rec. Aug. 6, 1810

p. 291-292 Jan. 3, 1807 Edward Arnett, son and heir-at-law of Edward Arnett desc, to Humphry Yarborough; for $40 sold 20 ac; border: E-Humphry Yarborough and William Edwards and by remainder of a tract on other sides; part of tract on S of Tygar R that Edward Arnett desc possessed. Witness George Divine and Thomas Martin. Signed Edward Arnett. Wit. oath Feb. 24, 1808 George Divine to Burrell Bobo. Rec. Aug. 6, 1810

p. 292 Jun. 7, 1810 James Hadden (Spartanburgh) to David White (same); for $200 sold 100 ac on Ben's Cr; border: Daniel McKie, William Gresham, Brushy fork, Alexander Wakefield, Jonah Leonard, and Thomas Hadden's old line. Witness John Bozwell and James Johnson. Signed James Hadden. Wit. oath Jun. 9, 1810 James Johnson to Danl McKie. Rec. Aug. 6, 1810

p. 292-293 Nov. 27, 1809 John Broockshier (NC) to James Quin (SC); for $400 sold 100 ac on N side Cherokee Cr; border: Blackburn Quin and a new road; part of grant to James Seamon. Witness James Trail and Richard Turner. Signed John Brookshier. Wit. oath Aug. 6, 1810 James Trail to Henry Turner. Rec. Aug. 6, 1810

p. 293-294 Jul. 25, 1806 Abraham Wyatt (Spartanburgh) to Lewis Cannon (same); for 40£ sold 100 ac on Pacolate R. Witness William Cannon and John Quarles. Signed Abraham Wyatt's mark. Wit. oath Jul. 26, 1806 John Quarles to Jno H Jones. Rec. Aug. 6, 1810

p. 294-295 Aug. 8, 1810 John Golightly sr (Spartanburgh) to John Golightly jr (same); for $700 sold 350 ac on both sides Lawson's fork of Pacolate R; grant to Mary Wood. Witness Elihu Golightly and Ransom Golightly. Signed John Golightly sr. Wit. oath Aug. 8, 1810 Elihu Golightly to A Benson. Rec. Aug. 8, 1810

p. 295-296 Feb. 26, 1810 Daniel McClaren (Bedford Co, Tenn) to John McClaren (Spartanburgh); for $20 sold (1) 53 ac and (2) (ac not given). Witness Wilson Nesbett and James Swanay. Signed Daniel McClaren. Wit. oath Aug. 15, 1810 Wilson Nesbett to A Benson. Rec. Aug. 15, 1810

p. 296-297 Apr. 10, 1809 John McClaren (Spartanburgh) to Samuel Nesbett (same); for $200 sold 200 ac on waters of Broad R; border: Daniel McClaren; grant to Daniel McClaren who sold to John McClaren. Witness Peter Gray, Herbt Hawkins, and James D

Johnson. Signed John McClaren. Wit. oath Apr. 10, 1809 Herbt Hawkins to John Collins. Rec. Aug. 15, 1810

p. 297-298 Dec. 22, 1809 Baylis Earle (Spartanburgh) to Asspasio Earle (Rutherford Co, NC); for $500 sold 150 ac on N side of N Pacolate R; border: heirs of Col. John Earle, George W Earle, Money Suthern, a line run today between Theron Earle and Asspasio Earle; part of 400 ac grant to Samuel Young who sold to Baylis Earle. Witness Gabriel Benson and C. W. McVay. Signed Baylis Earle. Wit. oath Sept. 3, 1810 Gabriel Benson to W Lancaster. Rec. Sept. 3, 1810

p. 298 Jan. 18, 1810 James Stone (tenn) to Jesse Brown (Spartanburgh); a bond of $330; Condition: James deeds Jesse by Dec. 25, 1811 77 ac on waters of Two Mile Cr; border: W-Jesse Brown, N-Spencer Colvert, and E-County Rd; except land within 20 feet of Two Mile Cr "for obstrusction of pond and waters of creek". Witness Caleb Woodruff and Rosannah Woodruff. Signed James Stone. Wit. oath Sept. 4, 1810 Caleb Woodruff to John Dean. Rec. Sept. 7, 1810

p. 298-299 Feb. 13, 1810 David McCarley (Spartanburgh) to James McCarley (same); for $165 sold 106 3/4 ac on Ford's Cr; border: waggon road; NE part of 213 ac grant May 2, 1785 to Elisha Ford. Witness James Selmon and Drury McAbee. Signed David McCarley's mark. Wit. oath Sept. 3, 1810 Drury McAbee to D. J. Puckett. Rec. Sept. 7, 1810

p. 299-300 May 20, 1809 David McCarley (Spartanburgh) to Thomas McCarley (same); for $150 sold 100 ac; border: Zachariah McDaniel and Thomas Underwood; NW part of grant Jan. 1, 1787 to Thomas Hightower. Witness James Selmon and James McCauly. Signed David McCarley's mark. Wit. oath Sept. 3, 1810 James McCauly to D. J. Puckett. Rec. Sept. 7, 1810

p. 300-301 Sept. 10, 1810 John Simmons to Joseph Simmons; to secure a note Oct. 18, 1800 to Nat Simmons for $34 and note transfered to Joseph Simmons and a second note May 3, 1808 to Joseph Simmons and their note Dec. 6, 1809 to Muse Tolleson for $13 and transfered to Joseph Simmons or total(?) of $70.25 now owed John Simmons sells all corn crop and fodder "as it now stands", a stack of oats, 10 hogs marked with cross and stape fork in each ear, a bed, bedstead, and furniture, 6 chairs, a 8 gallon pot, a 3 gallon pot, a dutch oven, a 1 gallon pot, 2 fish pans, and a frying pay; Condition: sale void if John Simmons pays debt by Dec. 25, 1811. Witness Herbt Hawkins and James Ward. Signed John Simmons. Wit. oath Sept. 20, 1810 (sic) James Ward to Hugh Means. Rec. Sept. 10, 1810

p. 301-303 Apr. 20, 1810 William Foster (Spartanburgh) to John Bankston (same); for $606 sold 204 ac on waters of N Tygar R; border: James Ballenger jr, Mr. Cree's old line, and Bankston's field; part of it granted Apr. 9, 1770 "Office" to Samuel Nesbett and grant Dec. 1, 1800 States Office to Hosea Camp and rest was granted Mar. 4, 1793 to William Ford. Witness Edmond Fowler, James Young, and James White. Signed William Foster. Wit. oath Apr. 28, 1810 Edmond Fowler to James Young. Rec. Sept. 22, 1810. Dower renounced Nancy Foster to James Young Apr. 28, 1810

p. 303-304 Aug. 20, 1809 John Gowen to Allantu and Daundas, daughters of Polly Saunders; give 100 ac each; Allantu's part borders "the" river at John Gowen's cross fence and running South; Daundas' part runs from river North; border: Bartholonew Grogan. Witness Theron Earle, C. W. McVay, and Wiley S Brown. Signed Jno Gowen. Wit. oath Jan. 8, 1810 Theron Earle to D. J. Puckett. Rec. Sept. 22, 1810

p. 304 Feb. 17, 1810 Nicholas Gentry (Spartanburgh) to George Brewton (same); for $100 sold 50 ac; border: N-Forgason's Cr, W-Broderick Mayson and George Brewton, and E-George Isom. Witness Zephaniah Posey, William Moore, and Mathew Patton. Signed Nicholas Gentry's mark. Wit. oath Sept. 3, 1810 Mathew Patton to John Brewton. Rec. Sept. 22, 1810

p. 304-306 Mar. 31, 1810 Thomas Porter (Laurence Dist) to William Calvert; for $500 and to secure debt of $1,800 by bond of Mar. 4, 1810 sold 142 ac on waters of Enoree R; border: Waldrop, Christopher Rhodes, Thos Farrow, N Durkie, and Robert Watson; part of tract where Nathaniel Durkie lives and where his Grist and Saw Mills are; Condition: sale void if Thomas pays debt. Witness Aaron Casey and Richard Allen. Signed Thomas Porter. Wit. oath Mar. 31, 1810 Aaron Casey to M Casey. Rec. Sept. 24, 1810

p. 306-307 Aug. 5, 1803 (Greenville Dist) Charles Dean (Greenville Dist) to James Pike (Spartanburgh); for $287 sold 230 ac on N side of Enoree R; border: James Rucker, Robert Wood, Robert Greyen (or Gregen); part of 469 ac grant Sept. 3, 1792 to Benjamin Kilgore jr. Witness Joshua Benson to Thomas Green. Signed Charles Dean. Wit. oath (Spartanburgh Dist (sic)) Aug. 5, 1803 Joshua Benson to James Kilgore. Rec. Sept. 27, 1810. Dower renounced (Greenville Dist) Margaret Dean to James Kilgore Aug. 5, 1803

p. 307-308 Oct. 1, 1810 Henry Brown to Edith Berry (Spartanburgh); for $300 sold 658 ac on waters of Pacolate R; grant in 1809 to John Nolen; if Edith loses land due to other claims,then Henry returns money. Witness Robert Legon and Lewis Brown. Signed Henry Brown. Wit. oath Oct. 1, 1810 Robert Legon to A Benson. Rec. Oct. 1, 1810

p. 308-309 Feb. 1, 1806 Joseph Woodruff (Spartanburgh) to John Arnold (same); for $1,000 sold 360 ac on N side of Enoree R; border: William Young. Witness William Shackelford, Thomas Stone, and Richard Harrison. Signed Joseph Woodruff's mark. Wit. oath Feb. 20, 1800 (sic) William Shackelford to John Brewton. Rec. Oct. 1, 1810. Dower renounced Anne Woodruff to Burrel Bobo Feb. 10, 1810

p. 309-310 Apr. 4, 1810 James Templeton (Spartanburgh) to William L Bishop (same); for $166 sold 50 ac where James Templeton lives; border: a bridge on waggon road from Court House to Edward Ballenger's; part of grant in Dec. 1768 North Carolina to Robert McMordie and sold by his heirs to John McMordie May 11, 1797 who sold to James Templeton and Samuel Miller Jan. 3, 1799 and Samuel Miller sold to James Templeton Nov. 18, 1800. Witness Peter Gray and Rachal Jamison. Signed Ja Templeton. Wit. oath Apr. 10, 1810 Peter Gray to Danl White. Rec. Oct. 1, 1810

p. 310-312 Jul. 20, 1810 James Templeton (Spartanburgh) to James Vernon (same); for $500 by bond Jul. 20, 1810 and to secure the bond sold "where he lives" including his house and improvements and all crop now in ground and "small" grain now cut and stacked, a Negro man Pompy, 2 horses, 2 cows, "some" young cattle; land borders: Abner Benson; land already sold to James Vernon excepted on N cormer of tract to Barney Bishop 43 ac on SW corner of tract and to William Bishop 50 ac adjoining Barney's; Condition: sale void if James Templeton pays debt in two years. Witness William Perrin and John Jordan. Signed James Templeton. Wit. oath Aug. 6, 1810 William Perrin to D. J. Puckett. Rec. Oct. 8, 1810

p. 312-313 Oct. 8, 1810 William Ross Smith (Spartanburgh) to James Smith (Union Dist); for $550 and James' share of estate of James Smith desc sold 940 ac on both sides Lawson's fork of

Pacolate R; including mill and house where William R Smith lives; border: William Bagwell. Witness William S Golightly, Reuben Harrison, and Micajah Barnett. Signed Wm Ross Smith. Wit. oath Oct. 8, 1810 William S Golightly to William Reid. Rec. Oct. 8, 1810

p. 313-314 Oct. (omitted), 1808 William Easley (Spartanburgh) to Armstead Bomar (Halifax Co, Va); for $1,512 sold 428 ac on S Pacolate R; border: mouth of Reuben Bomar Spring Br; part of grant to William Dickson. Witness James Blassingame and Reuben Bomar. Signed Wm Easley. Wit. oath Sept. 29, 1810 Reuben Bomar to James Young. Rec. Oct. 9, 1810

p. 314 Oct. 28, 1809 Michael Wood (Spartanburgh) to Thomas Wood (same); for $220 sold a Negro boy Moses 5 years old. Witness Theophelus Cannon and Tyrce Glenn. Signed Michael Wood's mark. Wit. oath Oct. 9, 1810 Tyrce Glenn to Drury McDaniel. Rec. Oct. 10, 1810

p. 314-315 Feb. 14, 1810 John Clark (Spartanburgh) to James Ridings (same); for $200 sold (1) 167 ac on waters of Alien Cr; grant May 13, 1799 Gov. Edward Rutledge to John Clark; and (2) 104 ac adjoining (1) and on waters of Alien's Cr; part of grant to James McClure who sold to John Clark. Witness Richard Carver and James Whitton. Signed John Clark. Wit. oath Nov. 5, 1810 Richard Carver to Andrew Furgason. Rec. Nov. 5, 1810

p. 315-317 Sept. 4, 1810 Isham Foster, sheriff (Spartanburgh) to Nathaniel Rochell (Union Dist); for $160 sold 412 ac on waters of Tygar and Enoree Rivers; border: Foster, Bobo, Langston, Legon, and Harmoning; sale due to writ from Spartanburgh Common Pleas Court suit Spencer Bobo vs Sally Bobo and other heirs of Sampson Bobo desc; Commissioners John Hobby, Nathaniel Langston, Isaac Crow sr, John Hughston, and Spencer Colbert to divide Sampson Bobo's land; land was divided as follows: to Sally (widow of Sampson) 620 ac and remainder of land sold half on 12 months credit and half on 2 years credit and recommendation became judgment of the court; sale at Isaac Crow's house on Sept. 4, 1810. Witness Thomas Allison and Muse Tolleson. Signed Ism Foster SSD. Wit. oath Nov. 6, 1810 Thomas Allison to A Benson. Rec. Nov. 6, 1810

p. 317-318 Aug. 7, 1810 William Underwood (Spartanburgh) to William Bush (same); for $260 sold 109½ ac; border: Obadiah Roberbert's (sic) old field. Witness James Young and Reuben Bomar. Signed William Underwood's mark. Wit. oath Nov. 6, 1810 Reuben Bomar to James Young. Rec. Nov. 6, 1810. Dower renounced Kezziah Underwood to James Young Aug. 7, 1810

p. 318-319 Apr. 15, 1807 William Renfro (Spartanburgh) to Benjamin Rollins (same); for $350 sold 109½ ac; border: Obed Robert's old field. Witness David Rolins and James Young. Signed William and Janny Renfro. Wit. oath Nov. 6, 1810 James Young to John Lipscomb. Rec. Nov. 6, 1810

p. 319-320 Jan. 27, 1807 Larken and Leonard Carden to Heardy Fletcker; for $100 sold 200 ac; border: Venable's crossroads, John Barnett, Curt Road Br, George Rowland, and School House Br; part of 890 ac survey Jan. 21, 1793 for Leonard Carden and granted by Gov. William Moultrie. Witness James Boid and Frances Watson. Signed Larken Carden and Leonard Carden. Wit. oath Nov. 6, 1810 Frances Watson to James Young. Rec. Nov. 6, 1810

p. 320-321 Mar. 6, 1807 John D and Susanna Neel (Spartanburgh) to William Woldrup (same); for $300 sold 252 ac on N side of Enoree R; border: William Woldrup, Wm Stewart, Widow Fuller, Richard Fryer, Christopher Rhodes sr, and Benjamin Rhodes; part of

557 ac grant to George Wright who sold to Pruk Cunningham who sold to Thomas Greger who sold to Henry Heerder(?) who sold to William Steward who sold to John Neel. Witness Aaron Casey and Chaney Bobo. Signed John D and Susanna Neel's marks. Wit. oath Feb. 1, 1808 Aaron Casey to Burrell Bobo. Rec. Nov. 6, 1810

p. 321-322 Oct. 24, 1809 William Dewberry (Spartanburgh) to Stephen White (same); for $50 sold 170 ac on waters of Thickety Cr; part of grant States Office to William Dewberry. Witness Thomas Betterton and Rolley Horton. Signed William Dewberry. Wit. oath Oct. 24, 1809 Rolly Horton to Henry Turner. Rec. Nov. 6, 1810

p. 322-323 Aug. 27, 1810 William Williams (Spartanburgh) to Willham Gilham (Rutherford Co, NC); for $400 sold 200 ac on Cherokee Cr of Broad R; border: John Arendel sr, Martin now Hester's, and Walker. Witness Fendal Robertson and Anthony Sarratt. Signed William Williams' mark. Wit. oath Oct. 5, 1810 Anthony Sarratt to John Lipscomb. Rec. Nov. 6, 1810. Dower renounced Candes Williams to John Lipscomb Oct. 5, 1810

p. 323-324 Sept. 6, 1809 William Murry (Spartanburgh) to George Poole (Rutherford Co, NC); for $200 sold 146 ac on Island Cr and Pacolate R; border: Leonard Adcock. Witness William Adcock and John Adcock. Signed William Murry's mark. Wit. oath Sept. 16, 1809 William Adcock to Leond Adcock. Rec. Nov. 16, 1810

p. 324-325 Nov. 2, 1808 William Grant (Spartanburgh) to William Powers (same); for $500 sold 157 ac on N side Tygar R; border: mouth of Motley's Cr, Drury Parham, Ridge path, Alexander Prewett, and Daniel Grant; part of two grants: (1) to Joseph Powers desc and (2) to Thomas Fletcher. Witness James Power and Joseph Power. Signed William Grant. Wit. oath Nov. 7, 1810 James Power to Samuel Morrow. Rec. Nov. 24, 1810

p. 325-327 Sept. 4, 1808 John Gray and wife Judith (Spartanburgh) to Casandra Gray (same); for $100 sold 73 ac in two parts: (1) 50 ac on S side of Pacolate R; part of 200 ac grant Nov. 14, 1771 Gov. Jesse Martin (NC) to James Alley; and (2) 23 ac on S side of Pacolate R; includes small houses and about half of Pacolate Springs; border: Poole and Brow; grant Feb. 4, 1805 Gov. Paul Hamilton to John Gray. Witness Elijah Herrin, David Quarles, and H. M. W. Gray. Signed John Gray and Judith's mark. Wit. oath Jul. 11, 1809 H. M. W. Gray to A Benson. Rec. Nov. 25, 1810

p. 327 Nov. 5, 1810 Thomas Dare and John Tolleson (Spartanburgh) to Masouree Catherine Fenney Tolleson, first and eldest daughter of Muse Tolleson and his wife; a bond to each give Masouree $500 when she is 12 years old; Condition: money goes to next eldest child of Muse if Masouree dies before she's 12 years old and bond is boid if there aren't any other children. Witness Wm R Smith and Vincent Bennett. Signed Thomas Dare and John Tolleson. Wit. oath Dec. 1, 1810 Wm R Smith to D. J. Puckett. Rec. Dec. 4, 1810

p. 327-328 Aug. 31, 1810 Austin Clayton (Barren Co, Ky) to Moses Foster (Spartanburgh); for $300 sold 382 ac on Mill Cr. Witness Drury Gooch, Thomas Wheasley, and Robert Clayton. Signed Augusten Clayton and Cayt's mark. Wit. oath Sept. 17, 1810 Drury Gooch to Drury McDaniel. Rec. Dec. 22, 1810

p. 328-330 Jul. 11, 1809 Casandra Gray (Spartanburgh) to James Brannon (same); for $15 sold 23 ac on Pacolate R; border: Pacolate Springs, Poole, and Brown; grant Feb. 4, 1805 Gov. Paul Hamilton to John Gray and sold by John Gray and wife Judith to Casandra Gray Sept. 4, 1808. Witness Muse Tolleson and William Robinson. Signed Casandra Gray. Wit. oath Dec. 3, 1810 Muse

Tolleson to A Benson. Rec. Dec. 28, 1810

p. 330-331 Jul. 2, 1810 Nehemiah Norton (Spartanburgh) to John Tolleson (same); for $17.18 and 3 milles sold 75 ac on N side Pacolate R; E part of grant to Laurence Ready; border: Thomas Hill and Samuel Wilkins. Witness Muse Tolleson and Peter Peterson. Signed Nehemiah Norton. Wit. oath Jan. 1, 1811 Muse Tolleson to A Benson. Rec. Jan. 1, 1811

p. 331-332 Jan. 4, 1811 Joshua Hareden (Spartanburgh) to Jesse Wenson (Union Dist); for $200 sold 216 ac on branch of Magney's Cr of N Pacolate R; grant to Thomas Goodaere who sold to Bartholomew Grogan who sold to Joshua Hareden. Witness David Moore and James Whitton. Signed Joshua Hareden. Wit. oath Jan. 4, 1811 David Moore to Andw Furgason. Rec. Jan. 5, 1811

p. 332-333 Jan. 4, 1811 Bartholomew Grogan to Joshua Hareden (Spartanburgh); for $100 sold 216 ac on branch of Magney's Cr of N Pacolate R; grant to Thomas Goodair who sold to Bartholomew Grogan. Witness David Moore and James Whitton. Signed Bartholomew Grogan's mark. Wit. oath Jan. 4, 1811 David Moore to Andrew Furgason. Rec. Jan. 5, 1811

p. 333-334 Aug. 1, 1806 William Harris jr (Spartanburgh) to Nathaniel Stokes (same); for $1,000 sold 673 ac on waters of N Tygar R. Witness Elisha Hadden and Jacob Hadden. Signed William Harris. Wit. oath Jan. 5, 1811 Jacob Hadden to Drury McDaniel Rec. Jan. 7, 1811

p. 334-335 May 1, 1809 Nathaniel Stokes (Spartanburgh) to Elisha Hedden (same); for $200 sold 673 ac on waters of N Tygar R. Witness Jacob Hedden and John Harris. Signed Nathl Stokes. Wit. oath Jan. 5, 1811 John Harris to Drury McDaniel. Rec. Jan. 7, 1811

p. 335-336 Apr. 1, 1807 William Dannely (Rutherford Co, NC) to Benjamin Hamet (Spartanburgh); for $600 sold (1) 60 ac on both sides Hollston's Cr; border: Henderson; grant Jan. 9, 1792 Gov. Bremar (sic) to John McGuire desc; and (2) 25 ac on both sides Holsom Cr of S Pacolate R; W side of 265 ac grant Aug. 2, 1802 to Willis Benson who sold to Robert Sloan who sold to William Dannely. Witness John Easterwood, Peter Fry, and James Ridings. Signed Wm Dannelly. Wit. oath Jan. 5, 1811 James Ridings to Andrew Furgason. Rec. Jan. 7, 1811

p. 336-337 Mar. 22, 1809 William L Allen (Spartanburgh) to Samuel Woodruff sr (same); for $200 sold 164 ac on James Cr of Tygar R; border: Nathl Woodruff and Joseph Woodruff. Witness Thomas Woodruff III, Josiah Woodruff sr and Robert Alexander. Signed Wm L Allen. Wit. oath Jan. 4, 1811 Thomas Woodruff III to John Dean. Rec. Jan. 7, 1811. Dower renounced (Laurence Dist) Mary Allen to Daniel Wright Jan. 5, 1811

p. 337-339 Aug. 17, 1810 Jesse Reams (Spartanburgh) to Shands Golightly (same); for $100 sold 555 ac; border: Brasher, Parson's Rd, Dry Pond Path, head of Lawson's fork Cr, Robert Kemble, and Ready Br; part of grant May 14, 1804 James B Richardson (SC) to Robert Kemble. Witness Robert Kemble, James Walleny, and Neddy Reams. Signed Jesse Reams. Wit. oath Nov. 6, 1810 Robert Kemble to W Lancaster. Rec. Jan. 7, 1811.

p. 339-340 Feb. 13, 1809 Nathaniel Woodruff and William L Allen (Spartanburgh) to Shands Golightly (same); for $22 sold 22 ac on branches of Jamey's Cr of Tygar R. Witness Wm Shachelford, Wm Lindsey, and James Wofford. Signed Nat Woodruff and Wm L Allen.

Wit. oath May 12, 1810 Wm Shackelford to John Brewton. Rec. Jan. 7, 1811

p. 340-341 Jan. 14, 1811 James Ward sr (Spartanburgh) to Samuel Ward and James Ward jr (same); for $40 sold 122 ac in two tracts on Fairforrest Cr: (1) 72 ac border: Benson, Tan trough Br, Walden, and Allison; (2) 50 ac adjoining (1) border: Thomson Fauset, Benson, and Ward. Witness John Lancaster and John Ward. Signed James Ward sr's mark. Wit. oath Jan. 14, 1811 John Lancaster to Jno H Jones. Rec. Jan. 14, 1811

p. 341-342 Oct. 25, 1810 Solomon Ward (Spartanburgh) to James Ward sr (same); for $50 sold 122 ac in two tracts on Fairforrest Cr: (1) 72 ac border: Benson, Tan trough Br, Walden, and Allison; and (2) 50 ac border: Thompson Fauset, Benson, and Ward. Witness Muse Tolleson and Henry Brown. Signed Solomon Ward's mark. Wit. oath Nov. 2, 1810 Muse Tolleson to D. J. Puckett. Rec. Jan. 14, 1811

p. 342-343 Jan. 5, 1811 William Smith and George Brewton (Spartanburgh), executors of will (dated Feb. 9, 1796) of Samuel Morrow (late of Spartanburgh) to Samuel Morrow jr (same); for 61£ sold 180 ac on Popular Br of Dutchman's Cr; where Samuel Morrow lived; Samuel Morrow sr died May 13, 1796 and will was proved Jul. 18, 1796 and executors qualified Aug. 10, 1796. Witness William N Morrow and Isaac Smith. Signed Wm Smith and George Brewton. Wit. oath Jan. 15, 1811 William N Morrow to Danl White. Rec. Jan. 15, 1811

p. 343-344 Nov. 7(?), 1808 Daniel McClaren (Spartanburgh) to Joseph Gist esq (Union Dist); for $50 sold (1) 300 ac; border: Cantrell and William Abbott; and (2) 100 ac; border: "the battle-ground", Scruggs, Hainey, Earl, and Williams; "including land sold Wilson Nesbett". Witness John Brown and Wilson Nesbett. Signed Daniel McClaren. Wit. oath Jan. 15, 1811 Wilson Nesbett to A Benson. Rec. Jan. 15, 1811

p. 344-345 Mar. 17, 1810 Jason Moore (Spartanburgh) to Samuel Moore (same); for $200 sold 50 ac on Ward's Cr; border: a waggon road; E part of grant May 4, 1775 to William Paden. Witness Zephaniah Posey and Jason Moore. Signed Jason Moore. Wit. oath Oct. 9, 1810 Zephaniah Posey to John Collins. Rec. Jan. 15, 1811

p. 345-347 Dec. 27, 1810 Samuel Colley (Spartanburgh) to Patrick Hoy (same); for $400 sold 166 ac on S side of S Tygar R; border: S-Peter Bragg, W-Wm Cook, and N-James Otts. Witness John Means, James Otts, and William Cook. Signed Samuel Cooley's mark. Wit. oath Dec. 31, 1810 William Cook to John Brewton. Rec. Jan. 15, 1811

p. 347-348 Dec. 31, 1810 William Cook (Spartanburgh) to Patrick Hoy (same); for $107 sold 80 ac on waters of S Tygar R; part of grant to Thomas Hightower. Witness Elijah McMillin and Robert Scott. Signed William Cook. Wit. oath Dec. 31, 1810 Elijah McMillin to John Brewton. Rec. Jan. 15, 1811

p. 348-349 Jan. 2, 1811 Joseph Woodruff sr (Spartanburgh) to John Woodruff (same); for $37 sold 2 cows and 3 yearlings, a sow and 3 shoats, 2 beds and furniture, 2 dishes and 7 pewter plates, 4 knives anf forks, 3 pots, an oven, 3 hoes, 3 axes, a matock, a framnell(?), a hand saw, a drawing knife, 4 chisels, 3 water vessels, a cotton wheel, 2 pair cotton cards, a hammer, an iron wedge, 4 barrels of corn, a stack of oats, 5 chairs, and 3 books; Condition: sale void if Joseph pays debt due to Archibald Young, merchant, (Laurence Dist) dated Dec. 27, 1810 for $25.22

for which John is security and $13 Joseph owes John and (total?) $35.25 Joseph owes John; all to be paid by Dec. 25, 1811 with interest. Witness George Leatherwood and William Shands. Signed Joseph Woodruff's mark. Wit. oath Jan. 2, 1811 William Shands to John Brewton. Rec. Jan. 2, 1811

p. 349-350 Jan. 15, 1811 Elizabeth Rainey (Spartanburgh) to son Uriah Rainey (same); for love and affection give a heifer cow of a "peard" (?) color, a more colt (sic), a feather bed and straw bed and bedstead and all furniture of bed, a black walnut chest, a pine chest, a large spinning wheel, a pair of cotton cards, a set of tea ware--a tea pot, 6 cups and sausers, a tea canister, a sugar box and tea spoons, 4 chairs, 7 earthen plates, a large earthen dish and a small kettle. Witness Jenny Rainey and J. W. Farrow. Signed Elizabeth Rainey's mark. Wit. oath Jan. 16, 1811 J. W. Farrow to A Benson. Rec. Jan. 16, 1811

p. 350-351 Jul. 19, 1809 John McKie to Robert Akin; for $500 sold 886 ac in two tracts on Proctor's fork of People's Cr: (1) 350 ac granted Dec. 8, 1774 to William Copeland "as county land"; and (2) 536 ac; border: Copeland; grant May 5, 1806 to John McKie. Witness Zacheriah Cooper and Margaret Camp. Signed Joseph Camp, agent for John McKie. Wit. oath Jan. 14, 1811 Zacheriah Cooper to John Lipscomb. Rec. Jan. 17, 1811

p. 351-352 Dec. 27, 1800 William Jones (Abbeville Co) to William Rickmon (Spartanburgh); for 18£ sterling sold 300 ac on People's Cr of Broad R; border: all vacant. Witness David Sloan and Henry Ledbetter. Signed William Jones' mark. Wit. oath May 11, 1801 (Pendleton Dist) Henry Ledbetter to John Vernon. Rec. Jan. 21, 1811

p. 352-353 Jan. 20, 1810 John Dodd (Spartanburgh) to Joseph Davis (same); for $350 sold 140 ac in two parts: (1) (ac not given) on both sides S Pacolate R; border: a waggon road; and (2) "a small piece"; border: James Ridings and former tract of John Henry; includes house where John Henry lived; part of 640 ac grant Feb. 3, 1775 to Mathew Harper sr. Witness Rice F Ross and David Moore. Signed John Dodd. Wit. oath Jun. 23, 1810 David Moore to Andw Furgason. Rec. Jan. 25, 1811

p. 353-354Jan. 12, 1807 Alfred S. E. Elkin (Spartanburgh) to Joseph Davis (Greenville Dist); for $350 sold (1) 318 ac on both sides of S Pacolate R; grant Jun. 5, 1786 to John McEube (or McEulre) sr; and (2) (ac not given); grant in 1800 Gov. John Drayton to Henry Young. Witness John B. E. Elkin, William Harris, and Abner Underwood. Signed A. S. E. Elkin. Wit. oath May 15, 1807 Abner Underwood to Daniel Wilbanks. Rec. Jan. 25, 1811

p. 354-355 Oct. 31, 1809 Charles Dean (Spartanburgh) to Benjamin Dun (SC); for $175 sold 97 ac on N side of Enoree R; border: Pike, an old road, and Benjamin Dun; part of grant to Benjamin Kilgore jr. Witness Nathaniel Davis and Sally Davis. Signed Charles Dean. Wit. oath Feb. 24, 1810 (Greenville Dist) Nathaniel Davis to P Hudson. Rec. Jan. 26, 1811. Dower renounced (Greenville Dist) Margaret Dean to Pleasant Hudson Feb. 24, 1810

p. 355-359 Jan. 1, 1810 Vincent Simmons (Spartanburgh) to Thomas Allison (same); for #22 sold 161 ac (sic) on Fairforrest Cr of Tygar R; in two tracts: (1) 67 ac granted Gov. William Moultrie to Thomas Brooks; and (2) 39 ac granted Gov. Paul Hamilton to Vincent Simmons; and sold 50 ac; part of grant to R Harrison; plat attached shows on Court House Road; plat dated Dec. 12, 1809 and signed Wm Ross Smith DS. Witness Isham Harrison, Thomas Wells, and Abner Benson. Signed Vinson Simmons. Wit. oath Jan. 26, 1811 Abner

Benson to John Gossett. Rec. Jan. 26, 1811. Dower renounced Elizabeth Simmons to D. J. Puckett Jan. 9, 1810

p. 359-360 Nov. 29, 1810 Marshal Piper (Spartanburgh) to Joseph Lanam (or Lanham) (same); for $500 sold 165 ac on both sides Ward's Cr of Tygar R; border: S & E-Jane Thomson, N-Jason Moore and Josiah Hatchet, W & S-William Moore, and S-John Otts and George Floyd. Witness Lewis Furguson, Ignatus Tweley, and Lawson Thomson. Signed Marshal Piper. Wit. oath Feb. 4, 1811 Lawson Thomson to John Collins. Rec. Feb. 4, 1811

p. 360-362 Jan. 30, 1811 Duglas J Puckett (Spartan Dist) to Muse Tolleson (same); for $350 sold 361½ ac; border: Wm Shaw, road from Spartanville to A Foster's, and Thomas Allison; part of 741 ac grant Jan. 6, 1794 to Isham Harrison who sold to Duglas J Puckett; if Muse is sued about the land, he is to give Duglas notice so Duglas can defend Muse. Witness Vincent Bennett and Jesse Cleveland. Signed D. J. Puckett. Wit. oath Feb. 8, 1811 Vincent Bennett to John Gossett. Rec. Feb. 8, 1811. Dower renounced Precella Puckett to John Gossett Feb. 8, 1811

p. 362-363 Jan. 2, 1807 Ephraim Story (Spartanburgh) to Benjamin Wooton (same); for $30 sold 40 ac on N side of Dutchman's Cr; border: William Prewett desc, Nathaniel Wooton, Charles Holt's old line, and Samuel Prewett; part of grant to Dudley Wooton. Witness Osburn West and James Hewett. Signed Ephraim Story's mark. Wit. oath Mar. 17, 1807 Osburn West to Samuel Lancaster. Rec. Feb. 9, 1811

p. 363-364 Apr. 9, 1804 Jesse Story (Spartanburgh) to Ephraim Story (same); for $35 sold 40 ac; border: William Prewett desc, Nathaniel Wotton, Charles Holt's old line, and Samuel Prewett; part of grant to Dudly Wolton (sic). Witness John Grist and James K Benson. Signed Jesse Story's mark. Wit. oath Dec. 7, 1805 James K Benson to Andrew Trarrence. Rec. Feb. 9, 1811

p. 364-365 Jan. 3, 1811 James Sarratt (Spartanburgh) to Richard Hewett (same); for $85 sold 70 ac on both sides of Ephraim Hill's Still House Br; border: Ephraim Hill; part of grant Jan. 5, 1789 to John Gray who sold Dec. 5(?), 1805 to William Burton who sold Feb. 15, 1806 to Samuel Smith who sold Jan. 19, 1807 to James Sarratt. Witness George T Sloan and Ezekiah Burrell. Signed James Sarratt's mark. Wit. oath Jan. 3, 1811 George T Sloan to Samuel Morrow. Rec. Feb. 13, 1811. Dower renounced Patsy Sarratt to Samuel Morrow Feb. 8, 1811

p. 365-367 Feb. 9, 1808 John Smith and wife Lettice to William Laurence jr (Spartanburgh); for 20£ sold 100 ac; border: Joel Smith (now Palmer's), head of John OShields' Spring Br, and John OShields; grant Mar. 2, 1789 to George Newmon. Witness John Hewett and Claymond Lancaster. Signed John Smith's mark. Wit. oath Feb. 9, 1808 John Hewett to Samuel Lancaster. Rec. Feb. 13, 1811

p. 367-368 Feb. (blank), 1811 John Tolleson (Spartanburgh) to Muse Tolleson (same); for $500 sold (1) 222 ac sold by Henry Brown to John Tolleson; on waters of Fairforrest Cr; (3) 102 ac sold by Edith Berry to John Tolleson; adjoins (1); on waters of Fairforrest Cr; border: Henry Brown and Reuben Daniel; and (3) 540 ac sold by Obadiah Watson to John Tolleson; on waters of Chinquepin Cr; except 63 ac claimed by Abner Benson and "a small peice" claimed by John Moorehouse (see deed Obadiah Watson to Moorehouse); adjoins Old Court House tract (see deed Samuel Miller to William Wells who sold to Obadiah Watson who sold to John Tolleson). Witness Abner Benson and John Gossett. Signed John Tolleson. Wit. oath Feb. 14, 1811 Abner Benson to John Gossett. Rec. Feb. 15, 1811

p. 368-369 Oct. 21, 1808 Zacheriah Green Cud (Spartanburgh) to John Covington (Rutherford Co, NC); for $150 sold 75 ac on Buck Cr of Pacolate R; grant Jan. 1, 1787 to Richard Saunders. Witness Archebell Nelson, John Nelson, and James Underson. Signed Zacheriah G and Elizabeth Cud's mark. Wit. oath May 17, 1801 (sic) Archebell Nelson to Leor Adcock. Rec. Feb. 15, 1811

p. 369-371 Sept. 4, 1810 Henry Freemon (Spartanburgh) to Isham Foster, sheriff; to secure a bond to Isham and his successors in office of $1,200 with $600 payable in 12 months and $600 payable in 2 years sold 266 ac on Two Mile Cr; border: Joseph Barnett, Spencer Bobert(?), and Bobo; sold by Isham Foster as property of Sampson Bobo desc for benefit of his heirs; Condition: sale void if Henry Freemon pays debt. Witness Nathaniel Rochell and Willis Bobo. Signed Henry Freemon. Wit. oath Feb. 14, 1811 Willis Bobo to M Casey. Rec. Feb. 20, 1811

p. 371-372 Sept. 4, 1810 George Robuck (Spartanburgh) to Isham Foster, sheriff; to secure notes to Isham Foster and his successors in office of $80.12 (sic) and 5 mils with $40.60 payable in 1 year and $40.60 payable in 2 years sold (total ac not given) in two tracts on Jamies Cr: (1) (ac not given) and (2) 60 ac border: John Caven, King, and Robuck; sold by Isham Foster to George Robuck by Spartanburgh Court order as property of Sampson Bobo desc for benefit of his heir; Condition: sale void if George pays the debt. Witness Nathaniel Rochell and Willis Bobo. Signed George Robuck. Wit. oath Jan. 14, 1811 Willis Bobo to M Casey. Rec. Feb. 20, 1811

p. 372-374 (date omitted) Burrell Bobo (Spartanburgh) to Isham Foster, sheriff; to secure notes to Isham and his successors in office of $110 with $55 payable in 1 year and $55 payable in 2 years sold 83 ac; land was sold by Isham Foster dut to Spartanburgh Court order as property of Sampson Bobo desc for benefit of his heirs; Condition: sale void if Burrell pays debt. Witness Nathaniel Rochell and Herbert Hawkins. Signed Burrell Bobo. Wit. oath Jan. 7, 1811 Herbert Hawkins to James Young. Rec. Feb. 20, 1811

p. 374-375 Sept. 4, 1810 William Wilder (Spartanburgh) to Isham Foster, sheriff; to secure notes to Isham and his successors in office of $150 with $75 due in 1 year and $75 due in 2 years sold 177 ac on waters of Tygar R; land sold by Isham Foster due to Spartanburgh Court order as property of Sampson Bobo desc for benefit of his heirs; Condition: sale void if William pays debt. Witness Nathaniel Rochell and Moses Casey. Signed Wm Wilder. Wit. oath Jan. 14, 1811 Moses Casey. Rec. Feb. 20, 1811

p. 375-376 Sept. 4, 1810 Nathaniel Rochell (Spartanburgh) to Isham Foster, sheriff; to secure notes to Isham and his successors in office of $160 with $80 payable in 1 year and $80 payable in 2 years sold 412 ac on waters of Tygar and Enoree Rivers; land sold by Isham Foster due to Spartanburgh Court order as property of Sampson Bobo desc for benefit of his heirs; Condition: sale void if Nathaniel pays debt. Witness Harbert Hawkins and Chaney Bobo. Signed N Rochell. Wit. oath Jan. 17, 1811 Harbert Hawkins to James Young. Rec. Feb. 20, 1811

p. 376-378 Sept. 4, 1810 Chaney Bobo (Spartanburgh) to Isham Foster, sheriff; to secure notes to Isham and his successors in office of $430 with $215 payable in 1 year and $215 payable in 2 years sold (1) 200 ac on Enoree R and (2) 375 ac on Seader Shoal Cr; border: Harmoning; sold by Isham Foster due to Spartanburgh Court Order as porperty of Sampson Bobo desc for benefit of his heirs; Condition: sale void if Chaney pays debt. Witness

Nathaniel Rochell and Willis Bobo. Signed Chaney Bobo. Wit. oath Jan. 14, 1811 Willis Bobo to M Casey. Rec. Feb. 20, 1811

p. 378-379 Dec. 13, 1809 William Patton (Spartanburgh) to Henry Golightly (same); for $300.75 sold 5 ac on waters of Dutchman's Cr; part of grant Nov. 7, 1785 to John Shands. Witness George West and Mary Golightly. Signed Wm Patton. Wit. oath Feb. 1, 1810 Mary Golightly to W Lancaster. Rec. Feb. 21, 1811

p. 379-380 Jun. 16, 1810 William Foster (Spartanburgh) to Sarah Barrot (same); for $160 sold 88 ac; border: Clabourn Johnson, Jones, and near Sarah Barrot's house; part of two grants: (1) Mar. 4, 1793 to William Ford and (2) Apr. 7, 1806 to John Dodd; on N fork of N Tygar R. Witness Henry Hutcherson and John M Collins. Signed William Foster. Wit. oath Mar. 4, 1811 Henry Hutcherson to James Young. Rec. Mar. 4, 1811

p. 380-381 Oct. 8, 1811 Daniel Wyatt (Spartanburgh) to John Old Hance (same); for $150 sold 160 ac on Ashworth Cr; border: Thomas Wyatt; part of 555 ac grant to Crenshaw Camp. Witness Samuel Haskins and Allen Sarratt. Signed Daniel Wyatt's mark. Wit. oath Oct. 8, 1810 Samuel Haskins to John Lipscomb. Rec. Mar. 4, 1811

p. 381-382 Feb. 28, 1805 Crenshaw Camp (Rutherford Co, NC) to Daniel Wyatt (Spartanburgh); for $120 sold 160 ac on Ashworth Cr; border: Thomas Wyatt; part of 555 ac grant to Crehshaw Camp. Witness George Camp esq and Thomas Wyatt. Signed Crenshaw Camp. Wit. oath Jul. 20, 1805 Thomas Wyatt to A Camp. Rec. Mar. 4, 1811

p. 382-383 Oct. 24, 1806 Huchen Forester (Spartanburgh) to Tounsen Robertson (same); for $75 sold 50 ac on branch of Buck Cr; border: Daniel Cantrell. Witness David Paris and Solomon Forrester. Signed Sut (sic) Forrest. Wit. oath Oct. 28, 1806 Solomon Forrester to Henry Turner. Rec. Mar. 4, 1811

p. 383-384 Sept. 8, 1810 Gean Henderson (Spartanburgh) to Samuel Haney (same); for $100 sold 100 ac on both sides Horse Cr of Broad R; part of 300 ac grant Jan. 1, 1787 States Office to Joseph Warren. Witness William Morrow and Ruth Morrow. Signed Gean Henderson's mark. Wit. oath Feb. 23, 1811 William Morrow and Leond Adcock. Rec. Mar. 4, 1811

p. 384 Jun. 8, 1808 John Harris (Pendleton Dist) to Townard (or Townsend) Robertson (Spartanburgh); for $50 sold 25 ac on little Buck Cr; border: Robertson and Adcock. Witness George Purtle and John Blackwell. Signed John Harris. Wit. oath John Blackwell to L Adcock Dec. 5, 1809. Rec. Mar. 4, 1811

p. 384-385 Oct. 18, 1810 Solomon Ward (Spartanburgh) to Thompson Faucet (same); for $50 sold 50 ac on Fairforrest Cr; border: the forrest. Witness Herbert Hawkins, Muse Tolleson, and Banister Hawkins. Signed Solomon and Melendy Ward's marks. Wit. oath Feb. 4, 1811 Herbert Hawkins to James Young. Rec. Mar. 4, 1811

p. 385-386 Mar. 12, 1808 George Campbell (Spartanburgh) to Samuel Fowler (same); for $40 sold 50 ac on Mollonex(?) Cr; border: John Owen, Nathen Pettet, Samuel Alexander, and Andrew Furgason. Witness John Owen and Demey Fowler. Signed George Campbell's mark. Wit. oath Mar. 2, 1811 Demey Fowler to Andrew Furgason. Rec. Mar. 4, 1811

p. 386-387 Dec. 16, 1810 Garner Self to James Seay sr; to secure notes of $50 sold a bay mare 11 years old, 2 cows, 2 fodder stacks, and 20 barrels of corn; Condition: sale void if Garner pays debt by Dec. 25, 1812. Witness Robert Benson and Henry Walden. Signed Garner Self. Wit. oath Mar. 13, 1811 Robert Benson to A Benson. Rec. Mar. 13, 1811

p. 387-388 Jan. 21, 1808 William Bandy (Spartanburgh) to David Adcock (same); for $100 sold 100 ac on S side of Buck Cr; border: Thomas Pope (or Posse), Oliver, "old road", "race paths", and Harris. Witness Leonard Adcock and Thomas Garret. Signed William Bandy's mark. Wit. oath Mar. 30, 1811 Thomas Garret to Leon Adcock. Rec. Apr. 8, 1811

p. 388-389 Dec. 22, 1806 Joseph Woods (Spartanburgh) to William Bandy (same); for $100 sold 100 ac on S side of Buck Cr; border: Thomas Pope, Oliver, old road, "rase paths", and Harris. Witness John Sutton (or Subton) jr and Thomas Garrett. Signed Joseph Woods' mark. Wit. oath Apr. 14, 1807 Thomas Garrett to L Adcock. Rec. Apr. 8, 1811

p. 389-390 Jun. 17, 1806(?) Zacheriah Arrowwood to Thomas Liles (Rutherford Co, NC); for $240 sold 240 ac on waters of Buck Cr; part of 476 ac grant to Zacheriah Arrowwood to James Smith. Witness David Lyles and James Lyles. Signed Zacheriah Arrowwood. Wit. oath Mar. 29, 1811 David Lyles to Leon Adcock. Rec. Apr, 8, 1811

p. 390-392 (blank), 1811 Absolem Roe (Spartanburgh) to Robert Belcher (same); for $70 sold 70 ac on W side Shoal Cr of Lawson's fork of Pacolate R; part of grant to John Pepes and given to daughter Sally Pepes, wife of Absolem Roe. Witness William F Piephoff and John Belcher. Signed Absolem Roe's mark. Wit. oath Apr. 9, 1811 (sic) William F Piephoff to John Gossett. Rec. Apr. 8, 1811

p. 392-393 Jun. 13, 1808 George Gilbert (Spartanburgh) to Thomas Liles (Rutherford Co, NC); for $100 sold 100 ac on waters of Buck Cr; part of grant Oct. 6, 1788 States Office to John Henderson. Witness Thomas Pope and Mashak Hall. Signed George Gilbert. Wit. oath Apr. 4, 1811 Thomas Pope to James Young. Rec. Apr. 8, 1811

p. 393-394 Jan. 22, 1807 Israel Morris (Spartanburgh) to John Morris (same); for $20 sold 30 ac on "back" Br of Buck Cr of Pacolate R; border: Greed, Joseph Morris, and John Morris. Witness Thomas Morris and Jordan Morris. Signed Israel Morris. Wit. oath Apr. 8, 1811 Jordan Morris to Henry Turner. Rec. Apr. 8, 1811

p. 394-395 Dec. 31, 1810 William Powers (Spartanburgh) to Frederick Parham (same); for $400 sold 147 ac on both sides Tygar R; border: mouth of Motley's Cr, John Robuck and wife, Joseph Power, Benjamin Grist, Drury Parham, Ridge path, Alexander Prewett, and Daniel Grant; part of two grants: (1) to Joseph Power desc and (2) to Thomas Fletcher. Witness Tilmon Bobo and Lewis Parham. Signed William Powers. Wit. oath Apr. 8, 1811 Lewis Parham to M Casey. Rec. Apr. 8, 1811

p. 395-396 Apr. 8, 1811 Isham Foster, late sheriff (Spartanburgh) to Justice Reynolds; for $10.25 sold 300 ac on waters of Lawson's fork; sale due to writ from Spartanburgh Common Pleas Court case John Gray vs Justice Reynolds; sale Nov. 5, 1810; in two tracts that were property of John Gray. Witness Herbert Hawkins and Elisha Bomar. Signed Ism Foster SSD. Wit. oath Apr. 8, 1811 Herbert Hawkins to James Young. Rec. Apr. 8, 1811

p. 396-398 Apr. 2, 1811 John Bankston (Spartanburgh) to Richard Morris (same); for $165 sold 200 ac on N side Pacolate

R; border: Mark Cantrell, Richard Morris, road from Cantrell's mill to Buck Creek Meeting House, Buck Cr, Hugh Warren's old line, John Cantrell, and John Morris; part of grant Aug. 23, 1774 States Office to Hugh Warren and part of grant Oct. 6, 1788 to Thomas Warren who sold to John Bankston. Witness John Cantrell, John Morres, and William Cantell. Signed John Bankston. Wit. oath Apr. 8, 1811 John Morres to Henry Turner. Rec. Apr. 8, 1811

p. 398-399 Apr. 2, 1811 John Bankston (Spartanburgh) to John Morris (same); for $165 sold 200 ac on N side of Pacolate R; border: John Morris, Richard Morris, John Cantrell, Abraham Cantrell, Burgess' old line, and Hugh Warren's old line; part of grant Aug. 23, 1774 States Office to Hugh Warren and Part of grant Oct. 6, 1788 to Thomas Warren and sold to John Bankston. Witness John Cantrell, Richard Morris, and William Cantrell. Signed John Bankston. Wit. oath Apr. 8, 1811 Richard Morris to Henry Turner. Rec. Apr. 8, 1811

p. 399-400 Jul. 5, 1809 Richard Thomson (Spartanburgh) to Henry Brown (same); for $85 sold ½ ac in village of Spartanburgh; border: Todd's stable and Tolleson. Witness John W Farrow and William Bostick. Signed Richard Thomson. Wit. oath Apr. 8, 1811 William Bostick to John Lipscomb. Rec. Apr. 8, 1811

p. 400-402 Nov. 13, 1809 Vincent Bennett, sheriff (Spartanburgh) to David Spears (Laurence Dist); for $50 sold 300 ac on waters of Two Mile Cr of Enoree R; where Thomas Leatherwood formerly lived; near Mountain Shoal on Enoree R; sold due to writ from Laurence Dist Common Pleas Court David Spears vs Thomas Leatherwood. Witness James Brannon and Gabriel Benson. Signed Vincent Bennett SSD. Wit. oath Apr. 8, 1811 Gabriel Benson to Drury McDaniel. Rec. Apr. 8, 1811

p. 402-403 Mar. 14, 1808 John P Poole (Spartanburgh) to Drury Couch (same); for $100 sold 50 ac; border: grant to Thomas Couch (now owned by Drury Couch) and by Thomas Stroud; part of grant to Charles Hunt and sold Sept. 23, 1796 Joseph Couch to John P Poole. Witness Aaron Casey and William Higgins. Signed John P Poole. Wit. oath Mar. 14, 1808 Aaron Casey to Burrell Bobo. Rec. Apr. 8, 1811. Dower renounced Elender Poole to Burrell Bobo Mar. 4, 1808 (sic)

p. 403-404 Oct. 14, 1808 Benjamin Rollins (Spartanburgh) to William Underwood (same); for $335 sold 109½ ac; border: Obed Roberts' old field. Witness David Lusk, Abner Rollans, and William Rollans. Signed Benjamin and Martha Rollins' mark. Wit. oath Jan. 14, 1811 William Rollans to Andw Furgason. Rec. Apr. 9, 1811

p. 404-405 Mar. 1, 1811 Jacob Chapmon (Spartanburgh) to Thomas Brannon (same); for $20 sold a bay filly "rising" 2 years old, 4 shoats marked with swallow fork in each ear and under keel in right ear--2 shoats are 16 months old and 2 about 6 or 7 months old; Condition: sale void if Jacob pays Thomas $20 by Mar. 1, 1812. Witness James Templeton and William F Piephoff. Signed Jacob Chapmon's mark. Wit. oath Apr. 9, 1811 William F Piephoff to John Gossett. Rec. Apr. 9, 1811

p. 405-406 Apr. 15, 1800 David Bruton (Spartanburgh) to James Bruton (same); for 50£ sterling sold 200 ac on Forgason's Cr of Tygar R; border: James Russell, Thomas Woodruff's Spring Br, Richard Harris, Henry Earnest, and James Wofford; part of two grants: (1) granted Oct. 23, 1756 to Robert Russell and recorded at Charleston Dec. 23, 1774 and (2) granted Nov. 7, 1785. Witness Thomas Underwood and Jaconias Langston. Signed David Bruton. Wit. oath Apr. 17, 1800 Jaconias Langston to J Bruton. Rec. Apr. 9, 1811

p. 406-408 Mar. 26, 1808 William Hase (Spartanburgh) to John Williams (same); for $250 sold (1) 257 ac on branch of Dutchman's Cr of Tygar R; border: Samuel Morrow; grant Jan. 21, 1785 to Ephraim Hill; and (2) 130 ac adjoining (1); border: Herum Herrelson; part of grant Mar. 25, 1790 to Ephraim Hill. Witness Samuel Burton and John Beard. Signed William Hase. Wit. oath Mar. 26, 1808 Samuel Burton to Samuel Lancaster. Rec. Apr. 9, 1811

p. 408-409 Dec. 8, 1807 John Beard (Spartanburgh) to John Williams (same); for $480 sold 200 ac on both sides Cain Cr of Tygar R; grant Aug. 2, 1781 Gov. William Moultrie to John Butler. Witness John Rodgers and Arthur Faulkner. Signed John Beard. Wit. oath Jan. 2, 1808 John Rodgers to William Lancaster. Rec. Apr. 9, 1811. Dower renounced Mary Beard to William Lancaster Jan. 2, 1808

p. 409-410 Jan. 19, 1811 James Ridings (Spartanburgh) to Robert Young (same); for $250 sold 350 ac on both sides Alect (or Alep?) Cr; border: Davis; part of four surveys. Witness James Whitten, Thomas Penney, and John Ridings. Signed James and Charety Ridings' marks. Wit. oath Apr. 5, 1811 James Whitten to Andw Furgason. Rec. Apr. 9, 1811

p. 410-411 Nov. 7, 1810 Mathew Harper (Smith Co, Tenn), executor of estate of Robert Harper, to Golden Tinsley (Spartanburgh); for $400 sold 240 ac; where Robert Harper desc formerly lived; border: Whitten, Molley's Cr, and S Pacolate. Witness Lemuel Stokes and James Whitten. Signed Mathew Harper. Wit. oath Mar. 6, 1811 James Whitten to Andrew Furgason. Rec. Apr. 9, 1811

p. 411-412 Nov. 9, 1804 Henry Young sr (Spartanburgh) to Robert Young (same); for $200 sold 100 ac on Meadow Cr of S Pacolate R; border: Benson, Gilbert, and McDaniel. Witness Jesse Dalton, Andrew Venable, and Samuel Venable. Signed Henry Young. Wit. oath Jun. 13, 1809 Jesse Dalton to Wm Kelso. Rec. Apr. 9, 1811

p. 412-413 Nov. 29, 1810 Golden Tinsley (Spartanburgh) to James Ridings (same); for $400 sold 240 ac; border: Whitten and S Pacolate R. Witness James Whitten, John Ridings, and Franklen Foster. Signed Golden Tinsly. Wit. oath Mar. 16, 1811 James Whitten to Andw Furgason. Rec. Apr. 9, 1811

p. 413-415 Sept. 18, 1806 John Lindsey sr (Spartanburgh) to Samuel Woodruff sr (same); for $500 sold 200 ac; border: William Castelberry, Amos Bryat, Woodruff Spring Br, and Two Mile Cr; NW part of grant Jan. 25, 1785 Gov. Benjamin Guerard to John Ford sr (?). Witness Wm L Allen, Samuel Woodruff, and Thomas Woodruff III. Signed John Lindsey sr. Wit. oath Nov. 16, 1810 Wm L Allen to Drury McDaniel. Rec. Apr. 9, 1811. Dower renounced Jemema Lindsey to Drury McDaniel Feb. 16, 1811

p. 415-416 Oct. 19, 1810 Thomas House (Spartanburgh) to Jacob Cooper (Laurence Dist); for $300 sold 130 ac on N side Enoree R; part of two grants: (1) to Thomas Childres and (2) to Robert Cooper; border: John Hamby's Spring Br. Witness Nancy Wright and John Wright. Signed Thomas House's mark. Wit. oath Oct. 19, 1810 John Wright to Danl Wright. Rec. Apr. 9, 1811. Dower renounced (Laurence Dist) Milley House to Daniel Wright Oct. 19, 1810

p. 416-417 Mar. 25, 1811 Margaret Blackwood (Spartanburgh) to Isabella Blackwood (same); for love and affection give a Negro boy Sam. Witness George Welch, Thomas Millican, and Jean Murckle. Signed Margaret Blackwood. Wit. oath Apr. 5, 1811 George Welch to Wm Kelso. Rec. Apr. 10, 1811

p. 417-419 Feb. 17, 1810 George Isom (Tenn) to Charles Gravell (Spartanburgh); for $225 sold 50 ac on Furgason Cr; border: Thomas Price and George Brewton. Witness Mathew Patton, David McCarley, and James Isom. Signed George Isom. Wit. oath Nov. 6, 1810 Mathew Patton to Drury McDaniel. Rec. Apr. 10, 1811

p. 419 Mar. 25, 1811 Margaret Blackwood (Spartanburgh) to daughter Ann Blackwood (same); for love and affection give a Negro woman Poll. Witness George Welch, Thomas Millican, and Jean Muckle. Signed Margaret Blackwood's mark. Wit. oath Apr. 5, 1811 George Welch to Wm Kelso. Rec. Apr. 11, 1811

p. 419-421 Mar. 21, 1811 John Underwood (Spartanburgh) to Jacob Utley (same); for 50£ sterling sold 250 ac on S side of Fairforrest Cr; border: Wm Benson, Widow White, and James Ward; where John Underwood use to live. Witness William Underwood and Micajah Barnett. Signed John Underwood. Wit. oath Mar. 21, 1811 William Underwood to Danl White. Rec. Apr. 12, 1811

p. 421-422 Mar. 5, 1811 Isham Foster (Spartanburgh) to Herbert Hawkins (same); for $300 sold 42 ac at head of Fairforrest Cr and on NE side of road from Maj William Foster to John Wingo's; border: Prince's old road; original survey by Gabriel Benson. Witness Edward Clement and Thomas Burton. Signed Ism Foster. Wit. oath Apr. 9, 1811 Edward Clement to John Lipscomb. Rec. Apr. 16, 1811

p. 422-423 Mar. 8, 1811 James Bright (Spartanburgh) to Bridget Bright (same); for $150 sold 50 ac on S Tygar R; border: Jacob Bright and Bridget Bright. Witness Page Rork and James Staggs. Signed James Bright. Wit. oath Apr. 6, 1811 James Staggs to John Collins. Rec. May 6, 1811

p. 423-424 Mar. 8, 1811 James Bright (Spartanburgh) to Charety Bright (same); for $150 sold 50 ac on S Tygar R; where Charety Bright lives. Witness Page Rork and James Staggs. Signed James Bright. Wit. oath Apr. 6, 1811 James Staggs to John Collins. Rec. May 6, 1811

p. 424-425 Nov. 30, 1810 Willis Allen (Spartanburgh) to James Campbell (same); for $320 sold 165 ac on S branch of Goucher's Cr; border: on S side of creek--William Roberson and Griffin Carter and on N side of Cr--Thomas Red, Jarret Patterson and others; sold by Jarret Patterson to Willis Allen. Witness Smith Lipscomb and Amos Austell. Signed Willis Allen's mark. Wit. oath Dec. 11, 1810 Smith Lipscomb to John Lipscomb. Rec. May 16, 1811. Dower renounced Sally Allen to John Lipscomb Jan. 12, 1811

p. 425-426 May 21, 1811 Shands Golightly (Spartanburgh) to Henry Golightly (same); for $10 sold 3 ac on waters of Kelso's Cr; part of grant to John Golightly; border: Henry Golightly. Witness Ephraim Roddy and Muse Tolleson. Signed Shands Golightly. Wit. oath May 22, 1811 Ephraim Roddy to A Benson. Rec. May 22, 1811

p. 426-427 Jan. 22, 1811 Andrew Ray (Spartanburgh) to William Garrett (same); for $11 sold 11 ac on both sides of Cass Cr of Pacolate R. Witness John Ray and Andrew Ray jr. Signed Andrew Ray. Wit. oath Jan. 22, 1811 John Ray to Henry Turner. Rec. May 27, 1811

p. 427-429 Jun. 3, 1811 Hancock Smith (Spartanburgh) to Mary, Elizabeth, Thomas, and Margaret Dezell (same); for $70 sold 85 ac on waters of Kelso's Cr of Fairforrest Cr; border: N-Micajah Barnett, S-Shands Golightly, and SE-David Golightly jr; includes improvements where "they" live. Witness Allen Lancaster and William

Lancaster. Signed Hancock Smith. Wit. oath Jun. 3, 1811 William Lancaster to William Read. Rec. Jun. 3, 1811

p. 429-430 Dec. 3, 1801 Silus Williams to Elihu Golightly (Spartanburgh); for $90 sold 100 ac on branches of Ford's Cr; border: Hurt, Golightly, waggon road, Duncan, and Beaver. Witness John Golightly sr and John Golightly jr. Signed Silus Williams. Wit. oath Jun. 3, 1811 John Golightly sr to A Benson. Rec. Jun. 3, 1811

p. 430-431 Aug. 31, 1810 John Hughes (Spartanburgh) to Samuel Miller (same); for $200 sold 43 ac on S side of N Tygar R and on Hughes Br; border: James Paden, Andw Berry, and William McDaniel. Witness James Hughes, Samuel Miller, and Rebeca Stafford. Signed John Hughes. Wit. oath Aug. 31, 1810 Samuel Miller to Drury McDaniel. Rec. Jun. 3, 1811. Dower renounced Sally Hughes to Drury McDaniel Sept. 6, 1810

p. 431-432 Aug. 31, 1810 James Hughes (Spartanburgh) to Samuel Miller (same); for $200 sold 100 ac between S and Middle Tygar R; border: James Miller and William McDaniel; part of 150(?) ac grant to James Hughes. Witness John Hughes, Samuel Miller BS, and Rebeca Stafford. Signed James Hughes. Wit. oath Aug. 31, 1810 John Hughes to Drury McDaniel. Rec. Jun. 3, 1811. Dower renounced Ann Hughes to Drury McDaniel Sept. 6, 1810

p. 432-434 Mar. 17, 1811 William Johnson, Roland Johnson, and John Wood (Spartanburgh) to Robert Foster (same); for $200 sold 267 ac; border: Joel Lewis and Elizabeth Bishop. Witness Fielding Foster, John Wood, and William Johnson. Signed Wm Johnson, Roaland Johnson, and John Wood. Wit. oath Jun. 3, 1811 Fielding Foster to James Young. Rec. Jun. 3, 1811

p. 434 Oct. 23, 1810 (Nachitoches Parish, Orleans Terr) James P Harrison (Nachitoches Par.) to Richard Harrison (Greenville Dist); power of attorney to sell his share of estate of Richard Harrison desc; land is on S side Fairforrest Cr; and to collect debts due him. Witness none. Signed James P Harrison. Wit. oath Oct. 23, 1810 James P Harrison to John C Carr, judge of Nachitoches Parrish. Rec. Jun. 3, 1811

p. 434-436 Dec. 26, 1810 Richard Harrison (Greenville Dist) to James Seay (Spartanburgh); for $300 sold 157 ac on S side of Fairforrest Cr; border: Walden's old line, Ward, Tinsley, Reuben Daniel; part of estate of Richard Harrison desc alloted to James Harrison, legate of estate; see "general plan" of plat made by James Smith desc. Witness Vincent (or Vinson) Simmons and Sophia Daniel. Signed Richard Harrison. Wit. oath Jun. 3, 1811 Vincent Simmons to A Benson. Rec. Jun. 3, 1811

p. 436-437 Dec. 17, 1810 Thomas Tinsley (Spartanburgh) to John Cook (same); for $60 sold (ac not given) on waters of Fairforrest Cr; border: N & W-Thomas Tinsley, S-Barnett, and E-Cook. Witness Robert Martin and Thomas James. Signed Tho Tinsley. Wit. oath May 17, 1811 Thomas James to Daniel White. Rec. Jun. 3, 1811

p. 437-438 Jan. 10, 1811 Richard Barnett (Spartanburgh) to James Cook (same); for $203 sold 3/4 ac and 36 poles on Fairforrest Cr; part of where Richard Barnett lives. Witness Daniel White and Laurence Hoots. Signed Richard Barnett. Wit. oath Jun. 3, 1811 Daniel White to William Reid. Rec. Jun. 3, 1811

p. 438-439 Feb. 25, 1811 Elisha James (Spartanburgh) to Robert Martin (same); for $30 sold 80 ac on S side of Fairforrest Cr; border: John Smith, James Fleming, and Tate; grant Aug. 1, 1785

Gov. William Moultrie to Charles Bruce. Witness James Barnett and Charles James jr. Signed Elisha James. Wit. oath Jun. 2, 1811 James Barnett to Danl White. Rec. Jun. 3, 1811

p. 439-440 Dec. 10, 1810 James Adams (Spartanburgh) to John Trail (same); for $100 sold 100 ac on waters of Dutchman's Cr; border: Thomas Rees; part of 200 ac grant Jul. 1, 1793 Gov. William Moultrie to William Lancaster. Witness Daniel Smith and Robert Page. Signed James Adams. Wit. oath Feb. 18, 1811 Daniel Smith to Samuel Morrow. Rec. Jun. 11, 1811. Dower renounced Catherine Adams to Samuel Morrow Jan. 13, 1811

p. 440-441 Feb. 20, 1802 Jesse Hammett (Spartanburgh) to William Adams (same); for $75 sold 100 ac on waters of Dutchman's Cr; border: land Jesse Hammett sold to Thomas Rees; part of grant Jul. 1, 1793 Gov. William Moultrie to William Lancaster. Witness Thomas Adams, Pricilla White, and James Adams. Signed Jesse Hammett. Wit. oath Aug. 7, 1802 Thomas Adams to I Harrison. Rec. Jun. 11, 1811

p. 441-442 Aug. 28, 1810 William Adams (Spartanburgh) to James Adams (same); for $75 sold 100 ac on waters of Dutchman's Cr; border: land William Adams sold to Thomas Rees; part of 200 ac grant Jul. 1, 1793 Gov. William Moultrie to William Lancaster. Witness David Trail and John Trail. Signed William Adams' mark. Wit. oath Jan. 23, 1811 John Trail to Samuel Morrow. Rec. Jun. 11, 1811

Book N 1811-1813

p. 1-3 Dec. 23, 1810 Duglas J Puckett (Spartanburgh) to Thomas Allison (same); for $380 sold 155 ac on E side Spartanburgh Court House on waters of Fairforrest Cr; border: a black on S side of road from Spartanburgh to Anthony Foster, William Shaw, and William Robertson; lower end of D. J. Puckett's land; part of grant Jan. 6, 1794 to Isham Harrison; plat attached for 186 ac including 31.3 ac taken by Wm Shaw's line leaving 154.7 ac. Witness Abner Benson and Walter Carrult. Signed D. J. Puckett. Wit. oath Jan. 26, 1811 Abner Benson to John Gosset. Rec. Jan. 26, 1811. Dower renounced Priscilla L Puckett to Drury McDaniel Jan. 10, 1810

p. 3-5 Feb. 19, 1811 Duglas Josephus Puckett (Spartanburgh) to Jesse Cleveland and Enoch Berry Benson (same); for $200 sold lots 8 and 9 of ½ ac each in village of Spartanburgh; border: E-Gabriel Benson, N & W-Richard Thompson, and S-Main St. Witness Charles McAbee and John P Benson. Signed D. J. Puckett. Wit. oath Feb. 26, 1811 John P Benson to John Gossett. Rec. Feb. 28, 1811. Dower renounced Priscilla L Puckett to John Gossett Feb. 26, 1811

p. 5-6 Feb. 12, 1811 James Rulley (Spartanburgh) to Henry Golightly (same); for #2 sold 204 ac on Fairforrest and Kelso's Creeks; border: Golightly and Handcock Smith's old line. Witness William Lancaster, Thomas Cook, and Moses Foster. Signed James Rulley. Wit. oath Feb. 27, 1811 Moses Foster to Samuel Morrow. Rec. Mar. 14, 1811. Dower renounced Mary Rulley to Samuel Morrow Feb. 27, 1811

p. 6-7 Oct. 29, 1810 John Duncan (Spartanburgh) to James Cook (same); for $200 sold 85 ac on Ford's Cr of Fairforrest Cr; border: N-Silus Williams and W-Frances Mason; sold by Nathan and George Wright to John Duncan. Witness Elizabeth Otts and Philip Otts. Signed John Duncan. Wit. oath Mar. 15, 1811 Philip Otts to Danl White. Rec. Mar. 16, 1811

p. 7-8 Sept. 24, 1808 George McWilliams (Spartanburgh) to James Young (same); for 5s sold 50 ac; border: Nathaniel McCarrell,

Obed's Cr, James Young, and Robert Wall. Witness Robert McDowell and John F Knight. Signed George McWilliams. Wit. oath Feb. 20, 1809 Robert McDowell to Wm Kelso. Rec. Mar. 18, 1811

p. 8-9 (blank), 1809 John Arnold (Spartanburgh) to Richard Shackelford (same); for $300 sold 150 (or 158) ac on N side Enoree R; border: part of same tract "laid off for" John Allen and by Wm Stone. Witness Richard Shackelford, James Arnold, and William Arnold. Signed John Arnold. Wit. oath Jan. 13, 1800 (sic) James Arnold to John Brewton. Rec. Apr. 1, 1811

p. 9-10 Oct. 15, 1793 Frances Marion (St John Parish, Berkley Co) to John Young (Spartanburgh); for (money omitted) sold 78 ac; border: on S side of S Pacolate R, S-Benjamin Clark, and W-John Young; part of grant to Peter Vedian and bequeathed to Mary Easter Marion, "present" wife of Frances Marion. Witness James Dillingham and John Daniel. Signed Frances Marion and Mary E Marion. Wit. oath Jan. 21, 1800 James Dillingham to William McDowell. Rec. Apr. 1, 1811

p. 10-11 Mar. 17, 1809 Zacheriah Green Cud (Spartanburgh) to Jonathan Green (same); for $50 sold 75 ac on Buck Cr of Pacolate R; part of grant Jan. 1, 1787 to Richard Saunders; border: Saunders and Greed. Witness John Covington and Hannah Crumly. Signed Zacheriah Green Cud's mark. Wit. oath Mar. 27, 1811 John Covington to Leon Adcock. Rec. Apr. 1, 1811

p. 11-13 Mar. 2, 1811 John Robnett and Margaret Bell Robnett (Spartanburgh) to John Ison sr (Union Dist); for $350 sold 175 ac; where "we" live; border: John Tolleson, Stephen Crew, Simpson, James Nesbett, and John Ison; part of 350 ac grant to Joseph Nesbett; plat attached shows border: John Ison, W. T. Simpson, and James Nesbett. Witness Daniel Wilbanks, John Ison jr, and Elizabeth Eison (or Ison). Signed John and Margaret B Robenett. Wit. oath (not dated) John Ison jr to John Gossett. Rec. Apr. 1, 1811

p. 13-14 Oct. 10, 1809 Samuel Woodruff III (Spartanburgh) to Richard Shackelford (same); for $200 sold 100 ac on N side Delden Cr; part of grant Jul. 10, 1769 Gov. Charles Granville to William Sims. Witness Wm Shackelford and John Arnold. Signed Samuel Woodruff. Wit. oath Jan. 13, 1810 Wm Shackelford to John Brewton. Rec. Apr. 1, 1811. Dower renounced Polly Woodruff to Daniel Wright Oct. 15, 1810

p. 14-15 Apr. 1, 1811 Robert Belcher (Spartanburgh) to son Jacob Belcher (same); "make over by bill of sale" 70 ac on Sholey Cr, a mair, 6 cattle, 10 sheep, 12 hogs, 3 feather beds and their furniture, 2 pots, 2 dutch ovens, 2 plows, 2 cratters(?), 4 axes, 5 weeding hoes, 2 sythes and craddles, all household furniture, 4 barrels of corn, 3 bedsteads, a blade stack, all his fodder, and all other things he possesses. Witness George Carruth and Banister Hawkins. Signed Robert Belcher's mark. Wit. oath Apr. 1, 1811 Banister Hawkins to A Benson. Rec. Apr. 1, 1811

p. 15-17 Sept. 12, 1810 Isham Foster, sheriff (Spartanburgh) to Henry Brown; for $22.50 sold 300 ac on waters of Pacolate R; sale due to writ from Spartanburgh Common Pleas Court suit Robert A Todd vs John Noland and James Carter. Witness D. J. Puckett and Herbert Hawkins. Signed Ism Foster SSD. Wit. oath Oct. 23, 1810 Herbert Hawkins to D. J. Puckett. Rec. Apr. 3, 1811

p. 17-18 Dec. 28, 1810 William Moore (Spartanburgh) to Samuel Burton (same); for $200 sold 200 ac in forks of N and S Tygar Rivers; border: Patton. Witness Samuel Moore and Ansel Hudings. Signed William Moore. Wit. oath Jul. 1, 1811 Samuel Moore to Drury

McDaniel. Rec. Jul. 1, 1811

p. 18-19 May 4, 1811 Samuel Culbertson (Spartanburgh) to Obediah Wingo (same); for $700 sold 341 ac on Dugan's Br of Fair-forrest Cr; where Samuel Culbertson lives; opposite Antioch Meeting House; border: O'Neill's Br, N-Hamilton Wilson and Willis Wingo, S-Joseph Kelso and David Johnson, E-Joseph Kelso and Willis Wingo, and W-Henry O'Neill. Witness Willis Wingo and William Lnacaster. Signed Saml Culbertson. Wit. oath Jul. 1, 1811 William Lancaster to Danl White. Rec. Jul. 1, 1811. Dower renounced Jun. 3, 1811 Sully Culbertson to James Young.

p. 19-21 Mar. 1, 1811 John Brown (Spartanburgh) to William Graham (Rutherford Co, NC); for $1,600 sold 999 ac on Sarratt's Cr of Broad R; grant to John Rickman who sold to Daniel McClaren who sold to John Brown; deed warranted May 2, 1811 by William Brown (Spartanburgh) and witnessed by Joseph Camp and Wilson Nesbett. Witness Robert Byars and Jonas Byars. Signed John Brown. Wit. oath May 22, 1811 Robert Byars to Joshua Richards. Rec. Jul. 12, 1811. Dower renounced Mar. 15, 1811 Roseannah Brown to John Lipscomb

p. 21-22 Mar. 3, 1811 John Robnett (Spartanburgh) to John Ison jr (same); for $200 or $300 sold 160 ac on Pacolate R. Witness Michael Loverender, Peggy Eison, and Wielt Bullard. Signed John and Margaret B. Robnett. Wit. oath Mar. 12, 1811 Wielt Bullard to John Gossett. Rec. Apr. 1, 1811. Dower renounced Mar. 12, 1811 Margaret B. Robnett to John Gossett

p. 22-24 Mar. 3, 1806 Isham Harrison, sheriff (Spartanburgh) to John Tollison (same); for $9.12 and 5 mills sold 93 ac on branches of Pacolate R; border: NE & SE-David Allen, SW-Howard, NW-Thomson; grant to George Murfed who sold to William Wells and company; sale due to writ from Spartanburgh Common Pleas Court suit Felix Warley vs William Wells. Witness Jacob Utley, Robert A Todd, and Thomas Lancaster. Signed I Harrison SSD. Wit. oath Mar. 6, 1810 Robert A Todd to A Benson. Rec. Jun. 15, 1811

p. 24-25 Jun. 22, 1811 James Burton to William Moore; "for value received" sold a bed and furniture, plates, knives, and forks, cups and saucers, a table, a coffee pot, a skillet, 150 sides of leather, 2 heiffers, a saddle and bridle and blanket, and a "riffle" gun. Witness James Brannon. Signed James Burton. Wit. oath Jul. 25, 1811 James Brannon to A Benson. Rec. Jul. 25, 1811

p. 25-26 Mar. 1, 1811 James Smith (Spartanburgh) to John Tolleson (same); for $100 sold 104 ac on both sides Big Br of Island Cr of Pacolate R; includes two dwelling houses; where John Reec lives; border: Abraham Markley's old line and William Murry; plat attached shows border: Abraham Markley and Smith and two 100 ac\tracts sold by Markely to Reece; part of grant Apr. 6, 1801 to James Smith. Witness Elisha Smith, Hancock Smith, Susanna Smith, and Lettice Smith. Signed Jas Smith. Wit. oath Jul. 24, 1811 Hancock Smith to A Benson. Rec. Jul. 24, 1811

p. 26-28 Apr. 11, 1811 Adam Kilby (Spartanburgh) to James White, Peter Hawkins, John Bishop, John Foster, and Edmond Clement, trustees (all Spartanburgh); for $1 spece sold 3 ac to build a house of worship for members of Methodist Episcopal Church in USA according to rules of the church general conference and hire a preacher; successors to trustees are to be members of the church one year and 21 years old and elected by majority of church members with minister breaking tie votes. Witness Venson (or Vincent) Simmons and James White. Signed Adam Kilby's mark. Wit. oath Aug. 5, 1811 Venson Simmons to Thos Poole. Rec. Aug. 5, 1811

p. 28-30 Jun. 19, 1810 George Poole (Rutherford Co, NC) to Samuel Gilbert (Spartanburgh); for $100 sold 250 ac on Casy Cr of Thomson Cr of Pacolate R; border: Samuel Sentell (formerly Joseph Venable), Mark Gilbert, William Canter, Thomas Kimboll, Suffiah's Br, and Gore; sold by John Lee to George Poole; except "parts" George has already sold to Mark Gilbert and Thomas Kimboll and company. Witness Edmond Bishop, Mark Gilbert, and Garves Gilbert. Signed George Pool. Wit. oath Jul. 27, 1811 Mark Gilbert to James Young. Rec. Aug. 5, 1811

p. 30-31 Feb. 18, 1811 John Trail sr (Spartanburgh) to John Trail jr (same); for $100 sold 100 ac on waters of Dutchman's Cr of Tygar R; border: Thomas Rees; part of grant Jul. 1, 1793 to William Lancaster. Witness Daniel Smith, David Trail, and Lawson Thomson. Signed John Trail's mark. Wit. oath Feb. 18, 1811 Daniel Smith to Saml Morrow. Rec. Aug. 5, 1811. Dower renounced Mar. 5, 1811 Clerecy Trail to Saml Morrow.

p. 31-32 Dec. 5, 1810 John Connell (Spartanburgh) to Elijah Barnett (same); for $500 sold 283 ac except half an ac "about the graves". Witness Anthony Foster and Reuben Harrison. Signed John Connell. Wit. oath May 6, 1811 Reuben Harrison to John Gossett. Rec. Aug. 5, 1811

p. 32-33 Dec. 12, 1810 Benjamin Hammett and wife Sally (Spartanburgh) to Daniel Hammett (same); for $100 sold 150 ac on waters of Pacolate R; border: Francis Brock; grant to John Hammett sr. Witness John Hammett and Mitild Hammett. Signed Benjamin and Sally Hammett's marks. Wit. oath Aug. 5, 1811 John Hammett to Jno H Jones. Rec. Aug. 5, 1811

p. 33-35 Dec. 6, 1809 David White (Spartanburgh) to James White (same); for $60 sold 160 ac on Foun Br; border: George Rowland, Edmond Clement, John Clement, and Abraham Markely. Witness Zachariah Wall and John Clement. Signed David White's mark. Wit. oath Aug. 5, 1811 John Clement to Thomas Poole. Rec. Aug. 5, 1811

p. 35-36 Aug. 12, 1811 Vincent Bennett (Spartanburgh) to Maj. John Tolleson; for $70 sold 200 ac on waters of Lawson's fork; border: Widow Bishop, Wm Ford, and George McDowell; sale due to writ from Spartanburgh Common Pleas Court suit Luke Burnett vs George Deavours; suit was when Gab. Benson was sheriff; sale Apr. 3, 1809. Witness Muse Tollison and Wm N Miller. Signed Vincent Bennett SSD. Wit. oath Aug. 20, 1811 Muse Tollison to A Benson. Rec. Aug. 20, 1811

p. 36-37 Aug. 12, 1811 Vincent Bennett, sheriff (Spartanburgh) to Maj. John Tolleson; for $57 sold 507 ac on both sides of Thickety Cr; grant to John G Bostick; sale due to writ from Spartanburgh Common Pleas Court suit John Tollison vs John G Bostick; suit when Gab Benson was sheriff; sale Apr. 3, 1809. Witness Muse Tollison and Wm N Miller. Signed Vincent Bennett SSD. Wit. oath Aug. 20, 1811 Muse Tollison to A Benson. Rec. Aug. 20, 1811

p. 37-38 Feb. 27, 1811 William and Thomas Willis (Spartanburgh) to John Poole (same); for $100 sold 40 ac on S side of Pacolate R; below Pacolate Springs; border: Henry Pettet and William Poole sr; where William and Thomas Willis live. Witness William Crocker, William Poole, and Sarah Gore. Signed William Willis and Thomas Willis' mark. Wit. oath Aug. 26, 1811 William Poole to Jno H Jones. Rec. Aug. 26, 1811

p. 38-40 Sept. 2, 1811 Vincent Bennett, sheriff (Spartanburgh) to Benjamin Wofford; for $132 sold 180 ac on Prater's Cr of Tygar R; border: N-George Bevin, NW-John Spears and heirs of Henry

Williamson desc, S-Wm Sexton, E-Humphry Yarborough and Wm Edwards; grant Aug. 31, 1774 to Wm Cleton; sale due to writ from Spartanburgh Common Pleas Court suit Humphry Yarborough vs John Spears; suit when Isham Foster was sheriff; sale Aug. 6, 1811. Witness William Lancaster and Thomas James. Signed Vincent Bennett SSD. Wit. oath Sept. 2, 1811 Thomas James to A Benson. Rec. Sept. 2, 1811

p. 40-41 Mar. 4, 1811 Daniel White (Spartanburgh) to Samuel Burton (same); for a debt from Daniel to Samuel of $413 principal and $54.88 interest sold 200 ac on Fairforrest Cr; where Daniel White lives; border: N-Thomas James, S-Joel Hurt, E-Thomas Tynsley, and W-Micajah Barnett. Witness Thomas Moore and John White. Signed Danl White. Wit. oath Aug. 31, 1811 Thomas Moore to Drury McDaniel. Rec. Sept. 2, 1811

p. 41 Jul. 9, 1811 Abraham Potter to Hugh Ewing; to secure the following debt sold a sorrel mare about 4 years old; mare is sold until Abraham Potter discharges cost of suit due to William Copland for which Hugh Ewing is security; Condition: sale void if Abraham pays the debt by Dec. 25, 1811. Witness John Ridings and Leonard Love. Signed Abraham Potter. Wit. oath Aug. 30, 1811 John Ridings to Andrew Furgerson. Rec. Sept. 4, 1811

p. 41-43 Sept. 16, 1811 Vincent Bennett, sheriff (Spartanburgh) to Samuel Farrow esq (same); for $23 sold 700 ac on Elijah's Cr; plat attached shows border: Samuel Bell, vacant, Thos McCrera, Jos Nerew, Sampson Bobo, Spencer Bobo, and Edwd Arnett; sale due to writ from Laurens Common Pleas Court suit Samuel Farrow vs John Beckler; sale Apr. 1, 1811. Witness J. W. Farrow and A Sloan. Signed Vinct Bennett. Wit. oath Sept. 16, 1811 J. W. Farrow to Thos Poole. Rec. Sept. 16, 1811

p. 43-45 May 7, 1811 Vincent Bennett, sheriff (Spartanburgh) to Golden (or Golding) Tinsley; for $10.25 sold 400 ac on waters of Tygar R where Golden Tinsley lives; sale due to writ from Spartanburgh Common Pleas Court suit Robert A Todd vs Arkillas Foster; sale Apr. 1, 1811. Witness Muse Tollison and William N. Miller. Signed Vincent Bennett SSD. Wit. oath Sept. 21, 1811 William N Miller to A Benson. Rec. Sept. 21, 1811

p. 45-46 Jul. 30, 1810 Leonard Carden (Spartanburgh) to Vincent Bennett (same); for $300 sold 250 ac on waters of Lawson's fork; border: a waggon road, John Wolf, John Burnett, and near Clemmon's old road; part of 840 ac survey Jan. 21, 1793 for Leonard Carden and granted by Gov. William Moultrie. Witness William Littlefield and Robert Moore. Signed Leonard Carden. Wit. oath Sept. 28, 1811 William Littlefield to A Benson. Rec. Sept. 26, 1811

p. 46-47 Jul. 24, 1809 Paul Cox (Spartanburgh) to Richard Bomar (same); for $173 sold 70 ac on S Pacolate R; border: Bomar; grant to William Dixon who sold to James Dixon who sold to Gabriel Benson and Paul Cox; part of land sold by Gabriel Benson to Paul Cox. Witness Jesse A Burton and William Ramsey. Signed Paul Cox. Wit. oath May 14, 1811 Jesse A Burton to James Young. Rec. Oct. 3, 1811

p. 47-48 May 14, 1811 Robert McDowell (Spartanburgh) to Reuben Bomar; for $40 sold 40 ac on S side of S Pacolate R; border: Dickson, James Gilmore's old line, and David McDowell. Witness William Ramsey and William McClure. Signed Robert McDowell. Wit. oath May 18, 1811 William Ramsey to James Young. Rec. Oct. 3, 1811

p. 48-49 Mar. 4, 1811 John Golightly jr (Spartanburgh) to John Vandike (same); for $168 sold 80 ac on Lawson's fork of Pacolate R; except Ruth Poole's dower. Witness Richard Vandike and Anderson Vandike. Signed John Golightly jr. Wit. oath Oct. 7, 1811 Anderson Vandike to A Benson. Rec. Oct. 7, 1811

p. 49-50 Feb. 13, 1808 Jesse Mathus (Spartanburgh) to William Willis (same); for $150 sold 270 ac on S side of Pacolate R; a small distance below Hammett's ford; border: John Gray. Witness Charles McAbee and John Jones. Signed Jesse Mathus. Wit. oath Feb. 13, 1808 John Jones to John H Jones. Rec. Oct. 9, 1811

p. 50-51 Jul. 22, 1811 William Willis (Spartanburgh) to Thomas Willis (same); for $150 sold 320 ac on S side of Pacolate R; a small distance below Hammett's ford. Witness Elijah Poole and Jno H Jones. Signed William Willis. Wit. oath Jul. 22, 1811 Elijah Poole to John H Jones. Rec. Oct. 9, 1811

p. 51-52 Jul. 3, 1811 Samuel Nesbett (Spartanburgh) to Andrew F. Nesbett (same); for $70 sold 45 ac on S side of Middle Tygar R; border: Buncomb Rd; part of 400 ac grant in Jun. 1774 to James Mayson who sold in Jun. 1775 to James Dyson who sold in Feb. 1797 to Samuel Nesbett. Witness James Gilleland and William Moore. Signed Samuel Nesbett. Wit. oath Sept. 5, 1811 James Gilleland to John Collins. Rec. Oct. 10, 1811

p. 52-54 Jun. 17, 1811 L Edmond Bishop (Spartanburgh) to Barney Bishop (same); for $116.25 sold 46½ ac on Standing Stone Br of Lawson's fork; border: William Bishop sr's Spring Br and James Templeton; part of tract sold in 1811 by James Templeton to L Edmond Bishop. Witness James Barrett and William Rollins. Signed L. E. Bishop's mark. Wit. oath Oct. 18, 1811 James Barrett to A Benson. Rec. Oct. 18, 1811

p. 54-55 Jun. 29, 1811 John King (Spartanburgh) to John Tolleson (same); for $150 sold 150 ac on Story's Mill Cr; border: John Lukeroy, William Crocker, Howard, a waggon road, and Poole; part of grant to Wm Crocker who sold to Page Puckett who sold to John King. Witness Muse Tolleson and Sally Tolleson. Signed John King. Wit. oath May 19, 1812 (sic) Muse Tolleson to A Benson. Rec. Nov. 5, 1811. Dower renounced Oct. 12, 1811 Sally King to John Gossett

p. 55-57 Sept. 13, 1810 Joseph Woodruff sr (Spartanburgh) to William Sparks (same); for $100 sold (1) 50 ac on Dildena's Cr; border: N-Stoutingburgh, E-Samuel Woodruff sr, S-Anderson Page, and W-Morgan Darnel; and (2) 40 ac; border: Samuel Woodruff, Robert Page, and Wm Stoutenburgh. Witness Thomas Woodruff III and Joseph Woodruff IV. Signed Joseph Woodruff sr's mark. Wit. oath Nov. 9, 1811 Thomas Woodruff III to John Dean. Rec. Nov. 11, 1811. Dower renounced Anny Woodruff to Daniel Wright Jul. 13, 1811

p. 57-58 Nov. 5, 1811 Abraham Moore, blacksmith (Spartanburgh) to James Moore (same); for $200 sold 147 ac in two parts: (1) 100 ac; part of 150 ac grant to Abraham Moore desc; and (2) 47 ac; part of 250 ac grant to William Smith; border: James Ham, Wm Smith, and Abraham Moore desc; (1) is on Willus fork of Duchman's Cr; land was left by will of Abraham Moore sr to his son Abraham Moore. Witness James Ham jr, John White, and James Ham sr. Signed Abraham Moore. Wit. oath Nov. 8, 1811 James Ham jr to Samuel Morrow. Rec. Nov. 11, 1811

p. 58-59 Nov. 7, 1809 James Smith (Union Dist) to Edward Fowler (Spartanburgh); for $40 sold 160 ac; except part taken by an "old survey" now belonging to Joseph Lively; grant in 1804 to James Smith. Witness Demcy Fowler and James Hany. Signed James Smith. Wit. oath Nov. 7, 1809 Demcy Fowler to (not signed). Rec. Nov. 11, 1811

p. 59 May 11, 1811 Joseph Daffren (or Daffron) to Samuel Sarratt; for $35.25 sold 11 ac and 7 chains on Broad R. Witness John Old Hance and Joseph Camp. Signed Joseph Daffron and Nancy's mark. Wit. oath Jul. 3, 1811 Joseph Camp to Joshua Richards. Rec. Nov. 11, 1811

p. 59-60 May 11, 1811 Joseph Daffron and wife (name omitted) to John Sarratt; for $40.25 sold 14 ac and 7 chains on Broad R. Witness John Old Hance and Joseph Camp. Signed Joseph Daffron and Nancy's mark. Wit. oath Jul. 13, 1811 Joseph Camp to Joshua Richards. Rec. Nov. 12, 1811

p. 60-61 Dec. 10, 1802 James Jordan (Spartanburgh) to Alexander Wikefield (same); for $150 sold 135 ac on branch of Been's Cr of Tygar R; border: survey for John Nesbett; where "he" lives; grant in 1786 to James Jordan; "half" of 250 ac "sold to" Alexander Wikefield by his father Moses Wickfield. Witness Alexander McCarter, Edward Stewart, and Moses Wickfield (or Wakefield). Signed James Jordan. Wit. oath Nov. 12, 1811 Alexander McCarter to John Collins. Rec. Nov. 12, 1811

p. 61-62 Oct. 22, 1811 Samuel Nesbett (Spartanburgh), attorney for James Johnston (Logan Co, Ky), to William Ford (Spartanburgh); for $100 sold 200 ac on S side of S Tygar R and on both sides of Piegon Roost Br; border: all vacant; grant Dec. 3, 1792 Gov. Charles Pickney to James Johnston. Witness Page Rork, William Cornwell, and Isaiah Bright. Signed Samuel Nesbett. Wit. oath Nov. 13, (omitted) Page Rork to Burrell Bobo. Rec. Nov. 13, 1811

p. 62-64 Apr. 27, 1811 Vincent Bennett, sheriff (Spartanburgh) to Isaac Young jr; for $63.75 sold 350 ac on waters of Island Cr of Pacolate R; sale due to writ from Spartanburgh Common Pleas Court suit Moses Wilkins vs Moses Cantrell; sale Apr. 1, 1811. Witness James Brannon, William Hughe, and John Golightly jr. Signed Vincent Bennett SSD. Wit. oath Oct. 7, 1811 James Brannon to Thos Poole. Rec. Nov. 13, 1811

p. 64-65 Apr. 27, 1811 William Patton (Spartanburgh) to John Ison jr (same); for $180 sold 108 ac on N side Duchman's Cr of Tygar R and on Dry Branch of Wilies fork; border John Shands and William Smith; part of 330 ac grant Apr. 3, 1811 to John Smith, blacksmith. Witness Henry Foster and Samuel Hays. Signed Wm Patton. Wit. oath Nov. 3, 1811 Samuel Hays to John Collins. Rec. Nov. 13, 1811

p. 65-66 Oct. 24, 1811 Bayles Earle (Spartanburgh Dist) to William Hembry (same); for $60 sold 100 ac on Wolf Cr of N Pacolate R; survey for John Lewis who sold to Bayles Earle; border: William Hembry. Witness Hugh Ewing and Crury Bomar. Signed Bayles Earle. Wit. oath Oct. 26, 1811 Hugh Ewing to Wm Kelso. Rec. Nov. 13, 1811

p. 66-67 Jan. 12, 1810 James Powell (Spartanburgh) to John Fowler (same); for $100 sold 150 ac on W side of Middle Tygar R; where "he" lives; border: SW-John Smith sr and SE & NE-vacant and Robert Philips' heirs; plat attached shows border: "Greenvile line". Witness Daniel Wilbanks and Thomas Moore. Signed James Powell. Wit. oath Feb. 15, 1810 Thomas Moore to Michl Miller. Rec. Nov. 13, 1811

p. 67-68 Mar. 9, 1811 Gabriel Benson (Spartanburgh) to Elizabeth Monroe (same); for $50 sold 70 ac on branches of S Pacolate R; border: W & S-Peterson Bonam, E-Cuningham, and N-Boman; part of grant to John Daniel. Witness Henry Monroe and Reuben Bomar. Signed Gal Benson. Wit. oath Nov. 12, 1811 Henry Monroe to James Young. Rec. Nov. 13, 1811

p. 68-69 Sept. 30, 1809 Penuel Wood (Spartanburgh) to Reuben Mayfield (same); for $100 sold 200 ac on Peney Rock Br of Abner's Cr of Enoree R; border: John Jones, John Wood, Benson, Dempson, and Cave. Witness John Jones and James Wood. Signed Penuel Wood's mark. Wit. oath Dec. 1, 1810 John Jones to Tyre Glenn. Rec. Nov. 13, 1811

p. 69-70 Oct. 17, 1804 James Johnston (Logan Co, Ky) to Samuel Nesbett (Spartanburgh); power of attorney to sell 200 ac on Pegeon Roost Br and to collect debts owed to James Johnston. Witness James Gilleland and William Wilson. Signed James Johnston. Wit. oath Oct. 21, 1811 James Gilleland to John Collins. Rec. Nov. 21, 1811

p. 70-71 Jul. 4, 1809 George Lewis (Spartanburgh) to Gabriel Benson (same); for $300 sold 2,000 ac in Tennessee on Chittahamah R of Tennessee R; part of 4,000 ac grant Dec. 18, 1789 Gov. Alexander Moultrie (NC) to George Lewis "agreeable to resolution of NC General Assembly; border: a tree marked "ML". Witness John Harrison, Richard Harrison, and Thomas Lancaster. Signed Geor Lewis. Wit. oath Dec. 3, 1811 Thomas Lancaster to Jno H Jones. Rec. Dec. 4, 1811

p. 71-72 Nov. (omitted), 1811 Ezekiel Swellivan (Spartanburgh) to John Tolleson (same); for $80 sold 70 ac on Bullock's fork of Thickety Cr. Witness Muse Tolleson and William N Miller. Signed Ezekiel Swellavan. Wit. oath Nov. 15, 1811 Muse Tolleson to John Gossett. Rec. Dec. 4, 1811

p. 72-73 Nov. 15, 1810 David Hubbard (Pendleton Dist) to John Rainwater; "for a riding chain" sold 165 ac which was lot 4 of W. T. Thomson's estate (desc). Witness William Rainwater and William West. Signed David Hubbard. Wit. oath Nov. 19, 1811 William Rainwater to A Benson. Rec. Dec. 4, 1811. Dower renounced (Pendleton Dist) Nov. 15, 1810 Martha Hubbard to John Wilson

p. 73-74 Dec. 14, 1811 Peter Hawkins to William Johnston; for $100 rent and lease for 66 years 97½ ac on Camp Br of Lawson's fork; part of tract leased by William Dunlap, trustee of Wadsworth free school, to Rolly Fauset and Rolly Fauset (sic) rented and leased it to William Johnston. Witness Charles McAbee and Abner Benson. Signed Peter Hawkins. Wit. oath Dec. 14, 1811 Charles McAbee to Thos Poole. Rec. Dec. 14, 1811

p. 74-76 Jun. 5, 1809 Phebe Thomason (Spartanburgh) to Abner Benson (same); for $180 sold 90 ac on waters of Lawson's fork; border: Alexander McKie, Heron, and below McKie's mill; part of 300 ac "laid out" to Phebe Thomason as widow of Turner Thomason, desc by Commissioners of Spartanburgh Common Pleas Court. Witness Wm R Smith, Franklin Foster, and John Thomason. Signed Phebe Thomason's mark. Wit. oath Dec. 14, 1811 Wm R Smith to Thos Poole. Rec. Dec. 14, 1811. Jun. 5, 1809 Franklin Foster and John Thomason relinquish their claims to land--witness by William Pollard

p. 76-77 Sept. 19, 1811 William Traylor (Spartanburgh) to John Wingo (same); for $100 sold 100 ac on S side of N Tygar R; part of two tracts: (1) 46 ac sold by John Pace to William Traylor and (2) 60 ac sold by Richard Pace to William Traylor; border: N-N Tygar R, E-Isaac Snoddy, S-Joseph Rodgers, and W-Joseph Collins. Witness Edmund Wood and Joseph Collins. Signed William Traylor. Wit. oath Oct. 11, 1811 Edmund Wood to Michl Miller. Rec. Dec. 16, 1811. Dower renounced Oct. 11, 1811 Mary Traylor to Michl Miller

p. 77-78 Feb. 6, 1804 Thomas Price and wife (not named) (Spartanburgh) to John Stone (same); for 4200 sold 100 ac on James Cr of Tygar R; grant Gov. William Bull to John Dunkins who sold to

William Caldwell who sold to Mark McCrory and by his will to Anthony Wilson who sold Feb. 23, 1795 to Thomas Price. Witness Caleb Stone and Longshorn Lamb. Signed Thomas Price. Wit. oath Jun. 30, 1804 Caleb Stone to A Casey. Rec. Dec. 17, 1811

p. 78-79 Jan. 6, 1812 David Burton (Spartanburgh) to Sarah Thomson; for $60 sold 29 ac on branch of N Tygar R; border: Jane Thomson. Witness Thomas Thornton and Lawson Thomson. Signed David Burton. Wit. oath Jan. 6, 1812 Lawson Thomson to William Reid. Rec. Jan. 6, 1812

p. 79-81 Nov. 21, 1811 Vincent Wyatt jr (Spartanburgh) to Richard Thomson (same); for $260 sold 260 ac on ridge between Peters Cr and Pacolate R; border: Old Green River Road and near Templemon's Still House; part of grant Dec. 3, 1787 to Jesse Connell. Witness John H Low and James Hayns. Signed Vincent Wyatt's mark. Wit. oath Dec. 26, 1811 John H Low to A Benson. Rec. Jan. 27, 1812. Dower renounced Dec. 1, 1811 Elizabeth Wyatt to Abner Benson

p. 81-83 Sept. 17, 1811 Richard Thomson (Spartanburgh) to Muse Tolleson (same); for $75 sold ½ ac in Spartanburgh, SC; border: Muse Tolleson's lot and "machine", Brown, and Todd. Witness W. N. Miller and Eli Tolleson. Signed Richard Thomson. Wit. oath Oct. 19, 1811 W. N. Miller to John Gossett. Rec. Jan. 27, 1812. Dower renounced Polly Thomson to John Gossett Nov. 4, 1811

p. 83-84 Oct. 15, 1811 James Hadden (Spartanburgh) to William Hoy (same); for $25 sold 10 ac (or 14 ac) on waters of Ben's Cr; border: William Brce and William Hoy. Witness Thomas Hadden and Alexander Evans. Signed James Hadden. Wit. oath Jan. 1, 1812 Alexander Evans to John Collins. Rec. Feb. 3, 1812

p. 84-85 Oct. 14, 1811 Thomas Hadden (Spartanburgh) to William Hoy (same); for $200 sold 140 ac on S side Ben's Cr of Tygar R. Witness William M McBrice and James McHughes. Signed Thomas Hadden. Wit. oath Feb. 3, 1812 William M McBrice to John Collins. Rec. Feb. 3, 1812

p. 85-86 Nov. 12, 1809 Joshua Edwards (Spartanburgh) to James Wofford (same); for $200 sold 250 ac on Ready fork Cr of S Tygar R; except 13 ac "square" on S side for Joshua Benson "forever back"; border: trees marked "WB" and "IW"; part of 300 ac grant Nov. 7, 1785 to Nathaniel Miller who sold to Joshua Edwards. Witness Nath Wofford, Isaac Wofford, and Samuel McHugh. Signed Joshua Edwards' mark. Wit. oath Nov. 29, 1809 Samuel McHugh to Drury McDaniel. Rec. Feb. 5, 1812. Dower renounced Nov. 29, 1809 Citurity (or Keturo) Edwards to Drury McDaniel

p. 86-87 Feb. 14, 1812 William Rickman to son Peter Rickman; for love and affection give 345 ac. Witness Michael Gaffney and Isaac Gorden. Signed William Rickman. Wit. oath Feb. 14, 1812 Michael Gaffney and Isaac Gordan to Joshua Richards. Rec. Feb. 20, 1812

p. 87-88 Feb. 22, 1802 Mary Hays to son Willis Hays; for (omitted) give a mare, saddle and bridle, a woman's saddle, 3 cattle, 7 hogs, a sow and pigs, 2 pots, a skillet, a table and cupboard, 3 beds and bedding, 2 bedstids, a chest, 4 chairs, 2 wheels and "reel", 10 geese, a looking glass, a canister, a bucket, a tea pot and teaward, a bason, a desk, 5 plates, etc. Witness Thomas Meredy and Samuel Noblet. Signed Mary Hays' mark. Wit. oath Feb. 23, 1812 Thomas Meredy to John Gossett. Rec. Feb. 24, 1812

p. 88 Nov. 12, 1811 Dower renounced Agness Broockshier to John Gossett for deed from John Broocksheir to Solomon Abbott. Rec. Mar.

2, 1812

p. 88-89 Feb. 11, 1809 Joel Hurt (Spartanburgh) to Johnson Beavers (same); for $160 sold 100 ac on waters of Ford's Cr. Witness William H Cook and Thomas Tinsley. Signed Joel Hurt. Wit. oath Feb. 11, 1809 Thomas Tinsley to Danl White. Rec. Mar. 2, 1812

p. 89-91 Oct. 17, 1811 John White (Spartanburgh) to Elisha James (same); for $90 sold 110 ac on Col. White's Br of Fairforrest Cr; border: Thomas Finch, Lancaster, James Finch, and John Smith; grant to John Smith who sold to Thomas Smith who sold to Daniel White esq who sold to Rowland Jennings who sold to John White. Witness John Rakestraw and William Lancaster. Signed John White. Wit. oath Mar. 2, 1812 William Lancaster to Drury McDaniel. Rec. Mar. 2, 1812

p. 91-92 Jan. 27, 1812 Thomas Cook (Union Dist) to John Little (same); for $125 sold 100 ac; border: vacant when granted; part of grant to Edward Kelly desc and by heirship to Mary and Martin Kelly and "leased" to William Chesney to Thomas Murry and to Thomas Cook. Witness John Hames sr and John Hames jr. Signed Thomas Cook. Wit. oath (Union Dist) Jan. 27, 1812 John Hames to Davis Goudelock. Rec. Mar. 2, 1812

p. 92-93 Sept. 13, 1811 James Cook (Spartanburgh) to William M. Golightly (same); for $151 sold 217 ac on ridge between branches of Fairforrest and Dutchman's Creeks; border: S-R Calbert, W-vacant, N-Thomas Cook, and E-Edward Barnett; part of grant to Fredreck (or Fredrut) Eisen. Witness Robert Martin and Lemuel Cook. Signed James Cook. Wit. oath Jan. 21, 1812 Lemuel Cook to Saml Morrow. Rec. Mar. 3, 1812. Dower renounced Feb. 26, 1812 Rohode Cook to Samuel Morrow

p. 93-94 Mar. 2, 1812 Nimrod Cantrell (Spartanburgh) to mother Mary Cantrell, widow (same); for love and affection give all household foods, all stock, and all plantation "afancs". Witness Mark Cantrell and Abraham Cantrell. Signed Nimrod Cantrell. Wit. oath Mar. 3, 1812 Mark Cantrell to Henry Turner. Rec. Mar. 7, 1812

p. 94-95 Nov. 13, 1811 Thomas Leatherwood and wife Mary (Spartanburgh) to David Spears (Laurens Dist); for $200 sold 94 ac; grant May 1, 1797 to James Langford jr. Witness John Woodruff and Jonathan Moore. Signed Thomas Leatherwood and Mary's mark. Wit. oath Nov. 22, 1811 Jonathan Moore to Drury McDaniel. Rec. Apr. 6, 1812. Dower renounced Mary Leatherwood to Drury McDaniel Nov. 22, 1811

p. 95-96 Feb. 1, 1809 John Gowan (Spartanburgh) to Jonathan Stokes (same); for $200 sold 242 ac on S side of S Pacolate R; border: Mouttow; N end of grant Jun. 5, 1786 to George Thompson; where Polly Saunders lives; and other end is part of grant Jul. 1, 1783 to John Gowen. Witness Lemuel Stokes and Willey S Brown. Signed Jno Gowen. Wit. oath Apr. 6, 1812 Lemuel Stokes to Andw Furgeson. Rec. Apr. 6, 1812

p. 96-98 Jan. 18, 1812 John Bearden sr to Benjamin Bearden; for $125 sold 75 ac at head of McElevaen's Br of Fairforrest Cr; part of 300 ac grant to William Thompson who sold to Ralph Smith and by his will to Zophar Smith. Witness Eber Smith and William Wofford. Signed John Bearden. Wit. oath Jan. 31, 1812 William Wofford to Samuel Morrow. Rec. Apr. 6, 1812

p. 98-99 Nov. 28, 1811 John Hurt (Spartanburgh) to Andrew B Fleming (same); for $10 sold 140 ac on N side of S branch of N Tygar R; part of grant to John Orr; border: W-Alexr. McCarter, E & N-

J Jordan, and S-J Vernon. Witness Joseph Hurt, Henry Hutcheson, and James Vernon. Signed John Hurt. Wit. oath Mar. 15, 1814 Henry Hutcheson to John Chapman. Rec. Apr. 6, 1812. Dower renounced Nov. 28, 1811 Esther Hurt to Michl Miller

p. 99-100 Mar. 3, 1812 Ephraim Lewis (Spartanburgh) to Abijah Lewis (same); for $100 sold 400 ac on N side of Lawson's fork; border: George Lewis; part of land sold by Clement to Ephraim Lewis. Witness George Lewis and Rachal Lewis. Signed Ephraim Lewis. Wit. oath Apr. 7, 1812 George Lewis to Andw Furgason. Rec. Apr. 7, 1812

p. 100-101 Nov. 22, 1811 Hugh Caldwell (Spartanburgh) to Andrew Caldwell (same); for $200 sold 120 ac on N side of N Tygar R; part of grant Aug. 10, 1774 to John Brown; border: Andrew Caldwell and Samuel Snoddy. Witness William Caldwell, Andrew Coan, John Crawford. Signed Hugh Caldwell. Wit. oath Apr. 7, 1812 John Crawford to John Collins. Rec. Apr. 7, 1812

p. 101-102 Jan. 6, 1809 Alexander Roddy (Spartanburgh) to Samuel Bowlin (same); for $150 sold 237 ac on both sides Beaverdam Cr of S Pacolate R; grant Aug. 4, 1794 Gov. William Moultrie to James Reavs. Witness John Roddy, son of Thomas, and John Roddy. Signed Alexr Roddy. Wit. oath Feb. 2, 1811 John Roddy to Andw Furgason. Rec. Apr. 7, 1812

p. 102-103 Nov. 22, 1811 James Ridings (Spartanburgh) to Samuel Bolane (same); for $100 sold 177 ac on waters of N Pacolate R; border: on N side of Grogan's Road; part of grant to James Ridings. Witness Abram Brock and David Moore. Signed James Ridings' mark. Wit. oath Apr. 4, 1812 David Moore to Andw Furgason. Rec. Apr. 7, 1812

p. 103-105 Jun. 21, 1811 David Johnson (Union Dist) to James Means (same); for $500 sold 794 ac on both sides Story's Cr of Fairforrest Cr; border at original survey: E-Hugh Gourley, Robert Erwen, and "old lines", S-Thomas Compton, W-Thomas Brandon, N-old line; grant Jan. 6, 1794to Thomas Brandon and resurveyed part in a grant owned and occupied by Josiah Thorton. Witness William Farnanders and Thomas Jackson. Signed David Johnson. Wit. oath (Union Dist) Jun. 20, 1811 Thomas Jackson to Wm Rice. Rec. Apr. 7, 1812. Dower renounced (Union Dist) Jun. 21, 1811 Barbara Johnson to Hugh Means

p. 105-106 Jul. 20, 1811 William West (Spartanburgh) to Drury Boman; for $140 sold 140 ac on N side of S Pacolate R and both sides Alexander Kilpatrick's Cr; grant Dec. 19, 1793 Gov. William Moultrie to (omitted). Witness William Ramsey and Mary Ramsey. Signed William West's mark. Wit. oath Mar. 28, 1812 William Ramsey to Wm Kelso. Rec. Apr. 7, 1812

p. 106-107 Mar. 9, 1812 Isham Foster (Spartanburgh) to Herbert Hawkins (same); for $100 sold (1) 94 ac on Mill Cr of N Tygar R; border: road from Maj. Wm Foster's to John Wingo's; part of grant to Gabl Benson; and (2) 7½ ac at head of Fairforrest Cr; border: Prince's old road and a road from Wm Foster's to John Wingo's; part of grant to Gabriel Benson. Witness David Foster and Armin Foster. Signed Ism Foster. Wit. oath Apr. 6, 1812 David Foster to Thos Poole. Rec. Apr. 7, 1812

p. 107-108 Mar. 14, 1812 Edward Stubblefield (Spartanburgh) to George Horton (same); for $50 sold 50 ac on waters of Pacolate R; part of where Edward Stubblefield lives; border: Burges and John Cantrill. Witness Richard Turner and Isaac Cantrell. Signed Edwd Stubblefield. Wit. oath Mar. 14, 1811 Isaac Cantrell to Henry Turner. Rec. Apr. 7, 1812

p. 108-109 Sept. 7, 1811 Robert Smith (Spartanburgh) to Henry Smith (same); for $300 sold 150 ac on S side Tygar R; border: English, John Ward, Jesse Crook, James Crook's Spring Br, Ephraim Drummon, and McCarter. Witness Peter Smith and Abner Watkins Legon. Signed Robert Smith. Wit. oath Sept. 18, 1811 Peter Smith to Danl White. Rec. Apr. 7, 1812. Dower renounced Mar. 14, 1812 Polly Smith to Drury McDaniel.

p. 109-110 Dec. 27, 1804 Jeremiah Stokes (Greenville Dist) to Jonathan Stokes (Spartanburgh); for $600 sold 267 ac on S Pacolate R; border: E & N-Samuel Hunt, W-John Kirtlan, and S-survey for Robert Harper; grant Sept. 6, 1803 Gov. James B. Richardson to Jeremiah Stokes. Witness James McClure and Aspasio Earle. Signed Jeremiah and Elizabeth Stokes. Wit. oath Apr. 4, 1812 Aspasio Earle to Andrew Furgason. Rec. Apr. 8, 1812

p. 110-111 Aug. 23, 1811 Gabriel Benson (Spartanburgh) to Jonathan Wall (same); for $40 sold 118 ac on branch of S Pacolate R; border: a waggon road, Young, and Daniel White; part of grant to James Dillingham. Witness James Brannon and Vincent Bennett. Signed Gal Benson. Wit. oath Apr. 8, 1812 James Brannon to Burrell Bobo. Rec. Apr. 8, 1812

p. 111-113 Mar. 15, 1799 Jesse Ford, attorney for James Ford (Shelby Co, Ky) to William Moore (Spartanburgh); for $1,300 sold 596 ac in four adjoining tracts--(1) 200 ac granted Nov. 27, 1771 SC governor to John Ford; (2) 50 ac granted Jun. 2, 1769 SC governor to John Ford; (3) 332 ac granted May 1, 1796 SC governor to Samuel Ford who sold to John Ford; and (4) 14 ac part of grant NC governor to Robert Miller who sold 14 ac to John Ford; on W side of N Tygar R; border: S-S Tygar R; includes a grist mill and houses; where John Ford lived. Witness Michael Barnett and Thomas Wright. Signed Jesse Ford, attorney for John Ford. Wit. oath Apr. 23, 1807 Thomas Wright to Drury McDaniel. Rec. Apr. 8, 1812

p. 113-115 Dec. 7, 1811 Obadiah Wingo (Spartanburgh) to Elijah Ballinger (same); for $425 sold 212 ac on waters of Fairforrest Cr; part of where Samuel Culbertson lives; part of grant to Samuel Culbertson and part of grant to George Galaspie who sold to Robert Dugan who sold to Samuel Culbertson sr who sold to Samuel Culbertson jr who sold to Obadiah Wingo; border: Still House Br and Henry ONiell. Witness Samuel Culbertson and Willis Wingo. Signed Obadiah Wingo. Wit. oath Dec. 7, 1811 Willis Wingo to Danl White. Rec. Apr. 8, 1812. Dower renounced Apr. 8, 1812 Obedience Wingo to Dan White

p. 115-116 Nov. 18, (1796?) Susanna Layton, executrix of will of John Layton desc, (late of Spartanburgh) to George Divine (Spartanburgh); for $200 sold 100 ac on S Tygar R; border: Prother Cr, S-John Spears, and other sides-Thomas Todd; where John Layton lived. Witness William Fennell and James Layton. Signed Susanna Layton's mark. Wit. oath Jan. 1, 1807 John Layton to A Casey. Rec.Apr. 8, 1812

p. 116-117 Jan. 25, 1812 William Brock (Spartanburgh) to Moses Wilkins (same); for $250 sold 187 ac; border: John Lipscomb. Witness John H Jones, Young Allen, and David Lipscomb. Signed William Brock's mark. Wit. oath Mar. 3, 1812 Young Allen to John Lipscomb. Rec. Apr. 8, 1812. Dower renounced Apr. 4, 1812 Martha Brock to John Lipscomb

p. 117-118 Jan. 25, 1812 William Brock (Spartanburgh) to Moses Wilkins (same); for $13 sold 13 ac. Witness John H

Jones, Young Allen, and David Lipscomb. Signed William Brock's mark. Wit. oath Mar. 31, 1812 Young Allen to John Lipscomb. Rec. Apr. 8, 1812. Dower renounced Apr. 4, 1812 Martha Brock to John Lipscomb

p. 118-120 Mar. 18, 1812 Robert Smith (Spartanburgh) to Edith Legon (same); for $200 sold (1) 57 ac on Kelso's Cr; border: Peter Smith; and (2) 63 ac; border: Shands Golightly. Witness Charles James jr and David Lynch. Signed Robert Smith. Wit. oath Mar. 18, 1812 Charles James jr to John Cook. Rec. Mar. 28, 1812

p. 120-121 Mar. 7, 1812 James Kendrick (Spartan Dist) to James Brannon (same); for $235 sold 120 ac on S side Lawson's fork; part of grant Gov. Edmund Rutledge to William Turner. Witness Willis W Smithwick and John Harden. Signed Jamed Kendrick's mark. Wit. oath Mar. 14, 1812 Willis W Smithwick to Thos Poole. Rec. Mar. 28, 1812

p. 121-122 Mar. 25, 1812 James Ridings (Spartanburgh) to James Loftis (same); for $260 sold 200 ac at ford of Molley Cr; border: Carver's path, an old road, Robert Harper's old line, on N side of S Pacolate R, and Whitten. Witness Thoddus Owen, John Owen, and John Wilkins. Signed James Ridings' mark. Wit. oath Apr. 1, 1812 John Owen to Michl Miller. Rec. Apr. 3, 1812

p. 122-123 Mar. 9, 1812 Jobe Loftis (Spartanburgh) to James Loftis (same); for $150 sold 94 ac. Witness Thaddes Owen and John Owen. Signed Jobe Loftis' mark. Wit. oath Apr. 1, 1812 John Owen to Michl Miller. Rec. Apr. 3, 1812

p. 123-124 Apr. 4, 1812 Peter Legon (Spartanburgh) to Abner W Legon (same); for $300 sold a large red cow, a small red cow and yearling, a gray horse 10 years old, a bay mare 10 years old, a bay horse 10 years old, 2 bedsteads, 3 feather beds and furniture, 2 small trunks, a set of blacksmith tools--an anvil, bellows, vice, hamers, and all utensils, a set of carpenter's tools--joiner, plain, jack plain, smoothing plane, hamers, chisels, draw knife, auger, and all utensils, a broad ax, a pole ax, a large oven, 3 pots, an earthen dish, 10 plates, knives, forks, cups, saucers, mugs, pitchers, sugar dishes, tin (or 10) pans, 2 pair of cards, a spinning wheel, a quantity of bason, barrels, lules(?), piggon, pails, a man's saddle, a Borman saddle, 2 collars, hames, traces, plows, and all household furniture and farming utensils etc. Witness Jesse Cleveland and Abner Benson. Signed Peter Legon. Wit. oath Apr. 4, 1812. Rec. Apr. 4, 1812

p. 124-125 Sept. 17, 1811 Elizabeth Caven (Spartanburgh) to Gideon Reynolds (same); for $20 sold 10 ac; part of where Elizabeth Caven lives; border: James W Reynolds, Samuel Crucks, Gideon Reynolds, and Samuel Enicker. Witness Benjamin Robuck, John Henry, and John Huckaby. Signed Elizabeth Caven's mark. Wit. oath Apr. 4, 1812 John Henry to John Bruton. Rec. Apr. 4, 1812

p. 125-126 Jan. 12, 1812 William Morris (Spartanburgh) to Jilson Oliver (same); for $50 sold 160 ac on Barton Cr of Pacolate R; border: Jilson Oliver and John Mason; grant May 13, 1802 States Office to William Morris. Witness John Littlefield, Gibson Oliver, and John Cantrell. Signed William Morris and Sally's mark. Wit. oath Mar. 13, 1812 Gibson Oliver to James Young. Rec. Apr. 6, 1812

p. 126-127 (blank), 1811 Martin Newmon (Spartanburgh) to Thomas G. Potter (same); for $300 sold 140 ac; border: NW-Thomas G Potter, SW-Reuben Newmon, SE-Nelur, and NE-Mary Wilson; part of 640 ac grant to Joo Sample sr and sold Jul. 9, 1790 by Jos Rainey to Stephen Wilson desc who sold to George Newmon who sold to Martin

Newmon. Witness Burrell Bobo and Wiley Casey Newmon. Signed Martin Newmon. Wit. oath Nov. 3, 1811 Burrell Bobo to M Casey. Rec. Apr. 7, 1812. Dower renounced Oct. 5, 1811 Charity Newmon to Burrell Bobo

p. 127-128 Nov. 7, 1809 James Cook (Spartanburgh) to David Golightly (same); for $24 sold 33 ac near head of Bufelo Lick Cr; border: S-Thomas Vaughan, E-David Golightly, and NW-Elemuel Cook. Witness Robert Martin and Lemuel Cook. Signed James Cook. Wit. oath Dec. 27, 1809 Robert Martin to W Lancaster. Rec. Apr. 8, 1812

p. 128-129 Jan. 1, 1812 Drewry Boman (Spartanburgh) to Thomas Jackson (same); for $50 sold 100 ac on N side Abner's Cr; border: grant to James Mutin; part of two surveys. Witness William Jackson, Samuel Jackson, and John Jackson. Signed Drewry Boman. Wit. oath Apr. 19, 1812 John Jackson to William Kelso. Rec. Apr. 20, 1812

p. 129-130 Oct. 31, 1811 Samuel Seay (Spartanburgh) to William Powell (same); for $100 sold (ac omitted); where "my" mother lives and formerly estate of Gideon Seay desc; Samuel Seay sells his "right and interest and title" to the land. Witness Thomas Bomar, William Bomar, and Robert Wood. Signed Samuel Seay's mark. Wit. oath Apr. 7, 1812 William Bomar to John Collins. Rec. Apr. 20, 1812

p. 130-131 Aug. 23, 1808 James Campbell (Spartanburgh) to Charles Smith (same); for $6 sold 6 ac; border: the big cane break; "part of Dart's and adjoining former purchase Smith made of Campbell". Witness William Smith and Betsey Smith. Signed James Campbell. Wit. oath Aug. 10, 1810 William Smith to W Lancaster. Rec. Apr. 23, 1812. Dower renounced Aug. 10, 1810 Molley Campbell to William Lancaster

p. 131-133 Mar. 11, 1811 Lorenzo Dow (Connecticut) to Seth Mead (Lynchburgh, Va); for $200 sold 800 ac; border: Island Cr and Spears; grant Apr. 2, 1804 to Lorenzo Dow. Witness James Wade, John Percevul, and Ann Wade. Signed Lorenzo Dow. Wit. oath (Court of Hastings, held for Corporation of Lynchburg, Va) Sept. 5, 1811 James Wade, Ann Wade, and John Percevul to Wm Norvell. Rec. Apr. 23, 1812. (not dated) John Schoolfield certifys William Norvell is clerk of Court of Hastings. Oct. 15, 1811 William Norvell certifys John Schoolfield is mayor due to election first Monday in Apr. 1811

p. 133-134 Dec. 4, 1811 Jonathan Stokes (Spartanburgh) to John Grogan (same); for $100 sold 25 ac on N side of S Pacolate R; part of grant Oct. 3, 1803 to Jeremiah Stokes. Witness Samuel Hunt and Andrew Furgason. Signed Jonathan Stokes. Wit. oath Apr. 25, 1812 Samuel Hunt to Wm Kelso. Rec. Apr. 30, 1812

p. 134-135 Apr. 18, 1812 William R Smith (Spartanburgh) to Abner Benson (same); for $20 sold ½ ac in village of Spartanburgh on S side of Main St; border: W-Abner Benson. Witness John W Farrow, Charles McAbee, and Thomas Poole. Signed Wm R Smith. Wit. oath Apr. 20, 1812 John W Farrow to Thos Poole. Rec. Apr. 20, 1812

p. 135 Nov. 16, 1811 Alexander McKie (Spartanburgh) to daughter Nancy McKie; for love and affection give a Negro girl Dinah about 10 years old. Witness William Thomson and Abner Benson. Signed Alexr McKie. Wit. oath Apr. 20, 1812 Abner Benson to Jno H Jones. Rec. Apr. 20, 1812

p. 135-136 Nov. 16, 1811 Alexander McKie (Spartanburgh) to daughters Sally, Narcissa, and Nancy McKie (same); for love and affection give a Negro boy Phil, another boy Mate (or Merte), and another boy Adam "all children". Witness William Thomson and Abner Benson. Signed Alexr McKie. Wit. oath Apr. 20, 1812 Abner Benson to Jno H Jones. Rec. Apr. 20, 1812

p. 136-137 Mar. 16, 1801 James Ford (Spartanburgh) to Zadock Ford esq; for $10 sold 310 ac on branch of Enoree R; grant Aug. 31, 1798. Witness James Chamblen, Henry Hambelton, and Zadock Ford. Signed James Ford. Wit. oath Mar. 4, 1812 James Chamblen to A Benson. Rec. May 4, 1812

p. 137-139 Dec. 15, 1800 John Pennington (Spartanburgh) to Zadock Ford; for $50 sold 100 ac on branch of Enoree R; border: "old North survey" and Zadock Ford; S part of grant Aug. 1, 1791. Witness James Ford, Barnet H Allgood, and John Power. Signed Jno Pennington. Wit. oath May 4, 1812 James Ford to Danl White. Rec. May 4, 1812. Dower renounced Jan. 10, 1806 Sarah Pennington to James Kilgore

p. 139-140 Oct. 19, 1811 Newbel Johnson (Spartanburgh) to William Beacham (same); for $150 sold 300 ac on both sides Buncomb Rd; border: William Beacham; part of 1,000 ac grant to Joel Dean. Witness James Hammett and Theophelus Cannon. Signed Newbel Johnson. Wit. oath Oct. 19, 1811 Theophelus Cannon to Tyrce Glenn. Rec. May 4, 1812

p. 140-141 Apr. 6, 1812 Rebeca Turner (SC), wife of John Turner to Mary Turner (SC); for $500 sold 470 ac; border: Nesbett; where "we" now live; grant Jan. 4, 1796 to Rebeca Turner. Witness Daniel Amos sr and Joseph Camp. Signed Rebeca Turner's mark. Wit. oath Apr. 13, 1812 Daniel Amos sr to Joshua Richards. Rec. May 7, 1812

p. 141-142 Jan. 31, 1812 John Jordan (Spartanburgh) to Edward Smith (same); for $350 sold (1) 96 ac on S side of Thompson's Beverdam Cr; where Joshua Edwards lived; border: McCoy; and (2) 40 ac on S side Thompson's Beverdam Cr; below John J Reynolds; grant to James Hall; sold by James Reynolds to James Hall who sold to James Jordan. Witness Alexander M Thompson and John Robbs. Signed John Jordan. Wit. oath Apr. 25, 1812 John Robbs to John Collins. Rec. May 16, 1811

p. 142-143 Dec. 3, 1811 Zacheriah Wyatt and wife Scythe (or Syphthy) (Spartanburgh) to James Spencer (same); for $100 sold 200 ac on Mayor's Br on S side Peter's Cr; grant Dec. 3, 1787 States Office of Jesse Connel who sold to Vincent Wyatt (deed Book B p. 397 and 391 (sic)) who sold to Zacheriah Wyatt. Witness Samuel Turner and John Lancaster. Signed Zacheri and Scythe Wyatt. Wit. oath May 23, 1812 John Lancaster to Thomas Poole. Rec. May 23, 1812

p. 143-144 Dec. 3, 1811 Zacheriah Wyatt and wife Syphthy (Spartanburgh) to James Spencer (same); for $200 sold 60 ac on Mayer's Br on S side of Peter's Cr; border: Mare Br; part of SW end of grant Dec. 3, 1787 Gov. Thomas Pinckney to Jesse Connell. Witness Samuel Turner and John Lancaster. Signed Zacheri and Scythe Wyatt. Wit. oath May 23, 1812 John Lancaster to Thos Poole. Rec. May 23, 1812

p. 144-146 Feb. 3, 1806 Isham Harrison, sheriff (Spartanburgh) to Abner Benson; for $36 sold 143 ac on branches of Fairforrest Cr of Tygar R; part of 447 ac grant to William Wells; sale due to writ from Spartanburgh Common Pleas Court suit Felix Warley vs William Wells. Witness William Ross Smith, John Jordan, and D. J. Puckett. Signed I Harrison SSD. Wit. oath Apr. 20, 1812 William R Smith to Thos Poole. Rec. May 23, 1812

p. 146 Dec. 30, 1811 Richard Hicks (Rutherford Co, NC) to Berry Hicks; for $122 sold 122 ac on branch of McKinney's Cr. Witness Robert Herden and Sally Haims. Signed Richard Hicks' mark. Wit. oath Feb. 6, 1812 Robert Harden to Henry Turner. Rec. May 27, 1812

p. 146-147 Apr. 13, 1812 Dan Gilbert (Spartanburgh) to Daniel White (same); for $15 sold 20 ac on waters of S Pacolate R; border: Dan Gilbert; grant to Amos Spence. Witness Henry White and Garves (or Jarves) Gilbert. Signed Dan Gilbert's mark. Wit. oath May 16, 1812 Henry White to James Young. Rec. Jun. 1, 1812

p. 147-148 Jan. 30, 1812 James White (Spartanburgh) to Daniel White (same); for $300 sold 117 ac on both sides Richland Cr; border: N-Jonathan Wall, S & W-Daniel White, and E-George Rowlen; part of grant to Daniel White and assigned to James White. Witness Zacheriah Wall and Elizabeth Simmons. Signed James White's mark. Wit. oath May 16, 1812 Zacheriah Wall to James Young. Rec. Jun. 1, 1812

p. 148-149 Jan. 30, 1812 James Kelby (Spartanburgh) to Daniel White (same); for $100 sold 65 ac on SW side of Pacolate R "just below the fork" and "just above the ford"; border: Gilbert and Philip Johnson; survey Mar. 21, 1804 for William Holly and grant by Gov. James B Richardson and "part of a tract belonging to Philip Johnson; "being" all of land formerly belonging to William Holly and Philip Johnson. Witness Zacheriah Wall and Adlai (or Edley) Austin. Signed James Kelby. Wit. oath May 16, 1812 Zacheriah Wall to James Young. Rec. Jun. 1, 1812

p. 149-150 May 2, 1807 James Boyd (Spartanburgh) to Peter Willis (Rutherford Co, NC); for $300 sold 150 ac on both sides Lawson's fork; border: Hickes, Foster, and Knight; part of two grants--(1) to James Ross and (2) to James McDowell. Witness James Jolley and Joseph Willis. Signed James and Elizabeth Boyd's marks. Wit. oath Dec. 9, 1811 James Jolley to Joshua Richards. Rec. Jun. 1, 1812

p. 150-152 Nov. 29, 1811 Thomas James (Spartanburgh) to Anthony Foster (same); for $400 sold 207 ac on both sides Fairforrest Cr; where Thomas James lives; border: Jefferies Br, George Connell's old line, John Golightly, and Daniel White; part of grant to John Gibbs who sold to Giles Connell and sold by John Connell, one of legatees of Giles Connell, to Thomas James. Witness Laurence Hoots and Elijah Barnett. Signed Thomas James. Wit. oath Nov. 29, 1811 Elijah Barnett to Danl White. Rec. Jun. 1, 1812. Dower renounced Jan. 8, 1812 Ann James to Danl White

p. 152-153 Jul. 20, 1810 Benjamin Hammett (Spartanburgh) to John Parks (same); for $150 sold 100 ac on N side Pacolate R and on Doctor's Br; border: Quales. Witness James Harrison and William Lipscomb. Signed Benjamin Hammett's mark. Wit. oath Jul. 14, 1810 James Harrison to John Lipscomb. Rec. Jul. 6, 1812. Dower renounced Dec. 8, 1810 Salley Hammett to John Lipscomb

p. 153-154 May 26, 1812 Richard Vandike (Spartanburgh) to John Golightly jr (same); for $300 sold 370 ac on Peter's Cr and Cherokee Cr of Pacolate R. Witness Isaac White and James Vandike. Signed Richard Vandike. Wit. oath Jul. 6, 1812 James Vandike to A Benson. Rec. Jul. 6, 1812

p. 154-155 Mar. 5, 1812 John Vandike (Spartanburgh) to Cleveland and Brown (same); for $200 sold 80 ac on Lawson's fork of Pacolette R. Witness William B Benson and John Golightly jr. Signed John Vandike. Wit. oath Jul. 29, 1812 William B Benson to

A Benson. Rec. Jul. 29, 1812

p. 155-156 Feb. 13, 1812 James Saunders Guignard (Columbia, SC) to William Caldwell (Spartanburgh); for $40 sold 85 ac between S and Middle Tygar Rivers; border: N-John Caldwell, W-William Caldwell, S-Isaac Uuger (or Thuger?), and E-Thomas Paden; survey Sept. 29, 1798 for William Caldwell and grant Dec. 2, 1799 to Ezias Earle who sold Mar. 10, 1800 to James S Guignard (see Union Dist Book A p. 147 & 148). Witness John R. E. Chisley and Robert H. Waring. Signed James S Guignard. Wit. oath (Richland Dist) (not dated) John R. E. Chisley to John (T?) Goodwyn. Rec. Jul. 29, 1812. Dower renounced (Richland Dist) Feb. 27,1812 Caroline Guignard to Benjamin Haile

p. 156-157 Jun. 6, 1806 Laurence Bankston (Spartanburgh) to John Martin; for $5 sold 75 ac on N side of Cases Cr; border: Isaac Cantrell desc, Templeman's Br, and Martin; grant Jan. 7, 1799 States Office to Laurence Bankston. Witness Sampson Cantrell and John Bankston. Signed Laurence Bankston. Wit. oath Apr. 18, 1812 John Bankston to Leonard Adcock. Rec. Jul. 29, 1812

p. 157-159 Oct. 22, 1811 Joseph Hurt (Spartanburgh) to James Vernon (same); for $100 sold 150 ac on N side of N Tygar R; border: E-Edmond Wood, W-Collins, N-Goodlett, and S-N Tygar R; part of two grants--(1) Apr. 4, 1767 and (2) Apr. 28, 1768 both by Gov. Tryon (NC) to Francis Dodds and sold by Shields (or Shulds) Bookter to Joseph Hurt. Witness Henry Hutcheson and William Pering. Signed Joseph Hurt. Wit. oath Aug. 3, 1812 Henry Hutcheson to Drury McDaniel. Rec. Aug. 3, 1812.

p. 159-160 Jan. 1, 1812 Edith Berry (Spartanburgh) to children Polly and Robert Harper Berry; for love and affection give 658 ac on Cases Cr of Pacolate R; grant Dec. 4, 1809 to John Nolen and sold by Spartanburgh sheriff to Henry Brown who sold to Edith Berry; and give a Negro man Jack about 25 years old, a Negro woman Mary 17 years old, a bay horse and all household and kitchen furniture--beds and furniture, plates, knives, forks, pots, and ovens, and all plantation tools, and all horses, cattle, sheep, and hogs. Witness Henry Brown, Abner W. Legon and James W Legon. Signed Edith Berry's mark. Wit. oath Aug. 27, 1812 James W Legon to A Benson. Rec. Aug. 27, 1812

p. 160-161 Jun. 16, 1804 Richard Collins, attorney for Thomas Hendrix (Ky) to Thomas Farrow (SC); for $350 sold 100 ac on Two Mile Cr; part of 400 ac grant to John Hendrix and "least" to George Lowther and Thomas Hendrix sued Thomas Farrow for the land in Spartanburgh Court and recovered judgment for land at March term 1804. Witness Robert McCord, Thomas Owen, and James Harrison. Signed Richard Collins. Wit. oath Aug. 7, 1812 Robert McCord to John Dean. Rec. Aug. 27, 1812

p. 161-162 Jan. 10, 1812 Amos Speace (Spartanburgh) to Edmond Cooley (same); for $1,000 sold 400 ac on both sides Cases Cr of Pacolate R; border: William Garrett, vacant, James Turner, and Richard Lee. Witness Luke Burnett and Hannah Burnett. Signed Amos Speace. Wit. oath Jan. 14, 1812 Luke Burnett to James Young. Rec. Aug. 27, 1812

p. 162-163 Feb. 14, 1812 Jonathan Low jr (Hancock Co, Ga) to Thomas Wyatt (Spartanburgh); for $100 sold 100 ac on Beck's Cr of Pacolate R; border: Jonathan Low sr. Witness William Dewberry and Daniel L Richardson. Signed Jonathan Low. Wit. oath Aug. 3, 1812 William Dewberry to Henry Turner. Rec. Aug. 31, 1812

p. 163 Apr. 18, 1812 Turner Hall to Thomas Willis; Turner sold his share of "crop that I am now making" to Thomas for Thomas to dispose of as he wants to; "mortgage" to be given up when Turner pays Thomas $14.50. Witness John H Jones. Signed Turner Hall's mark. Wit. oath Aug. 7, 1812 John H Jones to Thos Poole. Rec. Sept. 7, 1812

p. 163-165 Mar. 9, 1812 Drury and Thornton McDaniel (Spartanburgh) to Enoch Underwood (same); for $400 sold 100 ac on E side of S Tygar R at mouth of Island Pond; border: Enoch Underwood, Miller, Lowry McDaniel. Witness John Ward and William McDaniel. Signed Drury and Thornton McDaniel. Wit. oath Aug. 24, 1812 William McDaniel to Daniel White. Rec. Sept. 7, 1812. Dower renounced Aug. 24, 1812 Martha McDaniel, wife of Drury, to Daniel White

p. p. 165-166 Apr. 4, 1812 James Ridings (Spartanburgh) to Joseph Wilson (same); for $50 sold 25 ac on S side and W end of grant Nov. 9, 1774 to Mathew Harper; border: Wilson, Harper, Mollow's Cr, and Samuel Fowler's Mill path. Witness Neddy Reams and John Ridings. Signed James Ridings' mark. Wit. oath Apr. 7, 1812 Neddy Reams to Andw Furgason. Rec. Aug. 21, 1812

p. 166-167 May 28, 1811 Richard Barnett (Spartanburgh) to Thomas Greenwood (same); for $360 sold 125 ac on waters of Fairforrest Cr; border: William Moore and Legon's Br. Witness John Cook and Thomas James. Signed Richard Barnett. Wit. oath Nov. 11, 1811 John Cook to John Gossett. Rec. Aug. 21, 1812. Dower renounced Susannah Barnett to John Gossett Nov. 11, 1811

p. 167-168 Feb. 24, 1812 William Moore (Spartanburgh) to Thomas Greenwood (same); for $50 sold 18 ac on waters of Fairforrest Cr; where Thomas Greenwood lives; part of grant to Jesse Connell who sold to Robert Legon and sold by the sheriff as Robert Legon desc's property to John Cook who sold to William Moore; border: Legon Br. Witness Samuel Burton and Samuel Moore. Signed William Moore. Wit. oath Mar. 21, 1812 Samuel Burton to Drury McDaniel. Rec. Aug. 21, 1812

p. 168-169 Sept. 22, 1812 Jordan Ordom (Spartanburgh) to Samuel Jinkins (Union Dist); mortgage (for $70) a gray mare 13 years old, a brown horse 5 years old, a bay horse 10 years old, 300 bushels of corn, 2,000 bundles of fodder, a red cow with a white face, a poded cow and calf, 13 or 14 hogs, 4 feather beds and furniture, and all household and kitchen furniture; Condition: Jordan to pay Samuel $70 by Dec. 25, 1813. Witness William Cooper and William Odom. Signed Jordan Odom's mark. Wit. oath Sept. 22, 1812 William Cooper and A Benson. Rec. Sept. 22, 1812

p. 169-170 Jan. 18, 1806 Wilie Williford (Spartanburgh) to William Patton (same); for $180 sold 100 ac on N side Dutchman's Cr of Tygar R and on Dry Br of Wilies fork; border: John Shands and William Smith; part of 330 ac grant Apr. 3, 1786 to John Smith. Witness Samuel Archebald esq and William Wofford. Signed Wilie Wofford. Wit. oath Apr. 15, 1812 William Wofford to J Gossett. Rec. Sept. 22, 1812

p. 170-171 Apr. 13, 1812 John Smith (Spartanburgh) to William Wofford (same); for 25£ sold 110 ac; border: Hutchens' field, Thomas Williams, and Arthur Hutchens. Witness Clara Smith and John Palmer. Signed John Smith. Wit. oath May 15, 1812 John Palmer to Saml Archebald. Rec. Sept. 22, 1812. Dower renounced Aug. 8, 1812 Masey Smith to John Gossett

p. 171-173 Apr. 15, 1812 John Ison jr (Spartanburgh) to William Wofford (same); for $50 sold (1) 100 ac on waters of Dutchman's Cr; part of grant Nov. 17, 1785 to John Shan; border: William Smith; and (2) 100 ac on N side Dutchman's Cr; border:

John Shands and William Smith; part of 330 ac grant Apr. 3, 1786 to John Smith, blacksmith. Witness Deasten McHolder and Zepheniah Holmes. Signed John Ison jr. Wit. oath Apr. 15, 1812 Zepheniah Holmes to John Gossett. Rec. Sept. 22, 1812. Dower renounced Aug. 8, 1812 Nancy Ison to John Gossett

p. 173-174 Sept. 14, 1812 Isaac Young jr (Spartanburgh) to William Odum (same); for $300 sold 250 ac on Island Cr of Pacolate R; sold by Spartanburgh sheriff,as property of Moses Cantrell at suit of Moses Wilkins, to Isaac Young. Witness Whitney Henes and Patsey Odum. Signed Isaac C Young. Wit. oath Sept. 14, 1812 Whitney Henes to Leonard Adcock. Rec. Sept. 22, 1812

p. 174-175 Aug. 3, 1812 James Ward (Spartanburgh) to Richard Haney (same); for $214.50 sold 286 ac on Buck Cr, Suck Cr, and Island Cr of Pacolate R and Broad R; including the Battleground; James is to repay Richard 3s 6p per ac for land taken by older rights. Witness Floyd Turner and Reuben Warren. Signed James Ward's mark. Wit. oath Sept. 25, 1812 Reuben Warren to Henry Turner. Rec. Sept. 26, 1812

p. 175-176 Sept. 16, 1812 Daniel McKie (Spartanburgh) to Laban P. Poole (same); for $700 sold (1) 204 ac on S fork of Tygar R; and (2) 158 ac that adjoins (1). Witness John James Seay and Robert C Hanna. Signed Danl McKie. Wit. oath Sept. 16, 1812 John J Seay to Drury McDaniel. Rec. Oct. 5, 1812

p. 176-177 May 22, 1812 James W Darby (Union Dist) to Henry Brown (Spartanburgh); for $700 sold 250 ac on S Pacolate R. Witness William J Sempson and Thomas Haile. Signed James W Darby. Wit. oath May 22, 1812 (Union Dist) William J Sempson to David Johnson. Rec. Oct. 5, 1812. Dower renounced (Union Dist) Sept. 23, 1812 Mary Darby to David Johnson

p. 177-178 Oct. 11, 1810 Ruth, Thomas, William, and Jane Poole (Spartanburgh) to Jacob Land (same); for $30 sold 53 ac on Ridge between waters of Pacolate R and Fairforrest Cr; border: Crocker; "including oar banks which is excepted" (sic) and any "oare" that is found; part of two grants (1) Feb. 6, 1786 to Arthur Crocker and (2) Oct. 6, 1788 to William Crocker. Witness George Thomason and Allen Lancaster. Signed Ruth, Thomas, William, and Jeane Poole. Wit. oath Oct. 6, 1812 George Thomason to A Benson. Rec. Oct. 6, 1812

p. 178-179 Mar. 6, 1812 Jacob Land (Spartanburgh) to John Tollison (same); for $300 sold 53 ac between waters of Pacolate R and Fairforrest Cr; border: Crocker; "including the oar bank which is excepted" and any oar that is found; part of two grants (1) to Arthur Crocker and (2) to William Crocker. Witness Ely Tollison and Stephen Tollison. Signed Jacob Land. Wit. oath Aug. 31, 1812 Ely Tollison to John Gossett. Rec. (omitted)

p. 179-181 Sept. (blank), 1794 Page Puckett (Spartanburgh) to John King (same); for 25£ sterling sold 130 ac on Richland Cr of Pacolate R; border: John Lukroy, William Crocker, Howard, waggon road, and Poole; part of grant Oct. 6, 1788 Gov. Thomas Pinckney to William Crocker (415 ac) who sold 130 ac to Page Puckett. Witness Christopher Golightly and Nathan Whitley. Signed Page and Rebecah Puckett's marks. Wit. oath Oct. 2, 1811 Nathan Whitley to John Gossett. Rec. Oct. 6, 1812

p. 181 Apr. 21, 1812 Robert Legon (Spartanburgh) to Aaron Smith (same); for $50 sold 50 ac on E side Dutchman's Cr; border: W & N-Rolly Calvert, S-Thomas Moore, and E-unknown. Witness Charles Smith and Anny Alexander. Signed Robert Legon. Wit. oath Oct. 9,

BOOK N

1812 Charles Smith to Danl White. Rec. Oct. 12, 1812

p. 181-182 Apr. 17, 1812 William Moore (Spartanburgh) to James Cook; for $600 sold 179 ac on Fairforrest Cr; border: N-widow Legon, E-Thomas Greenwood, S-David Golightly, and W-Walter West. Witness Thomas Cook and Mary Cook. Signed William Moore. Wit. oath Oct. 13, 1812 Thomas Cook to John Cook. Rec. Oct. 13, 1812

p. 182-183 Jan. 21, 1812 Samuel Giddens (Spartanburgh) to Henry Smith (same); for $100 sold 50 ac on branches of Fairforrest Cr of Tygar R; border: Thomas Williamson, Griffith Middleton, and William Lary. Witness Samuel Colly and John Ward. Signed Samuel Giddens' mark. Wit. oath Aug. 1, 1812 John Ward to Drury McDaniel. Rec. Oct. 13, 1812

p. 183-184 May 21, 1812 John Tolleson (Spartanburgh) to Richard Kerby (same); for $150 sold 100 ac on Pacolate R; border: John Tolleson, ford of Troft Shoal Br, and Wm Stone. Witness Ely Tolleson and Berry Qunn. Signed John Tolleson. Wit. oath May 23, 1812 Berry Qunn to John Gossett. Rec. Oct. 13, 1812

p. 184-186 Jul. 27, 1811 Money Suthern (Spartanburgh) to Theron Earle (same); for $400 sold 70 ac on N side of N Pacolate R; border: road from Gilbert Bowman's to James Berry's, Bayles Earle, and "the" ford. Witness Bayles Earle, John Roddy, and Thomas Archer. Signed Money Sutherlan. Wit. oath Sept. 29, 1812 John Roddy to Wm Kelso. Rec. Oct. 14, 1812

p. 186-187 Nov. 9, 1799 William Poole (Spartanburgh) to son John Poole (same); for love and affection give 232 ac on N side of Pacolate R; about a mile from "the" springs; border: E-David Henrey, W-Hammett's old land, and other sides vacant; part of 312 ac grant Aug. 2, 1791 Gov. Charles Pinckney to Hugh Pearce; other 80 ac of grant was sold to John Henry and laid out by James Smith, surveyor. Witness John Mathus and Susanna Mathus. Signed William Poole. Wit. oath Oct. 12, 1809 John Mathus to John H Jones. Rec. Oct. 14, 1812

p. 187-188 May 9, 1812 Vincent Bennett, sheriff (Spartanburgh) to James Hodge; for $29.50 sold 200 ac on N side of Middle Tygar R; where John Smith lives or lived; sale due to writ from Spartanburgh Common Pleas Court suit John B. E. Elkin vs John Smith. Witness James Brannon and Anthony Foster. Signed Vincent Bennett SSD. Wit. oath Oct. 24, 1812 James Brannon to A Benson. Rec. Oct. 24, 1812

p. 188-189 Jul. 24, 1809 (Edgefield Dist) John Dishazo (Edgefield Dist) to Robert Dishazo sr (same); for $500 sold 600 ac on both sides S Pacolate R; border: S-Burton and Ralph Danger, N-Francis Pride and James McDaniel and William West, Samuel Carrell, and Thomas Jackson. Witness John Harvey and Robert Dishazo jr. Signed John Dishazo. Wit. oath (Edgefield Dist) Oct. 12, 1812 John Harvey to Shephard Spears. Rec. Nov. 3, 1812

p. 189-190 Oct. 20, 1808 Robert Henderson (Spartanburgh) and Thomas Henderson (Pendleton Dist) to John Dishazo (Edgefield Dist); for $200 sold 600 ac on both sides of S Pacolate R; border: S-Burton and Ralph Dangar, N-Francis Pride and James McDaniell, and William West, Samuel Carroll, and Thomas Jackson. Witness John Cansler (or Canselor) and Daniel Henderson. Signed Robert and Thos Henderson. Wit. oath (Pendleton Dist) Oct. 13, 1808 John Cansler to Wm Edmondson. Rec. Nov. 3, 1812. Dower renounced Oct. 13, 1808 (Pendleton Dist) Elizabeth Henderson, wife of Thomas, to Wm Edmondson

p. 190-191 Feb. 2, 1808 John Prest (Spartanburgh) to William Wells (same); for $300 sold 300 ac on Enoree R; border: Charles Pearson. Witness Lenoue (or Lencom) Westmoreland and Charles Pearson. Signed John Preast. Wit. oath Feb. 3, 1810 Charles Pearson to James Ford. Rec. Nov. 9, 1812

p. 191-192 Nov. 3, 1800 Isaac Hamby (Spartanburgh) to Henry Earnest (same); for $700 sold 300 ac on NE side of Enoree R; border: S-Enoree R and Bailey; grant Mar. 7, 1769 to William Lindsey. Witness James Wofford, Nathaniel Wofford, and Henry Hamilton. Signed Isaac Hamby. Wit. oath Jan. 4, 1812 James Wofford to Drury McDaniel. Rec. Nov. 9, 1812. Dower renounced Ellener Hamby to James Wofford (witness) Apr. 27, 1805

p. 192-193 Dec. 21, 1811 William Wells (Spartanburgh) to Henry Earnest (same); for $300 sold 260 ac on N side Enoree R and E side of Snolny Cr; part of grant to John Prest. Witness John Wells sr and Baretor (or Bastor) Fowler. Signed William Wells. Wit. oath Jan. 4, 1812 John Wells sr to Drury McDaniel. Rec. Nov. 9, 1812

p. 193-194 Nov. 7, 1803 Edward Arnold (Spartanburgh) to Henry Earnest (same); for $100 sold 40 ac on N side of Enoree R; border: Henry Earnest. Witness Benjamin Arnold and James Wofford. Signed Edward Arnold. Wit. oath Jan. 4, 1812 James Wofford to Drury McDaniel. Rec. Nov. 9, 1812

p. 194-196 Sept. 20, 1811 John Jean (Spartanburgh) to Tyre G Blackwell (NC); for $400 sold 80 ac on Pacolate R; part of two surveys. Witness Aspaseo Earle and John Ridings. Signed John Jean's mark. Wit. oath Oct. 13, 1812 John Ridings to Wm Kelso. Rec. Nov. 9, 1812. Dower renounced Dec. 23, 1811 Efereler Jean to James Young

p. 196-197 Jul. (blank), 1812 John Stroud (Spartanburgh) to Isaac Stroud (same); for $250 sold 100 ac on N side of Enoree R; border: E-Drury Couch and N & W-Benjamin Rhodes; part of 300 ac grant to Thos Couch and sold by John P Pool to John Stroud Mar. 14, 1808. Witness Aaron Casey and William Casey. Signed John Stroud. Wit. oath Jul. 9, 1812 Aaron Casey to Burrell Bobo. Rec. Nov. 9, 1812. Dower renounced Jul. 9, 1812 Rebecca Stroud to Burrell Bobo

p. 197-198 Jul. 23, 1811 Benjamin Wooton (Spartanburgh) to Samuel Pruett (same); for $35 sold 40 ac on N side Dutchman's Cr; border: William Pruett (or Ruett) desc and Nathaniel Wooton; part of grant Dudley Wooton; money for this sale received Jul. 29, 1811 by Rachel Wooton. Witness John Grist sr and John Grist jr. Signed Benjamin Wooton's mark. Wit. oath Feb. 25, 1812 John Grist sr to Samuel Morrow. Rec. Nov. 9, 1812

p. 198-200 Dec. 24, 1811 John Vice (Spartanburgh) to Gideon Harroldson (same); for $77 sold 27 ac on waters of Tygar R; border: George Vice, Nathaniel Vice, Gideon Harroldson, and Rheuben Vice. Witness Nathaniel Vice and Aaron Moore. Signed John Vice. Wit. oath Jan. 11, 1811 Aaron Moore to Saml Morrow. Rec. Nov. 9, 1812. Dower renounced Oct. 7, 1812 Franke Vice to Samuel Morrow

p. 200 Feb. 21, 1812 Isham Kendrick (Spartanburg) to Henry Wood (same); for $500 sold 200 ac on N side Rockey Field Cr of Enoree R; border: James Mellor; where Henry Wood lives. Witness Benjamin Wood and Page Rork. Signed Isham Kendrick. Wit. oath Mar. 11, 1812 Benjamin Wood to James Kilgore. Rec. Nov. 9, 1812

p. 200-201 Sept. 11, 1812 William Pool, taylor (Spartanburgh) to daughter Sarah Gore, widow (same); for love and affection give (ac omitted) on N side Lawson's fork and on Pacolate R; includes improvements where Thomas Gore desc lived. Witness Benjamin Poole, Elisha Pool, and David Lewis Pool. Signed William Pool. Wit. oath Nov. 8, 1812 Benjamin Pool to Jno H Jones. Rec. Nov. 10, 1812

p. 201-202 Aug. 25, 1812 Lawson Thomson (Spartanburgh) to William Rogers (same); for $600 sold 200 ac on both sides Ward's Cr of Tygar R; border: William Rogers and Charles Moore; grant North Carolina to Rev. Joseph Alexander. Witness John Ward and Theophelus Moore. Signed Lawson Thomson. Wit. oath Nov. 10, 1812 John Ward to Drury McDaniel. Rec. Nov. 10, 1812

p. 202-203 Nov. 9, 1812 William Pool (Spartanburgh, taylor to John Pool (same); for $200 sold (ac omitted) on S side Pacolate R; border: mouth of Pacolet Spring Br, Henry Pettet, and house Sara Gore lived in; where John Brown lived and where John Pool lives. Witness Bartholomew Stovall, William Gore, and Sarah Gore. Signed William Poole. Wit. oath Nov. 9, 1812 Bartholomew Stovall to Jno H Jones. Rec. Nov. 10, 1812

p. 203-204 Oct. 5, 1812 William Pool, taylor (Spartanburgh) to son Benjamin Pool (same); for love and affection give (ac omitted) on N side Lawson's fork; border: Pacolett Springs; part of William Pool's land where William lives; including a house. Witness Bartholomew Stovall, John Mathes, and Maryan(?) Pool. Signed William Pool. Wit. oath Nov. 8, 1812 John Mathes to Jno H Jones. Rec. Nov. 11, 1812

p. 204-205 Apr. 6, 1812 John House (Pendleton Dist) to Jacob Cooper (Laurens Dist); for $170 sold 100 ac on waters of Enoree R. Witness John Dunn and John C Aderhold. Signed John House. Wit. oath (Pendleton Dist) Apr. 6, 1812 John Dunn to Jno Cochran. Rec. Nov. 11, 1812. Dower renounced (Pendleton Dist) Apr. 6, 1812 Isabel House to Jno Cockran

p. 205 Jul. 18, 1812 Thomas Sherebert (Spartan Dist) to James Brannon (same); for $29 sold (ac omitted); willed by James Sherebert to Thomas Sherebert. Witness Joseph V Shanklin and Walter Carruth. Signed Thomas Sherebert's mark. Wit. oath Nov. 13, 1812 Joseph V Shanklin to A Benson. Rec. Nov. 12, 1812

p. 205-206 Jan. 15, 1810 Nathan Langstone (Spartanburgh) to William Langstone (same); for $110 sold 110 ac on Cooper's Br of Cedar Shoal Cr; border: Carlton Griyer, Thomas Witers, and William Wilbanks' heirs. Witness John Langstone and Hurain Goodwin. Signed Nathan Langstone. Wit. oath Oct. 15, 1812 John Langstone to Burrel Bobo. Rec. Oct. 19, 1812

p. 206-208 Nov. 18, 1812 Richard James (Spartanburgh) to Richard Thomson (same); for $900 sold 364 ac on both sides Brown's Br of Lawson's fork of Pacolette R and on a branch of Fairforrest Cr; where Richard James lives; border: a large pond and Brown's old line of 200 ac; two tracts granted to James Brown in (1) 1772 and (2) 1774 and 21 ac sold by James Cawell to Richard James; the two grants were mortgaged to Thomas Farrar and sold to Wells Griffeth who sold to Richard James; "P.S." land Richard Thomson "covers" is not warranted by Richard James. Witness Charles McAbee and John Simmons. Signed Richard James. Wit. oath Nov. 27, 1812 John Simmons to Danl White. Rec. Nov. 28, 1812. Dower renounced Elizabeth James to Daniel White Nov. 27, 1812

p. 208-209 Aug. 28, 1812 Vincent Bennett, sheriff (Spartanburgh) to Richard James; for $15 sold 125 ac on waters of Lawson's fork and Fairforrest Cr; part of grant to William Locock;

where Richard James lives; sale due to writ from Spartanburgh Common Pleas Court division dy Court Commissioners of land of James Smith desc; sold on 12 months credit; sale Apr. 6, 1812. Witness Muse Tollison and James Hunt. Signed V Bennett SSD. Wit. oath Nov. 28, 1812 James Hunt to A Benson. Rec. Nov. 28, 1812

p. 209-210 Nov. 5, 1812 Reuben Harrison (Spartanburgh) to James Harrison (same); for $110 sold 107 ac; except part taken by Locock's old survey near the high land pond. Witness John Connell and Richard James. Signed Reuben Harrison. Wit. oath Nov. 9, 1812 John Connell to Danl White. Rec. Nov. 30, 1812. Dower renounced Nov. 14, 1812 Nancy Harrison to John Lipscomb

p. 210-211 Nov. 30, 1812 Thomas, William, and Jean Poole, sons and daughter of William Poole desc, (Spartanburgh) to James Harrison (same); for $200 sold 383 ac on S side of Lawson's fork; grant Nov. 7, 1785 Gov. William Moultrie to William Poole desc. Witness Arkelles Foster and Richard Thomson. Signed Thomas, William, and Jane Poole. Wit. oath Nov. 30, 1812 Richard Thomson to A Benson. Rec. Nov. 30, 1812

p. 211-212 Nov. 23, 1812 Burjick McFearson (Spartanburgh) to son George and daughters Elizabeth, Nancy, Anne, Sally, and Winefred McFearson; since the children have "engaged" to maintain Burjick and wife Sydia during their lifetimes and since parents are old and very infirmed, Burjick gives: (1) to George part of Burjick's land (total 84 ac); the amount to be decided by three men chosed by George; and all corn and fodder and all farming utensels; (2) to Sally the other part of Burjick's land, a bed, and furniture; (3) to Elizabeth a bed and furniture; (4) to Nancy a bed and furniture; (5) to Anne a bed and furniture; (6) to Winefred a bed and furniture; all household and other furniture to be equally divided among the daughters. Witness Nathaniel Miller and Andrew B Miller. Signed Burjeck McFearson. Wit. oath Dec. 1, 1812 Andrew B Miller to Danl White. Rec. Dec. 5, 1812

p. 212 Dec. 1, 1812 James Brown jr and Thomas Reid to Joshua Richards JP; an oath that on the night of Nov. 15, 1812 they say Ambrus Hudgins bite off part of left ear of Henry Petet jr "which may be called an under Bit". Witness Joshua Richards. Signed James Brown and Thomas Reid. Rec. Dec. 7, 1812

p. 212-213 Nov. 12, 1811 John Poole (Spartanburgh) to James Quin (same); for $50 sold 71 ac on S side of Pacolate R; about a mile from Cotter's ford; border: E-Lee, N-Cantrel, W-James Turner, and S-Richard Cantrell. Witness Edward Turner and Andrew Red. Signed John Poole. Wit. oath Jun. 19, 1812 Edward Turner to Henry Turner. Rec. Dec. 14, 1812

p. 213-214 Oct. 20, 1812 Henry Gray (Spartanburgh) to Michael Miller (same); for $50 sold 23 ac on S side of Middle Tygar R; border: "the forge tract"; part of grant to Robert Nesbett jr. Witness Wilson Nesbett and Roddy Smith. Signed Henry Gray. Wit. oath Nov. 10, 1812 Wilson Nesbett to Wm Kelso. Rec. Dec. 16, 1812

p. 214-215 Nov. 30, 1812 Absolem Roe (Spartanburgh) to his children Simpson (the oldest), William, Marella, and Margaret Roe; for love and affection give 130 ac, 2 cows and 2 yearlings, a sorrel mare, a sow and 10 pigs, and all stock, all household furniture; stuff to be equally divided. Witness Robert Belcher sr and Robert Belcher jr. Signed Absolem Roe's mark. Wit. oath Dec. 15, 1812 Robert Belcher jr to Thos Poole. Rec. Dec. 18, 1812

p. 215-216 Sept. 4, 1812 Drury Boman (Spartanburgh) to Gilbert

Bowman; for $140 sold 140 ac on N side of S Pacolate R and both sides Alexr Kilpatrick's Cr; grant Dec. 19, 1793. Witness Muse Tolleson and James Hunt. Signed Drury Bowman. Wit. oath Dec. 21, 1812 James Hunt to A Benson. Rec. Dec. 21, 1812

p. 216-217 Sept. 14, 1811 Vincent Bennett, sheriff (Spartanburgh) to Henry Cuningham; for $33 sold 200 ac on waters of Dutchman's Cr; border: John Wofford; where William Patton lives; sale due to writ from Spartanburgh Common Pleas Court suit William Bond vs William Patton and Daniel Palmer; suit when Gabriel Benson was sheriff; sale Feb. 6, 1811. Witness Thomas Allison and Abner Benson. Signed Vincent Bennett SSD. Wit. oath Dec. 21, 1812 Thomas Allison to A Benson. Rec. Dec. 21, 1812

p. 217-219 Sept. 12, 1811 James Brannon (Spartanburgh, SC) to John Poole (Spartanburgh); for $100 sold 21 ac on S side of Pacolate R; border: John Poole and Pacolate Springs; James "received at law of John" this land in Spartanburgh Court of Common Pleas. Witness Abner Benson, Ephraim Roddy, and Benjamin Poole. Signed J Brannon. Wit. oath Dec. 21, 1812 Ephraim Roddy to A Benson. Rec. Dec. 21, 1812. Dower renounced Dec. 21, 1812 Sarah Brannon to Abner Benson

p. 219-220 Dec. 19, 1812 James Richards sr (province of E Florida) to "neffew" James Richards jr (Spartanburgh); for love and affection and $1 give 4 Negroes: Esaw, Burges, Milly, and Debaro. Witness Joshua Gorden, George Wood, and Joseph Richards. Signed Jas Richards. Wit. oath Dec. 24, 1812 George Wood and Joseph Richards to Joshua Richards. Rec. Dec. 25, 1812

p. 220 Nov. 28, 1812 Patrick Hogan to James Reams; for $100 sold (ac omitted) on N Tygar R; where Patrick Hogan lives; border: James Reams, Hogan's Spring Br, James Loftis, and Thomson Cleaton. Witness Robert Kimble and Neddy Reams. Signed Patrick Hogan's mark. Wit. oath Nov. 30, 1812 Robert Kimble to Andrew Furguson. Rec. Jan. 7, 1813

p. 220-222 Dec. 30, 1812 Joseph White (Spartanburgh) to William Broom (same); a bond for $40.50 payable in 12 months and to secure the bond Joseph sells 100 ac; border: James Kuns; part of grant to James Gibbs; Condition: sale void if Joseph pays the debt. Witness Joseph V Shanklin and James Adams. Signed Joseph White's mark. Wit. oath Dec. 30, 1812 James Adams to A Benson. Rec. Dec. 30, 1812

p. 222 Oct. 27, 1810 Edward McDaniel to Drury McDaniel JQ; Edward swears that Jeremiah Harris, commonly called Jerry, is free born Negro who was bound to him by court of Macklenburgh Co, Va and has served his time til age 21 and is now free. Witness Drury McDaniel JQ. Signed Edward McDaniel. Rec. Dec. 30, 1812

p. 222-223 Dec. 12, 1801 John Mathies (Spartanburgh) to George Hatfield (same); for $18 sold 30 ac on N side Pacolate R; border: Gray, Goore, and George Hatfield. Witness William Poole and William Willis. Signed John Mathies. Wit. oath Oct. 12, 1811 William Willis to Jno H Jones. Rec. Jan. 4, 1813

p. 223-224 Feb. 1, 1811 James Ridings and Charity Ridings (Spartanburgh) to James Whitten (same); for $500 sold 265 on S Pacolate R; border: Dood, Rase Paths, and Mollow's Cr; part of grant to Mathew Harper sr. Witness David Moore, Joseph Davis, and James Ridings jr. Signed James and Charity Ridings' marks. Wit. oath Apr. 6, 1811 David Moore to Andrew Furgason. Rec. Jan. 4, 1813

p. 224-225 Jan. (blank), 1813 Richard Thomson (Spartanburgh) to

Thomas Allison (same); for $175 sold 0.9 ac in Spartanburgh, SC; border: Thomas Allen's lot and Main St, blacksmith shop, and Farrow; W end of lots 15 and 16. Witness Vincent Bennett and Muse Tolleson. Signed Richard Thomson. Wit. oath Jan. 7, 1813 Vincent Bennet to A Benson. Rec. Jan. 7, 1813

p. 225-226 Feb. 12, 1807 Joshua Elliot (Spartanburgh) to Joseph Deason (same); a bond of $240 to deed Joseph Deason for 100 ac on head of Green's Cr of Pacolate R; border: David Jones, Howell, and Connell; deed to be made when money is paid. Witness Henry Littlejohn and Benjamin Deason. Signed Joshua Elliot. Wit. oath Oct. 15, 1811 Henry Littlejohn to John Lipscomb. Rec. Jan. 11, 1813

p. 226-227 Mar. 13, 1812 Thomas G Traylor (Spartanburgh) to Edward Bomar; for $150 sold 56 ac on N Tygar R; border: Edward Bomar and widow Traylor. Witness Jesse Traylor and Joel Traylor. Signed Thomas G Traylor. Wit. oath Sept. 1, 1812 Jesse Traylor to John Chapman. Rec. Jan. 16, 1818

p. 227-228 Mar. 20, 1811 (Greenville Dist) Benjamin Griffith, William Griffith, Hezekiah McDaniel, Hannah Carten, and Joseph Reed, legates of estate of Benjamin Griffith desc, to John Owens (Spartanburgh); for $600 sold 300 ac on N fork of Forgason's Cr of Tygar R; border: Middleton (two sides) and Frances Fowler (two sides). Witness John F. Hammett, Jonathan Shelton, Isaac Long, and Nimrod Underwood. Signed John Reed, Hezekiah McDaniel, and Hannah Carten's marks, B Griffith, and Wm Griffith. Wit. oath (Greenville Dist) Sept. 5, 1812 John F Hammett to B Griffith. Rec. Jan. 19, 1813

p. 228-229 Jan. 1, 1813 Isaac Young sr (Spartanburgh) to Ephraim Potter (same); for $120 sold 140 ac on both sides of Island Cr; border: William Abbett and Ephraim Potter. Witness John Cantrell and Samuel Sanders. Signed Isaac Young's mark. Wit. oath Jan. 1, 1813 Samuel Sanders to Henry Turner. Rec. Jan. 20, 1813

p. 229-231 Nov. 13, 1812 James Harrison (Spartanburgh) to Richard Thompson (same); for $150 sold 107 ac where Reuben Harrison formerly lived; border: near "high land pond"; W end of 383 ac grant Nov. 7, 1785 Gov. William Moultrie to William Pool. Witness V Bennett and Thomas Poole. Signed James Harrison. Wit. oath Nov. 30, 1812 V Bennett to A Benson. Rec. Jan. 20, 1813. Dower renounced Dec. 25, 1812 Rhoda Harrison to John Lipscomb

p. 231-232 Dec. 17, 1810 John Hammett and wife Sabra (Spartanburgh) to Daniel Hammett (same); for $100 sold 150 ac on waters of Pacolate R; border: Francis Brooks; grant to John Hammett sr. Witness William Brock and Anne Moore. Signed John Hammett and Sabra's mark. Wit. oath Feb. 1, 1813 William Brock to Thos Poole. Rec. Feb. 1, 1813

p. 232-233 Nov. 3, 1812 Jacob Cooper (Lawrence Dist) to John Cooper (same); for (money omitted) sold 100 ac on waters of Enoree R. Witness William Fowler and Henry Earnest. Signed Jacob Cooper. Wit. oath Nov. 5, 1812 Henry Earnest to Thomas Parks. Rec. Feb. 1, 1813

p. 233-234 Dec. 6, 1812 Richard James (Spartanburgh) to Charles McAbee (same); for $50 sold 283 ac on waters of Fairforrest Cr; border: N-Poole, W-Brown (now Richard Thompson), S-Loocock, and E-Elijah Barrett; known as Richard James' old place; survey Mar. 23, 1786; except land taken by Loocock's survey. Witness William James and Danl White. Signed Richard James. Wit. oath Feb. 1, 1813 William James to Jno H Jones. Rec. Feb. 1, 1813

p. 234 Jan. 12, 1813 Lucy Fowler (Spartanburgh) to Merica Fowler (Maddison Co, Tenn); for $100 sold "all my land", 2 feather beds and furniture, a loom, 2 spinning wheels, 5 chairs, a pot and oven, 2 cattle, a horse and saddle, 19 hogs, "a parcell" of pewter and earthenware; Condition: sale void if Lucy pays $100 to Merica by Dec. 25, 1815. Witness Absolem Blundell and Moses Fowler. Signed Lucy Fowler. Wit. oath Jan. 23, 1813 Absolem Blundell to James Hammett(?). Rec. Feb. 5, 1813

p. 234-236 Oct. 31, 1812 John Wells sr (Spartanburgh) to Stacy Cooper (same); for $400 sold 250 ac on waters of Fergerson's Cr of Tygar R; border: James Wofford, E-David More, SW-Martane Cole, NW-Thomas Garrett, NE-old survey, N-Paden, and SE-Aaron Arnold; part of grant to Daniel Obar. Witness Wm Cooper and Samuel Jenkins. Signed John Wells sr and Sarah's mark. Wit. oath Oct. 31, 1812 Wm Cooper to Drury McDaniel. Rec. Feb. 8, 1813

p. 236-237Mar. 25, 1809 Randolph Casey (Spartanburgh) to William Casey (same); for $200 sold 271 ac on waters of Enoree R and Cedar Shoal Cr; border: E-John Stone, N-Foster's great survey, W-Fuller, and S-remainder of grant; where Randolph Casey lives; grant to Willis Whittacer. Witness Jesse Casey and Miles Rainwaters. Signed Randolph Casey. Wit. oath Mar. 6, 1811 Jesse Casey to M Casey. Rec. Feb. 8, 1813

p. 237-239 Dec. 7, 1807 John F Harmming (Spartanburgh) to Randolph Casey (same); for $200 sold 271 ac on waters of Enoree R and Cedar Shoal Cr; border: E-John Stone and William Casey, N-Foster's big survey, W-Fuller's big survey, and S-remainder of grant now owned by William Casey; grant to Willis Whittecor. Witness Moses Casey jr and Thomas Berry. Signed John F Harmming. Wit. oath Oct. 7, 1809 Moses Casey jr to Burrell Bobo. Rec. Feb. 8, 1813

p. 239-240 Jun. 1, 1810 Moses Casey (Spartanburgh) to William Casey (same); for $200 sold 188 3/4 ac on SW side of Cedar Shoal Cr; plat attached shows border: Moses Casey, J Barker, R Fryer, and William Casey. Witness William Stone and Thomas Rhodes. Signed M Casey. Wit. oath Jun. 1, 1810 Thomas Rhodes to Burrell Bobo. Rec. Feb. 8, 1813. Dower renounced Jun. 1, 1810 Sarah Casey to Burrell Bobo

p. 240-242 Jun. 13, 1812 William Graham (Rutherford Co, NC) to Samuel Lowery esq (same); for $636 sold 1,000 ac on Sarratt's Cr of Main Broad R; border Clary, Holloway, Foster, and Sarratt; plat attached shows 1,054 ac and border: Forge tract, R Arnold, Charles Hester, Sarratt, Holloway, and Clary; includes where John Brown lived and bought from Maj. Daniel McClaren May 2, 1811 with plat signed by Joseph Camp DS; grant to John Rukman who sold to Daniel McClaren who sold to John Brown who sold to William Graham. Witness Vincent Bennett and Wilson Nesbett. Signed W Graham. Wit. oath Jan. 30, 1813 Wilson Nesbett to A Benson. Rec. Feb. 8, 1813

p. 242-243 Sept. 26, 1808 Isham Harrison (Spartanburgh) to D. J. Puckett (Spartanburgh, SC); for $100 and for a bond to Samuel Lancaster but now legally held by D. J. Puckett--bond dated Mar. 12, 1804 to convey 371½ac (half of tract sold to D. J. Puckett) --sell 741 ac near Spartanburgh, SC on branches of Fairforrest Cr of Tygar R; grant Jan. 6, 1794 Gov. William Moultrie to Isham Harrison. Witness Thomas Barnet, Elizabeth Harrison, and Lucy Harrison. Signed I Harrison. Wit. oath (Giles Co, Tenn) date omitted Thomas Barnet to M. W.(?) Buchanan JP for Giles Co and Wit. oath (Spartanburgh) Jan. 23, 1813 Thomas Barnet to Joshua Richards. Rec. Feb. 8, 1813

p. 243-244 Feb. 4, 1813 David Jones (Spartanburgh) to Young Allen (same); for $50 sold 27 ac on S side of Goocher's Cr; border: William Morris and William Patterson. Witness Agatha Lipscomb and Agner Lipscomb. Signed David Jones. Wit. oath Feb. 4, 1813 Agatha Lipscomb to John Lipscomb. Rec. Feb. 11, 1813

p. 244-245 Sept. 5, 1807 Robert Sloan (Spartanburgh) to Turner Hutcheson (same); for $215 sold 276 ac on Berd's (or Bud's) Cr of S Pacolate R; border: NE-James Alexander; grant Mar. 5, 1794 to Robert McDowell who sold to John Sloan jr who sold to Robert Sloan. Witness Esther Sloan and John Sloan. Signed Robert Sloan. Wit. oath (not dated) Esther Sloan, daughter of John and sister of Robert, to Michl Miller. Rec. Feb. 12, 1813

p. 245-246 Mar. 10, 1810 Samuel Crowder (Spartanburgh) to Howell Johnson (same); for $125 sold 156 ac; border: David Drummon and Daniel McKie. Witness William N Miller, George Miller, and Jesse Crook. Signed Samuel Crowder. Wit. oath Sept. 10, 1810 Jesse Crook to Drury McDaniel. Rec. Feb. 16, 1813

p. 246-247 Jul. 29, 1812 James Calvert (Spartanburgh) to Thomas Price (same); for $50 sold 30 ac on N side of N Tygar R; border: Josiah Hatchett, John Otts, and Ward's Cr. Witness Lawson Thomson and Zephaniah Posey. Signed James Calvert. Wit. oath Dec. 7, 1812 Lawson Thomson to John Cook. Rec. Feb. 18, 1813

p. 247-248 Dec. 26, 1811 Samuel Burton (Spartanburgh) to Joseph Landham (same); for $250 sold 100 ac on S side of N Tygar R. Witness Samuel Moore and Robert Miller. Signed Samuel Burton. Wit. oath Aug. 27, 1812 Robert Miller to Drury McDaniel. Rec. Feb. 18, 1813. Dower renounced Mar. 21, 1812 Rody Burton to Drury McDaniel

p. 248-249 Jan. 17, 1811 George Floyd to James Calvert (Spartanburgh); for $100 sold 30 ac on N side of N Tygar R; border: John Otts, Furgason, and Ward's Cr. Witness John Ward and John Otts. Signed George Floyd's mark. Wit. oath Nov. 10, 1812 John Ward to Drury McDaniel. Rec. Feb. 18, 1813

p. 249-250 Apr. 11, 1812 Joseph Lanham (Spartanburgh) to Thomas Price (same); for $250 sold (ac omitted) between forks of N and S Tygar R. Witness John Ward and Lydia Ward. Signed Joseph Lanham's mark. Wit. oath Apr. 11, 1802 John Ward to John Bruton. Rec. Feb. 18, 1813. Dower renounced May 28, 1812 Sally Lanham to Drury McDaniel

p. 250-252 May 22, 1812 Henry Brown (Spartanburgh) to James W Darby (same); to secure three notes for $700 payable one third on Dec. 25, 1812, one theid on Dec. 25, 1813, and one third on Dec. 25, 1814 and for $1 sold 250 ac on S Pacolate R; Condition: sale void if Henry Brown pays debt. Witness William J Thompson and Thomas Haile. Signed Henry Brown and James W Darby. Wit. oath Feb. 17, 1813 (Union Dist) William J Thompson to Batte Budsong. Rec. Feb. 18, 1813

p. 252-253 Jan. 7, 1813 Vincent Bennett, sheriff (Spartanburgh) to Maj. John Tolleson; for $30 sold 100 ac on waters of Pacolate R; sale due to writ from Spartanburgh Common Pleas Court suit John Tolleson vs James Robinson; sale Jan. 6, 1812. Witness Muse Tolleson and James Hunt. Signed Vincent Bennett SSD. Wit. oath Feb. 1, 1813 Muse Tolleson to A Benson. Rec. Mar. 1, 1813

p. 253-254 Jan. 7, 1813 Vincent Bennett, sheriff (Spartanburgh) to Maj. John Tolleson; for $81 sold 140 ac on waters of Lawson's fork; where John Thomason lives; sale due to writ from Spartanburgh Common Pleas Court suit Robert A Todd vs John Thomason and Clayborn Holt. Witness Muse Tolleson and James Hunt. Signed Vincent Bennett

SSD. Wit. oath Feb. 1, 1813 Muse Tolleson to A Benson. Rec. Mar. 1, 1813

p. 254-255 Feb. 12, 1813 Thomas Greenwood (Spartanburgh) to James Cook (same); for $10 quit claim to 18 ac where James Cook lives; on S and SW of tract where Thomas Greenwood lives; border: Legon Br and land sold by Richard Barnett to Thomas Greenwood. Witness Charles James and Walter West. Signed Thos Greenwood. Wit. oath Feb. 12, 1813 Walter West to Danl White. Rec. Mar. 1, 1813

p. 255 Jan. 8, 1813 Elizabeth Moore (Barren Co, Ky) to James Cook; for $10 sold her dower rights to 200 ac on waters of Fairforrest Cr; border: N-Edeth Legon, W-Thomas Tinsley, S-David Golightly, and E-Thomas Greenwood. Witness Samuel Moore and Thomas Cook. Signed Elizabeth Moore's mark. Wit. oath Feb. 18, 1813 Thomas Cook to John Cook. Rec. Mar. 1, 1813

p. 255-256 Nov. 22, 1811 Mary, William, Hugh, and Andrew Caldwell and John Coan, heirs and legates of estate of John Caldwell desc (Spartanburgh) to Samuel Caldwell (same); for $100 sold 250 ac in forks to Tygar R; border: S-Middle Tygar R, N-N Tygar R, W-Booye, and others vacant; belonged to John Caldwell's estate; grant Mar. 1, 1774 to John Caldwell desc. Witness John Crawford and Andrew Coan. Signed Mary's mark, Wm Cladwell, Hugh Caldwell, Andrew Caldwell, and John Coan. Wit. oath Mar. 1, 1813 John Crawford to Drury McDaniel. Rec. Mar. 1, 1813

p. 256-257 Aug. 13, 1811 John Parris to Judy Robertson; for $40 sold 65 ac on Suck Cr of Broad R; border: Moultrie and Williams; part of grant Sept. 11, 1795 to Jacob Dilbeck. Witness Peter Goslen and John Adcock. Signed John Parres. Wit. oath Aug. 13, 1811 Peter Goslen to Leond Adcock. Rec. Mar. 1, 1813

p. 257-260 Nov. 14, 1812 Lewis Brown (Spartanburgh) to James Younger (same); for $600 sold 300 ac; border: James Young, a tree branded "Y", John Nathaniel McCarrol, and creek of N Pacolate R. Witness Eaton Walker and William Bennett. Signed Lewis Brown. Wit. oath (not dated) William Bennett to James Young. Rec. Mar. 15, 1813. Dower renounced Mar. 12, 1813 Patsey Brown to James Young

p. 260-261 Aug. 25, 1808 Daniel French (Spartanburgh) to James Cook (same); for $200 sold 200 ac on Buffelow Br of Fairforrest Cr; border: N-Hampton's old tract, W-vacant, S-Calvert, and E-John Smith's old tract; grant to Frederk Eison. Witness Wm H Cook and Jos Thomas Cook. Signed Daniel French's mark. Wit. oath Dec. 2, 1809 J Thomas Cook to Danl White. Rec. Mar. 17, 1813

p. 261-262 Feb. 24, 1813 William Shaw (Columbia, SC) to Abner Benson (Spartanburgh); for $125 sold 100 ac; border: land where Court House stands; part of tract sold by Vincent Bennett, sheriff (Spartanburgh) due to execution as property of Jeremiah Walker and sold to William Shaw in copartnership with William Benson; William Shaw now sells his share. Witness Samuel Green and Simon P Gray. Signed W Shaw. Wit. oath Feb. 24, 1813 (Richland Dist) Samuel Green to James S Guignard, CCP and Not. Pub. Rec. Mar. 29, 1813

p. 262-263 Aug. 7, 1811 Isaac Cantrell sr (Spartanburgh) to Elijah Cantrell (same); for $120 sold 70 ac on Buck Cr; border: John Nelson, Johnson, Richard Morris, Elijah Cantrell, and Abraham Cantrell; grant Oct. 6, 1788 States Office to William Jordan. Witness Archibald Nelson and Ely Cantrell. Signed Isaac Cantrell and Charlote's mark. Wit. oath Aug. 31, 1811 Archibald Nelson to Leon Adcock. Rec. Mar. 30, 1813

p. 263-264 Oct. 26, 1812 John Mason sr (Spartanburgh) to Harvey Davis (same); for $200 sold 294 ac on waters of Burton's Cr. Witness Thomas Burton and James Ezell. Signed John Mason's mark. Wit. oath Mar. 29, 1813 Thomas Burton to Leon Adcock. Rec. Mar. 30, 1813

p. 264-265 Apr. 2, 1813 Thomas Bearden (Spartanburgh) to William Smith (same); to secure a note for $97.69 sold a sorrel horse, a featherbed and furniture, 2 cows and calves, a cupboard, a pot, a dutch oven, 2 plows, 2 axes, 2 pair of gers with iron traces, a frow, a mattock, a pine table; Condition sale void if Thomas pays the debt in 6 months; William can sell the stuff after 6 months after giving 20 days notice. Witness Joseph Smith and Jacob Ham. Signed Thos Bearden. Wit. oath Apr. 3, 1813 Jacob Ham and Saml Morrow. Rec. Apr. 5, 1813

p. 265-267 Oct. 27, 1807 John Couch sr (Spartanburgh) to Benjamin Couch (same); for (money not mentioned) sold 160 ac on N side of Enoree R at Sandy ford; border: land John Couch sold to Adam Farmer and land John Couch sold to William Camnel; part of 300 ac grant Mar. 9, 1773 to James Couch. Witness Henry Meredeth, Levi Couch, and William Cammell. Signed John Couch's mark. Wit. oath Apr. 3, 1813 Levi Couch to Burrell Bobo. Rec. Apr. 5, 1813. Dower renounced Feb. 13, 1808 Winny Couch to Burrell Bobo

p. 267-268 Jan. 24, 1804 John Couch and wife Winny (Spartanburgh) to Benjamin Couch (same); for $240 sold 100 ac on N side of Enoree R; border: William Campbell. Witness William Stewart and Davis Underwood. Signed John and Winny Couch's marks. Wit. oath Apr. 3, 1813 Davis Underwood to Burrell Bobo. Rec. Apr. 5, 1813. Dower renounced Feb. 13, 1808 Winny Couch to Burrell Bobo

p. 268-269 Feb. 24, 1809 Richard Young to Reubin Newman (Spartanburgh); for $100 sold 50 ac on S side of Tygar R below mouth of Jemey's Cr; part of grant to Benjamin Wofford sr; border: Richard Young. Witness William Young and Willis Williford. Signed Richard Young. Wit. oath Mar. 5, 1813 Willis Williford to M Casey. Rec. Apr. 5, 1813. Dower renounced May 8, 1809 Isabell Young to Burrell Bobo

p. 269-271 Sept. 9, 1801 Owen and Eleonor Forrester (Spartanburgh) to Reubin Newman (same); for $200 sold 75 ac on S side of Tygar R; border: Richard Young. Witness William Wilson and Anthony Shands. Signed Owen Forrester's mark. Wit. oath Mar. 5, 1813 Anthony Shands to M Casey. Rec. Apr. 5, 1813. Dower renounced Oct. 26, 1801 Elender Forrester to Wm Smith

p. 271-272 Apr. 5, 1813 Vincent Wyatt sr (Spartanburgh) to Vincent Wyatt jr (same); for $200 sold 80 ac on Peter's Cr; border: Drueour's Br and Vincent Wyatt jr's Spring Br. Witness William F Reynolds and Ephraim Elder. Signed Vincent Wyatt sr. Wit. oath Apr. 5, 1813 William F Reynolds to Henry Turner. Rec. Apr. 5, 1813

p. 272-273 Dec. 5, 1812 Patrick Hogan (Spartanburgh) to Thompson Clayton (same); for $50 sold 100 ac; part of where Patrick Hogan lives; border: N Tygar R, Thads Owens, and Thompson Clayton; grant to Alexander McCarter. Witness John Vaughan, Nancy Reams, and Mary Hogan. Signed Patrick Hogan's mark. Wit. oath Apr. 5, 1813 John Vaughan to Thos Poole. Rec. Apr. 5, 1813

p. 273-274 Feb. 17 (or 19), 1807 Ebenezer Moss (Spartanburgh) to John Moss (same); for $600 sold 250 ac on Two Mile Cr of Enoree R; border: Bumpass, Jesse Brown, Bussey, and Thomas Farrow. Witness James Moss, William Calvert, and Spencer Bobo. Signed Ebenezer and Agness Moss' marks. Wit. oath Jun. 3, 1807

(Laurens Dist) James Moss to Starling Tucker. Rec. Apr. 5, 1813

p. 274-275 Mar. 12, 1813 Jane Jordan (Spartanburgh) to Daniel and John Robertson (same); for $400 sold 189 ac on S side of S Tygar R; border: Joisha Benson, John Kennely, and Samuel Burns; grant to Wm Semons who sold to Jane Jordan. Witness James Swanzy and Robert Bailey. Signed Jane Jordan's mark. Wit. oath Mar. 12, 1813 James Swanzy to John Collins. Rec. Apr. 6, 1813

p. 275-276 Aug. 27, 1810 (Union Dist) Robert Akin (SC) to Thomas Hancock (Union Dist); for $300 sold (1) 350 ac on Proctor's fork of People's Cr and (2) 536 ac on NE of (1). Witness James Bice and Aquilla McJunkins. Signed Robert Akin. Wit. oath (not dated) (Union Dist) Aquilla McJunkins to James Mury(? or Meey). Rec. Apr. 6, 1813

p. 276-277 Sept. 28, 1812 Richard Haney (Spartanburgh) to James Dodd (Rutherford Co, NC); for $214 sold 286 ac on Buck, Suck, and Island Creeks of Pacolate and Broad Rivers; including the battleground; Note: if part is taken by older grants, then Richard pays 3s 6p per ac. Witness Samuel Frolenger and Townson Robertson. Signed Richard Haney's mark. Wit. oath Oct. 31, 1812 Samuel Frolenger to Leon Adcock. Rec. Apr. 6, 1813

p. 277-278 Mar. 19, 1806 Jean Jordan (Spartanburgh) to Samuel Burns (same); for $250 sold 115 ac on S side of S Tygar R; border: Samuel Burns' house; part of 280 ac grant Mar. 2, 1789 to William Simmons. Witness James Gilliland and Beverly Lewis. Signed Jean Jordan's mark. Wit. oath Mar. 2, 1811 James Gilliland to John Collins. Rec. Apr. 6, 1813

p. 278 Jan. 10, 1813 Hugh Moore, John Low jr, Henry Griffith, Mary Dewberry, Rosanna Low, and Dicey Low (all of Spartanburgh), legal "representation" of Jonathan Low desc (late of Ga) to John Low sr; for (money not mentioned) sold all rights by heirship to 164 ac on N side of Pacolate R and both sides of Old Post Road; border: SW-John Low sr, E-Carling and Sharbull, NE & S-John Low sr, and NW-Betterton; grant to Jonathan Low desc. Witness Samuel Turner and Thomas Wyatt. Signed Hugh Moore, John Low jr, and Henry Griffith, Mary Dewberry, Rosanna Low, and Dicey Low's marks. Wit. oath Apr. 6, 1813 Thomas Wyatt to John H Jones. Rec. Apr. 6, 1813

p. 278-279 Jun. 15, 1811 Reuben Warren (Spartanburgh) to John Low sr (same); for $19 sold 19 ac on branch of Island Cr of Pacolate R; border: Jonathan Low. Witness Lot Warren and Drury McMillin. Signed Reuben Warren. Wit. oath Oct. 8, 1812 Lot Warren to Henry Turner. Rec. Apr. 6, 1813

p. 279-280 Mar. 5, 1813 Thomas Farrow (Spartanburgh and John F Morss (same); a agreement on dividing of tract granted to John Farrow and sold to John Raney(?) "for purchase money"; the line is on a Public Road; John takes land on E and N side of line and Thomas takes land to W and S of line. Witness James Wofford and Joseph Woodruff. Signed Thomas Farrow and John F Morss. Wit. oath Apr. 6, 1813 James Wofford to John Collins. Rec. Apr. 6, 1813

p. 280-281 Aug. 19, 1809 Christopher Bell (Spartanburgh) to Richard Chesney (same); for $450 sold 250 ac on branch of Tygar R; border: S-John Meroney, W-John Raiman, David Dunsmore, and Jacob Earnest, E-John White and William Dunlap; part of grant May 4, 1775 Gov. William Bull to James Sloan. Witness Isaac Crow jr and Thomas Bell. Signed Christopher Bell. Wit. oath Sept. 11, 1812 Isaac Crow to Samuel Woodruff. Rec. Apr. 6, 1813. Dower renounced Sept. 17, 1812 (York Dist) Jane Bell to James A Whythe JQ

p. 281-282 Aug. 23, 1806 Alexander Dunlap (Newberry Dist), son of William Dunlap desc, to Richard Chesney (Spartanburgh); for $250 sold 200 ac on branch of Tygar R; border: W-John M Croney and James Sloan, E-William Bolding and Richard Fletcher, and others vacant; grant Jan. 25, 1773 Gov. William Bull to William Dunlap. Witness James Smith, John Leopard, and William Betton sr. Signed Alexander Dunlap. Wit. oath Nov. 15, 1808 James Smith to John Brewton. Rec. Apr. 6, 1813

p. 282-283 Dec. 9, 1809 Achiles Durham (Rutherford Co, NC) Daniel Cantrell (Spartanburgh); for $140 sold 100 ac on waters of Buck Cr. Witness John Martin, John Blackwell, and Dicy Hicks. Signed Achiles Durham. Wit. oath Aug. 18, 1812 John Blackwell to Leonard Adcock. Rec. Apr. 6, 1813

p. 283-284 Aug. 8, 1812 Henry Cunningham (Spartanburgh) to William Wofford (same); for $115 sold 120 ac on waters of Dutchman's Cr; border: Thomas Williams and William Wofford; part of 330 ac grant to John Smith, blacksmith. Witness John Wright and Judith Wright. Signed Henry Cunningham. Wit. oath Aug. 8, 1812 John Wright to John Gossett. Rec. Apr. 6, 1813

p. 284 (not dated) Moses and Elizabeth Cavin (Spartanburgh) to John Henry; for $250 sold 148 ac; part of land of John Cavin desc and where Elizabeth Cavin lives; border: James M (or W) Reynold, Gideon Reynolds, Samuel Enick, John Williams, Robert Rogers, and John Arnold. Wit. oath William Alexander and James W Reynolds. Signed Moses Cavin and Elizabeth's mark. Wit. oath Apr. 5, 1813 James W Reynolds to Jno H Jones. Rec. Apr. 6, 1813

p. 284-285 Oct. 7, 1807 Longshore Lamb (Spartanburgh) to Christopher Bell (same); for $450 sold 250 ac on branch of Tygar R; border: S-John Meroney, W-John Raman, David Dunsmore, and Jacob Earnest, and E-John White and Wm Dunlap; grant May 4, 1774 Gov. William Bull to James Sloan. Witness Isaac Crow jr and Samuel Bell. Signed Longshore Lamb. Wit. oath Apr. 6, 1813 Isaac Crow jr to Samuel Woodruff. Rec. Apr. 6, 1813. Dower renounced Sept. 3, 1810 (Caldwell Co, Ky) Sally Lamb to John Mercer JP and David James JP

p. 285-286 Jan. 1, 1808 Christopher Bell to Richard Young; for $130 sold (ac omitted); Condition: sale void if Christopher pays Richard $130 by Mar. 1, 1808. Witness Richard Chesney, William Crow, and Longshore Lamb. Signed Christopher Bell. Wit. oath none. Rec. Apr. 6, 1813

p. 286 Mar. 5, 1810 Edward Ballenger (Spartanburgh) to Peter Hawkins (same); for $60 sold 70 ac on S side of Camp Br of Lawson's fork of Pacolate R; survey Jul. 22, 1797 for Edward Ballenger and grant Jan. 7, 1799 Gov. Edward Rutledge to Larkin Ryley and assigned on back of grant Jun. 23, 1806 to Joshua Ingrine. Witness John Ballenger, James Ballenger, and Peggy Ballenger. Signed Edward Ballenger. Wit. oath Apr. 6, 1813 John Ballenger to James Young. Rec. Apr. 7, 1813

p. 286-287 Dec. 3, 1807 Owen Hembree (Spartanburgh) to William Hembree (same); for $40 sold 40 ac on SW side of Dutchman's Cr and both sides Blacktock's (sic) Rd; border: SW-Pinckney, N-Moore, and SE-where Owen Hembree lives; survey Oct. 18, 1806 for Owen Hembree and grant Mar. 2, 1807 Gov. Charles Pinckney to Owen Hembree. Witness John Morrow and William N Morrow. Signed Owen Hembree. Wit. oath Dec. 3, 1807 John Morrow to Samuel Morrow. Rec. Apr. 7, 1813

p. 287-288 Feb. 7, 1804 James Dickson (Craven Co, NC) to Robert McDowell (Spartanburgh); for $400 sold 200 ac on S side of S Pacolate R; border: Gabriel Benson and James McDowell; part of two grants to William Dickson. Witness David McDowell and Gabriel Benson. Signed James Dickson. Wit. oath Apr. 7, 1813 Gabriel Benson to Thomas Poole. Rec. Apr. 7, 1813

p. 288-289 Apr. 14, 1810 Mathew, Thomas, and William Patton, James P Meders, A. D. Thomson, Jenny O'Niell, and Moses White, heirs of Robert Patton desc (Union Dist), to Samuel Archibald (Spartanburgh); for $80 sold 57 ac; border: Samuel Archibald, George Story, E bank of Storey's Cr, and McElewan's Cr. Witness Col. Hugh Means and Adden(?) Chishol (or Chiskolure). Signed Mathew Patton, Thos Patton, Wm Patton, Jas P Meders, A. D. Thomson, Jenny O'Niell, and Moses White. Wit. oath Jul. 4, 1812 Hugh Means to Saml Morrow. Rec. Apr. 7, 1813

p. 289-290 Dec. 28, 1810 Samuel Burton (Spartanburgh) to William Hambrey (same); for $30 sold 45 ac; border: Purckuny(?) and Currey; part of 383 ac grant to Hopkins Bright. Witness Samuel Moore and Ancel Hudgins. Signed Samuel Burton. Wit. oath Jan.(?) 12, 1811 Ancel Hudgins to Saml Morrow. Rec. Apr. 7, 1813

p. 290 Dec. 23, 1811 William Moore (Spartanburgh) to Mathew Patton (same); for $300 sold 120 ac on N side of S Tygar R; border: Thornton McDaniel and Enock Underwood. Witness John Patton and Nath Burton. Signed William Moore. Wit. oath Feb. 11, 1813 John Patton to Drury McDaniel. Rec. Apr. 7, 1813

p. 290-291 Sept. 26, 1801 Stephen Hyde (Spartanburgh) to Thomas Price (same); for $30 sold 50 ac on branch of waters of Tygar R; border: John Jeffars, David Ander's old line, and Roberts. Witness Randolph Gravett and Margaret Floyd. Signed Stephen Hyde's mark. Wit. oath Mar. 29, 1813 Randolph Gravett to Drury McDaniel. Rec. Apr. 7, 1813

p. 291-292 Jan. 25, 1812 Ezekiel Sillavan (Spartanburgh) to Solomon Jackson; for $70 paid to Jesse Goun sold 70 ac. Witness (blank) Patterson and William Jackson. Signed Ezekiel Sillaven. Wit. oath Dec. 18, 1812 William Jackson to Jno H Jones. Rec. Apr. 8, 1812

p. 292 Apr. 9, 1813 Anthony Foster (Spartanburgh) to Thomas Weaver (same); for $100 sold 165 ac where Thomas Weaver lives on Lawson's fork; part of grant to Turner Thomason desc and by heirship to Salley Thomason and sold by Spartanburgh sheriff,as Franklin Foster's land (husband of Salley Thomason),to Anthony Foster. Witness Alexander McKie and John Thomason. Signed A Foster. Wit. oath Apr. 9, 1813 John Thomason to Danl White. Rec. Apr. 9, 1813

p. 292-293 Apr. 19, 1813 John Wood (Spartanburgh) to son James Wood; for love and affection give 70 ac on W side Wilson's Cr of Tygar R; border: Capt. Peter Gray. Witness Isham Foster, Banister Hawkins, and David Foster. Signed John Wood's mark. Wit. oath Apr. 19, 1813 Banister Hawkins to John Chapman. Rec. Apr. 30, 1813

p. 293-294 Dec. 5, 1812 James Miller (Spartanburgh) to William N. Miller (same); for $182.50 sold 830 ac on S side of Middle Tygar R; border: Wm Caldwell and unknown. Witness Samuel Miller, Richard Berry jr and Hugh W Berry. Signed James Miller. Wit. oath Apr. 27, 1813 Samuel Miller to Drury McDaniel. Rec. May 3, 1813

p. 294 Dec. 17, 1812 Andrew Red sr (Spartanburgh) to Andrew Red jr (same); for $132 sold 310 ac on Canes Cr of Pacolate R; escept part sold to William Garrott sr. Witness John Red and Elizabeth Red. Signed Andrew Red. Wit. oath Dec. 17, 1812 John Red to Leonard Adcock. Rec. May 3, 1813

p. 294-295 Apr. (blank), 1813 James Quinn (Spartanburgh) to Soloman Abbit (same); for $120 sold 120 ac on Cherokee Cr of Pacolate R; grant to James Stedmon. Witness Edward Turner and William Turner. Signed James Quinn. Wit. oath May 3, 1813 William Turner to Thomas Poole. Rec. May 3, 1813

p. 295-296 Mar. 23, 1812 Zachariah Blackwell (Spartanburgh) to Marvel Humphrey Smith (same); for $50 sold 70 ac on fork of Suck Cr; border: Wyatt. Witness Sarah Blackwell and Rachel Blackwell. Signed Zachariah Blackwell. Wit. oath Apr. 14, 1812 Rachel Blackwell to Henry Turner. Rec. May 3, 1813

p. 296-297 Oct. 18, 1810 John Stone (Caldwell Co, Ky) to John Thornton (Spartanburgh); for $200 sold 100 ac on Jamies Cr of Tygar R; grant Gov. William Bull to John Dunkin who sold to William Caldwell who sold to Martha McCrory and by her will to Anthony Wilson who sold to Thomas Price who sold to John Stone. Witness John Lancaster and John Huckabey. Signed John Stone. Wit. oath May 16, 1813 John Lancaster to Thomas Poole. Rec. May 20, 1813

p. 297 Feb. 11, 1813 Thomas Cook to James Foster (Spartanburgh); for $227 sold 227 ac on waters of Fairforrest Cr and Buffelick (sic) Cr; border: Alerey, Autrey, E-William Cook, Dd Golightly, and Ch Barnett, S-Dd Golightly's old survey, W-Philip Oats, and N-Wm Finch and Ed Autery. Witness Ralph Smith and Lemuel Cook. Signed Thomas Cook. Wit. oath May 8, 1813 Ralph Smith to John Chapmon. Rec. Jun. 3, 1813

p. 297-298 Oct. 9, 1805 Jesse Wells (Spartanburgh) to William Thomson (same); for $61 sold (ac omitted); border: Main St; lot 7 in Spartanburgh, SC. Witness Richard Thomson, Isham Harrison, Abner Benson. Signed Jesse Wells. Wit. oath Jun. 3, 1813. Richard Thomson to Thomas Poole. Rec. Jun. 4, 1813

p. 298-299 May 3, 1808 Owen J Bowen, for self and as agent for Henry Cannon (Ga), see power of attorney from Henry Cannon, Patrick Tylar, Hunlet Jones (Spartanburgh) to Caleb Jones (Spartanburgh); for $344.76 sold their "equal parts" of 194 ac belonging to Malachi Jones desc on S side of Pacolette R and at mouth of Lindsay Cr; where Caleb Jones lives. Witness Hugh Moore and Ezekiel Sillevan. Signed Owen J Bowen, O. J. Bowen as agent for Henry Cannon, Patrick M Tylar, and Jno H Jones. Wit. oath Apr. 7, 1812 Hugh Moore to John Gossett. Rec. Jun. 4, 1813

p. 299 Jun. 2, 1807 Thomas Burton (Spartanburgh) to Gabriel Benson (same); for $100 sold 118 ac on Fairforrest Cr; grant to Charles Benson; part of lot drawn by Eaton Walker as legate of William Benson desc and sold to Thomas Burton. Witness Robert A Todd and George Thomason. Signed Thomas Burton's mark. Wit. oath May 10, 1813 Robert A Todd to Thomas Poole. Rec. Jun. 4, 1813

p. 299-300 Apr. 6, 1813 Samuel Farrow (Spartanburgh) to Isaac Smith (same); for $300 sold ½ ac; lot 14 on S side Spartanburgh Court House; border: S-Thompson, W-Abner Benson, E-Thompson, and N-Publick tract. Witness N. E. Benson and R Criswell. Signed S Farrow. Wit. oath Jun. 7, 1813 N. E. Benson to A Benson. Rec. Jun. 7, 1813. Dower renounced Elizabeth Farrow to Charles J. Colcock Apr. 10, 1813

p. 300-301 Jan. 23, 1809 Thomas House (Spartanburgh) to Thomas Thornton (same); for $300 sold 250 ac on branches of Enoree R; SW part of 1,000 ac sold by Robert Gaddis to Thomas

House. Witness James Wofford and William Rhodes. Signed Thomas House's mark. Wit. oath May 22, 1813 James Wofford to David Moore. Rec. Jun. 4, 1813

p. p. 301-302 Mar. 10, 1812 William Moore (Spartanburgh) to Mathias Rush; for $478 sold (ac omitted) on S side of N Tygar R; border: Patton, Posey, and Miller. Witness William Rogers and Jason Moore. Signed William Moore. Wit. oath Jun. 7, 1813 William Rogers to Drury McDaniel. Rec. Jun. 7, 1813. Dower renounced Mar. 12, 1812 Elizabeth Moore to Drury McDaniel

p. 302-303 Apr. 14, 1809 Henry Wells (Logan Co, Ky) to John Barrett (Spartanburgh); for $200 sold 200 ac; border: Obediah Wingo's Spring Br, John Foster, Richard Foster, Elijah Barrett, and Richard Daniel. Witness Thomas Barnett and John Wells. Signed Henry Wells. Wit. oath Apr. 14, 1809 John Wells to Danl White. Rec. Jun. 7, 1813

p. 303-304 Apr. 29, 1813 John Chapman (Spartanburgh) to James Wood (same); for $30 sold 15 ac on branch of N Tygar R; border: Court House Road, Woods' Spring Br, Woods, and Gray; part of grant to William Goodlett. Witness Beverly Chapman and John Chapman jr. Signed John Chapman. Wit. oath Jun. 7, 1813 Beverly Chapman to Thomas Poole. Rec. Jun. 7, 1813

p. 304-305 Apr. 24, 1813 Thomas Kimbrell (Spartanburgh) to James Wood (same); for $600 sold 200 ac on both sides Thompson's Cr of Pacolate R; border: Thomas Burnett. Witness William Burnett and Milton Davis. Signed Thomas Kimbrell's mark. Wit. oath Jun. 7, 1813 Milton Davis to James Young. Rec. Jun. 7, 1813. Dower renounced Apr. 30, 1813 Nancy Kimbrell to James Young

p. 305 May 7, 1813 John Shippy to Drury Wood; for $280 sold 165 ac on Skelton's Cr of Thickety Cr; border: Johnson. Witness George Wood and Margaret Camp. Signed John Shippy. Wit. oath May 7, 1813 George Wood to J Camp. Rec. Jun. 7, 1813

p. 305-306 Mar. 27, 1813 (Union Dist) Jacob Puter (Union Dist) to John Shippy (Spartanburgh); for $40 sold 200 ac on both sides Skilton's Cr of Thickety Cr; grant to Leonard Anderson Cole; border: Obrian Smith. Witness George Boyd (or Bleoyd), Powell Ovonbey, and Jacob Greyton. Signed Jacob Puter. Wit. oath May 21, 1813 Jacob Greyton to John Lipscomb. Rec. Jun. 7, 1813

p. 306-307 Mar. 3, 1813 William Berry (Spartanburgh) to John Hobbey (same); for $300 sold 206 ac on Berry's Cr on N side of Enoree R; where William Berry lives; part of two grants--(1) Oct. 3, 1785 to Vincent Berry who sold Feb. 27, 1812 to William Berry and (2) sold Mar. 15, 1806 by James Langford to William Berry. Witness Josiah Woodruff, Samuel Jones, and James Langford. Signed William Berry. Wit. oath Mar. 3, 1813 James Langford to Samuel Woodruff. Rec. Jun. 7, 1813. Dower renounced Mar. 11, 1813 Frances Berry to Burrell Bobo

p. 307 Mar. 13, 1802 Daniel Allen (Spartanburgh) to James Cook (same); for $800 sold 200 ac on S side of N Tygar R at mouth of Mill Br; border: Ephraim Drummon, Daniel Davias, Raws(?), William Duncan, James Moore, John Massey; part of "Addaneschuks(?) Rawses deed William Duncan's" land. Witness Joseph Burton, Joseph Crook, and William Crook. Signed Daniel Allen. Wit. oath Dec. 18, 1802 Joseph Crook to Drury McDaniel. Rec. Jun. 7, 1813. Dower renounced Mar. 13, 1802 Sealy Allen to (omitted)

p. 307-308 Dec. 23, 1812 Hancock Smith (Spartanburgh) to Anthony Foster (same); for $200 sold 247 ac on Lawson's fork and

Fairforrest Cr; border: Foster's Spring Br, Richard Thompson, and Brown's Br; part of grant to William Loocock and by heirship to William Clarkson who sold to James Smith desc and by heirship to Hancock Smith. Witness Heram Bobo and Richard Barnett. Signed Hancock Smith. Wit. oath Dec. 23, 1812 Richard Barnett to Danl White. Rec. Jun. 7, 1813

p. 308-309 Aug. 6, 1802 William Garrott (Spartanburgh) to James Cantrell (same); for $80 sold 182 ac on Buck Cr of Pacolate R; border: Abraham Cantrell, Thomas Warren, and James Cantrell's Spring Br; Note: only 150 ac of land is warranted. Witness Isaac Young, James Garrott, and Benjamin Cantrell. Signed William Garrott. Wit. oath Mar. 16, 1805 Benjamin Cantrell to Ism Foster. Rec. Jun. 7, 1813

p. 309 Sept. 10, 1810 Isaac Young jr (Spartanburgh) to James Cantrell (same); for $100 sold 170 ac on both sides of Buck Cr; border: Webber's field. Witness Moses Cantrell and William Murry. Signed Isaac Young jr's mark. Wit. oath Sept. 10, 1810 Moses Cantrell to Henry Turner. Rec. Jun. 7, 1813

p. 309-310 Aug. 6, 1802 Elijah Thompson (Spartanburgh) to James Cantrell (same); for $100 sold 200 ac on branch of Buck Cr of Pacolate R; border: Isaac Young, Thomas Jordan, Elias Legett, and Abraham Cantrell; Elijah warrants land from himself. Witness Isaac Young, James Garrott, and Benjamin Cantrell. Signed Elijah Thompson. Wit. oath Mar. 16, 1805 Benjamin Cantrell to Ism Foster. Rec. Jun. 7, 1813

p. 310-311 Jun. 7, 1813 Reuben Warren (Spartanburgh) to Richard Proctor (same); for $60 sold 60 ac on branch of Island Cr of Pacolette R; border: Hiraim Proctor and Liltton (or Sutton) Young. Witness Elijah Sutterfield and Sutton Young. Signed Reuben Warren. Wit. oath Jun. 4, 1813 Elijah Sutterfield to Henry Turner. Rec. Jun. 7, 1813

p. 311 Aug. 1, 1810 John McClaren (Spartanburgh) to Charles Hester (same); for $20 sold 53 ac. Witness Joseph Dill and Isaac Dill. Signed John McClaren. Wit. oath Jan. 20, 1813 Joseph and Isaac Dill to Joshua Richards. Rec. Jun. 7, 1813

p. 311-312 Mar. 14, 1808 Josiah Watson (Spartanburgh), carpenter, to Ezekiel Dobbins (Rutherford Co, NC); for $200 sold 202 ac on Island Cr of Pacolate R; grant Jun. 4, 1804 to George Walker who sold to Josiah Watson. Witness Robert Benson and Drury Dobbins. Signed Josiah Watson. Wit. oath Sept. 10, 1808 Drury Dobbins to Leonard Adcock. Rec. Jun. 7, 1813

p. 312 Oct. 10 (or 16), 1812 Joshua Prout (NC) to Ezekiel Dobbins (Spartanburgh); for $30 sold 3/4 of 200 ac which is rights fo Joshua Prout and wife Sarah, Thomas Murry and wife Mary, and James S Hendricks and wife Mary, and Sarah Wood to the land; grant Apr. 28, 1768 Gov. William Tryon (NC) to Peter Howard. Witness William Dobbins and Richard Scruggs. Signed Joshua Prout. Wit. oath Mar. 13, 1813 Richard Scruggs to Leon Adcock. Rec. Jun. 7, 1813

p. 312-313 Feb. 15, 1813 Baylis Earle (Spartanburgh) to John McElrath (same); for $500 sold 1,000 ac on Pigeon Roost Br and head of Williams Cr of S Tygar R. Witness Theron Earle and Vanday Camp. Signed Baylis Earle. Wit. oath Feb. 15, 1813 Theron Earle to Michl Miller. Rec. Jun. 7, 1813

p. 313-314 Feb. 19, 1813 Abraham Cantrell (Spartanburgh) to John Morris (same); for $200 sold 110 ac on Buck Cr of Pacolette R; border: John Morris, Mark Forrest, and School House Br. Witness Thomas Morris, Jordan Morris, and James Scott. Wit. oath

Apr. 17, 1813 Thomas Morris to Henry Turner. Rec. Jun. 12, 1813

p. 314 Dec. 14, 1811 Lafford French (Spartanburgh) to William French (same); for $250 sold 70 ac on N side of N Pacolette R; part of grant Sept. 25, 1766 to George Alexander. Witness George Wilett and Lemuel Millican. Signed Lafford French. Wit. oath Jun. 16. 1813 George Wilett to Wm Kelso. Rec. Jun. 16, 1813

p. 314-315 May 21, 1813 William Bostick (Spartanburgh) to William Fowler Reynolds (same); for $96 sold 18 feet square in Spartanburgh, SC; border: Alexander McKie and street from Court House to James Seay's; formerly sold by Richard Thompson. Witness William Tracy and John Lipscomb. Signed William Bostick. Wit. oath May 21, 1813 William Tracy to Thomas Poole. Rec. Jun. 17, 1813

p. 315-317 Aug. 24, 1782 James Meser (96 Dist) to Thomas McCurkin (Camden Dist); for 100£ gold and silver coin agreeable to SC money sold 100 ac on Abner Cr of Enoree R; grant Dec. 12, 1768 Gov. Charles G Montague to Reuben Gilder who sold Jun. 2, 1774 to William Smith (recorded in Secretary's office Jan. 17, 1778) who sold Mar. 5,1780 to James Meser. Witness Benjn Ramey and Nathl Austen. Signed James Meser. Wit. oath Aug. 28, 1782 Benjn Ramey to James Jordan. Rec. Jun. 18, 1813

p. 317-319 Mar. 5, 1780 William Smith (Camden Dist) to James Meser (96 Dist); for 860£ SC money sold 100 ac on Abner Cr of Enoree R; grant Dec. 12, 1768 Gov. Charles G Montague to Reuben Gilder who sold Jun. 2, 1774 to William Smith (recorded in SC Secretary's office Jan. 17, 1778). Witness Benjn Ramey, Samuel Isaacks, and Jacob Gilder. Signed William Smith. Wit. oath Aug. 26, 1782 Benjn Ramey to James Jordan. Rec. Jun. 18, 1813

p. 319-321 Mar. 5, 1785 Thomas McCurkin (Camden Dist) to John Ridman (96 Dist); for 20£ 30s sterling sold 100 ac on Abner's Cr of Enoree R; border: vacant; grant Dec. 12, 1768 Gov. Charles G Montague to Reuben Gilder who sold to William Smith who sold to James Meser who sold to Thomas McCurkin. Witness Benjn Ramey and Bethiah Ramey. Signed Thomas McCurkin. Wit. oath Mar. 12, 1785 Benjn Ramey to Benjn Kilgore. Rec. Jun. 18, 1813

p. 321-322 Apr. 7, 1798 William Bowen (Laurens Co) to James Ridman (Spartanburgh); for $110 sold 102 ac; part of 500 ac on branch of Enoree R; survey Jan. 6, 1775 on warrant Dec. 8, 1774 and granted Oct. 15, 1784 to Daniel Huger esq and sold by Arnold Vanderhorst and Thomas Warring sr, executors of will of John Vanderhorst (late of Charleston, SC) desc, to William Bowen; border: John Ridman and Abner's Cr. Witness Gabriel Jones and Joseph Lyon. Signed William Bowen. Wit. oath Apr. 11, 1798 Gabriel Jones to Zadock Ford. Rec. Jun. 18, 1813. Dower renounced (Laurens Dist) Dec. 22, 1802 Mary Bowen to Daniel Wright

p. 322 Oct. 14, 1809 John Tate (Spartanburgh) to Samuel Jones (same); for $200 sold 200 ac on waters of Enoree R; border: Thomas Westmoreland. Witness John Kemp and Thomas Westmoreland. Signed John Tate. Wit. oath Jun. 28, 1813 Thomas Westmoreland to David Moore. Rec. Jul. 5, 1813

p. 322-323 Mar. 8, 1809 John Prust (Pendleton Dist) to George Thornton (Spartanburgh); for $200 sold 256 ac on branches of Enoree R; border: Thomas Westmoreland; part of 1,000 ac grant to John Prust. Witness Elijah Barnet and Elijah Dover. Signed John Priast. Wit. oath Mar. 9, 1809 (Pendleton Dist) Elijah Barnet to Wm Jamison. Rec. Jul. 5, 1813

p. 323 Jun. 7, 1813 John Wofford to Floyd Tanner; for $400 sold 326 ac on Beaverdam Cr of Fairforrest Cr; border: Foster; part of two grants to Henry Wells. Witness James Silevan and Richard Daniel. Signed John Wofford's mark. Wit. oath Jul. 5, 1813 Richard Daniel to Thos Poole. Rec. Jul. 5, 1813

p. 323-324 Mar. 17, 1812 Samuel Burton (Spartanburgh) to James Compton (same); for $750 sold 632 ac on both sides Owens Br of N Tygar R; border: Currey, Jane(?) Thomson, and Sarah Thomson. Witness Wm Powers and George Akidge. Signed Samuel Burton. Wit. oath Mar. 21, 1812 Wm Powers to Drury McDaniel. Rec. Jul. 5, 1813. Dower renounced Mar. 21, 1812 Rody Burton to Drury McDaniel

p. 324-325 Jul. 8, 1813 William Acre (Spartanburgh) to son Dandridge Acre; for love and affection give a Negro woman Luck, a bed and furniture, a bay horse called Sanp, a cow and calf, an ewe, an oven, a fish pan, 6 earthen plates, and a dish. Witness Charles Moore and John Ward. Signed William Acre. Wit. oath Jul. 12, 1813 Charles Moore to Saml Morrow. Rec. Jul. 12, 1813

p. 325 Jul. 9, 1813 William Acre (Spartanburgh) to son Dandridge Acre; for love and affection give 80 ac on W side of Wards Cr of Tygar R; border: N-Martin Otts, W-Charles Moore, S & SW-Robert Legon and Josiah Hatchell, and E-Wards Cr. Witness Charles Moore and Burton Acre. Signed Wm Acre. Wit. oath Jul. 12, 1813 Charles Moore to Saml Morrow. Rec. Jul. 12, 1813

p. 325-326 Jul. 8, 1813 William Acre (Spartanburgh) to daughter Peggy Acre; for love and affection give a Negro boy Amos, a bed anf furniture, a bay mare named Fly, a saddle, a cow and 2 yearlings, a sow and 6 shoats, an ewe, 6 earthen plates and a dish, 2 pewter basons, a pot, and an oven. Witness Charles Moore and J Ward. Signed Wm Acre. Wit. oath Jul. 12, 1813 Charles Moore to Saml Morrow. Rec. Jul. 12, 1813

p. 326 Jul. 8, 1813 William Acre (Spartanburgh) to son Burton Acre; for love and affection give a Negro named Bob, a bed and furniture, a bay horse named Dargan, a cow and 2 yearlings, a ewe and eaue(?), a sow and 4 pigs, a pot and fish pan, 6 pewter plates, and a dish. Witness Charles Moore and John Ward. Signed Wm Acre. Wit. oath Jul. 12, 1813 Charles Moore to Samuel Morrow. Rec. Jul. 12, 1813

p. 326-327 Jul. 9, 1813 William Acre (Spartanburgh) to son Burton Acre; for love and affection give 94 ac in two parts: (1) sold by Charles Moore to William Acre and (2) sold by Jesse Spencer to William Acre; on W side of Wards Cr; border: Dowell. Witness Charles Moore and Dandridge Acre. Signed Wm Acre. Wit. oath Jul. 12, 1813 Charles Moore to Saml Morrow. Rec. Jul. 12, 1813

p. 327-328 Jan. 1, 1813 Vincent Wyatt sr (Spartanburgh) to William Wyatt; for good will and affection for son Vincent (sic) give 128 ac; grant to William Wofford. Witness John Golightly jr and Spencer Wyatt. Signed Vincent Wyatt and Elizabeth's mark. Wit. oath May 19, 1813 Spencer Wyatt to Thomas Poole. Rec. Jul. 16, 1813

p. 328 May 15, 1813 William Camron (Spartanburgh) to John Cameron (same); for good causes and valuable consideration give all goods, chattles, and household stuff. Witness Theron Earle and John Roddy. Signed Wm Camron. Wit. oath Jul. 11, 1813 Theron Earle to Wm Kelso. Rec. Jul. 14, 1813

p. 328-329 Nov. 4, 1812 Daniel Bragg (Spartanburgh) to Andrew Coan (same); for $297.50 or 2 and 97.50 sold 119 ac on S side of Floyd's Br of Furgerson's Cr; border: Rogers bridge, S-Charles

Skinner and John King, N-Young Scott, E-John Skinner, and W-Daniel Bragg. Witness Patrick Hog (or Hoy), William Otts, and William Skinner. Signed Daniel Bragg. Wit. oath Jul. 13, 1813 William Skinner to Drury McDaniel. Rec. Jul. 16, 1813. Dower renounced Jul. 13, 1813 Elizabeth Bragg to Daniel McDaniel

p. 329-330 Jul. 14, 1813 John Harvey jr (Union Dist) to Henry Harvey; for $150 sold 115 ac on S side of Pacolette R; border: island in river, where Daniel fluallace(?) formerly lived, John Story, and Troft Shoal Br; part of grant to Maj. John Tolleson. Witness Richard Kearby and John Gossett. Signed John Harvey. Wit. oath Jul. 14, 1813 Richard Kearby to John Gossett. Rec. Jul. 24, 1813. Dower renounced Jul. 21, 1813 Patsey Harvey to John Gossett

p. 330-331 Feb. 27, 1809 John Low (Spartanburgh) to Samuel Sharbut (same); for $100 sold 100 ac on N side of Pacolette R; border: Thomas Dean and Dry Br. Witness Thomas Wyatt and William Murry. Signed John Low. Wit. oath Dec. 3, 1810 Thomas Wyatt to Henry Turner. Rec. Jul. 16, 1813

p. 331-332 Feb. 13, 1813 George and Fortunatus Legg (Spartanburgh) to Andrew B Moore (same); to secure a note of $784 by Andrew's own hand dated May 23, 1811 and with interest from Nov. 1, 1811 sold a Negro man Adam, Negro woman Deed(?), her two children Legis and Matilda, a stud horse "by value(?)" Buzzard; Condition: sale void if George and Fortunatus pay debt and interest by Feb. 13, 1814. Witness John Crawford. Signed George and Fortunatus Legg. Wit. oath Aug. 2, 1813 John Crawford to A Benson. Rec. Aug. 2, 1813

p. 332-333 Feb. 27, 1813 David Cook (Spartanburgh) to David Golightly sr (same); for $84 sold 84 ac on Bufulow Br of Fairforrest Cr; border: W & S-Wm Cook, E, N & W-David Golightly, and by Henry Ayres and Ephraim Elder; part of grant to Giles Tillett who sold to William Wofford who sold to John Gibbs who sold to James Gibbs who sold to Peter Elder who sold to Ephraim Elder who sold to Mark Swadley who sold to Robert Head who sold to George Connell who sold to John Cook who sold to David Cook. Witness William H Cook and William M Golightly. Signed David Cooke. Wit. oath Jul. 31, 1813 William H Cook to Danl White. Rec. Aug. 2, 1813. Dower renounced Jul. 31, 1813 Milley Cook to Daniel White

p. 333-334 Jul. 31, 1813 David Cook (Spartanburgh) to Moses Foster (same); for $550 sold 357 ac on Ready Br of Fairforrest Cr; border: James Foster, David Golightly, William Foster, and William Underwood. Witness William H Cook and Lemuel Cook. Signed David Cook. Wit. oath Jul. 31, 1813 William H Cook to Danl White. Rec. Aug. 2, 1813. Dower renounced Jul. 31, 1813 Milley Cook to Daniel White

p. 334-335 Apr. 7, 1813 Gabriel Benson (Greenville Dist) to John Burd (Spartanburgh); for $70 sold 130 ac on waters of Fairforrest Cr of Tygar R; part of 200 ac on both sides Fairforrest Cr granted to Benjamin Thomson. Witness W W Smithwick and Thompson Faucett. Signed Gal Benson. Wit. oath Jun. 7, 1813 W W Smithwick to James Young. Rec. Aug. 2, 1813

p. 335-336 Aug. 11, 1812 Peter Frye (Spartanburgh) to William Frye (same); for $200 sold 80 ac on N side of N Pacolette R and S side of Howard's Cr; border: E-Lot Adcock; part of where Peter Frye lives; grant Oct. 16 (or 6), 1767 Gov. William Tryon (NC) to James Howard who sold May 17, 1770 to Thomas Wade who sold May 29, 1773 to James Evins who sold Feb. 15, 1775 to Samued (sic) Jackson who sold to his son John Jackson who sold to Peter Frye; border: William Wade, George Welch, and Wolf pet(?) Br. Witness

Hugh Ewing and John Abram. Signed Peter Frye's mark. Wit. oath Aug. 11, 1812 Hugh Ewing to Wm Kelso. Rec. Aug. 2, 1813

p. 336-337 Jul. 27, 1812 John Dalton (Spartanburgh) to William Ramsey (same); for $200 sold 200 ac on both sides Mudow Cr of S Pacolett R; border: Robert Young, Ramsey, and Dalton; part of two grants to Henry Young who sold to James McDonald who sold to John Dalton. Witness Jabez Galt and William Durham. Signed John Dalton. Wit. oath Jul. 31, 1813 Jabez Galt to Andrew Furgerson. Rec. Aug. 2, 1813

p. 337 Oct. 12, 1812 Robert McDowell (Spartanburgh) to William Ramsey (same); for $500 sold 200 ac on S side of S Pacolett R; border: James McDowell and Paul Cox; part of grant to Wm Dickson. Witness Jabez Galt and Jesse A Burton. Signed Robert McDowell. Wit. oath Jul. 31, 1813 Jabez Galt to Andrew Furgerson. Rec. Aug. 2, 1813

p. 337-338 Feb. 27, 1813 Samuel Noblett (Spartanburgh) to John Tolleson (same); for $90 sold 164 ac on waters of Fair-forrest Cr; border: Joseph Ashe. Witness Ely Tolleson and Jonathan Low sr. Signed Saml Noblet. Wit. oath Jul. 7, 1813 Ely Tolleson to Jn Gossett. Rec. Aug. 2, 1813. Dower renounced Jun. 11, 1813 Salley Noblet to John Gossett

p. 338-339 Nov. 25, 1812 John Covinton to James Robens; for 40£ sold 100 ac on Buck Cr of Pacolett R; border: Johnson and Henderson. Witness William Butter and William Little. Signed John Covinton's mark. Wit. oath May 24, 1813 William Little to Leonard Adcock. Rec. Aug. 2, 1813

p. 339-340 May 10, 1813 John Meadows (Spartanburgh) to William Calvin (same); for $300 sold 125 ac on waters of N Tygar R. Witness Benjamin Nicholls and William Power. Signed John Meadows. Wit. oath Jul. 27, 1813 Benjamin Nicholls to Saml Morrow. Rec. Aug. 5, 1813. Dower renounced Jul. 27, 1813 Nancy Meadows to Samuel Morrow

p. 340-341 Apr. 10, 1813 James Powers (Spartanburgh) to Benjamin Nicholls (same); for $25 sold 4 ac on N side of Tygar R; border: Sherbet. Witness John Meadows and William Powers. Signed James Powers. Wit. oath Jul. 27, 1813 John Meadows to Saml Morrow. Rec. Apr. 5, 1813. Dower renounced Jul. 27, 1813 Lidey Powers to Samuel Morrow

p. 341 Feb. 10, 1809 John Prust (or Preast) (Pendleton Dist) to John Tate (Spartanburgh); for $200 sold 156 ac on N side Enoree R. Witness Levi Livingston and John C Aderhold. Signed John Prust. Wit. oath Feb. 10, 1809 (Pendleton Dist) Levi Livingston to Wm Jamison. Rec. Aug. 7, 1813

Book O 1813-1816

p. 1 Nov. 10, 1811 Francis Fowler (Spartanburgh) to George Jeremiah Ryal Miles Irey and Isaac Fowler (same); for $200 sold 156 ac on Enoree R; Condition: Francis and wife are to enjoy the land as long as they live. Witness Samuel Jones and Aillia Fowler. Signed Francis Fowler's mark. Wit. oath Jun. 28, 1813 Samuel Jones to David Moore. Rec. Aug. 7, 1813

p. 1-2 Oct. 19, 1809 John Tate (Spartanburgh) to Francis Folwer (same); for $200 sold 156 ac on Enoree R. Witness Isaac Hambey and Moses Fowler. Signed John Tate. Wit. oath Mar. 14, 1810 Isaac Hambey to James Ford. Rec. Aug. 7, 1813

p. 2-3 Apr. 6, 1803 Andrew Red (Spartanburgh) to Nathaniel Paris (same); for $100 sold 100 ac on Horse Cr of Broad R; border: Richard Paris; part of 305 ac grant Jan. 4, 1802 to Andrew Red. Witness Benjn Hicks and Lewis Paris. Signed Andrew Red. Wit. oath Aug. 22, 1803 Lewis Paris to Wm McDowell. Rec. Aug. 14, 1813

p. 3-4 Feb. 6, 1812 Pleasant Brannon (Spartanburgh) to William Copeland (same); for $326 sold 47½ ac on S side of N Pacolett R; part of grant to William Millican and part of where Pleasant Brannon lives. Witness Paddy Scott, George Welch, and James Berry. Signed Pleasant and Mary Brannon's marks. Wit. oath Aug. 2, 1813 James Berry to Wm Kelso. Rec. Aug. 24, 1813

p. 4-5 Nov. 6, 1812 John Ison sr (Union Dist) to John Ison jr (Spartanburgh); for $1,600 sold 575 ac in Union and Spartanburgh Dists; border: Robert Harris, Joseph Kelso, Samuel Kelso, William Burton, George Storey, and John Tolleson; part of two grants to George Storey. Witness Thomas Hurt and Jonathan Chasewood. Signed John Ison sr. Wit. oath Sept. 20, 1813 Thomas Hurt to William Ried. Rec. Sept. 20, 1813

p. 5-6 Jan. 31, 1812 John Ison (Union Dist) to Elizabeth Ison (Spartanburgh); for $350 sold 175 ac; border: Tolleson, Delphan, William T Simpson, James Nesbett, and Capt. John Ison; part of 350 ac grant to Joseph Nesbett; "all land on the creek excepted and belongs to Storey's tract". Witness Thomas Hart and Jonathan Chasewood. Signed John Ison sr. Wit. oath Sept. 20, 1813 Thomas Hart to William Ried. Rec. Sept. 20, 1813

p. 6-8 Dec. 17, 1811 Paul Casleberry (Spartanburgh) to Henry Castleberry (same); for $100 sold 60 ac on waters of Jeaney's Cr of Tygar R; border: John King; part of 100 ac grant to Jean McClearkin. Witness Thomas Castleberry and James Wofford. Signed Paul Castleberry. Wit. oath Oct. 8, 1812 Thomas Castelberry to Samuel Wofford. Rec. Sept. 22, 1813

p. 8-9 Jul. 28, 1813 Benjamin Poole (Spartanburgh) to James Crocker (same); for $100 sold (ac omitted) on S side of Lawson's fork; border: William Gore's barn, Solomon Crocker, James Crocker, and John Lee. Witness William Gore, James Crocker jr, and Arthur Crocker. Signed Benjamin Poole. Wit. oath Aug. 17, 1813 William Gore to John Gossett. Rec. Oct. 1, 1813. Dower renounced Sept. 24, 1812 Metildy Poole to John Gossett

p. 9 Jul. 15, 1813 Jacob Autrey (Spartanburgh) to James Foster (same); for $160 sold 73 ac on branch of Fairforrest Cr; border: N-David Cook, S-Edward Autrey, and E-James Foster. Witness William H Cook and Moses Foster. Signed Jacob Autrey. Wit. oath Aug. 2, 1813 Moses Foster to John Cook. Rec. Oct. 1, 1813

p. 9-10 Sept. 24, 1811 Benjamin Howard (Spartanburgh) to Anthony Bates (same); for $100 sold 100 ac; border: William Crocker and Arthur Crocker's old line. Witness Nathan Whitby and Thomas Mevidy. Signed Benjamin Howard. Wit. oath Oct. 9, 1811 Nathan Whitby to John Gossett. Rec. Oct. 1, 1813

p. 10-11 Jan. 13, 1806 Edmund Bishop (Spartanburgh) to James Leonard (same); for $230 sold 200 ac on Little Shoal Cr of Lawson's fork; border: S-John Kelso and others unknown; part of 467 ac survey Jan. 9, 1797 for Henry Mitchen and grantee by Gov. Charles Pinckney. Witness Absolem Roe and William Rollans. Signed Edmund Bishop's mark. Wit. oath Oct. 4, 1813 Absolem Roe to Thos Poole. Rec. Oct. 4, 1813

p. 11-12 Oct. 31, 1812 Blake Masingale (Stewart Co, Tenn) to James Leonard (Spartanburgh); for $200 sold 100 ac on Sholly Cr.

Witness George Thomason and Rebeckah Thomason. Signed Blake Masingale's mark. Wit. oath Oct. 4, 1813 George Thomason to Thomas Poole. Rec. Oct. 4, 1813

p. 12-13 Apr. 16, 1813 Jacob Autry (Spartanburgh) to William H Cook (same); for $200 sold 100 ac on waters of Fairforrest Cr; border: Buffelow Cr and David Cook. Witness Sarah Cook and Lemuel Cook. Signed Jacob Autry. Wit. oath Oct. 1, 1813 Lemuel Cook to John Cook. Rec. Oct. 4, 1813

p. 13-14 Dec. 8, 1812 Thads Owens (Spartanburgh) to James Beck (same); for $175 sold 167 ac on S fork of N Tygar R. Witness John Ballenger, John Owens, and Joseph Atkins. Signed Thads Owens. Wit. oath Aug. 19, 1813 John Ballenger to Michl Miller. Rec. Oct. 4, 1813. Dower renounced Sept. 27, 1813 Aner Owens to Michl Miller

p. 14-15 Sept. 25, 1813 Phoebe Thomason (Spartanburgh) to John Thomason (same); for $120 sold 120 ac on waters of Lawson's fork; border: Benson, Hering's old place, and Post road; part of 352 ac grant to William Turner Thomason. Witness William Poole and Moses Shields. Signed Phoebe Thomason's mark. Wit. oath Sept. 27, 1813 William Poole to Thomas Poole. Rec. Oct. 4, 1813

p. 15-16 Mar. 23, 1813 Henry Pettit (Spartanburgh) to James Vangant (or Vangant) (Rutherford Co, NC); for $700 sold 212 ac on N side Pacolette R above Castelberry Shoal Br; border: Potiton. Witness Bartholomew Stovall and William Rogers. Signed Henry Pettitt. Wit. oath Oct. 14, 1813 Bartholomew Stoval to John Gossett. Rec. Oct. 16, 1813. Dower renounced Oct. 14, 1813 Anna Pettit to John Gossett

p. 16-17 Jul. 23, 1813 William Hurt (Spartanburgh) to James Vernon (same); for $740 sold 330 ac on Brown's Cr; border: Abner Timmons, Samuel Timmons, Shields Booker, and John James (formerly Robert James). Witness E Roddy and N. E. Benson. Signed William Hurt. Wit. oath Jul. 23, 1813 E Roddy to A Benson. Rec. Oct. 21, 1813. Dower renounced Oct. 21, 1813 Jane Hurt to Abner Benson

p. 17-18 Sept. 2, 1808 James Cook (Spartanburgh) to James Thomas Cook (same); for $420 sold 400 ac on S side Fairforrest Cr and on Buffalow and Ready Branches; border: S-Daniel Fench, W-Elizabeth Autry, N-Jacob Autry and Wm Cook, and E-Edward Barnett. Witness Wm H Cook and Roland Joanis(?). Signed James Cook. Wit. oath Oct. 4, 1813 Wm H Cook to John Cook. Rec. Oct. 4, 1813

p. 18-19 Apr. 26, 1809 Isham Foster (Spartanburgh) to brother William Foster; for $82.50 sold 27½ ac on Fairforrest Cr; border: William Foster. Witness James Foster and David Foster. Signed Ism Foster. Wit. oath Jul. 3, 1809 James Foster to James Young. Rec. Oct. 25, 1813

p. 19-20 Jun. 14, 1811 Moses Foster, son of Robert Foster, (Spartanburgh) to William Foster (same); for $100 sold 44 ac on waters of N Tygar R; border: James Foster, Nimrod Benson, Robert Foster, and William Foster; part of grant to William Benson. Witness Thomas J Foster and Moses Foster. Signed Moses Foster. Wit. oath Sept. 3, 1811 Moses Foster [the witness] to James Young. Rec. Oct. 25, 1813

p. 20-21 Mar. 18, 1808 Pleasant Easley (Greenville Dist) to Joseph Lively (Spartanburgh); for $250 sold 100 ac on both sides S Pacolette R; border: Publick Road, Joseph Lively, John Henry, and S Pacolette Bridge; upper end of 640 ac grant Feb. 3, 1775 Gov. William Bull to Mathew Harper sr. Witness Anderson Lively and

Mary Henry. Signed Pleasant Easley. Wit. oath Apr. 20, 1809 Anderson Lively to Andrew Furgerson. Rec. Oct. 30, 1813

p. 21-22 Jul. 16, 1805 John Byrn (Spartanburgh) to Pleasant Easley (same); for $500 sold 365 ac on S side Pacolette R; part of grant to Mathew Harper and Part of grant to John Byrn. Witness Gabriel Benson and Jonathan Harper. Signed John Byrn. Wit. oath Nov. 6, 1810 Gabriel Benson to Jno H Jones. Rec. Oct. 30, 1813

p. 22-23 Mar. 30, 1813 James Younger (Spartanburgh) to William Bush (same); for $600 sold 300 ac; border: James Young, John Brown, branch of N Pacolette R, and McClures' old line. Witness Hugh McMillin, William Huddleston, and Ludy Canthorn. Signed James Younger's mark. Wit. oath Oct. 30, 1813 Hugh McMillin to James Young. Rec. Nov. 1, 1813

p. 23-24 Jan. 10, 1807 Jesse Davison (Spartanburgh) to Charles Wilkins (Rutherford Co, NC); for $300 sold 119 ac on Sarratt's Cr of Broad R; border: William Davison, William Hollaway, and Wilson's old line; part of two grants: (1) to Joseph Champin and (2) to Robert Warren. Witness William Blanton and Nancy Holloway. Signed Jesse Davison's mark. Wit. oath Nov. 18, 1812 William Blanton to Joshua Richards. Rec. Nov. 8, 1813

p. 24-25 May 28, 1813 John Arnold (Spartanburgh) to James Arnold (same); for $350 sold 128 (or 150) ac on branch of Tygar R; border: John Henry, Richard Willus, and Floyd. Witness Willis Arnold and William Arnold. Signed John Arnold. Wit. oath Nov. 8, 1813 William Arnold to John Dean. Rec. Nov. 8, 1813

p. 25-26 May 24, 1813 James Gowen (Greenville Dist) to Willey S Brown (Spartanburgh); for $500 sold 800 ac on both sides Mile Cr of S Pacolette R; border: Capt. John Lucas, Willey S Brown, and James Sutherland; includes field known as James aus (or aces) and shoal where saw mill is; part of grant Oct. 6, 1772 to Henry Bouredau (or Bouruau) and willed to James Gowen by his father John Gowen. Witness Julius Nichols and James Blasingame. Signed James Gowen. Wit. oath Sept. 25, 1813 Julius Nichols to Wm Kelso. Rec. Nov. 8, 1813. Dower renounced Jun. 7, 1813 (Greenville Dist) Elizabeth Gowen to John Whitten

p. 26-27 Aug. 10, 1813 Sarah Penny, wife of Thomas Penny,(Spartanburgh) to Robert McCrory (same); for $50 sold 125 ac on Middle Tygar R; border: Abner Wingo; part of grant in 1767 to Thomas Penny. Witness Samuel Brice and Sarah McMillin. Signed Sarah Penny's mark. Wit. oath Aug. 11, 1813 Samuel Brice to John Chapman. Rec. Nov. 8, 1813

p. 27-28 May 9, 1813 William Crow sr (Spartanburgh) to Isaac Crow jr (same); for $206.50 sold 104 ac on waters of Two Mile Cr; border: Spencer Calvert and Isaac Crow; part of grant to William Clayton. Witness James Crow and Sabrey Selvey. Signed William Crow sr's mark. Wit. oath Oct. 26, 1813 James Crow to Samuel Woodruff. Rec. Nov. 8, 1813. Mar. 23, 1795 William Crow received 14£ sterling from Isaac Crow payment in full for 100 ac. Signed William Crow's mark. Witness James Lanford. Wit. oath Oct. 26, 1813 James Lanford to Samuel Woodruff

p. 28-29 Sept. 12, 1812 Daniel Bragg (Laurens Dist) to David Bruton (Spartanburgh); for $50 sold 50 ac on N side of James Cr; border: E-David Bruton, N-Joseph Woodruff, W-Daniel Bragg, and S-George Leatherwood. Witness Caleb Woodruff and Phillip Brewton. Signed Daniel Bragg. Wit. oath Oct. 13, 1812 Phillip Brewton to John Brewton. Rec. Nov. 8, 1813

p. 29 May 7, 1813 James Compton (Spartanburgh) to Thomas Power (same); for $200 sold 112 ac on branch of N Tygar R; border: Sarah Thomson and Joseph Meders. Witness Lawson Thomson and William Powers. Signed James Compton. Wit. oath May 14, 1813 William Powers to M Casey. Rec. Nov. 9, 1813

p. 29-30 Aug. 24, 1811 Stephen White (Spartanburgh) to James Millwood (same); for $100 sold 320 ac on waters of Thickety Cr; border: N-formerly land of Lewis, NE-Lewis, SE-Dewberry, NW-Templemon, and SW-vacant. Witness John Prewett and Peter Prewett. Signed Stephen White. Wit. oath Sept. 28, 1811 John Prewett to Wm Ried. Rec. Nov. 9, 1813

p. 30-31 Oct. 14, 1810 Thomas Cook (Spartanburgh) to James Cook; for $200 sold (ac omitted) at head of Ford's Cr of Fair-forrest Cr; border: N-James Keens, W-James White, and S-Philip Otts; formerly land of John Finch. Witness Lemuel Cook and David Cook. Signed Jo Thomas Cook. Wit. oath Jul. 31, 1813 Lemuel Cook to Danl White. Rec. Nov. 9, 1813

p. 31-32 Apr. 27, 1812 Dorcas Crocker (Spartanburgh) to James Cudd (same); for $100 sold 100 ac on branch of Buck Cr; part of 640 ac grant Oct. 6, 1788 to William Dartton and eventually sold to Jonathan Cudd "party to these presents" (sic). Witness Jesse Burk and Benjamin Moss. Signed Dorcas Crocker's mark. Wit. oath May 7, 1812 Benjamin Moss to Leonard Adcock. Rec. Nov. 9, 1813

p. 32-33 Jul. 3, 1813 Thornton McDaniel (Spartanburgh) to Robert Miller (same); for $500 sold 340 ac on S Tygar R at mouth of Eiland Pond; where Thornton McDaniel lives; border: Jesse Crook, Patton, waggon road, Crook's bridge; and sold 3feather beds anf furniture, a cubbard and its furniture, 2 spinning wheels, 2 pair of cards, 2 chests, a cut real, a loom, a table, 4 pots, 2 dutch ovens, a pan, 10 stands of bees, all plantation tools, 10 hogsheads and barrels, 8 pewter plates, 2 dishes and basons, 24 spoons, all household furniture, a "mare filley" got by Florezell, 2 cows and calves, 34 hogs marked with cross in each ear, 10 sheep with same mark, all my corn, 12 stacks of wheat; Condition: sale void if Thornton pays Robert $100 in two years. Witness John Fielder and Asa Mitchell. Signed Thornton McDaniel. Wit. oath Jul. 3, 1813 John Fielder to Drury McDaniel. Rec. Nov. 9, 1813

p. 33-34 Oct. 23, 1813 Robert Rogers sr (Spartanburgh) to grandson Elias Rogers; for love and affection give to Elias unless he dies without heirs; then it goes to Thomas Rogers, son of William Rogers; 173 ac on S side of S Tygar R; border: NE-Jno Crow, SW-Caven, N-Clark, and others vacant. Witness John Ward and Robert Rogers. Signed Robt Rogers. Wit. oath Nov. 9, 1813 John Ward to M Casey. Rec. Nov. 9, 1813

p. 34-35 Jul. 22, 1813 Thomas Gilbert (Spartanburgh) to William Gilbert sr (same); for $90 sold 400 ac on both sides Batton's Cr of Pacolette R; border: McDowell's old path; where William Gilbert lives; part of grant to Thomas Gore; survey for James Huggins. Witness John Littlefield and Isaiah Gilbert. Signed Thomas Gilbert's mark. Wit. oath Nov. 9, 1813 John Littlefield to James Young. Rec. Nov. 9, 1813

p. 35-36 Oct. 29, 1813 Hugh Caldwell (Spartanburgh) to William Caldwell (same); for $120 sold 317 ac on N side of N Tygar R; part of grant Aug. 10, 1774 to John Brown. Witness James Swanzy, John Crawford, and John Collins. Signed Hugh Caldwell. Wit. oath Apr. 29, 1813 John Crawford to John Collins. Rec. Nov. 9, 1813

p. 36-38 Mar. (blank), 1810 (Smith Co, Tenn) James Stone (Smith Co,

Tenn) to Jesse Brown; for $180 sold 77 ac on Two Mile Cr; border: county road, Spencer Calvert, Sampson Bobo, and Jesse Brown; except land within 20 feet of creek for "ponding" the creek; part of two grants: (1) John Hendricks and (2) Richard Neely. Witness Simon Stone and William Stone. Signed James Stone and Pattey's mark. Wit. oath Jun. 7, 1810 (Smith Co, Tenn) James and Pattey Stone to Joseph W Allen, clerk. Rec. Nov. 10, 1813. Jun. 7, 1810 (Smith Co, Tenn) James Hebetts, "justice", certifys Joseph W Allen is clerk of court. Dower renounced Jun. 7, 1810 (Smith Co, Tenn) Patty Stone to William Moore, Richard Bailey, and John Lancaster

p. 38-39 Jan. 1, 1807 John Stokes jr (Union Dist) to Gabriel Benson (Spartanburgh); for $75 sold 100 ac on both sides Fairforrest Cr; border: Abner Benson, Zachariah Wingo, and David Tanner; part of 200 ac grant to Benjamin Thompson; "drawn" by Elizabeth Benson, one of legates of William Benson desc,who intermarried with John Stokes jr. Witness Thomas Moore and Thomas Greer jr. Signed John Stokes jr. Wit. oath Nov. 11, 1813 Thomas Moore to Thomas Poole. Rec. Nov. 11, 1813

p. 39-40 May 28, 1813 Obediah Wingo (Spartanburgh) to William Wingo (same); for $100 sold 83 ac on waters of Fairforrest Cr; border: Elijah Ballenger; where William Wingo lives; part of tract sold by Samuel Culbertson to Obediah Wingo. Witness Willis Wingo and Isaac Thornton. Signed Obediah Wingo. Wit. oath Jun. 7, 1813 Willis Wingo to James Young. Rec. Nov. 16, 1813. Dower renounced Sept. 25, 1813 Obedience Wingo to Daniel White

p. 40-41 Sept. 28, 1813 Aaron Templemon (Spartanburgh) to Tellotson Brookshear (same); for $100 sold 121 ac on Pole Bridge Br of Pacolette R and Barter's mare Br. Witness George Turner and William Brown. Signed Aaron Templemon's mark. Wit. oath Sept. 28, 1813 George Turner to Henry Turner. Rec. Nov. 22, 1813

p. 41-42 Apr. 19, 1813 William H Cook (Spartanburgh) to James Foster (same); for $355 sold 161½ ac on Buffalow lick Br of Fairforrest Cr. Witness Lemuel Cook and William Foster. Signed Wm H Cook. Wit. oath May 8, 1813 William Foster to John Chapman. Rec. Nov. 26, 1813. Dower renounced Sept. 26, 1813 Phebe Cook to Daniel White

p. 42-44May 16, 1810 James Hadden (Spartanburgh) to Daniel McKie (same); for $1,600 sold 600 ac on both sides Ben's Cr and S of Tygar R; where James Hadden lives; plat attached dated Jan. 14, 1810 by Jas Wofford DS shows border: John Basel, mouth of Shurdcer's(?) Br, Anderson, Durham, John, and includes a Mill house; part of three grants to: (1) William Moore, (2) John McDowell, and (3) Aaron Moore. Witness Labon P Poole, Marshall Leay, and Thomas Hadden. Signed James Hadden. Wit. oath May 17, 1810 Labon P Poole to Drury McDaniel. Rec. Nov. 27, 1813. Dower renounced Nov. 25, 1813 Sarah Hadden to Drury McDaniel

p. 44-45 Apr. 16, 1813 Catherine Traylor (Spartanburgh) to daughter Mary Traylor (same); for love and affection give a Negro girl Fempey about 18 months old. Witness Thomas Bomar and Elisha Bomar. Signed Catherine Traylor's mark. Wit. oath Dec. 6, 1813 Thomas Bomar to James Hammett. Rec. Dec. 6, 1813

p. 45-47 Oct. 30, 1807 Reuben Gunn (Spartanburgh) to Henry Brockman and Theophelus Cannon (Greenville Dist and Spartanburgh); for $600 sold 35 ac including Griss and Saw mill machines; on N side of Enoree R; border: "ridge of Proctor", Kevil, Tyrce Glen, and Abner's Cr; "part of border made by deed" Aug 5, 1801 Pennel Wood jr to Reuben Gunn; part of 500 ac grant to Thomas Scott esq and survey Feb. 27, 1775 by James Wofford and sold to Richard

Hampton who sold to Stephen Cantrell who sold to Thos Kevil who sold May 11, 1795 to Reuben Gunn. Witness James Hammett and Charles Gunn. Signed Reuben Gunn. Wit. oath Aug. 15, 1809 James Hammett to Tyrce Glenn. Rec. Dec. 6, 1813. Dower renounced Oct. 31, 1807 Mary Gunn to James Kilgore

p. 47-48 May 22, 1813 John Gowen, James Blasingame, Strut (or Street) Thurston, and Win G Gowen (all of Greenville Dist), executors of will of John Gowen desc, to Henry Grogan (Spartanburgh); for $100 sold 100 ac on both sides Beverdam Cr of S Pacolette R; border: John Grogan, Bartholomew Grogan, and Dormdas (or Doreudas); part of 450 ac grant Oct. 6, 1772 to Peter Vidion; where Henry Grogan lives. Witness Willey S Brown and John Lucas. Signed John Gowen, Jas Blasingame, Strut Thurston, and W. B. Gowen. Wit. oath Nov. 20, 1813 Willey S Brown to Andrew Furgurson. Rec. Dec. 6, 1813

p. 48-50 Oct. 30, 1807 Reuben Gunn (Spartanburgh) to Theophelus Cannon (same); for $400 sold 150 ac; where Reuben Gunn lives; border: Thomas Cowder, Hammett, Tyrce Glenn, Theophelus Cannon, and Henry Brockman; part of 500 ac grant to Thos Scotts esq, with survey Feb. 27, 1775 by James Wofford, and sold to Richard Hampton who sold to Stephen Cantrell who sold to Thomas Kevil who sold May 11, 1795 to Reuben Gunn. Witness James Hammett and Charles Gunn. Signed Reuben Gunn. Wit. oath Aug. 15, 1809 James Hammett to Tyrce Glenn. Rec. Dec. 6, 1813

p. 50-51 Dec. 23, 1812 Samuel Hunt (Spartanburgh) to John Grogan (same); for $8 sold 12 ac on N side of S Pacolette R and on Beaver Dam Cr; border: John Grogan; part of grant Jun. 6, 1803 to Samuel Hunt. Witness Julius Nichols and James Gowen. Signed Samuel Hunt. Wit. oath Dec. 23, 1812 James Gowen to Andrew Furgerson. Rec. Dec. 10, 1813

p. 51-52 Mar. 11, 1813 David Mosley to John Grogan (Spartanburgh); for $30 sold 5 ac on both sides Beaverdam Cr of S Pacolette R; border: E Houston, John Grogan, and Gowen. Witness James Whitten and James Southerland. Signed David Mosley's mark. Wit. oath Dec. 4, 1813 James Whitten to Andrew Furgerson. Rec. Dec. 10, 1813

p. 52-53 Feb. 24, 1813 James Cook (Spartanburgh) to John Cook (same); for $600 sold 179 ac on Fairforrest Cr; border: N-widow Legon, W-Thomas Tinsley, S-Walter West and David Golightly, and E-Thomas Greenwood; formerly belonged to Robert Legon desc. Witness Abner W Legon and Lemuel Cook. Signed James Cook. Wit. oath May 3, 1813 Lemuel Cook to Danl White. Rec. Dec. 13, 1813. Dower renounced Mar. 31, 1813 Rhoda Cook to Daniel White

p. 53-55 Dec. 15, 1813 James Brannon, sheriff (Spartanburgh) to John McClure jr; for $240 sold 240 ac on Obed's Cr on N side of S Pacolette R; where Richard Brown lives; sale due to writ from Spartanburgh Common Pleas Court suit William Allen vs Lewis and Richd Brown; sale Dec. 6, 1813. Witness E Roddy and Daniel White. Signed J Brannon SSD. Wit. oath Dec. 16, 1813 E Roddy to A Benson. Rec. Dec. 16, 1813

p. 55-56 Dec. 16, 1811 Samuel Woodruff (Spartanburgh) to John Arnold (same); for $150 sold 164 ac on James Cr of Tygar R; border: Nathaniel Woodruff and Joseph Woodruff. Witness William Shackelford, James Allen, and Samuel Woodruff. Signed Samuel Woodruff. Wit. oath Nov. 19, 1813 James Allen to John Dean. Rec. Dec. 16, 1813. Dower renounced Nancy Woodruff to Thomas Wright Nov. 19, 1813

p. 56-57 Dec. 29, 1813 Rebecka Arendale (Spartanburgh) to son Richard Arendale (same) and to son Bridges Arendale (Franklin Co,

Tenn); for love and affection give equally divided (at her death) all goods and chattels in her dwelling house, all stock, and three Negroes: Will, Morris, and Luke. Witness Elliot Hickman and John Arendale. Signed Rebecka Arendale's mark. Wit. oath Dec. 30, 1813 John Arendale to Joseph Camp. Rec. Jan. 3, 1814

p. 57-58 Sept. 14, 1811 Elisha Hedden (Spartanburgh) to Gen. Thomas Moore; for $11.25 sold 5 ac on W side of Middle Tygar R; border: Thomas Moore and "great road"; part of grant to James Alexander. Witness John Ward and Fortewaters H Legg. Signed Elisha Hedden. Wit. oath Oct. 3, 1811 John Ward to Drury McDaniel. Rec. Jan. 3, 1814

p. 58-59 Dec. 26, 1812 Jane Smith (Spartanburgh) to John Cook (same); for $20 sold 20 ac on waters of Fairforrest Cr; border: John Cook and Golightly; formerly belonged to her husband James Smith and came to Jane Smith by dowry right. Witness Henry White and Daniel White. Signed Jane Smith. Wit. oath May 3, 1813 Daniel White to Thos Poole. Rec. Jan. 3, 1814

p. 59-60 Apr. 25, 1811 William L Allen (Spartanburgh) to John Arnold (same); for $47 sold 80 ac on James Cr of Tygar R; border: John Woodruff, Susanna Hambry's old line, (Hiaid? or Sleaie) Golightly, Thomas Woodruff, George Leatherwood; sold at publick auction by Bennett to John Arnold (sic). Witness Caleb Allen, Salley Stone, and Richd Shackelford. Signed Wm L Allen. Wit. oath Nov. 19, 1813 Richd Shackelford to John Dean. Rec. Jan. 3, 1814. Dower renounced Nov. 19, 1813 Mary Allen to Thomas Wright

p. 60-61 Mar. 22, 1810 (Smith Co, Tenn) James Stone (Smith Co, Tenn) to Joseph Casey; for $165 sold 77 ac on Two Mile Cr; border: Joseph Casey, Samuel Crow, Spencer Calvert, and county road; part of two grants: (1) to John Hendricks and (2) to Richard Nolly. Witness Simon Stone and William Stone. Signed James Stone and Patsey's mark. Certified Jun. 7, 1810 (Smith Co, Tenn) by Joseph W Allen, clerk of court. Jun. 7, 1810 (Smith Co, Tenn) Joseph Hebell, justice, certifys Joseph W Allen is clerk of court. Rec. Jan. 3, 1814. Dower renounced Jun. 7, 1810 (Smith Co, Tenn) (or Wit. oath) Patty Stone to William Moore, Richard Baily and John Lancaster, each JP

p. 61-62 Nov. 8, 1813 Mary Crow to William Crow (Caldwell Co, Ky); power of attorney to collect what is due her by people living in South Carolina. Witness J Mercer and Longsher Lamb. Signed Mary Crow. Certified Nov. 18, 1813 (Caldwell Co, Ky) by John H Philips, clerk of court. Nov. 18, 1813 David James, presiding magistrate, certifys John H Philips is clerk of court. Rec. Jan. 3, 1814

p. 62-63 Jul. 13, 1813 Samuel Shearbutt (Spartanburgh) to Isaac Lender (same); for $150 sold 100 ac on N side of Pacolett R; border: Thomas James and Dry Branch. Witness Thomas Wyatt and George Cantrell. Signed Samuel Shearbutt. Wit. oath Dec. 9, 1813 Thomas Wyatt to Henry Turner. Rec. Jul. 3, 1814 (sic)

p. 63-65 Aug. 7 (or 20), 1807 Richard Barnett (Spartanburgh) to John Cook; for $300 sold 120 ac on waters of Fairforrest Cr; border: Smith; where Richard Barnett lives. Witness Micajah Barnett and Drusilla Barnett. Signed Richard Barnett. Wit. oath Nov. 11, 1811 Drusilla Barnett to John Gossett. Rec. Jan. 3, 1814 Dower renounced Nov. 11, 1811 Susannah Barnett to John Gossett

p. 65 Dec. 11, (or 16), 1813 John Alexander (Greenville Dist) to Isaac Hendrix (Spartanburgh); for $60 sold 50 ac on waters of Jamies Cr; part of 160 ac grant Nov. 6, 1786 Gov. William Moultrie to John Alexander. Witness Mathew Waldrop and John

Lewis. Signed John Alexander. Wit. oath Feb. 8, 1811 Mathew Waldrop to John Dean. Rec. Jan. 3, 1814

p. 65-67 Aug. 8, 1809 James Kilgore (Greenville Dist) to Jeremiah Pace (same); for $200 sold 200 ac on N side of Maple Swamp Cr of Tygar R; includes where Ellis Reynolds lives; part of 1,000 ac grant to Pennel Wood. Witness John Grier and Richard Lock. Signed James Kilgore. Wit. oath Aug. 8, 1809 (Greenville Dist) John Grier to James N McCrary. Rec. Jan. 3, 1814. Dower renounced Mar. 9, 1811 (Greenville Dist) Keziah Kilgore to Reuben Barrett

p. 67-68 Jan. 23, 1813 Robert Alexander (Spartanburgh) to William B Alexander (same); for $250 sold 202 ac on James Cr of Tygar R and between Enoree and Tygar Rivers; border: William Posey, John Bragg, Capt. George Robuck, and John Leatherwood; "originally" sold by John Chesney to Alexander Alexander. Witness John Herckeby and Presley Smith. Signed Robert Alexander. Wit. oath Jul. 9, 1813 Presley Smith to M Casey. Rec. Jan. 3, 1814. Dower renounced Dec. 18, 1813 Sarah Alexander to Burrell Bobo

p. 68-69 Feb. 2, 1813 William B Alexander (Spartanburgh) to Presley Smith (same); for $125 sold 101 ac on James Cr of Tygar R; sold by Robert Alexander to William B Alexander. Witness Resa Robuck and Sampon Robuck. Signed Wm B Alexander. Wit. oath Jul. 7, 1813 Resa Robuck to M Casey. Rec. Jan. 3, 1814. Dower renounced Dec. 18, 1813 Ailsey Alexander to Burrel Bobo

p. 69-70 Nov. 4, 1801 Benjamin Busey (Spartanburgh) to Joseph Casey (same); for $95 sold 42½ ac on Two Mile Cr of Tygar R; part of grant to James Hendrix. Witness Christopher Rodes, James Grizble, and Edward Busey. Signed Benjamin and Lucy Busey's marks. Wit. oath Feb. 6, 1811 Christopher Rodes to M Casey. Rec. Jan. 3, 1814

p. 70-71 Feb. 9, 1807 David Jones (Spartanburgh) to Thomas Hill (same); for $100 sold 100 ac; "laid out by" Christopher Golightly. Witness Young Allen and Moses Guyton. Signed David Jones. Wit. oath May 2, 1811 Young Allen to Joshua Richards. Rec. Jan. 10, 1803

p. 71-72 (blank), 1814 Elias Benson (Spartanburgh) to Zachariah Wingo (same); for $125 sold 100 ac on both sides Fairforrest Cr; border: Grindstone Br; part of grant May 5 (or fifth line day), 1772 to Benjamin Thomason and to Elias Benson as an heir of William Benson. Witness Thos Tensley, John Bird, and William Foster. Signed Elias Benson. Wit. oath Jan. 11, 1814 Thos Tensley to John Chapman. Rec. Jan. 11, 1814

p. 72 Dec. 1, 1812 Patrick Hogan (Spartanburgh) to son-in-law Alexander McCollam (same); for love and affection give 165 ac; border: Walling, Thompson Clayton, and Reames. Witness John Vaughan and Thompson Clayton. Signed Patrick Hogan's mark. Wit. oath Jan. 10, 1814 John Vaughan to Michl Miller. Rec. Jan. 11, 1814

p. 72-73 (blank) 9, 1807 John Parris to John Williams; for $75 sold 75 ac on Suck Cr of Broad R; border: Moultrie; plat attached shows also border: John Williams; part of grant Sept. 11, 1795 to Jacob Dilback. Witness Peter Gosnal and Jeremiah Gosnal. Signed John Parris. Wit. oath Aug. 9, 1811 Peter Gosnal to Leonard Adcock. Rec. Jan. 11, 1814

p. 73-74 May 7, 1806 William Patton (Spartanburgh) to Isaac Crow jr (same); for $150 sold 320 ac in four tracts on waters of Dutchman's Cr; border: N-William Wofford, W-Wm (or Mrs) Smith, S-Elsworth Moore, and E-James Wofford. Witness John Wright and

George Leatherwood. Signed Wm Patton. Wit. oath Jan. 10, 1814 George Leatherwood to Samuel Woodruff. Rec. Jan. 11, 1814

p. 74-75 Mar. 9, 1806 John McCarroll (Spartanburgh) to Jesse Duglass; for $200 sold 100 ac; border: near ford of Obed Robert Cr known as McCarroll's ford; part of grant to Obediah Roberts. Witness Henry Monroe and George McWilliams. Signed John McCarroll. Wit. oath Jan. 10, 1814 George McWilliams to Wm Kelso. Rec. Jan. 13, 1814

p. 75-76 Mar. 30, 1811 Thomas Crumley (Spartanburgh) to Jesse Duglass (same); for $200 sold 183 ac on Obed's Cr of Pacolette R; border: McClure, Galt, Young, and McCarroll; grant to Isaac Anderson. Witness Wm Monroe, Henry Morgan, and Benjamin Crumley. Signed Thomas Crumley. Wit. oath Jan. 10, 1814 Henry Morgan to Wm Kelso. Rec. Jan. 13, 1814

p. 76-77 Jan. (blank), 1814 Jesse Duglass (Spartanburgh) to Henry Brown (same); for $350 sold 250 ac on S side of N Pacolette R; border: SE-James Young, SW & NW-survey for Capt. William Anderson, N & NE-grant to Locock or John McClure and Obed Cr, and by Roberts; all of 183 ac grant Jan. 2, 1797 Gov. Charles Pinckney to Isaac Anderson and part of grant to Obediah Roberts and grant to James Young esq. Witness Jabez Galt and Solomon Royston. Signed Jesse Duglass. Wit. oath Jan. 10, 1814 Solomon Royston to James Young. Rec. Jan. 13, 1814

p. 77-78 Nov. 10, 1813 John Farmer (Greenville Dist) to Daniel and John Robettson (Spartanburgh); for $260 sold 103 ac on S Tygar R; grant to John Farmer. Witness John Vaughan, Nathan Farmer, and William Alkins. Signed John Farmer's mark. Wit. oath Jan. 10, 1814 John Vaughan to Michl Miller. Rec. Jan. 18, 1814

p. 78-79 Sept. 23, 1809 George Alexander (Blunt Co, Tenn) to John Owings (Spartanburgh); for $160 sold 150 ac on both sides Molley Cr; border: Easley's Cr and corner marked "ꟷC"; lower part of grant Jun. 6, 1785 to Robert Goodgion; except "situation" of a machine and dam to support it--not to exceet 6 ac--reserved for James Galt. Witness William Bishears, Nathan Peliett(?), and John Bouham. Signed George Alexander. Wit. oath Sept. 23, 1809 William Bishears to Andrew Furgerson. Rec. Jan. 26, 1814

p. 79-80 May 30, 1811 Hugh Moore (Spartanburgh) to Christopher Cook; for $1.50 per ac sold 39 3/4 ac on waters of Thickety Cr of Broad R; border: Dewberry's old corner; part of 500 ac grant to Bennett C Webster and sold to Hugh Moore. Witness Thomas Cook and James Haynes. Signed Hugh Moore. Wit. oath Jun. 15, 1811 Thomas Cook to John Lipscomb. Rec. Feb. 1, 1814

p. 80 Mar. 10, 1813 James Ridings (Spartanburgh) to Joseph Wilson (same); for $100 sold 120 ac on SW side of Motlow's Cr; part of grant Mar. 2, 1812 to James Ridings. Witness James Whitten and James Ridings jr. Signed James Ridings' mark. Wit. oath Feb. 5, 1814 James Whitten to Andrew Furgerson. Rec. Feb. 7, 1814

p. 80-81 Jan. 4, 1813 Alexander McCarter (Lincoln Co, Tenn) to James Ballinger (Spartanburgh); for $1,000 sold 300 ac on both sides N Tygar R. Witness Henry Hutcherson, John M Collins, and John L Ballinger. Signed Alexander McCarter. Wit. oath Jan. 26, 1814 John L Ballinger to John Chapman. Rec. Feb. 7, 1814

p. 81-82 Jul. 20, 1811 William Shackelford (Spartanburgh) to James Crow (same); for $300 sold 125 (or 100) ac on waters of James Cr of Tygar R; border: Wm Peason and Paul Castleberry. Witness John Smith jr and Miles Nash. Signed Wm Shackelford. Wit. oath

Apr. 4, 1812 John Smith jr to John Dean. Rec. Feb. 7, 1814. Dower renounced Nov. 19, 1813 Nancy Shackelford to Drury McDaniel

p. 82-83 Jan. 15, 1812 Moses Foster (Spartanburgh) to son Andrew Foster; for obedience and good will towards Andrew give all stock of horses, cattle, hogs, sheep, household furniture and farming utensils, reserving a horse, 2 cows and calves, 2 sows and their pigs, 2 sheep, a bed and furniture all reserved for Moses and his wife during their lives; Moses expects Andrew to support Moses and wife during their lifetime; "waggon" mentioned in Moses' will to be divided as specified. Witness Clary Lancaster and William Lancaster. Signed Moses Foster. Wit. oath Feb. 7, 1814 William Lancaster to John Lipscomb. Rec. Feb. 7, 1814

p. 83-84 Feb. 5, 1814 James Laurence (Spartanburgh) to children; for love and affection give (1) to James Laurence--a bay mare, a red cow and calf, 8 hogs, a man's saddle; (2) to Unity Laurence--a burided(?) cow and yearling and a bed and furniture; (3) to Asley Laurence--a Peded cow and calf and bed and furniture; (4) to Joseph Laurence--a man's saddle, a bay horse and sorrel filley, a red heded cow and calf; (5) Patsey Laurence--a bed and furniture, a loom, and hiruesses(?), a side saddle, and all balance of kitchen and household furniture; (6) to grandson John Ragan--a bed and furniture; (7) to Darby Ragan--a bed and furniture; (8) and to James Alexander Ragan--a cow and calf; grandchildren's property formerly ment for daughter Nancy. Witness John Mason, Elijah Bishop, and George Bishop. Signed James Laurence. Wit. oath Feb. 7, 1814 Elijah Bishop to Jno H Jones. Rec. Feb. 8, 1814

p. 84-85 Jan. 7, 1813 Vincent Bennett, sheriff (Spartanburgh) to John Cunningham; for $315 sold 350 ac on waters of S Pacolette R; border: N-formerly owned by Jesse Duglass, W-Henry Morgan, S & SW-Henry Brown and Armstead Bomar, and E-unknown; sale due to writ from Spartanburgh Common Pleas Court suit John Cunningham vs James Galt; sale Aug. 5, 1811. Witness Muse Tolleson and James Hunt. Signed Vincent Bennett SSD. Wit. oath Feb. 8, 1814 James Hunt to William Ried. Rec. Feb. 8, 1814

p. 85-86 Dec. 1, 1813 James Milwood (Spartanburgh) to Judah Pruitt (or Prewitt) (same); for $100 sold 160 ac on waters of Thickety Cr; border: William Dewberry's house; where James Milwood lives. Witness John Pruett and Samuel Milwood. Signed James Milwoos. Wit. oath Dec. 1, 1813 John Pruett to Henry Turner. Rec. Feb. 12, 1814

p. 86-87 Feb. 11, 1814 James Dodd (Spartanburgh) to Noble Hamilton (Rutherford Co, NC); for $191 sold 186 ac on Buck Cr, Suck Cr, and Island Cr of Pacolette and Broad Rivers; including the Battleground. Witness David Pope and William Adcock. Signed James Dodd. Wit. oath Feb. 14, 1814 William Adcock to Leonard Adcock. Rec. Feb. 14, 1814

p. 87-88 Sept. 28, 1812 Alexr Cunningham (Spartanburgh) to Hugh McMullin; for $75 sold 76 ac on waters of N Pacolette R; border: David Cunningham and Hugh McMullin. Witness Lurke Burnett and Henry Davis. Signed Alexr Cunningham. Wit. oath Feb. 18, 1814 Lurke Burnett to James Young. Rec. Feb. 19, 1814

p. 88 Aug. 30, 1813 Thomas Roseborough, Lina Merriman, Deticha Merriman, and Tabitha Merriman (Warren Co, Tenn) to Demcy Boner (Jackson Co, Ga); power of attorney to sell 220 ac on head waters of Sarratt's Cr. Witness Wm Barnett, James Merryman, and Ferraba Bonberry. Signed Thomas Roseborough's, Lina, Deticha, and Tabitha Merriman's marks. Wit. oath Dec. 31, 1813 Demcy Boner jr (sic) to Joseph Camp. Rec. Feb. 28, 1814

p. 88-89 Dec. 30, 1813 Demcy Boner, attorney for Thomas Roseborough and Lina, Dilitha, and Tabitha Merriman, to Briant Bonner; for $200 sold 200 ac on waters of Sarratt's Cr; border: Nesbett, Turner, and Holloway. Witness William C Camp jr and John Arendale. Signed Demcy Bonner's mark. Wit. oath Dec. 30, 1811 John Arendale to Joseph Camp. Rec. Feb. 28, 1814

p. 89-90 Nov. 12, 1813 William Holt (Spartanburgh) to William Brown (same); for $200 sold 200 ac on waters of Cherokee Cr; border: Walden; part of grant to James Stedman. Witness John Elder and Jeremiah McMullin. Signed William Holt. Wit. oath Nov. 12, 1813 John Elder to Henry Turner. Rec. Mar. 7, 1814

p. 90-91 Oct. 30, 1813 John Redman (Spartanburgh) to Bennett Wilson (same); for $60 "paid last old Christmas past was a year" sold 30 ac where Bennet Wilson lives; on N side Sims Fork of Abner's Cr; border: waggon ford and Wilson's field; deed evidently not made until now; John Redman is in "low state of health" but his memory is good. Witness Robert Green and Charles McClain. Signed John Redman's mark. Wit. oath Oct. 30, 1813 Robert Green to James Hammett. Rec. Mar. 7, 1814. Dower renounced Dec. 15, 1813 Rachel Redman to Drury McDaniel

p. 91-92 Jan. 15, 1814 Aaron Tempelton to William Low; for $100 sold 300 ac on N side Pacolette R. Witness Thomas Wyatt and Jonathan Low sr. Signed Aaron Tempelton's mark. Wit. oath Mar. 7, 1814 Thomas Wyatt to Jno H Jones. Rec. Mar. 7, 1814

p. 92-93 Jan. 22, 1814 Aaron Tempelton (Spartanburgh) to William Low (same); for $50 sold 100 ac on N side of Pacolette R; part of grant in 1787 to Francis Ballenger. Witness John Low jr and Thomas Wyatt. Signed Aaron Tempelton's mark. Wit. oath Mar. 7, 1814 Thomas Wyatt to Jno H Jones. Rec. Mar. 7, 1814

p. 93-95 Oct. 10, 1813 Mary Lee (Spartanburgh) to Levi Lee (same); to secure a bond of $350 (to pay $200 by Mar. 15, 1814 with interest from Mar. 1, 1814 (sic)) and for $10 sold (1) 284 ac on branch of Lawson's fork; grant to John Holcom; (2) 100 ac on S side of Lawson's fork; grant to Edward Dickson; (3) 60 ac part of grant to Disken Grant; (4) 100 ac on S side of Lawson's fork; (5) 100 ac; border: George Parkerson and Randolph Brown; (6) all land she owns and a bay mare, a sorrell horse, a black colt, 4 cows and 2 yearlings, 2 sows and 10 pigs, 3 feather beds and furniture, 3 bedsteads, a chest, table, a loom and 7 chairs; Condition: sale void if Mary pays debt. Witness James Ross and Sarah Ross. Signed Mary Lee's mark. Wit. oath Mar. 10, 1814 James Ross to A Benson. Rec. Mar. 10, 1814

p. 95-96 May 28, 1813 John Arnold (Spartanburgh) to William Arnold (same); for $250 sold 70 ac on branch of Tygar R. Witness Richard Shackelford and Willis Arnold. Signed John Arnold. Wit. oath Apr. 3, 1814 (sic) Willis Arnold to John Dean. Rec. Mar. 14, 1814

p. 96-97 Mar. 16, 1814 Daniel Wilbanks (Union Dist) to Moses White (Spartanburgh), carpenter; for $45 sold 113 ac in Spartanburgh and Union Districts on branches of McElwain's Cr; plat attached shows border: Will Archibald, Saml Archibald, Jas Hamon, Chas Goodwin, Lancaster Haselwood, Will Wofford, and Isaac Wofford. Witness John Storey and Joseph Wilbanks. Signed Daniel Wilbanks. Wit. oath Mar. 23, 1814 John Storey to Saml Archibald. Rec. Mar. 24, 1814

p. 97 Oct. 20, 1813 Jarrett Miller (Spartanburgh) to John Fielder (same); for $100 sold 95 ac on E side of Tygar R; border:

James Hughes and Samuel Miller. Witness John Mason and Jarrett Miller. Signed Jarrett Miller's mark. Wit. oath Jan. 13, 1814 Jarrett Miller to Drury McDaniel. Rec. Apr. 4, 1814

p. 97-98 Nov. 4, 1808 John Arendell (or Arnold) sr (Logan Co, Ky) to son John Arendell (Spartanburgh); for $100 sold 100 ac SW of where Bridges Arnold lives; border: William Williams. Witness Isaac Dill and Joseph Dill. Signed John Arendell. Wit. oath May 13, 1813 Joseph Dill to Joshua Richards. Rec. Apr. 4, 1814

p. 98-100 Jan. 10, 1806 John Pennington (Spartanburgh) to John Dickey (same); for $4,000 sold 470 ac on N side Enoree R; where John Dickey lives; border: Ford's Still House Br, Samuel Guilkey, and Ellener(?); part granted to Jacob Pennington, part of Zadock Ford, part to Samuel Guilkey and rest granted to John Pennington. Witness William Thackston sr and William Thackston jr. Signed Jno Pennington. Wit. oath Jan. 10, 1806 William Thackston sr to James Kilgore. Rec. Apr. 11, 1814. Dower renounced Jan. 10, 1806 Sarah Pennington to James Kilgore

p. 100-101 Dec. 15, 1800 Zadock Ford (Spartanburgh) to John Pennington (same); for $50 sold 250 ac on Suortree(?) Cr of Enoree R; border: James Ford, Thomas House, Drury Anderson, JP; grant Sept. 3, 1798. Witness James Ford, Barnett H Allgood, and John Powers. Signed Zadock Ford. Wit. oath Aug. 17, 1805 James Ford to Denny Anderson. Rec. Apr. 11, 1814. Dower renounced Jan. 10, 1806 Casander Ford (late wife of Zadock Ford desc) to James Kilgore

p. 101-102 Sept. 7, 1801 Denny Anderson (Spartanburgh) to John Pennington (same); for $5 sold "near" an ac; part of 250 ac grant Oct. 15, 1784 to Denny Anderson. Witness William Massy and Thomas Kevil. Signed Denny Anderson. Wit. oath May 18, 1807 Thomas Kevil to James Kilgore. Rec. Apr. 11, 1814

p. 102-103 Sept. 13, 1797 Zadock Ford esq and wife Casander (Spartanburgh) to John Pennington (same); for $30 sold 25 ac on both sides King's R (now known as Enoree R); border: John Pennington and Denny Anderson; part of grant Jun. 29, 1752 Gov. Mathew Rowan (NC) to Samuel Gilkey (600 ac); in SC grant book LNN (sic) p. 121 and sold to John Dickinson who sold to John Dalton who sold to Zadock Ford. Witness Jarrott Moss, Mary Ford, and Nancy Ford. Signed Zadock and Casander Ford. Wit. oath May 26, 1806 Nancy Ford to Denny Anderson. Rec. Apr. 11, 1814

p. 103-104 Dec. 15, 1813 John Sellivan (Spartanburgh) to Thomas Thomas (same); for $120 sold 200 ac; border: John Beley, Ezekiel Sellivan, and Webber; part of 974 ac grant to Ezekiel Sillivan. Witness Robert Coleman and Charles Seven Guyton. Signed John Sellivan. Wit. oath Jan. 10, 1814 Robert Coleman to John Lipscomb. Rec. Apr. 11, 1814

p. 104 Mar. 7, 1814 James Clayton (Spartanburgh) to Fielding Clayton (same); for $200 sold 100 ac on Fort Shoals Br of Enoree R; border: N & W-Drury Couch, S-Rachal Farrow, and E-James Clayton. Witness James Keating and William Clayton. Signed James Clayton. Wit. oath Mar. 7, 1814 James Keating to Burrell Bobo. Rec. Apr. 11, 1814

p. 104-105 Mar. 7, 1814 James Clayton (Spartanburgh) to William Clayton (same); for $300 sold 100 ac on Fort Shoals Cr of Enoree R; border: S-William Word, W-John Farrow, N-James Clayton, and E-Willis Bobo and John Bogan; part of two grants: (1) to Mathew Couch and (2) to Samuel Farrow. Witness James Keating and Fielding Clayton. Signed James Clayton. Wit. oath Mar. 7, 1814 James Keating to Burrell Bobo. Rec. Apr. 11, 1814

p. 105-106 Apr. 1, 1814 Mary Otts, widow of Martin Otts desc, Martin Otts, son of Martin Otts, desc, and Rachel Otts, daughter of Martin Otts desc (all of Spartanburgh) to Mary Otts, eldest daughter of Martin Otts desc; they relinquish and quit claim "lower part" of Martin Otts' land (ac omitted); border: branch running between two houses at Charles Moore's land, Rock Br, Samuel Otts, and Rogers. Witness Robert Legon and James Otts. Signed Mary Ann Otts, Martin Otts, and Rachel Otts. Wit. oath Apr. 11, 1814 Robert Legon to Danl White. Rec. Apr. 11, 1814

p. 106-107 Jun. 11, 1813 Willis and Polley Green (Spartanburgh) to Archibald Lester (Greenville Dist); for $100 sold 250(?) ac on both sides Green's Cr of Lawson's fork of Pacolette R; border: N & NW-George McDowell, NW & NE- Isaac Bishop, NE-West, and SW & SE-vacant; half of 500 ac grant Aug. 8, 1792 to William McDowell. Witness George Green and Philip Chester. Signed Willis and Polley Green. Wit. oath Apr. 9, 1814 (Greenville Dist) Philip Chester to Jas N McCrary. Rec. Apr. 11, 1814. Dower renounced Jun. 9, 1813 Polley Green to Drury McDaniel

p. 107-108 Nov. 9, 1801 Adam Sloan (Spartanburgh) to Charles Barry (same); for $490 sold 185 ac on W side of N Tygar R; border: Cannon; includes Adam Sloan's dwelling house; part of two grants--(1) E part adjoins River; grant Oct. 24, 1767 to William Neely who sold to John Ward who sold to Richd Barry who sold to Adam Sloan; and (2) W end is part of grant May 15, 1772 to Charles Moore who sold to Richard Barry who sold to Adam Sloan. Witness Chas Moore and Thos Moore. Signed Adam Sloan. Wit. oath Apr. 12, 1814 (sic) Chas Moore to Drury McDaniel. Rec. Apr. 11, 1814

p. 108-109 Apr. 7, 1813 Alexander McKie and Gabriel Benson (Spartanburgh) to Obediah Prewitt (same); for $100 sold 210 ac on Caney Cr of Tygar R; border: John Smith, blacksmith. Witness Robert Benson and Thomas Poole. Signed Alexr McKie and Gal Benson. Wit. oath Apr. 12, 1814 Thomas Poole to Jno H Jones. Rec. Apr. 12, 1814

p. 109-110 Feb. 3, 1814 Alexander McKie (Spartanburgh) to Hamilton Wilson (same); for $130 sold 150 ac on Fairforrest Cr; border: road from Spartanburgh Court House to Henry O'Niel's, an old saw mill seat, Thomas' old line, Tillet, Dugas Br, and John Martin. Witness Thomas Poole esq and John Arendale. Signed Alexr McKie. Wit. oath Mar. 12, 1814 Thomas Poole to Danl White. Rec. Apr. 12, 1814

p. 110 Feb. 18, 1814 William Ramsey (Spartanburgh) to John Dalton (same); for $18 sold 35 ac on both sides Meador's Cr; part of grant Nov. 5, 1810 to William Ramsey. Witness James Whitten and Richard Vandike. Signed Wm Ramsey. Wit. oath Apr. 12, 1814 James Whitten to Wm Kelso. Rec. Apr. 12, 1814

p. 110-111 Feb. 6, 1813 James Wofford (Spartanburgh) to Nathaniel Woodruff (same); for $300 sold 100 ac on S side of Furgerson's Cr of Tygar R; border: Fort Br and Driver's(?) Br. Witness Nathaniel Wofford, Samuel Woodruff, and Jonathan Moore. Signed James Wofford. Wit. oath Jul. 28, 1813 Jonathan Moore to Samuel Woodruff. Rec. Apr. 12, 1814. Dower renounced Mar. 3, 1813 Cathraine Wofford to Drury McDaniel

p. 111-112 Dec. 24, 1813 Benjamin Ellis (Spartanburgh) to Joshua Hearn; for $150 sold 50 ac on W side of Broad R. Witness John Lewis and James Campbell. Signed Benjamin Ellis. Wit. oath Jan. 29, 1814 John Lewis to Joseph Camp. Rec. Apr. 13, 1814

p. 112-113 Feb. 4, 1812 William Murry (Spartanburgh) to James Young (same); for $50 sold 50 ac; border: Bever house field, James Lard, Big Br, and Headen's ford; part of tract on E side of Island Cr of Pacolette R. Witness James Lard and William Garrett. Signed William Murry's mark. Wit. oath Feb. 6, 1812 James Lard to Henry Turner. Rec. Apr. 14, 1814

p. 113-114 Jan. 1, 1814 James Harrison (Spartanburgh) to Muse Tollison (same); to secure a $100 debt sold a bay horse 5 years old James bought from Jesse Griffin, a dark bay mare with one eye out "from" Benjamin Howard, a buirdle(?) cow and calf bought from Thomas Ried, a sow and 4 shoats unmarked, two barrows--one white and one blue marked with a cross and a half cross in right ear and cross and undirkeal in left ear, 3 feather beds, bedsteads and furniture, 8 chairs, 6 pewter plates, a pewter dish, a gallon pewter bason, a chest, a pine table, 2 pots, a dutch oven, a baker, a skillet, 2 shovel plows, a barshar(? or barslear) plow, 2 coutters, 4 weeding hoes, 2 parting(?) planes, a fore plane, 3 jack planes, 2 hand saws, 3 foot adze(?), 8 chisels, 2 broad axes, and 2 club axes; Condition: sale void if James pays $100 with interest by Jan. 1, 1815. Witness James Hunt and James Treveleon(?). Signed James Harrison. Wit. oath Apr. 4, 1814 James Hunt to Jno H Jones. Rec. Mar. 9, 1814

p. 114-115 Feb. 8, 1814 John McDowell (Charleston, SC) to Muse Tolleson (Spartanburgh); for $100 sold 160 ac on waters of Fairforrest Cr; border: SW-Armstrong and SE-Gov. Montague; plat attached with survey Jul. 30, 1782 by James Smith; part of land late property of Gov. Charles G Montague. Witness Vincent Tapp and Thomas Wright. Signed John McDowell. Wit. oath Apr. 16, 1814 Vincent Tapp to A Benson. Rec. Apr. 16, 1814

p. 115-116 Nov. 26, 1813 Elijah Barnett (Spartanburgh) to James W. Cooper (Union Dist); for $490 sold 294 ac on branches of Kelsoe's Cr of Fairforrest Cr; part of grants to (1) Charles Hammett and (2) Charles James; where Elijah Barnett lives; ½ ac "around the graves" excepted. Witness John Lancaster sr, Ralph Jackson, and Lawrence Lancaster. Signed Elijah Barnet. Wit. oath Dec. 3, 1813 John Lancaster jr to Daniel White. Rec. May 2, 1814. Dower renounced Feb. 12, 1814 Mary Barnett to Daniel White

p. 116-117 Oct. 1, 1808 Abner Underwood (Spartanburgh) to Polly Underwood (same); for $150 sold 350 ac on both sides Green's Cr of Lawson's fork of Pacolate R; grant to George McDowel. Witness William Underwood and Jesse Cannon. Signed Abner Underwood. Wit. oath May 2, 1814 William Underwood to Thomas Poole. Rec. May 2, 1814

p. 117-118 Jan. 26, 1813 John Owens (Spartanburgh) to Jesse Crook (same); for $400 sold 120 ac on N fork Forgeson's Cr of Tygar R. Witness James Wofford and William Crook. Signed John Owens. Wit. oath Nov. 3, 1813 William Crook to D McDaniel. Rec. May 2, 1814

p. 118-119 Apr. 30, 1814 John Thomason (Spartanburgh) to John Tollison (same); for $142 sold 142 ac on waters of Lawson's Cr; border: Stephen Thomason; part of tract alloted by Commissioners to John Thomason as his part of his father's real estate. Witness Muse Tollison and James Hunt. Signed John Thomason. Wit. oath May 2, 1810 Muse Tollison to A Benson. Rec. May 2, 1814

p. 119-120 Mar. 21, 1814 John Tollison (Spartanburgh) to Richard Kirby (same); for $55 sold 50 ac on waters of Pacolate R; border: mouth of Richard Kirby's Spring Br, where Ralph Lancaster formerly lived, Reubin Briant, and John Harvy. Witness Ely Tollison and Abraham Lancaster. Signed John Tollison. Wit. oath Mar. 21,

1814 Ely Tollison to John Gossett. Rec. May 13, 1814

p. 120-121 May 16, 1814 Aaron Wilkins (Spartanburgh) to William Cantrell (same); for $750 sold 175 ac on Pacolate R; border: S-William Wilkins and Hugh McMillen, W-George McWilliams and James Caps, and N & E-William Cantrell. Witness Moses Wilkins and George Wilkins. Signed Aron Wilkins. Wit. oath May 16, 1814 George Wilkins to John Lipscomb. Rec. May 20, 1814.

p. 121 Dec. 8, 1813 John Foster (Spartanburgh) to James Vernon (same); for $33 sold 11 ac; border: a ford and a country road. Witness Eaton Walker and William Pollard. Signed John Foster. Wit. oath (date omitted) William Pollard to John Chapman. Rec. May 23, 1814

p. 121-122 Feb. 1, 1814 Obediah Wingo (Spartanburgh) to Willis Wingo (same); for $152 sold 71 ac on waters of Fairforrest Cr; border: Hamilton Wilson, Willis Wingo, and Elijah Ballenger; part of tract sold by Samuel Culberson to Obediah Wingo. Witness William Wingo and Elijah Ballenger. Signed Obediah Wingo. Wit. oath May 2, 1814 William Wingo to John Chapman. Rec. May 24, 1814. Dower renounced May 2, 1814 Obedience Wingo to Michael Miller

p. 122-123 Mar. 5, 1814 Joseph Simmons (Spartanburgh) to Richard Thomson (same); for $40 sold 25 ac; border: Richard Thomson and Reubin Harrison; part of grant Sept. 7, 1789 to Reubin Mathus. Witness William G Davis, Jesse Simmons, and Jane Parker. Signed Joseph Simmons. Wit. oath Mar. 10, 1814 William G Davis to Danl White. Rec. May 24, 1814

p. 123-125 Sept. 19, 1811 Elisha Hadden (Spartanburgh) to George and Fortunatus H Legg (same); for $1,072.45 sold 478 ac on waters of Middle Tygar R; border: Gen. Thomas Moore, main road, and David Drummon. Witness Thomas Moore and Jacob Hadden. Signed Elisha Hadden. Wit. oath Nov. 28, 1811 Jacob Hadden to Drury McDaniel. Rec. Jun. 6, 1814

p. 125-126 Mar. 2, 1813 Abraham Cantrell (Spartanburgh) to Thomas Cantrell; for $100 sold 60 ac on S side of Buck Cr of Pacolate R; border: John Morris and "siad" Forest. Witness John Cantrell and Luke Demsey. Signed Abraham Cantrell. Wit. oath Feb. 2, 1813 (sic) John Cantrell to Henry Turner. Rec. Jun. 6, 1814

p. 126-127 Jun. 7, 1814 Henry Brown (Spartanburgh) to Richard Brown (same); for $350 sold 250 ac on S side of Obed's Cr of N Pacolate R; border: SE-James Young, SW & NW-survey for Capt. William Anderson, N & NE-grant to Locock or John McClure's land and Obed Cr and by Roberts; all of 183 ac grant Jan. 2, 1797 Gov. Charles Pinckney to Isaac Anderson and part of grant to Obediah Roberts and part of land belonging (sic) to James Young esq. Witness John Walker and William Walker. Signed Henry Brown. Wit. oath Jun. 7, 1814 William Walker and A Benson. Rec. Jun. 7, 1814

p. 127-129 Aug. 30, 1813 John Cook (Spartanburgh) to Elias Palmer (same); for $600 sold 179 ac on Fairforrest Cr; border: N-Widow Legon, W-Thomas Tinsley, S-Walter West and David Golightly, and E-Thomas Greenwood; land formerly owned by Robert Legon desc. Witness Lemuel Cook and John Palmer. Signed John Cook. Wit. oath Dec. 4, 1813 John Palmer to A Benson. Rec. Jun. 10, 1814. Dower renounced Dec. 13, 1813 Sally Cook to Daniel White

p. 129-130 Sept. 9, 1813 James Compton (Spartanburgh) to George Acridge (same); for $30 sold 34 ac on both sides branch of Ward's Cr of N Tygar R; part of 283 ac grant to Hopkins Bright. Witness Thomas Thornton and Lawson Thomson. Signed James Compton.

Wit. oath Oct. 21, 1813 Thomas Thornton to Drury McDaniel. Rec. Jun. 25, 1814

p. 130 Mar. 29, 1813 Edward Autry (Spartanburgh) to George Acridge; for $80 sold 100 ac on branch of Mill Cr of N Tygar R; border: Bush and John Foster. Witness John Ward and Thomas Moore. Signed Edward Autry's mark. Wit. oath Apr. 12, 1814 John Ward to Drury McDaniel. Rec. Jun. 25, 1814

p. 130-131 Jul. 24, 1814 Drury McMillon (Spartanburgh) to Tillotson Brookshear (same); for $100 sold 100 ac on N side Pacolette R and on Cool Spring Br; border: James Sanders, a road from the Cowpens to Coulter's ford, and Young. Witness Mathew Abbett and John Brookshear. Signed Drury McMillon's mark. Wit. oath Jul. 24, 1814 John Brookshear to Henry Turner. Rec. Jul. 26, 1814

p. 131-132 Jun. 22, 1814 George Acridge (Spartanburgh) to David McCarley (same); for $100 sold 100 ac on branches of Mill Cr of N Tygar R; border: NW-Parnear(?), NW & SE-Foster, and NE-Greenberry Leeg. Witness James McCarley and Drury McAbee. Signed George Acridge's mark. Wit. oath Jul. 4, 1814 James McCarley to James Hammett. Rec. Jul. 4, 1814

p. 132-133 Aug. 9, 1813 Jason Moore sr (Spartanburgh) to Jason Moore jr (same); for $50 sold 50 ac on branch of Ward's Cr of Tygar R; part of 100 ac grant May 4, 1775 Gov. William Bull to William Peden. Witness Green Meadows and Theophelus Moore. Signed Jason Moore sr. Wit. oath Jun. 3, 1814 Green Meadows to John Brewton. Rec. Jul. 4, 1814

p. 133-134 Feb. 28, 1805 Joseph Rogers (Spartanburgh) to Mrs. Nancy Posey and Jason Moore jr (same); for $200 sold 125 ac on N side of Tygar R and N side of Ward's Cr; border: Thomas Moore sr, Vicker's Spring Br, Jason Moore sr, and William Rodgers. Witness Andw B Moore and Samuel Otts. Signed Joseph Rodgers. Wit. oath Oct. 11, 1808 Samuel Otts to William Lancaster. Rec. Jul. 4, 1814

p. 134-135 Nov. (blank), 1813 Samuel Turner (Spartanburgh) to James Lackey (same); "for half the cost of providing a right from states office for 250 ac" sold 125 ac; border: Brice. Witness George Turner and John Low. Signed Samuel Turner. Wit. oath Apr. 11, 1814 George Turner to Henry Turner. Rec. Jul. 4, 1814

p. 135 Jun. 8, 1813 John Low sr (Spartanburgh) to John Low jr; for "a third of what he shall raise on the place during my lifetime and lifetime of my wife and third of profit of orchard and he is to clear ground and mend fences and improve plantation as far as his power lies" sold 250 ac; if he fails land returns to John Low sr when John repays what he receives; border: Thomas Wyatt, Shadrick Prewett, Bosey Low, Mary Dewberry, Reubin Warren, and Jonathan Low. Witness James Haynes and Hugh Moore. Signed John Low sr. Wit. oath Jul. 4, 1814 James Haynes to Henry Turner. Rec. Jul. 4, 1814

p. 135-136 Jan 29, 1814 John Owen (Spartanburgh) to Thompson Clayton (same); for $160 sold 150 ac on N side Motley's Cr; border: corner marked "IO". Witness Gowen Clayton sr, Thadious Owen, and John Davis. Signed John Owen. Wit. oath Apr. 2, 1814 John Davis to Andrew Furgeson. Rec. Jul. 4, 1814

p. 136-137 Jul. 9, 1812 Samuel Fowler (Spartanburgh) to William Jackson (same); for $46 sold 50 ac on Motley Cr; border: James Owens, Nathan Pettet, James Alexander, and Andrew Furgerson. Witness John Boliam, Edward Fowler and Martha Fowler. Signed Samuel Fowler's mark. Wit. oath Jul. 11, 1812 Edward Fowler to Andrew

Furgerson. Rec. Jul. 4, 1814

p. 137-138 Apr. 10, 1814 Reubin Bomar (Spartanburgh) to Thomas Jackson (same); for $7.50 sold 299 3/4 ac; border: Kelso (now Thomas Jackson's land) and Earles Machine. Witness Aewburn Boder, William West and James Center. Signed Reubin Bomar. Wit. oath Jul. 2, 1814 James Center to Wm Kelso. Rec. Jul. 4, 1814

p. 138-139 Jun. 28, 1814 John Woodruff (Spartanburgh) to Zacheriah Leatherwood; for ($?)100 sold 75 ac on branches of Fergerson's Cr of Tygar R. Witness Daniel McKie and James Leatherwood. Signed John Woodruff. Wit. oath Jun. 28, 1814 James Leatherwood to Samuel Woodruff. Rec. Jul. 4, 1814

p. 139-140 Nov. 11, 1811 Richard Roberds (Spartanburgh) to Nathaniel McElrath (same); for $200 sold 210 ac on Williams Cr of S Tygar R; border: Nisbett, McKie, Edwards, and Landford; grant Dec. 1, 1806. Witness Samuel N Evins and Alexander Evins. Signed Richard Roberds and Jane's mark. Wit. oath Nov. 15, 1811 Alexander Evins to John Collins. Rec. Jul. 4, 1814

p. 140-141 May 23, 1814 John Stone (Spartanburgh) to Young Fuller (same); for $150 sold 150 ac on Cherokee Cr of Pacolette R; border: mouth of Dugoway Cr and Solomon Abbott; part of grant to Robert Lee sr desc. Witness Christopher Golightly and William Golightly. Signed John Stone. Wit. oath Jul. 4, 1814 Christopher Golightly to A Benson. Rec. Jul. 4, 1814

p. 141-142 Aug. 10, 1803 Sarah Patton (Spartanburgh) to Nathaniel McElrath (same); for $180 sold 75 ac on S side of S Tygar R; border: Nathaniel McElrath; part of 400 ac grant to Francis Dodds who sold to Henry Leach who sold to John McElrath who sold to John Berry who sold to Sarah Patton. Witness Samuel Pearson, Jean Evins, and Alexander Evins. Signed Sarah Patton's mark. Wit. oath Jul. 4, 1814 Samuel Pearson to John Collins. Rec. Jul. 4, 1814

p. 142-143 Oct. 28, 1809 John Tate (Spartanburgh) to Daniel McKie (same); for $500 sold 555 ac on both sides Arnold's Cr of Enoree R; plat attached shows 560 ac (sic) and border: Sowell, now Samuel Jones, William Lindsey, George Thornton, Mirica Fowler, and William Shackelford (by resurvey Oct. 20, 1809 Jas Wofford DS); part of 972 ac grant Mar. 15, 1804 to John Tate sr; where John Tate sr and Noah Westmoreland lived. Witness A. M.(or N) Harrison and Richard Sowell. Signed John Tate. Wit. oath (Pendleton Dist) Mar. 17, 1814 Richard Sowell to John Keith. Rec. Jul. 4, 1814

p. 143 Apr. 1, 1814 John, James, William, Samuel, and Phillip Otts, Jesse Spencer, and Anne Miller, heirs of Martin Otts desc (all of Spartanburgh) to Mary Ann Otts, wife and widow of Martin Otts, and Martin Otts, younger son of Martin Otts desc, Rachell Otts, younger daughter of Martin Otts; the grantors give up (quit claim) all claim to all Martin Otts' real and personal estate. Witness Robert Legon and Samuel Otts. Signed John Otts, James Otts, William Otts, Samuel Otts, Phillip Otts, Jesse Spencer, and Anne Miller. Wit. oath Jun. 18, 1814 Samuel Otts to Danl White. Rec. Jul. 20, 1814

p. 143-144 Apr. 11, 1814 Mart Otts to Mary Ann Otts, Martin Otts, and Rachel Otts, heirs of Martin Otts; Mary quit claims to land that belonged to Mary's father, exclusive of part Mary Ann, Martin, and Rachel Otts assigned to Mary Otts; border: "a branch" and Sam Otts. Witness Robert Legon and Peggy Acrey. Signed Mary Otts. Wit. oath Jul. 16, 1814 Peggy Acrey to Danl White. Rec. Jul. 20, 1814

p. 144-145 Dec. 23, 1809 Thomas Rees (Spartanburgh) to Drury McMillon (same); for $100 sold 100 ac on Wolf Br on N side of Tygar R; border: James Sanders, a road from the Cowpens to Coulter's ford, and Young. Witness James Cantrell and James Trail. Signed Thomas Rees. Wit. oath Jan. 2, 1810 James Cantrell to Henry Turner. Rec. Jul. 26, 1814

p. 145-146 Apr. 8, 1814 Edith Legon (Spartanburgh) to Peter Smith (same); for $200 sold (1) 57 ac on Kelso's Cr of Fair-forrest Cr; border: Peter Smith; and (2) 63 ac; border: Shands Golightly; both (1) and (2) sold by Henry Smith to Robert Smith who sold to Edith Legon. Witness Henry Golightly to James White. Signed Edith Legon. Wit. oath Apr. 8, 1814 Henry Golightly to Danl White. Rec. Aug. 1, 1814

p. 146-147 Dec. 14, 1809 Daniel White (Spartanburgh) to Drury McAbee (same); for $125 sold 116 ac on both sides Ford's Cr of Fairforrest Cr; border: Thomas McCarely, Nathaniel Simmons, John Gideon, Ephraim Mason, William Barber, and James Selmon; formerly Henry Wells' land; on E side of road from William Wells' to Spartan-burgh Court House; where Richardson hucurt formerly lived. Witness Micajah Barnett to John Duncan. Signed Danl White. Wit. oath Aug. 1, 1814 Micajah Barnett to James Hammett. Rec. Aug. 1, 1814

p. 147-148 May 8, 1798 John McElrath (Spartanburgh) to Nathaniel McElrath (same); for $10 sold 150 ac on S side of S Tygar R; border: John Berry, William Rivers, Williams Cr, and James McHugh; part of grant Oct. 4, (omitted) Gov. William Tryon (NC) to Francis Dodds who sold in 1770 to Henry Leech who sold in 1773 to John McElrath. Witness Samuel Nisbett, Thomas McElrath, and Alexander Evins. Signed John McElrath. Wit. oath Aug. 1, 1814 Alexander Evins to James Hammett. Rec. Aug. 1, 1814

p. 148-149 Jan. 31, 1814 William Davis Thomas (Greenville Dist) to Joel and William Farmer (Spartanburgh); for $200 sold 192 ac on S side of S Tygar R; border: Stephen Phillips, grant to John Thomas jr, "ancient boundary line", and Wm Crane; where Joel and William Farmer live. Witness James R Marshall, Alexander M Thompson, and Lemuel Loftis. Signed W. D. Thomas. Wit. oath Jun. 25, 1814 Lemuel Loftis to James Hammett. Rec. Aug. 2, 1814

p. 149-150 Jan. 25, 1813 Mary Cantrell (Spartanburgh) to Abraham Cantrell (same); for $100 sold 78 ac on both sides Cases Cr of Pacolette R; border: John Martin, William Garrott, Bankston, and James Turner; grant States Office to William Garrott. Witness John Nolen and John Bankston. Signed Mary Cantrell's mark. Wit. oath Feb. 27, 1813 John Nolen to Leonard Adcock. Rec. Aug. 29, 1814

p. 150-151 Aug. 23, 1814 Abraham Cantrell (Spartanburgh) to Laurence Bankston (same); for $100 sold 78 ac on both sides Casey Cr of Pacolette R; border: John Martin, William Garrott, a road, Bankston, Mary Cantrell, and James Turner; grant States Office to William Garrott. Witness Mary Turner and James Turner. Signed Abraham Cantrell. Wit. oath Aug. 29, 1814 James Turner to Henry Turner. Rec. Aug. 29, 1814

p. 151-152 Feb. 5, 1814 Richard Morris (Spartanburgh) to William Lettel (same); for $190 sold 200 ac on branches of Buck Cr; border: Nolan Johnson, Dalton (or Datton), and Joseph Morris. Witness Samuel Trolanger and James Robins. Signed Richard Morris' mark. Wit. oath Feb. 22, 1814 James Robins to Leonard Adcock. Rec. Sept. 2, 1804

p. 152-154 Mar. 24, 1814 David Lynch (Spartanburgh) to Anthony Foster (same); to secure notes dated Sept. 15, 1813 for

$218.07 and 7 mills to be paid (1) in two days and (2) in 5 days sold 135 ac; border: near fork of Kelsey's Cr, James, Buffington, and Barnett; Condition: sale void if David Lynch pays debt by Mar. 1, 1815. Witness Collins Smith and Maiden Smith. Signed David Lynch. Wit. oath Aug. 27, 1814 Collins Smith to A Benson. Rec. Sept. 5, 1814

p. 154-155 Jun. 24, 1814 Peter Legon and wife Patsey (lately Patsey Ward) (Spartanburgh) to Richard Legon (Amelia Co, Va); for $140 sold (ac omitted) on Landry (or Saudry) Cr; "our distribution" shard; originally Samuel Ward desc's land; border: Rodophin Jeter, William Robertson, and Pleasant Gibbs. Witness John D Palmer and James Hunt. Signed Peter and Patsey Legon. Wit. oath Sept. 5, 1814 James Hunt to John Gossett. Rec. Sept. 5, 1814

p. 155-156 Jul. 23, 1814 John Ballenger, David Lewis, Edward Ballenger, Francis Ballenger, Elijah Ballenger, and William Ballenger, legatees of James Ballenger desc, to James Ballenger; for $450 sold 200 ac on both sides of Main N Tygar R; border: John Miller. Witness William Perrin, Laurence Bankston, and James Balenger. Signed John Ballenger, Edward Ballenger, Francis Ballenger, Elijah Ballenger, William Ballenger, and David Lewis. Wit. oath Sept. 5, 1814 William Perrin to John Chapman. Rec. Sept. 5, 1814

p. 156-157 Jan. 10, 1814 John Tucker (Greenville Dist) to James Vernon (Spartanburgh); for $25 sold 100 ac at head of Shoaley fork Cr of N Tygar R; border: Goodigion's Road; part of grant Feb. 4, 1804 to John Tucker. Witness Henry Hutchison, John Jordan, and Moses Ritcheson. Signed John Tucker's mark. Wit. oath Sept. 5, 1814 John Jordan to John Chapman. Rec. Sept. 5, 1814

p. 157-158 Sept. 3, 1814 John Jordan (Spartanburgh) to James Vernon (same); for $191 sold 71 ac on both sides of N fork of N Tygar R; border: Miller; part of grant to Alexander Red and by his will to his wife who later married Armstead Shumate who sold to John Jordan esq and at his death to John Jordan. Witness William Perrin and John James. Signed John Jordan. Wit. oath Sept. 5, 1814 William Perrin to John Chapman. Rec. Sept. 5, 1814

p. 158-159 Apr. 2, 1814 Benjamin Bonner (Spartanburgh) to Silas Yarbrough (same); for $100 sold 100 ac on Sarratt's Cr. Witness Thomas Whitaker and Briant Bonner. Signed Benjamin Bonner's mark. Wit. oath Jul. 5, 1814 Briant Bonner to J Camp. Rec. Sept. 6, 1814

p. 159-160 Aug. 3, 1807 William Thomson (Spartanburgh) to Gabriel Benson (same); for $60 sold ½ ac; lot 7 in Spartanburgh, SC; border: Main St. Witness John Guyton and John G Bostick. Signed William Thomson. Wit. oath Aug. 12, 1814 John G Bostick to Thos Poole. Rec. Sept. 12, 1814

p. 160-161 Dec. 4, 1802 Anthony Bates (Spartanburgh) to Nicholas Harris (same); for $130 sold 120 ac; border: Henry's Br, Golightly, Noblett, and Foster; part of grant to Wm Simpson esq. Witness Benjamin Howard and Richd Thomson. Signed Anthony Bates' mark. Wit. oath (not dated) Benjamin Howard to William Reid. Rec. Sept. 17, 1814

p. 161-162 May 16, 1812 Nicholas Harris (Union Dist) to Stephen Foster (Spartanburgh); for $130 sold 120 ac; border: Henry's Br, Golightly, Noblett, and Foster; part of grant to William Simpson esq. Witness John Lusk and Christopher Golightly. Signed N Harris. Wit. oath Apr. 6, 1813 Christopher Golightly to Thos Poole. Rec. Sept. 17, 1814

p. 162-163 Dec. 22, 1812 Joseph Camp and Saul Camp to Vardry Camp; for $530 sold 221 ac on McBee's Cr of Pacolette R; border: Baylis Earle, Thos Jackson, and Colley; where Vardry Camp lives. Witness Richard Arendel and Joseph Collins. Signed Joseph Camp and Saul Camp. Wit. oath May 10, 1813 Joseph Collins to J Camp. Rec. Sept. 20, 1814

p. 163-164 Nov. 16, 1805 Abishai Camp (Spartanburgh) to Vardry Camp; for $100 sold 406 ac on N(?) fork Thickety Cr; part of grant Oct. 7, 1803 to Abishai Camp. Witness William Holloway and John Cooper. Signed Abishai Camp. Wit. oath Mar. 6, 1806 John Cooper to John Lipscomb. Rec. Sept. 20, 1814

p. 164-166 Sept. 28, 1814 Alexander Ray (Spartanburgh) to James Vernon (same); for $200 sold 71 ac on both sides of N fork of N Tygar R; border: Brown; part of grant to Alexander Ray desc and by his will to son Alexander Ray. Witness Thomas Brice and William Perrin. Signed Alexander Ray. Wit. oath Sept. 29, 1814 William Perrin to Thomas Poole. Rec. Sept. 29, 1814

p. 166-167 Feb. 18, 1808 John Demsey (Spartanburgh) to Thomas Cave (same); for $280 sold 282 ac on both sides Abner's Cr of "Inoree R"; border: Barnett Demsey, James Woods, Jones, and John Cargill; part of 396 ac grant Jun. 5, 1797 to John Demsey; where Thomas Cave lives. Witness Jesse Demsey and William Willson. Signed John Demsey's mark. Wit. oath Mar. 1, 1808 Jesse Demsey to James Kilgore. Rec. Sept. 29, 1814

p. 167-168 Oct. 13, 1813 James Vernon and wife Peggy (Spartanburgh) to William Perrin (same); for $10 sold 127 ac on waters of N Tygar R; border: N-Alexr Roddy, E-John Bankston, S-Alexander Thompson, and W-John Jordan; part of tract sold by Samuel Farrow, sheriff, to James Jordan esq and divided as estate of James Jordan to Peggy Vernon. Witness Eaton Walker and William Pollard. Signed James and Peggy Vernon. Wit. oath Jul. 4, 1814 Eaton Walker to Michael Miller. Rec. omitted. Dower renounced Aug. 2, 1814 Peggy Vernon to Michael Miller

p. 168-170 Feb. 18, 1793 Zacheriah Carwiles (Spartanburgh) to Thomas Clark (same); for 100£ sterling sold 300 ac grant Jan. 18, 1788 Gov. Pinckney to Zacheriah Carwiles; border: Hugh McWilliams. Witness Starling Tucker, John Rodgers, and Carlton Lindsey. Signed Zacheriah Carwiles. Wit. oath Mar. 7, 1793 Carlton Lindsey to Thomas Farrow. Rec. Sept. 29, 1814

p. 170-171 Sept. 23, 1814 James Landford jr (Spartanburgh) to Thomas Clark (Laurens Dist); for $35 sold 90 ac on waters of Enoree R. Witness James Landford and Jonathan Crook. Signed James Landford. Wit. oath Sept. 23, 1814 Jonathan Crook to John Dean. Rec. Sept. 29, 1814

p. 171-172 Jan. 10, 1804 John Sims (Spartanburgh) to Thomas Clark (same); for 3£ sterling sold 40 ac; border: Thomas Clark and Berry; part of grant to Paul Schatters(?). Witness Sterling Tucker and John Clark. Signed John Sims. Wit. oath (Laurens Dist) Feb. 25, 1814 Sterling Tucker to William Cowan. Rec. Sept. 29, 1814

p. 172-173 Sept. 26, 1814 Frances Ballenger (Spartanburgh) to William Balenger (same); for $200 sold 121 ac on N Tygar R; sold by legates of James Balenger to Frances Ballenger. Witness John Bankston, William Perrin, and Laurence Banskston. Signed Frances Ballenger. Wit. oath Sept. 29, 1814 William Perrin to Thomas Poole. Rec. Sept. 29, 1814

p. 173-174 Nov. 20, 1811 Joseph Kelso (Spartanburgh) to John Ridings (same); for $85 sold 350 ac; border: Dalton and Wm Kelso; grant Feb. 1, 1802 Gov. John Drayton to Joseph Kelso. Witness Hugh Ewing and Arthur F Jackson. Signed Joseph Kelso. Wit. oath Nov. 20, 1811 Hugh Ewing to Wm Kelso. Rec. Sept. 29, 1814

p. 174-175 Jun. 6, 1810 Hugh Ewing (Spartanburgh) to John Ridings (same); for $26 sold 17 ac on N side of Pacolette R; border: Relpallrick (or Relssallrick); grant Gov. John Drayton to James Hooper and Wm Davis. Witness Arthur F Jackson and Joseph Kelso. Signed Hugh Ewing. Wit. oath Jun. 6, 1810 Arthur F Jackson to Wm Kelso. Rec. Sept. 29, 1814

p. 175-176 Jan. 17, 1814 Roaland Johnson and wife Milley (Spartanburgh) to John Ray (same); for $70 sold 8 ac; border: Miller and Alxr; part of grant to John Miller. Witness Alexander Ray and Samuel Johnson. Signed Roaland Johnson. Wit. oath Sept. 29, 1814 Samuel Johnson to A Benson. Rec. Sept. 29, 1814

p. 176 Oct. 31, 1811 Joseph Lannom (Spartanburgh) to Josiah Hatchell (same); for $220 sold (1) 29 ac granted to Lewis Furgason; (2) 36 ac granted to Francis Ward desc and sold by his son John Ward to Lewis Furgason; and (3) 100 ac granted to "old" McBarnett where Furgerson lives; border: N-Josiah Hatchell, W-Wm Moore, S-John Ottes, James Calvert, and George Floyd, and E-Lawson Thomson. Witness Robert Legon and John Hatchett. Signed Joseph Lannom's mark. Wit. oath Jan. 20, 1813 Robert Legon to Drury McDaniel. Rec. Sept. 29, 1814

p. 176-177 Jan. 16, 1802 Lod Dooling (Spartanburgh) to John Tarket (same); for $20 sold 6 ac on N side of Enoree R; border: Brown's old line and mouth of Tarkett's Br. Witness James Smith and Ephraim Moore. Signed Lod Dulin. Wit. oath Sept. 29, 1814 Samuel Otts to John Brewton. Rec. Sept. 29, 1814

p. 178-179 May 10, 1814 James Compton (Spartanburgh) to James Calvert (same); for $200 sold 133 ac; border: Pinckney Road, Currey, and Jane Thomson. Witness Thomas Thornton and Lawson Thomson. Signed James Compton. Wit. oath Oct. 10, 1814 Lawson Thomson to Samuel Woodruff. Rec. Oct. 11, 1814

p. 179-180 Apr. 28, 1814 Absolem Roe (Spartanburgh) to Edmond L. Bishop (same); for $150 sold 130 ac on W side Shoaly Cr of Lawson's fork of Pacolette R; border: Robert Belcher's part of said 200 ac tract; part of 200 ac deeded by John Pipes to daughter Sally Roe. Witness Ephraim Lewis and George Tucker. Signed Absolem Roe, Sally Roe's mark, and Benjamin Lewis (sic). Wit. oath Oct. 15, 1814 Ephraim Lewis to William Reid. Rec. Oct. 15, 1814

p. 180-182 Oct. 13, 1813 William Shackelford (Spartanburgh) to Samuel Woodruff (same); for $550 sold 150 ac on N side of Enoree R; border: Cool Spring Br, Joseph Woodruff, James Allen, and John Wells; part of grant to Wm Hamby. Witness Simson Lavender, Phillip Pilgrim, and Joseph Woodruff. Signed Wm Shackelford. Wit. oath Nov. 19, 1813 Simson Lavender to Burrell Bobo. Rec. Oct. 24, 1814. Dower renounced Oct. 12, 1813 Nancy Shackelford to Burrell Bobo

p. 182 Apr. 1, 1814 Isaac Young to James Cantrell; a mortgage for $28 to be paid by Jul. 1, 1814 for 225 ac on Island Cr. Witness Leonard Adcock and John Cantrell. Signed Isaac Young's mark. Wit. oath Oct. 12, 1814 John Cantrell to Leonard Adcock. Rec. Oct. 13, 1814

p. 182-183 May 17, 1813 James Quinn (Spartanburgh) to William Bealk (same); for $40 sold 50 ac. Witness Richard Turner and Presley Turner. Signed James Quinn. Wit. oath Jun. 24, 1813 Presley Turner to Henry Turner. Rec. Oct. 17, 1814

p. 183-184 Oct. 24, 1814 John Wadkins (Spartanburgh) to Shadrick Farmer (Grainger Co, Tenn); for $200 sold 93 ac on both sides N Tygar R; grant Mar. 4, 1805 to John Wadkins. Witness James Ridings and James Whitten. Signed John Wadkins' mark. Wit. oath Oct. 27, 1814 James Ridings to A Benson. Rec. Oct. 27, 1814

p. 184-185 Apr. 15, 1803 William Harris sr (Spartanburgh) to Elisha Hadden (same); for ($?)130 sold 100 ac on waters of Middle Tygar R; border: Elisha Hadden, Barry, and Hughes' old line. Witness William Harris jr and Gowen Harris. Signed William Harris. Wit. oath Jul. 16, 1814 William Harris jr to Samuel Woodruff. Rec. Oct. 28, 1814

p. 185-186 May 6, 1812 Thomas Burton (Spartanburgh) to Jesse Burton (same); for $300 sold 100 ac on N side of S Pacolette R; sold by James Allen to Thomas Burton; border: Jesse Burton. Witness John Ridings and James Ridings. Signed Thomas Burton's mark. Wit. oath May 6, 1812 John Ridings to Andrew Furgerson. Rec. Oct. 28, 1814

p. 186-187 Oct. 7, 1814 John Farrow to John Morso and wife Jinney; "since their marriage" give a Negro girl, "natural" mill, a bed and furniture and bedstead, sorrel horse, saddle, and bridle and all the other small articles John has let them have since their marriage. Witness John Brown. Signed John Farrow. Wit. oath (Laurens Dist) Nov. 2, 1814 John Brown to Starling Tucker. Rec. Nov. 7, 1814

p. 187 Jan. 22, 1814 William Low (Spartanburgh) to Thomas Wyatt (same); for $30 sold 50 ac on Belk's Br of Pacolette R; border: Jonathan Low's old line, ridge path, and Lender's mill path. Witness John Low jr and Jonathan Low sr. Signed William Low's mark. Wit. oath Sept. 29, 1814 John Low jr to Jno H Jones. Rec. Nov. 8, 1814

p. 187-189 Mar. 30, 1814 Thomas Moore (Spartanburgh) to Hammonds Elder (same); for $50 sold 100 ac on branches of Ward's Cr of Tygar R; border: Moore, Daniel Stevens, McGowen (now Wm Rodgers), and A. B. Moore. Witness John Ward and George Akridge. Signed Thomas Moore. Wit. oath Jun. 18, 1814 John Ward to Danl White. Rec. Nov. 8, 1814. Dower renounced (omitted), 1814 Edy Moore to Daniel White.

p. 189-190 Feb. 8, 1813 William Massey (Spartanburgh) to William Arnold (same); for $260 sold 120 ac on branches of Enoree R; grant to Edward Arnold who sold to William Massey. Witness William Cooper and Martin Cole. Signed William Massey. Wit. oath Oct. 5, 1814 Martin Cole to David Moore. Rec. Nov. 8, 1814

p. 190-191 Nov. 8, 1814 Reubin Warren (Spartanburgh) to Sutton Young; for $5 sold 100 ac on E side of Island Cr; border: Herden Procter. Witness Elijah Satterfield and Richard Procter. Signed Reubin Warren. Wit. oath Nov. 8, 1814 Elijah Satterfield to Henry Turner. Rec. Nov. 9, 1814

p. 191-192 May 12, 1814 Major Gossett (Spartanburgh) to Richard Kirby; to secure a bond of $53 sold 100 ac on Fairforrest Cr (sold by Maj. John Tollison to Major Gossett), a weaving loom and gear, a cotton wheel, a pine table, a walnut cubbard and its contents, 6 sitting chairs, a churn, a wheel churn, a walnut table, 2 flat irons, a looking glass, a black walnut chest, a trunk, 2 halts(?), a piggon, a tub, 2 pots, 2 pair of hooks, a fish pan, a

Ber(?) stand, 2 axes, 5 hoes, a mattock, 2 plows, a pair of drawing chains, a collar, 13 hogs, a sorrell stud colt, 5 geese, 12 ducks, 2 saddles, a straw bed and furniture, 2 feather beds and furniture and steads, a real(?), 5 geese, 2 sheep, a plow, 2 augers, a drawing knife and a piggin(?); Condition: sale void if Major Gossett pays debt. Witness Muse Tollison and Eli Tollison. Signed Major Gossett. Wit. oath Oct. 31, 1814 Eli Tollison to Jno Gossett. Rec. Nov. 9, 1814

p. 192-194 Sept. 30, 1811 Samuel Nesbitt (Spartanburgh) to Michael Miller (same); for $720 sold his part of 299 ac; part of two tracts: (1) 153 ac sold Aug. 15, 1805 by Solomon, William, and Robert Hill to Samuel Nesbitt and Michael Miller; on both sides Middle Tygar R; including a forge; grant May 1, 1786 to John Nicholl; (2) 146 ac adjoining (1); grant Apr. 3, 1786 to William Garrott and sold by Soloman Hill to Samuel Nesbitt and Michael Miller Aug. 15, 1805. Witness Wilson Nesbitt and Robert Bailey. Signed Samuel Nesbitt. Wit. oath Nov. 9, 1814 Wilson Nesbitt to James Hammett. Rec. Nov. 9, 1814

p. 194-195 Dec. 14, 1809 Reubin Warren (Spartanburgh) to James Lard (same); for $100 sold 100 ac on waters of Island Cr of Pacolette R. Witness John Low sr and Lot Warren. Signed Reubin Warren. Wit. oath Feb. 16, 1810 Lot Warren to Henry Turner. Rec. Nov. 18, 1814

p. 195-196 Nov. 5, 1813 William Garrott (Spartanburgh) to James Lard (same); for 5£ sterling sold 100 ac on N side Pacolette R; border: Richard Turner. Witness Reubin Warren and William Lackey. Signed William Garrott's mark. Wit. oath Jul. 21, 1814 Reubin Warren to Henry Turner. Rec. Nov. 18, 1814

p. 196-197 Jul. 23, 1814 John Ballenger, David Lewis, Edward Ballenger, James Ballenger, Elijah Ballenger, and William Ballenger, legates of estate of James Ballenger desc, to Frances Ballenger; for $700 sold 200 ac on N Tygar R; border: Alexander Ray and Alexr McCarter. Witness William Perrin, Laurence Bankston, and James Ballenger. Signed David Lewis, John Ballenger, Edward Ballenger, James Ballenger, Elijah Ballenger, and William Ballenger. Wit. oath Oct. 11, 1814 William Perrin to Michl Miller. Rec. Dec. 1, 1814. Dower renounced Nov. 15, 1814 Peggy Lewis, Alice Ballenger, Nancy Ballenger, Judith Ballenger, Polley Ballenger, and Polley Ballenger to Michael Miller [not mentioned which wife goes with which husband]

p. 197-198 Feb. 11, 1814 Richard Brown (Spartanburgh) to Michael McKie (same); for $200 sold 200 ac E of Rolly Br; border: Michael McKie; part of grant Jan. 21, 1785 Gov. Guerard to Wells Griffith; also border: George Downs, Holly Spring Br, a road by Joel Lewis formerly called Old Green River Rd, and George McDowell's old corner. Witness Hincher Ballard and James Young. Signed Richard Brown. Wit. oath Feb. 11, 1814 Hincher Ballard to James Young. Rec. Dec. 1, 1814

p. 198-199 May 18, 1814 Hugh Moore, agent for Thomas Deen (Spartanburgh), to John Tollison (same); for $164.78 sold 150 ac on waters of Pacolette R; border: Richardson Whitbey and Wm Gossett; includes 10 ac border: Lancaster and Richardson Whitbey; land was sold by John Lancaster to Thomas Deen. Witness Muse Tollison and Labon P Poole. Signed Hugh Moore, agent and attorney for Thos Deen. Wit. oath Dec. 5, 1814 Muse Tollison to A Benson. Rec. Dec. 5, 1814. May 18, 1814 Hugh Moore agrees to sell John Tollison the land and to sue John to recover the land if John leaves; Hugh Moore to pay cost of suit

p. 199-201 Nov. 23, 1814 William Carter (Spartanburgh) to Caleb

Carter (Pendleton Dist); for $100 sold 115 ac on E side of Thomson Cr of Pacolette R; grant to Greenham Crowder. Witness William Bennett and Thomas Kimbrel. Signed William Carter. Wit. oath Dec. 2, 1814 William Bennett to James Young. Rec. Dec. 5, 1814

p. 201-202 Feb. 10, 1814 James Branon (or Brannan) (Spartanburgh) to Cyrus Seay (same); for $70 sold 50 ac on waters of Lawson's fork; grant Nov. 25, 1774 Gov. William Bull to Stephen Miller. Witness William Johnson and Mathew Seay. Signed James Brannan and Sarh's mark. Wit. oath Nov. 7, 1814 Mathew Seay to John Chapman. Rec. Dec. 15, 1814

p. 202-203 Nov. 29, 1808 John A Gore (Spartanburgh) to James Carter (same); for $33 sold 33 ac; where James Carter lives. Witness William Carter and Caleb Carter. Signed John A Gore. Wit. oath May 17, 1809 Caleb Carter to Leon Adcock. Rec. Dec. 23, 1814

p. 203-204 Sept. 28, 1814 William Bennett (Spartanburgh) to Henry White (same); for $45 sold 80 ac on branches of S Pacolette R; part of grant to William Bennett; border: Sperce's (or Spuce) old corner, John Tapp, Thos Barnett, and survey for Amos Speice. Witness Thomas Kimbril and Vincent Kimbril. Signed William Bennett. Wit. oath Nov. 8, 1814 Vincent Kimbril to John Collins. Rec. Jan. 2, 1815

p. 204-205 Mar. 14, 1810 Thomas Young (Spartanburgh) to John Leatherwood (same); for $400 sold 100 on James Cr of Tygar R; border: George Crawford and William Young; grant Feb. 17, 1767 Gov. Charles G Montague to William Young jr who sold Apr. 4, 1795 to Thomas Young. Witness John Huston and William Young. Signed Thomas Young. Wit. oath Mar. 14, 1810 John Huston to Burrell Bobo. Rec. Jan. 2, 1815. Dower renounced Mar. 14, 1810 Mary Young to Burrell Bobo

p. 205-206 Sept. 27, 18(blank) Daniel White (Spartanburgh) to Henry White (same); for $300 sold 210 ac on S side of Pacolette R; border: Thomas Bennett and Mullesses Br; part of two grants to Amos Speice on S Pacolette R and at Wading Shoal Ford. Witness Zachariah Wall and Oney Wall. Signed Daniel White's mark. Wit. oath Nov. 8, 1814 Zachariah Wall to John Collins. Rec. Jan. 2, 1815

p. 206-207 Oct. 1, 1814 George Davis to Moses Wilkins; to secure a 12 month note for $27 sold 50 ac or "pledge, oblige, and make chargeable" (instead of sale); border: Robert Stacey, Austin Wright, and David Jones; no condition to sale. Witness Henry Littlejohn and James Spencer. Signed George Davis. Wit. oath Jan. 28, 1815 Henry Littlejohn to John Lipscomb. Rec. Jan. 30, 1815

p. 207-208 Dec. 30, 1813 William Ford (Spartanburgh) to Michael Miller (same); for $60 sold 100 ac at the Holly Spring; border: George Deavours, Lawson's fork, Isaac Bishop, McDowel, Boyers, and George McDowel. Witness Manley Ford and William Ford. Signed William Ford. Wit. oath Jan. 3, 1814 Manley Ford to Drury McDaniel. Rec. Jan. 30, 1815

p. 208-210 Nov. 12, 1810 Jesse Traylor, Robert Foster, Robert Wood, Richard Traylor, Joel Traylor, Thomas G Traylor, and Polly Traylor (Spartanburgh) to William Traylor (same); for $300 sold 120 ac on N side of N Tygar R; part of land formerly of Joel Traylor desc. Witness Edward Bomar, Stephen Powell, and Ludy Cauthorn. Signed Jesse, Thomas G, and Joel Traylor, Polley and Richard Traylor's marks, Robert Wood, and Robert Foster. Wit. oath Oct. 11, 1814 Edward Bomar to John Chapman. Rec. Feb. 6, 1815

p. 210-211 Dec. 31, 1814 Bridges Arendle (Spartanburgh) to Thomas Higs (same); for $200 sold 200 ac; border: Charles Hester, Gordan, John Arnold, and Standley. Witness James Hutcherson and James Cooper. Signed Bridges Arendel. Wit. oath Jan. 21, 1815 James Cooper to J Camp. Rec. Feb. 6, 1815

p. 211-212 Jan. 10, 1809 John Rodgers (Spartanburgh) to John Williams; for $80 sold 124 ac; border: Robert Rogers, John Cavan, Jacob Earnest, and William Sloan; grant Mar. 3, 1788 to James Crow. Witness Hiram Harelson and Robert Hindman. Signed John Rogers. Wit. oath Oct. 10, 1814 Robert Hindman to M Casey. Rec. Feb. 6, 1815

p. 212-213 Aug. 7, 1813 Buckner Smith (Spartanburgh) to John Williams (same); for $400 sold [179 ac] in two parts: (1) 78 ac on N side Tygar R; border: John Campbell and Timothy Toney; and (2) 101 ac on N side Tygar R; part of 249 ac grant Jul. 3, 1772 to Timothy Toney; border: SW-Tygar R, W-Joel Hembry, N-Samuel Cathcart, and E-Daniel Grant; N of Cain(?) Cr. Witness William Young and Richd Young. Signed Buckner Smith's mark. Wit. oath Dec. 31, 1813 Richd Young to M Casey. Rec. Feb. 6, 1815

p. 213-215 (blank), 1814 James Bennett sr (Spartanburgh) to Milton Davis (same); for $100 sold 100 ac on waters of Richland Cr of S Pacolette R; border: Thomas Bennett, William Bennett, and Milton Davis; where Milton Davis lives; part of grant to Greenham Crowder. Witness William Bennett and William Clemons. Signed James Bennett's mark. Wit. oath Feb. 6, 1815 William Bennett to Leonard Adcock. Rec. Feb. 6, 1815

p. 215-216 Aug. 15, 1814 Samuel Stewart (Spartanburgh) to Richard White and wife Amey; for (money not mentioned) sold 70 ac on S Tygar R; border: S-James Anderson and John Johnston and other sides-Samuel Stewart; part of grant to John Whitemore who sold to Robert Connl who sold to Samuel Stewart; plat attached shows land also on Redy fork. Witness James Swanzy, John Patton, and Samuel Pearson. Signed Samuel Stewart. Wit. oath Feb. 6, 1815 Samuel Pearson to David Moore. Rec. Feb. 6, 1815

p. 216-217 Jan. 21, 1815 Thomas Higs to John Arendle; for $200 sold 200 ac; border: Charles Hester, John Arendle, and Standley's old field. Witness Young Allen and James Cooper. Signed Thomas Higgs. Wit. oath Jan. 21, 1815 James Cooper to J Camp. Rec. Feb. 6, 1815

p. 217-218 Feb. 28, 1811 Britton George (Spartanburgh) to Jeremiah George; for $20 sold 100 ac on N side of Pacolette R; border: Robert Thomson, Charles Hammett, Dorton's Br, and Britton George jr. Witness David Thompson and Jonathan Chonwood. Signed Britton George's mark. Wit. oath Feb. 28, 1811 David Thompson to Jno H Jones. Rec. Feb. 20, 1815

p. 218-219 Jan. 14, 1815 William Bennett (Spartanburgh) to Zachariah Nance (Union Dist); for $750 sold 250 ac on both sides Thomson's Cr of Pacolette R; border: School House Br; part of grant to Thomas Bennett. Witness William Littlefield, William Littlefield jr, and Thomas Kimbrel. Signed William Bennett. Wit. oath Mar. 6, 1815 William Littlefield to Wm Reid. Rec. Mar. 7, 1815

p. 219-221 May 24, 1814 John Gowen, James Blasingame, Strut Thurston, and Wm B Gowen to Bartholomew Grogan (Spartanburgh); for $150 sold 100 ac on S side of S Pacolette R; border: Rice T Ross and John Lucas; known as James Braden's land; formerly land of John Gowen desc; grantors are executors of will of John Gowen. Witness Henry Wolf and Henry Grogan. Signed John Gowen, W. B. Gowen, Strut

Thurston, and Jno Blasingame. Wit. oath Feb. 16, 1815 Henry Grogan to Andrew Furgerson. Rec. Mar. 7, 1815

p. 221-222 Nov. 24, 1814 Culbert Burton, attorney for Samuel Burton, (Warren Co, Ky) to Kinsey West (Spartanburgh); for $500 paid to Samuel Burton (Robertson Co, Tenn) sold 130 ac on Fairforrest Cr; border: Cool Spring and ford opposite "the grave walled in with stone"; part of grant to Giles Connell and by heirship to his legates and sold to John Barnett who sold to Elijah Barnett who sold to Samuel Burton who sold to Daniel White and relinquished to Samuel Burton. Witness Benjamin Nicholls and Stephen West. Signed Culbert Burton. Wit. oath Nov. 26, 1814 Stephen West to Danl White. Rec. Mar. 6, 1815

p. 222-223 Sept. 26, 1814 Isaac Young jr (Spartanburgh) to Smith Lipscomb (same); for $29.18 sold 183 ac on waters of Pacolette R and branches of Buck Cr and Dog Br and Meadow Br. Witness David S Lipscomb and James Wood. Signed Isaac Young jr. Wit. oath Mar. 7, 1815 David S Lipscomb to A Benson. Rec. Mar. 7, 1815

p. 223-224 Nov. 12, 1812 Isaac Young sr (Spartanburgh) to Isaac Young jr (same); for $200 sold 183 ac on waters of Pacolette R and branch of Buck Cr and on Dog Br and Meadow Br. Witness James Cantrell and John Cantrell. Signed Isaac Young's mark. Wit. oath Nov. 13, 1812 John Cantrell to Henry Turner. Rec. Mar. 7, 1815

p. 224-226 Jan. 20, 1815 John Smith (Spartanburgh) to William Lancaster (same); for $75 sold 125½ ac on Col. White's Br of Fairforrest Cr; border: Thomas Finch, Lancaster, and James Finch; where Elisha James lives. Witness Thomas Smith, William Smith, and Isaac Smith. Signed John Smith. Wit. oath Feb. 15, 1815 Thomas Smith to Saml Archebald. Rec. Mar. 7, 1815. Dower renounced Feb. 17, 1815 Elizabeth Smith to Drury McDaniel

p. 226-227 Jan. 20, 1815 Martha Savage, executrix of will of William Savage (late of Charleston, SC), to James Crook (SC); for $300 sold 1,000 ac on branches of Furgerson's Cr of Tygar R; plat attached shows border: vacant, unknown, Wm Floyd, and David Crow; Martha doesn't warrant deed; Thomas Bee, esq desc was executor of William Savage's will and Martha is the surviving executrix. Witness Sarah H Savage and William Holmes esq. Signed Martha Savage. Wit. oath (Charleston) Feb. 24, 1815 William Holmes esq to L. W. Moore. Rec. Mar. 7, 1815

p. 227-228 Dec. 23, 1808 John Smith to Isaac Crow; for $38.50 sold (ac omitted) on Two Mile Cr; border: John Deen or Dean, Ford's old line, Isaac Crow, and John Smith's Spring Br. Witness Samuel Crow. Signed John Smith. Wit. oath Jan. 2, 1814 Samuel Crow to M Casey. Rec. Mar. 7, 1815

p. 228-229 Mar. 27, 1806 Charles Mathis and wife Nancy (Spartanburgh) to Elisha Lindsey (same); for $120 sold 365 ac on both sides waggon road from Hammett's ford of Pacolette R to old iron works on Lawson's fork and on branch of Lindsey's Cr. Witness Caleb Jones and Patrick Tyler. Signed Charles Mathis. Wit. oath Apr. 10, 1806 Patrick Tyler to Jno H Jones. Rec. Mar. 23, 1815. Dower renounced Mar. 28, 1809 Nancy Mathis to William Lancaster

p. 229-230 Sept. 13, 1814 Isaac S Pebworth (Spartanburgh) to Samuel Miller; for (see condition below) sold a box of carpenter's tools containing a complete "aportment" or set, 2 beds and furniture, a cow and calf, 5 hogs, all kitchen and household furniture, 3 sheep, my part of corn crop now growing; Condition: sale void if Isaac finishes house or building for Samuel in 18 months. Witness Nimrod

E Benson. Signed Isaac S Pebworth. Wit. oath Mar. 25, 1815 N. E. Benson to A Benson. Rec. Mar. 24, 1805

p. 230-231 Apr. 18, 1813 James Ridings (Spartanburgh) to Jesse Prewitt; for $40 sold 200 ac on N side Motlow's Cr; border: William Bishear and Thomas; part of grant to James Ridings. Witness Abram Brock and James Whitten. Signed James Ridings' mark. Wit. oath Aug. 1, 1812 Abram Brock to Andrew Furgerson. Rec. Mar. 24, 1815

p. 231-232 Sept. 16, 1812 Jesse Prewitt (Spartanburgh) to Benjamin Prewitt (same); for $150 sold 200 ac on N side Moltow's Cr; border: Wm Bishear and Thomas; grant to James Ridings who sold to Jesse Prewitt. Witness James Whitten and Assa(?) W. Crowder. Signed Jesse Prewitt's mark. Wit. oath Aug. 7, 1813 James Whitten to Wm Kelso. Rec. Mar. 24, 1815

p. 232-233 Jan. 17, 1814 Rachel and Ann Jamison (Spartanburgh) to Alexander Roddy (same); for $225 sold 77 ac on Wilson's Mill Cr of N Tygar R; border: Abner Timmons and Peter Gray; part of 100 ac grant Sept. 28, 1766 to John Nesbitt and at his death to his oldest son Frances Nesbett and sold by Frances Nesbett and wife Ann to Robert Jamison and willed to Rachel and Ann Jamison. Witness Samuel Jamison and James Roddy. Signed Rachel and Ann Jamison's marks. Wit. oath (not dated) James Roddy to John Chapman. Rec. Mar. 25, 1815

p. 233-234 Sept. 10, 1814 Leonard Adcock (Spartanburgh) to James Hews (Laurens Dist); for $120 sold 200 ac on waters of Horse Cr of Broad R; border: "North State line", road crosses the line from Andrew Ray's old place to Miner Cockreney fishery, and Sharp. Witness Thomas Neighbours and Isaac Adcock. Signed Leon Adcock. Wit. oath Oct. 11, 1814 Isaac Adcock to Henry Turner. Rec. Apr. 10, 1815

p. 234-236 Feb. 13, 1815 Jonathan Stokes (Spartanburgh) to John Rudesail (Lincoln Co, NC); for $100 sold (1) 267 ac on S side of S Pacolette R; border: Samuel Hurt; gant Oct. 3, 1803 to Jerh Stokes for 237 ac (sic); (2) 242 ac joining (1); border: Moultrie; part of two grants: (a) N end of grant Jun. 5, 1786 to George Thompson and (b) (omitted); and (3) 100 ac; border: N-Jerh Stokes, S-Samuel Fowler, W-vacant, and NE & E-Alston; part of 182 ac grant Jun. 7, 1790 to Robert Harper; total of 1, 2, & 3 is 570 ac (sic). Witness Rice F Ross and Willey S Brown. Signed Jonathan Stokes. Wit. oath Apr. 1, 1815 Rice F Ross to Andrew Furgerson. Rec. Apr. 11, 1815

p. 236-237 Sept. 24, 1814 Thomas Cole (Spartanburgh) to Thomas Cole jr (same); for 10£ sold 150 ac on waters of Beaverdam Cr; border: William Thompson, Capt. Gaffney, and Gordan. Witness William Dewberry and Obediah Cole. Signed Thomas Cole. Wit. oath Apr. 11, 1815 Obediah Cole to Jno H Jones. Rec. Apr. 12, 1815

p. 237-238 Sept. 24, 1814 Christopher Golightly (Spartanburgh) to William Lancaster (same); for $157.50(?) sold 35 ac on White's Br on S side Fairforrest Cr; border: Lancaster and James Finch; part of grant to James Tillet who sold to David Thomas who sold to Col. Henry White and mortgaged by the state and sold to Col. Thomas Taylor who sold to Christopher Golightly. Witness David Golightly jr and Samuel Noblet. Signed Christi Golightly. Wit. oath Feb. 15, 1815 David Golightly jr to Samuel Archibald. Rec. Apr. 12, 1815. Dower renounced Apr. 10, 1815 Jane Golightly to Samuel Golightly

p. 238-239 Dec. 5, 1809 Richard James (Spartanburgh) to Daniel

White (same); for $100 sold 240 ac on waters of Fairforrest Cr; border: Young, Lancaster, and Finch. Witness Ely Tollison and Elizabeth Tollison. Signed Richard James. Wit. oath Apr. 11, 1815 Ely Tollison to Saml Archibald. Rec. Apr. 12, 1815

p. 239-240 Apr. 14, 1815 Edward Smith (Spartanburgh) to sons Charles and Holman Smith (same); for love and affection give two Negro boys--Burrell and Randol; they get the Negroes at death of Edward and his wife and can divide (one a piece) the Negroes if they want to (wife not named). Witness William Smith and Moses Waters. Signed Edwd Smith. Wit. oath Apr. 17, 1815 William Smith to Thomas Poole. Rec. Apr. 17, 1815

p. 240-241 Oct. 1, 1814 William Frey (Spartanburgh) to John Jackson (same); for $200 sold 80 ac on N side of N Pacolette R and S side of Howard's Cr; border: E-Lot Adcock; grant (omitted) 26, 1767 Gov. William Tryon (NC) to James Howard who sold May 17, 1770 to Thomas Wade who sold May 29, 1773 to Jeben(?) Evins who sold Feb. 15, 1775 to Samuel Jackson and then to his son John Jackson who sold to Peter Fry desc who sold part to William Frey; remainder of border: William Wade, George Welsh, and Wolf Pet Br. Witness Thos Jackson, John Ridings, and Samuel L Ewing. Signed William Frey's mark. Wit. oath Apr. 24, 1815 John Ridings to Wm Kelso. Rec. Apr. 24, 1815

p. 241-242 Jun. 6, 1814 Daniel White (Spartanburgh) to William Lancaster esq (same); for $10 quit claim to 66 ac on E side of branch running through grant to Richard James that was sold to Daniel White and settled by Daniel's father Henry White desc; border: William Lancaster, Zacheriah McDaniel, James Finch, and John Martin. Witness John Walker and William R Smith. Signed Danl White. Wit. oath Feb. 15, 1815 William R Smith to James Hamm. Rec. May 1, 1815

p. 242-243 May 22, 1814 John Low sr (Spartanburgh) to Rosanna Low; quit claim to all his heirs except Rosanna for 50 ac on waters of Pacolette R; border: Ann Smith and Turner. Witness Samuel Turner and Richard Procter. Signed John Low. Wit. oath May 1, 1815 Samuel Turner to Thomas Poole. Rec. May 1, 1815

p. 243-244 Feb. 17, 1812 James Bishop (Spartanburgh) to John Windsor (York Dist); for $50 sold 150 ac on waters of Fairforrest Cr; land is warranted except for part William Hammett claims. Witness Edmond J Bishop, Barney Bishop, and R Benson. Signed James Bishop's mark. Wit. oath May 8, 1812 Edmond J Bishop to Wm Reid. Rec. May 8, 1815

p. 244-246 Jul. 28, 1813 Sarah Gore (Spartanburgh) to Benjamin Poole (same); for $100 sold 100 ac on S side of Pacolette R; border: on both sides Lawson's fork, Benjamin Poole's Spring, spring William Poole got water from "when they lived by the big walnut tree" that stands in the old field, Thomas, and corner made by Maj. Bullock, surveyor; includes where James Gore lived when he died. Witness William Gore, David C Poole, and James Poole. Signed Sarah Gore's mark. Wit. oath Feb. 13, 1815 James Poole to Jno H Jones. Rec. May 8, 1815

p. 246-247 Feb. 3, 1812 William McGowen (Spartanburgh) to Michael Gaffney (same); for $1,100 sold 400 ac on S side of Broad R; border: Beaty; grant Oct. 26, 1769 to Hugh Quin (of Tryon Co, NC). Witness John W Farrow and Vincent Bennett. Signed William McGowen. Wit. oath Jan. 2, 1814 John W Farrow to H. Means. Rec. May 8, 1815

p. 247 Apr. 3, 1815 Detithy Merriman (Bledso Co, Tenn) to Briant Bonner (Spartanburgh); for $100 sold 100 ac on Sarratt's Cr of Broad R; border: Silas Yarborough, Nathan Byars, path from Nathan

Byars to the Furnace, and Wilson Nesbitt. Witness Thomas Whitaker and Silas Yarborough. Signed Detithy Merriman's mark. Wit. oath May 8, 1815 Silas Yarborough to Joseph Camp. Rec. May 8, 1815

p. 247-248 Apr. 7, 1814 Thomas Cretchfield to Thomas Farmer; for $20.50 sold 20½ ac on Little Cherokee Cr of Broad R. Witness John Vincent. Signed Thomas and Mary Cretchfield's marks. Wit. oath Feb. 7, 1814 John Vincent to Joshua Richards. Rec. May 20, 1815

p. 248-249 Jan. 7, 1812 Major Hancock to James Page; for $150 sold 115 ac on Cherokee Cr of Broad R; border: John Hester, Ezekiel Stanley desc, Charles Hester, and Major Hancock. Witness James Richards and Joshua Richards. Signed Major Hancock. Wit. oath Jan. 10, 1814 Joshua Richards to John Lipscomb. Rec. May 20, 1815

p. 249-250 Nov. 15, 1813 James Page to Laurence Anderson (Spartanburgh); for $150 sold 115 ac on Cherokee Cr of Broad R; border: John Hester, Charles Hester, and Major Hancock. Witness Michael Gaffney and Major Hancock. Signed James Page's mark. Wit. oath Jan. 10, 1814 Michael Gaffney to John Lipscomb. Rec. May 20, 1815

p. 250-251 Apr. 8, 1815 John McClure (Spartanburgh) to son Thomas Boles McClure; for love and affection give a cow "of a second quality"--red cow marked with swallow fork in right ear and under bit on left ear and sawed horns. Witness William Copeland and James Berry. Signed John McClure. Wit. oath Jun. 10, 1814 William Copeland to Wm Kelso. Rec. Jan. 12(?), 1815. Andrew Kilpatric (Spartanburgh) was guardian for his apprentice Thomas B. McClure in exchange for red cow and her increase until Thomas' freedom, and he was to then return the cow and increase to Thomas, except some of them died by accident not by poverty. Witness William Copeland and James Berry. Signed John McClure and Andrew Kilpatric

p. 251-252 Feb. 27, 1815 John Ward (Spartanburgh) to Thornton Ward (same); for $100 sold 50 ac on branches on S side of S Tygar R; border: Robert Miller, Still House Br, and James Otts; where Thornton Ward lives. Witness Henry Ray Lanham and James Ottes. Signed John Ward. Wit. oath Feb. 27, 1815 Henry R Lanham to Drury McDaniel. Rec. Jun. 5, 1815

p. 252 (omitted), 1815 Alexander Cunningham to John Clark; for $228 sold 228 ac; border: McMeullins(?). Witness William Bennett, Thomas Kembrill, and Samuel Turner. Signed Alexr Cunningham. Wit. oath Jun. 5, 1815 William Bennett to Thomas Poole. Rec. Jun. 5, 1815

p. 252-253 Dec. 26, 1814 Alexander Cunningham (Spartanburgh) to Hugh McMillen (same); for $200 sold 177 ac on both sides of N Pacolette R; border: Barten. Witness Thomas Pope and John Clark. Signed Alexr Cunningham. Wit. oath Apr. 6, 1815 John Clark to James Young. Rec. Jun. 5, 1815

p. 253-254 Dec. 26, 1814 Alexander Cunningham (Spartanburgh) to Hugh McMillen (same); for $300 sold 100 ac on both sides of N Pacolette R. Witness Thomas Pope and John Clark. Signed Alexr Cunningham. Wit. oath Apr. 6, 1815 John Clark to James Young. Rec. Jun. 5, 1815

p. 254-255 May 9, 1812 Elisha Hedden (Spartanburgh) to Thomas Traylor (same); for $107 sold (ac omitted) on waters of N Tygar R; border: Woods, Foster, Timmons, Edn Bomar, and Thomas Bomar. Witness William T Tanner and Robert Miller. Signed Elisha

Hadden. Wit. oath Aug. 3, 1812 Robert Miller to Drury McDaniel. Rec. Jun. 5, 1815

p. 255-256 May 13, 1815 William Sentell (or Sentett) (Spartanburgh) to James Kendrick (SC); for $150 sold 125 ac on S side of S Pacolette R; border: Amos Spiece, Luke Burnett, John Clark, and Thomas Bennett; where James Kendrick lives; part of grant to Larkin Carden. Witness William Bennett and Polley Bush. Signed Wm Sentell. Wit. oath Jun. 5, 1815 William Bennett to Thomas Poole. Rec. Jun. 5, 1815

p. 256-257 Dec. 9, 1813 William Reynolds (Laurens Dist) to Henry Marler (Spartanburgh); power of attorney to collect money and debts owed William in SC and elsewhere. Witness Thomas Bell, Stephen J Casey, and M Casey. Signed William Reynolds' mark. Wit. oath Dec. 9, 1813 Thomas Bell to M Casey. Rec. Jun. 5, 1815

p. 257-258 Mar. 13, 1815 Henry Hines (Spartanburgh) to Edith Ray; quit claim to Negro girl Mary and at Edith's death to her children (that she has or may have) by Andrew Ray; if Edith has no children, Mary and her increase go "with said mother to said Berry children above mentioned (sic) to return to said heirs" and also a featherbed. Witness none. Signed Henry Hines. Edith Ray receives property and complys with agreement (not dated). Witness Henry Turner. Signed Edith Ray's mark. Wit. oath (not dated) Henry Turner to Leonard Adcock. Rec. Jun. 17, 1815

p. 258-261 Jan. 8, 1815 Sarah Parker (Charleston, SC), Caroline P. Edwards, Sarah P Scott, Elizabeth Scott, and Maria P Scott (Christ Church Parish, SC) to Andrew B Moore (Spartanburgh); for $800 ($400 to Sarah Parker, $100 to Caroline P Edwards, $100 to Sarah P Scott, $100 to Elizabeth Scott, and $100 to Maria P Scott) sold 1,000 ac on branches of Tygar R; Sarah sells half of land and the girls sell 1/8th each; see will of John Parker (St. James Goose Creek Parish, SC); plat attached shows border: SW, N & W-Charles Moore, NE-Lawson, SE-Parker, and SW-Jesse Connell; plat dated Oct. 16, 1772 by Wm Gist DS and was due to precept Jul. 20, 1772 by John Bremar esq, D Surv. Gen; plat was for John Parker esq; copy was certified Feb. 8, 1815 by Surv. Gen. Office, Columbia, SC by William Clark, Surv. Gen. Witness William H Parker and William Singetton. Signed Sarah Parker, Caroline P Edwards, Sarah P Scott, Elize Scott, and Maria P Scott. Wit. oath Jun. 8, 1815 William H Parker to James Jervey. Rec. Jun. 7, 1815. William Scott says he had "superentended" above sale for his four daughters (sic) Caroline, Sarah, Eliza, and Maris and saw them get their share of money (not dated). Jun. 8, 1815 Thomas Parker (Charleston, SC), executor of will of his father John Parker (St. James Goose Creek Parish) to Andrew B Moore--for 1¢ and for payment made to divisees sold 1,000 ac; Thomas is empowered to sell land for payment of debts or for a division between divisees of John Parker's will. Witness William H Parker and William Singetton. Signed Thomas Parker, executor of John Parker. Wit. oath Jun. 8, 1815 William H Parker to James Jervey JQ

p. 261-262 Oct. 9, 1812 Richard Cruse (Spartanburgh) to Nicholas Harris (Union Dist); for $200 sold (ac omitted) "all" of land Evan Lands sold to Richard Cruse except 120 ac sold to Anthony Bates on the open corner; on both sides Henry "Brens" of Fairforrest Cr. Witness Isabella Simpson and Jane Simpson. Signed Richard Cruse. Wit. oath Aug. 6, 1811 (Union Dist) Isabella Simpson to H Means. Rec. Jun. 23, 1815

p. 262-263 Nov. 9, 1813 Daniel McKie (Spartanburgh) to William Bozwell, son of John Bozwell; for $13 sold 13 ac; border: Brice and Hoy. Witness Robert Creswell and B. H. Saxon. Signed D. McKie. Wit. oath Nov. 10, 1813 Robert Creswell to Samuel Woodruff.

Rec. Jul. 1, 1815

p. 263-264 Jun. 14, 1806 Robert Kimble (Spartanburgh) to Jesse Reams (same); for $6 sold 550 ac (? or grant was 550 ac) on Ready Br; border: Jesse Reams, Bishear, and head of Lawson's fork; part of grant May 4, 1804 Gov. James B Richards to Robert Kimble. Witness John Davis, Moses Brooks, and Jesse Cooper. Signed Robert Kimble. Wit. oath Mar. 10, 1807 John Davis to Michl Miller. Rec. Jul. 1, 1815

p. 264-265 Oct. 11, 1804 William Traylor (Spartanburgh) to Thomas Bomar; for $575 sold 120 ac on N Tygar R; border: Crawford's Mill. Witness Elisha Bomar and Jesse Traylor. Signed William Traylor. Wit. oath Jan. 12, 1815 Elisha Bomar to John Chapman. Rec. Jul. 13, 1815 (sic)

p. 265-266 Jul. 15, 1809 Mary Garrott (Spartanburgh) to Laurence Bankston; Mary agrees to bind her son Philip to Laurence until Philip is 21 years old (he is now 1 year old last June); Laurence is to find Philip common dut(?) with suitable clothing and lodging; Philip is to serve Laurence faithfully and not to be absent without leave and to keep "his" secrest until age 21; Mary keeps the child until he is weaned and then is to give it up into "possession" of Laurence. Witness John Bankston. Signed Laurence Bankston and Mary Garrott's marks. Wit. oath Jul. 4, 1815 John Bankston to Henry Turner. Rec. Jul. 4, 1815

p. 266-267 Jan. 15, 1810 David Adcock (Spartanburgh) to John Cantrell, son of Isaac, (same); for $150 sold 100 ac on S side of Buck Cr; border: Oliver, old road, race paths, and Harris. Witness Isaac Cantrell sr and Leonard Adcock. Signed David Adcock. Wit. oath Mar. 1, 1814 Isaac Cantrell sr to (omitted). Rec. Jul. 4, 1815

p. 267-269 Feb. 22, 1815 Edmond Bishop, son of William Bishop, (Spartanburgh) to Gibson Oliver (same); for $70 sold (ac omitted) on waters of Pacolette R; border: William Morris. Witness William Morris, John Gilbert, and Sary Morris. Signed Edmond Bishop and Sary's mark. Wit. oath Jun. 14, 1815 William Morris to Leonard Adcock. Rec. Jul. 4, 1815

p. 269-270 Jul. 24, 1812 Hutchen Forrest (Spartanburgh) to Nimrod Cantrell (same); for $100 sold 50 ac on branch of Little Buck Cr of Pacolette R; part of grant to James Forrest; border: Townson Roberson and Nimrod Cantrell. Witness Isaac Adcock and Jeremiah Gosnal (or Gusnell). Signed Hutchen Forrest's mark. Wit. oath Aug. 29, 1813 Jeremiah Gosnal to Leonard Adcock. Rec. Aug. 4, 1815

p. 270 Aug. 2, 1815 dower renounced Polly Thomson to A Benson for deed from Richard Thomson to Thomas Allison. Rec. (omitted)

p. 270-271 Aug. 2, 1815 dower renounced Polly Thomson to A Benson for deed Richard Thomson to Thomas Allison. Rec. (omitted)

p. 271-272 Aug. 4, 1815 Samuel Farrow (Spartanburgh) to Negro slaves Christopher (a man about 35 years old) and Sarah (a woman about 45 years old); give their freedom. Witness B. W. Waters. Signed S Farrow. Wit. oath Aug. 7, 1815 B. W. Waters to A Benson. Rec. Aug. 7, 1815. Jun. 29, 1815 Wm Willbanks, B. W. Waters, Wm Farrow, Wm Parnel (or Camel), and Landon Waters gather at Landon Waters' house to examine Christopher and Sarah (slaves of Samuel Farrow) before Samuel frees them; group finds slaves capable of gaining sufficient honest livelyhood by their labour and are both of good character. Witness Burrell Bobo JQ. Signed Wm Willbanks, B. W. Waters, Wm Farrow, Wm Parnel (or Camel)'s mark, and Landon

Waters' mark

p. 272-273 May (blank), 1815 Richard Thomson (Spartanburgh) to Thomas Allison (same); for $100 sold 3 ac on S side of Main St; "back lot" at Spartanburgh Court House; border: SE-Nancy McKie. Witness E Roddy and Labon P Poole. Signed Richard Thomson. Wit. oath May 22, 1815 E Roddy to A Benson. Rec. Aug. 7, 1815. Dower renounced Aug. 2, 1815 Polly Thomson to A Benson

p. 273-275 Apr. 12, 1815 Henry Brown (Spartanburgh) to Christopher Golightly (same); for $900 sold 250 ac on S Pacolette R; border: below Garret's(?) Bridge; Henry Brown reserves for himself and heirs 8 feet square where his daughter Betsy was buried. Witness William Cantrell and William Lancaster esq. Signed Henry Brown. Wit. oath Apr. 12, 1815 William Lancaster to James Young. Rec. Aug. 7, 1815. Dower renounced Apr. 17, 1815 Susanna Brown to James Young

p. 275 Apr. 6, 1814 James Wofford to daughter Didamea Johnson; for good causes give a Negro girl Venus and her increase. Witness Isaac Wofford and Jacob Driver. Signed James Wofford. Wit. oath Jul. 24, 1814 Isaac Wofford to Drury McDaniel. Rec. Aug. 7, 1815

p. 275-277 Dec. 22, 1806 Zachariah Hembre (Spartanburgh) to John Smith (same); for $50 sold 80 ac on branch of Cain Cr on N side of Tygar R; grant Jun. 3, 1805 Gov. Paul Hamilton to Zachariah Hembre. Witness Eber Smith and Reuben Leonard. Signed Zacharia Hembre. Wit. oath Dec. 22, 1806 Eber Smith to Wm Smith. Rec. Aug. 7, 1815. Dower renounced Dec. 22, 1806 Rosy Hembree to William Smith

p. 277-278 Nov. 18, 1814 James Land (Spartanburgh) to Thomas Hackett (same); for $250 sold 170 ac on Pacolette R; border: Island Cr. Witness Samuel Turner and Margaret Turner. Signed James Land. Wit. oath Nov. 18, 1814 Samuel Turner. Rec. Aug. 7, 1815

p. 278-279 Jun. 20, 1815 Thomas Wyatt (Spartanburgh) to John Wyatt; for $50 sold 50 ac; border: Jonathan Low, old ridge path, Lee Linder's Mill path, and Beck's Br. Witness Reubin Warren and Mary Warren. Signed Thomas Wyatt. Wit. oath Aug. 8, 1815 Reubin Warren to Henry Turner. Rec. Aug. 9, 1815

p. 279-280 Jan. 31, 1815 Labon P Poole, sheriff (Spartanburgh) to Moses Wilkins (same); for $15.50 sold 150 ac on waters of Goochi Cr; where James Harrison lived; border: Moses Wilkins (on two sides), Henry Littlejohn, and George Davis; sale due to writ from Spartanburgh Common Pleas Court second Monday after fourth Monday in Mar. 1814 with suit Moses Wilkins asignee of George Davis vs James Harrison to levy $86.56½. Witness John Lipscomb and Patterson Thomson. Signed Labon P Poole. Wit. oath Jul. 14, 1815 Patterson Thomson to John Lipscomb. Rec. Aug. 10, 1815

p. 280-282 Dec. 14, 1813 James Brannon, sheriff (Spartan Dist) to Moses Wilkins; for $16 sold 100 ac on N side of Thickety Cr; sale Dec. 6, 1813 due to execution issued by Thomas Bomar esq, tax collector (Spartan Dist), for taxes against Jesse Connell. Witness E Roddy and N. E. Benson. Signed Ja Brannon SSD. Wit. oath Jan. 3, 1814 E Roddy to Jno H Jones. Rec. Aug. 16, 1815

p. 282-283 Jan. 12, 1815 Laurence Bankston (Spartanburgh) to Luke Demsy (same); for $85 sold 85 ac on Cases Cr of Pacolette R. Witness Stephen Groors and Nancy Demsey. Signed Laurence Bankston's mark. Wit. oath Jan. 12, 1815 Stephen Goors to Henry Turner. Rec. Aug. 17, 1815

p. 283-284 Jan. 19, 1815 John Harris (Pendleton Dist) to Towson Robertson (Spartanburgh); for $40 sold 50 ac on waters of Buck Cr; border: Towson Robertson, Herris, and Below. Witness James Turner and Anna Turner. Signed John Harris. Wit. oath Jan. 19, 1815 James Turner to Henry Turner. Rec. Aug. 26, 1815

p. 284-285 Jan. 11, 1815 Robert Armour sr (Spartanburgh) to Vincent Wyatt (same); power of attorney to sell land on Peter's Cr of Pacolette R. Witness Patrick Tylor and James Hayns. Signed Robert Armour. Wit. oath Sept. 4, 1815 Patrick Tylor to Jno H Jones. Rec. Sept. 4, 1815

p. 285-286 Jan. 11, 1815 Vincent Wyatt (Spartanburgh) to James Wyatt (same); for $200 sold 80 ac on Peter's Cr and Armour's Br; border: Vincent Wyatt jr Spring Br. Witness James Haynes and William Wyatt. Signed Vincent Wyatt's mark. Wit. oath Sept. 4, 1815 William Wyatt to Jno H Jones. Rec. Sept. 4, 1815

p. 286-287 Jul. 24, 1815 John Sparks (Spartanburgh) to James Tracy and Nathaniel Tracy (same); for $100 sold 50 ac on N side Pacolette R; border: Doctor's Br, Rn Hammett, and Charles Hammett. Witness Samuel Parks and Francis Parks. Signed John Sparks. Wit. oath Jul. 26, 1815 Samuel Parks to Jno H Jones. Rec. Sept. 4, 1815

p. 287-288 Mar. 10, 1815 Moses House (Spartanburgh) to Hilley House (same); for $200 sold 2 bay mares, 4 cattle, 2 sows and 7 pigs marked with cross and half cross in right ear and under keel in left ear, 2 feather beds and furniture, all household and kitchen furniture and plantation tools, and 3 sheep. Mary 10, 1815 Milley House says Moses can have property when he repays $200; if money is not repaid by time Milley dies, Moses gets property back anyway. Witness Henry G Vaughan and William Wade. Signed Moses House. Wit. oath Mar. 18, 1815 William Wade to Drury McDaniel. Rec. Sept. 9, 1815

p. 288-290 Sept. 6, 1815 (Union Dist) James W Darby, Commissioner of Pinckney Dist Equity Court, to William Thomson (called Gentleman Thomson); for $957 sold (1) 200 ac on N side Lawson's fork including Grist and Saw Mills; granted by North Carolina to (omitted) and sold to Wm Wofford who sold to Wells Griffith who sold to Justice Reynolds; and (2) (ac omitted) joining (1) on N side of Lawson's fork; part of 187 ac grant to Wells Griffith; sale due to Equity Court case at Union Court House for Pinckney Dist fourth Monday in Jun. 1814 Justice Reynolds vs Isham Harrison and Alexander McKie; Justice Reynolds to pay "balance on Commissioner's report" in three months or his land is to be sold; land was sold Sept. 5, 1815 on six months credit at Union Court House; land was confiscated by court at Feb. 1815 term. Witness James M Ckebbin esq, John Wright, and Daniel A Mitchell. Signed Jas W Darby. Wit. oath Sept. (omitted), 1815 (Union Dist) Daniel A Mitchell to David Johnson. Rec. Sept. 9, 1815

p. 290-292 Jan. 1, 1802 David Childres and Aries Childres (Spartanburgh) to William Hendricks (same); for 300 Spanish milled dollars sold 350 ac on branches of Abner's Cr of Enoree R; grant to Fennell Wilson (Pinckney Dist); 250 ac is from Fennell Wilson (sic) and 100 ac from Isaac Hendrix (sic); land maybe is now owned by David and Aries Childres. Witness William Tippens, William Medford, and Barnett Demsey. Signed David Childres and Aries' mark. Wit. oath Mar. 6, 1802 William Medford to Denny Anderson. Rec. Oct. 2, 1815

p. 292-293 Nov. 26, 1798 Fennel Willson (Spartanburgh) to William Hendrix (same); for 60£ sterling sold 106 ac on branches of Abner's Cr of Enoree R; border: Chamberlin Br; S part of 656 ac grant Aug. 5, 1793 to (omitted). Witness William Tippens, William Medford, and David Childers. Signed Fennel Willson and Sary's mark. Wit. oath Mar. 6, 1802 William Medford to Denny Anderson. Rec. Oct. 2, 1815

p. 293-294 Nov. 28, 1814 William Lancaster (Spartanburgh) to Zachariah McDaniel (same); for $93 sold 31 ac on S side of Fairforrest Cr and Tate's Br; border: Henry ONeill, Henry White, and James Tillett desc. Witness Christopher Golightly and David Golightly jr. Signed W Lancaster. Wit. oath Apr. 10, 1815 David Golightly jr to Drury McDaniel. Rec. Oct. 2, 1815

p. 294-295 Aug. 1, 1815 Rosannah Low (Spartanburgh) to Samuel Turner (same); for $17.50 sold 30 ac; border: John Low jr, Widow Smith, and part of John Low sr desc's land(?). Witness Charles Smith and William Wyatt. Signed Rosannah Low's mark. Wit. oath Aug. 31, 1815 William Wyatt to Henry Turner. Rec. Oct. 2, 1815

p. 295-297 Nov. 28, 1814 Christopher Golightly (Spartanburgh) to Zachariah McDaniel (same); for $47.50 sold 31 ac on S side of Fairforrest Cr; border: William Lancaster; part of grant to James Tillet who sold to Daniel Thomas who sold to Col. Henry White and mortgaged to state which sold to Col. Thomas Taylor who sold to Christopher Golightly. Witness David Golightly jr and Theron (or Heron) Lancaster. Signed Christi Golightly. Wit. oath Oct. 2, 1815 David Golightly jr to Drury McDaniel. Rec. Oct. 2, 1815

p. 297 Oct. 18, 1815 Charles McAbee to A Benson; swears he was present at fight at Spartanburgh Court House in 1814 between John Thomason and Thomas Ainsworth; and part of Thomas' ear was bit off and he believes it was Thomas' left ear. Witness A Benson JQ. Signed Charles McAbee. Rec. Oct. 18, 1815 (sic). Oct. 12, 1815 Elisha James to Danl White; swears that on Dec. 25, 1810 he took off a piece of Thomas Haynesworth's right ear in a fight. Witness Danl White JQ. Signed Elisha James

p. 297-299 May 27, 1815 James Miller (Spartanburgh) to John S Coan (same); for $212 sold 106 ac on N side of S Tygar R; border: Mill Br, Thomas Grisham, and John Patton. Witness John P. Evans, James Powers, and William Anderson. Signed James Miller. Wit. oath Oct. 2, 1815 John P Evans to John Collins. Rec. Oct. 2, 1815

p. 299-300 Sept. 29, 1814 James Ballenger (Spartanburgh) to Alexander Ray (same); for $250 sold 106 ac on E side of N Tygar R; border: W-N Tygar R, N-Roland Jomons, E-John Ray, and S-James Vernon. Witness William Perrin and James Vernon. Signed James Ballenger. Wit. oath Oct. 2, 1815 James Vernon to A Benson. Rec. Oct. 2, 1815

p. 300-302 Feb. 24, 1815 Reubin Warren (Spartanburgh) to Richard Proctor (same); for $10 sold 100 ac on W side of Island Cr; border: Henry Turner and Robert Thompson. Witness Hiram Proctor and Lewis Ballard. Signed Reuben Warren. Wit. oath Jul. 12, 1815 Hiram Proctor to Henry Turner. Rec. Oct. 2, 1815

p. 302-304 Jul. 29 (or 27), 1814 James Wofford (Spartanburgh) to Nathaniel Wofford (same); for $600 sold 350 ac on N side of Forgeson's Cr of Tygar R; border: tree marked NW and Sparks Br; where Nathaniel Wofford lives. Witness James Rhodes, Jesse Wofford, and John Wofford. Signed James Wofford. Wit. oath Sept. 14, 1815 Jesse Wofford to Drury McDaniel. Rec. Oct. 2, 1815

p. 304-306 Jan. 29, 1810 Thomas House (Spartanburgh) to Nathaniel

Wofford (same); for $30 sold 60 ac on branches of Fergeson's Cr of Tygar R; border: William Rhodes, Thomas Geast(?), and tree marked IW; SE part of 1,000 ac grant to George Savage who sold to Robert Gaddes who sold to Thomas House. Witness James Wofford, Isaac Wofford, and John Wofford. Signed Thomas House's mark. Wit. oath Feb. 19, 1812 John Wofford to Drury McDaniel. Rec. Oct. 2, 1815

p. 306-307 Jan. 7, 1815 Robert Armour (Tenn) to John Pettet (Spartanburgh); for $200 sold 222 ac on waters of Peter's Cr. Witness Sampson Soesbee and Enoch Ward. Signed Robert Armour. Wit. oath Jan. 7, 1815 Sampson Soesbee to Henry Turner. Rec. Oct. 3, 1815

p. 307-310 May 11, 1815 Richard Thomson (Spartanburgh) to James Hunt (same); for $250 sold ½ ac at Spartanburgh Court House on S side of "the public street" and below (on W side) Laurence R; border: SE & SW-Richard Thomson. Witness Muse Tollison and John D Palmer. Signed Richard Thomson. Wit. oath Oct. 4, 1815 John D Palmer to A Benson. Rec. Oct. 4, 1815. Dower renounced Aug. 2, 1815 Polly Thomson to A Benson

p. 310-312 May 15, 1815 Richard Thomson (Spartanburgh) to Muse Tollison (same); for $800 sold (1) 1 ac at Spartanburgh Court House on N side of Publick St (Main St); includes "top of the hill" on N side of Main St; and (2) ½ ac on S side of Main St. Witness N. E. Benson and John D Palmer. Signed Richard Thomson. Wit. oath Oct. 4, 1815 John D Palmer to A Benson. Rec. Oct. 4, 1815. Dower renounced Aug. 2, 1815 Polly Thomson to A Benson

p. 312-314 Jul. 17, 1813 Edward Autry to William Foster (Spartanburgh); for $176 sold 176 ac on S side of Fairforrest Cr; part of grant to Richard Hampton. Witness Wm H Cook and Lemuel Cook. Signed Edward Autry's mark. Wit. oath Aug. 2, 1813 Lemuel Cook to John Cook. Rec. Oct. 9, 1815

p. 314-315 Apr. 8, 1813 Thomas Cook (Spartanburgh) to Edward Autry (same); for $150 sold 176 ac on S side of Fairforrest Cr; part of grant to Richard Hampton. Witness Wm H Cook and Jacob Autry. Signed Thomas Cook. Wit. oath Aug. 2, 1813 Jacob Autry to John Cook. Rec. Oct. 9, 1815

p. 315-316 Oct. 4, 1815 George Storey (Burke, NC) to John Ison (Spartanburgh); for $150 sold 75 ac on waters of Fairforrest Cr; border: Burton and Samuel Kelso. Witness James Storey, Henry Storey, Joseph Kelso, and Wm N Morrow. Signed George Storey. Wit. oath Oct. 7, 1815 James Storey to Samuel Archibald. Rec. Oct. 13, 1815

p. 316-318 Dec. 6, 1813 Isaac Young (Spartanburgh) to Samuel Jinkins (Union Dist); for $350 sold 300 ac on Buck Cr on N side of Pacolate R; border: James Cantrell. Witness John Hughy, Moses Young, and Aron Odom. Signed Isaac Young's mark. Wit. oath Apr. 20, 1814 (Union Dist) Aron Odom to P(?) Williams. Rec. Oct. 20, 1815

p. 318-319 Aug. 23, 1815 James Cook (Spartanburgh) to Samuel Snoddy (same); agreement to quit claim to land called Savages big survey; (1) James gives rights to Samuel to cleared land inside Snoddy's fence; part of Snoddy's survey now purchased by James Cook; and (2) Samuel gives rights to James to 40 ac of wooded land that Samuel bought from John Duncan; part of Savages big survey on waters of and on S side of Tygar R. Witness Anna Snoddy and Peggy Snoddy. Signed James Cook and Samuel Snoddy. Wit. oath Aug. 23, 1815 Anna Snoddy to Drury McDaniel. Rec. Oct. 28, 1815 (sic)

p. 319-321 Aug. 26, 1815 John Onale (or Oneal) (Spartanburgh) [for love of children Clarenda G Onale and Henry Onale] to Dr Thomas Patton (Union Dist); in trust for children's benifit sold a Negro man Cato, 3 heifers, a 3 year old steer, 7 sheep, 9 one year old hogs, and 3 small pigs. Witness Ephraim Roddy and A Benson. Signed John Onale. Wit. oath Oct. 23, 1815 Ephraim Roddy to A Benson. Rec. Oct. 24, 1815

p. 321 Jun. 27, 1815 James Wofford to Isaac Wofford; for $600 sold two Negroes: boy Sam and girl Hanna. Witness Nathaniel Wofford and John Wofford. Signed James Wofford. Wit. oath Oct. 25, 1815 John Wofford to Drury McDaniel. Rec. Oct. 25, 1815

p. 321-322 Jun. 29, 1815 James Wofford to Jesse Wofford; for $300 sold a Negro boy Joe. Witness Thomas Drummonor and William Johnson. Signed James Wofford. Wit. oath Oct. 25, 1815 Thomas Drummonor to Drury McDaniel. Rec. Oct. 25, 1815

p. 322-323 Jun. 27, 1815 James Wofford to John Wofford; for $600 sold a Negro girl Clary. Witness Nathaniel Wofford and Isaac Wofford. Signed James Wofford. Wit. oath Oct. 25, 1815 Isaac Wofford to Drury McDaniel. Rec. Oct. 25, 1815

p. 323-325 Jan. 12, 1811 James Wofford (Spartanburgh) to Isaac Wofford (same); for $50 sold 50 ac on Forgerson's Cr of Tygar R; border: David Moore and William Rodes. Witness John Adams, Bailey Adams, and John Wofford. Signed James Wofford. Wit. oath Oct. 25, 1815 John Wofford to Drury McDaniel. Rec. Oct. 25, 1815

p. 325-327 Jul. 9, 1811 James Wofford (Spartanburgh) to Jesse Wofford (same); for $500 sold 220 ac on Forgeson's Cr of Tygar R; border: David Moore, William Burrow, and William Rodes; Note: James Wofford and wife (not named) to have use of land for their lifetimes. Witness William Rice and John Wofford. Signed James Wofford. Wit. oath Oct. 25, 1815 John Wofford to Drury McDaniel. Rec. (blank) 25, 1815

p. 327-328 Jul. 3, 1815 Jesse Wofford (Spartanburgh) to Isaac Wofford (same); for $30 sold 30 ac on branch of Forgeson's Cr of Tygar R; border: line laid off by James Wofford and Thomas Williamson. Witness John Wofford and Thomas Drummond. Signed Jesse Wofford. Wit. oath Oct. 25, 1815 Thomas Drummond to Drury McDaniel. Rec. Oct. 25, 1815

p. 328-330 Dec. 29, 1814 James Wofford (Spartanburgh) to Isaac Wofford (same); for $200 sold 250 ac on waters of Forgeson's Cr of Tygar R; border: John Owens, Ephraim Drummond, Thomas Williams, and John Wofford; part of 640 ac grant to James Wofford. Witness Thomas Drummond and John Wofford. Signed James Wofford. Wit. oath Oct. 25, 1815 Thomas Drummond to Drury McDaniel. Rec. Oct. 25, 1815

p. 330-332 Feb. 18, 1813 James Wofford (Spartanburgh) to John Wofford (same); for $300 sold 350 ac on N side Forgeson's Cr of Tygar R; border: John Owens, Williamson, and Nathaniel Wofford. Witness Jesse Wofford and William Wofford. Signed James Wofford. Wit. oath Mar. 3, 1813 Jesse Wofford to Samuel Woodruff. Rec. Oct. 25, 1815. Dower renounced Catherine Wofford to Drury McDaniel Oct. 20, 1815

p. 332-335 Nov. 13, 1814 Richard Thomson (Spartanburgh) to Peter Kerr McMecan (same); for $250 sold ½ ac at Spartanburgh Court House on S side of Publick Ground above the "cross" street; border: Wm Thomson; Note Richard to return money if court moves in five years. Witness Drury Wood and N. E. Benson. Signed Richard Thomson. Wit. oath Dec. 22, 1814 N. E. Benson to Thomas Poole. Rec. Oct. 5, 1815 (sic). Dower renounced Oct. 20, 1815 Polly Thomson to Abner Benson

p. 335-336 Jul. 15, 1815 Micajah Barnett to Frederick Williams; for $180 sold 104 ac on Beaverdam Br of Fairforrest Cr. Witness Elisha Bomar and Anthony Foster. Signed Macajah Barnett. Wit. oath Sept. 9, 1815 Elisha Bomar to Danl White. Rec. Nov. 3, 1815

p. 336-337 Jun. 30, 1815 Thomas Pope (Spartanburgh) to Charlotte Debery (same); for $1 sold 16 cattle, 4 horses(?), 10 hogs, 4 feather beds, and all household and kitchen furniture. Witness Thomas Barton and Harvy Davis. Signed Thomas Pope. Wit. oath Oct. 12, 1815 Thomas Barton to James Young. Rec. Nov. 6, 1815

p. 337-338 Jun. 30, 1815 Thomas Pope (Spartanburgh) to Charlotte Debery (same); for $100 sold (ac not known) on both sides Buck Cr; ac not known due to old "write" taking part from tract suppose to be 160 ac; where Thomas Pope lives; border: W-Thomas Henderson, S-Mack Williams and other sides-old tract formerly said to be Thomas Sabe's. Witness Harry Davis and Thomas Barton. Signed Thomas Pope. Wit. oath Oct. 12, 1815 Thomas Barton to James Young. Rec. Nov. 6, 1815

p. 338-341 Jul. 1, 1814 Randolph Johnson (Spartanburgh) to Willias Vaughan (same); for $300 sold 160 ac on Provis (or Rovis) Cr; border: John Durham, William Anderson, Robertson's Spring Br, and Page's Br. Witness John Waddle and William Wade. Signed Randolph Johnson's mark. Wit. oath Jul. 29, 1815 John Waddle to Drury McDaniel. Rec. Nov. 6, 1815. Dower renounced Sept. 23, 1815 Mary Johnston to Drury McDaniel

p. 341-343 Apr. 26, 1815 Jamimah Lindsey (Spartanburgh) to Matthew Allen (same); for $100 sold (ac omitted) between Tygar and Enoree Rivers and on both sides Two Mile Cr of Enoree R; border: S & W-Samuel Woodruff, N-Nathaniel Woodruff and Zachariah Leatherwood, E-Paul Castleberry; part of grant Feb. 5, 1787 Gov. William Moultrie to James McGowen. Witness Moses Woodruff, Levy Brown, and Micajah Brown. Signed Jamimah Lindsey's mark. Wit. oath Jul.(?) 8, 1815 Moses Woodruff to Samuel Woodruff. Rec. Nov. 7, 1815

p. 343-346 Nov. 7, 1815 Adam Carruth (Greenville Dist) to Charles Moore (Spartanburgh); for $400 sold a Negro woman Amy and her four children Lucy, Rebecca, Sampson, and Willis; sold Mar. 19, 1806 by Adam Sloan to Adam Carruth recorded in Greenville Dist Clerk's office; Charles Moore is to permit Catherine Sloan (during her lifetime), wife of Adam Sloan, to take the slaves and their issue; Adam Sloan or Catherine's future husbands can't interfer; after Catherine's death, her share of the slaves go to her children when they marry or become 21; if "eighte" child dies without issue, then that share goes to other child; Catherine can also sell the slaves. Witness Tho Moore and Andrew B Moore. Signed H Carruth. Wit. oath Nov. 7, 1815 Andrew B Moore to Samuel Woodruff. Rec. Nov. 7, 1815

p. 346-347 Sept. 23, 1815 James Philips (Rutherford Co, NC) to William Philips (same); for $50 sold 170 ac on both sides Ashworth Cr; border: N-North Carolina and S-Camp; upper end of 340 ac grant to Thomas Thomson surveyed Sept. 23, 1794. Witness James Philips (signature) and Reuben Philips. Signed James Philips' mark. Wit. oath Nov. 7, 1815 Reuben Philips to Leonard Adcock. Rec. Nov. 7, 1815

p. 347-348 Feb. 10, 1815 John Blackburn to Reuben Philips; for $30 sold 298 ac on middle fork of Suck Cr; border: Blackwele. Witness Charles Blackwell and Nimrod Horton. Signed John Blackburn's mark. Wit. oath Nov. 7, 1815 Nimrod Horton to Leonard Adcock. Rec. Nov. 7, 1815

p. 348-350 Feb. 5, 1813 Samuel Haney (Spartanburgh) to Richard Haney (Same); for 15£ sterling sold 181 ac on waters of Hors Cr of Broad R; border: N & E-Sharp, E(sic)-Parris, S-Thomas Haney, SW-Haney, and NE-William Adcock. Witness Shaderick Weaver and Samuel Trolinger. Signed Samuel Haney's mark. Wit. oath Dec. 18, 1813 Shaderick Weaver to Leonard Adcock. Rec. Nov. 7, 1815

p. 350-351 Jan. 12, 1813 John Parris to Reuben Philips; for $100 sold 100 ac on Suck Cr of Broad R; border: Juay (or Iuay) Robertson; part of grant Sept. 11, 1795 to Jacob Pack. Witness Nimrod Horton and Ezekiel Brothers. Signed John Parris. Wit. oath Nov. 7, 1815 Nimrod Horton to Leonard Adcock. Rec. Nov. 7, 1815

p. 351-353 Feb. 24, 1810 William Morrow (Spartanburgh) to William Adcock (same); for 30£ sterling sold 100 ac on both sides Hors Cr of Broad R; part of grant Jan. 1, 1787 States Office to Joseph Warren. Witness Lewis Parris and Isaac Young jr. Signed William Morrow. Wit. oath Oct. 16, 1810 Isaac Young jr to Leonard Adcock. Rec. Nov. 7, 1815

p. 353-355 Oct. 10, 1809 Jacob Dilback (Rutherford Co, NC) to John Parris (Spartanburgh); for $100 sold 227 ac on waters of Suck Cr of Broad R; border: Moutre, Williams, and D Chuck (or Cback). Witness Thomas Wyatt and Peter Gosnell. Signed Jacob Dilback's mark. Wit. oath Jun. 9, 1810 Thomas Wyatt to Leonard Adcock. Rec. Nov. 7, 1815

p. 355-356 Jan. 14, 1813 Samuel Fowler, administrator "to" John McGuire desc (SC), to John Mason (SC); for $100 sold 100 ac; border: Richd Carver, John Bonham, Robert Black, Andrew Ferguson, Holston's Cr, and Arnold filed; part of grant Feb. 6, 1792 to John McGuire. Witness Richd Carver and Bedwell Jaterfield. Signed Samuel Fowler's mark. Wit. oath Jan. 14, 1813 Richd Carver to Andrew Ferguson. Rec. Nov. 7, 1815

p. 356-358 Nov. 1, 1815 William McDaniel (Spartanburgh) to Thomas Miller (same); for $544 sold 340 ac between Middle and S Tygar Rivers; border: John Patten, Miller, Moore, and Daniel McKie; part of grant to William McDaniel desc. Witness Samuel Miller and John Fielden. Signed William McDaniel. Wit. oath Nov. 4, 1815 John Fielden to Drury McDaniel. Rec. Nov. 7, 1815

p. 358-359 Jul. 26, 1815 Gilbert Boman sr (Spartanburgh) to son Gilbert Boman jr; for love and affection give 30 ac; where Gilbert Boman sr lives; border: Thomas Earle (or Earlen), "the canal", and "the State line". Witness Henry Monroe, Drewery Boman, and Richard Sisemon. Signed Gilbert Boman's mark. Wit. oath Sept. 22, 1815 Drewery Boman to Wm Kelso. Rec. Nov. 7, 1815

p. 359-360 Jun. 10, 1815 Henry Geddis esq (Charleston Dist) to Col. William Austin (Greenville Dist); for $90 sold 380 ac on both sides Cub Br of Fairforrest Cr; grant Sept. 4, 1786 to Henry Geddis. Witness Caleb Hughes and George W Geddis. Signed Henry Geddis. Wit. oath Sept. 9, 1815 (Greenville Dist) Caleb Hughes to B Griffith. Rec. Nov. 7, 1815

p. 360-361 Aug. 30, 1815 Edmond J Bishop (Spartanburgh) to John Bishop (same); for $200 sold 100 ac on waters of Fairforrest Cr and Lawson's fork; border: Barney Bishop. Witness Wm Bishop, Edmund Bishop (short), and Soloman Bishop. Signed Edmd J. Bishop. Wit. oath Nov. 8, 1815 Edmund Bishop (short) to Thomas Poole. Rec. Nov. 8, 1815

p. 361-363 Sept. 13, 1815 James Wood (Spartanburgh) to Thomas Kimbril (same); for $30 sold 32 ac on both sides Sophia's Br of Thompson's Cr of Pacolete R; grant Jan. 7, 1799 Gov. Edward Rutledge to Larkin Rylie and by power of attorney to William D Thomas who sold to Thomas Kimbril but William "had not done" power of attorney dated May 11, 1799 see "records of Greenville". Witness William Bennett, Edmd Clement and James Young. Signed James Wood's mark. Wit. oath Jan. 4, 1816 William Bennett to James Young. Rec. Jan. 5, 1816

p. 363-364 Oct. 26, 1813 Britain George sr (Spartanburgh) to John Low; for $30 sold 150 ac on N side of Pacolette R and head of Doctor's Br; border: John Carmon, Bradley, and Smith. Witness John Parks and Samuel Parks. Signed Britain George's mark. Wit. oath Apr. 2, 1814 John Parks to Jno H Jones. Rec. Nov. 30, 1815

p. 364-365 Oct. 5, 1803 Francis Powers (Spartanburgh) to Lewrey Powers (same); for $100 sold 140 ac on S side of S Tygar R. Witness John Patton and William Powers. Signed Francis Powers. Wit. oath Feb. 10, 1815 William Powers to John Collins. Rec. Dec. 4, 1815

p. 365-366 Sept. 19, 1815 Jonathan Nesbitt (Spartanburgh) to John Nesbitt (Dickson Co, Tenn); for $100 sold 115 ac on S side of S Tygar R; border: Burns, Bright, and Ford; survey Jul. 23, 1785 by Andrew Thomson for Jonathan Nesbitt and granted Jan. 1, 1787 to Jonathan Nesbitt. Witness James Hadden, Alexander Thompson, and Any Morrow. Signed Jonathan Nesbitt. Wit. oath Oct. 9, 1815 James Hadden to John Collins. Rec. Dec. 4, 1815. Dower renounced Elizabeth Nesbitt to Drury McDaniel Oct. 7, 1815

p. 366-367 Jul. 28, 1815 Paul Cox and William Ramsey (Spartanburgh) to James Senter (same); for $200 sold 100 ac on S side of S Pacolete R; border: William Ramsey, James McDowell, Ralph Danger, and William Camron; part of grant to William Dickson. Witness James Burton and Uriah Bush. Signed Paul Cox and W Ramsey. Wit. oath Dec. 2, 1815 Jesse Burton to Andrew Fergerson. Rec. Dec. 4, 1815

p. 367-368 (blank), 1815 Amos Austill (Spartanburgh) to William Bostick (same); for $300 sold 340 ac; on both sides McBee's Cr; 69 ac excluded that is "held by" Hert's and McBee's old surveys; known as Tanner's place; grant Gov. William Moultrie to Josiah Tanner. Witness Joseph Willis, Littleberry Bostick, and John Dill. Signed Amos Austill. Wit. oath Dec. 4, 1815 Littleberry Bostick to Joseph Camp. Rec. Dec. 5, 1815

p. 368-369 Jan. 11, 1808 Caleb Jones (Spartanburgh) to Patrick Taylor (same); for $190 sold 118 ac on Lindsey's Cr of Pacolate R. Witness John H Jones and John Jones. Signed Caleb Jones. Wit. oath Jan. 20, 1808 John Jones to Jno H Jones. Rec. Dec. 8, 1815

p. 379-370 Aug. 18, 1809 David Millhanks (Spartanburgh) to Patrick Taylor (same); for $150 sold 83 ac on Turkey pine Br of Pacolete R and on S side of Pacolete R; border: Patrick Taylor, Jones, and fork of old road; part of grant to Joseph Lively. Witness Caleb Jones and Jno H Jones. Signed David Millhanks. Wit. oath Aug. 28, 1809 Caleb Jones to Jno H Jones. Rec. Dec. 8, 1815

p. 370-371 Jan. 29, 1807 Daniel Hammett (Spartanburgh) to Samuel Burton (same); for $60 sold 180 ac on S side of Pacolate R and both sides Lindsey's Cr; border: Caleb Jones, Jeremiah Walker, and Col. Henderson; grant "assigned by" Gov. Charles Pinckney to (omitted). Witness Reuben Jentry and Jesse Cannon. Signed Daniel Hammett. Wit. oath Jan. 31, 1807 Jesse Cannon to John Brewton.

Rec. Dec. 8, 1815

p. 371-372 Oct. 13, 1808 Samuel Burton (Spartanburgh) to Patrick Tylor (same); for $60 sold 180 ac on S side of Pacolete R and both sides Lindsey's Cr; border: Caleb Jones, Jeremiah Walker, and Col. Henderson; grant "assigned by" Gov. Charles Pinckney. Witness Leonard George and Ansel Hudgins. Signed Samuel Burton. Wit. oath Oct. 13, 1808 Leonard George to Jno H Jones. Rec. Dec. 8, 1815

p. 372-373 Dec. 6, 1806 William Hammett sr (Spartanburgh) to Daniel Hammett sr (same); for $60 sold 180 ac on S side of Pacolett R and both sides Lindsey's Cr; border: Caleb Jones; grant "assigned by" Gov. Charles Pinckney. Witness Sterling Hudgins, Lewis Ferguson, and Arthur Faulkner. Signed William Hammet. Wit. oath Dec. 8, 1806 Sterling Hudgins to Wm Smith. Rec. Dec. 8, 1815

p. 373-374 Feb. 25, 1803 Joseph Lively (Spartanburgh) to William Hammett (same); for 12£ sold 238 ac on S side of Pacolett R and both sides Lindsey's Cr; border: Caleb Jones; grant "assigned" by Gov. Charles Pinckney. Witness Reuben Simmons and Beven Patterson. Signed Joseph Lively. Wit. oath Oct. 24, 1803 Beven Patterson to William Lancaster. "entered before signed" Rec. Dec. 8, 1815

p. 374-375 Dec. 6, 1815 William R Smith (Spartanburgh) to Richard Thomson (same); for $173 sold 173 ac on waters of Kelso's Cr of Fairforrest Cr; border: Richard Thomson, Anthony Foster, and David Manl (or Marrl); part of grant to Wm Loocock. Witness Daniel White and William Bagwell. Signed Wm R Smith. Wit. oath Dec. 6, 1815 William Bagwell to Danl White. Rec. Dec. 9, 1815

p. 375-376 Nov. 18, 1814 William Brown (Spartanburgh) to James Robertson (same); for $600 sold 200 ac on N side of S Tygar R; border: Andrew F Nisbett and "the" road. Witness Page Rork and Daniel Robertson. Signed Wm and Nancy Brown. Wit. oath Nov. 18, 1814 Page Rork to Michl Miller. Rec. Dec. 18, 1815

p. 376-377 Dec. 8, 1815 Patrick Tylor (Spartanburgh) to Richard Thomson (same); for $300 sold 228 ac on both sides Lindsey's Cr of Pacolett R; border: Turkey pin Br, Jones, and Mare Br; part to two tracts: (1) grant Feb. 5, 1787 to Reuben Matthis and (2) grant Mar. 1, 1790 to Joseph Lively. Witness Elisha Bomar and Thomas Bomar. Signed Patrick Tylor. Wit. oath Dec. 8, 1815 Elisha Bomar to Danl White. Rec. Dec. 18, 1815. Dower renounced Dec. 18, 1815 Esther Tylor to Abner Benson

p. 377-378 Sept. 15, 1815 Henry Golightly (Spartanburgh) to Richard Barnett (same); for $400 sold 204 ac on Fairforrest and Kelso's Creeks; border: waggon road, Martin, Hancock Smith's old line. Witness Jesse Barnett and Elisha James. Signed Henry Golightly. Wit. oath Oct. 4, 1815 Elisha James to Danl White. Rec. Dec. 20, 1815. Dower renounced Oct. 4, 1815 Polly Golightly to Daniel White

p. 378-379 Feb. 29, 1814(sic) Thompson Clayton (Spartanburgh) to James Owen (same); for $150 sold 100 ac part of where Patrick Hogan lives; border: N Tygar R, Thads Owin, Big Br, and C Clayton; grant to Alexander McCarter. Witness Thadias Owin, Gowin Clayton jr and John Davis. Signed Thompson Clayton's mark. Wit. oath Nov. 4, 1815 Thadias Owin to Andrew Ferguson. Rec. Jan. 1, 1816

p. 379-380 Oct. 19, 1815 John Dill (Spartanburgh) to George Wood (same); for $385 sold 140 ac on N side of Beaverdam Cr of Thickety Cr; border: Wm Bostick, Thos Littlejohn, and Hort's old line; part of grant in 1773 to Wm Hort. Witness Smith Lipscomb and

James Richards. Signed John Dill's mark. Wit. oath Oct. 30, 1815 Smith Lipscomb to John Lipscomb. Rec. Jan. 1, 1816. Dower renounced Oct. 30, 1815 Mary Dill to John Lipscomb

p. 380-381 (date omitted) Stephen Foster (Spartanburgh) to John and Nancy Foster (same); for $94 sold 85 ac; border: Hen Colwell, Bagwell, McMaken, and McMaken's Br. Witness Joseph Selmon and William Foster. Signed Stephen Foster. Wit. oath Jan. 1, 1816 Joseph Selmon to Drury McDaniel. Rec. Jan. 1, 1816

p. 381-382 Sept. 30, 1815 James Wood (Spartanburgh) to Thomas Kimbrel (same); for $300 sold 140 ac on both sides of Thomson's Cr of Pacolett R; border: survey for Thomas Bennett, Vencent Kimbrel's cleared field, Thomas Kimbrel, and William Bennett. Witness James Young, Edm Clement, and William Bennett. Signed James Wood's mark. Wit. oath Jan. 4, 1816 William Bennett to James Young. Rec. Jan. 5, 1816

p. 382-383 Aug. 9, 1815 James Gilmore jr (Spartanburgh) to Charles and Alexander Copeland (same); for $400 sold (ac omitted) on N side of Pacolete R a small distance from mouth of Bare Cr; border: Calf pin Br, road from Iron works to Rutherford, the state line, Stillhouse Br, and Charles McKnight; part of grant to James Gilmore sr and part of grant to James Gilmore jr. Witness Alexander Copeland and William Copeland. Signed James Gilmore. Wit. oath Jan. 10, 1816 William Copeland to A Benson. Rec. Jan. 10, 1816

p. 383-384 Dec. 18, 1815 Samuel Jenkins (Spartanburgh) to John Hughey (same); for $350 sold 300 ac on Buck Cr on N side of Pacolete R; border: James Cantrell. Witness John Solter (or Sarlor) and John Hughey sr. Signed Samuel Jenkins' mark. Wit. oath Dec. 19, 1815 (Union Dist) John Hughey sr to Jno Hall. Rec. Jan. 29, 1816

p. 384-385 Nov. 30, 1815 Adam Kilby (Pennelton Dist) to Samuel Seay (Spartanburgh); for (money omitted) sold 200 ac on both sides Forw Br of Lawson's fork of Pacolett R; border: John Clemont and Markel; part of grant to John Burnett. Witness William Braman and William Rollans. Signed Adam Kilby's mark. Wit. oath Feb. 5, 1816 William Braman to Thomas Poole. Rec. Feb. 5, 1816

p. 385-386 Oct. 23, 1815 Jesse Morrow to Silas Cash; for "first cost States price and officer's fees" quit claim grant of 486 ac; surveyed by Gabl Benson Mar. 8, 1797 and granted in 1797. Witness James Dunaway and James Morrow. Signed Jesse Morrow. Wit. oath Jan. 27, 1816 James Dunaway to Henry Turner. Rec. Feb. 5, 1816

p. 386-387 Sept. 28, 1815 Samuel Hendrix (Spartanburgh) to William Lanford (SC); for $60 sold 50 ac on Two Mile Cr of Enoree R; border: William Lanford, Crow, Allen, and tree marked "JW"; where Samuel Hendrix lives. Witness James Lanford, Lewis Lanford, and Ammis Lanford. Signed Samuel Hendrix's mark. Wit. oath Oct. 10, 1815 Annis Hendrix (sic) to Drury McDaniel. Rec. Feb. 5, 1816. Dower renounced Oct. 10, 1815 Melina Hendrix to Drury McDaniel

p. 387-388 Jul. 15, 1815 John Hester (Spartanburgh) to Joseph Willis (same); for $200 sold 150 ac; Joseph Willis is now "in possession" of land; grant to Charles Miles and sold to Charles Hester by Spartanburgh sheriff and Charles sold to John Hester. Witness Anderson Willis and Obadiah Hester. Signed John Hester. Wit. oath Jul. 24, 1815 Anderson Willis to J Camp. Rec. Feb. 5, 1816

p. 388-389 Oct. 3, 1815 Samuel Woodruff (Spartanburgh) to Lewis Lanford (same); for $225 sold 150 ac; grant Gov. William Moultrie to John Hendrix and resurveyed Sept. 27, 1815 by Jesse

Wofford. Witness William Lanford, Joseph Woodruff, and Aaron Woodruff. Signed Samuel Woodruff. Wit. oath Oct. 10, 1815 William Lanford to Drury McDaniel. Rec. Feb. 5, 1816. Dower renounced Oct. 10, 1815 Nancy Woodruff to Drury McDaniel

p. 389-390 Oct. 13, 1812 James Cook to Francis Mason (Spartanburgh); for $3 sold 80 ac on waters of Fairforrest Cr; border: W-Wm Beaver, N-Elihu Golightly, E-Benjamin Rainwater, and S-Francis Mason. Witness Henry Walden and David McCarley. Signed James Cook. Wit. oath Apr. 7, 1813 Henry Walden to Thomas Poole. Rec. Feb. 5, 1816

p. 390-391 Apr. 12, 1808 James Mason (Spartanburgh) to Francis Mason (same); for $200 sold 100 ac on Ford's Cr; border: W-Francis Mason's old line, N-George Right and James Hurt, E-Benjamin Rainwater, and SE-John Underwood. Witness W. S. Golightly, Elias Corder, and Broadrick Mason. Signed James Mason. Wit. oath Apr. 12, 1808 Broadrick Mason to Danl Wilbanks. Rec. Feb. 5, 1816

p. 391-392 Jan. 24, 1816 Richard Fryer (Spartanburgh) to Charles Stewart and heirs of William Stewart desc; a bond for $300; Condition: bond void if Richard Fryer does <u>not</u> "call" a mortgage bond William Stewart gave Richard Fryer Feb. 23, 1807 for land on Enoree R; latter mortgage recorded in Spartanburgh Clerk's office. Witness Aaron Casey and Moses Couch. Signed Richard Fryer. Wit. oath Jan. 24, 1816 Aaron Casey to M Casey. Rec. Feb. 5, 1816

p. 392-393 Mar. 27, 1815 Thomas Grisham (Spartanburgh) to James Miller (same); for $87.75 sold 58½ ac on E side of S Tygar R. Witness J. P. Evins, James Anderson, and James Powers. Signed Thomas Grisham. Wit. oath Sept. 15, 1815 James Anderson to Drury McDaniel. Rec. Feb. 5, 1816

p. 393-394 Dec. 12, 1814 George Bennett (Spartanburgh) to Samuel Seay (same); for $50 sold 140 ac on waters of Thompson's Cr of Pacolett R; border: survey for John Mason, Leonard Carden, Joseph Venable, John Kimbrel, and Thos Bennett. Witness William Brannon and Cyrus Seay. Signed George Bennett's mark. Wit. oath Jul. 28, 1815 William Brannon to Thomas Poole. Rec. Feb. 5, 1816

p. 394-395 Mar. 28, 1811 Sarah Brekin (Spartanburgh) to James Miller (same); for $200 sold 50 ac on N side of S Tygar R; border: mouth of Mill Br, David Anderson, and James Chamblin. Witness Hiram Bennett, Moses Bobeter, and Simon West. Signed Sarah Brekin. Wit. oath Mar. 7, 1812 Hiram Bennett to Drury McDaniel. Rec. Feb. 5, 1816

p. 395-396 Sept. 19, 1815 Celia Meadows, widow of Joseph Meadows desc (Spartanburgh), to Green W Meadows (same); for $51 sold 46 ac on Cain Cr; her part of 141 ac where Joseph Meadows desc lived. Witness Joseph Powers and Lawson Thomson. Signed Celia Meadows' mark. Wit. oath Feb. 5, 1815 Lawson Thomson to M Casey. Rec. Feb. 5, 1816

p. 396-397 Jan. 6, 1816 Andrew Foster (Spartanburgh) to John Foster (same); for "lands deeded" to Andrew by John sold 50 ac; border: on N side of Kelso's Cr and John Foster; part of two tracts formerly land of Moses Foster desc. Witness Christopher Golightly, David Golightly jr, and Theron Lancaster. Signed Andrew Foster. Wit. oath Feb. 4, 1816 David Golightly jr to Wm Kelso. Rec. Feb. 5, 1816

p. 397-398 Jan. 6, 1816 John Foster (Spartanburgh) to Andrew Foster (same); for "lands deeded" to John by Andrew sold 39 ac; border: on E side of Kelso's Cr and Shands Golightly; part of where Andrew Foster lives. Witness Christopher Golightly, David Golightly jr and Theron Lancaster. Signed John Foster. Wit. oath Feb. 4, 1816 David Golightly jr to Wm Kelso. Rec. Feb. 5, 1816

p. 398-399 Dec. 26, 1815 Anthony McElwain, James McElwain, Mary McElwain, Sarah McElwain, and Elizabeth Smith (Union Dist), heirs of James McElwain jr desc and heirs of James McElwain sr desc, to Daniel Wilbanks (Union Dist); for $25 sold (ac omitted) that is their right to estate of James McElwain sr in Union and Spartanburgh Dists on McElwain's Cr; border: W & SW-James McElwain jr desc, S-James Story, NE & SE-William Patton, NE-James Donaldson, and NW-John Davidson. Witness Ephraim G Harris and Thomas Wilbanks. Signed Anthony McElwain, James McElwain, and Mary's, Sally's, and Elizabeth's marks. Wit. oath Feb. 12, 1816 Ephraim G Harris to Saml Archibald. Rec. Feb. 15, 1816

p. 399-400 Oct. 19, 1814 Leonard Carden (Spartanburgh) to John E. Smith; for $125 sold 150 ac on head waters of Thomson's Cr of Pacolett R; border: Samuel Sentel, Mark Gilbert, Mochaboy, and Nathan Sentell. Witness William Sentill and Jacob Belcher. Signed Leonard Carden. Wit. oath Feb. 23, 1816 Jacob Belcher to Thomas Poole. Rec. Feb. 24, 1816

p. 400 Nov. 23, 1815 Hosea Camp (Jackson Co, Ga) to James Vernon (Spartanburgh); for $240 sold 160 ac on N Tygar R; part of 400 ac grant to John Miller and sold by his heirs to Jas Jordan and drawn by Hosea Camp as lot #3 in Jas Jordan's estate. Witness Memory N Chapman and William F Piephoff. Signed Hosea Camp. Wit. oath Mar. 4, 1816 Memory N Chapman to Thos Poole. Rec. Mar. 4, 1816

Book P 1816-1818

p. 1-2 Mar. 14, 1812 Thomas Vaughan (Spartanburgh) to Sanford Smith (same); for $65 sold 100 ac on waters of Dutchman's Cr of Tygar R; where James Hickey lived; border: N & W-Thomas Vaughan and S & E-Lowns and Elijah Smith. Witness Britain Williford and William Lancaster esq. Signed Thomas Vaughan. Wit. oath Mar. 4, 1816 William Lancaster esq to Saml Archibald. Rec. Mar. 4, 1816

p. 2-3 Feb. 21, 1816 Fortunaius H Legg (Spartanburgh) to John Bazwell; for $40 sold 80 ac where John Bazwell lives. Witness David Drummon and Hays Bazwell. Signed Fortunaius H Legg. Wit. oath Mar. 14, 1816 (sic) Hays Bazwell to A Benson. Rec. Mar. 4, 1816

p. 3-4 Dec. 27, 1815 Sandford Smith (Spartanburgh) to Elijah Smith (same); for $100 sold 100 ac on branches of Dutchman's Cr of Tygar R. Witness Thos Hanna and John Bearden jr. Signed Sandford Smith. Wit. oath (omitted) 29, 1816 John Bearden jr to James Hamn. Rec. Mar. 4, 1816

p. 4-5 Dec. 27, 1815 Sandford Smith (Spartanburgh) to Elijah Smith (same); for $65 sold 100 ac on branches of Dutchman's Cr of Tygar R; border: Drury Smith, N & S-"said" Vaughan, and S & E-Elijah Smith. Witness Thos Hanna and John Bearden jr. Signed Sandford Smith. Wit. oath Jan. 29, 1816 John Bearden jr to Jas Hamn. Rec. Mar. 4, 1816

p. 5-6 Sept. 5, 1815 Legrand Palmer (Spartanburgh) to Ransom Foster; for $400 sold 382 ac on waters of Mill Cr of N Tygar R. Witness Wilson Foster and Floyd Tanner. Signed Legrand Palmer. Wit. oath Sept. 6, 1815 Floyd Tanner to Wm Underwood. Rec. Mar. 8, 1816

p. 6-7 Dec. 6, 1800 James Kindrick (Spartanburgh) to John Kimbrel (same); for $150 sold 130 ac on S side of S Pacolett R; where James Kindrick lives; border: Amos Spiece, Clark, Thomas Bennett, and William Bennett. Witness William Bennett, Thomas Kimbrel, and Vincent Kimbrel. Signed James Kindrick's mark. Wit. oath Jan. 4, 1816 William Bennett to James Young. Rec. Mar. 13, 1816. Dower renounced Feb. 15, 1816 Frances Kindrick to James Young

p. 7-8 Mar. 16, 1816 Zacheriah Wingo (Spartanburgh) to Thomson Fossett (same); for $61 sold 40.7 ac; border: Fairforrest Cr. Witness George Lewis and Kinsman Seay. Signed Zacheriah Wingo. Wit. oath Mar. 16, 1816 George Lewis to A Benson. Rec. Mar. 16, 1816

p. 8-9 Nov. 18, 1815 Thomas Cantwell (Spartanburgh) to Nimrod Cantrell (same); for $120 sold 60 ac on S side of Buck Cr of Pacolett R; border: John Morris and N Cantrell. Witness John Morris and John Cantrell. Signed Thomas Cantwell's mark. Wit. oath Mar. 18, 1816 John Morris to A Benson. Rec. Mar. 18, 1816

p. 9-10 May 21, 1814 "at office of William Payne #131 Broad St"(SC) Peter Smith (Charleston, SC) to Ephraim Drummond (SC); for $337.50 sold 500 ac on branch of Ferguson's Cr of Tygar R; border: S-William Prewett and vacant; Peter Smith is agent for estate of late Henry Middleton. Witness Richard Hrabowski and B. G. Bounitheaw. Signed Peter Smith. Wit. oath Feb. 20, 1816 (Charleston Dist) Richard Hrabowski to John Walton. Rec. Mar. 20, 1816

p. 10-11 Dec. 15, 1814 Peter Smith to Ephraim Drummond; a bond of $500; Peter sold Ephraim 500 ac on branch of S Tygar R and Mary Smith, Peter's wife, is "indisposed" and unable to relinquish her dower third of land; so condition of bond is that Peter defend Ephraim's right to land against Mary Smith's dower right, otherwise the bond if forfieted. Witness Nash Roach and V. M. Bounitheau QU. Singed Peter Smith. Wit. oath Dec. 16, 1814 (Charleston, SC) Peter Smith esq to V. M. Bounitheau. Rec. Mar. 20, 1816

p. 11-12 Mar. 14, 1810 Daniel Allen (Spartanburgh) to Ephraim Drummond (same); for $320 sold 320 ac on branches of N fork of Forgerson's Cr of Tygar R; E part of 640 ac grant to William Allen. Witness Jesse Wofford and Isaac Wofford. Signed Daniel Allen. Wit. oath Jan. 8, 1811 Isaac Wofford to Drury McDaniel. Rec. Mar. 20, 1816. Dower renounced Jan. 8, 1811 Sealy Allen to Drury McDaniel

p. 12-13 Jan. 4, 1816 Laban P Poole, sheriff (Spartanburgh) to John Westmoreland; for $3,016 sold 492 ac by resurvey on N side of Enoree R (formerly called Big Cain Break); sale due to writ from Spartanburgh Common Pleas Court "tested" Nov. 9, 1815; sald as property of John Dickie desc for benefit of heirs of desc. Witness Ephraim Roddy esq, S Westmoreland, and Thomas Hannon. Signed Laban P Poole SSD. Wit. oath Mar. 28, 1816 Thomas Hannon to A Benson. Rec. Mar. 28, 1816

p. 13-14 Jan. 4, 1816 John Westmoreland to Laban P Poole, sheriff (Spartanburgh); to secure bond John gave Laban for $3,016 due in two parts: (1) Jan. 1, 1817 and (2) Jan. 1, 1818 sold 592 ac (sic) by resurvey on N side of Enoree R; formerly called Big Cain Break; land was sold by Laban due to writ from Spartanburgh Court as property of John Dickie desc for benefit of heirs; Condition: sale void if John pays bond. Witness Ephraim Roddy esq and Thomas Hannon. Signed John Westmoreland. Wit. oath Mar. 28, 1816 Thomas Hannon to A Benson. Rec. Mar, 28, 1816

p. 14-15 Dec. 18, 1815 William Camp (York Dist) to Joseph Camp; for $1,000 sold 567 ac on Cherokee Cr. Witness Casper Webber and Thomas Camp. Signed Wm Camp. Wit. oath Mar. 22, 1816 Casper Webber to J Camp. Rec. Apr. 1, 1816

p. 15-16 Dec. 1, 1810 Thomas Hadden (Spartanburgh) to Charles McHugh (same); for $300 sold 120 ac; border: S Tygar R, Francis Powers, Nichols, and Widow Powers; part of 538 ac grant Mar. 6, 1786 South Carolina governor to Francis Powers. Witness Samuel McHugh and John McHugh. Signed Thomas Hadden. Wit. oath Apr. 1, 1816 Samuel McHugh to A Benson. Rec. Apr. 1, 1816

p. 16-17 May 14, 1814 David McCoy (Greenville Dist) to John McMeken (Spartanburgh); for $480 sold 233 ac on S Tygar R. Witness James Lewis and Alexander McMakin. Signed David McCoy. Wit. oath Apr. 20, 1815 Alexander McMakin to Michl Miller. Rec. Apr. 4, 1816. Dower renounced Jan. 30, 1815 (Greenville Dist) Susannah McCoy to Robert Cook JQ

p. 17-18 Mar. 11, 1816 Lewis Turner (Spartanburgh) to David Mosteller (Lincoln Co, NC); for $550 sold 317 ac in two tracts: (1) 242 ac on Lawson's fork of Pacolett R; part of 392 ac grant to William Turner; and (2) 75 ac on Buck Cr of Lawson's fork; grant to Lewis Turner. Witness Hugh Means and Samuel Sentell. Signed Lewis Turner's mark. Wit. oath Mar. 11, 1816 Hugh Means to Thomas Poole. Rec. Apr. 6, 1816. Dower renounced Mar. 18, 1816 Ann Turner to Abner Benson

p. 18-19 Jan. (blank), 1816 Charles Stewart, James Stewart, and Sarah Stewart (Spartanburgh) to William Waldrop (or Waldrip) (same); for $230 sold 84 ac at mouth of Canon Br; border: Niel's Still Br, Long Br and Waldrup. Witness A Casey and Hillen Waldrup. Signed Charles L Stewart, James Stewart, and Sarah's mark. Wit. oath (not dated) Hillen Waldrup to Burrell Bobo. Rec. Apr. 8, 1816. Dower renounced Feb. 22, 1816 Rebekah Stewart, wife of Charles, to Burrell Bobo

p. 19-20 Mar. 28, 1814 Miles Nash (SC) to James Lanford (SC); for $2 sold 8½ ac; border: James Lanford sr; part of where Miles Nash lives. Witness John Lanford and Joseph Barnett. Signed Miles Nash. Wit. oath Aug. 11, 1815 Miles Nash to John Dean. Rec. Apr. 8, 1816

p. 20-21 Feb. 3, 1813 David Owens (Spartanburgh) to James Lanford (same); for $50 sold 50 ac on branch of Two Mile Cr of Enoree R; border: James Lanford, John Dean, and a road. Witness Thomas Knighton and Jonathan Crow. Signed David Owens' mark. Wit. oath Aug. 11, 1815 Thomas Knighton to John Dean. Rec. Apr, 8, 1816

p. 21-22 Oct. 4, 1815 George Storey (Buncomb Co, NC) to Jean (or Jane) Foster (Spartanburgh); for $40 sold 20 ac; border: Henry Foster, Joseph Nesbitt, and John Ison; part of grant to George Storey; where Jean Foster lives; includes boundary George "laid off for him" by Mr. Richard Thomson. Witness James Storey, Henry Storey, Joseph Kelso, and Wm N Morrow. Signed George Storey. Wit. oath Oct. 7, 1815 James Storey to Samuel Archibald. Rec. Apr. 9, 1816

p. 22-23 Mar. 12, 1816 Paul Cox and William Ramsey (Spartanburgh) to Alexander Wilson (same); for $36 sold 134 ac on Clear Cr of S Pacolett R; border: Galt's road and Bowmer; E side of two tracts; where Alexander Wilson lives. Witness John Camron and Willey S Brown. Signed Paul Cox and W Ramsey. Wit. oath Mar. 12, 1816 Willey S Brown to Ephm Lewis. Rec. Apr. 9, 1816

p. 23-24 Mar. 14, 1814 Hugh Ewing (Spartanburgh) to Samuel L Ewing; "has taken into consideration to give" 70 ac on N side of N Pacolet R; part of where Hugh Ewing lives; sold by James Hooper to Henry Ewing. Witness John Ridings, Anny Ewing, and Patsey Ewing. Signed Hugh Ewing. Wit. oath Mar. 1, 1815 John Ridings to Wm Kelso. Rec. Apr. 9, 1816

p. 24-25 Feb. 24, 1816 Gilbert Bowman sr (Spartanburgh) to Gilbert Bowman jr (same); for $120 sold 20 ac on N side of N Pacolate R; border: Jackson and Gilbert Bowman jr; balance of tract that Gilbert Bowman sr gave to Gilbert Bowman jr. Witness Curtis Caldwell and George Welch. Signed Gilbert Bowman sr's mark. Wit. oath Mar. 20, 1816 George Welch to Wm Kelso. Rec. Apr. 16, 1816

p. 25-26 Mar. 28, 1813 William Holloway (Spartanburgh) to Nimrod Horton (same); for $100 sold 100 ac on waters of Ashworth Cr; border: Camp; part of 555 ac grant Oct. 6, 1788 to Crainshaw Camp. Witness James Walker and Leurey (or Lewsey) Bostick. Signed Wm Holloway. Wit. oath Jan. 26, 1815 James Walker to Joseph Camp. Rec. Apr. 17, 1816

p. 26-27 Apr. 8, 1816 William N Miller (Spartanburgh) to John Patton (same); for $833 sold 833 ac on S side of Middle Tyger R; border: James Miller and William Caldwell. Witness John P Evins and John D Palmer. Signed W. N. Miller. Wit. oath Apr. 8, 1816 John P Evins to John Collins. Rec. Apr. 18, 1816

p. 27-28 Dec. 3, 1810 John Oldhants to Jesse Prichard; for $75 sold 160 ac on Ashworth Cr; border: Thomas Wyatt; part of 555 ac grant to Crainshaw Camp. Witness Joseph Camp and Joseph Richards. Signed John Oldhants' mark. Wit. oath May 6, 1811 Joseph Camp to Joshua Richards. Rec. Apr. 22, 1816

p. 28-29 Oct. 9, 1815 Burrel Bobo to Randolph Palmer; for (money omitted) sold 300 ac on Dutchman's Cr and N side of Tygar R; border: Joseph Gowen's old line, old road formerly Blackstock's road, and Sanders (near the widow's house). "note: Blank relinquishment of dower on above deed". Witness John M Taylor and John Grist. Signed Burrel Bobo. Wit. oath Jan. 22, 1816 John M Taylor to M Casey. Rec. May 1, 1816

p. 29-30 Oct. 6, 1815 Burrel Bobo to John Withers; for $400 sold 200 ac on N side Enoree R; border: NW-Falling Br, Joseph Gowing, and R Sanders; "Note Enoree R should be Tygar". Witness John M Taylor and Peter Laggin. Signed Burrel Bobo. Wit. oath Jan. 22, 1816 John M Taylor to M Casey. Rec. May 1, 1816. Dower renounced Oct. 21, 1815 Elizabeth Bobo to J (F?) Grimke

p. 30-33 Oct. 12, 1815 Caleb Clarke (Fairfield Dist) and wife Julia Briscoe Clark, late Julia Briscoe Ross, widow of William W Ross (late of Lancaster Dist) desc, brother of James Ross (York Dist) desc and Alexander Love Ross (Mecklenburg Co, NC), brother of James Ross to Smith Lipscomb (Spartanburgh); for $2,000 (paid to Alexander L Ross) and $1 (paid to Caleb and Julia Clark) sold 1,800 ac on Miller's fork on N side of Thickety Cr of Broad R; 63 ac excepted that was taken by older survey; see plat made by Richard Thompson; grant Sept. 18, 1785 to Vardry McBee who sold Jun. 1, 1797 to James Ross; Caleb and Julia Clark don't warrant the deed. Witness John Buchanan jr, Albert Allison, and George Wood. Signed Caleb Clark, Julia B Clarke, and A. L. Ross. Wit. oath Apr. 9, 1816 George Wood to Thomas Poole. Rec. Apr, 9, 1816. Dower renounced Jan. 8, 1816 (Fairfield Dist) Julia B Clarke to James Elliott. Dower renounced Oct. 16, 1815 (York Dist) Rachel Ross, wife of Alexander, to Wm Hill

p. 33-34 Mar. 20, 1813 James Kilgore (Greenville Dist) to Benjamin Wood (Spartanburgh); for $200 sold 200 ac on both sides of Maple Swamp Cr of S Tygar R; border: Erasmus Nobles, Mill Shoal, Wm Miller, and Burns; part of 1,000 ac grant to Pennel Wood and "part to Daniel Woolbanks". Witness Bannister Stone and Charles Dun. Signed James Kilgore. Wit. oath Aug. 23, 1813 Charles Dun to James Hammett. Rec. May 6, 1816

p. 34-35 Feb. 17, 1816 James P Means (Spartanburgh) to James Ham (same); for $80 sold 120 ac on branches of Willy's fork; plat attached shows border: James Hamm, widow Mays, Wofford road, and Thomas Compton. Witness Isaac Thornton and James Moore. Signed J. P. Means. Wit. oath Apr. 9, 1816 James Moore to Samuel Archibald. Rec. May 6, 1816

p. 35-36 Feb. 1, 1808 John McCollester (Greenville Dist) to William Glenn (Laurens Dist); for $400 sold 202 ac between Enoree R and Abnor's Cr; border: Tyrce Glenn; part of 500 ac grant Oct. 15, 1784 to Daniel Huger esq. Witness James Hammett and John Herring. Signed John McCollester's mark. Wit. oath Feb. 1, 1808 James Hammett to James Kilgore. Rec. May 6, 1816. Dower renounced Feb. 1, 1808 Nancy McCollester to James Kilgore

p. 36-37 Apr. 20, 1816 Elizabeth M Leger and Elizabeth L Hutcherson (Charleston Dist) by attorney Robert Creswell (Laurens Dist) to Richard Thompson (Spartanburgh); for $90 sold 90 ac on branch of Fairforrest Cr; border: Locock; N part of 250 ac grant to Peter Leger and survey Dec. 22, 1772 for David Maul. Witness Absolom Lancaster and James W Cooper. Signed Elizabeth M Leger and Elizabeth L Hutcherson by Robert Creswell, attorney. Wit. oath Apr. 12, 1816 James W Cooper to Danl White. Rec. May 6, 1816

p. 37-38 Apr. 12, 1816 Elizabeth M Leger and Elizabeth L Hutcherson (Charleston Dist) to James Cooper (Spartanburgh); for $80 paid to attorney Robert Creswell sold 80 ac on Kelso's Cr of Fairforrest Cr; border: Wm R Smith, James Cooper, and Absalom Lancaster; part of 250 ac survey for David Maul and "elapsed by and granted to" Peter Leger and devised to Elizabeth M Leger and Elizabeth L Hutcherson. Witness Absolom Lancaster and Richard Thomson. Signed Elizabeth M Leger and Elizabeth L Hutcherson by Robert Creswell, attorney. Wit. oath Apr. 12, 1816 Richard Thomson to Danl White. Rec. May 6, 1816

p. 38-39 Mar. 5, 1816 William Arnold, James Arnold, Willis Arnold, Jonathan Crook, and Rich Shackelford, executors and heirs of John Arnold desc's estate (Spartanburgh), to Caleb Allen (same); for $170 sold 164 ac on Jord's Cr of Tygar R; border: Nathaniel Woodruff and Joseph Woodruff. Witness Joseph Crook, William Crook, and Jeremiah Crook. Signed William Arnold, James Arnold, Willis Arnold, Jonathan Crook, and Rich Shackelford. Wit. oath Mar. 30, 1816 Joseph Crook to John Collins. Rec. May 11, 1816. Dower renounced Mar. 6, 1816 (Laurens Dist) Nancy Arnold, wife of John, to Thomas Wright

p. 39-40 May 14, 1816 Labon P Poole, sheriff (Spartanburgh) to George Rowland (same); for $134 sold 130 ac; border: William Turner and Means; sale due to writ from Richland Dist Common Pleas Court (in Columbia) first Monday in Mar. 1816 suit Samuel Todd vs James Barrett; James Barrett assessed $45.25 and costs. Witness Mathew Seay and Nimrod E Benson. Signed Laban P Poole SSD. Wit. oath May 14, 1816 Mathew Seay to Danl White. Rec. May 14, 1816

p. 40-41 Apr. 17, 1816 Daniel Wilbanks (Spartanburgh) to John McCarter (same); for $7.50 sold (ac omitted) on Middle Tygar R; border: James Reynolds and Mary McMakin. Witness Ephraim Roddy and Thomas Hannon. Signed Danl Wilbanks. Wit. oath Apr. 27, 1816 Thomas Hannon to A Benson. Rec. May 16, 1816

p. 41-42 Apr. 9, 1808 Charles McAbee (Spartanburgh) to Jesse Matthis (same); for $117 sold 120 ac on S side of Pacolett R and on Hurrican Br; border: Robinson's Spring Br; W end of 671 ac grant Oct. 3, 1791 to Henry McCray and part of grant to Charles McAbee. Witness Elisha McAbee, William McAbee jr, and William

Cannon. Signed Charles McAbee. Wit. oath Nov. 7, 1809 Elisha McAbee to Hugh Means. Rec. May 22, 1816

p. 42-43 Apr. 20, 1816 Elizabeth Evins and John P Evins, administrators of Alexander Evins desc, to John Ballenger (Spartanburgh); for $135 sold 118 ac on branches of N Tygar R; border: James Ballinger; part of grant to Wm Ford. Witness Alexander McKings, Benjamin Farmer, and Nathan Bankston. Signed J. P. Evins and Elizabeth's mark. Wit. oath Apr. 20, 1816 Benjamin Farmer to Henry Turner. Rec. May 22, 1816

p. 43-44 Dec. 16, 1814 Garlen Calwell and wife Elizabeth (Spartanburgh) to Polly Hammett (same); for $45 sold 58 ac on Harrican Br of Pacolete R; border: Quarles and a waggon road. Witness Jesse Mathis and Samuel Parks. Signed Garlen and Elizabeth Calwell's marks. Wit. oath Jan. 19, 1815 Samuel Parks to Jno H Jones. Rec. May 23, 1816

p. 44-45 Jan. 18, 1813 Lacy McAbee (Spartanburgh) to son Elisha McAbee (same); for love and affection give 102 ac on N side of Lawson's fork; border: Richard Thomson and Cold Water Br; includes where Elisha McAbee lives; E end of 450 ac grant Jun. 2, 1772 to Lucy McAbee. Witness Charles McAbee and William McAbee. Signed Lucy McAbee's mark. Wit. oath Mar. 1, 1813 Charles McAbee to Danl White. Rec. May 25, 1816

p. 45-46 Nov. 22, 1815 John Low (Spartanburgh) to Mary Dewberry; for (money omitted) relinquished rights to 50 ac on waters of Pacolette R; border: Rosanna Low, Mary Dewberry, Samuel Turner, Reuben Warren, and Buck Br. Witness Richard Proctor and John Low jr. Signed John Low. Wit. oath Apr. 13, 1816 John Low jr to Henry Turner. Rec. Jun. 3, 1816

p. 46-47 Feb. 7, 1816 Samuel Turner (Spartanburgh) to Mary Dewberry (same); for $30 sold 50 ac; border: Mary Dewberry's Spring, widow Smith, and John Low; "lying in two tracts" (1) John Low's and (2) Samuel Turner's. Witness John Low sr and John Low jr. Signed Samuel Turner. Wit. oath Apr. 13, 1816 John Low jr to Henry Turner. Rec. Jun. 3, 1816

p. 47-48 Oct. 20, 1809 Levi Lee (Spartanburgh) to Caleb Jones (same); for $63 sold (1) 284 ac on waters of Lawson's fork; Levi Lee's part of estate of Basel Lee desc; grant to John Holcom; (2) 100 ac(?) on S side of Lawson's fork; Levi Lee's part of grant to Edward Dickson; (3) 60 ac; border: Harrison; Levi's part of grant to Desken Grant; (4) 100 ac on S side of Lawson's fork; Levi's part of land; (5) 100 ac; border: George Parkison and Randolph D Brown; Levi's part of land; total if all of Levi Lee's part of Basel Lee's estate. Witness Jonathan Low sr and John H Jones. Signed Levi Low. Wit. oath Jun. 3, 1816 Jno H Jones to Danl White. Rec. Jun. 3, 1816

p. 48-49 Feb. 28, 1806 John Thomas and wife Margaret (St. Clair Co, Ill) to Daniel Wilbanks (Union Dist); for $30 sold (ac omitted) on McElwain's Cr; part of 540 ac grant to John McElwain sr; all of land of late John McElwain sr desc in Union and Spartanburgh Dists. Witness Robert Thomas, Samuel Allen, and James D Thomas. Signed J and Margret Thomas. Wit. oath Feb. 28, 1816 (St. Clair Co, Ill) Robert Thomas to Risdon Moore. Rec. Jun. 10, 1816

p. 49 Oct. 19, 1815 Moses Tapp (Spartanburgh) to Benjamin High jr and Thomas Bomar (same); for $100 sold 300 ac on waters of Fairforrest Cr; "above" waggon road from Spartanburgh Court House to Greenville Court House; former owner was Peter Legon and land was sold due to an execution to (omitted). Witness George R Hunter and Benjamin High. Signed Moses Tapp. Wit. oath Apr. 16, 1816 Benjamin High to John Chapman. Rec. Jun. 11, 1816

p. 49-51 Dec. 22, 1813 John Couch (Spartanburgh) to Joel Lewis (same); for $150 sold 200 ac on both sides Holston Cr of S Pacolett R; border: Charleston Road, John Sloan, and Samuel Evans; part of two grants to (1) Thomas Pellorrow (or Pellarow) and (2) Robert Harper; where John Couch lives. Witness James Roddy and Frances Lewis. Signed John Couch's mark. Wit. oath Jan. 5, 1814 Frances Lewis to James Young. Rec. Jun. 12, 1816. Dower renounced Jan. 5, 1814 Winny Couch to James Young

p. 51-52 May 7, 1816 James Ballinger, Sarah Barrett, Henry Hutcheson, Richard Foster, William Foster, John M Collins, Thomas Foster, and Joel Foster (all of Spartanburgh) to Polly Lewis (same); for $1,050 sold 461 ac on Lawson's fork of Pacolett R. Witness Pressley Ballinger and Francis M Lewis. Signed William Foster, J. W. Collins, H Hutcheson, Thomas Foster, Richard Foster, Joel Foster, James Ballinger, and Sarah's mark. Wit. oath Jun. 12, 1816 Francis M Lewis to A Benson. Rec. Jun. 12, 1816. Dower renounced Jun. 1, 1816 Nancy Foster, wife of William, Edy Collins, wife of John, Judy Ballinger, wife of James, and Elizabeth Hutcheson, wife of Henry to James Young

p. 52-53 May 30, 1816 Drury Hutcheson (Spartanburgh) to Polly Lewis (same); for $300 sold 97½ ac on Twitty's Br; border: Meadow Cr. Witness Francis M Lewis and Pressley Ballinger. Signed Drury Hutcheson's mark. Wit. oath Jun. 12, 1816 Pressley Ballinger to A Benson. Rec. Jun. 12, 1816. Dower renounced Jun. 1, 1816 Mourning Hutcheson to James Young

p. 53-54 Mar. 19, 1806 John Walker (Greenville Dist) to James Wilson jr (Spartanburgh); $351 sold 404 ac on waters of S Tygar R in Greenville and Spartanburgh Dists; border: Forohock(?); part of 1,000 ac grant to John Thomas jr. Witness Ism Foster. Signed John Walker and Mary McMakin(sic)'s mark. Wit. oath Jun. 15, 1816 Ism Foster to John Chapman. Rec. Jun. 15, 1816. Dower renounced Mar. 18, 1806 Martha Walker, wife of John, to Ism Foster

p. 54-55 Feb. 19, 1810 Hugh Ewing (Spartanburgh) to Nathan Pettit (same); for $250 sold (1) 205 ac on both sides Molley's Cr; except 30 ac sold to George Campbell; part of grant Jun. 6, 1785 Gov. William Moultry(sic) to John Cleaton; and (2) 20 ac; border: John Cleaton, James Alexander, and James Mayson; part of grant Jun. 6, 1785 to Robert Godgion. Witness Will Camron, Samuel L Ewing, and Joseph Wilson. Signed Hugh Ewing. Wit. oath Mar. 13, 1810 Joseph Wilson to Andrew Fuguson. Rec. Jun. 22, 1816

p. 55-56 Nov. 27, 1813 Alexander Austin (Spartanburgh) to James White (same); for $100 sold 100 ac on E side of Lawson's fork; border: Cabbin Br, Wm Bishop, Abraham Markley, and James White. Witness Mathew Leay (or Seay) and William Morgan. Signed Alexr Austin. Wit. oath Nov. 27, 1813 Mathew Leay to James Young. Rec. Jul. 1, 1816

p. 56-57 Jan. 3, 1805 Thomas Jones (Barrow Co, Ky) and Henry Jones (Warren Co, Ky) to David Jones (Spartanburgh); for 50£ Virginia money sold (1) 421 ac and (2) 175 ac part of 350 ac. Witness William Toly and Mary Toly. Signed Thomas Jones and Henry Jones. Wit. oath Jan. 7, 1805 (Warren Co, Ky) William Toly to Robert Wallace. Rec. Jul. 27, 1815

p. 57-58 Nov. 14, 1815 Francis Littlejohn (Union Dist) to Isaac Dill (Spartanburgh); for $385 sold 130½ ac by resurvey on both sides Beaverdam Cr of Thickety Cr; grant May 1, 1786 Gov. William

Moultrie to Abraham Buy. Witness Smith Lipscomb and Joseph Dill. Signed Francis Littlejohn. Wit. oath Nov. 21, 1815 Smith Lipscomb to John Lipscomb. Rec. Jul. 29, 1816. Dower renounced Nov. 21, 1815 Elizabeth Littlejohn to John Lipscomb

p. 58-59 May 2, 1811 Thomas Hill (Spartanburgh) to Charles Crittendon (or Crillindon) (same); for $100 sold 100 ac; "laid out" by Christopher Golikely. Witness John Lipscomb and Bartlet Wright. Signed Thomas Hill's mark. Wit. oath May 2, 1816 John Lipscomb to William Reid. Rec. Jul. 31, 1816

p. 59-60 Sept. 5, 1811 David Jones (Spartanburgh) to Charles Crittendon (same); for $30 sold 24 ac; "laid out" by Joseph Kemp; border: N-Jones, NE-Deasence(?), S-unknown. Witness Aaron Wilkins and Benjamin Vinson. Signed David Jones. Wit. oath Jul. 18, 1812 Aaron Wilkins to John Lipscomb. Rec. Jul. 31, 1816

p. 60-61 Oct. (blank), 1814 Charles Crittenden (Spartanburgh) to Aaron Wilkins (same); for $300 sold 204 ac at head of Green's Cr of Pacolete R; border: E-John Rochell (bought from Charles Crittenden), S-Johnson Bryant (bought from Bartlett Wright), W-Griffin Carter, and N-Aaron Wilkins (bought from Charles Crittenden); in three parts: (1) 24 ac "laid out" by Joseph Camp and granted to David Jones; (2) 100 ac "laid out" by Christopher Golikely and granted to David Jones; and (3) 80 ac part of tract "laid out" by Jesse Connel and granted to James Brown sr. Witness William Brown and Cristian (or Crystian) Morris. Signed Charles Crittenden. Wit. oath Jan. 6, 1816 William Brown to John Lipscomb. Rec. Jul. 31, 1816

p. 61-62 Dec. 16, 1814 Denny Anderson (Spartanburgh) to Hiram Bennett (same); for $10 sold 221½ ac; part of 663 ac on Enoree R and Anderson's Cr; survey Apr. 8, 1801 by Jas Wofford and granted Jul. 22, 1801. Witness Edward Burnett, John Crocker, and Westwood Ford. Signed Denny Anderson. Wit. oath Dec. 17, 1814 Westwood Ford to David Moore. Rec. Aug. 5, 1816. Dower renounced Apr. 22, 1815 Elizabeth Anderson to Drury McDaniel

p. 62-63 Nov. 30, 1814 Amos Austill (Spartanburgh) to William Lipscomb (same); for $600 sold (1) 200 ac on both sides Thickety Cr; border: N-Smith Lipscomb and W-David Lipscomb; part of 400 ac grant to Thomas Nicols; (2) 30 ac on both sides Thickety Cr; border: W-Amos Austill, NE-David Lipscomb, E-William Wilkins, where Joseph Austill formerly lives, and"the main Road"; grant in 1792 to William Wilkins. Witness Patterson Thomson and Moses Williams. Signed Amos Austill. Wit. oath Nov. 30, 1814 Patterson Thomson to John Lipscomb. Rec. Aug. 5, 1816. Dower renounced Dec. 17, 1814 Lucy Austill to John Lipscomb

p. 63 Mar. 16, 1816 William Austin (Greenville Dist) to William Nantz (Union Dist); for $200 sold 97 ac; border: Robert McCollem, Robert Wood, Elisha Bomar, and Timmons. Witness Elisha Bomar and John Bomar. Signed Wm Austin. Wit. oath Aug. 4, 1816 Elisha Bomar to Wm Reid. Rec. Aug. 5, 1816

p. 63-64 Dec. 16, 1815 George Wilkins (Spartanburgh) to John Wilkins (same); for $550 sold 205 ac on waters of Thickety Cr; bequeathed by will of William Wilkins desc (Spartanburgh) to George Wilkins. Witness Robert Wilkins and Richard Thomson. Signed George Wilkins. Wit. oath Aug. 5, 1816 Robert Wilkins to Wm Reid. Rec. Aug. 5, 1816. Dower renounced May 24, 1816 Elizabeth Wilkins to John Lipscomb

p. 64-65 Jan. 11, 1816 Samuel Miller (Spartanburgh) to John Fielder (same); for $150 sold 100 ac on branch of S Tygar R and N side of S Tygar R; border: Thomas Alexander and vacant. Witness

Thomas Dean and Isaac S(or L) Pebroorth. Signed Samuel Miller. Wit. oath Jul. 27, 1816 Thomas Dean to James Hammett. Rec. Aug. 5, 1816

p. 65-66 Feb. 27, 1816 William Arnold (Spartanburgh) to James Mason (same); for $280 sold 70 ac on S side of Floyd's Br of Ferguson's Cr; border: W-J Skinner, S-P Arnold, E-S Floyd, and N-W Grant. Witness John Henry and Benjamin Robuck. Signed William Arnold. Wit. oath Aug. 3, 1816 Benjamin Robuck to James Hammett. Rec. Aug. 5, 1816

p. 66-67 Jun. 21, 1816 John Farrow (Spartanburgh) to Aaron Casey, William Ward, and Robert Creswell; "in persuance of agreement entered into by John Farrow to compromise a bill filed against John in Washington Equity Court for John's wife, Mary, by her next frund(sic) Bordywine Waters" and for $5 sold to Aaron, William, and Robert, in trust: 270 ac where Mary Farrow lives; border: Rachael Farrow, James Cleton, Benjamin Stone, and Enoree R; and sold 7 Negroes: Will about 24 years old, Man (or Mare) about 17 years old, Sampson about 12 years old, Frank about 12 years old, Jacob about 10 years old, Led about 8 years old, and Simon about 9 months old; 3 horses: Dave, Doctor, and Bedford, a mare called Flying filly, all cattle at the plantation, all hogs, half of sheep, a shot gun, all plantation tools anf farming utensils, carriage with a new seat of harness "which I am to furnish by next Christmas" has good a quality as the former set, 3 bee gums, a flax wheel, 2 spinning wheels, cards, and loom, 6 featherbeds and furniture, 4 bedsteads, all household and kitchen furniture, corn fodder, wheat, meat, and the crop now growing on the plantation; above sold to pay (1) half of debts owed by John Farrow except demand which Euphamia Brown may have against John after deducting half that is due to John, (2) for Mary Farrow's use during her lifetime, and (3) for benefit of Mary's five children after Mary's death: Thomas, John, Mary, Sarah, Hannah, and their heirs; John Farrow advanced to son John $106 and it is counted as part of his share of above. Witness Thomas M Bragg and William M Farrow. Signed John Farrow. Wit. oath Jul. 31, 1816 Thomas M Bragg to Burrell Bobo. Rec. Aug. 5, 1816

p. 67-68 Dec. 16, 1812 Jesse Burton (Spartanburgh) to Edward Fowler (same); for $200 sold 100 ac on N side of S Pacolete R; part of grant to James Alexander who sold to Thos Burton who sold to Jesse Burton. Witness Demcy Fowler and Hubard Quarles. Signed Jesse Burton. Wit. oath Dec. 17, 1812 Demcy Fowler to Andrew Ferguson. Rec. Aug. 5, 1816

p. 68-69 May 10, 1816 James Cook jr to Samuel Jamison; for $170 sold 85 ac; border: J Vernon and Jeffen's Br; grant to William Savage. Witness Joshua Tapp and Alla Connell. Signed James Crook. Wit. oath Jun. 8, 1816 Joshua Tapp to Thomas Poole. Rec. Aug. 5, 1816

p. 69 Oct. 10, 1814 Edward Fowler to Sarah Camp (Rutherford Co, NC); for $300 sold 100 ac on N side of S Pacolett R; part of grant to James Alexander who sold to Thomas Burton who sold to Jesse Burton who sold to Edward Fowler. Witness Hugh Ewing and Isaac Bishop. Signed Edward Fowler and Martha's mark. Wit. oath Oct. 10, 1814 Hugh Ewing to Wm Kelso. Rec. Aug. 5, 1816

p. 69-70 Jun. 14, 1816 John Wood (Spartanburgh) to John Means (same); for $300 sold 160 ac on S side of S Tygar R; border: English and Miller; part of grant Feb. 4, 1788 to John Brown; except "a part" border: Miller, Still House Br, and Ottey (or Otts). Witness Patrick Hoy and John Ward. Signed John Ward. Wit. oath Aug. 5, 1816 Patrick Hoy to James Hammett. Rec. Aug. 5, 1816

p. 70-71 Jul. 16, 1816 Sarah Camp (Spartanburgh) to two sons Albert and George Camp, now minors (same); for good offices and other reasons give (at Sarah's death) 100 ac on S side of S Pacolett R; border: Thos Burton; part of grant to Jas Alexander who sold to Thomas Burton who sold to Jesse Burton who sold to Edward Fowler who sold to Sarah Camp. Witness Rebecah Turner and James Whitten. Signed Sarah Camp's mark. Wit. oath Aug. 5, 1816 James Whitten to Danl White. Rec. Aug. 12, 1816

p. 71-72 Jan. 24, 1810 Gabriel Benson, late sheriff (Spartanburgh) to Robert Miller, agent for James Miller; for $360 sold 1,500 ac in two parts: (1) 1,000 ac and (2) 500 ac between S and Middle Tygar R; both parts granted to Gen. Isaac Huger; sale due to writ from Charleston Common Pleas Court suit Jacob Willimon vs administrators of Gen. Isaac Huger desc. Witness Laban P Poole and Vincent Bennett. Signed Gal Benson late SSD. Wit. oath Aug. 12, 1816 Laban P Poole to A Benson. Rec. Aug. 12, 1816

p. 72 Mar. 10, 1816 Charles McAbee (Spartanburgh) to Muse Tollison (same); for $100 sold 100 ac on waters of Pacolete R; border: Lindsey and Jesse Matthews. Witness John D Palmer and William N Miller. Signed Charles McAbee. Wit. oath Aug. 12, 1816 John D Palmer to A Benson. Rec. Aug. 12, 1816

p. 72-73 Feb. 5, 1816 John ONeill (Spartanburgh) to Muse Tollison (same); for $200 sold 200 ac on Mill Cr of Tygar R; known as hills furnace tract; formerly border: all vacant; part of grant Jun. 4, 1772 to John Snoddy who sold to Henry Hays "and so forth". Witness John D Palmer and Charlott Briant. Signed John Oneill. Wit. oath Apr. 12, 1816 John D Palmer to A Benson. Rec. Aug. 12, 1816

p. 73-74 Aug. 16, 1816 Aaron Templeman (Spartanburgh) to Lewis Cannon (same); for $200 sold 150 ac on both sides Thickety Cr; border: Rolla Horton, John Low, and Pruett. Witness Allen Lancaster and Abner Benson. Signed Aaron Templeman's mark. Wit. oath Aug. 16, 1816 Allen Lancaster to A Benson. Rec. Aug. 16, 1816

p. 74-75 Aug. 17, 1816 Jordan Odam (Spartanburgh) to William Odam; to secure a note Jordan gave William promising to pay $500 in 10 days sold a sorrel horse with ball face about 10 years old, a sorrel horse 6 years old, a ady(?) horse about 20 years old, 3 cows and calves, a bull marked with cross and half cross in right ear and swallow fork in left ear, 7 sheep of same mark, 25 hogs of same mark, 4 feather beds, bedstead and furniture, all household and kitchen furniture, plantation and farming tools, all geese and foul; Condition: sale void if Jordan pays debt in 10 days; promisary note added at bottom of the sale. Witness Abner Benson and Thomas Hannon. Signed Jordan Odam's mark. Wit. oath Aug. 17, 1816 Thomas Hannon to A Benson. Rec. Aug. 17, 1816

p. 75-76 Mar. 12, 1816 (Charleston Dist) Elizabeth M Leger and Elizabeth L Hutcherson (Charleston Dist) to Robert Creswell (Laurens Dist); power of attorney to "look up", resurvey and identify the following: (1) 300 ac in Berkly Co on waters of Little R when surveyed; border: NE, S & SE-John Dickey, SE-unknown, SE-Samuel Henderson, and other sides-vacant; survey Jan. 17, 1772 by Patrick Cunningham DS for George Ancrum and granted to Peter Leger; (2) 200 ac in Craven Co when surveyed on waters of Cain Cr; border: NE-James McGill, SW-Patrick Cunningham, SE-John Caldwell, and other sides-vacant; survey Mar. 17, 1773 by Patrick Cunningham DS for Thomas Carter and granted to Peter Leger; (3) 250 ac in Craven Co when surveyed; on NE side of Reybornes Cr; border: all vacant; survey Feb. 3, 1773 by Jonathan Downs DS for Samuel Dunlap and granted to Peter Leger; (4) 200 ac in Berkly Co when surveyed on waters of

Reyborn's Cr; border: all vacant; survey Jan. 11, 1770 by Patrick Cunningham DS for John McHug and granted to Peter Leger; (5) 150 ac in Craven Co when surveyed on Celsoe's Cr of Fairforrest Cr; border: SW-Robert Hammett, NW-James Hammett, and NE-Locock; survey Dec. 22, 1772 by William Gist DS for David Mault and granted to Peter Leger; (6) 250 ac in Craven Co when surveyed on N side of Saluda R nearly opposite "saluda old town"; border: NE-Wm Linkfield now William Turner, SW-John Dunanan, and other sides vacant; survey Jul. 19, 1769 by John Calwell DS for Peter Leger and granted to Peter Leger; (7) 250 ac in Greenville Co when surveyed on waters of Stephenson's Cr; border: all vacant; survey Mar. 4, 1771 by Patrick Cunningham DS for John McGuger and granted to Peter Leger; (8) 200 ac in Greenville Co when surveyed on branches of Stephenson's Cr; border: NW-Joel Crafford and other sides vacant; survey Apr. 15, 1772 by W Goode DS for Nicholas Minor and granted to Peter Leger; and (9) 4,000 ac in Craven Co when surveyed in St. Mark's Parish; on waters of Buck Cr of Pacolate R; border: N-state line, NE-Benjamin Huger esq, SW-Roberts, and other sides vacant; survey Aug. 5, 1772 by Jas Cook surv. for John Ward; Robert Creswell to prosecute anyone who lives on the land now and is to sell the land. Witness Mrs. B Abbott and William Allen. Signed Elizabeth M Leger and Elizabeth L Hutcherson. Wit. oath Mar. 12, 1816 (Charleston Dist) Mrs. B Abbott and William Allen to H Gray. Rec. Aug. 19, 1816

p. 76-78 Oct. 18, 1814 David Jones (Spartanburgh) to William Patterson (same); for $350 sold 200 ac; border: David Jones Spring Br, Carter, Cammel, William Patterson, and Young Allen. Witness Young Allen and John Vinsent. Signed David Jones. Wit. oath Apr. 29, 1815 YoungAllen to John Lipscomb. Rec. Aug. 24, 1816. Dower renounced Aug. 22, 1816 Ann Jones to John Lipscomb

p. 78-79 Jan. 1, 1811 Sally Bobo to Willis Bobo; for $500 sold 222 ac on S side of Cedar Shoal Cr; border: Farrow's old line, waggon road, Jas Clayton, and Bogan. Witness Spencer Bobo and Chaney Bobo. Signed Sally Bobo. Wit. oath Aug. 26, 1816 Chaney Bobo to M Casey. Rec. Aug. 26, 1816

p. 79-80 Jan. 23, 1811 Sally Bobo to Chaney Bobo; for $500 sold 215 ac on N side Cedar Shoal Cr; border: Farrow's old line and Burrel Bobo. Witness Spencer Bobo and Willis Bobo. Signed Sally Bobo. Wit. oath Aug. 26, 1816 Willis Bobo to M Casey. Rec. Aug. 26, 1816

p. 80-81 Apr. 8, 1815 Lucy Fowler (Spartanburgh) to Barnett Burnett (same); for $100 sold 65 ac on branches of Furguson's Cr of Tygar R. Witness John Paden and F. H. Legg. Signed Lucy Fowler's mark. Wit. oath Apr. 8, 1815 John Paden to James Hammet. Rec. Aug. 30, 1816

p. 81-82 Aug. 26, 1816 David Jones jr, heir of David Jones sr desc (Spartanburgh), to William Patterson (same); for $100 sold 296 ac(sic) half of (1) 421 ac and (2) 175 ac that is part of 350 ac. Witness Ephraim Roddy and William Hunt. Signed David Jones. Wit. oath Aug. 30, 1816 William Hunt to A Benson. Rec. Aug. 30, 1816

p. 82-83 Jan. 15, 1815 (Laurens Dist) William Glen (Laurens Dist) to Tyrce Glen (Spartanburgh); for $400 sold 202 ac between Enoree R and Abner Cr; border: Tyrce Glen; part of 500 ac grant Oct. 15, 1784 to Daniel Huger esq. Witness John Cook and Garland A Glen. Signed Wm Glen. Wit. oath Mar. 4, 1816 (Laurens Dist) Garland A Glen to Jas McMahin. Rec. Sept. 2, 1816. Dower renounced Apr. 27, 1816 Mary Glen to William Pollard

p. 83-84 Jul. 13, 1816 Edward Bomar, John Wood, Robert Wood, and Edmond Wood (Spartanburgh) to William Pollard (same); for

$76 sold 50 ac on branch of Lawson's fork; border: Jabez Galt, John Collins, Moultrie, and William Pollard. Witness Elisha Bomar and William E Wood. Signed Edward Bomar, John Wood, Robert Wood, and Edmund Wood. Wit. oath Sept. 2, 1816 Elisha Bomar to James Young. Rec. Sept. 2, 1816

p. 84-85 Oct. 19, 1815 Jonathan Low (Spartanburgh) to Samuel Millwood (same); for $25 sold 80 ac on N side of Pacolette R; border: John Low and Thomas Wyatt. Witness Shadrick Prewet and John Pruit. Signed Jonathan Low. Wit. oath Sept. 2, 1816 John Pruit to Henry Turner. Rec. Sept. 2, 1816

p. 85-86 Apr. 18, 1788 George Turner (Spartanburgh) to Richard Turner (same); for 5£ sold 140 ac on S side of Pacolete R; border: mouth of Cherokee Cr. Witness George Headen and Aaron Templeman. Signed George Turner. Wit. oath Sept. 2, 1816 Aaron Templeman to James Young. Rec. Sept. 2, 1816

p. 86-87 Jun. 3, 1811 Henry Golightly (Spartanburgh) to Shands Golightly (same); for $500 sold 234 ac on waters of Dutchman's Cr; border: William Smith, Williford, and Elsworth Moore; grant of 200 ac(sic) Nov. 7, 1785 to John Shands and part of two other grants: (1) 456 ac granted Nov. 6, 1786 to Britain Williford and (2) 240 ac granted Jan. 21, 1785 to Britain Williford. Witness James Gossett and Christi Golightly. Signed Henry Golightly. Wit. oath Sept. 2, 1816 Christi Golightly to William Reid. Rec. Sept. 2, 1816

p. 87-88 Jan. 27, 1815 John Allen sr (Spartanburgh) to Fountain Mosely (same); for $150 sold 38 ac on branch of Delden's Cr; border: Fountain Mosely; plat attached; W end of 671 ac grant Nov. 18, 1786 to Benjamin Busey. Witness Daniel McKie and James Page. Signed John Allen sr. Wit. oath Dec. 12, 1815 James Page to Samuel Woodruff. Rec. Sept. 3, 1816

p. 88-89 Aug. 9, 1816 Caleb May (Spartanburgh) to Henry Smith (same); for $700 sold 510 ac on branches of Mill Cr of Tygar R; known "by" Crossroads; border: NW-Foster and McKiely (or Kirby), NE-Robert Love, and SE-Blackstock Road; plat attached shows also on both sides of road to Pooleville. Witness Daniel Wilbanks and Reddick Rutland. Signed Caleb May. Wit. oath Sept. 3, 1816 Reddick Rutland to A Benson. Rec. Sept. 3, 1816. Dower renounced Sept. 3, 1816 Martha May to Abner Benson

p. 89-90 Jul. 20, 1816 Micajah Lindsey (Monroe Co, Miss) to Thomas Price (Spartanburgh); for $70 sold 65 ac on NW side of Bethel Meeting house Br of Enoree R; border: N-Hamby and Reeves, S-Amos Pilgrim and Elijah Hendrix, and W-William Moore. Witness Thomas Woodruff III and William L Allen. Signed Micajah Lindsey. Wit. oath Aug. 29, 1816 William L Allen to Samuel Woodruff. Rec. Sept. 5, 1816

p. 90-91 Dec. 16, 1815 James Smith (Union Dist) to William R Smith (Spartanburgh); for $1,500 sold 940 ac on both sides Lawson's fork of Pacolett R; border: William Bagwell. Witness James Bagwell and Henry White. Signed James Smith. Wit. oath Dec. 10, 1815 James Bagwell to Danl White. Rec. Sept. 7, 1816

p. 91-92 Jan. 7, 1811 Reddick Rutland (Spartanburgh) to Caleb May (same); for $500 sold 480 ac on SW side of Blackstock's Road and on branches of Mill Cr of Tygar R; part of grant Jul. 8, 1774 to Dr Saml Gravil. Witness Fielden Selmon and Thomas Js Foster. Signed Reddick Rutland. Wit. oath Sept. 16, 1816 Fielden Selmon to A Benson. Rec. Sept. 16, 1816. Dower renounced Sept. 3, 1816 Dorthy Rutland to Abner Benson

p. 92-93 Apr. 23, 1808 Joshua Smith (Franklin Co, NC) to Reddick Rutland (Spartanburgh); for $1,000 sold 1,000 ac on waters of Beaverdam fork of Fairforrest Cr of Tygar R; except 60 ac given to Richard Foster including his plantation, 50 ac given to William Wingo including his plantation, and 9 ac given to John Foster--"given to them as Jury directed in case of Joshua Smith vs John Foster, William Wingo, and Richard Foster"; grant Jul. 8, 1774 to Dr Saml Gravill. Witness James Selman and Jeremiah Selman. Signed Joshua Smith. Wit. oath Sept. 16, 1816 James Selman to A Benson. Rec. Sept. 16, 1816

p. 93-94 Apr. 30, 1811 Alexander Parkison (Chester Dist) to John Wylie (same); for $500 sold (ac omitted) all his land in whatever district of South Carolina. Witness Saml Machon and William Morray. Signed Alexander Parkison. Wit. oath Jul. 25, 1811 (Chester Dist) Saml Machon to P. S. Wylie. Rec. Sept. 16, 1816

p. 94-95 Sept. 2, 1816 Alexander Roddy (SC) to Eaton Walker (SC); for $200 sold 77 ac on Wilson Mill Cr of N Tygar R; border: Abner Timmons and Peter Gray. Witness Abner Benson, Ephraim Roddy, and William Walker. Signed Alexr Roddy. Wit. oath Sept. 18, 1816 Ephraim Roddy to A Benson. Rec. Sept. 18, 1816

p. 95-96 May 29, 1810 John Cantrill (Spartanburgh) to son Isaac Cantrill (same); for $100 sold 94 ac; where Isaac Cantrill lives; border: N-Bankston, W-M Forrest, S-Moses Cantrell, and E-JohnCantrell. Witness Isaac Cantrell and Jacob Cantrell. Signed John Cantrill. Wit. oath Sept. 14, 1810 Isaac Cantrell to Leonard Adcock. Rec. Sept. 19, 1816

p. 96-97 Dec. 19, 1813 Laurens Bankston (Spartanburgh) to Isaac Cantrell, son of John (same); for $20 sold 60 ac on waters of Maple Swamp Cr of Island Cr; border: road from Island ford of Broad R to Colter's ford on Pacolett R,Mark Forrester, and Whitney Henis. Witness Henry Turner and Leonard Adcock. Signed Laurens Bankston's mark. Wit. oath Jul. 27, 1810 Henry Turner to Leonard Adcock. Rec. Sept. 19, 1816

p. 97 Sept. 20, 1816 Joseph Wilbanks (Spartanburgh) to James Story jr (same); for $5 sold 15 ac on branch of Fairforrest Cr; border: SW-James Storey sr and Nancy Storey and NE-Joseph Kelso. Witness Daniel Wilbanks and Robert Morrow. Signed Joseph Wilbanks. Wit. oath Sept. 21, 1816 Daniel Wilbanks to A Benson. Rec. Sept. 21, 1816

p. 97-98 Mar. 10, 1807 Henry Smith (Spartanburgh) to Peter Smith jr (same); for $84 sold 56 ac on Kelso's Cr of Fairforrest Cr; where Peter Smith jr lives; part of grant South Carolina Proprietor's office to Peter Smith sr. Witness John Smith and Peter Smith sr. Signed Henry Smith. Wit. oath Jul. 28, 1807 John Smith to Danl White. Rec. Sept. 23, 1816

p. 98-99 Sept. 28, 1816 Samuel Ward (Spartanburgh) to Zacheriah Wingo (same); for $100 sold 50 ac on Fairforrest Cr; border: James Ward, Abner Benson, and Thomson Faunt. Witness Ephraim Roddy and Laban P Poole. Signed Samuel Ward. Wit. oath Sept. 28, 1816 Ephraim Roddy to A Benson. Rec. Sept. 28, 1816

p. 99-100 Sept. 18, 1816 William S McCarter (Spartanburgh) to James McCarter (same); for $200 sold 504 ac; where George McCarter desc lived; willed to James and Wm McCarter jointly by their father George McCarter. Witness Ephraim Roddy, Thomas Hannon, and William Hunt. Signed William S McCarter. Wit. oath Oct. 4, 1816 Thomas Hannon and A Benson. Rec. Oct. 4, 1816

p. 100-101 Oct. 4, 1816 Abner Benson (Spartanburgh) to Thomson Fossell (same); for $265 sold 265 ac on Fairforrest Cr; border: Shoaly Br and Grind Stone Br; grant Feb. 3, 1794 to William Benson. Witness Joel Lewis and Thomas Hannon. Signed A Benson. Wit. oath Oct. 4, 1816 Thomas Hannon to A Benson. Rec. Oct. 4, 1816

p. 101-102 Apr. 21, 1812 Richard Thomson (Spartanburgh) to Thomas Allison (same); for $30 sold ¼ ac at Spartanburgh Court House; border: Publick Square, Nancy McKie, and Thomas Allison's house and lot. Witness Abner Benson and William R Smith. Signed Richard Thomson. Wit. oath Oct. 5, 1816 William R Smith to A Benson. Rec. Oct. 5, 1816. Dower renounced Polly Thomson to A Benson Aug. 2, 1815

p. 102-103 Jan. 21, 1816 Nimrod E Benson (Spartanburgh) to Eaton Walker (same); for $500 sold 120 ac on Wilson's Mill Cr of Tygar R; "laid" out to Nimrod E Benson as heir of William Benson desc by the commissioners. Witness Jesse Cleveland and Abner Benson. Signed Nimrod E Benson. Wit. oath Oct. 5, 1816 Jesse Cleveland to A Benson. Rec. Oct. 5, 1816

p. 103-104 Nov. 15, 1814 Thomas Greenwood (Spartanburgh) to David Golightly (same); for $550 sold 145 ac; border: N-Legon's Spring Br, S-Fairforrest Cr, W-Elias Palmer, ENE-Isaac Smith and David Golightly. Witness Thomas Allison and Laban P Poole. Signed Thos Greenwood. Wit. oath Oct. 6, 1816 Laban P Poole to A Benson. Rec. Oct. 6, 1816. Dower renounced Nov. 27, 1814 Lydia Greenwood to Abner Benson

p. 104-105 May 7, 1813 James Templeton (Spartanburgh) to Abner and Robert Benson (same); for $735 sold 210 ac on N side of Standing Stone Br of Lawson's fork; border: court house road, bridge across Standing Stone Br, Prince's old road, Abner Benson, and Robert Benson; part of grant Dec. 23, 1768 North Carolina to Robert McMurdy. Witness William R Smith, Elijah Foster, and James Murray. Signed Jas Templeton. Wit. oath Oct. 7, 1816 James Murray to Thos Poole. Rec. Oct. 7, 1816

p. 105-106 Jan. 18, 1814 Burton Acrie (Spartanburgh) to Andrew B Moore (same); for $200 sold 94 ac on W side of Wards Cr of Tygar R. Witness Gen. Thomas Moore, Charles Moore, and Lawson Thomson. Signed Burton Acrie's mark. Wit. oath Oct. 7, 1816 Charles Moore to Thos Poole. Rec. Oct. 7, 1816

p. 106-107 Feb. 21, 1812 James Wofford (Spartanburgh) to Isham Kendrick (same); for $825 sold 360 ac on waters of Rockyfield Cr of Enoree R and branch of Maple Br of Tygar R; border: John McDaid, Wheller, Ford, and John Woods. Witness Page Rork and Daniel Wood. Signed James Wofford. Wit. oath Nov. 23, 1812 Page Rork to Michl Miller. Rec. Oct. 7, 1816

p. 107-108 Jan. 21, 1812 Michael McElrath (Spartanburgh) to Isham Kendrick (same); for $405 sold 162 ac on Middle and S Tygar Rivers and both sides of road from mountains to Charleston; where Robert Redmon lives; border: Blake Bright and James Bright; grant Jan. 5, 1795 to John Thomas; "laid out" to John Vanderhorst. Witness Bowin Griffin and William Brown. Signed Michael McElrath's mark. Wit. oath Jan. 21, 1812 Bowin Griffin to Michl Miller. Rec. Oct. 7, 1816

p. 108-109 Jan. 1, 1814 (Union Dist) Thomas Lusk to William Stone; Thomas promises to pay William $210.96 by Jan. 1, 1815; to secure that debt Thomas "pledges" to William a Negro girl Rachel about 11 or 12 years old. Witness Thomas Murray and John Lusk. Signed Thos Lusk. Apr. 13, 1816 Thomas borrows $54 from executors of William Stone desc. Witness Sary Lusk. Signed Tho Lusk. Wit. oath Jul. 4, 1815 Thomas Murray to William Reid. Rec. Oct. 7, 1816

p. 109-110 "May June" 23, 1816 Michael Allen (Spartanburgh) to James Leonard (same); for $20 sold 18 ac on waters of Two Mile Cr; border: Leonard's Spring Br, William Lanford, John Leatherwood, Samuel Busey, and James Leonard. Witness William L Allen and John Pearson. Signed Michael Allen's mark. Wit. oath Oct. 1, 1816 John Pearson to John Dean. Rec. Oct. 7, 1816

p. 110-111 Sept. 25, 1816 Jesse Traylor (Spartanburgh) to Andrew Gramling (same); for $500 sold 150 ac on N Tygar R; border: widow Snoddy, James Vernon, John Timmons, and Edward Bomar. Witness Elisha Bomar and John Bomar. Signed Jesse Traylor. Wit. oath Oct. 7, 1816 John Bomar to Wm Reid. Rec. Oct. 7, 1816. Dower renounced Oct. 7, 1816 Winny Traylor to William Reid

p. 111-112 Oct. 17, 1815 Lawson Thomson (Spartanburgh) to Dr Andrew B Moore (same); for $1,400 sold 400 ac on S side of N Tygar R; border: Robert Foster; part of grant Feb. 23, 1754 to Hugh Lawson. Witness Robert Legon and Mathias Rush. Signed Lawson Thomson. Wit. oath Oct. 7, 1816 Mathias Rush to Thomas Poole. Rec. Oct. 7, 1816

p. 112-113 Dec. 12, 1815 John Lanford (Spartanburgh) to James Leonard (same); for $250 sold 100 ac on Two Mile Cr of Enoree R; border: Kirk. Witness Jesse Leatherwood and Mary Lanford. Signed John Lanford's mark. Wit. oath Oct. 2, 1816 Jesse Leatherwood to John Dean. Rec. Oct. 7, 1816

p. 113-114 Sept. 17, 1816 Samuel Caldwell (Spartanburgh) to James Coan (same); for $300 sold 182½ ac between N and Middle Tygar Rivers. Witness William Otts and John Gramling. Signed Saml Caldwell. Wit. oath Oct. 7, 1816 John Gramling to A Benson. Rec. Oct. 7, 1816. Dower renounced Oct. 7, 1816 Anna Caldwell to Abner Benson

p. 114-115 Apr. 10, 1816 James Vanzant (Rutherford Co, NC) to Dr Thomas Hancock (Union Dist); for $625 sold (1) 200 ac on N side of Pacolette R; grant to Arthur Crocker; and (2) 12 ac adjoining (1); part of grant to Reuben Bryant; on N side of Pacolette R; border: Loure. Witness J Collins and William S Golightly. Signed James Vanzart. Wit. oath Oct. 7, 1816 William S Golightly to A Benson. Rec. Oct. 7, 1816

p. 115-116 Sept. 3, 1816 Edmund Bishop (Spartanburgh) to Richard Thomson (same); for $200 sold 200 ac on waters of Lawson's fork and Fairforrest Cr; border: John Windsor; where Edmund Bishop lives; part of grant to David Goodlett. Witness Silas Bell and Wm Misskelley. Signed Edmd Bishop "stat". Wit. oath Sept. 9, 1816 Silas Bell to A Benson. Rec. Oct. 7, 1816. Dower renounced Oct. 7, 1816 Delila Bishop to A Benson

p. 116-117 Oct. 4, 1816 Catherine Traylor (Spartanburgh) to John L Rast (same); for $286 sold 89 ac on waters of N Tygar R. Witness John Gramling and James Coan. Signed Catherine Traylor's mark. Wit. oath Oct. 7, 1816 John Gramling to Wm Reid. Rec. Oct. 7, 1816

p. 117-118 Sept. 25, 1816 Jesse Traylor (Spartanburgh) to John Gramling (Orangeburg Dist); for $450 sold 160 ac on N Tygar R; border: James Coan, John Crawford, Samuel Miller, Benjamin High, and JLR. Witness Elisha Bomar and John Bomar. Signed Jesse Traylor. Wit. oath Oct. 7, 1816 John Bomar to Wm Reid. Rec. Oct.

7, 1816. Dower renounced Oct. 7, 1816 Winney Traylor to Wm Reid

p. 118-119 Nov. 23, 1811 Moses Stubs (Spartanburgh) to William Quinn (same); for $100 sold 100 ac; border: Bullock, head of Lick Br, and Sparks; part of grant Feb. 2, 1801 Gov. John Drayton to Paterson Thomson. Witness William Quinn jr and Archibald Quinn. Signed Moses Stubs and Taby Stubs. Wit. oath Mar. 14, 1812 William Quinn to John Gossett. Rec. Oct. 8, 1816

p. 119-120 Mar. 30, 1816 Lewis Brown (Spartanburgh) to John Dodd (same); for $500 sold 300 ac; border: small part of original survey sold by Reuben Bomar or Gabriel Benson to Henry and William Monroe, Obed's Cr, N (sic) side of Pacolett R, and road from Cunningham's Mill to Galt's old store. Witness Herbert Hawkins, Coleman Wood, and Margaret Hawkins. Signed Lewis Brown. Wit. oath May 6, 1816 Herbert Hawkins to James Young. Rec. Oct. 8, 1816

p. 120-121 Oct. 27, 1815 James Younger (Spartanburgh) to Lewis Brown (same); for $500 sold 300 ac; border: small part of original survey sold by Reuben Bomar or Gabriel Benson to Henry and William Monroe, Obed's Cr, S side of N Pacolett R, and road from Cunningham's Mill to Galt's old store. Witness Edmund Hurley, Uriah Bush, and Thomas Miller. Signed James Younger's mark. Wit. oath Apr. 24, 1816 Thomas Miller to James Young. Rec. Oct. 8, 1816

p. 121-122 Dec. 30, 1805 Alexander Evins (Spartanburgh) to William Ford (same); for $400 sold 200 ac on S side of S Tygar R; half of 400 ac grant to William Sharp; survey May 23, 1767. Witness Samuel Nisbett, Hamilton Wilson, and Samuel Pearson. Signed Alexr Evins. Wit. oath Dec. 30, 1805 Samuel Nisbett to Michl Miller. Rec. Oct. 8, 1816

p. 122-123 Mar. 7, 1814 Laban P Poole (Spartanburgh) to Michael McKie (same); for $80 sold 150 ac on Standing Stone Br of Lawson's fork; border: NE-William Bishop, NW-Nevil Gee, and S & SW-remainder of grant; part of grant Dec. 1, 1788 to David Goodlett. Witness Thomas Woodruff III and Page Rork. Signed Laban P Poole. Wit. oath Mar. 7, 1814 Page Rork to James Hammett. Rec. Oct. 8, 1816

p. 123-124 May 28, 1816 John McElrath (Spartanburgh) to William Ford (same); for $600 sold 300 ac on Pugion Roost Br and the head of Williams Cr of S Tygar R; part of 1,000 ac grant to Baylis Earle who sold to John McElrath. Witness Michl Moore, Jacob Davison, and W. S. Moore. Signed John McElrath. Wit. oath May 28, 1816 Michl Moore to John Chapman. Rec. Oct. 8, 1816. Dower renounced May 28, 1816 Rachel McElrath to John Chapman

p. 124-125 Sept. 15, 1815 Michael McKie (Spartanburgh) to Edmund Bishop "short" (same); for $200 sold 200 ac on waters of Fairforrest and Lawson fork Creeks; border: William Bishop, Nevil Gee, William Foster, and David Goodlett. Witness Edmond J Bishop, William Messkelley, and Solomon Bishop. Signed Michael MeKie's mark. Wit. oath Sept. 7, 1816 Solomon Bishop to Ephm Lewis. Rec. Oct. 8, 1816

p. 125-126 Oct. 3, 1808 Richard Chesney (Spartanburgh) to John Chesney jr (same); for $250 sold 200 ac on branch of Tygar R; border: W-John Meroney and James Stone, E-Wm Balding and Richard Fletcher, S-Richard Chesney, and other sides vacant; grant Jan. 25, 1773 Gov. William Bull to Wm Dunlap. Witness Isaac Crow sr and Wm Braughton. Signed Richard Chesney's mark. Wit. oath Sept. 28, 1814 Wm Braughton to Burrel Bobo. Oct. 15, 1816. Dower renounced Sept. 28, 1814 Hester Chesney to Burrel Bobo

p. 126-127 (omitted), 1816 Samuel Turner (Spartanburgh) to William

Garrett (same); for $5 sold 8 ac in fork of Pacolete R and Island Cr. Witness Isaac Cantrill and William Smith. Signed Samuel Turner. Wit. oath Oct. 15, 1816 William Smith to Henry Turner. Rec. Oct. 15, 1816

p. 127-128 Jul. 26, 1816 (Green Co, Ga) Robert Corry, Andrew McCombs and wife Jane (formerly Jane Corry), and William Corry, a "Lunatic" by Alexander Corry, appointed guartian by Ordianry Court of Green Co to take care of estate of said "Lunatic" (all of Green Co, Ga), to William Robert (Spartanburgh); for $500 sold 300 ac on branch of N Tygar R; border when surveyed: all vacant; grant Aug. 24, 1770 to Robert Corry, Jane Corry, and William Corry. Witness Green W Meaders, Jason Moore jr, and Nancy Posey. Signed Robert Corry, Alexander Corry, Andrew McCombs, and Jane's mark. Wit. oath Oct. 15, 1816 Jason Moore jr to Danl White. Rec. Oct. 15, 1816

p. 128 Jul. 13, 1816 Peter Smith (Charleston, SC) to William Rogers (Spartanburgh); for $307 sold 500 ac on Dutchman's Cr; border when surveyed: E-Henry Middleton, W-survey "for the Irish", and others vacant; grant Sept. 9, 1774 to Henry Middleton. Witness Richard Hrabowski and William Roach jr. Signed Peter Smith. Wit. oath (not dated) (Charleston, SC) Richard Hrabowski to G. M. Bounetheau. Rec. Oct. 15, 1816

p. 128-129 Wit. oath (York Dist) Albert Allison to J. A. White dated Sept. 16, 1816 for deed Caleb Clark and wife Julia to Smith Lipscomb; other witness was John Buchanon

p. 129-130 May 15, 1816 Thomas Cantwell (Spartanburgh) to Charles Cantrill (same); for $80 sold 123 ac on waters of Buck Cr on N side of Pacolett R; border: Purtlis and Morris. Witness Leonard Adcock and Isaac Adcock. Signed Thomas Cantwell's mark. Wit. oath May 15, 1816 Isaac Adcock to Leonard Adcock. Rec. Oct. 15, 1816

p. 130-131 Aug. 24, 1815 Charles Smith (Spartanburgh) to Collins Smith (same); for $200 sold 245 ac on E side of Pacolett R; border: Harrican Shoal. Witness James Emerson and William Smith. Signed Charles Smith. Wit. oath Oct. 15, 1816 William Smith to Henry Turner. Rec. Oct. 16, 1816

p. 131-132 Jun. 27, 1815 James Wofford to Nathaniel Wofford; for $500 sold a Negro woman Jesse. Witness John Wofford and Isaac Wofford. Signed James Wofford. Wit. oath Oct. 14, 1816 John Wofford to John Brewton. Rec. Oct. 19, 1816

p. 132-133 Nov. 2, 1815 Samuel Farrow (Spartanburgh) to niece Rebecca Bogan; for (omitted) gave 150 ac on SW side Cedar Shoal Cr of Enoree R; border: road to Charleston, Solomon Smith, William Hitchcock; where Solomon Smith lived and where John Bogan lives; part of grant to Henry Hambleton. Witness Thos F Farrow and Mary Farrow. Signed S Farrow. Wit. oath Oct. 26, 1816 Mary Farrow to Burrel Bobo. Rec. Oct. 28, 1816

p. 133-134 Jan. 29, 1811 Solomon Crocker (Spartanburgh) to James and Benjamin Poole (same); for $5 sold 50 ac on N side of Lawson's fork; part of 997 ac grant to Solomon Crocker. Witness William Gore, Mark Crocker, and Elisha Poole. Signed Solomon Crocker's mark. Wit. oath Oct. 15, 1816 William Gore to Caleb Jones. Rec. Oct. 29, 1816

p. 134-135 Dec. 13, 1810 John Brookshear (Spartanburgh) to James Trail (same); for $50 sold 100 ac on waters of Pacolett R. Witness Mannering Brookshire and Jeremiah McMillian. Signed John Brookshire (sic). Wit. oath Dec. 13, 1810 Mannering Brookshire to Henry Turner. Rec. Oct. 30, 1816

p. 135-136 Dec. 28, 1812 James Trail (Spartanburgh) to Enoch Ward (same); for $30 sold 50 ac on waters of Cherokee Cr of Pacolate R. Witness Jeremiah McMillion and Richard Turner. Signed James Trail's mark. Wit. oath Dec. 28, 1812 Richard Turner to Henry Turner. Rec. Oct. 30, 1816

p. 136-137 May 24, 1815 James Crow (Spartanburgh) to Peter Hamilton (same); for $400 sold 125 ac on both sides of Jemmies Cr; border: Paul Castleberry and George Leatherwood. Witness Isaac Crow and Henry Marler. Signed James Crow's mark. Wit. oath Jul. 4, 1815 Henry Marler to M Casey. Rec. Nov. 2, 1816

p. 137-138 Aug. 9, 1816 William McM Brice (Spartanburgh) to Reuben Traylor (same); for $84 sold 56 ac on Jno Bazwell's Spring Br of Ben's Cr of S Tygar R; border: S & SE-William Brice and NE-Reuben Traylor. Witness Jesse Wofford and William Hoy. Signed Wm McM Brice. Wit. oath Nov. 4, 1816 William Hoy to James Hammett. Rec. Nov. 4, 1816

p. 138-139 Aug. 1, 1816 William Shaw (Pendleton Dist) to James Brannon (Spartanburgh); for $300 sold 200 ac near Spartanburgh Court House; border: Williford, Bull, and Thomson. Witness Jesse Cleveland and Nimrod E Benson. Signed Wm Shaw. Wit. oath Nov. 4, 1816 Jesse Cleveland to A Benson. Rec. Nov. 4, 1816

p. 139-140 Oct. 26, 1816 William McM Brice (Spartanburgh) to William Hoy (same); for $200 sold 180 ac on Camp Br of Ben's Cr of S Tygar R; border: Reuben Traylor, Jno Bazwell's Spring Br, William Hoy, Denny Anderson, and W-Wm Beacham. Witness John Means and David Morton. Signed Wm McM Brice. Wit. oath Nov. 4, 1816 John Means to James Hammett. Rec. Nov. 4, 1816

p. 140-141 Mar. 1, 1816 Isaac S Pebworth (Spartanburgh) to Thomas Dean; for $85 due in 18 months sold a box of carpenter's tools--"containing a complete assortment or set", 2 feather beds and furniture, a cow and calf, 5 hogs, all kitchen and household furniture, and a sheep; Condition: sale void if Isaac pays Thomas $85 in 18 months. Witness James Brannon "ackd". Signed Isaac S Pebworth. Wit. oath Nov. 6, 1816 James Brannon to A Benson. Rec. Nov. 6, 1816

p. 141-142 Jul. 13, 1806 Robert McDowell (Spartanburgh) to Andrew Austin (same); for 100£ sterling sold 150 ac on N side of Lawson's fork of Pacolete R. Witness James Lewis, Samuel Austin, and John Knight. Signed Robert McDowell. Wit. oath Aug. 7, 1806 Samuel Austin to Ism Foster. Rec. Nov. 7, 1816

p. 142-143 Feb. 10, 1795 Miles Nash (Spartanburgh) to James Lanford (same); for 40£ sterling sold 125 ac on Two Mile Cr of Enoree R; upper part of grant Jan. 20, 1773 to Daniel Mooring who sold to William Sargent who sold to Edward Nash who sold to Miles Nash. Witness Joseph Barnett, James Lanford jr, and Thomas Medford. Signed Miles Nash. Wit. oath May 13, 1801 Joseph Barnett to John Dean. Rec. Nov. 11, 1816

p. 143-144 Dec. 14, 1813 William Crow, by power of attorney from Mary Crow dated Nov. 8, 1813, to Jonathan Crow jr (Spartanburgh); for $110 sold 248 ac on waters of Two Mile Cr; formerly land of William Crow desc. Witness Mary Crow and John Dean. Signed William Crow. Wit. oath Oct. 14, 1816 John Dean to Samuel Woodruff. Rec. Nov. 11, 1816

p. 144-145 Dec. 14, 1813 William Crow, by power of attorney from

Mary Crow Nov. 8, 1813, to James Crow jr (Spartanburgh); for $100 sold 185 ac on waters of Two Mile Cr; formerly William Crow desc's land. Witness Mary Crow and John Dean. Signed William Crow. Wit. oath Oct. 14, 1816 John Dean to Samuel Woodruff. Rec. Nov. 11, 1816

p. 145-146 Dec. 14, 1813 Jonathan Crow, William Crow, Moses Crow, and Caleb Stone, heirs of William Crow desc (Spartanburgh), to James Crow jr (same); for $800 sold 185 ac on waters of Two Mile Cr; formerly land of William Crow desc. Witness Aaron Casey and John Dean. Signed William Crow, Caleb Stone, and Jonathan and Moses Crow's marks. Wit. oath Oct. 14, 1816 John Dean to Samuel Woodruff. Rec. Nov. 11, 1816

p. 146-147 Dec. 14, 1813 James Crow, William Crow, Moses Crow, and Caleb Stone, heirs of William Crow desc (Spartanburgh), to Jonathan Crow jr (same); for $1,000 sold 248 ac on Two Mile Cr; formerly land of William Crow desc. Witness Aaron Casey and John Dean. Signed William Crow, Caleb Stone, and James and Moses Crow's marks. Wit. oath Oct. 14, 1816 John Dean to Samuel Woodruff. Rec. Nov. 11, 1816

p. 147-148 Jul. 26, 1814 Smedley Lynch (Spartanburgh) to Benjamin Couch (same); for $400 sold 200 ac on branches of Elisha's Cr of Enoree R; originally border: all vacant and now border: W-Nathan Smith, N-R Oliphant and John Anderson, E-Spencer Bobo, and S-Samuel Farrow. Witness Davis Newman and William Cambell. Signed Smedley Lynch. Wit. oath Nov. 8, 1816 Davis Newman to Burrel Bobo. Rec. Nov. 11, 1816. Dower renounced Jul. 29, 1814 Mary Lynch to Burrel Bobo

p. 148-149 Feb. 28, 1814 Chany Bobo (Spartanburgh) to Smedley Lynch (same); for $250 sold 200 ac on branches of Elisha's Cr of Enoree R; originally border: all vacant and now border: W-Nathan Smith, N-R Oliphant and J Anderson, E-Spencer Bobo, and S-Samuel Farrow. Witness Burrel Bobo and Rhoda Bobo. Signed Chaney Bobo. Wit. oath Feb. 28, 1814 Rhoda Bobo to Burrel Bobo. Rec. Nov. 11, 1816. Dower renounced Mar. 2, 1814 Rachel Bobo to Burrel Bobo

p. 149-150 Oct. 18, 1816 (Franklin Co, Tenn) Richard Fondrin (Franklin Co, Tenn) to Jesse Fondrin; power of attorney to obrain his share of estate of Thomas Cole desc. Witness William Fondrin sr and William Fondrin jr. Signed Richard Fondrin's mark. Wit. oath Nov. 11, 1816 William Fondrin to J Camp. Rec. Nov. 11, 1816

p. 150-151 Mar. 8, 1797 Hugh McWilliams (Laurens Co) to John Sims (Spartanburgh); for 10£ sterling sold (ac omitted) on Bufalow Cr; border: Carns and Warters. Witness Starling Tucker and William Terry. Signed Hugh McWilliams' mark. Wit. oath May 13, 1814 (Laurens Dist) Starling Tucker to William Cowan. Rec. Nov. 12, 1816

p. 151-152 Jul. 27, 1816 William Morris (Spartanburgh) to Joseph Gibson Oliver (same); for $35 sold 35 ac on waters of Pacolate R; border: Joseph G Oliver and William McKinney. Witness Jarvis Gilbert and Joseph Stublefield. Signed William Morris. Wit. oath Oct. 26, 1816 Jarvis Gilbert to Leonard Adcock. Rec. Nov. 12, 1816

p. 152-153 Jun. 10, 1816 Joel Brewton (Spartanburgh) to Peter Bragg (same); for $88 sold 22 ac on N side of Ferguson's Cr. Witness William Otts and Dililah Otts. Signed Joel Brewton. Wit. oath Oct. 3, 1816 William Otts to John Brewton. Rec. Nov. 13, 1816

p. 153-154 Jun. 29, 1814 John Stone (Spartanburgh) to William Stone (same); for $400 sold 200 ac; border: Seth Lewis and Aaron Stone; where William Stone lives and part of where John Stone lives; part of grant to John Naile. Witness Hillory Stone and Thomas Murray. Signed John Stone. Wit. oath (no date) Thomas Murray to Wm Reid. Rec. Nov. 13, 1816

p. 154-155 Aug. 5, 1815 Daniel McKie (Spartanburgh) to Rutha Pilgrim (same); for $80 sold 56 ac on luk (sic) Cr of Enoree R; part of 400 ac grant to John Hamby who sold to John Arnold jr who sold to Stone who sold to Herring who sold to Daniel McKie. Witness Fountain Moseley and William Brooks. Signed Danl McKie. Wit. oath Nov. 18, 1815 Fountain Moseley to Samuel Woodruff. Rec. Nov. 13, 1816

p. 155-156 Aug. 24, 1816 James Ford (Spartanburgh) to Thomas Westmoreland jr; for $225 sold 100 ac on Snawbey Cr of Enoree R. Witness George Durham and Grisham Durham. Signed James Ford. Wit. oath Sept. 26, 1816 Grisham Durham to David Moore. Rec. Nov. 14, 1816

p. 156-157 Nov. 15, 1816 Benjamin Lewis to Edmond L Bishop; a bond of $500 because of judgment obtained against Absalom Roe by Larkin Carden with Benjamin Lewis "to preserve his property" agreed to "conjunction" with Edmond L Bishop to discharge "said debt"; Benjamin Lewis warants land formerly Absalom Roe's and now in Edmond L Bishop possession; bond void <u>unless</u> Edmond Bishop loses the land. Witness William Rollins and Banister Hawkins. Signed Benjamin Lewis. Wit. oath Nov. 15, 1816 Banister Hawkins to A Benson. Rec. Nov. 15, 1816

p. 157-158 Feb. 10, 1814 James Smith (Spartanburgh) to Charles James; for $46 sold 23 ac on Wilson's Cr and Thomson Br of Fairforrest Cr; border: Robert Smith, Micajah Barnett, Charles James, and Kelso's Cr; part of land that formerly belonged to her husband James Smith desc and was assigned to Jane "in Dowery" by a commission. Witness Shands Golightly and Charles James jr. Signed Jane Smith. Wit. oath Feb. 11, 1814 Shands Golightly to Danl White. Rec. Nov. 18, 1816

p. 158-160 Aug. 26, 1815 Elijah Johnson (Spartanburgh) to Reuben Traylor (same); for $300 sold 171 ac on Provy's Cr of S Tygar R; border: Aaron Moor, Philip Johnson, John Durham, Moorton, and Camp Br of Ben's Cr; includes where James Vaughan lives. Witness James Vaughan and William McM Brice. Signed Elijah Johnson. Wit. oath Sept. 16, 1815 William McM Brice to Drury McDaniel. Rec. Dec. 3, 1816. Dower renounced Sept. 16, 1815 Dicy Johnson to Drury McDaniel

p. 160 Jul. 22, 1816 Laurens Bankston and Robert Garrett (Spartanburgh) to Leonard Adcock, "Justice" (Spartanburgh); they swears on Mar. 8, 1816 they saw Mary Cantwell sell a Negro girl Suck for $200 to her son Mark Cantwell. Witness Leon Adcock JP. Signed Laurens Bankston and Robert Garrett's mark. Wit. oath none. Rec. Dec. 19, 1816

p. 160-161 Sept. 28, 1815 James Jordan (late of St Clair Co, Ill) and wife Mary, daughter of James McElwayn sr desc, to Daniel Wilbanks; for $25 sold all their rights to (ac omitted) known as McElwayn's old place and formerly land of James McElwayn sr desc; where Daniel Wilbanks lives. Witness Anthony W Thomas, Silas Bankston, and Samuel Allen. Signed James and Mary Jordan. Wit. oath Sept. 28, 1815 (St Clair Co, Ill) James and Mary Jordan to Benjamin Walls. Rec. Dec. 23, 1816

p. 161-163 Dec. 4, 1815 William Prince (Spartanburgh) to William

Pruitt (same); for $300 sold 101 ac on Cane Cr on N side of Tygar R; border: John Red, Richard Prince desc, Timothy Toney's old line, and Samuel Sheretrett(?)'s old line; part of 200 ac grant Nov. 20, 1772 Gov. G Montague to James Hembry. Witness Isaac Wofford jr, Samuel Pruitt, and Henry Palmer. Signed Wm Prince. Wit. oath Apr. 28, 1816 Henry Palmer to James Hamm. Rec. Dec. 23, 1816

p. 163-164 Dec. 2, 1816 John Thomason to Thomas Holt (Baldwin Co, Ga); for $250 sold 120 ac on waters of Lawson's fork; border: Benson and Herring's old line; part of 352 ac grant to William Turner Thomason. Witness Thomas Hannon and Abner Benson. Signed John Thomason. Wit. oath Dec. 31, 1816 Thomas Hannon to A Benson. Rec. Dec. 31, 1816

p. 164-165 Oct. 7, 1816 John and Carter Burnett (Spartanburgh) to Thomas Wells (same); for $170 sold 137 ac; border: Rowland, Healing Springs Road, and Leonard Cardin. Witness John H Jones and Richard Wells. Signed Carter Burnett and John Burnett's mark. Wit. oath Oct. 7, 1816 John H Jones to Wm Underwood. Rec. Jan. 1, 1817

p. 165-166 Oct. 3, 1812 John Smith (Spartanburg) to Alexander McDaniel (Greenville Dist); for $100 sold 200 ac on both sides Middle Tygar R; border: John McCree and Lowen. Witness Reuben Barrett, Reuben Barrett jr, and David Jackson. Signed John Smith's mark. Wit. oath Nov. 23, 1816 David Jackson to John Montgomery. Rec. Jan. 6, 1817

p. 166-167 Nov. 21, 1816 Edmund Foster (Spartanburgh) to Thomas Gore (same); for $800 sold 400 ac on Cedar Shoals Cr and Spears's Cr; between Enoree and Tygar Rivers; ¼ ac reserved for burying ground for Foster family and ¼ ac "in the old plantation" for use of Bobo family. Witness Thomas McClure and Joel Foster. Signed Edmund Foster. Wit. oath Dec. 24, 1816 Thomas McClure to Burrell Bobo. Rec. Jan. 6, 1817

p. 167-168 Jan. 9, 1807 John and James Young (Spartanburgh) to Peterson Bowrum (Edgefield Dist); for (money not mentioned) sold 297 ac on N side of S Pacolette R; border: N-Alexander Cunningham and Henry Munroe; part of two grants to (1) Peter Vedeun and (2) John Young. Witness Samuel Turner and Alexander Roe. Signed James Young and John Young. Wit. oath Nov. 4, 1816 Samuel Turner to Thomas Poole. Rec. Jan. 6, 1817. Dower renounced Nov. 7, 1816 Anne Young, wife of James, to James Young

p. 168-169 Sept. 21, 1807 James Young (Spartanburgh) to Peterson Bowrum (Edgefield Dist); for (money omitted) sold 15 ac on N side of S Pacolette R and in bend of river; part of grant to Peter Videan. Witness Iredell Cunningham and William Bennett. Signed James Young. Wit. oath Oct. 30, 1816 Iredell Cunningham to James Young. Rec. Jan. 6, 1817

p. 169-170 Oct. 23, 1816 Peterson Bowrum (Spartanburgh) to Richard Thomson (same); for $800 sold 312 ac on N side of S Pacolett R; where Peterson Bowrum lives; part of two grants (1) May 17, 1794 to Peter Vidcan and (2) to John Young sr. Witness Alexander Cunningham and William Bennett. Signed Peterson Bowrum. Wit. oath Oct. 23, 1816 Alexander Cunningham to James Young. Rec. Jan. 6, 1817. Dower renounced Nov. 1, 1816 Delilah Bowrum to James Young

p. 170-171 Sept. 16, 1816 Edmund Cooly (Spartanburgh) to Philip Johnson (same); for $100 sold 100 ac; border: Johnson, Tinhold Br, Thomas Gilbard, Barton's Cr, and McWilliams; near Pacolett R; part of survey by Spears. Witness William Johnson,

Thomas Barton, Wm Bennett, and Thomas Lankston. Signed Edmund Cooley. Wit. oath Oct. 31, 1816 Wm Bennett to James Young. Rec. Jan. 6, 1817

p. 171-173 Feb. 4, 1815 Philip Johnson (Rutherford Co, NC) to Russell Twitty (same); for $450 sold 340 ac on both sides N Pacolett R; border: William Barton, Spece, Gore's old line, Sink hole Br, Thomas Gilbert, "Mother", and McWilliams; part of two tracts of Thomas Gore and Amos Spece; if there is more than 340 ac, then Philip is to be paid at above rate (per ac). Witness John B Twitty and William Garret. Signed Philip Johnson and Mary's mark. Wit. oath Oct. 30, 1816 John B Twitty to James Young. Rec. Jan. 6, 1817

p. 173-174 Oct. 31, 1816 Russel Twitty (Rutherford Co, NC) to Richard Thomson (Spartanburgh); for $400 sold 350 ac on both sides of N Pacolett R; border: Matthis, McWilliams, and Speice; note added--"part of land granted to Thos Gore Nov. 7, 1796". Witness William Bennett and Thomas Barton. Signed Russell Twitty. Wit. oath Oct. 31, 1816 William Bennett to James Young. Rec. Jan. 6, 1817. Dower renounced Nov. 7, 1816 Polley Twitty to James Young

p. 174-176 May 11, 1811 Vincent Bennett, sheriff (Spartanburgh) to Thomas Wells; for $17 sold 200 ac at head waters of Lawson's fork; near where Robert Lockhart jr lives; sale due to writ from Spartanburgh Common Pleas Court suit Daniel Galt vs Robt Lockhart sr; sale Apr. 1, 1811. Witness Muse Tollison and William N Miller. Signed Vincent Bennett. Wit. oath Jan. 17, 1817 Muse Tollison to Thomas Poole. Rec. Jan. 17, 1817

p. 176-177 Nov. 4, 1816 Alexander Ray to Levi Lee (Spartanburgh); for $25 sold 500 ac on Lawson's fork; where Mary Lee lives; Alexander bought land at sheriff's sale as Mary Lee's land. Witness Muse Tollison and Charles McAbee. Signed Alexander Ray. Wit. oath Dec. 8, 1816 Muse Tollison to Caleb Jones. Rec. Jan. 17, 1817

p. 177-178 (omitted), 1803 James Young (Spartanburgh) to Alexr Cunningham (same); for $100 sold 200 ac; border: William Anderson. Witness William Bennett jr and William Lewis. Signed James Young. Wit. oath Aug. 17, 1805 William Lewis to William Kelso. Rec. Jan. 25, 1817

p. 178-180 Nov. 6, 1816 Alexander Cunningham (Spartanburgh) to Richard Thomson (same); for $150 sold 168 ac in fork of N and S Pacolette R and on S side of Obed's Cr; border: Sampson Brooks, survey for John Daniel, and land sold by Peterson Borraum to Richard Thomson; part of grant to James Young. Witness William Bennett and Peterson Borraum. Signed Alexr Cunningham. Wit. oath Nov. 30, 1816 William Bennett to James Young. Rec. Jan. 25, 1817. Dower renounced Nov. 30, 1816 Ruth Cunningham to James Young

p. 180-181 Jun. 10, 1815 Thomas Clark (Spartanburgh) to Jonathan Crook (same); for $500 sold 410 ac on branches of Enoree R; border: Thomas Farrow, Teary, Hobby, and McKie; part of two adjoining grants (1) Feb. 2, 1782 to Zacheriah Caruru (or Carevill) and (2) James Landford. Witness Joshua Tapp and William Terry. Signed Thomas Clark. Wit. oath Dec. 8, 1815 William Terry to John Dean. Rec. Feb. 1, 1817

p. 181-182 Mar. 5, 1816 William Arnold (Spartanburgh) to Jonathan Crook (same); for $680 sold 165 ac on Enoree R. Witness Caleb Allen and Joseph Crook. Signed Willis (sic) Arnold. Wit. oath Mar. 30, 1816 Caleb Allen to John Brewton. Rec. Feb. 1, 1817

p. 182-183 Jan. 14, 1817 William Quin jr (Spartanburgh) to Jesse

Griffin (Union Dist); for $100 sold 60 ac; border: S & W-Leven Sparks and E & N-Henry Fernandes. Witness Thomas Sparks and Joseph Collins. Signed William Quin. Wit. oath Jan. 23, 1817 Thomas Sparks to William Reid. Rec. Feb. 3, 1817

p. 183-184 Nov. 20, 1816 Reubin Briant (Spartanburgh) to Jesse Griffin (same); for $20 sold 8 ac; border: Norton's Spring, Ligh Sparks, and Fernandes. Witness John Rochelle and Thomas Sparks. Signed Reubin Briant's mark. Wit. oath Jan. 23, 1817 Thomas Sparks to Wm Reid. Rec. Feb. 3, 1817

p. 184-185 Nov. 16, 1816 Willis L Colvert to Nathaniel Burton; for $300 sold 125 ac on waters of Tygar R. Witness Edward Willis and William Hobby. Signed William (sic) L Colvert. Wit. oath Feb. 3, 1817 William Hobby to John Brewton. Rec. Feb. 3, 1817

p. 185-186 Nov. 6, 1816 William Perrin (Spartanburgh) to William Wingo (same); for $700 sold 127 ac on waters of N Tygar R; border: N-Maj. Alexr Roddy, E-John Bankston, S-Alexr Thomson, and W-John Jordan; part of tract bought by James Jordan esq at sheriff's sale and sold "by said Jordan by Samuel Farrow, sheriff (Spartanburgh)"; land was divided among the heirs of estate of "said" jordan; 127 ac was allotted to Peggy Vernon, heir of "said" Jordan and sold by James Vernon and wife Peggy to William Perrin. Witness Joseph Collins and James Vernon. Signed William Perrin. Wit. oath Feb. 3, 1817 Joseph Collins to Thomas Poole. Rec. Feb. 3, 1817. Dower renounced Nov. 7, 1816 Polly Perrin to A Benson

p. 186-188 Nov. 13, 1816 Mason Shumate (Spartanburgh) to Isaac Snoddy (same); for $1,000 sold 375 ac on waters of Tygar R; border: Anthony Pearson, James Vernon, and widow Wingo; part of three grants--(1) to Anthony Pearson desc, (2) to John Leach, and (3) to William Benson. Witness Charles McHugh, Anthony Pearson, and Henry How. Signed Mason Shumate. Wit. oath Feb. 3, 1817 Anthony Pearson to John Montgomery. Rec. Feb. 3, 1817. Dower renounced Dec. 2, 1816 Nancy Shumate to James Young

p. 188-189 Jan. 24, 1816 Edmund Clement (Spartanburgh) to William Clement (same); "give" 174 ac on waters of Lawson's fork; N of conditional line between Edmund Clement and Edmd Fowler and on E side of line made by Edmund Clement, "my" father to Wm Clement and John Clement; part of grant Oct. 14, 1785 to James Wood and sold by William Wood, his father, to Edmund Clement. Witness James McDowell and John Clement. Signed Edmund Clement. Wit. oath Apr. 17, 1816 James McDowell to James Young. Rec. Feb. 3, 1817

p. 189-190 Apr. 13, 1814 Elias Stone (Spartanburgh) to William Clement (same); for $500 sold 235 ac on E side Richland Cr of S Pacolett R; border: widow Clark, Benjamin Clark, Wolf trap Br, and Zack Wall; part of two grants--(1) to Samuel Spener and (2) to Thomas Bennett. Witness Zach Wall and James McDowell. Signed Elias Stone. Wit. oath Oct. 10, 1814 James McDowell to William Kelso. Rec. Feb. 3, 1817

p. 190-192 Mar. 3, 1812 Joseph Rogers (Spartanburgh) to Anthony Pearson (same); for $400 sold 172 ac on both sides Jemmies Cr of N Tygar R; border: Snoddy and "District" road; part of two grants--(1) May 4, 1769 "North patent" to John Leach and (2) to Anthony Pearson. Witness Willis Shumate, Saml Caldwell, and Samuel Pearson. Signed Joseph Rogers. Wit. oath Feb. 3, 1817 Samuel Pearson to John Montgomery. Rec. Feb. (omitted) 1817. Dower renounced Mar. 18, 1812 Sarah Rogers to Michl Miller

p. 192-193 Oct. 11, 1814 Leven Sparks (Spartanburg) to William Quinn jr (same); for $100 sold 60 ac; border: W & S-Leven Sparks and N & E-Henry Fernandas. Witness John Rochelle and Josiah Sparks. Signed Leven Sparks. Wit. oath Jan. 23, 1817 Josiah Sparks to Wm Reid. Rec. Feb. 3, 1817

p. 193-194 Sept. 4, 1815 Soloman (or Solamon) Jackson (Spartanburgh) to Ephra_m Jackson; for $60 sold 70 ac on Snud's (or Sneed's) Br; border: Green River Rd and Sellavert. Witness William W Sillaven and William Jackson. Signed Solomon Jackson. Wit. oath Apr. 19, 1816 William Jackson to James Camp. Rec. Feb. 3, 1817

p. 194-195 Feb. 11, 1815 Joseph Austell (Spartanburg) to Amos Austell (same); for $263.50 sold 175 ac; border: Hill Cr, Hunter, Grunton, Baustick, and Thomson; part of grant to Joseph Austell. Witness Fendal Robertson and John Brock. Signed Joseph Austell. Wit. oath May 12, 1815 Fendal Robertson to John Lipscomb. Rec. Feb. 3, 1817. Dower renounced Jul. 26, 1816 Nancy Austell to John Lipscomb

p. 195-196 Dec. 3, 1816 Jason Moore jr, Samuel Moore, and Nancy Posey (Spartanburg) to William Rogers (same); for $250 sold 146 ac; border: James McGowen and Carrey; 100 ac was granted in 1794 to William Paden and 46 ac was part of grant in 1786 to Thomas Moore. Witness William Posey and Daniel Alexander. Signed Jason Moore jr, Samuel Moore, and Nancy Posey. Wit. oath none. Rec. Feb. 10, 1817. Dower renounced Nancy Moore, wife of Jason jr, to Daniel White Dec. 4, 1816

p. 196-198 Nov. 25, 1816 Samuel Moore (Spartanburg) to William Rogers (same); for $200 sold 100 ac on branch of Ward's Cr of Tyger R; border: W-Andrew Fawan and others vacant; grant to Alexander Brown. Witness Greene Meadows and David Walker. Signed Samuel Moore. Wit. oath Nov. 12, 1816 Greene Meadows to Wm Reid. Rec. Feb. 10, 1817. Dower renounced Dec. 4, 1816 Elizabeth Moore to Daniel Moore

p. 198-199 Dec. 6, 1816 Abijah Lewis (Spartanburgh) to George Lewis (same); for $120 sold 50 ac on N side Lawson's fork; border: George Lewis sr; sold by Edward Clement to Ephraim Lewis. Witness Robert Langford and Joseph Blackwell. Signed Abijah Lewis. Wit. oath Dec. 6, 1816 Robert Langford to Eph Lewis. Rec. Mar. 3, 1817

p. 199-200 Mar. 10, 1816 Edward Clement (Spartanburgh) to George Lewis; for $100 sold 300 ac on both sides Sholy Cr of Lawson's fork; border: S-George Lewis and vacant, E-Robert Lankford and Joseph Lewis, N-Mavarick, and W-Ephraim Lewis; part of grant to Edward Clement. Witness Robert Lankford and John Rollins. Signed E Clement. Wit. oath Dec. 6, 1816 Robert Lankford to Eph Lewis. Rec. Mar. 3, 1817

p. 200-202 Nov. 1, 1816 (Laurens Dist) William H Durkie (Spartanburgh) to Robert Creswell (Laurens Dist); to secure a bond of $778.72 (condition to pay $389.36 as follows--$188.10 paid May 1, 1817 and $201.26 paid May 1, 1818) and for $5 sold 100 ac; above Mountain Shoals; where Augustus F Durkie lives; sold by Spartanburgh sheriff due to court order to foreclose a mortgage "in favor of" Samuel Young vs Nathaniel Durkie and Hugh Young and bought by William H Durkie; Condition: sale void if William pays debt. Witness John Cunningham and Tim F Stewart. Signed Wm H Durkie. Wit. oath Feb. 24, 1817 (Laurens Dist) John Cunningham to Chas Allen. Rec. Mar. 3, 1817

p. 202-203 Oct. 7, 1816 Ephraim Hembree (Spartanburgh) to Thomas Thomas; for (money omitted) sold 150 ac on both sides Rocky fork Cr; border: Tollison, Green River road, Smith,

Sellowen, Wolf Br, Spence, Ballard, and Jackson. Witness William W Sillavan and Abraham Hembree. Signed Ephraim Hembree. Wit. oath Feb. 15, 1817 William W Sillavan to Wm Reid. Rec. Mar. 3, 1817

p. 203-204 Nov. 4, 1815 Jonathan Nisbett (Spartanburgh) to Jacob Bridges (same); for $175 sold 70 ac on S side of Middle Tygar R. Witness James Swancey and Wilson Nisbett. Signed Jonathan Nisbett. Wit. oath Feb. 20, 1817 Wilson Nisbett to J Collins. Rec. Mar. 3, 1817. Dower renounced Feb. 17, 1817 Elizabeth Nisbett to Abner Benson

p. 204-205 Nov. 16, 1816 Even Watkins (Rutherford Co, NC) to Philip Davis; for $376 to 473 ac on both sides Suck Cr of Broad R. Witness William Watkins and James McDaniel. Signed Evan Watkins. Wit. oath Feb. 12, 1817 James McDaniel to A Benson. Rec. Mar. 3, 1817

p. 205-206 Nov. 20, 1816 John Bogan and wife Rebecca to James Burk; for $450 sold 150 ac on Cedar Shoal Cr of Enoree R; border: Moses Casey. Witness Joel Dean and Thomas F Farrow. Signed John and Rebekah Bogan. Wit. oath Nov. 20, 1816 Thomas F Farrow to Burrell Bobo. Rec. Mar. 3, 1817. Dower renounced Nov. 28, 1816 Rebekah Bogan to Burrell Bobo

p. 206-207 Oct. 1, 1816 John Low jr to John Low sr; for $20 sold 20 ac; border: Thomas Wyatt and S Wyatt. Witness Reubin Warren and Samuel Turner. Signed John Low. Wit. oath Mar. 3, 1817 Reubin Warren to Thomas Poole. Rec. Mar. 3, 1817

p. 207-208 Jan. 24, 1817 Nathaniel Burton (Spartanburgh) to Benjamin Nicholls (same); for $250 sold 125 ac on Opossom Br of N Tygar R. Witness Sterling Hudgins and Jonathan Craw. Signed Nathl Burton. Wit. oath Mar. 3, 1817 Jonathan Craw to Thomas Poole. Rec. Mar. 3, 1817

p. p. 208-209 Jul. 22, 1815 Jonathan Crow (Spartanburgh) to Benjamin Nicholls (same); for $1 sold 1/16 ac on S side of N Tyger R; part of where Jonathan Crow lives. Witness Willis L Colvert and Danl White. Signed Jonathan Crow. Wit. oath Apr. 18, 1816 Willis L Colvert to William Underwood. Rec. Mar. 3, 1817

p. 209-211 Nov. 23, 1816 John Meadows (Spartanburgh) to Benjamin Nicholls (same); for $282 sold 282 ac; border: John Trail; a;; of 200 ac grant to Obediah Edwards and part of grant to John Meadows. Witness James Power and Lawson Thomson. Signed John Meadows. Wit. oath Mar. 3, 1817 James Power to Thomas Poole. Rec. Mar. 3, 1817. Dower renounced Feb. 18, 1817 Nancy Meadows to John Brewton

p. 211-212 Nov. 24, 1809 Nathaniel Woodruff (Spartanburgh) to Josiah Woodruff (same); for $130 sold 74 ac on waters of Tyger R; border: "near the house", George Brewton, John Brenton, and Josiah Woodruff; NE part of grant Dec. 3, 1792 Gov. Charles Pinckney to Dennis Lindsey. Witness Joseph Woodruff, Josiah Woodruff, and Thomas Woodruff. Signed Nat Woodruff. Wit. oath Apr. 14, 1810 Thomas Woodruff to John Bruton. Rec. Mar. 3, 1817

p. 212 Dec. 22, 1807 Lewis Stanley and wife Adah (Spartanburgh) to Major Hancock (same); for $300 sold 230 ac on waters of Cherokee Cr on W side of Broad R; border: Ezekiel Stanley desc, Charles Hester, William Fondrin, Jesse Fondrin, and John Hester. Witness Daniel McCay and John Williams. Signed Lewis Stanley and Adah's mark. Wit. oath May 18, 1810 John Williams to John Lipscomb. Rec. Mar. 3, 1817

p. 212-216 Mar. 1, 1788 William Barnett (Spartanburgh) to George Kirk (same); for 80£ sterling sold 160 ac on Two Mile Cr of Enoree R; border: Jean McClearkin and Richard Chesney; N part of 640 ac grant Jun. 15, 1786 Gov. William Moultrie to William Barnett. Witness Samuel Busey, George Sisel, and James Wofford. Signed Wm Barnett. Wit. oath Feb. 13, 1817 Samuel Busey to John Dean. Rec. Mar. 4, 1817

p. 216-217 Jan. 24, 1816 George Kirk and John Kirk (Jackson Co, Ga) to Joseph Barnett (Spartanburgh); for $240 sold 120 ac on branch of Jamey's Cr; survey by James Wofford for William Barnett and granted Jul. 15, 1786 Gov. Moultrie to William Barnett. Witness Rebeka F Dean and John Dean. Signed George and John Kirk's marks. Wit. oath Nov. 25, 1816 Rebeka F Dean to John Dean. Rec. Mar. 4, 1817

p. 217-218 May 19, 1815 Spencer Bobo (Spartanburgh) to Joseph Barnett (same); for $150 sold 100 ac on branch of Two Mile Cr of Enoree R; border: Barnett, Spiller, Spencer Colvert, James Crow, and Isaac Crow. Witness William Barnett, Samuel Hendrix, and Sarah Barnett. Signed S Bobo. Wit. oath Aug. 11, 1815 William Barnett to John Dean. Rec. Mar. 4, 1817

p. 218-219 Nov. 4, 1816 Thomas Hill (Spartanburgh) to William Lockhart (Union Dist); for $500 sold 100 ac on branch of People's Cr; part of survey for Saml Sparks. Witness John Waters, Power Ownbey, and James Waters. Signed Thomas Hill's mark. Wit. oath Mar. 8, 1817 James Waters to John Lipscomb. Rec. Mar. 10, 1817

p. 219-220 Nov. 4, 1816 Thomas Hill (Spartanburgh) to William Lockhart (Union Dist); for $500 sold (ac omitted); border: near Cooper's fence, branch of Gilkey's Cr, and Samuel Sparks; part of survey for Samuel Sparks. Witness John Waters, James Waters, and Powell Ownbey. Signed Thomas Hill's mark. Wit. oath Mar. 8, 1817 James Waters to John Lipscomb. Rec. Mar. 10, 1817

p. 220-221 Nov. 4, 1816 Thomas Hill (Spartanburgh) to William Lockhart (Union Dist); for $500 sold (ac omitted) on head branches of Gilkey's Cr; border: Alexander Cooper; part of survey in 1784 for Isaac Chapman. Witness John Watters(sic), James Waters(sic), and Powell Ownbey. Signed Thomas Hill's mark. Wit. oath Mar. 8, 1817 James Watters to John Lipscomb. Rec. Mar. 10, 1817

p. 221-222 Mar. 10, 1808 Joroyal Barnett (Spartanburgh) to John Lancaster sr; for $250 sold 200 ac on Kelso's Cr of Fairforrest Cr; border: W-John Connell, S-Micajer Barnett and Wm Golightly, E & N-Eli Tollison and Absalem Lancaster. Witness Micajah Barnett and Absalem Lancaster. Signed Joroyal Barnett. Wit. oath Mar. 22, 1817 Micajah Barnett to Danl White. Rec. Mar. 24, 1817. Dower renounced Mar. 24, 1817 Agness Barnett to James Young

p. 222-223 Feb. 22, 1817 George Floyd (Spartanburgh) to Thomas Price (same); for $325 sold 115 ac at mouth of Ward's Cr; border: Josiah Hatchett, James W Reynolds, James Thomson, and N side of Tyger R; part of grant to Patrick Mark. Witness Amos Sanford and Thomas Wright. Signed George Floyd's mark. Wit. oath Mar. 28, 1817 Thomas Wright to Robert Ligon. Rec. Apr. 3, 1817

p. 223-224 Feb. 25, 1805 Crenshaw Camp (Rutherford Co, NC) to William Wyatt (Lincoln Co, NC); for $68 sold 100 ac at head of Ashworth's Cr; border: Thomas Wyatt and Peg's old field; part of 555 ac grant to Crenshaw Camp. Witness George Camp and Thomas Wyatt. Signed C C. Wit. oath Oct. 8, 1810 Thomas Wyatt to Henry Turner.

Rec. Apr. 4, 1817

p. 224-225 Oct. 5, 1810 William Wyatt (Spartanburgh) to James Wyatt (Lincoln Co, NC); for $97 sold 100 ac at head of Ashworth's Cr; border: Thomas Wyatt and Peg's old field; part of 555 ac grant to Cranshaw Camp. Witness Reubin Philips and Jacob Philips. Signed William Wyatt's mark. Wit. oath Jun. 1, 1811 Jacob Philips to Joshua Richards. Rec. Apr. 4, 1817

p. 225 Mar. 29, 1815 James Wyatt to son Elisha Jones Wyatt; for love and affection give "at James' death and not before" 200 ac; border: Peg's old field, Horton, and Walker. Witness Briant Bonner and Patrick Sanders. Signed James Wyatt. Wit. oath dated "29th" Patrick Sanders to J Camp. Rec. Apr. 4, 1817

p. 225-226 Dec. 10, 1815 William Shackelford to William Pearson; for $250 sold (ac not given) where William Pearson lives; William Shackelford relinquishes title to David Pearson, son of William Pearson. Witness Jonathan Moore and George Leatherwood. Signed Wm Shackelford. Wit. oath Feb. 5, 1816 Jonathan Moore to Drury McDaniel. Rec. Apr. 5, 1817

p. 226-227 Oct. 22, 1816 Thomas Hill (Spartanburgh) to William Lockhart (Union Dist); for $500 sold (ac omitted) "all Thomas' claim belonging to Wearing's (sic) claim in his survey". Witness John Waters and Jane Waters. Signed Thomas Hill. Wit. oath Apr. 7, 1817 John Waters to J Camp. Rec. Apr. 7, 1817

p. 227-228 Dec. 9, 1814 William Young, George Salman and wife Elizabeth, John Young (Greenville Dist), Saley Young, William Foster and wife Nancy, James Young (Spartanburgh), Boley Conner and wife Frances (Franklin Co, Ga), heirs of John and Margaret Young desc (late of Spartanburgh) to John Young, one of the legatees; for $657 sold 219 ac on S side of S Pacolett R; border: Alexander Kilpatrick, William Foster, and William Young; lot #3 (or Bear holes lot) of three lots that were all the property of John and Margaret Young that was sold at public sale Dec. 3, 1814. Witness Alsey Wall, Frances Walker, and John Walker. Signed George Salman, Elizabeth Salman, Sarah Young, Boley and Frances Conner, William and Nancy Foster, James Young, James(sic) and Hannah(sic) Dillingham, and William Young. Wit. oath Mar. 18, 1817 Alsey Wall to James Young. Rec. Apr. 7, 1817

p. 228 May 28, 1813 William Holaway (Spartanburgh) to James Walker (same); for $100 sold 100 ac on waters of Ashworth's Cr; border: Calvin and Camp; part of grant Oct. 6, 17088(sic) to Crenshaw Camp. Witness Nimrod Horton and Lewcy Bostick. Signed William Holaway. Wit. oath Jan. 26, 1815 Nimrod Horton to Joseph Camp. Rec. Apr. 7, 1817

p. 228-229 Sept. 5, 1816 John Otts (Spartanburgh) to Robert Goodgion (Greenville Dist); for $300 sold 245 ac on both sides Colley's Cr of N Pacolette R; part of 458 ac grant Mar. 5, 1792 to Jervis Cornwell. Witness Thomas Price and L Thomson. Signed John Otts. Wit. oath (not dated) L Thomson to John Brewton. Rec. Apr. 7, 1817

p. 229 Mar. 20, 1808 Thomas Hill (Spartanburgh) to Charles Crittenton (same); for $65 sold 80 ac; border: E-John Crittenton, S-Benjamin Hudgins, W-Griffin Carter, and N-Charles Crittenton bought from Thomas Hill. Witness Young Allen and Thomas Reid. Signed Thomas Hill's mark. Wit. oath Mar. 2, 1808 Young Allen to John Lipscomb. Rec. Apr. 7, 1817

p. 229-230 Nov. 22, 1816 Charles Hester to Major Hancock; for $55.50

sold 111 ac on waters of Cherokee Cr of Broad R. Witness Laurens Anderson and Joseph Collins. Signed Chs Hester. Wit. oath Mar. 7, 1817 Laurens Anderson to (not signed). Rec. Apr. 7, 1817

p. 230 Nov. 22, 1816 Charles Hester to Laurence Anderson; for $58.50 sold 117 ac on branch of Cherokee Cr of Broad R. Witness Joseph Collins and Major Hancock. Signed Chs Hester. Wit. oath Mar. 17, 1817 Major Hancock to John Lipscomb. Rec. Apr. 7, 1817

p. 230-231 Feb. 5, 1814 William W Sillaven (Anderson Co, Tenn) to Thomas Lipscomb (Spartanburgh); for $135 sold 100 ac on Snud's Br on S side of Thickety Cr; border: William George and Thomas Lipscomb; part of grant to Hezekiah Sillaven who sold to Thomas Sillaven. Witness William Jackson and Solomon Jackson. Signed William W Sillaven. Wit. oath Jul. 30, 1814 Solomon Jackson to John Lipscomb. Rec. Apr. 7, 1817

p. 231-232 Mar. 25, 1815 George and Mary Devine (Spartanburgh) to John Weathers jr (same); for $82 sold 27 ac on Divine's Spring Br of Prater's Cr; border: N-formerly Thomas Todd, E & S-John Weathers, and W-George Divine and part of same tract. Witness John M Traylor and James Sexton. Signed George Divine and Mary's mark. Wit. oath Apr. 1, 1817 James Sexton to M Casey. Rec. Apr. 7, 1817

p. 232-233 Nov. 27, 1816 Burton Forrester (Spartanburgh) to Elenor Morrow (same); for $35 sold 100 ac on waters of Little Beech(?) Cr; border: Whitney Hines' old tract, road from Island ford to Broad R to Coker's ford ("deed has part of paper torn so part of description cannot be given"), and Steedman's old line. Witness Solomon Forrester and Peter Gaumal (or Gausnal). Signed Burton Forrester's mark. Wit. oath Mar. 7, 1817 Peter Gaumal to William Hendrix. Rec. Apr. 7, 1817

p. 233-234 Nov. 28, 1816 James Younger (Spartanburgh) to James Young (same); for $200 sold 45 ac; border: J Young, Robert Wells, and Carrol's old line. Witness Christopher Golightly, Robert Wall, and Edmund Henley. Signed James Younger's mark. Wit. oath Mar. 20, 1817 Robert Wall to Wm Kelso. Rec. Apr. 8, 1817

p. 234-235 Feb. 13, 1817 James Campbell (Spartanburgh) to Thomas Lipscomb (same); for $495 sold 165 ac on S side Goucher's Cr--border: William Patterson and Griffin Carter and on N side of Goucher's Cr--border: Thomas Reid, Jarratt Patterson, and "others"; sold by Jarratt Patterson to Willis Allen who sold to James Campbell. Witness John H Jones and Ignatius Littlejohn. Signed James Campbell. Wit. oath Feb. 13, 1817 John H Jones and Ignatius Littlejohn to John Lipscomb. Rec. Apr. 8, 1817. Dower renounced Feb. 13, 1817 Molly Campbell to John Lipscomb

p. 235-236 Jan. 25, 1816 Jarratt Patterson (Spartanburgh) to Thomas Lipscomb (same); for $900 sold 450 ac; border: Hembre, James Campbell, Gocher Cr, William Patterson, Young Allen, David Lipscomb, John Lipscomb esq, Ezekiel Sillavan, and widow Griffin's Spring Br; part of grant in 1771 North Carolina to Hugh Moore; "part of grants to Hugh Moore, David Allen, Mallichi Jones, and Jonathan Griffin". Witness Moses Wilkins and Edward Lipscomb. Signed Jarret Patterson. Wit. oath Nov. 23, 1816 Edward Lipscomb to (not signed). Rec. Apr. 8, 1817. Dower renounced Nov. 23, 1816 Jean Patterson to John Lipscomb

p. 236-237 Oct. 12, 1816 Andrew McMakin (Spartanburgh) to Edward Smith (same); for $325 sold 100 ac on both sides Middle Tyger R; border: SW-John McCarter, SE-David Reynolds, and N & NW-lot #6; Andrew McMakin's lot 4 "as his dividend" of estate of his father Benjamin P McMakin desc. Witness Alexr M Thompson, Byrd Linthicum, and John McDaniel. Signed Andrew McMakin. Wit. oath Mar. 17, 1817 Alexr M Thompson to John Montgomery. Rec. Apr. 8, 1817

p. 237-238 Mar. 3, 1817 Pleasant Brannon (Spartanburgh) to William Copeland (same); for $450 sold 157½ ac on S side of N Pacolette R; border: William Copeland, James Milican, Moses Milican, and Margaret Jackson; part of land formerly belonging to William Milican desc and where Pleasant Brannon formerly lived; "balance" of tract Pleasant sold to William Copeland Feb. 6, 1812. Witness John Williams, Charles Copeland, and James Samerhill. Signed Pleasant Brannon's mark. Wit. oath Mar. 4, 1817 James Samerhill to Wm Kelso. Rec. Apr. 8, 1817. Dower renounced Mar. 4, 1817 Polley Brannon to James Young

p. 238-239 Feb. 2, 1815 James Hammett to James Brockman; for $300 sold 150 ac on both sides Abner's Cr of Enoree R; border: Henry Brockman, Tyrce Glenn, Hammett's Still house Br, and Herring; includes where James Hammett lives. Witness Thomas Wood and Josiah McClain. Signed James Hammett. Wit. oath Oct. 14, 1816 Thomas Wood to John Collins. Rec. Apr. 8, 1817. Dower renounced Aug. 24, 1815 Anna Hammett to Drury McDaniel

p. 239-240 Dec. 9, 1815 William Dalton (Spartanburgh) to William Morgan (same); for $150 sold (ac omitted) on waters of Obed's Cr of Pacolette R. Witness William Morgan and Moses Brooks. Signed William Dalton. Wit. oath Mar. 20, 1817 William Morgan to Wm Kelso. Rec. Apr. 8, 1817

p. 240 Oct. (blank), 1815 Robert Stacy and Jesse Tate to Michael Gaffney (Spartanburgh); for $700 sold 120 ac on both sides Cherokee Cr of Broad R; border: Michael Gaffney. Witness Hugh Quin and John Quin. Signed Robert Stacy and Jesse Tate. Wit. oath Oct. 5, 1816 John Quin to J Camp. Rec. Apr. 8, 1817

p. 240-241 Sept. 10, 1814 Samuel Oldhantz (Spartanburgh) to Michael Gaffney (same); for $30 sold 30 ac on People's Cr of Broad R; border: Wm Rickman; part of grant Sept. 5, 1791 to James Martin. Witness Saml G Huskins (or Hoskins) and Gibson Rickman. Signed Samuel Oldhantz's mark. Wit. oath Oct. 14, 1816 Gibson Rickman to John Lipscomb. Rec. Apr. 8, 1817

p. 241-242 Nov. 28, 1816 John Henry (Spartanburgh) to Miles Sumner (Union Dist); for $400 sold 146 3/4 ac; border: Caven's Spring Br, W-James W Reynolds, S-Gideon Reynolds and James Alexander, E-Robert Alexander and Robert Bogin, and N-Joseph Willis. Witness William Otts, James Mason, and Benjamin Robuck. Signed John Henry. Wit. oath Nov. 29, 1816 William Otts to John Brewton. Rec. Apr. 8, (omitted)

p. 242-243 Oct. 5, 1815 Brittain Williford (Spartanburgh) to John Cook (same); for $700 sold 471 ac on Wilder's fork of Dutchman's Cr; border: Richard Hewatt; part of two grants: (1) on Jan. 21, 1785 and (2) on Nov. 9, 1786 both to Brittain Williford. Witness Levi Lancaster, John C Cook, and Drury Parham. Signed Britn Williford. Wit. oath Oct. 9, 1815 John C Cook to Burrell Bobo. Rec. Apr. 8, 1817. Dower renounced Oct. 9, 1815 Lucy Williford to Burrell Bobo

p. 243-245 Dec. 9, 1814 William Young, George Salman and wife Elizabeth, John Young (Greenville Dist), Sally Young, William Foster and wife Nancy, James Young (Spartanburgh), Boley Conner and wife Frances (Franklin Co, Ga), heirs of John and Margaret Young (late of Spartanburgh) desc, to William Young, one of legatees;

for $1,075.50 sold 478 ac on N side of "Jakes to Bodley's Br" of S Pacolett R; border: Kilpatrick and Jonathan Walls; lot #1 of three lots divided from estate of John and Margaret Young and sold at public sale Dec. 3, 1814. Witness Alsey Wall and Frances Walker. Signed Geo and Elizabeth Salman, John Young, Sarh Young, Boley and Frances Conner, William and Nancy Foster, James Young, James(sic and Hannah(sic) Dillingham. Wit. oath Mar. 18, 1817 Alsey Wall to James Young. Rec. Apr. 8, 1817

p. 245 Feb. 13, 1816 Thomas Hill (Spartanburgh) to Henry Kenedy (same); for $100 sold 200 ac; border: Wheeler; part of grant Feb. 26, 1800 Gov. John Drayton to Samuel Drayton to Samuel Sparks. Witness Michl Gaffney and Isaac Hill. Signed Thomas Hill's mark. Wit. oath Apr. 9, 1817 Michl Gaffney to Wm Reid. Rec. Apr. 9, 1817

p. 245-246 Nov. 29, 1816 Henry Kenedy (Spartanburgh) to George Stacy (same); for $145 sold 200 ac; border: Hill and Wheeler; part of grant Feb. 26, 1800 Gov. John Drayton to Saml Sparks. Witness Michl Gaffney and Levin Dill. Signed Henry Kanady. Wit. oath Apr. 9, 1817 Levin Dill to Wm Reid. Rec. Apr. 9, 1817

p. 246-247 Jan. 2, 1817 Henry Kenedy (Spartanburgh) to Michael Gaffney (same); for $800 sold 200 ac on Popular Cr and Skelton's Cr of Broad R; border: Hill; part of grant Mar. 3, 1800 Gov. John Drayton to Samuel Sparks; and sold 200 ac "laid to said Sparks to Josiah Sparks"; border: W Bryan and Hill. Witness Levin Dill and Joseph Collins jr. Signed Henry Kanady. Wit. oath Apr. 9, 1817 Levin Dill to Wm Reid. Rec. Apr. 9, 1817

p. 247-248 Mar. (blank), 1817 William Holaway (Spartanburgh) to Robert B McGowen (same); for $150 sold 150 ac on Cherokee Cr; part of 300 ac. Witness Tindal Robertson and Richard Lee. Signed Wm Holaway. Wit. oath Apr. 9, 1817 Tindal Robertson to Danl White. Rec. Apr. 9, 1817. Dower renounced Apr. 9, 1817 Nancy Holaway to Daniel White

p. 248-249 Nov. 16, 1816 John Hester (Spartanburgh) to Tindal Robertson (same); for $200 sold 202 ac on Little Cherokee Cr; border: Vinesal; part of "large" survey by James Martin for Charles Miles. Witness John Surratt, John Cincett (or Cineset), and Anthony Surratt. Signed John Hester and Sarah's mark. Wit. oath Apr. 7, 1817 John Surratt to J Camp. Rec. Apr. 9, 1817

p. 249 Jan. 3, 1817 (Laurens Dist) John Spurgen (Laurens Dist) to John Paden (Spartanburgh); for $304.93 sold a Negro girl Cherre and her increase "otherwise called" Buffy about 14 years old; Condition John Paden can't move Negro and her increase outside South Carolina and is to give Negro sufficient provisions and clothing nad treat her with humanity and sale is void if John Spurgen pays $304.93 to John Paden by Jan. 3, 1824. Witness Henry C Young and George Fowler. Signed John Spurgen and John Paden. Wit. oath Mar. 27, 1817 George Fowler to Thomas Poole. Rec. Apr. 9, 1817

p. 249-250 Mar. 27, 1817 John Jordan (Spartanburgh) to Andrew B Fleming (same); for $250 sold 150 ac on both sides of branch of N Tygar R; border: Andrew B Fleming, Vernon, and Thompson; a third of land formerly belonged to James Jordan desc. Witness Page Rork and Joseph Collins. Signed John Jordan. Wit. oath Apr. 9, 1817 Joseph Collins to John Montgomery. Rec. Apr. 9, 1817

p. 250-251 Nov. 18, 1816 Spencer Colvert (Spartanburgh) to Moses Casey jr esq; power of attorney to recover legacy due Spencer Colvert from Danl McKey, John Leatherwood, and James Leatherwood, executors of estate of Zacheriah Leatherwood desc; see will of Zacheriah Leatherwood. Witness William Leatherwood and

Isaac Crow jr. Signed Spencer Colvert. Wit. oath Mar. 31, 1817 Isaac Crow jr to Samuel Woodruff. Rec. Apr. 9, 1817

p. 251-252 Jul. 28, 1816 John Withers jr (Spartanburgh) to Reubin Newman (same); for $500 sold 100 ac; border: Anthony Shand, Tyger R, Richard Young (bought from Owen Forister), and Reubin Newman. Witness Joseph Red and Enoch Anderson. Signed John Withers. Wit. oath Apr. 2, 1817 Joseph Red to Thomas Poole. Rec. Apr. 10, 1817. Dower renounced Oct. 18, 1816 Mary Withers to Burrell Bobo

p. 252-253 Mar. 27, 1817 Gabriel Gossett (Spartanburgh) to Spencer Tollison (same); for $150 sold 98 ac on branch of Fair-forrest Cr; where "he" lives. Witness James Smith and William King. Signed Gabriel Gossett. Wit. oath Apr. 4, 1817 James Smith to Thomas Poole. Rec. Apr. 14, 1817

p. 253-254 Sept. 26, 1801 William Turner to Samuel Turner; for $100 sold 100 ac on N side of Lawson's fork; part of 200 ac grant Sept. 25, 1766 Gov. William Tryon (NC) to Thomas Wilson. Witness Benjamin Lewis and Robert Foster. Signed William Turner. Wit. oath Sept. 26, 1801 William Turner to Ism Foster. Rec. Apr. 19, 1817. Dower renounced Sept. 20, 1816 Elizabeth Turner to James Young

p. 254-255 Mar. 27, 1817 William Morgan (Spartanburgh) to C C Duncan (same); for $150 sold (ac omitted) on waters of Obed's Cr of Pacolet R. Witness William S Morgan and James Trevilion. Signed Wm Morgan. Wit. oath Apr. 19, 1817 William S. Morgan to Ephm Lewis. Rec. Apr. 19, 1817

p. 255-256 Aug. 20, 1805 Abishae Camp (Spartanburgh) to Nathan Byars (same); for $50 sold 140 ac on branches of Turner's fork of Thickety Cr; border: Byars, Turner, and Crocker. Witness Joseph Camp and James Riding. Signed Abishae Camp. Wit. oath Aug. 30, 1806 Joseph Camp to John Lipscomb. Rec. May 5, 1817

p. 256-257 Jan. 13, 1817 Austin Wright (Spartanburgh) to Claburn Laurence (Union Dist); for $337.50 sold 112½ ac; border: Wilson Moraso; part of 200 ac survey in 1784 for Adam Thomson. Witness Q McKlimurry and John Laurence. Signed Austin Wright. Wit. oath Jan. 21, 1817 John Laurence to John Lipscomb. Rec. May 5, 1817

p. 257-258 (blank), 179(blank) Lewis Ogier (Charleston, SC), tailor(?) to Paul Hamilton (same); for $600 sold 250 ac in fork of Tygar R. Witness William Redleck and Samuel House. Signed L Ogier. Wit. oath none. Rec. May 5, 1817. Dower renounced Aug. 4, 1808 Susannah Ogier to Samuel House. Apr. 28, 1809 Paul Hamilton gave above to his son Paul Hamilton. Mar. 20, 1815 Paul J Hamilton "conveys" deed to Nathl Burton. Witness John Thornton and Spencer Leatherwood. Wit. oath Mar. 5, 1817 John Thornton to John Collins

p. 258-259 Sept. 18, 1813 Benjamin Bonner (Spartanburgh) to William Wilson; for $100 sold 100 ac on waters of Surat's Cr and head of Long Br; border: S-Wilson Nisbett and E-Benjamin Bonner. Witness William Collins and Henry Johnson. Signed Benjamin Bonner's mark. Wit. oath Nov. 27, 1816 William Collins to J Camp. Rec. May 5, 1817

p. 259-260 Nov. 27, 1816 William Wilson to Nathan Byars; for $100 sold 100 ac at head of Long Br of Sarrat's Cr; deed warranted for claims <u>after</u> titles of Daniel McClaron's grant. Witness William Collins and Joseph Richards. Signed William Wilson. Wit. oath Nov. 27, 1816 William Collins to J Camp. Rec. May 5, 1817

p. 260 Nov. 8, 1816 James Hammett (Spartanburgh) to Henry Brockman; Henry Brockman paid $800 to John and Charles Bulow (Charleston, SC) and to secure a debt James Hammett and Henry Brockman had with John and Charles Bulow sold three Negroes--a wench Susannah and two girls Aggy and Malinda; Condition: sale void if James Hammett pays Henry Brockman or John and Charles Bulow $800 with interest by Dec. 25, 1817. Witness Thomas Brockman and Harriet Brockman. Signed James Hammett. Wit. oath May 6, 1817 Thomas P Brockman to Thomas Poole. Rec. May 6, 1817

p. 260-261 Sept. 17, 1816 Alice Fowler (Spartanburgh) to Andrew Paden (same); for $100 sold 100 ac on waters of Enoree R; border: William Massy. Witness Grisham Durham and John Paden. Signed Alice Fowler's mark. Wit. oath May 10, 1817 John Paden to John Montgomery. Rec. May 12, 1817

p. 261-262 Apr. 20, 1817 James Paden (Greenville Dist) to Andrew Paden (Spartanburgh); for $300 sold 200 ac on waters of Fargsin Cr. Witness John S Paden and Wm Strange. Signed James Paden. Wit. oath May 10, 1817 Wm Strange to John Montgomery. Rec. May 12, 1817

p. 262-263 Mar. 15, 1817 Laban P Poole (Spartanburgh) to Hays Bagwell; for $200 sold 300 ac on waters of N Tyger R; "by and just above" Tanner's Mill; sold by sheriff Vincent Bennett due to a writ. Witness Elisha Bomar and George Thomason. Signed Laban P Poole. Wit. oath Jun. 2, 1817 Elisha Bomar to Thomas Poole. Rec. Jun. 2, 1817

p. 263-264 Nov. 28, 1817 Nancy and John Foster (Spartanburgh) to Hays Bagwell (same); for $150 sold 75 ac on waters of N Tyger R and on McMicken's Br. Witness F. H. Legg and Wm N Miller. Signed John Foster and Nancy's mark. Wit. oath May 29, 1817 Wm N Miller to F. H. Legg. Rec. Jun. 2, 1817

p. 264-265 Dec. 13, 1816 Green W Meadows (Spartanburgh) to John Meadows (same); for $50 sold 46 ac on waters of Cain Cr of Tyger R; a third of land owned by Joseph Meadows desc. Witness George Meadows and Benjamin Meadows. Signed Green W Meadows. Wit. oath May 29, 1817 George Meadows to James Hamm. Rec. Jun. 2, 1817

p. 265-267 Feb. 1, 1817 Joseph Kelso (Spartanburgh), "Hatter" to Elijah Ballenger (same); for $120 sold 100 ac on S side Fairforrest Cr; border: W-Elijah Ballenger, S-Willis Wingo, E-Joseph Kelso, S-James Means; part of grant to John Thomas who sold to Josiah Culbertson who sold to Joseph Kelso. Witness Willis Wingo and Hamilton Wilson. Signed Jos Kelso. Wit. oath Feb. 3, 1817 Willis Wingo to James Young. Rec. Jun. 2, 1817

p. 267-268 Feb. 1, 1817 Joseph Kelso (Spartanburgh) "Hatter" to James Hutchens (same), blacksmith; for $500 sold 487 ac on S side of Fairforest Cr; border: N-Obediah Wingo, S-Nancy Story, widow, E-James Story, and W-Willis Wingo; part of grant to John Thomas and Charles Kempton; John Thomas sold to Josiah Culbertson who sold to Joseph Kelso; Charles Kempton sold to John Foster who sold to Josiah Culbertson who sold to Joseph Kelso. Witness Willis Wingo and Hamilton Wilson. Signed Jos Kelso. Wit. oath Feb. 3, 1817 Willis Wingo to James Young. Rec. Jun. 2, 1817. Dower renounced May 10, 1817 Ann Kelso to William Reid

p. 268-270 Mar. (blank), 1817 William Nantz (Union Dist) to John Deavours (Spartanburgh); for $207 sold 97 ac; border: Robert McCollum, Robert Wood, E Bomar, road from Spartanburgh to Greenville Court House, and Timmons. Witness Nathl Gist and Thomas Scott. Signed William Nantz. Wit. oath Jul. 4, 1817 Thomas Scott to A Benson. Rec. Jul. 4, 1817

p. 270-272 Aug. 25, 1793 Benjamin Kilgore jr (Greenville Co) to Robert Wood (Spartanburgh); for 10£ sterling sold 100 ac on N side Enoree R; border: S-Old Indian boundary, N & W-Henry Woods, NW & NE-James Donalds and Robert Wood, and other sides-Enoree R and Capt. John Thomas; part of grant Sept. 3, 1792 Gov. Chas Pinckney to Benjamin Kilgore jr for 469 ac; Robert Wood loses out if older grant claims the land. Witness Pennewell Wood, Henry Woods, and Benjamin Kilgore. Signed (Aug. 31, 1793) Benjamin Kilgore jr. Wit. oath Feb. 25, 1807 Pennewell Wood to James Kilgore. Rec. Jul. 7, 1817

p. 272 Apr. 6, 1817 John Snoddy to Samuel Snoddy; for $100 sold 148 ac on Jemmies Br; grant to John Leach. Witness Saml Jamison, James Chamblin, and James Crook. Signed John Snoddy. Wit. oath May 2, 1817 James Chamblin to F. H. Legg. Rec. Jul. 7, 1817

p. 272-274 Aug. 31, 1816 Joshua Benson (Greenville Dist) to John Kirkpatrick and Patrick L Dunlap (same); for $1,200 sold 600 ac on both sides of S Tyger R. Witness James Mayfield, Thomas Mayfield, and Wm H Thirlkell. Signed Joshua Benson. Wit. oath Jun. 2, 1817 (Greenville Dist) James Mayfield to Thos Forgusan. Rec. Jul. 7, 1817. Dower renounced Oct. 19, 1816 (Greenville Dist) Rosannah Benson to Andrew McCrary

p. 274-276 Aug. 31, 1816 Joshua Benson (Greenville Dist) to John Kirkpatrick and Patrick Dunlap (same); for $2,500 sold (1) 1,000 ac on E side of Rocky field Cr; (2) 200 ac on S side of Rocky field Cr; (3) 98 ac on branch of Reid fork of Tyger R; and (4) 1 ac containing an ore bank that Joshua Benson now "occupies". Witness Thomas Mayfield, James Mayfield, and Wm H Thirlkeld. Signed Joshua Benson. Wit. oath Jun. 2, 1817 (Greenville Dist) James Mayfield to Thomas Forguson. Rec. Jul. 7, 1817. Dower renounced Oct. 19, 1816 (Greenville Dist) Rosannah Benson to Andrew McCrary

p. 276 Aug. 21, 1816 Joseph Laurence and Michael Walling (Spartanburgh) to John Pattison (Laurens Dist); for $180 sold (ac omitted); where Joseph Laurence lives; border: Davis and Goodlett. Witness Gowen Clayton and Joseph Wilson. Signed Joseph Laurence and Michael Walling. Wit. oath Jun. 20, 1817 Joseph Wilson to J Whitten. Rec. Jul. 21, 1817

p. 276-278 Aug. 12, 1815 William Reid (Spartanburgh) to William Hardy (same); for $50 sold 170 ac on waters of Pacolette R and Lawson's fork; border: S-William Golightly, E-Solomon Crocker, N-Wm R Smith, and S & SW-James Barnett, Joroyal Barnett, and William Bagwell. Witness Richard Lamaster and Richard Gordan. Signed William Reid. Wit. oath Jul. 11, 1817 Richard Lamaster to A Benson. Rec. Jul. 21, 1817

p. 278-279 Aug. 19, 1815 William Hardy (Spartanburgh) to John Tollison (same); for $250 sold 170 ac on waters of Pacolett R and Lawson's fork; border: S-William Golightly, E-Solomon Crocker, N-William R Smith, S & SW-James Barnett, Joroyal Barnett, and William Bagwell. Witness O Kirby and Abraham Lamaster. Signed William Hardy's mark. Wit. oath Jul. 21, 1817 Abraham Lamaster to A Benson. Rec. Jul. 21, 1817

p. 279-280 Nov. 9, 1816 William B Alexander (Spartanburgh) to Nancy Robuck (same); for $225 sold 100 ac on Jemmies Cr; border: George Robuck, John Bragg, William Posey, and Priestly Smith. Witness Benjamin Robuck and Nathaniel Floyd. Signed William B Alexander. Wit. oath Jul. 22, 1817 Benjamin Robuck to Thomas Poole.

Rec. Jul. 22, 1817

p. 280-281 Dec. 2, 1816 James Berry (SC) to John Williams (SC); for $700 sold (ac omitted); border: Wm Millican, Tate, Thomas Millican, and on N side of N Pacolette R; part of grant to Robert Tate. Witness George Welch and William Copeland. Signed James Berry's mark. Wit. oath May 28, 1817 George Welch to Wm Kelso. Rec. Jul. 23, 1817

p. 281-282 Nov. 18, 1809 Isaac Williams (Spartanburgh) to Robert Scruggs (same); for $80 sold 80 ac on waters of Thickety Cr of Broad R; adjoins the Cowpens; part of two tracts formerly belonging to Edward Williams desc. Witness Leonard Adcock and Drury Scruggs. Signed Isaac Williams. Wit. oath Nov. 18, 1809 Leonard Adcock to Henry Turner. Rec. Jul. 23, 1817

p. 282-283 Dec. 14, 1807 Jacob Crocker (Spartanburgh) to Joshua Gordan (Rutherford Co, NC); for (blank) sold 185 ac on waters of Quinn's Cr; border: Markley and Crocker; part of grant Jul. 7, 1802 to Jacob Crocker. Witness John Turner and William Davidson. Signed Jacob Crocker. Wit. oath Feb. 13, 1808 John Turner to Leonard Adcock. Rec. Jul. 23, 1817

p. 283-284 Oct. 13, 1812 Joshua Richards (Spartanburgh) to Edmund Chambers (York Dist); for $100 sold 51 ac on Cherokee Cr; border: Camp. Witness William Cockrum and James Richards. Signed Joshua Richards. Wit. oath Feb. 5, 1816 James Richards to Joseph Camp. Rec. Jul. 23, 1817

p. 284-285 Oct. 20, 1813 William Camp (York Dist) to Edmund Chambers (same); for $500 sold 210½ ac on Cherokee Cr; border: Cooper. Witness Zachariah Cooper and William Morgan. Signed Wm Camp. Wit. oath Jul. 11, 1816 William Morgan to J Camp. Rec. Jul. 23, 1817. Dower renounced Dec. 13, 1814 Rebeca Camp to Joshua Richards

p. 285-286 Aug. 5, 1804 Benjamin Bonner (Spartanburgh) to Daniel McClaren (same); for $500 sold 240 ac on waters of Sarratt's Cr of Broad R; border: Robertson and Turner. Witness William Walker and John McClarren. Signed Benjamin Bonner's mark. Wit. oath Aug. 10, 1804 John McClarren to John Rickman. Rec. Jul. 23, 1817

p. 286-287 Sept. 16, 1815 Joshua Gorden to William Amos; for $40 sold 85 ac; border: Nesbett. Witness Samuel Adams and Daniel Rollins. Signed Joshua Gorden's mark. Wit. oath Sept. 16, 1815 Samuel Adams to J Camp. Rec. Jul. 23, 1817

p. 287-288 May 26, 1813 John Turner to Matthias Turner; for $150 sold 150 ac on Cherokee Cr; part of 317 ac grant Dec. 16, 1806 to John Turner. Witness Jesse Turner and Thomas Robertson. Signed John Turner. Wit. oath May 26, 1813 Thomas Robertson to J Camp. Rec. Jul. 23, 1817

p. 288-289 Nov. 17, 1812 James Harrison to Wilson Nesbett; for $150 sold 350 ac on Leach Cr of Broad R; border: Turner. Witness William Holaway and William Camp jr. Signed James Harris (sic). Wit. oath Jul. 8, 1815 William Camp jr to J Camp. Rec. Jul. 23, 1817

p. 289-290 Dec. 11, 1812 Jacob Gorden to Wilson Nesbett; for $50 sold 100 ac on head branches of Quinn's Cr of Thickety Cr; border: Joseph Byars. Witness Samuel G Hoskins and Charles Amos. Signed Jacob Gorden's mark. Wit. oath Jul. 11, 1816 Charles Amos to J Camp. Rec. Jul. 23, 1817

p. 290-291 Nov. 19, 1813 William Morress (Spartanburgh) to Wilson Nesbett (same); for $250 sold 573 ac in two parts--(1) (ac omitted); border: Turner and Wilson Nesbett (bought from James Harrison); part of grant to John Bomar; and (2) 79 ac; border: Wilson Nesbett (bought from James Harrison, Wofford, and Turner; 23 ac excepted "where Spece's old line runs into (1)"; William Morress is to return money if older grant takes the land in 10 years. Witness William Camp jr and Nathan Byars. Signed William Morriss. Wit. oath Jul. 28, 1813 William Camp jr to J Camp. Rec. Jul. 23, 1817

p. 291-292 May 12, 1814 Brian Bonner (Spartanburgh) to Wilson Nesbett (same); for $200 sold 200 ac on waters of Surratt's Cr of Broad R; border: W-Holaway, Wilson Nesbett, and Turner. Witness William Camp jr and William Collins. Signed Brian Bonner. Wit. oath Jul. 8, 1815 William Collins jr(sic) to J Camp. Rec. Jul. 23, 1817

p. 292-293 Oct. 26, 1814 James Wells (Lincoln Co, NC) to Wilson Nesbett; for $60 sold 80 ac on waters of Suck Cr. Witness Daniel Byrns, Matthias Turner, and Clizby Cobb. Signed James Webb. Wit. oath Jul. 8, 1815 Matthias Turner to J Camp. Rec. Jul. 23, 1817

p. 293-294 Apr. 3, 1815 William Camp sr (York Dist) to Wilson Nesbett; for (money omitted) sold ½ ac on waters of Cherokee Cr; includes an ore bank known as Camp's bank. Witness William Camp jr and Thomas Camp. Signed Wm Camp. Wit. oath Feb. 19, 1816 William Camp jr to J Camp. Rec. Jul. 23, 1817

p. 294-295 Feb. 14, 1815 William Holoway (Spartanburgh) to Wilson Nesbett; for $892 sold 892 ac on Surratt's Cr of Broad R. Witness William Collins and Hugh Baily. Signed William Holoway. Wit. oath Jul. 8, 1815 William Collins to J Camp. Rec. Jul. 23, 1817

p. 295-296 Nov. 13, 1813 James Poole (Spartanburgh) to son Elijah Poole (same); for love and affection give 100 ac on Richland Cr and Rich Hill Br; where James Poole lives; land Col. William Dickson sold to James Poole; note: "the Spring I now fetch water out of is free from them who may live on either side of the Creek forever". Witness James Crocker, John Poole, and Benjamin Poole. Signed James Poole. Wit. oath Jan. 12, 1814 James Crocker to Jno H Jones. Rec. Aug. 4, 1817

p. 296-297 Feb. 1, 1817 Joseph Kelso (Spartanburgh), Hatter to Willis Wingo (same); for $220 sold 203 ac on S side of Fairforrest Cr; border: N-Obediah Wingo, S-James Means, E-Joseph Kelso, and W-Elijah Ballenger; part of grant to John Thomas who sold to Josiah Culbertson who sold to Joseph Kelso. Witness Hamilton Wilson and James Hutchens. Signed Joseph Kelso. Wit. oath Feb. 3, 1817 Hamilton Wilson to James Young. Rec. Aug. 4, (omitted). Dower renounced Ann Kelso to William Reid May 10, 1817

p. 297-299 Sept. 29, 1814 James Foster, son of Robert (Spartanburgh) to James Foster, son of William (same); for $400 sold (1) 130 ac on Wilson's Mill Cr of N Tyger R; border: William Foster and Nimrod Benson; and (2) 50 ac; border: tract (1) above; (1) and (2) were allotted to wife of James Foster, son of Robert, as an heir of William Benson desc. Witness Abner Benson and Thomas Hannon. Signed James Foster. Wit. oath Aug. 4, 1817 Abner Benson to James Young. Rec. Aug. 4, 1817

p. 299-300 Nov. 16, 1816 John Hester (Spartanburgh) to William Tate (same); for $280 sold 216 ac on Cherokee Cr; part of "large survey" by James Morton for "Charles". Witness Tindal Robertson and John Arendall. Signed John Hester and Sarah's mark. Wit.

oath Jun. 9, 1817 John Arendall to J Camp. Rec. Aug. 4, 1817

p. 300-301 Jan. 18, 1817 Richard Shackelford (Spartanburgh) to John Langford (same); for $200 sold 100 ac on N side of Dildine Cr; part of grant Jul. 10, 1769 Gov. Charles Gevell(sic) to William Sims. Witness Matthew Allen, Jonathan Crook, and Lewis Landford. Signed Richd Shackelford. Wit. oath Aug. 2, 1817 Lewis Landford to Samuel Woodruff. Rec. Aug. 4, 1817

p. 301-302 Dec. 14, 1816 Joseph Woodruff (Spartanburgh) to Caleb Allen (same); for $400 sold 160 ac on E side of South (or Suck) Cr of Enoree R. Witness William Otts and Elias Corder. Signed Joseph Woodruff's mark. Wit. oath Mar. 27, 1817 William Otts to Samuel Woodruff. Rec. Aug. 4, 1817

p. 302-303 Jan. 18, 1817 Richard Shackelford (Spartanburgh) to John Landford (same); for $250 sold 158 ac on N side of Enoree R; border: John Allen, Wm Stone, and tree marked "B Chops". Witness Matthew Allen, Lewis Landford, and Jonathan Crook. Signed Richard Shackelford. Wit. oath Aug. 2, 1817 Matthew Allen to Samuel Woodruff. Rec. Aug. 4, 1817

p. 303-304 May 30, 1817 Nathaniel Burton (Spartanburgh) to Ford Mason (same); for $365 sold 89 ac on fork of Tyger R; border: Nathl Gentry's Spring Br, S-J Crow, E-N Tyger R, N-N Gentry, and W-Nathaniel Burton. Witness Tollever Scott and Jonothan Crow. Signed Nathl Burton. Wit. oath Jun. 28, 1817 Tollever Scott to Robt Ligon. Rec. Aug. 4, 1817

p. 304-305 Apr. 11, 1817 Laurens Bankston (Spartanburgh) to James Turner (same); for $375 sold 150 ac on S side of Pacolett R at mouth of Buck Cr. Witness Nancy Turner and Fielding Turner. Signed Laurens Bankston's mark. Wit. oath Apr. 11, 1817 Fielding Turner to Henry Turner. Rec. Aug. 4, 1817

p. 305 May 2, 1817 Joel Brewton (Spartanburgh) to Peter Bragg (same); for $180 sold 80 ac on N side of Furgerson's Cr; border: S-Joel Brewton and Furgerson's Cr, W & N-Peter Bragg, and E-Broarick Masson. Witness William Otts and Philip Bruton. Signed Joel G Bruton. Wit. oath May 2, 1817 Philip Bruton to John Brewton. Rec. Aug. 4, 1817

p. 305-306 Mar. 22, 1817 James W Reynolds (Spartanburgh) to George Floyd (same); for $300 sold 88 ac; where "he" lives; border: Mills Sumner, Gideon Reynolds, John King, John Mason, Richard Jentry, Samuel Jentry, and Joseph Willis. Witness John Brewton and Thomas Wright. Signed James W Reynolds. Wit. oath Jul. 31, 1817 Thomas Wright to Robert Ligon. Rec. Aug. 4, 1817

p. 306-307 Mar. 20, 1817 William Lindsey (Spartanburgh) to Spencer Bobo (same); for $300 sold 200 ac; where William Lindsey lives; border: N-Spencer Bobo, E-Brewton, S-John Lindsey, and W-John Crocker. Witness John Lindsey and James Brewton. Signed William Lindsey's mark. Wit. oath none. Rec. Aug. 4, 1817. Dower renounced Apr. 25, 1807(sic) Rachel Lindsey to Drury McDaniel

p. 307-308 Aug. 2, 1817 Richard Vandike (Spartanburgh) to son John Vandike; power of attorney to recover from Samuel Long, J. M. Lewis, and Peter R Booker esqs a bond given by Samuel Long for $100 or 100 pounds of merchantable indigo; note was left in hands of Maj. J. M. Lewis for collection. Witness Laban P Poole and James Hammett. Signed Richard Vandike. Wit. oath Aug. 4, 1817 James Hammett to Henry Turner. Rec. Aug. 4, 1817

p. 308-309 Jul. 4, 1817 John Deavours (Spartanburgh) to Joel Mason (same); for $225 sold 97 ac; border: Robt McCollum, Robert Wood, E Bomar, road from Spartanburgh to Greenville Court House, and Timmons. Witness E Bomar and Thomas Scott. Signed John Deavours. Wit. oath (not dated) Thomas Scott to A Benson. Rec. Sept. 5, 1817

p. 309 Sept. 27, 1816 John Ridings (SC) to Joseph Kelso (same); for $50 sold (ac not given) on N side of N Pacolette R; border: William Kelso and near the graveyard. Witness William Kelso, John Blackwell jr, and Elizabeth Ridings. Signed John Ridings. Wit. oath Sept. 27, 1816 Elizabeth Ridings to William Kelso. Rec. Sept. 16, 1817

p. 309-310 Sept. 28, 1816 Joseph Kelso (SC) to William Kelso jr (SC); for $50 sold (ac omitted) on N side of N Pacolette R; border: William Kelso and near the graveyard. Witness William Kelso, Jane F Kelso and Martha Kelso. Signed Joseph Kelso. Wit. oath Sept. 30, 1816 Martha Kelso to William Kelso. Rec. Sept. 16, 1817

p. 310-311 Dec. 9, 1812 Daniel Morrow and wife Sally (Spartanburgh) to William Kelso jr (same); for $300 sold 60 ac; border: William Kelso sr; sold by Robt Davis to William Kelso sr who sold to Sally Davis. Witness William Jackson, John Ridings, Joseph Jackson jr. Signed Daniel Morrow and Sally's mark. Wit. oath Dec. 9, 1812 John Ridings to William Kelso. Rec. Sept. 16, 1817

p. 311-312 Jan. 6, 1817 James Walker (Spartanburgh) to John Wilson (Lincoln Co, NC); for $195 sold 194 ac on Ashworth's Cr of Broad R; border: near Peg's cabin and Camp; part of grant to Crenshaw Camp. Witness Jacob Philips and William Collins. Signed James Walker. Wit. oath Jul. 23, 1817 William Collins to J Camp. Rec. Sept. 24, 1817

p. 312-313 Feb. 14, 1797 Samuel Kelso (Spartanburgh) to Joseph Kelso sr (same); for 30£ sterling sold (ac omitted); border: James McElwain; part of grant Feb. 6, 1786 to Samuel Kelso; survey by Andrew Thompson. Witness James Story, John Storey, and William Watson. Signed Samuel Kelso. Wit. oath Apr. 15, 1817 James Story to Samuel Archibald. Rec. Sept. 28, 1817

p. 313-315 Sept. 3, 1816 William Williamson and Ann Williamson (Ohio), Thomas Alexander, James Alexander, Nancy Newton Alexander (Greenville Dist) to John Means (Spartanburgh); for $3,000 (sic) sold 1,025 ac on Furgerson's Cr of Tyger R; deed warranted only for land belonging to Thomas Williamson when he died; Thomas Williamson desc (late of Spartanburgh)'s will was proved in Spartanburgh Ordinary's office and appointed William Williamson and John Means executors; Thomas Williamson gave wife Ann Williamson one third of land not otherwise disposed of and the remaining two-thirds were to be sold by executors; legatees decided to sell all the land on Oct. 10, 1815 for $3,500. Witness John Paden, John S Paden, and Alexander Savage. Signed Ann Williamson (by attorney in fact), John Alexander, James Alexander, Thos W Alexander, Nancy N Alexander, and "Williams atty" for William Williamson. Wit. oath Mar. 27, 1817 John Paden to Thomas Poole. Rec. Sept. 1, 1817

p. 315-316 Feb. 26, 1811 James Wofford (Spartanburgh) to Spencer Bobo (same); for $600 sold 200 ac on S side of Furgerson's Cr; border: Thomas Williams, Jonas Brewton, Spencer Bobo, John Crocker, and Jonathan Moore. Witness William Rhodes and John Crocker. Signed James Wofford. Wit. oath Aug. 2, 1817 William Rhodes to John Dean. Rec. Sept. 1, 1817. Dower renounced Jul. 4, 1815 Catherine Wofford to Drury McDaniel

p. 316-317 Nov. 16, 1812 William Wilder (SC) to Thomas Miles (SC);

for $50 sold 17 ac on waters of Tyger R. Witness Burrell Bobo and Foster Folding. Signed Wm Wilder. Wit. oath Nov. 16, 1812 Foster Folding to Burrell Bobo. Rec. Sept. 1, 1817. Dower renounced Nov. 16, 1812 Sejerimah (or Sepremah) Wilder to Burrell Bobo

p. 317-318 Apr. 22, 1817 Samuel Turner to John Low sr; for $50 sold 80 ac; border: Wyatt, Warren, James Saterfield, and ridge path. Witness Reuben Warren and Robert Thomson. Signed Samuel Turner. Wit. oath Sept. 1, 1817 Reuben Warren to J Whitten. Rec. Sept. 1, 1817

p. 318-319 Oct. 6, 1816 Thomas Pinckney jr (Pendleton Dist) to Thomas Hunter (same); for $600 sold 750 ac in two parts--(1) 500 ac in Union Dist and (2) 250 ac in Spartanburgh Dist. Witness John T Lewis and John Baun. Signed Thomas Pinckney jr. Wit. oath Jan. 2, 1817 John T Lewis to Joseph Frisham. Rec. Sept. 1, 1817

p. 319-320 Oct. 9, 1810 Charles Cotesworth Pinckney (late Maj. Gen. of U. S. Army) to nephew Thomas Pinckney, eldest son of brother Major Pinckney; for $1 sold (1) 500 ac on waters of Brown's Cr; border: SE & SW-Daniel Huger, NE-Pierce Butler; grant Sept. 13, 1774 to Charles C Pinckney; and (2) 250 ac on branches of Tyger R; border: NW-Albert Bright (now Ane Burton); grant Sept. 13, 1774 to Charles C Pinckney. Witness Alexander Gorden (of Charleston, SC) and Nathaniel Heywood. Signed Charles Cotesworth Pinckney. Wit. oath (not dated) Alexander Gorden to Henry M Desausure. Rec. Sept. 1, 1817

p. 320-321 Mar. 2, 1813 dower renounced Susannah Graham, wife of William Graham, to Joshua Richards for deed from William Graham to Samuel Lowry; land is on Surratt's Cr. Rec. Oct. 3, 1817

p. 321 May 19, 1811 John Ward (Spartanburgh) to George Floyd (same); for $100 sold (ac omitted) on N side of N Tyger R and on branches of Ward's Cr; "covered with" grant to Patrick March and sold to Francis Ward. Witness John Otts and James Colvert. Signed John Ward. Wit. oath Aug. 30, 1817 John Otts to Robert Ligon. Rec. Oct. 6, 1817

p. 321-322 May 13, 1817 Nancy Saunders (Spartanburgh) to John Saunders (same); for $50 sold 100 ac on branch of Thickety Cr of Broad R; border: Samuel Dunaway (bought from Brown) and Doby. Witness William Saunders and Patrick Saunders. Signed Nancy Saunders' mark. Wit. oath May 13, 1817 William Saunders to Henry Turner. Rec. Oct. 6, 1817

p. 322-323 Feb. 18, 1813 Samuel Enicks (Spartanburgh) to James Alexander (same); for $170 (or $160) sold 63 ac. Witness William Posey and James Colvert. Signed Samuel Enicks. Wit. oath Jan. 10, 1814 William Posey to Samuel Woodruff. Rec. Oct. 6, 1817

p. 323-324 Oct. 4, 1815 John Williams (Spartanburgh) to Robert Alexander; for $80.75 sold 75½ ac; border: James Alexander, E-Richard Chesney, N-Robert Rogers and Nathaniel Burton, W-John Henry and James Alexander, and S-Robert Alexander. Witness William Otts and James Alexander. Signed John Williams. Wit. oath Oct. 6, 1817 James Alexander to Robt Ligon. Rec. Oct. 6, 1817

p. 324-325 Oct. 28, 1816 John Gramling (Spartanburgh) to John Crawford (same); for $322.50 sold 129 ac on Jemmies Cr of Tyger R; border: James Coan, John Crawford, Isaac Snoddy, and Samuel Miller. Witness James Coan and Andrew Coan. Signed John Gramling. Wit. oath none. Rec. Oct. 5, 1817. Dower renounced Sept. 20, 1817 Elizabeth Gramling to John Collins

p. 325-326 Apr. 3, 1817 Joseph Wofford to daughter Ann Tucker; for good causes give a Negro woman Feby and her boy Sam and her increase. Witness John Williams and Samuel Tucker. Signed Joseph Wofford. Wit. oath Sept. 9, 1817 Samuel Tucker to Danl White. Rec. Oct. 6, 1817

p. 326-327 Mar. 25, 1817 John Lancaster sr (Spartanburgh) to Richard Thomson (same); for $300 sold 179 ac on waters of Kelso's Cr of Fairforrest Cr; border: W-James Cooper, S-Micajah Barnett and Wm Golightly, N-John Lancaster jr, and W(sic)-Absalem Lancaster; where John Lancaster lives; part of two grants: (1) to David Lewis and (2) to Joroyal Barnett. Witness Micajah Barnett and Lewis Barnett. Signed John Lancaster sr. Wit. oath Apr. 8, 1817 Lewis Barnett to James Young. Rec. Oct. 10, 1817. Dower renounced Oct. 8, 1817 Abigail Lancaster to Daniel White

p. 327-328 Oct. 20, 1817 Isaac Hill (Spartanburgh) to William Lockhart (same); for $150 sold (ac omitted) at head of Scott's Cr of Broad R; border: Thomas Hill; part of 600 ac. Witness James Crutchfield and James Gilbert. Signed Isaac Hill. Wit. oath Oct. 21, 1817 James Crutchfield to James Camp. Rec. Oct. 28, 1817

p. 328-329 Aug. 20, 1817 Robert McCollum (Spartanburgh) to Andrew Gramling (same); for $650 sold 175 ac on waters of Tyger R on Cubb Br; border: Robert Wood. Witness Enoch George Foster and Joel Mason. Signed Robert McCollum. Wit. oath Oct. 13, 1817 Enoch G Foster to F. H. Legg. Rec. Nov. 3, 1817. Dower renounced Oct. 13, 1817 Nancy McCollum to F. H. Legg

p. 329-331 Aug. 7, 1811 Alexander Thompson (Spartanburgh) to James Hendrix (same); for $700 sold 260 ac on both sides Middle Tyger R and Beverdam Cr; border: Daniel Evans, John McCarter, Mary McMakin, John Reynolds, Edward Smith, Lemuel Loftis, McCoy, and John McMakin; part of two tracts: (1) 200 ac to Alexander Thompson as legate of John Leech desc and (2) 60 ac "granted by" Nathaniel Walker; includes 1 ac for a spring Shadrack Farmer used when he lived there. Witness Absalem Blundell and Michl Miller JQ (desc by time of Wit. oath). Signed Alexander Thompson. Wit. oath Aug. 9, 1817 Absalem Blundell to Thomas Wood. Rec. Nov. 3, 1817. Dower renounced Aug. 7, 1811 Agnes Thompson to Michael Miller

p. 331-333 Oct. 17, 1817 Joseph Dill (Spartanburgh) to Wyatt and Robert Lipscomb (Louisa Co, Va); for $1,650 sold 272 ac on both sides Cherokee Cr of Broad R; border: Green and Robertson; except the mill pond included in lines; where Joseph Dill lives. Witness Smith Lipscomb and William Ross. Signed Joseph Dill. Wit. oath Oct. 24, 1817 Smith Lipscomb to John Lipscomb. Rec. Nov. 3, 1817. Dower renounced Oct. 24, 1817 Mary Dill to John Lipscomb

p. 333-334 May 12, 1817 Thomas Dare to Wyatt and Robert Lipscomb; for $42 sold 7 ac including Thomas Dare's still house. Witness William Ross and Jesse Tate. Signed Thomas Dare. Wit. oath May 12, 1817 Jesse Tate to J Camp. Rec. Nov. 3, (omitted). Dower renounced Oct. 24, 1817 Lucy Dare to John Lipscomb

p. 334-335 Aug. 18, 1817 Levi Lancaster (Spartanburgh) to Isaiah Rhew (same); for $500 sold 100 ac on N side of Dutchman's Cr; part of grant to Samuel Lancaster esq desc and willed to Moses Lancaster who sold to Levi Lancaster Jan. 21, 1784 (or granted on Jan. 21, 1784?). Witness Richard Hewett and William Poole. Signed Levi Lancaster. Wit. oath Sept. 29, 1817 Richard Hewett to Saml Archibald. Rec. Nov. 10, 1817. Dower renounced Sept. 29, 1817 Amy Lancaster to Samuel Archibald

p. 335-336 Mar. 22, 1817 George Floyd to James W Reynolds (SC); for

$250 sold 10 3/4 ac; includes mill and "such of waters" as appears in the lines; where "he" lives. Witness Thomas Thornton and Robert Shearly. Signed George Floyd's mark. Wit. oath Oct. 11, 1817 Thomas Thornton to Robt Ligon. Rec. Nov. 10, 1817

p. 336 Oct. 20, 1817 Joel Lewis to M Casey; an oath that Joel was present on Oct. 8 at house of Isaac Crow jr (Spartanburgh) when a dispute took place between John Crow and Henry Marler (both of Spartanburgh) and they fought and John Crow bit off upper part of Henry Marler's right ear. Signed Joel Lewis. Rec. Nov. 10, 1817

p. 336-338 Dec. 19, 1815(sic) Hartwell Lester (Greenville Dist) to Edward Burnett; for $316 sold 107 ac on N side of Ben's Cr; part of estate of William Beacham desc and divided by Court's partition writ; this part went to Elizabeth Ann Lester, wife of Hartwell. Witness Lodwick Johnson and Thomas L Beacham. Signed Hartwell Lester. Wit. oath Dec. 26, 1812 Lodwick Johnson to Drury McDaniel. Rec. Nov. 10, 1817

p. 338-339 Oct. 11, 1817 James Lanford sr (Spartanburgh) to Abner Teague (Laurens Dist); for $650 sold 485 ac on Williams Cr of Tyger R; border: N & NW-Founal (or Fonnal) Wilson, NW-Barnett Demsey, SW & SE-old lines and Isaac Kendrix, W-Samuel Hendrix, and others unknown. Witness Samuel Busey, Nancy Busey, and James Leonard. Signed James Lanford. Wit. oath Oct. 11, 1817 James Leonard to John Dean. Rec. Nov. 10, 1817

p. 339-340 Jul. 31, 1816 Edward Burnett (Spartanburgh) to Daniel Beacham (Laurens Dist); for $350 sold 107 ac on N side of Ben's Cr; part of estate of William Beacham desc and divided by Court's partition writ; this part went to Elizabeth Ann Lester, wife of Hartwell Lester and was sold by Hartwell and Elizabeth Lester to Edward Burnett. Witness Thomas L Beacham and David Fowler. Signed Edward Burnett's mark. Wit. oath Nov. 10, 1817 Thomas L Beacham to F. H. Legg. Rec. Nov. 10, 1817

p. 340-341 (not dated) John Matthis (Spartanburgh) to daughter Darcus Stovaul Matthis; for love and affection give 3 beds and furniture, 2 cotton wheels, 3 pair of cotton cards, 2 pots, a bake pan, and a checkrul(?) and many other small articles. Witness Sarah Quinn, James Matthis, and Elisha Poole. Signed John Matthis. Wit. oath Nov. 3, 1817 James Matthis to Caleb Jones. Rec. Nov. 11, 1817

p. 341-343 Apr. 5, 1817 Turner Richardson, Commissioner of Washington Dist Equity Court (composed of Greenville, Laurens, and Newberry Dists) to Thomas Farrow sr; for $250 sold 200 ac; border: James Lanford, Thomas Farrow sr, Miles Nash, Jonathan Crook, and John Terry; on Feb. 17, 1817 Margaret Spears petitioned the court at Laurens Court House to show husband David Spears died intestate and had--200 ac in Spartanburgh Dist sold by Spartanburgh sheriff (sic) Thomas Leatherwood and wife to David Spears and David "recovered it" from John Terry; land could not be divided and so it was sold due to Commissioner's judgment Feb. term 1817; sale was on Apr. 5, 1817. Witness Caleb Woodruff and William Terry. Signed T Richardson CJW Dist. Wit. oath Nov. 10, 1817 Caleb Woodruff to Starling Tucker. Rec. Nov. 11, 1817

p. 343-344 Oct. 3, 1815 John Moss (Spartanburgh) to Patitlow Farrow (same); for 600 silver dollars sold 250 ac on Two Mile Cr of Enoree R; border: Main Rd, Bumpass, Jesse Brown, Ebenezer Moss, Benjamin Busey, and Thomas Farrow; part of two grants: (1) survey for John Hendrick and (2) for John Farrow; plat attached shows land includes John Hendrick's old line. Witness William Rhodes and John Brown. Signed John F Moss. Wit. oath Nov. 10, 1817 William Rhodes to Starling Tucker. Rec. Nov. 11, (omitted). Dower renounced Oct. 5, 1815 (Laurens Dist) Jeney F Moss to Starling Tucker

p. 344-345 Jan. 23, 1817 John Wofford sr (Spartanburgh) to George Wofford (same); for $400 sold 100 ac at head branch of Sugar Cr. Witness Isaac Varner and William Varner. Signed John Wofford sr's mark. Wit. oath Nov. 11, 1817 William Varner to Danl White. Rec. Nov. 11, 1817

p. 345-346 (not dated) Reubin Cantrell to Samuel Boyd; for $52 sold 90 ac on Long Br of Thickety Cr; border: Fed Gutery, Patrick Saunders, Robert Dunaway, and Elias Turner; where Reubin Cantrell lives; Condition: sale void if Reubin pays Samuel $52 by Jan. 1, "next". Witness John Padgett and Peter Green. Signed Reuben Cantrell. Wit. oath Aug. 29, 1817 John Padgett to Henry Turner. Rec. Nov. 11, 1817

p. 346-349 Jan. 27, 1791 George Scissel (Spartanburgh) to Samuel Busey (same); for 50£ sterling sold 170 ac on Buffaloe's Cr of Enoree R; E part of grant May 17, 1787 Gov. Thomas Pinckney to Benjamin Busey (675 ac) who sold to George Scissel. Witness Joseph Barnett, Miles Nash, and James Lanford. Signed George Scissel's mark. Wit. oath May 13, 1801 Joseph Barnett to John Dean. Rec. Nov. 11, 1817

p. 349-350 Mar. 20, 1797 Samuel Busey (SC) to James Lanford (SC); for $60 sold (ac omitted) on Buffaloe Cr of Enoree R; border: John Dean, Robert Page, John Allen, Hugh McWilliams, and Joseph Wofford. Witness James Lanford, Lydia Lanford, and John Lanford. Signed Samuel Busey's mark. Wit. oath Oct. 15, 1817 James Lanford to Samuel Woodruff. Rec. Nov. 11, 1817

p. 350-351 Jun. 6, 1808 James Lanford (Spartanburgh) to son Lewis Lanford (same); for love and affection give (ac omitted) on waters of Buffalow Cr; where Lewis Lanford lives. Witness William Terry, John Terry, and Robert Page. Signed James Lanford. Wit. oath Oct. 15, 1817 John Terry to Samuel Woodruff. Rec. Nov. 11, 1817

p. 351-353 Dec. 14, 1790 Benjamin Busey (Spartanburgh) to George Sissel (same); for 50£ sterling sold 170 ac on Buffalow Cr of Enoree R; E part of 675 ac grant May 7, 1787 Gov. Thomas Pinckney to Benjamin Busey. Witness Joseph Barnett, William Barnett, and John Cecill. Signed Benjamin Busey's mark. Wit. oath May 13, 1801 Joseph Barnett to John Dean. Rec. Nov. 11, 1817

p. 353-354 Aug. 13, 1816 Thomas Hill (Spartanburgh) to Henry Kenedy (same); for $100 sold 200 ac on waters of Gilkies Cr of Broad R; border: Si H Sparks and Isaac Hill. Witness Richard Arendle and Edward James. Signed Thomas Hill's mark. Wit. oath Nov. 12, 1817 Richard Arendle to Wm Reid. Rec. Nov. 12, 1818 (sic)

p. 354-355 Oct. 10, 1816 Michael Jones (Casey Co, Ky) to William Patterson (Spartanburgh); for 50¢ sold 200 ac on waters of Gocher Cr; border: W-Griffin Carter and James Campbell, N-William Patterson jr, NE-Young Allen, E-Austin Wright, "ES"-Davis and Aaron Wilkins, and S-Crittendon; land formerly belonged to David Jones sr(?) desc. Witness Edward Patterson and James Jones. Signed Michael Jones. Wit. oath Nov. 12, 1817 Edward Patterson to John Lipscomb. Rec. Nov. 12, 1817. Dower renounced Oct. 18, 1816 (Casey Co, Ky) Sally Jones to Ben W Napier and Collen McKinney

p. 355-357 Oct. 11, 1816 Malichi Monk and wife Mima (Harrison Co, Ind) to William Patterson (Spartanburgh); for $50 sold 500 ac on waters of Gocha Cr; border: N-Griffin Carter and James Campbell, S-William Patterson desc, NE-Young Allen, E-Austin Wright,

"ES"-Davis Wilkins and Aaron Wilkins, S-Criddenton; formerly land belonged to David Jones. Witness Edward Patterson and Samuel Monk. Signed Malichi and Mima Monk's marks. Wit. oath Nov. 12, 1817 Edward Patterson to John Lipscomb. Rec. Nov. 12, 1817. Dower renounced Oct. 12, 1816 (Harrison Co, Ind) Mima Monk to W H Tucker

p. 357-358 Dec. (blank), 1814 Benjamin Wofford (Spartanburgh) to Humphrey Yarborough (same); for $212 sold 99 ac; border: William Edwards' Spring Br, Prater's Cr, N-George Divine and Thomas Todd, W-part of same grant, Sham, Sexton, Humphrey Yarborough, and "others" Humphrey Yarborough(sic); part of grant to (blank) Clayton. Witness Abel Maulden, Elizabeth Molden, Golding Tinsley, and Isaac Miles. Signed Benjamin Wofford. Wit. oath Nov. 7, 1817 Isaac Miles to M Casey. Rec. Nov. 12, 1817

p. 358-359 Sept. 13, 1816 John Chesney (Spartanburgh) to William Young (same); for $500 sold 200 ac on S side of Tyger R; border: W-John McCrorey and James Sloane, E-William Rowland and Richard Fletcher, S-Richard Chesney, and others vacant; grant Jan. 15, 1773 Gov. William Bull to William Dunlap. Witness Richard Young and John B Leatherwood. Signed John Chesney. Wit. oath Sept. 28, 1816 John B Leatherwood to Burrell Bobo. Rec. Nov. 12, 1817. Dower renounced Nov. 7, 1816 Rebeccah Chesney to Burrell Bobo

p. 359-360 Nov. 12, 1817 Justus Reynolds (Spartanburgh) to Abram Crow and David Dicky (both of NC); for $340 sold 400 ac; border: William Hammett and Dishan Grant; where Justus Reynolds lives; part of 591 ac grant Dec. 3, 1792 Gov. Charles Pinckney to William Hammett. Witness James Galt and Charles Smith. Signed Justus Reynolds. Wit. oath Nov. 13, 1817 Charles Smith to Thomas Poole. Rec. Nov. 12, 1817

p. 360-362 Mar. 8, 1817 Nimrod Cantrell (Spartanburgh) to John Morress (same); for $88 sold 60 ac on S side of Buck Cr of Pacolett R; border: John Morress and John Cooper. Witness Lansford Cantrell and William Morris. Signed Nimrod Cantrell. Wit. oath Oct. 25, 1817 William Morris to Henry Turner. Rec. Nov. 13, 1817

p. 362-363 Jan. 1, 1817 George Lusher, merchant (Charleston, SC) to Judge John F Grimkee (same); for $400 sold 504 ac on both sides Robert's Cr of N Pacolett R; part of 2,000 ac grant to Lewis Dutarque (or Dutargue) and resurvey by Richard Thomson DS shows 1,593 ac; plat attached for resurvey dated Dec. 15, 1814 and Dec. 9, 1816 mentioned as sold 504 ac; plat shows 1,593 ac including 104 ac to Wm McClure and 161 ac and 504 ac to Judge Grimke; border: Evins and both sides of Mills Gap Rd. Witness J. F. Grimkee, Abram Nott, Langdon Cheves. Signed George Lusher attorney for heirs of Lewis Dutarque. Wit. oath Nov. 13, 1817 Abram Nott to A Benson. Rec. Nov. 14, 1817

p. 363-365 Sept. 13, 1817 Samuel Boling (Spartanburgh) to William Hannon (Rutherford Co, NC); for $200 sold 177 ac on waters of N Pacolett R; border: Grogin's Road, includes small part claimed by Robert Goodgion, and William Hannon looses that part if Robert Goodgion's claim holds up; part of grant to James Ridings who sold to Samuel Boling. Witness William Holcomb and Alfred Whitten. Signed Samuel Boling. Wit. oath Oct. 2, 1817 William Holcomb to T (or J) Whitten. Rec. Nov. 20, 1817

p. 365-366 May 13, 1817 Nathaniel Burton (Spartanburgh) to Toliver Scott (same); for $60 sold 29½ ac; border: below the old bridge, W-Toliver Scott, S-Jonathan, and E & N-Nathaniel Burton. Witness Ford Mason and Samuel Floyd. Signed Nathl Burton. Wit. oath Oct. 11, 1817 Ford Mason to (not signed). Rec. Nov. 27, 1817

p. 366 Oct. 26, 1816 Phebe Thomason (Spartanburgh) to daughter Delilah Turner; for love and affection give (at Phebe's death) a Negro girl Hannah about 5 years old. Witness Abner Benson. Signed Phebe Thomason's mark. Wit. oath Nov. 29, 1817 Abner Benson to Thomas Poole. Rec. Nov. 29, (omitted)

p. 366-368 Nov. 25, 1817 Larkin Carden (Spartanburgh) to Richard Thomson (same); for $700 sold 500 ac on both sides Sholy Cr of Pacolett R near the Boiling Spring; border: Taylor, Nathan Center's Spring Br, and Burnett; where Larkin Carden lives; part of 1,000 ac grant to Leonard Carden sr. Witness Woodson Burnett and Edmund Fowler. Signed Larken Carden. Wit. oath Dec. 1, 1817 Edmund Fowler to Thomas Poole. Rec. Nov. 2, 1817. Dower renounced Dec. 1, 1817 Betsy Cardin to Daniel White

p. 368 Mar. 3, 1817 Alexander McKie (Spartanburgh) to Andrew Foster (same); for $469 sold 134 ac on Kelso's Cr and Fairforest Cr; border: John Martin. Witness John White and Robert Martin. Signed Alexander McKie. Wit. oath Mar. 3, 1817 John White to Wm Reid. Rec. Dec. 2, 1817

p. 368-370 Nov. 15, 1817 Lewis and Delilah Turner (Spartanburgh) to Thomas Wells (same); for $101.25 sold 81 ac on branches of Walker's Cr of Lawson's fork; border: Thomas Wells. Witness Wm Hunt and Simpson Foster. Signed Lewis and Delilah Turner's marks. Wit. oath Dec. 1, 1817 Simpson Foster to Thomas Poole. Rec. Dec. 2, 1817

p. 370 Feb. 7, 1814 James Ward (Spartanburgh) to Rachel McBee (same); for $100 sold 200 ac on waters of Horse Cr of Broad R. Witness Peter Peterson and James Ezell. Signed James Ward's mark. Wit. oath Feb. 7, 1814 James Ezell to Henry Turner. Rec. Dec. 2, 1817

p. 370-371 (blank), 1814 Matthew McBee (Spartanburgh) to John McBee (same); for $100 sold 250 ac on waters of Macin's Cr of Broad R. Witness William Macbee and Matthew Macbee. Signed Matthew Macbee. Wit. oath Dec. 31, 1815 William Macbee to Wm Reid. Rec. Dec. 2, 1817

p. 371-372 Jul. 31, 1815 Matthew Macbee (Spartanburgh) to Anna McBee; for 10£ sterling sold 275 ac on branches of Pacolett R; border: George Poole and S-Wind. Witness William Macbee and Matthew Macbee. Signed Matthew McBee. Wit. oath Jul. 31, 1815 William Macbee to Wm Reid. Rec. Dec. 2, 1817

p. 372-373 Sept. 28, 1814 Leonard Cardin (Spartanburgh) to Larkin Cardin (same); for $400 sold 250 ac on waters of Sholy Cr; border: Samuel Sentell, Nathan Sentell, Larkin Cardin, and Ginyard; part of grant to Leonard Cardin sr. Witness William Sentell and Jacob Belcher. Signed Leonard and Caty Cardin. Wit. oath Dec. 1, 1817 Jacob Belcher to Eph Lewis. Rec. Dec. 2, 1817

p. 373-374 Jul. 11, 1817 (Greenville Dist) Branch J League (Greenville Dist) to Adam Carruth (same); for $660 sold 478 ac on N side Lawson's fork; border: S-widow Brannon and N-Alexander Austin. Witness James Cooly and Elias Carruth. Signed Branch J League. Wit. oath Dec. 10, 1817 Elias Carruth to Thomas Poole. Rec. Dec. 10, 1817

p. 374 Nov. 20, 1817 Rebecca Turner to son Matthias Turner; for $1,800 sold five Negroes: Joab, Reubin, Sarah, John, and Ephraim. Witness William Turner and John Turner. Signed Rebecca Turner's mark. Wit. oath Dec. 8, 1817 William Turner to J Camp. Rec. Dec. 17, 1817

p. 374-375 Nov. 3, 1817 Fortunatus H Legg (Spartanburgh) to John T Earle; for $300 sold ½ ac in Spartanburgh, SC; border: cross street, Todd's stable, and Tollison. Witness Wilson Nesbett and Danl Wilbanks. Signed Fortunatus H Legg. Wit. oath Dec. 20, 1817 Danl Wilbanks to Thomas Poole. Rec. Dec. 20, 1817

p. 375-376 Aug. 10, 1814 Nathaniel Rochell (Union Dist) to Nathan Smith (Spartanburgh); for $400 sold 410 ac on ridge between Tyger and Enoree Rivers; border: NW & NE-James Whiteker, NE-Sampson Bobo, NW, SE, SW, & S-Ezekiel Barkler, NW & SW-William Dod, and NW & SW-James Head; where Nathan Smith lives; grant Dec. 1, 1788 Gov. Thomas Pinckney to Sampson Bobo; also sold(?) by Robt Oliphant. Witness John Watson and Elijah Watson. Signed N and Sarah Rochell. Wit. oath Nov. 1, 1817 John Watson to Burrell Bobo. Rec. Dec. 22, 1817

p. 376-377 Oct. 31, 1815 William Dolton (Spartanburgh) to Peter Hawkins (same); for $300 sold 200 ac on S side of Obed's Cr and in fork of Pacolette R; border: John Anderson. Witness William Chapman, John McClure, and Henry Morgan. Signed Wm Dolton. Wit. oath (not dated) John McClure to James Young. Rec. Jan. 3, 1818

p. 377-378 Dec. 15, 1817 Agness Barnett, widow of Joroyal Barnett desc, Joseph Barnett, Martin Baily, Thomas Barnett, John Barnett, Nancy Blackwell, Betsey Barnett, Glen Barnett, and Polley Barnett (all of Spartanburgh except Joseph Barnett, Martin Baily, and John Barnett--Rutherford Co, NC) to Richard Thomson (Spartanburgh); for $400 sold 300 ac on waters of Lawson's fork; border: Iron Works Road; part of two grants: (1) 383 ac Nov. 7, 1785 to Wm Poole and (2) 500 ac to David Lewis. Witness Micajah Barnett, John Windsor, and Jacob Chapman. Signed Joseph Blackwell's mark, Joseph Barnett, John Barnett, Elizabeth Barnett, Thomas Barnett, Glenn Barnett, Charles Baily, Agnes Barnett's mark, Polly Barnett's mark, and Nancy Barnett's mark. Wit. oath Dec. 20, 1817 John Windsor to Thomas Poole. Rec. Jan. 5, 1818

p. 378-379 Jan. 1, 1818 John Dodd (Spartanburgh) to Stephen Huddleston (Halifax Co, Va); for $500 sold 300 ac except small part divided off originally survied by Reubin Bomar of Gabriel Benson to Henry and William Monroe; border: Obed's Cr, N Pacolette R, and road from Cunningham's Mills to Galt's old store. Witness Charles C Duncan, Armsted Bomar and Christopher Golightly. Signed John Dodd. Wit. oath Jan. 5, 1818 Armsted Bomar to John Montgomery. Rec. Jan. 5, 1818

p. 379-380 Dec. 3, 1817 Edmond Fowler (Spartanburgh) to Willis Seay; for (money omitted) sold 70 ac; border: John Clement and Edward Clement; part of tract sold by James Wood to Edmond Fowler. Witness Thomas Brannon and Lowry Burnett. Signed Edmond Fowler. Wit. oath Jan. 3, 1818 Lowry Burnett to Eph Lewis. Rec. Jan. 5, 1818

p. 380-381 Jan. 5, 1818 Matthew Seay (Spartanburgh) to son Willis Seay (same); for love and affection give (1) 250 ac on waters of Lawson's fork and Pacolette R; part of 500 ac divided by heirship between Sally and Rhody Brannon; and (2) give a sorrel mare, 5 cows and 4 yearlings, 10 sheep, 10 hogs, 2 beds and furniture, a cribb of corn, 4 stacks of fodder, and 2 rifle guns. Witness William Hughe, John B Lewis, and Edmund Fowler. Signed Matthew Seay. Wit. oath Jan. 5, 1818 Edmund Fowler to Eph Lewis. Rec. Jan. 5, 1818

p. 381 Jan. 5, 1818 W. N. Miller, administrator of Robet Miller desc, received from Thorton McDaniel $343.35 and 4 mills in full payment of "within" mortgage. Witness Danl Wilbanks. Signed W. N. Miller. Wit. oath Jan. 6, 1818 Danl Wilbanks to F. H. Legg. Rec. (omitted)

p. 381-383 Sept. 30, 1816 William French (Spartanburgh) to James Camp (same); for $600 sold 70 ac on N side of N Pacolett R; part of grant to George Alexander. Witness Peter Hawkins and Robert Milican. Signed William French. Wit. oath Dec. 30, 1817 Peter Hawkins to Wm Kelso. Rec. Jan. 10, 1818. Dower renounced Mar. 1, 1817 Bassna French to James Young

p. 383-384 Jun. 3, 1817 Hamilton Wilson (Spartanburgh) to Zacheriah McDaniel (same); for $100 sold 120 ac and 20 chains on S side of Fairforest Cr; border: Zacheriah McDaniel, Dugan's Br, and John Martin. Witness Robert Martin and John Martin. Signed Hamltn Wilson. Wit. oath Aug. 4, 1817 Robert Martin to F. H. Legg. Rec. Jan. 13, 1818. Dower renounced Dec. 2, 1817 Hanah Wilson to Samuel Archibald

p. 384 Nov. 14, 1812 Richard Brown (Spartanburgh) to Jabez Galt (same); for $400 sold 208 ac; border: widow Story, John McCollin, Rowland, and Lewis Brown; part of land "now belonging to John Wood Baptist". Witness William Bennett and Lewis Brown. Signed Richard Brown. Wit. oath Jan. 12, 1818 Lewis Brown to Wm Kelso. Rec. Jan. 15, 1818

p. 384-385 Apr. 13, 1807 Edmund Wood (Spartanburgh) to Robert Mason jr (same); for $300 sold 208 ac; border: widow Story, John Wood, Knox, and Rowland Johnson. Witness Lewis Brown and John Foster. Signed Edmund Wood. Wit. oath Jan. 12, 1818 Lewis Brown to Wm Kelso. Rec. Jan. 15, 1818

p. 385-386 Jan. 11, 1818 Matthew Seay (Spartanburgh) to daughter Polley Seay (same); for love and affection give a pot and oven, a skillet and bake pan, a chest, a spinning wheel, a table, a loom, a small quantity of pewter and crockery ware, and all plantation tools. Witness William Rollins, Elijah Fowler, and David Rollins. Signed Matthew Seay. Wit. oath Jan. 15, 1818 David Rollins to Eph Lewis. Rec. Jan. 15, 1818

p. 386-387 Apr. 6, 1816 Nimrod Cantrell (Spartanburgh) to John Stedman (same); for $85 sold 125 ac on waters of Buck Cr. Witness James Cudd and John Cooper. Signed Nimrod Cantrell. Wit. oath Nov. 9, 1816 James Cudd to Wm Adcock. Rec. Jan. 16, 1818

p. 387 Sept. 9, 1817 Andrew Foster (Spartanburgh) to Zacheriah McDaniel (same); for $10 sold 3/4 ac on N side of Fairforest Cr. Witness J. W. Cooper and William King. Signed Andrew Foster. Wit. oath Jan. 13, 1818 J. W. Cooper to Wm Underwood. Rec. Jan. 17, 1818

p. 387-388 Dec. 12, 1816 John Otts (Spartanburgh) to Thomas Thornton (same); for $200 sold 100 ac on waters of Ward's Cr of Tyger R; grant to Andrew Coan. Witness James Colvert and Lawson Thomson. Signed John Otts. Wit. oath Jan. 20, 1818 Lawson Thomson to Robt Ligon. Rec. Jan. 20, 1818

p. 388-390 Jan. 4, 1794 Thomas Lehre (Charleston, SC) to James Crook (Spartanburgh); for 12£ 10s sterling per 100 ac sold 390 ac in two tracts: (1) 320 ac and (2) 70 ac; part of 889 ac grant Dec. 4, 1786 Gov. William Moultry(sic) to Thomas Lehre. on both sides of S Tyger R. Witness Peter Cregier and Joseph Lewis. Signed (at Charleston) Thos Lehre. Wit. oath Dec. 16, 1817 (Charleston Dist) Peter Cregier to J. H. Mitchell. Rec. Jan. 24, 1818. Dower renounced Dec. 14, 1817 Susanna Lehre to John Hinckley Mitchell JQ

p. 390-391 Sept. 15, 1807 John Frederick Harmoning (Spartanburgh) to Moses Casey jr (same); for $400 sold 300 ac on Cedar Shoal Cr of Enoree R; border: E-James McDowell and Christopher Casey,

S-Thomas Rhodes, W-Richd Friar, and N-William Casey. Witness Aron Casey and Martin Newman. Signed John Frdr Harmoning. Wit. oath Aug. 24, 1809 Martin Newman to Burrell Bobo. Rec. Jan. 25, 1818. Dower renounced Oct. 8, 1807 Mary Harmoning to Burrell Bobo

p. 391-392 Jan. 24, 1818 Moses Casey sr (Spartanburgh) to Stephen Johnson Casey (same); for $300 sold 224 ac on Bright's Br of Cedar Shoal Cr of Enoree R; border: Burrell Bobo esq; grant to Thomas Jones. Witness Daniel Liles and Chaney Bobo. Signed Moses Casey sr. Wit. oath Jan. 24, 1818 Chaney Bobo to Moses Casey. Rec. Jan. 25, 1818

p. 392-394 Jan. 24, 1818 Moses Casey sr (Spartanburgh) to Randolph Casey jr (same); for $110 sold 191 ac on both sides of Sedar Shoal Cr; border: Mr Casey. Witness Daniel Liles and Chaney Bobo. Signed Moses Casey sr. Witness Jan. 24, 1818 Chaney Bobo to M Casey. Rec. Jan. 25, 1818

p. 394-395 Jan. 24, 1818 Moses Casey sr (Spartanburgh) to Moses Casey jr (same); for $200 sold 90 ac on both sides Cedar Shoal Cr; border: Aron Casey; grant to Christopher Casey. Witness Daniel Liles and Chaney Bobo. Signed Moses Casey sr. Wit. oath Jan. 24, 1818 Chaney Bobo to M Casey. Rec. Jan. 25, 1818

p. 395-396 Jan. 29, 1818 John Wingo to John Wood; for $27.50 sold 18 3/4 ac on branch of Mill Cr of N Tyger R; border: John Wood. Witness Marshall Covington, Herbertt Hawkins, and David Foster. Signed John Wingo sr. Wit. oath Jan. 29, 1818 Herbertt Hawkins to E Walker. Rec. Feb. 2, 1818

p. 396-397 Jan. 29, 1818 John Wood sr to John Wingo; for $40 sold 20 ac on waters of Mill Cr of N Tyger R; border: Pollard and William Laurence. Witness David Foster, Marshall Covington, and Herbert Hawkins. Signed John Wood sr's mark. Wit. oath Jan. 29, 1818 Herbertt Hawkins to E Walker. Rec. Feb. 2, 1818

p. 397-398 Apr. 4, 1816 James M Butler and wife Eliza, daughter of John Kennerly desc, (Edgefield Dist) to Josiah Kilgore (Richland Dist); for $150 sold 200 ac on Maple Swamp Br of S Tyger R; border: James Bright; grant Aug. 19, 1774 to John Kennerly. Witness John Caldwell and Abner Blacker. Signed J M and Eliza Butler. Wit. oath Jul. 17, 1816 (Edgefield Dist) Abner Blacker to Spencer J McCan (or JctCan). Rec. Feb. 2, 1818. Dower renounced Jun. 28, 1816 (Edgefield Dist) Eliza A Butler to Sampson Pope

p. 398-399 Oct. 20, 1814 William Hill (Spartanburgh) to Ignatius Littlejohn (same); for $120 sold 200 ac on N side of Pacolette R; border: Henry Petett, Abraham Hambree, "new" road, Joshua Petit, and Hatfield. Witness Bartholomew Stovaul and Nancy Stovaul. Signed William Hill's mark. Wit. oath Feb. 27, 1817 Bartholomew Stovaul to William Reid. Rec. Feb. 2, 1818

p. 399-400 Feb. 27, 1804 George Poole (Rutherford Co, NC) to David Pope (Spartanburgh); for $200 sold 300 ac on waters of Pacolett and Broad Rivers; grant Jul. 5, 1788 to Thomas Sabb. Witness Theophelus Thorn and William Barr. Signed George Pope. Wit. oath Apr. 25, 1811 Theophelus Thorn to Leonard Adcock. Rec. Feb. 2, (omitted)

p. 400-401 Sept. 29, 1817 John Kelso (Spartanburgh) to Administrator of estate of John Foster desc (same); for $39 sold 39 ac agreeable with contract made during John Foster's lifetime; border:John Foster. Witness David Golightly jr and James K Means. Signed John Kelso. Wit. oath Feb. 2, 1818 David Golightly jr to Danl White. Rec. Feb. 2, 1818

p. 401-402 Oct. 29, 1817 Joseph Crook (Spartanburgh) to Elizabeth Snoddy (same); for $425 sold 170 ac on S side of Tyger R. Witness Mary Coan, Peggy Snoddy, and Anna Snoddy. Signed Joseph Crook. Wit. oath Oct. 29, 1817 Peggy Snoddy to James Crook. Rec. Feb. 2, 1818

p. 402-403 Jan. 2, 1817 Matthew Patton (Spartanburgh) to Thomas Underwood (same); for $350 sold 120 ac on N side of S Tyger R; border: Thornton McDaniel, Enoch J Underwood, and Robt Ligon. Witness Enoch J Underwood and John Patton. Signed Matthew Patton. Wit. oath Feb. 2, 1818 Enoch J Underwood to Wm Underwood. Rec. Feb. (omitted), 1818

p. 403-404 Sept. 24, 1817 John Kelso (Spartanburgh) to Andrew Foster (same); for $174 sold (ac omitted) on Henry's Br of Fairforest Cr. Witness David Golightly jr and James K Means. Signed John Kelso. Wit. oath Feb. 2, 1818 David Golightly jr to Danl White. Rec. Feb. 2, 1818

p. 404-406 Aug. 16, 1817 William Patterson (Spartanburgh) to Francis Littlejohn (Union Dist); for $800 sold 300 ac; border: Jones' Methodist Meeting House; part of four tracts: (1) grant to John Elliott, (2) grant to David Allen desc and given to Drury Allen who sold to William Patterson, (3) grant in 1784 Gov. William Moultrie to David Jones, and (4) grant in 1794 Gov. William Moultrie to David Jones; (1) and (2) parts are 94 ac and (3) and (4) parts are 204 ac. Witness John Wilkins and Dolly Burton. Signed William Patterson's mark. Wit. oath Sept. 13, 1817 John Wilkins to John Lipscomb. Rec. Feb. 7, 1818. Dower renounced Sept. 13, 1817 Fanny Patterson to John Lipscomb

p. 406-407 Nov. 22, 1817 William Patterson (Spartanburgh) to James Lawrence (Union Dist); for $500 sold 300 ac on waters of Gocher Cr of Thickety Cr; border: Claburn Laurence, S-George Davis and Aron Wilkins, W-Aron Wilkins and Francis Littlejohn, and N-Young Allen; part of 421 ac grant Aug. 4, 1794 Gov. William Moultrie to David Jones sr who sold part of William Patterson; known as Jones' Place. Witness Francis Littlejohn and James Harrison. Signed William Patterson's mark. Wit. oath Nov. 22, 1817 Francis Littlejohn and James Harrison to John Lipscomb. Rec. Feb. 7, 1818. Dower renounced Dec. 8, 1817 Fanny Patterson to John Lipscomb

p. 407-408 Sept. 28, 1816 Barnett Burnett (Spartanburgh) to Elijah Johnson (same); for $130 sold 65 ac on branches of Furgerson's Cr of Tyger R. Witness Newbel Johnson and Thomas Burnett. Signed Barnett Burnett's mark. Wit. oath Mar. 26, 1817 Newbel Johnson to Thomas Wood. Rec. Feb. 11, 1818

p. 408-409 Jan. 20, 1818 George Leatherwood (Spartanburgh) to John Edwards (same); for $124 sold 62 ac on S side of Jemmie's Cr of Tyger R; border: William L Allen, J Edwards, and John Leatherwood. Witness Zacchariah Edwards and Henry Pearson. Signed George Leatherwood. Wit. oath Jan. 23, 1818 Zacchariah Edwards to Samuel Woodruff. Rec. Feb. 17, 1818

p. 409-410 Oct. 11, 1816 Nathaniel Woodruff sr, by attorney William L Allen (Spartanburgh) to John Edwards (same); for $120 sold 60 ac on branch of Jemmie's Cr of Tyger R; border: Shands Golightly. Witness Josiah Woodruff and Thomas Castleberry. Signed Nathaniel Woodruff, by attorney William L Allen. Wit. oath Jan. 25, 1818 Thomas Castleberry to Samuel Woodruff. Rec. Feb. 17, 1818

p. 410-411 Sept. 27, 1816 Paul Castleberry sr (Spartanburgh) to Peter Hamilton (same); for $30 sold 30 ac on branch of Jemmie's Cr. Witness James Leatherwood and Thomas Castleberry.

Signed Paul Castleberry's mark. Wit. oath Sept. 28, 1816 James Leatherwood to John Dean. Rec. Mar. 2, 1818

p. 411-412 Jan. 26, 1818 Alexander Roddy (Spartanburgh) to Beverly Chapman (same); for $285 sold 95 ac on waters of N Tyger R; border: John Chapman, John M Collins, Rowlan Johnson, and Henry Rhea. Witness John Chapman and James Roddy. Signed Alexr Roddy. Wit. oath Mar. 2, 1818 James Roddy to John Montgomery. Rec. Mar. 2, 1818

p. 412-413 Oct. 7, 1817 Isaac Linder (Spartanburgh) to Lee Linder (same); for $175 sold 100 ac on N side of Pacolette R; border: Ivey Br. Witness Thomas Wyatt and Richard Farrow. Signed Isaac Linder. Wit. oath Feb. 1, 1818 Thomas Wyatt to Caleb Jones. Rec. Mar. 2, 1818

p. 413-414 Jan. 2, 1818 John Low sr (Spartanburgh) to Lee Linder (same); for $50 sold (ac omitted) on N side of Pacolette R; border: Thomas Wyatt, Williams, Lee Linder, George Curling, Dry Br, and Isaac Linder. Witness Samuel Turner and Laurence Linder. Signed John Low sr. Wit. oath Feb. 2, 1818 Samuel Turner to Caleb Jones. Rec. Mar. 2, 1818

p. 414-415 Feb. 10, 1818 James Knox (Spartanburgh) to Ephraim Potter (same); for $200 sold 200 ac on waters of Island Cr; border: Ephraim Potter. Witness William Cantrell and Benjamin Gilbert. Signed James Knox. Wit. oath Feb. 12, 1818 William Cantrell to Henry Turner. Rec. Mar. 2, 1818. Dower renounced Feb. 18, 1818 Mary Ann Knox to Henry Turner

p. 415-416 Nov. 7, 1817 Isaac Young jr (Spartanburgh) to Ephraim Potter (same); for $5 sold 5.7 ac on Island Cr. Witness William Cantrell and Silas Cash. Signed Isaac Young. Wit. oath Nov. 7, 1817 William Cantrell to Henry Turner. Rec. Mar. 2, 1818

p. 416-417 Jan. 31, 1818 Richard Thomson (Spartanburgh) to Payton Simmons (same); for $49 sold 24 ac on branches of Fair-forest Cr; part of grant to Peter Legar; survey Dec. 22, 1772 for Daniel Maul. Witness James W Cooper and Absalem Lancaster. Signed Richard Thomson. Wit. oath Mar. 2, 1818 James W Cooper to Caleb Jones. Rec. Mar. 2, 1818

p. 417-418 Aug. 21, 1817 Nathl Burton (Spartanburgh) to John Brewton (same); for $600 sold 155 ac in fork of Tyger R; border: Jonathan Crow, S Tyger R below Shurley's old bridge, Ford, William Mason, Nathl Gentry, John Wright, and Tolliver Scott; "balance of land unsold by Nathl Burton". Witness William L Allen and David Burton. Signed Nathl Burton. Wit. oath Feb. 23, 1818 William L Allen to Samuel Woodruff. Rec. Mar. 2, 1818

p. 418-419 Aug. 20, 1817 Nathl Burton (Spartanburgh) to John Brewton (same); for $1,500 sold 440 ac; where Nathl Burton lives at fork of Tyger R; border: John Thornton Chesney, Robert Alexander, Robt Rogers, Richd Willis, S Tyger R, Jonathan Crow, and N Tyger R. Witness William L Allen and David Burton. Signed Nathl Burton. Wit. oath Feb. 28, 1818 William L Allen to Samuel Woodruff. Rec. Mar. 2, 1818

p. 419-420 Feb. 26, 1818 Philip and Jonas Brewton (Spartanburgh), executors of estate of David Brewton desc, to Susannah Brewton; for $100 sold 50 ac on N side of James Cr; border: E-Simpson Lavender, N-Susannah Powell, W-Susannah Brewton, and S-George Leatherwood; land was sold at public auction specified in David Brewton's will. Witness David Brewton and Elizabeth Brewton. Signed Jonas Brewton and Philip Brewton. Wit. oath Feb. 28, 1818 David

Brewton to John Brewton. Rec. Mar. 2, 1818

p. 420-421 May 6, 1815 William Willis (Spartanburgh) to son (sic) William Shores; for love and affection give 148 ac on S side of Pacolette R and Lawson's fork; where William Willis lives; border: William Poole; and give 2 gray mares and a sorrel horse, 2 guns, a saddle; and give to Nancy Shores a yound horse colt; and give to Betsy Shores a red cow called Swann; and give to Polly Shores a black heifer; 6 sheep to be divided by all the children and 30 hogs and rest of household furniture to be divided by children; and give to William Shores all working tools. Witness John H Jones and Thomas Willis. Signed William Willis. Wit. oath May 6, 1815 Thomas Willis to Jno H Jones. Rec. Mar. 2, 1818

p. 421 Aug. 9, 1817 Alexander Cunningham (Spartanburgh) to Iredell Cunningham; Alexander owes Iredell \$330.37½ and to secure payment sells all his goods and chattles to Iredell. Witness Thomas Barton and William Barton. Signed Alexr Cunningham. Wit. oath Feb. 6, 1818 Thomas Barton to James Young. Rec. Mar. 2, 1818

p. 421-422 Feb. 17, 1818 John Tollison (Spartanburgh) to John Vandiver (same); for \$100 sold 100 ac on Harican Br; border: Jesse Matthis, "James Robertson's former Spring Br", William Connor, and John Quarles. Witness James Vandiver and James Tollison. Signed John Tollison. Wit. oath Mar. 2, 1818 James Tollison to (omitted). Rec. Mar. 2, 1818

p. 422-423 Feb. 4, 1818 Robert McCrory (Spartanburgh) to Philip Bettis (same); for \$375 sold 125 ac on Middle Tyger R; border: Abner Wingo; half of 250 ac grant in 1767 to Thomas Penny. Witness John Sexton and William Sexton. Signed Robert McCrory. Wit. oath Feb. 14, 1818 William Sexton to John Collins. Rec. Mar. 2, 1818. Dower renounced Feb. 11, 1818 Martha McCrory to John Collins

p. 423-424 Apr. 17, 1812 Ellis Cannon (Spartanburgh) to John Vandiver (same); for \$80 sold 100 ac on Peter's Cr and Pacolette R; border: John Hammett. Witness Lewis Cannon and James Cannon. Signed Ellis Cannon. Wit. oath Mar. 2, 1818 James Cannon to William Reid. Rec. Mar. 2, 1818

p. 424-425 Jan. 8, 1812 James Haynes (Spartanburgh) to John Vandiver (same); for \$40 sold 30 ac on branch of Peter's Cr; border: old Post Road and Jesse Cannon. Witness Ellis Cannon and James Cannon. Signed James Haynes. Wit. oath Mar. 2, 1818 by Wm Reid. Rec. Mar. 2, 1818

p. 425-426 Nov. 14, 1817 James Poole (Spartanburgh) to son Elisha Poole (same); for love and affection give 100 ac; border: Machchine Br; part of tract where James Poole lives. Witness Bartholomew Stovaul, Elijah Poole, and Ezekiel Fuller. Signed James Poole. Wit. oath Mar. 2, 1818 Elijah Poole to Wm Reid. Rec. Mar. 2, 1818

p. 426-428 Feb. 5, 1818 William Covington, Elizabeth Selman, John L Selman, William P Selman, Fielding Selman, and Larkin Selman (Spartanburgh and Georgia) to James Selman (Spartanburgh); for \$103.22 sold 355 ac on waters of Tyger R and Fairforest Cr; border: Ford's old line, Blackstock's Road, Leech's old line, and Bethleham Meeting House; part of real estate of Jeremiah Selman desc. Witness William N (or V) Miller and Ransom Foster. Signed William Covington, Frederick Williams, Wm P Selman, Fielding Selman, John L Selman, Larkin Selman, and Elizabeth Selman. Wit. oath Mar. 2, 1818 William N Miller to Wm Underwood. Rec. Mar. 2, 1818

p. 428 Jan. 31, 1818 Absalem Lancaster (Spartanburgh) to Payton

Simmons (same); for $220 sold 78 ac on branches of Fairforest Cr; border: James W Cooper and Richard Thomson; part of grant to Peter Leger and survey Dec. 22, 1772 for David Maul. Witness Richard Thomson and James W Cooper. Signed Absalem Lancaster's mark. Wit. oath Mar. 2, 1818 James W Cooper to Caleb Jones. Rec. Mar. 2, 1818

p. 428-430 Feb. 28, 1818 David Bettis (Spartanburgh) to Hugh Gaston (same); for $150 sold 3 cattle, 2 beds, a set of smith's tools, a chest, 2 pots, an oxen, a skillet, a gun, a table, 5 chairs, a set of cups and sausers, a set of tin cups, 3 tin buckets, 2 tin pans, 2 sets of plates, one set of spoons, 2 dishes, a spinning wheel, a "clock real", 6 glass "tumbles", 3 bowls, 3 bottles, a looking glass, 2 pitchers, and 2 water pails; Condition: sale void if David pays Hugh $150 by Feb. 2, 1819. Witness Samuel Pearson. Signed David Bettis' mark. Wit. oath Mar. 2, 1818 Samuel Pearson to Thomas Poole. Rec. Mar. 2, 1818

p. 430 Jan. 12, 1818 Charles Hammett (Spartanburgh) to granddaughters Nancy and Cynthia Hammett; for love and affection give to Nancy a feather bed; to Cynthia a feather bed and furniture; and to (name omitted) feather bed and furniture. Witness Jesse Hammett and Daniel Hammett. Signed Charles Hammett's mark. Wit. oath Jan. 12, 1818 Jesse Hammett to Caleb Jones. Rec. Mar. 3, 1818

p. 430-431 Mar. 3, 1818 Jackson Neely to William Neely; for $125 sold a black horse, saddle, and bridle, and a silver watch; warrant the horse is free of disease. Witness William Hunt and Walter Carruth. Signed Jackson Neely. Wit. oath Mar. 3, 1818 Walter Carruth to A Benson. Rec. Mar. 2, 1818

p. 431-432 Oct. 20, 1817 Benjamin Robuck (Spartanburgh) to Richard Willis (same); for $350 sold 114 ac on N side of Jamie's Cr; border: E-Samuel Floyd, S-Richard Gentry, W-John Shinner, and N-James Mason. Witness Edward Willis and Starling Willis. Signed Benjamin Robuck. Wit. oath Mar. 9, 1818 Starling Willis to John Brewton. Rec. Mar. 30, 1818

p. 432-433 Oct. 13, 1817 Solomon Crocker (Spartanburgh) to James Crocker jr (Murry (sic) Co, Tenn); for $500 sold 200 ac on S side of Pacolet R; border: John Lee, mouth of Graveyard Hollow, Anthony Crocker, and Thomas Brown; part of grant to Solomon Crocker. Witness Samuel Noblet and Ezekiel Fuller. Signed Solomon Crocker's mark. Wit. oath Feb. 17, 1818 Samuel Noblet to Wm Reid. Rec. Apr. 2, 1818

p. 433-434 Jan. 20, 1813 William Dolton (Spartanburgh) to William Jackson (same); for $100 sold (ac omitted) on N side of Obed's Cr; part of tract sold by John Anderson to William Dolton. Witness William Kelso sr, Henry Monroe, and William Munrow. Signed Wm Dolton. Wit. oath Apr. 5, 1811(sic) William Kelso sr to William Kelso. Rec. Apr. 6, 1818

p. 434-435 Nov. 1, 1817 Joseph Wofford to daughter Martha White; for good cause give "an Intailment forever from one generation to another" a Negro girl Mary and her increase. Witness John Mullinax and Thomas Jones. Signed Joseph Wofford. Wit. oath Apr. 6, 1818 John Mullinax to James Hamm. Rec. Apr. 6, 1818

p. 435 Sept. 13, 1816 Joseph Wofford to son Joseph Wofford; for good cause give a Negro woman Rody and her increase and a Negro boy Isaac. Witness Samuel Tucker and John Tucker. Signed Joseph Wofford. Wit. oath Sept. 19, 1816 Samuel Tucker to John Dean. Rec. Apr. 6, 1818

p. 435-436 Jun. 5, 1817 John White (Spartanburgh) to Moses White (same): for $200 sold 46 ac; border: Dunlap; part of grant Jul. 7 1806 to John White. Witness Samuel Thomas and Abel Mauldin. Signed John White. Wit. oath Jun. 7, 1817 Samuel Thomas to John Brewton. Rec. Apr. 6, 1818

p. 436-437 Nov. 19, 1817 Thomas Farrow (Spartanburgh) to John Terry (same); for $60 sold 71 ac on waters of Two Mile Cr; border: Waggon Road and Terry; part of grant to Joseph Wofford. Witness Caleb Woodruff and James Leonard. Signed Thomas Farrow. Wit. oath Apr. 4, 1818 Caleb Woodruff to Wm Hendrix. Rec. Apr. 6, 1818

p. 437-438 Feb. 17, 1818 Jonathan Crook (Spartanburgh) to William Terry (same); for $192 sold 96 ac on branches of Enoree R; border: John Terry. Witness James Leonard, Joseph Crook, and Jeremiah Crook. Signed Jonathan Crook. Wit. oath Apr. 4, 1818 James Leonard to Samuel Woodruff. Rec. Apr. 6, 1818

p. 438-440 Feb. 19, 1818 Lewis Landford (Spartanburgh) to Samuel Woodruff jr (same); for $325 sold 150 ac; part of grant Gov. William Moultrie to John Hendrix and resurvey Sept. 27, 1815 by Jesse Wofford. Witness John Dean and Moses Woodruff. Signed Lewis Landford's mark. Wit. oath Apr. 4, 1818 Moses Woodruff to Samuel Woodruff. Rec. Apr. 6, 1818. Dower renounced Mar. 26, 1818 Mary Landford to John Brewton

p. 440-442 (p. 441 omitted) Feb. 1, 1806 Ebenezer Moss (Spartanburgh) to John Terry (same); for $180 sold 150 ac on branches of Enoree R; border: "the main road" and Waldrop. Witness Seth PettyPoole and James Moss. Signed Ebenezer Moss and Agnes' mark. Wit. oath Apr. 4, 1818 Seth PettyPoole to Samuel Woodruff. Rec. Apr. 6, 1818

p. 442-443 Sept. 20, 1813 Benjamin Wofford (Spartanburgh) to George Divine (same); for $10 sold 16 ac on S side of Tyger R; border: Prater's Cr, George Divine, and Humphrey Yarborough; grant to William Clyton. Witness Nancy Patterson and John Divine. Signed Benjamin Wofford. Wit. oath Oct. 23, 1816 John Divine to Burrell Bobo. Rec. Apr. 7, 1818

p. 443-444 Apr. 2, 1812 Bayles Earle (Spartanburgh) to Hugh Henderson (same); for (money omitted) sold 130 ac on waters of N Pacolette R; border: Wolf Cr, William Hembry, Greenville Road, and Henderson. Witness Theron Earle and John B Lewis. Signed Baylis Earle. Wit. oath Oct. 12, 1812 Theron Earle to Wm Kelso. Rec. Apr. 7, 1818

p. 444 (blank), 181(blank) John Varnal (Spartanburgh) to James Varnal (same); for $200 sold 112 ac on waters of Sugar Cr; border: Samuel Lancaster; grant Jan. 4, 1793 to Aron Lancaster. Witness John Wofford jr and William West. Signed J Varner(sic)'s mark. Wit. oath Jan. 12, 1818 John Wofford to Saml Archibald. Rec. Apr. 7, 1818

Book Q 1818-1820

p. 1-2 Dec. 27, 1817 John Crocker and Nathaniel Woodruff (Spartanburgh), executors of Joseph Woodruff desc (by his will) to Anne Woodruff (same); for $336 sold 138 ac on Jemmies Cr of Tyger R; plat attached shows border: Thomas Woodruff, Josiah Woodruff, Wm Hendricks, Wm Jones, and Wm L Allen; land was sold at publick auction. Witness Baily Adams and Caleb Allen. Signed John Crocker and Nathaniel Woodruff. Wit. oath Mar. 26, 1818 Caleb Allen to Samuel Woodruff. Rec. (omitted)

p. 2-3 Nov. 1, 1817 Joseph Wofford to daughter Rebecca Millinix; for good cause give "as an Intailment forever from one generation to another" a Negro girl Esther and her increase. Witness Moses White and Thomas Jones. Signed Joseph Wofford. Wit. oath Apr. 6, 1818 Moses White to James Hamm. Rec. Apr. 7, 1818

p. 3-5 Nov. 6, 1817 John Ward (Spartanburgh) to Henry Smith (same); for $250 sold 100 ac on Tyger R; border: Miller, Still House, and widow Otts; "leaving out 5 rods above the shoal in the River to 5 rods below the shoal and a rod wide". Witness Thornton McDaniel and Francis Ward. Signed John Ward. Wit. oath Mar. 6, 1818 Francis Ward to John Brewton. Rec. Apr. 7, 1818. Dower renounced Mar. 6, 1818 Mary Ward to John Brewton

p. 5-6 May 23, 1815 Alexander McMakin (Spartanburgh) to David Wheeler (same); for $200 sold 122 ac on branch of Middle Tyger R; border: Andrew McMakin (tract #4 for 100 ac), Peter C McMakin (tract #8 for 210 ac), Rachal McMakin (tract #5 for 121 ac), and survey for Clark and Reese; plat attached shows also border: Elizabeth McMakin (tract #3 for 98 ac); tract #6 Alexander McMakin drew as his part of his father's (not named) estate. Witness Danl Wilbanks and Andrew McMakin. Signed Alexr McMakin. Wit. oath Apr. 15, 1816 Andrew McMakin to John Montgomery. Rec. Apr. 7, 1818

p. 6-7 (blank), 1815 Fielding Sudduth and wife Rachel to David Wheeler (Spartanburgh); for $200 sold 121 ac that is tract #5 on branch of Middle Tyger R; border: Mary McMakin, John McCarter, Peter C McMakin (tract #8 for 210 ac), Alexander McMakin (tract #6 for 122 ac), and Elizabeth McMakin (tract #3 for 96 ac); plat attached shows also border: John McMakin (tract #2 for 96 ac) but does not show Mary McMakin. Witness James Hendricks and Mary McMakin. Signed Fielding Sudduth. Wit. oath Apr. 15, 1816 James Hendricks to John Montgomery. Rec. Apr. 7, 1818

p. 7-8 Mar. 21, 1817 John Tollison (Spartanburgh) to Austin Wright (same); for $107 sold 112½ ac on Gum Root Br; mortgage dated Mar. 16, 1808 for 112½ ac is now void. Witness James Smith and Patterson Thomson. Signed John Tollison. Wit. oath Oct. 23, 1817 Patterson Thomson to John Lipscomb. Rec. Apr. 7, 1818

p. 8-9 Feb. 28, (omitted) William Crain (Greenville Dist) to John Duncan (same); for $200 sold 200 ac; border: NW & NE-Thomas Potter, NW-John Rosson and vacant, S-W. D. Thomas, and SE-unknown; "laid out" Feb. 10, 1791 to William Crain. Witness Allen Marshall and John McMakin. Signed William Crain's mark. Wit. oath Mar. 14, 1818 John McMakin to John Montgomery. Rec. Apr. 7, 1818

p. 9-10 Mar. 14, 1818 William Arnold (Spartanburgh) to Samuel Jones (same); for $50 sold 120 ac on branches of Enoree R. Witness John Crocker and Baily Adams. Signed Wm Arnold. Wit. oath Apr. 7, 1818 John Crocker to James Hamm. Rec. Apr. 7, 1818

p. 10-11 Jan. 18, 1817 James Wood (Spartanburgh) to John Kimbrell (same); for $150 sold 100 ac on S side of Thomson's Cr of Pacolette R; border: survey for Thomas Bennett; part of grant to Robert Crawder; part of where Thomas Kimbrell lives. Witness William Bennett and William Jackson. Signed James Wood's mark. Wit. oath Apr. 17, 1818(sic) William Bennett to James Young. Rec. Apr. 7, 1818. Dower renounced Jan. 19, 1818 Susannah Wood to James Young

p. 11-12 Nov. 4, 1816 Alexander McKie (Spartanburgh) to John Martin (same); for $4 sold 1½ ac on Fairforest Cr; border: Andrew Foster; except part belonging to Hamilton Wilson. Witness Wm S Golightly, James Spencer, and John White. Signed Alexr McKie. Wit. oath Apr. 7, 1818 Wm S Golightly to J Whitten. Rec. Apr. 8, 1818

p. 12-13 Nov. 14, 1815 Spencer Bobo (Spartanburgh) to Absolem Bobo (same); a bond for $2,000; Condition: bond is void if Spencer deeds Absolem 261 ac; border: Sarah Freeman, Thomas Farrow, John Leatherwood, W-Miles Nash, and N-Spiller's place. Witness Joseph Barnett, Sarah Barnett, and Nancy Barnett. Signed S Bobo. Wit. oath Nov. 9, 1816 Joseph Barnett to John Dean. Rec. Apr. 8, 1818

p. 13-15 Feb. 25, 1814 Christopher Golightly (Spartanburgh) to John Martin (same), blacksmith; for $448 sold 200 ac; border: James Finch; grant to Tate (now John and Rob Martin); part of grant to James Tillet who sold to Danl Thomas who sold to Henry White and mortgaged to Commissioners of South Carolina Loan Office and sold by William Hort, treasurer of South Carolina, to Thomas Taylor due to act of Assembly and sold to Christopher Golightly. Witness Robert Martin, John White, and Ralph Compton. Signed Christe Golightly. Wit. oath Apr. 24, 1815 John White to Danl White. Rec. Apr. 8, 1818. Dower renounced Apr. 24, 1815 Jenny (or Jane) Golightly to Samuel Archibald

p. 15-16 Mar. 15, 1817 John Stedman (Spartanburgh) to James Cudd (same); for $45 sold 50 ac on waters of Buck Cr. Witness John Covington and William Little. Signed John Stedman. Wit. oath May 3, 1817 John Covington to Henry Turner. Rec. Apr. 8, 1818

p. 16-17 Nov. 19, 1817 Thomas Farrow (Spartanburgh) to Caleb Woodruff (same); for $50 sold 45½ ac on waters of Two Mile Cr; border: J Terry, waggon road, and Saunder's Br; part of grant to Joseph Woodruff. Witness William Terry and James Leonard. Signed Thomas Farrow. Wit. oath Apr. 4, 1818 William Terry to Wm Hendrix. Rec. Apr. 9, 1818

p. 17-18 Jan. 3, 1818 Samuel Camp and William Camp jr to Frederick Gutrey; for $110 sold (ac omitted) at head of Allgood's Cr of Thickety Cr; border: Green River road and Vardery Camp; if older claim takes some of the land in next 5 years, William Camp refunds money proportionally. Witness Jonathan Gutrey and Samuel Gutrey. Signed Saml Camp and Wm Camp jr. Wit. oath Mar. 16, 1818 Jonathan Gutrey to John Lipscomb. Rec. Apr. 9, 1818

p. 18 Sept. 21, 1814 Jonathan Gutry (Spartanburgh) to Frederick Gutry (same); for (money omitted) sold 71 ac on waters of Thickety Cr; border: Camp and vacant. Witness Samuel Gutry and Benjamin Gilbert. Signed Jonathan Gutry. Wit. oath Sept. 22, 1814 Samuel Gutry to Henry Turner. Rec. Apr. 9, 1818

p. 18-20 Feb. 28, 1818 George Davis (Ga) and Francis Wright and wife Polly (Union Dist) to Moses Wilkins (Spartanburgh); for $75 sold 47 ac on S side of Gum Root Br of Gocher Cr of Thickety Cr; border: Moses Wilkins and John Laurence. Witness Austin Wright and Benjamin Hudgins. Signed George Davis, Francis Wright, and Polly's mark. Wit. oath Apr. 3, 1818 Austin Wright to John Lipscomb. Rec. Apr. 9, 1818

p. 20-21 Apr. 1, 1817 Edmund Wood (Spartanburgh) to Burrell High (same); for $280 sold 100 ac on waters of N Tyger R; border: James Vernon and John James. Witness John Wingo and John James. Signed Edmund Wood. Wit. oath Jan. 20, 1818 Edmund Wood to Memory N Chapman. Rec. Apr. 14, 1818. Dower renounced Jan. 1, 1818 Matilda Wood to John Collins

p. 21-22 Nov. 18, 1817 George and Fortunatus H Legg (Spartanburgh) to Muse Tollison (same); for $2,500 sold 478 ac on waters of Middle Tyger R; border: Thomas Moore. Witness John D Palmer and W. V. Miller. Signed George Legg and Fortunatus H Legg. Wit. oath

Mar. 3, 1818 John D Palmer to Wm Reid. Rec. Apr. 30, 1818

p. 22-23 Apr. 8, 1818 Laban P Poole (Rutherford Co, NC) to Elizabeth Evins, John P Evins, and "rest of" legates of Alexander Evins desc (Spartanburgh); for $1,500 sold (1) 204 ac on N side of S Tyger R; and (2) 158 ac adjoining (1). Witness James Swanzy and James Anderson. Signed Laban Poole. Wit. oath Apr. 8, 1818 James Swanzy to Wm Reid. Rec. May 4, 1818

p. 23-24 May 20, 1818 John Owens sr (Spartanburgh) to son David Owens (same); for love and affection give 130 ac on Enoree R where John Owens sr lives, and give a Negro boy Toll, a Negro girl Rachel, two Negro winches Jude and Rose, a Negro boy Washington, two Negro children Jackson and Jacob, and all his goods and chattles and household and kitchen furniture, and 2 bay mares, a roan, a sorrel horse, a stud bay colt, 11 cattle, 14 sheep, and 20 hogs. Witness James Leonard, James Lanford, and Caty Redman. Signed John Owens' mark. Wit. oath May 20, 1818 James Lanford to Samuel Woodruff. Rec. May 21, 1818

p. 24-25 Feb. 5, 1807 Thomas Burgess (Spartanburgh) to Samuel Gilbert (same); power of attorney to rent or sell his land in Spartanburgh Dist; Thomas Burgess is about to leave Spartanburgh Dist. Witness John Bankston, Laurence Bankston, and Sarah Bankston. Signed Thos Burgess. Wit. oath Apr. 22, 1818 John Bankston to John Montgomery. Rec. May 4, 1818

p. 25-26 Jun. 8, 1808 James Lanford (Spartanburgh) to son James Lanford (same); for love and affection give (ac omitted) on S side of Two Mile Cr with dwelling house; where grantor lives. Witness William Terry and John Terry and Robert Page. Signed James Lanford. Wit. oath Apr. 4, 1818 John Terry and Samuel Woodruff. Rec. May 4, 1818

p. 26-27 Nov. 19, 1017(sic) Thomas Farrow (Spartanburgh) to James Lanford jr (same); for $45 sold 70 ac on waters of Two Mile Cr; border: Nash; part of grant to Joseph Wofford. Witness James Leonard, Caleb Woodruff, and William Terry. Signed Thos Farrow. Wit. oath Apr. 4, 1818 William Terry to Samuel Woodruff. Rec. May 4, 1818

p. 27-28 Dec. 29, 1817 Silas Yarborough (Spartanburgh) to Joseph Collins (Union Dist); for $100 sold 100 ac on Surratt's Cr of Broad R; border: Benj Bonner desc; where Silas Yarborough lives. Witness Thomas Collins jr and William Collins. Signed Silas Yarborough's mark. Wit. oath May 4, 1818 William Collins to Henry Turner. Rec. May 4, 1818

p. 28-29 Jun. 13, 1816 Asahel Beeson (Spartanburgh) to John Beeson (same); for $200 sold 33 ac on Jimmies Cr; NW corner of 200 ac grant to George Crafford. Witness Robert Alexander and John Huckeby. Signed Asahel Beeson's mark. Wit. oath Apr. 6, 1818 Robert Alexander to Samuel Woodruff. Rec. May 4, 1818

p. 29-30 Mar. 17, 1812 Archibald Smith to Isael Beeson; for $400 sold 66 3/4 ac on Jemmies Cr; NW corner of 200 ac grant to George Crawford. Witness Richard Young and William Young. Signed Archibald Smith's mark. Wit. oath Sept. 1, 1813 Richard Young to M Casey. Rec. May 4, 1818

p. 30-31 Aug. 24, 1808 Pennewell Wood (Spartanburgh) to John Jones (same); for (money omitted) sold 57 ac on waters of Abner's Cr of Enoree R; border: Benjamin Wood, John Jones, Markbe, Thomas Cave, and John Wood. Witness John Wood and James Wood. Signed Pennewell Wood. Wit. oath Dec. 1, 1810 James Wood to Tyre Glen.

BOOK Q

Rec. Jun. 1, 1818

p. 31-33 Feb. 18, 1808 James Kilgore (Greenville Dist) to John Jones (Spartanburgh); for 100£ sold 249 ac on branches of Abner's Cr of Enoree R; border: Thomas Cave and William Williamson. Witness Samuel Jones and William Mayfield. Signed James Kilgore. Wit. oath Dec. 1, 1810 William Mayfield to Tyrce Glenn. Rec. Jun. 1, 1818

p. 33-34 Dec. 23, 1817 Richard Barnett (SC) to Peter Smith (SC); for $200 sold 90½ ac on Kelso's Cr of Fairforest Cr; border: Robert Martin; part of grant to Peter Smith, father of grantee. Witness Ephraim Roddy and John D Palmer. Signed Richd Barnett. Wit. oath May 4, 1818 John D Palmer to Danl White. Rec. Jun. 1, 1818

p. 34-35 Jul. 30, 1812 Jobe Sosbee to son Sampson Sosbee; for love and affection give 100 ac on branches of Peter's Cr of Pacolate R. Witness John Golightly jr and Polly Sosbee. Signed Jobe Sosbee's mark. Wit. oath Nov. 9, 1815 Polly Sosbee to Thomas Poole. Rec. Jun. 1, 1818

p. 35-36 Jan. 9, 1814 Jobe Sosbee (Spartanburgh) to Sampson Sosbee (same); for $85 sold 85 ac on waters of Peter's Cr. Witness Thomas Sosebee and Richard Turner. Signed Jobe Sosbee's mark. Wit. oath Jan. 9, 1815 Thomas Sosebee to Henry Turner. Rec. Jun. 1, 1818

p. 36-37 Jun. 1, 1818 Thomas Burgess (formerly of Spartanburgh but now lives outside SC) by power of attorney to Samuel Gilbert sell to John Nolen (Spartanburgh); for $200 sold 130 ac on Pacolet R; border: John Cantril, George Horton, John Nolen, and Tolbert Gipson; part of tract sold by Edward Stubblefield to Thomas Burgess. Witness William Trimmier and Danl Wilbanks. Signed Samuel Gilbert's mark, attorney for Thos Burges. Wit. oath Jun. 1, 1818 William Trimmier to A Benson. Rec. Jun. 1, 1818

p. 37-39 Feb. 5, 1812 James Wofford (Spartanburgh) to William Morgan (same); for $200 sold 250 ac on Reedy fork Cr of S Tyger R; 13 rods square "on South side" excepted "for Joshua Benson's on bank"; part of 300 ac grant Nov. 7, 1785 to Nathaniel Miller who sold to Joshua Edwards who sold to James Wofford. Witness John Turner and Mary Turner. Signed James Wofford. Wit. oath Jun. 12, 1816 Mary Turner to J Camp. Rec. Jun. 1, 1818

p. 39-40 May 7, 1817 William R Smith (Spartanburgh) to Daniel Lynch (same); for $500 sold 202 ac on Kelso's Cr. Witness William Bagwell, James Bagwell, and Samuel Shurbutt. Signed Wm R Smith. Wit. oath Jun. 1, 1818 William Bagwell to Caleb Jones. Rec. Jun. 1, 1818

p. 40-41 Mar. 16, 1815 James Smith (Union Dist), an heir of Capt. James Smith desc, to William R Smith (same); for $500 sold 202 ac on Kelso's Cr; land is lot 7 in division of estate of James Smith desc. Witness James White and Lemuel White. Signed James Smith. Wit. oath Apr. 18, 1817 James White to Danl White. Rec. Jun. 1, 1818

p. 41-42 Jan. 26, 1818 Andw B Moore received from Geo Legg and F. H. Legg at "sundry" times $1,090 in payment of mortgage. Witness John P Evins. Signed Andw B Moore. Wit. oath Jan. 27, 1818 John P Evins to F. H. Legg. Rec. Jun. 1, 1818

p. 42-43 Apr. 19, 1817 George McWilliams (Spartanburgh) to Robert T Wall (same); for $110 sold 60 ac on waters of N Pacolate R; border: James Young and Robert T Wall. Witness William Wilkins and Zacchariah Wall. Signed George McWilliams. Wit. oath Jan. 12,

1818 Zacchariah Wall to Wm Kelso. Rec. Jun. 13, 1818

p. 43-44 May 4, 1810 George Curling (Spartanburgh) to Lee Linder (same); for 500 gal of "good merchantable" whiskey sold 230 ac on waters of Pacolet R and on Dry Br. Witness James Campbell and Aron Templeman. Signed Ge Curling. Wit. oath Aug. 10, 1811 James Campbell to Henry Turner. Rec. Jun. 18, 1818. Dower renounced Dec. 11, 1811 Ann M Curling to John Lipscomb

p. 44-46 Aug. 21, 1809 Aron Templeman (Spartanburgh) to Lee Linder (same); for $320 sold 200 ac on N side of Pacolet R. Witness Elijah Satterfield and Thomas Wyatt. Signed Aron Templeman's mark. Wit. oath Aug. 21, 1809 Thomas Wyatt to Henry Turner. Rec. Jun. 18, (omitted)

p. 46-47 Jun. 29, 1818 Abner Benson (Spartanburgh) to Daniel Faust (same); for $100 sold (1) ½ ac in Spartanburgh, SC on S side of Court House; border: S-Richard Thomson, W-Abner Benson's lot, E-Col. Isaac Smith's lot, and N-public street; and (2) ½ ac in Spartanburgh, SC on S side of Main St; adjoins (1) on West. Witness John T Earle and Elisha Bomar. Signed A Benson. Wit. oath Jun. 29, 1818 John T Earle to E Walker. Rec. Jun. 29, 1818 Jun. 29, 1818 Daniel Faust received from Abner Benson a deed dated May 26, 1804 from William Thomson to Abner Benson for lot (1) and a deed dated May 26, 1804 from William Thomson to William R Smith for lot (2) and a deed dated Apr. 18, 1812 from Wm R Smith to Abner Benson for lot (2). Witness John T Earle. Signed Daniel Faust

p. 47-48 May 30, 1817 Nathl Burton (Spartanburgh) to Jonathan Crow (same); for $207 sold 103½ ac on waters of Tyger R; border: old bridge. Witness Ford Mason and Tolliver Scott. Signed Nathl Burton. Wit. oath Apr. 14, 1818 Ford Mason to Robt Ligeon. Rec. Jul. 1, 1818

p. 48-50 Feb. 10, 1807 John Jones (Spartanburgh) to Eaton Walker (same); for $400 sold (1) 50 ac; border: Peter Gray, John Chapman, Robert Goodlet, and Robert Jamerson; sold Dec. 30, 1806 by Robert Haile to Matthias Rush who sold to Joseph Fleming who sold to William Wells who sold to John Jones; and (2) 9 ac adjoining (1) and sold Aug. 20, 1799 by John Chapman to Matthias Rush. Witness Isham Foster and James Goodlett. Signed John Jones. Wit. oath Apr. 7, 1818 James Goodlett to James Young. Rec. Jul. 1, 1818

p. 50-51 Oct. 15, 1804 Henry M Wood (Greenville Dist) to Saml Nesbitt (Spartanburgh); for $150 sold 140 ac on N side of S Tyger R; border: SE & NE-John McClerath, SE & S-vacant, and other sides-S Tyger R; grant Jan. 7, 1799 to Thomas Wood. Witness John Pace and John Spence. Signed H. M. Wood. Wit. oath Oct. 15, 1804 John Pace to Jas Kilgore. Rec. Jul. 1, 1818

p. 51-52 Mar. 22, 1814 Richard Barnett (Giles Co, Tenn) to Daniel White (Spartanburgh); for $300 sold 177 ac on waters of Kelso's Cr of Fairforest Cr; border: James Smith and James; where Daniel White lives; ¼ ac excepted including graves where Meeting House formerly stood; part of the old Meeting house tract; grant to Giles Connell who sold to John Cook who sold to Joseph Barnett desc and sold by "representatives" of Joseph Barnett to Richard Barnett; also border: E of "big" road to Spartanburgh Court House. Witness Wm Underwood and Henry White. Signed Richard Barnett. Wit. oath Apr. 6, 1818 Wm Underwood to Wm Reid. Rec. Jul. 6, 1818

p. 52-53 Apr. 13, 1813 Charles James (Spartanburgh) to Daniel White (same); for $9 sold 6 ac on both sides of Kelso's Cr; border: Daniel White, a waggon ford on the creek; and road formerly called Meeting House Road; part of grant to George Story. Witness Charles

James jr and Francis James. Signed Charles James. Wit. oath Feb. 21, 1818 F Barnett, late Francis James, to Wm Underwood. Rec. Jul. 6, 1818

p. 53-2nd 54 May 10, 1798 Henry Hughs (Augusta, Ga) to David Lewis (same); for $15 sold 375 ac; border: all vacant when surveyed. Witness Gabriel Benson, John Lewis, and Edward Ballenger. Signed Henry Hughs. Wit. oath Jul. 6, 1818 Edward Ballenger to Henry Turner. Rec. Jul. 6, 1818

p. 2nd 54-55 Mar. 8, 1817 Patrick Saunders (Spartanburgh) to Nancy Wood (same); for $124.50 sold 249 ac on Allgood's Br. Witness A Benson, William Wood, and John Wood. Signed Patrick Saunders' mark. Wit. oath Jan. 27, 1818 William Wood to A Benson. Rec. Jul. 6, 1818. Dower renounced Jan. 27, 1818 Susannah Saunders to A Benson

p. 55-56 Jul. 7, 1817 Young Fuller (Spartanburgh) to David Golightly jr (same); for $90 sold 150 ac on Cherokee Cr of Pacolate R; part of grant to Robert Lee sr desc; at mouth of Daggaway's Cr; border: Solomon Abbott. Witness William Lancaster and Robert Martin. Signed Young Fuller. Wit. oath Jul. 6, 1818 William Lancaster to Robt Ligon. Rec. Jul. 6, 1818

p. 56-57 May 14, 1817 James Powell to Richard Loftis; for $200 sold a Negro girl Grace. Witness John Cantrell. Signed James Powell's mark. Wit. oath Jul. 4, 1818 John Cantrell to John Montgomery. Rec. Jul. 6, 1818

p. 57-58 Sept. 21, 1816 Abram Cantrell (Spartanburgh) to William Bennett (same); for $100 sold 100 ac on Pacolate R; Abram Cantrell's share of land as heir of his mother, Mary Cantrell, when Mary Cantrell died. Witness Iredell Cunningham and Alfred Cunningham. Signed Abram Cantrell. Wit. oath Oct. 1, 1816 Alfred Cunningham to James Young. Rec. Jul. 6, 1818

p. 58-59 Apr. 4, 1818 George Floyd (Spartanburgh) to Thomas Price (same); for $150 sold 88 ac; border: Miles Sumner, Gideon Reynolds, John King, John Mason, Richard Gentry, and Joseph Willis. Witness Benjamin Robuck and Samuel Floyd. Signed George Floyd's mark. Wit. oath Jul. 2, 1818 Benjamin Robuck to John Brewton. Rec. Jul. 9, 1818

p. 59-60 Jan. 19, 1818 Henry William Desaussure, surviving acting trustee for estate of John Wearing (late of Charleston Dist) to William Lockhart; for "a small sum" ($300 sold 1,500 ac on Gilky's Cr of Thickety Cr; grant to John Wearing but "run out by other persons and claimed by them" and recovery would cost a lot; William Lockhart gest John Wearing's rights to the land. Witness Mary Caroline Blanding and Jesse Kilgore. Signed Henry Wm Desaussure. Wit. oath Jan. 19, 1818 Jesse Kilgore to James T Goodwyn. Rec. Jul. 13, 1818

p. 60-61 Jul. 20, 1818 William Willis (Spartanburgh) to son William Shoes (sic); for love and affection give a gray mare and her increase and a musket gun. Witness Zacchariah Hammett and William Brock. Signed William Willis. Wit. oath Jul. 20, 1818 Zacchariah Hammett to Caleb Jones. Rec. Jul. 20, 1818

p. 61-62 Jul. 20, 1818 William Willis to Barsheba Shores; for love and affection give 40 hogs and their increase, a red cow Swan and her increase, a loom and geer, and a spinning wheel and a pair of cards. Witness Zacchariah Hammett and William Brock. Signed William Willis. Wit. oath Jul. 20, 1818 Zacchariah Hammett to Caleb Jones. Rec. Jul. 20, 1818

p. 62-63 Jul. 20, 1818 William Willis (Spartanburgh) to daughter Nancy Shoes (sic); for love and affection give a bay horse named Silver, a bridle cow and calf and their increase, and a bed and furniture. Witness Zacchariah Hammett and William Brock. Signed William Willis. Wit. oath Jul. 20, 1818 Zacchariah Hammett to Caleb Jones. Rec. Jul. 20, 1818

p. 63-64 Jul. 20, 1818 William Willis (Spartanburgh) to daughters Polly Shores and Sally Shores (sic); for love and affection give 14 sheep, a black cow and her increase, a black heifer and her increase, 2 beds and furniture, and a spinning wheel and cards. Witness Zachariah Hammett and William Brock. Signed William Willis. Wit. oath Jul. 20, 1818 Zachariah Hammett to Caleb Jones. Rec. Jul. 20, 1818

p. 64-65 Jul. 20, 1818 William Willis (Spartanburgh) to son William Shoes(sic); for love and affection sold 151 ac where William Willis lives on S side of Pacolate R and Lawson's fork; border William Poole. Witness Zachariah Hammett and William Brock. Signed William Willis. Wit. oath Jul. 20, 1818 Zachariah Hammett to Caleb Jones. Rec. Jul. 20, 1818

p. 65-66 Oct. 12, 1807 Denny Anderson (Spartanburgh) to David Anderson (same); for $400 sold 450 ac on N side of S Tyger R; border: E-James Alexander and SE-William Hendrix and David Anderson; part of grant in 1774 Gov. William Bull to Benjamin Huger for 1,000 ac in Craven Co. Witness James Chamblin and John Johnson. Signed Denny Anderson. Wit. oath Oct. 12, 1807 James Chamblin to David Morton. Rec. Jul. 22, 1818. Dower renounced Oct. 20, 1807 Elizabeth Anderson to David Morton

p. 66-68 May 5, 1798 William Moore (Spartanburgh) to James Allen (same); for 10£ sterling sold 101 ac on branches of Lyck's Cr of Enoree R; border: SW & N-Isaac Hanly, SE-Enoch Hooper, and NE-Wm Hanly; grant Nov. 5, 1793 Gov. William Moultrie to William Moore. Witness Burrel Pace and Thomas Woodruff. Signed William Moore. Wit. oath Feb. 8, 1814 Thomas Woodruff to Samuel Woodruff. Rec. Jul. 27, 1818

p. 68-70 Jul. 6, 1818 James Hunt, sheriff (Spartanburgh) to Jane (or Sara) Bobo (same); for $50 sold 600 ac on Furguson's Cr; oath attached shows border: John Means, David Brewton, John Brewton, James Brewton, Wm Westmoreland, Wm Jones, Josiah Woodruff, Wm Hendricks, John Crocker, and Nathaniel Woodruff; sale due to writ from Spartanburgh Common Pleas Court suit Samuel Farrow vs Thomas Bragg, administrator of Spencer Bobo desc when Laban P Poole was sheriff; James Hunt is successor of L. P. Poole; sale Jul. 7, 1817. Witness William N Miller and David Golightly. Signed Jas Hunt. Wit. oath Jul. 7, 1818 W. N. Miller to A Benson. Rec. Jul. 27, 1818

p. 70-71 Dec. 19, 1816 Joseph Woodruff (Spartanburgh) to James Allen (same); for $300 sold 98 ac; border: Henderson, E-Lick Cr, S-J Woodruff, N-James Allen, W-Samuel Woodruff esq. Witness Samuel Woodruff and Thomas Woodruff. Signed Joseph Woodruff's mark. Wit. oath Jul. 25, 1818 Samuel Woodruff to Samuel Woodruff. Rec. Jul. 27, 1818

p. 71-73 May 5, 1817 Thomas Kelso (Spartanburgh) to Samuel Kelso (same); for $400 sold 116 ac on S side of Fairforest Cr; border: John Kelso; grant to George Story who sold to Joseph Kelso who willed to Thomas Kelso. Witness John Kelso and Joseph Kelso. Signed Thomas Kelso. Wit. oath May 10, 1817 Joseph Kelso to Wm Reid. Rec. Aug. 1, 1818. Dower renounced Sept. 13, 1817 Jean Kelso to Samuel Archibald

p. 73 Jun. 22, 1818 Philip Bettis (Spartanburgh) to James Vernon (same); for (money omitted) sold (ac omitted); quit claim to survey Oct. 7, 1816 for Philip Bettis and claimed by James Vernon. Witness Michael Mooren and John Sexton. Signed Philip Bettis' mark. Wit. oath Aug. 3, 1818 Michael Mooren to E Walker. Rec. Aug. 3, 1818

p. 73-75 Jun. 1, 1816 Goen Clayton (Spartanburgh) to James Vernon (same); for $50 sold 150 ac on Wolf Swamp Br of Middle Tyger R; border: James Vernon and Thompson; part of grant to Goen Clayton. Witness Andrew F Nesbett and David Henson. Signed Goen Clayton's mark. Wit. oath Aug. 3, 1818 Andrew F Nesbett to John Montgomery. Rec. Aug. 3, 1818

p. 75-76 Feb. 28, 1818 Thomas McCarley (Spartanburgh) to James Cook jr (same); for $150 sold 100 ac on waters of Furgerson's Cr; border: Henry U Smith and James Otts; NW part of grant Jan. 1, 1787 to Thomas Hightower. Witness Joshua Tapp and Moses Tapp. Signed Thomas McCarley. Wit. oath Aug. 3, 1818 Joshua Tapp to Thomas Wood. Rec. Aug. 3, 1818

p. 76-77 Feb. 23, 1818 James Chamblin, D Chamblin, Jeremiah Bobo, and Jean Chamblin to Willis Arnold (Spartanburgh); for $500 paid to Jean Chamblin sold 150 ac on Fulles Br of Cedar Shoal Cr of Enoree R; part of grant May 6, 1772 to Eliz Benson. Witness Jonathan Crook and Susan Simpson. Signed Jas Chamblin, D Chamblin, Jeremiah Bobo's mark, and Jane(sic) Chamblin's mark. Wit. oath Aug. 1, 1818 Jonathan Crook to Samuel Woodruff. Rec. Aug. 3, 1818

p. 77-78 Aug. 3, 1818 Alexander McKie (Spartanburgh) to Obadiah Wingo (same); for $394 sold (ac omitted) on S side of Fairforest Cr and Dangin's Br; border: Obadiah Wingo. Witness Muse Tollison and Berryman S Holder. Signed Alexn McKie. Wit. oath Aug. 3, 1818 Muse Tollison to Wm Reid. Rec. Aug. 3, 1818

p. 78-79 Feb. 26, 1816 Benjamin Robuck (Spartanburgh) to John Mason (same); for $300 sold 63 ac on N side of Jemmies Cr; border: E-Jno King, N-J. W. Reynolds, Mark Langston, and Richard Gentry, W-David King, and S-George Robuck. Witness William Posey and James Mason. Signed Benjamin Robuck. Wit. oath Aug. 3, 1818 William Posey to Wm Underwood. Rec. Aug. 3, 1818

p. 79-80 Aug. 15, 1817 Robert White and wife Anne (Spartanburgh) to James Anderson; for (money omitted) sold 70 ac on S Tyger R; border: S-James Anderson and John Johnson and other sides-Samuel Stewart and Reedy fork; part of grant to John Whitaman who sold to Robert Connell who sold to Samuel Stewart who sold to Robert and Anne White. Witness John Patton and Jonathan N Hadden. Signed Robert M White and Anne White. Wit. oath Aug. 3, 1818 John Patton to Thomas Poole. Rec. Aug. 3, 1818

p. 80-81 Jan. 26, 1814 David Anderson (Spartanburgh) to James Anderson (same); for $300 sold 183 ac on Ben's Cr of Tyger R; border: David Allen's old line, Rebun(?) Anderson, and Hugge. Witness Denny Anderson, William Anderson, and John Durham. Signed David Anderson. Wit. oath Aug. 3, 1818 John Durham to Thomas Poole. Rec. Aug. 3, 1818

p. 81-82 Dec. 1, 1817 Nathan Sentell (Spartanburgh) to Robert Belcher; for $25 sold 100 ac on E and W of Bartan's Br of Lawson's fork; border: Samuel Seay, Cardin, and Robert Belcher; part of 1,000 ac survey for Larkin Cardin. Witness Edmd Bishop, short and Larkin Cardin. Signed Nathan Sentell. Wit. oath Jul. 11, 1818 Edmd Bishop to Eph Lewis. Rec. Aug. 3, 1818

p. 82-83 Jan. 2, 1818 Robert Dunaway (Spartanburgh) to Samuel Dunaway jr (same); for $61 sold 61 ac on branches of Thickety Cr. Witness Jonathan Gutry and John Saunders. Signed Robert Dunaway. Wit. oath Jan. 2, 1818 Jonathan Gutry to Henry Turner. Rec. Aug. 3, 1818

p. 83-84 Jan. 2, 1818 Robert Dunaway (Spartanburgh) to William Saunders (same); for $64 sold 64 ac on branches of Thickety Cr. Witness Jonathan Gutry and John Saunders. Signed Robert Dunaway. Wit. oath Jan. 3, 1818 Jonathan Gutry to Henry Turner. Rec. Aug. 3, 1818

p. 84 Jan. 1, 1818 William Redman (Spartanburgh) to Bennett Wilson; for $66.50 sold rights to land from estate of his father John Redman. Witness James Hammett and Tyre Glen. Signed William Redman. Wit. oath Aug. 7, 1818 James Hammett to Thomas Wood. Rec. Aug. 15, 1818

p. 84-85 Jan. 21, 1818 John Redman jr (Spartanburgh), heir of John Redman desc (same), to Bennett Wilson (same); for $100 sold rights to land of estate of John Redman. Witness James Hammett and Starling Redman. Signed John Redman. Wit. oath Aug. 7, 1817 James Hammett to Thomas Wood. Rec. Aug. 15, 1818

p. 85-86 Jan. 1, 1818 Polly Redman (Spartanburgh) to Bennett Wilson (same); for $66.50 sold rights to land from estate of her father John Redman desc. Witness James Hammett and Tyre Glen. Signed Polly Redman. Wit. oath Aug. 7, 1818 James Hammett to Thomas Wood. Rec. Aug. 15, 1818

p. 86-87 Jan. 1, 1818 Rachel Redman, widow of John Redman desc, (Spartanburgh) to Bennett Wilson; for $300 sold rights to land from estate of her husband John Redman desc. Witness James Hammett and Tyre Glenn. Signed Rachel Redman's mark. Wit. oath Aug. 7, 1818 James Hammett to Thomas Wood. Rec. Aug. 15, 1818

p. 87-88 May 15, 1818 John Jordan (Spartanburgh) to John Vaughn; a bond for $600; Condition: bond void if John Jordan deeds John Vaughn (1) 300 ac in Greenville Dist on Middle Tyger R; border: Joseph Smith, Job Henson, District line, James Smith (near James Smith's Still House), and Mawhal; and (2) 40 ac part of grant to John McKie "on Spartanburgh Side" and sold to John Jordan; on E side of Indian boundary--"if the lines can be adentified" and otherwise void. Witness Frances Galt and Jabez Galt. Signed John Jordan. Wit. oath Aug. 22, 1818 Jabez Galt to E Walker. Rec. Aug. 22, 1818

p. 88-90 Aug. 22, 1818 Robert Martin (Spartanburgh) to John Murff (or Murph) (Orangeburgh Dist); for $1,554 sold 259 ac on both sides Fairforest Cr; border: John Martin, Rakestraw, D Golightly sr, and James Fleming; part of tract sold by Mr Tate to James Lusk and part of tract granted Aug. 11, 1785 to Charles Bruce. Witness Shands Golightly and Burdit L Evetts. Signed Robert Martin. Wit. oath Aug. 28, 1818 Burdit L Evetts to Danl White. Rec. Aug. 29, 1818. Dower renounced Aug. 27, 1818 Polly Martin to Danl White

p. 90-92 Aug. 22, 1818 Shands Golightly (Spartanburgh) to John Murph (Orangeburgh Dist); for $100 sold 302 ac on N side of Fairforest Cr; border: E & SE-P Smith, SW & SE-Andrew Foster, SW & NW-John Martin; resurvey May 28, 1818 by Robert Martin surv; plat attached shows border: Ben Smith, Sally Foster, Anr Foster, Jno Martin, Robert Martin, School House, and on both sides of Kelso's Cr and a road. Witness Robert Martin and Burdit L Evetts. Signed Shands Golightly. Wit. oath Aug. 28, 1818 Burdit L Evetts to Danl White. Rec. Aug. 29, 1818

p. 92-93 Aug. 26, 1815 John L Tippens (Spartanburgh) to Sterling Westmoreland (Greenville Dist); for $300 sold 220 ac on branches of Tyger R; border: Newbell Johnson. Witness John Westmoreland, Jesse Wofford, and Nathaniel Wofford. Signed Jno L Tippen. Wit. oath Aug. 24, 1818 John Westmoreland to Thomas Wood. Rec. Aug. 29, 1818

p. 93 Sept. 8, 1818 Anderson Williams to A Benson JP; an oath that on Sept. 2, 1818 a fight ensued between William Turner and Robert McMen and Robert lost a piece of his left ear and a peice of his upper lip. Witness A Benson JP. Signed Andrew Williams. Rec. Sept. 8, 1818

p. 93-95 Aug. 26, 1815 William Rhodes (Spartanburgh) to Starling L Westmoreland (Greenville Dist); for $205.50 sold 179 ac on branches of Furgerson's Cr of Tyger R; border: old muster ground. Witness Jno Westmoreland, Jesse Wofford, and Nathaniel Wofford. Signed Wm Rhodes. Wit. oath Aug. 24, 1818 Jno Westmoreland to Thos Wood. Rec. Aug. 29, 1818. Dower renounced Aug. 26, 1818 Rebecca Rhodes to Thomas Wood

p. 95-97 Aug. 26, 1818 John Owens (Spartanburgh) to Sterling L Westmoreland (same); for $75 sold 2 ac on N fork of Furgerson's Cr of Tyger R; border: W-Isaac Wofford and SE & N-John Owens. Witness Jesse Wofford and Warren Drummond. Signed John Owens. Wit. oath Aug. 26, 1818 Jesse Wofford to Thos Wood. Rec. Aug. 29, 1818. Dower renounced Aug. 26, 1818 Patsy Owens to Thomas Wood

p. 97-98 Aug. 25, 1817 Thomas Allison (Spartanburgh) to Muse Tollison (same); for $4,000 sold 4 ac, 1 rod, and 22 "perches" in Spartanburgh, SC on S side of Main St; border: NE-Thomas Allison's "Piaza", Blacksmith shop, and Public Square. Witness Jesse Cleveland, John T Earle and Simpson Foster. Signed Thomas Allison. Wit. oath Sept. 2, 1817 Jesse Cleveland to A Benson. Rec. Sept. 7, 1818. Dower renounced Aug. 23, 1818 Jane Allison to Burrell Bobo

p. 98-100 Aug. 25, 1817 Thomas Allison (Spartanburgh) to Muse Tollison (same); for $400 sold 154 ac on E side of Spartanburgh Court House and on Fairforest Cr; border: road from Court House to Anthony Foster's, lane from Thomas Allison to Muse Tollison's, James Brannon, and road from Court House to William Robertson's; part of grant Jan. 6, 1794 to Isham Harrison. Witness Jesse Cleveland, John T Earle, and Simpson Foster. Signed Thomas Allison. Wit. oath Sept. 2, 1817 Jesse Cleveland to A Benson. Rec. Sept. 7, (omitted). Dower renounced Aug. 23, 1818 Jane Allison to Burrel Bobo

p. 100-102 Aug. 25, 1817 Thomas Allison (Spartanburgh) to Muse Tollison (same); for $100 sold 171 ac(sic) on Fairforest Cr of Tyger R; in two(sic) tracts: (1) 77 ac grant Gov. William Moultrie to Thomas Brooks; (2) 39 ac grant Gov. Paul Hamilton to Vincent Simmons; and (3) 50 ac grant (governor unknown) to R Harrison; 7 or 8 ac (a small peice) excepted on N side of tract included in "junior" grant to Vincent Simmons and "a few ac" on SE side included in a "senior" grant to William Shaw, now owned by James Brannon. Witness Jesse Cleveland, John T Earle, and Simpson Foster. Signed Thomas Allison. Wit. oath Jesse Cleveland to A Benson Sept. 2, 1317. Rec. Sept. 7, 1318. Dower renounced Aug. 23, 1818 Jane Allison to Burrell Bobo

p. 102-103 May 3, 1818 Jonathan Nesbett (Spartanburgh) to Jacob Bridges (same); for $338.50 sold 97 ac on Tyger R. Witness Bowen Griffin and Rachel Griffin. Signed Jonathan Nesbett. Wit. oath Jul. 11, 1818 Bowen Griffin to John Montgomery. Rec. Sept. 7, 1818

p. 103-104 Dec. 26, 1816 William Wyatt and wife Judith (Spartanburgh) to Vincent Wyatt (same); for $200 sold 128 ac on Peter's Cr of Pacolette R; grant to William Wofford. Witness Sampson Sosbee and William Sosbee. Signed Wm Wyatt and Judith's mark. Wit. oath Dec. 26, 1816 Sampson Sosbee to Thomas Poole. Rec. Sept. 7, 1818

p. 104-105 Jun. 29, 1818 Vincent Wyatt and wife Elizabeth (Spartanburgh) to James Wyatt (same); for $200 sold 128 ac on Peter's Cr of Pacolate R; grant to William Wofford. Witness Jesse Cannon and James Cannon. Signed Vincent and Elizabeth Wyatt. Wit. oath Sept. 7, 1818 Jesse Cannon to Thomas Poole. Rec. Sept. 7, 1818

p. 105-107 Aug. 3, 1818 Peter Best (Lincoln Co, NC) to Vincent Wyatt (Spartanburgh); for $625 sold 1,000 ac on Lawson's fork Cr of Pacolate R. Witness James Cannon and James Wyatt. Signed Peter Best's mark. Wit. oath Sept. 7, 1818 James Wyatt to Thomas Poole. Rec. Sept. 7, (omitted)

p. 107-108 Nov. 19, 1817 Reuben Bomar (Spartanburgh) to Robert Bullington (Union Dist); for $1,500 sold 470 ac by resurvey on both sides S Pacolate R; border: Bomar's Bridge, Paul Cox, James McDowell, Dickson's old line, and Armstead Bomar; where Reuben Bomar lives. Witness Christopher Golightly, Thomas Howard, and Jesse Burton. Signed Reuben Bomar. Wit. oath Sept. 7, 1818 Christopher Golightly to Thomas Poole. Rec. Sept. 7, 1818. Dower renounced Feb. 12, 1818 Nancy Bomar to James Young

p. 108-109 Feb. 10, 1817 Joseph Wilson (Spartanburgh) to David Moore (same); for $125 sold 100 ac on S side of Motlow's Cr; border: James Ridings, James Whitton, Henderson, and Mill Road. Wit. oath Hubbard Quals and Alfred Whitten. Signed Joseph Wilson's mark. Wit. oath Jun. 4, 1818 Hubbard Quals to J Whitten. Rec. Sept. 7, (omitted)

p. 109-110 Dec. 12, 1817 John McBee (Spartanburgh) to Theophelus Thorn (same); for $50 sold 50 ac on waters of McKenney's Cr. Witness Whitney Hines and Elizabeth Hines. Signed John McBee's mark. Wit. oath Dec. 12, 1817 Whitney Hines to Henry Turner. Rec. Sept. 7, 1818

p. 110-111 Jun. 20, 1818 John Means (SC) to Jesse Crook (Spartanburgh); for $100 sold 50 ac; border: W-branch of Furgerson's Cr, S-formerly Thomas Williams, E & NE-formerly where John Means lived, and N-James Crook; grant to Drury McDaniel esq. Witness Andrew Barry, Jesse Wofford, and Richard Barry. Signed John Means. Wit. oath Jun. 20, 1818 Andrew Barry to James Brook. Rec. Sept. 7, 1818

p. 111-112 Jun. 20, 1818 John Means (Spartanburgh) to Jesse Crook (same); for $50 sold 24 ac on branches of Forguson's Cr of Tyger R; border: W-John Means and E-Peter Bragg. Witness Andrew Barry, Jesse Wofford, and Richard Barry. Signed John Means. Wit. oath Jun. 20, 1818 Andrew Barry to James Crook. Rec. Sept. 7, 1818

p. 112-113 Oct 27, 1816 Joseph Wofford (Spartanburgh) to Jeremiah Wofford (same); for $500 sold 100 ac on Jemmies Cr of Tyger R and on Rigefield Spring Br; border: William Pugh, Jeremiah Wofford, Thomas Young, John Hobby, Nancy Britain, and William Ervin; part of 300 ac grant Aug. 11, 1774 to Luke Viccory. Witness Joseph Wofford jr and John Tucker. Signed Joseph Wofford. Wit. oath Jul. 10, 1818 John Tucker to Benjamin Wofford. Rec. Sept. 7, (omitted)

p. 113-114 Mar. 9, 1818 Robert Hudson to Jeremiah Wofford; for $40 sold 40 ac; border: NW-Isaac Crow, NE-Miles Rainwater, SE-Jesse Casey; on branch of Cedar Shoal Cr; part of grant to William Casey who sold to Moses Casey who sold to Robert Hudson. Witness

Reubin Harris and Thomas Bell. Signed Robert Hudson. Wit. oath Aug. 4, 1818 Thomas Bell to Benjamin Wofford. Rec. Sept. 7, 1818

p. 114-115 Feb. 14, 1808 Isaac Crow to Joseph Wofford; for $250 sold 100 ac on S side of Tyger R; border: NW-Joseph Wofford jr and Samuel Jones and SW & SE-Samuel Tucker, and by grant to Delaney Carrol now owned by Joseph Wofford; grant to David Donamore. Witness John Ervin and Samuel Thomas. Signed Isaac Crow. Wit. oath Jun. 8, 1818 John Ervin to Benjamin Wofford. Rec. Sept. 7, 1818

p. 115-116 Aug. 6, 1818 Dower renounced Lucy Jordan to John Collins for deed from John Jordan desc to Andrew B Flemming. Rec. Sept. 7, 1818

p. 116-117 Aug. 11, 1818 John Vandike (Spartanburgh) to Vincent Wyatt (same); for $160 sold 80 ac on N side of Lawson's fork of Pacolate R; border: Peter Bess. Witness Elisha Bomar and J Brannon. Signed John Vandike. Wit. oath Sept. 10, 1818 Elisha Bomar to A Benson. Rec. Sept. 10, 1818

p. 117-118 Jul. 20, 1818 Frances L Walker, heir of Edward Walker desc, to John Walker (Spartanburgh); for $640 sold 1/5 of two tracts that total 714 ac granted to William Meyer who sold to Edward Walker; land in Richland Dist in fork of Cedar Cr and Black Swamp of Congaree R; border: NW-Isaac Raiford, Daniel Hoy, John White, and Col. Frances Goodwyn, S-survey for Hamilton and Vincent Simmons, SE-formerly land of Gen. Hampton, NE-Gen. Hampton known as Rutledge's Mill tract, SE-heirs of Robert Goodwyn esq, NE-Robert Howeles, and NW-William Fishburn esq. Witness George Tarrant and William Walker. Signed Frances L Walker. Wit. oath Jul. 21, 1818 William Walker to E Walker. Rec. Sept. 19, 1818

p. 118-119 Mar. 31, 1818 John Gowen, Winn B Gowen, Strut Thurston, and James Blassingame (all of Greenville Dist), appointed by will of John Gowen desc, to Thomas Grogan (Spartanburgh); for $150 sold 100 ac on N side of Pacolete R; border: Brown, ancient Indian Boundary, and Penington's Still House Br; where Thomas Grogan lives; part of 1,000 ac grant to Henry Bennson and part of real estate of John Gowen desc. Witness Asa W Crowder and Minon W Brown. Signed John Gowen, W. B. Gowen, Strut Thuston, and Jas Blassing(sic). Wit. oath Sept. 12, 1818 Minon W Brown to J Whitten. Rec. Sept. 19, 1818

p. 119-120 Sept. 20, 1815 Moses Tapp (Spartanburgh) to John McAbee (same); for $150 sold 100 ac on branches of N Tyger R; part of grant to William Ford. Witness Thomas Tinsley and James Haskins. Signed Moses Tapp. Wit. oath Nov. 7, 1815 James Haskins to Thomas Poole. Rec. Sept. 17, 1818

p. 120-122 Nov.18, 1800 Samuel Miller (Spartanburgh) to James Templeton (same); for $308 sold 300 ac on S side of Lawson's fork of Pacolate R and both sides of James' waggon road and both sides of Reedy Br; border: John Miller; grant in Dec. 1768 North Carolina to Robert McMordir and sold by his heirs to John McMordir May 11, 1797 who sold Jan. 3, 1799 to James Templeton and Samuel Miller. Witness Ism Foster, Isaac Snoddy, and Moses Timmons. Signed Saml Miller. Certified Nov. 18, 1800 by Ism Foster. Rec. Sept. 29, 1818

p. 122-123 Sept. 22, 1818 John Johnson (Spartanburgh) to James Anderson (same); for $900 sold 300 ac on Ben's Cr of Tyger R. Witness Jesse Wofford and William Anderson. Signed John Johnson. Wit. oath Oct. 5, 1818 William Anderson to John Collins. Rec. Oct. 6, 1818. Dower renounced Sept. 30, 1818 Sarah Johnson to

John Collins

p. 123-124 Apr. 25, 1815 James Wilson (Spartanburgh) to Peter Carr McMakin (same); for $100 sold 100 ac on Middle Tyger R; plat attached shows border: Andrew Nesbett, Benson, and James Wilson. Wit. oath Danl Wilbanks, John Wilson, and John Montgomery. Signed James Wilson's mark. Wit. oath Dec. 8, 1815 John Wilson to John Collins. Rec. Oct. 5, 1818. Dower renounced Sept. 12, 1818 Agnes Wilson to John Collins

p. 124-126 Feb. 13, 1810 James Wilson (Spartanburgh) to Peter Carr McMakin (same); for $100 sold 68 ac on ridge between Middle and N Tyger Rivers; includes Wilson's Racepath; plat attached shows border: grant to Thomas Wadsworth. Witness Francis Pace, Jeremiah S Faris, and William Wilson. Signed James Wilson's mark. Wit. oath Dec. 8, 1815 William Wilson to John Collins. Rec. Oct. 5, 1818. Dower renounced Sept. 12, 1818 Agnes Wilson to John Collins

p. 126-127 Jul. 8, 1800(sic or 42nd year of independence-1817) Jesse Reams (Spartanburgh) to Jno Robbs (same); for (money omitted) sold 272 ac. Witness James Reames and Robert Kimbrell. Signed Jesse Reams. Wit. oath Nov. 10, 1818 Robert Kimbrell to John Montgomery. Rec. Nov. 10, 1818

p. 127-1st 128 Feb. 21, 1812 James Wofford (Spartanburgh) to John Wood (same); for $100 sold 100 ac on branch of Maple Swamp Cr of Tyger R. Witness Page Rork and Daniel Wood. Signed James Wofford. Wit. oath Feb. 26, 1813 Daniel Wood to James Hammett. Rec. Oct. 5, 1818

p. 1st 128-1st 129 Nov. 19, 1817 Reuben Traylor (Spartanburgh) to William Grisham (same); for $300 sold 100 ac on Reedy fork of S Tyger R; border: William Grisham, Francis Powers, Jesse Wakefield's Spring Br, and Sol Steward. Witness William McM. Brice and John M Delany. Signed Reuben Traylor's mark. Wit. oath Sept. 26, 1818 John M Delany to John Collins. Rec. Oct. 5, 1818

p. 1st 129-2nd 128 Apr. 22, 1817 Thomas Hunter jr (Pendleton Dist) to Lawson Thomson (Spartanburgh); for $300 sold 230 ac on branches of N Tyger R; grant Sept. 30, 1774 to Charles Cotesworth Pinckney esq. Witness Dr Andrew B Moore and Adonijah Patterson. Signed Thomas Hunter jr. Wit. oath Nov. 10, 1817 Andrew B Moore to John Collins. Rec. Jan. 20, 1818(sic).

p. 2nd 128-2nd 129 Aug. 10, 1818 John Morris (Spartanburgh) and Joseph Morris (Edgefield Dist) to Jordan Morris (Edgefield Dist); for $200 sold 250 ac on waters of Buck Cr of Pacolate R; border: S-Thomas Cantwell, W-David Parris, N-John Steedman, and E-Charles Cantwell; part of John Morris' land and part of Joseph Morris' land. Witness Joseph Morris jr and John Jordan. Signed John Morris and Joseph Morris' mark. Wit. oath Aug. 27, 1818 (Abbeville Dist) Joseph Morris jr to Chs C Mayson. Rec. Oct. 9, 1818

p. 2nd 129-130 Jul. 3, 1818 James Crook sr (Spartanburgh) to James McDaniel (Greenville Dist); for $72 sold 70 ac on N side of S Tyger R; part of grant to Thomas Lehre. Witness William Crook and Nathaniel Woodruff. Signed James Crook. Wit. oath Oct. 12, 1818 Nathaniel Woodruff to Wm Hendrix. Rec. Oct. 13, 1818

p. 130-131 Dec. 10, 1816 James Miller (Spartanburgh) to Samuel Pearson (same); for $470.75 sold 307 ac on N side of S Tyger R and on Mill Br and Grissom's Spring Br; border: Cowen. Witness James Swanzy and John Patterson. Signed James Miller. Wit. oath Oct. 12, 1818 John Patterson to Thos Wood. Rec. Oct. 14, 1818

p. 131-132 Aug. 4, 1817 Joseph Gibson Oliver (Spartanburgh) to William Morris (same); for $150 sold 158 ac on N side of Pacolate R; border: Edmund Cooley. Witness John Morris and Jilson Oliver. Signed Joseph Gibson Oliver. Wit. oath Oct. 25, 1817 John Morris to Henry Turner. Rec. Oct. 14, 1818

p. 132-134 Oct. 24, 1817 William Odam (Spartanburgh) to George Bone (Lexington Dist); for $205 sold 150 ac on waters of Island Cr; border: an old road, George Cantrell, Evett, and race path. Witness Frederic Davis and Asa Bone. Signed William Odam. Wit. oath Oct. 24, 1817 Frederic Davis to Henry Turner. Rec. Oct. 31, 1818. Dower renounced Oct. 24, 1817 Tilby (or Tillethe) Odam to Henry Turner

p. 134-136 Jun. 10, 1818 Jesse Cleveland (Spartanburgh) and Enoch B Benson (Pendleton Dist) to Samuel Turner (Spartanburgh); for $400 sold 1 ac in Spartanburgh, SC; 3(sic or 2) lots--#8 and 9 of ½ ac each; border: E-lot formerly Gabriel Benson's and now Daniel Faust's, N & W-Richard Thomson, and S-Main St; includes a house. Witness Warren R Davis and John T Earle. Signed Jesse Cleveland and E. B. Benson. Wit. oath Dec. (blank), 1818 John T Earle to (not signed). Rec. Oct. 27, 1818. Dower renounced Jun. 29, 1818 (Pendleton Dist) Ester Benson, wife of Enoch B, to John T Lewis. Dower renounced Aug. 10, 1818 Mary Cleveland, wife of Jesse, to Daniel White

p. 136-137 Jul. 20, 1798 William King (Spartanburgh) to John King (same); for $100 sold 100 ac on branches of Jemmies Cr; border: Marthews; grant Feb. 6, 1786 to John King desc. Witness Zacchariah Grace and Charles Bragg. Signed William King's mark. Wit. oath Oct. 29, 1818 Charles Bragg to John Brewton. Rec. Nov. 8, 1818

p. 137-139 Nov. 2, 1818 William Rollins (Spartanburgh) to William Bennett (same); for $441 and 3/4¢(sic) which is amount William Rollins gave William Bennett in a note and to secure payment sold a Negro boy Paton between 5 and 6 years old black complexion and healthy and sound; Condition William Bennett is to give William Rollins the money if more than $404 and 3/4¢ is obtained if Paton is sold by Mar. 1, 1819 after giving 20 days notice at Spartanburgh Court House. Witness W Walker and Edmund Cooley. Signed (not signed). Wit. oath Nov. 2, 1818 Edmund Cooley to James Young. Rec. Nov. 2, 1818

p. 139-140 Apr. 8, 1818 John McElrath (Spartanburgh) to Philip Bettis (same); for $200 sold 100 ac on S side of Middle Tyger R. Witness Page Rork and John Sexton. Signed John McElrath. Wit. oath Oct. 3, 1818 John Sexton to John Collins. Rec. Nov. 2, 1818. Dower renounced Sept. 25, 1818 Rachel McElrath to John Collins

p. 140-141 Mar. 1, 1813 John King (Spartanburgh) to David King (same); for $200 sold 72 ac; border: Charles Skinner, William Pearson, David King, George Robuck, and Richard Gentrey. Witness Benjamin Robuck and Richard Gentry. Signed John King's mark. Wit. oath Dec. 4, 1813 Benjamin Robuck to John Dean. Rec. Nov. 2, 1818

p. 141-142 Nov. 22, 1810 David Lewis (Spartanburgh) to Ralph Danger (same); for $17 sold 131 ac on waters of Meadow's Cr. Witness George L Publes, William Copand, and William Ford. Signed David Lewis. Wit. oath Aug. 31, 1811 George L Publes to Andrew Ferguson. Rec. Nov. 2, 1818

p. 142-143 Nov. 22, 1810 Robert McDowell (Spartanburgh) to Ralph Danger (same); for $17 sold 250 ac on waters of Lawson's fork; border: William Foster and William Lewis; part of two grants from the King to (1) Frances Ross and (2) from South Carolina to Robert McDowell. Witness Lewis Shelton, Benjamin Rowland, and George L Publes. Signed Robert McDowell. Wit. oath Aug. 12, 1812 George L Publes to Andrew Ferguson. Rec. Nov. 2, 1818

p. 143-144 Nov. 22, 1810 John Lacky (Spartanburgh) to Ralph Danger (same); for $17 sold 82½ ac on waters of Lawson's fork; border: McDowell. Witness George Publes, Benjamin Rowland, and Lewis Shelton. Signed John Lacky's mark. Wit. oath Aug. 31, 1811 George L Publes to Andw Ferguson. Rec. Nov. 2, 1818

p. 144-146 Oct. 15, 1818 Bassel Compton (Spartanburgh) to James Moore (same); for $750 sold 150 ac on waters of Dutchman's Cr; border: Moore; part of 300 ac grant to Thomas Thornton. Witness Samuel Dorcas and James Hamm. Signed Basil Compton. Wit. oath Oct. 15, 1818 Samuel Dorcas to James Hamm. Rec. Nov. 7, 1818. Dower renounced Nov. 6, 1818 Sarah Compton to Samuel Archibald

p. 146-147 Feb. 11, 1818 Allen Sarratt (or Surratt) (Spartanburgh) to Joseph Richards; for $100 sold 200 ac on Turner's Cr of Thickety Cr; border: Crocker, Markley, Price, and Byars. Witness Thomas Whitaker and Edmund Chambers. Signed Allen Sarrett. Wit. oath Jul. 14, 1818 Edmund Chambers to A Benson. Rec. Nov. 7, 1818. Dower renounced Mar. 5, 1818 Elizabeth Sarratt to A Benson

p. 147-148 Apr. 4, 1818 James Hammett (Spartanburgh) to Eli Baldwin (Greenville Dist); for $693 sold 250 ac; border: Josiah McElwain, Abner's Cr, Hammett's Still House Br, Herring, James Brockman, and Hambey; 100½ ac was sold by McFadin to James Hammett, 100 ac was sold by Herring to James Hammett and remainder (49½ ac) was sold by Cannon to James Hammett. Witness Robert Wood and Mathew Vance. Signed James Hammett. Wit. oath Nov. 7, 1818 Robert Wood to Thomas Wood. Rec. Nov. 7, 1818

p. 148-150 Oct. 18, 1812 Solomon Littlefield (Spartanburgh) to Samuel Tucker (same); for $250 sold (1) 50 ac formerly part of James Beard's land and (2) 33 ac vacant land that Solomon "took up" adjoining (1); on Jemmies Cr of Tyger R; border: Samuel Jones. Witness Benjamin Wofford and Reuben Newman. Signed Solomon Littlefield's mark. Wit. oath Oct. 10, 1814 Benjamin Wofford to M Casey. Rec. Nov. 10, 1818. Dower renounced Oct. 23, 1812 Mary Littlefield to Samuel Morrow

p. 150-151 Jun. 9, 1803 John Gowen (Spartanburgh) to Robert Black (York Dist); for $402 sold 268 ac on S side of S Pacolet R; border: James Alexander; part of grant Gov. Thomas Pinckney to John Gowen. Witness Andrew Ferguson and Richard Venables. Signed Jno Gowen. Wit. oath Aug. 15, 1818 Andrew Ferguson to John Vernon(?). Rec. Nov. 11, 1818

p. 151-153 Feb. 15, 1816 William Brashears (Spartanburgh) to Etson Wilson (same); for $100 sold 150 ac on Fields Cr; border: T Reames, road to Miller's Mills, and Wadsworth. Witness Neddy Reams and David Moore. Signed William Brashears' mark. Wit. oath Oct. 29, 1818 Neddy Reams to Thomas Wood. Rec. Nov. 11, 1818

p. 153-154 Oct. 12, 1818 Abraham McMinn (Rutherford Co, NC) to Joseph Richards (Spartanburgh); for $80 sold 150 ac on Turner's fork of Thickety Cr of Broad R; border: Guttrey, Paice, and Mrs. Woods. Witness William Collins and Joseph Byars. Signed Abraham McMinn. Wit. oath Nov. 20, 1818 William Collins to A Benson. Rec. Nov. 12, 1818

p. 154-156 Mar. 2, 1797 Isham Pullum (Spartanburgh) to Joseph Carver jr (same); for 50£ sterling sold 441 ac on waters of Meadow Cr and Green Cr of Lawson's Cr; grant Aug. 3, 1795 to Isham Pullum. Witness Richard Carver and Joseph Carver. Signed Isham Pullum. Wit. oath Oct. 28, 1813 Richard Carver to Andrew Furguson. Rec. Nov. 12, 1818

p. 156-158 Nov. 13, 1818 William Young (Greenville Dist) to Moses Foster (Spartanburgh); for $1,075.50 sold (ac omitted) on N side of Jack's Br and Bodley's Br of S Pacolett R; border: Kilpatrick, Jonathan Wall, John Young, and William Foster. Witness Juliet G Young and Robert McDowell. Signed Wm Young. Wit. oath Nov. 13, 1818 Robert McDowell to James Young. Rec. Nov. 16, 1818

p. 158 Nov. 27, 1809 Jordan Cardin to Hugh Means JP; an oath that he saw Adaman Johnson sell Francis Watson land Adaman bought from Joseph James and also delivered Adaman's bond and also saw Francis pay Adaman; Watson's house was burned with bond in it. Witness Hugh Means JP. Signed Jordan Cardin. Rec. Nov. 18, 1818 Nov. 27, 1809 William Watson to Hugh Means JP; an oath that he saw Adaman Johnson deliver to Francis Watson Adaman's bond and he believes the bond was burned in "the house". Witness Hugh Means JP. Signed William Watson's mark

p. 158-160 Nov. 17, 1818 Francis Watson (Spartanburgh) to James Brannon (same); for $200 sold 270 ac on Shoaly Cr of Lawson's fork; grant to Thomas James; 2 ac excepted sold by Francis Watson to Jacob Belcher. Witness Patsey Williams and Darby Turner. Signed Francis Watson. Wit. oath Nov. 18, 1818 Darby Turner to Thomas Poole. Rec. Nov. 18, 1818

p. 160-161 Jan. 29, 1818 John Mathis (Spartanburgh) to Nimrod Cantrell (same); for $50 sold 187 ac on waters of Burton's (?) Cr of Pacolett R. Witness John Nelson and James Burnett. Signed John Mathis' mark. Wit. oath Oct. 31, 1818 John Nelson to Henry Turner. Rec. Dec. 7, 1818

p. 161-162 Apr. 9, 1817 Jesse Cleveland and Enoch B Benson (Spartanburgh) to John Vandike (same); for $200 sold 80 ac on Lawson's Fork of Pacolett R. Witness Richard Thompson, Alfred Cleveland, H Cleveland, and Js Cleveland. Signed Jesse Cleveland and E. N. Benson. Wit. oath Dec. 9, 1818 Alfred Cleveland to Thomas Poole. Rec. Dec. 9, 1818

p. 162-163 Jun. 18, 1818 Mary Cantrell (Spartanburgh) to grandchildren who are Nimrod Cantrell's heirs (same); for love and affection give all goods, household, stock, and plantation affairs now in Nimrod Cantrell's possession and are where Nimrod lives. Witness William Morris and George Horton. Signed Mary Cantrell's mark. Wit. oath Oct. 31, 1818 William Morris to Henry Turner. Rec. Dec. 9, 1818

p. 163-165 Nov. 27, 1818 James Hunt, sheriff (Spartanburgh) to Jane Bobo; for $95 sold 118 ac on N side of Enoree R and on E branch of Cedar Shoal Cr; sale due to writ from Spartanburgh Common Pleas Court suit Samuel Farrow vs Thomas M Bragg, administrator of Spencer Bobo desc; sale Aug. 3, 1818. Witness William Trimmier and Levi Lee. Signed Jas Hunt SSD. Wit. oath Nov. 27, 1818 William Trimmier to Thomas Poole. Rec. Dec. 12, 1818

p. 165-166 Feb. 7, 1816 James P Means (Spartanburgh) to Josiah Thornton (same); for $433 sold 325 ac on Story's Cr; plat attached shows border: James Martin, James Means, widow Mays, and Josiah Thornton. Witness James Hamm jr and James Moore. Signed J. P. Means. Wit. oath Apr. 3, 1817 James Moore to James Hamm. Rec. Dec. 9, 1818. Dower renounced Nov. (blank), 1818 Jane (or

Jenny) Means to Samuel Archibald

p. 166-167 Jul. 11, 1818 Moses Casey, son of William (Spartanburgh) to Jesse Cooper (Union Dist); for $128.43 sold 59 ac on Cedar Shoal Cr of Enoree R; border: NE-Wm Harris, SE-Uriah Casey, SW-Burrell Bobo, and W-Jesse Cooper; plat attached. Witness David Norman and William Martindale. Signed Moses Casey. Wit. oath (Union Dist) Dec. 11, 1818 David Norman to Caleb Green. Rec. Dec. 23, 1818. Dower renounced Sept. 30, 1818 Rebecca Casey to Burrell Bobo

p. 167-169 Sept. 11, 1818 James Miller (Spartanburgh) to William Anderson (same); for $583.33 and 3 mills sold 250 ac on N side of S Tyger R and on Mile Br. Witness William N Miller, James Selman, and Samuel Jameson. Signed James Millers. Wit. oath Dec. 23, 1818 Samuel Jameson to John Collins. Rec. Jan. 4, 1819. Dower renounced Dec. 23, 1818 Adinia Miller to John Collins

p. 169-171 Sept. 11, 1818 James Miller (Spartanburgh) to William Anderson (same); for $116.66 and 7 mills sold 50 ac on N side of S Tiger R and on Mile Br; border: David Anderson and James Chamblin. Witness William N Miller, James Selman, and Samuel Jameson. Signed James Miller. Wit. oath (not dated) Samuel Jameson to John Collins. Rec. Jan. 4, 1819

p. 171-172 Nov. 17, 1818 John Bazwell (Spartanburgh) to William Waddle; for $350 sold 159 ac on waters of Win's Cr; border: Bazwell's Spring and Hadden; includes 13 ac of Daniel McKie's land sold to John Bazwell that borders William Hoy and William Brice. Witness John Durham and Philip Johnson. Signed John Bazwell. Wit. oath Jan. 4, 1819 Philip Johnson to James Crook. Rec. Jan. 4, 1819

p. 172-173 Oct. 3, 1818 James Miller (Spartanburgh) to John S Coan (same); for $150 sold 30 ac on N side of S Tiger R; border: Thomas Grisham's Spring Br and Mile Br. Witness William N Miller, Richard Barry, and John Patton. Signed James Miller. Wit. oath Dec. 23, 1818 William N Miller to John Collins. Rec. Jan. 4, 1819

p. 173-175 Jan. 1, 1819 Nathaniel Wofford (Spartanburgh) to John Crocker (same); for $10 sold 199 ac on branches of Forgerson's Cr of Tyger R; border: Burrow. Witness Caleb Allen and James Rhodes. Signed Nathaniel Wofford. Wit. oath Jan. 1, 1819 Caleb Allen to Samuel Woodruff. Rec. Jan. 4, 1819

p. 175-176 Jan. 24, 1818 Elias Corder (Spartanburgh) to James Mason (same); for $75 sold 25 ac; border: Corder's Spring Br and Floyd's Br. Witness James Scott and William Otts. Signed Elias Corder. Wit. oath Sept. 25, 1818 William Otts to John Brewton. Rec. Jan. 4, 1819

p. 176-177 Aug. 6, 1819(sic) Daniel McKie (Spartanburgh) to James Anderson (same); for $1,000 sold 600 ac on S of Tyger R and both sides Ben's Cr; part of three grants: (1) to William Moore, (2) to John McDowell, and (3) to Aron More. Witness Jesse Wofford and John Miller. Signed Daniel McKie. Wit. oath Jan. 4, 1819 John Miller to John Montgomery. Rec. Jan. 4, 1819

p. 177-179 Jul. 23, 1818 James Crook sr (Spartanburgh) to William Crook (same); for $1,000 sold 401 ac on waters of Tyger R and on Drummond's Spring Br. Witness John H Owens and John H Strange. Signed James Crook sr. Wit. oath Jan. 4, 1819 John H Strange to James Crook. Rec. Jan. 4, 1819

p. 179-180 Nov. 20, (omitted) Reuben Traylor (Spartanburgh) to Jeremiah Burnett; for $250 sold 134 ac on Provis'(?) Cr and Camp Br; border: Brice. Witness George Johnson and Archibald McCravy. Signed Reuben Traylor's mark. Wit. oath Jan. 1, 1819 George Johnson to James Crook. Rec. Jan. 4, 1819

p. 180-181 Apr. 4, 1814 Joab Heflen and Fanny Heflen (Spartanburgh) to Joshua Layton; for $200 sold 134 ac on S side of Thickety Cr. Witness Mathew Gutrie and Benjamin Fowler. Signed Joab Heflen. Wit. oath Sept. 22, 1814 Mathew Gutrie to Henry Turner. Rec. Jan. 4, 1819

p. 181-182 Jun. 26, 1817 John Allen (Spartanburgh) to Jonathan Crook (same); for $15 sold 5 ac on N side of Enoree R; border: a road and Mr Allen. Witness Jeremiah Crook and Thomas Knighton. Signed John Anderson. Wit. oath Feb. 18, 1818 Jeremiah Crook to James Crook. Rec. Jan. 4, 1819

p. 182-184 Nov. 23, 1815 James Wheeler (Jackson Co, Ga) to John Waters (Spartanburgh); for $200 sold 194 ac on W side of Rockyfield Cr of Enoree R. Witness Daniel Wood and Henry Wood. Signed James Wheeler's mark. Wit. oath Nov. 8, 1816 Daniel Wood to James Hammett. Rec. Jan. 4, 1819

p. 184-186 Oct. 3, 1818 James McDaniel (Greenville Dist) to Samuel Miller (Spartanburgh); for $520 sold 135 ac on N side of S Tyger R; border: Underwood and Samuel Miller; belongs to estate of Drury McDaniel esq desc. Witness James Daniel and Samuel Miller. Signed James McDaniel. Wit. oath Jan. 4, 1819 Samuel Miller to F. H. Legg. Rec. Jan. 4, 1819. Dower renounced Jan. 1, 1818(sic) Hanah McDaniel to John Bruton

p. 186-187 Oct. 24, 1818 Presley Smith, Wm B Alexander, and John Chesney, heirs of Richard Chesney desc, (Spartanburgh) to Thomas Chesney (same); for $250 sold 208½ ac; border: SW-Asahel Beason, W-Nathaniel Chesney, N-John White, and E-William Young. Witness William Posey and Peter Bragg. Signed Presley Smith, Wm B Alexander, and John Chesney. Wit. oath Jan. 4, 1819 William Posey to Samuel Archibald. Rec. Jan. 4. 1819. Dower renounced Nov. 28, 1818 Hester Chesney, wife of Richard, to John Bruton

p. 187-189 Dec. 12, 1818 Thomas Underwood (Spartanburgh) to Enoch J Underwood (same); for $450 sold 120 ac on N side of S Tyger R; border: Thornton McDaniel, Enoch J Underwood, and Robert Ligon. Witness Thomas U Wells and Green Underwood. Signed Thomas Underwood. Wit. oath Dec. 24, 1818 Green Underwood to James Crook. Rec. Jan. 4, 1819. Dower renounced Dec. 28, 1818 Elizabeth Underwood to John Brewton

p. 189-190 Jul. 23, 1818 James Crook jr (Spartanburgh) to James Crook sr (same); for $100 sold 50 ac on waters of Tyger R and on Drummond's Spring Br; border: Lehre. Witness John H Owens and John H Strange. Signed James Crook jr. Wit. oath Aug. 8, 1818 John H Owens to Wm Hendrix. Rec. Jan. 4, 1819

p. 190-192 Aug. 7, 1818 Daniel McKie and James Allen hold jointly on N bank of Enoree R (ac omitted); Daniel has older grant: formerly granted to Zacheriah Gibbs; Daniel and James can't agree how to divide the land; so decision is left to Samuel Woodruff esq and Nathaniel Woodruff. Witness Samuel Woodruff sr and John Dean. Signed Daniel McKie and James Allen. Wit. oath Nov. 26, 1818 John Dean to John Brewton. Rec. Jan. 4, 1819
Aug. 7, 1818 Samuel Woodruff esq and Nathaniel Woodruff have "run a line" between Daniel McKie and James Allen. Signed Samuel Woodruff sr and Nathaniel Woodruff

p. 192-193 Jul. 16, 1817 Thomas Bomar (Spartanburgh) to John L Rast (same); for $650 sold (ac omitted) on N TygerR; border: Rush's Mill. Witness John Gramling and Little Berry. Signed Tho Bomar. Wit. oath Jul. 20, 1818 Little Berry to John Collins. Rec. Jan. 9, 1819. Dower renounced Jul. 6, 1818 Elizabeth Bomar to John Collins

p. 193-195 Feb. 24, 1815 Thomas Miller (Spartanburgh) to Samuel Miller (same); for $200 sold 95 ac between Middle and S Tyger R; border: Samuel Miller and N-Esq. McDaniel; part of grant to James Miller desc. Wit. oath Thomas Dean, Samuel Miller, and Casandra Miller. Signed Thomas Miller. Wit. oath Apr. 8, 1817 Thomas Dean to F. H. Legg. Rec. Jan. 9, 1819

p. 195-196 Sept. 25, 1817 John Crawford (Spartanburgh) to John L Rast; for $1,000 sold 139 ac on N Tyger R. Witness John Grambling and James Moore. Signed John Crawford. Wit. oath Aug. 27, 1818 John Grambling to John Collins. Rec. Jan. 9, 1819. Dower renounced Aug. 27, 1818 Mary Crawford to John Collins

p. 196-197 Oct. 13, 1812 Charles McAbee (Spartanburgh) to Elizabeth Mathias (same); for $75 sold 358 ac on Harrison's Br of Pacolett R; border: Lindsey and Jesse Matthews. Witness John H Low and Wm McAbee. Signed Charles McAbee. Wit. oath Oct. 13, 1812 Wm McAbee to Jno H Jones. Rec. Jan. 12, 1819

p. 197-198 Nov. 6, 1817 Richard Barnett (Spartanburgh) to Hancock Smith; for $500 sold a Negro girl Betty about 14 years old. Witness Catharine Smith. Signed Richard Barnett. Wit. oath Jan. 12, 1819 Catharine Smith to Daniel White. Rec. Jan. 12, 1819

p. 198-199 Oct. 8, 1815 Jane Smith (Spartanburgh) to Hancock Smith; for $500 sold a Negro boy Phill about 13 years old. Witness Isaac Smith. Signed Jane Smith. Wit. oath Jan. 12, 1819 Isaac Smith to Daniel White. Rec. Jan. 12, 1819

p. 199-200 Jan. 4, 1819 Sarah King, widow of John King desc, "for obligation given by Jemima King to Levingston Bobo" of $50 to be paid yearly for support of Sarah King sold (ac omitted); where Jemima King lives; left to Sarah King for her support by will of John King; Sarah gets to occupy house until Sept. 1, 1819. Witness Jonas Brewton and Mary McCarley. Signed Sarah King's mark. Wit. oath Jan. 4, 1819 Jonas Brewton to John Brewton. Rec. Jan. 12, 1819

p. 200-202 May 22, 1816 Garland Caldwell and wife Elizabeth (Spartanburgh) to Muse Tollison (same); for $175 sold 300 ac on Hurricane Br of Pacolett R; border: Old Iron Works Road. Witness Daniel Wilbanks and J. D. Palmer. Signed Garland Caldwell's mark. Wit. oath Jan. 19, 1819 J. D. Palmer to Thomas Poole. Rec. Jan. 19, 1819. Dower renounced Oct. 14, 1818 Elizabeth Caldwell to Daniel White

p. 202-204 Sept. 2, 1818 James Hunt, sheriff (Spartanburgh) to Muse Tolleson; for $101 sold 100 ac; border: Maj. John Tolleson, James McCarter, and George Hennett (or Kennett); where Major Gossett lives; sale due to writ from Spartanburgh Common Pleas Court suit Muse Tolleson vs Major Gossett; sale first Monday in June 1818. Witness Simpson Foster and Elisha Bomar. Signed Jas Hunt SSD. Wit. oath Sept. 3, 1818 Simpson Foster to A Benson. Rec. Jan. 12, 1819

p. 204-205 Jan. 7, 1797 Joel Lewis (Spartanburgh) to John Lewis (same); for 50£ sterling sold 300 ac on N side of Green's Cr; where Charles Martin lives. Witness David Lewis and Margarett

Lewis. Signed Joel Lewis. Wit. oath May 29, 1812 David Lewis to James Young. Rec. Jan. 18, 1819

p. 205-207 Sept. 25, 1818 Alexander Austin jr (Spartanburgh) to David Golightly (same); for $400 sold 245 ac on Lawson's fork of Pacolett R. Witness John S Rowland, Joel Lewis, and Mary Lewis. Signed Alexander Austin. Wit. oath Jan. 18, 1819 Joel Lewis to Thomas Poole. Rec. Jan. 18, 1819. Dower renounced Nov. 17, 1818 Isabella Austin to James Young

p. 207-208 May 5, 1813 Adam Kelly (Spartanburgh) to Alexander Austin (same); for $100 sold 200 ac; border: Wm Bishop, Abr (or Mr.) Markley, and Alexander Austin's old line. Witness Zacheriah Wall and Edmond Clement. Signed Adam Kelly's mark. Wit. oath May 16, 1812 Zacheriah Wall to William Kelso. Rec. Jan. 18, 1819

p. 208-209 Jan. 7, 1797 Joel Lewis (Spartanburgh) to John Lewis (same); for 38£ sterling sold 100 ac on branches of Green's Cr of Lawson's fork; "taking in" John Williams' improvements. Witness David Lewis and Margaret Lewis. Signed Joel Lewis. Wit. oath May 29, 1812 David Lewis to James Young. Rec. Jan. 18, 1819

p. 209-210 Jul. 4, 1818 Elenor Bagwell to Littleton Bagwell and George Bulman; "for great services and other good causes" and $200 sold half of land where Elenor Bagwell lives (550 ac); border: E-Smith and Lindsey, N-Wm Travy, and W-Travy and McBee; land given "during his life" and to "his" wife Rebecak as a life estate and then to Rebecak's children. Witness Dicy Sherbutt and James Smith. Signed Elenor Bagwell's mark. Wit. oath Jul. 7, 1818 James Smith to Caleb Jones. Rec. Jan. 13, 1819

p. 210-213 Dec. 5, 1818 Muse Tolleson (Spartanburgh) to John D Palmer (same); for $2,550 sold 478 ac on Middle Tyger R; border: Thomas Moore. Witness Wm Trimmier and Elisha West. Signed Muse Tolleson. Wit. oath Jan. 1, 1819 Elisha West to A Benson. Rec. Jan. 19, 1819. Dower renounced Jan. 1, 1819 Sarah Tolleson to Abner Benson

p. 213-215 Sept. 2, 1818 James Hunt, sheriff (Spartanburgh) to James Younger; for $345 sold 300 ac; border: Obed's Cr, Pacolett R, and waggon road from Cunningham's Mill to Galt's old store; part of grant was sold by Reuben Bomar or Gabriel Benson to Henry and Wm Monro; sold due to writ from Spartanburgh Common Pleas Court suit James Younger vs Lewis Brown; sale Apr. 7, 1818. Witness Thomas Hannon and Elisha Bomar. Signed Jas Hunt SSD. Wit. oath Jan. 20, 1819 Thomas Hannon to A Benson. Rec. Jan. 20, 1819

p. 215-216 Sept. 29, 1818 David Lynch (Spartanburgh) to Robert White (Union Dist); for $1,200 sold 331 ac on Kelso's Cr of Fairforest Cr; where David Lynch lives; border: Catherine Smith, Daniel White, Charles James, Cooper's Br, David M (blank)'s old line; part of two grants: (1) to James Smith and (2) to Joseph Buffington and mortgaged to "the loan office" and by order of Legislature sold to James Smith and descended to David Lynch by heirship. Witness Willis Foster and Payton Simmons. Signed David Lynch. Wit. oath Sept. 29, 1818 Payton Simmons to Danl White. Rec. Feb. 1, 1819. Dower renounced Oct. 19, 1818 Lettice Lynch to Daniel White

p. 216-217 Jan. 23, 1807 William Murry (Spartanburgh) to Benjamin Cash (same); for $150 sold 197 ac. Witness James Land and Osburn Reece. Signed William Murry's mark. Wit. oath Jan. 23, 1807 James Land to Henry Turner. Rec. Feb. 1, 1819

p. 217-218 Jun. 3, 1812 Elias Stone (Spartanburgh) to James Bishop (same); for $100 sold (ac omitted) on waters of Fair-forrest Cr; border: Wm Hammett, John Walker, and Drayton. Witness Barney Bishop and Robert Benson. Signed Elias Stone. Wit. oath Aub. 3, 1818 Barney Bishop to E Walker. Rec. Feb. 1, 1819

p. 218-219 Mar. 15, 1810 Matthias Rush (Spartanburgh) to James Bishop (same); for $50 sold 150 ac on Reedy Br of Fair-forrest Cr. Witness Peter Hawkins and John Bishop. Signed Mathias Rush. Wit. oath Aug. 3, 1818 John Bishop to E Walker. Rec. Feb. 1, 1819

p. 219-221 Dec. 29, 1818 Thomas Thornton (Spartanburgh) to Henry G Baughan (same); for $290 sold 120 ac on branches of Enoree R; border: David Moore and Wm Rhodes. Witness Zadock F Westmoreland and Starling L Westmoreland. Signed Thomas Thornton. Wit. oath Jan. 2, 1819 Zadock F Westmoreland to John Brewton. Rec. Feb. 1, 1819

p. 221-222 Feb. 20, 1818 George Acridge (Spartanburgh) to Lawson Thomson (same); for $150 sold 34 ac on both sides of branch of Ward's Cr of N Tyger R; part of 283 ac grant to Hopkins Bright. Witness James Compton, James Calvert, and James W Reynolds. Signed George Acridge's mark. Wit. oath Jul. 25, 1818 James Calvert to Robert Ligon. Rec. Feb. 1, 1819

p. 222 Aug. 3, 1818 Philip Johnson (Spartanburgh) to George Johnson (same); for $280 sold 100 ac; border: Durham's old line and waters of Bert's Cr of S Tyger R; sold by James Jordan esq to Philip Johnson. Witness Wm McBrice and Westwood Ford. Signed Philip Johnson's mark. Wit. oath Jan. 1, 1819 Westwood Ford to James Crook. Rec. Feb. 1, 1819

p. 222-224 Oct. 18, 1810 Spencer Bobo (Spartanburgh) to Philip Brewton (same); for $430 sold 98 ac on Furgerson's Cr; border: Williamson, Philip Brewton's Spring, and George Brewton; 75 ac is on N corner of grant to Robert Russel and 23 ac was granted to David Brewton. Witness George Brewton, Caty Brewton, and Casander Brewton. Signed S Bobo. Wit. oath Feb. 1, 1819 Caty Brewton to John Brewton. Rec. Feb. 1, 1819. Dower renounced Jul. 4, 1815 Jane Bobo to Drury McDaniel

p. 224-225 Feb. 1, 1819 John Tollison (Spartanburgh) to Benjamin Cash (same); for $400 "paid by John Tolleson" (sic) sold (1) 100 ac on Big Br of Island Cr; border: Markley's old line and Smith Murry; and (2) 104 ac; border: Abraham Markley, Big Br, and Murry; grant "from" James Smith sr. Witness William Brock and James Tolleson. Signed John Tolleson. Wit. oath Feb. 1, 1819 James Tolleson to Wm Reid. Rec. Feb. 1, 1819

p. 225-1st 226 Jun. 8, 1818 Josiah Woodruff, blacksmith (Spartanburgh) to Susannah Adkinson (same); for $300 sold 100 ac on waters of Jimmie's Cr; part of grant to George Brewton. Witness Lee Hendrix and Eli Cooper. Signed Josiah Woodruff. Wit. oath Jun. 8, 1818 Lee Hendrix to Wm Hendrix. Rec. Feb. 1, 1819. Dower renounced Jan. 4, 1819 Marget Woodruff to John Brewton

p. 1st 226-2nd 226 Aug. 6, 1818 George Arnold (Spartanburgh) to Isaac Wofford (same); for $123 sold 2 beds and furniture, a corner cupboard, all "my" crop of corn and cotton now growing, a bridle and saddle, a sorrel mare, a loom, 2 ovens, a pot, a skillet, 10 geese, a pair of chain traces harness and plow; Condition: sale void if George pays Muse Tolleson $23 and pays to Spartanburgh sheriff a debt ($65) and cost due to case of William Wofford vs George Arnold and Isaac Wofford. Witness John Powers.

Signed George Arnold. Wit. oath Jan. 4, 1819 John Powers to James Crook. Rec. Mar. 2, 1819

p. 2nd 226-228 Jul. 7, 1818 James Hunt, sheriff (Spartanburgh) to Richard Thomson; for $305 sold 348 ac on waters of Lawson's fork Cr; border: Richard Thomson, Richard James, grant to William Locock, and Anthony Foster; part of 500 ac grant Jul. 21, 1775 to William H Drayton; balance of grant after 160 ac deducted due to older grant to William Locock and 3 ac included in grant to Richard Thomson; sale due to writ from Charleston Common Pleas Court suit James Gregorie and Hugh Smith to John Drayton; sale Jul. 7, 1818. Witness William Trimmier and Wm N Miller. Signed Jas Hunt SSD. Wit. oath Mar. 1, 1819 Wm N Miller to E Bomar. Rec. Mar. 2, 1819

p. 228-229 Jan. 31, 1818 Jonathan Nesbitt (Spartanburgh) to Wm Elmore (same); for $357 sold 102 ac on N side of S Tyger R; border: Burris' Bridge. Witness Page Rork and James Robertson. Signed Jonathan Nesbitt. Wit. oath Mar. 12, 1819(sic) Page Rork to Wm Hendrix. Rec. Mar. 2, 1819

p. 229-231 Sept. 7, 1818 Peter C McMekin (Spartanburgh) to Jesse Cleveland (same); for $350 sold ½ ac at the Court House on S side of Publick ground; border: "Cross St" and William Thompson jr. Witness Alexander Thompson and Joseph Collins. Signed Peter C McMakin. Wit. oath Feb. 1, 1819 Alexander Thompson to John Collins. Rec. Mar. 2, 1819

p. 231-232 Feb. 3, 1819 John Low sr (Spartanburgh) to James Waters (same); for $150 sold 200 ac between Packolet R and Thickety Cr and on both sides of waggon road; where John Low sr lives; border: Chas Smith, Wyatt, ridge path, and Isaac Linder; "deeded" May 7, 1817 to Robert Thompson sr. Witness Charles Smith and Samuel Turner. Signed John Low sr. Wit. oath Feb. 20, 1819 Charles Smith to Caleb Jones. Rec. Mar. 2, 1819

p. 232-234 Jan. 20, 1819 (Pendleton Dist) William Henderson (Pendleton Dist) to James Whitten (Spartanburgh); for $300 sold 300 ac on N side of Motlow's Cr (called Cub Cr in original grant); border: Samuel Fowler; grant Dec. 23, 1768 to Richard Henderson who sold to Robert Henderson and by his will bequeathed to John, James, Robert, and William Henderson; now Robert Henderson and heirs of John and James Henderson by powers of attorney authorize William Henderson to sell their share of the land. Witness Jacob Gowen and Allen Patrick. Signed Wm Henderson. Wit. oath Jan. 20, 1819 (Pendleton Dist) Jacob Gowen to George Edmondson. Rec. Mar. 2, 1819

p. 234-235 Jan. 8, 1819 Burrel Bobo (Spartanburgh) to Jesse Cooper; for $150 sold 88 ac on Cedar Shoal Cr of Enoree R; plat attached shows border: J Cooper, J (or I) Hobby, and "bounded by land held by J". Witness Elisha Huston and David Norman. Signed Burrel Bobo. Wit. oath Mar. 9, 1819 David Norman to M Casey. Rec. Mar. 20, 1819

p. 234-236 Sept. 29, 1814 Edmond Wood (Spartanburgh) to John James (same); for $210 sold 64(?) ac; border: John James and James Vernon. Witness John Wingo and James Whitten. Signed Edmond Wood. Wit. oath Sept. 28, 1818 J Wingo to James Young. Rec. Mar. 2, 1819

p. 236-237 Mar. 1, 1819 Ransom Golightly (Spartanburgh) to Vincent Wyatt (same); for $200 sold 175 ac; in two parts: (1) (ac omitted) part of grant to Jesse Connel; border: Wyatt; and (2) (ac omitted) part of grant to Ransom Golightly; border: Wyatt.

Witness Jane Wyatt and John Golightly jr. Signed Ransom Golightly. Wit. oath Mar. 1, 1819 John Golightly jr to John Collins. Rec. Mar. 2, 1819

p. 237-239 Sept. 21, 1818 Eaton Walker to John James; for $1,500 sold (1) 120 ac on Wilson's Mill Cr of Tyger R; "laid out" to Nimrod Benson, heir of William Benson desc; and (2) 77 ac on Wilson's Mill Cr of Tyger R; border: John Foster. Witness Thomas Bomar, John Walker, and Elijah Foster. Signed Eaton Walker. Wit. oath Sept. 28, 1818 Elijah Foster to James Young. Rec. Mar. 2, 1819. Dower renounced Sept. 28, 1818 Nancy Walker to James Young

p. 239-240 Sept. 14, 1816 Alexander Ray (Spartanburgh) to Sarah Barrett (same); for $242 sold 75 ac on N side of N Tyger R and N side of branch that runs from William Johnson's to N Tyger R; part of tract between the branch, Claborn Johnson, and Sarah Barrett; other part of tract was sold by Alexander Ray to James Ballenger. Witness Joel Foster and William Perrin. Signed Alexander Ray. Wit. oath Nov. 10, 1818 Joel Foster to John Collins. Rec. Mar. 2, 1819

p. 240-242 Feb. 8, 1819 Andrew Gramling (Spartanburgh) to Isaac Snoddy (same); for $600 sold 150 ac on N Tyger R; border: Edward Bomar, Isaac Snoddy, James Vernon, and John Timmons. Witness Alexander Vernon and Enoch G Foster. Signed Andrew Gramling. Wit. oath Mar. 1, 1819 Alexander Vernon to John Collins. Rec. Mar. 2, 1819. Dower renounced Mar. 1, 1819 Rebecah Gramling to John Collins

p. 242-244 Nov. 1, 1817 James Mayes, Thomas Mayes, and Samuel Davidson (all of White Co, Ill) to Samuel Archibald (Spartanburgh); power of attorney to get any money due to them. Witness none. Signed James Mayes, Thomas Mayes, and Samuel Davidson. Wit. oath Nov. 1, 1817 (White Co, Ill) James Ratcliff, clerk of Court, certifies Daniel Hay is JP. Wit. oath Nov. 1, 1817 (White Co, Ill) James Mayes, Thomas Mayes, and Samuel Davidson to Daniel Hay JP. Nov. 1, 1817 (White Co, Ill) John C Slocumb, presiding judge, certifys James Ratcliff is clerk of court. Rec. Mar. 2, 1819

p. 244-245 Dec. 12, 1816 (Jasper Co, Ga) Mary Mayes, Elunor Ricks, John Reed, Samuel Mayes, John Thompson, Andrew Reed, Rotherford Mayes, Robert Mayes, Andrew Mayes, John Mayes, James Mayes, Thomas Mayes, and Saml Davidson, heirs of Andrew Mayes desc, to Samuel Archibald; power of attorney to sell 793 ac on Wiley's fork; part of estate of Andrew Mayes. Witness John Wilson and Hiram Glazier JIC. Signed Mary Mayes' mark, Elunor Ricks' mark, John Reed, Samuel Mayes, John Thompson, Andrew Reed, Rotherford Mayes, Robert Mayes, Andrew Mayes, John Mayes, James Mayes, Thomas Mayes, and Saml Davidson. Rec. Mar. 2, 1819. Dec. 12, 1816 (Jasper Co, Ga) John Willson, clerk of Inferior Court, certifies Hiram Glazier is judge of Inferior Court. Dec. 12, 1816 (Jasper Co, Ga) John Willson certifys there is "no official seal of office" of Jasper Co. Dec. 12, 1816 (Jasper Co, Ga) Hiram Glazier certifys John Willson is clerk of Inferior Court

p. 245-247 Sept. 21, 1816 Walter West (Spartanburgh) to Elias Palmer; for $189 sold (1) 56 ac where Walter West lives on Fairforest Cr; border: late John Barrett and Elias Palmer formerly Robert Legon; sold Apr. 22, 1803 by Robert Legon to Walter West; and (2) 7 ac adjoining (1); border: formerly John Barrett; sold Oct. 22, 1807 by Christopher Golightly to Walter West. Witness Isaac Smith and James W Ligon. Signed Walter West. Wit. oath Mar. 1, 1819 Isaac Smith to John Chapman. Rec. Mar. 3, 1819. Dower renounced Oct. 13, 1816 Nancy West to Daniel White

p. 247-248 Oct. 30, 1818 William Harris (Spartanburgh) to Jesse

Cooper (same); for $140 sold 40 ac on Cedar Shoal Cr on N side of Enoree R; border: Jesse Casey, Miles Rainwater, Isaac Crow, and Jesse Cooper; part of (grant?) to Wm Casey. Witness David Norman and Archibald Huston (or Hughston). Signed William Harris' mark. Wit. oath Mar. 9, 1819 David Norman to M Casey. Rec. Mar. 20, 1819

p. 248-250 Nov. 20, 1816 Jason Moore (Spartanburgh) to Samuel Otterey (same); for $300 sold (1) 175 ac; border: W-Ward's Cr, S-Josiah Hatchett and Jane Thompson, and E & N-William Rogers; part of grant to Jason Moore; and (2) 100 ac grant to Alexander Paden. Witness John Hatchett and Thomas Hatchett. Signed Jason Moore. Wit. oath Mar. 19, 1819 John Hatchett to Robert Ligon. Rec. Mar. 22, 1819

p. 250-251 Mar. 12, 1819 George Hughe (Spartanburgh) to William Hughe (same); for $50 sold 50 ac on Wolf Br of Lawson's fork; part of 108 ac grant in 1794 Gov. William Moultrie to Hance Harper who sold to George Hughe. Witness John Barnett and Amaziah Lewis. Signed George Hughe's mark. Wit. oath Mar. 12, 1819 John Barnett to Eph Lewis. Rec. Mar. 27, 1819

p. 251-252 Nov. 2, 1818 Ralph Danger to Henry Danger; for $1,000 sold 500 ac on Medow Cr; border: Clark Lewis and Joseph Carver; where Henry Danger lives and "originally run in this survey by" David Lewis, John Luckery, and "other" by Robert McDowel. Witness Charles C Duncan and Jesse Burton. Signed Ralph Danger's mark. Wit. oath Jan. 29, 1819 Charles C Duncan to (not signed). Rec. Mar. 28, 1819

p. 252-254 Nov. 20, 1816 Richard Thompson (Spartanburgh) to Muse Tolleson (same); for $1,300 sold 66 ac adjoining village of Spartanburgh; border: Muse Tolleson and Publick Street. Witness Daniel Wilbanks and John D Palmer. Signed Richard Thompson. Wit. oath Jan. 17, 1819 John D Palmer to Thomas Poole. Rec. Mar. 28, 1819. Dower renounced Mar. 11, 1819 Polly Thompson to Elisha Bomar

p. 254-255 Nov. 10, 1818 Moses Foster (Spartanburgh) to Joel Mason (same); for $400 sold 80 ac on branch of N Tyger R; border: Edward Clement, road from Greenville Road at Foster's Meeting House to Blackstocks Road, and Wm Foster. Witness Elijah Foster and Frederick Rast. Signed Moses Foster. Wit. oath Mar. 30, 1819 Elijah Foster to E Bomar. Rec. Mar. 30, 1819

p. 255-257 Feb. 3, 1819 John Dillard (Spartanburgh) to Joel Foster and Thomas Gore (same); for $831 sold 100 ac on Cedar Shoal Cr of Enoree R; known as Harmoning Saw Mill tract; Condition: sale void if John Dillard pays $831 to legates of J. F. Harmoning's estate; Joel Foster and Thomas Gore are "his" securities. Witness Edmond Foster, John Fred Harmoning, and Israel Simson. Signed John Dillard's mark. Wit. oath Feb. 19, 1819 John Fred Harmoning to M Casey. Rec. Apr. 7, 1819

p. 257-258 Jan. 12, 1819 William Morris (Spartanburgh) to Joseph Gibson (same); for $150 sold 158 ac on N side of Packolet R; border: Edmond Cooley. Witness Gibson Oliver and James Carter. Signed William Morris. Wit. oath Feb. 26, 1819 Gibson Oliver to Eph Lewis. Rec. Apr. 9, 1819

p. 258-259 Feb. 8, 1819 John Brewton (Spartanburgh) to James Corder (same); for $312 sold 104 ac in fork of Tyger R; border: Corder, E-Ford Mason, N & W-Tollive Scoot, S-Jonathan Crow, and N-Gentry; sold by Nathaniel Burton to John Brewton. Witness William Otts and Elias Corder. Signed John Brewton. Wit. oath Apr. 5, 1819 Elias Corder to James Cook. Rec. Apr. 9, 1819

p. 259-261 Aug. 27, 1816 Henry Morrow (Rutherford Co, NC) to John Jordan; for $200 sold 50 ac; border: James Ballinger; part of grant to William Ford. Witness Robert Jamison, Robert Kimbrol, and Solomon Loftis. Signed Henry Morrow. Wit. oath Nov. 9, 1818 Robert Jamison to Henry Turner. Rec. Apr. 8, 1819

p. 261-263 Dec. 3, 1796 Isaac Hendrix (Spartanburgh) to William Hendrix (same); for 70£ sold (ac omitted); border: Ward Tippen and Abner's Cr of Enoree R; part of 200 ac grant Apr. 2, 1792 Gov. Charles Pinckney to (omitted). Witness Jeremiah Snow, James Ford, and Zadock Ford. Signed Isaac Hendrix' mark. Witness Jan. 7, 1797 James Ford to Zadock Ford. Rec. Apr. 9, 1819

p. 263-264 Dec. 13, 1818 Arthur Clark and Samuel Ross to Alexander Davidson; for $137 sold 101 ac on waters of Surratt's Cr; border: Jesse Humphries and Davidson; where James Seratt formerly lives. Witness Joseph Camp, Jesse Humphries, and Moses Davidson. Signed Arthur Clark and Samuel S Ross. Wit. oath Mar. 19, 1819 Jesse Humphries to J Camp. Rec. Apr. 10, 1819

p. 264-265 Dec. 14, 1818 Alexander Davidson and William Humphries to Jesse Humphries; for $145 sold 84 ac on waters of Seratt's Cr; border: John Humphries. Witness John Humphries and James Humphries. Signed Alexander Davidson's and William Humphries' marks. Wit. oath Mar. 19, 1819 John Humphries to J Camp. Rec. Apr. 10, 1819

p. 265-267 Nov. 16, 1818 Thomas Chesney (Spartanburgh) to Moses White (same); for $71 sold 35½ ac; border: N-John Thornton, E-John White, W-Young, S-Thomas Chesney, and W-Robert Alexander. Witness William Otts and Delilah Otts. Signed Thomas Chesney. Wit. oath Mar. 31, 1819 William Otts to John Brewton. Rec. Apr. 10, 1819. Dower renounced Nov. 28, 1818 Caroline Chesney to John Brewton

p. 267-268 Dec. 22, 1818 William Garrett (Spartanburgh) to Edward Turner (same); for $200 sold 11 ac on both sides Casey's Cr of Pacolet R; including a mill and shoal on the creek. Witness James Turner and William Turner. Signed William Garrett's mark. Wit. oath Dec. 22, 1818 James Turner to Henry Turner. Rec. Apr. 10, 1819. Dower renounced Jan. 2, 1819 Sarah Garrett to Henry Turner

p. 268-270 Mar. 5, 1819 Samuel Archibald (Spartanburgh), attorney for Mary Mayes, widow of and the heirs of Andrew Mayes desc, to Theron Lancaster (same); for $1,000 sold 294 ac on Wilies fork of Fairforest Cr; border: Josiah Thornton, Andrew Mayes, Col Thomas Brandon, James Beardan, Sparling Thornton, N-Thornton, E-James Means or James Ham esq, S-John Beardan, and W-remainder of grant; part of grant to Col Thomas Beardon desc who sold to Andrew Mayes desc and Samuel Archibald is empowered by heirs to sell the land. Witness James H Archibald and Robert Archibald. Signed Saml Archibald atty. Wit. oath Apr. 6, 1819 James H Archibald and Robert Archibald to William Reid. Rec. Apr. 10, 1819

p. 270-272 Sept. 19, 1818 John Jeffres (Spartanburgh) to Samuel Jamerson; for $300 sold 100 ac on Provis Cr; border: Miller, Roberts' Spring Br, and Ram Br. Witness John Durham and George Durham. Signed John and Sally Jeffres' marks. Wit. oath Mar. 20, 1819 George Durham to Thomas Wood. Rec. Apr. 10, 1819

p. 272-273 Nov. 21, 1818 Stephen Wilson to John Fowler; for $310 sold 200 ac on S of Tyger R; border: E & N-Thomas Layton, S-King and Hooker, W-Heaton, and N-Grist; where Stephen Wilson lives; "granted" by Benjamin Hooper to Stephen Wilson. Witness Absalem Bobo, Miles Nask, and Joseph Barnett. Signed Stephen Wilson. Wit.

Mar. 24, 1819 Joseph Barnett to Samuel Woodruff. Rec. Apr. 10, 1819. Dower renounced Mar. 29, 1819 Nancy Wilson to John Brewton

p. 273-274 Mar. 31, 1819 Edmund W Chapman (SC) to Michael McKie (Spartanburgh); for $15 sold 20 ac on fork of Roddy's Cr (the fork leading to the Saluda Gap and the other fork to Mills Gap); border: Wm Johnson, Rodday, and Wood. Witness Edmund Bishop (short) and Nathaniel Danggar. Signed Edmund W Chapman. Wit. oath Apr. 5, 1819 Nathaniel Danggar to Daniel White. Rec. Apr. 10, 1819

p. 274-275 Mar. 31, 1819 Edmund W Chapman (Spartanburgh) to Michael McKie (same); for $80 sold 33 ac on head of branch of N Tyger R; border: Richardson; grant in 1774 Gov. William Bull to Rev. Robert Smith. Witness Edmund Bishop (short) and Nathaniel Danggar. Signed Edmund W Chapman. Wit. oath Apr. 5, 1819 Nathaniel Danggar to Daniel White. Rec. Apr. 10, 1819

p. 275-276 Mar. 5, 1819 Samuel Archibald (Spartanburgh), attorney for Mary Mayes, widow of and heirs of Andrew Mayes desc, to William Lancaster esq (same); for $1,000 sold 231 ac on Wilies fork of Fairforest Cr; border: Wilies fork, house where John White lives, S-John Bearden, Sparling Thornton, E-Theron Lancaster, William Lancaster, N-Thornton, W-Edward Lipscomb; part of grant to Col Thomas Beardon desc who sold to Andrew Mayes desc whose heirs empower Samuel Archibald to sell land. Witness James H Archibald and Robert Archibald. Signed Samuel Archibald atty. Wit. oath Apr. 6, 1819 Robert Archibald to William Reid. Rec. Apr. 10, 1819

p. 276-278 Mar. 3, 1819 William Lancaster (Spartanburgh) to Elijah Smith (same); for $100 sold 70 ac; border: Mountain tract; part of grant to Drewry Smith who sold to Arthur Hutchson who sold to Christopher Johnson and sold by sheriff to Judge David Johnson who sold to Lawson Thompson who sold to William Lancaster. Witness Henry White and Moses Smith. Signed W Lancaster. Wit. oath Mar. 3, 1819 Henry White to David White. Rec. Apr. 10, 1819

p. 278-279 Dec. 21, 1818 Lemuel Loftis (Greenville Dist) to Bird Linthecum (Spartanburgh); for $1,000 sold 200 ac on S side of Beaverdam Cr and N side of Tyger R and both sides Hampton's Br; border: Beaverdam Swamp. Witness Page Rork and Edmund Booker. Signed Lemuel Loftis' mark. Wit. oath Apr. 5, 1819 Edmund Booker to John Collins. Rec. Apr. 10, 1819

p. 279-281 Feb. 18, 1819 Lawson Thompson (Spartanburgh) to William Lancaster (same); for $355 sold (1) 280 ac; border: Charles Smith and mountain tract; where William West now lives; part of grant to Drewry Smith who sold to Arthur Hutchson who sold to Christopher John (sic) and sold by sheriff to Judge David Johnson who sold to Lawson Thompson; and (2) 75 ac adjoining (1) on S; border: Lownd, Charles Smith, and Elijah Smith; total of (1) and (2) is 280 ac (sic). Witness Wm West and Elijah Kelley. Signed Lawson Thompson. Wit. oath Mar. 3, 1819 Wm West to Daniel White. Rec. Apr. 10, 1819

p. 281-282 Mar. 15, 1819 Matthew Sparks (Spartanburgh) to Reuben Briant (same); for $400 sold 300 ac on N side of Pacolet R; grant Nov. 12, 1771 to John Butler esq who sold to James Turner and sold by his son James Turner jr to Matthew Sparks. Witness Samuel Whitly and Richerson Whitly. Signed Matthew Sparks' mark. Wit. oath Apr. 6, 1819 Samuel Whitly to Wm Reid. Rec. Apr. 10, 1819

p. 282-283 Sept. 26, 1818 Charles C Duncan to John Clark; for $300 sold 150 ac on both sides Lawson's fork; border: Hicks, Foster, and Night; part of two grants (1) to Francis Ross and (2) to James McDowel. Witness Perry E Duncan and William S Morgan.

Signed C C Duncan. Wit. oath Jan. 30, 1819 William S Morgan to Wm Kelso. Rec. Apr. 10, 1819

p. 283-284 Feb. 1, 1814 James Whitten (Spartanburgh) to Joseph Davis (same); for $15 sold 430 ac on both sides of S Pacolet R; plat attached shows border: Hunt and Anderson (or Ancherson) Liviley. Witness Abram Brock and Thomas Moore. Signed J Whitten. Wit. oath Mar. 30, 1816 Abram Brock to Andrew Furgerson. Rec. Apr. 17, 1819

p. 284-287 Jan. 29, 1793 Henry Petit (Spartanburgh) to William Poole, taylor (same); for 10£ sterling sold 46 ac on S side of Packolet R in fork below the Healing Springs; border: William Pooles's old line and land sold by Henry Petit to William Reid, schoolmaster; part of 246 ac grant Feb. 6, 1786 Gov. William Moultrie to (omitted). Witness Charles McAbee, John Poole, and Benjamin Poole. Signed Henry Petit. Wit. oath Sept. 30, 1809 John Poole to Jn H Jones. Rec. Apr. 13, 1819

p. 287-288 Jun. 25, 1818 John Pennington (same) to Leroy Burns (same); for $122 sold 122 ac on branch of Maple Swamp Cr of S Tyger R. Witness Isham Hendricks and Thomas Marks. Signed John Pennington. Wit. oath May 3, 1819 Capt. Page Rork (sic) to E Bomar. Rec. May 3, 1819

p. 288-289 May 3, 1819 Ann Means (Spartanburgh) to Jacob Chapman (same); for $500 sold 273 ac on Lawson's fork and Showly Cr; part of tract Wood sold to Hugh Means desc. Witness Josiah Blackwell and Jeston Childs. Signed Ann Means' mark. Wit. oath May 3, 1819 Josiah Blackwell to Wm Reid. Rec. May 3, 1819

p. 289-290 Oct. 19, 1818 David Moore (Spartanburgh) to James Whitten (same); for $175 sold 90 ac on S side of Motlow's Cr; border: James Whitten and Hammit's Mill Road; part of grant to James Ridings who sold to Wilson who sold to David Moore. Witness A Brock and Joseph Davis. Signed David Moore. Wit. oath Apr. 17, 1819 A Brock to W Bonnett. Rec. May 3, 1819

p. 290-291 Mar. 23, 1819 James Selman (Spartanburgh) to James McCarley (same); for $115 sold 46 ac; border: Ford's old line now James McCarley and a waggon road. Witness Drury McAbee and William N Miller. Signed Jas Selman. Wit. oath May 3, 1819 William N Miller to F. H. Legg. Rec. May 3, 1819

p. 291-293 Dec. 21, 1818 James Smith (Spartanburgh) to William F Reynolds (same); for $500 sold 354 ac on S side of Lawson's fork and Betsy's or Mold's Br. Witness Nancy Tracy and William Tracy. Signed James Smith. Wit. oath May 3, 1819 William Tracy to John Lipscomb. Rec. May 3, 1819

p. 293-294 May 22, 1819 Elisha Smith (Spartanburgh) to James Smith (same); for $50 sold 300 ac on S side of Pacolet R; border: Joseph Davis. Witness John Parks and Nancy Parks. Signed Elisha Smith's marks. Wit. oath May 22, 1819 John Parks to Thomas Poole. Rec. May 26, 1819

p. 294-295 Feb. 10, 1819 Elisha Smith (Spartanburgh) to Elisha Smith jr (same); for 5s sold 30 ac on branch of Pacolet R; border: Ellis Cannon, Lewis Cannon, and William Smith. Witness John Vandiver and Ellis Cannon. Signed Elisha Smith's mark. Wit. oath Apr. 6, 1819 John Vandiver to Caleb Jones. Rec. May 26, 1819

p. 295-296 May 2, 1819 Elizabeth Demsey (Spartanburgh) to Laurence Bankston (same); for $30 sold 40 ac on E side of Casey's Cr; border: James Turner and John Martin; part of where "said" widow

Demsey lives. Witness Peter Cantrell and Middleton Turner. Signed Elizabeth Demsey's mark. Wit. oath May 2, 1819 Peter Cantrell to Henry Turner. Rec. Jun. 7, 1819

p. 296-297 Jan. 22, 1819 Elisha Smith (Spartanburgh) to William Smith (same); for 5s sold 34 ac on S side of Pacolet R; border: Lewis Cannon and Templeman. Witness Ellis Cannon and Zachariah Cannon. Signed Elisha Smith's mark. Wit. oath Jun. 7, 1819 Ellis Cannon to Wm Reid. Rec. Jun. 7, 1819

p. 297-299 Feb. 15, 1819 David Mosteller (Greenville Dist) to Thomas Wells (Spartanburgh); for $600 sold (1) 242 ac on Lawson's fork of Pacolate R; part of 392 ac grant to William Turner; and (2) 75 ac on Buck Br of Lawson's fork; grant to Lewis Turner. Witness Thomas Cannon and Thomas U Wells. Signed David Mosteller. Wit. oath Jun. 1, 1819 Thomas Cannon to Peter Edwards. Rec. Jun. 7, 1819. Dower renounced Jun. 1, 1819 Susannah Mosteller to Peter Edwards

p. 299-300 May 24, 1815 William Hammett (Spartanburgh) to John Winsor (same); for $84 sold 72 ac on waters of Fairforest Cr; border: John Winsor, Boiling Springs Meeting House Road, James Bishop, Edmond Bishop, Reedy Br, and Seargus Seay; E corner of 1,640 ac survey in 1785 for William Foster. Witness John Lancaster and John Bishop. Signed Wm Hammett. Wit. oath Apr. 9, 1816 John Lancaster to Ephm Lewis. Rec. Jun. 7, 1819

p. 300-301 Aug. 12, 1816 James Martin (Spartanburgh) to James P Means (same); for $500 sold (1) (ac omitted) on both sides Stories Cr of Fairforest Cr; border: E, N & W-Henry Cunningham and Joseph Kelso, SE & S-David Johnson; sold by Joshua Thomas to John Wright; part of two grants: (a) 200 ac to Hugh Gamby and (b) to Joshua Thomas; and (2) 37 ac; border: H Cunningham and Joseph Kelso. Witness Robert Archibald and Washington Harris. Signed James Martin. Wit. oath Aug. 12, 1816 Robert Archibald to Saml Archibald. Rec. Jun. 7, 1819. Dower renounced Dec. 23, 1816 Hester Martin to Samuel Archibald

p. 301-302 May 10, 1819 John Crocker and Nathaniel Woodruff, esecutors of estate of Joseph Woodruff desc, (Spartanburgh) to James Allen (same); for $740 sold 130 ac on Enoree R and Lick Cr and Cool Springs Br; border: Daniel McKie and James Allen; sold at public auction due to will of Joseph Woodruff desc. Witness Caleb Allen and Thomas Woodruff. Signed John Crocker and Nathaniel Woodruff. Wit. oath Jun. 1, 1819 Caleb Allen to Samuel Woodruff. Rec. Jun. 7, 1819

p. 302-303 Jan. 29, 1817 Nimrod Cantrell (Spartanburgh) to John Mathis (same); for $50 sold 256 ac in Greenville Dist on both sides Goose Cr of Middle fork Saluda R. Witness James Dison jr and James Burnett jr. Signed Nimrod Cantrell. Wit. oath Apr. 17, 1819 James Burnett jr to W Bennett. Rec. Jun. 7, 1819

p. 303-305 Jun. 7, 1809 (sic 1819) Equity Court of Newberry Dist) Francis B Higgins, Commissioner of Newbery Dist Equity Court, to David Dantzler; for $305 sold 530 ac but resurvey "finds" 516 ac on waters of Tyger R; border: J Montgomery, James Loftis, R Ludson, Hugh Barnett, Jesse Wheeler; see Equity Court complaint Hannah Edson and Casper Edson vs William Turpin jr and "others" filed Jun. 1, 1818 to partition eight tracts in Spartanburgh, Laurens, Union, and Newberry Dists which Peter Brasselman and Cusman (?) Edson owned when they died; Commissioner recommended sale of land Feb. term of court 1819; terms of sale were: credit of 1 and 2 years from Oct. 1, 1818; sale for above land was Jun. 7, 1819 at Spartanburgh. Witness Andrew B Moore and Anthony Foster. Signed F. B. Higgins, Commissioner Equity Newberry Dist. Wit. oath Jun.

7, 1819 Andrew B Moore to Danl White. Rec. Jun. 7, 1819

p. 305-306 Dec. 25, 1816 (Union Dist) James Mayes, carpenter (Union Dist) to James P Means (Spartanburgh); for $200 sold 108 ac; part of grant to Robert Irvin. Witness Wm Patton and James K Means. Signed James Mayes. Wit. oath Dec. 25, 1816 Wm Patton to Saml Archibald. Rec. Jun. 7, 1819

p. 306-307 Nov. 12, 1818 John Deshazo (Edgefield Dist) to William Morgan (Spartanburgh); for $1,000 sold (1) 400 ac on both sides S Pacolate R; grant to John Clark; plat attached shows border: E-Camron, S-Dangard, W-Barton, and N-(2) which follows; and (2) 199 ac adjoining (1) on N side; grant to Robert Henderson; except "small part" taken off E end by John Dolton's land. Witness William Ramsey and Armsted Bomar. Signed John Deshazo. Wit. oath Mar. 6, 1819 William Ramsey to Wm Kelso. Rec. Jun. 7, 1819

p. 307-308 Feb. 1, 1819 John M Collins and Wm Laurence (Spartanburgh) to John Chapman jr (same); for $500 sold (ac omitted) on waters of N Tyger R; border: Blackstock's Road and Alexr Roddy. Witness Memory N Chapman and Calvin Foster. Signed Jno M Collins and Wm Laurence. Wit. oath Jun. 7, 1819 Memory N Chapman to John Rowland. Rec. Jun. 7, 1819

p. 308-309 Mar. 16, 1818 Henry Smith (Spartanburgh) to Richard Thomson (same); for $700 sold 510 ac on branches of Mill Cr of Tyger R and known "by" the Crossroads; on S and W side of Blackstocks Road; border: Ransom Foster; where Henry Smith lives; W end of grant Jul. 8, 1774 to Dr Samuel Gravel. Witness William Trimmier and E Bomar. Signed Henry Smith. Wit. oath Jun. 7, 1819 William Trimmier to E Bomar. Rec. Jun. 7, 1819

p. 309-310 Apr. 3, 1819 James Smith (Spartanburgh) to William P Gadberry (Union Dist); for $3,982 sold 885 ac on N side of Lawson's fork; border: Lindsey. Witness Lundsford Bagwell and Elisha Poole. Signed James Smith. Wit. oath Jun. 14, 1819 Lundsford Bagwell to Caleb Jones. Rec. Jun. 14, 1819

p. 310-313 Jun. 30, 1818 James Hunt, sheriff (Spartanburgh) to Richard Thomson; for $576 sold 400 ac in two parts--lots (200 ac each) "parts A & B"; on S side of Pacolate R opposite fork of Pacolet R and Lawson's fork; part of two grants: (1) to Robert Lee and (2) to Mathew McBee; border: Benjn Poole, Solomon Crocker, and John Pearce; sale due to writ from Spartanburgh Common Pleas Court John Calvert et al petitioned second Monday after fourth Monday in Oct. 1816 to divide real estate of Rolly Calvert desc; court appointed James Selman, James Foster, Elisha Ginnins, John Trail, and William Underwood esqs Commissioners for Petition; their return made second Monday after fourth Monday in Mar. 1818 saying real estate can't be divided between parties concerned and they recommend a sale; credit to be 12 months; sale on first Monday in Jun. 1818. Witness Wm Trimmier esq and Jesse Cleveland. Signed Jas Hunt SSD. Wit. oath Jun. 14, 1819 Wm Trimmier to E Bomar. Rec. Jun. 14, 1819

p. 313 Jun. 12, 1819 Alexander McKie (Spartanburgh) to Moses Shields (same); for $306 sold 204 ac on dividing ridge between Lawson's fork and Peter's Cr. Witness Memory N Chapman and Joel Lewis. Signed Alexr McKie. Wit. oath Jun. 14, 1819 Joel Lewis to Thomas Poole. Rec. Jun. 14, 1819

p. 313-314 Jan. 7, 1819 William Johnson to John Wingo; for $175 rent and lease for 63 years 97½ ac on Camp Br of Lawson's fork; part of tract leased by William Dunlap, trustee to Thomas Wadsworth, "free school" to Robert Fausett and Reubin Fausett.

Witness Presley Ballenger and William Weatherford. Signed William Johnson. Wit. oath Apr. 22, 1819 Presley Ballenger to John Chapman. Rec. Jun. 28, 1819

p. 314-316 Jan. 29, 1814 Hardy Fluker (Edgefield Dist) to Marmeduke Coate (Newberry Dist); for $90 sold 200 ac; border: Venable's Crossroads, John Burnet, Cart Road Br, George Rowlan, School House Br, and Leonard Cardin; part of 890 ac survey Jan. 21, 1793 for Leonard Cardin. Witness Henry Coate and Joel Bell. Signed Hardy Fluker. Wit. oath Jun. 17, 1815 (Newberry Dist) Joel Bell to Y. J. Harrington JQ. Rec. Jul. 2, 1819

p. 316 Jul. 5, 1819 John and Ann Means to Robert McMillen; for $1,092 sold three Negroes: Oney, Mary, and Minerva. Witness James Brannon. Signed John Means and Ann's mark. Wit. oath Jul. 22, 1819 James Brannon to E Bomar. Rec. Jul. 22, 1819

p. 316-317 Jan. 4, 1819 George and Leonard Hill and Sheldon Clark & Co (Spartanburgh) to Isaac Crow (same); for $1,210 sold (ac omitted) on S side of Tyger R; known as Mill tract; border: W-William Ervin and Jeremiah Wofford, S-Thomas and William Young, N & E-Tyger R; border agrees with that "laid down in deed this day made by IC to us"; Condition: deed void if George and Leonard Hill and Sheldon Clark pay Isaac Crow $1,210 by Jan. 20, 1821. Witness Samuel Smith and James Leonard. Signed George Hill, Leonard Hill, and Sheldon Clark. Wit. oath Apr. 23, 1819 James Leonard to Samuel Woodruff. Rec. Jul. 5, 1819

p. 317-318 Dec. 28, 1818 William Bomar (Spartanburgh) to Elisha Bomar (same); for $700 sold 153 ac on branch of N Tyger R; border: Robert Woods' Spring Br and by where John Foster sr formerly lived. Witness William W Bomar and John Walker. Signed Wm Bomar. Wit. oath Jan. 4, 1819 John Walker to James Crook. Rec. Jul. 5, 1819

p. 318-319 Dec. 28, 1818 Elisha Bomar (Spartanburgh) to John Bomar (same); for $700 sold 153 ac on branch of N Tyger R; border: Robert Woods' Spring Br and by where John Foster sr formerly lived. Witness William Bomar and Barbara Brown. Signed E Bomar. Wit. oath Jul. 5, 1819 William Bomar to John Chapman. Rec. Jul. 5, 1819

p. 319-320 May 22, 1815 Charles Mathis (Spartanburgh) to Reubin Mathis (same); for $200 sold 50 ac on waters of Lawson's fork; border: N-land Charles Mathis sold to William R Smith (part of same tract) and W & S-William Bagwell; grant to Charles Mathis. Witness Joseph Day and Jesse Mathis. Signed Charles Mathis. Wit. oath Jul. 5, 1819 Jesse Mathis to Caleb Jones. Rec. Jul. 5, 1819

p. 320-321 Dec. 7, 1818 Benjamin Wofford (Spartanburgh) to Nathaniel Gist (Union Dist); for $4,000 sold 60 ac on waters of Tyger R; where South Carolina Cotton Manufactory is now situated; includes all buildings. Witness Robert G. H. Farr and John Jones. Signed Benjm Wofford. Wit. oath Jun. 29, 1819 John Jones to William Reid. Rec. Jul. 23, 1819

p. 321-322 Dec. 25, 1818 Eli Couch (Spartanburgh) to Francis Glenn (Laurens Dist); for $1,000 sold 300 ac on NE side of Cedar Shoal Cr of Enoree R; border: N-Spencer Bobo, W-Nathan Langston, E-Jesse Couch and J. F. Harmoning, S-Samuel Farrow, and Musgrove's Road. Witness James Burk and Chancy Stone. Signed Eli Couch. Wit. oath May 10, 1819 James Burk to M Casey. Rec. Jul. 23, 1819. Dower renounced Dec. 21, 1818 Nancy Couch to Burrel Bobo

p. 322-324 (blank), 1798 William Hammett (Spartanburgh) to Justice

Reynolds (same); for 15£ sold 300 ac; border: NE & SE-Thomason and Hews, SW-Wyatt, SE-Poole, Elisha McAbee, Deskin Grant, Court House Road, and Iron Works Road; part of 591 ac grant Dec. 3, 1792 Gov. Charles Pinckney to William Hammett. Witness Henry Petit, Peter Peterson, and Anthony Bates. Signed William Hammett. Wit. oath Aug. 3, 1819 Henry Petit to Thomas Poole. Rec. Aug. 4, 1819

p. 324-325 Apr. 12, 1819 James Selman (Spartanburgh) to Robert Bullington (same); for $2,000 sold 400 ac on Meadows and Clear Creeks of S Pacolate R; border: E-Armstead Bomar, N-McWilliams, and W & S-Smith and Ramsey; part of grant Jun. 2, 1806 Gov. Paul Hambleton to James Selman. Witness Armstead Bomar and Christopher Golightly. Signed Jas Selman. Wit. oath Aug. 2, 1819 Christopher Golightly to Eph Lewis. Rec. Aug. 4, 1819

p. 325-326 Apr. 12, 1819 Thomas Dean (Bedford Co, Tenn) to Peggy Ford (Spartanburgh); for $500 sold 115 ac on S side of S Tyger R; border: Burns, Bright, Ellmore, Ford, and Sizemore; survey Jul. 20 (or 23), 1785 by Andrew Thompson for Jonathan Nesbett and granted Jan. 1, 1787 to Jonathan Nesbett who sold Sept. 19, 1815 to John Nesbett who sold Oct. 3, 1815 to Thomas Dean. Witness Manley Ford and James Burns. Signed Thos Dean. Wit. oath Jul. 28, 1819 Manley Ford to Thomas Wood. Rec. Aug. 4, 1819

p. 326-327 Apr. 14, 1818 Jesse Crook (Spartanburgh) to James Crook (same); for $2,000 sold 250 ac on S side of S Tyger R; border: English, Zacheriah McDaniel, and Ephraim Drummon; part of grant to Thomas English. Witness William Crook and Matthew R Evins. Signed Jesse Crook. Wit. oath Jan. 9, 1819 William Crook to Wm Hendrix. Rec. Aug. 4, 1819

p. 327-328 Sept. 21, 1816 Alexander Cunningham (Spartanburgh) to Capt Hugh McMillen (same); for $50 sold 50 ac on N side of Obed's Cr and on S side of N Pacolate R; border: David Cunningham, John Daniel, John Leech, and a line between Alexander Cunningham and Hugh McMillen marked out by Vincent Bennett; part of grant to John Leech. Witness William Bennett and Iredell Cunningham. Signed Alexr Cunningham. Wit. oath Aug. 2, 1819 William Bennett to John Rowland. Rec. Aug. 4, 1819

p. 328-329 Dec. 29, 1818 Robert McDowell (Spartanburgh) to Robert Bullington (same); for $244 sold 90 ac; border: Robert McDowell and James McDowell; one ac excepted for a graveyard. Witness Christopher Golightly, Thomas Burton, and Charles C Duncan. Signed Robert McDowell. Wit. oath Aug. 2, 1819 Christopher Golightly to Eph Lewis. Rec. Aug. 4, 1819

p. 329-330 Jul. 9, 1819 Nimrod Cantrell (Spartanburgh) to John Mathis (same); for $100 sold 187 ac on waters of Barton's Cr of Pacolate R; border: NW & SW-Nelson, SE-Thomas Gore, and NE-Harvy Davis. Witness William Gilbert and Harvey Davis. Signed Nimrod Cantrell. Wit. oath Jul. 10, 1819 William Gilbert to W Bennett. Rec. Aug. 5, 1819

p. 330-331 Oct. 22, 1818 Samuel Turner, George Turner, and James Lord (Spartanburgh) to Richard Proctor (same); for $210 sold 200 ac on waters of Island Cr; border: Warren, Prevley Turner, McBee, Bruise, and George Turner Spring. Witness Hiram Proctor and Richard Farrow. Signed George Turner, Samuel Turner, and James Lord. Wit. oath Hiram Proctor to Henry Turner. Rec. Aug. 5, 1819. Dower renounced Mar. 4, 1819 Hannah Turner, Sarah Turner, and Mary Lord to Henry Turner

p. 331-333 Aug. 2, 1819 Hugh Moore (Spartanburgh) to Wm H Gilliland (Charleston, SC); to secure a note dated Feb. 10, 1819 from Hugh Moore to Wm H Gilliland for $818.14 (or $818.84) "at 60 days" after that date and on Mar. 12, 1819 another note for $124.13 "at 60 days" after that date and for $5 sold (1) 500 ac on waters of Thickety Cr; grant to Hugh Moore; and (2) 524 ac on waters of Pacolate R; grant to Jonathan Low and sold to Hugh Moore; Condition: sale void if Hugh pays the notes. Witness Samuel C Hunt and James Hunt esq. Signed Hugh Moore. Wit. oath Aug. 17, 1819 James Hunt to E Bomar. Rec. Aug. 17, 1819

p. 333-335 Jul. 26, 1819 George W Parkison (Smith Co, Tenn) to James Hunt (Spartanburgh); for $50 sold (1) 284 ac on waters of Lawson's fork; grant to John Holcomb; George W Parkison's part of estate of Basel Lee desc; (2) 100 ac on S side of Lawson's fork; grant to Edward Dickson; (3) 60 ac; border: Harrison; part of grant to Diskin Grant; (4) 100 ac on S side of Lawson's fork; and (5) 100 ac; border: Randolph Brown; all the tracts are George W Parkison's part of Basel Lee's estate. Witness Levi Lee and Thomas J Underwood. Signed George W Parkison. Wit. oath Jul. 27, 1819 Thomas J Underwood to E Bomar. Rec. Aug. 5, 1819

p. 335-336 Feb. 6, 1819 Reubin Briant (Spartanburgh) to Jesse Griffin (same); for $40 sold 20 ac; border: Fernande and Jesse Griffin. Witness Thomas Kerby and David Reid. Signed Reubin Briant's mark. Wit. oath Feb. 6, 1819 Thomas Kerby to Wm Reid. Rec. Aug. 28, 1819

p. 336-339 Aug. (blank or 7), 1777 Luke Vickory (Tyger R, SC) to Joseph Wofford (same); for 1,000£ sold 300 ac on S side of Tyger R in Craven Co; border: S-William Young, W-Thomas Young, and others vacant; grant Aug. 11, 1774 Lt. Gov. William Bull to Luke Vickory. Witness Charles Smith and James Crow. Signed Luke Vickory. Wit. oath Aug. 14, 1777 James Crow to W Wofford. Rec. Aug. 31, 1819

p. 339-340 Nov. 22, 1809 William Wingo (Spartanburgh) to Robert Love (same); for $250 sold 244 ac on Beaverdam Cr of Fairforest Cr; border: Gravel and road from Spartanburgh Court House to Nicholas' old mill on Tyger R. Witness Joshua D Balinger, John Wingo and Hamilton Wilson. Signed William Wingo. Wit. oath Jul. 31, 1819 Hamilton Wilson to E Bomar. Rec. Sept. 6, 1819

p. 340-341 Nov. 9, 1818 John Wilson (Spartanburgh) to William Clary (same); for $275 sold 151 ac; border: E-William Humphries and Alexander Davidson, S-Major McClarrin (now Wilson Nesbett), and W & S-Frances Robertson; SE corner of grant Dec. 9, 1774 to Timothy Philips. Witness Hugh Quinn, Thomas Clary, and Benjamin Ellis. Signed John and Rebekah Wilson's marks. Wit. oath Mar. 19, 1819 Thomas Clary to J Camp. Rec. Sept. 6, 1819

p. 341-342 Apr. 23, 1819 Thomas Harrison to Thomas Harrison jr; for $150 sold 180 ac on Surratt's Cr; border: North Carolina; where Thomas Harrison lives. Witness Martin Harris and Balus Harris. Signed Thomas Harrison's mark. Wit. oath Apr. 23, 1819 Balus Harris to J Camp. Rec. Sept. 6, 1819

p. 342-343 Apr. 20, 1818 Isaiah Rhew (Spartanburgh) to James Meadows (same); for $500 sold 100 ac on N side ofDutchman's Cr; part of grant to Samuel Lancaster esq and willed Jan. 21, 1785 (or date granted) to Moses Lancaster. Witness Gabriel Philips sr and William Poole. Signed Isaiah Rhew. Wit. oath (Apr. 20, 1818?) Gabriel Philips sr to Robert Ligon. Rec. Sept. 6, 1819

p. 343-344 Apr. 2, 1819 Samuel Gentry (Spartanburgh) to Elisha Thornton (same); for $60 sold 15½ ac on branch of Furgason Cr of Tyger R; border: E-Joseph Willis, S-George Floyd,

W-Richard Jentry, and N-Benjamin Robuck. Witness Isaac Crow and Else Crow. Signed Samuel Gentry's mark. Wit. oath Sept. 11, 1819 Isaac Crow to Robert Ligon. Rec. Sept. 15, 1819

p. 344-345 Feb. 28, 1818 William Arnold (Madison Co, Miss) to Samuel Gentry (Spartanburgh); for $60 sold 15½ ac; border: W(sic)-Joseph Willis, S-George Floyd, W(sic)-Richard Gentry (sic) and Samuel Gentry, and N-Benjamin Robuck. Witness Isaac Crow and Benjamin Robuck. Signed William Arnold. Wit. oath Sept. 11, 1819 Isaac Crow to Robert Ligon. Rec. Sept. 15, 1819

p. 345 Mar. 4, 1816 (Greenville Dist) Robert Spence (Greenville Dist) to William S Dill (same); for $100 sold 125 ac on Middle Tyger R; part of 250 ac tract "to" Robert Spence. Witness William Kimbrell (or Kimbrol) and Matthew Garrett. Signed Robert Spence. Wit. oath Aug. 13, 1818 (Greenville Dist) Matthew Garrett to David Jackson. Rec. Sept. 21, 1819

p. 345-346 Mar. 23, 1819 (Greenville Dist) William S Dill (Greenville Dist) to Thomas Underwood (same); for $200 sold 125 ac on Middle Tyger R; part of 250 ac grant to Robert Spence. Witness Theron Underwood and Jonathan Farmer. Signed William S Dill. Wit. oath Sept. 18, 1819 Jonathan Farmer to John Montgomery. Rec. Sept. 21, 1819

p. 346-348 Feb. 1, 1819 James Hunt, sheriff (Spartanburgh) to John E Bobo (same); for $66 sold 30 ac on Two Mile Cr; border: widow Freeman, Ablsalem Bobo and (blank) Barnett; sale due to writ from Spartanburgh Common Pleas Court suit Samuel Farrow vs Thomas M Bragg, administrator of estate of Spencer Bobo desc; sale Oct. 6, 1817; James Hunt is the successor of Labon P Poole, who neglected to execute titles. Witness John T Earle and Simpson Foster. Signed James Hunt SSD. Wit. oath Sept. 24, 1819 Simpson Foster to E Bomar. Rec. Sept. 24, 1819

p. 348-349 Sept. 16, 1819 Alexander McKie (Spartanburgh) to Muse Tolleson (same); for $441 sold 157 ac on S side of Lawson's fork; border: mill tract; part of two tracts granted to (1) Diskin Grant who sold part to William Roberson who sold to Alexander McKie and (2) to William Wells who sold to Alexander McKie; plat attached. Witness Elisha Bomar and Joseph Carswell. Signed Alexr McKie. Wit. oath Sept. 16, 1819 Elisha Bomar to Daniel White. Rec. Sept. 16, 1819

p. 349-350 Dec. 28, 1814 James Beck (Spartanburgh) to Alexander Robbs (same); for $200 sold 105 ac in Spartanburgh and and Greenville Dists on S side of S Tyger R; border: James Wilson jr, David McCoy, and Heirs of David Moore desc; part of "large survey" grant to John Thomas jr who sold to James Beck. Witness Abraham Cantrell, James Robbs, and John Robbs. Signed James Beck. Wit. oath Sept. 10, 1816 Abraham Cantrell to James Hammett. Rec. Sept. 29, 1819

p. 350-353 Jul. 15, 1818 William G Davis (Charleston, SC) to Andrew McDowell and Alexander Black "under the firs of McDowell and Black" merchants of Charleston, SC; to secure a bond of $4,455.62 to pay $2,227.81 with interest sold four shares in South Carolina Cotton Manufactory in Spartanburgh Dist on Tyger R and all improvements, lands, buildings, negroes, stock, machinery, utensils, trade, debts, dues, obligations, and real and personal property; Condition: sale void if William G Davis pays debt. Witness N. W. Vincent and Samuel P Ripley. Signed Wm G Davis. Wit. oath Jul. 22, 1818 Samuel P Ripley to Saml Burger Not Pub. Rec. Sept. 29, 1819

p. 353-355 Jan. 3, 1814 John Cook (Spartanburgh) to Isaac Smith (same); for $320 sold 190 ac on waters of Fairforest Cr; border: Golightly and Smith; part of tract sold to John Cook by Richard Barnett and Jane Smith in two separate tracts. Wit. oath Jul. 9, 1814 William M Golightly, E Roddy, and Hancock Smith. Signed John Cook. Wit. oath Jul. 9, 1814 William M Golightly to Danl White. Rec. Sept. 29, 1819. Dower renounced Mar. 11, 1814 Sally Cook to Daniel White

p. 355-356 Feb. 2, 1819 Joel Morris (Amelia Co, Va) to William Pollard (Spartanburgh); gives (1) 150 ac on branch of Lawson's fork; border: SW-William Moultrie, SE-Harry Prince, and others vacant when granted; sold to William Pollard in trust for Nancy Pollard wife of Moses and "issue of her body"; and (2) give $500 to William Pollard as trustee for Nancy Pollard's benefit; Joel Morris is executor of will of Zaccheriah Morris desc. Witness E Roddy and Simpson Foster. Signed Joel Morris. Wit. oath Sept. 28, 1819 E Roddy to E Bomar. Rec. Sept. 29, 1819

p. 356-357 (blank) 2, 1819 William Pollard (Spartanburgh) to Joel Morris; for $50 sold 150 ac on branch of Lawson's fork; border: SW-William Moultrie, SE-Henry Prince, and others vacant when granted. Witness E Roddy and Simpson Foster. Signed William Pollard's mark. Wit. oath Sept. 28, 1819 E Roddy to E Bomar. Rec. Sept. 29, 1819

p. 357-358 Apr. 23, 1819 Thomas Harris (Spartanburgh) to Balus Harris (same); for $150 sold 150 ac on N fork of Sarratt's Cr; border: North Carolina line. Witness Thomas Harris and Martin Harris. Signed Thomas Harris' mark. Wit. oath Apr. 22, 1819 (sic) Thomas Harris to J Camp. Rec. Oct. 4, 1819

p. 358-359 Mar. 26, 1817 John Ray (Spartanburgh) to James Ballinger (same); for $500 sold 100 ac on N Tyger R; border: Rowland Johnson and Sauney Ray. Witness Frances Galt and Jabez Galt. Signed John Ray. Wit. oath Oct. 4, 1819 Jabez Galt to John Chapman. Rec. Oct. 4, 1819

p. 359-360 Apr. 23, 1819 Elisha Smith (Spartanburgh) to James Keene; for (money omitted) sold 15 ac on waters of Fairforest Cr; part of grant to Hancock Smith. Witness Ralph Smith and James Crocker jr. Signed Elisha Smith. Wit. oath May 3, 1819 Ralph Smith to E Bomar. Rec. Oct. 6, 1819

p. 360-361 Mar. 27, 1817 Andrew Coan jr (Spartanburgh) to William Skinner (same); for $200 sold 119 ac on S side of Floyd's Br of Furgeson's Cr; border: N of road from Rogers' Bridge, S-Charles Skinner and Sally Bragg, N-Young Scott, E-John Skinner, and W-Simeon Lavender. Witness William Otts and Delilah Otts. Signed Andrew Coan. Wit. oath Oct. 18, 1819 William Otts to Robert Ligon. Rec. Oct. 25, 1819

p. 361 May 18, 1816 William Amos to Wilson Nesbett; for $38 sold 85 ac on Quinn's Cr; border: Wilson Nesbett. Witness William Collins and Charles Amos. Signed William Amos' mark. Wit. oath May 25, 1818 William Collins to A Benson. Rec. Oct. 25, 1819

p. 361-363 Mar. 9, 1814 John Williams (Spartanburgh) to Wilson Nesbett (same); for $215 sold 214 ac in two parts on Suck Cr of Broad R: (1) 75 ac; border: Moultrie; grant Sept. 11, 1795 to Jacob Dilback; and (2) 139 ac at head branches of Suck Cr; part of grant to Isaac Williams who sold to John Williams. Witness W Camp sr and Briant Bonner. Signed John Williams. Wit. oath William Camp jr(sic) to Joshua Richards Mar. 9, 1814. Rec. Oct. 25, 1819

p. 363-364 Jul. 6, 1816 Matthis Turner jr to Wilson Nesbett (Spartanburgh); for $75 sold 150 ac on Cherokee Cr; border: Wilson Nesbett; part of grant to John Turner. Witness Thomas Hannon and William Collins. Signed Matthis Turner jr's mark. Wit. oath May 25, 1818 William Collins to A Benson. Rec. Oct. 25, 1814

p. 364-365 Nov. 2, 1814 Edmond Chambers (Spartanburgh) to Wilson Nesbett (same); for $520 sold 250 ac on Cherokee Cr; border: Cooper. Witness William Collins, John Williams, and Ralph Cobb. Signed Edmund Chambers. Wit. oath May 25, 1818 William Collins to A Benson. Rec. Oct. 26, 1814. Dower renounced Nov. 24, 1814 Elenor Chambers to Joshua Richards

p. 365-366 Feb. 15, 1812 William Morgan (Spartanburgh) to Wilson Nesbett (same); for $125 sold 250 ac; part of 300 ac grant Nov. 7, 1785 to Nathaniel Miller who sold to Joshua Edwards who sold to James Wofford who sold to William Morgan; except 13 rods square on S side for an ore bank for Joshua Benson. Witness William Collins and Briant Bonner. Signed William Morgan. Wit. oath May 25, 1818 William Collins to A Benson. Rec. Oct. 25, 1819

p. 366-367 (blank) 9, 1813 Thomas (or William) Hill (Spartanburgh) to Drury Wood (same); for $45 sold 100 ac; border: Grindal Shoal Road and Drury Wood (bought from John Shippy); part of grant Mar. 3, 1800 Lt. Gov. John Drayton to Samuel Sparks. Witness Smith Lipscomb and George Wood. Signed Thomas Hill's mark. Wit. oath Nov. 18, 1819 Smith Lipscomb to John Lipscomb. Rec. Nov. 19, 1819

p. 367-368 Sept. 17, 1818 Charles McDaniel (NC) to Sally Harris (Spartanburgh); for $35 sold 100 ac on Gum Spring Gully Br of Buck Cr; border: Pirtles old line and widow Crocker. Witness James Cudd and William Little. Signed Charles McDaniel's mark. Wit. oath Sept. 26, 1818 William Little to Henry Turner. Rec. Nov. 1, 1819

p. 368-369 May 3, 1819 John Timmons (Spartanburgh) to Edward Bomar (same); give "all" his property (ac omitted) on waters of N Tyger R; John Timmons' part of his father Samuel Timmons' land; and give a Negro boy Orange, all horse flesh and stock; all given to secure loan from Edward Bomar to John Timmons and sale void if John Timmons repays the money. Witness Andrew Gramling, Rebecca Gramling, and Adam Hemperley. Signed John Timmons. Wit. oath Nov. 1, 1819 Adam Hemperley to John Rowland. Rec. Nov. 1, 1819

p. 369-372 Jun. 7, 1719(sic) William Holoway (Spartanburgh) to Elijah Turner (York Dist); for $2,000 sold 547 ac in three parts on Surratt's Cr of Main Broad R: (1) 290 ac sold by Joseph Champion to William Holoway; (2) 290 ac; border: NW-William Holoway, NE & SE-William Davidson, and E, NE, N & S-vacant; grant to William Holoway; except 120 ac "for" William Davidson on N side of Halfway Br and 100 ac excepted that William Holoway sold to Anthony Surratt on S side of Halfway Br (this leaves 70 ac); and (3) 187 ac sold by Robert Meloore to William Holoway. Witness Fendal M Robertson and Charles Hooper. Signed Wm Holoway. Wit. oath Mar. 3, 1819 Fendal M Robertson to J Camp. Rec. Nov. 4, 1819. Dower renounced Nov. 4, 1819 Nancy Holoway to Elisha Bomar

p. 372-373 Sept. 15, 1819 John Means (Spartanburgh) to Jesse Crook (same); for $8,000 sold 1,330 ac on Furgeson's Cr of Tyger R; border: S-Jonas Brewton and Philip Brewton, E-Joel Brewton, Peter Bragg, and estate of James Otts desc, N-Major Crook and John Wofford, W-Nathaniel Wofford and estate of Spencer Bobo desc. Witness William Means, Nancy C Means, and Elizabeth Stripling. Signed John Means. Wit. oath Sept. 21, 1819 William Means to John Brewton. Rec. Nov. 11, 1819. Dower renounced Sept. 21, 1819 Anne or Nancy Means to John Brewton

p. 373-375 Jul. (blank), 1819 James M Hunter and Mary Hunter (Spartanburgh) to William Ross (same); for $500 sold (ac omitted) on Broad R; grant to John Tagert or Mary Seeper (sic) and sold by John Tagert to John Ross and sold to heirs of John Trimmier who sold to William Ross. Witness William Bostick, William Thomson, and Abraham Collins. Signed James M and Mary Hunter. Wit. oath Jul. 9, 1819 (York Dist) William Bostick to George Plaxco. Rec. Nov. 11, 1819. Dower renounced Sept. 24, 1819 (York Dist) Mary Hunter to George Plaxco

p. 375-376 Aug. 2, 1819 Thomas Gore (Spartanburgh) to John Fredk Harmining (same); for $41.62½ sold 11.89 ac; plat attached shows border: Harmining on two sides, Grist, and Gore; part of grant to Sampson Bobo. Witness Golding Tinsley and Willis Arnold. Signed Thomas Gore. Wit. oath Aug. 2, 1819 Golding Tinsley to M Casey. Rec. Nov. 11, 1819

p. 376-377 Feb. 4, 1812 Abner Wingo (Spartanburgh) to James Hunt (same); for $300 to be paid by Jan. 1, 1815 to James Hunt, Abner Wingo is to deed 200 ac on Holson's Br of Fairforest Cr; part of grant to David Goodlett; border: Roberson and Wm Moore (sold to Hill); Condition: payment void if deed for land made by Dec. 25, 1814. Witness Elisha Bomar and John Wingo. Signed Abner Wingo. Wit. oath Feb. 2, 1819 Elisha Bomar to A Benson. Rec. Nov. 11, 1819

p. 377-378 Oct. 16, 1818 Col. John Wilson (Spartanburgh) to Nesbett and Benson; for $195 sold 194 ac on Ashworth's Cr of Broad R; border: near Pegg's Cabbin and Camp; part of grant to Crenshaw Camp. Witness Richard Roberds and William Collins. Signed John Wilson. Wit. oath Oct. 13, 1819 Richard Roberds to W Bennett. Rec. Nov. 11, 1819

p. 378-379 May 18, 1819(?) Edward Hooker (Spartanburgh) to son Zadok Hooker (Abbeville Dist Cambridge); for love and affection give Negroes: (1) African named Dick about 45 or 50 years old, a boy Dick about 12 years old, a girl Hagar about 10 years odl and her increase, and a boy James about 7 years old, and (2) give all horses, cows, hogs, etc, all household and kitchen furniture. Witness Benjamin Hooker and Jesse Lamb. Signed Edward Hooker. Wit. oath Nov. 11, 1819 Jesse Lamb to M Casey. Rec. Nov. 15, 1819

p. 379-381 Nov. 22, 1819 (Eastern Circuit, SC) William Hasell Gibbs, Master Equity Court Southern Circuit (Charleston, SC) to Jesse Burton (Spartanburgh); for $375 sold 500 ac; grant Apr. 2, 1773 to Thomas Ferguson; border: S-William Bird, N-Richard Henderson, S-William Jamison, and E-vacant; Christopher Gadsden and "others", executors of will of Thomas Ferguson esq (late of Charleston, SC) on Sept. 7, 1791 had complaint in Charleston Equity Court against An Ferguson, the widow, and "the several" children to settle debts of estate; see "Bill" in Charleston Equity Court heard Sept. term 1797; Court decided to sell land; sale Nov. 22, 1819. Witness James Ferguson and William R Bee. Signed W Hasell Gibbes, Master in Equity. Wit. oath Nov. 23, 1819 James Ferguson to E Bomar. Rec. Nov. 23, 1819

p. 381-382 Sept. 26, 1817 James Smith to William R Smith; James gives a bond "to find" William 50 bushels of corn, 15 bushels of wheat, 15 bushels of rye, $20 of paper or silver, 20 gal of whiskey, and a comfortable house to live in to be "on the premises if possibel or within 5 miles"; all this "support" to be delivered at Smith's mill on Lawson's fork and house is to be on permanent "or buk(?) one place"; William is to deed James two tracts known as (1) the upper shoal tract and (2) borders: Lindsey; total ac not known; and William sells all his "other" property, household and kitchen furniture, farm tools, chattles, utensils, and "all other things profitable". Witness George Bullman and James Bagwell. Signed Wm R Smith and James Smith. Wit. oath Jan. 28, 1818 George Bullman to Caleb Jones. Rec. Nov. 23, 1819

p. 382 Sept. 26, 1817 William R Smith and James Smith; a bond of $2,000; Condition: bond void if James pays William $550 by Jan. 1, 1818 and William agrees to deed 940 ac known as lower mill or ironworks tract; granted to William R Smith who sold to James Smith who sold to William R Smith. Wit. oath George Bulman and James Bagwell. Signed Wm R Smith. Wit. oath Jan. 22, 1818 George Bulman to Caleb Jones. Rec. Nov. 23, 1819

p. 382-383 Oct. 13, 1805 John N Creese (Spartanburgh) to George Rowland (same); for $100 sold 50 ac on waters of S Pacolate R; border: Daniel White and George Rowland; part of grant May 5, 1794 Gov. William Moultrie to Daniel White. Witness Alexander McMillen and Elizabeth Rowland. Signed John N Creese. Wit. oath Apr. 6, 1811 Alexander McMillen to James Young. Rec. Nov. 23, 1819

p. 383-385 Aug. 23, 1816 Samuel Turner (Spartanburgh) to George Rowland (same); for $450 sold 178½ ac in three parts on N side of Lawson's fork: (1) 100 ac part of 200 ac grant Sept. 5, 1766 to Thomas Williamson; (2) 30 ac; border: E-Hugh Means, N-Darby Turner, W-Henry Childs, and S-Lawson's fork; grant Gov. William Moultrie to Henry Turner; and (3) 48½ ac; border: a waggon road and Hugh Means; part of grant to Thomas Wood. Witness Hugh Means, Jacob Sartain, and John Turner. Signed Samuel Turner. Wit. oath Aug. 23, 1816 Hugh Means to Thomas Poole. Rec. Nov. 23, 1819. Dower renounced Sept. 20, 1816 Nancy Turner to James Young

p. 385-387 Nov. 22, 1819 Sampson Sosbee (Spartanburgh) to Daniel Faust (same); for $200 sold 185 ac in two parts on waters of Peter's Cr of Pacolate R: (1) 85 ac and (2) 100 ac. Witness Thomas Poole and Enoch Bearden. Signed Sampson Sosbee. Wit. oath Nov. 25, 1819 Enoch Bearden to E Bomar. Rec. Nov. 25, 1819. Dower renounced Nov. 25, 1819 Elizabeth Sosbee to E Bomar

p. 387 Dec. 19, 1812 Joshua Richards (SC) to James Richards sr (Province of E Fla); for $1 sold a Negro boy Esaw about 15 years old. Witness Joshua Gorden, Joseph Richards, and George Wood. Signed Joshua Richards. Wit. oath Nov. 9, 1819 George Wood to J Camp. Rec. Nov. 25, 1819

p. 387-388 Feb. 1, 1819 William McAboy (Spartanburgh) to George Gipson Gilbert (same); for $120 sold 240 ac on S side of Pacolate R; border: Balaam Gilbert, Henry Hiner, and "others". Witness William Bennett and Henry Calffy Gilbert. Signed Wm McAbee. Wit. oath Apr. 6, 1819 Henry C Gilbert to Wm Reid. Rec. Dec. 6, 1819

p. 388-389 Dec. 16, 1819 Thomas Paden (Spartanburgh) to John Paden (same); for $200 sold 238 ac on branches of Furgeson's Cr of Tyger R. Witness David Morton and Thomas N Peden. Signed Thomas Peden. Wit. oath Dec. 16, 1819 Thomas N Peden to Wm Hendrix. Rec. Dec. 16, 1819

p. 389-390 Apr. 23, 1819 Thomas Harrison to Martin Harrison; for $150 sold 160 ac on Serratt's Cr of Broad R; part of where Thomas Harrison lives. Witness Thomas Harris and Balus Harris. Signed Thomas Harrison's mark. Wit. oath Apr. 23, 1819 Thomas Harris to J Camp. Rec. Dec. 6, 1819

p. 390-391 Apr. 23, 1819 Thomas Harris (Spartanburgh) to William Harris (same); for $150 sold 200 ac on waters of Sarratt's Cr; border: Roberson, Balus Harris, and North Carolina line. Witness

Balus Harris and Martin Harris. Signed Thomas Harris' mark. Wit. oath Apr. 23, 1819 Balus Harris to J Camp. Rec. Dec. 6, 1819

p. 391-394 Feb. 23, 1792 George West (Spartanburgh) to John West (same); for 60£ sterling sold 150 ac on N side of Lawson's fork; part of 300 ac belonging to George West and where George West lives; see deed Sept. 26, 1789 Christopher Long to George West (Spartanburgh Book B p. 362 (sic 361) rec. Sept. 8, 1790). Witness Charles West and John Young jr. Signed George and Ann West's marks. Wit. oath Nov. 6, 1819 (Greenville Dist) John Young to Geo W Earle. Rec. Dec. 7, 1819

p. 394-396 Nov. 25, 1818 Jesse Reams (Spartanburgh) to Benjamin Farmer (same); for $100 sold 67 ac. Witness John Ballinger, Elisha Harris, and Robert Kimbril. Signed Jesse Reams. Wit. oath Dec. 20, 1819 John Ballinger to E Bomar. Rec. Dec. 20, 1819. Dower renounced Nov. 1, 1819 Agnes Reams to E Bomar

p. 396-397 Feb. 3, 1819 William Finch (Spartanburgh) to James Keene (same); for $200 sold 107 ac on W side of Fairforest Cr; border: James Keene, Philip Otts, Thomas Cook, and Reedy Br. Witness Ralph Smith and Elial Williams. Signed William Finch's mark. Wit. oath Dec. 1, 1819 Ralph Smith to Wm Underwood. Rec. Jan. 3, 1820

p. 397-398 Aug. 9, 1811 Daniel Sims (Spartanburgh) to William Farmer (same); for $100 sold 100 ac on N side of Tyger R and both sides of Dutchman's Cr. Witness John Grist, Abner Center, and Daniel Meham. Signed Daniel Sims' mark. Wit. oath Oct. 11, 1811 John Grist to M Casey. Rec. Jan. 3, 1820

p. 398-399 May 11, 1807 Thomas Hancock (Union Dist) to Joseph Austell (Spartanburgh); for 5£ sold 200 ac on Miller's fork of Thickety Cr; border: Littlejohn, Arnold, and McBee; part of grant to Thomas Hancock. Witness Frances Littlejohn and Henry Littlejohn. Signed Thomas Hancock. Wit. oath Sept. 2, 1807 Frances Littlejohn to John Lipscomb. Rec. Jan. 4, 1820

p. 399-400 Jan. 1, 1820 Joseph Morris sr (Spartanburgh) to Jordan Morris (same); for $200 sold 150 ac on Back Br of Pacolate R; border: W-Berryman Hines, N-William Little and John Steedman, E-John Steedman, and S-Jordan Morris; part of grant in 1788 to Joseph Morris sr. Witness Joseph Morris jr and James Martin. Signed Joseph Morris sr's mark. Wit. oath Jan. 3, 1820 (Edgefield Dist) Joseph Morris jr to James Bell. Rec. Jan. 4, 1820

p. 400-401 Mar. 27, 1817 Major Gossett (Spartanburgh) to John Tollison (same); for $96 sold 64 ac on S side of Charleston Rd; border: Tollison and Kinnell. Witness James Tolleson and James Vandiver. Signed Major Gosset. Wit. oath Jan. 4, 1820 James Tolleson to F. H. Legg. Rec. Jan. 4, 1820

p. 401-402 (not dated) James McCarter (Spartanburgh) to John Tolleson (same); for $200 sold 20 ac; border: branch from Maj. John Tolleson's Quarter, James Means, Mill Cr, Bird's Br, Tolleson, and Quater Br. Witness James Tolleson and Jacob Land. Signed James McCarter. Wit. oath Dec. 29, 1819 James Tolleson to Danl White. Rec. Jan. 4, 1820

p. 402 Feb. 3, 1819 Nehemiah Norton (Spartanburgh) to John Tolleson (same); for $58.37½ sold 75 ac on Pacolate R; border: Thomas Hill and Samuel Wilkins; E side of grant to Laurence Reedy; Condition: sale void if Nehemiah pays John $58.37½ in 8 months. Witness James Tolleson and Charles McAbee. Signed Nehemiah Norton. Wit. oath Dec. 29, 1819 James Tolleson to Danl White. Rec. Jan. 4,

1820

p. 404-404 Sept. 27, 1819 Margaret Campbell, Elizabeth Campbell, Margaret Campbell (the younger), Washington Campbell, and Mary Campbell (all of Spartanburgh), Thomas Campbell (Greenville Dist), and Samuel Campbell (Rutherford Co, NC) to Thomas Cleaton (Spartanburgh); for $200 sold 200 ac on N side of Easley Cr near the fork; border: Wm D Thomas, Thomas Jackson, and Thomas Campbell; where Margaret Campbell (the older) lives; part of grant Jun. 6, 1785 to Robert Giodgion and deed is warranted against all except claims of William Campbell and Jeremiah Martin. Witness Demsey Fowler and James Whitten. Signed Thomas Campbell, Samuel Campbell, and Margaret, Elizabeth, Margaret, Washington, and Mary Campbell's marks. Wit. oath Sept. 27, 1819 Demsey Fowler to J Whitten. Rec. Jan. 4, 1820

p. 404 Dec. 8, 1819 William Rogers (Spartanburgh) to Daniel Alexander (same); for $90 sold 80 ac on W side of Ward's Cr of Tyger R; border: Otts, Moore, Ligon, and Hatchett. Witness Amos Martin and John Rogers. Signed William Rogers. Wit. oath Jan. 3, 1820 John Rogers to Robert Ligon. Rec. Jan. 4, 1820

p. 404-405 Dec. 22, 1818 Burrel Bobo to Vallentine Smith; for $135 sold 90 ac on branch of Jameis' Cr of Tyger R; border: Miles Rainwaters, J Hobby, E Stalleon, and Elisha Wells as shown on attached plat. Witness Joel Dean jr and Simson Bobo. Signed Burrel Bobo. Wit. oath Jan. 16, 1819 Simson Bobo to M Casey. Rec. Jan. 5, 1820

p. 405-406 Jan. 6, 1820 John Parker (Spartanburgh) to daughter Charity Parker; for love and affection give 2 mares: a black and a cream sorrel, a cow and calf, a bed anf furniture, and a saddle and bridle. Witness Joseph Carswell and Lunsford Bagwell. Signed John Parker's mark. Wit. oath Jan. 6, 1820 Joseph Carswell to Thos Poole. Rec. Jan. 10, 1820

p. 406-407 Oct. 19, 1819 William Campbell and Jeremiah Martin (Cook Co(sic), Tenn) to Thompson(sic) Cleaton (Spartanburgh); for $50 sold all rights to land (ac omitted) where "our" mother Margaret Campbell lives; left by desc father George Campbell to Margaret during her life and at her death to be divided amongst her children. Witness Washington Campbell and George Roberts. Signed William Campbell's mark and Jeremiah Martin. Wit. oath Oct. 27, 1819 Washington Campbell to J Whitten. Rec. Jan. 10, 1820

p. 407-408 Jul. 15, 1819 Susannah Adkinson (Spartanburgh) to John Brewton (same); to secure a note from Susannah to John for $49.75 with interest sold (ac omitted) on S side of Georgia Rd; border: N & E-John Brewton, S-Susannah Brewton, and W-D Moore; where Susannah Adkison lived and bought from Josiah Woodruff; Condition: sale void if Susannah pays debt. Witness Thomas Price and Ann Price. Signed Susannah Adkison's mark. Wit. oath Jan. 13, 1820 Thomas Price to Robert Ligon. Rec. Jan. 10, 1820

p. 408 Jan. 17, 1820 Dower renounced Rhoda Harrison to John Lipscomb for deed from James Harrison to Austin Wright. Rec. Apr. 17, 1820 (sic)

p. 408-409 Jul. 9, 1816 Thomas Barnett (Spartanburgh) to Anderson Vandike (same); for $300 sold 147 ac on N side of Lawson's fork; plat attached. Witness Josiah Blackwell and Richard Vandike. Signed Thomas Barnett. Wit. oath Sept. 17, 1819 Richard Vandike to Eph Lewis. Rec. Jan. 19, 1820

p. 409-410 Sept. 17, 1819 Anderson Vandike (Spartanburgh) to Ransom

Golightly (same); for $450 sold 147 ac on waters of Lawson's fork; border: mouth of Henry Childs' Spring Br and a waggon road. Witness Elihu Golightly and Elisha Bomar. Signed Anderson Vandike. Wit. oath Jan. 19, 1820 Elisha Bomar to W Hunt. Rec. Jan. 19, 1820

p. 410-411 Apr. 28, 1818 John Keene (Spartanburgh) to Tillman Bobo (same); for $336 sold 134 ac in Spartanburgh and Union Dists on Hacker's Cr of Tyger R; sold by Tillman Bobo to John Keene; Condition:sale void if John pays Tillman $336 by May 1, 1819 with interest. Witness Philip Weaver and Hancock Smith. Signed John Keene. Wit. oath Sept. 2, 1818 (Union Dist) Hancock Smith to Wm Rice. Rec. Jan. 6, 1820 (sic)

Book R 1820-1822

p. 1 Jan. 25, 1820 Reubin Mathis (Spartanburgh) to Anthony Foster; for $20 sold 50 ac on waters of Lawson's fork; border: N-land sold by Charles Mathis to Wm R Smith and W & S-William Bagwell; part of grant to Charles Mathis who sold to Reubin Mathis. Witness Joseph Keller and Simpson Foster. Signed Reubin Mathis' mark. Wit. oath Jan. 31, 1820 Simpson Foster to Daniel White. Rec. Feb. 1, 1820

p. 1-2 Feb. 3, 1819 William Hammett (Spartanburgh) to George Killick (same); for $1,000 sold 300 ac on waters of Fairforest Cr; border: SE-Gideon Seay desc and NW-Elias Stone; part of grant Sept. 5, 1785 Gov. William Moultrie to William Foster and now borders: John Winsor. Witness Fielding Foster and Frederick Rast. Signed Wm Hammett. Wit. oath Apr. 28, 1819 Fielding Foster to Thomas Poole. Rec. Feb. 1, 1820

p. 2-4 May 6, 1816 George Brewton (Union Dist) to John Brewton (Spartanburgh); for $600 sold 273 ac on waters of Furgerson's Cr; border: Young Scott, Josiah Woodruff, John Brewton, and Georgia Road; willed to George Brewton by his father George Brewton. Witness Joel G Brewton, Rhoda M Bragg, and Cassander Brewton. Signed George Brewton. Wit. oath Mar. 26, 1818 Joel G Brewton to Samuel Woodruff. Rec. Feb. 7, 1820. Dower renounced Oct. 23, 1819 (Union Dist) Catherine Brewton to William White

p. 4-5 Feb. 7, 1820 John Foster sr (Spartanburgh) to John Foster jr (same); for $900 sold 270 ac on Beaverdam Br of Fairforest Cr; border: NW-Reubin Daniels, NW-Henry Walden, SW-Utley, and SE-Rutland. Witness James Moss and Jesse Mason. Signed John Foster's mark. Wit. oath Feb. 7, 1820 James Moss to Thos Poole. Rec. Feb. 7, 1820

p. 5-6 Oct. 30, 1819 Joseph Austell to Lee Linder; for $960 sold 427 ac on Miller's fork of Thickety Cr. Witness Laurence Linder and Nathaniel Linder. Signed Joseph Austell. Wit. oath Nov. 9, 1819 Laurence Linder to Wm Reid. Rec. Feb. 7, 1820

p. 6 Dec. 7, 1809 John Huckaba (Spartanburgh) to Hezekiah Farmer (same); for $100 sold 88 ac on branch of Dutchman's Cr of Tyger R; part of grant Oct. 4, 1796 Gov. Arnoldus Vanderhurst to Dudly Wolton. Witness John Grist and Joseph Wofford. Signed John Huckaba's mark. Wit. oath Dec. 7, 1809 John Grist to Burrell Bobo. Rec. Feb. 7, 1820

p. 6-7 Jan. 21, 1819 Charles C Duncan (Spartanburgh), merchant to Christopher Golightly (same); for $552 sold 275 ac; border: Christopher Golightly and Jno McClure. Witness Claremont Bullington and William Golightly. Signed C C Duncan. Wit. oath Dec. 16, 1819 Claremont Bullington to E Lewis. Rec. Feb. 21, 1820

p. 7-8 Oct. 28, 1818 Reuben Seay, a blind and infirmed man, to Ephm

Lewis; an oath that David Hicks sold Reuben Seay land (ac omitted) 11 or 12 years ago and Reuben Seay gave three notes in payment: 2 notes of $33 each and the other for $34; Reuben says Mrs. Elizabeth Russel lived with David Hicks as his housekeeper and she didn't agree to leave with David unless David gave her her "right and property"; Reuben witnessed David giving Elizabeth Russel her property--a horse bridle and saddle and "the whole of cows", a bed and furniture, sheep, pots, pewter ware, and the above $34 note; David had previously moved to another "plantation" and "twas said" that David "was like to suffer for want of someone to keep house for him"; David made agreement with Elizabeth Russel to come and keep house with him and property to be brought with her "to support upon". Witness Eph Lewis JP. Signed Reuben Seay's mark. Rec. Feb. 22, 1820

p. 8 Oct. 12, 1818 Thomas Miles (Spartanburgh) to James Rainwaters; for $50 sold 25 ac on Rock Cr of Tyger R; plat attached shows border: J Rainwaters. Witness Landon Miles and Isaac Miles. Signed Thomas Miles. Wit. oath Oct. 12, 1818 Landon Miles to Burrell Bobo. Rec. Mar. 1, 1820

p. 8-9 Aug. 12, 1819 Miles Rainwater (Spartanburgh) to James Rainwater sr (same); for $200 sold 100 ac; plat attached; on Camp Br of James Creek; grant to John Hunt. Witness Jesse Casey and Valentine Smith. Signed Miles Rainwater. Wit. oath Nov. 27, 1819 Jesse Casey to M Casey. Rec. Mar. 1, 1820

p. 9-10 Jan. 10, 1820 William Harrison (Spartanburgh) to Philip Weaver and John Weaver (same); for $90 sold 15 ac on both sides of N prong of Prater's Cr; border: N-a waggon road, Weavers, George Divine, and S Prater's Cr; part of two tracts: (1) formerly owned by Benjamin Wofford and (2) by George Divine. Witness Thos M Bragg and William Relph. Signed William Harrison. Wit. oath Jan. 13, 1820 William Relph to M Casey. Rec. Mar. 3, 1820

p. 10-11 Jan. 10, 1820 Philip Weaver and John Weaver (Spartanburgh) to Thomas Slack (Rhode Island); for $3,000 sold 300 ac on E side of Tyger R; border: N-Drury Parham, E-Randolph Palmer, S-estate of Capt Reubin Sanders, and W-Tyger R; part of land formerly owned by Burrel Bobo esq. Witness William Relph and Alpheus Wilbur. Signed Philip Weaver and John Weaver. Wit. oath Jan. 13, 1820 William Relph to M Casey. Rec. Mar. 3, 1820

p. 11-12 Jan. 10, 1820 Philip Weaver and John Weaver (Spartanburgh) to Thomas Slack (same)(sic); for $500 sold 55 ac on W side of Tyger R; border: N-Benjamin Wofford, W-N fork of Prater's Cr and George Divine, S-William Harrison, E-S fork of Prater's Cr; formerly owned part by Benjamin Wofford and part by George Divine. Witness William Relph and Alpheus Wilbur. Signed Philip Weaver and John Weaver. Wit. oath Jan. 13, 1820 William Relph to M Casey. Rec. Mar. 3, 1820

p. 12-13 Jan. 10, 1820 Thomas Slack (Rhode Island) to Philip Weaver and John Weaver; for $15,000 sold (355 ac?) in two parts: (1) 300 ac on S side of Tyger R; border: N-Drury Parham, E-Randolph Palmer, S-estate of Capt Reuben Sanders, and W-Tyger R; formerly owned by Burrel Bobo esq; and (2) (ac omitted) on W side of Tyger R; border: E-Tyger R and S fork of Prater's Cr, S-William Harrison, W-George Divine and N fork Prater's Cr, and N-Benjamin Wofford; and sold all machinery and manufacturing utensils of South Carolina Cotton Manufactory--288 trostles spindles and 192 mule spindles, 6 cords, 4 drawing heads, 10 roping heads with all drums and "every kind of preperation"; Condition deed void if Thomas Slack pays Philip and John Weaver $12,000 by Jan. 1, 1825 with interest. Witness William Relph and Alpheus Wilbur. Signed Thomas Slack. Wit. oath Jan. 13, 1820 William Relph to M Casey. Rec. Mar. 3, 1820

p. 13-14 Aug. 14, 1819 John Withers (Columbia, SC) to Philip Weaver and Co, manufacturers (Spartanburgh); for $600 sold 300 ac on E side of Tyger R; border: N-Drury Parham, E-Randolph Palmer, S-estate of Capt Reubin Sanders, and W-Tyger R; part of land formerly owned by Burrel Bobo esq. Witness John G Danner and John Watson. Signed Jno Withers. Wit. oath Jan. 13, 1820 John G Danner to M Casey. Rec. Mar. 3, 1820. Dower renounced Aug. 19, 1819 (Richland Dist) Mary Withers to D. J. McCord

p. 14-15 Nov. 6, 1819 Samuel Neely (Spartanburgh) to Samuel Miller, sheriff (same); for $750 sold 116½ ac on N side of Tyger R having benefit of waters of Mill Cr. Witness Elias Palmer and William N Miller. Signed Samuel Neely. Wit. oath Nov. 15, 1819 Elias Palmer to F. H. Legg. Rec. Mar. 6, 1820. Dower renounced Nov. 15, 1819 Nancy Neely to F. H. Legg

p. 15-16 Jan. 16, 1820 John Tolleson (Spartanburgh) to Jacob Stotts (same); for $150 sold 142 ac on waters of Lawson's fork; formerly belonged to John Thomason, one of heirs of William T Thomason desc and was John's share of estate of W T Thomason; sold by writ from Spartanburgh Common Pleas Court suit Robert A Todd vs John Thomason and Claburn Hold; sold by Vincent Bennett, sheriff; Note: Jan. 6, 1820(sic) if part of land is lost "according to law", John Tolleson is to reduce price accordingly; signed James Tolleson, Levi Ward, and Wm Ward. Witness James Tolleson and Levi Ward. Signed John Tolleson. Wit. oath Mar. 6, 1820 Levi Ward to E Bomar. Rec. Mar. 6, 1820

p. 16-17 Feb. 21, 1818 John Patton (Spartanburgh) to Jacob Hedden (same); for $300 sold 197 ac. Witness Robert M White and Alston Drummond. Signed John Patton. Wit. oath Feb. 21, 1818 Alston Drummond to F. H. Legg. Rec. Mar. 6, 1820. Dower renounced Mar. 13, 1820 Jane (or Jinney) Patton to F. H. Legg

p. 17-18 Jun. 8, 1819 Joseph G Evetts (Spartanburgh) to Elemuel Powell (same); for $150 sold 100 ac on waters of Lawson's fork; border: George Bishop; part of tract sold by George McDowell and William McDowell, heirs of William McDowell desc, to John Beard (or Bard) who sold to William Bishop who sold to Joseph G Evetts. Witness Daniel White and Drury McAbee. Signed Joseph G Evetts. Wit. oath Mar. 6, 1820 Daniel White to Caleb Jones. Rec. Mar. 6, 1820

p. 18-19 Oct. 15, 1818 Andrew Rea jr (Spartanburgh) to James Foster (same); for $400 sold (1) 256 ac on Cases Cr of Packolet R; and (2) 49 ac adjoining (1); on both sides Cases Cr. Witness Robert Garrt and Wyatt E Hines. Signed Andrew Rea. Wit. oath none. Rec. Mar. 6, 1820

p. 19-20 Oct. 11, 1819 Jacob Chapman (Spartanburgh) to Josiah Blackwell (same); a bond for $300; Condition: to secure payment of $100 at Apr. court 1822, $100 at Apr. court 1823, and $100 at April court 1824 sold 273 ac on Lawson's fork and Sholah Cr; where Hugh Means esq desc lived; Josiah Blackwell is security for payment of money for the land; sale is void if Jacob Chapman pays the money; three notes for $100 each attached. Witness E Roddy and Simpson Foster. Signed Jacob Chapman's mark. Wit. oath Oct. 11, 1819 Simpson Foster to Thomas Poole. Rec. Mar. 6, 1820

p. 20-21 Jul. 31, 1819 Robert Love (Spartanburgh) to Joseph Carswell and Elisha West (same); for $150 sold 244 ac on Baverdam Cr of Fairforest Cr; border: Gravel's old line and road from Spartanburgh Court House to Nicholas' old mill on Tyger R. Witness William Trimmier and Memory N Chapman. Signed Robt Love. Wit. oath Sept. 15, 1819 Memory N Chapman to Thomas Poole. Rec. Mar. 6, 1820. Dower renounced Oct. 19, 1819 Nancy Love to E Bomar

p. 21-22 Aug. 15, 1818 Richard Thomson (Spartanburgh) to Muse Tolleson (same); for $320 sold ½ ac and 15 perches [rods] in Spartanburgh, SC; border: Muse Tolleson on S side of Main St. Witness William Hunt and William Trimmier. Signed Richard Thomson. Wit. oath Sept. 3, 1818 William Hunt to A Benson. Rec. Mar. 6, 1820. Dower renounced Feb. 7, 1820 Polly Thomson to Daniel White

p. 22-24 Sept. 27, 1819 John White (Spartanburgh) to Edward Lipscomb (same); for $500 sold 230 ac on boδh sides Willies fork of Tyger R; border: S-John Bearden and Sanford Smith, E-William Lancaster, W-widow Johnson or Thomson, and N-Charles Smith; where John White lives; grant May 3, 1813 to John White and John White jr. Witness Clary Lancaster and William Lancaster esq. Signed John White. Wit. oath Oct. 1, 1819 William Lancaster to William Underwood. Rec. Mar. 6, 1820. Dower renounced Dec. 25, 1819 Lettice White to Samuel Archibald

p. 24-25 Feb. 13, 1819 William Stone (Spartanburgh) to Samuel Green (Laurens Dist); for $600 sold 100 ac on N side of Cedar Shoal Cr; border: E-Robert Hanna, W-Whitaker, S-John Dillard, N-James Head, John Head, and Tilmon Bobo; part of two grants (1) Aug. 7, 1786 Gov. William Moultrie to William Hendrick and (2)(omitted). Witness John F Harmining and L. D. Bragg. Signed Wm Stone. Wit. oath Jan. 31, 1820 John F Harmining to Burrel Bobo. Rec. Mar. 6, 1820. Dower renounced Apr. 9, 1819 Jane Stone to Burrel Bobo

p. 25-26 May 29, 1819 William P Gadberry (Union Dist) to James Smith; to secure a bond for $3,982 by noted dated Dec. 4, 1819 sold (ac omitted) on Lawson's fork; border: Lindsey; Condition: sale void if William pays the notes. Witness John Rochell and Philip Littlefield. Signed W. P. Gadberry. Wit. oath Jan. 5, 1820 Philip Littlefield to Wm White. Rec. Mar. 10, 1820

p. 26-27 Mar. 10, 1820 James Hunt, sheriff (Spartanburgh) to Jabez Galt (same); for $311 sold 300 ac on waters of Lawson's fork; border: John Lewis, Mary Lewis, Robert Foster, John Wood, and William Turpin sr; sale due to writ from Spratanburgh Common Pleas Court on second Monday after fourth Monday in Mar. 1819 suit John Tollison jr, indorsee, and Co vs William Weatherford; levy was $73.55 from William Weatherford. Witness John T Earle and John Dickson. Signed Jas Hunt SSD. Wit. oath Mar. 10, 1820 John T Earle to E Bomar. Rec. Mar. 10, 1820

p. 27-20 Feb. 21, 1818 John Patton (Spartanburgh) to Alston Drummond (same); for $300 sold 197 ac. Witness Jacob Hedden and Robert M White. Signed John Patton. Wit. oath Feb. 21, 1818 Jacob Hedden to F. H. Legg. Rec. Mar. 13, 1820. Dower renounced Mar. 13, 1820 Jane (or Jenney) Patton to F. H. Legg

p. 29-30 Mar. 7, 1820 Elias Palmer, sole heir and esecutor of John D Palmer desc, to Muse Tolleson (Spartanburgh); for $2,500 sold 478 ac on waters of Middle Tyger R; border: Thomas Moore; sold by Muse Tolleson to John D Palmer and known as Poolesville tract. Witness John T Earle and Berryman S Holder. Signed Elias Palmer. Wit. oath Mar. 18, 1820 John T Earle to F. H. Legg. Rec. Mar. 18, 1820. Dower renounced Mar. 12, 1820 Mary M Palmer to F. H. Legg

p. 30-31 Dec. 10, 1809 John Blackwell (Spartanburgh) to Daniel Cantril (same); for $20 sold 100 ac on Little Buck Cr. Witness Nimrod Cantrell and Solomon Forest. Signed John Blackwell. Wit. oath Oct. 31, 1818 Solomon Forest to Henry Turner. Rec. Apr. 3, 1820

p. 31 Jan. 4, 1820 Matthew Patton (Spartanburgh) to Thomas Price (same); for $2,500 sold 300 ac on both sides of S Tyger R;

border: W-Broadrick Mason, W-Peter Bragg, E & S-Thomas Price, and N-Z Posey. Witness Peter Bragg and Broadrick Mason. Signed Matthew Patton. Wit. oath Feb. 15, 1820 Peter Bragg to Robert Ligon. Rec. Apr. 3, 1820

p. 31-32 Aug. 1, 1818 James Burk (Laurence Dist) to William Farrow (Spartanburgh); for $500 sold 100 ac on Cedar Shoals Cr of Enoree R; border: road from Charleston, a line made between Solomon Smith and William Hitchcock, N-Moses Casey, W-William Word, S-James Casey, and E-Cedar Shoal Cr; where Solomon Smith and John Bogan lived; grant (date blank) to Henry Hamilton. Witness Richard Farrow and Thomas Waters. Signed James Burk. Wit. oath Apr. 10, 1820 Richard Farrow to M Casey. Rec. Apr. 10, 1820. Dower renounced Aug. 1, 1818 Jane Buck and Burrel Bobo

p. 32-34 Nov. 23, 1818 Samuel Jones (Spartanburgh) to William Hendricks (same); for $270 sold 150 ac on S side of Reedy fork of Abner's Cr of Enoree R; border: Henry Wood, Benjamin Wood, Reuben Mayfield, William Hughes, and Lewis Jones. Witness James Hendricks and William Hughes. Signed Samuel Jones. Wit. oath Aug. 17, 1819 James Hendricks to Thomas Wood. Rec. Apr. 10, 1820. Dower renounced Nov. 24, 1818 Bethier Jones to Thomas Wood

p. 34-35 Nov. 29, 1819 Thomas Chesney (Spartanburgh) to Moses White; for $500 sold 173 ac; border: W-Robert Alexander, N-Moses White, S-Ahasel Beason and Hester Chesney, and William Young. Witness George Chumley and Spencer Bolton. Signed Thomas Chesney. Wit. oath Feb. 19, 1820 George Chumley to John Brewton. Rec. Apr. 10, 1820. Dower renounced Feb. 19, 1820 Caroline Chesney to John Brewton

p. 35 Nov. 18, 1819 Lawson Thomson (Spartanburgh) to Elias Corder (same); for $700 sold 300 ac on head waters of Ward's Br; border: "Currey Bounty survey"; part of two grants: (1) to Charles C Pinckney and (2) to Hopkins Bright. Witness Thomas Price and James Corder. Signed Lawson Thomson. Wit. oath Jan. 15, 1820 James Corder to John Brewton. Rec. Apr. 10, 1820

p. 35-36 Feb. 28, 1820 (Union Dist) Henry Farnandis (Union Dist) to Jesse Griffen (Spartanburgh); for $200 sold 98 ac in Union and Spartanburgh Dists. Witness Smith Lipscomb and William Littlejohn. Signed Henry Farnandis. Wit. oath Feb. 28, 1820 Smith Lipscomb to John Lipscomb. Rec. Apr. 10, 1820

p. 36-37 Feb. 19, 1819 John Golightly jr (Spartanburgh) to Ransom Golightly; for $600 sold 300 ac on both sides of Lawson's fork Cr; border: Bettey Green's Br and old mill pond; grant to Mary Wood. Witness Elihu Golightly and John Golightly sr. Signed John Golightly jr. Wit. oath Apr. 10, 1820 Elihu Golightly to Danl White. Rec. Apr. 11, 1820

p. 37-38 Apr. 10, (1820?) Armstead Shumate to James Cook; for $225 sold (ac omitted) on S Tyger R in Greenville Dist; part of survey by Alexr Ray desc and granted to Alexr Ray. Witness Margaret Hawkins and Hubert Hawkins. Signed Atd Shumate. Wit. oath Apr. 20, 1820 Hubert Hawkins to John Chapman. Rec. Apr. 11, 1820

p. 38-39 Apr. 7, 1820 (Spartanburgh and Union Dists) Leonard Sparks sr (Union Dist) to Jesse Griffin (Union Dist?); for $200 sold 75 ac; border: Headen and Bullock; part of grant to (1) Patterson Thomson and (2) Richard Joy. Witness William Littlejohn sr and Hugh Thomas. Signed Leonard Sparks' mark. Wit. oath Apr 7, 1820 William Littlejohn sr to William Reid. Rec. Apr. 11, 1820

p. 39 Mar. 19, 1819 Thomas Dare (Spartanburgh) to Fendal W Robertson and Henry Robertson, executors of will of Nathaniel Robertson desc; for $50 sold 50 ac on N side of Cherokee Cr; border: Wyatt Lipscomb, Robert Lipscomb, Nathaniel Robertson; part of tract known as Dare's Mill tract; sold by William Champion to Thomas Dare. Witness William Fondren and Wyatt Lipscomb. Signed Thomas Dare. Wit. oath Oct. 29, 1819 William Fondren to J Camp. Rec. Apr. 14, 1820

p. 39-40 Oct. 25, 1819 James Alexander (Spartanburgh) to William Mason (same); for $307 sold 63 ac. Witness William Posey and Zephaniah Posey. Signed James Alexander. Wit. oath Apr. 11, 1820 William Posey to John Brewton. Rec. Apr. 14, 1820. Dower renounced Apr. 8, 1820 Mary Alexander to John Brewton

p. 40-42 Feb. 13, 1819 Josiah Woodruff, merchant (Spartanburgh) to John Brewton (same); for $600 sold 237.6 ac on Ferguson's and James' Cr; border: Georgia Road, S-Susanna Adkeson, E-J Brewton, and N & W-Thomas Woodruff and James Leatherwood; where Josiah Woodruff formerly lived; includes Harris' old tract and land sold by John Woodruff to Josiah Woodruff. Witness James Corder and William Hendrix. Signed Josiah Woodruff. Wit. oath Feb. 13, 1819 James Corder to Wm Hendrix. Rec. Apr. 14, 1820. Dower renounced Mar. 22, 1820 Margaret Woodruff to Thomas Poole

p. 42 Nov. 11, 1817 William F Gist (Union Dist) to Richard Scruggs (Spartanburgh); for $10 sold 25 ac; border: "the" Battleground, Scruggs, Haney, Earle, and Williams; includes land sold by Daniel McClarin to Wilson Nesbitt. Witness Muse Tolleson and Jas Hunt. Signed Wm F Gist. Wit. oath Apr. 6, 1819 Muse Tolleson to George Camp. Rec. Apr. 14, 1820

p. 42-43 Feb. 16, 1820 John Leatherwood (Spartanburgh) to Miles Leatherwood (same); for $400 sold 99½ ac on branches of James' Cr of Tyger R; border: Paul Castleberry. Witness James Leonard and John Arnold. Signed John Leatherwood. Wit. oath Apr. 11, 1820 James Leonard to John Brewton. Rec. Apr. 14, 1820

p. 43-44 Nov. 17, 1816 (Newberry Dist) Edward Gore (Newberry Dist) to Charles H Miller (Spartanburgh); for $125 sold 120 ac on N side of S Tyger R; border: all vacant; grant to Edward Gore. Witness Thornton McDaniel and James Blackburn. Signed Edward Gore. Wit. oath May 17, 1817 Thornton McDaniel to F. H. Legg. Rec. Apr. 14, 1820

p. 44-45 Nov. 25, 1819 Archibald McCravy (Spartanburgh) to William Waddle; for $213.50 sold 61 ac on both sides Provies Cr. Witness John M Delany and John H Owens. Signed Archibald McCravy. Wit. oath Mar. 16, 1820 John M Delany to David Moon. Rec. Apr. 14, 1820

p. 45-47 Jan. 28 (or 21), 1819 Sarah Abbett, widow, Solomon Abbett, (both Spartanburgh), Drury Abbett, Matthew Abbett, John Abbett, William Abbett, James Knox, James Williamson, and William Cobb (all Pendleton Dist), widow and heirs of William Abbett desc (SC) to Jesse Scruggs (Spartanburgh); for $333.75 sold 267 ac on both sides Island Cr of Pacolet R; border: W-Young, N-Cantril, E-Knox and Morrow, and S-Potter; part of 455 ac grant Sept. 5, 1803 to William Abbett. Witness Henry Turner, Sibby Turner, John S Puttut, William Knox jr, and James Cantril. Signed Sarah Abbett's mark, Solomon Abbett's mark, Drury Abbett's mark, Matthew Abbett, John Abbett's mark, William Abbett, James Knox, James Williamson's mark, and William Cobb. Wit. oath (Pendleton Dist) Jan. 29, 1819 William Knox (for Sarah, John, and William Abbett, James Williamson and William Cob) to W Nicholson. Wit. oath Apr. 6, 1819 Sibby Turner (for Solomon Abbett and Solomon Abbett's signing for Drury

Abbett as his agent) to George Camp. Wit. oath Mar. 30, 1820 Isaac Young (for Matthew Abbett) to George Camp. Rec. Apr. 14, 1820

p. 47-48 May 18, 1818 Mary Taylor to George Divine; for $60 sold 12 ac on S side of Tyger R; plat attached shows border: Mary Taylor, Humphry Yarbrough, William Harrison, and Philip Wiam; grant Jul. 6, 1801 to Thomas Tod. Witness John Divine and William Harrison. Signed Mary Taylor's mark. Wit. oath Apr. 14, 1820 John Divine to W Hunt. Rec. Apr. 15, 1820

p. 48 Mar. 15, 1815 Thomas Tod to Mary Taylor; for $8.25 sold 12 ac on S side of Tyger R; plat attached shows border: Edmund Bearden, James Simple, Philip Mulkin, and Thos Tod; part of grant Jul. 6, 1801 to Thomas Tod. Witness George Divine and John Taylor. Signed Thos Tod. Wit. oath Apr. 29, 1818 George Divine to Burrell Bobo. Rec. Apr. 15 1820

p. 48-49 Dec. 14, 1819 Bartholomew Grogan sr (Spartanburgh) to Bartholomew Grogan jr (same); for $500 sold 100 ac on S side of S Pacolet R; border: Thomas Earle and William Holcomb; part of land of John Gowen desc; includes where Bartholomew Grogan sr lives. Witness Thomas Grogan and Willey S Brown. Signed Bartholomew Grogan's mark. Wit. oath Apr. 29, 1820 Thomas Grogan to J Whitten. Rec. May 1, 1820

p. 49-50 Apr. 11, 1820 Hamilton Wilson (Spartanburgh) to Zachariah McDaniel (same); for $5 sold ½ ac on Fairforest Cr; border: John Martin's old mill tract; part of grant to Giles Tillett who sold to John Thomas who sold to John Buffington and mortgaged to South Carolina Loan Office and sold for Loan Office's benefit by Spartanburgh Dist sheriff to Alexr McKie who sold to Hamilton Wilson. Witness David Golightly and R Golightly. Signed Hamilton Wilson. Wit. oath Apr. 11, 1820 David Golightly to James Crooke. Rec. May 4, 1820

p. 50-51 Mar. 4, 1820 (Madison Co, Ala) William Arnold, Samuel Allen, James Arnold, and Richard Shackleford (Madison Co, Ala) to Jonathan Crook (Spartanburgh); power of attorney to settle with William L Allen who is endebted to grantors due to 80 ac John Arnold "bid off" at sheriff's sale; 80 ac is on waters of James' Cr; border: John Arnold; Jonathan Crook can deed land for grantors, as "legatees" to the land and William Arnold gives Jonathan Crook power of attorney to get all money etc due to him. Witness Ezekiah Eastland, Ger Shackelford, and Wm Cook. Signed Richd Shackelford, James Arnold, Saml A Arnold, and William Arnold. Wit. oath Mar. 6, 1820 (Madison Co, Ala) W Arnold to Isaac Willbourn JP. Rec. May 4, 1820. Apr. 8, 1820 Thomas Brandon, clerk of Madison Co Court, certifys Isaac Willbourn is Justice of Peace

p. 51-52 Apr. 8, 1819 John W Farrow (Union Dist) to John Morrow (Spartanburgh); for $42 sold 42 1/3 ac in two parts: (1) 37 ac and (2) 5 1/3 ac on Dutchman's Cr; border: John Morrow and William Smith; part of 300 ac grant to Pierce Butler. Witness Sandford Smith, Isaac Smith, and H. A. Johnson. Signed J. W. Farrow, attorney for Julius Tavill. Wit. oath Apr. 6, 1819 Sandford Smith to Saml Archibald. Rec. May 5, 1820

p. 52-53 Dec. 16, 1817 Samuel Morrow (Spartanburgh) to John Morrow (same); for $560 sold (ac omitted) on Popular Br of Dutchman's Cr; granted in 1789 Gov. Charles Pinckney to Samuel Morrow sr and sold Jan. 5, 1811 by William Smith and George Brewton, executors of will of Samuel Morrow sr desc, to Samuel Morrow. Witness David Morrow and Robert Morrow. Signed Saml Morrow. Wit. oath Oct. 26, 1818 David Morrow to James Hamm. Rec. May 5, 1820

p. 53-54 Aug. 25, 1819 James Young (Spartanburgh) to Isaac Young (same); for $50 sold 50 ac; part of tract on E side of Island Cr of Pacolet R; border: Beaverpond field, James Land, the old path that crosses at Headen's ford. Witness George Bone and Randolph Cash. Signed James Young's mark. Wit. oath Aug. 25, 1819 George Bone to Henry Turner. Rec. May 8, 1820. Dower renounced Aug. 25, 1819 Cely Young to Henry Turner

p. 54-56 May 2, 1820 James Hunt, sheriff (Spartanburgh) to Josiah Blackwell; for $22 sold 50 ac on waters of Lawson's fork; border: Ransom Golightly, Josiah Blackwell, and George Lewis desc; sale due to drit from Spartanburgh Common Pleas Court on second Monday after fourth Monday in Mar. 1819; suit Muse Tolleson vs Robert Langford; levy from Robert Langford $45.77. Witness John T Earle and Memory N Chapman. Signed Jas Hunt SSD. Wit. oath May 2, 1820 Memory N Chapman to W Hunt. Rec. May 13, 1820

p. 56-57 Dec. 30, 1819 Robert Creswell (Laurens Dist) to John Wingo (Spartanburgh); for $300 sold 348 ac; plat attached shows border: Robert Creswell, John Wingo, and on Camping Br; part of 1,085 ac recovered by John Drayton from John Wingo and sold by Spartanburgh Dist sherif (as property of John Drayton) to Robert Creswell; except land recovered by John Wingo in "action" commenced by John Drayton "to try titles" to a "certain tract of land" and a small piece included in a North Carolina grant now claimed by John Dodd esq. Witness Richard Thomson and Coleman Wingo. Signed Robert Creswell. Wit. oath Mar. 6, 1820 Coleman Wingo to John Chapman. Rec. May 17, 1820

p. 57-58 Jan. 27, 1819 Jinny Milakin (Roane Co, Tenn) to Pleasant Brandon (same); power of attorney to sell land Jinny Milakin was left by her father William Milakin desc. Witness Thomas Blake and Thomas McMullin JP (Roane Co, Tenn). Signed Jinny Milikin's mark. Feb. 4, 1819 (Roane Co, Tenn) Henry Breazeale, clerk of Court of Pleas and Quarterly sessions, by John Purris, deputy clerk, certifies Thomas Blake and Thomas McMullin were Justices of Peace. Feb. 4, 1819 Samuel Eskridge, "Chairman" of Court of Pleas and Quarterly Sessions, certifies Henry Breazeale is clerk. Rec. May 18, 1820

p. 58-59 Jan. 6, 1820 Pleasant Brandon (Roane Co, Tenn) to Joseph Jackson (Spartanburgh); for $234 sold 60 ac that belongs to Jane Milakin and "drawn" by Robert Milakin as lot #3 "out of #1". Witness James Jackson and Samuel Kelso. Signed Pleasant Brandon's mark. Wit. oath May 17, 1820 Samuel Kelso to Wm Kelso. Rec. May 18, 1820

p. 59-60 Jan. 18, 1820 Fielding Foster (Spartanburgh) to Philip Keller (same); for $500 sold 133 ac; border: William Foster. Witness James Moss and George Killock. Signed F Foster. Wit. oath May 25, 1820 James Moss to Thomas Poole. Rec. May 25, 1820

p. 60-61 Apr. 25, 1820 Ransom Golightly (Spartanburgh) to James Brannon (same); for $500 sold 147 ac on Lawson's fork of Pacolet R; border: Henry Childs' Spring Br and a waggon road. Witness John T Earle and John Wilbanks. Signed R Golightly. Wit. oath May 1, 1820 John T Earle to W Hunt. Rec. May 25, 1820

p. 61-62 May 13, 1820 James Hunt, sheriff (Spartanburgh) to Manly Ford; for $500 sold 300 ac on Pidgeon Roost Br and head of Williams Cr of S Tyger R; part of 1,000 ac grant to Baylis Earle who sold to John McElrath; in Spartanburgh Common Pleas Court second Monday after fourth Monday in Mar. 1818 William Ford and others petitioned the court to divide real estate of William Ford desc; a writ to divide was issued by James Vernon,David Dantzler, Page

Rork, Isham Hendrick, and Thomas Dean esq; on second Monday after fourth Monday in Oct. 1818 they decided land couldn't be divided and should be sold; land was sold on first Monday in Jan. 1819. Witness Jesse Cleveland and Ransom Foster. Signed Jas Hunt SSD. Wit. oath May 13, 1820 Ransom Foster to Thomas Poole. Rec. May 25, 1820

p. 62-63 Mar. 11, 1820 Edmon Chapman to Maj John Tolleson; to secure a bond of $400 sold a sorrel horse, bridle and saddle, 6 cattle marked with cross and slit in each ear, 11 sheep 11 hogs marked as above, a shot gun, 2 feather beds and bedsteads and furniture, 3 bee stands, a hand saw, a box and cutting knife, all farming utensils, a walnut cupboard and furniture, a copper still, 9 stands singling and doubling casks, 200 weight of bacon, 3 whiskey barrels, 2 "blade stacks", 20 barrels of corn, all household and kitchen furniture, and a cart; Condition: sale void if Edmon Chapman pays debt. Witness James Tolleson and A Lancaster. Signed Edmon Chapman. Wit. oath Apr. 3, 1820 James Tolleson to W Hunt. Rec. May 25, 1820

p. 63-64 Dec. 28, 1818 Wineford and Levy Demsey (Spartanburgh) to George Hotzclaw (SC); for $240 sold 160 ac on branch of Abner's Cr of Enoree R; border: Philip Tippins, William Hendrake, Isham Wilson, and Levy Demsey; part of grant to Charles Wakefield. Witness William Hughes and Philip Tippens. Signed Wineford Demsey's mark and Levy Dempsey. Wit. oath Jul. 17, 1819 Philip Tippens to Thomas Wood. Rec. Jun. 5, 1820

p. 64-65 Oct. 27, 1818 James Cudd (Spartanburgh) to John Stedman (same); for $50 sold 50 ac on waters of Buck Cr. Witness William Little and James Robins. Signed James Cudd's mark. Wit. oath Oct. 31, 1818 William Little to Henry Turner. Rec. Jun. 5, 1820

p. 65 Jan. 29, 1817 John Coventon to John Stedman; for $150 sold 50 ac on N side of "main" Buck Cr; border: James Robus (or Robins) and Johnson. Witness William McKinney and Jordan Morris. Signed John Coventon's mark. Wit. oath Mar. 13, 1819 Jordan Morris to Henry Turner. Rec. Jun. 6, 1820

p. 65-66 Oct. 5, 1819 Ezekiel Johnson (Spartanburgh) to John Stedman (same); for $89 sold 65 ac; border: James Cudd, Little, Johnson, Robins, and Wofford; grant States Office to James Harwood. Witness L Berry Hines and James Robins. Signed Ezekiel Johnson's mark. Wit. oath May 13, 1820 James Robins to W Bennett. Rec. Jun. 5, 1820

p. 66-67 May 30, 1820 Joseph Carswell and Elisha West (Spartanburgh) to Thomas M Bragg (Union Dist); for $600 sold 244 ac on Beaverdam Cr of Fairforest Cr; border: Gravel's old line and a road from Spartanburgh Court House to Nichold's old mill on Tyger. Witness Muse Tolleson and Elias Palmer. Signed Joseph Carswell and E West. Wit. oath Elias Palmer to W Hunt Jun. 5, 1820. Rec. Jun. 5, 1820

p. 67-68 Aug. 15, 1816 Joel Foster (Union Dist) to James King (Spartanburgh); for $100 sold 250 ac on waters of Tyger R; plat attached shows border: Benj Wofford, Wm Saxton, Jacob Casey, and Benj Hooten. Witness Leviston Bobo and Shadrack Waldrip. Signed Joel Foster. Wit. oath Oct. 11, 1817 Leviston Bobo to Burrell Bobo. Rec. Jun. 7, 1820

p. 68-69 Sept. 5, 1818 James Clark (Lincoln Co, NC) to James Wood (Spartanburgh); for $300 sold 320 ac on both sides S Pacolet R; border: "the" lake, Dempsey Fowler, and Ferguson; part of 850 ac grant Jul. 7, 1800 to John Gowen; includes where Richd Venable lived. Witness Thomas Alexander and William Ramsey. Signed James Clark. Wit. oath May 16, 1820 William Ramsey to J Whitten. Rec. Jun. 10, 1820

p. 69-70 Dec. 14, 1819 William George (Spartanburgh) to Hugh Moore; to secure payment of $28.21 sold 50 ac; border: S-E Jackson, SE & E-Collins and Lands, N-Sullivant, and W-Wright; Condition: sale void if William George pays debt. Witness John Graham and James Smith. Signed William George. Wit. oath Jun. 7, 1820 John Grimes (sic) to Caleb Jones. Rec. Jun. 12, 1820

p. 70-71 Oct. 9, 1819 James Hunt, sheriff (Spartanburgh) to William Hunt esq (same); for $10 sold 279 ac on Shoaly Cr of Lawson's fork; border: S-Jacob Chapman, W-Justin Chiles and Darby Turner, N-Reuben Faucett, and E-Owens; sale due to writ from Spartanburgh Common Pleas Court on second Monday after fourth Monday in Oct. 1818; suit of Labon P Poole vs John Spears; judgment was levy from John Spears $50 with interest and costs. Witness Simpson Foster and Saml C Hunt. Signed Jas Hunt SSD. Wit. oath Oct. 9, 1819 Simpson Foster to Thomas Poole. Rec. Jun. 27, 1820

p. 71-73 Apr. 22, 1820 John Martin (Spartanburgh) to John Murph (same); for $3,012 sold 456 ac on Fairforest Cr; ½ ac excepted claimed by Zechariah McDaniel and sold to him by H Wilson; border: J Murph and James Finch; resurveyed Nov. 13, 1819; plat attached shows also on White's Br. Witness Zechariah McDaniel and Samuel Noblit. Signed John Martin. Wit. oath May 19, 1820 Zechariah McDaniel to Danl White. Rec. Jul. 3, 1820. Dower renounced May 19, 1820 Margaret (or Paggy) Martin to Daniel White

p. 73-75 May 16, 1820 John Murph (Spartanburgh) to John Oeland (Charleston, SC), merchant; for $3,012 sold 456 ac on Fairforest Cr; ½ ac excepted claimed by Zechariah McDaniel and sold to him by Hamilton Wilson; border: James Finch. Witness Zechariah McDaniel and James Hutchins. Signed John Murph. Wit. oath May 19, 1820 Zechariah McDaniel to Danl White. Rec. Jul. 3, 1820. Dower renounced Jun. 22, 1820 Mary Murph to Daniel White

p. 75-76 Mar. 6, 1820 John W Farrow (Union Dist) to Thomas Farrow (Spartanburgh); Thomas Farrow was sued and judgment obtained against him in U S District Court for $7,000 due to his securityship for John W Farrow as paymaster of late 18th Regt U S Infantry; so John W Farrow sold (1) 100 ac granted to John Hendrix; (2) 100 ac part of 250 ac grant to George Louther see deeds executed Oct. 8, 1808 by Thomas Farrow to John W Farrow; and sold the following: a Negro boy Ben about 20 years old, a Negro girl Patt about 8 years old, a bay horse or gelding 9 years old, 3 feather beds and their furniture--4 pair of sheets, 3 "bolsters", 5 pillows and their cases, a pair of rose blankets, a coverled, 2 bed quilts, 2 shite needle worked counterpanes, 2 checked counterpanes, a stand of bed surtains, 2 bed steads, a cott and matrass, a mahogany dining table, a small pine table, a "slab" with its furniture--2 Decanters, a dozen tumblers, a tea pot and a coffee pot, pepper box and salt cellar, 3 sets of earthen plates, half dozen knives and forks, 2 sets of cups and saucers, a dozen tea spoons, half dozen tablespoons, all kitchen furniture--3 pots, an oven, a frying pay, a water pail, 2 piggins, a washing tub, a man's saddle and bridle, a woman's saddle, a cow and calf, a shot gun, a pair of fire dogs, 4 trunks, a yellow and white spotted heifer 3 years old, a yearling calf, half dozen blue painted chairs, 4 red painted chairs, a paper case, a large looking glass, a waiter, a brass candlestick, a case of horseman's pistols, "all my library", a silver patent "lever" watch, and all John W Farrow's property; "words George to 1788 stricken and John Hendrix underlined before signed"; no condition on sale. Witness E Williamson and Sarah Williamson. Signed J. W. Farrow. Wit. oath May 22, 1820 (Newberry Dist) E Williamson to Jno B ONeall. Rec. Jul. 3, 1820

p. 76-77 Jun. 9, 1818 John McCarter, Amey McCarter (alias Evans), Joseph Brown, and Daniel Robertson (all of Spartanburgh), heirs of Alexander McCarter "(alias Evans) a minor" who died Jun. 26, 1815, to John M Collins (Spartanburgh); for $500 sold 200 ac known as Mc Elhaney tract on both sides of Middle Tyger R; border: James Reynolds and Edward Smith; part of grant to John Kur who sold to Lemuel Loftis who sold to Alexander McCarter. Witness James Hendricks and James Whitten esq. Signed John and Amey McCarter's marks, Joseph Brown's mark, and Daniel Robertson. Wit. oath Jul. 3, 1820 James Whitten to E Bomar. Rec. Jul. 3, 1820

p. 77-78 Jun. 20, 1807 James Sanders Guignard (Columbia, SC) to Edward Ballinger (Spartanburgh); for 5s sold 103 ac on branch on N side and S fork of Lawson's fork of Pacolet R; border: E-Miller, NE-William Brannon, NW-Elisabeth Lewis, W-Joel Lewis, and S-Ballinger, Wadsworth and Turpin; resurveyed Feb. 8, 1793 "for Edward Ballinger" and granted Feb. 6, 1804 to J. S. Guignard. Witness Jacob J Faust and Isaac T Cushing. Signed James S Guignard. Wit. oath (Richland Dist) Jacob J Faust to John Hooker, municipal warden of Columbia. Rec. Jul. 3, 1820

p. 78-79 Mar. 5, 1819 Jesse Wheeler (Spartanburgh) to John M Collins (same); for $300 sold (1) 69 ac; border: Jesse Wheeler and John M Collins; part of tract sold by Mary Makin to Jesse Wheeler; and (2) 13½ ac; border: tract (1). Witness John Burris, Henry Smith, and James Whitten. Signed Jesse Wheeler. Wit. oath Jul. 3, 1820 James Whitten to E Bomar. Rec. Jul. 3, 1820

p. 79-81 Jan. 4, 1819 Isaac Crow (Spartanburgh) to George Hill, Leonard Hill, and Shelden Clark & Co (same); for $1,210 sold 125 ac on S side of Tyger R; border: Jeremiah Wofford, J Leatherwood, and William Young. Witness Saml Smith and James Leonard. Signed Isaac Crow. Wit. oath Jan. 4, 1819 James Leonard to M Casey. Rec. Jul. 3, 1820. Dower renounced Apr. 3, 1820 Eliza Crow to Burrell Bobo

p. 81-82 May 12, 1819 Isaac Crow (Spartanburgh) to George Hill, Leonard Hill, and Shelden Clark (same); for $200 sold 13 ac on N side of Tyger R; below old Iron works. Witness John Ervin and Joseph Barnett. Signed Isaac Crow. Wit. oath May 12, 1819 John Ervin to Samuel Woodruff. Rec. Jul. 3, 1820. Dower renounced Apr. 3, 1820 Elese (or Liza) Crow to Burrell Bobo

p. 82-83 May 12, 1819 Joseph Wofford (Spartanburgh) to George Hill, Leonard Hill, and Shelden Clark (same); for $20 sold rights and title to islands and shoals in Tyger R--six islands of 5 ac total; border: near where lower Irons works was; see deed Feb. 4, 1793 from South Carolina Government to Joseph Wofford and plat Jan. 23, 1793. Witness John Ervin and Isaac Crow. Signed Joseph Wofford. Wit. oath May 12, 1819 John Ervin to Samuel Woodruff. Rec. Jul. 3, 1820. Dower renounced Jun. 16, 1820 Martha Wofford to John Brewton

p. 83-85 Apr. 13, 1820 Joseph Wofford (Spartanburgh) to George Hill, Leonard Hill, and Shelden Clark (same); for $525 sold 136 ac which is all the land Joseph Wofford gave his son-in-law John Mullenix except ½ ac where burying yard is reserved for intering the ded on S side of Tyger R; border: Carrol, Jeremiah Wofford, and Crow. Witness John Mullennix and William Walker. Signed Joseph Wofford. Wit. oath Jun. 16, 1820 William Walker to John Brewton. Rec. Jul. 3, 1820. Dower renounced Jun. 16, 1820 Martha Wofford to John Brewton.

p. 85-86 Apr. 4, 1820 John and James Davis (Spartanburgh) to James Cathcart; for $180 sold 104½ ac on N side of Cane Cr of Tyger R; border: Saml Cathcart, D Parham, John Oshield, and John Red. Witness James Newman and Asa Calicot. Signed John Davis and James Davis. Wit. oath Apr. 4, 1820 Asa Calicot to Burrell Bobo. Rec. Jul. 15, 1820. Dower renounced Apr. 4, 1820 Rebecca Davis, wife of James, and Sarah Davis, wife of John, to Burrell Bobo

p. 86-87 (not dated) Elijah Gossett (Spartanburgh) to Stephen Tolleson; for $85 sold 40 ac on waters of Fairforest Cr; border: Stephen Tolleson and Abraham Gossett. Witness James Tolleson and Jacob Land. Signed Elijah Gossett's mark. Wit. oath Apr. 7, 1820 James Tolleson to William Reid. Rec. Jul. 15, 1820

p. 87-88 Nov. 26, 1818 James Wyatt (Spartanburgh) to Charles Simmons (Rutherford Co, NC); for $500 sold (1) 128 ac on Peter's Cr of Packolet R; grant to William Wofford; and (2) 80 ac on Armour's Br of Peter's Cr and Vincent Wyatt's Spring Br; border: (1) above. Witness Wm Trimmier and Thomas Poole. Signed James Wyatt's mark. Wit. oath Jun. 19, 1820 Thomas Poole to W Hunt. Rec. Jul. 20, 1820

p. 88-89 Jun. 28, 1820 Samuel Cathcart (Spartanburgh) to son James Cathcart (same); for love and affection give 80 ac on Cane Cr; border: SW-Asa Calicot, NW-land Blassingame sold to James Cathcart, NE-Davis, S-land given to John Cathcart. Witness Asa Calicot, John Hindman, and John Ward. Signed Sam Cathcart. Wit. oath Jul. 8, 1820 John Hindman to James Hamm. Rec. Jul. 24, 1820

p. 89 Jun. 28, 1820 Samuel Cathcart to son James Cathcart; for love and affection give all my goods, chattles, debts, bonds, notes, and money. Witness Asa Calicot, John Hindman, and John Ward. Signed Samuel Cathcart. Wit. oath Jul. 8, 1820 Asa Calicot to James Hamm. Rec. Jul. 24, 1820

p. 89-90 Mar. 3, 1810 (or 1008 and 10) Daniel McClaren (Bedford Co, Tenn) to Arthur Clark and Samuel S Ross; for $1,000 sold 408 ac on waters of Sarratt's Cr of Broad R; border: North Carolina state line, William Bonner, Walker, William Holloway, Davison, and Thomas Clary. Witness William Sadler, Jacob Gage, John Allison, and William Collins. Signed Daniel McClaren. Wit. oath Feb. 6, 1818 John Allison to J Camp. Rec. Jul. 31, 1820

p. 90-92 Feb. 28, 1810 Daniel McClaren (Bedford Co, Tenn) to Samuel S Ross and Arthur Clark (both of Rutherford Co, NC); for $2,000 sold 604 ac on waters of Sarratt's Cr of Broad R; border: forge pond, Brown, and Arnold. Witness William Sadler, Jacob Gage, John Allison, and William Collins. Signed Daniel McClaren. Wit. oath Feb. 6, 1818 John Allison to J Camp. Rec. Jul. 31, 1820

p. 92-93 Apr. 17, 1816 Arthur Clarke (Spartanburgh) to Samuel S Ross (Rutherford Co, NC); for $600 sold half of 604 ac on Sarratt's Cr of Broad R; border: forge pond, Brown, Arnold, Ellis, and Clary. Witness Gen. John Carson and Col. William Porter. Signed Arthur Clarke. Wit. oath May 27, 1820 (Rutherford Co, NC) John Carson to Jas W Carson. Rec. Jul. 31, 1820. Jun. 15, 1820 (Rutherford Co, NC) Isaac Craton, clerk of Rutherford Co Court, certifys Jas W Carson is justice of peace

p. 93-94 Apr. 17, 1816 Arthur Clarke (Spartanburgh) to Samuel S Ross; for $200 sold 200 ac on waters of Sarratt's Cr of Broad R; border: North Carolina state line, William Bonner, Walker, William Holloway, Davison, and Thomas Clary; half of 400 ac tract. Witness Gen. John Carson and Col. William Porter. Signed Arthur Clarke. Wit. oath May 27, 1820 (Rutherford Co, NC) John Carson to Jas W Carson. Rec. Jul. 31, 1820. Jun. 15, 1820 (Rutherford Co, NC)

Isaac Craton, clerk of Rutherford Co Court, certifys Jas W Carson is justice of peace

p. 94-95 Apr. 5, 1820 Isaac Wofford (Spartanburgh) to Starling Willis (same); for $575 sold 147½ ac on Furgerson's Cr of Tyger R; border: Edwards. Witness Patrick Hoy and Nathaniel Wofford. Signed Isaac Wofford. Wit. oath Jun. 15, 1820 Patrick Hoy to John Brewton. Rec. Aug. 4, 1820

p. 95-96 Jun. 28, 1820 Samuel Cathcart (Spartanburgh) to son John Cathcart (same); for love and affection give 70 ac on Cane Cr; border: E & S-John Red and N-James Cathcart. Witness Asa Calicot, John Hindman, and John Ward. Signed Sam Cathcart. Wit. oath Jul. 8, 1820 Asa Calicot to James Hamm. Rec. Aug. 9, 1820

p. 96-97 Dec. 28, 1816 William Morris (Spartanburgh) to Edmund Cooley (same); for $280 sold 237 ac on Pacolet R; where William Morris lives; border: Gibson Oliver, Thomas Barton, and John Jordan (of Edgefield Dist); part of grant to (1) Thomas Barton and (2) to William Morris. Witness William Bennett and Samuel Wall. Signed William Morris. Wit. oath Apr. 19, 1817 William Bennett to James Young. Rec. Aug. 10, 1820. Dower renounced Mar. 22, 1817 Sarah Morris to James Young

p. 97-98 Aug. 15, 1817 James Wilson to James Vernon; for $1,300 sold a Negro woman Nancy, a Negro woman Thuray (daughter of Nancy), and her child Bob. Witness John Montgomery and Alexr McMakin. Signed James Wilson's mark. Wit. oath Aug. 12, 1820 John Montgomery to John T Rowland. Rec. Aug. 14, 1820

p. 98-99 Mar. 19, 1820 Alexander Copeland (Spartanburgh) to Charles Copeland (same); for $300 sold (ac omitted); half of land sold by James Gilmore to Alexander and Charles Copeland. Witness William Copeland and William H Chapman jr. Signed Alexander Copeland. Wit. oath Aug. 14, 1820 William Copeland to James Young. Rec. Aug. 16, 1820

p. 99-102 Feb. 10, 1798 Arnoldus Vanderhorst and Thomas Waring sr, executors of will of John Vanderhorst esq desc (late of Charleston, SC), to Andrew Boding (Richland Co, Camden Dist); for 446£ 7s 9p sterling sold (1) 640 ac on 18 Mile Cr; grant Feb. 6, 1786 to John Vanderhorst; (2) 200 ac on N of Saluda R of Broad R; border: SW-Christopher Sea and unknown; survey Jun. 9, 1785 for James Henny and granted May 1, 1786 to John Vanderhorst; (3) 579 ac on Rocky Cr; grant Nov. 7, 1785 to John Vanderhorst; (4) 363 ac on W side of Saluda R; border: NW-land newly marked and vacant; grant Oct. 15, 1784 to Simeon Theus; (5) 640 ac on Big Beaverdam Cr; border: SW-John Selles, SE-Thomas Lewis, Martin, and unknown, and vacant; survey Jan. 5, 1785 for George Warley and granted Feb. 6, 1786 to John Vanderhorst; (6) 500 ac on Enoree R; survey Jan. 9, 1775 on warrant dated Dec. 8, 1774 and granted Oct. 15, 1784 to Daniel Huger esq; (7) 500 ac on waters of Enoree R; survey Jan. 4, 1775 on warrant dated Dec. 8, 1774 and granted Oct. 15, 1784 to Daniel Huger esq; (8) 640 ac on W fork of 18 Mile Cr of Savannah R; border: NE-Robert Lusk, SW-John Frierson, SE-granted land, and vacant; grant Aug. 1, 1785 to John Jackson; (9) 529 ac in Camden Dist survey Nov. 2, 1784 for Thomas Stokes and granted Aug. 1, 1785 to Samuel Stedman; (10) 200 ac on Durban's Cr of Enoree R; border: SE-John Wallis and Isaac Gray, SW-Isaac Gray, NE-old survey and Daniel Welch, NW-Daniel Welch, and W-vacant; survey in Jan. 1775 for Daniel Huger and granted Oct. 15, 1784 to (omitted) and sold Jan. 13 and 14, 1785 to John Vanderhorst; and (11) 125 ac in Camden Dist on Broad R; late Joseph Robertson's land; border: W-Broad R and others vacant; sold by Commissioners of Forfieted Estates to John Vanderhorst Nov. 1 & 2, 1786. Witness Elias Horry, Benjamin

Bonncaw Simons, George Mathews, and Daniel Smith esq. Signed A Vanderhorst esq and Tho Waring sr esq. Wit. oath Jun. 11, 1798 B. B. Simons to Stephen Ravenel JQ. Wit. oath Jun. 19, 1798 Daniel Smith esq to Stephen Ravenel JQ. Rec. Sept. 4, 1820

p. 102 Oct. 28, 1818 Francis McClure, widow (Spartanburgh) to Thomas Gore (same); for $81 sold 20 ac on ridge between Enoree and Tyger Rivers; border: NW & NE-James Whiteker. Witness John F Harmening and Wm Dossey. Signed Francis McClure's mark. Wit. oath Sept. 1, 1820 John F Harmening to Burrel Bobo. Rec. Sept. 4, 1820

p. 102-104 Sept. 13, 1816 Nathan Smith (Spartanburgh) to Francis McClure (same); for $20 sold 20 ac on ridge between Enoree and Tyger Rivers; border: NW & NE-James Whitaker. Witness Edward Lynch and Robert Olephant. Signed Nathan Smith. Wit. oath Sept. 1, 1820 Robert Olephant to M Casey. Rec. Sept. 4, 1820. Dower renounced Oct. 2, 1816 Margaret Smith to J. F. Grimke

p. 104-105 Sept. 21, 1816 Abram Cantrell (Spartanburgh) to William Bennett (same); for $500 sold a Negro woman Polley between 20 and 30 and her increase; agreeable with the will of Isaac Cantrell desc and all Abram Cantrell's rights to mother Mary Cantrell's property (when she died)--a Negro, horse, beasts, cow and cow beast, hogs, sheep etc, beds and bed furniture, and all household and kitchen furniture and all his part of crops. Witness Iredell Cunningham and Alfred Cunningham. Signed Abram Cantrell. Wit. oath Oct. 1, 1816 Alfred Cunningham to James Young. Rec. Sept. 4, 1820

p. 105-106 Feb. 22, 1815 Elizabeth Knight, administrator of estate of Samuel Knight desc, James Knight, James Lewis, Samuel Knight, and John F Knight (Spartanburgh) to Robert McDowell (same); for $170 sold 170 ac on branches of Lawson's fork of Pacolet R; border: "Great Road", Wm Foster, unknown, David McDowell, and Miriry Br. Witness Peter Hawkins, Samuel Turner, and James Camron. Signed Elizabeth and James Knight's marks, J Lewis, Saml Knight, and John F Knight. Wit. oath Sept. 4, 1820 Samuel Turner to W Bennett. Rec. Sept. 4, 1820

p. 106-107 Aug. 12, 1818 Thomas M Bragg and Zebulin D Bragg (Spartanburgh) to Toliver Scott (same); for $150 sold (ac omitted) in fork of S Tyger R; border: W-Tyger R and other sides-Toliver Scott. Witness Chany Bobo and Burrell Bobo. Signed T M Bragg and Zebulin D Bragg. Wit. oath Aug. 12, 1818 Chany Bobo to Burrell Bobo. Rec. (omitted). Dower renounced Aug. 12, 1818 Rosannah Bragg, wife of Zebulon, to Burrell Bobo

p. 107-108 Feb. 1, 1820 James Corder (Spartanburgh) to Toliver Scott (same); for $183 sold 61 ac in forks of S Tyger R and on Miry Br; border: Jonathan Crow, Nathl Gentry, Capt. John Wright, and Toliver Scott. Witness Ford Mason and John Wright. Signed James Corder. Wit. oath May 27, 1820 John Wright to Robert Ligon. Rec. Sept. 4, 1820

p. 108-109 Feb. 15, 1820 Robert Rakestraw (Spartanburgh) to John Murph (same); for $101.31¼ sold a bay horse, 13 cattle, 20 hogs, all household and kitchen furniture, and plantation tools; Condition: sale void if Robert pays John $101.31¼ by Jan. 1, 1821 with interest or by Jun. 1, 1821. Witness Augustin Shands and Zaccheriah McDaniel. Signed Robert Rakestraw. Wit. oath Sept. 4, 1820 Zaccheriah McDaniel to James Crook. Rec. Sept. 4, 1820

p. 109 Nov. (blank), 1818 William Arrendell (Spartanburgh) to James Cooper (same); for $51 sold 51½ ac on waters of Thickety Cr; border: Charles Hester, branch of Beaverdam Cr, Matthew Cooper, and Cowpen Road. Witness Thomas Cole and Matthew Cooper. Signed William and Mary Arrendell's marks. Wit. oath Mar. 31, 1820 Matthew Cooper to J Camp. Rec. Sept. 4, 1820

p. 109-110 Jul. 30, 1817 Obadiah Cole to James Cooper; for $207 sold 207 ac on Beaverdam Cr; border: Gaffney and Thomas Cole. Witness Thomas Cole and Matthew Cooper. Signed Obadiah Cole and Mary Nichols Cole. Wit. oath Mar. 31, 1820 Matthew Cooper to J Camp. Rec. Sept. 4, 1820

p. 110-111 Sept. 2, 1820 Jonathan Crook (Spartanburgh) to Caleb Allen (same); for $160 sold 85 ac on James' Cr of Tyger R. Witness William Jones, SM, Joel G Brewton, and Thomas Woodruff. Signed Jonathan Crook. Wit. oath Sept. 4, 1820 Joel G Brewton to John Brewton. Rec. Sept. 4, 1820

p. 111 Aug. 1, 1820 William Ramsey (Spartanburgh) to Robert Smith (same); for $100 sold 500 ac on head branches of Obey's Cr of N Pacolate R; border: S-Whilleger, S(sic)-William Ramsey, and W-Bomar and Eli Bullington; part of grant to William Ramsey. Witness Wm Bush and Uriah Bush (or Rich). Signed Wm Ramsey. Wit. oath Sept. 4, 1820 Wm Rich to Thomas Poole. Rec. Sept. 4, 1820

p. 111-112 Aug. 18, 1820 Rowland Johnson (Spartanburgh) to James Ballinger (same); for $450 sold 100 ac on N Tyger R; border: Roddy and J Ballinger; part of grant Apr. 10, 1767 to John Willin (or Williu). Witness Wm Ballinger, Wm Weatherford, and William Weatherford (sic). Signed Rowland Johnson. Wit. oath William Weatherford to John Montgomery. Rec. Sept. 4, 1820

p. 112-114 Jul. 8, 1820 Jesse Reams (Spartanburgh) to Martin Ball; for $549 sold 366 ac on both sides of N fork of N Tyger R; border: Edward Reams; where James Higgins lives. Witness John Cantrell and Robert Kimbrel. Signed Jesse Reams. Wit. oath Jul. 29, 1820 John Cantrell to J Whitten. Rec. Sept. 4, 1820. Dower renounced Aug. 14, 1820 (Greenville Dist) Agnes Reams to Robert Nelson

p. 114-115 Apr. 12, 1816 Elizabeth M Ligon and Elizabeth L Hutcheson (Charleston Dist) to Absalem Lancaster (Spartanburgh); for $80 paid to their attorney, Robert Creswell, sold 80 ac on Kelso's Cr of Fairforest Cr; border: James Cooper, Richard Thomson, and Wm R Smith; survey for David Maul and granted to Peter Leger and willed to Elizabeth M Ligon and Elizabeth L Hutcheson. Witness James W Cooper and Richard Thomson. Signed Elizabeth M Leger and Elizabeth L Hutcheson by Robert Creswell attorney. Wit. oath Apr. 12, 1816 James W Cooper to Danl White. Rec. Sept. 4, 1820

p. 115 Jan. 8, 1808 John Harris (Pendleton Dist) to John Blackwell (Spartanburgh); for $50 sold 100 (ac?) on Little Buck Cr. Witness George Pertle and Abraham Nelson. Signed John Harris. Wit. oath Jan. 2, 1809 Abraham Nelson to Henry Turner. Rec. Sept. 4, 1820

p. 115-116 Sept. 6, 1819 Dower renounced Susannah Mathis to Daniel White for deed from Jesse Mathis to William Willis. Rec. Sept. 4, 1820

p. 116-117 Aug. 1, 1820 Anthony Foster (Spartanburgh) to James Duncan, son of Alexander (Union Dist); for $200 sold 50 ac on Lawson's fork; border: N-land sold by Charles Mathis to William R Smith and W & S-William Bagwell; part of grant to Charles Mathis who sold to Reuben Mathis who sold to Anthony Foster. Witness James Hunt and Simpson Foster. Signed A Foster. Wit. oath Aug. 1, 1820 Simpson Foster to Thos Poole. Rec. Sept. 21, 1820. Dower renounced Sept. 21, 1820 Elizabeth Foster to E Bomar

p. 117-118 Feb. 14, 1820 Keziah Kilgore and Henry Brockman, executors of will of James Kilgore desc (Greenville Dist) to Stephen Sizemore (Spartanburgh); for $140 sold (1) 90 ac on waters of Maple Swamp Cr; border: grant to Jonathan Nisbet (now owned by Margaret Ford), Manly Ford, Baylis Earle, James Ford, and Samuel Burne; and (2) 116 ac; border: Earle and James Ford. Witness William Wilson and Joel D Brockman. Signed Henry Brockman, Andrew McCrary (sic), and Keziah Kilgore's mark. Wit. oath Sept. 16, 1820 Joel D Brockman to Thomas Wood. Rec. Sept. 22, 1820

p. 118-119 Feb. 14, 1820 Keziah Kilgore, Henry Brockman, and Andrew McCrary, executors of will of James Kilgore desc (Greenville Dist) to Stephen Sizemore; for $85 sold 130 ac on waters of Maple Swamp Cr; border: Benjamin Wood, McDowell, Manly Ford, and Lucretia Demsey. Witness William Wilson and Joel D Brockman. Signed Henry Brockman, Andrew McCrary, and Keziah Kilgore's mark. Wit. oath Sept. 16, 1820 Joel D Brockman to Thomas Wood. Rec. Sept. 22, 1820

p. 119-120 Jan. 3, 1818 Henry Brockman, Andrew McCrary, and Keziah Kilgore, executor of will of James Kilgore desc (Greenville Dist) to Ephraim Sizemore (Spartanburgh); for $104 sold 104 ac on branch of Maple Swamp Cr on S side of S Tyger R; border: Burnes, Bright, and Page Rork. Witness James Kilgore and James Hammett. Signed Andrew McCrary, Henry Brockman, and Keziah Kilgore's mark. Wit. oath Sept. 16, 1820 James Hammett to Thomas Wood. Rec. Sept. 22, 1820

p. 120-121 Jun. 19, 1820 Samuel Burns (Spartanburgh) to James Burns (same); for $200 sold 61 ac on S side of S Tyger R. Witness Page Rork and James Staggs. Signed Samuel Burns' mark. Wit. oath Sept. 22, 1820 Page Rork to E Bomar. Rec. Sept. 22, 1820

p. 121-122 May 10, 1796 Thomas Foster (Spartanburgh) to Robert Wood (same); for 35£ sterling sold 193 ac on Cub Br of Tyger R; border: N-Robert Wood, S-Robertson, E-unknown, and John Foster and Isham Foster; part of 387 ac grant Jun. 5, 1786 Gov. William Moultrie to Thomas Crowder. Witness Ism Foster and John Foster. Signed Thomas Foster. Wit. oath May 10, 1796 Thomas Foster to Ism Foster. Rec. Sept. 23, 1820

p. 122-123 Jul. (blank), 1790 Thomas Crowder and wife Mary (Spartanburgh) "shoe waters" to Robert Wood (same); for 45£ sterling sold 200 ac on both sides of branch of Hannon's Br; border: John Foster and N-Thomas B Wyatt (now Robert Wood's land); where Thomas Crowder lives; part of grant Jan. 5, 1786 Gov. William Moultrie to Thomas Crowder. Witness David Goodlett, James (or Thomas) Adkerson, and Thomas Foster. Signed Thomas Crowder and Mary's mark. Certified Sept. 17, 1790 by D Goodlett. Rec. Sept. 23, 1820

p. 123-125 Feb. 27, 1820 Thomas Jackson sr to Capt. William Jackson jr; for $1 sold 600 ac (or 787 ac) on N side of S Pacolate R and both sides of Mick's Cr; border: Robert Henderson, William Bishop, Gilbert, Sterling Ingrim, Richard Venable, James Alexander, and John McMillen; grant May 7, 1774 to Jno Brody (resurveyed as 787 ac by Gabriel Benson esq) who sold to David Baty who sold to Thomas Tod who sold Oct. 6, 1791 to Edward Hooker who sold Oct. 15, 1791 to James McClure. Witness Samuel Jackson, James Jackson, and Moses White. Signed Thomas Jackson. Wit. oath Sept. 23, 1820 Moses White to Wm Kelso. Rec. Sept. 25, 1820

p. 125 Jul. 1, 1820 Thomas Gilbert (Spartanburgh) to Edmond Cooley (same); for $300 sold 248 ac on Barton's Cr of Pacolate R; border: NE-Harvy, E-Jilson Oliver, S-Lewis Barnett, W-Richard Thomson, and N-Jno Mathis. Witness Luke Burnett, George G Gilbert, and Moses

Brooks. Signed Thomas Gilbert's mark. Wit. oath Sept. 5, 1820 Luke Burnett to W Bennett. Rec. Oct. 2, 1820

p. 125-127 Dec. 14, 1818 John Morris (Spartanburgh) to John Cooper (same); for $450 sold 310 ac on N side of Pacolate R and on Buck Cr; border: Richard Morris, John Cantrell, Abraham Cantrell, Mark Forrest, widow Crocker, and Hugh Warren's old line. Witness Jesse Burk and John Parks. Signed John Moris. Wit. oath Dec. 19, 1818 Jesse Burk to Henry Turner. Rec. Oct. 2, 1820

p. 127-128 Dec. 19, 1818 John Cantrell (Spartanburgh) to John Cooper (same); for $400 sold 100 ac on Buck Cr; border: John Cooper, Richard Morris, Abraham Cantrell's Spring Br. Witness Richard Morris and Seth Lewis. Signed John Cantrell. Wit. oath Dec. 19, 1818 Richard Morris to Henry Turner. Rec. Oct. 2, 1820. Dower renounced Dec. 30, 1818 Elizabeth Cantrell to Henry Turner

p. 128-129 Oct. 20, 1819 David Fowler (Spartanburgh) to Lemuel Johnson (same); for $250 sold 145 ac on Ben's Cr of Tyger R; border: John Johnson, Thomas L Beachune, Lodwick Johnson, and Jonas Leonard. Witness James Leonard, S. L. Westmoreland, and John Johnson. Signed David Fowler's mark. Wit. oath Nov. 19, 1819 John Johnson to F. H. Legg. Rec. Oct. 2, 1820

p. 129-130 Sept. 9, 1820 John F Harmining (Spartanburgh) to Joseph Carswell (same); for $1,750 sold 196 ac; known as Cross Anchor; plat attached Jan. 29, 1820 by Joel Davis DS and Joseph Carswell and Gideon Shands, chain carriers, shows 196½ac and that land is part of grant Aug. 19, 1776 to Joseph Kershaw. Witness John T Earle and Daniel White. Signed John F Harmining. Wit. oath Sept. 9, 1820 John T Earle to M Casey. Rec. Oct. 2, 1820. Dower renounced Sept. 13, 1820 Martha Harmining to Burrell Bobo

p. 130-131 Sept. 1, 1820 Thomas Gore (Spartanburgh) to Joseph Carswell (same); for $85 sold 20 ac on ridge between Enoree and Tyger Rivers; border: James Whittier. Wit. oath Wm H Miles and Moses Casey. Signed Thomas Gore. Wit. oath Sept. 1, 1820 Wm H Miles to M Casey. Rec. Oct. 2, 1820. Dower renounced Sept. 30, 1820 Elizabeth Gore to Burrell Bobo

p. 131-133 Jul. 21, 1820 John Wilkins (Spartanburgh) to Robert Wilkins (same); for $276.76 sold 76.6 ac on N side of Goucher Cr of Thickety Cr; border: David Lipscomb.
John Lipscomb sr (Spartanburgh) to Robert Wilkins (same); for $12.98 sold 3.6 ac; border: Robert Wilkins and "below the creek". Witness Polly Wilkins and Joseph Camp. Signed John Wilkins and John Lipscomb sr. Wit. oath Jul. 21, 1820 Joseph Camp to John Lipscomb. Rec. Oct. 2, 1820. Dower renounced Oct. 7, 1820 Elizabeth Wilkins, wife of William desc, and Polly Wilkins, wife of John, to John Lipscomb

p. 133-134 Apr. 7, 1820 Clemuel Powell (Spartanburgh) to Zachariah McDaniel (same); Zachariah is security for $50 note payable to James Fleming due Dec. 25, 1820; to secure Zachariah, Clemuel mortgages 100 ac on waters of Lawson's fork of Pacolate R; border: George Bishop; part of tract sold by George and William McDowell, heirs of Wm McDowell desc, to John Beard who sold to William Bishop who sold to Joseph G Evatt who sold to Clemuel Powell. Witness Eliza Ann Herman and Thomas Posey. Signed Clemuel Powell's mark. Wit. oath Oct. (blank), 1820 Thomas Posey to Saml Archibald. Rec. Oct. 10, 1820

p. 134-135 Sept. 5, 1820 Alexander McKie (Spartanburgh) to John White (same); for $493 sold 246 ac on Fairforest and Kelso's Creeks; border: Obadiah Wingo's bridge, Willis Hays, rich hill, and Andrew Foster; part of grant to Zachariah Bullock and part of grant to Giles Tillet. Witness Robert Rakestraw and James Harrison. Signed Alexr McKie. Wit. oath Oct. 10, 1820 Robert Rakestraw to Wm Underwood. Rec. Oct. 10, 1820

p. 135-136 Sept. 26, 1820 James Leonard (Spartanburgh) to John Willis (same); for $450 sold 280 in three tracts on Sholy Cr of Lawson's fork of Pacolate R; (1) part of 476 ac sold by Edward L Bishop to James Leonard; (2) not described; (3) part of tract sold by Blake Massingale to James Leonard; border: Blake Massingale. Witness Richard Willis and Josiah Blackwell. Signed James Leonard's mark. Wit. oath Oct. 10, 1820 Josiah Blackwell to E Bomar. Rec. Oct. 10, 1820. Dower renounced Oct. 10, 1820 Tabitha Leonard to E Bomar

p. 136-137 Mar. 12, 1819 Iredell Cunningham (Spartanburgh) to John Clark (same); for $70 sold 10 ac on N side of W fork of Richland Cr of S Pacolate R; border: John Clark's old line and John Young; part of grant to Samuel Spencer. Witness Zacheriah Wall and Oney Wall. Signed Iredell Cunningham. Wit. oath Apr. 7, 1819 Zacheriah Wall to W Bennett. Rec. Oct. 10, 1820

p. 137-138 Jul. 5, 1820 Smith Lipscomb (Spartanburgh) to heirs of David Lipscomb desc (same); for $200 sold 300 ac; part of 400 ac on Blue Br of Thickety Cr; land was allotted to David Lipscomb desc from estate of William Lipscomb desc; grant in May 1774 to Daniel Burckmeyer. Witness William Lipscomb and Smith Lipscomb jr. Signed Smith Lipscomb. Wit. oath Jul. 5, 1820 William Lipscomb to John Lipscomb. Rec. Oct. 11, 1820

p. 138 Jul. 27, 1820 James Brown (Spartanburgh) to Thomas Brown (same); for $20 sold 12 ac; border: Thomas Brown and Stone. Witness Joseph Harmon and Jesse Hutchens. Signed James Brown. Wit. oath Oct. 10, 1820 Jesse Hutchens to William Reid. Rec. Oct. 12, 1820

p. 138-140 Sept. 6, 1820 Samuel Archibald, attorney for Mary Mays widow and heirs of Andrew Mays desc, (Spartanburgh) to William Lancaster (same); for $1,000 sold (1) sold 122 ac; border: James Beardin; (2) 231 ac; border: James Bearden, William Lancaster, Lipscomb, Sparling Thornton, and Thornton's Br; (1) and (2) are parts of grant Jan. 6, 1794 to Gen. Thomas Brandon who sold to Andrew Mays desc; on waters of Wiley's fork of Tyger R and waters of Fair-forest Cr. Witness Nancy Archibald and J. P. Means. Signed Saml Archibald, attorney. Wit. oath Oct. 10, 1820 J. P. Means to Wm Underwood. Rec. Oct. 12, 1820

p. 140 Oct. 10, 1820 Thomas Burton to daughter Mary McVay, wife of Clabron McVay (Giles Co, Tenn) and to grandchildren (children of Mary McVay); for paternal love give a Negro girl Sary 12 years old and her increase supposed to be worth $500; Sary is to "attend" to Mary during her lifetime and at her death to her children; Clabron can't dispose of the Negro. Witness Joseph Davis and Isaac S Whitten. Signed Thomas Burton's mark. Wit. oath Oct. 19, 1820 Joseph Davis to J Whitten. Rec. Oct. 19, 1820

p. 140-141 Feb. 8, 1794 Ellis Cannon and wife Alsebeth (Spartanburgh) to John Hammett (same); for 10£ sold 25 ac (or 75 ac) on Pacolet R; border: branch of Peter's Cr; grant Dec. 28, 1787 Gov. Thomas Pinckney to Ellis Cannon. Witness Mayson Cannon and Sarah Hammett. Signed Ellis Cannon. Wit. oath Mar. 26, 1805 Mayson Cannon to Dl White. Rec. Oct. 23, 1820

p. 141-142 Dec. 30, 1809 Samuel Sparks and wife Rachel (Spartanburgh) to John Hammett (same); for $200 sold 250 ac on waters of Pacolet R; grant to John Hammett sr. Witness Bartholomew Stovall, Nehemiah Norton, and Benjamin Hammett. Signed Samuel and Rachel

Sparks' marks. Wit. oath Nov. 6, 1810 Bartholomew Stovall to Henry Turner. Nov. 6, 1810. Rec. Oct. 23, 1820

p. 142-144 Oct. 10, 1820 David Quarles and wife Anna (Spartanburgh) to John Hammett (same); for $90 sold 65 ac on waters of Pacolet R; border: where John Low formerly lived and John Harris; part of survey by John Hammett sr. Witness Mayson Cannon and Levi Rainwaters. Signed David Quarles. Wit. oath (omitted) 12, 1808 (sic) Mayson Cannon to J. H. Jones. Rec. Oct. 23, 1820

p. 144-145 Jul. 21, 1807 Elisha Lindsey (Spartanburgh) to John Hammett (same); for $20 sold 20 ac on both sides Harriken Cr of Pacolet R; includes the shoals; border: William Brock and Jesse Matthews. Witness Zachariah Hammett and James Cannon. Signed Elisha Lindsey. Wit. oath Feb. 2, 1818 Zachariah Hammett to Danl White. Rec. Oct. 23, 1820

p. 145-146 Nov. 2, 1820 Josiah Belcher (Spartanburgh) to two daughters Louiza Belcher and Caroline Belcher; for love and affection give all "my personal property"--horses, cattle, hogs, plantation tools, household and kitchen furniture; property reserved to Josiah until the girls "arrive at the legal age". Witness William Trimmier and Jacob Belcher. Signed Josiah Blecher's mark. Wit. oath Nov. 2, 1820 Jacob Belcher to E Bomar. Rec. Nov. 2, 1820

p. 146-147 Nov. 18, 1815 Saul Camp (Rutherford Co, NC) to Abraham McMiun; for $100 sold 150 ac on Turner's fork of Thickety Cr of Broad R; border: Price, Mrs. Woods, and Guttre. Witness Jesse Reynolds, Thomas Harrison, and William Holloway. Signed Saul Camp. Wit. oath Mar. 19, 1819 William Holloway to J Camp. Rec. Nov. 2, 1820

p. 147-148 Jan. 4, 1808 Joseph Austill (Spartanburgh) to Moses Guyton (same); for 10£ sold 171 ac; border: Harris' Cr, Francis Littlejohn, and Bostick; grant to Joseph Austill. Witness William M Darwin, William Bostick, and John Amos. Signed Joseph Austill. Wit. oath Sept. 18, 1817 William Bostick to Caleb Jones. Rec. Nov. 4, 1820

p. 148-149 May 18, 1819 Edward Hooker (Spartanburgh) to son Zadoc (or Zadock) Hooker (Abbeville Dist); for love and affection give 250 ac between Enoree and Tyger Rivers; border: N-Kern, E-Benjamin Hooker, W & S-Austin Newman, and W-Richard Fryer; Condition: Zadoc to pay $100 annually for support of Edward during Edward's lifetime and land returns to Edward if Zadoc dies first with no heirs. Witness Benjamin Hooker and Jesse Lamb. Signed Edward Hooker. Wit. oath Nov. 11, 1819 Jesse Lamb to M Casey. Rec. Nov. 6, 1820

p. 149-150 Jan. 20, 1816 William Wilder (Spartanburgh) to Landon Miles (same); for $25 sold 29 ac on waters of Tyger R; plat attached shows border: J. D. Neburgh desc and Jas Agee (or Ogee). Witness Thomas M Bragg and William H Miles. Signed William Wilder. Wit. oath May 14, 1818 William H Miles to Burrell Bobo. Rec. Nov. 6, 1820. Dower renounced Dec. 27, 1818 Susannah Wilder to Burrel Bobo

p. 150-151 Apr. 3, 1807 Thomas M Bragg and Zebulon D Bragg (Spartanburgh), heirs of Zebulon Bragg desc, to Landon Miles (same); for $300 sold 100 ac on branches of Rock Cr of Tyger R; NE part of 300 ac grant Mar. 2, 1769 to Joseph Pack who sold to Thomas Miles who sold Oct. 25, 1794 to Zebulon Bragg (100 ac). Witness William H Miles and Isaac Edwards. Signed Thomas Bragg and Zebulon D Bragg. Wit. oath May 14, 1818 William H Miles to Burrel Bobo. Rec. Nov. 6, 1820

p. 151-152 Jul. 27, 1809 Thomas Miles (Spartanburgh) to son Landon Miles; for love and affection and to have Landon as a neighbor give 100 ac; border: Zebulon Bragg; part of grant to Joseph Pack who sold to Philomon Waters who sold to Thomas Miles; Condition: Landon can't sell the land during Thomas' lifetime. Witness Isaac Miles and Mary Miles. Signed Thomas Miles. Wit. oath Jul. 27, 1809 Isaac Miles to Burrel Bobo. Rec. Nov. 6, 1820

p. 152-153 Jul. 11, 1820 Lawson Thompson (Spartanburgh) to Capt. Matthias Rush (same); for $1,500 sold 400 ac on N Tyger R. Witness John Eskridge and George Meadows. Signed Lawson Thompson. Wit. oath Oct. 14, 1820 George Meadows to Robert Legon. Rec. Nov. 8, 1820

p. 153-154 Mar. 18, 1816 James White (Spartanburgh) to Branch J League (same); for $600 sold 300 ac on N side of Lawson's fork; border: S-widow Brannon and N-Alexander Austin. Witness William Walker and Edward Ballinger. Signed James White's mark. Wit. oath Nov. 8, 1820 William Walker to John S Rowland. Rec. Nov. 8, 1820

p. 154-155 Feb. 25, 1820 John B Hodgens (Spartanburgh) to Joshua Conner (Greenville Dist); for $60 sold 82 ac on both sides of Long Br of Maple Swamp Cr of S Tyger R; border: Nathan Farmer, James Robertson, John B Hodgens, Jesse Foster, and the Greenville line. Witness Philip A Lester and Walker Morgan. Signed John B Hodgens. Wit. oath Oct. 31, 1820 Philip A Lester to Thomas Ferguson. Rec. Nov. 9, 1820

p. 155-156 Sept. 29, 1820 Miles Rainwaters (Spartanburgh) to James Rainwaters sr (same); for $200 sold 100 ac on branch of James' Cr of Tyger R; border: Abner Wells, Leviston Bobo, land James Rainwaters bought from Miles Rainwaters, and Camp Br; part of 200 ac grant to John Hunt. Witness James Mason and John Thornton. Signed Miles Rainwaters. Wit. oath Sept. 29, 1820 James Mason to John Brewton. Rec. Nov. 10, 1820

p. 156-158 Nov. 10, 1820 James Hunt, sheriff (Spartanburgh) to Thomas Woodruff III (same); for $805 sold 1,000 ac on branch of Enoree R; border: NE & NW-Danl McKie and Amos Pilgrim, SE & SW-Woodruff and Burel Parris (or Barel Pane), Moore, Morgan, and Darnold(?); sale due to writ from Richland Dist fourth Monday of Mar. 1820 due to suit Eli Kenerly vs Zacariah Philips, administrator of A Bodden desc; levy was $913.72 and costs from Zacariah Philips. Witness John M Collins and Caleb Allen. Signed John Hunt SSD. Wit. oath Nov. 10, 1820 Caleb Allen to E Bomar. Rec. Nov. 10, 1820

p. 158-159 Sept. 2, 1817 Joseph Woodruff (Spartanburgh) to James Hendrix (same); for $100 sold 58 ac on E side of Lick Cr; border: William Hendrix. Witness John Dean and Thomas Woodruff III. Signed Joseph Woodruff's mark. Wit. oath Mar. 26, 1818 Thomas Woodruff III to William Hendrix. Rec. Nov. 10, 1820

p. 159 Oct. 2, 1820 Maj. John Tollison (Spartanburgh) to Ephraim Jackson (same); for $50 sold 50 ac on waters of Thickety Cr; border: Joseph Collins, Thomas Waters, and Ephraim Jackson. Witness James Tollison and Edmond Chapman. Signed John Tollison. Wit. oath Oct. 2, 1820 James Tollison to W Hunt. Rec. Nov. 16, 1820

p. 159-161 Nov. 25, 1816 John Brown (Spartanburgh) to John N Crease; for $650 sold (1) 120 ac on head waters of Thickety Cr of Broad R; border: James Dunaway, John Turner, a ford, Gilbert, and John Bess; and (2) 80 ac adjoining (1). Witness William Collins and Thomson Whitaker. Signed John Brown. Wit. oath Dec. 3, 1816 William Collins to Joseph Camp. Rec. Nov. 18, 1816

p. 161-162 Feb. 1, 1820 John Low sr (Spartanburgh) to Jacob Crocker (same); for $22 sold 286 ac; border: Deen's old corner. Witness Reuben Warren and Arthur Warren. Signed John Low sr. Wit. oath Feb. 1, 1820 Reuben Warren to Henry Turner. Rec. Nov. 18, 1820

p. 162-163 Nov. 24, 1820 John Tollison (Spartanburgh) to James T McCarter (same); for $200 sold 4 ac. Witness James Tollison and Daniel Faust jr. Signed John Tollison. Wit. oath Nov. 24, 1820 James Tollison to W Hunt. Rec. Nov. 24, 1820

p. 163-164 Jun. 30, 1820 William Turpin (Charleston, SC) to Presley Ballinger (Spartanburgh); for $700 sold 442 ac on S fork of Lawson's fork of Pacolet R; border when surveyed: NE-David Lewis, SE-Rowland Johnson, and SW-Joseph Rees and Bartlet Yancy; grant Dec. 11, 1786 to Wadsworth and Turpin; survey Oct. 13, 1786 by William Benson and Thomas Wadsworth sold his half to William Turpin; if land is less than 442 ac, no money is returned. Witness Joseph T Weyman and Jacob Barton. Signed William Turpin. Wit. oath Jun. 13, 1820 (sic) (New York) William Turpin esq to Jacob Barton, commissioner. Rec. Dec. 4, 1820

p. 164-165 Oct. 25, 1814 William Belk (Spartanburgh) to Benjamin Pope (same); for $40 sold 50 ac. Witness Nathaniel Floyd. Signed William Belk's mark. Wit. oath Dec. 9, 1820 Nathaniel Floyd to Wm Kelso. Rec. Dec. 4, 1820

p. 165-166 Sept. 18, 1820 Jesse Tate (Union Dist) to Michael Gaffney; for $1,120 sold 247 ac on Cherokee Cr and Broad R in Union and Spartanburgh Dists; border: Gaffney and Lick; grant to "Alexander Martin esq Rockingham Co, NC". Witness Charles Petty and Henry Johnson. Signed Jesse Tate. Wit. oath Sept. 18, 1820 Charles Petty to J Camp. Rec. Dec. 4, 1820

p. 166-167 Sept. 18, 1820 Isham Arendill (Franklin Co, Ala) to Jesse Tate (Union Dist); for $500 sold 248 ac on Cherokee Cr of Broad R; border: Little Cherokee Cr and Lipscomb. Witness Charles Petty and Henry Johnson. Signed Isham Arendill by Bridges Arendill attorney. Wit. oath Sept. 18, 1820 Henry Johnson to J Camp. Rec. Dec. 4, 1820

p. 167-168 Oct. 19, 1820 John White (Spartanburgh) to Robert Rakestraw (same); for $200 sold 100 ac on Fairforest Cr; border: Willis Hayes' old place, Wingo's bridge, and Andrew Foster; part of grant to Zachariah Bullock who sold to John Thomas who sold to Joseph Buffington and mortgaged to South Carolina Loan office and sold by General Assembly act to Alexander McKie who sold to John White. Witness Jesse Daniel and Hiram White. Signed John White. Wit. oath Oct. 30, 1820 Hiram White to Danl White. Rec. Jan. 1, 1821. Dower renounced Oct. 30, 1820 Agatha White to Daniel White

p. 168-169 Sept. 28, 1820 Henry Smith (Spartanburgh) to James Crook esq; for $200 sold 70 ac on branches on S side of Tyger R; border: Augusta road. Witness W. W. Hasten and Robert Scott. Signed Henry Smith. Wit. oath Oct. 9, 1820 W. W. Hasten to Wm Hendrix. Rec. Jan. 1, 1821

p. 169-170 Apr. 3, 1820 Jesse Rakestraw (Spartanburgh) to John Rakestraw (same); for $200 sold 50 ac on S side of Fairforest Cr; border: old mountain line, ridge path, Samuel Giddings, William Rakestraw, and John Smith. Witness Elisha James and Thomas Bell. Signed Jesse Rakestraw. Wit. oath Aug. 9, 1820 Elisha James to Danl White. Rec. Dec. 4, 1820

p. 170-171 May 25, 1820 John M Collins (Spartanburgh) to Edward

Smith (same); for $59 sold 13 ac on S side of Middle Tyger R; border: Calwell, John Carr, and Collins; part of 200 ac grant to John Carr. Witness Alex M Thompson, John Baily, and Perry Smith. Signed John M Collins. Wit. oath Sept. 9, 1820 Perry Smith to John Montgomery. Rec. Dec. 5, 1820

p. 171-172 Dec. 5, 1820 Henry White (Spartanburgh) to James Brannon (same); for $1,500 sold ½ ac in Spartanburgh, SC; border: Henry H Thompson and public land. Witness William Trimmier and William Hunt. Signed Henry White. Wit. oath Dec. 5, 1820 William Trimmier to W Hunt. Rec. Dec. 5, 1820

p. 172-174 Jan. 23, 1819 Thomas Wilson to Alpheus Wilber; for $187.50 sold 62½ ac on branch of Tyger R; border: wagon road, W-E Wells, S-J. F. Curus, and E-Edward Hooker and Benjamin Hooker. Witness Stephen Wilson and Moses Casey. Signed Thomas Wilson. Wit. oath Oct. 24, 1820 Stephen Wilson to Burrel Bobo. Rec. Jan. 1, 1821. Dower renounced Feb. 20, 1819 Jane Wilson to Burrel Bobo

p. 174-175 Sept. 22, 1819 Hannah Gray (Spartanburgh) to John James (same); for $98 sold 14 ac on Wilson Mill Cr of N Tyger R; border: Hannah Gray's Spring Br and John James. Witness Calvin Foster, Ann H Gray, and David Foster. Signed Hannah Gray. Wit. oath Dec. 23, 1820 Calvin Foster to James Young. Rec. Jan. 1, 1821

p. 175-176 Mar. 24, 1819 Daniel Beacham (Spartanburgh) to John Johnson (same); for $450 sold 107 ac on N side of Ben's Cr of Tyger R; part of estate of William Beacham desc and allotted to Elizabeth Ann Foster who sold to Daniel Beacham. Witness Lodwick W Johnson and John Johnson. Signed Daniel Beacham. Wit. oath Nov. 19, 1819 Lodwick W Johnson to F. H. Legg. Rec. Jan. 1, 1821. Dower renounced Nov. 19, 1819 Alia Beacham to F. H. Legg

p. 176-177 Nov. 16, 1818 Richard Thomson (Spartanburgh) to Thomas Poole (same); for $350 sold ½ ac on S side of Main St; lot #22 at Spartanburgh Court House; border: James Hunt and Jesse Cleveland. Witness William Poole and William Bagwell. Signed Richard Thomson. Wit. oath Oct. 28, 1820 William Bagwell to W Hunt. Rec. Jan. 5, 1821. Dower renounced Jun. 15, 1820 Polly Thomson to E Bomar

p. 177-178 Nov. 25, 1820 William B Alexander, Presly Smith, Thomas Chesney, Nathaniel Chesney, John Chesney, and George Chesney, heirs of Richard Chesney desc, to Robert Alexander (Spartanburgh); for $400 sold 208½ ac on ridge between James Cr and Tyger R; border: S-Robert Alexander, N-John Thornton, and (E?)-Moses White. Witness William Grant and Moses White. Signed Wm B Alexander, Presley Smith, Thomas Chesney, John Chesney, and Nahtaniel and George Chesney's marks. Wit. oath Dec. 30, 1820 William Grant to John Brewton. Rec. Jan. 11, 1821. Dower renounced Dec. 1, 1820 Heather Chesney, wife of Richard, to John Brewton

p. 178-180 Jul. 10, 1817 John Tollison (Spartanburgh) to Augustin Shands (same); for $200 sold 164 ac; where Gabriel Gossett lives; border: David Golightly, Hazle, John King, and Augustin Shands; grant Dec. 1, 1794 to Samuel Noblit who sold to John Tollison. Witness Samuel Noblitt and Richard Kirby. Signed John Tollison. Wit. oath Apr. 11, 1818 Richard Kirby to Wm Reid. Rec. Jan. 11, 1821. Dower renounced Jun. 13, 1818 Mary Tollison to Wm Reid

p. 180-181 Dec. 26, 1820 William Foster (Spartanburgh) to Z McDaniel (same); for $68.74 sold a cow and calf, a three year old heifer, a bay horse, a walnut table, an oven, a pot, a feather bed and furniture, all household and kitchen furniture, 20 barrels of good corn, 150 bundles of fodder, 2 sows and 9 shoats, 2 plows, 2 hoes, a cow tungue, 2 axes, and all land due William Foster from United States for service in "the late war"; Condition: sale void if William pays Z McDaniel $68.74 by Nov. 1, 1821. Witness W. W. Harris and Augustin Shands. Signed William Foster's mark. Wit. oath Dec. 26, 1820 Augustin Shands to D White. Rec. Jan. 11, 1821

p. 181-182 May 20, 1817 Christopher Golightly (Spartanburgh) to Augustin Shands (same); for $1,255.50 sold 558 ac; where Augustin Shands lives; border: S-David Golightly, NW-Wm Golightly, NE-James Poole and Benjamin Howard, and SE-John Kerr and John Tollison; part of grant in Nov. 1771 North Carolina governor to James Hammett. Witness Zacariah McDaniel and Mary Shands. Signed Christopher Golightly. Wit. oath Apr. 7, 1818 Zacariah McDaniel to Wm Reid. Rec. Jan. 11, 1821. Dower renounced Apr. 3, 1818 Jane (or Janey) Golightly to James Young

p. 182 Aug. 12, 1820 James W Reynolds (Spartanburgh) to Robert Legon (same); for $100 sold 10½ ac on waters of Ward's Cr; where James W Reynolds lives. Witness John Otts and Martin Otts. Signed James W Reynolds. Wit. oath Nov. 14, 1820 John Otts to John Brewton. Rec. Jan. 16, 1821

p. 182-184 Jan. 16, 1821 David Ulmer (Spartanburgh) to Edward Bomar (same); for $417 sold (ac omitted) on Cub Br of Tyger R; border: Edward Bomar, Mrs. Hunkerpiller Doigg and "others"; where David Ulmer lives; Condition: deed void if David pays Edward $417 by Jan. 1, 1822 with interest. Witness Thomas Bomar, William Bomar, and John Bomar jr. Signed David Ulmer. Wit. oath Jan. 17, 1821 John Bomar to E Bomar. Rec. Jan. 16, 1821

p. 184-185 Jan. 22, 1821 James Foster, son of Wm, (Spartanburgh) to Edmond W Chapman (same); for $600 sold (1) 130 ac on Wilson Mill Cr of N Tyger R; border: William Foster and Nimrod Benson; and (2) 50 ac adjoining (1); (1) and (2) "allowed" to wife of James Foster, son of Robt, heir of William Benson desc. Witness John Crawford and William Wilkins. Signed James Foster. Wit. oath Jan. 22, 1821 John Crawford to E Bomar. Rec. Jan. 22, 1821

p. 185-187 Jul. 6, 1818 James Hunt, sheriff (Spartanburgh) to Thomas Price; for $455 sold 160 ac on Jemmy's Cr; border: Asarel Beson, "widow", and Thomas Bell; lot #2 of estate of Richard Chesney; Presly Smith and wife petitioned Spartanburgh Common Pleas Court held second Monday after fourth Monday in Oct. 1817 to divide estate of Richard Chesney desc; court appointed William Posey, John Thornton, Asakel Beson, Lawson Thompson, and George Robuck esqs to partition the estate; they returned to court second Monday after fourth Monday in Mar. 1818 and said estate can't be divided and recommended sale with credit to be first payment first Monday in Jan. 1819, second payment Jan. 1, 1820, and third payment Jan. 1, 1821; sale was on first Monday in Jun. 1818. Witness Wm D (or V) Miller and William Rogers. Signed Jas Hunt SSD. Wit. oath Jan. 1, 1821 William Rogers to Robert Legon. Rec. Jan. 22, 1821

p. 187 Feb. 1, 1821 John McElrath (Spartanburgh) to Michael Moore (same); for $553.50 sold 123 ac on S side of Middle Tyger R; border: Philip Bettis, Wilson Nesbett, Michael Moore, and James Vernon. Witness Page Rork and James Nesbett jr. Signed John McElrath. Wit. oath Feb. 5, 1821 James Nesbett to E Bomar. Rec. Feb. 5, 1821

p. 187-188 Jan. 15, 1821 James Burns sr (Spartanburgh) to Michael Moore (same); for $800 sold 210 ac on N side of Middle Tyger R; border: James Vernon and Michael Moore desc. Witness James Swanzy, John Collins, and John Burns. Signed James Burns sr's mark. Wit. oath Jan. 15, 1820 James Swanzy to John Collins. Rec. Feb. 5, 1821

p. 188-189 Jan. 15, 1820 James Burns sr (Spartanburgh) to Michael Moore (same); for $200 sold 103 ac on S side of S Tyger R; border: David Dantzler, John McElrath, and Wilson Nesbett. Witness James Swanzy, John Collins, and John Burns. Signed James Burns sr's mark. Wit. oath Jan. 15, 1820 James Swanzy to John Collins. Rec. Feb. 5, 1821

p. 189-190 May 18, 1819 Wilson Nesbett (Spartanburgh) to Michael Moore (same); for $306 sold 102 ac on S Tyger R; border: David Dantzler, David Jordan, and Wilson Nesbett. Witness Jonathan Nesbett and Isaah Bright. Signed Wilson Nesbett. Wit. oath Jan. 15, 1820 Isaah Bright to John Collins. Rec. Feb. 5, 1821

p. 190-191 Sept. 7, 1820 Catharine Smith (Spartanburgh) to James Cooper, William Underwood, and William Lancaster, members of Cedar Springs Church, and rest of members and their successors; for good will and wish for prosperity of religion give 1 ac for church building; border: road West of present old meeting house. Witness William S Golightly and Daniel White. Signed Catherine Smith. Wit. oath Sept. 7, 1820 William S Golightly to Danl White. Rec. Feb. 5, 1821

p. 191-192 Jan. 8, 1818 Thornton McDaniel (Spartanburgh) to Edward Willis (same); for $425 sold 120 ac on waters of S Tyger R; border: a pond, Drury McDaniel, Addam Meeks' old line, William McDaniel, road from McDaniel's bridge to Hugh's, English, and William Allen; part of grant to Addam Meeks. Witness Wm N Miller and J. D. Palmer. Signed Thornton McDaniel. Wit. oath Jan. 8, 1817 (sic) J. D. Palmer to F. H. Legg. Rec. Feb. 5, 1821. Dower renounced Mar. 13, 1818 Keziah McDaniel to F. H. Legg

p. 192-193 Nov. 3, 1820 David Jordan to James Vernon; for $83 sold a sorrel mare, a sorrel filly, 4 cows and 6 small cattle, 18 hogs, a crib of corn, 1,400 bundles of fodder, "a parcel" of tobacco, 2 cupboards and furniture, 3 featherbeds and furniture, a chest, 3 bedsteads, 2 trunks, 2 small "(Ditto)", 3 tables, 6 chairs, 3 pots 3 ovens, a spider, a frying pan, a skellet, a loom, 2 spinning wheels, 4 flour barrels, a clock, a looking glass, 4 pails, a woman's saddle, a man's saddle, a dimijohn, 2 axes, 2 mattocks, 2 ploughs and a pair of gears; Condition: sale void if David pays James $83 by Jan. 1, 1821. Witness Michael Moore and Alexander Vernon. Signed David Jordan. Wit. oath Feb. 5, 1821 Alexander Vernon to E Bomar. Rec. Feb. 5, 1821

p. 193-194 Nov. 3, 1820 David Jordan (Spartanburgh) to James Vernon (same); for $250 sold 132 1/3 ac on S side of Middle Tyger R; border: Vanderhorst; part of grant to Robert Nesbett jr. Witness Michael Moore and Alexander Vernon. Signed D Jordan. Wit. oath Feb. 5, 1821 Alexander Vernon to E Bomar. Rec. Feb. 5, 1821

p. 194-195 Dec. 2, 1820 Robert White (Spartanburgh) to John Bullington (same); for $500 sold 131 ac on Kelso's Cr of Fairforest Cr; border: Katharine Smith, Daniel White, and Charles Jones; part of two grants: (1) to James Smith and (2) to Joseph Buffington; (2) was mortgaged to Loan Office and sold by legislative order to James Smith and by heirship went to David Lynch who sold to Robert White. Witness Benjamin White and Daniel White. Signed Robert White. Wit. oath Dec. 2, 1820 Benjamin White to Danl White. Rec. Feb. 5, 1821. Dower renounced Jan. 11, 1821 Mary G (or Polly) White to Daniel White

p. 195-196 Sept. 27, 1817 William House (Spartanburgh) to William W Hastings (same); for $290 sold 120 ac on N side of Enoree R; border: Jacob Cooper. Witness John Crocker and John Hasten. Signed William House. Wit. oath Oct. 9, 1820 John Hasten to James Crook. Rec. Feb. 5, 1821

p. 196-197 first Monday in Jan. 1817 (Jan. 6) Labon P Poole, sheriff (Spartanburgh) to Isaac Beardan; for $232 sold 188 ac; land was sold by Hiram Harrison to Osborn West; on second Monday after fourth Monday in Mar. 1816 David West in Spartanburgh Common Pleas Court asked Court to divide estate of Osborn West desc; Court appointed Wm Smith, James Hamm, James Salmon, Benjamin Peaks, and John Meadder esq to partition estate; they said estate can't be divided and should be sold with credit of 12 months; sale was on first Monday in Jan. 1817. Witness William Wafford and James Moore. Signed Labon P Poole SSD. Wit. oath Feb. 5, 1821 William Wafford to James Hamm. Rec. Feb. 5, 1821

p. 197-198 Apr. 4, 1812 Elias Stone (Spartanburgh) to Barney Bishop (same); for $150 sold 100 ac on waters of Fairforest Cr and Lawson's fork; border: Barney Bishop and Edmond J Bishop. Witness William L Bishop, Edmond J Bishop, and Robert Benson. Signed Elias Stone. Wit. oath Apr. 7, 1812 Edmond J Bishop to Thomas Poole. Rec. Feb. 5, 1821

p. 198-199 Oct. 15, 1818 Andrew Ray jr (Spartanburgh) to James Foster (same); for $400 sold (1) 256 ac on Cases' Cr of Pacolett R; and (2) 49 ac on both sides Cases' Cr. Witness Robert Garret and Wyatt E Hinez. Signed Andrew Rea. Wit. oath Feb. 4, 1821 Robert Garret to James Young. Rec. Feb. 5, 1821

p. 199-200 Jan. 9, 1821 John Parham (Union Dist) to James Cathcart (same); for $128 sold 110 ac on waters of Cane Cr of Tyger R; border: N-old Mr Cathcart, S-Oshealds, E-Walker, and Samuel Cathcart and Callico; part of grant in 1786 to J Blassingame and by power of attorney to John Parham to sell. Witness James Pruett and Samuel McCravy. Signed John Parham for Blassingame. Wit. oath Feb. 2, 1821 James Pruett to James Hamm. Rec. Feb. 5, 1821

p. 200-201 Jan. 4, 1821 John Vice (Spartanburgh) to James Duncan, son of Alexander (same); for $300 sold 168 ac on waters of Tyger R; border: Reuben Vice, Robert Rogers, Nathaniel Vice, and Gideon Hereldson; part of 640 ac grant Gov. William Moultrie to John Vice. Witness Eli Vice and Abner Vice. Signed John Vice. Wit. oath Jan. 15, 1821 Eli Vice to Burrel Bobo. Rec. Feb. 5, 1821. Dower renounced Jan. 15, 1821 Francis (or Franky) Vice to Burrel Bobo

p. 201-202 Oct. 25, 1819 Jacob Davis (Spartanburgh) to Philip Watkins (NC); for $65 sold 80 ac on waters of Suck Cr; border: James Stedmon, Motre, and Zachariah Blackwell. Witness Philip Davis and William Watkins. Signed Jacob Davis. Wit. oath Nov. 2, 1820 William Watkins to George Camp. Rec. (omitted)

p. 202-203 Jul. 28, 1820 George Davours (or George Bishop), Joseph Lawrence, Elizabeth Bishop, and Manly Ford (Ga), heirs of Elizabeth Bishop desc, to Isaac Bishop (Spartanburgh); for $300 sold (ac omitted) on waters of Lawson's fork of Pacolett R; border: Jonathan Newman; part of grant May 4, 1769 to Robert Henderson who sold to James Jordan who sold to heirs of Robert Bishop desc. Witness John Devours. Signed George Deavours, Joseph Laurence, Manly Ford, and Elizabeth Bishop's mark. Wit. oath Aug. 12, 1820 John Devours to John Montgomery. Rec. Feb. 5, 1821

p. 203-205 Feb. 16, 1821 Jesse Brown (Spartanburgh) to Caleb Woodruff (same); for $10 sold 177 ac in two parts: (1) 100 ac on waters of Two Mile Cr of Enoree R; border: Young Lowder, Isaac Hendrix, William Cleton, and Wm Willes; sold by Benjamin Busey to Jesse Brown; and (2) 77 ac on waters of Two Mile Cr of Enoree R; border: county road, Spencer Calvert, and Sampson Bobo; part of two grants: (a) to John Hendrix and (b) to Richard Nally; and sold two Negroes Pat and her child Gabriel; Condition: sales void if Jesse Brown pays bond to Simpson Foster, Commissioner for Spartanburgh Equity Court for $2,000 (Feb. 16, 1821) for which Caleb is security. Witness Elisha Bomar and James Hunt. Signed Jesse Brown's mark. Wit. oath Feb. 16, 1821 James Hunt to E Bomar. Rec. Feb. 16, 1821

p. 205-206 Oct. 1, 1820 Benjamin Ragan, Henry Danger, and Nathaniel Danger (Spartanburgh) to Ralph Danger (same); for $500 479 ac on both sides Bridge Br of S Pacolate R; "originally run" in survey by J Henderson (1) 120 ac and (2) 359 ac "run" (or grant?) by James Smith and runs partly around (1). Witness George L Peebles, Ause (or Ausbon) Body, and William West. Signed Nathaniel Danger, Henry Danger, and Benjamin Ragan's mark. Wit. oath Feb. 21, 1821 Ause Body to James Young. Rec. Feb. 24, 1821

p. 206-207 Jan. 1, 1820 Reuben and Rebecca Philips to James Moreland; for $550 sold (1) 100 ac on Suck Cr of Broad R; border: Turner and Judy Robertson; part of grant Sept. 11, 1796 to Jacob Dilback; and (2) 298 ac; border: Lidia Blackwell. Witness Philip Davis, Nimrod Horton, and John Turner. Signed Reuben Philips and Rebecca's mark. Wit. oath Feb. 10, 1821 Nimrod Horton to Joseph Camp. Rec. Mar. 2, 1821

p. 207-208 Oct. 31, 1821 Robert Rakestraw (Spartanburgh) to John Murph (same); for $106.75 sold 100 ac on Fairforest Cr; border: Willis Hay's old place, Wingo's bridge, and Andrew Foster; part of grant to Zachariah Buttock (sic) who sold to John Thomas who sold to Joseph Buffington and mortgaged to State Loan Office and sold by act of Assembly to Alexander McKie who sold to John White who sold to Robert Rakestraw; Condition: sale void if Robert pays John $106.75 with interest by Jan. 1, 1822. Witness Zachariah McDaniel to John White. Signed Robert Rakestraw. Wit. oath Mar. 5, 1821 Zachariah McDaniel to E Bomar. Rec. Mar. 5, 1821

p. 208-209 Jan. 1, 1821 Robert Wyatt (Spartanburgh) to Zachariah McDaniel (same); for $100 sold 75 ac where Robert Wyatt lives, 3 feather beds and furniture, 5 cattle, 35 hogs, a bay mare, a walnut cupboard, all farming utensils, and all household and kitchen furniture; Condition: sale void if Robert pays Zachariah $100 with interest by Jan. 1, 1822. Witness Hamilton Wilson and John Rakestraw. Signed Robert Wyatt. Wit. oath Mar. 5, 1821 John Rakestraw to Wm Underwood. Rec. Mar. 5, 1821

p. 209-210 (not dated) Daniel Rogers (Spartanburgh) to granddaughter Elizabeth Ann Carlton (same); for love and affection give all his goods and chattels: a cow and calf, 2 beds, 12 sheets, 2 bed covers, 5 bed quilts, 5 pillows, a dutch blanket, a sow and 4 pigs, a checkrell, a dresser, 2 puter dishes, a bason, 6 plates, 2 tin pans, 19 cups, 6 cups and saucers, a tea pot, a pitcher and mug, an earthen dish, a table tray, a barrel, a dutch oven and lid, a matock, a wedge, a plow clevis, swingle trees and traces, a covered trunk, a bee hive, and 3 chairs. Witness William Rogers and James Rogers. Signed Daniel Rogers' mark. Wit. oath Mar. 4, 1820 William Rogers to John Dean. Rec. Mar. 5, 1821

p. 210-211 Oct. 4, 1816 James Hindman (Spartanburgh) to Thos Pruett (same); for $212.50 sold 92 ac on waters of Tyger R; border: Thos Pruett and Samuel Kethcart; part of 174 ac grant Feb. 5, 1787 Gov. William Moultrie to Owen Foroster. Witness Isa Callicot and John Hindman. Signed James Hindman. Wit. oath Jan. 24, 1817 Isa Callicot to James Hamm. Rec. Mar. 5, 1821

p. 211-212 Mar. 4, 1821 Labon P Poole (Spartanburgh) to Robert Wier (same); for $230 sold 135 ac on S side of Middle Tyger R; border: Caldwell and James Gordan. Witness Ephraim Roddy and Abner Benson. Signed Labon P Poole. Wit. oath Mar. 6, 1821 (sic) Ephraim Roddy to Thos Poole. Rec. Mar. 5, 1821

p. 212-213 Aug. 8, 1820 David McKie (Spartanburgh) to Green Underwood; for $200 sold 140 ac; border: Enoch Underwood, Busy, and Wm McDaniel jr. Witness Enoch J Underwood and Drury Fowler. Signed Danl McKie. Wit. oath Nov. 7, 1820 Enoch J Underwood to Wm Underwood. Rec. Mar. 5, 1821

p. 213-214 Oct. 21, 1820 William Crook (Spartanburgh) to Isaac Snoddy (same); for $2,000 sold 395 ac on branches on S side of Tyger R; border: James Crook and Drummond's Spring Br. Witness Joseph Crook and William W Hastin. Signed William Crook. Wit. oath Oct. 21, 1820 William W Hastin to James Crook. Rec. Mar. 5, 1821

p. 214-215 Feb. 16, 1821 William Bishop sr (Spartanburgh) to Barney Bishop (same); for $65 sold 25 ac on waters of Standing Stone Br of Lawson's fork; border: Barney Bishop, Blackstock Road, and Ballinger Road from Spartanburgh; part of survey for Edmond Bishop sr and granted to William Bishop sr. Witness Edmond J Bishop and John Bishop. Signed William Bishop's mark. Wit. oath Mar. 5, 1831 John Bishop to W Hunt. Rec. Mar. 5, 1821

p. 215-216 Dec. 6, 1820 Henry White (Spartanburgh) to Muse Tollison (same); for $1,000 sold ½ ac in Spartanburgh, SC; border: S-public square, W-William P Gadbury, N-Maj. J. T. Earle, and NE-public road. Witness William Trimmier and Memory N Chapman. Signed Henry White. Wit. oath Mar. 7, 1821 Memory N Chapman to E Bomar. Rec. Mar. 7, 1821

p. 216-217 May 20, 1820 Richard Thomson (Spartanburgh) to Muse Tollison (same); for $400 sold 6¼ (or 6 1/14) ac in Spartanburgh, SC on S side of Main St; border: Tollison's shop. Witness Berryman S Holder and James Hunt, sheriff. Signed Richard Thomson. Wit. oath Jul. 5, 1820 James Hunt to W Hunt. Rec. Mar. 7, 1821. Dower renounced Mar. 5, 1821 Polly Thomson to Daniel White

p. 217-218 Dec. 5, 1820 James Brannon (Spartanburgh) to Henry White (same); for $1,000 sold ½ ac in Spartanburgh, SC; border: S-public square, W-Wm P Gadberry, N-Maj. J. T. Earle, and NE-publick road. Witness William Trimmier and William Hunt. Signed J Brannon. Wit. oath Dec. 5, 1820 William Trimmier to W Hunt. Rec. Mar. 16, 1821. Dower renounced Mar. 9, 1821 Sarah Brannon to E Bomar

p. 218-219 Mar. 18, 1812 Joseph Woodruff (Spartanburgh) to John Mullinax (same); for $400 sold 115 ac on Tyger R; border: John White, Chesney, and a dry pond. Witness Benjamin Wofford and Rebekah Mullinax. Signed Joseph Mullinax. Wit. oath Jan. 30, 1821 Benjamin Wofford to Burrell Bobo. Rec. Mar. 16, 1821

p. 219-220 Mar. 16, 1821 Job Sosebee (Spartanburgh) to Daniel Faust (same); for $100 sold 171 ac onPeter's Cr; border: Markly; part of two grants (1) to Job Sosebee and (2) to James Wyatt. Witness Elisha Bomar and John P Miller. Signed Job Sosebee's mark. Wit. oath Mar. 16, 1821 John P Miller to E Bomar. Rec. Mar. 16, 1821

p. 220-221 Nov. 22, 1820 John Tollison sr (Spartanburgh) to John McDowell jr (Union Dist); for $300 sold 150 ac in Spartanburgh and Union Dists; where William Hardey lives; border: Cruse, John McDowell sr, and John Eison, and Poole. Witness James Tollison and John McDowell sr. Signed John Tollison jr. Wit. oath Jan. 6, 1821 John McDowell sr to William Reid. Rec. Mar. 26, 1821

p. 221-222 May 11, 1820 Bartholomew Grogan (Spartanburgh) to Henry Grogan (same); for $270 sold 390 ac on both sides Beaverdam Cr of S Pacolett R; one part is where Henry Grogan lives and is 150 ac grant Nov. 5, 1771 to Abigail Terrell and other part is part of 483 ac grant Nov. 6, 1797 to Bartholomew Grogan. Witness Thomas Grogan and George W Manly. Signed Bartholomew Grogan's mark. Wit. oath Mar. 20, 1821 Thomas Grogan to J Whitten. Rec. Mar. 28, 1821

p. 222-223 Jul. 3, 1820 Anderson Vandike (Spartanburgh) to David Ulmer (same); for $200 sold 1,050 ac in two parts: (1) 743 ac on waters of Lawson's fork of Pacolett R and (2) 307 ac. Witness John W Leonard and Isaac Leonard. Signed Anderson Vandike. Wit. oath Oct. 2, 1820 Isaac Leonard to Thomas Poole. Rec. Mar. 29, 1821

p. 223-224 Apr. 1, 1821 Thomas Dare (Spartanburgh) to sons-in-law William Ross and Muse Tollison (same); for love and affection give all lands, utensils, goods and chattels: (1) 700 ac on Lawson's fork; (2) 340 ac on Little Cherokee Cr; 13 Negroes--Owen, Saul, Jaber, Vince, Manuel, Nelson, Bob, Jim, Clary, Pat, Hannah, Will, and Mary; "my" stud horse, 13 mares, geldings and colts, 70 meat cattle, 40 sheep, all my hogs, 5 featherbeds, all household and kitchen furniture, and plantation tools. Witness William Trimmier and Memory N Chapman. Signed Thomas Dare. Wit. oath Apr. 2, 1821 William Trimmier to E Bomar. Rec. Apr. 2, 1821

p. 224-225 Apr. 18, 1818 Chaney Bobo (Spartanburgh) to Bord W Waters (SC); for $200 sold 196 ac on Sandy Fork Rd below New Hope Meeting House; border: Chaney Bobo, Solomon Smith, Willis Arnold, and land formerly owned by John F Harmoning and Co; 3 ac excepted around New Hope Meeting House including spring and burial ground. Witness Margarett Waters and Aron Casey. Signed Chaney Bobo. Wit. oath Mar. 31, 1821 Aron Casey to M Casey. Rec. Apr. 2, 1821. Dower renounced Nov. 5, 1818 Rachel Bobo to Burrell Bobo

p. 225-226 Feb. 6, 1821 John Cooper (Spartanburgh) to Darkes Crocker (same); for $600 sold 125 ac on Buck Cr; border: John Cantrell (Miller), Richard Morris, Abraham Cantrell's Spring Br, and a road. Witness William Crocker and James Galt. Signed John Cooper. Wit. oath Mar. 17, 1821 James Galt to George Camp. Rec. Apr. 2, 1821

p. 226-227 Dec. 20, 1819 James Crook (Spartanburgh) to George Durham (same); for $425 sold 220 ac on Page's Spring Br; border: Savage, Stone's Br, and George Durham; part of grant to William Savage. Witness James Leonard and Grisham Durham. Signed James Crook. Wit. oath Dec. 20, 1819 Grisham Durham to James Crook. Rec. Apr. 2, 1821

p. 227-229 Mar. 9, 1820 James Hunt, sheriff (Spartanburgh) to Muse Tollison (same); for $66 sold 200 ac on Holston Br of Fairforest Cr; border: Roberson and William Moore (who sold to Hill); grant to David Goodlett; sale due to writ from Spartanburgh Common Pleas Court second Monday after fourth Monday in Oct. 1818 suit James Brannon vs James Hunt, carpenter; judgment was levy of $48.56 and costs from James Hunt, carpenter. Witness Berryman S Holder and Charles McAbee. Signed James Hunt SSD. Wit. oath Apr. 3, 1821 Berryman S Holder to E Bomar. Rec. Apr. 3, 1821

p. 229 Apr. 3, 1821 William P Gadberry (Spartanburgh) to Muse Tollison (same); for $506 sold ½ ac in Spartanburgh, SC on NW side of Main St; border: Tollison's old house and public square. Witness Memory N Chapman and William Hunt. Signed W. P. Gadberry. Wit. oath Apr. 3, 1821 Memory N Chapman to W Hunt. Rec. Apr. 3, 1821

p. 229-230 Aug. 23, 1820 John Bragg (Spartanburgh) to James Alexander for $10 sold 9½ ac on S side of Jemmes Cr of Tyger R; border: E-James Alexander, N & W-John Bragg, and S-William Posey. Witness Robert Alexander and Peter Bragg. Signed John Bragg. Wit. oath Mar. 26, 1821 Robert Alexander to Wm Young. Rec. Apr. 5, 1821

p. 230-232 Nov. 6, 1820 David Burton (Spartanburgh) to William Smithwick (same); for $1,000 sold 200 ac on N side of N Tyger R; border: N & W-Capt. Matthew Rush, NE-John Trail, and S & SW-Benjamin Nichols and Henry White. Witness Eber Smith and Robert Alexander. Signed David Burton. Wit. oath Apr. 2, 1821 Robert Alexander to W Hunt. Rec. Apr. 5, 1821. Dower renounced Nov. 18, 1820 Esther Burton to John Brewton

p. 232-233 Oct. 3, 1820 James Jordan McMicken, John McMicken, and Nancy McMicken (Spartanburgh) to John Crawford (same); for $600 sold 177 ac on N Tyger R and Middle Tyger R. Witness Robert Wier and John Caldwell. Signed Jas J McMiken and John and Nancy McMicken's marks. Wit. oath Apr. 3, 1821 Robert Wier to Thomas Poole. Rec. Apr. 10, 1821. Dower renounced Apr. 3, 1821 Rebecca McMicken, wife of James J, to Thomas Poole

p. 233-234 Mar. 23, 1819 Joshua H Brown (Spartanburgh) to Hase Bagwell (same); for $150 sold (ac omitted) on N side of N Tyger R; sold by power of attorney from Jane and Mary McMicken to Joshua H Brown; land was part of real estate of late James McMicken desc and alloted to Jane and Mary McMicken as legates of James; Joshua is also legate of James McMicken. Witness Aloan Dean and Samuel Miller. Signed Joshua H Brown attorney for Jane and Mary McMicken. Wit. oath Mar. 23, 1819 Samuel Miller to F. H. Legg. Wit. oath Apr. 10, 1821

p. 234-235 Dec. 28, 1820 Willy S Brown (Spartanburgh) to Minor Brown (same); for $300 sold 62 ac on N side of S Pacolett R; includes mouth of Mill Cr; border: John Lucas; lower end of tract sold to Willy S Brown by James Gowen and formerly part of his father John Gowen's estate. Witness Silas R Whitten and Alfred Whitten. Signed Willy S Brown. Wit. oath Apr. 7, 1821 Alfred Whitten to J Whitten. Rec. Apr. 10, 1821

p. 235-236 Aug. 20, 1820 Richard Gentry (Spartanburgh) to John Shurley (same); for $187 sold (ac omitted) at head of branches of Ferguson's and Jemme's Creeks; border: N & W-John Skinner and S & SE-widow King and Richard Gentry. Witness William Otts, Samuel Floyd, and James Barnett. Signed Richard Gentry's mark. Wit. oath Apr. 6, 1821 James Barnett to John Brewton. Rec. Apr. 10, 1821

p. 236-237 Jan. 15, 1821 Ann Price (Spartanburgh) to William B Alexander (same); for $455 sold 140 ac; border: S-Thomas Bell, W-James Alexander, N-Hester Chesney, and E-Asahel Beason. Witness David W Wilmot and Robert Pedan. Signed Ann Price, administrator of Thos Price. Wit. oath Mar. 10, 1821 Robert Pedan to Robert Legon. Rec. Apr. 10, 1821

p. 237-238 Mar. 26, 1821 William Lindsey (Spartanburgh) to Isaac Lindsey (same); for $125 sold 57 ac on branches on S side of Enoree R; border: John Childres and Samuel Jones; part of grant to John Tate who sold 57 ac to William Lindsey. Witness Chaney

Lindsey and John Pearson. Signed William Lindsey's mark. Wit. oath Mar. 27, 1821 Chaney Lindsey to James Ford. Rec. Apr. 10, 1821

p. 238-239 Sept. 22, 1820 James Leonard (Spartanburgh) to John Arnold (same); for $375 sold 120 ac on branches of Two Mile Cr of Enoree R; border: Wm Lanford. Witness Zachariah Edwards and Reuben Stone. Signed James Leonard. Wit. oath Sept. 23, 1820 Reuben Stone to John Dean. Rec. Apr. 10, 1821

p. 239 Jan. 29, 1821 Daniel Stephens (Spartanburgh) to son John Stephens; for love and affection give 100 ac; part of where Daniel Stephens lives; border: Rogers, Gibs, and Medoles Rotten. Witness Robert Ligon and A. B. Moore. Signed Daniel Stephens' mark. Wit. oath Apr. 9, 1821 Robert Ligon to Danl White. Rec. Apr. 10, 1821

p. 239-240 Jan. 26, 1821 (Union Dist) Anna Gibbs, executrix of James Gibbs desc, (Union Dist) to John Stephens (Spartanburgh); for $2 quit claim to (ac omitted); border: "N & NW of Jesse Spencer to 100 ac tract" that isn't otherwise sold by James Gibbs desc or joint executor, Zachariah Gibbs; grant in 1792 Gov (sic) Peter Bremar to James Gibbs. Witness Robert Ligon and William White. Signed Anna Gibbs' mark. Wit. oath Apr. 9, 1821 Robert Ligon to Danl White. Rec. Apr. 10, 1821

p. 240-241 Nov. 2, 1815 James Wilson (Spartanburgh) to son Carter Wilson (same); for $175 sold 100 ac; border: P. C. McMakin, Thomas Booker, and John Montgomery; part of where "he" lives; on lower side of grant Jun. 5, 1786 to James Wilson. Witness Alexander M Thompson, Joshua Ballenger, and Elisha Davis. Signed James Wilson's mark. Wit. oath Dec. 8, 1815 Alexander M Thompson to Andrew Ferguson. Rec. Apr. 12, 1821

p. 241-242 Feb. 26, 1820 James Ellis sr (Rutherford Co, NC) to Absalem Ellis (same); for $500 sold 100 ac on W side of main Broad R; border: Benjamin Ellis; part of James Ellis' survey. Witness Joseph Weber and John Weber. Signed James Ellis' mark. Wit. oath Apr. 9, 1821 Joseph Weber to Thomas Poole. Rec. Apr. 12, 1821

p. 242-243 Feb. 19, 1820 (Union Dist) Joseph Collins to William Turner (Spartanburgh); for $130 sold 100 ac on Tinet's Cr of Broad R; border: B Bonner; where Silas Yarborough lived. Witness James Harrison and James Kerby. Signed Jo Collins. Wit. oath Aug. 19, 1820 James Kerby to John Lipscomb. Rec. Apr. 12, 1821

p. 243-244 Oct. 28, 1816 Joshua Herrin (Rutherford Co, NC) to Absalem Ellis; for $150 sold 50 ac on W side of Broad R. Witness Joseph Weber and Casper Weber. Signed Joshua Herrin. Wit. oath Dec. 12, 1817 Joseph Weber to John Lipscomb. Rec. Apr. 12, 1821

p. 244-245 Nov. 2, 1815 James Wilson (Spartanburgh) to son John Wilson (same); for $175 sold (ac omitted); border: John McCarter; part of where "he" lives; grant Jun. 5, 1786 to James Wilson. Witness Alexander M Thompson, Thadeous Owen, and Alexander McCollum. Signed James Wilson's mark. Wit. oath Dec. 8, 1815 Alexander McCollum to Andrew Ferguson. Rec. Apr. 12, 1821

p. 245-246 Nov. 20, 1819 Charles Williamson to George Divine; for $50 sold 25 ac on Prater's Cr on S side of Tyger R; border: Yarbrough. Witness John Weaver and Philip Weaver. Signed Charles Williamson. Wit. oath Mar. 24, 1821 John Weaver to Benj Wofford. Rec. Apr. 13, 1821

p. 246-247 Mar. 1, 1820 Peter Hawkins (Spartanburgh) to William

Whitaker (same); for $400 sold 200 ac on S side of Obed's Cr between S and N Pacolett Rivers; part of 400 ac sold by Baylis Earle to John Anderson who sold to William Dalton. Witness Robert King, William Jackson, and John Ridings. Signed Peter Hawkins. Wit. oath Mar. 21, 1821 John Ridings to Wm Kelso. Rec. Apr. 13, 1821

p. 247-248 Jul. 11, 1817 Abner Benson (Spartanburgh) to James Tollison, Birdson Tollison, Josephus Berryman Tollison, and Alfred Tollison, sons of Maj. John Tollison, (same); for good will and affection give 9 beds, bedsteads and furniture, an eight day clock and case, a desk, book case and furniture, a side board and furniture, 2 walnut cupboards and furniture, a double walnut table and furniture, 2 walnut tables and furniture, a weaving loom and gears, all kitchen and household furniture about John Tollison's house, a copper still, flake stand, worn tub, 8 good bands, 24 chairs to set it, 2 trunks, 2 chests, a set of blacksmith tools, a rifle gun, a shot gun, a wagon and gears, a grindstone, a cross cut saw, and all farmer and carpenter tools about John Tollison's place. Witness Ralph Lemaster, Edmon Chapman, Fielder Gossett. Signed A Benson. Wit. oath Apr. 7, 1821 Fielder Gossett to William Reid. Rec. Apr. 19, 1821

p. 248-249 Jun. 10, 1819 Muse Tollison (Spartanburgh) to Alfred Tollison, son of John Tollison; for affection give, when Muse's father (John Tollison) dies, a Negro boy Milas and a mulatto girl Mary children of Negro woman Jane; both born as property of Muse's father; John Tollison has the Negroes now and is allowed to sell them in his lifetime but if John doesn't sell them then they go to Alfred. Witness James Tollison and Birdsong Tollison. Signed Muse Tollison. Wit. oath Apr. 7, 1821 James Tollison to William Reid. Rec. Apr. 19, 1821

p. 249-250 Dec. 16, 1818 Muse Tollison (Spartanburgh) to brothers James, Birdsong, and Josephus Berryman Tollison, sons of John Tollison; for love and affection give (1) 500 ac and "adjoining tracts" where John Tollison lives; (2) (as omitted) where Rosey West lives; except 10 ac in fork of branch given to Richard Kirby; above two tracts granted to John Tollison; (3) a tract granted to Mr Reid and Mr Haxon and sold by Wm Thompson and Mathias Bates to John Tollison; (4) a tract granted to Seth Lewis and granted to John McCoole(?) and sold by Wm Stone to John Tollison; (5) 5 ac sold by John Lemaster to John Tollison; and (6) a tract sold by Maj. Gossett to John Tollison who sold to Muse Tollison; sale is effective after death of John Tollison; if one of grantees dies before becoming of legal age, then his share goes to two survivors; also John Tollison can sell the land before he dies. Witness Stephen Tollison and Richard Kerby. Signed Muse Tollison. Wit. oath Apr. 10, 1821 Stephen Tollison to William Reid. Rec. Apr. 19, 1821

p. 250-251 Dec. 13, 1820 Jacob Chapman (Spartanburgh) to David Markley (same); for $600 sold 273 ac on Lawson's fork and Showley Cr; part of tract sold by Wood to Hugh Means desc. Witness William Tuck and Josiah Blackwell. Signed Jacob Chapman's mark. Wit. oath Dec. 18, 1820 William Tuck to W Hunt. Rec. Apr. 20, 1821. Dower renounced Apr. 20, 1821 Matilda Chapman to Elisha Bomar

p. 251-252 Oct. 31, 1820 Richard Roberts (Spartanburgh) to Michael Gaffney (same); for $100 sold 100 ac on waters of Suck Cr; border: S & E-Wilson Nesbett, W-Moreland, and N-Wm Turner; sold by Saml Boyd to Richard Roberts; originally half of Wm Turner's land; Condition: sale void if Richard pays Michael $100 by Jan. 1, 1822. Witness Drury Robertson and James Waters. Signed Ricahrd Roberts. Wit. oath Apr. 23, 1821 Drury Robertson to E Bomar. Rec.

Apr. 23, 1821

p. 252-253 Oct. 5, 1819 Nathaniel Danggar (Spartanburgh) to Benjamin Ragan; for $100 sold 210 ac on branches of S Pacolett R; border: SW & W-Robert McDowell and SE-survey for Burd or a road to Henderson's Bridge; survey Aug. 7, 1804 by George Peables (or Peabbs). Witness Henry Danggar and Osburn Body. Signed Nathaniel Danngar. Wit. oath Apr. 21, 1821 Henry Danggar to John L Rowland. Rec. Apr. 25, 1821

p. 253-254 Jun. 10, 1819 Muse Tollison (Spartanburgh) to Lucinda Tollison, daughter of John Tollison; for affections give, at descease of John Tollison, a Negro woman Jane and her child Ebyina (or Ebzina); Jane was sold by Norman Morrison to Maj. John Tollison, but John can sell Negro during his lifetime if he wants to; if John doesn't sell her, she goes to Lucinda and if Lucinda dies without issue then the Negro goes to James, Birdsong, Josephus B, and Alfred Tollison. Witness James Tollison and Birdsong Tollison. Signed Muse Tollison. Wit. oath Apr. 20, 1821 James Tollison to William Reid. Rec. May 1, 1821

p. 254-255 May 7, 1821 John Linder (Spartanburgh) to son Thomas Linder; for (omitted) give a Negro boy Jack. Witness Nathaniel Linder and Abraham Linder. Signed John Linder. Wit. oath May 7, 1821 Nathaniel Linder to E Bomar. Rec. May 7, 1821

p. 255 May 4, 1821 John Linder (Spartanburgh) to son Jacob Linder; for (omitted) give a Negro boy Jim. Witness Lee Linder and Elisha Bomar. Signed John Linder. Wit. oath May 5, 1821 Lee Linder to E Bomar. Rec. May 7, 1821

p. 255-256 May 6, 1821 John Linder (Spartanburgh) to son Lee Linder; for (omitted) give a Negro boy Daniel. Witness Elisha Bomar and Jacob Linder. Signed John Linder. Wit. oath May 5, 1821 Jacob Linder to E Bomar. Rec. May 7, 1821

p. 256 May 7, 1821 John Linder (Spartanburgh) to son Nathaniel Linder; for (omitted) give a Negro boy Dave. Witness Thomas Linder and Abraham Linder. Signed John Linder. Wit. oath May 7, 1821 Thomas Linder to E Bomar. Rec. May 7, 1821

p. 256-257 Nov. 13, 1820 John Timmons (Spartanburgh) to Alexander Vernon (same); for $800 sold 133 1/3 ac; border: Edward Bomar and John Foster; land was divided to John Timmons by his father Samuel Timmons desc. Witness Edward Ballenger and Page Rork. Signed John Timmons. Wit. oath May 7, 1821 Page Rork to John Chapman. Rec. May 7, 1821. Dower renounced Nov. 18, 1820 Temperance Timmons to Thomas Poole

p. 257-259 Dec. 13, 1813 William Bishop sr (Spartanburgh) to son Barney Bishop (same); for love and affection and for services Barney rendered to William give (1) 150 ac on Standing Stone Br of Lawson's fork; part of 250 ac grant to Edmond Bishop; border: John Bishop and Goodlett's old road; where William Bishop sr lives; and (2) 24 ac adjoining (1); border: Moultre and Robert McMurdy; part of 124 ac grant to Nathan Bishop. Witness Abner Benson and Nancy Evins. Signed William Bishop's mark. Wit. oath May 7, 1821 Abner Benson to E Bomar. Rec. May 7, 1821

p. 259-261 Jul. 6, 1818 James Hunt, sheriff (Spartanburgh) to James Alexander; for $441 sold 125 ac on waters of Jimmes Cr; lot #3 of estate of Richard Chesney; border: W-Robert Alexander, SE & SW-James Alexander and William Posey, E-Isaac Crow, and N-lots 1 and 2; Presley Smith and wife petitioned Spartanburgh Common Pleas Court second Monday after fourth Monday in Oct. 1817 to divide real estate of Richard Chesney desc; the Court appointed William Posey, John Thornton, Asarel Beson, Lawson Thomson, and George Robuck esqs to divide the land; but they said on second Monday after fourth Monday in Mar. 1818 that land can't be divided and recommended a sale with credit--first payment on first Monday in Jan. 1819, second payment Jan. 1, 1820, and third payment Jan. 1, 1821; sale was on first Monday in Jun. 1818. Witness William N Miller and William Rogers. Signed Jas Hunt SSD. Wit. oath May 7, 1821 William N Miller to Robert Ligon. Rec. May 7, 1821

p. 261-263 May 4, 1821 James Hunt, sheriff (Spartanburgh) to James K Means; for $1,563 sold 491 ac in Spartanburgh and Union Dists on both sides Fairfield (sic) Cr; border: Pointer's view and Fairforest Cr; Joseph Kelso and "others" petitioned Spartanburgh Common Pleas Court second Monday after fourth Monday in Mar. 1819 to divide estate of Saml Kelso desc; the Court appointed William Kelso, John Ison, James Means, Henry Cunningham, and John Thompson esqs to divide the land; on second Monday after fourth Monday in Oct. 1819 they said land can't be divided and recommended sale with credit of 12 months; sale was on first Monday in Jun. 1820. Witness John Wilbanks and William Kelso. Signed Jas Hunt. Wit. oath May 3, 1821 John Wilbanks to E Bomar. Rec. May 7, 1821

p. 263-264 Feb. 3, 1814 Spencer Bobo to Samuel Jones; for $210 sold 140 ac on James' Cr of Ferguson's Cr; border: Moore and Lindsey's Spring Br; includes a house and apple orchard. Witness William Jones and Samuel H Woodruff. Signed S Bobo. Wit. oath Mar. 31, 1821 William Jones to John Brewton. Rec. May 9, 1821. Dower renounced Jul. 4, 1815 Jane Bobo to Drury McDaniel

p. 264-266 Mar. 3, 1821 Josiah Woodruff (Spartanburgh) to William Jones (same); for $470 sold 150 ac; part of grant Gov. William Moultrie to John Hendrix; resurvey Sept. 27, 1815 by Jesse Wofford. Witness Thomas Woodruff III, Philip Pilgrim, and Eli Cox. Signed Josiah Woodruff. Wit. oath Apr. 5, 1821 Thomas Woodruff III to John Brewton. Rec. May 9, 1821. Dower renounced Mar. 16, 1821 Margaret Woodruff to John Brewton

p. 266 Jun. 20, 1819 John Tollison to Muse Tollison; for $1,200 sold a Negro woman Mill and Jane and her children Milas, Mary, and Ezina. Witness Charles McAbie and Matthew Norton. Signed John Tollison. Wit. oath Mar. 31, 1821 Charles McAbie to W Hunt. Rec. May 14, 1821

p. 266-267 May 17, 1821 Moses Fowler (Spartanburgh) to John Fowler (same); for $250 sold 200 ac on branch of Forgeson Cr of Tyger R; border: Thomas Peden, Francis Fowler's old tract, and Moses Fowler's old tract. Witness James Paden and William Strange. Signed Moses Fowler's mark. Wit. oath Mar. 17, 1821 William Strange to Thomas Wood. Rec. May 16, 1821

p. 267-268 Dec. 5, 1820 Thomas Dare to son Roland Dare; for affection give (ac omitted); known as Morgan's tract; sold by Reuben Morgan to Thomas Dare. Witness Wyatt Lipscomb and Benjamin Pennington. Signed Thomas Dare. Wit. oath Aug. 5, 1820 Wyatt Lipscomb to J Camp. Rec. May 22, 1821

p. 268-269 Dec. 7, 1820 Thomas Dare (Spartanburgh) to Abner Benson (same); for $1,600 sold 400 ac on both sides of Cherokee Cr; includes grist and saw mills; sold by William Champion to Thomas Dare; where Wyatt Lipscomb and Robert Lipscomb live. Witness Briant Bonner and William Rickman and Daniel White. Signed Thomas Dare. Wit. oath Dec. 8, 1820 Daniel White to E Bomar. Rec. May 22, 1821

p. 269-270 Oct. 3, 1820 James Hunt, sheriff (Spartanburgh) to William

D Young; for $40 sold 144 ac on waters of Thickety Cr; border: Benjamin Price, Samuel Dunaway, Nicholas Creace, and James Hodge; sale due to writ from Spartanburgh Common Pleas Court case second Monday after fourth Monday in Mar. 1820 suit Samuel Boyde vs Benjamin Fowler; levy was $21.68 and costs from Benjamin Fowler. Witness William Irby and Samuel C Hunt. Signed Jas Hunt SSD. Wit. oath Oct. 3, 1820 William Irby to W Hunt. Rec. May 29, 1821

p. 270-271 Dec. 23, 1820 William D Young (Spartanburgh) to William Irby (same); for $144 sold 144 ac on waters of Thickety Cr; border: Benjamin Price, Samuel Dunaway, Nicholas Crease, and James Hodge; formerly Benjamin Fowler's land and sold by Spartanburgh Dist sheriff due to suit "in favor of" James Land, indorsee (sic). Witness James Hunt and Levi Lee. Signed William D Young. Wit. oath Dec. 13, 1820 Levi Lee to E Bomar. Rec. May 29, 1821

p. 271-272 Dec. 30, 1820 William Irby (Spartanburgh) to William P Gadberry (same); for $300 sold 144 ac on waters of Thickety Cr; border: Benjamin Price, Samuel Dunaway, Charles Crean, and James Hodge; formerly Benjamin Fowler's land and sold by Spartanburgh Dist sheriff due to suit in favor of James Land indorsee (sic). Witness William Bomar and Elisha Bomar. Signed William Irby. Wit. oath May 29, 1821 Elisha Bomar to Wm Hunt. Rec. May 29, 1821

p. 272-273 Feb. 14, 1821 John Stephens (Spartanburgh) to Daniel Stephens (same); for love and affection give 60 ac; border: Otts, Zera Stephens (son of John), Daniel Stephens, and Roland Rd; N end of tract known as "rolling ginnings tract". Witness Rowland Ginnings and John Stephens. Signed John Stephens. Wit. oath May 26, 1821 John Stephens to Robert Ligon. Rec. Jun. 4, 1821

p. 273-274 Mar. 10, 1821 John Bishop (Spartanburgh) to James Hutchison (same); for $700 sold 200 ac on waters of Fairforest Cr and Lawson's fork; border: Barney Bishop, road from Edward Ballenger's to Spartanburgh Court House, Blackstock road, and Edmond J Bishop. Witness Barney Bishop and William L Bishop. Signed John Bishop. Wit. oath Jun. 4, 1821 Barney Bishop to W Hunt. Rec. Jun. 4, 1821. Dower renounced Mar. 17, 1821 Elizabeth Bishop to Barney and William L Bishop

p. 274-275 Feb. 13, 1821 Rhesa Robuck (Spartanburgh) to John Williams (same); for $260 sold 180 ac in two parts on waters of Cossen's fork of Pacolet R: (1) 100 ac part of grant to John Kerkennel; and (2) 80 ac adjoining (1); part of grant to Joseph Carver; border: Daniel Walling. Witness John Mayson and John Robuck. Signed Rhesea Robuck. Wit. oath Jun. 2, 1821 John Mayson to John Brewton. Rec. Jun. 4, 1821

p. 275-276 Apr. 12, 1819 James Selmon (Spartanburgh) to Armsted Bomar (same); for $150 sold 350 ac on Meeting House Spring Br of S Pacolett R; part of grant Jun. 2, 1806 Gov. Paul Hamilton to James Selmon. Witness Robert Bullington, Christopher Golightly, and Samuel Bullington. Signed Jas Selmon. Wit. oath Jun. 4, 1821 Christopher Golightly to E Lewis. Rec. Jun. 4, 1821

p. 276-277 Feb. 17, 1818 Reuben Bomar (Spartanburgh) to Armsted Bomar (same); for $10 sold 299 ac in fork of Pacolett R. Witness C. C. Duncan, Coleman Wood, and Lefford French. Signed Reuben Bomar. Wit. oath Apr. 10, 1821 Coleman Wood to E Lewis. Rec. Jun. 4, 1821

p. 277-278 May 23, 1821 Iredell Cunningham (Spartanburgh) to John Clark (same); for $50 sold 40 ac on N side of W fork of Richland Cr of S Pacolett R; border: Young, John Clark, and Wm Clement; part of grant to Samuel Spencer. Witness Luke Burnett and

Oliver Clark. Signed Iredell Cunningham. Wit. oath May 23, 1821 Luke Burnett to Wm Clement. Rec. Jun. 4, 1821

p. 278-279 Feb. 17, 1818 Reuben Bomar (Spartanburgh) to Armsted Bomar; for $10 sold 500 ac in forks of Pacolett R; border: Robert Young and David Walls; part of grant to Reuben Bomar. Witness C. C. Duncan, Lefford French, and Coleman Wood. Signed Reuben Bomar. Wit. oath Apr. 10, 1821 Coleman Wood to E Lewis. Rec. Jun. 4, 1821

p. 279-280 Feb. 14, 1821 John Stephens (Spartanburgh) to son Zira Stephens (same); for love and affection give 70 ac; border: sons Daniel and Zira Stephens; S end of land known as Rowland Ginnings tract. Witness John Stephens and Rowland Ginnings. Signed John Stephens. Wit. oath May 26, 1821 John Stephens to Robert Ligon. Rec. Jun. 4, 1821

p. 280-281 Dec. 23, 1818 Edward Bomar (Spartanburgh) to Andrew B Moore (same); for $150 sold 179 ac; part of grant Sept. 15, 1785 to William White. Witness Page Rork and John Bomar. Signed Edward Bomar. Wit. oath Jan. 14, 1819 Page Rork to John Collins. Rec. Jun. 4, 1821. Dower renounced Jan. 6, 1819 Mary Bomar to John Collins

p. 281-282 Sept. 20, 1820 Thomas Crumley (Buncomb Co, NC) to Sally Maclure (Spartanburgh); for $65 sold 300 ac on both sides of Obed's Cr of Pacolett R; border: David Frenkim, Thomas Evans' old line, and Robert Evans' old line; part of survey Oct. 4, 1784 for Thomas Evans. Witness Martin Lucas and Robert King. Signed Thomas Crumley. Wit. oath Jun. 4, 1821 Robert King to Wm Clement. Rec. Jun. 4, 1821

p. 282 Jun. 4, 1821 Z McDaniel received from William Foster $68. Witness M. N. Chapman and Garner Self. Signed Z McDaniel. Wit. oath Jun. 4, 1821 Garner Self to John Chapman. Rec. Jun. 4, 1821

p. 282-284 Dec. 28, 1819 Adam Gramling (Spartanburgh) to James Moss (same); for $1,400 sold 300 ac on waters of Hannon's Br; border: Fielding Foster and Elisha Bomar's Spring Br. Witness Fielding Foster and Joel Mason. Signed Adam Gramling. Wit. oath Feb. 7, 1820 Fielding Foster to F. H. Legg. Rec. Jun. 19, 1821. Dower renounced Mar. 15, 1820 Mary Gramling to F. H. Legg

p. 284-285 Dec. 31, 1819 Joel Mason (Spartanburgh) to James Moss (same); for $400 sold 80 ac on branch of N Tyger R; border: Edward Clement, Greenville Rd, Foster's Meeting House, Blackstocks Road, Wm Foster, Fielding Foster, and Ford Br. Witness Fielding Foster and Nancy Foster. Signed Joel Mason. Wit. oath Feb. 7, 1820 Fielding Foster to F. H. Legg. Rec. Jun. 19, 1821. Dower renounced Mar. 15, 1820 Mary Mason to F. H. Legg

p. 285-287 (p. 286 omitted) Aug. 22, 1820 James Brannon (Spartanburgh) to William P Gadberry (same); for $500 sold ½ ac in Spartanburgh, SC on NW side of Main St; border: Tollison's old house and public square. Witness Elisha Bomar and William Hunt. Signed J Brannon. Wit. oath Aug. 22, 1820 William Hunt to Daniel White. Rec. Jun. 21, 1821. Dower renounced Mar. 5, 1821 Sarah Brannon to Thomas Poole

p. 287-288 Sept. 16, 1820 James Brannon (Spartanburgh) to Josiah Blackwell (same); for $450 sold 147 ac on Lawson's fork of Pacolate R; border: Henry Child's Spring Br and waggon road. Witness William P Gadberry, John Wilbanks, and William Hunt. Signed J Brannon. Wit. oath Sept. 16, 1820 William Hunt to E Bomar. Rec.

Jun. 28, 1821. Dower renounced Jun. 25, 1821 Sarah Brannon to Elisha Bomar

p. 288-289 Jan. 29, 1821 Daniel Stephens (Spartanburgh) to John Stephens jr (same); for $100 sold (1) 100 ac; border: Wm Rogers, John Stephens jr, and John Stephens sr; (2) 129 ac; sold by Zacheriah Gibbs to John Otts who sold to Daniel Stephens; part of grant to Richard Hampton; at head waters of Ward's Cr; border: Philip Otts and John Finch; and (3) 50 ac; and at Daniel's death, John Stephens jr gets all Daniel's "other" property except John is to give his two sisters Sarah and Betsy each a feather bed and furniture complete, a cow and calf, 6 pewter plates, a large dish, and a set of knives and forks. Witness A. B. Moore, Anna A Moore, and Robert Ligon. Signed Daniel Stephens' mark. Wit. oath Jul. 2, 1821 Robert Ligon to Wm Underwood. Rec. Jul. 2, 1821

p. 289-290 Mar. 16, 1821 David Tanner (Spartanburgh) to Thomas Tinsley (same); for $1,000 sold 300 ac on both sides Fairforest Cr; includes Harrison's Mill; border: Case; part of two grants: (1) to Thomas Case and (2) to Richard Harrison, now desc. Witness William T Tanner, John Foster, and Floyd Tanner. Signed David Tanner. Wit. oath Jul. 2, 1821 William T Tanner to John Chapman. Rec. Jul. 2, 1821

p. 290-291 Jul. 4, 1821 Margaret Bagwell, widow of Hays Bagwell desc, George Bagwell, Amelia Bagwell, and Harriet Bagwell, heirs of estate of Hays Bagwell, to John Crawford (Spartanburgh). for $250 sold (ac omitted) that is all their shares of land sold by Joshua H Brown, attorney for Jane and Mary McMiken, heirs of estate of James McMiken desc, to Hays Bagwell desc Mar. 23, 1819 (see Book R p. 233 & 234); land on waters of and N side of N Tyger R. Witness Samuel Miller BS and Patrick C Caldwell. Signed Milly Bagwell and Margaret, George, and Harriet Bagwell's marks. Wit. oath Jul. 4, 1821 Samuel Miller BS to E Bomar. Rec. Jul. 4, 1821

p. 291-292 Jun. 25, 1821 Stephen Williams, taylor (Spartanburgh) to James Vernon (same); for a horse valued at $65 sold 490 ac in Appling Co, Ga second Dist #449; border: #462, #463, #510, and #498; land was drawn by lottery at Milledgeville, Ga by Stephen Williams (then living in Jefferson Co). Witness Alexander Vernon, Andrew McDavid, and George Gillard. Signed Stephen Williams. Wit. oath Jul. 4, 1821 George Gillard to E Bomar. Rec. Jul. 4, 1821

p. 292-293 Mar. 24, 1821 David Ulmer to John Rush jr; for $300 sold a note of Thomas Crumley of $45 with interest, note of George Smith $41, note of Henry Till $13, note of James Cross $2.84, note of Andrew Doigg $10, 12 cattle, a jearsey waggon, 3 beds and furniture, 6 hogs a trunk waggon, a clock and case, 2 horse colts; Condition: sale void if David pays John $300 by Jan. 1, 1822. Witness William Alexander Vernon and Henry Gramling. Signed David Ulmer. Wit. oath Jul. 4, 1821 Alexander Vernon to E Bomar. Rec. Jul. 4, 1821

p. 293-294 Dec. 30, 1820 Bayles Earle (Spartanburgh) to Benjamin Page (Chester Dist); for $100 sold (ac omitted) near Meeting House Spring; border: Wm Embry; N end of tract Bayles Earle owns. Witness Theron Earle and John Embry. Signed Baylis Earle. Wit. oath Jul. 28, 1821 John Embry to Thomas Poole. Rec. Aug. 4, 1821

p. 294-295 Jan. 30, 1821 Nicholas Gentry (Spartanburgh) to Samuel Eskridge (same); for $550 sold (ac omitted) on SW side of Ferguson's Cr; border: Joel G Brewton, Broadrick Mason, and William Otts' Spring Br. Witness William Otts and Joseph Willis. Signed Nicholas Gentry's mark. Wit. oath Aug. 6, 1821 William Otts and Joseph Willis. Signed Nicholas Gentry's mark. Wit. oath Aug. 6, 1821 William Otts to John Brewton. Rec. Aug. 6, 1821

p. 295-296 Feb. 21, 1818 Reuben Harris (Spartanburgh) to Miles Rainwaters (same); for $325 sold 200 ac on branch of Jamies Cr of Tyger R; grant to John Hunter. Witness Robert Hewett and Alfred Casey. Signed Reuben Harris. Wit. oath Feb. 21, 1818 Robert Hewett to M Casey. Rec. Aug. 6, 1821. Dower renounced Jul. 3, 1818 Polly Harris to Burrel Bobo

p. 296 Sept. 6, 1813 Samuel Earle (Pendleton Dist) to Aspasio Earle (Rutherford Co, NC); for $500 sold 300 ac on Bridge fork of Suck Cr of Broad R; grant Jun. 5, 1786 Gov. William Moultrie to Samuel Earle. Witness Theron Earle and John Roddy. Signed Samuel Earle. Wit. oath Aug. 6, 1821 Theron Earle to John Montgomery. Rec. Aug. 6, 1821

p. 296-298 Jan. 24, 1821 John Westmoreland (Greenville Dist) to Sterling L Westmoreland (Spartanburgh); for $316 sold 592.47 ac by resurvey on N side of Enoree R; border: N-D Anderson, E-Z. F. Westmoreland, S-Ford, and Samuel Gilkey's old line. Witness Zadoc F Westmoreland and Archibald McCravy. Signed John Westmoreland. Wit. oath Jul. 21, 1821 Zadoc F Westmoreland to James Ford. Rec. Aug. 6, 1821

p. 298-300 Dec. 7, 1820 Thomas Dare (Spartanburgh) to Abner Benson (same); for $5,000 sold (1) 318 ac on S side of Broad R; where Thomas Dare lives; border: Michael Gaffney; except 23 ac now owned by William Ross; grant to Francis Beatis who sold to William Tate and willed to James Tate and Elizabeth Tate (now Roberts) who sold to Thomas Dare; (2) 46 ac in two parts (a) sold by John Ross (now desc) to James Tate and sold to Thomas Dare; part of 200 ac grant to John Tygert; and (b) 200 ac part of grant Apr. 2, 1792 North Carolina governor (sic) to John Ross who sold to "said" Tate; border: McGowen, Tate's Mill tract, John Ross, and James Tate; (3) 57 ac in Union Dist on Pepleses Cr of Broad R; and (4) 140 ac in Union Dist on waters of Cherokee Cr; border: Levi Pennington, John Leek, William Cumberland, and Cherokee Rd. Witness William Rickman, Briant Bonner, and Daniel White esq. Signed Thomas Dare. Wit. oath May 19, 1821 Daniel White to E Bomar. Rec. May 19, 1821

p. 300-301 Jan. 1, 1821 John Chapman jr (Spartanburgh) to Coleman Wingo (same); for $500 sold 270 ac on waters of N Tyger R; border: William Laurence, John M Collins, Blackstock Road, North Carolina or Nesbett's furnace road, and Alexander Roddy. Witness Ransom Wingo and Berryman Foster. Signed John Chapman jr. Wit. oath Aug. 6, 1821 Ransom Wingo to John S Rowland. Rec. Aug. 6, 1821

p. 301-302 Jul. 10, 1821 Elizabeth Parker (Spartanburgh) to Augustin Shands (same); to secure payment of $2,200 in three notes: $733.33 payable in Mar. 1821, $733.33 payable Jan. 1, 1822 and $733.33 payable Jan. 1, 1823 sold (ac omitted) in two tracts--(1) (ac omitted) border: SW-David Golightly jr, NW-William S Golightly, NE-James Poole and Anthony Bates, and SE-John King; and (2) (ac omitted) border: David Golightly; grant to James Hammett and sold by Christopher Golightly to Augustin Shands who sold to Elizabeth Parker; and (3) (ac omitted) border: David Golightly, Hase, Ferguson, and John King; grant to Samuel Noblett who sold to John Tollison who sold to Augustin Shands who sold to Elizabeth Parker; Condition: sale void if Elizabeth pays the debt. Witness Green B Evans and Sarah Matthews. Signed Eliza Parker. Wit. oath Jul. 23, 1821 Green B Evans to Benj Wofford. Rec. Aug. 6, 1821

p. 302-303 Jul. 25, 1821 Robert Rogers to son Robert Rogers jr; for love and affection give 343 ac; where grantor lives;

grant Mar. 3, 1785; one ac excepted for burial ground; on Tyger R. Witness Amos Martin and William A Rogers. Signed Robert Rogers. Wit. oath Jul. 25, 1821 William A Rogers to Robert Ligon. Rec. Aug. 6, 1821

p. 303-304 Feb. 9, 1821 Sterling L Westmoreland (Spartanburgh) to Zadoc F Westmoreland (same); for $2,000 sold 346 ac on waters of Ferguson's and Ben's Creeks; border: SE & SW-Harris Ford and Sterling L Westmoreland and NE & NW-Anderson and Burnett. Witness Willis W Dickie and Richard Fowler. Signed Sterling L Westmoreland. Wit. oath Jul. 21, 1821 Willis W Dickie to James Ford. Rec. Aug. 6, 1821

p. 304-305 Jan. 17, 1821 John Durham sr (Spartanburgh) to Grisham Durham (same); for $50 sold 425 ac on Bushy fork Cr of S Tyger R; border: Jonas Leonard, Anderson, Powder fork, and Turner's old line. Witness Philip Johnson and John Durham jr. Signed John Durham. Wit. oath Aug. 6, 1821 John Durham jr to W Hunt. Rec. Aug. 6, 1821

p. 305-306 Jan. 1, 1820 William Brown (Spartanburgh) to Hugh Holt (Union Dist); for $160 sold 140 ac on Green Cr on N side of Pacolate R; border: Jesse Conell and James Brown; where Charles Criddinton lived. Witness Peter Peterson and James Briant. Signed William Brown and Nancy's mark. Wit. oath Aug. 3, 1821 Peter Peterson to Wm Reid. Rec. Aug. 6, 1821

p. 306-307 Dec. 13, 1820 William George (Spartanburgh) to Ephraim Jackson; for $150 sold 50 ac on Sneed's Br on S side of Thickety Cr; border: Thomas Lipscomb and Sullivan's old line; part of grant to Ezekiel Sullivan who sold to William Sullivan. Witness Hugh Moore and John Moore. Signed William George. Wit. oath Aug. 1, 1821 Hugh Moore to Caleb Jones. Rec. Aug. 6, 1821

p. 307-308 May 27, 1820 Jonathan Wall (Spartanburgh) to Samuel Wall; for $150 sold 100 ac on both sides of S Pacolate R; border: Philip Johnson, Amos Spencer, "place called burnt cabbin", Luke Burnett, Jordan Carden, Daniel White, "the wading shoal", and N Pacolate R; part of grant to Amos Speace. Witness David Bettes and Iredell Cunningham. Signed Jonathan Wall. Wit. oath Jul. 3, 1821 Iredell Cunningham to W Clemment. Rec. Aug. 6, 1821

p. 308 Jul. 28, 1821 Samuel Fowler (Spartanburgh) to son John Fowler (same); for extra attention given by John to Samuel and for parental affection give a Negro woman named Dark; Samuel reserves "authority and command of" Dark during his lifetime. Witness John W Lewis and John S Rowland. Signed Samuel Fowler's mark. Wit. oath Jul. 28, 1821 John S Rowland to J Whitten. Rec. Aug. 6, 1821

p. 308-309 Jul. 28, 1821 Samuel Fowler sr (Spartanburgh) to grandson Samuel Fowler jr, son of John Fowler, (same); for services rendered and attentioned paid to Samuel sr give a Negro boy Caleb, at Samuel sr's desc; Samuel sr reserves "authority to" Caleb during his lifetime. Witness John W Lewis and John S Rowland. Signed Samuel Fowler's mark. Wit. oath Jul. 28, 1821 John W Lewis to J Whitten. Rec. Aug. 6, 1821

p. 309-310 Jan. 31, 1821 John Whorton (Spartanburgh) to Samuel Moore (same); for $100 sold (1) 50 ac on E side of Beaverdam Cr of S Pacolate R; part of 200 ac survey for James G Reaves; border: William Duncan and John Duncan; and (2) 20 on W side of Beaverdam Cr; border: Martin Bowling and Agga Prewett; adjoins (1) and part of same survey. Witness John Grogan and Willey S Brown. Signed John Whorton's mark. Wit. oath Mar. 30, 1821 John Grogan to J Whitten. Rec. Apr. 2, 1821

p. 310-311 Jan. 15, 1821 Obadiah Prewett (Spartanburgh) to William Smith and John OShield (same); for $400 sold 210 ac on Cany Cr of Tyger R; border: John Smith and blacksmith. Witness Thomas Prewett and James Newman. Signed Obadiah Prewett. Wit. oath Aug. 17, 1821 James Newman to Wm Young. Rec. Aug. 18, 1821

p. 311 May 12, 1821 Solomon Crocker (Spartanburgh) to Thomas Chapman (same); for $200 sold 100 ac; border: Wells and Thomson. Witness Arthur Crocker jr and John Crocker. Signed Solomon Crocker's mark. Wit. oath Aug. 6, 1821 Arthur Crocker jr to William Reid. Rec. Aug. 27, 1821

p. 311-313 Sept. 3, 1821 James Hunt, sheriff (Spartanburgh) to Manly Ford; for $500 sold 200 ac on S side of S Tyger R; half of 400 ac grant May 23, 1767 to William Sharp; William Ford petitioned Spartanburgh Common Pleas Court second Monday after fourth Monday in Mar 1818 to divide estate of William Ford desc; court appointed James Vernon, David Dantzler, Page Rork, Isham Hendricks, and Thomas Deas esq to divide the estate; they said on second Monday after fourth Monday in Oct. 1818 that estate can't be divided and should be sold; credit is first payment in one year and second payment in 2 years; sale was on first Monday in Jan. 1819. Witness Page Rork and Toliver Scott. Signed Jas Hunt SSD. Wit. oath Sept. 3, 1821 Page Rork to J Whitten. Rec. Sept. 3, 1821

p. 313-314 Feb. 2, 1819 Robert Coleman (Spartanburgh) to Charles Petty (same); for $150 sold 118½ ac; border: John Amos, Amos Austill, and William Bostick; "two lots" were part of grant formerly owned by Moses Guiton desc and divided by court order as lots #2 and 3. Witness Michael Gaffney and Drury Wood. Signed Robert Coleman. Wit. oath Apr. 11, 1820 Michael Gaffney to John Lipscomb. Rec. Sept. 3, 1821. Dower renounced Feb. 11, 1819 Judith Coleman to John Lipscomb

p. 314-315 Feb. 10, 1821 Reuben Jentry (or Gentrey) to Isaac Crow (Spartanburgh); for $400 sold 125 ac on waters of Tyger R; part of where Reuben Jentry lives and sold by Burrel Bobo to Reuben Jentry. Witness Henry Marler and Cassander Johnson Jentry. Signed Reuben Jentry's mark. Wit. oath Aug. 9, 1821 Cassander J Jentry to John Dean. Rec. Aug. 11, 1821

p. 315-316 Aug. 11, 1821 Samuel Eskridge (Spartanburgh) to George Floyd jr (same); for $550 sold (ac omitted) on SW side of Furguson's Cr; border: Joel G Brewton, Mason, and Wm Otts' Spring Br. Witness David P Wilmott and Paul Combee. Signed Samuel Eskridge's mark. Wit. oath Sept. 3, 1821 David P Wilmott to Robert Ligon. Rec. Sept. 3, 1821

p. 316-317 Jan. 10, 1808 Joroyal Barnett (Spartanburgh) to Absalem Lancaster; for $80 sold 70 ac on waters of Kelso's Cr of Fairforest Cr; border: N & S-Joroyal Barnett, W-Thomas James, and E-John Tolleson; and on Bagwell's Br which borders main road and Reubin Harrison. Witness Thomas Barnett and Laurence Lancaster. Signed Joroyal Barnett. Wit. oath Feb. 16, 1808 Laurence Lancaster to William Lancaster. Rec. Sept. 3, 1821

p. 317-318 Sept. 3, 1821 John T Earle (Spartanburgh) to Muse Tolleson (same); for $350 sold ½ ac in Spartanburgh, SC; border: cross street, Todd's Stable, and Alleson. Witness William Trimmier and Joseph Carswell. Signed John T Earle. Wit. oath Sept. 4, 1821 William Trimmier to E Bomar. Rec. Sept. 4, 1821

p. 318-319 Feb. 18, 1817 William Wofford (Spartanburgh) to Isaac Wofford jr and George Wofford (same); for $90 sold 70 ac on S side of Dutchman's Cr; border: William Hembree, Osburn West,

Maj. William Smith's mill, and James Bennett; part of 440 ac grant to Sarah Elder. Witness Hosea Wofford and Isaac Wofford sr. Signed Wm Wofford. Wit. oath Aug. 30, 1821 Hosea Wofford to James Hamm. Rec. Sept. 4, 1821

p. 319 Aug. 7, 1821 John Golightly jr (Spartanburgh) to Elias Palmer (same); for $150 sold 427 ac on Peter's and Cherokee Crks of Pacolate R. Witness Wm Trimmier esq and Levi Lee. Signed John Golightly jr. Wit. oath Sept. 5, 1821 Wm Trimmier to E Bomar. Rec. Sept. 5, 1821

p. 319-321 Mar. 6, 1821 Job Sosbee (Spartanburgh) to Thomas Reese (same); for $500 sold 337 ac on both sides of Peter's Cr; border: Faust; where Job Sosbee lives; part of three (sic) grants: (1) to James Wyatt and (2) to Job Sosbee. Witness Craven Jinkins and Thomas Sosebee. Signed Job Sosbee's mark. Wit. oath Mar. 15, 1821 Craven Jinkins to Henry Turner. Rec. Sept. 13, 1821. Dower renounced Mar. 15, 1821 Elizabeth Sosebee to Henry Turner

p. 321 Apr. 1, 1821 Robert Hudson to Daniel McKie and Labon P Poole, of the firm of McKie, Poole & Co; for $100 (paid to Labon P Poole) sold 62½ ac on branch of Tyger R; border: waggon road, W-Elisha Wells, S-J. F. Kerne, and E-Edmd Hooker and Benjm Hooker. Witness E Roddy and D. P. McKie jr. Signed Robert Hudson. Wit. oath Sept. 19, 1821 E Roddy to E Bomar. Rec. Sept. 19, 1821

p. 321-322 Aug. 29, 1820 Alpheus H Wilbur to Robert Hudson; for $153 sold 62½ ac on branch of Tyger R; border: waggon road, W-Elisha Wells, S-J. F. Kerne, and E-Edmd Hooker and Benjm Hooker. Witness Levingston Bobo and Frederick Parham. Signed Alpheus H Wilbur. Wit. oath Levingston Bobo to M Casey Sept. 18, 1821. Rec. Sept. 21, 1821

p. 322-324 Oct. 29, 1819 (Eastern Circuit, SC) William Hasell Gibbs esq, Master of Equity Court of Southern Circuit (Charleston) to John Gossett (Spartanburgh); for $750 sold 500 ac near Fairforest Cr; grant Sept. 9, 1774 to Thomas Furguson in Craven Co; border: N, W & S-Col. William Thompson, Edward Cassen(?), and Robert Thomas and NE & SE-vacant, Hemet(?), David Brown, and James Meas; refer to Spartanburgh Common Pleas Court case John Horry Furguson and others vs John King; Christopher Gadsden "and others", executors of will of Thomas Furguson esq (late of Charleston) on Sept. 7, 1791 complained to Charleston Equity Court against Ann Furgeson, widow, and the "several" children of Thomas Furguson and against creditors and others; Christopher asked the Court to sell Thomas Furguson's real estate; case was heard in Sept. term 1791 and suit agrees to sell land; sale was Oct. 29, 1819. Witness James Ferguson and William R Bee. Signed Wm Hasell Gibbes, Master of Equity. Wit. oath Feb. 10, 1821 James Ferguson to Charles Tew(?). Rec. Oct. 1, 1821

p. 324-325 Dec. 24, 1813 Patrick Tylor (Spartanburgh) to John Grayham (same); for $75 sold 100 ac on waters of Lindsey's Cr and on Mare Br. Witness David Thompson and Robert Thompson. Signed Patrick Tylor. Wit. oath Dec. 24, 1813 Davie Thompson to Jno H Jones. Rec. Oct. 1, 1821

p. 325-327 Jan. 29, 1819 John L Rast (Spartanburgh) to Christina Rast, wife of Fredrick Rast (same); for $450 sold (ac omitted) on waters of Fairforest Cr; border: James Bishop, William Hammett, John Walker, and Drayton. Witness David Ulmer and Lewis Ulmer. Signed John L Rast. Wit. oath Apr. 17, 1820 Lewis Ulmer to Thomas Poole. Rec. Oct. 1, 1821. Dower renounced Sept. 26, 1821 Margaret Rast to Thomas Poole

p. 327-328 Jan. 19, 1819 Richard Cunningham (Charleston, SC) to Charles C Duncan, merchant (Spartanburgh); for $872 sold 436 ac; border: N-formerly Jesse Douglas' land, W-Henry Morgan, S & SW-Christopher Golightly and Armstead Bomar, and E-unknown; plat attaches shows also border: James Young and McClure. Witness John G Brown and Wilson Nesbett. Signed Richard Cunningham. Wit. oath Oct. 1, 1821 Wilson Nesbett to E Bomar. Rec. Oct. 1, 1821

p. 328-330 Sept. 14, 1818 Joel Mason (Spartanburgh) to Fredrick Rast (Orangeburgh Dist); for $400 sold 97 ac; border: Andrew Grambling, Robert Woods, E Bomar, road from Spartanburgh to Greenville Court House, and Timmons. Witness Andrew Grambling and John L Rast. Signed Joel Mason. Wit. oath Apr. 17, 1820 Andrew Grambling to Thomas Poole. Rec. Oct. 1, 1821. Dower renounced Sept. 27, 1821 Mary Mason to Thomas Poole

p. 330-331 Mar. 21, 1821 David Fowler (Spartanburgh) to Thomas B Brockman; for $40 sold 3 feather beds, a table, 5 chairs, a spinning wheel, a chest, a cupboard, 2 pots, an oven, a gridiron, 3 weeding hoes, 4 plow hoes, a bridle, a hand saw, 2 augers, a drawing knife, a pair of chain traces, a piggin, a pail, a bred tray, a tin bucket, a pewter dish, an umbrella, a smoothing iron, 9 ducks, a meal tub, a dozen cups and saucers, 3 bottles, 2 bed steads and furniture of the beds; Condition: sale void if David pays Thomas $40 with interest by Dec. 25, 1821. Witness James Hammett and William Beacham. Signed David Fowler's mark. Wit. oath Jul. 24, 1821 James Hammett to Thomas Wood. Rec. Oct. 1, 1821

p. 331-332 Dec. 1, 1820 George G Gilbert (Spartanburgh) to James Carter jr (same); for $100 sold 120 ac; border: James Carter sr and John Lee; part of where Henry Gilbert lives. Witness Wm Bennett and James Carter sr. Signed George G Gilbert. Wit. oath May 25, 1821 James Carter sr to Wm Clemment. Rec. Oct. 1, 1821

p. 332-333 Apr. 21, 1821 Thomas Slack (Spartanburgh) to Nathaniel Gist (Union Dist); for $3,000 sold (1) 300 ac on E side of Tiger R; border: N-Drury Parham, E-Randol Palmer, S-estate of Capt. Reuben Saunders, and W-Tiger R; part of land formerly owned by Burrell Bobo esq; and (2) (ac omitted) on W side of Tiger R; border: Prater's Cr, waggon road, and George Divin. Witness Hiram Colman and Allen King. Signed Thomas Slack. Wit. oath none. Rec. Oct. 4, 1821

p. 333-334 Oct. 18, 1811 Eli Tolleson and wife Elizabeth (Spartanburgh) to John Lancaster jr (same); for $100 sold 72 ac at head of Richland Cr of Pacolett R; border: Lauson, Joroyal Barnett, and John Lancaster jr. Witness John Lancaster sr and John Simmons. Signed Ely Tolleson. Wit. oath Apr. 12, 1821 John Lancaster sr to John Lipscomb. Rec. Oct. 4, 1821

p. 334-335 Oct. 9, 1821 Nemrod E Benson promises to pay Abner Benson $2,897.36 for "value received" to be paid Oct. 10. Witness E Roddy and Wilson Nesbett. Signed N. E. Benson.
Oct. 9, 1821 Nemrod E Benson to Abner Benson; to secure the foregoing payment with interest, sold a Negro Dick about 35 years old, Stephen about 22 years old, Alexander about 19 years old, Lot about 37 years old, Michael about 17 years old Moses about 14 years old, and Larkin about 20 years old; Condition: sale void if Nimrod pays the debt. Witness E Roddy and Wilson Nesbett. Signed N. E. Benson. Wit. oath Oct. 10, 1821 E Roddy to E Bomar. Rec. Oct. 10, 1821

p. 335-337 Sept. 24, 1821 Adam Carruth (Greenville Dist) to Elias Carruth (same); power of attorney to manage Adam's business in Spartanburgh Dist relating to suit of Adam Carruth vs Col. Wilson Nesbett in Equity Court; Elias is to collect what Adam is due and

Elias can hire a lawyer to help. Witness James McDaniel and William Choice jr. Signed A Carruth. Wit. oath Oct. 11, 1821 (Greenville Dist) William Choice jr to J. H. Goodlet. Rec. Oct. 18, 1821

p. 337-338 Oct. 22, 1821 Muse Tolleson (Spartanburgh) to Edward Autry (same); for $206 sold 103 ac on Mill Cr of Tyger R; border: W. T. Tanner; part of grant to John Swoddy. Witness William Trimmier and John Foster MC. Signed Muse Tolleson. Wit. oath Oct. 22, 1821 William Trimmier to John Chapman. Rec. Oct. 22, 1821

p. 338-339 Jun. 8, 1820 John Strickland (Spartanburgh) to Edmond Bishop, short, Edmd L Bishop, Joseph Gilbert, and Josiah Blackwell (same); for $59.87½ sold 100 ac on both sides Bartius Br of Lawson's fork; border: Larkin Carden, Pasimue Br, and furnace road. Witness John B Lewis and Abijah Lewis. Signed John Strickland. Wit. oath Dec. 7, 1820 John B Lewis to E Lewis. Rec. Oct. 25, 1821

p. 339-340 Oct. 20, 1821 Wiley Berry (Edgefield Dist) to Muse Tolleson (Spartanburgh); for 240 gal of whiskey sold ½ ac in Spartanburgh, SC on N side of Main St "below the jail"; part of lot #5. Witness Robert Walker and Agrippa Cooper. Signed Wiley Berry. Wit. oath Oct. 26, 1821 Agrippa Cooper to E Bomar. Rec. Oct. 27, 1821

p. 340-341 Oct. 26, 1821 Clayborn Holt (Spartanburgh) to Hugh Holt (same); for future care, protection, and provision to be given by Hugh sold 120 ac on Lawson's fork Cr; where Clayborn Holt lives; Hugh must furnish Clayborn and wife Elizabeth with comfortable clothing and lodging as long as Clayborn and Elizabeth Holt live. Witness Peter Peterson and William Hunt. Signed Clayborn Holt's mark. Wit. oath Oct. 26, 1821 Peter Peterson to W Hunt. Rec. Oct. 27, 1821

p. 341-342 Mar. 3, 1821 James Hunt, sheriff (Spartanburgh) to Ephraim Drummon jr (same); for $240 sold 122 ac in two tracts on branch of Jinnings Cr of Tyger R; border: Shans Golightly, William L Allen, J Edwards, John Leatherwood, and George Leatherwood; sale due to writ from Spartanburgh Common Pleas Court second Monday after fourth Monday in Oct. 1820 suit Elisha Bobo vs John Edwards; judgment was levy from John Edwards of $107 with interest. Witness John Dean and Dennis Lindsey. Signed Jas Hunt SSD. Wit. oath Nov. 8, 1821 Dennis Lindsey to John Brewton. Rec. Nov. 10, 1821

p. 342-343 Nov. 3, 1821 Elihu Golightly (Spartanburgh) to Joel Hurt (same); for (money omitted) sold (ac omitted) on Fairforest and Beverdam Creeks of Tyger R; on May 2, 1819 John Golightly (Spartanburgh) sold 430 ac to Francis Golightly, now wife of Joel Hurt, and Elihu Golightly; Elihu sells land E of Public Road from Wm Anthony Foster's to Tanner's Mills on Tyger R. Witness John Golightly jr and Christi Golightly. Signed Elihu Golightly. Wit. oath Nov. 3, 1821 Christi Golightly to E Bomar. Rec. Nov. 3, 1821

p. 343-344 Aug. 20, 1821 Susannah Walker to William Clary; for $200 sold 100 ac; grant to Hugh Quin who sold to William Walker and "fell" to George Walker and sold by sheriff to Susannah Walker. Witness Alexander Davidson and Joseph Camp. Signed Susannah Walker. Wit. oath Nov. 3, 1821 Alexander Davidson to Geo Camp. Rec. Nov. 10, 1821

p. 344-345 Jan. 11, 1819 Wilson Langley and wife Martha (Kershaw Dist) to Burrel Bobo; for $3,200 sold 2,500 ac on Cedar Shoal Cr of Enoree R and James Cr of Tyger R; except about 40 ac claimed by William Littlefield and about 300 ac claimed by Wm Casey. Witness John B Leatherwood and Eliza Dean. Signed Wilson and Martha

Langley. Wit. oath Nov. 7, 1821 John B Leatherwood to Wm Young. Rec. Nov. 10, 1821

p. 345-346 Sept. 29, 1821 Miles Rainwaters (Spartanburgh) to James Rainwaters sr (same); for $100 sold 88½ ac on E side of branch of Cedar Shoal Cr of Enoree R; plat attached shows border: Healing Spring. Witness James Rainwaters jr and John E Wilson. Signed Miles Rainwaters. Wit. oath Oct. 6, 1821 James Rainwaters jr to Wm Young. Rec. Nov. 10, 1821

p. 346-347 Jan. 17, 1821 James Childress (Spartanburgh) to William Hendrix (same); for $105 sold 93 ac on S side of Ready fork of Abner's Cr of Enoree R; border: Lewis Jones, John T King, William Hendrix, Wm Hugh, and William Jones; includes where James Childress lives. Witness William Hughes and Elizabeth Hughes. Signed James Childress. Wit. oath Feb. 20, 1821 William Hughes to Thomas Wood. Rec. Nov. 10, 1821

p. 347-349 Mar. 14, 1821 Abraham Nelson (Spartanburgh) to Charles Simmons (same); for $380 sold 380 ac on waters of Buck Cr. Witness Isaiah Johnson and John Covington. Signed Abraham Nelson. Wit. oath Mar. 14, 1821 Isaiah Johnson to Henry Turner. Rec. Nov. 10, 1821

p. 349-350 Jul. 16, 1821 John Vise (Spartanburgh) to Benjamin Wofford (same); for 80($?) sold 125 ac on N side of Tyger R; border: John Vise, Gideon Herelson, and Reuben Vise; part of 164 ac formerly belonged to Peter Laurence. Witness John Williams and Eli Vise. Signed John Vise. Wit. oath Nov. 7, 1821 John Williams to D White. Rec. Nov. 10, 1821

p. 350-351 Jan. 20, 1821 Thomas Prewett (Jiles(sic) Co, Tenn) to Benjamin Wofford (Spartanburgh); for $300 sold 174 ac on N side of Tyger R and waters of Cane Cr; grant Feb. 5, 1787 Gov. William Moultrie to Owen Forester. Witness Abner Vise and James Newman. Signed Thos Prewett. Wit. oath Oct. 30, 1821 James Newman to Wm Young. Rec. Nov. 10, 1821

p. 351-353 Oct. 1, 1821 Augustin Shands (Spartanburgh) to Phebe Shands (same); for $671 sold a Negro man Punch(?), a bay horse called Suip, 2 cows and calves, 2 bull yearlings, 3 saws, 11 pigs, all his carpenter tools; Condition: sale void if Augustin pays Phebe $671 with interest by Jan. 1, 1822. Witness Elijah Ballinger and Elijah Foster. Signed Augustin Shands. Wit. oath Nov. 6, 1821 Elijah Ballinger to James Hamm. Rec. Nov. 10, 1821

p. 353-354 Oct. 1, 1821 Augustin Shands (Spartanburgh) to Mary Shands (same); for $874 sold a Negro man Toney, a bay horse named Saph, a bay mare named Bonney, 6 cattle bought from James Head, 7 hogs bought from James Head, a "riding chair", and harnis, a feather bed and furniture, all household and kitchen furniture and all farming utensils; Condition: sale void if Augustin pays Mary $874 with interest by Jan. 1, 1822. Witness Elijah Ballinger and Elijah Foster. Signed Augustin Shands. Wit. oath Nov. 6, 1821 Elijah Ballinger to James Hamm. Rec. Nov. 10, 1821

p. 354-355 Feb. 14, 1820 Kesiah Kilgore, Henry Brockman, and Andrew McCrary, executors of will of James Kilgore desc (Greenville Dist), to Lucretia Dempsey (Spartanburgh); for $30 sold 124 ac on waters of Maple Swamp Cr; border: Stephen Sizemore and Ephraim Sizemore. Witness William Wilson and Joel D Brockman. Signed Henry Brockman, Andrew McCrary, and Kesiah Kilgore's mark. Wit. oath Mar. 27, 1820 William Wilson to Thomas Wood. Rec. Nov. 10, 1821

p. 355-356 Nov. 20, 1818 Manly Ford (Spartanburgh) to John Johnson jr (same); for $400 sold 350 ac on branches of Rocky field and Maple Swamp Creeks of Tyger and Enoree Rivers. Witness James Hammett and Newbel Johnson. Signed M Ford. Wit. oath Mar. 24, 1819 Newbel Johnson to James Crook. Rec. Nov. 10, 1821

p. 356-357 Mar. 3, 1821 Samuel Busey (Spartanburgh) to John Todd sr (Laurence Dist); for $40.76 sold 84 ac on branch of Two Mile Cr of Enoree R. Witness John S Todd and John Wallis sr. Signed Samuel Busey's mark. Wit. oath Nov. 2, 1821 (Laurens Dist) John S Todd to Starling Tucker. Rec. Nov. 10, 1821

p. 357-358 Feb. 13, 1819 (Greenville Dist) Andrew McCrary, Henry Brockman, and Keziah Kilgore, executors of James Kilgore desc (Greenville Dist), to John Johnson jr (Spartanburgh); for $140 sold 234 ac on Duncan's Br of Maple Swamp Cr; border: John Johnson jr. Witness Lodwick Johnson and Newbell Johnson. Signed Andrew McCrary, Henry Brockman, and Keziah Kilgore's mark. Wit. oath Mar. 24, 1819 Newbell Johnson to James Crook. Rec. Nov. 10, 1821

p. 358-359 May 4, 1821 Jesse Scruggs (Spartanburgh) to Richard Scruggs (same); for $333 sold 267 ac on both sides of Island Cr; border: W-Young, N-Cantrell, E-Knox and Marrow, and S-Potter; part of 455 ac grant Sept. 5, 1803 to William Abbott. Witness Robert Scruggs and Lewis Martin. Signed Jesse Scruggs. Wit. oath Nov. 2, 1821 Lewis Martin to Geo Camp. Rec. Nov. 10, 1821

p. 359-360 Feb. 16, 1816 William Robb (Sumpter Dist) to Samuel Saratt (Spartanburgh); for $373.75 sold 323 ac on W side of Broad R; border: NE-John Sarratt jr and SE-"said" Sarratt. Witness Anthony Sarratt and Charles Happer. Signed William Robb. Wit. oath Oct. 14, 1815 Anthony Sarratt to J Camp. Rec. Nov. 10, 1821

p. 360-361 Apr. 10, 1821 John Wofford to Fredrick Parham; John owes Fredrick $300 due "perhaps" 12 months past and note is now in possession of James Brannon; Richard Hewel and George Wofford were security for John for payment of the note; John gives a Negro boy Smart about 10 years old to Richard Hewel and George Wofford if they loose out due to security on John's debt. Witness John W Williams and Samuel Turner. Signed John Wofford's mark. Wit. oath Nov. 5, 1821 Samuel Turner to Thomas Poole. Rec. Nov. 10, 1821

p. 361-363 Dec. 5, 1818 Adam Henderson, John Henderson, and Isabela Henderson (Smith Co, Tenn), Robert Henderson, Mary Henderson, and Hanah Henderson (Pendleton Dist), and Robert Henderson (Jackson Co, Ga) to friend William Henderson (Pendleton Dist); power of attorney to sell 300 ac in Spartanburgh Dist on "in the greuiz" (or Hugreuiz) Cub Cr of S Pacolett R; grant to Richard Henderson who sold to Robert Henderson; grantors are heirs of Robert Henderson. Witness Allen Patrick, Isabella Henderson, and Samuel Henderson. Signed Adam Henderson, John Henderson, Isabella Henderson, Robert Henderson, Anne Henderson, Hannah Henderson, Robert Henderson, and Martha and Mary Henderson's marks. Wit. oath Jan. 20, 1819 (Pendleton Dist) Allen Patrick to George Edmondson. Wit. oath Mar. 25, 1819 (Pendleton Dist) Samuel Henderson to James McDill. Wit. oath (Jackson Co, Ga) by W. D. Martin JJC for Robert Henderson. Mar. 5, 1819 (Jackson Co, Ga) Joseph Diprest(?), clerk of Inferior Court, certifys William D Martin is Justice of Inferior Court. Mar. 5, 1819 (Jackson Co, Ga) David Will, JJC certifys Joseph Diprest is clerk of Court. Rec. Nov. 10, 1821

p. 363-364 Dec. 7, 1819 Abraham Brock (Spartanburgh) to James Whitten (same); for $200 sold 60 ac on N side of S Pacolate R; border: James Whitten and Joseph Davis; part of grant to James Whitten who sold to Abraham Brock. Witness David M Davis and James Loftis. Signed A Brock. Wit. oath Nov. 5, 1821 James Loftis to Wm Bennett.

Rec. Nov. 10, 1821

p. 364-365 Mar. 22, 1819 Hugh Ewing (Lincoln Co, NC) to Thomas Jackson sr (SC); for $1,500 sold (1) 250 ac on both sides of N Pacolate R; border: Alexander Kilpatrick; grant Apr. 27, 1767 Gov. William Trion to Saml Young and regranted May 4, 1775 Gov. William Bull (to Saml Young?); and (2) 97 ac on both sides of N Pacolate R; border: John Ridings; grant Jul. 6, 1801 Gov. John Drayton to Hugh Ewing and Wm Davis. Witness John Ridings, Samuel Jackson, and Thomas Jackson jr. Signed Hugh Ewing. Wit. oath Nov. 7, 1821 Samuel Jackson to J Whitten. Rec. Nov. 11, 1821

p. 365-367 Jun. 20, 1818 James Wilson (Spartanburgh) to Isham Wilson (same); for $150 sold 106 ac on branch of Abner's Cr of Enoree R; part of grant to Charles Wakefield. Witness William Hendricks and James Hendricks. Signed James Wilson's mark. Wit. oath Aug. 17, 1819 James Hendricks to Thomas Wood. Rec. Nov. 12, 1821. Dower renounced Oct. 13, 1818 Prudence Wilson to Thomas Wood

p. 367-368 (not dated) Henry Wade (Spartanburgh) to Matthew Jones (same); for $250 sold 203 ac(?) on both sides of Abner's Cr of Enoree R; includes where Henry Wade lives; border: Charles Baker, Lewis Jones, William Hughes, Levi Demsey, Isham Wilson, Joseph Hughes, and John Cargeles; part of (1) 282 ac and (2) 311 ac (part of 396 ac grant Jun. 5, 1797 to John Denis) and (3) 500 ac grant Jun. 23, 1774 to Robert Filas (or Filpes), 200 ac grant to John Dempsey and 3 ac grant to Robert Files. Witness William Hughes and Joseph Hughes. Signed Henry Wade's mark and Dicy Wade. Wit. oath Nov. 10, 1821 Joseph Hughes to Thomas Wood. Rec. Nov. 12, 1821

p. 368-369 Dec. 14, 1820 John Thomas (Spartanburgh) to John Murph (Spartanburgh); for $300 sold 114½ ac between Fairforest and Kelso's Creeks; where John Thomas lives; sold Oct. 1820 by Richard Barnett to John Thomas; also sold a bay mare, 2 cows and calves, 12 hogs and their increase; Condition: sale void if John Thomas pays John Murph $300 with interest by Jan. 1, 1822. Witness Daniel Zimmerman and Elizabeth Zimmerman. Signed John Thomas' mark. Wit. oath (Orangeburgh Dist) Daniel Zimmerman to John C Kennerly. Rec. Nov. 20, 1821

p. 369-370 Oct. 28, 1820 John T Rast (Spartanburgh) to John Mullinix (same); for $2,000 sold 380 ac on waters of N Tyger R; border: Edward Bomar, Ulmer, Traylor's old house, mill tract, White's Br, and Snoddy; includes 2 ac on S side of river. Witness Samuel Tucker and Jesse Williams. Signed John T Rast. Wit. oath Sept. 28, 1821 Jesse Williams to Benj Wofford. Rec. Nov. 24, 1821

p. 370-380 (p. 371-379 missing when microfilmed Jul. 22, 1971) Dec. 1, 1821 James Hunt, sheriff (Spartanburgh) to Benjamin Cash (same); for $20 sold 80 ac on Island Cr of Pacolate R; border: Reuben Warren, James Land sr, James Young, Benjamin Cook, and Daniel Cash; land was bought by Jesse Cleveland for Benjamin Cash; sale due to writ from Spartanburgh Common Pleas Court second Monday after fourth Monday in Mar. 1821 suit by Jesse Cleveland; judgment was levy of $39.05 with interest from Samuel Turner. Witness Richard Thomson and Benjamin Gilbert. Signed Jas Hunt SSD. Wit. oath Dec. 1, 1821 Benjamin Gilbert to Thomas Poole. Rec. Dec. 1, 1821

p. 380-381 Aug. 2, 1819 Robert McMillen (Spartanburgh) to Hugh McMillen (same); for $800 sold a Negro woman Oma and her two children Mary and Marilla. Witness John S Rowland and Luke Burnett. Signed Robert McMillen. Wit. oath Sept. 15, 1820 John S Rowland to James Young. Rec. Dec. 3, 1821

p. 381-382 Oct. 22, 1821 Hugh McMillen (Spartanburgh) to Robert

McMillen (same); for $200 sold 277 ac on both sides of N Pacolate R; border: Barton. Witness Benjamin D Pope and George B Camp. Signed Hugh McMillen. Wit. oath Oct. 30, 1821 Benjamin D Pope to E Lewis. Rec. Dec. 3, 1821

p. 382-383 Nov. 3, 1821 Elihu Golightly (Spartanburgh) to Ransom Golightly (same); for $1,020 sold 300 ac on both sides Beverdam Cr on S side of Fairforest Cr; border: ford of Fairforest Cr, road from Anthony Foster's and Tanner's Mills on Tyger R, and Richard Daniel; part of grant to John Golightly sr who sold to Elihu and Francis Golightly. Witness John Golightly jr and Christi Golightly. Signed Elihu Golightly. Wit. oath Dec. 20, 1821 John Golightly jr to E Bomar. Rec. Dec. 20, 1821

p. 383 Mar. 10, 1820 Moses Waters (Spartanburgh) to Thomas Waters; for (money omitted) sold 100 ac on both sides of Rocky fork Cr; border: Solomon Jackson, Green River Rd, Sprouse, and Wolf Br. Witness William Waters and William Hindman. Signed Moses Waters. Wit. oath Sept. 4, 1820 William Waters to Wm Reid. Rec. Dec. 21, 1821

p. 383-384 Mar. 10, 1820 Moses Waters (Spartanburgh) to Thomas Waters (same); for $600 sold 150 ac; 100 ac borders: William Bice and on S side of Thickety Cr; and 50 ac borders: on Rocky fork Cr and Jackson; 100 ac was sold in 1804 by Ephraim Jackson and 50 ac was sold in 1805 Edward Smith to Charles Smith who sold to Moses Waters. Witness William Waters and William Hindman. Signed Moses Waters. Wit. oath Sept. 4, 1821 William Waters to William Reid. Rec. Dec. 21, 1821

p. 384-385 Nov. 6, 1821 Elizabeth McCarry (Spartanburgh) to John Arnold (same); power of attorney to obtain her due from will of Edmond Chambers desc (Spartanburgh); her due is the land where Edmond Chambers lived, a Negro girl Leah, a horse, 2 coes and calves, 10 hogs, 5 sheep, the cupboard and its furniture, and other property left to her. Witness William Lancaster. Signed Elizabeth McCarry. Wit. oath Nov. 7, 1821 William Lancaster to J Whitten. Rec. Dec. 27, 1821

p. 385-386 Dec. 15, 1820 Ransom Golightly (Spartanburgh) to John Golightly jr (same); for $400 sold (ac omitted) on both sides of Lawson's fork Cr; border: Betty Green's Br and old mill pond and dam; grant to Mary Wood. Witness Zachariah Cannon and James Cummins. Signed R Golightly. Wit. oath Dec. 24, 1821 James Cummins to E Bomar. Rec. Dec. 27, 1821

p. 386-387 Dec. 17, 1821 Muse Tolleson (Spartanburgh) to William P Gadberry (same); to secure notes Muse gave when he bought the land from William sold 885 ac known as mill tract; formerly belonged to James Smith; sold the same day by William P Gadberry to Muse Tolleson. Witness William Trimmier and F. H. Legg. Signed Muse Tolleson. Wit. oath Dec. 17, 1821 William Trimmier to E Bomar. Rec. Dec. 27, 1821

p. 387-388 Apr. 15, 1820 William Clayton (Spartanburgh) to Benjamin Wofford (same); for $300 sold 100 ac on Fort Shoals Br of Enoree R; border: S-William Word, W-John Farrow, N-James Clayton, and E-Willis Bobo and John Bogan. Witness Joseph Wofford and Elias Corder. Signed Wm Clayton. Wit. oath Apr. 15, 1820 Elias Corder to John Brewton. Rec. Dec. 27, 1821

p. 388 (blank) 20, 1821 William Harrison (Spartanburgh) to Benjamin Wofford (same); for $200 sold 67 ac on Prater's Cr on S side of Tyger R; plat attached. Witness John Nesbett and Sarah Matthews. Signed William Harrison. Wit. oath Apr. 2, 1821 Sarah Matthews to Wm Young. Rec. Dec. 27, 1821

p. 388-390 Aug. 7, 1821 James Hunt, sheriff (Spartanburgh) to John Wolf (same); for $150 sold 100 ac on S Pacolate R near the forks; border: Luke Barnett, John Kimbrell, George Wolf, and Henry White; sale due to writ from Spartanburgh Common Pleas Court second Monday after fourth Monday in Mar. 1821 suit of Joseph Davis; judgment was levy of $30 with interest from John Trevillian and Samuel Wall; land was Samuel Wall's. Witness W Clemment and Jesse Cleveland. Signed Jas Hunt SSD. Wit. oath Aug. 7, 1821 Jesse Cleveland to W Clemment. Rec. Jan. 7, 1822

p. 390-391 Nov. 15, 1821 William Howard (Spartanburgh) to William Bennett (same); for $53.25 note William Howard is indebted to William Bennett and to secure the note sold a dark sorrel horse about 12 years old, cow and calf marked black and white, 4 feather beds and sheets, 6 bedquilts, 3 coverlets, 4 blankets, and 3 "under" beds; stuff is to be sold at the Court House Apr. 10, 1822 and if more than $53.25 and costs is received, then overage goes to William Howard. Witness Jesse Cleveland and Mathew Seay. Signed William Howard's mark. Wit. oath Dec. 11, 1821 Jesse Cleveland to E Bomar. Rec. Jan. 7, 1822

p. 391-392 Sept. 7, 1816 Andrew Ferguson (Spartanburgh) to James Wood (same); for $500 sold 100 ac on S side of S Pacolate R; border: Rice F Ross, Motlow's Cr, and Robert Black; grant Jun. 6, 1800 to John Gowen sr. Witness John Chapman and Coleman Wood. Signed Andrew Ferguson. Wit. oath Jan. 7, 1822 Coleman Wood to E Bomar. Rec. Jan. 7, 1822

p. 392-393 Mar. 15, 1817 Golden Tinsley (Spartanburgh) to Thomas Kelley; for $200 sold 200 ac on Public Road from Isaac Crow to Anthony Foster sr; between Tyger and Enoree Rivers; part of 1,000 ac grant to James Sample jr and sold by Rotty Sample, heir-at-law of James Sample, to John McCullock who sold to "said" Edward Hooker. Witness Edward Hooker and Isaac Tinsley. Signed Golding Tinsley. Wit. oath Aug. 23, 1817 Edward Hooker to M Casey. Rec. Jan. 7, 1822

p. 393 Nov. 18, 1821 George Floyd (Spartanburgh) to James Mason (same); for $160 sold 70 ac on SW side of Ferguson's Cr and on Floyd's Spring Br; border: SW-William Otts and Joel G Brewton, N-B Mason, and E-Ferguson's Cr and George Floyd. Witness William Otts and Willis Otts. Signed George Floyd. Wit. oath Dec. 7, 1821 William Otts to John Brewton. Rec. Jan. 7, 1822

p. 393-394 Dec. 29, 1821 Milton Davis (Spartanburgh) to children Elizabeth, Sophia, Polley, Ann, and Alesey Davis (same); for love and affection give 160 ac where Milton Davis lives and all horses, cattle, sheep, and hogs, all household furniture, and farming utensils. Witness John B Lewis and George Lewis. Signed Milton Davis. Wit. oath Jan. 7, 1822 George Lewis to James Young. Rec. Jan. 7, 1822

p. 394-395 Aug. 16, 1821 Solomon Crocker (Spartanburgh) to Daniel Tucker (same); for $450 sold 100 ac on S side of Lawson's fork; border: Thomas Weather; part of 997 ac grant to Solomon Crocker. Witness James Haynes and John Petit. Signed Solomon Crocker's mark. Wit. oath Jan. 7, 1822 James Haynes to Wm Underwood. Rec. Jan. 7, 1822

p. 395-396 Jul. 14, 1821 Robert Rogers sr and Elias Rogers (Spartanburgh) to Worshiping Congregation attending Unity Meeting House on S side of Tyger R; for "desire we have for prosperity of Zion" give 3 ac; border: Richard Willis; for burying ground and church (with monthly meetings). Witness William Posey and Joel Brewton. Signed Robert Rogers and Elias Rogers. Wit. oath Jul. 14, 1821 William Posey to Robert Ligon. Rec. (omitted)

p. 396-397 Dec. 27, 1821 William Whirley (Rutherford Co, NC) to Henry Hutcheson (Spartanburgh); for $150 sold all rights to estate of Drury Hutcheson (now living); William is heir because he married Hannah, daughter of Drury Hutcheson. Witness Lorenzo D Chapman and Peter F Gray. Signed Wm Whirley. Wit. oath Jan. 7, 1822 Lorenzo D Chapman to John Chapman. Rec. Jan. 7, 1822

p. 397-398 Nov. 3, 1821 Hanah Gray (Spartanburgh) to Henry Hutcheson (same); for $22.50 sold 5 ac 1 rod and 4 porches; border: the Smith's shop, Henry Hutcheson, "great road", David Foster, and Squire Chapman. Witness Ann F Vernon, Moses Richardson, and E. W. Chapman. Signed Hannah Gray. Wit. oath Jan. 7, 1822 E. W. Chapman to John Chapman. Rec. Jan. 7, 1822

p. 398-399 Oct. 13, 1821 James Hunt, sheriff (Spartanburgh) to John Kimbrell; for $1 sold 130 ac; border: Capt. James Lewis, John Clark, Charles C Duncan, and estate of James McDowell desc; Elizabeth Hicks and others petitioned Spartanburgh Common Pleas Court on second Monday after fourth Monday in Oct. 1819 to divide estate of David Hicks desc; Court appointed Page Rork, Thomas Kimbrell, Vincent Kimbrell, Tolbert Gibson, and George Gilbert esqs to partition the land; on second Monday after fourth Monday in Mar. 1820 they said estate can't be divided and should be sold; credit to be 12 months; sale was on first Monday in Apr. 1821. Witness John Bagwell and James E Henry. Signed Jas Hunt SSD. Wit. oath Jan. 7, 1822 James E Henry to W Bennett. Rec. Jan. 7, 1822

p. 399-400 Aug. 9, 1821 Thomas Hackett (Spartanburgh) to Tillotson Brookshear (same); for $200 sold 170 ac on E side of Pacolet R; border: Island Cr. Witness Lee Linder and James Lord. Signed Thomas Hackett's mark. Wit. oath Nov. 17, 1821 Lee Linder to Henry Turner. Rec. Jan. 15, 1822. Dower renounced Nov. 17, 1821 Alley Hackett to Henry Turner

p. 400-401 Nov. 5, 1819 George Wood (Spartanburgh) to John Guyton (same); for $600 sold 140 ac on N side of Beaverdam Cr of Thickety Cr; border: Wm Bostick, Thomas Littlejohn, and Hert's old line; part of grant in 1773 to Wm Hort. Witness Smith Lipscomb and David S Lipscomb. Signed George Wood. Wit. oath Dec. 28, 1821 Smith Lipscomb to John Lipscomb. Rec. Jan. 17, 1822

p. 401-402 Oct. 24, 1821 Mary Davidson, widow (Spartanburgh) to Zacheriah McDaniel (same); for $37.15 sold a cow and calf, 2 yearlings, a bed and furniture, a bedsted, 3 chairs, an oven, a large pot dross(?) and furniture; Condition: sale void if Mary pays Zacheriah $37.15 by Nov. 1, 1822. Witness John Murph and David Whetston. Signed Mary Davidson's mark. Wit. oath Nov. 2, 1821 John Murph to Augustin Shands. Rec. Jan. 17, 1822

p. 402-404 Sept. 3, 1821 Simpson Foster, commissioner of Equity Court (Spartanburgh) to Holeman Smith; for $220.50 sold 375 ac on Bullock's fork of Thickety Cr; part of grant to Irby Dewberry and all of grant to Edward Smith sr; Holeman Smith and others filed petition in Equity Court against William Smith on Jan. 1, 1820; they petitioned to divide estate of Edword Smith desc (late of Spartanburgh) and commissioners of Court recommended sale; sale was on Jul. 2, 1821. Witness Eber Smith and Willis Foster. Signed Simpson Foster CESD. Wit. oath Sept. 3, 1821 Eber Smith to Caleb Jones. Rec. Jan. 17, 1822

p. 404-405 Oct. 22, 1821 Hugh McMullen (Spartanburgh) to Robert McMullen (same); for $300 sold 100 ac on both sides of N Pacolate R. Witness Wm F Reynolds and David McMullen. Signed Hugh McMullen. Wit. oath Nov. 22, 1821 Wm F Reynolds to E Lewis. Rec. Jan. 17, 1822

p. 405 Jan. 21, 1822 Elizabeth Elder, Abigail Elder, Patience Elder, and Hammon Elder to William Jinnings; for good cause quit claim to 33 ac; SW corner of tract sold by James Calvert to "said" desceased; laid out by Capt. William Rogers, Capt. Charles Moore, John Stevens, Elisha Jennings, James Calvert, and Dr. A. B. Moore, "chosen for the purpose above mentioned"; plat attached. Witness J. W. Tucker and William Ginnings. Signed Hammon Elder and Elizabeth, Abigail, and Patience Elder's marks. Wit. oath Jun. 28, 1822 William Ginnings to Wm Underwood. Rec. Jan. 28, 1822

p. 405-407 Sept. 13, 1821 John Crawford, James Hunt, and Robert Jameson, guardians of minor children of John Jordan, to John Vaughan; due to bond given by John Jordan in his lifetime to John Vaughan, relinquish title to (1) (ac omitted) in Greenville Dist; border: Job Henson, Marchel, James Smith, and James Smith's Still house; and (2) 340 ac adjoining (1); grant to John Mcbre "on Spartanburgh side" and is the part John Mcbre sold to John Jordan on E side of old Indian Boundary. Witness Ephraim Roddy esq and S. C. Hunt. Signed Robert Jameson, guardian for Elizabeth, Samuel, and John Jordan, James Hunt, guardian for James Jordan, and John Crawford, guardian for Sarah Jordan. Wit. oath Jan. 17, 1822 Ephraim Roddy to E Bomar. Rec. Jan. 31, 1822. Dower renounced Jan. 17, 1822 Lucy Jordan (now Jamison) to E Bomar

p. 407-408 Jan. 15, 1822 Susannah Walling and son Michael Walling (Spartanburgh) to James Harrison (same); for $50 sold 5 ac on both sides N Tyger R; border: N & W-Saable, E-Wadsworth, mill pond, and road; part of survey for John Brooks. Witness Martin Lucas and James Tucker. Signed Michael Walling and Susannah Walling's mark. Wit. oath Feb. 2, 1822 Martin Lucas to Tho Poole. Rec. Feb. 2, 1822

p. 408-409 Jan. 1, 1822 William McWilliams (Spartanburgh) to Armsted Bomar (same); for $75 sold 30 ac on S side of S Pacolate R; border: W Bullington and Armsted Bomar. Witness William H Bullington and Christi Golightly. Signed William McWilliams. Wit. oath Feb. 4, 1822 William H Bullington to James Young. Rec. Feb. 4, 1822

p. 409 Oct. 13, 1818 Nancy Posey (Spartanburgh) to Theophelus Moore (same); for $75 sold 46½ ac; border: E-Jason Moore, N-heirs of Samuel Otts, W-Hatchett, and S-Solomon Autry; half of grant to Thomas Moore (Spartanburgh) who sold to Joseph Rogers who sold to Nancy Posey who sold to Jason Moore and divided by Nancy Posey and Jason Moore with W part going to Nancy. Witness John Hatchett and Polley Hatchett. Signed Nancy Posey. Wit. oath Jan. 30, 1819 John Hatchett to Robert Ligon. Rec. Feb. 4, 1822

p. 409-410 Nov. 30, 1819 Samuel Seay (Spartanburgh) to John Gideons (same); for (money omitted) sold 200 ac on both sides Faun Br of Lawson's fork of Pacolate R; border: John Clemments, Markley, and John Bennett; part of grant to John Burnett. Witness Joshua Tapp and Charles Darby. Signed Samuel Seay. Wit. oath Feb. 4, 1822 Joshua Tapp to Thomas Collins. Rec. Feb. 4, 1822

p. 410-411 Feb. 4, 1822 Daniel Amos (Spartanburgh) to Joshua Richards; for $3 sold 1 ac on waters of Thickety Cr; border: widow Woods and Joshua Richards; part of grant to Daniel Amos. Witness Michael Gaffney and Joshua Byars sr. Signed Daniel Amos. Wit. oath Feb. 4, 1822 Michael Gaffney to John Lipscomb. Rec. Feb. 4, 1822. Feb. 4, 1822 Daniel Amos and Joshua Richards agree that Saw Pit Br is dividing line between them. Witness Michael Gaffney and Joshua Byars. Signed Joshua Richards and Daniel Amos. Wit. oath Feb. 4, 1822 Michael Gaffney to John Lipscomb

p. 411-412 Dec. 12, 1819 Manly Ford (Spartanburgh) to John Wood (same);

for $50 sold 50 ac on branches of Maple Swamp Cr of Tyger R; border: McDowell; part of "grant" by James Wofford to Manly Ford. Witness Stephen Sisemore and Mavrick Ford. Signed Manly Ford. Wit. oath Mar. 21, 1820 Stephen Sisemore to Thomas Wood. Rec. Feb. 4, 1822

p. 412-412 Mar. 13, 1821 William Elmore (Spartanburgh) to David Dantzler (same); for $500 sold 102 ac on N side of S Tyger R; border: Burne's Bridge. Witness Michael Moore and John Wingo. Signed Wm Elmore. Wit. oath Feb. 4, 1822 John Wingo to Tho Poole. Rec. Feb. 4, 1822

p. 413-414 Nov. 5, 1821 William Morris (Spartanburgh) to William Lipscomb (same); for $1,100 sold (ac omitted); border: Robert Wilkins, David Lipscomb, William Thompson, Capt. Allen, John Laurence, and Thomson; part of "sundry" grants of both sides Gocher Cr. Witness Nathan Littlejohn and John Wilkins. Signed William Morris. Wit. oath Nov. 5, 1821 Nathan Littlejohn to John Lipscomb. Rec. Feb. 4, 1822. Dower renounced Dec. 12, 1821 Christian Morris to John Lipscomb

p. 414-415 Jan. 24, 1820 Shadrack Weaver (Spartanburgh) to John Pain (same); for $100 sold 92 ac on Horse Cr. Witness Jesse Weaver and George Bone. Signed Shadrick Weaver. Wit. oath Jan. 26, 1820 Jesse Weaver to Henry Turner. Rec. Feb. 4, 1822

p. 415-417 Dec. 17, 1821 William P Gadberry (Spartanburgh) to Muse Tolleson (same); for $4,500 sold 885 ac on N side of Lawson's fork. Witness William Trimmier and John S Young. Signed W. P. Gadberry. Wit. oath Feb. 8, 1822 William Trimmier to E Bomar. Rec. Feb. 8, 1822. Dower renounced Feb. 8, 1822 Juliet G Gadberry to E Bomar

p. 417 Dec. 16, 1817 Charles Amos to John Brown; for $110 sold 100 ac on Long Br of Broad R and Sarratt's Cr. Witness William Collins and William Harris. Signed Charles Amos. Wit. oath Dec. 28, 1818 William Collins to J Camp. Rec. Feb. 18, 1822

p. 417-419 Feb. 18, 1822 Samuel C Hunt, sheriff, successor of James Hunt, (Spartanburgh) to Abner Benson; for $25 sold 100 ac on waters of Sarratt's Cr and Long Br; Abner Benson indorsee of Wilson Nesbett, who was indorsee of Daniel McClarron, Joseph Collins, and William Collins "in company", issued from their attachments in Spartanburgh Common Pleas Court against John Brown; James Hunt levied on 100 ac; the court held at Apr. term 1820 said to sell the land on first Monday in Jun. 1820. Witness James Hunt and James Brannon. Signed Saml C Hunt SSD. Wit. oath Feb. 19, 1822 James Brannon to E Bomar. Rec. Feb. 19, 1822

p. 419-420 Jan. 1, 1822 Randolph Palmer (Spartanburgh) to Elias Palmer (same); for $3,000 sold 433 ac on N side of Tyger R and on Dutchman's Cr; known as Ball Hall plantation; border: Drury Parham, "the" manufacturing company, and Martha Saunders. Witness John S Young and William Trimmier. Signed Randolph Palmer. Wit. oath Feb. 22, 1822 William Trimmier to E Bomar. Rec. Feb. 22, 1822. Dower renounced Jan. 12, 1822 Susannah Palmer to Daniel White

p. 420-2nd 420 Feb. 23, 1822 George Gilbert (Spartanburgh) to William Littlefield (same); for $150 sold a bay mare, 2 cows, 2 yearlings, 3 feather beds with all their furniture, a cupboard with its contents: dishes, plates, bowls, mugs, pitchers, knives, and forks, a chest a tin trunk, a table, 2 bedsteads, 3 pots, 2 ovens, 4 chairs, 2 plows, 10 barrels of corn, 200 weight of bacon, 2 blade stacks, an axe, and a matox; William is to sell the stuff Dec. 25, 1824 and give George anything over $150. Witness Benjamin Evins and Obadiah Gilbert. Signed George Gilbert. Wit. oath Feb. 7, 1822

Benjamin Evins to W Clemment. Rec. Feb. 23, 1822

Book S 1822-1825
p. 1-2 Sept. 18 (or 20), 1794 Thomas Hunter (Spartanburgh) to Thomas Brown (same); for 20£ SC money sold 30 ac on S side of Pacolett R; border: Thomas Brown; part of grant Oct. 15, 1784 Gov. Benjamin Guerard to Jacob Holmes. Witness James Brown, Isaac Brown, and Isaac Holmes. Signed Thomas Hunter. Wit. oath Mar. 29, 1810 James Brown to Jno H Jones. Rec. Mar. 4, 1822

p. 2 Mar. 19, 1821 William McBee (SC) to Thomas Brown (Spartanburgh); for $100 sold 125 ac on Bullock's fork; grant to Malichi Jones; includes 25 ac sold by Warner Sherbut (or Shurbutt) to John Prewett see two deeds from Warner Sherbute to John Prewett. Witness James Brown and Jesse Hutchins. Signed William Mcbee. Wit. oath Dec. 19, 1821 James Brown to Thomas Poole. Rec. Mar. 4, 1822

p. 2-3 Oct. 14, 1821 Moses Fowler (Spartanburgh) to Thomas Fowler (same); for $600 sold 238 ac on Ferguson's Cr of Tiger R; border: Thomas Padon and Harris. Witness James Padon and William Strange. Signed Moses Fowler's mark. Wit. oath Jan. 10, 1822 William Strange to James Ford. Rec. Mar. 4, 1822

p. 3-4 Nov. 16, 1821 James Compton (Spartanburgh) to John Rogers (same); for $500 sold 300 ac; border: John Trail, Meadows, and Pinckny Rd. Witness James Selman and John Betterton. Signed James Compton. Wit. oath Mar. 4, 1822 James Selman to Robert Ligon. Rec. Mar. 4, 1822

p. 4-5 Sept. 17, 1821 Sparling Thornton (Spartanburgh) to Theron Lancaster (same); for $500 sold 86 ac on waters of Culberton's Br of Fairforest Cr; border: Josiah Thornton, Charles Smith, Andrew Mays, William Lancaster, and Edward Lipscomb. Witness J. P. Means, W. H. Lancaster, and William Lancaster esq. Signed Sparling Thornton's mark. Wit. oath Mar. 4, 1822 William Lancaster to John Chapman. Rec. Mar. 4, 1822. Dower renounced Sept. 23, 1821 Sally Thornton to James Hamm

p. 5-6 Sept. 17, 1821 Josiah Thornton (Spartanburgh) to Theron Lancaster (same); for $500 sold 50 ac on waters of Culbertson's Br of Fairforest Cr; border: Charles Smith, Sparling Thornton, Lancaster, Lipscomb, and Josiah Thornton. Witness J. P. Means, W. H. Lancaster, and William Lancaster esq. Signed Josiah Thornton's mark. Wit. oath Mar. 4, 1822 William Lancaster to John Chapman. Rec. Mar. 4, 1822. Dower renounced Sept. 23, 1821 Sally Thornton to James Hamm

p. 6-7 Apr. 7, 1820 Charles Smith to Sparling Thornton (same); for $100 sold 30 ac on Culbertson's Br of Fairforest Cr; border: Thornton. Witness Henry H Thornton and William Lancaster esq. Signed Charles Smith. Wit. oath Apr. 16, 1820 William Lancaster to William Underwood. Rec. Mar. 4, 1822

p. 7 Jan. 28, 1819 Samuel Archibald, attorney for Mary Mayes, widow, and heirs of Andrew Mayes desc (Spartanburgh) to Sparling Thornton (same); for $100 sold 56 ac on waters of Fairforest Cr; border: Public Road, N-Charles Smith and Thronton,E & S-William Lancaster and Edward Lipscomb; part of grant to Col. Thomas Brandon desc who sold to Andrew Mayes desc. Witness Wm Lancaster esq and John Bearden. Signed Saml Archibald atty. Wit. oath Mar. 10, 1820 William Lancaster to William Underwood. Rec. Mar. 4, 1822

p. 7-8 Nov. 3, 1821 Joel Hurt (Spartanburgh) to Elihu Golightly (same) give (ac omitted); on May 2, 1809 John Golightly sr (Spartanburgh) sold 430 ac on Fairforest and Beaverdam Creeks of Tyger R to Francis Golightly, wife of Joel Hurt, and Elihu Golightly; Joel now gives Elihu the land W of Public Road from Anthony Foster's "by the dwelling house of said premises" to Tanner's Mills on Tyger R. Witness Christopher Golightly and John Golightly jr. Signed Joel Hurt. Wit. oath Mar. 4, 1822 Christopher Golightly to Henry Turner. Rec. Mar. 4, 1822

p. 8-9 Feb. 10, 1822 Edmond Nelson to John Mathis; for $50 sold 84 ac on Nelson's Br of Buck Cr; border: Nelson and Big Br. Witness James Young and Jacob Elenburg. Signed Edmond Nelson. Wit. oath Feb. 10, 1822 Jacob Elenburg to James Young. Rec. Mar. 4, 1822

p. 9 Jun. 6, 1821 Newbell Johnson (Spartanburgh) to Benjamin Burrell (same); for $300 sold 100 ac on W side of Buncomb Road; border: E-estate of William Beacham desc and on other sides-Newbell Johnson. Witness Willis W Dickie and William Strange. Signed Newbell Johnson. Wit. oath Jul. 21, 1822 William Strange to David Moore. Rec. Mar. 4, 1822

p. 9-10 Oct. 13, 1821 Benjamin Poole (Spartanburgh) to James Parks sr (same); for $125 sold 38 ac on Lawson's fork of Pacolett R; border: Poole. Witness James White and Nehemiah Norton. Signed Benjamin Poole. Wit. oath Mar. 2, 1822 James White to D White. Rec. Mar. 4, 1822

p. 10-11 Sept. 11, 1821 Sarah Harris (Spartanburgh) to James Cantrell (same); for $37 sold 50 ac on Jumping Gully Br of Buck Cr; border: Pertle's old line, widow Crocker, and Charles Cantrell. Witness Charles Cantrell and Daniel Cantrell. Signed Sarah Harris' mark. Wit. oath Mar. 5, 1822 Charles Cantrell to Henry Turner. Rec. Mar. 6, 1822

p. 11-12 May 7, 1819 Thomas Wyatt (Spartanburgh) to Lee Linder (same); for $150 sold 100 ac on Bucks Branches of Pacolett R; border: Jonathan Low sr. Witness James Waters and John Low. Signed Thomas Wyatt. Wit. oath Jun. 7, 1819 James Waters to Caleb Jones. Rec. Mar. 18, 1822. Dower renounced Aug. 26, 1819 Nancy Wyatt to Henry Turner

p. 12-13 Jan. 17, 1822 William Low (Spartanburgh) to Lee Linder; for $150 sold (1) 100 ac on N side of Pacolett R; part of grant in 1807 to James Ballinger; and (2) 200 ac adjoining (1). Witness Thomas Wyatt and Aaron Templeman. Signed William Low. Wit. oath Jan. 22, 1822 Aaron Templeman to Henry Turner. Rec. Mar. 18, 1822. Dower renounced Jan. 30, 1822 Mary Low, wife of William, and Elizabeth Low, widow, to Hnery Turner

p. 13 Mar. 18, 1822 James Hutcheson (Spartanburgh) to William L Bishop (same); for $34.75 sold 40 ac on waters of Lawson's fork; border: Standing Stone Br, William L Bishop, Edmond Bishop, Barney Bishop; part of where James Hutcheson lives; Condition: sale void if James pays William $100 (sic) by Dec. 25, 1822. Witness William Trimmier and Barney Bishop. Signed James Hutcheson's mark. Wit. oath Mar. 18, 1822 Barney Bishop to E Bomar. Rec. Mar. 18, 1822

p. 13-14 Sept. 21, 1821 William Bennett (Spartanburgh) to Caleb Carter (Pendleton Dist); for $100 sold 40 ac; part of tract on SE side of Thompson Cr of Pacolett R; border: Back Br, Thomas Bennett, Caleb Carter, Lee, Thomas, and John Kimbrell. Witness John Kimbrell and Vincent Kimbrell. Signed W Bennett. Wit. oath Feb. 5, 1822 John Kimbrell to James Young. Rec. Mar. 25, 1822

p. 14-15 Mar. 25, 1822 Muse Tolleson (Spartanburgh) quit claim to property given to Muse Tolleson and William Ross in trust for heirs of Thomas Dare--700 ac on Lawson's fork, and all "other" land, Negroes, houses, cattle, stock, and tools. Witness William

Trimmier and William T Nicholas (or Nichols). Signed Muse Tolleson. Wit. oath Mar. 26, 1822 William Trimmier to E Bomar. Rec. Mar. 26, 1822

p. 15 Dec. 29, 1821 Jeremiah McBee (Spartanburgh) to Anna McBee (same); for $200 sold 244 ac; border: Crocker's Mill. Witness Mathew McBee and James Crocker jr. Signed Jeremiah McBee. Wit. oath Mar. 28, 1822 James Crocker to W Hunt. Rec. Mar. 28, 1822

p. 15-16 Apr. 7, 1821 William Ward (Spartanburgh) to Nathan Ward (same); for $100 sold 39½ ac on branch of Pacolett R; border: road from Canney's Meeting House, S-William Cannon, E-John Hammett, N-Mayson Cannon, and W-Jesse Cannon; grant to John Hammett. Witness Levi Ward and Soloman Ward. Signed Wm Ward. Wit. oath Nov. 17, 1821 Levi Ward to W Hunt. Rec. Mar. 28, 1822

p. 16-17 Sept. 21, 1821 William Bennett (Spartanburgh) to John Kimbrell (same); for $115 sold 75 ac; border: Thomas Kimbrell, John Kimbrell, Caleb Carter, Obed Gilbert (where William Littlefield jr now lives). Witness Caleb Carter and Thomas Kimbrell sr. Signed W Bennett. Wit. oath Feb. 5, 1822 Caleb Carter to James Young. Rec. Mar. 28, 1822

p. 17-18 Nov. 5, 1821 Edward Autry (or Aughtry) promises to pay Edward Bomar $194.13 on "day after date". Signed Edward Autry's mark
Nov. 5, 1821 Edward Autry to Edward Bomar to secure above sold 103 ac on Mill Cr of N Tyger R; sold by Muse Tolleson to Edward Bomar Oct. 22, 1821; mortgage lasts until Dec. 25, 1822 (Edward Autry to repay money by then). Witness John Bomar jr, Thomas Bomar, and Armstead Bomar. Signed Edward Autry's mark. Wit. oath Feb. 29, 1822 John Bomar jr to E Bomar. Rec. Mar. 29, 1822

p. 18 Jul. 17, 1820 Joseph Carswell to Elias Palmer; for (omitted) mortgage (ac omitted) "all land claimed by Joseph Carswell specified or unspecified"; known as Cross Anchor tract; Condition: Elias is security for Joseph for two notes (1) payable Jan. 25, 1825 and (2) payable Jun. 15, 1825; mortgage valid if Joseph fail to pay debt. Witness William Trimmier. Signed Joseph Carswell. Wit. oath Mar. 30, 1822 William Trimmier to E Bomar. Rec. Mar. 30, 1822

p. 18-19 Nov. 30, 1822 Daniel White and William S Golightly, esecutors of estate of Charles James desc, (late of Spartanburgh) to James W Cooper (same); for $43 sold 80 ac on Kelso's Cr of Fairforest Cr; border: David Whitstone (or Whiteton), Michjah Barnett, and Cooper. Witness Wm C. H. Smith and Lemuel White. Signed D White and W. S. Golightly. Wit. oath Mar. 30, 1822 Lemuel White to E Bomar. Rec. Mar. 30, 1822

p. 19-20 Nov. 5, 1821 John Payne (Spartanburgh) to Henry Cantrell (same); for $150 sold 92 ac on Horse Cr. Witness Samuel Ezell and Rachael Ezell. Signed John Payne and Philialphy's mark. Wit. oath Mar. 15, 1822 Samuel Ezell to Henry Turner. Rec. Apr. 1, 1822

p. 20-21 Oct. 30, 1816 Matthew Gore (Spartanburgh) to Thomas Kimbrell (same); for $50 sold 150 ac on waters of Pacolett R; border: James Carter. Witness William Bennett and Alfred Cunningham. Signed Matthew Gore. Wit. oath Oct. 13, 1819 William Bennett to E Lewis. Rec. Apr. 1, 1822. Dower renounced Nov. 30, 1816 Elizabeth Gore to James Young

p. 21 Nov. 19, 1821 Isaac Crow received $1,280.58 from Leonard Hills and John Clark in full satisfaction of mortgage. Witness Ansel Jacobs and Jasper Billings. Signed Isaac Crow. Wit. oath

Mar. 6, 1822 Jasper Billings to Wm Young. Rec. (omitted)

p. 21-22 Jan. 20, 1822 Michael McKie promises to pay Jesse Cleveland $60.66 "one day after date". Signed Michael McKie's mark Jan. 20 (or 24), 1822 Michael McKie (Spartanburgh) to Jesse Cleveland; to secure above debt sold 100 ac; border: Alexander Roddy, Adam Gramling, John Lewis, and Robert Foster; where Michael McKie lives; sold by Edmond W Chapman to Michael McKie; Condition: sale void if Michael pays Jesse by Oct. 15 (year omitted). Witness Richard Thompson and Elisha Bomar. Signed Michael McKie's mark. Wit. oath Mar. 11, 1822 Elisha Bomar to J. E. Henry. Rec. Apr. 3, 1822

p. 22-23 Jun. 21, 1820 Adam Carruth (Spartanburgh) to Larkin Ballinger (same); for $660 sold 478 ac on N side of Lawson's fork; border: S-widow Brannon and N-Alexander Austin. Witness James McDaniel and Andrew Barry. Signed A Carruth. Wit. oath Apr. 2, 1822 James McDaniel to B Griffith. Rec. Apr. 4, 1822

p. 23-24 Nov. 26, 1818 Henry Morgan (Spartanburgh) to Armstead Bomar (same); for $250 sold 138 ac in forks of Pacolett R; border: C. C. Duncan, road from Galt's bridge to Camp bridge, and Robt Bullington; where Henry Morgan lives. Witness Christopher Golightly, William Golightly, and Claremont (or Clary) Golightly (now Bullington). Signed Henry Morgan. Wit. oath Apr. 5, 1822 Christopher Golightly to James Young. Rec. Apr. 6, 1822

p. 24 Nov. 19, 1821 Isaac Crow received from George Hill, Leonard Hill, and John Clark $1,280.58 full satisfaction of mortgage. Witness Ansel Jacobs and Jasper Billings. Signed Isaac Crow. Wit. oath Mar. 6, 1822 Jasper Billings to Wm Young. Rec. (omitted)

p. 24-25 Apr. 12, 1822 Richard Thompson (Spartanburgh) to Henry Hopson jr (Christian Co, Ky); power of attorney to collect money owed Richard due to rent of land in Christian Co, Ky and to prosecute or defend any suit relating to land sold by Joshua Cates to Richard Thompson. Witness E Bomar. Signed Richard Thomson. Wit. oath Apr. 12, 1822 by Richard Thomson in General Sessions and Common Pleas Court. Rec. Apr. 12, 1822

p. 25-26 Jan. 8, 1822 William Kelso sr to Samuel Kelso (SC); for $500 sold 80 ac; border: Howard, pond, and swamp; part of tract sold by Robert Davis to William Kelso sr. Witness William Kelso jr, Mary Kelso, and William Berry. Signed William Kelso. Wit. oath Feb. 27, 1822 William Kelso jr to William Kelso. Rec. Apr. 9, 1822

p. 26 Sept. 17, 1821 Ransom Foster to Thomas Kimbel (or Kimbol); for $170 sold 85 ac on Mill Cr of Tyger R. Witness Herbert Hawkins and Jane Jones. Signed Ransom Foster. Wit. oath Apr. 9, 1822 Herbert Hawkins to William Underwood. Rec. Apr. 11, 1822

p. 26-27 Oct. 2, 1821 Thomas Collins to Saul Mize (Spartanburgh); for $100 sold 70 ac; border: Ephraim Jackson, Snudes(?) Br, and Willis Allen's Spring Br. Witness Hiram Allen and James Land. Signed Thomas Collins. Wit. oath Mar. 23, 1822 James Land to Thomas Poole. Rec. Apr. 11, 1822

p. 27 Apr. 30, 1821 Hannah Collins, widow (Spartanburgh) to grandson Harmon Ward Wilson; for love and affection give a horse colt 2 years old past of sorrel color. Witness James McDaniel and George Camp. Signed Hannah Collins' mark. Wit. oath Apr. 7, 1822 George Camp to D White. Rec. Apr. 11, 1822

p. 27-28 May 2, 1821 John Arndel to Jesse Tate; for $200 sold 100 ac on little Cherokee Cr; border: John Arndel and Gillon.

Witness Joseph Camp and Peter Q Camp. Signed John Arendel. Wit. oath Mar. 1, 1822 Joseph Camp to F. W. Robertson. Rec. Apr. 11, 1822

p. 28 Jan. 13, 1819 Leonard Smith, John Fredk Harming, and John Daniel Harmining, legates of estate of John (or Job) F Harmining desc (Spartanburgh), to William Stone; for $750 sold 100 ac on Cedar Shoal Cr; sold Jun. 1, 1802 by William Parker to John F Harmining (see Book H p. 243). Witness James E Henry and Aaron Casey. Signed Leonard Smith's mark, John Daniel Harmining, and John Fredk Harmining "for self and as guardian for Mary Harmining". Wit. oath Mar. 30, 1819 Aaron Casey to M Casey. Rec. Apr. 11, 1822

p. 28-29 Sept. 27, 1813 Joel Foster (SC) to William Stone (Spartanburgh); for $150 sold 75 ac on Cedar Shoal Cr of Enoree R; border: William Casey, Watson, Jessey Casey, and Miles Rainwaters; grant in 1772 to John Stone jr who sold to Joel Foster. Witness Aaron Casey and S. J. Casey. Signed Joel Foster. Wit. oath Mar. 30, 1819 Aaron Casey to M Casey. Rec. Apr. 11, 1822

p. 29-30 Apr. 2, 1822 William Clemment (Spartanburgh) to John Clemment (same); for $500 sold 120 ac on E side of Richland Cr of S Pacolett R; border: Benjamin Clark, Wolf Trap Br, Zachariah Wall, and George Wolf; part of two grants: (1) to Samuel Spencer and (2) to Thomas Bennett. Witness George Wolf and John Wolf. Signed William Clemment. Wit. oath Apr. 8, 1822 John Wolf to William Dobbins. Rec. Apr. 11, 1822

p. 30-31 Jun. 1, 1815 John Cooper (Spartanburgh) to William Johnson (same); for $260 sold 100 ac on waters of Enoree R; sold by John Han(?) to John Cooper. Witness David Moore JP and Jesse M Anderson. Signed John Cooper. Wit. oath Mar. 30, 1822 Jesse M Anderson to David Moor. Rec. Apr. 11, 1822

p. 31 Mar. 14, 1817 Ruthey Pilgrim (Spartanburgh) to William Johnson; for $150 sold 56 ac between Tyger and Enoree Rivers; part of grant to John (blank). Witness William Cooper and Larkin Hendrix. Signed Ruthey Pilgrim's mark. Wit. oath Mar. 30, 1822 William Cooper to David Moore. Rec. Apr. 11, 1822

p. 31-32 Feb. 16, 1816 William Robb (Sumpter Dist) to John Serratt jr (Spartanburgh); for $286 sold 229 ac on W side of Broad R. Witness Anthony Serratt and Charles Hopper. Signed William Robb. Wit. oath Mar. 23, 1821 Charles Hooper to Thomas Poole. Rec. Apr. 11, 1822

p. 32 Feb. 21, 1822 Muse Tolleson (Spartanburgh) to Joseph Carswell; to secure $600 Muse owes Joseph due Feb. 21, 1823 ($300) and Feb. 21, 1824 ($300) sold 196 ac known as Cross Anchor plantation that Joseph Carswell to Muse Tolleson; Condition: sale void if Muse pays debt. Witness William Trimmier. Signed Muse Tolleson. Wit. oath Apr. 9, 1822 William Trimmier to E Bomar. Rec. Apr. 11, 1822

p. 32-33 Nov. 9, 1815 Alexander Davidson (Spartanburgh) to Daberel (or Caben) McCraw; for $85 sold 92 ac on Surratt's Cr; border: North Carolina state line, Harris, and Caben McCraw. Witness Moses Davidson and Clabourn Humphries. Signed Alexander Davidson's mark. Wit. oath Mar. 16, 1823 Clabourn Humphries to F. W. Robertson. Rec. Apr. 11, 1822

p. 33-34 Sept. 28, 1820 William G Foster (Spartanburgh) to Moses Casey; for $600 sold 117 ac on S side of James' Cr of Tyger R; plat attached shows border: T Powers, John Hobby sr, Richard Young, L Littlefield, and J Bison. Witness Zachariah Hobby and Peter Hamilton. Signed W. G. Foster. Wit. oath Dec. 20, 1820 Zachariah Hobby to Burrell Bobo. Rec. Apr. 11, 1822. Dower renounced Nov. 16,

1820 Judith Foster to Burrell Bobo

p. 34-35 Apr. 3, 1822 Muse Tolleson (Spartanburgh) to Richard Kirby (same); to secure $1,217.54 Muse owes Richard mortgage 14 Negroes: Ned and wife Lucy and their children Mary, Jack, and Alexander, Cooper and wife Poll, Jeff, Jure(?) and wife Caty and son Dare and daughter Eliza, Sam and Big Ben, and mortgage 300 barrels of corn, 10,000 bundles of fodder, 2 sets of blacksmith tools, 3,000 pounds of iron; Condition: sale void if Muse pays $1,217.54 and interest of $704.87½ by Apr. 3, 1824 to Richard Kirby. Witness William Trimmier and James Quinn. Signed Muse Tolleson. Wit. oath Apr. 12, 1822 William Trimmier to E Bomar. Rec. Apr. 12, 1822

p. 35 Mar. 1, 1822 Muse Tolleson (Spartanburgh) to Berriman S Holder (same); for $20,000 sold (1) 1 ac in Spartanburgh, SC where Muse Tolleson lives; (2) 66 ac adjoining (1); (3) 540 ac called Watson's tract; (4) 3 lots (1½ ac total) in Spartanburgh, SC where there is store, law office, doctor shop, wagon makers, and blacksmith shop on S side of Main St; (5) 147 ac sold by Alexander McKie to Muse Tolleson; (6) 450 ac sold by D. J. Puckett and Thomas Alleson to Muse Tolleson; (7) 324 ac (sold by?) Edith Berry to Henry Brown who sold to John Tolleson who sold to Muse Tolleson; (8) 135 ac on Fairforest Cr; sold by Vincent Simmons to Thomas Alleson who sold to Muse Tolleson. Witness James Haynes, Joseph Keller, and James Hutcheson. Signed Muse Tolleson. Wit. oath Apr. 13, 1822 Joseph Keller to E Bomar. Rec. Apr. 13, 1822

p. 35-36 Aug. 25, 1821 Daniel Rogers (Spartanburgh) to Edmund Rogers; for $20 sold 50 ac; border: George Durham and William Crook. Witness George Durham and William Rogers. Signed Daniel Rogers' mark. Wit. oath Apr. 9, 1822 George Durham to James Crook. Rec. Apr. 16, 1822

p. 36-37 Oct. 20, 1821 Hannah Gray (Spartanburgh) to Alexander Vernon (same); for $100 sold 181 ac. Witness George Gilland, Peter F Gray, and John Rush. Signed Hannah Gray. Wit. oath Apr. 17, 1822 George Gilland to E Bomar. Rec. Apr. 17, 1822

p. 37-38 Feb. 9, 1822 James Hunt, sheriff (Spartanburgh) to James Brannon (same); for $31 sold 279 ac on Shoaly Cr of Lawson's fork; border: S-Jacob Chapman, W-Justin Childs and Darby Turner, N-Reuben Faucett, and E-Markley; sold due to writ from Spartanburgh Common Pleas Court on second Monday after fourth Monday in Oct. 1820 suit of Samuel Turner; judgment was levy $62 and costs from William Hunt. Witness John Bomar jr and Willis Foster. Signed Jas Hunt SSD. Wit. oath Apr. 20, 1822 John Bomar jr to E Bomar. Rec. Apr. 20, 1822

p. 38-39 Jan. 2, 1822 Muse Tolleson (Spartanburgh) to James McDowell (Charleston, SC); to secure $6,032 Muse owes James mortgage Negroes: Walter, Cloe, Daniel and wife Sarah, Ephraim and wife Mary, Joe Archibald, a 60 saw cotton jin, Reuben, Mill, Black Sarah, Little Bice, Lucinda, Tell, Calo and Charles, 4 road wagons and teams (4 horses or mules per team) and harness belonging to each, 2 mules, a 4 wheel carriage and harness, a stage wagon and harness, 110 cattle of different sizes and kinds, a cart and pair of oxen, a Jersey wagon and harness, 30 feather beds, steds, and furniture, a gig and harness, a mahogany side board and furniture, a walnut side board and furniture, 2 "beauroes", 2 sells walnut faining tables, an 8 day brass clock, a walnut desk and book case; Condition: sale void if Muse pays $6,032 and interest by Jan. 1, 1824 to James McDowell. Witness William Trimmier and James Hutcheson. Signed Muse Tolleson. Wit. oath Apr. 15, 1822 William Trimmier to E Bomar. Rec. Apr. 22, 1822

p. 39-40 Mar. 22, 1822 Muse Tolleson (Spartanburgh) to Daniel White esq (same); to secure $1,410 Muse owes Thomas Moore, administrator of estate of Ann Price desc, and Daniel White is security for debt, debt is due "first inst", sold (1) 4½ ac in lot on NE corner of Public Square in Spartanburgh, SC formerly owned by Thomas Allison; and to secure Daniel White from case in Spartanburgh Common Pleas Court second Monday in Apr. 1822 suit of George Miller (Charleston, SC) vs Muse Tolleson for $6,150, Muse mortgages (2) (ac omitted) all of "square" of land on NE corner of Public Square in Spartanburgh, SC where Muse Tolleson lived; and (3) 2 3/4 ac lot purchased "from Henry White, from W. P. Gadberry, J. T. Earle, and Wiley Berry"; Condition: mortgage void if Muse pays off $1,410 and Daniel White doesn't have to pay George Miller anything. Witness William Trimmier and Lemuel White. Signed Muse Tolleson. Wit. oath Apr. 22, 1822 Lemuel White to E Bomar. Rec. Apr. 22, 1822

p. 40-41 Oct. 9, 1815 Joseph Hays (Union Dist) to William C Evetts; for $300 sold 300 ac on Foster's Br of Fairforest Cr; where William C Evetts lives; grant to Matilda Buffington who sold to Joseph Hays. Witness Seth Poole, Richeson Whitby, and Nathan Whitby. Signed Joseph Hays. Wit. oath Oct. 9, 1816 Richeson Whitby to Wm Reid. Rec. Apr. 23, 1822

p. 41 Feb. 10, 1822 Muse Tolleson received from Berryman S Holder $800 full payment for: a Negro Stephen, a wagon, 5 horses and 5 pair of harnesses, a pair of stretchers, a log chain and "fifth chain". Witness Samuel White and Rolan Dare. Signed Muse Tolleson. Wit. oath Apr. 10, 1822 Rolan Dare to W Hunt. Rec. Apr. 23, 1822

p. 41 (omitted), 1822 John Linder (Spartanburgh) to daughter Tilitha Webster; for (not given) give a Negro boy Charles during her lifetime and at her death to her two sons Noah Webster and Ezekiel Webster. Witness Lee Linder and Polly Linder. Signed John Linder. Wit. oath Apr. 23, 1822 Lee Linder to E Bomar. Rec. Apr. 23, 1822

p. 41-42 Apr. 24, 1822 Hall Roddy (Spartanburgh) to friend John T Earle; for good will and affection give Hall Roddy's two favorite hound dags known as Rock and Fast; John T Earle to reward dogs for past services by kind and gentle usage. Witness William Trimmier and Jesse F Cleveland. Signed H Roddy. Wit. oath Apr. 24, 1822 William Trimmier to W Hunt. Rec. Apr. 24, 1822

p. 42-43 Feb. 9, 1819 William Sexton to Charles Williamson; for $36 sold 2 ac near Prater's Cr on S side of Tyger R; formerly James Layton's land. Witness Abner Marsh and Washington Simpson. Signed William Sexton. Wit. oath Mar. 27, 1819 Abner Marsh to Burrell Bobo. Rec. May 14, 1822

p. 43 Feb. 8, 1819 Benjamin Wofford to Charles Williamson; for $240 sold 120 ac on Prater's Cr on S side of Tyger R; border: Yarbrough; formerly John Spears' land. Witness Thomas G Potter and Thomas Layton. Signed Benjm Wofford. Wit. oath Mar. 29, 1819 Thomas G Potter to Burrell Bobo. Rec. May 14, 1822

p. 43-44 (not dated) Samuel P Kelso, Capt. Joseph Kelso, and John F Kelso (Dubois Co, Ind) to William Kelso (Spartanburgh), administrator of estate of Samuel Kelso, "our father", desc; power of attorney to get their due from their father's estate. Witness none. Signed Capt. Jos Kelso, Saml P Kelso, and John F Kelso. Wit. oath Sept. 10, 1821 (Dubois Co, Ind) Joseph, Samuel P, and John F Kelso to Thomas Scott JP. Sept. 10, 1821 (Dubois Co, Ind) Simon Morgan, clerk of Dubois Circuit Court, certifys Thomas Scott was Justice of Peace. Rec. (omitted)

p. 44-45 Apr. (omitted), 1822 Elizabeth Foster (Spartanburgh) to son William Foster (same); for love and affection give a Negro

Rachael and her two children Alford and Hanner. Witness James Polls, Tumpy Brown, and Jane Jones. Signed Elizabeth Foster's mark. Wit. oath May 20, 1822 Jane Jones to E Bomar. Rec. May 20, 1822

p. 45-46 Aug. 2, 1821 Edward W Chapman (Spartanburgh) to John James (same); for $100 sold 50 ac; border: John James and Willson's Mill Cr; spring excepted. Witness Mary Ann Young, Rebekeh W Wells, and Simpson Foster. Signed E. W. Chapman. Wit. oath May 21, 1822 Simpson Foster to E Bomar. Rec. May 21, 1822

p. 46-47 Feb. 9, 1822 James Hunt, sheriff (Spartanburgh) to Samuel Sarratt (same); for $279 sold 289 ac on waters of Broad R; border: Joseph Daffion, Wilson Nesbett, Charles Hester, and Samuel Serratt; sale due to writ from Spartanburgh Common Pleas Court on second Monday after fourth Monday in Mar. 1821 suits of W. J. Burham, John Serratt, and Michael Borders; judgment was levy $88.92 with interest from Robert Byars, administrator of William Byars desc; land was bought by Michael Gaffney for Samuel Sarratt. Witness Simpson Foster and James Edward Henry. Signed Jas Hunt SSD. Wit. oath May 21, 1822 Simpson Foster to E Bomar. Rec. May 21, 1822

p. 47 Oct. 20, 1821 Jesse Prichard to Nimrod Horton; for $100 sold 160 ac on Ashworth Cr; border: Thomas Wright; part of 555 ac grant to Cranshaw Camp. Witness Philip Davis and Philip Watkins. Signed Jesse Prichard. Wit. oath Mar. 14, 1822 Philip Davis to Geo Camp. Rec. Jun. 3, 1822

p. 47-48 Jan. 21, 1822 Elizabeth Elder, Abigail Elder, Hammon Elder, and William Ginnings to Patience Elder; quit claim to 33 ac; N side of tract sold by James Calvert to "said desc"; land laid out by Capt. William Rogers, Capt. Charles Moore, John Stephens, Elijah Jinnings, James Calvert, and Dr. A. B. Moore; grantors and grantee are legates of estate; plat attached. Witness William Rogers and William Ginnings. Signed William Ginnings, Hammon Elder, and Elizabeth and Abigail Elder's marks. Wit. oath May 25, 1822 William Rogers to Robert Ligon. Rec. Jun. 3, 1822

p. 48 Jan. 21, 1822 Elizabeth Elder, Abagail Elder, Patience Elder, and William Ginnings to Hammon Elder; quit claim to 34 ac; S part of estate of Hammon Elder desc; sold by Dr. A. B. Moore; this is Hammon Elder's part of the estate: land laid out by Capt. William Rogers, Capt. Charles Moore, James Calvert, Elisha Ginnings, John Stephens, and Dr. A. B. Moore; where "we" lived; plat attached shows border on Rogers' Still Br. Witness William Rogers and William Ginnings. Signed William Ginnings and Elizabeth, Abagail, and Patience Elder's marks. Wit. oath May 25, 1822 William Rogers to Robert Ligon. Rec. Jun. 3, 1822

p. 48-49 Jan. 21, 1822 Elizabeth Elder, Patience Elder, Hammon Elder, and William Ginnings to Abigail Elder; quit claim to 33 ac; in SE corner of tract sold by James Calvert to "sd desc"; laid out by Capt. William Rogers, Capt. Charles Moore, John Stephens, Elisha Ginnings, James Calvert, and Dr. A. B. Moore; plat attached. Witness Joseph W Tucker and William Ginnings. Signed Hammon Elder, William Jinnings, and Elizabeth and Patience Elder's marks. Wit. oath May 25, 1822 Joseph W Tucker to Robert Ligon. Rec. Jun. 3, 1822

p. 49 Jan. 21, 1822 Abigail Elder, Patience Elder, Hammon Elder, and William Ginnings to Elizabeth Elder, widow of Hammon Elder desc; quit claim to (ac omitted); laid out by Capt. William Rogers, Capt. Charles Moore, John Stephens, Elisha Ginnings, James Calvert, and Dr. A. B. Moore, "chosen by legatees of desc for that purpose"; plat attached. Witness William Rogers and William Ginnings. Signed Hammon Elder, William Ginnings, and Abigail and Patience Elder's marks. Wit. oath May 25, 1822 William Rogers to Robert Ligon. Rec. Jun.

3, 1822

p. 49-50 Mar. 1, 1822 William Land (Spartanburgh) to Zachariah McDaniel (same); for $100 sold a sorrel horse, 2 feather beds and furniture, a loom and geers, 2 pots, an oven, 2 axes, 2 plows, 2 pair of chains, and all household furniture; Condition: sale void if William Land pays Zachariah McDaniel $100 with interest by Jan. 1, 1823

p. 50-51 Feb. 11, 1818 Justus Reynolds (Spartanburgh) to William Tracy (same); for $400 sold (1) 244 ac on N side of Lawson's fork; border: Green River road; and (2) 200 ac; border: S-Elisha McAbee, SE-Littleton Bagwell, and NW-(1) above; both tracts granted to John Gray; tract (2) is where William Tracy lives. Witness William F Reynolds and Benjamin Poole. Signed Justus Reynolds. Wit. oath Jun. 3, 1822 William F Reynolds to W Hunt. Rec. Jun. 3, 1822

p. 51-52 May 3, 1819 John Hindman jr to John Hindman sr (Spartanburgh); for $40 sold 100 ac on branch on N side Tyger R; border: Meeting House Br, Coblers Br, and Thomas Wright; part of 400 ac; where John Hindman lives. Witness Gideon Harelson and David Hindman. Signed John Hindmand. Wit. oath Sept. 9, 1819 Gideon Harelson to James Hamm. Rec. Jun. 3, 1822. Dower renounced Jul. 10, 1821 Martha Hindman to Benjn Wofford

p. 52-53 Apr. 3, 1822 William C Evetts (Spartanburgh) to John Ison (same); for $300 sold 300 ac on Foster's Br of Fairforest Cr; grant to Matilda Buffington who sold to Joseph Hays who sold to William C Evetts. Witness Abel Lancaster and Elisha Bomar. Signed Will C Evetts. Wit. oath Jun. 3, 1822 Abel Lancaster to D White. Rec. Jun. 3, 1822. Dower renounced Jun. 3, 1822 Sally Evetts to Daniel White

p. 53-54 May 12, 1822 Drury Hutcheson (Spartanburgh) to Mary Lewis (same); for $100 sold 102 ac on waters of Meadow Cr; border: Lockart's Br, John S Rowland, M Lewis, and the ford. Witness John W Lewis and Frances M Rowland. Signed Drury Hutcheson's mark. Wit. oath May 12, 1822 John W Lewis to John S Rowland. Rec. Jun. 3, 1822

p. 54-55 Dec. 10, 1820 John Brewton (Spartanburgh) to Clemons McGanty (same); for $1,050 sold 440 ac at fork of N and S Tyger R; border: N-Johnathan Crow, S & W-John Thornton, Chesney, Robert Alexander, Elias Rogers, Richard Willis, and E-N Tyger R; where Nathaniel Burton formerly lived. Witness John Tornton and Spencer Leatherwood. Signed John Brewton. Wit. oath Feb. 27, 1822 Spencer Leatherwood to Benjn Wofford. Rec. Jun. 3, 1822. Dower renounced Feb. 23, 1822 Nancy Brewton to Benjamin Wofford

p. 55 May 7, 1821 John Linder (Spartanburgh) to son Abraham Linder; for (omitted) give a Negro boy Luke. Witness Thomas Linder and Nathaniel Linder. Signed John Linder. Wit. oath Jun. 3, 1822 Thomas Linder to Lee Linder. Rec. Jun. 3, 1822

p. 55-56 Apr. 25, 1822 Amos Cooper (Spartanburgh) to Nathaniel Linder (same); for $325 sold 100 ac on S side of Pacolett R above mouth of Cherokee Cr; border: Carter Bennett. Witness Firlden Turner and Abraham Linder. Signed Amos Cooper. Wit. oath May 1, 1822 Firlden Turner to Henry Turner. Rec. Jun. 27, 1822. Dower renounced (omitted) 1, 1822 Nancy Cooper to Henry Turner

p. 56-57 May 26, 1819 John Nolen (Spartanburgh) to Tolbert Gipson (same); for $30 sold 30 ac on S side of Pacolate R; border: Burgess' Spring Br, Burgess' Ridge, and Tolbert Gipson. Witness Sibby Turner and Henry Turner. Signed John Nolen. Wit. oath May

26, 1819 Sibby Turner to Henry Turner. Rec. Jun. 29, 1822

p. 57 Jan. 16, 1822 William Gore (Spartanburgh) to Tolbert Gipson (same); for $175 sold 354 ac on S side of Pacolate R; border: Gilbert, McCarter, Burgess. Witness James Ezell and Absalem Nolen. Signed William Gore. Wit. oath Apr. 27, 1822 James Ezell to James Foster. Rec. Jun. 29, 1822

p. 57-58 Apr. 27, 1811 John Nolen (Spartanburgh) to Tolbert Gipson (same); for $50 sold 329 ac on S side of Casey's Cr of Pacolate R; part of grant to John Nolen. Witness William Bennett, William Morris, and Daniel Cantrell. Signed John Nolen. Wit. oath Apr. 26, 1811 (sic) William Morris to Leonard Adcock. Rec. Jun. 29, 1822

p. 58-59 Feb. 4, 1822 John Powers (Spartanburgh) to Nathaniel McElrath (same); for $43.35 sold 2 feather beds and furniture, a pot, an oven and spider, a cotton wheel, a trunk and clothing, a skillet, a pair of cotton cards, a set of fire irons, 6 chairs, a water pail, a piggin, a bread tray, and a sifter. Witness John P Evins and Thomas Wood. Signed John Powers. Wit. oath Jul. 1, 1822 John P Evins to John Burns. Rec. Jul. 1, 1822

p. 59-60 Apr. 9, 1822 Elisha James (Spartanburgh) to Daniel White and William S Golightly, executors for Charles James desc; to secure debt of $45 with interest in two notes sold a waggon, 3 cows, 2 calves, 3 steers, a gray horse, a gray mare, a sorrel colt, 3 feather beds and furniture, a cupboard and furniture, a chest, a clock, 2 pots, and 2 ovens. Witness Henry White. Signed Elisha James. Wit. oath Jul. 1, 1822 Henry White to William Reid. Rec. Jul. 1, 1822

p. 60 Jan. 31, 1822 Philip Keller (Spartanburgh) to James Moss (same); for $200 sold (ac omitted); border: William Foster. Witness John Walker and Coleman Wood. Signed Philip Keller. Wit. oath Jun. 3, 1822 Coleman Wood to Wm Underwood. Rec. Jul. 4, 1822

p. 60 Mar. 4, 1822 William West to daughter Bathsheba West; for good causes give 4 beds with their furniture, 11 chairs, 2 pine tables, a walnut table, a spinning machine, a loom with its appentenances, 2 chests, female wearing apparrel, 3 books, with earthen hard and tin ware, a case of knives and forks, look glass and glass ware, a pail, piggin, 22 geese, washing tub, and 3 pair of cotton cards. Witness Juliet E Matthews and James J Richardson. Signed William West's mark. Wit. oath Apr. 4, 1822 Juliet E Matthews to Joseph Wofford. Rec. Jul. 4, 1822

p. 60-61 Mar. 4, 1822 William West to son William West; for good causes give a "mare colt", 3 cows and 4 yearlings, a riding chair, 2 hogs, 10 barrels of corn, a clock, 2 guns--a rifle and shotgun, a saddle and bridle, 2 plows, 2 pair of geers, 2 axes, and 2 hoes. Witness James J Richardson and Juliet E Matthews. Signed William West's mark. Wit. oath Apr. 4, 1822 James J Richardson to Joseph Wofford. Rec. Jul. 4, 1822

p. 61 Nov. 15, 1814 Casper K Weber (Knox Co, Tenn) to James Hunter; for $220 sold 147 ac on waters of Thickety Cr; border: Amos and Limekill Cr. Witness Joseph Weber and Moses Weber. Signed Casper K Weber. Wit. oath Dec. 30, 1814 Joseph Weber to Joseph Camp. Rec. Jul. 4, 1822

p. 61-62 Nov. 10, 1815 James Hunter (Spartanburgh) to Joseph Austell (same); for $200 sold 147 ac on waters of Thickety Cr; border: Limekill Cr and Amos. Witness William Weber and James Lockhart. Signed James Hunt. Wit. oath Oct. 23, 1817 William Weber to J Camp.

Rec. Jul. 4, 1822

p. 62-63 Oct. 4, 1820 Lee Linder to Joseph Austell; for $960 sold 427 ac on Wilson's fork of Thickety Cr. Witness John Linder and Amos Austell. Signed Lee Linder. Wit. oath Feb. 26, 1822 Amos Austell to F. W. Robertson. Rec. Jul. 4, 1822. Dower renounced Jul. 3, 1822 Polly Linder to Henry Turner

p. 63 Aug. 11, 1821 Joseph Austell (Spartanburgh) to William Austell (same); for $500 sold 200 ac on Thickety Cr; border: Limekill Cr, Amos, and Gaffney. Witness William Littlejohn, James Austell, and Nancy Austell. Signed Joseph Austell. Wit. oath Feb. 26, 1822 James Austell to F. W. Robertson. Rec. Jul. 4, 1822

p. 63-64 Nov. 5, 1821 John Nolen (Spartanburgh) to William Cantrell (same); for $300 sold 300 ac on Pacolate R; border: John Cantrell, George Horton, Edward Stubblefield, Joseph Stubblefield, and Carter Gibson. Witness William Turner and Middleton Turner. Signed John Nolen. Wit. oath Mar. 12, 1822 William Turner to Henry Turner. Rec. Jul. 4, 1822

p. 64-65 Feb. 14, 1822 John Foster (Spartanburgh) to Lee Linder (same); for $125 sold 224 ac on E side of Pacolate R; border: Turner, Island Cr, and Hackett. Witness Enoch G Foster and James Satterfield. Signed John Foster. Wit. oath Jun. 22, 1822 James Satterfield to Henry Turner. Rec. Jul. 8, 1822

p. 65-66 Jul. 10, 1822 Frederick Hickey (Spartanburgh), one of devisees of will of Joseph Hoover desc (Orangeburgh Dist), to Fortunatus H Legg (Spartanburgh); for $1,000 sold 4 Negroes: Charity about 20 years old, Paul about 13 years old, Nancy or Anna about 4 years old, and Joe about 3 years old; Negroes belonged to Joseph Hoover desc and Orangeburgh Dist Equity Court appointed Frederick Hickey as Negroes' "guardian". Witness Abel Lancaster and James Hunt. Signed Frederick Hickey's mark. Wit. oath Jul. 10, 1822 Abel Lancaster to E Bomar. Rec. Jul. 1, 1822. "John Frederick Hickey was born Jun. 29, 1801". Jul. 11, 1822 John Gramling swears to John Chapman that preceeding birth date is correct age of John F Hickey, son of Andrew Hickey (Orangeburgh Dist), as appears from examination of Bible Register in possession of Mrs. Christina Gramling (Spartanburgh)

p. 66 Oct. 3, 1818 Benjamin Poole and James Poole (Spartanburgh) to Benjamin Newton (same); for $200 sold 50 ac; border: Lawson's fork and Smith. Witness James Crocker and James Smith. Signed James Poole and Benjamin Poole. Wit. oath Feb. 1, 1819 James Crocker to Danl White. Rec. Jul. 12, 1822

p. 66-67 Feb. 9, 1822 James Hunt, sheriff (Spartanburgh) to George Weaver; for $20 sold 54 ac; one third of 162 ac "belonging to" John Rainwaters, Thomas Poole esq, Jesse Cannon, Alexander McKie, and Jacob Stotts (or Scotts); bought by Muse Tolleson for George Weaver; sold due to writ from Spartanburgh Common Pleas Court second Monday after fourth Monday in Oct. 1819 suit of Muse Tolleson; judgment was levy from William Ware of $62 and costs. Witness Simpson Foster and James Edward Henry. Signed Jas Hunt SSD. Wit. oath Jul. 12, 1822 James E Henry to E Bomar. Rec. Jul. 12, 1822

p. 67-68 May 2, 1822 James Morris (Spartanburgh) to William Morris (Edgefield Dist); for $300 sold 150 ac on Buck Cr of Pacolate R; border: road and Pumping Gully Br. Witness Joseph Morris and Thomas Cantwell. Signed John Morris. Wit. oath Jul. 18, 1822 Joseph Morris to E Bomar. Rec. Jul. 18, 1822

p. 68 Jul. 11, 1822 Thomas Poole, sheriff (Spartanburgh) to Reuben

Fausett (same); for $40 sold 89 ac on Sholy Cr of Lawson's fork; border: S-Darby Turner, E-Justen Childs, N-Lewis and Fausett, and W-Josiah Blackwell; land bought by Col. James Brannon for Reuben Fausett; sold due to writ from Spartanburgh Common Pleas Court second Monday after fourth Monday in Oct. 1821 suit Elisha Bomar vs Joseph Lewis; judgment was levy of $33.34 and costs from Joseph Lewis. Witness Jeston Childs and Samuel Reid. Signed Thomas Poole SSD. Wit. oath Jul. 10, 1822 Jeston Childs to E Bomar. Rec. Jul. 19, 1822

p. 68-69 Mar. 5, 1822 James V Miller (Spartanburgh) to Matthias Elmore (same); for $1,500 sold 223 ac on both sides of Middle Tyger R including a shoal where John Sloan erected a "blooming &c"; border: Bailey Gray, Michael Moore, John McElrath, estate of Michael Miller desc, Hugh McClemons, and Henry Gray; part of two grants: (1) 153 ac May 1, 1786 to John Nicoll and (2) 146 ac Apr. 3, 1786 to William Garrett. Witness William Hunt esq and Thomas Friar. Signed J. V. Miller. Wit. oath Mar. 5, 1822 William Hunt to E Bomar. Rec. Jul. 25, 1822. Dower renounced Jul. 25, 1822 Maria R Miller to E Bomar

p. 69-70 Apr. 23, 1822 Nathaniel Linder (Spartanburgh) to Jacob Linder; for "standing security" for Nathaniel for $350 Nathaniel owed to Amos Coper payable in 1823 mortgage a Negro boy Gary and Nathaniel's rights to estate of Aaron Templeman desc; Condition: sale void if Nathaniel pays debt. Witness Lee Linder and Patrick Saunders. Signed Nathaniel Linder. Wit. oath Apr. 23, 1822 Patrick Saunders to Lee Linder. Rec. Jul. 19, 1822

p. 70 Jan. 18, 1822 Henry Smith (Spartanburgh) to Ephraim Drummond (same); for $70 sold 50 ac on branches of Furgeson's Cr of Tyger R; border: Thomas Williamson, Griffith, Middleton, and William Lary. Witness W. W. Hasten and Ephraim Drummond jr. Signed Henry Smith. Wit. oath Ephraim Drummond jr to Robt Ligon Apr. 9, 1822. Rec. Aug. 5, 1822

p. 70-71 Jan. 24, 1822 Gilbert Fry (Ga) to John Jackson (Spartanburgh); for $500 sold 80 ac on N side of N Pacolate R; in Spartanburgh Dist and Rutherford Co, NC; border: John Jackson, Howard's Cr, John Abram, Dolton's old line, and Thomas Jackson; willed by Peter Fry desc (Spartanburgh) to son Gilbert Fry. Witness Samuel Jackson, Curtis Caldwell, and Gilbert Bowman. Signed Gilbert Fry's mark. Wit. oath Aug. 3, 1822 Samuel Jackson to Wm Kelso. Rec. Aug. 5, 1822

p. 71-72 Mar. 23, 1822 David Bettis (Spartanburgh) to William Bennett (same); for $100 sold 66 ac on Watson's Br of Mill Cr of Tyger R; border: Smith, John Foster, and Ransom Foster. Witness William F Reynolds and W. H. Bullington. Signed David Bettis' mark. Wit. oath Apr. 11, 1822 William F Reynolds to Thomas Poole. Rec. Aug. 5, 1822

p. 72 Dec. 4, 1815 John Brewton (Spartanburgh) to Philip Brewton (same); for $30 sold 4 ac on Ferguson's Cr; border: Philip Brewton; part of grant to George Brewton. Witness David Brewton, George Brewton, and Enoch Brewton. Signed John Brewton. Wit. oath Jul. 20, 1822 David Brewton to James Crook. Rec. Aug. 5, 1822

p. 72-73 Aug. 15, 1821 David Hudgings and wife Rebecca, heir of Saml Shurbutt sr desc (Spartanburgh), to William W Smithwick (same); for $80 sold (ac omitted) on N side of N Tyger R; border: S-Tyger R, N-Benjamin Nichols, E & SE-estate of Richd Willis jr desc, and W-Henry White; where Saml Shurbutt sr died. Witness Nathaniel Jentry and Ansel Hudgins. Signed David and Rebecca Hudgings' marks. Wit. oath Jul. 26, 1822 Ansell Hudgins to Robert Ligon. Rec. Aug. 5, 1822. Dower renounced Aug. 22, 1821 Rebecca Hudgins to John Brewton

p. 73-74 Jan. 18, 1820 John Low sr (Spartanburgh) to daughter Sally Low (same); for love and affection give a cow with no horns, a yearling and a calf with all her increase. Witness Arthur Dewberry. Signed John Low sr. Wit. oath Jun. 29, 1822 Arthur Dewberry to Lee Linder. Rec. Aug. 5, 1822

p. 74 Jan. 9, 1822 James White (Spartanburgh) to Robert White (same); for $100 sold 27 ac on Kelso's Cr of Fairforest Cr; border: David Whetstone and James W Cooper; grant to James White. Witness Daniel White and Henry White. Signed James White. Wit. oath Aug. 5, 1822 Daniel White to Wm Reid. Rec. Aug. 5, 1822

p. 74-75 Mar. 9, 1816 Shands Golightly (Spartanburgh) to Benjamin Smith (same); for $160 sold 159 ac on waters of Kelso's Cr on N side of Fairforest Cr; border: NW-Dodd (now Micajah Barnett), SE-land formerly Moses Foster's, S-Shands Golightly, and SW-Peter Smith; where Benjamin Smith lives. Witness Robert Rakestraw and Peter Smith. Signed Shands Golightly. Wit. oath Dec. 29, 1820 Peter Smith to Danl White. Rec. Aug. 5, 1822

p. 75-76 Oct. 10, 1821 Muse Tolleson (Spartanburgh) to Stephen Foster and Thomas Munday; a bond of $402; Condition: bond void if Stephen Foster and Thomas Munday get to keep the following land: John Gossett made deeds to Stephen Foster for 31 ac and Thomas Munday for 95 ac; land was "sold by" William Simpson esq to Stephen Foster and Thomas Munday and by suit of James Ferguson "gained from them" and John Gossett became purchasor. Witness David Golightly jr and John Gossett. Signed Muse Tolleson. Wit. oath Aug. 5, 1822 David Golightly jr to Wm Underwood. Rec. Aug. 5, 1822

p. 76 Oct. 10, 1821 John Gossett (Spartanburgh) to Stephen Foster (same); for $52.50 sold 39 ac; border: Thomas Mundy; part of claim by Thomas Fergeson "as a grant"; resurvey "by Thomas Fergeson by Richd Thomson" authorized surveyor for South Carolina. Witness Muse Tolleson and David Golightly jr. Signed John Gossett. Wit. oath Aug. 5, 1822 David Golightly jr to Wm Underwood. Rec. Aug. 5, 1822

p. 76-77 Oct. 10, 1821 John Gossett (Spartanburgh) to Thomas Meridy (sic) (same); for $142.50 sold (ac omitted); border: Ferguson; "claimed by Ferguson as agent"; resurvey for Thomas Ferguson by Richd Thomson, authorized surveyor for South Carolina. Witness Muse Tolleson and David Golightly jr. Signed John Gossett. Wit. oath Aug. 5, 1822 David Golightly jr to Wm Underwood. Rec. Aug. 5, (omitted)

p. 77 Aug. 2, 1822 Jacob Stotts (Spartanburgh) to Hugh Holt (same); for $164 sold (1) 120 ac on waters of Lawson's fork; land "formerly belonged" to Jacob Stotts; and (2) 44 ac on N side of tract (1). Witness Herndon McKie and Abel Lancaster. Signed Jacob Stotts. Wit. oath Aug. 5, 1822 Abel Lancaster to Wm Reid. Rec. Aug. 5, 1822

p. 77-78 Dec. 4, 1822 Hannah O'Neill, widow to daughter Hannah McDowell Wilson; "grant" 2 beds, 2 pillows, 2 counterpanes, a quilt, a silver scissor chain, 2 "bolsters", and 2 "counter". Witness Robert Love and John O'Niell Love. Signed Hannah ONeill "By consent". Wit. oath Aug. 26, 1822 Robert Love to E Bomar. Rec. Aug. 26, 1822

p. 78-79 Aug. 2, 1822 Zachariah Nance (Union Dist) to William Littlefield jr (Spartanburgh); for $300 sold 150 ac on W side of Thomson's Cr of Pacolate R; border: John Kimbrell, School House Br, and James Bennett; where George Gilbert and Benjamin Evins live; part of grant to Thomas Bennett. Witness Thomas Craven, Elizabeth Nance, and William B Nance. Signed Zachariah Nance. Wit. oath Aug.

2, 1822 Thomas Craven to Benjamin Wofford. Rec. Aug. 26, 1822

p. 79 Feb. 21, 1822 Joseph Carswell (Spartanburgh) to Muse Tolleson (same); for $3,000 sold 196 ac known as Cross Anchor. Witness William Trimmier and Lemuel White. Signed Joseph Carswell. Wit. oath Aug. 13, 1822 William Trimmior to J. E. Henry. Rec. Aug. 26, 1822

p. 79-80 Jan. 6, 1817 Laban P Poole, sheriff (Spartanburgh) to David Trail; for $377 sold 213 ac; David West petitioned Spartanburgh Common Pleas Court second Monday after fourth Monday in Mar. 1816 to divide estate of Osbourn West desc; Court appointed William Smith, James Hamm, James Selman, Benjamin Peak(?), and John Meadows esq to divide the land; but they said on second Monday after fourth Monday in Oct. 1816 the land can't be divided and should be sold with credit of 12 months; sale was on first Monday in Jan. 1817; land was sold by Clark to Osbourn West. Witness Samuel Turner and William G Clark. Signed Laban P Poole SSD. Wit. oath Nov. 5, 1822 Samuel Turner to Robert Ligon. Rec. Aug. 26, 1822

p. 80-81 Feb. 28, 1822 Muse Tolleson (Spartanburgh) to Fortunatus H Legg (same); for $1,500 sold 478 ac on waters of Middle Tyger R; border: Thomas Moore. Witness Howell Johnson and Wm L Johnson. Signed Muse Tolleson. Wit. oath Apr. 1, 1822 Howell Johnson to Thomas Poole. Rec. Aug. 26, 1822. Dower renounced Apr. 12, 1822 Sally Tolleson to E Bomar

p. 81-82 Oct. 18, 1821 Henry Cole (Spartanburgh) to Drury Cox (same); for $50 sold 25 ac (or 20 ac) on branches of Lick Cr of Enoree R. Witness William Hendrix and Charles Cox. Signed Henry Cole. Wit. oath Jan. 11, 1822 Charles Cox to David Moore. Rec. Aug. 26, 1822

p. 82-83 Oct. 18, 1821 William Hendrix (Spartanburgh) to Drury Cox (same); for $500 sold 105 ac on branches of Lick Cr of Enoree R. Witness Charles Cox and Henry Cole. Signed William Hendrix. Wit. oath Jan. 11, 1822 Charles Cox to David Moore. Rec. Aug. 26, 1822

p. 83 Mar. 22, 1821 William Lindsey (Spartanburgh) to John Childress (same); for $1,050 sold 57 ac on branch on E side of Enoree R; border: Samuel Jones and Henry Pearson; part of grant to John Tate who sold to William Lindsey. Witness James W Cantrell and Drury Cox. Signed William Lindsey's mark. Wit. oath Apr. 4, 1821 James W Cantrell to Thomas Wood. Rec. Aug. 26, 1822

p. 83-84 Aug. 6, 1822 William Hartgrave (Jefferson Co, Ala) to James Brown (Spartanburgh); for $100 sold 100 ac; border: Howell. Witness Young Allen and Smith Lipscomb jr. Signed William Hartgrave's mark. Wit. oath Aug. 6, 1822 Young Allen to John Lipscomb. Rec. Aug. 27, 1822

p. 84-85 Mar. 30, 1822 Robert Young to John Jackson (Spartanburgh); for $20 sold (1) 350 ac on both sides Alex Cr; border: Davis; and (2) 70 ac on waters of Beaverdam Cr; border: Grogan; part of widow Bolin's land. Witness William S Morgan and William Young. Signed Robert Young. Wit. oath Aug. 29, 1822 William Young to Wm Kelso. Rec. Aug. 29, 1822

p. 85-86 Aug. 16, 1822 Stephen Tolleson (Spartanburgh) to John Ison (same); for $2,600 mortgage all Stephen Tolleson's property real and personal: (1) 180 ac where Stephen Tolleson lives; (2) 150 ac where Jacob Land lived; (3) 700 ac (or half of it) sold by Mr. Ferguson to Stephen Tolleson's father (not named) and John Gossett; (4) land from Stephen Tolleson's father's estate; 8 (sic) Negroes--

Conkoe, Daysoe, old Tom, Dilse and three children; a machine, 2 stills and tubs, a waggon and geer, 4 horses, 16 cattle, 40 hogs, 10 sheep, 4 beds and furniture, 3 spinning sheels, 100 gal of brandy, "a quantity" of pots, dishes, pans, and plates, a cross cut saw, Stephen's crop of corn, fodder, and cotton, 30 bushels of wheat, 16 (bushels) of rye, "some" oats, 7 plows, 8 hoes, 3 mattocks, cupboard, chest, trunks, and a large grindstone; Condition sale void if Stephen Tolleson pays John Ison $2,600 with interest by Dec. 25, 1823. Witness Capt. Abraham Lancaster, James Gossett, and Zealy Stone. Signed Stephen Tolleson. Wit. oath Sept. 2, 1822 Abraham Lancaster to Caleb Jones. Rec. Sept. 2, 1822

p. 86-87 Apr. 3, 1822 John H Owens and Sterling L Westmoreland (Spartanburgh) to James Crook (same); for $1,400 sold 150 ac on N fork of Toguson's Cr of Tyger R; border: Jesse Crook, Wofford, and Warren Drummond. Witness A Drummond, Thomas Crymes, and W. W. Hastin. Signed John H Owens and S. L. Westmoreland. Wit. oath Apr. 9, 1822 A Drummond to Wm Underwood. Rec. Sept. 2, 1822

p. 87-88 Dec. 26, 1821 Josiah Thornton (Spartanburgh) to Enoch J Underwood (same); for $1,100 sold 425 ac on Stories Cr and Dugan's Br of Fairforest Cr; in two parts: (1) 175 ac granted to Gen. Thomas Brandon who sold to Josiah Thornton; border: James Rainwaters; and (2) 250 ac; border: Theron Lancaster. Witness William Lancaster and Joshua Hammond. Signed Josiah Thornton's mark. Wit. oath Sept. 2, 1822 William Lancaster to Wm Underwood. Rec. Sept. 2, 1822. Dower renounced Feb. 14, 1822 Sally Thornton to Daniel White

p. 88 Jul. 26, 1822 John N Crease (Spartanburgh) to James Burnett jr (same); for $200 sold a Negro woman Ailsa 27 years old. Witness Woodson Burnett. Signed John N Crease's mark. Wit. oath Sept. 2, 1822 Woodson Burnett to W Bennett. Rec. Sept. 2, 1822

p. 88-89 May 30, 1821 Jesse Smith (Spartanburgh) to Edward Patterson (same); for $35.81¼ sold 50 ac on N side of Pacolate R above mouth of Lawson's fork. Witness Isaac Lindsey and William Smith. Signed Jesse Smith. Wit. oath Aug. 20, 1821 Isaac Lindsey to Caleb Jones. Rec. Sept. 10, 1822

p. 89 Apr. 15, 1822 David Tanner to William T Tanner; for $1,500 sold 200 ac in fork between Middle and N Tyger Rivers and on N side of N Tyger R; border: S-Floyd Tanner and Gen. Moore, N-Jno Crawford, E-John Foster, and S-S Miller and B McFearson. Witness Floyd Tanner and Elizabeth Tanner. Signed David Tanner. Wit. oath Aug. 12, 1822 Floyd Tanner to Ransom Foster. Rec. Sept. 12, 1822

p. 89-90 Aug. 23, 1821 Isaac Young (Spartanburgh) to Ephraim Potter (same); for $50 sold 50 ac; part of tract on E side of Island Cr of Pacolate R; border: James Lard and Headen's ford. Witness Tillotson Brookshier and Elbert Blalock. Signed Isaac Young. Wit. oath Aug. 24, 1822 Tillotson Brookshier to Henry Turner. Rec. Sept. 12, 1822

p. 90-91 Mar. 9, 1821 Samuel Turner (Spartanburgh) to Ephraim Potter (same); for $106 sold 212 ac on both sides of Island Cr. Witness Benjamin Cash and Robert Garrett. Signed Samuel Turner. Wit. oath Mar. 9, 1821 Benjamin Cash to Henry Turner. Rec. Sept. 12, 1822

p. 91 Feb. 9, 1819 Thomas Moore (Spartanburgh) to Richard Barry jr (same); for $1 sold 20 ac on W side of N Tyger R; part of grant to Charles Moore who sold to Thomas Moore. Witness Charles H Moore and Charles M Barry. Signed Tho Moore. Wit. oath Sept. 26, 1822 Charles H Moore to F. H. Legg. Rec. Sept. 27, 1822

p. 91-92 Aug. 28, 1822 John Jordan (Edgefield Dist) to Joseph Morris, son of William Morris (Spartanburgh); for $200 sold 200 ac on S side of Buck Cr; border: Joseph Morris and John Morris. Witness Joseph Morris jr and Joseph Morris sr. Signed John Jordan's mark. Wit. oath Aug. 28, 1822 (Edgefield Dist) Joseph Morris jr to James Adams. Rec. Sept. 27, 1822

p. 92-93 Aug. 28, 1822 John Jordan (Edgefield Dist) to Joseph Morris, son of William Morris (Spartanburgh); for $100 sold 150 ac on waters of Buck Cr and Pacolate R; border: Wm Morris. Witness Joseph Morris sr and Joseph Morris jr. Signed John Jordan's mark. Wit. oath Aug. 28, 1822 Joseph Morris jr to James Adams. Rec. Sept. 27, 1822

p. 93 Aug. 5, 1822 William Howard to William Bennett; "mortgaged satisfied by the sale of property". Signed Thos Poole SSD. Rec. Oct. 7, 1822

p. 93-94 Aug. 2, 1822 Peter Smith (Spartanburgh) to John Murph (same); for $1,000 sold (1) 50 ac on Kelso's Cr of Fairforest Cr; (2) 63 ac; border: Shands Golightly; sold Sept. 18, 1811 by Henry Smith to Robert Smith who sold Mar. 18, 1812 to Edith Ligon who sold Apr. 8, 1814 to Peter Smith; (3) 90½ ac on Kelso's Cr; border: Jane Smith, Robt Martin, and tracts 1 & 2 above; part of grant to Peter Smith and sold (sic) Dec. 23, 1817 by Richd Barnett to Peter Smith; and (4) 56 ac; border: tract 3 above and Kelso's Cr; sold Mar. 10, 1807 by Henry Smith to Peter Smith; total of four tracts is 259½ ac. Witness John Oeland and David Whetstone. Signed Peter Smith. Wit. oath Sept. 9, 1822 John Oeland to Augustin Shands. Rec. Oct. 7, 1822. Dower renounced Sept. 4, 1822 Kesiah Smith to Daniel White

p. 94-95 Aug. 28, 1820 David S Lipscomb (Ala) to John H Lipscomb (Spartanburgh); power of attorney to sell 272 ac--lots 1 and 2 in Abbeville Dist from estate of William Lipscomb desc; David S Lipscomb is legatee of William Lipscomb; and John is to obtain money owed to David. Witness Simpson Foster and Allen Lancaster. Signed David S Lipscomb. Wit. oath Aug. 28, 1820 Simpson Foster to John Chapman. Rec. Oct. 7, 1822

p. 95-96 Mar. 23, 1822 Thomas Dare (Spartanburgh) to Wyatt Lipscomb and Robert Lipscomb (same); for $1,200 sold 400 ac on Cherokee Cr; includes saw and grist mills; see deed from William Champion to Thomas Dare. Witness Fendal W Robertson and George Haxies (or Kaxies). Signed Thomas Dare. Wit. oath Sept. 28, 1822 Fendal W Robertson to J Camp. Rec. Oct. 7, 1822. Dower renounced Apr. 9, 1822 Lucy Dare to Daniel White

p. 96-97 Mar. 12, 1822 Nicholas Gentry (Spartanburgh) to Richard Willis; for $55 sold 52 ac on N side of Tyger R; border: Richard Willis. Witness Polly W Crook and Amelia Crook. Signed Nicholas Gentry's mark. Wit. oath May 8, 1822 Polly W Crook to James Crook. Rec. Oct. 7, 1822. Dower renounced May 8, 1822 Sarah Gentry to James Crook

p. 97-98 Jan. 10, 1818 Edward Stewart (Greenville Dist) to Alexander Roddy (Spartanburgh); for $600 sold 270 ac on waters of N Tyger R; border: widow Darrott. Witness John Miller and George Miller. Signed Edward Stewart's mark. Wit. oath Mar. 25, 1818 John Miller to John Montgomery. Rec. Oct. 7, 1822

p. 98 Feb. 9, 1822 James Hunt, sheriff (Spartanburgh) to Edward Bomar; for $417.50 sold 350 ac on Cub Cr of N Tyger R; border: Edmond Bomar, Mrs. Hemkerpillar Doigg, and "others"; sale due to writ from Spartanburgh Common Pleas Court second Monday after fourth Monday in Oct. 1821 suit of William Bomar; judgment was levy from David Ulmer of $109 and costs. Witness Simpson Foster and James Edward Henry. Signed Jas Hunt SSD. Wit. oath Oct. 8, 1822 James Edward Henry to E Bomar. Rec. Oct. 8, 1822

p. 98-99 Oct. 31, 1821 Agrippa Cooper (Spartanburgh) to James Hunt (same); for $1,000 sold Negroes: fellow named Buck or Will, woman Milly and her child Elvira, and a girl child Mary about 10 or 11 years old. Witness Elisha Bomar and William Trimmier. Signed A Cooper. Wit. oath Oct. 8, 1822 Elisha Bomar to James E Henry. Rec. Oct. 8, 1822

p. 99-100 Oct. 13, 1807 David Anderson (Spartanburgh) to Denny Anderson (same); for $350 sold 250 ac on both sides Ben's Cr of Tyger R; grant Apr. 28, 1798 Gov. Tryon (NC) to David Anderson (then in Mecklinburgh Co, NC) and in South Carolina Memorial Book 11-L p. 242. Witness Samuel Jameson, James Chamblin, and William Anderson. Signed David Anderson. Wit. oath Oct. 14, 1807 James Chamblin to David Morton. Rec. Oct. 9, 1822. Dower renounced Oct. 20, 1807 Marion Anderson to David Morton

p. 100 Nov. 15, 1816 Leonard Adcock (Spartanburgh) to William McKinney (Rutherford Co, NC); for $350 sold 225 ac on Little Buck Cr of Pacolate R. Witness Charles Simmons and Deidamia Simmons. Signed Leonard Adcock. Wit. oath Oct. 14, 1822 Charles Simmons to E Bomar. Rec. Oct. 14, 1822

p. 100-101 Dec. 1, 1819 Frederic Davis (Spartanburgh) to William McKinney (NC); for $300 sold 328 ac on ridge between Horse and Buck Creeks; border: Reuben Warren and Drury Scruggs; part of 655 ac grant Dec. 2, 1793 States Office to Reuben Warren. Witness Abraham Davis and Drury Scruggs. Signed Frederic Davis. Wit. oath Dec. 28, 1821 Drury Scruggs to Geo Camp. Rec. Oct. 14, 1822

p. 101-102 Aug. 31, 1811 Basel Lee jr (Spartanburgh) to Caleb Jones (same); for $70 sold (1) Basel's part of 284 ac on waters of Lawson's fork of S Pacolate R; grant to John Holcom; (2) Basel's part of 100 ac on S side of Lawson's fork; grant to Edward Dixon; (3) Basel's part of 60 ac; border: Harrison; part of grant to Disken; (4) Basel's part of 100 ac on S side of Lawson's fork; and (5) Basel's part of 100 ac; border: George Parkeson and Randol (sic) Brown; total is 63 ac and is Basel's part of estate of Basel Lee desc. Witness John H Jones and James Lee. Signed Basel Lee. Wit. oath Aug. 31, 1811 James Lee to Jno H Jones. Rec. Oct. 14, 1822

p. 102-103 Mar. 8, 1814 James Lee (Spartanburgh) to Caleb Jones; for $75 sold all James' part of estate of Basel Lee desc: (1) James' part of 284 ac on waters of Lawson's fork; grant to John Holcom; (2) James' part of 100 ac on S side of Lawson's fork; grant to Edward Dickson; (3) James' part of 60 ac; part of grant to Disken; border: Harrison; (4) James' part of 100 ac on S side of Lawson's fork; and (5) James' part of 100 ac; border: George Parkeson and Randolph Brown. Witness Robert Jones and John H Jones. Signed James Lee. Wit. oath Aug. 4, 1817 John H Jones to Thomas Poole. Rec. Oct. 14, 1822

p. 103-104 Jun. 24, 1818 Robert Erwin (or Irwin) and Joab Alexander, executors of William Beaty desc, (Mecklenburgh Co, NC) to William McKinney (Rutherford Co, NC); for $175 sold 340 ac on Horse Cr of main Broad R below forks of creek; border: Bone. Witness Thomas Camp and Major R Alexander. Signed Robert Irwin and Joab Alexander. Wit. oath Oct. 1, 1821 Thomas Camp to Geo Camp. Rec. Oct. 14, 1822

p. 104-105 Sept. 10, 1821 Littleton Bagwell (Spartanburgh) to Levi Lee (same); to secure $300 with interest Littleton owes

Levi by May 1, 1822 and for $2 sold a bay mare, a black colt, a sorrel mare with fold, 3 dows and 16 pigs, a woman's saddle, a man's saddle, 3 feather beds and furniture, a pot, an oven, a spider, a table and 2 chairs, a wheel, 2 plows and geers, 4 weeding hoes, 2 axes, 2 stacks of fodder, 5 barrels of corn, a chest and furniture, and a rifle gun; Condition: sale void if Littleton pays Levi $300 with interest. Witness Sarah Parkison and John Bagwell. Signed Littleton Bagwell's mark. Wit. oath Sept. 28, 1822 John Bagwell to James E Henry. Rec. Oct. 14, 1822

p. 105-106 Mar. 27, 1821 William Clemment (Spartanburgh) to Edmond Clement (same); for $500 sold 174 ac on waters of Lawson's fork; border: N of Edmond Clement and Edmd Fowler and E-Wm Clement and John Clement; part of grant Oct. 14, 1785 to James Wood and sold by Wm Wood to Edmond Clement (sic). Witness Samuel Wall and Mahala Clement. Signed Wm Clement. Wit. oath Apr. 5, 1821 Samuel Wall to W Bennett. Rec. Oct. 14, 1822

p. 106-107 Apr. 2, 1821 William Clement (Spartanburgh) to John Clement (same); for $1,226 sold a Negro boy Kiah, Negro girl Matilday, a waggon, a riding chair, 2 sorrel mares, a sorrel filly, 10 cattle, 30 hogs, 3 feather beds steads and furniture, a black walnut desk, a pine cupboard, a quantity of earthen ware, a patent clock, 2 rifle guns, 2 shot guns, a side saddle, and all kitchen furniture. Witness George Wolf and John Wolf. Signed William Clement. Wit. oath Oct. 14, 1822 John Wolf to W Bennett. Rec. Oct. 14, 1822

p. 107 Mar. 2, 1822 Vardry Camp to Peter Hawkins; for $600 sold 221 ac on McBee's Cr of N Pacolate R; border: Theron Earle, Thomas Jackson, and Cally's old line; where Peter Hawkins lives. Witness Willey S Brown and Theron Earle. Signed Vardry Camp. Wit. oath Oct. 14, 1822 Willey S Brown to J Whitten. Rec. Oct. 14, 1822

p. 107-108 Sept. 23, 1820 Samuel Cantrell (Spartanburgh) to William Cantrell (same); for $150 sold 115 ac on Buck Cr; border: John Cantrell. Witness Mecheck Hall and Judah Terry. Signed Samuel and Polly Cantrell's marks. Wit. oath Oct. 15, 1822 Mecheck Hall to Geo Camp. Rec. Oct. 15, 1822

p. 108 Aug. 19, 1822 Daniel Amos sr (Spartanburgh) to Elijah Logan; for $200 sold 100 ac on Thickety Cr. Witness Thomas Byars and Daniel Amos jr. Signed Daniel Amos sr. Wit. oath Oct. 15, 1822 Thomas Byars to J Camp. Rec. Oct. 18, 1822

p. 108-109 Oct. 1, 1822 Jacob Utley (Spartanburgh) to Benjamin High (Rutherford Co, NC); for $600 sold 250 ac on S side of Fairforest Cr; border: William Benson, widow White (now Henry Walder), and James Ward. Witness James Hunt and Jesse Cleveland. Signed Jacob Utley. Wit. oath Oct. 1, 1822 Jesse Cleveland to E Bomar. Rec. Oct. 18, 1822

p. 109-110 Apr. 22, 1822 Larken Mathis to George Weaver; for $45 sold a horse, a cow, a feather bed, a straw bed, 2 saddles and 2 bridles, an oven, a dresser and furniture, 2 tubs and 2 pails, 2 chairs, a chest, a plough and a pair of geers, a gun and shot bag, a spinning wheel and a pair of cards; Condition: sale void if Larken pays George $45 with interest by Mar. 28, 1822. Witness John Mathis and Mathew Mathis. Signed Larken Mathis. Wit. oath Oct. 18, 1822 John Mathis to Caleb Jones. Rec. Oct. 21, 1822

p. 110-111 Oct. 29, 1822 Cassey West (Spartanburgh) to Moses Casey esq (same); for $500 sold 100 ac on Cedar Shoal Cr of Enoree R; border: W-William Farrow, S-William Wilbanks, E-Willis Arnold, on Meeting House Br, Bordwin Waters, and Farrow. Witness William C Allen and Avery Stone. Signed Cassey West. Wit. oath Oct.

31, 1822 William C Allen to Burrel Bobo. Rec. Oct. 31, 1822

p. 111 Sept. 16, 1822 Henry Cole (Spartanburgh) to son Osbon Cole (same); for love and affection give 200 ac on E side of Enoree R, 2 horse "brutes", all the cattle, hog, and sheep, household and kitchen furniture, and all Henry Cole's property. Witness Jesse Cole and John Wood. Signed Henry Cole. Wit. oath Nov. 2, 1822 (sic) John Wood to F. H. Legg. Rec. Nov. 1, 1822

p. 111-112 Apr. 27, 1821 Gideon Harrelson (Spartanburgh) to Meadows Harrelson (same); for $100 sold 27 ac on waters of Tyger R; border: George Vice, Nathaniel Vice, and Reuben Vice. Witness John Hindman and Daniel Hindman. Signed Gideon Harrelson. Wit. oath May 9, 1821 John Hindman to Benj Wofford. Rec. Nov. 4, 1822. Dower renounced Elizabeth Harrelson to Benj Wofford May 9, 1821

p. 112-113 Aug. 27, 1822 Thomas Poole, sheriff (Spartanburgh) to Thomas Brown (same); for $13.50 sold 125 ac on Bullocks fork of Thickety Cr; border: Cannon and Low; sale due to writ from Spartanburgh Common Pleas Court suit John Prewit vs William McBee on second Monday after fourth Monday in Oct. 1821; writ entered in Sheriff's Office Jan. 12, 1822 endorsed by Samuel C Hunt, then sheriff; Thomas Poole is successor of Samuel C Hunt; sale was on Apr. 1, 1822. Witness Col. James Brannon and B. S. Holder. Signed Thomas Poole SSD. Wit. oath Nov. 5, 1822 James Brannon to E Bomar. Rec. Nov. 5, 1822

p. 113-114 Apr. 12, 1821 Nancy Guyton to Charles Petty; for $69 sold 46 ac on branch of Beaverdam Cr of Broad R; "lot 1"; border: Petty, Bostick, "lot 2", and Amos. Witness William Weber sr and John Bolton. Signed Nancy Guyton's mark. Wit. oath Oct. 24, 1822 William Weber to F. W. Robertson. Rec. Nov. 15, 1822

p. 114 Dec. 14, 1818 Thomas Lipscomb to John Lipscomb jr; for $160 sold 358 ac. Witness John Lipscomb sr and Sally Lipscomb. Signed Thomas Lipscomb. Wit. oath Nov. 12, 1822 John Lipscomb sr to William Reid. Rec. Nov. 15, 1822. Dower renounced Nov. 29, 1821 Agness R Lipscomb to John Lipscomb

p. 114-115 May (blank), 1822 Hugh Stuart (Charleston Dist) to Aaron Casey (Spartanburgh); for $500 sold 237½ ac on branches of Cedar Shoal Cr; border: Thomas Gore, Joseph Carswell, widow Casey, and L Bobo. Witness James Reynolds and Saml Wharton. Signed Hugh Stuart. Wit. oath Aug. 23, 1822 James Reynolds to John Dean. Rec. Nov. 15, 1822

p. 115-116 May 10, 1813 James Vaughan (Spartanburgh) to Philip Johnson (same); for $80 sold 45 ac on Ben's Cr of Tyger R. Witness William Dickie and John Durham. Signed James Vaughan. Wit. oath May 16, 1814 John Durham to Drury McDaniel. Rec. Nov. 15, 1822. Dower renounced May 16, 1814 Hannah Pines Vaughan to Drury McDaniel

p. 116-117 Nov. 8, 1816 Charles Williamson, William Wileder, and Susannah Wileder to Abner Marsh; for $500 sold 158 ac on Prater's Cr on S side of Tyger R; border: Edward Arnett, E-John Spears, N-Benjamin Wofford, W-James Layton, and S-William Sexton. Witness Elisha Stattion and Thomas Layton. Signed Charles Williamson and William Wileder, and Susannah Wileder's mark. Wit. oath May 17, 1817 Thomas Layton to Burrel Bobo. Rec. Nov. 15, 1822. Dower renounced Dec. 7, 1816 Elizabeth Williamson to Burrell Bobo

p. 117 Mar. 5, 1822 Joseph Carswell (Spartanburgh) to Aaron Casey (same); for $200 sold 20 ac; "grant" by Thos Gore to Joseph Carswell. Witness William Wileder and Robert Oliphant. Signed

Joseph Carswell. Wit. oath Nov. 12, 1822 Robert Olephant to Wm Young. Rec. Nov. 15, 1822

p. 117-118 Nov. 4, 1821 Thomas Collins (Spartanburgh) to Thomas Landtrip (Union Dist); for $550 sold 200 ac on Thickety Cr; border: Collins Spring Br, Moses Guyton, Hunts' old line, Lipscomb, and William Thomson. Witness John Guyton and James Land. Signed Thomas Collins. Wit. oath Sept. 14, 1822 John Guyton to John Lipscomb. Rec. Nov. 15, 1822. Dower renounced Sept. 14, 1822 Margaret Collins to John Lipscomb

p. 118-119 Sept. 28, 1822 Joseph T Robertson (Spartanburgh) to James K Nance (same); for $229.50 sold (ac omitted) on waters of Fairforest Cr of Tyger R. Witness Ab Lancaster and Jas Hunt. Signed Joseph T Robertson. Wit. oath none. Rec. Nov. 22, 1822. Dower renounced Nov. 22, 1822 Renney Robertson to Elisha Bomar

p. 119-120 Jan. 16, 1821 Thornton Ward (Spartanburgh) to Henry W Smith (same); for $200 sold 50 ac on S side of Tyger R; border: near a still house, widow Otts, and Joseph Miller. Witness Presley Smith and Samuel Colley. Signed Thornton Ward. Wit. oath Jan. 16, 1821 Presley Smith to James Crook. Rec. Nov. 22, 1822

p. 120 Nov. 21, 1822 Jordan Morris (Spartanburgh) and William Morris (Edgefield Dist) to William McKinney (Rutherford Co, NC); for $237 sold 220 ac on Back Br and Jumping G Br. Witness Seth Russel and Alfred Brown. Signed Jordan Morris and William Morris. Wit. oath Nov. 22, 1822 Alfred Brown to James Young. Rec. Nov. 23, 1822

p. 120-121 Oct. 17, 1822 Labon P Poole to Samuel McHughs; for $200 sold 126 ac on S side of S Tyger R; resurvey Dec. 10, 1817 by Page Rork. Witness Henry G Shely and Eugene Brenan. Signed Labon P Poole. Wit. oath Oct. 18, 1822 (Edgefield Dist) Henry G Shely to Eugene Brenan Notary Public and JQ. Rec. Nov. 26, 1822. Dower renounced Oct. 18, 1822 (Edgefield Dist) Lettice P Poole to Eugene Brenan

p. 121-122 Oct. 17, 1822 Labon P Poole (Spartanburgh) to Alexander McHughs desc (same); for $70 sold 70 ac; border: Williamson's Cr, McElrath, and Daniel McKie; resurvey Dec. 12, 1816 by James Swanzy DS. Witness Henry G Shely and Eugene Brenan. Signed Labon P Poole. Wit. oath Oct. 18, 1822 (Edgefield Dist) Henry G Shely to E Brenan. Rec. Nov. 26, 1822. Dower renounced Oct. 18, 1822 (Edgefield Dist) Lettice P Poole to Eugene Brenan

p. 122-123 Sept. 28, 1822 Joseph T Robertson (Spartanburgh) to James K Nance (same); for $229.50 sold (ac omitted) on waters of Fairforest Cr of Tyger R. Witness Abel Lancaster and James Hunt. Signed Joseph T Robertson. Wit. oath Nov. 22, 1822 James Hunt to E Bomar. Rec. Nov. 28, 1822. Dower renounced Nov. 28, 1822 Renney Robertson to E Bomar

p. 123-124 Mar. 26, 1821 Henry Cole sr (Spartanburgh) to Jesse Cole (same); for $200 sold 128½ ac on E side of Enoree R; E part of grant to Robert Cooper who sold to Charles Saxon who sold to Henry Cole. Witness Jesse Wofford and Noel Wadel (or Waddle). Signed Henry Cole sr. Wit. oath Nov. 29, 1822 Jesse Wofford to David Moore. Rec. Dec. 2, 1822

p. 124 Nov. 29, 1822 Henry Cole (Spartanburgh) to John Cole (same); for $100 sold 58 ac on waters of Enoree R. Witness Ozbon Cole and John Wood. Signed Henry Cole. Wit. oath Nov. 30, 1822 John Wood to David Moore. Rec. Dec. 2, 1822

p. 124-125 Oct. 10, 1822 James Wood (Spartanburgh) to Robert Stacy (same); for $100 sold 178 ac on branch of Lawson's fork. Witness Findal W Robertson and Amos Stacy. Signed James Wood's mark. Wit. oath Nov. 30, 1822 Amos Stacy to F. W. Robertson. Rec. Dec. 2, 1822

p. 125-126 Dec. 28, 1820 Findal W Robertson (Spartanburgh) to Robert Stacy sr (same); for $300 sold 202 ac on Little Cherokee Cr; border: Voinset. Witness John Lefever and George Stacy. Signed Findal W Robertson. Wit. oath Oct. 8, 1822 George Stacy to J Camp. Rec. Dec. 2, 1822. Dower renounced Nov. 27, 1821 Elizabeth Robertson to John Lipscomb

p. 126-127 Apr. 10, 1822 Edmond Rogers (Spartanburgh) to George Durham; for $30 sold 50 ac; border: George Durham, Williams Cr, and Crook; where Edmond Rogers lives; part of Daniel Rogers' land. Witness John Durham jr and John Durham sr. Signed Edmond Rogers' mark. Wit. oath Dec. 7, 1822 John Durham jr to James Crook. Rec. Dec. 9, 1822

p. 127 Sept. 9, 1822 Jane Smith, widow (Spartanburgh) to Hancock Smith (same); for $800 sold 400 ac between Fairforest and Kelso's Creeks; border: N-lately Charles James "now desc Whetstone", W-White and Smith, S-Golightly and Flemming, and E-Thomas and Murph; where Jane Smith lives; Jane's distribution of estate of her husband James Smith desc. Witness Isaac Smith and Richard Lee. Signed Jane Smith. Wit. oath Nov. 12, 1822 Isaac Smith to D White. Rec. Dec. 11, 1822

p. 127-128 Mar. 21, 1822 John Golightly jr (Spartanburgh) to Vincent Wyatt (same); for $50 sold 20 ac on E side of Lawson's fork; border: road from Spartanburgh to Coulter's ford on Pacolate and Peter Bess. Witness Spencer Wyatt and James Cannon. Signed John Golightly jr. Wit. oath Dec. 11, 1822 Spencer Wyatt to E Bomar. Rec. Dec. 11, 1822

p. 128-129 Nov. 20, 1821 Stephen Cruse (Spartanburgh) to James T McCarter; for $1,200 sold 363 ac on waters of Fairforest Cr. Witness Samuel Reid and Elander Reid. Signed Stephen Cruse. Wit. oath Nov. 20, 1821 Samuel Reid to William Reid. Rec. Dec. 17, 1822. Dower renounced Dec. 17, 1822 Hannah Cruse to E Bomar

p. 129 Nov. 4, 1822 Thomas Poole, sheriff (Spartanburgh) to James Cantrell (same); for $25 sold 80 ac on Buck Cr; border: Young, Hines, and Daniel Cantrell; sale due to writ from Spartanburgh Common Pleas Court second Monday after fourth Monday in Mar. 1822 suit of William Cantrell; judgment was levy of $198 and costs from John Nolen. Witness James Brannon and Hiram White. Signed Thomas Poole SSD. Wit. oath Dec. 23, 1822 James Brannon to E Bomar. Rec. Dec. 23, 1822

p. 129-130 Nov. 23, 1822 William Wingo (Spartanburgh) to John Wingo (same); for $500 sold (1) 75 ac on waters of N Tyger R; border: S-Alexander Thompson, W-Robert Jameson, E-Thomas Wingo and James Ballinger, and N-Alexander Roddy; and (2) 52 ac; total of both tracts is 127 ac; (2) tract was "released by William Wingo and Fanny Wingo to John Wingo" at death of William and Fanny Wingo; part of estate of James Jordan allotted to Peggy Vernan and sold by Samuel Farrow, sheriff (Spartanburgh) to James Jordan esq. Witness Thomas Wingo and Laurence Bankston. Signed William Wingo. Wit. oath Jan. 6, 1822(sic) Thomas Wingo to E Bomar. Rec. Jan. 6, 1823

p. 130-131 Jan. 22, 1822 James Smith (Spartanburgh) to William Tracy (same); for $300 sold 475 ac; border: Linder, Wooldridge, Champion, and Gibbs. Witness John Parks and James Smith. Signed James Smith. Wit. oath Dec. 13, 1822 James Smith to W Hunt. Rec.

Jan. 6, 1823

p. 131-132 Sept. 26, 1822 Abner Benson (Spartanburgh) to Michael Gaffney (same); for $3,000 sold (1) 318 ac where Abner Benson lives; on S side of Broad R; border: Thomas Dare and Michael Gaffney; except 23 ac owned by William Ross; sold by Thomas Dare to Abner Benson; and (2) 246 ac in two parts; (a) border: grant to Beatie; 46 ac that is part of 200 ac grant to John Tygert; sold by John Ross (sic) to (Abner Benson?); and (b) (ac omitted); border: Michael Gaffney (formerly McGowen), Tate's Mill tract, Ross, and Tate; sold by Thomas Dare to Abner Benson. Witness Findle W Robertson and Wm R Bostick. Signed A Benson. Wit. oath Oct. 14, 1822 Wm R Bostick to F. W. Robertson. Rec. Jan. 6, 1822

p. 132-133 Dec. 3, 1821 William Rickman (Spartanburgh) to Michael Gaffney (same); for $576 sold 921 ac; part of two tracts: (1) on waters of People's Cr on W side of Broad R; grant as 392 ac Feb. 6, 1785 to Thomas Warren and (2) 640 ac granted to George Taylor; "subject to deduction" of 345 ac laid off to Peter Rickman. Witness Findal W Robertson and Zachariah Blackwell. Signed William Rickman. Wit. oath Oct. 14, 1822 Findal W Robertson to J Camp. Rec. Jan. 6, 1823. Dower renounced Dec. 12, 1822 Mary Rickman to John Lipscomb

p. 133-134 Sept. 30, 1822 William Rickman (Spartanburgh) to Michael Gaffney; for $300 sold 300 ac on People's Cr of Broad R; border: on all sides Michael Gaffney. Witness Charles Petty and Peter Rickman. Signed William Rickman. Wit. oath Oct. 14, 1822 Peter Rickman to F. W. Robertson. Rec. Jan. 6, 1823. Dower renounced Dec. 12, 1822 Mary Rickman to John Lipscomb

p. 134-135 Dec. 3, 1821 Peter Rickman (Spartanburgh) to Michael Gaffney (same); for $345 sold 345 ac on People's Cr of Broad R; "laid off to Peter Rickman by his father William Rickman". Witness Findal W Robertson and Zachariah Blackwell. Signed Peter Rickman's mark. Wit. oath Oct. 14, 1822 Findal W Robertson to J Camp. Rec. Jan. 6, 1832. Dower renounced Sally Rickman to John Lipscomb Dec. 12, 1823

p. 135 Jan. 6, 1832 Peter F Gray (Spartanburgh) to John Chapman jr (same); for $360 sold 53 ac on Mill Cr of N Tyger R; border: David Foster and "above the old machine"; Peter F Gray's share of his father Peter Gray's estate that Commissioners laid out. Witness Saml N Evins and M. P. Evins. Signed Peter F Gray. Wit. oath Jan. 6, 1832 M. P. Evins to F. H. Legg. Rec. Jan. 6, 1823

p. 135-136 Feb. 10, 1820 Sutton Young (Spartanburgh) to Arthur Warren; for $150 sold 100 ac on E side of Island Cr; border: Hiram Procter. Witness Samuel Turner and Turner W Warren. Signed Sutton Young's mark. Wit. oath Jan. 15, 1832 Turner Warren to Henry Turner. Rec. Jan. 27, 1823

p. 136-137 May 28, 1822 David Foster (Spartanburgh) to John Chapman jr (same); for $600 sold 152 ac on W side of Wilson's Cr; border: Laurence Br, John Chapman sr, road from widow McMiken to the Court House, Blackstock road, and widow Gray; 42½ ac was David Foster's share ("lot #3") of estate of Peter Gray desc laid off by Commissioners. Witness Ann Chapman and Peter F Gray. Signed David Foster. Wit. oath Jul. 11, 1822 Ann Chapman to F. H. Legg. Rec. Jan. 6, 1823. Dower renounced Jul. 11, 1822 Frances W Foster to F. H. Legg

p. 137-138 Apr. 27, 1822 James Ballinger to Thomas Wingo; for $120 sold 50 ac on N Tyger R; border: Laurence and Bankston. Witness William Ballinger, John Ballinger, and Elijah Ballinger. Signed James Ballinger. Wit. oath Jan. 6, 1822 John Ballinger to E Bomar. Rec. Jan. 3, 1823

p. 138-139 Jul. 19, 1821 John Bankston (Spartanburgh) to Thomas Wingo (same); for $600 sold 119½ ac on waters of N Tyger R; border: William Wingo and Bankston's Spring Br; part was granted Apr. 9, 1770 "office" to Samuel Nesbett and rest was granted Mar. 4, 1793 to William Ford. Witness Laurence Bankston, Joseph Pearson, and Joseph Barrett. Signed John Bankston. Wit. oath Jan. 6, 1823 Laurence Bankston to E Bomar. Rec. Jan. 6, 1823

p. 139-140 Jan. 8, 1823 Thomas Poole, sheriff (Spartanburgh) to Abner Benson; for $5 sold 111 ac; half of 222 ac on waters of Fairforest Cr; sold by James R Benson to Alexander McKie and Abner Benson; sold due to writ from Newberry Equity Court fourth Monday in Jun. 1822 suit of Daniel McKie, surviving administrator of Michael McKie desc; judgment was levy of $923 and costs from Alexander McKie. Witness Jesse Cleveland and Ephraim Roddy. Signed Thomas Poole SSD. Wit. oath Jan. 8, 1823 Ephraim Roddy to E Bomar. Rec. Jan. 8, 1823

p. 140-141 Nov. 23, 1814 Samuel Jones (Spartanburgh) to John King (same); for $90 sold 165 ac on N side of Ried fork of Abner Cr of Enoree R; border: John Jones, Caves, William Nelson, Penman, William Johnson, and William Williamson. Witness James Hendricks and William Jones. Signed Samuel Jones. Wit. oath Jan. 5, 1815 James Hendricks to James Hammett. Rec. Jan. 10, 1823. Dower renounced Dec. 29, 1814 Bethyer Jones to Drury McDaniel

p. 141-142 Jan. 11, 1823 Thomas Poole, sheriff (Spartanburgh) to James Brannon (same); for $5 sold 224 ac on Little Shoaly Cr of Lawson's fork; where John Speers formerly lived; border: E-Owen, N-Faucett, W-Childs, S-Markly and Turner; sale due to writ from Spartanburgh Common Pleas Court second Monday after fourth Monday in Oct. 1822 suit of James Brannon; judgment was levy of $16.07 and 6 mills and costs from William Turpin. Witness Jesse F Cleveland jr and John Poole. Signed Thomas Poole SSD. Wit. oath Dec. 11, 1823 (sic)John Poole to E Bomar. Rec. Jan. 11, 1823

p. 142 Sept. 10, 1822 Ephraim Lewis (Spartanburgh) to grandson Ephraim Lewis, son of Alijah Lewis (same); for love and affection give a brown mare and sorrel horse colt, a white and red spotted cow and her calf "of male kind" red with white face; following added: a brown mare with glass eyes called "about 9 years old" with large star on her forehead and 4 white feet, a horse colt with glass eye, a large blaze down "her" face bright sorrel colour with 3 white feet about 3 months old, a cow chiefly white with red spots about 4 years old, calf stear red with white face. Witness Wiley Fowler and Alesy Burnett. Signed Eph Lewis. Wit. oath Nov. 12, 1822 Wiley Fowler to John S Rowland. Rec. Jan. 18, 1822

p. 142-143 Jan. 11, 1823 James Brannon (Spartanburgh) to Lewis Turner (same); for $450 sold 274 ac on Little Shoaly Cr; border: E-Owens, N-Faucett, W-Childs, and E-Marklay. Witness James Edward Henry and Samuel Turner. Signed J Brannon. Wit. oath Jan. 22, 1823 James E Henry to E Bomar. Rec. Jan. 22, 1823. Dower renounced Jan. 18, 1823 Sarah Brannon to E Bomar

p. 143-144 (omitted) 25, 1822 James Lard sr (Spartanburgh) to Lee Linder (same); for $400 sold 200 ac on both sides of Island Cr; border: William Morrow and Leonard Adcock. Witness James Lard (signature) and Thomas Hackett. Signed James Lard sr's mark. Wit. oath Oct. 26, 1822 James Lard (signature) to Henry Turner. Rec. Jan. 27, 1823

p. 144-145 Jan. 12, 1822 James Hunt, sheriff (Spartanburgh) to Alexander Roddy sr (same); for $118 sold 120 ac on N Tyger R; border: William Davis, Alexander Roddy jr, and John Davis; sale due to writ from Spartanburgh Common Pleas Court second Monday after fourth Monday in Mar. 1820 suit of Herbert Hawkins; judgment was $27.37 and 5 mills and costs from John Davis. Witness E Roddy and John Bomar jr. Signed James Hunt. Wit. oath Jan. 27, 1823 John Bomar jr to E Bomar. Rec. Jan. 27, 1823

p. 145-146 Jan. 27, 1823 David Markley (Spartanburgh) to Darby Turner (same); for $100 sold (ac omitted) on Shoaly Cr of Lawson's fork; border: Darby Turner and a public road. Witness William Trimmier and William C Evets. Signed David Markley. Wit. oath Jan. 27, 1823 William Trimmier to E Bomar. Rec. Jan. 27, 1823

p. 146-147 Sept. 13, 1822 John B Hendrix (Spartanburgh) to John T Owen (same); for $200 sold 120 ac between Broad and Pacolett Rivers and on Buck Cr; part of "grant" from Thomas Salb (or Sabb) to Robert Lee who sold to James Wofford who sold to Isaac Wofford who sold to John B Hendrix. Witness George Gilland and William Bomar. Signed John B Hendrix. Wit. oath Feb. 1, 1823 George Gilland to Ransom Foster. Rec. Feb. 3, 1823

p. 147-148 Aug. 18, 1817 Benjamin Pennington (Spartanburgh) to William Surratt (same); for $150 sold 40 ac on N side of People's Cr; border: William Cumberland and Levi Pennington. Witness Edmond James and Henry Wilson. Signed Benjamin Pennington. Wit. oath Dec. 21, 1822 Henry Wilson to F. W. Robertson. Rec. Feb. 3, 1823

p. 148-149 Mar. 23, 1822 William Mayfield (Spartanburgh) to William Grisham (same); for $400 sold 358 ac on both sides Buncomb road at head of branch of Abner's Cr; border: Bayles Earle and William Nellson. Witness William Hughes and Thomas Grisham. Signed William and Jane Mayfield's marks. Wit. oath May 13, 1822 Thomas Grisham to F. H. Legg. Rec. Feb. 3, 1823. Dower renounced Jul. 3, 1822 Jane Mayfield to Thomas Wood

p. 149-150 Dec. 12, 1822 John Childres (Spartanburgh) to John Cooper (same); for $260 sold 57 ac on branch on E side of Enoree R; border: Henry Pearson and Saml Jones; part of grant to John Tate who sold to William Linsey who sold to John Childres. Witness William Linsey and Rachel Linsey. Signed John Childres. Wit. oath Jan. 27, 1823 William Linsey to Thomas Wood. Rec. Feb. 3, 1823. Dower renounced Jan. 27, 1823 Catharine Childres to Thomas Wood

p. 150-151 Nov. 22, 1822 George Thornton (Spartanburgh) to John Cooper (Lawrence Dist); for $380 sold 153 ac on waters of Enoree R; border: Daniel McKie, John Childres, Robert Westmoreland, and Francis Fowler. Witness Isaac Linsey and Real Fowler. Signed George Thornton. Wit. oath Jan. 27, 1823 Real Fowler to Thomas Wood. Rec. Feb. 3, 1823. Dower renounced Jan. 27, 1823 Sarah Thornton to Thomas Wood

p. 151 Jan. 9, 1817 Isaac Wofford (Spartanburgh) to John B Hendrix; for $125 sold 120 ac between Broad and Pacolett Rivers; part of grant to Thomas Sab. Witness John Crocker and Nicy Crocker. Signed Isaac Wofford. Wit. oath Feb. 3, 1823 John Crocker to James Young. Rec. Feb. 3, 1823

p. 151-152 Jan. 21, 1823 Susannah Walker (Spartanburgh) to Briant Bonner (same); for $100 sold 225 ac on Island Cr; part of grant to James Knox. Witness Abner Benson and William Martin. Signed Susannah Walker's mark. Wit. oath Feb. 3, 1823 Abner Benson to E Bomar. Rec. Feb. 3, 1823

p. 152-153 Apr. 8, 1820 David West (Spartanburgh) to Cassy West (same); for $500 sold (ac omitted) on waters of Cedar Shoal Cr of Enoree R; border: W-William Farrow, S-William Wilbanks,

E-widow Shamblen (now owned by Willis Arnold), and on Meeting House Br, and Bordurm Waters. Witness Willis Arnold and Johnson Martin. Signed David West. Wit. oath Nov. 3, 1820 Johnson Martin to Burrell Bobo. Rec. Feb. 4, 1823

p. 153 Jan. 17, 1818 (York Dist) Gordon Moore and wife Sally (York Dist) to Thompson Barlow Collins, son of Joseph and Nancy Collins; for $912 paid by Joseph Collins (Union Dist) sold ½ ac in Spartanburgh, SC on S side of public ground; includes a house next to the Court House and a framed house known as the Old Court House; also border: Cross street. Witness William T Nucholls and William Thomson. Signed Gordon Moore. Wit. oath Feb. 3, 1823 William Thomson to E Bomar. Rec. Feb. 3, 1823

p. 153-154 Dec. 18, 1818 William Davis (Spartanburgh) to John Davis (same); for $250 sold 119 ac on both sides of branch of N Tyger R; part of where William Davis' father lived when the father died. Witness James Whitten, Joshua D Ballinger, and John Ballinger. Signed William Davis. Wit. oath Feb. 3, 1823 Joshua D Ballinger to John Burns. Rec. Feb. 4, 1823

p. 154-156 (p. 155 not in book) Nov. 22, 1820 David Morton (Spartanburgh) to William Crook (same); for $2,000 sold 500 ac E half of 1,000 ac on branch of Fergason's Cr of Tyger R. Witness John M Delany and George Durham. Signed David Morton. Wit. oath Feb. 1, 1823 John M Delany to James Crook. Rec. Feb. 5, 1823

p. 156-157 Feb. 20, 1823 Robert M Young (Spartanburgh) to James Brannon (same); for $400 sold 0.4 ac in Spartanburgh, SC; border: James Brannon's lot (bought from Henry White) and NE corner of public square. Witness James E Henry and John T Earle. Signed Robert M Young. Wit. oath Feb. 21, 1823 James E Henry to E Bomar. Rec. Feb. 21, 1823

p. 157 Nov. 6, 1822 Jacob Land (Spartanburgh) to Henry White (same); to secure a debt to Henry White of $45.50 and $15 on book account due Jan. 1, 1823 sold a sorrel stud horse about 6 or 8 years old, a riding chair or gigg, 16 hogs, and a clock. Witness James White. Signed Jacob Land. Wit. oath Feb. 15, 1823 James White to Danl White. Rec. Feb. 17. 1823

p. 157-158 Nov. 26, 1822 John Bragg (Spartanburgh) to Charles Bragg (same); for $200 sold 90 ac on both sides Jamies Cr; border: E-John Clark and James Alexander, N-G Reynolds, W-George Robuck, and S-widow Robuck and William Posey. Witness William Otts, Charles Bragg, and Thomas Bragg. Signed John Bragg. Wit. oath Dec. 4, 1822 Thomas Bragg to John Brewton. Rec. Feb. 3, 1823

p. 158 Sept. 10, 1812 William Poole (Spartanburgh) to Joshua Petit (same); for $20 sold (300 ac?) on E side of Pacolate R; "between lines of" 500 ac "run out" by Richd Thompson, surveyor, for John Brown out of a 777 ac tract granted to William Poole, taylor. Witness Benjamin Poole and Elijah Poole. Signed William Poole. Wit. oath Oct. 15, 1816 Elijah Poole to Henry Turner. Rec. Feb. 3, 1823

p. 158-159 Jan. 2, 1819 William Herring (Spartanburgh) to Joshua Petit (same); for $200 sold 150 ac on N side of Pacolate R; border: Joshua Petit's 100 ac, John Gray, and Skaggs; part of 777 ac grant to William Poole; includes 25 ac "in Skaggs" and "extending into" what is called Binon(?) Patterson. Witness William Gore, Elisha McAbee, and Nathan Petit. Signed William Herring. Wit. oath Feb. 3, 1823 William Gore to John Lipscomb. Rec. Feb. 3, 1823

p. 159-160 Jan. 2, 1802 William Poole (Spartanburgh) to daughter

Judith Petit (same); for love and affection give 100 ac on N side of Pacolate R; border: John Henry and John Gray; part of 777 ac laid out by Jesse Connel(?) for William Poole; includes Joshua Petit's improvements on the river where he formerly lived. Witness Thomas Gore and John Gore. Signed William Poole. Wit. oath Mar. 23, 1802 Thomas Gore to John Lipscomb. Rec. Feb. 3, 1823

p. 160 Sept. 29, 1809 William Scaggs and wife Mary (Spartanburgh) to Joshua Petit (same); for $135 sold 70 ac on N side of Pacolate R; border: Gray, Kennady, William Land, and Joshua Petit. Witness William Poole, John Poole, and Polley Poole. Signed William Scaggs. Wit. oath Oct. 21, 1809 William Poole to John Lipscomb. Rec. Feb. 3, 1823. Dower renounced Oct. 21, 1809 Mary Scaggs to John Lipscomb

p. 160-161 Nov. 13, 1822 David Norman (Spartanburgh) to Elisha Hughston (same); quit claim to legacy of estate of Elizabeth Hughston desc. Witness Robert McCord and Jesse Cooper. Signed David Norman. Wit. oath Dec. 8, 1822 Robert McCord to Burrel Bobo. Rec. Feb. 3, 1823

p. 161 Mar. 2, 1821 Edward W Lynch (Lincoln Co, Tenn) to Robert Oliphant and/or Westwood L Waters (Spartanburgh); power of attorney to obtain from Dora Ducker (Spartanburgh) the money due Edward W Lynch by virtue of a note Robert Oliphant has or power of attorney to sell the bond. Witness Leonard Smith and Francis Fincher. Signed Edward W Lynch. Wit. oath Apr. 27, 1821 Leonard Smith to M Casey. Rec. Feb. 21, 1823

p. 161-162 Feb. 11, 1823 James Turner (Spartanburgh) to Samuel Turner and James Foster (same); for love and affection of daughter Elizabeth Martin give a Negro girl Oney about 10 or 12 years old and her increase, 2 feather beds, bedsteads, and furniture, a cow and calf, 2 pots, an oven, a skillet, a trunk, a dish, 6 pewter plates, 6 earthen plates, a set of knives and forks, 6 cups and saucers, an earthen bowl, a water pail, a bred tray, and a tin pan; stuff is given as a trust for Elizabeth Martin. Witness John T Earle and C. H. Moore. Signed James Turner. Wit. oath Feb. 12, 1823 John T Earle to E Bomar. Rec. Mar. 5, 1823

p. 162-163 Oct. 29, 1812 Benjamin Champion (Spartanburgh) to Joel Martin (same); for $200 sold 100 ac on N fork of Thickety Cr of Broad R; border: Francis King, Joel Martin, Lackey's Br, and Miry Br; part of grant in 1787 to James Clark. Witness William King and James King. Signed Benjamin Champion and Margaret's mark. Wit. oath Mar. 11, 1813 Francis King (sic) to John Lipscomb. Rec. Mar. 1, 1823. Dower renounced Dec. 14, 1816 Margaret Champion to Henry Turner

p. 163-164 Mar. 9, 1813 John Tolleson (Spartanburgh) to Joel Martin (same); for $53 sold 53 ac on waters of Thickety Cr; border: King, Champion's Cr, and Lackey's Br. Witness Eli Tolleson and Abraham Lancaster. Signed John Tolleson. Wit. oath Mar. 10, 1813 Eli Tolleson to John Gossett. Rec. Mar. 1, 1823

p. 164 Sept. 10, 1822 Ephraim Lewis (Spartanburgh) to John B Lewis; for $150 sold 50 ac; part of 74 ac grant Dec. 7, 1795 to Edmond Bishop who sold to George Bishop and sold to Ephraim Lewis. Witness Abjah Lewis and Wiley Fowler. Signed Eph Lewis. Wit. oath Feb. 22, 1823 Wiley Fowler to W Clement. Rec. Mar. 3, 1823

p. 164-165 Sept. 28, 1822 William Caldwell (Spartanburgh) to Andrew Caldwell (same); for $500 sold 217 ac on branches of N Tyger R. Witness Matthew P Evins and Ransom Seay. Signed William Caldwell. Wit. oath Nov. 6, 1820 Matthew P Evins to F. H. Legg. Rec. Mar. 3, 1823. Dower renounced Feb. 26, 1823 Margaret Caldwell to F. H. Legg

p. 165-166 Jan. 11, 1823 William Weber sr (Spartanburgh) to Nancy Wood (same); for $4.87½ sold 16 ac on S side of Thickety Cr; part of grant Jun. 4, 1821 Gov. Thomas Bennett to William Weber sr. Witness Smith Lipscomb and William Walker Weber. Signed Wm Weber. Wit. oath Feb. 28, 1823 Smith Lipscomb to John Lipscomb. Rec. Mar. 3, 1823

p. 166-167 Oct. 16, 1821 Elisha Thornton (Spartanburgh) to Samuel Jentry (same); for $60 sold 15½ ac; border: W-Joseph Willis, S-Gideon Reynolds, W(sic)-Richd Jentry and Samuel Jentry, and N-Benjamin Robuck. Witness Robert Alexander and John Gentry. Signed Elisha Thornton. Wit. oath Feb. 22, 1823 John Gentry to Robert Ligon. Rec. Oct. 3, 1823(sic)

p. 167 Jan. 14, 1823 George Poole (Burk Co, NC) to Ephraim Potter (same); for $150 sold 146 ac on Island Cr; border: Adcock and Murry. Witness Fielden Turner and John Turner. Signed George Poole. Wit. oath Jan. 17, 1823 Fielden Turner to Henry Turner. Rec. Mar. 3, 1823

p. 167-168 Sept. 30, 1819 William Tucker (Greenville Dist) to Benjamin Prewett (Spartanburgh); for $70 sold 280 ac on both sides Spencey's Br of Middle Tyger R; border: Absolem Guthrey; part of grant Dec. 8, 1774 to Andrew Carson. Witness Soloman Dill and David Jackson. Signed William Tucker. Wit. oath Jan. 18, 1820 (Greenville Dist) Soloman Dill to Abs Thompson. Rec. Mar. 5, 1823

p. 168-169 Jan. 20, 1823 Richard Thomson (Spartanburgh) to Peyton Simmons (same); for $70 sold 78 ac; near Peyton Simmons' house; border: James Cooper and Absalem Lancaster; part of two grants: (1) 383 ac to William Poole and (2) to Peter Leger. Witness William H Thomson and Isaac Neighbours. Signed Richard Thomson. Wit. oath Feb. 3, 1823 William H Thomson to Wm Underwood. Rec. Mar. 8, 1823

p. 169-170 Mar. 26, 1823 Elias Palmer (Spartanburgh) to Hervey Palmer (same); for discharging the following eleven debts sold 1,098 ac as described below: Elias Palmer owes (1) James McDowell $333 with interest due to suit amount unknown, (2) Peell, Smith and Co $166 with interest due to suit amount unknown, (3) William H Gilliland $600 with interest due to suit, (4) Goodman and Weyman and Co $187 with interest due to suit, (5) William Swift $5 with interest due to suit, (6) George Miller $400 with interest due to suit (all of Charleston), (7) Saml Todd (Laurens Dist) $300 with interest, (8) Randolph Palmer $2,600 (late of Spartanburgh), (9) estate of Frederick Parham (late of Spartanburgh) $75 and to his widow Fanny Ann Parham $80, (10) Joyce Underwood (Spartanburgh) $130 with interest; (11) William Walker (Spartanburgh) $125 with interest for a total of about $4,375 with interest; sold (a) 179 ac where Elias Palmer lives; border: N-Ligon, W-Thomas Tinsbey, S-David Golightly, and E-formerly owned by Edith Ligon; parts of sundry tracts; sold by John Cook (formerly Spartanburgh) to Elias Palmer; (b) 427 ac on waters of Peters and Cherokee Creeks of Pacolate R; sold by John Golightly sr to Elias Palmer on Aug. 7, 1821; (c) 57 ac adjoining where Elias Palmer lives; sold by Walter West to Elias Palmer; (d) 433 ac where Randolph Palmer formerly lived in Spartanburgh and Union Dists on both sides of Dutchman's Cr of Tyger R; border: SE-Martha Saunders, SW-Drury Parham, and S-the Manufacturing Company; if land is not "sufficient according to the contract between Elias and Hervey Palmer", Elias is to sell Hervey personal property: a Negro Adam, a Negro Humphry, Negro woman Silvy and her 3 sons--Alexander, Johnson, and Titus, Negro boy Toney, boy Samuel, boy Stephen, a road wagon and horse team, 2 colts and their future increase (that is the mares), 50 cattle with their future increase, all household and kitchen furniture. Witness John Bullington and Daniel White jr. Signed Elias Palmer. Wit. oath Mar. 26, 1823 JohnBullington to D White. Rec. Apr. 4, 1823

p. 170-171 Dec. 11, 1821 Andrew McDowell and Alexander Black (Charleston, SC), merchants to James McDowell; power of attorney; by "sale" Dec. 3 James McDowall sold Andrew McDowell and Alexander Black, merchants (Charleston) and copartners in firm McDowell and Black (sale in trust) all James McDowall's notes, bonds, etc; to help Andrew McDowell and Alexander Black recover debts due James McDowall, James appointed Andrew McDowell and Alexander Black power of attorney to recover debts; now Alexander and Andrew give James power of attorney to collect debts of Andrew McDowell and Alexander Black. Witness John W Vinre. Signed Andw McDowall and Alexr Black. Wit. oath Apr. 10, 1823 James Blocker(sic) to E Bomar. Rec. Apr. 10, 1823

p. 171-172 Sept. 14, 1820 John Hobby (Spartanburgh) to Thomas Hobby (same); for $362 sold 206 ac on Berry Cr on N side of Enoree R; part of two grants (1) Oct. 3, 1785 to Gennet Berry and (2) to James Lanford. Witness Joseph Crook, John Dean, and Robert C Hanna. Signed John Hobby. Wit. oath Sept. 14, 1820 Joseph Crook to John Dean. Rec. Apr. 9, 1823

p. 172-173 Feb. 12, 1823 Ransom Golightly (Spartanburgh) to Richard Daniel sr (same); for $800 sold 300 ac on both sides Beaverdam Cr on S side of Fairforest Cr; border: Richard Daniel and a road from Anthony Foster's to Tanner's Mills on Tyger R; part of grant to John Golightly sr who sold to Elihu and Francis Golightly and Elihu Golightly's half was sold to Ransom Golightly. Witness William H Harris and E Golightly. Signed R Golightly. Wit. oath Feb. 19, 1823 E Golightly to James E Henry. Rec. Mar. 4, 1823. Dower renounced Mar. 4, 1823 Mary R Golightly to Elisha Bomar

p. 173-174 Oct. 12, 1822 Thomas Poole, sheriff (Spartanburgh) to Thomas Jackson jr (same); for $103 sold 350 ac on Ellick's Cr of Pacolate R; border: David Hall, William Jackson jr, and Elisha Yarborough; sale due to writ from Spartanburgh Common Pleas Court second Monday after fourth Monday in Mar. 1821 suit of Muse Tolleson; judgment was levy of $25.66 and costs from Robert Young. Witness E Roddy and Daniel McKie. Signed Thomas Poole SSD. Wit. oath Mar. 18, 1823 E Roddy to E Bomar. Rec. Mar. 18, 1823

p. 174-175 Sept. 27, 1822 James Poole (Spartanburgh) to Joseph Hardy, a man of colour (same); for $100 sold 60 ac on Mire Br on S side of Pacolate R; border: Joseph Hardy; part of 1,000 ac grant to Soloman Crocker. Witness Elisha Poole and James Crocker. Signed James Poole. Wit. oath Oct. 2, 1822 James Crocker to William Reid. Rec. Mar. 20, 1823. Dower renounced Oct. 28, 1822 Rebecca Poole to William Reid

p. 175 Apr. 13, 1821 Larken Carden (Monroe Co, Tenn) to Sarah Owen (Spartanburgh); for $100 sold 50 ac on branch of Sholey Cr of Lawson's fork; border: Frances Watson, Strickland, the furnace road, Ginard, and Robert Belcher; part of 1,000 ac grant to Larken Carden. Witness Wm Trimmier, James Lewis, and James E Henry. Signed Larken Carden. Wit. oath Mar. 23, 1823 James E Henry to E Bomar. Rec. Mar. 28, 1823

p. 175-176 Mar. 6, 1818 Absalem Blundell (Spartanburgh) to Daniel McKie (same); for $500 sold 600 ac; known as Green Ponds where (blank) Swinney formerly lived "since Richard Roberds" on Buncomb road; part of 1,000 ac grant to Absalem Blundell. Witness James Brockman and A. W. Padin. Signed Absalem Blundell. Wit. oath Apr. 6, 1819 James Brockman to Benjamin Wofford. Rec. Mar. 28, 1823

p. 176-177 Oct. 6, 1819 James Hunt, sheriff (Spartanburgh) to John Todd (Laurence Dist); for $11 sold 100 ac on Enoree R; border: E-William Waldrip and David Neel, N-Elijah Watson, and NW-Tillman Bobo; sale due to writ from Spartanburgh Common Pleas Court second Monday after fourth Monday in Mar. 1817 suit of James Todd vs James Stewart; judgment was levy of $41.94 from James Stewart. Witness E Roddy and Elisha Bomar. Signed Jas Hunt SSD. Wit. oath Mar. 27, 1823 E Roddy to W Hunt. Rec. Mar. 28, 1823

p. 177-178 Sept. 1, 1817 William F Reynolds (Spartanburgh) to Ephraim Roddy (same); for $50 sold 18 feet square in Spartanburgh, SC; border: formerly Alexander McKie's lot (now Maj. Joseph Collins) and street from Court House to James Seay's; sold by Richard Thomson to William Bostick who sold to William F Reynolds. Witness John S. B. Foster and Wm Hunt. Signed Wm F Reynolds. Wit. oath Mar. 27, 1823 Wm Hunt to E Bomar. Rec. Mar. 28, 1823

p. 178 Oct. 30, 1817 Lewis Turner (Spartanburgh) to Thomas Wells (same); for $101.25 sold 81 ac on Wilke's Cr of Lawson's fork; border: Thomas Wells. Witness Elisha Bomar and William Hunt. Signed Lewis Turner's mark. Wit. oath Mar. 27, 1823 William Hunt to E Bomar. Rec. Mar. 28, 1823

p. 178-179 Jan. 5, 1810 John Tolleson (Spartanburgh) to Isham Briant (same); for $250 sold 258 ac on N side of Pacolate R; border: Peter Peterson, George Riner, James Brown, Jones, Howard, Robert Thomson, Henry Petit, and James Wilkins. Witness Bartholemew Stoval and Abraham Lancaster. Signed John Tolleson. Wit. oath Jun. 12, 1810 Abraham Lancaster to John Gossett. Rec. Apr. 5, 1823

p. 179-180 Nov. 6, 1822 Thomas Poole, sheriff (Spartanburgh) to Samuel Auterson (Union Dist); for $61 sold 153 ac on N side of Lawson's fork; sold by Edward Herring to Alexander McKie; sale due to writ from Newberry Equity Court fourth Monday in Jun. 1822 suit of Daniel McKie, surviving administrator of Michael McKie desc; judgment was levy of $923 from Alexander McKie. Witness M. N. Chapman and E Bomar. Signed Thomas Poole SSD. Wit. oath May 6, 1823 M. N. Chapman to E Bomar. Rec. May 6, 1823

p. 180-181 Apr. 5, 1823 William W Hembree (Spartanburgh) to Enoch Smith (same); for $150 sold 50 ac; border: Pickney and Curry's bounty survey; part of 383 ac grant to Hopkins Bright. Witness Jesse Vaughan and Robert Page. Signed Wm W Hembree. Wit. oath Apr. 21, 1822 Jesse Vaughan to Wm Underwood. Rec. Apr. 25, 1823

p. 181 Nov. 19, 1817 William Grisham (Spartanburgh) to John M Delaney (same); for $150 sold 50 ac on N side of Ben's Cr of S Tyger R; border: Alexander Wakefield's Spring Br and Thomas Pearson; where John M Delaney lives. Witness John Brazwell and Wm McM Brice. Signed William Grisham. Wit. oath Mar. 15, 1823 Wm McM Brice to Thomas Wood. Rec. Apr. 25, 1823

p. 181-182 Jan. 5, 1819 Joseph G Evitts (Spartanburgh) to Shadrack Weaver (same); for $250 sold 150 ac on waters of Island Cr; border: Coulter's Rd, an old road, Bellow, Cantrell, and Odam. Witness George Cantrell and William Foster. Signed Joseph G Evetts. Wit. oath Feb. 20, 1823 George Cantrell to Henry Turner. Rec. Apr. 7, 1823

p. 182-183 Jan. 15, 1823 Grisham Durham (Spartanburgh) to John Bazwell (same); for $550 sold 425 ac on Brushy fork Cr of S Tyger R; border: Josiah Leonard, Anderson, Powder fork, and Toomar. Witness Lemuel Johnson and Westley Waters. Signed Grisham Durham. Wit. oath Jan. 25, 1823 Lemuel Johnson to Thomas Wood. Rec. Apr. 7, 1823. Dower renounced Jan. 25, 1823 Catharine Durham to Thomas Wood

p. 183-184 Sept. 12, 1822 William B Alexander (Spartanburgh) to William Mason (same); for $650 sold 140 ac; border: S-Thomas Bells Rand (or road), W-James Alexander, N-Hester Chesney, and E-Asahel Beason. Witness Wm Posey and John Mason. Signed Wm B Alexander. Wit. oath Apr. 9, 1823 Wm Posey to Wm Underwood. Rec. Apr. 11, 1823. Dower renounced Dec. 11, 1822 Ellasa Alexander to Burrel Bobo

p. 184-185 Aug. 2, 1820 Charles James (Spartanburgh) to David Whetstone; for $1,600 sold 377 ac; border: Robt Smith, branch of Kelso's Cr, Thompson's Br, and Micajah Barnett; part of "several tracts" grant to (1) George Story for 200 ac Mar. 1, 1775 on Kelso's Cr on N side of Fairforest Cr, (2) 150 ac granted Nov. 7, 1785 to Charles James adjoining (1) with plat drawn Aug. 27, 1784, and 23 ac sold Feb. 13, 1814 by Jane Smith to Charles James. Witness John Murph, Elisha James, and Absalem Lancaster. Signed Charles James. Wit. oath Aug. 21, 1820 John Murph to Danl White. Rec. Apr. 11, 1823

p. 185-186 Apr. 6, 1820 Jeremiah Wofford to Burrel Bobo; for $600 sold 124 ac on James Cr on S side of Tyger R; plat attached shows border: John Leatherwood, J Wofford, and Manufacturing; where Jeremiah Wofford lives. Witness Thomas Waters and William H Torrans. Signed Jeremiah Wofford. Wit. oath Feb. 26, 1823 Thomas Waters to Benjamin Wofford. Rec. Apr. 11, 1823. Dower renounced Apr. 7, 1820 Elizabeth Wofford to John Brewton

p. 186-187 Jun. 5, 1822 Burrel Bobo to George Hill, Leonard Hill, and John Clark; for $150 sold 31½ ac on James Cr of Tyger R; plat attached shows border: J Leatherwood and Manufacturing Co. Witness John B Leatherwood and Thos Young. Signed Burrel Bobo. Wit. oath Jun. 5, 1822 John B Leatherwood to Burrel Bobo. Rec. Apr. 11, 1823. Dower renounced Feb. 25, 1823 Elizabeth Bobo to Benjamin Wofford

p. 187-2nd 187 Oct. 18, 1820 Elias Rogers (Spartanburgh) to James Corder (same); for $500 sold 173 (or 170) ac; grant to Robert Rogers; except 3 ac where Meeting House stands. Witness Vincent Tapp and Paul Combe. Signed Elias Rogers. Wit. oath Oct. 18, 1822 Paul Combe to Robert Ligon. Rec. Apr. 14, 1823. Dower renounced Apr. 12, 1823 Sarah Rogers to John Brewton

p. 2nd 187 Jan. 3, 1823 Jennett Miller (Spartanburgh) to son John Miller (same); for $800 sold (ac omitted) in fork of Tyger R; part of where Jennett Miller lives; on SW side of a wagon road. Witness William Miller and Joseph Miller. Signed Jennett Miller's mark. Wit. oath Mar. 26, 1823 Joseph Miller to Robert Ligon. Rec. Apr. 14, 1823

p. 2nd 187-188 Oct. 18, 1822 Elias Corder (Spartanburgh) to Elias Rogers (same); for $700 sold 300 ac on head waters of Ward's Cr; border: Correy bounty survey; grant to Charles C Pinckney and part of grant to Hopkins Bright. Witness Vincent Tapp and Paul Combee. Signed Elias Corder. Wit. oath Oct. 18, 1822 Vincent Tapp to Robert Ligon. Rec. Apr. 17, 1823. Dower renounced Apr. 12, 1823 Anna Corder to John Brewton

p. 188-189 Feb. 18, 1822 Thomas Collins to John Thomas; for $200 sold 100 ac on Sneed's Br of Thickety Cr; border: Land. Witness Joseph Collins and William Littlejohn. Signed Thomas Collins. Wit. oath Jul. 3, 1822 William Littlejohn to F. W. Robertson. Rec. Apr. 19, 1823. Dower renounced Aug. 28, 1822 Margaret Collins to John Lipscomb

p. 189 Nov. 27, 1822 John Brown (Rutherford Co, NC) to William F

Reynolds; to secure $400 note mortgaged 354 ac on S side of Lawson's fork and on Betty's Br. Witness Wm Tracy and James Smith. Signed John Brown's mark. Wit. oath Apr. 19, 1823 Wm Tracy to W Hunt. Rec. Apr. 19, 1823

p. 189-190 Dec. 28, 1814 James Layton to William Sexton; for $90 paid Dec. 26 sold 65 ac on Prater's Cr on S side of Tyger R; border: Edwards, N-Henry Hoof and Todd, W-King, S-William Sexton, and E-Arnett and Spears; grant to William Clayton. Witness Charles William and John Smith. Rec. James Layton. Wit. oath Apr. 1, 1817 John Smith to M Casey. Rec. Apr. 19, 1823

p. 190-191 Aug. 1, 1808 Thomas Martin (SC) to William Sexton (Spartanburgh); for $50 sold 100 ac on S side of Tyger R; border: S-John Spears. Witness Anthony Shands and James Sexton. Signed Thomas and Mary Martin's marks. Wit. oath Mar. 14, 1823 James Sexton to M Casey. Rec. Apr. 19, 1823

p. 191-192 Apr. 4, 1823 Thomas Clary (SC) to Lewis Clary (SC); for $500 sold 292 ac on Surratt's Cr on S side of Broad R; border: N-North Carolina line, S-William Davison, and W-Samuel S Ross; grant Oct. 6, 1788 Gov. Thomas Pinckney to Reuben Blanton. Witness Samuel S Ross to John Allison. Signed Thomas Clary's mark. Wit. oath Apr. 19, 1823 John Allison to Samuel S Ross. Rec. Apr. 25, 1823

p. 192-193 Jan. 29, 1822 Lowry Burnett (Spartanburgh) to Woodson Burnett (same); for $125 sold 101 ac on both sides Fawn Br of Lawson's fork; part of grant to John or James Burnett or John <u>and</u> James Burnett; half of tract given by will of John Burnett (late of Spartanburgh) to Lowry Burnett. Witness Wiley Fowler and Carter Burnett. Signed Lowry Burnett. Wit. oath Jan. 29, 1822 Wiley Fowler to W Burnett. Rec. Apr. 26, 1823

p. 193 Mar. 13, 1823 Woodson Burnett and Sarah Burnett, widow of John Burnett desc (Spartanburgh), to Hezekiah Seay (same); for $250 sold 200 ac on both sides of Fawn Br of Lawson's fork; border: James Burnett; grant to John Burnett. Witness Mitchell Tillotson, James Templeman, and Mathew Seay. Signed Woodson Burnett. Wit. oath (to Woodson Burnett's signature) Apr. 8, 1823 Mathew Seay to John S Rowland. Wit. oath (to Sarah Burnett's signing (sic)) James Templeman to John S Rowland. Rec. Apr. 27, 1823. Dower renounced Apr. 8, 1823 Susannah Burnett, wife of Woodson, to John S Rowland

p. 193-194 Jan. 28, 1823 William Smith (Union Dist) to Reuben Daniel (Spartanburgh); for $1,500 sold five Negroes: a woman Milly and her four children--James, Hannah, David, and Peter, a horse, bridle and saddle, 2 feather beds and furniture, a chest, 2 cows and calves. Witness Martha Daniel. Signed William Smith. Wit. oath Feb. 20, 1823 Martha Daniel to E Bomar. Rec. May 2, 1823

p. 194 May 7, 1823 Philip Johnson (Spartanburgh) to Hiram Johnson (same); for $20 sold 45 ac on Ben's Cr of Tyger R; border: Jerry Burnett. Witness John Durham and John Durham (sic). Signed Philip Johnson's mark. Wit. oath May 17, 1823 (sic) John Durham to Thomas Wood. Rec. May 2, 1823

p. 194-195 Mar. 7, 1823 David Whetstone (Spartanburgh) to John Oreland (same); to secure payment of $565 debt mortgaged (1) 200 ac on Kelso's Br on N side of Fairforest Cr; (2) 150 ac adjoining (1); plat dated Aug. 27, 1784 and granted Nov. 7, 1785 to Charles James; and (3) 23 ac on branch of Kelso's Cr; border: Robert Smith, Thomson's Br, and Micajah Barnett; sold Feb. 13, 1814 by Jane Smith to Charles James; Condition: sale void if David Whetstone pays John Oreland $565 with interest by Mar. 7, 1824. Witness John

Glass and Z McDaniel. Signed David Whetstone. Wit. oath Apr. 11, 1823 John Glass to William Reid. Rec. May 5, 1823

p. 195-196 Feb. 1, 1823 (Giles Co, Tenn) Shands Golightly (Giles Co, Tenn) to Christopher Golightly (Spartanburgh); power of attorney to sell (1) 150 ac on waters of Enoree R; and (2) 800 ac on N Tyger R; sold by Reves and Kimble to Sell or SM. Witness John B Armstrong JP and John Laird JP. Signed Shands Golightly. Feb. 3, 1823 (Giles Co, Tenn) Nelson Patterson, "chairman" of Quarterly Sessions Court, certifies German Lester is clerk of court. Feb. 3, 1823 (Giles Co, Tenn) German Lester, clerk of Quarterly Sessions Court, certifies John B Armstrong and John Laird are justices of peace. Rec. May 12, 1823

p. 196-197 Nov. 3, 1822 Matthias Elmore (Spartanburgh) to Samuel K Elmore (same); for $1,000 sold 223 ac on Middle Tyger R; border: Michael Moore, John McElrath, estate of Michael Miller desc, and Wilson Nesbett. Witness James Burns jr and James Wilson. Signed Matthias Elmore. Wit. oath May 3, 1823 James Burns jr to John Burns. Rec. May 17, 1823

p. 197 Jul. 28, 1820 Thomas Miles (Spartanburgh) to daughter Sally Martindale; for love and affection and $1 give a Negro girl Clary (or Clara) about 13 years old. Witness Thomas M Bragg and James E Henry. Signed Thomas Miles. Wit. oath May 20, 1823 James E Henry to E Bomar. Rec. May 20, 1823

p. 197-199 Jul. 10, 1821 Thomas Gore (Spartanburgh) to William Martindale (same); for $660 sold 200 ac; 1 ac excepted as burying ground for Bobo family; border: SW-J Red and Livingston Bobo, SE-J. F. Harmoning, NE-Thomas Gore, and NW-William Wilder; between Enoree and Tyger Rivers and on Ceder Shoal and Speargin's Creeks. Witness William H Miles and David Norman. Signed Thomas Gore. Wit. oath May 16, 1823 William H Miles to Burrell Bobo. Rec. May 20, 1823. Dower renounced Oct. 4, 1821 Elizabeth Gore to Burrell Bobo

p. 199-200 May 2, 1823 Johnson Hembree (Spartanburgh), planter and cooper to William Smith (same), merchant; to secure payment of two notes for $111 with interest sell a sorrel horse, a red cow and yearling, 4 hogs and their increase, 4 beds, bedsteads, and furniture, a pine cupboard, all "my" earthenware and pewter, a pot, 2 ovens, 2 plow stocks and double set of irons to each, a pair of geers, six weeding hoes and 2 mattocks, a sprouting hoe, a set of cooper's tools, 5 club axes, 2 pine chests, a man's saddle, a woman's saddle, 10 chairs, a pair of saddle bags, 2 stone jugs, 2 water pails, a piggin, a washing tub, 2 tile caoks (or cooks), 3 open barrels, a set of stone tools, 2 "spinning", 2 pair cotton cards, a reel, a rifle gun, and a shot gun; Condition: sale void if Johnson Hembree pays debt. Witness Isaac Smith and Polley M Smith. Signed Johnson Hembree. Wit. oath Jun. 2, 1823 Isaac Smith to F. H. Legg. Rec. Jun. 4, 1823

p. 200-201 May 12, 1823 Thomas Miles to William Martindale; for $600 sold 107 ac on branches of Tyger R; plat attached shows border: William Martindale, William Blackstock, G Tinsley, and Thomas Miles. Witness Joel Dean and Isaac Tinsley. Signed Thomas Miles. Wit. oath May 16, 1823 Isaac Tinsley to Burrell Bobo. Rec. May 20, 1823

p. 201 Jul. 28, 1815 John F Grimkee to William Martindale (Spartanburgh); for $65.50 sold 26½ ac on Rocky Cr of Tyger R; plat attached shows border: William Martindale, Joseph Pock, William Blackstock, and "Judge" Grimkee; part of 204 ac laid off for Benjamin Guerrey see partition in Union Dist Common Pleas Court. Witness William H Miles and Isaac Miles. Signed J. F. Grimkee. Wit. oath

May 16, 1823 William H Miles to Burrell Bobo. Rec. May 20, 1823

p. 201-202 Dec. 20, 1822 Thomas Westmoreland (Spartanburgh) to Andrew Westmoreland (SC); for $300 sold 95 ac on branches of Enoree R. Witness Nimrod Linsey and George Thornton. Signed Thomas Westmoreland's mark. Wit. oath Mar. 15, 1823 Nimrod Linsey to James Ford. Rec. May 22, 1823

p. 202-203 Feb. 1, 1823 Thomas Westmoreland jr (Spartanburgh) to John Westmoreland (same); for $300 sold 102 ac on branches of Enoree R. Witness Nimrod Lindsey and Robert Westmoreland. Signed Thomas Westmoreland's mark. Wit. oath Mar. 15, 1823 Nimrod Lindsey to James Ford. Rec. May 22, 1823

p. 203 Mar. 1, 1823 James Smith (Spartanburgh) to Jacob Esler (same); for $100 sold 100 ac on N side of Little Cherokee Cr; border: Solomon Abbott. Witness Alfred Breedlove and Jobe Sosebee. Signed James Smith's mark. Wit. oath Mar. 3, 1823 Jobe Sosebee to Lee Linder. Rec. May 22, 1823

p. 203-204 Dec. 20, 1822 George Thornton (Spartanburgh) to Robert Westmoreland (same); for $300 sold 103 ac on branches of Enoree R. Witness Nimrod Lindsey and Andrew Westmoreland. Signed George Thornton and Sarah's mark. Wit. oath Mar. 14, 1823 Nimrod Lindsey to James Ford. Rec. May 22, 1823

p. 204-205 Jan. 28, 1823 William Hendrix (Spartanburgh) to James Hendrix (same); for $200 sold 100 ac on waters of Lick Cr of Enoree R; border: Philip Pilgrim and Trap (or Shap). Witness Thomas Woodruff III and Daniel Hinds. Signed Wm Hendrix. Wit. oath Jun. 2, 1823 Thomas Woodruff III to James Crook. Rec. Jun. 2, 1823

p. 205 Dec. 27, 1822 Edmond W Chapman to Herbertt Hawkins (Spartanburgh); for $400 sold (1) 150 ac on Wilson's Mill Cr of Tyger R; border: William Foster and John James; and (2) 50 ac adjoining (1); sold by James Foster, son of William, to Edmond W Chapman. Witness Nathaniel Dodd and Beverly R Chapman. Signed Edmond W Chapman. Wit. oath Mar. 8, 1823 Nathaniel Dodd to Ransom Foster. Rec. Jun. 2, 1823

p. 205-206 Oct. 6, 1810 Stephen Wilson to Reuben Newman; for $175 sold 135 ac on branches on S side of Tyger R; border: Sample's old line, William Lindsey, Thomas Wilson, and School House Br; part of grant to James Sample. Witness Austin Newman and Anthony Shands. Signed Stephen Wilson. Wit. oath May 27, 1823 Austin Newman to Wm Young. Rec. Jun. 2, 1823

p. 206-207 Oct. 28, 1820 John Mullenix (Spartanburgh) to John L Rast (same); for $800 sold 115 ac on S side of Tyger R; border: John White, Jeremiah Wofford, Chesney, Joseph Wofford. Witness Samuel Tucker and Jesse Williams. Signed John Mullenix. Wit. oath Oct. 16, 1822 Jesse Williams to Benj Wofford. Rec. Jun. 2, 1823. Dower renounced Aug. 6, 1822 Rebekah Mullenix to Benjamin Wofford

p. 207-208 Feb. 3, 1817 Samuel Lancaster (Spartanburgh) to Isaac Wofford, administrator for James W Wofford desc (same); for $90 sold 100 ac at head of Cain Cr on N side of Tyger R; part of grant Jan. 7, 1793 to William Smith. Witness William Smith jr and John Wofford jr. Signed Smauel Lancaster. Wit. oath Jun. 2, 1823 John Wofford to John Lipscomb. Rec. Jun. 2, 1823

p. 208-209 Feb. 3, 1817 Samuel Lancaster (Spartanburgh) to Isaac Wofford jr, administrator of James W Wofford desc (same); for $20 sold 61 ac at head of Cain Cr on N side of Tyger R; part of grant Jan. 7, 1805 to Willis Williford. Witness William Smith jr and John Wofford jr. Signed Saml Lancaster. Wit. oath Jun. 2, 1823 John Wofford jr to John Lipscomb. Rec. Jun. 3, 1823

p. 209-210 Apr. 16, 1823 Charles C Duncan (Spartanburgh) to John Dodd (same); for $1,250 sold 200 ac on waters of S Pacolate R; plat attached shows border: J McClure, Christopher Golightly, and Armstead Bomar; drawn Apr. 16, 1823 by Herbert Hawkins, surveyor; where Charles C Duncan lives. Witness Herbert Hawkins, Christopher Golightly, and Robert M McDowell. Signed C. C. Duncan. Wit. oath Apr. 23, 1823 Christopher Golightly to James Young. Rec. Jun. 2, 1823. Dower renounced Apr. 23, 1823 Milly Duncan to James Young

p. 210-211 Apr. 5, 1823 William Hendrix (Spartanburgh) to Samuel Jameson (SC); for $1,100 sold 325 ac on branches of Enoree R. Witness James Allen, James Hendrix, and Moses Fuller. Signed Wm Hendrix. Wit. oath Apr. 5, 1823 James Hendrix to James Crook. Rec. Jun. 4, 1823. Dower renounced Apr. 5, 1823 Nancy Hendrix to James Crook

p. 211-212 Apr. 9, 1822 Nathaniel Gist (Union Dist) to Gabriel Gossett (Spartanburgh); for $360 sold 180 ac on Fairforest Cr; border: the Meeting House, John Ison, Thomson, and Turguson; part of grant to Joseph Ashe. Witness Danl White and Samuel Whitbey. Signed Nathl Gist. Wit. oath Feb. 2, 1823 Samuel Whitbey to William Reid. Rec. Jun. 4, 1823. Dower renounced Mar. 18, 1823 Elizabeth L Gist to William Reid

p. 212-213 Nov. 6, 1818 John Low jr to Hugh Moore (Spartanburgh); for $160 sold 160 ac; border: Mary Dewberry, Warren, Wyatt, and Beck Br; part of 409 ac grant Dec. 6, 1811 to Jonathan (or John) Low jr and sold by his heirs to John Low sr who sold to John Low jr. Witness John Low sr and Dicy Shurbutt. Signed John Low jr. Wit. oath Jun. 1, 1822 John Low sr to Lee Linder. Rec. Jul. 7, 1823

p. 213 Jan. 20, 1823 Robert Smith (Spartanburgh) to Benjamin Smith (same); for $1,000 sold 500 ac on head branches of Oby's Cr of N Pacolate R; border: N-Whitteger, S-William Ramsey, W-Bomar, and E-Bullington; part of grant to William Ramsey. Witness William P Smith and John A Smith. Signed Robert Smith. Wit. oath Feb. 22, 1823 William P Smith to D White. Rec. Jul. 7, 1823

p. 213-214 Jun. 27, 1823 James P Means (Spartanburgh) to Augustin Shands (same); for $1,500 sold 723 ac on both sides Story's Cr of Fairforest Cr; where James P Means lives; border: W-James Rainwaters and Theron Lancaster, S-James Hamm and John Picken Pack (formerly Thomas Compton's land), E-Joseph Park and Henry Cunningham, and N-Joshua Hammond (formerly T Kelso's old tract); part of (1) grant to Thomas Brandon and sold due to Court order by Gabriel Benson, sheriff (Spartanburgh) to David Johnson esq (Union Dist) who sold to James P Means and part of (2) grant to Robert Irwin and sold by Hudson Dudley, Joseph Park, and Wm Findley to Robert Summorvill who sold to James Mayes who sold to James P Means and part of (3) grant to Hugh Gourbey (or Gorby) who sold to John Thomas who sold to John Wright who sold to James Martin who sold to James P Means and (4) a tract sold by Joseph T Kelso to John Wright who sold to James Martin who sold to James P Means. Witness Henry Cunningham and Robert Cunningham. Signed J. P. Means. Wit. oath Jul. 5, 1823 Henry Cunningham to Benjamin Wofford. Rec. Jul. 7, 1823. Dower renounced Jul. 5, 1823 Jane Means to Benjamin Wofford

p. 214-215 Mar. 1, 1823 Jacob Casey to Burrell Bobo; for $75 sold 50 ac; border: Benjamin Hooker, Burrell Bobo, and James King; where Jacob Casey lives; Condition sale void if Jacob Casey pays following note to Burrell Bobo by Christmas 1823--note payable to Joseph Carswell dated Mar. 26, 1822 and pay interest due Dec. 25, 1824. Witness Thomas Martin and Moses Anderson. Signed Jacob Casey. Wit. oath Jul. 3, 1823 Moses Anderson to Benj Wofford. Rec. Jul. 7, 1823

p. 215-216 Mar. 1, 1823 Jacob Casey (Spartanburgh) to Burrell Bobo (same); to secure note Mar. 26, 1822 for $75 to Burrell Bobo payable next Christmas(sic) sold a bay colt 3 years old, a sorrel horse, a sorrel mare, sorrel colt 6 months old, a "dun" colored cow marked (blank) and "half red no hound" cow marked 2 smooth crosses and under keel in right ear, a brindle cow and calf marked slope off the right ear and swallow fork in the left, a white faced cos, "calf black" swallow fork in the right and under bit in the left, a dun colored bull with same mark, 17 hogs marked same and reverse or under swallow fork in the left and under keel in the right, 2 feather beds, bedsteads, and furniture--a large and a small, 2 ovens, 2 pails, a piggin, a wash tub, walnut table, loom, 2 slays and harness, a pine chest, 2 mattocks, 4 axes, 2 shovel plows, 2 scooter plows, 2 plow stocks, 2 sets of traces, harness, collars, 3 clevises, 6 hoes, a man's saddle, a shot gun, 4 spinning sheels, a reel, 6 chairs, and a number of other articles of household and kitchen furniture; property is to remain with Jacob Casey until Dec. 25, 1824 and if money is not paid, Burrell Bobo can get property then. Witness Thomas Martin and Moses Anderson. Signed Jacob Casey. Wit. oath Jul. 3, 1823 Moses Anderson to Benj Wofford. Rec. Jul. 7, 1823

p. 216-217 Nov. 18, 1822 William Morris (Edgefield Dist) to Jordan Morris (Spartanburgh); for $400 sold 150 ac on Buck Cr of Pacolate R and on Jumping Gulley Br. Witness Joseph Morris and Thomas Cantwell. Signed William Morris. Wit. oath Jul. 7, 1823 Joseph Morris to E Bomar. Rec. Jul. 7, 1823

p. 217-218 Feb. 6, 1823 Thomas Poole, sheriff (Spartanburgh) to Floyd Tanner (same); for $2,027 sold 335 ac in fork of Middle and N Tyger Rivers; bought by A. B. Moore for Floyd Tanner; sold due to writ from Spartanburgh Common Pleas Court second Monday after fourth Monday in Oct. 1821 suit of William N Miller; judgment was levy of $3,924 and costs from David Tanner and Floyd Tanner. Witness M. N. Chapman and Wm T Tanner. SignedThomas Poole SSD. Wit. oath Jul. 7, 1823 Wm T Tanner to Wm Underwood. Rec. Jul. 7, 1823

p. 218-219 Jan. 5, 1818 Labon P Poole, sheriff (Spartanburgh) to David Tanner (same); for $3,270 sold 335 ac in fork of Middle and N Tyger Rivers; border: Gen. Thomas Moore and David Tanner; George and Nathaniel Miller petitioned Spartanburgh Common Pleas Court second Monday after fourth Monday in Mar. 1817 to divide real estate of Robert Miller desc; Court appointed John Foster, James Foster, Samuel Neely, and Andrew Barry esqs to divide the land; on second Monday after fourth Monday in Oct. 1817 they said land can't be divided and should be sold; sale first Monday in Jan. 1818 with credit in three annual installments--starting Jan. 1, 1818 (sic); buyers are to give bond to William N Miller, administrator of estate of Robert Miller desc. Witness Thomas Moore, John Roddy, and Elisha Bomar. Signed Labon P Poole SSD. Wit. oath Jul. 7, 1823 Elisha Bomar to Wm Underwood. Rec. Jul. 7, 1823

p. 219-220 Jan. 29, 1813 John Owen (Spartanburgh) to David Owen; for $50 sold 100 ac on branch of Buffaloe Cr and branch of Two Mile Cr of Enoree R; border: John Dean, James Lanford, Lewis Lanford, and Thomas Clark. Witness James Lanford, Thomas Knighton, and Eli Jackson. Signed John Owen's mark. Wit. oath Jul. 15, 1823 James Lanford to John Dean. Rec. Jul. 19, 1823

p. 220-221 May 24, 1823 Reuben Warren promises to pay Jesse Cleveland

$136.56; May 24, 1823 Reuben Warren (Spartanburgh) to Jesse Cleveland; to secure payment of above mortgaged 500 ac; border: Robert Thompson, Tolleson, Proctor's Br, widow Edward, and Low's Br; where Reuben Warren lives; Condition: mortgage void if Reuben pays Jesse $136.56 by Jan. 1, 1824. Witness Jesse F Cleveland and James E Henry. Signed Reuben Warren. Wit. oath Jul. 10, 1823 Jesse F Cleveland to E Bomar. Rec. Jul. 9, 1823

p. 221-222 Jan. 9, 1823 Robert Martin (Spartanburgh) to Richard Roberts jr; for love and affection give a still and vessels, 2 cows and calves and a heifer which has been in possession of his father Richard Roberts sr; cattle are: a cow of dunn color with only one horn with swallow fork in left ear and slit and overkeel in right, her calf--red and white, a black cow marked with swallow fork in right ear and under bit out of left ear, her calf--black and white unmarked, a red and white heifer marked with a slit out of left ear and smooth cross out of right ear. Witness William Harris and John Davis. Signed Robert Martin. Wit. oath Jul. 27, 1823 William Harris to Geo Camp. Rec. Aug. 4, 1823

p. 222-223 May 31, 1823 Muse Tolleson (Spartanburgh) to wife Sarah Tolleson, Benjamin S Holder, trustee; Muse has been unfortunate in trade and to secure Sarah Muse allows Sarah to carry on her own trade for her lifetime and to invest or spend her money or sell property. Witness Willis Foster, Benjamin L Goodman, and William F Reynolds. Signed Muse Tolleson. Wit. oath May 31, 1823 William F Reynolds to E Bomar. Rec. Aug. 4, 1823

p. 223-224 Jul. 23, 1823 Thomas Poole, sheriff (Spartanburgh) to Samuel Harmon (same); for $90.50 sold 100 ac; border: Samuel Harmon, John Gossett, and Abner Gossett; sale due to writ from Spartanburgh Common Pleas Court second Monday after fourth Monday in Oct. 1822 suit of John Ison vs Stephen Tolleson; judgment was levy of $460 and costs from Stephen Tolleson. Witness Fortunatus H Legg and Memery N Chapman. Signed Thomas Poole. Wit. oath Jul. 25, 1823 Memery N Chapman to E Bomar. Rec. Aug. 4, 1823

p. 224-225 Sept. 7, 1821 Thomas Rees (Spartanburgh) to Richard Turner (same); for $400 sold 337 ac on both sides of Peter's Cr; border: Job Sosbee jr and Daniel Faust; where Thomas Rees lives; part of three(sic) grants to (1) James Wyatt and (2) to Job Sosbee sr. Witness John Scott and Elizabeth Scott. Signed Thomas Rees. Wit. oath Aug. 4, 1823 John Scott to E Bomar. Rec. Aug. 4, 1823. Dower renounced Polley Rees to E Bomar May 6, 1822

p. 225 Sept. 4, 1823 Augustin Shands received from Mrs. Elizabeth Parker balance of mortgage given by Mrs. Elizabeth Parker Jul. 10, 1821. Witness John Glass. Signed Augustin Shands. Wit. oath Sept. 11, 1823 John Glass to E Bomar. Rec. Sept. 11, 1823

p. 225-226 Jul. 22, 1823 James Crook (Spartanburgh) to Elizabeth Snoddy (same); for $1,000 sold 512 ac on branches of S Tyger R; border: Page's Br, N-Snoddy, W-Durham and Vaughan, S-Drummond, and E-E Drummond and Snoddy. Witness William Otts and Isaac Snoddy. Signed James Crook. Wit. oath Sept. 20, 1823 Isaac Snoddy to Thomas Wood. Rec. Aug. 6, 1823

p. 226-227 Nov. 21, 1811 Joel Foster (Spartanburgh) to Aaron Casey (same); for $500 sold 238 ac on waters of Cedar Shoal Cr of Enoree R; plat attached shows border: Benjamin Wofford, Wilder, A Bobo, and Richard Fryer. Witness Burrel Bobo. Signed Joel Foster. Wit. oath (date omitted) Burrel Bobo esq to (not signed). Rec. Aug. 4, 1823. Dower renounced Nov. 21, 1811 Joeinah (or Sinai) Foster to Burrel Bobo

p. 227-228 Jul. 23, 1823 Thomas Poole, sheriff (Spartanburgh) to John Oeland (same); for $83 sold 3/4 ac in Spartanburgh, SC; lot #5; on N side of Main Street opposite the Jail; where Muse Tolleson's family lived; sold due to writ from Spartanburgh Common Pleas Court second Monday after fourth Monday in Mar. 1820 suit of Abraham Lemasters vs Muse Tolleson and Birdsong Tolleson, administrators of John Tolleson desc. Witness John Pickeypack and Memory N Chapman. Signed Thomas Poole SSD. Wit. oath Jul. 23, 1823 John Pickeypack to E Bomar. Rec. Aug. 4, (omitted)

p. 228-229 Jul. 14, 1823 Thomas Poole, sheriff (Spartanburgh) to Richard Thomson (same); for $976 sold 300 ac on N side of Tyger R; border: SE-Martha Sanders, SW-Drury Parham, S-"lower" Manufacturing Co known as Bell Hall tract; see deed from Randolph Palmer to Elias Palmer; sale due to writ from Spartanburgh Common Pleas Court second Monday after fourth Monday in Oct. 1822 suit of Peet Smith and Co vs Elias Palmer, executor of John D Palmer desc; judgment was levy of $211.60 and costs from Elias Palmer. Witness John Poole and M. N. Chapman. Signed Thomas Poole SSD. Wit. oath Jul. 16, 1823 John Poole to E Bomar. Rec. Aug. 4, 1823

p. 229 Apr. 5, 1823 Samuel Prewett (Spartanburgh) to Daniel Prewett jr (same); for $800 sold 160 ac on both sides Dutchman's Cr; border: Danl Pruitt's Spring Br and Joseph Betterton. Witness Jorial Pruitt, Basel Shaw, and Martha Pruitt. Signed Samuel Pruitt. Wit. oath Apr. 25, 1823 Basel Shaw to Benj Wofford. Rec. Aug. 9, 1823

p. 229-230 Mar. 15, 1823 Thomas Brice (Spartanburgh) to James Vernon (same); for $532 sold (ac omitted); where Thomas Brice lives; border: Greenville Road; grant Oct. 24, 1767 to Thomas Penney and sold by Thomas Penney and wife Sarah to Daniel Brice who sold to his son Thomas Brice; 4 ac added on side where Thomas Brice and his brother Samuel Brice live. Witness Joseph Haggett, Polley C Vernon, and James Swanzey. Signed Thomas Brice. Wit. oath Aug. 7, 1823 James Swanzey to Thomas B Collins. Rec. Aug. 9, 1823

p. 230-231 Aug. 12, 1823 John McElrath (Spartanburgh) to Philip Bettis (or Batis) (same); for $236 sold 59 ac on Middle Tyger R. Witness Simpson Foster and E Roddy. Signed John McElrath. Wit. oath Aug. 12, 1823 E Roddy to E Bomar. Rec. Aug. 12, 1823

p. 231-232 Feb. 22, 1821 Daniel McKie (Spartanburgh) to Samuel Woodruff sr (same); for $100 sold 95½ ac on Dildine's Cr; part of tract "called" William Stonlnburgh's(?). Witness Vincent Johnson (or Johnston) and Herndon McKie. Signed Daniel McKie. Wit. oath Apr. 5, 1821 Herndon McKie to John Brewton. Rec. Aug. 16, 1823

p. 232 Feb. 14, 1821 Thomas Woodruff (Spartanburgh) to Samuel Woodruff sr (same); for $125 sold 102 ac on waters of Dildine's Cr of Enoree R. Witness Josiah Woodruff, Caleb Allen, and Philip Pilgrim. Signed Thomas Woodruff. Wit. oath Apr. 5, 1821 Philip Pilgrim to John Brewton. Rec. Aug. 12, 1823

p. 232-233 Aug. 14, 1823 Thomas Poole, sheriff (Spartanburgh) to John Vandike (same); for $106 sold 200 ac on Standing Stone Cr of Lawson's fork; border: Barney Bishop, William L Bishop, and Richard Thompson; bought by Samuel C Hunt for John Vandike; sold due to writ from Spartanburgh Common Pleas Court second Monday after fourth Monday in Oct. 1822 suit of Jesse Cleveland; judgment was levy of $45 and costs from James Hutcherson. Witness John Hooper and John Poole. Signed Thomas Poole SSD. Wit. oath Aug. 18, 1823 John Hooper to E Bomar. Rec. Aug. 18, 1823

p. 233-234 Feb. 1, 1822 Benjamin Nichols (Spartanburgh) to Clemmins McGarity (Union Dist); for $200 sold 4 ac on N side of Tyger R; border: Shurbutt. Wit. oath Mark Bennett and Wm Lancaster. Signed Benjamin Nicholls. Wit. oath Mar. 8, 1823 Mark Bennett to Wm Smith. Rec. Aug. 18, 1823

p. 234-235 Feb. 1, 1822 Benjamin Nichols (Spartanburgh) to Clemmins McGarity (Union Dist); for $50 sold 1/16 ac on S side of S Tyger R; border: Crow's Spring; part of land did belong to Jonathan Crow and was sold to Benjamin Nichols. Witness Mark Bennett and Wm Lancaster. Signed Benjamin Nichols. Wit. oath Mar. 8, 1823 Mark Bennett to Wm Smith. Rec. Aug. 18, 1823

p. 235-236 Mar. 17, 1823 William White, executor of estate of Clemmins McGarity (late of Union Dist), to Toliver Scott; for $270 sold (1) 4 ac on N side of N Tyger R; border: Sherbutt; includes grist and saw mills known as Nichols' Mills; and (2) 1/16 ac on S side of N Tyger R; border: Crow's Spring; formerly Jonathan Crow's who sold to Nichols. Witness Benjamin Nichols and Absalom Wright. Signed Wm White. Wit. oath Aug. 18, 1823 Benjamin Nichols to John Brewton. Rec. Aug. 18, 1823

p. 236-237 Jun. 6, 1823 Zadock Ford (Spartanburgh) to William Ford (same); to secure note of $416 sold a slave Pomp; Condition: sale void if Zadock Ford pays debt. Witness Craddock Dickie. Signed Zadock Ford. Wit. oathAug. 25, 1823 Craddock Dickie to James Ford. Rec. Sept. 1, 1823

p. 237 Dec. 6, 1818 John Tolleson (Spartanburgh) to Muse Tolleson (same); for $800 sold (1) 500 ac; where John Tolleson lives; granted to John Tolleson; "and adjoining tracts" granted to Seth Lewis and John McCoole and sold by William Stone to John Tolleson; (2) (ac omitted); grant to Bird and Thaxton and sold by Mathew Bates and Wm Thomson; (3) 5 ac sold by John Lancaster to John Tolleson; (4) (ac omitted); sold by Major Gossett to John Tolleson; and (5) 100 ac where Rosey West lives; except 10 ac in fork of branch "given" by John Tolleson to Richard Kirby; border: Richard Kirby. Witness Stephen Tolleson and Richard Kerby. Signed John Tolleson. Wit. oath Apr. 23, 1821 Stephen Tolleson to Thomas Poole. Rec. Sept. 1, 1823

p. 237-238 Apr. 4, 1823 Adam Sloan (Spartanburgh) to Richard Barry, "son of R" (same); for $100 sold all household stuff and furniture and all other chattels: 3 feather beds, bedsteads, and furniture, a pine chest and its contents, "all my library", a man's saddle, and a woman's saddle; Condition: sale void if Adam pays Richard $100 by May 15, 1823 due to note dated Mar. 22, 1822. Witness Andrew Barry and C. H. Moore. Signed Adam Sloan. Wit. oath Sept. 1, 1823 Andrew Barry to Thomas B Collins. Rec. Sept. 1, 1823

p. 238-239 Mar. 3, 1823 William W Smithwick (Spartanburgh) to James Duncan, son of Alexand (same); for $100 sold (ac omitted) on N side of Tyger R; border: S-Tyger R, N-Benjamin Nicholls, E & SE-estate of Richd Willis desc, and W-Henry White; part of where Samuel Shubut desc lived; part of land belonging to David Hudgins and wife who sold to William W Smithwick. Witness Wm Trimmier and Wm Hunt. Signed Wm W Smithwick. Wit. oath Mar. 3, 1823 Wm Trimmier to W Hunt. Rec. Sept. 1, 1823

p. 239-240 Dec. 30, 1815 Malkijah Bush (Spartanburgh) to Edward Hemperley; for $180 sold 100 ac on Mill Cr of Tyger R; border: Ransom Foster. Witness Floyd Tanner, Ransom Foster, and John Foster. Signed Malkija Bush. Wit. oath Jan. 6, 1817 John Foster to Thomas Poole. Rec. Sept. 1, 1823

p. 240-241 Sept. 3, 1823 Augustin Shands (Spartanburgh) to John Wearing Parker (Charleston Dist); for $600 sold 164 ac; border: David Golightly, Hazle, John King, and John Wearing Parker; where Gabriel Gossett formerly lived; grant Dec. 1, 1794 to Samuel Noblett who sold to John Tolleson; sold as John W Parker trustee for Elizabeth Parker for her lifetime; like John W Parker's holding of land called Hopewell in Edgefield Dist sold to James Longstreet (Edgefield Dist) and part of proceeds are hereby invested; after Elizabeth Parker dies land is to be divided as per will of Benjamin Maryek (late of St James Parish) desc. Witness John Glass and Z McDaniel. Signed Augustin Shands. Wit. oath Sept. 5, 1823 John Glass to J. W. Farrow. Rec. Sept. 5, 1823

p. 241-242 Sept. 3, 1823 Augustin Shands (Spartanburgh) to John Warring Parker (Charleston Dist) as trust for Elizabeth Parker; for $1,600 sold 558 ac; border: SW-David Golightly jr, NW-Mr. G Golightly, NE-James Poole and Antony Bates, SE-James King; where Elizabeth Parker lives; part of grant in Nov. 1711(sic) North Carolina governor to James Hammett; land to be used as land called Hopewell John W Parker held for Elizabeth Parker in Edgefield Dist and sold to James Longstreet (Edgefield Dist) and part of proceeds are hereby invested; at Elizabeth Parker's death land to be divided according to will of Benjamin Maryek (late of St. James Parish) desc. Witness John Glass and Z McDaniel. Signed Augustin Shands. Wit. oath Sept. 5, 1823 John Glass to J. W. Farrow. Rec. Sept. 5, 1823

p. 242-243 Apr. 4, 1823 Edward Autrey (Spartanburgh) to Edward Bomar; for $210 sold 103 ac on Mill Cr of Tyger R; border: T Tanner; part of grant to John Snoddy. Witness W. T. Tanner, Adam Hemperley, and John Brooks. Signed Edward Autrey's mark. Wit. oath Apr. 8, 1823 Adam Hemperley to F (or T) Collins. Rec. Sept. 6, 1823

p. 243-244 Jul. 18, 1823 Thomson Fausett (Spartanburgh) to Adam Hemperley (same); for $520.50 sold 347 ac on waters of Fairforest Cr; border: Grindstone Br. Witness John Bomar jr and Edward Hemperley. Signed Thompson Fausett. Wit. oath Jul. 18, 1823 Edward Hemperley to E Bomar. Rec. Oct. 6, 1823. Dower renounced Sept. 1, 1823 Polly Fausett to Elisha Bomar

p. 244-245 Dec. 28, 1822 Casper Weber (Knox Co, Tenn) to Lethy and Rebeckah Bostick (Spartanburgh); for $400 sold 260 ac on N side of Pacolate R and mouth of Buck Cr; border: Isaac Young. Witness Richard Potter and Ephraim Elder. Signed Casper Weber. Wit. oath Dec. 28, 1822 Richard Potter to Henry Turner. Rec. Oct. 6, 1823

p. 245 Sept. 10, 1823 Towsend Robertson (Rutherford Co, NC) to brother's daughter Jude Robertson; for love and affection give a gray mare, 3 cows and calves, and a 2 year old heifer. Witness George Camp and Robert Scruggs. Signed Towsend Robertson's mark. Wit. oath Sept. 10, 1823 Robert Scruggs to Geo Camp. Rec. Oct. 6, 1823

p. 245-246 Jul. 1, 1823 Thomas Miles (Spartanburgh) to grandson Thomas Pinckney Miles, son of William H Miles (same); for love and affection give 100 ac; border: William Martendale, Humphrey Yarborough, Landon Miles, William Wilder, and Golding Tinsley; where Thomas Miles lives; except "part" given to daughter Mary Miles; Thomas P Miles gets land when Thomas Miles dies; Thomas M Bragg is nominated guardian for Thomas P Miles until he is "lawful age"; Thomas M Bragg can rent or lease the land with money going to educate Thomas P Miles; William H Miles gave Thomas Miles $1 for Thomas P Miles. Witness Thomas M Bragg and Mary Miles. Signed Thomas Miles. Wit. oath Sept. 8, 1823 Mary Miles to James

E Henry. Rec. Oct. 6, 1823

p. 246-247 Jun. 4, 1823 Thomas Poole, sheriff (Spartanburgh) to Thomas West (same); for $70 sold 100 ac; belongs to John Wofford sr and where John lives; border: Thomas Posey, William Wofford and George Wofford; sale due to writ from Spartanburgh Common Pleas Court second Monday after fourth Monday in Mar. 1823 suit of William Smith vs John Wofford sr, George Wofford, and John C Cook; judgment was levy of $122.68 and costs from (omitted). Witness William Tracy and Memory N Chapman. Signed Thomas Poole SSD. Wit. oath Jun. 4, 1823 Memory N Chapman to James E Henry. Rec. Oct. 6, 1823

p. 247-248 Mar. 25, 1823 Nathaniel Gist (Union Dist) to Elijah Gossett sr; for $220 sold 110 ac on waters of Fairforest Cr; grant to Joseph Ash. Witness John Eison. Signed Nathl Gist. Wit. oath Apr. 8, 1823 John Eison to William Reid. Rec. Oct. 6, (omitted). Dower renounced Oct. 4, 1823 Elizabeth L Gist to William Reid

p. 248-249 Jan. 17, 1822 John Fisher (Spartanburgh) to James A Page (Chester Dist); for $216 sold 216 ac on branches of Magey Cr of N Pacolate R; granted to Thomas Goodacre who sold to Bartholomew Grogan who sold to Jesse Winson who sold to John Fisher. Witness William Owen and William Embrey (or Emry) jr. Signed John Fisher's mark. Wit. oath Sept. 29, 1823 William Embrey to J Whitten. Rec. Oct. 16, 1823

p. 249 Mar. 31, 1823 Allen Lancaster and his mother Sarah Lancaster (Spartanburgh) to Jesse Cleveland (same); for $28.50 sold 9½ ac on Chinchequpin Cr; SE part of 273 ac grant to Thomas Lehre; survey Mar. 5, 1787 to Bassel Lee. Witness Abel Lancaster and Jesse F Cleveland. Signed Allen Lancaster and Sarah Lancaster. Wit. oath Apr. 17, 1823 Jesse F Cleveland to E Bomar. Rec. Oct. 17, 1823

p. 249-250 Oct. 16, 1816 Thomas Price (Spartanburgh) to Joseph Lannum (same); for $107 sold (ac omitted) on N side of N Tyger R; border: Josiah Hatchett, Otts, and Ward's Cr. Witness Vincent Tapp and Joseph Johnston. Signed Thomas Price. Wit. oath Dec. 31, 1818 Joseph Johnston to Robert Ligon. Rec. Oct. 17, 1823

p. 250-251 Jan. 8, 1819 Joseph James (Spartanburgh) to Josiah Blackwell (same); for $100 sold 70 ac on S side of Camp Br of Lawson's fork of Pacolet R; survey Jul. 22, 1797 for Edward Ballenger and granted Jan. 7, 1799 Gov. Edward Ballenger (sic Rutledge) to Larkin Rily (or Rindley) and assigned by Larkin Rily to Joshua Ingrim Jun. 28, 1806. Witness Edmond J Bishop and Barney Bishop. Signed Joseph James. Wit. oath Jul. 5, 1819 Edmond J Bishop to Thomas Poole. Rec. Oct. 24, 1823

p. 251 Apr. 17, 1821 Ralph Lemaster (Spartanburgh) to Abraham Lemaster (same); for $150 sold 40 ac; formerly owned by Ralph Lemaster's father Ralph Lemaster and to grantor by heirship. Witness William Hunt esq and John McDowell. Signed Ralph Lemaster. Wit. oath Apr. 17, 1821 William Hunt to William Reid. Rec. Oct. 25, 1823

p. 251-252 Mar. 31, 1823 Allen Lancaster and mother Sarah Lancaster (Spartanburgh) to Richard Thomson (same); for $25 sold 8½ ac on S side of Chinquepin Cr; border: Jesse Cleveland; part of 273 ac grant to Thomas Lehre and surveyed Mar. 5, 1787 "for" Basel Lee. Witness E Roddy and Abel Lancaster. Signed A Lancaster and Sarah's mark. Wit. oath Oct. 30, 1823 E Roddy to E Bomar. Rec. Oct. 30, 1823

p. 252-253 Mar. 3, 1823 Frederick Steading, Ann Wilmot, Paul Combee, and Rachel Stealing, heirs and representatives of Thomas Price desc, to Joseph Lanham; for $360 sold 100 ac; money was paid to Thomas Price during his lifetime; Joseph Lanham filed in Spartanburgh Equity Court against Frederick Steading, his wife, and "others" on Jan. 28, 1822 to execute title from grantors for land Joseph Lanham bought from Thomas Price in his lifetime; land is in fork of Tyger R; border: SE-John Thomas, N-N Tyger R and Joseph Johnson, and W-Matthew Patten. Witness Robert Ligon and Edith Ligon. Signed Frederick Steading, Rachel Steading, Paul Combee, and Ann Wilmot's mark. Wit. oath Oct. 17, 1823 Robert Ligon to E Bomar. Rec. Nov. 3, 1823

p. 253-254 Apr. 17, 1821 Richard Lemaster (Spartanburgh) to Abraham Lemaster (same); for $20 sold 20 ac; part of land of Richard's father Ralph Lemaster and to Richard by heirship. Witness William Hunt and James T McCarter. Signed Richard Lemaster. Wit. oath Apr. 17, 1821 William Hunt to William Reid. Rec. Nov. 3, 1823

p. 254-255 Oct. 24, 1816 Willis Bobo (Spartanburgh) to Moses Casey, son of Aaron (same); for $1,000 sold 290 ac on Cedar Shoal Cr; plat attached shows 290.8 ac. Witness Aaron Casey and Chaney Bobo. Signed Willis Bobo. Wit. oath Sept. 22, 1820 Chaney Bobo to M Casey. Rec. Nov. 3, 1823. Dower renounced Oct. 28, 1816 Delilah Bobo to Burrell Bobo

p. 255-256 Jan. 30, 1822 Pennel Wood (Greenville Dist) to James McClain (same); for $500 sold 204 ac on N side Enoree R and on Rocky field Cr; border: Robert Green, Tyre Glenn, Benjamin Green, and Kilgore; part of 334 ac grant Aug. 7, 1786 to David Quarles who sold Sept. 21 & 24, 1792 to Robert Wood; resurvey Jan. 21, 1822 by Josiah Kilgore DS. Witness James Hammett and Josiah McClain. Signed Pennel Wood. Wit. oath Nov. 27, 1822 Josiah McClain to Thomas Wood. Rec. Nov. 3, 1823. Dower renounced Oct. 18, 1822 Elizabeth Wood to Thomas Wood

p. 256-258 Apr. 6, 1820 James Hunt, sheriff (Spartanburgh) to Richard Thomson (same); for $25 sold 166 ac; one third of 500 ac at head of Sholy Cr of Lawson's fork and branches of Peter's and Casey Creeks of Pacolet R; border: W-Sholy Cr and Joseph Hutchins and others vacant; grant in 1772 to William Saunders; sold due to writ from Edgefield Dist Common Pleas Court first Monday in Oct. 1819 suit of Abner Blocker vs Martha Sprat, administrix of Thomas Sprat desc; judgment was levy of $60 and costs from Martha Sprat. Witness Randolph Palmer and Elihu Golightly. Signed Jas Hunt. Wit. oath Nov. 14, 1823 Elihu Golightly to E Bomar. Rec. Nov. 3, 1823

p. 258 Feb. 12, 1820 James Spratt, Rachel Spratt, and Martha Spratt, heirs of John Spratt desc (Edgefield Dist) to Richard Thomson (Spartanburgh); for $300 sold 500 ac on Sholy Cr and Casey's Cr of Pacolate R; grant in 1772 to WilliamSaunders. Witness Lewis B Holloway and James Holloway. Signed James Spratt and Rachel and Martha Spratt's marks. Wit. oath Feb. 12, 1820 (Edgefield Dist) Lewis B Holloway to Jeff Blocker. Rec. Nov. 3, 1823

p. 258-259 Apr. 7, 1821 John Gossett (Spartanburgh) to Abraham Lemaster (same); for $47 sold 47 ac on head waters of Story's Mill Cr; formerly owned by John Gossett's father-in-law, Ralph Lemaster and by heirship to John Gossett. Witness Daniel White and James T McCarter. Signed John Gossett. Wit. oath Apr. 7, 1821 James T McCarter to William Reid. Rec. Nov. 3, 1823

p. 259-260 Mar. 15, 1823 Francis Mason (Spartanburgh) to William Baber (same); for $180 sold 45 ac on both sides Ford's Cr of Fairforest Cr; border: William Baber. Witness William Foster and James Foster. Signed Francis Mason. Wit. oath Apr. 8, 1823 James Foster to Ransom Foster. Rec. Nov. 3, 1823

p. 260-261 Nov. 6, 1823 Josiah Woodruff (Spartanburgh) to Daniel Woodruff (same); for $1,000 sold 75 ac on branches of Enoree R; border: Augusta Road, S & E-Thomas Woodruff, and N & W-Esq. Hendrix; 12½ ac excepted for use of Bethel Meeting House leaving 75 ac. Witness Simeon Lavender and Isaac Leatherwood. Signed Josiah Woodruff. Wit. oath Nov. 3, 1823 Simeon Lavender to John Brewton. Rec. Nov. 8, 1823

p. 261 Nov. 6, 1823 Josiah Woodruff (Spartanburgh) to Daniel Woodruff (same); for $800 sold 289 ac on waters of Ferguson's and Jamie's Creeks; border: Lindsey's Br, N-Daniel Woodruff and Jonas Brewton, W-Capt. Jameson, S-Thomas Woodruff, and E-Eli Cox. Witness Simeon Lavender and Isaac Leatherwood. Signed Josiah Woodruff. Wit. oath Nov. 8, 1823 Simeon Lavender to John Brewton. Rec. Nov. 8, 1823

p. 261-262 Jan. 18, 1813 Nathan Farmer (Spartanburgh) to William Miller (same); for $50 sold 20 ac; border: William Miller and a road; part of tract granted (sic) by Sam Crane(?) to Nathan Farmer. Witness Manly Ford and Ellis Reynolds. Signed Nathan Farmer's mark. Wit. oath Aug. 31, 1821 Ellis Reynolds to Thomas Wood. Rec. Nov. 12, 1823

p. 262-263 Jan. 1, 1816 Jeremiah Pace (Buncomb Co, NC) to William Miller (Spartanburgh); for $300 sold 200 ac on N side Maple Swamp Cr of S Tyger R; border: William Miller and a wagon road; part of 1,000 ac grant to Pennel Wood. Witness Benjamin Wood and John Wood. Signed Jeremiah R Pace. Wit. oath Aug. 20, 1821 Benjamin Wood to Thomas Wood. Rec. Nov. 12, 1823

p. 263-264 Jun. 2, 1821 William Miller (Spartanburgh) to Edmond Miller (Greenville Dist); for $220 sold (1) 200 ac on N side Maple Swamp Cr of S Tyger R; part of 1,000 ac grant to Pennel Wood; and (2) 20 ad adjoining (1); border: William Miller, Nathan Farmer, and a post road; part of "grant" to Nathan Farmer. Witness Ellis Reynolds and Henry Wood. Signed William Miller. Wit. oath Aug. 31, 1821 Ellis Reynolds to Thomas Wood. Rec. Nov. 12, 1823. Dower renounced Nov. 8, 1823 (Greenville Dist) Patsey Miller to Caleb Green

p. 264-265 Mar. 1, 1823 Drury Cox (Laurens Dist) to Joseph Allen (Spartanburgh); for $60 sold 25 ac on ridge between Lick Cr and Enoree R; part of land formerly owned by John Hanaby and sold by Henry Cole sr to Drury Cox. Witness James Allen and Archibald Young. Signed Drury Cox. Wit. oath Nov. 5, 1823 James Allen to James Ford. Rec. Nov. 13, 1823

p. 265-266 Nov. 7, 1823 Lewis Parris (Spartanburgh) to William McKinney sr (Broad R, Rutherford Co, NC); for $200 sold 181 ac on waters of Horse Cr of Broad R; border: N-Sharp, E-Stock, S-Haney, and Black; grant Dec. 5, 1808 to Samuel Haney. Witness John Paris and James Tramel. Signed Lewis and Elizabeth Parris' marks. Wit. oath Nov. 7, 1823 John Paris to Geo Camp. Rec. Nov. 13, 1823. Dower renounced Nov. 7, 1823 Elizabeth Paris to Geo Camp

p. 266 Mar. 1, 1823 Drury Cox (Laurens Dist) to Joseph Allen (Spartanburgh); for $315 sold 105 ac on branches of Lick Cr of Enoree R; part of land formerly owned by John Handly and sold by William Hendrix esq to Drury Cox. Witness James Allen and Archibald Young. Signed Drury Cox. Wit. oath Nov. 5, 1823 James Allen to James Ford. Rec. Nov. 13, 1823

p. 266-267 Sept. 4, 1823 John Bazwell to Lemuel Johnson; for $193 sold 425 ac; where John Bazwell lives; border: A Wakefield, James Leonard, Jonas Leonard, Solomon Burnett, Green Pond tract, and Wm Anderson "&C"; Condition: sale void if John Bazwell pays notes to Grisham Durham--$96.50 due Christmas 1823 and $96.40 due Christmas 1824 for which Lemuel Johnson is security. Witness William Ford and James Leonard. Signed John Bazwell. Wit. oath Sept. 20, 1823 William Ford to Thomas Wood. Rec. Nov. 13, 1823

p. 267-268 May 30, 1823 Isaac Crow to Penelope Broughton (Spartanburgh); for $100 sold 60 ac on N side of Tyger R; border: John Vixe, Thomas Rite, and John Hindman. Witness George Hill and John Clark. Signed Isaac Crow. Wit. oath Oct. 27, 1823 John Clark to Joseph Wofford. Rec. Nov. 13, 1823

p. 268-269 May 10, 1823 James A McDowell and Robert McDowell sr (Spartanburgh) to Oliver Clark (same); for $720 sold 132 ac on waters of N Pacolate R; where James McDowell lives; on road from Spartanburgh and Greenville Court Houses to Galt's Bridge; border: William McWilliams and Bullington. Witness Christopher Golightly, John Golightly, and John McDowell. Signed James A McDowell and Robert McDowell. Wit. oath Sept. 20, 1823 Christopher Golightly to James Young. Rec. (omitted)

p. 269-270 Aug. 2, 1823 Robert Ligon to John Clark (Spartanburgh); for $450 sold 205 ac partly on Jammies Cr; border: Ginnings Cr and James Alexander; Robert Ligon's wife's part of real estate of Alexander Alexander desc except 22½ ac sold to Gideon Reynolds that borders Charles Bragg. Witness Mathias Rush and John Mason. Signed Robert Ligon. Wit. oath Oct. 25, 1823 John Mason to John Brewton. Rec. Nov. 14, 1823. Dower renounced Esther Ligon to John Brewton Sept. 20, 1823

p. 270 Oct. 8, 1816 Silas Cooper (SC) to Mathew Cooper (Spartanburgh); for $500 sold 160 ac on "Dam" Cr of Broad R. Witness Joshua Richards and Polley Cooper. Signed Silas and Rachel Cooper's marks. Wit. oath Jan. 10, 1817 Joshua Richards to J Camp. Rec. Nov. 14, 1823

p. 270-271 Apr. 5, 1823 Benjamin Poole (Spartanburgh) to James Poole (same); for $1,200 sold 310 ac on S side of Pacolate R; border: above Island ford on Pacolate R, line made by William Poole desc between Benjamin Poole and John Poole, and Lawson's fork; where Benjamin Poole lives. Witness William Poole, John S Poole, and Bartholomew Stoval. Signed Benjamin Poole. Wit. oath none. "Probate will be found on p. 274". Rec. Nov. 14, 1823. Dower renounced Nov. 13, 1823 Matildy Poole to William Reid

p. 271-272 Dec. 6, 1810 Thomas Penny (Spartanburgh) to James Ridings (same); for $100 sold 150 ac on N side of Alex Cr; border: grant to John Clark and McMullin's Cr. Witness Joseph Davis and Abram Brock. Signed Thomas Penny. Wit. oath Apr. 2, 1814 Abram Brock to Andrew Ferguson. Rec. Nov. 17, 1823

p. 272-273 Sept. 12, 1822 William Mason (Spartanburgh) to John Clark (same); for $310 sold 63 ac; border: W-Gideon Reynolds, N-Mills Sumner, E-Robert Alexander, and S-John Clark. Witness William Posey and John Mason. Signed Wm Mason. Wit. oath Aug. 9, 1823 John Mason to Robert Ligon. Rec. Nov. 17, 1823

p. 273-274 Jan. 8, 1823 John Brown (Burk Co, NC) to William Petit (Spartanburgh); for $12 sold (ac omitted) on N side of Pacolate R; border: Joshua Petit, David Allen, and Smith; part of grant to William Poole. Witness John Petit and Joshua Petit. Signed John Brown's mark. Wit. oath Nov. 29, 1823 John Petit to Caleb Jones. Rec. Dec. 1, 1823

p. 274 Apr. 7, 1823 Wit. oath Bartholomew Stovall to William Reid for deed from Benjamin Poole to James Poole; other witness was John S Poole

p. 274-275 Mar. 28, 1822 Nathan Ward sr (Spartanburgh) to Nathan Ward jr (same); for $250 sold (1) 140 ac; border: old Green River road and Nathan Ward sr's Spring Br; and (2) 100 ac adjoining (1); border: Reuben Lawson. Witness Jacob Stotts (or Slotts) and James Smith. Signed Nathan Ward sr's mark. Wit. oath Apr. 1, 1822 Jacob Stotts to W Hunt. Rec. Dec. 1, 1823

p. 275-276 Jan. 6, 1821 William Frasure (Stuart Co (sic), Tenn) to Alexander Wakefield (Spartanburgh); for $270 sold 135 ac on waters of Ben's Cr of S Tyger R; border: Leonard, Brushy fork Cr, John Durham, G Durham, Wm Anderson, and Alexander Wakefield. Witness John M Delany and George Durham. Signed William Frasure. Wit. oath Oct. 14, 1823 John M Delany to Thomas Wood. Rec. Dec. 1, 1823

p. 276 Mar. 12, 1823 Constant Wood (Spartanburgh) to John Hudson; for $500 sold all her rights to her husband's land. Witness John D Smith and Lucretia Demsey. Signed Constant Wood's mark. Wit. oath Oct. 7, 1823 John D Smith to Andrew McClain. Rec. Jan. 5, 1824

p. 276 Oct. 2, 1820 (Gwinnett Co, Ga) Dennis Tippins to John Hudson; for $600 sold a Negro woman Conann and her child Green (or Grun). Witness Benjamin Tippins. Signed Dennis Tippins. Wit. oath Nov. 25, 1823 (Greenville Dist, SC) Benjamin Tippins to Wm Mason. Rec. Jan. 5, 1824

p. 276-277 Apr. 21, 1803 William and Isaac Muzyck (Charleston, SC) to George Brewton (SC); for $500 sold 1,058 ac on waters of Farguson's Cr and Tyger R; border: N-George Brewton, John Patton, and David Prewett, W-Thomas Woodruff, Isaac Lockheart, and Joseph Brown, S-John Highleor, and E-Withers and unknown; grant as 1,000 ac to William Mazyck but contains 1,058 by resurvey in Sept. 1789 by John Hunter. Witness Stephen Ravenel and David James Ravenel. Signed William Mazyck and Isaac Mazyck. Wit. oath Apr. 22, 1803 David J Ravenel to Daniel Huger. Rec. (omitted). Dower renounced Apr. 22, 1803 Elizabeth Mazyck, wife of William, to Daniel Huger

p. 277-278 Jul. 21, 1823 John Cantrell (Spartanburgh) to Berryman Cantrell (same); for $200 sold 133 ac on Pacolate R; border: Mary Cantrell, old road, Horton's path, Lansford Cantrell, and Burgess. Witness William Cantrell and Martin Cantrell. Signed John Cantrell's mark. Wit. oath Dec. 5, 1823 William Cantrell to James Young. Rec. Jan. 5, 1824

p. 278 Nov. 20, 1820 Robert Dunaway to James Dunaway; for $50 sold 50 ac on branch of Thickety Cr of Broad R; border: Samuel Dunaway and Champion. Witness John Dunaway and Wm Gilbert. Signed Robert Dunaway. Wit. oath Jul. 4, 1821 John Dunaway to Wm Clement. Rec. Jan. 5, 1824

p. 279-280 Oct. 11, 1819 Mary Dunaway, William Dunaway, Robert Dunaway, and Richard Proctor (Spartanburgh) to James Dunaway (same); for $130 sold 120 ac on waters of Thickety Cr. Witness Lee Linder and John Saunders. Signed William Dunaway, Robert Dunaway, and Mary Dunaway's and Richard Proctor's marks. Wit. oath Oct. 11, 1819 Lee Linder to Henry Turner. Rec. Jan. 5, 1824

p. 280 May 6, 1823 Christopher Golightly (Spartanburgh), attorney for Shands Golightly (now Giles Co, Tenn), to Ephraim Drummond (same); for $150 sold 140 ac on waters of Jamies Cr of Tyger and Two Mile Cr of Enoree R; border: road from Thos Woodruff's to Dirkie's Br on Enoree R. Witness Jared Drummond and Warren Drummond. Signed Christi Golightly. Wit. oath Dec. 2, 1823 Jared Drummond to James Crook. Rec. Jan. 5, 1824

p. 280-281 Sept. 24, 1823 James Haskins, Sally Haskins, Elizabeth Haskins, and Peter Haskins (Spartanburgh) to Joshua Tapp; for $100 sold 47 ac; border: Lawson and Lick Cr; tract was "granted" by James Hammett sr to William Haskins. Witness William Smith and William Tapp. Signed James Haskins, Peter Haskins, and Sally and Elizabeth Haskins' marks. Wit. oath Jan. 5, 1824 William Tapp to E Bomar. Rec. Jan. 5, 1824

p. 281-282 Sept. 25, 1823 Benjamin High (Spartanburgh) to James Tapp; for $250 sold 150 ac; half of grant to Peter Ligon and sold by Labon P Poole, sheriff (Spartanburgh) to (omitted). Witness Thomas Bomar and John C Coon. Signed Benjamin High. Wit. oath Jan. 5, 1824 Thomas Bomar to Ransom Foster. Rec. Jan. 5, 1824

p. 282 Feb. 27, 1806 Samuel Crane (Pendleton Dist) to Nathan Farmer (Spartanburgh); for $105 sold 125 ac on S fork of Middle Tyger R; border: Roddy Smith and Potter. Witness Alexander M Thompson and William Crane. Signed Samuel Crane's mark. Wit. oath Dec. 18, 1821 Alexander M Thompson to John Montgomery. Rec. Jan. 5, 1824

p. 282-284 Sept. 13, 1811 Elijah McBee (Spartanburgh) to Rolly Calvert (same); for $500 sold 115 ac on S side Pacolate R opposite fork of Pacolate R and Lawson's fork. Witness Clary Lancaster and William Lancaster. Signed Elijah McBee. Wit. oath Mar. 20, 1812 William Lancaster to John Gossett. Rec. Jan. 11, 1824. Dower renounced May 21, 1813 Patsy McBee to John Gossett

p. 284-285 Mar. 8, 1814 John Lee (Spartanburgh) to heirs of Rolly Calvert desc (same); for $250 paid by Rolly Calvert and for $90 paid by James Pool, administrator for Rolly Calvert, sold 175 ac; border: Solomon Crocker; part of grant to John Lee's father Robert Lee desc and willed to John Lee. Witness Theron Lancaster, Juliet Lancaster, and William Lancaster. Signed John Lee's mark. Wit. oath Mar. 10, 1814 William Lancaster to J. H. Jones. Rec. Jan. 11, 1824. Dower renounced Jul. (blank), 1814 Elizabeth Lee to John Gossett

p. 285-286 Dec. 25, 1823 Hannah McBee (Monroe Co, Miss) to son Vandry McBee (Lincoln Co, NC); power of attorney to recover her dower right to land known as Lime kiln tract on waters of Thickety Cr and to land in South Carolina as widow of Vardry McBee sr (late of Spartanburgh) desc. Witness Bartlet Sims, Silas L McBee, and John Roberts. Signed Hannah McBee. Wit. oath Jan. 15, 1824 John Roberts to James Ed Henry. Rec. Jan. 15, 1824

p. 286-287 Jan. 18, 1822 William Grisham (Spartanburgh) to Abner Wakefield (same); for $400 sold 125 ac on waters of Reedy fork of S Tyger R; border: widow Stewart, Francis Powers, Robert Gaston, Jesse Wakefield, and James Anderson. Witness James Leonard and Alexandria (or Alexander) Wakefield. Signed William Grisham. Wit. oath Jan. 8, 1824 Alexandria Wakefield to Thomas Wood. Rec. Jan. 17, 1824. Dower renounced Jan. 8, 1824 Sary Grisham to Thomas Wood

p. 287-288 Aug. 21, 1823 James Poole (Spartanburgh) to John Poole (same); for $800 sold 200 ac; border: Lawson's fork; part of tract formerly belonging to William Poole desc. Witness Robert C Poole, George W Poole, and Jesse Mason. Signed James Poole. Wit. oath Jan. 28, 1824 Robert C Poole to William Reid. Rec. Jan. 27,

1824. Dower renounced Jan. 28, 1824 (sic) Rebecca Poole to William Reid

p. 288-289 Apr. 17, 1823 Thomas Poole, sheriff (Spartanburgh) to Fortunatus H Legg (same); for $630 sold ½ ac in Spartanburgh, SC; border: S-Public Square, N & W-Jesse Cleveland, and NE-Public Road; sale due to writ from Spartanburgh Common Pleas Court second Monday after fourth Monday in Oct. 1822 suit of James H Irby; judgment was levy of $772.50 and costs from Muse Tolleson. Witness John T Earle and M. N. Chapman. SignedThomas Poole SSD. Wit. oath Apr. 19, 1823 M. N. Chapman to E Bomar. Rec. Jan. 27, 1824

p. 289-290 Jan. 5, 1824 Jane and Hancock Smith (Spartanburgh) to Henry Murph (same); for $500 sold 250 ac on Fairforest and Kelso's Creeks; where Jane Smith lives; border: David Whetstone, White, Isaac Smith, David Golightly, William Smith's grant, John Thomas, John Murph, and Thomson's Br; part of three grants (1) to William Smith, (2) to Peter Smith, and (3) to Giles Connell who sold to James Smith desc and assigned to Jane Smith by Commissioners as her dower sare of James Smith's estate; plat attached. Witness Zechariah McDaniel and Benjamin Poole. Signed Jane Smith and Hancock Smith. Wit. oath Jan. 10, 1824 Zechariah McDaniel to E White. Rec. Feb. 5, 1824

p. 290-291 May 19, 1821 (Charleston Dist) Archibald McLachlaw, assignee of Peter C Graff, (Charleston Dist) to William Turpin jr (Newberry Dist); for $500 sold 1,770 ac in Spartanburgh Dist on Greenville Dist line, Mill Cr, Wolf Cr Swamp, and branches of Middle Tyger R; border: "old Pointers"; half of share assigned to Peter C Graff by Union Dist Equity Court; part of grants to Graff, Subles, and Braselman--12 grants dated Mar. 3, 1788 and certified Jul. 18, 1787 by WilliamD Thomas DS. Witness William Smith and Duke Goodman. Signed A McLachlan, assignee of P. C. Graff. Wit. oath May 19, 1821 Duke Goodman to J. W. Mitchell. Rec. Feb. 5, 1824

p. 291-292 Feb. 2, 1824 Mathias Rush (Spartanburgh) to William Rogers (same); for $500 sold 137 ac on both sides E branch of Ward's Cr of N Tyger R; border: Reynolds Mill; part of grant to Andw Thompson. Witness Philip Brewton and William Compton. Signed Mathias Rush. Wit. oath Feb. 2, 1824 Philip Brewton to Robert Ligon. Rec. Feb. 5, 1824. Dower renounced Feb. 2, 1824 Elizabeth Rush to John Brewton

p. 292-293 Jan. 12, 1824 John Gramling (Spartanburgh) to James Coan (same); for $650 sold 150 ac on N Tyger R; border: James Coan, Mills Gap road, Samuel Miller, Thomas Bomar, and John Mullinax. Witness James Selman and James Foster. Signed John Gramling. Wit. oath Jan. 17, 1824 James Selman to Ransom Foster. Rec. Feb. 5, 1824. Dower renounced Jan. 21, 1824 Elizabeth Gramling to F. H. Legg

p. 293-294 Jan. 27, 1824 James Norris (Union Dist) to Jesse Griffin (Spartanburgh); for $60 sold 40 ac on N side of Pacolet R; border: ridge road from Bullock's old place or Thompson's Quarter on Pacolet R to wagon road at John Duncan's, Griffin, Dillard's old cabin, and Henry Littlejohn. Witness William Orr and Samuel Littlejohn. Signed James Norris. Wit. oath Jan. 31, 1824 Samuel Littlejohn to John Lipscomb. Rec. Feb. 5, 1824

p. 294 Sept. 16, 1812 Robert Belcher sr (Spartanburgh) to grandson Isaac Lewis "otherwise called Belcher" (same); for love and affection give 2 beds and furniture. Witness Ephraim Lewis esq and Robert Belcher jr. Signed Robert Belcher sr's mark. Wit. oath Jan. 5, 1824 Ephraim Lewis to Jno Chapman. Rec. Feb. 5, 1824

p. 294-295 Feb. 4, 1824 Thomas Poole, sheriff (Spartanburgh) to

Thomas Tinsley (same); for $255.25 sold 222 ac on ridge between Lawson's fork and Fairforest Cr; border: Thomas Tinsley and Mary Lee; sold by Henry Brown to John Tolleson who sold to Muse Tolleson; sale due to writ from Spartanburgh Common Pleas Court second Monday after fourth Monday in Oct. 1822 suit of Joseph Collins, assignee; judgment was levy of $235 and costs from Muse Tolleson. Witness Jesse Cleveland and John Poole. Signed Thomas Poole. Wit. oath Feb. 17, 1824 John Poole to F. H. Legg. Rec. Feb. 17, 1824

p. 295-296 Feb. 18, 1824 Green Lee (Jackson Co, Ala) to David Thomson (same); for $100 sold number of ac "not yet ascertained" on E side of Spartanburgh Court House; Green Lee's share as heir of Basel Lee desc; where Green Lee's mother Mary Lee lives. Witness Simpson Foster, Simpson Bobo, and E Roddy. Signed Green W Lee. Wit. oath Feb. 18, 1824 Simpson Foster to James E Henry. Rec. Feb. 18, 1824

p. 296-297 Sept. 5, 1823 (Lawrence Co, Ala) Samuel J Adams (Lawrence Co, Ala) to William Thomas (Spartanburgh); for $200 sold 100 ac on Thickety Cr; border: Jonathan Hifflin and Joseph Collins; sold by John Ross to Samuel J Adams. Witness John H Lipscomb and John Littlejohn. Signed Samuel J Adams. Wit. oath Oct. 12, 1823 John H Lipscomb to John Lipscomb. Rec. Feb. 27, 1824

p. 297 Sept. 9, 1823 Robert Jamison to James Vernon and John Roddy (Spartanburgh); to secure debt of $1,350 to S Foster, Commissioner of Spartanburgh Equity Court, with James Vernon and John Roddy as security sold (ac omitted) on N side of fork of Middle Tyger R; and sold a Negro girl Phebe and Negro boy David; Condition: sale void if Robert Jamison pays debt by Feb. 1, 1824. Witness John Nance and Alexr Roddy jr. Signed Robt Jamison. Wit. oath Feb. 22, 1824 Alexr Roddy jr to John Burns. Rec. Feb. 27, 1824

p. 297-298 Oct. 1, 1823 William Wilder (Spartanburgh) to Thomas Kelley (same); for $900 sold 288 ac; 3 ac excepted for Mr(?) Ann Jolly's use while she is single with liberty of the water; 3 ac goes to Thomas Kelley when Ann Jolly moves. Witness Golding Tinsley and Elisha Statterns. Signed Wm Wilder. Wit. oath Feb. 6, 1824 Golding Tinsley to Benj Wofford. Rec. Mar. 1, 1824

p. 298-299 Aug. 20, 1819 Robert Love (Spartanburgh) to Thomas Finch (same); for $600 sold 600 ac on Mill Cr of Tyger R; border: Gravel's old line. Witness Theron Lancaster and James Finch. Signed Robert Love. Wit. oath Jan. 3, 1820 James Finch to Wm Underwood. Rec. Mar. 1, 1824. Dower renounced Aug. 26, 1820 Nancy Love to Daniel White

p. 299-300 Feb. 5, 1823 Benjamin Page (Spartanburgh) to Thomas Worthy (Chester Dist); for $200 sold 100 ac; border: Meeting House Spring and Wm Embrey; N end of "a tract". Witness Abner Raley and James Page. Signed Benjamin Page. Wit. oath Jan. 26, 1824 Abner Raley to J Whitten. Rec. Mar. 1, 1824

p. 300 Jul. 17, 1823 James Doigg (Spartanburgh) to John Brooks (same); for $169.34½ sold 82 ac; part of 179 ac grant Sept. 15, 1785 to William White who sold to Edward Bomar who sold to A. B. Moore who sold to James and Andw Doigg. Witness John Lewis and A. B. Moore. Signed James Doigg's mark. Wit. oath Aug. 4, 1823 A. B. Moore to F. H. Legg. Rec. Mar. 1, 1824. Dower renounced Feb. 2, 1824 Elizabeth Doigg to John S Rowland

p. 300-301 Jan. 24, 1824 Adam Gramling to John Brooks; for $60 sold 50 ac on waters of White's Br. Witness Enoch G Foster and Joel Mason. Signed Adam Gramling. Wit. oath Feb. 2, 1824 Joel Mason to John S Rowland. Rec. Mar. 1, 1824. Dower renounced Feb.

7, 1824 Mary Gramling to John S Rowland

p. 301-302 Sept. 3, 1823 James Crocker (Spartanburgh) to Edward Patterson (same); for $287 sold 200 ac on S side of Pacolet R; border: John Lee, Richland Cr, Graveyard hallow, Solomon Crocker, graveyard, Anthony Crocker, and Thomas Brown; where James Crocker lives. Witness Arthur Crocker sr and Charles Arnold. Signed James Crocker. Wit. oath Sept. 3, 1823 Arthur Crocker sr to D White. Rec. Mar. 1, 1824

p. 302-303 Mar. 25, 1823 Mathew Jones (Spartanburgh) to Isham Willson (same); for $90 sold 60 ac on Abner's Cr of Enoree R; part of grant to John Demsey(?). Witness James Leonard and William Hughes. Signed Mathew Jones. Wit. oath Jan. 30, 1824 William Hughes to Thomas Wood. Rec. Mar. 1, 1824. Dower renounced Jan. 30, 1824 Elizabeth Jones to Thomas Wood

p. 303-304 Mar. 1, 1824 Alston Drummond (Spartanburgh) to Walters J Drummond (same); for $103 sold 197 ac; Condition: sale void if Alston pays Walters J $103 by Dec. 25, 1824. Witness F. H. Legg and F. J. Drummond. Signed A Drummond. Wit. oath (date omitted) F. H. Legg to Jno Chapman. Rec. Mar. 1, 1824

p. 304 Nov. 9, 1822 Agness Prewit (Spartanburgh) to Robert Bellington (same); for $50 sold 80 ac on waters of Beaverdam Cr of Pacolet R; in two parts: (1) 50 ac and (2) 30 ac that borders: Boling and tract (1). Witness Moses Brooks and James Turner. Signed Agness Prewit's mark. Wit. oath Dec. 15, 1823 James Turner to James Young. Rec. Mar. 1, 1824

p. 304-306 Feb. 4, 1824 Thomas Poole, sheriff (Spartanburgh) to George Jones (Rutherford Co, NC); for $135 sold 350 ac; border: James Brannon and Thomas Tinsley; sold by D. J. Puckett to John Tolleson who sold to Muse Tolleson; sold due to writ from Spartanburgh Common Pleas Court second Monday after fourth Monday in Oct. 1822 suit of John Cannon; judgment was levy of $1,050 and costs from Muse Tolleson. Witness John Poole and Memory N Chapman. Signed Thomas Poole SSD. Wit. oath Mar. 4, 1824 John Poole to E Bomar. Rec. Mar. 4, 1824. Dower renounced Mar. 4, 1824 Sarah Tolleson to Elisha Bomar

p. 306-307 Feb. 4, 1824 Thomas Poole, sheriff (Spartanburgh) to George Jones (Rutherford Co, NC); for $331 sold 66 ac; border: lot where Muse Tolleson lives in Spartanburgh, SC, Ephraim Roddy, Sarah Lancaster, Daniel Faust, and Richard Thompson; sold due to writ from Spartanburgh Common Pleas Court second Monday after fourth Monday in Oct. 1822 suit of Fortunatus H Legg; judgment was levy of $2,865 and costs from Muse Tolleson; sold to Jesse Cleveland (Spartanburgh) for George Jones. Witness John Poole and Memory N Chapman. Signed Thomas Poole SSD. Wit. oath Mar. 4, 1824 John Poole to E Bomar. Rec. Mar. 4, 1824. Dower renounced Mar. 4, 1824 Sarah Tolleson to Elisha Bomar

p. 307-308 Apr. 17, 1823 Thomas Poole, sheriff (Spartanburgh) to Jesse Cleveland (same); for $90 sold ½ ac in Spartanburgh, SC; border: Cross street and Todd's stable; where John W Farrow lives; sold due to writ from Spartanburgh Common Pleas Court second Monday after fourth Monday in (omitted), 1822 suit of James H Irby; judgment was levy of $690 and costs from Muse Tolleson. Witness E Roddy and Richard Underwood. Signed Thomas Poole SSD. Wit. oath Apr. 17, 1823 Richard Underwood to E Bomar. Rec. Mar. 4, 1824

p. 308-309 Mar. 2, 1824 Thomas Poole, sheriff (Spartanburgh) to Benjamin Wofford (same); for $30 sold 50 ac on Tyger R; border: E-George Divine, S-Charles Williamson, and W-Abner Marsh;

sale due to writ from Spartanburgh Common Pleas Court second Monday after fourth Monday in Oct. 1822 suit of John W Farrow vs administrators of John Spear desc; judgment was levy of $32 and costs from John Spear desc's estate. Witness John Poole and Memory N Chapman. Signed Thomas Poole SSD. Wit. oath Mar. 4, 1824 John Poole to E Bomar. Rec. Mar. 4, 1824

p. 309 Oct. 25, 1823 James Finch (Spartanburgh) to son William Finch; for $200 sold 58 ac on waters of Fairforest Cr; border: William Lancaster, John Oeland, Isaac Finch, and White's Br; where James Finch lives. Witness Isaac Finch and Daniel White. Signed James Finch's mark. Wit. oath Nov. 13, 1823 Daniel White to Wm Underwood. Rec. Mar. 6, 1824

p. 309-310 Feb. 11, 1824 James Seay, Elizabeth Wingo, and Nancy Seay (Spartanburgh) to William Bomar (same); for $125 sold 200 ac on N side of Fairforest Cr; part of land formerly of Gideon Seay desc. Witness Joel Foster and Elijah McMullin. Signed James Seay and Elizabeth Wingo's and Nancy Seay's marks. Wit. oath Mar. 1, 1824 Joel Foster to Geo Camp. Rec. (omitted)

p. 310-311 Mar. 1, 1823 Thomas Poole, sheriff (Spartanburgh) to Jesse Cleveland (same); for $332 sold 147 ac; border: N-Allen Lancaster, S-Richard Thomson, E-William Thomson, W-Ephraim Roddy and Muse Tolleson; land belonged to Muse Tolleson; sale due to writ from Spartanburgh Common Pleas Court second Monday after fourth Monday in Oct. 1822 suit of Joseph T Wayman; judgment was levy of $1,000 and costs from Muse Tolleson and Berryman S Holder. Witness Richard Thomson and Memory N Chapman. Signed Thomas Poole SSD. Wit. oath Apr. 17, 1823 Memory N Chapman to E Bomar. Rec. Mar. 8, 1824

p. 311-312 Mar. 1, 1823 Thomas Poole, sheriff (Spartanburgh) to Jesse Cleveland (same); for $140 sold ½ ac; border: Tolleson's old house and public square; sold due to writ from Spartanburgh Common Pleas Court second Monday after fourth Monday in Oct. 1822 suit of James H Irby; judgment was levy of $751 anc costs from Muse Tolleson. Witness Richard Thomson and Memory N Chapman. Signed Thomas Poole SSD. Wit. oath Apr. 17, 1823 Memory N Chapman to E Bomar. Rec. Mar. 8, 1824. Dower renounced Feb. 16, 1824 Sarah Tolleson to James E Henry

p. 312-313 Aug. 16, 1822 Richard Thomson (Spartanburgh) to "agents for the state of South Carolina"; for $100 sold (ac omitted) in Spartanburgh,SC; border: on SW corner of Jesse Cleveland's lot and SE corner of William Thomson's lot; allowing for 50 foot wide street and E Roddy's office. Witness James Hunt and James E Henry. Signed Richard Thomson. Wit. oath Aug. 16, 1822 James Hunt to E Bomar. Rec. Mar. 8, 1824. Dower renounced Mar. 8, 1824 Polly Thomson to Elisha Bomar

p. 313-314 Feb. 18, 1824 Mathias Elmore sr (Spartanburgh) to son-in-law Reason Hilburn (same); for love and affection give Negroes: Prunus 22 years old, Isham 16 years old, and George 2 years old. Witness James Atkins and Daniel Atkins. Signed Mathias Elmore. Wit. oath Feb. 28, 1824 James Atkins to Thos Collins. Rec. Mar. 15, 1824

p. 314 Mar. 13, 1824 James Turner (Spartanburgh) to son Samuel Turner and son-in-law James Foster (same); for love and affection of daughter Tamer Brown give Samuel Turner and James Foster in trust for Tamer Brown a Negro girl Charity 9 years old and her increase, 100 ac on S side of Casey's Cr of Pacolet R; border: James Turner, Edmund Fowler, and land formerly of Amos Speace; and give a cow and claf, a feather bed and furniture, an oven, a pot,

2 skillets, a trunk, 6 pewter plates, a pewter dish, a pewter basin, and a spinning wheel. Witness E Roddy and Memory N Chapman. Signed James Turner. Wit. oath Mar. 13, 1824 Memory N Chapman to W Hunt. Rec. Mar. 15, 1824

p. 314-315 Apr. 2, 1821 Richard Thomson (Spartanburgh) to Robert M Young and William Trimmier (same); for $175 sold 0.4 ac in Spartanburgh, SC; border: Col. James Brannon (bought from Henry White) and NE corner of public square. Witness James Brannon and John Walker. Signed Richard Thomson. Wit. oath Mar. 15, 1824 James Brannon to E Bomar. Rec. Mar. 15, 1824. Dower renounced Mar. 8, 1824 Polly Thomson to E Bomar

p. 315-316 Aug. 20, 1822 Richard Thomson (Spartanburgh) to James Hunt (same); for $150 sold 2 ac in Spartanburgh, SC; S of James Hunt's house and on Cross Street. Witness Jesse F Cleveland and E Bomar. Signed Richard Thomson. Wit. oath Mar. 15, 1824 Jesse F Cleveland to E Bomar. Rec. Mar. 15, 1824. Dower renounced Mar. 8, 1824 Polly Thomson to Elisha Bomar

p. 316-318 Mar. 2, 1824 (Spartanburgh Equity Court) Simpson Foster, Commissioner of Spartanburgh Equity Court, to John Harrison and John H Joice; for $1,500 sold 4 ac 1 rod and 22 perches at Spartanburgh Court House on S side of Main St; border: "my piazo", blacksmith shop, and public square; Daniel White filed in Spartanburgh Equity Court vs Muse Tolleson on Dec. 2, 1822 to foreclose Muse's mortgage given to Daniel White; sale was on Mar. 1, 1824. Witness Ephraim Roddy, Abel Lancaster, and Simpson Bobo. Signed S Foster CESD. Wit. oath Mar. 18, 1824 Simpson Bobo to E Bomar. Rec. Mar. 18, 1824

p. 318-319 Aug. 20, 1822 Richard Thomson (Spartanburgh) to Thomas Poole (same); for $150 sold 2.1 ac in Spartanburgh, SC on S side of Poole's house; border: James Brannon's stables, Jas Hunt, "back" street,and Jesse Cleveland. Witness Jesse F Cleveland and Elisha Bomar. Signed Richard Thomson. Wit. oath Mar. 15, 1824 Jesse F Cleveland to E Bomar. Rec. Mar. 18, 1824. Dower renounced Mar. 8, 1824 Polly Thomson to Elisha Bomar

p. 319-320 Nov. 24, 1823 Richard Thomson (Spartanburgh) to John Bomar (same); for $800 sold 1¼ ac in Spartanburgh, SC on N side of Main St and adjoins NE end of public ground and is opposite Jas Hunt's lot; border: Cross Street, Muse Tolleson, and Brannon. Witness James E Henry and James Brannon. Signed Richard Thomson. Wit. oath Mar. 15, 1824 James Brannon to E Bomar. Rec. Mar. 18, 1824. Dower renounced Mar. 8, 1824 Polly Thomson to Elisha Bomar

p. 320-321 Dec. 26, 1823 Richard Thomson (Spartanburgh) to John Vandike (same); for $205 sold 200 ac on waters of Lawson's fork and Fairforest Cr; border: John Windsor; where Edmund Bishop formerly lived; part of grant to David Goodlett. Witness Jas Brannon and Ephraim Roddy. Signed Richard Thomson. Wit. oath Mar. 16, 1824 Jas Brannon to E Bomar. Rec. Mar. 18, 1824

p. 321-322 Feb. 5, 1824 Thomas Poole,sheriff (Spartanburgh) to Jesse Cleveland (same); for $294 sold 640 ac; in two parts: (1) 500 ac known as Watson's tract; border: E Roddy, Lancaster, Buleau, and Thomson; and (2) 140 ac known as Allison's tract; border: E Roddy, J Cleveland, Mary Lee, and George Jones; sold due to writ from Spartanburgh Common Pleas Court second Monday after fourth Monday in Oct. 1822 suit of Fortunatus H Legg and John Cannon; judgment was levy of $3,333 and costs from Muse Tolleson. Witness John Poole and Memory N Chapman. Signed Thomas Poole SSD. Wit. oath Mar. 18, 1824 Memory N Chapman to E Bomar. Rec. Mar. 18, 1824

p. 322-323 Nov. 13, 1822 Abner Benson (Spartanburgh) to Theron Earle (same); for $800 sold 62½ ac on N side of Fairforest Cr of Tyger R; near Spartanburgh Court House; grant Mar. 6, 1786 to William Williamson and then border: vacant. Witness George Thomson and George V Miller. Signed A Benson. Wit. oath Mar. 18, 1824 George V Miller to E Bomar. Rec. Mar. 18, 1824

p. 323-324 Nov. 25, 1822 Richard Thomson (Spartanburgh) to Elisha Bomar (same); for $150 sold 2½ ac in Spartanburgh, SC; border: public street, David Faust, Cross St, Main St, and road from Spartanburgh to Greenivlle Court House. Witness William Trimmier and Richard M Young. Signed Richard Thomson. Wit. oath Mar. 19, 1824 Richard M Young to James E Henry. Rec. Mar. 8, 1824

p. 324-325 Feb. 26, 1823 Wilson Nesbett to Abner Benson, Andrew B Moore, Ephraim Roddy, and esecutor of Thomas Moore; to secure grantees from paying bond from Bank of South Carolina (bond for benefit of Wilson Nesbett) sold Negroes: Simon about 40 years old, Jacob about 35 years old, Jack about 25 years old, Landon about 25 years old, Saul about 40 years old, Nury about 45 years old, and Will about 20 years old; Condition: sale void if Wilson pays debt; if Negroes are sold, money above amount of bond goes to Wilson Nesbett. Witness Elisha Bomar and James E Henry. Signed Wilson Nesbett. Wit. oath Mar. 18, 1824 Elisha Bomar to J. W. Farrow. Rec. Mar. 18, 1824

p. 325 Dec. 21, 1822 Charles Hammet (Spartanburgh) to Daniel Hammet (same); for $130 sold 50 ac on waters of Pacolet R; border: Thompson and Common. Witness Isaiah Hembree and Mary Hembree. Signed Charles Hammet's mark. Wit. oath Jul. 16, 1823 Isaiah Hembree to Caleb Jones. Rec. Mar. 30, 1824

p. 325-326 Feb. 16, 1822 Henry Grogan (Spartanburgh) to John Fisher; for $300 sold 100 ac on both sides Beaverdam Cr of S Pacolate R; border: John Grogan, Bartholomew Grogan, and Dorinda; part of 450 ac grant Oct. 6, 1772 to Peter Videau. Witness James Owen and John Waldrop. Signed Henry Grogan's mark. Wit. oath Apr. 3, 1824 James Owen to J Whitten. Rec. Apr. 5, 1824

p. 326-327 Mar. 31, 1824 John Eison sr (Spartanburgh) to daughter Elizabeth Poole (same); for love and affection give a Negro girl Silbe and her increase. Witness Hiram White. Signed John Eison. Wit. oath Mar. 31, 1824 Hiram White to J. P. Thomson. Rec. Apr. 5, 1824

p. 327 Oct. 8, 1823 Daniel White (Spartanburgh) to Henry White (same); Henry White has agreed with Daniel White by bond payable to heirs of Charles James desc (Daniel is executor of Charles James desc's will); bond is to pay $1,600 which Daniel has "converted to his own use" and Henry is to pay $1,600 to heirs when they become of age; because of bond Daniel sold Henry 215 ac where Daniel White lives on waters of Fairforest Cr; border: SW-Isaac Smith, SE-Jane Smith, E-David Whetstone, and N-John Bullington; Daniel also sells to Henry a Negro man Will, Negro woman Lucy, and her two sons Charles and Moses. Witness Lemuel White and Daniel White jr. Signed D White. Wit. oath Apr. 6, 1824 Lemuel White to Caleb Jones. Rec. Apr. 6, 1824

p. 327-328 Jan. 19, 1824 William Walkermerryman (Rhea Co, Tenn) to Clabourn Humphries (late of Spartanburgh); for $1 per ac sold 125 ac on N side of Cherokee Cr; border: little Cherokee Cr. Witness Briant Bonner and Thomas Farmer. Signed William Walker-merryman. Wit. oath Mar. 10, 1824 Thomas Farmer to F. W. Robertson. Rec. Apr. 6, 1824

p. 328-329 Sept. 26, 1823 (Tenn) Thomas Gore (Franklin Co, Tenn) to Joshua Gore (same); for $600 sold 187½ ac; border: William Martindale, John Harmoning, and Golden Tinsley. Witness Mary Smith and Charles Gillaspie. Signed Thomas Gore. Wit. oath Nov. 12, 1823 Mary Smith to William Young. Rec. Apr. 6, 1824

p. 329 Dec. 15, 1823 William Walkermerryman (Rhea Co, Tenn) to Thomas Farmer (Spartanburgh); for $50 sold 20 ac on waters of little Cherokee and big Cherokee Cr; border: Gillum and Thomas Farmer; part of land sold by Gabriel Benson and Susanah Walker (Spartanburgh) to William Walkermerryman. Witness Lawrence Anderson, Clabourn Humphries "late", and Joshua Richards. Signed William Walkermerryman. Wit. oath Mar. 10, 1824 Clabourn Humphries to F. W. Robertson. Rec. Apr. 6, 1824

p. 329-330 Nov. 13, 1821 Joseph Johnston (Spartanburgh) to Mathias Rush (same); for $791 sold 155 ac on W side of N Tyger R and part of waters of S Tyger R; sold by Samuel Burton to Joseph Johnson. Wit. oath Robert Ligon and John Mason. Signed Joseph Johnston. Wit. oath (blank), 1824 Robert Ligon to E Bomar. Rec. Apr. 6, 1824 Dower renounced Apr. 3, 1824 Anna Johnston to John Brewton

p. 330-331 Nov. 26, 1823 Thomas Cole (Spartanburgh) to Michael Gaffney (same); for $87.50 sold 87½ ac on waters of Thickety Cr; border: Michael Gaffney; where Thomas Cole lives; grant by Gov. Charles Pinckney to Samuel and William Omelvany. Witness Charles Petty and James Cooper. Signed Thomas Cole. Wit. oath Apr. 5, 1824 Charles Petty to F. W. Robertson. Rec. Apr. 7, 1824

p. 331 Jul. 8, 1823 Isaac Gordon (Spartanburgh) to Michael Gaffney (same); for $120 sold 123 ac; border: E-Isaac Gordon's son Isaac, N-son Sterling, W-son John, and S-Michael Gaffney; where Isaac Gordon lives; part of lot "as a dividend to my son Abraham". Witness Abner Benson and Abraham Gordon. Signed Isaac Gordon. Wit. oath Apr. 6, 1824 Abner Benson to John Lipscomb. Rec. Apr. 7, 1824

p. 331-332 Feb. 18, 1823 Harvey Davis (Spartanburgh) to Robert Mince (same); for $300 sold 294 ac on Barton's Cr. Witness Thomas Barton and Philip Brisco. Signed Harvey Davis. Wit. oath Apr. 7, 1824 Thomas Barton to Geo Camp. Rec. Apr. 7, 1824

p. 332-333 Nov. 18, 1823 John Brown to Dr Thomas Hancock; to secure five notes: (1) $100 payable by Feb. 20, 1824, (2) $200 payable Feb. 20, 1825, (3) $200 payable Feb. 20, 1826, (4) $200 payable Feb. 20, 1827, and (5) $200 payable Feb. 20, 1828 with interest on (4) from Feb. 20, 1827 and for $1 sold (1) 200 ac on N side of Pacolate R; grant to Arthur Crocker; and (2) 12 ad adjoining (1) on N of Pacolate R; part of Reuben Briant's land; Condition: sale void if John Brown pays notes. Witness James Poole and Peter Peterson. Signed John Brown's mark. Wit. oath Apr. 6, 1824 Peter Peterson to J Whitten. Rec. Apr. 7, 1824

p. 333-334 Oct. 14, 1822 Thomas Collins (Spartanburgh) to James Austell (same); for $400 sold 200 ac; border: little Snead Br or Fall Br of Thickety Cr and John Thomas; part of grant to Thomas Collins. Witness William Austell and Green A Pinks. Signed Thomas Collins. Wit. oath Oct. 16, 1822 William Austell to F. W. Robertson. Rec. Apr. 7, 1824

p. 334-335 Mar. 27, 1824 Thomas Poole, sheriff (Spartanburgh) to Memory N Chapman (same); for $206 sold ½ ac in Spartanburgh, SC on S side of Main St; border: E lot sold by sheriff to James E Henry, S-Richard Thomson, W-James Hunt, and N-Main St; where there is a house occupied as doctor's shop and law office; sold due to writ from Spartanburgh Common Pleas Court second Monday after fourth Monday in Mar. 1823 suit of James Cohen; judgment was levy of $224 and costs from Muse Tolleson. Witness Robert M Young and Isaac Smith. Signed Thomas Poole SSD. Wit. oath Apr. 13, 1824(sic) Robert M Young to D White. Rec. Apr. 12, 1824

p. 335 Nov. 19, 1818 Edward Ballinger (Spartanburgh) to William Brannon (same); for $126 sold 63 ac; border: William Brannon and a wagon road; part of grant Feb. 6, 1804 to James S Guignard. Witness Richard Thomson and Matthew Seay. Signed Edward Ballinger and Pleasant's mark. Wit. oath Jan. 20, 1821 Matthew Seay to Wm Clement. Rec. Apr. 17, 1824

p. 335-336 Mar. 2, 1824 Thomas Poole, sheriff (Spartanburgh) to James Tolleson (same); for $14.06½ sold 150 ac on waters of Fairforest Cr; border: James McCarter, George Kennet, and estate of John Tolleson desc; sold due to writ from Spartanburgh Common Pleas Court second Monday after fourth Monday in Oct. 1822 suit of John Cannon vs Muse Tolleson; judgment was levy of $885 and costs from Muse Tolleson. Witness Richard Kirby and Memory N Chapman. Signed Thomas Poole SSD. Wit. oath Apr. 19, 1824 Richard Kirby to E Bomar. Rec. Apr. 19, 1824

p. 336-337 Jan. 24, 1824 Thomas Poole, sheriff (Spartanburgh) to William Tracy (same); for $55.25 sold 500 ac on waters of Pacolet R; border: W-William Tracy, N-Qualls, E-Jones and Thomson, and S-Linsey and Ison; sold due to writ from Spartanburgh Common Pleas Court second Monday after fourth Monday in Oct. 1822 suit of James Keen (or Kun); judgment was levy of $142 and costs from Muse Tolleson. Witness Simpson Foster and John Poole. Signed Thomas Poole SSD. Wit. oath Apr. 19, 1824 John Poole to W Hunt. Rec. Apr. 19, 1824

p. 337-338 Feb. 7, 1824 Thomas Poole, sheriff (Spartanburgh) to James Hunt (same); for $406 sold ½ ac in Spartanburgh, SC; corner lot on S side of Main St; border: N-Main St, W-Cross St between James Hunt and said lot, S-Richard Thompson, and E-lot bought by M. N. Chapman; opposite where Muse Tolleson lives; sold due to writ from Spartanburgh Common Pleas Court second Monday after fourth Monday in Oct. 1823 suit of Nathan Hort; judgment was levy of $1,117 and costs from Muse Tolleson. Witness James Brannon and John Poole. Signed Thomas Poole SSD. Wit. oath Apr. 19, 1824 John Poole to E Bomar. Rec. Apr. 19, 1824

p. 338-339 Dec. 12, 1816 John Findley (Spartanburgh) to John Linder (same); for $400 sold 202 ac on waters of Thickety Cr; border: Headen and Piolar. Witness Lee Linder and John Wooldridge. Signed John and Jane Findley's marks. Wit. oath Lee Linder to Henry Turner. Rec. Apr. 28, 1824. Dower renounced Apr. 6, 1817 Jane Findley to Wm Reid

p. 339-340 Sept. 25, 1822 James Templeman, Carter Burnet, Abraham Linder, Nathaniel Linder, Tillotson Brookshier, Lee Linder, and Lewis Cannon, heirs of Aaron Templeman desc (Spartanburgh), to Jacob Linder; for $306 sold 150 ac on S side of Pacolet R; border: James Templeman and Mill Pond. Witness Samuel Kennedy and Mary Templeman. Signed James Templeman, Carter Burnet, Abraham Linder, Nathaniel Linder, Lee Linder, Tillotson Brookshier, and Lewis Cannon. Wit. oath none. Rec. Apr. Apr. 28, 1824. Dower renounced Mar. 1, 1823 Mary Templeman, wife of Abraham (sic) desc, to Lee Linder

p. 340 Apr. 24, 1824 Philip Bettis (Spartanburgh) to Joseph McMillen; quit claim to 125 ac on N side of Middle Tyger R; survey Sept. 24, 1816 for Philip Bettis and granted Oct. 7, 1816; where

Joseph McMillen lives; "originally granted to Thomas Penny and sold Mar. 1, 1803 to Joseph McMillen". Witness John P Evins and Samuel Brice. Signed Philip and Sally Bettis' marks. Wit. oath May 3, 1824 Samuel Brice to John Chapman. Rec. May 3, 1824

p. 340-341 Jan. 15, 1824 Barney Bishop (Spartanburgh) to William L Bishop (same); for $325 sold 100 ac on Fairforest and Lawson's fork Creeks; border: Edmund T Bishop. Witness George Lewis and John Vandike. Signed Barney Bishop. Wit. oath May 3, 1824 John Vandike to E Bomar. Rec. May 3, 1824

p. 341 Jul. 26, 1823 Vincent Wyatt (Spartanburgh) to James Cannon jr (same); for $250 sold 212 ac on Betty Green Cr; border: Cannon. Witness Bird Low and Spencer Wyatt. Signed Vincent Wyatt. Wit. oath May 3, 1824 Spencer Wyatt to Caleb Jones. Rec. May 3, 1824

p. 341-342 Oct. 3, 1811 Tyre G Blackwell (Rutherford Co, NC) to Humphrey Paris (same); for $350 sold 80 ac on Pacolate R; part of two surveys. Witness James Blackwell and Thomas Miller. Signed Tyre G Blackwell. Wit. oath Jun. 7, 1823 James Blackwell to Wm Kelso. Rec. May 3, 1824

p. 342-343 Feb. 25, 1822 John Adams (Spartanburgh) to William Jackson; for $500 sold 80 ac on Pacolate R; part of two surveys. Witness Joseph Jackson, William Kelso and A. F. Jackson. Signed John Adams. Wit. oath Apr. 3, 1824 A. F. Jackson to William Kelso. Rec. May 3, 1824. Dower renounced Jan. 2, 1823 Lydia Adams to James Young

p. 343 Mar. 20, 1820 Humphrey Parish (Rutherford Co, NC) to John Abrams (Spartanburgh); for $350 sold 80 ac on Pacolate R; part of two surveys. Witness William Wade and Edmund Booker. Signed Humphrey Parish. Wit. oath Apr. 3, 1824 William Wade to William Kelso. Rec. May 3, 1824

p. 343-344 Apr. 1, 1824 John Bozwell to Samuel J Anderson; John promises to pay Samuel $110.50 by Dec. 25, 1825. Signed John Bozwell.
John Bozwell to Samuel J Anderson; to secure above, John mortgages a black mare, a bay mare, a bay horse, 9 cattle, and 3 feather beds and furniture. Witness T. J. Deen and James G Johnson. Signed John Bozwell. Wit. oath Apr. 6, 1824 James G Johnson to Thomas Wood. Rec. May 3, 1824

p. 344-345 Dec. 29, 1823 Nancy Pope (Spartanburgh) to John Burnett sr (same); for $60 sold 50 ac; border: Edward Turner; where Nancy Pope formerly lived. Witness John Kimbrill and Vincent Kimbrill. Signed Nancy Pope's mark. Wit. oath Jan. 5, 1824 John Kimbrill to W Bennett. Rec. May 3, 1824

p. 345-346 May 1, 1818 (Laurens Dist) John Frederick Kern (Laurens Dist) to Livingston Bobo (Spartanburgh); for $770 sold 440 ac on waters of Tyger R; grant Dec. 12, 1788 to John Daniel Kern and resurveyed Mar. 13, 1818 by Gen. Elmore. Witness Tillman Bobo and P. D. Kern. Signed John Frederick Kern. Wit. oath Apr. 5, 1824 Tillman Bobo to James Hamm. Rec. May 3, 1824. Dower renounced May 5, 1818 (Laurens Dist) Elizabeth Kern to John A Elmore

p. 346 Feb. 20, 1824 Abner Benson (Spartanburgh) to Robert H Goldthwaite (late of Lexington Dist); for $1 sold (1) 5 ac on waters of Chuquapin Br of Lawson's fork; and (2) 20 ac on waters of Chuquapin Br of Lawson's fork; border: Lincoln Road to Spartanburgh Court House. Witness James Hunt and B. L. Goodman. Signed Abner Benson. Wit. oath Feb. 20, 1824 B. L. Goodman to James Ed Henry. Rec. May 15, 1824

p. 346-347 Feb. 20, 1824 Abner Benson (Spartanburgh) to Robert H Goldthwaite (late of Lexington Dist); for $1,000 sold 100 ac on branch of Chinquepin Cr of Lawson's fork. Witness James Hunt and B. L. Goodman. Signed Abner Benson. Wit. oath Feb. 20, 1824 B. L. Goodman to James Ed Henry. Rec. May 15, 1824

p. 347-348 Mar. 1, 1824 Richard Thomson (Spartanburgh) to Robert H Goldthwaite (Spartanburgh); for $75 sold 1 ac near Spartanburgh, SC; border: Robert H Goldthwait's house; on corner of grant to Thomas Williamson. Witness John Poole and Thomas Poole. Signed Richard Thomson. Wit. oath Mar. 8, 1824 John Poole to James Ed Henry. Rec. May 15, 1824. Dower renounced Mar. (omitted), 1824 Polly Thompson (sic) to James Ed Henry

p. 348-349 Feb. 20, 1824 Ephraim Roddy (Spartanburgh) to Robert H Goldthwaite (Spartanburgh); for $3,000 sold 187 ac; border: road from the Court House to McKie's Mill, Dr Young, and branch of Chinquepin Cr. Witness James Hunt and B. L. Goodman. Signed E Roddy. Wit. oath Feb. 20, 1824 B. L. Goodman to James Ed Henry. Rec. May 15, 1823

p. 349 Nov. 13, 1823 James Burnett jr (Spartanburgh) to Enoch Brannon and Thomas Brannon (same); for $350 sold 160 ac; border: Samuel Sentell; where William Davis lives; (grant?) to Leonard Carden sr and Jordan Corden. Witness John Burnett sr and W Bennett. Signed James Burnett jr's mark. Wit. oath Apr. 25, 1824 John Burnett sr to W Clement. Rec. May 15, 1824

p. 349-350 Aug. 20, 1822 Richard Thomson (Spartanburgh) to Jesse Cleveland (same); for $200 sold 3½ ac in Spartanburgh, SC; border: S of Jesse Cleveland's house allowing 50 feet for a street between lots, Joal lot, and Thomas Boole(sic). Witness Jesse F Cleveland and Elisha Bomar. Signed Richard Thomson. Wit. oath Apr. 20, 1824 Jesse F Cleveland to E Bomar. Rec. May 20, 1824. Dower renounced Mar. 8, 1824 Polly Thomson to James Ed Henry

p. 350-351 Feb. 16, 1822 John McAbee (Spartanburgh) to Joshua Tapp; for $280 sold 63 ac on waters of N Tyger R; border: N-Joshua Tapp, S-Dr A. B. Moore, E-James McAbee, and NE-Joshua Tapp. Witness William Trimmier esq and Elisha Bomar. Signed John McAbee. Wit. oath Feb. 16, 1824 William Trimmier to E Bomar. Rec. May 21, 1824

p. 351-352 Oct. 12, 1816 Robert William (Spartanburgh) to Hugh McBride (same); for $1,500 sold 230 ac on N Pacolate R; where Robert William lives; of which 170 ac was grant to Robert William and 60 ac was grant to Andrew Millican who sold to Robert Millican. Witness Christopher Golightly, Isaac McBride, and Thomas Millican. Signed Robert Millican. Wit. oath Mar. 12, 1824 Christopher Golightly to J Whitten. Rec. May 25, 1824. Dower renounced Mar. 1, 1817 Nancy Millican to James Young

p. 352-353 Oct. 6, 1823 Thomas Poole, sheriff (Spartanburgh) to Dr John P Evins (same); for $53 sold 140 ac on waters of Tyger R; border: W-McHug, E-David Tippen, and SE-Thomas Gaston; land was William Pearson's; bought by Blake Carlton for Dr John P Evins; sold due to writ from Spartanburgh Common Pleas Court second Monday after fourth Monday in Mar. 1822 suit Anthony Pearson vs William Pearson; judgment was levy of $123 and costs from William and Joseph Pearson. Witness John T Earle and Theron Earle. Signed Thomas Poole SSD. Wit. oath May 28, 1824 John T Earle to E Bomar. Rec. May 28, 1824

p. 353-354 Jan. 1, 1824 Isaac Johnson (Spartanburgh) to James Nesbitt (same); for $50 sold 16 ac on James Nesbitt's Spring Br;

border: Aries Brown (now Isaac Johnson), Joseph Collins, and James Nesbitt. Witness James Chamblin and Samuel Pearson. Signed Isaac Johnson. Wit. oath Jan. 2, 1824 James Chamblin to F. H. Legg. Rec. May 29, 1824. Dower renounced Jan. 2, 1824 Nancy Johnson to F. H. Legg

p. 354 Jan. 1, 1824 Isaac Johnson (Spartanburgh) to James Nesbitt (same); for $900 sold 100 ac on Middle Tyger R; border: John Collins, James Nesbitt, and Joseph Collins; plat certified Jul. 25, 1786 by Andrew Thompson (not attached). Witness James Chamblin and Samuel Pearson. Signed Isaac Johnson. Wit. oath Jan. 2, 1824 James Chamblin to F. H. Legg. Rec. May 29, 1824. Dower renounced Jan. 2, 1824 Nancy Johnson to F. H. Legg

p. 354-357 (p. 355 & 356 omitted from book) Sept. 28, 1821 Moses Tapp (Spartanburgh) to John Gideons (same); for $225 sold 100 ac; border: Blackstocks Road, John Hammett, and Selmon. Witness James Yates and Thomas McCarley. Signed Moses Tapp. Wit. oath Mar. 13, 1824 James Yates to Ransom Foster. Rec. Jun. 4, 1824

p. 357-358 Sept. 28, 1821 Moses Tapp (Spartanburgh) to Joshua Tapp (same); for $240 sold 120 ac; border: John Hemmett, Moses Tapp, James Haskins, Smith, and McAbee. Witness James Yates and Thomas McCarley. Signed Moses Tapp. Wit. oath Mar. 13, 1824 James Yates to Ransom Foster. Rec. Jun. 4, 1824

p. 358 Sept. 28, 1821 Moses Tapp (Spartanburgh) to James Haskins (or Hoskins) (same); for $250 sold 110 ac; border: Joshua Tapp, Smith, Blackstock's Road, and Richason Vincent. Witness James Yates and Thomas McCarley. Signed Moses Tapp. Wit. oath Mar. 13, 1824 James Yates to Ransom Foster. Rec. Jun. 4, 1824

p. 358-359 Jan. 31, 1824 Samuel N Evans (Spartanburgh) to Howel Johnson (same); for $100 sold 156 ac; border: David Drummond and James Miller. Witness Charles H Moore and Isaac Snoddy. Signed Samuel N Evins. Wit. oath Jun. 7, 1824 Charles H Moore to Wm Underwood. Rec. Jun. 7, 1824

p. 359-360 Jan. 24, 1824 William McKinney (Rutherford Co, NC) to Abraham Crow (Spartanburgh); for $500 sold 225 ac on little Buck Cr of Pacolate R. Witness Lewis Brown and Jonathan McKinney. Signed Wm McKinney. Wit. oath Apr. 5, 1824 Lewis Brown to Robert Ligon. Rec. Jun. 7, 1824

p. 360 Mar. 5, 1822 John McElrath (Spartanburgh) to John Smith (same); for $219 sold 108 ac on N side of Middle Tyger R; part of grant Dec. 24, 1772 to Elias Foison who sold to James Smith who sold Feb. 20, 1805 to John McElrath. Witness William Smith and William McElrath. Signed John McElrath. Wit. oath Jul. 6, 1822 William Smith to John Burns. Rec. Jun. 7, 1824

p. 360-361 Feb. 28, 1824 John Cathcart (Spartanburgh) to John Williams; for $310(sic) in three notes dated Nov. 24, 1821--first payable in 13 months ($150), second payable in 25 months ($114.58), and third payable in 37 months ($182.37½) and to secure payment sold 179 ac on N side of Tyger R; "granted" Nov. 24, 1824 John Williams to John Cathcart; Condition: sale void if John Cathcart pays debt. Witness John Clark and Moses White. Signed John Cathcart. Wit. oath Jun. 5, 1824 Moses White to Joseph Wofford. Rec. Jun. 7, 1824

p. 361-362 Jan. 24, 1824 Jesse Delany (or John M Delany) (Spartanburgh) to John Johnson sr; for $80 sold 2 cows and a rearling, 2 feather beds and furniture--consisting of 4 coverlets, 5 red quilts, 2 bed blankets, 7 sheets, 4 pillows, 2 bedsteds and cords, 3 sheep, a pine cupboard, 6 earthen plates, 4 pewter plates, 8 bowls, 5 basons, a set of tea ware, a large pitcher, 2 cream pots, a mug, a coffee mill, 4 glasses, a coffee pot, 2 decanters, a dish, a bread water, a brass candlestick, a set of knives and forks, a chest, a table, tub, pail, piggin, pot, oven, 3 chears, a wheel and cords,a "sad" iron, and a frying pan; Condition: sale void if Jesse Delany pays debt by Dec. 25, 1825. Witness Thomas H Bennett and Samuel Johnson. Signed Jesse Delany. Wit. oath Jan. 28, 1824 Samuel Johnson to Thomas Wood. Rec. Jun. 7, 1824

p. 362-363 Jan. 31, 1824 Howell Johnson (Spartanburgh) to Matthew P Evins (same); for $300 sold 156 ac; border: David Drummond, Samuel N Evins, and Miller. Witness Charles H Moore and Isaac Snoddy. Signed Howell Johnson. Wit. oath Feb. 2, 1824 Charles H Moore to F. H. Legg. Rec. Jun. 7, 1824. Dower renounced Feb. 2, 1824 Holly Johnson to F. H. Legg

p. 363-364 Jan. 12, 1824 John Burnett (Spartanburgh) to Edward Turner shoemaker (same); for $60 sold (ac omitted) on waters of Pacolate R. Witness Turner W Warren and Carter Burnett. Signed John Burnett. Wit. oath Jun. 11, 1824 Turner W Warren to James Foster. Rec. Jul. 5, 1824

p. 364 Nov. 8, 1823 Clemuel Powell (Spartanburgh) to Adam Grambling (same); for $35 sold 100 ac on waters of Lawson's fork; border: George Bishop; part of tract sold by George and William McDowell, heirs of William McDowell desc, to John Burd who sold to William Bishop who sold to Joseph Evitts who sold to Clemuel Powell. Witness John Murph and Zachariah McDaniel. Signed Clemuel Powell's mark. Wit. oath Mar. 5, 1824 Zachariah McDaniel to A Shands. Rec. Jul. 5, 1824. Dower renounced (omitted), 1824 Nancy Powell to (not signed)

p. 364-365 Jul. 21, 1823 Henry Smith (Spartanburgh) to James Crook esq; for $731.25 sold 295½ ac on S(sic) side of Tyger R; border: Augusta Road, W, N & NE-James Crook, W-Tyger R, and S-Joseph Miller and widow Otts. Witness William Otts, Mathias Rush, and Hoseah J Dean. Signed Henry W Smith. Wit. oath Jul. 5, 1824 Mathias Rush to Robert Ligon. Rec. Jul. 5, 1824

p. 365 Feb. 14, 1824 Jordan Morris (Spartanburgh) to Reuben Gilbert (same); for $300 sold 220 ac on Buck Cr of Pacolate R; border: Joseph Morris, William Jordan, Back Br, and John Morris. Witness Joseph B Morris and Joa Haynes. Signed Jordan Morris. Wit. oath Mar. 6, 1824 Joseph B Morris to Wm Dobbins. Rec. Jul. 5, 1824

p. 365-366 Jul. 14, 1826 Thomas Poole, sheriff (Spartanburgh) to Edmund Cooley (same); for $21 sold 100 ac on Bird's Cr of Pacolate R; border: James Lawrence sr; sold due to writ from Spartanburgh Common Pleas Court second Monday after fourth Monday in Mar. 1822 suit of Michael Moore vs James Lawrence jr and Peggy Ford; judgment was levy of $45 and costs from James Lawrence jr. Witness Memory N Chapman and Richard Thompson. Signed Thomas Poole SSD. Wit. oath Jul. 6, 1824 Memory N Chapman to J. W. Farrow. Rec. Jul. 6, 1824

p. 366-367 Sept. 13, 1823 Isaac Pennington (Spartanburgh) to Sarah Cayle (same); for $40 sold 68 ac on People's Cr of Broad R; border: Worshman, Gaffney, and McKie; grant Apr. 6, 1815 to Isaac Pennington. Witness Isaac Peeter and Catherine Colewell. Signed Isaac Pennington and wife Judith's mark. Wit. oath Jan. 3, 1824 Isaac Peeter to J Camp. Rec. Jul. 6, 1824

p. 367-368 Mar. 31, 1824 Isaac Lindsey and wife Elizabeth to Benjamin Poole; to secure note of $105 and interest dated Dec. 25,

1823 sold a dark colored cow, 2 feather beds, bedsteads, and furniture, 2 rose blankets, a large oven, 2 pots, a set of fire irons, a spinning sheel, a saddle, a blanket, 4 chairs, a shot gun, a chest, 2 water pails, a washing tub, 2 hogsheads, a loom, 2 small hogs, a set of "shelow", 5 plates, a pitcher, 2 bowls, a pewter dish, 3 cups and saucers, and a stand of curtains; Condition: sale void if Isaac Lindsey and Elizabeth pay debt. Witness John Parks and James Smith. Signed Isaac Lindsey and Elizabeth's mark. Wit. oath Jun. 15, 1824 James Smith to Caleb Jones. Rec. Jul. 6, 1824

p. 368 Feb. 5, 1821 John Low sr promises to pay Felix Dewberry $31.12½ in three days. Witness Reuben Warren. Signed John Low. Feb. 5, 1824 John Low sr (Spartanburgh) to Felix Dewberry; to secure payment of above, mortgage 120 ac; border: Mary Dewberry, Warren, Wyatt, and Buck's Br. Witness Hugh Moore sr and Reuben Warren sr. Signed John Low. Wit. oath Jul. 5, 1824 Hugh Moore sr to Lee Linder. Rec. Jul. 6, 1824

p. 368-369 Jan. 16, 1824 Patrick Sanders (Spartanburgh) to William Thomas (same); for $32 sold 13 ac on W side of Thickety Cr. Witness Moses Weber and Jeremiah Sanders. Signed Patrick Sanders' mark. Wit. oath Feb. 28, 1824 Moses Weber to J Camp. Rec. Jul. 8, 1824

p. 369-370 Dec. 27, 1823 Floyd Tanner (Spartanburgh) to Joel Yates (same); for $625 sold 500 ac on waters of Holson Br of Fairforest Cr; grant to John Evins. Witness John Foster MC, William Yates, and John Rutland. Signed Floyd Tanner. Wit. oath Jan. 7, 1824 John Foster MC to F. H. Legg. Rec. Jul. 18, 1824. Dower renounced Jun. 7, 1824 Judith Tanner to F. H. Legg

p. 370-371 Dec. 10, 1821 John Lucas (Spartanburgh) to James Whitten (same); for $400 sold 116 ac on S side of S Pacolate R; border: B Grogan. Witness Kinsey Lucas, Richard Coggins, and John Lucas jr. Signed John Lucas. Wit. oath Jul. 7, 1824 John Lucas jr to Wm Holcombe. Rec. Jul. 12, 1824

p. 371 Nov. 8, 1823 Zachariah McDaniel received full amount of mortgage from Clemuel Powell. Witness none. Signed Z McDaniel. Wit. oath Apr. 20, 1824 John Murph to D White. Rec. Jul. 12, 1824

p. 371-372 Jan. 13, 1824 Hugh Moore sr to John Low sr (Spartanburgh); for "given in part payments of a military tract of 2,560 ac in Tennessee" which John Low sr is entitled to for Revolutionary service sold (ac omitted or maybe 409 ac); border: Mary Dewberry, Warren, Wyatt, Buck Br, and path from John Low sr to Mary Dewberry; part of (409? ac) grant to Jonathan Low jr and sold by heirs to John Low sr who sold to John Low jr who sold to Hugh Moore sr. Witness Lee Linder and John Linder. Signed Hugh Moore sr. Wit. oath Jan. 13, 1824 John Linder to Lee Linder. Rec. Jul. 27, 1824

p. 372 Mar. 8, 1824 Enoch Smith (Spartanburgh) to Orinah Hembree (same); for $130 sold 50 ac; border: Coverey's county survey; part of 383 ac grant to Hopkins Bright who sold to Burton who sold to William Hembree who sold to Enoch Smith. Witness William W Hembree and Jesse Vaughan. Signed Enoch Smith. Wit. oath Mar. 20, 1824 William W Hembree to John Brewton. Rec. Jul. 28, 1824. Dower renounced Jul. 17, 1824 Abigail Smith to John Brewton

p. 372-373 Feb. 5, 1824 Jesse Cleveland (Spartanburgh) to Thomas Poole (same); for $84 sold 140 ac; border: W-E Roddy, N-Jesse Cleveland, E-Mary Lee, and S-George Jones; sold by Thomas Allison to Muse Tollison. Witness James Hunt and Memory N Chapman. Signed Jesse Cleveland. Wit. oath Jul. 29, 1824 James Hunt to James E Henry. Rec. Jul. 29, 1824

p. 373-374 Aug. 2, 1824 Sarah Bishop (Spartanburgh) to Lovely Bishop (female) (same); for love and affection give a bed and furniture, household and kitchen furniture, stock: a cow and her increase, 6 hogs, and the part of land where Sarah Bishop lives. Witness Joseph Keller and James Bishop. Signed Sarah Bishop's mark. Wit. oath Aug. 2, 1824 Joseph Keller to J Whitten. Rec. Aug. 2, 1824

p. 374 Feb. (blank), 1820 William White (Union Dist) to James Gossett (Spartanburgh); for $700 sold 188 ac on Harris' Cr of Fairforest Cr; border: Cruise and Robert Donaldson; grant in 1784 to (omitted). Witness Robert White and Fielding Gossett. Signed William White. Wit. oath Dec. 31, 1823 Robert White to William Ried. Rec. Aug. 2, 1824

p. 374-375 Feb. 9, 1824 Willis Vaughan (Spartanburgh) to Asa Vaughan; for $50 sold 30 ac on waters of Ben's Cr; border: John Durham, Denny Anderson, William Anderson, Anderson's Road, and the Main Road. Witness Philip Johnson and John Durham. Signed Willis Vaughan's mark. Wit. oath Jun. 3, 1824 Philip Johnson to James Ford. Rec. Aug. 2, 1824

p. 375 Jan. 14, 1824 Jacob Crocker (Spartanburgh) to Thomas Thomas (same); for $50 sold 211 ac; border: James Crocker and Jeremiah Martin. Witness Nathan Byars and Shadrick Weer. Signed Jacob Crocker. Wit. oath Jan. 14, 1824 Nathan Byars to Joseph Camp. Rec. Aug. 2, 1824

p. 375-376 Aug. 15, 1822 Richard Jentry (Spartanburgh) to John Mason (same); for $56 sold 14 ac; border: N & E-Richard Jentry, S-John Mason, and W-Jemima King. Witness William Otts and William Mason. Signed Richard Jentry's mark. Wit. oath Mar. 13, 1824 William Mason to John Dean. Rec. Aug. 2, 1824

p. 376 Aug. 2, 1824 Joel Yates (Spartanburgh) to William Yates; for $125 sold 100 ac on waters of Fairforest Cr; part of tract Floyd Tanner sold to Joel Yates. Witness William Tapp and Martin Otts. Signed Joel Yates. Wit. oath Aug. 2, 1824 William Tapp to W Hunt. Rec. Aug. 2, 1824

p. 376-377 Feb. 11, 1824 Elizabeth Wingo and Nancy Seay (Spartanburgh) to George Killock (same); for $100 sold 115 ac on N side of Fairforest Cr; part of land formerly belonging to Gideon Seay desc. Witness Joel Foster, Elijah McMillin, and Daniel Brice. Signed John J Seay and Nancy and Elizabeth Wingo's marks. Wit. oath Aug. 3, 1824(sic) Joel Foster to F. H. Legg. Rec. Aug. 2, 1824

p. 377-378 Apr. 6, 1824 Isaac Crow (Spartanburgh) to Benjamin Wofford; to secure debt of $449.60 due to notes dated Feb. 25, 1824 and due Dec. 25, 1824 sold 952 ac; on Main Charleston Road and branches of James and Two Mile Creeks; where Isaac Crow lives; Condition: sale void if Isaac Crow pays debt. Witness Thomas Craven and James King jr. Signed Isaac Crow. Wit. oath Jul. 9, 1824 James King jr to Wm Young. Rec. Aug. 2, 1824

p. 378-379 Feb. 23, 1824 Joel Lewis (Spartanburgh) to brother-in-law Thomas Green (late of Philadelphia); for consideration Joel Lewis "knows" leased for 20 years 20 ac on side of Lochart's Br; border: about 385 or 390 yards below ford of Lochart's Br above Robin Lochart's old cabin, Mary Lewis, road to Peggy Lewis', and near where Thomas Green lives; Thomas Green can clear and cultivate as much as he wants and make improvements; Joel Lewis gets land back if Thomas Green leaves in less than 20 years. Witness John Lewis and Catharine Lewis. Signed Joel Lewis. Wit. oath Jul. 5, 1824 John Lewis to John S Rowland. Rec. Aug. 2, 1824

p. 379-380 Feb. 22, 1819 John McElrath (Spartanburgh) to John Smith (same); for $328 sold 175 ac on N side of Middle Tyger R; part of grant Dec. 24, 1772 to Edward Blake who sold Mar. 2, 1774 to Thomas Woodward who sold Jan. 8, 1793 to John McElrath. Witness William McElrath and William Smith. Signed John McElrath. Wit. oath Nov. 2, 1819 William McElrath to John Collins. Rec. Aug. 2, 1824. Dower renounced Nov. 9, 1819 Rachael McElrath to John Collins

p. 380-381 Feb. 5, 1824 Thomas Grisham (Spartanburgh) to John S Coan (same); for $130 sold 30 ac on N side of S Tyger R. Witness R. N. Hadden and Sally Patton. Signed Thomas Grisham. Wit. oath May 8, 1824 R. N. Hadden to F. H. Legg. Rec. Aug. 2, 1824. Dower renounced Jun. (blank), 1824 Jane Grisham to F. H. Legg

p. 381-382 Feb. 5, 1824 John Collins esq (Spartanburgh) to John S Coan (same); for $597 sold 199 ac on N side of S Tyger R; border: NE & NW-John Collins and SE-Samuel Pearson and Thomas Grisham; part of grant Apr. 2, 1773 to Daniel Heyward; resurveyed Feb. 16, 1808 by Wm Dunlap. Witness Thomas Grisham, James Swanzy, and R. N. Hadden. Signed John Collins. Wit. oath May 8, 1824 R. N. Hadden to F. H. Legg. Rec. Aug. 2, 1824. Dower renounced Jun. 1, 1824 Elizabeth Collins to F. H. Legg

p. 382-383 Jul. 23, 1824 Catharine Gossett, Fielder Gossett, Sunbury Gossett, Asbury Gossett, and Elijah Gossett (Spartanburgh), widow and sons of James Gossett (late same), to David R Burns (same); for $500 sold 188 ac in Union and Spartanburgh Dists on Harris Cr of Fairforest Cr; border: Cruce and Robert Donaldson; grant in 1784 to (omitted). Witness Jonathan Chosewood, David Reed, and John Harmon. Signed Catharine Gossett's mark, Gielder Gossett, Sonbury Gossett, Asbury Gossett, and Elijah Gossett. Witness Jul. 27, 1824 Jonathan Chosewood to William Ried. Rec. Aug. 2, 1824

p. 383-384 Mar. 8, 1824 Richard Thomson (Spartanburgh) to Miles Furgason (Lawrence Dist); for $1,500 sold 400 ac on Tyger R near the Factory; known as Bell hall plantation; "held by" Elias Palmer and sold by sheriff. Witness James Ed Henry and J Sprowl. Signed Richard Thomson. Wit. oath Mar. 8, 1824 James Ed Henry to E Bomar. Rec. Aug. 23, 1824. Dower renounced Mar. 8, 1824 Polly Thomson to E Bomar

p. 384-385 Mar. 3, 1824 William and Abraham Cantrill, administrators of estate of John Cantrill desc (one from Spartanburgh and the other from Warren Co, Tenn) to Mark Cantrill (Spartanburgh); for $50 sold 30 ac on Pacolate R. Witness Martin Cantrill and John Calvert. Signed Wm Cantrill and Abraham Cantrill. Wit. oath Aug. 28, 1824 John Calvert to James Foster. Rec. Aug. 31, 1824

p. 385 Mar. 3, 1824 William and Abraham Cantrill, administrators of estate of John Cantrill desc (one of Spartanburgh and other of Warren Co, Tenn) to Mark Cantrill (Spartanburgh); for $100 sold 100 ac on branch of Pacolate R. Witness Martin Cantrill and John Calvert. Signed Wm Cantrill and Abraham Cantrill. Wit. oath Aug. 28, 1824 John Calvert to James Foster. Rec. Aug. 31, 1824

p. 385-386 Mar. 15, 1824 Susannah Barnett (Spartanburgh), widow to John Murph (same); for $50 sold dower rights to 90½ ac on Kelso's Cr of Fairforest Cr; border: formerly Jane Smith's corner and formerly Robt Martin's field. Witness John Harmon and Abedingo Felkel. Signed Susannah Burnett. Wit. oath Sept. 4, 1824 John Harmon to Augustin Shands. Rec. Sept. 6, 1824

p. 386-387 Aug. 16, 1824 Moses Simmons (Rutherford Co, NC) to Lewis Peoples (same); for $200 sold 118 ac on W side of Buck Cr; border: formerly Thomas Gore's and John Nelson's lines and road to Camp's Bridge. Witness Daniel Blackwell and Edward Simmons. Signed Moses Simmons. Wit. oath Aug. 16, 1824 Edward Simmons to Geo Camp. Rec. Sept. 6, 1824. Dower renounced Aug. 16, 1824 Mary Simmons to George Camp.

p. 387-388 Jun. 20, 1824 John Foster jr (Spartanburgh) to Joel Foster (same); for $100 sold 100 ac on Mill Cr of Tyger R; border: Bagwell, Tanner, and Miller. Witness W. T. Tanner and Mariah Timmons. Signed John Foster. Wit. oath Sept. 6, 1824 W. T. Tanner to W Hunt. Rec. Sept. 6, 1824

p. 388-389 Sept. 29, 1823 William Thomas (Spartanburgh) to John Eison (same); for $70 sold 160 ac on both sides Foster's Cr on N side Fairforest Cr; border: N-Henry Foster, S-Henry Foster and John Eison jr, E-George Story, and W-Joseph Hays; of which 40 ac was grant to Joseph Wade and 120 ac was grant to William Burton who sold to Joseph Wade and 160 ac sold to William Thomas, grandson of Joseph Wade. Witness Mitchell Jackson and Jno(?) Kinningham. Signed William Thomas' mark. Wit. oath Sept. 29, 1823 (Franklin Co, Tenn) J. C. Pryor JP. Sept. 29, 1823 (Franklin Co, Tenn) Edmond Russell,clerk of Quarterly Sessions Court, certifys J. C. Pryor is Justice of Peace. May 3, 1824 (Tenn) James Sharp, presiding justice of Quarterly Sessions Court, certifys Edmond Russell is clerk. Rec. Sept. 6, 1824

p. 389-390 Aug. 7, 1824 William Grant (Spartanburgh) to daughter Rachal Clark, wife of John Clark (same); for good causes give a (ink blotch) colored boy Briant, 2 horses, a cow and calf, all his hogs, 3 beds and furniture, 2/3 of William Grant's corn crop, all household furniture, farming utensils, and kitchen furniture. Witness William Posey and James Powers. Signed Wm Grant. Wit. oath Sept. 6, 1824 James Powers to John Brewton. Rec. Sept. 6, 1824

p. 390 Aug. 13, 1824 Richard Daniel jr (Spartanburgh) to Kinsmon Seay (same); for $131 sold 63 ac on waters of Fairforest Cr; border: James Seay. Witness Richard Thomson and Wm N Story. Signed Richard Daniel jr. Wit. oath Sept. 6, 1824 Wm N Story to E Bomar. Rec. Sept. 6, 1824

p. 390-391 Jun. 5, 1824 Elias Corder (Spartanburgh) to Thomas Thomas; for $300 sold 100 ac on waters of Forgerson's Cr; border: William Otts, Young Scott, John Skinner, James Mason, James Scott, Georgia Road, Floyd's Br, and Corder's Spring Br. Witness James Nesbitt and John Skinner. Signed Elias Corder. Wit. oath Sept. 6, 1824 James Nesbitt to J Whitten. Rec. Sept. 6, 1824. Dower renounced Aug. 14, 1824 Ann Corder to John Brewton

p. 391-392 Jan. 14, 1824 Reuben Warren (Spartanburgh) to Arthur Warren; for $78.78 sold 50 ac on Low's Br of Pacolate R; border: John Low Tollison, and Linder. Witness John Low sr and John Low jr. Signed Reuben Warren. Wit. oath Sept. 1, 1824 John Low jr to Lee Linder. Rec. Sept. 6, 1824

p. 392-393 Jan. 12, 1824 Reuben Warren and Lott Warren (Spartanburgh) to Arthur Warren; for $81.94 sold 100 ac on W side Island Cr of Pacolate R; border: William Lackey. Witness Reuben Warren jr and Felix Dewberry. Signed Reuben Warren and Lott Warren. Wit. oath Aug. 31, 1824 Felix Dewberry to Lee Linder. Rec. Sept. 6, 1824

p. 393 May 25, 1824 William Caldwell (Newberry Dist) to Ephraim Drummond (Spartanburgh); for $571.75 sold 321 ac on waters of Enoree R; border: Burrell, John Shands, and Samuel Woodruff; tract was 324 ac but 3 ac was sold by Samuel Woodruff sr; grant Jun. 23, 1774 by Edward Penman (sic) to Robert Philip who sold to Alexander McDowell and sold by representatives of McDowell "say" (or to?)

William Caldwell. Witness Mathew Allen and Samuel Woodruff sr. Signed Wm Caldwell jr. Wit. oath Jul. 10, 1824 Mathew Allen to James Crook. Rec. Sept. 6, 1823

p. 393-394 Feb. 9, 1822 James Hunt, sheriff (Spartanburgh) to Daniel McKie (same); for $170 sold 200 ac on waters of Enoree R; border: Daniel McKie and James Ford; sold by Daniel McKie to Henry Pearson; sold due to writ from Spartanburgh Common Pleas Court second Monday after fourth Monday in Mar. 1821 suit of Daniel McKie; judgment was levy of $414 and costs from Henry Pearson. Witness John Bomar jr and Willis Foster. Signed Jas Hunt SSD. Wit. oath Sept. (omitted), 1824 John Bomar jr to James E Henry. Rec. Sept. 6, 1824

p. 394-395 Jan. 29, 1823 John Payne (Spartanburgh) to Moses Simmons (Rutherford Co, NC); for $300 sold 118 ac on W side of Buck Cr; border: Thomas Gore, John Nelson, and Camp's bridge. Witness Charles Simmons, Edward Simmons, and Richard Scrugs. Signed John Payne and Philadelphia's mark. Wit. oath Edward Simmons to Geo Camp Aug. 16, 1824. Wit. oath Aug. 14, 1824 Charles Simmons to Geo Camp. Rec. Sept. 6, 1824

p. 395-397 Jun. 5, 1824 Thomas Poole, sheriff (Spartanburgh) to David Golightly sr; for $1 sold 333 ac in two parts: (1) 133 ac; border: mouth of Buffalow Cr of Fairforest Cr; (2) 200 ac; border William Lancaster; bought by William W Harris for David Golightly sr; sold due to writ from Spartanburgh Common Pleas Court second Monday after fourth Monday in Oct. 1823 suit of John Dunlap; judgment was levy of $33 from William T Broderick. Witness John Poole and Memory N Chapman. Signed Thomas Poole SSD. Wit. oath Sept. 18, 1824 John Poole to E Bomar. Rec. Sept. 18, 1824

p. 397-398 May 18, 1816 John Oneill (Spartanburgh) to Robert Love (same); for $400 sold (1) 207 ac on waters of Fairforest Cr; border: tree marked "ƗC"; where his mother Hannah Oneill lives; John Oneill owns land after Hannah dies; part of grant Feb. 23, 1854 to George Gillaspy and "audited" in South Carolina Auditor General Books Feb. 27, 1775 and sold to his father Henry ONeill and willed to Hannah during her lifetime and at her death to John Oneill; and (2) 25½ ac "descended as above"; on Culbertson's Still House Br; border: Samuel Culbertson and Henry ONeill. Witness Daniel White esq and Willis Wingo. Signed John ONeill. Wit. oath Aug. 21, 1824 Daniel White to John Eison. Rec. Sept. 29, 1824

p. 398-399 Sept. 9, 1824 Thomas Poole, sheriff (Spartanburgh) to Reuben Daniel (same); for $60 sold 102 ac on waters of Fairforest Cr; border: Reuben Daniel and Thomas Tinsley; known as the Berry tract; bought by John Wells for Reuben Daniel; sold due to writ from Spartanburgh Common Pleas Court second Monday after fourth Monday in Oct. 1822 suit of Adam Buis; judgment was levy of $49 and costs from Muse Tollison. Witness Jesse F Cleveland and Simpson Bobo. Signed Thomas Poole SSD. Wit. oath Oct. 4, 1824 Jesse F Cleveland to E Bomar. Rec. Oct. 4, 1824

p. 399-400 Aug. 21, 1824 Thomas Poole, sheriff (Spartanburgh) to James E Henry (same); for $80 sold ½ ac in Spartanburgh, SC on S side of Main St; border: N-Main St, W-½ ac lot bought by M. N. Chapman, and S & E-Richard Thomson; sold due to writ from Spartanburgh Common Pleas Court second Monday after fourth Monday in Oct. 1822 suit of James Keene; judgment was levy of $143 from Muse Tollison. Witness Jesse F Cleveland to Thomas Gray. Signed Thomas Poole SSD. Wit. oath Sept. 23, 1824 Thomas Gray to J. W. Farrow. Rec. Oct. 4, 1824

p. 400-401 May 24, 1824 William Cantrill (Spartanburgh) to William

Jackson (same); for $1,500 sold 175 ac on N Pacolate R; border: S-William Wilkins and Hugh McMullin, W-George McWilliams and James Camp, and N & E-William Cantrill. Witness William Cantrell jr and James Jackson. Signed William Cantrell. Wit. oath Jan. 13, 1824 William Cantrell jr to James Young. Rec. Oct. 4, 1824 Dower renounced Elizabeth Cantrell to James Young Jan. 13, 1824

p. 401-402 Aug. 6, 1824 Catharine Smith (Spartanburgh) to Robert Creswell and Elihu Creswell, Nathaniel Marion, John Black, William Caldwell, James Sprowl, and James Shackelford; for $700 sold 138 ac; includes Cedar Springs; part of which was assigned to Catharine Smith by Partition Commissioner from her father's land (lot #6). Witness Robert White and Mary G White. Signed Catharine Smith. Wit. oath Oct. 4, 1824 Robert White to E Bomar. Rec. Oct. 4, 1824

p. 402 Jan. 3, 1824 Paul Combee and Ann P Wilmott (SC) to Robert Ligon (Spartanburgh); for $500 sold 1/3 of their interest in extate of Ann Price desc; "formerly" estate of Thomas Price desc. Witness Paul Castleberry and William Glassy. Signed Paul Combee and Ann Wilmott's mark. Wit. oath Apr. 9, 1824 William Glassy to Ransom Foster. Rec. Oct. 4, 1824

p. 402-403 Sept. 6, 1824 Paul Combee to Robert Ligon (SC); for $300 sold his interest (or 1/3 of Paul Combee's claims) in estate of Ann Price desc; Paul's interest is land N of Georgia road on both sides of Crook's roads; Ann Price (late of Spartanburgh) left Ann Caster, Rachel Stedding, and Paul Combee as only relations; if Paul gets nothing, Robert Ligon loses the money anyway. Witness John Wright and John D Murphy. Signed Paul Combee. Wit. oath Oct. 4, 1824 John Wright to James Crook. Rec. Oct. 4, 1824

p. 403-404 Sept. 6, 1824 Ann P Wilmott to Robert Ligon (SC); for $350 sold all Ann P Wilmott's interest in estate of Ann Price on SW of Forgason's Cr; Ann Price desc (late of Spartanburgh) died with only relations being Ann Caster, Rachel Stedding, and Paul Combee; Robert Ligon loses the money if Ann P Wilmott gets nothing from estate. Witness John Wright and John D Murphy. Signed Ann P Wilmott's mark. Wit. oath Oct. 4, 1824 John Wright to James Crook. Rec. Oct. 4, 1824

p. 404 Oct. 9, 1824 John Linder sr (Spartanburgh) to son John Linder jr; for (omitted) give a Negro girl Viney after John Linder dies. Witness Samuel Linder and Reuben Bowden. Signed John Linder. Wit. oath Oct. 9, 1824 Samuel Linder to Lee Linder. Rec. Oct. 11, 1824

p. 404-405 Apr. 13, 1824 Lewis Vaughan to John Baldwin; for $23.60 due to John Baldwin that remains in arrers for last year's rent on land where Lewis Vaughan lives mortgaged a sorrel mare with a blaze face, a sorrel horse colt, 2 "likely" red cows, all his sheep, all household and kitchen furniture, all farming tools, and all chattles; Condition: sale void if Lewis Vaughan pays debt to John Baldwin by Jan. 1, 1825. Witness Jeremiah Gleen. Signed Lewis Vaughan. Wit. oath Oct. 11, 1824 Jeremiah Gleen to James Ford. Rec. Oct. 12, 1824

p. 405-406 Oct. 13, 1821 Griffin Carter (Spartanburgh) to Joshua Draper (same); for $600 sold 175 ac; NW half of 350 ac grant to David Jones. Witness John Woods and Samuel Wilkins. Signed Griffin Carter. Wit. oath Oct. 13, 1821 John Woods to John Lipscomb. Rec. Oct. 12, 1824. Dower renounced Nov. 5, 1821 Nancy Carter to John Lipscomb

p. 406 Apr. 2, 1824 William Crook (Spartanburgh) to Jeremiah Burnett (same); for $50 sold 50 ac at head of Provies Cr; border: Paden and William Waddle. Witness William Anderson and Elijah Johnson. Signed William Crook. Wit. oath Jul. 17, 1824 William Anderson to Thomas Wood. Rec. Oct. 12, 1824

p. 406-407 Aug. 2, 1824 John Gideans (Spartanburgh) to Hezekiah Seay (same); for (omitted) sold 200 ac on both sides Faun Br of Lawson's fork of Pacolate R; border: John Clement, Markley, Hezekiah Seay, and John Burnett; meeting house and use of spring excepted. Witness Mathew Seay and Cyrus Seay. Signed John Gideans' mark. Wit. oath Aug. 2, 1824 Mathew Seay to W Clement. Rec. Oct. 15, 1824

p. 407 Jan. 31, 1824 Solomon Crocker (Spartanburgh) to Samuel Elsworth (same); for $100 sold 100 ac on waters of Lawson's fork on S side of Pacolet R; border: Wofford's old corner, Rainwaters, old ridge road, Thomas Chapman, Thomas Wells, and Stotte (or Slotte). Witness William Gore to John Crocker. Signed Solomon Crocker's mark. Wit. oath Oct. 12, 1824 William Gore to William Reid. Rec. Oct. 19, 1824

p. 407-408 Mar. 17, 1824 Nathan Hamby (Spartanburgh) to Thomas P Brockman (Greenville Dist); for $177.81¼ sold 175 ac on Rocky Cr on N side Enoree R; border: James Redman; where Nathan Hamby lives; part of 400 ac grant Feb. 9, 1787 to James Cantrill. Witness Andrew McCrary and Henry Brockman. Signed Nathan Hamby's mark. Wit. oath (omitted) 11, 1824 Andrew McCrary to Wm Austin. Rec. Oct. 21, 1824

p. 408-409 Oct. 21, 1824 Peter Haskins (Spartanburgh) to John Gideans (same); for $180 sold 29½ ac on N branches of Tyger R; border:Haskins' Spring Br. Witness John P Miller and James Haskins. Signed Peter Haskins. Wit. oath Oct. 21, 1821 James Haskins to J. W. Farrow. Rec. Oct. 21, 1824

p. 409-410 Dec. 27, 1821 John Hammett sr (Spartanburgh) to Peter Haskins (same); for $500 sold 29½ ac on N branches of Tyger R; border: Hammett's Spring Br. Witness James Haskins and John Gideans. Signed John Hammett. Wit. oath Oct. 20, 1824 John Gideans to Ransom Foster. Rec. Oct. 21, 1824

p. 410-411 Sept. 5, 1820 Mary Ann Otts and son Martin Otts to Andrew Stevens (Spartanburgh); for $120 sold 50 ac on waters of Ward's Cr of Tiger R; border: Capt. Charles Moore and Mary Otts (also legatee of Martin Otts); grant Dec. 17, 1766 to John Miller who sold to Martin Otts desc and to Mary Ann and Martin Otts as his legatees. Witness Daniel Stevens, William Pennings "2nd jr", and John Peace. Signed Martin Otts and Mary Ann's mark. Wit. oath Sept. 6, 1820 John Peace to Wm Underwood. Rec. Oct. 22, 1824

p. 411-412 Aug. 11, 1824 Thomas Poole, sheriff (Spartanburgh) to David R Burns (Union Dist); for $50 sold 130 ac; border: James T McCarter, Elijah Gassett, and Spartanburgh-Union Dist line; sold due to writ from Spartanburgh Common Pleas Court second Monday after fourth Monday in Mar. 1824 suit of Muse and Stephen Tolleson, executors; judgment was levy of $392.38 from Fielder, James, Sunbury, and Elijah Gossett. Witness Jonathan Low and John Poole. Signed Thomas Poole SSD. Wit. oath Oct. 28, 1824 Jonathan Low to E Bomar. Rec. Oct. 29, 1824

p. 412-413 Sept. 14, 1824 Thomas Poole, sheriff (Spartanburgh) to Robert H Goldthwaite (same); for $17.25 sold 140 ac on ridge between Lawson's fork and Pacolate R; border: Moses Shields, Thomas Poole, George Thomason, and estate of William Poole desc; land was Mary Foster's share of "her father's" estate; sold due to writ from Spartanburgh Common Pleas Court second Monday after fourth Monday in Mar. 1824 suit of Hugh Holt; judgment was levy of $42.93 and costs from Mary Foster. Witness John Bomar jr and John Poole. Signed Thomas Poole SSD. Wit. oath Oct. 23, 1824 John Bomar jr to E Bomar. Rec. Oct. 29, 1824

p. 413 Dec. 26, 1823 William Lancaster (Spartanburgh) to son William Harvey Lancaster (same); for good will and affection give 210 ac; border: Charles Smith and Elijah Smith; "includes 75 ac S of the above"; sold by Lawson Thompson to William Lancaster; "respect being paid" to graveyard and Philadelphia Church; "after dividing 70 ac sold to Elijah Smith; the 75 ac borders Charles Smith, Elijah Smith, and the 210 ac tract; total was formerly 280 ac(sic). Witness Theron Lancaster, Ambrose Stone, and Elijah Ballinger. Signed W Lancaster. Wit. oath Nov. 1, 1824 Theron Lancaster to W Hunt. Rec. Nov. 1, 1824

p. 413-414 Jul. 16, 1824 Miller & Poole and John D. A. Murphrey (Columbia, SC) to William Harrison (Spartanburgh); for (omitted) sold (ac omitted) in two parts both of which are part of survey Dec. 4, 1803 for John Hundman and granted Dec. 1, 1823 to Miller & Poole and John D. A. Murphrey; (1) borders: Nesbitt, William Harrison, Bryce (formerly Robinson), and W. B. Gurner; and (2) borders: Nesbitt and Harrison. Witness Briant Bonner and W. B. Turner. Signed Miller & Poole and John D. A. Murphrey, attorney for Miller & Poole. Wit. oath Jul. 23, 1824 W. B. Turner to George Camp. Rec. Nov. 8, 1824

p. 414-415 Oct. 11, 1819 Mathew Jones (Spartanburgh) to Black Isaac, "that formerly belonged to Joshua Benson" (same); for $225 sold 156 ac on branches of Abner's Cr of Enoree R; border: Elijah (a black) and William Williamson. Witness William Hughs and Benjamin Wood. Signed Mathew Jones. Wit. oath Dec. 27, 1820 Benjamin Wood to Thomas Wood. Rec. Nov. 9, 1824. Dower renounced Oct. 20, 1819 Elizabeth Jones to Thomas Wood

p. 415-416 Apr. 15, 1824 John Johnson (Spartanburgh) to Newbell Johnson; for $50 sold a cow and calf, 4 hogs, 2 feather beds and furniture, all other household furniture, 2 axes, 2 mattocks, and 2 ploughs; Condition: sale void if John Johnson pays Newbell Johnson $50 by Dec. 25, 1824. Witness Lemuel Johnson and John Johnson. Signed John Jonnson. Wit. oath Apr. 20, 1824 Lemuel Johnson to Thomas Wood. Rec. Nov. 9, 1824

p. 416 Nov. 18, 1823 Thomas Hancock (Union Dist) to John Brown (Spartanburgh); for $900 sold (1) 200 ac on N side of Pacolate R; grant to Arthur Crocker; and (2) 12 ac adjoining (1); part of grant to Reuben Briant on N side of Pacolate R. Witness James Poole and Peter Peterson. Signed Thomas Hancock. Wit. oath Nov. 10, 1824 James Poole to William Reid. Rec. Nov. 10, 1824

p. 416-417 Jun. 4, 1824 Charles Hester to Michael Sellers; for $100 sold 100 ac on Cherokee Cr; border: Walker. Witness Joseph Daffron and Starling Gardon. Signed Charles Hester. Wit. oath Jun. 4, 1824 Joseph Daffron to Joseph Camp. Rec. Nov. 11, 1824. Dower renounced Oct. 11, 1824 Martha Hester to John Lipscomb

p. 417-418 Oct. 16, 1824 Daniel P Woodruff (Spartanburgh) to James H Leatherwood (same); for $400 sold 108 ac on branch of Fougerson's Cr of Tyger R; border: Harris' old corner and Laxton's old corner. Witness Zechariah Edwards and Paul C Leatherwood. Signed Daniel P Woodruff. Wit. oath Oct. 30, 1824 Zechariah Edwards to John Brewton. Rec. Nov. 11, 1824. Dower renounced Oct. 30, 1824 Sarah Woodruff to John Brewton

p. 418-419 Aug. 6, 1824 Arthur Hutchins (Spartanburgh) to John Eison; quit claim to 85 ac claimed by John Eison due to sale by William Thomas (Tenn) to John Eison; John Eison brought a suit against Arthur Hutchins and this settles the suit. Witness John White and Daniel White. Signed Arthur Hutchins' mark. Wit. oath Aug. 12, 1824 Daniel White to F. H. Legg. Rec. Nov. 14, 1824

p. 419 Sept. 6, 1824 George Lewis (Spartanburgh) to Wiley Fowler (same); for $130 sold 32 ac on Wolf Br of Lawson's fork; border: Elijah Fowler (part of same tract), John Taylor (late deeded to "said" Elijah and John), NE-"George and Elijah", NW-"George" and John Taylor, and E & S-original grant lines; lower end of 115 ac grant to George Lewis. Witness Elijah Fowler and John Hughey. Signed George Lewis. Wit. oath Sept. 6, 1824 Elijah Fowler to Wm Trimmier. Rec. Nov. 15, 1824

p. 419-420 Jan. 29, 1823 John Collins (Spartanburgh) to Thomas Grisham (same); for $67 sold 96 ac on N side of S Tyger R; border: Thomas Grisham and John Patton; part of grant to Daniel Heyward. Witness Willis S Wingo and Mark Sexton. Signed John Collins. Wit. oath Jan. 29, 1823 Willis S Wingo to Thomas Collins. Rec. Nov. 19, 1824

p. 420-421 Jun. 9, 1824 Thomas Poole, sheriff (Spartanburgh) to James T McCarter (same); for $15 sold 17 ac on waters of Fairforest Cr; border: James T McCarter, James Means, and Abram Gossett; sold due to writ from Spartanburgh Common Pleas Court second Monday after fourth Monday in Mar. 1824 suit of "Missourie" C. F. Tollison; judgment was levy of $521 and costs from estate of John Tolleson. Witness Jesse F Cleveland and Memory N Chapman. Signed Thomas Poole SSD. Wit. oath Nov. 26, 1824 Jesse F Cleveland to E Bomar. Rec. Nov. 26, 1824

p. 421-422 Mar. (omitted), 1820 Hugh Bailey and Hugh McClimons (Greenville Dist) to James Mayfield (same); for $333 sold 111 ac on S side of Rockyfield Cr. Witness John Mayfield and Thomas Taylor. Signed Hugh Bailey and Hugh McClimons. Wit. oath Dec. 27, 1820 John Mayfield to Thomas Wood. Rec. Dec. 6, 1824. Dower renounced Dec. 27, 1820 Elizabeth Baley and Jane McClimons to Thomas Wood

p. 422-423 Dec. 10, 1823 John McElrath (Spartanburgh) to John Smith (same); for $115 sold 126 ac on N side of Middle Tyger R; part of grant Dec. 24, 1772 to Edward Blake. Witness William McElrath and Michael Moore. Signed John McElrath. Wit. oath Oct. 11, 1824 Michael Moore to Tho Collins. Rec. Dec. 6, 1824

p. 423 Jan. 1, 1822 Jacob Bridges (Spartanburgh) to Henry Howe (same); for $400 sold 200 ac on S side of N Tyger R and on James Cr; grant May 5, 1769 to Daniel Brice who sold to Thomas Davis who sold to Frederick Isham who sold to John Sloan who sold to Wm and Solomon Hill who sold to Charles Moore who sold Sept. 1, 1804 to Jacob Bridges. Witness Thomas McElrath, Samuel McElrath, and William Smith. Signed Jacob Bridges. Wit. oath Nov. 21, 1822 William Smith to John Burns. Rec. Dec. 6, 1824

p. 423-424 Nov. 6, 1824 William Finch (Spartanburgh) to John Oeland (same); for $150 sold 58 ac on waters of Fairforest Cr; border: William Lancaster, John Oeland, and Isaac Finch; where William Finch lives; sold by James Finch to William Finch. Witness Andrew Gramling and Zachariah McDaniel. Signed William Finch. Wit. oath Dec. 6, 1824 Zachariah McDaniel to E Bomar. Rec. Dec. 6, 1824. Dower renounced Dec. 4, 1824 Charity Finch to Daniel White

p. 424-425 Jun. 14, 1824 Samuel K Elmore (Spartanburgh) to John B ONeill (Newberry Dist); for $123 sold (1) 223 ac on Middle

Tyger R; border: Michael Moore, John McElrath, Michael Miller desc, and Wilson Nesbett; sold Nov. 3, 1822 by Mathias Elmore to Samuel K Elmore; (2) 50 ac on Middle Tyger R adjoining (1); and (3) 30 ac on Gap Creek Road; border: Andrew McDavid, David Dansler, and Mrs. Kendrick; Condition: sale void if Samuel K Elmore pays John B ONeill $123 by Dec. 25, 1824. Witness Philip Schoppert and Hugh ONeall. Signed Saml K Elmore. Wit. oath Nov. 20, 1824 (Newberry Dist) Philip Schoppert to F. B. Higgins. Rec. Dec. 11, 1824

p. 425-426 Jan. 3, 1823 William Littlefield jr (Spartanburgh) to Benjamin Evans (same); for $125 sold 50 ac on Thomson's Cr; where Benjamin Evans lives; part of grant to Thomas Bennett. Witness Vincent Kimbrell and Jason Evans. Signed William Littlefield's mark. Wit. oath Nov. 26, 1824 Jason Evans to W Clement. Rec. Dec. 15, 1824

p. 426-427 Oct. 7, 1824 William H Tarrans (Spartanburgh) to Robert Oliphant in trust for wife Frances Tarrans; William has been unfortunate in trade and wants to secure wife Frances; so Frances can do her own trading and invest as she pleases and have her own will. Witness William Hunt and Jane Wilson. Signgd William H Farrow(sic). Witness Oct. 7, 1824 Jane Wilson to W Hunt. Rec. Feb. 20, 1824

p. 427-428 Jul. 9, 1824 (Perry Co, Ala) Gabriel Benson (Perry Co, Ala) to Alexander Roddy sr (Spartanburgh); power of attorney to sell Gabriel Benson's land in Spartanburgh Dist, SC and Rutherford Co, NC. Witness none. Signed Gab Benson. Wit. oath Jul. 9, 1824 (Perry Co, Ala) Benjamin Burton, JP for Perry Co. Jul. 9, 1824 Samuel H Nelms, clerk of Perry Co Court, certifys Benjamin Burton is JP. Jul. 9, 1824 George W Braim, Judge of Perry Co Court, certifys Samuel H Nelms is clerk. Rec. Jan. 3, 1825

p. 428-429 Oct. 19, 1816 George Knight (Spartanburgh) to James Johnson (same); for $50 sold 50 ac on N fork of Forgeson's Cr of Tyger R. Witness Jesse Wofford and Isaac Wofford. Signed George Knight. Wit. oath Sept. 11, 1824 Isaac Wofford to David Moore. Rec. Jan. 3, 1825

p. 429 Sept. 11, 1824 Jesse Wofford (Spartanburgh) to James Johnson (same); for $50 sold 100 ac on Forgeson's Cr of Tyger R; border: Richard Berry. Witness Ephraim Drummond and Lewis T Wade. Signed Jesse Wofford. Wit. oath Sept. 11, 1824 Ephraim Drummond to David Moore. Rec. Jan. 3, 1825

p. 429-430 Sept. 11, 1824 Isaac Wofford (Spartanburgh) to James Johnson (same); for $200 sold 127 ac; border: Knight and Hanna. Wit. oath Ephraim Drummond and Lewis T Wade. Signed Isaac Wofford. Wit. oath Sept. 11, 1824 Ephraim Drummond to David Moore. Rec. Jan. 3, 1825

p. 430 Jul. 19, 1824 Joseph Collins to John Thomas; for $300 sold 333 ac on Thickety Cr of Broad R; border: Wm Weber, John Thomas, Joshua Layton, and "others"; part of grant to Thomas Collins. Witness Zarah Sparks and Samuel Hodge. Signed Jos Collins. Wit. oath Oct. 15, 1824 Zarah Sparks to William Reid. Rec. Jan. 3, 1825

Book T 1825-1827
p. 1 Dec. 12, 1824 Redrick Rutland (Spartanburgh) to David McCarley (same); for $140 sold 60 ac on waters of Beaverdam Cr; border: Blackstock Road. Witness James P Woodson and Thomas Kimbril. Signed Redrick Rutland. Wit. oath Dec. 15, 1824 James P Woodson to W Hunt. Rec. Jan. 3, 1825

p. 1-2 Dec. 31, 1823 Sarah Freeman, Zachariah Edwards, Nancy Edwards,

Elizabeth F. Bobo, Daniel P Woodruff, and Sarah M Woodruff (all of Spartanburgh) to John E Bobo (same); for $291.50 sold 90 ac on Two Mile Cr of Enoree R; border: NW-Nash, SE-Absalem Bobo, and NE-J. E. Bobo and Joseph Barnett; grant to Wm Spiller. Witness Peter N Bragg and William Mason. Signed Sarah Freeman, Zachariah Edwards, Nancy Edwards, Elizabeth F Bobo, Daniel P Woodruff, and Sarah M Woodruff. Wit. oath Dec. 4, 1824 William Mason to Burrell Bobo. Rec. Jan. 3, 1825. Dower renounced Apr. 2, 1824 Nancy Edwards and Sarah M Woodruff to Burrell Bobo

p. 2-3 Jul. 2, 1824 John Lucas (Spartanburgh) to Alfred Camp; for $700 sold 220 ac on both sides S Pacolate R; border: Wm Archer. Witness Charles Lucas and John Stokes. Signed John Lucas. Wit. oath Aug. 28, 1824 John Stokes to J Whitten. Rec. Jan. 3, 1825

p. 3-4 Dec. 31, 1823 Zachariah Edwards, Nancy Edwards, Elizabeth F Bobo, Daniel P Woodruff, and Sarah M Woodruff (all of Spartanburgh) to John E Bobo (same); for $750 sold 299 ac on Two Mile Cr of Enoree R; border: S-Thomas Farrow and Jesse Brown, E-James Crow ("of Wm"), N-James Crow and Green B Evans and Spiller, and W-Absalem Bobo. Witness Peter N Bragg and William Mason. Signed Zachariah Edwards, Nancy Edwards, Elizabeth F Bobo, Daniel P Woodruff, and Sarah M Woodruff. Wit. oath Dec. 4, 1824 William Mason to Burrell Bobo. Rec. Jan. 3, 1825. Dower renounced Apr. 2, 1824 Nancy Edwards and Sarah M Woodruff to Burrell Bobo

p. 4 Dec. 18, 1820 William Webber (Spartanburgh) to Joshua Layton (same); for $75 sold 48 ac on W side of Thickety Cr; border: Hart and Nesbett. Witness Nancy Guyton and Patrick Sanders. Signed Wm Webber. Wit. oath May 5, 1821 Nancy Guyton to Henry Turner. Rec. Jan. 3, 1825

p. 4-5 Nov. 3, 1824 Josiah and Daniel Woodruff (Spartanburgh) to Willis W Dickie (same); for $1,000 sold 289 ac on waters of Furgason's and Jammies Creeks; border: Mrs. Woodruff, Lindsey's Br, Horse head Br, N-Daniel Woodruff and Jonas (or James) Brewton, W-Capt. Jamison, S- T Woodruff, and E-Eli Cox. Witness William Otts and Philip Brewton. Signed Josiah Woodruff and Daniel Woodruff. Wit. oath Nov. 11, 1824 William Otts to John Brewton. Rec. Jan. 3, 1825. Dower renounced Nov. 12, 1824 Margaret Woodruff, wife of Josiah, and Sarah M Woodruff, wife of Daniel, to John Brewton

p. 5-6 Oct. 19, 1816 John Patton (Spartanburgh) to Robert Dickson (same); for $200 sold 134 ac on S side of Middle Tyger R; border: William Caldwell. Witness James Powers, J. N. Hadden, and Thomas Grisham. Signed John Patton. Wit. oath Nov. 23, 1824 Thomas Grisham to F. H. Legg. Rec. Jan. 3, 1825. Dower renounced Nov. 23, 1824 Jane Patton to F. H. Legg

p. 6-7 Dec. 7, 1824 Benjamin High (Spartanburgh) to Samuel Ward (same); for $250 sold 167 ac on S side of Fairforest Cr; border: Walden, Ward's Br of Fairforest Cr, Wingo's Br, Tanner, and Ransom White. Witness John Chapman jr and Richard Barry "son of R". Signed Benjamin High. Wit. oath Jan. 3, 1825 John Chapman jr to W Hunt. Rec. Jan. 3, 1825

p. 7-8 Nov. 3, 1824 Josiah Woodruff and Daniel Woodruff (Spartanburgh) to Willis W Dickie (same); for $1,000 sold 75 ac at head of two branches of Enoree R; border: Augusta Road, S & E-Thomas Woodruff, and N & W-Esq Hendrix; 12½ ac removed for Bethel Meeting house leaving 75 ac. Witness William Otts and Philip Brewton. Signed Josiah Woodruff and Daniel Woodruff. Wit. oath Nov. 11, 1824 William Otts to John Brewton. Rec. Jan. 3, 1825. Dower renounced Nov. 12, 1824 Margaret Woodruff, wife of Josiah, and Sarah M Woodruff, wife of Daniel, to John Brewton

p. 8-9 Jan. 10, 1825 David McCearley sr (Spartanburgh) to David McCearley jr; for $300 sold 325 ac on waters of Beaverdam Br of Fairforest Cr; border: SW-Richard Daniel sr, NE & NW-Richard Foster, SE-John Foster, and NE, SE & SW-Richard Daniel jr. Witness James P Woodson and George W Johnson. Signed David McCearley's mark. Wit. oath Jan. 10, 1825 James P Woodson to W Hunt. Rec. Jan. 10, 1825

p. 9 Mar. 13, 1824 Andrew B Miller (Spartanburgh) to James P Woodson (same); for $60 sold 50 ac on branches of McMicken's Cr; border: Caldwell and Finch. Witness David McCearley jr and Lewis Autry. Signed Andrew B Miller. Wit. oath Mar. 20, 1824 David McCearley jr to W Hunt. Rec. Jan. 11, 1825

p. 9-10 Apr. 15, 1824 Richard Thomson, Smith Lipscomb, and Elijah Dawkins, executors of will of William Thompson desc (Spartanburgh and Union Dist) to Amos Austell (Spartanburgh); for $410 sold 300 ac on branches of Beaverdam Cr of Thickety Cr; border: S-Thomas Cole, W-Mathew Cooper, and E-Michael Gaffney; grant to Josiah Tanner who sold to William Thompson desc. Witness William Austell and Thomas Thompson. Signed Richard Thompson, Smith Lipscomb, and Elijah Dawkins. Wit. oath Aug. 6, 1824 William Austell to Joseph Camp. Rec. Jan. 11, 1825

p. 10 Oct. 16, 1824 Isaac Gorden jr (Spartanburgh) to Michael Gaffney (same); for $186 sold 124 ac; border: Gaffney and Starling; where Isaac Gorden jr lives; part of land Isaac Gorden sr gave his son Isaac. Witness Sterling Gorden and William Petty. Signed Isaac Gorden. Wit. oath Jan. 10, 1825 Sterling Gorden to J Camp. Rec. Jan. 12, 1825

p. 10-12 Sept. 30, 1824 William Hammett (Spartanburgh) to James Spencer (same); for $346.66 2/3 sold 14 ac and adjoining mill pond on Peter's Cr of Pacolate R; border: old Green River Road and James Spencer. Witness T. J. Underwood and Elisha Bomar. Signed Wm Hammett. Wit. oath Jan. 13, 1825 (sic) E Bomar to John S Rowland. Rec. Jan. 12, 1825. Dower renounced Dec. 6, 1824 Martha Hammett to Daniel White

p. 12 Dec. 30, 1824 Dower renounced Sarah Tolleson to Elisha Bomar for deed from Muse Tolleson to James Hunt. Rec. Jan. 17, 1825

p. 12 Oct. 30, 1824 Dower renounced Sarah Tolleson to Elisha Bomar for deed from Muse Tolleson to James Hunt. Rec. Jan. 17, 1825

p. 12-13 Dec. 30, 1824 Thomas Poole, sheriff (Spartanburgh) to James Hunt (same); for $88 sold 135 ac on Fairforest Cr; border: Richard Thomson, James Ward, and James Seay; sold due to writ from Spartanburgh Common Pleas Court second Monday after fourth Monday in Oct. 1822 suit of Joseph T Weymon; judgment was levy of $2,388 and costs from Muse Tolleson and Berryman S Holder. Witness Elisha Bomar and John Poole. Signed Thomas Poole SSD. Wit. oath Dec. 30, 1824 John Poole to E Bomar. Rec. Jan. 17, 1825

p. 13-14 Jan. 18, 1825 Sarah Scott (Spartanburgh) to John Scott (same); for good causes give all goods, chattles, and household stuff "and increase" that John Scott "granted" to Sarah Scott Feb. 28, 1810. Witness William Trimmier and Margaret Trimmier. Signed Sarah Scott's mark. Wit. oath Jan. 19, 1825 William Trimmier to E Bomar. Rec. Jan. 19, 1825

p. 14-15 Jul. 31, 1824 William Littlefield (Spartanburgh) to Benjamin Wofford (same); to secure payment of $348 note dated Feb. 19, 1824 and due Dec. 25, 1825 sold 153 ac on branch of James Cr of Tyger R; part of 2,500 ac grant to Alexander Foster desc; border:

E-William Hindmond and W-Thomas Bell; Condition: sale void if William Littlefield pays debt. Witness Philip Littlefield and Moses White. Signed Wm Littlefield. Wit. oath Jan. 13, 1825 Philip Littlefield to Joseph Wofford. Rec. Jan. 24, 1825

p. 15 Oct. 15, 1824 Judith Gray (Monroe Co, Miss), widow of John Gray desc (Morgan Co, Ala), to Elijah Herrin (Hall Co, Ga); power of attorney to obtain her dower right to land in Spartanburgh Dist and recover a note executed by Justice Reynolds (Spartanburgh) to John Gray desc. Witness none. Signed Judith Gray's mark. Wit. oath Oct. 15, 1824 Barlett Sims, Justice of Pleace Monroe Co, Miss. Oct. 16, 1824 (Monroe Co, Miss) Stephen Cooke, clerk of Monroe Co Court, certifys Barlett Sims is Justice of Peace. Oct. 19, 1824 Robert D Haden, chief justice of Monroe Co Court, certifys Stephen Cooke is clerk. Rec. Jan. 24, 1825

p. 15-16 Jan. 18, 1825 John Foster (Spartanburgh) to son Welden Foster (same); for $1 sold 170 ac; border: Richard Foster; land goes to Welden when John dies; where John Foster now lives. Witness Ralph Smith, James Selmon, and William Hunt. Signed John Foster's mark. Wit. oath Jan. 18, 1825 Ralph Smith to W Hunt. Rec. Jan. 24, 1825

p. 16-17 Jan. 19, 1825 Jesse Cleveland (Spartanburgh) to John W Farrow (same); for $150 sold ½ ac in Spartanburgh, SC; border: Todd's stable; where J.W. Farrow lives. Witness R. H. Goldthwaite and Collins Smith. Signed Jesse Cleveland. Wit. oath Jan. 18, 1825 Collins Smith to E Bomar. Rec. Jan. 24, 1825. Dower renounced Jan. 18, 1825 Mary Cleveland to Elisha Bomar

p. 17-18 Jan. 29, 1825 Elijah Herrin (Hall Co, Ga), for self and heirs and widow of John Gray desc, to Mathew Mathias (Spartanburgh); for $100 sold 58 ac; border: Anthony Foster, Buffington, and Loockok; part of grant to Phebe Buffington who sold to John Gray desc. Witness Elisha McAbee and B. L. Goodman. Signed Elijah Herrin. Wit. oath Jan. 29, 1825 Elisha McAbee to E Bomar. Rec. Jan. 29, 1825

p. 18-19 Dec. 29, 1815 George Lusher, attorney for heirs of Lewis Dutargue desc (Charleston, SC), to William McClure and Charles McClure (Spartanburgh); for $100 sold 104 ac on branches of N Pacolate R; border: Thomas Shurley and Underwood; part of grant to Lewis Dutargue. Witness J. F. Grimky and Abram Nott. Signed George Lasher, attorney for Lewis Dutargue. Wit. oath Nov. 14, 1823 Abram Nott to James Young. Rec. Feb. 7, 1825

p. 19 Sept. 13, 1824 William Clement (Spartanburgh) to John Wolf (same); for $500 sold (ac omitted) on E side of Richland Cr and both sides of Wolf trap Br; border: Z Wall, G Wolf, a still house, and Cunningham. Witness Jesse Cleveland and Zachr Wall. Signed W Clement. Wit. oath Feb. 7, 1825 Jesse Cleveland to J. S. Rowland. Rec. Feb. 7, 1825

p. 19-20 Sept. 6, 1824 George Lewis (Spartanburgh) to Elijah Fowler (same); for (omitted) sold 57 ac on waters of Lawson's fork; part of grant Apr. 3, 1815 Gov. David R Williams to George Lewis. Wit. oath Wiley Fowler and John Hughe. Signed George Lewis. Wit. oath Sept. 6, 1824 Wiley Fowler to Wm Trimmier. Rec. Feb. 7, 1825

p. 20-21 Nov. 22, 1822 Joel Dean sr (Spartanburgh) to Hiram Bennett (same); for $191 sold 82 ac on branch of Enoree R; border: Hiram Bennett and Newbell Johnson. Witness Thomas P Brockman and Penail Wood jr. Signed Joel Dean. Wit. oath Mar. 6, 1824 Thomas P Brockman to Thomas Wood. Rec. Feb. 7, 1825. Dower renounced Dec. 14, 1822 Mary Dean to Thomas Wood

p. 21-22 Oct. 21, 1824 James Norris (Union Dist) to Jesse Griffin (Spartanburgh); for $800 sold 200 ac on waters of Pacolate R; border: N-Jesse Griffin, S & W-part of same tract, and W-Henry Littlejohn; on Farmer's Br; part of tract sold by Henry Farnandis to James Norris. Witness John Littlejohn and Samuel Littlejohn. Signed Jas Norris. Wit. oath Nov. 18, 1824 Samuel Littlejohn to John Lipscomb. Rec. Feb. 7, 1825. Dower renounced Nov. 24, 1824 Sally Norris to John Lipscomb

p. 22-23 Sept. 25, 1824 Rhesa Robuck and Mary Robuck (Spartanburgh) to William Grant (same); for $500 sold 117 ac on branch of James Cr; border: E-James Hobby, W-Glasby, N-Castleberry, and S-Arnold; part of survey by James Wofford for William Barnett and granted Jul. 15, 1786 Gov. Motrie(sic) to William Barnett. Witness John Robuck and Thomas Bragg. Signed Rhesa Robuck and Mary's mark. Wit. oath Jan. 11, 1825 Thomas Bragg to Burrell Bobo. Rec. Feb. 7, 1825

p. 23 Sept. 11, 1824 James Johnson (Spartanburgh) to Jared Drummond (same); for $1,500 sold 325 ac on N side of Forgeson's Cr of Tyger R. Witness Ephraim Drummond and Jesse Wofford. Signed James Johnson's mark. Wit. oath Oct. 7, 1824 Ephraim Drummond to James Crook. Rec. Feb. 7, 1825. Dower renounced Oct. 7, 1824 Diadama Johnson to James Crook

p. 23-24 Aug. 2, 1824 Daniel McKie (Spartanburgh) to Thomas Davis (same); for $1,500 sold 500 ac; border: Enoree R, Robert Hannah, Thomas Hobbs, widow Sims, and John Tackett; known as Dooling place. Witness John Wofford jr and Robert Creswell. Signed Danl McKie. Wit. oath Aug. 2, 1824 Robert Creswell to E Bomar. Rec. Feb. 7, 1825

p. 24-25 Nov. 19, 1824 Thomas Grisham (Spartanburgh) to James Anderson (same); for $300 sold 116 ac on N side of S Tyger R; border: SE & NE-John S Coan, N-Samuel Pearson, and E-a branch. Witness John Gilchrist and A Drummond. Signed Thomas Grisham. Wit. oath Nov. 22, 1824 A Drummond to F. H. Legg. Rec. Feb. 10, 1825. Dower renounced Nov. 22, 1824 Jane Grisham to F. H. Legg

p. 25-26 Nov. 9, 1819 James Moss (Spartanburgh) to John Patton (same); for $1,000 sold 100 ac on N Tyger R; border: William Clayton and Samuel Miller. Witness Samuel Pearson, Alexander Vernon, and James Anderson. Signed James Moss. Wit. oath Nov. 19, 1824 James Anderson to F. H. Legg. Rec. Feb. 10, 1825. Dower renounced Dec. 4, 1824 Emily Moss to F. H. Legg

p. 26-27 Nov. 19, 1824 John Patton (Spartanburgh) to Samuel Miller, sheriff (Spartanburgh); for $900 sold 100 ac on N Tyger R; border: Wm Clayton and Samuel Miller. Witness James Anderson and Thomas J Cean. Signed John Patton. Wit. oath Nov. 19, 1824 James Anderson to F. H. Legg. Rec. Feb. 10, 1825. Dower renounced Nov. 22, 1824 Jane Patton to F. H. Legg

p. 27-28 Jul. 17, 1824 Alexander Vernon (Spartanburgh) to James Vernon (same); for $800 sold 133 1/3 ac; border: Snoddy, Edward Bomar, and John Foster; devised by Samuel Timmons to son John Timmons who sold to Alexander Vernon. Witness W Perrin, Mary C Vernon, and Sarah Jordan. Signed Alexr Vernon. Wit. oath Nov. 24, 1824 Mary C Vernon to John Chapman. Rec. Feb. 10, 1825. Dower renounced Jan. 4, 1825 Ann H Vernon to F. H. Legg

p. 28-29 Feb. 16, 1825 Thomas Poole, sheriff (Spartanburgh) to James Roddy; for $181.50 sold 100 ac on waters of N Tyger R; border: Adam Grambling, John W Lewis, Alexander Roddy, and Robert Foster; bought by Alexander Roddy for James Roddy; sold due to writ from Spartanburgh Common Pleas Court second Monday after fourth Monday in Oct. 1823 suit of Jesse Cleveland; judgment was levy of $73 and costs from Michael McKie. Witness James V Miller and John Poole. Signed Thomas Poole. Wit. oath Feb. 16, 1825 James V Miller to James E Henry. Rec. Feb. 19, 1825

p. 29 Dec. 15, 1824 William Ross (Spartanburgh) to Thomas Dare (same); quit claim to his share of deed of gift from Thomas Dare to William Ross and Muse Tolleson. Witness Abner Benson and Michael Gaffney. Signed W Ross. Wit. oath Feb. 18, 1825 Abner Benson to W Trimmier. Rec. Feb. 19, 1825

p. 29-30 Feb. 11, 1825 William West sr (Spartanburgh) to William West jr (same); for $135 sold (ac omitted) in McNary Co, Tenn on Cypress Cr of Hatchee R in 9th Surveyor's Dist Range 3 and Section 3; border: three mile post. Witness John Moore and Henry West. Signed William West's mark. Wit. oath Feb. 21, 1825 John Moore to E Bomar. Rec. Feb. 21, 1825. Dower renounced Feb. 19, 1825 Margaret West to James Hamm

p. 30-32 Jan. 29, 1818 James Foster (Spartanburgh) to William W Harris (same); for $750 sold 398 ac on W side of Buffalow Lick Cr on E side of Ready Br; border: Hindman. Witness David Golightly, Robert Wyatt, and Simpson West Harris. Signed James Foster. Wit. oath Feb. 19, 1825 David Golightly to D White. Rec. Feb. 21, 1825. Dower renounced Feb. 19, 1825 Patience Foster to Daniel White

p. 32 Mar. 28, 1823 John Golightly (Spartanburgh) to William W Harris (same); for $400 sold 250 ac on both sides Lawson's fork of Pacolate R; border: Wyatt; part of grant to Mary Wood. Witness James Foster and Wm D Mitchell. Signed John Golightly. Wit. oath Feb. 19, 1825 James Foster to D White. Rec. Feb. 21, 1825

p. 32-33 Feb. 17, 1824 Mary Barrett (Spartanburgh) to William W Harris (same); for $100 sold 117 ac on head waters of Buffalow Cr; border: David Golightly, W. W. Harris, and Thomas Vaughan. Witness Josiah Hort and James Foster. Signed Mary Barrett's mark. Wit. oath Feb. 19, 1825 James Foster to D White. Rec. Feb. 21, 1825

p. 33-34 Dec. 28, 1824 Thomas Poole and Jane Poole (Spartanburgh) and William Poole (Richland Dist) to Zachariah Hammett (Spartanburgh); for $177 sold 118 ac on waters of Lawson's fork; border: road from Spartanburgh Court House to Coulter's ford on Pacolate R; part of 500 ac grant Oct. 3, 1786 to William McDowell. Witness Samuel Reid, John Poole, and Ben Sherbutt. Signed Thomas Poole, Jane Poole, and William Poole. Wit. oath Dec. 31, 1824 Ben Sherbutt to E Bomar. Rec. Feb. 24, 1825

p. 34-35 Sept. 1, 1823 Abner Benson (Spartanburgh) to Thomas Dare (same); for $500 sold (1) 200 ac on Lawson's fork; sold by Edmond Bishop to Abner Benson and Robert Benson; (2) 100 ac on Lawson's fork; part of 200 ac sold by Edmond Bishop to Abner and Robert Benson; (3) 23 ac on Lawson's fork; sold by George Hughey to Abner and Robert Benson; (4) 5 ac on branch of Camp Br of Lawson's fork; sold by James Templeton to Abner and Robert Benson; (5) 210 ac on Standing Stone Br of Lawson's fork; sold by James Templeton to Abner and Robert Benson; (6) rent or lease for 70 years from Oct. 11, 1807 97½ ac on Camp Br of Lawson's fork; rented or leased by heirs of Rolley Fossett desc to Abner and Robert Benson. Witness E Roddy, Abel Lancaster, and Wilson Nesbitt. Signed A Benson. Wit. oath Feb. 24, 1824 Abel Lancaster to E Bomar. Rec. Mar. 3, 1825

p. 35-36 Oct. 26, 1824 John Cantrill (Spartanburgh) to Jacob Cooper

(Laurens Dist); for $3,000 sold 500 ac; border: John Westmoreland, Earnest, and William Childres; includes mill and houses where John Cantrill lives. Witness Joshua Gilbert and Moses Hughes. Signed John Cantrill. Wit. oath Jan. 10, 1825 (Lawrence Dist) Joshua Gilbert to Joseph Brown. Rec. Mar. 7, 1825. Dower renounced Jan. 5, 1825 (Lawrence Dist) Mary Cantrill to Thomas Wright

p. 36-37 Feb. 26, 1825 Rowland Dare (Spartanburgh) to Thomas Dare (same); for $400 sold 344 ac on Little Cherokee Cr; border: Jesse Tate, James Jeffries, and Michael Gaffney; sold by Reuben Morgan to Thomas Dare(sic). Witness A Benson, John Walker, and A Lancaster. Signed Rowland Dare's mark. Wit. oath Mar. 7, 1825 John Walker to James Crook. Rec. Mar. 7, 1825

p. 37 Dec. 3, 1824 Samuel Fowler (Spartanburgh) to Henry Childs (Lancaster Co(sic), NC); for $100 sold 52 ac on N side of Samuel Fowler's Mill Cr; border: Elisha Russell; where Elisha Russell lives; part of grant to Samuel Fowler. Witness Elisha Russel and Willey S Brown. Signed Samuel Fowler's mark. Wit. oath Mar. 1, 1825 Willey S Brown to John S Rowland. Rec. Mar. 7, 1825

p. 37-39 Dec. 2, 1822 Thomas Meredith (Davies Co, Ind) to David Golightly (Spartanburgh); power of attorney to sell 51 ac (or 151 ac?); border: Stephen Foster and waters of Fairforest Cr; where Thomas Meredith lived and now "in the care of" David Golightly. Witness Jas Waurer and Parminas Palmer JP. Signed Thomas Meredith's mark. Wit. oath Dec. 2, 1822 (Davies Co, Ind) Parminas Palmer JP. Dec. 2, 1822 (Davies Co, Ind) Emanuel Vantrees, clerk of Davies Co Court, certifys Parminas Palmer is justice of peace. Dec. 2, 1822 Eph Thompson, associate Justice, certifys Emanuel Vantrees is clerk. Rec. Mar. 7, 1825

p. 39-40 Mar. 6, 1820 James Hunt, sheriff (Spartanburgh) to James Foster; for $500 sold 353 ac on Reedy Br of Fairforest Cr; border: James Kun, William Harris, David Golightly, and William Underwood; sold on first Monday in Jun. 1818; Mary Foster petitioned Spartanburgh Common Pleas Court on second Monday after fourth Monday in Oct. 1817 to divide estate of Moses Foster desc; court appointed Robert Martin, William Underwood, William Foster, Joseph Hurt, and William Harris esqs to divide the land; on second Monday after fourth Monday in Mar. 1818 they said land couldn't be divided and should be sold. Witness Caleb Jones and William Walker. Signed Jas Hunt. Wit. oath Mar. 27, 1824 Caleb Jones to Ransom Foster. Rec. Mar. 12, 1825

p. 40 Mar. 14, 1825 Dower renounced Sarah Tolleson to Elisha Bomar for sale from Muse Tolleson to Thomas Tinsley. Rec. Mar. 14, 1825

p. 40-41 Aug. 16, 1811 Thomas Crumly (Spartanburgh) to William Underwood (same); for $400 sold 300 ac on both sides Obed's Cr; border: S-John McClure and W, N & E-McWilliams; grant to Thomas McKnight. Witness Henry Monroe, William Millican, and Henry Morgan. Signed Thomas Crumly. Wit. oath Jan. 8, 1816 H Morgan to James Young. Rec. Mar. 14, 1825

p. 41-42 Mar. 16, 1825 Samuel Ward (Spartanburgh) to James K Nance (same); for $80 sold 43 ac on Fairforest Cr; border: Ransom White, Wm Yates, James K Nance, Samuel Ward, and Zachariah Wingo; part of grant to Thomas Hayes. Witness Henry J Rowland and William Trimmier. Signed Samuel Ward. Wit. oath Mar. 16, 1825 William Trimmier to W Hunt. Rec. Mar. 16, 1825

p. 42-43 Aug. 23, 1824 William Wofford sr (Spartanburgh) to John Wofford jr (same); for $300 sold 200 ac on waters of McClure's

Cr of Fairforest Cr in Spartanburgh and Union Dists; border: Larken Lancaster, Wofford road, Brownley, Isaac Wofford jr, Wilbanks, Archibald, Donaldson, and Thomas Haselwood; where John Wofford jr lives; grant Dec. 3, 1810 Gov. John Drayton to William Wofford sr. Witness Isaac Wofford jr, William West, and Mark Bennett. Signed Wm Wofford sr. Wit. oath Mar. 12, 1825 Isaac Wofford jr to Wm Smith. Rec. Mar. 17, 1825

p. 43 Apr. 16, 1821 (York Dist) William Furgeson (York Dist) to William Cantrill; for $230 sold 400 ac on E side of Pacolate R; border: S & SW-William Furgeson; SE of line drawn by Wm Furgeson and George McWilliams; William Furgeson's part of grant to William Furgeson and George McWilliams. Witness James Lewis and Robert McDowell. Signed Wm Furgeson. Wit. oath Aug. 4, 1823 Robert McDowell to James Young. Rec. Mar. 18, 1825

p. 43-44 Mar. 18, 1825 Dower renounced Sarah Tolleson to Elisha Bomar for deed from Muse Tolleson to Reuben Daniel. Rec. Mar. 18, 1825

p. 44 Sept. 5, 1807 Isaac Cantrell (Spartanburgh) to David Parris (same); for $200 sold 100 ac on both sides of Buck Cr; border: Joseph Morris, David Parris, Abraham Nelson, Bangley Br, and William Morrow; part on one side of creek granted States Office to William Jordan and other side of creek grant Oct. 6, 1788 States Office to Joseph Morris. Witness William Morrow, Abraham Nelson, and Edmond Nelson. Signed Isaac Cantrell. Wit. oath Apr. 12, 1808 Abraham Nelson to L Adcock. Rec. Mar. 24, 1825

p. 44-45 Nov. 4, 1824 Hugh Holt (Spartanburgh) to Jacob Stotts (same); for $164 sold (1) 120 ac on waters of Lawson's fork; sold Aug. 2, 1822 Jacob Stotts to Hugh Holt; and (2) 44 ac on N side of tract (1). Witness David McDowell and Washington Bomar. Signed Hugh Holt. Wit. oath Mar. 24, 1825 Washington Bomar to J. W. Farrow. Rec. Mar. 25, 1825

p. 45-46 Nov. 6, 1824 Thomas Hobby (Spartanburgh) to William Stone (same); for $900 sold 206 ac on N side of Enoree R; border: Daniel McKie; part of two grants: (1) Oct. 3, 1785 to Jennet Berry who sold to William Berry and (2) sold by James Lanford to "said" Barry and sold by William Berry to John Hobby who sold to Thomas Hobby. Witness William Jones SM and William Terry jr. Signed Thomas Hobby. Wit. oath Nov. 6, 1824 William Jones SM to John Brewton. Rec. Mar. 26, 1825. Dower renounced Nov. 6, 1824 Sally Hobby to John Brewton

p. 46-47 Nov. 1, 1823 Anthony Foster (Spartanburgh) to Daniel White, Isaac Smith, James Cooper, Richard Thompson, Robert Creswell, and Elihu Creswell; for building an Academy or house for purpose of keeping a school near Cedar Springs give 5 ac where Academy now is erecting by Henry White; grantees get to use the Academy. Witness Thomas Poole and James Hunt. Signed A Foster. Wit. oath Mar. 29, 1825 James Hunt to E Bomar. Rec. Mar. 29, 1825

p. 47-48 Jan. 19, 1825 William Trimmier, Commissioner of Spartanburgh Equity Court, to Mrs. Nancy Poole; for $100 sold 100 ac on Dutchman's Cr of Tyger R; border: Thomas Reese; part of grant Jul. 1, 1793 to William Lancaster; David Golightly complained Jul. 24, 1823 to Equity Court against Joseph Smith and asked to forclose mortgage for 100 ac; case was heard in Feb. term (year omitted) and Court said to sell the land; sale first Monday in Mar. 1825. Witness John Poole and Thomas Poole. Signed William Trimmier. Wit. oath Mar. 30, 1825 John Poole to E Bomar. Rec. Mar. 30, 1825

p. 48-49 Dec. 1, 1823 Francis Mason to William Jennings (Spartanburgh) for $200 sold 125 ac on Ford's Cr of Fairforest Cr; border: Barber. Witness Elisha Jennings and Jesse Mason. Signed Francis Mason. Wit. oath Jun. 7, 1824 Jesse Mason to Robert Ligon. Rec. Mar. 30, 1825

p. 49-50 Sept. 30, 1824 David Drummond (Spartanburgh) to T. J. Drummond (same); for $150 sold 157 ac; border: F. H. Legg; where David Drummond formerly lived and part of where Berryman W Tate lived. Witness John Drummond and A. M. Drummond. Signed David Drummond's mark. Wit. oath Dec. 13, 1824 A. M. Drummond to F. H. Legg. Rec. Apr. 1, 1825. Dower renounced Mar. 31, 1825 Nancy Drummond to F. H. Legg

p. 50-51 Dec. 6, 1824 Benjamin Wood (Spartanburgh) to William J Wood (same); for $148 sold 74 ac; where "he" lives. Witness Wiley D Wood and Sarah Wood. Signed Benjamin Wood. Wit. oath Feb. 17, 1825 Wiley D Wood to Thomas Wood. Rec. Apr. 4, 1825

p. 51-52 Feb. 12, 1825 William Grant and wife Mary (Spartanburgh) to John Clark (same); for $500 sold 117 ac on branch of James Cr; border: Castleberry, Rhesa Roebuck, James Hobby, and Galasby; part of survey by James Wofford for William Barnett and granted Jul. 15, 1786 Gov. Montreal(sic) to William Barnett. Witness William Posey, Thomas Bragg, and Charles Bragg. Signed Wm Grant and Mary's mark. Wit. oath Apr. 3, 1825 William Posey to James E Henry. Rec. Apr. 4, 1825

p. 52-53 Aug. 25, 1823 Moses Casey (Spartanburgh) to son Thomas Jefferson Casey; for parental affection give 80 ac on waters of Enoree R; border: Aaron Casey sr, William Casey, and post road on Stoney ridge; where Moses Casey lives; grant in 1775 to Thomas Todd. Witness Jonathan Fryer and Stephen Wilson. Signed M Casey. Wit. oath Apr. 7, 1825 Jonathan Fryer to Wm Young. Rec. Apr. 11, 1825

p. 53-54 Dec. 21, 1824 William Bryce (Union Dist) to Elisha Bridges (Rutherford Co, NC); for $150 sold 100 ac; border: Robertson's old line, Bonner, and William Clary. Witness John Bridges and William Clary. Signed Wm Bryce. Wit. oath Dec. 21, 1824 John Bridges to J Camp. Rec. Apr. 12, 1825. Dower renounced Jan. 6, 1825 (Union Dist) Mary Bridges to Daniel White

p. 54-55 Oct. 13, 1813 William Shackelford (Spartanburgh) to Josiah Woodruff (same); for $250 sold 14 3/4 ac; border: Joseph Woodruff (on all sides), an old stonhouse, and Thomas Woodruff. Witness Simon Lavender, Philip Pilgrim, and Samuel Woodruff. Signed Wm Shackelford. Wit. oath Oct. 13, 1813 Simon Lavender to Samuel Woodruff. Rec. Apr. 12, 1825. Dower renounced Dec. 11, 1813 Nancy Shackelford to Thomas Wright

p. 55 Sept. 20, 1820 Martin Cole (SC) to Henry and Archibald Cole (SC); for $500 sold 160 ac; border: William Cooper, William Rhodes, and Thomas Garrett. Witness Clabourn Waddel and William Cooper. Signed Martin Cole. Wit. oath Dec. 27, 1824 Clabourn Waddel to James Crook. Rec. Apr. 12, 1825

p. 55-56 Apr. 2, 1824 Solomon Crocker (Spartanburgh) to Arthur Crocker (same); for $300 sold 100 ac on both sides Richland Cr on S side of Pacolate R; border: James Crocker, Big Br, William Crocker, Anthony Bait's old corner, and Arthur Crocker's Spring Br; Solomon Crocker gets to keep plantation during his lifetime. Witness William Crocker and John Crocker. Signed Solomon Crocker's mark. Wit. oath Oct. 12, 1824 William Crocker to William Reid. Rec. Apr. 12, 1825

p. 56-57 Oct. 8, 1824 James Dillard (Spartanburgh) to John Kirby, son of Richard Kirby (same); for $300 sold (1) 103 ac where James Dillard lives; and (2) 17 ac adjoining (1); sold by George W Lawrence; border: G. W. Lawrence and Joshua Drapers. Witness B. S. Holder and David Easterwood. Signed James Dillard. Wit. oath Apr. 12, 1825 B. S. Holder to W Hunt. Rec. Apr. 12, 1825

p. 57 Sept. 14, 1815 Willis Williford (Spartanburgh) to John Wethers jr (same); for $50 sold 100 ac; border: Anthony Shands, Tyger R, Richard Young (bought from Owen Forrester), and Reuben Newman. Witness William Young and John M Taylor. Signed Willis Williford. Wit. oath Apr. 9, 1825 William Young to Joseph Wofford. Rec. Apr. 13, 1825. Dower renounced Oct. 30, 1815 Polly Williford to Burrell Bobo

p. 57-58 Apr. 2, 1819 Pickney Horry (blank) to Joisah Kilgore (Greenville Dist); for $300 sold 300 ac on S side of Middle Tyger R; grant in 1773 to Pinckney's father Daniel Horry esq desc. Witness C. C. Pinckney jr and Fredk Rutledge. Signed Pinckney Horry, by attorney Harriott Horry. Wit. oath Apr. 6, 1819 (Charleston Dist) C. C. Pinckney jr to Robert Ogden. Rec. Apr. 13, 1825

p. 58-59 Oct. 25, 1823 Anthony Shands to Reuben Newman; for $150 sold 100 ac S of Tyger R and on branches of James Cr; border: S, E & N-Reuben Newman and W-Richard Young; all the land sold by Stephen Wilson desc to son William Wilson and "transfered" to Anthony Shands. Witness Reuben Newman jr and Austen Newman. Signed Anthony Shands. Wit. oath Apr. 9, 1825 Reuben Newman jr to Wm Young. Rec. Apr. 13, 1825

p. 59 Feb. 7, 1825 Jesse Godfrey to Thomas Wood JP; an oath that Jesse Fodfrey has owned a mulatto girl Susannah Tate since her infancy and she was always called a free born person and is 18 or 19 years old. Signed Jesse Godfrey's mark. Rec. Apr. 25, 1825

p. 59-60 Sept. 14, 1815 Richard Young and wife Isabel (Spartanburgh) to son-in-law Willis Williford and our daughter (and his wife) Polly Williford (same); for good will give 100 ac on S side of Tyger R; border: Anthony Shands, land Richard Young bought from Owen Forrester, and Reuben Newman; part of two grants: (1) to Benjamin Wofford and (2) to Joshua Smith. Witness William Young and Thomas Young. Signed Richd Young and Isabel's mark. Wit. oath Apr. 9, 1825 William Young to Joseph Wofford. Rec. Apr. 13, 1825

p. 60-61 Apr. 12, 1825 Elias Carder to Josiah Kilgore; to secure three notes of $849 in three equal payments beginning Apr. 1, 1826 sold 377 ac on S side of Middle Tyger R; border: David Wheeler, Hilborn, and Robert Bailey; grant Jun. 23, 1776 to Daniel Horry; Condition: sale void if Elias Carder pays the debt. Witness James Corder and Thomas Thomas. Signed Elias Corder and Josiah Kilgore. Wit. oath Apr. 12, 1825 James Corder to Philip Brewton. Rec. Apr. 13, 1825

p. 61-62 Apr. 22, 1823 John Clark (Spartanburgh) to William Bush (same); for $518 sold 259 ac on waters of Obed's Cr of N Pacolate R. Witness Oliver Clark, William Bush jr and Christopher Golightly. Signed John Clark. Wit. oath Jul. 31, 1823 William Bush jr to James Young. Rec. Apr. 13, 1825. Dower renounced Apr. 12, 1825 Polly Clark to Thomas Young

p. 62-63 Feb. 9, 1822 James Hunt, sheriff (Spartanburgh) to Zachariah Hobby (same); for $5 sold 100 ac on waters of Tyger R; border: Livingston Bobo, Abner Wells, and Elisha Wells; sold due to writ from Spartanburgh Common Pleas Court second Monday after fourth Monday in Mar. 1821 suit of Zachariah Hobby; judgment was levy of

$15.56 and 3 mills and costs from Robert Hutson. Witness Simpson Foster and James Edward Henry. Signed Jas Hunt. Wit. oath Apr. 14, 1825 James E Henry to D White. Rec. Apr. 14, 1825

p. 63-64 Feb. 24, 1825 Robert McDowell (Spartanburgh) to James McDowell (same); for $550 sold 307 ac on waters of S Pacolate R. Witness Samuel Bullington and James McWilliams. Signed Robert McDowell. Wit. oath Mar. 2, 1825 Samuel Bullington to James Young. Rec. Apr. 18, 1825

p. 64 Apr. 22, 1825 Rose Barry (Spartanburgh) to Isaac Smith (same); power of attorney to get Rose Barry's share of will of Vilet Watson (York Dist) (female), administrator of will is John Barry (York Dist). Witness David Golightly. Signed Rose Barry. Wit. oath Apr. 23, 1825 David Golightly to E Bomar. Rec. Apr. 28, 1825

p. 64-65 Jan. 3, 1824 Shadrack Waldrip, Eli Waldrip, and Ira Waldrip to Thomas Farrow; for $500 sold 48½ ac on N side of Enoree R; plat attached shows border: David McKie, Thomas Farrow, and Ira Waldrip; part of 150 ac grant to Shadrack Waldrip sr desc. Witness James Rhodes and John E Casey. Signed Shadrack, Eli, and Ira Waldrip's marks. Wit. oath Dec. 31, 1824 James Rhodes to John Dean. Rec. Apr. 28, 1825. Dower renounced Jan. 3, 1824 Rachel Waldrip, wife of Shadrack, Sarah Waldrip, wife of Eli, and Rebecca Waldrip, wife of Ira, to Burrell Bobo. Dower renounced Jan. 3, 1824 Polly Waldrip, wife of Shadrack sr desc, to Burrell Bobo

p. 65-66 May 30, 1817 Nathaniel Burton (Spartanburgh) to Nathaniel Gentry (same); for $160 sold 74 ac on S side of N Tyger R. Witness Ford Mason and Samuel Floyd. Signed Nath Burton. Wit. oath May 31, 1817 Ford Mason to Robert Ligon. Rec. Apr. 25, 1825

p. 66-67 Oct. 29, 1822 Muse Tolleson (Spartanburgh) to John Tolleson jr (same); for $500 John Tolleson sr left Muse Tolleson sold 1,000 ac on waters of Fairforest and Two Mile Creeks above the Court House on both sides of Main Road; formerly owned by old Mr Gray; bought by Elias Palmer for John Tolleson sr's estate and sold by Muse Tolleson, as executor of estate, to John Tolleson jr as John Tolleson jr's part of his father's (John Tolleson sr) estate. Witness Mordica W Hutcheson and Missouri C. F. Tolleson. Signed Muse Tolleson. Wit. oath Apr. 18, 1825 Mordica W Hutcheson to W Hunt. Rec. Apr. 29, 1825

p. 67 Dec. 17, 1824 Josiah Hatchett (Spartanburgh) to John Hatchett (same); for $500 sold 100 ac on N side of Pinckney Road; border: Mathias Rush, Thomas Hatchett, and Robert Ligon; on N side of Tyger R. Witness Martin Otts and Josiah Hatchett sr. Signed Josiah Hatchett's mark. Wit. oath Apr. 29, 1825 Josiah Hatchett sr to Philip Brewton. Rec. May 2, 1825

p. 67-68 Mar. 26, 1825 Cyrus Seay (Spartanburgh) to Burrel Wingo (same); for $152 sold 76 ac on both sides Fairforest Cr; includes shoals where "the" county road crosses; border: James Nance and Spartanburgh Road. Witness Paschal Wingo and John Burns. Signed Cyrus Seay. Wit. oath Apr. 12, 1825 Paschal Wingo to William Reed. Rec. May 2, 1825

p. 68 May 2, 1825 Paul Combee (Spartanburgh) to Robert Ligon esq (same); power of attorney to obrain Paul Combee's share of estate of Ann Price desc. Witness Charles Moore and William W Smithwick. Signed Paul Combee. Wit. oath May 2, 1825 William W Smithwick to W Hunt. Rec. May 2, 1825

p. 68-69 Oct. 28, 1824 Josiah Hatchett and wife Tabitha (Spartanburgh) to Thomas Hatchett (same); for $500 sold 186 ac on Furgason's

Cr; border: S-John Otts, E-William Rogers, N-Solomon Autrey's old tract and Josiah Hatchett, and W-Robert Ligon. Witness Martin Otts and John Hatchett. Signed Josiah Hatchett. Wit. oath Apr. 29, 1825 John Hatchett to Philip Brewton. Rec. May 2, 1825

p. 69-70 Feb. 15, 1825 William McWilliams (Spartanburgh) to Thomas S Rice (same); for $340 sold 226 ac on both sides of S Pacolate R; border: Armsted Bomar, William McWilliams, and widow Turner; part of grant to William McWilliams. Witness Jabez Galt, George Heatherington, and Armsted Bomar. Signed William McWilliams. Wit. oath May 2, 1825 Armsted Bomar to James Young. Rec. May 2, 1825. Dower renounced May 2, 1825 Elizabeth McWilliams to James Young

p. 70-71 Feb. 15, 1825 Robert McDowell (Spartanburgh) to Thomas S Rice (same); for $50 sold 18 ac on waters of S Pacolate R; border: Oliver Clark and a waggon road; part of grant to Capt. David McDowell. Witness Jabez Galt, George Heatherington, and Armsted Bomar. Signed Robert McDowell. Wit. oath May 2, 1825 Armsted Bomar to J Whitten. Rec. May 2, 1825

p. 71 Aug. 26, 1824 John Trail (Spartanburgh) to John Hatchett (same); for $235 sold 200 ac; border: Pinckney Rd. Witness James Calvert and Adonijah Patterson. Signed John Trail. Wit. oath Apr. 29, 1825 James Calvert to Philip Brewton. Rec. May 2, 1825

p. 71-72 Nov. 1, 1815 Samuel Farrow (Spartanburgh) to niece Miss Charlotte Farrow (same); for affectionate respect give 150 ac in Spartanburgh and Union Dists on W side of Elishi's Cr of Enoree R; sold by Spencer Bobo to William Langston and Mark Langston who sold to Samuel Farrow; except part known as Groves Yarborough's place where Thomas Waters lives; part of grant to John Head. Witness William Farrow and Richard Farrow. Signed S Farrow. Wit. oath Apr. 7, 1825 William Farrow to Burrell Bobo. Rec. May 14, 1825

p. 72-73 Jan. 6, 1825 Thomas Poole, sheriff (Spartanburgh) to William Lipscomb (same); for $20 sold 90 ac; border: NE & S-Thomas Reid and S-Thomas Hancock; sold due to writ from Spartanburgh Common Pleas Court second Monday after fourth Monday in Mar. 1823 suit of C. F. Tolleson; judgment was levy of $520 and costs from John Tolleson desc. Witness John Bomar jr and J Dickson. Signed Thomas Poole SSD. Wit. oath May 14, 1825 John Bomar jr to E Bomar. Rec. May 14, 1825

p. 73-74 Dec. 24, 1822 Joshua Durham (Spartanburgh) to Soloman Burnett (same); for $125 sold 181 ac on Brushy fork Cr of S Tyger R; border: Toomer and Jonah Leonard. Witness Jeremiah Burnett and John Durham jr. Signed Joshua Durham. Wit. oath Mar. 6, 1823 John Durham jr to Thomas Wood. Rec. May 16, 1825

p. 74 Feb. 4, 1820 William Waddel (Spartanburgh) to Barnett Burnett; for $350 sold 159 ac on Ben's Cr; border: Bazwell's Spring and Haden; includes 13 ac of Daniel McKie's land that Daniel sold to William Bazwell; border: Hoy (or Hay). Witness Philip Johnson and John Durham. Signed William Waddel. Wit. oath Jul. 15, 1820 Philip Johnson to Thomas Wood. Rec. May 16, 1825

p. 74-75 Feb. 22, 1825 James Varner (Spartanburgh) to John Varner (same); for $64.94 sold a bay horse 4 years old, 3 feather beds and furniture, a cupboard and furniture, a dresser, 2 pewter dishes, 2 pewter plates, a pewter bason, a loom, 13 chairs, 10 barrels of corn, 2 pots, 2 ovens, a skillet, a pan, "40 dozen of oats", 10 hogs, 2 axes, 2 pair of chains, 3 ploughs, a log chain, a mattock, 2 spinning sheels, and a pair of cards; Condition: sale void if James pays John $64.94 by Mar. 1, 1826. Witness James Nesbitt and John Ward. Signed James Vernon. Wit. oath Mar. 10, 1825 James Nesbitt to F. H. Legg. Rec. May 17, 1825

p. 75-76 May 19, 1825 John Neal, heir at law of John Neal desc who served as private in Capt. Turner's Company in North Carolina Line of Regulars in Revolutionary War, to Josiah Hall (Henderson Co, Tenn); power of attorney to obtain from Secretary of State of North Carolina or "Military Land Committee of Univ. of North Carolina" military land warrant of John Neal desc. Witness Joshua Richards and John S Hall. Signed John Neal's mark. Wit. oath May 20, 1825 Joshua Richards and John S Hall to John W Farrow and Joseph Camp. Rec. May 20, 1825

p. 76-77 Nov. 30, 1824 David Tanner (Spartanburgh) to William Yates (same); for $300 sold 150 ac on Heleson Br of Fairforest Cr; grant Jun. 5, 1786 Gov. William Moultrie to James Johnson. Witness Felix Green and Polly Tanner. Signed David Tanner. Wit. oath Apr. 20, 1825 Polly Tanner to F. H. Legg. Rec. May 23, 1825. Dower renounced Apr. 20, 1825 Nancy Tanner to F. H. Legg

p. 77 Mar. (blank), 1825 John Rainwaters (Spartanburgh) to grandson John D Nebughr (same); for love and affection give a sorrel mare with blaze face about 6 years old next Spring and her future offspring. Witness John Brooks. Signed John Rainwaters' mark. Wit. oath May 23, 1825 John Brooks to W Hunt. Rec. May 24, 1825

p. 77-78 Apr. 5, 1825 Thomas Poole, sheriff (Spartanburgh) to Elisha Poole (same); for $30 sold 43 ac on Richland Cr of Pacolate R; border: Anthony Baits, James Poole, Elisha Poole, and Crocker; sold to Daniel White for Elisha Poole; sold due to writ from Spartanburgh Common Pleas Court second Monday after fourth Monday in Oct. 11824 suit of Ephraim Jackson; judgment was levy of $30 and costs from William Crocker. Witness John Nance and John Poole. Signed Thomas Poole. Wit. oath May 24, 1825 John Poole to Caleb (or Jaleb) Jones. Rec. May 24, 1825

p. 78-79 Oct. 16, 1823 Thomas Dezell, John Martin, Margaret Martin, George Killock, Mary Killock, and Elizabeth Dezell (Spartanburgh) to John Murph (same); for $192 sold 96½ ac; in two adjoining tracts: (1) 85 ac on waters of Kelso's Cr of Fairforest Cr; border: N-Macajah Barnett, S-Shands Golightly, SE-David Golightly jr; and (2) 11½ ac; grant May 4, 1812 to Jane Dezell then border: SE-Shands Golightly, E & N-David Golightly, and SW-Jane Dezell by plat dated Feb. 28, 1812. Witness George Bails, Benjamin Smith, William Bomar, and Edward Bomar. Signed Thomas Dezell, Elizabeth Dezell, John Martin, Margaret Martin, George Killock, and Mary Killock. Wit. oath Mar. 31, 1825 George Bails (for Thomas and Elizabeth Dezell, John and Margaret Martin, and Mary Killock) to E Bomar. Wit. oath May 30, 1825 Edward Bomar (for George Killock) to E Bomar. Rec. May 30, 1825

p. 79-80 Dec. 20, 1824 Seth Lewis (Spartanburgh) to Lewis Turner (same); for $30 sold 7½ ac on waters of Showly Cr; border: Lewis Turner, Reuben Fossett, and Justin Childs. Witness Samuel Turner and William Trimmier. Signed Seth Lewis. Wit. oath May 31, 1825 William Trimmier to E Bomar. Rec. May 31, 1825

p. 80 Jan. 4, 1825 Memory N Chapman (Spartanburgh) to Robert M Young (same); for $350 sold ½ ac in Spartanburgh, SC on S side of Main St; border: E-James E Henry, S-Richard Thomson, W-James Hunt, and N-Main St. Witness W. T. Nicholls and Willis Foster. Signed M. N. Chapman. Wit. oath Jun. 2, 1825 Willis Foster to E Bomar. Rec. Jun. 2, 1825

p. 80-81 Jan. 8, 1822 William W Smithwick (Spartanburgh) to James Duncan, son of Alexander (same); for $1,000 sold 200 ac on N side of N Tyger R; border: N & W-Joseph Johnson and John Trail, E-Benjamin Nicholls and Henry White, and S-N Tyger R. Witness

Meadows Harrelson and Nancy Harrelson. Signed Wm W Smithwick. Wit. oath May 5, 1823 Meadows Harrelson to E Bomar. Rec. Jun. 6, 1825

p. 81-82 Feb. 7, 1825 Robert Ligon (Spartanburgh) to William Tapp and James Tapp; for $109 sold 107 ac (by calculation of James Silmon) on both sides of Fairforest Cr; border: James Tapp and Bomar; plat attached shows also border: William Tapp; grant to Henry Brown. Witness Ransom Foster and John Bomar. Signed Robert Ligon. Wit. oath Jun. 6, 1825 Ransom Foster to W Hunt. Rec. Jun. 6, 1825

p. 82-83 Oct. 29, 1824 David Foster (Spartanburgh), one of heirs (and son of) of estate of John Foster desc, to Herbertt Hawkins (same); for $500 sold (1) 180 ac on Mill Cr of N Tyger R; border: N-estate of John Word desc, W-John Chapman jr, and other sides-Herbertt Hawkins; see deed from Gabriel Benson to John Foster desc; where David Foster's mother, Holly Foster, lives and willed by John Foster desc to David Foster after Holly's death; see John Foster's will at Spartanburgh Ordinary's Office; and (2) 7 ac; border: Herbertt Hawkins and tract (1); sold by Edmond W Chapman to David Foster. Witness John Wingo and Robert Foster. Signed David Foster. Wit. oath Jun. 9, 1825 John Wingo to J. W. Farrow. Rec. Jun. 9, 1825

p. 83 Mar. 1, 1825 William Gillaspie (Spartanburgh) to Willis W Dickie (same);for $293.18 3/4 sold 120½ ac on James Cr of Furgeson's Cr; known as Jones tract; Condition: sale void if William Gillaspie pays Willis W Dickie $293.18 3/4 by Dec. 25, 1826. Witness Eli Cox, William L Allen, and Matthew Allen. Signed William Gillaspie. Wit. oath Jun. 4, 1825 Eli Cox to Philip Brewton. Rec. Jun. 20, 1825

p. 83-84 Apr. 13, 1824 Matthew V Jones (Spartanburgh) to Lester and McCrary (Greenville Dist); for $100 sold 150 ac on Abner's Cr of Enoree R; border: William McHughs, William Hendrix jr, William Mayfield, John Cargale, Joseph Hughs sr, Isham Wilson, and "others"; part of tract sold by Henry Wade to Matthew V Jones. Witness William Hughes and John Duncan. Signed Matthew V Jones. Wit. oath Apr. 15, 1825 William Hughes to Jesse Hammett. Rec. Jun. 24, 1825

p. 84-85 Jun. 21, 1825 James Burnett sr (Spartanburgh) to James Burnett jr; for $600 sold two Negro boys Spencer about 12 years old and Willis about 17 years old. Witness William Clement and Zachariah Wall. Signed James Burnett's mark. Wit. oath Jul. 4, 1825 William Clement to W Bennett. Rec. Jul. 4, 1825

p. 85 Jun. 21, 1825 James Burnett sr (Spartanburgh) to Mathew Burnett; for $800 sold three Negroes: a man John age 40, woman Dilse 47 years old, and girl Ambriler 5 years old. Witness William Clement and Zachariah Wall. Signed James Burnett's mark. Wit. oath Jun. 21, 1825 Zachariah Wall to W Clement. Rec. Jul. 4, 1825

p. 85-86 Feb. 18, 1822 Benjamin High (Spartanburgh) to Moses Tapp; for $150 sold 260 ac on waters of Fairforest Cr; grant Mar. 23, 1818 to Benjamin High. Witness James Selman and Joshua Tapp. Signed Benjamin High. Wit. oath Jul. 4, 1825 Joshua Tapp to W Hunt. Rec. Jul. 4, 1825

p. 86-87 May 12, 1825 John Vice (Spartanburgh) to Nathaniel Vice (same); for $222.50 sold 300 ac; border: Meadows Harrelson and James Duncan; part of grant of 600 ac to John Vice. Witness Robert Rogers jr, Eli Vice, and Abner Vice. Signed John Vice. Wit. oath Jun. 4, 1825 Robert Rogers jr to James Hamm. Rec. Jul. 4, 1825. Dower renounced Jun. 8, 1825 Francis Vice to James Hamm

p. 87 Feb. 24, 1825 Philip Tippins (Spartanburgh) to Thomas P Brockman

(Greenville Dist); for $98.25 sold 3 sorrel mares, 2 sorrel colts, 2 feather beds and furniture, 10 hogs, 5 cattle, a loom, and all household and kitchen furniture; Condition: sale void if Philip Tippins pays Thomas P Brockman $98.25 by Jan. 1, 1826. Witness James B Hudson and Benjamin Tippins. Signed Philip Tippins. Wit. oath Jul. 1, 1825 James B Hudson to James McDaniel. Rec. Jul. 18, 1825

p. 87-88 Oct. 4, 1819 Thomas Wright to Vincent Tapp (Spartanburgh); for $200 sold 100 ac on fork of Tyger R; border: Nathaniel Jentry and Broton Tommas. Witness Robert Ligon and John Thornton. Signed Thomas Wright. Wit. oath Jan. 3, 1825 Robert Ligon to D White. Rec. Jul. 18, 1825

p. 88 Dec. 12, 1823 Larkin Cardin (Monroe Co, Tenn) to John A Cunningham (Spartanburgh); for $35 sold 100 ac on N side of S Pacolate R; border: Luke Burnett; part of grant to Larkin Cardin. Witness A Cunningham and R. L. Cunningham. Signed Larkin Cardin. Wit. oath Jul. 22, 1825 A Cunningham to W Clement. Rec. Jul. 20, 1825

p. 88-89 Mar. 14, 1825 John Ward (Spartanburgh) to Hudson Lanham (same); for $200 sold (ac omitted) on NE side of S Tyger R; border: Zep Posey and Hudson Lanham; sold Jan. 26, 1825 by Robert Ligon to John Ward. Witness Samuel B Bragg and James Nesbitt. Signed J Ward. Wit. oath May 28, 1825 James Nesbitt to Philip Brewton. Rec. Jul. 21, 1825

p. 89 Jan. 26, 1825 Robert Ligon (Spartanburgh) to John Ward (same); for $100 quit claim to (ac omitted) on NE side of S Tyger R; part of grant to John Ward "at the sitting" of the Legislature; part was cultivated last year by Joseph Lannum; between Lanham and Posey; and quit claim rights to Robert Ligon by Frederick Steding. Witness Mathias Rush and James Enock. Signed Robert Ligon. Wit. oath May 28, 1825 Mathias Rush to Philip Brewton. Rec. Jul. 21, 1825

p. 89-90 Jan. 31, 1825 David Golightly jr (Spartanburgh), attorney for Thomas Merreda (Davis Co, Ind), to Stephen Foster (Spartanburgh); for $138 sold 138 ac on waters of Fairforest Cr; border: Stephen Foster, heirs of John Foster desc, Andrew Foster, William Kirby, John Gossett, and Mry P Parker. Witness Christi Golightly and Henry O Golightly. Signed David Golightly jr, attorney for Thomas Meredah. Wit. oath Jul. 21, 1825 Christi Golightly to E Bomar. Rec. Jul. 21, 1825

p. 90-91 Mar. 8, 1824 Joseph Lanham (Spartanburgh) to Hudson Lanham (same); for $363 sold 83 ac on fork of N & S Tyger R and on Chyncapin Cr of N Tyger R; border: N-Mathias Rush, W-Maj. Patton, and S & E-John Thomas. Witness William Otts, Martin Otts, and Henry R Lanham. Signed Joseph Lanham's mark. Wit. oath Mar. 26, 1825 Henry R Lanham to James Crook. Rec. Jul. 21, 1825

p. 91-92 May 31, 1825 Moses Casey (Spartanburgh) to Simpson C Newmon (same); for $100 sold 50 ac on Cedar Shoals Cr of Enoree R; border: William Casey and Richard Fryer. Witness Aaron F Casey and Eliza S Casey. Signed M Casey. Wit. oath May 4, 1825 Aaron F Casey to Burrell Bobo. Rec. Aug. 1, 1825

p. 92 Feb. 23, 1815 Jonathan Wall (Spartanburgh) to Nancy Kilby and Elsey and Sarah Wall (same); for $500 sold 300 ac on both sides Jacob's Cr and Bodley's Br; border: Young, a road, and Daniel White. Witness William Foster and William Clement. Signed Jonathan Wall. Wit. oath Apr. 11, 1825 William Foster to James Young. Rec. Aug. 1, 1825

p. 92-93 Jun. 25, 1825 James Burnett sr (Spartanburgh) to son-in-law Woodson Burnett (same); for love and affection give a Negro boy Simpson in his eighth year of age. Witness W Bennett and Mathew Burnett. Signed James Burnett sr's mark. Certified Jul. 6, 1825 by W Bennett. Rec. Aug. 1, 1825

p. 93-94 Feb. 1, 1825 Elias Rogers (Spartanburgh) to Nancy Poole (same); for $82 sold 23½ ac on waters of N Tyger R; part of grant to Charles C Pinckney. Witness John Hatchett and Gideon Harelson. Signed Elias Rogers. Wit. oath Jul. 18, 1825 John Hatchett to W Hunt. Rec. Aug. 1, 1825. Dower renounced Apr. 30, 1825 Sarah Rogers to James Hamm

p. 94 Mar. 10, 1824 Moses Tapp (Spartanburgh) to A. B. Moore (same); for $208.71 sold (1) 175 ac where Moses Tapp lives; and (2) 200 ac on Fairforest Cr; see deed for (2) on Apr. 24, 1824 Thomas Bomar to Moses Tapp and "transfered" to A. B. Moore. Witness A Barry and Joshua Tapp. Signed Moses Tapp. Wit. oath Aug. 1, 1825 A Barry to E Bomar. Rec. Aug. 1, 1825

p. 94-95 Dec. 20, 1822 Moses Tapp (Spartanburgh) to William Tapp (same); for $350 sold 175 ac on Big Br; on S side of Blackstock's Road; where "he" now lives. Witness James Yates and William Calvert. Signed Moses Tapp. Wit. oath Aug. 4, 1823 James Yates to Ransom Foster. Rec. Aug. 1, 1825

p. 95-96 Mar. 1, 1825 Fortunatus H Legg (Spartanburgh) to James Brannon (same); for $900 sold ½ ac in Spartanburgh, SC; border: S-Public Square, W-Jesse Cleveland, N-John W Farrow, and NE-Public road. Witness John Dickson and Ransom Seay. Signed F. H. Legg. Wit. oath Mar. 1, 1825 John Dickson to James E Henry. Rec. Aug. 9, 1825. Dower renounced Mar. 9, 1825 Mary Legg to John S Rowland

p. 96-97 Feb. 22, 1822 Susanna Atkenson (Spartanburgh) to Simon Lavendar (same); for $125 sold 50 ac on E side of branch of James' Cr; border: W-Jesse Moor, S-Susannah Brewton, and N-Georgia Road. Witness William Otts and Charles Skinner. Signed Susanna Atkenson's mark. Wit. oath Aug. 22, 1825 William Otts to Philip Brewton. Rec. Aug. 22, 1825

p. 97 Feb. 24, 1825 Leonard Sparks (Spartanburgh) to William Wood (Union Dist); to secure two notes (1) to William Wood for $21.50 dated Feb. 5, 1825 due one day after and note to James Norris for $34.76 due Dec. 25, 1825 and dated Feb. 4, 1825 "witness Joel Kirby, endorsed pay to William Wood for value received Feb. 4, 1825 John Norris" sold to William Wood 100 ac on N side of Pacolate R; border: Thomas Norton and Norris; Condition: sale void if Leonard Sparks pays William Wood by Dec. 25, 1825. Witness Thomas Wyatt and Nehemiah Sparks. Signed Leonard Sparks. Wit. oath none. Rec. Aug. 12, 1825

p. 97-98 Feb. 24, 1825 Leonard Sparks (Spartanburgh) to William Wood (Union Dist); to secure note to William Wood of $21.50 dated Feb. 5, 1825 and due Feb. 6, 1825 and second note to James Norris for $34.76 dated Feb. 4, 1825 and due Dec. 25, 1825 "witness by Joel Kirby and endorsed to pay William Wood for value recieved Feb. 4, 1825 James Norris" sold a bay horse, sorrel cold, 2 cows and calves, 2 beds and furniture, and 2 pots and an oven; Condition: sale void if Leonard Sparks pays William Wood by Dec. 25, 1825. Witness Thomas Wyatt and Nehemiah Sparks. Signed Leonard Sparks. Wit. oath Aug. 12, 1825 Thomas Wyatt to William Reid. Rec. Aug. 12, 1825

p. 98 Apr. 14, 1821 Thomas Bomar (Spartanburgh) to Moses Tapp; for $175 sold 200 ac (according to "late" survey of James Silmon) on Fairforest Cr; border: William Bomar, Benjamin High, and "others"; part of land formerly owned by Peter Ligon and sold by Labon P Poole, sheriff (Spartanburgh) to Moses Tapp who sold to Benjamin High and Thomas Bomar "cojointly". Witness Elial Williams and Ransom Foster. Signed Tho Bomar. Wit. oath Aug. 15, 1825 Elial Williams to E Bomar. Rec. Aug. 15, 1825

p. 98-99 Dec. 4, 1811 James Cook (Spartanburgh) to James Kean (same); for $50 sold 50 ac on waters of Fairforest Cr; border: Kean's Spring Br; part of grant Gov. Josiah Martin (NC) to Richard Hampton who sold to James Gibbs and sold by Zachariah Gibbs, executor of James Gibbs desc, to John Finch who sold to Micajah Barnett or Richard Barnett who sold to Thomas Cook who sold to James Cook. Witness Philip Otts and Solomon Autry. Signed James Cook. Wit. oath Mar. 4, 1812 Solomon Autry to Danl White. Rec. Aug. 15, 1825

p. 99-100 Mar. 21, 1825 Alexander Roddy (Spartanburgh), attorney for Gabriel Benson (Ala), to Cyrus Seay (Spartanburgh); for $422 sold 211 ac on both sides Fairforest Cr; includes shoal and county road. Witness Peter Haskins and Burrel Wingo. Signed Gabriel Benson and Alexr Roddy, attorney for Gabriel Benson. Wit. oath Aug. 16, 1825 Peter Haskins to J. W. Farrow. Rec. Aug. 16, 1825

p. 100 Apr. 2, 1824 Hugh Moore (Spartanburgh) to Patrick Moore (same); for $5,000 paid partly by note sold 1,451 ac on waters of Thickety Cr of Broad R; border: John Little; where Hugh Moore lives. Witness John Moore and Charles Petty. Signed Hugh Moore. Wit. oath Feb. 16, 1825 Charles Petty to F. W. Robertson. Rec. Aug. 29, 1825

p. 100-101 Mar. 15, 1825 Nephphatha Roe (Spartanburgh) to Samuel McCrary and Philip C Lester (Greenville Dist); for $87 sold 196 ac on branch of Rocky field Cr of Enoree R and Penny Rock Br; border: Bailey, Lucretia Demsey, Benjamin Woods, William Hendricks, and William Hughes; where Nephphatha Roe lives; Condition: sale void if Naphphatha Roe pays McCrary $50.81¼ and Lester $36.18 3/4 (total $87) by Dec. 15, 1825. Witness Joel Hammett and Walker Morgan. Signed Nephphatha Roe. Wit. oath Sept. 1, 1825 (Greenville Dist) Walker Morgan to Jesse Hammett. Rec. Sept. 3, 1825

p. 101-103 Jul. 22, 1820 William B Sheldon (Union Dist) to John Clerk (Spartanburgh); for $500 sold W. B. Sheldon's share in following property: (1) (ac omitted) on S side of Tyger R; called Mill tract; tract Isaac Crow sold to George Hill, Leonard Hill, Sheldon, and Clark Jan. 4, 1819; (2) (ac omitted) on N side of Tyger R; sold by Isaac Crow to George Hill, Leonard Hill, Sheldon, and Clark May 12, 1819; (3) "priviledge" of shoals of Tyger R that Joseph Wofford sold to George Hill, Leonard Hill, Sheldon,and Clark May 12, 1819; (4) (ac omitted) on S side of Tyger R; border: E-tract (1); sold by Joseph Wofford to George Hill, Leonard Hill, Sheldon, and Clark Apr. 13, 1820; and for $1,000 sold W. B. Sheldon's share in "a mule unfurnished" which when assembled has 180 spindles, 2 trastle frames containing 84 spindles each, 4 finishers, 2 breakers, 8 heads of drawing, 8 head of roping, and "preparations" belonging to each for spinning cotton, a roler lathe, a hand lathe for turning iron, a small wood lathe, a cutting engine, a fluttering engine, a vice and all other tools for making machinery, carpenter's tools, a cotton gin and "preparation" thereto, all grains, flour, cotton, cotton yarn, lumber of all kinds, and "other property" owned by George Hill, Leonard Hill, Sheldon, and Clark. Witness Sarah P Hill and George Hill. Signed William B Shelton. Wit. oath May 27, 1822 George Hill to Wm Young. Rec. Sept. 5, 1825. Dower renounced Jul. 16, 1825 Anna H Sheldon to Benjamin Wofford

p. 103 Jan. 31, 1821 William Arnold (Spartanburgh) to Henry Earnest (same); for $200 sold 26 ac on branches of Enoree R. Witness William Johnson and Jesse Wofford. Signed William Arnold. Wit. oath

Apr. 5, 1821 William Johnson to David Moor. Rec. Sept. 5, 1825

p. 103-104 May 12, 1821 Alexander Roddy (Spartanburgh) to Peter C McMakin (same); for $1,000 sold 132 ac on waters of N Tyger R with gris and saw mills; part of grant in (1) 1784 to John Brooks and (2) Oct. 3, 1804 to John McDowel. Witness William Wilson and James Wilson. Signed Alexr Roddy. Wit. oath Dec. 11, 1824 William Wilson to John Montgomery. Rec. Sept. 4, 1825

p. 104-105 Aug. 18, 1825 James Keen (Spartanburgh) to grandson Thomas Finch (same); for love and affection give 15 Negroes: Amos, Isaac, Amy, Sally, Susy, Alfred, Miles, Nerva, Nancy, Jacob, Noah, Amos, Harriet, Benjamin, and Isham; Thomas gets slaves when James dies; Thomas to provide wholesome food, clothing, and washing and lodging for John Finch and Jane Finch, parents of Thomas Finch, during their lifetimes; provided John and Jane Finch consent to move to Thomas' place; Thomas has to deliver to his brother William Finch in 6 months after James Keen dies a Negro boy slave of value $200 or $200 cash; if Thomas refuses then other folks can sue. Witness William Trimmier and John Bomar jr. Signed James Keen's mark. Wit. oath Sept. 4, 1825 William Trimmier to W Hunt. Rec. Sept. 5, 1825

p. 105-106 Aug. 17, 1824 Byrd Linthicum (Laurence Co, Ala) to John McMikin (Spartanburgh); for $600 sold 200 ac on Hampton's Br of S Tyger R; border: S-Alexander Robbs desc's heirs, W-William Robbs sr, N-Alexander Thompson, and E-Edward Smith. Witness Alexander McMakin and Neal McDale. Signed Byrd Linthicum. Wit. oath Apr. 9, 1825 Alexander McMakin to John Chapman. Rec. Sept. 5, 1825

p. 106-107 Aug. 16, 1825 John D Cannon (Spartanburgh) to Benjamin A Markley; to secure bond of $300 condition to pay $140 and for $300 sold 200 ac on Peter's Cr; border: S & E-Jesse Cannon, N-"rest of land sold to Jesse Cannon", and W-David Patterson; part of 332 ac; 200 ac was "lately" sold by Benjamin A Markley to John D Cannon; Condition: sale void if John D Cannon pays Benjamin A Markley $140 and interest. Witness James Spencer and David Patterson. Signed John D Cannon. Wit. oath Sept. 5, 1825 James Spencer to E Bomar. Rec. Sept. 5, 1825

p. 107-108 Aug. 16, 1825 Benjamin A Markley (Charleston, SC) to Jesse Cannon (Spartanburgh); for $132 sold 132 ac on Peter's Cr of Pacolate R; border: S & E-Jesse Cannon, N-Richard Thompson, and W-David Patterson; N end of 332 ac grant to Abraham Markley; (other part of tract?) sold to John Cannon; Abraham Markley desc (Charleston, SC)'s will appointed son Benjamin A Markley and sons-in-law William Lee and Ezekiel Noble executors and Abraham Markley said to sell his property; Benjamin was only executor who qualified. Witness James Spencer and David Patterson. Signed Benjamin A Markley, by his attorney Wm Ellison. Wit. oath Sept. 5, 1825 James Spencer to Caleb Jones. Rec. Sept. 5, 1825

p. 108 Dec. 9, 1815 David Davis (Spartanburgh) to Peter C McMakin (same); for $150 sold 61 ac on both sides branch of N Tyger R; border: John Montgomery and Alexander Keller; plat attached shows also border: Jas Miller; part of grant to Joseph Alexander who sold to David Davis sr and given to David Davis. Witness Alexander McCollum, James Hodge, and Richard Hanson. Signed David Davis' mark. Wit. oath Jan. 27, 1823 Richard Hanson to John Burns. Rec. Sept. 5, 1825

p. 108-109 Aug. 16, 1825 Benjamin A Markley (Charleston, SC) to John D Cannon (Spartanburgh); for $250 sold 200 ac on Peter's Cr; border: line between John D Cannon and his father Jesse Cannon, S & E-Jesse Cannon, N-Richard Thompson, and W-David Patterson; part of grant to Abraham Markley; Abraham Markley desc's will appointed son Benjamin A Markley and sons-in-law William Lee and Ezekiel Noble executors and Benjamin was only one who qualified; Abraham Markley's will said to sell the land. Witness James Spencer and David Patterson. Signed Benj A Markley, by his attorney Wm Ellison. Wit. oath Sept. 5, 1825 James Spencer to Caleb Jones. Rec. Sept. 5, 1825

p. 109-110 Sept. 6, 1825 Thomas Poole, sheriff (Spartanburgh) to William Rice esq (Union Dist); for $3,000 sold 2,000 ac on Enoree R; where Daniel McKie lives; sold due to writ from Charleston Dist Common Pleas Court Feb. 12, 1825 suit of Isaac Bowell (or Barrett) and Co; judgment was levy of $3,111.71 and costs from Daniel McKie and Labon P Poole. Witness William T Nicholls and James Hunt. Signed Thomas Poole. Wit. oath Sept. 6, 1825 William T Nicholls to E Bomar. Rec. Sept. 6, 1825

p. 110-111 Aug. 5, 1825 James Keen to wife's (Martha) brother-in-law Philip Brewton; because his wife desires it and for $100 give Martha's share of her father's estate: a Negro woman Suckey, who has had increase Ruth about 18 years old and a child Jonas about 1 year old, Reuben 16 years old, Massey 14 years old, Cassey 12 years old, Betsey 10 years old, Mat 7 years old, and Decey 2 years old; the $100 was paid to James Keen "sometime since" by Dr Eber Smith and Philip Brewton is to pay $62.50--the balance of James Keen's account with Dr Eber Smith for medical services on Martha and family of Negroes; Philip Brewton has agreed to maintain James Keen's "mathin law" Elizabeth Autry during her lifetime provided she chooses to live with Philip Brewton. Witness Thomas Bomar, John Brooks, and W. T. Tanner. Signed James Keen's mark. Wit. oath Sept. 12, 1825 W. T. Tanner to James Crook. Rec. Sept. 12, 1825

p. 111-112 Mar. 6, 1821 William Dewberry (Spartanburgh) to Francis Little (same); for $200 sold 397 ac; part of 567 ac grant Feb. 2, 1807 by(sic) John Bynum to William Dewberry. Witness Charles Smith and William Waters. Signed William Dewberry. Wit. oath Apr. 10, 1821 William Waters to Caleb Jones. Rec. Sept. 20, 1825. Dower renounced Apr. 7, 1821 Betsy Dewberry to John Lipscomb

p. 112 Mar. 3, 1824 Samuel Gentry (Spartanburgh) to Richard Willis; for $60 sold 20 ac on S side of Tyger R; border: Richard Willis, Joseph Willis, Gideon Reynolds, and Richard Gentry. Witness John Thornton and James Mason. Signed Samuel Gentry's mark. Wit. oath Sept. 26, 1825 John Thornton to Robert Ligon. Rec. Sept. 26, 1825

p. 112-113 Feb. 26, 1825 Robert Alexander (Spartanburgh) to Richard Willis; for $17 sold 5 ac on S side Tyger R. Witness John Thornton and William Thornton. Signed Robert Alexander. Wit. oath Sept. 26, 1825 John Thornton to Robert Ligon. Rec. Sept. 26, 1825

p. 113-114 Jul. 3, 1819 John Williams (Spartanburgh) to Thomas Wright (same); for $100 sold 10 ac on Cain Cr on N side Tyger R. Witness Gideon Harrelson and Reuben Fowler. Signed John Williams. Wit. oath Dec. 15, 1824 Gideon Harrelson to James Hamm. Rec. Oct. 3, 1825. Dower renounced Dec. 15, 1824 Margaret Harrelson to James Hamm

p. 114-115 Nov. 11, 1823 (Equity Court) J. S. Sims, commissioner of Union Dist Equity Court, to William W Smithwick; for $401 sold 440 ac on Tyger R; border: N-Jonathan Crow, S & W-John Thornton, Chesny, Robert Alexander, Elias Rogers, and Richard Willis, and E-N Tyger R; William White, executor of will of Cemina McCarily desc, complained to Union Dist Equity Court against Mary McCarity and others on Aug. 11, 1823; he saked to sell part of Cemina McCarily's property; sale was on Nov. 10, 1823 at Union Court House and was sold (for?) $100 (debt?). Witness William T Nicholls and Robert M Young. Signed J. S. Sims CEUD. Wit. oath Oct. 3, 1825 William T Nicholls to William Hunt. Rec. Sept. 3, 1825

p. 115-116 Apr. 18, 1825 Redrick Rutland (Spartanburgh) to Ransom Foster (same); for $400 sold 440 ac on Beaverdam Cr of Fairforest Cr; border: W-Blackstock road and Richard Thomson, S-David McCarley, SE-Richard Foster, E-John Rutland, NE-John Foster "(mill creek)", and N-Joel Yates and Thomas McCarley; grant to Samuel Gravell who sold to Joshua Smith who sold to William Smith who sold part of 1,000 ac Sept. 30, 1805 to Redrick Rutland. Witness William Yates and Joel Yates. Signed Reddrick Rutland. Wit. oath Jul. 4, 1825 William Yates to John S Rowland. Rec. Oct. 3, 1825. Dower renounced Apr. 20, 1825 Dorithy Rutland to F. H. Legg

p. 116-117 Apr. 12, 1825 Josiah Kilgore (Greenville Dist) to Elias Corder (Spartanburgh); for $1,131 sold 377 ac on S side of Middle Tyger R; border: David Wheeler, Hilborn, and Robert Bailey; grant Jun. 23, 1774 to Daniel Horry. Witness Thomas Thomas and James Corder. Signed Josiah Kilgore. Wit. oath Apr. 12, 1825 James Corder to Philip Brewton. Rec. Oct. 3, 1825

p. 117 Jun. 2, 1825 Isaac Finch (Spartanburgh) to John J Bagwell (same); for $5 sold 26 ac on waters of Fairforest Cr; border: Bagwell; grant to Thomas Finch who sold to Isaac Finch. Witness Alexander Flemming and Daniel White. Signed Isaac Finch. Wit. oath Oct. 3, 1825 Alexander Flemming to W Hunt. Rec. Oct. 3, 1825

p. 117-118 Jul. 1, 1824 Ezekiel Sillavan (Ray Co (or Roy), Tenn) to Vincent Sprouce (Spartanburgh); for $200 sold 204 ac; part of 970 ac grant to Ezekiel Sillavan. Witness William Littlejohn and Young Allen. Signed Ezekiel Sillaven. Wit. oath Oct. 3, 1825 Young Allen to Caleb Jones. Rec. Oct. 3, 1825

p. 118-119 Jan. 22, 1824 Nathaniel Dangger (Spartanburgh) to David Clark (same); for $343 sold 332 ac on W side of Meadow Cr; border: Henry Gramling. Witness Lemuel S Walters and John Clark. Signed Nathaniel Dangger. Wit. oath Jan. 22, 1825 Lemuel S Walters to John S Rowland. Rec. Oct. 3, 1825. Dower renounced May 13, 1825 Maryann Danggar to James Young

p. 119-120 Oct. 17, 1816 John Frederick Kern (Laurence Dist) to Jacob Dorner (Spartanburgh); for $285.50 sold 285½ ac on waters of Tyger R and Dutchman's Cr; border: O'Sheald; grant in 1787 to John Danl Kern desc (Laurens Dist); resurveyed by Gen. John A Elmore Aug. 1, 1816. Witness William Liles and Pariden Danl Kern. Signed John Fredk Kern. Wit. oath Mar. 31, 1825 (Lawrence Dist) Pariden Danl Kern to Robert Long. Rec. Oct. 3, 1825. Dower renounced Mar. 31, 1825 (Laurence Dist) Elizabeth Kern to Robert Long

p. 120-121 May 1, 1824 Benjamin Wofford to trustees of "Pasonage for Enoree Circuit"; for $300 sold 1 ac; land is where Passonage house stands; plat attached shows border: Benj Wofford on all sides; trustees are James Mahew, Sheldon Swift, F. J. Potter, and William Wright esqs. Witness Anthony Shands and Isaac Miles. Signed Benjamin Wofford. Wit. oath Aug. 25, 1825 Isaac Miles to Burrell Bobo. Rec. Oct. 4, 1825

p. 121-122 May 7, 1817 Benjamin Wofford and wife Anna (Spartanburgh) to Thomas G Potter, Isaac Miles, Golden Tinsley, Benjamin Wofford, and Anthony Shands, trustees (Spartanburgh); for $5 sold 1½ ac to erect a house of worship for Methodist Episcopal Church in USA according to rules of the General Conference of USA. Witness Gideon Shands and Isaac Tinsley. Signed Benjm Wofford. Wit. oath Aug. 25, 1825 Isaac Tinsley to Burrell Bobo. Rec. Oct. 4, 1825

p. 122 Sept. 8, 1824 John Bomar jr (Spartanburgh) to George Jones (Rutherford Co, NC); for $800 sold 1½ ac in Spartanburgh, SC on N side of Main St; adjoins NE corner of Public Square; opposite

James Hunt's lot; border: Muse Tolleson and Brannon. Witness Daniel Faust and William F Jones. Signed John Bomar jr. Wit. oath Oct. 4, 1825 William F Jones to E Bomar. Rec. Oct. 4, 1825

p. 122-124 Aug. 2, 1825 Thomas Poole, sheriff (Spartanburgh) to George Jones (Rutherford Co, NC); for $2,100 sold 1 ac and "parallel line of 30 feet" annexed on East square in Spartanburgh, SC on N side of Main St; border: W-Cross St, N-George Jones, E-Richard Thompson, and S-Main St; sold due to writ from Spartanburgh Common Pleas Court second Monday after fourth Monday in Oct. 1822 suit of Joseph T Weyman; judgment was levy of $2,388 and costs from Muse Tolleson. Witness James Ed Henry and John Poole. Signed Thomas Poole. Wit. oath Oct. 11, 1825 James Ed Henry to E Bomar. Rec. Oct. 4, 1825. Dower renounced Oct. 4, 1825 Sarah Tolleson to James E Henry. Wit. oath to dower Oct. 4, 1825 James E Henry to E Bomar

p. 124-125 Oct. 12, 1825 James Brannon (Spartanburgh) to John Willis and Edward Willis (same); for $465 sold 235 ac on Little Showly Cr; border: N-Fausett, E-Owens, W-Chiles, and S-Turner. Witness William Trimmier and John Dickson. Signed J Brannon. Wit. oath Oct. 24, 1825 John Dickson to E Bomar. Rec. Oct. 24, 1825. Dower renounced Oct. 24, 1825 Sarah Brannon to Elisha Bomar

p. 125 Sept. 21, 1825 Vincent Wyatt and Spencer Wyatt (Spartanburgh) to Zachariah Hammett (same); for $100 sold 53 ac on Lawson's fork; border: Hammett's Spring Br and Poole. Witness William Ellison and Elijah Mathis. Signed Vincent Wyatt and Spencer Wyatt. Wit. oath Oct. 29, 1825 Elijah Mathis to E Bomar. Rec. Oct. 29, 1825

p. 125-126 Sept. 21, 1825 Zachariah Hammett (Spartanburgh) to Vincent Wyatt (same); for $100 sold 53 ac on Lawson's fork. Witness William Ellison and Elijah Mathis. Signed Zachariah Hammett. Wit. oath Oct. 29, 1825 Elijah Mathis to E Bomar. Rec. Oct. 29, 1825

p. 126 Jul. 18, 1825 James Burnett sr (Spartanburgh) to granddaughter Margaret Johnson (same); for love and affection give a Negro girl Clarinda now in the third year of her age and her increase. Witness W Bennett and Mathew Bennett. Signed James Burnett sr's mark. Certified Jul. 20, 1825 W Bennett. Rec. Oct. 29, 1825

p. 126-128 Aug. 5, 1815 John Low jr (Spartanburgh) to Caleb Jones (same); for $60 sold (ac omitted) on Lawson's fork of S Pacolate R; John Low jr's part of estate of Bassel Lee desc: (1) 284 ac grant to John Holcome; (2) 100 ac grant to Edward Dixon on S side of Lawson's fork; (3) 60 ac; part of grant to Deskin; border: Harrison; (4) 100 ac on S side of Lawson's fork; (5) 100 ac; border: George Parkison and Randol Brown. Witness Robert Jones and Jane Jones. Signed John Low jr's mark. Wit. oath Oct. 19, 1822 Jane Jones to Ransom Foster. Rec. Oct. 30, 1825

p. 128 Nov. 4, 1825 John Lucas (Spartanburgh) to Thomas Grogan (same); for $215 sold 50 ac on N side of S Pacolate R; border: ridge road and Brown; where Thomas Campbell lived; part of tract sold by executors of Maj. John Gowen desc to John Lucas. Witness William B Archer and Willey S Brown. Signed John Lucas. Wit. oath Nov. 7, 1825 Willey S Brown to John Montgomery. Rec. Nov. 7, 1825

p. 128-129 Dec. 23, 1823 Davis Turner and wife Jude to Nancy Ray (Spartanburgh); for $65 sold 65 ac on Suck Cr of Broad R; border: Gausnel and Williams; part of grant Sept. 11, 1795 to Josiah Dilback. Witness George Camp and Andrew Wray. Signed Davis and Jude Turner's marks. Wit. oath May 22, 1824 Andrew Wray to Geo Camp. Rec. Nov. 7, 1825

p. 129-130 Dec. 7, 1824 Nancy Ray (Spartanburgh) to James Moreland (same); for $65 sold 65 ac on Suck Cr of Broad R; border: Gausnel and Williams; part of grant Sept. 11, 1795 to Jacob(sic) Dilback. Witness Daniel Blackwell and Andrew Wray. Signed Nancy Ray's mark. Wit. oath Dec. 7, 1824 Daniel Blackwell to Geo Camp. Rec. Nov. 7, 1825

p. 130 Aug. 29, 1825 Robert Goodgion (Greenville Dist) to John Otts (Spartanburgh); for $250 sold 300 ac in Greenville Dist on both sides Green's Cr of S Pacolate R; border: Stephen Johnson and John Evans; part of grant (1) Jun. 5, 1786 to Lynch and (2) Jul. 1, 1793 to Richard Brasill. Witness Jacob Kytle (or Kitle), William Butler, and Martin Otts. Signed Robt Goodgion. Wit. oath Aug. 29, 1825 (Greenville Dist) William Butler to Thoa Stanford. Rec. Nov. 9, 1825

p. 130-131 Nov. 5, 1825 Dower renounced Alethia Backler to Burrell Bobo; widow of John Backler desc; land willed to Rosannah Huff by Samuel Farrow desc; "within the Backler tract". Rec. Nov. 9, 1825

p. 131 Nov. 5, 1825 Dower renounced Alethia Backler to Burrell Bobo; widow of John Backler desc; for 50 ac willed by Samuel Farrow to Sarah Waters, wife of Thomas Waters. Rec. Nov. 9, 1825

p. 131 Nov. 5, 1825 Dower renounced Alethia Backler, widow of John Backler desc, to Burrell Bobo; for 150 ac given by Samuel Farrow desc to Sharlotte Arnold, wife of Willis Arnold. Rec. Nov. 9, 1825

p. 131-132 Oct. 17, 1822 Bartholomew Grogan jr to Thomas Grogan; for $400 sold 100 ac on S side of S Pacolate R; border: Theron Earle and William Halcomb; sold by Bartholomew Grogan jr's father to Bartholomew. Witness Polley S Brown and Willey S Brown. Signed Bartholomew Grogan. Wit. oath Oct. 7, 1814 Polley S Borwn to J Whitten. Rec. Nov. 10, 1825

p. 132 Sept. 18, 1824 Alexander Keller (Spartanburgh) to John Montgomery; "to swap" 56 ac on N Tyger R with (omitted); part of grant to John McCarter. Witness John M Collins, James Ballinger, David Loftis. Signed Alexander Keller's mark. Wit. oath Nov. 8, 1825 James Ballinger to James Foster. Rec. Nov. 12, 1825

p. 132-133 May 11, 1822 Joel Fowler (Laurence Dist) to John Owens (Spartanburgh); for $1,500 sold 300 ac on Enoree R. Witness Jonathan Crook and Lucy B Crook. Signed Joel Fowler. Wit. oath May 11, 1823 Jonathan Crook to (not signed). Rec. Nov. 12, 1825. Dower renounced May 11, 1823 Sarah Fowler to James Crook

p. 133-134 Oct. 7, 1824 John Ownes (Spartanburgh) to James Johnson (same); for $1,600 sold 300 ac on Enoree R. Witness Joseph Crook and Isaac Wofford. Signed John Owens. Wit. oath Nov. 18, 1824 Joseph Crook to James Crook. Rec. Nov. 12, 1825. Dower renounced Nov. 18, 1824 Patsey Owens to James Crook

p. 134-135 Mar. 28, 1825 Susannah Brewton (Spartanburgh) to great granddaughter Rebecca Addeline Cochran; for love and affection give a feather bed and teester, bedsted, 8 counterpins, 8 bedquilts, an "oven leds", a pine table, an oven and lid (sic), a frying pan, a cupboard, 2 pewter plates, 5 earthen plates, 2 pitchers, 2 mugs, 6 earthen bowls, a spinning wheel, a black chest, and a set of canapies; Susannah Brewton keeps the stuff until she dies. Witness Josiah Woodruff, Harrison Woodruff, and Thomas Woodruff III. Signed Susannah Brewton's mark. Wit. oath Nov. 4, 1825 Thomas Woodruff III to Philip Brewton. Rec. Nov. 12, 1825

p. 135 Oct. 24, 1825 Thomas Thomas and Nathan Byars to Cabred McCraw; for $131.25 sold 211 ac on waters of Island Cr of Pacolate R; except what is in Bonner's tract. Witness John Martin and Sterling Gorden. Signed Thomas Thomas and Nathan Byars. Wit. oath Oct. 24, 1824 John Martin to J Camp. Rec. Nov. 12, 1825. Dower renounced Oct. 31, 1825 Nancy Thomas to Geo Camp

p. 135-137 Nov. 3, 1825 John Dashields (Spartanburgh) to Joel Foster, trustee for Abigail Dashields, wife of John Dashields; John Dashields has been unfortunate in business and to secure Abigail, he allows Abigail to do her own business and Abigail can invest her own money and sell her property, if any. Witness Fielding Foster and Franklin W Foster. Signed John Dayshields. Wit. oath Nov. 3, 1825 Fielding Foster to W Hunt. Rec. Nov. 12, 1825

p. 137-138 Nov. 22, 1825 Jesse Cleveland (Spartanburgh) to Thomas Poole (same); for $200 sold 3½ ac in Spartanburgh, SC; S of Jesse Cleveland's store house lot allowing for a 50 foot street between lots; border: Jail lot and Thomas Poole. Witness Abner Benson and John Poole. Signed Jesse Cleveland. Wit. oath Nov. 23, 1825 John Poole to James Ed Henry. Rec. Nov. 23, 1825. Dower renounced Nov. 22, 1825 Mary Cleveland to James Ed Henry

p. 138 Nov. 28, 1825 Dower renounced Ellender Mason to Elisha Bomar for deed from Francis Mason to William Jinnings. Rec. Nov. 28, 1825

p. 138-139 Dec. 1, 1825 James E Henry (Spartanburgh) to Robert M Young (same); for $250 sold (ac omitted) in Spartanburgh, SC on S side of Main St; border: N-Main St, S- back street, W-Robert M Young, and E-Richard Thomson; formerly owned by Muse Tolleson and sold by sheriff to James E Henry. Witness James Norris and Jesse Cleveland. Signed James E Henry. Wit. oath Dec. 2, 1825 James Norris to E Bomar. Rec. Dec. 2, 1825

p. 139 Jul. 16, 1824 John Cooper (Spartanburgh) to Hiram Jones (same); for $388.50 sold 111 ac on waters of Enoree R. Witness Amos Cooper and Henry Turner. Signed John Cooper. Wit. oath Jul. 24, 1824 Amos Cooper to Henry Turner. Rec. Dec. 5, 1825. Dower renounced Jul. 24, 1824 Nicy Cooper to Henry Turner

p. 139-140 May 7, 1824 John Lucas (Spartanburgh) to John Lucas jr; for $500 sold 100 ac on N side of S Pacolate R; border: Alfred Camp; includes a house and land where John Lucas lives; part of land formerly owned by Maj. John Gowen and sold by his executors to John Lucas. Witness Benja C Dillingham and Willey S Brown. Signed John Lucas. Wit. oath Mar. 1, 1825 Willey S Brown to John S Rowland. Rec. Dec. 5, 1825

p. 140-141 Jan. 8, 1825 Sarah Foster, widow of Thomas Foster and guardian for Lucretia, George, James, Jesse, Berryman, Moses, Ransom, Elizabeth, and Sarah Foster jr, heirs of Thomas G Foster desc, to Claybourn Waddle (Greenville Dist); for $400 sold 180 ac on S side of Maple Swamp Cr of S Tyger R; border: Greenville-Spartanburgh county line, a county road, and Greenville road; part of grant to Thomas Farr jr who sold to John McDowell who sold to Thomas G Foster. Witness George W Bagwell and Philip C Lester. Signed Sarah Foster's mark, Jesse Foster, Berryman Foster, Moses Foster, Ransom Foster, Sarah jr Foster, and Elizabeth Foster's mark. Wit. oath May 2, 1825 (Greenville Dist) Philip C Lester to James Lester. Rec. Dec. 9, 1825

p. 141-142 Oct. 28, 1816 Jesse Traylor (Spartanburgh) to Edward Bomar (same); for $20 sold 30 ac on N Tyger R; border: Edward Bomar, Andrew Gramling, land formerly belonging to John Snoddy desc, and Benjamin High; part of survey by Jesse Traylor and Edward Bomar "in Co". Witness Thomas Bomar and Reuben Gramling. Signed Jesse Traylor. Wit. oath Dec. 10, 1825 Thomas Bomar to E Bomar. Rec. Dec. 10, 1825

p. 142 Apr. 26, 1816 Richard Posey (Spartanburgh) to Patrick Hoy; for $380 sold (ac omitted) on both sides of S Tyger R; border: mouth of Thomas Posey's Spring Br. Witness William Otts, Ford Mason, and William Coan. Signed Richard Posey. Wit. oath Dec. 20, 1825 William Coan to James Crook. Rec. Dec. 10, 1825

p. 142-143 Sept. 21, 1825 Benjamin A Markley (Charleston, SC) to Elijah Mathis (Spartanburgh); for $200 sold 200 ac on waters of Lawson's fork; border: SW-William Poole, W-James Cannon, E-Vincent Wyatt, and NE-Job Sarsby; plat attached; part of 419 ac belonging to Abraham Markley's estate; Abraham Markley (late of Charleston, SC) by his will appointed son Benjamin A Markley and sons-in-law William Lee and Ezekiel Noble executors and Benjamin was only one who qualified; Abraham Markley said to sell his land. Witness Zachariah Hammett and Spencer Wyatt. Signed Benjamin A Markley by attorney Wm Ellison. Wit. oath Oct. 29, 1825 Spencer Wyatt to E Bomar. Rec. Dec. 28, 1825

p. 143-145 Sept. 21, 1825 Benjamin A Markley (Charleston, SC) to Vincent Wyatt (Spartanburgh); for $140 sold 219 ac on waters of Lawson's fork and on road from Harris' saw mill; border: SW-Elijah Mathis, NE-Job Sorsby, and other sides-William Pool; plat attached; Abraham Markley (late of Charleston, SC) by his will appointed son Benjamin A Markley and sons-in-law William Lee and Ezekiel Noble executors and Benjamin was only one who qualified; Abraham said in the will to sell the land. Witness Zachariah Hammett and Elijah Mathis. Signed Benjamin A Markley, by attorney Wm Ellison. Wit. oath Oct. 29, 1825 Elijah Mathis to E Bomar. Rec. Dec. 28, 1825

p. 145 Dec. 28, 1825 Sarah Tolleson (Spartanburgh), widow of Muse Tolleson, to Thomas Poole (same); for $50 sold her interest and dower rights to 140 ac; border: W-R. H. Goldthwate, N-Jesse Cleveland, E-Mary Lee, and S-George Jones; sold by Thomas Allison to Muse Tolleson. Witness Elisha Bomar and Willis Foster. Signed Sarah Tolleson. Wit. oath Dec. 28, 1825 Willis Foster to J. W. Farrow. Rec. Dec. 28, 1825

p. 145-146 Dec. 30, 1825 Sarah Tolleson (Spartanburgh), widow of Muse Tolleson, to John W Farrow (same); for $50 sold her interest in and dower rights to 3/4 ac in Spartanburgh, SC; border: Cross St and Col. Brannon; where John W Farrow lives. Witness Thomas Poole and John Land. Signed Sarah Tolleson. Wit. oath Dec. 30, 1825 Thomas Poole to E Bomar. Rec. Dec. 30, 1825

p. 146 Jun. 12, 1819 James Burnes sr (Spartanburgh) to John Burns and James Burns jr (same); for $1,000 sold 300 ac on N Tyger R in three tracts; see deed Mar. 5, 1819 from Edwd Ballinger to James Burns sr. Witness Edmund Booker and Joseph Thompson. Signed James Burns sr's mark. Wit. oath Apr. 15, 1820 Edmund Booker to John Montgomery. Rec. Jan. 2, 1826

p. 146-147 Nov. 7, 1825 Gabriel Benson (Perry Co, Ala) to James McDaniel (Greenville Dist); for $100 sold ½ ac in Spartanburgh, SC; lot #7; see deed from (omitted) to Gabriel Benson. Witness Alexander Evins, Samuel N Evins, and Elias Benson. Signed Gab Benson. Wit. oath Jan. 2, 1826 Samuel N Evins to E Bomar. Rec. Jan. 2, 1826

p. 147-148 Dec. 16, 1825 Joseph Crook (Spartanburgh) to William Wright (same); for $150 sold 50 ac on branches of Enoree R; border: Thomas Farrow. Witness Willis Robuck, James Lanford, and

William Jones SM. Signed Joseph Crook. Wit. oath Dec. 30, 1825 James Lanford to John Dean. Rec. Jan. 2, 1826

p. 148 Feb. 5, 1824 John Crocker (Spartanburgh) to Zachariah Edwards (same); for $900 sold 180ac on waters of Fergerson's Cr; border: Nathaniel Wofford, Nathaniel Woodruff, and widow Bobo. Witness William Cooper and Archibald Cole. Signed John Crocker. Wit. oath Dec. 22, 1825 Archibald Cole to David Moore. Rec. Jan. 2, 1826

p. 148-149 Oct. 29, 1825 James Turner (Spartanburgh) to Middleton Turner (same); for $375 sold 150 ac on S side of Pacolate R and at mouth of Buck Cr. Witness Wyatt E Hines and Edward Turner. Signed James Turner. Wit. oath Oct. 29, 1817 Wyatt E Hines to James Foster. Rec. Jan. 2, 1826

p. 149-150 Jun. 17, 1819 Laurence Bankston (Spartanburgh) to Middleton Turner (same); for $34.50 sold 40 ac on E side of Cases Cr; border: James Turner and John Martin; part of widow Demcy's tract of land. Witness James Turner, Edward Turner and Samuel Hunt. Signed Laurence Bankston's mark. Wit. oath Oct. 29, 1825 Edward Turner to James Foster. Rec. Jan. 2, 1826

p. 150-151 Oct. 1, 1825 John Wofford (Spartanburgh), constable, to William Smith (same), merchant; for $145.54 sold 368 ac in Spartanburgh and Union Dists on waters of Fairforest Cr; border: Lancaster, Haslewood, Wilbanks, Hosea Wofford, and Wofford's road; where John Wofford lives; Condition: sale void if John Wofford pays William Smith $145.54. Witness Johnson Hembree, William Lee, and Elihu P Smith. Signed John Wofford. Wit. oath Dec. 30, 1825 William Lee to James Hamm. Rec. Jan. 2, 1826

p. 151 May 28, 1824 William Jackson (Spartanburgh) to Elijah Alverson (same); for $1,200 sold 880 ac on N side of S Pacolate R and on both sides Abner's Cr; border: Morgan, Senter, Wood, Fowler, and Green; part of ten surveys. Witness Col. William Wilkins and Patsey Wilkins. Signed William Jackson. Wit. oath Feb. 11, 1825 William Wilkins to James Young. Rec. Jan. 2, 1826. Dower renounced Feb. 11, 1825 Jane Jackson to James Young

p. 151-152 Jun. 8, 1824 Stephen Sizemore (Spartanburgh) to Joseph Carman (same); for $260 sold 116 ac; border: Earle and James Ford. Witness William Grisham and Jacob Hughes. Signed Stephen Sizemore's mark. Wit. oath Jun. 8, 1824 Jacob Hughes to Thomas Wood. Rec. Jan. 2, 1826. Dower renounced Dec. 19, 1824 Margory Sizemore to Thomas Wood

p. 152-153 Apr. 18, 1825 James Poole (Spartanburgh) to Matthias Bates (same); for $52.93 3/4 sold 30 ac; border: Anthony Bates, Burk, and Golightly's old line; part of grant to Benjamin Howard and James Poole. Witness Benjamin White and Elisha Poole. Signed James Poole. Wit. oath Elisha Poole to Caleb Jones. Rec. Jan. 2, 1826

p. 153-154 (blank), 1817 Henry Story (Spartanburgh) to James Story jr, William Mitchell Story, John Story, and George Story jr (same); for $100 sold 80 ac on Story's Cr of Fairforest Cr; border: Capt. Henry Cunningham. Witness John Kelso, Robert Story, and James Story. Signed Henry Story sr. Wit. oath Aug. 18, (omitted) Robert Story to Saml Archibald. Rec. Jan. 2, 1826

p. 154-155 Jan. 18, 1822 Samuel Turner (Spartanburgh) to William M Story (same); for $300 sold (1) 41 ac on branches of Fairforest Cr about a mile from Spartanburgh Court House; border: Richard Thomson and road to Greenville Court House; and (2) two ½ ac each lots (#8 & 9) in Spartanburgh, SC; border: E-Gabriel Benson, N & W-Richard Thomson, and S-Main St. Witness William Trimmier and

Memory N Chapman. Signed Saml Turner. Wit. oath Jan. 12, 1825 William Trimmier to E Bomar. Rec. Jan. 12, 1826. Dower renounced Jan. 4, 1826 Mahalah Turner to John Chapman jr

p. 155-156 Mar. 12, 1825 Thomas Kelley (Spartanburgh) to Nathan Chandler; for $300 sold 200 ac between Tyger and Enoree Rivers; on road from Isaac Crow's to Anthony Foster sr's; part of 1,000 ac grant to James Sample jr and sold by Ratty Sample, heir-at-law to James, to John McCullock who sold to Edward Hooper who sold Thomas Kelley. Witness William Williams and Elijah Stallons. Signed Thomas Kelley. Wit. oath Mar. 12, 1825 William Williams to Benjamin Wofford. Rec. Jan. 12, 1826. Dower renounced Mar. 12, 1825 Selah Kelley to Benj Wofford

p. 156 Mar. 1, 1825 Zadock Hooker (Union Dist) to William Wilder; for $600 sold 155 ac on ridge between Enoree and Tyger Rivers and on Main Buncom Road; plat attached shows border: Kelley, Thos Darby, Livingston Bobo, Jesse Lamb, and Benjamin Hooker. Witness Nathan Chandler and W. M. Thomson. Signed Z Hooker. Wit. oath Jan. 12, 1826 Nathan Chandler to J. W. Farrow. Rec. Jan. 12, 1826

p. 156-157 Jan. 2, 1824 James King to Elisha Stallians; for $310 sold 103½ ac on Prater's Cr of Tyger R; plat attached shows border: Tho Layton, Wm Lartan, Burrell Bobo, Benj Hooker, and John Fowler. Witness John Darby and Benjamin Hooker. Signed James King's mark. Wit. oath Jan. 2, 1824 John Darby to Burrell Bobo. Rec. Jan. 12, 1826. Dower renounced Jan. 2, 1824 Rachael King to Burrell Bobo

p. 157-158 Oct. 5, 1825 Thomas Poole, sheriff (Spartanburgh) to Patrick Moore (same); for $161 sold 319 ac on waters of Thickety Cr; border: Ignatious Littlejohn, Joshua Pettit, Thomas Lipscomb, and estate of David Lipscomb desc; sold due to writ from Spartanburgh Common Pleas Court second Monday after fourth Monday in Mar. 1823 suit of Joseph Gist; judgment was levy of $130 and costs from John Tolleson desc. Witness John Moore and John Poole. Signed Thomas Poole. Wit. oath Jan. 9, 1826 John Moore to Caleb Jones. Rec. Jan. 13, 1826

p. 158-159 Dec. 24, 1825 Patrick Moore (Spartanburgh) to John P Petet (same); for $300 sold 345 ac on waters of Goucher Cr; border: Gore; grant in 1788 to David Allen desc and sold as Abraham Hembree's land at suit of John Tolleson desc (sold by Thomas Poole, sheriff of Spartanburgh). Witness Robert Moore, Joshua Petit, and Hugh Moore jr. Signed Patrick Moore. Wit. oath Jan. 9, 1826 Joshua Petit to Caleb Jones. Rec. Jan. 13, 1826

p. 159-160 Dec. 24, 1825 William W Smithwick (Spartanburgh) to Richard Daniel sr (same); for $700 sold 440 ac on S side of lower (sic) fork of Tyger R; border: N-Jonathan Crow, S & W-John Thornton, Robert Alexander, Elias Rogers, and Richard Willis, and E-N Tyger R; where William W Smithwick lives. Witness John Snoddy and Robert M Daniel. Signed Wm W Smithwick. Wit. oath Jan. 2, 1826 John Snoddy to D White. Rec. Jan. 14, 1826

p. 160 Jun. 15, 1825 Thomas Poole, sheriff (Spartanburgh) to Robert M Young (same); for $54 sold ½ ac in Spartanburgh, SC on N side of Main St; near the ole Jail; border: N & E-Richard Thomson, W-Cross St, and S-Main St; sold due to writ from Spartanburgh Common Pleas Court second Monday after fourth Monday in Oct. 1822 suit of James H Irby; judgment was levy of $696.89 and costs from Muse Tolleson. Witness William Trimmier and Collins Smith. Signed Thomas Poole. Wit. oath Jan. 16, 1826 William Trimmier to E Bomar. Rec. Jan. 16, 1826

p. 160-161 Jan. 12, 1826 Robert M Young (Spartanburgh) to John Bomar (same); for $55 sold ½ ac in Spartanburgh, SC on N side of Main St; below the old Jail; part of lot #5. Witness R. H. Goldthwaite and L. A. Mills. Signed R. M. Young. Wit. oath Jan. 16, 1826 L. A. Mills to E Bomar. Rec. Jan. 16, 1826

p. 161-162 Aug. 26, 1823 Andrew Gramling (Spartanburgh) to Francis G Mason (same); for $650 sold 196 ac on waters of N Tyger R and on Cub Br; border: Robert Woods. Witness Joel Mason and Howard Owen. Signed Andrew Gramling. Wit. oath Nov. 11, 1823 Joel Mason to Wm Reid. Rec. Jan. 23, 1826. Dower renounced Jan. 3, 1825 Rebeccah Gramling to James Hamm

p. 162-163 Dec. 15, 1825 (Marian Co, Ala) Nathaniel Miller (Marian Co, Ala) to son James Miller (same); power of attorney to get Nathaniel Miller's share of estate of Thomas Miller (late of Spartanburgh) and any money owed to Nathaniel Miller. Witness none. Signed Nathaniel Miller. Wit. oath Dec. 15, 1825 (Marian Co, Ala) Nathaniel Miller to Francis Shoemake, clerk of county court. Dec. 15, 1825 (Marian Co, Ala) DeLee F Roydon, judge of county court, certifies Francis Shoemake is clerk. Rec. Jan. 23, 1826

p. 163-164 Sept. 21, 1825 Vincent Wyatt (Spartanburgh) to Benjamin A Markley, executor of will of Abraham Markley; to secure a bond of $240 due Jan. 1, 1828 and for $3 sold 219 ac on waters of Lawson's fork; part of 419 ac sold by Benjamin A Markley to Vincent Wyatt; Condition: sale void if Vincent Wyatt pays bond with interest. Witness Elijah Mathis and Zachariah Hammett. Signed Vincent Wyatt. Wit. oath Jan. 28, 1826 Elijah Mathis to E Bomar. Rec. Jan. 28, 1826

p. 164 Oct. 22. 1825 Lewis Turner (Spartanburgh) to Darby Turner (same); for $65 sold 30 ac on Shoally Cr; border: Darby Turner, Mrs. Susan Owens, John Willis, and David Markley. Witness William Trimmier and Samuel Turner. Signed Lewis Turner's mark. Wit. oath Jan. 30, 1826 William Trimmier to E Bomar. Rec. Jan. 30, 1826

p. 164-165 Aug. 10, 1821 Hannah Barton (SC) to Philip Brisco (Spartanburgh); for $200 sold 200 ac on both sides of Pacolet R; border: Philip Brisco; grant Dec. 24, 1793 to Thomas Gore. Witness William Gilbert, Mary Gilbert, and William Mince. Signed Hannah Barton's mark. Wit. oath Jan. 7, 1822 William Gilbert to James Young. Rec. Feb. 6, 1826

p. 165-166 Nov. 25, 1825 William Black and wife Mesina and Samuel Black (York Dist) to Archibald Nelson (Spartanburgh); for $700 sold 210 ac on S side of S Pacolate R; border: James Wood, Jesse Burton, and Thomas Burton. Witness Nathaniel Enloe and William Erwin. Signed William Black, Samuel Black, and Mesina's mark. Wit. oath Jan. 18, 1826 (York Dist) Nathaniel Enloe to G Enloe. Rec. Feb. 6, 1826. Dower renounced Jan. 3, 1826 (York Dist) Mesina Black, wife of William, to Samuel Turner

p. 166-167 Apr. 2, 1825 Josiah Woodruff and Daniel P Woodruff (Spartanburgh) to Willis W Dickie (same); for $1,000 sold 86½ ac on two branches of Enoree R; except 12½ ac for Bethel Meeting House or total of 74 ac; border: Thomas Woodruff and fork of Augusta Rd; plat attached shows also border: Buncomb Rd, road to Columbia, Pilgrim, and Wm Hendricks; includes Dickie's house. (not dated) Thomas Woodruff (Spartanburgh) says he was present when lines were drawn by his land and agrees to the line. Witness Isaac Wofford and James Page. Signed Josiah Woodruff and Daniel Woodruff. Wit. oath Apr. 2, 1825 James Page to Philip Brewton. Rec. Feb. 6, 1826. Dowers renounced Jan. 4, 1826 Margaret Woodruff, wife(?) of Josiah, and Sarah M Woodruff, wife(?) of Daniel P, to James Crook

p. 167-168 Nov. 8, 1813 William Camp to Joseph Collins; for $150 sold 166 2/3 ac on Cherokee Cr of Broad R; border: Zachariah

Cooper and Joseph Camp. Witness John Copeland and Thomas Camp. Signed Wm Camp. Wit. oath Nov. 25, 1813 Thomas Camp to Joseph Camp. Rec. Feb. 6, 1826

p. 168-169 Dec. 14, 1820 Joseph Collins to Joseph Camp; for $333 sold 166½ ac (sic) on Cherokee Cr of Broad R; border: Chaney Turner. Witness Joseph Byars and Peter Q Camp. Signed Joseph Collins. Wit. oath Dec. 14, 1821 Joseph Byars to J Camp. Rec. Feb. 6, 1826. Dower renounced Feb. 20, 1821 (York Dist) Anny Collins to Geo Plaxco

p. 169-170 Aug. 26, 1824 Daniel Amos jr to Joseph Camp; for $400 sold 214 ac on Thickety Cr; border: Nancy Woods, Richards, Saward's still house Br; Blanton, Lipscomb, William Weber, Sarah Adams, and Logan; where Daniel Amos jr lives. Witness Polly Ann Camp and Thomas Byars. Signed Daniel Amos. Wit. oath Feb. 6, 1826 Polly Ann Camp to J. W. Farrow. Rec. Feb. 6, 1826. Dower renounced Oct. 11, 1824 Orapa Amos to John Lipscomb

p. 170 Jul. 25, 1825 Joseph Gibson Oliver (Spartanburgh) to Lewis Mathis (same); for $200 sold 158 ac on N side of Pacolate R; border: Edmond Cooley. Witness William Morris and George G Gilbert. Signed Joseph G Oliver's mark. Wit. oath Nov. 14, 1825 George G Gilbert to W Clement. Rec. Feb. 6, 1826

p. 170-171 Mar. 19, 1821 William Turner (Spartanburgh) to John Turner; for $200 sold 191 ac on SW side of Lawson's fork and on both sides of Court House Road; border: Golightly; where John Turner lives; grant to William Turner. Witness R Golightly and Elihu Golightly. Signed William Turner. Wit. oath Feb. 6, 1826 Elihu Golightly to Caleb Jones. Rec. Feb. 6, 1826

p. 171-172 Jan. 24, 1824 Tillman Bobo (Union Dist) to James Bragg (Spartanburgh); for $200 sold 100 ac on branches of Tyger R; part of grant Nov. 11, 1788 to John Daniel Kern and Co; survey Apr. 1, 1818 by Gen. J. A. Elmore. Witness Thomas Bragg and Livingston Bobo. Signed Tilman Bobo. Wit. oath Feb. 1, 1826 Thomas Bragg to Benj Wofford. Rec. Feb. 6, 1826

p. 172-173 Oct. 5, 1818 William Moore (Spartanburgh) to Henry How (same); for $200 sold 119½ ac on S Tyger R; border: Francis Powers, Nicholls, and widow Powers; part of 538 ac grant Mar. 7, 1786 South Carolina governor to Francis Powers. Witness John W Moore, William Pearson, and John Smith. Signed William Moore's mark. Wit. oath Nov. 10, 1818 William Pearson to John Collins. Rec. Feb. 6, 1826

p. 173 Jan. 4, 1826 John Rogers (Spartanburgh) to son James Rogers; for affection give 155 ac; border: Meadows. Witness B. S. Goodman and Robert Ligon. Signed John Rogers. Wit. oath Feb. 6, 1826 Robert Ligon to W Clement. Rec. Feb. 6, 1826

p. 173-174 Aug. 20, 1825 Thomas Wells (Spartanburgh) to son Thomas U Wells (same); for love and affection give 317 ac in two tracts: (1) 242 ac on Lawson's fork of Pacolet R; part of 392 ac grant to William Turner; and (2) 75 ac on Buck Br of Lawson's fork; grant to Lewis Turner. Witness Elisha Poole and Abner J Wells. Signed Thomas Wells. Wit. oath Feb. 6, 1826 Elisha Poole to Caleb Jones. Rec. Feb. 6, 1826

p. 174-175 Apr. 28, 1825 John E Bobo (Union Dist) to James Crow, "of Wm" (Spartanburgh); for $60 sold 15 ac on waters of Two Mile Cr; border: E-James Crow, W-John E Bobo, and S-Jesse Brown. Witness Moses A Crow. Signed John E Bobo. Wit. oath Feb. 1, 1826 Moses A Crow to Benj Wofford. Rec. Feb. 6, 1826

p. 175 Feb. 28, 1825 Isaac Crow (Spartanburgh) to James Crow (same);

for $34 sold 10 ac; border: W-James Crow, SW-John L Rast, S-Christopher Rhodes, and E-Isaac Crow; W part of where Isaac Crow lives. Witness Zachariah Hobby and Robert Wood. Signed Isaac Crow. Wit. oath Feb. 1, 1826 Zachariah Hobby to Benj Wofford. Rec. Feb. 6, 1826. Dower renounced Feb. 1, 1826 Martha Crow to Benjm Wofford

p. 175-176 Sept. 16, 1825 Isaac Crow (Spartanburgh) to Thomas J Underwood and Ralph Smith; for $1,200 sold 218 ac on branches of Two Mile Cr and Jemmies Cr; border: E & N-Isaac Crow, W-John L Rast and James Crow, and S-Christopher Rhodes. Witness James Nesbett and Charles Bragg. Signed Isaac Crow. Wit. oath Feb. 1, 1826 Charles Bragg to Benj Wofford. Rec. Feb. 6, 1826. Dower renounced Feb. 1, 1826 Martha Crow to Benjamin Wofford

p. 176-177 Jul. 7, 1825 (McMinn Co, Tenn) Barnard Seay and Allen Seay McMinn Co, Tenn) to John J Seay (Spartanburgh); power of attorney to sell (ac omitted) on Fairforest Cr; part of estate of Gideon Seay desc; Barnard and Allen Seay are heirs thereof. Witness none. Signed Allen Seay and Barnard Seay. Wit. oath Sept. 14, 1825 (McMinn Co, Tenn) Barnard and Alley Seay to Robert Cowan and James McRaney JP. Sept. 14, 1825 Young Colville, clerk of Quarterly Sessions Court, certifys Robert Cowan and James McRaney are justices of peace. Rec. Feb. 6, 1826

p. 177-178 Oct. 14, 1825 Barnard Seay (McMinn Co, Tenn), one of heirs of estate of Gideon Seay desc (late of Spartanburgh), to George Killock (Spartanburgh); for $50 sold 115 ac on N side of Fairforest Cr; part of Gideon Seay's land. Witness C. G. Steele and C. H. Moore. Signed Barnard Seay. Wit. oath Oct. 14, 1825 C. H. Moore to F. H. Legg. Rec. Feb. 6, 1826

p. 178 Oct. 14, 1825 Barnard Seay (McMinn Co, Tenn), one of heirs of Gideon Seay's estate (late of Spartanburgh), to William Bomar (Spartanburgh); for $50 sold 200 ac on N side of Fairforest Cr; part of Gideon Seay's land. Witness C. G. Steele and C. H. Moore. Signed Barnard Seay. Wit. oath Oct. 14, 1825 C. H. Moore to F. H. Legg. Reb. 6, 1826

p. 178-179 Oct. 17, 1825 John James Seay (Spartanburgh), attorney for Allen Seay (McMinn Co, Tenn), one of heirs of Gideon Seay (late of Spartanburgh), to William Bomar (Spartanburgh); for $50 sold 200 ac on waters of Fairforest Cr. Witness Joel Faster and Barnard Seay. Signed John J Seay, attorney for Allen Seay. Wit. oath Feb. 6, 1826 Joel Faster to James Young. Rec. Feb. 6, 1826

p. 179-180 (date in question) William W Smithwick (Spartanburgh) to James Duncan, son of Alexr; for $700 received "this" Jul. 31, 1822 and $300 received "this" Oct. 7, 1822 sold "a tract" where William W Smithwock lives and David Barton lived; William gives up the land Jan. 1, 1823. Witness Jesse Pinson. Signed Wm W Smithwick. Wit. oath Feb. 13, 1826 Jesse Pinson to E Bomar. Rec. Feb. 13, 1826

p. 180 Aug. 4, 1819 John E Wilson to Thomas Darby; for $200 sold 100 ac on ridge between Enoree and Tyger Rivers and on branches of Cedar Shoal Cr; border: Austin Newman and Kelley. Witness Thomas Kelley and Humphrey Yarborough. Signed John E Wilson. Wit. oath Sept. 24, 1819 Thomas Kelley to Burrell Bobo. Rec. Feb. 18, 1826. Dower renounced Jan. 28, 1825 Salley Wilson to Benj Wofford

p. 180-181 Aug. 4, 1819 Austin Newman to Thomas Darby; for $300 sold 114 ac on ridge between Enoree and Tyger Rivers and waters of Cedar Shoal Cr. Witness Thomas Kelley and Humphrey Yarborough. Signed Austin Newman. Wit. oath Sept. 24, 1819 Thomas Kelley to Burrell Bobo. Rec. Feb. 18, 1826. Dower renounced Sept. 24, 1819 Sarah Newman to Burrell Bobo

p. 181-182 Apr. 25, 1825 William W Smithwick (Spartanburgh) to Zachariah Moore (same); for $100 sold 10 ac on Cain Cr; where Wright's mill formerly stood. Witness John Thornton and William Thornton. Signed Wm W Smithwick. Wit. oath Jul. 9, 1825 John Thornton to James Hamm. Rec. Feb. 22, 1826. Dower renounced Jul. 9, 1825 Francis Smithwick to James Hamm

p. 182-183 Feb. 15, 1813 Lemuel Stokes (Spartanburgh) to Jesse Burton (same); for $250 sold 236 ac on both sides Bird's Cr of S Pacolate R; border: John Carner; grant Mar. 3, 1794 to Robert McDowell who sold to John Stone jr who sold to Robert Stone who sold to Turner Hutcheson who sold to Lemuel Stokes. Witness Thomas Burton and Andrew Furguson. Signed Lemuel Stokes. Wit. oath Feb. 25, 1826 Thomas Burton to James Young. Rec. Feb. 27, 1826

p. 183-184 Sept. 29, 1817 Jonathan Stokes (Greenville Dist) to Thomas Burton (Spartanburgh); for $100 sold 100 ac on Holston's Cr of S Pacolate R; border: Richard Carver, Robert Black, Andrew Ferguson, and John Banham; part of grant Feb. 6, 1792 to John McGuin. Witness Archard Burton and Samuel Knight. Signed Jonathan Stokes. Wit. oath Feb. 25, 1826 Archard Burton to James Young. Rec. Feb. 27, 1826

p. 184 Jul. 7, 1812 Turner Hutcheson (Spartanburgh) to Lemuel Stokes (same); for $300 sold 276 ac on both sides Bird's Cr of S Pacolate R; border: NE-Thomas Burton; grant Mar. 3, 1794 to Robert McDowel who sold to John Stone jr who sold to Robert Stone who sold to Turner Hutcheson. Witness Archard Burton and Jonathan Stokes. Signed Turner Hutcheson's mark. Wit. oath Feb. 25, 1826 Archard Burton to James Young. Rec. Feb. 27, 1826

p. 184-185 Apr. 12, 1825 Alexander Roddy sr (Spartanburgh) to Berdett L Evitts (same); for $5 sold 4 ac; near "the" school house where Berdett L Evitts teaches. Witness Michael Gamling and Alexander Roddy jr. Signed Alexr Roddy. Wit. oath Mar. 2, 1826 Alexander Roddy jr to John Burns. Rec. Mar. 4, 1826

p. 185-186 Mar. 1, 1826 Alexander Roddy jr (Spartanburgh) to Burdett L Evitts (same); for $200 sold 50 ac on branches of Tyger R; near the school house; border: Jamison, Wingo, and T Wingo; part of 340 ac grant Jan. 5, 1824 Gov. John L Wilson to Alexander Roddy sr who sold to Alexander Roddy jr. Witness Thomas Wingo and James C Ballinger. Signed Alexr Roddy jr. Wit. oath Mar. 1, 1826 Thomas Wingo to John Burns. Rec. Mar. 4, 1826

p. 186-187 Dec. 10, 1825 Mathew Jones (Spartanburgh) to Archibald Holtzclaw and Elijah Holtzclaw (same); for $150 sold 150 ac (sic); where Mathew Jones lives; border: Charles Barker, William Hendrix, William Hughes, James Hendrix, John Wilson, Joseph Hughs, and John Cargile; part of 311 ac that is (1) part of 396 ac grant Jan. 5, 1797 to John Demsey and (2) part of 500 ac grant Jun. 23, 1774 to Robert Felps; "200 ac on tract (1) and 3 ac of (2) or 203 ac total on both sides Abner's Cr of Enoree R". Witness William Hughes and William J Wood. Signed Mathew Jones. Wit. oath Dec. 10, 1825 William Hughes to Thomas Wood. Rec. Mar. 6, 1826. Dower renounced Dec. 10, 1825 Elizabeth Jones to Thomas Wood

p. 187 (not dated) Thomas Cave (Spartanburgh) to William Jones (same); for $300 sold 282 ac on both sides of Abner's Cr of Enoree R; includes where Thomas Cave lives; border: Barnett Demsey, William Hughes, Jones, and John Cargile; grant Jun(sic) 5, 1797 to John Demsey. Witness William Hughes and Lewis Jones. Signed Thomas Cave and Elizabeth's mark. Wit. oath Dec. 16, 1825 William Hughes to Thomas Wood. Rec. Mar. 6, 1826

p. 187-189 Feb. 8, 1826 Thomas Poole, sheriff (Spartanburgh) to William Skinner; for $300 sold 70 ac on waters of Tyger R; border: road from Roger's bridge, S-John Pearson and King, E-John Skinner, N-W Skinner and S Bragg, and W-Simon Lavender; William Skinner filed petition in Spartanburgh Ordinary Court against Broughton Thomas on Jul. 18, 1825 to distribute estate of Charles Skinner desc; Ordinary told sheriff to sell the land first Monday in Nov. 1825; sale Nov. 7, 1825. Witness John Poole and Thomas J Dean. Signed Thomas Poole. Wit. oath Mar. 6, 1826 John Poole to James Crook. Rec. Mar. 6, 1826

p. 189 Dec. 15, 1825 James Keen (Spartanburgh) to grandson William Finch (same); for love and affection gave 107 ac; border: Philip Otts, Thomas Cook, and Reedy Br; where William Finch lives; sold by William Finch to James Keen. Witness W W Harris and James Foster. Signed James Keen's mark. Wit. oath Mar. 6, 1826 W W Harris to E Bomar. Rec. Mar. 6, 1826

p. 189-190 Feb. 16, 1826 James Keen (Spartanburgh) to grandson William Finch (same); for love and affection gave (1) 40 ac on Reedy Br of Fairforest Cr; sold by Elizabeth Autry to James Keen; and (2) 50 ac adjoining (1); sold by James Cook to James Keen. Witness W W Harris and James K Finch. Signed James Keen's mark. Wit. oath Mar. 6, 1826 W W Harris to E Bomar. Rec. Mar. 6, 1826

p. 190-191 Nov. 6, 1825 John Arnold (Spartanburgh) to Price Skinner (same); for $100 sold 18 1/3 ac on waters of James' Cr; border: S-James Arnold, N-Price Skinner, Charleston Road, E-James Hobby, and W-William and A M Arnold. Witness James Arnold and Absalam W Arnold. Signed John Arnold. Wit. oath Feb. 20, 1826 Absalam W Arnold to John Dean. Rec. Mar. 6, 1826

p. 191 (not dated) William Jones (Spartanburgh) to Henry Wade (same); for $250 sold 282 ac; includes where Henry Jenkins lives; border: John Cargele, Lewis Jones, William Hughes, Lucy Demsey, James Willson, and Joseph Hughes; part of 311 ac that is part of (1) 396 ac grant Jun. 5, 1797 to John Demsey and (2) part of 500 ac grant Jun. 23, 1774 to Robert Felps; "200 ac of tract (1) and 30(sic) ac of tract (2) on both sides of Bner's(sic) Cr of Enoree R". Witness William Hughes and George Barker. Signed William and Avarilla Jones' marks. Wit. oath Dec. 16, 1825 William Hughes to Thomas Wood. Rec. Mar. 6, 1826

p. 191-192 Oct. 29, 1825 James Turner (Spartanburgh) to William Turner (same); for $250 sold 150 ac on waters of Pacolate R; border: Nesbett's Road, Coulter's ford, and Edward Turner. Witness Middleton Turner and Edward Turner. Signed James Turner. Wit. oath Oct. 29, 1825 Middleton Turner to James Foster. Rec. Mar. 6, 1826

p. 192-193 Oct. 21, 1825 Isaac Crow (Spartanburgh) to James Alexander (same); for $600 sold 170 ac on branches of James Cr; border: McClukin, E-Jacob Rast, N-Benjamin T Crow, E-William Posey, S-Ralph Smith, Thomas J Underwood and Co, and Zachariah Hobby. Witness William Otts and Robert Alexander. Signed Isaac Crow. Wit. oath Jan. 16, 1826 Robert Alexander to Robert Ligon. Rec. Mar. 9, 1826. Dower renounced Jan. 16, 1826 Martha Crow to Robert Ligon

p. 193 Nov. 11, 1823 William Staggs (Spartanburgh) says Bowen Griffen (same) is innocent of horse stealing; William had Bowen arrested on that charge but conference between them has settled matters. Witness William Choice jr and Philip C Lester. Signed William Staggs. Wit. oath Dec. 1, 1823 William Choice jr to Richd Thurston. Rec. Mar. 20, 1826

p. 193-195 Sept. 29, 1825 William Scibles (or Scibels) (Edgefield Dist) to John McCreless (Richland Dist); to secure note Oct. 20, 1820 payable to Thomas T Willson for $650 with interest and endorsed by Thomas T Willson to John McCreless and for $1 sold 2,850 ac; part of grant to Graffs Scibel and Braselman; land is William's share in division of land of William Scibles, Sarah Scibels, and Henry Scibels and was bought by William Scibels from Sarah and Henry Scibels; Condition: sale void if William Scibels pays debt with interest. Witness John Collem and John T Scibels. Signed William Scibels. Wit. oath Mar. 16, 1826 (Richland Dist) John T Scibels to Benj Rawls. Rec. Mar. 25, 1826. Sept. 29, 1825 William Scibels revokes power of attorney to Claiborn C Clifton (Columbia, SC) since Claiborn didn't sell the land. Witness John T Scibels

p. 195-196 Oct. 14, 1825 Alexander Vernon (Spartanburgh) to Samuel Turner (same); for $256 sold 263 ac on waters of Tyger R; border: John Chapman, Wilson's Cr, Mr. James, and Mrs. Gray; "known formerly as two districts and separate tracts" (1) lately occupied by Mrs. Hannah Gray and (2) by Henry Hutcheson; the two tracts are now consolidated. Witness Beverly R Chapman and M. N. Chapman. Signed Alexander Vernon. Wit. oath Oct. 14, 1825 Beverly R Chapman to John Chapman. Rec. Mar. 24, 1826. Dower renounced Mar. 14, 1826 Ann H Vernon to F. H. Legg

p. 196-197 Nov. 21, 1823 James Senter (Spartanburgh) to Parker M Rice (same); for $550 sold 181 ac on S side of S Pacolate R; border: William Ramsey, McDowell, and Dangar; where James Senter lives. Witness Christopher Golightly and Nathaniel Dodd. Signed James Senter. Wit. oath Jun. 25, 1825 Nathaniel Dodd to James Young. Rec. Mar. 24, 1826

p. 197-198 Dec. 5, 1825 Elijah Gossett and wife Sidney (late Sidney Donaldson) (Spartanburgh) to Capt. William Black (Union Dist); for $250 sold 72 ac on Harris' Cr of Story's Cr, otherwise called Mill Cr, of Fairforest Cr; border: James McCarter, George Kennett, David R Burns, and William Hardy, a free man of color; part of grant to Hugh Donaldson sr who sold to Robert Donaldson, father of Sidney Gossett, and to Sidney by will of Robert Donaldson. Witness Hugh Donaldson and James A McDowell. Signed Elijah Gossett and Sidney's mark. Wit. oath Feb. 11, 1826 James A McDowell to William Reid. Rec. Mar. 25, 1826. Dower renounced Feb. 7, 1826 Sidney Gossett to William Reid

p. 198-199 Dec. 31, 1825 Alston Drummond (Spartanburgh) to James Anderson (same); for $1,000 sold 197 ac. Witness S. N. Evins, James Chamblin, and A. B. Moore. Signed A Drummond. Wit. oath Jan. 3, 1826 James Chamblin to F. H. Legg. Rec. Apr. 3, 1826. Dower renounced Jan. 11, 1826 Lucinda Mary Drummond to F. H. Legg

p. 199-200 May 14, 1825 John Montgomery and Theron Earle (Spartanburgh), executors of Michael Miller desc, to James Anderson (same); for $1,100 sold 550 ac on N side of Middle Tyger R; border: old forge tract; "late" survey by James Swansey. Witness Thos Holland and John Crawford. Signed Theron Earle and John Montgomery. Wit. oath May 14, 1825 John Crawford to John Montgomery. Rec. Apr. 3, 1826

p. 200 Mar. 14, 1826 Henry Walding sr (Spartanburgh) to William Walding (same); for $100 sold 100 ac. Witness James Selman, William White, and W Hunt. Signed Henry Walding sr's mark. Wit. oath Mar. 14, 1826 James Selman to W Hunt. Rec. Apr. 3, 1826

p. 200-201 Mar. 29, 1826 Robert Jamison (Spartanburgh) to John Wingo (same); for $79 sold 36 ac; border: School House Br, Big Br, Alexander Thompson, John Wingo, and Mrs. Jamison; part of grant to Robert McCrea. Witness Alexander Miller and James C Ballinger. Signed Robt Jamison. Wit. oath Mar. 31, 1826 James C Ballinger to

John Burns. Rec. Apr. 3, 1826

p. 201 Mar. 29, 1826 Robert Jamison (Spartanburgh) to Alexander Miller (same); for $436 sold 118 ac; border: Alexander Thompson; part of grant to Robert McCrea. Witness John Wingo and James C Ballinger. Signed Robt Jamison. Wit. oath Mar. 31, 1826 James C Ballinger to John Burns. Rec. Apr. 3, 1826

p. 201-202 Aug. 29, 1825 Robert Goodgion (Greenville Dist) to John Otts (Spartanburgh); for $300 sold 245 ac on both sides Colley's Cr of N Pacolate R; part of 458 ac grant Mar. 5, 1792 to Jervis Carnnell (or Carnwell). Witness Jacob Kitle and Martin Otts. Signed Robt Goodgion. Wit. oath Aug. 29, 1825 Martin Otts to Thos Stanford. Rec. Apr. 10, 1826

p. 202-203 Feb. 9, 1825 Isaac Williams to Edward Williams; for $100 sold 190 ac on Suck Cr of Broad R; where Edward Williams lives. Witness Robert Martin and John Martin. Signed Isaac Williams. Wit. oath Mar. 3, 1825 John Martin to Wm Dobbins. Rec. Apr. 10, 1826

p. 203-204 Mar. 25, 1826 Archibald Nelson (Spartanburgh) to Robert D Talley (same); for $725 sold 205 ac on S side of S Pacolate R; border: James Wood, land formerly of Jesse Bruton, and Thomas Bruton; grant to John Gowen who sold to Robert Black and given to his two sons William and Samuel Black who sold to Archibald Nelson. Witness Thomas Jackson jr, John Jackson, and Archey Burton. Signed Archibald Nelson. Wit. oath Mar. 25, 1826 Thomas Jackson jr to W. T. Morgan. Rec. Apr. 11, 1826. Dower renounced Apr. 1, 1826 Elizabeth Nelson to W. T. Morgan

p. 204-205 Oct. 21, 1825 Henry White (Spartanburgh) to Toliver Scott (same); for $150 sold 100 ac N of Tyger R; border: David Brewton, Benjamin Nickolls, Shearbutt, and Benjamin Nickolls' mill; part of grant to William Shirley. Witness John Trail and Enoch Floyd. Signed Henry White. Wit. oath Mar. 25, 1826 Enoch Floyd to Philip Brewton. Rec. Apr. 11, 1826

p. 205 Nov. 11, 1825 Ebsworth Moore (Spartanburgh) to Nathan Vice (same); for $1 sold 48 ac on S side of Cain Cr and N side of Tyger R; border: Francis Bremar and Nicholls; part of grant Dec. 4, 1794 Gov. William Moultrie to Joel Hembree who sold to Herndon Meadows who sold to Ebsworth Moore. Witness Thomas Robers and Robert Page. Signed Ebsworth Moore. Wit. oath Mar. 22, 1826 Robert Page to James Hamm. Rec. Apr. 11, 1826

p. 205-206 Dec. 3, 1825 Isaac Leatherwood (Spartanburgh) to William Scott (same); for $550 sold 100 ac on S side of James Cr of Tyger R. Witness Peter N Bragg and William Jones SM. Signed Isaac Leatherwood. Wit. oath Jan. 23, 1826 Peter N Bragg to James Crook. Rec. Apr. 11, 1826. Dower renounced Jan. 23, 1826 Delilah Leatherwood to James Crook

p. 206-208 Jan. 13, 1826 William Hays (Spartanburgh) to Daniel McHam (same); to secure debt of $29.75 sold a bay mare, a sow and 6 pigs, 2 feather beds and furniture, a loom, a spinning wheel, 2 pine chests, a table, 3 pots, an oven and skillet, 2 ploghs, 2 hoes and gears, an axe, 10 barrels of corn, 400 bundles of fodder, a cupboard and furniture; Condition: sale void if William Hays pays debt. Witness John Grist and Elijah Smith. Signed Wm Hays. Wit. oath Apr. 11, 1826 John Grist to Augustin Shands. Rec. Apr. 11, 1826

p. 208-209 Dec. 13, 1825 Isaac Crow (Spartanburgh) to Foley Brown and John King; for $337.06½ sold 100 ac on branches of Two Mile Cr of Enoree R; border: Buncomb Road. Witness Zachariah Leatherwood and Peter Bragg. Signed Isaac Crow. Wit. oath Feb. 1, 1826 Peter

Bragg to Benj Wofford. Rec. Apr. 11, 1826. Dower renounced Feb. 1, 1826 Martha Crow to Benj Wofford

p. 209-210 Feb. 24, 1826 (Union Dist) William Rice (Union Dist) to Robert Creswell (Laurens Dist); for $352.50 sold 1,729 ac (dut to "late" survey by Thomas Wright); border: James Allen, Caleb Allen, Woodruff, James Page, Allen Johnson, and Enoree R; where Daniel McKie lives; sold as forfiet of Daniel McKie's land by Spartanburgh sheriff to William Rice in Sept. 1825. Witness Abraham Spencer and James McKibbin. Signed Wm Rice. Wit. oath Feb. 24, 1826 (Union Dist) Abraham Spencer to J McKibbin. Rec. Apr. 11, 1826. Dower renounced Feb. 24, 1826 (Union Dist) Sarah P Rice to James McKibbin. Dower renounced Mar. 8, 1826 Fanny McKie, wife of Daniel, to James Crook

p. 210-211 Mar. 22, 1825 William S Morgan and wife Cinthy (Spartanburgh) to Thomas Jackson jr (same); for $750 sold (1) (ac omitted) on N side of S Pacolate R; border: Elijah Alversan; grant to John Clark; (2) 199 ac border: N-tract (1); grant to Robert Henderson; (3) 150 ac; border: Elijah Alversan; part of grant Oct. 12, 1784 to Carrell (or Cawell); except a small portion on E end of (2) taken by John Dalton. Witness James Jackson and Archey Burton. Signed Wm S Morgan. Wit. oath Mar. 27, 1826 James Jackson to James Young. Rec. Apr. 12, 1826. Dower renounced Mar. 27, 1826 Sinthy Morgan to James Young

p. 211-212 Jan. 14, 1826 James and Clabourn D Lawrence (Union Dist) to Robert Wilkins (Spartanburgh); for $500 paid to John B Lawrence (Spartanburgh) sold 137 ac on Gum Root Br of Goucher Cr of Thickety Cr; border: E & S-Moses Wilkins, W-Green Laurence, and N-William Lipscomb; where John B Lawrence lived; part of grant to James Thomson. Witness William Blakely and Green Lawrence. Signed Jas Lawrence and C. D. Lawrence. Wit. oath Mar. 10, 1826 Green Lawrence to John Lipscomb. Rec. Apr. 12, 1826. Dower renounced Apr. 3, 1826 Catharine Lawrence to John Lipscomb

p. 212-213 Nov. 6, 1824 Thomas Crutchfield (Spartanburgh) to John Sarratt (same); for $175 sold 70 ac; border: Edmond Green, George Walker, Clabourn Umphres, little Cherokee Cr, and Vineset; part of "large" survey belonging to Charles Hester. Witness William G Clark to John Lemans. Signed Thomas Crutchfield's mark. Wit. oath Mar. 4, 1826 William G Clark to Joseph Camp. Rec. Apr. 12, 1826

p. 213-124 Apr. 12, 1825 Alexander Roddy (Spartanburgh) to William Hammett (same); for $1,112 sold 410 ac; border: Michael Gramling. Witness Michl Gramling and Alexander Roddy jr. Signed Alexr Roddy. Wit. oath Mar. 16, 1826 Michl Gramling to John Burns. Rec. Apr. 12, 1826

p. 214 Oct. 13, 1825 James Duncan, son of Alexander, (Spartanburgh) to Meadows Harrelson (same); for $195 sold 54 ac on waters of Tyger R; border: Nathaniel Vice and Harrelson's old line; where James Duncan lives; part of 114 ac tract. Witness John Clark and Gideon Harrelson. Signed James Duncan, son of Alexr. Wit. oath Mar. 31, 1826 John Clark to Wm Smith. Rec. Apr. 12, 1826

p. 214-215 Dec. 7, 1826(sic) John Arnold (Spartanburgh) to Francis Miller (same); for $375 sold 120 ac on branches of Two Mile Cr of Enoree R; border: Wm Lanford. Witness James Powers and William Skinner. Signed John Arnold. Wit. oath Apr. 12, 1826 William Skinner to Philip Brewton. Rec. Apr. 12, 1826

p. 215-126 Apr. 12, 1810 William G Foster (Spartanburgh) to Elisha Wells; for $130 sold 50 ac on branch of Jemey's Cr; border: NE-Keley and Kern; part of 250 ac grant Apr. 3, 1786 to Jonathan Senard(sic). Witness Thomas G Potter and Thomas Layton. Signed William

G Foster. Wit. oath Mar. 24, 1826 Thomas G Potter and Thomas Layton to Wm Young. Rec. Apr. 15, 1826. Dower renounced Oct. 5, 1823 Judah Foster to Burrell Bobo

p. 216-217 Oct. 4, 1808 Thomas Wilson (Spartanburgh) to Elisha Wells (same); a bond for $350; Condition: bond void if Thomas deeds Elisha 76 ac on E side of tract "of" James Cr; border: N-Young, W-Foster, and S-Leonard. Witness Thomas G Potter. Signed Thomas Wilson. Wit. oath Mar. 24, 1826 Thomas G Potter to Wm Young. Rec. Apr. 15, 1826

p. 217 Sept. 28, 1809 Thomas Wilson (Spartanburgh) to Abner Marsh (same); a bond for $350; Condition: bond void if Thomas deeds Abner 70 ac; border: W-Elisha Wells, N-a branch and Young, and E-Nebur. Witness Thomas Layton. Signed Thomas Wilson. Wit. oath Mar. 24, 1826 Thomas Layton to Wm Young. Rec. Apr. 15, 1826

p. 217-218 Jan. 20, 1826 John Hobby (Spartanburgh) to Zachariah Hobby; for $250 sold 83 3/4 ac on branches of Two Mile Cr of Enoree R; border: Zachariah Hobby; note: purchase price to be taken out of Zachariah Hobby's share of John Hobby's estate when John dies. Witness William Posey and Robert McCord. Signed John Hobby. Wit. oath Feb. 1, 1826 William Posey to (not signed) Feb. 1, 1826. Rec. Apr. 15, 1826. Dower renounced Feb. 1, 1826 Elizabeth Hobby to Benj Wofford

p. 218-219 Jan. 20, 1826 Isaac Crow to Zachariah Hobby (Spartanburgh); for $300 sold 73 ac on branch of Jamey's Cr of Tyger R; border: E-Thomas Bell, N-Benjamin Chain, W-James Alexander, and S-George Chumbler. Witness William Posey and Robert McCord. Signed Isaac Crow. Wit. oath Feb. 1, 1826 William Posey to Benj Wofford. Rec. Apr. 15, 1826. Dower renounced Feb. 1, 1826 Martha Crow to Benj Wofford

p. 219-220 Mar. 4, 1826 William Trimmier, Commissioner of Spartanburgh Equity Court, to Mrs. Nancy Poole; for $100 sold 100 ac on Dutchman's Cr of Tyger R; border: Thomas Reese; part of grant Jul. 1, 1793 to William Lancaster; David Golightly on Jul. 24, 1823 complained to Equity Court against Joseph Smith to foreclose mortgage on land; case was heard in Feb. term and Court ordered sale of land. Witness John Poole and Thomas J Dean. Signed Wm Trimmier. Wit. oath Mar. 11, 1826 John Poole to E Bomar. Rec. Apr. 20, 1826

p. 220-221 Mar. 23, 1826 Elijah Alverson (Spartanburgh) to Pleasant Alverson (same); for $200 sold 100 ac on N side of S Pacolate R and SW side of Alexander Cr; border: J Jackson, Green, and Fowler; part of two surveys. Witness Thomas Jackson jr and John King. Signed Elijah Alverson's mark. Wit. oath Mar. 30, 1826 Thomas Jackson jr to W. T. (or S) Morgan. Rec. Apr. 29, 1826

p. 221-222 Oct. 31, 1825 Henry Grogan (Spartanburgh) to William Page (Chester Dist); for $320 sold 390 ac on both sides Beaverdam Cr of S Pacolate R; includes where Henry Grogan lives; grant of 150 ac Nov. 5, 1771 to Abigail Tenell and part of 483 ac grant Mar. 6, 1797 to Henry Grogan. Witness John W Hunt and James A Page. Signed Henry Grogan's mark. Wit. oath Feb. 25, 1826 John W Hunt to W. T. (or S) Morgan. Rec. Apr. 29, 1826

p. 222-223 Apr. 13, 1821 William Farmer (Spartanburgh) to James B Shields (same); for $172 sold 90 ac; border: Philips, Joel Farmer, and Thomas; where William Farmer lives. Witness John Brown, Joseph Brown, and Robert Kimble. Signed William Farmer and Elizabeth's mark. Wit. oath Jan. 14, 1822 Robert Kimble to John Chapman. Rec. May 1. 1826

p. 223 Dec. 12, 1820 John Robbs (Spartanburgh) to James B Shields (same); for $120 sold 95 ac on waters of N Tyger R; border: John Montgomery esq, David Davis, Mary McMikins, and John Robbs; part of 272 ac grant to Jesse Reames. Witness Watson Robbs, William Porter, and Alexander Robbs. Signed John Robbs. Wit. oath Jan. 3, 1821 William Porter to John Montgomery. Rec. May 1, 1826

p. 223-224 Dec. 3, 1825 Isaac Snoddy jr (Spartanburgh) to John M Delany (same); for $521.50 sold 150 ac on Jamey's Cr of N Tyger R; part of grant to John Luck. Witness James Leonard and Andrew Snoddy. Signed Isaac Snoddy jr. Wit. oath Apr. 12, 1826 Andrew Snoddy to Thomas Wood. Rec. May 1, 1826

p. 224-225 May 8, 1826 Thomas Poole, sheriff (Spartanburgh) to Elleanor Mayson (same); for $20 sold 103 ac on Mill Cr of Tyger R; border: Finch; sold due to writ from Spartanburgh Common Pleas Court second Monday after fourth Monday in Mar. 1822 suit of John Rush jr; judgment was levy of $143.28 and costs from Joel Mayson. Witness Jesse Mason and James Rainwaters. Signed Thomas Poole. Wit. oath Mar. 8, 1826 Jesse Mason to E Bomar. Rec. May 8, 1826

p. 225-226 May 8, 1826 Thomas Poole, sheriff (Spartanburgh) to Elleanor Mayson; for $50 sold 200 ac on Ford's Cr of Fairforest Cr; border: William Baber, Joseph Hurt, Benjamin Rainwaters, and Jesse Mayson; where Joel Mayson formerly lived; sold due to writ from Spartanburgh Common Pleas Court second Monday after fourth Monday in Mar. 1822 suit of John Rush jr; judgment was levy of $143.28 and costs from Joel Mayson. Witness Jesse Mayson and James Rainwaters. Signed Thomas Poole. Wit. oath May 8, 1826 Jesse Mayson to E Bomar. Rec. May 8, 1826

p. 226-227 May 12, 1826 Thomas Poole, sheriff (Spartanburgh) to Leonard Hill and John Clark (same); for $13 sold 184 ac on waters of Pacolate R; border: Richard Kirby, Richard Lemaster, George Kennett, and Joseph Tolleson; sold due to writ from Spartanburgh Common Pleas Court second Monday after fourth Monday in Oct. 1825 suit of Muse Bryant; judgment was levy of $124 and costs from John Tolleson desc. Witness Thomas J Dean and John Poole. Signed Thomas Poole. Wit. oath May 13, 1826 John Poole to E Bomar. Rec. May 13, 1826

p. 227-228 Feb. 2, 1826 Thomas Poole, sheriff (Spartanburgh) to Leonard Hill and John Clark (same); for $155 sold 184 ac on waters of Pacolate R; border: Richard Kirby, Richard Lemaster, Geroge Kennett, and Josephus Tolleson; bought by George Hill for Leonard Hill and John Clark; sold due to writ from Spartanburgh Common Pleas Court second Monday after fourth Monday in Mar. 1825 suit of Hill and Clark; judgment was levy of $553 and costs from Birdsong Tolleson. Witness John Poole and Thomas J Dean. Signed Thomas Poole. Wit. oath May 13, 1826 John Poole to E Bomar. Rec. May 13, 1826

p. 228-229 Jul. 12, 1822 William Littlejohn (Spartanburgh) to Elizabeth Lipscomb (same); for $600 sold 116 ac on S side of Brice's fork of Thickety Cr; border: Elizabeth Lipscomb and a waggon road. Witness John H Lipscomb and Smith Lipscomb. Signed William Littlejohn. Wit. oath Smith Lipscomb to John Lipscomb. Rec. May 22, 1826. Dower renounced Oct. 8, 1825 Elizabeth Littlejohn to John Lipscomb

p. 229-230 May 31, 1809 Thomas Paden (Spartanburgh) to John Paden (same); for $60 sold 140 ac on branches of Ferguson's Cr of Tyger R; plat attached shows border: Thomas Paden, Andrew Paden, and John Wells; survey May 19, 1809 by Jas Wofford. Witness Moses W Paden and James Paden. Signed Thomas Paden. Wit. oath May 22, 1826 James Paden to James Crook. Rec. May 22, 1826

p. 230-231 Jan. 3, 1818 David S Lipscomb (Spartanburgh) to Elizabeth Lipscomb (same); for $675 sold 85 ac on both sides Byces fork of Thickety Cr; border: Thomson, Elizabeth Lipscomb jr, and William Wood; "laid out by Commissioners and drawn by David S Lipscomb". Witness Smith Lipscomb and John H Lipscomb. Signed David S Lipscomb. Wit. oath Oct. 17, 1823 Smith Lipscomb to John Lipscomb. Rec. May 22, 1826

p. 231-232 Jan. 3, 1818 William Wood (Spartanburgh) to Elizabeth Lipscomb sr (same); for $550 sold 85 ac on N side of Byce's fork of Thickety Cr; border: Thomas Littlejohn, Thomson, and David S Lipscomb; "laid out by Commissioners and drawn by William Wood". Witness Smith Lipscomb and John H Lipscomb. Signed William Wood. Wit. oath Oct. 17, 1823 Smith Lipscomb to John Lipscomb. Rec. May 22, 1826. Dower renounced Oct. 17, 1823 Nancy Wood to John Lipscomb

p. 232 May 24, 1826 Thomas Tinsley sr (Spartanburgh) to Sir Paton Tinsley (same); for $500 sold #2 and #3 (56½ ac each) on waters of Fairforest Cr; #2 was formerly sold to John Foster (sic) and #3 was formerly sold to James Harrison (sic). Witness Elisha West and John Foster. Signed Thomas Tinsley. Wit. oath May 24, 1826 Elisha West to Jas Ed Henry. Rec. May 23, 1826

p. 232-233 Oct. 8, 1825 Thomas Hanna (Spartanburgh) to David Trail (same); for $93 sold 93 ac on waters of Dutchman's Cr of Tyger R; part of grant to Henry Middleton. Witness Zepheniah Posey and Joicy Bearden. Signed Thos Hanna. Wit. oath Mar. 28, 1826 Zepheniah Posey to Robert Ligon. Rec. Jun. 5, 1826. Dower renounced Nov. 4, 1825 Catharine Hanna to James Hamm

p. 233-234 Feb. 2, 1826 James Wofford (Spartanburgh) to Mark Bennett (same); to secure a note dated Feb. 7, 1823 sold a young iron gray horse 4 years old and saddle and bridle; Condition: sale void if James Wofford pays debt. Witness Isaac Wofford jr and Sarrah Wofford. Signed James Wofford. Wit. oath Mar. 25, 1826 Isaac Wofford jr to James Hamm. Rec. Jun. 5, 1826

p. 234-235 Jan. 2, 1826 Jacob Domer (or Dorner) (Spartanburgh) to John Eison (same); for $50 sold 160 ac on Blackstock road; border: Daniel Prewett, Drury Parham, Zephiniah O'Shealds, John Grist, and Wm Farmer; where Jacob Domer lives; grant to John F Kerns who sold to Jacob Domer. Witness Benjamin Wofford and Young Terry. Signed Jacob Domer. Wit. oath Apr. 11, 1826 Young Terry to James Young. Rec. Jun. 5, 1826

p. 235-236 Mar. 20k 1826 David Golightly (Spartanburgh) to Celia Lee (same); for $114.75 sold 51 ac (or 50 ac) on branch of S side of Fairforest Cr; border: Rakestraw and Hancock Smith; part of grant to John Smith who sold to Henry Smith who sold to David Golightly. Witness Isaac Smith, Henry Murph, and Robert James. Signed D Golightly. Wit. oath Jun. 5, 1826 Isaac Smith to E Bomar. Rec. Jun. 5, 1826

p. 236-237 May 12, 1826 Thomas Poole, sheriff (Spartanburgh) to John Garlington (Laurens Dist); for $20 sold 250 ac on waters of Tyger R; border: S-Alexander Roddy, E-James Weatherford, N-Elijah Bishop, and W-William Davis; bought by John Brannan for John Garlington; sold due to writ from Laurence Dist Common Pleas Court on third Monday after fourth Monday in Oct. 1823 suit of John Garlington; judgment was levy of $207.30 and costs from John Patterson. Witness Thomas J Dean and John Poole. Signed Thomas Poole. Wit. oath Jun. 14, 1826 John Poole to E Bomar. Rec. Jun. 14, 1826

p. 237-238 May 12, 1826 Thomas Poole, sheriff (Spartanburgh) to John Garlington (Laurence Dist); for $20 sold 517 ac on Lawson's fork; border: E-Elijah Bishop and W-survey by Jesse Rheams;

bought by James Brannon for John Garlington; sold due to writ from Laurence Dist Common Pleas Court third Monday after fourth Monday in Oct. 1823 suit of John Garlington; judgment was levy of $207.30 and costs from John Patterson. Witness Thomas J Dean and John Poole. Signed Thomas Poole. Wit. oath Jun. 14, 1826 John Poole to E Bomar. Rec. Jun. 14, 1826

p. 238 Jan. 6, 1826 William W Smithwick (Spartanburgh) to John Shurley (same); for $250 sold 100 ac on S Tyger R and N Tyger R; border: Jonathan Crow. Witness John Ward and John Gentry. Signed Wm W Smithwick. Wit. oath Jun. 23, 1826 John Ward to Robert Ligon. Rec. Jul. 3, 1826

p. 238-239 Oct. 13, 1825 Nathaniel Gentry (Spartanburgh) to John Shurley (SC); for $205 sold 75 ac on N Tyger R; border: mouth of Tapp's Spring Br and Solomon Autrey's Spring Br. Witness James Nesbett and John Gentry. Signed Nathaniel Gentry's mark. Wit. oath Jun. 25, 1826 James Nesbett to Robert Ligon. Rec. Jul. 3, 1826

p. 239-240 Jan. 6, 1826 John Shurley (Spartanburgh) to John Gentry (same); for $400 sold 100 ac in fork of Tyger R; border: Jonathan Crow. Witness James Nesbett and John Ward. Signed John Shurley. Wit. oath Jun. 23, 1826 James Nesbett to (not signed). Rec. Jul. 3, 1826. Dower renounced Jun. 23, 1826 Fanny Shurley to Robert Ligon

p. 240-241 Apr. 3, 1826 John S Coan (Spartanburgh) to John Anderson (same); for $408 sold 136 ac in two parts of Tyger R-- (1) 106 ac and (2) 30 ac; border: Robert Anderson, Saml Pearson, James Anderson, John S Coan, and SW-S Tyger R. Witness Willis Foster and Simpson Bobo. Signed John S Coan. Wit. oath Jun. 13, 1826 Willis Foster to F. H. Legg. Rec. Jul. 3, 1826. Dower renounced Jun. 14, 1826 Jane Coan to F. H. Legg

p. 241-242 Jun. 24, 1826 Robert McDowell sr (Spartanburgh) to Lucy Kelso (same); for $340 sold 170 ac on both sides Lawson's fork; border: Miry Br, Jno Clark, Jno S Rowland, and James A McDowell; where Lucy Kelso lives. Witness Christi Golightly, William Bullman, and Sarah Kelso. Signed Robert McDowell. Wit. oath Jul. 21, 1826 Christi Golightly to E Bomar. Rec. Jul. 21, 1826. Dower renounced Jul. 4, 1826 Mary McDowell to James Young

p. 242-243 Oct. 19, 1825 William M Story (Spartanburgh) to Robert M Young (same); for $300 sold (1) 40 ac on branches of Fairforest Cr; about a mile from the Court House; border: Richard Thomson and Greenville road; (2) lots 8 and 9 (½ ac each) in Spartanburgh, SC; border: E-Gabriel Benson, N & W-Richard Thomson, and S-Main St. Witness J Brannan, James J Vernon, and D. J. Goodlett. Signed W. M. Storey. Wit. oath Jan. 7, 1826 D. J. Goodlett to James Ed Henry. Rec. Jul. 25, 1826. Dower renounced Jan. 13, 1826 Susannah Story to James Ed Henry

p. 243-244 Oct. 6, 1823 Thomas Poole, sheriff (Spartanburgh) to Abner Benson (same); for $1,500 sold 700 ac on Lawson's fork; where Thomas Dare lives; sold by Abner Benson to Thomas Dare; sold due to writ from Spartanburgh Common Pleas Court second Monday after fourth Monday in Mar. 1823 suit of Abner Benson; judgment was levy of $1,457 and costs from Thomas Dare. Witness Jesse F Cleveland and T. J. Underwood. Signed Thomas Poole. Wit. oath (not dated) T. J. Underwood to James Ed Henry. Rec. Jul. 25, 1826. Feb. 15, 1826 Thomas Dare to Abner Benson (Spartanburgh); for $650 Thomas Dare agrees to discontinue Spartanburgh Equity Court case. Witness Michael Gaffney and Wilson Nesbett. Signed Thomas Dare. Wit. oath (not dated) Wilson Nesbett to James Ed Henry

p. 244-245 Mar. 2, 1824 William Bostick to son William Rice Bostick; for love and affection give 340 ac on Harris Br of Thickety Cr; grant Gov. Moultrie to Josiah Tanner except part covered by McBee's and Hart's old surveys. Witness Amos Austell, Thomas Cole, and Joseph Camp. Signed William Bostick. Wit. oath Jan. 11, 1826 Amos Austell to J Camp. Rec. Jul. 26, 1826

p. 245-246 Apr. 29, 1826 William Rice Bostick to Amos Austell; for $600 sold 340 ac on Harris' Br of Thickety Cr; grant Gov. Moultrie to Josiah Tanner except part covered by McBee's and Hart's old surveys. Witness William Austell and Peter Quin Camp. Signed Wm R Bostick. Wit. oath May 10, 1826 Peter Q Camp to Joseph Camp. Rec. Jul. 26, 1826

p. 246 Nov. 6, 1822 John Gowen and Winn B Gowen (Greenville Dist), executors of estate of John Gowen desc, to John Lucas (Spartanburgh); for $200 sold 120 ac on N side of S Pacolate R; border: Willey S Brown, James Gowen, Jamison, and Thomas Grogan. Witness Benajah Durham and John Stokes. Signed John Gowen and W. B. Gowen. Wit. oath (not dated) (Greenville Dist) Benajah Durham to Richd Thurston. Rec. Aug. 7, 1826

p. 246-247 Dec. 1, 1821 John Gowen and Winn B Gowen (Greenville Dist), executors of father John Gowen desc, to John Lucas (Spartanburgh); for $1,000 sold 1,357 ac in Spartanburgh and Greenville Dists on both sides S Pacolate R; border: Barthow Grogan, William Archer, and W. S. Brown; includes where John Lucas lives. Witness John Gowen jr and Ambrose Williams sr. Signed John Gowen and W. B. Gowen. Wit. oath Dec. 20, 1822 Ambrose Williams to J Whitten. Rec. Aug. 7, 1826

p. 247-248 Mar. 27, 1826 James Vernon (Spartanburgh) to Robert Jamison (same); for $404 sold 219 ac on waters of N Tyger R; border: Alexander Thompson, Alexander Miller, John Wingo, B. L. Evetts, and John Ballinger; sold in Jun. 1825 by Thos Poole to (omitted). Witness Wm Perrin and Elijah McMillen. Signed James Vernon. Wit. oath Aug. 7, 1826 Wm Perrin to James Crook. Rec. Aug. 7, 1826

p. 248-249 Jul. 18, 1826 Charles Bragg sr (Spartanburgh) to John Clark ("lest"); for $200 sold 90 ac on both sides of James Cr; border: E-John Clark and James Alexander, N-Gideon Reynolds, W-G Robuck, and S-widow Robuck and William Posey. Witness Thomas Bragg and James Bragg. Signed Charles Bragg. Wit. oath Aug. 5, 1826 Thomas Bragg to Philip Brewton. Rec. Aug. 7, 1826

p. 249-250 Jan. 6, 1826 Susannah Owen and Patsey Owen (Spartanburgh) to Jacob Chapman (same); for $300 sold 223 ac; border: Betty Green Br, Thomas Wood, Buck Br, and Mary Woods; where Jacob Chapman lives; part of grant to William Turner. Witness James Cummins, Joseph Tucker, and Priscilla Walden. Signed Susannah and Patsey Owen's marks. Wit. oath Jan. 6, 1826 James Cummins to W Bennett. Rec. Aug. 7, 1826

p. 250-251 Dec. 15, 1824 Isaac Crow to Zachariah Hobby; for $250 sold 122½ ac on branch of James Cr of Tyger R; border: road from Buncomb to Columbia; plat attached shows border: George (blank), Zachariah Hobby, Isaac Crow, and Wm Posey. Witness Jesse Williams and Chaney R Bobo. Signed Isaac Crow. Wit. oath Aug. 4, 1826 Chaney R Bobo to Joseph Wofford. Rec. Aug. 7, 1826. Dower renounced Dec. 28, 1824 Martha Crow to Daniel White

p. 251-252 Feb. 8, 1826 Thomas Poole, sheriff (Spartanburgh) to Isaac Snoddy; for $399.75 sold 108 ac on waters of Tyger R; part of 158 ac grant Feb. 5, 1787 to John William; Silas Stone petitioned Spartanburgh Ordinary Court vs Sally Stone, Pheby Stepp, Nimrod Arnold and wife Mary, Susannah Stone, Lydia Hammond, John Stone,

Volly Stone, Thomas Stone, Stephen Stone, and Polly Stone on Jul. 14, 1825; Silas asked to distribute estate of Thomas Stone desc among aforesaid legatees anc Court ordered sale first Monday in Nov. 1825; sale was on Nov. 7, 1825. Witness John Poole and Thomas J Dean. Signed Thomas Poole. Wit. oath Aug. 7, 1826 Thomas J Dean to Philip Brewton. Rec. Aug. 7, 1826

p. 252-253 Feb. 14, 1826 William Wood (Union Dist) to Green Mitchell (Spartanburgh); for $52 sold 52 ac on Janes' Cr; border: Davis S Lipscomb and John Lipscomb; drawn by William Wood in division of William Lipscomb sr desc's estate. Witness John Duncan and Samuel Littlejohn. Signed William Wood. Wit. oath Mar. 25, 1826 (Union Dist) Samuel Littlejohn to Wm Goudelock. Rec. Aug. 7, 1826

p. 253 Mar. 8, 1826 (Union Dist) James Lawrence (Union Dist) to Green Mitchell (same); for $425 paid to Henry Littlejohn by Green Mitchell sold 165 ac on waters of Gum Root Br of Goucher Cr of Thickety Cr; border: Joshua Draper and John Kirby; part of grant to David Jones sr and sold by David Jones jr to William Patterson who sold to James Lawrence. Witness Henry Littlejohn and Richard Lawrence. Signed Jas Lawrence. Wit. oath Mar. 25, 1826 (Union Dist) Henry Littlejohn to Wm Goudelock. Rec. Aug. 7, 1826

p. 253-254 Jul. 31, 1809 Thomas Wilson, son of Stephen Wilson desc, to Thomas G Potter; for $200 sold 100 ac on S side of Tyger R; border: Thos Todd, John E Wilson, Wilson's Meeting house, and Reuben Wilson; willed by Stephen Wilson to Thomas Wilson. Witness James Chambers and Stephen Wilson. Signed Thomas Wilson. Wit. oath Jul. 15, 1826 Stephen Wilson to Benj Wofford. Rec. Aug. 18, 1826

p. 254-255 Mar. 1, 1826 Thomas Poole, sheriff (Spartanburgh) to James Vernon (same); for $520 sold 219 ac on waters of Tyger R; where Robert Jamison lives; border: Alexander Thomson, Alexander Miller, John Wingo, B. L. Evetts, and James Ballinger; sold due to writ from Spartanburgh Common Pleas Court second Monday after fourth Monday in Oct. 1822 suit of Alexander Vernon; judgment was levy of $88 and costs from Robert Jamison. Witness John Poole and Thomas J Dean. Signed Thomas Poole. Wit. oath Aug. 30, 1826 John Poole to E Bomar. Rec. Aug. 30, 1826

p. 255-256 May 12, 1826 Thomas Poole, sheriff (Spartanburgh) to Richard Kirby (same); for $32 sold 100 ac on waters of Pacolate R; border: John Cannon, William Lackey, Mary Dewberry, and Lee Linder; sold due to writ from Spartanburgh Common Pleas Court second Monday after fourth Monday in Mar. 1823 suit of Missouri C. F. Tolleson; judgment was levy of $523 and costs from John Tolleson desc. Witness Thomas J Dean and John Poole. Signed Thomas Poole. Wit. oath Aug. 30, 1826 John Poole to E Bomar. Rec. Aug. 30, 1826

p. 256-257 Aug. 21, 1821 (Equity Court) Simpson Foster, Commissioner of Spartanburgh Equity Court, to Alexander Miller; for $285 sold 115 ac on branch of N side of N fork of Middle Tyger R; border: W-Joseph James and others vacant; land is lot #3; known as Morgan's tract; Robert Jamison complained to Equity Court vs John Crawford, guardian, and others on Feb. 5, 1821; Robert asked to divide estate of John Jordan desc and Court said to sell lots 2 and 3; sale was on Aug. 6, 1821. Witness J Brannon and Thomas Poole. Signed Simpson Foster. Wit. oath Jul. 30, 1826 Thomas Poole to E Bomar. Rec. Aug. 30, 1826

p. 257-259 Apr. 29, 1826 James Norris (Spartanburgh) to William Norris (Union Dist); for $3,500 sold 969 ac in Spartanburgh and Union Dists on N side of Pacolate R; border: Thomson (formerly Bullock), Sparks, Griffen, the Quarter Road, Littlejohn's old corner, Leonard Sparks sr, Thos Sparks, Reed, Norton, and Leonard Sparks jr;

sold by Richard Bullock to Henry Farnandes who sold to James Norris; except part James Norris sold Jesse Griffen and adjoining part belonging to James Norris. Witness Richard Thomson and Joseph Collins. Signed Jas Norris. Wit. oath Jul. 25, 1826 Joseph Collins to E Bomar. Rec. Aug. 31, 1826. Dower renounced Aug. 31, 1826 Sally Norris to Elisha Bomar

p. 259-260 Aug. 16, 1826 James Norris and wife Sarah Norris (late Sarah Farnandes) (Spartanburgh) to William Norris (Union Dist); for $3,500 sold 50 ac in Spartanburgh and Union Dists; includes shoals, mill seat and store house at Easterwood's ford on Pacolate R; given by Henry Fernandes desc to James and Sarah Norris subsequent to their marriage and before Henry's death. Wit. oath John J Tuller and A Baird. Signed Jas Norris and Sally Norris. Wit. oath Aug. 30, 1826 A Baird to E Bomar. Rec. Aug. 31, 1826. Dower renounced Aug. 30, 1826 Sally Norris to Elisha Bomar

p. 260 Dec. 31, 1824 William Willis (Spartanburgh) to Thomas Willis (same); for $148 sold 54 ac on S side of Pacolate R; border: still house, Jones' big Spring, and Petetis (or Petit's). Witness James Crocker and James Smith. Signed William Willes. Wit. oath Sept. 4, 1826 James Crocker to William Reid. Rec. Sept. 4, 1826

p. 260-261 Apr. 19, 1826 Jacob Stotts to George Weaver; power of attorney to sell 150 ac; grant to Henry Walker; border: Thos Wells; and power of attorney to collect judgment in sheriff's hands against estate of John Tolleson desc. Witness Absalom McBee and Wm McBee. Signed Jacob Stotts' mark. Wit. oath Sept. 4, 1826 Absalom McBee to Jas Ed Henry. Rec. Sept. 4, 1826

p. 261-262 May 12, 1826 Isaac Compton and wife Barbary (formerly Barbary Smith) and Franklin Smith (Giles Co, Tenn) to James Moore (Spartanburgh); power of attorney to sell land that came to Barbary and Franklin Smith by will of Charles Smith desc (Spartanburgh); on waters of Fairforest Cr; part of where Charles Smith lived. Witness none. Signed Isaac Compton, Barbary Compton, and Franklin Smith. Certified May 13, 1826 by John B Armstrong and John Laird. May 15, 1826 (Giles Co, Tenn) German Lester, clerk of Quarterly Sessions Court, certifies John B Armstrong and John Laird are justices of peace. Jun. 8, 1826 (Giles Co, Tenn) Edward D Jones, JP of Quarterly Sessions Court, certifys German Lester is clerk. Rec. Sept. 4, 1826

p. 262-263 Jul. 18, 1826 Vincent Tapp (Spartanburgh) to Joseph Lanham (same); for $200 sold 100 ac on S side of N Tyger R; border: John Shirley, Bronton Thomas, and waggon road. Witness James Mason and Paul Cambee. Signed Vincent Tapp. Wit. oath Sept. 2, 1826 Paul Cambee to Robert Ligon. Rec. Sept. 4, (omitted). Dower renounced Sept. 2, 1826 Fanny Tapp to Robert Ligon

p. 263-264 Nov. 15, 1825 James Corder (Spartanburgh) to Jorial Barnett (same); for $500 sold 173 ac; grant to Robert Rogers; except 3 ac where meeting house stands and was laid out for public worship or 170 ac sold. Witness Benjamin Robuck and George Vice. Signed James Corder. Wit. oath Apr. 9, 1826 Benjamin Robuck to Joseph Wofford. Rec. Sept. 4, 1826. Dower renounced May 20, 1826 Elizabeth Corder to Robert Ligon

p. 264-265 Dec. 7, 1825 Alexander Roddy (Spartanburgh) to Thomas Wingo (same); for $870 sold (1) 290 ac; border: Wingo and Evetts; and (2) 8 or 9 ac; W corner of tract formerly belonged to John Roddy and surveyed by Jonathan Newman. Witness John Burns and John Wingo. Signed Alexander Roddy. Wit. oath Sept. 4, 1826 John Wingo to E Bomar. Rec. Sept. 4, 1826. Dower renounced Mar. 17, 1826 Martha Roddy to Thomas Wood

p. 265 Sept. 30, 1824 John Windsor to Mary Covil (Spartanburgh); for $80 sold 80 ac on waters of Fairforest Cr; border: NW-John Vandyke and Barney Bishop, S-Henry Bishop, SE-David Dantzler, and E-Sarjus Seay. Witness A Lancaster and Barney Bishop. Signed John Windsor's mark. Wit. oath Sept. 4, 1826 Barney Bishop to E Bomar. Rec. Sept. 4, 1826

p. 265-266 Apr. 21, 1826 John Oeland received from David Whetstone all mortgage due. Witness John Murph. Signed John Oeland. Wit. oath Sept. 4, 1826 John Murph to Elisha Bomar. Rec. Sept. 4, 1826

p. 266 Aug. 6, 1826 John Crow (Spartanburgh) to William Brooks (same); to secure payment of debt mentioned below sold 135 ac; border: James Langford, Lewis Langford, John Terry, and "others"; where John Crow lives; and sold a sorrell horse (Dick) about 6 years old, a bay colt, 2 cows and a calf, and 2 beds and furniture; Condition: sale foid if John Crow pays William Brooks $273 with interest that John owes William; interest is figured from Jan. 1, 1826; in annual installments: $100 due Jan. 1, 1827, $100 due Jan. 1, 1828, and $73 due Jan. 1, 1829. Witness Benjamin L Goodman and James Tapp. Signed John Crow's mark. Wit. oath Sept. 15, 1826 Benjm L Goodman to E Bomar. Rec. Sept. 15, 1826

p. 266-267 Jan. 29, 1821 Daniel Stephens (Spartanburgh) to Andrew Stephens (same); for $100 sold 140 ac; survey for Frederick Eison and granted Apr. 16, 1785 (to Frederick Eison?). Witness Dr. A. B. Moore and Robert Ligon. Signed Daniel Stephens' mark. Wit. oath Nov. 1, 1824 A. B. Moore to W Hunt. Rec. Sept. 21, 1826

p. 267-268 Sept. 15, 1826 (Clark Co, Ga) David Lynch (Clark Co, Ga) to Thomas J Lynch (same); for $1,000 sold 270 ac on waters of Kelsey's Cr and near Cedar Springs; border: White and "others"; lot #7 drawn by Lettice Lynch, wife of David, in division of her father, James Smith desc's, estate. Witness Joseph T Clark and Ulysses R Lynch. Signed David Lynch. Wit. oath Sept. 15, 1826 (Clark Co, Ga) Ulysses R Lynch to William Clark JJC. Rec. Sept. 22, 1826. Dower renounced Sept. 15, 1826 (Clark Co, Ga) Lettice Lynch to William Clark

p. 268-269 Sept. 22, 1826 Robert M Young (Spartanburgh) to William Trimmier (same); for $370 sold 1 ac in Spartanburgh, SC; lots # 8 & 9; border: Richard Thomson, John H Harrison, and Main St. Witness Elisha Bomar and Saml C Hunt. Signed R. M. Young. Wit. oath Sept. 22, 1826 Saml C Hunt to E Bomar. Rec. Sept. 22, 1826

p. 269-270 Feb. 24, 1826 Miles Nash (Spartanburgh) to John Dean (same); for $239.25 sold 300 ac on Two Mile Cr; border: SW-James Lanford, NW-James Lanford and William Lanford, and other sides-Joseph Barnett and John E Bobo; where Miles Nash lives; part of grant to Daniel Marine. Witness William Nash and Hosea J Dean. Signed Miles Nash. Wit. oath Sept. 7, 1826 (Laurens Dist) Hosea J Dean to John G Klinch. Rec. Sept. 25, 1826

p. 270 Aug. 12, 1826 Jonathan Nesbett (Spartanburgh) to son James Nesbett (same); for love and affection and $1 sold 439 ac on NE side of Middle Tyger R; border: Andrew McElrath, Giney Jarvis, Michael Miller desc, Andrew F Nesbett, and by Jonathan Nesbett's own land on SE side of Middle Tyger R; part of three grants to Jonathan Nesbett. Witness Tolliver Scott, John Ward, and James Cathcart. Signed Jonathan Nesbett. Wit. oath Oct. 2, 1826 John Ward to E Bomar. Rec. Oct. 2, 1826

p. 270-271 Oct. 5, 1826 James Hunt (Spartanburgh) to David Thompson (same); for $100 sold James Hunt's share of Bassel Scott's estate which is the share of George Parkerson and wife Patsey (late Patsey Lee, heir of Bassel Scott); land was sold by George Parkerson to James Hunt Jul. 26, 1819 see Book Q p. 333. Witness Elisha Bomar and G. W. Bomar. Signed Jas Hunt. Wit. oath Oct. 5, 1826 G. W. Bomar to E Bomar. Rec. Oct. 5, 1826

p. 271-272 Oct. 1, 1825 Elisha Bridges to Nathaniel Jones; for $250 sold 100 ac on Jumping Br of Sarratt's Cr; border: Bonner and Robertson. Witness William Clary and Alexander Davidson. Signed Elisha Bridges. Wit. oath Alexander Davidson to Joseph Camp Dec. 30, 1825. Rec. Oct. 10, 1826

p. 272 Oct. 9, 1826 Samuel McDade (Spartanburgh) to John Vaughn (same); for $700 sold 495 ac, a gray horse, 8 cattle, 5 hogs, a feather bed and furniture, 2 bedsteds, a trunk and its contents, all his corn, fodder, and cotton, and a chest and its contents. Witness Martin Lucas, John McDade, and William Kimble. Signed Samuel McDade. Wit. oath Oct. 9, 1826 Martin Lucas to John Burns. Rec. Oct. 10, 1826

p. 272-273 Oct. 20, 1825 Henry Walden (Spartanburgh) to Asa Walden (same); for $300 sold 100 ac on branch of Fairforest Cr; border: Henry Walden, Foster, and White. Witness John Foster MC, William Walden, and Nathan Walden. Signed Henry Walden. Wit. oath Nov. 8, 1825 Nathan Walden to David Moore. Rec. Oct. 16, 1826

p. 273-274 Oct. 14, 1826 Asa M Walden (Spartanburgh) to Robert M Young (same); for (omitted) sold (1) 100 ac on waters of Fairforest Cr; border: Henry Walden, White, and Foster; and (2) 27 ac adjoining (1); and (3) 5 ac border: tract (1) and "the big road". Witness James Ed Henry and Thomas N Dawkins. Signed Asa M Walden. Wit. oath Oct. 14, 1826 Thomas N Dawkins to Jas Ed Henry. Rec. Oct. 16, 1826. Dower renounced Oct. (blank), 1826 Polly Walden to James Edward Henry

p. 274-276 Mar. 11, 1825 William Trimmier and wife Margaret (Spartanburgh) to John Hammett (same); for $400 sold 178½ ac on Lawson's fork; known as Woods Fort; border: William Turner, Darby Turner, Henry Childs, and John Tuck; in three parts: (1) 100 ac, (2) 30 ac grant to Henry Turner, and (3) 48½ ac border: Hugh Means and Saml Turner and granted to Thomas Wood. Witness A Lancaster, George Thomason, "W. T. Ackd, the others I seen" and J Dickson. Signed Wm Trimmier and Margaret Trimmier. Wit. oath Oct. 17, 1826 George Thomason to E Bomar. Rec. Oct. 17, 1826. Dower renounced Mar. 30, 1825 Margaret Trimmier to J. W. Farrow

p. 276 Mar. 31, 1825 James Brannon quit claim to John Hammett for land James Brannon bought at sheriff's sale. Witness William C Evetts and Jonathan Low. Signed J Brannon. Wit. oath Oct. 16, 1826 Jonathan Low to E Bomar. Rec. Oct. 17, 1826

p. 276-277 Mar. 25, 1826 James Brannon (Spartanburgh) to John Hammett (same); for $400 sold 178 ac on waters of Lawson's fork; border: William Turner desc; sold by Samuel Turner to George Rowland and "lately owned" by Wm Trimmier esq (same) and "lately" sold by sheriff to James Brannon. Witness John Dickson and James Fondren. Signed J Brannon. Wit. oath Mar. 25, 1826 James Fondren to J. W. Farrow. Rec. Oct. 17, 1826

p. 277-278 Aug. 26, 1826 Alexander Vernon, sheriff (Spartanburgh) to John Hammett (same); for $295 sold 178 ac on Lawson's fork; border: John Tuck, Darby Turner, and Henry Childs; sold Mar. 8, 1825 to James Brannon for John Hammett; sold due to writ from Spartanburgh Common Pleas Court second Monday after fourth Monday in Mar. 1824 suit of Jesse Cleveland vs William Trimmier; suit was entered in sheriff's office Apr. 28, 1824 endorsed by Thomas Poole, sheriff and Alexander Vernon is Thomas Poole's successor. Witness Thomas Poole and John Poole. Signed Alexander Vernon. Wit. oath Oct. 16, 1826 John Poole to E Bomar. Rec. Oct. 17, 1826

p. 278-279 Aug. 2, 1825 Charles Ferguson (Laurens Dist) to Phillemon M Waters (Spartanburgh); for $750 sold 180 ac in Spartanburgh and Union Dists; border: N & E-Aaron Stornes, S-Enoree R, and W-Drury Farrler (or Fowler) and Aaron Staines(sic); resurvey Nov. 28, 1804 by J. A. Elmore. Witness Drury Fowler and Robert Hastings. Signed Charles Ferguson. Wit. oath Jun. 3, 1826 Drury Fowler to Joel Dean. Rec. Oct. 30, 1826. Dower renounced Aug. 11, 1825 (Laurens Dist) Elizabeth Ferguson to Robert Lang

p. 279-280 Sept. 22, 1826 William Weber sr to daughter Anna, alias Nanna Linder, and husband Samuel Linder; for love and affection give 698 ac on Rocky fork of Thickety Cr. Witness Moses Weber and William W Weber. Signed Wm Weber. Wit. oath Oct. 9, 1826 Moses Weber to Joseph Camp. Rec. Oct. 30, 1826

p. 280-281 Apr. 29, 1801 William McDaniel (Spartanburgh) to William McDaniel jr (same); for love and affection give 300 ac on branches on E side of S Tyger R; border: William Allen, James Miller, Col. Thomas Moore, Andrew Berry, and Malashi Eskridge; part of grant to Moses Ward and grant to William McDaniel. Witness Jesse Crook, James Crook jr, and Henry Cannon. Signed William McDaniel and Judith's mark. Wit. oath Apr. 29, 1801 Jesse Crook to Drury McDaniel. Rec. Oct. 30, 1826

p. 281-282 Nov. 4, 1826 John Land to James Brannon; James is security for $75 bond from John Land to Richard Thomson; to secure James from loss John sells ½ ac on SE side of Spartanburgh, SC; sold by Richard Thomson to John Land; Condition: sale void if John Land pays debt. Witness John Dickson and J Cunningham. Signed John Land. Wit. oath Nov. 4, 1826 John Dickson to Jas Ed Henry. Rec. Nov. 4, 1826

p. 282-283 Dec. 1, 1825 George Hill (Spartanburgh) to Leonard Hill and John Clark (same); for $4,500 sold bands, executions, judgments, notes, account books, receipts, and papers, 3 thrastle frames containing 84 spindles each, bobbins and other preperations attached for spinning cotton, a mule containing 180 spindles with bobbins and other preperations attached for spinning cotton yarn i.e. "woof" 8 cards for breaking and preparing cotton for drawing frame, drawing and roping frames, 8 water looms, reeds, hernesses, a spooling machine, a warping machine, spools etc and other preperations for looms etc, a "moting" machine and preperations for it, 2 cotton gins and preperations for them, a hand lathe for turning iron, a small wood lathe, a cutting engine, a flutting engine, drums, pullies, belts and all preperations, carpenter's tools, turning tools, axes, farming tools and all other tools, a pair of mill stones in unfinished state, a saw mill saw, a screw bail and pins for raising a mill stone to pick etc, a Negro boy Gilbert, 2 horses, 2 horse waggons, 4 sets of harnesses for same--2 single ones and 2 double ones, a pain (or pair) of waggon wheels new with running geers etc, fodder, corn, oats, wheat, rye, cotton yarn, cotton cloth, seed, and ginned cotton, a smith's vice, lumber, iron, nails, leather and all other articles the late firm of Hill and Clark owned jointly; George Hill relinquishes his claim to above stuff. Witness Jasper Billings and William Philips. Signed George Hill. Wit. oath Jul. 1, 1826 William Philips to Wm Young. Rec. Nov. 6, 1826

p. 283-284 Dec. 1, 1825 George Hill (Spartanburgh) to Leonard Hill and John Clark (same); for $1,000 sold (1) 125 ac on S side of Tyger R; called mill tract; sold Jan. 4, 1819 by Isaac Crow to George Hill, Leonard Hill, Sheldon, and Clark; (2) 13 ac on N side of Tyger R; sold May 12, 1819 Isaac Crow to George Hill, Leonard Hill, Sheldon, and Clark; (3) 5 ac in six islands in shoals of Tyger R;

sold May 12, 1819 by Joseph Wofford to George Hill, Leonard Hill, Sheldon, and Clark; (4) 136 ac on S side of Tyger R; border: E-tract (1); sold Apr. 13, 1820 by Joseph Wofford to George Hill, Leonard Hill, Sheldon, and Clark; and (5) 31½ ac on S side of Tyger R; border: E-tract (1); sold Jun. 5, 1822 by Burrell Bobo to George Hill, Leonard Hill, Sheldon, and Clark. Witness Jasper Billings and William Philips. Signed George Hill. Wit. oath Jul. 1, 1826 William Philips to Wm Young. Rec. Nov. 6, 1826

p. 284-285 Aug. 29, 1826 Moses Casey to Rolley Bainbridge and Jane Ann Sofpona(?), son and daughter of Casey West (Spartanburgh); for good causes give 53 ac on waters of Enoree R; border: W Wilbanks, Col. Wm Farrow, and Moses Casey; given for their support until they come of age and afterwards given forever. Witness James Casey and Jacinthia M Casey. Signed M Casey. Wit. oath Oct. 17, 1826 Jacinthia M Casey to Joel Dean. Rec. Nov. 6, 1826

p. 285-286 Jan. 10, 1815 John Vice (Spartanburgh) to Thomas Wright; for $100 sold 96 ac on N side of Tyger R; where Thomas Wright lives. Witness Eli Vice and George Vice. Signed John Vice. Wit. oath Oct. 22, 1824 Eli Vice to Joseph Wofford. Rec. Nov. 6, 1826

p. 286-287 Oct. 22, 1824 Thomas Wright (Spartanburgh) to William W Smithwick (same); for $300 sold 96 ac; border: N & W-John Vice, E-John Hinman, and S-Isaac Crow. Witness Eli Vice and Meadows Harrelson. Signed Thomas Wright. Wit. oath Sept. 12, 1826 Meadows Harrelson to Wm Young. Rec. Nov. 6, 1826. Dower renounced Dec. 15, 1824 Elizabeth Wright to James Hamm

p. 287-288 Aug. 25, 1826 William W Smithwick (Spartanburgh) to Jasper Billings (same); for $200 sold 96 ac; border: N & W-John Vice, E-John Hinman, and S-Isaac Crow. Witness Hiram Tucker and John Clark. Signed Wm W Smithwick. Wit. oath Sept. 12, 1826 John Clark to Wm Young. Rec. Nov. 6, 1826

p. 288-289 Mar. 1, 1825 Willis W Dickie (Spartanburgh) to William Gillaspie (same); for $486 sold 121 ac on N side of James' Cr; border: Holland Leatherwood's Spring Br. Witness Mathew Allen, William L Allen, and George Leatherwood. Signed Willis W Dickie. Wit. oath Aug. 6, 1825 William L Allen to Philip Brewton. Rec. Nov. 7, 1826

p. 289 Apr. 4, 1826 Daniel P McKie, attorney for Daniel McKie (Laurence Dist), to John Pearson (Spartanburgh); for $500 sold 200 ac; border: E-Fowler, N-J Ford, W-H Earnest, and S-rest of tract (now Saml Jones'); sold "lately" by Spartanburgh sheriff as Henry Pearson's land due to suit of Daniel McKie vs Henry Pearson; bought by Daniel McKie from John Tate(sic). Witness Peter N Bragg and Willis W Dickie. Signed Daniel McKie, by Daniel P McKie, attorney. Wit. oath Jun. 3, 1826 Peter N Bragg to Philip Brewton. Rec. Nov. 7,(omitted)

p. 289-290 Oct. 11, 1826 James H Leatherwood (Spartanburgh) to William Clayton (same); for $330 sold 100 ac on branch of Forguson's Cr of Tyger R; border: Thomas Laxton, John Woodruff, and Harris' old corner. Witness Willis W Dickie and Peter N Bragg. Signed James H Leatherwood. Wit. oath Nov. 3, 1826 Peter N Bragg to James Crook. Rec. Nov. 7, 1826

p. 290-291 Oct. 11, 1826 William Gillaspie (Spartanburgh) to William Clayton (same); for $435 sold 121 ac on N side of James Cr; border: Holland Leatherwood's Spring Br, S-Thos Woodruff, and by W W Dickie and Mrs. Bobo. Witness Willis W Dickie and Peter N Bragg. Signed William Glaspy. Wit. oath Nov. 3, 1826 Peter N Bragg to James Crook. Rec. Nov. 7, 1826. Dower renounced Nov. 3, 1826 Lavcina Gillaspie to James Crook

p. 291-292 Dec. 4, 1819 Abraham Nelson, Archibald Nelson, John Nelson, Edmond Nelson, James Nelson, Lucretia Nelson, Nancy Nelson, Sally Nelson, Betsey Nelson, Jinney Nelson, Michael Steadman and wife Milley (late Milly Nelson) to Thomas Nelson; for $50 sold 56 ac on Buck Cr; border: Archibald Nelson and James Nelson. Witness Jacob Cantrell and James Smith. Signed Abraham Nelson, Archd Nelson, John Nelson, Edmond Nelson, Michael Stedman, and James, Sally, Luc, Nancy, Betsey, Jenny, and Milly's marks. Wit. oath Jan. 10, 1820 James Smith to J Whitten. Rec. Nov. 8, 1826

p. 292-293 Sept. 16, 1826 Thomas Nelson (Spartanburgh) to Lewis Peiples (same); for $150 sold 56 ac on Buck Cr; border: Archibald Nelson and James Nelson. Witness Mary Ann Young and Maden Young. Signed Thomas Nelson's mark. Wit. oath Sept. 16, 1826 Maden Young to James Young. Rec. Nov. 8, 1826. Dower renounced Sept. 16, 1826 Billanna Nelson to James Young

p. 293-294 Mar. 15, 1810 Edward Fowler (Spartanburgh) to Anderson Lively (same); for $100 sold 160 ac; except part taken by old survey now belonging to Joseph Lively and grant in 1804 to James Smith (latter grant actually relates to 160 ac instead of "old survey"). Witness Hugh Ewing and James Lawrence. Signed Edward Fowler. Wit. oath Mar. 15, 1810 Hugh Ewing to Andrew Ferguson. Rec. Nov. 9, 1826

p. 294-295 Sept. 30, 1816 Joseph Lively sr (Spartanburgh) to Anderson Lively (same); for $100 sold 80 ac on both sides of Pacolate R; border: Anderson Lively, a bridge, and John Henry; part of grant Feb. 3, 1775 Lt. Gov. William Bull to Mathew Harper sr. Witness Andrew Ferguson and Joseph Lively jr. Signed Joseph Lively. Wit. oath Sept. 30, 1816 Joseph Lively jr to Andrew Ferguson. Rec. Nov. 9, 1826

p. 295-296 Mar. 5, 1822 William Littlejohn, son of Charles, and wife Elizabeth (Spartanburgh) to John Lipscomb jr (same); for $50 sold 52 ac on N side of Thickety Cr; lot #6 that was allotted to Elizabeth Lipscomb, now Littlejohn. Witness Smith Lipscomb and William Wood. Signed William Littlejohn and Elizabeth's mark. Wit. oath Mar. 5, 1822 Smith Lipscomb to John Lipscomb. Rec. Nov. 10, 1826. Dower renounced Dec. 6, 1822 Elizabeth Littlejohn to John Lipscomb

p. 296-297 Nov. 18, 1822 William Odem (Spartanburgh) to Jeremiah Martin (same); for $140 sold 140 ac on both sides Maple Swamp Cr of Pacolate R; border: Bone, Jesse Scruggs, Crocker, and John Cantrell. Witness Jesse Scruggs and Isaac Young. Signed William Odem and Tibitha Odem. Wit. oath Nov. 12, 1823 Jesse Scruggs to Wm Dobbins. Rec. Nov. 11, 1826

p. 297-298 Mar. 1, 1826 James Pierce (Spartanburgh) to John Lee (same); for $30 sold 150 ac; border: John Lee, Richard Thomson, and Pacolate R; John Pearce (late of Spartanburgh) died intestate and left James and eight other heirs equal shares of land on S side of Pacolate R; James is selling his share (1/9th) of land to John Lee. Witness W Trimmier and Jesse Cleveland. Signed James Pierce's mark. Wit. oath Nov. 8, 1826 Jesse Cleveland to Caleb Jones. Rec. Nov. 14, 1826

p. 298 Aug. 13, 1826 Robert Pearce (Spartanburgh) to John Lee (same); for $30 sold his share (1/9th) of 150 ac on Pacolate R; border: John Lee and Richard Thomson; land was formerly owned by John Pearce (late of Spartanburgh) desc who died and left Robert and eight other heirs. Witness Elisha Poole and David L Poole. Signed Robert Pearce's mark. Wit. oath Nov. 8, 1826 Elisha Poole to Caleb Jones. Rec. Nov. 14, 1826

p. 298-299 Nov. 8, 1826 James Hutchens (Spartanburgh) to James Brannon (same); for $496.09 sold 373 ac on waters of Fairforest Cr;

border: Henry C Borough and widow Foster. Witness Wm W Harris and Daniel White. Signed James Hutchins. Wit. oath Nov. 8, 1826 Wm W Harris to Henry Turner. Rec. Nov. 15, 1826. Dower renounced Nov. 13, 1826 Mary Hutchens to Daniel White

p. 299-300 Aug. 17, 1825 William Pollard (Spartanburgh) to Hezekiah Pollard (same); for $400 sold 194 ac on waters of Lawson's fork of Tyger R; border: Wm Laurence, John Wingo, Moses Pollard, and Isaac Pollard. Wit. oath John Machen and Jabez Galt. Signed William Pollard. Wit. oath May 13, 1826 Jabez Galt to James Young. Rec. Nov. 15, 1826

p. 300-302 Jan. 15, 1820 Nathaniel Wofford (Spartanburgh) to Nathaniel Woodruff (same); for $500 sold 140 ac on both sides Fort Br of Farguson's Cr of Tyger R; border: James Rhodes, Wm Ward, Wm Hendrix, and John Crocker. Witness Joseph Wofford, Jeremiah Wofford, and Nathaniel Wofford jr. Signed Nathaniel Wofford. Wit. oath Nov. 13, 1826 Jeremiah Wofford to James Crook. Rec. Nov. 20, 1826. Dower renounced Nov. 18, 1826 Cumfort Wofford to James Crook

p. 302-303 Apr. 28, 1825 James Crow, son of Wm,(Spartanburgh) to John E Bobo (Union Dist); for $60 sold 16 ac on waters of Two Mile Cr; border: NW-J. L. Rast, NE-James Crow, and other sides-John E Bobo. Witness Moses A Crow and S. T. Higgins. Signed James Crow's mark. Wit. oath Jul. 4, 1826 Moses A Crow to Joel Dean. Rec. Nov. 22, 1826. Dower renounced May 13, 1825 Martha Crow to Burrell Bobo

p. 303-304 Aug. 12, 1826 Alexander Vernon, sheriff (Spartanburgh) to Edward Bomar (same); for $100 sold 103 ac on Mill Cr on N Tyger R; border: N & E-Thomas Finch, W-David Tanner, and S-John Foster; where Edward Autrey lives; sold due to writ from Spartanburgh Common Pleas Court second Monday after fourth Monday in Oct. 1824 suit of Muse Tolleson; judgment was levy of $40.64 and costs from Edward Autrey. Witness Thomas Poole and John Poole. Signed Alexander Vernon SSD. Wit. oath Nov. 29, 1826 John Poole to E Bomar. Rec. Nov. 30, 1826

p. 304-305 Feb. 15, 1825 Thomas Poole, sheriff (Spartanburgh) to Simpson Bobo (same); for $60 sold 18 feet square in Spartanburgh, SC near the new Jail; border: W-Cross St from Court House to the Jail and N-William Thomson; bought by Alexander Roddy sr for Simpson Bobo; sold due to writ from Spartanburgh Common Pleas Court second Monday after fourth Monday in Oct. 1823 suit of William Swift; judgment was levy of $1,450 and costs from Ephraim Roddy. Witness J. W. Farrow and John Poole. Signed Thomas Poole. Wit. oath Nov. 30, 1826 John Poole to E Bomar. Rec. Nov. 30, 1826

p. 305-306 Aug. 21, 1826 Robert Daniel jr (Spartanburgh) to William Otts (same); for $655 sold 270 ac on branches on N side of S Tyger R; border: the Latin School house Spring Br; S-E Underwood and W Coan, E-J Miller and Gen. T Moore, N-A Barry, and W-E Underwood. Witness Aquila (or A Quilar) Miles and Charles P Woodruff. Signed Richard Daniel jr. Wit. oath Aug. 21, 1826 Aquila Miles to James Crook. Rec. Nov. 30, 1826. Dower renounced Aug. 21, 1826 Sarah Daniel to James Crook

p. 306-307 Oct. 26, 1825 Richard Thomson (Spartanburgh) to Jesse Cleveland (same); for $125 sold 1½ ac in Spartanburgh, SC; border: Main St, public ground, Tolleson's old lot, and John Bomar. Witness John Wilbanks and John M Roberts. Signed Richard Thomson. Wit. oath Oct. 26, 1826 John M Roberts to James E Henry. Rec. Dec. 1, 1826. Dower renounced Nov. 28, 1826 Polly Thomson to James E Henry

p. 307-308 Nov. 18, 1825 Elizabeth Harrelson to William Rogers; for

$320 sold Elizabeth's rights to estate of Gideon Harrelson desc. Witness Sarah A Rogers and Jacob Ginnings. Signed Elizabeth Harrelson's mark. Wit. oath Dec. 4, 1826 Sarah A Rogers to Robert Ligon. Rec. Dec. 4, 1826

p. 308-309 Feb. 26, 1821 Samuel Woodruff jr (Spartanburgh) to Josiah Woodruff (same); for $470 sold 150 ac; grant Gov. William Moultrie to John Hendrix; resurvey Sept. 27, 1815 by Jesse Wofford. Witness Eli Cox, James Hendrix, Thomas Woodruff III. Signed Samuel Woodruff. Wit. oath Dec. 2, 1826 Thomas Woodruff III to John Dean. Rec. Dec. 4, 1826. Dower renounced Mar. 16, 1821 Mary Woodruff to John Brewton

p. 309-310 Dec. 8, 1826 John Vandyke (Spartanburgh) to Barney Bishop (same); for $700 sold (1) 200 ac on waters of Fairforest Cr and Lawson's fork; border: Henry Bishop; grant to David Goodlett; where Edmond Bishop lived; sold by "him" to Richard Thomson who sold to John Vandyke; and (2) 200 ac on waters of Lawson's fork adjoining (1); border: Barney Bishop, road from Spartanburgh Court House to Ballingers, Black Stock Road, and Edmon J Bishop; sold by John Bishop to James Hutcheson and sold by Thomas Poole, sheriff, as James Hutchenson's property, to Abner Benson and Samuel C Hunt "who directed sheriff to make titles to" John Vandyke. Witness W. L. Bishop and A Lancaster. Signed John Vandyke. Wit. oath Dec. 8, 1826 A Lancaster to E Bomar. Rec. Dec. 8, 1826

p. 310-311 Dec. 8, 1826 Robert Ligon to daughter Edith Goodman, formerly Edith Ligon; for love and affection give four Negroes (not named) value $1,200 and "other property" valued at $750 for a total of $1,950; and to put children on equal standing in division of his estate give to son Robert and daughters Jane and Nancy Ligon for love and affection--give to Robert Ligon four Negroes--man George, boy Ben, girl Louisa (wife of George), and her child (not named) and $750 (to be given when Robert becomes of age); to Jane Ligon give four Negroes--boy Sam, Phebe (his wife), Kitty, and her youngest child Kitty and $750 (to be given when Jane marries or comes of age); to Nancy Ligon give four Negroes--a boy Charles, girl Betsey, girl Dianna, and girl Judith and $750 (to be given when Nancy becomes of age or marries); property remains with Robert Ligon (grantor) until he dies or children become 21 years old. Witness William Bomar and William Trimmier. Signed Robert Ligon. Wit. oath Dec. 18, 1826 William Trimmier to E Bomar. Rec. Dec. 18, 1826

p. 311-312 Sept. 30, 1824 Malkijah Bush (Spartanburgh) to Miles J Pope (Rutherford Co, NC); for $228 sold (1) 111 ac on W side of Beaverdam Cr of S Pacolate R; border: Samuel Hunt, Saml Moore, and R Young; and (2) 77 ac adjoining (1); part of "several" tracts sold by Samuel Hunt sr (to Malkijah Bush?). Witness Uriah Bush and Bennett Pope. Signed Malkijah Bush. Wit. oath Sept. 30, 1824 Bennett Pope to Geo Camp. Rec. Dec. 19, 1826. Dower renounced Oct. 8, 1824 Elender Bush to James Young

p. 312-313 Dec. 15, 1826 Hugh McMillin (Spartanburgh) to David McMillin (same); for $500 sold 571 ac on both sides of N Pacolate R; border: William Cantrell, Edmund Cooley, Joseph Wilks, William Bush, James Foster, and Love McMillin. Wit. oath Benjamin Padgett and Francis W Cunningham. Signed Hugh McMillin. Wit. oath Dec. 19, 1826 Francis W Cunningham to James Young. Rec. Dec. 19, 1826

p. 313-314 Oct. 6, 1804 James Wood (Spartanburgh) to son Harry Wood (same); for love and affection give 150 ac on N side of Pacolate R; border: a lake and Demsey Fowler. Witness Henry Dodd and Hugh McDowell. Signed James Wood. Wit. oath Oct. 11, 1824 Hugh McDowell to W Bennett. Rec. Dec. 26, 1826

p. 314-315 Dec. 4, 1826 "articles of marriage" Berryman S Holder (Spartanburgh) and Sarah Tolleson (Franklin Co, W Tenn) to Mordicai W Hutcheson (Franklin Co, W Tenn); for $1 sold everything Sarah Tolleson has--(1) 174 ac on Cumberland R in Wilson Co, W Tenn; and (2) dower rights to property of late husband Muse Tolleson; and a Negro woman Delila and her child Clarentine, road waggon and harness, 8 horses, 14 cattle, a gig, 5 beds and furniture, framing tools, household and kitchen furniture, cash, and debts due to her; Sarah Tolleson plans to marry Berryman S Holder; sale made with consent of Berryman; property sold in trust for Sarah Tolleson's benefit during her lifetime and then equally divided equally among her children (not named). Witness James V Miller, Moses Foster, and Stephen Foster. Signed B. S. Holder, Sarah Tolleson, and M. W. Hutcheson. Wit. oath Dec. 23, 1826 James V Miller to E Bomar. Rec. Dec. 26, 1826

p. 315-316 Oct. 3, 1826 James Winsor (Spartanburgh) to Henry Bishop (same); for $250 sold (1) 150 ac on waters of Fairforest Cr; where John Winsor lives; and (2) 72 ac; border: tract (1), Boiling Spring Road, Killock, Rush, Vandike, and Hamett. Witness A Benson and J. G. Harris. Signed James Winsor's mark. Wit. oath Dec. 25, 1826 A Benson to E Bomar. Rec. Dec. 26, 1826. Dower renounced Aug. 19, 1826 Anna Winsor to E Bomar

p. 316-317 Sept. 20, 1826 John Wofford jr (Spartanburgh) to Zephaniah Posey (same); for $307 sold 307 ac on waters of McClure's Cr of Fairforest Cr; in Spartanburgh and Union Dists; border: Haselwood, Moses, and Wofford's Road; part of grant to William Wofford sr. Witness Elihugh P Smith and James Hermon. Signed John Wofford jr. Wit. oath Oct. 9, 1826 Elihugh P Smith to James Hamm. Rec. Jan. 1, 1827. Dower renounced Oct. 24, 1826 Lucy Wofford to James Hamm

p. 317-318 May 23, 1826 John E Bobo (Spartanburgh) to Miles Nash (same); for $2 sold 2.1 ac on Two Mile Cr; border: John E Bobo and Miles Nash. Witness William Nash and Edward L Nash. Signed John E Bobo. Wit. oath Dec. 9, 1826 William Nash to Philip Brewton. Rec. Jan. 1, 1827

p. 318-319 Aug. 16, 1826 Woodson Burnett (Spartanburgh) to William Bennett (same); for $200 sold 200 ac on both sides N fork of Shoaly Cr of Lawson's fork; border: Larkin Cardin, Thomson, Saml Sentell, Joseph Venable, Hardy Fluker, and Milton Davis; where Woodson Burnett lives; part of two grants--(1) to Leonard Cardin sr and (2) to (blank) Cardin. Witness Eph Lewis and John B Lewis. Signed Woodson Burnett. Wit. oath Nov. 7, 1826 John B Lewis to W Clement. Rec. Jan. 1, 1827

p. 319-320 Aug. 6, 1826 Elleanor Mayson, Moses H Smith, James Rainwaters, and James Mason, heirs of Francis Mayson desc (Spartanburgh), to Jesse Mayson (same); for $300 paid to Francis Mayson desc sold 125 ac on waters of Ford's Cr of Fairforest Cr; border: James Aytes' crib. Witness Thomas Poole and David Posey. Signed Elleanor's mark, Moses H Smith, James Rainwaters, and James Mason. Wit. oath Jan. 2, 1827 Thomas Poole to Geo Camp. Rec. Jan. 2, 1827

p. 320 Dec. 27, 1826 David Drummond (Spartanburgh) to John Drummond (same); for $139 sold 57 ac. Witness M. P. Evins and A. M. Drummond. Signed David Drummond's mark. Wit. oath Jan. 4, 1857 A. M. Drummond to F. H. Legg. Rec. Jan. 6, 1827. Dower renounced Dec. 30, 1826 Nancy Drummond to F. H. Legg

p. 320-321 Dec. 30, 1826 John Drummond (Spartanburgh) to James M Anderson (same); for $110 sold 57 ac; border: Jacob Heddin. Witness James Chamblin and Thos J Drummond. Signed John Drummond.

Wit. oath Jan. 4, 1827 Thos J Drummond to F. H. Legg. Rec. Jan. 6, 1827. Dower renounced Dec. 30, 1826 Maneria Drummond to F. H. Legg

p. 321-322 Dec. 25, 1826 Thomas J Drummond (Spartanburgh) to Samuel N Evins (same); for $200 sold 137 ac; border: Fortunatus H Legg; where David Drummond lived and part of where Perunan W Tate lived. Witness M. P. Evins to J. J. McMicken. Signed T. J. Drummond. Wit. oath Jan. 4, 1827 J J McMicken to F. H. Legg. Rec. Jan. 6, 1827. Dower renounced Margaret Drummond to F. H. Legg Jan. 4, 1827

p. 322-323 Feb. 18, 1819 Alexander McDaniel (Greenville Dist) to Solomon Dill (same); for $400 sold 200 ac on both sides of Middle Tyger R; border: John M Cree and "Greenville line". Witness William S Dill, Lemuel Loftis, and D Jackson. Signed Alexander McDaniel's mark. Wit. oath (Greenville Dist) Nov. 30, 1826 Lemuel Loftis to J. H. Goodlett. Rec. Jan. 12, 1827

p. 323-324 Nov. 30, 1826 Solomon Dill (Greenville Dist) to Samuel Crayton (same); for $1,000 sold 200 ac on both sides of Middle Tyger R; border: John McCree and "Greenville line". Witness John H Goodlett and James H Randolph. Signed Solomon Dill. Wit. oath Dec. 27, 1826 (Greenville Dist) John H Goodlett to J. H. Goodlett. Rec. Jan. 12, 1827

p. 324-325 Sept. 30, 1807 James Bright (Spartanburgh) to Richard Willis jr (same); for $300 sold 150 ac on E side of Tyger R and below Thomson's Br; border: Tobias Bright and Robert Rogers; part of two tracts--(1) 450 ac grant Apr. 7, 1788 Gov. Thomas Pinckney to William Shurley and (2) 300 ac grant May 15, 1772 to Michael Prewett. Witness Drury Burton and Nathaniel Burton. Signed James Bright. Wit. oath Oct. 1, 1807 Drury Burton to John Brewton. Rec. Jan. 16, 1827

p. 325-326 Aug. 21, 1826 John Covington (Rutherford Co, NC) to George Cantrell (Spartanburgh); for $80 sold 100 ac on N side of Pacolate R; border: Elizabeth Cantrell, George Cantrell's old line, and John Morris. Witness William Morris and Alfred Brown. Signed John Covington's mark. Wit. oath Sept. 2, 1826 William Morris to Henry Turner. Rec. Jan. 17, 1827

p. 326 Jan. 20, 1825 Robert McDowell (Spartanburgh) to Oliver Clark (same); for $74 sold 19 ac on W side of road from Spartanburgh; border: E & N-William McWilliams, W-Bullington, and S-Oliver Clark; part of grant to David McDowell. Witness Samuel Bullington and James A McDowell. Signed Robert McDowell. Wit. oath Jul. 21, 1826 Samuel Bullington to Wm Kelso. Rec. Jan. 17, 1827

p. 326-328 Nov. 20, 1826 Alexander Vernon, sheriff (Spartanburgh) to Benjamin Nicholls (same); for $150 sold (ac omitted) on E side of Tyger R below mouth of Thomson's Br; border: Tobias Bright and Robert Rogers; corner of 450 ac; Armstead G Wier, guardian for minor children of Richard Willis desc, petitioned Spartanburgh Ordinary Court Aug. 11, 1826 to divide estate of Richard Willis jr desc; court sets sale for first Monday in Nov. 1826 on credit until Mar. 1, 1828; sale was on Nov. 7, 1826. Witness J. W. Farrow and John Poole. Signed Alexander Vernon. Wit. oath Jan. 22, 1827 John Poole to E Bomar. Rec. Jan. 22, 1827

p. 328 Nov. 11, 1825 Henry Clyne to Wade Regan (Spartanburgh); for $140 bond Henry Clyne is to deed 75 ac to Wade Regan; border: S-Jno Bonnam, E-Saml Fowler, N-John Rudisel, and W-unknown; where Wade Regan lives; given in place of deed left for record at Spartanburgh Court House. Witness George L Publes and Ephraim Banham. Signed Henry Clyne. Wit. oath Jan. 3, 1827 Ephraim Banham to W. S.

Morgan. Rec. Jan. 24, 1827

p. 328-329 Oct. 12, 1826 Elisha Wells (Spartanburgh) to Henry M Wells; for $200 sold 100 ac on S Tyger R on Wallas Br; border: Willis L Wells, Hoby, William Durham, William Curam, Ironwork road, and Sinuard's old line. Witness Ford Mason and John E Wilson. Signed Elisha Wells. Wit. oath Feb. 2, 1827 Ford Mason to J Cooper. Rec. Feb. 5, 1827

p. 329 Feb. 8, 1826 Elisha Wells to son Willis Wells; for love and affection give 77 ac on S side Nalley's Br of Tyger R; border: Neeber, Elisha Wells, Young, and Fowler. Witness Ford Mason and Novis Compton. Signed Elisha Wells. Wit. oath Feb. 2, 1827 Ford Mason to J Cooper. Rec. Feb. 5, 1827

p. 329-330 Aug. 19, 1826 Woodson Burnett (Spartanburgh) to William Bennett (same); mortgage 100 ac on NW side of Thompson's Cr and W side of William Bennett's Spring Br for payment of $300 due to W Bennett in notes dated Aug. 17, 1826--(1) due Dec. 1, 1826, (2) due Dec. 1, 1827, and (3) due Dec. 1, 1828; border: Henry White and School House Br; sold Aug. 16, 1826 by W Bennett to W Burnett; land can be sold first Monday in May 1829 if debt is not paid. Witness Ephraim Lewis to John B Lewis. Signed Woodson Burnett. Wit. oath Nov. 7, 1826 John B Lewis to W Clement. Rec. Feb. 5, 1827

p. 330-332 Feb. 13, 1827(sic) William McElrath and Adam McElrath (Spartanburgh) to heirs of Michael Moore desc (Winifred S Moore, widow, and four children--Adeline, John, Mary B, and Alfred L Moore); for $530 paid by John Moore, executor of Michael Moore desc, sold 265 ac on N side of Middle Tyger R; border: John Smith and estate of Michael Moore desc. Witness William P Moore jr and Willis S Wingo. Signed Wm McElrath and Adam McElrath. Wit. oath Feb. 2, 1827 Willis S Wingo to Thomas Wood. Rec. Feb. 5, 1827. Dower renounced Feb. 2, 1827 Jane McElrath, wife of William, and Rebecca McElrath, wife of Adam, to Thomas Wood

p. 332 Apr. 28, 1826 Paul Castleberry (Spartanburgh) to Peter Hamilton (same); for $100 sold 14 ac on both sides James' Cr; border: N & E-widow King, S-widow Castleberry, and W-Paul Castleberry. Witness William Otts and Zachariah Leatherwood. Signed Paul Castleberry's mark. Wit. oath Jun. 17, 1826 Zachariah Leatherwood to James Crook. Rec. Feb. 5, 1827. Dower renounced Jun. 17, 1826 Nancy Castleberry to James Crook

p. 332-333 Sept. 26, 1822 James Sexton ("place") to Ford Mayson; for $450 sold 76 ac on James' Br of Tyger R; border: Littlefield, Foster, Elisha Stalion, and William Durham. Witness William Wileder and Daniel Durham. Signed James Sexton. Wit. oath Dec. 15, 1823 Daniel Durham to M Casey. Rec. Feb. 5, 1827

p. 333-334 Feb. 1, 1827 Moses Biter (Spartanburgh) to Elizabeth Snoddy (same); for $700 sold 100 ac on N side of S Tyger R; border: NW-James Vernan, NE-Samuel Evans, and other sides-S Tyger R. Witness James Leonard and Isaac Snoddy jr. Signed Moses Biter's mark. Wit. oath Feb. 3, 1827 Isaac Snoddy jr to James Crook. Rec. Feb. 27, 1827

p. 334-335 Oct. 11, 1826 Alexander Keller (Spartanburgh) to David Dantzler; for $1,000 sold 362 ac; where Alexander Keller lives; border: Wilson's old house. Witness Alexr Thompson and Barbary Dantzler. Signed Alexander Keller's mark. Wit. oath Oct. 11, 1826 Alexr Thompson to John Burns. Rec. Feb. 5, 1827. Dower renounced Oct. 26, 1826 Hannah Keller to Thomas Wood

p. 335 Feb. 19, 1820 Isaiah Bright (Spartanburgh) to David Dantzler (same); for $500 sold 200 ac on N side of S Tyger R. Witness

James Nesbett jr and Michl Moore. Signed Isaiah Bright. Wit. oath Mar. 4, 1820 James Nesbett to John Collins. Rec. Feb. 5, 1827. Dower renounced Feb. 26, 1820 Cararine Bright to John Collins

p. 335-336 Jun. 29, 1816 Elizabeth Bragg, Rhodo M Bragg, Abigail W Bragg, William Clayton, Catharine G Bragg, and George B Bragg, widow and heirs of Danl Bragg (late of SC), to Simeon Lavinder; for $55 paid to Danl Bragg by Simeon Lavinder and $243 "balance to be obligated for said Danl Bragg" sold 149 ac; border: Wm Skinner Br; where Simeon Lavinder lives. Witness David Bruton and Joel G Brewton. Signed Elizabeth Bragg, Rhodo M Bragg, Abigail W Bragg, Catharine G Bragg, George B Bragg, and Wm Clayton. Wit. oath Nov. 2, 1826 Joel G Brewton to Philip Brewton. Rec. Feb. 5, 1827

p. 336-337 Dec. 27, 1826 Simeon Lavinder (Spartanburgh) to Philip Brewton (same); for $600 sold 149 ac; border: Wm Skinner's old Spring Br, S-John Pearson, W-Susannah Brewton, N-John Brewton and Young Scott, and E-William Skinner; where Simeon Lavinder lives. Witness John Brewton and William Clayton. Signed Simeon Lavinder. Wit. oath Jan. 11, 1827 John Brewton to James Crook. Rec. Feb. 5, 1827. Dower renounced Feb. 11, 1827 Mary Lavinder to James Crook

p. 337-338 Nov. 25, 1826 Sarah Tolleson (Franklin Co, Tenn) to Benjamin S Holder (Spartanburgh); power of attorney to do her business especially concerning her dower rights. Witness James Smith and Josiah Bagwell. Signed Sarah Tolleson. Wit. oath Feb. 5, 1827 Josiah Bagwell to E Bomar. Rec. Feb. 5, 1827

p. 338 Aug. 17, 1826 Benjamin Wofford (Spartanburgh) to James Cleaton (same); for $220 sold 100 ac on Fort Shoal Br of Enoree R; border: S-Carter Harris, W-John Farrow, N-James Cleaton, and E-Jane Bobo and M Casey. Witness Samuel Hindman and Jesse Watson. Signed Benj Wofford. Wit. oath Nov. 9, 1826 Samuel Hindman to Wm Young. Rec. Feb. 12, 1827

p. 338-339 Sept. 21, 1826 Reuben Newman and Sabrey Walker agree to marriage contract concerning their property: Reuben Newman relinquishes right to Sabrey's property she had before "they came together" and Sabrey Walker relinquishes right to Reuben's property he had "before they came together" and "leaves it to his good will" to leave Sabrey Newman what thinks best if he dies first. Witness Thos G Potter and Elizabeth Potter. Signed Sabrey Walker's mark and Reuben Newman. Wit. oath Feb. 2, 1827 Thos G Potter to Benj Wofford. Rec. Feb. 14, 1827

p. 339 Nov. 10, 1806 Robert McFaden (Spartanburgh) to John Herrin (same); for $200 sold 100 ac on N side of Enoree R; border: Thomas Lowden, Francis Hamby, and Reuben Gunn; includes where John Floyd and Mishack Hamby live; part of 500 ac grant to Thomas Scotae esq and sold "to Richard Hamton to Stephen Cantrell and Thomas Kevil" and sold by Thomas Kevil to Robert McFaden. Witness James Hammett and Nathaniel McElrath. Signed Robert McFaden. Wit. oath Mar. 22, 1813 James Hammett to Drury McDaniel. Rec. Feb. 19, 1827

p. 339-340 Jul. 3, 1824 John Herring to John Baldwin; for $300 sold 100 ac on N side of Enoree R; border: Thomas Lowder, Francis Hamby, and Reuben Gunn; border is by "lines and corners known in 1806"; part of 500 ac grant to Thomas Scotae esq and sold "to Richard Hampton to Stephen Cantrell and Thomas Kevil" and sold by Thomas Kevil to Robert McFaden who sold to John Herring. Witness Tyrce Glenn jr and Jeremiah Glenn. Signed John Herring. Wit. oath Feb. 11, 1827 Tyrce Glenn to John Ford. Rec. Feb. 19, 1827

p. 340-341 Dec. 30, 1826 Eli Baldwin (Greenville Dist) to John Baldwin (same) (sic); for $340 sold 100½ ac on N side of Enoree R;

border: Josiah McClain, Abner's Cr, Hammett's still house Br, formerly Herring's corner, James Brockman, and Hamby (formerly called Cowden's); where James Hammett lived. Witness Sylvanus Baldwin and Nathaniel Thackston. Signed Eli Baldwin. Wit. oath Feb. 19, 1827 Sylvanus Baldwin to James Ford. Rec. Feb. 19, 1827

p. 341 Feb. 14, 1827 Jesse Lamb (Spartanburgh) to Thomas Darby (same); for $245 sold 125 ac on Prator's Cr; border: W-Livingston Bobo, N & E-Thos Layton (or Seyton) and Elisha Wells, and S-S Anderson; Condition: sale void if Jesse Lamb pays Thomas Darby $245 and interest by Oct. 1, 1827. Witness Nathan Chandler and Joel Dean. Signed Jesse Lamb. Wit. oath Feb. 19, 1827 Nathan Chandler to Joel Dean. Rec. Feb. 21, 1827

p. 341-342 Feb. 16, 1827 Polly Bruce (Spartanburgh) to brother Samuel Bruce; power of attorney to obtain her share of estate of father Ignatious Bruce desc from executors in Burk Co, NC. Witness Mary B Moore and Editha Goodman. Signed Polly Bruce's mark. Wit. oath Feb. 16, 1827 Mary B Moore to Robert Ligon. Rev. Feb. 24, 1827

p. 342 Feb. 22, 1827 Dennis Lindsey (SC) to Benjamin L Goodman (Spartanburgh); for $400 sold 100 ac on Ferguson's Cr; border: SW-William Rhodes and SE-Nathaniel Wofford. Witness William Otts and Thomas Bragg. Signed Dennis Lindsey. Wit. oath Feb. 22, 1827 William Otts to Philip Brewton. Rec. Feb. 26, 1827. Dower renounced Feb. 22, 1827 Anna Lindsey to Robert Lindsey

p. 342-343 Sept. 27, 1824 John Burrough, attorney for Elizabeth and William Burrough (Decatur Co, Ala), to Nathaniel Wofford (Spartanburgh); for $840 sold 115 ac on S side Ferguson's Cr of Tyger R; border: Fort Br. Witness Dennis Lindsey and John Haston. Signed John Burrough. Wit. oath Sept. 27, 1824 John Haston to John Brewton. Rec. Feb. 26, 1827

p. 343-344 Feb. 1, 1819 Elizabeth Burrow (or Burrough), John Burrow, and William Burrow (Madison Co, Ala) to Nathaniel Wofford (Spartanburgh); for $800 sold 115 ac on S side of Ferguson's Cr of Tyger R; border: Fort Br. Witness Philip Brewton and Jesse Wofford. Signed Elizabeth Burrough. Wit. oath Feb. 26, 1827 Philip Brewton to James Crook. Rec. Feb. 26, 1827

p. 344-345 Feb. 12, 1827 William H Thomson (York Dist) to John S Rowland (Spartanburgh); for $650 sold ½ ac at Spartanburgh Court House; border: Jesse Cleveland's store lot, Cross St, and Bostick; lot #20 that is corner lot on S side of Court House. Witness John Poole and Geo W Bomar. Signed Wm H Thomson. Wit. oath Feb. 28, 1827 Geo W Bomar to E Bomar. Rec. Feb. 28, 1827. Dower renounced Feb. 22, 1827 Margaret Thomson to Elisha Bomar

p. 345 Sept. 14, 1826 Willis Hammett, agent for William Hammett, to Jesse Mason (Spartanburgh); for $20 sold William Hammett's interest in 124 ac on waters of Tyger R; belonged to estate of John Hammett and subject to partition among William Hammett and "others". Witness William Trimmier and Mathew Seay. Signed Willis Hammett, agent for William Hammett. Wit. oath Feb. 28, 1827 William Trimmier to E Bomar. Rec. Feb. 28, 1827

p. 345-346 Sept. 4, 1826 Anderson Hammett, for self and as guardian for heirs of Jesse(sic) Hammett desc, to Jesse Mason (Spartanburgh); for $20 sold interest in 124 ac on waters of Tyger R; belonged to estate of John Hammett desc and subject to division among the heirs. Witness William Trimmier and Mathew Seay. Signed Anderson Hammett, for self and as guardian of heirs of Jesse Hammett. Wit. oath Feb. 28, 1827 William Trimmier to E Bomar. Rec. Feb. 28,

1827

p. 346 Nov. 4, 1826 Samuel Turner (Spartanburgh) to Lewis Turner (same); for $294 sold 247 ac on Shoally Cr of Lawson's fork. Witness A Baird and William Trimmier. Signed Samuel Turner. Wit. oath Feb. 28, 1827 William Trimmier to E Bomar. Rec. Feb. 28, 1827

p. 346-347 Feb. 5, 1827 (Clark Co, Ga) David Lynch and wife Lettice (Clark Co, Ga) to Thomas J Lynch; for $1,000 sold (ac omitted) on waters of Kelsey's Cr near Cedar Springs; border: White and "others"; lot #7 drawn by Lettice Lynch in division of father's (James Smith desc) estate. Witness William B. P. Adams and Ulysses R Lynch. Signed David Lynch and Lettice Lynch. Wit. oath Feb. 6, 1827 (Clark Co, Ga) Ulysses R Lynch to William Clark. Feb. 22, 1827 (Clark Co, Ga) Robert Ligon, clerk of Inderior Court, certifys William Clark is justice of Inferior Court. Rec. Mar. 3, 1827. Dower renounced Feb. 21, 1827 (Clark Co, Ga) Lettice Lynch to William Clark

p. 347-348 Mar. 17, 1824 John Trail and wife Sarah (Spartanburgh) to James Otts (same); for $600 sold 160 ac; border: S-Benjm Nicholls, E-John Trail and widow Meadows, and N & W-John Trail. Witness William Otts and Adanijah Patterson. Signed John Trail and Sarah Trail. Wit. oath Dec. 9, 1825 Abanijah Patterson to Robert Ligon. Rec. Mar. 5, 1827

p. 348-349 Jan. (blank), 1826 James Otts (Spartanburgh) to John Hatchett (same); for $700 sold 160 ac on N side of Tyger R; border: S & SE-Benjm Nicholls, NE-widow Meadows, and others-John Trail. Witness Iasiah Hatchett and Isaiah Kelly. Signed John Otts. Wit. oath Sept. 22, 1826 Iasiah Hatchett to Philip Brewton. Rec. Mar. 5, 1827

p. 349 Dec. 12, 1826 Miles Nash (Spartanburgh) to David Brewton (same); for $1,600 sold 249 ac on Two Mile Cr of Enoree R; border: James Landford's Spring Br, S-J Bobo, N-W Leatherwood, and W-William Landford and James Landford. Witness James Brewton and Philip Brewton. Signed Miles Nash. Wit. oath Jan. 15, 1827 Philip Brewton to James Crook. Rec. Mar. 5, 1827. Dower renounced Jan. 19, 1827 Elizabeth Nash to James Crook

p. 349-350 Feb. 1, 1827 Reuben Daniel (Spartanburgh) to son-in-law Amos Liles (same); for love and affection and $325 "in advancement of" Reuben Daniel's estate give 217 ac; where Amos Liles lives; border: S & E-Anthony Foster, NW-Thomas Wells, and W-"intended" for Jesse Daniel; on Poison Br and Foster's Still house Br. Witness Christi Golightly and Richard Daniel. Signed Reuben Daniel. Wit. oath Mar. 5, 1827 Christi Golightly to E Bomar. Rec. Mar. 5, 1827

p. 350-351 Mar. 5, 1827 Robert Ligon (Spartanburgh) to Patrick Hoy (same); for $20 sold 2 ac at mouth of Colly field ditch Br; plat attached shows on Hoy's mill pond and S Tyger R and "Chequepin". Witness Mordicia Brown and William Skinner. Signed Robert Ligon. Wit. oath Mar. 5, 1827 William Skinner to William Reid. Rec. Mar. 5, 1827

p. 351-352 Aug. 28, 1826 James Wood (Spartanburgh) to William Golightly (same); for $600 sold 200 ac on S Pacolate R; border: N & NW-Henry Wood, Demsey Fowler, and Abram Brock, SW-James Loftis, and SE-Robert D Tolly. Witness Nathaniel Dodd, Henry Wood, and Richard H Golightly. Signed James Wood's mark. Wit. oath Mar. 5, 1827 Nathaniel Dodd to E Bomar. Rec. Mar. 5, 1827. Dower renounced Feb. 22, 1827 Susannah Wood to Wm S Morgan

p. 352 Aug. 25, 1825 Isaac Crow to Ann Hindman; agree to give 60 ac on Two Mile Cr of Enoree R; border: John Todd, George Hound,

Wm Littlefield; known as Draper tract; deed given "in consequence" of illegitimate child Ann Hindman has and "lays to" Isaac Crow and a suit now in court against Isaac Crow for marriage contract and condition of sale is that Ann is to keep Isaac "harmless"; otherwise sale is void. Witness Simeon Lavinder and William Skinner. Signed Isaac Crow. Wit. oath Mar. 1, 1827 William Skinner to Robert Ligon. Rec. Mar. 5, 1827

p. 352-353 Oct. 29, 1825 James Turner (Spartanburgh) to James Foster (same); for $50 sold 100 ac on Casis Cr of Pacolate R. Witness Wyatt E Hines and Ephraim Potter. Signed James Turner. Wit. oath Mar. 5, 1827 Ephraim Potter to Jas W Martin. Rec. Mar. 5, 1827

p. 353 Mar. 5, 1827 Abner Benson (Spartanburgh) to Peter Haskins (same); for $150 sold 66 ac on N side of Fairforest Cr; border: Greenville Road from Spartanburgh Court House, Hemperley, and Anderson Wingo; part of grant to Benson and Hays. Witness Burnell High, Paschal Wingo, and David Tinsley. Signed A Benson. Wit. oath Mar. 5, 1827 Paschal Wingo to D White. Rec. Mar. 5, 1827

p. 353-354 Mar. 5, 1827 Abner Benson (Spartanburgh) to Anderson Wingo (same); for $150 sold 68 ac on N side of Fairforest Cr; border: Peter Haskins and Greenville Road from Spartanburgh Court House; part of grant to Benson and Hays. Witness Burnell High, Paschal Wingo, and David Tinsley. Signed A Benson. Wit. oath Mar. 5, 1827 Paschal Wingo to Wm Dobbins. Rec. Mar. 5, 1827

p. 354-355 Aug. 8, 1812 James Cook (Spartanburgh) to Keen Finch; for $107 paid by William Finch, father of Keen, sold 107 ac; border: James Keen, Philip Otts, Thos Cook, and Reedy Br. Witness Robert Martin and Polly Martin. Signed James Cook. Wit. oath May 3, 1813 Robert Martin to John Cook. Rec. Mar. 5, 1827

p. 355-356 Aug. 14, 1826 James Johnson (Spartanburgh) to Elizabeth Farrow (same); to secure three notes--(1) to pay Elizabeth Farrow $263 Jan. 1, 1828, (2) to pay Elizabeth $228 Jan. 1, 1829, and (3) to pay Elizabeth $214 Jan. 1, 1830 and for $10 sold 314 ac on Enoree R; border: Robert Creswell, John Lanford, and Enoree R; and sold Negro man Peter; Condition: sale void if James Johnson pays debt. Witness Robert Creswell and Mary G Griffin. Signed James Johnson's mark. Wit. oath Mar. 11, 1827 Robert Creswell to E Bomar. Rec. Mar. 11, 1827

p. 356 Oct. 16, 1826 Thomas Burgess (Spartanburgh) to firm of Brannon and White (same); to secure notes of (1) $55.43 dated Oct. 16, 1826 and due Dec. 17, 1826 and (2) to give on demand for $21.80 dated Jun. 1, 1826 with interest from Jan. 1, 1826 sold 120 ac on creek of Fairforest Cr; where Thomas Burgess lives; border: S-James Means, E-Jas T McCarter, N-Jas Tolleson, and W-Saml Harman. Witness B. S. Holder, James Tolleson, and Manantrie Gossett. Signed Thomas Burgess. Wit. oath Feb. 5, 1827 James Tolleson to D White. Rec. Mar. 19, 1827

p. 356-357 Sept. 2, 1826 John Nelson (Spartanburgh) to Thomas Cantwell (same); for $175 sold 191 ac on Nelson's Br of Buck Cr; border: John Mathis. Witness William Little and Edmund Thorn. Signed John Nelson. Wit. oath Sept. 2, 1826 William Little to Wm Reid. Rec. Mar. 31, 1827. Dower renounced Mar. 12, 1827 Nancy Nelson to Geo Camp

p. 357-358 Nov. 18, 1825 William McWilliams to William Ferguson; for $25 sold (ac omitted) on N Pacolate R; border: George McWilliams, Wm McClure, Hugh McBride, and Thomas Bryan; grant to James McWilliams desc. Witness Robert McDowell and David McDowell. Signed W McWilliams. Wit. oath Mar. 24, 1827 Robert McDowell to W Clement. Rec. Apr. 2, 1827

p. 358-359 Jul. 15, 1826 Sterling L Westmoreland (Spartanburgh) to William Beacham (same); for $55 sold 54 ac on waters of Ben's Cr; border: SE & SW-Amos Ray and Z. F. Westmoreland and NE & NW-Wm Beacham and Burnett. Witness B. C. Wilkinson and William Leonard. Signed S. L. Westmoreland. Wit. oath Jul. 15, 1826 B. C. Wilkinson to Thomas Wood. Rec. Apr. 7, 1827

p. 359 Dec. 19, 1826 Joseph Wofford, sr (Spartanburgh) to Moses White (same); for $200 sold 150 ac on waters of Tyger R; border: "the big road", Methodist Meeting House, James Williams, John Beson, J Leatherwood, Hill, and Clark. Witness Thomas Taylor and John Smith. Signed Joseph Wofford. Wit. oath Dec. 19, 1826 Thomas Taylor to Benj Wofford. Rec. Apr. 9, 1827

p. 359 May 5, 1826 Thomas Westmoreland (Spartanburgh) to Jesse Westmoreland (same); for $50 sold 55 ac on Enoree R. Witness Rial Fowler and Dennis Westmoreland. Signed Thomas Westmoreland's mark. Wit. oath May 5, 1826 Dennis Westmoreland to James Ford. Rec. Apr. 9, 1827

p. 359-360 (blank), 1827 John Pearson (Spartanburgh) to Thomas Pearson (same); for $300 sold 115 ac on waters of Enoree R; border: John Pearson, Isaac Lindsey, Moses Fowler and John Fowler and "others"; sold by Daniel McKie jr, attorney for Daniel McKie sr to John Pearson. Witness William L Allen and William Jones. Signed John Pearson. Wit. oath Mar. 23, 1827 William Jones to James Ford. Rec. Apr. 9, 1827

p. 360-361 Sept. 7, 1826 Samuel Guthree to William McCraw; for $207 for 115 ac on branch of Thickety Cr of Broad R. Witness Edmund Guthree and Pleasant McCraw. Signed Samuel Guthree. Wit. oath Sept. 7, 1826 Pleasant McCraw to Joseph Camp. Rec. Apr. 9, 1827

p. 361 Feb. 17, 1827 William Brice (Ga) to Thomas Harris (Spartanburgh); for $100 sold 136 ac on waters of Sarratt's Cr of Broad R; border: Balas Havis. Witness Andrew Banner and Nathaniel Jones. Signed Wm Bryce. Wit. oath Apr. 4, 1827 Andrew Banner to J Camp. Rec. Apr. 9, 1827

p. 361-362 Sept. 19, 1825 William W Millican (Roan Co, Tenn) to Thomas Brian (Spartanburgh); for $331.25 sold 83 ac on S side of N Pacolate R; where Thomas Brian lives; lot #1 that descended to William W Millican from his father William Millican desc. Witness Henry Utley and Christopher Golightly. Signed William W Millican. Wit. oath Mar. 18, 1826 Christopher Golightly to James Young. Rec. Apr. 9, 1827

p. 362 Nov. 22, 1826 Richard Daniel (Spartanburgh) to George Floyd jr (same); for $400 sold 350 ac on Tyger R; border: John Gentry. Witness John Ward and Francis Ward. Signed Richard Daniel. Wit. oath Apr. 7, 1827 John Ward to Robert Ligon. Rec. Apr. 9, 1827

p. 362-363 Mar. 1, 1826 John Lucas (Spartanburgh) to Benjamin C Dillingham (same); for $150 sold 20 ac on both sides of S Pacolate R; border: Benjamin C Dillingham; part of land formerly of Maj. John Gowen desc and sold by his executors to John Lucas. Witness Lemuel Lucas and Willey S Brown. Signed John Lucas. Wit. oath Apr. 4, 1827 Lemuel Lucas to Thos Grogan. Rec. Apr. 9, 1827

p. 363-364 Mar. 28, 1827 Humphrey Yarborough (Spartanburgh) to Hiram Yarborough (same); for $500 sold 200 ac on Rock Cr on S side of Tyger R; border: S-Landon Miles and Thomas Miles, E-William Martinale(?) and Dehay, N-Tilman Bobo, and W-Hiram Yarborough; grant Aug. 11, 1774 to Edmund Beardan who sold to Thomas Miles who sold to James Rainwaters "and part of Lanly Miles" and sold by James Rainwaters and Lanly Miles to Humphrey Yarborough. Witness John Yarborough and Stephen Yarborough. Signed Hy Yarborough. Wit. oath Apr. 9, 1827 John Yarborough to Benj Wofford. Rec. Apr. 7, 1827

p. 364 Nov. 8, 1826 Aspasio Earle (Rutherford Co, NC) to Henry Grogan (same); for $200 sold 300 ac on waters of N Pacolate R; border: David Blackwell; except "a few ac" claimed by David Blackwell. Witness Dennis Marshall and Benjamin Page. Signed Aspasio Earle. Wit. oath Mar. 21, 1827 Benjamin Page to Thos Grogan. Rec. Apr. 9, 1827

p. 364-365 Oct. 26, 1826 Jacob Chapman (Spartanburgh) to George B Bishop (same); for $350 sold 170 ac on both sides Buck Br of Lawson's fork; part of grant to William Turner. Witness Wm Bennett esq and Susan Turner. Signed Jacob Chapman's mark. Wit. oath Mar. 5, 1827 Wm Bennett esq to W Clement. Rec. Apr. 20, 1827

p. 365-366 Jan. (blank), 1826 John Lucas to Lemuel Lucas; for $660 sold 150 ac on both sides of S Pacolate R; border: bridge "made by him", Theron Earle, Whitten, Thomas Grogan, and Willey S Brown; part of tract sold by Maj. John Gowen to John Lucas. Witness Benjamin C Dillingham and Willey S Brown. Signed John Lucas. Wit. oath Apr. 4, 1827 Benjamin C Dillingham to Thos Grogan. Rec. Apr. 9, 1827

p. 366 Feb. 22, 1827 Minor W Brown (Hall Co, Ga) to Benjamin C Dillingham (Spartanburgh); for $300 sold (ac omitted) on N side of S Pacolate R; border: ford between Benjamin C Dillingham and Hoel Lucas; part of tract sold by James Gowen to Minor W Brown's father (name omitted). Witness Lemuel Lucas and Willey S Brown. Signed Minor W Brown. Wit. oath Apr. 4, 1827 Lemuel Lucas to Thos Grogan. Rec. Apr. 9, 1827

p. 366-367 Dec. 27, 1825 James Foster (Spartanburgh) to Samuel Miller, sheriff (same); for $279.37½ sold 40 ac on N side of N Tyger R; border: N & E-Samuel Miller, S & E(sic)-Ransom Foster, and NE-James Foster. Witness Joshua Tapp and Ransom Foster. Signed James Foster. Wit. oath Apr. 9, 1827 Joshua Tapp to Joel Dean. Rec. Apr. 9, 1827

p. 367-368 Mar. 15, 1824 Michael Wood (Spartanburgh) to son Abraham Wood; for love and affection and $1 sold 200 ac on waters of Abner's Cr of Enoree R; border: W-Josiah McClain "part of the above tracts", S-John Herring, E-Thomas Taylor "part of above surveys", N & NW-G A Glenn, Bennet Wilson and "others"; includes all Michael Wood's land where "he" lives; part of grant Mar. 3, 1794 to Michael Wood and part of grant Mar. 21, 1792 to David Qualls and "a small tract" sold by John Redman to Michael Wood. Witness Thomas P Brockman and Thomas Taylor. Signed Michael Wood's mark. Wit. oath Apr. 9, 1827 Thomas Taylor to James Ford. Rec. Apr. 11, 1827

p. 368 Apr. 1, 1826 John Duncan (Spartanburgh) to Samuel Duncan (same); for $200 sold 200 ac where John Duncan lives. Witness John Wood and Walker Morgan. Signed John Duncan's mark. Wit. oath Mar. 17, 1827 Walker Morgan to Jesse Hammett. Rec. Apr. 10, 1827

p. 368-369 Oct. 28, 1826 James B Shields (Spartanburgh) to Samuel Duncan; for $150 sold 90 ac; border: Philips, Joel Farmer, Thomas, and Wm Croan; where Wm Farmer lived now occupied by James Duncan. Witness Reason Hillburn and Bowen Griffin. Signed J. B. Shields. Wit. oath Apr. 10, 1827 Bowen Griffin to John Burns. Rec. Apr. 10, 1827

p. 369 Jan. 16, 1827 James Newman (Spartanburgh) to William Young; for $200 sold a Negro boy Glousester about 13 years old;

Condition: sale void if James Newman pays William Young $200 by Oct. 1, 1827. Witness Thomas Young. Signed Jas Newman. Wit. oath Apr. 9, 1827 Thos Young to Joel Dean. Rec. Apr. 10, 1827

p. 369-370 Feb. 9, 1827 Elizabeth Hayward to John B Hudgans (or Hodgen) (Spartanburgh); for $365 sold 365 ac on Long Br of Maple Swamp Cr; part of 1,250 ac grant Jul. 20, 1772 to Thomas Hayward. Witness Philip C Lester and John R Wood. Signed Elizabeth Hayward by attorney Josiah Kilgore. Wit. oath Apr. 10, 1827 Philip C Lester to Ransom Foster. Rec. Apr. 10, 1827

p. 370 Aug. 21, 1826 Willey S Brown to Benjamin C Dillingham; for $4 sold 16 ac; border: ridge road; where "he" lives. Witness John T Hannan and Alfred Camp. Signed Willey S Brown. Wit. oath Apr. 10, 1827 Alfred Camp to Thos Grogan. Rec. Apr. 10, 1827

p. 370-371 Feb. 1, 1826 John Hatchett (Spartanburgh) to Josiah Hatchett (same); for $500 sold 100 ac; border: Rush's Mill, Mathias Rush, Thomas Hatchett, Mrs. Hatchett, and Robert Ligon. Witness John Otts and Martin Otts. Signed Josiah Hatchett. Wit. oath Apr. 10, 1827 Martin Otts to Philip Brewton. Rec. Apr. 10, 1827

p. 371 Dec. 29, 1821 Anna McBee (Spartanburgh) to Jeremiah McBee; for $400 sold 275 ac; border: George Poole's land and S-Winn. Witness Mathew McBee and James Crocker jr. Signed Anna McBee's mark. Wit. oath Nov. 24, 1826 James Crocker to William Reid. Rec. Apr. 10, 1827

p. 371-372 Jan. 4, 1827 George Floyd (Spartanburgh) to John D Scott (same); for $108.30 sold 72.2 ac on S side of S Tyger R and on Still House Br. Witness W. B. Otts and Martin Otts. Signed George Floyd. Wit. oath Apr. 10, 1827 Martin Otts to Robert Ligon. Rec. Apr. 10, 1827

p. 372 Jun. 8, 1826 (Providence, RI) Dower renounced Mary Hill to Thomas Mann, chief justice of Providence Common Pleas Court, for deed from George Hill to Leonard Hill and John Clark. Witness Sarah P Hill. Rec. omitted. Providence, RI Feb. 27, 1827 Wm S Patten, clerk of Common Pleas Court, certifys Thomas Mann is chief judge

p. 372-373 Apr. 3, 1826 (Union Dist) Nathaniel Gist (Spartanburgh) to Barrum Bobo (same); for $2,500 sold (1) 40 ac on S side Tyger R; "late" Weaver's Manufacturing; and (2) 60 ac on S side Tyger R; where late Carolina Manufacturing was; and (3) 304 ac on N side Tyger R; opposite late cotton manufactury; border: Richard Thomson. Witness E. M. Bobo and Hese Rice. Signed Nathl Gist. Wit. oath (not dated Union Dist) E. M. Bobo to Danl Thomas. Rec. Apr. 11, 1827. Dower renounced Jul. 17, 1826 (Union Dist) Elizabeth L Gist to John P Thomson

p. 373-374 Mar. 12, 1827 David Moore (Spartanburgh) to Josiah Woodruff (Dallis Co, Ala); for $27 sold 27 ac on branches of Jimmey's Cr of Tyger R. Witness Thomas Woodruff III, William Woodruff, and John Leatherwood. Signed David Moore. Wit. oath Apr. 11, 1827 Thomas Woodruff III to Philip Brewton. Rec. Apr. 11, 1827

p. 374 Feb. 17, 1827 Newman Wilson (Spartanburgh) to Thomas P Brockman (Greenville Dist); for $82 sold 100 ac on Vine's fork of Abner's Cr; border: grant to Pennell Wood, grant to Augustus Attrrick, George Holtzclaw, and Robert Greer. Witness Thomas Goldsmith and Josiah Kilgore. Signed Newman Wilson's mark. Wit. oath Feb. 17, 1827 (Greenville Dist) Josiah Kilgore to Andrew McCrary. Rec. Apr. 11, 1827

p. 374-375 Jan. 9, 1827 James Hindman (Spartanburgh) to William West sr (same); for $82 sold 50 ac on W side of Reedy Br; part of tract sold by Jas Foster to James Hindman. Witness Joshua Tapp and Samuel B Elder. Signed James Hindman. Wit. oath Apr. 12, 1827 Joshua Tapp to D White. Rec. Apr. 12, 1827

p. 375 Mar. 22, 1827 David McCarley (Spartanburgh) to James McCarley (same); for $150 sold 60 ac on Beaverdam Cr of Fairforest Cr; border: Blackstock's Road and NE-Foster. Witness Thomas McCarley and Drury McAbee. Signed David McCarley. Wit. oath Apr. 10, 1827 Thomas McCarley to W Hunt. Rec. Apr. 13, 1827. Dower renounced Apr. 7, 1827 Catharine McCarley to J. W. Farrow

p. 375-376 Oct. 5, 1826 Charles H Miller (Spartanburgh) to William Coan (same); for $850 sold 179 ac on S Tyger R; border at time of grant: vacant; border now: W-John Miller and Richard Berry, S-Francis Miller, James Miller and Robert Ligon, and N-Thomas Miller and John Miller; grant to Edward Gore who sold to Charles H Miller. Witness Robert Ligon and Simon West. Signed Charles H Miller. Wit. oath Apr. 9, 1827 Robert Ligon to James Crook. Rec. Apr. 14, 1827

p. 376 Dec. 11, 1826 Robert Ligon to Henry R Lanham; for $214 sold 50 ac; border: James Miller, William Coan, and Enoch Underwood; on E side of S Tyger R; "leaving out a rod in back and one in front a certain shoal that Mc Daniel once began a mill on". Witness Charles Moore and C. H. Moore. Signed Robert Ligon. Wit. oath Apr. 10, 1827 Charles Moore to Philip Brewton. Rec. Apr. 14, 1827

p. 376-377 Jan. 8, 1826 John Turner (Spartanburgh) to Francis Little (same); for $750 sold 696 ac on S side of Lawson's fork; border: Moultrie; sold by Ordinary as distribution of estate of William Turner desc to John Turner. Witness James Brannon and Thomas Wells. Signed John Turner's mark. Wit. oath Jan. 8, 1827 James Brannon to Jas Ed Henry. Rec. Apr. 23, 1827. Dower renounced Apr. 10, 1827 Anna Turner to Henry Turner

p. 377-378 Mar. 28, 1827 Robert Penden (Spartanburgh) to Patrick Hoy (same); for $159 sold 99 ac on N(sic) side of S Tyger R and on Chyncopin Cr; border: N-P Salman, E-widow Hanna and widow Miller, S-Patrick Hoy, and W-S Tyger R. Witness Charles M Bragg and John B Bragg. Signed Robert Peden. Wit. oath Mar. 28, 1827 John B Bragg to James Crook. Rec. Apr. 24, 1827. Dower renounced Apr. 11, 1827 Polly Peden to James Crook

p. 378 Dec. 10, 1811 James George (Spartanburgh) to Jesse Cannon (same); for $80 sold 100 ac on S side of Pacolate R "in bludding shoal called Herican Shoal"; border: Caleb Jones, Patrick Taylor, and Quall. Witness John Parks and James Cannon. Signed James George's mark. Wit. oath Apr. 9, 1827 James Cannon to Danl White. Rec. Apr. 30, 1827. Dower renounced Jan. 6, 1812 Gemima George to John Gossett

p. 378-379 Mar. 9, 1820 Abraham Crow and David Dickey (Rutherford Co, NC) to Jesse Cannon (Spartanburgh); for $320 sold 400 ac; border: William Hammett and Dishan Grant; where Justice Runnels lived; part of 591 ac grant Dec. 3, 1792 Gov. Charles Pinckney to William Hammett. Witness James Cannon and John Cannon. Signed Abraham Crow and D Dickey. Wit. oath May 1, 1822 James Cannon to Henry Turner. Rec. Apr. 30, 1827

p. 379-380 Dec. 28, 1826 Matthew P Evins (Spartanburgh) to Samuel N Evins (same); for $300 sold 154 ac; border: David Drummond, Samuel N Evins, and Miller. Witness Ransom Seay and J. J. McMiken. Signed M. P. Evins. Wit. oath Dec. 28, 1826 J. J. McMiken to F. H. Legg. Rec. May 7, 1827. Dower renounced Dec. 28, 1826 Ann Evins to

F. H. Legg

p. 380 Feb. 21, 1827 Feb. 21, 1827 Reuben Daniel (Spartanburgh) to son Jesse Daniel (same); for love and affection and $500 advancement on Reuben Daniel's estate give 271 ac; border: S-A Foster, W-Reuben Daniel, NW-Wells, and E-Amos Liles; on Poison Br of Fairforest Cr and Belcher's Br and Foster's Still house Br; where Jesse Daniel lives. Witness Christi Golightly, Nancy W. High, and Martha Daniel. Signed Reuben Daniel. Wit. oath Apr. 26, 1827 Martha Daniel to James W Cooper. Rec. May 7, 1827

p. 380-381 Apr. 7, 1827 Jeremiah McBee (Spartanburgh) to John Kimbrell (same); for $110 sold 275 ac on both sides Casey's Cr of Pacolate R; border: George Poole and Winn; grant to Sabb and Lee. Witness James Poole and Richard Findly. Signed Jeremiah McBee. Wit. oath Apr. 7, 1827 James Poole to W Bennett. Rec. May 7, 1827. Dower renounced May 5, 1827 Sally McBee to Geo Camp

p. 381-382 Mar. 5, 1827 Jesse Mason (Spartanburgh) to James Yates (same); for $200 sold 50 ac on waters of Ford's Cr; border: William Ginnings, Kerkling's old line, Thomas Hurt, and Georgia Rd; part of where Jesse Mason lived. Witness O Vice and M Foster. Signed Jesse Mason. Wit. oath May 7, 1827 O Vice to E Bomar. Rec. May 7, 1827

p. 382 Nov. 11, 1826 Joseph Betterton (Spartanburgh) to Joseph Smith (same); for $500 sold 129 ac on W side of Dutchman's Cr; border: McHam's Spring Br; part of grant to John Blasingame. Witness John Grist and John Betterton. Signed Joseph Betterton. Wit. oath Jan. 4, 1827 John Grist to James Hamm. Rec. May 7, 1827. Dower renounced Nov. 18, 1826 Ann Beddeton(sic) to James Hamm

p. 382-383 Jul. 28, 1826 John Thornton (Spartanburgh) to Zachariah Moore (same); for $700 sold 242½ ac on S side of Tyger R; border: Burton's still house Br, N-Smithwick, the bridge road, Thornton's still house Br, W-Robert Alexander and Elbert Casey, and E(sic)-Tyger R. Witness William Otts and Isaac Wofford. Signed John Thornton. Wit. oath Jul. 28, 1826 William Otts to Robert Ligon. Rec. May 7, 1827. Dower renounced Jul. 28, 1826 Elizabeth Thornton to Robert Ligon

p. 383-384 Apr. 14, 1827 Berryman S Holder (Wilson Co, Tenn), attorney for Sarah Tolleson, widow of Muse Tolleson, (now Sarah Holder), to James Brannon; for $150 sold Sarah's dower rights to ½ ac in Spartanburgh, SC; border: S-Public squard, W-Jesse Cleveland, N-John W Farrow, and NE-public road. Witness E Bomar and G. W. Bomar. Signed B. S. Holder, attorney for Sarah Holder. Wit. oath May 10, 1827 G. W. Bomar to E Bomar. Rec. May 10, 1827

p. 384 Apr. 20, 1827 Berryman S Holder (late of Spartanburgh and now Wilson Co, Tenn) to Dr. Robert M Young; for $16 sold Mrs. Sarah Holder's, late Mrs. Sarah Tolleson, dower claim to (omitted). Witness John Wilbanks and James J Vernon. Signed B. S. Holder, attorney for Sarah Holder. Wit. oath May 10, 1827 John Wilbanks to E Bomar. Rec. May 10, 1827

p. 384-385 Apr. 20, 1827 Berryman S Holder (late of Spartanburgh now Wilson Co, Tenn), by power of attorney from Mrs. Sarah Holder, late Sarah Tolleson, to Dr. Robert M Young; for $50 sold Sarah's dower claim to (omitted). Witness John Wilbanks and James J Vernon. Signed B. S. Holder, attorney for Sarah Holder. Wit. oath May 10, 1827 John Wilbanks to E Bomar. Rec. May 10, 1827

p. 385-386 Apr. 28, 1824 Thomas Poole, sheriff (Spartanburgh) to John Oeland (same); for $55 sold 1 ac on N side of Main

St in Spartanburgh, SC near old jail; where Muse Tolleson lived; border: lot "lately" bought by John Oeland at sheriff's sale, W & N-Richard Thomson, and E-½ ac lot of John W Farrow; sold due to writ from Spartanburgh Common Pleas Court second Monday after fourth Monday in Oct. 1822 suit of Abram Lemaster; judgment was levy of $125 and costs from Muse Tolleson. Witness John Pickenpack and John Poole. Signed Thomas Poole. Wit. oath May 10, 1827 John Pickenpack to E Bomar. Rec. May 10, 1827

p. 386 Jan. 3, 1827 Berryman S Holder, attorney and husband of Sarah Tolleson now Sarah Holder, widow of Muse Tolleson desc, to John Oeland; for $18 sold Sarah's dower claim to "within described lot". Witness E Bomar and G. W. Bomar. Signed B. S.Holder, attorney for Sarah Holder. Wit. oath May 10, 1827 G. W. Bomar to E Bomar. Rec. May 10, 1827

p. 386-387 Nov. 27, 1826 Elijah Fowler (Spartanburgh) to Wiley Fowler (same); for (money omitted) sold 57½ ac on waters of Lawson's fork; border: Samuel Maverick and Guinvarel(?); sold by George Lewis to Elijah Fowler; part of grant to George Lewis. Witness John Barnett and David Rollins. Signed Elijah Fowler and Elizabeth's mark. Wit. oath Apr. 10, 1827 David Rollins to W Bennett. Rec. May 14, 1827

p. 387 Mar. 28, 1827 Thomas Davis (Spartanburgh) to daughter Margaret S Davis (same); for past services and assistance and continued assistance to Thomas Davis and his wife when they need it give all personal property: horses, cattle, hogs, plantation tools, household and kitchen furniture, notes, and accounts and money that Thomas Davis has at his death. Witness W.T. Tanner and Thomas Finch. Signed Thos Davis. Wit. oath May 14, 1827 Thomas Finch to Philip Brewton. Rec. May 14, 1827

p. 387-388 Feb. 5, 1827 Green Mitchell (Spartanburgh) to Henry Littlejohn (Union Dist); for $425 sold (ac omitted) on waters of Gum Root Br of Gocher's Cr of Thickety Cr; border: Joshua Iraper (or Jraper), John Kirby, and David Jones; Condition: sale void if Green Mitchell pays Henry Littlejohn $425 by Dec. 25, 1827. Witness Wm A Steen and Johnson Shippey. Signed Green Mitchell. Wit. oath Mar. 19, 1827 (Union Dist) Johnson Shippey to Wm Goudelock. Rec. May 22, 1827

p. 388-389 Mar. 10, 1827 Alexander Vernon, sheriff (Spartanburgh) to Jesse Wakefield; for $25 sold 125 ac on Ben's Cr of S Tyger R; border: grant to John Nesbett; where "he" lives; grant in 1786 to James Jordan; half of 250 ac sold to Moses and his son Alexander Wakefield and divided by them; Jesse Wakefield petitioned Spartanburgh Ordinary Court vs Hester Delaney and "others" Jan. 11, 1827 to partition estate of Moses Wakefield desc and Court ordered a sale; sale was on Mar. 5, 1827 with credit of 12 months. Witness Patrick White and John Dickson. Signed Alexander Vernon. Wit. oath May 14, 1827 John Dickson to E Bomar. Rec. May 24, 1827

p. 389 Dec. 23, 1826 James Mason jr (Spartanburgh) to Brodrick Mason (same); for $200 sold 70 ac on SW side of Ferguson's Cr; border: SW-Wm Otts and Joel G Brewton, N-B Mason, and E-Ferguson's Cr and James Mason jr. Witness James Nesbett and Paul Cambee. Signed James Mason jr. Wit. oath Mar. 5, 1827 James Nesbett to Philip Brewton. Rec. May 28, 1827

p. 389-390 Nov. 22, 1826 George Floyd (Spartanburgh) to James Mason (same); for $300 sold 75 ac on SW side of Ferguson's Cr; border: SW-William Otts, Floyd's Spring Br, Big Br, and E-Ferguson's Cr and land formerly of Thos Rice. Witness James Nesbett and Eber Bragg. Signed George Floyd. Wit. oath Feb. 24, 1827 Eber Bragg to Robert Ligon. Rec. May 28, 1827. Dower renounced Mar. 31, 1827

Jane Floyd to Robert Ligon

p. 390-391 May 15, 1827 Margaret McElrath, late Margaret Ford, guardian for minor kids of William Ford desc., to Jonathan Nesbett; to secure Jonathan Nesbett from harm due to Jonathan being security for Margaret McElrath as guardian sold 118 ac where Margaret lives; grant to Jonathan Nesbett; and sold three Negroes--Anaca, Rose, and Resta (or Repta); Condition: sale void if Jonathan Nesbett doesn't lose anything due to security for guardianship. Witness M Ford and James Nesbett jr. Signed Margaret McElrath's mark. Wit. oath May 28, 1827 James Nesbett jr to E Bomar. Rec. May 28, 1827

p. 391-392 Mar. 15, 1827 David Owen (Spartanburgh) to John Owen (same); for $500 sold 118 ac on N side of Enoree R; border: E-Thomas Farrow, John Owen sr, N & W-Robert Hannah, and S-Enoree R. Witness Zachariah Lanford and William Lanford. Signed David Owen's mark. Wit. oath Apr. 14, 1827 William Lanford to John Dean. Rec. Jun. 4, 1827

p. 392-393 May 26, 1827 Thomas Waters (Spartanburgh) to Dorah Ducker and Davis Newman (SC); for $2 and for love and affection for wife Sarah Waters sold a brown cow and lands and goods Sarah Waters may acquire for her benefit and make Sarah Waters "a sole trader". Witness Drury Fowler and Leroy Campbell. Signed Thomas Waters, Sarah Waters, Dorah Ducker, and Davis Newman. Wit. oath May 28, 1827 Drury Fowler to Benj Wofford. Rec. Jun. 8, 1827

p. 393 Mar. 2, 1801 David Anderson (Spartanburgh) to William Anderson (same); for 20£ sterling sold 163 ac on S side of S Tyger R; border: Provey's Cr and Ben's Cr. Witness John Durham, John Crawford, and Samuel Jamerson. Signed David Anderson. Wit. oath Mar. 2, 1801 John Durham to Drury McDaniel. Rec. Jun. 11, 1827

p. 393-394 Feb. 16, 1827 David D Anderson (Spartanburgh) to Michael Dickson (same); for $650 sold 145 ac on E Side of Mile Br of S Tyger. Witness James Chamblin and James Rodgers. Signed David D Anderson. Wit. oath Feb. 17, 1827 James Chamblin to Thomas Wood. Rec. Jun. 25, 1827. Dower renounced Feb. 17, 1827 Ann Anderson to Thomas Wood

p. 394-395 Feb. 8, 1827 William Anderson (Spartanburgh) to Michael Dickson (same); for $400 sold 165 ac on N side of S Tyger R; border: David Anderson sr, Jas Chamblin, and Mile Br. Witness Robert Gaston and James Rodgers. Signed Wm Anderson. Wit. oath Mar. 6, 1827 Robert Gaston to Saml Pearson. Rec. Jun. 25, 1827. Dower renounced Feb. 17, 1827 Martha Anderson to Thomas Wood

p. 395-396 Aug. 25, 1823 Moses Casey (Spartanburgh) to Aaron F Casey and Jeremiah F Casey (same); for $500 sold 150 ac on both sides Cedar Shoal Cr of Enoree R; border: Aaron Casey, Richd Fryer, and William Casey; grant to Christopher Casey and Thomas Todd. Witness Jonathan Fryer and Stephen Wilson. Signed M Casey. Wit. oath Apr. 7, 1825 Jonathan Fryer to Wm Young. Rec. Jun. 30, 1827

p. 396 Jan. 25, 1827 Abraham Lemaster (Spartanburgh) to James Tolleson (same); to secure a note from Abraham Lemaster to James Tolleson for $105 dated Apr. 4, 1825 and due Dec. 25, 1825 sold 6 cattle, 4 cows and 2 yearlings, 6 hogs, 7 barrels of corn. 300 lb of bacon, a sorrel horse, 400 bundles of fodder, a chest, a pot, an oven, 2 shovel ploughs, 2 cow tung plows, 3 hoes, 3 jack plains, 2 fore plains, 2 smoothing planes, a joiner, a foot atz, a rabit plain, and a square. Witness Henry White and J. B. Tolleson. Signed A Lemasters. Wit. oath Jul. 2, 1827 Henry White to W Hunt. Rec. Jul. 2, 1827

p. 396-397 Feb. 27, 1827 Hugh Davitt and Charles Berry; for $1,125.92

sold three Negroes--a boy Alonzo about 16 years old, a malottoe girl Becca about 21 or 22 years old, a girl Patsey about 14 years old; Condition: Hugh Davitt is indebted to Charles Berry as agent for John Means jointly with John Rochell, who is now insolvent; debt is $140 with interest from Dec. 1822 or total of $180.83; and Hugh Davitt indebted to "him" as agent for his father William Davitt for $525 with interest from Jan. 1, 1823 in note received from Charles Berry and William S James due to William Davitt (money was received by Hugh Davitt and hasn't be accounted for); and Hugh Davitt owes Charles Berry for $150 with interest from Mar. 1, 1824 paid by Charles Berry to William Davitt for Hugh's benefit; and Hugh Davitt owes Charles Berry $65 with interest from Feb. 24, 1827 in note Charles "holds on" Hugh; total debt is $1,125.92 and sale is void if Hugh Davitt pays Charles Berry $1,125.92 by Feb. 1, 1828. Witness Charles Moore. Signed Hugh Davitt. Wit. oath Jun. 15, 1827 Charles Moore to Robert Ligon. Rec. Jul. 2, 1827

p. 397-398 Feb. 23, 1827 John Divine to Benjamin Wofford esq; for $52 sold 25 3/4 ac on branch on S side of Tyger R; plat attached shows border: Benjamin Wofford. Witness Joel Dean and William Harrison. Signed John Divine. Wit. oath Feb. 23, 1827 William Harrison to Joel Dean. Rec. Jul. 2, 1827. Dower renounced Mar. 1, 1827 Margaret Divine to Moses Casey

p. 398 Mar. 27, 1827 Norris Compton (Spartanburgh) to Zachariah Hobby; for $32.20 sold 2 cows, a yearling, 21 hogs, 11 geese, a bed and furniture, a chest, 2 tables, 5 chairs, and a writing desk; Condition: sale void if Norris Compton pays Zachariah Hobby $32.20 and interest by Dec. 1, 1827. Witness Samuel Tucker and Thomas Cannon. Signed N Compton. Wit. oath May 10, 1827 Samuel Tucker to Benj Wofford. Rec. Jul. 4, 1827

p. 398-399 Dec. 13, 1825 William Rogers (Spartanburgh) to Elizabeth Herilson (same); for $196 sold 112 ac. Witness Hamman Elder and Thomas Rogers. Signed William Rogers. Wit. oath May 30, 1827 Hamman Elder to Robert Ligon. Rec. Jul. 4, 1827. Dower renounced May 30, 1827 Elizabeth Rogers to Robert Ligon

p. 399-400 Feb. 9, 1827 John B Hodgen (Spartanburgh) to Philip C Lester; for $288.83 sold 365 ac on Long Br of Maple Swamp Cr; where John B Hodgen lives; Condition: sale void if John B Hodgen pays Philip C Lester $288.83 by Dec. 25, 1827. Witness Josiah Kilgore and John K Wood. Signed John B Kilgore. Wit. oath Jul. 6, 1827 (Greenville Dist) John B Hodgen to Jesse Hammett. Rec. Jul. 11, 1827

p. 400 May 10, 1825 Hugh Baily and Hugh McClemons (both of Greenville Dist) to Philip C Lester (same); for $28 sold 5.8 ac in Greenville Dist(?) on both sides of State Road near head of branches of Morgan's Cr and Maple Swamp Cr of Enoree R and S Tyger R; part of tract known as "the bealt tract"; border: Philip C Lester. Witness John Crymes and Isaac Morgan. Signed Hugh Balay and Hugh McClemans. Wit. oath Jul. 6, 1827 (Greenville Dist) Isaac Morgan to Jesse Hammett. Rec. Jul. 11, 1827

p. 400-401 Dec. 25, 1826 Samuel McDade (Spartanburgh) to Philip C Lester (Greenville Dist); for $92.50 sold 495 ac on waters of Middle Tyger R; border: John Loftis, John M Collins, David Dantzler, and Sebles; where Samuel McDade lives; grant Sept. 4, 1820 to Samuel McDade; Condition: sale void if Samuel McDade pays Philip C Lester $46.25 by Jan. 10, 1827. Witness Asa Cunningham and Samuel McCravy. Signed Saml McDade. Wit. oath Jul. 6, 1827 (Greenville Dist) Asa Cunningham to Jesse Hammett. Rec. Jul. 11, 1827

p. 401 May 28, 1827 Philip Bettis (Spartanburgh) to Abner Benson and

Andrew B Moore (same); for $61.50 sold 20½ ac on Middle Tyger R. Witness Simpson Bobo and Anthony Pearson. Signed Philip Bettis' mark. Wit. oath May 27, 1827 Simpson Bobo to E Bomar. Rec. Jul. 17, 1827

p. 401-402 Apr. 29, 1826 Amos Austill to William Rice Bostick; for $600 sold 300 ac on Beaverdam Cr of Thickety Cr; border: S-Thomas Cole, W-Mathew Cooper, and E-Michael Gaffney; grant to Josiah Tanner who sold to William Thomson desc and sold by William Thomson's executors to Amos Austill. Witness William Austell and Peter Quinn Camp. Signed Amos Austell. Wit. oath May 10, 1826 Peter Q Camp to Joseph Camp. Rec. Jul. 18, 1827

p. 402-403 Mar. 1, 1827 Moses Casey (Spartanburgh) to Benjamin Wofford esq (same); for $100 sold 53½ ac on Cedar Shoal Cr of Enoree R; border: W-Col. William Farrow, S-Wilbanks, E-"part of said tract" where Casander West lives, and N-"part of said tract" and B. W. Waters "agreeable to" survey by Joel Dean esq. Witness S. C. Newman and Nancy Tucker. Signed M Casey. Wit. oath Jul. 11, 1827 Nancy Tucker to Joseph Wofford. Rec. Jul. 23, 1827

p. 403-404 Feb. 1, 1823 (Giles Co, Tenn) Robert A Hewatt (Giles Co, Tenn) to Richard Hewatt (same); power of attorney to sell Robert A Hewatt's land and collect money owed him. Witness none. Signed Robert A Howatt. Certified by John B Armstrong JP and John Laird JP (not dated). Feb. 3, 1823 (Giles Co, Tenn) German Lester, clerk of Quarterly Sessions Court, certifys John B Armstrong and John Laird are justices of peace. Feb. 3, 1823 (Giles Co, Tenn) Nelson Patterson, "chairman" of Quarterly Sessions Court, certifys German Lester is clerk of court. Rec. Jul. 27, 1827

p. 404 Nov. 13, 1826 Martin Ball (Laurens Dist) to Robert Kimble and Archy Kimble; for $75 sold 75 ac on N side of N fork of N Tyger R; border: Kimble. Witness Lucy Burns and William C Evitts jr. Signed Martin Ball. Wit. oath Nov. 13, 1826 Lucy Burns to John Burns. Rec. Jul. 27, 1827

p. 404-405 Jan. 27, 1823 Joseph Harris (Union Dist) to Moses Fowler (Spartanburgh); for $500 sold 250 ac on waters of Ferguson's Cr of Tyger R; border: NW & NE-Wm Moore and other sides vacant; W end of 304 ac grant Nov. 7, 1791 to Thomas House. Witness Harris Brewton, John Fowler, and Alexander D Peden. Signed Joseph Harris. Wit. oath Jan. 27, 1823 Alexander D Peden to Thomas Wood. Rec. Jul. 30, 1827

p. 405 Apr. 30, 1827 Benjamin A Markley received $145.68 3/4 from John D Cannon by hands of Thomas Poole in full satisfaction of mortgage. Witness Peter Hamilton and Henry White. Signed Benj A Markley. Wit. oath Aug. 6, 1827 Henry White to Caleb Jones. Rec. Aug. 6, 1827

p. 405 Aug. 6, 1827 Dower renounced Nancy Vandyke to Elisha Bomar for deed from John Vandyke to Barney Bishop. Rec. Aug. 6, 1827

p. 405-406 Feb. 1, 1822 William Durham (Spartanburgh) to William Young; for $250 sold 75 ac on branch of James' Cr on S side of Tyger R; part of tract formerly of Elisha Stallions. Witness Thomas Young and Michael W Dycus. Signed William Durham. Wit. oath Aug. 4, 1827 Thomas Young to J Cooper. Rec. Aug. 6, 1827

p. 406-407 Apr. 2, 1827 William Young (Spartanburgh) to Michael W Dichus; for $250 sold 75 ac on branch of James' Cr on S side of Tyger R; part of tract fromerly of Elisha Stallions. Witness James D Callicott and Phebe S Smith. Signed Wm Young. Wit. oath Aug. 4, 1827 James D Callicott to J Cooper. Rec. Aug. 6, 1827

p. 407 Apr. 2, 1824 Solomon Crocker (Spartanburgh) to John Crocker (same); for $200 sold 100 ac on both sides of Richland Cr on S side of Pacolate R; border: Anthony Crocker's Spring Br, James Crocker, Graveyard hollow, John Lee, Big Br, Dunkin, and William Crocker; Solomon Crocker gets to use the land for his lifetime. Witness William Crocker and Arthur Crocker jr. Signed Solomon Crocker's mark. Wit. oath May 6, 1827 William Crocker to Caleb Jones. Rec. Aug. 6, 1827

p. 407-408 Feb. 6, 1827 Leonard Sparks jr (Spartanburgh) to firm of Brannon and White (same); to secure a note for $97.90 sold (1) 100 ac on N side of Pacolate R; where Leonard Sparks jr lives; and (2) 20 ac adjoining (1); "lately" sold by Wm Norris to Leonard Sparks jr; (1) and (2) border: E & N-Wm Norris, W-Wm Reid, and S-Pacolate R. Witness James Tolleson and Elihu Sparks. Signed Leonard Sparks. Wit. oath Aug. 6, 1827 James Tolleson to D White. Rec. Aug. 6, 1827

p. 408 Mar. 23, 1827 Peter Bragg (Spartanburgh) to John Bragg jr (same); for $236 sold 59 ac on N side of Ferguson's Cr; border: Grace's Spring Br, S-Joel G Brewton, W-Maj. Crook, and others-Peter Bragg. Witness William Otts and A Bragg. Signed Peter Bragg. Wit. oath Mar. 23, 1827 William Otts to Philip Brewton. Rec. Aug. 6, 1827

p. 408-409 Jul. 20, 1827 (Charleston, SC) Mary Grimkie, executrix of will of Honorable John F Grimkie desc, to Charles F Grimkie; power of attorney to collect from Muse Tolleson's estate, Joseph Carswell or Burrell Bobo what is owed Mary Grimkie. Witness none. Signed Mary Grimkie, executor. Wit. oath Aug. 14, 1827 Charles F Grimkie to Jas Ed Henry. Rec. Aug. 14, 1827

p. 409 Jul. 27, 1826 (Greenville Dist) James McDaniel to John H Harrison (Greenville Dist); for $200 sold (ac omitted); land was sold by Gabl Benson to James McDaniel. Witness Tandy Walker and B. F. Perry. Signed Jas McDaniel. Wit. oath May 28, 1827 B. F. Perry to E Bomar. Rec. Aug. 14, 1827

p. 409-410 Jan. 27, 1824 Hugh Donoldson (Spartanburgh) to William Hardy, a man of color (same); for $200 sold 82 ac on Ham's Cr of Fairforest Cr; border: Cruse, McCarter, Sidney Donoldson, and Gossett; Hugh Donoldson's share in distribution with Sidney Donoldson only heirs of Robert Donoldson desc. Witness James Donoldson and Darcas Donoldson. Signed Hugh Donoldson. Wit. oath May 13, 1824 James Donoldson to John Eison. Rec. Aug. 20, 1827

p. 410-411 Apr. 4, 1827 David Golightly sr (Spartanburgh) to William W Harris; for $200 sold 160 ac on both sides Buffalow Lick Cr of Fairforest Cr; border: David Golightly and William W Harris. Witness Patience Foster and James Foster. Signed D Golightly. Wit. oath Aug. 2, 1827 James Foster to E Bomar. Rec. Aug. 20, 1827

p. 411 Sept. 17, 1825 James Hindman (Spartanburgh) to William W Harris; for $92 sold 46 ac; border: David Golightly, William W Harris, and "others"; plat attached. Witness James Foster and Julia G Harris. Signed James Hindman. Wit. oath Aug. 20, 1827 James Foster to E Bomar. Rec. Aug. 20, 1827

p. 411-412 Jan. (blank), 1819 David Anderson (Spartanburgh) to William Anderson (same); for $600 sold 200 ac on Powder fork of S Tyger R and on Prudy fork. Witness William Hoy and J. N. Haddin. Signed David Anderson. Wit. oath Aug. 21, 1827 William Hoy to James Crook. Rec. Aug. 21, 1827

p. 412 Aug. 22, 1826 Elizabeth Smith, James Moore (attorney for Isaac Compton) and wife Barbara, late Barbara Smith, and Franklin

Smith (Giles Co, Tenn)) (but "we both" of Spartanburgh) to Andrew Huffman (Spartanburgh); for $153.50 sold 100 ac on waters of Ferguson's Cr; border: Henry White and Hervey Lancaster; part of grant in 1785 to Charles Smith and by his will given to children of his son William Smith desc, who are Barbara Compton, Elizabeth Smith, and Franklin Smith. Witness John Murph and John A(?) Smith. Signed Elizabeth Smith and James Moore. Wit. oath Aug. 22, 1826 John Murph to D White. Rec. Aug. 23, 1827

SLAVE INDEX

PLACE INDEX

CREEK and BRANCH INDEX

www.ingramcontent.com/pod-product-compliance
Lightning Source LLC
LaVergne TN
LVHW090252210926
848480LV00001B/5